Glencoe Physical Science

Contents in Brief

Teacher Wraparound Edition

Correlations and Standards

Program Resources

Support for All Learners

Classroom Activities and Materials

Student Edition

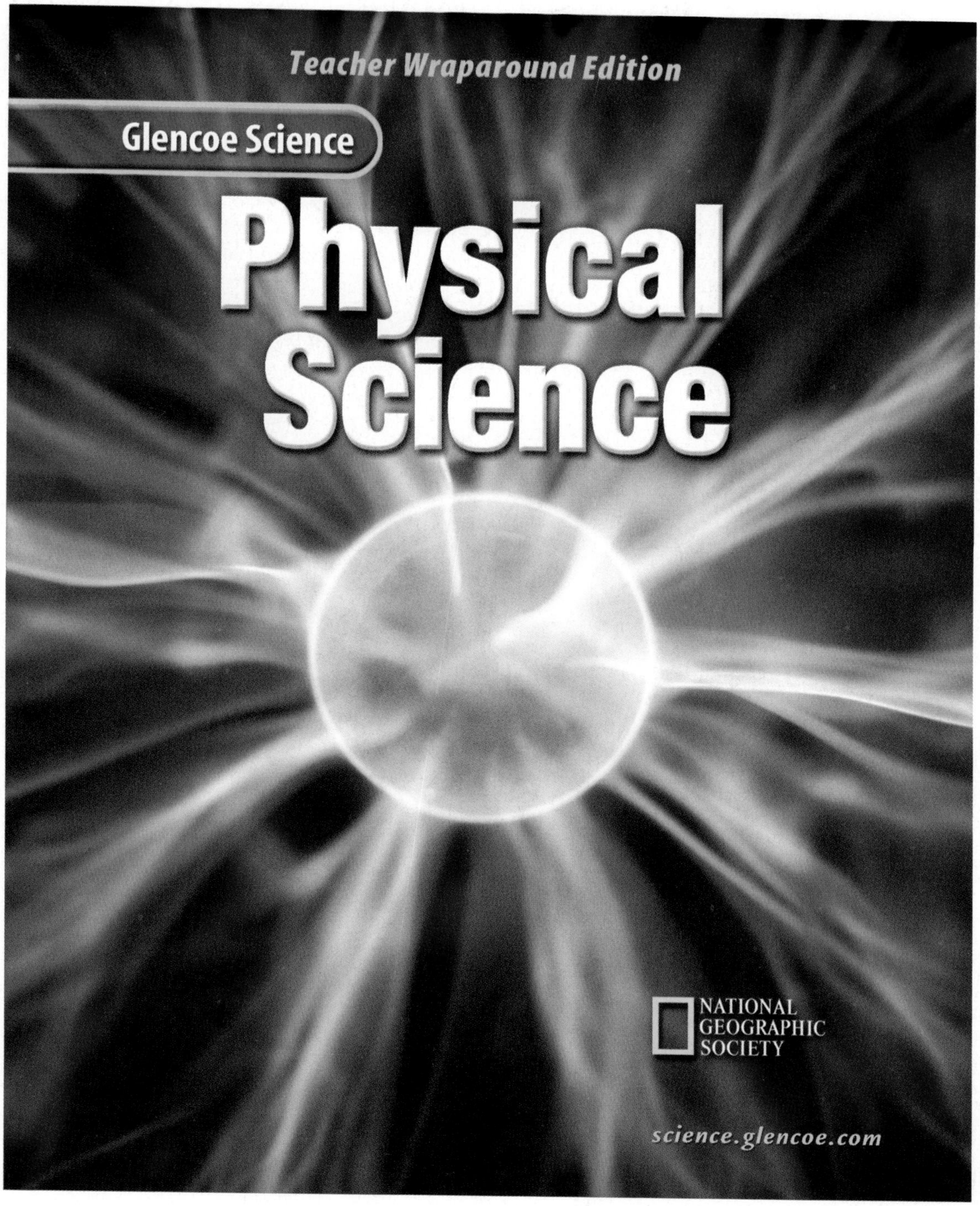

Teacher Wraparound Edition

Glencoe Science

Physical Science

NATIONAL GEOGRAPHIC SOCIETY

science.glencoe.com

New York, New York Columbus, Ohio Woodland Hills, California Peoria, Illinois

GLENCOE
PHYSICAL SCIENCE

Student Edition
Teacher Wraparound Edition
Interactive Teacher Edition CD-ROM
Interactive Lesson Planner CD-ROM
Lesson Plans
Content Outline for Teaching
Directed Reading for Content Mastery
Foldables: Reading and Study Skills
Assessment
Chapter Review
Chapter Tests
ExamView Pro Test Bank Software
Assessment Transparencies
Performance Assessment in the Science Classroom
The Princeton Review Test Practice Booklet
Spanish Directed Reading for Content Mastery
Spanish Resources
Reinforcement
Enrichment
Activity Worksheets
Section Focus Transparencies
Teaching Transparencies
Laboratory Activities
Science Inquiry Labs
Critical Thinking/Problem Solving
Reading and Writing Skill Activities
Mathematics Skill Activities
Cultural Diversity
Laboratory Management and Safety
Mindjogger Videoquizzes and Teacher Guide
Interactive Explorations and Quizzes CD-ROM
Puzzlemaker Software
Cooperative Learning
Environmental Issues in the Science Classroom
Home and Community Involvement
Using the Internet in the Science Classroom

"Test-Taking Tip," "Study Tip," and Test practice features in this book were written by The Princeton Review, the nation's leader in test preparation. Through its association with McGraw-Hill, The Princeton Review offers the best way to help students excel on standardized assessments.

The Princeton Review is not affiliated with Princeton University or Educational Testing Service.

Glencoe/McGraw-Hill

A Division of The ***McGraw-Hill*** *Companies*

The "Science and Society" and the "Science and History" features that appear in this book were designed and developed by TIME for Kids, a division of TIME Magazine.

Send all inquiries to:

Glencoe/McGraw-Hill
8787 Orion Place
Columbus, OH 43420

ISBN 0-07-822746-1

Printed in the United States of America

1 2 3 4 5 6 7 8 9 10 071/055 10 09 08 07 06 05 04 03 02 01

Authors, Reviewers, and Consultants

for the *Teacher Wraparound Edition*

Authors

Charles William McLaughlin, PhD
Senior Lecturer
University of Nebraska
Lincoln, Nebraska

Marilyn Thompson
Assistant Professor, College of Education
Arizona State University
Tempe, Arizona

Peter Rillero, PhD
Professor of Science Education
Arizona State University West
Phoenix, Arizona

Dinah Zike
Educational Consultant
Dinah-Might Activities, Inc.
San Antonio, Texas

Reviewers

Gilbert Naizer, PhD
Assistant Professor of Elementary Education
Texas A&M University
Commerce, Texas

Kimberly S. Roempler, PhD
Associate Director
Eisenhower National Clearinghouse
for Math and Science
The Ohio State University
Columbus, Ohio

Cultural Diversity Consultants

Nedaro Bellamy
Associate Director,
Rice Model Science Laboratory
Lanier Middle School, Houston ISD
Houston, Texas

Joyce Hilliard-Clark, PhD
Director, Imhotep Academy
North Carolina State University
Raleigh, North Carolina

Inclusion Strategies Consultant

Barry Barto
Special Education Teacher
John F. Kennedy Elementary School
Manistee, Michigan

National Science Education Standards

"The* National Science Education Standards *are premised on a conviction that all students deserve and must have the opportunity to become scientifically literate. The* Standards *look toward a future in which all Americans, familiar with basic scientific ideas and processes, can have fuller and more productive lives."

—National Science Education Standards

About the Standards

This book, published by the National Research Council, represents the contributions of thousands of educators and scientists, and offers a comprehensive vision of a scientifically literate society. The standards describe what all students should know at the end of grades 4, 8, and 12, and offer guidelines for science teaching and assessment.

How *Glencoe Physical Science* Aligns with *The National Science Education Standards*

Content Standards

The correlations that follow show the close alignment between ***Glencoe Physical Science*** and the grade-appropriate standards. ***Glencoe Physical Science*** allows students to discover concepts within each of the content standards and gives students opportunities to make connections among the science disciplines. Hands-on activities and inquiry-based lessons reinforce the science processes emphasized in the standards.

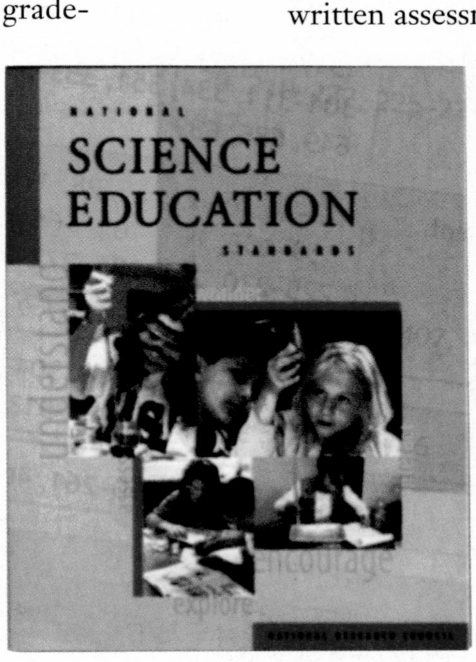

Teaching Standards

Glencoe Physical Science provides activities and discussions that allow students to discover science concepts through inquiry and to apply the knowledge they've constructed to their own lives. The ***Teacher Wraparound Edition*** supports this endeavor with an abundance of effective strategies for guiding students of different ability levels and interests as they explore science.

Assessment Standards

Glencoe Physical Science provides many opportunities in many different formats to assess students' understanding of important concepts. Ideas for portfolios, performance activities, and written assessments accompany every section. Glencoe's Professional Series booklet *Performance Assessment in the Science Classroom* contains rubrics and Performance Task Assessment Lists. This booklet also contains information about evaluating cooperative work. Learning outcomes improve for students of all ability levels in a cooperative learning environment.

Correlation to National Science Education Standards

The following chart illustrates how *Glencoe Physical Science* addresses the National Science Education Standards.

Content Standard	Chapter and Section
(UCP) Unifying Concepts and Processes	
1. Systems, order, and organization	5-2, 5-3, 6-3, 21-4
2. Evidence, models, and explanation	6-1, 7-1, 8-1, 8-2, 8-3, 11-1, 11-2, 11-3, 12-1, 12-3, 15-1, 15-2, 15-3, 17-1, 18-1, 18-3, 19-1, 21-3, 23-1, 23-2, 23-3, 23-4
3. Change, constancy, and measurement	1-1, 1-2, 1-3, 2-1, 2-2, 2-3, 3-1, 3-2, 3-3, 4-1, 4-2, 5-1, 5-2, 5-3, 6-2, 7-2, 7-3, 9-1, 9-2, 9-3, 9-4, 10-1, 10-2, 1-3, 12-2, 13-1, 13-2, 13-3, 16-1, 16-2, 16-3, 18-2, 19-2, 19-3, 24-1, 24-2, 24-3, 24-4, 25-1, 25-2, 25-3
4. Evolution and equilibrium	16-1, 16-2, 16-3, 17-2
5. Form and function	12-4, 14-1, 14-2, 14-3, 14-4, 20-1, 20-2, 20-3, 21-1, 21-2, 22-1, 22-2, 22-3
(A) Science as Inquiry	
1. Abilities necessary to do scientific inquiry	1-1, 1-2, 1-3, 5-1, 5-2, 5-3, 6-2, 6-3, 7-1, 7-2, 7-3, 8-1, 8-3, 9-2, 9-4, 10-1, 11-2, 11-3, 14-1, 14-2, 14-3, 15-1, 15-2, 15-3, 17-1, 17-2, 18-1, 18-2, 18-3, 19-2, 19-3, 20-1, 20-2, 20-3, 21-1, 21-2, 21-3, 21-4, 22-1, 22-2, 22-3, 23-1, 23-2, 23-4, 24-1, 24-4, 25-1, 25-2, 25-3
2. Understandings about scientific inquiry	1-1, 1-2, 1-3, 2-1, 2-3, 3-1, 3-2, 3-3, 4-1, 4-2, 5-3, 10-3, 12-1, 12-2, 12-3, 12-4, 13-1, 13-2, 13-3, 16-1, 16-2, 16-3, 19-1
(B) Physical Science (Grades 9–12)	
1. Structure of atoms	9-1, 9-2, 9-3, 9-4, 10-2, 18-1, 18-2, 18-3,
2. Structure and properties of matter	1-2, 8-1, 8-2, 8-3, 8-1, 8-2, 8-3, 9-1, 9-2, 9-3, 9-4, 14-2, 15-1, 15-2, 15-3, 16-1, 16-2, 16-3, 17-1, 17-2, 18-1, 18-2, 18-3, 19-1, 19-2, 19-3, 20-1, 20-2, 20-3, 21-1, 21-2, 21-3, 21-4, 22-1, 22-2, 22-3, 23-1, 23-2, 23-3, 23-4, 25-1, 25-2, 25-3
3. Chemical reactions	17-1, 17-2, 19-1, 19-2, 19-3, 20-2, 20-3, 23-1, 23-2, 23-3, 23-4, 24-1, 24-2, 24-3, 24-4, 25-1, 25-2, 25-3
4. Motion and forces	2-1, 2-2, 2-3, 3-1, 3-2, 3-3, 5-1, 5-2, 5-3, 16-2, 16-3
5. Conservation of energy and increase in disorder	4-1, 4-2, 6-1, 11-1, 11-2, 11-3, 16-1, 17-2, 23-1, 23-2, 23-3, 23-4, 24-1, 24-2, 24-3, 24-4
6. Interactions of energy and matter	4-1, 4-2, 6-1, 6-2, 6-3, 7-1, 7-2, 7-3, 8-1, 8-2, 8-3, 8-1, 8-2, 8-3, 10-1, 10-2, 10-3, 11-1, 11-2, 11-3, 12-1, 12-2, 12-3, 12-4, 13-1, 13-2, 13-3, 14-1, 14-2, 14-3, 16-1, 16-3, 17-2, 21-4, 22-3
(C) Life Science (Grades 9–12)	
5. Matter, energy, and organization in living systems	12-2, 14-2, 15-2, 21-4
(D) Earth and Space Science (Grades 9–12)	
1. Energy in the earth system	16-1, 16-2, 16-3
(E) Science and Technology	
1. Abilities of technological design	1-1, 5-2, 5-3, 6-2, 6-3, 10-3, 15-1, 15-2, 15-3, 16-2
2. Understandings about science and technology	1-1, 4-1, 4-2, 5-3, 6-2, 6-3, 8-2, 8-3, 9-2, 9-4, 10-2, 10-3, 13-1, 13-2, 13-3, 14-2, 14-3, 14-4, 15-1, 15-2, 15-3, 16-2, 20-3, 21-2, 21-3, 22-1, 22-2, 22-3, 23-4, 24-4, 25-1, 25-2, 25-3
(F) Science in Personal and Social Perspectives (Grades 9–12)	
1. Personal and community health	2-3, 5-3, 9-4, 12-1, 12-2, 12-3, 13-2, 15-2, 21-4
2. Population growth	21-3
3. Natural resources	10-1, 10-2, 10-3, 14-3, 21-3, 24-4,
4. Environmental quality	10-1, 10-2, 10-3, 21-3, 24-4
5. Natural and human-induced hazards	2-3, 10-1, 10-2, 10-3, 12-2, 13-2, 14-3, 21-4, 24-4, 25-4
6. Science and technology in local, national, and global challenges	4-2, 5-3, 6-2, 6-3, 8-2, 8-3, 10-1, 10-2, 10-3, 12-4, 13-1, 13-2, 13-3, 14-3, 14-4, 15-3, 20-3, 21-3, 22-1, 22-2, 22-3, 24-4, 25-1, 25-2, 25-3, 25-4
(G) History and Nature of Science	
1. Science as a human endeavor	1-3, 5-3, 7-3, 9-4, 12-3, 12-4, 14-4, 19-3, 24-4
2. Nature of science	1-1, 1-2, 1-3, 9-4, 18-1, 19-3, 21-4, 24-4
3. History of science	8-3, 9-1, 11-3, 18-3, 20-3, 22-3

National Council of Teachers of Mathematics
Principles and Standards for School Mathematics

High school students often make personal, educational, and career choices on their own that can influence the rest of their lives. Throughout their school years, they acquire skills that help them make these decisions. The development of keen mathematical skills can ensure that students have a wide variety of life options.

Principles and Standards for School Mathematics of the National Council of Teachers of Mathematics describes the foundation of mathematical concepts and applications that can provide students with the necessary mathematical skills to help achieve their life goals.

The ten categories of mathematical concepts and applications, as shown in the table below, include a broad range of topics that build on previous knowledge. They also allow students to increase their abilities to visualize, describe, and analyze situations in mathematical terms.

In Glencoe ***Physical Science***, each Math Skill Activity and Problem-Solving Activity provides students with the opportunity to practice and apply some of the mathematical concepts and applications described in the Standards. These activities serve to reinforce mathematical skills in real-life situations, thus, preparing students to meet their needs in an ever-changing world.

Correlation of *Glencoe Physical Science* to NCTM Standards Grades 9–12

Standard	Chapter-Section
1. Number and Operations	1-2, 1-3, 2-1, 3-1, 4-1, 5-1, 7-3, 8-1, 9-3, 11-2, 12-4, 13-1, 15-2, 16-2, 17-2, 18-2, 19-3, 20-3, 21-4, 23-1, 24-3
2. Algebra	1-2, 1-3, 2-1, 3-1, 4-1, 5-1, 7-3, 9-3, 11-2, 12-4, 15-2, 16-2, 17-2, 20-3, 23-1, 24-3
3. Geometry	1-3, 23-1
4. Measurement	1-2, 2-1, 16-2, 23-1
5. Data Analysis and Probability	1-3, 8-1, 15-2, 18-2, 20-3, 21-4, 22-2
6. Problem Solving	1-3, 2-1, 3-1, 4-1, 5-1, 7-3, 8-1, 9-3, 10-2, 13-1, 15-2, 16-2, 18-2, 19-3, 20-3, 21-4, 22-2, 23-1, 24-3, 25-3
7. Reasoning and Proof	8-1, 10-2 19-3
8. Communication	8-1, 10-2, 12-4, 15-2, 18-2, 19-3, 21-4, 22-2, 23-1, 25-3
9. Connections	1-2, 1-3, 2-1, 3-1, 4-1, 5-1, 7-3, 8-1, 9-3, 10-2 11-2, 12-4, 13-1, 15-2, 16-2, 17-2, 18-2, 19-3, 20-3, 21-4, 22-2, 23-1, 24-3, 25-3
10. Representation	1-3, 8-1, 9-3, 13-1, 18-2, 19-3, 20-3, 21-4, 24-3

Benchmarks for Science Literacy

Benchmarks for Science Literacy is a publication by the American Association for the Advancement of Science that describes how students should progress toward science literacy. People who are science literate are "equipped with knowledge and skills they need to make sense of how the world works, to think critically and independently, and to lead interesting, responsible, and productive lives in a culture increasingly shaped by science and technology."

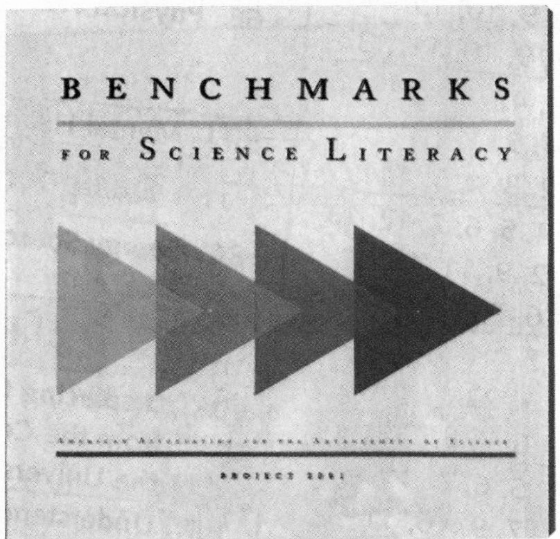

Benchmarks was the culmination of Project 2061, the work of scientists, mathematicians, engineers, and educators to develop benchmarks, or statements, of what *all* students should know or be able to do in science, mathematics, and technology by the end of grades 2, 5, 8, and 12.

Glencoe Physical Science is aligned with ***Benchmarks*** in the following ways:

- Concepts are presented in ways that help students understand the how and why of science, not just requiring them to learn facts that they commit to short-term memory.
- Science concepts are related to students' daily experiences.
- Teachers are provided strategies for encouraging students in independent work and for addressing the needs of students of varied abilities.
- Specific strategies are provided for identifying and addressing student misconceptions.

IDENTIFYING Misconceptions

Educators are becoming increasingly aware of the importance of identifying and addressing misconceptions—prescientific or naïve ideas—that students may hold about science. Students often develop these from their experiences as a way to make sense of the world.

A one-page feature, Identifying Misconceptions, is found on the F interleaf pages preceding selected chapters in the ***Teacher Wraparound Edition.*** This feature provides specific teaching strategies to find out what students think about a particular concept, to help them understand the concept, and to assess the accuracy of their understanding after learning the concept. These strategies were developed by Peter Rillero, Ph.D., Professor of Science Education at Arizona State University.

Correlation to **Benchmarks**

Glencoe Physical Science **address many of the Benchmarks for Science Literacy**

Benchmark	Chapter(s)
3 The Nature of Technology	
3A. Technology and Science	All Science and Technology Features
3B. Design and Systems	All Science and Technology Features
3A. Issues in Technology	All Science and Technology Features
4 The Physical Setting	
4D. Structure of Matter	16, 17, 18, 19, 20, 21, 22, 23, 24, 25
4E. Energy Transformation	4, 5, 6, 9, 10, 12, 13, 14, 15, 16, 19, 23, 24
4F. Motion	2, 3, 5, 11, 12
4G. Forces of Nature	3, 7, 8
8 The Designed World	
8B. Materials and Manufacturing	22
8C. Energy Sources and Use	6, 7, 8, 9, 10
10 Historical Perspectives All Science and History Features	
10C. Relating Matter and Energy and Time and Space	3, 4
10F. Understanding Fire	24
10G. Splitting the Atom	9, 18
10J. Harnessing Power	5, 7, 8, 9, 10
12 Habits of Mind	
12A. Values and Attitudes	1, All Science and Language Arts Features
12B. Computation and Estimation	All chapters, 1–25
12D. Communication Skills	All Activities and Skill Builders

Planning Your Course

Glencoe Physical Science **is a flexible program that allows you to decide the pace at which you cover the content and which topics to present, based on the needs of your students and on district requirements. The** ***Glencoe Interactive Lesson Planner*** **integrates the** ***Teacher Classroom Resources*** **with an electronic lesson planner to make your job easier.**

Pacing Options

Two approaches to covering all content are provided in the Planning Guide.

- A **traditional, full-year** course comprises 180 periods of approximately 45 minutes each.
- A **block scheduling** approach involves covering the same information in fewer days but in longer class periods.

Chapter Organizers

A two-page organizer (A–B pages) precedes every chapter in the teacher edition. These organizers include:

- pacing information and objectives.
- correlations to standards.
- lists of activities and the materials needed.
- lists of reproducible resources, assessments, and technologies with page or booklet references.

Interactive Lesson Planner

This easy-to-use CD-ROM allows you to:

- plan daily, weekly, monthly, or yearlong lessons in a versatile calendar format.
- select or customize a built-in plan, or make a new plan.
- print lesson plans.
- access all print components of the *Teacher Classroom Resources* through a convenient pop-up menu.
- print student pages and answer keys from the resource list or from the lesson plan.

Unit	Chapter/Section	Single-Class (180 days*)	Block (90 days*)
1	**Energy and Motion**	**40**	**20**
	1 The Nature of Physical Science	5	2
	2 Motion and Speed	7	4
	3 Forces	7	4
	4 Energy	7	4
	5 Work and Machines	7	3
	6 Thermal Energy	7	3
2	**Electricity and Energy Resources**	**30**	**15**
	7 Electricity	8	4
	8 Magnetism and Its Uses	9	4.5
	9 Radioactivity and Nuclear Reactions	7	3.5
	10 Energy Sources	6	3
3	**Energy on the Move**	**30**	**15**
	11 Waves	6	3
	12 Sound	6	3
	13 Electromagnetic Waves	6	3
	14 Light	6	3
	15 Mirrors and Lenses	6	3
4	**The Nature of Matter**	**35**	**17.5**
	16 Solids, Liquids, and Gases	10	5
	17 Classification of Matter	7	3.5
	18 Properties of Atoms and the Periodic Table	9	4.5
	19 Chemical Bonds	9	4.5
5	**Diversity of Matter**	**20**	**10**
	20 Elements and Their Properties	8	4
	21 Organic Compounds	8	4
	22 New Materials Through Chemistry	4	2
6	**Interactions of Matter**	**25**	**12.5**
	23 Solutions	8	4
	24 Chemical Reactions	8	4
	25 Acids, Bases, and Salts	9	4.5

**The suggested number of days are the recommended maximum number of days needed to thoroughly cover a chapter. Individual planning will vary.*

Student Edition Features

Glencoe Physical Science was designed so that the Science Processes TEKS are reinforced in _every_ chapter.

Feature	Location and Suggestions For Use
Design Your Own Experiment	• Find near end of chapter where concept is taught. • Promote inquiry learning through open-ended activities. • Reinforce understanding of scientific methods.
Use the Internet	• Find near end of chapter where concept is taught. • Strengthen skills in collecting, organizing, and sharing data. • Integrate the Internet into your class easily.
Model and Invent	• Find near end of chapter where concept is taught. • Reinforce the use of models to represent relationships or abstract ideas, and to predict outcomes. • Strengthen investigative skills.
Other Full-Length Activities	• Find near end of chapter where concept is taught. • Strengthen lab skills. • Reinforce understanding of science process
Mini LAB Try at Home Mini LAB	• Find in every chapter. • Do as a demonstration. • Involve parents in the student's learning. • Reinforce that science is not restricted to the classroom.
Explore Activity	• Find at beginning of each chapter. • Stimulate curiosity for the topic and focus students' attention.
Problem-Solving Skills Math Skills Activity	• Find one in every chapter at the point where the concept is taught. • Use after reading or other work to strengthen critical thinking and math skills.
Science Online	• Find in every chapter. • Focus students' Internet time with predetermined links.

Program Resources

Feature	Location and Suggestions For Use
Skill Builders	• Find at the end of every Section Assessment. • Assign as homework or class work.
Foldables Reading & Study Skills	• Find on every Chapter Opener and Chapter Study Guide. • Provide a purpose for reading with these fun, simple, hands-on activities. • Encourage students to use as a study tool for review of chapter content.
Interdisciplinary Connections	• Find one of these five features in every chapter.
Oops! Accidents in Science	• Stimulate students' interest by studying science-related events that are out of the ordinary.
Science and Language Arts	• Advance reading and writing skills through literature connected to science.
Science Stats	• Show students the fun side of mathematics and how it is an integral part of science.
TIME Science & History	• Illustrate how scientific phenomena, discoveries, and inventions shape history.
TIME Science & Society	• Connect science to people's everyday lives.
National Geographic Visualizing	• Find in every chapter. • Use the discussion and activities to teach science content.
Career Connection	• Find in every Science & Language Arts feature. • Point out that people of all ages, ethnicities, and training work in science.
Field Guide	• Find in the back of the student text. • Promote interest and independent study. • Teach students how to use a classification key.
Science, Technology, and Math Skill Handbooks	• Find at the back of the student and teacher editions. • Use to teach students scientific processes. • Use to teach students how to organize information. • Refer students to handbooks for assistance.

Teacher Wraparound Edition Features

This table will help you locate features of the Teacher Wraparound Edition that will help you develop your lesson plans.

Program Resources

Component	Where and How Many	What It Provides
Teacher to Teacher	Every Unit Opener	Teaching tip that relates to teaching unit content or activities.
Chapter Organizer	A and B pages preceding every chapter	• Objectives • Occurrence of activities and other features within each section • List of materials needed for each activity • List of materials from the *Teachers Classroom Resources* box • List of technology resources
Science Content Background	In every chapter on E page and F page where an Identifying Misconceptions feature does not appear	• Helps you prepare for the lesson by giving you more information about each section • Assists you with questions the students might ask
IDENTIFYING Misconceptions	F page of some chapters	Strategies to • determine misconceptions students may hold • promote understanding of concept • assess understanding
Key to Teaching Strategies	B page preceding every chapter	Coding to assist in planning for individual needs
Three-Step Teaching Cycle 1 Motivate 2 Teach 3 Assess	Every chapter	• Help for a first-year teacher • Help for experienced teacher in the first year in a new program
Resource Manager	C and D pages of every chapter Every two pages throughout each chapter	**C and D pages:** • List of transparencies • List of chapter teacher resources **Throughout chapter:** • List of reproducible resources • List of technology resources
Activity	Throughout all chapters in side wrap	Reinforces science concepts

Component	Where and How Many	What It Provides
Quick Demo	Throughout all chapters in side wrap	Idea to illustrate a concept; performed in a short amount of time, using available materials
LAB DEMONSTRATION	Throughout all chapters in bottom wrap	Teacher-performed activity, more complex than Quick Demo, often involving students
Extension	Throughout all chapters in side wrap	An activity idea for: • more advanced students • students who finish their work early • students who want to learn more about the topic
Teacher FYI	Throughout all chapters in side wrap	Additional information about a concept
Visual Learning	Throughout all chapters in side and bottom wrap	Idea for discussion or activity related to a graphic
Fun Fact	Throughout all chapters in side and bottom wrap	Interesting science content to share with students
Make a Model	Throughout all chapters in side wrap	Idea for model that students can make to clarify or illustrate abstract concepts
Use an Analogy	Throughout all chapters in side wrap	Way to make abstract concepts more concrete
Curriculum Connection	Throughout all chapters in bottom wrap	Way that science ties in with other curricular areas
Cultural Diversity	Throughout all chapters in bottom wrap	Current or historical background on a custom or belief associated with a science concept
Use Science Words	Throughout all chapters in side wrap	Strategies for students to learn word origins, meanings, and uses
Active Reading Strategies	Throughout all chapters in bottom wrap	Strategies to help students read and understand content
Science Journal	Throughout all chapters in bottom wrap	Writing exercises that promote writing and critical thinking skills
Assessment **Section Assessment** **Chapter Assessment** **Assessment Resources**	 First page of every section Chapter Assessment page Chapter Assessment page	• Location of Portfolio, Performance, and Content Assessments in the section • Ideas for Portfolio and Performance Assessments • List of Reproducible Masters, CD-ROMs, and other technologies for assessment

Program Resources

Glencoe Science is also online at mhln.com

The Interactive E-Textbook that will change the way you teach!

The McGraw-Hill Learning network is an online learning space connecting parents, teachers, and students.

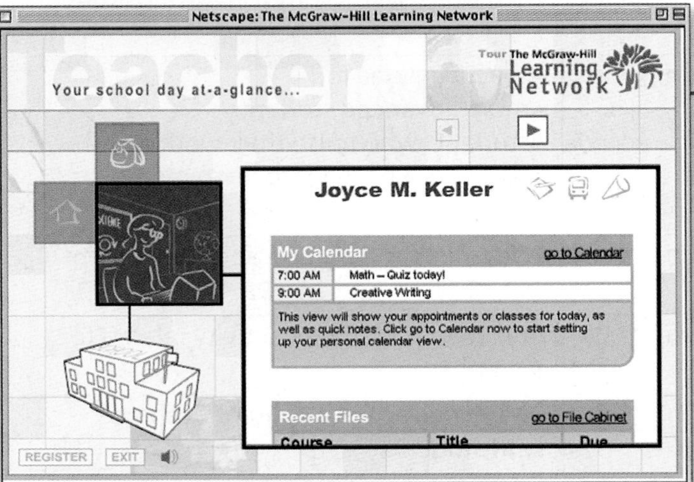

For Teachers

- Online Lesson Planner
- Calendar/Class Organizer
- Assignment Creator (Teachers can create, grade and send assignments to students.)
- Grade Book/Class Roster
- And much more . . .

There's a ton of helpful tools such as a website builder and thousands of educational weblinks.

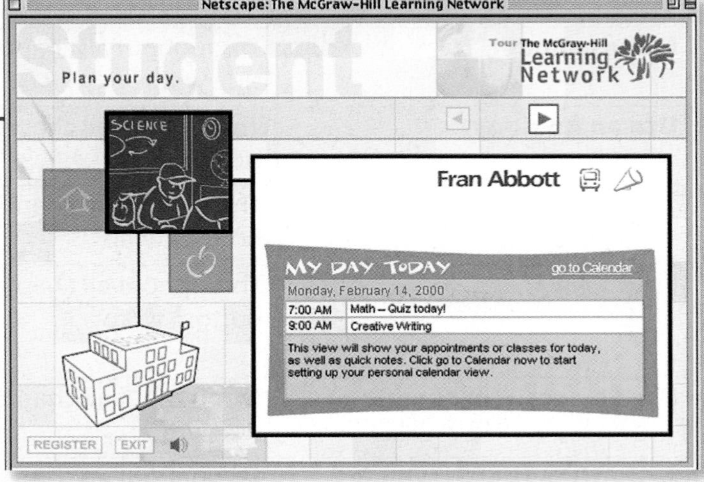

For Students

- Interactive games
- 24–hour homework help
- Online planner
- Instant feedback with diagnostic assessments
- Unlimited practice
- And much more . . . including movies, animations, sound, weblinks, and an online encyclopedia

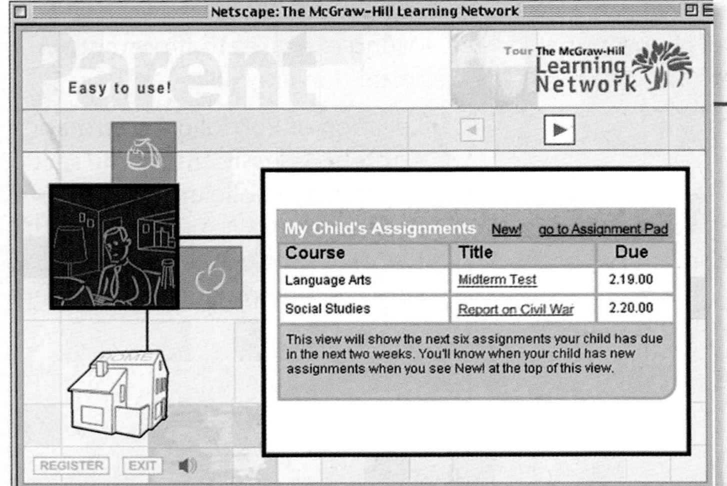

For Parents

- Tips to help their child succeed in school
- Instant access to textbooks, homework assignments, and progress

Online Science

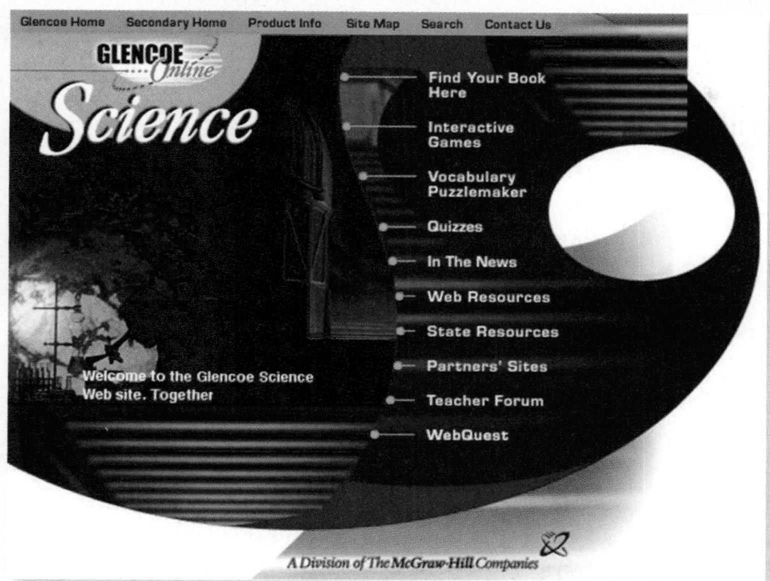

The Glencoe Science Web site is an invaluable resource for all teachers and students.

Teachers can:

- share ideas on Teacher Bulletin Board.
- access current scientific information on your textbooks updates.

Students can:

- access previewed web links.
- record information on printable Internet log worksheets.
- review chapter content with the Interactive Tutor.
- prepare for tests using Interactive Quizzes.
- share data with students worldwide using our exclusive Internet Activities.

Interactive Explorations, Quizzes, and Presentation CD-ROM Program

Provides students the opportunity to:

- develop hypotheses.
- manipulate variables.
- build presentations.
- review content.
- think critically.

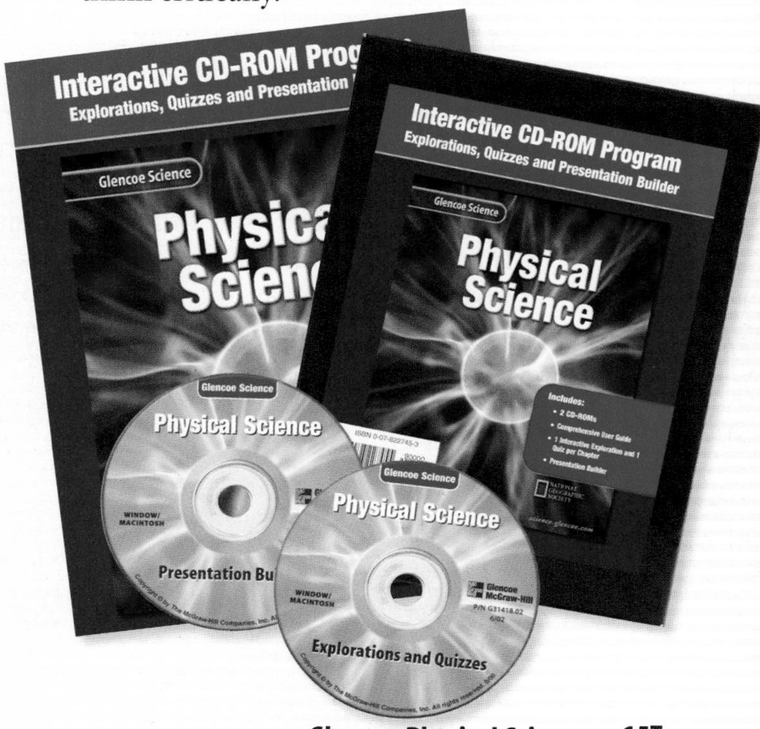

Program Resources

ExamView Pro Computer TestMaker Software

You can design and create your own test instruments in minutes, using Glencoe Physical Science ExamView Pro Testmaker software. This versatile program allows you to create paper tests as well as tests that can be used on your school LAN system, or posted on your class Web site. Choose and edit questions from a question bank, or write your own.

Interactive Lesson Planner

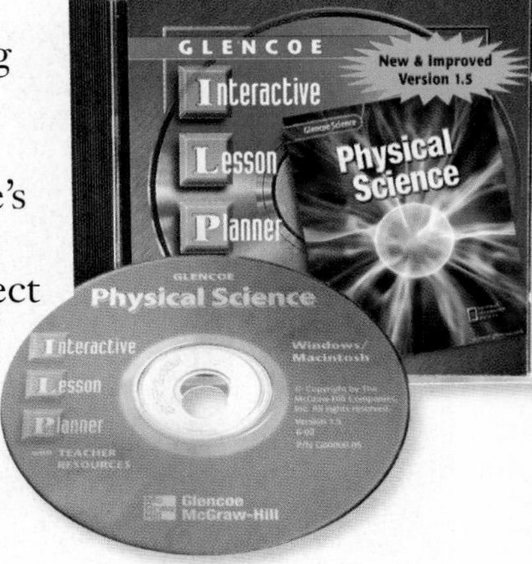

Need help planning your lessons and organizing you resources? Glencoe's Interactive Lesson Planner is the perfect solution. All you need to do is to identify your length of course and number of class days and the program automatically places all the materials available for each day for each chapter into the calendar. Every page of your Teacher Classroom Resources are available to you at the click of a mouse.

Interactive Teacher Edition

Imagine having your entire Teacher Edition and all your Teacher Classroom Resources available to you on one CD-ROM. That is what the Interactive Teacher Edition provides for you. The program allows you to view all teacher material and the student text on your computer screen. You can export all worksheet masters to your own word processor for editing.

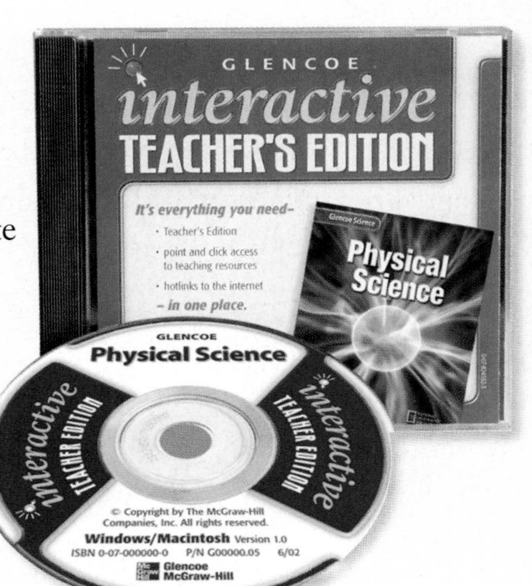

MindJogger Videoquizzes

The interactive quiz-show format of the Glencoe Physical Science Mindjogger Videoquizzes provides fun for your students while reviewing key concepts for every chapter. The three levels of increasing difficulty add to the drama and excitement of the game, and help you assess your students' understanding of the concepts.

Guided Reading Audio Program

English/Spanish

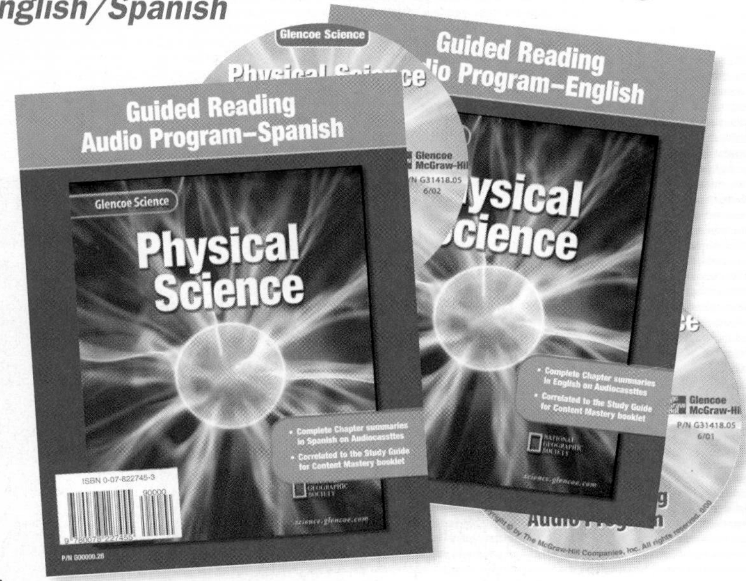

Complete chapter text read in English and Spanish provides another way for students who are auditory learners, or for ELL students, to access chapter content. Students can listen individually in class or at home. They can also choose to read along with their texts to improve reading skills. Tie to the Directed Reading for Content Mastery in the *Chapter Resources* booklets to give students a way to check their understanding of the material. The Guided Reading program is provided in CD format.

Vocabulary PuzzleMaker Software

This software program allows you to create crossword puzzles, jumble puzzles, or word searches in minutes to review chapter vocabulary. The puzzles can be printed or played on the computer screen.

Teacher Classroom Resources

Chapter Resources

We've organized all of the materials you need for each chapter into chapter-based booklets. The cover of each booklet becomes a file folder to help you stay organized.

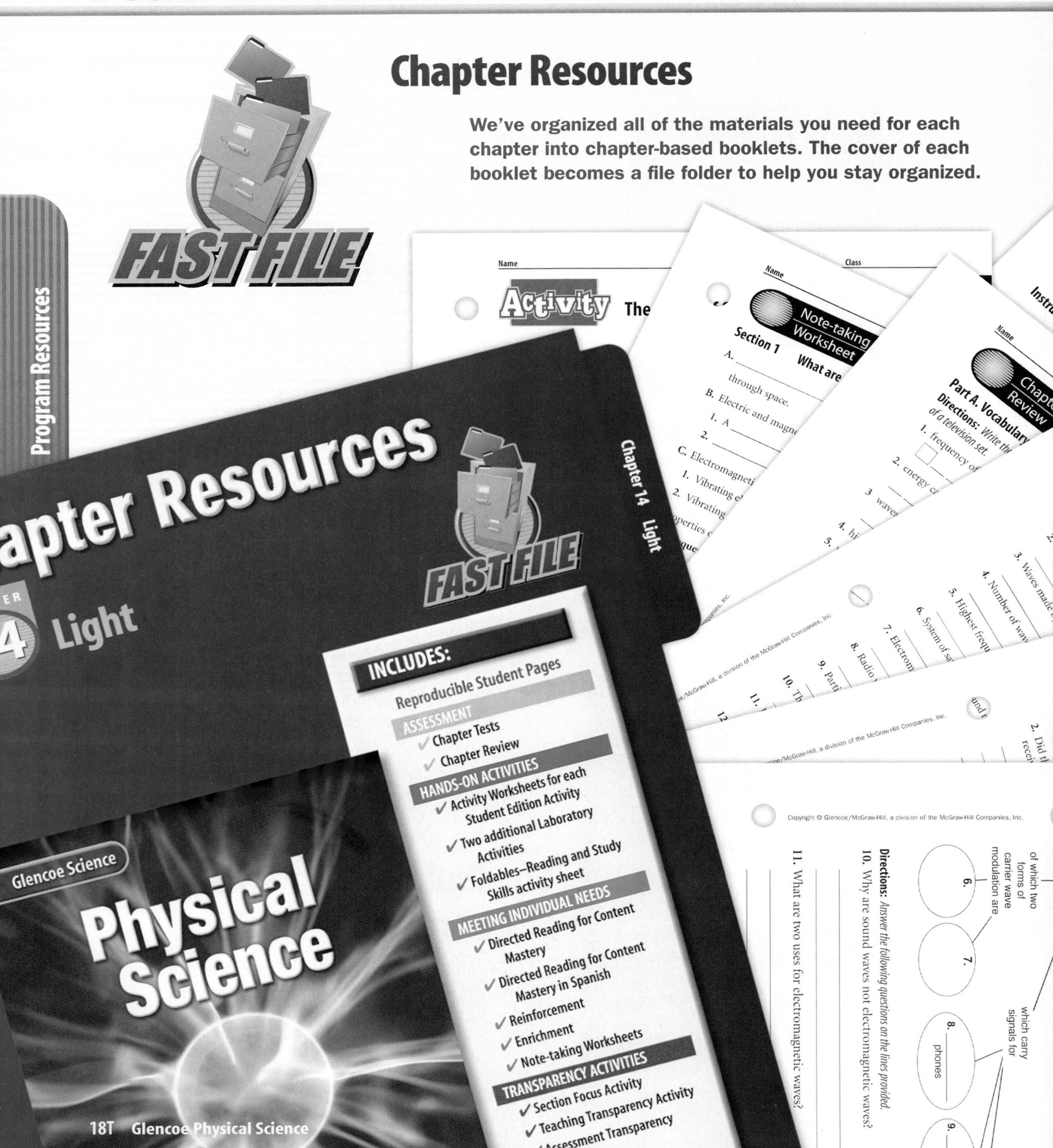

Reproducible Student Pages

Assessment
- Chapter Review
- Chapter Test

Hands-On Activities
- Activity Worksheets for each activity in the *Student Edition*
- Two additional laboratory activities
- Foldables: Reading and Study Skills

Meeting Individual Needs
- Extension and Intervention
- Directed Reading for Content Mastery
- Directed Reading for Content Mastery *in Spanish*
- Reinforcement
- Enrichment
- Note-taking Worksheets

Transparency Activities
- Section Focus Activity
- Teaching Transparency Activity
- Assessment Transparency Activity

Teacher Support and Planning
- Content Outline for Teaching
- Spanish Resources
- Teacher Guide and Answers

Program Resources

Additional Resources

These resources are available as stand-alone booklets to give you the flexibility to decide when to use them.

Transparencies

Section Focus Transparencies
Teaching Transparencies
Assessment Transparencies

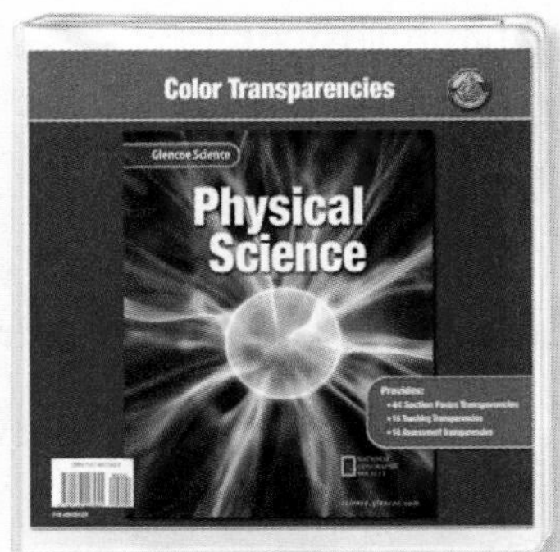

Content Outlines for Teaching

Lesson Plans

Laboratory Activities *SE*

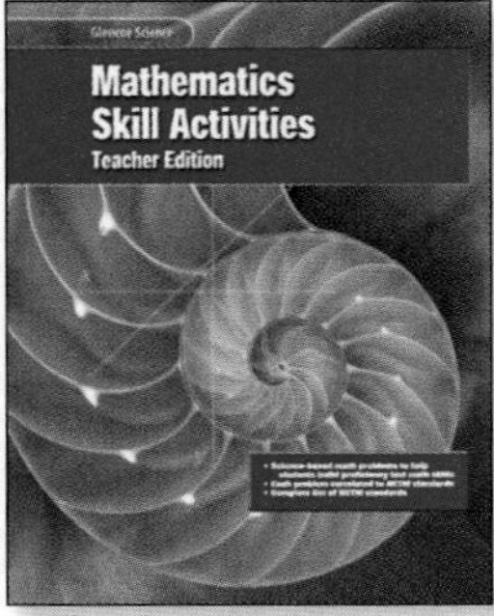

Math Skills Activities *(SE and TE)*

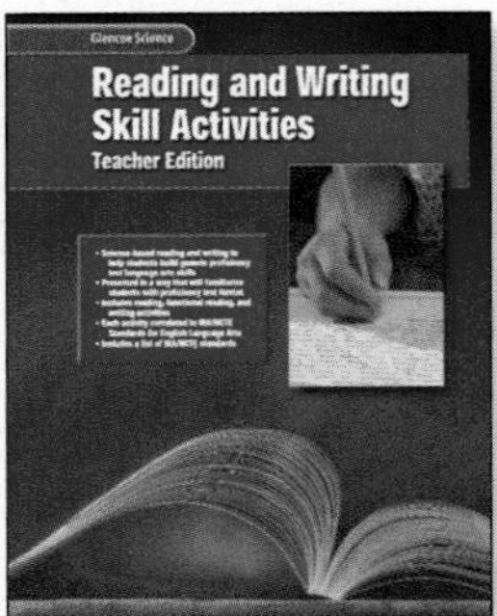

Reading and Writing Skills Activities *(SE and TE)*

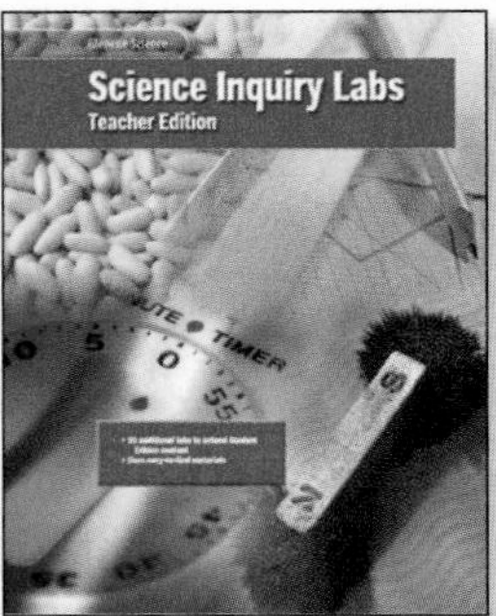

Science Inquiry Labs *(SE and TE)*

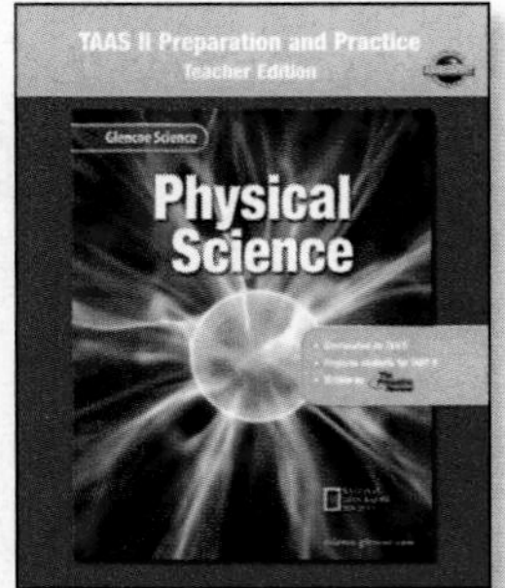

Standardized Test Practice *(SE and TE)*

Critical Thinking/ Problem Solving

Physical Science

Home and Community Involvement

Laboratory Management and Safety

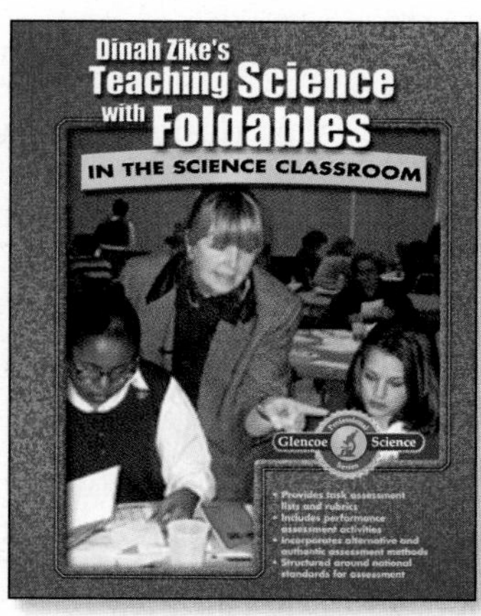

Dinah Zike's Teaching Science with Foldables

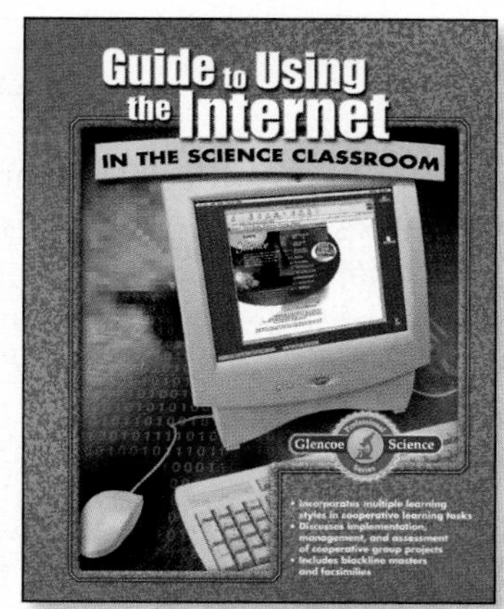

Guide to Using the Internet in the Science Classroom

Cooperative Learning

Cultural Diversity

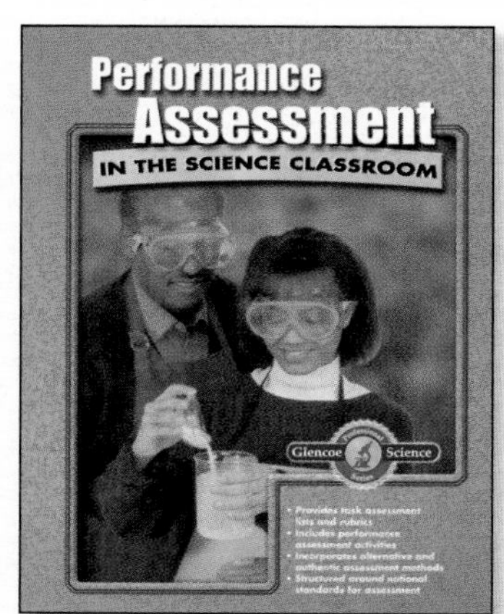

Performance Assessment in the Science Classroom

Program Resources

Meeting Individual Needs

Each student brings his or her unique set of abilities, perceptions, and needs into the classroom. *Glencoe Physical Science Teacher Wraparound Edition* offers you a variety of strategies so that your students can learn science concepts through many different methods.

Strategy	Designation
Ability Levels Activities are provided that accommodate students of all ability levels.	L1 Basic activities that reinforce the concepts for lower-ability students L2 Application activities that give all students an opportunity for practical application of concepts L3 Challenging activities that allow students to expand their perspectives on the basic concepts
English-Language Learners These strategies focus on overcoming a language barrier. It is important not to confuse ability in speaking/reading English with academic ability or "intelligence."	ELL These activities reinforce content and aid in the development of science vocabulary.
Learning Styles A variety of instructional strategies help students to learn science concepts through their preferred learning styles. Students generally display more than one of these styles. You may want to assign activities to students that accommodate their strongest learning styles, but assign other activities that help to develop their weaker styles.	LS Look for these bold-faced designations wherever you see this logo: • **Kinesthetic** learners learn through touch, movement, and manipulating objects. • **Visual-Spatial** learners think in terms of images, illustrations, and models. • **Logical-Mathematical** learners understand numbers easily and have highly-developed reasoning skills. • **Linguistic** learners write clearly and easily understand the written word. • **Auditory-Musical** learners remember spoken words and can create rhythms and melodies. • **Interpersonal** learners understand and work well with other people. • **Intrapersonal** learners can analyze their own strengths and weaknesses and may prefer to work on their own.

Strategy	Designation
Inclusion Strategies Inclusion strategies provide you with additional support for helping students with special needs.	Look for these bold-faced designations and strategies wherever you see the **Inclusion** Strategies • **Learning Disabled**—ideas for additional concept review • **Behaviorally Disordered**—activities for helping to keep students on task • **Physically Challenged**—tips for adjusting activities to accommodate students who have less mobility or dexterity than others • **Visually Impaired** or **Hearing Impaired**—ideas for aiding these students in grasping concepts • **Gifted**—challenging activities and research projects that extend chapter concepts
Cooperative Learning In cooperative learning, students work together in small groups to learn content and interpersonal skills. Group members learn that each is responsible for accomplishing an assigned group task as well as for learning the material. Cooperative learning fosters academic, personal, and social success for all students.	COOP LEARN Strategies with this designation are suitable for group work that will help students to: • develop positive attitudes toward science and school; • build respect for others, regardless of race, ethnic origin, or gender; and • increase their sensitivity to and tolerance of diverse perspectives.
Cultural Diversity Classrooms in the United States reflect the rich and diverse cultural heritage of the American people. Students come from different ethnic backgrounds and different cultural experiences into a common classroom that must assist all of them in learning.	Cultural **Diversity** The Cultural Diversity features provide insights into unique ways in which different people have approached science or adapted to their environments. The intent of these features is to build awareness and appreciation for the global community in which we live.
Misconceptions Students have had many experiences outside the science classroom that have shaped their understandings of the natural world. Unfortunately, interpretations based on casual observation are not always accurate. For example, based on their observations, some students might think that the Sun moves around Earth. As a science teacher, you need strategies to help replace these naive conceptions with scientific facts.	IDENTIFYING **Misconceptions** This one-page feature provides ideas about the types of misconceptions your students may have. It provides you with teaching strategies to uncover misconceptions and to help students understand concepts. You can find these preceding many chapters on the F interleaf pages of the Teacher Wraparound Edition. In addition, you will find several misconceptions stated, followed by the correct information, in the teacher wrap throughout each chapter.

Reading and Writing in the Content Area

***Glencoe Physical Science* is designed to increase science literacy through improving reading comprehension and deepening students' understanding of ideas and concepts. The reading strategies are active, constructive, and engaging.**

In the Student Edition

Pre-Reading Activities on each Unit Opener prepare students to read by helping them focus on important content before reading and studying the chapter. Previewing the chapters' visuals, questions, vocabulary, and captions will set a purpose for reading the material for all students.

> **Pre-Reading Activity**
>
> Have students read the objectives for each section, and search for charts and pictures that relate to each objective.

Reading Checks throughout each chapter stimulate quick recall to keep students focused on main ideas and important details.

> **Reading Check**
>
> *What type of chemical reaction is burning?*

The Before You Read and After You Read Activities in every chapter set a purpose for reading and help students to construct a graphic organizer to use for learning content and as a study aide.

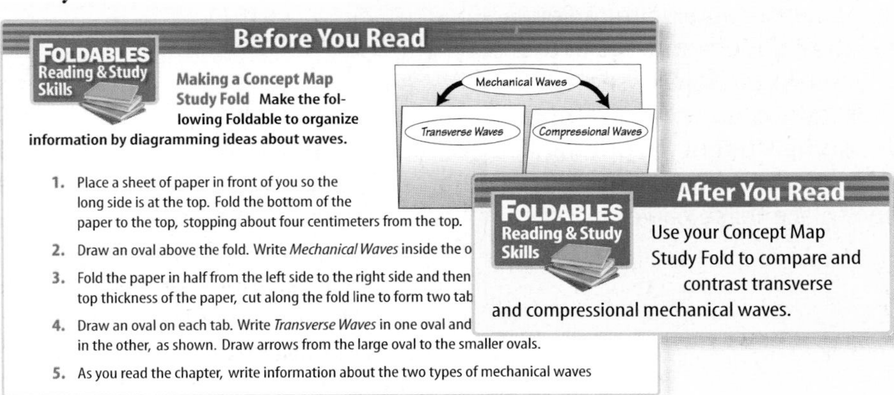

Before You Read
FOLDABLES Reading & Study Skills
Making a Concept Map Study Fold Make the following Foldable to organize information by diagramming ideas about waves.
Mechanical Waves
Transverse Waves
Compressional Waves
1. Place a sheet of paper in front of you so the long side is at the top. Fold the bottom of the paper to the top, stopping about four centimeters from the top.
2. Draw an oval above the fold. Write Mechanical Waves inside the o
3. Fold the paper in half from the left side to the right side and then top thickness of the paper, cut along the fold line to form two tab
4. Draw an oval on each tab. Write Transverse Waves in one oval and in the other, as shown. Draw arrows from the large oval to the smaller ovals.
5. As you read the chapter, write information about the two types of mechanical waves
After You Read
FOLDABLES Reading & Study Skills
Use your Concept Map Study Fold to compare and contrast transverse and compressional mechanical waves.

Skill Builder Activities in each Section Assessment often include questions that directly address reading and writing skills. Students are referred to the *Science Skill Handbook* for help.

> **Communicating** Watch carefully as you travel home from school or walk down your street. What examples of wave reflection and refraction do you notice? Describe each of these in your Science Journal and explain your reasons. **For more help, refer to the** Science Skill Handbook.

Caption Questions throughout each chapter help students to comprehend what they have read through interpreting the visual. This is especially useful for less proficient readers.

> **Figure 6**
>
> **After a golf ball is thrown, it follows a curved path toward the ground.** *How does this curved path show that the ball is accelerating?*

Support for All Learners

Print and **Technology Resources** to Promote **Reading** and **Writing** in the Content Area

Ancillaries

Chapter Resources

- Directed Reading for Content Mastery pages *(in English and Spanish)*
- Foldables: Reading and Study Skills Worksheets
- Note-taking Worksheets

Dinah Zike's Teaching Science with Foldables

Reading and Writing Skill Activities

Technology

Guided Reading Audio Program *(English and Spanish)*

MindJogger VideoQuizzes

Interactive CD-ROM

Vocabulary PuzzleMaker

Glencoe Science Online

Glencoe Exclusive

Foldables: Improving Reading and Study Skills

Students love Foldables because they're fun. Teachers love them because they're effective.

What is a Foldable?

FOLDABLES Reading & Study Skills

Foldables are three-dimensional, interactive graphic organizers. As students fold paper, cut tabs, write, and manipulate what they have made, they are kinesthetically involved in learning. These unique, hands-on tools for studying and reviewing were created exclusively for Glencoe Science by teaching specialist Dinah Zike.

Foldables are Useful!

Reading in the Content Area

Foldables help students develop ways of organizing information that are fun and creative. These useful activities help students practice basic writing skills, find and report main ideas, organize information, review key vocabulary terms, and much more!

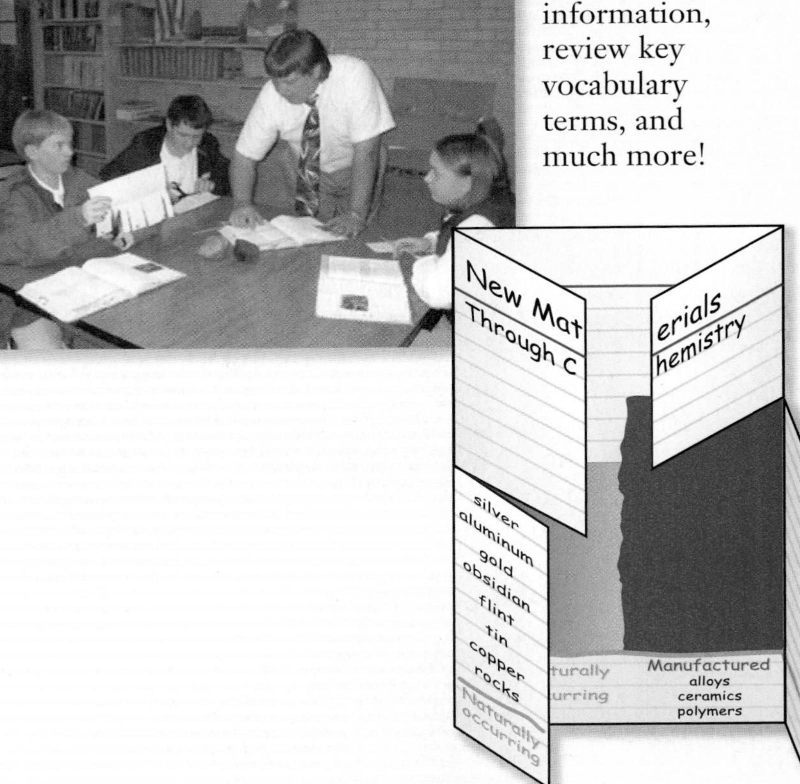

Every chapter begins with a Foldable activity. Students make the physical structure of a Foldable that incorporates one of many prereading strategies. Then, as students read through the chapter and do the activities, students record information as they learn it in the appropriate part of the foldable. In the Chapter Study Guide, the After You Read feature gives students a strategy for using the fold they made to help them review the chapter concepts.

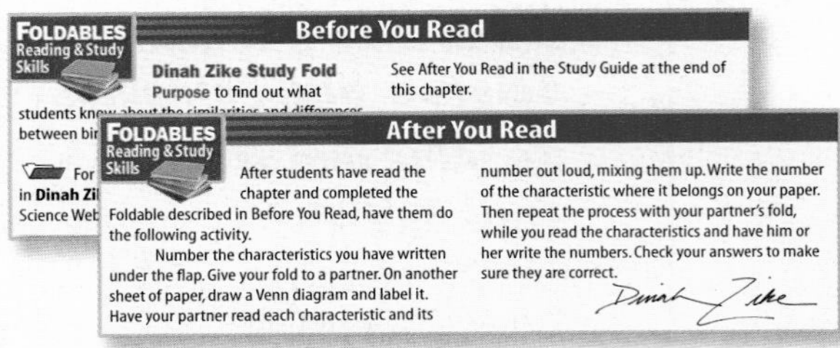

FOLDABLES Reading & Study Skills

Before You Read

Dinah Zike Study Fold

Purpose to find out what students kn[...] between bir[...]

For [...] in **Dinah Zi**[...] Science Web[...]

See After You Read in the Study Guide at the end of this chapter.

FOLDABLES Reading & Study Skills

After You Read

After students have read the chapter and completed the Foldable described in Before You Read, have them do the following activity.

Number the characteristics you have written under the flap. Give your fold to a partner. On another sheet of paper, draw a Venn diagram and label it. Have your partner read each characteristic and its number out loud, mixing them up. Write the number of the characteristic where it belongs on your paper. Then repeat the process with your partner's fold, while you read the characteristics and have him or her write the numbers. Check your answers to make sure they are correct.

Dinah Zike

Review One advantage of Foldables is that they result in an organized study guide. The Foldables then can be used not only while preparing for the chapter test, but they can also be used for reviewing for unit tests, end of course exams, and even standardized tests.

Assessment Foldables present an ideal opportunity for you to probe the depth of your students' knowledge. You'll get detailed feedback on exactly what they know and what misconceptions they may have.

Foldables are Easy!

Anyone who has paper, scissors, and maybe a stapler or some glue can implement Foldables in the classroom. Glencoe's Foldables have been tested with teachers and middle school students to make sure the directions are easy for both students and teachers. After doing a couple of them, your class will quickly become seasoned experts. Don't be surprised if you find them inventing their own for use in projects and reports in all of their classes!

A message from **the creator of Foldables,** Dinah Zike

You might not know my name or me, but I bet you have seen at least one of my graphic organizers or folds used in supplemental programs or teacher workshops. Today, my graphic organizers and manipulatives are used internationally. I present workshops and keynote presentations to over 50,000 teachers a year, sharing the manipulatives I began inventing, designing, and adapting over thirty years ago. Around the world, students of all ages are using them as daily work, note-taking activities, student-directed projects, forms of alternative assessment, science lab journals, quantitative and qualitative observation books, graphs, tables, and more. But through all my years of teaching, designing, and publishing, my materials had never been featured in a middle school textbook. When Glencoe/McGraw-Hill approached me to share some of my three-dimensional, manipulative graphic organizers with you in this new and innovative science series, I was thrilled.

Working with Glencoe, we all had the vision that Foldables should be an integral part of the curriculum, not simply tacked on. What we ended up with was a strategy that will help students read and learn science concepts. One of the advantages of using the same manipulative repeatedly is that students are immersed in what they are learning. It is not out of sight and out of mind. How long is your average student actively involved with a duplicated activity sheet? Ten minutes? Fifteen? Students will use the Foldable at the beginning of each chapter, before reading the chapter, during reading, and after reading. That's a lot of immersion!

Dinah Zike

Reading and Writing in the Content Area

In the Teacher Edition

Science & Language Arts

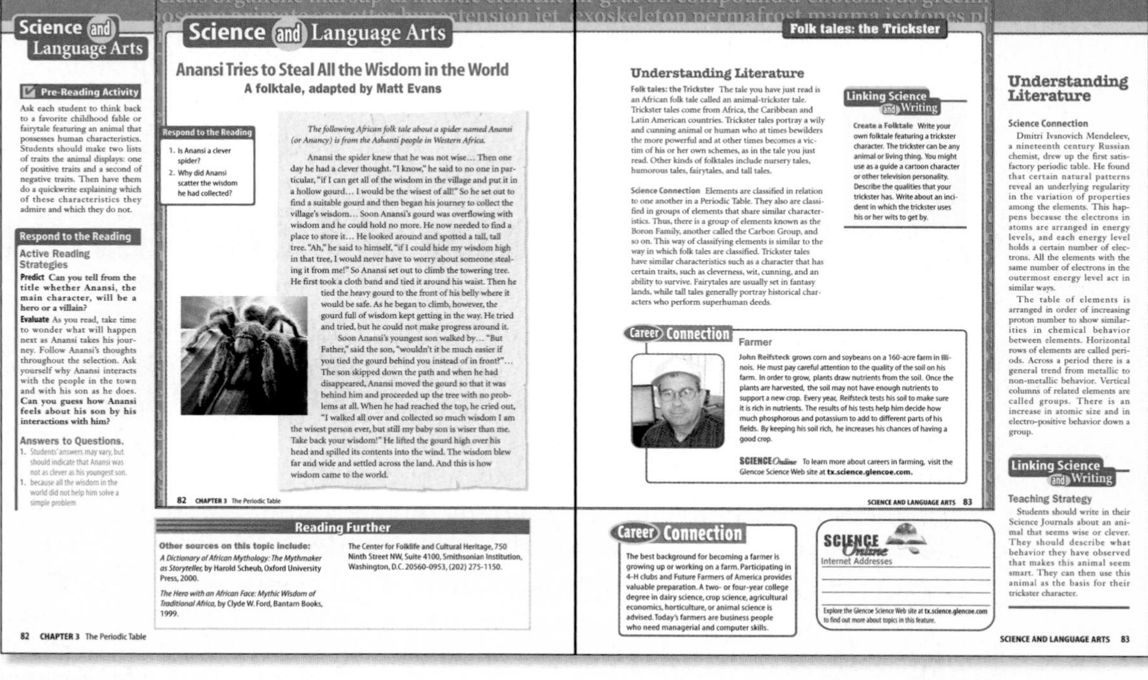

Science and Language Arts

Pre-Reading Activity

Ask each student to think back to a favorite childhood fable or fairytale featuring an animal that possesses human characteristics. Students should make two lists of traits the animal displays: one of positive traits and a second of negative traits. Then have them do a quickwrite explaining which of these characteristics they admire and which they do not.

Respond to the Reading

Active Reading Strategies

Predict **Can you tell from the title whether Anansi, the main character, will be a hero or a villain?**

Evaluate As you read, take time to wonder what will happen next as Anansi takes his journey. Follow Anansi's thoughts throughout the selection. Ask yourself why Anansi interacts with the people in the town and with his son as he does. **Can you guess how Anansi feels about his son by his interactions with him?**

Answers to Questions.

1. Students' answers may vary, but should indicate that Anansi was not as clever as his youngest son.
1. because all the wisdom in the world did not help him solve a simple problem

Science and Language Arts

Anansi Tries to Steal All the Wisdom in the World

A folktale, adapted by Matt Evans

Respond to the Reading

1. Is Anansi a clever spider?
2. Why did Anansi scatter the wisdom he had collected?

The following African folk tale about a spider named Anansi (or Anancy) is from the Ashanti people in Western Africa.

Anansi the spider knew that he was not wise… Then one day he had a clever thought. "I know," he said to no one in particular, "if I can get all of the wisdom in the village and put it in a hollow gourd… I would be the wisest of all!" So he set out to find a suitable gourd and then began his journey to collect the village's wisdom… Soon Anansi's gourd was overflowing with wisdom and he could hold no more. He now needed to find a place to store it… He looked around and spotted a tall, tall tree. "Ah," he said to himself, "if I could hide my wisdom high in that tree, I would never have to worry about someone stealing it from me!" So Anansi set out to climb the towering tree. He first took a cloth band and tied it around his waist. Then he tied the heavy gourd to the front of his belly where it would be safe. As he began to climb, however, the gourd full of wisdom kept getting in the way. He tried and tried, but he could not make progress around it.

Soon Anansi's youngest son walked by… "But Father," said the son, "wouldn't it be much easier if you tied the gourd behind you instead of in front?"… The son skipped down the path and when he had disappeared, Anansi moved the gourd so that it was behind him and proceeded up the tree with no problems at all. When he had reached the top, he cried out, "I walked all over and collected so much wisdom I am the wisest person ever, but still my baby son is wiser than me. Take back your wisdom!" He lifted the gourd high over his head and spilled its contents into the wind. The wisdom blew far and wide and settled across the land. And this is how wisdom came to the world.

82 CHAPTER 3 The Periodic Table

Reading Further

Other sources on this topic include:

A Dictionary of African Mythology: The Mythmaker as Storyteller, by Harold Scheub, Oxford University Press, 2000.

The Hero with an African Face: Mythic Wisdom of Traditional Africa, by Clyde W. Ford, Bantam Books, 1999.

The Center for Folklife and Cultural Heritage, 750 Ninth Street NW, Suite 4100, Smithsonian Institution, Washington, D.C. 20560-0953, (202) 275-1150.

82 CHAPTER 3 The Periodic Table

Folk tales: the Trickster

Understanding Literature

Folk tales: the Trickster The tale you have just read is an African folk tale called an animal-trickster tale. Trickster tales come from Africa, the Caribbean and Latin American countries. Trickster tales portray a wily and cunning animal or human who at times bewilders the more powerful and at other times becomes a victim of his or her own schemes, as in the tale you just read. Other kinds of folktales include nursery tales, humorous tales, fairytales, and tall tales.

Science Connection Elements are classified in relation to one another in a Periodic Table. They also are classified in groups of elements that share similar characteristics. Thus, there is a group of elements known as the Boron Family, another called the Carbon Group, and so on. This way of classifying elements is similar to the way in which folk tales are classified. Trickster tales have similar characteristics such as a character that has certain traits, such as cleverness, wit, cunning, and an ability to survive. Fairytales are usually set in fantasy lands, while tall tales generally portray historical characters who perform superhuman deeds.

Linking Science and Writing

Create a Folktale Write your own folktale featuring a trickster character. The trickster can be any animal or living thing. You might use as a guide a cartoon character or other television personality. Describe the qualities that your trickster has. Write about an incident in which the trickster uses his or her wits to get by.

Career Connection

Farmer

John Reifsteck grows corn and soybeans on a 160-acre farm in Illinois. He must pay careful attention to the quality of the soil on his farm. In order to grow, plants draw nutrients from the soil. Once the plants are harvested, the soil may not have enough nutrients to support a new crop. Every year, Reifsteck tests his soil to make sure it is rich in nutrients. The results of his tests help him decide how much phosphorous and potassium to add to different parts of his fields. By keeping his soil rich, he increases his chances of having a good crop.

SCIENCE *Online* To learn more about careers in farming, visit the Glencoe Science Web site at **tx.science.glencoe.com.**

SCIENCE AND LANGUAGE ARTS 83

Career Connection

The best background for becoming a farmer is growing up or working on a farm. Participating in 4-H clubs and Future Farmers of America provides valuable preparation. A two- or four-year college degree in dairy science, crop science, agricultural economics, horticulture, or animal science is advised. Today's farmers are business people who need managerial and computer skills.

SCIENCE *Online*

Internet Addresses

Explore the Glencoe Science Web site at tx.science.glencoe.com to find out more about topics in this feature.

Understanding Literature

Science Connection

Dmitri Ivanovich Mendeleev, a nineteenth century Russian chemist, drew up the first satisfactory periodic table. He found that certain natural patterns reveal an underlying regularity in the variation of properties among the elements. This happens because the electrons in atoms are arranged in energy levels, and each energy level holds a certain number of electrons. All the elements with the same number of electrons in the outermost energy level act in similar ways.

The table of elements is arranged in order of increasing proton number to show similarities in chemical behavior between elements. Horizontal rows of elements are called periods. Across a period there is a general trend from metallic to non-metallic behavior. Vertical columns of related elements are called groups. There is an increase in atomic size and in electro-positive behavior down a group.

Linking Science and Writing

Teaching Strategy

Students should write in their Science Journals about an animal that seems wise or clever. They should describe what behavior they have observed that makes this animal seem smart. They can then use this animal as the basis for their trickster character.

SCIENCE AND LANGUAGE ARTS 83

Pre-Reading Activity helps students draw upon their personal experience and sets a purpose for reading.

Respond to the Reading provides active reading strategies that provide a variety of ways for students to respond to the feature through listening, speaking, and writing activities. It also provides students with an opportunity to make connections to the theme.

Linking Science and Writing provides options that all students can use to respond in writing to the feature.

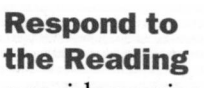

Use Science Words

Word Usage The distinction between distance and displacement can be confusing. Have students use each of these words correctly in a sentence. Possible response: When I go to school and then back home, my displacement is zero, even though the distance from home to school is 2 km. L2 LS **Linguistic**

Use Science Words appears throughout each chapter and provides three types of reading strategies. Students structurally analyze root words (Word Origin), develop vocabulary (Word Meaning), or apply their knowledge of science terms (Word Usage).

Science Journal

Cathode-Ray Tube Ask students to pretend that they are coworkers with Crookes at the time of his experiments with a cathode-ray tube. Have students write letters in their Science Journals to a fellow scientist telling about the exciting results they obtained and how they interpreted the results. L2 LS **Linguistic**

Science Journals throughout each chapter provide opportunities for students to write responses to questions that require critical thinking; to conduct research and write about it; or to practice creative writing skills.

Active Reading Strategies

A variety of active reading strategies are provided throughout the *Teacher Wraparound Edition*. These strategies utilize a variety of learning styles, and encourage cooperative learning and intrapersonal reflection on chapter content.

Active Reading

Think-Pair Share This strategy encourages students to think first before discussing their ideas or thoughts about a topic. Ask students to respond to a question by writing a response. After thinking for a few minutes, partners share responses to the question. Finally, ask the students to share responses with the class. Have students become involved in a Think-Pair Share about cathode rays.

Making Concept Maps and Charts

Bubble Map Students brainstorm and organize words in clusters to describe concepts.

Double-Bubble Map Students compare concepts using two bubble maps.

Flow Chart Students logically analyze and draw a sequence of events.

Cause and Effect Chart Students visually represent the causes and effects of an event or process.

Supporting Idea Chart Students make a concept map to analyze the relationship between a whole and its parts.

Using the Science Journal

Double Entry Journal Students read and record ideas, then reflect on the text and respond to the ideas.

Metacognition Students analyze what and how they have learned.

Learning Journal Students write and reflect on notes about content.

Problem-Solution Journal Students analyze problems and suggest workable solutions.

Speculation About Effects/ Prediction Journal Students examine events and speculate about their possible long-term effects.

Synthesis Journal Students reflect on a project, a paper, or a performance task and plan how to apply what they have learned to their own lives.

Reflective Journal Students identify what they learned in an activity and record responses.

Quickwrites Students use spontaneous writing to discover what they already know.

Collaborative Learning Strategies

Pair of Pairs Partners respond to a question and compare their response to that of other pairs and to the class.

Write-Draw-Discuss Students write about and draw a picture of a concept, then share it with the class.

Four-Corner Discussion The class works in four groups to debate a complex issue.

Jigsaw Students work in groups to become experts on a portion of text and share their expertise with their "home" group.

Buddy Interviews Students interview one another to find out what helps them to understand what they are reading.

Reciprocal Teaching Students take turns reading the text and retelling it in their own words, then asking one another questions.

News Summary Students are given several minutes to summarize, retell, or analyze an activity for a "TV" audience.

ReQuest The teacher reads aloud an article or story. Student pairs then construct discussion questions and review the content.

Concept Maps

Helping students understand concepts through visuals

Concept maps are visual representations or graphic organizers of relationships among particular concepts. Concept maps can be generated by individual students, small groups, or an entire class. Four types of concept maps that are most applicable to studying science are developed and reinforced in this program. Students can learn how to construct each of these types of concept maps by referring to the Skill Handbook in the ***Student Edition.***

Concept maps can be used to increase understanding of science concepts, to strengthen reading skills, to promote cooperative learning, and to assess learning. When evaluating concept maps, look for the conceptual strength of student responses, not absolute accuracy.

- **Science Concepts** Concept mapping helps students to understand science concepts through analyzing relationships among ideas and reinforcing those relationships by visualizing them.
- **Reading Skills** Concept maps can help students preview a chapter's content by visually relating the concepts to be learned and aiding students to read with purpose. Students learn key science terms by choosing the terms to use, supplying connecting words, or by placing terms and connecting words when provided by the teacher. To further develop concept mapping skills, the *Chapter Resources* booklet for each chapter contains concept maps in the reproducible student pages Directed Reading for Content Mastery.
- **Cooperative Learning** Construction of concept maps using cooperative learning strategies allows students to practice interpersonal skills as they work together to build the map.
- **Review and Assessment** As a review, constructing concept maps reinforces main ideas and clarifies their relationships. As an assessment tool, concept maps can be constructed by students or students can fill in the terms. Look for concept mapping assessment in the Chapter Assessment section of every chapter.

Network Tree

- Order information from general to specific.
- Show a hierarchy.
- Use branching procedures.
- Explain relationships with connecting terms.

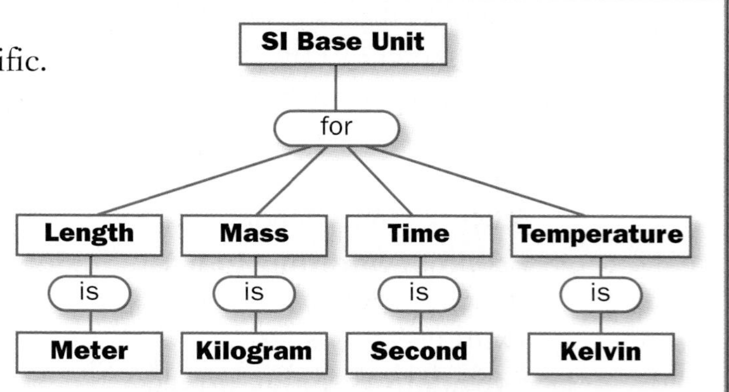

Support for All Learners

Events Chain

- Describe the stages of a process.
- Order the steps in a linear procedure.

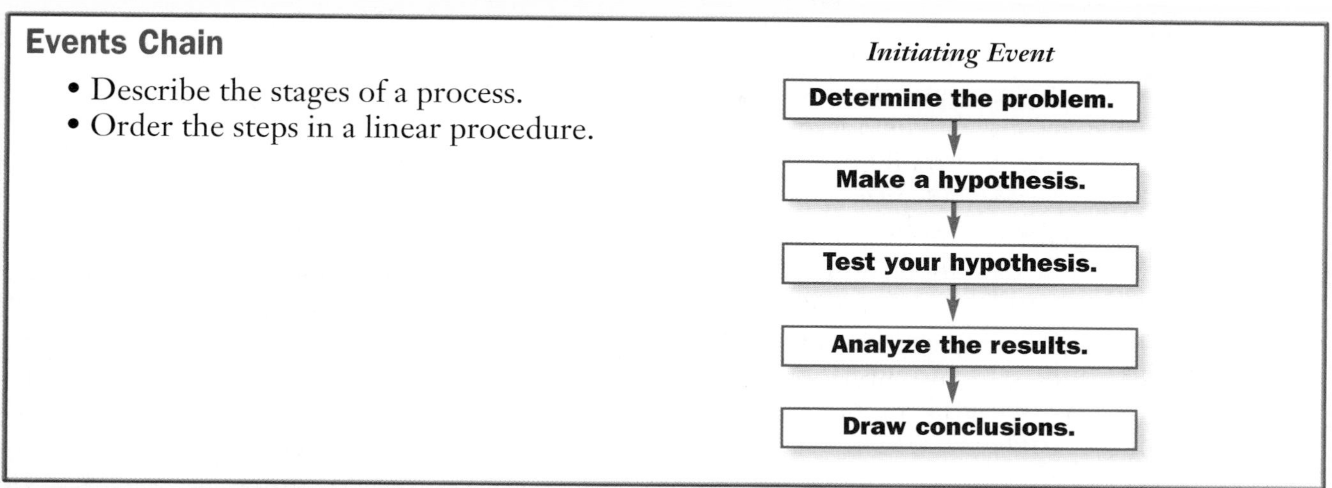

Cycle Concept Map

- Show how a series of events interact.
- Depict how the last event relates to the initiating event.

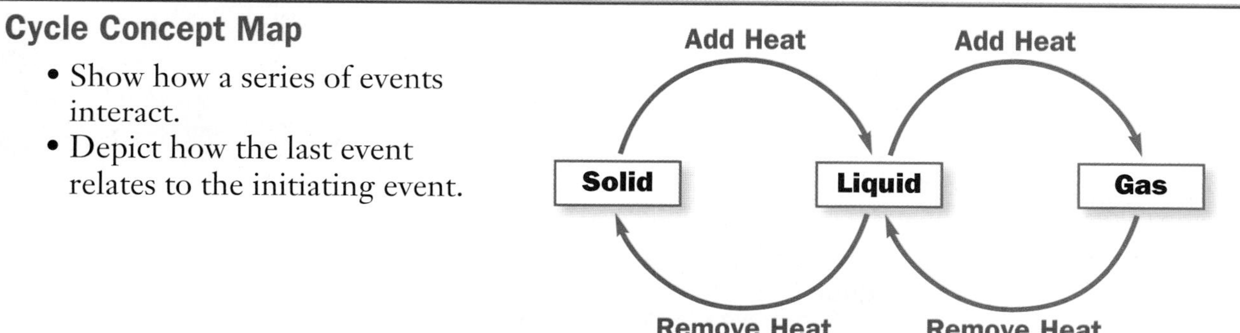

Spider Concept Map

- Use for brainstorming.
- Separate and group unrelated terms.
- Show relationship of nonrelated terms to a central idea.

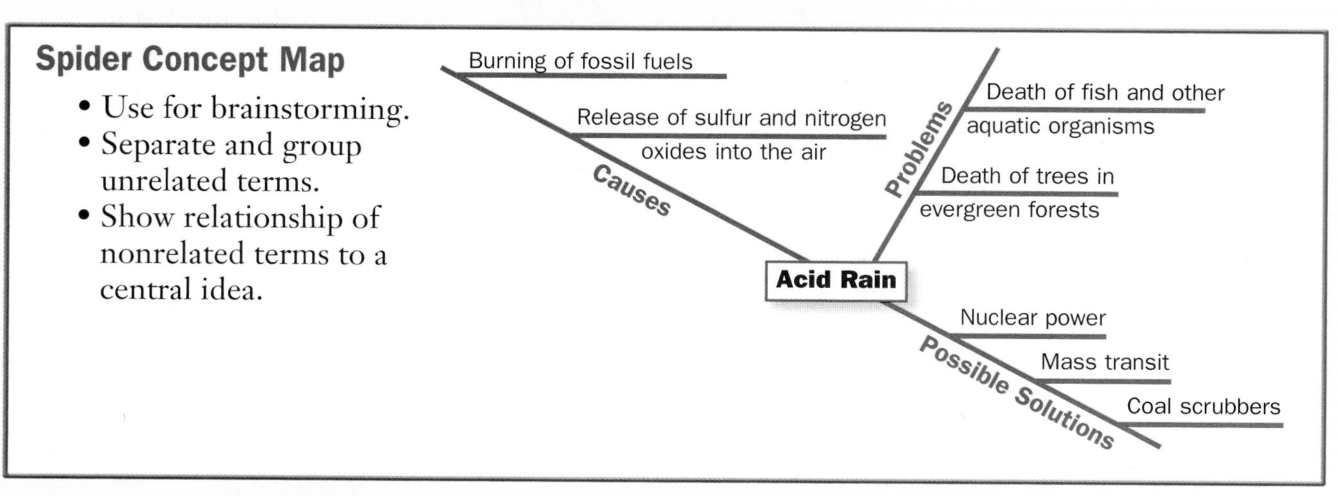

Assessment Support

Glencoe Physical Science **offers the Glencoe Assessment Advantage, a system of assessment options designed to give you the flexibility and tools to conduct standardized test preparation, and content and performance assessment.**

Glencoe has partnered with *The Princeton Review*, a nationally renowned company that helps students prepare for state and national tests. This partnership has resulted in the Study Tips and Test Practice questions at the end of each Chapter Assessment in the ***Student Edition***. Test practice booklets help prepare students for success on standardized tests.

Content Assessment

- **Section Assessment** questions and **Skill Builder Activities** appear in every chapter of the ***Student Edition***.
- A **Study Guide** at the end of each chapter in the ***Student Edition*** allows you to determine whether reteaching is needed.
- The **Chapter Assessment** questions in the ***Student Edition*** help you evaluate students' knowledge and ability to apply science concepts.

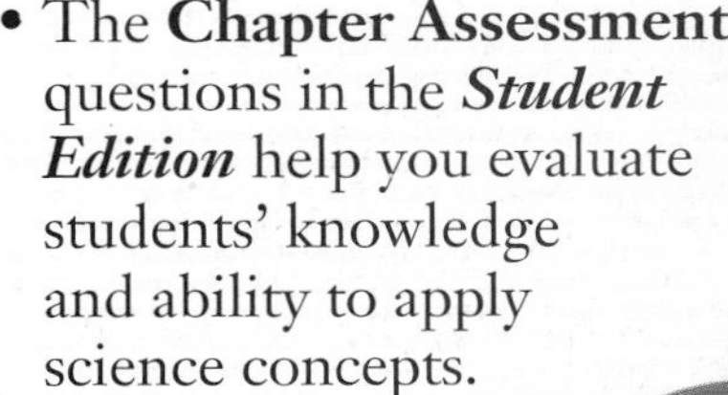

- **Assessment—Chapter Tests** in the *Chapter Resources* booklets assess recognition, recall of vocabulary and facts, and ability to interpret information and relationships.
- **MindJogger Videoquizzes** offer interactive videos that provide a fun way for your students to review chapter concepts.
- The **Interactive CD-ROM/DVD** provides quizzes that can be used as a whole-class presentation or as a review for individual students. These materials also are available on the Glencoe Science Web site.
- **ExamView Pro Test Bank Software (English/Spanish)** Software for Macintosh and Windows provides an easy way to make, edit, and print tests. You can add your own questions and graphics.

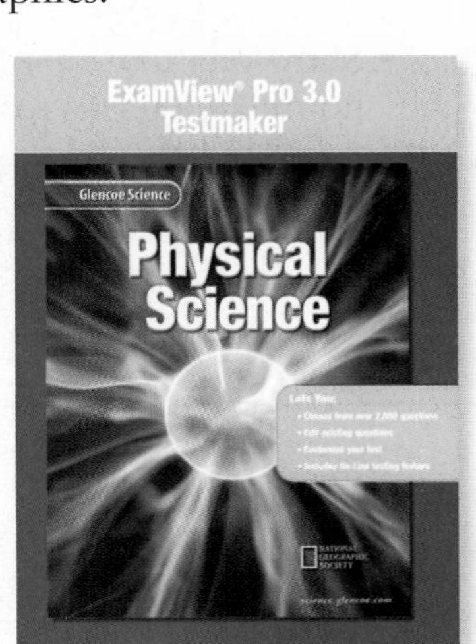

Performance Assessment

Performance Assessment refers to the strategies used to assess students' level of science literacy. Performance Assessment is based on judging the quality of a student's response to a performance task. A performance task is constructed to require the use of important concepts with supporting information, work habits important to science, and one or more of the elements of scientific literacy.

Performance Task Assessment Lists

Performance Assessments accompany **Activities** and **Chapter Assessments** in the ***Glencoe Physical Science Student Edition***. Task Assessment Lists are provided in Glencoe's *Performance Assessment in the Science Classroom*. Both the teacher and the student assess the work and assign points based on the well-defined categories and possible points for each category. These task lists were developed for the summative performance tasks included in the booklet.

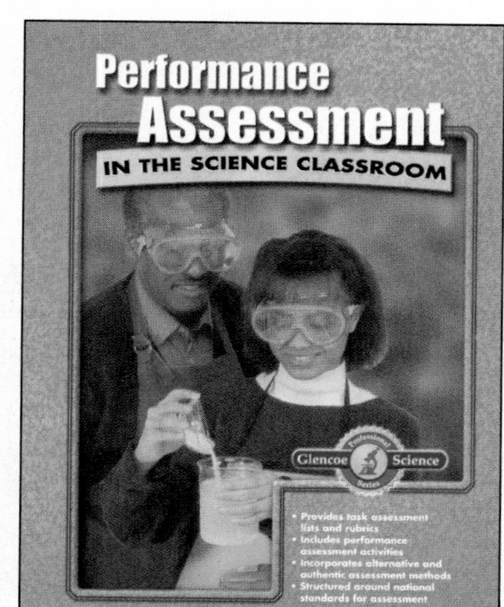

Assessing Student Work with Rubrics

A rubric is a set of descriptions of the quality of a process and a product. The set of descriptions includes a continuum of quality from excellent to poor. Rubrics for various types of assessment products are provided in the Glencoe Professional Development Series booklet *Performance Assessment in the Science Classroom*. In addition to sample rubrics, blank rubric forms allow teachers to customize assessment methods. The booklet also provides a step-by step model showing teachers how to use the materials most effectively.

Portfolios

Portfolio suggestions are featured throughout each chapter in the *Glencoe Physical Science Teacher Wraparound Edition*. The Portfolio should help the student see the big picture of how he or she is performing in gaining knowledge and skills and how effective his or her work habits are. The performance portfolio is not a complete collection of all worksheets and other assignments but rather a collection that reflects the student's growth in concept attainment and skill development. Writings and drawings from the student's **Science Journal**, featured in the ***Student Edition*** and the ***Teacher Wraparound Edition***, often are suggested to include in portfolios.

Group Assessment

All students benefit from a cooperative learning environment. Research has shown that student-learning outcomes improve for students of all ability levels. An example, along with information about evaluating cooperative work, is provided in the booklet *Performance Assessment in the Science Classroom*.

Lab Safety

The activities in *Glencoe Physical Science* in the laboratory and have been reviewed by safety consultants. Even so, there are no guarantees against accidents. For additional help, refer to the *Laboratory Management and Safety* booklet, which contains safety guidelines and masters to test students' lab and safety skills.

General Guidelines

- Post safety guidelines, fire escape routes, and a list of emergency procedures in the classroom. Make sure students understand these procedures. Remind them at the beginning of *every* lab session.

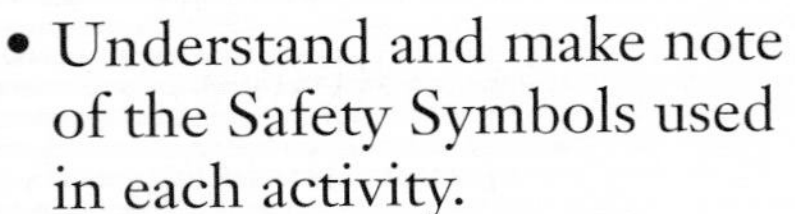

- Understand and make note of the Safety Symbols used in each activity.

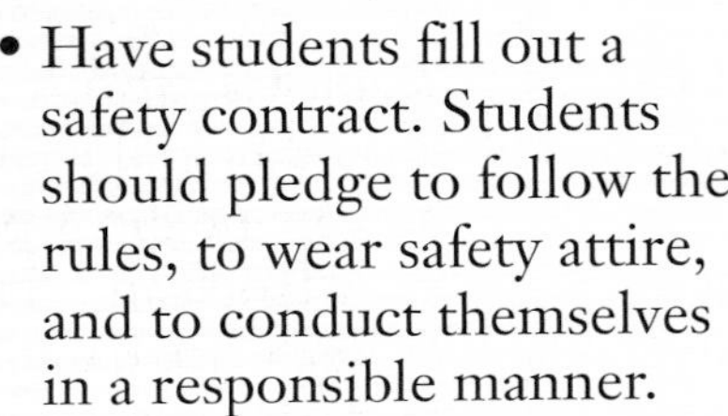

- Have students fill out a safety contract. Students should pledge to follow the rules, to wear safety attire, and to conduct themselves in a responsible manner.
- Know where emergency equipment is stored and how to use it.
- Supervise students at all times. Check assembly of all setups.
- Perform all activities before you allow students to do so.
- Instruct students to follow directions carefully.
- Make sure that all students are wearing proper safety attire: goggles and aprons when using chemicals, a heat source, or a hammer. They should secure long hair and loose clothing. Do not permit wearing contact lenses, even with safety glasses; splashing chemicals could infuse under a lens and cause eye damage.

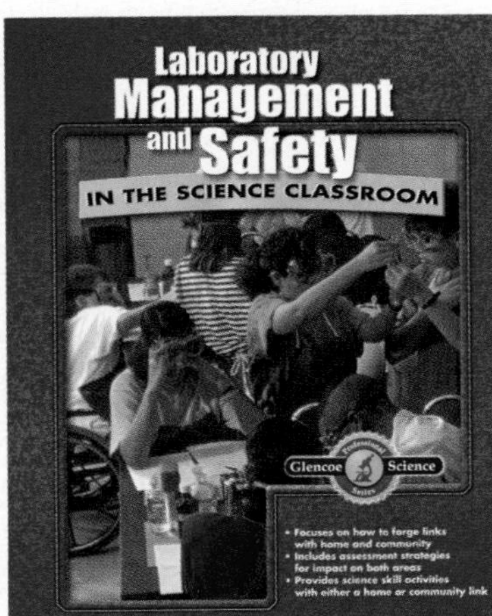

Handling Chemicals

- Handle chemicals carefully at all times. Always wear safety goggles, gloves, and an apron when handling chemicals. Treat all chemicals as potentially dangerous.
- Never ingest chemicals. Use proper techniques to smell solutions.
- Use a fume hood when handling chemicals that are poisonous or corrosive or that give off a vapor.
- *Always add acids to water, never the reverse.*
- Prepare solutions by adding the solid to a small amount of distilled water and then diluting with water to the volume listed. If you use a hydrate that is different from the one specified in a particular preparation, you will need to adjust the amount of hydrate to obtain the correct concentration.
- Consider purchasing premixed solutions from a scientific supply house to reduce the amount of chemicals on hand.
- Maintain appropriate MSDS (Materials Safety Data Sheets) in the laboratory.

Chemical Storage and Disposal

The following are some commonly used guidelines for chemical storage and disposal, but your school or local government may have additional requirements for handling chemicals. It is your responsibility to be informed of the rules governing chemical storage and disposal in your area.

- Use wood shelving rather than metal. All shelving should be firmly attached to the wall and have antiroll edges.
- Store only those chemicals you intend to use. Do not store chemicals above eye level.
- Store chemicals in labeled containers that indicate the contents, concentration, source, date purchased (or prepared), safety precautions for handling, and expiration date.
- Separate chemicals by reaction type. Store acids in one place and bases in another. Oxidants should be stored away from easily oxidized materials, for example.
- Dispose of outdated or waste chemicals properly.
- Follow regulations for storing hazardous chemicals.

Disposal of Chemicals

Local, state, and federal laws regulate the disposal of chemicals. Consult these laws before attempting to dispose of any chemicals. The following resource provides some general guidelines for handling and disposing of chemicals: *Prudent Practices in the Laboratory: Handling and Disposal of Chemicals*. Washington, DC: National Academy Press, 1995. Current laws in your area supersede the information in this book.

Disclaimer

Glencoe/McGraw-Hill makes no claims to the completeness of this discussion of laboratory safety and chemical storage. The material presented is not all-inclusive, nor does it address all of the hazards associated with handling, storage, and disposal of chemicals, or with laboratory management.

Activity Materials

Glencoe Physical Science **makes it easy for you to plan and facilitate activities in your classrooms.**

- You'll find a variety of hands-on activities, from short to long, from directed to open-ended.
- Many activities use common, inexpensive materials.
- Activities are easy to manage, with clearly numbered steps and illustrations.
- All MiniLABS have been teacher tested.

All laboratory activities have been thoroughly reviewed by a safety expert.

All full-length labs were bench tested by Science Kit to ensure quality and safety.

It's Quick and Easy to Order

Glencoe and Science Kit, Inc., have teamed up to make materials for ***Glencoe Physical Science*** easier with an activity-materials folder. This folder contains two convenient ways to order materials and equipment for the program—the **Activity Plan Checklist** and the **Activity Materials List** master. Call Science Kit at 1-800-828-7777 to get your folder.

Materials Support Provided by

Science Kit® & Boreal®
Laboratories
Your Classroom Resource
777 East Park Drive
Tonawanda, NY 14151-5003
Phone: 800-828-7777
Fax 800-828-3299
www.sciencekit.com

List of Activity Materials

It is assumed that goggles, laboratory aprons, tap water, textbooks, paper, calculators, pencils, and pens are available for all activities.

Non-Consumables

Item	Explore Activity Page	Mini LAB Page	Activity Chapter/Section
Aluminum chimney		293	
Aluminum nail			8-2
Aluminum rod			8-2
Aluminum, sample	737		20-1
Ammeter			8-1
Aquarium gravel		679	
Balance			1-1, 3-2, 4-1, 5-1
Balance, electronic			2-1
Balance, triple beam			2-1
Baseball		555	3-2
Battery	193		7-1
Battery, 6-V, dry cell			7-2
Battery, D-cell	99	204	8-2
Beaker	517, 671	274, 293	
Beaker(s)		397, 498, 506, 528	16-1, 24-1
Beaker, 100 mL	705, 765		22-1
Beaker, 250 mL		768	21-2, 22-1, 23-1, 23-2
Beaker, 500 mL			6-1
Beaker, large	487		
Beakers, 400 mL			6-2
Board(s)		54	2-2
Book(s)		54, 229, 392	13-1
Book, large			2-1
Bowl		592	
Bowl, deep		612	
Bowl, small, parabolically shaped			13-1
Broom handle	125		
Bucket		81	
Bulb holder			7-1
Bulb(s)	193	204	
Bunsen burner			16-1

Classroom Activities and Materials

Non-Consumables *continued*

Item	Explore Activity Page	MiniLAB Page	Activity Chapter/Section
Burner	607, 639, 671		6-1, 6-2, 19-2
Can opener, manual		134	
Carbon, sample			20-1
Cart		54	
Chair		359	
Coffe can (black)	289		
Coffe can lids	289		
Coffee can (white)	289		
Coiled spring toy, small			11-1
Compact disc	419		
Compact disc player			12-2
Compass, magnetic			8-2
Conductivity tester		673	20-1
Container, clear, rectangular			14-1
Container, clear-plastic		521	
Copper wire			17-1, 23-1
Cup, opaque		423	
Desk		359	
Dime		555	5-1
Dishes, for samples	737		20-1
Dominoes			9-1
Double pulleys (2)			5-2
Dropper		715	25-1, 25-2
Drum			12-2
Evaporating dish, small			17-2
Eyepiece lens, concave			15-2
Eyepiece lens, convex			15-2
Feather		555	
Fences, wooden			12-2
Fiberglass composite rods			22-2
Flashlight	193, 419		13-1, 14-2
Flashlight bulb			7-1
Flourescent bulb		431	

Non-Consumables *continued*

Item	Explore Activity Page	Mini LAB Page	Activity Chapter/Section
Galvanometer			8-1
Glass		392	
Glass prism	419		
Glasses, drinking, medium		710	
Glasses, drinking, small			
Gloves	125		
Golf ball		555	
Graduated cylinder			16-2, 22-1, 23-2
Graduated cylinder, 10 mL			17-2, 21-1, 21-2, 24-1
Graduated cylinder, 100 mL	573	19	1-1
Graduated cylinder, 25 mL			25-2
Gravel		521	
Hair dryer		592	
Hammer, small			20-1
Hand lens			17-2
Hanging laundry			12-2
Heat-proof surface	671, 705		
Horn			12-2
Hose, long			11-2
Hot plate	487, 517, 705		6-1, 6-2, 16-2, 17-2, 21-2, 23-1, 23-2, 24-1
Incandescent bulb		431	
Insulated wire			7-1
Jars, baby-food		397	
Knife, butter		229	
Knife, paring			6-2
Lamp			14-2
Lid		471	
Light source		455	14-1
Lights, small, with sockets (3)			7-2
Magnesium, sample			20-1
Magnet		612	
Magnet, bar	225	229	8-1

Activity Materials

Non-Consumables *continued*

Item	Explore Activity Page	MiniLAB Page	Activity Chapter/Section
Mallet		347	
Marble(s)	325	274, 555	16-2
Measuring cup			1-1
Measuring tablespoon			1-1
Measuring teaspoon			1-1
Metal object		359	
Meterstick	37, 257	40	2-2, 3-1, 3-2, 4-1, 4-2, 11-2, 12-2, 22-2
Metric ruler		71, 134	5-1
Metric tape measure			12-2
Microwave		397	
Miscellaneous objects for standards			1-2
Nail, iron	737		
Nail, iron, 16-penny			8-2
Needle, sewing		231	
Nickel coin		103	5-1
Objective lens, convex			15-2
Pan		333	
Pan, metal		392	
Paper clip(s)	225, 607	112, 229, 673, 555, 653	2-1, 15-1
Paper clips, non-coated	99		
Paper clips, steel			8-2
Paper towel		715	
Parked cars			12-2
Pebbles, small		679	
Penny		423, 555, 715	
Pie plate		333	
Plane mirrors (2)			15-1
Plastic freezer bag			17-1
Plate		231	
Polarizing filters (3)			14-2
Power supply, 0-6 v DC			8-2
Protractor			15-1

Non-Consumables *continued*

Item	Explore Activity Page	MiniLAB Page	Activity Chapter/Section
Quarter, coin		555	5-1
Racquetball			3-2
Radio		366	12-2
Ramps			2-2
Reference-Periodic table			19-1
Ring clamp			16-1
Ring stand		229	4-2, 6-2, 16-1, 21-2, 23-1, 23-2
Rock/Mineral-granite			
Rock/Mineral-rock		71	
Rope, heavy	125		11-1
Rope, light			11-1
Rope, long			11-2
Rubber ball, large			3-2
Rubber hammer		592	
Ruler	357		16-2, 18-1
Sand		397, 521, 679	24-1
Scissors	289		1-2, 3-1, 6-2, 7-2, 8-1, 5-2, 20-2, 25-1
Softball	67		
Soil		521	
Sound meter			12-2
Spatula			20-1
Spoon		455	
Spoon, metal		169	13-1
Spoon, wooden		169	
Spring scale 0-12-kg range			22-2
Spring scale 0-2kg range			22-2
Spring scale, 0 - 10 N range			5-2
Spring scale, 10-N			2-1
Spring, long			11-2
Springs			2-2
Stairs		129	

Non-Consumables *continued*

Item	Explore Activity Page	MiniLAB Page	Activity Chapter/Section
Stand/Support for pulleys			5-2
Steel composite rods			22-2
Steel nut		498	
Steel wire	671		
Steel wool	99		
Stop block		54	
Stopper		471	21-1
Stopwatch	37, 67, 157	40	2-2, 3-1, 3-2, 9-1, 11-1, 11-2, 16-2, 19-2
Sulfur, sample			20-1
Support for board, 10 cm high			
Support rod, 30 cm			4-2
Support-rod clamp, right angle			4-2
Surface, flat		547	
Table		423	
Tape measure	487		2-2
Television		392	
Television remote control		392	
Tennis ball	67		3-2, 4-1
Test tube(s)	639	471, 618, 752	12-1, 19-2, 25-1, 24-1, 25-2
Test tube, large			6-2, 21-1, 23-2
Test tube, medium			21-2
Test-tube clamp			6-2
Test-tube holder	639		21-2, 23-2
Test-tube holder, wire			19-2
Test-tube rack			12-1, 23-2
Test-tube stand			24-1
Textbook	325, 451		2-1
Thermal mitts	705		6-2
Thermometer(s)	289	25, 431	6-2, 10-1, 16-1, 21-2
Thermometer, celsius			23-1, 23-2
Timer with second hand		768	25-1
Tin, sample			20-1

Non-Consumables *continued*

Item	Explore Activity Page	Mini LAB Page	Activity Chapter/Section
Tongs	607, 671		
Toy car		40	2-2
Tray, metal		71	
Tray, plastic		71	
Tuning fork(s)		347	
Walls, brick			12-2
Walls, concrete			12-2
Walls, stone			12-2
Watch with second hand			10-1
Weight, 9.8 N (1kg mass)			5-2
Window exposed to direct sunlight		168	
Wire	193		
Wire gauze			6-2
Wire mesh			16-1
Wire, insulated, 22-gauge			8-2
Wire, thin, insulated			8-1
Wood block		71	
Wood composite rods			22-2
Wooden board, 40 cm long			5-2

Consumables

Item	Explore Activity Page	Mini LAB Page	Activity Chapter/Section
Agar gel	737		
Aluminum foil	517	229, 498	7-2, 13-1, 17-1
Balloon	487	506, 584	
Bead, plastic		169, 673	
Borax laundry soap			22-1
Candle		293	6-1
Cardboard			25-1
Cardboard boxes, small			4-1, 10-1
Cardboard tube			8-1
Cardboard tube, 3-cm diameter			15-2
Cardboard tube, 4-cm diameter			15-2
Cardboard, flat			20-2
Chalk	765		17-1
Clay		274, 521	14-1, 15-2
Cloth		306, 366	
Cloth, cotton		555	
Cloth, heavy			11-1
Cloth, light			11-1
Construction paper, red	389		
Craft stick			22-1
Crayon		555	
Cup(s), foam		25, 231, 431	6-2
Dish detergent			16-2
Dishwashing liquid	419		
Envelope	543		
Eraser		71	

Consumables *continued*

Item	Explore Activity Page	Mini LAB Page	Activity Chapter/Section
Fabric		229	
Food coloring	157, 517, 573	498	
Food-baking soda		781	17-2
Food-black pepper			6-1
Food-bread	639		
Food-brown rice			9-2
Food-butter		169	
Food-can of food		134	
Food-candies, red		267	
Food-candies, yellow		267	
Food-colored candies			9-2
Food-corn meal			1-1
Food-corn syrup		498	16-2
Food-dried beans	543		1-1, 9-2
Food-dried rice			1-1
Food-fortified cereal, cold, dry		612	
Food-grape juice, purple		781	
Food-gumdrops, small		643	20-2
Food-milk		555	
Food-molasses			
Food-orange juice		555	
Food-pancake syrup			16-2
Food-potato flakes			1-1
Food-raisins		643	
Food-salt			17-1, 19-2, 23-1
Food-soda		555	
Food-soft drinks, various colors			25-2

Consumables *continued*

Item	Explore Activity Page	MiniLAB Page	Activity Chapter/Section
Food-spaghetti, thin			20-2
Food-sugar	257		19-2
Food-sugar cubes		710	
Food-vegetable oil	573	498	1-1, 16-2
Food-vinegar			1-1, 16-2
Food-vinegar, white		781	
Food-white rice			9-2
Food-whole peppercorn		498	
Fur		584	
Glue			9-2, 10-1
Glue, white		679	22-1
Graph paper			2-2, 4-2, 22-2
Hair, small strand		555	
Ice	157	71	6-2, 16-1
Ice, crushed			19-2
Index cards		741	19-1
Ink pen		673	
Leaf		555	
Markers, colored			18-1
Marking pen			1-2
Motor oil			16-2
Note card		471	
Paper	67, 257, 639	471, 555, 673	3-1, 5-1, 7-2, 18-1
Paper filter	765		
Paper, blue		547	
Paper, colored		653	10-1
Paper, flash sheet	67		

Consumables *continued*

Item	Explore Activity Page	MiniLAB Page	Activity Chapter/Section
Paper, orange		547	
Paper, red		547	
Paper, typing			25-1
Pen	325		
Pencil	325	40, 555, 612, 673	4-1, 17-1
Pencil, unsharpened		19	
Pencils, colored			18-1
pH paper			25-1
Plaster of Paris		592	
Plastic bag		612	
Plastic wrap	451	431	
Polystyrene sheets, thin			20-2
Popsicle stick			22-1
Poster board		455	9-2
Ribbon			11-1
Rubber ball			4-1
Rubber band(s)		54, 103	
Rubber band, long			11-1
Rubber stopper, medium, 2 hole			4-2
Rubbing alcohol		715	
Shampoo			16-2
Shoe box			4-1
Solution samples	705		
Spoon, plastic		169	
String		359	1-2, 2-2, 4-2, 5-2, 11-1
Sugar water in a vial			17-1
Tape	99	40, 200, 231, 612	10-1

Consumables *continued*

Item	Explore Activity Page	MiniLAB Page	Activity Chapter/Section
Tape, cellophane			15-2
Tape, duct			8-2, 15-2
Tape, masking			1-2, 3-1, 3-2, 4-1, 15-1
Tape, transparent			7-2
Teaspoon, plastic			24-1
Thread		229	
Toothpicks		643	
Water	157, 289, 419, 451, 487, 517, 573	25, 81, 90, 293, 333, 423, 471, 498, 521, 528, 584, 592, 715, 752, 768	1-1, 6-1, 14-1, 16-2
Water, carbonated	765		
Water, cold	671		
Water, distilled		618, 710	23-1
Water, drinking		618	
Water, hot			24-1
Water, iced		506	
Water, warm			22-1
Wax		169	
Wooden splint			24-1
Wool		584	

Chemical Supplies

Item	EXPLORE ACTIVITY Page	Mini LAB Page	Activity Chapter/Section
0.01M potassium permanganate solution			21-1
1% Phenophthalein indicator solution			25-2
3% Hydrogen peroxide			24-1
6M sodium hydroxide solution			21-1
Acetic acid, dilute			25-1
Chloride standard solution		618	
Copper(II)bromide		752	
Copper(II)sulfate	607		
Ethanol			21-1
Hydrochloric acid (HCl)		768	17-2
Hydrochloric acid (HCl), dilute			25-1
Indicators, general	737		
Manganese dioxide			24-1
Methyl alcohol			21-2
NaOH solution, dilute			25-2
Potassium permanganate		528	
Salicylic acid			21-2
Sodium hydrogen sulfate		528	
Sulfuric acid, concentrated			21-2
Universal indicator		768	

Suppliers

Scientific Suppliers

Carolina Biological Supply Company
2700 York Road
Burlington, NC 27215
800-334-5551
www.carolina.com

Fisher Scientific Educational
485 South Frontage Road
Burr Ridge, IL 60521
800-955-1177
www.fisheredu.com

Fisher Scientific Company
4500 Turnberry Drive
Hanover Park, IL 60103
800-766-7000
www.fishersci.com

Flinn Scientific
P.O. Box 219
770 N. Raddant Road
Batavia, IL 60510
800-452-1261
www.flinnsci.com

Frey Scientific
100 Paragon Road
Mansfield, OH 44903
800-225-3739
www.freyscientific.com

Sargent-Welch/Cenco
P.O. Box 5229
911 Commerce Court
Buffalo Grove, IL 60089
800-727-4368
www.sargentwelch.com

Science Kit & Boreal Laboratories
777 East Park Drive
Tonawanda, NY 14150
800-828-7777
www.sciencekit.com

Ward's Natural Science Establishment, Inc.
P.O. Box 92912
5100 Henrietta Road
Rochester, NY 14692
800-962-2660
www.wardsci.com

Software Distributors

(AIT) Agency for Instructional Technology
Box A
Bloomington, IN 47402-0120
800-457-4509
www.ait.net

Educational Activities, Inc.
1937 Grand Avenue
Baldwin, NY 11510
800-645-3739
www.edact.com

IBM Educational Systems
Department PC
4111 Northside Parkway
Atlanta, GA 30327
800-426-4968
www.IBM.com

Microphys
12 Bridal Way
Sparta, NJ 07871
800-832-6591
www.microphys.com

Queue, Inc.
338 Commerce Drive
Fairfield, CT 06432
800-335-0906
www.queueinc.com

School Division of The Learning Company
6160 Summit Drive
Minneapolis, MN 55430
www.learningcompanyschool.com

Ventura Educational Systems
P.O. Box 425
Grover Beach, CA 93483
2782 Sevada
Arroyo, CA 93420
800-336-1022
www.venturaES.com

Audiovisual Distributors

Aims Multimedia
9710 Desoto Avenue
Chatsworth, CA 91311-4409
800-367-2467
www.amismultimedia.com

BFA Educational Media
2349 Chaffee Drive
St. Louis, MO 63146
800-221-1274
www.phoenixcoronet.com

CRM Films
2215 Faraday Avenue
Carlsbad, CA 92008
800-421-0833
www.crmfilms.com

Encyclopedia Britannica Educational Corp (EBEC)
310 S. Michigan Avenue
Chicago, IL 60604
800-554-9862 ext. 7007
www.ebec.com

Hawkill Associates, Inc.
125 E. Gilman Street
Madison, WI 53703
800-422-4295
www.hawkill.com

Lumivision
877 Federal Boulevard.
Denver, CO 80204
303-446-0400
www.lumivision.com

National Geographic School Publishing
P.O. Box 10579
De Moines, IA 50340
17th and "M" Streets, NW
Washington, DC 20009
800-368-2728
www.nationalgeographic.com\education

Time-Life Education
P.O. Box 8502
Richmond, VA 23285
800-449-2010
www.timelifeedu.com

Video Discovery
Suite 600
1700 Westlake Avenue, N
Seattle, WA 98109
800-548-3472
www.videodiscovery.com

Glencoe Science

Physical Science

NATIONAL GEOGRAPHIC SOCIETY

science.glencoe.com

New York, New York Columbus, Ohio Woodland Hills, California Peoria, Illinois

GLENCOE PHYSICAL SCIENCE

Student Edition
Teacher Wraparound Edition
Interactive Teacher Edition CD-ROM
Interactive Lesson Planner CD-ROM
Lesson Plans
Content Outline for Teaching
Directed Reading for Content Mastery
Foldables: Reading and Study Skills
Assessment
- *Chapter Review*
- *Chapter Tests*
- *ExamView Pro Test Bank Software*
- *Assessment Transparencies*
- *Performance Assessment in the Science Classroom*
- *The Princeton Review's Standardized Test Practice Booklet*

Directed Reading for Content Mastery in Spanish
Spanish Resources
English/Spanish Audiocassettes
Reinforcement
Enrichment
Activity Worksheets
Section Focus Transparencies
Teaching Transparencies
Laboratory Activities
Science Inquiry Labs
Critical Thinking/Problem Solving
Reading and Writing Skill Activities
Mathematics Skill Activities
Cultural Diversity
Laboratory and Safety in the Science Classroom
Mindjogger Videoquizzes and Teacher Guide
Interactive Explorations and Quizzes CD-ROM
Puzzlemaker Software
Cooperative Learning in the Science Classroom
Environmental Issues in the Science Classroom
Home and Community Involvement
Using the Internet in the Science Classroom

The "Study Tip" and the "Test Practice" features in this book were written by The Princeton Review, the nation's leader in test preparation. Through its association with McGraw-Hill, The Princeton Review offers the best way to help students excel on standardized assessments.

The Princeton Review is not affiliated with Princeton University or Educational Testing Service.

Glencoe/McGraw-Hill

A Division of The ***McGraw-Hill*** *Companies*

The "Science and Society" and the "Science and History" features that appear in this book were designed and developed by TIME for Kids, a division of TIME Magazine.

Cover Images: electrical discharges inside a plasma globe

Send all inquires to:
Glencoe/McGraw-Hill
8787 Orion Place
Columbus, OH 43240

ISBN 0-07-822745-3
Printed in the United States of America.
1 2 3 4 5 6 7 8 9 10 027/043 06 05 04 03 02 01

Authors

Charles William McLaughlin, PhD
Senior Lecturer
University of Nebraska
Lincoln, Nebraska

Marilyn Thompson, EdD
Assistant Professor, College of Education
Arizona State University
Tempe, Arizona

Contributing Authors

Nancy Ross-Flanigan
Science Writer
Detroit, Michigan

Margaret K. Zorn
Science Writer
Yorktown, Virginia

Content Consultants

Alan Bross, PhD
High Energy Physicist
Fermilab
Batavia, Illinois

Madelaine Meek, MEd
Physics Consultant
Editor
Lebanon, Ohio

Michael A. Hoggarth, PhD
Department of Life and Earth Sciences
Otterbein College
Westerville, Ohio

Teresa Anne McCowen, MS
Chemistry Instructor
Heartland Community College
Normal, Illnois

Carl Zorn, PhD
Staff Scientist
Jefferson Laboratory
Newport News, Virginia

Math Consultant

Michael Hopper, D.Eng
Manager of Aircraft Certification
Raytheon Company
Greenville, Texas

Safety Consultants

Malcolm Cheney, PhD
OSHA Chemical Safety Officer
Hall High School
West Hartford, Connecticut

Sandra West, PhD
Associate Professor of Biology
Southwest Texas State University
San Marcos, Texas

Reading Consultants

Elizabeth Babich, MEd
Special Education Teacher
Mashpee Public Schools
Mashpee, Massachusetts

Barry Barto
Special Education Teacher
John F. Kennedy Elementary
Manistee, Michigan

Rachel Swaters, MEd
Science Teacher
Rolla Middle Schools
Rolla, Missouri

Series Activity Testers

José Luis Alvarez, PhD
Math/Science Mentor Teacher
Yseleta ISD
El Paso, Texas

Nerma Coats Henderson
Teacher
Pickerington Jr. High School
Pickerington, Ohio

Mary Helen Mariscal-Cholka
Science Teacher
William D. Slider Middle School
Socorro ISD
El Paso, Texas

José Alberto Marquez
TEKS for Leaders Trainer
Yseleta ISD
El Paso, Texas

Science Kit and Boreal Laboratories
Tonawanda, New York

Reviewers

Sharla Adams
McKinney High School North
McKinney ISD
McKinney, Texas

Desiree Bishop
Baker High School
Mobile, Alabama

Nora M. Prestinari Burchett
Saint Luke School
McLean, Virginia

Mary Helen Mariscal-Cholka
William D. Slider Middle School
Socorro ISD
El Paso, Texas

Patricia Croft
Westside High School
Martinez, Georgia

Anthony DiSipio
Octorana Middle School
Atglen, Pennsylvania

George Gabb
Great Bridge Middle School
Chesapeake, Virginia

Maria Kelly
St. Leo School
Fairfax, Virginia

Eddie K. Lindsay
Vansant Middle School
Grundy, Virginia

H. Keith Lucas
Stewart Middle School
Fort Defiance, Virginia

Thomas E. Lynch Jr.
Northport High School
East Northport, New York

Linda Melcher
Woodmont Middle School
Piedmont, South Carolina

Annette Parrott
Lakeside High School
Atlanta, Georgia

Meredith Pickett
Memorial Middle School
Spring Branch ISD
Houston, Texas

Pam Starnes
North Richland Middle School
Birdville ISD
Fort Worth, Texas

Clabe Webb
Sterling City High School
Sterling City ISD
Sterling City, Texas

Alison Welch
William D. Slider Middle School
Socorro ISD
El Paso, Texas

Kim Wimpey
North Gwinnett High School
Suwanee, Georgia

Contents in Brief

UNIT 1 Energy and Motion — 2

CHAPTER 1

The Nature of Science — 4

CHAPTER 2

Motion and Speed — 36

CHAPTER 3

Forces — 66

CONTENTS

Contents

CHAPTER 4 Energy — 98

CHAPTER 5 Work and Machines — 124

CHAPTER 6 Thermal Energy — 156

UNIT 2 Electricity and Energy Resources — 190

CHAPTER 7

Electricity — 192

CHAPTER 8

Magnetism and Its Uses — 224

CHAPTER 9

Radioactivity and Nuclear Reactions — 256

Energy Sources — 288

UNIT 3 Energy on the Move — 322

Waves — 324

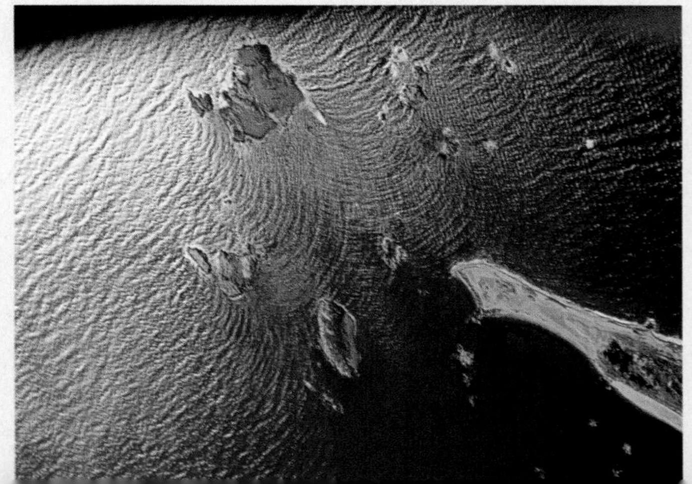

Sound — 356

Electromagnetic Waves — 388

Light — 418

Mirrors and Lenses — 450

UNIT 4 The Nature of Matter — 484

Solids, Liquids, and Gases — 486

Classification of Matter — 516

CONTENTS

Organic Compounds — 638

CHAPTER 22

New Materials Through Chemistry — 670

UNIT 6 Interactions of Matter — 702

CHAPTER 23 Solutions — 704

CHAPTER 24 Chemical Reactions — 736

CHAPTER 25 Acids, Bases, and Salts — 764

Interdisciplinary Connections

NATIONAL GEOGRAPHIC Unit Openers

NATIONAL GEOGRAPHIC VISUALIZING

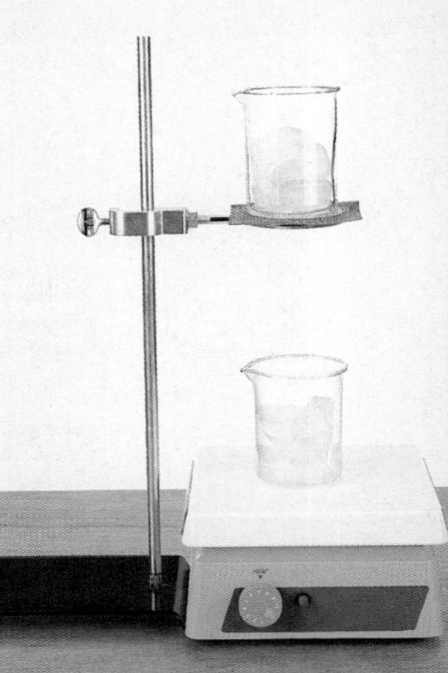

Interdisciplinary Connections

TIME

Science and Society

Science and History

Oops! Accidents in Science

Science and Language Arts

Science Stats

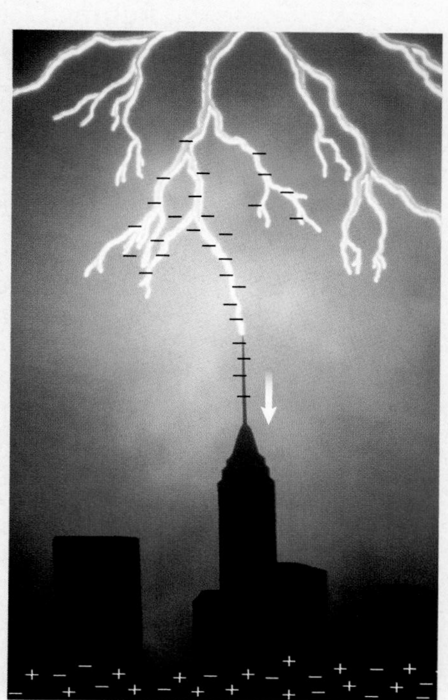

Activities

Feature Contents

Full Period Labs

Mini
LAB

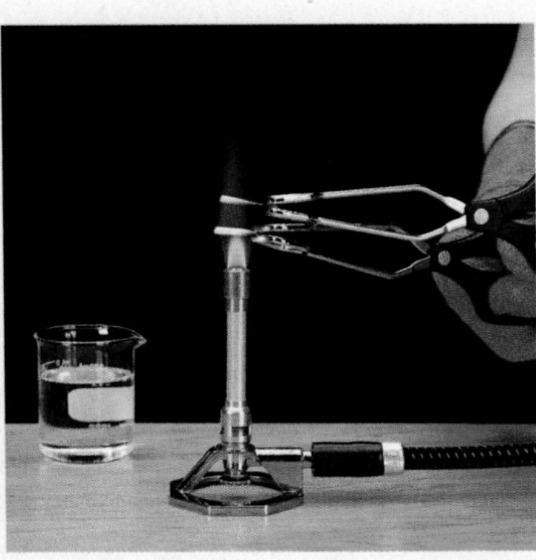

Activities

Explore Activity

Problem Solving Activities

Math Skills Activities

Activities

Feature Contents

Skill Builder Activites

Science:

Math:

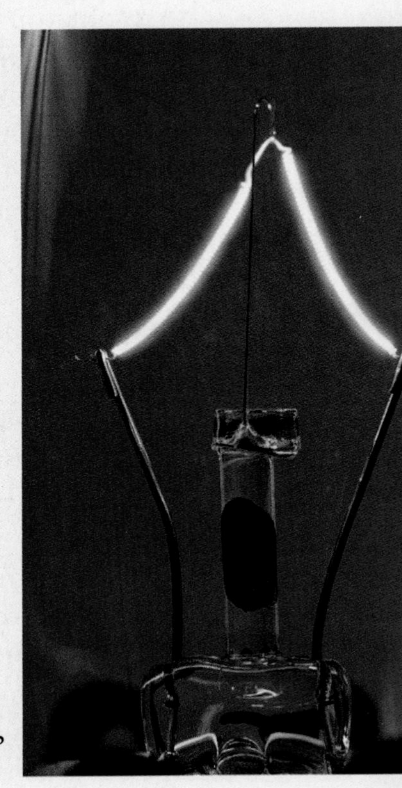

Technology:

Science INTEGRATION

SCIENCE *Online*

UNIT 1

Unit Contents

Pre-Reading Activity

Have students look at illustrations and photographs that depict different forms of energy.

UNIT 1

Energy and Motion

How Are Waffles & Running Shoes Connected?

2

Teacher to Teacher

"When examining compound machines, have students search the classroom, the school, or magazines to identify the compound machine that includes the greatest number of simple machines. Have them identify each simple machine they find."

Kevin Finnegan, Teacher
McCord Middle School
Worthington, OH

For centuries, shoes were made mostly of leather, cloth, or wood. These shoes helped protect feet, but they didn't provide much traction on slippery surfaces. In the early twentieth century, manufacturers began putting rubber on the bottom of canvas shoes, creating the first "sneakers." Sneakers provided good traction, but the rubber soles could be heavy—especially for athletes. One morning in the 1970s, an athletic coach stared into the waffles on the breakfast table and had an idea for a rubber sole that would be lighter in weight but would still provide traction. That's how the first waffle soles were born. Waffle soles soon became a world standard for running shoes.

SCIENCE CONNECTION

FRICTION Waffle soles improve traction by increasing friction—the force that opposes motion between two surfaces. At school or in a bicycle shop, examine and sketch the treads on different kinds of bicycle tires. Draw conclusions about how each type of tread increases or decreases friction between the tire and the ground. Then create a poster showing three different tire treads with an explanation about how each type of tread might suit a tire to particular riding conditions.

Introducing the Unit

How Are Waffles & Running Shoes Connected?

- Ask students how many of them have slipped when wearing an old pair of running or tennis shoes because the tread was worn.
- Have students compare the tread pattern in several pairs of their shoes and hypothesize how each increases friction. Ask them how the intended surface affects what type of tread is on a shoe.

SCIENCE CONNECTION

Activity

Before students create their posters, have their conclusions confirmed by a bicycle expert. Pamphlets relating tread to riding conditions might also be available from tire or bicycle manufacturers. Encourage creativity, but be sure posters depict accurate relationships.

SCIENCE Online

Internet Addresses

Explore the Glencoe Science Web site at **science.glencoe.com** to find out more about topics in this unit.

Section/Objectives	Standards		Activities/Features
	National	State/Local	
Chapter Opener	See p. 37T for a Key to Standards.		**Explore Activity:** Discover how long a foot is, p. 5 **Before You Read,** p. 5
Section 1 The Methods of Science 1 session .5 block 1. **Identify** the steps scientists often use to solve problems. 2. **Describe** why scientists use variables. 3. **Compare and contrast** science and technology.	National Content Standards: UCP3, A1, A2, E1, E2, G2		**Science Online,** p. 7 **Life Science Integration,** p. 9 **Earth Science Integration,** p. 11 **Science Online,** p. 12
Section 2 Standards of Measurement 2 sessions 1 block 1. **Name** the prefixes used in SI and indicate what multiple of ten each one represents. 2. **Identify** SI units and symbols for length, volume, mass, density, time, and temperature. 3. **Convert** related SI units.	National Content Standards: UCP3, A1, A2, B1 (5–8), B2 (9–12), G2		**Math Skills Activity:** Connecting Units of Measure, p. 16 **Earth Science Integration,** p. 17 **Science Online,** p. 18 **MiniLAB:** Determining the Density of a Pencil, p. 19 **Visualizing SI Dimensions,** p. 20
Section 3 Communicating with Graphs 2 sessions 1 block 1. **Identify** three types of graphs and explain the ways they are used. 2. **Distinguish** between dependent and independent variables. 3. **Analyze** data using the various types of graphs.	National Content Standards: UCP3, A1, A2, G1, G2		**Math Skills Activity:** Line Graphing, p. 24 **MiniLAB:** Observing Change Through Graphing, p. 25 **Activity:** Converting Kitchen Measurements, p. 27 **Activity:** Setting High Standards for Measurement, pp. 28–29 **Science and Language Arts:** Thinking in Pictures and other reports from my life with autism, pp 30–31

Activity Materials	Reproducible Resources	Section Assessment	Technology
	Chapter Resources Booklet Foldables Worksheet, p. 17 Note-taking Worksheets, pp. 33–34	GLENCOE'S ASSESSMENT ADVANTAGE	
Need materials? Contact Science Kit at 1-800-828-7777 or www.sciencekit.com on the Internet.	**Chapter Resources Booklet** Transparency Activity, p. 44 Enrichment, p. 30 Reinforcement, p. 27 Directed Reading, p. 20 **Cultural Diversity,** p. 29 **Science Inquiry Labs,** p. 47	**Portfolio** Earth Science Integration, p. 34 **Performance** Skill Builder Activities, p. 13 **Content** Section Assessment, p. 13	Section Focus Transparency Interactive CD-ROM/DVD Guided Reading Audio Program
MiniLAB: pencil, 100-mL graduated cylinder, 90 mL water	**Chapter Resources Booklet** Transparency Activity, p. 45 MiniLAB, p. 3 Enrichment, p. 31 Reinforcement, p. 28 Directed Reading, p. 20 Lab Activity, pp. 9–12	**Portfolio** Extension, p. 15 **Performance** Math Skills Activity, p. 16 MiniLAB, p. 19 Skill Builder Activities, p. 21 **Content** Section Assessment, p. 21	Section Focus Transparency Interactive CD-ROM/DVD Guided Reading Audio Program
MiniLAB: thermometer, plastic foam cup of hot water, plastic lid **Activity:** balance, 100-mL graduated cylinder, measuring cup, measuring teaspoon, measuring tablespoon, corn meal, dried beans, dried rice, potato flakes, water, vinegar, salad oil **Activity:** string, scissors, marking pen, masking tape, miscellaneous objects for standards	**Chapter Resources Booklet** Transparency Activity, p. 46 MiniLAB, p. 4 Enrichment, p. 32 Reinforcement, p. 29 Directed Reading, pp. 21, 22 Activity Worksheet, pp. 5–6, 7–8 Transparency Activity, pp. 47–48 Lab Activity, pp. 13–16	**Portfolio** Science Journal, p. 24 **Performance** Math Skills Activity, p. 24 MiniLAB, p. 25 Skill Builder Activities, p. 26 **Content** Section Assessment, p. 26	Section Focus Transparency Teaching Transparency Interactive CD-ROM/DVD Guided Reading Audio Program

End of Chapter Assessment

GLENCOE'S ASSESSMENT ADVANTAGE

Blackline Masters	Technology	Professional Series
Chapter Resources Booklet Chapter Review, pp. 37–38 Chapter Tests, pp. 39–42 **Standardized Test Practice by The Princeton Review,** pp. 8–11	MindJogger Videoquiz CD-ROM Explorations and Quizzes Vocabulary Puzzle Makers ExamView Pro Test Bank Interactive Lesson Planner Interactive Teacher's Edition	Performance Assessment in the Science Classroom (PASC)

Transparencies

Section Focus

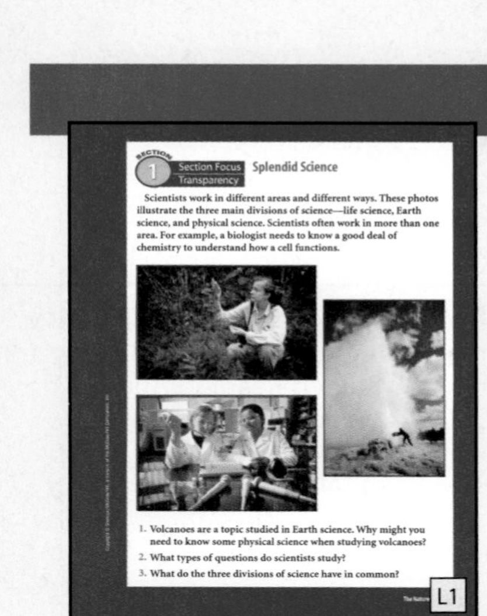
Section 1 Section Focus Transparency — Splendid Science

Scientists work in different areas and different ways. These photos illustrate the three main divisions of science—life science, Earth science, and physical science. Scientists often work in more than one area. For example, a biologist needs to know a good deal of chemistry to understand how a cell functions.

1. Volcanoes are a topic studied in Earth science. Why might you need to know some physical science when studying volcanoes?
2. What types of questions do scientists study?
3. What do the three divisions of science have in common?

L1

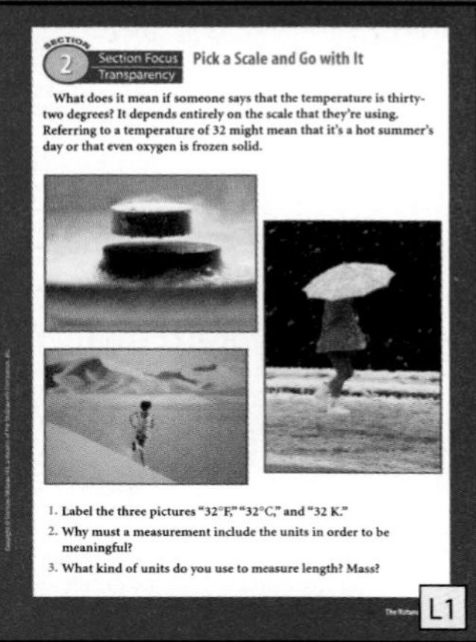
Section 2 Section Focus Transparency — Pick a Scale and Go with It

What does it mean if someone says that the temperature is thirty-two degrees? It depends entirely on the scale that they're using. Referring to a temperature of 32 might mean that it's a hot summer's day or that even oxygen is frozen solid.

1. Label the three pictures "32°F," "32°C," and "32 K."
2. Why must a measurement include the units in order to be meaningful?
3. What kind of units do you use to measure length? Mass?

L1

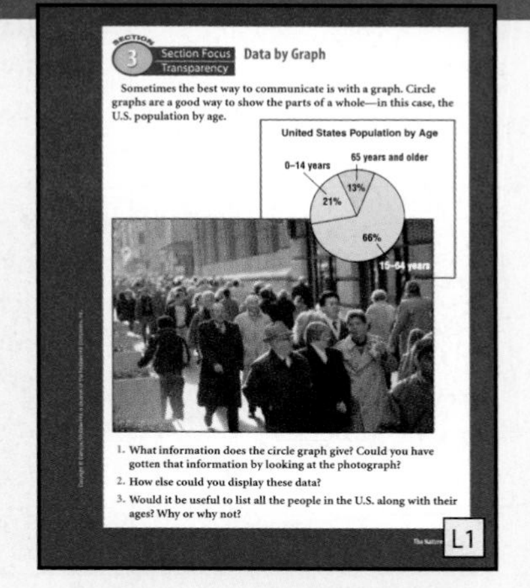
Section 3 Section Focus Transparency — Data by Graph

Sometimes the best way to communicate is with a graph. Circle graphs are a good way to show the parts of a whole—in this case, the U.S. population by age.

1. What information does the circle graph give? Could you have gotten that information by looking at the photograph?
2. How else could you display these data?
3. Would it be useful to list all the people in the U.S. along with their ages? Why or why not?

L1

Assessment

Assessment Transparency — The Nature of Science

Directions: *Carefully review the table and answer the following questions.*

Time (s)	Speed (m/s)	Time (s)	Speed (m/s)
0	0	6	60
1	10	7	70
2	20	8	80
3	30	9	90
4	40	10	100
5	50	11	?

1. The above data were collected during an experiment to find out the speed of a ball dropped from a tall building. Which type of graph would be the best way to display this information?
   A bar graph
   B pie graph
   C circle graph
   D line graph
2. According to these data, about how fast would the ball be dropping after 11 seconds?
   F 90 m/s
   G 100 m/s
   H 110 m/s
   J 120 m/s
3. In this data, the independent variable is the ___.
   A time
   B speed
   C ball
   D graph

L1

Teaching

Section 3 Teaching Transparency — Reading Graphs

Classroom Size (January 20, 2001)

Number of Classrooms: 0, 1, 2, 3, 4, 5, 6

Number of students: 20, 21, 22, 23, 24, 25, 26, 27

L1

This is a representation of key blackline masters available in the Teacher Classroom Resources. See Resource Manager boxes within the chapter for additional information.

Key to Teaching Strategies

The following designations will help you decide which activities are appropriate for your students.

L1 Level 1 activities should be appropriate for students with learning difficulties.

L2 Level 2 activities should be within the ability range of all students.

L3 Level 3 activities are designed for above-average students.

ELL ELL activities should be within the ability range of English Language Learners.

COOP LEARN Cooperative Learning activities are designed for small group work.

LS Multiple Learning Styles logos are used throughout to indicate strategies that address different learning styles.

P These strategies represent student products that can be placed into a best-work portfolio.

Hands-on Activities

Activity Worksheets

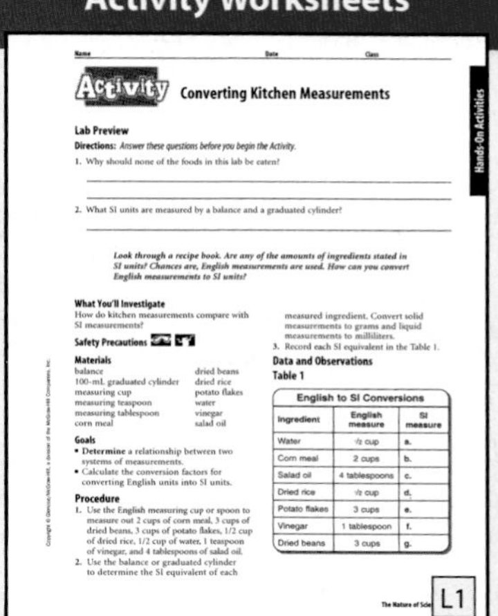
Name Date Class

Activity — Converting Kitchen Measurements

Hands-On Activities

Lab Preview

Directions: *Answer these questions before you begin the Activity.*

1. Why should none of the foods in this lab be eaten?
2. What SI units are measured by a balance and a graduated cylinder?

Look through a recipe book. Are any of the amounts of ingredients stated in SI units? Chances are, English measurements are used. How can you convert English measurements to SI units?

What You'll Investigate

How do kitchen measurements compare with SI measurements?

Safety Precautions

Materials

balance, 100-mL graduated cylinder, measuring cup, measuring teaspoon, measuring tablespoon, corn meal, dried beans, dried rice, potato flakes, water, vinegar, salad oil

Goals

- **Determine** a relationship between two systems of measurements.
- Calculate the conversion factors for converting English units into SI units.

Procedure

1. Use the English measuring cup or spoon to measure out 2 cups of corn meal, 3 cups of dried beans, 3 cups of potato flakes, 1/2 cup of dried rice, 1/2 cup of water, 1 teaspoon of vinegar, and 4 tablespoons of salad oil.
2. Use the balance or graduated cylinder to determine the SI equivalent of each measured ingredient. Convert solid measurements to grams and liquid measurements to milliliters.
3. Record each SI equivalent in the Table 1.

Data and Observations

Table 1

English to SI Conversions

Ingredient	English measure	SI measure
Water	1/2 cup	a.
Corn meal	2 cups	b.
Salad oil	4 tablespoons	c.
Dried rice	1/2 cup	d.
Potato flakes	3 cups	e.
Vinegar	1 tablespoon	f.
Dried beans	3 cups	g.

L1

Laboratory Activities

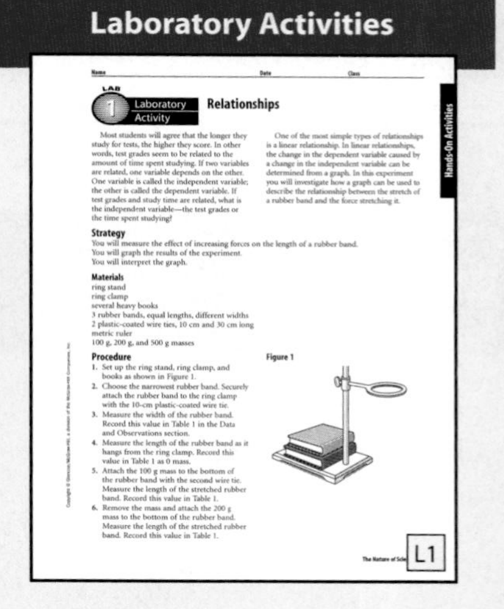
Name Date Class

LAB 1 Laboratory Activity — Relationships

Hands-On Activities

Most students will agree that the longer they study for tests, the higher they score. In other words, test grades seem to be related to the amount of time spent studying. If two variables are related, one variable depends on the other. One variable is called the independent variable; the other is called the dependent variable. If test grades and study time are related, what is the independent variable—the test grades or the time spent studying?

One of the most simple types of relationships is a linear relationship. In linear relationships, the change in the dependent variable caused by a change in the independent variable can be determined from a graph. In this experiment you will investigate how a graph can be used to describe the relationship between the stretch of a rubber band and the force stretching it.

Strategy

You will measure the effect of increasing forces on the length of a rubber band.
You will graph the results of the experiment.
You will interpret the graph.

Materials

ring stand
ring clamp
several heavy books
3 rubber bands, equal lengths, different widths
2 plastic-coated wire ties, 10 cm and 30 cm long
metric ruler
100 g, 200 g, and 500 g masses

Procedure

1. Set up the ring stand, ring clamp, and books as shown in Figure 1.
2. Choose the narrowest rubber band. Securely attach the rubber band to the ring clamp with the 10-cm plastic-coated wire tie.
3. Measure the width of the rubber band. Record this value in Table 1 in the Data and Observations section.
4. Measure the length of the rubber band as it hangs from the ring clamp. Record this value in Table 1 as 0 mass.
5. Attach the 100 g mass to the bottom of the rubber band with the second wire tie. Measure the length of the stretched rubber band. Record this value in Table 1.
6. Remove the mass and attach the 200 g mass to the bottom of the rubber band. Measure the length of the stretched rubber band. Record this value in Table 1.

Figure 1

L1

Meeting Different Ability Levels

Content Outline

Note-taking Worksheet — The Nature of Science

Section 1 The Methods of Science

L1

Reinforcement

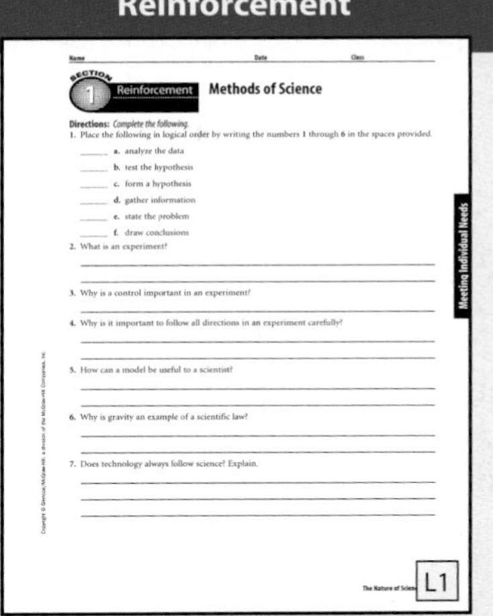
Section 1 Reinforcement — Methods of Science

L1

Directed Reading

Directed Reading for Content Mastery — Overview: The Nature of Science

L1

Enrichment

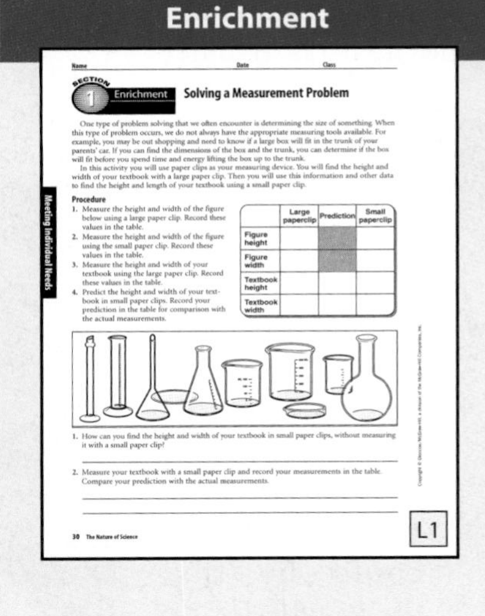
Section 1 Enrichment — Solving a Measurement Problem

L1

Spanish Directed Reading

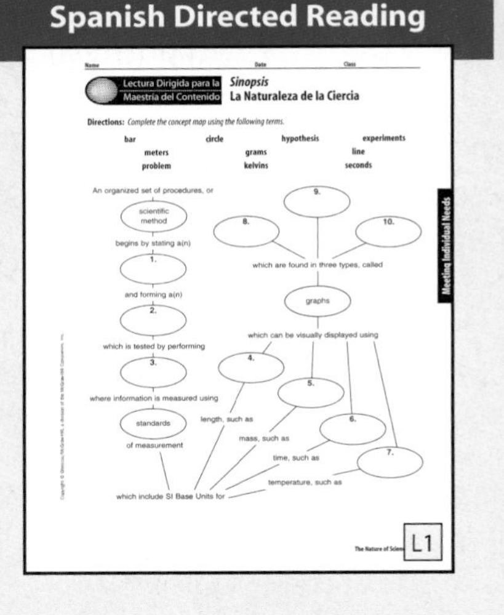
Lectura Dirigida para la Maestría del Contenido — Sinopsis: La Naturaleza de la Ciercia

L1

Assessment

Chapter Tests

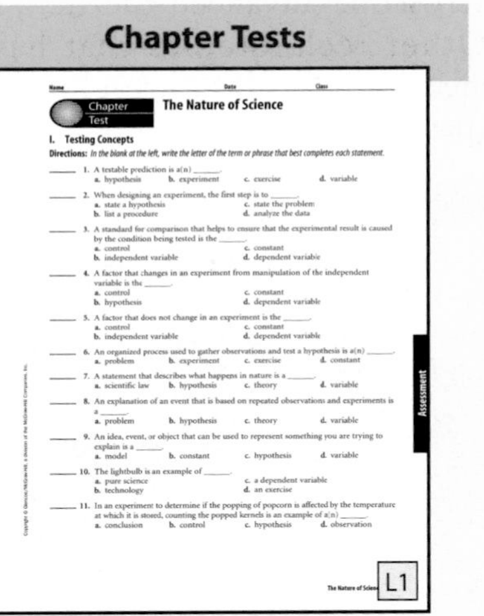
Chapter Test — The Nature of Science

L1

Test Practice Workbook

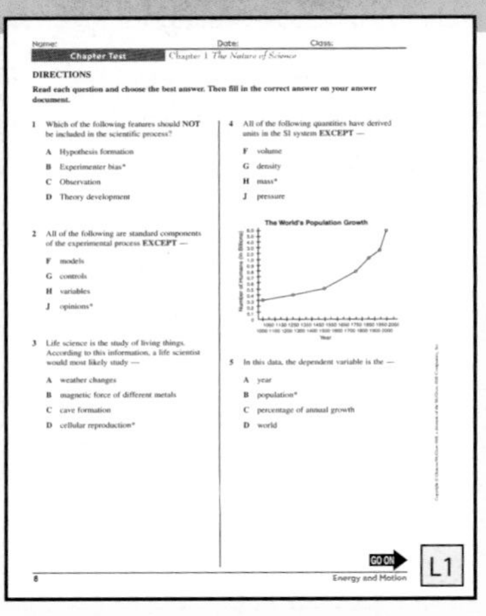
Chapter Test — Chapter 1: The Nature of Science

L1

Chapter Review

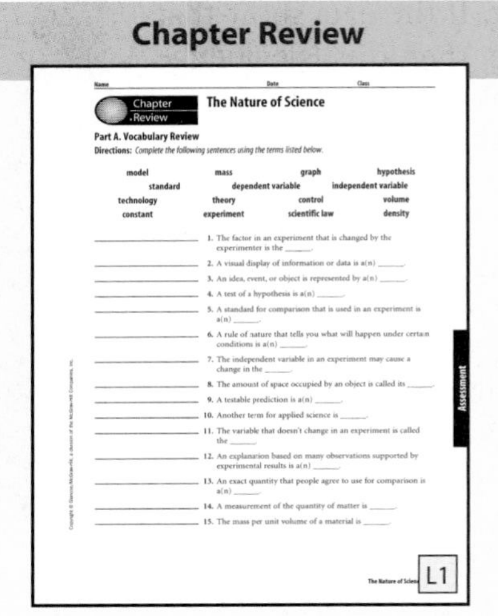
Chapter Review — The Nature of Science

L1

Science Content Background

SECTION 1

The Methods of Science

Scientific Methods

Many science educators are no longer using the term "The Scientific Method." This is because there is really no one method; an astronomer works in ways that are very different from those of a medical researcher. Also, science does not always proceed in the linear manner described by "The Scientific Method." The term "scientific methods" indicates that a variety of approaches are employed in scientific inquiry.

Investigations will sometimes use a null hypothesis. This null hypothesis is usually the opposite of the scientist's hypothesis for what will happen in the investigation. Thus if a medical researcher thinks Drug PR will help cure disease PQ, a null hypothesis could be that there will be no difference in symptoms between people who received PR and those who didn't receive it. If the data show that the null hypothesis is false, then this is evidence that the original hypothesis may be correct.

Fun Fact

In some scientific studies, neither the doctor nor the patients in the control and treatment groups know whether the given medication is the experimental drug or the placebo. These experiments, called "double-blind" experiments, help assure unbiased, statistically reliable results.

The term *experiment* should be reserved for occasions when scientists or students manipulate a variable to see the result. The independent variable is the thing or variable that is changed. This is done to see the effect on the dependent variable.

In human drug experiments, a drug is given to a treatment group and a placebo is given to a control group. A placebo is something, such as a sugar pill, that resembles medication but contains no drug. It is given because people often get better just because they believe they are taking something that will help even though they are not. The people in the drug experiment don't know whether they are taking the new drug or the placebo.

Using Science—Technology

Pure science is often contrasted with applied science. Pure science seeks knowledge just for the sake of knowledge. Applied science seeks to develop technologies that improve people's lives.

While science certainly leads to the development of technologies, technologies also lead to the development of science. The invention of the light microscope advanced the field of cell biology. Other technologies that have influenced science include gel electrophoresis, telescopes, and particle accelerators.

Barry L. Runk/Grant Heilman Photography, Inc.

Standards of Measurement

Measurement Systems

The SI system of measurement allows easy conversions among SI units. The SI system stops being easy when measurements are converted into English units. A gram is approximately the mass of one regular size paper clip. A kilometer is 2.5 times around an Olympic track. A liter is just a bit more than a quart of milk.

Measuring Distance

A common metric unit for area is the hectare. One hectare is equal to 10,000 square meters.

Measuring Time and Temperature

Three systems of units are commonly used for temperature. Almost all the people in the world use the Celsius system. People in the United States use the Fahrenheit system. While United States scientists typically use the Celsius or Kelvin system, many United States meteorologists use Fahrenheit. The Kelvin is the official SI unit for temperature.

Measuring Matter

Water has a density of 1 g/cm^3, so if you didn't have a scale you could measure 5 g of water by using a graduated cylinder to measure 5 cm^3, which is 5 mL, of water. Objects that have a density greater than 1 g/cm^3 sink in water and those with a lower density float.

Communicating with Graphs

SECTION 3

Choosing the Right Graph

Line graphs are appropriate for continuous data. This is numerical data that have a continuous range of values such as time of travel, growth in height of a plant, or current flow in a wire. Bar graphs are appropriate for categorical or nominal data. This is data that fall into defined categories or that have specific names such as boys and girls; types of primates; or types of fruits.

For additional content background on this topic, go to the Glencoe Science Web site at science.glencoe.com.

Spencer Grant/PhotoEdit

Fun Fact

Temperatures on the Celsius scale can be converted to equivalent temperatures on the Fahrenheit temperature scale by multiplying the Celsius temperature by $\frac{9}{5}$ and adding 32° to the result, according to the formula $(\frac{9}{5})C + 32 = F$.

The Nature of Science

Chapter Vocabulary

scientific method
hypothesis
experiment
variable
dependent variable
independent variable
constant
control
bias
model
theory
scientific law
technology
standard
SI
volume
density
mass
graph

What do you think?

Science Journal This photograph shows numbers on the hull of a ship that indicate how low in the water the ship is riding. If the ship is carrying too much cargo, it will ride too low in the water and be more likely to sink.

CHAPTER 1

The Nature of Science

Stacy Dragila of the United States won the women's pole vault event at the 2000 summer Olympics. The winner was decided through careful measurement of the jumps. In this chapter, you will learn how measurements are important to scientists. You also will learn about the methods scientists use to conduct their studies and how they communicate findings with graphs.

What do you think?

Science Journal Look at the picture below with a classmate. Discuss what this might be. Here's a hint: *Shipping authorities rely on these numbers for safety reasons.* Write your answer or best guess in your Science Journal.

Theme Connection

Systems and Interactions Scientific methods provide a system for observing interactions in the world, testing those observations, and forming hypotheses, theories, and laws about how and why interactions occur and have the consequences they do.

During a track meet, one athlete ran 1 mile in 5 min and another athlete ran 5,000 m in 280 s. The two runners used different units to describe their races, so how can you compare them? Do the following activity to explore how choosing different units can make it difficult to compare measurements.

Discover how long a foot is

1. Measure the distance across your classroom using your foot as a measuring device.
2. Record your measurement and name your measuring unit.
3. Now, have your partner measure the same distance using his or her foot as the measuring device. Record this measurement and make up a different name for the unit.

Observe

In your Science Journal, explain why you think it might be important to have standard, well-defined units to make measurements.

Before You Read

Making a Question Study Fold **Asking yourself questions helps you stay focused and better understand scientific processes when you are reading the chapter.**

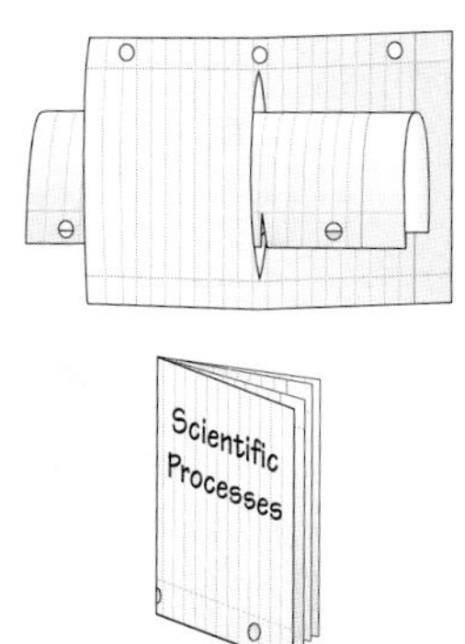

1. Stack two sheets of notebook paper in front of you so the long sides are at the top. Fold both in half from the left side to the right side. Unfold and separate.
2. Cut one sheet along the fold line, from one margin line to the other.
3. Place the second sheet in front of you so the long side is at the top. Cut along the fold line from the bottom of the paper to the margin line and then from the top of the paper to the margin line.
4. Insert the second sheet of paper into the cut of the first paper. Unfold it and align the cuts along the folds.
5. Title your book *Scientific Processes.* Before you read the chapter, write a question about something in your daily life on each page.

5

Before You Read

FOLDABLES Reading & Study Skills

Dinah Zike Study Fold

Purpose Students make a Foldable booklet and write questions in it from everyday life. They use these questions to help them stay focused and better understand scientific processes as they read the chapter.

For additional help, see Foldables Worksheet, p. 17 in **Chapter Resources Booklet,** or go to the Glencoe Science Web site at **science.glencoe.com.** See After You Read in the Study Guide at the end of this chapter.

EXPLORE ACTIVITY

Purpose Use the Explore Activity to introduce students to nonstandard measuring units. L1 ELL COOP LEARN IS Interpersonal

Materials Do not make standard measuring devices, such as metersticks, available.

Teaching Strategy Have students repeat the activity, measuring a different distance.

Observe

Only measurements made using the same standard can be easily compared. Standard units of measurement make it possible to compare measurements by different people in different locations.

Oral Have students draw cartoons that explain the limitations of the measurements they made. It is difficult to measure fractions of units accurately and to compare data from groups that use different units. Use **Performance Assessment in the Science Classroom,** p. 133.

SECTION

The Methods of Science

1 Motivate

Bellringer Transparency

Display the Section Focus Transparency for Section 1. Use the accompanying Transparency Activity Master. L2 ELL

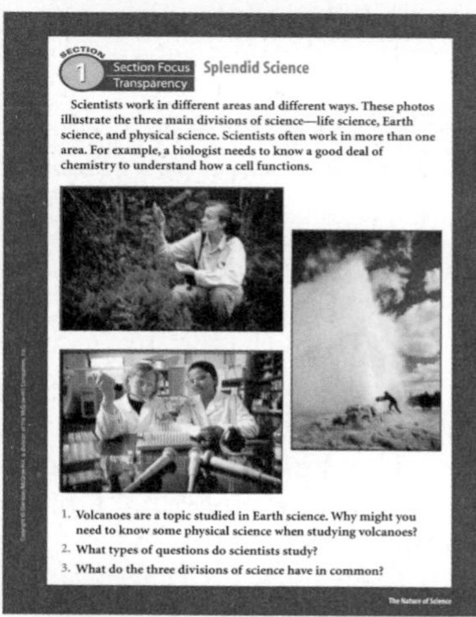

SECTION 1 Section Focus Transparency **Splendid Science**

Scientists work in different areas and different ways. These photos illustrate the three main divisions of science—life science, Earth science, and physical science. Scientists often work in more than one area. For example, a biologist needs to know a good deal of chemistry to understand how a cell functions.

1. Volcanoes are a topic studied in Earth science. Why might you need to know some physical science when studying volcanoes?
2. What types of questions do scientists study?
3. What do the three divisions of science have in common?

The Nature of Science

Tie to Prior Knowledge

Discuss with students what they believe science to be. Have them compare their ideas with the definition of science given in the text.

SECTION

The Methods of Science

As You Read

What You'll Learn

- **Identify** the steps scientists often use to solve problems.
- **Describe** why scientists use variables.
- **Compare and contrast** science and technology.

Vocabulary

scientific method, hypothesis, experiment, variable, dependent variable, independent variable, constant, control, bias, model, theory, scientific law, technology

Why It's Important

Using scientific methods will help you solve problems.

What is science?

Science is not just a subject in school. It is a method for studying the natural world. After all, science comes from the Latin word *scientia*, which means "knowledge." Science is a process that uses observation and investigation to gain knowledge about events in nature.

Nature follows a set of rules. Many rules, such as those concerning how the human body works, are complex. Other rules, such as the fact that Earth rotates once every 12 h, are simpler. When you study these natural patterns, you are using science.

Major Categories of Science Science covers many different topics that can be classified according to three main categories. (1) Life science deals with living things. (2) Earth science investigates Earth and space. (3) Physical science deals with matter and energy. In this textbook, you will study mainly physical science. Sometimes, though, a scientific study will overlap the categories. One scientist, for example, might study the motions of the human body to understand how to build better artificial limbs. Is this scientist studying energy and matter or how muscles operate? She is studying both life science and physical science. It is not always clear what kind of science you are using, as shown in **Figure 1.**

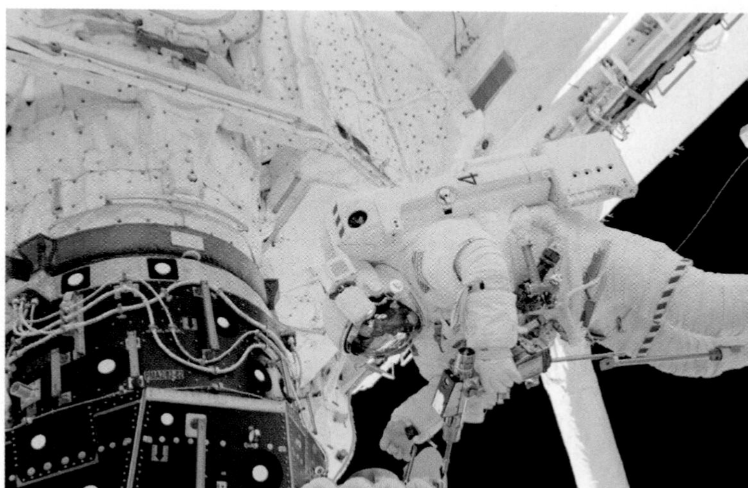

Figure 1
Astronaut Michael Lopez-Alegria uses a pistol grip tool on the *International Space Station.* *What evidence do you see of the three main branches of science in the photograph?*

Section Assessment Planner

PORTFOLIO
Earth Science Integration, p. 11

PERFORMANCE ASSESSMENT
Skill Builder Activities, p. 13
See page 34 for more options.

CONTENT ASSESSMENT
Section, p. 13
Challenge, p. 13
Chapter, pp. 34–35

Science Explains Nature Scientific explanations help you understand the natural world. Sometimes these explanations must be modified. As more is learned about the natural world, some of the earlier explanations might be found to be incomplete or new technology might provide more accurate answers.

For example, look at **Figure 2.** In the late eighteenth century, most scientists thought that heat was an invisible fluid with very little mass. Heat seems to flow like a fluid. It also moves away from a warm body in all directions, just as a fluid moves outward when you spill it on the floor.

However, the heat fluid idea did not explain everything. If heat were an actual fluid, an iron bar that had a temperature of 1,000°C should have more mass than it did at 100°C because it would have more of the heat fluid in it. The eighteenth-century scientists thought they just were not able to measure the small mass of the heat fluid on the balances they had. When more precise balances were invented and no difference in mass was detected, scientists had to change the explanation.

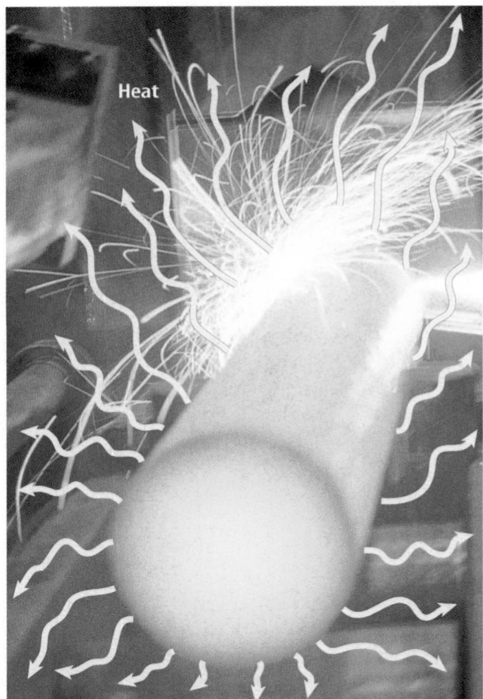

Figure 2
Many years ago, scientists thought that heat, such as this in the metal rod, was a fluid. *How does heat act similar to a fluid?*

Investigations How do scientists learn more about the natural world? Scientists learn new information by performing investigations, which can be done many different ways. Some investigations involve simply observing something that occurs and recording the observations, perhaps in a journal. Other investigations involve setting up experiments that test the effect of one thing on another. Some investigations involve building a model that resembles something in the natural world and then testing the model to see how it acts. Often, a scientist will use something from all three ways when attempting to learn about the natural world.

Reading Check *Why do scientific explanations change?*

Research Visit the Glencoe Science Web site at **science.glencoe.com** for information about why leaves change color in the autumn. Make a prediction about why this occurs. Support your answer with evidence.

Scientific Methods

Although scientists do not always follow a rigid set of steps, investigations often follow a general pattern. An organized set of investigation procedures is called a **scientific method.** Six steps often found in scientific methods are shown in **Figure 3.** A scientist might add new steps, repeat some steps many times, or skip other steps altogether when doing an investigation.

2 Teach

What is science?

Activity

Have students work as a class or in large groups. Have each group make a Venn diagram representing the three main branches of science. Place three overlapping circles on a large sheet of paper or a bulletin board and label each circle with one major category of science. Have them use pictures from newspapers and magazines to fill in the areas on the diagram. Be sure the overlap areas of the circles are large enough to accommodate examples that apply to more than one branch of science. Be sure students can justify each placement. L1 ELL COOP LEARN LS **Visual-Spatial**

SCIENCE Online
Internet Addresses

Explore the Glencoe Science Web site at **science.glencoe.com** to find out more about topics in this section.

Resource Manager

Chapter Resources Booklet
Transparency Activity, p. 44
Note-taking Worksheets, pp. 33–34
Enrichment, p. 30

Visual Learning

Figure 2 Discuss with students ways scientists study heat. Point out that scientists study the structure of the materials through which heat travels, why heat travels through them, and what heat really is. L1 LS **Logical-Mathematical**

Caption Answers

Figure 1 physical science—pistol grip tool and other instruments; Earth science—event taking place in space; life science—space suit that allows a human body to survive in space

Figure 2 It flows from one location to another.

Answer Scientists learn new information.

Scientific Methods

Use an Analogy

Ask students to describe how they found their different classrooms on the first day of school in this building. Explain that their methods are analogous to the way the scientific methods discussed in this section are used.

Use Science Words

Word Origin The word *experiment* is from the Latin word *experimentum*, which means "proof or test." Have students write entries in their Science Journals explaining how the meaning of the word reflects the meaning of its root. L2 LS **Linguistic**

Fun Fact

Experiments can be done to confirm a hypothesis about how an independent variable affects a dependent variable. They can also be done to confirm a null hypothesis. A null hypothesis states that the independent variable does not affect the dependent variable.

Discussion

Why are results that do not confirm a hypothesis important? These experimental results can help scientists adjust and restate hypotheses. L2

LS **Logical-Mathematical**

Figure 3
The series of procedures shown below is one way to use scientific methods to solve a problem.

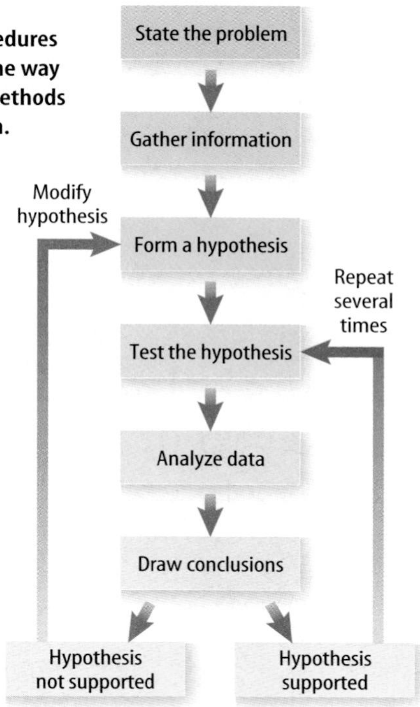

State the problem
Gather information
Form a hypothesis
Test the hypothesis
Analyze data
Draw conclusions
Hypothesis not supported
Hypothesis supported
Modify hypothesis
Repeat several times

Stating a Problem Many scientific investigations begin when someone observes that an event in nature repeats itself and wonders why this is true. Then the question of "why" is the problem. Sometimes a statement of a problem arises from an activity that is not working. Some early work on guided missiles showed that the instruments in the nose of the missiles did not always work. The problem statement involved finding a material to protect the instruments from the harsh conditions of flight.

Later, National Aeronautics and Space Administration (NASA) scientists made a similar problem statement. They wanted to build a new vehicle—the space shuttle—that could carry people to outer space and back again. Guided missiles did not have this capability. NASA needed to find a material for the outer skin of the space shuttle that could withstand the heat and forces of reentry into Earth's atmosphere.

Researching and Gathering Information Before testing a hypothesis, it is useful to learn as much as possible about the background of the problem. Have others found information that will help determine what tests to do and what tests will not be helpful? The NASA scientists gathered information about melting points and other properties of the various materials that might be used. In many cases, tests had to be performed to learn the properties of new, recently created materials.

Forming a Hypothesis A **hypothesis** is an educated guess using what you know and what you observe. NASA scientists knew that a ceramic coating had been found to solve the guided missile problem. They hypothesized that a ceramic material also might work on the space shuttle.

Testing a Hypothesis Some hypotheses can be tested by making observations. Others can be tested by building a model and relating it to real-life situations. One common way to test a hypothesis is to perform an experiment. An **experiment** tests the effect of one thing on another using controlled conditions.

Cultural Diversity

Shamanic Medicine Principles of science have been used to solve problems throughout the world and throughout history. In the rain forests of Central and South America, shamans do much of the healing. For thousands of years these shamans have observed and tested local plants and learned which ones can be used for medicines. Today scientists from industries that specialize in manufacturing prescription drugs are working with these shamans to identify the materials in the plants that have medicinal value.

Variables An experiment usually contains at least two variables. A **variable** is a quantity that can have more than a single value. You might set up an experiment to determine which of three fertilizers helps plants to grow the biggest. Before you begin your tests, you would need to think of all the variables that might cause the plants to grow bigger. Possible variables include plant type, amount of sunlight, water used, room temperature, type of soil, and type of fertilizer.

In this experiment, the amount of growth is the **dependent variable** because its value changes according to the changes in the other variables. The variable you change to see how it will affect the dependent variable is called the **independent variable.**

Constants and Controls To be sure you are testing to see how fertilizer affects growth, you must keep the other possible variables the same for each test, or trial. A variable that does not change when other variables change is called a **constant.** You might set up four trials, using the same soil and type of plant. Each plant is given the same amount of sunlight and water and is kept at the same temperature. These are constants. Three of the plants receive a different type of fertilizer. Fertilizer is the independent variable.

The fourth plant is not fertilized. This plant is a control. A **control** is the standard by which the test results can be compared. Suppose that after several days, the three fertilized plants grow between 2 and 3 cm. If the unfertilized plant grows 1.5 cm, you know the growth of the fertilized plants was due to the fertilizers.

How might the NASA scientists set up an experiment to solve the problem of the damaged tiles shown in **Figure 4?** What are possible variables, constants, and controls?

Reading Check *Why is a control used in an experiment?*

Life Science INTEGRATION

Through observations of living organisms, scientists have designed a classification system. The system groups organisms according to variables such as habits and physical and chemical features. As new organisms are discovered, scientific methods are used to determine their classification.

Figure 4
NASA has had an ongoing mission to improve the space shuttle. A technician is replacing tiles damaged upon reentry into Earth's atmosphere.

Activity

Organize the class into teams and give each team a large index card on which to write a problem for an experiment. Have teams exchange their cards. Each team should generate a hypothesis for the question they hold and write it on the card. Have students exchange cards with a different group. Ask each team to devise an experiment based on the question and hypothesis on the card the team now has. Students should be sure to identify the constants, independent variable, dependent variable, and control in the experiment. L2 COOP LEARN

LS **Logical-Mathematical**

Text Question Answer

They might make tiles of many different materials and subject them all to the heat and other stresses encountered by the shuttle. The variables would be the materials used, the constants would be the conditions to which the tiles were subjected, and scientists could use tiles from the first shuttle as controls.

Life Science INTEGRATION

The science that deals with the naming and classifying of organisms is called taxonomy. Taxonomists continually collect and analyze data, sometimes changing the way organisms are classified as a result of their findings. Fungi, for example, were classified as plants until data convinced scientists to put fungi in their own kingdom.

Reading Check

Answer A control is a standard to which test results can be compared.

Active Reading

ReQuest To improve listening skills, have students listen carefully as you read the discussion of scientific methods in this section. After the reading, have students construct questions to be discussed in class. You can have students reread the section and participate in the questioning with other students.

Resource Manager

Reading and Writing Skill Activities, p. 37
Cultural Diversity, p. 29
Science Inquiry Labs, p. 47

Scientific Methods, continued

Use Science Words

Word Meaning Some of the terms used when analyzing data are *mean*, *mode*, *median*, and *average*. These terms have slightly different meanings and can be confusing. Have students define each one. *mean:* a value that is computed by dividing the sum of a set of values by the number of values; *mode:* the most frequent value of a set of data; *median:* a value in an ordered set of values below and above which there is an equal number of values or, if there is no one middle number, a value which is the arithmetic mean of the two middle values; *average:* same as mean. L2 ELL LS **Linguistic**

Extension

When analyzing the results of many different trials, scientists use the methods of statistics. One of the most useful tools of statistics is normal distribution. Have students find out what this tool is and describe situations in physical science in which it might be used. A normal distribution is a distribution of values that produces a symmetrical bell-shaped curve. It shows the distribution of values that results from many random variables. L3 LS **Logical-Mathematical**

Fun Fact

It is impossible for any experiment to be completely objective and free from bias. The questions asked include an inherent bias. Scientists work to minimize bias and to be as aware as possible of the bias they introduce.

Reading Check

Answer A bias occurs when what the scientist expects changes how the results are viewed.

Figure 5
An exciting and important part of investigating something is sharing your ideas with others, as this student is doing at a science fair.

Analyzing the Data A part of an experiment includes recording observations and organizing the test data into easy-to-read tables and graphs. Later in this chapter you will study ways to display data. When you are making and recording observations, you should include all results, even unexpected ones. Many important discoveries have been made from unexpected occurrences.

Interpreting the data and analyzing the observations is an important step. If the data are not organized in a logical manner, wrong conclusions can be drawn. No matter how well a scientist communicates and shares that data, someone else might not agree with the data. Scientists share their data through reports and conferences. In **Figure 5** a student is displaying her data.

Drawing Conclusions Based on the analysis of your data, you decide whether or not your hypothesis is supported. When lives are at stake, such as with the space shuttle, you must be very sure of your results. For the hypothesis to be considered valid and widely accepted, the experiment must result in the exact same data every time it is repeated. If your experiment does not support your hypothesis, you must reconsider the hypothesis. Perhaps it needs to be revised or your experiment needs to be conducted differently.

Being Objective Scientists also should be careful to reduce bias in their experiments. A **bias** occurs when what the scientist expects changes how the results are viewed. This expectation might cause a scientist to select a result from one trial over those from other trials. Bias also might be found if the advantages of a product being tested are used in a promotion and the drawbacks are not presented.

Scientists can lessen bias by running as many trials as possible and by keeping accurate notes of each observation made. Valid experiments also must have data that are measurable. For example, a scientist performing a global warming study must base his or her data on accurate measures of global temperature. This allows others to compare the results to data they obtain from a similar experiment. Most importantly, the experiment must be repeatable. Findings are supportable when other scientists perform the same experiment and get the same results.

Reading Check *What is bias in science?*

Curriculum Connection

Language Arts Emphasize to students that being objective is important in reporting information in all areas. Have them search through magazines and newspapers and find articles in which the writer's bias has influenced the article. L2 LS **Linguistic**

Visualizing with Models

Sometimes, scientists cannot see everything that they are testing. They might be observing something that is too large, too small, or takes too much time to see completely. In these cases, scientists use models. A **model** represents an idea, event, or object to help people better understand it.

Models in History Models have been used throughout history. One scientist, Lord Kelvin, who lived in England in the 1800s, was famous for making models. To model how atoms behaved in a fluid, he put balls into a bowl of jelly and encouraged people to move the balls around with their hands. Kelvin's work to explain the nature of temperature and heat still is used today.

High-Tech Models Scientific models don't always have to be something you can touch. Today, many scientists use computers to build models. NASA experiments involving space flight would not be practical without computers. The complex equations would take far too long to calculate by hand, and errors could be introduced much too easily.

Another type of model is a simulator, like the one shown in **Figure 6.** An airplane simulator enables pilots to practice problem solving with various situations and conditions they might encounter when in the air. This model will react the way a plane does when it flies. It gives pilots a safe way to test different reactions and to practice certain procedures before they fly a real plane.

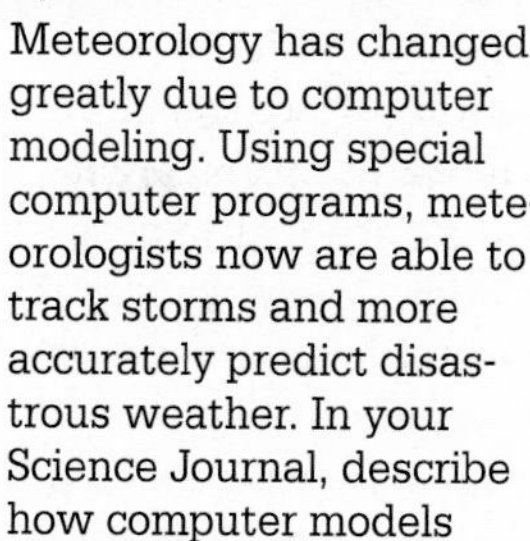

Earth Science INTEGRATION

Meteorology has changed greatly due to computer modeling. Using special computer programs, meteorologists now are able to track storms and more accurately predict disastrous weather. In your Science Journal, describe how computer models might help save lives.

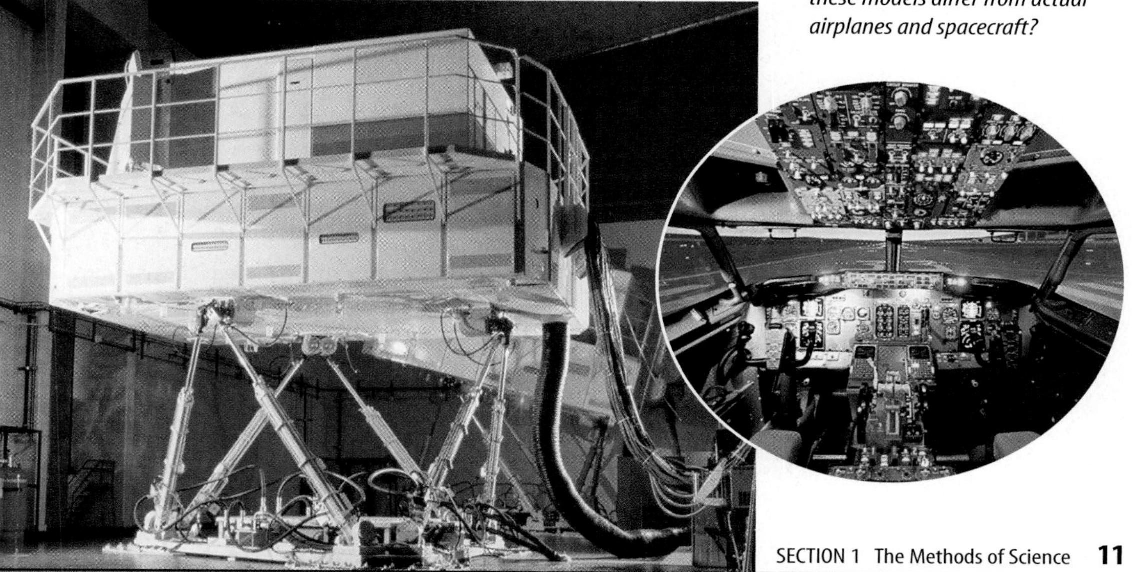

Figure 6
Pilots and astronauts use flight simulators for training. *How do these models differ from actual airplanes and spacecraft?*

Visualizing with Models

Earth Science INTEGRATION

Journal entries should include that predictions of severe weather, such as tornadoes, hurricanes, and flooding rains, can warn residents of an area to take precautions or evacuate the area. P

Activity

Have students make posters showing situations in which models are used to study something too large to study directly, too small to be studied directly, and too dangerous to be studied directly. Possible answers: the solar system, which is too large to be studied directly; the tiny particles that make up matter, which are too small to be studied directly; and a plane crash, which is too dangerous to be studied directly L2 **Visual-Spatial**

Caption Answer

Figure 6 They are idealized and not real, so they don't always mimic the real situation exactly. They also don't cause any damage to people or materials when the pilot makes a mistake and crashes.

Discussion

Why are computers useful for modeling situations? Computers can slow down or speed up action and can show how a process changes over time. They also can be programmed to make predictions based on data put into them. L2 **Logical-Mathematical**

Resource Manager

Chapter Resources Booklet

Directed Reading for Content Mastery, p. 20

Life Science Critical Thinking/Problem Solving, p. 1

Earth Science Critical Thinking/Problem Solving, p. 14

Visual Learning

Figure 6 Ask students whether they have used a driving simulator in a video game. Ask them to explain what it taught them about driving and why it does not really equip them to drive. The simulation might give them practice in steering, accelerating, and stopping, but it does not involve roadway experience with other cars. L2 **Visual-Spatial**

Scientific Theories and Laws

science.glencoe.com
Access this Web site for activities and the **Content Mastery** booklet to reinforce chapter content and vocabulary.

Reading Check

Answer A theory can change if its supporting data changes. A law is assumed to be true and doesn't change. Also, a law tells what happens but does not explain why. Theories try to explain why things happen.

The Limitations of Science

Caption Answer

Figure 7 no

Using Science—Technology

Teacher FYI

Many materials or processes commonly used are spin-offs of scientific research. That is, they result from scientific research done to solve another problem. For example, ceramic cookware that will withstand extremes in temperature is the result of research on ceramic tiles to be used on spacecraft. Aspartame, an artificial sweetener, was accidentally discovered while another substance was being researched.

SCIENCE Online

Research Visit the Glencoe Science Web site at **science.glencoe.com** to find out about Archimedes principle. Would you classify this principle as a scientific theory or scientific law? Communicate to your class what you learn.

Scientific Theories and Laws

A scientific **theory** is an explanation of things or events based on knowledge gained from many observations and investigations. It is not a guess. If scientists repeat an investigation and the results always support the hypothesis, the hypothesis can be called a theory. Just because a scientific theory has data supporting it does not mean it will never change. Recall that the theory about heat being a fluid was discarded after further experiments. A theory accepted today might at some time in the future also be discarded.

A **scientific law** is a statement about what hapens in nature and that seems to be true all the time. Laws tell you what will happen under certain conditions, but they don't explain why or how something happens. Gravity is an example of a scientific law. The law of gravity says that any one mass will attract another mass. To date, no experiments have been performed that disprove the law of gravity.

A theory can be used to explain a law. For example, many theories have been proposed to explain how the law of gravity works. Even so, there are few theories in science and even fewer laws.

Reading Check *What is the difference between a scientific theory and a scientific law?*

Figure 7
Science can't answer all questions. *Can anyone prove that you like this artwork?*

The Limitations of Science

Science can help you explain many things about the world, but science cannot explain or solve everything. Although it's the scientist's job to make guesses, the scientist also has to make sure his or her guesses can be tested and verified. But how do you prove that people will like a play or a piece of music? You cannot and science cannot.

Most questions about emotions and values are not scientific questions. They cannot be tested. You might take a survey to get people's opinions about such questions, but that would not prove that the opinions are true for everyone. A survey might predict that you will like the art in **Figure 7,** but science cannot prove that you or others will.

Resource Manager

Chapter Resources Booklet
Reinforcement, p. 27
Cultural Diversity, p. 49

Science Journal

Universal Theories Have students investigate theories about the origin of the universe and explain why these theories are not scientific laws. The current main theory is the Big Bang Theory. This theory is not a law because it tries to explain how or why something happens. A law simply describes a pattern. L2
LS **Logical-Mathematical**

Using Science—Technology

Many people use the terms *science* and *technology* interchangeably, but they are not the same. **Technology** is the application of science to help people. For example, when a chemist develops a new, lightweight material that can withstand great amounts of heat, this is science. When that material is used on the space shuttle, it is technology. **Figure 8** shows other examples of technology.

Technology doesn't always follow science, however. Sometimes the process of discovery can be reversed. One important historic example of science following technology is the development of the steam engine. The inventors of the steam engine had little idea of how it worked. They just knew that steam from boiling water could move the engine. Because the steam engine became so important to industry, scientists began analyzing how it worked. James Prescott Joule and Sadi Carnot, who lived in the 1800s, learned so much from the steam engine that they developed revolutionary ideas about the nature of heat.

Do science and technology always produce positive results? Some people don't think so. The benefits of some technological advances, such as nuclear technology and genetic engineering, are subjects of debate. Being more knowledgeable about science can help society address these issues as they arise.

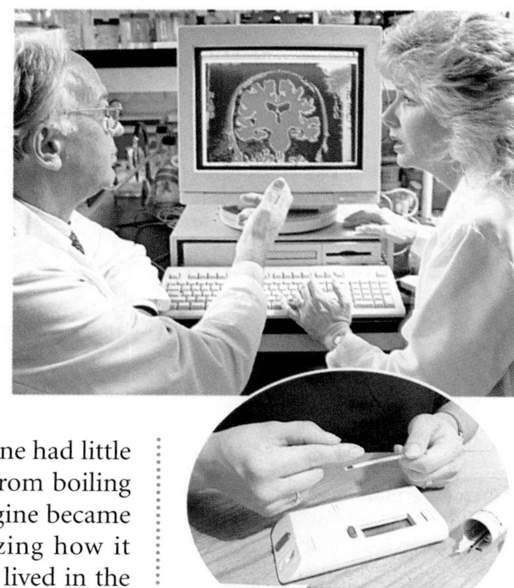

Figure 8
Technology is the application of science. *What type of science (life, Earth, or physical) is applied in these examples of technology?*

Section 1 Assessment

1. What is the first step a scientist usually takes to solve a problem?
2. What is the dependent variable in an experiment that shows how the volume of gas changes with changes in temperature?
3. Explain why a control is needed in a valid experiment.
4. How is science different from technology?
5. **Think Critically** You water your houseplant every Saturday. On Wednesday you notice its leaves are drooping. You give it some water, and the leaves perk up. You conclude you need to water twice a week. Was this a valid experiment? Explain.

Skill Builder Activities

6. **Forming Hypotheses** You don't have enough money to buy the music CD you want. Form a hypothesis about what you could do to solve the problem. How could you test your hypothesis before putting your plan in action? **For more help, refer to the Science Skill Handbook.**
7. **Communicating** You need to design a container to hold a new irregularly shaped device. Write the steps of the method you plan to use to help your team find the solution. **For more help, refer to the Science Skill Handbook.**

Caption Answer

Figure 8 The top picture shows applications of physical science (computer) and life science (medical image). The lower picture shows the application of physical science (instruments) and life science (measuring levels of sugar in blood).

3 Assess

Reteach

Ask students to design an experiment that will determine whether hot water freezes faster than cold water does. Make sure that constants include the amount of water, the size and kind of container, the amount of time in the freezer, and the freezer used. L2

LS **Logical-Mathematical**

Challenge

Have students imagine that a chemist has made some observations about a new type of plastic that may biodegrade in acidic soils. Have them state a possible hypothesis about these findings and explain how the hypothesis could be tested. L3

LS **Logical-Mathematical**

Assessment

Performance Have students perform an experiment to determine whether microwave popcorn pops better when it has been frozen. Have them identify constants, variables, and a control for the experiment. Use **Performance Assessment in the Science Classroom,** p. 95.

Answers to Section Assessment

1. Identify the problem.
2. volume of gas
3. to provide a standard against which test results can be compared
4. Science is a method for studying the natural world, and technology is the application of science to help people.
5. No; there was no control, and conditions other than the independent variable were not kept constant. Also, it did not last long enough.
6. Answers will vary but might include that the student could mow two lawns. The hypothesis could be tested by finding out how much is paid for lawn mowing.
7. Accept all reasonable answers.

SECTION

Standards of Measurement

1 Motivate

Bellringer Transparency

Display the Section Focus Transparency for Section 2. Use the accompanying Transparency Activity Master. L2 ELL

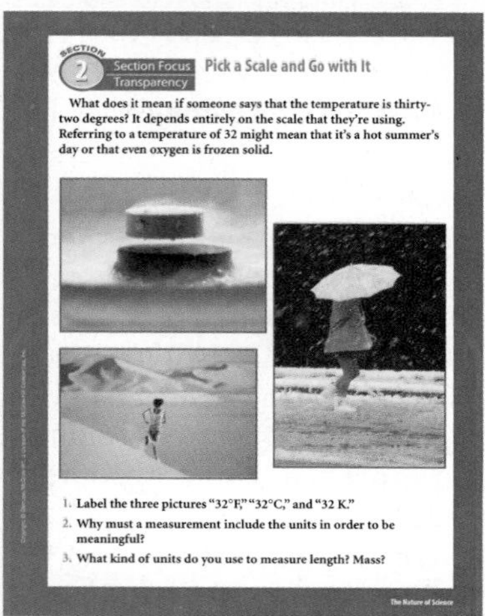
Section 2 Section Focus Transparency

Pick a Scale and Go with It

What does it mean if someone says that the temperature is thirty-two degrees? It depends entirely on the scale that they're using. Referring to a temperature of 32 might mean that it's a hot summer's day or that even oxygen is frozen solid.

1. Label the three pictures "32°F," "32°C," and "32 K."
2. Why must a measurement include the units in order to be meaningful?
3. What kind of units do you use to measure length? Mass?

The Nature of Science

Tie to Prior Knowledge

Students are familiar with measurements. Ask them to name the units they commonly use to measure length, mass, volume, and temperature.

SECTION

Standards of Measurement

As You Read

What You'll Learn

- **Name** the prefixes used in SI and indicate what multiple of ten each one represents.
- **Identify** SI units and symbols for length, volume, mass, density, time, and temperature.
- **Convert** related SI units.

Vocabulary

standard
SI
volume
density
mass

Why It's Important

By using uniform standards, nations can exchange goods and compare information easily.

Units and Standards

Accurate measurement is needed in a valid experiment. Accuracy depends upon standards. A **standard** is an exact quantity that people agree to use for comparison. Measurements made using the same standard can be compared to each other.

Look at **Figure 9.** Suppose you and a friend want to make some measurements to find out whether a desk will fit through a doorway. You have no ruler, so you decide to use your hands as measuring tools. Using the width of his hands, your friend measures the doorway and says it is 8 hands wide. Using the width of your hands, you measure the desk and find it is 7¾ hands wide. Will the desk fit through the doorway? You can't be sure. What if your hands are wider than your friend's hands? The distance equal to 7¾ of your hands might be greater than the distance equal to 8 of your friend's hands.

What went wrong? Even though you both used hands to measure, you didn't check to see whether your hands are the same width as your friend's. In other words, you didn't use a measurement standard, so you can't compare the measurements.

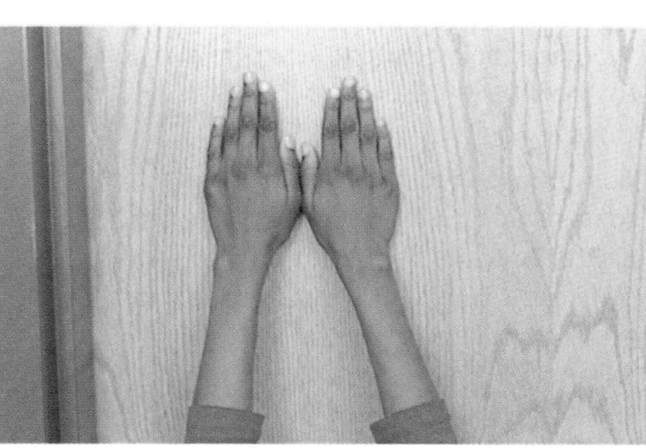

Figure 9
Hands are a convenient measuring tool, but using them can lead to misunderstanding.

Measurement Systems

Suppose the label on a ball of string indicates that the length of the string is 150. What is the length of the string? It could be 150 feet, 150 m, or 150 cm. In order for a measurement to make sense, it must include a number and a unit.

Your family might buy lumber by the foot, milk by the gallon, and potatoes by the pound. These measurement units are part of the English system of measurement, which is most commonly used in the United States. Most other nations use the metric system, which is a system of measurement based on multiples of ten. The metric system was devised by a group of scientists in the late 1700s.

Section Assessment Planner

PORTFOLIO
Extension, p. 15

PERFORMANCE ASSESSMENT
Math Skills Activity, p. 16
MiniLAB, p. 19
Skill Builder Activities, p. 21
See page 34 for more options.

CONTENT ASSESSMENT
Section, p. 21
Challenge, p. 21
Chapter, pp. 34–35

International System of Units In 1960, an improved version of the metric system was devised. Known as the International System of Units, this system is often abbreviated SI, from the *French Le Systeme Internationale d'Unites.* All **SI** standards are universally accepted and understood by scientists throughout the world. The standard kilogram, which is kept in Sèvres, France, is shown in **Figure 10.** All kilograms used throughout the world must be exactly the same as the kilogram kept in France.

Each type of SI measurement has a base unit, such as the meter. The meter is the fundamental unit of length. Every type of quantity measured in SI has a base unit and a symbol for that unit. These names and symbols are shown in **Table 1.** All other SI units are obtained from the seven units.

Figure 10
The standard for mass, the kilogram, and other standards are kept at the International Bureau of Weights and Measures in Sèvres, France. *What is the purpose of a standard?*

SI Prefixes The SI system is easy to use because it is based on multiples of ten. Prefixes are used with the names of the units to indicate what multiple of ten should be used with the units. For example, the prefix *kilo-* means "1,000." That means that one kilometer equals 1,000 meters. Likewise, one kilogram equals 1,000 grams. Because *deci-* means "one-tenth," one decimeter equals one tenth of a meter. A decigram equals one tenth of a gram. The most frequently used prefixes are shown in **Table 2.**

Reading Check *How many base units is 1 km? How many base units is 1 cg?*

Table 1 SI Base Units

Quantity Measured	Unit	Symbol
Length	meter	m
Mass	kilogram	kg
Time	second	s
Electric Current	ampere	A
Temperature	kelvin	K
Amount of Substance	mole	mol
Intensity of Light	candela	cd

Table 2 Common SI Prefixes

Prefix	Symbol	Multiplying Factor
Kilo-	k	1,000
Deci-	d	0.1
Centi-	c	0.01
Milli-	m	0.001
Micro-	μ	0.000 001
Nano-	n	0.000 000 001

2 Teach

Measurement Systems

IDENTIFYING Misconceptions

Students may think that SI is more precise than the English system because scientists use it. Point out that both systems can yield equally precise measurements. For instance, a micrometer used by machinists can measure the diameters of bolts to the nearest 0.000, 1 inch. Scientists use SI because it is easier to use and easier to convert units. Have students measure the length of their textbook using a metric ruler and a ruler calibrated in inches. Have them compare results and note that both measurements can be precise.

Caption Answer

Figure 10 It provides an accepted and understood value for a base unit.

Extension

Have students research the standardization of currency. When did it occur? Why? They can compare the need for standard units of measurement discussed in the chapter with the need for standard currency. It is believed that the first standard coins were produced in Lydia, part of present-day Turkey, in the 600s B.C. The coins were standardized so people knew the exact value of the metal pieces. This allowed them to trade money instead of goods. L3  Linguistic P

Reading Check

Answer 1,000; 1/100

Science Journal

Standards Have students record in their Science Journals the physical standards for mass, length, and time. The standard mass is the 1 kg of platinum shown in **Figure 10.** The standard length, 1 meter, is defined as the distance light travels in a vacuum in 1/299,792,458 of a second. The standard time, 1 second, is defined as 9,192,631,770 periods of the radiation of cesium-133 atoms. L3

Resource Manager

Chapter Resources Booklet
Transparency Activity, p. 45
Enrichment, p. 31
Directed Reading for Content Mastery, p. 20

Measurement Systems, continued

Caption Answer

Figure 11 31 mm

Make a Model

Model a new metric measurement system. Organize the class into groups and have each group choose an object to be the basis for its new metric standard of length. Have students make or draw models showing a unit, a deciunit, a centiunit, and a kilounit. L2 **Visual-Spatial**

Extension

Point out to students that while in SI the units for time less than 1 second are divided into multiples of 10 (the millisecond, nanosecond, etc.), the units for time greater than 1 second are not. Have each student devise a metric system for measuring the amount of time in a day. Accept all responses in which time is divided into units that are multiples of 10. L3 **Logical-Mathematical**

Math Skills Activity

National Math Standards

Correlation to Mathematics Objectives

1, 2, 3, 4, 5, 6, 9, 10

Answer to Practice Problem

? mm = 11 cm × 10 mm/cm

11 cm × 10 mm/cm = 110 mm

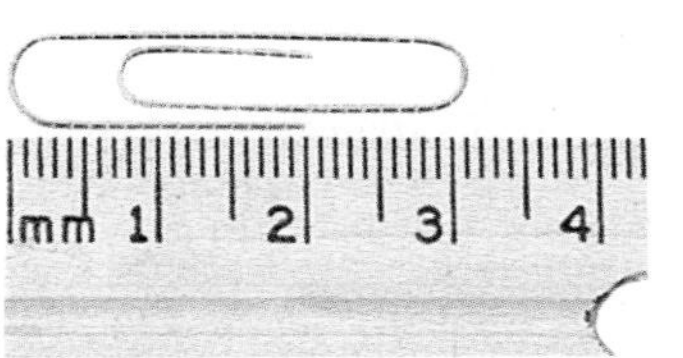

Figure 11
One centimeter contains 10 mm. *How many millimeters long is the paper clip?*

Converting Between SI Units Sometimes quantities are measured using different units. Conversion factors are used to change one unit to another. A conversion factor is a ratio that is equal to one. For example, there are 1,000 mL in 1 L, so 1,000 mL = 1 L. If both sides in this equation are divided by 1 L, the equation becomes:

$$\frac{1{,}000 \text{ mL}}{1 \text{ L}} = 1$$

The left side of this equation is a ratio equal to one and, therefore, is a conversion factor. You can make another conversion factor by placing 1L in the numerator and 1,000 mL in the denominator. The ratio still is equal to one.

To convert units, you multiply by the appropriate conversion factor. For example, to convert 1.255 L to mL, multiply 1.255 L by a conversion factor. Use the conversion factor with new units (mL) in the numerator and the old units (L) in the denominator.

$$1.255 \text{ L} \times \frac{1{,}000 \text{ mL}}{1 \text{ L}} = 1.255 \text{ mL}$$

The unit L cancels in this equation, just as if it were a number.

Math Skills Activity

Converting Units of Measure

Example Problem

You have a length of rope that measures 3,075 mm. How long is it in centimeters?

1. *This is what you know:* 1 m = 10 dm = 100 cm = 1,000 mm
2. *This is what you need to know:* 3,075 mm = ? cm
3. *This is the equation you need to use:* $? \text{ cm} = 3{,}075 \text{ mm} \times \frac{100 \text{ cm}}{1{,}000 \text{ mm}}$
4. *Cancel units and multiply:* $3{,}075 \cancel{\text{mm}} \times \frac{1\cancel{00} \text{ cm}}{10\cancel{00} \cancel{\text{mm}}} = 307.5 \text{ cm}$

Check your answer by multiplying your answer by $\frac{1{,}000 \text{ mm}}{100 \text{ cm}}$. *Do you calculate the original length in millimeters?*

Practice Problem

Your pencil is 11 cm long. How long is it in millimeters?

For more help, refer to the Math Skill Handbook.

Curriculum Connection

Math The SI prefix *pico-* is used for tiny measurements. The diameter of a hydrogen nucleus is about 100 picometers. Have students find out what *pico-* means and find the diameter of a hydrogen atom in meters. The prefix means one-trillionth. A hydrogen atom has a diameter of 100 trillionths (100×10^{-12}) of a meter. L2 **Logical-Mathematical**

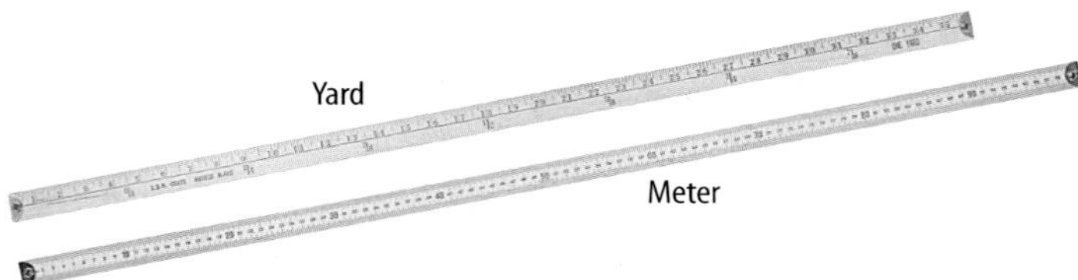

Figure 12
One meter is slightly longer than 1 yard and 100 m is slightly longer than a football field. *Would you expect your time for a 100-m dash to be slightly more or less than your time for a 100-yard dash?*

Measuring Distance

The word *length* is used in many different ways. For example, the length of a novel is the number of pages or words it contains. In scientific measurement, however, length is the distance between two points. That distance might be the diameter of a hair or the distance from Earth to the Moon. The SI base unit of length is the meter, m. A baseball bat is about 1 m long. Metric rulers and metersticks are used to measure length. **Figure 12** compares a meter and a yard.

Choosing a Unit of Length As shown in **Figure 13,** the size of the unit you measure with will depend on the size of the object being measured. For example, the diameter of a shirt button is about 1 cm. You probably also would use the centimeter to measure the length of your pencil and the meter to measure the length of your classroom. What unit would you use to measure the distance from your home to school? You probably would want to use a unit larger than a meter. The kilometer, km, which is 1,000 m, is used to measure these kinds of distances.

By choosing an appropriate unit, you avoid large-digit numbers and numbers with many decimal places. Twenty-one kilometers is easier to deal with than 21,000 m. And 13 m is easier to use than 0.000 13 m.

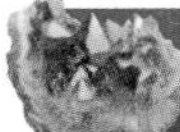

Earth Science INTEGRATION

The standard measurement for the distance from Earth to the Sun is called the astronomical unit, AU. The distance is about 150 billion (1.5×10^{11}) m. In your Science Journal, calculate what 1 AU would equal in km.

Figure 13
The size of the object being measured determines which unit you will measure in. A tape measure measures in meters. The micrometer, shown at the left measures in very small lengths. *What unit do you think it measures in?*

Measuring Distance

Caption Answer

Figure 12 slightly more

Activity

Distribute metric rulers and have students identify the millimeter, centimeter, and decimeter markings on the ruler. Have them measure common objects. As they are measuring, have each student choose an object that best represents a centimeter. Allow them to make estimations and use their rulers to check their estimations. L2

Kinesthetic

Earth Science INTEGRATION

Venus is 0.38 AU from the Sun and Pluto is 39.44 AU from the Sun. 1 AU is about 1.5×10^{8} km = 150,000,000 km.

Quick Demo

Use a meterstick to measure the circumference of a round object. Repeat the measurement with a metric tape measure. Ask students to explain why the measurement made with the tape measure is more accurate. The meterstick can't bend to accurately measure the curved surface. L1 ELL

Logical-Mathematical

Caption Answer

Figure 13 micrometers

Cultural Diversity

Length Through Time Accurate length measurement was important for ancient engineering projects, such as the Nazca lines, the pyramids in Central America and Africa, and the great public buildings found in many cultures. Have students identify some of the units of length used in the ancient world. Lengths used include the cubit and the Roman mile. L2 **Linguistic**

Resource Manager

Physical Science Critical Thinking/Problem Solving, p. 2

Mathematics Skill Activities, p. 61

Measuring Volume

SCIENCE Online

Internet Addresses

Explore the Glencoe Science Web site at **science.glencoe.com** to find out more about topics in this section.

Extension

Tell students that in many countries, gasoline is sold by the liter. If one liter is approximately the same volume as one quart, have them find the approximate cost of one gallon of gasoline if it costs 60 cents per liter. $2.40/gal [L2]

[LS] **Logical-Mathematical**

Activity

Provide a number of irregularly-shaped containers and a graduated cylinder. Have each student make a hypothesis about the relative volumes of the containers and write down the hypothesis. Then have students test their hypotheses by measuring the volume of each container. Tell them to fill each container completely with water, pour the water into the graduated cylinder and measure the amount the container held. [L2]

[LS] **Kinesthetic**

Caption Answer

Figure 14 1000 cm^3 are in 1 dm^3.

SCIENCE Online

Research Visit the Glencoe Science Web site at **science.glencoe.com** for more information on finding the volume of irregular objects using water displacement. Communicate to your class what you learn.

Measuring Volume

The amount of space occupied by an object is called its **volume**. If you want to know the volume of a solid rectangle, such as a brick, you measure its length, width, and height and multiply the three numbers and their units together ($V = l \times w \times h$). For a brick, your measurements probably would be in centimeters. The volume would then be expressed in cubic centimeters, cm^3. To find out how much a moving van can carry, your measurements probably would be in meters, and the volume would be expressed in cubic meters, m^3, because when you multiply you add exponents.

Measuring Liquid Volume How do you measure the volume of a liquid? A liquid has no sides to measure. In measuring a liquid's volume, you are indicating the capacity of the container that holds that amount of liquid. The most common units for expressing liquid volumes are liters and milliliters. These are measurements used in canned and bottled foods. A liter occupies the same volume as a cubic decimeter, dm^3. That is, 1 L is the same volume as a cube that is 1 dm, 10 cm on each side, as in **Figure 14.**

Look at **Figure 14.** One liter is equal to 1,000 mL. A cubic decimeter, dm^3 is equal to 1,000 cm^3. Because 1 L = 1 dm^3, it follows that:

$$1\ mL = 1\ cm^3.$$

Sometimes, liquid volumes such as doses of medicine are expressed in cubic centimeters.

Suppose you wanted to convert a measurement in liters to cubic centimeters. You use conversion factors to convert L to mL and then mL to cm^3.

$$1.5\ \cancel{L} \times 1{,}000\ \cancel{mL}/1\ \cancel{L} \times 1\ cm^3/1\ \cancel{mL} = 1{,}500\ cm^3$$

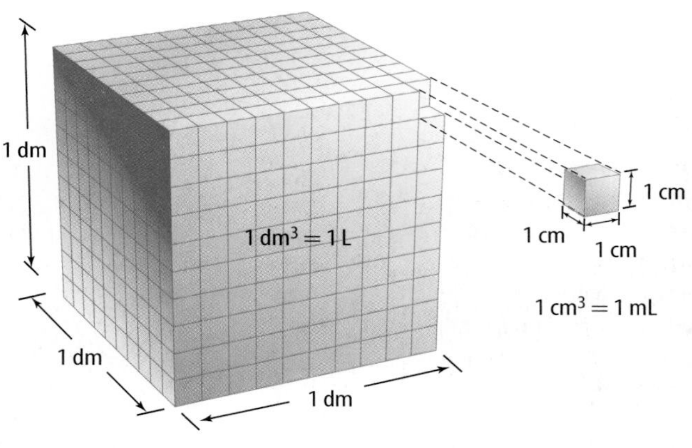

Figure 14
The large cube has a volume of 1 dm^3, which is equivalent to 1 L. *How many cubic centimeters (cm^3) are in the large cube?*

Curriculum Connection

Math Have students find and record the equations for determining the volumes of shapes such as a cylinder, sphere, square pyramid, and cone. The equation for calculating the volume of a cylinder is $\pi r^2 h$. The equation for the volume of a sphere is $\frac{4}{3}\pi r^3$. The equation for the volume of a square pyramid is $\frac{1}{3}$ bh. The equation for the volume of a cone is $\frac{1}{3}\pi r^2 h$. [L3]

[LS] **Logical-Mathematical**

Table 3 Densities of Some Materials at 20°C

Material	Density (g/cm^3)	Material	Density (g/cm^3)
hydrogen	0.000 09	aluminum	2.7
oxygen	0.001 3	iron	7.9
water	1.0	gold	19.3

Measuring Matter

A table-tennis ball and a golf ball have about the same volume. But if you pick them up, you notice a difference. The golf ball has more mass. **Mass** is a measurement of the quantity of matter in an object. The mass of the golf ball, which is about 45 g, is almost 13 times the mass of the table-tennis ball, which is about 3.5 g. A bowling ball has a mass of about 5,000 g. This makes its mass roughly 100 times greater than the mass of the golf ball and more than 1,400 times greater than the table-tennis ball's mass. To visualize SI units, see **Figure 15** on the following page.

Density A cube of polished aluminum and a cube of silver that are the same size not only look similar but also have the same volume. The mass and volume of an object can be used to find the density of the material the object is made of. **Density** is the mass per unit volume of a material. You find density by dividing an object's mass by the object's volume. For example, the density of an object having a mass of 10 g and a volume of 2 cm^3 is 5 g/cm^3. **Table 3** lists the densities of some familiar materials.

Derived Units The measurement unit for density, g/cm^3, is a combination of SI units. A unit obtained by combining different SI units is called a **derived unit.** An SI unit multiplied by itself also is a derived unit. Thus the liter, which is based on the cubic decimeter, is a derived unit. A meter cubed, expressed with an exponent—m^3—is a derived unit.

Measuring Time and Temperature

It is often necessary to keep track of how long it takes for something to happen, or whether something heats up or cools down. These measurements involve time and temperature.

Time is the interval between two events. The SI unit for time is the second. In the laboratory, you will use a stopwatch or a clock with a second hand to measure time.

Mini LAB

Determining the Density of a Pencil

Procedure

1. Measure the mass of a **pencil** (unsharpened) in grams.
2. Put 90 mL of **water** into a 100-mL **graduated cylinder.** Lower the pencil, eraser end down, into the cylinder. Push the pencil until it is just submerged. This is known as water displacement. Hold it there and read the new volume to the nearest tenth of a milliliter.

Analysis

1. Calculate the pencil's density by dividing its mass by the change in volume of the water level.
2. Is the density of the pencil greater than or less than the density of water? How do you know?

Measuring Matter

Purpose Students measure the mass and volume of a pencil and use these data to find its density. L1 ELL

LS **Logical-Mathematical**

Materials water, 100-mL graduated cylinder, unsharpened pencil, balance

Teaching Strategy The mass measurement should be made using a dry pencil.

Analysis

1. Students should use the equation $d = m/v$. Remind them that 1 mL $= 1\ cm^3$.
2. Because the pencil floats, its density is less than that of water. Also, its calculated density is less than that of water—1.0.

✓Assessment

Performance Have students use the same procedure to test the density of another object such as a cork or a rubber stopper. If possible, they could compare their results with the density given in **Table 3** on this page or another density table. Use **Performance Assessment in the Science Classroom,** p. 97.

Inclusion Strategies

Behaviorally Disordered Have these students read through the lab a day or two before the class does it. Show them how it works and ask them whether they have any questions. Make sure they understand the purpose of the water. When they do the activity, pair them with students who work well in the lab.

Resource Manager 

Chapter Resources Booklet
MiniLAB, p. 3
Lab Activity, pp. 9–12

Reading and Writing Skill Activities, p. 41

NATIONAL GEOGRAPHIC

Visualizing SI Dimensions

Have students examine the pictures and read the captions. Then ask the following questions.

- **In what units would you measure your height?** meters **The distance a runner covered in a marathon?** kilometers **The mass of pencil?** grams
- **Why wouldn't you measure the distance from Dallas, Texas to Miami, Florida in millimeters?** The number of millimeters would be an extremely large number, too big to be able to visualize. **What unit should you use?** kilometers

Activity

Set up three stations and allow groups to rotate through them. One station should have a balance and several objects that students can mass. Another station should have several containers of liquids and a graduated cylinder so they can measure volumes. The third station should have a metric ruler and meter stick and several objects whose lengths students can determine. Have students measure the objects and compare their measurements when all have finished. L1

LS **Kinesthetic**

Extension

Students could develop and make a board game based on using the proper and best SI units to measure different objects. L3

LS **Logical-Mathematical**

NATIONAL GEOGRAPHIC **VISUALIZING SI DIMENSIONS**

Figure 15

The characteristics of most of these everyday objects are measured using an international system known as SI dimensions. These dimensions measure length, volume, mass, density, and time. Celsius is not an SI unit but is widely used in scientific work.

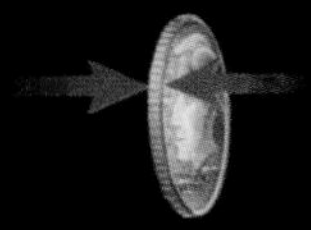

MILLIMETERS A dime is about 1 mm thick.

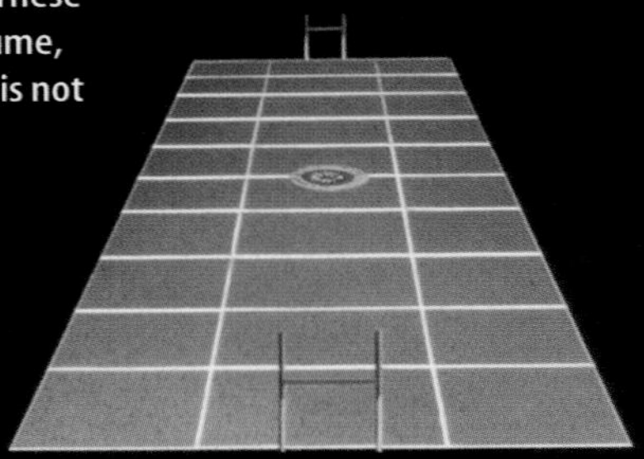

METERS A football field is about 91 m long.

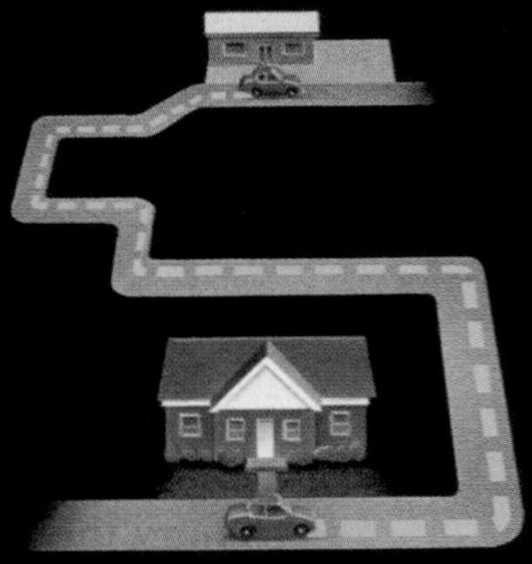

KILOMETERS The distance from your house to a store can be measured in kilometers.

LITERS This carton holds 1.98 L of frozen yogurt.

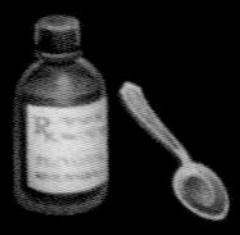

MILLILITERS A teaspoonful of medicine is about 5 mL.

GRAMS/METER This stone sinks because it is denser—has more grams per cubic meter—than water.

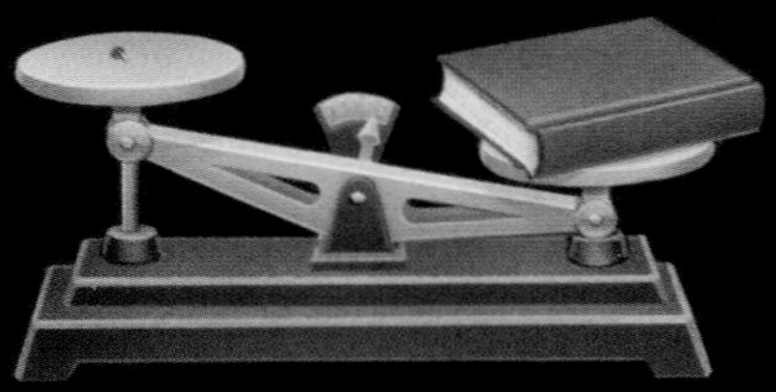

GRAMS The mass of a thumbtack and the mass of a textbook can be expressed in grams.

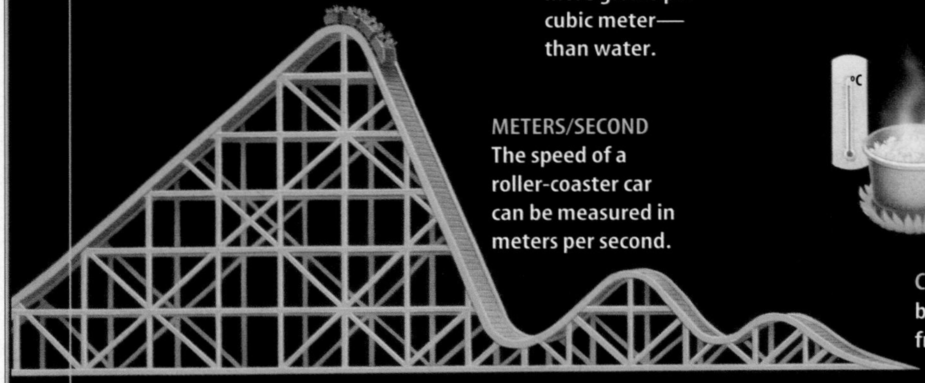

METERS/SECOND The speed of a roller-coaster car can be measured in meters per second.

CELSIUS Water boils at 100°C and freezes at 0°C.

Resource Manager

Chapter Resources Booklet
Reinforcement, p. 28

Reading and Writing Skill Activities, p. 13

Science Inquiry Labs, p. 11

What's Hot and What's Not You will learn the scientific meaning of temperature in a later chapter. For now, think of temperature as a measure of how hot or how cold something is.

Look at **Figure 16.** For most scientific work, temperature is measured on the Celsius (C) scale. On this scale, the freezing point of water is 0°C, and the boiling point of water is 100°C. Between these points, the scale is divided into 100 equal divisions. Each one represents 1°C. On the Celsius scale, average human body temperature is 37°C, and a typical room temperature is between 20°C and 25°C.

Kelvin and Fahrenheit The SI unit of temperature is the kelvin (K). Zero on the Kelvin scale (0 K) is the coldest possible temperature, also known as absolute zero. That is equal to −273°C, which is 273° below the freezing point of water.

Most laboratory thermometers are marked only with the Celsius scale. Because the divisions on the two scales are the same size, the Kelvin temperature can be found by adding 273 to the Celsius reading. So, on the Kelvin scale, water freezes at 273 K and boils at 373 K. Notice that degree symbols are not used with the Kelvin scale.

The temperature measurement you are probably most familiar with is the Fahrenheit scale, which was based roughly on the temperature of the human body.

 *What is the relationship between the Celsius scale and the Kelvin scale?*

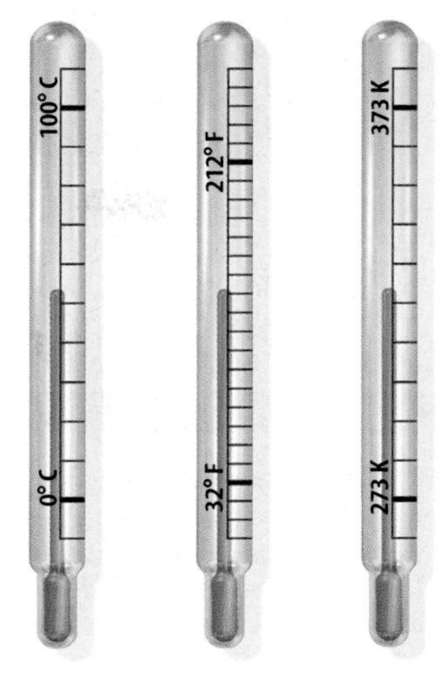

Figure 16
These three thermometers illustrate the scales of temperature between the freezing and boiling points of water. *How do the scales compare at the boiling point?*

Section  Assessment

1. Why is it important to have standards of measurement that are exact?
2. What are the SI prefixes for 0.001, 1,000, 0.1, and 0.01?
3. Make the following conversions—100 cm to meters and 27°C to K, 20 dg to milligrams, and 3 m to decimeters.
4. Explain why density is a derived unit.
5. **Think Critically** What is the density of an unknown metal that has a mass of 158 g and a volume of 20 mL? Use **Table 3** to identify this metal.

Skill Builder Activities

6. **Concept Mapping** Make a network-tree concept map displaying the SI base units used to measure quantities of length, mass, time, and temperature. **For more help, refer to the** Science Skill Handbook.
7. **Using Math** Use a metric ruler to measure a shoe box and a pad of paper. Find the volume of each ($V = w \times l \times h$) in cubic centimeters. Then convert the units to mL. **For more help, refer to the** Math Skill Handbook.

Answers to Section Assessment

1. They provide a consistent, known, and accepted value for a base unit.
2. milli-, kilo-, deci-, centi-
3. 1.0 m; 300 K; 2,000 mg; 30 dm
4. Density is mass/volume. Mass is a base unit, and volume is a derived unit, so density is also a derived unit.
5. 158.0 g/20.0 mL = 7.90 g/mL; iron
6. Concept maps should show that the meter is the base unit of length; kilogram, mass; second, time; and Kelvin, temperature.
7. Check students' work.

Measuring Time and Temperature

Caption Answer

Figure 16 The boiling point of water is 373 K, 100°C, and 212°F.

Reading Check

Answer The units are the same size, but zero on the Kelvin scale is 273 units lower than zero on the Celsius scale.

3 Assess

Reteach

Have each student calculate his or her mass in kilograms. Tell students that at Earth's surface, an object weighing 1 pound has a mass of 0.45 kg. Sample: A student weighing 120 pounds has a mass of 54 kg. L2 IS **Logical-Mathematical**

Challenge

Have students find the high temperature for the day in Fahrenheit, Celsius, and Kelvin. They can obtain the temperature, probably in Fahrenheit, from a weather report. Have them use the following equations: $C = 5(F - 32)/9$; $C + 273 = K$. L2 IS **Logical-Mathematical**

Assessment

Performance Have students develop their own standards and units for measuring time. Have them evaluate their units in terms of how easy it is to replicate results using their standards. Use **Performance Assessment in the Science Classroom,** p. 117.

SECTION 3

Communicating with Graphs

1 Motivate

Bellringer Transparency

Display the Section Focus Transparency for Section 3. Use the accompanying Transparency Activity Master. L2 ELL

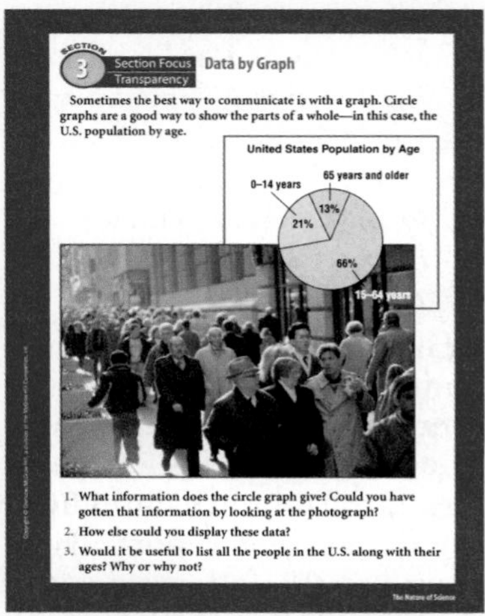
Section 3 Section Focus Transparency — Data by Graph

Sometimes the best way to communicate is with a graph. Circle graphs are a good way to show the parts of a whole—in this case, the U.S. population by age.

United States Population by Age: 0–14 years 21%; 65 years and older 13%; 15–64 years 66%

1. What information does the circle graph give? Could you have gotten that information by looking at the photograph?
2. How else could you display these data?
3. Would it be useful to list all the people in the U.S. along with their ages? Why or why not?

Tie to Prior Knowledge

Assign students to find graphs in newspapers and magazines and bring them to class. Have student groups develop a classification system for the graphs. L1 LS **Interpersonal**

SECTION 3

Communicating with Graphs

As You Read

***What* You'll Learn**

- **Identify** three types of graphs and explain the ways they are used.
- **Distinguish** between dependent and independent variables.
- **Analyze** data using the various types of graphs.

Vocabulary
graph

***Why* It's Important**

Graphs are a quick way to communicate a lot of information in a small amount of space.

A Visual Display

Scientists often graph the results of their experiments because they can detect patterns in the data easier in a graph than in a table. A **graph** is a visual display of information or data. **Figure 17** is a graph that shows a girl walking her dog. The horizontal axis, or the *x*-axis, measures time. Time is the independent variable because as it changes, it affects the measure of another variable. The distance from home that the girl and the dog walk is the other variable. It is the dependent variable and is measured on the vertical axis, or *y*-axis.

Graphs are useful for displaying numerical information in business, science, sports, advertising, and many everyday situations. Different kinds of graphs—line, bar, and circle—are appropriate for displaying different types of information.

Reading Check *What are three common types of graphs?*

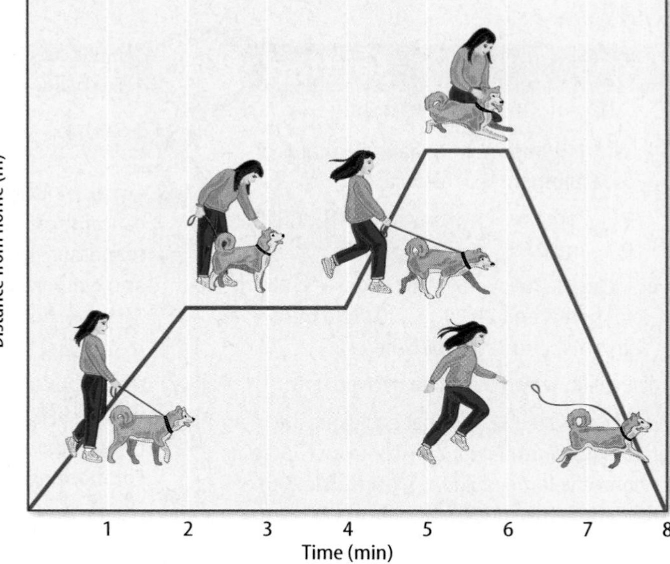

Figure 17
This graph tells the story of the motion that takes place when a girl takes her dog for an 8-min walk.

Section Assessment Planner

PORTFOLIO	CONTENT ASSESSMENT
Science Journal, p. 24	Section, p. 26
PERFORMANCE ASSESSMENT	Challenge, p. 26
Math Skills Activity, p. 24	Chapter, pp. 34–35
Try at Home MiniLAB, p. 25	
Skill Builder Activities, p. 26	
See page 34 for more options.	

Line Graphs

A line graph can show any relationship where the dependent variable changes due to a change in the independent variable. Line graphs often show how a relationship between variables changes over time. You can use a line graph to track many things, such as how certain stocks perform or how the population changes over any period of time—a month, a week, or a year.

You can show more than one event on the same graph as long as the relationship between the variables is identical. Suppose a builder had three choices of thermostats for a new school. He wanted to test them to know which was the best brand to install throughout the building. He installed a different thermostat in classrooms A, B, and C. He set each thermostat at 20°C. He turned the furnace on and checked the temperatures in the three rooms every 5 min for 25 min. He recorded his data in **Table 4.**

Table 4 Room Temperature

Time*	Classroom Temperature (°C) A	B	C
0	16	16	16
5	17	17	16.5
10	19	19	17
15	20	21	17.5
20	20	23	18
25	20	25	18.5

*minutes after turning on heat

The builder then plotted the data on a graph. He could see from the table that the data did not vary much for the three classrooms. So he chose small intervals for the *y*-axis and left part of the scale out (the part between 0° and 16°). See **Figure 18.** This allowed him to spread out the area on the graph where the data points lie. You can see easily the contrast in the colors of the three lines and their relationship to the black horizontal line. The black line represents the thermostat setting and is the control. The control is what the resulting room temperature of the classrooms should be if the thermostats are working efficiently.

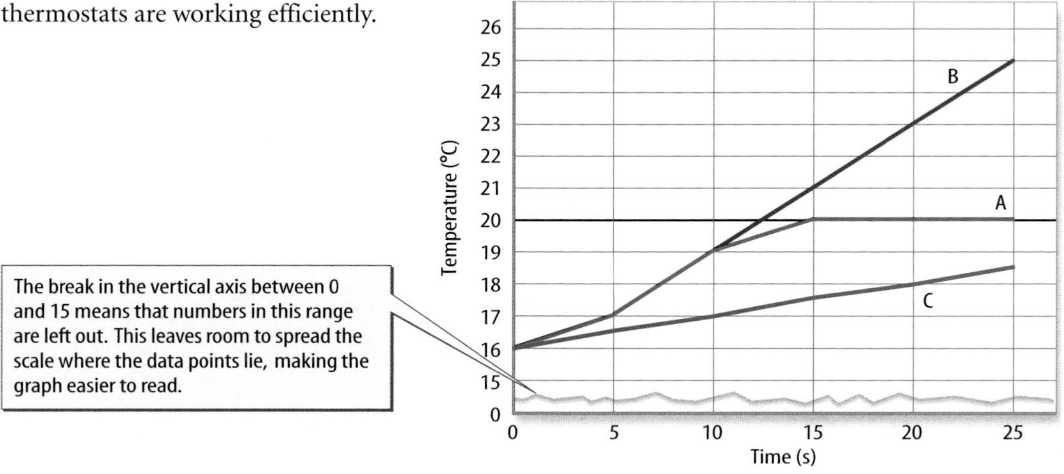

The break in the vertical axis between 0 and 15 means that numbers in this range are left out. This leaves room to spread the scale where the data points lie, making the graph easier to read.
Temperature (°C)
26
25
24
23
22
21
20
19
18
17
16
15
0
B
A
C
0
5
10
15
20
25
Time (s)

Figure 18
The room temperatures of classrooms A, B, and C are shown in contrast to the thermostat setting of 20°C. ***Which classroom had the most efficient thermostat?***

2 Teach

A Visual Display

Reading Check

Answer line, bar, and circle graphs

Line Graphs

Discussion

Explain to students that interpolation is reading graph values between data points, and extrapolation is reading graph values beyond data points. Ask students which process is likely to produce more error. Extrapolation; it goes beyond what has actually been measured in an experiment. L3

LS **Logical-Mathematical**

Caption Answer

Figure 18 thermostat A

Extension

Graphs are not always a completely objective presentation of data. Graphs are frequently used in advertising to conceal or distort data. Have students find examples from actual ads of graphs that distort data. Ask them to think of ways that information could be emphasized or underplayed on a graph. A stretched-out vertical scale would emphasize highs and lows. A compressed vertical scale would conceal them. L2

ELL LS **Logical-Mathematical**

Visual Learning

Figure 18 Have students practice interpolation (finding data between reference points) and extrapolation (finding data past the range of the reference points) by examining the data provided. Ask them what they would expect the temperature to be in the classroom using thermostat A after 8 minutes and after 30 minutes. 18°C and 20°C L3 ELL LS **Visual-Spatial**

Resource Manager

Chapter Resources Booklet

Transparency Activity, p. 46

Directed Reading for Content Mastery, pp. 21, 22

Reading and Writing Skill Activities, p. 47

Line Graphs, continued

Math Skills Activity

National Math Standards

Correlation to Mathematics Objectives

L4.1, L5.1

Answer to Practice Problem

1. Students could use either bar graphs or line graphs to represent this data. In either case, running time should be on the *y*-axis and year should be on the *x*-axis.

Bar Graphs

Quick Demo

Use students' clothing or shoes to demonstrate how to make a data table. For example, you could collect data such as shoe type, shoe color, sleeve length, or clothing type. After completing the data table, complete a bar graph of the information. Reinforce the idea that a bar graph rather than a line graph would be used because a line graph must contain two sets of numbers, while a bar graph can use categories. L2 ELL

LS **Visual-Spatial**

Figure 19
Graphing calculators are valuable tools for making graphs.

Building Line Graphs Besides choosing a scale that makes a graph readable, as illustrated in **Figure 18,** other factors are involved in building useful graphs. The most important factor in making a line graph is always using the *x*-axis for the independent variable. The *y*-axis always is used for the dependent variable. Because the points in a line graph are related, you connect the points.

Another factor in building a graph involves units of measurement. For example, you might use a Celsius thermometer for one part of your experiment and a Fahrenheit thermometer for another. But you must first convert your temperature readings to the same unit of measurement before you make your graph.

In the past, graphs had to be made by hand, with each point plotted individually. Today, scientists use a variety of tools, such as computers and graphing calculators like the one shown in **Figure 19,** to help them draw graphs.

Math Skills Activity

Line Graphing

Example Problem

In an experiment, you check the air temperature at certain hours of the day. At 8 A.M., the temperature is 27°C; at noon, the temperature is 32°C; and at 4 P.M., the temperature is 30°C. Graph the results of your experiment.

Solution

1. *This is what you know:* independent variable = time
   dependent variable = temperature
2. *Set up your graph:* Graph time on the *x*-axis and temperature on the *y*-axis. Mark the increments on the graph to include all measurements.
3. *Graph:* Plot each point on the graph by finding the time on the *x*-axis and moving up until you find the recorded temperature on the *y*-axis. Place a point there. Then connect the points from left to right.

Practice Problem

As you train for a marathon, you compare your previous times. In year one, you ran it in 5.2 h; in year two, you ran it in 5 h; in year three, you ran it in 4.8 h; in year four, you ran it in 4.3 h; and in year five you ran it in 4 h. Graph the results of your marathon races.

For more help, refer to the Math Skill Handbook.

Science Journal

Birth Months Take a class survey of the month in which each student's birthday occurs, and tally these data on the board. Have students record this information in their Science Journals. Ask each student to make both a bar graph and a circle graph to show the information. L2

LS **Logical-Mathematical** P

Resource Manager

Chapter Resources Booklet

MiniLAB, p. 4
Enrichment, p. 32
Transparency Activity, pp. 47–48

Bar Graphs

A bar graph is useful for comparing information collected by counting. For example, suppose you counted the number of students in every classroom in your school on a particular day and organized your data as in **Table 5.** You could show these data in a bar graph like the one shown in **Figure 20.** Uses for bar graphs include comparisons of oil, or crop productions, costs, or as data in promotional materials. Each bar represents a quantity counted at a particular time, which should be stated on the graph. As on a line graph, the independent variable is shown on the x-axis and the dependent variable is plotted on the y-axis.

Recall that you might need to place a break in the scale of the graph to better illustrate your results. For example, if your data were 1,002, 1,010, 1,030, and 1,040 and the intervals on the scale were every 100 units, you might not be able to see the difference from one bar to another. If you had a break in the scale and started your data range at 1,000 with intervals of ten units, you could make your comparison more accurately.

Reading Check ***Describe possible data where using a bar graph would be better than using a line graph.***

TRY AT HOME **Mini LAB**

Observing Change Through Graphing

Procedure

1. Place a **thermometer** in a **plastic foam cup** of hot, but not boiling, **water.**
2. Measure and record the temperature every 30 s for 5 min.
3. Repeat the experiment with freshly heated water. This time, cover the cup with a **plastic lid.**

Analysis

1. Make a line graph of the changing temperature from step 2, showing time on the *x*-axis and temperature on the *y*-axis. Then plot the changing temperature from step 3 on the same graph.
2. Use the graph to describe the cooling process in each of the trials.

Table 5 Classroom Size

Number of Students	Number of Classrooms
20	1
21	3
22	3
23	2
24	3
25	5
26	5
27	3

Figure 20
The height of each bar corresponds to the number of classrooms having a particular number of students.

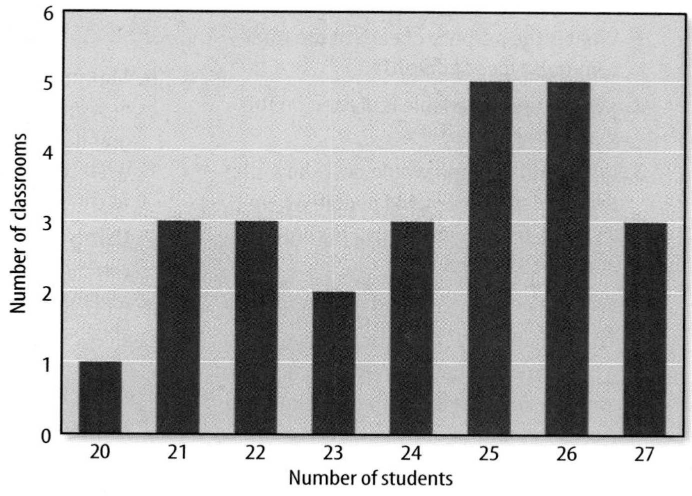

TRY AT HOME **Mini LAB**

Purpose Students measure the change in temperature over time and graph the data. L1 ELL LS **Visual-Spatial**

Materials plastic foam cup, matching lid with straw hole, thermometer, graph paper, timer with second hand, hot water

Teaching Strategy Show students how to estimate a reading between marks on the thermometer.

Analysis

1. The slopes of both graphs will be negative and steeper at the beginning. The first graph will be steeper than the second.
2. The temperature decreases most rapidly when it is highest. Adding a lid significantly reduces the rate at which temperature decreases.

Process Have students sketch a graph of what they probably would observe if they reversed the process and heated the water in an open glass container. The slope would be positive. Use **PASC,** p. 127.

Reading Check

Answer Answers will vary but might include the number of points scored by the local football team for each game of the season.

LAB DEMONSTRATION

Purpose to show students how to draw circle graphs

Preparation Write the following data on the board: Of the people who attended a play, 42 were under 10 years old; 27 were from 11 to 20, and 11 were over 21.

Procedure Determine what percentage of the whole each part represents (percentage = part ÷ whole × 100%). For those under 10, this is $\frac{42}{80}$ × 100% = 52%. A circle contains 360°. To find the number of degrees needed to show each percentage, change the percentage to a decimal number and multiply it by 360°. For those under 10, 360° × 0.52 = 187°.

Assessment

What percentage of the audience were from 11 to 20? $\frac{27}{80}$ × 100% = 34% from 11 to 20 **Over 21?** $\frac{11}{80}$ × 100% = 14% **How many degrees of the circle graph are required for each of these groups?** 360° × 0.34 = 122° from 11 to 20; 360° × 0.14 = 50° over 21

3 Assess

Reteach

Stick ten birthday cake candles in holders in a long piece of plastic foam. Light the second candle and let it burn for only 5 s. Light the remaining candles in turn, letting the third candle burn for 10 s, the fourth for 15 s, etc. Remove the candles from the holders, clip their wicks, and place them side-by-side, bases aligned, on an overhead projector. Discuss with students what the silhouette displays. L2

LS **Visual-Spatial**

Challenge

Tell students that four students scored a D on a test, ten scored a C, seven scored a B, and four scored an A. Ask students what kinds of graphs could be used to display this data. circle graph or bar graph Have each student make a bar graph and a circle graph of the data, choose the graph he or she prefers, and explain the choice. L2 LS **Logical-Mathematical**

Assessment

Process If students find line graphs for question 6 in the Section Assessment, have them identify the dependent and independent variables. For circle graphs, have them check that the percentages total 100 percent. Use **Performance Assessment in the Science Classroom,** p. 101.

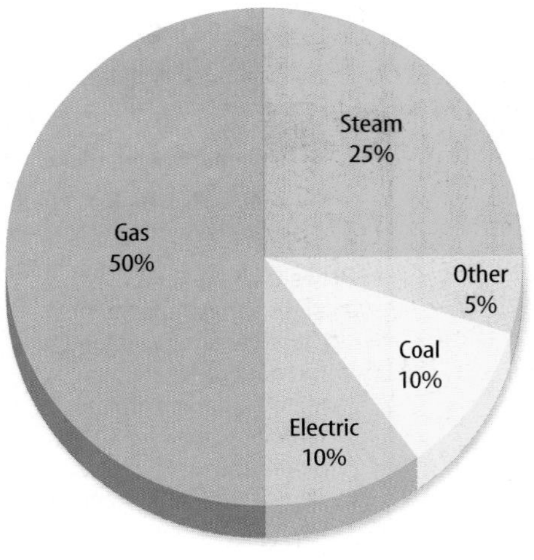

Figure 21
A circle graph shows the different parts of a whole quantity.

Circle Graphs

A circle graph, or pie graph, is used to show how some fixed quantity is broken down into parts. The circular pie represents the total. The slices represent the parts and usually are represented as percentages of the total.

Figure 21 illustrates how a circle graph could be used to show the percentage of buildings in a neighborhood using each of a variety of heating fuels. You easily can see that more buildings use gas heat than any other kind of system. What else does the graph tell you?

To create a circle graph, you start with the total of what you are analyzing. **Figure 21** starts with 72 buildings in the neighborhood. For each type of heating fuel, you divide the number of buildings using each type of fuel by the total (72). You then multiply that fraction (percent) by 360° to determine the angle that the fraction makes in the circle. Eighteen buildings use steam. Therefore, $18 \div 72 \times 360° = 90°$ on the circle graph. You then would measure 90° on the circle with your protractor to show 25 percent.

When you use graphs, think carefully about the conclusions you can draw from them. You want to make sure your conclusions are based on accurate information and that you use scales that help make your graph easy to read.

Section 3 Assessment

1. What is the purpose of each of the three common types of graphs?
2. Which type of variable is plotted on the *x*-axis? The *y*-axis?
3. What kind of graph would best show the results of a survey of 144 people where 75 ride a bus, 45 drive cars, 15 carpool, and 9 walk to work?
4. Why are points connected in a line graph?
5. **Think Critically** Describe one way that a bar graph is different from a circle graph and one way that a bar graph is similar to a circle graph.

Skill Builder Activities

6. **Making and Using Graphs** Find a graph in a newspaper or magazine. Identify the kind of graph you found and write an explanation of what the graph shows. **For more help, refer to the Science Skill Handbook.**
7. **Using an Electronic Spreadsheet** Some computer programs make creating data tables and making graphs an easier task. Use a spreadsheet and a graphing program to make a data table and a line graph of the data you collected in the Try at Home MiniLAB. **For more help, refer to the Technology Skill Handbook.**

Answers to Section Assessment

1. line graph—shows any relationship in which one variable changes due to a change in another variable; bar graph—shows quantities counted at a particular time; circle graph—shows parts of a whole
2. The independent variable is shown on the x-axis and the dependent variable is shown on the y-axis.
3. circle graph
4. Points are connected because they are related.
5. A circle graph shows how parts relate to a whole while a bar graph does not. Both a bar graph and a circle graph can show the relationship between a set of numerical data and a set of non-numerical data.
6. Check students' explanations for accuracy.
7. Students' computer graphs should match the graphs produced in the MiniLAB.

Activity

Converting Kitchen Measurements

Look through a recipe book. Are any of the amounts of ingredients stated in SI units? Chances are, English measurements are used. How can you convert English measurements to SI measurements?

What You'll Investigate

How do kitchen measurements compare with SI measurements?

Safety Precautions

Materials

- balance
- 100-mL graduated cylinder
- measuring cup
- measuring teaspoon
- measuring tablespoon
- corn meal
- dried beans
- dried rice
- potato flakes
- water
- vinegar
- salad oil

Goals

- **Determine** a relationship between two systems of measurements.
- Calculate the conversion factors for converting English units to SI units.

English to SI Conversions

Ingredient	English Measure	SI Measure
Water	½ cup	118 mL
Corn Meal	2 cups	295 g
Salad Oil	4 tablespoons	118 mL
Dried Rice	½ cup	90 g
Potato Flakes	3 cups	168 g
Vinegar	1 teaspoon	10 mL
Dried Beans	3 cups	510 g

Procedure

1. Copy the data table into your Science Journal.
2. Use the English measuring cup or spoon to measure out 2 cups of corn meal, 3 cups of dried beans, ½ cup of dried rice, ½ cup of water, 1 teaspoon of vinegar, and 4 tablespoons of salad oil.
3. Use the balance or graduated cylinder to determine the SI equivalent of each measured ingredient. Convert solid measurements to grams and liquid measurements to milliliters.
4. Record each SI equivalent in your data table.

Conclude and Apply

1. **Calculate** the conversion factors for finding the equivalents using math instead of making measurements. Do they match the measurements recorded in your data table? Explain..
2. Compare the number of kitchen devices used to measure English volume with the number of devices used to measure volume in SI units.
3. **Predict** how kitchen equipment would change if all recipes were in SI units.
4. **Explain** benefits and problems in changing all recipes to SI units.

Communicating Your Data

Write a recipe used in your home converting all the English units to SI units.

Activity

Purpose Students will compare English and metric measurements used in kitchen utensils.

Process Skills comparing, contrasting, predicting, inferring

Time Required 30 minutes

Safety Precautions Instruct students to wear safety goggles. Caution students to never eat or drink anything in science class.

Teaching Strategy Have dishwashing liquid available for students to use for clean up.

Troubleshooting Review metric and English units before starting the activity.

Answers to Questions

1. Liquid measure: 1 cup = 8 oz = about 237 mL; 1 Tbsp = 1/16 of a cup = about 15 mL; 1 tsp = 1/3 of a Tbsp = about 5 mL. For solid measure, in which cups, teaspoons, and tablespoons are converted to grams, there is no conversion factor, since conversion will depend on the density of the material measured.
2. The English system has three and the metric system has one.
3. People would need kitchen scales to measure masses of ingredients instead of volumes.
4. The metric system uses only one unit for volume; the English system uses three volume units. English measurements often use fractions; metric measurements do not.

Resource Manager

Chapter Resources Booklet

- Lab Activity, pp. 13–16
- Activity Worksheet, pp. 5–6, 7–8
- Lab Management and Safety, p. 71

Communicating Your Data

Have students trade recipes and take them home and make the dishes to test whether or not the conversions were done correctly.

Assessment

Oral Ask students to write metric/English unit conversion questions and quiz each other aloud. Use **Performance Assessment in the Science Classroom,** p. 169.

Activity BENCH TESTED

Recognize the Problem

Purpose

Students will design and carry out an experiment to show the necessary components of an acceptable measurement system.

L1 COOP LEARN LS **Interpersonal**

Process Skills

measuring, collecting and organizing data, making and using tables, separating and controlling variables, communicating, forming operational definitions, making models, using numbers, classifying, observing and inferring

Time Required

one class period to brainstorm; one-half to one class period to complete the activity and summarize results

Materials

Have various colors of string available.

Form a Hypothesis

Possible Hypothesis

Students may hypothesize that using a defined measurement standard will make it possible for other students to measure objects consistently.

Activity **Design Your Own Experiment**

Setting High Standards for Measurement

To develop the International System of Units, people had to agree on set standards and basic definitions of scale. If you had to develop a new measurement system, people would have to agree with your new standards and definitions. In this activity, your team will use string to devise and test its own SI (String International) system for measuring length.

Recognize the Problem

What are the requirements for designing a new measurement system using string?

Form a Hypothesis

Based on your knowledge of measurement standards and systems, state a hypothesis about how exact units help to keep measuring consistent.

Possible Materials

string
scissors
marking pen
masking tape
miscellaneous objects for standards

Safety Precautions

Goals

- **Design** an experiment that involves devising and testing your own measurement system for length.
- **Measure** various objects with the string measurement system.

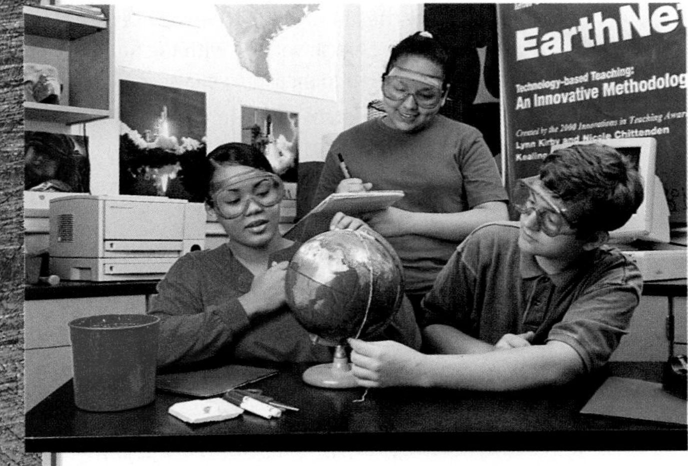

Test Your Hypothesis

Possible Procedures

Choose an object such as a piece of chalk, a paper clip, or a book as the standard. Mark the units on the string with a marker or tape. Try several different-sized scale divisions of the base unit to measure halves, quarters, and tenths of units.

Test Your Hypothesis

Plan

1. As a group, agree upon and write out the hypothesis statement.
2. As a group, list the steps that you need to take to test your hypothesis. Be specific, describing exactly what you will do at each step.
3. Make a list of the materials that you will need.
4. **Design** a data table in your Science Journal so it is ready to use as your group collects data.
5. As you read over your plan, be sure you have chosen an object in your classroom to serve as a standard. It should be in the same size range as what you will measure.
6. Consider how you will mark scale divisions on your string. Plan to use different pieces of string to try different-sized scale divisions.
7. What is your new unit of measurement called? Come up with an abbreviation for your unit. Will you name the smaller scale divisions?
8. What objects will you measure with your new unit? Be sure to include objects longer and shorter than your string. Will you measure each object more than once to test consistency? Will you measure the same object as another group and compare your findings?

Do

1. Make sure your teacher approves your plan before you start.
2. Carry out the experiment as it has been planned.
3. **Record** observations that you make and complete the data table in your Science Journal.

Analyze Your Data

1. Which of your string scale systems will provide the most accurate measurement of small objects? Explain.
2. How did you record measurements that were between two whole numbers of your units?

Draw Conclusions

1. When sharing your results with other groups, why is it important for them to know what you used as a standard?
2. **Infer** how it is possible for different numbers to represent the same length of an object.

Communicating Your Data

Compare your conclusions with other students' conclusions. **For more help, refer to the Science Skill Handbook.**

Teaching Strategy

Use heavy string to make handling easy. Be sure metersticks and other standard measuring devices are not available to students. Encourage students to use common classroom objects as standards.

Expected Outcome

Students will devise and test a measuring system that other groups can use to make consistent measurements. They may encounter errors due to stretching of the string and estimating between units.

Analyze Your Data

1. the system with the smallest divisions, because it is the most precise
2. Accept all reasonable answers.

Error Analysis

Have students analyze how errors could result from the method used to mark their string into smaller units.

Draw Conclusions

1. so they can reproduce your results
2. When the size of the unit of measurement varies, the number of units used to measure an object also must vary.

Assessment

Portfolio Tape a sample of your measuring string to an explanation of your standard and measuring system. Discuss any problems you solved in the process of developing this system. Include this paper in your portfolio. Use **Performance Assessment in the Science Classroom,** p. 159. P

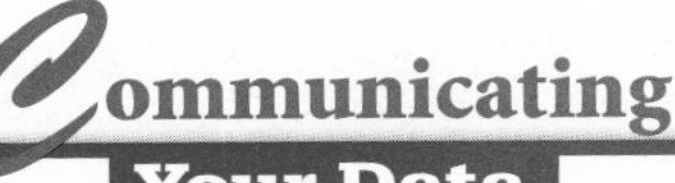

To test their measurement systems, have students exchange strings and use them to measure the same item.

Science and Language Arts

Pre-Reading Activity

Ask students to write down step-by-step instructions and draw rough sketches for something they have built or designed. Items could be as complex as model airplanes, or as simple as a peanut butter and jelly sandwich.

Respond to the Reading

Active Reading Strategies

Question Ask studetns if they understand the difference between visual thinking and language-based thinking. Suggest they go back and reread the sentences discussing the differences between these two kinds of thinking.

Review Ask students to review the selection, paying attention to the ways the writer applies visual thinking to her job. Have students consider what kind of thinker they are.

Answers to Questions

1. They think in pictures.
2. photographs at the cow's eye level
3. kites and model airplane

Science and Language Arts

Thinking in Pictures: and other reports from my life with autism[1]

By Temple Grandin

Respond to the Reading

1. How do people with autism think differently than other people?
2. What did the author use to see from a cow's point of view?
3. What did the author use for models to design things when she was a child?

Temple Grandin is an animal scientist and writer who also happens to be autistic. People with autism are said to think in pictures. For instance, an autistic person might think of a "dog" by visualizing a specific dog that he or she has seen rather than the word "dog."

I think in pictures. Words are like a second language to me. I translate both spoken and written words into full-color movies, complete with sound, which run like a VCR tape in my head. When somebody speaks to me, his words are instantly translated into pictures. Language-based thinkers often find this phenomenon difficult to understand, but in my job as equipment designer for the livestock industry, visual thinking is a tremendous advantage.

. . . I credit my visualization abilities with helping me understand the animals I work with. Early in my career I used a camera to help give me the animals' perspective as they walked through a chute for their veterinary treatment. I would kneel down and take pictures through the chute from the cow's eye level. Using the photos, I was able to figure out which things scared the cattle.

Every design problem I've ever solved started with my ability to visualize and see the world in pictures. I started designing things as a child, when I was always experimenting with new kinds of kites and model airplanes.

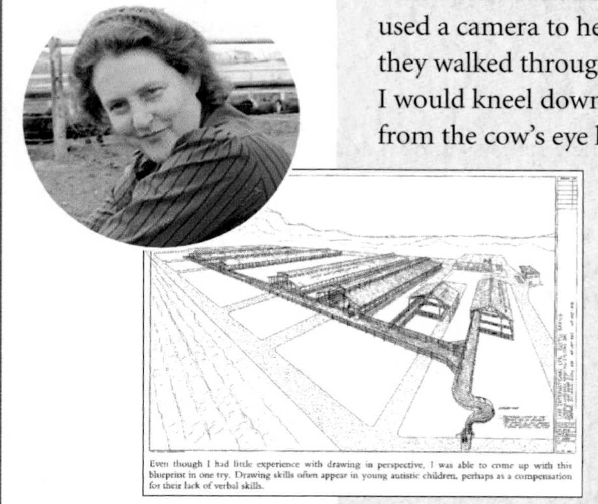

Even though I had little experience with drawing in perspective, I was able to come up with this blueprint in one try. Drawing skills often appear in young autistic children, perhaps as a compensation for their lack of verbal skills.

The author drew this blueprint of a cattle barn in one try.

[1] Autism is a complex developmental disability that usually appears during the first three years of life. Children and adults with autism typically have difficulties in communicating with others and relating to the outside world.

Reading Further

Other works by this author include:

Dr. Temple Grandin Video-Visual Thinking of a Person with Autism, by Temple Grandin, Future Horizons, 1999

Other sources on this topic include:

Unraveling the Mystery of Autism and Pervasive Development Disorder: A Mother's Story of Research and Recovery, by Karyn Seroussi and Bernard Rimland Ph.D., Simon & Shuster, 2000

An Anthropologist on Mars: Seven Paradoxical Tales, by Oliver W. Sacks, Vintage Books, 1996

Identifying the Main Idea

Understanding Literature

Identifying the Main Idea The most important idea expressed in a paragraph or essay is the main idea. The main idea in a reading might be clearly stated, but sometimes the main idea is implied. In other words, sometimes the reader has to summarize the contents of a reading in order to determine its main idea. What do you think is the main idea of the passage above? Look closely at the contents of the first and third paragraphs to help you summarize and determine the main idea.

Science Connection In this chapter you learned that models are important tools for scientists. Models enable scientists to see things that are too big, too small, or take too much time to see completely. Scientists might build models of DNA, atoms, airplanes, or other equipment. Temple Grandin excels at building models because she is a visual thinker. Her visual thinking and ability to make models enables her to predict how things will work when they are put together.

Linking Science and Writing

Summarizing Research a magazine or newspaper article about the use of a scientific model. The model can be a blueprint design like that of Temple Grandin's. Write a paragraph that summarizes what you learned. Your summary should organize the information you learned by stating the main ideas and listing supporting details.

Career Connection

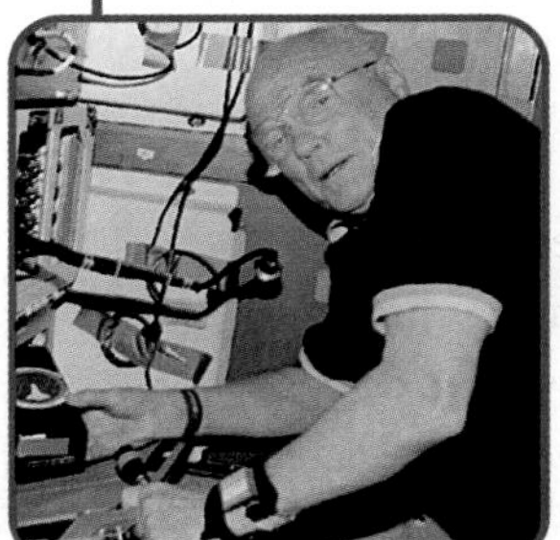

Astronaut

John Glenn, Jr. made history twice. In 1962 he became the first American to orbit Earth. In 1998, at age 77, he became the oldest person to fly in space. During Glenn's first mission, NASA learned how to place a craft into Earth's orbit and track its location. This mission also taught NASA the basics about how the human body reacts to weightlessness. On his second mission, Glenn studied the similarities between the effects of space flight and the effects of aging. After his retirement from the Marine corps in 1965, Glenn went on to serve four terms as U.S. Senator from Ohio.

SCIENCE *Online* To learn more about a career as an astronaut, visit the Glencoe Science Web site at **science.glencoe.com.**

Understanding Literature

Answers to Questions

Possible answer: The main idea of this selection is that thinking in pictures—has allowed Temple Grandin to solve design problems as an equipment designer.

Science Connection

The design and use of models can help people predict the characteristics of any system. Because a model can be built, tested, and modified at a reasonably low cost, scientists, architects, and other designers use models to predict the performance of a prototype. If the results obtained from a model are to be applicable to the prototype, a strict set of conditions must be met by the model or the deviations from these conditions must be considered when predicting the behavior of the prototype.

Linking Science and Writing

Teaching Strategies

Remind students that maps and pictures can be models as well as three-dimensional objects.

Career Connection

An astronaut candidate must meet three requirements: be a jet pilot with a thousand hours of flying time; have a bachelor's degree in engineering, physical or biological sciences, or mathematics; and be between five feet four inches and six feet four inches tall. Graduation from an armed forces test pilot school is common. While in orbit, astronauts conduct experiments and gather information.

Internet Addresses

Explore the Glencoe Science Web site at **science.glencoe.com** to find out more about topics in this feature.

SCIENCE AND LANGUAGE ARTS 31

Chapter 1 Study Guide

Reviewing Main Ideas

Preview

Students can answer the questions in their Science Journals. Discuss the answers as you go through the chapter. LS **Linguistic**

Review

Students can write their answers, then compare them with those of other students. LS **Interpersonal**

Reteach

Students can look at the illustrations and describe details that support the main ideas of the chapter. LS **Visual-Spatial**

Answers to Chapter Review

Section 1

2. They involve winds that move clouds in spirals. They occur over Florida.

Section 2

4. 451.9 m; 0.4519 km

Chapter 1 Study Guide

Reviewing Main Ideas

Section 1 The Methods of Science

1. Science is a way of learning about the natural world through investigation.
2. Scientific investigations can involve making observations, testing models, or conducting experiments. *What do you observe about hurricanes from the photo?*

3. Scientific experiments investigate the effect of one variable on another. All other variables are kept constant.
4. Scientific laws are repeated patterns in nature. Theories attempt to explain how and why these patterns develop.

Section 2 Standards of Measurement

1. A standard of measurement is an exact quantity that people agree to use as a basis of comparison.
2. When a standard of measurement is established, all measurements are compared to the same exact quantity—the standard. Therefore, all measurements can be compared with one another.
3. The most commonly used SI units include: length—meter, volume—liter, mass—kilogram, and time—second.
4. In SI, prefixes are used to make the base units larger or smaller by multiples of ten. *The Petronas Twin Towers in Malaysia is the world's tallest building, standing at 45,190 cm. Use a conversion factor to find out how many meters this is. How many kilometers?*

5. Any SI unit can be converted to any other related SI unit by multiplying by the appropriate conversion factor.

Section 3 Communicating With Graphs

1. Line graphs show continuous changes between related variables. Bar graphs are used to show data collected by counting. Circle graphs show how a fixed quantity can be broken into parts.
2. In a line graph, the independent variable is always plotted on the horizontal *x*-axis. The dependent variable is always plotted on the vertical *y*-axis.

FOLDABLES Reading & Study Skills

After You Read

Using the information in this chapter, determine if the questions on your Question Study Fold can be answered by scientific processes. Then review your questions on the foldable and write the answers.

FOLDABLES Reading & Study Skills

After You Read

After students have read the chapter and completed the Foldable described in Before You Read, have them do the activity on the student page.

Dinah Zike

Visualizing Main Ideas

Complete the following concept map on scientific methods.

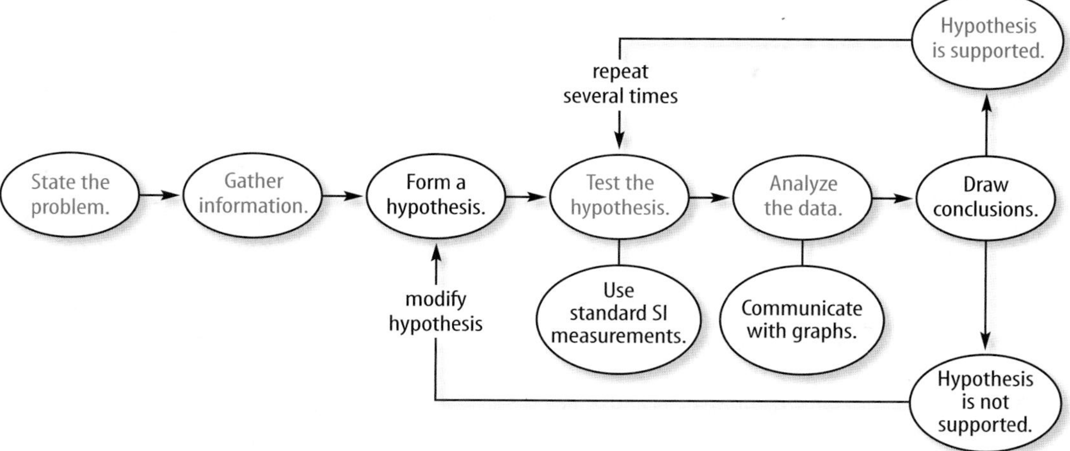

Vocabulary Review

Vocabulary Words

a. bias
b. constant
c. control
d. density
e. dependent variable
f. experiment
g. graph
h. hypothesis
i. independent variable
j. mass
k. model
l. scientific law
m. scientific method
n. SI
o. standard
p. technology
q. theory
r. variable
s. volume

Study Tip

THE PRINCETON REVIEW

If you're not sure of the relationship between terms in a question, try making a concept map of the terms and see how they fit together.

Using Vocabulary

Match each phrase with the correct term from the list of vocabulary words.

1. the modern version of the metric system
2. the amount of space occupied by an object
3. an agreed-upon quantity used for comparison
4. the amount of matter in an object
5. a variable that changes as another variable changes
6. a visual display of data
7. a test set up under controlled conditions
8. a variable that does NOT change as another variable changes
9. mass per unit volume
10. an educated guess using what you know and observe

Chapter 1 Study Guide

Visualizing Main Ideas

See student page.

Vocabulary Review

Using Vocabulary

1. SI
2. volume
3. standard
4. mass
5. dependent variable
6. graph
7. experiment
8. constant
9. density
10. hypothesis

Chapter 1 Assessment

Checking Concepts

1. B
2. B
3. A
4. D
5. D
6. A
7. C
8. B
9. B
10. D

Thinking Critically

11. **a.** 1.5 L **b.** 200,000 cm **c.** 580 mg **d.** 295 K
12. Possible answer: The next king's arm would be a different length.
13. **a.** nanometer, nm **b.** meter, m **c.** millimeter, mm **d.** centimeter, cm
14. A line graph; time would be the independent variable and temperature would be the dependent variable.
15. Possible advantages: SI is based on powers of 10, conversion is easy because the same prefixes are used for all types of measurements, most countries use it. Possible disadvantages: Conversion to SI would be expensive, people are reluctant to change from a familiar system.

Chapter  Assessment

Checking Concepts

Choose the word or phrase that best answers each question.

1. Which of the following questions CANNOT be answered by science?
   A) How do birds fly?
   B) Is this a good song?
   C) What is an atom?
   D) How does a clock work?
2. Which is an example of an SI unit?
   A) foot **C)** pound
   B) second **D)** gallon
3. Which system of measurement is used by scientists around the world?
   A) SI **C)** English system
   B) Standard system **D)** Kelvin system
4. Which of the following is SI based on?
   A) inches **C)** English units
   B) powers of five **D)** powers of ten
5. One one-thousandth is expressed by which prefix?
   A) kilo- **C)** centi-
   B) nano- **D)** milli-
6. What is the symbol for deciliter?
   A) dL **C)** dkL
   B) dcL **D)** Ld
7. What does the symbol μg stand for?
   A) nanogram **C)** microgram
   B) kilogram **D)** milligram
8. Which is the distance between two points?
   A) volume **C)** mass
   B) length **D)** density
9. Which of the following is NOT a derived unit?
   A) dm^3 **C)** cm^3
   B) m **D)** g/ml
10. Which of the following is NOT equal to 1,000 mL?
    A) 1 L **C)** 1 dm^3
    B) 100 cL **D)** 1 cm^3

Thinking Critically

11. Make the following conversions.
    a. 1,500 mL to L **c.** 5.8 dg to mg
    b. 2 km to cm **d.** 22°C to K
12. Standards of measurement used during the Middle Ages often were based on such things as the length of the king's arm. What would you say to convince people to use a different system of standard units?
13. List the SI units of length you would use to express the following. Refer to **Table 1** in Section 2.
    a. diameter of a hair
    b. width of your classroom
    c. width of a pencil lead
    d. length of a sheet of paper

14. Suppose you set a glass of water in direct sunlight for 2 h and measure its temperature every 10 min. What type of graph would you use to display your data? What would the dependent variable be? The independent variable?
15. What are some advantages and disadvantages of adopting SI in the United States?

Developing Skills

16. **Comparing and Contrasting** Compare and contrast the ease with which conversions can be made among SI units versus conversoins among units in the English system.

Chapter Assessment Planner

Portfolio Encourage students to place in their portfolios one or two items of what they consider to be their best work. Examples include:

- Earth Science Integration, p. 11
- Extension, p. 15
- Science Journal, p. 24
- Assessment, p. 29

Performance Additional performance assessments, Performance Task Assessment Lists, and rubrics for evaluating these activities can be found in Glencoe's **Performance Assessment in the Science Classroom.**

17. **Forming Hypotheses** A metal sphere is found to have a density of 5.2 g/cm^3 at 25°C and a density of 5.1 g/cm^3 at 50°C. Propose a hypothesis to explain this observation. How could you test your hypothesis?

18. **Measuring in SI** Not all objects have a volume that is measured easily. If you were to determine the mass, volume, and density of your textbook, a container of milk, and an air-filled balloon, how would you do it?

19. **Interpreting Scientific Illustrations** The illustrations show the items needed for an investigation. Which item is the independent variable? Which items are the constants? What might the dependent variable be?

Performance Assessment

20. **Making Observations and Inferences** In the two-page activity, suppose you needed to measure five times the quantities. Compare the difficulty of multiplying the English measurements five times with multiplying the SI measurements five times.

Technology

Go to the Glencoe Science Web site at **science.glencoe.com** or use the **Glencoe Science CD-ROM** for additional chapter assessment.

Test Practice

A student made measurements of several items using units from both the English system of measurement and the SI system of measurement to determine how units of the two systems were related. Using these data, the student determined unit conversion factors that allow one unit to be converted into another. These conversion factors and their related units are shown below.

Measurement Units

Measurement	English System Unit	SI Unit	Conversion Factor
Length	Foot	Meter	1 foot = 0.305 m
Mass	Slug	Kilogram	1 slug = 1.46 kg
Volume	Gallon	Liter	1 gallon = 3.78 L
Time	Second	Second	N/A

Study the table and answer the following questions.

1. According to this table, about how many liters are there in a gallon?
   A) ¼ **C)** ½
   B) 4 **D)** ⅔

2. How many kilograms are equal to two slugs?
   F) 4.28 **H)** 3.04
   G) 1.16 **J)** 2.92

3. Which unit is the same in both the English and SI systems of measurement?
   A) meter **C)** gallon
   B) slug **D)** second

Assessment Resources

Reproducible Masters

Chapter Resources Booklet
Chapter Review, p. 37
Chapter Tests, p. 39
Assessment Transparency Activity, p. 49

Glencoe Science Web site
Interactive Tutor
Chapter Quizzess

Glencoe Technology
Assessment Transparency
Interactive CD-ROM Chapter Quizzes
ExamView Pro Test Bank
Vocabulary PuzzleMaker Software
MindJogger Videoquiz DVD/VHS

Chapter 1 Assessment

Test Practice

The Test-Taking Tip was written by The Princeton Review, the nation's leader in test preparation.

1. B
2. J
3. D

Developing Skills

16. SI measurements are based on powers of ten. There are many different divisions in the English system. Thus it is easier to convert in SI than in the English system.
17. The metal expands when heated. The hypothesis can be tested by measuring the volume of the ball at the two temperatures.
18. Textbook volume could be determined by multiplying its length, width, and height. The volume of the balloon could be determined by measuring the volume of water it displaces. The volume of any irregular object, such as the milk carton, must be determined indirectly. If the object is not harmed by water, volume can be measured by water displacement.
19. Independent variable: pot; constant: vegetables; dependent variable: water, heat

Performance Assessment

20. SI measurements are easily multiplied. English measurements are not, if fractions are involved. Use PASC, p. 101.

Section/Objectives	Standards		Activities/Features
	National	State/Local	
Chapter Opener	See p. 37T for a Key to Standards.		**Explore Activity:** Calculate your speed, p. 37 **Before You Read,** p. 37
Secton 1 **Describing Motion** 2 sessions 1 block 1. **Distinguish** between distance and displacement. 2. **Explain** the difference between speed and velocity. 3. **Interpret** motion graphs.	National Content Standards: UCP3, A2, B2 (5–8), B4 (9–12)		**Astronomy Integration,** p. 39 **MiniLAB:** Describing the Motion of a Car, p. 40 **Science Online,** p. 41 **Math Skills Activity:** Calculating Time from Speed, p. 42 **Science Online,** p. 43
Secton 2 **Acceleration** 1 session 1 block 1. **Identify** how acceleration, time, and velocity are related. 2. **Explain** how positive and negative acceleration affect motion. 3. **Describe** how to calculate the acceleration of an object.	National Content Standards: UCP3, B2 (5–8), B4 (9–12),		**Life Science Integration,** p. 48 **Visualizing Acceleration,** p. 49
Secton 3 **Motion and Forces** 4 sessions 2 blocks 1. **Explain** how force and velocity are related. 2. **Describe** what inertia is and how it is related to Newton's first law of motion. 3. **Identify** the forces and motion that are present during a car crash.	National Content Standards: UCP3, B2 (5–8), B4 (9–12), F1, F5 (5–8), F1, F5 (9–12), G1		**Science Online,** p. 53 **MiniLAB:** Observing Inertia in Action, p. 54 **Activity:** Force and Acceleration, p. 57 **Activity:** Comparing Motion from Different Forces, p. 58 **Science and Language Arts:** A Brave and Startling Truth, p. 60

Activity Materials	Reproducible Resources	Section Assessment	Technology
Explore Activity: meterstick, stopwatch	**Chapter Resources Booklet** Foldables Worksheet, p. 17 Note-taking Worksheets, pp. 33–35	GLENCOE'S ASSESSMENT ADVANTAGE	
MiniLAB: tape, toy car, stopwatch, pencil, meterstick	**Chapter Resources Booklet** Transparency Activity, p. 44 MiniLAB, p. 3 Enrichment, p. 30 Reinforcement, p. 27 Directed Reading, p. 20 Lab Activity, pp. 9–12 Transparency Activity, pp. 47–48	**Portfolio** Activity, p. 42 **Performance** MiniLAB, p. 40 Math Skills Activity, p. 42 Skill Builder Activities, p. 46 **Content** Section Assessment, p. 46	Section Focus Transparency Teaching Transparency Interactive CD-ROM/DVD Guided Reading Audio Program
Need materials? Contact Science Kit at 1-800-828-7777 or www.sciencekit.com on the Internet.	**Chapter Resources Booklet** Transparency Activity, p. 45 Enrichment, p. 31 Reinforcement, p. 28 Directed Reading, p. 21 Lab Activity, pp. 13--15	**Portfolio** Challenge, p. 51 **Performance** Skill Builder Activities, p. 51 **Content** Section Assessment, p. 51	Section Focus Transparency Interactive CD-ROM/DVD Guided Reading Audio Program
MiniLAB: board, textbooks, stop block, small object, cart, rubber bands **Activity:** tape, paper clip, 10-N spring scale, large book, this science book, triple beam balance **Activity:** small toy car, ramps or boards of different lengths, springs, stopwatch, meterstick or tape measure, graph paper	**Chapter Resources Booklet** Transparency Activity, p. 46 MiniLAB, p. 4 Enrichment, p. 32 Reinforcement, p. 29 Directed Reading, p. 21, 22 Activity Worksheet, pp. 5–6, 7–8	**Portfolio** Activity, p. 55 **Performance** MiniLAB, p. 54 Skill Builder Activities, p. 56 **Content** Section Assessment, p. 56	Section Focus Transparency Interactive CD-ROM/DVD Guided Reading Audio Program

GLENCOE'S ASSESSMENT ADVANTAGE

End of Chapter Assessment

Blackline Masters	Technology	Professional Series
Chapter Resources Booklet Chapter Review, pp. 37–38 Chapter Tests, pp. 39–42 **Standardized Test Practice by The Princeton Review,** pp. 12–15	MindJogger Videoquiz CD-ROM Explorations and Quizzes Vocabulary Puzzle Makers ExamView Pro Test Bank Interactive Lesson Planner Interactive Teacher's Edition	Performance Assessment in the Science Classroom (PASC)

Transparencies

Section Focus

Section 1 Section Focus Transparency — How about a rematch?

In Aesop's fable "The Tortoise and the Hare," a tortoise and a hare have a race. The hare bounds far ahead of the tortoise and then, sure that he will win the race, lies down to rest under a tree. The tortoise passes the resting hare and wins the race.

1. Which animal ran faster?
2. Explain the difference between the average speed over the whole race and the speed at any one instant of the race.

L1

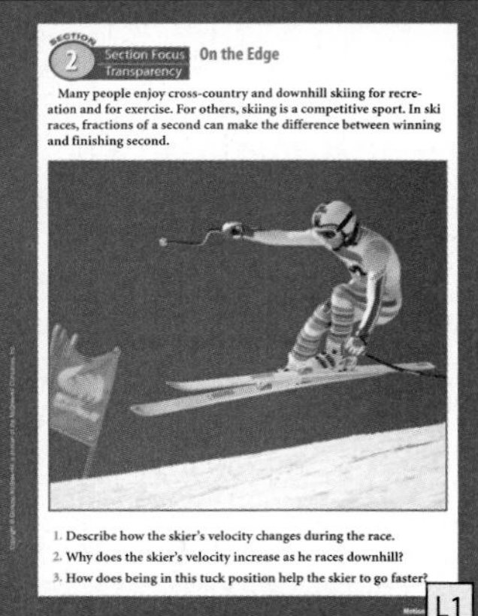

Section 2 Section Focus Transparency — On the Edge

Many people enjoy cross-country and downhill skiing for recreation and for exercise. For others, skiing is a competitive sport. In ski races, fractions of a second can make the difference between winning and finishing second.

1. Describe how the skier's velocity changes during the race.
2. Why does the skier's velocity increase as he races downhill?
3. How does being in this tuck position help the skier to go faster?

L1

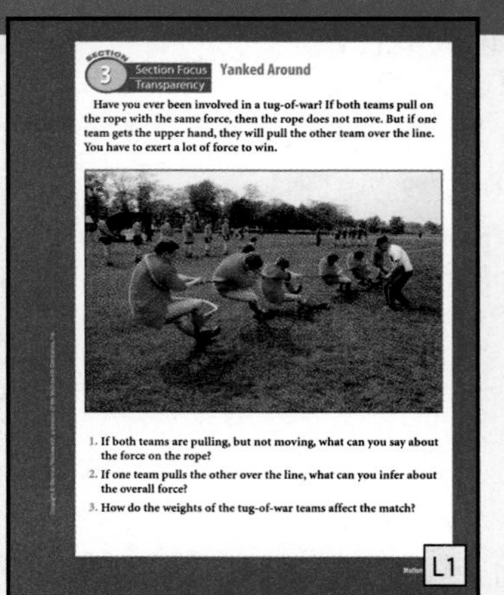

Section 3 Section Focus Transparency — Yanked Around

Have you ever been involved in a tug-of-war? If both teams pull on the rope with the same force, then the rope does not move. But if one team gets the upper hand, they will pull the other team over the line. You have to exert a lot of force to win.

1. If both teams are pulling, but not moving, what can you say about the force on the rope?
2. If one team pulls the other over the line, what can you infer about the overall force?
3. How do the weights of the tug-of-war teams affect the match?

L1

Assessment

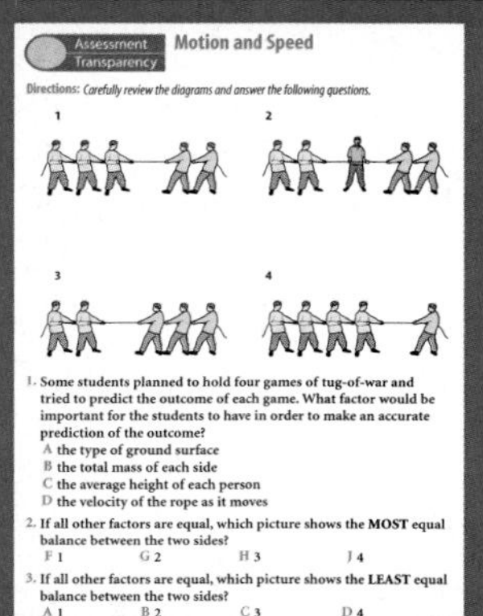

Assessment Transparency — Motion and Speed

Directions: Carefully review the diagrams and answer the following questions.

1. Some students planned to hold four games of tug-of-war and tried to predict the outcome of each game. What factor would be important for the students to have in order to make an accurate prediction of the outcome?
A the type of ground surface
B the total mass of each side
C the average height of each person
D the velocity of the rope as it moves
2. If all other factors are equal, which picture shows the MOST equal balance between the two sides?
F 1 G 2 H 3 J 4
3. If all other factors are equal, which picture shows the LEAST equal balance between the two sides?
A 1 B 2 C 3 D 4

L1

Teaching

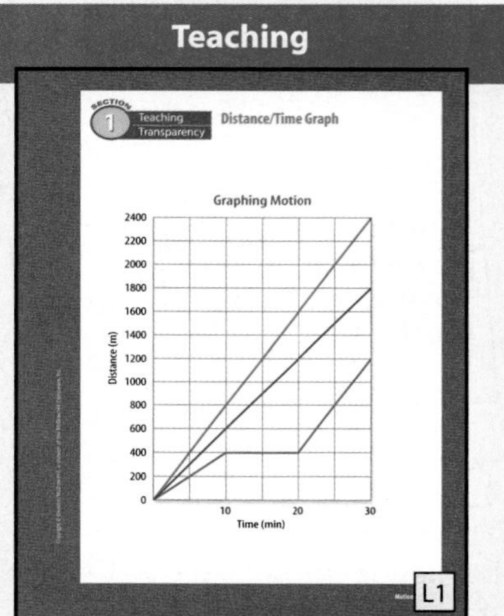

Section 1 Teaching Transparency — Distance/Time Graph

L1

This is a representation of key blackline masters available in the Teacher Classroom Resources. See Resource Manager boxes within the chapter for additional information.

Key to Teaching Strategies

The following designations will help you decide which activities are appropriate for your students.

- L1 Level 1 activities should be appropriate for students with learning difficulties.
- L2 Level 2 activities should be within the ability range of all students.
- L3 Level 3 activities are designed for above-average students.
- ELL ELL activities should be within the ability range of English Language Learners.
- COOP LEARN Cooperative Learning activities are designed for small group work.
- LS Multiple Learning Styles logos are used throughout to indicate strategies that address different learning styles.
- P These strategies represent student products that can be placed into a best-work portfolio.

Hands-on Activities

Activity Worksheets

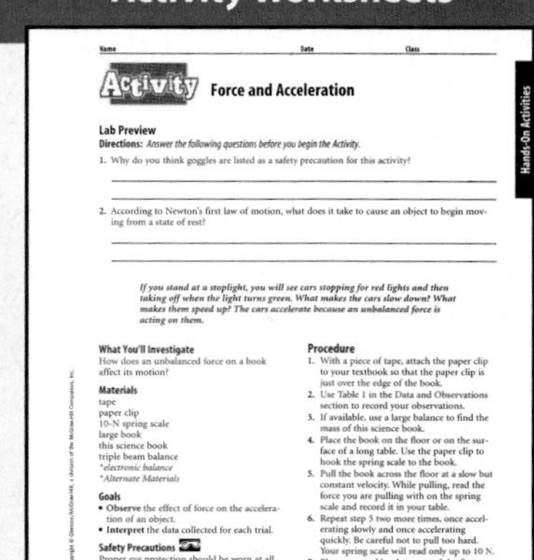

Activity — Force and Acceleration

Lab Preview

Directions: Answer the following questions before you begin the Activity.

1. Why do you think goggles are listed as a safety precaution for this activity?
2. According to Newton's first law of motion, what does it take to cause an object to begin moving from a state of rest?

L1

Laboratory Activities

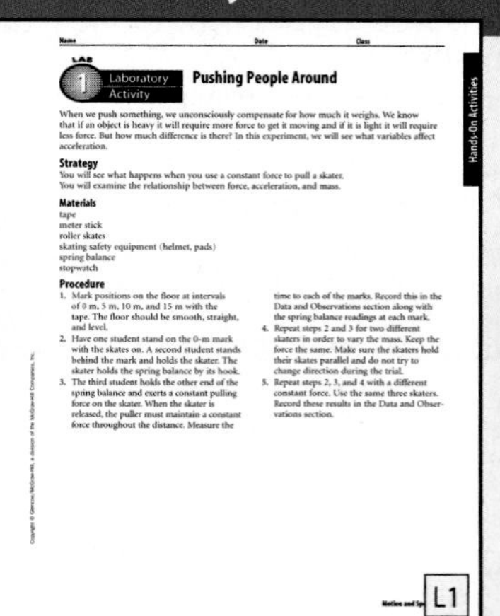

Laboratory Activity 1 — Pushing People Around

Strategy

Materials

Procedure

L1

Meeting Different Ability Levels

Content Outline

Reinforcement

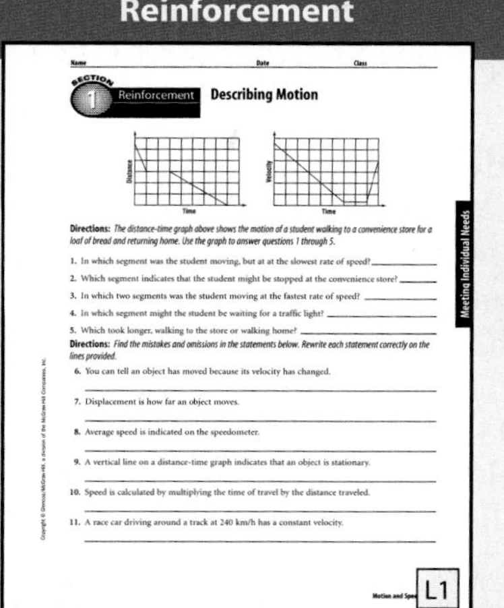

Directed Reading

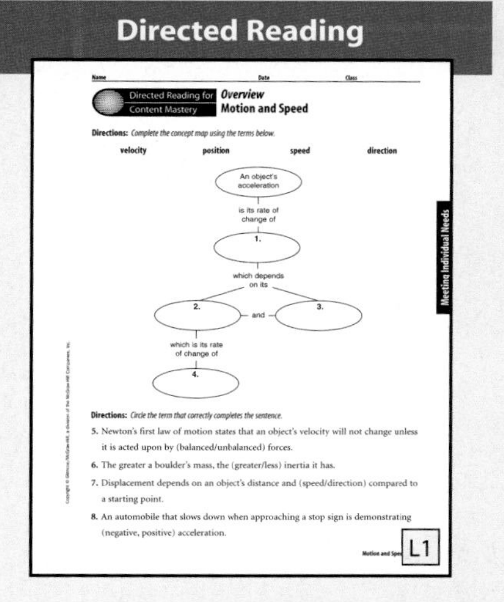

Enrichment

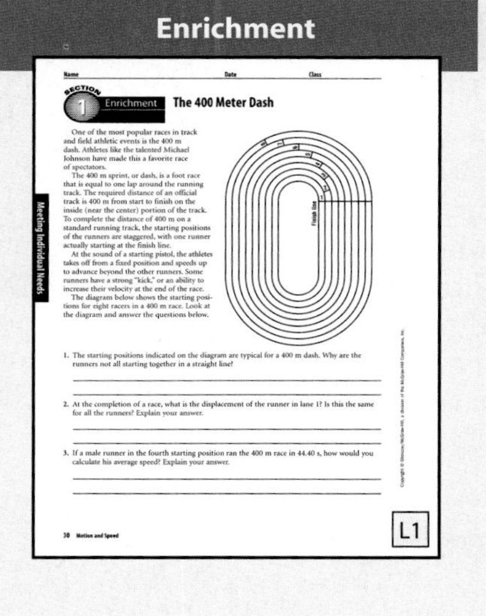

Spanish Directed Reading

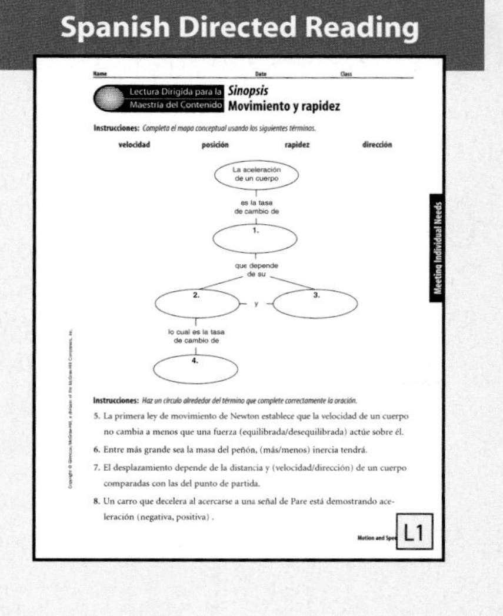

Assessment

Chapter Tests

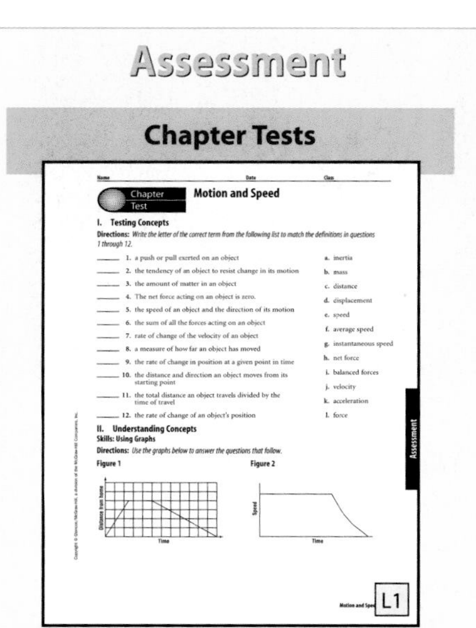

Test Practice Workbook

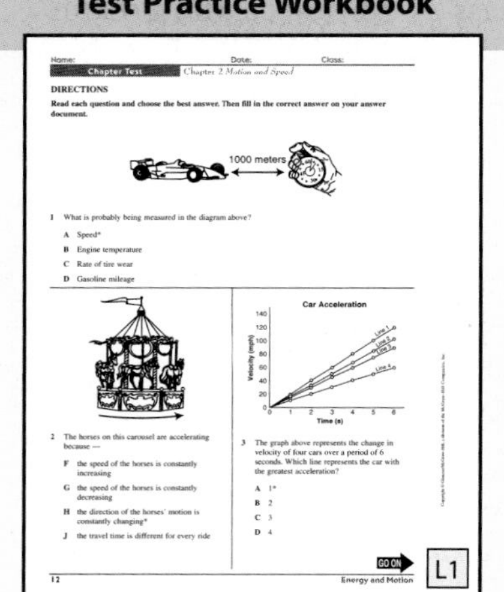

Chapter Review

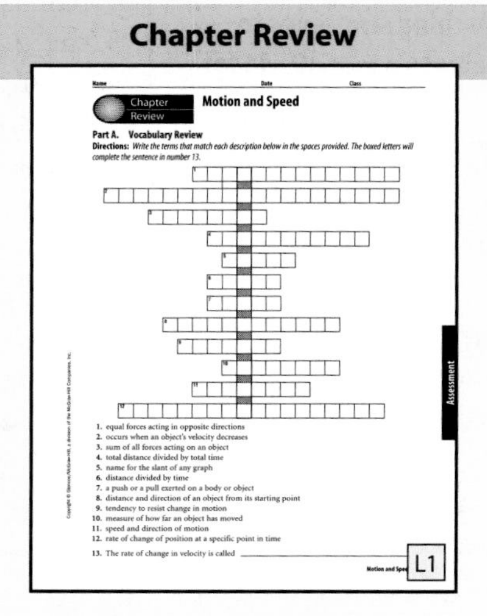

Science Content Background

SECTION 1 Describing Motion

Distance Versus Displacement

A vector quantity has both magnitude and direction, such as a displacement of 15 km east and a velocity of 7 m/s west. Scalar quantities have magnitude only, such as a distance of 5 km and a speed of 6 m/s. The terms *distance* and *displacement* have different meanings. Consider a car going around a round racetrack. The distance the car travels can be read from its odometer, but the car's displacement is its straight-line distance and direction from its starting point. For each lap the odometer increases. But for each lap its displacement at first increases, and then decreases and becomes zero as it returns to the starting point. Speed and velocity also can be contrasted easily. The car traveling around the track may have a constant speed, but its velocity is constantly changing because its direction is constantly changing.

Student Misconception

Students may think that distance and displacement are the same. They may also think that speed and velocity are the same.

Refer to the facing page for teaching strategies to address this misconception. Refer to pages 39–44 for content related to this topic.

SECTION 2 Acceleration

Acceleration, Speed, and Velocity

An object will tend to move in straight-line motion unless a force acts on it. A planet orbiting a star experiences the force of gravity between the star and the planet. This force causes the object to accelerate toward the star and not fly off in straight-line motion. So even though the planet moves with constant speed, it is accelerating.

Acceleration units show changes in velocity divided by time. If velocity is expressed as meters/second and time in seconds, then acceleration is expressed with units of meters per second per second. This is equivalent to m/s/s or (m/s x 1/s) or m/s^2.

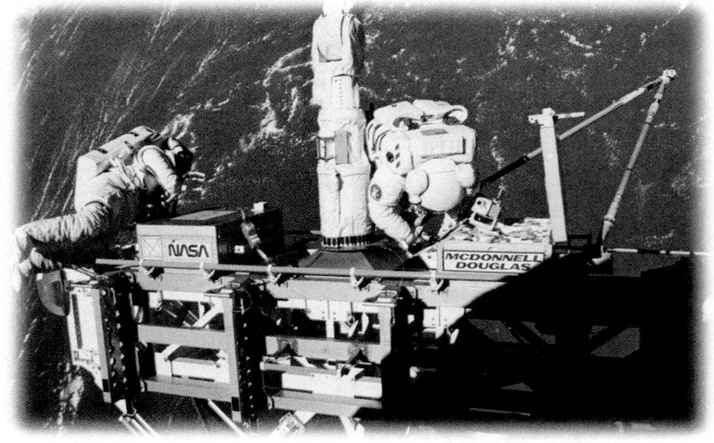

Corbis

SECTION 3 Motion and Forces

Inertia and Mass

Astronauts in weightless conditions would still have a harder time moving a massive object like a bowling ball than moving a tennis ball. This is because the greater the mass of an object, the greater is its inertia. In the weightless condition, if the bowling ball were not moving, it would be just as hard to push it down as to pick it up.

For additional content background on this topic, go to the Glencoe Science Web site at science.glencoe.com.

IDENTIFYING Misconceptions

Find Out What Students Think

Students may think that . . .

- **Distance and displacement are the same thing.**
- **Speed and velocity are the same thing.**

Students are familiar with scalar quantities and vector quantities, but terms such as *displacement* and *velocity* may cause confusion. Also the term *velocity* is frequently used as though it were the same thing as *speed*. Finally, the terms *displacement* and *distance* sound similar, and this may cause confusion between them.

Discussion

Tell students that a turtle and a hare start a race at the same time. The turtle goes straight to the finish line. The hare starts off and deviates along the way. They both finish the race at the same time. Discuss which had the greatest average speed during the race.

Promote Understanding

Activity

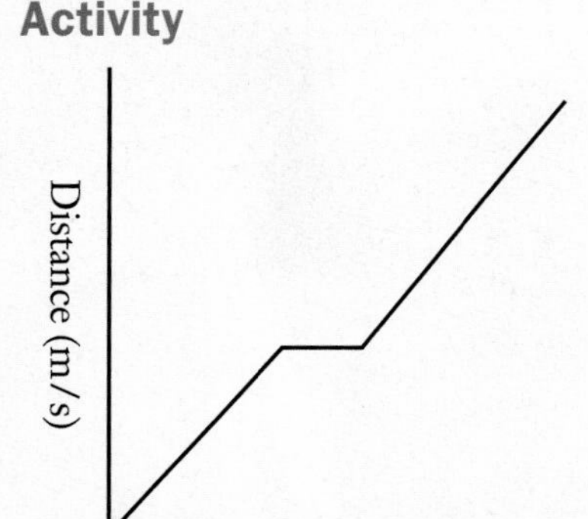

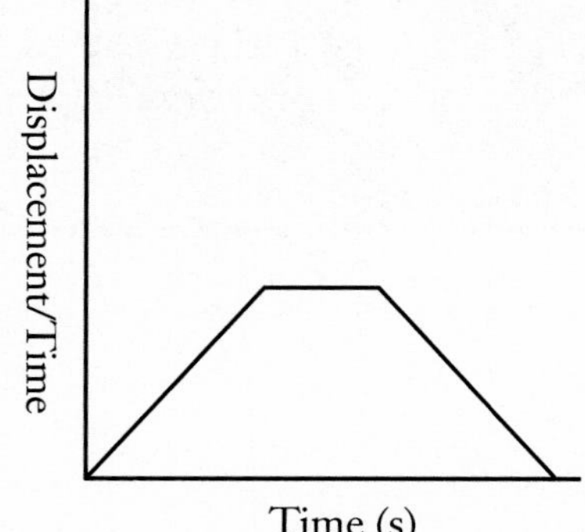

- Draw Figures 1 and 2 on the board. Explain that the distance-time graph and the displacement-time graph each show Samantha's walking motion after she left her house.
- Ask students to supply a possible story to describe her motion. Ask them what she might be doing when the lines of both graphs are horizontal.
- Students should see that the distance-time graph and the displacement-time graph for the same motion look very different. In this case the distance traveled is how far Samantha actually walked. Her displacement shows how far she is from her house.
- A plausible story for both graphs has Samantha walk with constant speed directly away from her house, then rest a bit, and then walk with constant speed directly back to her house.

Assess

After completing the chapter, see *Identifying Misconceptions* in the Study Guide.

CHAPTER 2

Motion and Speed

Chapter Vocabulary

distance
displacement
speed
average speed
instantaneous speed
velocity
acceleration
force
net force
balanced force
inertia

What do you think?

Science Journal The photo shows the treads on an automobile tire.

CHAPTER 2

Motion and Speed

When you think of amusement parks, do you automatically think about roller coasters? Do you remember your last roller coaster ride? Do you recall the fast speeds, sharp turns, and plunging hills that cause your senses and balance to be in a state of total confusion. At this moment, it is doubtful that you are thinking about motion, the laws of gravity, or how to describe motion. In this chapter, you will learn about motion and speed—what they are and how to describe them.

What do you think?

Science Journal Look at the picture below with a classmate. Discuss what you think this is or what is happening. Here's a hint: *Without these on your car, it would slide on a dry road.* Write your answer or best guess in your Science Journal.

36

Theme Connection

Stability and Change An object will maintain its inertia unless the object is acted upon by an outside force.

A cheetah can run at a speed of 112 km/h, and is the fastest runner in the world. A horse can reach a speed of 64 km/h; an elephant's top speed is about 30 km/h, and the fastest snake slithers at a speed of less than 10 km/h. The speed of an object is calculated by dividing the distance the object travels by the time it takes it to move that distance. How does the speed of a human compare to these animals?

Calculate your speed

1. Use a meterstick to mark off a 10-m distance.
2. Have your partner use a stopwatch to determine how fast you run 10 m.
3. Divide 10 m by your time in seconds to calculate your speed in m/s.
4. Multiply your answer by 3.6 to determine your speed in km/h.

Observe

Compare your speed with the maximum speed of a cheetah, horse, elephant, snake, and the fastest human. Could you win a race with any of them?

Before You Read

FOLDABLES Reading & Study Skills

Making a Question Study Fold **Asking yourself questions helps you stay focused and better understand motion and speed when you are reading the chapter.**

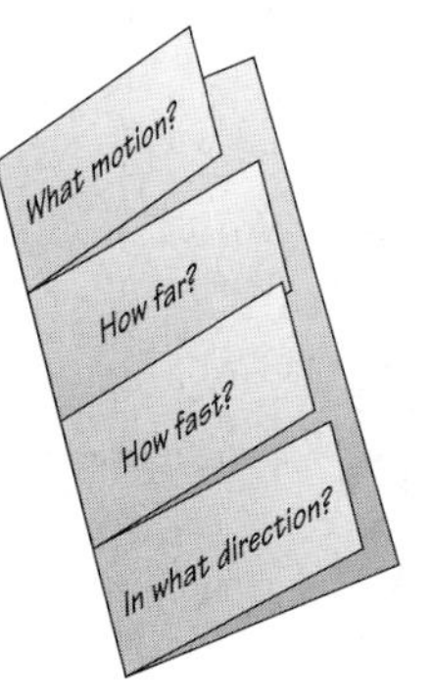

1. Place a sheet of paper in front of you so the short side is at the top. Fold the paper in half from the left side to the right side.
2. Now fold the paper in half from top to bottom. Then fold it in half again top to bottom. Unfold the last two folds that you did.
3. Label the four sections *What motion?, How far?, How fast?,* and *In what direction?* as shown.
4. Through one thickness of paper, cut along each of the fold lines to form four tabs as shown.
5. Before you read the chapter, select a motion you can observe and write it on the front of the top tab. As you read the chapter, write answers to the other questions under the correct tab.

EXPLORE ACTIVITY

Purpose Use the Explore Activity to introduce students to the relationship between motion and speed. L2 LS **Kinesthetic**

Preparation Find a location outside where groups of students will have room to mark off their 10 m distances. Assign each group a specific location.

Materials meterstick, stopwatch, calculator

Teaching Strategies Stage a contest between the five students with the greatest speeds to determine the fastest student in the class. Post the top speeds on a classroom bulletin board.

Observe

Students will lose races with a cheetah, horse, and the fastest human and will win races with the snake. Some students will have greater speed than the elephant.

Oral Have students infer a formula for determining the speed of moving objects Use **Performance Assessment in the Science Classroom,** p. 89.

Before You Read

FOLDABLES Reading & Study Skills

Dinah Zike Study Fold

Purpose Have students make a Foldable and use it to record an observed motion and to answer the following questions—How far? How fast? What direction?

For additional help, see Foldables Worksheet, p. 17 in **Chapter Resources Booklet,** or go to the Glencoe Science Web site at **science.glencoe.com.** See After You Read in the Study Guide at the end of this chapter.

SECTION

Describing Motion

1 Motivate

Bellringer Transparency

Display the Section Focus Transparency for Section 1. Use the accompanying Transparency Activity Master. L2 ELL

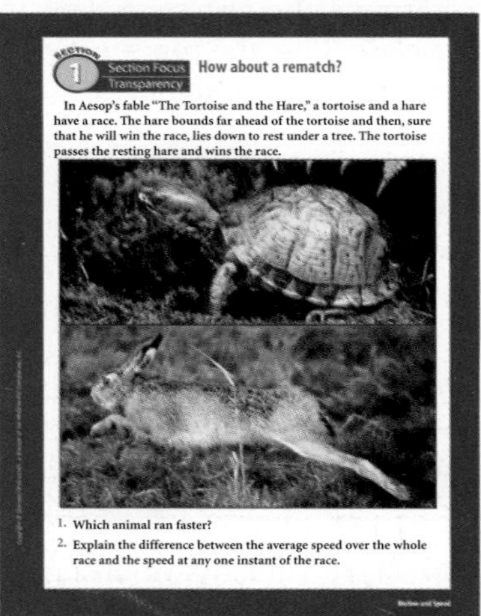

Section Focus Transparency — How about a rematch?

In Aesop's fable "The Tortoise and the Hare," a tortoise and a hare have a race. The hare bounds far ahead of the tortoise and then, sure that he will win the race, lies down to rest under a tree. The tortoise passes the resting hare and wins the race.

1. Which animal ran faster?
2. Explain the difference between the average speed over the whole race and the speed at any one instant of the race.

Tie to Prior Knowledge

Ask students to name the speed limits near their school, on the road in front of their homes, or on an interstate highway. Discuss with students the units, such as miles per hour and kilometers per hour, used in speed limits. Tell students they will learn about measuring speed in this section.

SECTION

Describing Motion

As You Read

What **You'll Learn**

- **Distinguish** between distance and displacement.
- **Explain** the difference between speed and velocity.
- **Interpret** motion graphs.

Vocabulary

distance, displacement, speed, average speed, instantaneous speed, velocity

Why **It's Important**

Understanding the nature of motion and how to describe it helps you understand why motion occurs.

Motion

Are distance and time important in describing running events at the track and field meets in the Olympics? Would the winners of the 5-km race and the 15-km race complete the run in the same length of time?

Distance and time are important. In order to win a race, you must cover the distance in the shortest amount of time. The time required to run the 15-km race should be longer than the time needed to complete the 5-km race because the first distance is longer. How would you describe the motion of the runners in the two races?

Motion and Position You don't always need to see something move to know that motion has taken place. For example, suppose you look out a window and see a mail truck stopped next to a mailbox. One minute later, you look out again and see the same truck stopped further down the street. Although you didn't see the truck move, you know it moved because its position relative to the mailbox changed.

Motion occurs when an object changes its position. To know whether the position of something has changed, you need a reference point such as the mailbox in **Figure 1.** A reference point also helps you determine how far the truck moved.

Figure 1
This mail truck is in motion.
How would you describe this motion to a friend?

Section Assessment Planner

PORTFOLIO
Activity, p. 42

PERFORMANCE ASSESSMENT
MiniLAB, p. 40
Skill Builder Activities, p. 46
See page 64 for more options.

CONTENT ASSESSMENT
Section, p. 46
Challenge, p. 46
Chapter, pp. 64–65

Relative Motion Not all motion is as obvious as that of a truck that has changed its position. Even if you are sitting in a chair reading this book, you are moving. You are not moving relative to your desk or your school building, but you are moving relative to the other planets in the solar system and the Sun.

Distance In track and field events, have you ever run a 50-m dash? A distance of 50 m was marked on the track or athletic field to show you how far to run. An important part of describing the motion of an object is to describe how far it has moved, which is **distance.** The SI unit of length or distance is the meter (m). Longer distances are measured in kilometers (km). One kilometer is equal to 1,000 m. Shorter distances are measured in centimeters (cm). One meter is equal to 100 centimeters.

Astronomy INTEGRATION

Using the Sun as your reference point, you are moving about 30 km through space every second. How many meters are in 30 km? What is this speed in meters per second? Record your answers in your Science Journal.

Displacement Suppose a runner jogs to the 50-m mark and then turns around and runs back to the 20-m mark, as shown in **Figure 2.** The runner travels 50 m in the original direction (north) plus 30 m in the opposite direction (south), so the total distance she ran is 80 m. How far is she from the starting line? The answer is 20 m. Sometimes you may want to know not only your distance but also your direction from a reference point, such as from the starting point. **Displacement** is the distance and direction of an object's change in position from the starting point. The runner's displacement in **Figure 2** is 20 m north.

The size of the runner's displacement and the distance traveled would be the same if the runner's motion was in a single direction. If the runner ran from the starting point to the finish line in a straight line, then the distance traveled would be 50 m and the displacement would be 50 m north.

Reading Check *How do distance and displacement differ?*

Speed

Think back to the example of the mail truck's motion in **Figure 1.** We now could describe the movement by the distance traveled and by the displacement from the starting point. You also might want to describe how fast it is moving. To do this, you need to know how far it travels in a given amount of time. **Speed** is the distance an object travels per unit of time.

Figure 2
Distance and displacement are not the same. The runner's displacement is 20 m north of the starting line. However, the total distance traveled is 80 m.

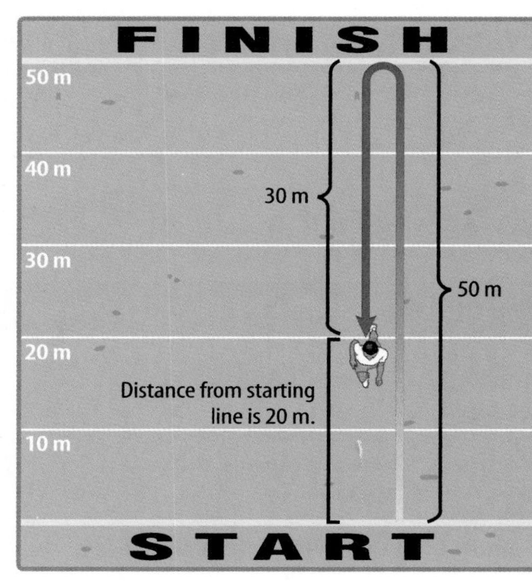

Displacement = 20 m north of starting line
Distance traveled = 50 m + 30 m = 80 m

2 Teach

Motion

Caption Answer

Figure 1 Possible answer: stops, starts, speeds up, slows down

Use Science Words

Word Usage Students may have difficulty with the term *relative* when it is used to describe an object's motion or position. Have them discuss what the word means. Possible answers are "dependent upon" or "with reference to." L1 ELL **Linguistic**

IDENTIFYING Misconceptions

Students may think that distance and displacement are the same. They may also think speed and velocity are the same. Refer to page 36F for teaching strategies that address this misconception.

Reading Check

Answer Distance describes how far an object has moved; displacement includes distance and direction of an object's change in position from its starting point.

Speed

Astronomy INTEGRATION

about 30,000 m/s The distance Earth travels around the Sun in one year is about 942 billion meters. One year has approximately 31,540,000 seconds. Have students use these numbers to calculate Earth's speed. 942 billion m ÷ 31,540,000 s = 29,848 m/s L3 **Logical-Mathematical**

Resource Manager 

Chapter Resources Booklet
- Transparency Activity, p. 44
- Directed Reading for Content Mastery, p. 20
- Note-taking Worksheets, pp. 33–35

Visual Learning

Figure 2 Help students understand the information presented in **Figure 2.** As you read the description from the text, have these students follow the path of the runner with their fingers. Then ask students how far the runner ran and how far she is from the starting line. 80 m; 20 m

Speed, continued

Activity

Review the concept of rate by having students measure their breathing rates. Discuss other rates, such as heart rate (pulse) and interest rates. Discuss the units that describe these rates and point out similarities in the units. They are all a number of something per time. L2 LS Logical-Mathematical

Purpose Students will calculate the average speed and velocity of a car's motion. L1 COOP LEARN LS **Interpersonal**

Materials tape, cart or toy car, stopwatch, meterstick

Teaching Strategy Try to use carts or cars that will travel approximately in a straight line when pushed gently.

Analysis

Average speed = distance/time. The speed would be the same if the car traveled in the opposite direction.

Process Have students use their observations to hypothesize why the car eventually comes to a rest. Use **Performance Assessment in the Science Classroom,** p. 93.

Text Question Answers

- Possible answer: cm/year
- Possible answers: the hands on an analog clock, the rotation of Earth about its axis

Describing the Motion of a Car

Procedure

1. Mark your starting point on the floor with **tape.**
2. At the starting line, give your **toy car** a gentle push forward. At the same time, start your **stopwatch.**
3. Stop timing when the car comes to a complete stop. Mark the spot at the front of the car with another **pencil.** Record the time for the entire trip.
4. Use a **meterstick** to measure the distance to the nearest tenth of a centimeter and convert it to meters.

Analysis

Calculate the speed. How would the speed differ if you repeated your experiment in exactly the same way but the car traveled in the opposite direction?

Rate Any change over time is called a rate. For example, your rate of growth is how much your height changes over a certain period of time, such as a year. If you think of distance as the change in position, then speed is the rate at which distance is traveled or the rate of change in position.

Calculating Speed Speed is related to the distance traveled and the time needed to travel the distance as follows:

$$\text{speed} = \frac{\text{distance}}{\text{time}}$$

If s = speed, d = distance, and t = time, this relationship can be written as follows:

$$s = \frac{d}{t}$$

Suppose you ran 2 km in 10 min. Your speed, or rate of change of position, would be found using the following equation:

$$s = \frac{d}{t} = \frac{2\text{ km}}{10\text{ min}} = 0.2\text{ km/min}$$

Because speed is calculated as distance divided by time, the units in which speed is measured always include a distance unit over a time unit. The SI unit for distance is the meter and the SI unit of time is the second (s), so in SI, units of speed are measured in meters per second (m/s). Speed also can be expressed in other units of distance and time, such as kilometers per hour (km/h) or centimeters per second (cm/s). **Table 1** shows some rates that show the range in which motion can occur. What units would you use to describe your rate of growth?

Motion with Constant Speed Suppose you are in a car traveling on a nearly empty freeway. You look at the speedometer and see that the car's speed hardly changes. If the car neither slows down nor speeds up, the car is traveling at a constant speed. Can you think of other examples of something moving at constant speed? If you are traveling at a constant speed, you can measure your speed over any distance interval from millimeters to light years.

Table 1 Examples of Units of Speed

Unit of Speed	Examples of Uses	Approximate Speed
km/s	rocket escaping Earth's atmosphere	11.2 km/s
km/h	car traveling at highway speed	100 km/h
cm/yr	geological plate movements	2 cm/yr–17 cm/yr

Science Journal

How Far Do They Move? Have students calculate how far each object in **Table 1** moves in one hour and put their calculations and their answers in their Science Journals. rocket: 40,320 km; car: 100 km; geological plate: 0.0002 cm–0.002 cm L2 LS **Logical-Mathematical**

Curriculum Connection

Geography Geographers use lines of latitude and longitude to help them describe displacement on Earth. Have students find out how early seafarers determined their latitude and longitude. To find their latitude they used the positions of the stars and the Sun. They had no way to determine longitude until an accurate chronometer was developed in the mid-1700s. L3 LS **Linguistic**

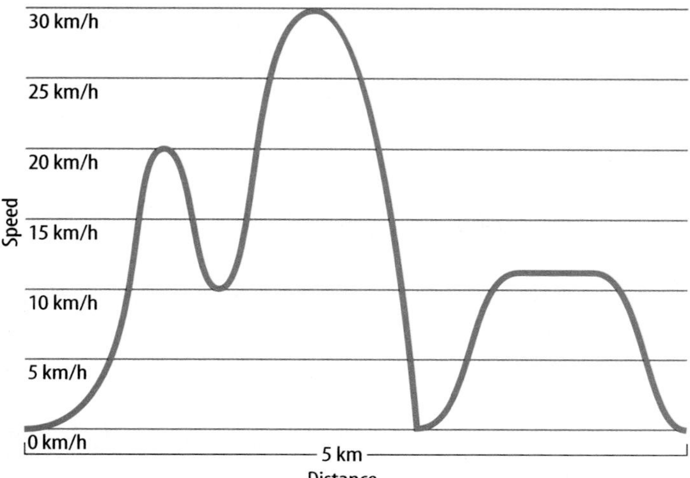

Figure 3
The cyclist is undergoing continuous speed changes.
How do you describe the speed of an object when the speed is changing continually?

Research Visit the Glencoe Science Web site at **science.glencoe.com** for interesting facts about running speeds. In your Science Journal describe how running fast benefits the survival of animals in the wild.

Changing Speed Much of the time, the speeds you experience are not constant. Think about riding a bicycle for a distance of 5 km as in **Figure 3.** As you start out, your speed increases from 0 km/h to, say, 20 km/h. You slow down to 10 km/h as you pedal up a steep hill and speed up to 30 km/h going down the other side of the hill. You stop for a red light, speed up again, and move at a constant speed for a while. As you near the end of the trip, you slow down and then stop. Checking your watch, you find that the trip took 15 min, or one-quarter of an hour. How would you express your speed on such a trip? Would you use your fastest speed, your slowest speed, or some speed between the two?

Average Speed Average speed describes speed of motion when speed is changing. **Average speed** is the total distance traveled divided by the total time of travel. It can be calculated using the relationship among speed, distance, and time. For the bicycle trip just described, the total distance traveled was 5 km and the total time was 1/4 h, or 0.25 h. The average speed was:

$$s = \frac{d}{t} = \frac{5\text{ km}}{0.25\text{ h}} = 20\text{ km/h}$$

Instantaneous Speed Suppose you watch a car's speedometer, like the one in **Figure 4,** go from 0 km/h to 60 km/h. A speedometer shows how fast a car is going at one point in time or at one instant. The speed shown on a speedometer is the instantaneous speed. **Instantaneous speed** is the speed at a given point in time.

Figure 4
The speed shown on the speedometer gives the instantaneous speed—the speed at one instant in time.

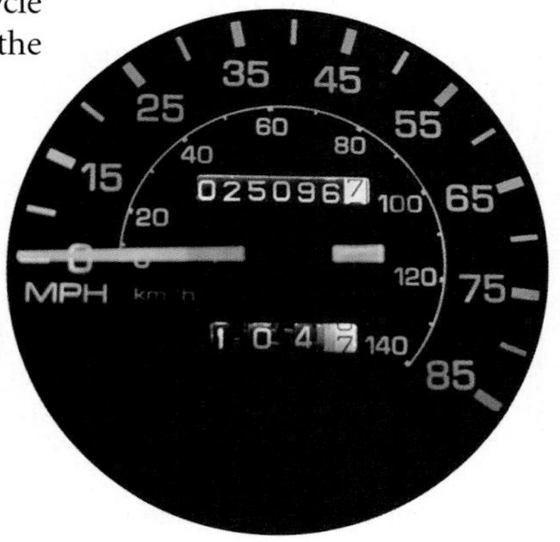

Caption Answer

Figure 3 either in great detail or by the average speed

Discussion

Remind students that when the equation for speed is rearranged, we have $t = d/v$. **How do time units emerge from this equation?** m ÷ (m/s) = m × (s/m) = s L2

LS **Logical-Mathematical**

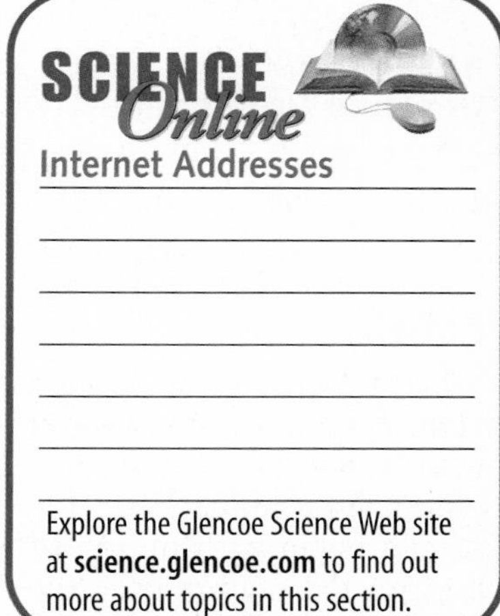

Activity

Make three ramps of various lengths, each at least 2 m long. Have a volunteer start a toy car rolling down one of the ramps while another volunteer times the car's motion. Ask a third volunteer to measure the distance covered by the car. Write the distance traveled and time elapsed on the board. Repeat the activity with each of the three ramps. Have students determine the average speed for the three runs by dividing the total distance traveled by the total time. L2 ELL LS **Kinesthetic**

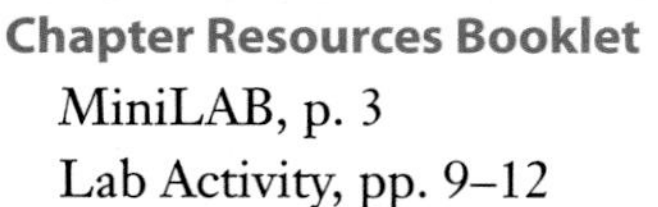

Chapter Resources Booklet
MiniLAB, p. 3
Lab Activity, pp. 9–12
Science Inquiry Labs, pp. 27, 41

Inclusion Strategies

Learning Disabled Perform the calculations for determining average speed on the board to help students understand the process before doing it themselves. After you have done the procedure several times, ask students to do the calculations on their own.

Speed, continued

Reading Check

Answer possible responses: driving a car in town, riding a bicycle

Math Skills Activity

National Math Standards

Correlation to Mathematics Objectives

1, 2, 4, 6, 9

Answers to Practice Problems

1. about 27.4 s
2. 0.25 hr or 15 min

Activity

Have each student make a table showing all of the speed limits between his or her home and school. The table should begin with the speed limit of the road outside the home and should also give the distance that speed limit is in effect. The table should then give the next speed limit and the distance it is in effect, and so on. Students can then use the formula $t = d/v$ to determine the time it would take them to get to school if they traveled the exact speed limit all the way to school. L2 ELL

LS **Logical-Mathematical** P

Extension

Have students use the information in the Math Skills Activity to calculate how far a lightning strike is from them if they see the lightning strike 5 seconds before they hear the thunder. $v = d \div t$, therefore $d = vt$; $d = 330 \text{ m/s} \times 5 \text{ s} = 1{,}650 \text{ m} = 1.65 \text{ km}$ L3

LS **Logical-Mathematical**

Changing Instantaneous Speed When something is speeding up or slowing down, its instantaneous speed is changing. The speed is different at every point in time. If an object is moving with constant speed, the instantaneous speed doesn't change. The speed is the same at every point in time.

Reading Check ***What are two examples of motion in which the instantaneous speed changes?***

Math Skills Activity

Calculating Time from Speed

Example Problem

Sound travels at a speed of 330 m/s. If a lightning bolt strikes the ground 1 km away from you, how long will it take for the sound to reach you?

Solution

1. *This is what you know:*
   distance: $d = 1$ km
   speed: $s = 330$ m/s
2. *This is the equation you need to use to find time,* t:
   $$s = \frac{d}{t}$$
3. *Because you know* d *and* s, *rewrite the equation as:*
   $$t = \frac{d}{s}$$
4. *Substitute the known values, and then solve the equation for* t:
   $$t = \frac{1 \text{ km}}{330 \text{ m/s}} = \frac{1{,}000 \text{ m}}{330 \text{ m/s}} = 3.03 \text{ s}$$

Practice Problems

1. A passenger elevator operates at an average speed of 8 m/s. If the 60th floor is 219 m above the first floor, how long does it take the elevator to go from the first floor to the 60th floor?
2. A motorcyclist travels an average speed of 20 km/h. If the cyclist is going to a friend's house 5 km away, how long does it take the cyclist to make the trip?

For more help, refer to the Math Skill Handbook.

Cultural Diversity

The Olympics Runners from all over the world participate in track and field events in the Olympics every four years. Have students research the winners and their times and speeds for a track event of their choice for the past five summer Olympics. They should combine their research into a bulletin board and creatively relate it to information in this chapter.

Resource Manager

Chapter Resources Booklet
Enrichment, p. 30

Mathematics Skill Activities, p. 11

Physical Science Critical Thinking/Problem Solving, p. 2

Graphing Motion

A distance-time graph makes it possible to display the motion of an object over a period of time. For example, the graph in **Figure 5** shows the motion of three swimmers during a 30-min workout. The straight red line represents the motion of a swimmer who swam 800 m during each 10-min period. Her speed was constant at 80 m/min.

The straight blue line represents the motion of a swimmer who swam with a constant speed of 60 m/min. Notice that the line representing the motion of the faster swimmer is steeper. The steepness of a line also is called the slope. On a distance-time graph, the slope of the line representing the motion of an object is the speed. Because the first swimmer has a greater speed, her line has a larger slope.

Changing Speed The green line represents the motion of a third swimmer, who did not swim at a constant speed. She covered 400 m during the first 10 min at a constant speed, rested for the next 10 min, and covered 800 m during the final 10 min. During the first 10 min, she swam a shorter distance than the other two swimmers, so her line has a smaller slope. During the middle period her speed is zero, so her line over this interval is horizontal and has zero slope. During the last time interval, she swam as fast as the first swimmer so her line has the same slope.

Reading Check *What was the average speed of each swimmer over the 30-min period?*

Plotting a Distance-Time Graph Plotting a distance-time graph is simple. The distance is plotted on the vertical axis and the time on the horizontal axis. Each axis must have a scale that covers the range of numbers you are working with. For instance, the total distance that the swimmers traveled was 2,400 m. The scale for distance must range from 0 to 2,400 m. The total time the swimmers worked out was 30 min. Therefore, the time scale must range from 0 to 30 min. Then each axis must be divided into equal intervals to represent the data correctly. Once the scales for each axis are in place, the data points can be plotted. After plotting the data points, draw a line connecting the points.

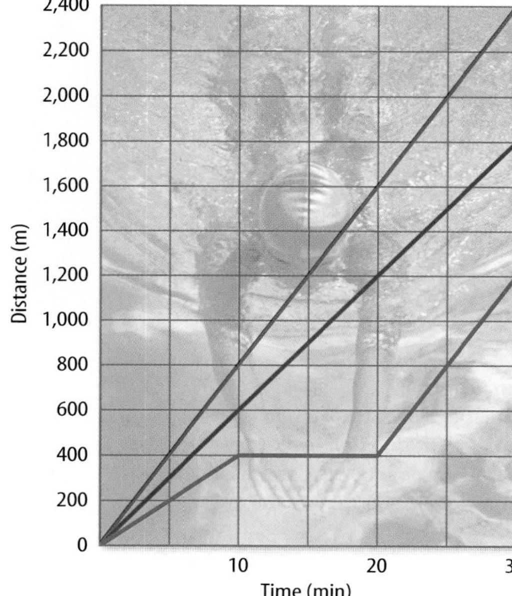

Figure 5
The slope of a distance-time graph gives the velocity of the object in motion.

SCIENCE Online

Research Visit the Glencoe Science Web site at **science.glencoe.com** for information about the speed of Olympic swimmers for the past 60 years. Communicate to your class what you learn.

Graphing Motion

IDENTIFYING Misconceptions

Students sometimes interpret the height of a distance-time graph as its slope. The steepness of the straight line of a distance-time graph is the slope. This shows the average speed. The height of the line is the farthest distance the object has traveled in the positive direction.

Visual Learning

Figure 5 In addition to finding the average speed over the entire 30-minute period, students can find the average speed over any time period by dividing the change in distance during the period by the amount of time. **What is the average speed of the third swimmer during the period 15 min to 25 min?** 40 m/min Students should also notice that the instantaneous speed at any point in time is the slope of the line at that point. **What is the instantaneous speed of the first swimmer at *t* = 5 min?** 80 m/min L2

LS **Visual-Spatial**

Reading Check

Answer red, 80 m/min; blue 60 m/min; green, 40 m/min

SCIENCE Online

Internet Addresses

Explore the Glencoe Science Web site at **science.glencoe.com** to find out more about topics in this section.

Teacher FYI

It is impossible to have a true vertical line on a distance-time graph. The vertical line would mean the object moved a distance in zero time. To do this, the object would have to go infinitely fast.

Velocity

Discussion

Describe the velocity of an object that travels north 6.9 m in 3 s, then turns and travels south 2.8 m in 4 s. velocity = 2.3 m/s north then 0.7 m/s south L2 LS **Logical-Mathematical**

Reading Check

Answer Velocity includes direction; speed does not.

Quick Demo

Swing a ball on a string around your head at a constant speed. Ask students whether the velocity of the ball is constant or changing. changing, because the direction varies L1 ELL LS **Visual-Spatial**

Extension

Have students explore relative velocity. For example, suppose you ride on a train that is going 80 km/h. If you walk toward the front of the train at a speed of 1.2 km/h, your velocity relative to the ground is 81.2 km/h in the direction that the train is moving. If, instead, you walk toward the back of the train at a speed of 1.2 km/h, your velocity relative to the ground is 78.8 km/h in the direction that the train is moving. Have students describe other situations that demonstrate the concept of relative velocity. L3 LS **Logical-Mathematical**

Teacher FYI

Distance is how far something moves, but displacement includes distance and direction. Velocity measures displacement, so average velocity is the total displacement divided by the time.

Figure 6
The speed of a storm is not enough information to plot the path. The direction the storm is moving must be known, too.

Velocity

You turn on the radio and hear the tail end of a news story about a tornado sighting in a storm. The storm, moving at a speed of 60 km/h, has just left a town 10 km north of your location, as shown in **Figure 6.** Should you be worried?

Unfortunately, you don't have enough information to figure out the answer. Knowing only the speed of the storm isn't much help. Speed describes only how fast something is moving. To decide whether you need to move to a safer area, you also need to know the direction that the storm is moving. In other words, you need to know the velocity of the storm. **Velocity** includes the speed of an object and the direction of its motion.

Escalators like the one shown in **Figure 7A** are found in shopping malls and airports. The two sets of passengers are moving at constant speed, but in opposite directions. The speeds of the passengers are the same, but their velocities are different because the passengers are moving in different directions.

Because velocity depends on direction as well as speed, the velocity of an object can change even if the speed of the object remains constant. For example, look at **Figure 7B.** A race car has a constant speed of 100 km/h and is going around an oval track. Even though the speed remains constant, the velocity changes because the direction of each car's motion is changing constantly.

Reading Check *How are velocity and speed different?*

Figure 7
For an object to have constant velocity, speed and direction must be the same.

A These two escalators have the same speed. However, their velocities are different because they are traveling in opposite directions.

B The speed of these cars might be constant, but the velocity is not constant because the direction of movement is always changing.

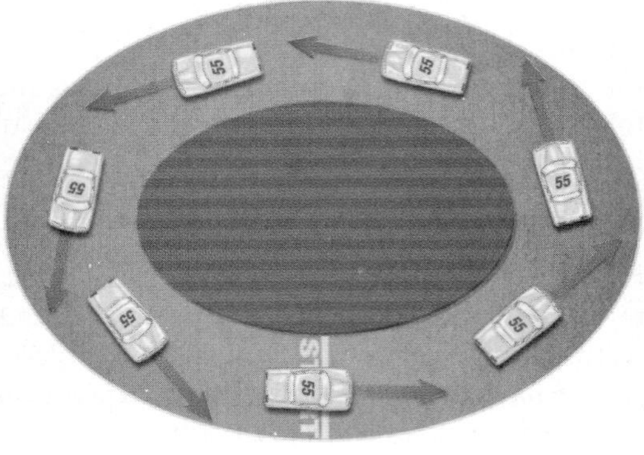

Science Journal

Changing Velocity Have students write brief paragraphs in their Science Journals describing several situations in which speed is constant but velocity is changing. a person walking up and down the aisles of a grocery store at a constant speed, a glider moving up and down in the air at constant speed L2 LS **Linguistic**

Active Reading

ReQuest Have students listen carefully as you read an interesting story or newsworthy item aloud. After the reading, students, alone or in groups, can formulate questions to discuss. Have students participate in a ReQuest related to Motion and/or Acceleration and the Forces attendant.

Motion of Earth's Crust

Can you think of something that is moving so slowly you cannot detect its motion, yet you can see evidence of its motion over long periods of time? As you look around the surface of Earth from year to year, the basic structure of the planet seems the same. Mountains, plains, lakes, and oceans seem to remain unchanged over hundreds of years. Yet if you examined geological evidence of what Earth's surface looked like over the past 250 million years, you would see that large changes have occurred. **Figure 8** shows how, according to the theory of plate tectonics, the locations of landmasses have moved during this time. Changes in the landscape occur constantly as continents drift slowly over Earth's surface. However, these changes are so gradual that you do not notice them.

Figure 8
Geological evidence suggests that continents have moved slowly over time.

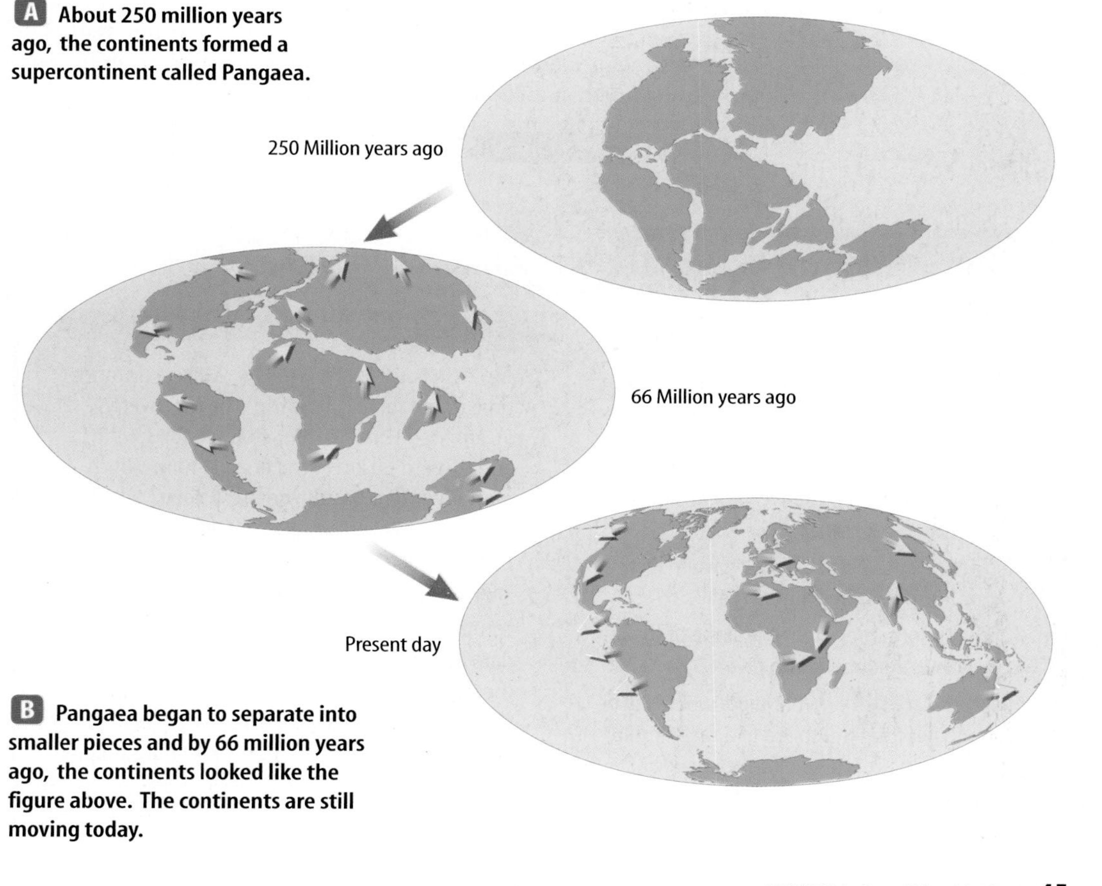

A About 250 million years ago, the continents formed a supercontinent called Pangaea.

B Pangaea began to separate into smaller pieces and by 66 million years ago, the continents looked like the figure above. The continents are still moving today.

Motion of Earth's Crust

Activity

When two of Earth's plates move past each other, scientists describe their speeds relative to each other. Use tape to mark two side-by-side tracks on the floor, each 3 m long. Have a student stand at each end of the tracks, and have other students with timers ready to record how long it takes balls to roll from one end of the track to the other end. When you say "go," the students at the ends of the tracks should roll the balls toward each other. The class can then determine the velocity (relative to the floor) of a ball going in one direction and the velocity of the ball going in the other direction. Explain that adding these numbers will give the speed of the balls relative to each other, similar to the speed of two of Earth's plates moving past each other. L2 ELL IS **Kinesthetic**

Earth Science INTEGRATION

In the early 1900s, Alfred Wegener, a German meteorologist, developed the theory that all Earth's continents were once part of a single landmass called *Pangaea*. Have students research and discuss evidence that supports this theory. Possible answers: similarities in fossils, glacial sediments, rock layers, structure of the ocean floor between continents L3 IS **Linguistic**

Resource Manager

Chapter Resources Booklet
- Reinforcement, p. 27
- Transparency Activity, pp. 47–48

Life Science Critical Thinking/Problem Solving, p. 14

Motions of the Earth's Crust

Reading Check

Answer The lithosphere is broken into plates that slide slowly on the more viscous, putty-like layers beneath them.

3 Assess

Reteach

Have students calculate the average speed of a windup or battery-operated toy car using metersticks and a wall clock. L2 LS **Logical-Mathematical**

Challenge

Suppose a bicyclist rides her bike along a straight road from one city to another and back again, and her speed is constant the entire trip. You've learned in this section that her distance-time graph would be a diagonal line. **What would her displacement-time graph look like and why?** An inverted V; the upward slope is the trip there, and the downward slope is the trip back. L3 LS **Visual-Spatial**

Assessment

Process Provide students with the following problem: Suppose a bus is traveling along the highway. It travels 100 km in the first 2 hours and 120 km in the second 2 hours. It stops for one hour, then it finishes the trip by going 100 km in two hours. Draw a distance-time graph of the bus's motion. Use **PASC,** p. 111.

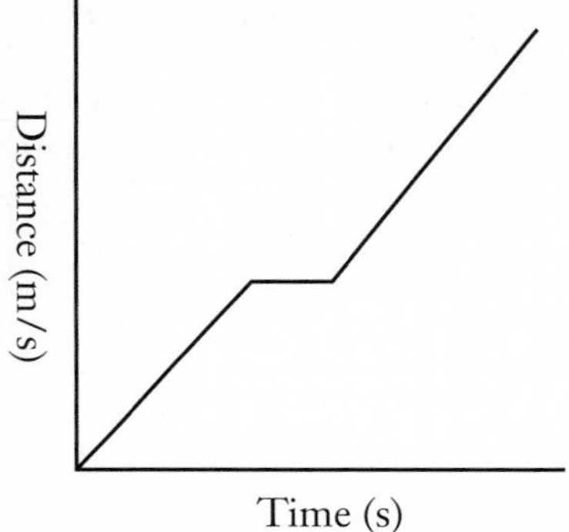

Figure 9
Earth's crust floats over a puttylike interior.

Moving Continents How can continents move around on the surface of Earth? Earth is made of layers, as shown in **Figure 9.** The outer layer is the crust, and the layer just below the crust is called the upper mantle. Together the crust and the top part of the upper mantle are called the lithosphere. The lithosphere is broken into huge sections called plates that slide slowly on the puttylike layers just below. If you compare Earth to an egg, these plates are about as thick as the eggshell. These moving plates cause geological changes such as the formation of mountain ranges, earthquakes, and volcanic eruptions.

Plates move so slowly that their speeds are given in units of centimeters per year. In California, two plates slide past each other along the San Andreas Fault with an average relative speed of about 2 cm per year. The Australian Plate's movement is one of the fastest, pushing Australia north at an average speed of about 17 cm per year.

Reading Check *How do the continents drift?*

Section  Assessment

1. How does displacement differ from distance? Give an example of displacement and distance.
2. You bike from your house to school, covering a distance of 3 km in 15 min. What is your average speed? Give your answer in kilometers per hour.
3. What do speed and velocity have in common? How do they differ?
4. What information does the slope of the line in a distance-time graph give?
5. **Think Critically** What units would you use to describe the speed of a car? Would you use different units for the speeds of runners in a school race? Explain.

Skill Builder Activities

6. **Making and Using Graphs** Make a distance-time graph for a 2-h car trip. The car covered 50 km in the first 30 min, stopped for 30 min, and covered 60 km in the final 60 min. Which graph segment has the greatest slope? What was the car's average speed? **For more help, refer to the** Science Skill Handbook.
7. **Using an Electronic Spreadsheet** Use a computer to construct a data table. Using the data in problem 6, list the distance and time measurements at 5-min intervals. Use a spreadsheet program to make a data table and, if possible, re-create the graphs. **For more help, refer to the** Technology Skill Handbook.

Answers to Section Assessment

1. Distance is how far an object is from something else. Displacement is the distance and direction between two objects. Possible example: The distance I travel from home to school is 5 km. When I get home my displacement is zero.
2. 12 km/hr
3. Both tell how fast something moves; velocity also tells direction.
4. velocity of the object in motion
5. Km/h; yes, m/s; the race would have short distances and short periods of time.
6. See graph. The graph segment of the first 30 minutes slopes the most. The average speed is 55 km/h.
7. Data in table should be consistent with data in problem 6.

SECTION 2

Acceleration

Acceleration, Speed, and Velocity

You're sitting in a car at a stoplight when the light turns green. The driver steps on the gas pedal and the car starts moving faster and faster. Just as speed is the rate of change of position, **acceleration** is the rate of change of velocity. When the velocity of an object changes, the object is accelerating.

Remember that velocity includes the speed and direction of an object. Therefore, a change in velocity can be either a change in how fast something is moving or a change in the direction it is moving. Acceleration occurs when an object changes its speed, its direction, or both.

Speeding Up and Slowing Down When you think of acceleration, you probably think of something speeding up. However, an object that is slowing down also is accelerating.

Imagine a car traveling through a city. If the speed is increasing, the car has positive acceleration. The car also is accelerating when it slows down. In this case the speed is decreasing and the car has negative acceleration. In both cases the car is accelerating because its speed is changing.

An acceleration has a direction, just as a velocity does. If the acceleration is in the same direction as the velocity, as in **Figure 10A,** the speed increases and the acceleration is positive. If the speed decreases, the acceleration is in the opposite direction from the velocity, and the acceleration is negative for the car shown in **Figure 10B.**

As You Read

***What* You'll Learn**

- **Identify** how acceleration, time, and velocity are related.
- **Explain** how positive and negative acceleration affect motion.
- **Describe** how to calculate the acceleration of an object.

Vocabulary
acceleration

***Why* It's Important**

Acceleration occurs all around you as objects speed up, slow down, or change direction.

Figure 10
These cars are accelerating because their speed is changing.

A **The speed of this car is increasing. The car has positive acceleration.**

B **The speed of this car is decreasing. The car has negative acceleration.**

Section Assessment Planner

PORTFOLIO
Challenge, p. 51

PERFORMANCE ASSESSMENT
Skill Builder Activities, p. 51
See page 64 for more options.

CONTENT ASSESSMENT
Section, p. 51
Challenge, p. 51
Chapter, pp. 64–65

SECTION 2

Acceleration

1 Motivate

Bellringer Transparency

Display the Section Focus Transparency for Section 2. Use the accompanying Transparency Activity Master. L2 ELL

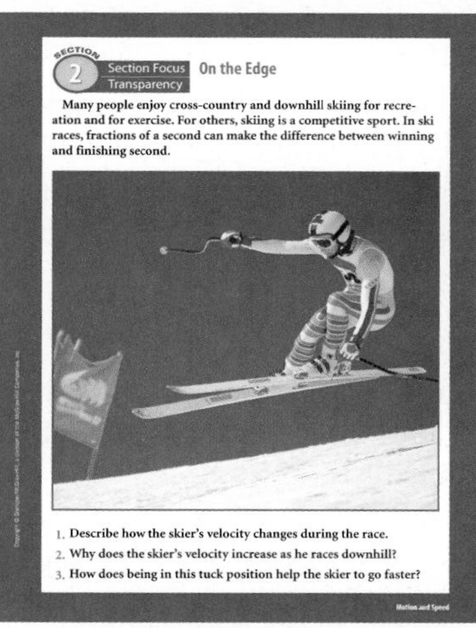

SECTION 2 Section Focus Transparency **On the Edge**

Many people enjoy cross-country and downhill skiing for recreation and for exercise. For others, skiing is a competitive sport. In ski races, fractions of a second can make the difference between winning and finishing second.

1. **Describe how the skier's velocity changes during the race.**
2. **Why does the skier's velocity increase as he races downhill?**
3. **How does being in this tuck position help the skier to go faster?**

Motion and Speed

Tie to Prior Knowledge

Have a student explain the phrase "stepping on the gas." Relate the function of the accelerator to the motion of a car.

Resource Manager

Chapter Resources Booklet
Transparency Activity, p. 45

2 Teach

Acceleration, Speed, and Velocity

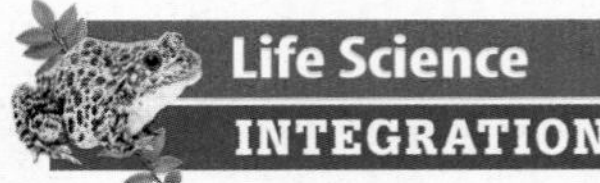

Life Science INTEGRATION

Our bodies are aware of acceleration because of structures in our ears called semicircular canals and the small sacs behind them. When a person moves, a liquid in the canals and sacs moves, bending tiny hairs and activating nerve cells, which send a message to the brain. Loss of orientation can occur if the body is spun around, such as on an amusement ride. Answers will vary. L2 ELL

LS **Kinesthetic**

Calculating Acceleration

Extension

Tell students that, as in the case of speed and velocity, acceleration can be constant or changing, and one can measure instantaneous acceleration as well as average acceleration. Have students give examples of constant acceleration, instantaneous acceleration, and average acceleration. constant acceleration: free fall; instantaneous acceleration: the acceleration of a falling rock after it has been falling for 3 s; average acceleration: final velocity of the falling rock when it hits the ground divided by the total time it was falling L3

LS **Logical-Mathematical**

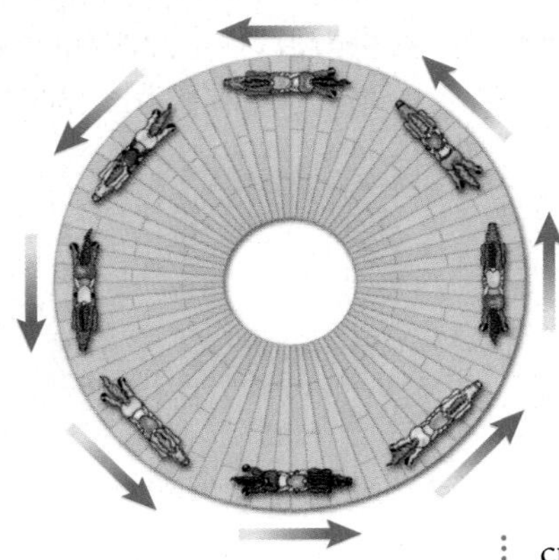

Figure 11
The speed of the horses in this carousel is constant, but the horses are accelerating because their direction is changing constantly.

Changing Direction A change in velocity can be either a change in how fast something is moving or a change in the direction of movement. Any time a moving object changes direction, its velocity changes and it is accelerating. Think about a horse on a carousel. Although the horse's speed remains constant, the horse is accelerating because it is changing direction constantly as it travels in a circular path, as shown in **Figure 11.** In the same way, Earth is accelerating constantly as it orbits the Sun in a nearly circular path.

Graphs of distance versus time can provide information about accelerated motion. The shape of the plotted curve shows when an object is speeding up or slowing down. **Figure 12** describes how motion graphs are constructed.

Calculating Acceleration

Remember that acceleration is the rate of change in velocity. To calculate the acceleration of an object, the change in velocity or speed is divided by the length of the time interval over which the change occurred. Another way to write this relationship is as follows:

$$\text{Acceleration} = \frac{\text{change in velocity}}{\text{time}}$$

How is the change in velocity calculated? Always subtract the initial velocity—the velocity at the beginning of the time interval—from the final velocity—the velocity at the end of the time interval. Let v_i stand for the initial velocity and v_f stand for the final velocity. The change in velocity is as follows:

$$\text{Change in velocity} = \text{final velocity} - \text{initial velocity} = v_f - v_i$$

Then the relationship between acceleration, velocity, and time is as follows:

$$a = \frac{(v_f - v_i)}{t}$$

If the motion is in a single direction or a straight line, velocity is equivalent to speed. Then the change in velocity is the final speed minus the initial speed.

In the equation above, the unit of acceleration is a unit of velocity divided by a unit of time. The SI unit for velocity is meters/second (m/s), and the SI unit for time is seconds (s). So, the unit for acceleration is meters/second/second. This unit is written as m/s^2 and is read "meters per second squared."

Life Science INTEGRATION

Your body is sensitive to acceleration. Much of the thrill of riding a roller coaster is due to the way your body feels while accelerating in different ways. Write a paragraph describing three situations in which you can feel accelerations while riding in a car.

Curriculum Connection

Physical Education Most sports rely on the ability of people to make quick changes in acceleration. Have students find out some of the equipment used in different sports to make acceleration easier. starting blocks for runners and swimmers; cleats on shoes for runners, soccer players, football players, and baseball players; rubber-soled shoes for basketball players; special clothing for reducing wind resistance for all racers

Teacher FYI

In the aerospace industry, the accelerations experienced by astronauts and pilots are often expressed as multiples of *g*. The acceleration, caused by gravity (*g*), acting on an object falling freely near Earth's surface is about 9.8 m/s^2. Headward (vertical) accelerations as low as 3 *g* can cause pilots to black out.

NATIONAL GEOGRAPHIC **VISUALIZING ACCELERATION**

Figure 12

Acceleration can be positive, negative, or zero depending on whether an object is speeding up, slowing down, or moving at a constant speed. If the speed of an object is plotted on a graph, with time along the horizontal axis, the slope of the line is related to the acceleration.

Ⓐ The car in the photograph on the right is maintaining a constant speed of about 90 km/h. Because the speed is constant, the car's acceleration is zero. A graph of the car's speed with time is a horizontal line.

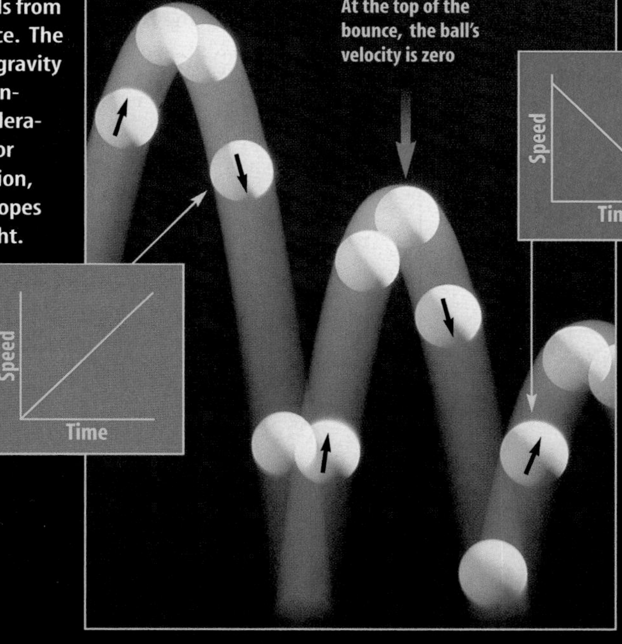

Ⓑ The green graph shows how the speed of a bouncing ball changes with time as it falls from the top of a bounce. The ball speeds up as gravity pulls the ball downward, so the acceleration is positive. For positive acceleration, the plotted line slopes upward to the right.

Ⓒ The blue graph shows the change with time in the speed of a ball after it hits the ground and bounces upward. The climbing ball slows as gravity pulls it downward, so the acceleration is negative. For negative acceleration, the plotted line slopes downward to the right.

Visualizing Acceleration

Have students examine the pictures and read the captions. Then ask the following questions.

In the graphs for A, B, and C, how are the slopes of the lines and the accelerations of the objects related? The slope of the line is positive if acceleration is positive, negative if acceleration is negative, and zero if there is no acceleration.

In the graph for B, what is the numerical value of the acceleration of the ball? The numerical value is the same as the acceleration due to gravity, 9.8 m/s^2.

What is the relation between the graphs for B and C? The acceleration of both balls is due to the pull of gravity. Graph B has a positive acceleration due to gravity or +9.8 m/s^2 and graph C has a negative acceleration due to gravity or −9.8 m/s^2.

Activity

Have students work in pairs to make up rap songs containing descriptions of the relationship between different types of acceleration and their corresponding graphs. L2 LS **Auditory-Musical**

Extension

Challenge students to find out what type of information can be obtained by finding the area under a speed-time graph. Explain why this could be a useful tool for scientists. The numerical value of the area under a speed-time graph is the distance traveled by the object. L3 LS **Logical-Mathematical**

Resource Manager

Chapter Resources Booklet

Enrichment, p. 31
Lab Activity, pp. 13–15
Directed Reading for Content Mastery, p. 21

Calculating Acceleration, continued

Visual Learning

Figure 13 Review with students the graphs in Figures 13A and B. Then ask a volunteer to draw on the board the velocity-time graph for a car that starts at 0 km/h, accelerates to 30 km/h over a period of 2 minutes, runs at 30 km/h for 10 minutes, then takes 30 seconds to stop.

Text Question Answer

zero acceleration

Amusement Park Acceleration

Answer steel

Resource Manager

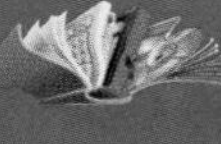

Chapter Resources Booklet
Reinforcement, p. 28

Performance Assessment in the Science Classroom, p. 37

Calculating Positive Acceleration How is the acceleration for an object that is speeding up different from that of an object that is slowing down? Suppose the jet airliner in **Figure 13A** starts at rest at the end of a runway and reaches a speed of 300 m/s in 20 s. The airliner is traveling in a straight line down the runway, so its speed and velocity are the same. Because it started from rest, its initial speed was zero. Its acceleration can be calculated as follows:

$$a = \frac{(v_f - v_i)}{t} = \frac{(300 \text{ m/s} - 0 \text{ m/s})}{20 \text{ s}} = 15 \text{ m/s}^2$$

The airliner is speeding up, so the final speed is greater than the initial speed and the acceleration is positive.

Calculating Negative Acceleration Now imagine that the skateboarder in **Figure 13B** is moving in a straight line at a speed of 20 m/s and comes to a stop in 2 s. The final speed is zero and the initial speed was 20 m/s. The skateboarder's acceleration is calculated as follows:

$$a = \frac{(v_f - v_i)}{t} = \frac{(0 \text{ m/s} - 20 \text{ m/s})}{2 \text{ s}} = -10 \text{ m/s}^2$$

The skateboarder is slowing down, so the final speed is less than the initial speed and the acceleration is negative. The acceleration always will be positive if an object is speeding up and negative if the object is slowing down. What is the acceleration if an object moves with constant velocity?

Figure 13
A velocity-time graph tells you if an object is speeding up or slowing down.

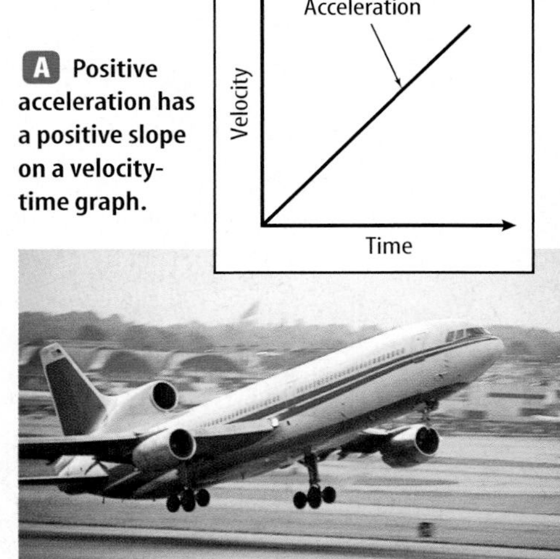

A Positive acceleration has a positive slope on a velocity-time graph.

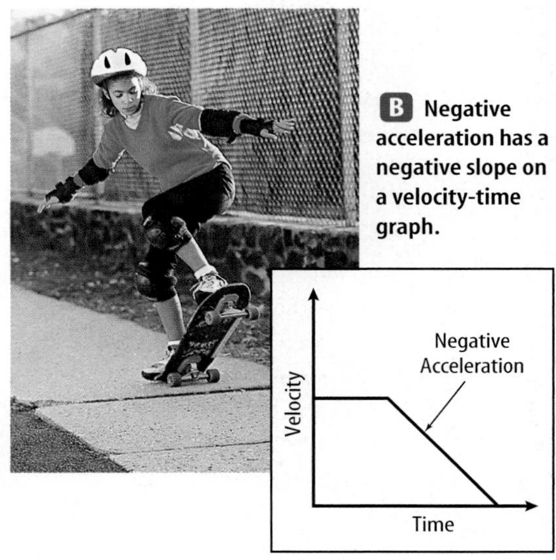

B Negative acceleration has a negative slope on a velocity-time graph.

LAB DEMONSTRATION

Purpose to demonstrate making a table and graph from distance-time measurements

Materials 8 socks, clock with second hand, meterstick

Preparation Mark a starting place where you have room to walk.

Procedure Start walking at the starting line. Have a student call out every 3 s. Begin walking slowly then steadily increase your speed. Drop a sock every 3 s. Measure the distance from t he starting line to each sock. On the board, make a table and a distance-time graph of the data.

Expected Outcome The distance between socks will increase for each 3-second interval.

Assessment

What is the slope of the line after 6 s? The slope will vary with the data. **What does this show?** the velocity

Amusement Park Acceleration

Riding roller coasters in amusement parks can give you the feeling that you are in danger—but these rides are safe. Engineers use the laws of physics to provide a thrilling but harmless ride. Roller coasters are constructed of wood or steel. Wooden roller coasters do not have the high velocities and accelerations that steel roller coasters do. Wood is not as rigid as steel. Therefore, these roller coasters do not have steep hills or inversion loops that propel the rider at high speeds. However, wooden roller coasters can have a swaying movement that steel roller coasters do not have. This swaying motion can give the rider a different type of thrill.

Steel roller coasters can offer multiple steep drops and inversion loops, which give the rider fast accelerations. As the rider moves down a steep hill or an inversion loop, he or she will accelerate toward the ground at 9.8 m/s^2 due to gravity. When riders go around a sharp turn, they also are accelerated. This acceleration makes them feel as if a force is pushing them toward the side of the car. The table in **Figure 14** shows the four fastest roller coasters in the United States. The fastest roller coaster goes from 0 to 160.9 km/h in 7 s.

 **Reading Check** ***What material are roller coasters with the steepest hills made from?***

Four of the Fastest Roller Coasters in the United States

Location	Top Speed (km/h)
Valencia, CA	160.9
Sandusky, OH	148
Valencia, CA	136.8
Primm, NV	128.7

Figure 14
This roller coaster is the fastest roller coaster in the world. Riders reach a speed of 160.9 km/h.

Section 2 Assessment

1. How are velocity, time, and acceleration related mathematically?
2. A swimmer speeds up from 1.1 m/s to 1.3 m/s during the last 20 s of a workout. What is the swimmer's acceleration during this time interval?
3. While walking to school, you approach an intersection and slow down from 2 m/s to a stop in 3 s. What was your acceleration during this time interval?
4. Explain the term *negative acceleration.*
5. **Think Critically** Describe three ways to change your velocity while riding a bicycle.

Skill Builder Activities

6. **Making and Using Graphs** In the graph shown in **Figure 13A,** is the velocity increasing or decreasing? Explain. Is the velocity increasing or decreasing in **Figure 13B?** Explain. Describe how the graph would look for a jet airplane cruising at a constant speed. **For more help, refer to the** Science Skill Handbook.
7. **Communicating** In your Science Journal, explain why streets and highways have speed limits rather than velocity limits. Where might a velocity limit be used? **For more help, refer to the** Science Skill Handbook.

Answers to Section Assessment

1. $a = \frac{(v_f - v_i)}{t}$
2. 0.01 m/s^2
3. about –0.67 m/s^2
4. An object undergoes negative acceleration when it slows down. At this time, its acceleration is in the opposite direction from its velocity.
5. speed up, slow down, change direction
6. Increasing; a positive acceleration indicates that the final velocity is greater than the initial velocity. Decreasing; a negative acceleration indicates that the initial velocity is greater than the final velocity. The graph would show a straight line , as there is no acceleration.
7. Going around curves changes velocity, so to have a velocity limit, you would have to specify the limit of speed for every curve. Speed is the important parameter, regardless of the direction in which you are moving.

3 Assess

Reteach

Have students demonstrate three ways to accelerate while walking. speeding up, slowing down, changing direction L1 LS **Kinesthetic**

Challenge

Have students work in groups to discuss acceleration experienced by a tennis ball as it is dropped and bounces. When the ball is falling the acceleration is positive and constant (9.8 m/s2) due to gravity. When the ball hits the floor, it experiences first negative acceleration as it stops, then positive acceleration as the kinetic energy of the ball pushes it up again. As it continues to moves up, it experiences negative acceleration as the force of gravity opposes its upward motion. This pattern repeats on each bounce, until the ball stops bouncing. Have students make a labeled poster illustrating the tennis ball's positive then negative acceleration cycle; a pattern that repeats itself with each bounce. L3

COOP LEARN LS **Interpersonal** P

Assessment

Process Think about how motion is affected by gravitational acceleration. Water on Earth falls from a waterfall with an acceleration of 9.8 m/s^2. The gravity of Mars is four-tenths that of Earth. **If water were on the surface of Mars, would water fall from a waterfall faster, more slowly, or at the same speed?** more slowly Use **PASC,** p. 89.

SECTION

Motion and Forces

1 Motivate

Bellringer Transparency

Display the Section Focus Transparency for Section 3. Use the accompanying Transparency Activity Master. L2 ELL

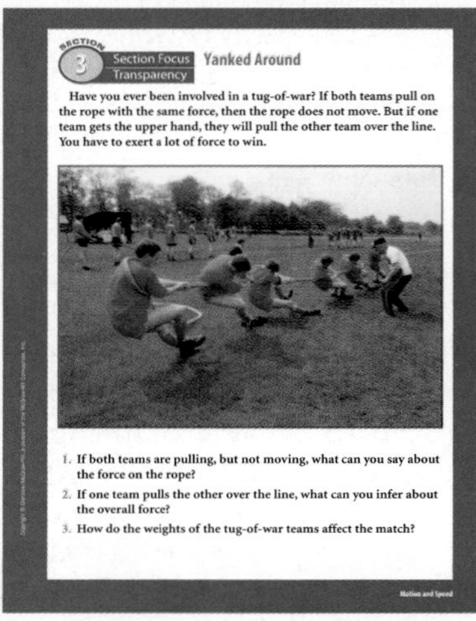

SECTION 3 Section Focus Transparency **Yanked Around**

Have you ever been involved in a tug-of-war? If both teams pull on the rope with the same force, then the rope does not move. But if one team gets the upper hand, they will pull the other team over the line. You have to exert a lot of force to win.

1. If both teams are pulling, but not moving, what can you say about the force on the rope?
2. If one team pulls the other over the line, what can you infer about the overall force?
3. How do the weights of the tug-of-war teams affect the match?

Motion and Speed

Tie to Prior Knowledge

Ask students to describe things they could do to change the velocity of a soccer ball. Point out that in each case, they are using a push or a pull to change the ball's motion. Tell students that pushes and pulls are forces, and this section discusses how forces change an object's motion.

SECTION

Motion and Forces

As You Read

***What* You'll Learn**

- **Explain** how force and velocity are related.
- **Describe** what inertia is and how it is related to Newton's first law of motion.
- **Identify** the forces and motion that are present during a car crash.

Vocabulary

force
net force
balanced force
inertia

***Why* It's Important**

Force and motion are directly linked—without force, you cannot have motion.

What is force?

Passing a basketball to a team member or kicking a soccer ball into the goal are examples of applying force to an object. A **force** is a push or pull that one body exerts on another. In both examples, the applied force results in the movement of the ball. Sometimes it is obvious that a force has been applied. But other forces aren't as noticeable. For instance, are you conscious of the force the floor exerts on your feet? Can you feel the force of the atmosphere pushing against your body or gravity pulling on your body?

Think about all the forces you exert in a day. Every push, pull, stretch, or bend results in a force being applied to an object.

Changing Motion What happens to the motion of an object when you exert a force on it? A force can cause the motion of an object to change. Think of hitting a ball with a racket, as in **Figure 15.** The racket strikes the ball with a force that causes the ball to stop and then move in the opposite direction. If you have played billiards, you know that you can force a ball at rest to roll into a pocket by striking it with another ball. The force of the moving ball causes the ball at rest to move in the direction of the force. In these cases, the velocities of the ball and the billiard ball were changed by a force.

Figure 15
This ball is hit with a force. The racket strikes the ball with a force in the opposite direction of its motion. As a result, the ball changes the direction it is moving.

Section Assessment Planner

Portfolio
Activity, p. 55

Performance Assessment
Try at Home MiniLAB, p. 54
Skill Builder Activities, p. 56
See page 64 for more options.

Content Assessment
Section, p. 56
Challenge, p. 56
Chapter, pp. 64–65

Figure 16
Forces can be balanced and unbalanced.

→ + ← = →
Net Force = →

B **These students are pushing on the box with unequal forces in opposite directions. The box will be moved in the direction of the larger force.**

→ + ← = 0
Net Force = 0

A **These students are pushing on the box with an equal force but in opposite directions. Because the forces are balanced, the box does not move.**

→ + → = →
Net Force = →

C **These students are pushing on the box in the same direction. The combined forces will cause the box to move.**

Balanced Forces Force does not always change velocity. In **Figure 16A,** two students are pushing on opposite sides of a box. Both students are pushing with an equal force but in opposite directions. When two or more forces act on an object at the same time, the forces combine to form the **net force.** The net force on the box in **Figure 16A** is zero because the two forces cancel each other. Forces on an object that are equal in size and opposite in direction are called **balanced forces.**

Unbalanced Forces Another example of how forces combine is shown in **Figure 16B.** When two students are pushing with unequal forces in opposite directions, a net force occurs in the direction of the larger force. In other words, the student who pushes with force will cause the box to move in the direction of the force. The net force that moves the box will be the difference between the two forces because they are in opposite directions or they are considered to be unbalanced forces.

In **Figure 16C,** the students are pushing on the box in the same direction. These forces are combined or added together because they are exerted on the box in the same direction. The net force that acts on this box is found by adding the two forces together.

✔ Reading Check *What is an unbalanced force?*

Research Visit the Glencoe Science Web site at **science.glencoe.com** for information about unbalanced forces along fault lines in the Earth's crust. In your Science Journal describe the significant activity that occurs along these fault lines.

2 Teach

What is force?

SCIENCE Online

Internet Addresses

Explore the Glencoe Science Web site at **science.glencoe.com** to find out more about topics in this section.

Quick Demo

Hold up a spring scale and hang objects of different masses from it. Have a student read the force required to hold up each object. Explain that the upward force exerted by the spring of the spring scale balances the downward gravitational force of the object. L2 IS **Visual-Spatial**

IDENTIFYING Misconceptions

Students often assume no motion means no force, but an object's lack of motion is because the forces acting on it are balanced. Students also may assume that an object in motion has an external force acting on it. Explain that motion may be caused by unbalanced forces, or it may be the result of inertia.

✔ Reading Check

Answer a force that is not balanced by another force

Resource Manager 

Chapter Resources Booklet

Transparency Activity, p. 46
Directed Reading for Content Mastery, pp. 21, 22
Enrichment, p. 32

Visual Learning

Figure 16 Tell students that the net force acting on an object is called the resultant force. In **Figure 16A,** the forces are equal and in opposite directions, so the resultant force is zero. In **Figure 16B,** you can calculate the resultant force by subtracting the smaller force from the larger one. **How would you calculate the resultant force in Figure 16C?** Add the two forces together. L2 IS **Visual-Spatial**

Inertia and Mass

Purpose Students will observe the effect of inertia. L2

LS Kinesthetic

Materials board, notebooks, block, small object, cart, rubber bands

Teaching Strategy

Analysis

1. Without rubber bands the forces are gravity and the force exerted by the cart on the object. When the cart hits the wall, the object continues moving until the stop block exerts a force on it. The rubber bands exert an additional force on the object. Because the rubber bands can stretch, the object slows down over a longer period of time, reducing the stopping force.
2. In a crash, seat belts reduce the stopping force and decrease damage to passengers.

Process Ask students to make diagrams of each run of the cart. Have them use labeled arrows to indicate the forces. Use **Performance Assessment in the Science Classroom,** p. 127.

Extension

Have students prepare a diagram showing the four forces acting on an ice skater skating forward. Explain why the skater is able to move forward for a relatively long period of time. Possible answer: The four forces are gravity pushing down, the ice pushing up, the skater's force pushing forward, and friction pulling the skater back. Since the ice provides relatively little friction, the skater's inertia keeps him or her moving forward for a relatively long time. L3

LS Logical-Mathematical

Observing Inertia in Action

Procedure

1. Create an inclined plane between 25° and 50° using a **board** and **textbooks.** Place a **stop block** (brick or other heavy object) at the end of the plane.
2. Place a **small object** in a **cart** and allow both to roll down the plane. Record the results in your journal.
3. Secure the object in the cart with **rubber bands** (seat belts). Allow both to roll down the plane again. Record the results.

Analysis

1. Explain the forces acting on the object in both runs.
2. Explain why it is important to wear seat belts in a car.

Inertia and Mass

The car in **Figure 17** is sliding on an icy road. This sliding car demonstrates the property of inertia. **Inertia** (ihn UR shuh) is the tendency of an object to resist any change in its motion. If an object is moving, it will keep moving at the same speed and in the same direction unless an unbalanced force acts on it. In other words, the velocity of the object remains constant unless a force changes it. If an object is at rest, it tends to remain at rest. Its velocity is zero unless a force makes it move.

Does a bowling ball have the same inertia as a table-tennis ball? Why is there a difference? You couldn't change the velocity of a bowling ball much by swatting it with a table-tennis paddle. However, you easily could change the velocity of the table-tennis ball. A greater force would be needed to change the velocity of the bowling ball because it has greater inertia. Why is this? Recall that mass is the amount of matter in an object, and a bowling ball has more mass than a table-tennis ball does. The inertia of an object is related to its mass. The greater the mass of an object is, the greater its inertia.

Newton's First Law of Motion Forces change the motion of an object in specific ways. The British scientist Sir Isaac Newton (1642–1727) was able to state rules that describe the effects of forces on the motion of objects. These rules are known as Newton's laws of motion. They apply to the motion of all objects you encounter every day such as cars and bicycles, as well as the motion of planets around the Sun.

Figure 17
On an icy road, it is hard to turn or stop a car because the car has no traction. Because of its inertia, the car tends to move in a straight line with constant speed.

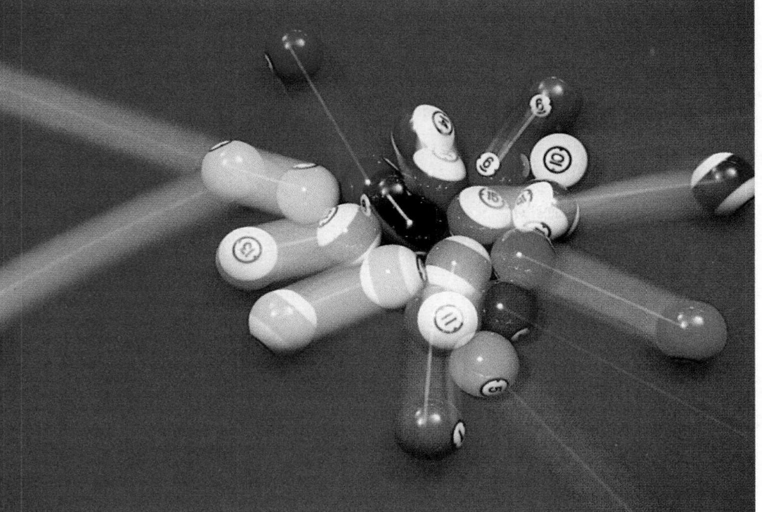

Figure 18
The cue ball is exerting a force on these billiard balls. The force of the cue ball has overcome the inertia of the stationary balls, resulting in motion.

The Law of Inertia According to Newton's first law of motion, an object moving at a constant velocity keeps moving at that velocity unless a net force acts on it. If an object is at rest, it stays at rest unless a net force acts on it. Does this sound familiar? It is the same as the earlier discussion of inertia. This law is sometimes called the law of inertia. You probably have seen and felt this law at work without even knowing it. **Figure 18** shows a billiard ball striking the other balls in the opening shot. What are the forces involved when the cue ball strikes the other balls? Are the forces balanced or unbalanced? How does this demonstrate the law of inertia?

Reading Check *What is Newton's first law?*

What happens in a crash?

The law of inertia can explain what happens in a car crash. When a car traveling about 50 km/h collides head-on with something solid, the car crumples, slows down, and stops within approximately 0.1 s. Any passenger not wearing a seat belt continues to move forward at the same speed the car was traveling. Within about 0.02 s (1/50 of a second) after the car stops, unbelted passengers slam into the dashboard, steering wheel, windshield, or the backs of the front seats, as in **Figure 19.** They are traveling at the car's original speed of 50 km/h—about the same speed they would reach falling from a three-story building.

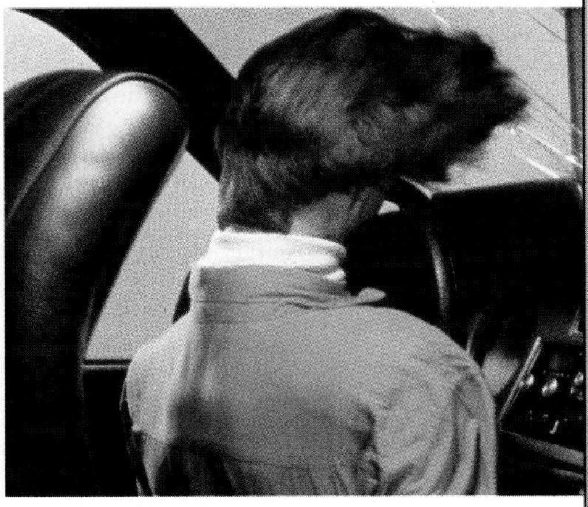

Figure 19
The crash dummy is not restrained in this low-speed crash. Consider the injuries that would occur to a real person traveling at highway speeds.

Fun Fact

Although the law of inertia is called Newton's first law, Galileo formulated it before Newton was born. In his writings, Newton credited Galileo for the idea.

Text Question Answer

Force of stick hitting cue ball, force of cue ball hitting other balls, force of balls hitting each other; no; balls are at rest, then move when a force acts on them.

Reading Check

Answer law of inertia

What happens in a crash?

Activity

Contact your local state patrol office to have an officer speak to the class about the advantages of wearing seat belts. Tell the officer ahead of time that you are studying the forces experienced by a person during a crash so that topic can be addressed. Afterward, have students write in their Science Journals about what they learned from the officer. L2
LS **Auditory-Musical** P

Discussion

How do air bags help prevent injuries during a car crash? Air bags increase the time over which a force acts to slow the motion of a body. The increased time decreases the force required to stop the body, thus reducing the chance for serious injury.
L3 LS **Logical-Mathematical**

Resource Manager

Chapter Resources Booklet
MiniLAB, p. 4
Reinforcement, p. 29
Home and Community Involvement, p. 41

Internet Addresses

Explore the Glencoe Science Web site at **science.glencoe.com** to find out more about topics in this section.

3 Assess

Reteach

Tie a string around a book and suspend it. Cut the string. Ask students to describe the forces acting on the book before and after you cut the string. Before the string was cut, the force of gravity was pulling down on the book. The string exerted an equal upward force on the book. Since these forces were equal and opposite in direction, the book was at rest. After the string was cut, there was no upward force on the book. The force of gravity was not opposed, so the book fell to the floor. L1 ELL

LS **Visual-Spatial**

Challenge

When astronauts are preparing for a space flight, part of their training involves riding in an airplane that is descending so quickly that the astronauts seem to float inside, similar to how they would in a weightless environment. Use what you have learned about forces to explain this effect. Normally in an airplane, the force of the plane pushing up opposes the force of gravity pulling down. During free fall, there is no force to oppose gravity, so people seem to float inside the airplane. L3

LS **Logical-Mathematical**

Oral Have students discuss the forces that enable a kite to stay in the air. Gravity pulls down on the kite. The upward force of the wind and the large surface area available for the wind to act upon results in an upward net force on the kite. This upward net force allows the kite to overcome gravity and fly. The tension (force) in the string prevents the kite from flying away. Use **Performance Assessment in the Science Classroom**, p. 89.

Figure 20
These crash dummies were restrained safely with seat belts in this low-speed crash. Usually humans would have fewer injuries if they were restrained safely during an accident.

Seat belts The crash dummy wearing a seat belt in **Figure 20** will be attached to the car and will slow down as the car slows down. The force needed to slow a person from 50 km/h to zero in 0.1 s is equal to 14 times the force that gravity exerts on the person. The belt loosens a little as it restrains the person, increasing the time it takes to slow the person down. This reduces the force exerted on the person. The seat belt also prevents the person from being thrown out of the car. Car-safety experts say that about half the people who die in car crashes would survive if they wore seat belts. Thousands of others would suffer fewer serious injuries.

Section 3 Assessment

1. When a soccer player kicks a ball, the ball accelerates. Explain what causes this acceleration in terms of forces.
2. Explain which has greater inertia—a speeding car or a jet airplane sitting on a runway.
3. Do forces always cause motion? Explain.
4. While trying to explain a physics concept, a student said, "Stuff keeps doing what it's doing unless something messes with it." What law was this student summarizing? Explain your answer.
5. **Think Critically** Describe three examples from sports in which a force changes the velocity of an object or a person.

Skill Builder Activities

6. **Researching Information** Many states have passed seat belt laws requiring all passengers in cars to wear seat belts. Research whether your state has such a law and when it became a law. Record your answer in your Science Journal. **For more help, refer to the Science Skill Handbook.**
7. **Communicating** Inertia plays an important role in most sports. In your Science Journal, write a paragraph describing the role of inertia in your favorite sport. Write another paragraph describing how the sport would be different without inertia. **For more help, refer to the Science Skill Handbook.**

Answers to Section Assessment

1. The force exerted by the soccer player's foot is greater than the force of the ball. Therefore, the resultant force is in the direction of the greater force, the kick.
2. The jet airplane; inertia is related to mass, not speed.
3. No, forces only cause motion if they are unbalanced.
4. Newton's first law; an object remains at rest or in motion unless an unbalanced force acts on it.
5. Possible answers: catching a football, sliding into base, and diving into water
6. Students' answers will reflect the seat belt laws in your state.
7. Possible answer: A soccer ball tends to keep moving after it is kicked, but friction slows it down.

Activity

Force and Acceleration

If you stand at a stoplight, you will see cars stopping for red lights and then taking off when the light turns green. What makes the cars slow down? What makes them speed up? The cars accelerate because an unbalanced force is acting on them.

What You'll Investigate

How does an unbalanced force on a book affect its motion?

Materials

tape	this science book
paper clip	triple beam balance
10-N spring scale	**electronic balance*
large book	**Alternate materials*

Goals

- **Observe** the effect of force on the acceleration of an object.
- **Interpret** the data collected for each trial.

Safety Precautions

Proper eye protection should be worn at all times while performing this lab.

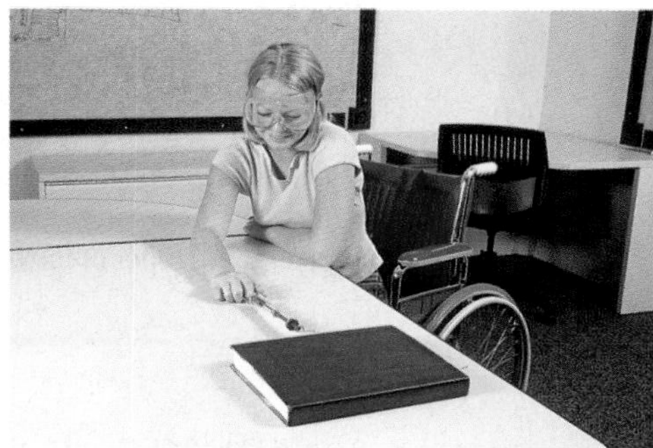

Procedure

1. With a piece of tape, attach the paper clip to your textbook so that the paper clip is just over the edge of the book.
2. Prepare a data table with the following headings: Force, Mass.
3. If available, use a large balance to find the mass of this science book.
4. Place the book on the floor or on the surface of a long table. Use the paper clip to hook the spring scale to the book.
5. Pull the book across the floor at a slow but constant velocity. While pulling, read the force you are pulling with on the spring scale and record it in your table.
6. Repeat step 5 two more times, once accelerating slowly and once accelerating quickly. Be careful not to pull too hard. Your spring scale will read only up to 10 N.
7. Place a second book on top of the first book and repeat steps 4 through 6.

Conclude and Apply

1. **Organize** the pulling forces from greatest to least for each set of trials. Do you see a relationship between force and acceleration? Explain your answer.
2. How did adding the second book change the results? Explain your answer.

Communicating Your Data

Compare your conclusions with those of other students in your class. **For more help, refer to the Science Skill Handbook.**

Activity

BENCH TESTED

Purpose Students will observe the relationship between mass, force, and acceleration.

Process Skills observing, comparing, inferring

Time Required 40 minutes

Materials tape (approximately 3 inches per group), paper clip, 10-N spring scale, large book, science textbook, triple beam or electronic balance

Safety Precautions Students should wear safety goggles while this activity is in progress.

Teaching Strategies Remind students that the spring scale only reads up to 10-N, so they must not pull too hard.

Answers to Questions

1. As force increased, so did the acceleration.
2. When the second book was added, the force should have increased. If the second book has approximately the same mass as the first book, the force should have doubled.

Resource Manager

Chapter Resources Booklet
Activity Worksheet, pp. 5–6

Earth Science Critical Thinking/Problem Solving, p. 9

Cultural Diversity, p. 63

Assessment

Process Ask students to infer how the pulling force would be different if a book with less mass were pulled. Less force would be required. **How would it be different if three of the science books were pulled?** More force would be required. Use **Performance Assessment in the Science Classroom,** p. 89.

Communicating Your Data

Have students discuss with one another any differences in their results and possible reasons for the differences.

Activity BENCH TESTED

Recognize the Problem

Purpose

Demonstrate how the motion of a toy car is affected by different forces. L2 LS **Kinesthetic**

Process Skills

forming a hypothesis, designing an experiment, separating and controlling variables, interpreting data, measuring, using numbers, observing, inferring, comparing and contrasting, recognizing cause and effect, communicating, making and using tables, making and using graphs

Time Required

30 minutes to plan the experiment and 45 minutes to make measurements and graph data

Materials

Use thin springs with loose windings so that they can be easily retracted and released to push the car forward. The string can be used to sharply tug the car.

Alternate Materials

Small springs used in molecular model sets can be used to propel the cars by flipping one end of the spring against the car while holding the other end securely. Rubber bands can be used, but they will provide less momentum.

Activity Design Your Own Experiment

Comparing Motion from Different Forces

Think about a small ball. How many ways could you exert a force on the ball to make it move? You could throw it, kick it, roll it down a ramp, blow it with a large fan, etc. Do you think the distance and speed of the ball's motion will be the same for all of these forces? Do you think the acceleration of the ball would be the same for all of these types of forces?

Recognize the Problem

How will the motion of a small toy car vary when different forces are applied to it?

Form a Hypothesis

Based on your reading and observations, state a hypothesis about which force that is exerted will cause the toy car to go fastest.

Possible Materials

small toy car
ramps or boards of different lengths
springs
string
stopwatch
meterstick or tape measure
graph paper

Safety Precautions 

Goals

- **Identify** several forces that you can use to propel a small toy car across the floor.
- **Demonstrate** the motion of the toy car using each of the forces.
- **Graph** the position versus time for each force.
- **Compare** the motion of the toy car resulting from each force.

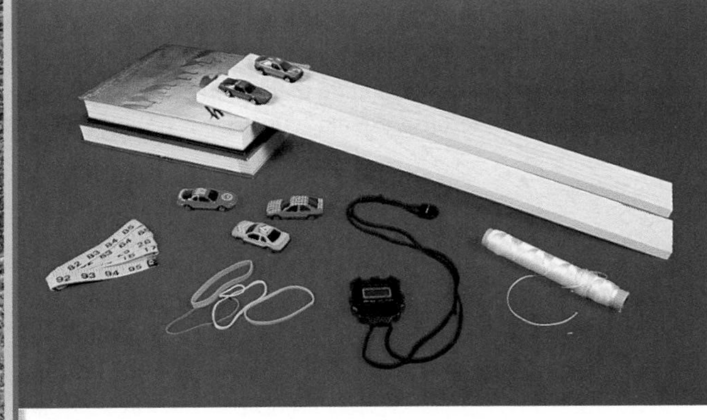

Data Table:

Force Used	Distance	Time	Speed
Force 1			
Force 2			
Force 3			
Force 4			

Resource Manager 

Chapter Resources Booklet
Activity Worksheet, pp. 7–8

Physical Science Critical Thinking/Problem Solving, p. 3

Earth Science Critical Thinking/Problem Solving, p. 10

Test Your Hypothesis

Plan

1. As a group, agree upon the hypothesis and decide how you will test it. Identify what results will confirm the hypothesis that you have written.
2. **List** the steps you will need to test your hypothesis. Be sure to include a control run. Be specific. Describe exactly what you will do in each step. List your materials.
3. Prepare a data table in your Science Journal to record your observations.
4. **Read** over the entire experiment to make sure all steps are in logical order and will lead to a conclusion.
5. **Identify** all constants, variables, and controls of the experiment. Keep in mind that you will need to have measurements at multiple points. These points are needed to graph your results. You should make sure to have several data points taken after you stop applying the force and before the car starts to slow down. It might be useful to have several students taking measurements, making each responsible for one or two points.

Do

1. Make sure your teacher approves your plan before you start.
2. Carry out the experiment as planned.
3. While doing the experiment, record your observations and complete the data tables in your Science Journal.

Analyze Your Data

1. **Graph** the position of the car versus time for each of the forces you applied. How can you use the graphs to compare the speeds of the toy car?
2. **Calculate** the speed of the toy car over the same time interval for each of the forces that you applied. How do the speeds compare?

Draw Conclusions

1. Did the speed of the toy car vary depending upon the force applied to it?
2. For any particular force, did the speed of the toy car change over time? If so, how did the speed change? Describe how you can use your graphs to answer these questions.
3. Did your results support your hypothesis? Why or why not?

Compare your data to those of other students. **Discuss** how the forces you applied might be different from those others applied and how that affected your results.

Form a Hypothesis

Possible Hypothesis

Students might hypothesize that the force of the spring will cause the car to go fastest.

Test Your Hypothesis

Possible Procedures

Position students with stopwatches at points along a track to determine when the car reaches there. One student will provide the initial force to the car by releasing a spring against it, tugging it with a string, etc.

Teaching Strategies

Encourage students to provide a sufficient force to enable the car to travel the entire length of the track they have made.

Expected Outcome

Although results will vary greatly, students should be able to determine the average speed of the car for each force.

Analyze Your Data

1. Some graphs will show a slight increase in speed. Others will show a decrease in speed.
2. Students should calculate the average speed using $v = d \times t$.

Error Analysis

Ask students to compare their results with other groups and discuss ways the differences could be minimized.

Draw Conclusions

1. yes
2. Answers will vary.
3. Answers will depend on student hypotheses.

Assessment

Process Ask students to draw diagrams showing how friction, gravity, and inertia influenced the motion of the car. Use **Performance Assessment in the Science Classroom,** p. 127.

Have students use graphics software to prepare a poster explaining their experiment and the results. Posters should contain sketches showing forces on the car. They might also include graphs of the data.

Science and Language Arts

Pre-Reading Activity

Students should work in groups to research the natural and human-made wonders of the world. Each group should present an oral report to the class, using visual aids.

Respond to the Reading

Active Reading Strategies

Visual Ask students to imagine the wonders of the world and form pictures in their minds. Have them pay attention to the details the writer gives about her impressions of the world.

Connect Point out to students that the selection may remind them of thoughts or feelings they have had that made them feel special. Ask them to think about an accomplishment or event that made them feel like "the true wonder of the world." Discuss whether or not the accomplishments of individuals are more or less wondrous than the accomplishments of the universe or of nature.

Respond to the Reading

1. small, lonely, minuscule, kithless, wayward, floating
2. Pyramids, Gardens of Babylon, Grand Canyon
3. people

Science and Language Arts

A Brave and Startling Truth

by Maya Angelou

We, this people, on a small and lonely planet
Traveling through casual space
Past aloof stars, across the way of indifferent suns
To a destination where all signs tell us
It is possible and imperative that we learn
A brave and startling truth...

When we come to it.
Then we will confess that not the Pyramids
With their stones set in mysterious perfection
Nor the Gardens of Babylon
Hanging as eternal beauty
In our collective memory
Not the Grand Canyon
Kindled into delicious color
By Western sunsets
These are not the only wonders of the world...

When we come to it
We, this people, on this minuscule and kithless[1] globe...
We this people on this mote[2] of matter

When we come to it
We, this people, on this wayward[3], floating body
Created on this earth, of this earth
Have the power to fashion for this earth
A climate where every man and every woman
Can live freely without sanctimonious piety[4]
Without crippling fear

When we come to it
We must confess that we are the possible
We are the miraculous, the true wonder of the world
That is when, and only when
We come to it.

[1] to be without friends or neighbors
[2] small particle
[3] wanting one's own way in spite of the advice or wishes of another
[4] a self-important show of being religious

Respond to the Reading

1. What adjectives does the poet use to describe Earth?
2. What wonders of the world does the poet name?
3. What does the poet believe are the true wonders of the world?

Reading Further

Other works by this author include:

On the Pulse of Morning from *The Complete Collected Poems of Maya Angelou,* Maya Angelou, Random House, Inc., 1994.

Other sources on this topic include:

Space Travel, edited by Ben Bova with Anthony R. Lewis, Writer's Digest Books, 1997.

Roller Coaster, by David Bennett, Chartwell Books, 1998.

Timelines of the Ancient World, editor-in-chief Chris Scarre, Dorling Kindersley, 1993

Understanding Literature

Descriptive Writing This poem is full of images of Earth moving through space. But the adjectives the author uses to describe Earth are from the perspective of the universe. This description from the point of view of the universe gives the impression that Earth is small and insignificant.

The poet also names some special places on Earth. These places, although marvelous, fall short of being really wonderful. Angelou contrasts Earth's position within the universe to emphasize the importance of people. The power that people have to make changes for better lives is more significant than the universe and the special places people have built on Earth.

Science Connection Sometimes a person doesn't need to see movement to know that something has moved. Even though we don't necessarily see Earth's movement, we know Earth moves because of reference points such as the Sun. We know Earth moves because the Sun appears to change its position in the sky. The poem describes Earth's movement from the point of view of the universe. The universe serves as a reference point for detecting Earth's movement.

Linking Science and Writing

Write a Poem In the poem you just read, Maya Angelou describes Earth's movement from the point of view of the universe. Write a six-line poem that describes Earth's movement from the point of view of the Moon. How might the Moon's point of view toward Earth be different from that of remote stars and suns?

Career Connection

Roller Coaster Designer and Engineer

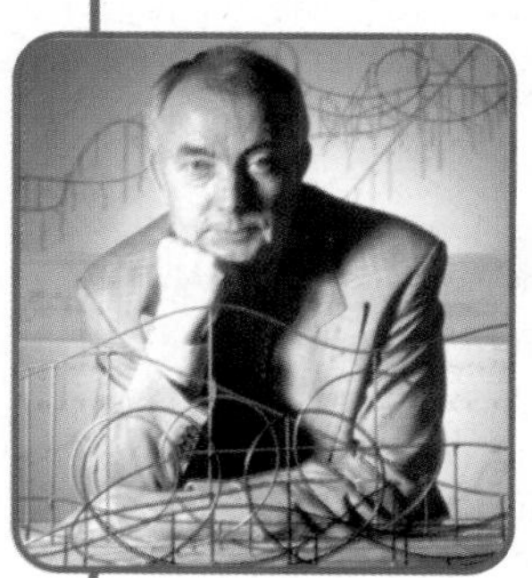

Ancient engineers designed the pyramids. Today, engineers design everything from can openers to cars. Werner Stengle and his team has designed and engineered more than 200 roller coasters. They compute the forces that react on roller coaster passengers. They also analyze the kind and amount of stress the roller-coaster structure will have to bear. Stengel has worked with safety committees and research groups to make sure that amusement park rides are safe for their riders.

SCIENCE *Online* To learn more about careers in engineering, visit the Glencoe Science Web site at **science.glencoe.com.**

Understanding Literature

Science Connection

Up until the Middle Ages, people thought Earth stood still and that the sky moved around Earth. It is now known that the daily movement of the stars is due to Earth's rotation on its axis. This can be proven by focusing a camera on the North Star and leaving the shutter open for several hours. At the same time that Earth rotates, it revolves about the Sun. Earth follows the Sun in its wanderings through the heavens. The Sun revolves around the center of the Milky Way. Earth, a satellite of the Sun, takes part in this journey.

Linking Science and Writing

Writing Strategies

Remind students that the Moon revolves around Earth. Therefore, their poems should describe how the Moon might see the Sun come and go as it moves around Earth. Students need to decide whether the narrator of the poem understands its own relationship to the Sun or not. Suggest that some students write poems as if the Moon does not understand that it orbits Earth while the Earth orbits the Sun. Other students should write poems as if the Moon *does* understand its position in relationship to Earth and the Sun.

Career Connection

To be a roller coaster designer and engineer requires a diverse background. Not only should students obtain a bachelor's degree focused on mathematics and the sciences, but they also need a sense of creativity, a grasp of psychology, and entrepreneurial skills. The ability to work as part of a team is also important. Engineers must take a state examination and be licensed to practice.

Internet Addresses

Explore the Glencoe Science Web site at **science.glencoe.com** to find out more about topics in this feature.

Chapter 2 Study Guide

Reviewing Main Ideas

Preview

Students can answer the questions in their Science Journals. Discuss the answers as you go through the chapter. LS **Linguistic**

Review

Students can write their answers, then compare them with those of other students. LS **Interpersonal**

Reteach

Students can look at the illustrations and describe details that support the main ideas of the chapter. LS **Visual-Spatial**

Answers to Chapter Review

Section 1

1. The shot moves in a straight line straight ahead of the shot putter. Initially it rises, then it falls until it hits the ground.

Section 2

2. negative acceleration as it is stopping; positive acceleration as it begins to move forward

Section 3

4. Gravity is pulling it to Earth and friction is slowing it down.

Chapter 2 Study Guide

Reviewing Main Ideas

Section 1 Describing Motion

1. Motion is a change of position of a body. Distance is the measure of how far an object moved. Displacement is the distance and direction of an object's change in position from the starting point. *In the figure above, how can the motion of this shot put be described correctly?*
2. Average speed is the total distance traveled divided by the total time of travel.
3. Instantaneous speed is the speed at a given instant of time.
4. Velocity describes the speed and direction of a moving object.

Section 2 Acceleration

1. Acceleration is the rate of change of velocity for any object.
2. Any time the velocity of an object changes, the object must be accelerated. *In the figure below, describe the type of acceleration that occurs when the car stops for the red light and when it moves again for a green light.*

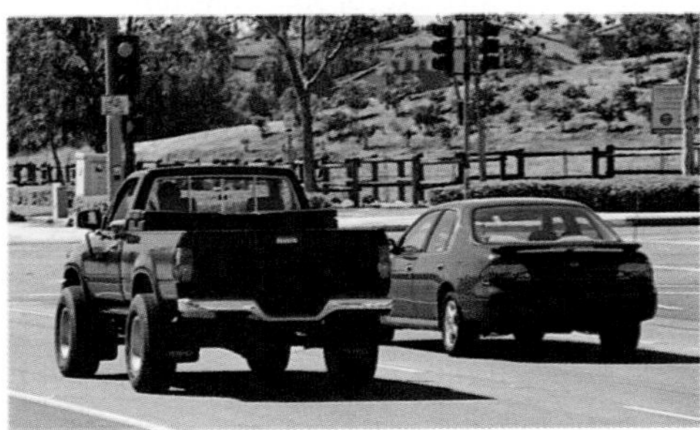

3. Acceleration occurs if an object speeds up, slows down, or changes direction.

Section 3 Motion and Forces

1. A force is a push or a pull one body exerts on another.
2. Balanced forces acting on a body do not change the motion of the body. Unbalanced forces result in a net force, which always changes the motion of a body.
3. Inertia is the resistance of an object to a change in its motion.
4. Newton's first law says an object's motion will not change unless a net force acts on it. *In the figure below, describe the forces that are acting on the car.*

FOLDABLES Reading & Study Skills — After You Read

To help you review the characteristics of motion, use the Foldable you made at the beginning of this chapter. Use the Foldable to review for quizzes, chapter tests, and semester exams.

FOLDABLES Reading & Study Skills — After You Read

After students have read the chapter and completed the Foldable described in Before You Read, have them do the activity on the student page.

Dinah Zike

Visualizing Main Ideas

Complete the following concept map about motion.

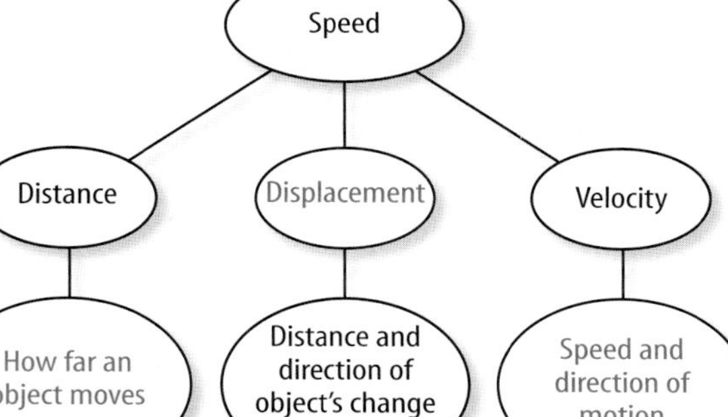

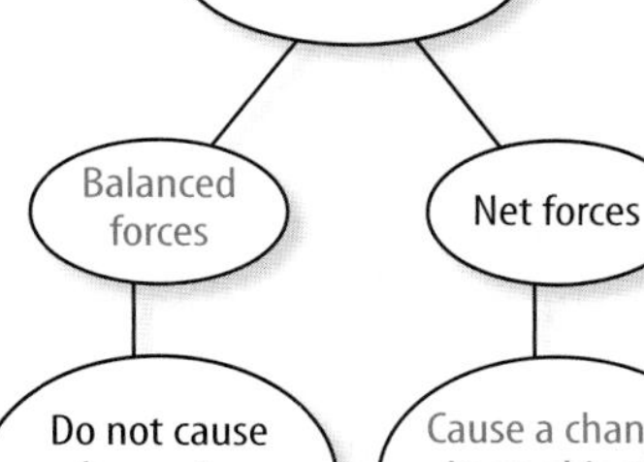

Vocabulary Review

Vocabulary Words

- **a.** acceleration
- **b.** average speed
- **c.** balanced force
- **d.** displacement
- **e.** distance
- **f.** force
- **g.** inertia
- **h.** instantaneous speed
- **i.** net force
- **j.** speed
- **k.** velocity

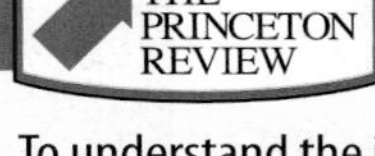

Study Tip

To understand the information on a graph, write a sentence that talks about the relationship between the *x*-axis and *y*-axis in the graph.

Using Vocabulary

Compare and contrast the following pairs of vocabulary words.

1. speed, velocity
2. distance, displacement
3. average speed, instantaneous speed
4. balanced force, net force
5. force, inertia
6. acceleration, velocity
7. velocity, instantaneous speed
8. force, net force
9. force, acceleration

IDENTIFYING Misconceptions

Assessment

After students have done the activity on page 36F and completed the chapter, have them perform this activity.

Materials protractor, paper, ruler, string

Procedure Have each student use the protractor to draw a large circle and label four points 9 degrees apart A, B, C and D. Have them place an object at point A, and tell them the object will travel around the circle. Their mission is to find the object's distance traveled and displacement at points B, C, and D. Tell them the top of the paper is North.

Expected Outcome Ways to find the distance traveled include using the string to measure the circle or using the formula for a perimeter of a circle.

Chapter 2 Study Guide

Visualizing Main Ideas

See student page.

Vocabulary Review

Using Vocabulary

1. Both tell how distance changes with time. Velocity includes the direction.
2. Displacement is distance and direction from a starting point. Distance is how far an object is from something.
3. Both describe rate of change in position. Average speed refers to total distance moved divided by total time elapsed. Instantaneous speed refers to speed at a given point in time.
4. Balanced forces are forces on an object that cancel each other out. Net force is the sum of all forces acting on an object.
5. Force is a push or a pull that one body exerts on another. Inertia is the tendency of an object to resist change in motion.
6. Velocity is the speed and direction of an object. Acceleration is how the velocity changes with time.
7. Velocity is the speed and direction of an object. Instantaneous speed is how fast an object moves at a given point in time.
8. Force is a push or a pull. Net force is the sum of all forces acting on an object.
9. Force is a push or a pull. Acceleration is the change in velocity of an object when an unbalanced force acts on it.

Chapter 2 Assessment

Checking Concepts

1. A
2. D
3. C
4. B
5. A
6. B
7. C
8. A
9. B
10. B

Thinking Critically

11. Time = 800 km/16 km/h = 50 h; at 8 h/day, total time is 6 days 2 hours.
12. about -83.3 m/s^2
13. 22.5 km/h; displacement is 0
14. time there is 1.75 hours; time back is 2.25 hours; velocity there is 25.7 km/h; velocity back is -20 km/h.

Chapter 2 Assessment

Checking Concepts

Choose the word or phrase that best answers the question.

1. What is the easiest way to calculate the rate of motion of an object that changes speed several times during the time of interest?
   A) average speed
   B) constant speed
   C) variable speed
   D) instantaneous speed
2. What is the tendency for an object to resist any change in its motion called?
   A) net force **C)** balanced force
   B) acceleration **D)** inertia
3. Which of the following is a proper unit of acceleration?
   A) s/km^2 **C)** m/s^2
   B) km/h **D)** cm/s
4. Which of the following is not used in calculating acceleration?
   A) initial velocity **C)** time interval
   B) average speed **D)** final velocity
5. In which of the following conditions does the car not accelerate?
   A) A car moves at 80 km/h on a flat, straight highway.
   B) The car slows from 80 km/h to 35 km/h.
   C) The car turns a corner.
   D) The car speeds up from 35 km/h to 80 km/h.
6. Which term below best describes the forces on an object with a net force of zero?
   A) inertia **C)** acceleration
   B) balanced forces **D)** unbalanced forces
7. How can speed be defined?
   A) acceleration/time
   B) change in velocity/time
   C) distance/time
   D) displacement/time
8. Which of the following objects has the greatest inertia?
   A) a car parked on the side of the road
   B) a baseball during a pop fly
   C) a computer sitting on a desk
   D) a woman running on a track
9. A man drives 3 km east from home to the store and then 2 km west to a friend's house. What is his displacement from his starting point at home?
   A) 1 km west **C)** 5 km west
   B) 1 km east **D)** 5 km east
10. Which answer best describes why a passenger who is not wearing a seat belt will likely hit the windshield in a head-on collision?
    A) forces acting on the windshield
    B) inertia of the unbelted person
    C) acceleration of the car
    D) gravity taking over

Thinking Critically

11. A cyclist must travel 800 km. How many days will the trip take if the cyclist travels 8 h/day at an average speed of 16 km/h?
12. A satellite's original velocity is 10,000 m/s. After 1 min, it is 5,000 m/s. What is the satellite's acceleration?
13. A cyclist leaves home and rides due east for a distance of 45 km. She returns home on the same bike path. If the entire trip takes 4 h, what is her average speed? What is her displacement?

14. The return trip of the cyclist in question 13 took 30 min longer than her trip east, although her total time was still 4 h. What was her velocity in each direction?

Chapter Assessment Planner

Portfolio Encourage students to place in their portfolios one or two items of what they consider to be their best work. Examples include:
- Activity, p. 42
- Challenge, p. 51
- Activity, p. 55

Performance Additional performance assessments, Performance Task Assessment Lists, and rubrics for evaluating these activities can be found in Glencoe's **Performance Assessment in the Science Classroom.**

Developing Skills

15. **Measuring in SI** Which of the following represents the greatest speed: 20 m/s, 200 cm/s, or 0.2 km/s? Here's a hint: *Express all three in m/s and then compare.*

16. **Recognizing Cause and Effect** Acceleration can occur when a car is moving at constant speed. What must cause this acceleration?

17. **Making and Using Graphs** The following data were obtained for two runners. Make a distance-time graph that shows the motion of both runners. What is the average speed of each runner? Which runner stops briefly? During what time interval do Sally and Alonzo run at the same speed?

Distance-Time for Runners

Time (s)	1	2	3	4
Sally's Distance (m)	2	4	6	8
Alonzo's Distance (m)	1	2	2	4

Performance Assessment

18. **Poster** Research the current safety features available in cars, including seat belts, improved door locks, collapsible steering columns, and air bags. Use this information, along with the statistics you found in the Science Online Feature regarding safety in cars, to make a poster on the benefits of using seat belts.

TECHNOLOGY

Go to the Glencoe Science Web site at **science.glencoe.com** or use the **Glencoe Science CD-ROM** for additional chapter assessment.

Test Practice

Four runners ran for 30 min. The following table represents the distance each runner covered in that time:

Runners' Distances

Runner Name	Distance Covered (km)
Rosemarie (R)	12.5
Sam (S)	8.9
Jake (J)	10.5
Theresa (T)	7.8

Study the table and answer the following questions.

1. Which of these graphs best represents these data?

A) **C)**

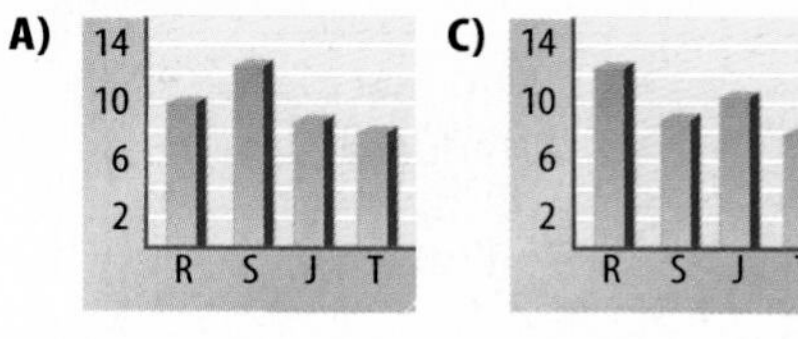

B)

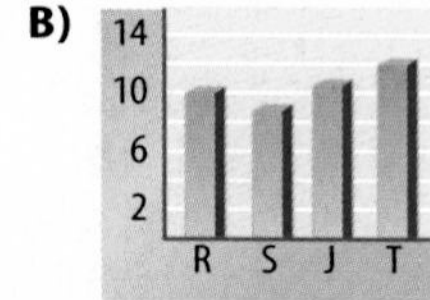

D)

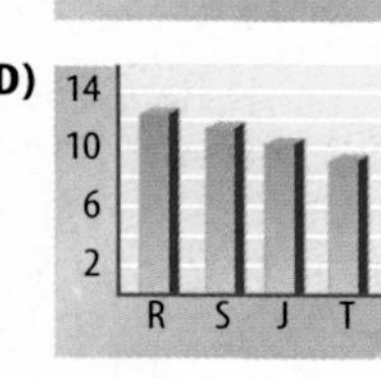

2. The average speed of each runner can be determined by dividing the total distance by the total travel time. Which runner most likely has the fastest average speed?

F) Rosemarie **H)** Jake
G) Sam **J)** Theresa

Chapter 2 Assessment

Test Practice

The Test-Taking Tip was written by The Princeton Review, the nation's leader in test preparation.

1. C
2. F

Developing Skills

15. 0.2 km/s
16. change in direction
17. Sally's average speed is 2 m/s and Alonzo's is 1 m/s. Alonzo stops briefly; they run at same speed from 3 s to 4 s.

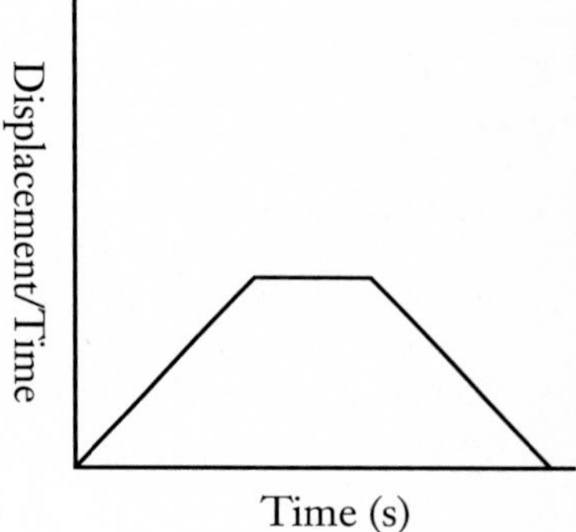

Performance Assessment

19. Posters might describe the force required to quickly stop a person traveling at various speeds in a car, what happens to a person not wearing a seat belt, and the percentage of people who die in crashes who would have survived if they had been wearing seat belts. Use **PASC**, p. 145

Assessment Resources

 **Reproducible Masters**

Chapter Resources Booklet
Chapter Review, pp. 37–38
Chapter Tests, pp. 39–42
Assessment Transparency Activity, p. 49

Glencoe Science Web site
Interactive Tutor
Chapter Quizzess

Glencoe Technology
- Assessment Transparency
- Interactive CD-ROM Chapter Quizzes
- ExamView Pro Test Bank
- Vocabulary PuzzleMaker Software
- MindJogger Videoquiz DVD/VHS

Section/Objectives	Standards		Activities/Features
	National	State/Local	
Chapter Opener	See p. 37T for a Key to Standards.		**Explore Activity:** Observe free-falling objects, p. 67 **Before You Read,** p. 67
Section 1 Newton's Second Law 2 sessions 1 block 1. **Explain** how force, mass, and acceleration are related. 2. **Describe** the three different types of friction. 3. **Observe** the effects of air resistance on falling objects.	National Content Standards: UCP3, A2, B2 (5–8), B4 (9–12)		**Science Online,** p. 69 **Math Skills Activity:** Calculating Acceleration, p. 69 **MiniLAB:** Comparing Friction, p. 71
Section 2 Gravity 2 sessions 1 block 1. **Describe** gravitational force. 2. **Distinguish** between mass and weight. 3. **Explain** why objects that are thrown or shot will follow a curved path. 4. **Compare** motion in a straight line with circular motion.	National Content Standards: UCP3, A2, B2 (5–8), B4 (9–12)		**Science Online,** p. 76 **Earth Science Integration,** p. 79 **MiniLAB:** Observing Centripetal Force, p. 81
Section 3 The Third Law of Motion 3 sessions 2 blocks 1. **Identify** when action and reaction forces occur. 2. **Calculate** momentum. 3. **Demonstrate** how momentum is conserved.	National Content Standards: UCP3, A2, B2 (5–8), B4 (9–12)		**Health Integration,** p. 84 **Visualizing Rocket Motion,** p. 85 **Activity:** Measuring the Effects of Air Resistance, p. 89 **Activity:** The Momentum of Falling Objects, pp. 90–91 **Science Stats:** Moving and Forcing, pp. 92–93

Activity Materials	Reproducible Resources	Section Assessment	Technology
Explore Activity: stopwatch, softball, tennis ball, a piece of crumpled paper, and a flat sheet of paper	**Chapter Resources Booklet** Foldables Worksheet, p. 17 Note-taking Worksheets, pp. 33–34	GLENCOE'S ASSESSMENT ADVANTAGE	
MiniLAB: ice cube, rock, eraser, wood block, square of aluminum foil, metal or plastic tray, metric ruler	**Chapter Resources Booklet** Transparency Activity, p. 44 MiniLAB, p. 3 Enrichment, p. 30 Reinforcement, p. 27 Directed Reading, p. 20 Lab Activity, pp. 9–12 **Reading and Writing Skill Activities,** p. 35	**Portfolio** Science Journal, p. 73 **Performance** Math Skills Activity, p. 69 MiniLAB, p. 71 Skill Builder Activities, p. 74 **Content** Section Assessment, p. 74	Section Focus Transparency Interactive CD-ROM/DVD Guided Reading Audio Program
MiniLAB: bucket filled with 3 cm water *Need materials?* Contact Science Kit at 1-800-828-7777 or www.sciencekit.com on the Internet.	**Chapter Resources Booklet** Transparency Activity, p. 45 MiniLAB, p. 4 Enrichment, p. 31 Reinforcement, p. 28 Directed Reading, p. 20 Transparency Activity, pp. 47–48 **Life Science Critical Thinking/Problem Solving,** p. 14 **Earth Science Critical Thinking/Problem Solving,** p. 5 **Cultural Diversity,** p. 25	**Portfolio** Curriculumn Connection, p. 79 Reteach, p. 82 **Performance** MiniLAB, p. 81 Skill Builder Activities, p. 82 **Content** Section Assessment, p. 82	Section Focus Transparency Teaching Transparency Interactive CD-ROM/DVD Guided Reading Audio Program
Activity: 4 equal size sheets of paper, scissors, meterstick, stopwatch, masking tape **Activity:** meterstick, large, light-weight rubber ball, racquetball, tennis ball, baseball, stopwatch, masking tape, balance	**Chapter Resources Booklet** Transparency Activity, p. 46 Enrichment, p. 32 Reinforcement, p. 29 Directed Reading, pp. 21, 22 Activity Worksheet, pp. 5–6, 7–8 Lab Activity, pp. 13–16 **Home and Community Involvement,** p. 49	**Portfolio** Extension, p. 86 **Performance** Skill Builder Activities, p. 88 **Content** Section Assessment, p. 88	Section Focus Transparency Interactive CD-ROM/DVD Guided Reading Audio Program

End of Chapter Assessment

GLENCOE'S ASSESSMENT ADVANTAGE

Blackline Masters	Technology	Professional Series
Chapter Resources Booklet Chapter Review, pp. 37–38 Chapter Tests, pp. 39–42 **Standardized Test Practice by The Princeton Review,** pp. 15–19	MindJogger Videoquiz CD-ROM Explorations and Quizzes Vocabulary Puzzle Makers ExamView Pro Test Bank Interactive Lesson Planner Interactive Teacher's Edition	Performance Assessment in the Science Classroom (PASC)

Transparencies

Section Focus

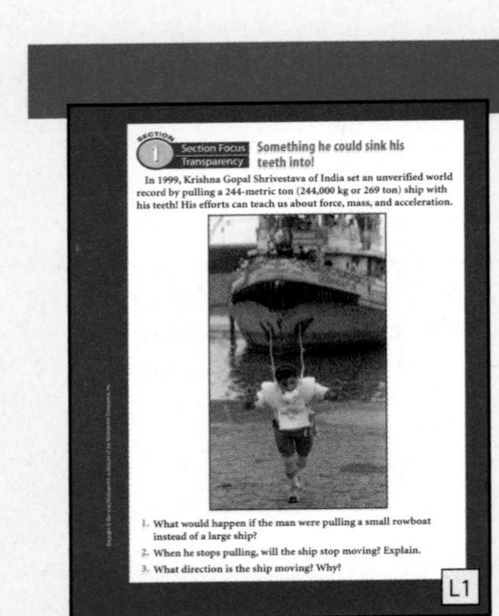
Section 1 Section Focus Transparency
Something he could sink his teeth into!
In 1999, Krishna Gopal Shrivestava of India set an unverified world record by pulling a 244-metric ton (244,000 kg or 269 ton) ship with his teeth! His efforts can teach us about force, mass, and acceleration.
1. What would happen if the man were pulling a small rowboat instead of a large ship?
2. When he stops pulling, will the ship stop moving? Explain.
3. What direction is the ship moving? Why?
L1

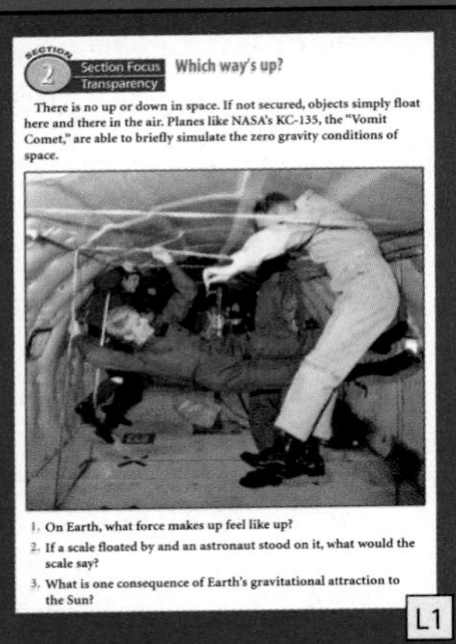
Section 2 Section Focus Transparency
Which way's up?
There is no up or down in space. If not secured, objects simply float here and there in the air. Planes like NASA's KC-135, the "Vomit Comet," are able to briefly simulate the zero gravity conditions of space.
1. On Earth, what force makes up feel like up?
2. If a scale floated by and an astronaut stood on it, what would the scale say?
3. What is one consequence of Earth's gravitational attraction to the Sun?
L1

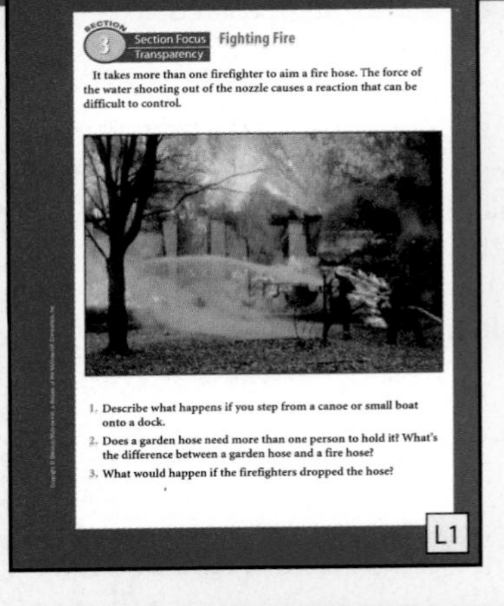
Section 3 Section Focus Transparency
Fighting Fire
It takes more than one firefighter to aim a fire hose. The force of the water shooting out of the nozzle causes a reaction that can be difficult to control.
1. Describe what happens if you step from a canoe or small boat onto a dock.
2. Does a garden hose need more than one person to hold it? What's the difference between a garden hose and a fire hose?
3. What would happen if the firefighters dropped the hose?
L1

This is a representation of key blackline masters available in the Teacher Classroom Resources. See Resource Manager boxes within the chapter for additional information.

Assessment

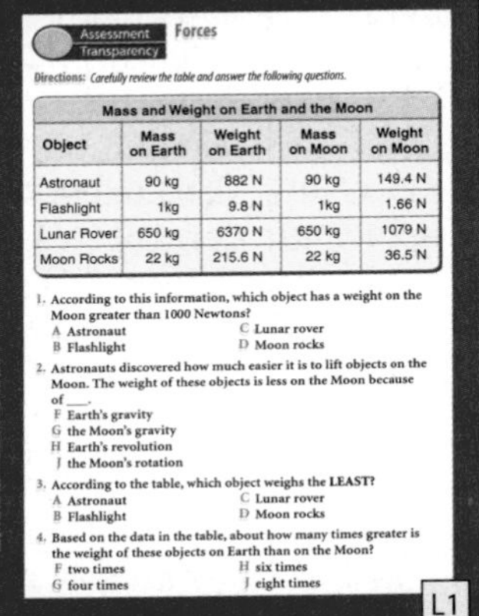
Assessment Transparency
Forces
Directions: Carefully review the table and answer the following questions.

Mass and Weight on Earth and the Moon				
Object	Mass on Earth	Weight on Earth	Mass on Moon	Weight on Moon
Astronaut	90 kg	882 N	90 kg	149.4 N
Flashlight	1kg	9.8 N	1kg	1.66 N
Lunar Rover	650 kg	6370 N	650 kg	1079 N
Moon Rocks	22 kg	215.6 N	22 kg	36.5 N

1. According to this information, which object has a weight on the Moon greater than 1000 Newtons?
A Astronaut C Lunar rover
B Flashlight D Moon rocks
2. Astronauts discovered how much easier it is to lift objects on the Moon. The weight of these objects is less on the Moon because of ___.
F Earth's gravity
G the Moon's gravity
H Earth's revolution
J the Moon's rotation
3. According to the table, which object weighs the LEAST?
A Astronaut C Lunar rover
B Flashlight D Moon rocks
4. Based on the data in the table, about how many times greater is the weight of these objects on Earth than on the Moon?
F two times H six times
G four times J eight times
L1

Teaching

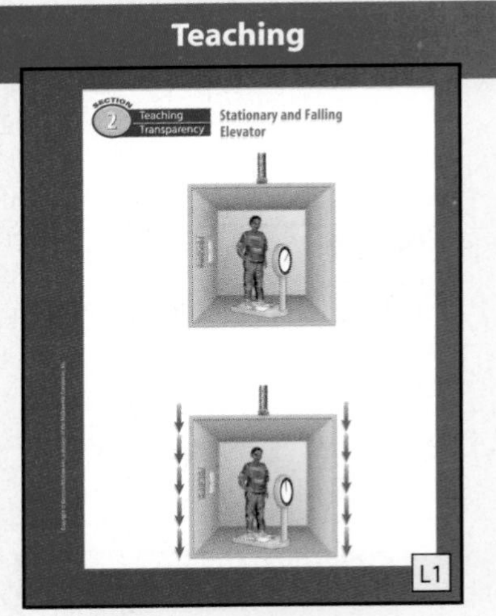
Teaching Transparency 2
Stationary and Falling Elevator
L1

Key to Teaching Strategies

The following designations will help you decide which activities are appropriate for your students.

L1 Level 1 activities should be appropriate for students with learning difficulties.

L2 Level 2 activities should be within the ability range of all students.

L3 Level 3 activities are designed for above-average students.

ELL ELL activities should be within the ability range of English Language Learners.

COOP LEARN Cooperative Learning activities are designed for small group work.

LS Multiple Learning Styles logos are used throughout to indicate strategies that address different learning styles.

P These strategies represent student products that can be placed into a best-work portfolio.

Hands-on Activities

Activity Worksheets

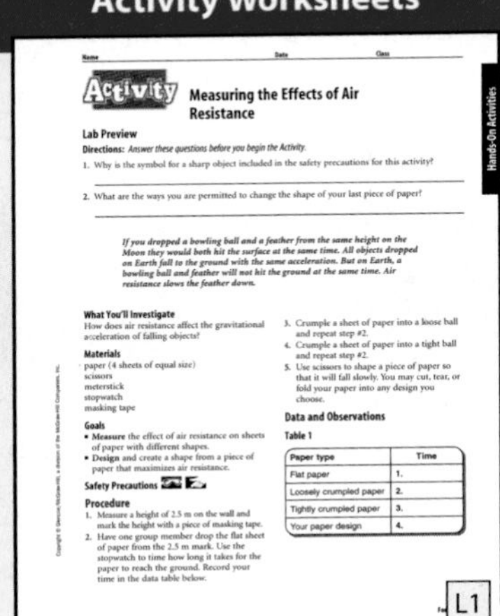
Activity
Measuring the Effects of Air Resistance
Lab Preview
Directions: Answer these questions before you begin the Activity.
1. Why is the symbol for a sharp object included in the safety precautions for this activity?
2. What are the ways you are permitted to change the shape of your last piece of paper?

If you dropped a bowling ball and a feather from the same height on the Moon they would both hit the surface at the same time. All objects dropped on Earth fall to the ground with the same acceleration. But on Earth, a bowling ball and feather will not hit the ground at the same time. Air resistance slows the feather down.

What You'll Investigate
How does air resistance affect the gravitational acceleration of falling objects?
Materials
paper (4 sheets of equal size)
scissors
meterstick
stopwatch
masking tape
Goals
• Measure the effect of air resistance on sheets of paper with different shapes.
• Design and create a shape from a piece of paper that maximizes air resistance.
Safety Precautions
Procedure
1. Measure a height of 2.5 m on the wall and mark the height with a piece of masking tape.
2. Have one group member drop the flat sheet of paper from the 2.5 m mark. Use the stopwatch to time how long it takes for the paper to reach the ground. Record your time in the data table below.
3. Crumple a sheet of paper into a loose ball and repeat step #2.
4. Crumple a sheet of paper into a tight ball and repeat step #2.
5. Use scissors to shape a piece of paper so that it will fall slowly. You may cut, tear, or fold your paper into any design you choose.
Data and Observations
Table 1

Paper type	Time
Flat paper	1.
Loosely crumpled paper	2.
Tightly crumpled paper	3.
Your paper design	4.

L1

Laboratory Activities

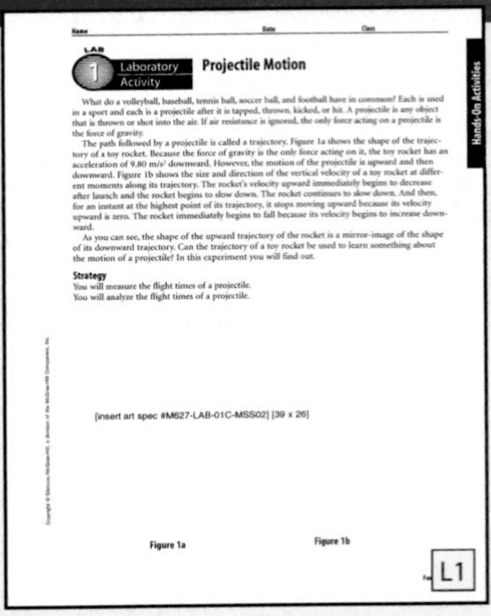

Lab 1 Laboratory Activity
Projectile Motion
Strategy
You will measure the flight times of a projectile.
You will analyze the flight times of a projectile.
Figure 1a Figure 1b
L1

Meeting Different Ability Levels

Content Outline

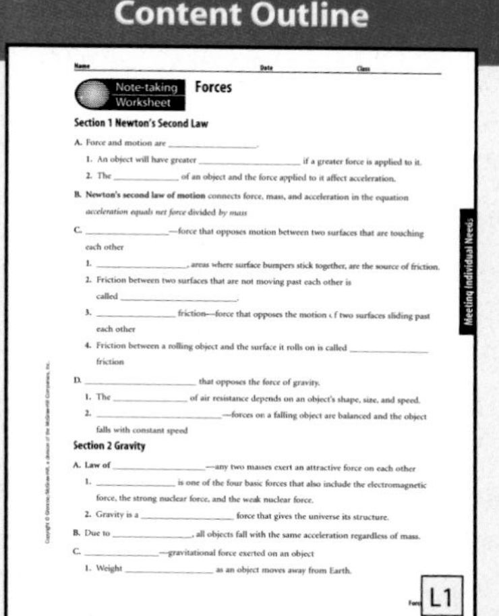

Reinforcement

Directed Reading

Assessment

Chapter Tests

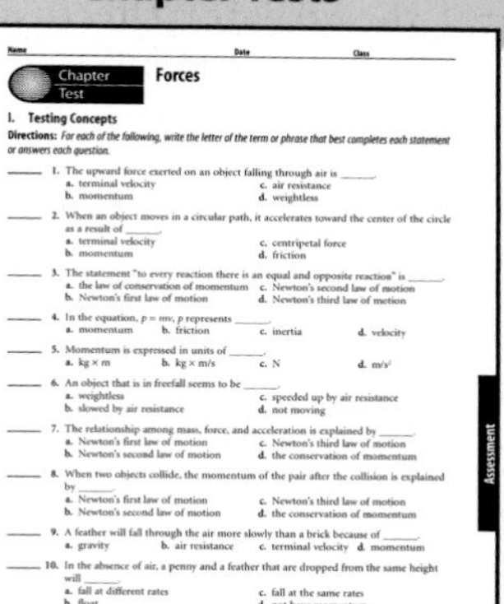

Enrichment

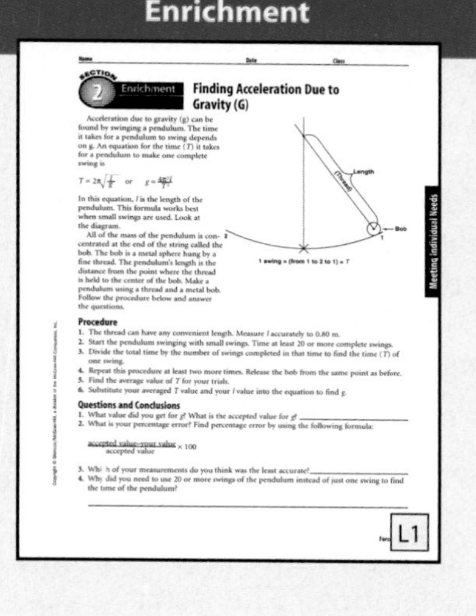

Spanish Directed Reading

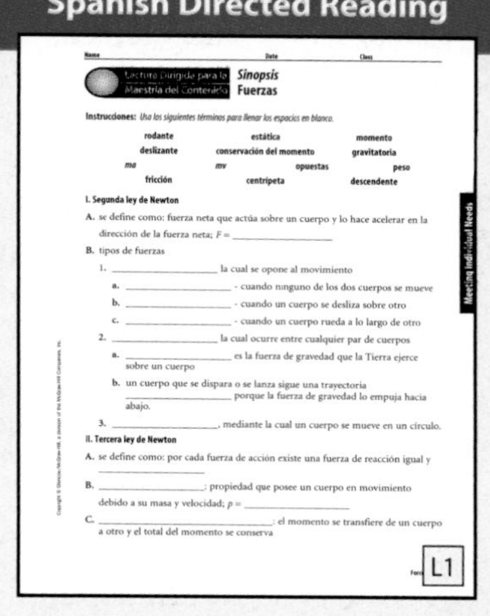

Test Practice Workbook

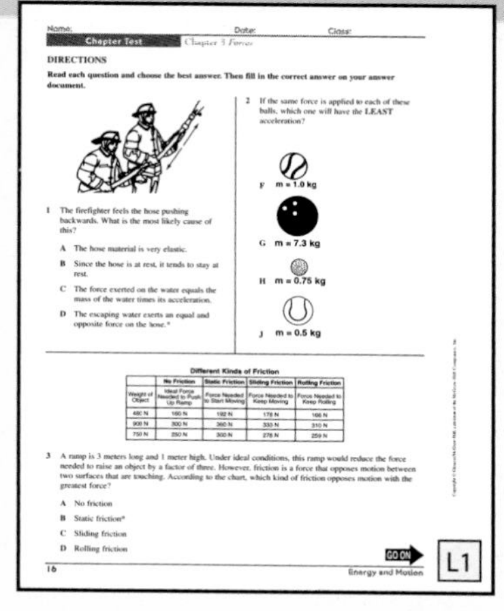

Chapter Review

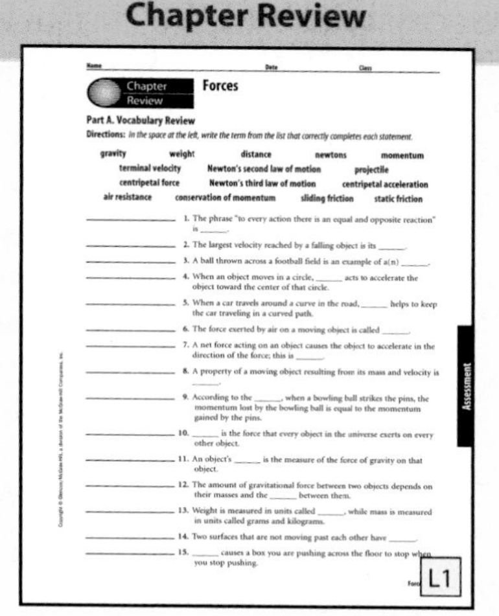

Science Content Background

SECTION 1 Newton's Second Law

Force, Mass, and Acceleration

Dynamics is the study of motion produced by forces. It comes from the Greek word *dynamis*, which means "strength or power." Words such as *dynamite* and *dynamo* share these origins.

Newton's Second Law

It follows from this law that if an object is accelerating, there must be force acting on it. Engines produce forces to make cars positively accelerate. The brakes produce forces to cause negative acceleration. A planet moving with constant speed around a star is constantly changing direction and therefore is accelerating toward the star. This acceleration is due to the force of gravity between the star and the planet.

A force of one Newton is equal to one kilogram–meter per second squared (1N = 1 kg m/s^2). Thus when dividing mass into force the kg units cancel leaving the acceleration units of m/s^2.

Air Resistance

When people jump out of high-altitude airplanes they don't keep accelerating. The faster they fall the greater the air resistance acting on them, so their acceleration decreases as they fall. Eventually a sky diver stops accelerating and achieves a constant velocity called the terminal velocity. For humans, terminal velocity is about 53 m/s or 190 km/h. It's a good thing velocity slows to only 5 to 10 m/s after the parachute opens!

SECTION 2 Gravity

The Law of Gravitation

Newton described the relationships between the masses of two objects and the distance between them with the following equation: force of gravity = G x $(\text{mass}_1) \times (\text{mass}_2)/(\text{distance between them})^2$. "G" is the universal gravitational constant. If the mass of one of the objects quadruples the force of gravity quadruples. If the distance between the objects quadruples, the force of gravity is reduced by one-sixteenth.

Gravitational Acceleration

The average acceleration due to gravity on Earth is 9.8 m/s^2. This value varies slightly with location. In general the greater the distance from Earth's center the lower the value, which means acceleration is smaller on a mountain than in a valley. The acceleration at the equator tends to be less than at the poles. This is because Earth is not a perfect sphere; its poles are somewhat pushed together. The acceleration due to gravity on Mercury is 3.8 m/s^2, while on Jupiter it is 25.8 m/s^2.

Newton's second law can be used to explain why all objects, regardless of mass, fall with the same acceleration due to gravity. Objects with a large mass do have a greater gravitational force acting on them. However, while the force is greater, so is the mass. These offset each other, causing all objects to fall with the same acceleration.

Centripetal Force

An object in circular motion was often said to be experiencing centrifugal force, which really doesn't exist. Water in a bucket seems to be pushed outward but this is due to the water's inertia. It tends to move in straight-line motion while the bucket is pulled in by the centripetal force of a string. This causes the water to remain at the bottom of the bucket.

SECTION 3

The Third Law of Motion

Newton's Third Law

The recoil of a rifle is an interesting application of Newton's Laws. When fired, the rifle "kicks back" into the shoulder of the shooter. If the rifle hurts the shoulder, should the shooter use a more massive or a less massive gun? If the guns are firing the same bullets with the same acceleration, the more massive gun will give less kick back. The recoil force will be the same, but the more massive gun will not accelerate as much ($a = F/m$).

Fun Fact

Squids and octopuses use Newton's third law as a means of propulsion. They take in water and forcibly expel it through a siphon in a sudden spurt that pushes them through the water. Squids are very streamlined and can achieve speeds of 23 miles per hour.

Finding Planets with Newton's Laws

Newton's third law is now being used to find planets in other solar systems. The planets are not directly seen, but their presence is inferred from the behavior of the star in that solar system. Fifty planets in other solar systems have been found in this way.

Momentum

To hit a home run, a softball player must impart the maximum momentum from his or her body and the bat to the ball. To do this each player must find the bat that gives him or her the best combination of mass and speed. A heavier bat has more mass but the player may not be able to swing it as fast as a lighter bat.

A force applied over time, also called an impulse, can change momentum. The formula describing this relationship is $F \times t = m\,\Delta V$. In softball, following through on a swing can increase the amount of time the bat stays in contact with the ball and this causes a greater velocity gain by the ball.

SCIENCE Online

For additional content background on this topic, go to the Glencoe Science Web site at science.glencoe.com.

David Young-Wolff/PhotoEdit

CHAPTER 3

Forces

Chapter Vocabulary

Newton's second law of motion
friction
law of gravitation
weight
centripetal acceleration
centripetal force
Newton's third law of motion
momentum

What do you think?

Science Journal The photograph shows the spirograph nebula, taken by the Hubble Space Telescope. This nebula is about 2,000 light years from Earth. It was formed by a star similar to the Sun during the last stages of its life. The star had become a red giant that ejected its outer layer. This ejected material forms the nebula.

CHAPTER 3

Forces

Crash! What brought this vehicle to its sudden stop? How did the impact affect the car and its driver? Automobile manufacturers consider factors like mass and acceleration to determine the forces on a driver during a crash. This helps them predict whether the driver would survive or be injured. In this chapter you will learn how forces affect motion, and what causes forces like gravity and friction.

What do you think?

Science Journal Look at the picture below with a classmate. Discuss what this might be or what is happening. Here's a hint: *gravity gives this object its structure.* Write your answer or best guess in your Science Journal.

66

Theme Connection

Stability and Change Newton established his three laws of motion by considering common patterns of change in all motion. Newton's laws can be used to analyze and predict changes in the motion of objects.

What holds you to Earth, pulls footballs back to the ground, and keeps the Moon in orbit? The force of gravity, of course. But did you know that the force of gravity causes all objects to fall with the same acceleration? If this is true, why do bowling balls fall faster than feathers? Explore free-falling objects for yourself in this activity.

Observe free-falling objects

1. Drop a softball from a height of 2.5 m and use a stopwatch to measure the time it takes for the softball to fall the given distance.
2. Repeat the procedure using a tennis ball, a piece of paper crumpled into a ball, and a flat sheet of paper.

Observe

In your Science Journal, write a paragraph comparing the time it took for the four items to drop the 2.5 m. Infer why the crumpled paper fell faster than the flat sheet of paper even though they have the same mass.

Before You Read

FOLDABLES Reading & Study Skills

Making a Compare and Contrast Study Fold **Make the following Foldable to help you see how the three types of friction are similar and different.**

1. Place a sheet of paper in front of you so the short side is at the top. Fold the top of the paper down and the bottom up.
2. Open the paper and label the three rows *Static Friction, Sliding Friction,* and *Rolling Friction.*
3. Before you read the chapter, write the definition of each type of friction next to it. As you read the chapter, write more information about each type.

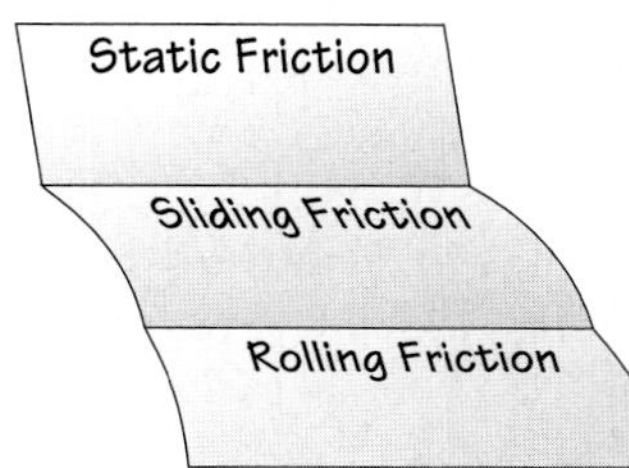

67

EXPLORE ACTIVITY

Purpose Use the Explore Activity to introduce students to the seemingly paradoxical phenomenon that, neglecting air resistance, objects with different masses fall with the same velocities. L2

LS **Visual-Spatial**

Preparation Find a suitable location, such as a stairwell, from which students can drop the balls. Measure a distance of 2.5 m above the floor, and mark the height with a piece of tape.

Materials softball, meterstick, tennis ball, paper

Teaching Strategy Have students do this activity in pairs so one student can drop the balls while the other observes and determines which object hit the ground first.

Observe

Although they differ in mass, the softball, tennis ball, and crumpled paper ball will fall at nearly the same velocity. Wind resistance prevents the flat paper from falling with the same velocity as the crumpled paper ball.

✓Assessment

Process Have students make bar graphs of the data they obtained in this activity. Use **Performance Assessment in the Science Classroom,** p. 111.

Before You Read

FOLDABLES Reading & Study Skills

Dinah Zike Study Fold

Purpose Students make and use a Foldable to determine what they know about forces before reading the chapter, and to provide a place for collecting data about forces as they read.

For additional help, see Foldables Worksheet p. 17 in **Chapter Resources Booklet,** or go to the Glencoe Science Web site at **science.glencoe.com.** See After You Read in the Study Guide at the end of this chapter.

SECTION

Newton's Second Law

1 Motivate

Bellringer Transparency

Display the Section Focus Transparency for Section 1. Use the accompanying Transparency Activity Master. L2 ELL

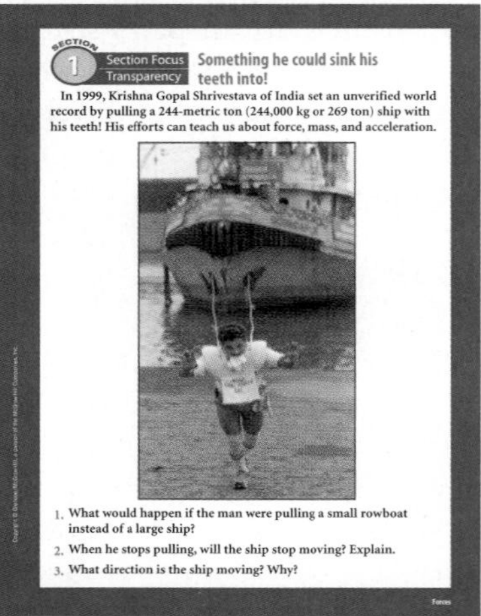

SECTION 1 Section Focus Transparency **Something he could sink his teeth into!**

In 1999, Krishna Gopal Shrivestava of India set an unverified world record by pulling a 244-metric ton (244,000 kg or 269 ton) ship with his teeth! His efforts can teach us about force, mass, and acceleration.

1. **What would happen if the man were pulling a small rowboat instead of a large ship?**
2. **When he stops pulling, will the ship stop moving? Explain.**
3. **What direction is the ship moving? Why?**

Forces

Tie to Prior Knowledge

Ask students what they do when they have heavy objects they need to move. In this section they will learn how the mass of an object affects how fast they can move it, and why some objects keep moving while others stop.

SECTION

Newton's Second Law

As You Read

***What* You'll Learn**

- **Explain** how force, mass, and acceleration are related.
- **Describe** the three different types of friction.
- **Observe** the effects of air resistance on falling objects.

Vocabulary

Newton's second law of motion
friction

***Why* It's Important**

Newton's second law explains why some objects move and some objects don't.

Force, Mass, and Acceleration

Newton's first law of motion states that the motion of an object changes only if a net force acts on it. Force and motion are connected. How does force cause motion to change?

Force and Acceleration What's different about throwing a ball as hard as you can and tossing it gently? When you throw hard, you exert a much greater force on the ball. How is the motion of the ball different in each case?

In both cases, the ball was at rest in your hand before it began to move. However, when you throw hard, the ball has a greater velocity when it leaves your hand than it does when you throw gently. Thus the hard-thrown ball has a greater change in velocity, and the change occurs over a shorter period of time. Recall that acceleration is the change in velocity divided by the time it takes for the change to occur. So, a hard-thrown ball has a greater acceleration than a gently thrown ball.

For any object, the greater the force that's applied to it, the greater its acceleration will be. This is true for anything from the blood cells swirling through your body to the galaxies swirling through outer space. Why would the student in **Figure 1** want to hit the volleyball as hard as possible?

Figure 1
A hard hit is just the thing needed to get the volleyball over the net.

Force and Mass If you throw a softball and a baseball as hard as you can, why don't they have the same speed? The difference is due to their masses. The softball has a mass of about 0.20 kg, but a baseball's mass is about 0.14 kg. With a larger mass, the softball has less velocity after it leaves your than the baseball does, even though you exerted the same force. If it took the same amount of time to throw both balls, the softball has less acceleration. The acceleration of an object depends on its mass as well as the force exerted on it. Force, mass, and acceleration are connected.

Resource Manager

Chapter Resources Booklet
Transparency Activity, p. 44
Note-taking Worksheets, pp. 33–34

Section Assessment Planner

PORTFOLIO
Science Journal, p. 73

PERFORMANCE ASSESSMENT
Math Skills Activity, p.69
MiniLAB, p. 71
Skill Builder Activities, p. 74
See page 96 for more options.

CONTENT ASSESSMENT
Section, p. 74
Challenge, p. 74
Chapter, pp. 96–97

Newton's Second Law

Newton's second law of motion describes how force, mass, and acceleration are connected. Recall that if more than one force acts on an object, the forces combine to form a net force. According to **Newton's second law of motion,** the net force acting on an object causes the object to accelerate in the direction of the net force. The acceleration of an object is determined by the size of the net force and the mass of the object according to the equation:

$$\text{acceleration} = \frac{\text{net force}}{\text{mass}}$$

If a stands for the acceleration, F for the net force, and m for the mass, Newton's second law can be written as follows:

$$a = \frac{F}{m}$$

In SI units, the unit of mass is the kilogram (kg), and the unit of acceleration is meters per sescond squared (m/s^2). So, according to the second law of motion, force has the units kg $\times$ m/s^2. The unit kg $\times$ m/s^2 is called the newton (N).

Research Visit the Glencoe Science Web site at **science.glencoe.com** for information about how athletic trainers analyze the motions of athletes so they make the best use of Newton's second law. Select a sport and report to your class about some of the findings in that sport.

Math Skills Activity

Calculating Acceleration

You are pushing a friend on a sled. You push with a force of 40 N. Your friend and the sled together have a mass of 80 kg. Ignoring friction, what is the acceleration of your friend on the sled?

1. *This is what you know:* force: $F = 40$ N; mass: $m = 80$ kg
2. *This is what you need to know:* acceleration: a
3. *This is the equation you need to use:* $a = F/m$
4. *Substitute the known values:* $a = 40\text{ N}/80\text{ kg} = 0.5\text{ m/s}^2$

Check your answer by multiplying it by the mass. Do you calculate the same force that was given?

Practice Problem

A student pedaling a bicycle applies a net force of 200 N. The mass of the rider and the bicycle is 50 kg. What is the acceleration of the bicycle and the rider?

For more help, refer to the Math Skill Handbook.

2 Teach

Force, Mass, and Acceleration

Text Question Answer

The harder the ball is hit, the faster it will move.

Discussion

Ask students whether they have ever used a "medicine ball." This heavier-than-normal ball is often used during training to build muscle strength and coordination. **In order to give the medicine ball the same acceleration as a basketball, how must the force you use when throwing the ball be different?** You must use a greater force because the mass of the medicine ball is greater. L2

IN **Logical-Mathematical**

Newton's Second Law

Quick Demo

Show how mass affects acceleration with a constant force. Place a flexed ruler next to a golf ball and release the ruler. Have students observe the motion of the ball. Repeat using a ping-pong ball. Be sure to bend the ruler the same amount each time. L2 ELL IN **Visual-Spatial**

Math Skills Activity

National Math Standards

Correlation to Mathematics Objectives

1, 2, 6, 9

Answer to Practice Problem

1. 4 m/s^2

Internet Addresses

Explore the Glencoe Science Web site at **science.glencoe.com** to find out more about topics in this section.

Teacher FYI

Newton's second law fails for particles moving close to the speed of light. At these speeds, a particle's mass increases significantly as velocity increases. This effect is important in particle accelerators. Newton's second law also does not apply in areas of extremely high gravity.

Friction

IDENTIFYING Misconceptions

It would seem that friction should increase as the size of the areas in contact increases. In fact friction is nearly independent of the surface area in contact. Friction depends on the microscopic contact areas on the microscopic welds that form when the surfaces are pushed together. If the macroscopic contact area increases, more welds are formed. However, because pressure equals force divided by area, the pressure pushing the surfaces together decreases. This causes the contact area on each weld to become smaller such that the total microscopic contact area remains nearly unchanged.

Reading Check

Answer kinds of surfaces and force pressing them together

Make a Model

Students can use modeling clay to show how two surfaces that appear to be smooth and in complete contact are, in fact, microscopically rough. The models should show the bumps and dips on the surfaces and how the surfaces touch only at the bumps. L2 LS **Kinesthetic**

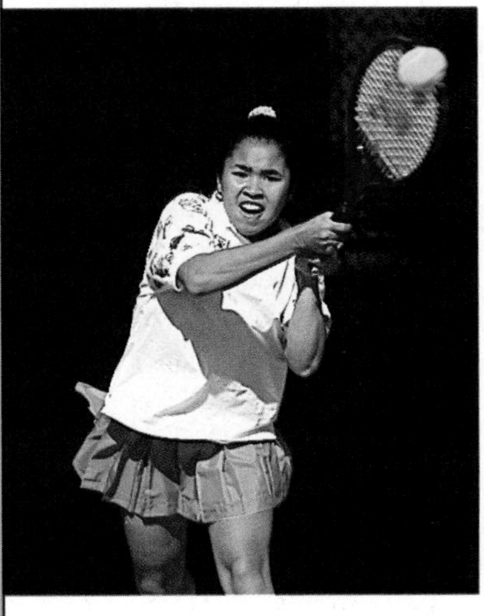

Figure 2
The force exerted on the ball by the tennis racket may be more than 500 times greater than the ball's weight.

Using Newton's Second Law The second law tells how to calculate the acceleration of an object when a net force acts on it. For example, a tennis ball like the one in **Figure 2** is accelerated by a tennis racket only during the few thousandths of a second the racket is in contact with the ball. Because this time period is so short, a ball that leaves the racket at a speed of 100 km/h, would have an acceleration of about 5,500 m/s^2. How much force would the tennis racket have to exert to give the ball this acceleration? The ball has a mass of 0.06 kg, so by Newton's second law the force would have to be:

$$F = ma = (0.06\ \text{kg})(5{,}500\ \text{m/s}^2) = 330\ \text{N}$$

Friction

Suppose you give a skateboard a push with your hand. According to Newton's first law of motion, if no forces are acting on a moving object, it continues to move in a straight line with constant speed. What happens to the motion of the skateboard after it leaves your hand? Does it continue to move in a straight line with constant speed?

You know the answer. The skateboard gradually slows down and finally stops. Recall that when an object slows down, its velocity changes. If its velocity changes, it is accelerating. And if an object is accelerating, a net force must be acting on it.

The force that slows the skateboard and brings it to a stop is friction. **Friction** is the force that opposes motion between two surfaces that are touching each other. The amount of friction between two surfaces depends on two factors—the kinds of surfaces and the force pressing the surfaces together.

Reading Check *The amount of friction between two objects depends on what two factors?*

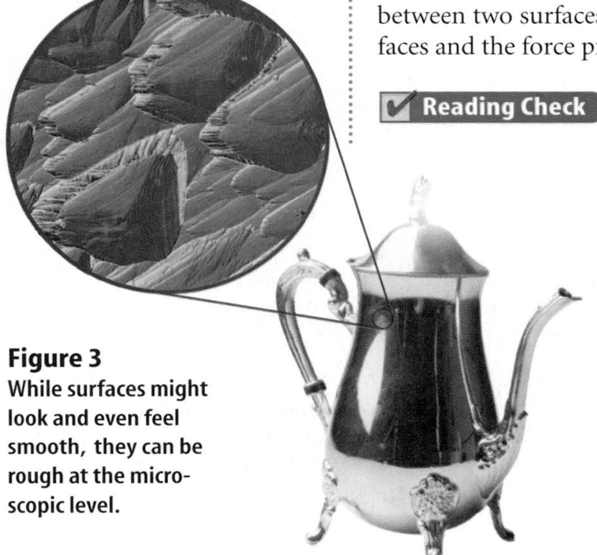

Figure 3
While surfaces might look and even feel smooth, they can be rough at the microscopic level.

What causes friction? Would you believe the surface of a highly polished piece of metal is rough? **Figure 3** shows a microscopic view of the dips and bumps on the surface of a polished silver teapot. If two surfaces, such as two pieces of silver, are pressed tightly together, welding, or sticking, occurs in those areas where the highest bumps come into contact with each other. These areas where the bumps stick together are called microwelds and are the source of friction.

LAB DEMONSTRATION

Purpose to observe properties of friction

Materials 2 heavy blocks, spring scale, tape, string, smooth and rough surfaces

Preparation Tape one end of the string to a block and the other end to the spring scale.

Procedure Use the spring scale to pull the block across a smooth surface. Record the force required. Repeat on a rough surface. Next, pull the block with another block on top of it. Finally, turn one block on its end and pull it.

Expected Outcome There is more friction on a rough surface. Friction doubles if the mass doubles. The area of contact doesn't affect friction.

Assessment

What would happen if a third block were put on top of the second block? The frictional force would be triple. **What did this activity show about the relation between static and sliding friction?** Static friction is greater than sliding friction.

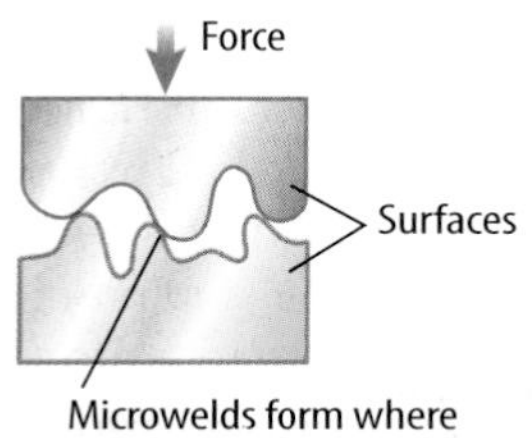

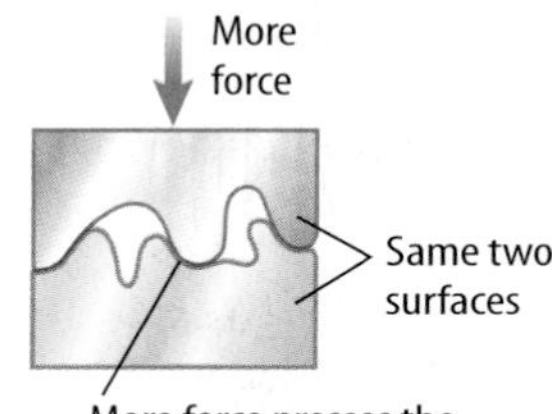

Figure 4
Friction is due to microwelds formed between two surfaces. The larger the force pushing the two surfaces together, the stronger microwelds will be.

Sticking Together The stronger the force pushing the two surfaces together is, the stronger these microwelds will be, because more of the surface bumps will come into contact, as shown in **Figure 4.** To break these microwelds and move one surface over the other, a force must be applied.

Static Friction Suppose you have filled a cardboard box, like the one in **Figure 5,** with books, and want to move it. It's too heavy to lift, so you start pushing on it, but it doesn't budge. Is that because the mass of the box is too large? If the box doesn't move, then it has zero acceleration. According to Newton's second law, if the acceleration is zero, then the net force on the box is zero. Another force that cancels your push must be acting on the box. That force is friction due to the microwelds that have formed between the bottom of the box and the floor. This type of friction is called static friction. Static friction is the friction between two surfaces that are not moving past each other. In this case, your push is not large enough to break the microwelds, and the box remains stuck to the floor.

Mini LAB

Comparing Friction

Procedure

1. Position an **ice cube, rock, eraser, wood block,** and square of **aluminum foil** at one end of a **metal** or **plastic tray.**
2. Slowly lift the end of the tray with the items.
3. Have a partner use a **metric ruler** to measure the height at which each object slides to the other end of the tray. Record the heights in your **Science Journal.**

Analysis

1. List the height at which each object slid off the tray.
2. Why did the objects slide off at different heights?
3. What type of friction acted on each object?

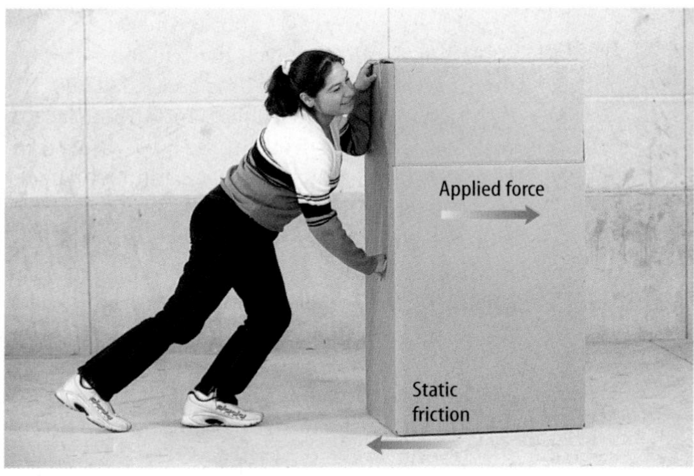

Figure 5
The box doesn't move because static friction cancels the applied force.

Purpose Students observe the effect of friction on several materials L2 LS **Kinesthetic**

Materials ice cube, rock, eraser, wood block, square of aluminum foil, metal or plastic tray, metric ruler

Teaching Strategies Have an empty jar or beaker available for the ice cubes.

Analysis

1. The ice cube should slide first, followed by the aluminum foil, rock, wood block, and eraser
2. The amount of friction between the tray and each object varied.
3. sliding friction and static friction

Oral Ask students to list several ways to increase the friction between tires and ice. Put chains on tires, make tires with steel grips, add sand or some other abrasive to ice, add weight to the car. Use **PASC,** p. 93.

Extension

In general, the smoother two surfaces are, the less friction there is between them. However, if surfaces are extremely smooth, they actually have more friction between them. Have students rub two new glass slides together and compare this to the resistance felt when rubbing older, scratched slides together. Ask them to explain this effect. Extremely smooth surfaces have a greater true contact area (more bumps are in contact). L3 LS **Kinesthetic**

Resource Manager

Chapter Resources Booklet
MiniLAB, p. 3
Enrichment, p. 30
Reading and Writing Skill Activities, p. 35

Visual Learning

Figure 4 The number of bumps where the two surfaces touch is actually quite small. If pressure on the surface is increased, the area over which the surfaces touch increases, so friction increases. Have students demonstrate the effect of increasing pressure on friction with various objects.

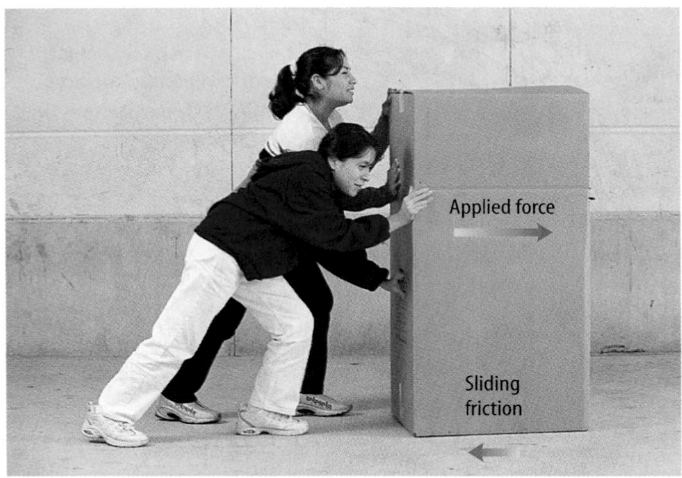

Figure 6
Sliding friction acts in the direction opposite the motion of the sliding box.

Sliding Friction To help you move the box, you ask a friend to push with you, as in **Figure 6.** Pushing together, the box starts to move, but it doesn't move easily. Also, if you stop pushing, it quickly comes to a stop. It might even seem as if someone is pushing on it from the opposite direction. But, by exerting enough force, you have broken the microwelds and started the box moving. However, as the box slides across the floor, another force—sliding friction—opposes the motion of the box. Sliding friction is the force that opposes the motion of two surfaces sliding past each other. To keep the box moving, you must continually apply a force to overcome sliding friction. How do you know that sliding friction isn't usually as strong as static friction?

Reading Check *What's the difference between sliding friction and static friction?*

Rolling Friction You might have watched a car stuck in snow, ice, or mud spinning its wheels. The driver steps on the gas, but the wheels just spin without the car moving. The car doesn't move when the wheels are on the slippery surface because there is not enough friction between the tires and the snow, ice, or mud. One way to make the car move might be to spread sand or gravel under the wheels. By spreading sand or gravel, the friction between the tires and the surface is increased. The friction between a rolling object and the surface it rolls on is rolling friction. As you can see in **Figure 7,** because of rolling friction, the wheels of the train rotate when they come in contact with the track rather than sliding over it. When a wheel rolls over a surface, rolling friction is caused by the wheel flattening out slightly and forming a slight indentation in the surface. Rolling friction is usually much less than static or sliding friction. This is why it's easier to pull a load in a wagon rather than dragging it along the ground.

Figure 7
Rolling friction is what makes a train's wheels turn on the tracks or a car's wheels turn on the road.

Friction, continued

Use Science Words

Word Origin Have students find the origin of the word *friction.* The word *friction* comes from the Latin word *fricare,* which means "to rub." L2 **Linguistic**

Extension

A force of 10 N is needed to produce an acceleration of 2.0 m/s^2 on a 3.0-kg wooden block sliding across a table. **What is the force of friction acting on the sliding block? What is its direction?** The force of 10 N applied to the block resulted in a net force of 3 kg × 2 m/s^2 = 6 N moving the block forward. This means that the force of friction is 10 N − 6 N, or 4 N in the direction opposite the direction of movement. L3 **Logical-Mathematical**

Text Question Answer

It is more difficult to start an object moving than to keep the object moving.

Reading Check

Answer Sliding friction is between two surfaces sliding past each other. Static friction is between two nonmoving surfaces.

Activity

Provide students with an assortment of toy cars. Have them examine the cars and roll them around and then identify all the sources of friction in the cars that hinder the cars' movement. Ask them to suggest ways to decrease the friction so the cars will roll more easily. Suggestions might include adding lubrication, making the contacting surfaces smoother, using different materials for the contacting surfaces, and adding ball bearings. L2 **Kinesthetic**

Visual Learning

Figure 6 Tell students that scientists use a number called the coefficient of static friction to describe the amount of friction between two stationary surfaces. The coefficient of static friction is equal to the force needed to start a body moving across a surface divided by the weight of the body being moved. **If the students in the picture had to push with a force of 400 N to start the 900 N box moving, what is the coefficient of static friction between the box and the floor?** $\frac{400\text{ N}}{900\text{ N}} = 0.44$ L3 **Logical-Mathematical**

Air Resistance

Acceleration due to Earth's gravity is the same for all objects, regardless of mass. This means that if no force other than gravity is present, all objects accelerate at the same rate. But do they fall at the same speed? Imagine dropping two identical plastic bags except that one is crumpled into a ball and one is spread out. The crumpled bag falls faster than the spread-out bag. So, the acceleration of the spread-out bag must be less than that of the crumpled bag. Therefore, the net force acting on the spread-out bag is less because a force is acting on it that opposes the force of gravity. This force is air resistance.

Air resistance affects anything that moves in Earth's atmosphere. Like friction, air resistance acts in the direction opposite to that of the object's motion. In the case of the two falling bags, air resistance is pushing up as gravity is pulling down, as shown in **Figure 8.**

The amount of air resistance on an object depends on the speed, size, and shape of the object. Air resistance, not the amount of mass in the object, is why feathers, leaves, and pieces of paper fall more slowly than pennies, acorns, and bowling balls. If no air resistance is present, then a feather and an apple fall at the same rate, as shown in **Figure 9.**

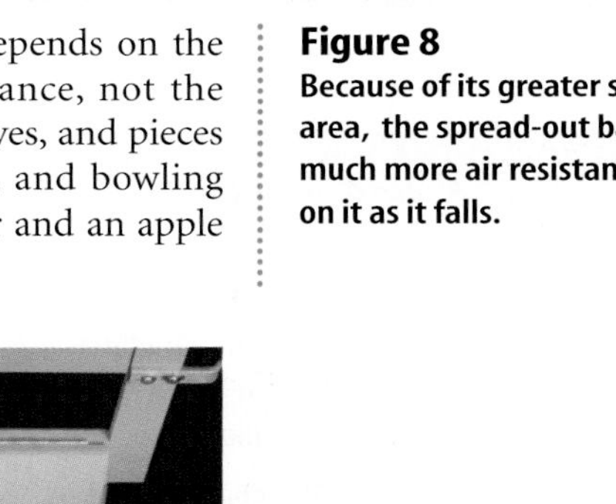

Figure 8
Because of its greater surface area, the spread-out bag has much more air resistance acting on it as it falls.

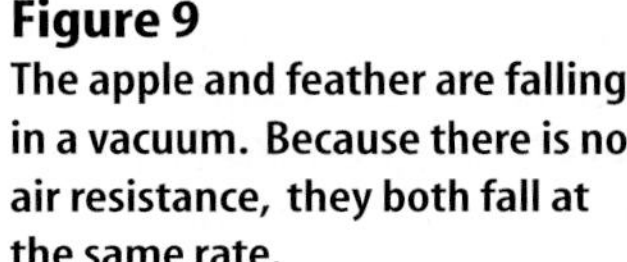

Figure 9
The apple and feather are falling in a vacuum. Because there is no air resistance, they both fall at the same rate.

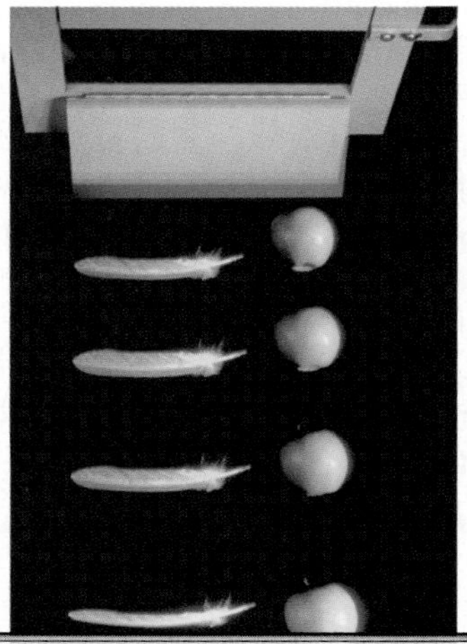

Air Resistance

Discussion

Why does using a parachute make it possible for skydivers to jump safely out of an airplane? The parachute has a large surface area. This causes a great deal of air resistance, which makes the skydiver fall slowly enough to land safely. L2

LS **Logical-Mathematical**

Activity

Have students show how air resistance affects the way an object falls by making a parachute out of string and cloth and attaching it to a small object. Suggest that students compare the rates at which the object falls when it is attached to the parachute and when it is not. L1 ELL LS **Kinesthetic**

Visual Learning

Figure 9 On August 2, 1971, during the *Apollo 15* mission, astronaut David Scott dropped a hammer and a feather onto the Moon's surface. This demonstration proved Galileo's conjecture that two objects would fall at the same rate in a vacuum, regardless of their mass.

Resource Manager

Chapter Resources Booklet

- Reinforcement, p. 27
- Directed Reading for Content Mastery, p. 20
- Lab Activity, pp. 9–12

Science Journal

Falling Objects Have students describe in their Science Journals how the velocity and acceleration of an object change as it falls from a tall building. Initially, velocity increases causing the air resistance force to increase until it equals the force of gravity at the object's terminal velocity. The velocity is then constant and acceleration is zero until the object hits the ground. L2

LS **Logical-Mathematical** P

Air Resistance, continued

Discussion

What happens to an object's velocity and acceleration when the object reaches terminal velocity? After reaching terminal velocity, the object's velocity remains constant, so its acceleration is zero.

3 Assess

Reteach

Have students demonstrate how rolling friction is less than sliding friction by pulling a rubber band attached to a toy car. If the car is pulled on its wheels, the rubber band barely extends. If the car is pulled on its top, the rubber band extends much more. L2 ELL IS **Kinesthetic**

Challenge

Have students show how Newton's first law can be derived from Newton's second law. According to Newton's second law, force equals mass times acceleration. If the force equals zero, the acceleration is zero. In other words, an object has zero acceleration, maintaining a constant velocity, if the net force acting on it is zero. L2 IS **Logical-Mathematical**

✔Assessment

Oral Have students work in small groups to discuss various sports they enjoy. They should explain how static, sliding, and rolling friction are important for the sport. Use **Performance Assessment in the Science Classroom,** p. 169.

Figure 10
The sky diver eventually will reach a terminal velocity and continue falling at a constant speed.

Terminal Velocity The force of air resistance increases with speed. As an object falls, it accelerates and its speed increases. So the force of air resistance increases until it becomes large enough to cancel the force of gravity. Then the forces on the falling object are balanced, and the object no longer accelerates. It then falls with a constant speed called the terminal velocity. This terminal velocity is the highest velocity that a falling object will reach. A low terminal velocity enables a sky diver, such as the one shown in **Figure 10,** to land safely on the ground.

Section  1 Assessment

1. What is Newton's second law of motion?
2. Why does a heavier object need more force to give it the same acceleration that a lighter object gets from a smaller force?
3. What is the difference between static friction, sliding friction, and rolling friction?
4. A squirrel runs across a branch on an oak tree and knocks an acorn and a leaf loose. Why does the acorn hit the ground first?
5. **Think Critically** To reduce the friction in a metal door hinge, you might try coating it with oil. Why does oil reduce friction?

Skill Builder Activities

6. **Drawing Conclusions** Boxes of equal size are resting on the floor. Applying the same force on each box, you find that you can accelerate the first one 1 m/s^2, the second 4 m/s^2, and the third 6 m/s^2. What can you infer about the total mass of each box? What other factors might have influenced your results? **For more help, refer to the** Science Skill Handbook.
7. **Communicating** Describe activities in which friction would be useful. **For more help, refer to the** Science Skill Handbook.

Answers to Section Assessment

1. Acceleration equals net force divided by mass.
2. F = ma; as mass increases, the amount of force needed to accelerate it increases.
3. Static friction is between two non-moving surfaces. Sliding friction is between two surfaces sliding past each other. Rolling friction is between a rolling object and the surface it rolls on.
4. The leaf has a larger surface area than the acorn, so it encounters more air resistance, which makes it fall more slowly.
5. The oil provides a smooth layer between the bumps and dips of the surfaces, which reduces the microwelding.
6. The first box has the greatest mass. The third box has the least mass. The surface friction also might have affected the acceleration.
7. Possible answers: A lot of friction is good for riding a bike, walking, or playing soccer.

SECTION 2

Gravity

The Law of Gravitation

There's a lot about you that's attractive. At this very moment, you are exerting a force on everything around you—your desk, your classmates, even the planet Jupiter millions of miles away. It's the attractive force of gravity.

Anything that has mass is attracted by the force of gravity. According to the **law of gravitation,** any two masses exert an attractive force on each other. The attractive force depends on the mass of the two objects and the distance between them, as shown in **Figure 11A.** This force increases as the mass of either object increases. Also, **Figure 11B** shows that the force of gravity increases as the objects move closer.

You can't feel any gravitational attraction between you and this book because the force is weak. Only Earth is close enough and has a large enough mass that you can feel its gravitational attraction. While the Sun has much more mass than Earth, the Sun is too far away to exert a noticeable gravitational attraction on you. And while this book is very close, it doesn't have enough mass to exert an attraction you can feel.

Gravity—A Basic Force Gravity is one of the four basic forces. The other basic forces are the electromagnetic force, the strong nuclear force, and the weak nuclear force. The nuclear forces only act on particles in the nuclei of atoms. Electricity and magnetism are caused by the electromagnetic force. Chemical interactions between atoms and molecules also are due to the electromagnetic force.

As You Read

***What* You'll Learn**

- **Describe** gravitational force.
- **Distinguish** between mass and weight.
- **Explain** why objects that are thrown or shot will follow a curved path.
- **Compare** motion in a straight line with circular motion.

Vocabulary
law of gravitation
weight
centripetal acceleration
centripetal force

***Why* It's Important**

No matter where you might be in the universe, gravity will have some effect on you.

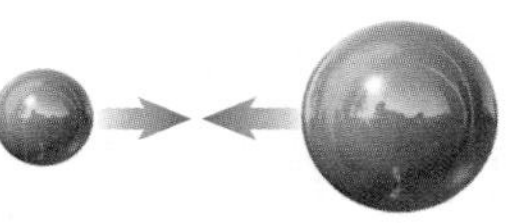

A If the mass of either of the objects increases, the gravitational force between them increases.

B If the objects are closer together, the gravitational force between them increases.

Figure 11
The gravitational force between two objects depends on their masses and the distance between them.

SECTION

Gravity

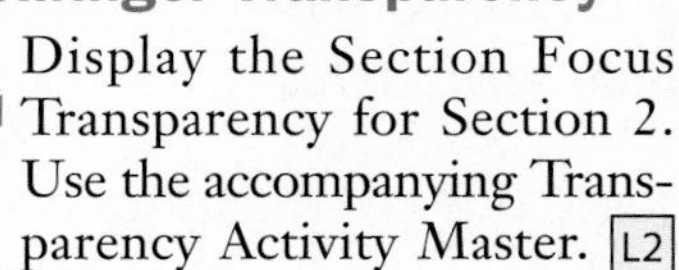

Bellringer Transparency

Display the Section Focus Transparency for Section 2. Use the accompanying Transparency Activity Master. L2 ELL

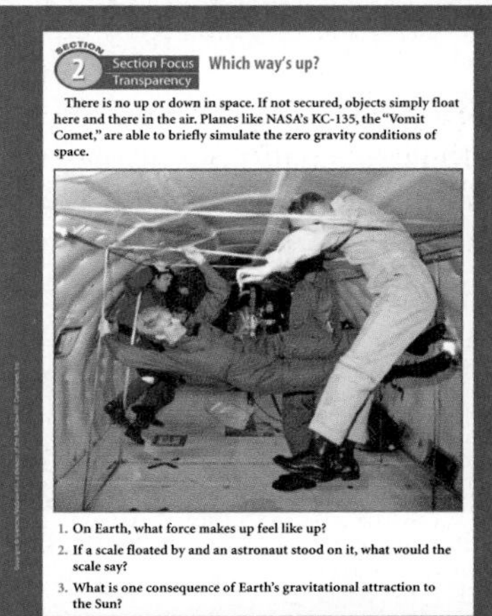

There is no up or down in space. If not secured, objects simply float here and there in the air. Planes like NASA's KC-135, the "Vomit Comet," are able to briefly simulate the zero gravity conditions of space.

1. On Earth, what force makes up feel like up?
2. If a scale floated by and an astronaut stood on it, what would the scale say?
3. What is one consequence of Earth's gravitational attraction to the Sun?

Tie to Prior Knowledge

Ask students to describe how a football must be thrown for a long pass. Explain that in this section they will learn how the force of gravity affects the motion of projectiles such as a football.

Section Assessment Planner

Portfolio
Curriculum Connection, p. 79
Reteach, p. 82

Performance Assessment
Try at Home MiniLAB, p. 81
Skill Builder Activities, p. 82
See page 96 for more options.

Content Assessment
Section, p. 82
Challenge, p. 82
Chapter, pp. 96–97

Resource Manager

Chapter Resources Booklet
Transparency Activity, p. 45
Directed Reading for Content Mastery, p. 20

2 Teach

The Law of Gravitation

Caption Answer

Figure 12 Gravitational attraction keeps the stars from flying off into space.

Gravitational Acceleration

Text Question Answers

The bowling ball and the marble would hit the water at the same time. They have the same acceleration, so their velocities are the same as they fall.

Quick Demo

Make a small hole in the bottom of a foam plastic cup. While holding the hole shut, fill the cup with water. Hold the cup as high as you can, and drop it into a bucket placed directly beneath it on the floor. Have students observe that no water ran from the cup as it fell because both the cup and water were in free fall. L2 ELL IS **Visual-Spatial**

Fun Fact

Newton's law of gravitation states that the gravitational attraction between two objects is $F = \frac{G(m_1m_2)}{d^2}$, where d is the distance between the two objects and G is the universal gravitational constant. In 1797, Henry Cavendish showed that the value of G is 6.67×10^{-11} $m^3/kg \cdot s^2$.

Figure 12
Gravity is at work in the formation of galaxies like this spiral galaxy. *How does gravity influence the shape of this galaxy?*

The Range of Gravity You might think that a star in another galaxy is too far away to exert a gravitational force on you, but you'd be wrong. Despite the distance between two objects, the gravitational attraction between them never disappears. Gravity is a long-range force. All the stars in a galaxy, such as the one shown in **Figure 12,** exert a gravitational force on each other. These forces help give the galaxy its shape. In fact, a gravitational force exists between all matter in the universe. Gravity is the force that gives the universe its structure.

SCIENCE Online

Data Update Visit the Glencoe Science Web site at **science.glencoe.com** for data comparing the gravitational accelerartions objects experienced on different planets. Discuss with your class why the gravitational acceleration is greater on some planets than on others.

Gravitational Acceleration

Near Earth's surface, the gravitational attraction of Earth causes all falling objects to have an acceleration of 9.8 m/s^2. Recall Newton's second law—the net force, mass, and acceleration are related according to the following formula:

$$F = ma$$

According to the second law, the force on an object that has an acceleration of 9.8 m/s^2 is as follows:

$$F = m \times 9.8 \text{ m/s}^2$$

This is the force of gravity on an object near Earth's surface. This force depends only on the object's mass. A force has a direction associated with it. The force of Earth's gravity is always downward.

When an object is influenced only by the force of gravity, it is said to be in free fall. Suppose you were to drop a bowling ball and a marble from a bridge at the same time. Which would hit the water below first? Would it be because the bowling ball has more mass?

Science Journal

Lower Gravity Ask students to imagine that, during the next few days, the gravitational force of Earth gradually becomes half of what it is now. Have students write in their Science Journals about the sort of changes that would take place. Students might describe slow-moving waterfalls, soaring tennis balls, or a thinner atmosphere. L2 IS **Linguistic**

Internet Addresses

Explore the Glencoe Science Web site at **science.glencoe.com** to find out more about topics in this section.

76 CHAPTER 3 Forces

Inertia and Gravity It's true that the force of gravity would be greater on the bowling ball because of its larger mass. But the larger mass also means the bowling ball has more inertia, so more force is needed to change its velocity. The gravitational force on the marble is smaller because it has less mass, but the inertia of the marble is smaller, too, so less force is needed to change its velocity. As a result, all objects fall with the same acceleration, no matter how large or small their mass is. Although the blue ball in **Figure 13** is more massive than the green one, they fall at the same rate.

Weight

If you are standing on the floor of your classroom, your acceleration is zero. According to Newton's second law, if your acceleration is zero, the net force on you must be zero. Does this mean Earth's gravitational attraction for you has disappeared? No. Earth still pulls you downward, but the floor also exerts an upward force that keeps you from falling.

Whether you are standing, jumping, or falling, Earth exerts a gravitational force on you. The gravitational force exerted on an object is called the object's **weight.** The symbol *W* stands for the weight. You can find gravitational force, or weight, using Newton's second law, as follows:

$$\text{gravitational force} = \text{mass} \times \begin{bmatrix}\text{acceleration} \\ \text{due to gravity}\end{bmatrix}$$

Because the gravitational force is the same as the weight and the acceleration due to gravity on Earth is 9.8 m/s^2, this equation can be written as follows:

$$W = m \times 9.8\ \text{m/s}^2$$

In other words, a mass of 1 kg weighs 1 kg $\times$ 9.8 m/s^2, or 9.8 N. You could calculate your weight in newtons if you knew your mass. For example, a person with a mass of 50 kg would have a weight of 490 N. On Earth, a cassette tape weighs about 0.5 N, a backpack full of books weighs about 40 N, and a jumbo jet weighs about 3.4 million N.

Reading Check *How much does a person with a mass of 70 kg weigh on Earth?*

Losing Weight What would happen to your weight if you were far from Earth? Recall that the gravitational attraction between two objects becomes weaker as they move farther apart. So if you were to travel away from Earth, your weight would decrease.

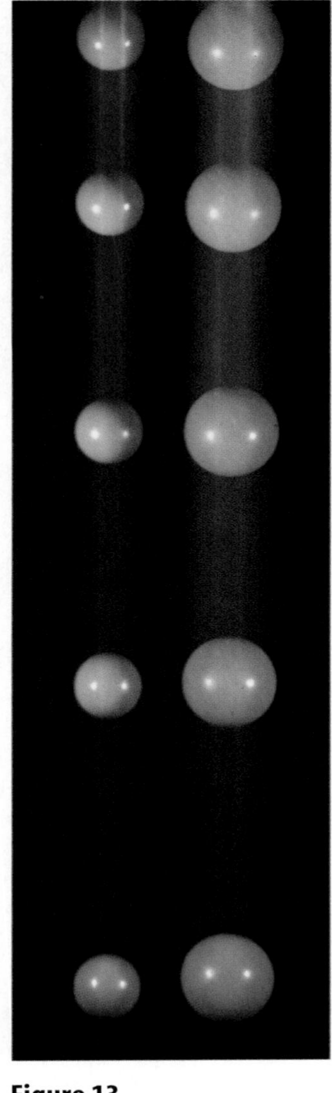

Figure 13
High-speed photography shows that two balls of different masses fall at the same rate.

Quick Demo

Bring to class a golf ball and a table tennis ball. Have volunteers determine the mass of each ball and write it on the board. Then drop both from the same height for the class to observe. L2 **Visual-Spatial**

Weight

Misconceptions

People in Europe and other places that use SI units usually express their weight in kilograms. This is technically incorrect, as the kilogram is a unit of mass, not weight.

Activity

Have students calculate their mass in kilograms, then use their answers to calculate their weight in newtons. Make sure students know that there are 2.2 pounds in one kilogram. L2 **Logical-Mathematical**

Answer 686 N

Resource Manager

Chapter Resources Booklet
Transparency Activity, pp. 47–48

Life Science Critical Thinking/ Problem Solving, p. 14

Earth Science Critical Thinking/ Problem Solving, p. 5

Inclusion Strategies

Gifted Ask students to identify the force that opposes gravity and enables objects to float in water. The buoyant force of the water acts on an object with a force equal to the weight of the water displaced by the object. If the buoyant force is greater than the force of gravity pulling on the object, the object will float. This occurs when the object is less dense than water. L3 **Logical-Mathematical**

Discussion

Why is it that an object has mass in and of itself but must interact with another object in order to have weight? Mass is a measure of the amount of matter an object contains. Weight is a measure of gravitational force, which only occurs between objects.
L2 LS **Logical-Mathematical**

Activity

To help students become familiar with the relationship between an object's mass and its weight on Earth, have groups of students work together to make a table listing the weights and masses of various objects. Students first should use a balance to determine the object's mass in kilograms, and then calculate its weight by multiplying the mass by 9.8 m/s^2. L2 ELL LS **Kinesthetic**

Answer Weight equals mass times acceleration due to gravity.

Weightlessness and Free Fall

Quick Demo

One way to overcome weightlessness in space is to build a large, doughnut-shaped ring called a torus. If the torus is set spinning in outer space, the centripetal force causes objects to feel as if they are being pushed toward the outer wall, simulating gravity. Demonstrate this to students by swirling a marble in a shallow pan. L3 LS **Visual-Spatial**

Figure 14
The astronaut was able to take longer steps on the Moon because the gravitational attraction on him there is less than on Earth.

Weight and Mass Weight and mass are not the same. Weight is a force, and mass is a measure of the amount of matter an object contains. However, weight and mass are related. The greater an object's mass is, the stronger the gravitational force between the object and Earth. So, the more mass an object has, the more it will weigh.

The weight of an object usually means the gravitational force between the object and Earth. But objects can have different weights, depending on what's pulling on them. For example, a person weighing about 480 N on Earth would weigh only about 80 N on the Moon. If you suddenly found yourself on another planet, what effect would this have on you? Because mass remains constant, the astronaut in **Figure 14** had the same inertia on the Moon as he had on Earth. How did this affect the way he moved? **Table 1** shows how an object's weight depends upon the object's location.

Reading Check *How are weight and mass related?*

Weightlessness and Free Fall

You've probably seen pictures of astronauts and equipment floating inside the space shuttle. Any item that is not fastened down in the shuttle floats throughout the cabin. They are said to be experiencing the sensation of weightlessness.

To be nearly weightless, the astronauts would have to be very far from Earth to be significantly free from the effects of its gravity. Even while orbiting 400 km above Earth, the force of gravity pulling on the shuttle is still about 90 percent as strong as it is at Earth's surface. So, they are not really weightless.

Table 1 Weight Comparison Table

Weight on Earth (N)	Weight on Other Bodies in the Solar System (N)				
	Moon	Venus	Mars	Jupiter	Saturn
75	12.5	67.5	28.5	190.5	87.0
100	16.7	90.0	38.0	254.0	116.0
125	20.8	112.5	47.5	317.5	145.0
150	25.0	135.0	57.0	381.0	174.0
2,000	333.3	1,800.0	760.0	5,080.0	2,320.0

Teacher FYI

Near Earth's surface, acceleration due to gravity (g) is approximately 9.8 m/s^2. This value differs only a fraction of a percent even at Mount Everest. The value of g decreases as you travel away from Earth's surface. At a height of 1,000 km, it is about 3/4 the value at Earth's surface.

Active Reading

Reflective Journal In this strategy, students record things they learned from and responses to activities. Have students divide sheets of paper into several columns. Have them record their thoughts under headings such as "What I did," "What I learned," "Questions I have," "What surprised me," and "Overall response." Have students write a Reflective Journal entry for the activities about gravity and weight in this section.

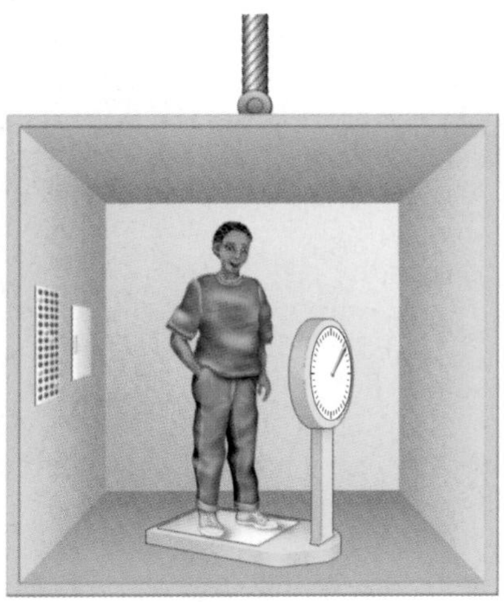

A When the elevator is stationary, the scale shows the boy's weight.

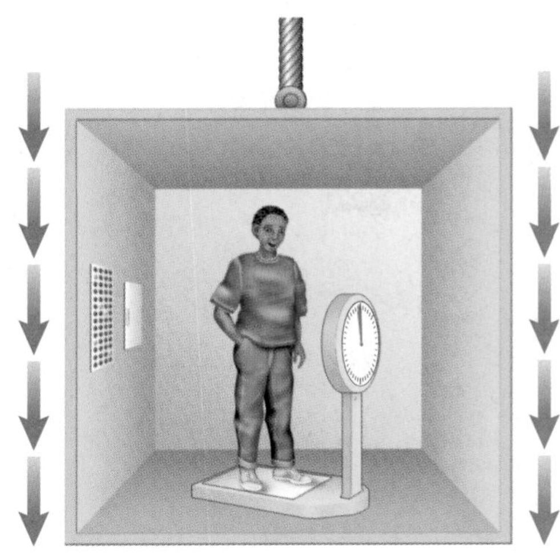

B If the elevator were falling, the scale would show a smaller weight. *Why do you sometimes feel almost weightless in an elevator?*

Figure 15
When two objects are falling at the same rate, they exert less force on each other.

Floating in Space So what does it mean to say that something is weightless in orbit? Think about how you measure your weight. When you stand on a scale, as in **Figure 15A,** you are at rest and the net force on you is zero. So the scale supports you and balances your weight by exerting an upward force. The dial on a scale shows the upward force exerted by the scale, which is your weight. Now suppose you stand on a scale in an elevator that is falling, as in **Figure 15B.** If you and the scale are both in free fall, then you no longer push down on the scale at all. The scale dial would say you have zero weight, even though the force of gravity on you hasn't changed.

Everything in the orbiting space shuttle is falling downward toward Earth at the same rate, in the same way you and the scale were falling in the elevator. Because all objects in the shuttle have no force supporting them, they seem to be floating.

Projectile Motion

If you've tossed a ball to someone, you probably noticed that thrown objects don't always travel in straight lines. They tend to curve downward. That's why quarterbacks, dart players, and archers aim above their targets. Anything that's thrown or shot through the air is called a projectile. Because of Earth's gravitational pull and their own inertia, projectiles follow a curved path. This is because they have horizontal and vertical velocities.

Earth Science INTEGRATION

Apart from simply keeping your feet on the ground, gravity is important for life on Earth for other reasons, too. Because Earth has a sufficient gravitational pull, for example, it can hold around it the oxygen/nitrogen atmosphere necessary for sustaining life. Research other ways in which gravity has played a role in the formation and look of Earth.

Caption Answer

Figure 15 You and the elevator are falling so you aren't pushing down on the elevator as much as when it is stationary.

Activity

Have students hang an object from a spring scale to determine its weight. Next, have them compare this with the force recorded on the scale when the object is moved rapidly up and rapidly down. Have students explain the results. The force recorded on the spring scale is greater than the object's weight when the object is pulled up because the net force on the object is the force of gravity plus the force of the student pulling up. The force recorded on the spring scale is less than the object's weight when the object is moving down because both the object and the spring scale are falling. L3 LS **Logical-Mathematical**

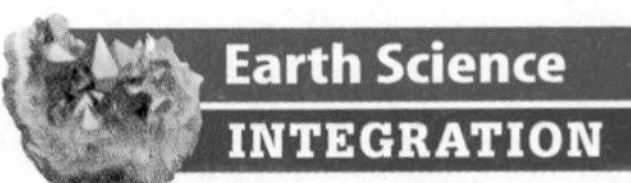

Earth Science INTEGRATION

Possible areas for research include current theories about the formation of Earth and the forces that give mountains and oceans their forms. Point out that gravity pulls all Earth's matter toward the center, giving Earth its round shape.

Projectile Motion

Use Science Words

Word Origins Ask students to find the origin of the word *projectile.* The word *projectile* comes from the Latin prefix *pro-,* which means "forward," and the Latin verb *jacere,* which means "to throw." L2 LS **Linguistic**

Resource Manager 

Chapter Resources Booklet
Enrichment, p. 31

Cultural Diversity, p. 25

Curriculum Connection

Health Pictures of objects floating around in a spaceship make weightlessness look like fun, but weightlessness can have an adverse effect on the health of astronauts. Have students research this problem and use a word processor to prepare a report about some effects. Some problems astronauts experience are loss of bone density and muscle atrophy. L2 LS **Linguistic** P

Activity

Have students work in groups of three to demonstrate the property shown in **Figure 17.** One student should throw a ball outward horizontally, the second student should drop an identical ball from the same height, and the third student should tell them when to begin and should observe the balls' impacts. Suggest that students change positions and repeat the process so each student has a chance to perform all three roles. L2 ELL LS **Kinesthetic**

Extension

Have students work in small groups to design experiments that show how the horizontal distance traveled by a projectile is affected by its initial angle. Be sure students realize that the force applied to the projectile must be kept constant. They might create a slingshot by stretching a rubber band between two nails. This will propel an object with a constant force. If this is constructed on a board, the initial angle can be varied by raising or lowering the end of the board. Students should plot the results of their experiment on a graph showing angle versus horizontal distance. Caution students to be careful not to aim the projectiles at one another or at easily breakable objects. L3
LS **Logical-Mathematical**

Text Question Answer

The ball would go farther before hitting the ground.

Figure 16
The pitcher gives the ball a horizontal motion. Gravity, however, is pulling the ball down. The combination of these two motions causes the ball to move in a curved path.

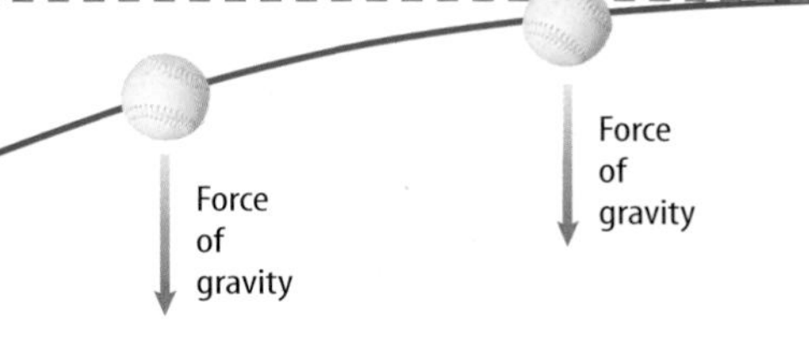

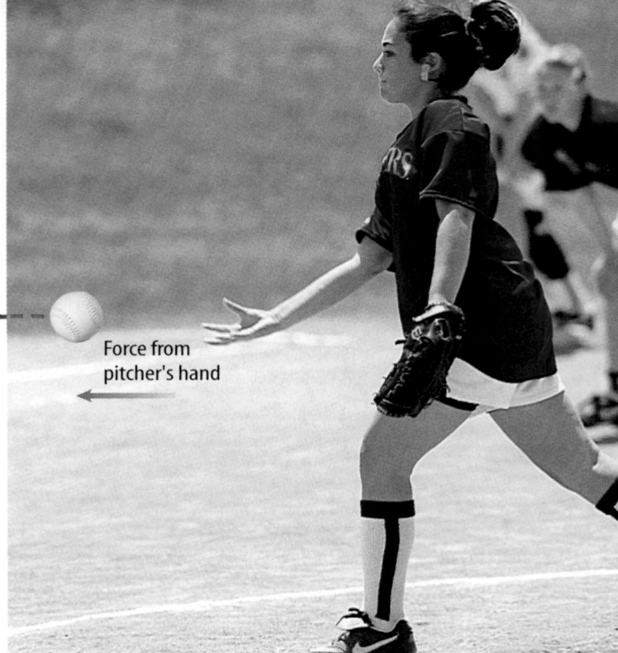

Figure 17
Time photography shows that each ball has the same acceleration downward, whether it's thrown or dropped.

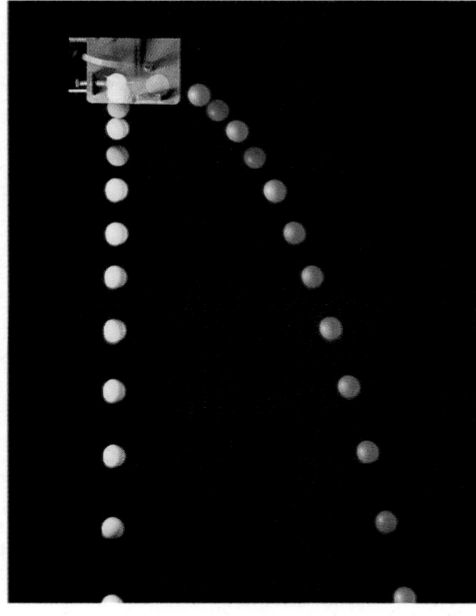

Horizontal and Vertical Motions When you throw a ball, like the pitcher in **Figure 16,** the force from your hand makes the ball move forward. It gives the ball horizontal motion or motion parallel to Earth's surface. After you let go of the ball, no other force accelerates it forward, so its horizontal velocity is constant, if you ignore air resistance.

However, when you let go of the ball, something else happens. Gravity can now pull it downward, giving it vertical motion, or motion perpendicular to Earth's surface. Now the ball has constant horizontal velocity but increasing vertical velocity. Gravity exerts an unbalanced force on the ball, changing the direction of its path from only forward to forward and downward. The result of these two motions is that the ball appears to travel in a curve, even though its horizontal and vertical motions are completely independent of each other.

If you were to throw a ball as hard as you could from shoulder height in a perfectly horizontal direction, will it take longer to reach the ground than if you dropped a ball from the same height? Surprisingly, it won't. A thrown ball and one dropped will hit the ground at the same time. If you have a hard time believing this, **Figure 17** might help. The two balls have the same acceleration due to gravity—9.8 m/s^2 downward. How would a thrown ball's path look on the Moon?

Resource Manager

Chapter Resources Booklet
MiniLAB, p. 4
Reinforcement, p. 28

Visual Learning

Figure 17 Point out that the spacing of the balls with respect to horizontal is identical. This shows that the balls have the same vertical acceleration. Ask students what the result would be if one of the balls had greater mass. The result would be the same. L2 LS **Visual-Spatial**

Centripetal Force

Recall that acceleration is a rate of change in velocity caused by a change in speed, direction, or both. Now, look at the path the ball follows as it travels through the pipe maze in **Figure 18.** The ball may accelerate in the straight sections of the pipe maze if it speeds up or slows down. However, when the ball enters a curve, even if its speed does not change, it is accelerating because its direction is changing. When the ball goes around a curve, the change in the direction of the velocity is toward the center of the curve. Acceleration toward the center of a curved or circular path is called **centripetal acceleration.** The word *centripetal* means to "move toward the center."

For the ball to be accelerating toward the center, an unbalanced force, called **centripetal force,** must be acting on it in a direction toward the center. The centripetal force acting on the ball running through the maze is exerted by the outside wall pushing against it and keeping it from going straight.

When a car rounds a sharp curve on a highway, the centripetal force is the friction between the tires and the road surface. If the road is icy or wet and the tires lose their grip, the centripetal force might not be enough to overcome the car's inertia. Then the car would keep moving in a straight line in the direction that it was traveling at the spot where it lost traction. Anything that moves in a circle, such as the cars in this amusement park ride in **Figure 19,** is doing so because a centripetal force is accelerating it toward the center.

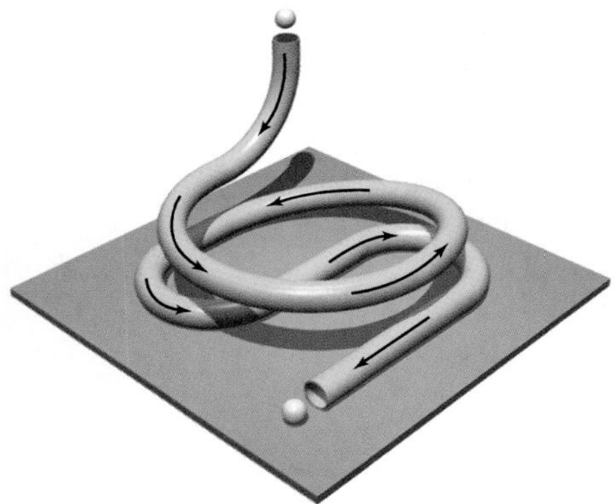

Figure 18
When the ball moves through the circular portions of the maze, it is accelerating because its velocity is changing. *Would you expect the ball to be traveling faster or slower if more curves were in the maze?*

Figure 19
Centripetal force keeps these riders moving in a circle.

Observing Centripetal Force

Procedure
1. Fill a **bucket** that has a secure handle with **water** to a level of about 3 cm.
2. Go outside and stand several meters away from any person or object.
3. Swing the bucket quickly in a circle. It should be upside down for just an instant.

Analysis
1. Why didn't you get wet?
2. What force did the bottom of the bucket exert on the water when you swung the bucket above you?
3. What would happen if you swung the bucket slowly?

Centripetal Force

Use Science Words

Word Usage Have students explain how the definition of the word *centripetal* describes the force exerted on a ball on a string that you swing around your head. *Centripetal* means "moving toward the center." The tension in the string pulls the ball toward the center. L2 IS **Linguistic**

Caption Answer

Figure 18 slower

Extension

In order to orbit Earth and not fall into it, an object needs to be moving with at least a minimum velocity. Have students find out what that velocity is. 28,150 km/h (17,500 mi/h) L3 IS **Logical-Mathematical**

Purpose to observe the effect of centripetal force

Materials bucket, water

Teaching Strategies Advise students to first try the activity with just a couple of spoonfuls of water if they are fearful of getting wet.

Analysis
1. Inertia kept the water in the bucket.
2. centripetal force
3. The water would fall out of the bucket.

Process Show students a picture of a satellite in orbit. Ask them to explain how centripetal force acts on the satellite. The centripetal force of Earth's gravity pulls the satellite toward Earth. Use **PASC,** p. 89.

Inclusion Strategies

Learning Disabled Make sure students realize that as an object moves in a circle, its change in direction is toward the center of the circle. Students can show this by moving a brick along the edge of a large circle. Every time they move the brick, they must twist it a bit so it fits on the circle. This twist shows the change in direction.

3 Assess

Reteach

Have students measure the distance that either of the two balls shown in **Figure 13** fell between each flash. They can use a bar graph to show distance fallen versus flash number. Ask them to explain how this graph supports the idea that the balls are accelerating downward. The ball falls farther between each succeeding two flashes. L2 ELL IS **Visual-Spatial** P

Challenge

If a bullet is dropped at the same time that a gun using an identical bullet is fired horizontally, the bullets will hit the ground at the same time. If the gun is fired at an upward angle, the bullets will not hit the ground at the same time. Explain this. When the gun is fired horizontally, both bullets start with zero vertical speed. When the gun is fired at an upward angle, it has an initial upward velocity, so the bullet will hit the ground later than the dropped bullet. L2 IS **Logical-Mathematical**

Assessment

Oral Ask students to explain why the astronauts and everything else in the space shuttle behave as if they were weightless. Everything in the shuttle is in free fall as the shuttle orbits the Earth. Use **Performance Assessment in the Science Classroom,** p. 89.

Figure 20
The Moon would move in a straight line except that Earth's gravity keeps pulling it toward Earth. This gives the Moon its circular orbit.

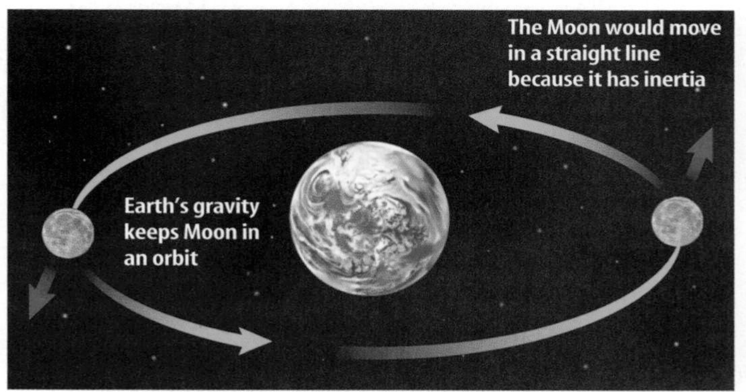

The Moon Is Falling A satellite is anything that moves around another body in a generally circular path called an orbit. Earth and the other planets are satellites because they orbit the Sun. The Moon is a natural satellite of Earth. The *International Space Station* is another of Earth's satellites. Because it was made here on Earth, it is an artificial satellite. Why do satellites move the way they do?

Imagine whirling an object tied to a string above your head. The string exerts a centripetal force on the object that keeps it moving in a circular path. In the same way, Earth's gravity exerts a centripetal force on the Moon that keeps it moving in a circular orbit, as shown in **Figure 20.**

Section  Assessment

1. What is gravity, and how does the size of two objects and the distance between them affect the gravitational force?
2. How is an object's mass different from its weight? Do objects always weigh the same? Explain.
3. What two motions contribute to the path of a projectile?
4. How do the planets stay in orbit around the Sun?
5. **Think Critically** The exit ramps on highways are sometimes sharp curves. Why are the exit ramps constructed at an angle, or banked?

Skill Builder Activities

6. **Using a Word Processor** Use a computer to make a table showing important characteristics of projectile motion, circular motion, and free fall. Table headings should include: *Kind of Motion, Shape of Path,* and *Laws or Forces Involved.* You can add other headings. **For more help, refer to the Technology Skill Handbook.**
7. **Communicating** Write a paragraph describing a situation in which you experienced something close to free fall or a feeling of weightlessness. Think about amusement park rides, elevators, athletic events, or even movie scenes. **For more help, refer to the Science Skill Handbook.**

Answers to Section Assessment

1. Gravity is a force exerted by every object on every other object. It increases as the mass of one or both objects increases, and it decreases as the distance between the objects increases.
2. Mass is a measure of the amount of matter an object contains. Weight is a measure of the force of gravity on an object. Weight changes if the gravitational force changes.
3. vertical motion and horizontal motion
4. The Sun's gravitational force combines with the planets' straight-line motion to keep them in orbit.
5. A banked road provides a centripetal force that helps keep cars from sliding off.
6. Check students' work.
7. Paragraphs might describe a roller coaster ride or going over a steep hill on a bicycle.

SECTION 3

The Third Law of Motion

Newton's Third Law

Push against a wall and what happens? If the wall is sturdy enough, usually nothing happens. Now, think about what would happen if you pushed against a wall while wearing roller skates. You would go rolling backwards, of course. The harder you pushed, the more you would roll backwards. Your action on the wall produced a reaction—movement backwards. This is a demonstration of Newton's third law of motion.

Newton's third law of motion describes action-reaction pairs this way: When one object exerts a force on a second object, the second one exerts a force on the first that is equal in size and opposite in direction. Another way to say this is "to every action force there is an equal and opposite reaction force."

Action and Reaction When a force is applied in nature, a reaction to it occurs. When you jump on a trampoline, for example, you exert a downward force on the trampoline. The trampoline then exerts an equal force upward, sending you high into the air.

Action and reaction forces are acting on the two skaters in **Figure 21.** The male skater is pulling upward on the female skater, while the female skater is pulling downward on the male skater. The two forces are equal, but in opposite directions.

As You Read

***What* You'll Learn**

- **Identify** when action and reaction forces occur.
- **Calculate** momentum.
- **Demonstrate** how momentum is conserved.

Vocabulary
Newton's third law of motion
momentum

***Why* It's Important**

From walking across the floor to a rocket speeding through space, all motion occurs because every action has a reaction.

Figure 21
According to Newton's third law of motion, the two skaters exert forces on each other. The two forces are equal, but in opposite directions.

SECTION

The Third Law of Motion

1 Motivate

Bellringer Transparency

Display the Section Focus Transparency for Section 3. Use the accompanying Transparency Activity Master. L2 ELL

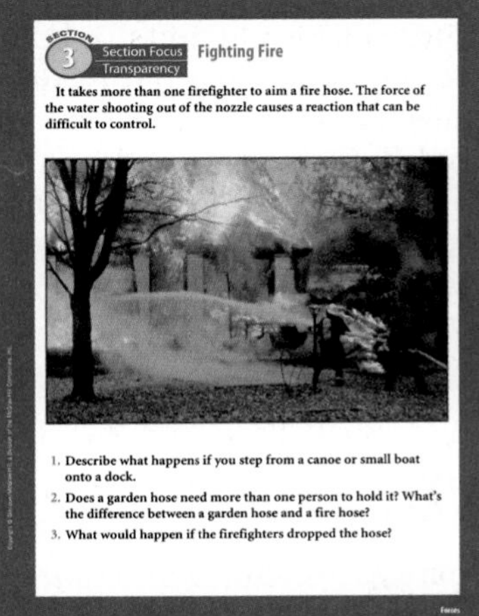

Section Focus Transparency 3 — Fighting Fire

It takes more than one firefighter to aim a fire hose. The force of the water shooting out of the nozzle causes a reaction that can be difficult to control.

1. Describe what happens if you step from a canoe or small boat onto a dock.
2. Does a garden hose need more than one person to hold it? What's the difference between a garden hose and a fire hose?
3. What would happen if the firefighters dropped the hose?

Tie to Prior Knowledge

Have students recall the motion of an untied, inflated balloon and the motion of a rocket. Tell them that the motions of the balloon and the rocket are governed by Newton's third law of motion. In this section they will learn more about Newton's third law.

Resource Manager

Chapter Resources Booklet
Transparency Activity, p. 46
Directed Reading for Content Mastery, pp. 21, 22

Section Assessment Planner

PORTFOLIO
Extension, p. 86

PERFORMANCE ASSESSMENT
Skill Builder Activities, p. 88
See page 96 for more options

CONTENT ASSESSMENT
Section, p. 88
Challenge, p. 88
Chapter, pp. 96–97

2 Teach

Newton's Third Law

Text Question Answer
The force of the tide pushes against the swimmer.

Health INTEGRATION

Some scientists think that living in outer space may arrest the spread of arthritis and be beneficial because stress on bones is much smaller than on Earth. Medical research is being carried out in outer space that could lead to a better understanding of diseases such as sicle cell anemia.

Reading Check

Answer The swimmer pushes against the water, and the water pushes back.

Visual Learning

Figure 22 Review with students the forces that move the car shown here. Draw the car on the board, and indicate the particles of air inside the rocket engine. Make sure students understand that the action force is the force of the rocket engine pushing the air and the reaction force is the force of the air against the rocket engine. L2 LS **Visual-Spatial**

Quick Demo

Demonstrate the propulsion of rockets using a toy water-powered rocket. Students will observe how water rushing out of the bottom of the rocket causes the rocket to rise. L2 LS **Visual-Spatial**

Health INTEGRATION

Astronauts who stay in outer space for extended periods of time may develop health problems. Their muscles, for example, may begin to weaken because they don't have to exert as much force to get the same reaction as they do on Earth. A branch of medicine called space medicine deals with the possible health problems that astronauts may experience. Research some other health risks that are involved in going into outer space. Do trips into outer space have any positive health benefits?

How You Move If action and reaction forces are equal, you might wonder how some things ever happen. For example, how does a swimmer move through the water in a pool if each time she pushes on the water, the water pushes back on her? An important point to remember when dealing with Newton's third law is that *action-reaction forces are acting on different objects.* Thus, even though the forces are equal, they are not balanced because they act on different objects. In the case of the swimmer, as she "acts" on the water, the "reaction" of the water pushes her forward. Thus, a net force, or unbalanced force, acts on her so a change in her motion occurs. Why is it harder for a swimmer to swim against a tide?

Reading Check *How is a swimmer able to move in the water?*

Rocket Propulsion Suppose you were standing on skates holding a softball. You exert a force on the softball when you throw the softball. According to Newton's third law, the softball exerts a force on you. This force pushes you in the direction opposite the softball's motion. Rockets use the same principle to move even in the vacuum of outer space. In the rocket engine, burning fuel produces hot gases. The rocket engine exerts a force on these gases and causes them to escape out the back of the rocket. By Newton's third law, the gases exert a force on the rocket and push it forward. The car in **Figure 22** uses rocket engines to propel it forward. **Figure 23** shows how rockets move through space.

Figure 22
If more gas is thrown from the rocket, or expelled at a greater velocity, the rocket engine will push the car faster.

84 CHAPTER 3 Forces

Science Journal

Newton's Third Law Have students use Newton's third law to describe the similarities between a person walking on a sidewalk and a fish swimming in the ocean. A person exerts a force on the sidewalk, and the sidewalk pushes back on the person, moving the person forward. A fish pushes on water, and the reaction force of the water on the fish propels the fish forward. L1 LS **Linguistic**

Cultural Diversity

And the Rockets' Red Glare Centuries ago, the Chinese invented gunpowder. Although it was first used during celebrations, gunpowder was quickly adapted for war purposes. By the fourteenth century, Chinese armies were using it in rockets. When the gunpowder ignited, it expelled superheated gas, which propelled the rockets forward.

NATIONAL GEOGRAPHIC **VISUALIZING ROCKET MOTION**

Figure 23

On the afternoon of July 16, 1969, *Apollo 11* lifted off from Cape Kennedy, Florida, bound for the Moon. Eight days later, the spacecraft returned to Earth, splashing down safely in the Pacific Ocean. The forces that carried the spacecraft to the Moon and back are governed by Newton's laws of motion.

▲ As *Apollo* rises, it burns fuel and ejects its rocket booster engines. This decreases its mass, and helps *Apollo* move faster. This is Newton's second law in action: As mass decreases, acceleration can increase.

◀ *Apollo 11* roars toward the Moon. At launch, a rocket's engines must produce enough force and acceleration to overcome the pull of Earth's gravity. A rocket's liftoff is an illustration of Newton's third law: For every action there is an equal and opposite reaction.

▶ The lunar module uses other engines to slow down and ease into a soft touchdown on the Moon. A day later, the same engines lift the lunar module again into outer space.

▲ After the lunar module returns to *Apollo,* the rocket fires its engines to set it into motion toward Earth. The rocket then shuts off its engines, moving according to Newton's first law. As it nears Earth, the rocket accelerates at an increasing rate because of Earth's gravity.

Visualizing Rocket Motion

Have students examine the pictures and read the captions. Then ask the following questions.

- **When Apollo 11 was launched, what were the equal and opposite forces?** The thrust from the rocket engines pushed on the rocket and the rocket pushed back.
- **As Apollo ejected its spent rocket booster, what equation described the relationship between mass and acceleration?** $F = ma$
- **As the rocket returns to Earth, why is the rocket able to shut off its engines?** The rocket will continue to move toward Earth after the engines are turned off because of inertia.

Activity

Have the students write a poem about the Apollo 11 mission and Newton's laws of motion. L2 LS **Linguistics.**

Extension

Challenge the students to research the Apollo 13 mission. Students should find out how the astronauts used Newton's law to safely return to Earth after a potentially life-threatening disaster occurred on board. Have the students make multimedia presentations to the class about what they learned.

Resource Manager 

Chapter Resources Booklet

Lab Activity, pp. 13–16

Enrichment, p. 32

Home and Community Involvement, p. 49

Finding Planets with Newton's Laws

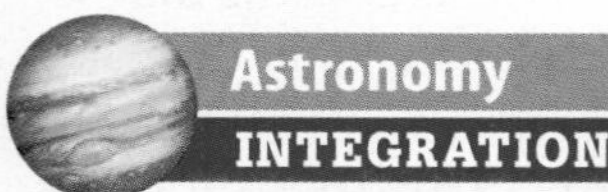

Pluto was discovered in 1930, having been predicted by deviations in the orbit of Neptune. Scientists soon determined that Pluto's mass alone wasn't large enough to cause these deviations. We now know that these deviations are caused by Pluto in conjunction with a number of other objects called Plutinos that are similar in size to Pluto.

Momentum

Discussion

Momentum is important to football players, who use it to stop players on the other team. **What can a football player do to increase his momentum?** run faster or increase his mass

Extension

Newton actually worded his second law to state that force equals the change in momentum divided by the change in time, $F = \frac{p}{t}$. Explain how this is equivalent to the definition given in the text, F = ma. $p = mv; F = \frac{p}{t} = \frac{mv}{t} = m(\frac{v}{t}); \frac{v}{t} = a$, so F = ma L3

LS Logical-Mathematical P

Figure 24
The location of the planet Neptune was correctly predicted using Newton's laws.

Finding Planets with Newton's Laws

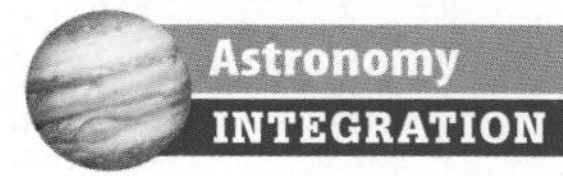

The gravitational force between Earth and the Sun causes Earth to orbit the Sun. However, Earth's orbit is also affected by the gravitational pulls of the other planets in the solar system. Each planet pulls on Earth with a force determined by its mass and its distance from Earth. In the same way, the orbit of every planet in the solar system is affected by the gravitational pulls from all the other planets.

In the 1840s the most distant planet known was Uranus. The astronomers Urbain Jean Leverrier and John Adams noticed that its orbit couldn't be explained by the forces exerted by the Sun and the other known planets. They concluded that there must be another planet affecting the orbit of Uranus that hadn't been discovered. Using Newton's laws of motion, they calculated where it must be located. Astronomers found the planet, shown in **Figure 24,** where Leverrier and Adams said it would be, and named it Neptune.

Momentum

You know that a slow-moving bicycle is easier to stop than a fast-moving one. Also, a slow-moving bicycle is easier to stop than a car traveling at the same speed. Increasing either the speed or mass of an object makes it harder to stop.

A moving object has a property called momentum that is related to how much force is needed to change its motion. The momentum of an object is the product of its mass and velocity. Momentum is given the symbol p and can be calculated with this equation

$$\text{momentum} = \text{mass} \times \text{velocity}$$
$$p = m \times v$$

The unit for momentum is kg m/s. Notice that momentum has a direction because velocity has a direction.

The two cars trucks in **Figure 24** might have the same velocity, but the bigger truck has more momentum because of its greater mass. An archer's arrow can have a large momentum because of its high velocity, even though its mass is small. A walking elephant may have a low velocity, but, because of its large mass, it has a large momentum at almost any speed.

Teacher FYI

The momentum transferred to an object depends on two factors: the size of the net force acting on the object and the time interval during which the net force acts. Many people pushing for a short time and a few people pushing for a longer time will cause equal changes in an object's momentum.

Resource Manager

Chapter Resources Booklet
Activity Worksheet, pp. 5–6, 7–8
Reinforcement, p. 29

Performance Assessment in the Science Classroom, p. 36

Force and Changing Momentum If you catch a fast-moving baseball, your hand might sting, even if you use a baseball glove. Your hand stings because the baseball exerted a force on your hand when it came to a stop, and its momentum changed.

Recall that acceleration is the difference between the initial and final velocity, divided by the time. Also, from Newton's second law, the net force on an object equals its mass times its acceleration. By combining these two relationships, Newton's second law can be written in this way:

$$F = m\,(v_f - v_i)/t$$

In this equation mv_f is the final momentum and mv_i is the initial momentum. So the equation says that the net force exerted on an object can be calculated by dividing its change in momentum by the time over which the change occurs. When you catch a ball, your hand exerts a force on the ball that stops it. Here the final velocity is zero. The force depends on the speed of the ball, and how long it takes to come to a stop.

Law of Conservation of Momentum The momentum of an object doesn't change unless its mass, velocity, or both change. Momentum, however, can be transferred from one object to another. Consider the game of pool shown in **Figure 26.** Before the game starts, all the balls are motionless. The total momentum of the balls is, therefore, zero. No momentum can exist because none of the balls has a velocity.

What happens when the cue ball hits the group of balls that are motionless? The cue ball slows down and the rest of the balls begin to move. If you measured the total momentum of all the balls before and after the collision, you would find it was the same. The momentum the group of balls gained is equal to the momentum that the cue ball lost. If no other forces act on the balls, their total momentum is conserved—it isn't lost or created. This is the law of conservatoin of momentum.

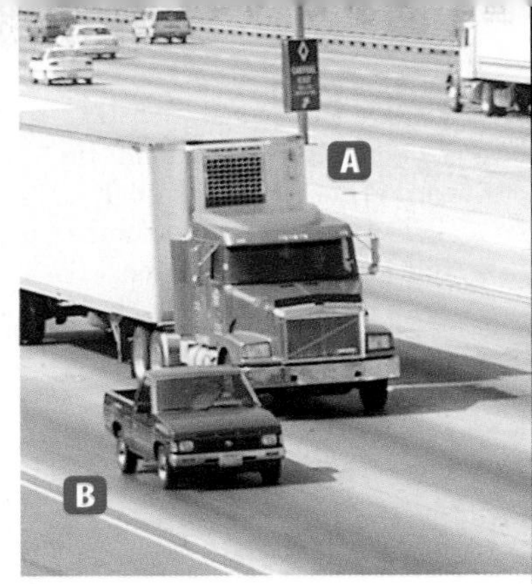

Figure 25
Truck A has more momentum than the smaller truck B because it has more mass.
How could the smaller truck have a momentum greater than the big truck?

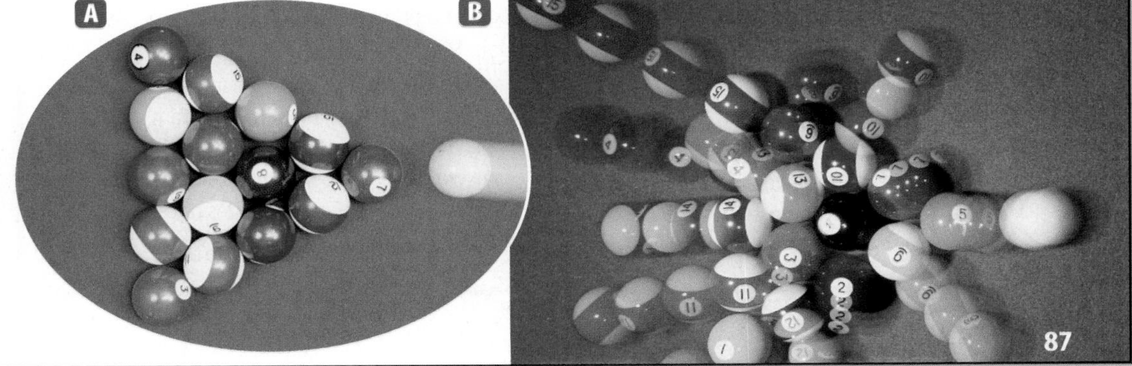

Figure 26
Transferring momentum
A At the start, the cue ball has all the momentum. The other balls have no momentum because they are not moving.
B When the cue ball strikes the other balls, it transfers some of its momentum to them.

87

Caption Answer

Figure 25 if its velocity were greater

Quick Demo

Demonstrate conservation of momentum using two identical marbles. Use superglue to attach a string to one marble. Fasten the string to a ring stand so the marble hangs just above the tabletop. Place the second marble on the table next to the first marble. Pull back the first marble, making sure the string is taut, and release it toward the other marble. The momentum of the first marble is transferred to the second. L2

LS **Visual-Spatial**

Use an Analogy

Conservation of momentum can be compared with the use of money to buy and sell things. People may exchange money back and forth with each other, but unless more is minted by the government, the amount of money remains constant.

Discussion

In a circus, a 50-kg clown is shot out of a cannon at 20 m/s. **What is the recoil speed of the cannon if it has a mass of 250 kg?** Because momentum is conserved, the momentum of the cannon will be equal to the momentum of the clown. The momentum of the clown is 50 kg × 20 m/s = 1,000 kg·m/s. For the cannon, therefore, mv = 1,000 kg m/s = (250 kg)v. Solving for v, we find that v = (1,000 kg·m/s) ÷ 250 kg = 4 m/s. L2 LS **Logical-Mathematical**

Visual Learning

Figure 26 Point out that the balls scatter left and right as they are deflected by the cue ball. Tell students that momentum is conserved separately in each direction. The sum of the forward velocities of the balls equals the cue ball's initial velocity. The sum of the left velocities is equal to the sum of the right velocities. **Why do the balls eventually slow and stop?** friction

Caption Answer

Figure 27 They will move away from each other with the same speed.

Visual Learning

Figure 27 Tell students that to apply conservation of momentum you must define the system you are referring to. Have them define the system shown in **Figure 27.** the table and the pucks. L2 LS **Visual-Spatial**

3 Assess

Reteach

Ask students to draw and explain action/reaction force arrows for a box sitting on the ground and for a person running. L2 LS **Visual-Spatial**

Challenge

Suppose you drop a rock to the ground and it stays, without bouncing, in the spot it hits. **What happens to the momentum of the rock?** By conservation of momentum, the momentum must be transferred to Earth. However, because Earth is so large, the change in its velocity is negligible. L3 LS **Logical-Mathematical**

Assessment

Process Provide students with photographs of various types of activities or collisions. Have them describe how momentum is conserved in each situation. Use **Performance Assessment in the Science Classroom,** p. 89.

Figure 27
A When the first puck hits the second puck from behind, it gives the second puck momentum in the same direction.
B If the pucks are speeding toward each other with the same speed, the total momentum is zero. *How will they move after they collide?*

A

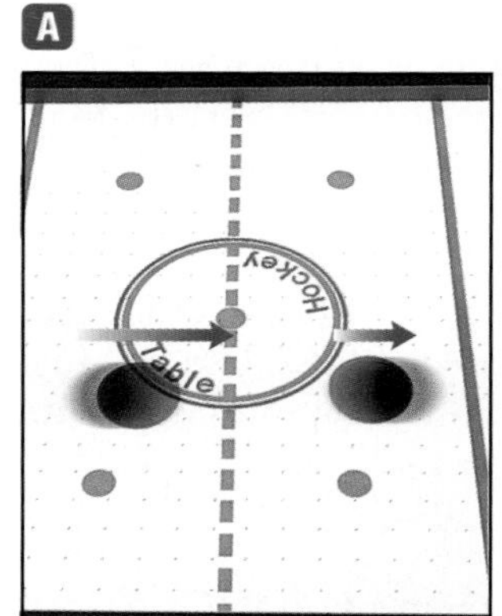

B

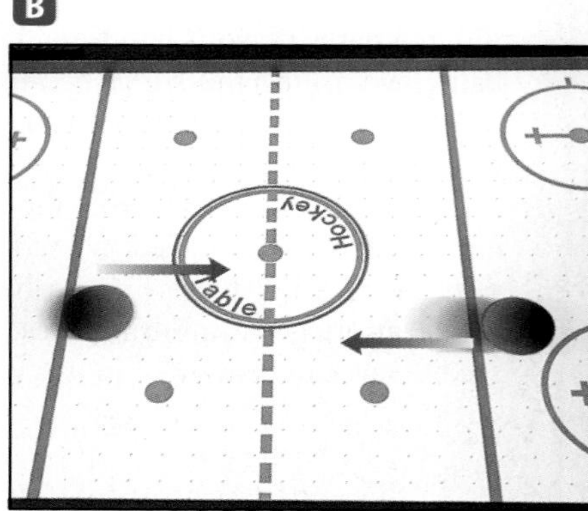

When Objects Collide Look at the pictures of the air-hockey table in **Figure 27.** Suppose one of the pucks was moving along the table in one direction and another struck it from behind. The puck that was struck would continue to move in the same direction but more quickly. The second puck has given it additional momentum in the same direction. What if the two pucks had the same mass and were moving toward each other with the same speed? Each would have the same momentum, but in opposite directions. So the total momentum would be zero. After the pucks collided, they would reverse direction, and move with the same speed. The total momentum would again be zero.

Section 3 Assessment

1. What is Newton's third law of motion?
2. How can a rocket move through outer space where no matter exists for it to push on?
3. Compare the momentums of a 50-kg dolphin swimming 16.4 m/s and a 6,300-kg elephant walking 0.11 m/s.
4. When two pool balls collide, what happens to the momentums of each?
5. **Think Critically** Some ballet directors assign larger dancers to perform slow, graceful steps and smaller dancers to perform quick movements. Does this plan make sense? Why?

Skill Builder Activities

6. **Predicting** You are a crane operator using a wrecking ball to demolish an old building. You can choose to use a 100-kg ball or a 150-kg ball. Which ball would knock the walls down faster? Which ball would be easier for you to control? Explain. **For more help, refer to the** Science Skill Handbook.
7. **Communicating** In your Science Journal, use the law of conservation of momentum to explain the results of a particular collision you have witnessed. For example, think of games, sports, or amusement park rides or contests. **For more help, refer to the** Science Skill Handbook.

Answers to Section Assessment

1. To every action force, there is an equal and opposite reaction force.
2. The rocket ejects gas molecules. These push against the rocket.
3. The dolphin's momentum is $p = (50\ kg)(16.4\ m/s) = 820\ kg{\cdot}m/s$. The elephant's momentum is $p = (6{,}300\ kg)(0.11\ m/s) = 693\ kg{\cdot}m/s$.
4. The two balls exchange momentum.
5. Yes; it takes less force for a person with less mass to move quickly than for a person with more mass to do so.
6. The ball with greater mass would knock the walls down faster. The ball with less mass would be easier to control.
7. Possible answer: A tennis racquet transfers momentum to a ball, changing the ball's velocity and direction. When two ice hockey players collide, they bounce off each other, changing their speeds and directions.

Activity

Measuring the Effects of Air Resistance

If you dropped a bowling ball and a feather from the same height on the Moon, they would both hit the surface at the same time. All objects dropped on Earth fall to the ground with the same acceleration. But on Earth, a bowling ball and feather will not hit the ground at the same time. Air resistance slows the feather down.

What You'll Investigate

How does air resistance affect the gravitational acceleration of falling objects?

Materials

paper (4 sheets of equal size)
scissors
meterstick
stopwatch
masking tape

Goals

- **Measure** the effect of air resistance on sheets of paper with different shapes.
- **Design** and create a shape from a piece of paper that maximizes air resistance.

Safety Precautions 

Procedure:

1. Copy the data table above in your Science Journal, or create it on a computer.
2. Measure a height of 2.5 m on the wall and mark the height with a piece of masking tape.
3. Have one group member drop the flat sheet of paper from the 2.5 m mark. Use the stopwatch to time how long it takes for the paper to reach the ground. Record your time in your data table.
4. Crumple a sheet of paper into a loose ball and repeat step # 3.

Effects of Air Resistance

Paper Type	Time
Flat paper	
Loosely crumpled paper	Answers
Tightly crumpled paper	will
Your paper design	vary.

5. Crumple a sheet of paper into a tight ball and repeat step # 3.
6. Use scissors to shape a piece of paper so that it will fall slowly. You may cut, tear, or fold your paper into any design you choose.

Conclude and Apply

1. **Compare** the falling times of the different sheets of paper.
2. **Infer** the relationship between the falling time of each sheet of paper and the effect their shapes had on their accelerations.
3. **Explain** why the different shaped papers fell at different speeds.
4. **Explain** how your design maximized the effect of air resistance on your paper's gravitational acceleration.
5. **Infer** why a sky diver will fall in a spread eagle position before opening her parachute.

Communicating Your Data

Compare your paper design with the designs created by your classmates. As a class, compile a list of characteristics that increase air resistance.

ACTIVITY 89

Activity

Purpose Students will observe the effect of air resistance on the gravitational acceleration of different shaped sheets of paper.

L2 LS **Kinesthetic**

Process Skills measuring, recognizing cause and effect, formulating models, comparing, inferring

Time Requirement 30 minutes

Safety Precautions Caution students to be careful when standing on chairs.

Teaching Strategies

- Stage a contest to determine which design maximizes the effect of air resistance.
- Have students practice timing the falling paper before entering data in their tables.

Conclude and Apply

1. The tightly crumpled paper will fall fastest; the flat paper will fall slowest.
2. The time is inversely proportional to the effect on gravitational acceleration.
3. Shapes with greater exposed surface areas will create more air resistance and fall more slowly.
4. Answers will vary.
5. A spread eagle position increases the surface area of the diver allowing more air resistance to slow her fall.

Assessment

Process Show students several photographs of falling skydivers and ask them to analyze the sky diver's body positions and infer the order of their velocities. Use **Performance Assessment in the Science Classroom,** p. 89.

Communicating Your Data

Encourage students to electronically represent their design using the appropriate software.

Activity

BENCH TESTED

What You'll Investigate

Purpose

Students will observe the effects of mass and velocity on the momentum of rolling objects. L2 LS **Kinesthetic**

Process Skills

observing, measuring, comparing, using numbers, using space/time relationship, sequencing, recognizing cause and effect, inferring

Time Required

one class period

Alternate Materials

A foam rubber ball, golf ball, or hockey ball could replace the tennis ball and racquetball.

Safety Precautions

Caution students never to throw the balls during the activity and to roll the baseball only when other students are clear of the ball's path.

Procedure

Teaching Strategies

Have students practice rolling the balls at different speeds and rolling the balls into the rubber ball. Clear away floor space in your room or take students outside to provide enough space for each group.

Activity

The Momentum of Colliding Objects

Many scientists believe dinosaurs became extinct 65 million years ago when a comet slammed into Earth. The comet's diameter was probably no more than 10 km. Earth's diameter is more than 12,700 km. How could an object that size change Earth's climate enough to cause the extinction of animals that had dominated life on Earth for 140 million years? The comet could because it was traveling at a velocity of 253,000 km/h, and had a huge amount of momentum. The combination of an object's velocity and mass will determine how much force it can exert. Explore how mass and velocity determines an object's momentum during this activity.

What You'll Investigate

How do the mass and velocity of a moving object affect its momentum?

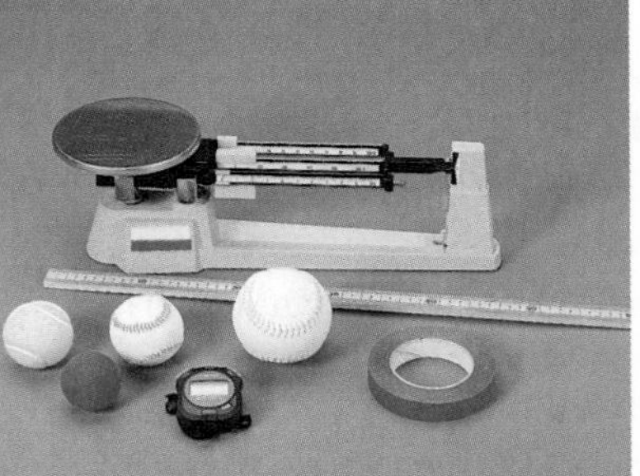

Materials

meterstick
large, light-weight rubber ball
racquetball
tennis ball
baseball
stopwatch
masking tape
balance

Goals

- **Observe and calculate** the momentum of different balls.
- **Measure and compare** the actions of the balls' different momentums based on the reactions they cause.

Safety Precautions 

Momentum of Colliding Balls

Action	Time	Velocity	Mass	Momentum	Distance ball moved rubber ball
Racquetball rolled slowly			0.04		
Racquetball rolled quickly			0.04		
Tennis ball rolled slowly	Answers will vary.	Answers will vary.	0.06	Answers will vary.	Answers will vary.
Tennis ball rolled quickly			0.06		
Baseball rolled slowly			0.14		
Baseball rolled quickly			0.14		

90

Active Reading

Synthesis Journal In this strategy, students reflect on a project, a paper, or a performance task and plan for personal application. Have each student divide a sheet of paper in three sections and record "What I did," "What I learned," and "How I can use it." Have students write a Synthesis Journal related to this activity.

Procedure

1. Copy the data table on the previous page in your Science Journal.
2. Use the balance to measure the mass of the racquetball, tennis ball, and baseball. Record these masses in your data table.
3. Use your meterstick to measure a 2 m distance on the floor. Mark this distance with two pieces of masking tape.
4. Place the rubber ball on one piece of tape. Starting from the other piece of tape, slowly roll the racquetball the 2 m distance so that it hits the rubber ball squarely.
5. Use a stopwatch to time how long it takes the racquetball to roll the 2 m distance and hit the rubber ball. Record this time in your data table.
6. Measure the distance the racquetball moved the softball. Record this distance in your data table.
7. Repeat steps 4-6, rolling the racquetball quickly and then slowly.
8. Repeat steps 4-6, rolling the tennis ball quickly and then slowly.
9. Repeat steps 4-6, rolling the baseball quickly and then slowly.

Conclude and Apply

1. Using the formula $p = mv$, **calculate** the momentum for each type of ball and action. Record your calculations in the data table.
2. **Compare** the momentums you calculated. Which action had the greatest momentum? Which had the smallest momentum?
3. **Infer** the relationship between the momentum of each ball and the distance the rubber ball was moved.
4. **Explain** why the baseball will have a greater momentum than the tennis ball even if both are traveling with an equal velocity.
5. **Explain** how you observed Newton's third law of motion occurring during this activity.

Communicating Your Data

Stage a classroom momentum contest to determine who can produce the greatest momentum by rolling a tennis ball a distance of 10 m. Post the names of the winners and the momentums they achieved on the science room bulletin board.

Tie to Prior Knowledge

Students will be aware that more massive moving objects and objects traveling with greater speeds will produce more force.

Expected Outcome

The high velocity baseball will have the greatest momentum, and the slow velocity racquetball will have the least momentum.

Conclude and Apply

1. Check students' work.
2. The high velocity baseball had the greatest momentum, and the slow velocity racquetball had the least momentum.
3. The more momentum, the more the rubber ball was moved.
4. The baseball has more mass.
5. The third law says that for every action there is an equal and opposite reaction. In this case, each time the tennis ball, baseball, or racketball hit the rubber ball, it pushed on the rubber ball and the rubber ball pushed back with an equal and opposite force.

Error Analysis

Ask student groups to compare their data with those of other groups and list possible explanations for differences. Ask students to identify possible sources of measurement errors or procedural errors.

Assessment

Oral Ask students if it is possible for an object to have a negative value for momentum. No; neither mass nor velocity can have a negative value. Use **Performance Assessment in the Science Classroom,** p. 89.

Communicating Your Data

Students may want to decorate their tennis ball entries to resemble racehorses or Nascar racing cars.

Science Stats

Content Background

The relationship between distance, speed, and time, d = vt, can be used to explain the Sun's movement from New York to Los Angeles and Nolan Ryan's pitch.

Newton's first and second laws of motion apply in all of the features. Newton's first law is known as the law of inertia. This law can be used to explain why the ocean waves destroyed the breakwaters, why it takes so much force to accelerate the massive space shuttle to escape velocity, and why it requires so much force to stop a huge 747 jumbo jet. In general, it requires force to change the movement of an object.

Discussion

Where does the force come from that accelerated the baseball? the pitcher's arm

Tell students that 10,000 kg is the total mass of water that covers each square meter of shoreline over the entire winter. Remind students that 1 g of water occupies 1cm^3 of space. **If all this water covered the shoreline at one time, how high would this wave be?** 10 m

Activity

Have students make a model of a breakfront. Students should calculate how much mass the water flowing at a certain rate will have as it strikes the breakfront and use the information to design a breakfront that will hold up to the force of the water.

Science Stats

Moving and Forcing

Did you know...

Nolan Ryan

...The fastest baseball pitch on record was thrown at 162.3 km/h. This superfast pitch was thrown by the California Angels' Nolan Ryan during a major league game in 1974.

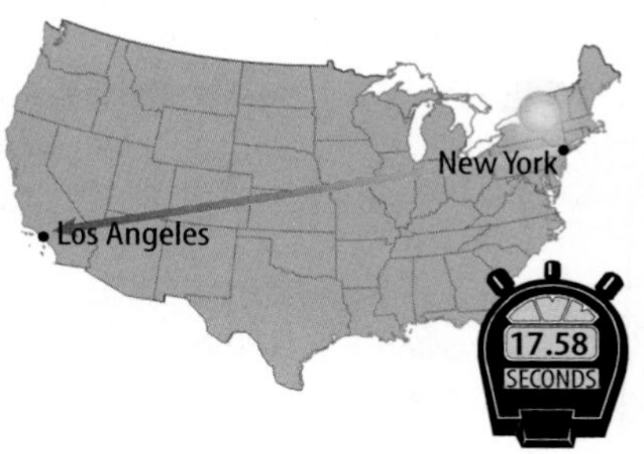

...The Sun moves in a circular path around the center of the galaxy at about 250 km/s. At this rate, the Sun could make a trip from New York to Los Angeles in about 18 s.

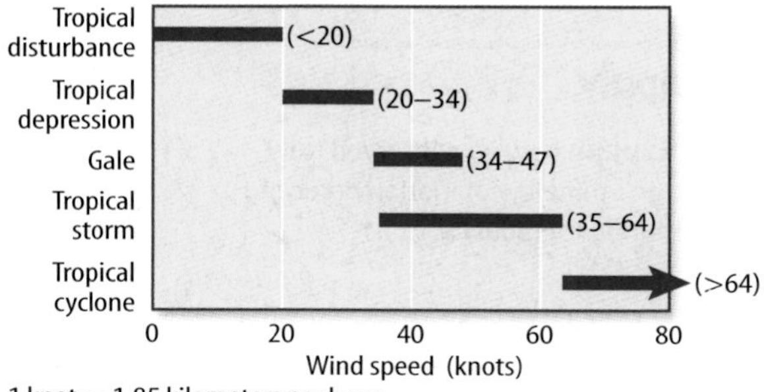

...Ocean waves are powerful. The Atlantic hurls an average of 10,000 kg of water per square meter at the shore in winter. During one storm, the waves ripped away a 1,496,880-kg steel-and-concrete portion of a breakwater. During a later storm, its 2,358,720-kg replacement met with the same fate.

SCIENCE Online
Internet Addresses

Explore the Glencoe Science Web site at **science.glencoe.com** to find out more about topics in this feature.

Space shuttle

Connecting To Math

...The force exerted by the space shuttle's solid rocket booster engines when lifting off from Earth equals the force exerted by the engines of thirty-five jumbo jets. To escape Earth's gravity, a spacecraft must reach a speed through the atmosphere of over 40,320 km/h. This is about 455 times faster than a typical highway speed limit of 88.5 km/h.

747 jumbo jet

...The force needed to stop a jumbo jet is equal to the frictional force applied by 1 million automobile brakes. Even so, the airplane has to travel a distance of almost 1 km before it comes to a complete stop.

Do the Math

1. What is the distance from New York to Los Angeles?
2. How far does the Sun travel in 5 min?
3. The following is a list of the masses of several types of balls: volleyball, 280 g; tennis ball, 58.5 g; baseball, 155.9 g; football, 425 g; basketball, 650 g; and softball, 198.4 g. Make a bar graph that compares the masses of these balls.

Go Further

Write Newton's first, second, and third laws of motion on three separate sheets of paper. Under each, write a paragraph or make a sketch that shows that law at work in some common situation.

Connecting To Math

Do the Math

Teaching Strategies

- Review the distance formula to assist students with question one.
- Remind students to look at the units in question two.
- Discuss which units should be used to mark the y-axis on the bar graph for the third question.
- Provide graph paper to assist the students with question three.

Answers

1. 250 km/s × 18 × = 4,500 km
2. 250 km/s × 5 min × 60 s/min = 75,000 km
3. Check students' graphs.

Go Further

The students may need to review Newton's laws of motion in the text to remind them what each law states. This may help them find common examples.

Visual Learning

The momentum of an object is the product of an object's mass in kg and velocity in m/s. The mass and velocity of an object are used to determine how much force is needed to change the object's motion. **How much momentum did Nolan Ryan's baseball have? Use the mass of the baseball given in Do the Math.** momentum = (0.1559 kg)(162,300 m/h) (1h/3,600s) = 7.0 kg · m/s

SCIENCE Online

Internet Addresses

Explore the Glencoe Science Web site at **science.glencoe.com** to find out more about topics in this feature.

Chapter 3 Study Guide

Reviewing Main Ideas

Preview

Students can answer the questions in their Science Journals. Discuss the answers as you go through the chapter. **LS Linguistic**

Review

Students can write their answers, then compare them with those of other students. **LS Interpersonal**

Reteach

Students can look at the illustrations and describe details that support the main ideas of the chapter. **LS Visual-Spatial**

Answers to Chapter Review

Section 1

2. static friction

Section 2

2. the force of the string on the ball

Section 3

2. If all the objects are moving with about the same speed, the object with the largest mass, the bus, has the greatest momentum.

Chapter 3 Study Guide

Reviewing Main Ideas

Section 1 Newton's Second Law

1. Newton's second law of motion states that a net force causes an object to accelerate in the direction of the net force, with an acceleration equal to the net force divided by the mass.
2. Friction is caused by the microwelds that develop between the microscopic bumps on two surfaces. The three types of friction are static, sliding, and rolling. *What type of friction is at work in this picture?*

3. All objects fall to Earth with the same acceleration. Air resistance exerts an upward force on objects falling through the atmosphere.

Section 2 Gravity

1. Gravity is the force of attraction that exists between any two objects having mass. The size of the gravitational force is determined by the mass of the objects and their distance from each other.
2. Projectiles have a horizontal and a vertical motion that makes them travel in a curved path. Circular motion is caused by a centripetal, or center-seeking force. *What's the center-seeking force at work in the photo?*

3. Weight is the measure of the gravitational force exerted on an object by Earth. Weight is expressed in newtons, N. You use the following equation to caculate weight:

$$W = m \times 9.8 \text{ m/s}^2$$

m is the mass of the object.

Section 3 The Third Law of Motion

1. Newton's third law of motion states that for every action there is an equal and opposite reaction.
2. Momentum is a property that an object has because of its mass and velocity. Momentum can be calculated by the equation $p = mv$. *Which object in this photo has the greatest momentum?*

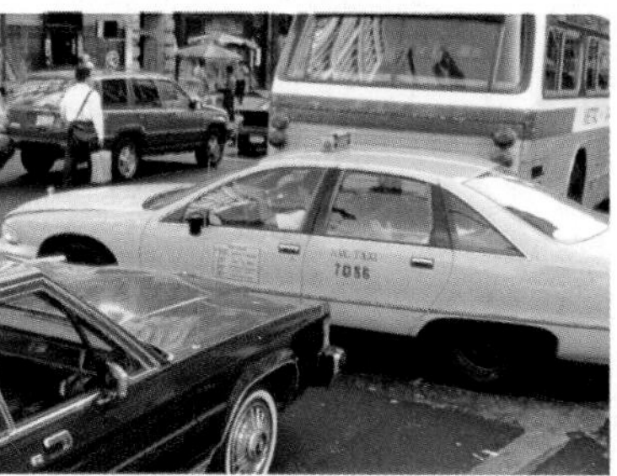

3. When two objects collide, momentum is conserved. Some of the momentum from one object is transferred to the other.

After You Read

Foldables Reading & Study Skills

Use the information on your Foldable to compare and contrast the types of friction. Write similarities and differences on the back of your Foldable.

After You Read

Foldables Reading & Study Skills

After students have read the chapter and completed the Foldable described in Before You Read, have them do the activity on the student page.

Dinah Zike

Visualizing Main Ideas

Complete the following concept map on forces.

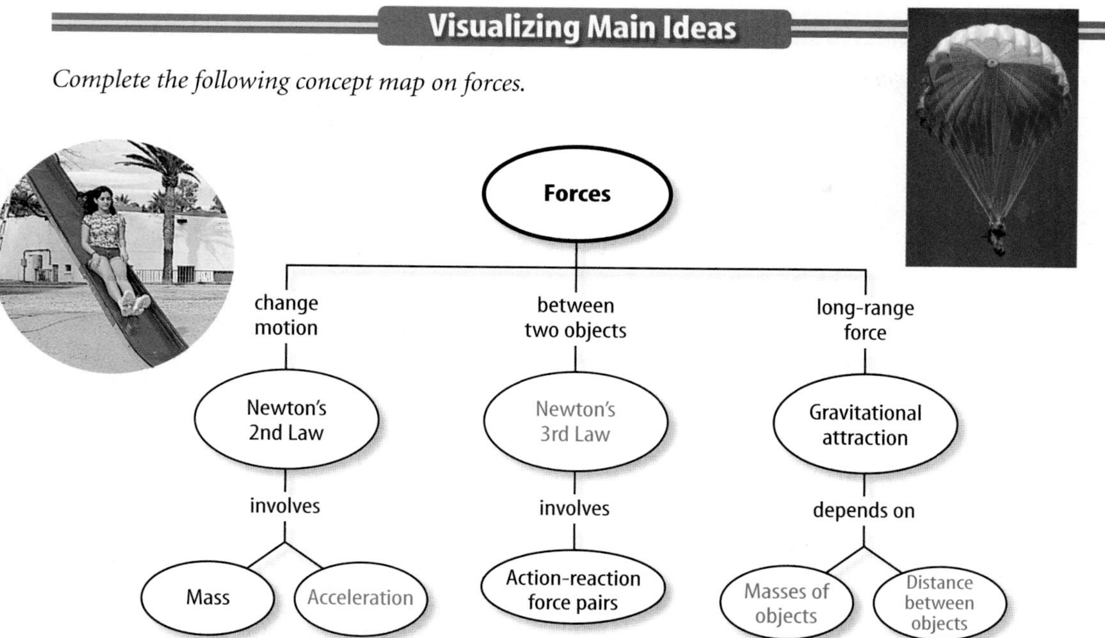

Vocabulary Review

Vocabulary Words

a. centripetal acceleration
b. centripetal force
c. friction
d. law of gravitation
e. momentum
f. Newton's second law of motion
g. Newton's third law of motion
h. weight

Study Tip

Make a note of anything you can't understand so that you'll remember to ask your teacher about it.

Using Vocabulary

Using the vocabulary words list, replace the underlined words with the correct words.

1. <u>The microwelds that form between the surfaces of two objects</u> sometimes make objects hard to move.
2. The Moon's <u>acceleration toward the center of its circular path</u> is caused by Earth's gravity.
3. <u>For every action, there is an equal and opposite reaction</u>.
4. The <u>force of gravity</u> exerted on an object is different on different planets.
5. The <u>combined mass and velocity</u> of the runaway train made it dangerous.
6. It takes only a little <u>pull toward the center</u> to keep a yo-yo spinning.

Chapter 3 Study Guide

Visualizing Main Ideas

See student page.

Vocabulary Review

Using Vocabulary

1. friction
2. centripetal acceleration
3. Newton's third law of motion
4. weight
5. momentum
6. centripetal force

Chapter 3 Assessment

Checking Concepts

1. C
2. D
3. D
4. C
5. C
6. A
7. B
8. C
9. A
10. C

Thinking Critically

11. 637 N
12. The chains help provide traction on ice and snow by increasing the amount of friction between the tires and the ice and snow.
13. Answers could include bolting down items, using Velcro fasteners, or keeping them tethered to the astronauts.
14. The action force is the wheels pushing against the street or sidewalk. The reaction force is the Earth (street or sidewalk) pushing back.
15. The elephant has much more momentum than the baseball because of its large size. The jumbo jet has no momentum because it's standing still.

Chapter 3 Assessment

Checking Concepts

1. What will happen to an object when a net force acts on it?
A) fall
B) stop
C) accelerate
D) go in a circle

2. Which is the expression for Newton's second law?
A) $F = 1/2ma^2$
B) $F = 2\ ma$
C) $p = mv$
D) $a = F/m$

3. What is the force of gravity on an object known as?
A) centripetal force
B) friction
C) momentum
D) weight

4. Which of the following is NOT a type of friction?
A) static
B) sliding
C) center-seeking
D) rolling

5. What's true about an object falling toward Earth?
A) It falls faster the heavier it is.
B) It falls faster the lighter it is.
C) Earth's gravity pulls on it, and it pulls on Earth.
D) It has no weight.

6. Why do projectiles follow a curved path?
A) They have a horizontal and a vertical motion.
B) They have centripetal force.
C) They have momentum.
D) They have inertia.

7. What is the product of mass and velocity known as?
A) gravity
B) momentum
C) friction
D) weight

8. Which body exerts the weakest gravitational force on Earth?
A) the Moon
B) Mars
C) Pluto
D) Venus

9. When a leaf falls, what force opposes gravity?
A) air resistance
B) terminal velocity
C) friction
D) weight

10. In circular motion, the centripetal force is in what direction?
A) forward
B) backwards
C) toward the center
D) toward the side

Thinking Critically

11. What is the weight on Earth of a person with a mass of 65 kg?

12. Some people put chains on their tires in the winter. Why?

13. List some ways an astronaut could keep her supplies from floating away from her while she is in orbit around Earth.

14. As you in-line skate around the block, what action and reaction forces keep you moving?

15. Which one of the following would have the most momentum—a charging elephant, a jumbo jet sitting on the runway, or a baseball traveling at 100 km/h? Explain.

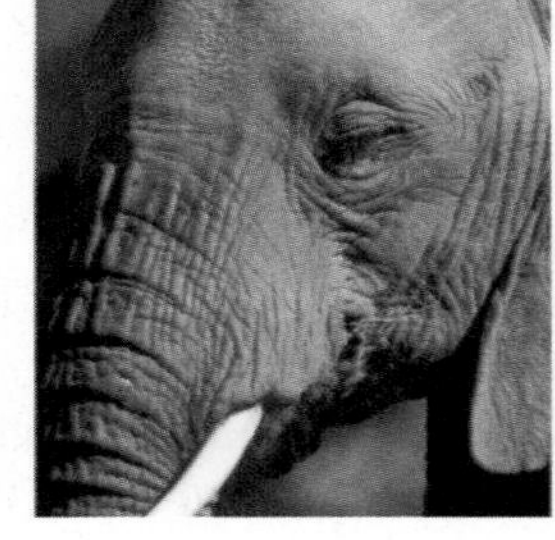

Developing Skills

16. Classifying Classify the following as examples of static, sliding, or rolling friction: sledding down a hill, sitting in a chair, pushing a grocery cart, standing on a steep slope, and rowing a boat.

Chapter Assessment Planner

Portfolio Encourage students to place in their portfolios one or two items of what they consider to be their best work. Examples include:
- Science Journal, p. 73
- Curriculum Connection, p. 79
- Reteach, p. 82
- Extension, p. 86

Performance Additional performance assessments, Performance Task Assessment Lists, and rubrics for evaluating these activities can be found in Glencoe's **Performance Assessment in the Science Classroom.**

17. Drawing Conclusions You drop a feather from the top of a ladder. Partway down, the feather begins to drift slowly toward the ground. What happened?

18. Recognizing Cause and Effect Suppose you stand on a scale next to a sink. What happens to the reading on the scale if you push down on the sink?

19. Interpreting Data The following table contains data about four objects that were dropped to Earth at the same time.

a. Which object fell fastest? Slowest?
b. Which object has the greatest weight?
c. Is air resistance stronger on A or B?
d. Why are the times different?

Time of Fall for Dropped Objects

Object	Mass (g)	Time of Fall (s)
A	5.0	2.0
B	5.0	1.0
C	30.0	0.5
D	35.0	1.5

Performance Assessment

20. Poem Write a poem about gravity. Include the terms *gravity, free fall, air resistance,* and *terminal velocity.*

21. Oral Presentation Prepare a presentation to explain Newton's third law of motion to a group of first grade students.

Technology

Go to the Glencoe Science Web site at **science.glencoe.com** or use the **Glencoe Science CD-ROM** for additional chapter assessment.

THE PRINCETON REVIEW Test Practice

Tiffany learned that the acceleration of a free-falling body is 9.8 m/s^2. She wanted to find out what speed a sky diver reaches after several seconds. Her calculations are shown in the table below.

Speed of a Falling Sky Diver

Time (s)	Speed (m/s)
0	0
1	9.8
2	19
3	29.4
4	39.2
5	?

Study the table and answer the following questions.

1. According to these data, about how fast will the speed of a falling sky diver be after 5 s?
A) 39.8 m/s
B) 44.2 m/s
C) 49.0 m/s
D) 54.0 m/s

2. Which of these causes falling sky divers to accelerate?
E) gravity
G) rotation of Earth on its axis
F) inertia
G) rotation of Earth on its axis
H) the tilt of Earth on its axis

3. If Tiffany extended her table, what would the sky diver's speed be after 14s?
A) 107.8 m/s
B) 78.4 m/s
C) 147.0 m/s
D) 137.2 m/s

THE PRINCETON REVIEW Test Practice

The Test-Taking Tip was written by The Princeton Review, the nation's leader in test preparation.

1. C
2. F
3. D

Developing Skills

16. sliding, static, rolling, static, sliding
17. The feather accelerated towards the ground until the air resistance on it canceled the force of gravity. Once the feather reached its terminal velocity, it drifted toward the ground at a constant speed.
18. If you push down on the sink the reading on the scale will decrease.
19. a. object C; object A; b. object D; c. object A; d. The times are different because air resisitance acted differently on the four objects.

Performance Assessment

20. Students can share their poems with the class. Use **PASC,** p. 151
21. Encourage students to work in groups on their presentations. Use **PASC,** p. 143

Assessment Resources

Reproducible Masters

Chapter Resources Booklet
Chapter Review, pp. 37–38
Chapter Tests, pp. 39–42
Assessment Transparency Activity, p. 49

Glencoe Science Web site
Interactive Tutor
Chapter Quizzess

Glencoe Technology
Assessment Transparency
Interactive CD-ROM Chapter Quizzes
ExamView Pro Test Bank
Vocabulary PuzzleMaker Software
MindJogger Videoquiz DVD/VHS

Section/Objectives	Standards		Activities/Features
	National	State/Local	
Chapter Opener	See p. 37T for a Key to Standards.		**Explore Activity:** Model how a light bulb works, p. 99 **Before You Read,** p. 99
Section 1 The Nature of Energy 3 sessions 2 blocks 1. **Distinguish** between kinetic and potential energy. 2. **Recognize** different ways that energy can be stored.	National Content Standards: UCP3, A2, B3 (5–8), B5, B6 (9–12), E2		**Science Online,** p. 102 **MiniLAB:** Interpreting Data from a Slingshot, p. 103 **Math Skills Activity:** Calculating Gravitational Potential Energy, p. 104 **Earth Science Integration,** p. 104 **Activity:** Bouncing Balls, p. 106
Section 2 Conservation of Energy 4 sessions 2 blocks 1. **Describe** how energy is conserved when changing from one form to another. 2. **Apply** the law of conservation of energy to familiar situations.	National Content Standards: UCP3, A2, B3 (5–8), B5, B6 (9–12), E2, F5 (5–8), F6 (9–12)		**Visualizing Energy Transformations,** p. 110 **Earth Science Integration,** p. 111 **MiniLAB:** Transforming Energy Using a Paper Clip, p. 112 **Science Online,** p. 113 **Activity:** Swing Energy, pp. 116–117 **Science and Society:** The Impossible Dream, pp. 118–119

Activity Materials	Reproducible Resources	Section Assessment	Technology
Explore Activity: 2 D-cell batteries, 2 non-coated paper clips, tape, steel wool	**Chapter Resources Booklet** Foldables Worksheet, p. 17 Note-taking Worksheets, pp. 31–32	GLENCOE'S ASSESSMENT ADVANTAGE	
MiniLAB: rubber band, nickel **Activity:** tennis ball, rubber ball, balance, meterstick, masking tape, cardboard box *Need materials?* Contact Science Kit at 1-800-828-7777 or www.sciencekit.com on the Internet.	**Chapter Resources Booklet** Transparency Activity, p. 42 MiniLAB, p. 3 Enrichment, p. 29 Reinforcement, p. 27 Directed Reading, p. 20 Activity Worksheet, pp. 5–6 Lab Activity, pp. 9–12 Transparency Activity, pp. 45–46 **Reading and Writing Skill Activities,** p. 35	**Portfolio** Curriculum Connection, p. 102 **Performance** MiniLAB, p. 103 Skill Builder Activities, p. 105 **Content** Section Assessment, p. 105	Section Focus Transparency Teaching Transparency Interactive CD-ROM/DVD Guided Reading Audio Program
MiniLAB: paper clip **Activity:** ring stand and ring, support-rod clamp (right angle), 30-cm support rod, 2-hole, medium rubber stopper, 1m string, metersticks, graph paper	**Chapter Resources Booklet** Transparency Activity, p. 43 MiniLAB, p. 4 Enrichment, p. 30 Reinforcement, p. 28 Directed Reading, pp. 21, 22 Activity Worksheet, pp. 7–8 Lab Activity, pp. 13–15 **Home and Community Involvement,** p. 36 **Cultural Diversity,** p. 53	**Portfolio** Visula Learning, p. 114 **Performance** MiniLAB, p. 112 Skill Builder Activities, p. 115 **Content** Section Assessment, p. 115	Section Focus Transparency Interactive CD-ROM/DVD Guided Reading Audio Program

End of Chapter Assessment

GLENCOE'S ASSESSMENT ADVANTAGE

Blackline Masters	Technology	Professional Series
Chapter Resources Booklet Chapter Review, pp. 35–36 Chapter Tests, pp. 37–40 **Standardized Test Practice by The Princeton Review,** pp. 20–23	MindJogger Videoquiz CD-ROM Explorations and Quizzes Vocabulary Puzzle Makers ExamView Pro Test Bank Interactive Lesson Planner Interactive Teacher's Edition	Performance Assessment in the Science Classroom (PASC)

Transparencies

Section Focus

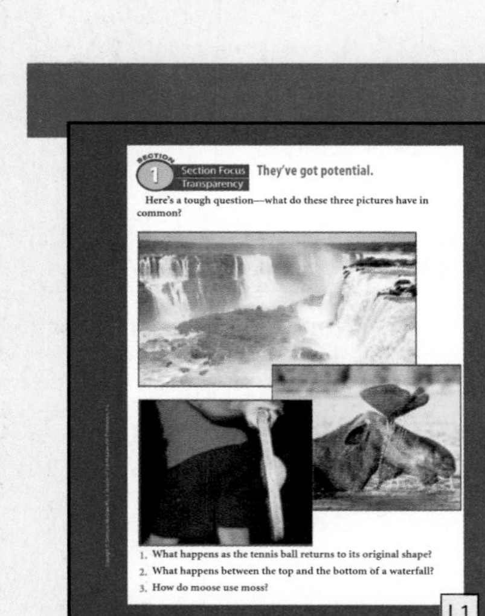
Section 1 Section Focus Transparency — They've got potential.

Here's a tough question—what do these three pictures have in common?

1. What happens as the tennis ball returns to its original shape?
2. What happens between the top and the bottom of a waterfall?
3. How do moose use moss?

L1

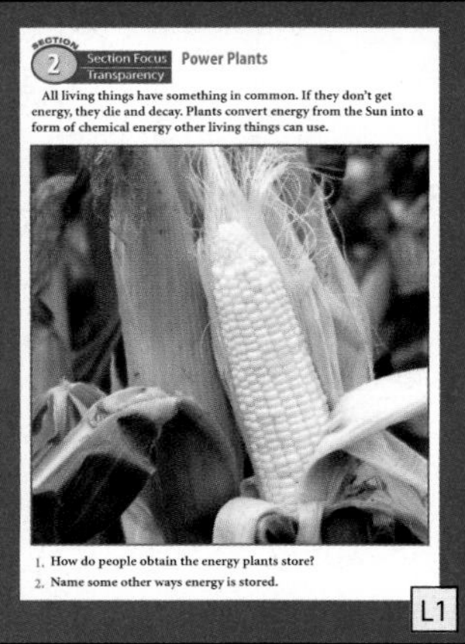
Section 2 Section Focus Transparency — Power Plants

All living things have something in common. If they don't get energy, they die and decay. Plants convert energy from the Sun into a form of chemical energy other living things can use.

1. How do people obtain the energy plants store?
2. Name some other ways energy is stored.

L1

This is a representation of key blackline masters available in the Teacher Classroom Resources. See Resource Manager boxes within the chapter for additional information.

Assessment

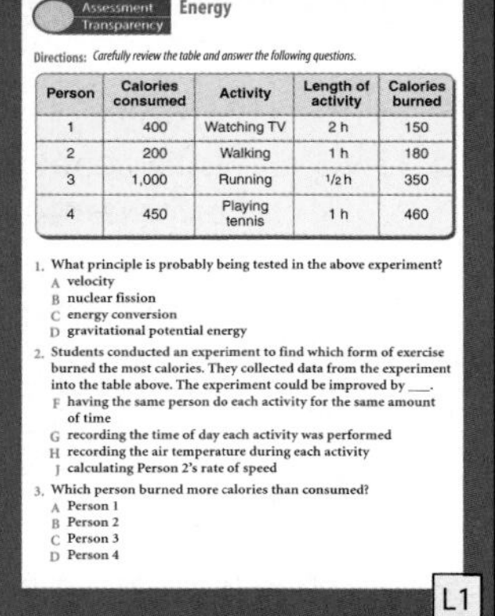
Assessment Transparency — Energy

Directions: *Carefully review the table and answer the following questions.*

Person	Calories consumed	Activity	Length of activity	Calories burned
1	400	Watching TV	2 h	150
2	200	Walking	1 h	180
3	1,000	Running	1/2 h	350
4	450	Playing tennis	1 h	460

1. What principle is probably being tested in the above experiment?
   A velocity
   B nuclear fission
   C energy conversion
   D gravitational potential energy
2. Students conducted an experiment to find which form of exercise burned the most calories. They collected data from the experiment into the table above. The experiment could be improved by ___.
   F having the same person do each activity for the same amount of time
   G recording the time of day each activity was performed
   H recording the air temperature during each activity
   J calculating Person 2's rate of speed
3. Which person burned more calories than consumed?
   A Person 1
   B Person 2
   C Person 3
   D Person 4

L1

Teaching

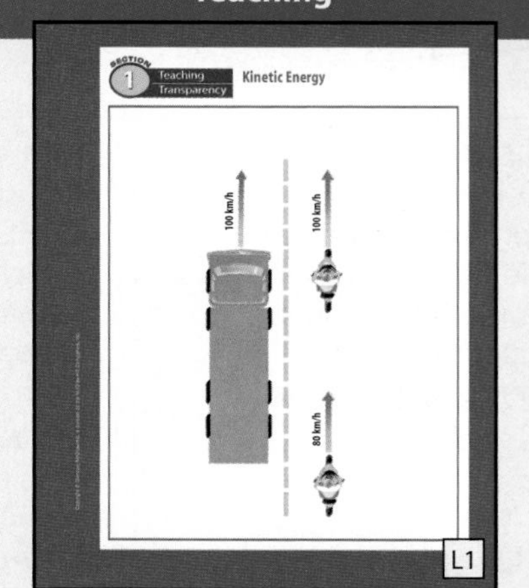
Section 1 Teaching Transparency — Kinetic Energy

L1

Key to Teaching Strategies

The following designations will help you decide which activities are appropriate for your students.

- L1 Level 1 activities should be appropriate for students with learning difficulties.
- L2 Level 2 activities should be within the ability range of all students.
- L3 Level 3 activities are designed for above-average students.
- ELL ELL activities should be within the ability range of English Language Learners.
- COOP LEARN Cooperative Learning activities are designed for small group work.
- LS Multiple Learning Styles logos are used throughout to indicate strategies that address different learning styles.
- P These strategies represent student products that can be placed into a best-work portfolio.

Hands-on Activities

Activity Worksheets

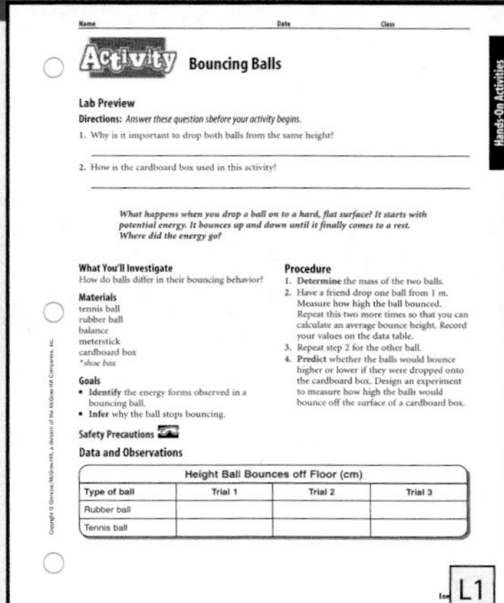
Name Date Class

Activity — Bouncing Balls

Lab Preview

Directions: *Answer these question sbefore your activity begins.*

1. Why is it important to drop both balls from the same height?
2. How is the cardboard box used in this activity?

What happens when you drop a ball on to a hard, flat surface? It starts with potential energy. It bounces up and down until it finally comes to a rest. Where did the energy go?

What You'll Investigate
How do balls differ in their bouncing behavior?

Materials
tennis ball
rubber ball
balance
meterstick
cardboard box
*shoe box

Goals
- **Identify** the energy forms observed in a bouncing ball.
- **Infer** why the ball stops bouncing.

Safety Precautions

Procedure
1. **Determine** the mass of the two balls.
2. Have a friend drop one ball from 1 m. Measure how high the ball bounced. Repeat this two more times so that you can calculate an average bounce height. Record your values on the data table.
3. Repeat step 2 for the other ball.
4. **Predict** whether the balls would bounce higher or lower if they were dropped onto the cardboard box. Design an experiment to measure how high the balls would bounce off the surface of a cardboard box.

Data and Observations

Height Ball Bounces off Floor (cm)			
Type of ball	Trial 1	Trial 2	Trial 3
Rubber ball			
Tennis ball			

Hands-On Activities

L1

Laboratory Activities

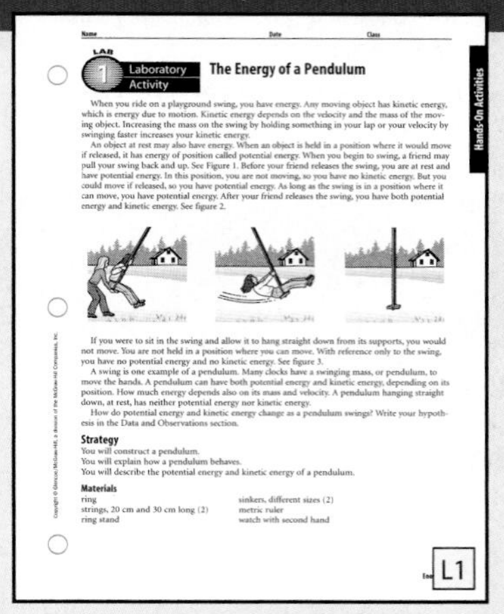
Name Date Class

Lab 1 Laboratory Activity — The Energy of a Pendulum

When you ride on a playground swing, you have energy. Any moving object has kinetic energy, which is energy due to motion. Kinetic energy depends on the velocity and the mass of the moving object. Increasing the mass on the swing by holding something in your lap or your velocity by swinging faster increases your kinetic energy.

An object at rest may also have energy. When an object is held in a position where it would move if released, it has energy of position called potential energy. When you begin to swing, a friend may pull your swing back and up. See Figure 1. Before your friend releases the swing, you are at rest and have potential energy. In this position, you are not moving, so you have no kinetic energy. But you could move if released, so you have potential energy. As long as the swing is in a position where it can move, you have potential energy. After your friend releases the swing, you have both potential energy and kinetic energy. See figure 2.

If you were to sit in the swing and allow it to hang straight down from its supports, you would not move. You are not held in a position where you can move. With reference only to the swing, you have no potential energy and no kinetic energy. See figure 3.

A swing is one example of a pendulum. Many clocks have a swinging mass, or pendulum, to move the hands. A pendulum can have both potential energy and kinetic energy, depending on its position. How much energy depends also on its mass and velocity. A pendulum hanging straight down, at rest, has neither potential energy nor kinetic energy.

How do potential energy and kinetic energy change as a pendulum swings? Write your hypothesis in the Data and Observations section.

Strategy
You will construct a pendulum.
You will explain how a pendulum behaves.
You will describe the potential energy and kinetic energy of a pendulum.

Materials
ring
strings, 20 cm and 30 cm long (2)
ring stand
sinkers, different sizes (2)
metric ruler
watch with second hand

Hands-On Activities

L1

Meeting Different Ability Levels

Content Outline

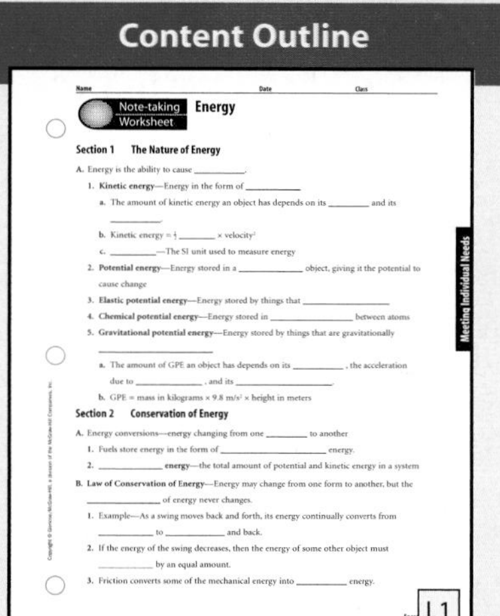

Name Date Class

Note-taking Worksheet **Energy**

Section 1 The Nature of Energy

A. Energy is the ability to cause __________.

1. **Kinetic energy**—Energy in the form of __________

a. The amount of kinetic energy an object has depends on its ________ and its ________

b. Kinetic energy = ½ ________ × velocity²

c. __________—The SI unit used to measure energy

2. **Potential energy**—Energy stored in a __________ object, giving it the potential to cause change

3. **Elastic potential energy**—Energy stored by things that __________

4. **Chemical potential energy**—Energy stored in __________ between atoms

5. **Gravitational potential energy**—Energy stored by things that are gravitationally __________

a. The amount of GPE an object has depends on its ________, the acceleration due to ________, and its ________

b. GPE = mass in kilograms × 9.8 m/s² × height in meters

Section 2 Conservation of Energy

A. Energy conversions—energy changing from one ________ to another

1. Fuels store energy in the form of __________ energy.

2. __________ energy—the total amount of potential and kinetic energy in a system

B. Law of Conservation of Energy—Energy may change from one form to another, but the __________ of energy never changes.

1. Example—As a swing moves back and forth, its energy continually converts from ________ to ________ and back.

2. If the energy of the swing decreases, then the energy of some other object must ________ by an equal amount.

3. Friction converts some of the mechanical energy into ________ energy.

Meeting Individual Needs

L1

Reinforcement

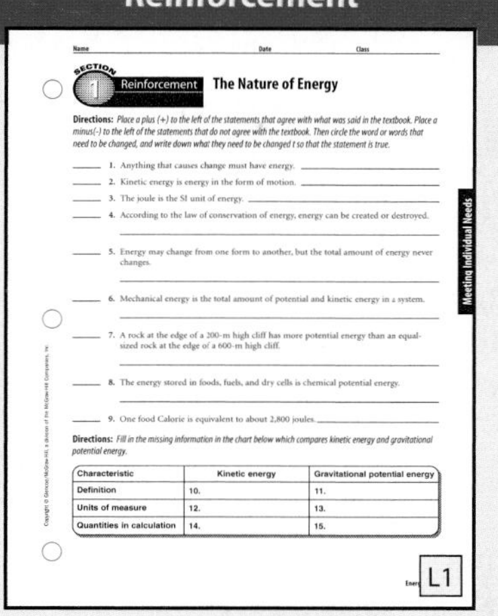

Name Date Class

Section 1 Reinforcement **The Nature of Energy**

Directions: *Place a plus (+) to the left of the statements that agree with what was said in the textbook. Place a minus (-) to the left of the statements that do not agree with the textbook. Then circle the word or words that need to be changed, and write down what they need to be changed to so that the statement is true.*

_____ 1. Anything that causes change must have energy.

_____ 2. Kinetic energy is energy in the form of motion.

_____ 3. The joule is the SI unit of energy.

_____ 4. According to the law of conservation of energy, energy can be created or destroyed.

_____ 5. Energy may change from one form to another, but the total amount of energy never changes.

_____ 6. Mechanical energy is the total amount of potential and kinetic energy in a system.

_____ 7. A rock at the edge of a 200-m high cliff has more potential energy than an equal-sized rock at the edge of a 600-m high cliff.

_____ 8. The energy stored in foods, fuels, and dry cells is chemical potential energy.

_____ 9. One food Calorie is equivalent to about 2,800 joules.

Directions: *Fill in the missing information in the chart below which compares kinetic energy and gravitational potential energy.*

Characteristic	Kinetic energy	Gravitational potential energy
Definition	10.	11.
Units of measure	12.	13.
Quantities in calculation	14.	15.

Meeting Individual Needs

L1

Directed Reading

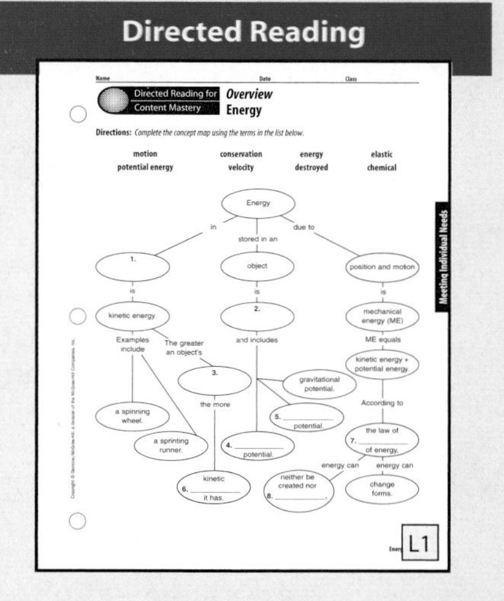

Name Date Class

Directed Reading for Content Mastery *Overview* **Energy**

Directions: *Complete the concept map using the terms in the list below.*

motion	conservation	energy	elastic
potential energy	velocity	destroyed	chemical

Meeting Individual Needs

L1

Enrichment

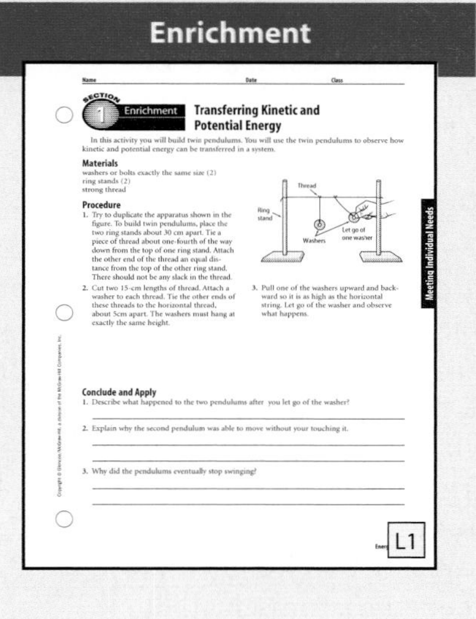

Name Date Class

Section 1 Enrichment **Transferring Kinetic and Potential Energy**

In this activity you will build twin pendulums. You will use the twin pendulums to observe how kinetic and potential energy can be transferred in a system.

Materials

washers or bolts exactly the same size (2)
ring stands (2)
strong thread

Procedure

1. Try to duplicate the apparatus shown in the figure. To build twin pendulums, place the two ring stands about 30 cm apart. Tie a piece of thread about one-fourth of the way down from the top of one ring stand. Attach the other end of the thread an equal distance from the top of the other ring stand. There should not be any slack in the thread.
2. Cut two 15-cm lengths of thread. Attach a washer to each thread. Tie the other ends of these threads to the horizontal thread, about 5cm apart. The washers must hang at exactly the same height.
3. Pull one of the washers upward and backward so it is as high as the horizontal string. Let go of the washer and observe what happens.

Conclude and Apply

1. Describe what happened to the two pendulums after you let go of the washer?
2. Explain why the second pendulum was able to move without your touching it.
3. Why did the pendulums eventually stop swinging?

Meeting Individual Needs

L1

Spanish Directed Reading

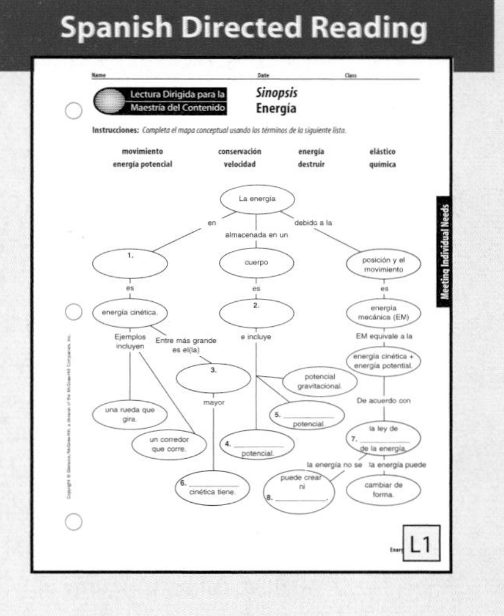

Nombre Fecha Clase

Lectura Dirigida para la Maestría del Contenido *Sinopsis* **Energía**

Instrucciones: *Completa el mapa conceptual usando los términos de la siguiente lista.*

movimiento	conservación	energía	elástico
energía potencial	velocidad	destruir	química

Meeting Individual Needs

L1

Assessment

Chapter Tests

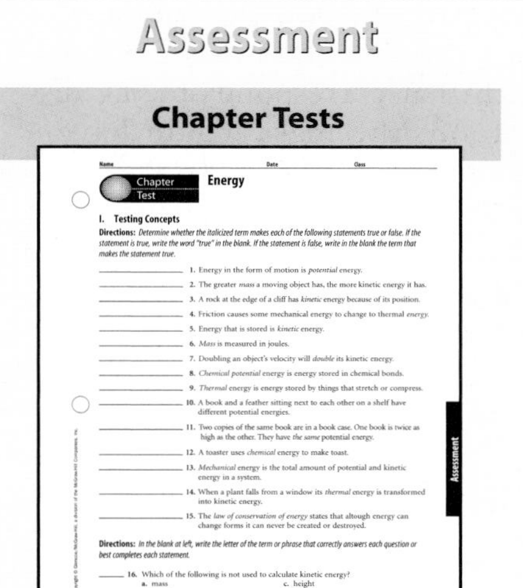

Name Date Class

Chapter Test **Energy**

I. Testing Concepts

Directions: *Determine whether the italicized term makes each of the following statements true or false. If the statement is true, write the word "true" in the blank. If the statement is false, write in the blank the term that makes the statement true.*

__________ 1. Energy in the form of motion is *potential* energy.

__________ 2. The greater mass a moving object has, the more kinetic energy it has.

__________ 3. A rock at the edge of a cliff has *kinetic* energy because of its position.

__________ 4. Friction causes some mechanical energy to change to thermal energy.

__________ 5. Energy that is stored is *kinetic* energy.

__________ 6. *Mass* is measured in joules.

__________ 7. Doubling an object's velocity will *double* its kinetic energy.

__________ 8. *Chemical potential* energy is energy stored in chemical bonds.

__________ 9. *Thermal* energy is energy stored by things that stretch or compress.

__________ 10. A book and a feather sitting next to each other on a shelf have different potential energies.

__________ 11. Two copies of the same book are in a book case. One book is twice as high as the other. They have the *same* potential energy.

__________ 12. A toaster uses *chemical* energy to make toast.

__________ 13. *Mechanical* energy is the total amount of potential and kinetic energy in a system.

__________ 14. When a plant falls from a window its *thermal* energy is transformed into kinetic energy.

__________ 15. The *law of conservation of energy* states that athough energy can change forms it can never be created or destroyed.

Directions: *In the blank at left, write the letter of the term or phrase that correctly answers each question or best completes each statement.*

_____ 16. Which of the following is not used to calculate kinetic energy?
a. mass c. height
b. speed d. velocity

_____ 17. Which of the following is not used to calculate potential energy?
a. mass c. height
b. gravitational acceleration d. velocity

Assessment

L1

Test Practice Workbook

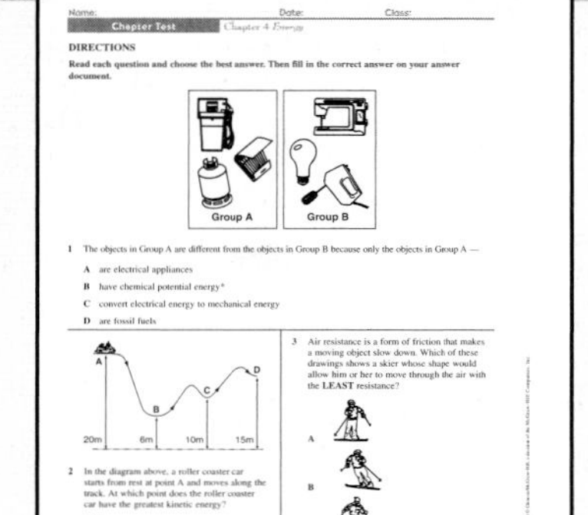

Name: Date: Class:

Chapter Test *Chapter 4 Energy*

DIRECTIONS

Read each question and choose the best answer. Then fill in the correct answer on your answer document.

1 The objects in Group A are different from the objects in Group B because only the objects in Group A —

A are electrical appliances
B have chemical potential energy*
C convert electrical energy to mechanical energy
D are fossil fuels

2 In the diagram above, a roller coaster car starts from rest at point A and moves along the track. At which point does the roller coaster car have the greatest kinetic energy?

F A
G B*
H C
J D

3 Air resistance is a form of friction that makes a moving object slow down. Which of these drawings shows a skier whose shape would allow him or her to move through the air with the LEAST resistance?

A
B
C
D

GO ON

20 Energy and Motion

L1

Chapter Review

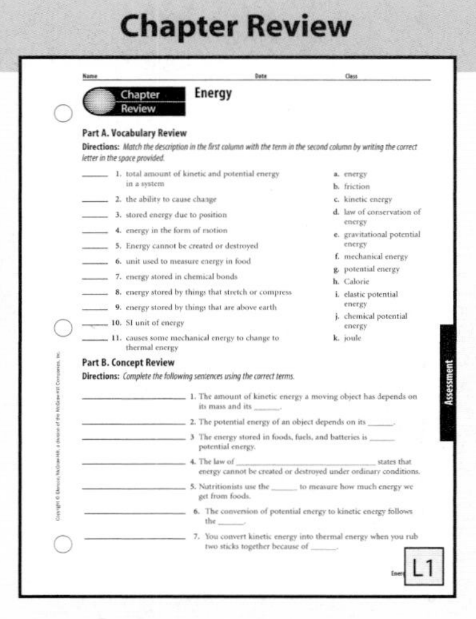

Name Date Class

Chapter Review **Energy**

Part A. Vocabulary Review

Directions: *Match the description in the first column with the term in the second column by writing the correct letter in the space provided.*

_____ 1. total amount of kinetic and potential energy in a system
_____ 2. the ability to cause change
_____ 3. stored energy due to position
_____ 4. energy in the form of motion
_____ 5. Energy cannot be created or destroyed
_____ 6. unit used to measure energy in food
_____ 7. energy stored in chemical bonds
_____ 8. energy stored by things that stretch or compress
_____ 9. energy stored by things that are above earth
_____ 10. SI unit of energy
_____ 11. causes some mechanical energy to change to thermal energy

a. energy
b. friction
c. kinetic energy
d. law of conservation of energy
e. gravitational potential energy
f. mechanical energy
g. potential energy
h. Calorie
i. elastic potential energy
j. chemical potential energy
k. joule

Part B. Concept Review

Directions: *Complete the following sentences using the correct terms.*

__________ 1. The amount of kinetic energy a moving object has depends on its mass and its ______.

__________ 2. The potential energy of an object depends on its ______.

__________ 3. The energy stored in foods, fuels, and batteries is ______ potential energy.

__________ 4. The law of __________ states that energy cannot be created or destroyed under ordinary conditions.

__________ 5. Nutritionists use the ______ to measure how much energy we get from foods.

__________ 6. The conversion of potential energy to kinetic energy follows the ______.

__________ 7. You convert kinetic energy into thermal energy when you rub two sticks together because of ______.

Assessment

L1

Science Content Background

SECTION 1 The Nature of Energy

What is energy?

Energy is not matter. Electromagnetic energy can exist independent of matter. Other forms of energy, such as chemical and kinetic energy, can only exist with matter.

Kinetic Energy

The equation for kinetic energy states that $E = 1/2mv^2$. This means that as an object's velocity doubles its kinetic energy quadruples.

Kinetic comes from a Greek word for movement. The word *cinema*—used to describe moving pictures or movies—shares the same root word.

Fun Fact

Mitochondria are organelles that convert chemical energy into forms usable by cells. For this reason, they are called the powerhouses of the cell. Mitochondria have their own DNA, separate from the DNA in the nucleus. The mitochondria we have come from only our mothers, not our fathers.

Potential Energy

Potential energy is energy due to an object's position or condition. A rock on a cliff has potential energy due to its position, while the energy stored in a starch molecule is due to the condition of the bonds between the atoms in that molecule.

Hooke's law describes the relationship between stress and strain in a spring. The amount of force is directly proportional to the stretching of the spring. The amount of potential energy depends on the amount of stretching and the elasticity of the spring.

Without friction, the work done to lift an object is equal to the object's gain in potential energy. Consider the two equations: Work = Force × Distance and Potential Energy = mass × gravity × height. The force needed to lift an object is equivalent to the object's *mass* × *gravity*. The distance traveled is the height. So in this case, these two equations are equivalent.

If you took a one-kilogram mass to a distance from Earth that corresponds to the distance to the Moon, the mass would have a potential energy to Earth of 62,000,000 joules or 62 mega-joules. This is small compared to the one-kilogram mass' potential energy to the Sun, which would be 190,000 mega-joules.

Albert Copley/Visuals Unlimited

SECTION 2

Conservation of Energy

Changing Forms of Energy

In our common experiences on Earth, energy is neither created nor destroyed, but is often transformed from one form into another. People use these energy transformations to do work. In most energy transformations, heat is produced.

Energy is not recycled in ecosystems like matter is recycled. Much of the energy that flows through ecosystems is lost to heat. As energy flows from organism to organism, more and more is lost as heat. This flow of energy can be visually represented as food chains. The Sun supplies new energy to plants, which start almost all food chains.

Conversions Between Kinetic and Potential Energy

As an object falls, its gravitational potential energy is converted into kinetic energy. Therefore, if you know the falling object's initial potential energy, you can calculate the velocity it attains just before it hits the ground using the equation $PE = mgh$. A 0.06 kg tennis ball dropped from a height of 2.9 m starts with 1.7 J of energy. Solving the kinetic energy equation for v gives 7.54 m/s.

The joule is the SI unit of energy and work. It is in the units $kg \cdot m^2/s^2$. In work calculations a joule is sometimes called a newton-meter. Since a newton is composed of the units $kg \cdot m/s^2$, multiplying newtons by meters, results in $kg \cdot m^2/s^2$, or joules.

The Law of Conservation of Energy

The law of conservation of energy works for most of our calculations, but Einstein suggested that mass could be converted to energy and energy into mass. Einstein's famous equation, $E=mc^2$ shows the relationship between mass and energy and explains the incredible power unleashed by atomic bombs. So the law of conservation of energy should more accurately be called the law of conservation of energy and mass.

Frank Rossotto/The Stock Market

For additional content background on this topic, go to the Glencoe Science Web site at science.glencoe.com.

Energy

Chapter Vocabulary

kinetic energy
joule
potential energy
elastic potential energy
chemical potential energy
gravitational potential energy
mechanical energy
law of conservation of energy

What do you think?

Science Journal The photograph shows the filaments in a lightbulb. Electrical energy has been converted into light and heat.

Energy

Snowboarding down the side of a mountain is an exhilarating experience. With little effort, you can easily reach speeds well over 50 km/h using nothing other than a snowboard, the slope, and a lot of snow. How do snowboarders achieve such high speeds? What supplies the energy to move them so fast? The answers to these questions can be found by studying energy and energy conservation.

What do you think?

Science Journal Look at the picture below with a classmate. Discuss what you think this might be or what is happening. Here's a hint: *It's used every day and allows people to work and play at any hour.* Write your answer or best guess in your Science Journal.

98

Theme Connection

Energy This chapter focuses on different forms of energy and energy conversions. The law of conservation of energy is explained and applied to various systems.

One of the most useful inventions of the nineteenth century was the electric lightbulb. Being able to light up the dark allows for extended work and recreation. A lightbulb uses electricity to produce light, but heat also is produced. To observe the conversion of electricity to light and heat, do the following activity.

1. Obtain two D-cell batteries, two non-coated paper clips, tape, and some steel wool. Separate the steel wool into thin strands and straighten the paper clips.
2. Tape the batteries together and then tape one end of each paper clip to the battery terminals as shown in the photograph.
3. With the strands of steel wool, briefly connect the other ends of the paper clips.

WARNING: *Steel wool can become hot—connect to battery only for a brief time.*

Observe

Describe in your Science Journal what you saw. Touch the steel wool. What changes are you observing?

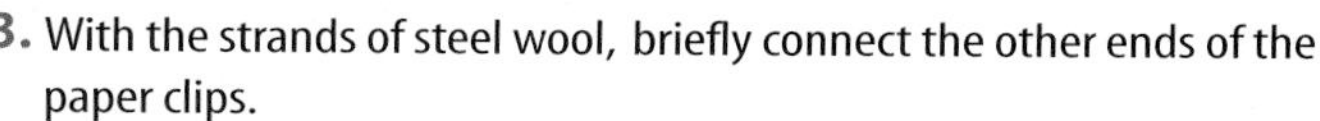

FOLDABLES Reading & Study Skills

Making a Know-Want-Learn Study Fold **Make the following Foldable to help identify what you already know and what you want to know about energy.**

1. Place a sheet of paper in front of you so the short side is at the top. Fold the paper in half from top to bottom.
2. Fold both sides in to divide the paper into thirds. Unfold the paper so three sections show.
3. Through the top thickness of paper, cut along each of the fold lines to the topfold, forming three tabs. Label the tabs *Know, Want,* and *Learned,* as shown.

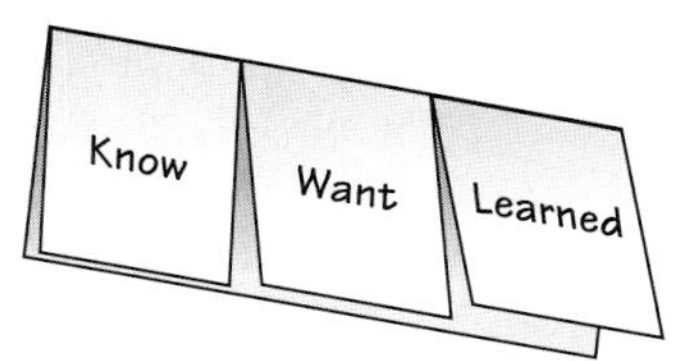

4. Before you read the chapter, write what you know about energy under the left tab and what you want to know under the middle tab.
5. As you read the chapter, write what you learn about energy under the right tab.

Before You Read

FOLDABLES Reading & Study Skills

Dinah Zike Study Fold

Purpose This assignment provides students with an opportunity to review what they know about energy and instructs them to list what they would like to know about energy. Their results can be used as an assessment tool at the end of the chapter to determine what they have learned.

For additional help, see Foldables Worksheet, p. 17 in **Chapter Resources Booklet,** or go to the Glencoe Science Web site at **science.glencoe.com.** See After You Read in the Study Guide at the end of this chapter.

Explore Activity

Purpose Use the Explore Activity to introduce students to the conversion of electricity to light and heat. L1 COOP LEARN

LS **Kinesthetic**

Materials 2 D-cell batteries, 2 non-coated paper clips, tape, steel wool

Teaching Strategy Inform students that the steel wool can become quite hot.

Observe

The steel wool will give off light and heat.

Assessment

Content Have students investigate how a light bulb works and write a paragraph comparing it with the model they made in this activity. Use **Performance Assessment in the Science Classroom,** p. 157. P

SECTION

The Nature of Energy

1 Motivate

Bellringer Transparency

Display the Section Focus Transparency for Section 1. Use the accompanying Transparency Activity Master. L2 ELL

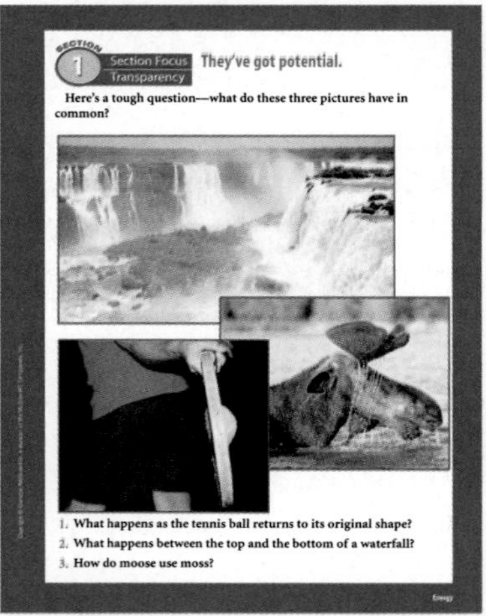

Section Focus Transparency

1 They've got potential.

Here's a tough question—what do these three pictures have in common?

1. What happens as the tennis ball returns to its original shape?
2. What happens between the top and the bottom of a waterfall?
3. How do moose use moss?

Tie to Prior Knowledge

Ask students to describe how the word *energy* is commonly used. They might mention fuel energy or energy from the Sun. Explain that in this section they will learn the scientific definition of energy.

SECTION

The Nature of Energy

As You Read

What You'll Learn

- **Distinguish** between kinetic and potential energy.
- **Recognize** different ways that energy can be stored.

Vocabulary

kinetic energy
joule
potential energy
elastic potential energy
chemical potential energy
gravitational potential energy

Why It's Important

Understanding energy helps you understand how your environment is changing.

What is energy?

Wherever you are sitting as you read this, changes are taking place—lightbulbs are heating the air around them, the wind might be rustling leaves, or sunlight might be glaring off a nearby window. Even you are changing as you breathe, blink, or shift position in your seat.

Every change that occurs—large or small—involves energy. Imagine a baseball flying through the air. It hits a window, causing the glass to break as shown in **Figure 1.** The window changed from a solid sheet of glass to a number of broken pieces. The moving baseball caused this change—a moving baseball has energy. Even when you comb your hair or walk from class to class, energy is involved.

Change Requires Energy When something is able to change its environment or itself, it has energy. Energy is the ability to cause change. The moving baseball had energy. It certainly caused the window to change. Anything that causes change must have energy. You use energy to arrange your hair to look the way you want it to. You also use energy when you walk down the halls of your school between classes or eat your lunch. You even need energy to yawn, open a book, and write with a pen.

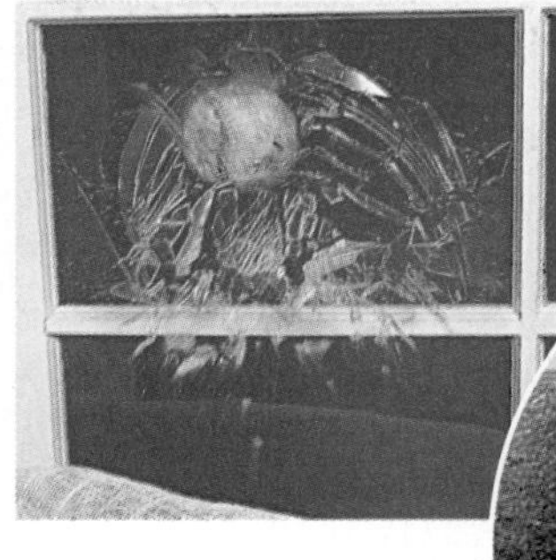

Figure 1
Each photo shows changes occurring.
How do these photos demonstrate energy?

Section Assessment Planner

PORTFOLIO
Curriculum Connection, p. 102

PERFORMANCE ASSESSMENT
MiniLAB, p. 103
Math Skills Activity, p. 104
Skill-Builder Activities, 105
See p. 122 for more options.

CONTENT ASSESSMENT
Section, p. 105
Challenge, p. 105
Chapter, pp. 122–123

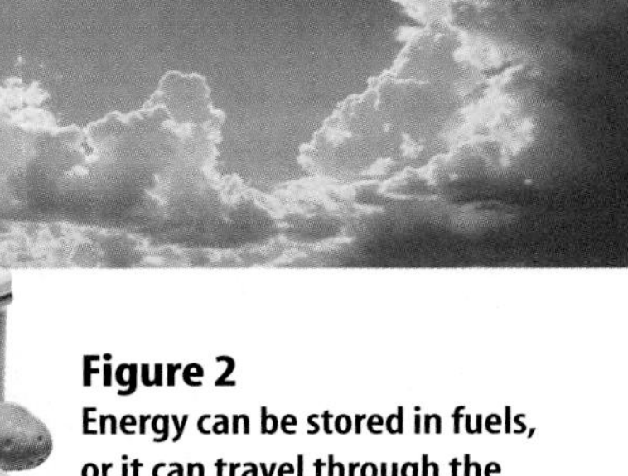

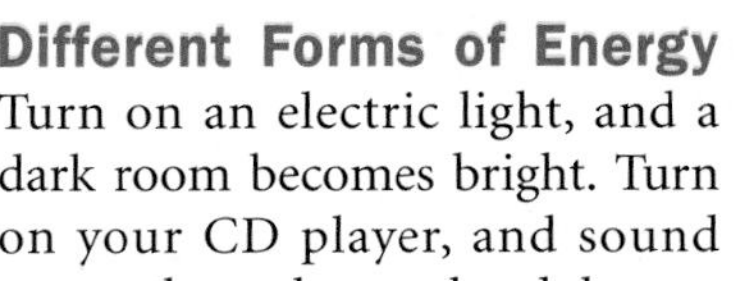

Figure 2
Energy can be stored in fuels, or it can travel through the environment. *Which objects are storing energy? Where is movement of energy occurring?*

Different Forms of Energy Turn on an electric light, and a dark room becomes bright. Turn on your CD player, and sound comes through your headphones. In both situations, energy transfers from one place to another. These changes seem to differ from each other and differ from a baseball shattering a window. This is because energy has several different forms, such as electrical, chemical, and thermal.

Figure 2 shows some examples of everyday situations in which you might notice energy. Is the chemical energy stored in food the same as the energy that comes from the Sun or the energy stored in gasoline? Energy from the Sun travels a vast distance through space to Earth, warming the planet and providing energy that enables green plants to grow. When you make toast in the morning, you are using electrical energy to heat the bread. In short, energy plays a role in every activity that you do.

An Energy Analogy Money can be used in an analogy to help you understand energy. If you have $100, you could store it in a variety of forms—cash in your wallet, a bank account, travelers' checks, or gold or silver coins. You could transfer that money to different forms. You could deposit your cash into a bank account or trade the cash for gold. Regardless of its form, money is money. The same is true for energy. Energy from the Sun that warms you and energy from the food that you eat are only different forms of the same thing.

Reading Check *How is energy like money?*

2 Teach

What is energy?

Caption Answers

- **Figure 1** Window breaks, hair is smoothed, students change location.
- **Figure 2** Energy is stored in the gasoline and in the food. Energy is moving from the Sun to Earth.

Discussion

Name some objects that store energy and some examples of energy in motion. Possible answers: stored—springs, muscles in our bodies; motion—bouncing ball, spinning top, baseball flying through the air L1 IN **Linguistic**

Extension

Students often have difficulty understanding that sound is a form of energy. Have interested students research this topic and present their findings in oral reports to the class.
L3 IN **Linguistic**

Reading Check

Answer When money is transferred from one person or place to another it can change form but it remains money. When energy is transferred, it can change form but it still remains energy.

Resource Manager

Chapter Resources Booklet
Transparency Activity, p. 42
Note-taking Worksheets, pp. 31–32

Science Journal

Different Forms of Energy Have students make a list in their Science Journals of the different types of energy mentioned in the text. Have them list several examples of how they use each form of energy every day.
L2 IN **Linguistic**

Kinetic Energy

Use Science Words

Word Origin Have students look up the words *kinetic* and *potential* in the dictionary. *Kinetic* comes from the Greek root *kinein* (to move) and *potential* from the Latin root *potere* (to be powerful). Ask a volunteer to state how the words *kinetic* and *potential* reflect the meanings of their roots. Possible answer: Kinetic energy is energy of movement. Potential energy is stored energy due to position, almost like a powerful force waiting to be unleashed. L1 LS **Linguistic**

Quick Demo

Show students two balls, one heavy and one light. Roll the balls across a table at about the same speed. **Which ball has greater kinetic energy?** Since the velocity of both balls is the same, the ball with greater mass has greater kinetic energy. Next show students two balls with the same mass. Roll the balls across a table, but roll one ball faster than the other. **Which ball has greater kinetic energy?** the ball with greater speed L1 LS **Logical-Mathematical**

Use an Analogy

Suggest to students that potential energy is analogous to money in a savings account. The money is not in use now, but it's ready for you to use when needed.

SCIENCE Online

Collect Data Visit the Glencoe Science Web site at **science.glencoe.com** for more information about the kinetic energy of various animals. Communicate to your class what you learn.

Kinetic Energy

Usually, when you think of energy, you think of action—or some sort of motion taking place. **Kinetic energy** is energy in the form of motion. A spinning bicycle wheel, a sprinting runner, and a football passing through the goalposts all have kinetic energy, but the amounts differ depending on two quantities—the mass of the moving object and its velocity.

The more mass a moving object has, the more kinetic energy it has. Similarly, the greater an object's velocity is, the more kinetic energy it has. **Figure 3** shows a truck and a motorcycle that are moving at 100 km/h. Which vehicle has more kinetic energy? Although they have the same velocity, the truck has more kinetic energy because it has a greater mass than the motorcycle. **Figure 3** also shows two motorcycles—one moving at 100 km/h and one moving at 80 km/h. Which motorcycle has more kinetic energy? Assuming that the motorcycles have the same mass, the one moving at 100 km/h has a greater kinetic energy than the one moving at 80 km/h.

Calculating Kinetic Energy The kinetic energy of an object can be calculated using the following relationship.

$$\text{kinetic energy} = \frac{1}{2}\,\text{mass} \times \text{velocity}^2$$

$$KE\ (\text{J}) = \frac{1}{2} m\ (\text{kg}) \times v^2\ (\text{m}^2/\text{s}^2)$$

The **joule** (JEWL) is the SI unit of energy. It is named after the nineteenth-century British scientist James Prescott Joule. To calculate kinetic energy in joules (J), mass is measured in kilograms, and velocity is measured in meters per second.

Because velocity is squared in the equation for kinetic energy, increasing the velocity of an object can produce an especially large change in its kinetic energy. Without changing the mass of an object, doubling its velocity will quadruple its kinetic energy.

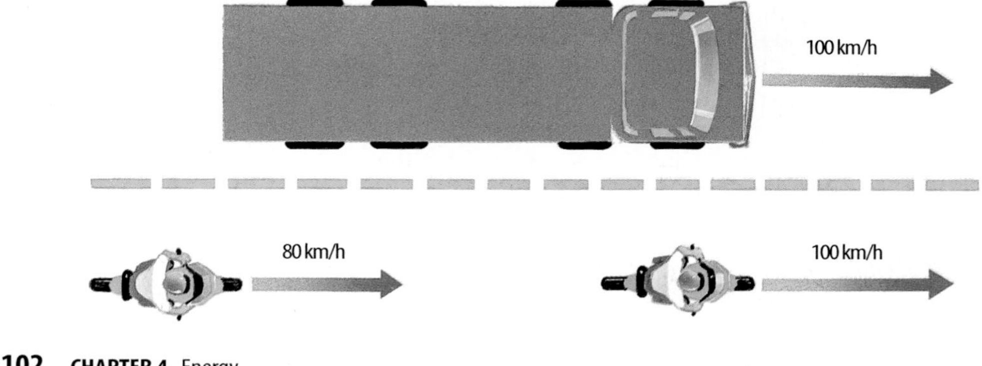

Figure 3
The kinetic energy of each vehicle is different because kinetic energy depends on an object's mass and its velocity.

Curriculum Connection

Geography On May 18, 1980, Mount St. Helens in the state of Washington erupted in a devastating volcanic explosion. The tremendous energy of the eruption hurled hot ash and rock more than 16 kilometers. Have students do research to discover other geologic events in history that have involved large amounts of energy. Have each student make a table listing the examples they find and where each event occurred. Possible events: earthquakes in 1964 in Alaska, in 1991 in southern California, in 1995 in Kobe, Japan, and in 2001 in India; and eruptions of the volcanoes Krakatau in 1883 and Mount Vesuvius in 79 A.D. L2 LS **Visual-Spatial** P

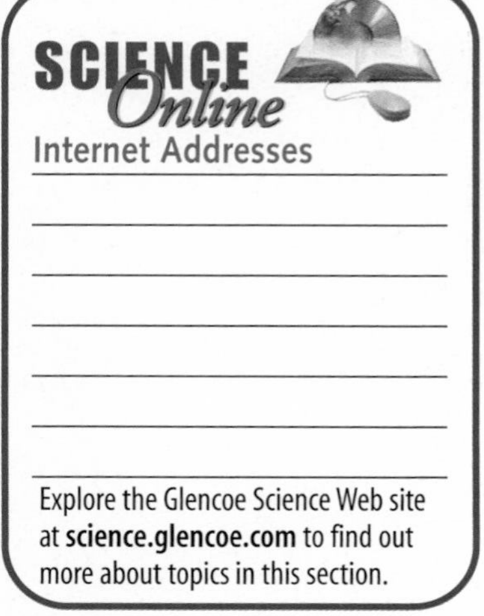

102 CHAPTER 4 Energy

Figure 4
As natural gas burns, it combines with oxygen to form carbon dioxide and water. In this chemical reaction, chemical potential energy is released.

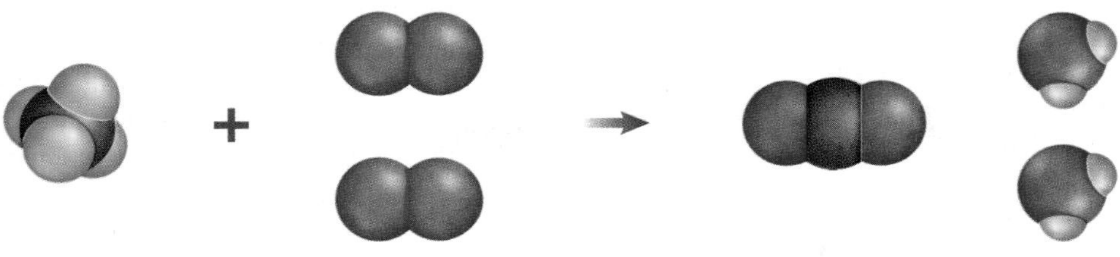

Potential Energy

Energy doesn't have to involve motion. Even motionless objects can have energy. This energy is stored in the object. Therefore, the object has potential to cause change. A hanging apple in a tree has stored energy. When the apple falls to the ground, a change occurs. Because the apple has the ability to cause change, it has energy. The hanging apple has energy because of its position above Earth's surface. Stored energy due to position is called **potential energy.** If the apple stayed in the tree, it would maintain the stored energy due to its height above the ground. If it falls, that stored energy of position is converted to energy of motion.

Elastic Potential Energy Energy can be stored in other ways, too. If you stretch a rubber band and let it go, it sails across the room. As it flies through the air, it has kinetic energy due to its motion. Where did this kinetic energy come from? Just as the apple hanging in the tree had potential energy, the stretched rubber band had energy stored as elastic potential energy. **Elastic potential energy** is energy stored by things that stretch or compress, like rubber bands or springs.

Chemical Potential Energy The cereal you eat for breakfast and the sandwich you eat at lunch also contain stored energy. Gasoline stores energy in the same way as food stores energy—in the chemical bonds between atoms. Energy stored in chemical bonds is **chemical potential energy. Figure 4** shows a molecule of natural gas. Energy is stored in the bonds that hold the carbon and hydrogen atoms together and is released when the gas is burned.

Reading Check *How is elastic potential energy different from chemical potential energy?*

Mini LAB

Interpreting Data from a Slingshot

Procedure

1. Using two fingers, carefully stretch a **rubber band** on a table until it has no slack.
2. Place a **nickel** on the table, slightly touching the midpoint of the rubber band.
3. Push the nickel back 0.5 cm and release. Measure the distance the nickel travels.
4. Repeat step 3, each time pushing the nickel back an additional 0.5 cm.

Analysis

1. How did the takeoff speed of the nickel seem to change relative to the distance that you stretched the rubber band?
2. What does this imply about the kinetic energy of the nickel?

Potential Energy

Purpose Students observe the relationship between the elastic potential energy and kinetic energy of an object. L1 COOP LEARN LS **Kinesthetic**

Materials nickel, rubber band, meterstick

Teaching Strategy Have students work in pairs and take turns making the measurements.

Troubleshooting Be sure students don't pull the rubber band back too far. The nickel can quickly travel a long distance.

Analysis

1. The farther you stretch the band, the faster the nickel takes off.
2. The greater the speed of the nickel, the greater its kinetic energy.

Process Have students predict how their results would differ on a rough surface. Have them test their hypotheses by repeating the activity on sandpaper. Use **Performance Assessment in the Science Classroom,** p. 93.

Reading Check

Answer Elastic potential energy is energy stored by things that stretch or compress. Chemical potential energy is energy stored in chemical bonds.

Resource Manager

Chapter Resources Booklet
MiniLAB, p. 3
Directed Reading for Content Mastery, p. 20
Reading and Writing Skill Activities, p. 35

Visual Learning

Figure 4 What forms of energy are given off when natural gas burns? light and heat (thermal energy)

Potential Energy, continued

Earth Science INTEGRATION

Possible answers: Kinetic—wind, ocean waves, avalanches, and erupting volcanoes; potential—water at the top of a waterfall, acorns hanging from a tree

Quick Demo

Demonstrate the idea of gravitational potential energy. Place three tennis balls on level surfaces at different heights. Ask students to compare the gravitational potential energy (GPE) of the balls. GPE increases with height. So the ball that is highest has the greatest GPE and the ball nearest the ground has the lowest GPE. L1 LS **Logical-Mathematical**

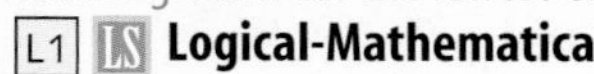

Math Skills Activity

National Math Standards

Correlation to Mathematics Objectives

1, 2, 6, 9

Answers to Practice Problems

1. Solve the equations: 0.06 kg $\times$ 9.8 m/s^2 $\times$ 2.5 m = 1.47 J for Bjorn's tennis ball 0.06 kg $\times$ 9.8 m/s^2 $\times$ 5 m = 2.94 J for Billie Jean's tennis ball Billie Jean's tennis ball has 2.94 J − 1.47 J = 1.47 J more energy than Bjorn's

Earth Science INTEGRATION

Fast-flowing rivers and slow-moving glaciers have kinetic energy. A rock balanced on a hill contains potential energy. What are some other examples of kinetic and potential energy in nature?

Gravitational Potential Energy Gravity caused the apple to fall from the tree. Anything that can fall has stored energy called gravitational potential energy. **Gravitational potential energy** (GPE) is energy stored by things that are above Earth. The amount of gravitational potential energy stored depends on three things—the mass of the object, the acceleration due to gravity, and the height above the ground. The acceleration of gravity on Earth is 9.8 m/s^2, and the height is measured as height in meters.

The amount of gravitational potential energy an object has can be calculated using the following equation.

$$GPE = \text{mass} \times 9.8\ \text{m/s}^2 \times \text{height}$$

$$GPE\ (\text{J}) = m\ (\text{kg}) \times 9.8\ \text{m/s}^2 \times h\ (\text{m})$$

Just like kinetic energy, gravitational potential energy is measured in joules. All energy, no matter which form it is in, can be measured in joules.

Math Skills Activity

Calculating Gravitational Potential Energy

Example Problem

A 0.06-kg tennis ball starts to fall from a height of 2.9 m. How much gravitational potential energy does the ball have at that height?

Solution

1. *This is what you know:* mass of tennis ball: m = 0.06 kg; height of the tennis ball: h = 2.9 m; acceleration of gravity: 9.8 m/s^2
2. *This is what you want to find:* gravitational potential energy: GPE
3. *This is the equation you use:* $GPE = m \times 9.8\ \text{m/s}^2 \times h$
4. *Solve the equation by substituting the known values:* $GPE = 0.06\ \text{kg} \times 9.8\ \text{m/s}^2 \times 2.9\ \text{m} = 1.7\ \text{J}$

Check your answer by substituting it and the known values into the original equation. Do you get the same result?

Practice Problem

Bjorn is holding a tennis ball outside a second-floor window (2.5 m from the ground) and Billie Jean is holding one outside a third-floor window (5 m from the ground). How much more gravitational potential energy does Billie Jean's tennis ball have? (Each tennis ball has a mass of 0.06 kg.)

For more help, refer to the Math Skill Handbook.

Cultural Diversity

Working with Energy During World War II, O.S. (Ozzie) Williams became the first African American aeronautical engineer hired by Republic Aviation, Inc. Later, his work included the application of solar and wind energy to the needs of Africa. Have students find other scientists who have spent much of their careers working with energy. Ask students to present their findings in oral reports to the class. L2 LS **Interpersonal**

Changing GPE Look at the objects on the bookshelf in **Figure 5.** Which of these objects has the most gravitational potential energy? According to the equation for gravitational potential energy, the GPE of an object can be increased by increasing its height above the ground. If two objects are at the same height, then the object with the larger mass has more gravitational potential energy.

In **Figure 5,** suppose the vase on the first shelf and the vase on the fourth shelf have the same mass. Then the vase that is on the fourth shelf has more gravitational potential energy because it is higher above the ground.

Imagine what would happen if the two vases were to fall. As they fall and begin moving, they have kinetic energy as well as gravitational potential energy. As the vases get closer to the ground, their gravitational potential energy decreases. At the same time they are moving faster, so their kinetic energy increases. The vase that initially had more gravitational potential energy will be moving faster when it hits the floor.

Do the books on the second shelf have more gravitational potential energy than the vase below it? That depends on the mass of the books. Even though they are twice as high as the vase, their gravitational potential energy also depends on their mass. If the mass of the books is less than half the mass of the vase, then the books have less gravitational potential energy, even though they are at a greater height.

Reading Check *What does GPE depend on?*

Figure 5
An object's gravitational potential energy increases with increased height. *Which vase has more gravitational potential energy? Which one will have more kinetic energy when it strikes the ground?*

Section 1 Assessment

1. Two books with different masses fall off the same bookshelf. As they fall, which has more kinetic energy and why?
2. How can the gravitational potential energy of an object be changed?
3. How is energy stored in food? Is the energy stored in food different from the energy stored in gasoline? Explain.
4. Contrast potential and kinetic energy.
5. **Think Critically** The food you eat supplies energy for your body. Suggest ways your body might make use of this energy.

Skill Builder Activities

6. **Comparing and Contrasting** Compare and contrast elastic potential energy, chemical potential energy, and gravitational potential energy. **For more help, refer to the Science Skill Handbook.**
7. **Solving One-Step Equations** An 80-kg diver jumps off a 10-m platform. Calculate how much gravitational potential energy the diver has at the top of the platform and halfway down. **For more help, refer to the Math Skill Handbook.**

Caption Answer

Figure 5 The vase highest off the ground has the highest GPE and will also have the greatest kinetic energy just before it strikes the ground.

Reading Check

Answer height and mass

3 Assess

Reteach

Perform several tasks, such as clapping your hands, walking across the room, tossing a ball across the room, or turning on a light. Ask students to identify the energy transformations that occur during each task. L1 ELL
LS **Visual-Spatial**

Challenge

The kinetic energy of a falling object is greatest just before the object hits the ground. The kinetic energy of the object immediately after falling is zero. **What happens to the kinetic energy?** It changes into other forms of energy, such as heat or sound. L3
LS **Logical-Mathematical**

Process Tell students that a 5 kg bowling ball is on a rack 1.5 m above the ground. Have them calculate the GPE of the ball. $5\text{ kg} \times 9.8\text{ m/s}^2 \times 1.5\text{ m} = 73.5\text{ J}$ Use **PASC,** p. 101.

Answers to Section Assessment

1. The book with the larger mass; kinetic energy depends on an object's mass as well as its velocity.
2. by changing the height of the object
3. in chemical bonds; no
4. Potential energy is stored energy due to an object's position. Kinetic energy is energy due to motion.
5. Possible answers: for walking, swimming, playing
6. All are stored energy due to position. To acquire elastic potential energy, an object is compressed or stretched. Chemical potential energy is due to the positions of atoms relative to one another. Gravitational potential energy is due to an object's height above the ground.
7. at the top, GPE. = 7,840 J; halfway down, GPE. = 3,920 J

Resource Manager

Chapter Resources Booklet
Lab Activity, pp. 9–12
Enrichment, p. 29
Reinforcement, p. 27

Activity

BENCH TESTED

Purpose Students observe how the GPE of a falling ball is converted to kinetic energy and elastic potential energy, enabling the ball to bounce. L2 COOP LEARN **Kinesthetic**

Process Skills observing and inferring, predicting, comparing, recognizing cause and effect

Time Required 30 minutes

Alternate Materials table tennis ball, book

Teaching Strategy Explain that it is only possible to measure the approximate height of the ball's bounce.

Conclude and Apply

1. Use the formula: GPE = m (kg) × 9.8 m/s^2 × h (m).
2. GPE decreases; kinetic energy increases. Most of their kinetic energy is converted to elastic potential energy.
3. Average height = sum of heights ÷ number of trials. Answers will vary.
4. The balls don't bounce as high on the box. Some of the kinetic energy the ball has when it hits the box is transferred to the box, causing the box to vibrate. This energy is then unavailable to help propel the ball up.
5. When a ball hits the ground, most of its kinetic energy is converted to elastic potential energy. This becomes kinetic energy as the ball rebounds. Some balls store more elastic potential energy than others.

Activity

Bouncing Balls

What happens when you drop a ball onto a hard, flat surface? It starts with potential energy. It bounces up and down until it finally comes to a rest. Where did the energy go?

What You'll Investigate

How do balls differ in their bouncing behavior?

Materials

tennis ball
rubber ball
balance
meterstick
masking tape
cardboard box
**shoe box*

**Alternate materials*

Goals

- **Identify** the energy forms observed in a bouncing ball.
- **Infer** why the ball stops bouncing.

Safety Precautions 

Procedure

1. **Determine** the mass of the two balls.
2. Have a friend drop one ball from 1 m. Measure how high the ball bounced. Repeat this two more times so that you can calculate an average bounce height. Record your values on the data table.
3. Repeat step 2 for the other ball.
4. **Predict** whether the balls would bounce higher or lower if they were dropped onto the cardboard box. Design an experiment to measure how high the balls would bounce off the surface of a cardboard box.

Conclude and Apply

1. **Calculate** the gravitational potential energy of each ball before dropping them.

Bounce Height

Type of Ball	Surface	Trial	Height (cm)
Tennis	Floor	1	36
Tennis	Floor	2	34
Tennis	Floor	3	37
Rubber	Floor	1	54
Rubber	Floor	2	56
Rubber	Floor	3	56
Tennis	Box	1	29

2. As the balls fall, what happens to their gravitational potential energy and their kinetic energy? What happens to their kinetic energy when they hit the floor?
3. **Calculate** the average bounce height for the three trials under each condition. Describe your observations.
4. How did the bounce heights compare when dropped on a cardboard box instead of the floor? Why? Hint: *Did you observe any movement of the box when the balls bounced?*
5. Use elastic potential energy to explain why the balls bounced to different heights.

Communicating Your Data

Meet with three other lab teams and compare average bounce heights for the tennis ball on the floor. Discuss why your results might differ. **For more help, refer to the** Science Skill Handbook.

Resource Manager 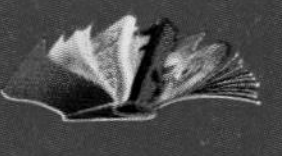

Chapter Resources Booklet
Transparency Activity, pp. 45–46
Activity Worksheet, pp. 5–6

Assessment

Process Demonstrate how the bounce height of a ball becomes lower and lower each time it bounces. Have students infer why this happens. Each time the ball bounces, part of its energy is converted to other forms of energy, such as thermal energy and sound. Use **PASC,** p. 89.

Communicating Your Data

Students can use a computer graphics program to prepare a display of their activity results. They should be allowed freedom to make their own design, but the picture should clearly show how the balls bounced higher off the floor than off the box.

SECTION 2

Conservation of Energy

Changing Forms of Energy

Unless you were specifically talking about potential energy, you probably wouldn't think of the book on top of a bookshelf as having much to do with energy, that is, until it fell. You'd be more likely to think of energy as a moving car burns fuel or as your body uses energy from food to help it move, or as the Sun warms your skin on a summer day. You might be thankful for electrical energy as you play a favorite CD. These situations involve energy changing from one form to another form. Energy is most noticeable as it transforms from one type to another.

Transforming Electrical Energy You use many devices every day that convert one form of energy to other forms. For example, you might be reading this page in a room lit by lightbulbs. The lightbulbs transform electrical energy into light so you can see. The warmth you feel around the bulb is evidence that some of that electrical energy is turned into thermal energy, as illustrated in **Figure 6.** What other devices have you used today that make use of electrical energy? You might have been awakened by an alarm clock, styled your hair, made toast, listened to music, or played a video game. What form or forms of energy is electrical energy converted to in these examples?

As You Read

What You'll Learn

- **Describe** how energy is conserved when changing from one form to another.
- **Apply** the law of conservation of energy to familiar situations.

Vocabulary

mechanical energy
law of conservation of energy

Why It's Important

Conservation of energy is a universal principle that can explain how energy changes occur.

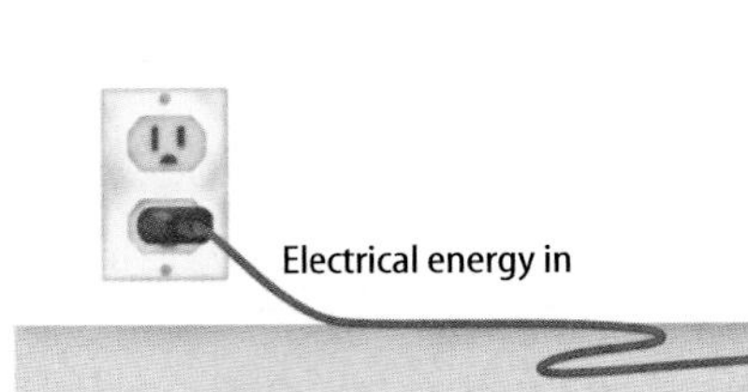

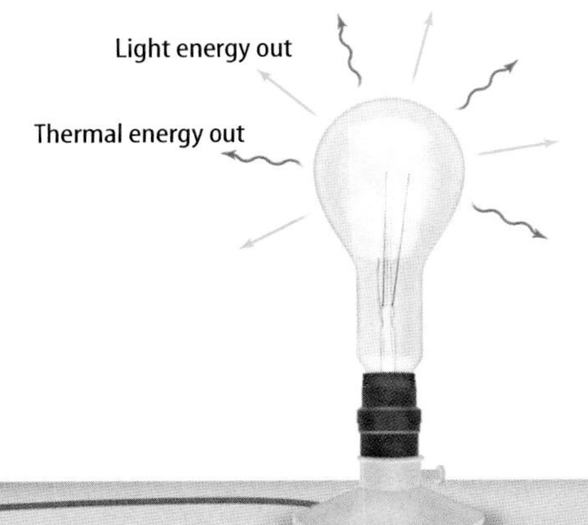

Figure 6
A lightbulb is a device that transforms electrical energy into light energy and thermal energy. *What other energy-transformation devices do you commonly use?*

Section Assessment Planner

PORTFOLIO
Visual Learning, p. 114

PERFORMANCE ASSESSMENT
Try At Home MiniLAB, p. 112
Skill-Builder Activities, p. 115
See p. 122 for more options.

CONTENT ASSESSMENT
Section, p. 115
Challenge, p. 115
Chapter, pp. 122–123

SECTION

Conservation of Energy

1 Motivate

Bellringer Transparency

Display the Section Focus Transparency for Section 2. Use the accompanying Transparency Activity Master. L2 ELL

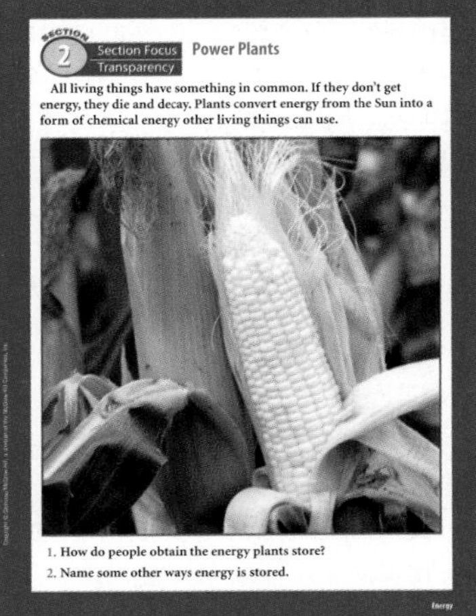

Section 2 Section Focus Transparency — Power Plants

All living things have something in common. If they don't get energy, they die and decay. Plants convert energy from the Sun into a form of chemical energy other living things can use.

1. How do people obtain the energy plants store?
2. Name some other ways energy is stored.

Tie to Prior Knowledge

Discuss the various forms of energy involved in skateboarding.

Text Question Answer

alarm clock—sound; hair styler—heat or kinetic; toaster—heat; music—sound; video game—light

Caption Answer

Figure 6 Possible answers: cars, televisions, bicycles

2 Teach

Changing Forms of Energy

Visual Learning

Figure 7 Review the energy conversions at work in an internal combustion engine. Then discuss how a diesel engine works. In a diesel engine, the air in the cylinder is compressed to a high pressure and becomes very hot. When the fuel is sprayed into the cylinder, it ignites in the hot air without the need of a spark plug. **What energy conversions take place in a diesel engine?** Chemical potential energy is converted to thermal energy and then to kinetic energy. L2

LS **Logical-Mathematical**

Conversions Between Kinetic and Potential Energy

Make a Model

Have students work in groups to make models that show the conversion from potential energy to kinetic energy. They might choose to use a spring, windup car, or ball to demonstrate the idea. L1 COOP LEARN

LS **Kinesthetic**

Extension

Have students research the imaginary inventions of cartoonist Rube Goldberg. Have them bring a picture of one invention they find to class and discuss the energy conversions illustrated by the contraption. L2 LS **Visual-Spatial**

Figure 7

A In a car, a spark plug fires, initiating the conversion of chemical potential energy into thermal energy.

B As the hot gases expand, thermal energy is converted into kinetic energy.

Fuel to Energy For many purposes, a convenient source of energy is fuel. Fuel stores energy in the form of chemical potential energy. For example, the car or bus that might have brought you to school this morning probably runs on gasoline. The engine transfers the chemical potential energy stored in gasoline into the kinetic energy of a moving car or bus. Several energy conversions occur in this process, as shown in **Figure 7.** An electrical spark ignites a small amount of fuel. The burning fuel produces heat or thermal energy. So chemical energy is changed to thermal energy. The thermal energy causes gases to expand and move parts of the car, producing kinetic energy.

Some energy transformations are less obvious because they do not result in visible motion, sound, heat, or light. Every green plant you see converts light energy from the Sun into energy stored in chemical bonds in the plant. If you eat an ear of corn, the chemical potential energy in the corn is transformed yet again when it is in your body.

Conversions Between Kinetic and Potential Energy

You have experienced many situations that involve conversions between potential and kinetic energy. Bicycles, roller coasters, and swings can be described in terms of potential and kinetic energy. Even something as simple as launching a rubber band or using a bow and arrow involves energy conversions. To understand the energy conversions in these activities, it is helpful to identify the mechanical energy of a system. **Mechanical energy** is the total amount of potential and kinetic energy in a system and can be expressed by this equation.

$$\text{mechanical energy} = \text{potential energy} + \text{kinetic energy}$$

In other words, mechanical energy is energy due to the position and the motion of an object. What happens to the mechanical energy of an object as potential and kinetic energy are converted into each other?

Inclusion Strategies

Gifted Remind students that work is the transfer of energy, is measured in the same units as energy, and can be calculated using the formula W = F × d. Provide students the following scenario: The kinetic energy of a hockey puck is 20 J as it moves from ice onto the cement surrounding the rink. **By how much is its energy decreased if it stops on the cement?** 20 J **If the cement causes a frictional force of 10 N on the puck, how far does it slide?** -10 N · d = -20 J, therefore d = 2.0 m **What happens to this energy?** It is converted into heat. L3

LS **Mathematical**

Falling Objects Standing under an apple tree can be hazardous. Here is an explanation of why this is true using energy terms. An apple on a tree, like the one in **Figure 8,** has gravitational potential energy due to Earth pulling down on it. The apple does not have kinetic energy while it hangs from the tree. However, the instant the apple comes loose from the tree, it accelerates due to gravity. As it falls, it loses height so its gravitational potential energy decreases. This potential energy is not lost. Rather, it is transformed into kinetic energy as the velocity of the apple increases.

Look back at the equation for mechanical energy. If the potential energy is being converted into kinetic energy, then the mechanical energy of the apple doesn't change as it falls. The potential energy that the apple loses is gained back as kinetic energy. The form of energy changes, but the total amount of energy remains the same.

Reading Check ***What happens to the mechanical energy of the apple as it falls from the tree?***

Energy transformation also occurs when a baseball is hit into the air. Look at **Figure 9.** When the ball leaves the bat, it has mostly kinetic energy. As the ball rises, its velocity decreases, so its kinetic energy must decrease, too. However, the ball's gravitational potential energy increases as it goes higher. At its highest point, the baseball has the maximum amount of gravitational potential energy. The only kinetic energy it has at this point is due to its forward motion. Then, as the baseball falls, gravitational potential energy decreases while kinetic energy increases as the ball moves faster. Once again, the mechanical energy of the ball remains constant as it rises and falls.

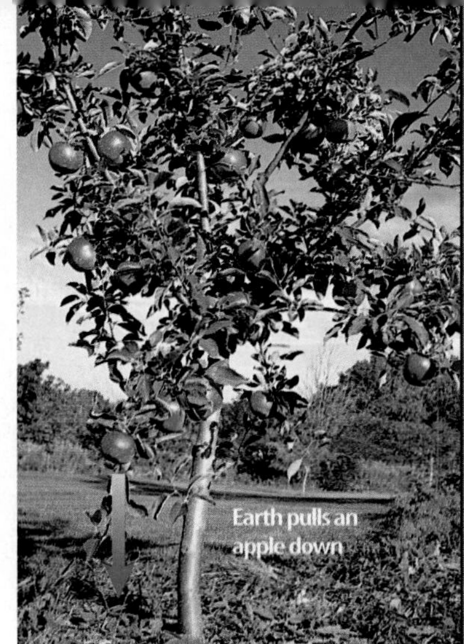

Figure 8
Objects that can fall have gravitational potential energy. *What objects around you have gravitational potential energy?*

Figure 9
A ball hit into the air illustrates how kinetic energy and gravitational potential energy are converted into each other.

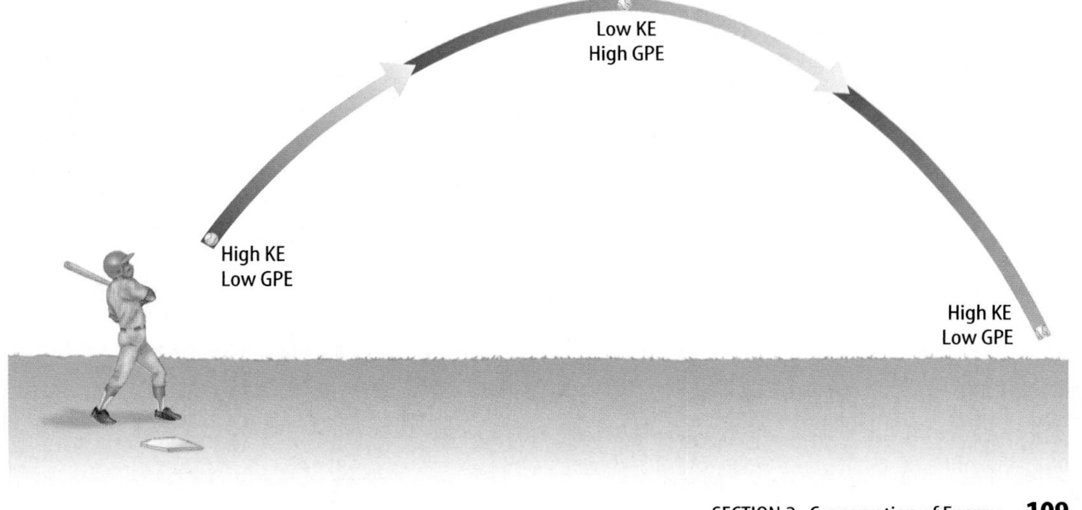

Reading Check

Answer Potential energy decreases; kinetic energy increases; total mechanical energy remains constant.

Caption Answer

Figure 8 Any objects that are elevated have GPE.

Discussion

You are riding in an elevator. **How do your kinetic and potential energy relative to the elevator change as you go up?** Neither changes. L1

Teacher FYI

If there is no air resistance, then two objects that start falling at the same time from the same height will hit the ground at the same time. The rate of free fall does not depend on mass. But an object with larger mass has more GPE before it falls and has more kinetic energy as it falls. In other words, it will hurt more when it hits your head.

Identifying Misconceptions

Some students may not realize that when the bob of a pendulum reaches its maximum height, it momentarily stops, and when it is at its lowest part of its swing, its velocity is highest. Sketch a pendulum on the board and use arrows to show movement. Explain that the bob must briefly stop to change directions. Because it has no velocity, it has no kinetic energy at this point.

Resource Manager

Chapter Resources Booklet
- Directed Reading for Content Mastery, pp. 21, 22
- Transparency Activity, p. 43

Cultural Diversity, p. 53

Curriculum Connection

History Students have probably heard the tale of Isaac Newton discovering gravity when an apple fell from a tree onto his head. Have students investigate this story to determine if it is a myth or a true occurrence. Have students share their findings with the class. Newton is purported to have said himself that the fall of the apple "occasioned" his "notion of gravitation." L3 LS **Interpersonal**

Visualizing Energy Transformations

Have students examine the pictures and read the captions. Then ask the following questions.

- **As the student goes from point A to B, why is her kinetic energy increasing?** because her velocity is increasing
- **What force accelerates the student as she goes from point A to the lowest point and slows down the student as she goes from the lowest point to point D?** gravity

Activity

The movement of the swing is similar to the movement of a pendulum. Provide students with a 1-meter piece of string with a large washer tied to the end of it. Ask students to simulate the movement of the swing or a pendulum using the string and washer. Have students experiment to see if the length of the string has any relationship to the time it takes the washer to make one complete period, going from point A on the diagram to point D and back to point A again.

Extension

Challenge students to learn how a pendulum clock works and prepare posters diagramming what they find.

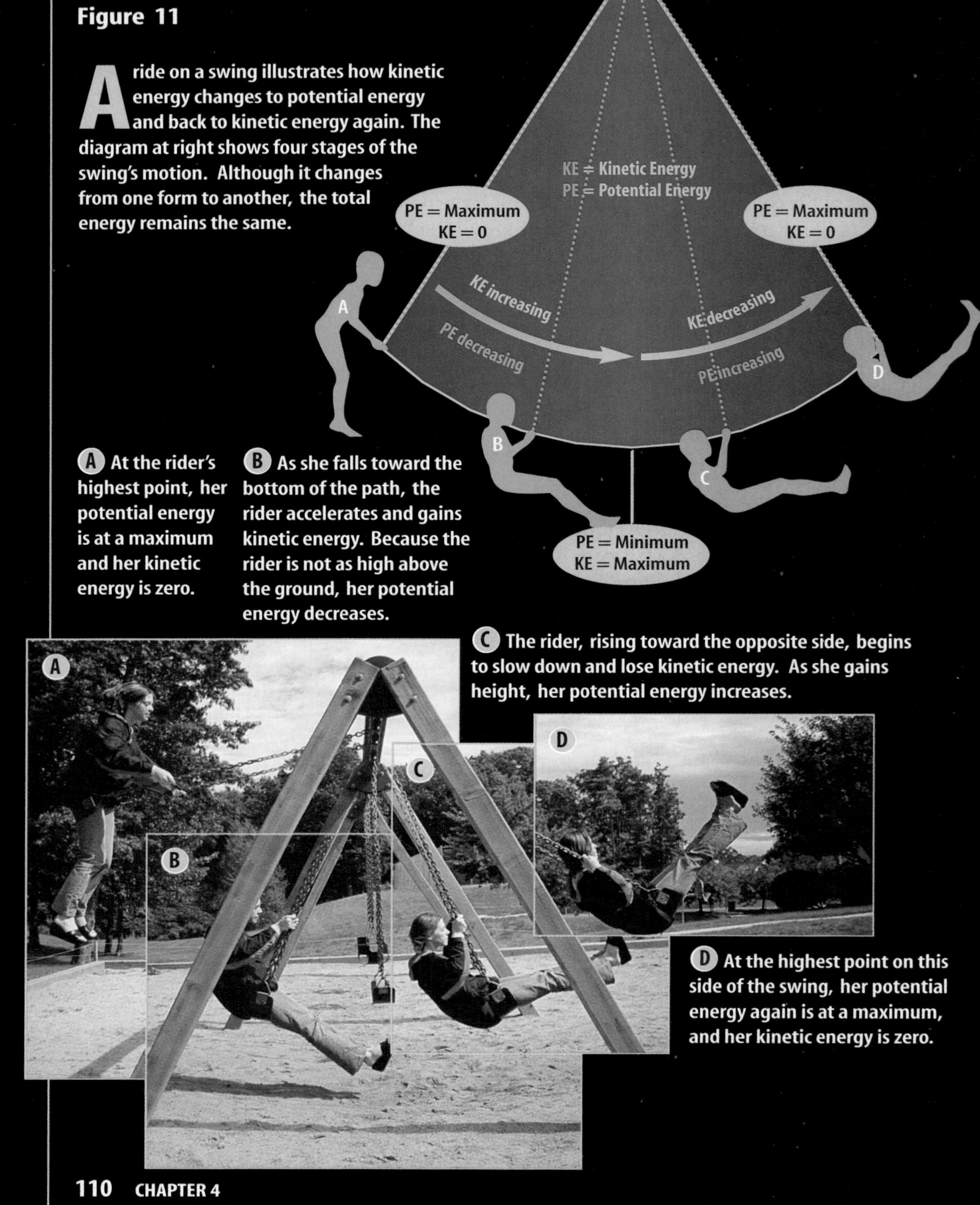

Figure 11

A ride on a swing illustrates how kinetic energy changes to potential energy and back to kinetic energy again. The diagram at right shows four stages of the swing's motion. Although it changes from one form to another, the total energy remains the same.

(A) At the rider's highest point, her potential energy is at a maximum and her kinetic energy is zero.

(B) As she falls toward the bottom of the path, the rider accelerates and gains kinetic energy. Because the rider is not as high above the ground, her potential energy decreases.

(C) The rider, rising toward the opposite side, begins to slow down and lose kinetic energy. As she gains height, her potential energy increases.

(D) At the highest point on this side of the swing, her potential energy again is at a maximum, and her kinetic energy is zero.

LAB DEMONSTRATION

Purpose to demonstrate the conservation of mechanical energy

Materials 1-m plastic tubing, 2 ring stands with clamps, marble

Preparation Form a U-shaped tunnel by clamping each end of the tubing to a ring stand. The ends should be at identical heights.

Procedure Hold a marble slightly above one end of the tubing. Have students predict the height the marble will reach on the opposite side. Release and discuss the result. Rearrange the tubing to form various shaped tunnels and repeat the activity.

Expected Outcome There should be a slight loss in mechanical energy.

✔Assessment

How was the mechanical energy affected as the marble traveled along the tubing? The mechanical energy decreased. **What are possible causes of this?** air resistance and friction from the tubing

Swinging Along When you ride on a swing, like the one shown in **Figure 10,** part of the fun is the feeling of almost falling as you drop from the highest point to the lowest point of the swing's path. Think about energy conservation to analyze such a ride.

The ride starts with a push that gets you moving, giving you some kinetic energy. As the swing rises, you lose speed but gain height. In energy terms, kinetic energy changes to gravitational potential energy. At the top of your path, potential energy is at its greatest. Then, as the swing accelerates downward, potential energy changes to kinetic energy. At the bottom of each swing, the kinetic energy is at its greatest and the potential energy is at its minimum. As you swing back and forth, energy continually converts from kinetic to potential and back to kinetic. What happens to your mechanical energy as you swing?

The Law of Conservation of Energy

When a ball is thrown into the air or a swing moves back and forth, kinetic and potential energy are constantly changing as the object speeds up and slows down. However, mechanical energy stays constant. Kinetic and potential energy simply change forms and no energy is destroyed.

This is always true. Energy can change from one form to another, but the total amount of energy never changes. Even when energy changes form from electrical to thermal and other energy forms as in the hair dryer shown in **Figure 11,** energy is never destroyed. Another way to say this is that energy is conserved. This principle is recognized as a law of nature. The **law of conservation of energy** states that energy cannot be created or destroyed. On a large scale, this law means that the total amount of energy in the universe remains constant.

Reading Check *What law states that the total amount of energy never changes?*

You might have heard about energy conservation or been told to conserve energy. These ideas are related to reducing the demand for electricity and gasoline, which lowers the consumption of energy resources such as coal and fuel oil. The law of conservation of energy, on the other hand, is a universal principle that describes what happens to energy as it is transferred from one object to another or as it is transformed.

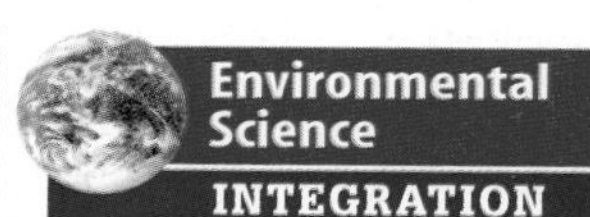

Environmental Science INTEGRATION

One way energy enters ecosystems is when green plants transform radiant energy from the Sun into chemical potential energy in the form of food. Energy moves through the food chain as animals that eat plants are eaten by other animals. Some energy leaves the food chain, such as when living organisms release thermal energy to the environment. Diagram a simple biological food chain showing energy conservation.

Figure 11
The law of conservation of energy requires that the total amount of energy going into a hair dryer must equal the total amount of energy coming out of the hair dryer. *Which object has kinetic energy ?*

Resource Manager

Chapter Resources Booklet
Lab Activity, pp. 13–15
Enrichment, p. 30
Home and Community Involvement, p. 36

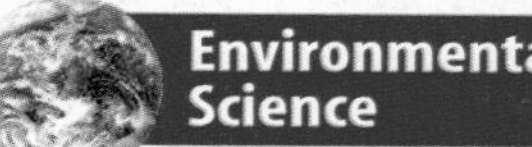

Environmental Science INTEGRATION

In a food chain, arrows show the direction in which energy moves from one organism to the next. Possible food chain: grass → rabbit → fox

Use Science Words

Word Meaning The word *conservation* means to keep from being lost or wasted. Discuss why this is an appropriate word to use for the principle of conservation of energy. Possible answer: It is appropriate because energy is never lost. It is not appropriate because some forms of energy are more valuable than others. L2 **Linguistic**

The Law of Conservation of Energy

Extension

Use a yo-yo to show the conservation of energy. The initial GPE changes to rotational kinetic energy (and translational kinetic energy) as the yo-yo falls. At the lowest point, the energy begins to change back to gravitational potential energy. Have students investigate the energy of a yo-yo and use computer graphics software to present their results. L2 **Visual-Spatial**

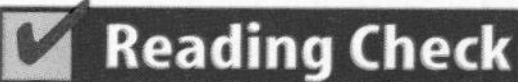

Reading Check

Answer the law of conservation of energy

The Law of Conservation of Energy, continued

Caption Answer

Figure 12 in the seat; in the support lines

Purpose Students observe how kinetic energy can change into thermal energy. L1

LS **Intrapersonal**

Materials paper clip

Teaching Strategy Have students use uncoated clips that are not too thick or brittle to easily bend.

Safety Precaution Students should be careful of the sharp ends of the paper clip when bending it.

Analysis

1. It went up. Some mechanical energy from the paper clip was converted to thermal energy.
2. Chemical energy from the body is converted to kinetic energy that is transferred to the paper clip. Mechanical energy is converted to thermal energy by collisions of the molecules.

Oral Have students discuss other examples of the process modeled by this activity. Possible answer: bicycle or car tires heat up as they roll along the road. Use **PASC,** p. 89.

Figure 12
Mechanical energy is transformed into thermal energy as the swing and the rider push on the air. *Where else is mechanical energy transformed into thermal energy?*

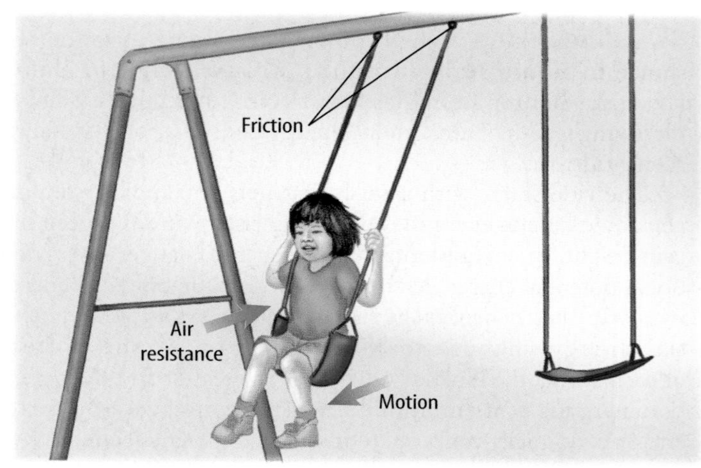

TRY AT HOME Mini LAB

Transforming Energy Using a Paper Clip

Procedure

1. Straighten a **paper clip.** While holding the ends, touch the paper clip to the skin just below your lower lip. Note whether the paper clip feels warm, cool, or about room temperature.
2. Quickly bend the paper clip back and forth five times. Touch it below your lower lip again. Note whether the paper clip feels warmer or cooler than before.

Analysis

1. What happened to the temperature of the paper clip? Why?
2. As you bend the paper clip, explain all the energy conversions that take place.

Friction and the Law of Conservation of Energy You might be able to think of situations where it seems like energy is not conserved. For example, while coasting along a flat road on a bicycle, you know that you will eventually stop if you don't pedal. If energy is conserved, why wouldn't your kinetic energy stay constant so that you would coast forever? In many situations, it might seem that energy is destroyed or created. Sometimes it is hard to see the law of conservation of energy at work.

Following Energy's Trail You know from experience that if you don't continue to pump the swing or be pushed by somebody else, your arcs will become lower and you eventually will stop swinging. In other words, the mechanical (kinetic and potential) energy of the swing seems to decrease, as if the energy were being destroyed. Is this a violation of the law of conservation of energy?

It can't be—it's the law! If the energy of the swing decreases, then the energy of some other object must increase by an equal amount to keep the total amount of energy the same. What could this other object be that experiences an energy increase? To answer this, you need to understand friction. With every movement, the swing's ropes or chains rub on their hooks and air pushes on the rider, as illustrated in **Figure 12.** Friction and air resistance cause some of the mechanical energy of the swing to change to thermal energy. With every pass of the swing, the temperature of the hooks and the air increases a little, so the mechanical energy of the swing is not destroyed. Rather, it is transformed into thermal energy. The total amount of energy always stays the same, obeying the law of conservation of energy.

Fun Fact

Many people have tried to develop a perpetual motion machine, a device which, once set in motion, would forever make more energy than it uses. Conservation of energy means that such a machine is impossible.

Inclusion Strategies

Learning Disabled To help students see how friction affects the velocity and therefore the kinetic energy of objects, have them roll marbles across a smooth table and then across a piece of carpet. Explain that the marbles move more slowly on the carpet because they lose kinetic energy to friction. L1 LS **Kinesthetic**

Converting Mass into Energy You might have wondered how the Sun unleashes enough energy to light and warm Earth from so far away. A special kind of energy conversion—nuclear fusion—takes place in the Sun and other stars. During this process a small amount of mass is transformed into a tremendous amount of energy. Two hydrogen nuclei come together and combine, or fuse, to form one helium nucleus as shown in **Figure 13A.**

Nuclear Fission Another process involving the nuclei of atoms, called nuclear fission, converts a small amount of mass into enormous quantities of energy. In this process, nuclei do not fuse—they are broken apart, as shown in **Figure 13B.** In either process, fusion or fission, mass is converted to energy. You must think of mass as energy when applying the law of conservation of energy to processes involving nuclear reactions. Here, as in all cases, the total amount of mass and energy is conserved. The process of nuclear fission is used by nuclear power plants to generate electrical energy. The fission process occurs in a nuclear reactor, and the heat released changes water to steam. The steam is used to spin an electric generator.

Research Visit the Glencoe Science Web site at **science.glencoe.com** for more information about the role of friction in the design of automobiles. Communicate to your class what you learn.

Figure 13
Mass is converted to energy in the processes of fusion and fission. But the change in mass is different.

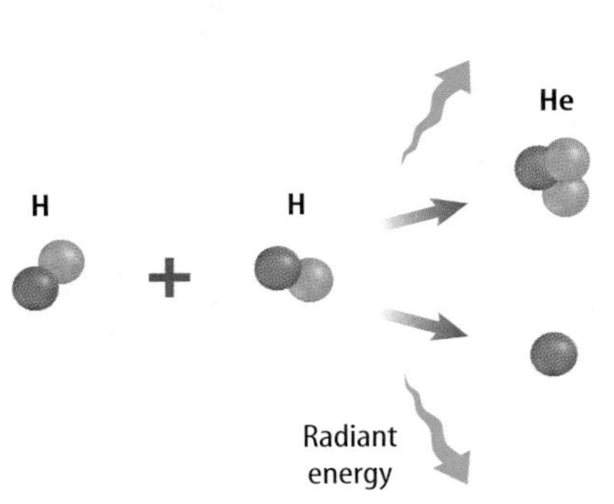

Mass **H** + **H** > Mass **He**

A **In nuclear fusion, the combined mass of the two hydrogen nuclei, H, is greater than the mass of the helium nucleus, He.**

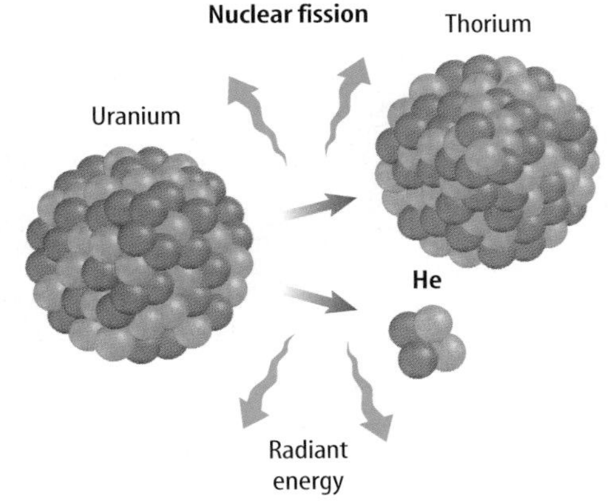

Mass Uranium > Mass Thorium + Mass **He**

B **In nuclear fission, the mass of the large nucleus on the left is greater than the combined mass of the other two nuclei.** *Why aren't the masses equal?*

Teacher FYI

In the process of fission, neutrons are released. They initiate further fission, beginning a chain reaction. For the chain reaction to continue, sufficient fissionable material must be present. The amount of material to sustain a chain reaction is known as the critical mass.

Use Science Words

Word Meaning Have students use a dictionary to look up the words *fusion* and *fission*. Ask them to explain why these are appropriate terms for the nuclear processes discussed in this section. Fusion is combining of things—in nuclear fusion, nuclei combine. Fission is splitting apart of things—in nuclear fission, nuclei split apart. L1 LS **Linguistic**

Caption Answer

Figure 13B Some of the mass has been converted to energy.

Resource Manager

Chapter Resources Booklet
MiniLAB, p. 4
Physical Science Critical Thinking/Problem Solving, p. 17
Cultural Diversity, p. 53

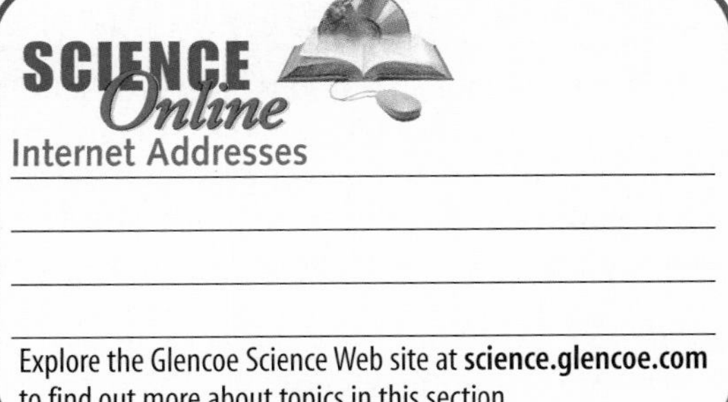

Explore the Glencoe Science Web site at **science.glencoe.com** to find out more about topics in this section.

The Human Body—Balancing the Energy Equation

IDENTIFYING Misconceptions

Students may confuse energy transformations with changes in matter. Some may state that food is converted into energy in the body. During digestion, chemical compounds in food are converted into compounds that muscle cells use to enable muscles to move.

Use Science Words

Word Origin The word *calorie* originates from the eighteenth-century word *caloric*, which was a hypothetical weightless fluid that scientists thought flowed from hot objects to cold objects. Ask students to find out how caloric theory contributed to the idea of conservation of energy. Scientists realized that caloric was neither gained nor lost during experiments. They gradually realized that caloric was the flow of energy. L2 LS **Linguistic**

Caption Answer

Figure 14 7 to 8 hours depending on body type

Visual Learning

Table 1 Have students think back over the past 24 hours and make a list of the things they did. Have them use the table to find out about how many Calories of energy they used. P

The Human Body—Balancing the Energy Equation

What forms of energy discussed in this chapter can you find in the human body? With your right hand, reach up and feel your left shoulder. With that simple action, stored potential energy within your body was converted to the kinetic energy of your moving arm. Did your shoulder feel warm to your hand? Some of the potential energy stored in your body is used to maintain a nearly constant internal temperature. A portion of this energy also is converted to the excess heat that your body gives off to its surroundings. Even the people shown standing in **Figure 14** require energy conversions to stand still.

Energy Conversions in Your Body The complex chemical and physical processes going on in your body also obey the law of conservation of energy. Your body stores energy in the form of fat and other chemical compounds. This chemical potential energy is used to fuel the processes that keep you alive, such as making your heart beat and digesting the food you eat. Your body also converts this energy to heat that is transferred to your surroundings, and you use this energy to make your body move. **Table 1** shows the amount of energy used in doing various activities. To maintain a healthy weight, you must have a proper balance between energy contained in the food you eat and the energy your body uses.

Figure 14
The runners convert the energy stored in their bodies more rapidly than the spectators do.
*Use **Table 1** to calculate how long a person would need to stand to burn as much energy as a runner burns in 1 h.*

Cultural Diversity

Energy in Martial Arts Karate, which means "empty hand," originated on Okinawa in the 17th century. A trained karateka can break a thin concrete block with his or her hand. Have students research the meanings of the names of other forms of martial arts and where they originated. Possible martial arts include judo, aikido, and tae kwon do. L2 LS **Intrapersonal**

Active Reading

Learning Journal Have students draw a vertical line down each page of a Learning Journal and record research notes, lecture notes, or vocabulary terms in the left column. In the right column, they respond to, interpret, question, or analyze the left column entries. Students can write a Learning Journal while reading about conservation of energy.

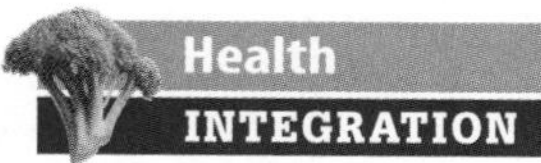

Food—Your Chemical Potential Energy

Energy Your body has been busy breaking down your breakfast into molecules that can be used as fuel. These fuel molecules, such as sugar, supply all the cells in your body with the energy they need to function. If you did not eat breakfast this morning, your body will convert energy stored in fat for its immediate needs until you eat again. The food Calorie (C) is a unit used by nutritionists to measure how much energy you get from various foods—1 C is equivalent to about 4,180 J. Every gram of fat a person consumes can supply 9 C of energy. Carbohydrates and proteins each supply about 4 C of energy per gram. The next time you go grocery shopping, look on the packages and notice how much energy each product eventually will supply to you.

Table 1 Calories Used in 1 h

Type of Activity	Body Frames		
	Small	Medium	Large
Sleeping	48	56	64
Sitting	72	84	96
Eating	84	98	112
Standing	96	112	123
Walking	180	210	240
Playing tennis	380	420	460
Bicycling (fast)	500	600	700
Running	700	850	1,000

Section 2 Assessment

1. Define the term *mechanical energy.* Describe the mechanical energy of a roller-coaster car immediately before it begins traveling down a long track.
2. What is the law of conservation of energy?
3. Applying bicycle brakes as you ride down a long hill causes the brake pads and the wheel rims to feel warm. Explain.
4. What is the source of the large amounts of energy released in nuclear reactors and in the Sun? Are the same processes occurring in the Sun and in reactors? Explain.
5. **Think Critically** Much discussion has focused on the need to drive more efficient cars and use less electricity. If the law of conservation of energy is true, why are people concerned about energy usage?

Skill Builder Activities

6. **Communicating** Suppose you drop a tennis ball out of a second-floor window. The first bounce will be the highest. Each bounce after that will be lower until the ball stops bouncing. Write a description of the energy conversions that take place, starting with dropping the ball. Accompany your description with an appropriate illustration. **For more help, refer to the** Science Skill Handbook.
7. **Communicating** Your body used energy as you walked into your school today. Where did this energy come from? In your Science Journal, write a paragraph describing where you acquired this energy. Trace it back through as many transformations as you can. **For more help, refer to the** Science Skill Handbook.

3 Assess

Reteach

Show students pictures of people performing various activities, such as those listed in **Table 1.** Ask students to order the pictures according to how quickly they burn Calories. Students should also identify types of energy conversion in each activity. L1 LS **Visual-Spatial**

Challenge

Have students use models to demonstrate nuclear fission and nuclear fusion. Students could use marbles for neutrons and protons, with clay to hold them together. L2 LS **Kinesthetic**

Assessment

Process Have students draw diagrams illustrating some of the changing forms of energy involved in bouncing a basketball. Chemical energy from the body changes to kinetic energy to lift the ball. This energy is transferred to the ball as potential energy. As the ball falls, this changes to kinetic energy. As the ball hits the floor, part of the energy changes to sound, part is transferred to the floor, and most is returned to the ball as elastic potential energy, enabling the ball to bounce. Use **Performance Assessment in the Science Classroom,** p. 127.

Answers to Section Assessment

1. the sum of potential and kinetic energy in a system; mostly potential energy
2. Energy cannot be created or destroyed.
3. Because of friction, kinetic energy is converted to thermal energy.
4. Mass changes to energy; no, nuclear fusion in the Sun, fission in reactors.
5. Much of the energy we use is converted to non-reusable forms.
6. The initial potential energy changes to kinetic during the fall. At the ground, kinetic energy becomes elastic potential energy, sound, thermal energy, and kinetic energy in the ground. This lost energy means the ball won't bounce as high each time.
7. Possible answers: conversion of radiant energy from the Sun to chemical energy in plants, conversion of chemical energy to mechanical energy for walking

Resource Manager

Chapter Resources Booklet
Activity Worksheet, pp. 7–8
Reinforcement, p. 28

Activity

BENCH TESTED

Recognize the Problem

Purpose

Construct a pendulum to compare the exchange of potential and kinetic energy. L2

COOP LEARN LS Kinesthetic

Process Skills

measuring, collecting and organizing data, observing and inferring, communicating, making and using tables, comparing and contrasting, recognizing cause and effect, forming a hypothesis, designing an experiment, using numbers, separating and controlling variables

Time Required

one class period

Materials

Have additional materials available (string, extra ring stands, banner paper, masking tape).

Safety Precautions

Students should wear safety goggles when swinging the stoppers.

Form a Hypothesis

Possible Hypothesis

Students may suggest that the crossarm's interference halfway up the length of the string will cause the maximum height to decrease by one half. In fact, the shape of the pendulum's path will change, but the height on the opposite end should still be close to the original height.

Activity

Design Your Own Experiment

Swinging Energy

Imagine yourself swinging on a swing. What would happen if a friend grabbed the swing's chains as you passed the lowest point? Would you come to a complete stop or continue rising to your previous maximum height?

Recognize the Problem

How would you design an experiment to answer the questions in the situation described above?

Form a Hypothesis

Examine the diagram on this page. How is it similar to the situation in the introductory paragraph? Hypothesize what will happen to the pendulum's motion and final height if its swing is interrupted.

Goals

- **Construct** a pendulum to compare the exchange of potential and kinetic energy when a swing is interrupted.
- **Measure** the starting and ending heights of the pendulum.
- Use the law of conservation of energy to explain observations.

Possible Materials

ring stand and ring
support-rod clamp, right angle
30-cm support rod
2-hole, medium rubber stopper
string (1 m)
metersticks
graph paper

Safety Precautions

Be sure the base is heavy enough or well anchored so that the apparatus will not tip over.

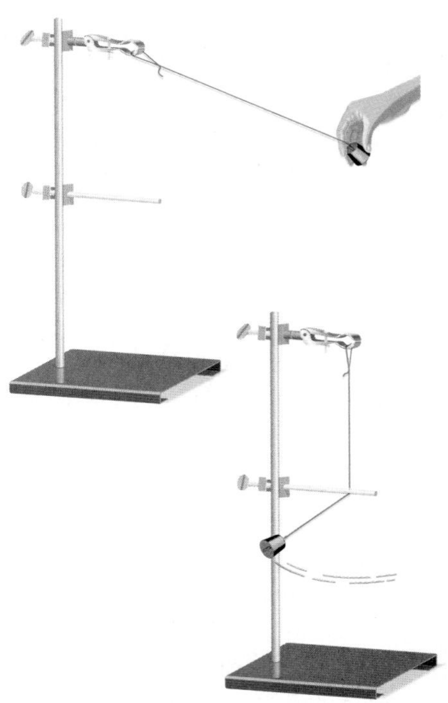

Inclusion Strategies

Gifted Have students determine the loss of energy from friction after the pendulum has swung 10 times. Have them measure the mass of the stopper, calculate its initial potential energy, using its initial height, and calculate its ending potential energy using the height after 10 swings. The difference is the amount of energy lost. Have them do this exercise both with and without cross-arm interference. L3 LS **Kinesthetic**

Data Table

	Trial 1	Trial 2	Trial 3
Initial Height			
Height with crossarm			

Test Your Hypothesis

Plan

1. As a group, write your hypothesis and list the steps that you will take to test it. Be specific. Also list the materials you will need.
2. **Design** a data table and place it in your Science Journal.
3. Set up an apparatus similar to the one shown in the diagram.
4. **Devise** a way to measure the starting and ending heights of the pendulum. Record your starting and ending heights in a data table. This will be your control.
5. **Decide** how to release the stopper from the same height each time.
6. Be sure you test your swing, starting it above and below the height of the cross arm. How many times should you repeat each starting point?

Do

1. Make sure your teacher approves your plan before you start.
2. Carry out the approved experiment as planned.
3. While the experiment is going on, write any observations that you make and complete the data table in your Science Journal.

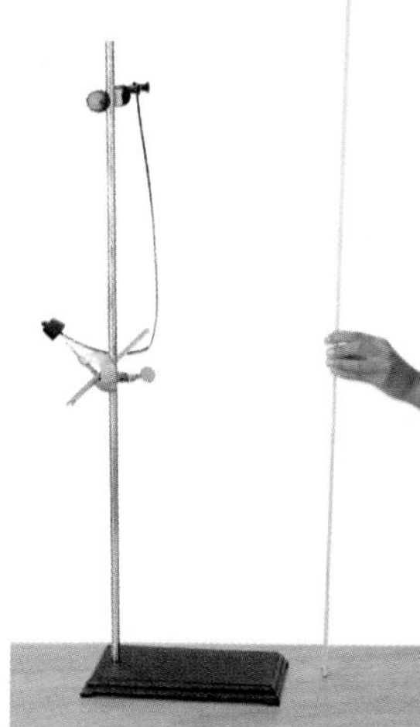

Analyze Your Data

1. When the stopper is released from the same height as the cross arm, is the ending height of the stopper exactly the same as its starting height? Use your data to support your answer.
2. **Analyze** the energy transfers. At what point along a single swing does the stopper have the greatest kinetic energy? The greatest potential energy?

Draw Conclusions

1. Do the results support your hypothesis? Explain.
2. **Compare** the starting heights to the ending heights of the stopper. Is there a pattern? Can you account for the observed behavior?
3. Do your results support the law of conservation of energy? Why or why not?
4. What happens if the mass of the stopper is increased? Test it.

Compare your conclusions with those of the other lab teams in your class. **For more help, refer to the Science Skill Handbook.**

Test Your Hypothesis

Possible Procedures

Set up the pendulum and start it moving. Measure the height at which the stopper was released to start the pendulum. When the pendulum is on the far side of its swing, insert the crossarm. Measure the height to which the pendulum swings after it hits the crossarm.

Teaching Strategies

Tape white paper to a wall behind the pendulum for marking stopper height.

Troubleshooting

The swing of the pendulum will be irregular if the crossarm inhibits movement of only one side of the pendulum's swing. Suggest students find a way to have the cross arm limit swing in both directions.

Expected Outcome

Students will observe that even with the crossarm, the approximate original height is reached.

Analyze Your Data

1. no
2. Kinetic is greatest at the bottom; potential is greatest at the top.

Draw Conclusions

1. Answers will vary with results.
2. Ending heights are lower. Friction slows the stopper and removes some energy from the system.
3. Yes; the apparent loss of energy is due to friction.
4. Kinetic and potential energy increase; the person must pull harder to stop the swing.

Assessment

Process When started from the same height, a pendulum without interference from a crossarm will remain in motion longer than a pendulum with an arm. Ask students to discuss and explain this. Some energy transfers to the crossarm. Use **Performance Assessment in the Science Classroom**, p. 89. L2 IS **Interpersonal**

Have students use a word processing program to write a short description of their experiment. They may wish to use a computer graphics program to make sketches that help explain the results.

Content Background

The laws of nature discussed in the Student Edition are the first and second laws of the thermodynamics. Thermodynamics also has a third law and a zeroth law. These laws deal with absolute zero and thermal equilibrium, respectively.

Perpetual motion machines have been around at least since Villand de Honnecourt made drawings of one in the 13th century. Between 1635 and 1903, 600 patents were granted for purported free-energy machines. Their claimants loved impressing people with their patents, but the granting of a patent does not guarantee a machine will work. Frauds and scams in the history of perpetual motion machines. John Worrel Keely of Keely Motors fooled scientists with a machine that appeared to run on water. He raised five million dollars of investor money; quite a large sum by 19th century standards. The machine was based on hidden air pressure tubes. In spite of the massive fraud that was found, there are still believers in his "technology" today.

More recently, Stanley Meyer claimed to have a water-powered car. Meyer was found guilty of fraud after his Water Fuel Cell was tested before an Ohio judge in 1996. It is rare for inventors to be prosecuted for inventions that don't work. Meyer was prosecuted because he was selling dealerships and offering investors the right to do business in Water Fuel Cell Technology.

TIME SCIENCE AND HISTORY

SCIENCE CAN CHANGE THE COURSE OF HISTORY!

The Impossible Dream

A machine that keeps on going? It has been tried for hundreds of years.

Science is a bit like an easy-going parent—it doesn't lay down a lot of laws. Those laws that do exist, however, are hard to get around. Just ask the hundreds of people who have tried throughout history—and failed—to build perpetual-motion machines.

In theory, a perpetual-motion machine would run forever and do work without a continual source of energy. You can think of it as a car that you could fill up once with gas, and with that single tankful, the car would run forever. Sound impossible? It is!

Artist M.C. Escher drew this never-ending staircase. You could walk on it perpetually!

118

Visitors look at the Keely Motor, the most famous perpetual-motion machine fraud of the later 1800s.

Resources for Teachers and Students

"Exploiting Zero-Point Energy", by Philip Yam. *Scientific American*, (December 1997).

Perpetual Motion: The History of An Obsession. by Arthur W.J.G. OrdHume. Barnes and Noble Books 1998.

Science Puts Its Foot Down

For hundreds of years, people have tried to create perpetual-motion machines. But these machines won't work because they go against two of nature's laws. The first law, the law of conservation of energy, states that energy cannot be created or destroyed. It can change form—say, from mechanical energy to electrical energy—but you always end up with the same amount of energy that you started with.

How does that apply to perpetual-motion machines? When a machine does work on an object, the machine transfers energy to the object. Unless that machine gets more energy, it can't keep doing work. If it did, it would be creating energy.

The second law states that heat by itself always flows from a warm object to a cold object. Heat will only flow from a cold object to a warm object if work is done. In the process, some heat is always lost. The hood of a car, for instance, feels hot when the car is running. That's lost heat, or energy, that has escaped from the system.

To make up for these energy losses, a machine needs more energy. Otherwise, it stops. No perpetual motion. No free electricity. No devices that generate more energy than they use. No engine motors that run forever without fuel. No lights that shine or ships that sail without a continual source of energy. Some laws just can't be broken.

Losing Battles

For more than 300 years, people have tried to build a perpetual-motion machine that works. Nobody has ever succeeded. In fact, the U.S. Patent Office, which studies inventions to see if they can work, refuses to look at these machines unless they have been working for a year. So far, none has.

Some laws just can't be broken.

CONNECTIONS Analyze Using your school or public library resources, locate a picture or diagram of a perpetual-motion machine. Figure out why it won't run forever. Explain to the class what the problem is.

SCIENCE Online
For more information, visit tx.science.glencoe.com

Discussion

What are the two laws of energy that make perpetual motioin machines impossible? Energy cannot be created or destroyed; it can only change form, and heat will only flow from a warm object to a cold object.

Historical Significance

Divide students into four or five groups and give each group a marble, a foam cup, a grooved ruler, a tongue depressor, and a paper and pencil.

Assign students the task of using their materials to transfer energy in such a way that their marble moves the greatest distance when they release it from a designated starting point. Inform them that throwing the marble or pushing it along the course is not permitted. They must simply release it from the starting point, and, using as many energy transfers as possible, cause it to travel as far as possible before stopping on its own.

After all groups have completed this task, a "play-off" may be held between groups to determine the best overall class set-up. Invite the winning group to explain the energy transfers involved in their set-up.

CONNECTIONS Ask students to think about how perpetual motion machines might be helpful to science and technology if the laws of thermodynamics did not exist. Start a dialogue addressing the thousands of scam artists who have tried in vain to sell their perpetual motion machines.

SCIENCE Online

Internet Addresses

Explore the Glencoe Science Web site at **science.glencoe.com** to find out more about topics in this feature.

Chapter 4 Study Guide

Reviewing Main Ideas

Preview

Students can answer the questions in their Science Journals. Discuss the answers as you go through the chapter. LS **Linguistic**

Review

Students can write their answers, then compare them with those of other students. LS **Interpersonal**

Reteach

Students can look at the illustrations and describe details that support the main ideas of the chapter. LS **Visual-Spatial**

Answers to Chapter Review

Section 1

2. Radiant energy from the Sun, mechanical energy of the windmill, chemical potential energy in the grass
4. Check that students use the formula GPE $= m \times 9.8\ m/s^2 \times h$, with GPE in joules, m in kg, and h in meters.

Section 2

3. Potential energy is being converted to kinetic energy and to thermal energy from friction; energy is always conserved.

Chapter  Study Guide

Reviewing Main Ideas

Section 1 The Nature of Energy

1. Energy is the ability of an object to cause change.
2. Energy can take a variety of different forms. *What are some of the forms of energy illustrated in the photograph below?*

3. Moving objects have kinetic energy that depends on the mass of the object and the velocity of the object.
4. Potential energy is stored energy. Objects that can fall have gravitational potential energy—the amount depends on their weight and height above the ground. *Estimate the amount of gravitational potential energy stored in Balanced Rock in Arches National Park.*

Section 2 Conservation of Energy

1. Energy can change from one form to another. You observe many energy transformations every day.
2. The law of conservation of energy states that energy never can be created or destroyed. Because of friction, energy might seem to be lost, but it has changed into thermal energy.
3. Falling, flying, and swinging objects all involve transformations between potential and kinetic energy. The total amount of potential and kinetic energy is called mechanical energy. *What energy transformations are taking place in the figure below? Is energy being conserved?*

4. Mass can be converted into energy in nuclear fusion and fission reactions. Fusion and fission involve atomic nuclei and release tremendous amounts of energy.

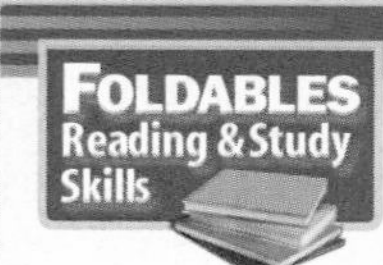

FOLDABLES Reading & Study Skills — **After You Read**

To help review what you've learned about energy and energy conservation, use the Foldable you made at the beginning of the chapter.

FOLDABLES Reading & Study Skills — **After You Read**

After students have read the chapter and completed the Foldable described in Before You Read, have them do the activity on the student page.

Dinah Zike

Chapter 4 Study Guide

Visualizing Main Ideas

Complete the concept map below using the following terms: nuclear fusion/fission, potential energy, friction, joules, kinetic energy.

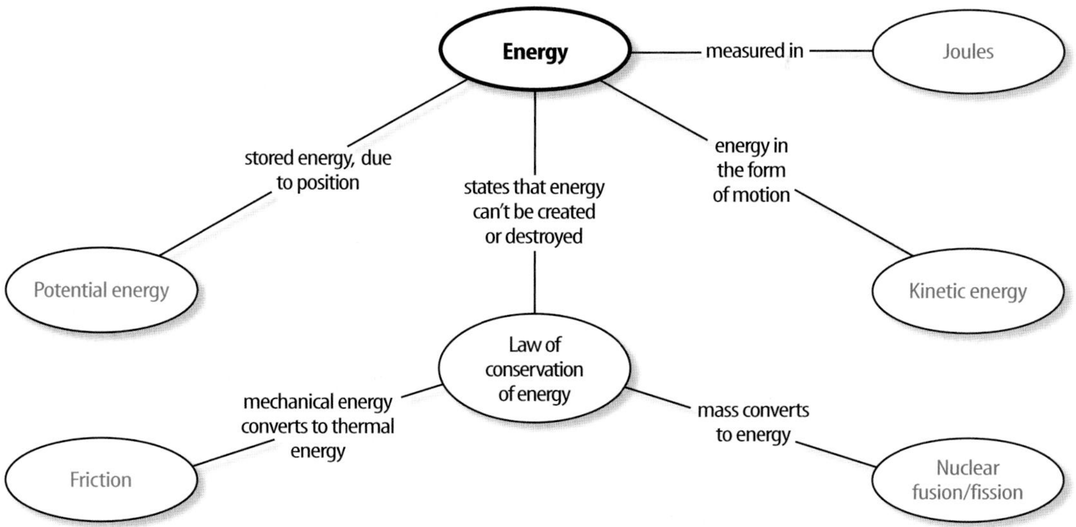

Vocabulary Review

Vocabulary Words

a. chemical potential energy
b. elastic potential energy
c. gravitational potential energy
d. joule
e. kinetic energy
f. law of conservation of energy
g. mechanical energy
h. potential energy

Study Tip

Be a teacher! Get together a group of friends and assign each person a section of the chapter to teach. When you teach you remember and understand information thoroughly.

Using Vocabulary

Using the list of vocabulary words, replace the underlined words with the correct science term.

1. In describing the energy changes of a bouncing ball, <u>the total amount of kinetic and potential energy</u> must be conserved.
2. The <u>energy due to stretching</u> of a bow can be used to propel an arrow forward.
3. Snow on the side of a mountain has <u>energy due to Earth pulling down on it</u>.
4. The <u>fact that energy cannot be created</u> means that dynamite does not create energy when it explodes.
5. The muscles of a runner transform chemical potential energy into <u>energy of motion</u>.

Chapter 4 Study Guide

Visualizing Main Ideas

See student page.

Vocabulary Review

Using Vocabulary

1. mechanical energy
2. elastic potential energy
3. gravitational potential energy
4. law of conservation of energy
5. kinetic energy

Checking Concepts

1. D
2. A
3. A
4. A
5. C
6. C
7. D
8. A
9. B
10. B

Thinking Critically

11. At the highest point, a pendulum has only potential energy. As it falls this changes to kinetic energy. At the lowest point, the pendulum has only kinetic energy. Friction slows the pendulum by converting mechanical energy to thermal energy.
12. Accept all reasonable answers.
13. Potential and kinetic energy are exchanged as the rider moves up and down along the roller coaster.
14. Under certain conditions, mass can be converted to energy and energy can be converted to mass.
15. 812.5 J

Chapter 4 Assessment

Checking Concepts

Choose the word or phrase that best answers the question.

1. When energy is transferred from one object to another, what must occur?
A) an explosion
B) a chemical reaction
C) nuclear fusion
D) a change

2. Which has more kinetic energy, a lightbulb shining brightly or a feather fluttering in the wind?
A) the fluttering feather
B) the shining lightbulb
C) both have the same kinetic energy
D) need more information to answer

3. What energy transformations occur when a lump of clay is dropped?
A) $GPE \rightarrow KE \rightarrow$ thermal energy
B) $KE \rightarrow$ chem $PE \rightarrow$ thermal energy
C) $KE \rightarrow GPE \rightarrow$ thermal energy
D) $GPE \rightarrow KE \rightarrow$ elastic PE

4. Suppose a juggler is juggling oranges. At an orange's highest point, what form of energy does it have?
A) mostly potential energy
B) mostly kinetic energy
C) no potential or kinetic energy
D) equal amounts of both

5. The gravitational potential energy of an object depends on which of the following?
A) velocity and height
B) velocity and weight
C) weight and height
D) weight and acceleration

6. Which idea is central to the law of conservation of energy?
A) Friction produces thermal energy.
B) People must conserve energy.
C) The total amount of energy is constant.
D) Energy is the ability to cause change.

7. To what property of an object is kinetic energy directly related?
A) volume
B) height
C) position
D) mass

8. Friction frequently causes some of an object's mechanical energy to be changed to which of the following forms?
A) thermal energy
B) nuclear energy
C) gravitational potential energy
D) chemical potential energy

9. What is the process of breaking apart large atomic nuclei into smaller nuclei called?
A) nuclear fusion
B) nuclear fission
C) atomic fracture
D) transformation

10. Green plants store energy from the Sun in what form?
A) light energy
B) chemical potential energy
C) gravitational potential energy
D) electrical energy

Thinking Critically

11. Briefly describe the energy changes in a swinging pendulum. Explain how energy is conserved, even as a pendulum slows.

12. Describe four ways elastic potential energy is used in the community around you.

13. Describe the energy conversions that take place during a roller-coaster ride.

14. Explain why the law of conservation of energy must include mass.

15. A 15-kg bicycle carrying a 50-kg boy is traveling at a speed of 5 m/s. What is the kinetic energy of the bicycle (including the boy)?

Chapter Assessment Planner

Portfolio Encourage students to place in their portfolios one or two items of what they consider to be their best work. Examples include:
- Curriculum Connection, p. 102
- Visual Learning, p. 114

Performance Additional performance assessments, Performance Task Assessment Lists, and rubrics for evaluating these activities can be found in Glencoe's **Performance Assessment in the Science Classroom.**

Developing Skills

16. Making and Using Tables Make a table that reports the kinetic energy of a 1-kg object moving at various speeds. Compute the kinetic energy at speed increments of 1 m/s, from 0 m/s to 10 m/s.

Energy of a Moving Object

Mass (kg)	Speed (m/s)	KE (J)
1	0	0
1	1	1
1	2	4
1	10	100

17. Making and Using Graphs Make a graph to show how kinetic energy changes as speed increases. Using the data from question 16, plot speed on the x-axis and kinetic energy on the y-axis. What shape does the graph have? How would you describe the relationship between speed and kinetic energy?

Performance Assessment

18. Poster Make an educational poster that highlights the law of conservation of energy. Include examples of energy conservation in your daily life.

19. Oral Presentation Research one type of alternative fuel. Find out the advantages and disadvantages of using the fuel. Present your findings to your class.

Technology

Go to the Glencoe Science Web site at **science.glencoe.com** or use the **Glencoe Science CD-ROM** for additional chapter assessment.

Test Practice

A team of students conducted an experiment in energy conversion and collected their data in a table.

Trial	Mass of Toy Car	Length of Ramp	Time to Travel Ramp(s)	Speed
1	7.5	1	1.0	1
	7.5	2	2.0	1
2	7.5	1	0.5	2
	7.5	2	1.0	2

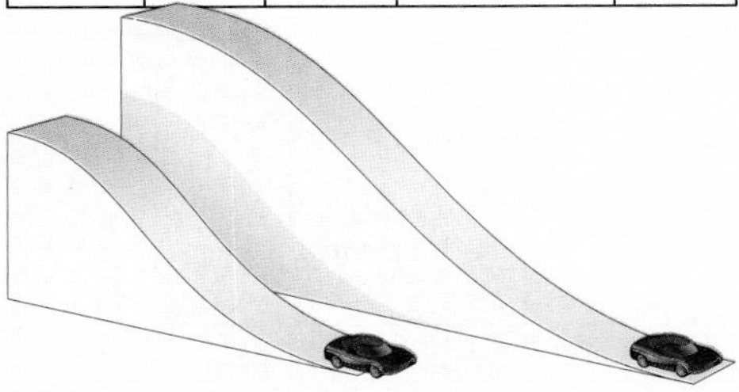

Study the experiment and the table above and answer the following questions.

1. The illustration above shows how these data were collected. Recording which one of the following would improve the experiment?

A) owner of the toy cars
B) weather conditions
C) height of incline
D) brand of the toy cars

2. At the beginning of the experiment, a toy car is at rest at the top of a ramp. In this position, what form of energy is stored in the car?

F) kinetic energy
G) fission
H) potential energy
J) mass

Assessment Resources

 **Reproducible Masters**

Chapter Resources Booklet
Chapter Review, pp. 35–36
Chapter Tests, pp. 37–40
Assessment Transparency Activity, p. 47

Glencoe Science Web site
Interactive Tutor
Chapter Quizzess

Glencoe Technology
Assessment Transparency
Interactive CD-ROM Chapter Quizzes
ExamView Pro Test Bank
Vocabulary PuzzleMaker Software
MindJogger Videoquiz DVD/VHS

Chapter 4 Assessment

Test Practice

The Test-Taking Tip was written by The Princeton Review, the nation's leader in test preparation.

1. C
2. H

Developing Skills

16. (Kinetic energy in joules) 0, 0.5, 2, 4.5, 8, 12.5, 18, 24.5, 32, 40.5, 50

17. an increasing curve; the kinetic energy changes as the square of the speed

Performance Assessment

18. Possible answers: walking (potential energy changes to kinetic energy and this changes to elastic potential energy); swimming (chemical potential energy in the swimmer changes to kinetic energy and thermal energy); cooking (electrical energy changes to thermal energy). Use **PASC**, p. 145.

19. Presentations should include alternative fuels, and their advantages and disadvantages. Use **PASC**, p. 143.

Section/Objectives	Standards		Activities/Features
	National	State/Local	
Chapter Opener	See p. 37T for a Key to Standards.		**Explore Activity:** Construct a pulley, p. 125 **Before You Read,** p. 125
Secton 1 Work 2 sessions 1 block 1. **Explain** the meaning of work. 2. **Explain** how work and energy are related. 3. **Calculate** work. 4. **Calculate** power.	National Content Standards: UCP1, UCP3, A1, B2 (5–8), B4 (9–12)		**MiniLAB:** Calculating Your work and Power, p. 129 **Science Online,** p. 130 **Math Skills Activity:** Calculating Power Given Work and Time, p. 130
Secton 2 Using Machines 2 sessions .5 blocks 1. **Explain** how machines make work easier. 2. **Calculate** mechanical advantage. 3. **Calculate** efficiency. 4. **Explain** ideal mechanical advantage.	National Content Standards: UCP1, UCP3, A1, B2 (5–8), B4 (9–12), E1		**MiniLAB:** Machines Multiplying Force, p. 134 **Chemistry Integration,** p. 136
Secton 3 Simple Machines 3 sessions 1.5 blocks 1. **Describe** the six types of simple machines. 2. **Calculate** the ideal mechanical advantage for different types of simple machines.	National Content Standards: UCP1, UCP3, A1, A2, B2 (5–8), B4 (9–12), E1, E2, F1 (5–8), F1 (912), F5 (5–8), F6 (9–12), G1		**Visualizing Levers in the Human Body,** p. 140 **Activity:** Levers, p. 147 **Activity:** Work Smarter, p. 148 **Science and Society:** The Science of Very Small Machines, p. 150

Activity Materials	Reproducible Resources	Section Assessment	Technology
Explore Activity: rope, broom handle, metric ruler, work or garden gloves	**Chapter Resources Booklet** Foldables Worksheet, p. 19 Note-taking Worksheets, pp. 35–37		
MiniLAB: stairs, stopwatch	**Chapter Resources Booklet** Transparency Activity, p. 46 Enrichment, p. 32 Reinforcement, p. 29 Directed Reading, p. 22 **Cultural Diversity,** p. 63 **Mathematics Skill Activities,** p. 11 MiniLAB, p. 3	**Portfolio** Assessment, p. 129 Assessment, p. 131 **Performance** MiniLAB, p. 129 Math Skills Activity, p. 130 Skill Builder Activities, p. 131 **Content** Section Assessment, p. 131	Section Focus Transparency Interactive CD-ROM/DVD Guided Reading Audio Program
MiniLAB: can of food, manual can opener, metric ruler	**Chapter Resources Booklet** Transparency Activity, p. 47 Enrichment, p. 33 Reinforcement, p. 30 Directed Reading, p. 22 MiniLAB, p. 4 **Physical Science Critical Thinking/Problem Solving,** p. 3	**Portfolio** Curriculum Connection, p. 134 **Performance** MiniLAB, p. 134 Skill Builder Activities, p. 137 **Content** Section Assessment, p. 137	Section Focus Transparency Interactive CD-ROM/DVD Guided Reading Audio Program
Activity: 8 1/2 X 11" sheet of paper, 1 quarter, 1 dime, 1 nickel, balance, metric ruler **Activity:** spring scale (1–10 N range), 9.8 N weight (1 kg mass), double pulleys (2), string for pulleys, stand for pulleys, board (40 cm long), support for board (10 cm high)	**Chapter Resources Booklet** Transparency Activity, p. 48 Activity Worksheet, pp. 5–6, 7–8 Enrichment, p. 34 Reinforcement, p. 31 Directed Reading, pp. 23, 24 Lab Activity, pp. 9–11, 13–18 Transparency Activity, pp. 49–50 **Home and Community Involvement,** p. 35 **Physical Science Critical Thinking/Problem Solving,** pp. 6, 7	**Portfolio** Extension, p. 144 **Performance** Skill Builder Activities, p. 146 **Content** Section Assessment, p. 146	Section Focus Transparency Teaching Transparency Interactive CD-ROM/DVD Guided Reading Audio Program

GLENCOE'S ASSESSMENT ADVANTAGE

End of Chapter Assessment		
Blackline Masters	**Technology**	**Professional Series**
Chapter Resources Booklet Chapter Review, pp. 39–40 Chapter Tests, pp. 41–44 **Standardized Test Practice by The Princeton Review,** pp. 24–27	MindJogger Videoquiz CD-ROM Explorations and Quizzes Vocabulary Puzzle Makers ExamView Pro Test Bank Interactive Lesson Planner Interactive Teacher's Edition	Performance Assessment in the Science Classroom (PASC)

Transparencies

Section Focus

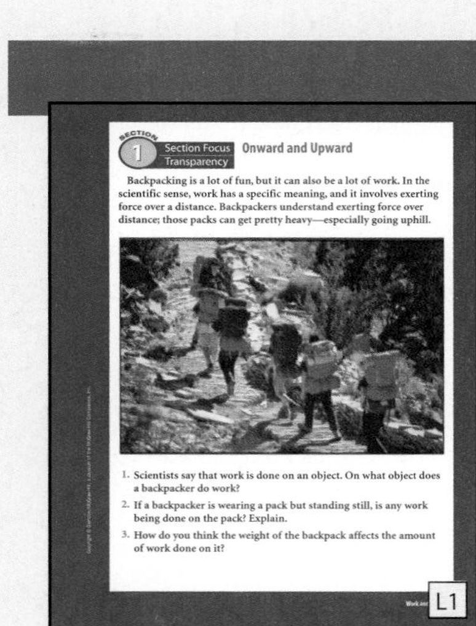
Section 1 Section Focus Transparency — Onward and Upward

Backpacking is a lot of fun, but it can also be a lot of work. In the scientific sense, work has a specific meaning, and it involves exerting force over a distance. Backpackers understand exerting force over distance; those packs can get pretty heavy—especially going uphill.

1. Scientists say that work is done on an object. On what object does a backpacker do work?
2. If a backpacker is wearing a pack but standing still, is any work being done on the pack? Explain.
3. How do you think the weight of the backpack affects the amount of work done on it?

L1

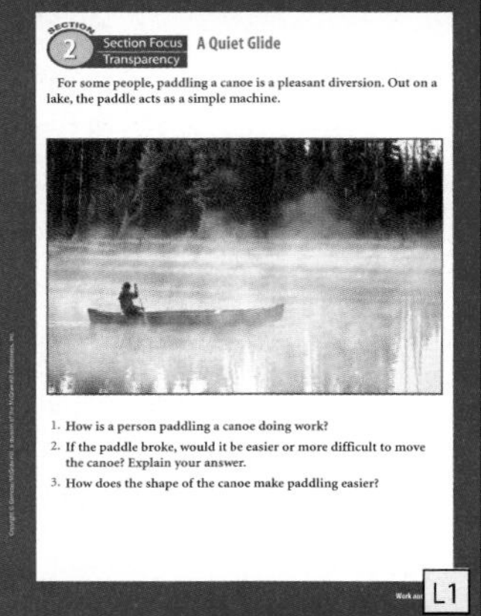
Section 2 Section Focus Transparency — A Quiet Glide

For some people, paddling a canoe is a pleasant diversion. Out on a lake, the paddle acts as a simple machine.

1. How is a person paddling a canoe doing work?
2. If the paddle broke, would it be easier or more difficult to move the canoe? Explain your answer.
3. How does the shape of the canoe make paddling easier?

L1

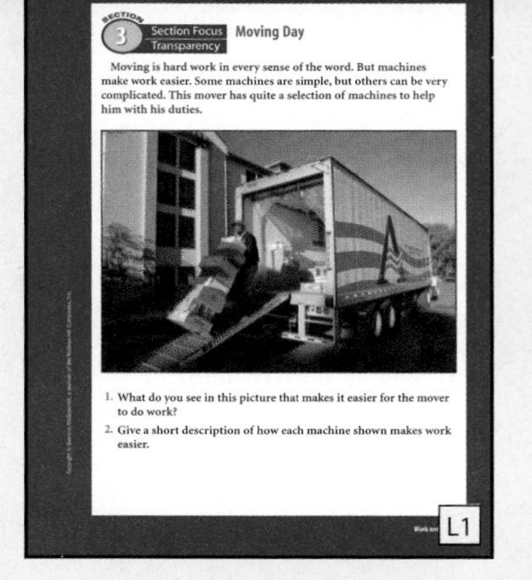
Section 3 Section Focus Transparency — Moving Day

Moving is hard work in every sense of the word. But machines make work easier. Some machines are simple, but others can be very complicated. This mover has quite a selection of machines to help him with his duties.

1. What do you see in this picture that makes it easier for the mover to do work?
2. Give a short description of how each machine shown makes work easier.

L1

Assessment

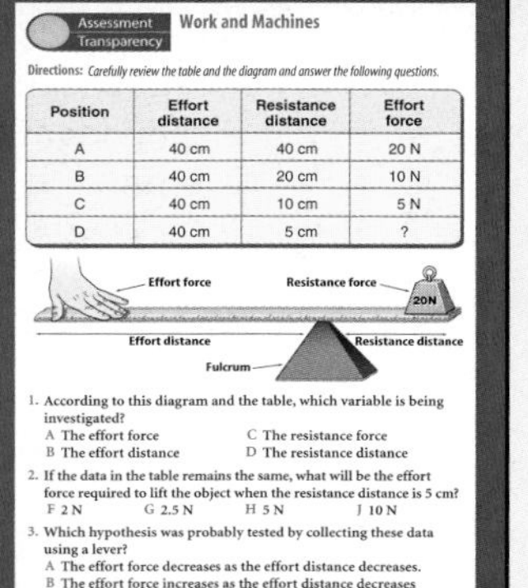
Assessment Transparency — Work and Machines

Directions: *Carefully review the table and the diagram and answer the following questions.*

Position	Effort distance	Resistance distance	Effort force
A	40 cm	40 cm	20 N
B	40 cm	20 cm	10 N
C	40 cm	10 cm	5 N
D	40 cm	5 cm	?

1. According to this diagram and the table, which variable is being investigated?
   A The effort force
   B The effort distance
   C The resistance force
   D The resistance distance
2. If the data in the table remains the same, what will be the effort force required to lift the object when the resistance distance is 5 cm?
   F 2 N
   G 2.5 N
   H 5 N
   J 10 N
3. Which hypothesis was probably tested by collecting these data using a lever?
   A The effort force decreases as the effort distance decreases.
   B The effort force increases as the effort distance decreases.
   C The effort force decreases as the resistance distance decreases.
   D The effort force increases as the resistance distance decreases.

L1

Teaching

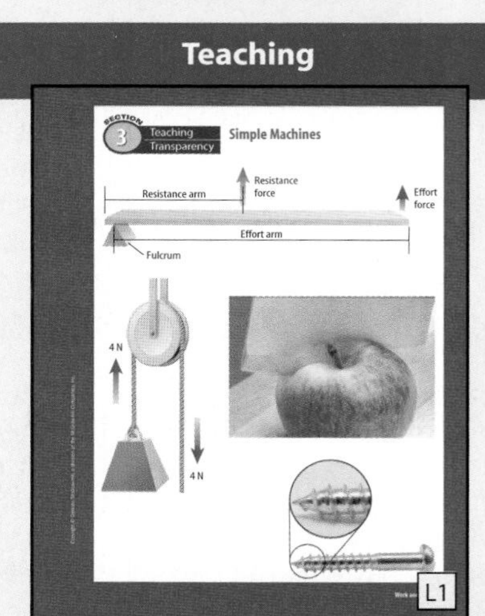
Section 3 Teaching Transparency — Simple Machines

L1

This is a representation of key blackline masters available in the Teacher Classroom Resources. See Resource Manager boxes within the chapter for additional information.

Key to Teaching Strategies

The following designations will help you decide which activities are appropriate for your students.

- L1 Level 1 activities should be appropriate for students with learning difficulties.
- L2 Level 2 activities should be within the ability range of all students.
- L3 Level 3 activities are designed for above-average students.
- ELL ELL activities should be within the ability range of English Language Learners.
- COOP LEARN Cooperative Learning activities are designed for small group work.
- LS Multiple Learning Styles logos are used throughout to indicate strategies that address different learning styles.
- P These strategies represent student products that can be placed into a best-work portfolio.

Hands-on Activities

Activity Worksheets

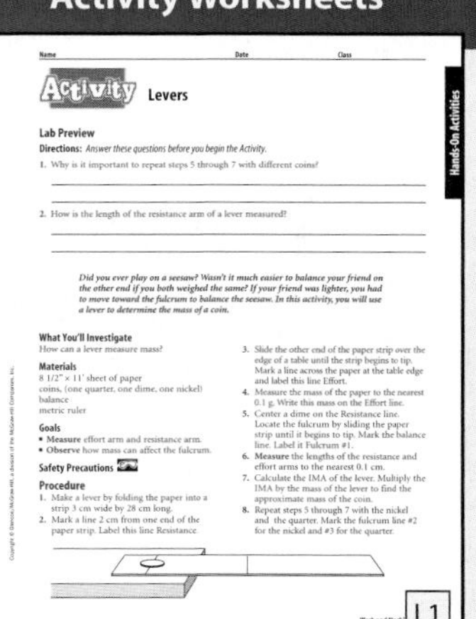
Name Date Class

Activity — Levers

Lab Preview

Directions: *Answer these questions before you begin the Activity.*

1. Why is it important to repeat steps 5 through 7 with different coins?
2. How is the length of the resistance arm of a lever measured?

Did you ever play on a seesaw? Wasn't it much easier to balance your friend on the other end if you both weighed the same? If your friend was lighter, you had to move toward the fulcrum to balance the seesaw. In this activity, you will use a lever to determine the mass of a coin.

What You'll Investigate
How can a lever measure mass?

Materials
8 1/2" × 11' sheet of paper
coins, (one quarter, one dime, one nickel)
balance
metric ruler

Goals
- **Measure** effort arm and resistance arm.
- **Observe** how mass can affect the fulcrum.

Safety Precautions

Procedure
1. Make a lever by folding the paper into a strip 3 cm wide by 28 cm long.
2. Mark a line 2 cm from one end of the paper strip. Label this line Resistance.
3. Slide the other end of the paper strip over the edge of a table until the strip begins to tip. Mark a line across the paper at the table edge and label this line Effort.
4. Measure the mass of the paper to the nearest 0.1 g. Write this mass on the Effort line.
5. Center a dime on the Resistance line. Locate the fulcrum by sliding the paper strip until it begins to tip. Mark the balance line. Label it Fulcrum #1.
6. **Measure** the lengths of the resistance and effort arms to the nearest 0.1 cm.
7. Calculate the IMA of the lever. Multiply the IMA by the mass of the lever to find the approximate mass of the coin.
8. Repeat steps 5 through 7 with the nickel and the quarter. Mark the fulcrum line #2 for the nickel and #3 for the quarter.

Hands-On Activities

L1

Laboratory Activities

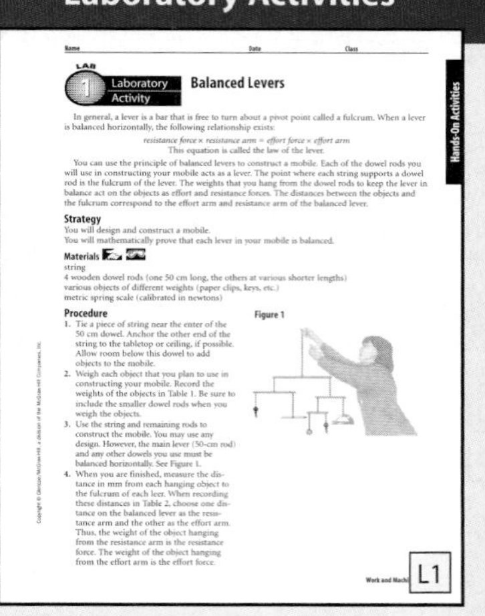
Name Date Class

Lab 1 Laboratory Activity — Balanced Levers

In general, a lever is a bar that is free to turn about a pivot point called a fulcrum. When a lever is balanced horizontally, the following relationship exists:

resistance force × resistance arm = effort force × effort arm

This equation is called the law of the lever.

You can use the principle of balanced levers to construct a mobile. Each of the dowel rods you will use in constructing your mobile acts as a lever. The point where each string supports a dowel rod is the fulcrum of the lever. The weights that you hang from the dowel rods to keep the lever in balance act on the objects as effort and resistance forces. The distances between the objects and the fulcrum correspond to the effort arm and resistance arm of the balanced lever.

Strategy
You will design and construct a mobile.
You will mathematically prove that each lever in your mobile is balanced.

Materials
string
4 wooden dowel rods (one 50 cm long, the others at various shorter lengths)
various objects of different weights (paper clips, keys, etc.)
metric spring scale (calibrated in newtons)

Procedure
1. Tie a piece of string near the enter of the 50 cm dowel. Anchor the other end of the string to the tabletop or ceiling, if possible. Allow room below this dowel to add objects to the mobile.
2. Weigh each object that you plan to use in constructing your mobile. Record the weights of the objects in Table 1. Be sure to include the smaller dowel rods when you weigh the objects.
3. Use the string and remaining rods to construct the mobile. You may use any design. However, the main lever (50-cm rod) and any other dowels you use must be balanced horizontally. See Figure 1.
4. When you are finished, measure the distance in mm from each hanging object to the fulcrum of each leer. When recording these distances in Table 2, choose one distance on the balanced lever as the resistance arm and the other as the effort arm. Thus, the weight of the object hanging from the resistance arm is the resistance force. The weight of the object hanging from the effort arm is the effort force.

Figure 1

Hands-On Activities

L1

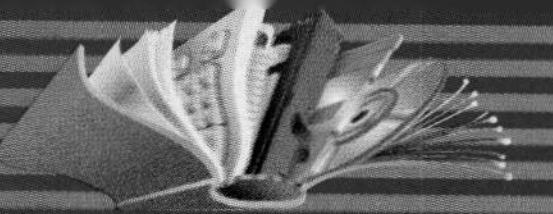

Meeting Different Ability Levels

Content Outline

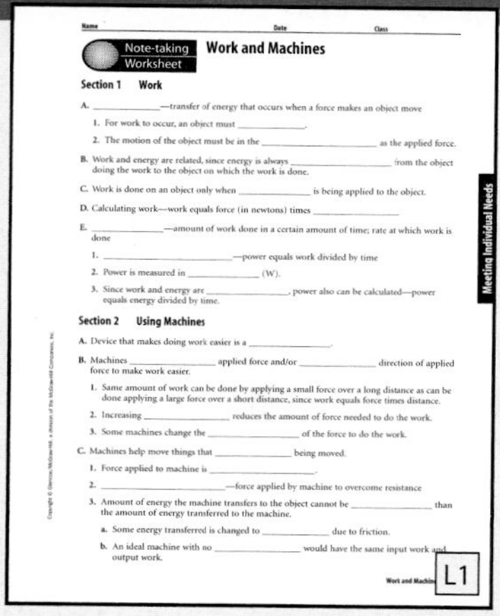

Note-taking Worksheet — Work and Machines

Section 1 Work

Section 2 Using Machines

L1

Reinforcement

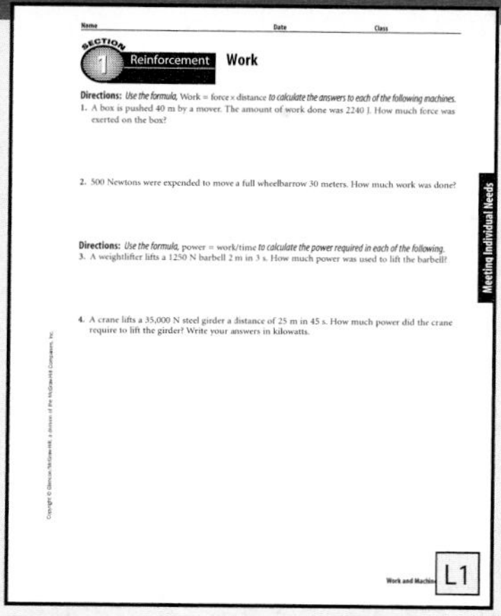

Section 1 Reinforcement — Work

L1

Directed Reading

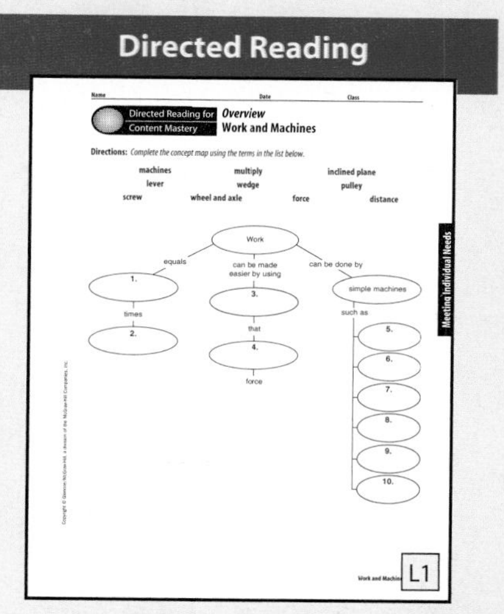

Directed Reading for Content Mastery — Overview: Work and Machines

L1

Assessment

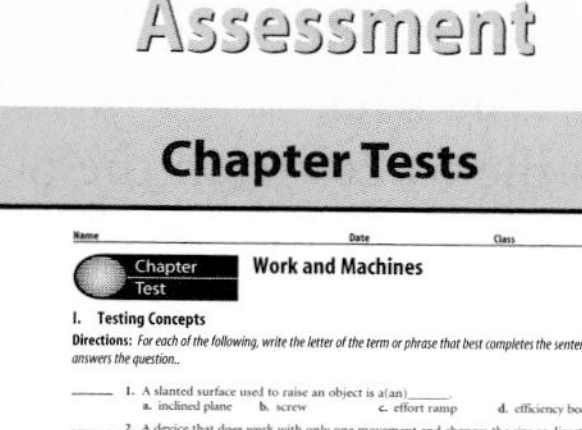

Chapter Tests

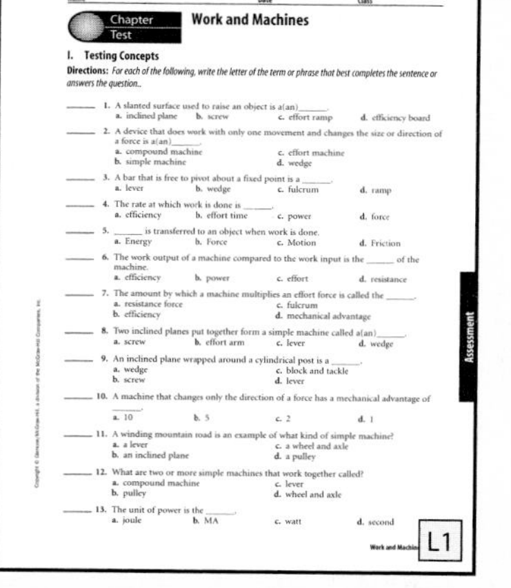

Chapter Test — Work and Machines

L1

Enrichment

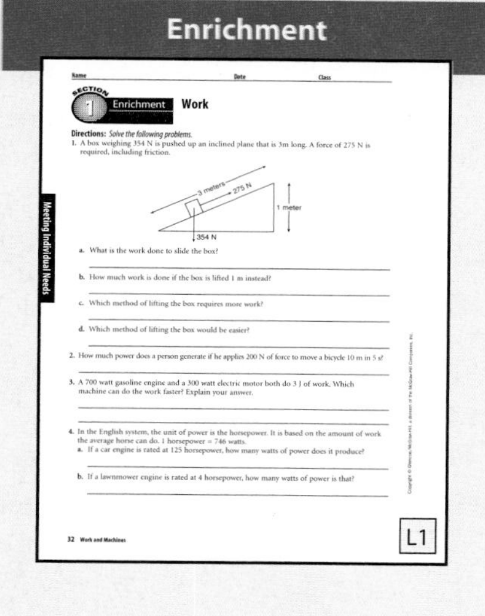

Section 1 Enrichment — Work

L1

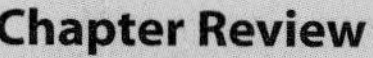

Spanish Directed Reading

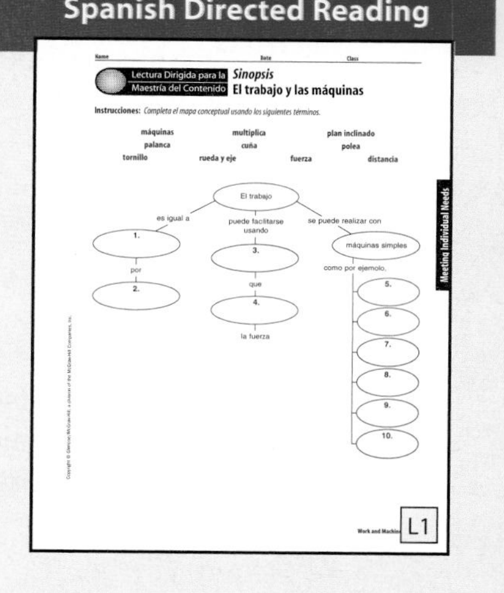

Lectura Dirigida para la Maestría del Contenido — Sinopsis: El trabajo y las máquinas

L1

Test Practice Workbook

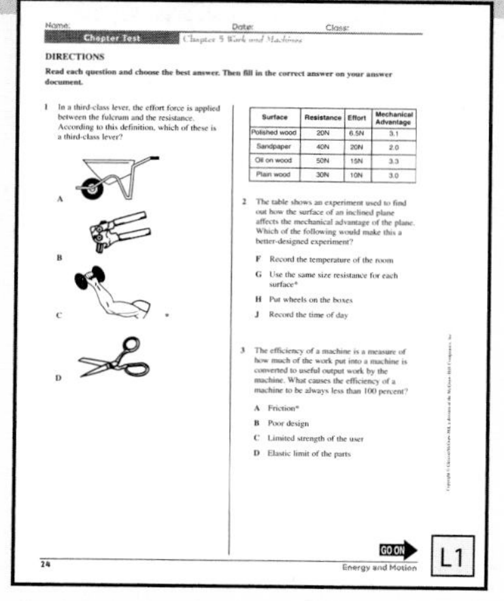

Chapter Test — Chapter 5 Work and Machines

L1

Chapter Review

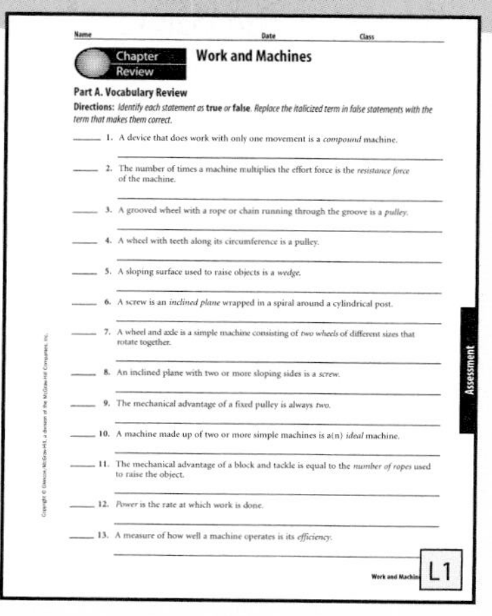

Chapter Review — Work and Machines

Part A. Vocabulary Review

L1

Science Content Background

SECTION 1

Work

Power

The horsepower is a common, although nonmetric, unit of power. It was originally created by James Watt to compare his steam engines to the power of a horse. It is equivalent to 760 watts.

SECTION 2

Using Machines

Making Work Easier

Many simple machines allow a person to use less effort to produce an effect such as lifting an engine or opening a soda bottle. These machines do not save work, as the smaller force supplied must be applied over a greater distance to produce the effect.

Student Misconception

A simple machine allows us to do less work.

Refer to the facing page for teaching strategies to address this misconception. Refer to pages 136–146 for content related to this topic.

Jeff J. Daly/Visuals Unlimited

Efficiency

New electrical appliances often have yellow stickers on them that state their efficiency in terms that the consumer can appreciate easily—how much the appliance will cost per year to operate. This expression of efficiency is loosely related to but not identical to efficiency as defined in the text. The more efficient an appliance as defined in the text, the less it costs to operate.

SECTION 3

Simple Machines

Pulleys

When counting the number of ropes supporting a load to determine mechanical advantage, the rope that is actually pulled is not counted. An easier means for determining mechanical advantage of a block and tackle system is to count the number of pulleys.

Wheel and Axles

Not all wheels with axles are simple machines. For example, the front wheel of a bicycle is not a simple machine. An area where a force is applied is needed. Thus the back wheel of bicycle, because it receives the forces from the pedals, is a simple machine.

Wedges

While considered a type of inclined plane, the wedge takes advantage of the relationships between force, pressure, and area as described by the equation $P = F/A$. The small area of the sharp front of a wedge multiples the force exerted on the larger back of the wedge so the front edge exerts a higher pressure.

For additional content background on this topic, go to the Glencoe Science Web site at science.glencoe.com.

Misconceptions

Find Out What Students Think

Students may think that . . .

- **A simple machine allows us to do less work.**

The term *machine* often makes people think of things such as cars and power tools. By using fuel or electrical energy to do work, these machines do allow people to do less work. This conception of machines may create the misconception that simple machines also allow people to do less work. Additionally, the force used on a simple machine provides an immediate sensation to the worker. Using a simple machine to do a task often feels easier than doing the task without the machine, and this may contribute to the idea less work is being done.

Activity

Ask students to write explanations of why people use simple machines such as the lever, pulley, and inclined plane. Have a few students read their explanations to the class. Then have the class try to decide which is the best explanation.

Promote Understanding

Activity

Show students a picture of movers pushing a large object up a ramp into the truck. Why do they use this ramp? Lead the discussion so students debate whether the movers do it to do less work or to use less effort. Have students do the following activity to find the answer. Organize the class into groups and give each group a spring scale, ruler, wooden plank, wood block with hook, and string. Tell them follow these steps:

- Use the spring scale to lift the block from the floor to a chair, and note the reading from the scale as it rises.
- Measure the height of the chair, and multiply force times distance to obtain the work done lifting the block.
- Rest the plank on the chair so it rises at about a 45° angle from the ground. Pull the block up the plane to the chair, and measure the effort used by reading the scale while the block is moving
- Measure the distance the block traveled and calculate the amount of work done.
- Compare the amounts of effort used and the amounts of work done in the two situations.

The results show that the simple machine made it easier to lift the load, but the amount of work students did with the ramp was the same or greater than the work done just lifting the block.

Assess

After completing the chapter, see *Identifying Misconceptions* in the Study Guide.

CHAPTER 5

Work and Machines

Chapter Vocabulary

work
power
machine
effort force
resistance force
mechanical advantage
efficiency
simple machine
lever
pulley
wheel and axle
inclined plane
screw
wedge
compound machine

What do you think?

Science Journal The photograph shows the claw end of a hammer pulling out a nail.

CHAPTER 5

Work and Machines

Paola Pezzo couldn't have won a gold metal in the 2000 Summer Olympic Games without a machine—her mountain bike. Can you imagine your life without machines? Think of all the machines you use every day—in-line skates, staplers, pencil sharpeners. Machines make work easier. Many machines are simple. Others, such as mountain bikes and automobiles, are combinations of many simple machines. What kinds of machines are in a mountain bike? In this chapter, you will learn about simple and compound machines and how they change forces to make work easier.

What do you think?

Science Journal Look at the picture below with a classmate. Discuss what you think is happening. Here's a hint: *This makes a carpenter's work easier.* Write your answer or best guess in your Science Journal.

124

Theme Connection

Systems and Interactions A simple machine is a system that has work done on it. It, in turn, does work on an object or another system.

Before the hydraulic lift, mechanics used a pulley to raise cars off the ground. The pulley had many grooved wheels and a long chain threaded through them. The mechanic had to pull several meters of chain just to raise the car a few centimeters. In this activity, make your own pulley and experience the advantage of using simple machines.

Construct a Pulley

1. Tie a rope several meters in length to the center of a broom handle. Have one student hold both ends of the handle.
2. Have another student hold the ends of a second broom handle and face the first student. The two handles should be parallel, a meter apart.
3. Have a third student loop the free end of the rope around the second handle. Continue wrapping, making six or seven loops.
4. Wearing gloves, the third student should stand to the side of one of the handles and pull on the free end of the rope. The two students holding the broom handles should prevent the handles from coming together.

Observe

Write a paragraph in your Science Journal describing what happened when the rope was pulled. How far did the rope have to be pulled to bring the handles together?

Before You Read

FOLDABLES Reading & Study Skills

Making a Compare and Contrast Study Fold **Make the following foldable to see how work and machines are similar and different.**

1. Place a sheet of paper in front of you so the long side is at the top. Fold the paper in half from the left side to the right side and unfold.
2. Through the top thickness of paper, cut along the middle fold line to form two tabs. Label *Work with Machines* and *Work without Machines*.
3. List examples of work you do without machines under its tab. As you read the chapter, rate the work you did without machines on a scale of 1 (little force) to 10 (great force). Write it next to the work.

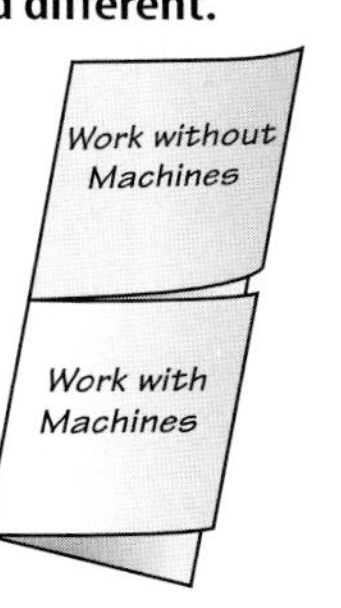

Before You Read

FOLDABLES Reading & Study Skills

Dinah Zike Study Fold

Purpose Students make and use a Foldable to collect information on doing work with and without machines. They use this information to compare and contrast the two.

For additional help, see Foldables Worksheet, p. 19 in **Chapter Resources Booklet,** or go to the Glencoe Science Web site at **science.glencoe.com.** See After You Read in the Study Guide at the end of this chapter.

EXPLORE ACTIVITY

Purpose Use the Explore Activity to introduce students to the force multiplying power of simple machines. L2 IS **Kinesthetic**

Preparation Cut 6-m lengths of rope and collect two broom handles for each group.

Materials 2 broom handles, 6-mlength of rope, pair of gloves for each group

Teaching Strategy Tell the students holding the broom handles that they must keep the handles parallel to each other and they cannot place their hands or fingers on the rope.

Observe

The third group member should easily pull the broom handles together despite the resistance of the other two members.

Assessment

Performance Ask each group to predict how the results of the activity would have differed if the rope had been wrapped only twice around the poles. Ask students to test their predictions. The pulley will have far less mechanical advantage, and the student pulling on the rope will not be able to pull the two handles together as easily. Use **Performance Assessment in the Science Classroom,** p. 93.

SECTION 1

Work

1 Motivate

Bellringer Transparency

Display the Section Focus Transparency for Section 1. Use the accompanying Transparency Activity Master. L2 ELL

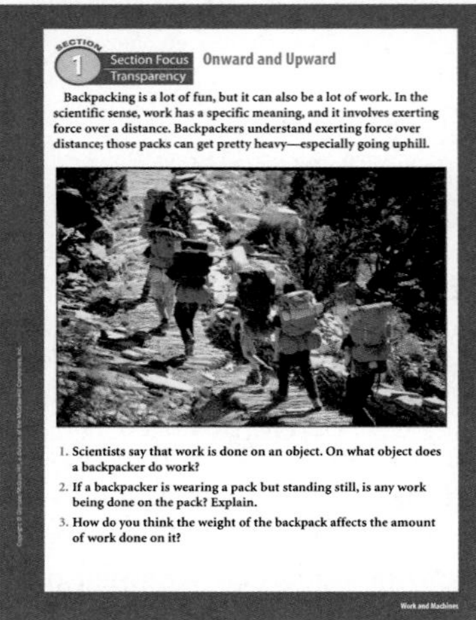

SECTION 1 Section Focus Transparency **Onward and Upward**

Backpacking is a lot of fun, but it can also be a lot of work. In the scientific sense, work has a specific meaning, and it involves exerting force over a distance. Backpackers understand exerting force over distance; those packs can get pretty heavy—especially going uphill.

1. Scientists say that work is done on an object. On what object does a backpacker do work?
2. If a backpacker is wearing a pack but standing still, is any work being done on the pack? Explain.
3. How do you think the weight of the backpack affects the amount of work done on it?

Work and Machines

Tie to Prior Knowledge

Ask students what types of work they do. They might mention cutting grass, taking out garbage, or caring for a younger sibling. In this section they will learn that the scientific definition of work is different from the everyday definition.

Work

As You Read

What You'll Learn

- **Explain** the meaning of work.
- **Explain** how work and energy are related.
- **Calculate** work.
- **Calculate** power.

Vocabulary

work
power

Why It's Important

Learning the scientific meaning of work is a key to understanding how machines make life easier.

What is work?

Press your hand against the surface of your desk as hard as you can. Although your muscles might start to feel tired, you haven't done any work. Most people feel that they have done work if they push or pull something. However, the scientific meaning of work is more specific. **Work** is the transfer of energy that occurs when a force makes an object move. Recall that a force is a push or a pull. For work to be done, a force must make something move. If you push against the desk and nothing moves, you haven't done any work.

Doing Work Two conditions have to be satisfied for work to be done on an object. One is that the object has to move, and the other is that the motion of the object must be in the same direction as the applied force. For example, if you pick up a pile of books from the floor as in **Figure 1,** you do work on the books. The books move upward in the direction of the force you are applying. If you hold the books in your arms without moving, you are not doing work on the books. You're still applying an upward force to keep the books from falling, but no movement is taking place.

Figure 1
When you lift a stack of books, your arms apply a force upward and the books move upward. Because the force and distance are in the same direction, your arms have done work on the books.

Section Assessment Planner

PORTFOLIO
MiniLAB Assessment, p. 129
Assessment, p. 131

PERFORMANCE ASSESSMENT
Math Skills Activity, p. 128
Try at Home MiniLAB, p. 129
Skill Builder Activities, p. 131

See page 154 for more options.

CONTENT ASSESSMENT
Section, p. 131
Challenge, p. 131
Chapter, pp. 154–155

Direction of Motion Now suppose you start walking as in **Figure 2.** The books are moving horizontally, but your arms still do no work on the books. The force exerted by your arms is still upward, and is at right angles to the direction the books are moving. It is your legs that are exerting the force that causes you and the books to move forward. It is your legs not your arms that cause work to be done on the books.

Reading Check *What must you ask to determine if work is being done?*

Figure 2
If you hold a stack of books and walk forward, your arms are exerting a force upward. However, the distance the books move is horizontal. Therefore your arms are not doing work on the books. *Does this mean no work is done on the books? Explain.*

Work and Energy

How are work and energy related? When work is done, a transfer of energy always occurs. This is easy to understand when you think about how you feel after carrying a heavy box up a flight of stairs. Remember that when the height of an object above Earth's surface increases, the potential energy of the object increases. You transferred energy from your moving muscles to the box and increased its potential energy by increasing its height.

You may recall that energy is the ability to cause change. Another way to think of energy is that energy is the ability to do work. If something has energy, it can transfer energy to another object by doing work on that object. When you do work on an object, you increase its energy. If you do work, such as the person carrying the box in **Figure 3,** your energy decreases. Energy is always transferred from the object that is doing the work to the object on which the work is done.

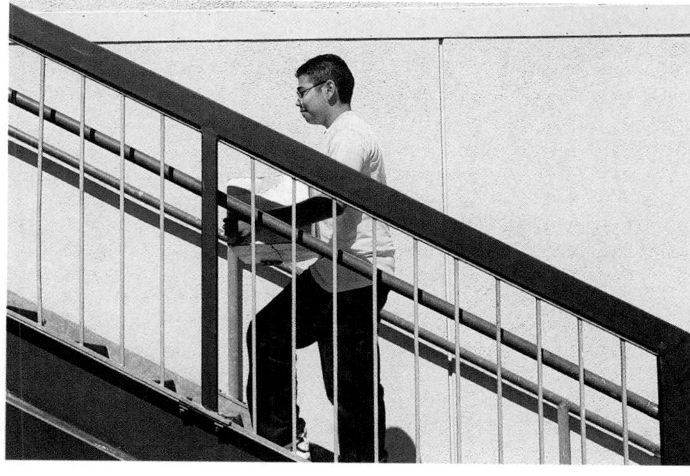

Figure 3
By carrying a box up the stairs, you are doing work. You transfer some of your energy to the box. *How is work done on the box?*

2 Teach

What is work?

Activity

Have a volunteer press against the wall. Ask students whether or not the person is doing work on the wall. no Repeat this demonstration for various other activities, such as raising an object vertically or carrying an object horizontally. If there is more than one force involved, help students analyze which forces are doing work and which are not. L2 LS **Kinesthetic**

Caption Answer

Figure 2 no; your legs not your arms cause work to be done on the books

Reading Check

Answer Does the object move, and is the motion in the same direction as the applied force?

Work and Energy

Caption Answer

Figure 3 The student is using force to move the box.

Science Journal

Relating Work and Energy Have students write descriptions in their Science Journals of situations they have seen or been a part of in which work has been done or energy has been transferred. Ask them to include at least one example of a situation in which energy was transferred but no work was done. L2
LS **Linguistic**

Resource Manager 

Chapter Resources Booklet
Transparency Activity, p. 46
Directed Reading for Content Mastery, p. 22
Note-taking Worksheets, pp. 35–37

Calculating Work

Quick Demo

Hook a spring scale to a 1-kg mass. Using the spring scale, raise the mass 1 m over a period of 1 second. Give students the opportunity to read the spring scale, which should read approximately 1 N. Tell students you have just done 1 J of work. Give students the opportunity to repeat your demonstration. L2

LS **Visual-Spatial**

Activity

The unit in which work is expressed is the joule. Ask students to express a joule in terms of the basic SI units that make it up. $W = F \times d = m \times a \times d$; therefore, $1\ J = 1\ kg \cdot \frac{m^2}{s^2}$ L2

LS **Logical-Mathematical**

Math Skills Activity

National Math Standards

Correlation to Mathematics Objectives

L4.1, L5.1

Answer to Practice Problem

1. $W = F \times d = 75N \times 25m = 1{,}875\ J$

Discussion

Suppose you used a force of 50 N to shoot an arrow, and the arrow flew 25 meters. As you shot the arrow, the bow string moved the arrow 1 meter. **Did you do 1,250 J of work or 50 J of work? Explain.** You did 50 J of work, because after the arrow left the bow, it was flying loose in the air and was not experiencing any force from you.

L2 LS **Logical-Mathematical**

Calculating Work

Which of these tasks would involve more work—lifting a pack of gum or a pile of books from the floor to waist level? Would you do more work if you lifted the books from the floor to your waist or over your head? You probably can guess the answers to these questions. You do more work when you exert more force and when you move an object a greater distance. In fact, the amount of work done depends on two things: the amount of force exerted and the distance over which the force is applied.

When a force is exerted and an object moves in the direction of the force, the amount of work done can be calculated as follows.

$$Work = force \times distance$$
$$W = F \times d$$

In this equation, force is measured in newtons (N) and distance is measured in meters. Work, like energy, is measured in joules. One joule is about the amount of work required to lift a medium-sized apple from your knees to your mouth.

Math Skills Activity

Calculating Work Given Force and Distance

Example Problem

You move a 75-kg refrigerator 35 m. This requires a force of 90 N. How much work, in joules, was done while moving the refrigerator?

Solution

1. *This is what you know:* force: $F = 90$ N; distance: $d = 35$ m; 1 newton-meter (N·m) = 1 joule (J)
2. *This is what you need to find:* Work W
3. *This is the equation you need to use:* $W = F \times d$
4. *Substitute the known values:* $W = (90\ N) \times (35\ m) = 3{,}150\ N{\cdot}m = 3{,}150\ J$

Check your answer by dividing the work you calculated by the given distance. Did you calculate the force that was given?

Practice Problem

When you and a friend move a 45-kg couch to another room, you exert a force of 75 N over 25 m. How much work, in joules, did you do?

For more help, refer to the Math Skill Handbook.

Curriculum Connection

History James Prescott Joule was a British scientist who lived from 1818 to 1889. Ask students to find out why the unit of work was named for him. Joule established the relationship between heat and mechanical energy, called the mechanical equivalent of heat.

L2 LS **Linguistic**

Figure 4
A softball pitcher exerts a force on the ball to throw it to the catcher. After the ball leaves her hand, she no longer is exerting any force on the ball. The only work she does on the ball is moving it from the back of the pitch to the release.

When is work done? Suppose you give a book a push and it slides along a table for a distance of 1 m before it comes to a stop. The distance you use to calculate the work you did is how far the object moves while the force is being applied. Even though the book moved 1 m, you do work on the book only while your hand is in contact with it. The distance in the formula for work is the distance the book moved while your hand was pushing on the book. As **Figure 4** shows, work is done on an object only when a force is being applied to the object.

Power

Suppose you and another student are pushing boxes of books up a ramp to load them into a truck. To make the job more fun, you make a game of it, racing to see who can push a box up the ramp faster. The boxes weigh the same, but your friend is able to push a box a little faster than you can. She moves a box up the ramp in 30 s. It takes you 45 s. You both do the same amount of work on the books because the boxes weigh the same and are moved the same distance. The only difference is the time it takes to do the work.

In this game, your friend has more power than you do. **Power** is the amount of work done in a certain amount of time. It is a rate—the rate at which work is done.

Reading Check *How is power related to work?*

Calculating Your Work and Power

Procedure
1. Find a set of **stairs** that you can safely walk and run up. Measure the total height of the stairs in meters.
2. Record how many seconds it takes you to walk and run up the stairs.
3. Calculate the work you did in walking and running up the stairs using $W = F \times d$. For force, use your weight in newtons (your weight in pounds $\times$ 4.5).
4. Use the formula $P = W/t$ to calculate the power you needed to walk and run up the stairs.

Analysis
1. Is the work you did walking and running the steps the same?
2. Which required more power—walking or running up the steps? Why?

Power

Purpose Students measure work and power. L2
LS Kinesthetic
Materials stairs, timer or clock
Teaching Strategy Suggest students work in pairs so one can time while the other climbs the stairs.
Safety Precautions Caution students to choose a set of stairs that they can run up without slipping.
Analysis
1. Yes; the work is independent of speed.
2. More power is used running than walking, because you do the same amount of work in less time.

Assessment

Content Have students work in small groups to write short rhymes to help them remember the relationships between force, distance, work, and power. Use **Performance Assessment in the Science Classroom**, p. 151. P

Reading Check

Answer Power is the amount of work done in a certain amount of time.

Teacher FYI

The metric unit of power is the watt, or joule/sec. The power of heating and cooling units is often given in British thermal units (Btu) per second. One Btu per second is about 1,055 watts. The power of motors and engines is usually given in horsepower. One horsepower is equal to about 746 watts.

Inclusion Strategies

Physically Challenged Students in wheelchairs can do the MiniLab by using a ramp instead of stairs. Students can time themselves going up the ramp at a slow rate, and then time themselves going up the ramp as quickly as they can. Point out that in order to calculate the force, students will need to know the weight of the wheelchair.

Resource Manager 

Chapter Resources Booklet
MiniLAB, p. 3
Enrichment, p. 32
Mathematics Skill Activities, p. 11

Power, continued

Discussion

Suppose two students are asked to unpack identical cartons of books. One student completes the job in ten minutes, while the other takes twenty minutes. **Which student did more work?** Both students did the same amount of work. **Which student used more power?** the one who finished in ten minutes L2

LS **Logical-Mathematical**

Use Science Words

Word Usage The word *power* is often used in the context of politics. Ask students to explain how this usage of the word *power* is analogous to the scientific use of the term. The more power a politician has, the shorter the period of time he or she needs to cause changes. L2 LS **Linguistic**

Explore the Glencoe Science Web site at **science.glencoe.com** to find out more about topics in this section.

Math Skills Activity

National Math Standards

Correlation to Mathematics Objectives
1, 2, 6, 9

Answer to Practice Problem

1. 550 Watts

$$P = \frac{W}{t} = \frac{5{,}500\text{J}}{10\text{s}} = \frac{550\text{J}}{\text{s}} = 550\text{W}$$

Research Visit the Glencoe Science Web site at **science.glencoe.com** for more information about energy-efficient devices. Communicate to your class what you learn.

Calculating Power To determine the power you deliver by pushing a box up the ramp, you need a way to calculate power. To calculate power, divide the work done by the time that is required to do the work.

$$\text{Power} = \text{work/time}$$
$$P = W/t$$

Power is measured in watts, named for James Watt, who invented the steam engine in the eighteenth century. A watt (W) is 1 J/s. A watt is fairly small—about equal to the power needed to raise a glass of water from a table to your mouth in 1 s. Because the watt is such a small unit, large amounts of power often are expressed in kilowatts. One kilowatt (kW) equals 1,000 W. If you were to run up a flight of steps in about 1.5 s, it would take about 1 kW of power.

Math Skills Activity

Calculating Power Given Work and Time

Example Problem

It took five minutes to move a refrigerator. You did 3,150 joules of work in the process. How much power was required to move the refrigerator?

Solution

1. *This is what you know:* Work: $W = 3{,}150$ J; Time: $t = 5$ min $= 300$ s; 1 J/s = 1 W
2. *This is what you need to find:* Power (P)
3. *This is the equation you need to use:* $P = W/t$
4. *Substitute the known values:* $P = 3{,}150$ J/300 s $= 10.5$ J/s $= 10.5$ W

Check your answer by multiplying the power you calculated by the time given in the problem. Did you calculate the same work that was given?

Practice Problem

How much power is required to push a car for 10 seconds if the amount of work done during that time is 5,500 joules?

For more help, refer to the Math Skill Handbook.

130 CHAPTER 5 Work and Machines

Curriculum Connection

Health Nutritionists recommend a daily diet of about 9,000,000 J (2,100 Cal) to maintain health. Have students calculate the average power that this diet would generate in a 24-hour period. There are 60 × 60 × 24 = 86,400 seconds in 24 hours. Therefore, the amount of power is 9,000,000 ÷ 86,400 = 104 watts. L2 LS **Logical-Mathematical**

Resource Manager

Chapter Resources Booklet
Reinforcement, p. 29

Cultural Diversity, p. 63

Power and Energy Doing work is a way of transferring energy from one object to another. Remember that energy can be transferred in other ways that don't involve doing work. For example, a lightbulb like the one in **Figure 5** uses electrical energy to produce heat and light, but no work is done. Power is produced or used any time energy is transferred from one object to another. Power is the energy transferred divided by the time needed for the transfer to occur. Anytime energy is transferred from one object to another, power can be calculated from the following equation.

$$\text{Power} = \text{energy}/\text{time}$$
$$P = E/t$$

Changing Energy by Doing Work What happens to the energy of a book when you lift it off your desk? You changed the height of the book, so its potential energy increased. Where did this increase in energy come from? You transferred energy to the book by doing work on the book when you lifted it. You can also increase the kinetic energy of an object by doing work on it, as when you push furniture from one place to another. In another example, think about using sandpaper on a piece of wood. Feel the wood and you will notice that it is warm. The energy of the wood has increased in the form of heat from friction. Anytime you do work on an object, you cause its energy to increase.

Figure 5
This 100 W lightbulb uses energy at 100 J/s, converting electrical energy into light and heat. *Even though energy is being transferred, why is no work done?*

Section  Assessment

1. Explain how the scientific definition of work is different from the everyday meaning.
2. How are work and energy related?
3. A person pushed a bowling ball 20 m. The amount of work done was 1,470 J. How much force did the person exert?
4. How are power, work, and time related?
5. **Think Critically** In which of the following situations is work being done? Explain.
   - A person shovels snow off a sidewalk.
   - A worker lifts bricks, one at a time, from the ground to the back of a truck.
   - A roofer's assistant carries a bundle of shingles across a construction site.

Skill Builder Activities

6. **Measuring in SI** A passenger weighing 500 N is inside an elevator weighing 24,500 N that rises 30 m in exactly 1 min. How much power is needed for the elevator's trip? **For more help, refer to the** Science Skill Handbook.
7. **Communicating** In your Science Journal, write down everything you did today that would be considered work in the everyday sense. From this list, choose one task that also fits the scientific description of work. Write a paragraph explaining how the task fits the scientific and the everyday descriptions. **For more help, refer to the** Science Skill Handbook.

Caption Answer

Figure 5 There is no force making an object move in the direction of the force.

3 Assess

Reteach

Ask students to name various activities they enjoy. Have the class discuss the work done and the amount of power used while performing each activity. L2
LS **Interpersonal**

Challenge

Power is defined as work divided by time. Have students use the definition of work to define power in terms of velocity, or how fast a force is applied. Ask students to relate this to the power of a car. $P = \frac{W}{t} = \frac{(F \times d)}{t} = F \times (\frac{d}{t}) = F \times v$, where v is the speed at which the force is applied. A powerful car is one that is fast. L3 LS **Logical-Mathematical**

Assessment

Portfolio Have students make posters that define the SI units for force, work, and power and illustrate the relationships among them. Use **Performance Assessment in the Science Classroom,** p. 145. P

Answers to Section Assessment

1. The scientific definition requires that a force act on an object, and that the object move in the direction of that force. The everyday meaning requires that an effort be exerted.
2. Work is one way of transferring energy.
3. $F = W \div d = 1{,}470\ \text{N·m} \div 20\ \text{m} = 73.5\ \text{N}$
4. Power equals work divided by time.
5. Work is done in the first two situations. The force from the person's arms moves the snow. Force from the worker's arms raises the bricks.
6. $P = W \div t = (F \times d) \div t = [(24{,}500\ \text{N} + 500\ \text{N}) \times 30\ \text{m}] \div 60\ \text{s} = 12{,}500\ \text{W}$
7. Possible answers: Everyday work includes doing homework, raking leaves, and straightening up a room. Raking leaves fits the scientific definition because the force from your arms causes the leaves to move.

SECTION 2

Using Machines

1 Motivate

Bellringer Transparency

Display the Section Focus Transparency for Section 2. Use the accompanying Transparency Activity Master. L2 ELL

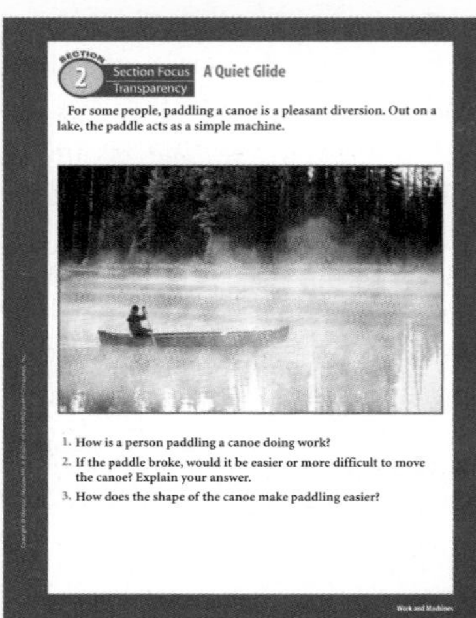
Section 2 Section Focus Transparency **A Quiet Glide**

For some people, paddling a canoe is a pleasant diversion. Out on a lake, the paddle acts as a simple machine.

1. How is a person paddling a canoe doing work?
2. If the paddle broke, would it be easier or more difficult to move the canoe? Explain your answer.
3. How does the shape of the canoe make paddling easier?

Work and Machines

Tie to Prior Knowledge

Ask students to name ways that machines make work easier. They might mention that a shovel makes lifting dirt easier, and a hammer makes pushing a nail into wood easier. In this section, students will use the scientific definition of work to learn how machines make accomplishing work easier.

Text Question Answer

Possible answers: pliers, screwdriver.

SECTION 

Using Machines

As You Read

***What* You'll Learn**

- **Explain** how machines make work easier.
- **Calculate** mechanical advantage.
- **Calculate** efficiency.
- **Explain** ideal mechanical advantage.

Vocabulary

machine
effort force
resistance force
mechanical advantage
efficiency

***Why* It's Important**

Complex devices are made up of simpler parts called simple machines. Even your body contains simple machines.

What is a machine?

How many machines did you use today? Did you cut your food with a knife? Or maybe you used a pair of scissors? If you did, you used a machine. A **machine** is a device that makes doing work easier. When you think of a machine you may picture a device with an engine and many moving parts. But not all machines are complicated or powered by engines or electric motors. Machines can be simple, and can be powered by a force applied by a person. Some, like knives, scissors, and doorknobs, are used everyday to make doing work easier.

Making Work Easier

Machines can make work easier by increasing the force that can be applied to an object. A bottle opener increases the force you can apply to a bottle cap, causing the cap to bend. A car jack enables you to lift a heavy automobile. A second way that machines can make work easier is by increasing the distance over which a force can be applied. A leaf rake is an example of this type of machine. Machines can also make work easier by changing the direction of an applied force. When you open window blinds by pulling on a cord, the downward force on the cord is changed to an upward force that opens the blinds.

Figure 6
A car jack works by increasing your force.

Increasing Force Nobody could lift a car to change a flat tire without help. A car jack, like the one in **Figure 6,** is an example of a machine that multiplies your force.

Remember that work is the product of force and distance. You can do the same amount of work by applying a small force over a long distance as you can by applying a large force over a short distance. For example, the distance you push the handle of a car jack downward is longer than the distance the car moves upward, and the upward force exerted by the jack is greater than the downward force you exert on the handle. Can you think of other machines that multiply force?

Section Assessment Planner

PORTFOLIO
Curriculum Connection, p. 134

PERFORMANCE ASSESSMENT
Try at Home MiniLAB, p. 134
Skill Builder Activities, p.137
See page 154 for more options.

CONTENT ASSESSMENT
Section, p. 137
Challenge, p. 137
Chapter, pp. 154–155

Figure 7
Whether the mover slides the chair up the ramp or lifts it directly into the truck, she will do the same amount of work. Doing the work over a longer distance allows her to use less force.

Increasing Distance Why does the mover in **Figure 7** push the heavy furniture up the ramp instead of lifting it directly into the truck? It is easier for her because less force is needed to move the furniture.

The work done in lifting an object depends on the change in height of the object. The same amount of work is done whether the mover pushes the furniture up the long ramp or lifts it straight up. If she uses a ramp to lift the furniture, she moves the furniture a longer distance than if she just raised it straight up. If work stays the same and the distance is increased, then less force will be needed to do the work.

Changing Direction Some machines change the direction of the force you apply. When you use the car jack, you are exerting a force downward on the jack handle. The force exerted by the jack on the car is upward. The direction of the force you applied is changed from downward to upward. Some machines change the direction of the force that is applied to them in another way. The wedge-shaped blade of an ax is one example. When you use an ax to split wood, you exert a downward force as you swing the ax toward the wood. As **Figure 8** shows, the blade changes the downward force into a horizontal force that splits the wood apart.

Figure 8
An ax blade changes the direction of the force from vertical to horizontal.

Reading Check *What are three ways machines make work easier?*

2 Teach

What is a machine?

Discussion

Ask students to name devices that make work easier but aren't what normally would be called machines in everyday conversations. Some examples are a bicycle, a can opener, and a rake. Discuss how each device makes work easier. L1 LS **Linguistic**

Making Work Easier

Extension

Point out that in both the car jack and the ramp, force is traded for distance. This means that in both cases, work is made easier because the amount of force required is less than it would have been without the machine, but the force is applied over a longer distance. **What is the difference in the way the two machines use the force applied to them?** When you use a car jack, you are applying your force to the lever, and it is translated into another force on the car. When you use a ramp, you apply your force directly to the object you are moving, and it is not translated into another force. L3 LS **Logical-Mathematical**

Activity

Have students experiment with lifting a load using a simple fixed pulley and using a screwdriver to pry the lid off a can. For each activity, also have students try to do the job without changing the direction of force. L2 LS **Kinesthetic**

Reading Check

Answer increasing force, increasing distance, changing direction

Inclusion Strategies

Learning Disabled Have students push a heavy box up a gentle ramp. Keep the ramp the same height, but make it shorter and therefore steeper. Then ask students to push the box again. Do this several times with increasingly shorter and steeper ramps to help students understand the relationship between the distance the box moves and the force required to move it.

Resource Manager 

Chapter Resources Booklet

Transparency Activity, p. 47
Directed Reading for Content Mastery, p. 22

The Work Done by Machines

Purpose Students observe how machines multiply a person's force of effort. L2
Kinesthetic

Materials can of food, manual can opener, metric ruler

Teaching Strategy Explain to students that the length of the can opener handle is the diameter of the circle or "wheel" that they must turn the handle around to be able to move the small circle or "axle" of the cutting blade. The can opener functions as a wheel and axle. To gain force from the cutting blade, they must move the handle a greater distance.

Analysis

1. The can opener easily opens the can, but the can would be impossible to open using just the cutting blade.
2. Answers will vary, but cutting blades generally measure 2 cm while the diameter of the circle formed by turning the handle ranges from 8 to 10 cm.
3. The added distance the student must turn the handle multiplies the amount of force applied by the cutting blade to the can.

Assessment

Process Show students a door handle and ask them to infer how the handle multiplies the force of the person opening the door. Like the can opener, the door handle works as a wheel and axle. The handle is the large "wheel" that easily turns the metal rod or "axle" inserted into the door lock. Use **PASC,** p. 89.

Figure 9
A crowbar increases the force you apply and changes its direction.

TRY AT HOME Mini LAB

Machines Multiplying Force

Procedure

1. Open a **can of food** using a **manual can opener.** Manual can openers are a type of simple machine, but electric can openers are not.
2. Use a **metric ruler** to measure the diameter of the cutting blade of the can opener.
3. Measure the length of the handle you turn.

Analysis

1. Compare how difficult it is to open the can using the can opener with how difficult it would have been to open the can by turning the cutting blade with your fingers.
2. Compare the diameter of the cutting blade with the diameter of the circle formed by turning the can opener's handle.
3. Infer why a can opener makes it easier to open a metal can.

The Work Done by Machines

To pry the lid off a wooden crate with a crowbar, you'd slip the end of the crowbar under the edge of the crate lid and push down on the handle. By moving the handle downward, you do work on the crowbar. As the crowbar moves, it does work on the lid, lifting it up. **Figure 9** shows how the crowbar increases the amount of force being applied and changes the direction of the force.

When you use a machine such as a crowbar, you are trying to move something that resists being moved. For example, if you use a crowbar to pry the lid off a crate, you are working against the friction between the nails in the lid and the crate. You also could use a crowbar to move a large rock. In this case, you would be working against gravity—the weight of the rock.

Effort and Resistance Forces Two forces are involved when a machine is used to do work. You exert a force on the machine, such as a bottle opener, and the machine then exerts a force on the object you are trying to move, such as the bottle cap. The force applied to the machine is called the **effort force.** F_e stands for the effort force. The force applied by the machine to overcome resistance is called the **resistance force,** symbolized by F_r. When you try to pull a nail out with a hammer as in **Figure 10,** you apply the effort force on the handle. The resistance force is the force the claw applies to the nail.

Two kinds of work need to be considered when you use a machine—the work done by you on the machine and the work done by the machine. When you use a crowbar, you do work when you apply force to the crowbar handle and make it move. The work done by you on a machine is called the input work and is symbolized by W_{in}. The work done by the machine is called the output work and is abbreviated W_{out}.

Science Journal

Work In and Work Out Ask students to choose two pieces of work they do using person-powered, not electrically powered, machines. For each, have them write a short paragraph in their Science Journals describing the work they do on the machine and the work the machine does. Machines used might include shovel, bicycle, broom, screw driver, scissors L2 **Linguistic**

Curriculum Connection

Art Leonardo da Vinci is famous for such well-known paintings as *Mona Lisa* and *The Last Supper.* However, he was also the inventor of an extraordinary collection of machines. Have students research Leonardo da Vinci and prepare a computer presentation showing how his work with mechanical devices inspired much of the technology we use today. L2 **Visual-Spatial** P

134 CHAPTER 5 Work and Machines

Conserving Energy Remember that energy is always conserved. When you do work on the machine, you transfer energy to the machine. When the machine does work on an object, energy is transferred from the machine to the object. Because energy cannot be created or destroyed, the amount of energy the machine transfers to the object cannot be greater than the amount of energy you transfer to the machine. A machine cannot create energy, so W_{out} is never greater than W_{in}.

However, the machine does not transfer all of the energy it receives to the object. In fact, when a machine is used, some of the energy transferred changes to heat due to friction. The energy that changes to heat cannot be used to do work, so W_{out} is always smaller than W_{in}.

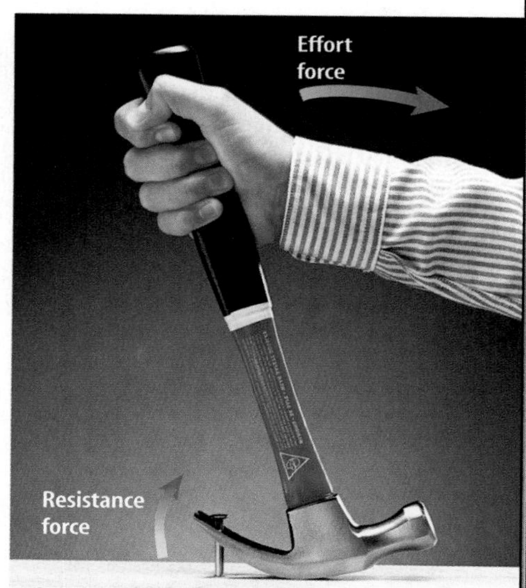

Figure 10
When prying a nail out of a piece of wood with a claw hammer, you exert the effort force on the handle of the hammer, and the claw exerts the resistance force.

Ideal Machines Remember that work is calculated by multiplying force by distance. The input work is the product of the effort force and the distance over which the effort force is exerted. The output work is the product of the resistance force and the distance that force moves the object.

Suppose a perfect machine could be built in which there was no friction. None of the input work or output work would be converted to heat. For such an ideal machine, the input work equals the output work. So for an ideal machine,

$$W_{in} = W_{out}$$

Suppose the ideal machine increases the force applied to it. This means that the resistance force, F_r, is greater than the effort force F_e. Recall that work is equal to force times distance. If F_r is greater than F_e, then W_{in} and W_{out} can be equal only if the effort force is applied over a greater distance than the resistance force is exerted over.

For example, suppose the hammer claw in **Figure 10** moves a distance of 0.10 m to remove a nail. If a resistance force of 1,500 N is exerted by the claw of the hammer, and you move the handle of the hammer 0.5 m, you can find the effort force as follows.

$$\begin{aligned} W_{in} &= W_{out} \\ F_e \times d_e &= F_r \times d_r \\ F_e \times (0.5\text{ m}) &= (1{,}500\text{ N}) \times (0.1\text{ m}) \\ F_e \times (0.5\text{ m}) &= 150\text{ N·m} \\ F_e &= 300\text{ N} \end{aligned}$$

Because the distance you move the hammer is longer than the distance the hammer moves the nail, the effort force is less than the resistance force.

Use an Analogy

Sometimes people resist new tasks or new situations. When this happens, they have to make an effort to overcome the resistance and do what the situation requires. This is analogous to a machine in which an effort force overcomes a resistance force in order to perform the task for which it is used.

Quick Demo

Bring to class a piece of wood with a nail pounded almost all the way into it. In front of the class, use a claw hammer to pull the nail out of the wood. Invite students to touch the nail to feel how some of the work done on the nail has been converted to heat energy, causing the nail to heat up. L2 LS **Kinesthetic**

Extension

One type of ideal machine is called a perpetual motion machine. Have students find out more about perpetual motion machines and prepare posters describing them and explaining why they are impossible. A perpetual motion machine is a device that either can deliver more work than is put into it or can continue to work with no energy input other than that which was used to start it. L3 LS **Linguistic**

Visual Learning

Figure 10 Point out the fact that although this hammer is not an ideal machine, most of the effort force applied is translated to work done on the nail. This means that $W_{in} \approx W_{out}$. Since work = force × distance, if the hammer handle is moved a large distance with a small force, then the claw, which moves a short distance, will exert a large force. Have students draw a diagram to show this relationship. L2 LS **Visual-Spatial**

Resource Manager

Chapter Resources Booklet
MiniLAB, p. 4
Enrichment, p. 33

Mechanical Advantage

Activity

Ask students to calculate the mechanical advantage of a crowbar to which you apply 100 N of force to lift a 250-N rock. MA = resistance force ÷ effort force = 250 N ÷ 100 N = 2.5 L2

LS **Logical-Mathematical**

Fun Fact

Mechanical advantage also can be determined by dividing the effort distance (d_e) by the resistance distance (d_r).

Efficiency

IDENTIFYING Misconceptions

Students may think that simple machines allow us to do less work. See page 124F for teaching strategies that address this misconception.

Chemistry INTEGRATION

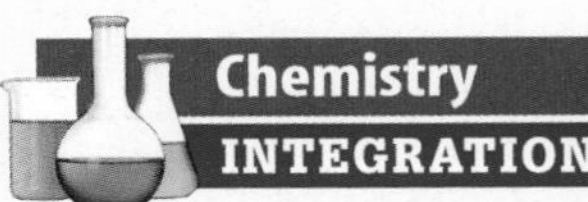

Graphite is composed of carbon atoms formed into linked hexagonal molecules. These molecules are arranged in weakly bonded layers. Graphite is useful as a lubricant because the layers can slide easily over one another. When graphite is applied to the moving parts of machines, the sliding of the layers reduces the effects of friction.

Reading Check

Answer by comparing its output work to its input work

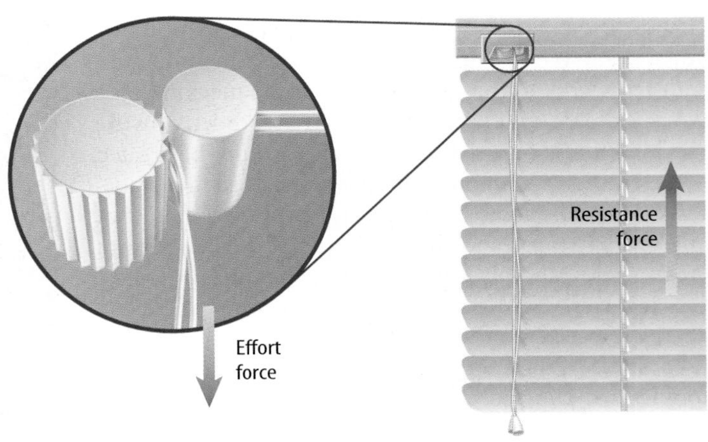

Figure 11
Mini blinds are a familiar example of a simple machine that changes the direction of a force. When you pull down on the cord, the direction of your force is changed upward. Because the effort force and resistance force remain the same, the MA of the mini blinds is 1.

Chemistry INTEGRATION

A material called graphite is sometimes used as a lubricant to increase the efficiency of machines. Find out what element graphite is made of and infer why graphite eases the movement of machines.

Mechanical Advantage

Think again about the crowbar example. The crowbar increases the force you apply, so the force exerted on the crate lid is greater than the force you exert on the handle. In other words, the resistance force is greater than the effort force. However, just as for the hammer, the effort distance you move the crowbar handle is greater than the distance the crowbar moves the lid. The machine multiplies your effort, but you must move the handle a greater distance.

The number of times a machine multiplies the effort force is the **mechanical advantage (MA)** of the machine. To calculate mechanical advantage, you divide the resistance force by the effort force. Some machines simply change the direction of the effort force, such as the window blinds in **Figure 11.** When only the direction of the force changes, the effort force and resistance force are equal, so the mechanical advantage is 1.

Efficiency

When you use a hammer to pull a nail out of a piece of wood, the friction between the wood and the nail causes the nail to get warm as it's pulled out. For real machines, some of the energy put into a machine is always lost as heat produced by friction. For that reason, the output work of a machine is always less than the work put into the machine. Machines that lose less energy to friction are said to be more efficient.

Efficiency is a measure of how much of the work put into a machine is changed into useful output work by the machine. A machine with high efficiency produces less heat from friction so more of the input work is changed to useful output work.

Reading Check *How is a machine's efficiency measured?*

Teacher FYI

Mechanical advantage (MA) is resistance force divided by effort force. If MA is less than 1, then the machine increases either the distance moved by the object or its speed. If MA is equal to 1, the machine changes the direction of the effort force. If MA is greater than 1, the machine increases the effort force.

Resource Manager

Chapter Resources Booklet
Reinforcement, p. 30

Physical Science Critical Thinking/Problem Solving, p. 3

Calculating Efficiency To calculate the efficiency of a machine, the output work is divided by the input work. Efficiency is usually expressed as a percentage by this equation:

$$\text{efficiency} = \left(\frac{W_{out}}{W_{in}}\right) \times 100\%$$

Because friction causes the output work to always be less than the input work, the efficiency of a real machine is always less than 100 percent. Because no machine is 100 percent efficient, the actual mechanical advantage is always less than the ideal mechanical advantage.

Machines can be made more efficient by reducing friction. This usually is done by adding a lubricant, such as oil or grease, to surfaces that rub together, as shown in **Figure 12.** When a lubricant is used in a machine, it fills in the gaps between the atoms. Because lubricants are usually liquids, the atoms are free to move around each other. This allows the two surfaces to slide more easily across each other, reducing friction and increasing efficiency. Eventually, dirt will build up on the lubricant, and it will lose its effectiveness. The dirty lubricant should be wiped off and replaced with clean oil or grease.

You might have heard some household appliances or automobiles described as being energy efficient. By using less energy to do work, these machines cost less to operate. They also help conserve resources that are used to produce fuel and electricity.

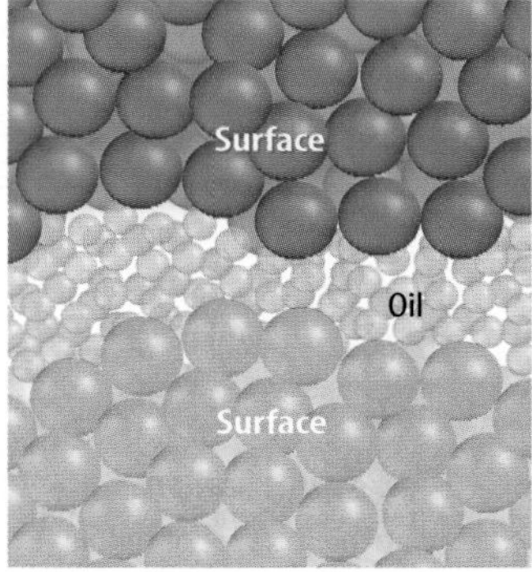

Figure 12
Oil reduces the friction between two surfaces. Oil fills the space between the surfaces so high spots don't rub against each other.

Section  Assessment

1. Explain how machines can make work easier without violating the law of conservation of energy.
2. A claw hammer is used to pull a nail from a board. If the claw exerts a resistance of 2,500 N to the applied effort force of 125 N, what is the MA of the hammer?
3. Explain why W_{out} is always less than W_{in}.
4. How would you calculate the efficiency of a machine?
5. **Think Critically** Give an example of a machine you've used recently. How did you apply effort force? How did the machine apply resistance force?

Skill Builder Activities

6. **Recognizing Cause and Effect** When you operate a machine, it's often easy to observe cause and effect. For example, when you turn a doorknob, the latch in the door moves. Give five examples of machines and describe one cause-and-effect pair in the action of each machine. **For more help, refer to the** Science Skill Handbook.
7. **Solving One-Step Equations** Suppose you want to use a machine to lift a 6,000-N log. What effort force will you need if your machine has a mechanical advantage of 25? 15? 1? Show your calculations. **For more help, refer to the** Math Skill Handbook.

Answers to Section Assessment

1. Machines can multiply force or change the direction of the force. When a machine multiplies force, the distance the force must travel is greater than the distance traveled by the resistance force, so the amount of work is not increased.
2. $MA = F_r \div F_e = 2{,}500\text{ N} \div 125\text{ N} = 20$
3. Friction always causes output work to be less than the input work.
4. $\text{efficiency} = \frac{W_{out}}{W_{in}} \times 100\%$
5. Accept all reasonable answers.
6. Possible answers: Pressing down on a bottle opener causes the bottle cap to pop up. Pushing together the handles of a pair of scissors causes the blades to cut. Pressing down on a shovel handle lifts dirt. Pulling the cord of window blinds raises the blinds. Pressing a bicycle pedal turns the wheels.
7. $F_e = \frac{F_r}{MA}$; $F_e = 6{,}000\,\frac{N}{25} = 240$ N; $F_e = 6{,}000\,\frac{N}{15} = 400$ N; $F_e = 6{,}000\,\frac{N}{1} = 6{,}000$ N

3 Assess

Reteach

Bring in various simple machines for students to examine. For each one, have students decide whether the machine works by increasing force, increasing distance, changing the direction of the force, or some combination of the three. L2 LS **Visual-Spatial**

Challenge

Tell students that some machines have a mechanical advantage that is less than 1. Have them find out what happens when this is the case and why these machines are still useful. In these machines the effort force is greater than the resistance force. These machines can be useful if they increase the distance an object moves or its speed. L3 LS **Logical-Mathematical**

Assessment

Process Have each student choose a machine and prepare a presentation showing different ways to reduce friction in the machine and increase its efficiency. Possible ways of reducing friction include using bearings, wheels, or a lubricant. Use **Performance Assessment in the Science Classroom,** p. 143.

SECTION 3

Simple Machines

1 Motivate

Bellringer Transparency

Display the Section Focus Transparency for Section 3. Use the accompanying Transparency Activity Master. L2 ELL

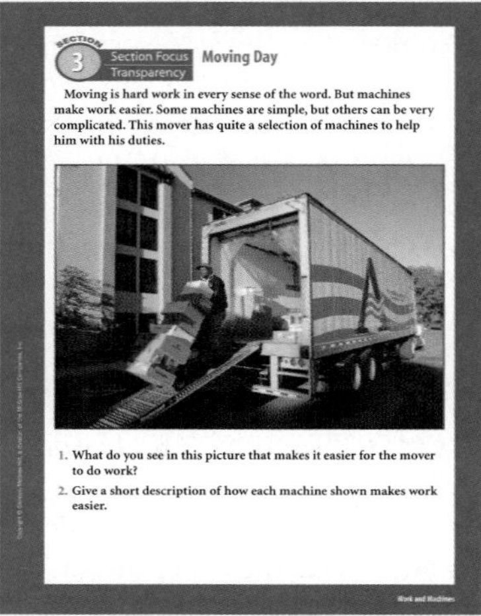
Section 3 Section Focus Transparency Moving Day

Moving is hard work in every sense of the word. But machines make work easier. Some machines are simple, but others can be very complicated. This mover has quite a selection of machines to help him with his duties.

1. What do you see in this picture that makes it easier for the mover to do work?
2. Give a short description of how each machine shown makes work easier.

Tie to Prior Knowledge

Ask students to define mechanical advantage. the number of times a machine multiplies the effort force applied to it Tell them that in this section they will learn how the design of a simple machine affects its mechanical advantage.

SECTION 

Simple Machines

As You Read

***What* You'll Learn**

- **Describe** the six types of simple machines.
- **Calculate** the ideal mechanical advantage for different types of simple machines.

Vocabulary

simple machine, lever, pulley, wheel and axle, inclined plane, screw, wedge, compound machine

***Why* It's Important**

If you know the principles behind simple machines, you'll make better use of everyday tools.

Types of Simple Machines

Without realizing it, you use many simple machines every day. A **simple machine** is a machine that does work with only one movement. The six types of simple machines are: lever, pulley, wheel and axle, inclined plane, screw, and wedge. As you'll see, the pulley and wheel and axle are modified forms of the lever, and the screw and wedge are modified forms of the inclined plane.

Reading Check *All simple machines are variations of which two basic machines?*

Levers

You probably won't try to pry the cap off a soft drink bottle with your fingers. Instead you would use a bottle opener to remove the cap. A bottle opener like the one in **Figure 13** is an example of a lever. A **lever** is a bar that is free to pivot, or turn, about a fixed point. The fixed point on the lever is called the fulcrum. The part of the lever on which the effort force is applied is called the effort arm. The part of the lever that exerts the resistance force is called the resistance arm.

There are three different classes of levers. The differences are based upon the positions of the effort force, resistance force, and fulcrum.

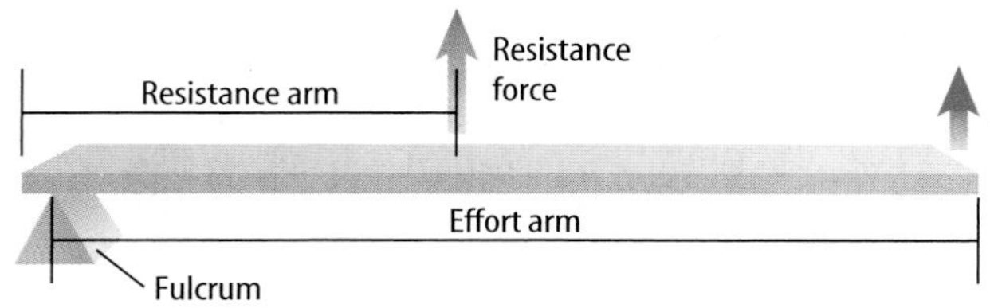

Figure 13
When you push up on the bottle opener (effort force), the opener bends the cap up (resistance force). *What acts as the fulcrum in a bottle opener?*

Section Assessment Planner

Portfolio
Extension, p. 144

Performance Assessment
Skill Builder Activities, p. 146
See page 155 for more options.

Content Assessment
Section, p. 146
Challenge, p. 146
Chapter, pp. 154–155

138 CHAPTER 5 Work and Machines

Figure 14
Levers are classified by the location of the effort force, resistance force, and the fulcrum.

A For a first-class lever, the fulcrum is between the effort force and resistance force.

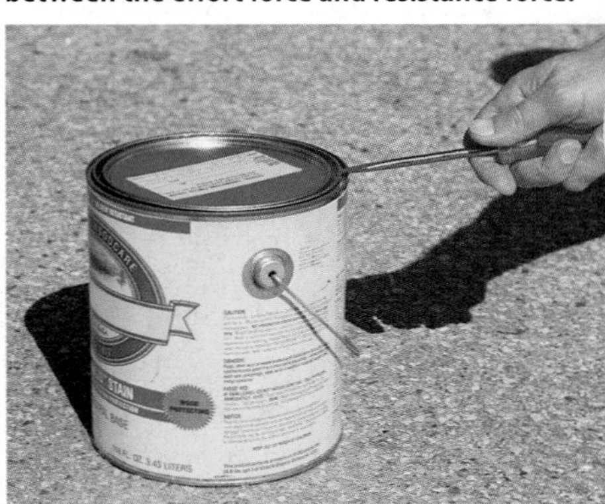

B For a second-class lever, the resistance force is between the effort force and the fulcrum.

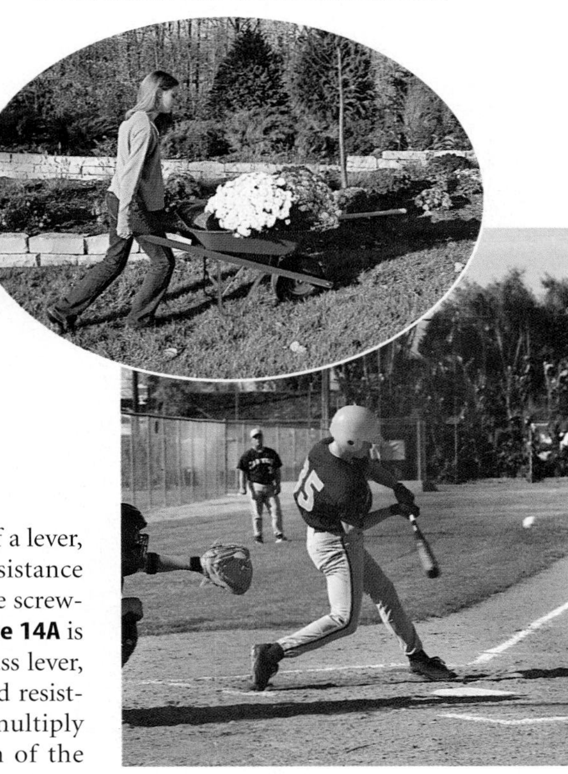

C For a third-class lever, the effort force is between the resistance force and the fulcrum.

Types of Levers To determine the class of a lever, you need to know where the effort and resistance forces are exerted relative to the fulcrum. The screwdriver used to open the can of paint in **Figure 14A** is an example of a first-class lever. In a first-class lever, the fulcrum is located between the effort and resistance forces. A first-class lever is used to multiply force, and it always changes the direction of the applied force.

In a second-class lever, the resistance force is located between the effort force and fulcrum. Look at the wheelbarrow in **Figure 14B.** You provide the effort force at the end, and the wheel acts as the fulcrum. The load you are lifting, the resistance force, is located in between. Second-class levers always multiply force.

Many pieces of sports equipment are examples of third-class levers. In a third-class lever, the effort force is located between the resistance force and fulcrum. Think about swinging a baseball bat like the one in **Figure 14C.** If you are righthanded, you hold the base of the bat with your left hand—the fulcrum. You use your right hand to apply the effort force and swing the bat. The resistance force is provided by the baseball when it hits the bat. Third-class levers cannot multiply force because the effort arm is always smaller than the resistance arm. Instead they increase the distance over which the resistance force is applied

Every lever can be placed into one of these classes. Each class can be found in your body, as shown in **Figure 15,** on the next page.

2 Teach

Types of Simple Machines

Reading Check

Answer lever and inclined plane

Levers

Caption Answer

Figure 13 the top of the bottle cap

Quick Demo

Display several examples of each of the three classes of levers for students to examine and handle. Some first-class levers are pliers and crowbars. Some second-class levers are nutcrackers, wheelbarrows, and bottle openers. Some third-class levers are tweezers and fishing poles. L2 LS **Kinesthetic**

Extension

Tell students that some levers can be different classes, depending on how they are used. Have students demonstrate how a broom can be two different kinds of levers. Hold the broom in one hand (H_1) near the top and another hand (H_2) near the middle. If H_1 moves while H_2 remains still, the broom is a first-class lever. If H_1 remains still while H_2 moves, the broom is a third-class lever. L3 LS **Kinesthetic**

Use Science Words

Word Origin Have students look up the word *fulcrum* in a dictionary to determine its origin. Ask a volunteer to explain how the meaning of the word reflects its root. The word *fulcrum* comes from the Latin root *fulcire,* meaning "to prop." A fulcrum acts as a prop around which a lever moves. L1 LS **Linguistic**

Cultural Diversity

Chinese Wheelbarrow The wheelbarrow, a second-class lever, was invented in China sometime in or before the first century B.C. The Chinese called their wheeled devices such things as wooden goat, wooden sheep, wooden ox, and gliding horse. **How does a wheelbarrow give a worker more power?** It allows the worker to do more work in a shorter amount of time. L2 LS **Logical-Mathematical**

Resource Manager

Chapter Resources Booklet
- Transparency Activity, p. 48
- Directed Reading for Content Mastery, pp. 23, 24

Physical Science Critical Thinking/Problem Solving, p. 6

Visualizing Levers in the Human Body

Have students examine the pictures and read the captions. Then ask the following questions.

- **Newborn babies are not able to support their heads and they must be carefully supported. Why is this?** The unborn baby floats in fluid and does not gave to support its own head. After birth, theses muscles must be strengthened.
- **Explain why your forearm becomes more muscular when you do curls with a dumbbell.** When you increase the resistance force (the dumbbell), your effort force (muscle in your forearm) must also increase, repeating curls increases the muscle mass in your forearm over time.

Activity

Find other levers in your body. Make a poster showing the various kinds that you find. For each example, mark the fulcrum, effort force, and resistance force. L2 LS **Visual-Spatial**

Extension

Levers have been a tool that mankind has used for centuries. Research how the ancient Egyptians used levers to build their pyramids. Report to your class the information that you learn. L3 LS **Linguistic**

Figure 15

All three types of levers—first-class, second-class, and third-class—are found in the human body. The forces exerted by muscles in your body can be increased by first-class and second-class levers, while third-class levers increase the range of movement of a body part. Examples of how the body uses levers to help it move are shown here.

▲ Fulcrum
▼ Effort force
▲ Resistance force

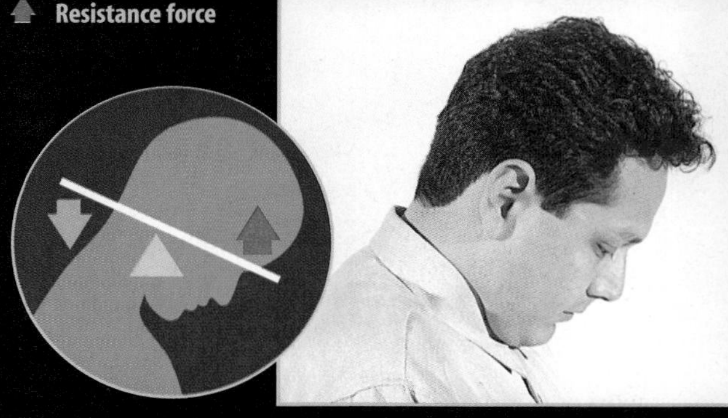

▲ FIRST-CLASS LEVER The fulcrum lies between the effort force and the resistance force. Your head acts like a first-class lever. Your neck muscles provide the effort force to support the weight of your head.

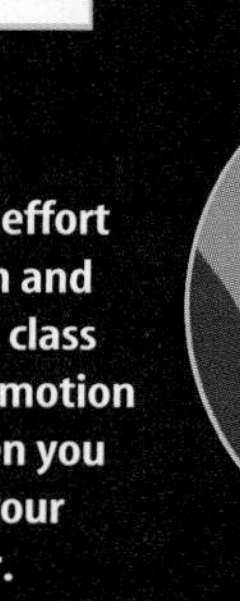

◀ SECOND-CLASS LEVER The resistance force is between the fulcrum and the effort force. Your foot becomes a second-class lever when you stand on your toes.

▶ THIRD-CLASS LEVER The effort force is between the fulcrum and the resistance force. A third class lever increases the range of motion of the resistance force. When you do a curl with a dumbbell, your forearm is a third-class lever.

140 CHAPTER 5 Work and Machines

Figure 16
A fixed pulley is another form of the lever. *What are the lengths of the effort arm and resistance arm in a pulley?*

Mechanical Advantage of a Lever The bottle opener makes work easier by multiplying your effort force and changing the direction of your force. To calculate the ideal mechanical advantage (IMA) of the lever, you can use the lengths of the arms of the lever. The distance from the fulcrum to the place you exert your force is the effort arm. The resistance arm is the distance from the fulcrum to the point the resistance force is applied. Assuming no friction, the IMA is as follows:

$$\text{IMA} = \frac{\text{length of effort arm}}{\text{length of resistance arm}} = \frac{L_e}{L_r}$$

Making the effort arm longer increases the ideal mechanical advantage.

Pulleys

What causes an elevator to rise? A cable attached to the elevator is wrapped around a pulley, allowing the elevator to be raised and lowered. A **pulley** is a grooved wheel with a rope, chain, or cable running along the groove. A fixed pulley is a modified first-class lever, as shown in **Figure 16.** The axle of the pulley acts as the fulcrum. The two sides of the pulley are the effort arm and resistance arm. A pulley can multiply the effort force, but all pulleys can change the direction of the effort force.

Fixed Pulleys An elevator has a fixed pulley that is lifted upward when a motor pulls down on the cable. A fixed pulley, such as the one in **Figure 17,** is attached to something that doesn't move, such as a ceiling or wall. Because a fixed pulley changes only the direction of force, the effort force is not multiplied and the IMA is 1.

Figure 17
A fixed pulley changes only the direction of your force. You still need to apply 4 N of force to lift the weight.

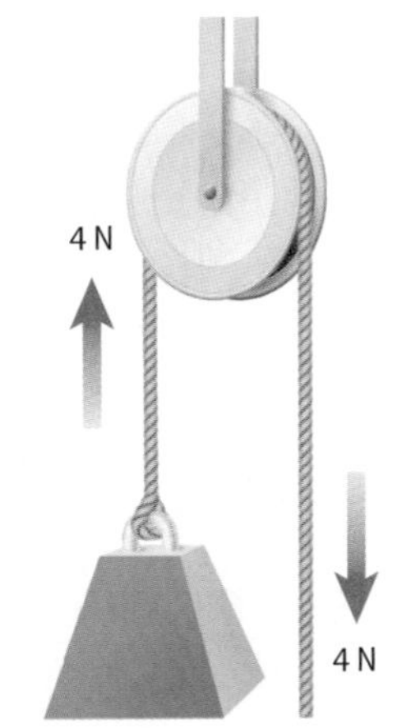

Activity

Ask students to calculate the IMA of a lever whose resistance arm is 1 m long and whose effort arm is 80 cm long. **What class of lever is this?** IMA = 0.8 m ÷ 1.0 m = 0.8; this must be a third-class lever. L2
LS **Logical-Mathematical**

Pulleys

Caption Answer

Figure 16 the radius of the pulley

Make a Model

Some pulleys, such as drive pulleys in automobiles, consist of two or more grooved wheels connected by a circular belt. Have students work in pairs to make models of a belt pulley. One student can hold two spools with pencils through the holes. Have students connect the spools with a large rubber band. The other student can turn the spools to show how turning one rotates the other in the same direction. If possible, use one small spool and one large spool. The students then can see that the speed of the pulleys is inversely related to their diameter. L3 LS **Kinesthetic**

Discussion

The IMA of a single fixed pulley is 1. **What is the benefit of using a fixed pulley?** A fixed pulley allows a person to take advantage of the force of gravity and use downward force to raise an object. Also, fixed pulleys may be used to raise objects to high places while the person stays at ground level. L2 LS **Logical-Mathematical**

Visual Learning

Figure 16 Point out that a fixed pulley, like that shown in **Figure 16,** is a type of first-class lever because the fulcrum is between the effort force and the resistance force. A movable pulley, like that shown on the next page, is a type of second-class lever. The point where the rope is attached to the ceiling is the fulcrum, and the resistance force is between the fulcrum and the effort force. L2 LS **Visual-Spatial**

Resource Manager

Chapter Resources Booklet
Transparency Activity, pp. 49–50
Lab Activity, pp. 9–11

Physical Science Critical Thinking/Problem Solving, p. 7

Pulleys, continued

✔ Reading Check

Answer by increasing the distance you must pull

Discussion

A person uses a block and tackle to lift an automobile engine that weighs 1,800 N. The person must exert a force of 300 N to lift the engine. **How many ropes support the engine? Explain how you know.** Six; the IMA is 1,800 N ÷ 300 N = 6, and in a pulley system, the IMA equals the number of supporting ropes.

Figure 18
The fixed pulley does not multiply force, while a movable pulley and block and tackle do.

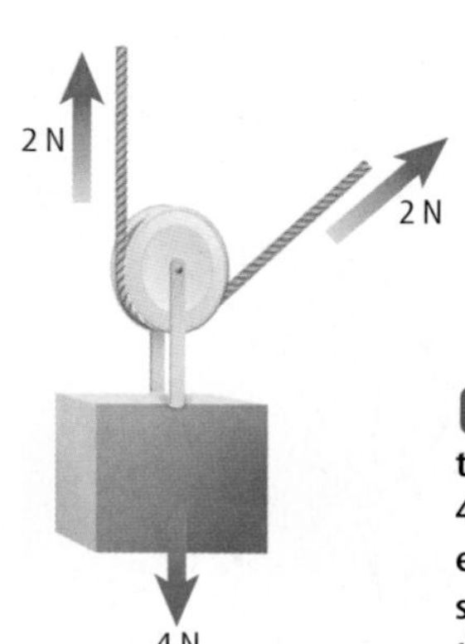

A With a movable pulley, the attached side of the rope supports half of the 4-N weight.

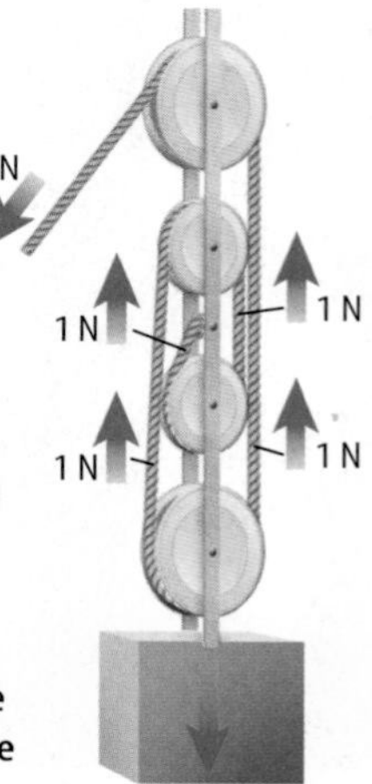

B In a block-and-tackle system, the 4-N weight is divided equally among each supporting rope. In this case, four ropes are used, so you have to use only a 1-N force to lift the weight.

Movable Pulleys A pulley in which one end of the rope is fixed and the wheel is free to move is called a movable pulley. Unlike a fixed pulley, a movable pulley does multiply force. Suppose a 4-N weight is hung from the movable pulley in **Figure 18A.** The ceiling acts like someone helping you to lift the weight. The string attached to the ceiling will support half of the weight—2 N. You need to exert only the other half of the weight—2 N—in order to support and lift the weight. Since the resistance force is 4 N and your effort force is 2 N, the IMA of the fixed pulley will be 2.

Because the movable pulley increases your effort force, the distance must increase to conserve energy. The IMA is 2, so the distance you pull must be twice as large as the resistance distance.

✔ Reading Check *How does a movable pulley multiply the effort force?*

The Block and Tackle A system of pulleys consisting of fixed and movable pulleys is called a block and tackle. **Figure 18B** shows a block and tackle made up of two fixed pulleys and two movable pulleys. If a 4-N weight is suspended from the movable pulley, each rope supports one fourth of the weight, reducing the effort force to 1 N. The IMA of a pulley system is equal to the number of ropes that support the resistance weight. A block and tackle can have a large mechanical advantage. When designing a block and tackle you must keep in mind that the more pulleys that are involved, the effects of friction are greater, which will reduce the overall mechanical advantage.

LAB DEMONSTRATION

Purpose to measure the mechanical advantage of various pulley systems

Materials one small, single sheave pulley; two small, 2-ring tandem pulleys; cord; 1-kg mass; 10-N spring scale

Procedure Use a single fixed pulley and the spring scale to measure the force required to lift the 1-kg mass. Next, attach one end of the cord to a fixed position, and with the spring scale measure the force needed to lift the mass using a single movable pulley. Finally, measure the force needed to lift the mass using a block and tackle.

Expected Outcome The IMAs are, respectively, 1, 2, and 4.

✔Assessment

Which system(s) increased force? movable pulley and block and tackle **Which system(s) changed direction of the force?** single fixed pulley and block and tackle **Which system(s) increased force and changed direction?** block and tackle

Figure 19
If the handle on the pencil sharpener were removed, you would be unable to sharpen your pencil.

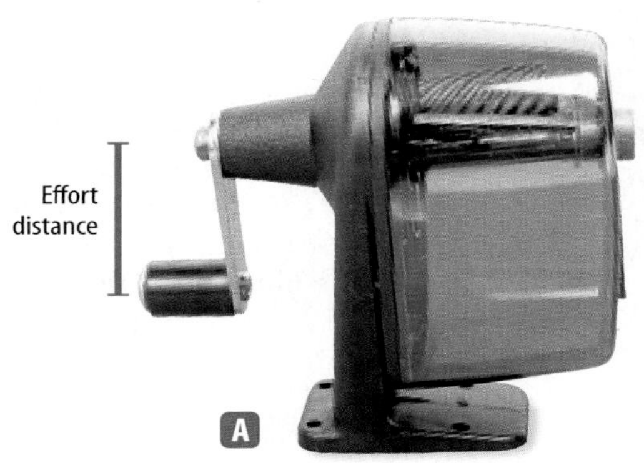

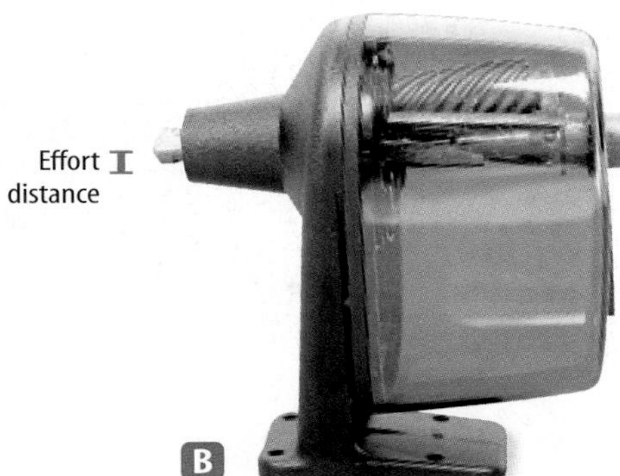

Wheel and Axle

Could you use the pencil sharpener in **Figure 19** if the handle weren't attached? The handle on the pencil sharpener is an example of a wheel and axle. A **wheel and axle** is a machine consisting of two wheels of different sizes that rotate together.

When you think of a wheel and axle, you might picture something like a bicycle tire, both parts of a wheel and axle move in a circle. Even though the handle of a pencil sharpener doesn't roll, it moves in a circular path just as the bicycle wheel does. Usually, effort force is exerted on the larger wheel. The smaller wheel, the axle, usually exerts the resistance force. Doorknobs and faucet handles are machines that use a wheel and axle.

The wheel and axle is another modified form of a lever. On the pencil sharpener, the point where the handle connects to the sharpening mechanism acts as the fulcrum. The length of the handle is the effort arm, or the wheel. The radius of the wheel inside is the resistance arm, or the axle.

Mechanical Advantage of the Wheel and Axle

Remember that the IMA of a lever can be calculated by dividing the effort arm by the resistance arm. In a wheel and axle, each travels in a circular path, so the effort arm is the same as the radius of the wheel. Likewise, the resistance arm is the same as the radius of the axle. Thus, the IMA can be calculated as follows.

$$\text{IMA} = \frac{\text{radius of wheel}}{\text{radius of axle}} = \frac{r_w}{r_a}$$

The mechanical advantage of a wheel and axle can be increased by making the radius of the wheel larger.

Wheel and Axle

IDENTIFYING Misconceptions

The wheel and axle on a skateboard or a pair of in-line skates is not the simple machine known as the wheel and axle. In the simple machine, the wheel and axle rotate together. Usually a small force is applied to the wheel and is translated to a larger force moving over the smaller distance of the axle. The wheels and axles on skateboards and in-line skates are rollers that help the vehicles move with less friction.

Extension

Look at a bicycle. **Is the front wheel a wheel and axle simple machine? Why?** No; it does not transfer energy. It is a roller. **Is the rear wheel? Why?** Yes; the force with which the rider pedals is transferred to the axle of the rear wheel by the chain. This force from the chain is transferred by the axle to the wheel. L3 LS **Logical-Mathematical**

Curriculum Connection

Math Supply students with several common wheels and axles, such as doorknobs or beaters from an electric mixer. Have them measure the radius of the wheel and the radius of the axle for each item and calculate its IMA. L2
LS **Logical-Mathematical**

Resource Manager

Chapter Resources Booklet
Enrichment, p. 34
Lab Activity, pp. 13–18

Home and Community Involvement, p. 35

Wheel and Axle, continued

Fast Fact

A system of two or more gears, like that shown in **Figure 20,** is called a gear train. The gear to which the effort force is applied is called the driven gear, and the other gears are called the driving gears.

Extension

Have students prepare posters showing various types of gears, such as helical, bevel, planetary, and worm gears. Give students time to explain to the class how the different gears work and what they are used for. L3 IS **Visual-Spatial** P

Inclined Planes

Activity

Create an inclined plane by resting a board against a stack of books. Have students measure the effort and resistance distances and calculate the IMA. Then ask students to use a spring scale to measure the force required to lift a toy car vertically and the force required to drag it up the ramp. Have them use the numbers they measured for distance and force and calculate the amount of work done pulling the toy car along the ramp and lifting it vertically. **Are the two amounts of work the same? Why or why not?** The two amounts of work should be close. Any difference is due to inaccurate measurements and loss of energy to friction. L2 ELL IS **Kinesthetic**

Figure 20
When one gear turns, the teeth that are interlocked with the other gear make it turn.

Gears A modified form of the wheel and axle that you may be familiar with is a gear. A gear usually consists of two wheels of different sizes with interlocking teeth along their circumferences. When one of the wheels is turned, the teeth force the other wheel to turn.

If the larger wheel is the effort gear one turn of the effort gear can result in many turns of the resistance gear, because it has more teeth than the smaller wheel. A system of gears in which the effort gear is larger reduces the effort force.

Gears also may change the direction of the force. Notice that when the effort gear in **Figure 20** is rotated clockwise, the resistance gear rotates counterclockwise. You may have noticed this when you use a can opener. As you twist the handle in one direction, the can revolves in the opposite direction.

Inclined Planes

Why do the roads and paths on mountains zigzag? Would it be easier to climb directly up a steep incline or walk a longer path gently sloped around the mountain? You have learned that it takes less force to lift something if you use a ramp. A sloping surface, such as ramp that reduces the amount of force required to do work, is called an **inclined plane.**

Mechanical Advantage of an Inclined Plane You do the same work by lifting a box straight up or sliding it up a ramp. But the ramp, an inclined plane, reduces the amount of force required by increasing the distance over which the force is applied. You can calculate the IMA of an inclined plane by dividing the length of the ramp by the height of the ramp.

$$\text{IMA} = \frac{\text{effort distance}}{\text{resistance distance}} = \frac{\text{length of slope}}{\text{height of slope}} = \frac{l}{h}$$

As the ramp is made longer and less steep, less force is required to push the object up the ramp.

When you think of an inclined plane, you normally think of moving an object up a ramp—you move and the inclined plane remains stationary. The screw and the wedge, however, are variations of the inclined plane in which the inclined plane moves and the object remains stationary.

Visual Learning

Figure 20 Point out that the teeth on the gears must be the same size in order to rotate smoothly. Tell students that the ratio of the number of teeth on the gears determines the speed that the gears turn and the IMA. **If the small gear has 24 teeth and the large gear has 72 teeth, how much faster will the small gear turn? What is the IMA?** The large gear will make one-third of a turn for each full turn of the small gear, so the small gear will turn three times faster. The IMA is 3. L2 IS **Logical-Mathematical**

Figure 21
A screw has an inclined plane that wraps around the post of the screw.

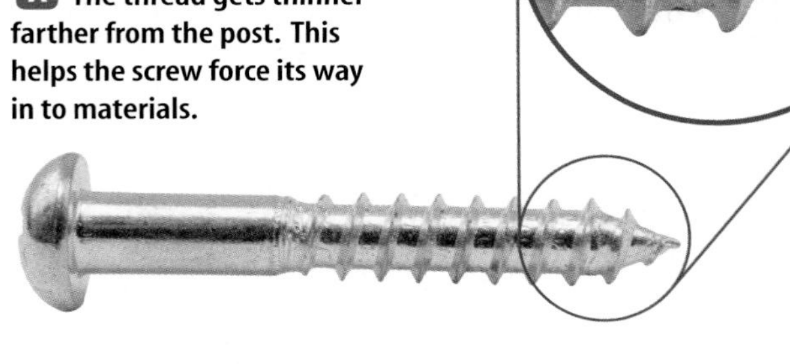

A The thread gets thinner farther from the post. This helps the screw force its way in to materials.

B Many lids, such as those on peanut butter jars, also contain threads.

The Screw

You normally think of a screw as a carpenter's tool like the one in **Figure 21A.** A **screw** is an inclined plane wrapped in a spiral around a cylindrical post. If you look closely at the screw in **Figure 21A,** you'll see that the threads form a tiny ramp that runs upward from its tip. As you turn the screw, the threads seem to pull the screw into the wood. The wood seems to slide up the inclined plane. Actually, the plane slides through the wood.

There are many other examples of the screw that you encounter every day. How do you remove the lid off a jar of peanut butter, like in **Figure 21B?** If you look closely, you see the threads similar to the ones in **Figure 21A.** Where else can you find examples of a screw?

Figure 22
A knife blade is an example of a sharp wedge. As you cut through the apple, it pushes the halves of the apple apart.

The Wedge

Like the screw, the wedge is also a simple machine where the inclined plane moves through an object or material. A **wedge** is an inclined plane with one or two sloping sides. It changes the direction of the effort force.

Look closely at the knife in **Figure 22.** One edge is extremely sharp, and it slopes outward at both sides, forming an inclined plane. As it moves through the apple in a downward motion, the force is changed to a horizontal motion, forcing the apple apart.

The Screw

Text Question Answer

Possible answer: light bulb.

Make a Model

An Archimedes' screw is a type of revolving screw used to lift water. This simple device was invented in the third century B.C. by the Greek scientist Archimedes. Have interested students make a model of an Archimedes' screw, using plastic sheeting attached to a dowel. L3
LS **Kinesthetic**

Teacher FYI

The threads of a screw are the windings. The pitch is the distance from a point on one thread to a point directly above it on the next thread. The pitch determines the force you must exert to turn a screw.

The Wedge

Activity

The ideal mechanical advantage of a wedge is calculated by dividing the length of one side of the wedge by the width of the wedge at the thick end. Ask students to calculate the mechanical advantage of a wedge that is 12 cm long and 5 cm wide. MA = 12 cm ÷ 5 cm = 2.4 L3
LS **Logical-Mathematical**

Active Reading

Write–Draw–Discuss This strategy encourages students to actively participate in reading and lectures, assimilating content creatively. Have students write about the different simple machines, clarify their ideas, and then make illustrations or drawings of the machines and how they work. Ask students to share responses with the class and display several examples.

Resource Manager

Chapter Resources Booklet
Reinforcement, p. 31
Activity Worksheet, pp. 5–6, 7–8

Performance Assessment in the Science Classroom, p. 37

Compound Machines

Fun Fact

In a compound machine, the output force of one of its simple machines becomes the input force of another. For a compound machine made of two simple machines, $MA = MA_2 \times MA_1$.

3 Assess

Reteach

From construction paper, cut three arrows, about 10, 20, and 30 cm long. Make a similar set in another color. Label the first set of arrows F_e and the second set F_r. Collect examples of simple machines. Ask volunteers to each choose a machine and use the arrows to show the direction and relative sizes of F_e and F_r. L2 ELL LS **Visual-Spatial**

Challenge

Some gear systems use a chain to connect the gears instead of having interlocking teeth. Have students draw diagrams on the board showing why gears used with a chain rotate in the same direction. L3 LS **Visual-Spatial**

Assessment

Process Ask students to compare and contrast pulleys and gears. Both use wheels. Gears have teeth, but pulleys don't. Pulleys use a cord to move the wheels. Gears are pulled by interlocking teeth or a chain. Use **Performance Assessment in the Science Classroom,** p. 89.

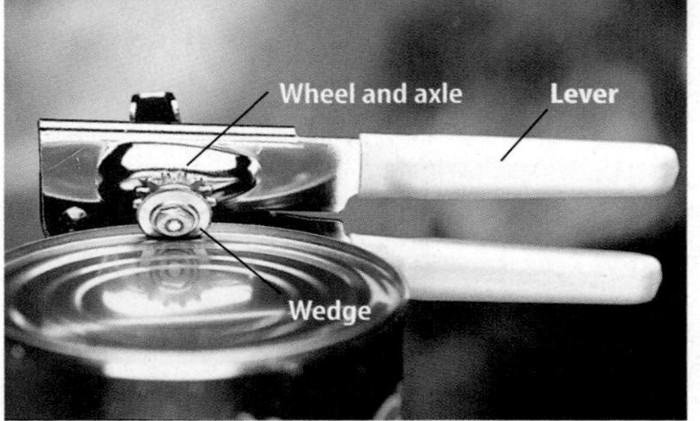

Figure 23
A compound machine, such as a can opener, is made up of many simple machines.

Compound Machines

Some of the machines you use every day are made up of several simple machines. When two or more simple machines are used together, it is called a **compound machine.**

Look at the can opener in **Figure 23.** To open the can you first squeeze the handles together. The handles act as a lever and increase the force applied on a wedge, which then pierces the can. You then turn the handle, a wheel and axle, to open the can. The overall mechanical advantage of a compound machine is related to the mechanical advantages of all the machines involved.

A car is also a compound machine. Burning fuel in the cylinders of the engine causes the pistons to move up and down. This up-and-down motion makes the crankshaft rotate. The force exerted by the rotating crankshaft is transmitted to the wheels through other parts of the car, such as the transmission and the differential. Both of these parts contain gears, which are simple machines. When a large and a small gear are in contact, the larger gear rotates a shorter distance, but the force it exerts is increased. In this way, these gears can change the rate at which the wheels rotate, the force exerted by wheels, and even reverse the direction of rotation.

Section 3 Assessment

1. Give one example of each kind of simple machine. Use examples different from the ones in the text.
2. Explain why the six kinds of simple machines are variations of two basic machines.
3. Suppose you are using a screwdriver to pry the lid off a paint can. Identify the fulcrum, the effort arm, and the resistance arm.
4. A 6-m ramp runs from a ground-level sidewalk to a porch. The porch is 2 m off the ground. What is the ideal mechanical advantage of the ramp?
5. **Think Critically** When would the friction of an inclined plane be useful?

Skill Builder Activities

6. **Making and Using Tables** Organize information about the six kinds of simple machines into a table. Include the type of machine, an example of each type, and a brief description of how it works. You may include other information, such as mechanical advantage, if you wish. **For more help, refer to the** Science Skill Handbook.
7. **Using a Word Processor** Using a word processor, write a separate paragraph about each class of lever. Describe at least two examples of each class, identifying the effort force, resistance force, and fulcrum for each. Use **Figure 15** for reference. **For more help, refer to the** Technology Skill Handbook.

Answers to Section Assessment

1. Possible answers: seesaw (lever), ski lift (pulley), hand-cranked pepper mill (wheel and axle), playground slide (inclined plane), swivel stool (screw), teeth (wedge)
2. The axle of a pulley and a wheel and axle act as a lever's fulcrum. A screw is an inclined plane wound around a post. A wedge is a two-sided inclined plane.
3. The fulcrum is the can's edge. The effort arm is the distance from your hand on the screwdriver to the fulcrum. The resistance arm is the distance from the fulcrum to the end of the screwdriver that is prying against the can.
4. $IMA = 6 \text{ m} \div 2 \text{ m} = 3$
5. Possible answer: to prevent slipping when rolling a wheelchair up a ramp.
6. Check students' work.
7. Check student's work. Paragraphs should reflect the information shown in **Figure 15.**

Activity

Levers

Did you ever play on a seesaw? Wasn't it much easier to balance your friend on the other end if you both weighed the same? If your friend was lighter, you had to move toward the fulcrum to balance the seesaw. In this activity, you will use a lever to determine the mass of a coin.

What You'll Investigate

How can a lever measure mass?

Materials

$8\frac{1}{2}" \times 11"$ sheet of paper
coins (one quarter, one dime, one nickel)
balance
metric ruler

Goals

- **Measure** effort arm and resistance arm.
- **Observe** how mass can affect the fulcrum.

Safety Precautions

Procedure

1. Make a lever by folding the paper into a strip 3 cm wide by 28 cm long.
2. Mark a line 2 cm from one end of the paper strip. Label this line Resistance.
3. Slide the other end of the paper strip over the edge of a table until the strip begins to tip. Mark a line across the paper at the table edge and label this line Effort.
4. **Measure** the mass of the paper to the nearest 0.1 g. Write this mass on the Effort line.
5. Center a dime on the Resistance line. Locate the fulcrum by sliding the paper strip until it begins to tip. Mark the balance line. Label it Fulcrum #1.
6. **Measure** the lengths of the resistance and effort arms to the nearest 0.1 cm.
7. Calculate the IMA of the lever. Multiply the IMA by the mass of the lever to find the approximate mass of the coin.
8. Repeat steps 5 through 7 with the nickel and the quarter. Mark the fulcrum line #2 for the nickel and #3 for the quarter.

Conclude and Apply

1. What provides the effort force?
2. What does it mean if the IMA is less than 1.0?
3. The calculations are done as if the entire weight of the paper is located at what point?
4. **Infer** why mass units can be used in place of force units in this kind of problem.

Communicating Your Data

Compare your results with those of other students in your class. **For more help, refer to the Science Skill Handbook.**

Activity

BENCH TESTED

Purpose Students calculate the mechanical advantage of levers. L1 LS **Logical-Mathematical**

Process Skills measuring, using numbers, interpreting data, classifying, observing and inferring, comparing and contrasting, recognizing cause and effect, forming operational definitions, interpreting scientific illustrations

Time Required 40 minutes

Teaching Strategies

- Have students draw the effective lever and fulcrum between the effort and resistance lines. The rest of the paper is not part of the lever but provides effort force and support.
- The following equations are needed for step 7:
  $IMA = L_e \text{ (paper)} \div L_r \text{ (coin)}$
  $IMA = F_r \text{ (coin)} \div F_e \text{ (paper)}$
- Mass and force are proportional, so
  $m_r \text{ (coin)} = m_e \text{ (paper)} \times IMA.$

Answers to Questions

1. gravity
2. The force to move the lever is more than the weight that is moved.
3. the paper's center of gravity
4. The forces on both ends of the lever are caused by gravity acting with the same ratio of force to mass.

Oral Evaluate student understanding of the lever design by having them explain to the class how they performed the calculations. Use **Performance Assessment in the Science Classroom,** p. 101.

Communicating Your Data

Have students use graphics software to draw diagrams that explain the activity and illustrate their results.

Activity

BENCH TESTED

What You'll Investigate

Purpose

Students will make models of different simple machines to lift a weight, and compare the forces used. L2 COOP LEARN

LS **Kinesthetic**

Process Skills

observing, using numbers, communicating, measuring, inferring, comparing and contrasting, recognizing cause and effect, interpreting data, formulating models, making and using tables

Time Required

one class period

Materials

The block and tackle can be difficult to set up unless the pulleys and string sizes are matched. The pulleys should be made for block and tackle use. The small pulleys typically available from hardware stores will work, but can be difficult to handle as they don't usually have the needed fastening points on both top and bottom.

Activity Model and Invent

Work Smarter

You are the contractor on a one-story building with a large air-conditioner. The lower the force, the easier the job for your crew. What ways can you think of to get the air conditioner to the roof?

Recognize the Problem

How can you minimize the force needed to lift an object? What machines could you use?

Thinking Critically

Is a lever practical for this job? Why? Consider a fixed pulley with ideal mechanical advantage (IMA) $=$ 1, a moveable pulley with IMA $=$ 2, a block and tackle with one fixed double pulley and one moveable double pulley with IMA $=$ 4, and an inclined plane with IMA $=$ slope / height $=$ 4. The latter two machines may differ in efficiency. How can you find the efficiency of machines?

Goals

- **Model** lifting devices based on a block and tackle and on an inclined plane.
- **Calculate** the output work that will be accomplished.
- **Measure** the force needed by each machine to lift a weight.
- **Calculate** the input work and efficiency for each model machine.
- **Select** the best machine for your job based on force required.

Possible Materials

Spring scale, 0 – 10 N range
9.8 N weight (1 kg mass)
Two double pulleys
String for pulleys
Stand or support for the pulleys
Wooden board, 40 cm long
Support for board, 10 cm high

Problem Data

	Control	Inclined Plane	Block and Tackle
Ideal Mechanical Advantage, IMA	1	4	4
Effort Force, F_e, N	Will vary	Will vary	Will vary
Effort Distance, d_e, m	0.10	0.40	0.10
Resistance Force, F_r, N	9.8	9.8	9.8
Resistance Distance, d_r, m	0.10	0.10	0.10
$Work_{in} = F_e \times d_e$, Joules	Will vary	Will vary	Will vary
$Work_{out} = F_r \times d_r$, Joules	0.98	0.98	0.98
% Efficiency, $(Work_{out} / Work_{in}) \times 100$	Will vary	Will vary	Will vary

Thinking Critically

Discussion

Aside from the amount of force needed, what are some of the advantages and disadvantages of each type of machine? The inclined plane would take up a large amount of space and would need supports under it at various places. It probably wouldn't be safe to walk on. The pulley would need a strong support from which it could be hung.

Planning the Model

1. Work in teams of at least two. **Collect** all the needed equipment.
2. Sketch a model for each lifting machine. **Model** the inclined plane with a board 40 cm long and raised 10 cm at one end. Include a control in which the weight is lifted while being suspended directly from the spring scale.
3. Make a table for data.

Check the Model Plans

1. Is the pulley support high enough that the block and tackle can lift a weight 10 cm?
2. Obtain your teacher's approval of your sketches and data table before proceeding.

Making the Model

1. Tie the weight to the spring scale and measure the force required to lift it. Record the effort force in your data table under control, along with the 10-cm effort distance.
2. Assemble the inclined plane so that the weight may be pulled up the ramp at a constant rate. The 40-cm board should be supported so that one end is 10 cm higher.
3. Tie the string to the spring scale and measure the force required to move the weight up the ramp at a constant speed. Record this effort force under inclined plane in your data table. Record 40 cm as the effort distance for the inclined plane.
4. Assemble the block and tackle using one fixed double pulley and one moveable double pulley.
5. Tie the weight to the lower pulley and tie the spring scale to the string at the top of the upper pulley.
6. **Measure** the force required to lift the weight with the block and tackle. Record this effort force.
7. **Measure** the length of string that must be pulled to raise the weight 10 cm. Record this effort distance.

Analyzing and Applying Results

1. **Calculate** the output work for all three methods of lifting the 9.8 N weight 10 cm.
2. **Calculate** the input work and the efficiency for the control, the inclined plane, and the block and tackle.
3. Which machine used the lowest force to raise the weight? How do you account for the observed differences in efficiencies? How could you improve the efficiency for each?

Make a poster showing how the best machine would be used to lift the air conditioner to the roof of your building.

Planning the Model

Teaching Strategy

When students pull on the weight using the spring scale, make sure they pull slowly, smoothly, and at constant speed. Jerky pulling will lead to the use of unnecessarily large forces.

Troubleshooting

Teams of two will be required to simplify assembly of apparatus and measurements.

Making the Model

Expected Outcome

Students will build models of three simple machines and use them to model lifting an air conditioner to a roof.

Analyzing and Applying Results

1. Output work is the same for all three, 0.98 Nm
2. Answers will vary.
3. The block and tackle require the lowest force. The reason for the efficiency difference is probably the difference in the friction between the ramp and the block and tackle. You could improve both by lubricating the ramp and the pulleys.

Assessment

Process Have students make bar graphs of the different amounts of force used and work done using each machine. Use **Performance Assessment in the Science Classroom,** p. 111.

Have students compare their posters. Did they all agree on the best machine? Display student posters in the classroom.

Content Background

Nanotechnology is a very broad term used to describe various scientific studies that involve the manipulation of materials at the atomic and molecular levels. Dr. Richard Feynman first examined the concept in a 1959 address to the American Physical Society. The current vision of nanotechnology and its possible uses was formulated by Dr. K. Eric Drexler in 1986. He envisioned the precise construction of advanced materials from chemically pure ingredients, eliminating the toxic byproducts of conventional manufacturing. The long-term goals for molecular manufacturing range from ultra-small computers and space construction to the alleviation of disease, hunger and pollution. At first nanotechnology appeared more like science fiction than serious science. However, when IBM scientists re-created the company logo using individual xenon atoms on a nickel surface in 1989, nanotechnology achieved widespread legitimacy. Many organizations, including NASA and Xerox, are now committed to research in this field. The development of new materials and the tools to manipulate them at the molecular level has paved the way for the creation of the first crude nano scale devices. As developments increase at a rapid pace, many questions arise concerning the possible use and misuse of the new technology.

THE SCIENCE

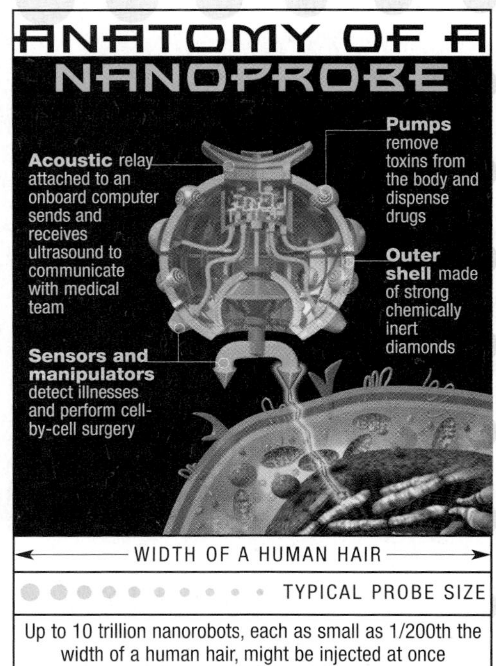
ANATOMY OF A NANOPROBE
Pumps remove toxins from the body and dispense drugs
Acoustic relay attached to an onboard computer sends and receives ultrasound to communicate with medical team
Outer shell made of strong chemically inert diamonds
Sensors and manipulators detect illnesses and perform cell-by-cell surgery
WIDTH OF A HUMAN HAIR
TYPICAL PROBE SIZE
Up to 10 trillion nanorobots, each as small as 1/200th the width of a human hair, might be injected at once

Imagine an army of tiny robots, each no bigger than a bacterium, swimming through your bloodstream. One type of robot takes continuous readings of blood pressure in different parts of your body. Another type monitors cholesterol. Still others measure your blood sugar, the beginnings of possible blockages in arteries leading to your heart, and your general health.

Welcome to the world of nanotechnology—the science of creating molecular-sized machines. The machines, called nanobots, are each about one one billionth of a meter in size. The prefix *nano* refers to a billionth part of a unit, and comes from *nanos*, the Greek word for "dwarf." These machines are so small they can skillfully control matter one atom at a time.

Nanotechnology uses microscopic machines to do microscopic work. By combining engineering and biology, scientists might actually be able to reorganize atoms and molecules to create new objects. For example, nanobots could create diamonds from coal—all they'd need to do is rearrange a few atoms.

150

Resources for Teachers and Students

Integrated Project Team on Devices and Nanotechnology NASA Ames Research Center, Moffett Field, CA 94035

Foresight Institute, PO Box 61058, Palo Alto, CA 94306

Engines of creation by K. Eric Drexler, Garden City, N.Y.: Anchor Press/Doubleday, 1986.

A spider mite, which is not visible to the human eye, crawls across a mirror assembly, a part used in micromachines.

OF VERY, VERY SMALL

One day you might have robots swimming through your bloodstream

Nanobots also could be used to clean up oil spills and toxic waste sites. Toxic wastes usually are made up of harmless atoms that are arranged into noxious molecules. Nanobots will be able to break down these poisonous molecules, converting dangerous waste into harmless forms. Nanobots will have all sorts of uses in nature, in the body, and in the workplace.

Small, Smaller, Smallest

Within a few decades, nanotechnologists are predicting they will be creating machines that can do just about anything, as long as it's small. Already, nanotechnologists have built gears 10,000 times thinner than a human hair. They've also built tiny molecular "motors" only 50 atoms long. At Cornell University, nanotechnologists created the world's smallest guitar. It is appoximately the size of a white blood cell and it even has six strings.

This is the smallest guitar in the world. It is about as big as a human white blood cell. Each of its six silicon strings is 100 atoms wide. You can see the guitar only with an electron microscope.

Of course, the tiny guitar isn't meant to be played—only to illustrate the reality of the "science of the small," and to give us a glimpse into what lies ahead.

And getting back to those nanobots in your body—in the future, they might transmit your internal vital signs to a nanocomputer, which might be implanted under your skin. There the data could be analyzed for signs of disease.

Nanomachines then could be sent to scrub your arteries clean of dangerous blockages, or mop up cancer cells, or even vaporize blood clots with tiny lasers. These are just some of the possibilities in the imaginations of those studying the new science of nanotechnology.

CONNECTIONS Design **Think up a very small simple or complex machine that could go inside the body and do something. What would the machine do? Where would it go? Share your diagram or design with your classmates.**

SCIENCE Online For more information, visit science.glencoe.com

Discussion

What would be the advantage of having nanobots perform medical tasks now done by drugs or surgery? Possible answer: By acting on a cell-by-cell basis nanobots can avoid damaging healthy cells and reduce recovery time. L2 LS **Logical-Mathematical**

Activity

Divide the class into groups of three or four. Assign a word to each group. Students in each group will use four different ways to spell out the word using sand on black paper, each time making the word as small as possible. The first time students put on gloves, the second time they will use their bare fingers to move the sand. For the third time, have them use an implement such as a craft stick to move the sand to make the word, and finally, provide students with tweezers and a magnifying glass. Ask students in each group to measure their smallest word and compare their with 500 nanometers. L2 LS **Kinesthetic**

Investigate the Issue

Have students research the most recent advances in nanotechnology. Discuss the tools scientists use to see and manipulate objects on the molecular level and how they are similar to and different from the tweezers and magnifying glass.

CONNECTIONS Debate Provide time for students to give short presentations of their designs to the class. Ask each student to describe why the tiny machine would do the job better than current technology.

SCIENCE Online

Internet Addresses

Explore the Glencoe Science Web site at **science.glencoe.com** to find out more about topics in this feature.

Chapter 5 Study Guide

Reviewing Main Ideas

Preview

Students can answer the questions in their Science Journals. Discuss the answers as you go through the chapter. **LS Linguistic**

Review

Students can write their answers, then compare them with those of other students. **LS Interpersonal**

Reteach

Students can look at the illustrations and describe details that support the main ideas of the chapter. **LS Visual-Spatial**

Answers to Chapter Review

Section 1

2. Yes; it pushes them up against the force of gravity.

Section 2

1. The hammer is a first class lever that multiplies the force applied to it.

Section 3

3. wedges and levers

Chapter 5 Study Guide

Reviewing Main Ideas

Section 1 Work

1. Work is the transfer of energy when a force makes an object move.
2. Work is done only when force produces motion in the direction of the force. *Does this forklift do work by lifting these crates? Explain.*

3. Power is the amount of work, or the amount of energy transferred, in a certain amount of time.

Section 2 Using Machines

1. A machine makes work easier by changing the size of the force applied, by increasing the distance an object is moved, or by changing the direction of the applied force. *How is work made easier for the person pulling the nail from a board?*

2. The number of times a machine multiplies the force applied to it is the mechanical advantage of the machine. The actual mechanical advantage is always less than the ideal mechanical advantage.
3. The efficiency of any machine is a ratio of the work done by the machine to the work put into the machine. No machine can be 100 percent efficient.

Section 3 Simple Machines

1. A simple machine is a machine that can do work with a single movement.
2. A simple machine can increase an applied force, or change its direction, or both.
3. A lever is a bar that is free to pivot about a fixed point called a fulcrum. A pulley is a grooved wheel with a rope running along the groove. A wheel and axle consists of two different-sized wheels that rotate together. An inclined plane is a sloping surface used to raise objects. The screw and wedge are special types of inclined planes.
4. A combination of two or more simple machines is called a compound machine. *What simple machines make up a pair of scissors?*

FOLDABLES Reading & Study Skills — After You Read

On your Foldable, list work you would do with machines under its tab. Now compare and contrast work with and without machines.

FOLDABLES Reading & Study Skills — After You Read

After students have read the chapter and completed the Foldable described in Before You Read, have them do the activity on the student page.

Dinah Zike

Visualizing Main Ideas

Complete the concept map for simple machines using the following terms: inclined plane, lever, lever types, pulley, screw, wedge, and wheel and axle.

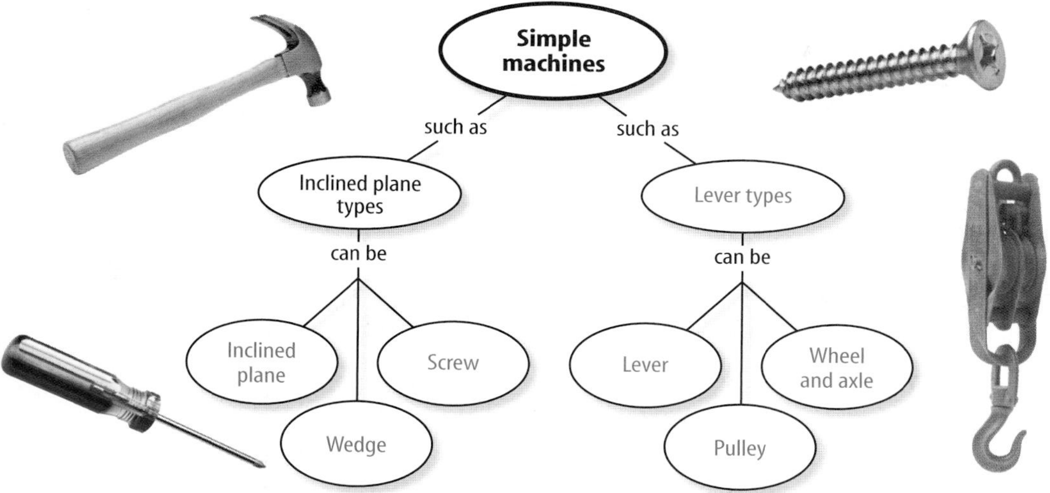

Vocabulary Review

Vocabulary Words

a. compound machine
b. efficiency
c. effort force
d. inclined plane
e. lever
f. machine
g. mechanical advantage
h. power
i. pulley
j. resistance force
k. screw
l. simple machine
m. wedge
n. wheel and axle
o. work

THE PRINCETON REVIEW Study Tip

When you encounter new vocabulary, write it down in a sentence. This will help you understand, remember, and use new vocabulary words.

Using Vocabulary

Replace the underlined words with the correct vocabulary word(s).

1. A combination of two or more simple machines is an ideal machine.
2. A wedge is another form of a wheel and axle.
3. The amount by which a machine multiplies your force is called efficiency.
4. The force that you exert on a lever is called the resistance force.
5. An inclined plane is a grooved wheel with a rope or chain running through it.
6. Efficiency is the rate at which work is done.
7. Power is when a force causes an object to move in the direction of the force.

IDENTIFYING Misconceptions

Assess

After students have done the activity on page 124F and completed the chapter, have them answer the following question.

Julio lifted a box onto a desk. Joshua pushed an identical box up an inclined plane onto the desk. A little bit of friction on the inclined plane opposes Joshua's push. **Which boy probably used more force in lifting the boxes?** Julio **Which boy did more work?** They did the same amount of work.

Expected Outcome Students should develop the understanding that simple machines may reduce the amount of force people exert; however, they do not decrease the amount of work people do.

Chapter 5 Study Guide

Visualizing Main Ideas

See student page.

Vocabulary Review

Using Vocabulary

1. compound machine
2. inclined plane
3. mechanical advantage
4. effort force
5. pulley
6. Power
7. Work

Chapter 5 Assessment

Checking Concepts

1. C
2. B
3. A
4. B
5. C
6. A
7. C
8. A
9. B
10. B

Thinking Critically

11. The fulcrum should be moved toward the adult to increase the length of the effort arm of the child's lever. This will multiply the effort force exerted by the child.
12. efficiency $= \frac{W_{out}}{W_{in}} \times 100\%$ $W_{out} = 2{,}000 \text{ N} \times 2 \text{ m} = 4{,}000 \text{ J}$; $W_{in} = 1{,}250 \text{ N} \times 6 \text{ m} = 7{,}500 \text{ J}$. $\frac{W_{out}}{W_{in}} = \frac{4{,}000 \text{ J}}{7{,}500 \text{ J}} \times 100\% = 53\%$
13. $P = \frac{W}{t}$; $W = F \times d = 500 \text{ N} \times 3\text{m} = 1{,}500 \text{ J}$; $P = \frac{1{,}500\text{J}}{5\text{s}} = 300 \text{ W}$
14. The one with the fat handle; the screwdriver is being used as a wheel and axle, with the handle acting as the wheel. The screwdriver with the fat handle will therefore have a greater MA. The length is irrelevant.

Chapter 5 Assessment

Checking Concepts

Choose the word or phrase that best answers the question.

1. Using the scientific definition, which of the following is true of work?
   A) It must be difficult.
   B) It must involve the transfer of money.
   C) It must involve the transfer of energy.
   D) It must be done with a machine.

2. How many types of simple machines exist?
   A) three **C)** eight
   B) six **D)** ten

3. In an ideal machine, which of the following is true?
   A) Work input is equal to work output.
   B) Work input is greater than work output.
   C) Work input is less than work output.
   D) Work input is independent of work output.

4. Which of these cannot be done by a machine?
   A) multiply force
   B) multiply energy
   C) change direction of a force
   D) work

5. What term indicates the number of times a machine multiplies the effort force?
   A) efficiency
   B) power
   C) mechanical advantage
   D) resistance

6. How could you increase the IMA of an inclined plane?
   A) increase its length
   B) increase its height
   C) decrease its length
   D) make its surface smoother

7. How far must the effort rope of a single fixed pulley move to raise a resistance 4 m?
   A) 1 m **C)** 4 m
   B) 2 m **D)** 8 m

8. In a wheel and axle, which of the following usually exerts the resistance force?
   A) the axle **C)** the gear ratio
   B) the larger wheel **D)** the pedals

9. What is the IMA of an inclined plane 8 m long and 2 m high?
   A) 2 **C)** 8
   B) 4 **D)** 16

10. Which of the following increases as the efficiency of a machine increases?
    A) work input **C)** friction
    B) work output **D)** IMA

Thinking Critically

11. An adult and a small child get on a seesaw that has a movable fulcrum. When the fulcrum is in the middle, the child can't lift the adult. How should the fulcrum be moved so the two can seesaw? Explain.

12. Using a ramp 6 m long, workers apply an effort force of 1,250 N to move a 2,000-N crate onto a platform 2 m high. What is the efficiency of the ramp?

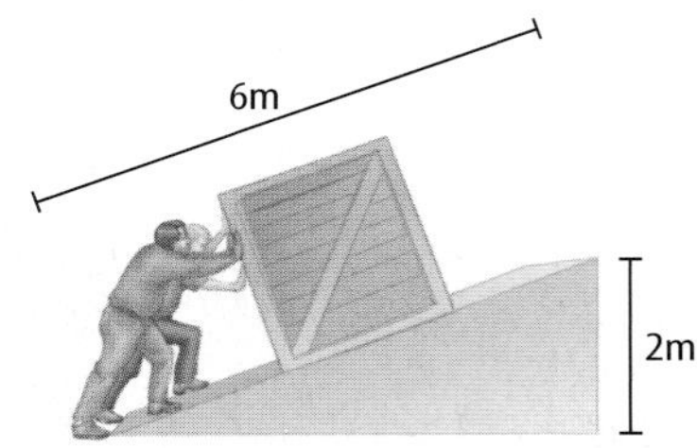

13. How much power does a person weighing 500 N need to climb a 3-m ladder in 5 s?

Chapter Assessment Planner

Portfolio Encourage students to place in their portfolios one or two items of what they consider to be their best work. Examples include:

- MiniLAB Assessment, p. 129
- Assessment, p. 131
- Curriculum Connection, p. 134
- Extension, p. 144

Performance Additional performance assessments, Performance Task Assessment Lists, and rubrics for evaluating these activities can be found in Glencoe's **Performance Assessment in the Science Classroom.**

154 CHAPTER ASSESSMENT

14. You have two screwdrivers. One is long with a thin handle, and the other is short with a fat handle. Which would you use to drive a screw into a board? Explain.

Developing Skills

15. Concept Mapping Complete the concept map of simple machines using the following terms: *compound machines, mechanical advantage, resistance force, work.*

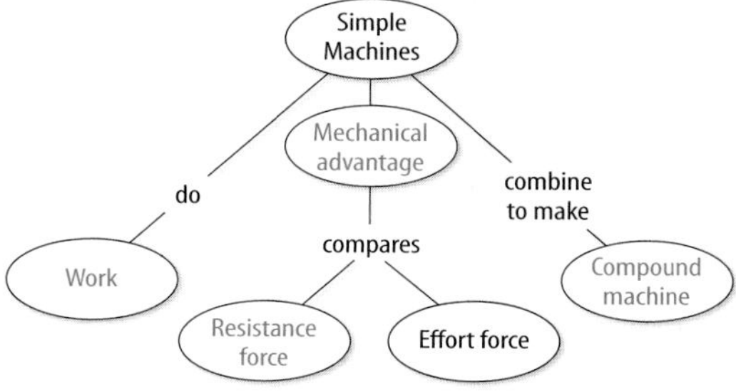

16. Communicating A pair of scissors is a compound machine. Draw a diagram of a pair of scissors and label the simple machines you can identify. Explain to a classmate the purpose of each simple machine in this device.

Performance Assessment

17. Invention Design a human-powered machine of some kind. Describe the simple machines used in your design, and tell what each of these machines does.

Technology

Go to the Glencoe Science Web site at **science.glencoe.com** or use the **Glencoe Science CD-ROM** for additional chapter assessment.

Test Practice

Maria went to the library to do some research on inventions that made it easier to perform everyday tasks. Some of the pictures that she photocopied are shown in the diagram below.

Study the diagram and answer the following questions.

1. What do these simple machines have in common?

A) They are all made of metal.
B) They are all levers.
C) All were invented in the United States.
D) They are all recent inventions.

2. The larger scissors can cut through a thick object because _____.

F) levers with longer effort arms are easier to hold
G) levers with longer effort arms multiply force more
H) levers with longer effort arms multiply her force less
J) levers with longer effort arms are made of stronger materials

Assessment Resources

Reproducible Masters

Chapter Resources Booklet
Chapter Review, pp. 39–40
Chapter Tests, pp. 41–44
Assessment Transparency Activity, p. 51

Glencoe Science Web site
Interactive Tutor
Chapter Quizzess

Glencoe Technology
Assessment Transparency
Interactive CD-ROM Chapter Quizzes
ExamView Pro Test Bank
Vocabulary PuzzleMaker Software
MindJogger Videoquiz DVD/VHS

Test Practice

The Test-Taking Tip was written by The Princeton Review, the nation's leader in test preparation.

1. B
2. G

Developing Skills

15. See student page.
16. Diagrams should show that scissors are two levers and two wedges. Each handle is an effort arm. Each blade is a resistance arm. The screw holding the levers together is the fulcrum for both levers. The blades are wedges.

Performance Assessment

17. Accept any reasonable design. Make sure they identify and describe all simple machines used. Use the Performance Task Assessment List for Invention in **PASC,** p. 117.

CHAPTER  THERMAL ENERGY

Section/Objectives	Standards		Activities/Features
	National	State/Local	
Chapter Opener	See p. 37T for a Key to Standards.		**Explore Activity:** Observe the effects of molecules at different temperatures, p. 157 **Before You Read,** p. 157
Section 1 Temperature and Heat 2 sessions 1 block 1. **Explain** the difference between heat and temperature. 2. **Define** thermal energy. 3. **Explain** the meaning of specific heat.	National Content Standards: UCP2, B3 (5–8), B6 (9–12)		**Science Online,** p. 160 **Chemistry Integration,** p. 162 **Math Skills Activity:** Calculating Changes in Thermal Energy, p. 162
Section 2 Transferring Thermal Energy 2 sessions 1 block 1. **Compare and contrast** thermal energy transfer by conduction, convection, and radiation. 2. **Compare and contrast** conductors and insulators. 3. **Explain** how insulation affects the transfer of energy.	National Content Standards: UCP3, A1, B3 (5–8), B6 (9–12), E1, E2, F5 (5–8), F6 (9–12)		**Visualizing Convection Currents,** p. 166 **MiniLAB:** Observing Heat Transfer by Radiation, p. 168 **MiniLAB:** Comparing Thermal Conductors, p. 169 **Activity:** Convection in Gases and Liquids, p. 171
Section 3 Using Heat 3 sessions 1 block 1. **Compare and contrast** three types of conventional heating systems. 2. **Distinguish** between passive and active solar heating systems. 3. **Describe** how internal combustion engines work. 4. **Explain** how a heat mover can transfer thermal energy in a direction opposite to that of its natural movement.	National Content Standards: UCP1, A1, B3 (5–8), B6 (9–12), E1, E2, F5 (5–8), F6 (9–12)		**Science Online,** p. 175 **Earth Science Integration,** p. 176 **Activity:** Conduction in Gases and Liquids, p. 180 **Science Stats:** Thermal Energy, p. 182

Activity Materials	Reproducible Resources	Section Assessment	Technology
Explore Activity: water, ice, 2 beakers, food coloring, stopwatch	**Chapter Resources Booklet** Foldables Worksheet, p. 17 Note-taking Worksheets, pp. 33–35	GLENCOE'S ASSESSMENT ADVANTAGE	
Need materials? Contact Science Kit at 1-800-828-7777 or www.sciencekit.com on the Internet.	**Chapter Resources Booklet** Transparency Activity, p. 44 Enrichment, p. 30 Reinforcement, p. 27 Directed Reading, p. 20 Lab Activity, pp. 9–12 **Reading and Writing Skill Activities,** p. 33 **Mathematics Skill Activities,** p. 11	**Portfolio** Science Journal, p. 160 **Performance** Math Skills, p. 162 Skill Builder Activities, p. 163 **Content** Section Assessment, p. 163	Section Focus Transparency Interactive CD-ROM/DVD Guided Reading Audio Program
MiniLAB: direct sunlight, window exposed to direct sunlight **MiniLAB:** plastic, metal, and wooden spoons; 3 plastic beads; butter or wax; beaker; boiling water **Activity:** burner or hot plate, water, candle, 500-mL beaker, pepper, matches	**Chapter Resources Booklet** Transparency Activity, p. 45 MiniLAB, pp. 3, 4 Enrichment, p. 31 Reinforcement, p. 28 Directed Reading, p. 20 Activity Worksheet, pp. 5–6 Lab Activity, pp. 13–15 **Texas Lab Management and Safety,** p. 44	**Portfolio** Extension, p. 167 **Performance** MiniLAB, p. 168 MiniLAB, p. 169 Skill Builder Activities, p. 170 **Content** Section Assessment, p. 170	Section Focus Transparency Interactive CD-ROM/DVD Guided Reading Audio Program
Activity: 3 thermometers, 2 foam cups, 400-mL beakers (2), burner or hot plate, paring knife, 2 thermal mitts, large test tube, ring stand, test-tube clamp, wire gauze, scissors, ice	**Chapter Resources Booklet** Transparency Activity, p. 46 Enrichment, p. 32 Reinforcement, p. 29 Directed Reading, pp. 21, 22 Activity Worksheet, pp. 7–8 Transparency Activity, pp. 47–48 **Science Inquiry Labs,** p. 21	**Portfolio** Activity, p. 173 Assessment, p. 179 **Performance** Skill Builder Activities, p. 179 **Content** Section Assessment, p. 179	Section Focus Transparency Teaching Transparency Interactive CD-ROM/DVD Guided Reading Audio Program

End of Chapter Assessment

GLENCOE'S ASSESSMENT ADVANTAGE

Blackline Masters	Technology	Professional Series
Chapter Resources Booklet Chapter Review, pp. 37–38 Chapter Tests, pp. 39–42 **Standardized Test Practice by The Princeton Review,** 28–31	MindJogger Videoquiz CD-ROM Explorations and Quizzes Vocabulary Puzzle Makers ExamView Pro Test Bank Interactive Lesson Planner Interactive Teacher's Edition	Performance Assessment in the Science Classroom (PASC)

Transparencies

Section Focus

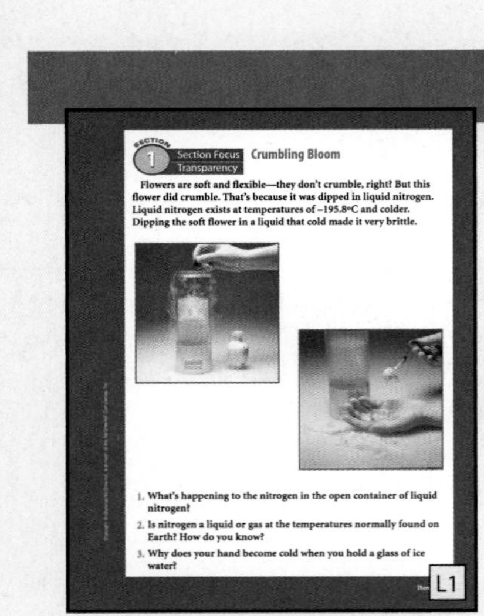
Section 1 Section Focus Transparency — Crumbling Bloom

Flowers are soft and flexible—they don't crumble, right? But this flower did crumble. That's because it was dipped in liquid nitrogen. Liquid nitrogen exists at temperatures of –195.8°C and colder. Dipping the soft flower in a liquid that cold made it very brittle.

1. What's happening to the nitrogen in the open container of liquid nitrogen?
2. Is nitrogen a liquid or gas at the temperatures normally found on Earth? How do you know?
3. Why does your hand become cold when you hold a glass of ice water?

L1

Section 2 Section Focus Transparency — A Spectacular Reentry

This is the return of Apollo 8 to Earth. In 1968, Apollo 8 became the first piloted vehicle to orbit the Moon. As you can see from the picture, the exterior of the space craft gets very hot on reentry to the atmosphere. The astronauts inside the craft need to be protected from the high temperatures outside the craft.

1. If a metal pan with a metal handle sits on a lit burner for a long time, what happens to the handle?
2. When it's really cold out, why does a jacket help you stay nice and warm?
3. How might the space craft be protected from the heat of reentry?

L1

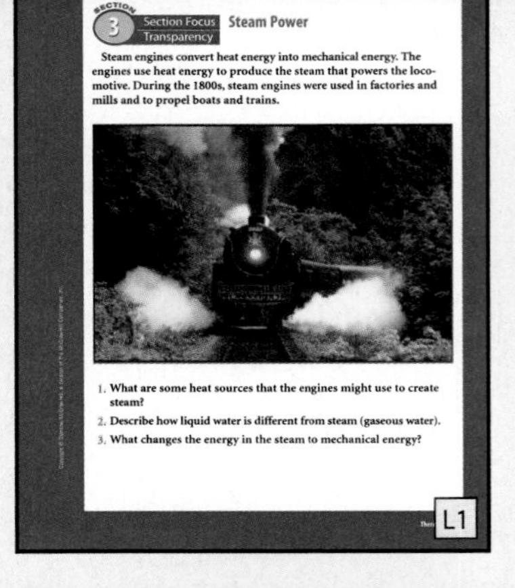
Section 3 Section Focus Transparency — Steam Power

Steam engines convert heat energy into mechanical energy. The engines use heat energy to produce the steam that powers the locomotive. During the 1800s, steam engines were used in factories and mills and to propel boats and trains.

1. What are some heat sources that the engines might use to create steam?
2. Describe how liquid water is different from steam (gaseous water).
3. What changes the energy in the steam to mechanical energy?

L1

This is a representation of key blackline masters available in the Teacher Classroom Resources. See Resource Manager boxes within the chapter for additional information.

Assessment

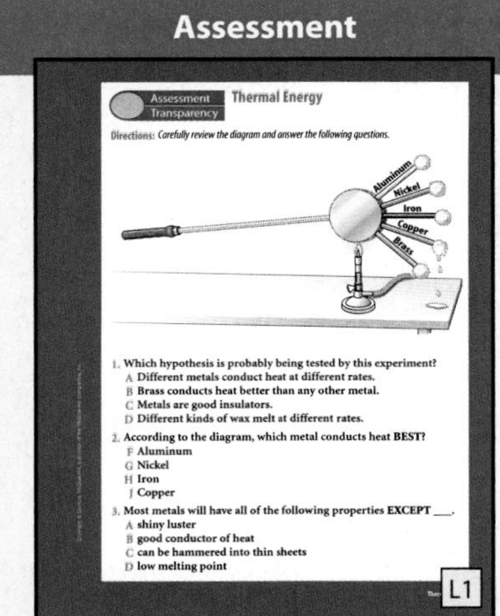
Assessment Transparency — Thermal Energy

Directions: Carefully review the diagram and answer the following questions.

1. Which hypothesis is probably being tested by this experiment?
   A Different metals conduct heat at different rates.
   B Brass conducts heat better than any other metal.
   C Metals are good insulators.
   D Different kinds of wax melt at different rates.
2. According to the diagram, which metal conducts heat BEST?
   F Aluminum
   G Nickel
   H Iron
   J Copper
3. Most metals will have all of the following properties EXCEPT ___.
   A shiny luster
   B good conductor of heat
   C can be hammered into thin sheets
   D low melting point

L1

Teaching

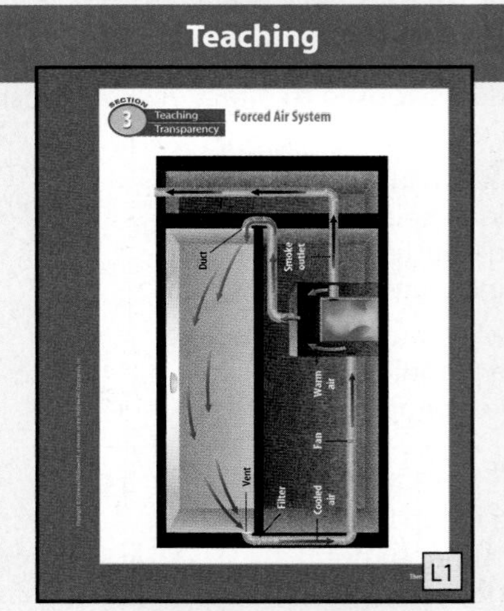
Section 3 Teaching Transparency — Forced Air System

L1

Key to Teaching Strategies

The following designations will help you decide which activities are appropriate for your students.

- L1 Level 1 activities should be appropriate for students with learning difficulties.
- L2 Level 2 activities should be within the ability range of all students.
- L3 Level 3 activities are designed for above-average students.
- ELL ELL activities should be within the ability range of English Language Learners.
- COOP LEARN Cooperative Learning activities are designed for small group work.
- LS Multiple Learning Styles logos are used throughout to indicate strategies that address different learning styles.
- P These strategies represent student products that can be placed into a best-work portfolio.

Hands-on Activities

Activity Worksheets

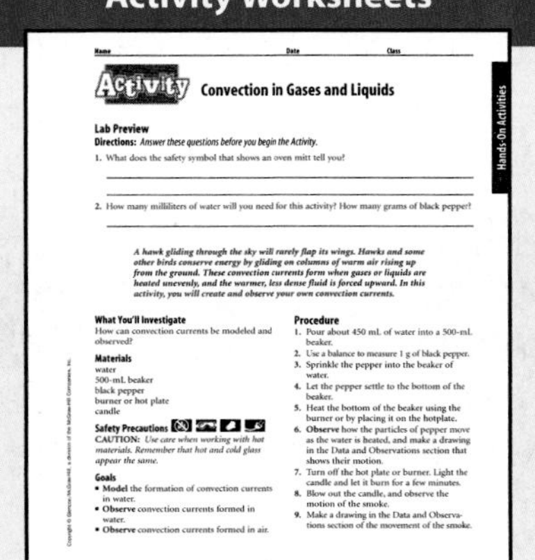
Name ______ Date ______ Class ______

Activity Convection in Gases and Liquids

Lab Preview

Directions: *Answer these questions before you begin the Activity.*

1. What does the safety symbol that shows an oven mitt tell you?
2. How many milliliters of water will you need for this activity? How many grams of black pepper?

A hawk gliding through the sky will rarely flap its wings. Hawks and some other birds conserve energy by gliding on columns of warm air rising up from the ground. These convection currents form when gases or liquids are heated unevenly, and the warmer, less dense fluid is forced upward. In this activity, you will create and observe your own convection currents.

What You'll Investigate

How can convection currents be modeled and observed?

Materials

water
500-mL beaker
black pepper
burner or hot plate
candle

Safety Precautions

CAUTION: *Use care when working with hot materials. Remember that hot and cold glass appear the same.*

Goals

- **Model** the formation of convection currents in water.
- **Observe** convection currents formed in water.
- **Observe** convection currents formed in air.

Procedure

1. Pour about 450 mL of water into a 500-mL beaker.
2. Use a balance to measure 1 g of black pepper.
3. Sprinkle the pepper into the beaker of water.
4. Let the pepper settle to the bottom of the beaker.
5. Heat the bottom of the beaker using the burner or by placing it on the hotplate.
6. **Observe** how the particles of pepper move as the water is heated, and make a drawing in the Data and Observations section that shows their motion.
7. Turn off the hot plate or burner. Light the candle and let it burn for a few minutes.
8. Blow out the candle, and observe the motion of the smoke.
9. Make a drawing in the Data and Observations section of the movement of the smoke.

Hands-On Activities

L1

Laboratory Activities

Name ______ Date ______ Class ______

LAB 1 Laboratory Activity — **Specific Heats of Metals**

The amount of heat needed to change the temperature of a metal is much less than that needed to change the temperature of a similar amount of other materials. You probably were aware of this fact if you ever tried to cool a can of soft drink quickly in the freezer. Metal cans tend to cool more quickly than their contents.

A measure of how much energy is needed to change the temperature of a material is called specific heat. The specific heat, C_p, is the amount of heat needed to change the temperature of 1 kilogram of a substance by 1 degree Celsius. As you recall, the specific heat of water is 4190 J/kg·°C, which is often expressed as 4.19 J/k·°C. The specific heat of a substance is a physical property of that substance. Therefore, a substance can be identified by its specific heat.

Strategy

You will use a calorimeter to determine the specific heat of a piece of metal.
You will identify the metal by its specific heat.

Materials

250-mL beaker
one-hole paper punch
metric balance
paper towels
2 plastic cups with lids
plastic pipette
rubber band
test tube, thick walled
test-tube holder
test-tube rack
thermometer
sample of unknown metal X, Y, or Z
water

Procedure

Part A—Building a Calorimeter

1. Place about 50 mL of water in the 250-mL beaker and allow the temperature of the water to come to room temperature.
2. Punch a hole for the thermometer in one of the lids of the plastic cups with a paper punch.
3. Wrap a rubber band around one of the plastic cups.
4. Place this cup inside the second plastic cup. Assemble the calorimeter as shown in Figure 1.
5. Measure the mass of the calorimeter. Record this value in the Data and Observations section.

Lid with hole
Plastic cup
Rubber band
Assembled calorimeter

Hands-On Activities

L1

Meeting Different Ability Levels

Content Outline

Note-taking Worksheet — Thermal Energy

L1

Reinforcement

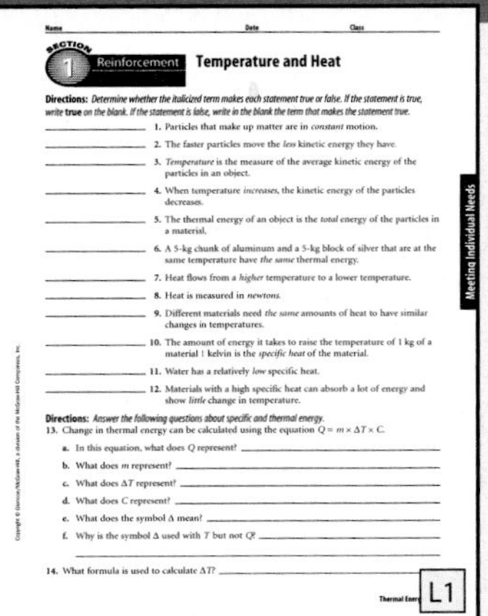

Reinforcement — Temperature and Heat

L1

Directed Reading

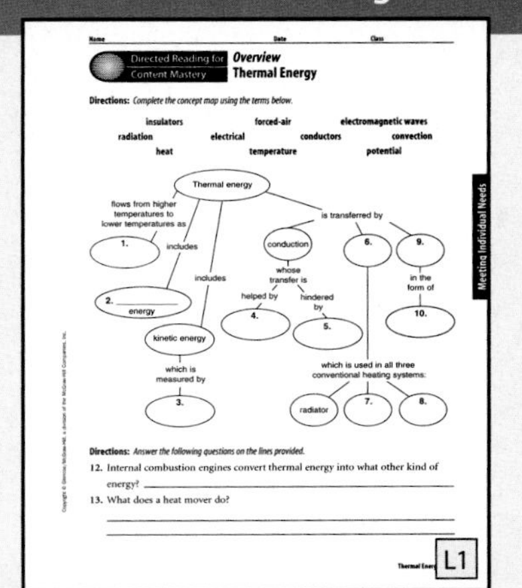

Directed Reading for Content Mastery — Overview — Thermal Energy

L1

Enrichment

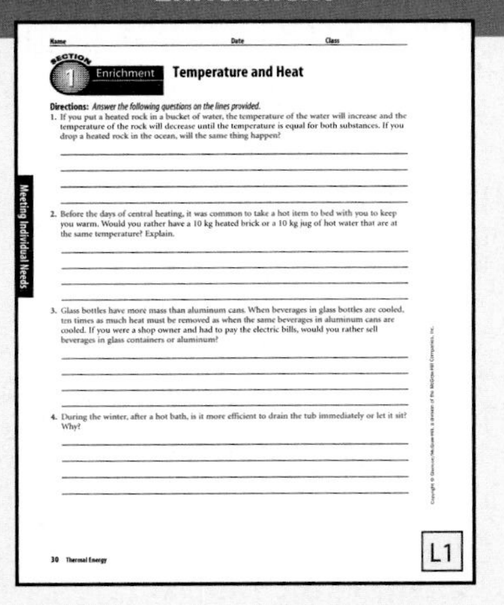

Enrichment — Temperature and Heat

L1

Spanish Directed Reading

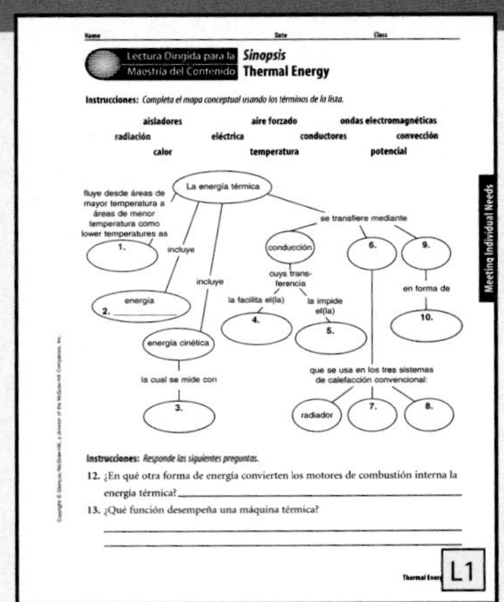

Lectura Dirigida para la Maestría del Contenido — Sinopsis — Thermal Energy

L1

Assessment

Chapter Tests

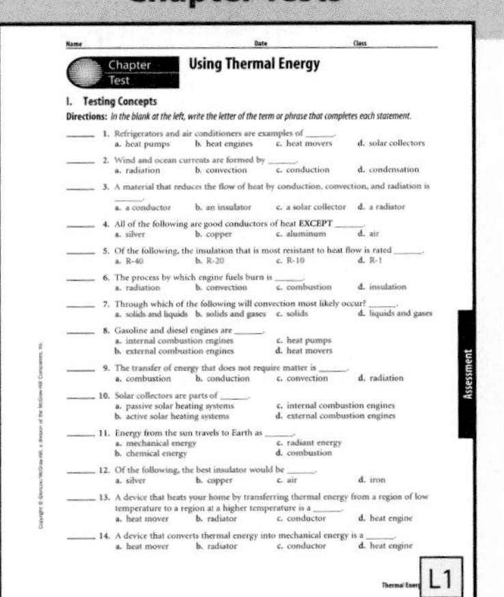

Chapter Test — Using Thermal Energy

L1

Test Practice Workbook

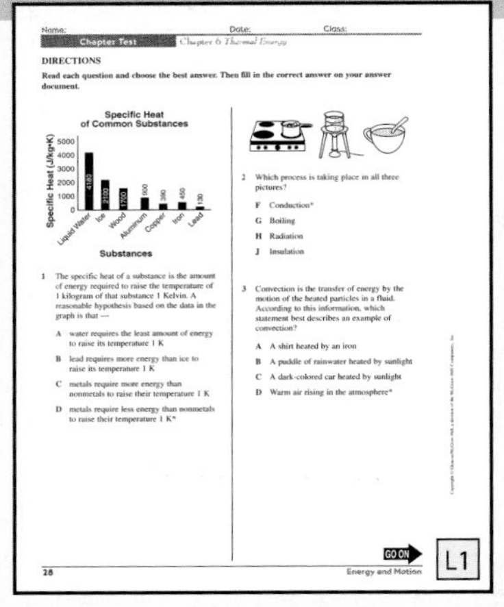

Chapter Test — Chapter 6 Thermal Energy

L1

Chapter Review

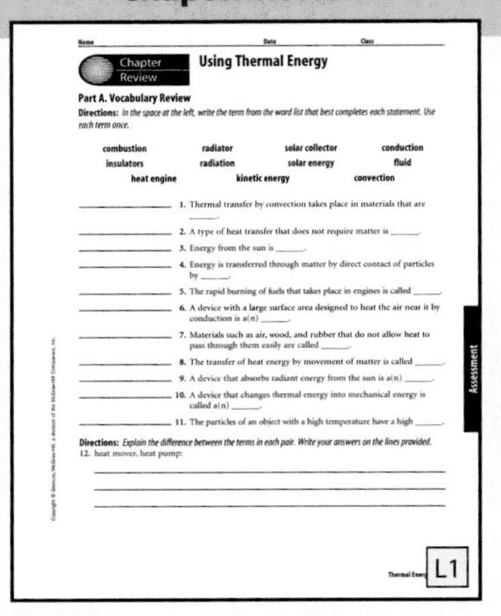

Chapter Review — Using Thermal Energy

L1

Science Content Background

SECTION 1 Temperature and Heat

Temperature

It is important to differentiate between temperature and thermal energy. A small nail at a temperature of 100°C has less thermal energy than a large hammer at a temperature of 90°C.

The common thermometer is a glass tube filled with colored alcohol or mercury, which expands with increasing heat to give a reading of temperature. Digital thermometers, such as those put into children's ears, rely on the increase in electrical resistance with higher temperature to ascertain temperatures.

Three temperature scales are commonly used around the world. The Celsius system is used by almost all the people in the world and in most scientific work. The Fahrenheit system, the oldest system, is used by people in the United States. The Kelvin is the official SI unit for temperature. This system, used exclusively by scientists, is based on absolute zero—the lowest possible temperature. Zero K is a theoretical value not yet observed.

Fun Fact

Water is weird when it comes to thermal energy. Unlike most materials that expand when heated, water at temperatures of 1°, 2°, or 3°C contracts when heated. Water is most dense at 4°C. This property allows ice to float in your glass of water, and keeps ponds from freezing from the bottom up.

Thermal Energy

Which contains more thermal energy, liquid water at 100°C water or steam at 100°C? Anyone who has been burned by steam knows the correct answer—steam! Thermal energy is the sum of both kinetic and potential energy. The steam, although at the same temperature as the liquid water, has more potential, or latent energy. This is the energy it absorbed in the phase change from a liquid to a gas.

Properties of materials can change as they gain or lose thermal energy. For example: most substances expand when they are heated, resistance in wire increases with rises in temperature, the color of some materials is influenced by temperature, and some chemical reactions occur only at specific temperatures.

Heat

The SI unit of thermal energy is the joule. Calorie is another unit frequently used. One calorie, equal to 4.184 joules, is the amount of heat needed to raise one gram of water one degree Celsius. This amount is so small that with food energy, we use units of kilocalories. We still call them *Calories*, but with a capital C. So if the packages says that chocolate contains 150 Calories, it really has 150,000 calories, or 627,600 joules, of energy.

David Young-Wolff/PhotoEdit

Specific Heat

Water has a very high specific heat. If you have one gram of water and one gram of aluminum and you add one calorie of heat to each, the water will increase in temperature by one degree and the aluminum will increase in temperature by five degrees. The high specific heat of water has important influences on climate. Large bodies of water tend to keep their temperatures longer than smaller bodies of water. So areas near the ocean often have milder winters and milder summers.

SECTION 2 Transferring Thermal Energy

Conduction

The term *thermodynamics* comes from Latin words that mean "heat flow." The first law of thermodynamics is simply the law of conservation of energy applied to thermal energy. Thermal energy doesn't just magically disappear or appear, it is transferred to or from other objects or it is created by work.

Things don't share coldness, but they do share heat. So the ice isn't giving cold to your drink, but the ice is absorbing heat from the beverage. If you touch a piece of wood and a piece of metal that are both at the same temperature, the metal feels colder. The metal conducts the heat away from your finger, giving it a cold sensation.

SECTION 3 Using Heat

Solar Heating

Passive solar heating usually features large windows facing south to let the sunlight in during the winter. Materials with high specific heats, such as concrete walls, water barrels, and tile floors, are frequently placed so that they are exposed to the sunlight. The Sun warms these materials, and then during the night, they slowly release the heat to the room.

Using Heat to do Work

No engine can be completely efficient. Heat is created from the mechanical motion and is lost from the system.

For additional content background on this topic, go to the Glencoe Science Web site at science.glencoe.com.

Bob Daemmrich/The Image Works

CHAPTER 6

Thermal Energy

Chapter Vocabulary

temperature
thermal energy
heat
specific heat
conduction
convection
radiation
insulator
radiator
solar energy
solar collector
heat engine
internal combustion engine
heat mover

What do you think?

Science Journal This photograph shows perspiration on a person's skin—one of the ways the body responds to heat.

CHAPTER 6

Thermal Energy

You probably couldn't shape a piece of cold steel unless it is very thin like a wire. But if the steel is heated enough, it melts, and the liquid steel can be poured into molds, as shown in this picture. In the mold, the steel cools and again becomes a solid, this time in the desired shape. In this chapter you will learn how heat and temperature are related, and how thermal energy is transferred. You will also learn how the flow of heat can be controlled.

What do you think?

Look at the picture below with a classmate. Discuss what this might be or what is happening. Here's a hint: *You can do this, but a dog can't.* Write your answer or your best guess in your Science Journal.

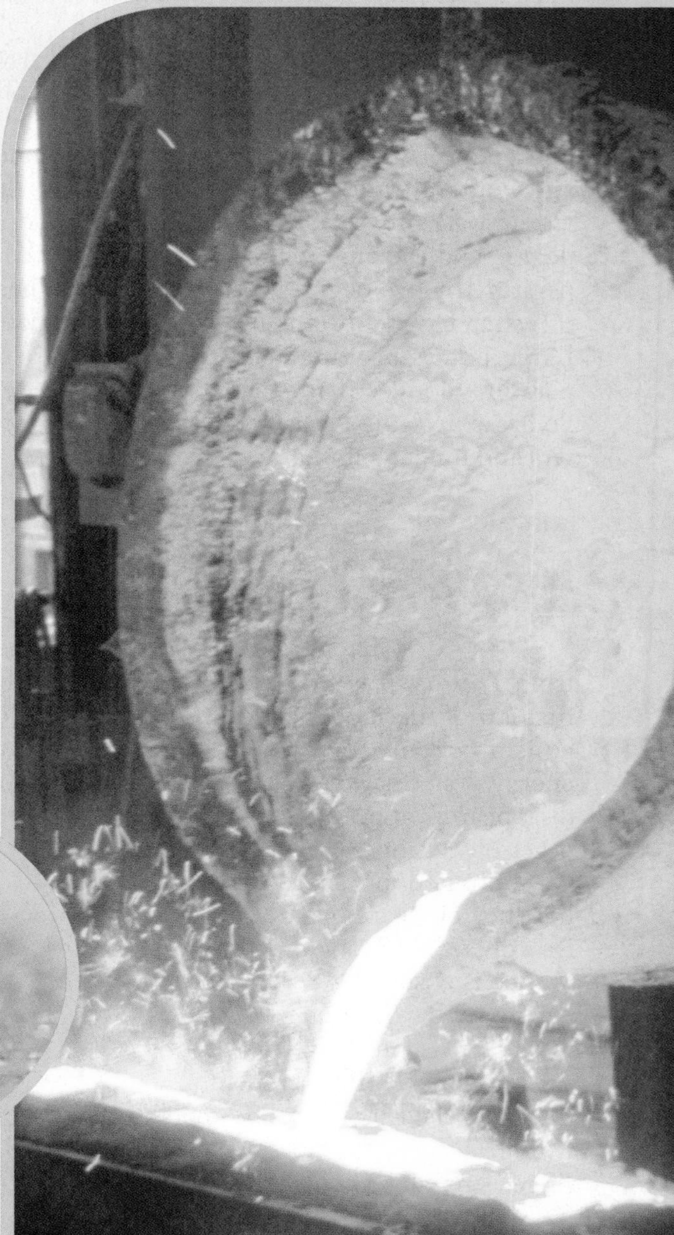

156

Theme Connection

Energy Thermal energy is the kinetic energy of the molecules, ions, and atoms that make up matter. We feel thermal energy as heat. Thermal energy can be transferred by conduction, convection, and radiation, and can be converted into mechanical energy to do work.

Why does hot water burn your skin but warm water does not? Molecules move faster and have more energy at a higher temperature than at a lower temperature. The energy of moving molecules is called kinetic energy. When fast-moving molecules of hot water touch your skin, they trigger nerve cells to send pain signals to your brain. Warm water molecules have less energy and cause no pain. In this activity, observe and compare the effects of fast-moving and slow-moving water molecules.

Observe the effects of molecules at different temperatures

1. Pour 200 mL of room-temperature water into a beaker.
2. Pour 200 mL of water in a beaker and add some ice.
3. Put one drop of food dye into each beaker.
4. Use a stopwatch to measure the time it takes for the food dye to change the color of the water in each beaker.

Observe

Write a paragraph in your Science Journal describing the results of your experiment. Infer why the food dye spread throughout the water in the two beakers at different rates.

Before You Read

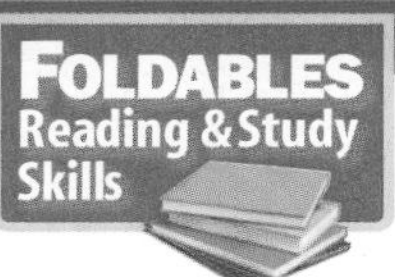

Making a Compare and Contrast Study Fold **Make the following Foldable to help you see how temperature and heat are similar and different.**

1. Place a sheet of paper in front of you so the long side is at the top. Fold the paper in half from top to bottom. Fold from the left side to the right side and crease. Then unfold.
2. Through the top thickness of paper, cut along the middle fold line to form two tabs. Label the tabs *Temperature* and *Heat*.
3. Before you read the chapter, write what you know about temperature and heat under the tabs. As you read the chapter, add to and correct what you have written.

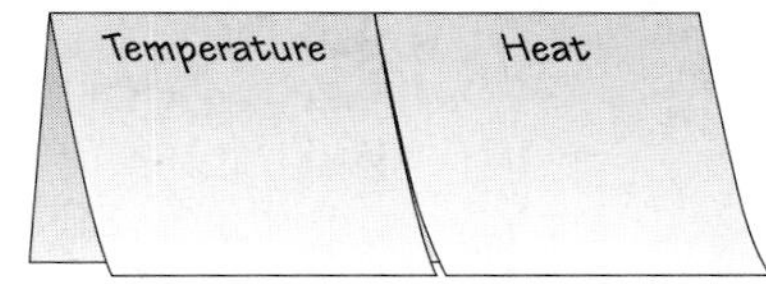

157

EXPLORE ACTIVITY

Purpose Use the Explore Activity to introduce students to the kinetic theory of matter. L2 ELL
LS **Kinesthetic**

Preparation Obtain enough ice for the class and keep it in a freezer until just prior to the time when students do this activity.

Materials 2 beakers, water, ice, food coloring, stopwatch

Teaching Strategies Suggest students repeat the experiment several times, waiting different amounts of time between adding the ice to the beaker and adding the food coloring.

Observe

The dye spread faster in the room temperature water than it did in the water with ice. In the warmer water the molecules move faster and collide more often with the dye molecules making them move faster.

Portfolio Have students draw colored sketches showing the water in each beaker every minute until all the water in each beaker has changed color. Make sure they label each sketch with the time. Use **Performance Assessment in the Science Classroom,** p. 127. P

Before You Read

FOLDABLES Reading & Study Skills

Dinah Zike Study Fold

Purpose Students make and use a Foldable to collect information on thermal energy and then use what they have learned to compare and contrast temperature and heat.

For additional help, see Foldables Worksheet, p. 17 in **Chapter Resources Booklet,** or go to the Glencoe Science Web site at **science.glencoe.com.** See After You Read in the Study Guide at the end of this chapter.

SECTION 

Temperature and Heat

1 Motivate

Bellringer Transparency

Display the Section Focus Transparency for Section 1. Use the accompanying Transparency Activity Master. L2 ELL

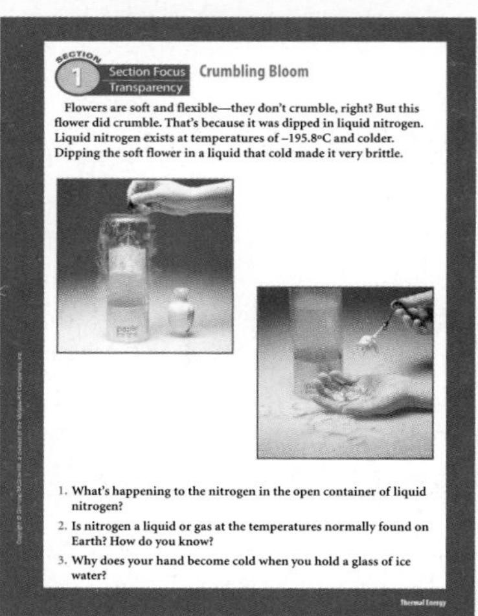
Section Focus Transparency 1 — Crumbling Bloom

Flowers are soft and flexible—they don't crumble, right? But this flower did crumble. That's because it was dipped in liquid nitrogen. Liquid nitrogen exists at temperatures of –195.8°C and colder. Dipping the soft flower in a liquid that cold made it very brittle.

1. What's happening to the nitrogen in the open container of liquid nitrogen?
2. Is nitrogen a liquid or gas at the temperatures normally found on Earth? How do you know?
3. Why does your hand become cold when you hold a glass of ice water?

Thermal Energy

Tie to Prior Knowledge

Ask students whether they have ever noticed that some materials heat up faster than others do. Tell students that the amount of heat it takes to make a substance warm up is called its specific heat, one of the things they will learn about in this section.

SECTION 

Temperature and Heat

As You Read

***What* You'll Learn**

- **Explain** the difference between heat and temperature.
- **Define** thermal energy.
- **Explain** the meaning of specific heat.

Vocabulary

temperature, thermal energy, heat, specific heat

***Why* It's Important**

If you know the difference between temperature and heat, you can understand why heat flows.

Temperature

The words hot and cold are commonly used to describe the temperature of a material. Although the terms *hot* and *cold* are not very precise, they still are useful. Everyone understands that hot indicates high temperature and that cold indicates low temperature. But what is temperature and how is temperature related to heat?

Matter in Motion All matter is made of tiny particles—atoms and molecules. Molecules are made of atoms held together by chemical bonds. Atoms and molecules are so small that a speck of dust has trillions of them. However, in all materials—solids, liquids, or gases—these particles are in constant motion.

Like all objects that are moving, these moving particles have kinetic energy. The faster these particles move, the more kinetic energy they have. **Figure 1** shows how molecules are moving in hot and cool objects.

Figure 1
The atoms in an object are in constant motion.

A **When the horseshoe is hot, the particles in it move very quickly.**

B **When the horseshoe has cooled, its particles are moving more slowly.**

Section Assessment Planner

PORTFOLIO
Science Journal, p. 160

PERFORMANCE ASSESSMENT
Math Skills Activity, p. 162
Skill Builder Activities, p. 163
See page 186 for more options.

CONTENT ASSESSMENT
Section, p. 163
Challenge, p. 163
Chapter, pp. 186–187

Temperature Why do some objects feel hot and others feel cold? The **temperature** of an object is related to the average kinetic energy of the atoms or molecules. The faster these particles are moving, the more kinetic energy they have, and the higher the temperature of the object is. Think about a cup of hot tea and a glass of iced tea. The temperature of the hot tea is higher because the molecules in the hot tea are moving faster than those in the iced tea. In SI units, temperature is measured in degrees kelvin (K), and degrees on the Kelvin and Celsius scales are the same size.

Thermal Energy

If you let cold butter sit at room temperature for a while, it warms and becomes softer. Because the air in the room is at a higher temperature than the butter, molecules in air have more kinetic energy than butter molecules. Collisions between butter and molecules in air transfer energy from the faster-moving molecules in air to the slower-moving butter molecules. The butter molecules then move faster and the temperature of the butter increases.

Molecules in the butter can exert attractive forces on each other. Recall that Earth exerts an attractive gravitational force on a ball. When the ball is above the ground, the ball and Earth are separated, and the ball has potential energy. In the same way, atoms and molecules that exert attractive forces on each other have potential energy when they are separated. The sum of the kinetic and potential energy of all the molecules in an object is the **thermal energy** of the object. Because the kinetic energy of the butter molecules increased as it warmed, the thermal energy of the butter increased.

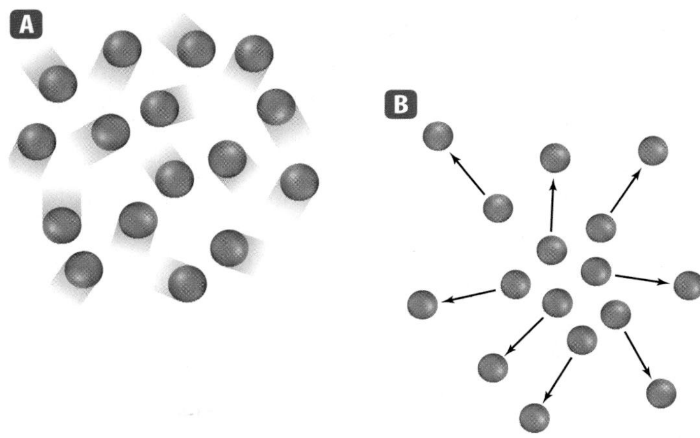

Figure 2
The thermal energy of a substance is the sum of the kinetic and potential energy of its molecules. A The kinetic energy increases as the molecules move faster. B The potential energy increases as the molecules move farther apart.

2 Teach

Temperature

Visual Learning

Figure 1 Point out to students that the horseshoe in **Figure 1A** bends easily while the one in **Figure 1B** is rigid. Why is the horseshoe in **Figure 1A** more malleable than the horseshoe in **Figure 1B?** When the horseshoe is hot, its quickly moving particles easily realign into new positions. When it has cooled down its particles are moving more slowly and resist realigning into new positions. L2
LS **Visual-Spatial**

Thermal Energy

Teacher FYI

One way the human body maintains its internal temperature is through rapid vibration known as shivering.

Resource Manager

Chapter Resources Booklet
Transparency Activity, p. 44
Note-taking Worksheets, pp. 33–35
Enrichment, p. 30

Active Reading

Quickwrites This strategy, sometimes called freewrite, lets students use spontaneous writing to discover what they already know. Have students write a list of ideas about heat and then share these ideas with the class. Next, have students write about these ideas freely without worrying about punctuation, spelling, and grammar. Have students use a Quickwrite to share ideas about thermal energy and heat.

Thermal Energy, continued

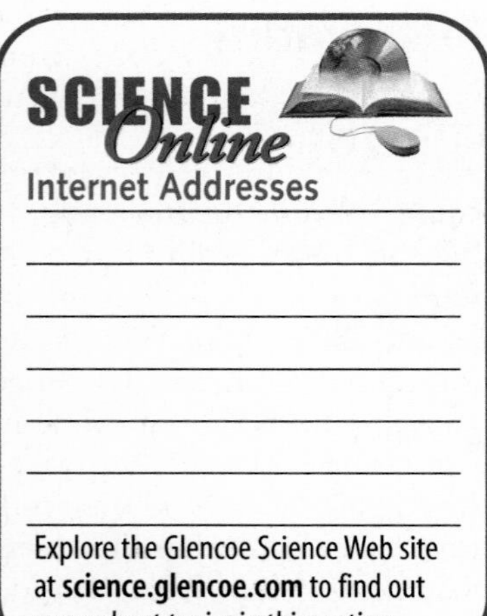

Heat

During cold weather, people often close doors and windows to keep the cold out. Since cold is the absence of heat, they are actually attempting to keep the heat inside, not keep the cold out.

Visual Learning

Figure 3 Why does the ice cream maker turn? Turning allows the ice cream mix to cool evenly and more quickly.

Reading Check

Answer Heat is thermal energy that flows from something with a higher temperature to something with a lower temperature.

SCIENCE Online

Research Visit the Glencoe Science Web site at **science.glencoe.com** for information about how weather satellites use thermal energy. Communicate to your class what you learn.

Thermal Energy and Temperature Thermal energy and temperature are related. When the temperature of an object increases, the average kinetic energy of the molecules in the object increases. Because thermal energy is the total kinetic and potential energy of all the molecules in an object, the thermal energy of the object increases when the average kinetic energy of its molecules increases. Therefore, the thermal energy of an object increases as its temperature increases.

Thermal Energy and Mass Suppose you have a glass and a beaker of water that are at the same temperature. The beaker contains twice as much water as the glass. The water in both containers is at the same temperature, so the average kinetic energy of the water molecules is the same in both containers. But there are twice as many water molecules in the beaker as there are in the glass. So the total kinetic energy of all the molecules is twice as large for the water in the beaker. As a result, even though they are at the same temperature, the water in the beaker has twice as much thermal energy as the water in the glass does. If the temperature doesn't change, the thermal energy in an object increases if the mass of the object increases.

Heat

Can you tell if someone has been sitting in your chair? Perhaps you've noticed that your chair feels warm, and maybe you concluded that someone has been sitting in it recently. The chair feels warmer because thermal energy from the person's body flowed to the chair and increased its temperature.

Heat is thermal energy that flows from something at a higher temperature to something at a lower temperature. Heat is a form of energy, so it is measured in joules—the same units that energy is measured in. Heat always flows from warmer to cooler materials. How did the ice cream in **Figure 3** become cold? Heat flowed from the warmer liquid ingredients to the cooler ice-and-salt mixture. The liquid ingredients lost enough thermal energy to become cold enough to be solid ice cream. Meanwhile, the ice-and-salt solution gained thermal energy, causing some of the ice to melt.

Figure 3
Heat flows from the warmer ingredients inside the container to the ice-and-salt mixture.

How are heat and thermal energy related?

Curriculum Connection

History Have a group of students report on the experiments of James Joule that quantitatively related thermal energy and work. Joule used falling weights to turn paddles that stirred water and raised its temperature. He calculated the mechanical energy of the falling weights and the heat energy from the increase in temperature of the water. L2 COOP LEARN
LS **Linguistic**

Science Journal

Body Heat Have students describe in their Science Journals how thermal energy flows when an oral thermometer is used to take someone's temperature. The thermometer should begin at a temperature lower than that of a human body, 37°C (98.6°F). In the mouth, thermal energy moves from the body to the thermometer, raising the temperature of the material in the thermometer. L2 LS **Logical-Mathematical** P

Specific Heat

If you are at the beach in the summertime, you might notice that the ocean seems much cooler than the air or sand. Even though the Sun is transferring energy to the air, sand, and water at the same rate, the temperature of the water has changed less than the temperature of the air or sand has.

As a substance absorbs heat, its temperature change depends on the nature of the substance, as well as the amount of heat that is added. For example, compared to 1 kg of sand, the amount of heat that is needed to raise the temperature of 1 kg of water by 1°C is about six times greater. So the ocean water at the beach would have to absorb six times as much heat as the sand to be at the same temperature. The amount of heat that is needed to raise the temperature of 1 kg of some material by 1°C or 1 K is called the **specific heat** of the material. Specific heat is measured in joules per kilogram kelvin [J/(kg K)]. **Table 1** shows the specific heats of some familiar materials.

Table 1 Specific Heat of Some Common Materials

Substance	Specific Heat [J/(kg K)]
Water	4,184
Alcohol	2,450
Carbon (graphite)	710
Sand	664
Iron	450

Water as a Coolant Compared with the other common materials in **Table 1,** water has the highest specific heat, as shown in **Figure 4.** Because water can absorb heat without a large change in temperature, it is useful as a coolant. A coolant is a subtance that is used to absorb heat. For example, water is used as the coolant in the cooling systems of automobile engines. As long as the water temperature is lower than the engine temperature, heat will flow from the engine to the water. Compared to other materials, water can absorb more heat from the engine before its temperature rises. Because it takes water longer to heat up compared with other materials, it also takes water longer to cool down.

Figure 4
The specific heat of water is high because water molecules form strong bonds with each other.

A When heat is added, some of the added heat has to break some of these bonds before the molecules can start moving faster.

B In metals, electrons can move freely. When heat is added, no bonds have to be broken before the electrons can start moving faster.

A

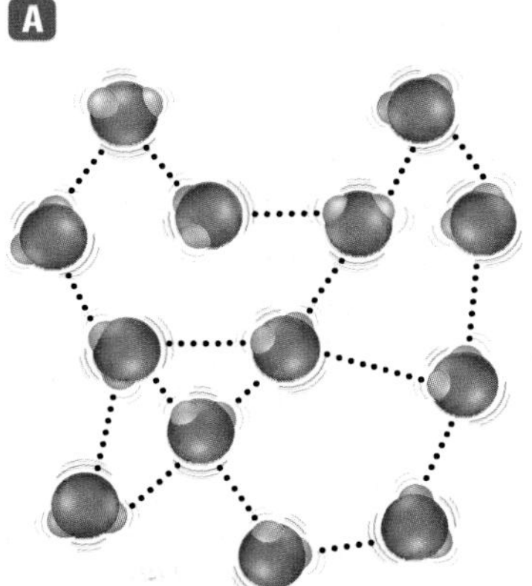

B

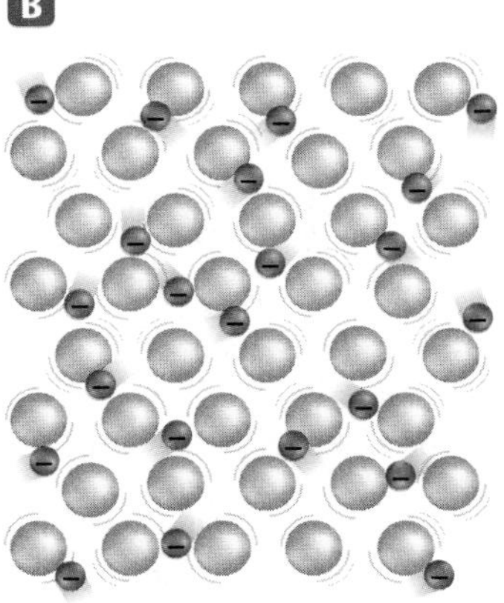

Specific Heat

Activity

To give students practice working with SI, have them convert the specific heats given in **Table 1** from units of $\frac{J}{(kg\ K)}$ to $\frac{J}{(g\ K)}$. water $4.184 \frac{J}{(g\ K)}$, alcohol $2.450 \frac{J}{(g\ K)}$, carbon $0.710 \frac{J}{(gK)}$, sand $0.664 \frac{J}{(g\ K)}$, iron $0.450 \frac{J}{(g\ K)}$

L2 IS **Logical-Mathematical**

Use an Analogy

Liken specific heat to the money a student must save so he or she can buy a bicycle. When enough money (heat) is accumulated, the bicycle can be bought (the temperature rises). Different substances have different specific heats, just as different bicycles have different prices.

Resource Manager

Chapter Resources Booklet

Directed Reading for Content Mastery, p. 20

Reading and Writing Skill Activities, p. 33

Mathematics Skill Activities, p. 11

Visual Learning

Figure 4 Explain that the attractive forces between water molecules are very strong, which means they have a lot of energy. These forces must be overcome to allow water molecules to gain kinetic energy and heat up. The atoms of the metal don't have the same strong attractive forces between them, so it takes less energy to make them move and heat up. L2 IS **Visual-Spatial**

Calculating Changes in Thermal Energy

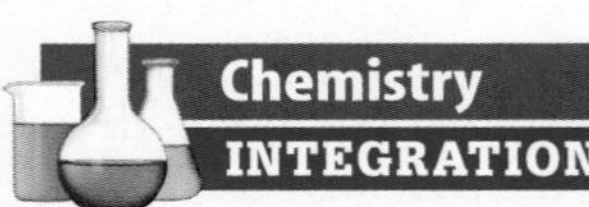

Since her earlobe remained cooler than the earring, her earlobe must have a higher specific heat. This is consistent with the specific heats given in **Table 1**, which shows that the specific heat of water is greater than that of metal. Discuss with students other situations in which two different materials subjected to the same heat source reach different temperatures. You might consider various objects in the Sun on a hot day. L2 LS **Naturalist**

Use Science Words

Word Origin Have students use their dictionaries to identify the origin of the word *thermal.* The word *thermal* comes from the Greek word *therme,* meaning "heat." Many English words derive from this root, including thermos, which insulates hot and cold beverages. L2 LS **Linguistic**

Math Skills Activity

Teaching Strategy

This is what you know: mass of brass sculpture, $m = 45$ kg; initial temperature, $T_i = 28°C$; final temperature, $T_f = 40°C$; change in thermal energy, $Q = 180{,}480$ J. This is what you want to find: specific heat of brass, C. This is the equation you need to use: $C = Q \div [m \times (T_f - T_i)] = 180{,}480\text{ J} \div [45\text{ kg }(40°C - 28°C) = 334\text{ J/(kg·K)}$

Answer to Practice Problem

1. 334 J (kg · k)

While Karen was blow-drying her hair, she noticed that her silver earring had become uncomfortably hot. If her earring was about the same mass as her earlobe, infer which of the two had the higher specific heat. Assuming a human earlobe is composed largely of water, find data from **Table 1** to support your inference and record it in your Science Journal.

Calculating Changes in Thermal Energy

The thermal energy of an object changes when heat flows into or out of it. The heat flow or the change in thermal energy is related to the mass of the object, its specific heat, and its change in temperature in this way:

$$\text{Change in thermal energy} = \text{mass} \times \text{change in temperature} \times \text{specific heat}$$

The change in temperature is the initial temperature subtracted from the final temperature, $T_{\text{final}} - T_{\text{initial}}$

If Q is the change in thermal energy, m is the mass, and C is the specific heat, then the change in thermal energy can be calculated from this formula:

$$Q = m \times (T_{\text{final}} - T_{\text{initial}}) \times C$$

Math Skills Activity

Calculating Changes in Thermal Energy

Example Problem

A 32-g silver spoon heats from 20°C to 60°C. What is the change in its thermal energy?

Solution

1. *This is what you know:* mass of spoon, $m = 32\text{ g} = 0.032\text{ kg}$; specific heat of silver, $C = 235\text{ J/(kgK)}$; initial temperature, $T_{\text{initial}} = 20°C$; final temperature, $T_{\text{final}} = 60°C$
2. *This is what you want to find:* change in thermal temperature, Q
3. *This is the equation you need to use:* $Q = m \times (T_{\text{final}} - T_{\text{initial}}) \times C$
4. *Solve the equation for Q:* $Q = 0.032\text{ kg} \times (60°C - 20°C) \times 235\text{ J/(kgK)}$; $Q = 301$ J; The spoon gains 301 J of thermal energy as it heats

Check your answer by dividing it by the change in temperature then by the specific heat of silver. Did you get the original mass of the spoon?

Practice Problem

1. A 45-kg brass sculpture gains 180,480 J of thermal energy as its temperature increases from 28°C to 40°C. What is the approximate specific heat of brass?

For more help, refer to the Math Skill Handbook.

Inclusion Strategies

Learning Disabled To help students calculate changes in thermal energy, make sure they know what each variable in the formula means, and show the places where numerical values are put in. Be sure to clarify that the change in temperature must be calculated by subtracting two other numbers.

Resource Manager

Chapter Resources Booklet
- Reinforcement, p. 27
- Lab Activity, pp. 9–12

Earth Science Critical Thinking/Problem Solving, p. 10

Thermal Energy and Temperature Changes

When the temperature of an object changes, the amount of thermal energy it contains changes also. When heat flows into an object its temperature usually increases. So T_{final} is greater than $T_{initial}$ and the change in temperature is a positive number. According to the formula for the change in thermal energy, if the change in temperature is a positive number, then Q is a positive number. Therefore, when the temperature increases, heat flows into an object, and Q is positive.

In the same way, when heat flows out of an object its temperature usually decreases. Then the temperature of an object decreases, the change in temperature is a negative number, and Q is also negative.

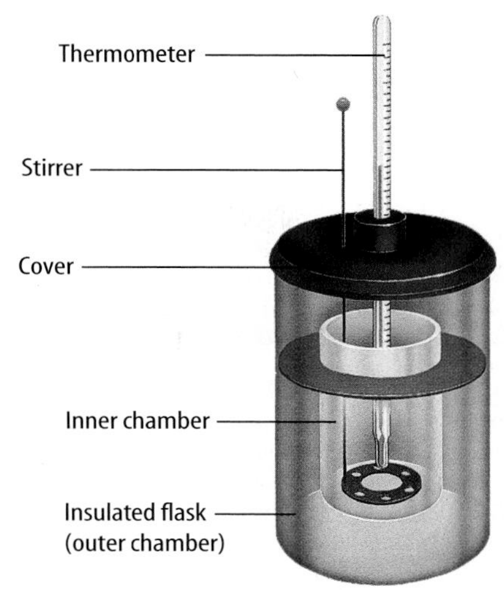

Figure 5
A calorimeter can be used to measure the specific heat of materials. The sample is placed in the inner chamber.

Measuring Specific Heat The specific heat can be measured using a device called a calorimeter, shown in **Figure 5.** To do this, the mass of the water in the calorimeter and its temperature are measured. Then a sample of a material of known mass is heated and its temperature measured. The heated sample is then placed in the calorimeter. Heat flows from the sample to the water until they both reach the same temperature. Then the increase in thermal energy of the water can be calculated. This is equal to the thermal energy lost by the sample. Because the mass of the sample, its change in temperature, and change in thermal energy are known, the sample's specific heat can be calculated.

Section  Assessment

1. Explain the difference between heat and temperature.
2. What is thermal energy and what causes it to change?
3. How is heat transferred between two objects?
4. What is specific heat?
5. **Think Critically** Using your knowledge of heat, explain what happens when you heat a pan of soup on the stove, and then put some of the leftover warm soup in the refrigerator.

Skill Builder Activities

6. **Interpreting Data** Equal amounts of iron, water, and sand with the same initial temperature were placed in an oven and heated briefly. Use the data in **Table 1** to match each final temperature with the appropriate material: 51.5°C, 25°C, and 66°C. **For more help, refer to the Science Skill Handbook.**
7. **Solving One-Step Equations** Calculate the change in thermal energy of 30 g of sand that cools from 100°C to 30°C. **For more help, refer to the Math Skill Handbook.**

3 Assess

Reteach

Ask students to look at specific heat values from their book and think about cooking food on top of a stove. Ask them why an iron or copper pan is used to heat food. These materials have low specific heats, which means that they heat up quickly, since a small amount of heat is needed for each degree of temperature change. These materials therefore can heat food quickly. L2

LS Logical-Mathematical

Challenge

The Dulong-Petit law, developed in 1819 by two French scientists, relates specific heat to atomic weight. Have students learn more about this law and how it has been used. According to the law, the specific heat of a solid element is inversely related to its atomic weight. For all the solid elements, multiplying specific heat by atomic weight yields a constant. The atomic weights of some elements were initially determined using this formula. Modern scientists apply this law only to metallic elements, and not at very low temperatures. L3

LS Linguistic

Assessment

Process Ask students to imagine that equal masses of water and alcohol are put into identical pans and heated for ten minutes. **Assuming that neither boils, which would have the higher temperature? Why?** The alcohol; it has a lower specific heat. For any given amount of thermal energy added, the temperature of alcohol will rise more than that of water. Use **PASC**, p. 89.

Answers to Section Assessment

1. Temperature is a measure of the average kinetic energy of all the particles in an object. Heat is thermal energy that flows from something with a higher temperature to something with a lower temperature.
2. Thermal energy is the total kinetic and potential energy of the particles in a material. It changes when energy is added that makes the particles move more.
3. from warmer materials to cooler materials
4. the energy needed to raise the temperature of 1 kg of a substance 1 K
5. Heat goes from the stove into the pan, then to the soup, and then into the cool refrigerator.
6. 25°, water; 51.5°, sand; 66°, iron
7. 1,394 J; grams must be changed to kg since specific heat has units of $\frac{J}{(kg\ K)}$.

SECTION 2

Transferring Thermal Energy

1 Motivate

Bellringer Transparency

Display the Section Focus Transparency for Section 2. Use the accompanying Transparency Activity Master. L2 ELL

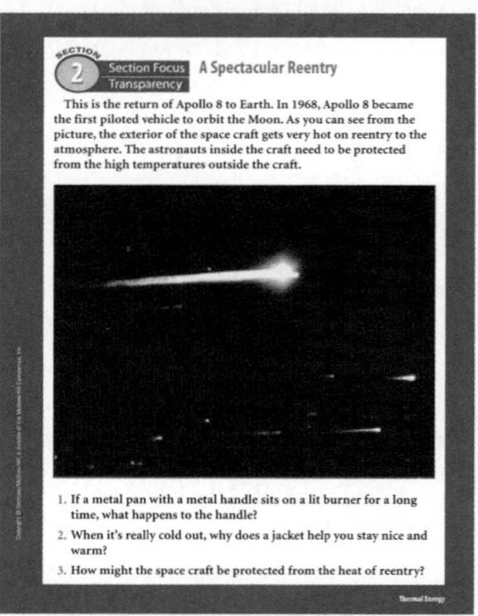
SECTION 2 Section Focus Transparency **A Spectacular Reentry**

This is the return of Apollo 8 to Earth. In 1968, Apollo 8 became the first piloted vehicle to orbit the Moon. As you can see from the picture, the exterior of the space craft gets very hot on reentry to the atmosphere. The astronauts inside the craft need to be protected from the high temperatures outside the craft.

1. If a metal pan with a metal handle sits on a lit burner for a long time, what happens to the handle?
2. When it's really cold out, why does a jacket help you stay nice and warm?
3. How might the space craft be protected from the heat of reentry?

Thermal Energy

Tie to Prior Knowledge

Ask students to recall whether they have ever been burned by touching a hot object. What type of material was the hot object made of? It probably was made of a good conductor that transferred its thermal energy to the student's hand by conduction.

Resource Manager

Chapter Resources Booklet
Transparency Activity, p. 45

Life Science Critical Thinking/Problem Solving, p. 10

Science Inquiry Labs, p. 39

SECTION 2

Transferring Thermal Energy

As You Read

What You'll Learn

- **Compare and contrast** thermal energy transfer by conduction, convection, and radiation.
- **Compare and contrast** conductors and insulators.
- **Explain** how insulation affects the transfer of energy.

Vocabulary

conduction
convection
radiation
insulator

Why It's Important

Understanding how thermal energy is transferred can help you use energy more efficiently.

Conduction

Thermal energy travels as heat from a material at a higher temperature to a material at a lower temperature. When you pick up a handful of snow to make a snowball, thermal energy from your hand is transferred to the snow, causing the snow to begin melting and your hand to get a little colder. When you come back indoors, the opposite happens if you hold a cup of hot chocolate. The thermal energy from the cup moves to your hand, making it warmer and the cup cooler. Direct contact is one way that heat can travel from one place to another. The transfer of thermal energy through matter by the direct contact of particles is called **conduction.** Conduction occurs because all matter is made of atoms and molecules that are in constant motion.

Transfer by Collisions Think about what happens when you grasp a handful of snow. The slower-moving molecules in the snow come into contact with the faster-moving molecules in your warm hand. These particles then collide with one another, and some of the kinetic energy from the faster-moving particles is transferred to the slower-moving particles. This causes the slower-moving particles to speed up and the faster-moving particles to slow down. As the collisions continue, thermal energy gets transferred from your bare hand to the snow. As a result, your hand gets colder and the snow melts.

Heat can be transferred by conduction from one material to another or through one material. What happens to a metal ladle that's used to stir a pot of simmering soup? The hot soup transfers thermal energy to the part of the ladle sitting in the soup. At first, this end of the ladle is hotter than the rest. Eventually, however, the entire ladle becomes hot. Thus, heat was transferred from the soup to the ladle—from one material to another—and through the length of the ladle—through one material. **Figure 6** shows how heat is transferred by conduction.

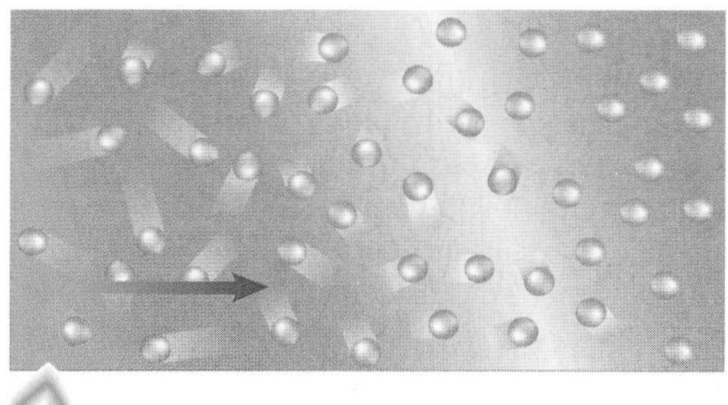

Figure 6
Conduction quickly transfers heat from the flame through the bar.

Section Assessment Planner

PORTFOLIO
Extension, p. 167

PERFORMANCE ASSESSMENT
Try at Home MiniLAB, p. 168
MiniLAB, p.169
Skill Builder Activities, p. 170
See page 186 for more options.

CONTENT ASSESSMENT
Section, p. 170
Challenge, p. 170
Chapter, pp. 186–187

Heat Conductors Although conduction can occur in solids, liquids, and gases, solids usually conduct heat much more effectively. The particles in a solid are usually much closer together than they are in liquids and gases, so they collide with one another more often. The loosely held electrons in a metal make them especially good heat conductors. In a metal, electrons can move easily, and they readily transfer kinetic energy to other nearby particles. Silver, copper, and aluminum are among the best heat conductors. Wood, plastic, glass, and fiberglass are poor conductors of heat. Why do you think cooking pots are made of metal, but the handles usually are not?

Convection

One way liquids and gases differ from solids is that they can flow. Any material that flows is a fluid. The ability to flow allows fluids to transfer heat in another way—convection. **Convection** is the transfer of energy by the motion of the heated particles in a fluid. In conduction, heated particles collide with each other and transfer their energy. In convection, however, the more energetic fluid particles move from one location to another, and carry their energy along with them.

As the particles move faster, they tend to be farther apart. In other words, the fluid expands as its temperature increases. Recall that density is the mass of a material divided by its volume. When a fluid expands, its volume increases, but its mass doesn't change. As a result, its density decreases. The same is true for parts of a fluid that have been heated. The density of the warmer fluid, therefore, is less than that of the surrounding cooler fluid.

Heat Transfer by Currents How does convection occur? Look at the lamp shown in **Figure 7.** The lamp contains two fluids—oil and alcohol. When the oil is cool, its density is greater than the alcohol, and it sits at the bottom of the lamp. When the two liquids are heated, the oil becomes less dense than the alcohol. Because it is less dense than the alcohol, it rises to the top of the lamp. As it rises, it loses heat by conduction to the cooler fluid around it. When the oil reaches the top of the lamp, it has become cool enough that it is denser than the alcohol, and it sinks. This rising-and-sinking action is a convection current. Convection currents transfer heat from warmer to cooler parts of the fluid. In a convection current, both conduction and convection transfer thermal energy.

Reading Check *How are conduction and convection different?*

Figure 7
The heat from the light at the bottom of the lamp causes one fluid to expand more than the other. This creates convection currents in the lamp.

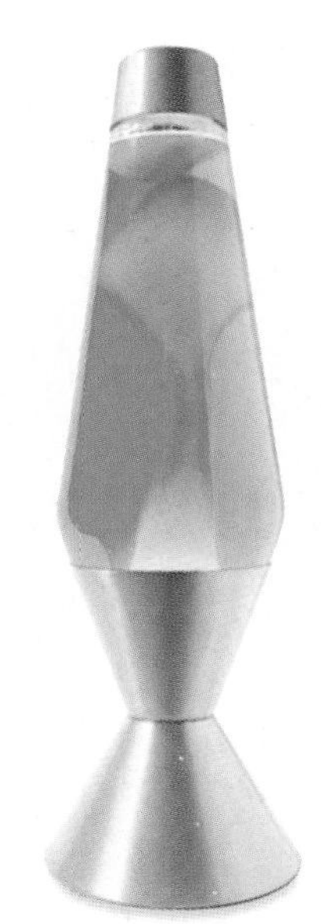

2 Teach

Conduction

Use an Analogy

Explain that transferring energy to a soccer ball by kicking it is similar to transferring thermal energy through a material by conduction. Both the soccer ball and the molecules in the material are given energy as they collide with something else.

Text Question Answer

The metal pot is a good conductor that easily transmits thermal energy from the stove to the food. The handle is made of an insulator, so when you pick up the pot you do not get burned.

Convection

Reading Check

Answer In conduction, heated particles collide with each other and transfer their energy. In convection, fluid particles move from one location to another, and carry their energy with them.

LAB DEMONSTRATION

Purpose to observe the effect of temperature on convection

Materials three 250-mL beakers, one 600-mL beaker, food coloring, dropper, hot plate, ice

Procedure Fill the 600-mL beaker two-thirds full of ice. Heat the hot plate. Put water in the small beakers and allow them to stand. Using the dropper, gently place a drop of food coloring in the bottom of each beaker. Place one beaker on the hot plate, one on the ice, and one in your hand.

Expected Outcome The food coloring will move in the heated beakers because heat causes convection. Greater heat causes more convection.

Assessment

Why did the food coloring disperse only in some beakers? The hot plate and hand warmth caused convection. No convection occurred in the cold water. **Why didn't the heated water rise to the top and stay there?** The heated water cooled and sank.

Visualizing Convection Currents

Have students examine the pictures and read the captions. Then ask the following questions.

- **Why does the air lose its moisture as it rises and cools at the equator?** Cool air cannot hold as much moisture as warm air.
- **Why does the dry air create a zone of deserts at the tropics?** The dry air pulls the moisture out of the ground. Since there is a continuous stream of hot, dry air that blows across the land, any water on the ground is vaporized and carried away. In addition to this drying process, there is insufficient rainfall to replenish the moisture.

Activity

Have students obtain or draw a world map. Ask students to locate and mark the equator and both tropics. Have them find the major rain forests and deserts of the world and mark them on their map. L2 ELL
LS **Visual-Spatial**

Extension

Challenge students to research the living conditions of the peoples in the desert areas discussed in this feature. Students should find out how they obtain food, shelter, and how they cope with their harsh conditions. Ask students to report their findings to their class.

Figure 8

When the Sun beats down on the equator, warm, moist air begins to rise. As it rises, the air cools and loses its moisture as rain that sustains rain forests near the equator. Convection currents carry the now dry air farther north and south. Some of this dry air descends at the tropics, where it creates a zone of deserts.

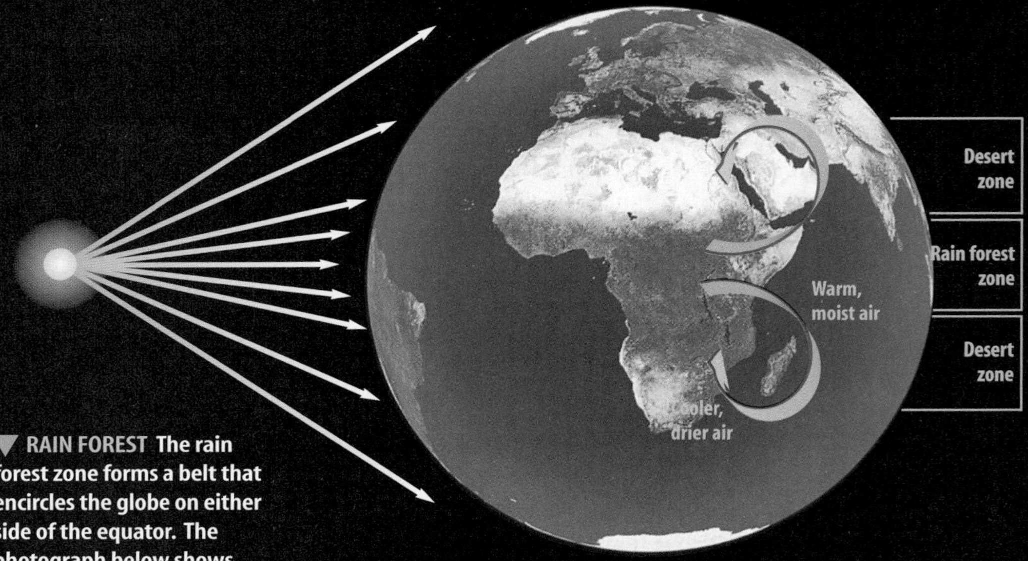

Desert zone

Rain forest zone

Desert zone

Warm, moist air

Cooler, drier air

▼ RAIN FOREST The rain forest zone forms a belt that encircles the globe on either side of the equator. The photograph below shows a rain forest near the Congo River in central Africa.

▲ DESERT Like many of the great desert regions of the world, the Sahara, in northern Africa, is largely a result of atmospheric convection currents. Here, a group of nomads gather near a dried-up river in Mali.

166 CHAPTER 6

Resource Manager

Chapter Resources Booklet

Directed Reading for Content Mastery, p. 20

Physical Science Critical Thinking/Problem Solving, p. 2

Life Science Critical Thinking/Problem Solving, p. 12

Desert and Rain Forests Earth's atmosphere is made of various gases and is a fluid. The atmosphere is warmer at the equator than it is at the north and south poles. Also, the atmosphere is warmer at Earth's surface than it is at higher altitudes. These temperature differences create convection currents that carry heat to cooler regions. **Figure 8** shows how these convection currents create rain forests and deserts over different regions of Earth's surface.

Radiation

Earth gets heat from the Sun, but how does that heat travel through space? Almost no matter exists in the space between Earth and the Sun, so heat cannot be transferred by conduction or convection. Instead, the Sun's heat reaches Earth by radiation.

Radiation is the transfer of energy by electromagnetic waves. These waves can travel through space even when no matter is present. Energy that is transferred by radiation often is called radiant energy. When you stand near a fire and warm your hands, much of the warmth you feel has been transferred from the fire to your hands by radiation.

Radiant Energy and Matter When radiation strikes a material, some of the energy is absorbed, some is reflected, and some may be transmitted through the material. **Figure 9** shows what happens to radiant energy from the Sun as it reaches Earth. The amount of energy absorbed, reflected, and transmitted depends on the type of material. Materials that are light-colored reflect more radiant energy, while dark-colored materials absorb more radiant energy. When radiant energy is absorbed by a material, the thermal energy of the material increases. Radiant energy can be transmitted through solids and liquids that are transparent.

Radiation in Solids, Liquids, and Gases The transfer of energy by radiation is most important in gases. In a solid, liquid or gas, radiant energy can travel through the space between molecules. Molecules can absorb this radiation and radiate some of the energy they absorbed. This energy then travels through the space between molecules, and is absorbed and re-radiated by other molecules.

In solids and liquids, molecules are much closer to each other than in gases and collide with each other more often. These collisions cause molecules to absorb the radiant energy rather than re-emit it. As a result, gases absorb less radiant energy and transmit more radiant energy than solids or liquids.

Figure 9
Not all of the Sun's radiation reaches Earth. Some of it is reflected by the atmosphere. Some of the radiation that does reach the surface is also reflected.

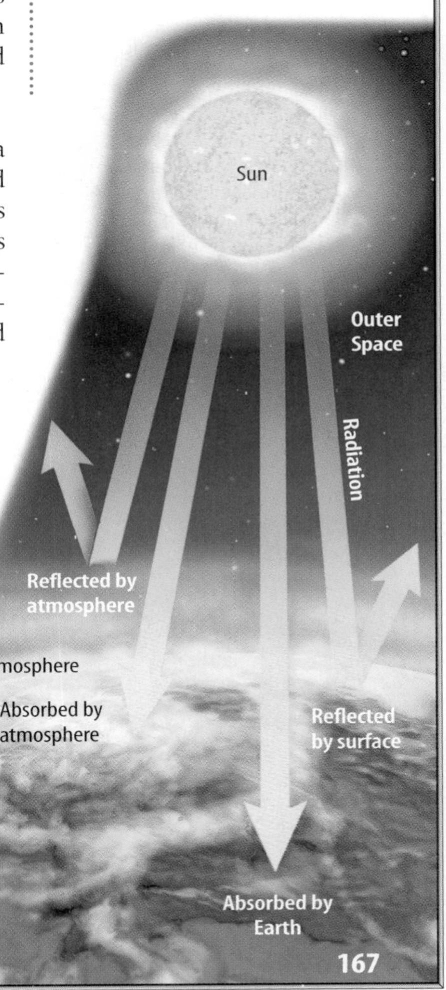

Extension

Although most of Earth's rain forests are located near the equator, the west coast of the Pacific Northwest receives great annual rainfall and has some rain forest areas. The western coasts of Vancouver Island and the Olympic Peninsula, for example, contain rain forests. Have students research this phenomenon and draw maps showing the heat flow patterns that cause moderate temperatures and substantial rainfall in the region. L2 LS **Visual-Spatial**

Radiation

Use Science Words

Word Origin Have students look up the origins of the words *conduction*, *convection*, and *radiation* in a dictionary. Students should find that the words come from the Latin roots *conducere* (to lead) and *convehere* (to bring together), and *radius* (ray), respectively. Ask volunteers to connect the meaning of each word with its root. L2 ELL LS **Linguistic**

IDENTIFYING Misconceptions

Students may confuse radiation as a form of heat transfer with nuclear radiation or radioactivity. Both types of radiation involve the sending out of energy as waves or particles. In nuclear radiation, radioactive nuclei of atoms break down and emit particles or waves. In thermal radiation, matter sends out electromagnetic energy as photons.

Curriculum Connection

Social Studies Very large cities can be measurably warmer than the surrounding countryside—as much as six or eight degrees warmer on a hot summer day. The main reason for these urban heat islands is thought to be their combination of paved land and tall, crowded buildings. Concrete, tar, and brick have lower specific heat than grass and trees, so they become hotter in the sun. They are good heat conductors, and at night the tall buildings radiate heat back and forth between them, rather than letting it escape quickly. Cities also generate their own heat through vehicles, factories, and even air conditioners. Have students draw diagrams showing heat flow in a large city and heat flow in the countryside. L2 LS **Visual-Spatial**

Controlling Heat Flow

Text Question Answer

Possible answer: Animals of a given species are generally larger in colder climates. This gives them a smaller surface area-to-volume ratio, making it easier for them to retain heat.

Answer Possible answers: antarctic fur seal's thick fur, emperor penguin's thick layer of blubber, scaly skin of the desert spiny lizard, black feathers on a penguin's back

TRY AT HOME Mini LAB

Purpose Students observe the effect of glass on heat from the Sun. L2 LS **Kinesthetic**

Materials window in sunlight

Teaching Strategies Make sure students find a window in a place where results won't be affected by heating or air conditioning.

Safety Precautions Advise students not to look directly at the Sun.

Analysis

1. by radiation
2. Answers will vary, depending on outdoor temperature, wind, and indoor climate control.
3. Yes; the student can feel the effect of the Sun's heat inside the window.

Process Have each student write up the procedure used and results obtained for this MiniLAB in lab report. Use **PASC**, p. 119.

Observing Heat Transfer by Radiation

Procedure

1. On a sunny day, go outside and place the back of your hand in **direct sunlight** for two min.
2. Go inside and find a **window exposed to direct sunlight.**
3. Place the back of your hand in the sunlight that has passed through the window for two min.

Analysis

1. Explain how heat was transferred from the Sun to your skin when you were outside.
2. Compare how warm your skin felt inside and outside.
3. Was thermal energy transferred through the glass in the window? Explain.

Controlling Heat Flow

You might not realize it, but you probably do a number of things every day to control the flow of heat. For example, when its cold outside, you put on a coat or a jacket before you leave your home. When you reach into an oven to pull out a hot dish, you might put a thick, cloth mitten over your hand to keep from being burned. In both cases, you used various materials to help control the flow of heat. Your jacket kept you from getting cold by reducing the flow of heat from your body to the surrounding air. And the oven mitten kept your hand from being burned by reducing the flow of heat from the hot dish.

As shown in **Figure 10,** almost all living things have special features that help them control the flow of heat. For example, the antarctic fur seal's thick coat and the emperor penguin's thick layer of blubber help keep them from losing heat. This helps them survive in a climate in which the temperature is often below freezing. In the desert, however, the scaly skin of the desert spiny lizard has just the opposite effect. It reflects the Sun's rays and keeps the animal from becoming too hot. An animal's color also can play a role in keeping it warm or cool. The black feathers on the penguin's back, for example, allow it to absorb as much radiant energy as possible. Can you think of any other animals that have special adaptations for cold or hot climates?

Reading Check *What are two animal adaptations that control the flow of heat?*

Figure 10
Animals have different features that help them control heat flow.

A **The antarctic fur seal grows a coat that can be as much as 10 cm thick.**

B **The emperor penguin has a thick layer of blubber and thick, closely grown feathers, which help reduce the loss of body heat.**

C **The scaly skin of the desert spiny lizard reflects the rays of the Sun. This prevents it from losing water to evaporation in an environment where water is scarce.**

Resource Manager

Chapter Resources Booklet
MiniLAB, pp. 3, 4
Enrichment, p. 31

Science Journal

Wet Blanket Have students describe in their journals whether they think a wet blanket would keep them as warm as a dry blanket and why. Responses might include that a dry blanket has air trapped among the fibers, and air is a poor heat conductor. The wet blanket would absorb heat from their skin as the water evaporates. L2 LS **Logical-Mathematical**

Figure 11
The tiny pockets of air in fleece make it a good insulator. They help prevent the jogger's body heat from escaping.

Insulators

A material that doesn't allow heat to flow through it easily is called an **insulator.** A material that is a good conductor of heat, such as a metal, is a poor insulator. Materials such as wood, plastic, and fiberglass are good insulators and, therefore, are poor conductors of heat.

Gases, such as air, are usually much better insulators than solids or liquids. Some types of insulators contain many pockets of trapped air. These air pockets conduct heat poorly and also keep convection currents from forming in the gas. Fleece jackets, like the one shown in **Figure 11,** work in the same way. When you put the jacket on, the fibers in the fleece trap air and hold this air next to you. This air slows down the flow of your body heat to the colder air outside the jacket. Gradually, the air trapped by the fleece is warmed by your body heat, and underneath the jacket you are wrapped in a blanket of warm air.

Reading Check *Why does trapped air make a material like fleece a good insulator?*

Insulating Buildings Insulation, or materials that are insulators, helps keep warm air from flowing out of buildings in cold weather and from flowing into buildings in warm weather. Building insulation is usually made of some fluffy material, such as fiberglass, that contains pockets of trapped air. The insulation is packed into a building's outer walls and attic, where it reduces the flow of heat between the building and the surrounding air.

Insulation helps furnaces and air conditioners work more effectively, saving energy. In the United States, about 20 percent of all energy that is consumed is used to heat and cool buildings.

Mini LAB

Comparing Thermal Conductors

Procedure
1. Obtain a **plastic spoon,** a **metal spoon,** and a **wooden spoon** with similar lengths.
2. Stick a small **plastic bead** to the handle of each spoon with a dab of **butter or wax.** Each bead should be the same distance from the tip of the spoon.
3. Stand the spoons in a beaker, with the beads hanging over the edge of the beaker.
4. Carefully pour about 5 cm of boiling water in the beaker holding the spoons.

Analysis
1. In what order did the beads fall from the spoons?
2. Describe how heat was transferred from the water to the beads.
3. Rank the spoons in their ability to conduct heat.

Insulators

Purpose Students observe the thermal conductivity of a metallic alloy, plastic, and wood.

Materials Each group will need: metallic, plastic, and wooden spoons (similar length), three small plastic beads, and three small dabs of butter, beaker, and boiling water.

Teaching Strategies Have students place their beakers on paper towels to catch butter drips.

Safety Precautions Students should be careful when handling boiling water.

Analysis
1. metal, plastic, then wood
2. by conduction through the spoons and by conduction and convection through the steam
3. metal, plastic, wood

Process Have students draw cartoons explaining why items in the kitchen are made of insulators or conductors. Use **PASC,** p. 133.

Visual Learning

Figure 11 Discuss with students how the light jacket can keep the jogger warm, despite the snow and the wintry temperatures. **Is the jacket producing heat?** No; because the skier is warm-blooded, she generates her own heat, which does not escape easily through the fleece jacket. L2

LS **Visual-Spatial**

Teacher FYI

Asbestos is an effective insulator. It has been used to insulate hot water pipes, to make safety clothing for firefighters, and to protect brake linings. Scientists have discovered that the disease asbestosis can result from breathing in asbestos fibers, so its use has been significantly decreased.

Reading Check

Answer Air is a good insulator.

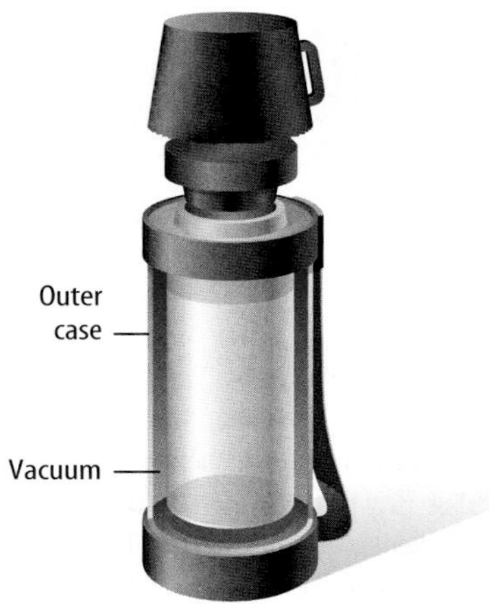

Figure 12
The vacuum layer of the thermos bottle is a very poor conductor of heat.

Using Insulators You might have used a thermos bottle, like the one in **Figure 12,** to carry hot soup or iced tea. The vacuum layer in the thermos helps keep your soup hot by reducing the heat flow due to conduction, convection, and radiation. Thermos bottles don't use a thick layer of material to reduce heat flow, instead they use nothing. A thermos bottle has two glass layers with a vacuum between the layers. The vacuum between the two layers contains almost no matter, and so prevents heat transfer either by conduction or by convection.

To reduce heat transfer by radiation, the inside and outside glass surface of a thermos bottle is coated with aluminum to make each surface highly reflective. This causes the electromagnetic waves that carry heat energy by radiation to be reflected at each surface. The inner coating prevents electromagnetic waves from leaving the bottle, and the outer coating prevents them from entering the bottle.

Think about the things you do to stay warm or cool. Sitting under a shady umbrella reduces the heat energy transferred to you by radiation. Also, wearing light-colored or dark-colored clothing changes the amount of heat you absorb due to radiation. To change the amount of heat transferred by convection, you can open and close windows. Putting on a sweater reduces the heat transferred from your body by conduction and convection. In what other ways do you control the flow of heat?

Section 2 Assessment

1. What are the three ways thermal energy can be transferred?
2. What are some good heat insulators? Conductors?
3. How is heat transfer by radiation different from conduction and convection?
4. Explain why we insulate our homes.
5. **Think Critically** Why is winter clothing generally darker than summer clothing? Why does wearing two or three layers of clothing help keep you warmer in cold weather than wearing one thick layer?

Skill Builder Activities

6. **Testing a Hypothesis** Design an experiment to find out which material makes the best insulation: plastic foam pellets, shredded newspaper, or crumpled plastic bags. Remember to state your hypothesis and indicate what factors must be held constant. **For more help, refer to the Science Skill Handbook.**
7. **Concept Mapping** Make a concept map showing the three types of thermal energy transfer and ways you can control the flow of heat in each type. **For more help, refer to the Science Skill Handbook.**

3 Assess

Reteach

Have students quiz one another on the three means by which thermal energy is transferred. Conduction occurs by collisions between particles and is usually most effective in solids. Convection transfers energy through movement of particles in a fluid. Radiation involves electromagnetic waves and doesn't require a medium. L2 LS **Linguistic**

Challenge

Which method of heat transfer would most concern an astronaut floating in a space suit? Conduction from the astronaut's body to the suit itself may be important, but heat radiation between the suit and outer space would be of serious concern. L3
LS **Logical-Mathematical**

Assessment

Oral Have students describe the forms of thermal energy transfer they might experience when they go to a beach or pool on a hot summer day. **How might they use insulation to increase their comfort?** Answers might include conduction from hot sand or concrete, convection while in the water, and radiation from the Sun. Insulators could include sandals and a towel. Use **PASC,** p. 89.

Resource Manager

Chapter Resources Booklet
Activity Worksheet, pp. 5–6
Lab Activity, pp. 13–15
Reinforcement, p. 28

Answers to Section Assessment

1. conduction, convection, radiation
2. insulators: air, plastic; conductors: metal, water
3. Radiation can travel through empty space, but convection and conduction require a medium through which to travel.
4. Buildings are insulated to keep warm air inside in cold weather and warm air outside during hot weather.
5. Dark colors absorb more light and keep you warmer. The layers trap air inside, and air is a good insulator.
6. Obtain a source of heat. A cup or plastic bag of warm water would work. Use the various materials to insulate the heat source. Place a thermometer on the side of the material away from the heat source, and monitor the temperature change.
7. Check students' work.

Activity

Convection in Gases and Liquids

A hawk gliding through the sky will rarely flap its wings. Hawks and some other birds conserve energy by gliding on columns of warm air rising up from the ground. These convection currents form when gases or liquids are heated unevenly, and the warmer, less dense fluid is forced upward. In this activity, you will create and observe your own convection currents.

What You'll Investigate

How can convection currents be modeled and observed?

Materials

burner or hot plate
water
candle
500-mL beaker
black pepper

Safety Precautions 

WARNING: *Use care when working with hot materials. Remember that hot and cold glass appear the same.*

Goals

- **Model** the formation of convection currents in water.
- **Observe** convection currents formed in water.
- **Observe** convection currents formed in air.

Procedure

1. Pour about 450 mL of water into a 500-mL beaker.
2. Use a balance to measure 1 g of black pepper.
3. Sprinkle the pepper into the beaker of water.
4. Let the pepper settle to the bottom of the beaker.
5. Heat the bottom of the beaker using the burner or by placing it on the hotplate.
6. **Observe** how the particles of pepper move as the water is heated, and make a drawing showing their motion in your Science Journal.
7. Turn off the hot plate or burner. Light the candle and let it burn for a few minutes.
8. Blow out the candle, and observe the motion of the smoke.
9. Make a drawing of the movement of the smoke in your Science Journal.

Conclude and Apply

1. **Describe** how the particles of pepper moved as the water became hotter.
2. How is the motion of the pepper particles related to the motion of the water?
3. **Explain** how a convection current formed in the beaker.
4. **Explain** why the motion of the pepper changed when the heat was turned off.
5. **Predict** how the pepper would move if the water were heated from the top.
6. **Describe** how the smoke particles moved when the candle was blown out.
7. **Explain** why the smoke moved as it did.

Communicating Your Data

Compare your conclusions with other students in your class. **For more help, refer to the** Science Skill Handbook.

Activity

Purpose Students will model and observe convection currents. L2 LS **Kinesthetic**

Process Skills modeling, observing

Time Required one class period.

Alternate Materials Other fine grained spices that are insoluble in water can replace the black pepper.

Safety Precautions Caution students never to taste foods during science class. Caution them not to touch the hot plate when it is on.

Teaching Strategy Ask students to bring in insoluble particles from home to be used during their experiments.

Conclude and Apply

1. The particles swirled upward.
2. As the water heated, the convection currents in the water carried the black pepper upwards.
3. The water was hotter in the bottom of the beaker because it was nearer the heat source. The hot water rose in the beaker and the cool water dropped.
4. There was no longer a temperature gradient in the beaker so convection stopped.
5. The pepper would stay on the top because hot water is less dense than cool water.
6. The smoke rose as long as there was a heat source. The rise of the smoke became slower as the wick cools.
7. When the heat source is turned off, the temperature gradient becomes less as the wick cools and convection slows down.

Assessment

Process Ask each student to make an events chain for each of the convection currents observed. Use **Performance Assessment in the Science Classroom,** p. 163.

Communicating Your Data

Have each group observe the convection current patterns created by the experiments of other groups. Ask students to explain any differences in results.

SECTION 3

Using Heat

1 Motivate

Bellringer Transparency

Display the Section Focus Transparency for Section 3. Use the accompanying Transparency Activity Master. L2 ELL

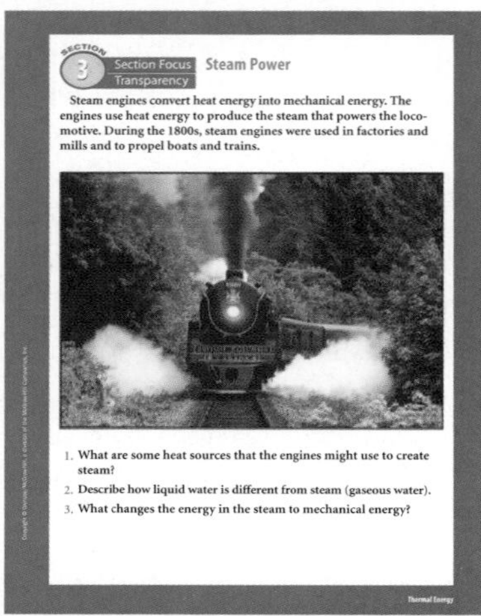

Tie to Prior Knowledge

Have students identify the energy sources and the types of energy used in their home heating systems. From a class poll, rank the energy sources from most used to least used. Compare and contrast some of the common ones mentioned.

SECTION 3

Using Heat

As You Read

What You'll Learn

- **Compare and Contrast** three types of conventional heating systems.
- **Distinguish** between passive and active solar heating systems.
- **Describe** how internal combustion engines work.
- **Explain** how a heat mover can transfer thermal energy in a direction opposite to that of its natural movement.

Vocabulary

solar energy
solar collector
heat engine
internal combustion engine
heat mover

Why It's Important

Heat is used to heat homes and operate vehicles.

Heating Systems

Almost everywhere in the United States air temperatures at some time become cold enough that a source of heat is needed. As a result, most homes and public buildings contain some type of heating system. No one heating system is best in all conditions. The best heating system for any home or building depends on the local climate and how the building is constructed.

All heating systems require some source of energy. In the simplest and oldest heating system, wood or coal is burned in a stove. The heat that is produced by the burning fuel is transferred from the stove to the surrounding air by conduction, convection, and radiation. One disadvantage of this system is that heat transfer from the room in which the stove is located to other rooms in the building can be slow.

Forced-Air Systems The most common type of heating system in use today is the forced-air system, shown in **Figure 13.** In this system, fuel is burned in a furnace and heats a volume of air. A fan then blows the warm air through a series of large pipes called ducts. The ducts lead to openings called vents in each room. Cool air returns to the furnace through additional vents, where it is reheated.

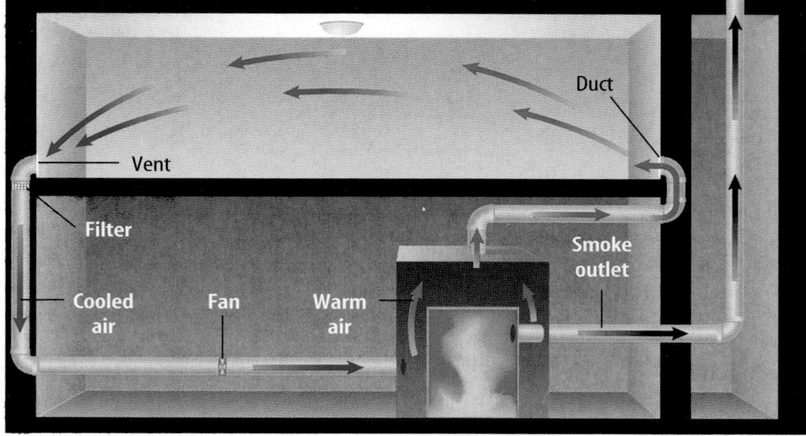

Figure 13
In forced-air systems, air heated by the furnace gets blown through ducts that usually lead to every room.

Section Assessment Planner

Portfolio
Activity, p. 173

Performance Assessment
Skill Builder Activities, p. 179
See page 186 for more options.

Content Assessment
Section, p. 177
Challenge, p. 177
Chapter, pp. 186–187

Radiator Systems Before forced-air systems were widely used, many homes and buildings were heated by a system of radiators. A radiator is a closed metal container that contains hot water or steam. The thermal energy contained in the hot water or steam is transferred to the air surrounding the radiator by conduction. This warm air then moves through the room by convection.

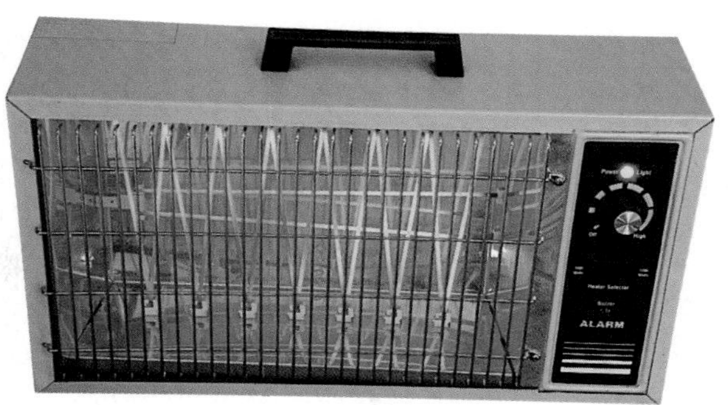

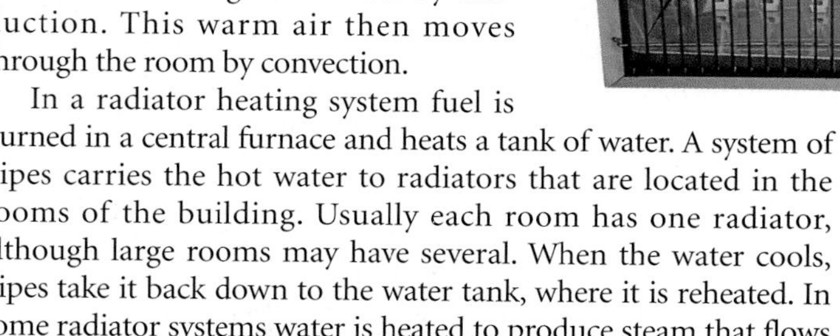

In a radiator heating system fuel is burned in a central furnace and heats a tank of water. A system of pipes carries the hot water to radiators that are located in the rooms of the building. Usually each room has one radiator, although large rooms may have several. When the water cools, pipes take it back down to the water tank, where it is reheated. In some radiator systems water is heated to produce steam that flows to the radiators. As the steam cools, it condenses into water and flows back to the tank.

You might have seen some radiators like the one in **Figure 14** that are not connected to a central furnace. These radiators contain metal coils that are heated when an electric current passes through them. The hot coils then transfer thermal energy to the room, mainly by radiation. This type of radiator often is used to provide heat in rooms that do not receive enough heat from the central heating system.

Figure 14
Radiators like this one convert electric energy to thermal energy. They are used in areas and rooms where heat from central systems might not reach.
What might stop hot air from central systems from reaching these areas?

Reading Check *What are two ways that heat is transferred from a radiator?*

Electric Heating Systems An electric heating system has no central furnace as forced-air and radiator systems do. Instead, it uses electrically heated coils placed in ceilings and floors to heat the surrounding air by conduction. Convection then distributes the heated air through the room. Electric heating systems are not as widely used as forced-air systems. In many areas, electric heating systems cost more to use. However, the walls and floors of some buildings might not be thick enough to include the pipes and ducts that forced-air and radiator systems require. Then an electric heating system might be the only practical way to provide heat.

Electric heating systems may seem to be a pollution-free way to provide heat. However, most power plants that produce electric energy burn fossil fuels, producing various pollutants. Also, it is much more efficient to burn fuels to produce heat rather than generate electricity. As a result, less fuel is needed to heat a house using a conventional furnace.

2 Teach

Heating Systems

Discussion

Why is water rather than other fluids used in home heating systems? The specific heat of water is high compared with that of other fluids. Thus, it carries more heat per unit of mass and loses it more slowly, keeping the room warm longer. L2 IS **Logical-Mathematical**

Caption Answer

Figure 14 In large rooms, heat may dissipate before it reaches the entire room. Heat may be blocked by large furniture or by a wall. An area may not have a heat vent.

Reading Check

Answer Conduction, convection, and radiation are all correct.

Activity

Have students work in small groups to draw diagrams of the movement of thermal energy from a radiator. Have them add arrows and labels to show the types of thermal energy transfer taking place. L2 COOP LEARN IS **Visual-Spatial** P

Resource Manager

Chapter Resources Booklet
Transparency Activity, p. 46
Home and Community Involvement, p. 38
Cultural Diversity, p. 41

Cultural Diversity

Home Heating Have students find out how the Inuit use convection currents to regulate heat inside their houses. The Inuit make the entranceways to their igloos lower than the inside. Since cold air sinks, the entranceway fills with cold outside air. The warmer air inside the igloo stays in because it is unable to move through cold, trapped air. L2 IS **Linguistic**

Solar Heating

Extension

Have students research the greenhouse effect. **Which gases in Earth's atmosphere increase the greenhouse effect, and how do they do it? How is this similar to heat flow in a man-made greenhouse?** Gases that increase the greenhouse effect include carbon dioxide and water. These gases, like the glass in a greenhouse, allow light to pass through them, but they absorb the reradiated infrared radiation, keeping it inside the atmosphere where it warms Earth. L3 LS **Linguistic**

Caption Answer

Figure 15 sunny climates

Solar Heating

Radiant energy from the Sun can make a greenhouse warm. The windows of the greenhouse allow the Sun's radiant energy to be transferred inside the greenhouse where materials absorb the radiant energy and become warmer. As they become warmer, the greenhouse heats up. The windows now keep the thermal energy from being transferred to the air outside, so the greenhouse stays warm.

The energy from the Sun is called **solar energy.** Solar energy is not only free, it is also available in a seemingly endless supply. Just as solar energy can heat a greenhouse, it also can be used to help heat homes and buildings.

Passive Solar Heating Two types of solar heating systems—passive and active—are available. In passive solar heating systems, solar energy heats rooms inside a building, but no mechanical devices are used to move heat from one area to another. Just as in a greenhouse, materials such as water or concrete inside a building absorb radiant energy from the Sun during the day and heat up. At night when the building begins to cool, the thermal energy absorbed by these materials helps keep the room warm.

Figure 15 shows a room in a house that uses passive solar heating. The south side of buildings usually receive the most solar energy. Homes that are heated by passive solar systems often have a wall of windows on the south side of the house. Walls of windows receive the maximum amount of sunlight possible during the day. The other walls are heavily insulated and have no windows to help reduce the loss of heat.

Figure 15
Passive solar heating systems make use of many materials' ability to hold heat. *In what climates would these systems work well?*

Cultural Diversity

Solar Brick-Making Passive solar heating can be used to make buildings as well as warm them. In the ancient Near East and Egypt, and still among some Native Americans of the desert Southwest, solar heat has been used to harden adobe clay into brick. Adobe is a particular type of clay found in combination with quartz and other minerals. Native Americans mix it with straw, form it into bricks, and bake the bricks in the Sun for one to two weeks. The bricks are sturdy enough to make multistory buildings, and some adobe structures have lasted for several centuries. Have students look up photos of Taos Pueblo (New Mexico) or cliff dwellings. L2 LS **Visual-Spatial**

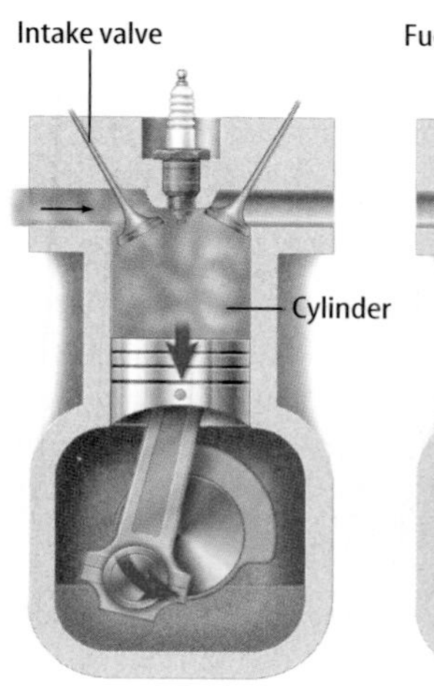

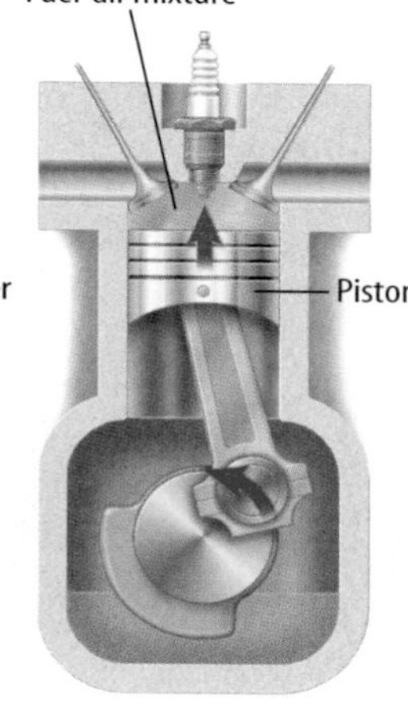

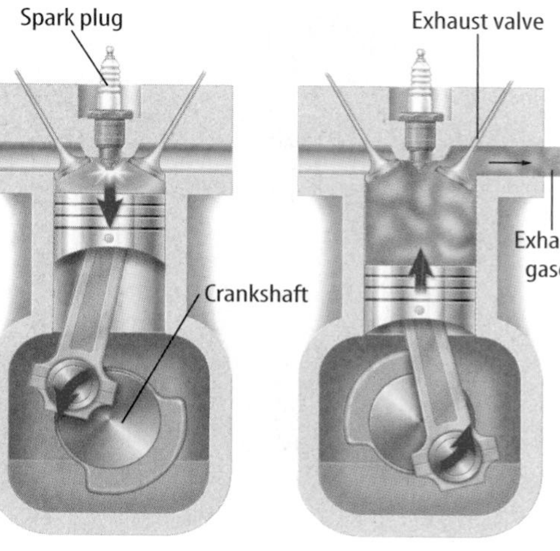

A Intake stroke
The intake valve opens as the piston moves downward, drawing a mixture of gasoline and air into the cylinder.

B Compression stroke
The intake valve closes as the piston moves upward, compressing the fuel-air mixture.

C Power stroke
The spark from a spark plug ignites the fuel-air mixture. As the mixture burns, hot gases expand, pushing the piston down.

D Exhaust stroke
As the piston moves up, the exhaust valve opens, and the waste gases from burning the fuel-air mixture are pushed out of the cylinder.

Figure 18
Automobile engines are usually four-stroke engines. Each four-stroke cycle converts thermal energy to mechanical energy.

Hot Engines If you've opened the hood of a car after it has been driven, you know the engine is too hot to touch. In an internal combustion engine, only part of the thermal energy that is produced by the burning fuel is converted into mechanical energy. Some of the thermal energy from the burning fuel has made the engine and other car parts hotter. So much heat is transferred to the engine that a cooling system is needed to keep the engine from becoming too hot to run properly. Gasoline automobile engines convert only about 26 percent of the chemical energy in the fuel to mechanical energy.

Heat Movers

How can the inside of a refrigerator stay cold? Heat should flow from the warmer room into the refrigerator until the room and refrigerator are at the same temperature. Instead, a refrigerator moves thermal energy out of the refrigerator into the warmer room. Heat can be made to flow from the cool refrigerator to the warm room only if work is done. The energy to do the work comes from the electricity that powers the refrigerator. A refrigerator is an example of a heat mover. A **heat mover** is a device that removes thermal energy from one location and transfers it to another location at a different temperature.

Fun Fact

The maximum efficiency possible for any heat engine is called the ideal efficiency and depends only on the temperature of the input materials and temperature of the output materials. The ideal efficiency of a four-cycle gasoline engine such as those used in automobiles is between 40 and 50%. This means that no matter how the engine is designed, it can never be more efficient than this.

Extension

Ask students to find out how internal combustion engines are cooled. Most automobile engines are cooled by water or a coolant fluid. Some automobile engines and most airplane engines are cooled by air.
L3 IN **Linguistic**

Heat Movers

Extension

The statement that heat can be made to flow from the cool refrigerator to the warm room only if work is done is one way to state the second law of thermodynamics. Have students find out who first stated the second law of thermodynamics and how he stated it. The second law of thermodynamics was first stated by Rudolph Clausius and Lord Kelvin and was based on work done by Sadi Carnot. Clausius' version of the second law says it is impossible for any self-acting machine to convey heat continuously from one body to another at a higher temperature.
L3 IN **Linguistic**

Resource Manager

Chapter Resources Booklet
Directed Reading for Content Mastery, pp. 21, 22

Performance Assessment in the Science Classroom, p. 41

Visual Learning

Figure 18 Read aloud the descriptions of each of the cycles in a four-cycle engine. Ask students to trace on the diagram each process as you read it. L2 IN **Auditory-Musical**

Heat Movers, continued

Reading Check

Answer It gets warmer.

Make a Model

Have students work in small groups to look up heat pumps and then draw two diagrams: one showing how a heat pump cools during warm weather, and the second showing how a heat pump warms during cool weather. L2 LS **Visual-Spatial**

Teacher FYI

To regulate body temperature, blood flow to the skin is automatically adjusted. When the environment is too cold, blood is drawn away from the skin and sent to more vital organs. When the environment is hot, more blood is sent to the skin so that its heat can be exchanged with the environment.

Life Science INTEGRATION

Evaporation explains why you shiver when you get out of a lake or pool, even on a hot day, or when you get out of the bathtub even into a warm room. It also explains why it's important to drink liquids when you're exercising or the day is hot. As your body sweats to cool off, you can become dehydrated.

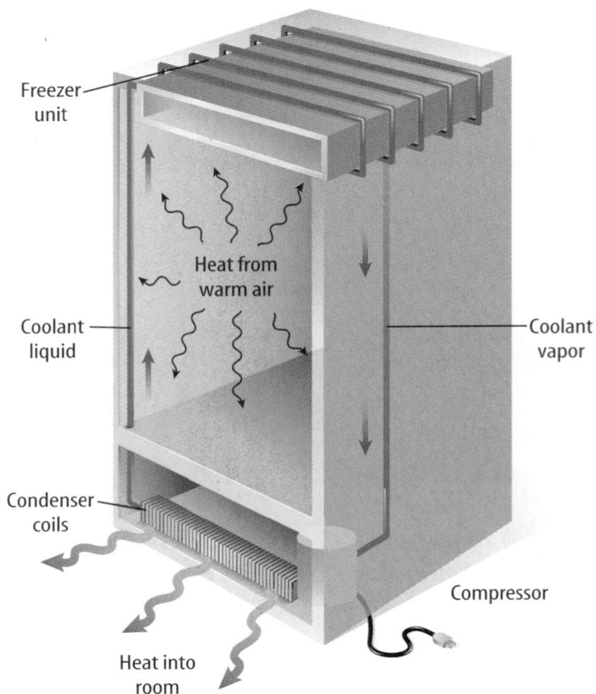

Figure 19
In refrigeration systems, the coolant that flows through the pipes absorbs heat from the food that is stored inside. It then condenses and releases the heat into the room.

Refrigerators A refrigerator contains a coolant that is pumped through pipes on the inside and outside of the refrigerator. The coolant is a special substance that evaporates at a low temperature. **Figure 19** shows how a refrigerator operates. Liquid coolant is pumped through a device where it evaporates and changes into a gas. When the coolant evaporates, it cools. The cold gas is pumped through pipes inside the refrigerator, where it absorbs thermal energy. The inside of the refrigerator cools.

The gas then is pumped to a compressor that does work by compressing the gas, which makes the gas warmer than the temperature of the room. The warm gas is pumped through the condenser coils. Because the gas is warmer than the room, thermal energy flows from the gas to the room. Some of this heat is the thermal energy that the coolant gas absorbed from the inside of the refrigerator. As the gas gives off heat, it cools and changes to a liquid. The gas then is made to evaporate, and the cycle is repeated.

Reading Check *What happens to a coolant when it is compressed?*

Air Conditioners and Heat Pumps An air conditioner is another type of heat mover. It operates like a refrigerator, except that warm air from the room is forced to pass over tubes containing the evaporating coolant. The warm air is cooled and passes back into the room. The thermal energy that is absorbed by the coolant is transferred to the air outdoors. Refrigerators and air conditioners are heat engines working in reverse—they use mechanical energy supplied by the compressor motor to move thermal energy from cooler to warmer areas.

A heat pump is a special two-way heat mover. In warm weather, it operates like an air conditioner—the warm air is cooled and returned to the house. In cold weather the evaporation and condensation processes are reversed. The cool coolant gas is pumped through tubes outside the house. Because the coolant is colder than the outside air, it absorbs heat. This heat is released inside the house when the coolant is compressed.

Curriculum Connection

Health Sweat glands exist in the dermis, the inner layer of skin lying below the epidermis. Although sweat itself has little smell, it contains bacteria that produce ammonia. Have students find out how deodorants work. Some deodorants kill the bacteria, while others cover the smell with perfume. Antiperspirants block the pores to prevent the secretion of sweat. L2 LS **Linguistic**

Resource Manager 

Chapter Resources Booklet
Reinforcement, p. 29

The Human Coolant After exercising on a warm day, you might feel hot and be drenched with sweat. But if you were to take your temperature, you would probably find that it's close to your normal body temperature of 37°C. How does your body stay cool in hot weather?

Your body uses evaporation to keep its internal temperature constant. When a liquid changes to a gas, energy is absorbed from the liquid's surroundings. As you exercise, your body generates sweat from tiny glands within your skin. As the sweat evaporates, it carries away heat, making you cooler, as shown in **Figure 20.** The thermal energy that is lost by your body becomes part of the thermal energy of your evaporated sweat.

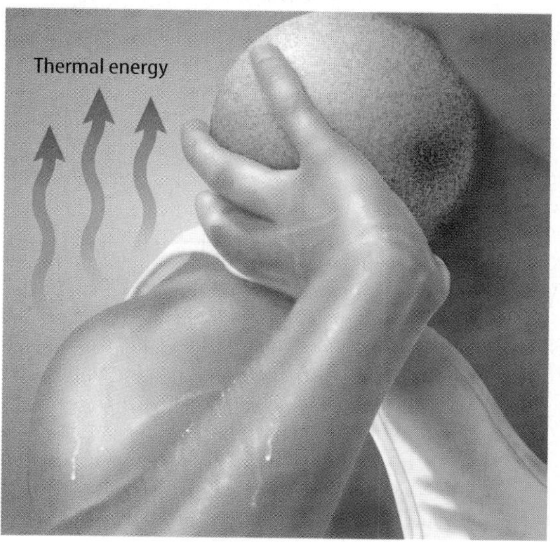

Figure 20
As perspiration evaporates from your skin, it carries heat away, cooling your body.

Why do humid days feel hotter? To most people humid days feel warmer than drier days, even when the temperature is the same. On humid days, more water vapor is in the air around you. Because there is more water vapor in the air, your sweat doesn't evaporate as quickly. As a result, you lose heat more slowly. Many animals can't sweat like humans do. Dogs, for example, only produce sweat between their toes, so they must pant to cause evaporation from their respiratory systems. Animals with heavy fur coats also can raise their fur on warm days to allow more heat to be released from their bodies. Most living things have some method for retaining and releasing heat.

Section 3 Assessment

1. Compare and contrast electrical, radiator, and forced-air heating systems.
2. Compare and contrast active and passive solar heating systems.
3. Describe how internal combustion engines work.
4. What is a heat mover?
5. **Think Critically** How does a heat mover get heat from cold air?

Skill Builder Activities

6. **Making and Using Tables** In a table, organize information about heating systems. **For more help, refer to the** Science Skill Handbook.
7. **Communicating** Only a small part of the chemical energy of gasoline is used to move your car. In your Science Journal, describe ways to improve an engine's efficiency. **For more help, refer to the** Science Skill Handbook.

3 Assess

Reteach

Have students make flash cards with the names of the strokes of the four-stroke cycle of an internal combustion engine. On the reverse side of each card, have them write descriptions of the stroke. Partners can then test each other by shuffling the cards and sequencing them by both name and description. L1 LS **Interpersonal**

Challenge

Have students work in small groups to think of as many ways as they can to keep a house warmer in the winter and then to categorize those ways according to energy source.
L2 LS **Interpersonal**

Assessment

Portfolio Have students make posters or drawings showing heat flow in any of the heating or cooling systems or engines studied. Some may be simpler than others, but all should show areas of high and low temperature and direction of heat flow. Use **Performance Assessment in the Science Classroom,** p. 145. P

Answers to Section Assessment

1. All three use an energy source to produce heat, which is distributed by conduction, convection, and radiation. Electrical systems do not have a central furnace; they radiate heat from coils within the room. A radiator system relies on a central furnace to heat water or steam, which is piped to different rooms, where the heat transfers to the air. In a forced-air system, centrally heated air is piped through a building and blown through vents into the rooms.
2. Passive systems simply absorb radiant energy from the Sun. Active systems collect that energy and distribute it.
3. Thermal energy from burning fuel is converted into mechanical energy.
4. a device that removes thermal energy from one location and transfers it to another location at a different temperature
5. by doing work
6. Systems could be organized by source of heat, heat transfer method, active/passive, conventional/solar, and so on.
7. Possible answers: low-friction gears, thermal insulation, complete burning of fuel

Activity BENCH TESTED

What Youíll Investigate

Purpose

Students will observe how heat is transferred by conduction in liquids and gases. L2 LS **Kinesthetic**

Process Skills

collecting data, measuring, making and using tables, recording data, making and using graphs, interpreting data

Time Required

80 minutes

Materials

Wire gauze is available in hardware stores or home centers. Ice can be stored in an ice chest for the day, if ice is not available in the building.

Safety Precautions

Students should be careful while handling hot liquids. Caution them to use care while cutting the wire gauze, the gauze will have sharp points on it.

Procedure

Teaching Strategy

Have small squares of wire gauze precut to save time during the lab.

Activity

Conduction in Gases and Liquids

Does smog occur where you live? If so, you may have experienced a temperature inversion. Usually the Sun warms the ground, and the air above it. When the air near the ground is warmer than the air above, convection occurs. This convection also carries smoke and other gases emitted by cars, chimneys, and smokestacks upward into the atmosphere. If the air near the ground is colder than the air above, convection does not occur. Then smoke and other pollutants can be trapped near the ground, sometimes forming smog. In this activity you will use a temperature inversion to investigate the conduction of heat in air and water.

What You'll Investigate

How is heat transferred by conduction in liquids and gases?

Goals

- **Measure** temperature changes in air near a heat source.
- **Observe** conduction of heat in air.
- **Observe** conduction of heat in water.

Materials

Thermometers (3)	test tube (large)
2 foam cups	ring stand
400-mL beakers (2)	test-tube clamp
burner or hot plate	wire gauze
paring knife	scissors
thermal mitts (2)	ice

Safety Precautions

WARNING: *Use care when handling hot water. Pour hot water using two hands. Make sure the test tube does not point at anyone.*

Procedure

1. Using the paring knife, carefully cut the bottom from one foam cup.
2. Use a pencil or pen to poke holes about 2 cm from the top and bottom of each foam cup.
3. Turn both cups upside down, and poke the ends of the thermometers through the upper holes and lower holes, so both thermometers are supported horizontally. The bulb end of both thermometers should extend into the middle of the bottomless cup.

Science Journal

Central Heat Ask students to explain in their Science Journals why it is not a good idea to put central heating vents in the ceiling when trying to heat a room. L2 LS **Logical-Mathematical**

Resource Manager

Chapter Resources Booklet

Activity Worksheet, pp. 7–8

Transparency Activity, pp. 47–48

Using Scientific Methods

4. Heat about 350 mL of water to about 80°C in one of the beakers.
5. Place an empty 400-mL beaker on top of the bottomless cup. Record the temperature of the two thermometers in your data table.
6. Add about 100 mL of hot water to the empty beaker. After one minute, record the temperatures of the thermometers in a data table like the one shown here.
7. Continue to record the temperatures every minute for 10 min. Add hot water as needed to keep the temperature of the water at about 80°C.
8. With scissors cut a piece of wire mesh slightly larger than the diameter of the test tube.
9. Place ice in the bottom of the test tube and push the mesh into the tube against the ice.
10. Attach a test-tube clamp to the ring stand and clamp the test tube so it is nearly vertical.
11. Fill the test tube with cold water to within 2 cm of the top, and carefully heat the water near the top of the test tube with the burner.

Air Temperatures in Foam Cup

Time (min)	Upper Thermometer (°C)	Lower Thermometer (°C)
0	22	22
1	23	27
2	23	30
3	24	33

Conclude and Apply

1. **Explain** whether convection can occur in the foam cup if it's being heated from the top.
2. **Describe** how heat was transferred through the air in the foam cup.
3. **Graph** the temperatures measured by the upper and lower thermometers, with time on the horizontal axis.
4. **Explain** why the temperature of the two thermometers changed differently.
5. **Explain** why the ice in the test tube didn't melt.
6. **Predict** how the ice would behave if the water in the tube were replaced by an aluminum rod.

Tie to Prior Knowledge

Remind students that heat transfer by conduction occurs by touch. The molecules have to touch in order for conduction to occur.

Expected Outcome

In both instances, the heat source is at the top of the container. Heat transfer by convection cannot occur, therefore the heat transfer must occur by conduction.

Conclude and Apply

1. No, heat transfer will be by conduction.
2. by conduction
3. check students' graphs
4. Conduction occurs faster in a liquid than in a gas because the molecular density is greater.
5. Heat conduction to the ice did not occur fast enough.
6. The ice would melt because heat would transfer through the solid much faster than it did through the liquid.

Error Analysis

Have each group compare its results with those of another group. If the data disagree, have students list reasons for the discrepancy.

Assessment

Oral Ask students to use the kinetic theory to explain why heat transfers in the following order: from fastest to slowest solids, liquids, and gases. Use **Performance Assessment in the Science Classroom,** p. 89.

Have students compare results with other groups and discuss differences noted. Why might these differences have occurred?

ACTIVITY 181

Science Stats

Content Background

The energy in the Sun is generated by the fusion of hydrogen atoms to form helium. Since the Sun is composed primarily of hydrogen atoms, the fuel for this reaction is readily available. The energy radiated from the Sun provides Earth with an environment that can support life, as we know it. The Sun provides energy for photosynthesis to occur, which provides a food source for many organisms. It provides heat, which combined with our atmosphere and water sources, provides a moderate temperature range that supports life. Despite all of these uses of solar energy a large portion of the energy that arrives on Earth's surface is not used. Scientists are attempting to develop technology that will enable people to use more of the Sun's energy.

Discussion

What role does the Sun play in maintaining life on Earth? The Sun is the source of the energy in all food on Earth. It provides energy for photosynthesis, which provides food for plants. These plants are eaten by animals, which in turn are eaten by other animals. The Sun also provides the heat necessary for the chemical reactions that take place in organisms.

Activity

Have students research the various ways people use solar energy. Students should make oral presentations to share their information with their class.

Science Stats

Surprising Thermal Energy

Did you know...

. . . The average amount of solar energy that reaches the United States each year is about 600 times greater than the nation's annual energy demands.

. . . Energy travels from the Sun to Earth at the speed of light—299,274 km/s. Nothing on Earth—not the fastest plane or car or train—goes nearly that fast!

. . . A lightning bolt heats the air in its path to temperatures of about 25,000°C. That's about 4 times hotter than the average temperature on the surface of the Sun.

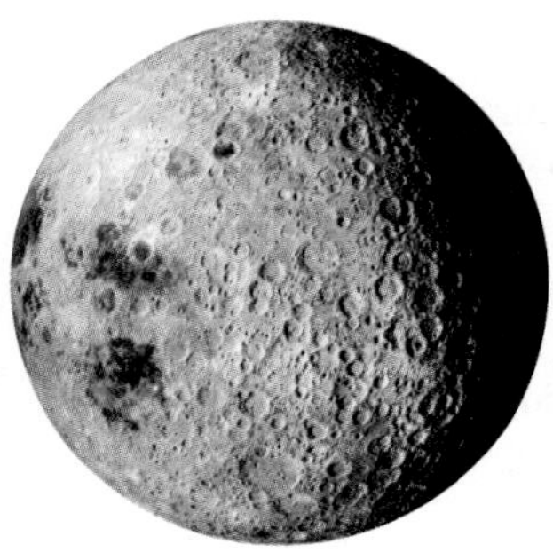

. . . Without energy from the Sun, Earth's average temperature would be −240°C. Earth would be like the side of the Moon that never sees the Sun. There could be no life at such frigid temperatures. The lowest recorded temperature on Earth is −89°C.

SCIENCE Online

Internet Addresses

Explore the Glencoe Science Web Site at **science.glencoe.com** to find out more about topics found in this feature.

Connecting To Math

. . . About 67 percent of the average home's energy is used for temperature control. This includes your refrigerator, heating, air-conditioning, and hot-water heater.

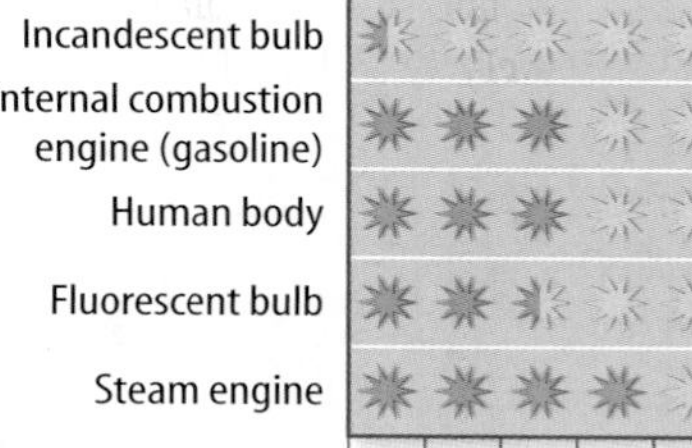

. . . When a space shuttle reenters Earth's atmosphere at more than 28,000 km/h, its outer surface is heated by friction to nearly 1,650°C. This temperature is high enough to melt steel.

Do the Math

1. The highest recorded temperature on Earth is 58°C and the lowest is −89°C. What is the range between the highest and lowest recorded temperatures?
2. What is the average temperature of the surface of the Sun? Draw a bar graph comparing the temperature of a lightning bolt to the temperature of the surface of the Sun.
3. The Sun is almost 150 million km from Earth. How long does it take solar energy to reach Earth?

Go Further

Use the library and the Glencoe Science Web site at **science.glencoe.com** to research how much energy is used in the United States. How much of the energy used comes from the Sun?

Connecting To Math

Do the Math

Teaching Strategies

- Review with students how to find range for question one in Do the Math.
- Discuss which units should be used to mark the y-axis on the bar graph for the second question in the Do the Math.
- Provide graph paper to assist the students with question two in the Do the Math.

Answers

1. 147° C
2. 6,250° C. Check students' graphs.
3. 501 s = 8 min

Go Further

Ask students to make a table of the data in the Energy Efficiency bar graph. For each item have them list the percentage of energy used and the percentage of energy wasted.

Visual Learning

Energy from the Sun travels at 299,274 km/s. Express this number in scientific notation using three significant digits. 3.00×10^5 km/s Express this number in m/s using three significant digits and scientific notation. 3.00×10^8 m/s

Chapter 6 Study Guide

Reviewing Main Ideas

Preview

Students can answer the questions in their Science Journals. Discuss the answers as you go through the chapter. LS **Linguistic**

Review

Students can write their answers, then compare them with those of other students. LS **Interpersonal**

Reteach

Students can look at the illustrations and describe details that support the main ideas of the chapter. LS **Visual-Spatial**

Answers to Chapter Review

Section 1

2. from the room to the outside

Section 2

3. conductors: aluminum foil, metal pan insulators: cup, cotton, sponge

Section 3

5. The water on the student's body is evaporating, conducting away a large amount of heat and cooling the student.

Chapter 6 Study Guide

Reviewing Main Ideas

Section 1 Temperature and Heat

1. The temperature of a material is a measure of the average kinetic energy of the molecules in the material.
2. Heat is thermal energy that flows from a higher to a lower temperature. *How is heat flowing in the photo at the right?*

3. The thermal energy of an object is the total kinetic and potential energy of the molecules in the object.
4. The specific heat is the amount of heat needed to raise the temperature of 1 kg of a substance by 1 K.

Section 2 Transferring Thermal Energy

1. Thermal energy is transferred by conduction, convection, and radiation.
2. Conduction and convection can occur only when matter is present.
3. Heat can flow easily through materials that are conductors. Heat flows more slowly through insulators. *What materials below are conductors, and which are insulators?*

Section 3 Using Heat

1. Conventional heating systems use air, hot water, and steam to transfer thermal energy through a building.
2. A solar heating system converts radiant energy from the Sun to thermal energy. Active solar systems use solar collectors to absorb the thermal radiant energy.
3. Heat engines convert thermal energy produced by burning fuel into mechanical energy. In an internal combustion engine, fuel is burned inside the engine in cylinders.
4. Heat movers, like refrigerators and air conditioners, move thermal energy from one place and release it somewhere else.
5. Sweating helps humans cool their bodies through evaporation. *Why is this person shivering after getting out of a pool, even though it is a warm day?*

FOLDABLES Reading & Study Skills — After You Read

Use what you learned and write how temperature and heat are related but different on the front of your Foldable.

FOLDABLES Reading & Study Skills — After You Read

After students have read the chapter and completed the Foldable described in Before You Read, have them do the activity on the student page.

Dinah Zike

Chapter 6 Study Guide

Visualizing Main Ideas

Complete the following concept map of thermal energy transfer.

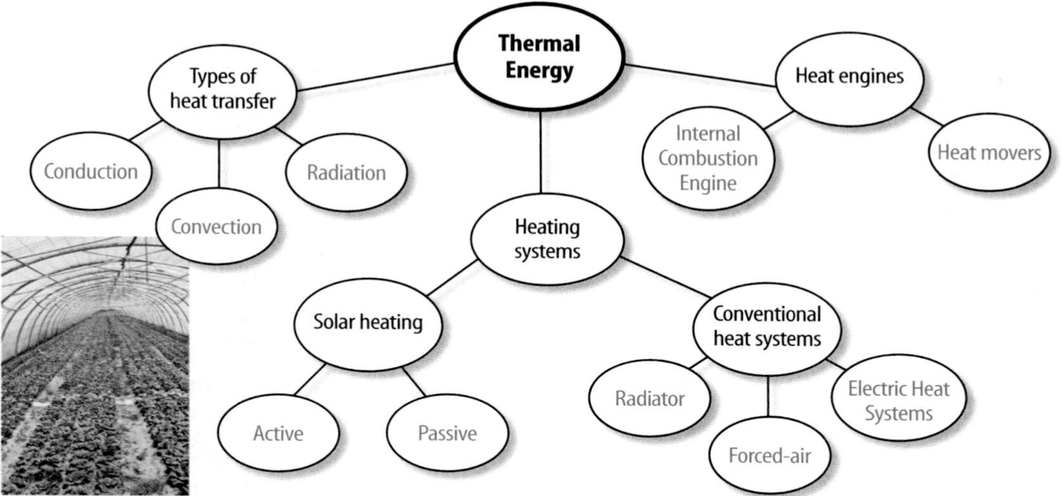

Vocabulary Review

Vocabulary Words

a. conduction
b. convection
c. heat
d. heat engine
e. heat mover
f. insulator
g. internal combustion engine
h. radiation
i. specific heat
j. solar collector
k. solar energy
l. temperature
m. thermal energy

Study Tip

Make a plan. Before you start your homework, write out a checklist of what you need to do for each subject. As you finish each item, check it off.

Using Vocabulary

Using the vocabulary words, change the incorrect terms to make the sentences read correctly.

1. A heat mover is a device that converts thermal energy into mechanical energy.
2. Solar energy is energy that is transferred from warmer to cooler materials.
3. A heat engine is a device that absorbs the Sun's radiant energy.
4. The energy required to raise the temperature of 1 kg of a material 1 K is a material's thermal energy.
5. Heat is a measure of the average kinetic energy of the particles in a material.
6. Convection is energy transfer by electromagnetic waves.

Chapter 6 Study Guide

Visualizing Main Ideas

See student page.

Vocabulary Review

Using Vocabulary

1. A heat *engine* is a device that converts thermal energy into mechanical energy.
2. *Heat* is energy that is transferred from warmer to cooler materials.
3. A *solar collector* is a device that absorbs the Sun's radiant energy.
4. The energy required to raise the temperature of 1 kg of a material 1 K is a material's *specific heat.*
5. *Temperature* is a measure of the average kinetic energy of the particles in a material.
6. *Radiation* is energy transfer by electromagnetic waves.

Chapter 6 Assessment

Checking Concepts

1. B
2. A
3. D
4. A
5. B
6. C
7. A
8. A
9. C
10. D

Thinking Critically

11. Place many balls together on a flat surface. Bump one, and the energy is transferred to others.
12. The copper bowl; its specific heat is greater.
13. Use good insulators. Use many layers that trap air, a good insulator. Make clothing waterproof so that water doesn't conduct heat away from the person. Use dark-colored exteriors to absorb more energy. Use reflective interiors to reflect energy back to the person.
14. You need to know the size of the layer of ice and the cup and the temperatures of both to give the answer.
15. As liquid coolant moves through the air conditioner, it evaporates, removing energy from the interior of the car. This energy is then released to the warmer air outside the car. This process requires work to be done by the car's engine.

Chapter  Assessment

Checking Concepts

Choose the word or phrase that best answers the question.

1. Which is NOT a method of heat transfer?
   A) conduction **C)** radiation
   B) specific heat **D)** convection
2. In which of the following devices is fuel burned inside chambers called cylinders?
   A) internal combustion engines
   B) radiators
   C) heat pumps
   D) steam engines
3. During which phase of a four-stroke engine are waste gases removed?
   A) power stroke
   B) intake stroke
   C) compression stroke
   D) exhaust stroke
4. Which material is a poor insulator of heat?
   A) iron **C)** air
   B) feathers **D)** plastic
5. Which of the following devices is an example of a heat mover?
   A) steam engine
   B) refrigerator
   C) combustion engine
   D) four-stroke engine
6. Which term describes the measure of the average kinetic energy of the particles in an object?
   A) potential energy **C)** temperature
   B) thermal energy **D)** specific heat
7. Which of these is NOT used to calculate change in thermal energy?
   A) volume
   B) temperature change
   C) specific heat
   D) mass
8. Which of these does NOT require the presence of particles of matter?
   A) radiation **C)** convection
   B) conduction **D)** combustion
9. What must occur to radiant energy for it to be changed to thermal energy?
   A) It must be reflected.
   B) It must be conducted.
   C) It must be absorbed.
   D) It must produce a convection current.
10. Which device changes thermal energy into mechanical energy?
   A) conductor **C)** solar collector
   B) refrigerator **D)** heat engine

Thinking Critically

11. Energy transfer by conduction takes place at the particle level of matter. Thus, the transfer of energy cannot be observed directly. Make a model to demonstrate the process of conduction.
12. A copper bowl and a silver bowl of equal mass were heated from 27°C to 100°C. Which required more heat? Explain.

Specific Heat (J/kg K)	
Copper	385
Silver	235
Tin	228

13. Design a line of clothing to be used on an arctic expedition. Describe the articles of clothing and explain why each will keep the wearer warm in extremely cold conditions.
14. Which has the greater amount of thermal energy, a layer of ice on a pond or a cup of hot water? Explain.
15. Describe how an automobile air conditioner works. Why must the engine be running for the air conditioner to work?

Chapter Assessment Planner

Portfolio Encourage students to place in their portfolios one or two items of what they consider to be their best work. Examples include:

- Science Journal, p. 160
- Extension, p. 167
- Activity, p. 173
- Assessment, p. 179

Performance Additional performance assessments, Performance Task Assessment Lists, and rubrics for evaluating these activities can be found in Glencoe's **Performance Assessment in the Science Classroom.**

Developing Skills

16. **Classifying** Order the events that occur in the removal of heat from an object by a refrigerator. Show the complete cycle, from the placing of a warm object in the refrigerator to the changes in the coolant.

17. **Recognizing Cause and Effect** Describe the problems that might occur if the following events occurred in a gasoline engine. Indicate the engine stroke that will be affected: exhaust valve stuck closed, bad spark plug, and intake valve will not close.

18. **Concept Mapping** Complete the following events chain to show how an active solar heating system works.

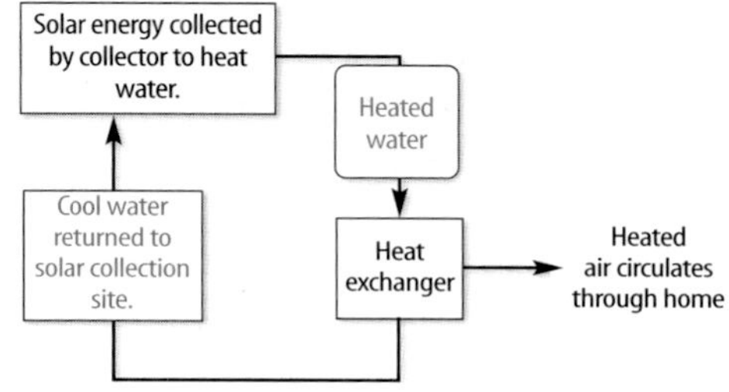

Performance Assessment

19. **Making Observations and Inferences** Identify the building materials that are used in or on the walls, ceilings, or attic space in your home and school. Which ones are good heat insulators?

Technology

Go to the Glencoe Science Web site at **science.glencoe.com** or use the **Glencoe Science CD-ROM** for additional chapter assessment.

Test Practice

Pierre's science class did an experiment involving heat. The setup for the experiment is shown in the diagram below. Pierre took temperature readings every 2 min for 20 min. For the first 10 min, the light was turned on. For the last 10 min, the light was turned off.

Study the diagram and answer the following questions.

1. What is probably being measured in the setup in the diagram?
   A) the rate at which electricity affects the temperature of soil and water
   B) the rate at which soil and water evaporate
   C) the rate at which soil and water absorb heat energy
   D) the effect of light on plant growth in soil and water

2. How could Pierre improve his experiment?
   F) by putting soil in both containers
   G) by taking temperature readings every 5 min
   H) by using more or less water
   J) by moving the lamp so that it heats both beakers equally

Chapter 6 Assessment

Test Practice

The Test-Taking Tip was written by The Princeton Review, the nation's leader in test preparation.

1. C
2. J

Developing Skills

16. Liquid coolant evaporates, removing thermal energy from the warm object; the coolant gas is compressed, which raises its temperature; thermal energy flows from the coolant gas to the exterior air, causing it to condense to a liquid; then the cycle repeats.
17. (a) Exhaust gases will not be removed during the exhaust stroke, which will limit the amount of fuel-air mixture entering during the intake stroke.
    (b) The fuel-air mixture will not be properly ignited, thus reducing the power stroke.
    (c) The fuel-air mixture that enters during the intake stroke will be pushed out of the stuck valve during the compression stroke, thus reducing the power stroke.
18. See student page.

Performance Assessment

19. Answers could include bricks, plaster, drywall, wood, glass, shingles, siding, insulation, pockets of air, and so on. Of these, insulation, wood, and air are good insulators. Use **PASC**, p. 89

Assessment Resources

Reproducible Masters

Chapter Resources Booklet
Chapter Review, pp. 37–38
Chapter Tests, pp. 39–42
Assessment Transparency Activity, p. 49

Glencoe Science Web site
Interactive Tutor
Chapter Quizzes

Glencoe Technology

- Assessment Transparency
- Interactive CD-ROM Chapter Quizzes
- ExamView Pro Test Bank
- Vocabulary PuzzleMaker Software
- MindJogger Videoquiz DVD/VHS

Standardized Test Practice

Reading Comprehension

QUESTION 1: B

Students need to use the information in the passage to identify which answer choice is the best supported conclusion. Information such as, *there are different types of rubber polymers—if the polymer chains are tightly linked, they do not deform much and thus they bounce high*, will help them identify choice B as the best supported conclusion. **Objective 5**

QUESTION 2: F

Students need to use context clues to identify the meaning of the underlined word. Rereading the sentences surrounding the underlined word will help them locate these clues, which include *which means that its molecules deform but quickly regain their original shape, making the ball bounce*. Only choice F is supported by the passage. **Objective 1**

Teaching Tip

Students should always look for important information in the passage.

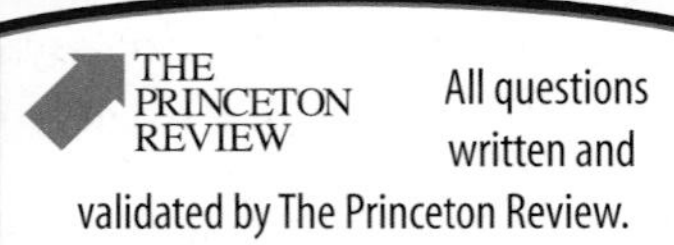

All questions written and validated by The Princeton Review.

Standardized Test Practice

Reading Comprehension

Read the passage. Then read each question that follows the passage. Decide which is the best answer to each question.

Bouncing Back

Have you ever noticed that the balls you use for different sports bounce differently? If you played baseball with a tennis ball, the ball would probably fly way out into the outfield without much effort when you hit it with your bat. In contrast, if you used a baseball in a tennis match, the ball probably would not bounce high enough for your opponent to hit it very well. The difference in the way balls bounce depends upon the materials that make up the balls and the way in which the balls are constructed.

A ball drops to the floor as a result of gravity. As the ball drops, it gathers speed. When the ball hits the floor, the energy that it has gained goes into deforming the ball, changing it from its round shape. As the ball changes shape, the molecules within it stretch farther apart in some places and squeeze closer together in other places. The strength of the bonds between molecules determines how much they stretch apart and squeeze together. This depends on the chemical composition of the materials in the ball.

Most balls are made of rubber. Rubber is elastic, which means that its molecules deform but quickly regain their original shape, making the ball bounce. Rubber is made of long chains of polymer molecules. When these molecules hit a surface, they stretch but then reform. There are different types of rubber polymers—if the polymer chains are tightly linked, they do not deform much and thus they bounce high. Some of the ball's kinetic energy is converted into thermal energy, which is why balls sometimes feel warm after they have been dropped.

Test-Taking Tip Make a list of the important details in the passage.

Sometimes a ball's kinetic energy is converted into thermal energy, making it warm to the touch.

1. According to information in the passage, it is probably accurate to conclude that _____.

A) all rubber balls bounce the same, no matter what they are made of

B) the way rubber balls bounce depends upon the polymers that they are made of

C) baseballs are better for playing tennis than tennis balls are for playing baseball

D) the higher a ball bounces, the more thermal energy that is produced

2. In the context of this passage, the word elastic means _____.

F) able to bounce

G) inflexible

H) tightly linked

J) deformed

188 STANDARDIZED TEST PRACTICE

Standardized Test Practice

Reasoning and Skills

Read each question and choose the best answer.

1. Latifah wanted to figure out which race car had the most kinetic energy during a competition. She researched the different race cars to find out their masses. Her experiment could be improved by _____.
   A) writing down a list of observations during the competition
   B) finding out the velocity of each race car during the competition
   C) weighing the cars after the competition
   D) researching motorcycles as well as race cars

Test-Taking Tip Consider how mass and velocity affect an object's kinetic energy.

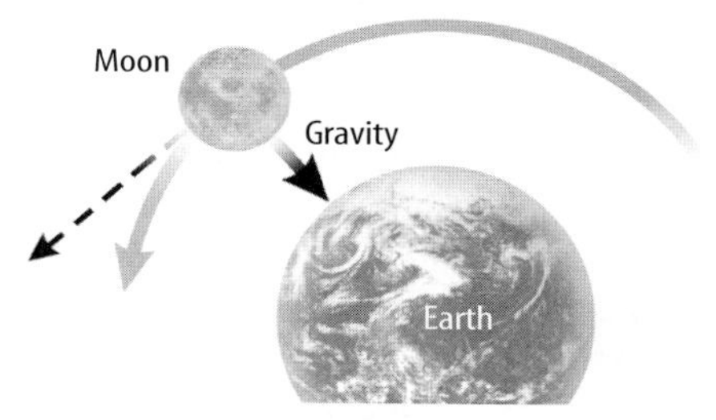

Centripetal Force

2. Which kind of scientist would most likely use this picture?
   F) geologist
   G) physicist
   H) chemist
   J) zoologist

Test-Taking Tip Consider the type of information presented by the picture.

Training record

End of Day	Maximum Speed (m/s)
1	10
2	8
3	6
4	?

3. These data were collected while an athlete trained for a marathon. If everything remains the same, what will be the maximum speed of the athlete at the end of the fourth day?
   A) 1 m/s
   B) 2 m/s
   C) 3 m/s
   D) 4 m/s

Test-Taking Tip Carefully consider the information in both the chart and the question in order to identify the trend.

Consider this question carefully before writing your answer on a separate sheet of paper.

4. Explain the similarities and differences between simple and complex machines.

Test-Taking Tip Recall examples of simple and complex machines from everyday life.

Standardized Test Practice

Reasoning and Skills

Question 1: B

Students need to use their understandings of mass, velocity, and kinetic energy to identify the correct answer choice. Students should be familiar with considering how to improve scientific experiments. Only choice B will improve Latifa's experiment in finding out the kinetic energy of race cars.

Question 2: G

Students need to carefully consider the information in the picture and its title to identify the correct answer choice. Students can use the information *centripetal force* to identify choice G as the correct answer.

Question 3: D

Students need to detect a trend in the data in the table and make a prediction based on that trend. Students should observe that the athlete's acceleration decreases by 2 m/s^2 every day. Using this information, students should be able to identify choice D as the correct answer.

Question 4: Answers will vary.

Students need to use their understanding of simple and complex machines in order to write a thorough response.

Teaching Tip

Students should review these test practice questions as they prepare for the test.

UNIT 2

Unit Contents

Pre-Reading Activity

Have students look at pictures and describe the ways they see electricity being used.

UNIT 2 Electricity and Energy Resources

How Are Clouds & Toasters Connected?

190

Teacher to Teacher

"While discussing chemical reactions, you can illustrate the wide range of energies involved with various reactions by having the students compare the relatively small amounts of energy released in the combustion of wood or coal to the large amounts of energy released during a space shuttle launch."

Cathy Mariotti Ezrailson, Teacher
Oak Ridge High School
Conroe, TX

NATIONAL GEOGRAPHIC

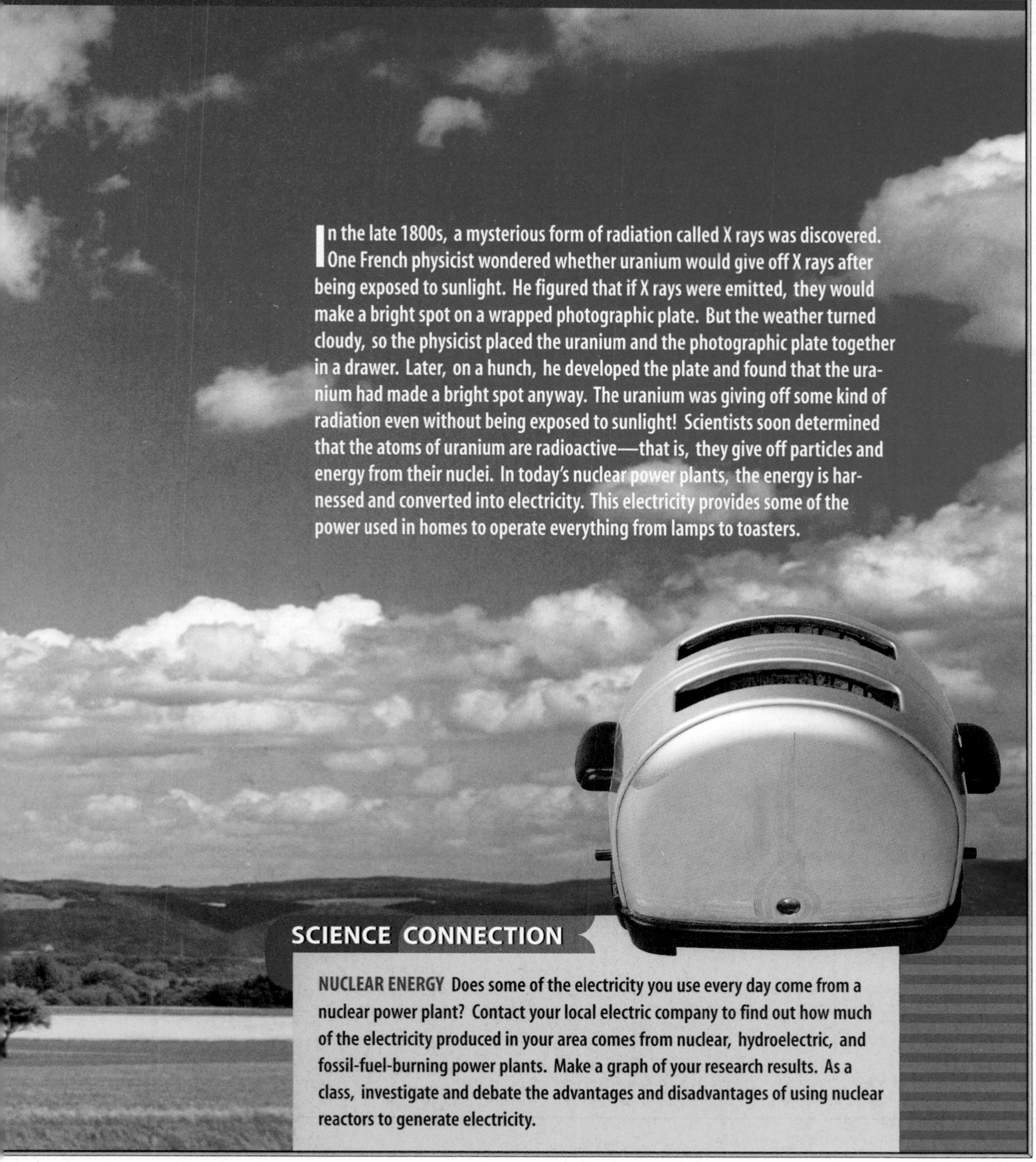

In the late 1800s, a mysterious form of radiation called X rays was discovered. One French physicist wondered whether uranium would give off X rays after being exposed to sunlight. He figured that if X rays were emitted, they would make a bright spot on a wrapped photographic plate. But the weather turned cloudy, so the physicist placed the uranium and the photographic plate together in a drawer. Later, on a hunch, he developed the plate and found that the uranium had made a bright spot anyway. The uranium was giving off some kind of radiation even without being exposed to sunlight! Scientists soon determined that the atoms of uranium are radioactive—that is, they give off particles and energy from their nuclei. In today's nuclear power plants, the energy is harnessed and converted into electricity. This electricity provides some of the power used in homes to operate everything from lamps to toasters.

SCIENCE CONNECTION

NUCLEAR ENERGY Does some of the electricity you use every day come from a nuclear power plant? Contact your local electric company to find out how much of the electricity produced in your area comes from nuclear, hydroelectric, and fossil-fuel-burning power plants. Make a graph of your research results. As a class, investigate and debate the advantages and disadvantages of using nuclear reactors to generate electricity.

Introducing the Unit

How Are Clouds & Toasters Connected?

- Students might start this activity with negative ideas about nuclear energy. Have them make a two-column table they can use to list the positive and negative aspects of nuclear energy as they learn more about it.
- Ask students to list the connections from clouds to toasters. You might want them to use a concept map to relate one step to another.
- Ask students to brainstorm what geographic areas might most likely use nuclear power to produce electricity. areas that don't have a close or convenient source of coal or running water for hydroelectric power

SCIENCE CONNECTION

Activity

As consumers now can choose a source of electricity for their homes, students should check with an adult in their family to find out what company supplies their electricity. Because sources might differ, have students compare their results and determine the advantages and disadvantages of different companies.

SCIENCE Online

Internet Addresses

Explore the Glencoe Science Web site at **science.glencoe.com** to find out more about topics in this unit.

Section/Objectives	Standards		Activities/Features
	National	State/Local	
Chapter Opener	See p. 37T for a Key to Standards.		**Explore Activity:** How many ways?, p. 193 **Before You Read,** p. 193
Section 1 Electric Charge 2 sessions 1 block 1. **Describe** the properties of static electricity. 2. **Distinguish** between conductors and insulators. 3. **Recognize** the presence of charge in an electroscope.	National Content Standards: UCP2, A1, B3 (5–8), B6 (9–12)		**Science Online,** p. 198 **Visualizing Lightning,** p. 199 **MiniLAB:** Investigating Charged Objects, p. 200
Section 2 Electric Current 3 sessions 1.5 blocks 1. **Describe** how electric current is different from static electricity. 2. **Explain** how a dry cell provides a source of voltage difference. 3. **Describe** the relationship among voltage difference, resistance, and current.	National Content Standards: UCP3, A1, B3(5–8), B6 (9–12)		**MiniLAB:** Investigating Battery Addition, p. 204 **Health Integration,** p. 207 **Activity:** Identifying Conductors and Insulators, p. 208
Section 3 Electrical Energy 3 sessions 1.5 blocks 1. **Describe** the difference between series and parallel circuits. 2. **Recognize** the function of circuit breakers and fuses. 3. **Explain** and calculate electrical power.	National Content Standards: UCP3, A1, B3, (5–8), B6 (9–12), F5 (5–8), G1		**Earth Science Integration,** p. 210 **Science Online,** p. 214 **Math Skills Activity:** Calculating Energy, p. 214 **Activity:** Comparing Series and Parallel Circuits, p. 216 **Science and Language Arts:** The Invisible Man, p. 218

Activity Materials	Reproducible Resources	Section Assessment	Technology
Explore Activity: battery, flashlight bulb, wire	**Chapter Resources Booklet** Foldables Worksheet, p. 15 Note-taking Worksheets, pp. 31–33	Glencoe's Assessment Advantage	
MiniLAB: roll of tape	**Chapter Resources Booklet** Transparency Activity, p. 42 MiniLAB, p. 3 Enrichment, p. 28 Reinforcement, p. 25 Directed Reading, p. 18 **Science Inquiry Labs**, p. 9	**Portfolio** Science Journal, p. 195 **Performance** MiniLAB, p. 200 Skill Builder Activities, p. 201 **Content** Section Assessment, p. 201	Section Focus Transparency Interactive CD-ROM/DVD Guided Reading Audio Program
MiniLAB: 2 bulbs, 2 D-cell batteries **Activity:** battery, flashlight bulb, bulb holder, insulated wire	**Chapter Resources Booklet** Transparency Activity, p. 43 MiniLAB, p. 4 Enrichment, p. 29 Reinforcement, p. 26 Directed Reading, p. 19 Activity Worksheet, pp. 5–6 Lab Activity, pp. 9–12	**Portfolio** Assessmsent, p. 204 **Performance** MiniLAB, p. 204 Skill Builder Activities, p. 207 **Content** Section Assessment, p. 207	Section Focus Transparency Interactive CD-ROM/DVD Guided Reading Audio Program
Activity: 6-V dry-cell battery, 3 small lights with sockets, aluminum foil, transparent tape, scissors, paper *Need materials?* Contact Science Kit at 1-800-828-7777 or www.sciencekit.com on the Internet.	**Chapter Resources Booklet** Transparency Activity, p. 44 Enrichment, p. 30 Reinforcement, p. 27 Directed Reading, pp. 19, 20 Transparency Activity, pp. 45–46 Lab Activity, pp. 13–14 Activity Worksheet, pp. 7–8 **Mathematics Skill Activities**, p. 9	**Portfolio** Earth Science Integration, p. 210 **Performance** Math Skills Activity, p. 214 Skill Builder Activities, p. 215 **Content** Section Assessment, p. 215	Section Focus Transparency Teaching Transparency Interactive CD-ROM/DVD Guided Reading Audio Program

End of Chapter Assessment

Glencoe's Assessment Advantage

Blackline Masters	Technology	Professional Series
Chapter Resources Booklet Chapter Review, pp. 35–36 Chapter Tests, pp. 37–40 **Standardized Test Practice by The Princeton Review**, pp. 32–35	MindJogger Videoquiz CD-ROM Explorations and Quizzes Vocabulary Puzzle Makers ExamView Pro Test Bank Interactive Lesson Planner Interactive Teacher's Edition	Performance Assessment in the Science Classroom (PASC)

Transparencies

Section Focus

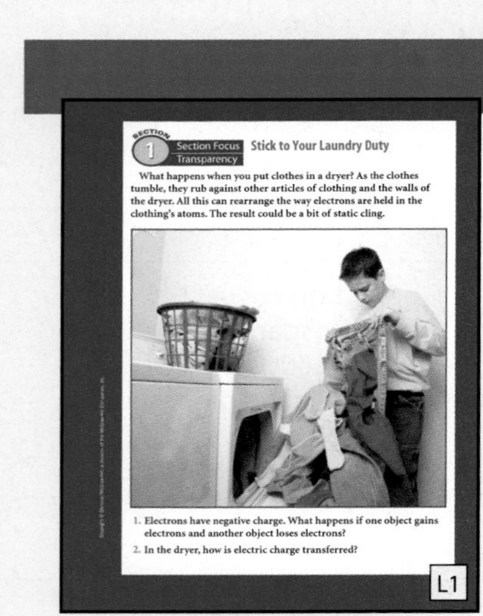

Section 1 Section Focus Transparency **Stick to Your Laundry Duty**

What happens when you put clothes in a dryer? As the clothes tumble, they rub against other articles of clothing and the walls of the dryer. All this can rearrange the way electrons are held in the clothing's atoms. The result could be a bit of static cling.

1. Electrons have negative charge. What happens if one object gains electrons and another object loses electrons?
2. In the dryer, how is electric charge transferred?

L1

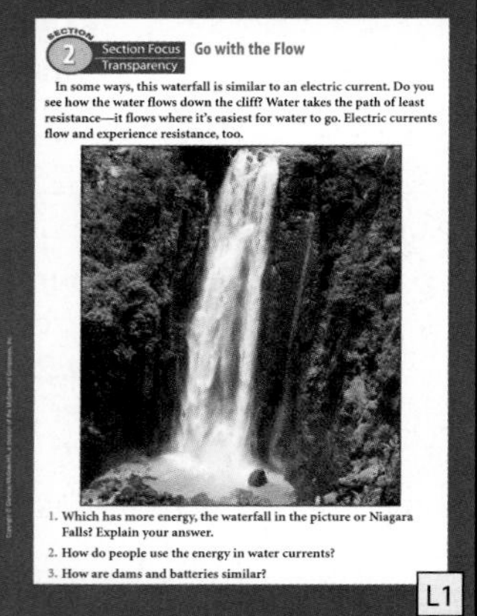

Section 2 Section Focus Transparency **Go with the Flow**

In some ways, this waterfall is similar to an electric current. Do you see how the water flows down the cliff? Water takes the path of least resistance—it flows where it's easiest for water to go. Electric currents flow and experience resistance, too.

1. Which has more energy, the waterfall in the picture or Niagara Falls? Explain your answer.
2. How do people use the energy in water currents?
3. How are dams and batteries similar?

L1

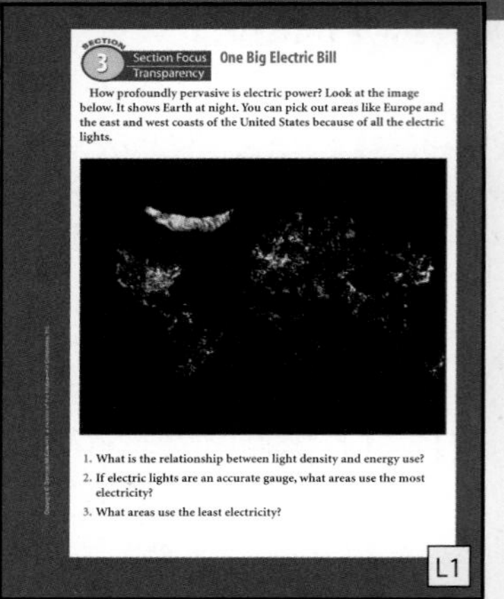

Section 3 Section Focus Transparency **One Big Electric Bill**

How profoundly pervasive is electric power? Look at the image below. It shows Earth at night. You can pick out areas like Europe and the east and west coasts of the United States because of all the electric lights.

1. What is the relationship between light density and energy use?
2. If electric lights are an accurate gauge, what areas use the most electricity?
3. What areas use the least electricity?

L1

This is a representation of key blackline masters available in the Teacher Classroom Resources. See Resource Manager boxes within the chapter for additional information.

Assessment

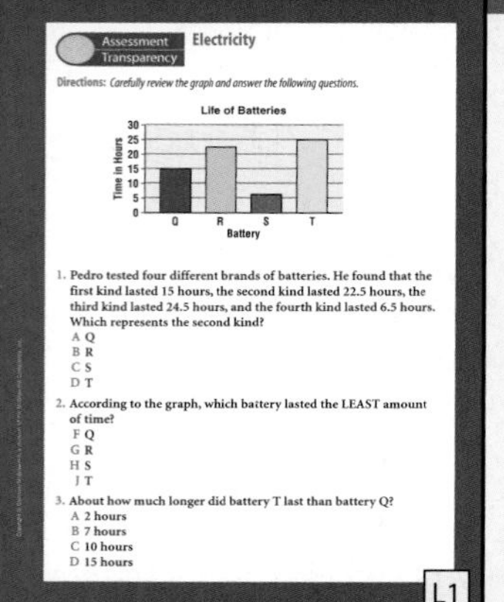

Assessment Transparency **Electricity**

Directions: *Carefully review the graph and answer the following questions.*

1. Pedro tested four different brands of batteries. He found that the first kind lasted 15 hours, the second kind lasted 22.5 hours, the third kind lasted 24.5 hours, and the fourth kind lasted 6.5 hours. Which represents the second kind?
   A Q
   B R
   C S
   D T
2. According to the graph, which battery lasted the LEAST amount of time?
   F Q
   G R
   H S
   J T
3. About how much longer did battery T last than battery Q?
   A 2 hours
   B 7 hours
   C 10 hours
   D 15 hours

L1

Teaching

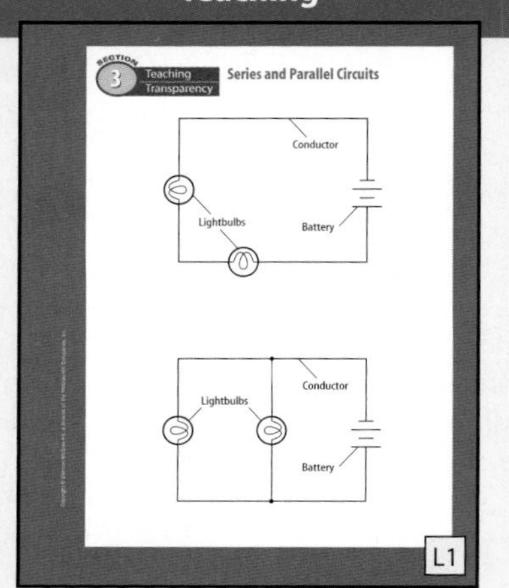

Section 3 Teaching Transparency **Series and Parallel Circuits**

L1

Key to Teaching Strategies

The following designations will help you decide which activities are appropriate for your students.

- L1 Level 1 activities should be appropriate for students with learning difficulties.
- L2 Level 2 activities should be within the ability range of all students.
- L3 Level 3 activities are designed for above-average students.
- ELL ELL activities should be within the ability range of English Language Learners.
- COOP LEARN Cooperative Learning activities are designed for small group work.
- LS Multiple Learning Styles logos are used throughout to indicate strategies that address different learning styles.
- P These strategies represent student products that can be placed into a best-work portfolio.

Hands-on Activities

Activity Worksheets

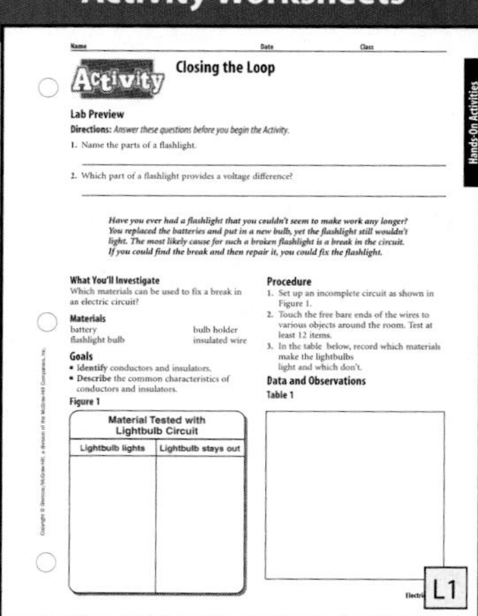

Name Date Class

Activity **Closing the Loop**

Lab Preview

Directions: *Answer these questions before you begin the Activity.*

1. Name the parts of a flashlight.
2. Which part of a flashlight provides a voltage difference?

Have you ever had a flashlight that you couldn't seem to make work any longer? You replaced the batteries and put in a new bulb, yet the flashlight still wouldn't light. The most likely cause for such a broken flashlight is a break in the circuit. If you could find the break and then repair it, you could fix the flashlight.

What You'll Investigate

Which materials can be used to fix a break in an electric circuit?

Materials

battery, flashlight bulb, bulb holder, insulated wire

Goals

- **Identify** conductors and insulators.
- **Describe** the common characteristics of conductors and insulators.

Figure 1

Material Tested with Lightbulb Circuit	
Lightbulb lights	Lightbulb stays out

Procedure

1. Set up an incomplete circuit as shown in Figure 1.
2. Touch the free bare ends of the wires to various objects around the room. Test at least 12 items.
3. In the table below, record which materials make the lightbulbs light and which don't.

Data and Observations

Table 1

Hands-On Activities

L1

Laboratory Activities

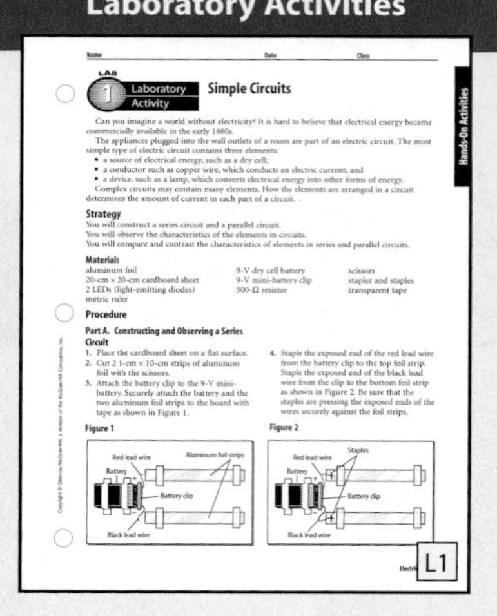

Name Date Class

Lab 1 Laboratory Activity **Simple Circuits**

Can you imagine a world without electricity? It is hard to believe that electrical energy became commercially available in the early 1880s.

The appliances plugged into the wall outlets of a room are part of an electric circuit. The most simple type of electric circuit contains three elements:

- a source of electrical energy, such as a dry cell;
- a conductor such as copper wire, which conducts an electric current; and
- a device, such as a lamp, which converts electrical energy into other forms of energy.

Complex circuits may contain many elements. How the elements are arranged in a circuit determines the amount of current in each part of a circuit.

Strategy

You will construct a series circuit and a parallel circuit.
You will observe the characteristics of the elements in circuits.
You will compare and contrast the characteristics of elements in series and parallel circuits.

Materials

aluminum foil, 20-cm × 20-cm cardboard sheet, 2 LEDs (light-emitting diodes), metric ruler, 9-V dry cell battery, 9-V mini-battery clip, 500-Ω resistor, scissors, stapler and staples, transparent tape

Procedure

Part A. Constructing and Observing a Series Circuit

1. Place the cardboard sheet on a flat surface.
2. Cut 2 1-cm × 10-cm strips of aluminum foil with the scissors.
3. Attach the battery clip to the 9-V mini-battery. Securely attach the battery and the two aluminum foil strips to the board with tape as shown in Figure 1.
4. Staple the exposed end of the red lead wire from the battery clip to the top foil strip. Staple the exposed end of the black lead wire from the clip to the bottom foil strip as shown in Figure 2. Be sure that the staples are pressing the exposed ends of the wires securely against the foil strips.

Figure 1

Figure 2

Hands-On Activities

L1

Meeting Different Ability Levels

Content Outline

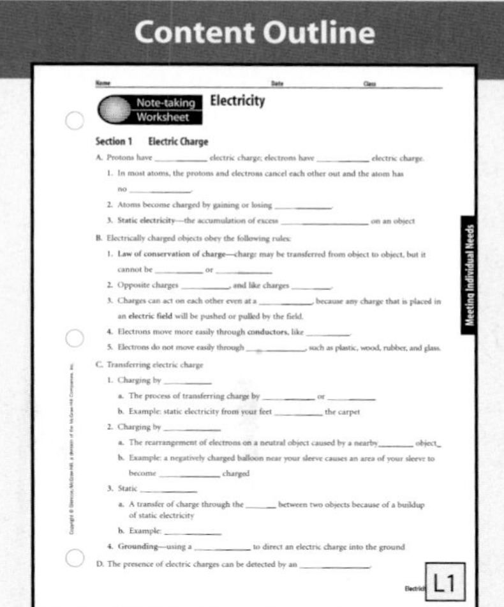

Reinforcement

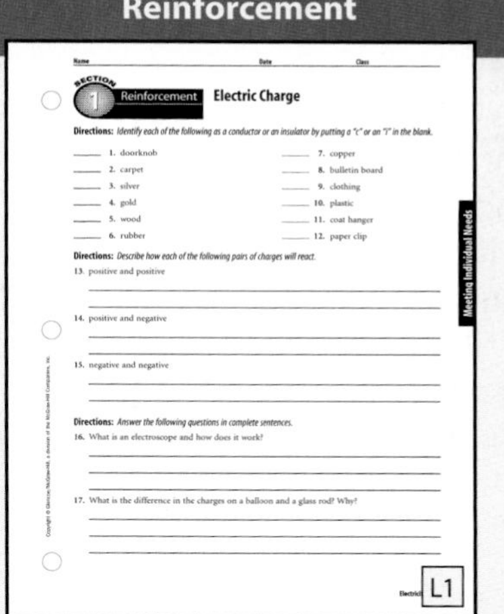

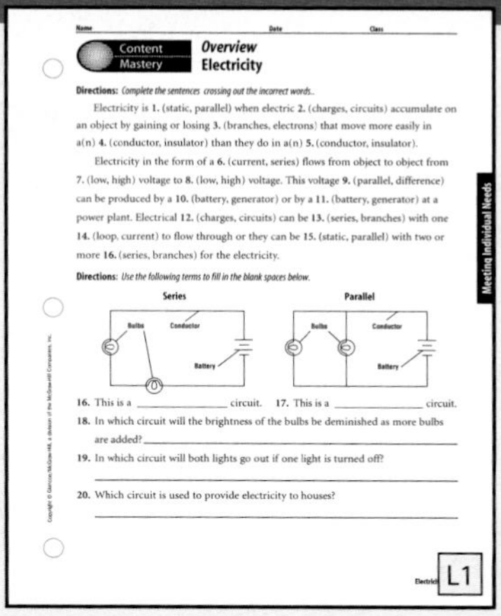

Directed Reading

Enrichment

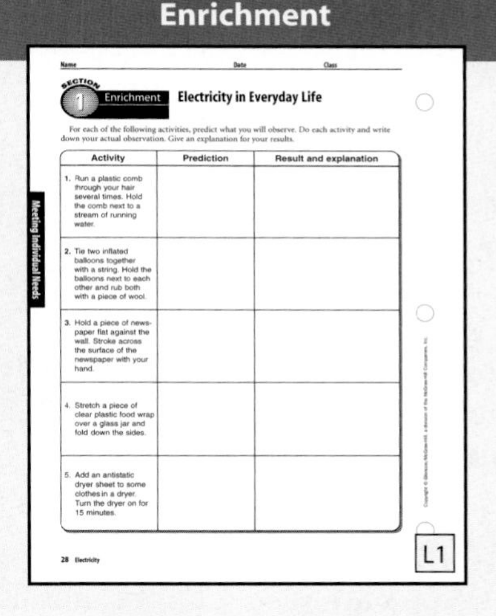

Spanish Directed Reading

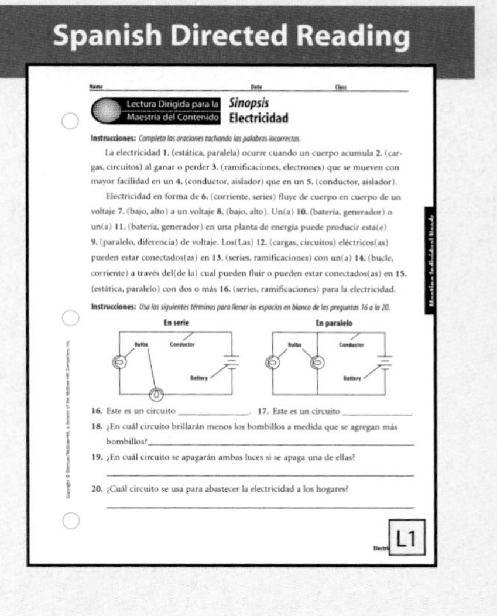

Assessment

Chapter Tests

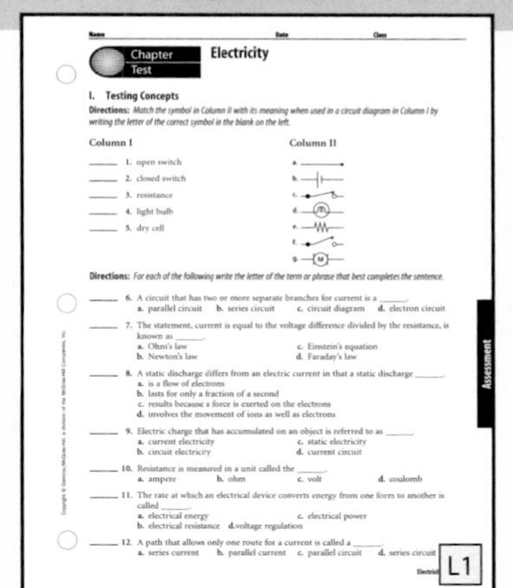

Test Practice Workbook

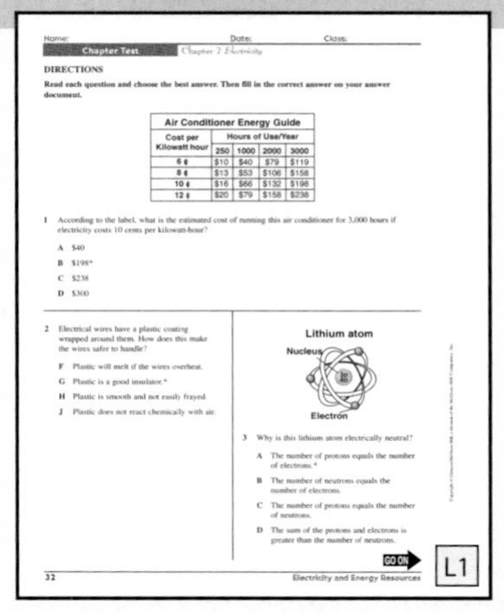

Chapter Review

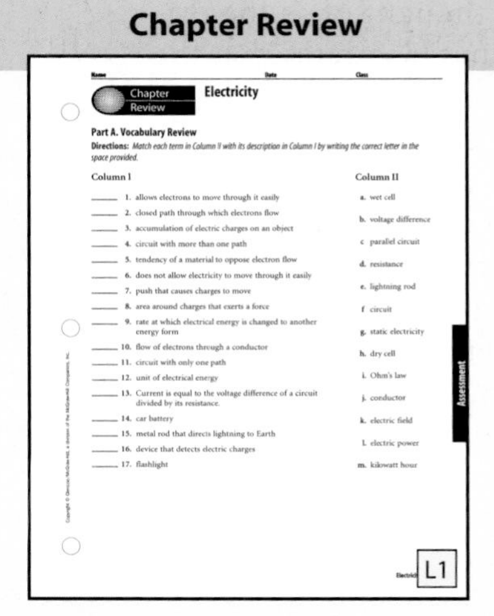

Science Content Background

SECTION 1

Electric Charge

Static Electricity

In static electricity large voltages may be built up but very little current flows.

Waterfalls produce airborne negative charges. Some people believe these charges make us feel happy and healthy. Ion machines were created to produce negative charges in houses and offices.

Transferring Electric Charge

If a neutral object is grounded in the presence of a charged object, the neutral object may gain or lose electrons. If the ground is removed and then the charged object is removed the once neutral object will have a charge opposite that of the original charged object.

Benjamin Franklin invented the lightning rod to protect homes. It was a metal rod that was grounded through a wire. The top of the rod was sharpened to a point. In the year 2000 it was discovered that the rods actually work better if they are not sharpened at the top.

SECTION 2

Electric Current

Charge on the Move

Voltage, or potential difference, is always measured across two points. One volt is defined as one joule per coulomb. Voltage is often thought of as the driving force for current. Ohm's law states that the greater the voltage, the greater the current, with the quantity of current determined by the resistance to the current flow. Resistance converts electrical energy to other forms of energy and lowers the voltage of current passing through. The best way to view voltage is as the amount of energy carried by electricity. Current is a measure of charge flow with units of coulombs per second. Voltage is a measure of how much energy is carried by each coulomb with units of joules per coulomb. This view makes it easy to see that voltage supplies a push for current and that voltage reflects the loss of electrical energy as charges move through a resistor.

Student Misconception

Voltage is the same at different places in a circuit and it exists only when current flows.

Refer to the facing page for teaching strategies to address this misconception. Refer to pages 202–207 for content related to this topic.

Electric current has the unit of the ampere, which is defined as one coulomb per second. One coulomb is equivalent to the charge of 6.25 x 1018 electrons.

SECTION 3

Electrical Energy

Electric Circuits

We pay the electric company for our use of electrical energy. The electrons that transfer electrical energy are not used up in the process; they keep flowing.

In a series circuit with three different resistors, the current at all points in the circuit is the same but the voltage across each resistor is different. In a parallel circuit with three different resistors, the voltage across the resistors is the same but the current is different.

Electrical Power

Electrical power is found by multiplying current (coulombs/second) times voltage (joules/coulomb), giving units of joules/second, which is equivalent to a watt.

SCIENCE Online

For additional content background on this topic, go to the Glencoe Science Web site at science.glencoe.com.

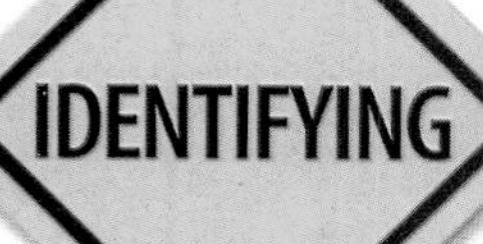

Misconceptions

Find Out What Students Think

Students may think that . . .

- **Voltage is the same at different places in a circuit and it exists only when current flows.**

Because electrons and the flow of charge that make up electricity cannot be seen directly, electricity can be difficult to understand and terms such as voltage, current, power, and energy can be confusing. Of all these terms, voltage is the most abstract and can be the most difficult to grasp. Because of the omnipresence of batteries, students are probably familiar with the volt as a unit of measure. This may conceal their misconceptions about voltage. They may confuse relationships between voltage and current and may come to the wrong conclusion that voltage is a consequence of current and not the cause of it. They also may have inaccurate conceptions of how voltages in a circuit vary.

Activity

Draw the circuit shown in Figure 1 on the board, and ask students to predict and write what the voltages will be between the points A–B, A–C, A–D, B–C, B–D, and C–D.

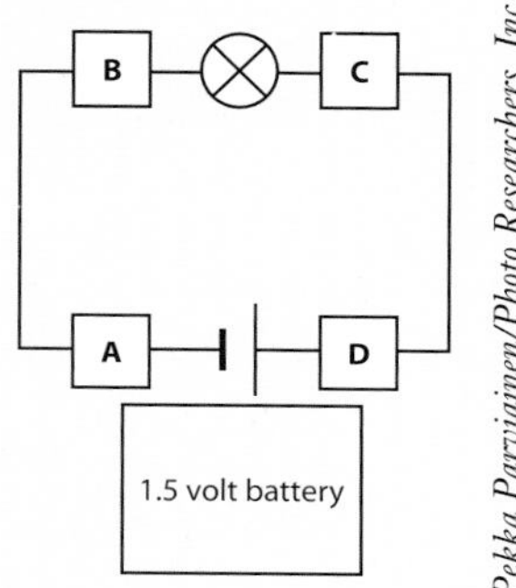

Pekka Parviainen/Photo Researchers, Inc.

Promote Understanding

Activity

Give each group of students four wires, a flashlight bulb in a socket, a D battery in a battery holder, and a voltmeter. Ask students to make a circuit using the battery, bulb, and two wires.

- Instruct them in the use of the voltmeter. Then have them refer to Figure 1 and record the voltages between points A–B, A–C, A–D, B–C, B–D, and C–D.
- The experimental results should show a voltage of approximately 1.5 volts across points A–C, A–D, B–C, and B–D, and an approximate voltage of zero across points A–B and C–D.
- Have them compare their experimental results with the predictions they made in the previous activity.
- Remove the lightbulb and socket from a circuit to leave a gap in the circuit.
- Ask students what they think the voltage across points B–C will now be. Have them share their thoughts and then test their ideas.
- The voltage across the gap should be approximately 1.5 volts.

Assess

After completing the chapter, see *Identifying Misconceptions* in the Study Guide.

CHAPTER 7

Electricity

Chapter Vocabulary

static electricity
law of conservation of charge
conductor
insulator
charging by contact
charging by induction
voltage difference
circuit
electric current
resistance
Ohm's law
series circuit
parallel circuit
electrical power
kilowatt-hour

What do you think?

Science Journal The girl's hair is being affected by static electricity. She has her hand on a Van de Graaff generator. Negative charges transferred to her from the dome of the generator cause her hair to stand on end.

CHAPTER 7

Electricity

A city at night. Lights of every color and size reflect from windows and the river's glassy surface. What makes the lights so bright? Electricity. It not only provides us with light, but also heat, refrigeration, and power to run the countless electrical devices we use every day. Where does electricity come from? How does it get into our homes, schools, and offices? And how can you control it by flicking a switch or pushing a button? In this chapter, you will learn the answers to these questions.

What do you think?

Science Journal Look at the picture below with a classmate. Discuss what this might be or what is happening. Here's a hint: *What force might cause her hair to behave this way?* Write your answer or best guess in your Science Journal.

192

Theme Connection

Energy This chapter explores the fundamental nature of electrical energy—how it is produced, measured, transmitted, and transformed into other forms of energy.

Imagine life before electricity. CD players, refrigerators, dishwashers, TVs, and dozens of other things that make your life comfortable and enjoyable would be impossible without electricity. You wouldn't even have lightbulbs and would have to use candles or oil lamps to provide light at night. So how do these electrical devices work? Explore how electric lights work during this activity.

How many ways?

1. Obtain a battery, a flashlight bulb, and some wire.
2. Arrange the materials so that the lightbulb lights.
3. Record all the ways that you were able to light the bulb.
4. Record a few of the ways that didn't work.
5. Can you light the bulb using only one wire and one battery?

Observe

In your Science Journal, write a paragraph describing the requirements to light the bulb. Write out a procedure for lighting the bulb and have a classmate follow your procedure.

Before You Read

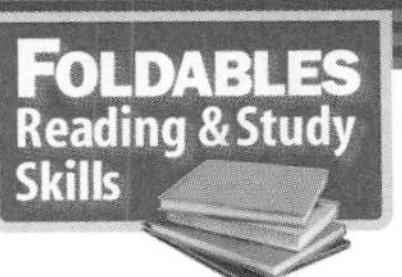

Making a Know-Want-Learn Study Fold **Make the following Foldable to help identify what you already know and what you want to know.**

1. Place a sheet of paper in front of you so the short side is at the top. Fold the paper in half from top to bottom.
2. Fold both sides in to divide the paper into thirds. Unfold the paper so three sections show.
3. Through the top thickness of paper, cut along each of the fold lines to the topfold, forming three tabs. Label the tabs *Know, Want,* and *Learned,* as shown.
4. Before you read the chapter, write what you know under the left tab and what you want to know under the middle tab.
5. As you read the chapter, add to or correct what you have written under the tabs.

Know Want Learned

193

Explore Activity

Purpose The Explore Activity allows students to experiment to make a working circuit. L2 ELL LS **Kinesthetic**

Preparation Strip insulation off the ends of the wire.

Materials C-battery, flashlight bulb, insulated wire, electrical tape or battery holder

Teaching Strategy If battery holders are used, demonstrate how to attach the wires to the clips. If not, show students how to tape the stripped ends of the wires to the battery.

Observe

In order to light the bulb, a continuous circle must be made from the battery, through a wire, to the bottom of the bulb. The circle must then lead from the side of the bulb, through another wire, and back to the battery.

Process Have students make a list of configurations that did NOT light the bulb. Have them infer what was wrong in each. Use **Performance Assessment in the Science Classroom,** p. 109.

Before You Read

Dinah Zike Study Fold

Purpose Use this activity to allow students to review what they know about electricity and list what they would like to know. The resulting Foldable can be used as an assessment tool at the end of the chapter to determine what students have learned.

For additional help, see Foldables Worksheet, p. 15 in **Chapter Resources Booklet,** or go to the Glencoe Science Web site at **science.glencoe.com.** See After You Read in the Study Guide at the end of this chapter.

SECTION

Electric Charge

1 Motivate

Bellringer Transparency

Display the Section Focus Transparency for Section 1. Use the accompanying Transparency Activity Master. L2 ELL

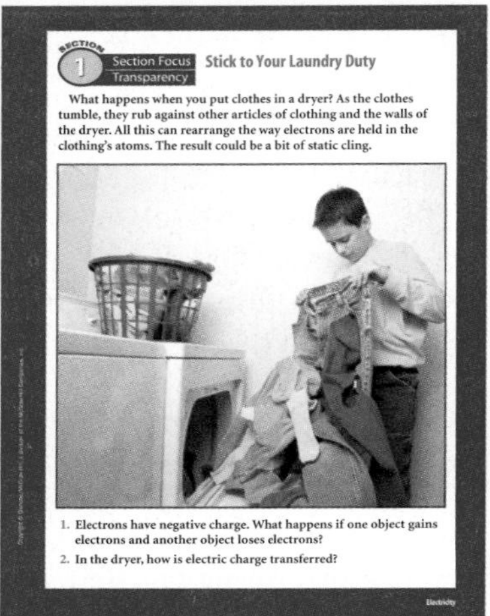

SECTION 1 Section Focus Transparency **Stick to Your Laundry Duty**

What happens when you put clothes in a dryer? As the clothes tumble, they rub against other articles of clothing and the walls of the dryer. All this can rearrange the way electrons are held in the clothing's atoms. The result could be a bit of static cling.

1. Electrons have negative charge. What happens if one object gains electrons and another object loses electrons?
2. In the dryer, how is electric charge transferred?

Electricity

Tie to Prior Knowledge

Ask students whether they have ever noticed clothes sticking together when they are taken out of the dryer. Explain that this is caused by the attractive nature of static electricity, the topic of this section.

SECTION 1

Electric Charge

As You Read

What You'll Learn

- **Describe** the properties of static electricity.
- **Distinguish** between conductors and insulators.
- **Recognize** the presence of charge in an electroscope.

Vocabulary

static electricity
law of conservation of charge
conductor
insulator
charging by contact
charging by induction

Why It's Important

Static electricity can damage electrical equipment and be lethal to humans.

Static Electricity

You know from experience that walking across a carpeted floor and touching something can often result in a shocking experience. What causes this startling and sometimes painful phenomenon?

Electric Charges When your feet rub on the carpet, some of the atoms in the carpet are disturbed. Atoms contain particles called protons, neutrons, and electrons, as shown in **Figure 1.** Protons and electrons have a property called electric charge, and neutrons have no electric charge.

No one knows exactly what electric charge is, but there are two different types of electric charge. Protons have positive electric charge, and electrons have negative electric charge. The amount of positive charge on a proton is exactly equal to the amount of negative charge on an electron. An atom contains equal numbers of protons and electrons, so the positive and negative charges cancel out and an atom has no net electric charge. Objects such as shoes and carpets are made of atoms and usually have no net electric charge. Objects with no net charge are said to be neutral.

Building Up Charge Some atoms hold their electrons more tightly than other atoms. For example, atoms in your shoes hold their electrons more tightly than atoms in the carpet. As you walk on carpet, some electrons that are loosely held by the atoms in the carpet are transferred to your shoes. Your shoes gain electrons and then have more electrons than protons. Because your shoes have an excess of negative charge, your shoes are said to be negatively charged. The carpet loses electrons and has more protons than electrons. Because the carpet has an excess of positive charge, it is positively charged. This is an example of static electricity. **Static electricity** is the accumulation of excess electric charges on an object. Can you think of other examples of static electricity?

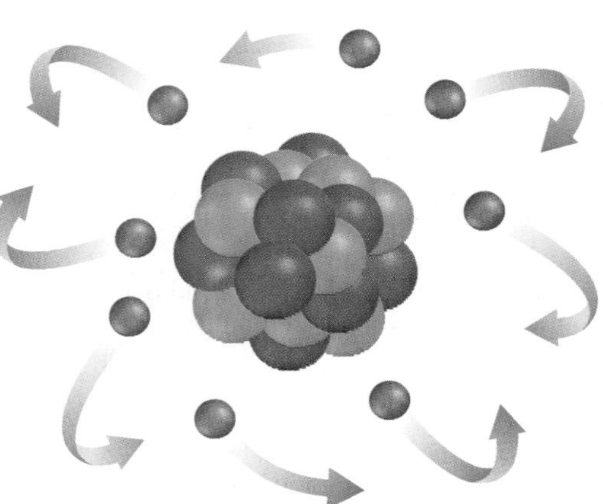

Figure 1
The center of an atom contains protons (orange) and neutrons (blue). Electrons (red) swarm around the atom's center.

Section Assessment Planner

Portfolio
- Science Journal, p. 195

Performance Assessment
Try at Home MiniLAB, p. 200
Skill Builder Activities, p. 201
See page 222 for more options.

Content Assessment
Section, p. 201
Challenge, p. 201
Chapter, pp. 222–223

A Before rubbing

B After rubbing

Figure 2
A Before the shoes scuff against the carpet, the shoes and the carpet have equal numbers of electrons and protons. This balance means the shoes and the carpet have no net charge. B Later, as electrons move from the carpet to the shoes, the shoes become negatively charged and the carpet becomes positively charged.

Conservation of Charge It is important to remember that when an object becomes charged, charge is neither created nor destroyed. Electrons simply have moved from one object to another. For example, before you rub your shoes against the carpet, your shoes and the carpet have equal numbers of electrons and protons. Your shoes and the carpet have no net charge and are electrically neutral, as shown in **Figure 2A.** After rubbing the carpet, your shoes gain electrons from the carpet and become negatively charged. The carpet, which now has more protons than electrons, is positively charged, as shown in **Figure 2B.** According to the **law of conservation of charge,** charge can be transferred from object to object, but it cannot be created or destroyed. In every case, when an object becomes charged, electric charges have moved.

Reading Check *How does an object acquire charge?*

Opposites Attract As shown in **Figure 3,** electrically charged objects obey two rules—opposite charges attract, and like charges repel. Have you noticed how clothes sometimes cling together when removed from the drier? While the clothes tumble around, electrons are transferred from fabrics that hold their electrons loosely to those that hold their electrons tightly. Clothes that gain electrons become negatively charged and cling to clothes that have lost electrons and are positively charged. Clothes that are oppositely charged attract each other and stick together.

Figure 3
The only two kinds of electric charge are positive and negative. *How do charged objects interact with each other?*

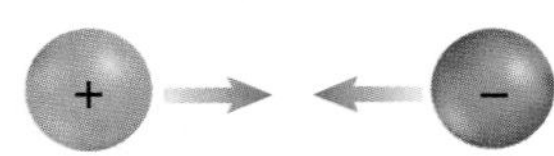

Opposite charges attract

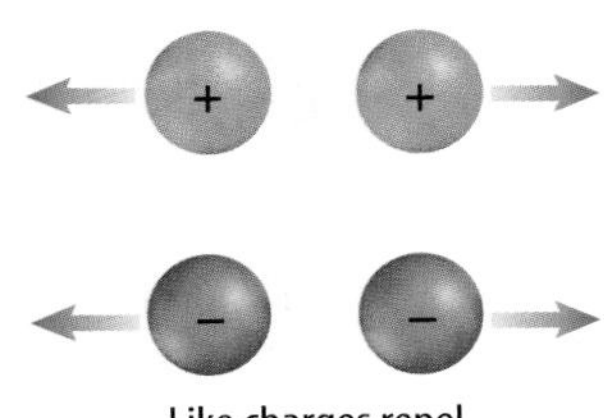

Like charges repel

2 Teach

Static Electricity

Text Question Answer

Possible answers: the charge on computer and television screens, "flyaway" hair on a dry day

Activity

Have students use balloons, glass rods, polystyrene, puffed cereal, and pieces of silk and wool cloth to explore the ideas of positive and negative charge and the law of conservation of charge. L2 ELL IS **Kinesthetic**

Use an Analogy

Reinforce the idea that electrons, not atoms, move to cause electricity by describing an atom as being like a swarm of bees (the electrons) around honey (the tightly held protons and neutrons). L1 IS **Visual-Spatial**

Caption Answer

Figure 3 Objects with like charge repel each other; objects with opposite charge attract each other.

Reading Check

Answer Electrons move from one object to another. The object that gains electrons becomes negatively charged. The one that loses electrons becomes positively charged.

Resource Manager

Chapter Resources Booklet
Transparency Activity, p. 42
Note-taking Worksheets, pp. 31–33
Directed Reading for Content Mastery, p. 18

Science Journal

Flyaway Hair Have students write a paragraph in their journals in which they use conservation of charge to explain why hair combed on a dry day may become "flyaway hair." Before combing, both the comb and hair have equal numbers of positive and negative charges. Combing causes hair to lose electrons to the comb. The hairs then have like charges on them and repel one another. This makes them fly away. P

Conductors and Insulators

Discussion

Explain that, when substances are categorized as conductors, semiconductors, and insulators, they are being ranked according to the ease with which electrons move around in them (their conductivity). Then have students explain, in terms of electrons, the two extreme limits of conductivity; that is, what would zero conductivity mean and what would the maximum possible conductivity mean? Zero conductivity means that no charge carriers can move. Maximum conductivity means that all charge carriers are free to move.
L2 IS **Logical-Mathematical**

Use Science Words

Word Meaning Students may have heard the word *semiconductor.* A semiconductor is a material, such as silicon or germanium, that is neither a good insulator nor a good conductor, but becomes a good conductor when a tiny impurity is added to it. Have students find what semiconductors are used for. Semiconductors are used in computer chips and to make electronic components such as transistors and diodes.
L3 IS **Linguistic**

Figure 4
Surrounding every charge is an electric field. Through the electric field, a charge is able to push or pull on another charge.

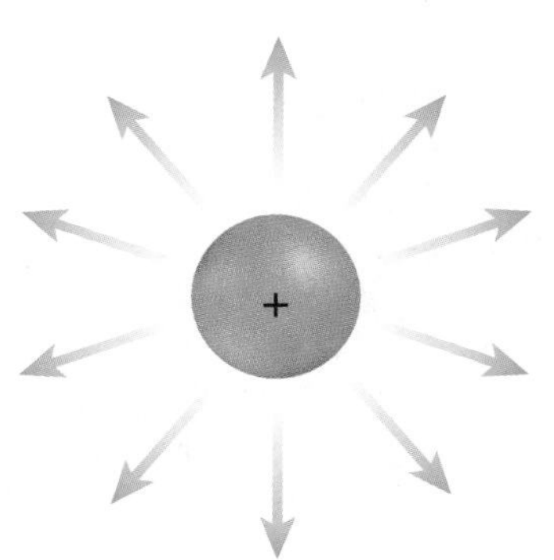

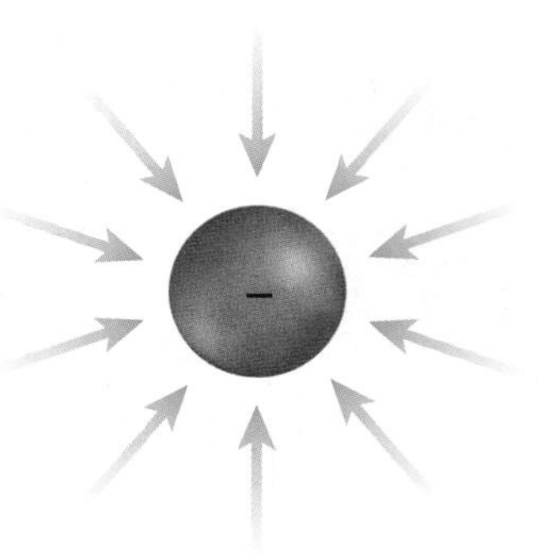

Force at a Distance You might have seen bits of tissue paper fly up and stick to a charged balloon. The balloon didn't even have to touch the bits of paper. The force of gravity behaves in the same way. A football in the air does not need to touch Earth for gravity to act on it. Likewise, the bits of paper do not need to touch the charged balloon for an electric force to act on them. If the balloon and the paper are not touching, what causes the paper to move?

An electric field surrounds every electric charge, as shown in **Figure 4.** The electric field exerts the force that causes other electric charges to move. Any charge that is placed in an electric field will be pushed or pulled by the field. Electric fields are represented by lines with arrows drawn away from positive charges and toward negative charges. The arrows show how the electric field would make a positive charge move.

Figure 5
As you walk across a carpeted floor, your body builds up a static charge. When you reach for a metal doorknob, the charges flow between your hand and the doorknob and you feel a shock.

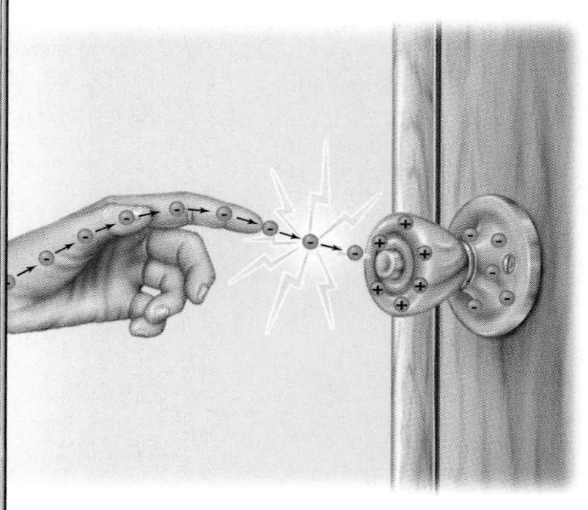

Conductors and Insulators

If you reach for a metal doorknob after walking across a carpet, you could feel a shock and see a spark. The spark is caused by excess electrons moving from your hand to the doorknob. Excess electrons were transferred from the carpet to your shoes. How did excess electrons move from your shoes to your hand?

Conductors Look at **Figure 5.** An excess of electrons can move more easily through some materials, called **conductors,** than through others. Electrons on your shoes repel each other and some are pushed onto your skin. Because your skin is a conductor, the electrons spread out over your skin and onto your hand. The metal doorknob is also a conductor.

Curriculum Connection

Ancient Greeks and Electricity Have students research what ancient Greeks knew about electricity. Ancient people knew that if amber was rubbed, it would become charged. Elektron is Greek for amber. L2 IS **Linguistic**

Visual Learning

Figure 5 On a dry day, bring in pieces of wool carpeting to have students reproduce the effects shown. Have them explain the transfer of charges that occur. L1 ELL IS **Visual-Spatial**

Metallic Conductors Excellent conductors of electricity are metals. The atoms in metals have electrons that are able to move easily through the material. For this reason, electric wires usually are made of metals, such as copper, which is one of the best conductors. Gold and silver wire are also excellent conductors of electricity but are much more expensive than copper.

Insulators Wires in cords attached to telephones and other household appliances are coated with some type of insulating material. An **insulator** is a material that doesn't allow electrons to move through it easily. Most plastics are insulators. Electrons are held strongly to atoms in insulating materials. The plastic coating around electric wires prevents a dangerous electrical shock when you touch the wire, as shown in **Figure 6.** In addition to plastic, other good insulators are wood, rubber, and glass.

Reading Check *What is an insulator?*

Transferring Electric Charge

Objects can become charged in several ways. Perhaps the most familiar situations are a static charge resulting from contact. For example, you probably have felt a charge on your own body after combing your hair on a dry day. You might have noticed socks being attracted to each other after they have been rubbed together in a clothes drier. Rubbing two materials together can result in a transfer of electrons between the objects. Then one object is left with a positive charge and the other with an equal amount of negative charge. The process of transferring charge by touching or rubbing is called **charging by contact.**

Figure 6
The plastic coating around wires is an insulator. A damaged electrical cord is hazardous when the conducting wire is exposed.

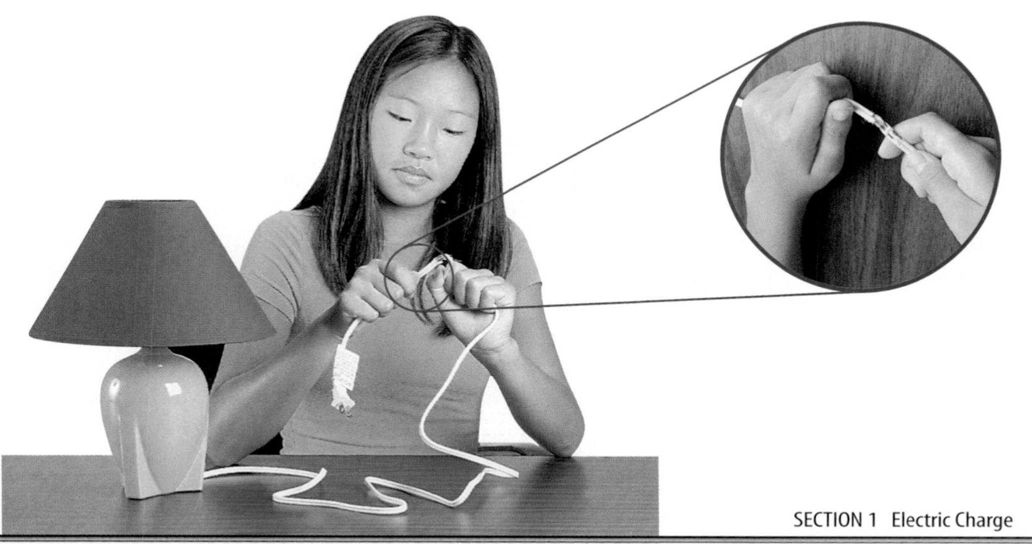

Extension

Have students investigate various conductors and insulators. Suggest that they design and make a circuit to test these objects. They also should make a chart to show which items are conductors and which are insulators. L3 **Kinesthetic**

Reading Check

Answer a material that doesn't allow electrons to move through it easily

Transferring Electric Charge

Fun Fact

The process of charging by contact is known as *triboelectricity*. The triboelectric properties of materials are of significant interest to scientists working on missions to Mars. The dry, windy conditions on Mars provide an ideal environment for triboelectric charging.

Extension

Have students research and report on how fabric softeners prevent excess electric charge on clothes. Fabric softeners coat laundry with chemicals that reduce wrinkling. The chemicals also help laundry retain moisture, which allows excess charge to dissipate. L3 **Linguistic**

Teacher FYI

The process of charge transfer by rubbing is often called *charging by friction.* This term can be misleading because the process requires only close contact, not friction. The rubbing, however, does increase the area of contact, thereby enhancing the charge transfer.

Active Reading

Cause-and Effect Chart This strategy is used to focus on cause-and-effect relationships. Have students design a Cause-and-Effect Chart for static electricity. In the center, students write the topic that they are trying to understand, in this case, static electricity. To the left, they write the apparent causes of static electricity. On the right, they write the apparent effects of static electricity.

Resource Manager 

Chapter Resources Booklet
Enrichment, p. 28

Transferring Electric Charge, continued

Caption Answer

Figure 7 from the sweater to the balloon

Discussion

Why are you more likely to get shocked when you touch a door handle in the winter than in the summer? In winter, the air in homes and buildings is often dry. Dry air is an insulator and doesn't easily discharge the excess charge on your body. The charge is therefore more likely to discharge to door handles.

Use Science Words

Word Meaning Ask students to look up the word *static* and tell one reason that this word is appropriate for the term *static electricity* and one reason that the word is misleading. The word static means "not moving." It is true that static electricity is not in continual motion like current electricity. However, a static discharge is far from motionless; it is a very rapid, though noncontinuous, transfer of charge. LS **Linguistic**

IDENTIFYING Misconceptions

Students may have heard the tale of Benjamin Franklin's kite being struck by lightning. Fortunately, the kite was *not* struck by lightning, but sparks Franklin observed during the experiment enabled him to show (as French scientists had done a month before) the relation between lightning and electricity.

Figure 7
The negatively charged balloon induces a positively charged area in the sleeve by repelling electrons from the surface. *What is the direction of the force between the balloon and the sweater?*

Charging at a Distance
Because electrical forces act at a distance, charged objects brought near a neutral object will cause electrons to rearrange their positions on the neutral object. Suppose you charge a balloon by rubbing it with a cloth. If you bring the negatively charged balloon near your sleeve, the extra electrons on the balloon repel the electrons in the sleeve. The electrons near the sleeve's surface move away from the balloon, leaving a positively charged area on the surface of the sleeve, as shown in **Figure 7.** As a result, the negatively charged balloon attracts the positively charged area of the sleeve. The rearrangement of electrons on a neutral object caused by a nearby charged object is called **charging by induction.** The sweater was charged by induction. The balloon will now cling to the sweater, being held there by an electrical force.

Lightning Have you ever seen lightning strike Earth? Lightning is a large static discharge. A static discharge is a transfer of charge through the air between two objects because of a buildup of static electricity. A thundercloud is a mighty generator of static electricity. As air masses move and swirl in the cloud, areas of positive and negative charge build up. Eventually, enough charge builds up to cause a static discharge between the cloud and the ground. As the electric charges move through air, they collide with atoms and molecules. These collisions cause the atoms and molecules in air to emit light. You see this light as a spark, as shown in **Figure 8.**

Thunder Not only does lightning produce a brilliant flash of light, it also generates a tremendous shock wave. The electrical energy in a lightning bolt rips electrons off atoms in the atmosphere and produces great amounts of heat, warming the surrounding air to temperatures as high as 30,000°C—several times hotter than the Sun's surface. The heat causes air in the bolt's path to expand rapidly, producing sound waves that you hear as thunder.

The sudden discharge of so much energy can be dangerous. It is estimated that Earth is struck by lightning more than 100 times every second. It can cause power outages, injury, loss of life, and fires.

SCIENCE Online

Collect Data Visit the Glencoe Science Web site at **science.glencoe.com** for an online update of lightning strikes each day. Communicate to your class what you learn.

SCIENCE Online
Internet Addresses

Explore the Glencoe Science Web site at **science.glencoe.com** to find out more about topics in this section.

Science Journal

Thunderstorm Safety You often hear the warning, "Don't stand near a tree during a thunderstorm." Ask students to explain the reasoning behind this warning based on what they have learned in this section. Trees are more susceptible to lightning strikes because they are often the tallest objects around. If you are near the tree, you are more likely to be charged by induction and suffer static discharge from the tree.

Figure 8

Storm clouds form when humid, sun-warmed air rises to meet a colder air layer. As these air masses churn together, the stage is set for the explosive electrical display we call lightning. Lightning strikes when negative charges at the bottom of a storm cloud are attracted to positive charges on the ground.

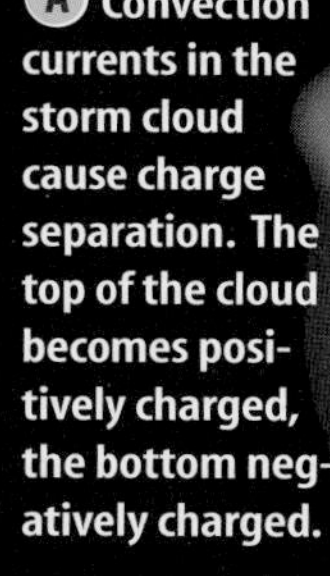

A Convection currents in the storm cloud cause charge separation. The top of the cloud becomes positively charged, the bottom negatively charged.

B Negative charges on the bottom of the cloud induce a positive charge on the ground below the cloud by repelling negative charges in the ground.

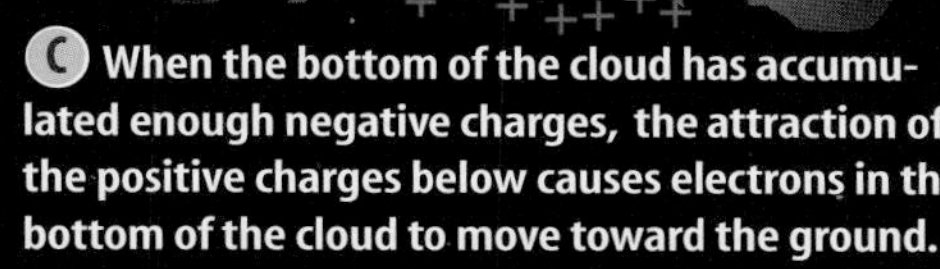

C When the bottom of the cloud has accumulated enough negative charges, the attraction of the positive charges below causes electrons in the bottom of the cloud to move toward the ground.

D When the electrons get close to the ground, they attract positive charges that surge upward, completing the connection between cloud and ground. This is the spark you see as a lightning flash.

INTRA-CLOUD LIGHTNING can occur ten times more often in a storm than cloud-to-ground lightning and never strikes Earth.

199

Visualizing Lightning

Have students examine the pictures and read the captions. Then ask the following questions.

- **When the warm humid air rises to meet the cold air, what causes the air masses to churn together?** convection currents
- **What electrical property causes the negative charges in the cloud to be attracted to the positive charges in the ground?** like charges repel and unlike charges attract
- **Why does the ground below a cloud have a concentration of positive charges?** because the negative charges in the bottom of the cloud repel the negative charges in the ground and attract the positive charges

Activity

Have students research the different types of lightning and have them make posters illustrating them. If possible, students also could include statistical data involving the number of strikes that occur per year in their area. L2

LS **Visual-Spatial**

Extension

Challenge students to find out more about storm chasers. These professionals intentionally go to areas where tornadoes, hurricanes, typhoons, etc. are occurring to study them. Students should report to the class what they learn.

Resource Manager

Science Inquiry Labs, p. 9

Transferring Electric Charge, continued

Text Question Answer

Possible answers: faucet (if plumbing is metal), electrical outlet ground

Detecting Electric Charge

Purpose Students analyze how charged objects interact with each other. L1 ELL

LS **Kinesthetic**

Materials transparent tape

Teaching Strategy Cellophane tape often works, but transparent tape is better.

Analysis

1. The tapes attracted each other because they had opposite charges. When pulled apart, one became positively charged and one became negatively charged.
2. The pieces of tape repelled each other because they had like charges. Pulling both strips off the surface charged each the same.

Process Have students write up the procedures and results for this MiniLAB as lab reports. Use **Performance Assessment in the Science Classroom,** p. 119.

Figure 9
A lightning rod directs the charge from a lightning bolt safely to the ground.

Investigating Charged Objects

Procedure

1. Fold over about 1 cm on the end of a **roll of tape** to make a handle. Tear off a strip of tape about 10 cm long.
2. Stick the strip on a clean, dry, smooth surface, such as a countertop. Make another identical strip and stick it directly on top of the first.
3. Pull both pieces off the counter together and pull them apart. Then bring the nonsticky sides of both tapes together. What happens?
4. Now stick the two strips of tape side by side on the smooth surface. Pull them off and bring the nonsticky sides near each other again.

Analysis

1. What happened when you first brought the pieces close together? Were they charged alike or opposite? What might have caused this?
2. What did you observe when you brought the pieces together the second time? How were they charged? What did you do differently that might have changed the behavior?

Grounding The sensitive electronics in a computer can be harmed by large static discharges. A discharge can occur any time that charge builds up in one area. Providing a path for charge to reach Earth prevents any charge from building up. Earth is a large, neutral object that is also a conductor of charge. Any object connected to Earth by a good conductor will transfer any excess electric charge. Connecting an object to Earth with a conductor is called grounding. For example, buildings often have a metal lightning rod that provides a conducting path from the highest point on the building to the ground to prevent damage by lightning, as shown in **Figure 9.**

Plumbing fixtures, such as metal faucets, sinks, and pipes, often provide a convenient ground connection. Look around. Do you see anything that might act as a path to the ground?

Detecting Electric Charge

The presence of electric charges can be detected by an electroscope. One kind of electroscope is made of two thin, metal leaves attached to a metal rod with a knob at the top. The leaves are allowed to swing freely from the metal rod. When the device is not charged, the leaves hang straight down, as shown in **Figure 10A.**

Suppose a negatively charged balloon touches the knob. Because the metal is a good conductor, electrons travel down the rod into the leaves. Both leaves become negatively charged as they gain electrons, as shown in **Figure 10B.** Because the leaves have similar charges, they repel each other.

If a glass rod is rubbed with silk, electrons are pulled from the atoms in the glass rod and build up on the silk. The glass rod becomes positively charged.

Visual Learning

Figure 9 The lightening rod's long, narrow shape causes charges induced into it to bunch together and repulse one another. This strong repulsion discharges onto nearby air molecules producing an effect known as a *corona discharge.* Excess electrical charge is thereby dissipated, and the likelihood of a lightening strike reduced. Look for lightening rods on buildings in your area. L2 LS **Visual-Spatial**

Resource Manager

Chapter Resources Booklet

MiniLAB, p. 3

Reinforcement, p. 25

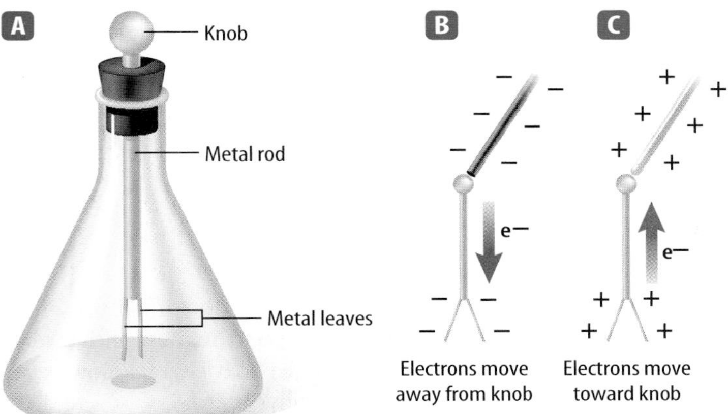

Figure 10
Notice the position of the leaves on the electroscope when they are A uncharged, B negatively charged, and C positively charged. *How can you tell whether an electroscope is positively or negatively charged?*

When the positively charged glass rod is brought into contact with the metal knob of an uncharged electroscope, electrons flow out of the metal leaves and onto the rod. The leaves repel each other because each leaf becomes positively charged as it loses electrons, as shown in **Figure 10C.**

Think of any other examples of static electricity that you have seen. Can you explain them in terms of like or opposite charges? How do objects become charged, and what happens when they discharge?

Section 1 Assessment

1. What is static electricity?
2. Distinguish between electrical conductors and insulators and give an example of each.
3. How is lightning produced?
4. How do like charges affect each other? Unlike charges? What could you use to detect the presence of electric charges?
5. **Think Critically** Assume you have already charged an electroscope with a positively charged glass rod. Hypothesize what would happen if you touched the knob again with another positively charged object.

Skill Builder Activities

6. **Drawing Conclusions** Suppose you observe that the individual hairs on your arm rise up when a balloon is placed near them. Using the concept of induction and the rules of static electricity, what could you conclude about the cause of this phenomenon? **For more help, refer to the Science Skill Handbook.**
7. **Communicating** Moist air is a better conductor than dry air. It is more difficult to observe events related to static electricity, such as clothes clinging or hair standing out, on humid days when the air is moist. In your Science Journal, explain how humidity affects static electricity. **For more help, refer to the Science Skill Handbook.**

Caption Answer

Figure 10 by the charge on the material in contact with the knob

Text Question Answer

Possible answers: In a television set, a negative charge on the inside of the cathode-ray tube induces a net positive charge on the outside of the screen. Objects become charged by contact with a charged object or by induction. When they discharge, there is a very rapid, noncontinuous transfer of charge.

3 Assess

Reteach

Use an electroscope to touch various objects, some of which are charged. Have students discuss the results based on what they have learned. L1 ELL

LS **Visual-Spatial**

Challenge

Electrons and protons are electrically attracted to each other. However, all particles with mass are gravitationally attracted to each other. **Why do we ignore gravitational effects when we discuss the attraction of electrons and protons?** The masses of the particles are so small that the gravitational attraction is insignificant compared to the electrical attraction. L3

LS **Logical-Mathematical**

Content Have students create posters showing different methods of transferring electric charge. Use **PASC,** p. 145.

Answers to Section Assessment

1. the accumulation of excess electric charge on an object
2. A conductor, such as copper, allows electrons to move easily through it; an insulator, such as wood or glass, doesn't allow electrons to pass easily through it.
3. Lightning occurs when excess negative charge in clouds discharges to regions of positive charge on the ground or in other clouds. This heats the nearby air, causing it to rapidly expand, producing sound waves we call thunder.
4. Like charges repel each other; unlike charges attract each other; a charged object.
5. The leaves would move farther apart.
6. The charged balloon induces an opposite charge on the hairs.
7. Humidity allows continual conduction of charge, so there is less chance of excess charge on objects, and thus less static electricity.

SECTION 2

Electric Current

1 Motivate

Bellringer Transparency

Display the Section Focus Transparency for Section 2. Use the accompanying Transparency Activity Master. L2 ELL

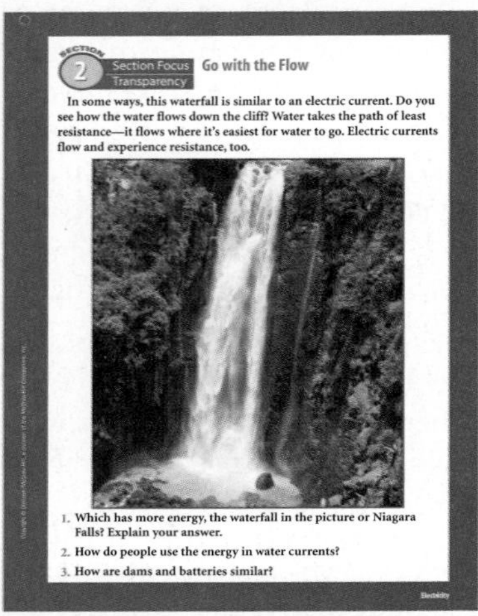

SECTION 2 Section Focus Transparency **Go with the Flow**

In some ways, this waterfall is similar to an electric current. Do you see how the water flows down the cliff? Water takes the path of least resistance—it flows where it's easiest for water to go. Electric currents flow and experience resistance, too.

1. **Which has more energy, the waterfall in the picture or Niagara Falls? Explain your answer.**
2. **How do people use the energy in water currents?**
3. **How are dams and batteries similar?**

Electricity

Tie to Prior Knowledge

Ask students if they have ever tried to play a CD in a portable CD player only to find that the batteries were dead. Ask students what they know about what happens when a battery dies. Explain that when it dies, the battery stops producing enough electric current to operate the CD player. Tell students that in this section, they will learn what an electric current is and how it is produced.

SECTION 2

Electric Current

As You Read

What You'll Learn

- **Describe** how electric current is different from static electricity.
- **Explain** how a dry cell provides a source of voltage difference.
- **Describe** the relationship among voltage difference, resistance, and current.

Vocabulary

voltage difference
circuit
electric current
resistance
Ohm's law

Why It's Important

Without electric current, many devices would not exist, including telephones, personal computers, and lighting.

Charge on the Move

You just learned that if you touch a conductor after building up a negative charge on your body, electrons will move from you to the conductor. You also learned that charges flow easily through a conductor. Do you know why?

Electrical Pressure To understand this question, think about water. Why does water flow? To answer, you might develop a rule—water will flow from a place where the pressure is high to a place where the pressure is low, as in **Figure 11A.** Air also follows this rule, as wind always blows from a high-pressure region to a lower-pressure region. For water or air to flow, a pressure difference must exist. To explain why charges flow, a similar rule can be developed. Charges flow from high-voltage areas to low-voltage areas. Voltage is like an electrical pressure that pushes charge. Just as water or air must have a pressure difference to flow, a voltage difference must be present for electric charges to flow, as shown in **Figure 11B.** A **voltage difference** is the push that causes charges to move and is measured in volts (V).

Reading Check *What do electric charges need in order to flow?*

Look at **Figure 12A.** The water flows because the pump supplies pressure to push water through the loop. The turbine makes use of the flowing water to do work. The turbine might turn gears in a machine or connect to a generator to produce electricity.

Figure 11
Water pressure and voltage are similar.

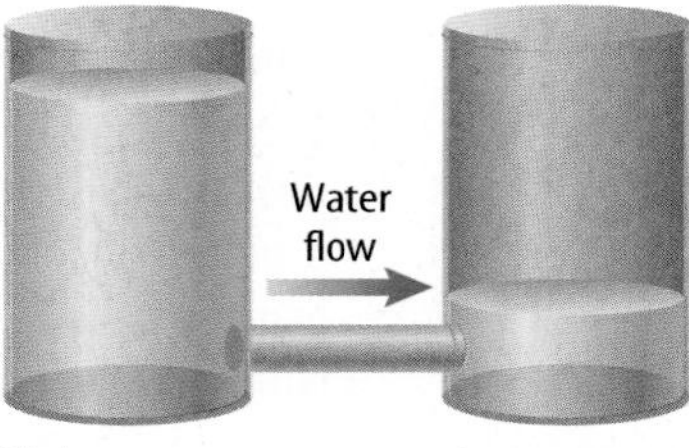

A **A pressure difference causes water to flow.**

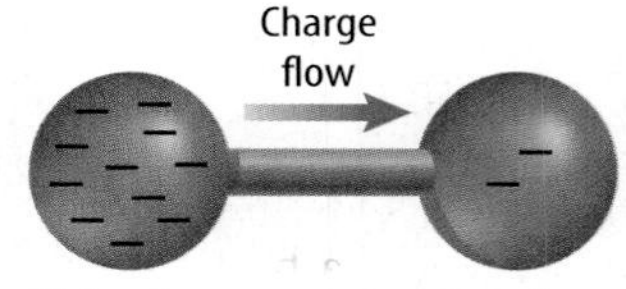

B **A voltage difference causes charge to flow.**

Section Assessment Planner

PORTFOLIO
Assessment, p. 204

PERFORMANCE ASSESSMENT
MiniLAB, p. 204
Skill Builder Activities, p. 207
See page 222 for more options.

CONTENT ASSESSMENT
Section, p. 207
Challenge, p. 207
Chapter, pp. 222–223

Figure 12
Although the systems are not exactly alike, the similarities between a water pipe and an electrical circuit are helpful to consider.

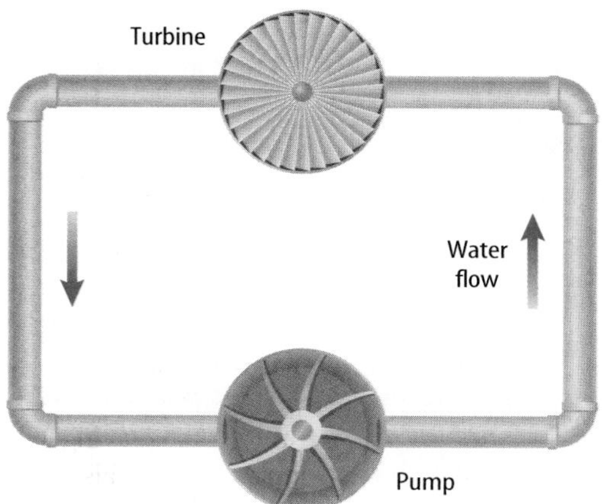

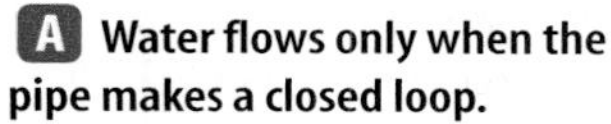

A **Water flows only when the pipe makes a closed loop.**

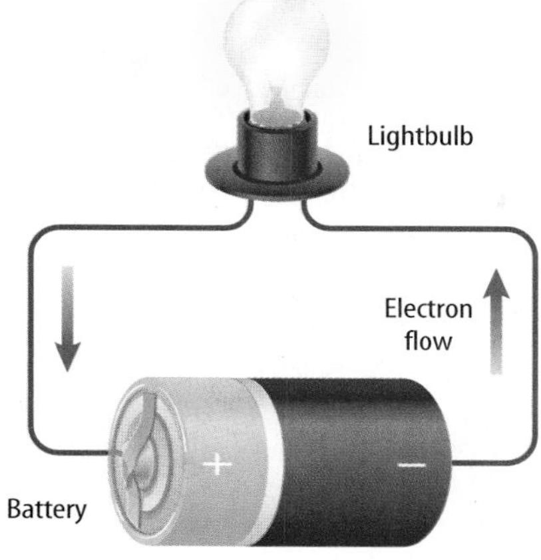

B **Electric charge flows only when the wire makes a closed loop.**

Closed Loop In **Figure 12A,** what would happen if the pipe broke? Rather quickly the water would stop flowing. For water to continue to flow, the pipe must always make a closed loop. The same must be true for charges flowing in a wire. For charges to flow, the wire must always be connected in a closed loop, or circuit. A **circuit** is a closed, conducting path, as shown in **Figure 12B.**

The flow of charges through a wire or any conductor is called **electric current.** The electric current in a circuit is measured in amperes (A). Current is almost always the flow of electrons. Protons have charge, but they are locked deep within the center of atoms and do not move. Only the outer, loosely held electrons are free to move.

Batteries

In a static discharge, charges move from one place to another in a short period of time. In order to keep the current moving continuously through a circuit, a device must be present that maintains a voltage difference. One common source of a voltage difference is a battery. Portable radios and flashlights use the voltage difference provided by batteries for power. Batteries also are used to provide the energy needed to start a car. How do batteries cause an electric current to flow?

Resource Manager

Chapter Resources Booklet
- Transparency Activity, p. 43
- Directed Reading for Content Mastery, p. 19

Home and Community Involvement, p. 25

Teacher FYI

A 9-volt battery is actually composed of six small 1.5-volt batteries connected in series. A 12-volt car battery is a series of six 2-volt batteries.

2 Teach

Charge on the Move

IDENTIFYING Misconceptions

Students may believe that positive charges flow through wires. Early researchers labeled the direction of current flow from the positive terminal of a battery to the negative terminal. This established the convention. After the discovery of the electron, researchers realized that the electrons actually move from the negative terminal to the positive terminal. Today we talk about conventional current, which is the direction of the hypothetical flow of positive ions, yet we realize that electron flow is a better representation of what happens in a wire. It is important for students to learn these distinctions and to realize that positive charges do not flow through the wire.

Reading Check

Answer a voltage difference

Batteries

Quick Demo

Place a strip of copper and a strip of zinc (or silver) into a glass containing lemon juice, tomato juice, or vinegar. Fasten an alligator clip to each electrode and attach these to a sensitive voltmeter (0–1 V DC). Have a student read the voltage difference that is established between the two electrodes. L1 ELL **Visual-Spatial**

Batteries, continued

Purpose Students discover the effect of adding an additional cell to a circuit. L2 COOP LEARN

LS **Logical-Matematical**

Materials two D-cells, two 3-volt bulbs and sockets, three pieces of connecting wire

Safety Precautions Caution students to leave the bulbs burning only long enough to make observations, and to not touch a hot bulb.

Troubleshooting Hooking up more than two cells per lamp in series will shorten the bulb's life or cause it burn out.

Analysis

1. 1.5 volts, 3.0 volts
2. As the voltage difference increases across the lamp, the charge flowing through it increases.

Performance Have students design and label several possible arrangements showing how to light a bulb at different levels of brightness. Have them demonstrate each method. Use **PASC**, p. 127, P

Text Question Answers

- a chemical reaction
- portable stereos, flashlights, some remote controls

Caption Answer

Figure 13 Each has a positive and a negative terminal surrounded by a chemical that conducts charge.

Mini LAB

Investigating Battery Addition

Procedure

1. Make a circuit by linking two bulbs and one **D-cell battery** in a loop. Observe the brightness of the bulbs.
2. Assemble a new circuit by linking two bulbs and two D-cell batteries in a loop. Observe the brightness of the bulbs.

Analysis

1. What is the voltage difference of each D cell? Add them together to find the total voltage difference for the circuit you tested in step 2.
2. Assuming that a brighter bulb indicates a greater current, what can you conclude about the relationship between the voltage difference and current?

Dry-Cell Batteries The individual batteries you are most familiar with are dry cells. Look at the dry cell shown in **Figure 13A.** The zinc container of the dry cell surrounds a moist chemical paste with a solid carbon rod suspended in the middle. Can you locate the positive and negative terminals of the dry cell in the diagram? A dry cell produces a voltage difference between the positive and negative terminals. What causes this voltage difference?

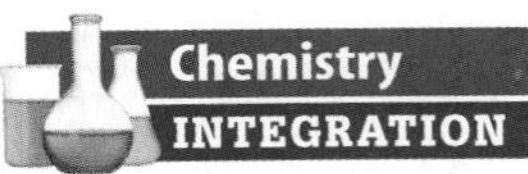

When the two terminals of a standard D-cell battery are connected in a circuit, such as in a flashlight, a reaction involving zinc and several chemicals in the paste occurs. The carbon rod does not take part in the reaction. Instead, it serves as a conductor to transfer electrons. Electrons are transferred between some of the compounds in this chemical reaction. As a result, the carbon rod becomes positive, forming the positive (+) terminal. Electrons accumulate on the zinc, making it the negative (−) terminal.

The voltage difference between these two terminals causes current to flow through a closed circuit, such as when you turn on a portable CD player. You make a battery when you connect two or more cells together to produce a higher voltage difference. Can you think of a device in your home or school that requires more than one battery to operate?

Wet Cells Another type of battery that is used commonly is the wet-cell battery. A wet cell, like the one shown in **Figure 13B,** contains two connected plates made of different metals or metallic compounds in a conducting solution.

Figure 13
A The dry cell can be connected with other dry cells to form a battery. A single dry cell also is called a battery. B The car battery is a series of wet cells. *How are these devices similar?*

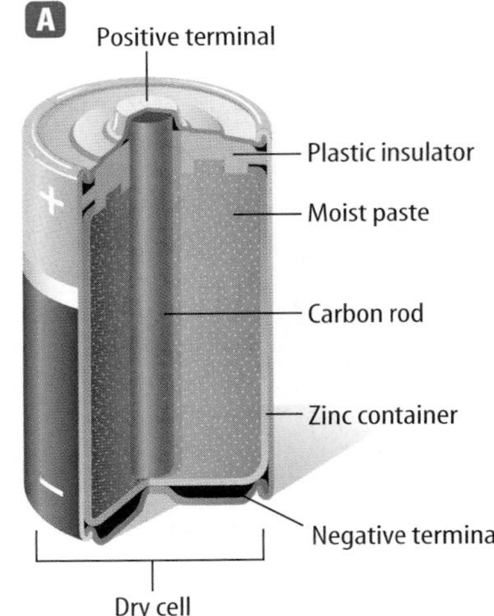

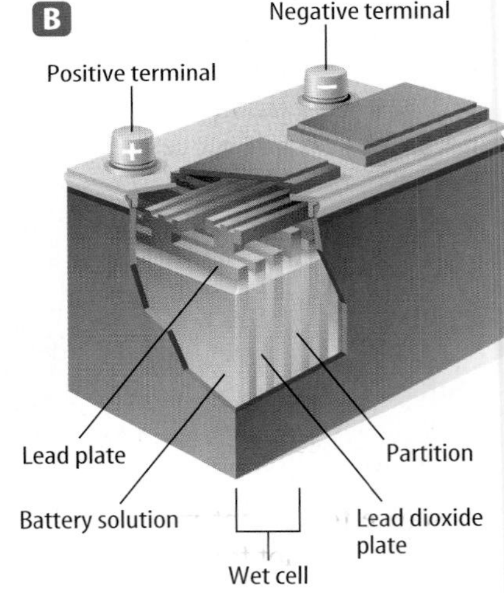

Visual Learning

Figure 13 Each cell of a battery has an *electrolyte* (a chemical that conducts charge) and two *electrodes* (terminals). One electrode provides electrons to the electrolyte. The other electrode takes electrons from the electrolyte. In dry cells the electrolyte is a paste, and in wet cells it is a liquid. **What are the electrodes in this figure?** In the dry cell, they are the carbon rod and the zinc container. In the wet cell, they are the lead dioxide and lead plates.

Providing Voltage Most car batteries, also called lead-storage batteries, contain a series of six wet cells made up of lead and lead dioxide plates in a sulfuric acid solution. The chemical reaction in each cell provides a voltage difference of about 2 V, giving a total voltage difference of 12 V. As a car is driven, the alternator recharges the battery by sending current through the battery in the opposite direction to reverse the chemical reaction.

In addition to batteries, a voltage difference is provided at electrical outlets, such as a wall socket. Most types of household devices are designed to use the voltage difference supplied by a wall socket. In the United States, the voltage difference across the two holes in a wall socket is usually 120 V. Some wall sockets supply 240 V, which is required by electric ranges and clothes dryers.

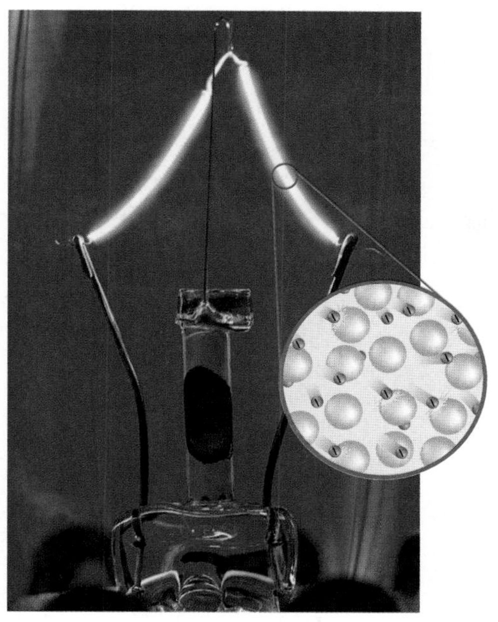

Figure 14
As electrons move through the filament in a lightbulb, they bump into metal atoms. Due to the collisions, the metal heats up and starts to glow.

Resistance

One function of the car battery is to light various lightbulbs in the car's electric circuits. What makes a lightbulb glow? Look at the lightbulb in **Figure 14.** Part of the circuit through the bulb contains a thin wire called a filament. As the electrons flow through the filament, they bump into the metal atoms that make up the filament. As these collisions occur, some of the electrical energy of the electrons is converted into thermal energy. Eventually, the metal filament becomes hot enough to glow, producing radiant energy that can light up a dark room.

Oppose the Flow Electric current loses energy as it moves through the filament because the filament resists the flow of electrons. **Resistance** is the tendency for a material to oppose the flow of electrons, changing electrical energy into thermal energy and light. With the exception of a few substances that become superconductors at low temperatures, all materials have some electrical resistance. Electrical conductors have much less resistance than insulators. Resistance is measured in ohms (Ω).

Copper is an excellent conductor and has low resistance to the flow of electrons. Copper is used in household wiring because little electrical energy is converted to thermal energy as current passes through the wires. In contrast, tungsten wire glows white-hot as current passes through it. Tungsten's high resistance to current makes it suitable for use as filaments in lightbulbs but not for carrying current through a house.

Curriculum Connection

Math In a car battery, the following chemical reaction occurs:
$Pb + PbO_2 + H_2SO_4 \rightarrow PbSO_4 + H_2O$. Use coefficients to balance this equation. $Pb + PbO_2 + 2H_2SO_4 \rightarrow 2PbSO_4 + 2H_2O$

Resource Manager

Chapter Resources Booklet
MiniLAB, p. 4
Enrichment, p. 29
Science Inquiry Labs, p. 45

IDENTIFYING Misconceptions

Students sometimes think that voltage is the same at different places in a circuit and it exists only when current flows. See page 192F for teaching strategies that address this misconception.

Quick Demo

Set up a wet cell and show that it produces a current by connecting it to an ammeter. There are a number of wet cells possible. A simple one consists of copper metal in a copper sulfate solution connected to zinc in a zinc chloride solution. Connect the two electrodes through an ammeter and place a salt bridge between the beakers of the two solutions. A salt bridge can be made by filling a U-shaped tube with a salt solution and loosely plugging both ends with cotton. L2
LS **Visual-Spatial**

Resistance

Use an Analogy

You can describe resistance by building on the analogy of charge flow being similar to water flow. Suppose a jug of water has a large hole in one side and a small hole in the other side. More water will flow out of the large hole. Similarly, a wire with a large diameter has less resistance and therefore carries greater current than a smaller-diameter wire.

Discussion

Should the heating elements on a stove top be made of high-resistance or low-resistance material? high-resistance

Resistance, continued

Reading Check

Answer Possible answer to produce light in filaments in lightbulbs

Control the Flow

IDENTIFYING Misconceptions

When it comes to electricity and our bodies, it is often true that high voltages are dangerous and low voltages are safer. Students are frequently not aware of a common situation where this is not true. In many static electricity situations, such as walking across a carpet, sparks are generated starting around 1,000 volts. No damage occurs to our bodies because there is little actual current flow.

Extension

Have students find out why *Electrophorus electricus* is commonly called the electric eel. **How does it produce its electrical current?** It has numerous cell membranes connected in parallel, enabling it to produce a 1-A current at 600 V. L2 IN **Linguistic**

Caption Answer

- **Figure 16A** It decreases the voltage difference
- **Figure 16B** It is brighter.

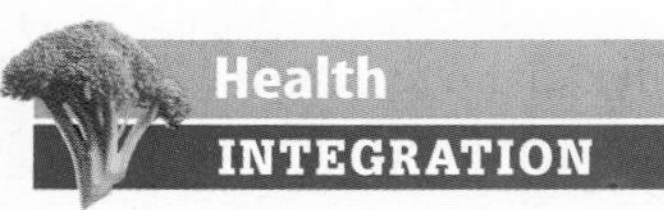

Health INTEGRATION

Currents lower than 0.5 mA cause a slight shock to a person. Higher currents cause increasing degrees of pain and loss of muscle control. Currents higher than about 150 mA will likely result in death.

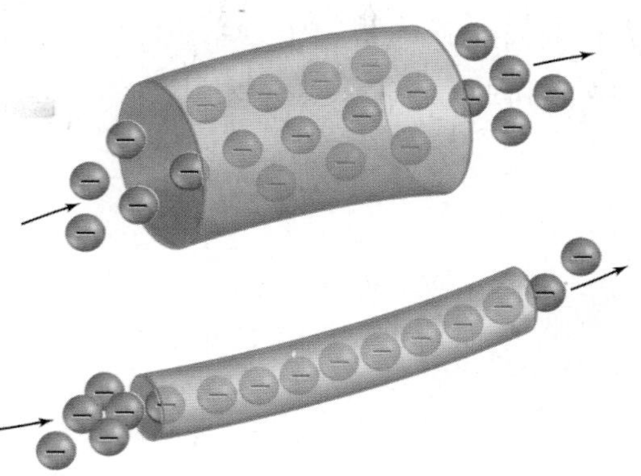

Figure 15
The resistance of a short, thick piece of wire is less than the resistance of a long, thin piece of wire.

Resistance in Wires The size of a wire also affects its resistance. **Figure 15** illustrates how electrons move more efficiently through thick wires than thin wires. In wires of the same length and material, thinner wires have greater resistance to electron flow. Making a wire longer causes the resistance to increase because more collisions occur as electrons flow through the longer wire. In most conductors, the resistance also increases as the temperature increases.

Reading Check *Why might you want to use a material with high resistance?*

Control the Flow

So far, you have learned two ways that the flow of charges, or current, in a circuit can be changed. A voltage difference causes the charges to flow, and an electrical resistance restricts the movement of charges. To help visualize this, think of water flowing in a pipe. If you increase the water pressure, the water flows faster and the water current increases. On the other hand, if you place obstructions in the pipe, the water current decreases.

Figure 16
The amount of current flowing through a circuit is related to the amount of resistance in the circuit.

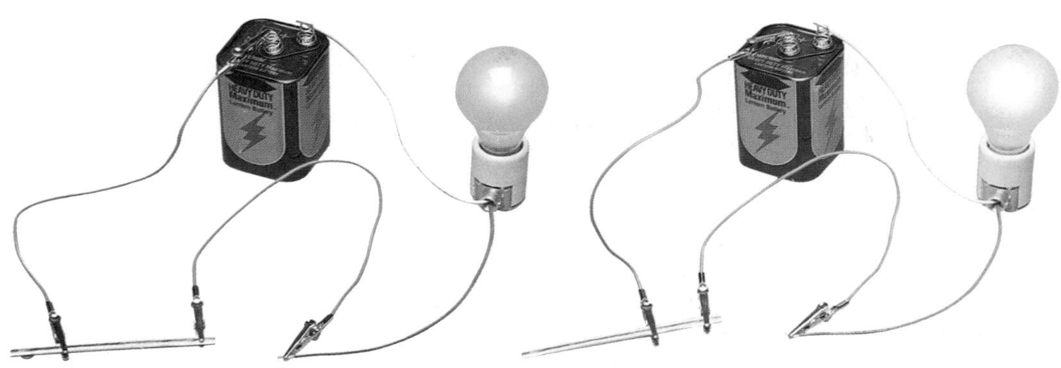

A **By changing the length of the graphite rod that the current must pass through, the resistance of the circuit can be changed. Recall that longer wires of a given material have higher resistances than shorter wires.** *How does changing the resistance affect the voltage difference of the circuit?*

B **Notice that here the current flows through a shorter section of the graphite rod. This decreases the total resistance of the circuit, while the voltage difference produced by the battery remains the same.** *How does the brightness of the bulb compare to the brightness of the bulb in the first photo?*

Teacher FYI

Conductivity depends on temperature. A higher temperature causes more movement of atoms and, generally, results in lower conductivity. However, the increased movement of atoms in some substances, such as carbon and semiconductors, frees electrons so that higher temperatures for these substances means higher conductivity.

Resource Manager

Chapter Resources Booklet
Lab Activity, pp. 9–12
Reinforcement, p. 26
Mathematics Skill Activities, p. 3

Ohm's Law For water flowing in a pipe, increasing the resistance causes the current to decrease, while increasing the pressure causes the current to increase. A similar relationship is true for electric current and is called Ohm's law.

$$\text{current} = \frac{\text{voltage difference}}{\text{resistance}}$$

$$I\,(\text{A}) = \frac{V\,(\text{V})}{R\,(\Omega)}$$

According to **Ohm's law,** the current in a circuit equals the voltage difference divided by the resistance. Consequently, as the resistance in a circuit increases, the current decreases. This inverse relationship is shown in **Figure 16.** The graphite rod resists the flow of current in the circuit. As the length of the graphite rod increases, the resistance in the circuit increases, and the current through a lightbulb decreases. As a result, the bulb becomes less bright. On the other hand, from Ohm's law the current increases if the voltage difference increases.

By multiplying both sides of the above equation by the resistance, R, Ohm's law also can be written as follows.

$$V = IR$$

Health INTEGRATION

Harm from electricity is due to high current. Wet skin has a much lower resistance than dry skin. According to Ohm's law, low resistance means high current. Research the effects of high current on the human body.

Section  Assessment

1. How does a current traveling through a circuit differ from a static discharge?
2. Briefly describe how a carbon-zinc dry cell supplies electric current for your CD player.
3. Describe three factors that affect the resistance of a copper wire.
4. Compare and contrast the flow of water through a pipe and the flow of electrons through a wire.
5. **Think Critically** Calculate the voltage difference across a 25-Ω resistor if a 0.3-A current is flowing through it. What happens to the voltage difference if the current is doubled?

Skill Builder Activities

6. **Interpreting Data** Suppose you connect three copper wires of unequal length to a 1.5-V dry cell. The following currents flow in the wires: wire 1, 1.2 A; wire 2, 1.4 A; wire 3, 1.1 A. Use Ohm's law to calculate the resistance of each wire. Make a graph of current versus resistance. Describe the shape of the line on your graph. **For more help, refer to the** Science Skill Handbook.
7. **Using Fractions** Suppose you place a bulb with a resistance of 60 Ω in a circuit with a 12-V battery. What is the current through this circuit? How does the current change if you add one more bulb? Two more bulbs? **For more help, refer to the** Math Skill Handbook.

Answers to Section Assessment

1. A circuit has a continuous current provided by a voltage source. A static discharge is a very rapid, noncontinuous transfer of charge.
2. A chemical reaction causes a negative charge on the zinc terminal and a positive charge on the carbon rod. This creates a voltage difference that allows a current to flow when the terminals are connected in a circuit through the tape player.
3. length, diameter, and temperature of the wire
4. Materials flow through both. The larger the diameter of the wire or pipe, the more material that can flow through at one time.
5. 7.5 V; it doubles.
6. 1.3 ohms, 1.1 ohms, 1.4 ohms
7. 0.2 A; it is cut in half to 0.1 A; it is cut in one-third to 0.07 A.

3 Assess

Reteach

Use the diagram below to help students remember how to rearrange Ohm's law. When the desired variable is covered, the other two variables are in proper mathematical order. L2

LS **Visual-Spatial**

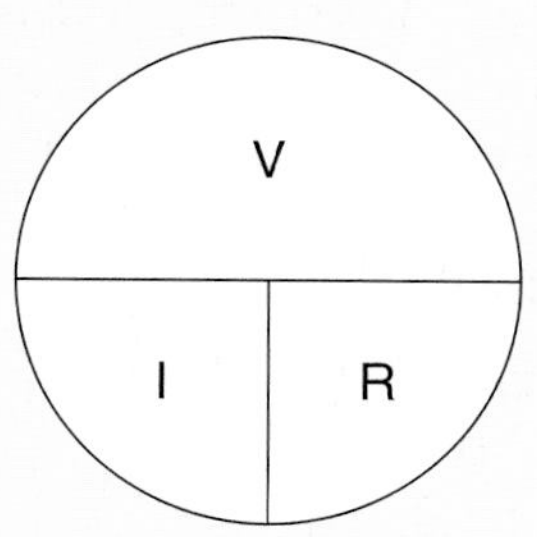

Challenge

Suppose you have a circuit with a battery attached to a lamp using two wires. The terminals on the battery are marked positive and negative. **If you have another battery with the same voltage but unmarked terminals, how can you distinguish positive and negative terminals?** Put the second battery in the circuit. The lamp only lights if terminals of opposite polarity are connected L2

LS **Logical Mathematical**

Performance Ask students to assume that the three wires in the Interpreting Data question are made of the same material and have the same diameter. Have them predict the relative lengths (longest, medium length, shortest) of the wires. Wire 1 is medium length, wire 2 is shortest, and wire 3 is longest. Use **Performance Assessment in the Science Classroom,** p. 89.

Activity

BENCH TESTED

Purpose Students will compare the conductivity of various materials. L2 LS **Kinesthetic**

Process collecting data, making and using tables, recording observations, drawing conclusions

Time Required 40 minutes

Teaching Strategy Have a collection of items ready for students to test but let students offer additional items to be tested.

Troubleshooting Make sure all connections in the circuit have good contact.

Answers to Questions

1. Answers will vary but should include that items that are metallic will conduct current.
2. They are metallic.
3. They are nonmetallic.
4. Materials that allow the lightbulb to light have metallic bonding. Materials that do not allow the lightbulb to light are nonmetallic.
5. Metallic materials will conduct electricity; bad connections will prevent the lightbulb from lighting.
6. Answers will vary.

Assessment

Process Silicon is an element that is nonconductive. Have students make posters illustrating how scientists treat silicon to alter its conductivity and how the altered silicon is used. Use **PASC,** p. 145

Activity

Identifying Conductors and Insulators

Have you ever had a flashlight that you couldn't seem to make work any longer? You replaced the batteries and put in a new bulb, yet the flashlight still wouldn't light. The most likely cause for such a broken flashlight is a break in the circuit. If you could find the break and then repair it, you could fix the flashlight.

What You'll Investigate

Compare the ability of different materials to conduct a current.

Materials

battery
flashlight bulb
bulb holder
insulated wire

Goals

- **Identify** conductors and insulators.
- **Describe** the common characteristics of conductors and insulators.

Procedure

1. Set up an incomplete circuit as pictured in the photograph.
2. Touch the free bare ends of the wires to various objects around the room. Test at least 12 items.
3. In a table like the one below, record which materials make the lightbulb light and which don't.

Material Tested with Lightbulb Circuit	
Lightbulb Lights	**Lightbulb Stays Out**
paper clip	tabletop
faucet	fabric
coin	paper

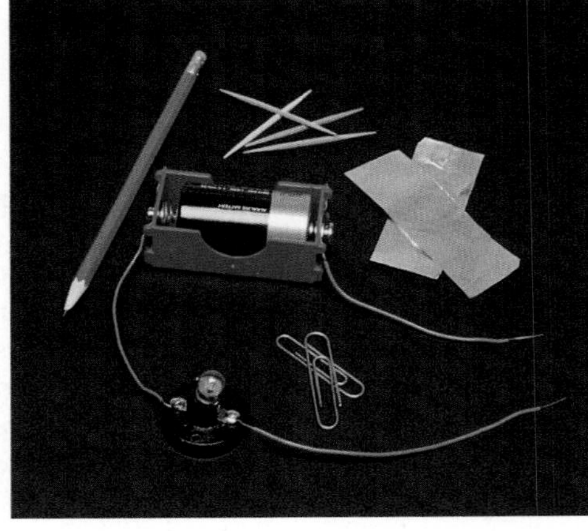

Conclude and Apply

1. Is there a pattern to your data?
2. Do all or most of the materials that light the lightbulb have something in common?
3. Do all or most of the materials that don't light the lightbulb have something in common?
4. **Explain** why a material may allow the lightbulb to light and what will prevent the lightbulb from lighting.
5. **Predict** what other materials will allow the lightbulb to light and what will prevent the lightbulb from lighting.
6. **Classify** all the materials you have tested as conductors or insulators.

Communicating Your Data

Compare your conclusions with those of other students in your class. **For more help, refer to the Science Skill Handbook.**

208 CHAPTER 7 Electricity

Communicating Your Data

Students should discuss why their conclusions did or did not agree. They can cite references to support their arguments.

Resource Manager

Chapter Resources Booklet
Activity Worksheet, pp. 5–6

Science Inquiry Labs, p. 55

SECTION 3

Electrical Energy

Electric Circuits

Look around. How many electrical devices such as lights, clocks, stereos, and televisions do you see that are plugged into wall outlets? These devices rely on a source of electrical energy and wires to complete an electric circuit. Circuits typically include a voltage source, a conductor such as a wire, and one or more devices that use the electrical energy to do work.

Consider, for example, a circuit that includes an electric hair drier. The drier must be plugged into a wall outlet to operate. A generator at a power plant produces a voltage difference across the outlet, causing the charge to move when the circuit is complete. The drier and the circuit in the house contain conducting wires to carry current. The hair drier turns the electrical energy into thermal energy and mechanical energy. When you unplug the hair drier or turn off its switch, you open the circuit and break the path of the current. To use electrical energy, a complete circuit must be made. Several kinds of circuits exist.

Series Circuits One kind of circuit is called a series circuit. In a **series circuit,** the current has only one loop to flow through, as shown in **Figure 17.** Series circuits are used in flashlights and some holiday lights.

Reading Check *How many loops are in a series circuit?*

As You Read

***What* You'll Learn**

- **Describe** the difference between series and parallel circuits.
- **Recognize** the function of circuit breakers and fuses.
- **Explain and calculate** electrical power.

Vocabulary
series circuit
parallel circuit
electrical power
kilowatt-hour

***Why* It's Important**

The convenience and safety of household electricity depend on how the electric circuits in your home are designed.

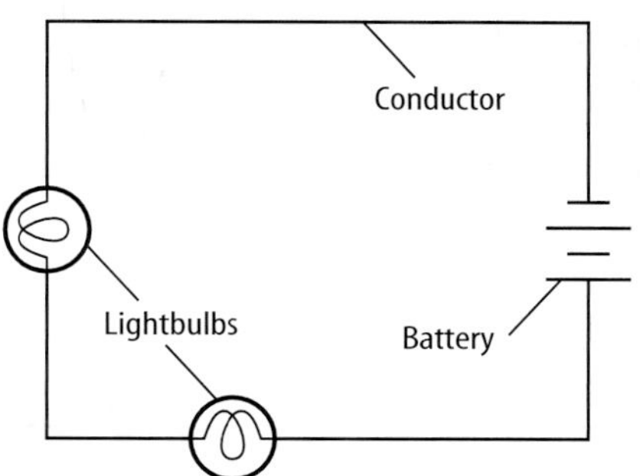

Figure 17
A series circuit provides only one path for the current to follow.
What happens to the brightness of each bulb as more bulbs are added?

Section Assessment Planner

Portfolio
Earth Science Integration, p. 210
Performance Assessment
Math Skills Activity, p. 214
Skill Builder Activities, p. 215
See page 222 for more options.

Content Assessment
Section, p. 215
Challenge, p. 215
Chapter, pp. 222–223

SECTION

Electrical Energy

1 Motivate

Bellringer Transparency

Display the Section Focus Transparency for Section 3. Use the accompanying Transparency Activity Master. L2 ELL

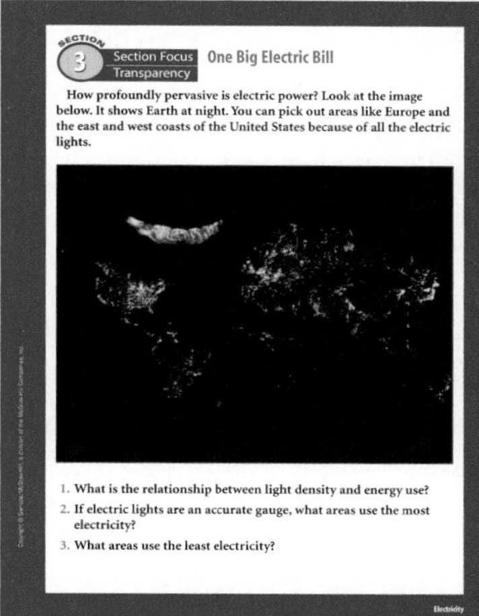

Section Focus Transparency — One Big Electric Bill

How profoundly pervasive is electric power? Look at the image below. It shows Earth at night. You can pick out areas like Europe and the east and west coasts of the United States because of all the electric lights.

1. What is the relationship between light density and energy use?
2. If electric lights are an accurate gauge, what areas use the most electricity?
3. What areas use the least electricity?

Tie to Prior Knowledge

Discuss with students what they learned in the last section about how resistance, voltage, and current are related. Tell them that this section will apply those terms to circuits in real devices.

Reading Check

Answer one

Caption Answer

Figure 17 The brightness decreases.

2 Teach

Electric Circuits

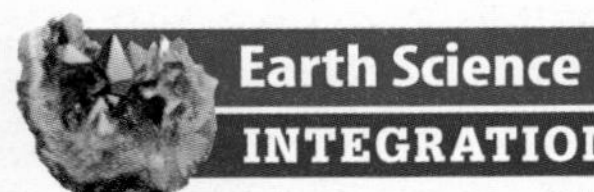

This is analogous to a parallel circuit. The change in potential energy is the same in both branches, and the branches rejoin with the same current as before the split. P

Activity

Have several small devices with electrical circuits, partially taken apart, in the room for students to examine. Possible displays include a small radio, a flashlight, and a telephone. L3 ELL LS **Kinesthetic**

Extension

Have students find out why a bird can sit on a high-voltage wire without getting electrically shocked. The bird's body has so much more resistance than the wire that no current flows through it. Also, there is no voltage difference across the bird. L3 LS **Logical-Mathematical**

Caption Answer

Figure 18 It is the same.

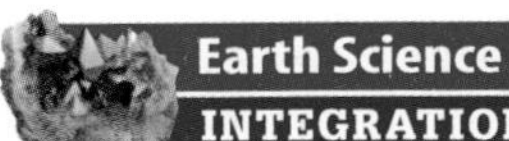

Rivers sometimes form different branches that separate and then rejoin, making an island. Write a paragraph describing which kind of circuit this is most like and why.

Open Circuit If you have ever decorated a window or a tree with a string of lights, you might have had the frustrating experience of trying to find one burned-out bulb. How can one faulty bulb cause the whole string to go out? Because the parts of a series circuit are wired one after another, the amount of current is the same through every part. When any part of a series circuit is disconnected, no current flows through the circuit. This is called an open circuit. The burned-out bulb causes an open circuit in the string of lights.

Parallel Circuits What would happen if your home were wired in a series circuit and you turned off one light? This would cause an open circuit, and all the other lights and appliances in your home would go out, too. This is why houses are wired with parallel circuits. **Parallel circuits** contain two or more branches for current to move through. Look at the parallel circuit in **Figure 18.** The current splits up to flow through the different branches. Because all branches connect the same two points of the circuit, the voltage difference is the same in each branch. Then, according to Ohm's law, more current flows through the branches that have lower resistance.

Parallel circuits have several advantages. When one branch of the circuit is opened, such as when you turn a light off, the current continues to flow through the other branches. Houses, automobiles, and most electrical systems use parallel wiring so individual parts can be turned off without affecting the entire circuit.

Figure 18
In parallel circuits, the current follows more than one path. *How will the voltage difference compare in each branch?*

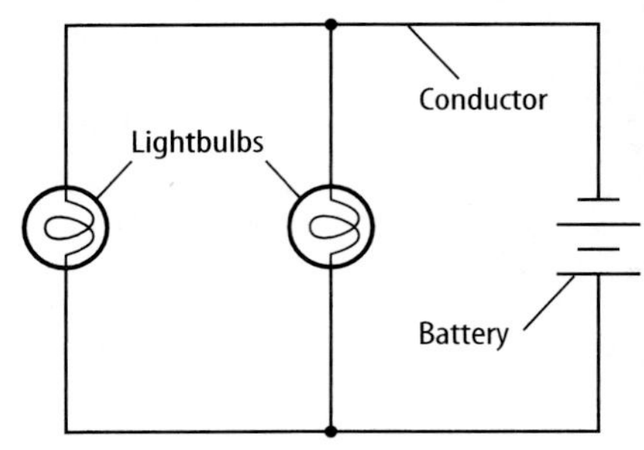

LAB DEMONSTRATION

Purpose to demonstrate series and parallel circuits

Materials battery, 2 small lightbulbs, 2 ammeters, wire

Procedure Set up a series circuit with the two lightbulbs. Include ammeters in two places in the circuit. Disconnect one lamp so the circuit is broken. Do the same for a parallel circuit.

Expected Outcome In the series circuit, current is the same everywhere, but the entire circuit is broken when the lamp is disconnected. For the parallel circuit, current is not the same everywhere, and the circuit is only broken in the branch with the disconnected lamp.

Assessment

Why do results differ for the two circuits? Series-current has only one path so it is the same everywhere; parallel-current has two paths, so it is split between the paths. An open circuit in one branch doesn't hinder current through the other branch.

Figure 19
The wiring in a house must allow for the individual use of various appliances and fixtures.
What type of circuit is most common in household wiring?

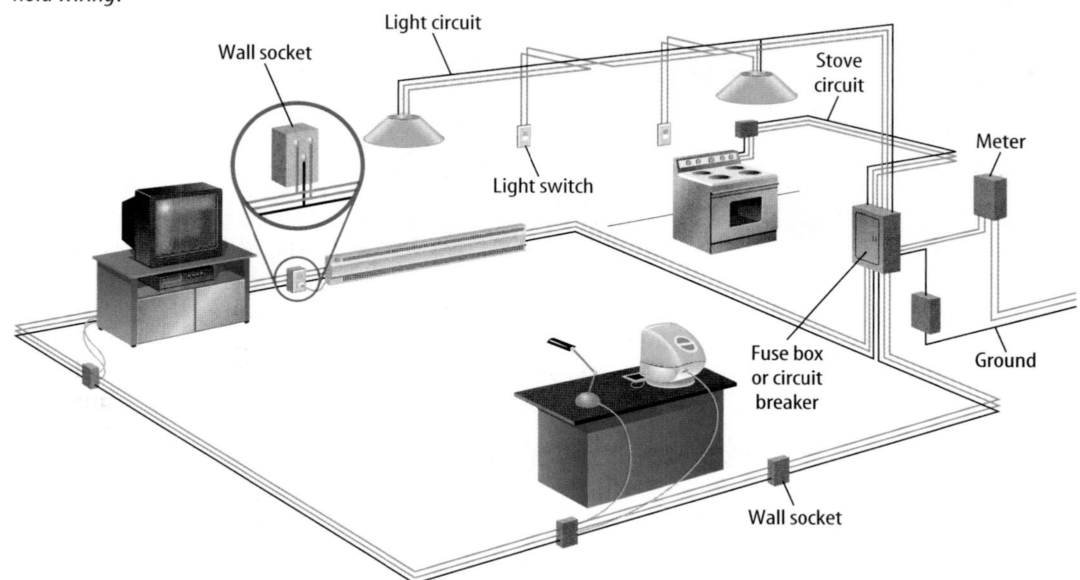

Household Circuits

Count how many different things in your home require electrical energy. You don't see the wires because most of them are hidden behind the walls, ceilings, and floors. This wiring is made up mostly of a combination of parallel circuits connected in an organized and logical network. **Figure 19** shows how electrical energy enters a home and is distributed. Each branch receives the standard voltage difference from the electric company, which is 120 V in the United States. The main switch and circuit breaker or fuse box serve as an electrical headquarters for your home. Parallel circuits branch out from the breaker or fuse box to wall sockets, major appliances, and lights.

In a house, many appliances draw current from the same circuit. If more appliances are connected, more current will flow through the wires. As the amount of current increases, so does the amount of heating in the wires. If the wires get too hot, the insulation can melt and the bare wires can cause a fire. To protect against overheating of the wires, all household circuits contain either a fuse or a circuit breaker.

Quick Demo

Use milk cartons filled with water to demonstrate how charge will not flow when any part of a series circuit is disconnected, but it will flow if one path of a parallel circuit is disconnected. Punch a hole near the bottom of one carton, and punch two holes on opposite sides of the other carton. Fill the cartons with water and show that when the hole in the first carton is closed (the circuit is open), the water (charge) doesn't flow. When one hole in the second carton is closed, the water continues to flow through the other path.

Activity

Draw several circuit diagrams on the board and have students identify them either as series circuits or as parallel circuits. At this point, avoid combination series/parallel circuits. L2

LS **Visual-Spatial**

Household Circuits

Caption Answer

Figure 19 parallel circuit

Teacher FYI

Resistance In a series circuit, total resistance is equal to the sum of the individual resistances: $R_{total} = R_1 + R_2 + \ldots$ The voltage difference across any resistance is equal to the current times that specific resistance. In a parallel circuit, the total resistance is calculated as follows: $1/R_{total} = 1/R_1 + 1/R_2 + \ldots$ The total resistance is less than any single resistance in a parallel circuit.

Resource Manager

Chapter Resources Booklet
- Transparency Activity, p. 44
- Enrichment, p. 30
- Directed Reading for Content Mastery, pp. 19, 20

Visual Learning

Figure 19 Students should notice that all wiring in the house first runs through the fuse box or circuit breaker for protection. **Why are three lines shown in the wiring?** One line is ground; the other two are forward and reverse current.

Household Circuits, continued

Caption Answer

Figure 20 a circuit breaker because it can be easily reset, whereas a fuse must be replaced

Make a Model

Students can learn about the behavior of fuses by constructing a simple circuit containing a battery and a lightbulb. To model a fuse, include as part of the circuit's wiring a strip of aluminum foil about 3 cm long. The strip should have a thin middle section that is about 1 mm wide. When the circuit is completed, the thin part of the foil will quickly melt, opening the circuit, and the light will go out, as occurs when a real fuse blows. L2 IS **Kinesthetic**

Reading Check

Answer to protect against overheating and possible fire if the current in a wire becomes too high

Electrical Power

Text Question Answer

They convert electrical energy into thermal energy through resistance in their wires. This drains the current, so a greater level of power is needed.

A

B

Figure 20
Two useful devices to prevent electric circuits from overheating are A fuses and B circuit breakers. *Which device, a fuse or a circuit breaker, seems more convenient to have in the home?*

Fuses When you hear that somebody has "blown a fuse," it means that the person has lost his or her temper. This expression comes from the function of an electrical fuse, **Figure 20A,** which contains a small piece of metal that melts if the current becomes too high. When it melts, it causes a break in the circuit, stopping the flow of current through the overloaded circuit. To fix this, you must replace the blown fuse with a new one. However, before you replace the blown fuse, you should unplug some of the appliances. Too many appliances in use at the same time is the most likely cause for the overheating of the circuit.

Circuit Breaker A circuit breaker, **Figure 20B,** is another guard against overheating a wire. A circuit breaker contains a piece of metal that bends when it gets hot. The bending causes a switch to flip and open the circuit, stopping the flow of current. Circuit breakers usually can be reset by moving the switch to its "on" position. Again, before you reset a circuit breaker, you should turn off or unplug some of the appliances from the overloaded circuit.

Reading Check ***What is the purpose of fuses and circuit breakers in household circuits?***

Electrical Power

The reason that electricity is so important to your everyday life is that electrical energy is converted easily to other types of energy. For example, electrical energy is converted to mechanical energy as the blades of a fan rotate to cool you. Electrical energy is converted to light energy in lightbulbs. A hair drier changes electrical energy into thermal energy. The rate at which electrical energy is converted to another form of energy is called **electrical power.**

The electrical power used by appliances varies. Appliances often are labeled with a power rating that describes how much power the appliance uses. Appliances that have electric heating elements, such as ovens and hair driers, have a large power rating. Why might ovens and hair driers require a high power rating?

Cultural Diversity

Electrical Lighting Lewis H. Latimer, the son of a former slave, taught himself to be a draftsman when he was a teenager. In 1879, Latimer was hired by the United States Electric Lighting Company, where he invented the first carbon-filament electric lamp and an inexpensive way to produce the filaments. In 1883, he joined Thomas Edison, and in 1890, he published the first textbook on electrical lighting—*Incandescent Electric Lighting*. In 1918, the Edison Pioneers organization was formed to honor some of the people who worked with Thomas Edison as the "creators of the electric industry." One member was Lewis H. Latimer.

Calculating Power Appliances with high power ratings can be supplied with the electrical power they need by increasing the amount of charge flowing into the appliance or increasing the electrical pressure on the charge that is flowing already. The relationship among power, voltage, and current can be expressed as follows.

$$\text{power} = \text{current} \times \text{voltage difference}$$
$$P\,(\text{watts}) = I\,(\text{amperes}) \times V\,(\text{volts})$$

Electrical power is expressed in watts (W). For example, a hair drier might draw 10 A of current at a voltage difference of 120 V. The power rating of the hair drier is then 10 A times 120 V, or 1,200 W.

Power Rating Every electrical appliance comes with a label that shows how much power it uses. **Figure 21** shows the power-rating label for a typical hair drier, and **Table 1** lists the power requirements of some appliances. Which appliance requires the most electrical power to operate? You can tell by looking at the number of watts listed for that appliance under the Power Rating column.

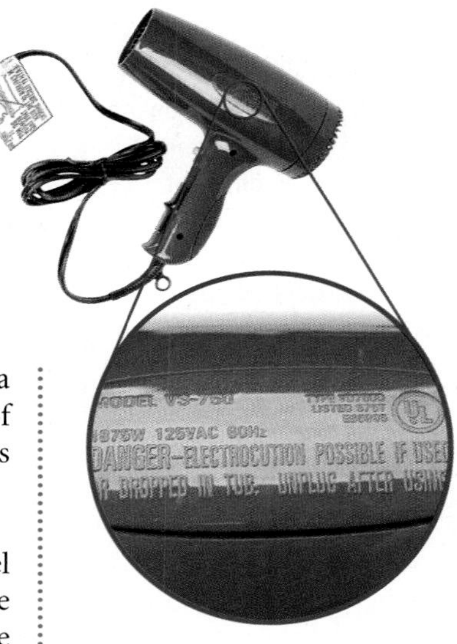

Figure 21
All appliances come with a power rating. *Why is a power rating important?*

Table 1 Energy Used by Home Appliances

Appliance	Time of Usage (h/day)	Power Rating (W)	Energy Usage (kWh/day)
Hair drier	0.25	1,000	0.25
Microwave oven	0.5	700	0.35
Stereo	2.5	109	0.27
Range (oven)	1	2,600	2.60
Refrigerator/freezer (15 ft^3, frostless)	10	615	6.15
Television (color)	3.25	200	0.65
Electric toothbrush	0.08	7	0.0006
100-W lightbulb	6	100	0.60
40-W fluorescent lightbulb	1	40	0.04

Use Science Words

Word Origin Many units of measurement in science are named for people who did related research. Have students investigate the origins of the words *ampere*, *watt*, and *volt*. The ampere is named after André Marie Ampère, who proposed the relationship between electricity and magnetism. The watt is named after James Watt, who created the steam engine and first used the word horsepower. The volt is named after Alessandro Volta, who observed that a conducting liquid produced a continuous transfer of electrons, a phenomenon later called electric current. L2
LS **Linguistic**

Caption Answer

Figure 21 possible answer: to keep people from overloading circuits

Visual Learning

Table 1 Have students make a list of appliances they have in their home. Then have them use the values in the table to calculate how much energy these appliances use in one week. As an extension, have students keep track of the actual time these appliances are used and recalculate their energy use. L2
LS **Logical-Mathematical**

Resource Manager

Chapter Resources Booklet
Lab Activity, pp. 13–14
Transparency Activity, pp. 45–46
Mathematics Skill Activities, p. 9

Science Journal

Power, Voltage, Current, and Resistance
Remind students that they have been given two mathematical formulas about electricity: Ohm's law, and the formula for electrical power. Have them write both formulas in their Science Journals and combine them to relate power to resistance. $I = V/R$; $P = IV$; therefore $P = V/R \times V = V^2/R$; also, $V = IR$, so $P = I \times IR = I^2R$. L2 LS **Logical-Mathematical**

Electrical Energy

Fun Fact

Benjamin Franklin was first to use the terms *positive* and *negative* to describe charged objects. He also invented the lightning rod.

Math Skills Activity

National Math Standards

Correlation to Mathematics Objectives

1, 2, 6, 9

Teaching Strategies

P = 100W/1000 = 0.10kW

E = .10kW × 5h = 0.50kWh

P = 1000W/1000 = 1kW

E = 1kW × 0.20h = 0.20kWh

Answers to Practice Problems

1. 0.50kWh
2. 0.20kWh

Internet Addresses

Explore the Glencoe Science Web site at **science.glencoe.com** to find out more about topics in this section.

SCIENCE Online

Data Update For an online update about the current energy costs in different communities across the United States, visit the Glencoe Science Web site at **science. glencoe.com** and select the appropriate chapter.

Electrical Energy

Do you leave the light on or the stereo playing in your room when you aren't there? Consider that any electrical energy you use costs money. Furthermore, most electrical energy is produced from natural resources, such as oil and coal, which are in limited supply.

The amount of electrical energy you use depends on two things. One is the power required by appliances in your home, and the other is how long they are used. Many appliances with high power ratings, such as hair driers, are used for such a short amount of time that the total amount of electrical energy they require in a given month is small. Appliances that run constantly, such as refrigerators, usually use more total energy. The last column of **Table 1** shows typical energy usage per day for various household appliances.

Math Skills Activity

Calculating Energy

Example Problem

You use your fan for 3 h each day. It has a power rating of 50 W. How much energy does it use? Express your answer in kilowatt-hours.

Solution

1. *This is what you know:* time: $t = 3$ h; power: $P = 50$ W
2. *This is what you need to find:* energy: E
3. *This is the equation you need to use:* $E = P \times t$
4. *To calculate energy, the unit of power must be kW. So convert* P *from W to kW by dividing by 1,000:* $P = \dfrac{50 \text{ W}}{1{,}000 \text{ W/kW}} = 0.05 \text{ kW}$
5. *Substitute the known values:* $E = 0.05 \text{ kW} \times 3 \text{ h}$; $E = 0.15 \text{ kWh}$

Check your answer by solving the original equation, E = P × t, *for* t. *Then substitute* E *and* P. *Do you calculate the same time that was given?*

Practice Problems

1. A 100-W lightbulb has a power rating of 100 W. How much energy in kWh is used when you leave it on for 5 h?
2. Find the power rating for a hair drier on **Table 1.** How much energy is used if you run it for 12 min (0.20 h)?

For more help, refer to the Math Skill Handbook.

Inclusion Strategies

Gifted Have students work in pairs to research and build a Leyden jar, an early form of a capacitor, a device used to store electric energy. Students should create their own design, but one simple method is to use a plastic film canister and aluminum foil. **CAUTION:** *Warn students not to use any flammable materials in their construction.*

Resource Manager

Chapter Resources Booklet

Activity Worksheet, pp. 7–8

Reinforcement, p. 27

Calculating Energy You can calculate the amount of energy an appliance uses in a day by multiplying the power required by the amount of time it uses that power.

$$\text{energy} = \text{power} \times \text{time}$$
$$E\,(\text{kWh}) = P\,(\text{kW}) \times t\,(\text{h})$$

Notice that to calculate energy, power is expressed in kilowatts. One kilowatt is 1,000 W. The unit of electrical energy is the **kilowatt-hour** (kWh). One kilowatt-hour is 1,000 W of power used for 1 h. The electric company charges you periodically for each kilowatt-hour you use. You can figure your electric bill by multiplying the energy used by the cost per kilowatt-hour. **Table 2** shows some sample costs of running electrical appliances. For example, to determine the cost of using a 100-W lightbulb for 20 h, the following calculation is made.

$$\text{cost} = 0.1\text{ kW} \times 20\text{ h} \times \$0.09/\text{kWh} = \$0.18$$

Table 2 Cost of Using Home Appliances

Appliance	Hair Drier	Stereo	Color Television
Average power in watts	1,000	109	200
Hours used daily	0.25	2.5	2.5
Hours used monthly	7.5	75.0	75.0
Monthly watt-hours	7,500	8,175	15,000
kWh used monthly	7.5	8.175	15.000
Rate charge	$0.09	$0.09	$0.09
Monthly cost	$0.68	$0.74	$1.35

Section  Assessment

1. What is electrical power? What is electrical energy? How are the two related?
2. Compare and contrast fuses and circuit breakers. Which is easier to use? Why?
3. Do appliances with the highest power ratings always use the most energy per month? Use examples to explain why or why not.
4. How does a series circuit differ from a parallel circuit? Sketch an example of each.
5. **Think Critically** How much energy would be needed for brushing your teeth with an electric toothbrush daily for the month of May? How much would it cost at $0.09 kWh?

Skill Builder Activities

6. **Concept Mapping** Prepare a concept map that shows the steps that are followed in calculating the energy used in operating an electrical device with known voltage difference and current for a known amount of time. **For more help, refer to the Science Skill Handbook.**
7. **Using an Electronic Spreadsheet** On a spreadsheet, list the appliances your family uses daily, the estimated hours per day, and, from **Table 1,** the power usage. Multiply the power usage by the hours per day to find the electrical energy used daily for each appliance. Which appliance uses the most energy? **For more help, refer to the Technology Skill Handbook.**

Teacher FYI

In the United States, the power of car engines is rated using the British unit horsepower (hp). One horsepower is equal to 746 watts.

3 Assess

Reteach

Bring in an energy rating label from a new appliance. Have students use the energy specifications of the appliance to determine the energy it will use and its power.
L2 LS **Logical-Mathematical**

Challenge

Have students draw a simple diagram of the electrical circuit in the classroom. The diagram should be similar to that shown in **Figure 19.** Students should be careful to show that the wiring is in parallel. L3 LS **Visual-Spatial**

Assessment

Process Ask students to write paragraphs that compare and contrast series and parallel circuits. Charge flows through both types of circuits. A series circuit has only one loop through which charge can flow; a parallel circuit has more than one. Use **Performance Assessment in the Science Classroom,** p. 157.

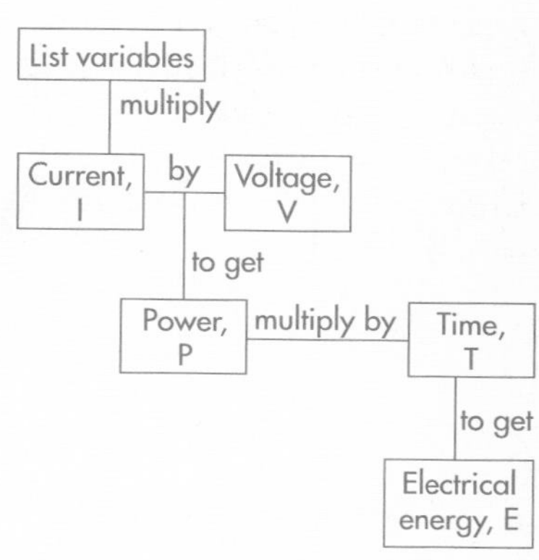

Answers to Section Assessment

1. Power is the rate at which electrical energy (the energy produced by the flow of moving electrons) is converted to another form of energy. The amount of electrical energy used is the power times the time the power is used.
2. Both break overloaded circuits. Fuses melt and must be replaced. Circuit breakers bend to flip a switch that can be easily reset, and thus are easier to use.
3. No; energy usage also depends on the amount of time the appliance is used.
4. A series circuit has one loop for the electrons to flow through. A parallel circuit has many loops. Thus, if an appliance on one loop stops functioning, the others remain functional.
5. 0.0186 kWh; about $0.0017
6. See side column.
7. The spreadsheet should look similar to Table 1, but will reflect individual usage.

Activity

BENCH TESTED

Recognize the Problem

Purpose

Students design and test parallel and series circuits. L1 COOP LEARN

LS Logical-Mathematical

Process Skills

observing, communicating, classifying, comparing and contrasting, recognizing cause and effect, interpreting data, using numbers, experimenting, hypothesizing

Time Required

one class period

Materials

The lightbulb current requirements should closely match the current expected in the circuit so bulbs don't burn out quickly.

Alternate Materials

Obtain economical low-voltage lightbulbs by cutting apart a string of Christmas minilights. Insulated wire may be used instead of foil.

Safety Precautions

To avoid overheating the wire, students should hook up the battery only long enough to make observations.

Form a Hypothesis

Possible Hypothesis

If a bulb is removed from a series circuit, all lights will go out. In a parallel circuit, the remaining bulbs will stay lit. Lights shine brightest in the parallel circuit.

Activity **Design Your Own Experiment**

Comparing Series and Parallel Circuits

Imagine what a bedroom might be like if it were wired in series. For an alarm clock to keep time and wake you in the morning, your lights and anything else that uses electricity would have to be on. Fortunately, most outlets in homes are wired on separate branches of the main circuit. Can you design simple circuits that have specific behaviors and uses?

Recognize the Problem

How do the behaviors of series and parallel circuits compare?

Form a Hypothesis

Predict what will happen to the other bulbs when one bulb is unscrewed from a series circuit and from a parallel circuit. Also, write a hypothesis predicting in which circuit the lights shine the brightest.

Possible Materials

6-V dry-cell battery
small lights with sockets (3)
aluminum foil
transparent tape
scissors
paper

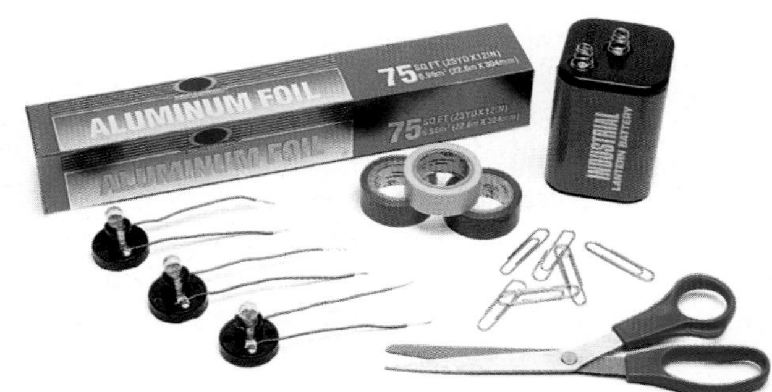

Goals

- **Design and construct** series and parallel circuits.
- **Compare and contrast** the behaviors of series and parallel circuits.

Safety Precautions

Some parts of circuits can become hot. Do not leave the battery connected or the circuit closed for more than a few seconds at a time. Never connect the positive and negative terminals of the dry-cell battery directly without including at least one bulb in the circuit.

Test Your Hypothesis

Possible Procedures

Series circuits should have a single path with lights in a chain. Parallel circuits should have the lights on three separate paths.

Inclusion Strategies

Visually Impaired Instead of using lamps, this activity can be performed using buzzers in the circuits. A visually impaired student could be paired with a sighted student to aid in circuit construction.

Test Your Hypothesis

Plan

1. As a group, agree upon and write the hypothesis statement.
2. Work together determining and writing the steps you will take to test your hypothesis. Include a list of the materials you will need.
3. How will your circuits be arranged? On a piece of paper, draw a large parallel circuit of three lights and the dry-cell battery as shown. On the other side, draw another circuit with the three bulbs arranged in series.
4. Make conducting wires by taping a 30-cm piece of transparent tape to a sheet of aluminum foil and folding the foil over twice to cover the tape. Cut these to any length that works in your design.

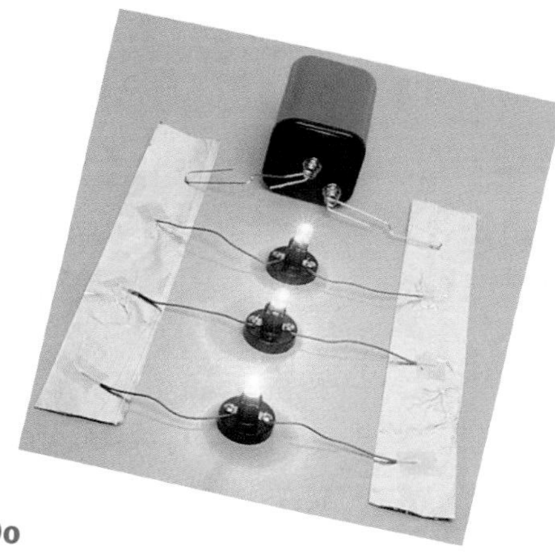

Do

1. Make sure your teacher approves your plan before you start.
2. Carry out the experiment. **WARNING:** *Leave the circuit on for only a few seconds at a time to avoid overheating.*
3. As you do the experiment, record your predictions and your observations in your Science Journal.

Analyze Your Data

1. **Predict** what will happen in the series circuit when a bulb is unscrewed at one end. What will happen in the parallel circuit?
2. **Compare** the brightness of the lights in the different circuits. Explain.
3. **Predict** what happens to the brightness of the bulbs in the series circuit if you complete it with two bulbs instead of three bulbs. Test it. How does this demonstrate Ohm's law?

Draw Conclusions

1. Did the results support your hypothesis? Explain by using your observations.
2. Where in the parallel circuit would you place a switch to control all three lights? Where would you place a switch to control only one light? Test it.

Communicating Your Data

Prepare a poster to highlight the differences between a parallel and a series circuit. Include possible practical applications of both types of circuits. **For more help, refer to the Science Skill Handbook.**

Teaching Strategy

Troubleshooting Students may design a circuit having two lightbulbs in parallel that are wired in series with the third light. Although interesting, this will not help students completely explore the behavior of each of the circuits independently.

Expected Outcome

When a light in series is removed, all the lights go out. In a parallel circuit, when a light is removed, others remain lit.

Analyze Your Data

1. In series, the current will stop and all bulbs will go out. In parallel, the charge will flow through other branches and the other bulbs will remain lit.
2. The lights are brighter in parallel because each loop has less resistance than the loop with three bulbs in a series circuit.
3. It will be brighter because of less resistance in the circuit.

Error Analysis

Have students analyze their circuits for possible sources of errors. dead batteries, burned-out bulbs, poor connections with the aluminum foil

Draw Conclusions

1. Answers depend on student hypotheses.
2. between the battery and a wire leading to one side of the lights; along the wire that goes to only one of the lights

Assessment

Oral Ask students to discuss why houses and buildings are wired in parallel and not in series. In a series circuit, all lights and appliances would have to be on at the same time; if one is off or burned out, no charge flows anywhere in the circuit. Use **Performance Assessment in the Science Classroom**, p. 143.

Communicating Your Data

Have students use a computer graphics program to draw sketches of circuits for their posters. They can also use the computer to write any explanations they wish to include on their posters.

Science and Language Arts

Pre-Reading Activity

Ask students to do a clustering of terms that define who they are or as Ralph Ellison says "confirms my reality." Each student should put his or her name in the center of a cluster that inlcudes elements that define his or her identity such as ethnic heritage, extracurricular activities, and family members.

Respond to the Reading

Active Reading Strategies

Connect Ask students if they can remember a time they were unfairly judged or misunderstood simply because their outward appearance was different from others around them.

Respond Tell students to be aware of their responses as they read about the invisible man. His description of himself might make them think that anyone who is judged by others is an outsider. Ask students if the invisible man has a positive view of himself and how the text conveys that it is important for a person to have a positive view of himself or herself.

Answers to Questions

1. Ectoplasm is the outer layer of a part of the cell. Epidermis is the outer layer of skin.
2. The narrator says he is "a man of substance, of flesh and bone, fiber and liquids."
3. because he has wired his ceiling with 1,369 lights

Science and Language Arts

The Invisible Man

by Ralph Ellison

Respond to the Reading

1. Sometimes you can figure out the meaning of words by their contexts. A word's context refers to the other words in a sentence or phrase that shed light on that word's meaning. Can you guess the meaning of the words *ectoplasm* and *epidermis* by their contexts?
2. What clues does the narrator give that he is not really invisible?
3. Why does the narrator believe he is in the "great American tradition of tinkers"?

I am an invisible man. No, I am not a spook like those who haunted Edgar Allan Poe; nor am I one of your Hollywood-movie ectoplasms.[1] I am a man of substance, of flesh and bone, fiber and liquids—and I might even be said to possess a mind. I am invisible, understand, simply because people refuse to see me. . . . Nor is my invisibility exactly a matter of biochemical accident to my epidermis.[2] That invisibility to which I refer occurs because of a peculiar disposition of the eyes of those with whom I come in contact. A matter of the construction of their *inner* eyes . . .

. . . Now don't jump to the conclusion that because I call my home a "hole" it is damp and cold like a grave. . . . Mine is a warm hole.

My hole is warm and full of light. Yes, *full* of light. I doubt if there is a brighter spot in all New York than this hole of mine, and I do not exclude Broadway. . . . Perhaps you'll think it strange that an invisible man should need light, desire light, love light. Because maybe it is exactly because I *am invisible.* Light confirms my reality, gives birth to my form. . . . I myself, after existing some twenty years, did not become alive until I discovered my invisibility.

. . . In my hole in the basement there are exactly 1,369 lights. I've wired the entire ceiling, every inch of it. . . . Though invisible, I am in the great American tradition of tinkers. That makes me kin to Ford, Edison and Franklin.

Ralph Ellison

[1]The outer layer of a part of the cell.
[2]The outer layer of skin.

Reading Further

Other works by this author include:
Juneteenth, by Ralph Ellison, Vintage Books, 1999.

Other sources on this topic include:
The African American Century, by Henry Louis Gates, Jr. and Cornel West, The Free Press, 2000.

Understanding Literature

Prologue The passage you have just read is a prologue to a novel. A prologue is an introduction to a novel, play, or other work of literature. Often a prologue contains useful information about events to come in the story. In a prologue to a play, an actor addresses the audience directly and tells them what the play will be about or describes the setting of the play.

Foreshadowing is the use of clues by the author to prepare readers for events that will happen.

The prologue of *The Invisible Man*, likewise, sets the stage for the reader by foreshadowing two themes that will reoccur in the novel: invisibility and light.

Science Connection The narrator of *The Invisible Man* says that he has strung 1,369 lights in his basement room. How were this many bulbs wired together? If all the bulbs were all wired together in a series circuit, the electrical resistance in the circuit would be high. By Ohm's law, the current in the circuit would be low and the bulbs wouldn't glow. If all the bulbs were wired in a parallel circuit, so much current would flow in the circuit that the connecting wires would melt. For the bulbs to light, the narrator must have wired them in many independent circuits.

Linking Science and Writing

Prologue Write a prologue to a make-believe book describing Edison's invention of the light bulb. Recall that a prologue is not a summary of the book. The prologue can state general themes that the work of literature will address, or it can set the stage or describe the setting of the story. You might want to discuss what was happening in the world during Edison's time or foreshadow the character and personality traits that enabled him to be a great inventor.

Career Connection

Electrical Engineer

At the age of 10, **Hans Moravec** wired up a tin can man and started building animate things out of inanimate objects. Since 1980, he has been a Principal Research Scientist at the Robotics Institute of Carnegie Mellon University in Pittsburgh. He and his team have built several mobile robots—the latest one is being designed to "see" in three dimensions and to move in crowded spaces without going bump in the night. By 2010, he expects robots, with the improved computers of that time, to be doing many simple tasks.

SCIENCE*Online* To learn more about careers in electrical engineering, visit the Glencoe Science Web site at **science.glencoe.com**.

Understanding Literature

Science Connection

All conductors offer some resistance. Conductors in a circuit may be connected in a series or in parallel. In a series circuit, the current passes through different resistances, one after the other, and then returns the main current. A parallel circuit is one in which the appliances are supplied by separate resistances from the same circuit, side by side.

Linking Science and Writing

Writing Strategies

Further discussion about what a prologue is will help students focus on the writing activity. Reading samples of prologues in other works also will help them focus on the task. If students are writing a prologue for a work of fiction, suggest that they might either set the stage by describing the town, country, or other setting in the book. If they are writing a prologue for a biography or autobiography, they might start by giving information about the subject that is not included in the book. If students are writing prologues for nonfiction works, suggest that they provide general information that will help introduce the topic.

Career Connection

Students interested in electrical engineering should study mathematics and the sciences. A bachelor's degree in engineering is the minimum requirement. All states require licensing of engineers whose work affects the general public. Electrical engineers may work with power generation, machinery controls, computers, and communications equipment, among other areas.

Internet Addresses

Explore the Glencoe Science Web site at **science.glencoe.com** to find out more about topics in this feature.

Chapter 7 Study Guide

Reviewing Main Ideas

Preview

Students can answer the questions in their Science Journals. Discuss the answers as you go through the chapter. LS **Linguistic**

Review

Students can write their answers, then compare them with those of other students. LS **Interpersonal**

Reteach

Students can look at the illustrations and describe details that support the main ideas of the chapter. LS **Visual-Spatial**

Answers to Chapter Review

Section 1

1. They have opposite charge.

Section 2

1. Just as water flows faster if moving down a steep incline, the flow of electrical charge is greater if it is moving through a large-diameter wire.

Section 3

4. Possible answer: Many devices would not exist, such as televisions, computers, and electric lights.

Chapter 7 Study Guide

Reviewing Main Ideas

Section 1 Electric Charge

1. There are two types of electric charge—positive charge and negative charge. Like charges repel and unlike charges attract. *Why are the towels clinging together?*

2. Electric charge is conserved. Charges cannot be created or destroyed.
3. An electrical conductor allows electrons to move through it easily. An electrical insulator doesn't allow electrons to move through it easily.
4. Objects can be charged by contact or by induction. Charging by induction occurs when a charged object is brought near an electrically neutral object.

Section 2 Electric Current

1. Charges flow through a conductor due to a voltage difference. *How is the flow of water similar to the flow of electric charge?*

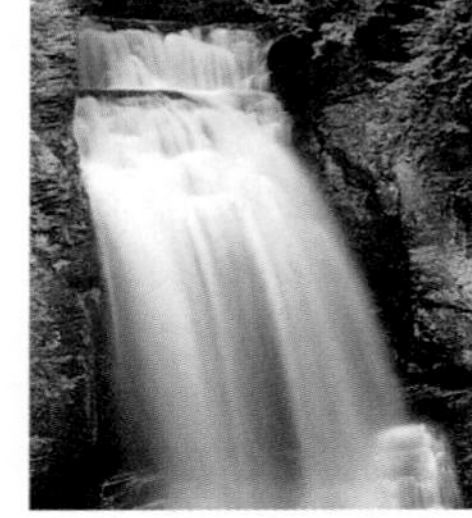

2. Electric current is the movement of electric charges. A circuit is a closed conducting loop through which electric charges can move.
3. A battery establishes a voltage difference in a circuit by separating positive and negative charges.
4. In an electric circuit, increasing the voltage difference increases the current. Increasing the resistance decreases the current. These relations are known as Ohm's law.

Section 3 Electrical Energy

1. Current has only one path in a series circuit and more than one path in a parallel circuit.
2. Circuit breakers and fuses are safety devices that prevent excessive current from flowing in a circuit.
3. Electrical power is the rate at which electrical energy is used.
4. Utility companies sell electrical energy by the kilowatt-hour, which is 1,000 W of power used for 1 h. *How would your life change if electrical energy were no longer available?*

FOLDABLES Reading & Study Skills — After You Read

Reflect on what you have learned about electricity in this chapter. Record your thoughts under the Learned tab of your Know-Want-Learn Study Fold.

FOLDABLES Reading & Study Skills — After You Read

After students have read the chapter and completed the Foldable described in Before You Read, have them do the activity on the student page.

Dinah Zike

Chapter 7 Study Guide

Visualizing Main Ideas

Use the following terms to complete the concept map: voltage difference, attract, conductor, repel, law of conservation of charge, insulator.

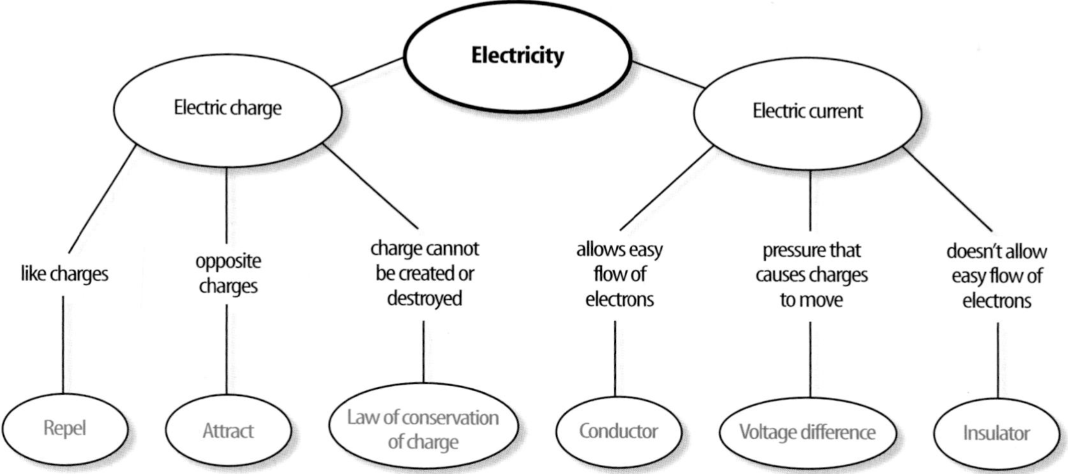

Vocabulary Review

Vocabulary Words

a. charging by contact
b. charging by induction
c. circuit
d. conductor
e. electric current
f. electrical power
g. insulator
h. kilowatt-hour
i. law of conservation of charge
j. Ohm's law
k. parallel circuit
l. resistance
m. series circuit
n. static electricity
o. voltage difference

Study Tip

Find a quiet place to study, whether you are at home or at school. Turn off the television or radio and give your full attention to your lessons.

Using Vocabulary

Distinguish between the terms in each of the following groups of words.

1. law of conservation of charge, Ohm's law
2. electric current, static electricity
3. current, voltage difference, electrical power
4. series circuit, parallel circuit
5. conductor, insulator
6. electrical power, kilowatt-hour
7. charging by contact, charging by induction
8. open circuit, closed circuit
9. current, voltage difference, resistance
10. kilowatt, watt

IDENTIFYING Misconceptions

Assess

After students have done the activity on page 192F and completed the chapter, have them perform this activity.

Materials For each group, one D-battery, one flash light bulb in socket, one switch, five wires, and one voltmeter.

Procedure Have each group set up a circuit with the battery, bulb, switch, and wires. Ask students to predict the voltage beteen the two sides of the switch when it is open and when it is closed. Have students use the voltmeters to test their predictions.

Expected Outcome Voltage varies across different points in a circuit and can exist without current flow. A voltage exists across the two sides of the switch when it is open. When the switch is closed that voltage approaches zero.

Chapter 7 Study Guide

Visualizing Main Ideas

See student page.

Vocabulary Review

Using Vocabulary

1. The law of conservation of charge states that charge can be neither created nor destroyed. Ohm's law relates voltage, resistance, and current.
2. Electric current is a continuous flow of charge. Static electricity is the accumulation of excess electric charge on an object.
3. Current is the flow of charges through a wire or conductor. The voltage difference is the push that causes electrons to move. Electrical power is the rate at which electrical energy is converted to another form of energy.
4. In a series circuit, current has only one possible path. In a parallel circuit, current has more than one path.
5. A conductor is a material through which charge moves easily. An insulator is a material through which charge cannot easily flow.
6. Electrical power is the rate at which electrical energy is converted to other forms of energy. A kilowatt-hour is a unit of electrical energy, equal to 1000 watts of power used for one hour.
7. Charging by contact requires that objects touch or rub. For charge by induction, objects only have to be close to each other.
8. In an open circuit, part of the path is disconnected so that no current can flow. In a closed circuit, the path is complete so current can flow.
9. Current is the flow of charges through a wire or conductor. The voltage difference is the push that causes electrons to move. Resistance is the tendency for a material to oppose the flow of electrons.
10. A kilowatt is 1,000 watts.

Chapter 7 Assessment

Checking Concepts

1. A
2. A
3. B
4. C
5. B
6. D
7. D
8. C
9. D
10. D

Thinking Critically

11. Lightning rods are grounded conductors. Because they are higher than the roof of a building, they are struck first. They discharge the electric charges of a lightning strike into Earth.
12. First, place a positive charge on the electroscope so that the leaves separate. Next, bring the object near the charged electroscope. If the object is negatively charged, the leaves will begin to move closer together.
13. $I = 3\ V/2\ \Omega = 1.5\ A$
14. $P = (120\ V)(2\ A) = 240\ W = 0.240\ kW$ and $E = (0.240\ kW)\ (4\ h) = 0.96\ kWh$
15. The appliances should be connected in parallel so if one appliance goes out, the others still work. The circuit should include either a fuse or circuit breaker, which would disconnect the current before it could get hot enough to start a fire.

Chapter 7 Assessment

Checking Concepts

Choose the word or phrase that best answers the question.

1. An object becomes positively charged when which of the following occurs?
   A) loses electrons **C)** gains electrons
   B) loses protons **D)** gains neutrons
2. How do two negative charges interact when they are brought close together?
   A) repel **C)** no interaction
   B) attract **D)** ground
3. What is a common source for a voltage difference?
   A) circuits **C)** wires
   B) batteries **D)** lightning
4. Which of the following is an insulator?
   A) copper **C)** wood
   B) silver **D)** salt water
5. What is the process of connecting an object to Earth with a conductor called?
   A) charging **C)** draining
   B) grounding **D)** induction
6. What is the SI unit used to measure the difference in voltage between two places?
   A) amperes **C)** ohms
   B) coulombs **D)** volts
7. What is the rate at which appliances consume energy?
   A) kilowatt-hour **C)** current
   B) resistance **D)** power
8. Resistance in wires causes electrical energy to be converted to what energy form?
   A) chemical energy **C)** thermal energy
   B) nuclear energy **D)** sound
9. Which of the following wires would tend to have the least amount of resistance?
   A) long **C)** hot
   B) fiberglass **D)** thick
10. What SI unit measures electrical energy?
    A) volts **C)** kilowatts
    B) newtons **D)** kilowatt-hours

Thinking Critically

11. How do lightning rods protect buildings from lightning?
12. Explain how an electroscope could be used to detect a negatively charged object.
13. A toy car with a resistance of 2 Ω is connected to a 3 V battery. How much current flows through the car?
14. The current flowing through an appliance connected to a 120-V source is 2 A. How many kilowatt-hours of electrical energy does the appliance use in 4 h?
15. You are asked to connect a stereo, a television, a VCR, and a lamp in a single, complete circuit. Would you connect these appliances in parallel or in series? How would you prevent an electrical fire? Draw a diagram of your circuit.

Developing Skills

16. **Making and Using Graphs** The resistance in a 1-cm length of copper wire at different temperatures is shown below. One microohm equals one millionth of an ohm. Construct a line graph for the data. Is copper a better conductor on a cold day or a hot day?

Copper Wire Resistance

Resistance in Microohms	Temperature (°C)
2	50
3	200
5	475

Chapter Assessment Planner

Portfolio Encourage students to place in their portfolios one or two items of what they consider to be their best work. Examples include:

- Science Journal, p. 195
- Assessment, p. 204
- Earth Science Integration, p. 210

Performance Additional performance assessments, Performance Task Assessment Lists, and rubrics for evaluating these activities can be found in Glencoe's **Performance Assessment in the Science Classroom.**

17. Concept Mapping Make a network concept map sequencing the events that occur when an electroscope is brought near a positively charged object and a negatively charged object. Indicate which way electrons flow and the charge and responses of the leaves.

18. Identifying and Manipulating Variables and Controls Design an experiment to test the effect on current and voltage differences in a circuit when two identical batteries are connected in series. What is your hypothesis? What are the variables and control?

19. Interpreting Scientific Illustrations The diagram below shows a series circuit containing a lamp connected to a standard wall outlet. Using the information in the diagram, compute the current in the circuit shown.

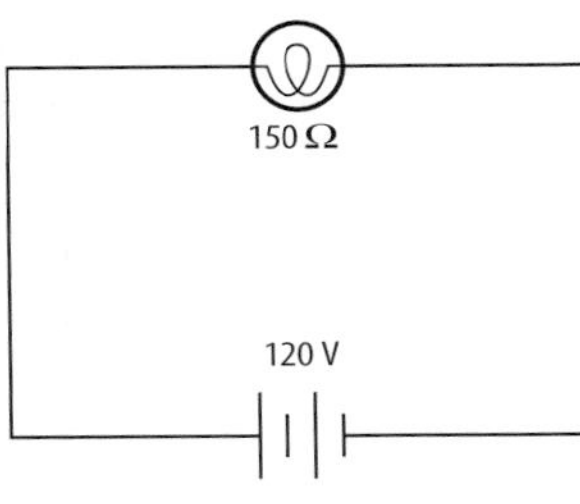

Performance Assessment

20. Poster You probably have seen warnings about contacting overhead power lines. However, birds can perch safely on power lines. Find out how this is possible. Share the information you learn by making a poster for your classroom.

Technology

Go to the Gle... Science Web site at **science.gl...om** or use the **Glencoe Sc... -ROM** for additional chapter ass...

THE PRINCETON REVIEW Test Practice

The local electric company did a study of the amount of power used by some common appliances. The results of this study are shown in the chart below.

Power Used by Common Appliances

Appliance	Power Used (watts)	Appliance	Power Used (watts)
Clock	3	Stove/oven	2,600
Microwave oven	1,450	Dishwasher	2,300
Clothes drier	4,000	Refrigerator/ freezer	600
Radio	100	Hair drier	1,000
Color TV	300	Toaster	700

Study the chart and answer the following questions.

1. According the chart, which appliance used the least amount of power?
A) toaster
B) clock
C) radio
D) color television

2. According to this information, which appliance uses more than 3,000 W of power?
F) dishwasher
G) microwave oven
H) clothes drier
J) stove/oven

Assessment Resources

Reproducible Masters

Chapter Resources Booklet
Chapter R...
Chapter T...
Assessment ...ctivity, p. 47

Glencoe Science Web site
Interacti...
Chapter ...

Glencoe Technology
Assessment Transparency
Interactive CD-ROM Chapter Quizzes
ExamView Pro Test Bank
Vocabulary PuzzleMaker Software
MindJogger Videoquiz DVD/VHS

Chapter 7 Assessment

THE PRINCETON REVIEW Test Practice

The Test-Taking Tip was written by The Princeton Review, the nation's leader in test preparation.

1. C
2. H

Developing Skills

16. Copper is a better conductor on a cold day because its resistance decreases with temperature.

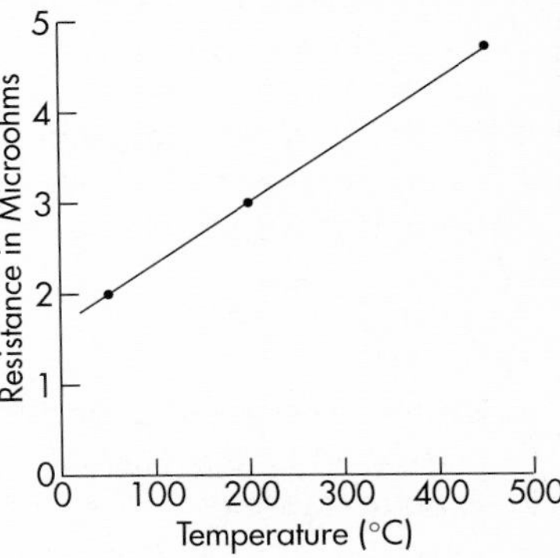

17. Maps should show that positively charged objects attract electrons away from the leaves, so they repel each other. For negatively charged objects, electrons flow toward the leaves and they repel each other.

18. Answers will vary, but the variable should be the number of batteries and the constants should include the materials in the circuit and the type of circuit (series or parallel).

19. $120\text{V}/150\Omega = 0.8$ A

Performance Assessment

20. Birds are not grounded. All parts of the bird are a similar high voltage. Also, the bird's body has much more resistance than the power line, so no current flows through it. Use **PASC**, p. 145

CHAPTER ASSESSMENT 223

Section/Objectives	Standards		Activities/Features
	National	State/Local	
Chapter Opener	See p. 37T for a Key to Standards.		**Explore Activity:** Observe the strength of a magnet, p. 225 **Before You Read,** p. 225
Section 1 Magnetism 2 sessions 1 block 1. **Describe** the properties of temporary and permanent magnets. 2. **Explain** how a magnet exerts a force on an object. 3. **Explain** why some materials are magnetic and others are not. 4. **Model** magnetic behavior using magnetic domains.	National Content Standards: UCP2, A1, B1 (5–8), B2, B6 (9–12)		**MiniLAB:** Observing Magnetic Interference, p. 229 **Life Science Integration,** p. 230 **Problem-Solving Activity:** How can magnetic parts of a junk car be salvaged?, p. 230 **MiniLAB:** Making Your Own Compass, p. 231
Section 2 Electricity and Magnetism 2 sessions 1 block 1. **Understand** the relationship between electric current and magnetism. 2. **Explain** how electromagnets are constructed. 3. **Describe** how electromagnets are used. 4. **Describe** how an electric motor operates.	National Content Standards: UCP2, B1 (5–8), B2, B6 (9–12), E2, F5 (5–8), F6 (9–12)		**Science Online,** p. 237
Section 3 Producing Electric Current 5 sessions 2.5 blocks 1. **Describe** how a generator produces an electric current. 2. **Distinguish** between alternating current and direct current. 3. **Explain** how a transformer can change the voltage of an alternating current.	National Content Standards: UCP2, A1, B1 (5–8), B2, B6 (9–12), E2, F5 (5–8), F6 (9–12), G3		**Environmental Science Integration,** p. 242 **Visualizing Motors and Generators,** p. 243 **Science Online,** p. 244 **Activity:** Electricity and Magnetism, p. 247 **Activity:** Putting Electromagnets to Work, p. 248 **Science and History:** Body Art, p. 250

Activity Materials	Reproducible Resources	Section Assessment	Technology
Explore Activity: bar magnet, paper clips	**Chapter Resources Booklet** Foldables Worksheet, p. 17 Note-taking Worksheets, pp. 33–35	GLENCOE'S ASSESSMENT ADVANTAGE	
MiniLAB: bar magnet, ring stand, thread, paper clip, book, aluminum foil, fabric, butter knife **MiniLAB:** plastic foam cup, sewing needle, tape, plate, water	**Chapter Resources Booklet** Transparency Activity, p. 44 MiniLAB, pp. 3, 4 Enrichment, p. 30 Reinforcement, p. 27 Directed Reading, p. 20 Lab Activity, pp. 9–12 **Mathematics Skill Acitivities,** p. 47	**Portfolio** Curriculum Connection, p. 229 **Performance** MiniLAB, p. 229 Problem-Solving Activity, p. 230 MiniLAB, p. 231 Skill Builder Activities, p. 232 **Content** Section Assessment, p. 232	Section Focus Transparency Interactive CD-ROM/DVD Guided Reading Audio Program
Need materials? Contact Science Kit at 1-800-828-7777 or www.sciencekit.com on the Internet.	**Chapter Resources Booklet** Transparency Activity, p. 45 Enrichment, p. 31 Reinforcement, p. 28 Directed Reading, p. 21 Lab Activity, pp. 13–16 **Physical Science Critical Thinking/Problem Solving,** p. 17 **Science Inquiry Labs,** p. 9	**Portfolio** Curriculum Connection, p. 238 **Performance** Skill Builder Activities, p. 239 **Content** Section Assessment, p. 239	Section Focus Transparency Interactive CD-ROM/DVD Guided Reading Audio Program
Activity: cardboard tube; scissors; bar magnet; thin, flexible, insulated wire; galvanometer or ammeter **Activity:** 22–gauge insulated wire, 16–penny iron nail, aluminum rod or nail, 6 v DC power supply, 1.5 v D-cells (3), steel paper clips, magnetic compass, duct tape	**Chapter Resources Booklet** Transparency Activity, p. 46 Enrichment, p. 32 Reinforcement, p. 29 Directed Reading, pp. 21, 22 Transparency Activity, pp. 47–48 Activity Worksheet, pp. 5–6, 7–8 **Cultural Diversity,** p. 53 **Science Inquiry Labs,** p. 55 **Home and Community Involvement,** p. 37 **Performance Assessment in the Science Classroom,** p. 53	**Portfolio** Curriculum Connection, p 242 **Performance** Skill Builder Activities, p. 246 **Content** Section Assessment, p. 246	Section Focus Transparency Teaching Transparency Interactive CD-ROM/DVD Guided Reading Audio Program

End of Chapter Assessment

GLENCOE'S ASSESSMENT ADVANTAGE

Blackline Masters	Technology	Professional Series
Chapter Resources Booklet Chapter Review, pp. 37–38 Chapter Tests, pp. 39–42 **Standardized Test Practice by The Princeton Review,** pp. 36–39	MindJogger Videoquiz CD-ROM Explorations and Quizzes Vocabulary Puzzle Makers ExamView Pro Test Bank Interactive Lesson Planner Interactive Teacher's Edition	Performance Assessment in the Science Classroom (PASC)

Transparencies

Section Focus

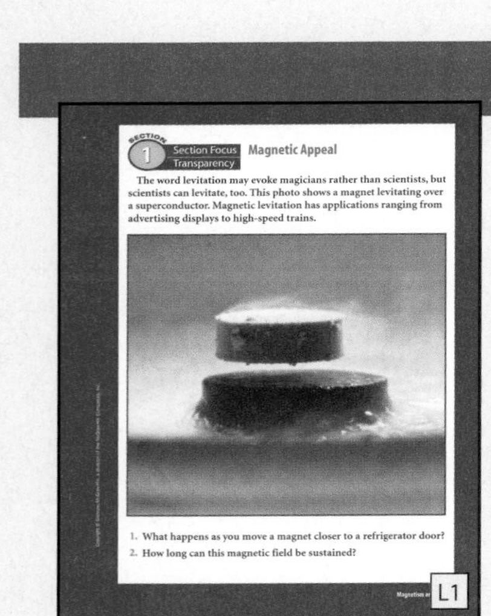
SECTION 1 Section Focus Transparency **Magnetic Appeal**

The word levitation may evoke magicians rather than scientists, but scientists can levitate, too. This photo shows a magnet levitating over a superconductor. Magnetic levitation has applications ranging from advertising displays to high-speed trains.

1. What happens as you move a magnet closer to a refrigerator door?
2. How long can this magnetic field be sustained?

L1

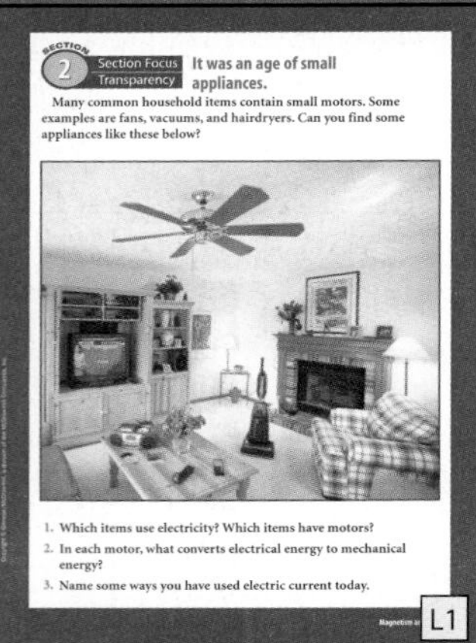
SECTION 2 Section Focus Transparency **It was an age of small appliances.**

Many common household items contain small motors. Some examples are fans, vacuums, and hairdryers. Can you find some appliances like these below?

1. Which items use electricity? Which items have motors?
2. In each motor, what converts electrical energy to mechanical energy?
3. Name some ways you have used electric current today.

L1

SECTION 3 Section Focus Transparency **Flowing Current**

Electricity is often generated at power plants by burning fossil fuels. But fossil fuels are nonrenewable resources that, when burned, can cause pollution. There are, however, nonpolluting sources of energy.

1. What is the source of energy for this hydroelectric power plant?
2. How does the source of energy translate into electrical energy?
3. What are the advantages of hydroelectric power? Disadvantages?

L1

Assessment

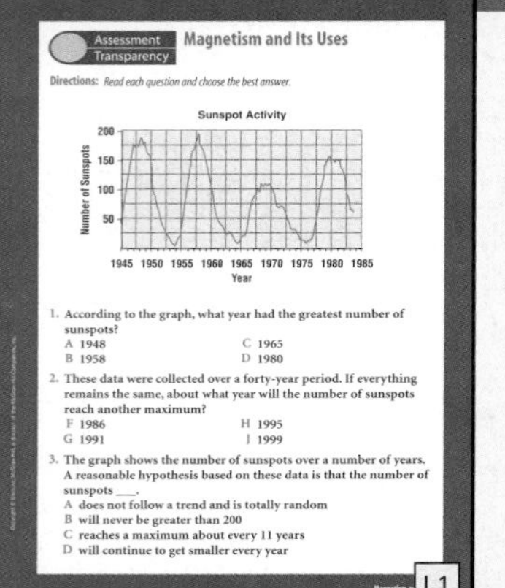
Assessment Transparency **Magnetism and Its Uses**

Directions: *Read each question and choose the best answer.*

1. According to the graph, what year had the greatest number of sunspots?
   A 1948 C 1965
   B 1958 D 1980
2. These data were collected over a forty-year period. If everything remains the same, about what year will the number of sunspots reach another maximum?
   F 1986 H 1995
   G 1991 I 1999
3. The graph shows the number of sunspots over a number of years. A reasonable hypothesis based on these data is that the number of sunspots ___.
   A does not follow a trend and is totally random
   B will never be greater than 200
   C reaches a maximum about every 11 years
   D will continue to get smaller every year

L1

Teaching

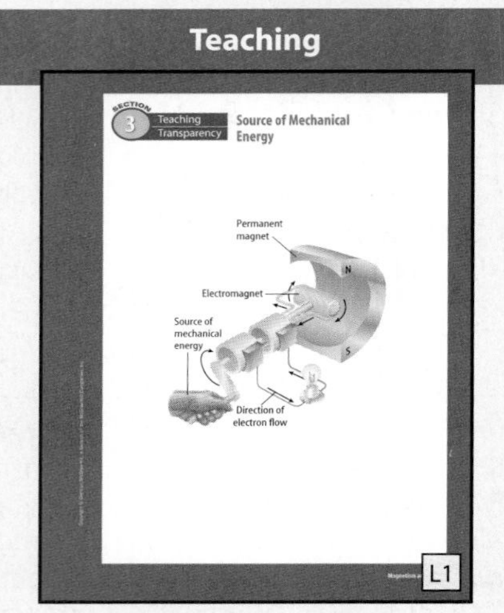
SECTION 3 Teaching Transparency **Source of Mechanical Energy**

L1

This is a representation of key blackline masters available in the Teacher Classroom Resources. See Resource Manager boxes within the chapter for additional information.

Key to Teaching Strategies

The following designations will help you decide which activities are appropriate for your students.

- L1 Level 1 activities should be appropriate for students with learning difficulties.
- L2 Level 2 activities should be within the ability range of all students.
- L3 Level 3 activities are designed for above-average students.
- ELL ELL activities should be within the ability range of English Language Learners.
- COOP LEARN Cooperative Learning activities are designed for small group work.
- LS Multiple Learning Styles logos are used throughout to indicate strategies that address different learning styles.
- P These strategies represent student products that can be placed into a best-work portfolio.

Hands-on Activities

Activity Worksheets

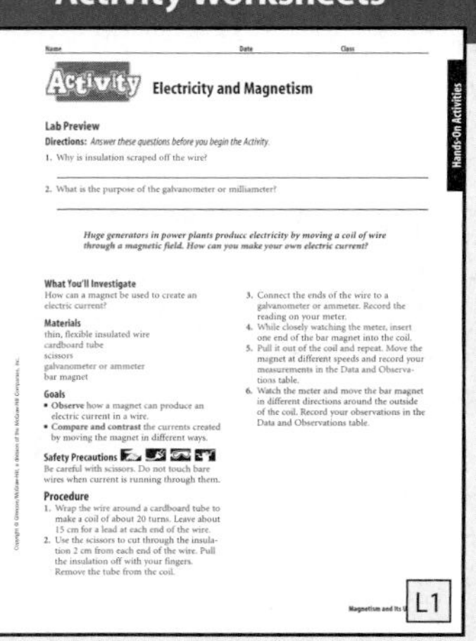
Name Date Class

Hands-On Activities

Activity Electricity and Magnetism

Lab Preview

Directions: *Answer these questions before you begin the Activity.*

1. Why is insulation scraped off the wire?
2. What is the purpose of the galvanometer or milliameter?

Huge generators in power plants produce electricity by moving a coil of wire through a magnetic field. How can you make your own electric current?

What You'll Investigate

How can a magnet be used to create an electric current?

Materials

thin, flexible insulated wire
cardboard tube
scissors
galvanometer or ammeter
bar magnet

Goals

- **Observe** how a magnet can produce an electric current in a wire.
- **Compare and contrast** the currents created by moving the magnet in different ways.

Safety Precautions

Be careful with scissors. Do not touch bare wires when current is running through them.

Procedure

1. Wrap the wire around a cardboard tube to make a coil of about 20 turns. Leave about 15 cm for a lead at each end of the wire.
2. Use the scissors to cut through the insulation 2 cm from each end of the wire. Pull the insulation off with your fingers. Remove the tube from the coil.
3. Connect the ends of the wire to a galvanometer or ammeter. Record the reading on your meter.
4. While closely watching the meter, insert one end of the bar magnet into the coil.
5. Pull it out of the coil and repeat. Move the magnet at different speeds and record your measurements in the Data and Observations table.
6. Watch the meter and move the bar magnet in different directions around the outside of the coil. Record your observations in the Data and Observations table.

L1

Laboratory Activities

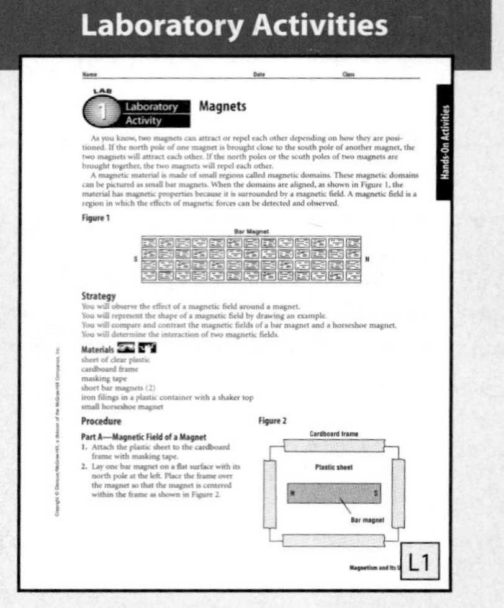
Name Date Class

Hands-On Activities

LAB 1 Laboratory Activity **Magnets**

As you know, two magnets can attract or repel each other depending on how they are positioned. If the north pole of one magnet is brought close to the south pole of another magnet, the two magnets will attract each other. If the north poles or the south poles of two magnets are brought together, the two magnets will repel each other.

A magnetic material is made of small regions called magnetic domains. These magnetic domains can be pictured as small bar magnets. When the domains are aligned, as shown in Figure 1, the material has magnetic properties because it is surrounded by a magnetic field. A magnetic field is a region in which the effects of magnetic forces can be detected and observed.

Figure 1

Strategy

You will observe the effect of a magnetic field around a magnet.
You will represent the shape of a magnetic field by drawing an example.
You will compare and contrast the magnetic fields of a bar magnet and a horseshoe magnet.
You will determine the interaction of two magnetic fields.

Materials

sheet of clear plastic
cardboard frame
masking tape
short bar magnets (2)
iron filings in a plastic container with a shaker top
small horseshoe magnet

Procedure

Part A—Magnetic Field of a Magnet

1. Attach the plastic sheet to the cardboard frame with masking tape.
2. Lay one bar magnet on a flat surface with its north pole at the left. Place the frame over the magnet so that the magnet is centered within the frame as shown in Figure 2.

Figure 2

L1

Meeting Different Ability Levels

Content Outline

Note-taking Worksheet — Magnetism and Its Uses

L1

Reinforcement

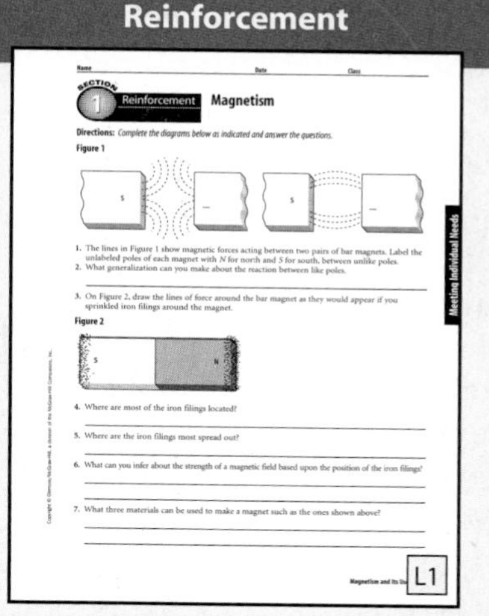
Reinforcement — Magnetism

L1

Directed Reading

Directed Reading for Content Mastery — Overview: Magnetism and Its Uses

L1

Assessment

Chapter Tests

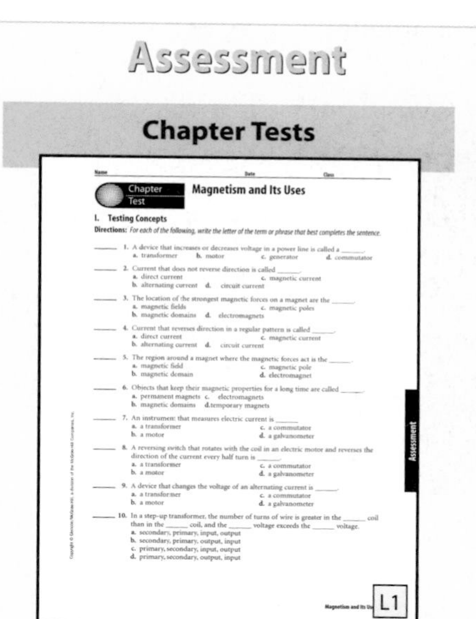
Chapter Test — Magnetism and Its Uses

L1

Enrichment

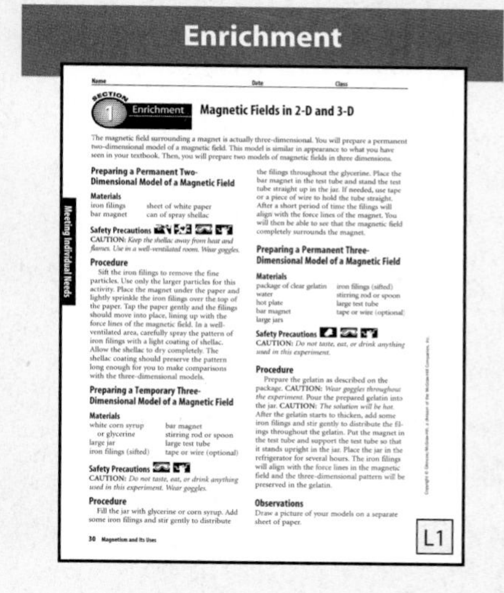
Enrichment — Magnetic Fields in 2-D and 3-D

L1

Spanish Directed Reading

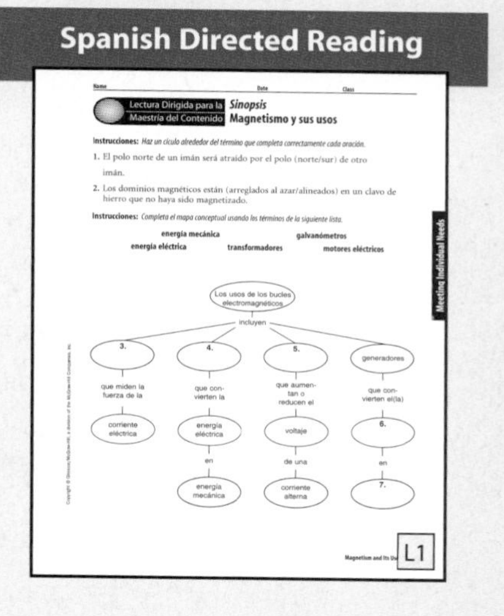
Lectura Dirigida para la Maestría del Contenido — Sinopsis: Magnetismo y sus usos

L1

Test Practice Workbook

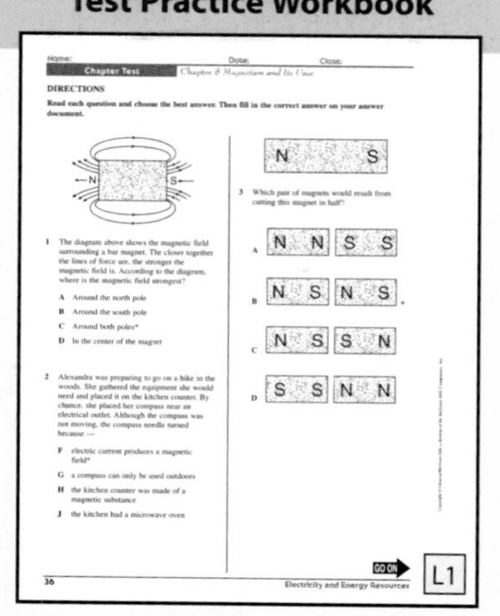
Chapter Test — Chapter 8 Magnetism and Its Uses

L1

Chapter Review

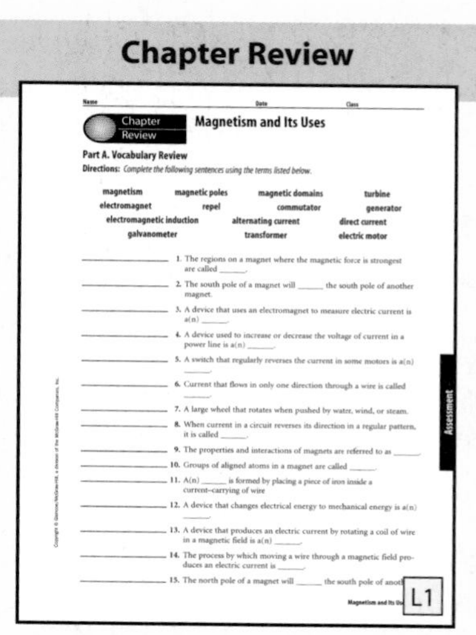
Chapter Review — Magnetism and Its Uses

L1

Science Content Background

SECTION 1

Magnetism

Magnets

In 1269 Petrus Peregrinus published an article describing the properties of lodestone. He reported that if it is hung freely, lodestone orients in a north-south plane but does not point exactly to true North. He also noted that like poles repel and unlike poles attract, and that iron can be magnetized by contact with it.

Magnetic Materials

A common definition of magnetism is the ability to attract iron. Steel is composed of iron and carbon molecules that form a strong material used in many common products. Steel is magnetic because it contains iron. This property allows cars to be lifted by electromagnets in junkyards and soup can lids to be held by the magnet on a can opener. Cobalt and nickel are also attracted to magnets. Iron, nickel, and cobalt are called ferromagnetic materials.

Student Misconception

Students may think that all metals are magnetic.

Refer to the facing page for teaching strategies to address this misconception. Refer to pages 230–232 for content related to this topic.

SECTION 2

Electricity and Magnetism

Electric Current and Magnetism

Most forces we experience interact in the same or in opposite directions. For example, air resistance on a car traveling north acts toward the south. In the case of electric current, the magnetic field acts at right angles to the direction of the current. The right-hand rule shows the direction of the magnetic field in a wire. The thumb points in the direction of the conventional current, or the way a positive charge would flow in a wire. The fingers then show the direction of the magnetic field.

SECTION 3

Producing Electric Current

From Mechanical to Electrical Energy

Niagara Falls generates significant tourism and electricity. In order to keep the tourism industry vibrant, only about 20% of the water that goes over the falls is diverted into turbines in the daytime; at night this amount is increased to 50%.

Tony Freeman/PhotoEdit

Transformers

The ability of alternating current (AC) to be transformed into higher and lower voltages gives it an advantage over direct current (DC) in electrical power distribution. Increasing the voltage does not create energy because current decreases as voltage increases. This increase does, however, result in more efficient transmission. This efficiency becomes significant as electricity travels through miles of wire.

For additional content background on this topic, go to the Glencoe Science Web site at science.glencoe.com.

IDENTIFYING Misconceptions

Find Out What Students Think

Students may think that . . .

- **All metals are magnetic.**

Students are aware of common properties of metals such as good the fact that they are good conductors of electricity and heat. It is natural for students to extend these similarities to magnetism and think that all metals can be attracted by a magnet. Lack of first-hand experience with magnets and metals makes this misconception common, even in adults. In addition, iron alloys are omnipresent, so people's limited experiences with magnets may lead them to believe that all metals are magnetic.

Activity

Ask students to draw two columns on their papers and label one **Attracted to a Magnet** and the other **Not Attracted to a Magnet.** Then ask that they place the following words into the appropriate columns: *iron*, *lead*, *plastic*, *copper*, *steel*, *aluminum*, *nickel*, *cobalt*, *oxygen*, and *wood*. Have students form groups and discuss any differences in opinion about which items belong in each column. The iron, steel, nickel, and cobalt are attracted to a magnet, and the lead, plastic, copper, aluminum, oxygen and wood are not.

Promote Understanding

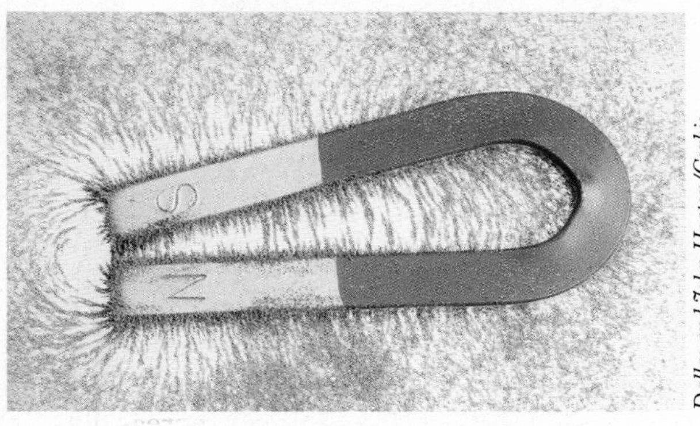

Dallas and John Heaton/Corbis

Activity

Provide students with different metals and nonmetals and with magnets with which to test them. The materials should include easily obtainable ferromagnetic materials such as iron and steel as well as nonferromagnetic metals such as aluminum and copper. Make sure to include nonmetals, even though most students will realize that these are not magnetic.

- Have students use the magnets to test for attraction and sort materials that are and are not magnetic.
- On the board, make a class list of the results.
- Help students realize that iron (Fe) is a magnetic material, so things made from iron, including steel, are attracted to magnets.
- Explain that cobalt (Co) and nickel (Ni) are also magnetic materials.
- Have students locate iron, cobalt, and nickel on a periodic table of the elements. Point out that on the periodic table, these metals are in the same row and are next to each other.

Assess

After completing the chapter, see *Identifying Misconceptions* in the Study Guide.

CHAPTER 

Magnetism and Its Uses

Chapter Vocabulary

magnetism
magnetic pole
magnetic domain
electromagnet
galvanometer
electric motor
electromagnetic induction
generator
turbine
direct current (DC)
alternating current (AC)
transformer

What do you think?

Science Journal The photograph shows a magnetic cube that is being repelled by a superconducting disk.

CHAPTER 

Magnetism and Its Uses

A giant solar flare erupts from the Sun, spewing high energy particles and other forms of radiation toward Earth. Fortunately, Earth's magnetic field deflects most of these particles so they don't damage you and other living creatures. In this chapter, you will learn how magnetism and electricity are related, and how some common devices use magnetism.

What do you think?

Look at the picture below with a classmate. Discuss what this might be or what is happening. Here's a hint: *The force holding up this cube also spins electric motors.* Write your answer or your best guess in your Science Journal.

Theme Connection

Systems and Interactions Electricity and magnetism interact as a system. Electrical flow causes magnetic effects, and moving magnets are used to produce electrical energy.

Magnets can do more than hold papers on a refrigerator door. Did you know that they are used in TVs, computers, stereo speakers, and electric motors? Magnets play an important role in making the electricity you use at home. Magnetism also is used to make images of the organs and tissues inside the human body. What properties of magnets make them so useful? This activity will help you find out.

Observe the strength of a magnet

1. Hold a bar magnet horizontally and suspend a paper clip from one end of it. Continue adding paper clips to make a chain until the magnet will hold no more. Record the number of paper clips the magnet held.
2. Repeat step 1 three times. First, suspend the paper clips about 2 cm from the end of the magnet, then near the center of the magnet, and finally at the other end of the magnet.

Observe

In your Science Journal, compare the number of clips suspended from each point on the magnet. Infer which part of the magnet has the strongest attraction for the paper clips.

Before You Read

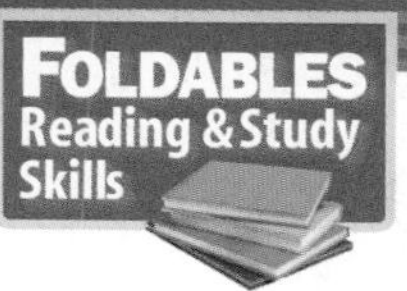

Making a Question Study Fold **Asking yourself questions helps you to stay focused and better understand magnets when you are reading the chapter.**

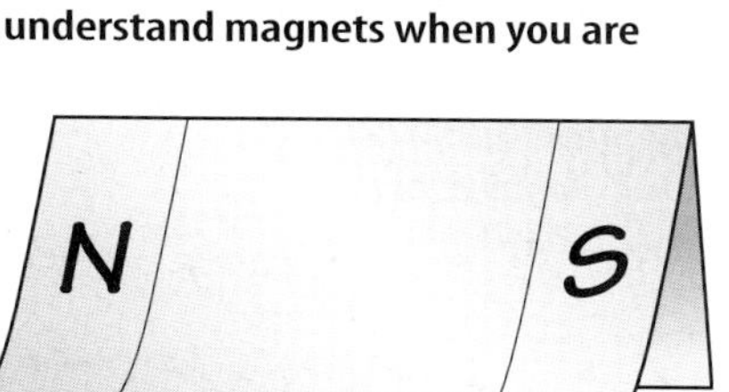

1. Place a sheet of paper in front of you so the long side is at the top. Fold the paper in half from top to bottom.
2. Make the front and back look like a magnet by writing *N* for north on the left side and *S* for south on the right side as shown.
3. Before you read the chapter write two questions about magnets inside the flaps.
4. As you read the chapter, write answers to your questions.

Explore Activity

Purpose Use the Explore Activity to illustrate the fact that the strength of a magnetic field varies over the length of a bar magnet. L2 ELL LS **Kinesthetic**

Preparation Test the bar magnets to see approximately how many paper clips each team will need. Small clips make it easier to observe differences in field strength.

Materials bar magnet, many small paper clips of the same size

Teaching Strategies If you have a variety of bar magnets, have the class compare results after finishing the activity. Ask students why the paper clips need to be the same size. so you can compare the numbers picked up

Observe

The two ends of the magnet are equally strong. The middle is weaker. Some magnets will not hold any clips there.

Process Have students sketch a graph showing how the strength of the magnetic field changes over the length of the magnet. Use **Performance Assessment in the Science Classroom,** p. 127.

Before You Read

FOLDABLES Reading & Study Skills

Dinah Zike Study Fold

Purpose Get students thinking about magnetism before they read the chapter by asking them to pose questions that guide their reading. The resulting question and answer Foldable becomes a simple study guide.

For additional help, see Foldables Worksheet, p. 17 in **Chapter Resources Booklet,** or go to the Glencoe Science Web site at **science.glencoe.com.** See After You Read in the Study Guide at the end of this chapter.

SECTION

Magnetism

1 Motivate

Bellringer Transparency

Display the Section Focus Transparency for Section 1. Use the accompanying Transparency Activity Master. L2 ELL

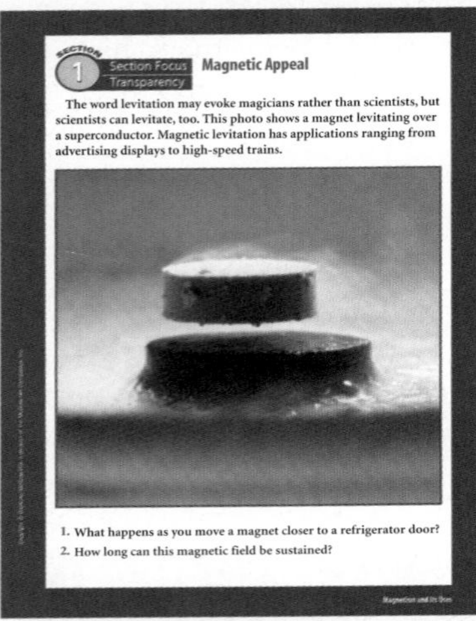

Tie to Prior Knowledge

Discuss with students places where they have seen or used magnets. Most will have used magnets on refrigerator doors and in science classes. Explain that magnets are also used in such items as stereo speakers, television screens, and floppy disks.

SECTION

Magnetism

As You Read

***What* You'll Learn**

- **Describe** the properties of temporary and permanent magnets.
- **Explain** how a magnet exerts a force on an object.
- **Explain** why some materials are magnetic and others are not.
- **Model** magnetic behavior using magnetic domains.

Vocabulary

magnetism
magnetic pole
magnetic domain

***Why* It's Important**

Without magnets, you could not use computers, CD players, or even the lights in your home.

Magnets

You may be familiar with magnets because they help display artwork on refrigerators, but magnets also fascinated early Greek and Chinese cultures long before refrigerators were invented. The Greeks discovered a mineral, shown in **Figure 1,** that was a natural magnet. They found the mineral in a region called Magnesia, so the Greeks called the mineral magnetic. More than 2,000 years later, magnets play an important role in business, medicine, transportation, and science. Today, the word **magnetism** refers to the properties and interactions of magnets.

Reading Check *Why did the Greeks use the term magnetic?*

Magnetic Force You probably have played with magnets to attract a metal object. You might have noticed that two magnets also exert a force on each other. Depending on which ends of the magnets are close together, the magnets either repel or attract each other. You probably noticed that the interaction between two magnets can be felt even before the magnets touch. This interaction is called magnetic force. Its strength increases as magnets move closer together and decreases as the distance between the magnets increases.

Figure 1
The Greeks found a mineral, now called magnetite, with natural magnetic properties. *What explanations do you think they gave for the behavior of magnetite?*

Section Assessment Planner

Portfolio
Curriculum Connection, p. 229

Performance Assessment
MiniLAB, p. 229
Problem-Solving Activity, p. 230
Try At Home MiniLAB, p. 231
Skill Builder Activities, p. 232
See page 254 for more options.

Content Assessment
Section, p. 232
Challenge, p. 232
Chapter, pp. 254–255

A

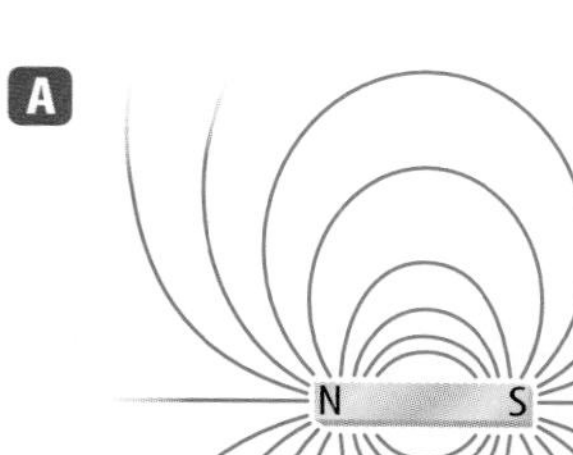

B

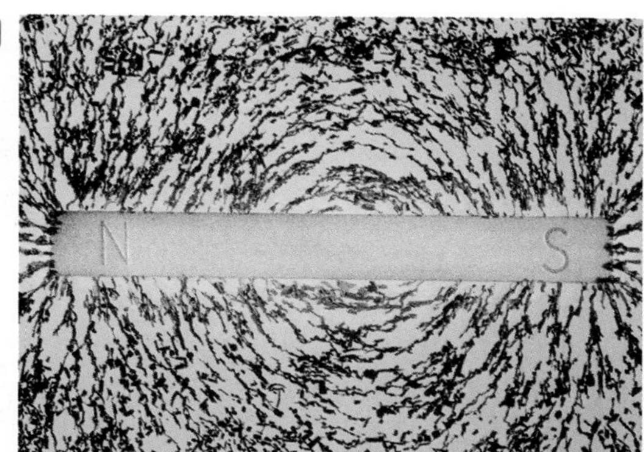

Magnetic Field A magnet is surrounded by a magnetic field that exerts the magnetic force. The magnetic field forms curved lines called magnetic field lines. When objects made of iron or another magnet is placed in this magnetic field, it reacts to the magnetic force. The magnetic field is strongest close to the magnet and weakest far away. **Figure 2** shows the magnetic field surrounding a bar magnet.

Figure 2
A magnet is surrounded by a magnetic field. A Magnetic field lines trace the shape of a magnet's magnetic field. B Iron filings sprinkled around a magnet line up along the magnetic field lines.

Magnetic Poles Look again at **Figure 2.** Do you notice that the magnetic field lines are closest together at the ends of the bar magnet? These regions, called the **magnetic poles,** are where the magnetic force exerted by the magnet is strongest. All magnets have a north pole and a south pole. For a bar magnet, the north and south poles are at the opposite ends. If a bar magnet is suspended so it turns freely, the north pole of the magnet will point north. Even magnets with more complicated shapes have north and south poles, as **Figure 3** shows. The two ends of a horseshoe-shaped magnet are the north and south poles. A magnet shaped like a disk has opposite poles on the top and bottom of the disk. Magnetic field lines always start at the north pole of a magnet and end on the south pole.

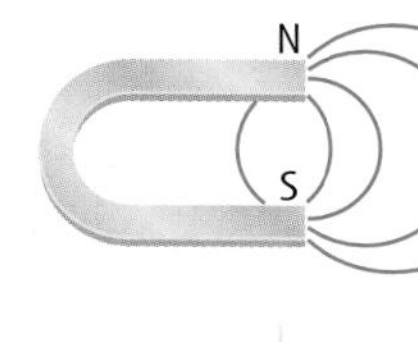

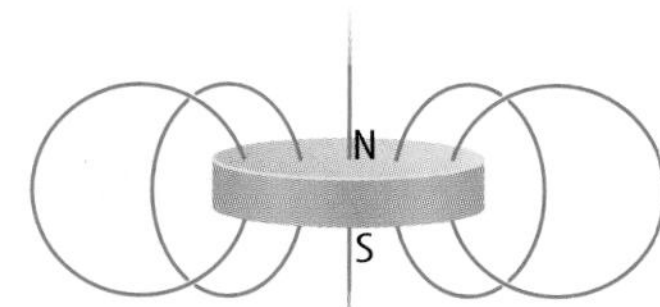

Figure 3
The magnetic field lines around horseshoe and disk magnets are closest together at the magnets' poles. ***Where would a horseshoe magnet have the weakest attraction for metal objects?***

2 Teach

Magnets

Caption Answers

Figure 1 Possible responses: magnetite has a natural tendency to orient toward the north; it has an affinity for the north star.

Reading Check

Answer They found the magnetic minerals in Magnesia.

Use an Analogy

A magnet's field, like a gravitational field, affects objects without touching them, even at a great distance. The faraway north magnetic pole attracts a compass needle, like the distant Sun holds Earth in orbit.

Use Science Words

Word Meaning Have students find out what *field* means in physics. A field is a region of space with a physical property (such as gravitational force, fluid pressure, etc.) that has a definite value at every point in the region. Compare and contrast this with other meanings of *field.* Other meanings also refer to areas, such as a meadow, a playing field, a background region, or even an area of interest. L3 LS **Linguistic**

Caption Answer

Figure 3 in the curve

Resource Manager

Chapter Resources Booklet

Transparency Activity, p. 44
Directed Reading for Content Mastery, p. 20
Note-taking Worksheets, pp. 33–35

Inclusion Strategies

Visually Impaired For students who cannot see the field lines in the illustrations and demonstrations, provide an opportunity to experiment with strong magnets. Make sure these students can feel the forces of attraction and repulsion between the magnets. L1 LS **Kinesthetic**

Caption Answer

Figure 4 When held in an oval, with ends facing, they will attract if opposite poles align, and repel if like poles align. The curved centers would show little interaction.

Visual Learning

Figure 5 What do you think happens to the magnetic force in the gaps between the lines? The force is continuous even though the lines don't show it.

Quick Demo

Show magnetic fields on the overhead projector. Make iron filings by rubbing a metal file on an iron nail. Place the iron filings in a covered petri dish or between two overhead sheets. Place different magnets on top of the filings on the projector. Then show the fields between attracting and repelling poles, and how the fields change as you move the magnets slowly toward or away from each other. This demonstrates how field strength diminishes with distance. L2 ELL **Visual-Spatial**

Reading Check

Answer Like poles repel each other; unlike poles attract.

Teacher FYI

Earth's magnetic poles do not perfectly align with Earth's geographic poles, the points about which Earth rotates. Also, Earth's magnetic field is not fixed. The north magnetic pole has traveled about 10 km/year over the past century, and, many times in the past, magnetic north and south have switched places.

A

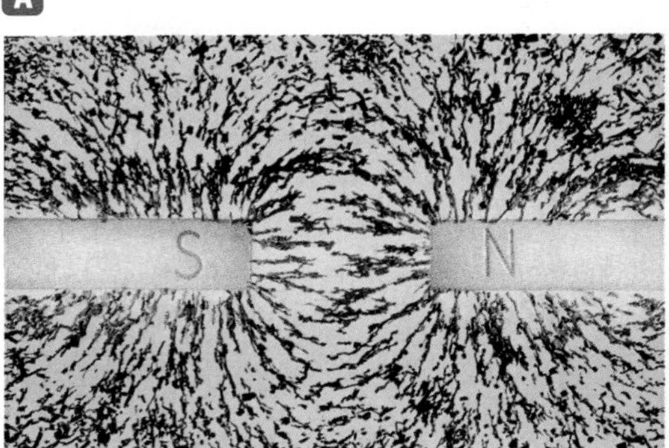

B

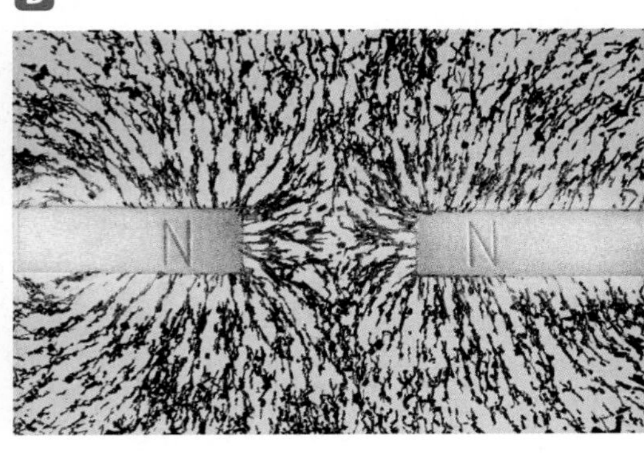

Figure 4
Magnets can attract or repel each other. A Unlike poles attract. When unlike poles are brought together, their magnetic field lines seem to connect with each other. B Like poles repel. When like poles are brought together, their magnetic field lines seem to push away from each other. *How would two horseshoe magnets interact?*

How Magnets Interact Two magnets can either attract or repel each other. If you try to bring the two north poles or the two south poles of two magnets close to each other, you can feel a force preventing the magnets from touching. However, north poles always attract south poles. When two magnets are brought close to each other, their magnetic fields can combine to produce a new magnetic field. **Figure 4** shows the magnetic field that results when like poles and unlike poles of bar magnets are brought close to each other.

Reading Check *How do magnetic poles interact with each other?*

A Compass Needle A magnet that is free to rotate can turn when it is placed in a magnetic field. A compass contains a needle, a small bar magnet, that can freely rotate. If you place a small compass near a bar magnet, the compass needle will turn so that the north pole of the needle points toward the south pole of the bar magnet. The compass needle also lines up along the magnetic field lines that pass near it. **Figure 5** shows how compass needles placed at several positions around a bar magnet are aligned along the magnetic field lines.

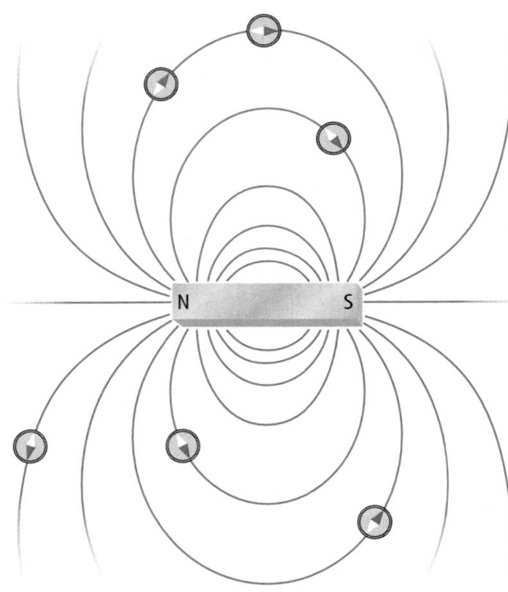

Figure 5
Compass needles rotate to line up with the magnetic field lines of a bar magnet.

228 CHAPTER 8 Magnetism and Its Uses

Fun Fact

Earth's magnetic field lines are not parallel to the surface. A delicately balanced magnetized needle can be used to measure the dip of the magnetic field, as well as its direction.

Cultural Diversity

Compasses Compasses were invented in China. By the ninth century A.D., the Chinese had discovered that magnetic north does not exactly coincide with geographic north. The compass was used for navigation at sea starting about 1,000 years ago (850–1050 A.D.). Before that they were used for a type of divination based on geographic features.

Earth's Magnetic Field Imagine you are in a boat in the middle of an ocean. Without landmarks nearby, how could you tell in which direction you were traveling? A compass would help determine your direction because the north pole of the compass needle always points north. This is because Earth acts like a giant bar magnet and is surrounded by a magnetic field that extends into space. Just as with a bar magnet, the compass needle aligns with Earth's magnetic field lines, as shown in **Figure 6.**

Earth's Magnetic Poles The north pole of a magnet is defined as the end of the magnet that points toward the geographic north. Sometimes the north pole and south pole of magnets are called the north-seeking pole and the south-seeking pole. Because opposite magnetic poles attract, the north pole of a compass is being attracted by a south magnetic pole. So Earth is a like a bar magnet with its south magnetic pole near its geographic north pole.

The location of Earth's south magnetic pole currently is in northern Canada about 1,500 km from the geographic north pole. So if you were north of the south magnetic, your compass needle would point south, away from the geographic north pole.

No one is sure what produces Earth's magnetic field. Earth's core is made of a solid ball of iron and nickel, surround by a liquid layer of molten iron and nickel. According to one theory, circulation of the molten iron and nickel caused by heat produces Earth's magnetic field.

Mini LAB

Observing Magnetic Interference

Procedure

1. Clamp a **bar magnet** to a **ring stand.** Tie a **thread** around one end of a **paper clip** and stick the paper clip to one pole of the magnet.
2. Anchor the other end of the thread under a **book** on the table. Slowly pull the thread until the paper clip is suspended below the magnet but not touching the magnet.
3. Without touching the paper clip, slip a piece of paper between the magnet and the paper clip. Does the paper clip fall?
4. Try other materials, such as **aluminum foil, fabric,** or a **butter knife.**

Analysis

1. Which materials caused the paper clip to fall? Why do you think these materials interfered with the magnetic field?
2. Which materials did not cause the paper clip to fall? Why do you think these materials did not interfere with the magnetic field?

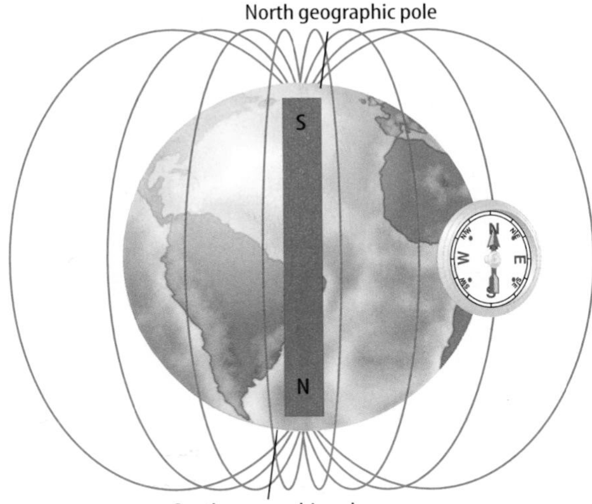

Figure 6
A compass needle aligns with the magnetic field lines of Earth's magnetic field. *Which way would a compass needle point if you held it while you stood directly over the south magnetic pole?*

Mini LAB

Purpose Students observe that magnetic fields extend beyond the magnet and through barriers, and that some materials can affect the field. L2 ELL LS **Kinesthetic**

Materials bar magnet, ring stand, 50 cm of thread, paper clip, tape, book, paper, other thin materials

Teaching Strategy Have students compare magnetic force to gravitational force. Remind students that gravitational force also acts through barriers.

Analysis

1. Some metals cause the paper clip to fall. These metals can be magnetized, so they affect the magnetic field.
2. Paper, glass, and plastic do not affect the field. The magnetic force is not affected by materials that cannot be magnetized.

Assessment

Process Have students examine the refrigerator door at home. Does it appear to be metal, or another material? Relate this to the lab. The plastic coating on some refrigerator doors does not interfere with the attraction between a magnet and the underlying metal. Use **PASC,** p. 89.

Caption Answer

Figure 6 straight down

Resource Manager

Chapter Resources Booklet

MiniLAB, p. 3
Enrichment, p. 30
Lab Activity, pp. 9–12

Curriculum Connection

History The compass was an important invention for navigation at sea. Have students research and write reports about some of the sea routes used before and after the invention of the compass. Most European exploration occurred after the adoption of the compass. Polynesian islanders and Vikings managed long sea voyages without the compass, depending on knowledge of the skies and the sea to find their way. L2 LS **Linguistic** P

Magnetic Materials

Life Science INTEGRATION

Cow magnets are shaped like capsules, just as some pills for humans are. Scrap metal can inflame the lining of the cow's digestive system and surrounding organs. This decreases milk production in dairy cows and impedes weight gain in beef cattle.

Problem-Solving Activity

National Math Standards

Correlation to Mathematics Objectives

1, 5, 6, 7, 8, 9, 10

Answers

1. A magnet will be sure to attract about 65% of the total mass of the car. We can only be sure of this amount because other metals (such as aluminum and copper) are not as magnetic as steel and iron are.
2. As cars become more plastic, we will have to rely less and less on magnets to separate materials. Cars might only need to be shredded. The magnet will be much less important.

IDENTIFYING Misconceptions

Students may think that all metals are magnetic. See p. 224F for teaching strategies that address this misconception.

Life Science INTEGRATION

Some animals may use Earth's magnetic field to help find their way around. Some species of birds, insects, and bacteria have been shown to contain small amounts of the mineral magnetite. Research how one species uses Earth's magnetic field, and report your findings to your class.

Magnetic Materials

You might have noticed that a magnet will not attract all metal objects. For example, a magnet will not attract pieces of aluminum foil. Only a few metals such as iron, cobalt, or nickel are attracted to magnets or can be made into permanent magnets. What makes these elements magnetic? Remember that every atom contains electrons. Electrons have magnetic properties. In the atoms of most elements, the magnetic properties of the electrons cancel out. But in the atoms of iron, cobalt, and nickel, these magnetic properties don't cancel out. Each atom in these elements behaves like a small magnet and has its own magnetic field.

Even though these atoms have their own magnetic fields, objects made from these metals are not always magnets. For example, if you hold an iron nail close to a refrigerator door and let go, it falls to the floor. However, you can make the nail behave like a magnet temporarily.

Problem-Solving Activity

How can magnetic parts of a junk car be salvaged?

Every year, over 10 million cars are scrapped. Magnets are often used to help retrieve valuable materials from these cars for recycling. Once the junk car has been fed into a shredder, big magnets can easily separate many of its metal parts from its nonmetal parts. How much of the car does a magnet actually help separate? Use your ability to interpret a circle graph to find out.

Percentage weight of materials in a car

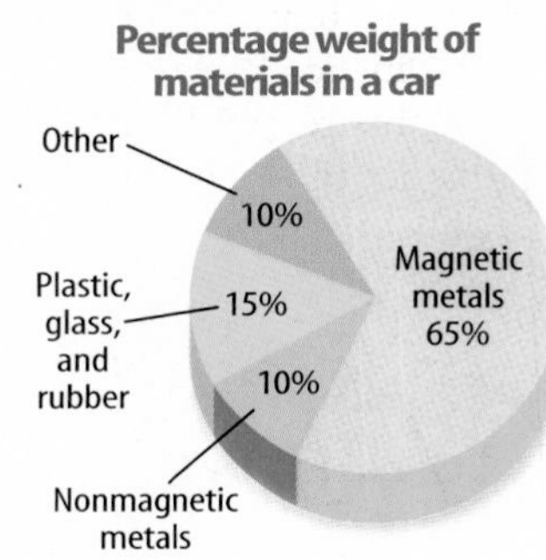

Identifying the Problem

The graph at the right shows the average percent by weight of the different materials in a car. Included in the magnetic metals are steel and iron. The nonmagnetic metals refer to aluminum, copper, lead, zinc, and magnesium. According to the chart, how much of the car can a magnet separate for recycling?

Solving the Problem

1. What percent of the car's weight will a magnet recover? Explain your answer.
2. Plastics are replacing steel in many new cars. How might this affect the future of car recycling?

LAB DEMONSTRATION

Purpose to show how a hard blow can magnetize a steel rod aligned with Earth's magnetic field

Materials compass, steel rod, hammer, paper clips, protractor

Preparation Use the compass to mark a line on the ground running north–south.

Procedure Position the rod along the north-south line as shown. Sharply rap the south end of the rod with a hammer.

Expected Outcome The rod becomes magnetized and will pick up a few clips. Repeat if needed, as this effect depends on hitting the rod just right.

Assessment

What happened to the magnetic domains in the steel rod when it was struck with the hammer? They were jolted and could realign. Enough of the magnetic domains realigned along Earth's field lines to make a magnet.

Magnetic Domains—A Model for Magnetism In iron, cobalt, nickel, and other magnetic materials, the magnetic field created by each atom exerts a force on the other nearby atoms. Because of these forces, groups of atoms align their magnetic poles so that all like poles point in the same direction. The groups of atoms with aligned magnetic poles are called **magnetic domains.** Each domain contains billions of atoms, yet the domains are too small to be seen with your naked eye. Because the magnetic poles of the individual atoms in a domain are aligned, the domain itself behaves like a magnet with a north pole and a south pole.

Lining Up Domains An iron nail contains an enormous number of these magnetic domains, so why doesn't the nail behave like a magnet? Even though each domain behaves like a magnet, the north poles of all the domains are arranged randomly and point in different directions, as shown in **Figure 7A.** As a result, the magnetic fields from all the domains cancel each other out.

If you place a magnet against the same nail, the atoms in the domains orient themselves in the direction of the nearby magnetic field, as shown in **Figure 7B.** The like poles of all the domains point in the same direction and no longer cancel each other out. The nail now acts as a magnet itself. But when the external magnetic field is removed, the constant motion and vibration of the atoms bump the magnetic domains out of their alignment. The magnetic domains in the nail return to random arrangement. For this reason, the nail is a temporary magnet. Paper clips and other objects containing iron also can become temporary magnets.

Making Your Own Compass

Procedure

WARNING: *Use care when handling sharp objects.*

1. Cut off the bottom of a **plastic foam cup** to make a polystyrene disk.
2. Magnetize a **sewing needle** by continuously stroking the needle in the same direction with a magnet for 1 min.
3. **Tape** the needle to the center of the foam disk.
4. Fill a **plate** with **water** and float the disk, needle side up, in the water.
5. Bring the magnet close to foam disk.

Analysis

1. What happened to the needle and disk when you placed them in the water? Explain.
2. How did the needle and disk move when the magnet was brought near it? Explain.

Figure 7
Magnetic materials contain magnetic domains.

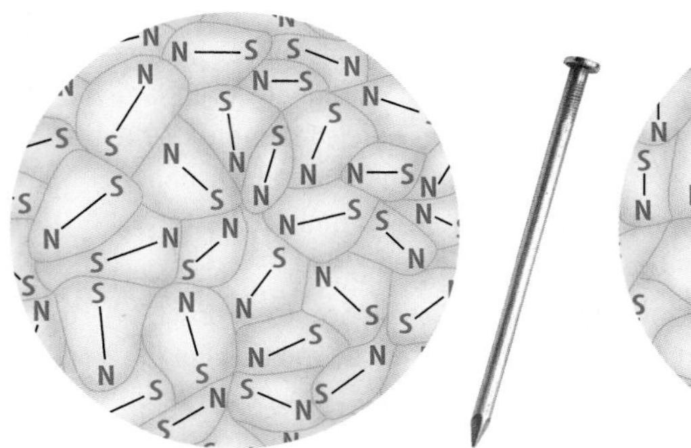

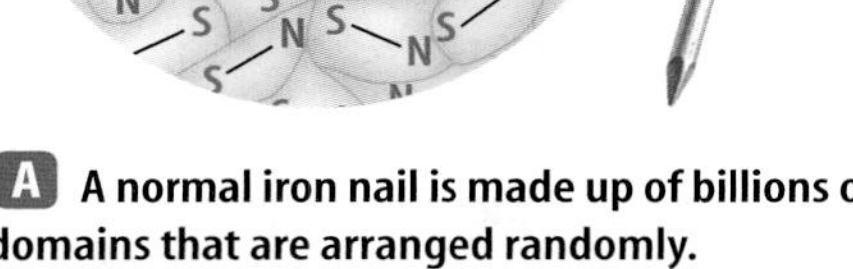

A **A normal iron nail is made up of billions of domains that are arranged randomly.**

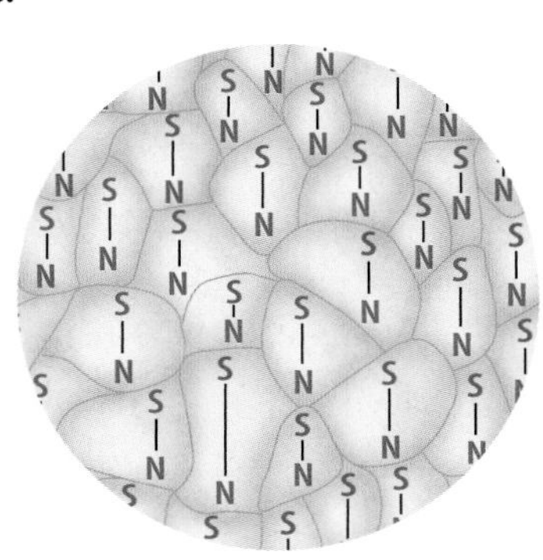

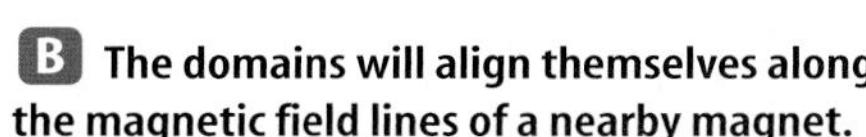

B **The domains will align themselves along the magnetic field lines of a nearby magnet.**

Use an Analogy

Lining up magnetic domains is like getting a group of people to pull together on one end of a rope. If each person pulls the rope in a different direction, the pulls cancel each other and nothing happens. If they all pull together in one direction, the individual forces add together.

Purpose Students will make a compass. L2 LS **Kinesthetic**

Materials plastic foam cup, magnet, sewing needle, tape, plate, water

Teaching Strategy Remind students that the sewing needle contains, or is made of, iron.

Safety Precautions Caution students to handle the needle with care.

Analysis

1. The needle aligned with Earth's north and south poles.
2. The needle swung around to point toward the magnet. The magnet's field is stronger than the Earth's at that distance, so the needle tries to line up with the magnet's north and south poles.

Assessment

Oral What causes the needle to become magnetic when you stroke it with the magnet? The magnet rearranges the domains so that they line up and make the needle magnetic. Use **Performance Assessment in the Science Classroom,** p. 89.

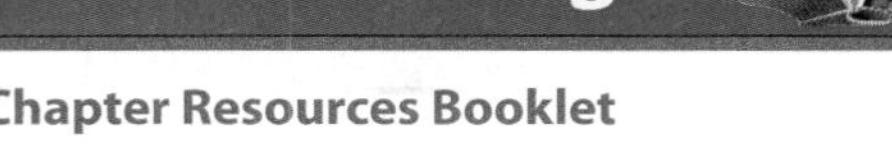

Resource Manager

Chapter Resources Booklet
MiniLAB, p. 4
Reinforcement, p. 27
Mathematics Skill Activities, p. 47

Teacher FYI

Iron minerals in some rocks (such as basalt) align themselves with Earth's magnetic field if the rock forms under the right conditions. This provides a record of Earth's changing magnetic field, which is studied by geologists and those hoping to determine Earth's past climates.

Magnetic Materials, continued

3 Assess

Reteach

Hang a nail, by the flat head, from the end of a bar magnet. Next, place the nail and a compass on the overhead to show that the nail has N and S poles. LS **Visual-Spatial**

Challenge

Ask students if cooling a magnet would reduce its magnetic properties. No; as objects cool, there is less atomic motion, and so there would be less opportunity for the magnetic domains to rearrange. L3 LS **Logical-Mathematical**

Performance Ask students to use a compass to map the magnetic field of a large horseshoe magnet. Use **Performance Assessment in the Science Classroom,** p. 97.

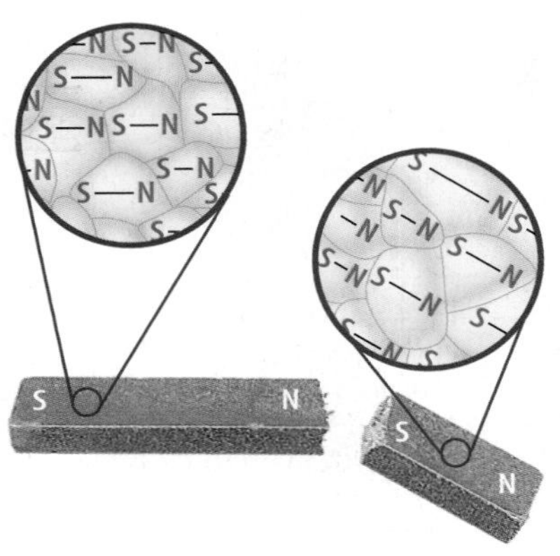

Figure 8
Each piece of a broken magnet still has a north and a south pole.

Permanent Magnets A permanent magnet can be made by placing a piece of magnetic material, such as iron, cobalt, or nickel, in a strong magnetic field. The strong magnetic field causes a large number of the magnetic domains in the material to line up. The magnetic fields of these aligned domains add together and create a magnetic field inside the material that may be several thousand times larger than the magnetic field outside the material. This then prevents the constant motion of the atoms from bumping all the domains out of alignment. The material is then a permanent magnet, and it can retain its magnetic properties for a long time.

But even permanent magnets can lose their magnetic behavior if they are heated or dropped. Heating causes atoms to move faster, so they can jostle magnetic domains out of alignment. If the material is heated enough, its atoms may be moving fast enough to jostle all the domains out of alignment. Then the material is no longer a magnet.

Can a pole be isolated? What happens when a magnet is broken in two? Can one piece be a north pole and one piece be a south pole? Look at the domain model of the broken magnet in **Figure 8.** Recall that even individual atoms of magnetic materials act as tiny magnets. Because every magnet is made of many aligned smaller magnets, even the smallest pieces have a north pole and a south pole. As a result, a magnetic pole cannot be isolated.

Section 1 Assessment

1. Describe what happens when you bring two like magnetic poles together. Draw a picture to illustrate your answer.
2. If a compass is placed in a magnetic field, how does the compass needle move?
3. Why aren't all materials magnetic?
4. What would happen to the properties of a bar magnet if it were broken in half? In thirds? Explain your answer.
5. **Think Critically** Use the magnetic domain model to explain why a magnet sticks to a refrigerator door.

Skill Builder Activities

6. **Forming Hypotheses** Your younger brother or sister played with a bar magnet. Afterward, you noticed that it was barely magnetic. Write a hypothesis to explain what might have happened to your magnet. **For more help, refer to the** Science Skill Handbook.
7. **Communicating** In your Science Journal, make a list of all the uses you can think of for magnets. Write a paragraph describing what these magnets seem to have in common. **For more help, refer to the** Science Skill Handbook.

Answers to Section Assessment

1. The poles repel one another.
2. It aligns itself along the field lines.
3. In the atoms of most materials, the magnetic properties of the electrons cancel out.
4. The properties would remain the same (though repeated breakage would weaken the magnet). Magnetic force is due to the alignment of all the atoms in the magnet, so each piece would retain its magnetic properties.
5. The metal in the door contains magnetic domains that are randomly oriented. When one pole of a magnet is close to the door, the magnetic domains in that section align with the magnet's field. That part of the door is magnetized, and holds the magnet.
6. The magnet may have been banged a lot, disturbing the orientation of some of the magnetic domains. To remagnetize it, align it with the field of a strong magnet.
7. Possible responses: cupboard latch, lid lifter of an electric can opener, compass, crane for lifting metal objects, attaching bottle opener or note clip to the refrigerator; all use a magnet's characteristic of attracting certain materials.

SECTION

Electricity and Magnetism

Electric Current and Magnetism

Even in science, it can help to be lucky. In 1820, Hans Christian Oersted, a Danish physics teacher, accidentally found that electricity and magnetism are related. While demonstrating the operation of electric circuits to his class, he happened to have a compass near a piece of wire. When current flowed through the wire, he noticed that the compass needle was turned, or deflected. When the current was reversed, he saw that the compass needle was deflected in the opposite direction. The compass needle returned to its normal position when he stopped the current in the wire. Oersted hypothesized that the electric current must produce a magnetic field around the wire, and the direction of the field changes with the direction of the current.

Moving Charges and Magnetic Fields It is now known that moving charges, like those in an electric current, produce magnetic fields. Oersted's hypothesis that passing electric current through a wire creates a magnetic field was correct. The magnetic field around a current-carrying wire forms a circular pattern about the wire, as shown in **Figure 9.** The direction of the field depends on the direction of the current. The strength of the magnetic field depends on the amount of current flowing in the wire. When no current flows in a wire, the magnetic field disappears. This discovery of the connection between electricity and magnetism has led to many useful devices.

As You Read

What You'll Learn

- **Understand** the relationship between electric current and magnetism.
- **Explain** how electromagnets are constructed.
- **Describe** how electromagnets are used.
- **Describe** how an electric motor operates.

Vocabulary

electromagnet
galvanometer
electric motor

Why It's Important

Many of the devices you use every day use the relationship between electricity and magnetism to operate.

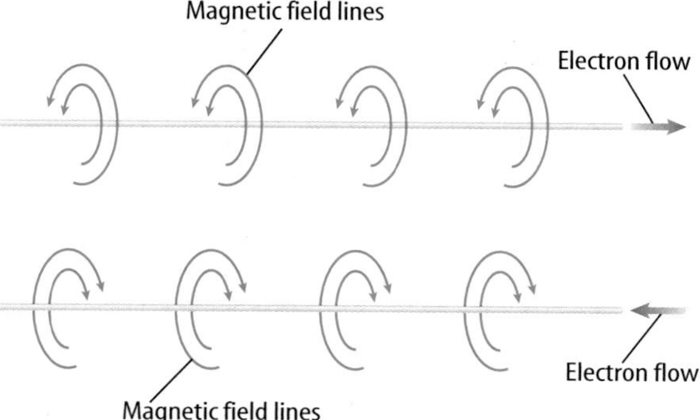

Figure 9
When electric current flows through a wire, a magnetic field forms around the wire. The direction of the magnetic field depends on the direction of the current in the wire.

SECTION

Electricity and Magnetism

1 Motivate

Bellringer Transparency

Display the Section Focus Transparency for Section 2. Use the accompanying Transparency Activity Master. L2 ELL

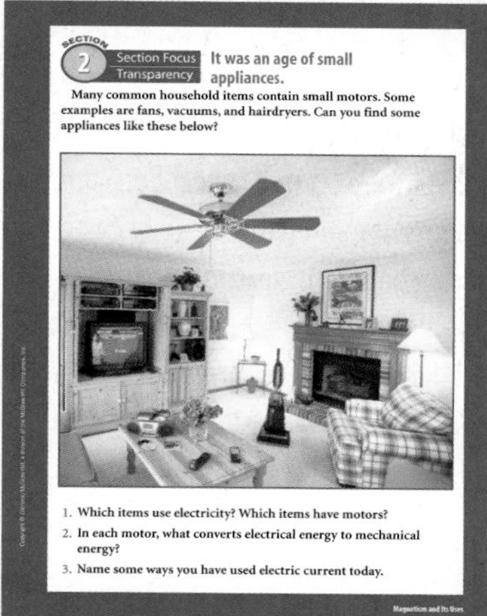
Section Focus Transparency It was an age of small appliances.

Many common household items contain small motors. Some examples are fans, vacuums, and hairdryers. Can you find some appliances like these below?

1. Which items use electricity? Which items have motors?
2. In each motor, what converts electrical energy to mechanical energy?
3. Name some ways you have used electric current today.

Tie to Prior Knowledge

Ask students to name some items that run by electric motors. Possible answers: fan, CD player, tape player. Explain that this section describes how electricity and magnetism work together in electric motors to make things move.

Section Assessment Planner

Portfolio
Curriculum Connection, p. 238
Performance Assessment
Skill Builder Activities, p. 239
See page 254 for more options.

Content Assessment
Section, p. 239
Challenge, p. 239
Chapter, pp. 254–255

Resource Manager

Chapter Resources Booklet
Transparency Activity, p. 45
Directed Reading for Content Mastery, p. 21

2 Teach

Electric Current and Magnetism

Quick Demo

Make a simple circuit of a battery and a bulb, arranging the parts so the wire forms a circle. Use a compass to map the magnetic field. Point out that if the outside of the loop is always north, for example, and you have a stack of loops, their individual magnetic fields will combine. L2 LS **Visual-Spatial**

Fun Fact

The source of Earth's magnetic field is still not well understood. One hypothesis is that convection currents of molten rock deep in Earth's core generate electric currents, which in turn generate a magnetic field, just like the current in a wire.

Electromagnets

Discussion

Explain that a crane can have a grabbing end to pick up an object, or it can use an electromagnet. **Compare the two cranes.** Possible responses: the electromagnet will only work on certain types of metals, while the mechanical crane can lift anything it can wrap around. The strength of the mechanical crane depends on the materials it is made from and how they are attached; the strength of the electromagnet crane depends on these factors plus the number of turns in the coil and the strength of the current running through it. L2 **Logical-Mathematical**

Caption Answer

Figure 10B The direction of the magnetic field would change.

Electromagnets

One of the most important devices that uses the connection between electricity and magnetism is the electromagnet (ih lek troh MAG nut). An **electromagnet** is a temporary magnet made by placing a piece of iron inside a current-carrying coil of wire. When a current flows through a circular loop of wire, magnetic-field lines form all around the wire as shown in **Figure 10A.** If more loops of wire are added to make a coil, the magnetic-field lines formed around each loop will overlap and add together, as shown in **Figure 10B.** As a result, the magnetic field inside the coil is made stronger. If an iron core is inserted into the coil as in **Figure 10C,** the magnetic field inside the coil causes the iron core to become magnetized. When a magnetized iron core and a coil are combined this way, the magnetic field comes mostly from the iron core.

Properties of Electromagnets Electromagnets are temporary magnets because the magnetic field is present only when current is flowing in the wire coil. The strength of the magnetic field can be increased by adding more turns to the wire coil or by increasing the current passing through the wire.

An electromagnet behaves like any other magnet when current flows through the wire coil. One end of the electromagnet is a north pole and the other end is a south pole. If placed in a magnetic field, an electromagnet will align itself along the magnetic field lines, just as a compass needle will. An electromagnet also will attract magnetic materials and be attracted or repelled by other magnets. What makes electromagnets so useful is that their magnetic properties can be controlled by changing the electric current flowing through the wire coil.

When current flows through the electromagnet and it moves toward or away from another magnet, it converts electric energy into mechanical energy to do work. Electromagnets do work in various devices such as stereo speakers and electric motors. They also can lift large metal objects.

Figure 10
An electromagnet is made from a current-carrying wire.

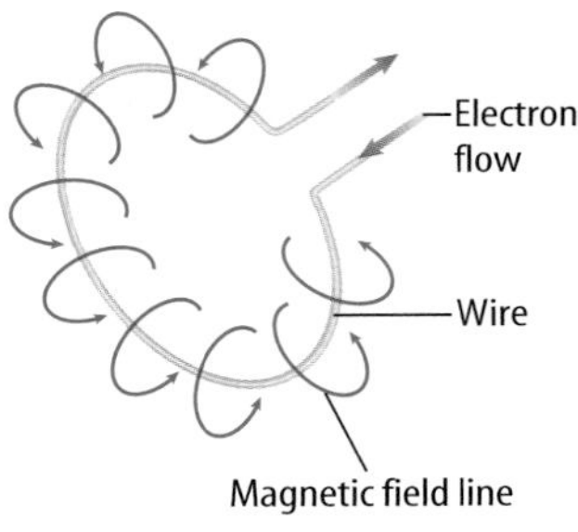

A Magnetic field lines circle around a loop of current-carrying wire.

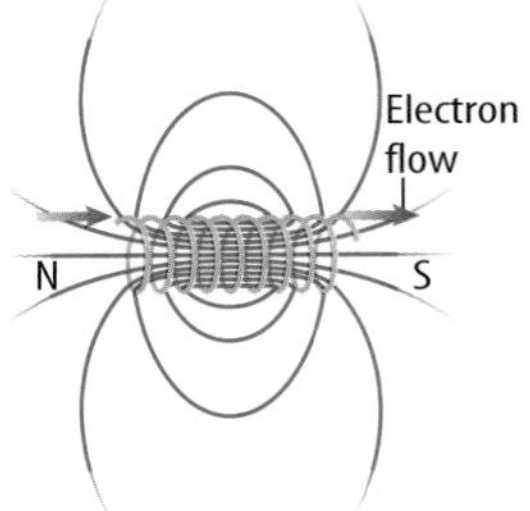

B When many loops of current-carrying wire are formed into a coil, the magnetic field is increased inside the coil. The coil has a north pole and a south pole. *What would happen if you switched the direction of the current in the coil?*

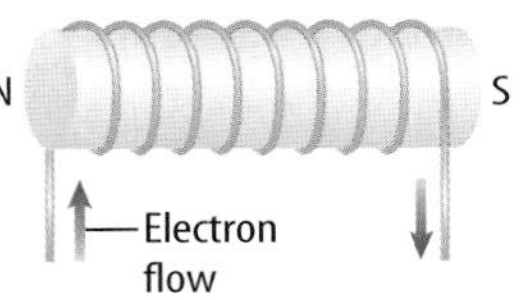

C An iron core inserted into the coil becomes a magnet.

234 CHAPTER 8 Magnetism and Its Uses

Inclusion Strategies

Learning Disabled For students who have difficulty following diagrams and complex descriptions, focus on the basic definitions—for example, that a motor converts electricity into motion. Provide a chance for students to observe, handle, and take apart a simple motor or generator. L1 LS **Kinesthetic**

Teacher FYI

Each electron in an atom acts like a tiny electromagnet—the electron orbiting the nucleus is a loop of electric current, just like electrons moving in a wire. An electron also has "spin,"—a quantum physics characteristic that contributes to the magnetic field generated by the electron.

Music to Your Ears—Stereo Speakers How does musical information stored on a CD become sound you can hear? The sound is produced by a stereo speaker that contains an electromagnet. The electromagnet changes electrical energy to mechanical energy that vibrates parts of the speaker to produce sound.

Reading Check *How does an electromagnet allow a stereo speaker to produce sound?*

When you listen to a CD, the CD player produces an electric current that changes according to the musical information on the CD. This varying electric current passes through a coiled wire inside the speaker that is part of an electromagnet, as in **Figure 11.** A magnetic field is generated in the electromagnet. This magnetic field changes depending on the varying characteristics of the electric current. The electromagnet is then attracted to or repelled by a permanent, fixed magnet, making the electromagnet move back and forth. This movement vibrates the speaker's flexible surface and produces sound. The vibration of the speaker cone reproduces the original musical information stored on the CD.

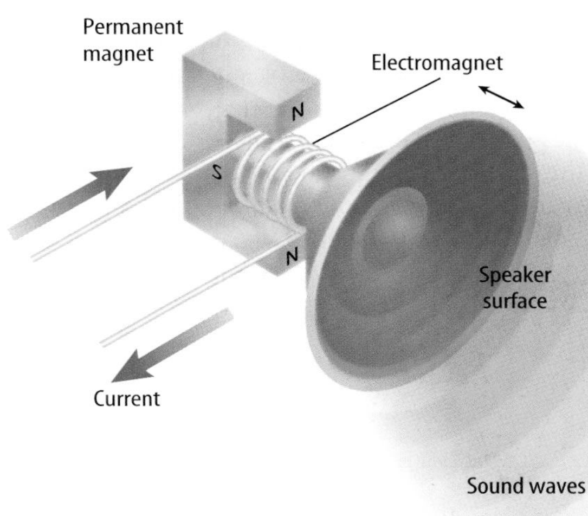

Figure 11
The electromagnet in a speaker turns electrical energy into movement to produce sound.

Quick Demo

Make an electromagnet by connecting a battery to a wire coiled 20 times around a large nail. Demonstrate that the nail picks up no paper clips before the wire is connected and several when it is connected. When the power is cut, the paper clips should fall. However, the nail will still be slightly magnetized and may pick up one or two paper clips after the current is turned off. **CAUTION:** The wire will heat up if it is left connected, so disconnect the battery as soon as you are done. L2 LS **Visual-Spatial**

Visual Learning

Figure 11 Have students analyze the diagram of the speaker. Review step by step the process in which electrical energy is converted to sound energy. Make sure students understand that the changing electrical signal causes a changing magnetic field in the electromagnet, and that the interaction of that magnetic field with the magnetic field of the permanent magnet causes the electromagnet to move.

Reading Check

Answer The electromagnet changes electrical energy to mechanical energy that vibrates parts of the speaker to produce sound.

Resource Manager

Chapter Resources Booklet
Lab Activity, pp. 13–16
Physical Science Critical Thinking/ Problem Solving, p. 17

Curriculum Connection

History Have students find out how Alexander Graham Bell used an electromagnet in the first telephone and make present their findings to the class. L2 LS **Linguistic**

Electromagnets, continued

Discussion

Have students describe all the dials with pointers they can find in their homes, school, cars, etc. **Which ones are galvanometers?** A galvanometer is used to measure current, or to measure something that can be measured with current. A clock is an example of a motorized measuring device that is not a galvanometer. L3 LS **Logical-Mathematical**

Caption Answer

Figure 13 Yes; if you are using direct current, when the current is reversed the electromagnet will rotate in the opposite direction to a different scale reading.

Reading Check

Answer electric current

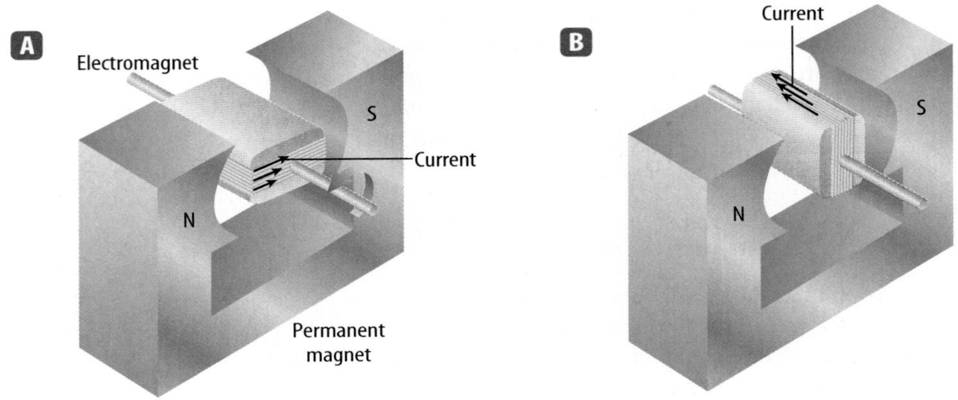

Figure 12
A When current flows through the coil, an electromagnet is formed that is attracted to and repelled by the poles of the permanent magnet. B The magnetic forces on the coil cause it to rotate aligning it with the field of the permanent magnet.

Galvanometers You've probably noticed the gauges in the dashboard of a car. One gauge shows the amount of gasoline left, another shows the engine temperature, and another shows the oil pressure. How does a change in the amount of gasoline in a tank or the water temperature in the engine make a needle move in a gauge on the dashboard? These gauges are **galvanometers** (gal vuh NAHM ut urs), which are devices that use an electromagnet to measure electric current. For example, a temperature sensor in the engine sends an electric current to the temperature gauge. This current changes as the engine temperature changes. The needle of the temperature gauge is connected to an electromagnet. This electromagnet is suspended so it can rotate between the poles of a permanent, fixed magnet. When current flows through the coil, the electromagnet rotates so that its north and south poles are aligned along the magnetic-field lines of the permanent magnet, as shown in **Figure 12.**

Reading Check *What is measured by a galvanometer?*

Figure 13
A galvanometer includes a permanent magnet, an electromagnet that rotates against a spring, and a scale that gives a measurement of the current. *Would it matter which way you hooked up the galvanometer to the two terminals of the circuit you were testing? Why?*

Cultural Diversity

China The first dial and pointer devices were made in China, using compass needles. A description of a type of abacus using indicator needles dates from the sixth century A.D. Modern dials and pointers, including galvanometers, descend from these early Chinese devices.

Resource Manager 

Chapter Resources Booklet
Enrichment, p. 31
Science Inquiry Labs, p. 9

Using Galvanometers If the coil is connected to a small spring, then the coil can act as a galvanometer. If the current through the coil is small, only a weak magnetic field is produced in the electromagnet. Then the magnetic force between the electromagnet and the permanent magnet is weak. The coil can rotate only a small amount against the resistance of the spring, and the needle moves by only a small amount. When a large current flows in the coil, the magnetic force between the electromagnet and the permanent magnet is stronger. The coil rotates further, and the needle moves further along the scale. To be used as a gauge, a galvanometer must be calibrated by sending a known current through the coil and seeing how much the needle is deflected. **Figure 13** shows an example of a galvanometer.

Research Visit the Glencoe Science Web site at **science.glencoe.com** for more information about how motors do work in electric devices. In your Science Journal, summarize the similarities among the motors you learn about.

Electric Motors

On sizzling summer days, do you ever use an electric fan to keep cool? A fan uses an **electric motor,** which is a device that changes electrical energy into mechanical energy. The motor in a fan turns the fan blades, moving air past your skin to make you feel cooler.

Like a galvanometer, an electric motor contains an electromagnet that is free to rotate between the poles of a permanent, fixed magnet. The coil in the electromagnet is connected to a source of electric current, such as a battery, as shown in **Figure 14.** When a current flows through the electromagnet, a magnetic field is produced in the coil.

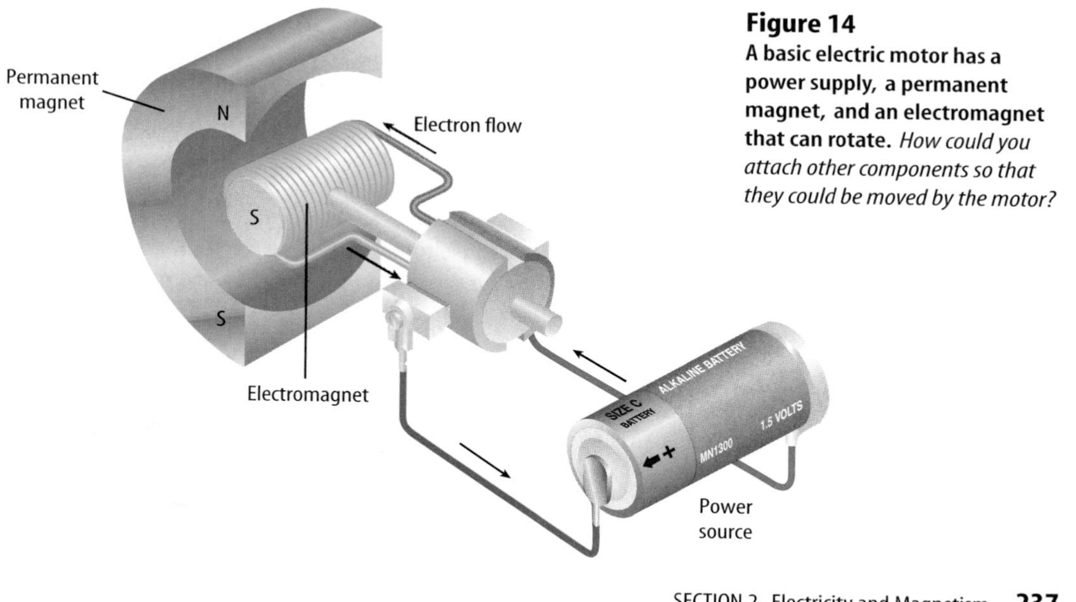

Figure 14
A basic electric motor has a power supply, a permanent magnet, and an electromagnet that can rotate. *How could you attach other components so that they could be moved by the motor?*

Visual Learning

Figure 14 Have students look at the diagram and point to each part of the motor (power supply, permanent magnet, electromagnet) as you name it. Ask a volunteer to use the diagram to show the movement that occurs when current is applied to the motor. The electromagnet rotates. L1 ELL IS **Visual-Spatial**

Electric Motors

SCIENCE Online

Internet Addresses

Explore the Glencoe Science Web site at **science.glencoe.com** to find out more about topics in this section.

Use Science Words

Word Origin Have students use a dictionary to find the origin of the word *motor.* It is derived from the Latin word for move. L2 IS **Linguistic**

Caption Answer

Figure 14 A component attached to the shaft that goes to the middle of the electromagnet will rotate. Gears can be used to change the rotation to other types of motion.

Quick Demo

Bring a direct current electric motor to class. Take it apart in class and show students the different parts. L2 ELL **Visual-Spatial**

Electric Motors
continued

Use an Analogy

An electric motor is like a waterwheel. A force (running water, magnetism) applied to a wheel (paddle of wheel, end of magnet) turns an axle. In either case, things can be attached to the axle to use the mechanical energy produced.

Extension

Have students find out more about how the commutator in an electric motor works. The commutator rotates with the electromagnet and alternately contacts the positive and negative terminals of the power source. The reversing current causes the poles of the rotating electromagnet to switch and rotate toward the opposite pole of the permanent magnet. L2
LS **Logical-Mathematical**

Make a Model

Have students use **Figures 14** and **15** as guides to make models of simple electric motors. L3 LS **Kinesthetic**

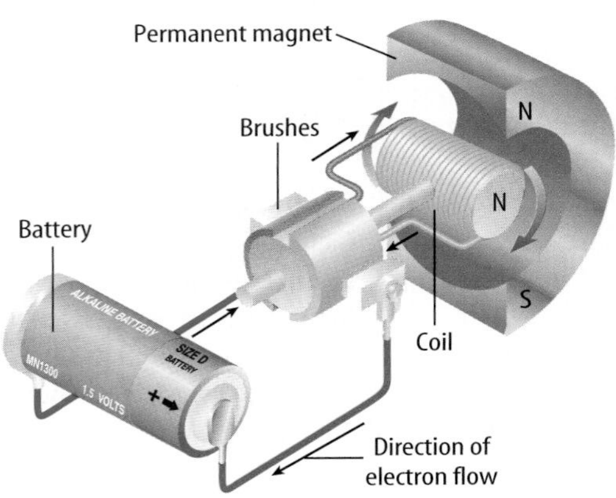

A A motor contains a fixed, permanent magnet and an electromagnet that is free to rotate.

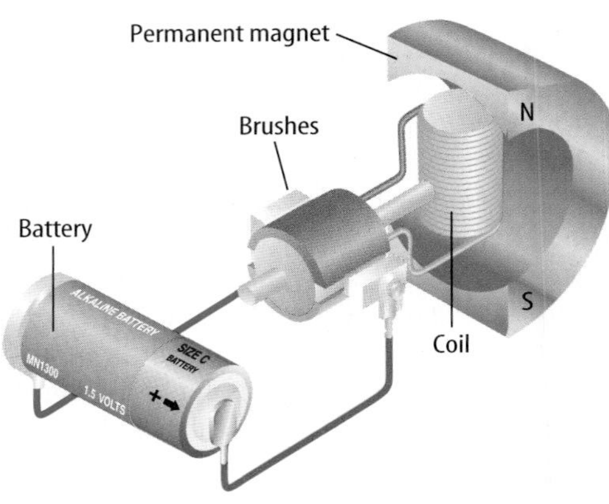

B Unlike poles of the two magnets attract each other, while the like poles repel. This causes the coil to rotate until the opposite poles are next to each other.

Figure 15
The shaft of an electric motor is made to rotate by the forces between magnets.

Switching Poles **Figures 15A** and **15B** show how the magnetic force between the electromagnet and the permanent magnet causes the coil to turn. Just as in a galvanometer, the coil in an electric motor turns so that its north and south poles are aligned along the magnetic-field lines of the permanent magnet.

However, once the coil is aligned, there is no longer a force that will keep the coil rotating. Now suppose that the magnetic field in the coil is flipped so the north and south poles switch ends. The direction of the coil's magnetic field can be flipped by reversing the direction of the electric current in the coil. Then the like poles of the coil and magnet will be next to each other.

After flipping the field, the coil will be repelled and will rotate further, as shown in **Figures 15C** and **15D**. The coil will then rotate until it is once again aligned along the field lines of the permanent magnet. Then the current is reversed again. In this way, the coil is kept rotating.

In some motors a switch called a commutator reverses the current in the coil. Other motors don't need a commutator because they use household alternating current, which reverses direction 120 times a second.

Controlling Electric Motors Electric motors can be more useful if their rotation speed can be controlled. One way to do this is to vary the amount of current flowing through the coil. Because the coil is an electromagnet, its magnetic field becomes stronger if more current flows through the coil. This causes the magnetic force between the coil and the permanent magnet to increase. As a result, the coil turns faster.

Curriculum Connection

History Have students research the history of the development of electric motors. Have them present their findings in the form of a poster. The first electric motor was a reversible DC electrical generator built in the early 1870s by Zénobe-Théophile Gramme. The first practical AC motor was built in 1888 by Nikola Tesla.
L2 LS **Linguistic** P

Resource Manager 

Chapter Resources Booklet
Reinforcement, p. 28

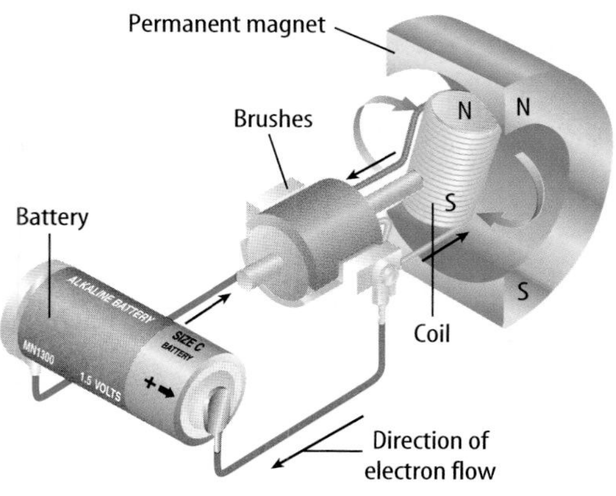

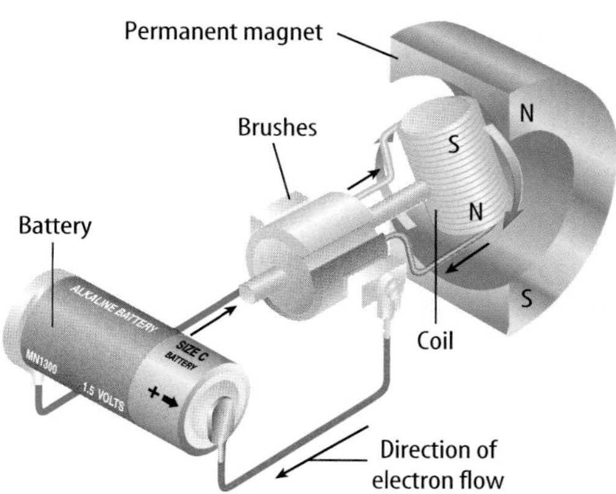

Figure 15

C If the current in the coil is switched, the direction of the coil's magnetic field also switches. The north and south poles of the magnet trade places.

D The coil is repelled by and attracted once again to the poles of the permanent magnet. The coil rotates until it is again aligned with the permanent magnet's field.

Using Electric Motors The first electric motor to be widely used was developed in 1873. This motor used direct current. The first motor to use alternating current was invented in 1888. Since that time many additional developments have made electric motors smaller, more powerful, and more efficient. Today electric motors are used everywhere. Almost every appliance with moving parts uses an electric motor. Can you find an electric motor in every room of your home?

Section  Assessment

1. Does a straight wire or a looped wire have a stronger magnetic field when both carry the same amount of current? Explain.
2. How is the magnetic field of an electromagnet controlled?
3. What are galvanometers used for?
4. How does an electric motor rotate once its electromagnet is aligned along the magnetic field of its permanent magnet?
5. **Think Critically** Could an electromagnet use a nickel core in the coil of wire instead of iron? Why or why not?

Skill Builder Activities

6. **Comparing and Contrasting** Compare and contrast galvanometers and electric motors. **For more help, refer to the Science Skill Handbook.**
7. **Using an Electronic Spreadsheet** Take an inventory of all the devices in your home or school that use an electric motor. Organize your inventory using a database or spreadsheet to indicate the following: *name of the device, the place you found it, the power source used, and which parts the motor causes to move.* **For more help, refer to the Technology Skill Handbook.**

3 Assess

Reteach

Make two electromagnets from iron nails wrapped in wire. Wrap the first one with only a few coils, the second one with many coils. Have students compare the strength of the two electromagnets as you attempt to pick up a number of paper clips. L2 LS **Visual-Spatial**

Challenge

Divide the class into groups. Provide each group with D-cell batteries, a few meters of insulated wire, and iron bolts. Ask the groups to construct electromagnets. **CAUTION:** The bolt cores will become hot if the current is left connected. Make sure students disconnect the wire from the battery when they are not using the electromagnet. L2 ELL COOP LEARN LS **Kinesthetic**

Assessment

Oral Demonstrate the different speeds on a fan or mixer. Ask students how they think the speed is varied. To make the appliance rotate faster, the amount of current passing through the coil of the electric motor is increased. To slow down the appliance, the amount of current is decreased. Use **PASC,** p. 89.

Answers to Section Assessment

1. The magnetic field around each bit of wire has the same strength, but when the wire is looped, the fields are added together, making a stronger field.
2. by varying the electric current passing through it
3. to measure electric current and to use varying electric current to measure such things as engine temperature and the amount of gas in the gas tank
4. by reversing the direction of the current to the electromagnet
5. yes, because nickel is a magnetic material
6. Both use an electric current to produce motion. A galvanometer is used to produce a one-time rotation, while an electric motor produces steady rotational motion.
7. Generally, anything that converts electrical energy to motion has an electric motor. Items include electric fans, electric mixers, vacuum cleaners, tape or CD players, electric tooth brushes, hair dryers, and automobiles.

SECTION

Producing Electric Current

1 Motivate

Bellringer Transparency

Display the Section Focus Transparency for Section 3. Use the accompanying Transparency Activity Master. L2 ELL

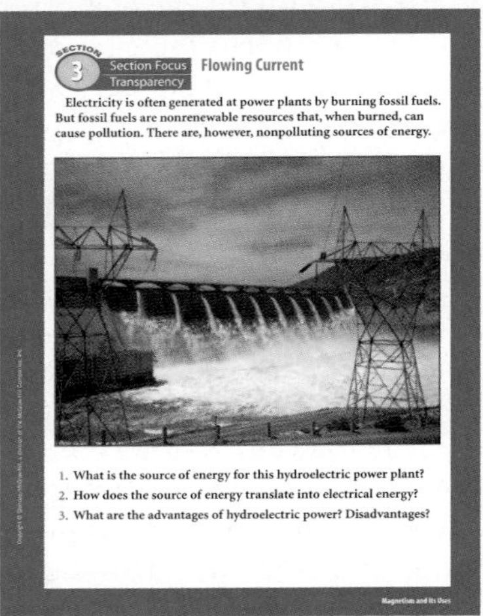

SECTION 3 Section Focus Transparency **Flowing Current**

Electricity is often generated at power plants by burning fossil fuels. But fossil fuels are nonrenewable resources that, when burned, can cause pollution. There are, however, nonpolluting sources of energy.

1. What is the source of energy for this hydroelectric power plant?
2. How does the source of energy translate into electrical energy?
3. What are the advantages of hydroelectric power? Disadvantages?

Magnetism and Its Uses

Tie to Prior Knowledge

Ask students if they have ever seen a windmill. Refer them to **Figure 19** and have them describe the motion of the blades and what the force of the wind is doing to the generators that they are connected to.

SECTION

Producing Electric Current

As You Read

***What* You'll Learn**

- **Describe** how a generator produces an electric current.
- **Distinguish** between alternating current and direct current.
- **Explain** how a transformer can change the voltage of an alternating current.

Vocabulary

electromagnetic induction
generator
turbine
direct current (DC)
alternating current (AC)
transformer

***Why* It's Important**

Power plants use electromagnetic induction to generate electricity for you to use at home and school.

From Mechanical to Electrical Energy

After it was discovered that an electric current could produce a magnetic field, some people wondered whether the opposite could happen: could a magnetic field produce an electric current? Working independently in 1831, Michael Faraday in Britain and Joseph Henry in the United States found that moving a loop of wire through a magnetic field caused an electric current to flow in the wire. They also found that moving a magnet through a loop of wire produces a current. In both cases the mechanical energy associated with the motion of the wire loop or the magnet is converted into electrical energy associated with the electrical current in the wire. Producing an electric current by moving a loop of wire through a magnetic field or moving a magnet through a wire loop is called **electromagnetic induction** (ihn DUK shun). The discovery of electromagnetic induction has led to many applications.

Generators How is the electricity that comes to your home and school produced? Most of the electricity you use each day is produced by generators using electromagnetic induction. A **generator** produces electric current by rotating a coil of wire in a magnetic field. Just as in a galvanometer or an electric motor, the wire coil is wrapped around an iron core and placed between the poles of a permanent magnet. The coil is rotated by an outside source of mechanical energy, as shown in **Figure 16.** As the coil turns within the magnetic field of the permanent magnet, an electric current flows through the coil.

Reading Check *How does a generator use electromagnetic induction?*

Figure 16
The electromagnet in a generator is rotated by some outside source of mechanical energy. In this setup, a student can rotate a crank to turn the electromagnet.

Section Assessment Planner

Portfolio
Curriculum Connection, p. 242

Performance Assessment
Skill Builder Activities, p. 246
See page 254 for more options.

Content Assessment
Section, p. 246
Challenge, p. 246
Chapter, pp. 254–255

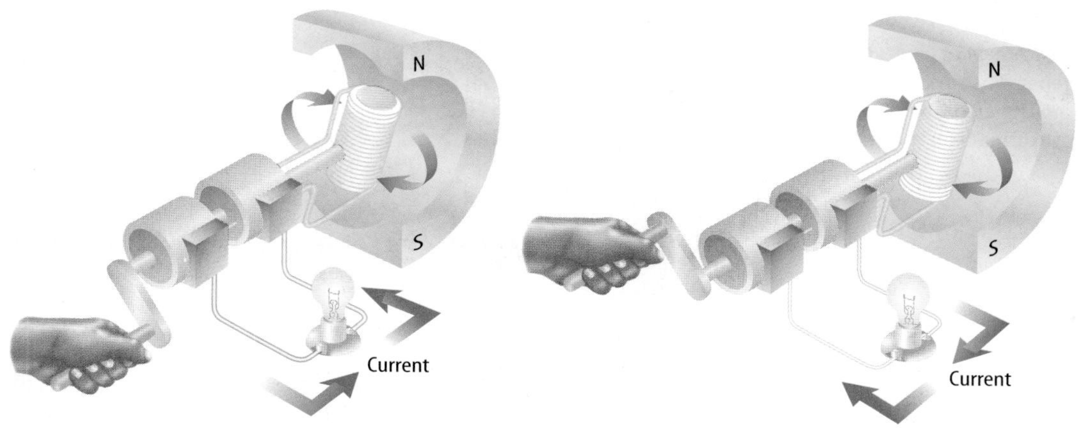

Figure 17
The direction that current flows in a wire coil depends on how the wire coil is aligned with the permanent magnet. *Would a generator still work if the electromagnet were held steady and the permanent magnet moved around it? Explain.*

Switching Direction As the generator's wire coil rotates through the magnetic field of the permanent magnet, current flows through the coil. After the wire coil makes one half of a revolution, the ends of the coil are moving past the opposite poles of the permanent magnet. This causes the current to change direction. Remember that the current flowing to a motor must switch directions periodically so the electromagnetic coil can keep turning. In a generator, as the electromagnetic coil continuously turns, the current that is produced periodically changes direction, as **Figure 17** shows. The direction of the current in the coil changes twice with each revolution. The frequency with which the current changes direction can be controlled by regulating the rotation rate of the generator. In the United States, current is produced by generators that rotate 60 times a second, or 3,600 revolutions per minute.

Using Electric Generators The type of generator shown in **Figure 17** is used in a car, where it is called an alternator. The alternator provides electrical energy to operate lights and other accessories. Spark plugs in the car's engine also use this electricity to ignite the fuel in the cylinders of the engine. Once the engine is running, it provides the mechanical energy that is used to turn the coil in the alternator.

Suppose instead of using mechanical energy to rotate the coil in a generator, the coil was fixed, and the permanent magnet rotated instead. In fact the current generated would be the same as when the coil rotates and the magnet doesn't move. The huge generators used in electric power plants are made this way. The current is produced in the stationary coil, and mechanical energy is used to rotate the magnet.

2 Teach

From Mechanical to Electrical Energy

Caption Answer

Figure 17 Yes, it doesn't matter which magnet moves and which is still; what matters is that they are in motion relative to each other.

Reading Check

Answer A generator rotates a coil of wire in a magnetic field. An electric current is produced in the coil by electromagnetic induction.

IDENTIFYING Misconceptions

Some students may think that a magnetic field alone is enough to produce a current. Emphasize that the magnetic field must be changing to induce a current in the wire coil. A stationary magnet and loop will not generate a current.

Use Science Words

Word Meaning The expression *electromagnetic induction* is related to the word *induce.* Have students find the common meaning of induce and use it in a sentence. Induce means to move to a course of action, to cause; Sample sentence: The king induced his knights to follow his lead. L2 LS **Linguistic**

Extension

Have students write paragraphs on the meaning of relative motion and how it relates to the generators shown in **Figure 17.**

Resource Manager

Chapter Resources Booklet
- Transparency Activity, p. 46
- Directed Reading for Content Mastery, pp. 21, 22

Science Inquiry Labs, p. 55

Science Journal

History of Technology A generator transforms straight-line motion into rotational motion. One of the oldest means of transforming motion this way is the waterwheel. Have students write paragraphs in their Science Journals comparing the design of a waterwheel with that of a hydroelectric turbine. L2 LS **Linguistic**

From Mechanical to Electrical Energy, continued

Discussion

Why is electricity usually generated at a few large plants, rather than many small ones? Possible answer: Generating plants are often located near rivers, dams, or other energy sources. Multiple small plants would require redundant resources and numerous turbines and coils, which are large and expensive items. L3

LS **Logical-Mathematical**

Environmental Science INTEGRATION

Show pictures of dams to the class, so they can see how large a dam is and how much of the landscape is altered by a dam. Dams affect both the area upstream that is flooded and areas downstream that may receive less water than before. Dams are often important for flood control and for ensuring a reliable water supply.

Caption Answer

Figure 19 Sample response: advantages: clean, usually quiet, easy to set up; disadvantages: depends on steady wind, may affect wildlife habitats

Visual Learning

Figure 19 In the 1920s and 1930s, before rural areas had access to electricity from power plants, people sometimes used small windmills to run water pumps or household generators. The windmills shown are much larger, of course. Windmills on "wind farms," such as the one shown in the figure, can be as big as 50 meters in diameter and stand several building stories high.

Figure 18
Electric power plants use huge generators such as the ones shown here to produce the electric current you use every day.

Environmental Science INTEGRATION

A dam can be placed on a river to create a lake. Water can then be released slowly from the dam to turn the turbines in a generator. Discuss with your classmates what effects a dam would have on the environment.

Generating Electricity for Your Home You probably do not have a generator in your home that supplies all the electricity you need to watch television or wash your clothes. Your electricity comes from a power plant with huge generators like the one in **Figure 18.** The electromagnets in these generators are made of many coils of wire wrapped around huge iron cores. The coils usually are connected to a **turbine** (TUR bine)—a large wheel that rotates when pushed by water, wind, or steam.

For example, some power plants first produce thermal energy by burning fossil fuels or using the heat produced by nuclear reactions. This thermal energy is used to heat water and produce steam. Thermal energy is then converted to mechanical energy as the steam pushes the turbine blades. The generator then changes the mechanical energy of the rotating turbine into an electric current that flows to your home. In some areas, fields of windmills like those in **Figure 19** can be used to capture the mechanical energy in wind to turn generators. Other power plants use the mechanical energy in falling water to drive the turbine. Look at **Figure 20** to compare and contrast the characteristics of generators and motors.

Figure 19
These windmills harness the energy in wind so it can be transformed into electrical energy by a generator. *What are some advantages and disadvantages of using windmills?*

Curriculum Connection

Geography Solar power can be used to generate electricity. A very large array is needed to generate enough electricity for a city, and only very sunny sites will do. Ask students to research and report on areas in the United States that are suitable for such solar generators. Large solar arrays have been proposed for the Southwest's deserts particularly those in California. L2 LS **Linguistic** P

Resource Manager

Chapter Resources Booklet
Transparency Activity, pp. 47–48
Home and Community Involvement, p. 37
Cultural Diversity, p. 53

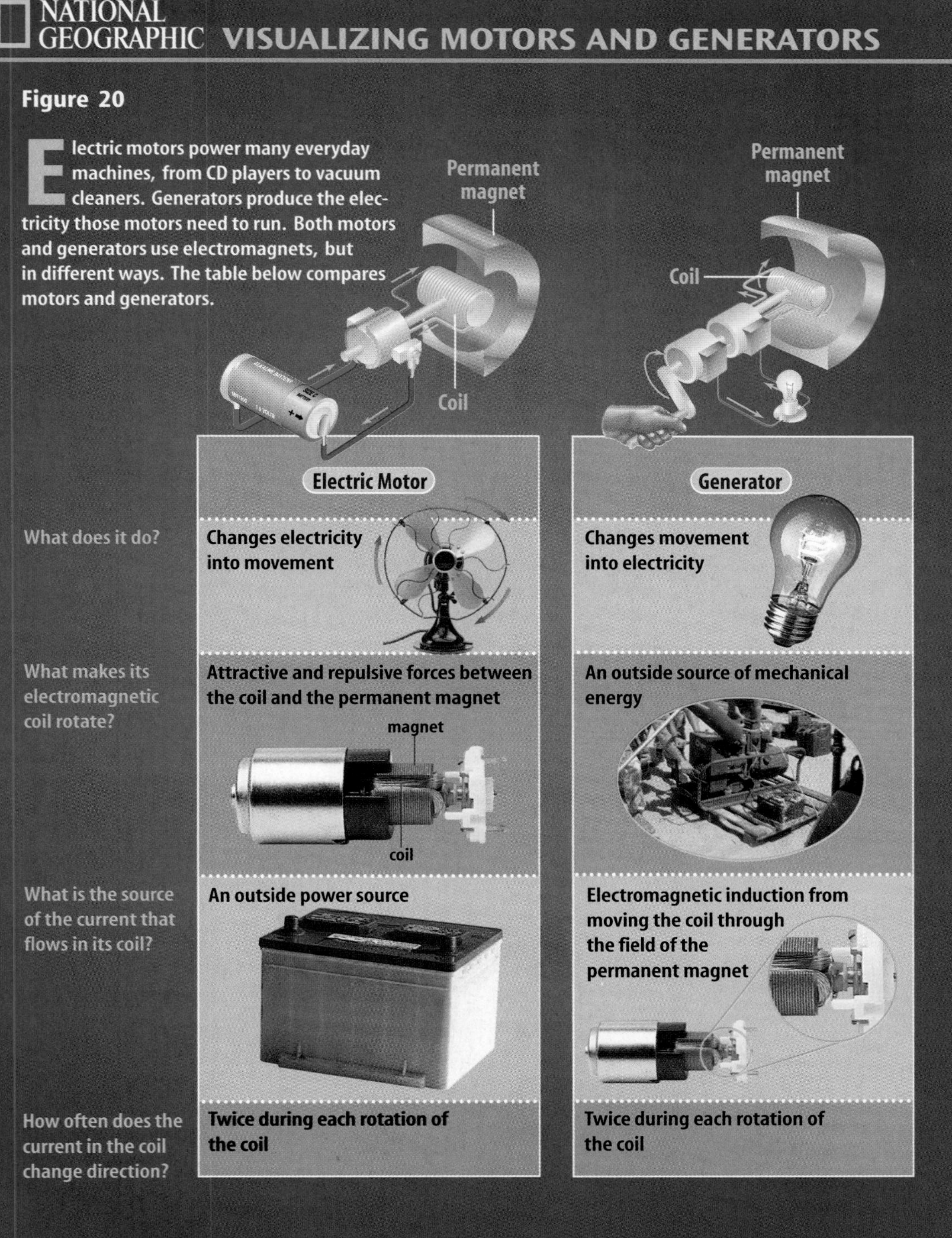

NATIONAL GEOGRAPHIC VISUALIZING MOTORS AND GENERATORS
Figure 20
Electric motors power many everyday machines, from CD players to vacuum cleaners. Generators produce the electricity those motors need to run. Both motors and generators use electromagnets, but in different ways. The table below compares motors and generators.
Permanent magnet
Coil
Permanent magnet
Coil
Electric Motor
Generator
What does it do?
Changes electricity into movement
Changes movement into electricity
What makes its electromagnetic coil rotate?
Attractive and repulsive forces between the coil and the permanent magnet
magnet
coil
An outside source of mechanical energy
What is the source of the current that flows in its coil?
An outside power source
Electromagnetic induction from moving the coil through the field of the permanent magnet
How often does the current in the coil change direction?
Twice during each rotation of the coil
Twice during each rotation of the coil
243

From Mechanical to Electrical Energy, continued

Visualizing Motors and Generators

Have students examine the pictures and read the captions. Then ask the following questions.

- **In what way is an electric motor the opposite of a generator? In what way is the same?** Opposite: A motor changes electricity into movement, while a generator changes movement into electricity. Same: The current in the coil changes direction twice during each rotation of the coil.
- **What kind of movement produces the electricity in hydroelectric generators?** moving water **In windmills?** moving air **In a bicycle generator?** moving bicycle wheel

Activity

Have small groups of students research power supplies used for camping or emergency situations that produce electricity from a hand-cranked generator. These devices include flashlights, lanterns, and radios. Have students make oral presentations about how these devices work and in what situations they would be most useful. L2 COOP LEARN **LS Logical-Mathmatical**

Extension

Students could research the differences between AC and DC generators and make labeled posters illustrating the differences between these two types of electricity. L3 **LS Visual-Spatial**

Direct and Alternating Currents

Internet Addresses

Explore the Glencoe Science Web site at **science.glencoe.com** to find out more about topics in this section.

Caption Answer

Figure 21 Sometimes a clock or VCR is briefly without AC power. The batteries let it continue running, so you don't need to reset everything when the AC power is reconnected.

Teacher FYI

Thomas Edison advocated the use of DC electricity. One of his workers, Nikola Tesla, argued that an AC system would be better. Edison and Tesla parted ways, and Tesla went to work for Edison's competitor, the Westinghouse Company. Today, all major systems in the United States use AC.

SCIENCE Online

Research Visit the Glencoe Science Web site at **science.glencoe.com** for more information about how transformers are used in transmitting electric current. Communicate to your class what you learned.

Direct and Alternating Currents

Modern society relies heavily on electricity. Just how much you rely on electricity becomes obvious during a power outage. Out of habit you might walk into a room and flip on the light switch. You might try to turn on a radio or television or check the clock to see what time it is. Because power outages occur, some electrical devices, like the one in **Figure 21,** use batteries as a backup source of electrical energy. Is the current produced by a battery the same as the current from a generator? Both devices cause electrons to move through a wire. However, the currents produced by these electric sources are different from each other in an important way.

A battery produces a direct current. **Direct current** (DC) flows in only one direction through a wire. When you plug your CD player or any other appliance into a wall outlet, you are using alternating current. **Alternating current** (AC) reverses the direction of the current flow in a regular way. In North America, generators produce alternating current at a frequency of 60 cycles per second, or 60 Hz. The electric current produced by a generator changes direction twice during each cycle or each rotation of the coil. So a 60-Hz alternating current changes direction 120 times each second.

Transformers

The current that flows in an electric circuit carries electrical energy. This electrical energy is related to the voltage in the circuit. The alternating current traveling through power lines is at an extremely high voltage. Before alternating current from the power plant can enter your home safely, its voltage must be decreased. The voltage is decreased by passing the current through a transformer. A **transformer** is a device that increases or decreases the voltage of an alternating current.

A transformer is made of two coils of wire called the primary and secondary coils. These coils are wrapped around the same iron core. As an alternating current passes through the primary coil, the iron core becomes an electromagnet. The current changes direction many times each second, so the magnetic field of the iron core also changes direction. This changing magnetic field induces an alternating current in the secondary coil.

Figure 21
Some devices can use either direct or alternating current.
Why might it be a good idea to keep batteries in a clock or a VCR?

Science Journal

Nikola Tesla Tell students that the inventor Nikola Tesla brought alternating current into wide usage. Have students find out where he was from, when he lived and how he spread the use of alternating current, and write their findings in their Science Journals. Tesla lived from 1856 to 1943. He was Serbian, born in Croatia. He sold George Westinghouse the idea of alternating current. L2 LS **Linguistic**

Stepping Up and Stepping Down If the secondary coil in a transformer has more turns of wire than the primary coil does, then the transformer increases, or steps up, voltage. For example, the secondary coil of the step-up transformer in **Figure 22A** has two times more turns than the primary coil has. This means than an input voltage in the primary coil of 60 V would increase by two times to 120 V in the secondary coil.

A transformer that reduces voltage is called a step-down transformer. **Figure 22B** shows how the output voltage of a transformer is decreased if the number of turns in the secondary coil is less than the number of turns in the primary coil. If the secondary coil of a transformer has half as many turns as the primary coil does, the output voltage will be half the input voltage.

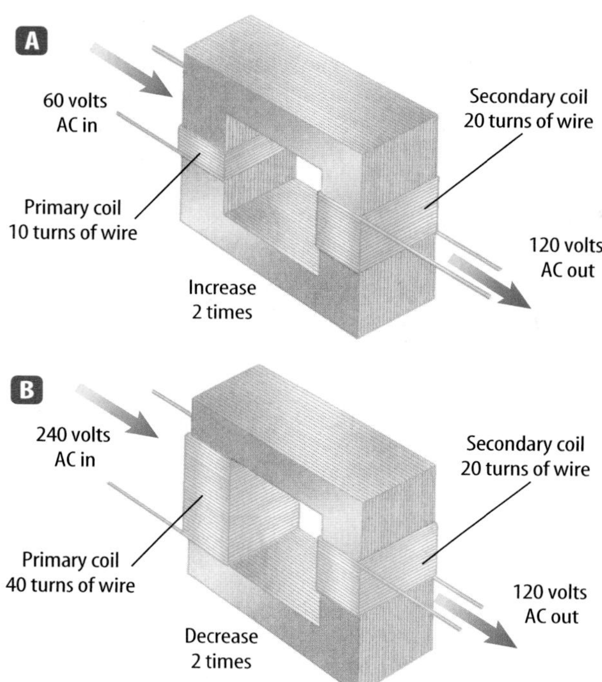

Figure 22
Transformers can increase or decrease voltage.
A A step-up transformer increases voltage. The secondary coil has more turns than the primary coil does.
B A step-down transformer decreases voltage. The secondary coil has fewer turns than the primary coil does.

Reading Check ***What type of transformer has more turns of wire in the secondary coil than the primary coil?***

Transmitting Alternating Current When an electric current flows in a wire, some of the energy carried by the current is lost as heat. This heat loss is due to the resistance of the wire and increases as the wire is made longer. If the current produced by a power plant is transmitted over long distances, as much as ten percent of the electrical energy can be lost as heat. This energy loss can be reduced greatly by transmitting the power at high voltages. Power plants commonly produce alternating current because the voltage can be increased or decreased with transformers. In the United States, some power lines carry power at voltages as high as 750,000 V—high voltage indeed although most power lines you see carry lower voltages.

Such high voltage is dangerous and cannot be used in home appliances. Step-down transformers reduce the voltage of the alternating current to 120 V before it enters your home. You can then operate devices such as microwaves and hair dryers with 120-V household current.

Transformers

Teacher FYI

Eddy currents can be generated in transformers by the changing magnetic field around the core. Because the magnetic fields generated by the eddy current oppose the original field, power is lost. The cores of transformers are often made out of many thin, laminated strips of metal instead of one big iron loop. Insulating glue between the strips restricts the eddy currents to individual strips, where they cannot grow very large. This makes the transformer more efficient.

Activity

Take students outside and find the transformers leading into the school. Ask students to find the transformers near their homes as well, and compare them. Caution students to not touch or get too close to the transformers. L1 ELL **Visual-Spatial**

Reading Check

Answer step-up transformer

Active Reading

Write-Draw-Discuss This strategy encourages students to actively participate in reading and lectures, assimilating content creatively. Have students write about electric motors, generators, and transformers, clarify their ideas, then make illustrations or drawings. Ask students to share responses with the class and display several examples.

Resource Manager

Chapter Resources Booklet
Enrichment, p. 32

Performance Assessment in the Science Classroom, p. 53

Transformers, Continued

Caption Answer

Figure 23 The step-up transformer and step-down transformer

3 Assess

Reteach

Use **Figure 20** to tie the electric generator to the electric motor. Have students explain what each is used for and how each uses the connection between electricity and magnetism. L2 LS **Visual-Spatial**

Challenge

Ask students to explore and explain the differences between the connections for a generator of direct current and the connections for a generator of alternating current. A high school text or popular science book may have illustrations. In a DC generator you need a commutator to straighten out the current. L3 LS **Logical-Mathematical**

Assessment

Content Ask students to work in teams to design a human-powered device for generating electrical energy. A device similar to a stationary bicycle would work—you may even find one in a science museum. Use **Performance Assessment in the Science Classroom,** p. 117.

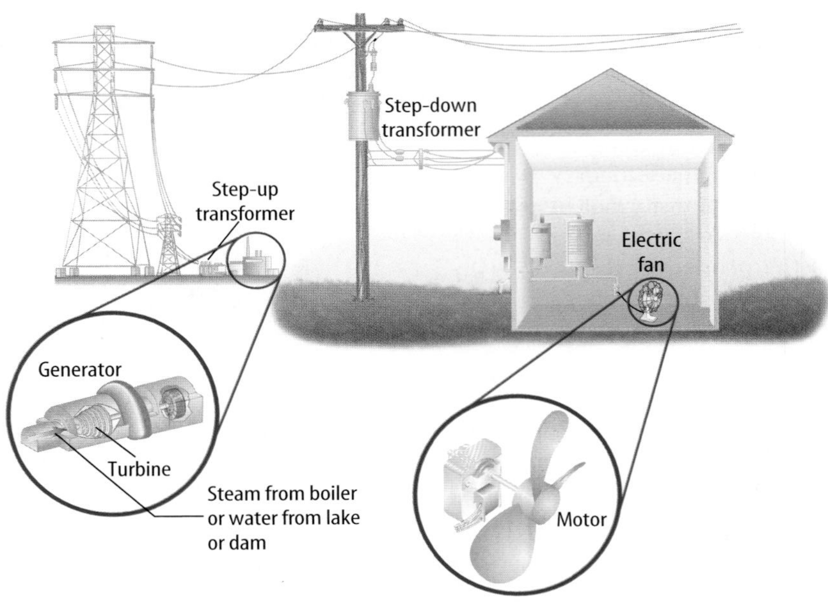

Figure 23
Many steps are involved in the creation, transportation, and use of the electric current in your home. *Which steps involve electromagnetic induction?*

Electric current in your home Think back over this section. You have learned how electromagnetic induction, generators, alternating current, and transformers all work together to make your electric fan operate. **Figure 23** illustrates the series of steps used in producing, transporting, and delivering alternating current to your home in a form that you can use safely.

Section 3 Assessment

1. How does a generator use electromagnetic induction to produce a current?
2. A transformer in a neon sign contains 20 turns in the primary coil and 80 turns in the secondary coil. Which is greater—the output voltage or the input voltage?
3. Contrast alternating and direct current.
4. What type of current do power plants produce? Why is it convenient?
5. **Think Critically** Why can't a transformer step up the voltage in a direct current?

Skill Builder Activities

6. **Concept Mapping** Prepare an events chain concept map to show how electricity is produced by a generator. **For more help, refer to the Science Skill Handbook.**
7. **Using Proportions** An alternating current in a wire has a voltage of 2,800 V. It needs to be reduced to 70 V. The wire makes 120 turns in the primary coil of a step-down transformer. How many turns of wire need to be in the secondary coil? **For more help, refer to the Math Skill Handbook.**

Answers to Section Assessment

1. A generator rotates a coil of wire in a magnetic field. An electric current is produced in the coil by electromagnetic induction.
2. the output voltage
3. Both are types of electric current. Direct current flows in one direction, while alternating current changes direction at regular intervals.
4. alternating current, because it can be transmitted at high voltage, which is more efficient
5. a direct current does not produce the changing electrical field needed to make a transformer work
6. Mechanical energy causes a wire loop to rotate in a magnetic field, which induces an alternating current in the loop.
7. Three

Activity

Electricity and Magnetism

Huge generators in power plants produce electricity by moving a coil of wire through a magnetic field. How can you make your own electric current?

What You'll Investigate

How can a magnet be used to create an electric current?

Materials

cardboard tube
scissors
bar magnet
thin, flexible, insulated wire
galvanometer or ammeter

Goals

- **Observe** how a magnet can produce an electric current in a wire.
- **Compare and contrast** the currents created by moving the magnet in different ways.

Safety Precautions

Be careful with scissors. Do not touch bare wires when current is running through them.

Procedure

1. Wrap the wire around a cardboard tube to make a coil of about 20 turns. Leave about 15 cm for a lead at each end of the wire.
2. Use the scissors to cut through the insulation 2 cm from each end of the wire. Pull the insulation off with your fingers. Remove the tube from the coil.
3. Connect the ends of the wire to a galvanometer or ammeter. Record the reading on your meter.
4. While closely watching the meter, insert one end of the bar magnet into the coil.

5. Pull the magnet out of the coil and repeat. Record the reading on the meter. Move the magnet at different speeds and record your measurements.
6. Watch the meter and move the bar magnet in different directions around the outside of the coil. Record your observations.

Conclude and Apply

1. Which circumstances that you tested generated the greatest current?
2. Does the current you generate by moving the magnet always move in the same direction? How do you know?
3. **Predict** what would happen if you tried the experiment with a coil made with fewer turns of wire.
4. **Infer** whether a current would have been generated if the cardboard tube were left in the coil. Why or why not? Try it.

Communicating Your Data

Compare the currents generated by different members of the class. **For more help, refer to the** Science Skill Handbook.

Activity

BENCH TESTED

Purpose Students observe electromagnetic induction of a current. L1 LS **Kinesthetic**

Process Skills observing and inferring, interpreting data, drawing conclusions, recognizing cause and effect, comparing and contrasting, making models

Time Required 45 minutes

Alternate Materials One end of a horseshoe magnet can replace the bar magnet.

Teaching Strategy Be sure the galvanometer is on the most sensitive scale and that students form complete circuits.

Answers to Questions

1. Faster motion produces more current, as does moving the magnet in the coil rather than outside it.
2. No; the needle was deflected in different directions depending on whether the magnet moved in or out of the coil.
3. A smaller current would be induced.
4. Yes; cardboard is not affected by electric or magnetic fields.

Assessment

Performance Ask each student to make a poster that shows the design of the experiment they used and explains what each piece of equipment does. To one side, they should list how changes in the setup change the current induced. Use **Performance Assessment in the Science Classroom,** p. 145.

Communicating Your Data

Ask students to include suggestions for how they could make a stronger current. Possible answers: increase the number of coils; make the coils closer to the moving magnet; produce a stronger field; use a stronger magnet

Resource Manager

Chapter Resources Booklet
Reinforcement, p. 29
Activity Worksheet, pp. 5–6, 7–8

Activity BENCH TESTED

Recognize the Problem

Purpose

Students will assemble an electromagnet and then attempt to control its strength by changing its construction. L2 LS **Kinesthetic**

Process Skills

forming a hypothesis, identifying and manipulating variables, making and using tables, observing

Time Required

60 minutes

Materials

Iron 16-penny nails are available through science supply companies. If nails are purchased locally, make sure they are made of iron.

Alternate Materials

Students can use either an electric power supply or batteries for the electric current in their electromagnets. A knife switch can be included for easier current control.

Safety Precautions

Closely monitor students who are using an electric power supply to ensure that they do not apply more than 6v.

Form a Hypothesis

Possible Hypothesis

The more loops that are used in the construction of the electromagnet the stronger the magnetic field it will generate.

Activity *Design Your Own Experiment*

Putting Electromagnets to Work

You have learned that a current flowing through loops of wire around an iron core forms an electromagnet. You use electromagnets every day in electric motors, stereo speakers, power door locks and many other devices. To make electromagnets work in these devices, you must be able to control the strength of their magnetic fields. When might you want to make a magnet stronger? When would you want to make it weaker?

Recognize the Problem

How can you control the strength of an electromagnet?

Form a Hypothesis

Think about how an electromagnet is constructed. As a group, write down the components of an electromagnet which might affect the strength of its magnetic field. Which component could have the most effect on the strength of the electromagnet? Which could be easiest to control? Form a hypothesis about the best way to control an electromagnet's strength.

Goals

- **Make** electromagnets.
- **Measure** relative strengths of electromagnets.
- **Modify** electromagnets to change their strength.
- **Determine** which factors affect the strength of an electromagnet.
- **Determine** which factor has the most effect on its strength.
- **Describe** how you could control the strength of an electromagnet.

Possible Materials

22-gauge insulated wire
16-penny iron nail
Aluminum rod or nail
0-6 v DC power supply
Three 1.5 v "D" cells
Steel paper clips
Magnetic compass
Duct tape (to hold "D" cells together)

Safety Precautions

Do not leave the electromagnet connected for a long time because the battery will run down. Magnets with only a few turns of wire will get very hot. Use caution in handling them when current is flowing through the coil. Do not apply voltages higher than 6 v to your electromagnets.

Inclusion Strategies

Learning Disabled Assign the students that make up each lab group. Put learning disabled students into groups that can assist these students in performing the lab. Suggest that this student be the data recorder, in addition to other tasks.

Inclusion Strategies

Gifted Have students research how a simple electric motor is made. Students should prepare a diagram explaining how it works and present it to the class.

Using Scientific Methods

Test Your Hypothesis

Plan

1. Write your hypothesis for the best way to control the strength of an electromagnet.
2. As a group, decide how you will assemble and test the electromagnets. Which features will you change to determine effect on the strength of the magnetic fields? How many changes will you need to try? How many electromagnets do you need to build?
3. Decide how you are going to test the strength of your electromagnets. Several ways are possible with the materials listed. Which way would be the most sensitive? Be prepared to change test methods if necessary.
4. Write your plan of investigation. Make sure your plan tests only one variable at a time.

Do

1. Before you begin to build and test the electromagnets, make sure your teacher approves of your plan.
2. Carry out your planned investigation. Record your results.

Analyze Your Data

1. **Make a table** showing the strength of your electromagnet relative to changes you made in its construction or operation.
2. **Examine** the trends shown by your data. Are there any data points which seem out of line? How can you account for them?

Draw Conclusions

1. Did the strength of the electromagnet change with changes in its construction or operation?
2. Which feature of the electromagnet's construction had the greatest effect on its strength? Which do you think would be easiest to control?
3. How might you use your electromagnet to make a doorbell? Would it work with both AC and DC?
4. Did your results support your hypothesis? Why or why not?

Communicating Your Data

Compare your group's results with those of other groups. Did any other group use a different method to test the strength of the magnet? Did you get the same results?

Test Your Hypothesis

Possible Procedures

Assemble a simple circuit that includes the power source and the coiled nail in the circuit. A knife switch can be added if desired. Vary the number of coils on the nail to vary the magnetic field strength. The number of paper clips that can be picked up by the electromagnet can be used as the strength indicator.

Teaching Strategy

Remind students that the polarity of the electromagnetic can be reversed by changing the direction of the current flow.

Expected Outcome

Most results will show that increasing the number of loops in the electromagnet increases the strength of the magnetic field.

Analyze Your Data

1. Check each group's table
2. Answers will vary

Error Analysis

Have students compare their results and their hypotheses and explain why differences occurred.

Draw Conclusions

1. The strength of the magnetic field increased when the number of loops increased.
2. number of loops; number of loops
3. Answers will vary
4. Answers will vary

Assessment

Process Students should research how a doorbell works and make drawings illustrating how what they find. Use **Performance Assessment in the Science Classroom,** p. 127.

Communicating Your Data

When comparing various methods used to test the strength of the magnet, students should consider the masses of the objects used and their composition.

TIME SCIENCE AND HISTORY

Content Background

Magnetic resonance imaging (MRI) is a noninvasive diagnostic technique that uses nuclear magnetic resonance (NMR) to image the structure of the body. Unhampered by bone and capable of producing images in a variety of planes, MRI is used in the diagnosis of brain tumors and disorders, spinal disorders, multiple sclerosis, and cardiovascular diseases. The procedure is considered to be without risk to the patient.

Types of magnetic resonance include electron paramagnetic resonance (EPR), also known as electron spin resonance (ESR), involving the magnetic effect of electrons, and nuclear magnetic resonance (NMR), involving the magnetic effects of protons and neutrons in the nuclei of atoms. The NMR resonant frequency provides information about the molecular material in which the nuclei reside.

NMR also is used in chemistry and physics to analyze samples of solids and liquids, as well as in medicine to analyze tissues removed from the body.

TIME SCIENCE AND HISTORY

SCIENCE CAN CHANGE THE COURSE OF HISTORY!

Body Art

The invention of a machine that uses magnetism means better lives for many

The year is 1975. A surgeon stands facing an exposed human brain. She has already removed part of the patient's skull and is looking for a growth on the brain. From the patient's symptoms, the surgeon can only infer where to find the tumor. But can she find it and remove it without causing more damage than the tumor was causing? "We're going in," the doctor says. She puts out her hand to the nurse. "Scalpel."

Flash forward to the present day. The surgeon turns the computer screen so the patient can see it. Pointing to a dark area on a colorful image of the patient's brain, she reassures the worried patient. "This MRI shows exactly where your tumor is. We can remove it with very little danger to you." "Thank goodness for the MRI," the patient says in relief.

MRI for the Soft Stuff

MRI stands for "magnetic resonance imaging." It's a way to take 3-D pictures of the inside of your body. Before the 1980s, doctors could X ray solid tissue like bones, but had no way to see soft tissue like the brain. Well, they had one way—surgery, which sometimes caused injury and infection, risking a patient's health.

MRIs were originally used to identify substances in chemistry and physics labs.

These are MRI scans of brains from different people. The colors help doctors read the scans more easily, and detect any problems.

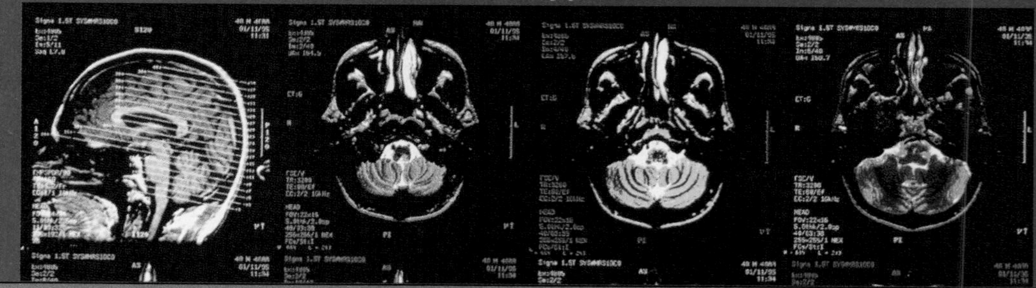

250

Resources for Teachers and Students

Functional MRI (Medical Radiology) by C.T.W. Moonen (Editor) and P.A. Bandettini (Editor). Springer Verlag. 2000.

Looking Within: How X-ray, Ct, Mri, Ultrasound, and Other Medical Images are Created, and How They Help Physicians Save Lives by Anthony B. Wolbarst and Gordon Cook (Illustrator). University Of California Press. 1999.

Naked to the Bone: Medical Imaging in the Twentieth Century by Bettyann Kevles. Perseus Press. 1998.

Then after research and modifications in the method, doctors began to use MRIs to make images of the tissues inside the human body.

MRI uses a strong magnet and radio waves. Tissues in your body contain water molecules that are made of oxygen and hydrogen atoms. The nucleus of a hydrogen atom is a proton, which behaves like a tiny magnet. A strong magnetic field inside the MRI tube makes these proton magnets line up in the direction of the field. Radio waves are then applied to the body. The protons absorb some of the radio-wave energy, and flip their direction.

When the radio waves are turned off, the protons realign themselves with the magnetic field and emit the energy they absorbed. Different tissues in the body absorb and emit different amounts of energy. The emitted energy is detected, and a computer uses this information to form images of the body.

A girl gets ready for an MRI scan. It doesn't hurt!

Your Brain Is Getting Bigger!

MRI has been most useful in finding and treating tumors. But it has also turned into an important research tool. For example, Elizabeth Sowell's research team at the University of California, Los Angeles, used MRIs to study the brain growth of middle school students. She and other researchers have found that the brain grows rapidly during adolescence. Before this groundbreaking research, people thought that the brain stopped growing in childhood. MRI has proved that adolescents are getting bigger brains all the time.

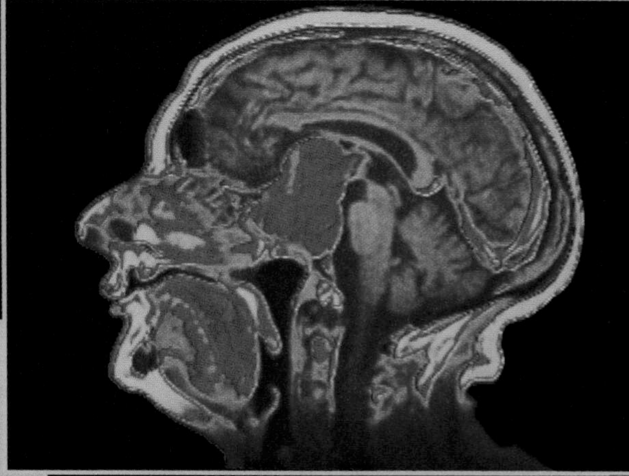

An MRI scan of a brain shows a tumor on the pituitary gland. The gland is the large pink area in the middle of the photo.

CONNECTIONS Interview As an oral history project, interview a retired physician or surgeon. Ask him or her to discuss with you how tools such as the MRI changed during his or her career. Make a list of the tools and how they have helped improve medicine.

SCIENCE *Online*
For more information, visit science.glencoe.com

Discussion

How are X-rays used differently from MRI? Possible Answer: X-rays are used for the diagnosis of problems in hard tissue areas of the body while MRI is used to diagnose soft tissue disorders. L2 **Logical-Mathematical**

Historical Significance

Make sure students understand that MRI has only been developed in the last twenty-five years, which is a very short period of time in the span of history. Start a discussion that will get students to think about the medical advances that have been made possible by MRI. For example, because of MRI doctors are now able to diagnose birth defects and operate on babies in the womb.

CONNECTIONS If any of the students' parents work in the health field, ask them for suggestions of people students can interview. Also, make available to your students any lists of local medical professionals who could help them find a source for their oral histories. Conduct a brainstorming session to establish questions for the students to ask during their interviews to help them focus on relevant facts. Encourage them to write down their questions before the interview to ease this process.

SCIENCE *Online*

Internet Addresses

____

____

____

Explore the Glencoe Science Web site at **science.glencoe.com** to find out more about topics in this section.

Chapter 8 Study Guide

Reviewing Main Ideas

Preview

Students can answer the questions in their Science Journals. Discuss the answers as you go through the chapter. **LS Linguistic**

Review

Students can write their answers, then compare them with those of other students. **LS Interpersonal**

Reteach

Students can look at the illustrations and describe details that support the main ideas of the chapter. **LS Visual-Spatial**

Answers to Chapter Review

Section 1

1. The refrigerator contains metal that can be magnetized; the wooden cupboard door cannot be magnetized.

Section 2

3. The electromagnet rotates in response to the electric current in a wire that changes with temperature. This moves the indicator on the temperature gauge.

Section 3

2. The dam lets water through at a calculated rate, providing mechanical energy to power the generator.

Chapter 8 Study Guide

Reviewing Main Ideas

Section 1 Magnetism

1. A magnetic field surrounds a magnet and exerts a magnetic force. *Why is this magnet attracted to the refrigerator but not to the cupboard?*
2. All magnets have two poles: a south pole and a north pole.
3. Opposite poles of magnets attract; like poles repel.
4. Groups of atoms with aligned magnetic poles are called magnetic domains.

Section 2 Electricity and Magnetism

1. An electric current flowing through a wire produces a magnetic field.
2. An electric current passing through a coil of wire can produce a magnetic field inside the coil. The coil becomes an electromagnet. One end of the coil is the north pole, and the other end is the south pole.
3. The magnetic field produced by an electromagnet depends on the current and the number of coils. *How is an electromagnet used in this temperature gauge from a car?*

4. An electric motor contains a rotating electromagnet that converts electrical energy to mechanical energy.

Section 3 Producing Electric Current

1. By moving a magnet near a wire, you can create an electric current in the wire. This is called electromagnetic induction.
2. A generator produces electric current by rotating a coil of wire in a magnetic field. *How does the dam in the picture below help make electricity?*

3. Direct current flows in one direction through a wire. Alternating current reverses the direction of current flow in a regular pattern.
4. The number of turns of wire in the primary and secondary coils of a transformer determines whether it increases or decreases voltage.

FOLDABLES Reading & Study Skills — After You Read

To help you review what you've learned about magnets, use the Question Study Fold you made at the beginning of this chapter.

FOLDABLES Reading & Study Skills — After You Read

After students have read the chapter and completed the Foldable described in Before You Read, have them do the activity on the student page.

Dinah Zike

Chapter 8 Study Guide

Visualizing Main Ideas

Complete the following concept map on how an electric motor works.

Place electromagnet between poles of a permanent, fixed magnet.

↓

Connect coil of electromagnet to source of electric current.

↓

Coil turns in order to align its north and south poles to magnetic field lines of permanent magnet.

↓

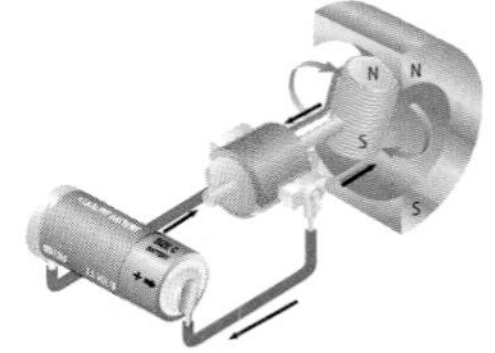

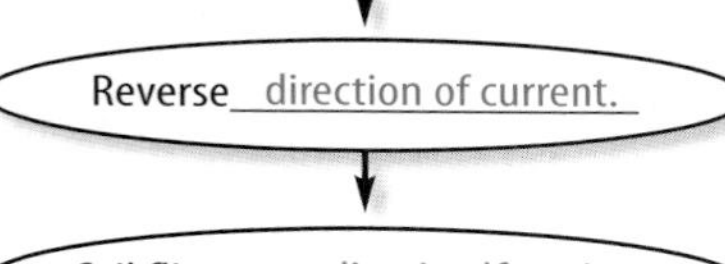

Reverse direction of current.

↓

Coil flips to align itself again.

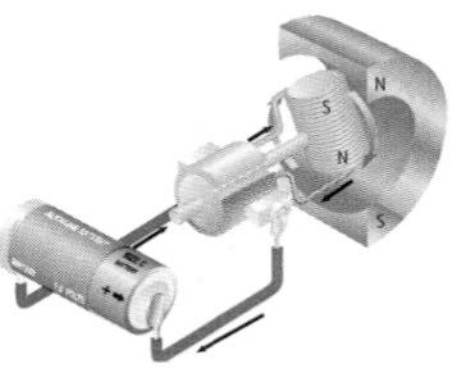

Vocabulary Review

Vocabulary Words

- **a.** alternating current (AC)
- **b.** commutator
- **c.** direct current (DC)
- **d.** electric motor
- **e.** electromagnet
- **f.** electromagnetic induction
- **g.** galvanometer
- **h.** generator
- **i.** magnetic domain
- **j.** magnetic pole
- **k.** magnetism
- **l.** transformer
- **m.** turbine

Study Tip

Study the material you *don't* understand as well first! It's easy to review the material you know, but harder to force yourself to really go over the tough stuff.

Using Vocabulary

Each of the following sentences is false. Make the sentence true by replacing the underlined word with a vocabulary word.

1. An electric motor can be used to change the voltage of an alternating current.
2. Flat current does not change direction.
3. A magnetic domain is the region where the magnetic force of a magnet is strongest.
4. Current flows in the coil of a galvanometer because of electromagnetic induction.
5. The properties and interactions of magnets are called electricity.
6. A transformer can rotate in a magnetic field when a current passes through it.
7. A generator uses alternating current to produce an electric current.

Chapter 8 Study Guide

Visualizing Main Ideas

See student page.

Vocabulary Review

Using Vocabulary

1. transformer
2. Direct current
3. magnetic pole
4. generator
5. magnetism
6. electromagnet
7. electromagnetic induction

IDENTIFYING Misconceptions

Assess

After students have done the activity on page 224F and completed the chapter, have them perform this activity.

Materials PVC pipe, aluminum or copper pipe, circular magnet

Procedure Drop a circular magnet down a length of PVC pipe and note how long it takes to get to the bottom. Now drop the magnet down an aluminum or copper pipe of the same length and note how long it takes to reach the bottom.

Expected Outcome The magnet travels more slowly down the metal tube, not because it is attracted to the pipe, but because the falling magnet creates an electric current in the pipe, which creates a magnetic field that opposes the magnet and slows it down.

Chapter 8 Assessment

Checking Concepts

1. A
2. C
3. D
4. B
5. B
6. A
7. C
8. B
9. C
10. C

Thinking Critically

11. Possible answer: suspend it by the middle so it can rotate; the south end should be attracted to magnetic north.
12. No, the current needed in the machine would be out of sync with that supplied.
13. The strong magnetic field would change the domains on the tape or disk.
14. 10 turns
15. Possible answer: No, they would not work as currently designed. The coil of wire in these devices is placed so that it passes through the strongest part of the field, that is, at the poles. You would need to redesign the devices.

Chapter  8 Assessment

Checking Concepts

Choose the word or phrase that best answers the question.

1. Where is the magnetic force exerted by a magnet strongest?
   A) both poles **C)** north pole
   B) south pole **D)** center
2. What happens to the magnetic force as the distance between two magnetic poles decreases?
   A) stays constant **C)** increases
   B) decreases sharply **D)** decreases slightly
3. What type of magnetic poles do the domains at the north pole of a magnet have?
   A) north magnetic poles only
   B) south magnetic poles only
   C) no magnetic poles
   D) north and south magnetic poles
4. Which of the following would not change the strength of an electromagnet?
   A) increasing the amount of current
   B) changing the current's direction
   C) inserting an iron core inside the coil
   D) increasing the number of loops
5. Which of the following would not be part of a generator?
   A) turbine **C)** electromagnet
   B) battery **D)** permanent magnet
6. Which conversion does an electric motor make?
   A) electrical energy to mechanical energy
   B) thermal energy to wind energy
   C) mechanical energy to electrical energy
   D) wind energy to electrical energy
7. Which of the following describes the direction of the electric current in AC?
   A) remains constant **C)** changes regularly
   B) is direct **D)** changes irregularly
8. Before current in power lines can enter your home, what must it pass through?
   A) step-up transformer
   B) step-down transformer
   C) commutator
   D) motor
9. A generator creates a 40-Hz alternating current. How many times does the current change direction every second?
   A) 40 times **C)** 80 times
   B) 60 times **D)** 20 times
10. When current flows through a wire, what is created around the wire?
    A) an electromagnet **C)** a magnetic field
    B) a galvanometer **D)** a direct current

Thinking Critically

11. How could you use a horseshoe magnet to find the direction north?
12. In Europe, generators produce alternating current at a frequency of 50 Hz. Would an appliance you use in North America work if you plugged it into an outlet in Europe? Why or why not?
13. Audiotapes, computer disks and audio CDs are recorded using magnets, and their information is coded magnetically. Why would it be harmful to a tape, computer disk or CD to expose it to a strong magnetic field?
14. A step-down transformer reduces a 1,200-V current to 120 V. If the primary coil has 100 turns, how many must its secondary coil have?
15. Suppose the magnetic fields of magnets were not strongest at the magnets' poles. Would motors, galvanometers, and generators still work? Why or why not?

Chapter Assessment Planner

Portfolio Encourage students to place in their portfolios one or two items of what they consider to be their best work. Examples include:
- Curriculum Connection, p. 229
- Curriculum Connection, p. 238
- Curriculum Connection, p. 242

Performance Additional performance assessments, Performance Task Assessment Lists, and rubrics for evaluating these activities can be found in Glencoe's **Performance Assessment in the Science Classroom.**

16. **Comparing and Contrasting** Compare and contrast electric and magnetic forces.

17. **Forming Hypotheses** A compass needle will point north due to the magnetic field of Earth. When a bar magnet is brought near the compass, the needle is attracted or repelled by the bar magnet. Propose a hypothesis about the relative strengths of a bar magnet and Earth's magnetic field.

18. **Interpreting Scientific Illustrations** Review **Figure 14** and describe the function of each labeled part of the motor.

19. **Comparing and Contrasting** Compare and contrast electromagnetic induction and the formation of electromagnets.

20. **Concept Mapping** Complete the following Venn diagram of AC generators and DC motors.

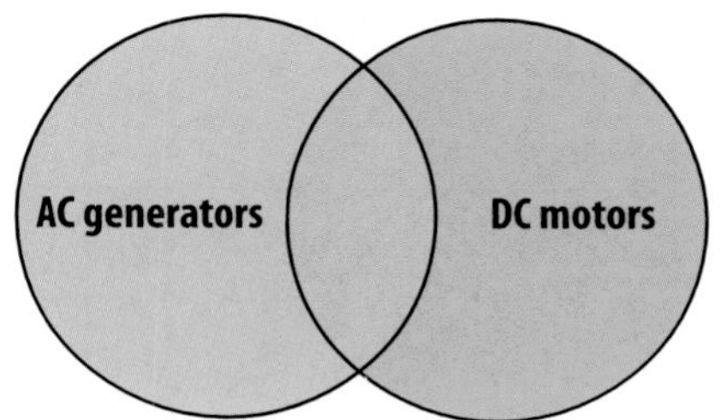

Performance Assessment

21. **Invention** Invent a device that uses an electric motor. Describe it to your class.

Technology

Go to the Glencoe Science Web site at **science.glencoe.com** or use the **Glencoe Science CD-ROM** for additional chapter assessment.

Test Practice

The diagram below is taken from the instructions that come with a blank videocassette.

Proper Storage

Avoid exposing cassettes to:

Direct sunlight and heat

Dust

Strong magnetic fields

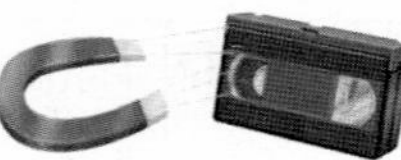

Humidity

Study the diagram and answer the following questions.

1. Why do videocassettes come with a warning to avoid strong magnetic fields?
   A) The videocassette will be turned into a powerful magnet.
   B) The information on the videocassette will be damaged.
   C) The videocassette's case will become electrically charged.
   D) The videocassette will melt.

2. According to this diagram, all of the following could be harmful to a videocassette **EXCEPT**______.
   F) air conditioning
   G) moisture
   H) direct sunlight and heat
   J) dust

Assessment Resources

Reproducible Masters

Chapter Resources Booklet
Chapter Review, pp. 37–38
Chapter Tests, pp. 39–42
Assessment Transparency Activity, p. 49

Glencoe Science Web site
Interactive Tutor
Chapter Quizzess

Glencoe Technology
Assessment Transparency
Interactive CD-ROM Chapter Quizzes
ExamView Pro Test Bank
Vocabulary PuzzleMaker Software
MindJogger Videoquiz DVD/VHS

THE PRINCETON REVIEW Test Practice

This Test-Taking Tip was written by The Princeton Review, the nation's leader in test preparation.

1. B
2. F

Developing Skills

16. Both have two opposing parts (north/south, positive/negative) for which likes repel and unlikes attract. Both act through fields, which become weaker with distance. Both affect some materials differently from others.
17. Earth's magnetic field is weaker than the field close to most bar magnets.
18. The electromagnet produces a magnetic field in the coil. The permanent magnet and the electromagnet share a magnetic force that turns the coil. The coil turns so that its N and S poles are aligned on the field. The power source provides electric current, creating continuous motion of this cycle.
19. In electromagnetic induction, a changing magnetic field induces a changing electric current. In electromagnets, a direct current induces a static magnetic field.
20. Both use a coil, an electromagnet, and a permanent magnet; in both cases the magnets move relative to one another. In an AC generator, a force turns one of the magnets, generating alternating electric current in the electromagnet. In a DC motor electricity causes a magnet to turn, thereby turning whatever is attached to it.

Performance Assessment

21. Inventions should show students' understanding that an electric motor produces motion. Use **PASC,** p. 117.

Section/Objectives	Standards		Activities/Features
	National	State/Local	
Chapter Opener	See p. 37T for a Key to Standards.		**Explore Activity:** Model the space inside an atom, p. 257 **Before You Read,** p. 257
Section 1 Radioactivity 1 session .5 block **1. Describe** the structure of an atom and its nucleus. **2. Explain** what radioactivity is. **3. Contrast** properties of radioactive and stable nuclei. **4. Discuss** the discovery of radioactivity.	National Content Standards: UCP3, B1, (5–8), B1, B2 (9–12), G3		**Science Online,** p. 262
Section 2 Nuclear Decay 1 session .5 block **1. Compare and contrast** alpha, beta, and gamma radiation. **2. Define** the half-life of a radioactive material. **3. Describe** the process of radioactive dating.	National Content Standards: UCP3, A2, B1, (5–8), B1, B2 (9–12), D2, E2		**MiniLAB:** Candy Nuclei, p. 267
Section 3 Detecting Radioactivity 2 sessions 1 block **1. Describe** how radioactivity can be detected in cloud and bubble chambers. **2. Explain** how an electroscope can be used to detect radiation. **3. Explain** how a Geiger counter can measure nuclear radiation.	National Content Standards: UCP3, B1, (5–8), B1, B2 (9–12)		**Math Skills Activity,** p. 270 **Earth Science Integration,** p. 271
Section 4 Nuclear Reactions 3 sessions 1.5 blocks **1. Explain** nuclear fission and how it can begin a chain reaction. **2. Discuss** how nuclear fusion occurs in the Sun. **3. Describe** how radioactive tracers can be used to diagnose medical problems. **4. Discuss** how nuclear reactions can help treat cancer.	National Content Standards: UCP3, A2, B1, (5–8), B1, B2 (9–12), D2, E2, F1(5–8), F1 (9–12), G1, G2		**MiniLAB:** Modeling a Nuclear Reaction, p. 274 **Science Online,** p. 275 **Chemistry Integration,** p. 276 **Visualizing Pet Scans,** p. 277 **Activity:** Chain Reactions, p. 279 **Activity:** Modeling Transmutation, pp. 280–281 **Oops! Accidents in Science:** X-Ray Surprise, p. 282

Activity Materials	Reproducible Resources	Section Assessment	Technology
Explore Activity: grains of sugar, piece of paper, ruler	**Chapter Resources Booklet** Foldables Worksheet, p. 17 Note-taking Worksheets, pp. 35–37	Glencoe's Assessment Advantage	
	Chapter Resources Booklet Transparency Activity, p. 46 Enrichment, p. 31 Reinforcement, p. 27 Directed Reading, p. 20	**Portfolio** Activity, p. 261 **Performance** Skill Builder Activities, p. 262 **Content** Section Assessment, p. 262	Section Focus Transparency Interactive CD-ROM/DVD Guided Reading Audio Program
MiniLAB: 88 yellow candies, 138 red candies, ruler	**Chapter Resources Booklet** Transparency Activity, p. 47 MiniLAB, p. 3 Enrichment, p. 32 Reinforcement, p. 28 Directed Reading, p. 20 Lab Activity, pp. 9–12, 13–16 Transparency Activity, pp. 51–52	**Portfolio** Science Journal, p. 265 **Performance** MiniLAB, p. 267 Skill Builder Activities, p. 267 **Content** Section Assessment, p. 267	Section Focus Transparency Teaching Transparency Interactive CD-ROM/DVD Guided Reading Audio Program
Need materials? Contact Science Kit at 1-800-828-7777 or www.sciencekit.com on the Internet.	**Chapter Resources Booklet** Transparency Activity, p. 48 Enrichment, p. 33 Reinforcement, p. 29 Directed Reading, p. 21 **Mathematics Skill Activities,** p. 31	**Portfolio** Challenge, p. 272 **Performance** Skill Builder Activities, p. 272 **Content** Section Assessment, p. 272	Section Focus Transparency Interactive CD-ROM/DVD Guided Reading Audio Program
MiniLAB: 32 marbles with attached lumps of clay, large beaker **Activity:** dominoes, stopwatch **Activity:** brown rice, white rice, colored candies, dried beans, dried seeds, glue, poster board	**Chapter Resources Booklet** Transparency Activity, p. 49 MiniLAB, p. 4 Enrichment, p. 34 Reinforcement, p. 30 Directed Reading, pp. 21, 22 Activity Worksheet, pp. 5–6, 7–8 **Home and Community Involvement,** p. 37	**Portfolio** Science Journal, p. 274 **Performance** MiniLAB, p. 274 Skill Builder Activities, p. 278 **Content** Section Assessment, p. 278	Section Focus Transparency Interactive CD-ROM/DVD Guided Reading Audio Program

End of Chapter Assessment

Glencoe's Assessment Advantage

Blackline Masters	Technology	Professional Series
Chapter Resources Booklet Chapter Review, pp. 39–40 Chapter Tests, pp. 41–44 **Standardized Test Practice by The Princeton Review,** pp. 40–43	MindJogger Videoquiz CD-ROM Explorations and Quizzes Vocabulary Puzzle Makers ExamView Pro Test Bank Interactive Lesson Planner Interactive Teacher's Edition	Performance Assessment in the Science Classroom (PASC)

Transparencies

Section Focus

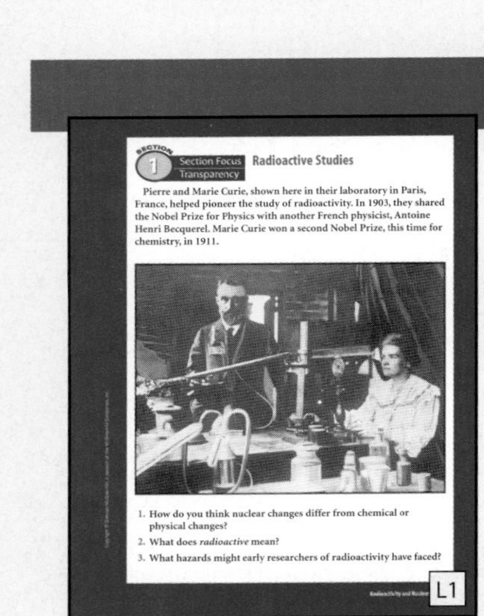
Section 1 Section Focus Transparency **Radioactive Studies**

Pierre and Marie Curie, shown here in their laboratory in Paris, France, helped pioneer the study of radioactivity. In 1903, they shared the Nobel Prize for Physics with another French physicist, Antoine Henri Becquerel. Marie Curie won a second Nobel Prize, this time for chemistry, in 1911.

1. How do you think nuclear changes differ from chemical or physical changes?
2. What does *radioactive* mean?
3. What hazards might early researchers of radioactivity have faced?

L1

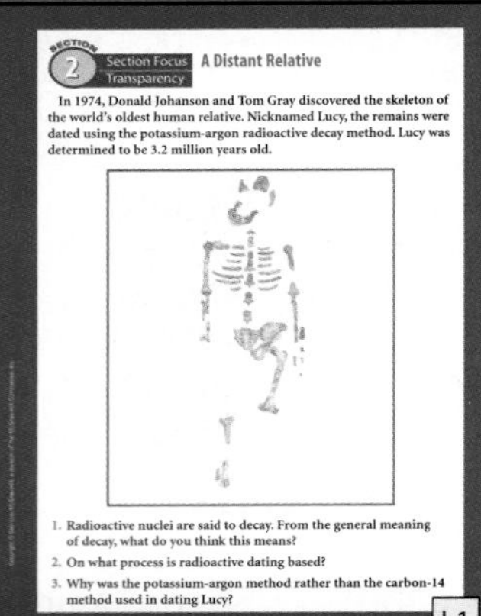
Section 2 Section Focus Transparency **A Distant Relative**

In 1974, Donald Johanson and Tom Gray discovered the skeleton of the world's oldest human relative. Nicknamed Lucy, the remains were dated using the potassium-argon radioactive decay method. Lucy was determined to be 3.2 million years old.

1. Radioactive nuclei are said to decay. From the general meaning of decay, what do you think this means?
2. On what process is radioactive dating based?
3. Why was the potassium-argon method rather than the carbon-14 method used in dating Lucy?

L1

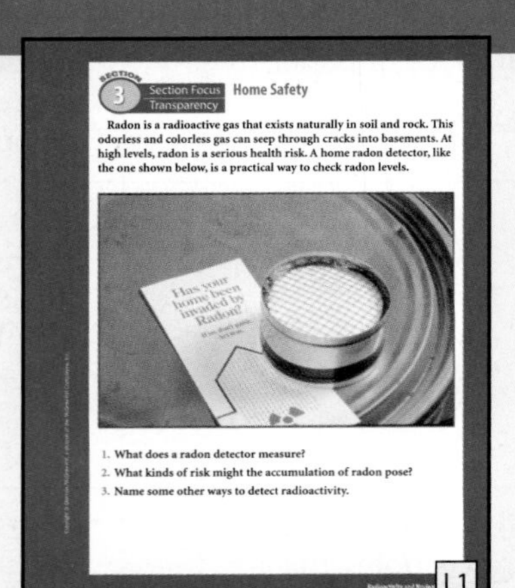
Section 3 Section Focus Transparency **Home Safety**

Radon is a radioactive gas that exists naturally in soil and rock. This odorless and colorless gas can seep through cracks into basements. At high levels, radon is a serious health risk. A home radon detector, like the one shown below, is a practical way to check radon levels.

1. What does a radon detector measure?
2. What kinds of risk might the accumulation of radon pose?
3. Name some other ways to detect radioactivity.

L1

Assessment

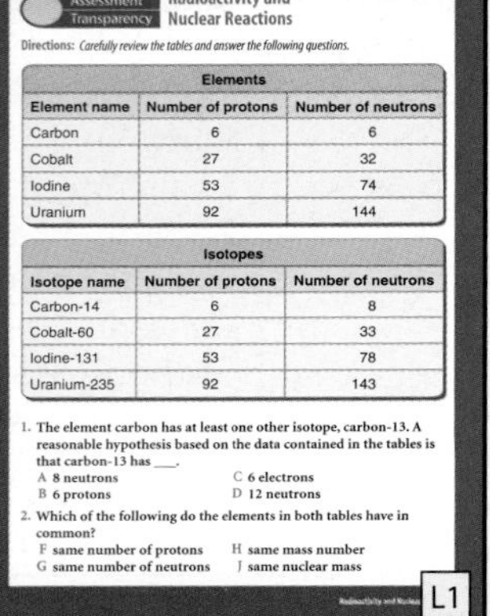
Assessment Transparency **Radioactivity and Nuclear Reactions**

Directions: Carefully review the tables and answer the following questions.

Elements		
Element name	Number of protons	Number of neutrons
Carbon	6	6
Cobalt	27	32
Iodine	53	74
Uranium	92	144

Isotopes		
Isotope name	Number of protons	Number of neutrons
Carbon-14	6	8
Cobalt-60	27	33
Iodine-131	53	78
Uranium-235	92	143

1. The element carbon has at least one other isotope, carbon-13. A reasonable hypothesis based on the data contained in the tables is that carbon-13 has ___.
   A 8 neutrons C 6 electrons
   B 6 protons D 12 neutrons
2. Which of the following do the elements in both tables have in common?
   F same number of protons H same mass number
   G same number of neutrons J same nuclear mass

L1

Teaching

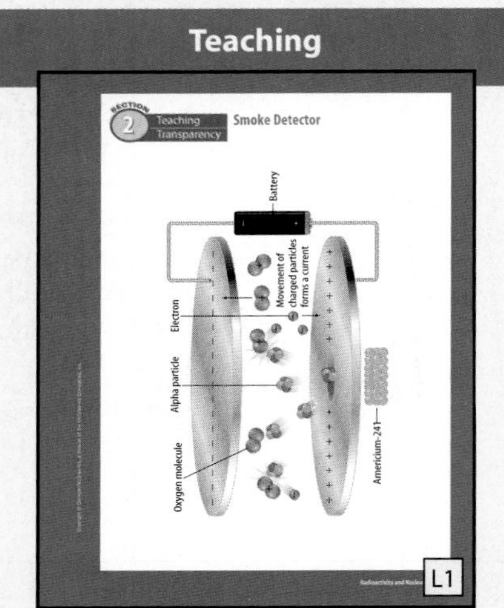
Section 2 Teaching Transparency **Smoke Detector**

L1

This is a representation of key blackline masters available in the Teacher Classroom Resources. See Resource Manager boxes within the chapter for additional information.

Key to Teaching Strategies

The following designations will help you decide which activities are appropriate for your students.

- L1 Level 1 activities should be appropriate for students with learning difficulties.
- L2 Level 2 activities should be within the ability range of all students.
- L3 Level 3 activities are designed for above-average students.
- ELL ELL activities should be within the ability range of English Language Learners.
- COOP LEARN Cooperative Learning activities are designed for small group work.
- LS Multiple Learning Styles logos are used throughout to indicate strategies that address different learning styles.
- P These strategies represent student products that can be placed into a best-work portfolio.

Hands-on Activities

Activity Worksheets

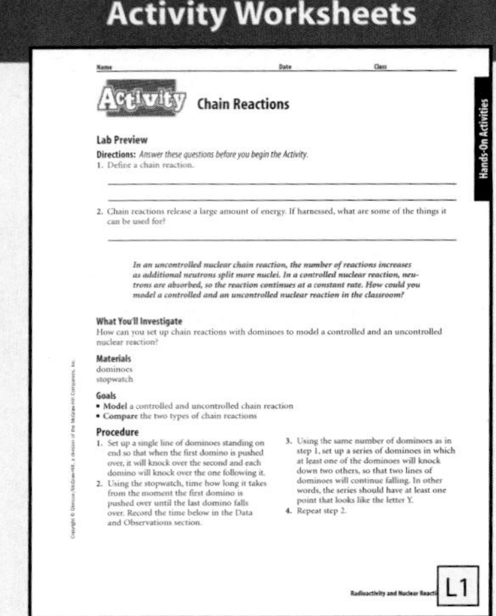
Name Date Class

Activity **Chain Reactions**

Hands-On Activities

Lab Preview

Directions: *Answer these questions before you begin the Activity.*

1. Define a chain reaction.
2. Chain reactions release a large amount of energy. If harnessed, what are some of the things it can be used for?

In an uncontrolled nuclear chain reaction, the number of reactions increases as additional neutrons split more nuclei. In a controlled nuclear reaction, neutrons are absorbed, so the reaction continues at a constant rate. How could you model a controlled and an uncontrolled nuclear reaction in the classroom?

What You'll Investigate

How can you set up chain reactions with dominoes to model a controlled and an uncontrolled nuclear reaction?

Materials

dominoes
stopwatch

Goals

- **Model** a controlled and uncontrolled chain reaction
- **Compare** the two types of chain reactions

Procedure

1. Set up a single line of dominoes standing on end so that when the first domino is pushed over, it will knock over the second and each domino will knock over the one following it.
2. Using the stopwatch, time how long it takes from the moment the first domino is pushed over until the last domino falls over. Record the time below in the Data and Observations section.
3. Using the same number of dominoes as in step 1, set up a series of dominoes in which at least one of the dominoes will knock down two others, so that two lines of dominoes will continue falling. In other words, the series should have at least one point that looks like the letter Y.
4. Repeat step 2.

L1

Laboratory Activities

Name Date Class

LAB 1 Laboratory Activity **The Effect of Radiation on Seeds**

Hands-On Activities

When seeds are exposed to nuclear radiation, many changes may be observed. Seeds contain genetic materials that determines the characteristics of the plants produced from them. Radiation can alter this genetic material. The type of seeds and the amount of radiation absorbed determine the extent of this alteration.

Strategy

You will grow plants from seeds that have been exposed to different amounts of nuclear radiation.
You will observe and record the growth patterns of the plants during a period of a week.
You will use the results of your experiment to discuss some of the possible effects of exposure to nuclear radiation.

Materials

seeds that have received different amounts of radiation
a few seeds that have not been irradiated
potting soil
boxes or containers for planting

Procedure

1. It is important that all seeds are planted and grown under the same conditions. Plant the seeds according to your teacher's instructions. Plant one container of untreated seeds. Label this container *1*. Carefully label each of the remaining containers. In Table 1, record the number of each container and the amount of radiation the seeds planted in it received.
2. Place the containers in a location away from drafts where they can receive as much light as possible. Keep the soil moist, but not wet, at all times.
3. As soon as the first seeds sprout, start recording your observations in Table 2. Observe the seeds at regular intervals for several weeks. If necessary, continue Table 2 on a separate sheet of paper. Watch for variations in sprouting and growth rates and differences in size, color, shape, number, and location of the stems and leaves. Remember, it is important to make an entry in the table for each container at every observation date, even if you report no change.
4. In the space provided in the Data and Observations section, make sketches of your plants and show any variation in growth patterns.

Data and Observations

Table 1

Container number	Amount of radiation
1	no radiation

L1

Meeting Different Ability Levels

Content Outline

Note-taking Worksheet — Radioactivity and Nuclear Reactions

L1

Reinforcement

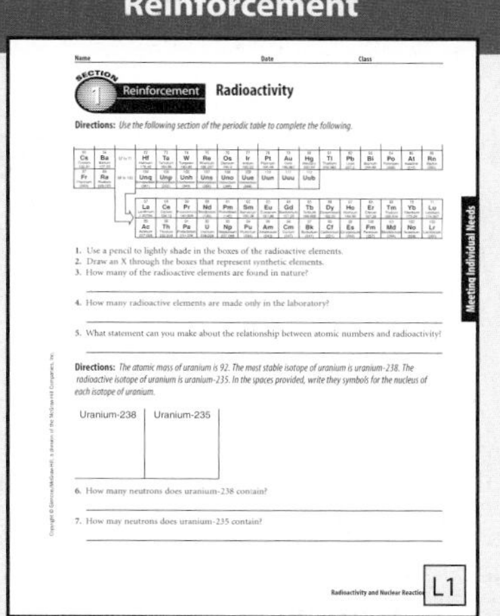

L1

Directed Reading

Directed Reading for Content Mastery — Overview: Radioactivity and Nuclear Reactions

L1

Enrichment

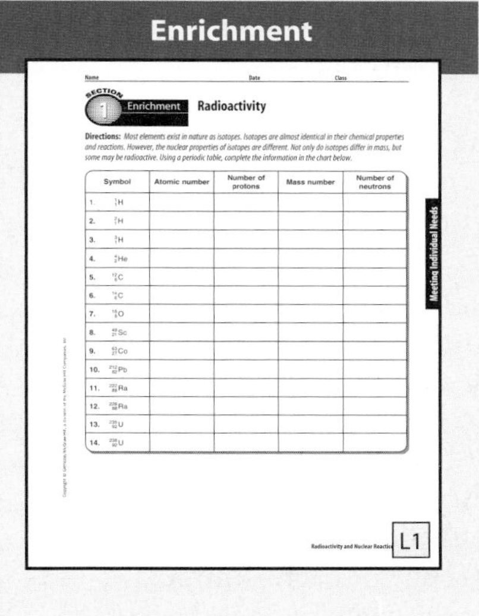

L1

Spanish Directed Reading

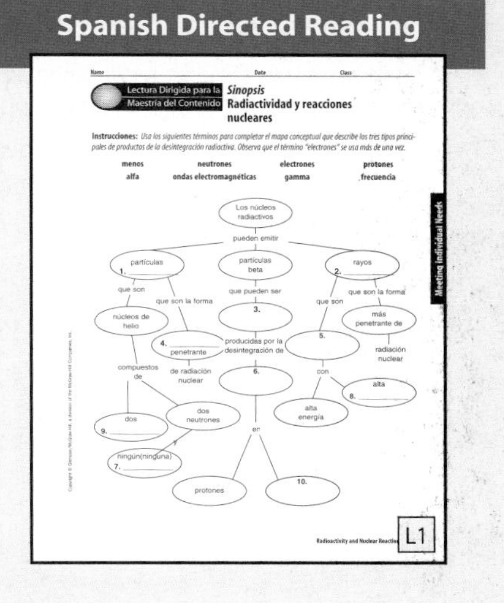

L1

Assessment

Chapter Tests

Chapter Test — Radioactivity and Nuclear Reactions

L1

Test Practice Workbook

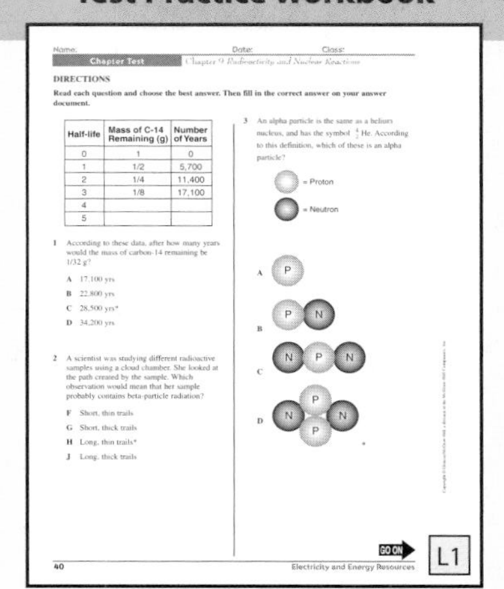

L1

Chapter Review

Chapter Review — Radioactivity and Nuclear Reactions

L1

Science Content Background

SECTION 1

Radioactivity

The Nucleus

There are six "flavors" of quarks—the fundamental components of matter. The up, charm, and top quarks have a charge of +2/3. The down, strange, and bottom quarks have a charge of −1/3. Protons are made of two up quarks and one down quark. Neutrons are made of one up quark and two down quarks. Quarks are bound tightly together by the strong force so they are not observed as free particles.

In periodic tables the atomic mass of an element is usually not written as a whole number. For example, silicon is shown as having an atomic mass of 28.086. The atomic mass on the periodic table is the average of the masses of all of the isotopes of an element weighted by the relative occurrence of each isotope. Carbon is the standard for the atomic mass of elements. It is defined as having a mass of 12 Atomic Mass Units.

Fun Fact

Marie Curie won two Nobel Prizes. In 1903 she won the Nobel Prize in physics with her husband, Pierre Curie, and Henri Becquerel for their research in radiation. In 1911 Marie was awarded the Nobel Prize in chemistry for the isolation of radium and polonium. In 1935 the Curie family won another Nobel Prize in chemistry. The Curie's daughter, Irene, and her husband were recognized for the synthesis of new radioactive elements.

Discovery of Radioactivity

Initial investigators of radioactivity were not aware of the long-term health risks associated with the handling of radioactive materials. Unfortunately this may have resulted in the death of Marie Curie due to leukemia in 1934.

SECTION 

Nuclear Decay

Gamma Rays

Gamma rays penetrate human tissue. Some cellular necrosis is not a problem as most cells can be replaced. The larger threat is from gamma rays that pass through tissues and change DNA. These changes can make a cell function less efficiently. When the cell reproduces, it produces more cells with less than optimal functioning. Aging is caused by the buildup of these kinds of cells. In rarer circumstances DNA is damaged in a way that results in a malfunction in the control of the growth of the cell, resulting in rapid cell growth and division—a condition known as cancer.

Putting food into sealed bags and exposing it to gamma rays can reduce the need for chemical preservatives or canning procedures. Many people object, however, to food irradiation. Some believe it will make food radioactive, which is not true. Others are concerned with the effects of eating foods with ionized molecules and with how the radioactive sources of the gamma rays are handled and disposed of.

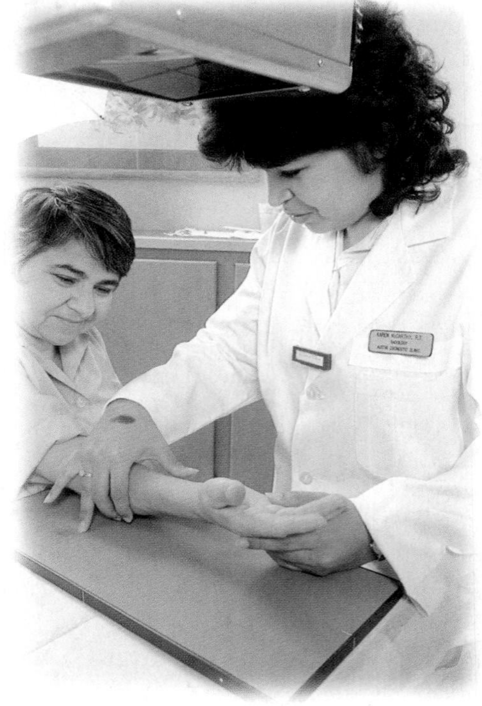

B. Daemmrich/The Image Works

SECTION 3

Detecting Radioactivity

Measuring Radiation

Many radiation detectors use the tendency of radiation to ionize atoms as a means for detection. Ionization can be as simple as knocking an electron off an atom or it might involve the more complex breakup of a molecule into positive and negative pieces.

Health care workers who use X rays and people who work with radioactivity often wear radiation badges and carry pocket dosimeters. The badges are worn for periods of one to three months and then analyzed to assess how much radiation the person has received during that period. Pocket dosimeters tell the wearer how much radiation he or she has received in a shorter time period such as one day of work.

Health physicists help nuclear power plant workers monitor and reduce their exposure to radiation. For introductory jobs, salaries range from $28,000 to $45,000 per year.

Background Radiation

Cosmic radiation in space is an obstacle that must be overcome before astronauts can spend longer periods in space. The majority of cosmic rays are protons, but heavier nuclei are common. Some cosmic rays exist as gamma rays.

While gamma rays can wreak havoc on our DNA, most of the DNA damage is routinely repaired by enzymes in cells.

SECTION 4

Nuclear Reactions

Nuclear Fusion

Fusion would be a great way to generate electricity. Unlike conventional nuclear reactions, fusion does not generate radioactive materials. The problem with fusion is that it needs great heat to make it happen. Researchers are seeking the secret to "cold fusion" to provide a clean and powerful source of energy.

Fun Fact

Magnetic resonance imaging (MRI) relies on radio waves to produce computer images that show biochemical and structural information about human tissues. Since an MRI machine uses radio waves, it is considered much safer to humans than are X rays or gamma rays. Today MRIs are widely used in the diagnosis of a number of conditions, including early-stage cancers.

For additional content background on this topic, go to the Glencoe Science Web site at science.glencoe.com.

Telegraph Colour Library/FPG International

Radioactivity and Nuclear Reactions

Chapter Vocabulary

strong force
radioactivity
alpha particle
transmutation
beta particle
gamma ray
half-life
cloud chamber
bubble chamber
Geiger counter
nuclear fission
chain reaction
critical mass
nuclear fusion
tracer

What do you think?

Science Journal The photograph shows a smoke detector. Smoke detectors give off alpha particles that ionize the surrounding air. Normally, an electric current flows through this ionized air to form a circuit. If smoke particles enter the ionized air, they absorb the alpha particles, causing fewer ions to form. This causes less current, signaling the alarm to go off.

CHAPTER 9

Radioactivity and Nuclear Reactions

The Sun gives off tremendous amounts of energy from day to day, year to year. The Sun's energy comes from nuclear reactions in which the nuclei of atoms are either split apart or fused together. In this chapter, you will learn about unstable atoms and how they emit different types of radiation. You will also learn how this radiation can be used to determine the age of objects, produce energy, or treat diseases.

What do you think?

Science Journal Look at the picture below with a classmate. Discuss what you think this is or what is happening. Here's a hint: *There's probably one of these on the ceiling.* Write your answer or best guess in your Science Journal.

256

Theme Connection

Stability and Change Although the nucleus of an atom is stable during normal chemical reactions, it undergoes profound changes during nuclear reactions. These can be so profound that they change the identity of the element.

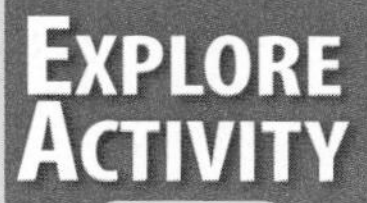

Do you realize you are mostly made up of empty space? Your body is made of atoms, and atoms are made of electrons whizzing around a small nucleus of protons and neutrons. The electrons are in motion far from the nucleus, and there is nothing but empty space between the nucleus and the electrons. During this activity you will find out just how far away these electrons are.

Model the space inside an atom

1. Go outside and pour several grains of sugar onto a sheet of paper.
2. Choose a tiny grain of sugar with a diameter equal to the width of one of the lines on a ruler. This sugar grain represents the nucleus of an atom.
3. Brush the rest of the sugar off the paper and place the sugar grain in the center of the paper.
4. Use a meterstick to measure a 10 m distance away from the sugar grain.

Observe

Write a paragraph in your Science Journal explaining how you modeled the large amount of empty space inside an atom.

Before You Read

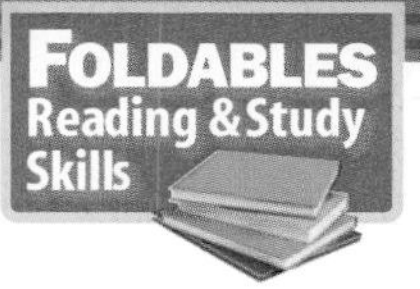

Making a Main Ideas Study Fold **Make the following Foldable to help you identify the major topics about radioactivity and nuclear reactions.**

1. Place a sheet of paper in front of you so the long side is at the top. Fold the paper in half from top to bottom and then unfold.
2. Fold in to the centerfold line to divide the paper into fourths.
3. Label the flaps *Radioactivity,* and *Nuclear Reactions.*
4. As you read the chapter, write what you learn about radioactivity and nuclear reactions under the flaps.

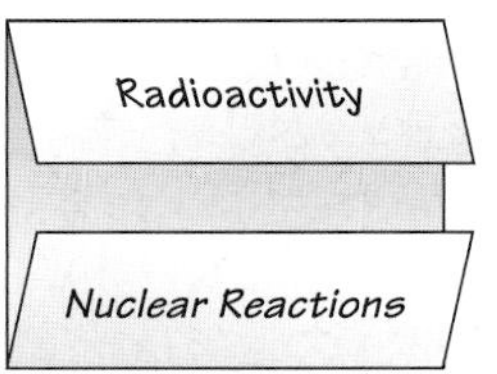

257

Explore Activity

Purpose Use this Explore Activity to introduce students to what the interior of an atom is like. Explain that they will learn how the atom is involved in radioactivity and nuclear reactions.

Preparation Choose an outdoor location that will safely accommodate all the groups. To avoid confusion, assign a location for each group.

Materials A meterstick, sugar, and sheet of paper for each group.

Teaching Strategies Ask one student to be a group leader and assign the tasks of choosing and measuring the sugar grain and measuring the 10-m distance to group members.

Observe

The sugar grain represents the nucleus of the atom, and the 10-m distance represents the radius of the atom. Aside from tiny electrons orbiting the nucleus, this space inside an atom is empty.

Assessment

Content Ask students to write songs describing what would happen to them if every electron of every atom in their bodies suddenly stopped moving. Without moving electrons, the students would appear to disappear because only the nuclei of their atoms would remain, which would occupy less space than the head of a pin. Use **Performance Assessment in the Science Classroom,** p. 151.

Before You Read

FOLDABLES Reading & Study Skills

Dinah Zike Study Fold

Purpose Have students use this Foldable to define, list examples of, and explain the uses of radioactivity and nuclear reactions. Students should then use what they have learned to predict future uses of nuclear power.

For additional help, see Foldables Worksheet, p. 17 in **Chapter Resources Booklet,** or go to the Glencoe Science Web site at **science.glencoe.com.** See After You Read in the Study Guide at the end of this chapter.

SECTION

Radioactivity

1 Motivate

Bellringer Transparency

Display the Section Focus Transparency for Section 1. Use the accompanying Transparency Activity Master. L2 ELL

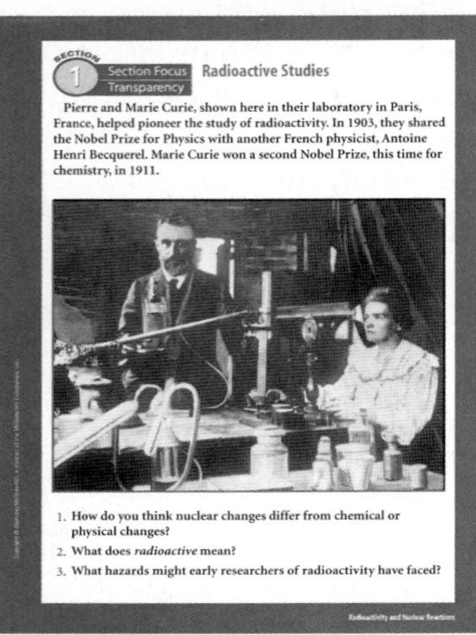

SECTION 1 Section Focus Transparency — Radioactive Studies

Pierre and Marie Curie, shown here in their laboratory in Paris, France, helped pioneer the study of radioactivity. In 1903, they shared the Nobel Prize for Physics with another French physicist, Antoine Henri Becquerel. Marie Curie won a second Nobel Prize, this time for chemistry, in 1911.

1. How do you think nuclear changes differ from chemical or physical changes?
2. What does *radioactive* mean?
3. What hazards might early researchers of radioactivity have faced?

Radioactivity and Nuclear Reactions

Tie to Prior Knowledge

Ask students to recall the parts of an atom. Students are probably aware that an atom is composed of electrons swirling around a nucleus of protons and neutrons. In this section they will learn about the force that holds the nucleus together, and how this force can be overcome to produce radioactive nuclei.

SECTION

Radioactivity

As You Read

What You'll Learn

- **Describe** the structure of an atom and its nucleus.
- **Explain** what radioactivity is.
- **Contrast** properties of radioactive and stable nuclei.
- **Discuss** the discovery of radioactivity.

Vocabulary

strong force
radioactivity

Why It's Important

The characteristics of atomic nuclei determine whether or not they will undergo radioactive decay.

The Nucleus

Every second you are being bombarded by energetic particles. Some of these particles come from unstable atoms in soil, rocks, and the atmosphere. What types of atoms are unstable? What type of particles do unstable atoms emit? The answers to these questions begin with the nucleus of an atom.

You remember that atoms are composed of protons, neutrons, and electrons. The nucleus of an atom contains the protons, which have a positive charge, and neutrons, which have no electric charge. The total amount of charge in a nucleus is determined by the number of protons, which also is called the atomic number. You might remember that an electron has a charge that is equal but opposite to a proton's charge. Atoms usually contain the same number of protons as electrons. Negatively charged electrons are electrically attracted to the positively charged nucleus and swarm around it.

Protons and Neutrons in the Nucleus Protons and neutrons are packed together tightly in a nucleus. The region outside the nucleus in which the electrons are located is large compared to the size of the nucleus. As **Figure 1** shows, the nucleus occupies only a tiny fraction of the space in the atom. If an atom were enlarged so that it was 1 km in diameter, its nucleus would have a diameter of only 1 cm. But the nucleus contains almost all the mass of the atom, because the mass of one proton or neutron is almost 2,000 times greater than the mass of an electron.

Figure 1
The size of a nucleus in an atom can be compared to a marble sitting in the middle of an empty football stadium.

258

Section Assessment Planner

Portfolio
Activity, p. 261

Performance Assessment
Skill Builder Activities, p. 262
See page 286 for more options.

Content Assessment
Section, p. 262
Challenge, p. 262
Chapter, pp. 286–287

Figure 2
The particles in the nucleus are attracted to each other by the strong force.

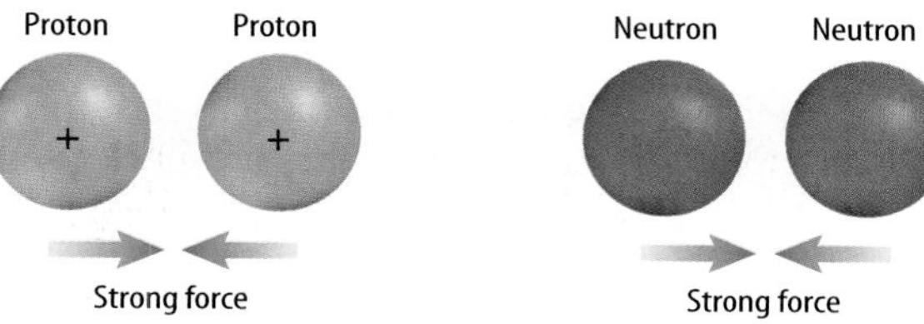

The Strong Force

How do you suppose protons and neutrons are held together so tightly in the nucleus? Positive electric charges repel each other, so why don't the protons in a nucleus push each other away? Another force, called the **strong force,** causes protons and neutrons to be attracted to each other, as shown in **Figure 2.**

The strong force is one of the four basic forces, and is about 100 times stronger than the electric force. The attractive forces between all the protons and neutrons in a nucleus keep the nucleus together. However, protons and neutrons have to be close together, like they are in the nucleus, to be attracted by the strong force. The strong force is a short-range force that quickly becomes extremely weak as protons and neutrons get farther apart. The electric force is a long-range force, so protons that are far apart still are repelled by the electric force, as shown in **Figure 3.**

Reading Check *What causes the attraction between protons and neutrons?*

Figure 3
The total force between two protons depends on how far apart they are.

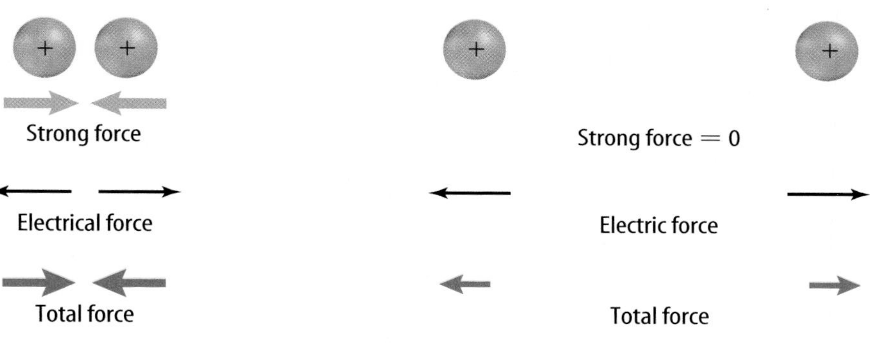

A When protons are close together, they are attracted to each other. The attraction due to the short-range strong force is much stronger than the repulsion due to the long-range electric force.

B When protons are too far apart to be attracted by the strong force, they still are repelled by the electric force between them. Then the total force between them is repulsive.

2 Teach

The Nucleus

Activity

To review atomic structure, display a periodic table. Have students choose an element and draw its structure on the board, using different colors for protons, neutrons, and electrons. Tell students that physicists often refer to the number of protons (atomic number) as "Z." L1 ELL LS **Visual-Spatial**

The Strong Force

Make a Model

The strong force is significant only for a distance that is less than the width of a few protons and neutrons. Have students model the nucleus of a nitrogen atom by drawing closely packed circles as nucleons. (Tracing around a penny works well.) Students should draw 7 neutrons and 7 protons, randomly placed and colored differently. By multiplying the diameter of a circle by 3, they can see about how far the strong force can be felt. L2 ELL LS **Kinesthetic**

Reading Check

Answer the strong force

Resource Manager

Chapter Resources Booklet

Note-taking Worksheets, pp. 35–37
Transparency Activity, p. 46
Directed Reading for Content Mastery, p. 20

Teacher FYI

Scientists have identified four fundamental forces of nature. The strong force holds neutrons and protons together; the electromagnetic force acts between protons and electrons; the weak force is involved in the neutron decay process; and the weakest force is gravity.

The Strong Force, continued

Visual Learning

Figure 4 Point out to students that in the large nucleus, the protons near the center of the nucleus feel a slightly greater strong force than those near the edge of the nucleus. Protons near the edge have no neighbors on the outer side of the nucleus to pull on them. This can be a source of instability in the nucleus. L2 LS **Visual-Spatial**

Quick Demo

Use magnets to review the concepts of repulsion and attraction. With magnetism, like poles repel and unlike poles attract. Similarly, two protons (both positively charged) repel each other. With the strong force, however, the charge doesn't matter; all nucleons attract one another at very short distances. L2 ELL LS **Visual-Spatial**

Radioactivity

Discussion

Why is there an end to the periodic table? As the number of protons in the nucleus increases, the relative effect of the electromagnetic repulsion between protons increases, causing large nuclei to be unstable. Beyond a certain point, the force makes large nuclei too unstable to exist. L3 LS **Logical-Mathematical**

Extension

Have students find out how elements are synthesized. by bombarding heavy nuclei with neutrons or alpha particles or by fusing the nuclei of lighter elements L3 LS **Linguistic**

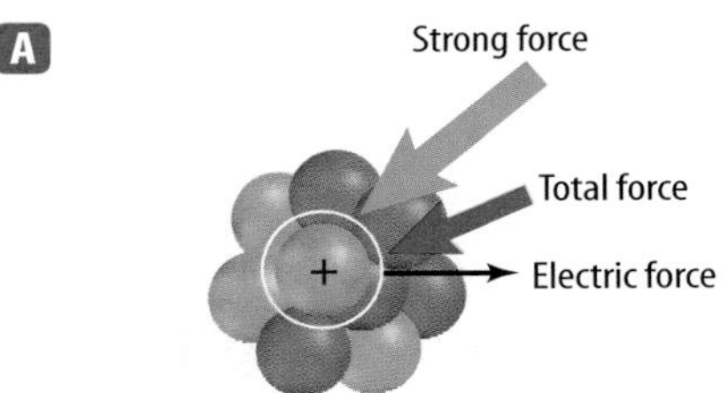

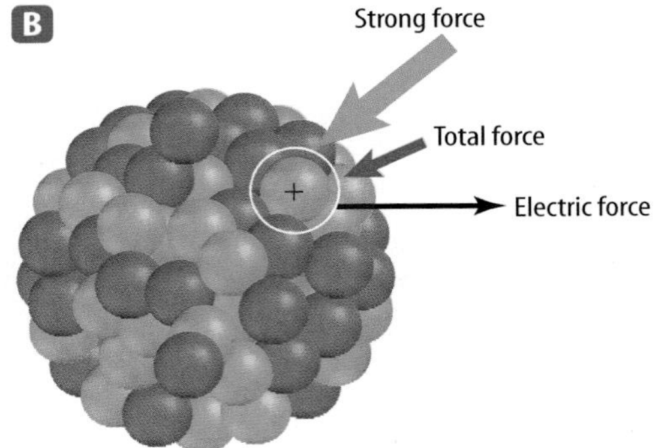

Figure 4
Protons and neutrons are held together less tightly in large nuclei. The circle shows the range of the attractive strong force. A Small nuclei have few protons, so the repulsive force on a proton due to the other protons is small. B In large nuclei, the attractive strong force is exerted only by the nearest neighbors, but all the protons exert repulsive forces. The total repulsive force is large.

Attraction and Repulsion Some atoms, such as uranium, have many protons and neutrons in their nuclei. These nuclei are held together less tightly than nuclei containing only a few protons and neutrons. To understand this, look at **Figure 4A.** If a nucleus has only a few protons and neutrons, they are all close enough together to be attracted to each other by the strong force. Because only a few protons are in the nucleus, the total electric force causing protons to repel each other is small. As a result, the overall force between the protons and the neutrons attracts the particles to each other.

Forces in a Large Nucleus However, if nuclei have many protons and neutrons, each proton or neutron is attracted to only a few neighbors by the strong force, as shown in **Figure 4B.** The other protons and neutrons are too far away. Because only the closest protons and neutrons attract each other in a large nucleus, the strong force holding them together is about the same as in a small nucleus. However, all the protons in a large nucleus exert a repulsive electric force on each other. Thus, the electric repulsive force on a proton in a large nucleus is larger than it would be in a small nucleus. Because the attractive force is about the same in a large or small nucleus, but the repulsive force increases in a large nucleus, protons and neutrons are held together less tightly in a large nucleus.

Radioactivity

In many nuclei the strong force is able to keep the nucleus permanently together, and the nucleus is stable. When the strong force is not large enough to hold a nucleus together tightly, the nucleus can decay and give off matter and energy. This process of nuclear decay is called **radioactivity.**

Large nuclei tend to be unstable and can break apart or decay. Radioactivity is most common in atoms with many protons in the nucleus. In fact, all elements with more than 84 protons in the nucleus are radioactive. However, even some elements with only a few protons have radioactive nuclei.

Elements with more than 93 protons don't exist naturally on Earth. They have been produced only in laboratories and are called synthetic elements. These synthetic elements are unstable, and some decay soon after they are created.

Cultural Diversity

Hideki Yukawa In 1949 Japanese scientist Hideki Yukawa received the Nobel Prize in physics for his work on nuclear forces. In 1935 he predicted the existence of particles he called mesons that would transfer energy between protons and neutrons and hold the nucleus together. His theory also stated that the nuclear force must be stronger over short distances than electromagnetic forces in order to overcome the repulsion between protons. The mesons Yukawa predicted, now known as pions, were discovered in 1937.

Stable and Unstable Nuclei The atoms of an element all have the same number of protons in the nucleus. For example, the nucleus of all carbon atoms contains six protons. However, not all carbon nuclei have the same numbers of neutrons. Some carbon nuclei have six neutrons, some have seven, and some have eight neutrons. Nuclei that have the same number of protons but different numbers of neutrons are called isotopes. The element carbon has three isotopes that occur naturally. The atoms of all isotopes of an element have the same number of electrons, and have the same chemical properties.

Isotopes of elements differ in the ratio of neutrons to protons, as shown in **Figure 5.** This ratio is related to the stability of the nucleus. In less massive elements, an isotope is stable if the ratio is about 1 to 1. Isotopes of the heavier elements are stable when the ratio of neutrons to protons is about 3 to 2. However, the nuclei of any isotopes that differ much from these ratios are unstable, whether the elements are light or heavy. In other words, nuclei with too many or too few neutrons compared to the number of protons are radioactive. Radioactive isotopes are sometimes called radioisotopes.

Nucleus Numbers A nucleus can be described by the number of protons and neutrons it contains. The number of protons in a nucleus is called the atomic number. Because the mass of all the protons and neutrons in a nucleus is nearly the same as the mass of the atom, the number of protons and neutrons is called the mass number.

A nucleus can be represented by a symbol that includes its atomic number, mass number, and the symbol of the element it belongs to, as shown in **Figure 6.** The symbol for the nucleus of the stable isotope of carbon is shown as an example.

$$\text{mass number} \rightarrow {}^{12}_{6}\text{C} \leftarrow \text{element symbol}; \quad \text{atomic number} \rightarrow 6$$

This isotope is called carbon-12. The number of neutrons in the nucleus is the mass number minus the atomic number. So the number of neutrons in the carbon-12 nucleus is $12 - 6 = 6$. Carbon-12 has six protons and six neutrons. Now, compare the isotope carbon-12 to this radioactive isotope of carbon:

$$\text{mass number} \rightarrow {}^{14}_{6}\text{C} \leftarrow \text{element symbol}; \quad \text{atomic number} \rightarrow 6$$

The radioactive isotope is carbon-14. How many neutrons does carbon-14 have?

Reading Check *What is the atomic number of a nucleus?*

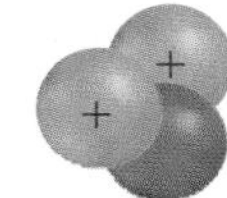

Figure 5
These two different isotopes of helium each have the same number of protons, even though they have different numbers of neutrons. *What is the ratio of protons to neutrons in each of these isotopes of helium?*

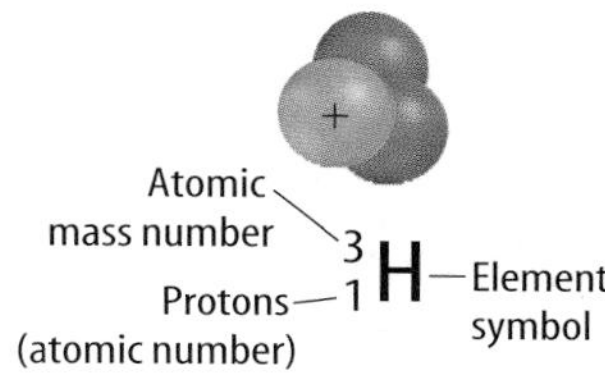

Figure 6
A simple way to indicate the atomic mass of an isotope is to use a symbol like this one for hydrogen. *How many neutrons are in this isotope?*

Caption Question Answers

- **Figure 5** Helium-3: 2 protons and 1 neutron; Helium-4: 2 protons and 2 neutrons
- **Figure 6** two

Students may think that radioactive materials glow. Explain that energy is given off, but not in the form of light. Radiation can, however, induce fluorescence in some materials.

Text Question Answer

8

Reading Check

Answer the number of protons

Discovery of Radioactivity

Activity

With students, make a class time line of the important events in nuclear radiation, beginning with Henri Becquerel's discovery of radioactivity. The time line could include contributions by Pierre and Marie Curie, Ernest Rutherford, Irène and Frédéric Joliot-Curie, Kasimir Fajans, Leo Szilard, Otto Hahn, Fritz Strassman, and Lise Meitner. L3
LS **Visual-Spatial** P

Resource Manager

Chapter Resources Booklet
Enrichment, p. 31
Reinforcement, p. 27

Visual Learning

Figure 6 After reviewing with students the symbols and numbers for hydrogen, have them practice using the format of Figure 6 to write the comparable information for other elements such as ${}^{5}_{2}\text{He}$, ${}^{8}_{3}\text{Li}$, ${}^{14}_{7}\text{N}$, ${}^{16}_{8}\text{O}$, and ${}^{56}_{26}\text{Fe}$. L2 ELL
LS **Visual-Spatial**

Discovery of Radioactivity, continued

Text Question Answer

uranium, 92; polonium, 84; radium, 88

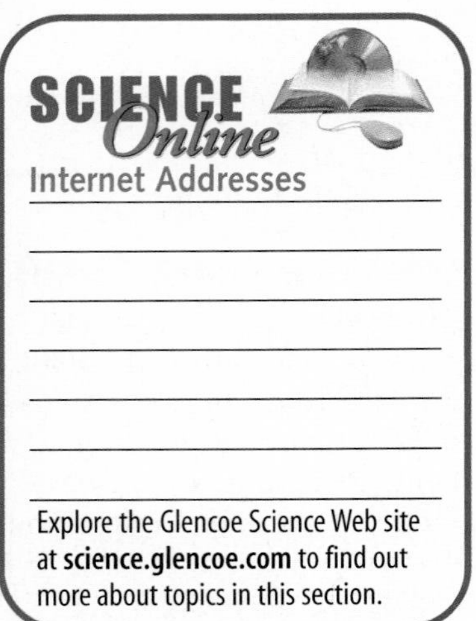

Explore the Glencoe Science Web site at science.glencoe.com to find out more about topics in this section.

3 Assess

Reteach

Write on the board the chemical symbol, atomic mass, and atomic number of an isotope. Have students tell the number of protons and neutrons the element has and predict whether the isotope is radioactive. Do this for several isotopes. L2 ELL
LS **Visual-Spatial**

Challenge

Why don't elements with atomic numbers greater than 92 exist naturally on Earth? because they are so unstable that if they are created, they decay almost immediately L3
LS **Logical-Mathematical**

Content Have students work in groups to create games that teach about radioactive elements. Games should reinforce the concept that unstable nuclei cause radioactivity. Use **PASC,** p. 169.

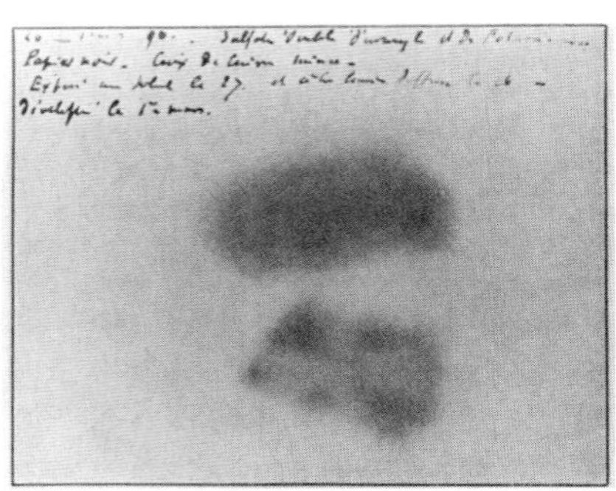

Figure 7
Henri Becquerel found outlines of uranium salt on a photographic plate.

SCIENCE Online

Research Visit the Glencoe Science Web site at **science.glencoe.com** for more information about the scientists who discovered and developed applications for radioactivity. Create a time line that shows key events and people in the use of radioactivity.

Discovery of Radioactivity

Look around the room. Can you detect any evidence of radioactivity? You can't see, hear, taste, touch, or smell radioactivity. Do you realize that small amounts of radioactivity are all around you, even inside your body? How was radioactivity first discovered if it can't be detected by your senses?

Henri Becquerel accidentally discovered radioactivity in 1896 when he left uranium salt in a desk drawer with a photographic plate. Later, when he removed the plate and developed it, he found an outline of the clumps of the uranium salt like in **Figure 7.** He hypothesized that the uranium had given off some invisible energy, or radiation, and exposed the film. Two years after Becquerel's discovery, Marie and Pierre Curie discovered the elements polonium and radium. These elements are even more radioactive than uranium. What are the atomic numbers of these elements?

Section 1 Assessment

1. What force keeps stable nuclei permanently together?
2. What is radioactivity?
3. Why are large nuclei unstable?
4. Identify the contributions of the three scientists who discovered the first radioactive elements.
5. **Think Critically** What is the ratio of protons to neutrons in lead-214? Explain whether you would expect this isotope to be radioactive or stable.

Skill Builder Activities

6. **Comparing and Contrasting** Compare and contrast stable and unstable nuclei. **For more help, refer to the** Science Skill Handbook.
7. **Communicating** In your Science Journal, make a list of the first things you think of when you hear the word *radioactivity.* Write one paragraph describing your positive thoughts about radioactivity and another describing your negative thoughts. **For more help, refer to the** Science Skill Handbook.

Answers to Section Assessment

1. the strong force
2. the decay of atomic nuclei to give off matter and energy
3. Large nuclei have so many protons that the strong force, having only a short-range effect, is unable to overcome the total electromagnetic repulsion.
4. Becquerel found that uranium salt emitted radiation. Marie and Pierre Curie discovered polonium and radium.
5. 82/132 = 0.62; it is likely to be radioactive because the ratio of protons to neutrons differs from the 2-to-3 (0.67) ratio for stable heavy elements.
6. Stable nuclei retain their identity while unstable nuclei decay.
7. Positive responses may include medical uses of radioactivity and using radioactivity to produce energy. Negative responses may include nuclear waste and health risks.

SECTION

Nuclear Decay

Nuclear Radiation

When an unstable nucleus decays, particles and energy are emitted from the decaying nucleus. These particles and energy are called nuclear radiation. The three types of nuclear radiation are alpha, beta (BAYT uh), and gamma radiation. Alpha and beta radiation are particles. Gamma radiation is a wave that is similar to light but of much higher frequency.

Alpha Particles

When alpha radiation occurs, an alpha particle is emitted from the decaying nucleus. An **alpha particle** is made of two protons and two neutrons, as shown in **Table 1.** Notice that the alpha particle is the same as a helium nucleus. The symbol for an alpha particle is the same as for the helium nucleus, $^{4}_{2}He$. An alpha particle has an electrical charge of +2 and an atomic mass of 4.

Reading Check *What does an alpha particle consist of?*

Damage from Alpha Particles Compared to beta and gamma radiation, alpha particles are much more massive. They also have the most electric charge. As a result, alpha particles lose energy more quickly when they interact with matter than the other types of nuclear radiation do. When alpha particles pass through matter, they exert an electric force on the electrons in atoms in their path. This force pulls electrons away from atoms and leaves behind charged ions. Alpha particles lose energy quickly during this process. As a result, alpha particles are the least penetrating form of nuclear radiation. Alpha particles cannot even pass through a sheet of paper.

However, alpha particles can be dangerous if they are released by radioactive atoms inside your body. Biological molecules inside your body are large and easily damaged. A single alpha particle can damage many fragile biological molecules. Damage from alpha particles can cause cells in your body to no longer function properly, leading to illness and disease.

As You Read

***What* You'll Learn**

- **Compare and contrast** alpha, beta, and gamma radiation.
- **Define** the half-life of a radioactive material.
- **Describe** the process of radioactive dating.

Vocabulary

alpha particle, transmutation, beta particle, gamma ray, half-life

***Why* It's Important**

Different types of nuclear radiation are used in medicine and for calculating the ages of artifacts.

Table 1 Alpha Particles

Symbol	$^{4}_{2}He$
Mass	4
Charge	+2

Section Assessment Planner

PORTFOLIO
Science Journal, p. 265

PERFORMANCE ASSESSMENT
Try At Home MiniLAB, p. 267
Skill Builder Activities, p. 267
See page 286 for more options.

CONTENT ASSESSMENT
Section, p. 267
Challenge, p. 267
Chapter, pp. 286–287

SECTION

Nuclear Decay

1 Motivate

Bellringer Transparency

Display the Section Focus Transparency for Section 2. Use the accompanying Transparency Activity Master. L2 ELL

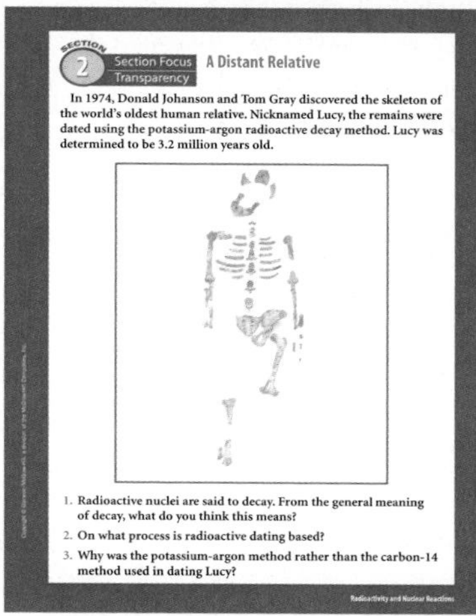

Section Focus Transparency — A Distant Relative

In 1974, Donald Johanson and Tom Gray discovered the skeleton of the world's oldest human relative. Nicknamed Lucy, the remains were dated using the potassium-argon radioactive decay method. Lucy was determined to be 3.2 million years old.

1. Radioactive nuclei are said to decay. From the general meaning of decay, what do you think this means?
2. On what process is radioactive dating based?
3. Why was the potassium-argon method rather than the carbon-14 method used in dating Lucy?

Tie to Prior Knowledge

Tell students that gamma radiation is one kind of radiation emitted during radioactive decay.

Resource Manager

Chapter Resources Booklet
Transparency Activity, p. 47

Alpha Particles

Reading Check

Answer two protons and two neutrons

Visual Learning

Figure 8 The black plastic cylinder shown in the figure is the ionization chamber. The metal plate on top serves as shielding for the radioactive source inside. Bring in a smoke detector that uses americium-241. Light some flash paper or a candle to produce enough smoke to make the smoke detector beep. L2 ELL
LS **Visual-Spatial**

Caption Answer

Figure 9 yes

Figure 8
When alpha particles collide with molecules in the air, positively-charged ions and electrons result. The ions and electrons move toward charged plates, creating a current in the smoke detector.

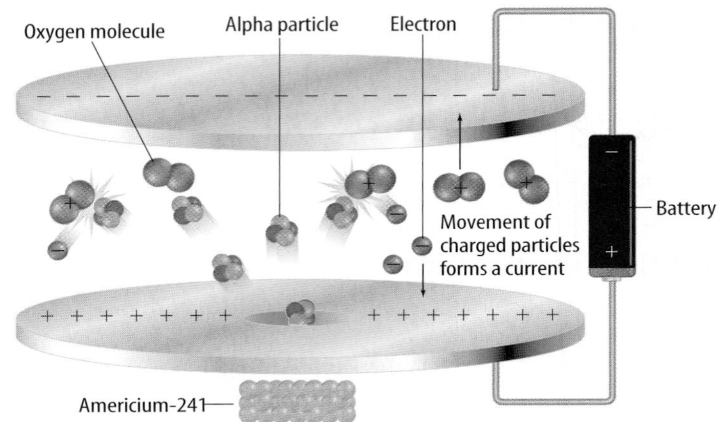

Smoke Detectors Some smoke detectors give off alpha particles that ionize the surrounding air. Normally, an electric current flows through this ionized air to form a circuit, as in **Figure 8.** But if smoke particles enter the ionized air, they will absorb the ions and electrons. The circuit is broken and the alarm goes off.

Transmutation When an atom loses an alpha particle, it no longer has the same number of protons, so it no longer is the same element. **Transmutation** is the process of changing one element to another through nuclear decay. In alpha decay, two protons and two neutrons are lost from the nucleus, so the new element formed has an atomic number two less than that of the original element. The atomic mass number of the new element is four less than the original element. The nuclear equation in **Figure 9** shows a nuclear transmutation caused by alpha decay. Notice in the equation that the charge of the original nucleus equals the sum of the charges of the nucleus and the alpha particle that are formed.

Figure 9
In this transmutation, polonium emits an alpha particle and changes into lead. *Do the charges and masses of the products add up to the charge and mass of the polonium nucleus?*

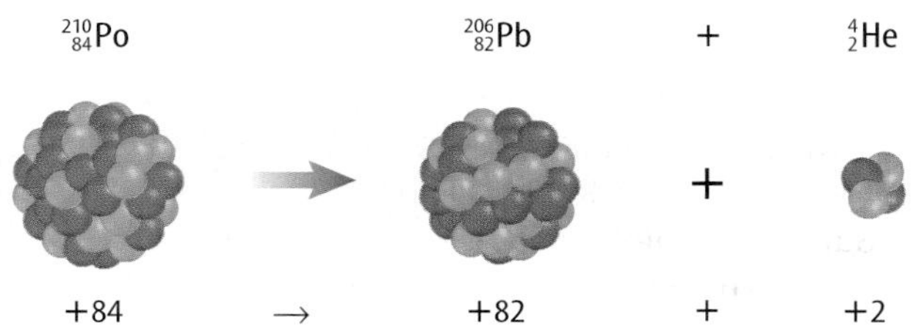

LAB DEMONSTRATION

Purpose to test the shielding of radiation

Materials Geiger counter; sources of α, β, and γ radiation, shielding (paper, aluminum foil, lead sheet)

Procedure Slowly bring the α source from far away to near, but not touching, the Geiger counter. Do this three more times, each time holding one type of radiation shielding between the detector and the source. Repeat the procedure for the β and γ sources.

Expected Outcome Students will observe how the detector responds to radiation and how paper blocks alpha particles, foil blocks beta particles, and lead blocks gamma radiation.

Assessment

When you shield the Geiger counter from the radioactive sources, it continues to register, although at a very low rate. Why? It is responding to cosmic rays—radioactive particles from the sun, distant stars, and other cosmological sources.

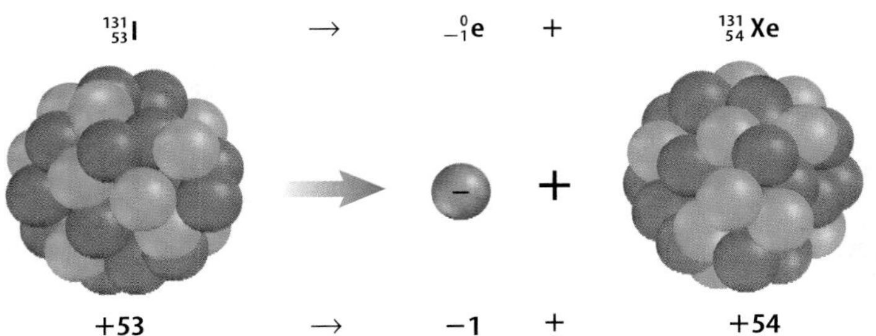

Figure 10
Nuclei that emit beta particles undergo transmutation. In this process, iodine changes to xenon. *Show how the charges and masses of the products add up to the charge and mass of the iodine nucleus.*

Beta Particles

A second type of radioactive decay is called beta decay, which is summarized in **Table 2.** Sometimes in an unstable nucleus a neutron decays into a proton and emits an electron. The electron is emitted from the nucleus and is called a **beta particle.** Beta decay is caused by another basic force called the weak force.

Because the atom now has one more proton, it becomes the element with an atomic number one greater than that of the original element. Atoms that lose beta particles undergo transmutation. However, because the total number of protons and neutrons does not change during beta decay, the atomic mass number of the new element is the same as that of the original element. **Figure 10** shows a transmutation caused by beta decay.

Damage from Beta Particles Beta particles are much faster and more penetrating than alpha particles. They can pass through paper but are stopped by a sheet of aluminum foil. Just like alpha particles, beta particles can damage cells when they are emitted by radioactive nuclei inside the human body.

Table 2 Beta Particles

Symbol	β
Mass	0.0005
Charge	−1

Gamma Rays

The most penetrating form of radiation is not made of protons, neutrons, or electrons. **Gamma rays** are a form of radiation called electromagnetic waves. Like water and sound waves, gamma rays carry energy. They have no mass and no charge, and they travel at the speed of light. They usually are released along with alpha or beta particles. The characteristics of gamma rays are summarized in **Table 3.**

Thick blocks of dense materials, such as lead and concrete, are required to stop gamma rays. However, gamma rays cause less damage to biological molecules as they pass through living tissue. Suppose an alpha particle and a gamma ray travel the same distance through matter. The gamma ray produces far fewer ions because it has no electric charge.

Table 3 Gamma Radiation

Symbol	γ
Mass	0
Charge	0

Beta Particles

Caption Answer

Figure 10 The charge of the xenon nucleus is +54 while the charge of the electron is −1, so the total charge of the products is +53. The mass of the xenon nucleus is 131 and the mass of the electron is essentially 0, so the total mass of the products is 131.

IDENTIFYING Misconceptions

Students might assume that electrons, protons, and neutrons are the smallest possible particles. Explain that electrons are fundamental particles, but that protons and neutrons are composite particles made up of subatomic particles called quarks. Nuclear decay is possible because of the creation, destruction, or exchange of these and other fundamental particles.

Extension

Have students find out more about the forces and radiation involved in beta decay. Beta decay involves the weak force and is accompanied by the release of particles called neutrinos, which have high energy but no mass. L3 IN **Linguistic**

Gamma Rays

Discussion

Have students summarize the effect on an atom's atomic mass (A) and atomic number (Z) if the atom emits an alpha particle, a beta particle, or a gamma ray. When an alpha particle is released, A decreases by four and Z decreases by two. When a beta particle is released, A is unchanged and Z increases by one. When gamma rays are released, A and Z are unchanged. L2
IN **Logical-Mathematical**

Resource Manager

Chapter Resources Booklet
Lab Activity, pp. 9-12, 13–16
Transparency Activity, pp. 51–52
Enrichment, p. 32

Science Journal

Radiation Have students find out who chose alpha, beta, and gamma to name different kinds of radiation, why, and when, and write this information in their journals. Ernest Rutherford gave these names to these types of radiation for, as he said, simplicity. He named alpha and beta radiation between 1895 and 1898 and gamma rays in 1903. L2 IN **Linguistic** P

Radioactive Half-Life

Fun Fact

The rate of radioactive decay is nearly impossible to change which makes it ideal for radioactive dating. Attempts to change it by alteration of temperature and pressure conditions, use of other chemical reactions, or exposure to electric and magnetic fields have been unsuccessful.

Caption Question Answer

Figure 11 one

Use an Analogy

Tell students to each hold up a large sheet of paper. Measure ten seconds, and have students tear their sheets of paper in half and place one half on their desks. During the next ten seconds, have them tear off half of the part that is left and place it on the desk. Continue counting ten-second intervals while students continue tearing their papers in half until they can no longer continue. Explain that, like the ever-smaller pieces of paper, decaying radioactive isotopes never completely lose their radioactivity but just get smaller and smaller.
L2 ELL LS **Kinesthetic**

Reading Check

Answer the nucleus left after the isotope decays

Radioactive Dating

Discussion

Scientists find two bones. The first bone has half as much radioactive carbon as a new bone, and the second bone has one-fourth as much radioactive carbon. **How old is each bone?** The first is 5,730 years old; the second is 11,460 years old. L2
LS **Logical-Mathematical**

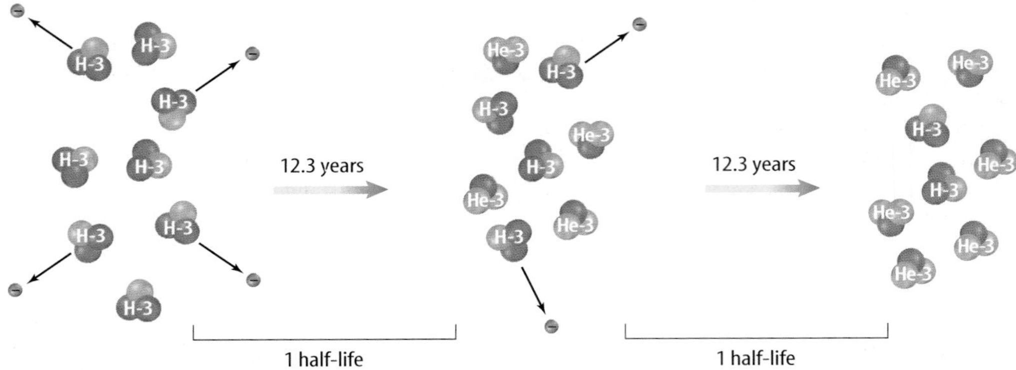

Figure 11
The half-life of $^{3}_{1}H$ is 12.3 years. During each half-life, half of the atoms in the sample decay into helium. *How many helium atoms will be left in the sample after the next half-life?*

Radioactive Half-Life

If an element is radioactive, how can you tell when its atoms are going to decay? Some radioisotopes decay to stable atoms in less than a second. However, the nuclei of certain radioactive isotopes require millions of years to decay. A measure of the time required by the nuclei of an isotope to decay is called the half-life. The **half-life** of a radioactive isotope is the amount of time it takes for half the nuclei in a sample of the isotope to decay. The nucleus left after the isotope decays is called the daughter nucleus. **Figure 11** shows how the number of decaying nuclei decreases after each half-life.

Half-lives vary widely among the radioactive isotopes. For example, polonium-214 has a half-life of less than a thousandth of a second, but uranium-238 has a half-life of 4.5 billion years. The half-lives of some other radioactive elements are listed in **Table 4.**

Reading Check *What is a daughter nucleus?*

Table 4 Sample Half-Lives

Isotope	Half-Life
$^{3}_{1}H$	12.3 years
$^{212}_{82}Pb$	10.6 hr
$^{14}_{6}C$	5,730 years
$^{194}_{84}Po$	0.7 s
$^{235}_{92}U$	7.04×10^{8} years
$^{131}_{53}I$	8.04 days

Radioactive Dating

Some geologists, biologists, and archaeologists, among others, are interested in the ages of rocks and fossils found on Earth. The ages of these materials can be determined using radioactive isotopes and their half-lives. First, the amounts of the radioactive isotope and its daughter nucleus in a sample of material are measured. Then, the number of half-lives that need to pass to give the measured amounts of the isotope and its daughter nucleus is calculated. The number of half-lives is the amount of time that has passed since the isotope began to decay. It is also usually the amount of time that has passed since the object was formed, or the age of the object. Different isotopes are useful in dating different types of materials.

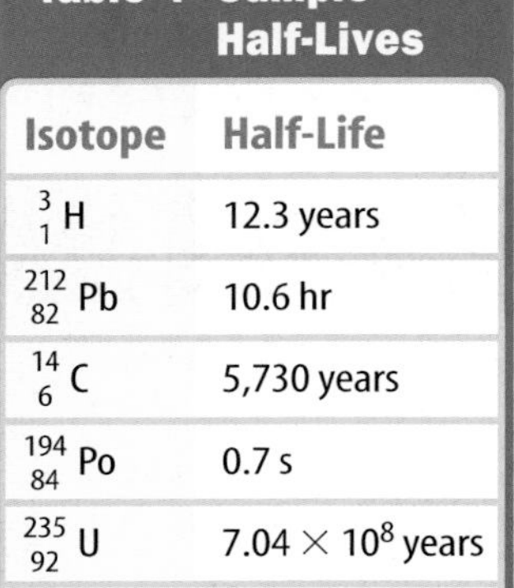

Curriculum Connection

History Have students do research to learn how radioactive dating has been used to determine the ages of artifacts found in archaeological digs. Students might research Pompeii, China's terra-cotta army, or Easter Island. L3 LS **Linguistic**

Resource Manager

Chapter Resources Booklet
MiniLAB, p. 3
Reinforcement, p. 28

Mathematics Skill Activities, p. 3

Carbon Dating The radioactive isotope carbon-14 often is used to find the ages of objects that were once living. Carbon-14 is found in molecules throughout the environment, including some carbon dioxide molecules plants take in as they carry out photosynthesis. Carbon-14 atoms behave chemically just like nonradioactive carbon-12 atoms, so all living plants contain some carbon-14. When animals eat plants, they ingest some of the radioactive carbon-14.

An atom of carbon-14 eventually will decay into nitrogen-14. The half-life of carbon-14 is 5,730 years. The amount of carbon-14 in living plants and animals remains fairly constant as decaying carbon-14 is replaced constantly by new carbon-14 when an animal eats or a plant makes food. However, when an organism dies, its carbon-14 atoms decay without being replaced. By measuring the amount of carbon-14 in a sample and comparing it to the amount of carbon-12, scientists can determine the approximate age of the material. Only the remains of plants and animals that lived within the last 50,000 years contain enough carbon-14 to measure.

Uranium Dating Radioactive dating also can be used to estimate the ages of rocks. Some rocks contain uranium, which has two radioactive isotopes with long half-lives. Each of these uranium isotopes decays into a different isotope of lead. The amount of these uranium isotopes and their daughter nuclei are measured. The ratio of these amounts gives the number of half lives since the rock was formed.

Candy Nuclei

Procedure

1. Use 88 **yellow candies** to represent protons and 138 **red candies** for neutrons.
2. Model a stable helium nucleus with two red and two yellow candies in a tight circle.
3. Measure and record the distance between the centers of the two protons.
4. In another tight circle, mix 86 yellow and 136 red candies to model an unstable radon nucleus. Measure and record the distance between the two farthest protons.

Analysis

1. Compare the distances.
2. Why is the helium nucleus stable and the radon nucleus unstable?

Section  Assessment

1. Describe three types of radiation.
2. Write a nuclear equation to show how radon-222 decays to give off an alpha particle and another element. What is the other element?
3. What is a half-life?
4. How is radioactivity useful in determining the age of material that was once part of a living organism?
5. **Think Critically** Is it possible for an isotope to decay to an element with a higher atomic number? Explain.

Skill Builder Activities

6. **Using an Electronic Spreadsheet** Write a short program that allows you to input the mass and the half-life of a radioactive sample and calculate what mass remains after a certain number of half-lives. **For more help, refer to the** Technology Skill Handbook.
7. **Using Fractions** The half-life of iodine-131 is about eight days. Calculate how much of a 40-g sample will be left after eight days, after 16 days, and after 32 days. **For more help, refer to the** Math Skill Handbook.

Answers to Section Assessment

1. alpha particles (2 protons, 2 neutrons), low penetrating power; beta particles (electrons), more penetrating power; gamma rays (electromagnetic waves), most penetrating power
2. $^{222}_{86}Rn \rightarrow ^{218}_{84}Po + ^{4}_{2}He$; polonium
3. time required for half of the atoms in a sample of a radioactive isotope to decay
4. By comparing the amount of certain radioactive elements in the organism with the original amount, you can find how much of the element has decayed and how long it has been since the organism died.
5. Yes; in beta decay, a neutron decays into an electron and a proton, thereby increasing the atomic number by one.
6. Programs should allow input of mass, half-life, and number of half-lives. Output should be remaining mass.
7. 20 g, 10 g, 2.5 g

Purpose Students will construct a model to discover why the nucleus of a radon atom is unstable. L2 IN **Kinesthetic**

Materials 88 yellow m & m's and 138 red m & m's, metric ruler, poster board

Analysis

1. The distance between protons is much greater in radon than in helium.
2. The small distance between the helium protons enables nuclear forces to hold them together. The distances between the radon protons are too great for nuclear forces to hold them all together.

Assessment

Process Show students a drawing of a uranium nucleus and ask them whether or not the nucleus is stable. It is not stable—it is too large. Use **PASC,** p. 89.

3 Assess

Reteach

Have students tell how long it would take for three-fourths of a sample of each isotope listed in **Table 3** to decay. For each isotope, the time would be twice the listed half-life. L2 IN **Logical-Mathematical**

Challenge

Have students use a computer graphics program to create a slide presentation showing how various radioactive isotopes decay. L2 IN **Visual-Spatial**

SECTION 3

Detecting Radioactivity

1 Motivate

Bellringer Transparency

Display the Section Focus Transparency for Section 3. Use the accompanying Transparency Activity Master. L2 ELL

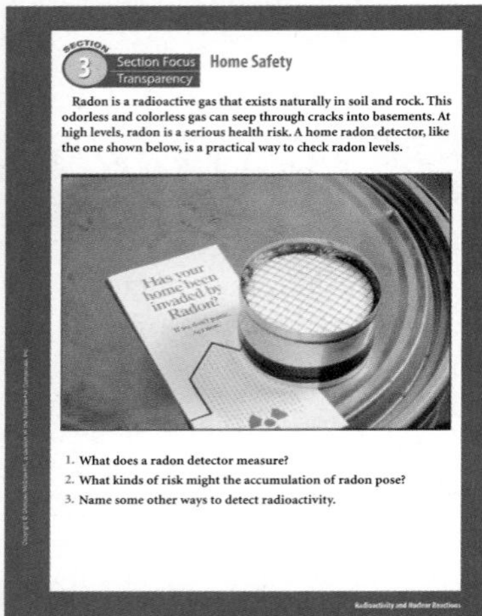

SECTION 3 Section Focus Transparency **Home Safety**

Radon is a radioactive gas that exists naturally in soil and rock. This odorless and colorless gas can seep through cracks into basements. At high levels, radon is a serious health risk. A home radon detector, like the one shown below, is a practical way to check radon levels.

1. **What does a radon detector measure?**
2. **What kinds of risk might the accumulation of radon pose?**
3. **Name some other ways to detect radioactivity.**

Radioactivity and Nuclear Reactions

Tie to Prior Knowledge

Our five senses allow us to see, hear, smell, taste, and feel, but none of our senses can tell us when we are being exposed to radioactivity. In this section, students will learn about four methods scientists have devised for detecting radiation.

SECTION 

Detecting Radioactivity

As You Read

What You'll Learn

- **Describe** how radioactivity can be detected in cloud and bubble chambers.
- **Explain** how an electroscope can be used to detect radiation.
- **Explain** how a Geiger counter can measure nuclear radiation.

Vocabulary

cloud chamber
bubble chamber
Geiger counter

Why It's Important

Devices to detect and measure radioactivity are needed to monitor exposure to humans.

Radiation Detectors

Because you can't see or feel alpha particles, beta particles, or gamma rays, you must use instruments to detect their presence. Some tools that are used to detect radioactivity rely on the fact that radiation forms ions in the matter it passes through. The tools detect these newly formed ions in several ways.

Cloud Chambers A **cloud chamber,** shown in **Figure 12,** can be used to detect alpha or beta particle radiation. A cloud chamber is filled with water or ethanol vapor. When a radioactive sample is placed in the cloud chamber, it gives off charged alpha or beta particles that travel through the water or ethanol vapor. As each charged particle travels through the chamber, it knocks electrons off the atoms in the air, creating ions. It leaves a trail of ions in the chamber. The water or ethanol vapor condenses around these ions, creating a visible path of droplets along the track of the particle. Beta particles leave long, thin trails, and alpha particles leave shorter, thicker trails.

Reading Check *Why are trails produced by alpha and beta particles seen in cloud chambers?*

Figure 12
If a sample of radioactive material is placed in a cloud chamber, a trail of condensed vapor will form along the paths of the radioactive particles.

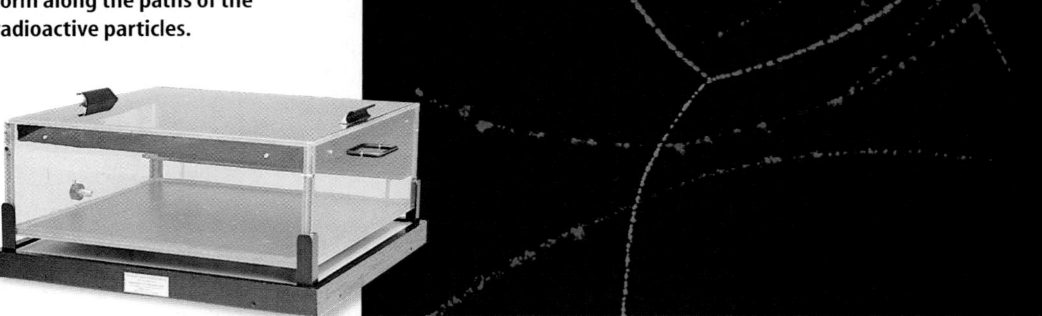

Section Assessment Planner

PORTFOLIO
Challenge, p. 272

PERFORMANCE ASSESSMENT
Math Skills Activity, p. 270
Skill Builder Activities, p. 272
See page 286 for more options.

CONTENT ASSESSMENT
Section, p. 272
Challenge, p. 272
Chapter, pp. 286–287

268 CHAPTER 9 Radioactivity and Nuclear Reactions

Bubble Chambers Another way to detect and monitor the paths of nuclear particles is by using a bubble chamber. A **bubble chamber** holds a superheated liquid, which doesn't boil because the pressure in the chamber is high. When a moving particle leaves ions behind, the liquid boils along the trail. The path shows up as tracks of bubbles, like the ones in **Figure 13.**

Electroscopes Do you remember how an electroscope can be used to detect electric charges? When an electroscope is given a negative charge, its leaves repel each other and spread apart, as in **Figure 14A.** They will remain apart until their extra electrons have somewhere to go and discharge the electroscope. The excess charge can be neutralized if it combines with positive charges. The air near an electroscope can become positively charged when nuclear radiation moves through the air and removes electrons from air molecules, as shown in **Figure 14B.** When this occurs near the leaves of the electroscope, some positively charged molecules in the air can come in contact with the electroscope and attract the electrons from the leaves, as **Figure 14C** shows. As these negatively charged leaves lose their charges, they move together. **Figure 14D** shows this last step in the process. When you see the charged leaves of the electroscope gradually come together, you know that they have lost their charge because of radioactive particles.

Figure 13
Particles of nuclear radiation can be detected as they leave trails of bubbles in a bubble chamber.

Figure 14
An electroscope can be used to detect radioactivity.

A Electroscope is charged with negative charge.

B Radioactive particles create positive ions.

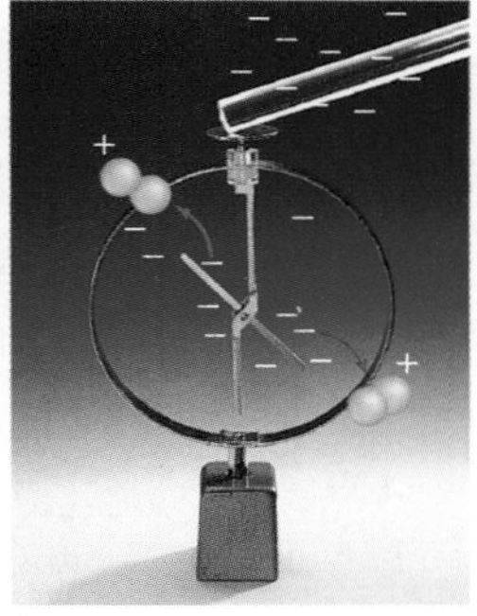

C Electroscope leaves transfer negative charges to positively charged ions.

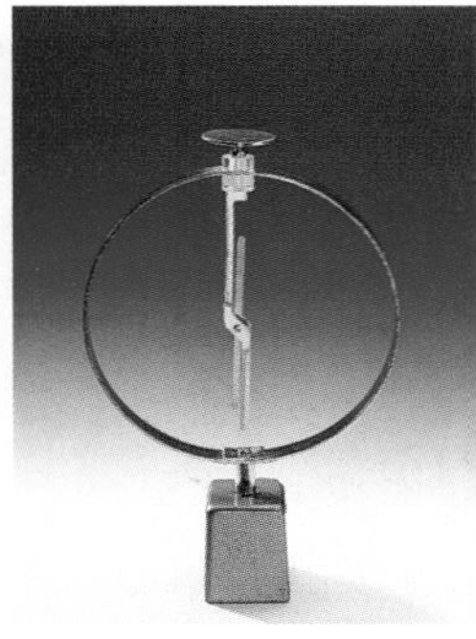

D The electroscope leaves lose their negative charge and come together.

2 Teach

Radiation Detectors

Use an Analogy

Tell students that the vapor trails sometimes seen behind jet airplanes are made up of water droplets that have condensed around the jet's exhaust fumes. Like the trails in cloud chambers, vapor trails provide a visual record of the path of the object that caused them.

Reading Check

Answer The charged particles knock electrons off atoms in the air, leaving a trail of ions. The vapor condenses around these ions.

Visual Learning

Figure 13 Point out to students that at the lower part of this bubble chamber photograph, particles collide and create a spray of charged particles. A magnetic field perpendicular to the page deflects the particles so that those curling to the left must have an opposite charge to those curling to the right. Note that only charged particles are visible.

Resource Manager

Chapter Resources Booklet
- Directed Reading for Content Mastery, p. 21
- Transparency Activity, p. 48

Mathematics Skill Activities, p. 31

Teacher FYI

The bubble chamber, developed in the 1950s, was used by scientists for many years to observe the particles in matter. It has since been replaced by newer, more complex, detectors that are capable of detecting the newest particles currently being studied by physicists.

Measuring Radiation

Quick Demo

People whose work involves possible exposure to radiation are required to wear film badges that record the amount of radiation the person has received. You can obtain one of these badges from the radiation laboratory at a hospital. Explain to students that a small piece of film is encased in a plastic holder. The casing is light-tight so the film responds only to alpha, beta, and gamma radiation, not visible light. Every month, the film is removed and the amount of radiation it (and therefore the wearer) has received is measured. New film is then inserted in the holder. L3 LS **Visual-Spatial**

Math Skills Activity

National Math Standards

Correlation to Mathematics Objectives

1, 2, 6, 9, 10

Teaching Strategy This is what you know: half-life of uranium-238 = 4.5 billion years; 94% of uranium-238 atoms have decayed

This is what you want to find: age of the rock

Set up a pattern to help solve: follow format of table in the text.

Answer to Practice Problem

After four half-lives, approximately 6.25% of the uranium-238 atoms will remain and about 93.75% of the atoms will be lead-206. Four half-lives is 18 billion years.

Measuring Radiation

Large doses of radiation are harmful to living tissue. If you worked or lived in an environment that had potential for exposure to high levels of radiation—for example, a nuclear testing facility—you might want to know exactly how much radiation you were being exposed to. You could measure the radiation with a Geiger (GI gur) counter. A **Geiger counter** is a device that measures radioactivity by producing an electric current when radiation is present.

Math Skills Activity

How can radioactive half lives be used to measure geological time?

Example Problem

The time it takes for half of the atoms of one element in a piece of rock to change into another element is called its half-life. Scientists use the half-lives of radioactive isotopes to measure geological time. Potassium-40 has a half-life of 1.24 billion years before it produces the stable daughter product argon-40. If three-fourths of the potassium-40 atoms in a rock had changed into atoms of argon-40, how old would you predict the rock to be?

Solution

1. *This is what you know:*
   half-life of potassium-40 = 1.24 billion years
   75% of potassium-40 atoms have decayed
2. *This is what you want to find:*
   age of the rock
3. *Set up a pattern to help solve:*

The age of the rock would be 2.48 billion years old.

Rate of Decay

Time	% Potassium-40	% Argon-40
1.25 billion years	50%	50%
2.5 billion years	25%	75%
3.75 billion years	12.5%	87.5%

Practice Problem

Uranium-238 has a half-life of 4.5 billion years before half of the atoms change into lead-206. Determine the age of a rock in which approximately 94% of the atoms are lead-206.

For more help, refer to the Math Skill Handbook.

Teacher FYI

There are several units for measuring radiation. The curie and the becquerel are based on the number of disintegrations per second. The roentgen, the rad, and the gray measure the effect radiation has on the absorbing material. The rem is used to measure biological damage to humans.

Active Reading

Metacognition Journal In this strategy, each student analyzes his or her own thought processes. Have students divide a sheet of paper in half. On the left, have them record what they have learned about radiation detection. On the right, have them record the reason they learned it.

Figure 15
Electrons that are stripped off gas molecules in a Geiger counter move to a positively charged wire in the device. This causes current to flow in the wire. The current then is used to produce a click or a flash of light.

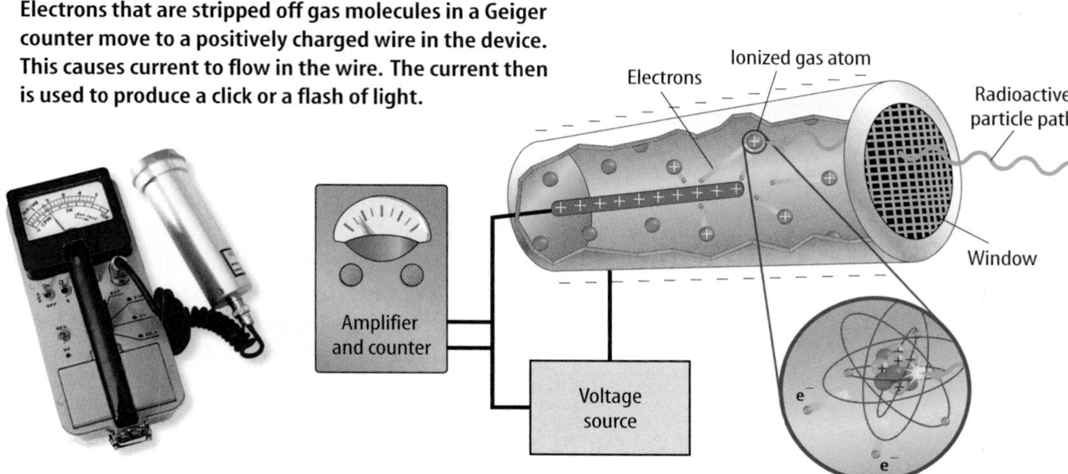

Geiger Counters **Figure 15** shows a Geiger counter. A Geiger counter has a tube with a positively charged wire running through the center of a negatively charged copper cylinder. This tube is filled with gas at a low pressure. When radiation enters the tube at one end, it knocks electrons from the atoms of the gas. These electrons then knock more electrons off other atoms in the gas, and an "electron avalanche" is produced. The free electrons are attracted to the positive wire in the tube. When a large number of electrons reaches the wire, a short, intense current is produced in the wire. This current is amplified to produce a clicking sound or flashing light. The intensity of radiation present is determined by the number of clicks or flashes of light each second.

Reading Check *How does a Geiger counter indicate that radiation is present?*

Background Radiation

It might surprise you to know that you are bathed in radiation that comes from your environment. This radiation, called background radiation, is not produced by humans. Instead it is low-level radiation emitted mainly by naturally occurring radioactive isotopes found in Earth's rocks, soils, and atmosphere. Building materials such as bricks, wood, and stones contain traces of these radioactive materials. Traces of naturally occurring radioactive isotopes are found in the food, water, and air consumed by all animals and plants. As a result, animals and plants also contain small amounts of these isotopes.

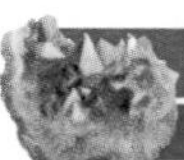
Earth Science INTEGRATION

Cloud chamber activity is a lot like what happens in a cloud when it begins to rain. Clouds contain droplets of supercooled water. Rain forms when ice crystals come near these droplets causing them to condense into ice, which falls to the ground as rain or snow. In the past fifty years or so, scientists have tried to create rain by throwing ice crystals into clouds to make the water in them condense. Research some attempts at artificial rainmaking and report your findings to the class.

Earth Science INTEGRATION

Scientists have tried three ways to make artificial rain. The first is spraying water into warm clouds, the second is dropping dry ice into cold clouds, and the third is seeding clouds with silver iodide crystals or other similar crystals. None of these techniques have been very successful.

Extension

In addition to the instruments described in this section, scientists often use other detectors. Have students research one of these detectors and prepare a poster about it. Detectors students might research include drift chambers, scintillation detectors, cherenkov detectors, spark chambers, and calorimeters. L3  **Visual-Spatial**

Reading Check

Answer by a clicking sound or flashing light

Background Radiation

Activity

Have students do research to find out about sources of background radiation in their community. L2 LS **Linguistic**

Teacher FYI

The Geiger counter was invented by a German physicist named Hans Geiger. In 1928, Geiger, along with Walther Müller, improved the detector, so it is often called the Geiger-Müller counter, or simply the G-M counter.

Resource Manager 

Chapter Resources Booklet
Enrichment, p. 33
Reinforcement, p. 29

Background Radiation, continued

Visual Learning

Figure 16 According to this circle graph, how much of the background radiation received by an average person in the United States comes from natural sources outside the body? at least 71%

3 Assess

Reteach

Have students explain why radiation occurs naturally in the human body. Radioactive isotopes of elements used by the body occur in nature and are picked up and used in the same way as the stable isotopes of the same elements. L2

LS Logical-Mathematical

Challenge

Ask students to draw sketches of pictures that might be obtained with a cloud chamber and a bubble chamber. For each sketch, have the students explain the lines they have drawn and which type of particle would cause that type of line. L2

LS Visual-Spatial P

Assessment

Process Have students create a concept map for each of the four methods of radiation detection mentioned in this section. Use **Performance Assessment in the Science Classroom,** p. 161.

Sources of Background Radiation

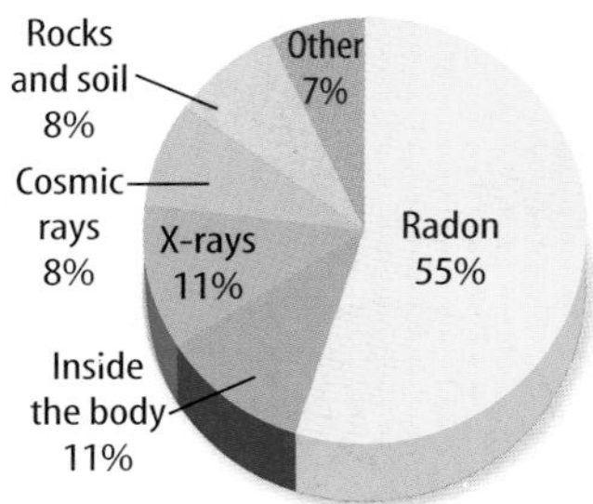

Figure 16
This circle graph shows the amount of background radiation received on average by a person living in the United States.

Sources of Background Radiation Background radiation comes from several sources, as shown in **Figure 16.** The largest source comes from the decay of radon gas. Radon is produced in Earth's crust by the decay of uranium-238 and emits an alpha particle when it decays. Radon gas can seep into houses and basements from the surrounding soil and rocks and can be inhaled.

Some background radiation comes from high-speed nuclei, called cosmic rays, that hit the top of Earth's atmosphere. They produce showers of particles, including alpha, beta, and gamma radiation. Most of this radiation is absorbed by the atmosphere. As you go higher, less atmosphere is above you to absorb this radiation. Therefore, the background radiation from cosmic rays increases with elevation.

Radiation in Your Body Naturally occurring radiation also is found inside your body. Some of the elements in your body that are essential for life have naturally occurring radioactive isotopes. For example, about one out of every trillion carbon atoms is carbon-14, which emits a beta particle when it decays. With each breath, you inhale about 3 million carbon-14 atoms.

The amount of background radiation a person receives can vary greatly. The amount depends on the type of rocks underground, the type of materials used to construct the person's home, and the elevation at which the person lives, among other things. However, because it comes from naturally occurring processes, background radiation never can be eliminated.

Section  Assessment

1. What are four ways that radioactivity can be detected?
2. How are cloud and bubble chambers similar? How are they different?
3. How can an electroscope be used to detect nuclear radiation?
4. Briefly explain how a Geiger counter operates.
5. **Think Critically** Which device would be used to check the amount of radiation present in your home? What are the possible sources of the radiation?

Skill Builder Activities

6. **Drawing Conclusions** You are observing the presence of nuclear radiation with a bubble chamber and see two kinds of trails. Some trails are short and thick, and others are long and thin. What type of nuclear radiation might have caused each trail? **For more help, refer to the** Science Skill Handbook.
7. **Comparing and Contrasting** How are alpha and beta radiation similar to background radiation? How are they different? **For more help, refer to the** Science Skill Handbook.

Answers to Section Assessment

1. cloud chamber, bubble chamber, electroscope, Geiger counter
2. Both show the paths of ions created by radiation. In bubble chambers a liquid boils along the trail of the ions. In cloud chambers, vapor condenses around the ions.
3. When a nuclear particle moves through air, it ionizes air molecules. This induces a negative charge on the electroscope, causing the leaves to separate.
4. Radiation enters the tube, pulling ions from air. These electrons cause an electron avalanche that causes a current to produce a sound or light.
5. A geiger counter; radon, background radiation, cosmic radiation
6. Alpha particles would produce the shorter trails. Beta particles are much smaller, have higher penetrating ability, and would produce the long, thin trails.
7. Alpha and beta radiation can be part of background radiation but also can occur under other circumstances.

SECTION 4

Nuclear Reactions

Nuclear Fission

Do you know what the first step in a game of pool is? One player shoots the cue ball into a triangle of densely packed billiard balls. If the cue ball hits the triangle right on, the balls spread apart, or break. In 1938, two physicists named Otto Hahn and Fritz Strassmann found that a similar result occurs when a neutron is shot into the large nucleus of a uranium-235 atom. The nucleus is split.

Lise Meitner was the first to offer a theory to explain the splitting of a nucleus. She concluded that the neutron fired into the nucleus disturbs and distorts the uranium-235 nucleus. The nuclear strong force is no longer enough to overcome the electrical repulsion within the nucleus, causing it to split into two nuclei, as in **Figure 17.** The process of splitting a nucleus into two nuclei with smaller masses is called **nuclear fission.** The word *fission* means "to divide."

Reading Check *What initiates nuclear fission of a uranium-235 nucleus?*

Only large nuclei with atomic numbers above 90 can undergo nuclear fission. The products of a fission reaction usually include several individual neutrons in addition to the smaller nuclei. The total mass of the products is slightly less than the mass of the original nucleus and the neutron. This small amount of missing mass is converted to a tremendous amount of energy during the fission reaction.

As You Read

***What* You'll Learn**

- **Explain** nuclear fission and how it can begin a chain reaction.
- **Discuss** how nuclear fusion occurs in the Sun.
- **Describe** how radioactive tracers can be used to diagnose medical problems.
- **Discuss** how nuclear reactions can help treat cancer.

Vocabulary

nuclear fission, chain reaction, critical mass, nuclear fusion, tracer

***Why* It's Important**

Radiation from nuclear reactions can be used to generate power and diagnose and treat medical problems.

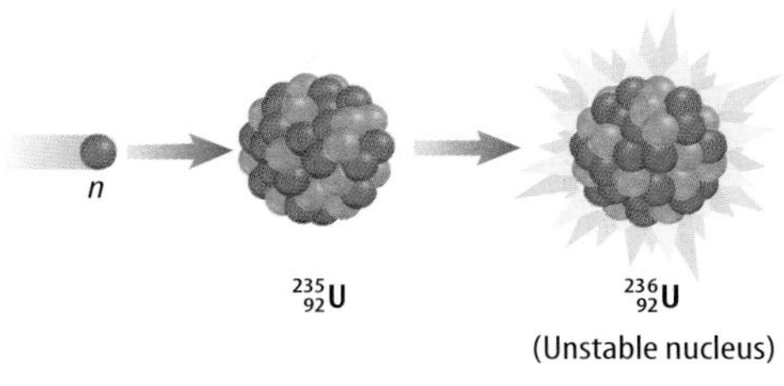

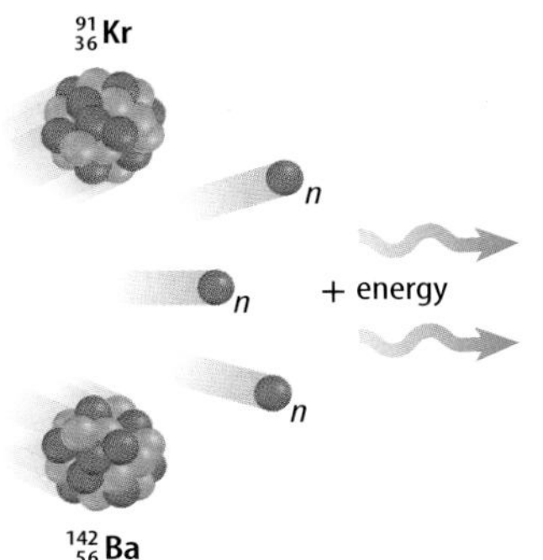

Figure 17
When a neutron hits a uranium-235 nucleus, the uranium nucleus splits into two smaller nuclei and two or three free neutrons. Energy also is released.

Section Assessment Planner

PORTFOLIO
Science Journal, p. 274

PERFORMANCE ASSESSMENT
MiniLAB, p. 274
Skill Builder Activities, p. 278
See page 286 for more options.

CONTENT ASSESSMENT
Section, p. 278
Challenge, p. 278
Chapter, pp. 286–287

SECTION

Nuclear Reactions

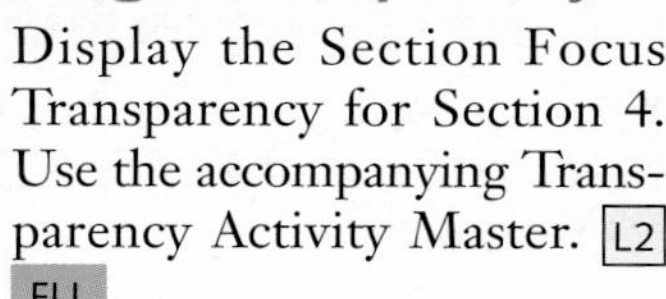

1 Motivate

Bellringer Transparency

Display the Section Focus Transparency for Section 4. Use the accompanying Transparency Activity Master. L2 ELL

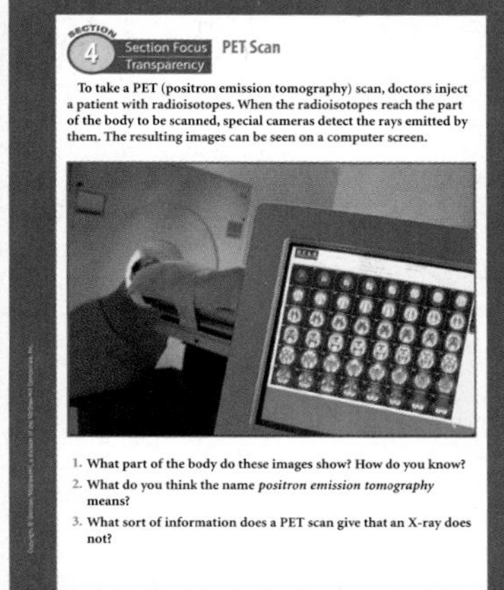

Section Focus Transparency — PET Scan

To take a PET (positron emission tomography) scan, doctors inject a patient with radioisotopes. When the radioisotopes reach the part of the body to be scanned, special cameras detect the rays emitted by them. The resulting images can be seen on a computer screen.

1. What part of the body do these images show? How do you know?
2. What do you think the name *positron emission tomography* means?
3. What sort of information does a PET scan give that an X-ray does not?

Tie to Prior Knowledge

Tell students that fission means breaking things apart and fusion means putting things together. Ask them to give examples of processes they know that fit these definitions. Tell them that in this section they will learn about nuclear fission and nuclear fusion.

Resource Manager

Chapter Resources Booklet
Transparency Activity, p. 49

Reading and Writing Skill Activities, p. 47

2 Teach

Nuclear Fission

Reading Check

Answer A neutron fired into the nucleus causes it to split.

Mini LAB

Purpose Students model a nuclear reaction. L2 ELL Kinesthetic

Materials marbles, beaker, modeling clay

Teaching Strategy Emphasize that the marbles taken out represent nuclei that decay but do not disappear; they change into nuclei of a different element.

Analysis

1. It produces a large amount of radioactive waste.
2. The waste is radioactive, so no one wants it located nearby, and it may remain radioactive for a long time.

Assessment

Oral What was the half-life of the marbles with clay? How many were left after 5 minutes? 1 minute; one Use **PASC,** p. 101.

Extension

Have students find out how fission chain reactions are controlled in nuclear power plants. Control rods made of nonfissionable material that can absorb neutrons are moved in and out of the fissionable material to control the rate of the chain reaction. L3 Logical-Mathematical

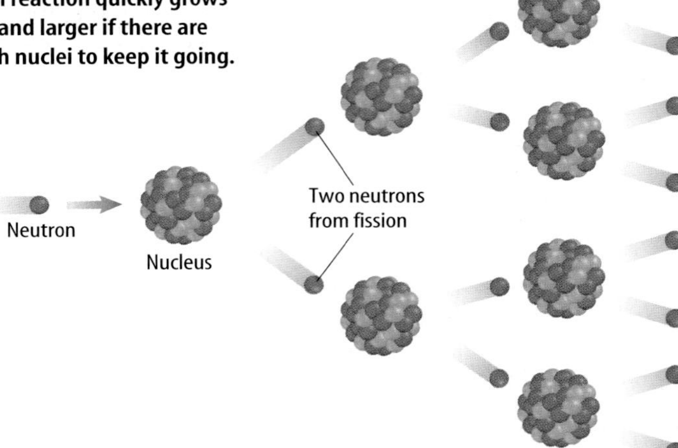

Figure 18 A chain reaction quickly grows larger and larger if there are enough nuclei to keep it going.

Mini LAB

Modeling a Nuclear Reaction

Procedure

1. Put **32 marbles,** each with an attached lump of **clay,** into a large **beaker.** These marbles with clay represent unstable atoms.
2. During a 1-min period, remove half of the marbles and pull off the clay. Place the removed marbles into another beaker and place the lumps of clay into a pile. Marbles without clay represent stable atoms. The clay represents waste from the reaction—smaller atoms that still might decay and give off energy.
3. Repeat this procedure four more times.

Analysis

1. How does this model show one of the main problems that is associated with using nuclear power to make electricity?
2. Why is it difficult to find a place for waste products from nuclear reactions?

Chain Reactions The energy released in a nuclear fission reaction is much greater than the energy released by the natural, spontaneous decay of a radioactive isotope. The neutrons produced in the fission reaction can then bombard and split other nuclei in the sample. These reactions each release more neutrons. If some other material is not present to absorb some of these neutrons as they are released, an uncontrolled chain reaction can result. A **chain reaction,** represented in **Figure 18,** is an ongoing series of fission reactions. Billions of reactions occur each second during a chain reaction, resulting in the release of tremendous amounts of energy.

When controlled, the large amounts of energy released in nuclear fission reactions can be used to generate electricity. Nuclear fission reactions also are used in nuclear weapons.

Critical Mass To be useful, chain reactions cannot grow out of control or die out. Especially when chain reactions are used to produce electricity, they should run at a relatively constant rate. How can the rate of chain reactions be controlled when they involve so much energy? Chain reactions can be controlled if the number of neutrons that are available to start additional fission reactions is controlled carefully. This can be done by adding materials that absorb neutrons. If enough neutrons are absorbed, the chain reaction will continue at a constant rate. The **critical mass** is the amount of fissionable material required so that each fission reaction produces approximately one more fission reaction. If less than the critical mass of reaction material is present, a chain reaction will not occur.

Science Journal

Nuclear Energy? Advocates claim that nuclear reactors are a safe, clean method of producing electricity. Opponents argue that because of the danger from spent nuclear fuel and nuclear waste, reactors should be permanently shut down. Have students write their opinions on this issue in their Science Journals. L2 Linguistic P

Inclusion Strategies

Physically Disabled Pair students who cannot manipulate the marbles with students who can. Have the disabled student in each pair calculate the number of marbles to be processed during each one-minute period, and keep track of the number of marbles processed.

Nuclear Fusion

Now you know that tremendous amounts of energy can be released in nuclear fission. In fact, splitting one uranium-235 nucleus produces about 200 million times more energy than chemically reacting one molecule of dynamite. Even more energy can be released in another type of nuclear reaction, called nuclear fusion. In **nuclear fusion,** two nuclei with low masses are combined to form one nucleus of larger mass. Fusion fuses atomic nuclei together, and fission splits nuclei apart.

Temperature and Fusion For nuclear fusion to occur, positively charged nuclei must get close to each other. However, all nuclei repel each other because they have the same positive electric charge. If nuclei are moving fast, they can have enough kinetic energy to overcome the repulsive electrical force between them and get close to each other.

Remember that the kinetic energy of atoms or molecules increases as their temperature increases. Only at temperatures of millions of degrees Celsius are nuclei moving so fast that they can get close enough for fusion to occur. These extremely high temperatures are found in the center of stars, including the Sun.

Nuclear Fusion and the Sun The Sun is composed mainly of hydrogen. Most of the energy given off by the Sun is produced by a process involving the fusion of hydrogen nuclei. This process occurs in several stages, and one of the stages is shown in **Figure 19.** The net result of this process is that four hydrogen nuclei are converted into one helium nucleus. As this occurs, a small amount of mass is changed into an enormous amount of energy. Earth receives some of this energy as heat and light.

As the Sun ages, the hydrogen nuclei are used up as they are converted into helium. So far, only about one percent of the Sun's mass has been converted into energy. Eventually, no hydrogen nuclei will be left, and the fusion reaction that changes hydrogen into helium will stop. However, it is estimated that the Sun has enough hydrogen to keep this reaction going for another 5 billion years.

Research Visit the Glencoe Science Web site at **science.glencoe.com** for more information about scientists' research involving nuclear fusion. Communicate to your class what you learn.

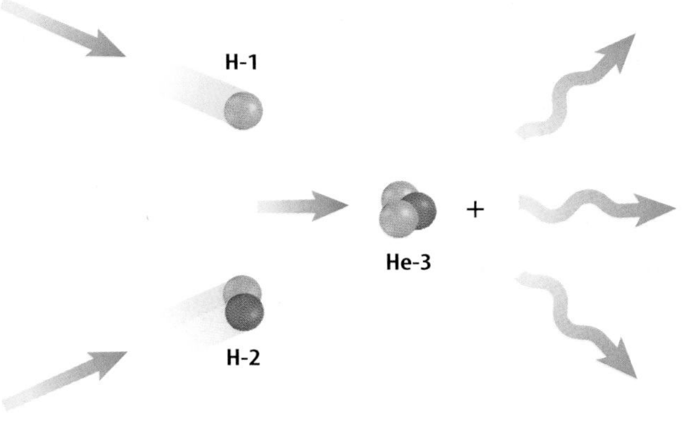

Figure 19
The fusion of hydrogen to form helium takes place in several stages in the Sun. One of these stages is shown here. An isotope of helium is produced when a proton and the hydrogen isotope H-2 undergo fusion.

Nuclear Fusion

Make a Model

Have students model fusion by using small balls of clay to show how two nuclei can join to become one larger nucleus. They should use different colors of clay to represent protons and neutrons. An easy reaction to model is the one in which a deuterium nucleus (hydrogen with one neutron) and a tritium nucleus (hydrogen with two neutrons) combine to form a helium nucleus and one neutron. Point out that when the number of protons changes, a nucleus of a new element is formed. L2 LS **Kinesthetic**

Teacher FYI

Scientists have been unable to achieve controlled fusion because the high temperature needed to initiate the reaction creates plasma that is difficult to contain. A hydrogen bomb, however, uses uncontrolled fusion. Inside the hydrogen bomb's casing, an atomic bomb uses fission to create the extreme temperatures needed to start the fusion reaction.

Use Science Words

Word Meaning Have students explain why the fusion of hydrogen nuclei on the Sun is called a thermonuclear reaction. *Thermo-* comes from a Greek word meaning "heat." Forcing hydrogen nuclei to fuse requires extreme heat. L3 LS **Linguistic**

Resource Manager 

Chapter Resources Booklet
- MiniLAB, p. 4
- Directed Reading for Content Mastery, pp. 21, 22

Home and Community Involvement, p. 37

SCIENCE Online
Internet Addresses

Explore the Glencoe Science Web site at **science.glencoe.com** to find out more about topics in this section.

One way a uranium-235 atom can fission, or break apart, is into barium and krypton. Use a periodic table to find the atomic numbers of barium and krypton. What do they add up to? A uranium-235 atom can fission in several other ways such as producing neodymium and another element. What is the other element?

Using Nuclear Reactions in Medicine

If you were going to meet a friend in a crowded area, it would be easier to find her if your friend told you that she would be wearing a red hat. In a similar way, scientists can find one molecule in a large group of molecules if they know that it is "wearing" something unique. Although a molecule can't wear a red hat, if it has a radioactive atom in it, it can be found easily in a large group of molecules, or even a living organism. Radioactive isotopes can be located by detecting the radiation they emit.

When a radioisotope is used to find or keep track of molecules in an organism, it is called a **tracer.** Scientists can use tracers to follow where a particular molecule goes in your body or to study how a particular organ functions. Tracers also are used in agriculture to monitor the uptake of nutrients and fertilizers. Examples of tracers include carbon-11, iodine-131, and sodium-24. These three radioisotopes are useful tracers because they are important in certain body processes. As a result, they accumulate inside the organism being studied.

Reading Check *What use do tracers have in agriculture?*

Iodine Tracers in the Thyroid The thyroid gland is located in your neck and produces chemical compounds called hormones. These hormones help regulate several body processes, including growth. Because the element iodine accumulates in the thyroid, the radioisotope iodine-131 can be used to diagnose thyroid problems. As iodine-131 atoms are absorbed by the thyroid, their nuclei decay, emitting beta particles and gamma rays. The beta particles are absorbed by the surrounding tissues, but the gamma rays penetrate the skin. The emitted gamma rays can be detected and used to determine whether the thyroid is healthy, as shown in **Figure 20.** If the detected radiation is not intense, then the thyroid has not properly absorbed the iodine-131 and is not functioning properly. This could be due to the presence of a tumor. **Figure 21** shows how radioactive tracers are used to study the brain.

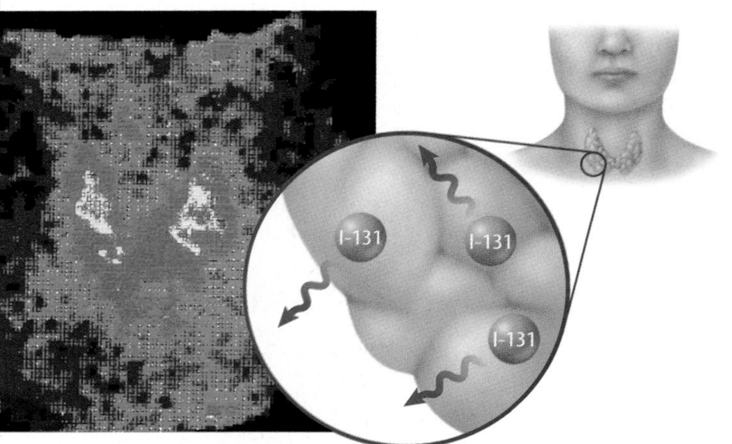

Figure 20
Radioactive iodine-131 accumulates in the thyroid gland and emits gamma rays, which can be detected to form an image of a patient's thyroid. *What are some advantages of being able to use iodine-131 to form an image of a thyroid?*

Using Nuclear Reactions in Medicine

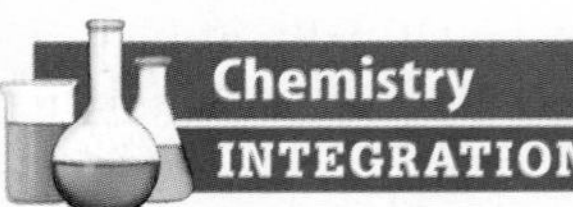

The atomic number of barium is 56 and the atomic number of krypton is 36. These add up to 92. Uranium-235 breaks into neodymium (atomic number 32) and germanium (atomic number 60).

Discussion

How is the use of tracers similar to the use of radio collars in tracking wild animals? The collars emit an electromagnetic signal that can be detected with an antenna and receiver. This allows scientists to determine the movement of the animal. Similarly, a radioactive tracer emits radiation, which allows physicians to track its movement in the body. L2 LS **Logical-Mathematical**

Reading Check

Answer to monitor the uptake of nutrients and fertilizers

Caption Question Answer

Figure 20 Iodine is naturally taken up by the thyroid. Also, it allows doctors to determine how well the thyroid is functioning without having to actually look at it.

Inclusion Strategies

Gifted Have students investigate other ways that tracers are used in medicine and prepare a report on one method. If possible, they should interview a physician who uses tracers to find out drawbacks and benefits of the procedure. Possible topics are tracers used to detect problems with the heart, kidneys, or digestion. L3 LS **Linguistic**

Visual Learning

Figure 20 Point out that the picture to the left shows the thyroid after the person has ingested the iodine-131 tracer. The red and orange colors indicate areas in which the iodine is well absorbed. Have students each find his or her thyroid gland, which is located in the neck between the larynx and the trachea. L2 LS **Visual-Spatial**

276 CHAPTER 9 Radioactivity and Nuclear Reactions

Figure 21

The diagram below shows an imaging technique known as Positron Emission Tomography, or PET. Positrons are emitted from the nuclei of certain radioactive isotopes when a proton changes to a neutron. PET can form images that show the level of activity in different areas of the brain. These images can reveal tumors and regions of abnormal brain activity.

A When positrons are emitted from the nucleus of an atom, they can hit electrons from other atoms and become transformed into gamma rays.

B The radioactive isotope fluorine-18 emits positrons when it decays. Fluorine-18 atoms are chemically attached to molecules that are absorbed by brain tissue. These compounds are injected into the patient and carried by blood to the brain.

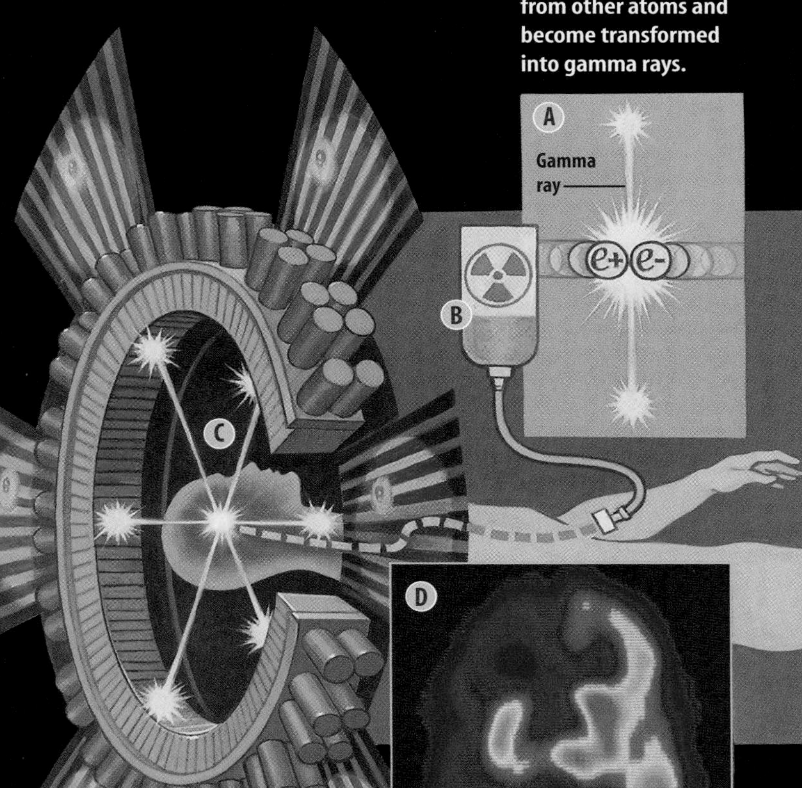

C Inside the patient's brain, the decay of the radioactive fluorine-18 nuclei emits positrons that collide with electrons. The gamma rays that are released are sensed by the detectors.

D A computer uses the information collected by the detectors to generate an image of the activity level in the brain. This image shows normal activity in the right side of the brain (red, yellow, green) but below-normal activity in the left (purple).

Visualizing PET Scans

Have students examine the pictures and read the captions. Then ask the following questions.

- **What is a positron?** A positron has the same mass as an electron but a positive charge. It can be considered a positively charged electron.
- **What is formed when a positron and electron combine?** a gamma ray
- **Why is it important for the fluorine-18 to be chemically attached to substances that are normally absorbed by the brain?** The fluorine-18 needs to be absorbed in the brain tissue because that is the area that is being studied.

Activity

Have the students research how positrons are formed. Suggest students make posters illustrating their findings and present their posters to the class. L2 LS **Visual-Spatial**

Extension

Challenge students to research the types of injuries that can cause brain inactivity similar to the type shown in Figure 21D. Have them find out if there are treatments for this type of injury and report their findings to the class.
L3 LS **Linguistic**

Resource Manager

Chapter Resources Booklet
Enrichment, p. 34

3 Assess

Reteach

Have students discuss why a critical mass is necessary to keep a fission reaction going but not to keep a fusion reaction going. In a fission reaction, a particle bombards a nucleus and splits it into two nuclei plus some extra particles. If the extra particles hit other fissionable nuclei, those nuclei will split and produce new particles. This chain reaction will continue as long as there is enough fissionable material nearby. The amount needed to keep the reaction going is the critical mass. A fusion reaction is not a chain reaction. L2

LS **Logical-Mathematical**

Challenge

Ask students to explain why chain reactions do not occur in naturally existing material. Fission occurs only for certain rare isotopes. The percentage of these isotopes in naturally existing material is so low that a chain reaction is unlikely.

LS **Logical-Mathematical**

Content Many benefits result from nuclear applications in medicine, but there are disadvantages, too. Ask students to write newspaper articles explaining how radiation can cause as well as treat cancer. Possible answers: It can cause mutations in cell structures, leading to tumor formation, or it can kill cancer cells by ionizing them. Use **Performance Assessment in the Science Classroom,** p. 141.

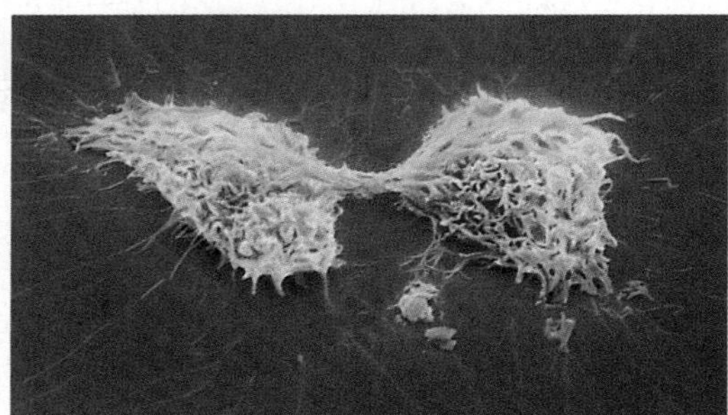

Figure 22
Cancer cells, such as the ones shown here, can be killed with carefully-measured doses of radiation.

Treating Cancer with Radioactivity

When a person has cancer, a group of cells in that person's body grows out of control and forms a tumor. Radiation can be used to stop some types of cancerous cells from growing. Remember that the radiation that is given off during nuclear decay is strong enough to ionize nearby atoms. If a source of radiation is placed near cancer cells, atoms in the cells can be ionized. If the ionized atoms are in a critical molecule, such as the DNA or RNA of a cancer cell, then the molecule might no longer function properly. The cell then could die or stop growing, as shown in **Figure 22.**

When possible, a radioactive isotope such as gold-198 or iridium-192 is implanted within or near the tumor. Other times, tumors are treated from outside the body. Typically, an intense beam of gamma rays from the decay of cobalt-60 is focused on the tumor for a short period of time. The gamma rays pass through the body and into the tumor. How can physicians be sure that only the cancer cells will absorb radiation? Because cancer cells grow quickly, they are more susceptible to absorbing radiation and being damaged than healthy cells are. However, other cells in the body that grow quickly also are damaged, which is why cancer patients who have radiation therapy sometimes experience severe side effects.

Section  Assessment

1. Why is critical mass important in some applications of nuclear fission?
2. Explain why it would be difficult to start a fusion reaction on Earth.
3. How might a tracer be used to diagnose a digestive problem?
4. Why does nuclear radiation cause damage to living cells?
5. **Think Critically** During nuclear fission, large nuclei with high masses are split into two nuclei with smaller masses. During nuclear fusion, two nuclei with low masses are combined to form one nucleus of larger mass. How are the two processes similar?

Skill Builder Activities

6. **Concept Mapping** Make a concept map to show how a chain reaction occurs when U-235 is bombarded with a neutron. Show how each of the three neutrons given as products begins another fission reaction. **For more help, refer to the** Science Skill Handbook.
7. **Identifying a Question** Suppose you had a medical problem and the doctor suggested a diagnostic test that involved a radioactive tracer. Using what you have learned about medical applications of radioactivity, write a set of questions you might ask your doctor. **For more help, refer to the** Science Skill Handbook.

Neutron
hits
U-235 nucleus
and forms: Ba-141, Kr-92
and releases: Neutron, Neutron, Neutron
which hits / which hits / which hits
U-235 nucleus / U-235 nucleus / U-235 nucleus

Answers to Section Assessment

1. to control the rate of the reaction
2. Starting a fusion reaction requires too much energy.
3. A doctor can have the patient swallow a radioactive substance that is not absorbed and trace it through the digestive system.
4. It ionizes them so they die or stop growing.
5. Both processes transmute atoms and release large amounts of energy.
6. See side column.
7. Possible answers: Will it damage healthy cells? How long will it remain in my body?

Activity

Chain Reactions

In an uncontrolled nuclear chain reaction, the number of reactions increases as additional neutrons split more nuclei. In a controlled nuclear reaction, neutrons are absorbed, so the reaction continues at a constant rate. How could you model a controlled and an uncontrolled nuclear reaction in the classroom?

What You'll Investigate

How can you set up chain reactions with dominoes to model a controlled and an uncontrolled nuclear reaction?

Materials

dominoes
stopwatch

Goals

- **Model** a controlled and uncontrolled chain reaction
- **Compare** the two types of chain reactions

Procedure

1. Set up a single line of dominoes standing on end so that when the first domino is pushed over, it will knock over the second and each domino will knock over the one following it.
2. Using the stopwatch, time how long it takes from the moment the first domino is pushed over until the last domino falls over. Record the time.
3. Using the same number of dominoes as in step 1, set up a series of dominoes in which at least one of the dominoes will knock down two others, so that two lines of dominoes will continue falling. In other words, the series should have at least one point that looks like the letter Y.
4. Repeat step 2.

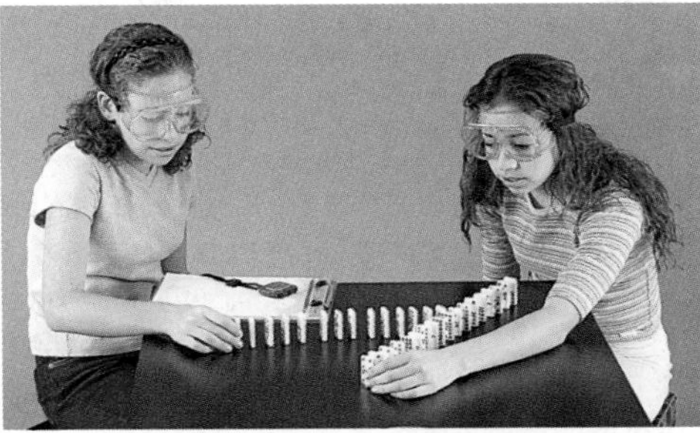

Conclude and Apply

1. **Compare** the amount of time it took for all of the dominoes to fall in each of your two arrangements.
2. Were the same number of dominoes falling at a particular time in both domino arrangements? Explain.
3. Which of your domino arrangements represented a controlled nuclear reaction? Which represented an uncontrolled nuclear reaction?
4. **Describe** how the concept of critical mass was represented in your model of a controlled chain reaction.
5. Assuming that they had equal amounts of material, which would finish faster—a controlled or uncontrolled nuclear fission reaction? Explain.

Communicating Your Data

Explain to friends or members of your family how a controlled nuclear chain reaction can be used in nuclear power plants to generate electricity.

Resource Manager

Chapter Resources Booklet

Activity Worksheet, pp. 5–6, 7–8
Reinforcement, p. 30

Communicating Your Data

Students should prepare an illustration of a controlled and an uncontrolled reaction to help explain what is taking place.

Activity

BENCH TESTED

Purpose Students model a controlled and uncontrolled nuclear reaction. L2 LS **Kinesthetic**

Process Skills collecting data, making models, comparing and contrasting, drawing conclusions

Time Required 40 minutes

Teaching Strategy Students can collect additional data by forming large groups and using all of their dominoes to form longer chains.

Answers to Questions

1. The Y-shaped arrangement fell faster.
2. No, in the Y-shaped arrangement some places had two dominoes falling at once.
3. The straight arrangement represented a controlled reaction because any neutron that split off was absorbed. The Y-shaped arrangement represented an uncontrolled reaction.
4. Critical mass was represented in the straight-line configuration because one domino caused only one other domino to fall.
5. An uncontrolled reaction would finish faster because a single reaction could produce two reactions which could produce four reactions and so.

Assessment

Content Have students write and perform a skit that demonstrates controlled and uncontrolled reactions. Use **PASC,** p. 147.

Activity

BENCH TESTED

Recognize the Problem

Purpose

Students will model the decay of a uranium atom through the process of transmutation. L2

LS **Kinesthetic**

Process Skills

making a model, comparing, constructing, identifying, and inferring

Time Required

one 45-minute class period

Thinking Critically

Discussion

Ask students to think about radioactive substances such as uranium and plutonium. Have them consider the exposure to radiation some people have been exposed to such as after nuclear testing or the Chernobyl accident. Why is radiation dangerous? Where does radiation come from? What effects would come from having radioactive materials in their homes? What radioactive substance might be found in their basements (Radon)?

Possible Materials

Students can use any small objects in place of the rice, beans, or candy. A strong bonding glue should be used when constructing the model.

Activity Model and Invent

Modeling Transmutation

Imagine what would happen if the oxygen atoms around you began changing into nitrogen atoms. Most of the elements familiar to you are stable and will not easily change into other elements, but the atoms of other elements have unstable nuclei and will decay. When an unstable nucleus decays, an alpha or beta particle is thrown out of its nucleus, and the atom becomes a new element. A uranium-238 atom, for example, will undergo eight alpha decays and six beta decays to eventually become lead. This process of one element changing into another element is called transmutation. You will model this decay process during this activity.

Recognize the Problem

How could you create a model of a uranium-238 atom and the decay process it undergoes during transmutation?

Thinking Critically

What types of materials could you use to represent the protons and neutrons in a U-238 nucleus? How could you use these materials to model transmutation?

Possible Materials

- brown rice
- white rice
- colored candies
- dried beans
- dried seeds
- glue
- poster board

Safety Precautions

Never eat foods used in the lab.

Data Source

Refer to your textbook for general information about transmutation.

Inclusion Strategies

Physically Challenged If students cannot manipulate the materials, have them design a model, and ask other students to work with them to make the model.

Planning the Model

1. **Choose** two materials of different colors or shapes for the protons and neutrons of your nucleus model. Choose a material for the negatively charged beta particle.
2. **Decide** how to model the transmutation process. Will you create a new nucleus model for each new element? How will you model an alpha or beta particle leaving the nucleus?
3. **Create** a transmutation chart to show the results of each transmutation step of a uranium-238 atom with the identity, atomic number, and mass number of each new element formed and the type of radiation particle emitted at each step. A uranium-238 atom will undergo the following decay steps before transmuting into a lead-206 atom: alpha decay, beta decay, beta decay, alpha decay, alpha decay, alpha decay, alpha decay, alpha decay, beta decay, beta decay, alpha decay, beta decay, beta decay, alpha decay.

Check the Model Plans

1. **Describe** your model plan and transmutation chart to your teacher and ask how they can be improved.
2. **Present** your plan and chart to your class. Ask classmates to suggest improvements in both.

Making the Model

1. Construct your model of a uranium-238 nucleus showing the correct number of protons and neutrons.
2. Using your nucleus model, demonstrate the transmutation of a uranium-238 nucleus into a lead-206 nucleus by following the decay sequence outlined in the previous section.
3. Show the emission of an alpha particle or beta particle between each transmutation step.

Analyzing and Applying Results

1. **Compare** how alpha and beta decay change an atom's atomic number.
2. **Compare** how alpha and beta decay change the mass number of an atom.
3. **Infer** how the universe would differ if all the elements were radioactive and readily underwent transmutation.
4. Alchemists living during the Middle Ages spent much time trying to turn lead into gold. Identify the decay processes needed to accomplish this task.

Show your model to the class and explain how your model represents the transmutation of U-238 into Pb-206.

Encourage students to use electronically designed diagrams to accompany their models.

Planning the Model

Teaching Strategies

Have references available for students to use that show the transmutation of uranium into lead.

Making the Model

Expected Outcome

Students will build a model that demonstrates the transmutation of uranium.

Analyzing and Applying Results

1. Alpha decay decreases the atomic number by 2; beta decay increases the atomic number by 1.
2. Alpha decay decreases the mass number by 4; beta decay causes no change in the mass number.
3. Answers will vary. Stars would still exist since they are composed primarily of hydrogen and helium, but everything else from planets to people would eventually degrade into alpha and beta particles.
4. Two alpha decays and one beta decay would be required to turn an atom of lead into an atom of gold.

Process Ask students to make pamphlets identifying ways the transmutation of uranium and plutonium are used. nuclear power plant, nuclear weapons, nuclear submarines, and spacecraft Use **Performance Assessment in the Science Classroom,** p. 129.

Oops!

Oops! Accidents in SCIENCE

SOMETIMES GREAT DISCOVERIES HAPPEN BY ACCIDENT!

Content Background

X rays are produced when high-energy electrons strike a material that abruptly slows them down, causing them to release radiant energy at the X ray wavelength. Since X rays easily pass through many materials, they cannot be focused like regular light waves can. Instead, metal tubes must be used to guide the X rays to the desired location. Their very short wavelengths also have made X rays the ideal tool for analyzing the structures of molecules. Almost as amazing as the discovery of X rays was how quickly they came into general use. Within weeks of Roentgen's announcement, X rays were being used in hospitals.

Discussion

There is no doubt that others had produced X rays before Roentgen. They either didn't realize it or didn't communicate it. Roentgen did a lot of experiments with X rays before he announced his discovery. **Why might this have been a wise thing for Roentgen to do?** Possible answer: He had to be sure of what he was seeing. He then could more reasonably describe the strange phenomenon to those who might be skeptical about it.

X-Ray Surprise

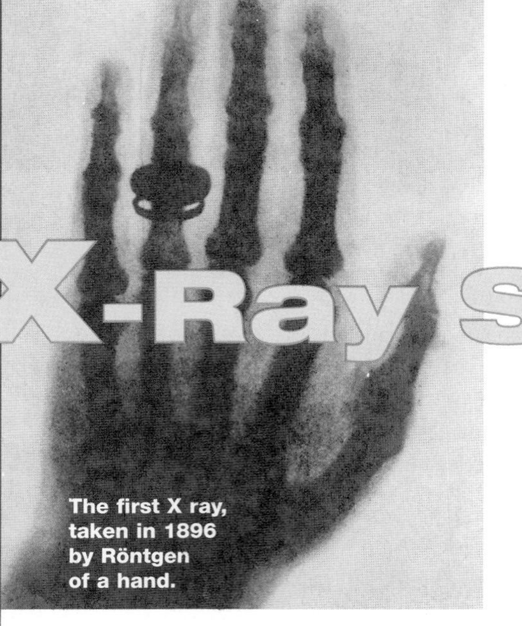

The first X ray, taken in 1896 by Röntgen of a hand.

The image on the X-ray screen looked like a metal box with wires attached to it. The airport security guard blinked, but her expression didn't change. "Excuse me, sir, could you step over here?" The passenger cooperated and the mysterious metal box turned out to be a tackle box tangled up with wires from a miniature radio headset. "Next time you fly, please bring a plastic tackle box," the guard advised. "It won't set off any alarms!"

Today, X rays of people and objects are fairly routine. But back in 1895, in Germany, an X ray was unknown and about to be discovered. Physics professor Wilhelm Röntgen was experimenting with a glass tube from which most of the air had been removed.

He sent a jolt of electricity from one end of the tube to the other and tried to observe the results. "What's wrong?" he asked himself. There was too much light in the room to see what was happening in the tube. So Röntgen darkened the room, put black paper around the tube, and restarted the electricity. The tube glowed. And in the dark room, a screen also glowed. Röntgen knew that something besides light must be coming from the tube, but what? He hadn't a clue. So he called these mysterious, unknown rays, X rays.

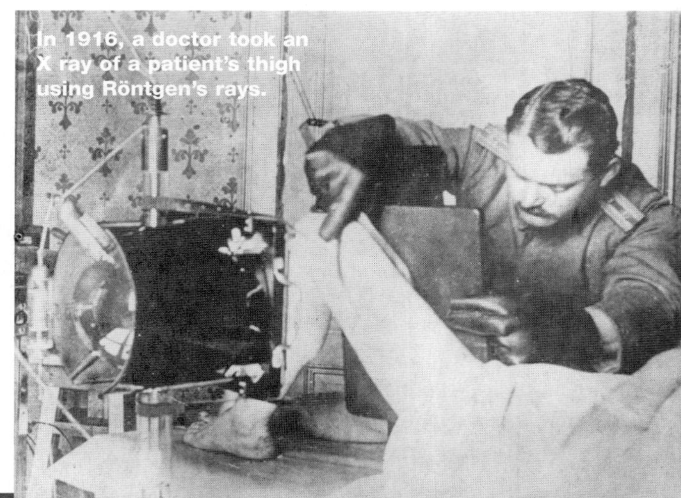

In 1916, a doctor took an X ray of a patient's thigh using Röntgen's rays.

282

Resources for Teachers and Students

Bettyann Holtzmann Kevles, *Naked to the Bone: Medical Imaging in the Twentieth Century*, Helix Books, 1997.

Kathy Svitil, "In the Beginning, All was Blackness," in *Discover*, April 2000, vol 21, issue 4, p. 16.

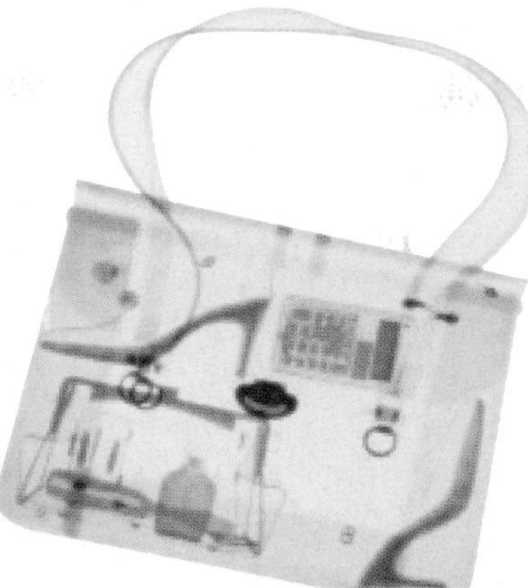

An X ray of a suitcase, a briefcase, and a handbag reveals their contents. What objects can you identify?

Medical Breakthrough

What Röntgen didn't know at the time is that X-ray radiation is a part of the electromagnetic spectrum with a shorter wavelength than light. X rays are created in an X-ray machine when a tungsten target is hit with electrons. The radiation produced passes easily through soft body tissues and materials, but is stopped by dense materials, such as metal and bone. X rays that pass through the soft material can be captured on film, leaving an outline of the dense material—an X ray.

Thanks to Röntgen's accidental discovery, doctors can look inside the human body. Fractured bones can be spotted, and certain diseases detected. However, too much exposure to X rays is dangerous to the body. But even this downside has been put to use, as radiation treatment to destroy cancerous cells.

An airport security check

X-Ray Visions

New uses for X rays continue to emerge. For example, one powerful type of X ray can look through vehicles and buildings to identify terrorists. Another new use of X rays is in identifying land mines so they can be safely removed from war zones. Other scientists are trying to focus X-ray radiation in the same way that light is focused in a laser beam. These "xasers" will allow biologists to study the structure of proteins. The most far out use is far out in space. Astronomers are using satellites to study sources of X rays from black holes deep in outer space.

CONNECTIONS **Research** Investigate the jobs of radiologists and radiology technicians. What training do they receive? How do they contribute to keeping people healthy?

SCIENCE Online For more information, visit science.glencoe.com

Activity

In recent years, other imaging methods have been developed to analyze the inside workings of the body. Ask students to research some of these newer methods and make a table describing each and how it is used to diagnose problems in the body. **Judging from your research, do you think X rays are still necessary?** Possible answer: Yes; X rays are still the quickest, simplest way to check to see if someone has a broken bone. L2

LS **Logical-Mathematical**

Analyze the Event

Wilhelm Roentgen was the kind of scientist who did not like to draw conclusions quickly. He believed that a scientist should refrain from having a well-conceived idea of what he or she wanted to find before carrying out an experiment. **How do you think this way of thinking made Roentgen better able to discover X rays?** Possible answers: His thinking wasn't clouded by what he expected to see. He had an open mind, so when he saw something strange, he didn't dismiss it because it didn't fit into his theories.

CONNECTIONS **Radiologists**

Radiologists are doctors who are experts in reading X rays of the body. In addition to normal medical training, radiologists spend a number of years learning how to read X rays and other medical images. Radiological technologists actually take the X rays. They are experts in determining just how much radiation to use on a patient and how to position the patient to get the best X ray images.

SCIENCE Online

Internet Addresses

Explore the Glencoe Science Web site at **science.glencoe.com** to find out more about topics in this feature.

Chapter 9 Study Guide

Reviewing Main Ideas

Preview

Students can answer the questions in their Science Journals. Discuss the answers as you go through the chapter. **LS Linguistic**

Review

Students can write their answers, then compare them with those of other students. **LS Interpersonal**

Reteach

Students can look at the illustrations and describe details that support the main ideas of the chapter. **LS Visual-Spatial**

Answers to Chapter Review

Section 1

1. The electromagnetic force acts as a repulsive force between the protons.

Section 2

4. carbon-14, because the bone was once living

Section 4

1. to generate electricity or for nuclear weapons

Chapter  Study Guide

Reviewing Main Ideas

Section 1 Radioactivity

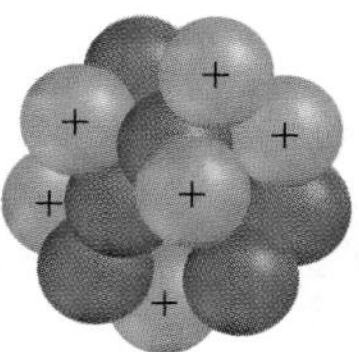

Nucleus

1. The protons and neutrons in an atomic nucleus are held together by the strong force. *What other force acts among particles in the nucleus?*
2. The ratio of protons to neutrons indicates whether a nucleus will be stable or unstable. Large nuclei tend to be unstable.
3. Radioactivity is the emission of energy or particles from an unstable nucleus.
4. Radioactivity was discovered accidentally by Henri Becquerel about 100 years ago.

Section 2 Nuclear Decay

1. The three common types of radiation emitted from a decaying nucleus are alpha particles, beta particles, and gamma rays. In alpha and beta decay, particles are given off. In gamma decay, energy is released.
2. Alpha and beta decay cause transmutation where the nucleus of one element changes into the nucleus of another element.
3. Half-life is the amount of time that it takes for half of the atoms in a radioactive sample to decay.
4. The half-lives of radioactive carbon and uranium isotopes can be used to calculate the ages of objects that contain these substances. *Would you use carbon-14 or uranium dating to find the age of a bone?*

Section 3 Detecting Radioactivity

1. Radioactivity can be detected with a cloud chamber, a bubble chamber, an electroscope, or a Geiger counter.
2. A Geiger counter indicates the intensity of radiation with a clicking sound or a flashing light that increases in frequency as more radiation is present.
3. Background radiation is low-level radiation emitted by naturally occurring isotopes found in Earth's rocks and soils, the atmosphere, and inside your body.

Section 4 Nuclear Reactions

1. Nuclei are split during fission and combined during fusion. In each reaction, large amounts of energy are released. *What are two ways that this energy can be used?*
2. Neutrons released from a nucleus during fission can split other nuclei, leading to a chain reaction.
3. Radioactive tracers can go to targeted areas of the body and then be detected to diagnose some health problems.
4. Some radiation can kill cancer cells.

FOLDABLES Reading & Study Skills 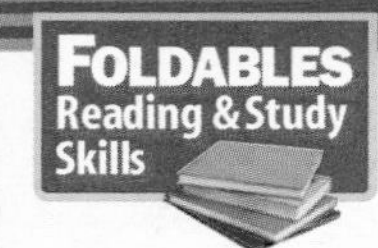

After You Read

On the inside center section of your Main Ideas Study Fold, list positive and negative uses of radioactive materials and nuclear reactions.

284 CHAPTER STUDY GUIDE

FOLDABLES Reading & Study Skills

After You Read

After students have read the chapter and completed the Foldable described in Before You Read, have them do the activity on the student page.

Chapter 9 Study Guide

Visualizing Main Ideas

Complete the following concept map on radioactivity.

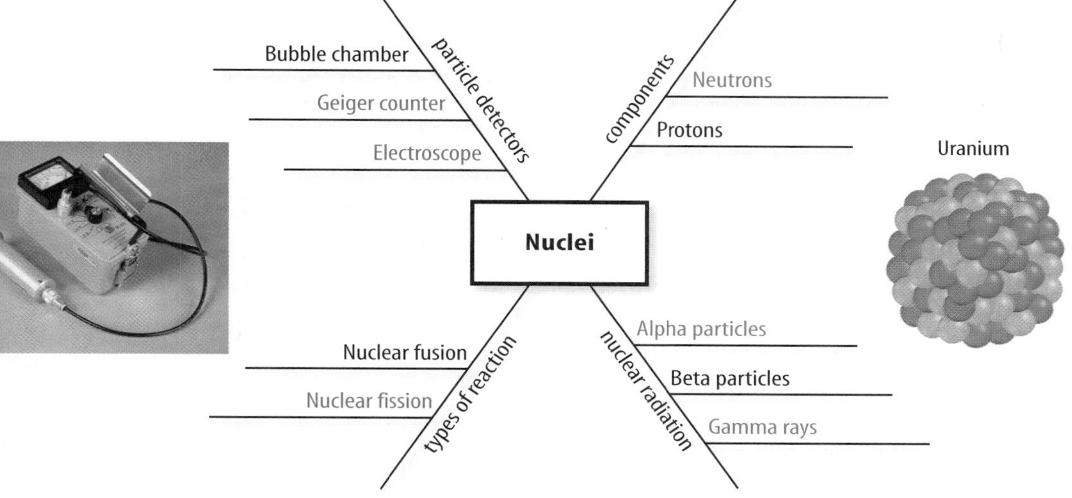

Vocabulary Review

Vocabulary Words

a. alpha particle
b. beta particle
c. bubble chamber
d. chain reaction
e. cloud chamber
f. critical mass
g. gamma ray
h. Geiger counter
i. half-life
j. nuclear fission
k. nuclear fusion
l. radioactivity
m. strong force
n. tracer
o. transmutation

Study Tip

Make a study schedule for yourself. If you have a planner, write down exactly which hours you plan to spend studying and stick to it.

Using Vocabulary

Use what you know about the vocabulary words to explain the differences in the following sets of words. Then explain how the words are related.

1. cloud chamber, bubble chamber
2. chain reaction, critical mass
3. nuclear fission, nuclear fusion
4. radioactivity, half-life
5. alpha particle, beta particle, gamma ray
6. Geiger counter, tracer
7. nuclear fission, transmutation
8. electroscope, Geiger counter
9. strong force, radioactivity

Chapter 9 Study Guide

Visualizing Main Ideas

See student page.

Vocabulary Review

Using Vocabulary

1. Both are used to detect subatomic particles. In both, charged particles create ions. In a cloud chamber, vapor condenses around these ions. In a bubble chamber, a liquid boils along the trail of ions.
2. A chain reaction is an ongoing series of fission reactions. Critical mass is the amount of fissionable material required to maintain a fission chain reaction at a constant rate.
3. Nuclear fission is the splitting of a nucleus. Nuclear fusion is the combining of two nuclei.
4. Radioactivity is the emission of high-energy radiation or particles from the nucleus of a radioactive atom. Half-life is the time required for half of a sample of radioactive material to decay.
5. An alpha particle is made of two protons and two neutrons. A beta particle is a high-speed electron. A gamma ray is high-energy electromagnetic radiation. All are types of radiation.
6. A Geiger counter is a device that measures radioactivity by producing an electric current when radiation is present. A tracer is a radioactive isotope that is used to keep track of molecules in an organism.
7. Nuclear fission is the splitting of a nucleus. Transmutation is the process of changing one element to another. Transmutation occurs during nuclear fission.
8. An electroscope detects radiation by responding to ionization of the surrounding air, which causes its leaves to separate. In a Geiger counter, electric current is produced when the instrument encounters radiation.
9. The strong force binds atomic nuclei together. In radioactivity nuclei come apart.

Chapter 9 Assessment

Checking Concepts

1. A
2. A
3. B
4. A
5. A
6. B
7. A
8. C
9. A
10. D

Thinking Critically

11. It stays the same.
12. Alpha particles lose energy quickly as they interact with matter, pulling electrons away from atoms and leaving charged ions behind. Inside the body, they can damage fragile biological molecules.
13. Background radiation comes from several sources, and the sources do not contain the same amount of radiation. Everyone is not exposed to the same sources or to the same amount of radiation in those sources.
14. Radioisotopes can be placed in the soil of lab plants. Using radiation detectors, scientists can monitor how the radioisotopes are taken up by the plant.
15. If a patient ingests radioactive tracers and they do not detect intense gamma rays being emitted from a patient's thyroid, the thyroid is not functioning properly.

Chapter 9 Assessment

Checking Concepts

Choose the word or phrase that best answers the question.

1. What keeps particles in a nucleus together?
   A) strong force **C)** electrical force
   B) repulsion **D)** atomic glue

2. What are the atomic numbers of elements that have been produced artificially?
   A) greater than 92 **C)** 83 through 92
   B) greater than 83 **D)** 90 through 111

3. What is an electron that is produced when a neutron decays called?
   A) an alpha particle **C)** gamma radiation
   B) a beta particle **D)** a negatron

4. Which of the following describes an isotope's half-life?
   A) a constant time interval
   B) a varied time interval
   C) an increasing time interval
   D) a decreasing time interval

5. For which of the following could carbon-14 dating be used?
   A) a Roman scroll **C)** dinosaur fossils
   B) a marble column **D)** rocks

6. Which device would be most useful for measuring radiation in a nuclear laboratory?
   A) a cloud chamber **C)** an electroscope
   B) a Geiger counter **D)** a bubble chamber

7. Which term describes an ongoing series of fission reactions?
   A) chain reaction **C)** positron emission
   B) decay reaction **D)** fusion reaction

8. Which process is responsible for the tremendous energy released by the Sun?
   A) nuclear decay **C)** nuclear fusion
   B) nuclear fission **D)** combustion

9. Which radioisotope acts as an external source of ionizing radiation in the treatment of cancer?
   A) cobalt-60 **C)** gold-198
   B) carbon-14 **D)** technetium-99

10. Which of the following is a common medical application of radiation?
    A) assist breathing **C)** heal broken bones
    B) ease pain **D)** treat cancers

Thinking Critically

11. When a nucleus emits gamma radiation, what happens to the atomic number?

12. How do the properties of alpha particles make them harmful? Explain.

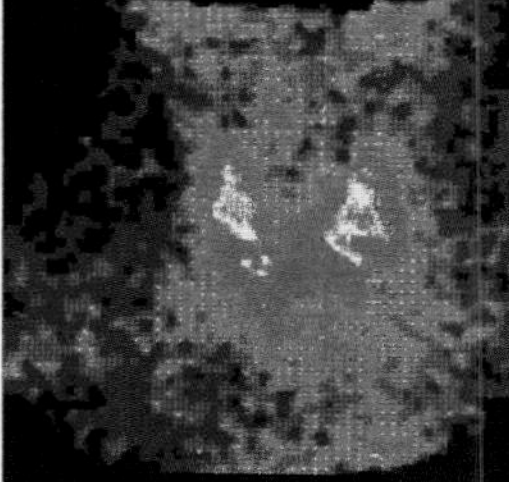

13. Why does the amount of background radiation a person receives vary greatly?

14. Explain how radioisotopes could be used to study how plants take up nutrients from the soil.

15. How can doctors tell if a patient's thyroid is not working correctly by using iodine tracers?

Developing Skills

16. **Communicating** Prepare a presentation to explain how a Geiger counter works.

17. **Making and Using Tables** Construct a table summarizing the characteristics of each of the three common types of radiation. Include the symbol for the radiation, what type of particle or energy it produces, and what it can penetrate.

Chapter Assessment Planner

Portfolio Encourage students to place in their portfolios one or two items of what they consider to be their best work. Examples include:
- Activity, p. 261
- Science Journal, p. 265
- Challenge, p. 272
- Science Journal, p. 274

Performance Additional performance assessments, Performance Task Assessment Lists, and rubrics for evaluating these activities can be found in Glencoe's **Performance Assessment in the Science Classroom.**

18. **Predicting** Predict what type of radiation will be emitted during each of the following nuclear reactions:
  a. uranium-238 decays into thorium-234
  b. potassium-40 decays into argon-40

19. **Interpreting Data** Using the data below, construct a graph plotting the mass numbers versus. the half-lives of radioisotopes. Is it possible to use your graph to predict the half-life of a radioisotope given its mass number?

Isotope Half-Lives

Radioisotope	Mass Number	Half-Life
Radon	222	4 days
Thorium	234	24 days
Iodine	131	8 days
Bismuth	210	5 days
Polonium	210	138 days

20. **Recognizing Cause and Effect** Describe nuclear fission chain reactions. How are these chain reactions controlled? What might happen if they were not controlled?
For more help, refer to the Science Skill Handbook.

Performance Assessment

21. **Oral Presentation** Research the causes and effects of radon pollution in the home. Report your findings to the class.

Technology

Go to the Glencoe Science Web site at **science.glencoe.com** or use the **Glencoe Science CD-ROM** for additional chapter assessment.

THE PRINCETON REVIEW **Test Practice**

In 1903, Ernest Rutherford placed radioactive uranium ore in a lead box with a small pinhole. He aimed it so that radiation escaping from the hole passed through an electric field to reach a photographic plate.

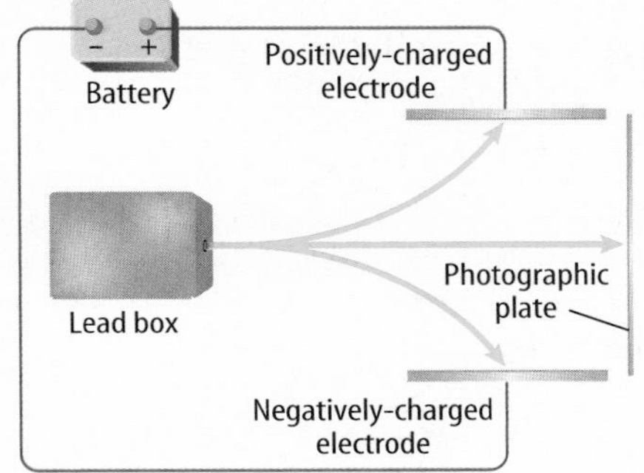

Study the diagram and answer the following questions.

1. In this experiment, beta particles were deflected toward the positive electrode while alpha particles were deflected toward the negative electrode because:
  A) Beta particles are negatively charged and alpha particles are positively charged.
  B) Beta particles have a negative charge and a larger mass than alpha particles.
  C) Beta particles have a positive charge and alpha particles are negative.
  D) Beta particles have a positive charge and a larger mass than alpha particles.

2. Why were gamma rays not deflected by the charged plates in this experiment?
  F) Gamma rays have negative charge.
  G) Gamma rays have positive charge.
  H) Gamma rays have no charge.
  J) Gamma rays travel too fast.

Assessment Resources

Reproducible Masters

Chapter Resources Booklet
Chapter Review, pp. 39–40
Chapter Tests, pp. 41–44
Assessment Transparency Activity, p. 53

Glencoe Science Web site
Interactive Tutor
Chapter Quizzess

Glencoe Technology
Assessment Transparency
Interactive CD-ROM Chapter Quizzes
ExamView Pro Test Bank
Vocabulary PuzzleMaker Software
MindJogger Videoquiz DVD/VHS

THE PRINCETON REVIEW **Test Practice**

The Test-Taking Tip was written by the Princeton Review, the nation's leader in test preparation.

1. A
2. H

Developing Skills

16. Encourage students to include diagrams in their presentations.
17. Check students' work.
18. a. alpha particle; b. beta particle
19. The graph shows no correlation between mass number and half-life.
20. In a nuclear fission chain reaction, the neutrons produced in the first reaction are used to start new reactions. These reactions are controlled by adding materials that absorb neutrons. If the reactions were not controlled, fission chain reactions would release huge amounts of energy and radiation in a short amount of time, as occurs in nuclear weapons.

Performance Assessment

21. Student reports should mention radon gas from the ground. Since radon is a source of alpha radiation, effects might include the possibility of lung damage from inhaling the gas. Use **PASC**, p. 143.

<table>
<tr><th rowspan="2">Section/Objectives</th><th colspan="2">Standards</th><th rowspan="2">Activities/Features</th></tr>
<tr><th>National</th><th>State/Local</th></tr>
<tr><td>Chapter Opener</td><td>See p. 37T for a Key to Standards.</td><td></td><td>Explore Activity: Observe solar heating, p. 289
Before You Read, p. 289</td></tr>
<tr><td>Section 1 Fossil Fuels
2 sessions
1 block
1. Discuss properties and uses of the three main types of fossil fuels.
2. Explain how fossil fuels are formed.
3. Describe how the chemical energy in fossil fuels is converted into electrical energy.</td><td>National Content Standards: UCP3, A1, B3 (5–8), B6 (9–12), E2, F3, F5 (5–8), F6 (9–12)</td><td></td><td>Visualizing the Formation of Fossil Fuels, p. 292
MiniLAB: Designing an Efficient Water Heater, p. 293</td></tr>
<tr><td>Section 2 Nuclear Energy
1 session
0.5 block
1. Outline the steps in the operation of a nuclear reactor.
2. Compare the advantages and disadvantages of using nuclear energy to produce electricity.
3. Discuss nuclear fusion as a possible energy source.</td><td>National Content Standards: UCP3, B1, B3 (5–8), B1, B6 (9–12), E2, F1, F2, F3, F4, F5 (5–8), F5, F6 (9–12)</td><td></td><td>Life Science Integration, p. 300
Earth Science Integration, p. 301
Science Online, p. 302
Problem-Solving Activity, p. 303</td></tr>
<tr><td>Section 3 Renewable Energy Sources
3 sessions
1.5 blocks
1. Analyze the need for alternate energy sources.
2. Describe alternate methods of generating electricity.
3. Compare the advantages and disadvantages of various alternate energy sources.</td><td>National Content Standards: UCP3, A2, B3 (5–8), B6 (9–12), E1, F3, F4, F5 (5–8), F4, F5, F6 (9–12)</td><td></td><td>MiniLAB: Using Solar Power, p. 306
Science Online, p. 309
Activity: Solar Heating, p. 311
Activity: How much does this energy really cost?, pp. 312–313
Science and Society: Reacting to Nuclear Energy, pp. 314–315</td></tr>
</table>

Activity Materials	Reproducible Resources	Section Assessment	Technology
Explore Activity: scissors, 2 coffee can lids, thermometer	**Chapter Resource Booklet** Foldables Worksheet, p. 17 Note-taking Worksheets, pp. 33–35	GLENCOE'S ASSESSMENT ADVANTAGE	
MiniLAB: candle, 50 mL water, beaker, aluminum chimney	**Chapter Resource Booklet** Transparency Activity, p. 44 MiniLAB, p. 3 Enrichment, p. 30 Reinforcement, p. 27 Directed Reading, p. 20	**Portfolio** Curricululm Connection, p. 291 Activity, p. 296 **Performance** MiniLAB, p. 293 Skill Builder Activities, p. 297 **Content** Section Assessment, p. 297	Section Focus Transparency Interactive CD-ROM/DVD Guided Reading Audio Program
Need materials? Contact Science Kit at 1-800-828-7777 or www.sciencekit.com on the Internet.	**Chapter Resource Booklet** Transparency Activity, p. 45 Enrichment, p. 31 Reinforcement, p. 28 Directed Reading, p. 20 Transparency Activity, pp. 47–48 **Mathematics Skill Activities,** p. 47	**Portfolio** Reteach, p. 304 **Performance** Skill Builder Activities, p. 304 **Content** Section Assessment, p. 304	Section Focus Transparency Teaching Transparency Interactive CD-ROM/DVD Guided Reading Audio Program
MiniLAB: cloth, scissors **Activity:** small cardboard boxes, black, white, and colored paper, tape or glue, thermometer, watch with a second hand **Activity:** Internet or other resources on energy costs	**Chapter Resource Booklet** Transparency Activity, p. 46 MiniLAB, p. 4 Enrichment, p. 32 Reinforcement, p. 29 Directed Reading, pp. 21, 22 Activity Worksheets, pp. 5–6, 7–8 Lab Activities, pp. 9–12, 13–16 **Reading and Writing Skill Activities,** p. 19 **Home and Community Involvement,** p. 42	**Portfolio** Challenge, p. 310 **Performance** MiniLAB, p. 306 Skill Builder Activities, p. 310 **Content** Section Assessment, p. 310	Section Focus Transparency Interactive CD-ROM/DVD Guided Reading Audio Program

End of Chapter Assessment

GLENCOE'S ASSESSMENT ADVANTAGE

Blackline Masters	Technology	Professional Series
Chapter Resources Booklet Chapter Review, pp. 37–38 Chapter Tests, pp. 39–42 **Standardized Test Practice by The Princeton Review,** pp. 44–47	MindJogger Videoquiz CD-ROM Explorations and Quizzes Vocabulary Puzzle Makers ExamView Pro Test Bank Interactive Lesson Planner Interactive Teacher's Edition	Performance Assessment in the Science Classroom (PASC)

Transparencies

Section Focus

Section 1 Section Focus Transparency **For Peat's Sake**

Dried peat has been used as fuel in many parts of the world for hundreds of years. Given enough time and pressure, peat will form a fossil fuel you are probably more familiar with—coal!

1. How might peat be used for energy?
2. Peat comes from bogs. What do you think it is composed of?

L1

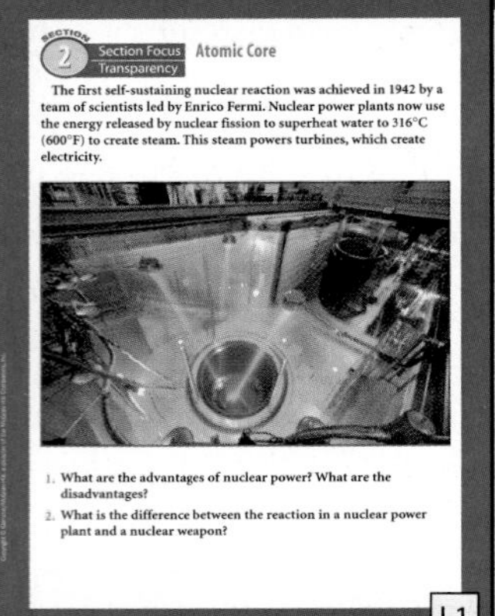
Section 2 Section Focus Transparency **Atomic Core**

The first self-sustaining nuclear reaction was achieved in 1942 by a team of scientists led by Enrico Fermi. Nuclear power plants now use the energy released by nuclear fission to superheat water to 316°C (600°F) to create steam. This steam powers turbines, which create electricity.

1. What are the advantages of nuclear power? What are the disadvantages?
2. What is the difference between the reaction in a nuclear power plant and a nuclear weapon?

L1

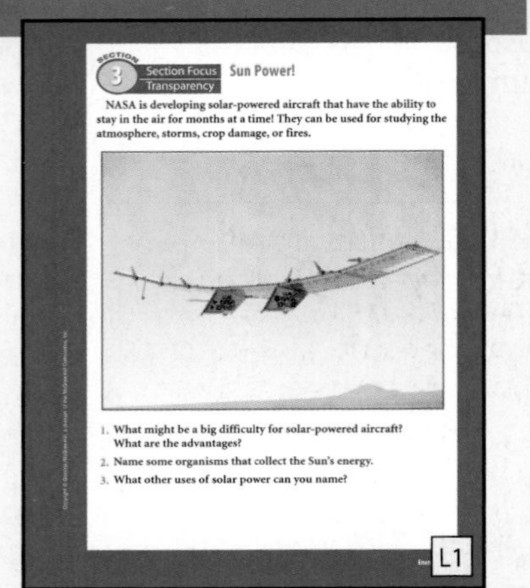
Section 3 Section Focus Transparency **Sun Power!**

NASA is developing solar-powered aircraft that have the ability to stay in the air for months at a time! They can be used for studying the atmosphere, storms, crop damage, or fires.

1. What might be a big difficulty for solar-powered aircraft? What are the advantages?
2. Name some organisms that collect the Sun's energy.
3. What other uses of solar power can you name?

L1

Assessment

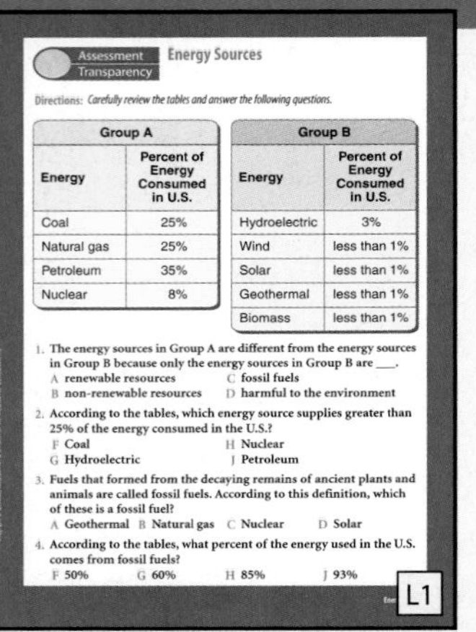
Assessment Transparency **Energy Sources**

Directions: Carefully review the tables and answer the following questions.

Group A	
Energy	Percent of Energy Consumed in U.S.
Coal	25%
Natural gas	25%
Petroleum	35%
Nuclear	8%

Group B	
Energy	Percent of Energy Consumed in U.S.
Hydroelectric	3%
Wind	less than 1%
Solar	less than 1%
Geothermal	less than 1%
Biomass	less than 1%

1. The energy sources in Group A are different from the energy sources in Group B because only the energy sources in Group B are ___.
   A renewable resources C fossil fuels
   B non-renewable resources D harmful to the environment
2. According to the tables, which energy source supplies greater than 25% of the energy consumed in the U.S.?
   F Coal H Nuclear
   G Hydroelectric J Petroleum
3. Fuels that formed from the decaying remains of ancient plants and animals are called fossil fuels. According to this definition, which of these is a fossil fuel?
   A Geothermal B Natural gas C Nuclear D Solar
4. According to the tables, what percent of the energy used in the U.S. comes from fossil fuels?
   F 50% G 60% H 85% J 93%

L1

Teaching

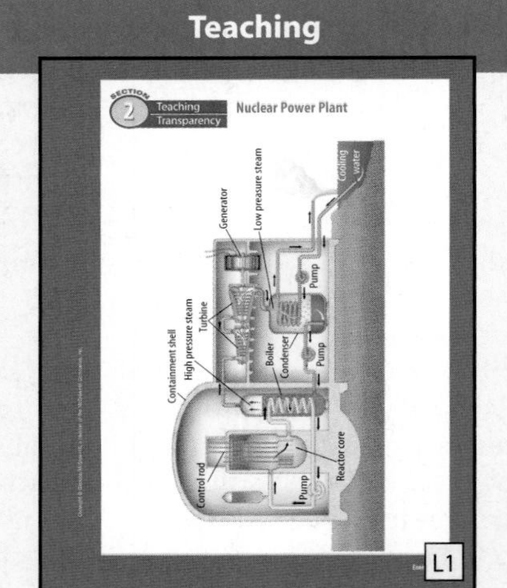
Section 2 Teaching Transparency **Nuclear Power Plant**

L1

This is a representation of key blackline masters available in the Teacher Classroom Resources. See Resource Manager boxes within the chapter for additional information.

Key to Teaching Strategies

The following designations will help you decide which activities are appropriate for your students.

L1 Level 1 activities should be appropriate for students with learning difficulties.

L2 Level 2 activities should be within the ability range of all students.

L3 Level 3 activities are designed for above-average students.

ELL ELL activities should be within the ability range of English Language Learners.

COOP LEARN Cooperative Learning activities are designed for small group work.

LS Multiple Learning Styles logos are used throughout to indicate strategies that address different learning styles.

P These strategies represent student products that can be placed into a best-work portfolio.

Hands-on Activities

Activity Worksheets

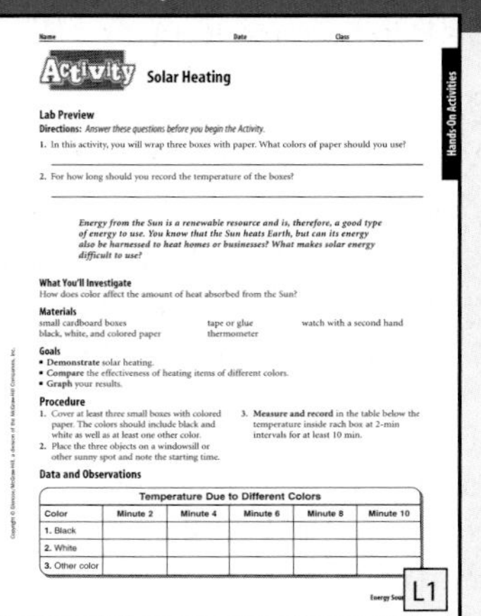
Name Date Class

Activity **Solar Heating**

Lab Preview

Directions: *Answer these questions before you begin the Activity.*

1. In this activity, you will wrap three boxes with paper. What colors of paper should you use?
2. For how long should you record the temperature of the boxes?

Energy from the Sun is a renewable resource and is, therefore, a good type of energy to use. You know that the Sun heats Earth, but can its energy also be harnessed to heat homes or businesses? What makes solar energy difficult to use?

What You'll Investigate

How does color affect the amount of heat absorbed from the Sun?

Materials

small cardboard boxes
black, white, and colored paper
tape or glue
thermometer
watch with a second hand

Goals

- **Demonstrate** solar heating.
- **Compare** the effectiveness of heating items of different colors.
- **Graph** your results.

Procedure

1. Cover at least three small boxes with colored paper. The colors should include black and white as well as at least one other color.
2. Place the three objects on a windowsill or other sunny spot and note the starting time.
3. **Measure and record** in the table below the temperature inside rach box at 2-min intervals for at least 10 min.

Data and Observations

Temperature Due to Different Colors

Color	Minute 2	Minute 4	Minute 6	Minute 8	Minute 10
1. Black					
2. White					
3. Other color					

Hands-On Activities

L1

Laboratory Activities

Name Date Class

LAB 1 Laboratory Activity **Solar Cells**

The sun's radiant energy drives the weather and water cycles of the Earth. This energy is necessary to sustain life on Earth. It may also be powering your pocket calculator or providing the hot water for your next shower.

Many pocket calculators contain solar cells. A solar cell is a device that converts radiant energy into electrical energy. In a circuit, a solar cell can produce an electric current. In this experiment you will investigate the power output of solar cells.

Strategy

You will determine the power of output of a solar cell.
You will describe how the power output of a solar cell is related to the power rating of its energy source.
You will compare sunlight and artificial sources of radiant energy.

Materials

25-, 60-, 75-, and 100-W lightbulbs
4 10-cm lengths of insulated wire
light socket and cord
utility clamp
ring stand
meterstick
masking tape
solar cell
DC voltmeter
DC ammeter
switch

Procedure

Part A—Artificial Sources of Light

1. Place the 25-W lightbulb into the light socket.
2. Attach the utility clamp to the ring stand. Use the utility clamp to position the light socket so that the bulb is 50 cm above the desk top. **CAUTION:** *Tape the socket's electrical cord onto the desk top so that no one can trip over the cord or topple the ring stand.*
3. Place the solar cell parallel to the desk and directly beneath the bulb.
4. Connect the voltmeter, ammeter, switch, and solar cell with the insulated wires as shown in Figure 1.
5. Plug the socket cord into an electrical outlet. Darken the room.

Figure 1

Hands-On Activities

L1

Meeting Different Ability Levels

Content Outline

Note-taking Worksheet — Energy Sources

Section 1 Fossil Fuels

L1

Reinforcement

Reinforcement — Fossil Fuels

L1

Directed Reading

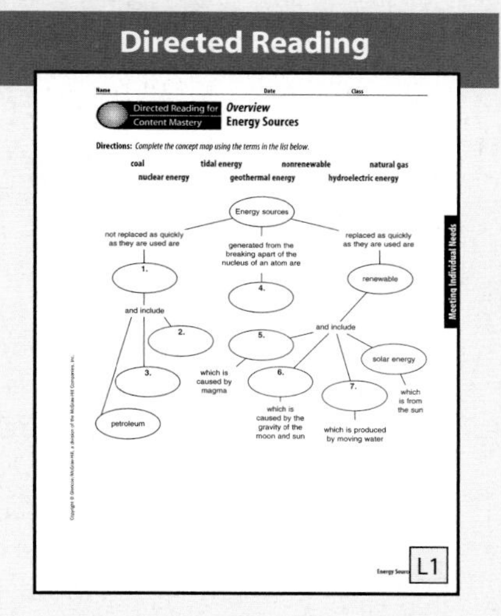

Directed Reading for Content Mastery — Overview: Energy Sources

L1

Enrichment

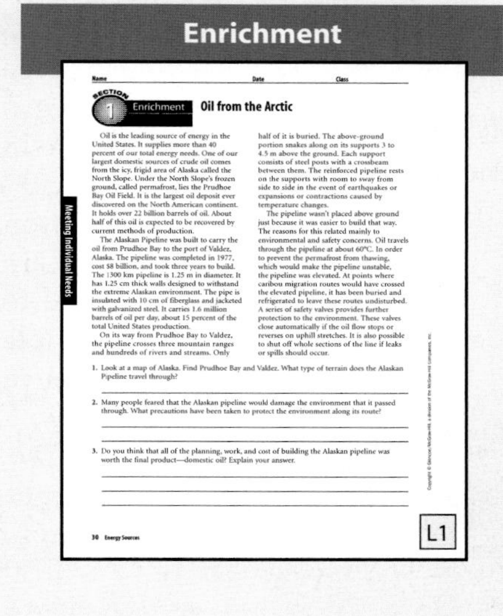

Enrichment — Oil from the Arctic

L1

Spanish Directed Reading

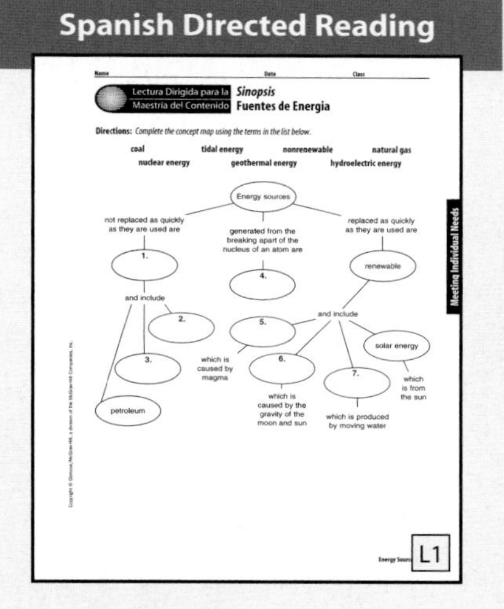

Lectura Dirigida para la Maestría del Contenido — Sinopsis: Fuentes de Energía

L1

Assessment

Chapter Tests

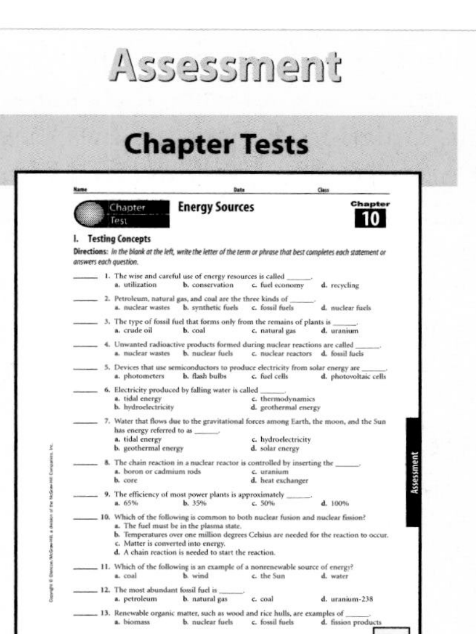

Chapter Test — Energy Sources — Chapter 10

L1

Test Practice Workbook

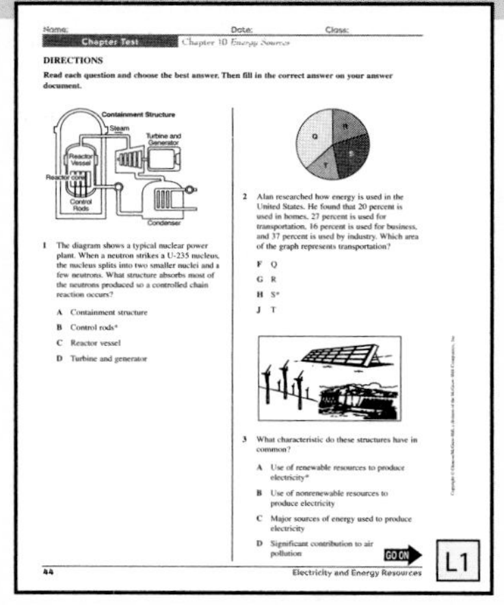

Chapter Test — Chapter 10 Energy Sources

L1

Chapter Review

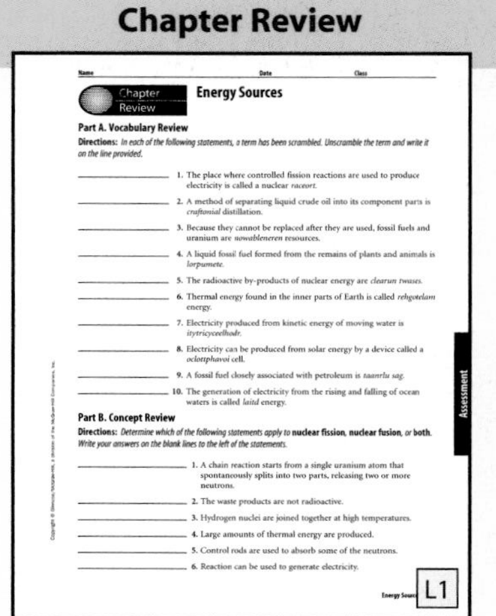

Chapter Review — Energy Sources

L1

Science Content Background

SECTION 1

Fossil Fuels

Making Fossil Fuels

Fossil fuels were once living organisms that obtained energy directly or indirectly from the Sun and can therefore be considered a type of solar energy. Unlike the direct use of solar energy, burning fossil fuels produces carbon dioxide gas and other pollutants.

Kerosene was once the most important product from petroleum because of its use in kerosene lanterns. Kerosene is now used mainly for jet fuel and as a carrier in insecticide sprays.

Generating Electricity

Whether using fossil fuels, geothermal energy, or nuclear power, the generation of electricity involves heating water to produce steam to turn turbines. Hydropower, wind, and tidal energy turn turbines, but water is not heated to produce steam.

A.J. Copley/Visuals Unlimited

Fun Fact

Fossil fuels currently supply nearly 90 percent of all the energy consumed by the industrially developed nations of the world

Nuclear Energy

Using Nuclear Energy

The law of conservation of energy was assumed to be true until Einstein suggested that mass could be converted into energy and energy into mass. Einstein's famous equation, $E=mc2$, shows that a small amount of matter can be converted into an astonishing amount of energy.

Gamma ray exposure is sometimes compared to the equivalent exposure in X-rays. For example, a nuclear weapons worker may have had a yearly dose that is equivalent to one chest X-ray. While the amount of radiation received may be the same, the gamma rays are more energetic, resulting in more ionization and greater risks of biological damage.

France is the world leader in electrical power generation from nuclear fission. Approximately three-quarters of France's electrical energy is generated by this process.

The only approved permanent storage site for radioactive wastes is Yucca Mountain in Nevada. Some scientists believe this is a good site because it is far from major populations, it has low levels of rainfall, and the water table is very deep.

SECTION 3

Renewable Energy Sources

Energy from the Sun

The materials required to generate electricity from solar energy are expensive. The materials to use the sun's energy for heating are, however, relatively inexpensive. Piping and a box with a glass roof are the fundamental parts of many solar water heaters. Unfortunately, only one million homes in the United States use solar water heating. Some states, such as North Carolina and Arizona, give tax incentives for the installation of solar water heaters. Passive solar heating of spaces in houses is another low cost way to use the sun's energy. New houses are increasingly being designed with windows facing the south to absorb the sun's energy in wintertime. Overhangs on the houses prevent the Sun's entry in the summertime.

Energy from Inside Earth

You don't need to live near a volcano to use geothermal energy. Heat pumps, in use in 400,000 United States homes, take advantage of fairly constant below ground temperatures. The temperature range in the first ten feet of soil is 10° to 15.5°C (50° to 60°F). This usually means the soil is warmer than the winter air and cooler than the summer air. In a heat pump, air either gains or loses heat to the ground before entering a heating or cooling unit.

Alternative Fuels

When animal manure is decomposed by anaerobic fermentation or digestion, methane gas is produced. This can be collected and used as a source of fuel for, among other things, generating electricity. Farms with 800 head of cattle can produce enough methane to supply the farm's electrical needs with enough left over to sell extra electricity to the local electric company. Methane is a greenhouse gas, and this process helps prevent additional methane from entering the atmosphere.

Fun Fact

Iceland leads the world in the use of geothermal energy for heating. Almost 90% of Iceland's buildings are warmed using water heated by hot magma below the surface of the Earth. Major towns have outdoor swimming pools heated by water, enabling people to swim even in the cold winters.

For additional content background on this topic, go to the Glencoe Science Web site at science.glencoe.com.

Bill Banaszewski/Visuals Unlimited

CHAPTER 

Energy Sources

Chapter Vocabulary

fossil fuels
petroleum
nonrenewable resource
nuclear reactor
nuclear waste
renewable resource
photovoltaic cell
hydroelectricity
geothermal energy
biomass

What do you think?

Science Journal The photograph shows a solar cell. This device converts energy from the sun into electricity.

CHAPTER 10

Energy Sources

It takes energy to build a car. The welding torches use energy. The robots that operate the torches require energy. The assembly line runs on energy. And the car, when it is finished, will need energy to be driven. Energy heats and cools your home, refrigerates and cooks your food, pumps your water, and turns on your lights. Where does all that energy come from? How does it get to your home? Will we ever run out of energy? In this chapter, you will learn about different energy sources, how they produce energy, and how they affect the environment.

What do you think?

Science Journal Look at the picture below with a classmate. Discuss what you think this is or what is happening. Here's a hint: *It can be used to operate a calculator.* Write your answer or best guess in your Science Journal.

Theme Connection

Energy People use energy from many different sources. Fossil fuels are the primary source of energy, but nuclear reactions, solar power, hydroelectric power, and geothermal power also are used.

Explore Activity

The Sun constantly bathes our planet with enormous amounts of energy, and this energy can be captured and used to make electricity, heat homes, and provide hot water. In this activity, you will explore a way to capture the Sun's energy to heat water.

Observe solar heating

1. Use scissors to poke a small hole in the center of two coffee can lids.
2. Fill a coffee can that is painted black with water at room temperature. Snap on the lid, and push a thermometer through the hole in the lid. Record the temperature.
3. Fill a coffee can that is painted white with water at room temperature. Snap on the lid, and push a thermometer through the hole in the lid. Record the temperature.
4. Place both cans in direct sunlight for 15 min.

Observe

Write a paragraph in your Science Journal explaining why the temperature change differed between the two cans.

Before You Read

Foldables Reading & Study Skills

Making a Concept Map Study Fold Make the following Foldable to help you organize information by diagramming ideas about energy sources.

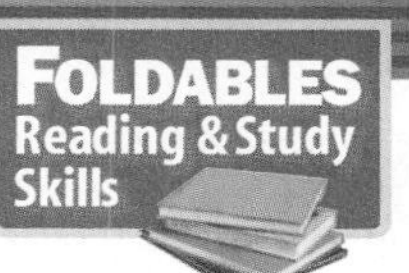

1. Place a sheet of paper in front of you so the long side is at the top. Fold the bottom of the paper up, stopping about four centimeters from the top.
2. Draw an oval above the fold. Write *Energy* in the oval.
3. Fold both sides in. Unfold. Through the top thickness of the paper, cut along each of the fold lines to form three tabs. Draw an oval on each tab and draw arrows from the large oval to the smaller ovals.
4. Write *Fossil Fuels, Nuclear Energy,* and *Renewable* Energy Sources in the ovals. Draw three smaller ovals, but don't write in them yet.
5. As you read the chapter, write about each source of energy under the tabs.

Explore Activity

Purpose Use the Explore activity to show students how one form of energy can be transformed into another form that we can use. L2 ELL LS **Kinesthetic**

Preparation To save time, you may want to paint coffee cans and cut holes in the lids ahead of time.

Materials scissors, coffee cans with lids, white paint, black paint, water, thermometer

Teaching Strategy Identify a place that gets direct sunlight where students can leave the cans for 15 minutes.

Observe

The temperature change will be greater in the black can because the color black absorbs heat and the color white reflects heat away. Drawings will vary, but could include a large, black container of water exposed to direct sunlight.

Assessment

Process Ask students to make data tables and to record in the tables the temperature readings for each can every two minutes. Use **Performance Assessment in the Science Classroom,** p. 109.

Before You Read

Foldables Reading & Study Skills

Dinah Zike Study Fold

Purpose Students make a Foldable concept map to help them define, collect data on, and list examples of three energy sources—fossil fuels, nuclear energy, and alternative sources.

For additional help, see Foldables Worksheet, p. 17 in **Chapter Resources Booklet,** or go to the Glencoe Science Web site at **science.glencoe.com.** See After You Read in the Study Guide at the end of this chapter.

SECTION

Fossil Fuels

1 Motivate

Bellringer Transparency

Display the Section Focus Transparency for Section 1. Use the accompanying Transparency Activity Master. L2 ELL

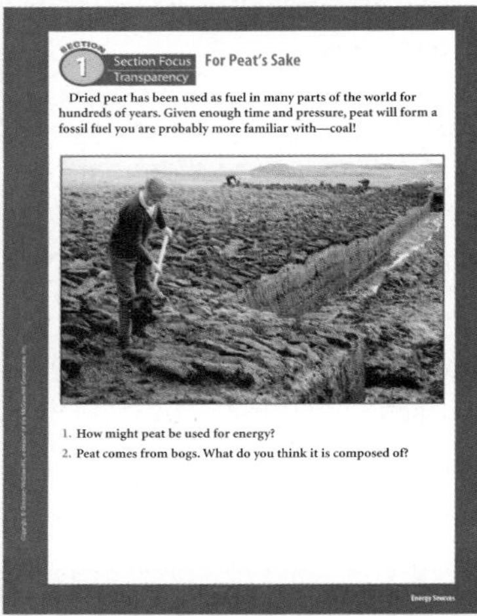

Section 1 Section Focus Transparency **For Peat's Sake**

Dried peat has been used as fuel in many parts of the world for hundreds of years. Given enough time and pressure, peat will form a fossil fuel you are probably more familiar with—coal!

1. How might peat be used for energy?
2. Peat comes from bogs. What do you think it is composed of?

Tie to Prior Knowledge

Ask students to name the last time they rode in a bus or car. Tell them that the energy that made the vehicle move came from fossil fuels. In this section, they will learn about various types of fossil fuels that are useful sources of energy.

SECTION 1

Fossil Fuels

As You Read

What You'll Learn

- **Discuss** properties and uses of the three main types of fossil fuels.
- **Explain** how fossil fuels are formed.
- **Describe** how the chemical energy in fossil fuels is converted into electrical energy.

Vocabulary

fossil fuels
petroleum
nonrenewable resource

Why It's Important

Fossil fuels are widely used to generate electricity.

Using Energy

How many different ways have you used electricity today? You can see energy being used in many ways, throughout the day, such as those shown in **Figure 1.** Furnaces and stoves use thermal energy to heat buildings and cook food. Air conditioners use electrical energy to move thermal energy outdoors. Cars and other vehicles use mechanical energy to carry people and materials from one part of the country to another.

Transforming Energy According to the law of conservation of energy, energy cannot be created or destroyed. Energy can only be transformed, or converted, from one form to another. To use energy means to transform one form of energy to another form of energy that can perform a useful function. For example, energy is used when the chemical energy in fuels is transformed into thermal energy that is used to heat your home.

Sometimes energy is transformed into a form that isn't useful. For example, when an electric current flows through power lines, about 10 percent of the electrical energy is changed to thermal energy. This reduces the amount of useful electrical energy that is delivered to homes, schools, and businesses.

Figure 1
Energy is used in many ways.

A A steel plant uses energy to make steel products.

B Automobiles burn gasoline to provide energy.

C Power lines like these carry the electrical energy you use everyday.

Section Assessment Planner

PORTFOLIO
Curriculum Connection, p. 291
Activity, p. 296

PERFORMANCE ASSESSMENT
MiniLAB, p. 293
Skill Building Activities, p. 297
See page 318 for more options.

CONTENT ASSESSMENT
Section, p. 297
Challenge, p. 297
Chapter, pp. 318–319

290 CHAPTER 10 Energy Sources

Energy Use in the United States More energy is used in the United states than in any other country in the world. **Figure 2A** shows how energy is used in the United States. About 20 percent of the energy is used in homes for heating and cooling, to run appliances, and to provide lighting and hot water. About 27 percent is used for transportation to power vehicles such as cars, trucks, and aircraft. Another 16 percent is used by businesses to heat, cool, and light stores, shops, and office buildings. Finally, about 37 percent of this energy is used by industry and agriculture to manufacture products and produce food. **Figure 2B** shows the main sources of the energy used in the United States. Almost 85 percent of the energy used in the United States comes from burning petroleum, natural gas, and coal. Nuclear power plants provide about eight percent of the energy used in the United States.

Energy Usage

Residential 20%
Industrial 37%
Business 16%
Transportation 27%
A

Sources of Energy

Hydroelectric 3%
Biomass 4%
Petroleum 39%
Nuclear 8%
Coal 23%
Natural gas 23%
B

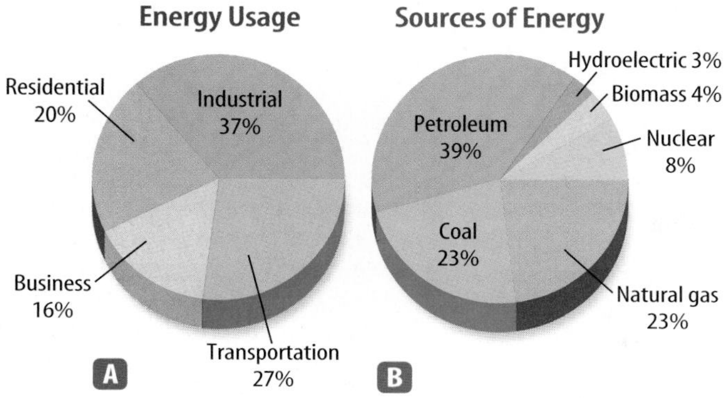

Figure 2
A This circle graph shows the percentages of energy in the United States used by homes, businesses, transportation and industry. B This circle graph shows the sources of the energy used in the United States.

Making Fossil Fuels

Electricity travels through power lines at lightning-fast speed. It may be hard to believe that it took millions of years to make the fuels that are used to produce electricity, provide heat, and transport people and materials. **Figure 4** on the next page shows how coal, petroleum, and natural gas are formed by the decay of ancient plants and animals. Fuels such as petroleum, or oil, natural gas, and coal are called **fossil fuels** because they are formed from the decaying remains of ancient plants and animals.

Concentrated Energy Sources When fossil fuels are burned, carbon and hydrogen atoms combine with oxygen molecules in the air to form carbon dioxide and water molecules. This process converts the chemical energy that is stored in the chemical bonds between atoms to heat and light. Compared to other fuels such as wood, the chemical energy that is stored in fossil fuels is more concentrated. For example, burning 1kg of coal releases two to three times as much energy as burning 1 kg of wood. **Figure 3** shows the amount of energy that is produced by burning different fossil fuels.

Figure 3
The bar graph shows the amount of energy contained in one gram of four different fuels. ***Which fuel is least efficient when it is burned?***

Energy Content of Fuels

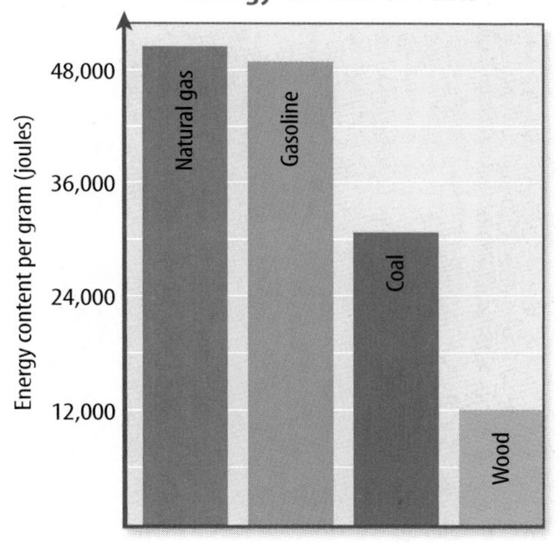

2 Teach

Using Energy

Teacher FYI

The Organization of Petroleum Exporting Countries (OPEC) is a group of thirteen countries that own most of the world's crude oil reserves. They work together to coordinate petroleum policy. Member nations are Algeria, Ecuador, Gabon, Indonesia, Iran, Iraq, Kuwait, Libya, Nigeria, Qatar, Saudi Arabia, the United Arab Emirates, and Venezuela.

Extension

Ask students to find out how much energy is used per person in other developed nations, compared with the amount used in the United States. In other developed nations, about half as much energy is used per person as is used in the United States. L3 LS **Logical-Mathematical**

Caption Answer

Figure 3 wood

Making Fossil Fuels

Discussion

Are fossil fuels still being made today? The physical and chemical processes that made fossil fuels are still acting on decaying organic matter on Earth's crust. However, the rate at which new fuel is being made is tiny compared with the rate at which it is being used. Also, less organic matter like that which created fossil fuels is dying and decaying today. L3 LS **Logical-Mathematical**

Resource Manager

Chapter Resources Booklet
- Transparency Activity, p. 44
- Note-taking Worksheets, pp. 33–35
- Directed Reading for Content Mastery, p. 20

Curriculum Connection

Language Arts Power outages sometimes occur because of severe snowstorms, flooding, or other natural disasters. Have each student write a story about how he or she would survive an imaginary week-long loss of electricity, natural gas, and gasoline. Students should describe their daily routines and include ideas for alternate sources of energy. L2 LS **Linguistic** P

Visualizing the Formation of Fossil Fuels

Have students examine the pictures and read the captions. Then ask the following questions.

- **Do you think coal is being formed now? Explain.** Yes, coal is still being formed in areas where peat from partially decomposed vegetation is being covered by sediment.
- **Why do oil and gas sometimes bubble to the surface, while coal never does?** Oil (a liquid) and natural gas (a gas) are less dense than the surrounding rock. Coal is a solid and its density is not low enough for it to rise to the surface.

Activity

Divide the class into three groups. Assign each group a different fossil fuel: coal, oil, and natural gas. Have students in each group research the locations of deposits of the fuel and plot the distribution on an outline map of the world. Display the three maps and discuss which parts of the world have the largest concentrations of each fossil fuel. L2

LS **Visual-Spatial**

Extension

Have students research the discoveries of bog mummies that have been made by peat cutters in northern Europe where peat is still sometimes used as a fuel. Have students write reports on the conditions that caused the peat bogs to form and that also mummified the bodies. L3

LS **Linguistic**

NATIONAL GEOGRAPHIC VISUALIZING THE FORMATION OF FOSSIL FUELS

Figure 4

Oil and natural gas form when organic matter on the ocean floor, gradually buried under additional layers of sediment, is chemically changed by heat and crushing pressure. The oil and gas may bubble to the surface or become trapped beneath a dense rock layer. Coal forms when peat—partially decomposed vegetation—is compressed by overlying sediments and transformed first into lignite (soft brown coal) and then into harder, bituminous (buh TYEW muh nus) coal. These two processes are shown below.

HOW OIL AND NATURAL GAS ARE FORMED

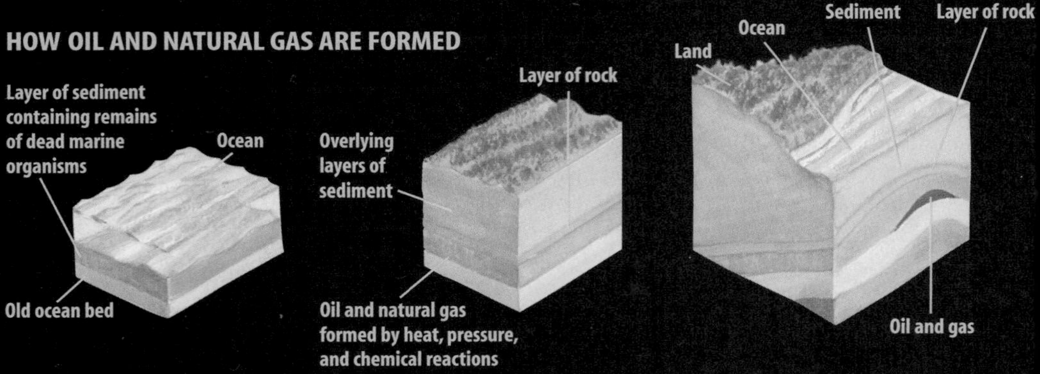

Layer of sediment containing remains of dead marine organisms

Ocean

Old ocean bed

Overlying layers of sediment

Layer of rock

Oil and natural gas formed by heat, pressure, and chemical reactions

Land

Ocean

Sediment

Layer of rock

Oil and gas

HOW COAL IS FORMED

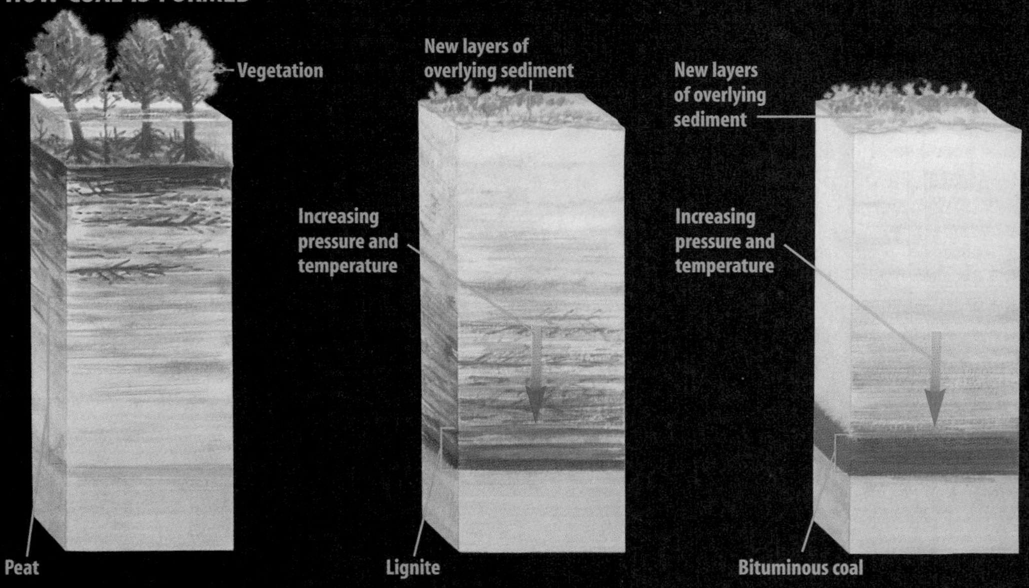

Vegetation

Peat

New layers of overlying sediment

Increasing pressure and temperature

Lignite

New layers of overlying sediment

Increasing pressure and temperature

Bituminous coal

Resource Manager 

Chapter Resources Booklet
MiniLAB, p. 3

Life Science Critical Thinking/Problem Solving, p. 12

Physical Science Critical Thinking/Problem Solving, p. 14

Petroleum

Millions of gallons of petroleum or crude oil are pumped every day from wells drilled deep into Earth's crust. **Petroleum** is a thick, greenish-brown, highly flammable liquid formed by decayed ancient organisms, such as microscopic plankton and algae. Petroleum is a mixture of thousands of chemical compounds. Most of these compounds are hydrocarbons, which means they contain only carbon and hydrogen.

Separating Hydrocarbons The different hydrocarbon molecules found in petroleum have different numbers and arrangements of carbon and hydrogen atoms. The composition and structure of hydrocarbons determines their properties.

The many different compounds that are found in petroleum are separated in a process called fractional distillation. This separation occurs in the tall towers of oil-refinery plants. First, crude oil is pumped into the bottom of the tower and heated. The chemical compounds in the crude oil boil and vaporize according to their individual boiling points. Materials with the lowest boiling points rise to the top of the tower as vapor and are collected. Hydrocarbons with high boiling points, such as asphalt and some types of waxes, remain liquid and are drained off through the bottom of the tower.

✔ Reading Check *What is fractional distillation used for?*

Other Uses for Petroleum Not all of the products obtained from petroleum are burned to produce energy. About 16 percent of the petroleum-based substances that are used in the United States go toward nonfuel uses. Look around at the materials in your home or classroom. Do you see any plastics? In addition to fuels, plastics and synthetic fabrics are made from the hydrocarbons found in crude petroleum. Also, lubricants such as grease and motor oil, as well as the asphalt used in surfacing roads, are obtained from petroleum. Some synthetic materials produced from petroleum are shown in **Figure 5.**

Mini LAB

Designing an Efficient Water Heater

Procedure

1. Measure and record the mass of a **candle.**
2. Measure 50 mL of **water** into a **beaker.** Record the temperature of the water.
3. Use the lighted candle to increase the temperature of the water by 10°C. Put out the candle and measure its mass again.
4. Repeat steps 1 to 3 with an **aluminum chimney** surrounding the candle to help direct the heat upward.

Analysis

1. Compare the mass change in the two trials. Does a smaller or larger mass change in the candle show greater efficiency?
2. Gas burners are used to heat hot-water tanks. What must be considered in the design of these heaters?

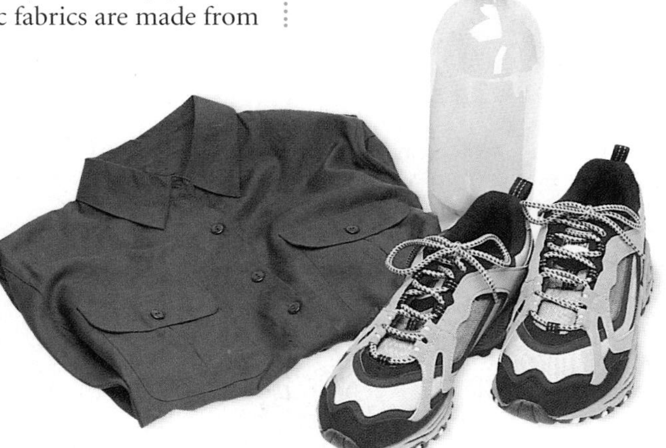

Figure 5
The objects shown here are made from chemical compounds found in petroleum.

Petroleum

Mini LAB

Purpose Students determine how heating efficiency can be improved. L1 ELL
LS **Kinesthetic**

Materials candle, water, foil, 100-mL beaker, thermometer, ring stand and ring, balance, wire gauze, graduated cylinder

Teaching Strategies

- Demonstrate how to set up the equipment. Place wire guaze between the ring stand and the beaker for more even heating.
- Encourage students to experiment with chimney size, shape, and location. Soot on the beaker improves the efficiency of heating.

Analysis

1. The mass changes less when the chimney is used. A smaller change in mass shows greater efficiency.
2. directing the flow of heat, controlling heating so that water will not turn to steam and expand

✔ Assessment

Oral How would the results differ if the temperature of the water were increased by 30° in each case? There would be a greater change in the candle's mass, especially if the chimney were not used. **Use Performance Assessment in the Science Classroom, p. 89.** P

Cultural Diversity

Oil-Rich Countries More than 65% of the world's oil reserves are in the Middle East. Have students research some of the changes that have occurred in these countries since oil was discovered in them. Possible answer: the economies of these countries are now based on income from the sale of oil. They have better health care, roads, schools, and other public facilities than they had before. L3 LS **Linguistic** P

Curriculum Connection

History In 1973, the Arab oil embargo caused an energy crisis in the United States that forced people to carefully examine their dependence on oil. Have groups of students research this topic and create computer presentations about related major events since that time. Topics might include the economic recession caused by the oil crisis or causes of the Persian Gulf War. L3 LS **Interpersonal**

✔ Reading Check

Answer to separate the many different compounds found in petroleum

Natural Gas

Fun Fact

Natural gas is often transported and stored as a liquid. By cooling natural gas until it becomes a liquid, 600 L can be reduced to 1 L.

Discussion

Natural gas has no odor. Why might natural gas distributors add an odorant to the gas? so you can tell if there is a gas leak L2 LS **Logical-Mathematical**

Coal

Extension

Fluidized-bed combustion of coal burns coal more efficiently and produces fewer pollutants than conventional coal boilers. Have students find out more about this technology. In fluidized-bed combustion, powdered coal is mixed with crushed limestone and suspended by a stream of hot air blown over it. The hot air removes the sulfur dioxide and some of the nitrogen oxide, so the coal burns more cleanly and more efficiently. Fluidized-bed combustion of coal is being used in Europe and China. L3 LS **Logical-Mathematical**

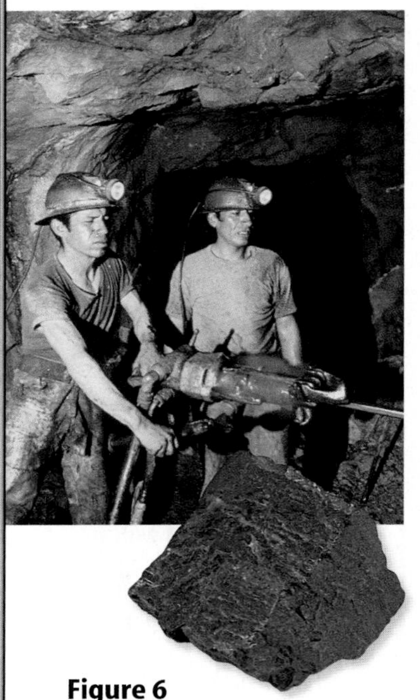

Figure 6
Coal mines usually are located deep underground.

Natural Gas

The chemical processes that produce petroleum as ancient organisms decay also produce gaseous compounds called natural gas. These compounds rise to the top of the petroleum deposit and are trapped there. Natural gas is composed mostly of methane, CH_4, but it also contains other hydrocarbon gases such as propane, C_3H_8, and butane, C_4H_{10}. Natural gas is burned to provide energy for cooking, heating, and manufacturing. About one fourth of the energy consumed in the United States comes from burning natural gas. There's a good chance that your home has a stove, furnace, hot-water heater, or clothes drier that uses natural gas.

Natural gas contains more energy per kilogram than petroleum or coal does. It also burns more cleanly than other fossil fuels, produces fewer pollutants, and leaves no residue such as ash.

Coal

Coal is a solid fossil fuel that is found in mines underground, such as the one shown in **Figure 6.** In the first half of the twentieth century, most houses in the United States were heated by burning coal. In fact, during this time, coal provided more than half of the energy that is used in the United States. Now almost two-thirds of the energy used comes from petroleum and natural gas, and only about one fourth comes from coal. About 90 percent of all the coal that is used in the United States is burned by power plants to generate electricity.

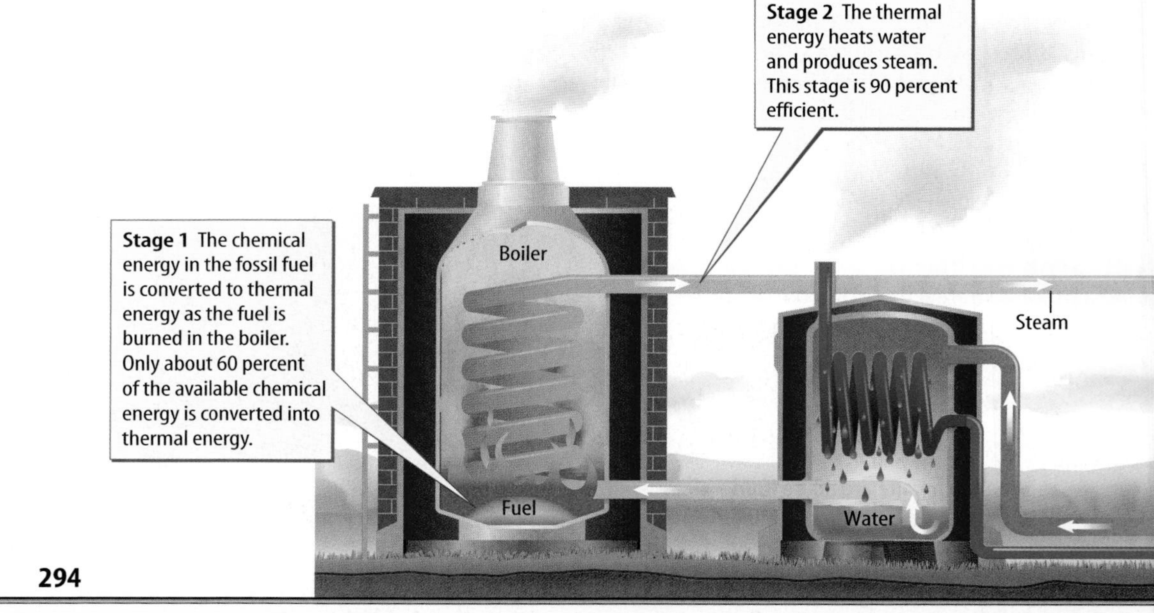

Stage 2 The thermal energy heats water and produces steam. This stage is 90 percent efficient.
Stage 1 The chemical energy in the fossil fuel is converted to thermal energy as the fuel is burned in the boiler. Only about 60 percent of the available chemical energy is converted into thermal energy.
Boiler
Steam
Fuel
Water

294

Visual Learning

Figure 8 Review with students the stages in producing electricity from fossil fuels. Which stage is least efficient? Stage 1 Discuss with students why this is the least efficient stage in the process. Possible reasons include incomplete combustion of the fuel and side reactions that use up thermal energy. L2 LS **Logical-Mathematical**

Teacher FYI

The four largest coal reserves in the United States are the Four Corners Region near northern New Mexico, the Powder River Basin in Montana and Wyoming, the Eastern Interior Region around Illinois, and the Appalachian Region from Pennsylvania to Alabama.

Origin of Coal Coal mines were once the site of ancient swamps where large, fernlike plants grew. Coal formed from this plant material. Worldwide, the amount of coal that is potentially available is estimated to be 20 to 40 times greater than the supply of petroleum.

Coal also is a complex mixture of hydrocarbons and other chemical compounds. Compared to petroleum and natural gas, coal contains more impurities, such as sulfur. As a result, more pollutants, such as sulfur dioxide, are produced when coal is burned.

Generating Electricity

Figure 7 shows that almost 70 percent of the electrical energy used in the United States is produced by burning fossil fuels. How is the chemical energy contained in fossil fuels converted to electrical energy in an electric power station?

The process is shown in **Figure 8.** In the first stage, fuel is burned in a boiler or combustion chamber, and it releases thermal energy. In the second stage, this thermal energy heats water and produces steam under high pressure. In the third stage, the steam strikes the blades of a turbine, causing it to spin. The shaft of the turbine is connected to an electric generator. In the fourth stage, electric current is produced when the spinning turbine shaft rotates magnets inside the generator. In the final stage, the electric current is transmitted to homes, schools, and businesses through power lines.

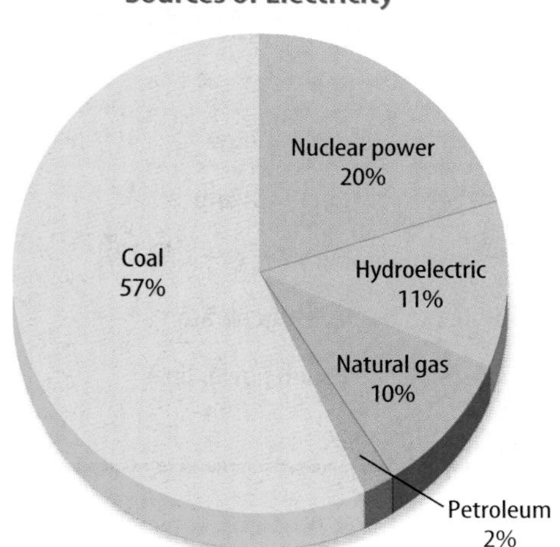

Figure 7
This circle graph shows the percentage of electricity generated in the United States that comes from various energy sources.

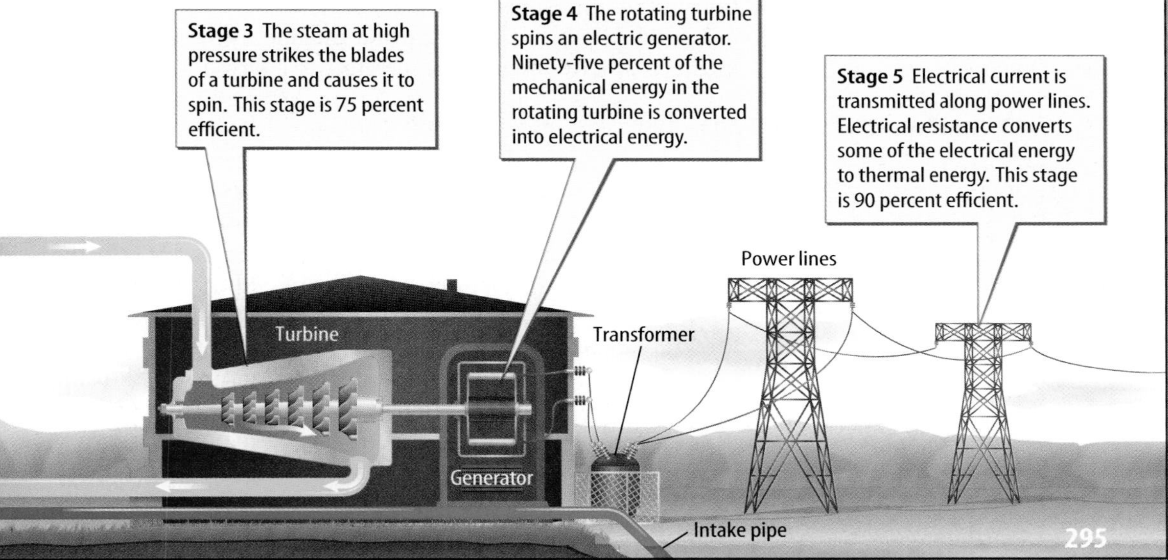

Stage 3 The steam at high pressure strikes the blades of a turbine and causes it to spin. This stage is 75 percent efficient.
Stage 4 The rotating turbine spins an electric generator. Ninety-five percent of the mechanical energy in the rotating turbine is converted into electrical energy.
Stage 5 Electrical current is transmitted along power lines. Electrical resistance converts some of the electrical energy to thermal energy. This stage is 90 percent efficient.
Power lines
Turbine
Transformer
Generator
Intake pipe
295

Figure 8
Fossil fuels are burned to generate electricity in a power plant.

Quick Demo

Bring to class some peat and samples of the four different types of coal for students to examine. Explain that the four types of coal are distinguished by the pressure that produced them. Lignite is produced when rock and soil pressed down on buried peat, causing it to dry out and harden. Further pressure produces subbituminous coal, then bituminous coal, and finally anthracite. L2 LS **Visual-Spatial**

Generating Electricity

Discussion

Electricity became the major source of power in the United States during the twentieth century. **What were the sources of power before that?** Possible answers include running water and steam. L2 LS **Logical-Mathematical**

Visual Learning

Figure 7 Review with students the information shown in Figure 7. What are the percentages of the three energy sources that are fossil fuels? What do they add up to? Coal 57%, natural gas 10%, and petroleum 2%. These add up to 69%. L2 LS **Visual-Spatial**

Resource Manager

Chapter Resources Booklet
Enrichment, p. 30
Cultural Diversity, p. 45
Science Inquiry Labs, p. 33

Curriculum Connection

History Electricity has been a major source of power in the United States for less than 100 years. Have students research the early history of the use of electricity in the United States. The first central power plant opened in California in 1879. In 1882, Edison opened an electric power plant that lit light bulbs. The first electric power was direct current. Power plants now produce alternating current. L3 LS **Linguistic**

Efficiency of Power Plants

Discussion

What is the primary way in which energy is lost in power plants? Energy is lost as heat.

The Costs of Using Fossil Fuels

Extension

In 1997, leaders from around the world met in Japan to consider the Kyoto Protocol for reducing harmful fossil fuel emissions. Have students write reports about the Protocol. The Kyoto Protocol would require participating countries to reduce harmful fossil fuel emissions by an average of 5% below their 1990 level. Some countries refused to ratify the Protocol because of the negative impact it would have on their economies. L3 LS **Linguistic**

Activity

Have students draw diagrams showing how burning fossil fuels causes pollution. Diagrams might illustrate smog formed when fossil fuels are burned, and the effects of ozone near Earth's surface. Students might also draw plants using devices that remove the pollutants before they can reach the air. L3 LS **Visual-Spatial** P

Nonrenewable Resources

Discussion

What might happen when readily available fossil fuels are used up? Possible answers: Alternative energy sources will be developed; companies will exploit more expensive sources of fossil fuels; people's way of life will change because energy will not be available. L2 LS **Logical-Mathematical**

Table 1 Efficiency of Fossil Fuel Conversion

Process	Efficiency (%)
Chemical to thermal energy	60
Conversion of water to steam	90
Steam-turning turbine	75
Turbine spins electric generator	95
Transmission through power lines	90
Overall efficiency	35

Efficiency of Power Plants

When fossil fuels are burned to produce electricity, not all the chemical energy in the fuel is converted to electrical energy. Energy is lost in every stage of the process. No stage is 100 percent efficient.

The overall efficiency of the entire process is given by multiplying the efficiencies of each stage. If you were to do this, you'd find that the resulting overall efficiency is only about 35 percent. This means that only about 35 percent of the energy contained in the fossil fuels is delivered to homes, schools and businesses as electrical energy. The other 65 percent is lost as the chemical energy in the fuel is transformed into electrical energy and delivered to energy users. **Table 1** shows the amount of energy converted at each stage.

The Costs of Using Fossil Fuels

Although fossil fuels are a useful source of energy for generating electricity and providing the power for transportation, their use has some undesirable side effects. When petroleum products and coal are burned, smoke is given off that contains small particles called particulates. These particulates may cause breathing problems for some people. Burning fossil fuels also releases carbon dioxide. **Figure 9** shows how the carbon dioxide concentration in the atmosphere has increased from 1957 to 1999. The increased concentration of carbon dioxide in the atmosphere might cause Earth's surface temperature to increase.

Figure 9
The carbon dioxide concentration in Earth's atmosphere has been measured since 1957 at Mauna Loa in Hawaii. From 1957 to 1999 the carbon dioxide concentration has increased by about 16 percent.

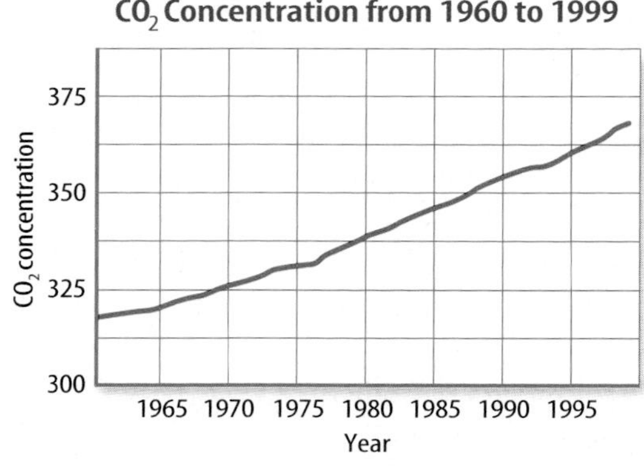

Using Coal The most abundant fossil fuel is coal, but coal contains even more impurities than oil or natural gas. Many electric power plants that burn coal remove some of these pollutants before they are released into the atmosphere. Removing sulfur dioxide, for example, helps to prevent the formation of compounds that might cause acid rain. Mining coal also can be dangerous. Miners risk being killed or injured, and some suffer from lung diseases caused by breathing coal dust over long periods of time.

Inclusion Strategies

Learning Disabled To help students understand the math involved in finding the total efficiency of a power plant, discuss a two-step process in which the efficiency of the first step is 50% and the efficiency of the second step is 50%. Fill a beaker with water. Pour off half (100% × 50% = 50%). Then pour off half again (50% × 50% = 25%).

Resource Manager

Chapter Resources Booklet
Reinforcement, p. 27

Cultural Diversity, p. 49

Performance Assessment in the Science Classroom, p. 48

Nonrenewable Resources

It's a safe bet that almost any time you use an electrical appliance or ride in a car, some type of fossil fuel is the energy source that is being used. All fossil fuels are **nonrenewable resources,** which means they are resources that cannot be replaced by natural processes as quickly as they are used. Therefore, fossil fuel reserves are decreasing as population and industrial demands are increasing. **Figure 10** shows that at the current rate of consumption, the world could be out of oil in less than one century. As the production of energy from fossil fuels continues, the remaining reserves of fuel will decrease. Fossil fuels will become more difficult to obtain, causing them to become more costly in the future.

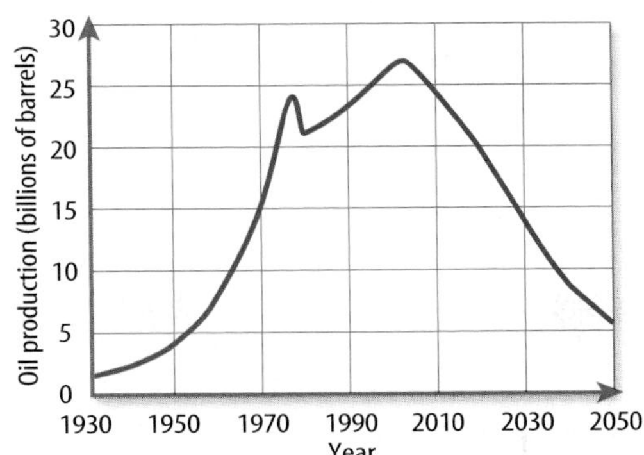

Figure 10
Some predictions show that worldwide oil production will peak by 2005 and then decline rapidly over the following 50 years.

Conserving Fossil Fuels

Even as reserves of fossil fuels decrease and they become more costly, the demand for energy continues to increase as the world's population increases. To meet these energy demands, the use of fossil fuels must be reduced and energy must be obtained from other sources. One way to reduce the use of fossil fuels is to make vehicles that are more fuel efficient. You can help reduce the demand for energy by not wasting energy in your daily activities.

Reading Check *Why is it important to conserve nonrenewable resources?*

Section 1 Assessment

1. Describe the three main forms of fossil fuels.
2. What are the advantages and disadvantages of using coal to generate electricity?
3. How are the different chemicals in crude oil separated?
4. Give three examples of different products derived from chemicals in crude oil.
5. **Think Critically** If fossil fuels are still forming, why are they considered to be nonrenewable resources?

Skill Builder Activities

6. **Comparing and Contrasting** Compare and contrast the different fossil fuels. Include the advantages and disadvantages of using each as a source of energy. **For more help, refer to the** Science Skill Handbook.
7. **Communicating** In your Science Journal, make a list of areas in your school where energy use could be reduced. **For more help, refer to the** Science Skill Handbook.

Answers to Section Assessment

1. Petroleum, a liquid, is made mostly of hydrocarbons. Natural gas is mostly methane. Coal, a solid, is formed from plant material.
2. An advantage is that coal is relatively abundant. Disadvantages include the fact that burning coal pollutes the air and mining coal deforms the land.
3. They are separated by fractional distillation, in which each compound vaporizes at its own boiling point, rises, and is collected.
4. Possible answers: plastics, grease, gasoline, asphalt
5. We are using fossil fuels faster than they are being replaced.
6. Possible answers: Petroleum is nonrenewable. Coal is inexpensive but can pollute the air and is nonrenewable. Natural gas burns more cleanly than coal but is also nonrenewable.
7. Possible answer: Insulate windows and around doors, turn off some lights.

Conserving Fossil Fuels

Activity

Have students work in small groups to make posters about energy waste. One half of each poster should show ways that energy is wasted, and the other half of each poster should show ways this energy could be conserved. L2 **Visual-Spatial**

Reading Check

Answer They cannot be replaced as quickly as they are being used.

3 Assess

Reteach

Organize the class into teams of three. Have each team consider the advantages and disadvantages of using petroleum, natural gas, and coal. Have the teams combine their lists and report their conclusions. L2 COOP LEARN **Interpersonal**

Challenge

The location of accessible fossil fuels around the world has a major political impact. Have students identify areas of the world rich in oil, natural gas, and coal. Have then identify a way this has affected the area. L3 **Intrapersonal**

Assessment

Process Have students make a bulletin board comparing and contrasting the ways people obtain petroleum and coal. Petroleum is a liquid, so it is pumped from wells drilled deep into Earth's crust. Coal also comes from underground, but it is a solid, so it must be mined. Use **PASC,** p. 131.

SECTION 2

Nuclear Energy

1 Motivate

Bellringer Transparency

Display the Section Focus Transparency for Section 2. Use the accompanying Transparency Activity Master. L2 ELL

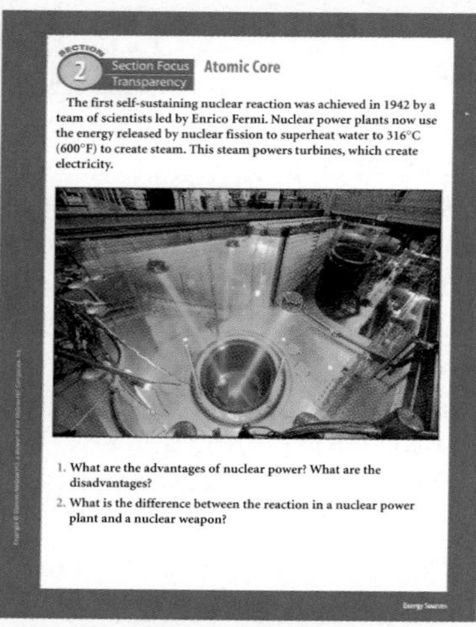

Section 2 Section Focus Transparency **Atomic Core**

The first self-sustaining nuclear reaction was achieved in 1942 by a team of scientists led by Enrico Fermi. Nuclear power plants now use the energy released by nuclear fission to superheat water to 316°C (600°F) to create steam. This steam powers turbines, which create electricity.

1. What are the advantages of nuclear power? What are the disadvantages?
2. What is the difference between the reaction in a nuclear power plant and a nuclear weapon?

Energy Sources

Tie to Prior Knowledge

Ask students to name ways that nuclear energy is used. Possible answers: diagnose and treat illnesses, nuclear weapons.

SECTION 2 Nuclear Energy

As You Read

What You'll Learn

- **Outline** the steps in the operation of a nuclear reactor.
- **Compare** the advantages and disadvantages of using nuclear energy to produce electricity.
- **Discuss** nuclear fusion as a possible energy source.

Vocabulary

nuclear reactor
nuclear waste

Why It's Important

Nuclear energy can help reduce the use of fossil fuels, but its use may cause environmental problems.

Using Nuclear Energy

Over the past several decades, electric power plants have been developed that generate electricity without burning fossil fuels. These power plants, such as the one shown in **Figure 11,** convert nuclear energy to electrical energy. Energy is released when the nucleus of an atom breaks apart. In this process, called nuclear fission, an extremely small amount of mass is converted into an enormous amount of energy. Today almost 20 percent of all the electricity produced in the United States comes from nuclear power plants. Overall, nuclear power plants produce about eight percent of all the energy consumed in the United States. Currently, there are 109 nuclear power plants in the United States, with 6 more under construction.

Nuclear Reactors

A **nuclear reactor** uses the energy from controlled nuclear reactions to generate electricity. Although nuclear reactors vary in design, all have some parts in common, as shown in **Figure 12.** They contain a fuel that can be made to undergo fission; they contain control rods that are used to control the nuclear reactions; and they have a cooling system that keeps the reactor from being damaged by the heat produced. The actual fission of the radioactive fuel occurs in a relatively small part of the reactor known as the core.

Figure 11
A nuclear power plant generates electricity using the energy released in nuclear fission. The dome in the center of the photo contains the reactor core. A cooling tower is on the left.

Section Assessment Planner

PORTFOLIO
Reteach, p. 304

PERFORMANCE ASSESSMENT
Problem-Solving Activity, p. 303
Skill Builder Activities, p. 304
See page 318 for more options.

CONTENT ASSESSMENT
Section, p. 304
Challenge, p. 304
Chapter, pp. 318–319

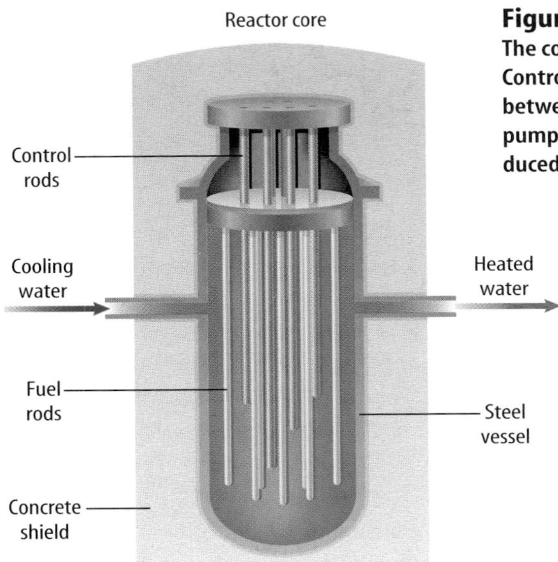

Figure 12
The core of a nuclear reactor contains the fuel rods. Control rods that absorb neutrons are inserted between the fuel rods. Water or another coolant is pumped through the core to remove the heat produced by the fission reaction.

Nuclear Fuel Only certain elements have nuclei that can undergo fission. Naturally occurring uranium contains an isotope, U-235, whose nucleus can split apart. As a result, the fuel that is used in a nuclear reactor is usually uranium dioxide. Naturally occurring uranium contains only about 0.7 percent of the U-235 isotope. In a reactor, the uranium is enriched so that it contains three percent to five percent U-235.

Figure 13
Nuclear fuel pellets are stacked together to form fuel rods. The fuel rods are bundled together, and the bundle is covered with stainless steel.

The Reactor Core The reactor core contains uranium dioxide fuel in the form of tiny pellets like the ones in **Figure 13.** The pellets are about the size of a pencil eraser and are placed end to end in a tube. The tubes are then bundled and covered with stainless steel, as shown in **Figure 13.** The core of a typical reactor may contain several hundred thousand kilograms of uranium contained in hundreds of fuel rods. For every kilogram of uranium that undergoes fission in the core, 1 g of matter is converted into energy. The energy released by this gram of matter is equivalent to the energy released by burning about 3 million kg of coal.

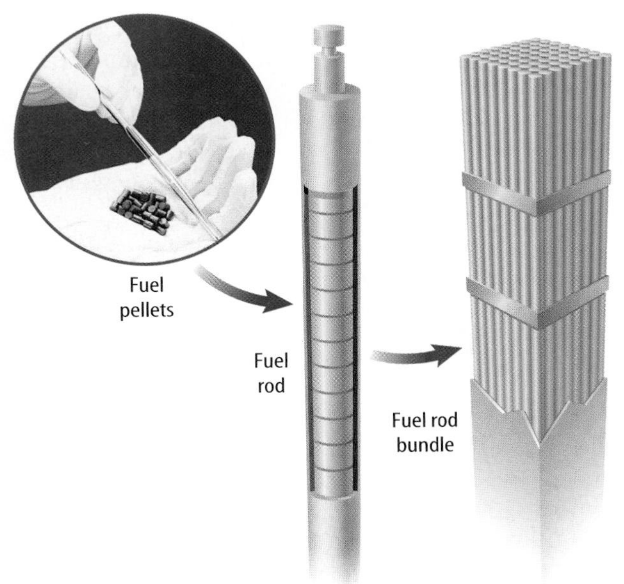

2 Teach

Nuclear Reactors

Teacher FYI

In an average American's lifetime, more than 1.5 million kg of coal would be needed to supply the person's energy needs. In contrast, if nuclear reactors were used instead of coal, only about 2.5 uranium fuel pellets would be needed to supply the same amount of energy.

Visual Learning

Figure 12 The distance the control rods extend between the fuel rods controls the reaction. If the control rods are inserted completely, they absorb too many neutrons and the reaction halts. If they are removed completely, the reaction is uncontained. **How do you think control rods are programmed to respond in an emergency?** They insert completely to stop the reaction. L2 LS **Logical-Mathematical**

Discussion

Why do you think the fuel and control used in the reactor are rod-shaped? to allow the water to flow freely around them and provide cooling L2 LS **Visual-Spatial**

Resource Manager

Chapter Resources Booklet
- Transparency Activity, p. 45
- Directed Reading for Content Mastery, p. 20
- Transparency Activity, pp. 47–48

Curriculum Connection

Social Studies The use of nuclear reactions in commercial power plants to produce electricity has been the subject of intense controversy. Organize the class into two teams and have them debate the issue. Arguments for nuclear power include its efficiency and nonreliance on fossil fuels. Arguments against nuclear power include safety hazards and disposal of nuclear waste. L3 LS **Logical-Mathematical**

Nuclear Reactors, continued

Use an Analogy

If rabbits live and breed in an environment rich in rabbit food but in which there are no rabbit predators, the rabbit population will boom very quickly. This is analogous to the uncontrolled chain reaction that can occur in a nuclear reactor. The introduction of foxes into the rabbit environment controls the size of the rabbit population just as the introduction of control rods controls the number of neutrons available to participate in the nuclear reaction.

Reading Check

Answer a nuclear reaction in which the products of one reaction start another reaction

Make a Model

Have students work in pairs to make models of the core of a nuclear reactor. Models should include some fuel rods, some control rods, and a coolant. One possible model could use test tubes filled with different substances to represent the fuel rods and the control rods, a test tube rack to represent the core, and water as the coolant. L2

LS **Kinesthetic**

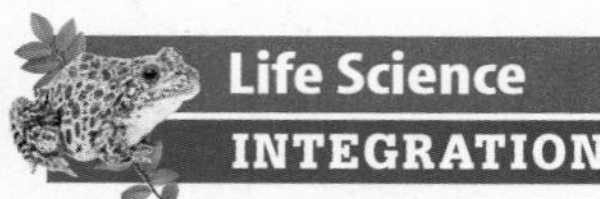

Nuclear power is promoted in various ways, such as on the Internet and with magazine advertising.

Figure 14
When a neutron strikes the nucleus of a U-235 atom, the nucleus splits apart into two smaller nuclei. In the process two or three neutrons also are emitted. The smaller nuclei are called fission products.

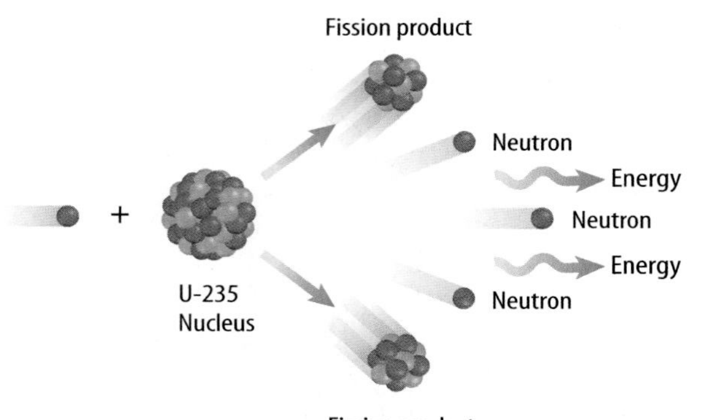

Life Science INTEGRATION

Nuclear reactions can be harmful if they aren't carefully controlled. An accident at the Chernobyl nuclear power plant in the Ukraine in 1986 caused radiation sickness in many poeple and a worldwide concern about nuclear power. Research how the nuclear power industry has attempted to reduce concern about nuclear power. What type of promotional material exists for nuclear power?

Nuclear Fission How does the nuclear reaction proceed in the reactor core? Neutrons that are produced by the decay of U-235 nuclei are absorbed by other U-235 nuclei. When a U-235 nucleus absorbs a neutron, it splits into two smaller nuclei, and two or three additional neutrons, as shown in **Figure 14.** These neutrons strike other U-235 nuclei, causing them to release two or three more neutrons each when they split apart.

Because every uranium atom that splits apart releases neutrons that cause other uranium atoms to split apart, this process is called a nuclear chain reaction. In the chain reaction involving the fission of uranium nuclei, the number of nuclei that are split can more then double at each stage of the process. As a result, an enormous number of nuclei can be split after only a small number of stages. For example, if the number of nuclei involved doubles at each stage, after only 50 stages more than a quadrillion nuclei might be split.

Nuclear chain reactions take place in a matter of milliseconds. If the process isn't controlled, the chain reaction will release an ever-increasing amount of energy each millisecond, rather than releasing energy at a constant rate.

Reading Check *What is a nuclear chain reaction?*

Controlling the Chain Reaction To control the chain reaction, some of the neutrons that are released when U-235 splits apart must be prevented from striking other U-235 nuclei. These neutrons are absorbed by rods containing boron or cadmium that are inserted into the reactor core. Moving these control rods deeper into the reactor allows them to absorb more neutrons and slow down the chain reaction. Eventually, only one neutron per fission reacts with a U-235 atom to produce another fission, and energy is released at a constant rate.

Visual Learning

Figure 14 The tremendous energy from the fission process shown here is mostly transferred to the smaller nuclei and the neutrons, but part of the energy is released as gamma radiation. **What are two ways a chain reaction can be avoided?** by introducing materials that absorb neutrons and by decreasing the amount of U-235 so there aren't enough atoms to continue the process L2

LS **Logical-Mathematical**

Active Reading

Think-Pair Share This strategy encourages students to think first before discussing their ideas or thoughts about a topic. Students are asked to respond to a question by writing a response. After thinking for a few minutes, partners share responses to the question. Finally, ask students to share responses with the class. Have students become involved in a Think-Pair Share about the use of nuclear energy.

Nuclear Power Plants

Nuclear fission reactors produce electricity in much the same way that conventional power plants do. **Figure 15** shows how a nuclear reactor produces electricity. The thermal energy released in nuclear fission is used to heat water and produce steam. This steam then is used to drive a turbine that rotates an electric generator. To transfer thermal energy from the reactor core to heat water and produce steam, the core is immersed in a fluid coolant. The coolant absorbs heat from the core and is pumped through a heat exchanger. There thermal energy is transferred from the coolant and boils water to produce steam. The overall efficiency of nuclear power plants is about 35 percent, similar to that of fossil fuel power plants.

The Risks of Nuclear Power

Producing energy from nuclear fission has some environmental advantages over burning fossil fuels. Fission produces no air pollution, but burning coal and petroleum creates nearly 20 million kg of pollutants each day. Also, nuclear power plants don't produce carbon dioxide.

The nuclear generation of electricity, however, has its problems. The mining of the uranium can cause environmental damage. Water that is used as a coolant in the reactor core must cool before it is released into streams and rivers. Otherwise, the excess heat could harm fish and other animals and plants in the water.

Earth Science INTEGRATION

Uranium is used to determine the age of rocks in which it occurs. As uranium decays into lead at a constant rate, the age of a rock can be found by comparing the amount of uranium to the amount of lead produced. Uranium-Lead dating is used by scientists to date rocks as old as 4.6 billion years. Research other methods used to determine the age of rocks.

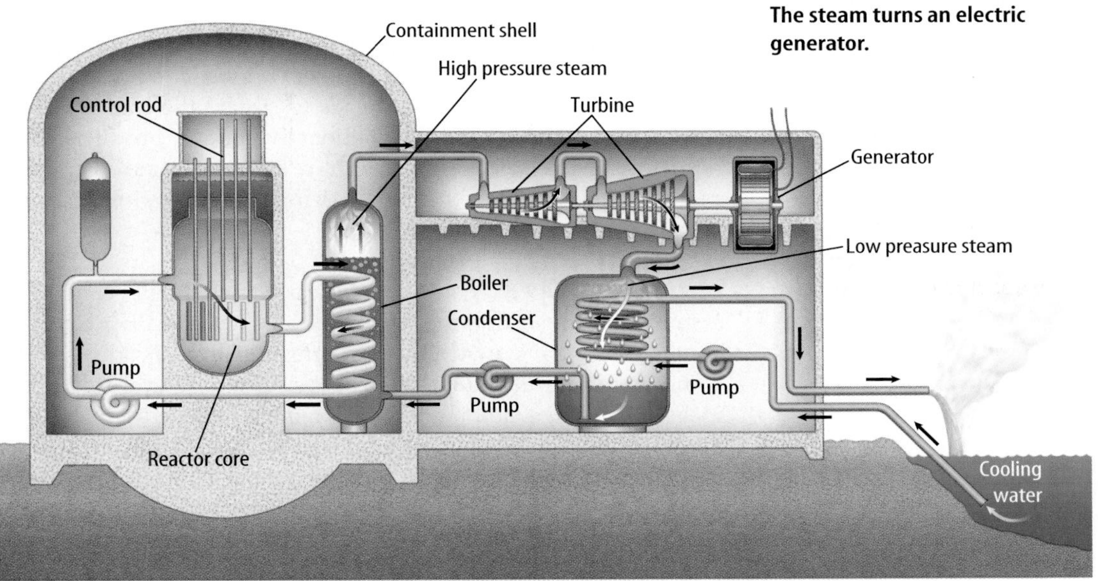

Figure 15
A nuclear power plant uses the heat produced by nuclear fission in it's core to produce steam. The steam turns an electric generator.

Nuclear Power Plants

Earth Science INTEGRATION

The thorium-230 to uranium -234 activity ratio has been used to date calcium carbonate. Rocks are also dated from the fossils they contain.

IDENTIFYING Misconceptions

The water that is used as a coolant in reactor cores becomes contaminated with radioactive material. This water is not the same water that is cooled and released into streams and rivers. The water that is released into the environment does not come into direct contact either with the reactor core or with the water that cools the reactor core. It exchanges heat with the contaminated water through a heat exchanger.

The Risks of Nuclear Power

Extension

A particularly controversial type of nuclear reactor is called a breeder reactor. Have students find out how this type of reactor works and why it is so controversial. In addition to generating energy, a breeder reactor produces more nuclear fuel than it uses, which is a more efficient use of fuel. However, breeder reactors are cooled with liquid sodium, which catches fire when it leaks from the plant, and these reactors produce plutonium-239, which can be used in nuclear weapons. L3

LS **Logical-Mathematical**

Resource Manager

Chapter Resources Booklet
Enrichment, p. 31

Earth Science Critical Thinking/Problem Solving, p. 2

Cultural Diversity, p. 59

Science Journal

Nuclear Power Plants Ask students to identify the nuclear power plant located closest to their community and write their findings in their Science Journals. Have them include the plant's name and location, when it began operation, how much electricity it generates, and its operating history. Answers will depend on the location of their community. L3 LS **Linguistic**

The Risks of Nuclear Power, continued

Teacher FYI

After the Chernobyl accident in 1986, people all over the world became concerned about the safety of nuclear reactors. Although all reactors have some risks, reactors in the United States are far safer than the one in Chernobyl. Most important, the Chernobyl reactor had a poor containment structure that was unable to prevent the escape of radioactive materials.

Extension

On March 28, 1979, an accident occurred at the Three Mile Island Nuclear Plant near Harrisburg, Pennsylvania. Have students find out more about this incident and report their findings to the class. The accident partially melted the reactor core. Emergency cooling systems eventually contained the problem, but some radiation was released. This accident focused the nation's attention on the potential dangers of nuclear reactors. L3 LS **Linguistic**

The Disposal of Nuclear Waste

Activity

Ask students to generate ideas for nuclear waste disposal. Remind them to consider short-term and long-term effects as well as the various types of waste. Have students share their ideas in small groups and arrive at a class consensus about the best methods of disposal. L2 LS **Interpersonal**

Figure 16
An explosion occurred at the Chernobyl reactor in the Ukraine after graphite control rods caught fire. The explosion shattered the containment shell.

The Release of Radioactivity

One of the most serious risks of nuclear power is the escape of harmful radiation from power plants. The fuel rods contain radioactive elements with various half-lives. Some of these elements could cause damage to living organisms if they were released from the reactor core. Nuclear reactors have elaborate systems of safeguards, strict safety precautions, and highly trained workers in order to prevent accidents. In spite of this, accidents have occurred.

For example, in 1986 in Chernobyl, Ukraine, an accident occurred when a reactor core overheated during a safety test. Materials in the core caught fire and caused a chemical explosion that blew a hole in the reactor, as shown in **Figure 16.** This resulted in the release of radioactive materials that were carried by winds and deposited over a large area. As a result of the accident, 31 people died of acute radiation sickness. It is possible that 260,000 people might have been exposed to levels of radiation that could affect their health.

In the United States, power plants are designed to prevent accidents such as the one that occurred at Chernobyl. But many people still are concerned that similar accidents are possible.

SCIENCE Online

Research Visit the Glencoe Science Web site at **science.glencoe.com** for a link to more information about storing nuclear wastes. Communicate to your class what you learn.

The Disposal of Nuclear Waste

After about three years, not enough fissionable U-235 is left in the fuel pellets in the reactor core to sustain the chain reaction. The spent fuel contains radioactive fission products in addition to the remaining uranium. **Nuclear waste** is any radioactive by-product that results when radioactive materials are used.

Low-Level Waste Low-level nuclear wastes usually contain a small amount of radioactive material. They usually do not contain radioactive materials with long half-lives. Products of some medical and industrial processes are low-level wastes, including items of clothing used in handling radioactive materials. Low-level wastes also include used air filters from nuclear power plants and discarded smoke detectors. Low-level wastes usually are sealed in containers and buried in trenches 30 m deep at special locations. When dilute enough, low-level waste sometimes is released into the air or water.

SCIENCE Online
Internet Addresses

Explore the Glencoe Science Web site at science.glencoe.com to find out more about topics in this section.

Resource Manager

Chapter Resources Booklet
Reinforcement, p. 28

Cultural Diversity, p. 69

Mathematics Skill Activities, p. 47

High-Level Waste High-level nuclear waste is generated in nuclear power plants and by nuclear weapons programs. After spent fuel is removed from a reactor, it is stored in a deep pool of water, as shown in **Figure 17.** Many of the radioactive materials in high-level nuclear waste have short half-lives. However, the spent fuel also contains materials that will remain radioactive for tens of thousands of years. For this reason, the waste must be disposed of in extremely durable and stable containers.

Figure 17
Spent nuclear fuel rods are radioactive and are placed underwater after they are removed from the reactor core. The water absorbs the nuclear radiation and prevents it from escaping into the environment.

 *What is the difference between low-level and high-level nuclear wastes?*

One method proposed for the disposal of high-level waste is to seal the waste in ceramic glass, which is placed in protective stainless-steel containers. The containers then are buried hundreds of meters below ground in stable rock formations or salt deposits. It is hoped that this will keep the material from contaminating the environment for thousands of years.

Problem-Solving Activity

Can a contaminated radioactive site be reclaimed?

In the early 1900s with the discovery of radium, extensive mining for the element began in the Denver, Colorado, area. Radium is a radioactive element that was used to make watch dials and instrument panels that glowed in the dark. After World War I, the radium industry collapsed. The area was left contaminated with 97,000 tons of radioactive soil and debris containing heavy metals and radium, which is now known to cause cancer. The soil was used as fill, foundation material, left in place, or mishandled.

Radium
88
Ra
226.025

Identifying the Problem

In the 1980s one area became known as the Denver Radium Superfund Site and was cleaned up by the Environmental Protection Agency. The land then was reclaimed by a local commercial establishment.

Solving the Problem

1. The contaminated soil was placed in one area and a protective cap was place over it. This area was also restricted from being used for residential homes. Explain why it is important for the protective cap to be maintained and why homes could not be built in this area.
2. The advantages of cleaning up this site are economical, environmental, and social. Give an example of each.

Discussion

What are some problems that must be addressed when deciding on a site for nuclear waste? Safe transportation from other sites, possible terrorist plans for theft, political changes on policies and funding, proper storage capability to prevent the risk of radioactive materials from entering the environment L2
LS **Logical-Mathematical**

Reading Check

Answer Low level wastes usually contain a small amount of nuclear waste with short half-lives. High level wastes include spent fuel from a reactor, some of which has very long half-lives.

Problem-Solving Activity

Answers

1. The cap has to be maintained to prevent contaminated soil from reaching people. Homes can't be built in this area because all of the contaminated soil may not have been removed and some contamination may have reached the groundwater.
2. Advantages: Economic: jobs, revenue for the community, tax for the state, increase in property values. Environmental: elimination of long term risks for contaminated material, prevention of the migration of metals through the soil, protection of the public from contaminated land and water. Social: improvement of the aesthetic quality of the land, commercial buildings can be built.

LAB DEMONSTRATION

Purpose to demonstrate how shielding decreases radiation levels

Materials source of radiation such as gas lantern mantle, cloisonne jewelry, orange-glazed ovenware; Geiger counter; lead sheets

Procedure Place the radiation source about 10 cm from the Geiger counter. Note the intensity measured by the counter when the radiation source is unshielded. Next, insert first one, then two, three, four, and five sheets of lead between the source and the counter, measuring the intensity each time.

Expected Outcome The intensity of radiation decreases with additional shielding.

Assessment

How were measurements affected by the amount of shielding? Increased shielding meant less radiation was measured. **Did the lead become radioactive? Why or why not?** No; materials do not become radioactive by being struck by radiation.

Nuclear Fusion

Fun Fact

Nuclear fusion produces more energy than nuclear fission. The nuclear fusion of hydrogen to form helium releases about ten times the amount of energy as does the nuclear fission of uranium-235.

3 Assess

Reteach

Have each student make a simple sketch of a nuclear reactor, showing the major parts of the reactor and describing the function of each of them. L2 LS **Visual-Spatial** P

Challenge

Plutonium-239 is a by-product of nuclear reactors, and its half-life is about 24,000 years. If 50 g of it were stored as nuclear waste, about how much would remain after 120,000 years? Have students use a computer graphing program to display this decay process. About 1.56 g would remain. L3 LS **Logical-Mathematical**

Assessment

Content Nuclear fission is a chain reaction. Have students draw diagrams showing the chain reaction and how it is controlled in nuclear power plants. Use **Performance Assessment in the Science Classroom,** p. 163.

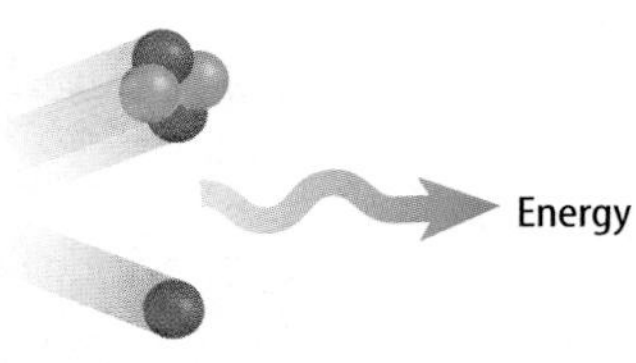

Figure 18
In nuclear fusion, two smaller nuclei join together to form a larger nucleus. Energy is released in the process. In the reaction shown here, two isotopes of hydrogen come together to form a helium nucleus.

Nuclear Fusion

Imagine the amount of energy the Sun must give off to heat Earth from 150 million kilometers away. It gets this energy from thermonuclear fusion. Thermonuclear fusion is the joining together of small nuclei at high temperatures, as shown in **Figure 18.** In this process, a small amount of mass is converted into energy. Fusion is the most concentrated energy source known.

An advantage of producing energy from fusion is that the fuel it uses, hydrogen, is the most abundant element in the universe. Hydrogen can be obtained from water in the oceans in practically limitless amounts. Another advantage is that the fusion reaction produces helium gas, which is not radioactive and is chemically nonreactive.

However, fusion reactions occur only at temperatures of millions of degrees Celsius. The biggest challenge lies in creating and maintaining the high temperatures fusion requires. To do this requires enormous amounts of energy in order to start the fusion reaction. Because of these and other problems, the use of fusion as an energy source remains in the future.

Section 2 Assessment

1. How is the rate of fission controlled in a nuclear reactor?
2. Explain the major obstacles in controlling nuclear fusion.
3. What types of environmental hazards do nuclear reactors produce?
4. In what way are nuclear power plants similar to those that burn fossil fuels?
5. **Think Critically** In a research project, a scientist has generated a 10-g sample of nuclear waste. The materials have a short half-life and are not present in a significant amount. How would you classify this waste, and how will it likely be disposed of?

Skill Builder Activities

6. **Concept Mapping** Using a computer, design an events-chain concept map for the generation of electricity in a nuclear fission reactor. Begin with the bombarding neutron and end with electricity in overhead lines. **For more help, refer to the** Science Skill Handbook.
7. **Using an Electronic Spreadsheet** Create a table with two divisions for the advantages and disadvantages of nuclear power. Type as many entries under each as you can. Do you think nuclear power is or isn't a good idea? Explain. **For more help, refer to the** Technology Skill Handbook.

Answers to Section Assessment

1. Control rods are used to absorb excess neutrons.
2. It is difficult to maintain the high temperatures that are necessary and contain fusion.
3. thermal pollution, possible release of harmful radiation into the air and onto land, nuclear waste
4. They heat water to produce steam that drives turbines and rotates generators.
5. It is low-level waste that should be sealed in an insulated container and buried in a repository.
6. Maps might show U-235 splitting and producing energy to heat water. The water produces steam that drives a turbine. The turbine rotates a generator that produces electricity.
7. Advantages include low pollution and availability of fuel. Disadvantages include waste disposal and risk of thermal and radioactive pollution.

SECTION

Renewable Energy Sources

Energy Options

The demand for energy increases continually, but supplies of fossil fuels are decreasing. Using more nuclear reactors to produce electricity will produce more high-level nuclear waste that has to be disposed of safely. As a result, sources of energy that can meet Earth's increasing demands and not damage the environment are being developed. A number of possible energy sources are renewable resources. A **renewable resource** is an energy source that is replaced nearly as quickly as it is used. Although no completely adequate energy source has been found, some promising options exist.

As You Read

***What* You'll Learn**

- **Analyze** the need for alternate energy sources.
- **Describe** alternate methods of generating electricity.
- **Compare** the advantages and disadvantages of various alternate energy sources.

Vocabulary

renewable resource
photovoltaic cell
hydroelectricity
geothermal energy
biomass

***Why* It's Important**

Our primary energy sources are nonrenewable, so alternative energy sources need to be explored.

Energy from the Sun

The amount of solar energy that falls on the United States in one day, on average, is more than the total amount of energy used in the United States in one year. Because the Sun is expected to continue to supply energy for several billion years, solar energy cannot be used up like fossil fuels. Solar energy is a renewable resource that can provide a source of energy for the foreseeable future. Even if a small fraction of this solar energy could be used, it could significantly reduce the consumption of fossil fuels.

Solar Cells

The radiant energy from the Sun can be used to heat homes and provide hot water. This energy also can be converted directly into electricity. A device that is used to convert solar energy into electricity is the **photovoltaic cell,** which also is called a solar cell. Do you own a solar-powered calculator, like the one shown in **Figure 19?** It contains solar cells.

Figure 19
This calculator uses a solar cell to produce the electricity it needs to operate.

What does a photovoltaic cell do?

Section Assessment Planner

Portfolio
Challenge, p. 310

Performance Assessment
Try at Home MiniLAB, p. 306
Skill Builder Activities, p. 310
See page 318 for more options.

Content Assessment
Section, p. 310
Challenge, p. 310
Chapter, pp. 318–319

SECTION

Renewable Energy Sources

1 Motivate

Bellringer Transparency

Display the Section Focus Transparency for Section 3. Use the accompanying Transparency Activity Master. L2 ELL

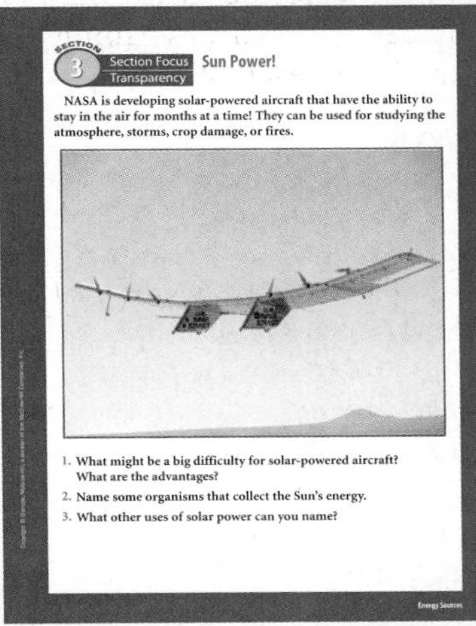

Section Focus Transparency 3 — Sun Power!

NASA is developing solar-powered aircraft that have the ability to stay in the air for months at a time! They can be used for studying the atmosphere, storms, crop damage, or fires.

1. What might be a big difficulty for solar-powered aircraft? What are the advantages?
2. Name some organisms that collect the Sun's energy.
3. What other uses of solar power can you name?

Tie to Prior Knowledge

Every day we turn on lights and ride in cars. Ask students what it would be like if suddenly our sources of fossil fuels ran out. Explain that this section describes alternative sources of energy.

Reading Check

Answer converts solar energy into electricity

Resource Manager

Chapter Resources Booklet
Transparency Activity, p. 46

2 Teach

Solar Cells

Use Science Words

Word Meaning Why are solar cells also known as photovoltaic cells? *Photo* - means "light," and *voltaic* refers to electricity. L2
LS **Linguistic**

TRY AT HOME
Mini LAB

Purpose to analyze the use of solar energy L2 ELL
LS **Kinesthetic**

Materials piece of cloth, watch or clock

Analysis

1. Answers will vary, but the shirts in direct sunlight should dry faster.
2. Answers will vary depending on the season and weather conditions. Factors such as temperature, wind velocity, cloudiness, humidity will affect the time needed.
3. Hang clothes in the sun to dry instead of using an electric drier. Open shades and curtains to warm a room with direct sunlight in cool weather, and close shades and curtains to cool a room in warm weather.

Assessment

Oral Ask students to identify the dependent and independent variables and the constants in this experiment. The dependent variable was drying time and the independent variable was location of the clothesline. Constants include size, color, and fabric of the T-shirts, as well as the way in which the shirts were treated before being hung on the clotheslines. Use **PASC**, p. 95.

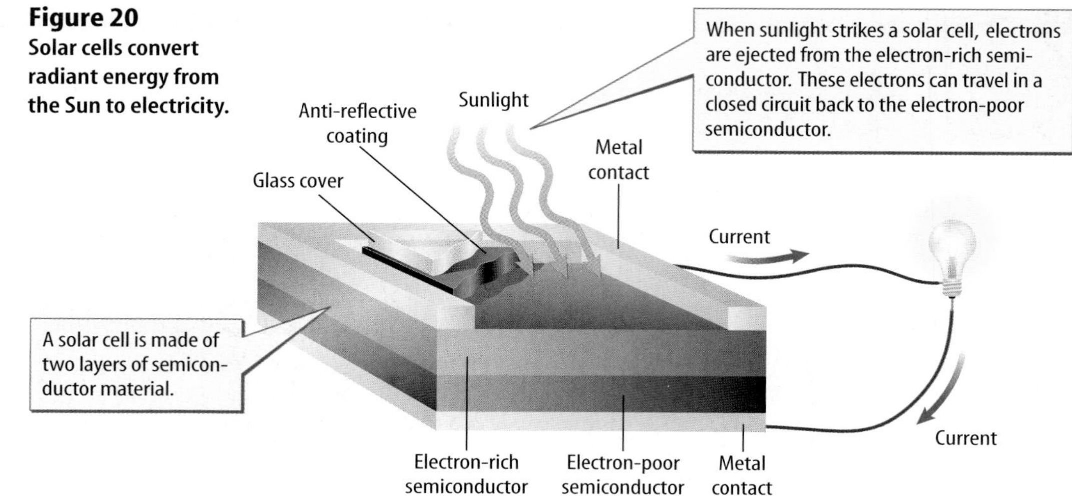

When sunlight strikes a solar cell, electrons are ejected from the electron-rich semiconductor. These electrons can travel in a closed circuit back to the electron-poor semiconductor.
Sunlight
Anti-reflective coating
Glass cover
Metal contact
Current
A solar cell is made of two layers of semiconductor material.
Electron-rich semiconductor
Electron-poor semiconductor
Metal contact
Current

Figure 20
Solar cells convert radiant energy from the Sun to electricity.

TRY AT HOME Mini LAB

Using Solar Power at Home

Procedure

1. Cut a piece of **cloth** into four equal sized pieces.
2. Wet the pieces and wring them out so they are the same dampness.
3. Spread the pieces out to dry—two pieces inside and two pieces outdoors. One piece of each set should be in direct sunlight and one piece should be in the shade.
4. In your **Science Journal,** record the time it takes for each cloth piece to dry.

Analysis

1. How long did it take for each cloth piece to dry?
2. What conditions determined how quickly the cloth dried?
3. Infer how you can use solar energy in your home to conserve electricity.

Making Electricity Solar cells are made of two layers of semiconductor materials sandwiched between two layers of conducting metal, as shown in **Figure 20.** One layer of semiconductor is rich in electrons, while the other layer is electron poor. When sunlight strikes the surface of the solar cell, electrons flow through an electrical circuit from the electron-rich semiconductor to the electron-poor material. This process of converting radiant energy from the Sun directly to electricity is only about 15 percent to 20 percent efficient.

Using Solar Energy Producing electricity using solar cells is, however, more expensive on a large scale than the use of nonrenewable fuels is. The cost of electricity produced by a conventional fossil-fuel power plant is about 8 cents to 10 cents per kilowatt-hour. In 1998, the cost of electricity generated by solar cells was about 28 cents per kilowatt-hour. However, in remote areas the difference in cost drops if the cost of building transmission lines to those areas is considered.

One disadvantage of using solar cells to generate electricity is that the Sun's rays do not strike any place on Earth every hour of every day. Therefore, the electricity generated by solar cells when the Sun is shining must be stored in batteries to be used when the Sun isn't out. However, a large amount of energy is needed to manufacture batteries, and large batteries contain heavy metals such as lead that are environmental hazards. In spite of this disadvantage, solar energy is an energy resource that is becoming more economical as solar technology improves. One of the world's largest and most productive solar energy plants is located in California.

Visual Learning

Figure 20 The semiconductor layers of this solar cell form a diode, a device that allows current to flow in only one direction. Thin metal strips on top of the cell serve as contacts for collecting the current. An anti-reflective coating reduces energy loss. One advantage of solar cells is that they have no moving parts. **Why does this make them attractive for use on satellites in space?** Solar cells require no maintenance and no fuel.

Inclusion Strategies

Learning Disabled Have students bring in devices that use solar cells, such as toys and calculators. Show how the devices stop working if the solar cell's light source is blocked. L1 ELL
LS **Visual-Spatial**

Energy from Water

Just as the expansion of steam can turn an electric generator, a river's rapidly moving water can, as well. The energy carried by water can be increased if the water is retained by a high dam. This increases the gravitational potential energy of the water. This potential energy is released when the water flows through tunnels near the base of the dam. **Figure 21** shows how the rushing water spins a turbine, which rotates the shaft of an electric generator to produce electricity. Dams built for this purpose are called hydroelectric dams.

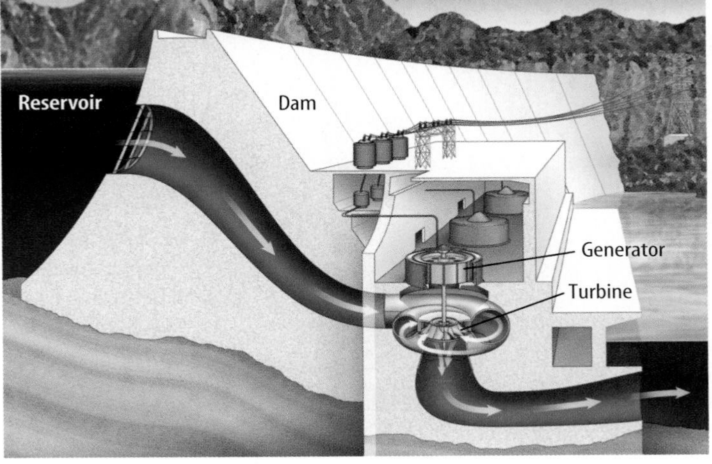

Figure 21
The potential energy contained in water stored behind the dam is converted to electrical energy in a hydroelectric power plant.

Using Hydroelectricity Electricity produced from the energy of moving water is called **hydroelectricity.** Currently about 4 percent of the electrical energy used in the United States is produced by hydroelectric power plants. Hydroelectric power plants are an efficient way to produce electricity with almost no pollution. Because no exchange of heat is involved in producing steam to spin a turbine, hydroelectric power plants are almost twice as efficient as fossil fuel or nuclear power plants.

Another advantage is that the bodies of water held back by dams can form lakes that can provide water for drinking and crop irrigation. These lakes also can be used for boating and swimming. Also, after the initial cost of building a dam and a power plant, the electricity is relatively cheap.

However, artificial dams can disturb the balance of natural ecosystems. Some species of fish that live in the ocean migrate back to the rivers in which they were hatched to breed. This migration can be blocked by dams, which causes a decline in the fish population. Fish ladders, such as those shown in **Figure 22,** have been designed to enable fish to migrate upstream past some dams. Also, some water sources suitable for a hydroelectric power plant are not near the people needing the power.

Figure 22
Fish ladders enable fish to migrate upstream past dams.

Reading Check ***Could your area use a hydroelectric power plant? Explain.***

Energy from Water

Teacher FYI

Waterwheels probably first provided energy around 200 B.C. They have been used to turn levers and run machines, such as sawmills and grain grinders. Falling water was first harnessed to provide electricity at Niagara Falls in 1879.

Discussion

Water is a free and renewable resource. Why, then, doesn't it supply more of our energy needs? Most sites suitable for developing hydroelectric power are already in use. Hydroelectric plants cannot be built in other locations because they disrupt the natural ecosystems. L2 **LS Logical-Mathematical**

IDENTIFYING Misconceptions

Students may think that because an alternative energy source isn't economical on a large scale that it isn't useful. Explain that many alternative energy sources, such as hydroelectricity, solar power, and wind power, are ideal for use on a small scale in rural areas or in developing societies.

Reading Check

Answer The answer will be yes if the community is near falling water.

Resource Manager

Chapter Resources Booklet
- MiniLAB, p. 4
- Enrichment, p. 32
- Directed Reading for Content Mastery, pp. 21, 22

Home and Community Involvement, p. 42

Cultural Diversity

The Amish and Electricity The Amish people in the United States avoid modern technology and focus on a simple life based on family, church, and community. Have students find out more about how the Amish use technology. The Amish will use such things as telephones and cars without owning them. They have their own electrical generators, but do not tap into public power supplies. L3 **LS Linguistic**

Energy from the Tides

Extension

Ask students to find out where the Annapolis Royal tidal energy plant is located and why it is located there. The plant is located on the Bay of Fundy between New Brunswick and Nova Scotia in Canada, which has tides up to 17 meters high. These are the highest tides in the world. L3 LS **Linguistic**

Discussion

Why do some coastal areas have higher tides than others? The height of the tide is increased by geographical features, such as the shapes of bays and inlets and the slope of the ocean floor.

Fun Fact

Tidal energy is possible only if the difference between high and low tides is more than 5 m. A higher tide difference means the plant can produce more electricity at a lower cost. A dam is needed to hold back the water at high tide. The dam's high construction cost makes it cheaper to build tidal plants on narrow inlets.

Harnessing the Wind

Extension

Have students research and write descriptions of the various forces that affect wind. They might write about the effects of temperature and pressure, surface obstacles, Earth's rotation, sea breezes, and mountain breezes. L3 LS **Logical-Mathematical**

Figure 23
This tidal energy plant at Annapolis Royal, Nova Scotia, generates 20 megawatts of electric power.

Energy from the Tides

The gravity of the Moon and Sun causes bulges in Earth's oceans. As Earth rotates, the two bulges of ocean water move westward. Each day, the level of the ocean on a coast rises and falls continually. Hydroelectric power can be generated by these ocean tides. As the tide comes in, the moving water spins a turbine that generates electricity. The water is then trapped behind a dam. At low tide the water behind the dam flows back out to the ocean, spinning the turbines and generating electric power.

Tidal energy is nearly pollution free. The efficiency of a tidal power plant is similar to that of a conventional hydroelectric power plant. However, only a few places on Earth have large enough differences between high and low tides for tidal energy to be a useful energy source. The only tidal power station in use in North America is at Annapolis Royal, Nova Scotia, shown in **Figure 23.** Tidal energy probably will be a limited, but useful, source of energy in the future.

Harnessing the Wind

You might have seen a windmill on a farm or pictures of windmills in a book. These windmills use the energy of the wind to pump water. Windmills also can use the energy of the wind to generate electricity. Wind spins a propeller that is connected to an electric generator. Usually, areas that make use of wind power have several hundred windmills working together, as shown in **Figure 24.**

Figure 24
Wind energy is converted to electricity as the spinning propeller turns a generator.

However, only a few places on Earth consistently have enough wind to rely on wind power to meet energy needs. Also, windmills are only about 30 percent efficient. Research is underway to improve the design of wind generators and increase their efficiency. Wind generators do not consume any resources. They do not pollute the atmosphere or water. However, they can be noisy and do change the appearance of a landscape. Also, they can disrupt the migration patterns of some birds. Still, wind energy can be a useful source of energy in some areas.

308

Teacher FYI

The world's first and largest tidal power plant began operating in 1966 at the Rance River in France, with a capacity of 240 MW. The Annapolis Royal plant in Canada has a 20 MW capacity, and the tidal plant near Murmansk in Russia has a capacity of 0.4 MW.

Inclusion Strategies

Gifted Have students research wave power, a form of hydroelectric power in which the kinetic energy of water waves is converted into electricity. Various countries (Norway, Japan, Scotland), have investigated wave power. In 1995, Scotland began operation of the world's first power plant to use the power of waves. The plant was damaged by waves and destroyed by a storm. L3 LS **Logical-Mathematical**

Energy from Inside Earth

Earth Science INTEGRATION Earth is not completely solid. Heat is generated within Earth by the decay of radioactive elements. This heat is called geothermal heat. Geothermal heat causes the rock beneath Earth's crust to soften and melt. This hot molten rock is called magma. The thermal energy that is contained in hot magma is called **geothermal energy.**

In some places, Earth's crust has cracks or thin spots that allow magma to rise near the surface. Active volcanoes, for example, permit hot gases and magma from deep within Earth to escape. Perhaps you have seen a geyser, like Old Faithful in Yellowstone National Park, shooting steam and hot water. The water that shoots from the geyser is heated by magma close to Earth's surface. In some areas, this hot water can be pumped into houses to provide heat.

Reading Check *What two natural phenomena are caused by geothermal heat?*

SCIENCE Online

Research Visit the Glencoe Science Web site at **science.glencoe.com** for a link to more information about geothermal energy. Communicate to your class what you learn.

Geothermal Power Plants

Geothermal energy also can be used to generate electricity, as shown in **Figure 25.** Where magma is close to the surface, the surrounding rocks are also hot. A well is drilled and water is pumped into the ground, where it makes contact with the hot rock and changes into steam. The steam then returns to the surface, where it is used to rotate turbines that spin electric generators.

The efficiency of geothermal power plants is about 80 percent—similar to that of hydroelectric plants. Although geothermal energy can release some sulfur compounds from gases within Earth, pumping the water and steam back into Earth can control this pollution. However the use of geothermal energy is limited to areas where magma is relatively close to the surface.

Figure 25
A geothermal power plant converts geothermal energy to electrical energy. Water is changed to steam by the hot rock, and the steam is pumped to the surface where it turns a turbine attached to an electric generator.

Energy from Inside Earth

Discussion

Most sources of geothermal energy are in areas with high volcanic activity. Geothermal energy is used on a large scale only in Japan, Iceland, Italy, New Zealand, and California. **Is geothermal energy renewable? Explain?** On the one hand, heat from a particular reservoir can be used up faster than it can be replaced, so it is not renewable. On the other hand, radioactive decay will provide a constant heat source for millions of years. L3 IS **Logical-Mathematical**

Use Science Words

Word Meaning Why is heat from Earth called "geothermal"? *Geo* means "Earth," and *thermal* means "heat." L2 IS **Linguistic**

Answer volcanoes and geysers

Visual Learning

Figure 25 In a geothermal plant such as the one shown here, after the steam has turned the turbine, the steam is condensed and returned to the rock through the injection well. **Why is the water returned to the rock formation?** to maintain the supply of water needed to produce steam L2 IS **Logical-Mathematical**

Resource Manager

Chapter Resources Booklet
Reinforcements, p. 29

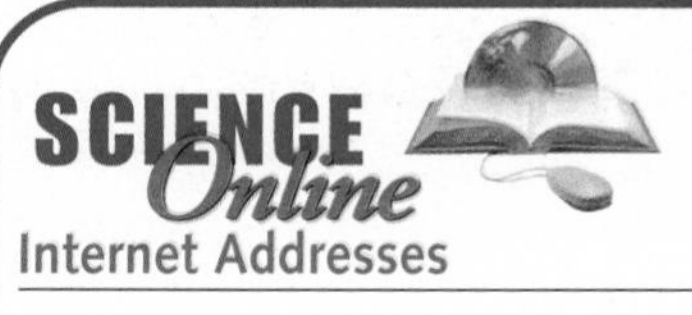

SCIENCE Online
Internet Addresses

Explore the Glencoe Science Web site at **science.glencoe.com** to find out more about topics in this section.

Alternative Fuels

Discussion

Using biomass and other alternative fuels reduces dependence on foreign oil. Why is this desirable? Political disagreements could reduce access to foreign oil because of strained relations with some countries. L3

LS Logical-Mathematical

3 Assess

Reteach

Ask students to list the six energy sources discussed in this section. Once the students have a complete list, ask them to write a sentence about each source, describing how it can be used to provide energy. L2

LS Linguistic

Challenge

Have students select one of the energy resources discussed in this section and draw up a plan describing how it could be used in their community. L3

LS Logical-Mathematical P

Performance Have students work in small groups to design and create a system for heating water using solar power. Use **Performance Assessment in the Science Classroom,** p. 117.

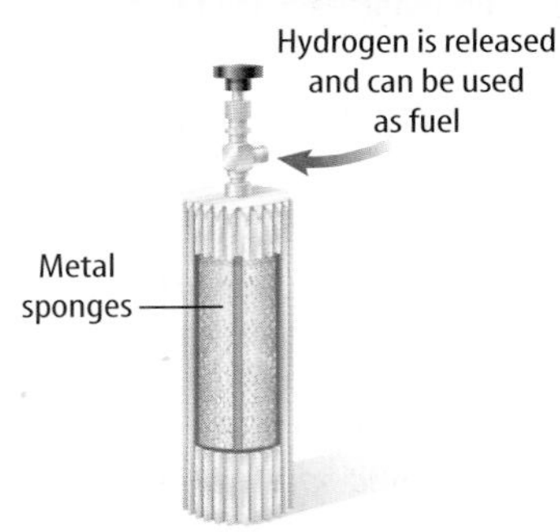

Figure 26
The hydrogen car might one day replace gasoline automobiles. One possible way of storing hydrogen is to use a metal sponge that will hold the hydrogen until it is ready to be used.

Alternative Fuels

More than two thirds of the petroleum used in the United States powers cars and other vehicles. The use of fossil fuels would be greatly reduced if cars could run on other fuels or sources of energy. For example, cars have been developed that use electrical energy supplied by batteries as a power source. Other designs use both electric motors and gasoline engines.

Hydrogen gas is another possible alternative fuel. It produces only water vapor when it burns and creates no pollution. The oceans contain an almost limitless supply of hydrogen that is combined with oxygen in water molecules. The hydrogen in water can be released by passing an electric current through the water. Producing the electric current, however, requires more energy than can be generated by burning the hydrogen gas that is produced. Other ways of producing hydrogen from water are being studied and might be useful in the future. **Figure 26** shows one possible way to store the fuel.

Biomass Fuels Fossil fuels and nuclear fission produce electricity by heating water. Could any other materials be used to heat water and produce electricity? **Biomass,** for example, is renewable organic matter, such as wood, sugarcane fibers, rice hulls, and animal manure. It, too, can be burned in the presence of oxygen to convert the stored chemical energy to thermal energy. In fact, burning biomass is probably the oldest use of natural resources for meeting human energy needs.

Section 3 Assessment

1. Why do humans need to develop and use alternative energy sources?
2. Describe three ways that solar energy can be used.
3. How is the generation of electricity by hydroelectric, tidal, and wind sources similar to each other? How is it similar to fossil fuel and nuclear power?
4. Why is geothermal energy unlikely to become a major energy resource?
5. **Think Critically** What single resource do most energy alternatives depend on, either directly or indirectly?

Skill Builder Activities

6. **Classifying** On a computer, draw a chart of the fuel sources in this section. List the advantages and disadvantages of each. Which source do you feel is most promising? Why? **For more help, refer to the** Science Skill Handbook.
7. **Using Percentages** U.S. sources of energy follow: 39 percent petroleum, 23 percent natural gas, 23 percent coal, 8 percent nuclear, and 7 percent other. If the percent of nuclear energy was shown with a 1-m strip of paper, how long would the other strips be? **For more help, refer to the** Math Skill Handbook.

Resource Manager

Chapter Resources Booklet
Activity Worksheet, pp. 5–6, 7–8
Lab Activities, pp. 9–12, 13–16

Answers to Section Assessment

1. Many present fuels are nonrenewable resources. Fossil fuels are in limited supply and cause pollution. Nuclear waste disposal is another problem.
2. Possible answers: Let the sun warm and light rooms. Use solar panels for heating water or air. Use photovoltaic cells to produce electricity.
3. Each of these spins a turbine to rotate the shaft of an electric generator.
4. It is limited to areas where magma is relatively close to the surface.
5. the Sun
6. Possible answers: Solar energy is the most abundant but can't be obtained at night. Water energy can generate power all the time, but isn't available everywhere.
7. petroleum, 4.9 m; natural gas, 2.9 m; coal, 2.9 m; other, 0.9 m

Activity

Solar Heating

Energy from the Sun is a renewable resource and is, therefore, a good type of energy to use. You know that the Sun heats Earth, but can its energy also be harnessed to heat homes or businesses? What makes solar energy difficult to use?

What You'll Investigate

How does color affect the amount of heat absorbed from the Sun?

Materials

small cardboard boxes
black, white, and colored paper
tape or glue
thermometer
watch with a second hand

Goals

- **Demonstrate** solar heating.
- **Compare** the effectiveness of heating items of different colors.
- **Graph** your results.

Procedure

1. Cover at least three small boxes with colored paper. The colors should include black and white as well as at least one other color.
2. Copy the following data table into your Science Journal. Replace "Other color" with whatever color you are using.
3. Place the three objects on a windowsill or other sunny spot and note the starting time.
4. **Measure and record** the temperature inside each box at 2-min intervals for at least 10 min.

Conclude and Apply

1. **Graph** your data using a line graph.
2. **Describe** what you can learn from your graph. What color heated up the most? The least?
3. **Explain** why the colored boxes heated at different rates.
4. Suppose you wanted to heat a tub of water using solar energy. Based on what you discovered in this activity, what color would you want the tub to be? Explain.
5. **Explain** why you might want to wear a white or light-colored shirt on a hot, sunny, summer day.

Communicating Your Data

Compare your results with those of other students in your class. Discuss any differences found in your graphs, particularly if different colors were used by different groups.

Temperature Due to Different Colors

Color	Minute 2	Minute 4	Minute 6	Minute 8	Minute 10
Black					
White		Answers will vary			
Other color					

Activity

BENCH TESTED

Purpose Students demonstrate how various colors absorb solar energy differently and graph the results. L2 LS **Kinesthetic**

Process Skills observing, inferring, comparing and contrasting, recognizing cause and effect, communicating, making and using tables, making and using graphs, interpreting data

Time Required 45 minutes

Teaching Strategy Suggest students work in pairs to make measurements. One student can read the thermometer as the other student fills in the data table. Have students work individually to prepare their graphs.

Troubleshooting Students should cover each box in a way that does not allow heat to escape.

Answers to Questions

1. Suggest students use a different color line for each color of paper.
2. Black heated the most. White heated the least.
3. Black absorbs light, which makes it heat faster, and white reflects light, which makes it heat more slowly.
4. Because black absorbs light and heats up faster, you would want the tub to be black.
5. You would want to wear a white or light-colored shirt because it reflects light and wouldn't heat up as quickly.

Assessment

Oral Have students make cartoons illustrating situations in which the color of something is important to its temperature. For example, dark colored car seats are hotter in summer than those with a light color. Use **Performance Assessment in the Science Classroom**, p. 133.

Communicating Your Data

Have students use a computer graphing program to prepare their graphs. Encourage them to make their graphs as clear as possible so that others can understand the results easily. Remind students that a clear presentation of data is important to help others benefit from their work.

Activity

BENCH TESTED

Recognize the Problem

Internet Students will use Internet sites that can be accessed through the Glencoe Science Web site at **science.glencoe.com**. They will investigate the costs and environmental impacts of different energy sources.

Non-Internet Sources Product information publications often have comparison data for energy sources such as batteries, as well as energy efficiency ratings for appliances.

Time Required

about three days

Preparation

Internet Access the Glencoe Science Web site at **science.glencoe.com** to run through the steps students will follow.

Non-Internet Sources Collect magazines and periodicals that list efficiencies of energy sources and appliances.

Form a Hypothesis

Possible Hypotheses A portable CD player runs least expensively when powered by non-rechargeable batteries.

Test Your Hypothesis

Teaching Strategy

Remind students that they should consider how different energy sources, such as rechargeable batteries and disposable batteries, affect the environment.

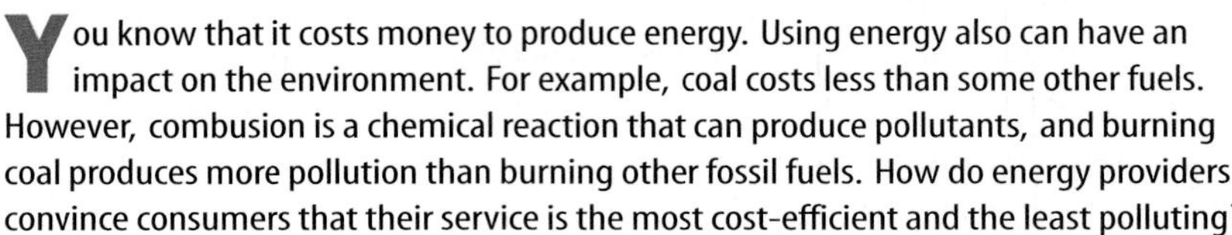

How much does energy really cost?

You know that it costs money to produce energy. Using energy also can have an impact on the environment. For example, coal costs less than some other fuels. However, combustion is a chemical reaction that can produce pollutants, and burning coal produces more pollution than burning other fossil fuels. How do energy providers convince consumers that their service is the most cost-efficient and the least polluting?

Recognize the Problem

What are the costs and environmental impacts of various energy-producing sources?

Form a Hypothesis

Form a hypothesis about which energy source you think will have the lowest cost and which will have the least impact on the environment.

Goals

- **Identify** three energy sources that people use.
- **Determine** the cost of each source.
- **Describe** the environmental impact of each source.
- **Describe** which energy source is most cost-efficient as well as the one which causes the least environmental impact.

Data Source

SCIENCE*Online* Go to the Glencoe Science Web site at **science.glencoe.com** to get more information about various energy sources and services and for data collected by other students.

Internet Addresses

Explore the Glencoe Science Web site at **science.glencoe.com** to find out more about topics in this activity.

Using Scientific Methods

Test Your Hypothesis

Plan

1. Think about the various sources of power used in different areas of the United States and make a list of possible energy sources to investigate.
2. Find out the cost of using three of these energy sources for 1 h.
3. Determine if any of your sources has a negative impact on the environment. Which sources are renewable? Do any of the sources harm the environment?
4. Use your data to create a table of energy sources, costs, and impacts.
5. Write a summary describing which of your three energy sources is the best for producing 1 h of energy. Consider the cost of the energy and the environmental impact. Provide facts from your research to support your conclusions.

Energy Sources

Energy Source	Cost for 1 h of Energy	Environmental Impacts
Energy source 1		
Energy source 2		
Energy source 3		

Do

1. Make sure your teacher approves your plan before you start.
2. Go to the Glencoe Science Web site at **science.glencoe.com** to post your data.

Analyze Your Data

1. Of the energy sources you investigated, which is the most expensive to use? The least expensive?
2. Which energy source do you think has the most impact on the environment? The least impact?

Draw Conclusions

1. Find this *Use the Internet* activity on the Glencoe Science Web site at **science.glencoe.com.** Post your data in the table provided. Compare your data to that of other students.
2. Of the energy sources you investigated, which is the least expensive energy source? Which is the best choice to use? Why or why not?
3. Of the energy sources you investigated, how did the environmental impact of that power influence your choice of the best energy solution?
4. What data support your decision?

Communicating Your Data

Make a poster of magazine pictures to illustrate impact on the enviroment for each of the three energy sources.

Analyze Your Data

1. Remind students to consider the costs of producing energy sources as they evaluate the cost of using each source.
2. Answers may vary. Students should evaluate different environmental impacts of energy sources, such as water pollution and toxins released into the ground.

Draw Conclusions

1. Ask students to investigate any major discrepancies between their data and data posted by other students.
2. To support their answers, ask students to provide specific facts to explain why an energy source is the least expensive or the most expensive.
3. Student responses should describe how the chosen energy source affects the environment.
4. Information from scientific and energy industry sources may provide data to support students' hypothesis.

Assessment

Process Have students make displays describing their findings. Displays should include the items that were investigated, students' hypotheses, different energy sources that could be used to operate the items, and the cost and environmental impact of each energy source. Displays should also describe whether the data supported their hypothesis and their conclusions. Use **PASC,** p. 135.

Communicating Your Data

Have them design a rating system to evaluate the environmental impact of the energy sources for the different sources. One criterion might be whether or not the energy source is renewable. After analyzing each energy source for each criterion, students can make bar graphs representing their results.

Content Background

Nuclear energy is a complicated subject. Images of the devastation from atomic explosions and sensational accounts of the dangers of radiation have created fear regarding anything labeled *nuclear*. The abstract nature of the subject offers little comfort to the layman.

Advocates of nuclear power dismiss people's fears as irrational and excessive. Advocates and opponents of nuclear power both present conflicting evidence from respectable scientists. The average person is usually left confused, frightened or both.

Radiation occurs when an unstable atom ejects particles or energy from its nucleus in the process of becoming stable. Fission, the splitting of an atom into two smaller atoms, releases neutrons at very high speeds. These neutrons collide with other atoms, destabilizing them and causing a chain reaction. The high energy impacts of fission also release high energy electromagnetic radiation called gamma rays, which can only be blocked by lead or thick concrete.

TIME SCIENCE AND Society

SCIENCE ISSUES THAT AFFECT YOU!

Reacting to

Solar panels help power homes in this development.

The power of the wind is harnessed by these wind turbines in California.

Most people agree that thanks to energy sources, we have many things that make our quality of life better. Energy runs our cars, lights our homes, and powers our appliances. What many people don't agree on is where that energy should come from. Nuclear energy is a topic that stirs up strong opinions in people. As you read the summaries of the issues given here, think about your own opinions.

A Question of the Environment

Almost all of the world's electric energy is produced by thermal power plants. Most of these plants burn fossil fuels—such as coal, oil, and natural gas—to produce energy. Nuclear energy is produced by fission, which is the splitting of an atom's nucleus. People in favor of nuclear energy argue that, unlike fossil fuels, nuclear energy is nonpolluting. When coal is burned, it releases large amounts of sulfur and other pollutants into the air. These pollutants contribute to serious environmental problems such as smog and acid rain. Uranium, the key fuel for nuclear reactors, releases no chemical or solid pollutants into the air during use.

Opponents counter, though, that the poisonous radioactive waste created in nuclear reactors qualifies as pollution—and will be lingering in the ground and water for hundreds of thousands of years.

Supporters of nuclear energy also cite the spectacular efficiency of nuclear energy—one metric ton of nuclear fuel produces the same amount of energy as up to 3 million tons of coal. Opponents point out that uranium is in very short supply and, like fossil fuels, is likely to run out in the next 100 years.

314

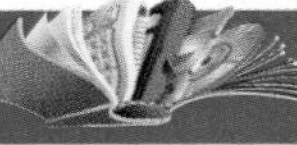

Resources for Teachers and Students

American Nuclear Society, 555 North Kensington Avenue, LaGrange Park, Illinois 60526 USA

Quarks and Sparks: The Story of Nuclear Power (Science and Society Series), by J. S. Kidd and Renee A. Kidd, New York: Facts on File (1999)

American Wind Energy Association, 122 C Street, NW, Suite 380, Washington, DC 20001

Nuclear Energy

A Question of Health & Safety

Opponents of nuclear energy point out the health dangers associated with mining and processing nuclear fuel. *Radiation sickness* is the term for a variety of symptoms that result when a person is exposed to damaging amounts of radiation. Exposure to high levels of radiation may cause lasting illness or even death. Opponents worry that as utilities come under less government regulation, safety standards will be ignored in the interest of profit. This could result in more accidents like the one that occurred at Chernobyl in the Ukraine. There, an explosion in the reactor core released radiation over a wide area.

Supporters counter that it will never be in the best interests of those running nuclear plants to relax safety standards since those safety standards are the best safeguard of workers' health. They cite the overall good safety record of nuclear power plants.

Radioactivity caused by a leak at a Ukraine nuclear power plant has given this baby physical problems.

Nuclear power plants give off "clean" energy.

A Third Side of the Coin

Others argue that the solution to energy woes lies elsewhere. They say nuclear energy and fossil fuels are both non-renewable and produce dangerous by-products—and that investments should be made in sources of energy that are renewable and safe.

They argue that if the same amount of money that has been spent to develop nuclear energy were spent to develop alternative energy sources, such as hydroelectric and solar power, many of the problems associated with these alternatives would have been solved by now.

This view is challenged by those who say that some alternative energy sources are not always available to people. For example, tidal energy isn't available everywhere, nor will solar power work well in an area in which the Sun doesn't shine very brightly.

CONNECTIONS Debate **Divide the class into three teams and assign each one of the views presented here. If you need more information, go to the Glencoe Science Web site. "Debrief" after the debate. Did the arguments change your understanding of the issues?**

SCIENCE *Online*
For more information, visit science.glencoe.com

Discussion

Are there any drawbacks to wind, hydroelectric, or tidal power technologies? Possible answers: Wind and tide generation are variable and restricted to a localized area. Hydroelectric power requires building dams, which then have an impact on wildlife habitats. Wind and hydro power use much more land area per kilowatt than the others.

Activity

Divide the class into teams. Have one team member record data and one or two take measurements and be spotters. Give the other students on the team equal weights. Have team members measure the height of each lifter both standing and squatting. The difference will be the lift distance. The lifters will then do as many squats as possible in 1 minute, holding the weight. The teams will then multiply the weight in pounds by the lift distance in feet and divide by 33 x 103 to determine the lifter's Horsepower. The electrical equivalent of 1HP is 746 watts. Average the students' HP and calculate the number of students it would take to equal the school's electrical consumption. L2 LS **Kinesthetic**

Investigate the Issue

Have students research the feasibility of power sources not discussed in the article such as fusion and fuel cells. Discuss whether any of these might replace current available sources.

CONNECTIONS Have the teams use the knowledge they gained from the activity and investigation above to help them investigate the cost per kilowatt of one of the technologies discussed. Remind students to keep in mind the amount and type of pollution caused by each technology and by processing its fuel. Ask teams for recommendations about future energy production.

SCIENCE *Online*

Internet Addresses

Explore the Glencoe Science Web site at **science.glencoe.com** to find out more about topics in this feature.

Chapter 10 Study Guide

Reviewing Main Ideas

Preview

Students can answer the questions in their Science Journals. Discuss the answers as you go through the chapter. LS **Linguistic**

Review

Students can write their answers, then compare them with those of other students. LS **Interpersonal**

Reteach

Students can look at the illustrations and describe details that support the main ideas of the chapter. LS **Visual-Spatial**

Answers to Chapter Review

Section 1

2. synthetic fabrics and plastics

Section 2

2. The bedrock would keep the waste from reaching the water supply.

Section 3

3. water

Chapter 10 Study Guide

Reviewing Main Ideas

Section 1 Fossil Fuels

1. Fossil fuels include oil, natural gas, and coal. They formed from the buried remains of plants and animals.
2. Fossil fuels can be burned to supply energy for generating electricity. Petroleum has other uses, as well. *What materials in this picture have been made from petroleum?*

3. Fossil fuels are nonrenewable energy resources. They can be replaced but it takes millions of years.

Section 2 Nuclear Energy

1. A nuclear reactor uses the energy from a controlled nuclear chain reaction to generate electricity.
2. Nuclear wastes must be contained and disposed of carefully so radiation from nuclear decay will not leak into the environment. *What makes the area in this picture a suitable place for storing nuclear wastes?*

3. Nuclear fusion releases energy when two nuclei combine. Fusion only occurs at high temperatures that are difficult to produce in a laboratory.

Section 3 Renewable Energy Sources

1. Alternate energy resources can be used to supplement or replace nonrenewable energy resources.
2. Other sources of energy for generating electricity include hydroelectricity and solar, wind, tidal, and geothermal energy. Each source has its advantages and disadvantages. Also, some of these sources can damage the environment.
3. Although some alternate energy sources produce less pollution than fossil fuels do, and are renewable, their use often is limited to the regions where the energy source is available. *What type of alternate energy might provide power for the area in this photo?*

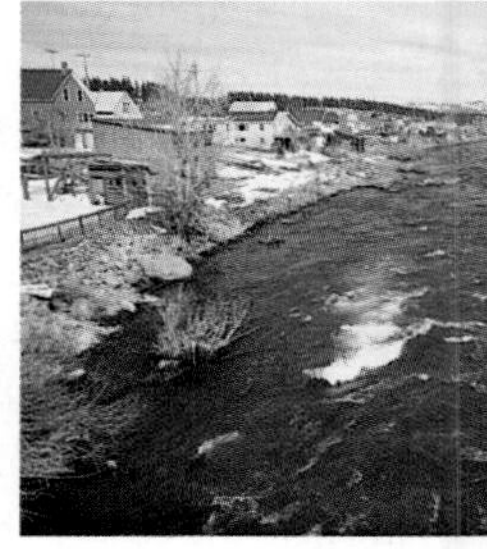

4. It's possible that humans might one day drive hydrogen-powered cars. Biomass is an alternate fuel that has been used for thousands of years.

FOLDABLES Reading & Study Skills — After You Read

Using information from the chapter, list an example of each energy source in the smaller ovals on the front of your Concept Map Study Fold.

FOLDABLES Reading & Study Skills — After You Read

After students have read the chapter and completed the Foldable described in Before You Read, have them do the activity on the student page.

Dinah Zike

Chapter 10 Study Guide

Visualizing Main Ideas

Complete the following concept map on energy resources.

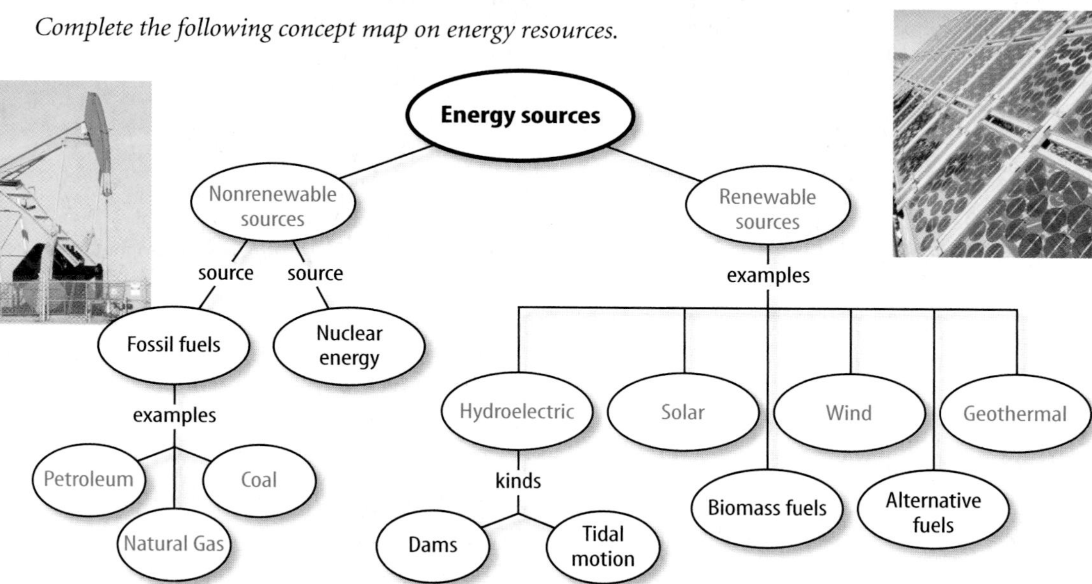

Vocabulary Review

Vocabulary Words

- **a.** biomass
- **b.** fossil fuel
- **c.** geothermal energy
- **d.** hydroelectricity
- **e.** nonrenewable resource
- **f.** nuclear reactor
- **g.** nuclear waste
- **h.** petroleum
- **i.** photovoltaic cell
- **j.** renewable resource

Study Tip

Listening is a learning tool, too. Record a reading of your notes on tape and listen to it several times each week.

Using Vocabulary

Change the incorrect terms so that the sentences read correctly. Underline your changes.

1. A nuclear reactor separates the hydrocarbons in crude oil.
2. Hydroelectricity makes use of thermal energy inside Earth.
3. Energy produced by the rise and fall of ocean levels is a nonrenewable resource.
4. Petroleum includes the following: oil, natural gas, and coal.
5. Fossil fuels are a renewable resource because they are being used up faster than they are being made.
6. Special caution should be taken in disposing of a photovoltaic cell.

Chapter 10 Study Guide

Visualizing Main Ideas

See student page.

Vocabulary Review

Using Vocabulary

1. Fractional distillation separates the hydrocarbons in crude oil.
2. Geothermal energy makes use of thermal energy inside Earth.
3. Energy produced by the rise and fall of ocean levels is tidal energy.
4. Fossil fuel includes the following: oil, natural gas, and coal.
5. Fossil fuels are a nonrenewable resource because they are being used up faster than they are being made.
6. Special caution should be taken in disposing of nuclear waste.

CHAPTER STUDY GUIDE 317

Chapter 10 Assessment

Checking Concepts

1. A
2. C
3. C
4. A
5. C
6. D
7. B
8. B
9. C
10. D

Thinking Critically

11. Alternative energy resources are not widely used because the necessary technology does not yet exist, is too expensive, or has limited applicability.
12. a. wind energy, hydroelectricity, tidal energy; b. geothermal energy; c. nuclear fission; d. fossil fuels, biomass; e. solar energy
13. It is too difficult to create and maintain the high temperatures required.
14. renewable: solar energy, hydroelectricity, tidal energy, geothermal energy, wind energy; nonrenewable: fossil fuels, nuclear fission
15. These new sources would still be non-renewable. Decreasing use would make them last longer.

Chapter 10 Assessment

Checking Concepts

Choose the word or phrase that best answers the question.

1. How much energy in the United States comes from burning petroleum, natural gas, and coal?
   A) 85% **C)** 65%
   B) 35% **D)** 25%
2. What do hydrocarbons react with when fossil fuels are burned?
   A) carbon dioxide **C)** oxygen
   B) carbon monoxide **D)** water
3. Why are fossil fuels considered to be nonrenewable resources?
   A) They are no longer being produced.
   B) They are in short supply.
   C) They are not being produced as fast as they're being used.
   D) They contain hydrocarbons.
4. To generate electricity, what product do fossil fuels and nuclear fission produce?
   A) steam **C)** plutonium
   B) carbon dioxide **D)** water
5. What is a major disadvantage of using nuclear fusion reactors?
   A) use of hydrogen as fuel
   B) less radioactivity produced
   C) extremely high temperatures required
   D) use of only small nuclei
6. Which is NOT a source of nuclear waste?
   A) products of fission reactors
   B) materials with short half-lives
   C) some medical and industrial products
   D) products of coal-burning power plants
7. To what can all of Earth's energy resources ultimately be traced?
   A) plants **C)** magma
   B) the Sun **D)** fossil fuels
8. How are high-level nuclear wastes usually disposed of?
   A) releasing them into water
   B) releasing them into a deep, insulated pool of water
   C) burying them at the reactor site
   D) releasing them into the air
9. What characteristic would enable photovoltaic cells to be used more widely?
   A) pollution free **C)** less expensive
   B) nonrenewable **D)** larger
10. What energy source uses water that is heated naturally by Earth's internal heat?
    A) hydroelectricity **C)** tidal energy
    B) nuclear fission **D)** geothermal energy

Thinking Critically

11. Why aren't alternate energy resources more widely used?
12. Match each of the energy resources described in the chapter with the proper type of energy conversion listed below.
    a. kinetic energy to electricity
    b. thermal energy to electricity
    c. nuclear energy to electricity
    d. chemical energy to electricity
    e. light energy to electricity
13. Why isn't fusion currently used as a source of energy?

14. Classify the energy resources discussed in this chapter and in the photo as renewable or nonrenewable.
15. Suppose new reserves of fossil fuels and a way to burn them cleanly were found. Why would it still be a good idea to decrease use of them as a source of energy?

Chapter Assessment Planner

Portfolio Encourage students to place in their portfolios one or two items of what they consider to be their best work. Examples include:
- Curriculum Connection, p. 291
- Activity, p. 296
- Reteach, p. 304
- Challenge, p. 310

Performance Additional performance assessments, Performance Task Assessment Lists, and rubrics for evaluating these activities can be found in Glencoe's **Performance Assessment in the Science Classroom.**

Developing Skills

16. **Communicating** Describe the steps that must occur before you can use the Sun's energy to power a car.
17. **Drawing Conclusions** Discuss whether or not alternate energy sources could have negative effects on the environment.
18. **Recognizing Cause and Effect** Complete the table describing possible effects of changes in the normal operation of a nuclear reactor.

Reactor Problems

Cause	Effect
The cooling water is released hot.	Pollution of the environment results.
The control rods are removed.	More heat is produced in the core.
The cooling system fails.	The reactor core overheats and meltdown occurs.

19. **Using Percentages** What is the overall efficiency of a power plant whose stages have efficiencies of 65, 75, 90 percents, and 70 percent?

Performance Assessment

20. **Newspaper Article** Write a newspaper article to raise public awareness of current energy problems and solutions. In your article, discuss the economic and environmental costs of various energy sources.

Technology

Go to the Glencoe Science Web site at **science.glencoe.com** or use the **Glencoe Science CD-ROM** for additional chapter assessment.

THE PRINCETON REVIEW Test Practice

Concerned about air pollution, Andrew gathered information about compressed natural gas-powered cars. He made a graph comparing emissions from a compressed natural gas (CNG)-powered car to its gasoline-powered counterpart.

Emissions

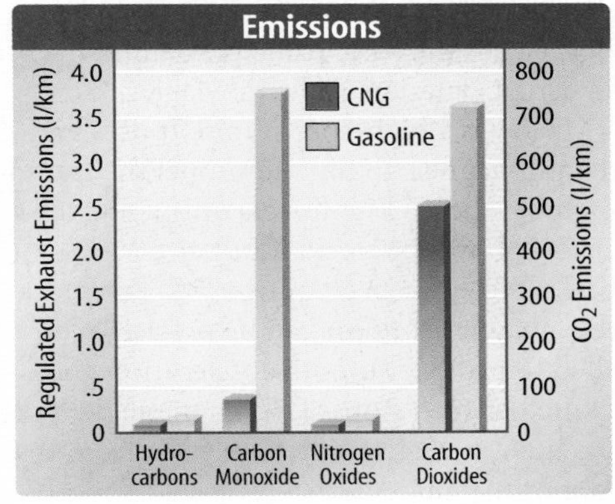

Study the graph and answer the following questions.

1. According to the graph, which pollutant is emitted into the air in the greatest amount?
   A) hydrocarbons
   B) carbon monoxide
   C) nitrogen oxides
   D) carbon dioxide
2. Based on the data in the graph, which is the greatest benefit of using cars that are powered by compressed natural gas?
   F) better gas mileage when traveling on highways
   G) fewer carbon monoxide emissions
   H) increased carbon dioxide emissions
   J) use of non-combustible fuel reclaimed?

Assessment Resources

Reproducible Masters

Chapter Resources Booklet
Chapter Review, pp. 37–38
Chapter Tests, pp. 39–42
Assessment Transparency Activity, p. 49

Glencoe Science Web site
Interactive Tutor
Chapter Quizzess

Glencoe Technology
Assessment Transparency
Interactive CD-ROM Chapter Quizzes
ExamView Pro Test Bank
Vocabulary PuzzleMaker Software
MindJogger Videoquiz DVD/VHS

Chapter 10 Assessment

THE PRINCETON REVIEW Test Practice

The Test-Taking Tip was written by The Princeton Review, the nation's leader in test preparation.

1. B
2. G

Developing Skills

16. Solar energy must be converted to electrical energy by photovoltaic cells and stored in batteries.
17. Possible answer: Tidal power plants could disrupt marine life.
18. See student page.
19. 31%

Performance Assessment

20. Problems may include pollution and exhaustion of nonrenewable resources. Use **PASC**, p. 141.

Standardized Test Practice

Reading Comprehension

Question 1: B
Students need to consider all the information in the passage in order to identify which answer choice is the best summary. Choices A, C, and D are details from the passage. Only choice B is a summary of the passage.

Question 2: F
Students need to use context clues in the passage in order to identify the correct answer choice. Students should reread the sentences surrounding the underlined word in order to locate clues. Only choice F is supported by information in the passage.

Teaching Tip

Students can use information in the passage in order to identify the correct answer choice as well as to eliminate incorrect answer choices.

All questions written and validated by The Princeton Review.

Standardized Test Practice

Reading Comprehension

Read the passage. Then read each question that follows the passage. Decide which is the best answer to each question.

Magnetic Levitation Train

One of the first things people learn about magnets is that like magnetic poles repel each other. This is the basic principle behind the Magnetic Levitation Train, or Maglev.

Maglev is a high-speed train. It uses high-strength magnets to lift and propel the train to incredible speeds as it hovers only a few centimeters above the track. A full-size Maglev in Japan achieved a speed of over 500 km/h! Its electromagnetic motor can be precisely controlled to provide smooth acceleration and braking between stops. The magnetic field prevents the vehicle from drifting away from the center of the guideway.

Because there is no friction between wheels and rails, Maglevs eliminate the principal limitation of <u>conventional</u> trains, which is the high cost of maintaining the tracks to avoid excessive vibration and wear that can cause dangerous derailments. Critics point out that Maglevs require enormous amounts of energy. However, studies have shown that Maglevs use 30 percent less energy than other high-speed trains traveling at the same speed. Others worry about the dangers from magnetic fields; however, measurements show that humans are exposed to magnetic fields no stronger than those from toasters or hair dryers.

In Japan, a series of Maglev vehicles are slated to begin tests later this year on a 27-mile demonstration line. In Germany, a 180-mile Maglev line between Berlin and Hamburg is scheduled to go into service in 2005. Perhaps, in the not-too-distant future, Maglev trains will transport commuters to and from work or school here in the United States.

Test-Taking Tip After you read the passage, write a one-sentence summary of the main idea for each paragraph.

This is a Maglev train test in Japan.

1. Which of these is the best summary of this passage?
   A) Maglev transportation is currently in use in Germany and Japan.
   B) Maglev is a high-speed transport system of the future.
   C) Maglevs use more energy than conventional high-speed trains.
   D) Maglevs can reach high speeds because there is no friction.

2. In this passage, the word <u>conventional</u> means _____.
   F) customary
   G) innovative
   H) political
   J) unusual

Standardized Test Practice

Reasoning and Skills

Read each question and choose the best answer.

1. Voltage gets stepped up when the secondary coil in a transformer has more turns of wire than the primary coil. Which of the following steps up voltage the most?

A)

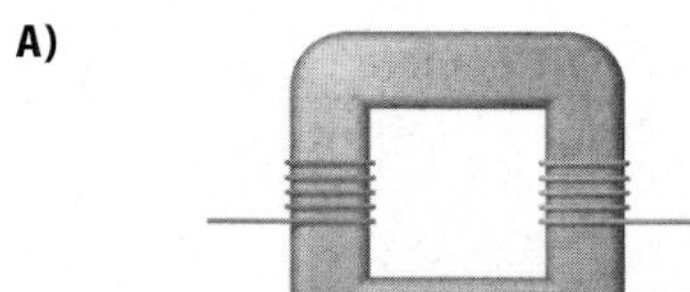

B)

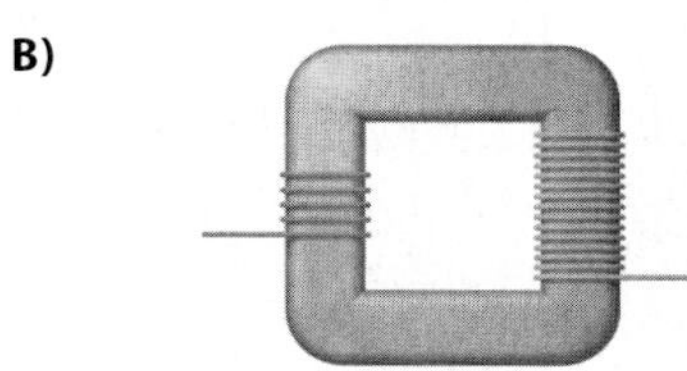

C)

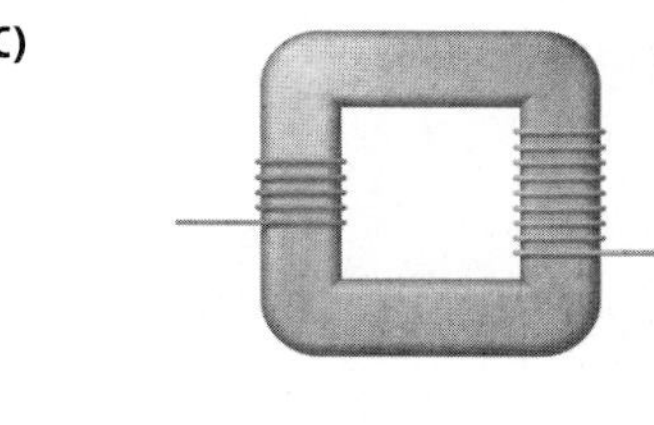

D)

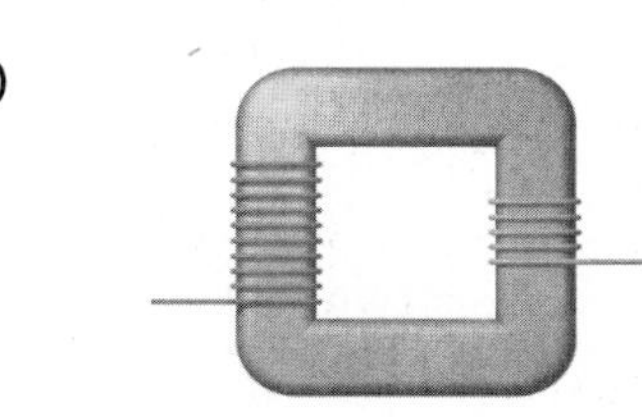

Test-Taking Tip Use the information provided in the question to closely consider each answer choice.

2. Nuclear decay produces radiation, which can ionize nearby atoms. How could this radiation benefit human health?
   F) Absorbing excess hormones produced by the thyroid.
   G) Increasing an organ's absorption of radioactive isotopes.
   H) Destroying cells in cancerous tumors.
   J) Boosting the immune system.

Test-Taking Tip Review information about cancer treatments that use radiation.

3. Shahid wanted to pick up pieces of metal with a magnet. Which observation would mean that the magnet would NOT allow Shahid to pick up the pieces of metal?
   A) The metal pieces were small and far away from the magnet.
   B) The magnet was brand new.
   C) The metal pieces were made out of aluminum foil.
   D) The metal pieces and the magnet have the same magnetic poles.

Test-Taking Tip Review what you know about magnetic materials.

Consider this question carefully before writing your answer on a separate sheet of paper.

4. Recall what you know about the production of current. Explain the similarities and differences between direct current (DC) and alternating current (AC).

Test-Taking Tip Use the clues *direct* and *alternating* to guide your answer.

Standardized Test Practice

Reasoning and Skills

QUESTION 1: B

Students should carefully read the question in order to use the statement *voltage gets stepped up when the secondary coil in a transformer has more turns of wire than the primary coil* to identify the correct answer choice. Choices A, C, and D do not follow the information in the above statement. Only answer choice B illustrates a secondary coil with more turns of wire than a primary coil.

QUESTION 2: H

Student need to use their understanding of cancer treatments and nuclear radiation in order to locate the correct answer.

- Choice F: No; this is an inaccurate statement.
- Choice G: No; this is not necessarily beneficial to human health, and it is not an accurate statement.
- Choice H: Yes; this is beneficial to human health, and it is an accurate statement.
- Choice J : No; this is an inaccurate statement.

QUESTION 3: C

Students need to use their understanding of magnets in order to identify the correct answer.

- Choice A: No; although this could have an affect on the magnet, it is not the best answer.
- Choice B: No; this should have no affect on the magnet.
- Choice C: Yes; aluminum has properties that resist magnetism.
- Choice D: No; this should have no affect on the magnet.

QUESTION 4: Answers will vary.

Students need to use their understanding of direct current (DC) and alternating current (AC) in order to write a thorough response.

UNIT 3

Unit Contents

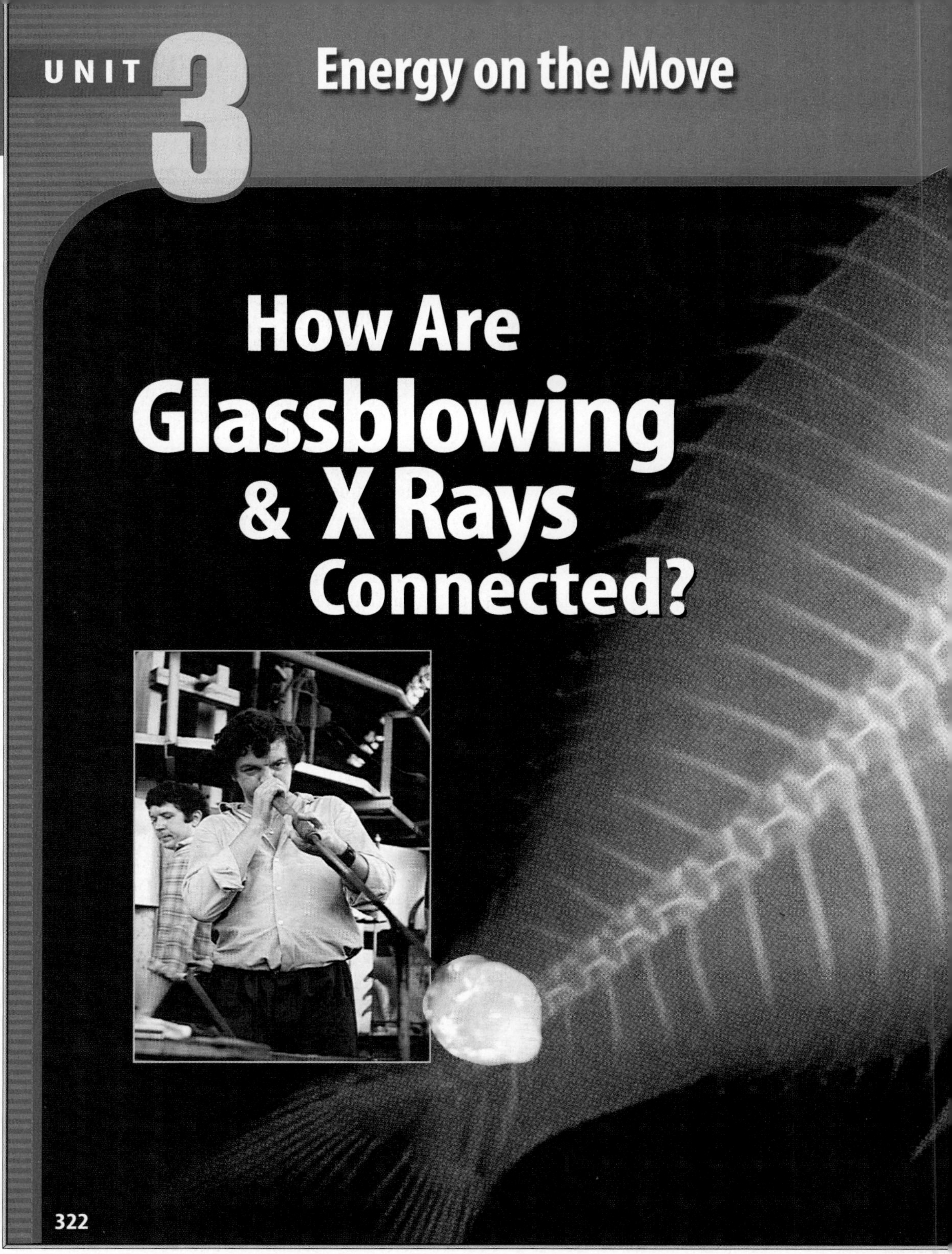

Pre-Reading Activity

Have students find pictures of optical instruments and machines and challenge them to name as many as they can.

UNIT 3 Energy on the Move

How Are Glassblowing & X Rays Connected?

322

Teacher to Teacher

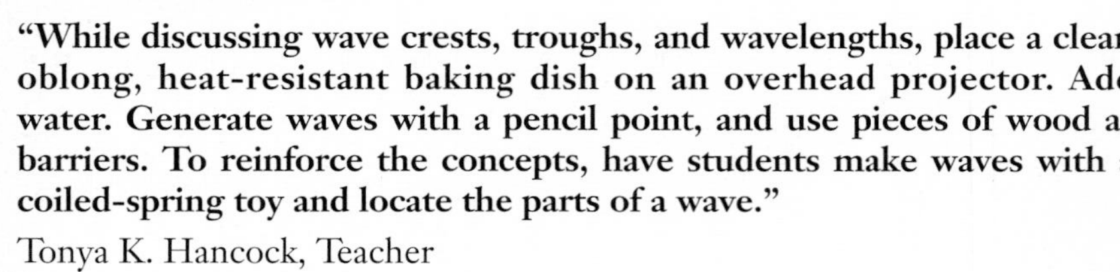

"While discussing wave crests, troughs, and wavelengths, place a clear, oblong, heat-resistant baking dish on an overhead projector. Add water. Generate waves with a pencil point, and use pieces of wood as barriers. To reinforce the concepts, have students make waves with a coiled-spring toy and locate the parts of a wave."

Tonya K. Hancock, Teacher
Davis Drive Middle School
Raleigh, NC

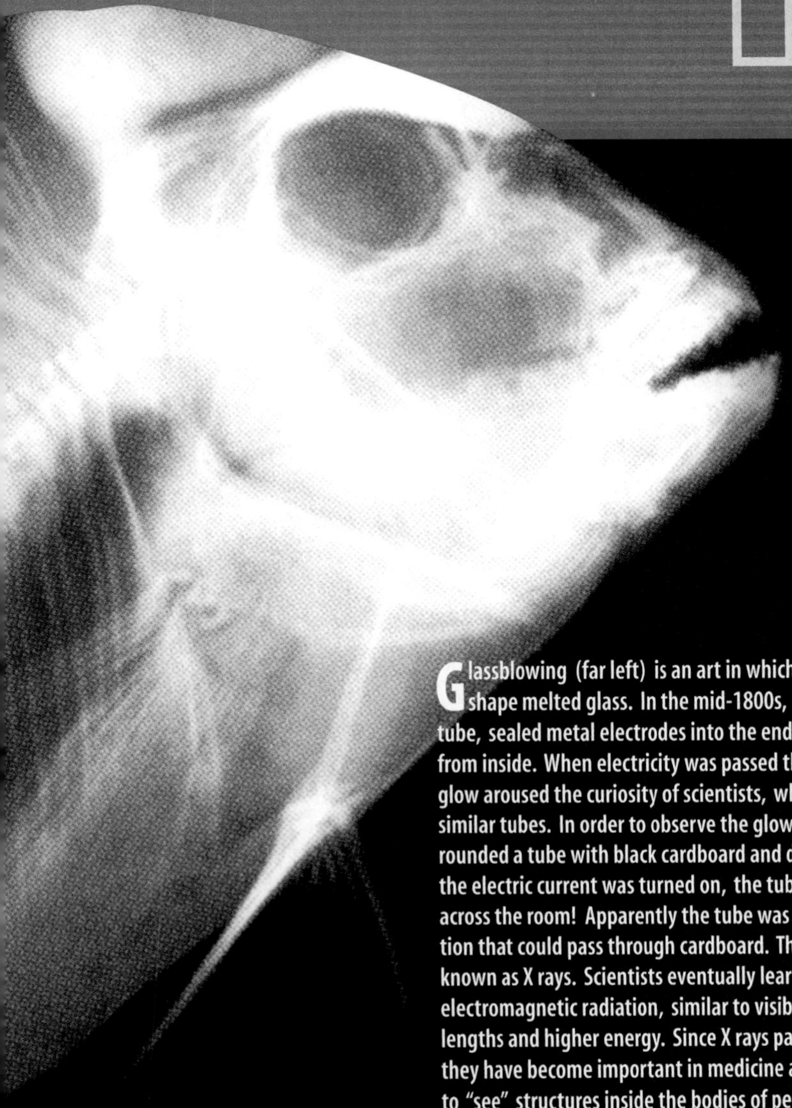

NATIONAL GEOGRAPHIC

Glassblowing (far left) is an art in which air is blown through a tube to shape melted glass. In the mid-1800s, a glassblower created a glass tube, sealed metal electrodes into the ends, and removed most of the air from inside. When electricity was passed through the tube, it glowed. The glow aroused the curiosity of scientists, who began experimenting with similar tubes. In order to observe the glow more closely, one physicist surrounded a tube with black cardboard and darkened the laboratory. When the electric current was turned on, the tube glowed—but so did an object across the room! Apparently the tube was emitting some kind of radiation that could pass through cardboard. The mysterious radiation became known as X rays. Scientists eventually learned that X rays are a form of electromagnetic radiation, similar to visible light but with shorter wavelengths and higher energy. Since X rays pass through many substances, they have become important in medicine and science, making it possible to "see" structures inside the bodies of people—and also fish.

SCIENCE CONNECTION

X RAYS AND BODY STRUCTURES X rays are used routinely by doctors to examine bones and some other structures inside the body. On a piece of drawing paper, use a pencil to trace around one of your hands, including all the fingers. Inside the outline, sketch what you think an X ray image of your hand might look like. Compare your drawing to a real X ray of a human hand. What types of body structures are most visible in X rays? What types of body structures are hard to see?

SCIENCE Online

Internet Addresses

Explore the Glencoe Science Web site at **science.glencoe.com** to find out more about topics in this unit.

Introducing the Unit

How Are Glassblowing & X Rays Connected?

- Tell students that X rays can be used on things that are not living. For example, they are helpful in locating cracks and overstressed areas in buildings and other structures.
- Ask students to brainstorm as many examples of energy on the move as they can. In addition to X rays and other types of electromagnetic radiation, such as visible light, lists might include transfer of heat from one place to another or the movement of an object, such as a bouncing ball.

SCIENCE CONNECTION

Activity

Students should notice that hard tissue, such as bone, is most visible. Soft tissue, such as skin and muscle, can be seen but not as clearly. Ask students to share times that they or someone in their families have had X rays taken. Be sure students understand that not all medical procedures that produce images involve X rays.

Section/Objectives	Standards		Activities/Features
	National	State/Local	
Chapter Opener	See p. 37T for a Key to Standards.		**Explore Activity:** Demonstrating Energy Transfer, p. 325 **Before You Read,** p. 325
Section 1 The Nature of Waves 1 session .5 block 1. **Recognize** that waves carry energy but not matter. 2. **Define** mechanical waves. 3. **Distinguish** between transverse waves and compressional waves.	National Content Standards: UCP2, B3 (5–8), B5, B6 (9–12)		**Visualizing Formation of Ocean Waves,** p. 330 **Science Online,** p. 331
Section 2 Wave Properties 2 sessions 1 block 1. **Compare and contrast** transverse and compressional waves. 2. **Describe** the relationship between frequency and wavelength. 3. **Calculate** wave speed.	National Content Standards: UCP2, A1, B3 (5–8), B5, B6 (9–12)		**MiniLAB:** Observing Wavelength, p. 333 **Earth Science Integration,** p. 335 **Math Skills Activity:** Calculating Wave Speed, p. 335 **Activity:** Waves in Different Mediums, p. 338
Section 3 The Behavior of Waves 3 sessions 1.5 blocks 1. **Identify** the law of reflection. 2. **Recognize** what makes waves bend. 3. **Explain** how waves combine.	National Content Standards: UCP2, A1, B3 (5–8), B5, B6 (9–12), G3		**Science Online,** p. 343 **Health Integration,** p. 345 **MiniLAB:** Experimenting with Resonance, p. 347 **Activity:** Measuring Wave Properties, p. 348 **Science and History:** Making Waves, p. 350

Activity Materials	Reproducible Resources	Section Assessment	Technology
Explore Activity: 4 marbles, textbook	**Chapter Resources Booklet** Foldables Worksheet, p. 17 Note-taking Worksheets, pp. 33–35	GLENCOE'S ASSESSMENT ADVANTAGE	
Need materials? Contact Science Kit at 1-800-828-7777 or www.sciencekit.com on the Internet.	**Chapter Resources Booklet** Transparency Activity, p. 44 Enrichment, p. 30 Reinforcement, p. 27 Directed Reading, p. 20 **Cultural Diversity,** p. 43 **Science Inquiry Labs,** p. 31 **Reading and Writing Skill Activities.** p. 7	**Portfolio** Assessment, p. 331 **Performance** Skill Builder Activities, p. 331 **Content** Section Assessment, p. 331	Section Focus Transparency Interactive CD-ROM/DVD Guided Reading Audio Program
MiniLAB: pie plate, water **Activity:** metal and plastic coiled spring toys, light and heavy rope, string, long rubber band, strip of towel, strip of pantyhose, ribbon, stopwatch	**Chapter Resources Booklet** Transparency Activity, p. 45 MiniLAB, p. 3 Enrichment, p. 31 Reinforcement, p. 28 Directed Reading, p. 20 Activity Worksheet, pp. 5–6 Lab Activity, pp. 9–11 Transparency Activity, pp. 47–48 **Mathematics Skill Activities,** p. 9	**Portfolio** Math Skills Activity, p. 335 **Performance** MiniLAB, p. 333 Math Skills Activity, p. 335 Skill Builder Activities, p. 337 **Content** Section Assessment, p. 337	Section Focus Transparency Teaching Transparency Interactive CD-ROM/DVD Guided Reading Audio Program
MiniLAB: 3 tuning forks, mallet **Activity:** long spring, rope, or hose; meterstck, stopwatch	**Chapter Resources Booklet** Transparency Activity, p. 46 MiniLAB, p. 4 Enrichment, p. 32 Reinforcement, p. 29 Directed Reading, pp. 21, 22 Activity Worksheet, p. 7–8 Lab Activity, pp. 13–16 **Reading and Writing Skill Activities,** p. 33 **Home and Community Involvement,** p. 38 **Cultural Diversity,** p. 61	**Portfolio** Science Journal, p. 340 Curriculum Connection, p.343 **Performance** MiniLAB, p. 347 Skill Builder Activities, p. 347 **Content** Section Assessment, p. 347	Section Focus Transparency Interactive CD-ROM/DVD Guided Reading Audio Program

End of Chapter Assessment

GLENCOE'S ASSESSMENT ADVANTAGE

Blackline Masters	Technology	Professional Series
Chapter Resources Booklet Chapter Review, pp. 37–38 Chapter Tests, pp. 39–42 **Standardized Test Practice by The Princeton Review,** pp. 48–51	MindJogger Videoquiz CD-ROM Explorations and Quizzes Vocabulary Puzzle Makers ExamView Pro Test Bank Interactive Lesson Planner Interactive Teacher's Edition	Performance Assessment in the Science Classroom (PASC)

Transparencies

Section Focus

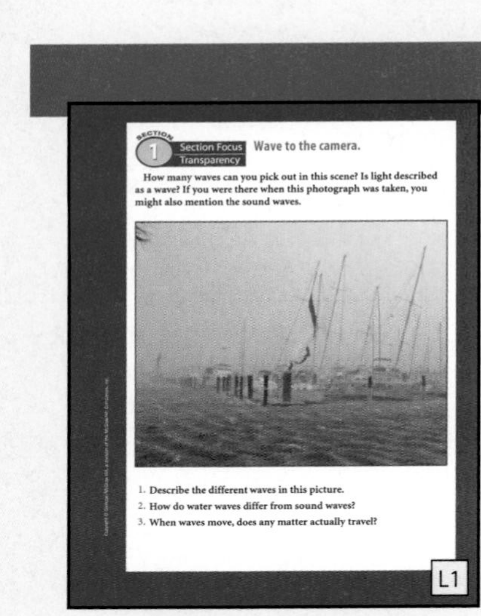
Section 1 Section Focus Transparency — Wave to the camera.

How many waves can you pick out in this scene? Is light described as a wave? If you were there when this photograph was taken, you might also mention the sound waves.

1. Describe the different waves in this picture.
2. How do water waves differ from sound waves?
3. When waves move, does any matter actually travel?

L1

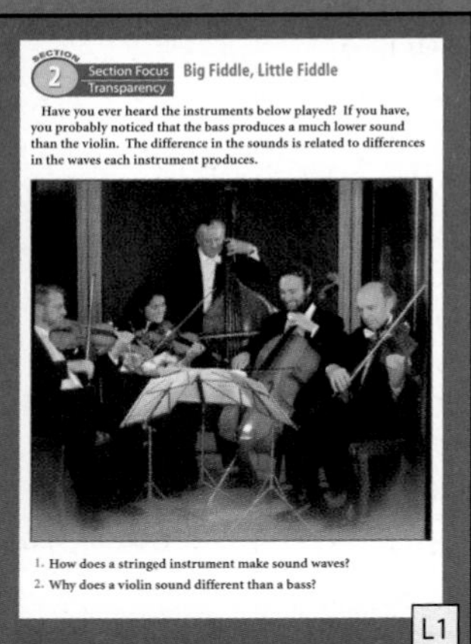
Section 2 Section Focus Transparency — Big Fiddle, Little Fiddle

Have you ever heard the instruments below played? If you have, you probably noticed that the bass produces a much lower sound than the violin. The difference in the sounds is related to differences in the waves each instrument produces.

1. How does a stringed instrument make sound waves?
2. Why does a violin sound different than a bass?

L1

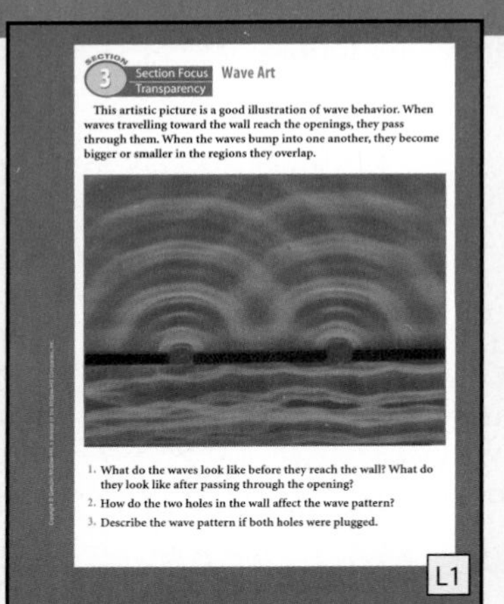
Section 3 Section Focus Transparency — Wave Art

This artistic picture is a good illustration of wave behavior. When waves travelling toward the wall reach the openings, they pass through them. When the waves bump into one another, they become bigger or smaller in the regions they overlap.

1. What do the waves look like before they reach the wall? What do they look like after passing through the opening?
2. How do the two holes in the wall affect the wave pattern?
3. Describe the wave pattern if both holes were plugged.

L1

This is a representation of key blackline masters available in the Teacher Classroom Resources. See Resource Manager boxes within the chapter for additional information.

Assessment

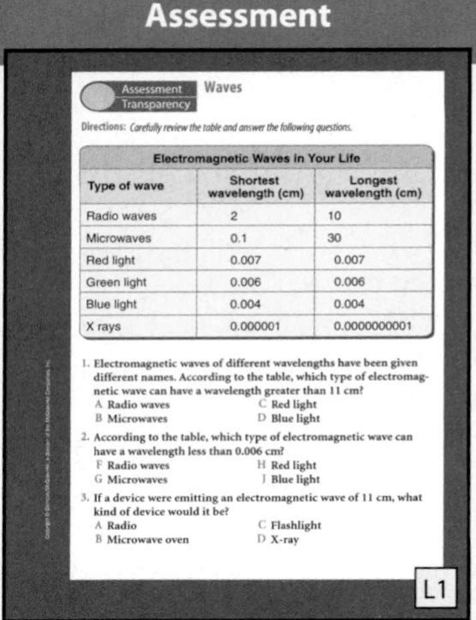
Assessment Transparency — Waves

Directions: Carefully review the table and answer the following questions.

Electromagnetic Waves in Your Life

Type of wave	Shortest wavelength (cm)	Longest wavelength (cm)
Radio waves	2	10
Microwaves	0.1	30
Red light	0.007	0.007
Green light	0.006	0.006
Blue light	0.004	0.004
X rays	0.000001	0.0000000001

1. Electromagnetic waves of different wavelengths have been given different names. According to the table, which type of electromagnetic wave can have a wavelength greater than 11 cm?
   A Radio waves C Red light
   B Microwaves D Blue light
2. According to the table, which type of electromagnetic wave can have a wavelength less than 0.006 cm?
   F Radio waves H Red light
   G Microwaves J Blue light
3. If a device were emitting an electromagnetic wave of 11 cm, what kind of device would it be?
   A Radio C Flashlight
   B Microwave oven D X-ray

L1

Teaching

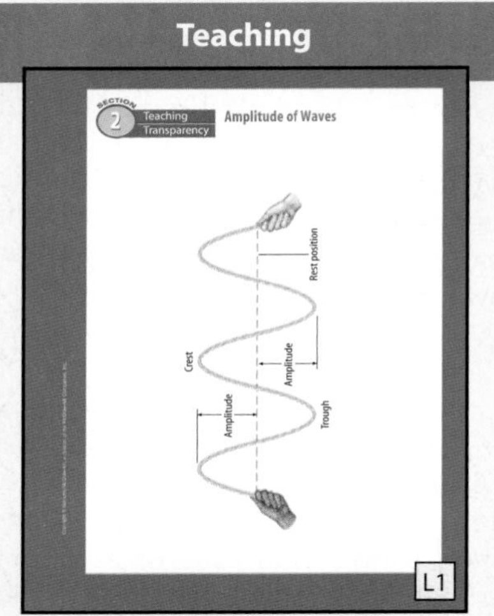
Section 2 Teaching Transparency — Amplitude of Waves

L1

Key to Teaching Strategies

The following designations will help you decide which activities are appropriate for your students.

- L1 Level 1 activities should be appropriate for students with learning difficulties.
- L2 Level 2 activities should be within the ability range of all students.
- L3 Level 3 activities are designed for above-average students.
- ELL ELL activities should be within the ability range of English Language Learners.
- COOP LEARN Cooperative Learning activities are designed for small group work.
- LS Multiple Learning Styles logos are used throughout to indicate strategies that address different learning styles.
- P These strategies represent student products that can be placed into a best-work portfolio.

Hands-on Activities

Activity Worksheets

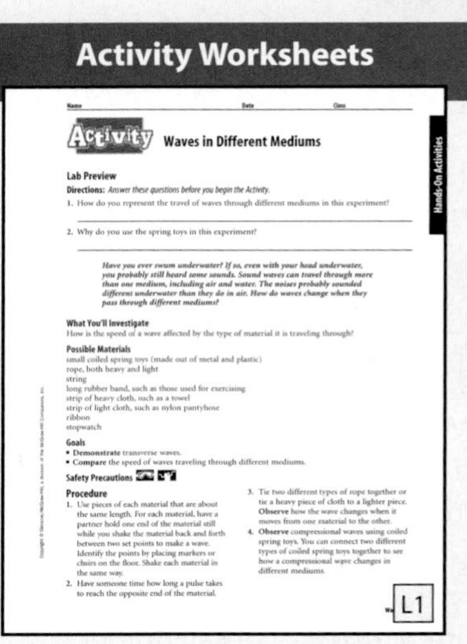
Name Date Class

Activity — Waves in Different Mediums

Hands-On Activities

Lab Preview

Directions: *Answer these questions before you begin the Activity.*

1. How do you represent the travel of waves through different mediums in this experiment?
2. Why do you use the spring toys in this experiment?

Have you ever swum underwater? If so, even with your head underwater, you probably still heard some sounds. Sound waves can travel through more than one medium, including air and water. The noises probably sounded different underwater than they do in air. How do waves change when they pass through different mediums?

What You'll Investigate

How is the speed of a wave affected by the type of material it is traveling through?

Possible Materials

small coiled spring toys (made out of metal and plastic)
rope, both heavy and light
string
long rubber band, such as those used for exercising
strip of heavy cloth, such as a towel
strip of light cloth, such as nylon pantyhose
ribbon
stopwatch

Goals

- **Demonstrate** transverse waves.
- **Compare** the speed of waves traveling through different mediums.

Safety Precautions

Procedure

1. Use pieces of each material that are about the same length. For each material, have a partner hold one end of the material still while you shake the material back and forth between two set points to make a wave. Identify the points by placing markers or chairs on the floor. Shake each material in the same way.
2. Have someone time how long a pulse takes to reach the opposite end of the material.
3. Tie two different types of rope together or tie a heavy piece of cloth to a lighter piece. **Observe** how the wave changes when it moves from one material to the other.
4. **Observe** compressional waves using coiled spring toys. You can connect two different types of coiled spring toys together to see how a compressional wave changes in different mediums.

L1

Laboratory Activities

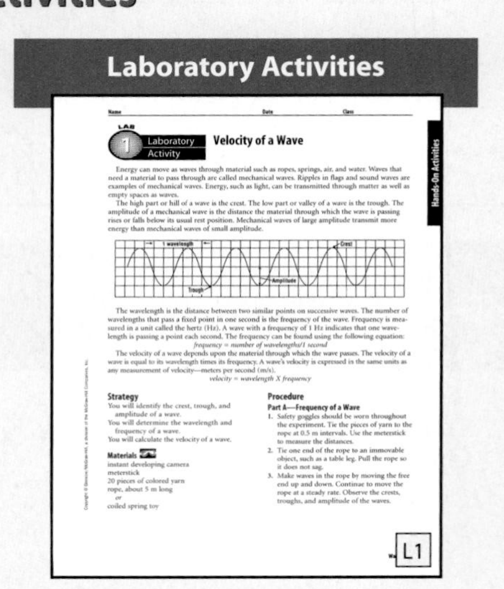
Name Date Class

Lab 1 Laboratory Activity — Velocity of a Wave

Hands-On Activities

Energy can move as waves through material such as ropes, springs, air, and water. Waves that need a material to pass through are called mechanical waves. Ripples in flags and sound waves are examples of mechanical waves. Energy, such as light, can be transmitted through matter as well as empty spaces as waves.

The high part or hill of a wave is the crest. The low part or valley of a wave is the trough. The amplitude of a mechanical wave is the distance the material through which the wave is passing rises or falls below its usual rest position. Mechanical waves of large amplitude transmit more energy than mechanical waves of small amplitude.

The wavelength is the distance between two similar points on successive waves. The number of wavelengths that pass a fixed point in one second is the frequency of the wave. Frequency is measured in a unit called the hertz (Hz). A wave with a frequency of 1 Hz indicates that one wavelength is passing a point each second. The frequency can be found using the following equation:

frequency = number of wavelengths/1 second

The velocity of a wave depends upon the material through which the wave passes. The velocity of a wave is equal to its wavelength times its frequency. A wave's velocity is expressed in the same units as any measurement of velocity—meters per second (m/s).

velocity = wavelength X frequency

Strategy

You will identify the crest, trough, and amplitude of a wave.
You will determine the wavelength and frequency of a wave.
You will calculate the velocity of a wave.

Materials

instant developing camera
meterstick
20 pieces of colored yarn
rope, about 5 m long
or
coiled spring toy

Procedure

Part A—Frequency of a Wave

1. Safety goggles should be worn throughout the experiment. Tie the pieces of yarn to the rope at 0.5 m intervals. Use the meterstick to measure the distances.
2. Tie one end of the rope to an immovable object, such as a table leg. Pull the rope so it does not sag.
3. Make waves in the rope by moving the free end up and down. Continue to move the rope at a steady rate. Observe the crests, troughs, and amplitude of the waves.

L1

Meeting Different Ability Levels

Content Outline

Name Date Class

Note-taking Worksheet **Waves**

Section 1 The Nature of Waves

A. Wave—a repeating disturbance or movement that transfers ________ through matter or space
1. Molecules pass energy on to ________ molecules.
2. Waves carry energy without transporting ________.
3. All waves are produced by something that ________.
4. Medium—a ________ through which a wave travels.
   a. May be solid, liquid, or ________
   b. Not all waves need a medium to travel through. Example: ________

B. Mechanical waves—waves that can travel only through ________
1. Transverse waves—matter in the medium moves back and forth ________ the direction that the wave travels. Example: ________
2. Compressional waves—matter in the medium moves ________ that the wave travels. Example: ________
3. Combinations—not purely transverse or compressional. Examples: water waves, ________ waves

Section 2 Wave Properties

A. Ways waves differ
1. How much ________ they carry
2. How ________ they travel
3. How they look
   a. ________ waves have crests—the highest points—and troughs—the lowest points.
   b. Compressional waves have dense regions called ________ and less dense regions called ________.

B. Wavelength—the distance between one point in the wave and ________

Meeting Individual Needs

L1

Reinforcement

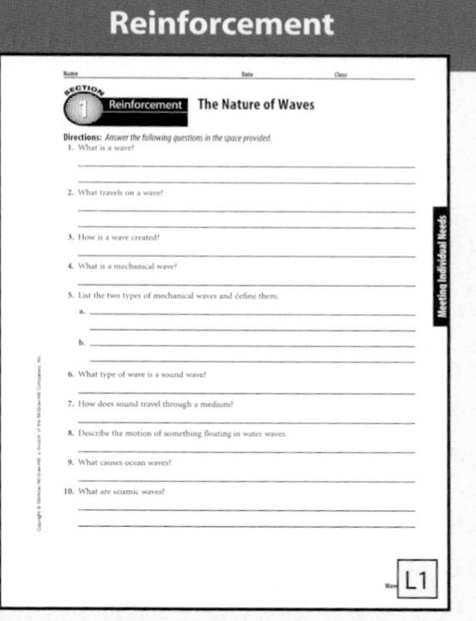

Name Date Class

Section 1 Reinforcement **The Nature of Waves**

Directions: Answer the following questions in the space provided.

1. What is a wave?
2. What travels on a wave?
3. How is a wave created?
4. What is a mechanical wave?
5. List the two types of mechanical waves and define them.
   a.
   b.
6. What type of wave is a sound wave?
7. How does sound travel through a medium?
8. Describe the motion of something floating in water waves.
9. What causes ocean waves?
10. What are seismic waves?

Meeting Individual Needs

L1

Directed Reading

Name Date Class

Directed Reading for Content Mastery *Overview* **Waves**

Directions: Complete the concept map using the terms in the list below.

repeating, reflection, medium, transverse, incidence, energy, waves, mechanical, space

1. — that need a — 2. — are called — 3. ________ waves — which are — compressional — if the medium moves in the same direction or — 4. — if the medium moves at right angles

are — 5. ________ disturbances — that transfer — 6. — through — matter or 7. ________

obey the — law of 8. ________ — which states that — the angle of 9. ________ — equals — the angle of reflection

Meeting Individual Needs

L1

Assessment

Chapter Tests

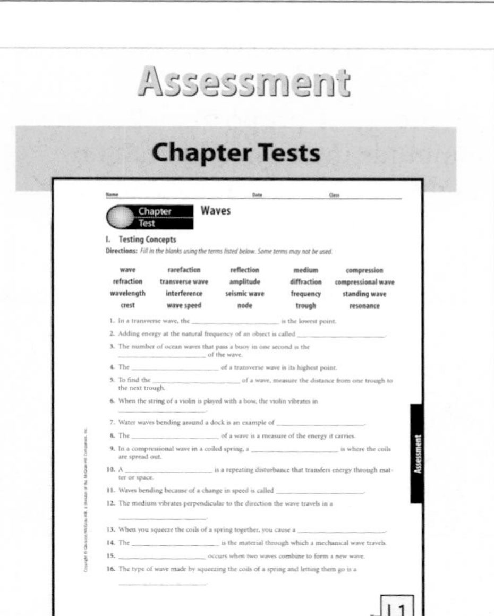

Name Date Class

Chapter Test **Waves**

I. Testing Concepts

Directions: Fill in the blanks using the terms listed below. Some terms may not be used.

wave	rarefaction	reflection	medium	compression
refraction	transverse wave	amplitude	diffraction	compressional wave
wavelength	interference	seismic wave	frequency	standing wave
crest	wave speed	node	trough	resonance

1. In a transverse wave, the ________ is the lowest point.
2. Adding energy at the natural frequency of an object is called ________.
3. The number of ocean waves that pass a buoy in one second is the ________ of the wave.
4. The ________ of a transverse wave is its highest point.
5. To find the ________ of a wave, measure the distance from one trough to the next trough.
6. When the string of a violin is played with a bow, the violin vibrates in ________.
7. Water waves bending around a dock is an example of ________.
8. The ________ of a wave is a measure of the energy it carries.
9. In a compressional wave in a coiled spring, a ________ is where the coils are spread out.
10. A ________ is a repeating disturbance that transfers energy through matter or space.
11. Waves bending because of a change in speed is called ________.
12. The medium vibrates perpendicular to the direction the wave travels in a ________.
13. When you squeeze the coils of a spring together, you cause a ________.
14. The ________ is the material through which a mechanical wave travels.
15. ________ occurs when two waves combine to form a new wave.
16. The type of wave made by squeezing the coils of a spring and letting them go is a ________.

Assessment

L1

Enrichment

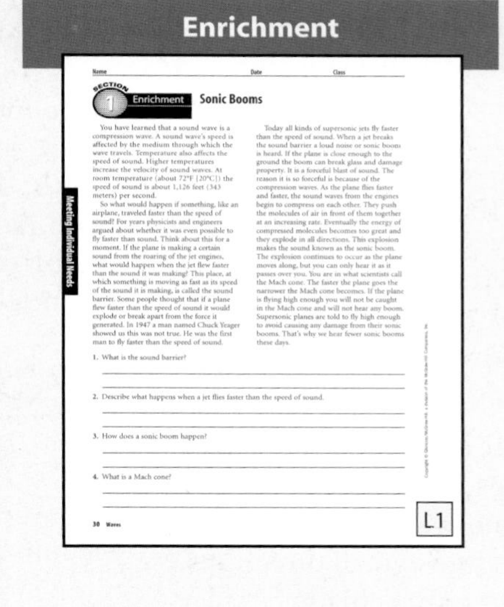

Name Date Class

Section 1 Enrichment **Sonic Booms**

You have learned that a sound wave is a compression wave. A sound wave's speed is affected by the medium through which the wave travels. Temperature also affects the speed of sound. Higher temperatures increase the velocity of sound waves. At room temperature (about 72°F [20°C]) the speed of sound is about 1,126 feet (343 meters) per second.

So what would happen if something, like an airplane, traveled faster than the speed of sound? For years physicists and engineers argued about whether it was even possible to fly faster than sound. What would happen at the moment when the plane is moving as fast as its speed of sound? ... In 1947 a man named Chuck Yeager showed us this was not true. He was the first man to fly faster than the speed of sound.

Today all kinds of supersonic jets fly faster than the speed of sound. When a jet breaks the sound barrier a loud noise or sonic boom is heard. ... Supersonic planes are told to fly high enough to avoid causing any damage from their sonic booms. That's why we hear fewer sonic booms these days.

1. What is the sound barrier?
2. Describe what happens when a jet flies faster than the speed of sound.
3. How does a sonic boom happen?
4. What is a Mach cone?

30 Waves

Meeting Individual Needs

L1

Spanish Directed Reading

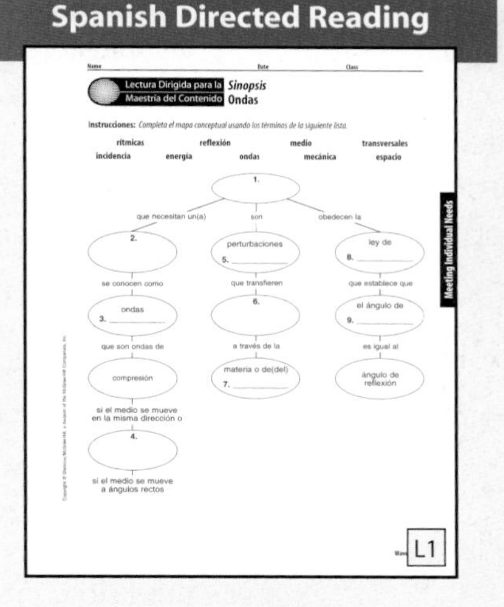

Nombre Fecha Clase

Lectura Dirigida para la Maestría del Contenido *Sinopsis* **Ondas**

Instrucciones: Completa el mapa conceptual usando los términos de la siguiente lista.

rítmicas, reflexión, medio, transversales, incidencia, energía, ondas, mecánica, espacio

1. — que necesitan un(a) — 2. — se conocen como — 3. ondas — que son ondas de — compresión — si el medio se mueve en la misma dirección o — 4. — si el medio se mueve a ángulos rectos

son — perturbaciones 5. — que transfieren — 6. — a través de la — materia o de(del) 7.

obedecen la — ley de 8. — que establece que — el ángulo de 9. — es igual al — ángulo de reflexión

Meeting Individual Needs

L1

Test Practice Workbook

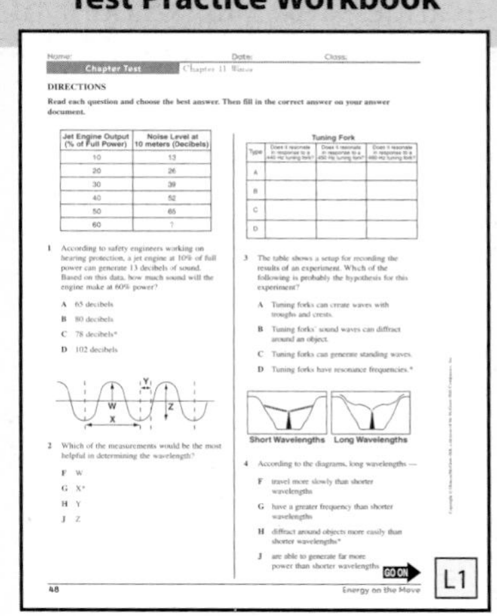

Name: Date: Class:

Chapter Test — Chapter 11 Waves

DIRECTIONS

Read each question and choose the best answer. Then fill in the correct answer on your answer document.

Jet Engine Output (% of Full Power)	Noise Level at 10 meters (Decibels)
10	13
20	26
30	39
40	52
50	65
60	?

1 According to safety engineers working on hearing protection, a jet engine at 10% of full power can generate 13 decibels of sound. Based on this data, how much sound will the engine make at 60% power?
A 65 decibels
B 80 decibels
C 78 decibels*
D 102 decibels

2 Which of the measurements would be the most helpful in determining the wavelength?
F W
G X*
H Y
J Z

3 The table shows a setup for recording the results of an experiment. Which of the following is probably the hypothesis for this experiment?
A Tuning forks can create waves with troughs and crests.
B Tuning forks' sound waves can diffract around an object.
C Tuning forks can generate standing waves.
D Tuning forks have resonance frequencies.*

4 According to the diagrams, long wavelengths —
F travel more slowly than shorter wavelengths
G have a greater frequency than shorter wavelengths
H diffract around objects more easily than shorter wavelengths*
J are able to generate far more power than shorter wavelengths

Short Wavelengths Long Wavelengths

GO ON

48 Energy on the Move

L1

Chapter Review

Name Date Class

Chapter Review **Waves**

Part A. Vocabulary Review

Directions: From the word list, choose the correct term and write it in the space beside each definition.

amplitude	compression	diffraction	compressional wave
destructive interference	crest	frequency	interference
law of reflection	medium	rarefaction	reflection
refraction	resonance	seismic waves	standing wave
transverse wave	trough	wavelength	waves

1. when a wave strikes an object and bounces off
2. repeating disturbances that transfer energy through matter or space
3. highest point of a transverse wave
4. region where the medium is crowded and dense in a compressional wave
5. wave that makes matter in the medium move back and forth at right angles to the direction the wave travels
6. ability of two or more waves to combine and form a new wave
7. lowest point of a transverse wave
8. material through which a wave transfers energy
9. the bending of waves around a barrier
10. less dense region of a compressional wave
11. vibrations from the breaking of Earth's crust that transmit energy outward
12. ability of an object to vibrate by absorbing energy at its natural frequency
13. wave in which matter in the medium moves back and forth in the same direction the wave travels
14. distance between one point in a wave and the nearest point just like it
15. measure of how many wavelengths pass a fixed point each second
16. the angle of incidence is equal to the angle of reflection
17. measure of the energy in a wave
18. a special type of wave pattern that forms when waves of equal wavelength and amplitude traveling in opposite directions continuously interfere with each other

Assessment

L1

Science Content Background

SECTION 1 The Nature of Waves

What's in a wave?

From radio waves to light waves to sound waves, we are immersed in a world of waves.

Student Misconception

When a wave travels through a medium, particles of the medium travel along with the wave.

Refer to the facing page for teaching strategies to address this misconception. Refer to pages 327–329 for content related to this topic.

Waves transfer energy from one place to another. Mechanical waves such as sound and water need a medium to travel through. These waves create disturbances or vibrations as they travel. The particles, however, do not move with the wave as it travels through the medium.

- Water waves may appear as plane waves, like a wall, or circular waves, as when a rock is thrown into water. Plane waves move in one direction; circular waves move in all directions. Waves on the top of water are actually circular waves that resemble transverse waves. Waves below the surface are compressional waves.

SECTION 2 Wave Properties

Wavelength

A great deal of variation exists in the wavelengths of electromagnetic waves. Radio waves are the longest, and they range in length from 20 cm to 20 m. Light wavelengths range from 400 to 700 nanometers. One nanometer is 0.000000001 m or 10^{-9} m.

Frequency

Frequency and period are different but related. Frequency is how often something happens in a given time. Period is the time for something to happen. Thus for a wave, frequency is equal to the reciprocal of the period. Frequency is expressed as cycles per second, and period is seconds per cycle.

Period = 1/frequency

Frequency = 1/period

Amplitude and Energy

Amplitude can be thought of as the maximum negative or positive displacement of a wave medium from its resting position. At times, such as when considering interference, the amplitude of one section of a wave is measured.

The energy in ocean waves can erode shorelines. The energy is proportional to the square of the amplitude multiplied by the wavelength. Thus, higher and longer waves produce more damage. For the same wavelength, every doubling in the height of the wave makes potential damage four times greater.

SECTION 3 The Behavior of Waves

Refraction and Diffraction

Optical density refers to the speed of light in a material. A vacuum is defined as having an optical density of one. The optical density is given for the following materials: air, 1.0003; water, 1.333; and diamonds, 2.417. For refraction to occur, light must pass from one material into a material with a different optical density. The amount of diffraction is proportional to the size of the wavelength. The longer the wavelength, the greater the amount of diffraction.

SCIENCE Online

For additional content background on this topic, go to the Glencoe Science Web site at science.glencoe.com.

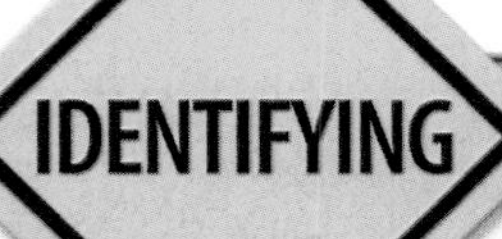

Misconceptions

Find Out What Students Think

Students may think that . . .

- **When a wave travels through a medium, particles of the medium travel along with the wave.**

Students have probably seen water waves hit land and flow up the beach. They may even have felt the force of an ocean wave pushing them towards the beach. Because these waves encounter the shore, they move differently from normal waves. But they do form lasting impressions. Thus, it is understandable that students would think that the medium travels with the wave.

Demonstration

Draw Figure 1 on the board. Tell students to imagine a rock is dropped into the water at Point A. Ask students to predict where each of the floating bobs will end up after ten waves go by the bobs.

1

4 A 2

3

Promote Understanding

Activity

Students make two models of waves, one that is incorrrect and one that is correct.

Model 1 (incorrect): Place on the floor alternating strips of green and red tape 2 m apart so they form the outline of a large circle. Have students walk slowly around the circle. Tell them to duck down when they get to a strip of green tape and to walk on their toes when they get to a strip of red tape. Thus as students rise up and down as they walk around the room.

Model 2 (correct): This resembles the "wave" done by fans at sporting events. Have students stand in a circle and not leave their positions. Start the wave by having a student reach up high, pause, duck down low, pause, and return to normal standing. After the first person rises, the second person rises and does the same thing. Each person in turn passes the wave around the circle.

Ask students to analyze the two models of waves and write which one they think is the better model and why.

Assess

After completing the chapter, see *Identifying Misconceptions* in the Study Guide.

Waves

Chapter Vocabulary

wave
medium
transverse wave
compressional wave
crest
trough
rarefaction
wavelength
frequency
amplitude
refraction
diffraction
interference
standing wave
resonance

What do you think?

Science Journal This is a picture of the Oakland highway. It was destroyed by the powerful seismic waves of an earthquake.

CHAPTER 11

Waves

The lights flash, guitar strings vibrate, keyboards wail, and the beat of the drums makes you want to get up and dance. All the sights and sounds of this concert are brought to you by waves. Waves are all around you. Some, like water and light waves, you can see. Others, like sound and radio waves, you cannot see. In this chapter, you will learn what waves are and how they travel. You will learn about the different kinds of waves and the things all waves have in common. You also will find out how waves interact to transform energy into bright lights and spectacular sound.

What do you think?

Science Journal Look at the picture below with a classmate. Discuss what this might be. Here's a hint: *They make movies out of events like this.* Write your answer or best guess in your Science Journal.

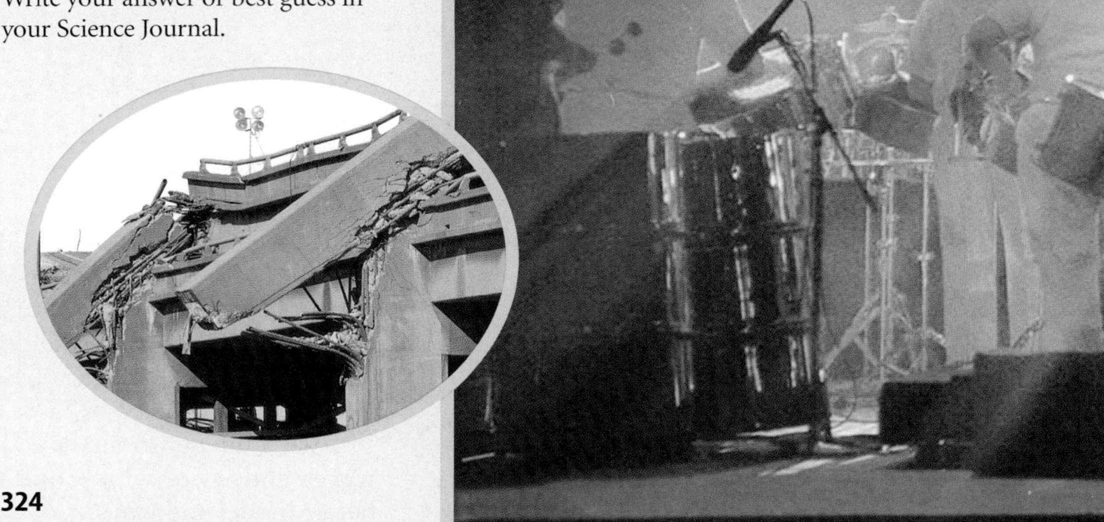

324

Theme Connection

Energy Waves are rhythmic disturbances that carry energy. As the amplitude of a wave increases, the energy it carries also increases.

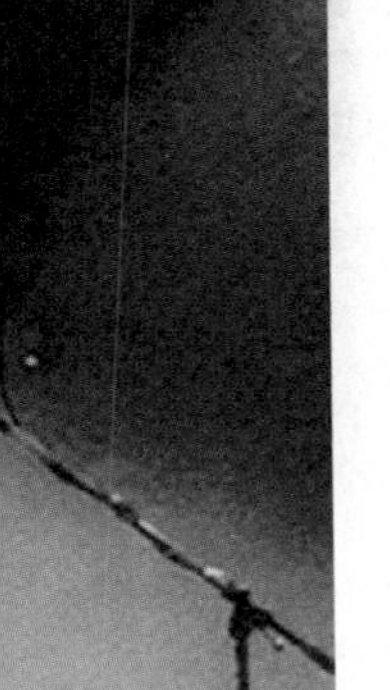

Light enters your eyes and sound strikes your ears, enabling you to sense the world around you. Light and sound are waves that carry energy from one place to another. What else gets transferred from place to place when a wave carries energy? Does a wave transfer matter as well as energy? In this activity you'll observe one way that waves can transfer energy.

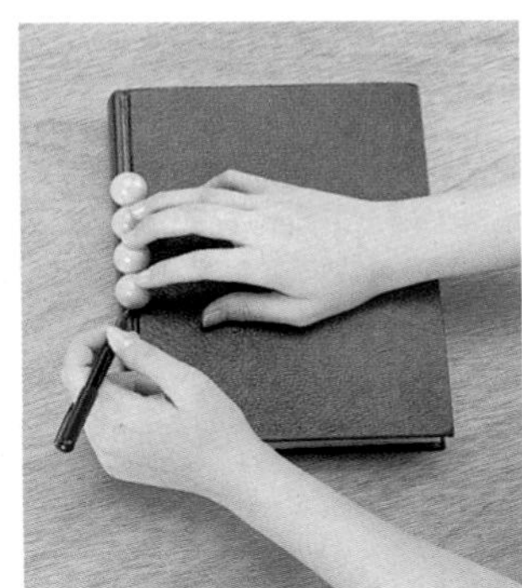

Demonstrating energy transfer

1. Line up four marbles on the groove formed by the spine of your textbook so that the marbles are touching each other.
2. Hold the first three marbles in place using three fingers of one hand.
3. Use your other hand to tap the first marble with a pen or pencil.
4. Observe what happens to the fourth marble.

Observe

Write a paragraph in your Science Journal explaining how the fourth marble reacted to the pen tap. Draw a diagram showing the energy transfer through the marbles.

Before You Read

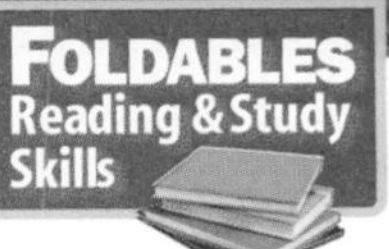

Making a Venn Diagram Study Fold **Make the following Foldable to compare and contrast two types of waves.**

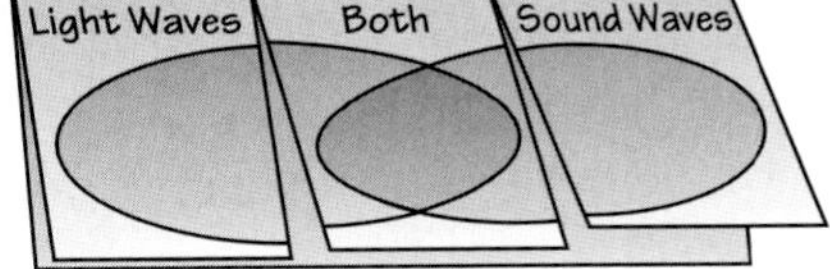

1. Place a sheet of paper in front of you so the long side is at the top. Fold the paper in half from top to bottom.
2. Fold both sides in. Unfold the paper so three sections show.
3. Through the top thickness of paper, cut along each of the fold lines to the topfold, forming three tabs. Label *Light Waves, Sound Waves,* and *Both* and draw ovals across the front of the foldable, as shown.
4. As you read the chapter, write characteristics of light and sound waves under the left and right tabs. Under the middle tab, write what light and sound waves have in common.

Before You Read

FOLDABLES Reading & Study Skills

Dinah Zike Study Fold

Purpose Students each make a Venn diagram Foldable to help them determine what they also know about waves as they identify the similarities and differences between light and sound waves.

For additional help, see Foldables Worksheet, p. 17 in **Chapter Resources Booklet,** or go to the Glencoe Science Web site at **science.glencoe.com.** See After You Read in the Study Guide at the end of this chapter.

Explore Activity

Purpose Use the Explore Activity to illustrate for students energy moving through matter. L2 LS **Kinesthetic**

Preparation Obtain enough marbles of the same size so that each student can have four.

Materials marbles, textbook

Teaching Strategies Instruct students to make sure books are on a flat surface. Make sure students hold the marbles so they are touching one another.

Observe

Energy is transferred through the first three marbles causing the fourth marble to move without matter being transferred

Performance Have students write short paragraphs explaining what happens if the marbles aren't touching each other and why. After the first marble hits the second marble nothing happens. This is because the energy of the first marble is transferred to the air, which doesn't transfer it to the next marble. Use **Performance Assessment in the Science Classroom,** p. 157.

SECTION

The Nature of Waves

1 Motivate

Bellringer Transparency

Display the Section Focus Transparency for Section 1. Use the accompanying Transparency Activity Master. L2 ELL

Section Focus Transparency — Wave to the camera.

How many waves can you pick out in this scene? Is light described as a wave? If you were there when this photograph was taken, you might also mention the sound waves.

1. Describe the different waves in this picture.
2. How do water waves differ from sound waves?
3. When waves move, does any matter actually travel?

Tie to Prior Knowledge

Review the idea of energy and have students give examples of waves. Emphasize to students that waves transfer energy but not matter.

Resource Manager

Chapter Resources Booklet

Transparency Activity, p. 44
Directed Reading for Content Mastery, p. 20
Note-taking Worksheets, pp. 33-35

SECTION

The Nature of Waves

As You Read

What **You'll Learn**

- **Recognize** that waves carry energy but not matter.
- **Define** mechanical waves.
- **Distinguish** between transverse waves and compressional waves.

Vocabulary

wave
medium
transverse wave
compressional wave

Why **It's Important**

You hear and see the world around you because of the energy carried by waves.

What's in a wave?

A surfer bobs in the ocean waiting for the perfect wave, microwaves warm up your leftover pizza, and sound waves from your CD player bring music to your ears. Do these and other types of waves have anything in common with one another?

A **wave** is a repeating disturbance or movement that transfers energy through matter or space. For example, ocean waves disturb the water and transfer energy through it. During earthquakes, energy is transferred in powerful waves that travel through Earth. Light is another type of wave that can travel through empty space to transfer energy from one place to another, such as from the Sun to Earth.

Waves and Energy

Kerplop! A pebble falls into a pool of water and ripples form. As **Figure 1** shows, the pebble causes a disturbance that moves outward in the form of a wave. Because it is moving, the falling pebble has energy. As it splashes into the pool, the pebble transfers some of its energy to nearby water molecules, causing them to move. Those molecules then pass the energy along to neighboring water molecules, which, in turn, transfer it to their neighbors. The energy moves farther and farther from the source of the disturbance. What you see is energy traveling in the form of a wave on the surface of the water.

Figure 1
Falling pebbles transfer their kinetic energy to the particles of water in a pond, forming waves.
Where else have you seen waves?

Section Assessment Planner

Portfolio
Assessment, p. 331

Performance Assessment
Skill Builder Activities, p. 331
See page 354 for more options.

Content Assessment
Section, p. 331
Challenge, p. 331
Chapter, pp. 354–355

326 CHAPTER 11 Waves

Waves and Matter Imagine you're in a boat on a lake. Approaching waves bump against your boat, but they don't carry it along with them as they pass. The boat does move up and down and maybe even a short distance back and forth because the waves transfer some of their energy to it. But after the waves have moved on, the boat is still in the same place. The waves don't even carry the water along with them. Only the energy carried by the waves moves forward. All waves have this property—they carry energy without transporting matter from place to place.

Reading Check *What do waves carry?*

Making Waves A wave will travel only as long as it has energy to carry. For example, when you drop a pebble into a puddle, the ripples soon die out and the surface of the water becomes still again.

Suppose you are holding a rope at one end, and you give it a shake. You would create a pulse that would travel along the rope to the other end, and then the rope would be still again, as **Figure 2** shows. Now suppose you shake your end of the rope up and down for a while. You would make a wave that would travel along the rope. When you stop shaking your hand up and down, the rope will be still again. It is the up-and-down motion of your hand that creates the wave.

Anything that moves up and down or back and forth in a rhythmic way is vibrating. The vibrating movement of your hand at the end of the rope created the wave. In fact, all waves are produced by something that vibrates.

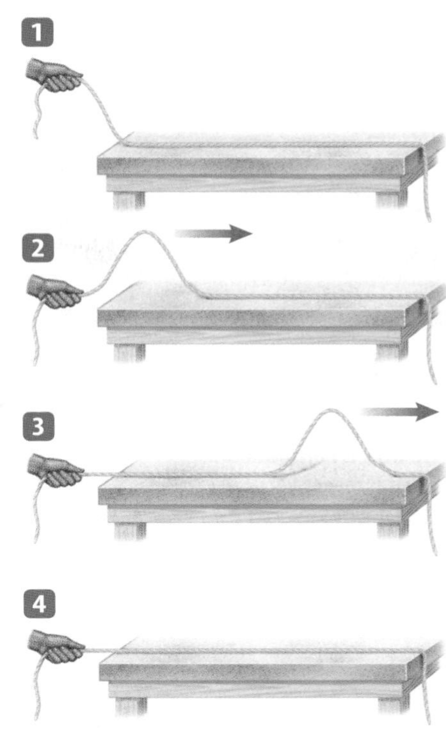

Figure 2
A wave will exist only as long as it has energy to carry. *What happened to the energy that was carried by the wave in this rope?*

Mechanical Waves

Sound waves travel through the air to reach your ears. Ocean waves move through water to reach the shore. In both cases, the matter the waves travel through is called a **medium.** The medium can be a solid, a liquid, a gas, or a combination of these. For sound waves the medium is air, and for ocean waves the medium is water. Not all waves need a medium. Some waves, such as light and radio waves, can travel through space. Waves that can travel only through matter are called mechanical waves. The two types of mechanical waves are transverse waves and compressional waves.

2 Teach

What's in a wave?

Caption Answer

Figure 1 Possible answers: ocean, bathtub, swimming pool

Waves and Energy

Quick Demo

Place a table tennis ball in a wide pan of water about halfway between the center and the edge of the pan. When the water is still, drop a rock into the pan. The ball moves up and down, but not horizontally in the direction in which the wave moves. L2 **Visual-Spatial**

Reading Check

Answer energy

Caption Answer

Figure 2 It left the wave.

Mechanical Waves

Students may think that when a wave travels through a medium, particles of the medium travel along with the wave. See page 324F for teaching strategies that address this misconception.

LAB DEMONSTRATION

Purpose to demonstrate the movement of a wave through matter

Materials rope, broom

Preparation Tie the end of a rope to the handle of a broom.

Procedure Rest the broom upright in the corner of the room. Send a wave through the rope.

Expected Outcome Students will see the wave travel through the rope and cause the broom to shake or fall down.

Assessment

Where did the energy that caused the broom to shake or fall come from? from the hand moving the rope **How did the energy get to the broom?** It traveled along the rope in a wave.

Mechanical Waves, continued

Use Science Words

Word Meaning Tell students that the word *transverse* means "acting, lying, or being across; set crosswise." **What makes a transverse wave transverse?** When a transverse wave travels through a medium, the particles of the medium move crosswise to the direction in which the wave moves. L2 LS **Linguistic**

Extension

Have students hypothesize how transverse waves will travel in different kinds of ropes. Then, have students check their hypotheses using different ropes. **Will a thick rope carry waves as easily as a thin rope?** A thick rope will carry waves but may require more energy to get the waves started than a thin rope will. L2 ELL LS **Kinesthetic**

Activity

Have students use a coiled spring toy to make both transverse and compressional waves. Have them compare and contrast how the waves look and the different things they did to make the two different types of waves. L1 ELL LS **Kinesthetic**

Teacher FYI

Compressional waves are also known as longitudinal waves.

Caption Answer

Figure 4 Possible answer: sound wave

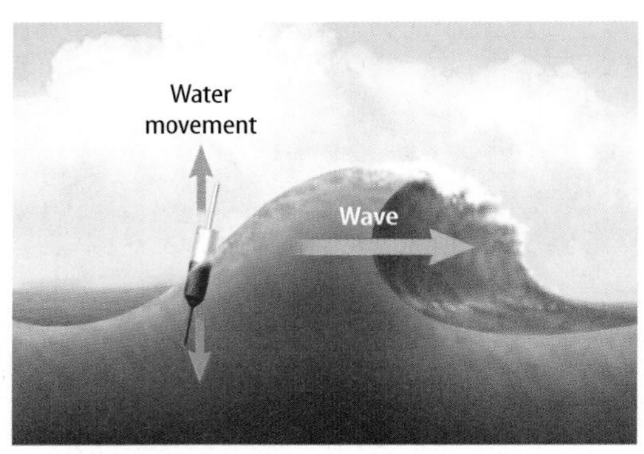

Figure 3
A water wave is an example of a transverse wave. The wave travels horizontally as the water moves vertically up and down.

Transverse Waves In a **transverse wave,** matter in the medium moves back and forth at right angles to the direction that the wave travels. For example, **Figure 3** shows how a wave in the ocean moves horizontally, but the water that the wave passes through moves up and down. When you shake one end of a rope while your friend holds the other end, you are making transverse waves. The wave and its energy travel from you to your friend as the rope moves up and down.

Compressional Waves In a **compressional wave**, matter in the medium moves back and forth in the same direction that the wave travels. You can model compressional waves with a coiled spring toy, as shown in **Figure 4.** Squeeze several coils together at one end of the spring. Then let go of the coils, still holding onto coils at both ends of the spring. A wave will travel along the spring. As the wave moves, it looks as if the whole spring is moving toward one end. However, if you could focus on just one coil, you would see that it moves back and forth as the wave passes, then stops moving after the wave has passed. The wave carries energy, but not matter, forward along the spring.

Sound Waves Sound waves are compressional waves. When a noise is made, such as when a locker door slams shut and vibrates, nearby air molecules are pushed together by the vibrations. The air molecules are squeezed together like the coils in a coiled spring toy are when you make a compressional wave with it. The compressions travel through the air to make a wave.

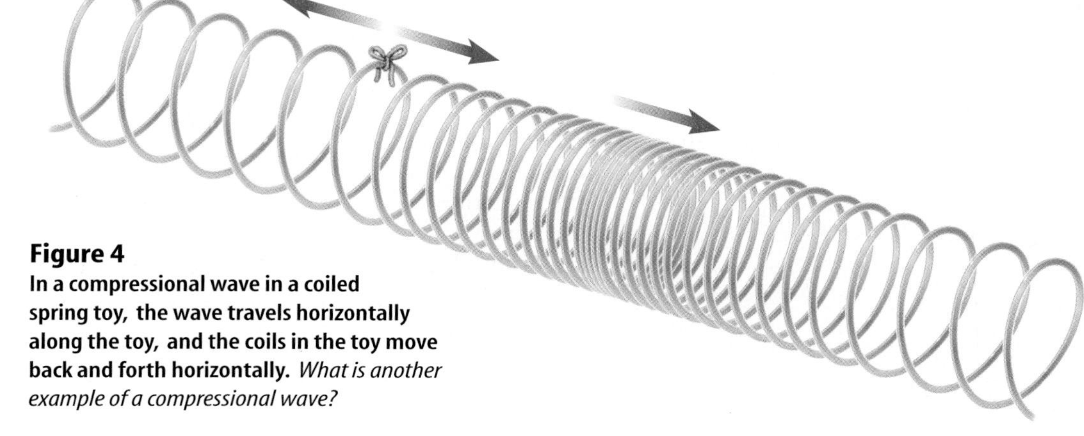

Figure 4
In a compressional wave in a coiled spring toy, the wave travels horizontally along the toy, and the coils in the toy move back and forth horizontally. *What is another example of a compressional wave?*

Inclusion Strategies

Visually Impaired Help these students feel what they have difficulty seeing. Have each visually impaired student place a hand on a section of a rope or spring toy. Make waves in the rope or spring toy. Ask each student to describe how the section he or she is touching moves. Does it move up or down, backwards or forwards? Does it travel from one place to another? L1 ELL COOP LEARN LS **Kinesthetic**

Science Journal

Wave Diary Have students list in their Science Journals the kinds of waves they see in a typical day, classifying each wave as transverse or compressional. Have them identify the effects each wave's energy produces. L2 LS **Linguistic**

Sound in Other Materials Sound waves also can travel through other mediums, such as water and wood. Particles in these mediums also are pushed together and move apart as the sound waves travel through them. When a sound wave reaches your ear, it causes your eardrum to vibrate. Your inner ear then sends signals to your brain, and your brain interprets the signals as sound.

Reading Check *How do sound waves travel in solids?*

Water Waves Water waves are not purely transverse waves. The surface of the water moves up and down as the waves go by. But the water also moves a short distance back and forth. This movement happens because the low part of the wave can be formed only by pushing water forward or backward toward the high part of the wave, as in **Figure 5A.** Then as the wave passes, the water that was pushed aside moves back to its initial position, as in **Figure 5B.** In fact, if you looked closely, you would see that the combination of this up-and-down and back-and-forth motion causes water at the surface to move in circles. Anything floating on the surface of the water absorbs some of the waves' energy and bobs in a circular motion.

Ocean waves are formed most often by wind blowing across the ocean surface. As the wind blows faster and slower, the changing wind speed is like a vibration. The size of the waves that are formed depends on the wind speed, the distance over which the wind blows, and how long the wind blows. **Figure 6** on the next page shows this process.

Figure 5
When a wave passes, the surface of the water does not move only up and down.

A **The low point of a water wave is formed when water is pushed aside and up to the high point of the wave.**

B **The water that is pushed aside returns to its initial position.**

Reading Check

Answer Particles in the solid are pushed together and move apart as sound waves travel through them.

Extension

When people go to the beach on a windy day, they see ocean waves moving in and out and breaking along the shore. Have students find out what causes these waves to break and move as they do. As waves of water move into the increasingly shallow area near the shore, the particles of water can no longer move in circles and are forced to move in shallower and shallower ellipses. The wave breaks when it hits the ground as it tries to complete its elliptical path. The energy of the wave dissipates as the water moves up the beach and then falls back into the ocean. L3 **LS Logical-Mathematical**

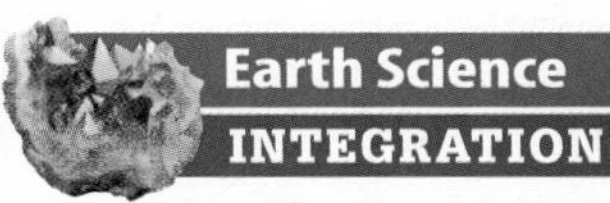

Earth Science INTEGRATION

Earthquakes produce three types of waves, all of which move out in concentric circles from the focus of the earthquake. Primary waves, known as P waves, are compressional waves that travel deep inside Earth. These waves travel the fastest. Secondary waves, called S waves, are transverse waves that can travel only through solids. They also travel deep inside Earth. Most of the damage from earthquakes is caused by L waves, which travel along Earth's surface. L waves are transverse waves that can move back and forth and up and down.

Resource Manager

Chapter Resources Booklet
Enrichment, p. 30

Reading and Writing Skill Activities, p. 7

Earth Science Critical Thinking/Problem Solving, p. 9

Visual Learning

Figure 5 When you throw a stone into the water, how does it start the motion of the wave? When the stone hits the water, it pushes down on the water. **Why does the wave spread out as it moves?** It spreads because it moves in all directions from its point of origin. L2 **LS Visual-Spatial**

Visualizing Formation of Ocean Waves

Have students examine the pictures and read the captions. Then ask the following questions.

- **What happens to the surface area of water exposed to the wind as waves build up?** The surface area increases. **How does this affect the waves?** The greater surface area means that there is more contact area between the air and water, providing an increased area to which to transfer energy.

Activity

Use a wave tank or large flat pan such as a cake pan partially filled with water to observe waves. Students can blow across the surface or a fan can be provided to simulate the wind. Students should try to duplicate the four types of seas presented. L2 **LS Kinesthetic**

Extension

Challenge students to research and find the impact to the shoreline when ocean waves repeatedly strike the shore. Have them find out what some of the measures that are being taken to keep the shoreline unchanged.

VISUALIZING FORMATION OF OCEAN WAVES

Figure 6

When wind blows across an ocean, friction between the moving air and the water causes the water to move. As a result, energy is transferred from the wind to the surface of the water. The waves that are produced depend on the length of time and the distance over which the wind blows, as well as the wind speed.

▲ Wind causes ripples to form on the surface of the water. As ripples form, they provide an even larger surface area for the wind to strike, and the ripples increase in size.

▲ Waves that are higher and have longer wavelengths grow faster as the wind continues to blow, but the steepest waves break up, forming whitecaps. The surface is said to be choppy.

▲ The shortest-wavelength waves break up, while the longest-wavelength waves continue to grow. When these waves have reached their maximum height, they form fully developed seas.

▲ After the wind dies down, the waves lose energy and become lower and smoother. These smooth, long-wavelength ocean waves are called swells.

Resource Manager

Chapter Resources Booklet
Reinforcement, p. 27
Cultural Diversity, p. 43
Science Inquiry Labs, p. 31

SCIENCE Online
Internet Addresses

Explore the Glencoe Science Web site at **science.glencoe.com** to find out more about topics in this section.

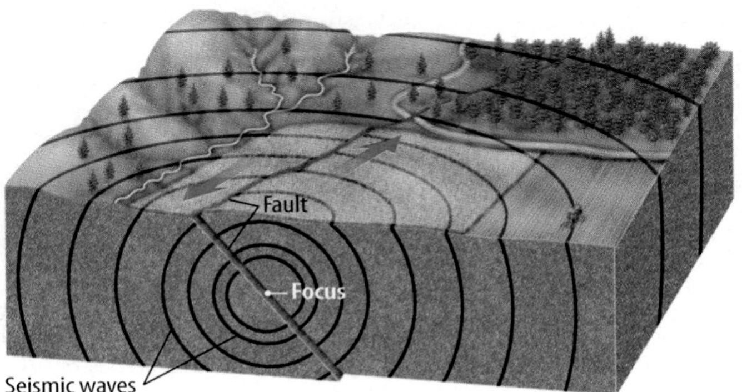

Figure 7
When Earth's crust breaks, the energy that is released is transmitted outward, causing an earthquake. *Why are earthquakes mechanical waves?*

Seismic Waves If you pulled too hard on a guitar string, the string would break and you would hear a noise. The noise occurs because the string vibrates for a short time after it breaks, and creates a sound wave. In a similar way, forces in Earth's crust can cause regions of the crust to shift, bend, or even break. The breaking crust vibrates, creating seismic (SIZE mihk) waves that carry energy outward, as shown in **Figure 7.** Seismic waves are a combination of compressional and transverse waves. They can travel through Earth and along Earth's surface. When objects on Earth's surface absorb some of the energy carried by seismic waves, they move and shake. The more the crust moves during an earthquake, the more energy is released.

Research Seismic waves generated by earthquakes are used to map the interior of Earth. Visit the Glencoe Science Web site at **science.glencoe.com** to find out more about interpreting seismic waves. Write a summary of what you learn.

Section 1 Assessment

1. Give one example of a transverse wave and one example of a compressional wave.
2. Why doesn't a boat on a lake move forward when a water wave passes? Describe the boat's motion.
3. Describe how to model compressional waves using a coiled spring toy.
4. What is a mechanical wave?
5. **Think Critically** If ocean waves do not carry matter forward, why do boats need anchors?

Skill Builder Activities

6. **Comparing and Contrasting** Compare and contrast transverse and compressional waves. What does each type of wave carry? How does matter in the medium move? **For more help, refer to the Science Skill Handbook.**
7. **Communicating** In your Science Journal, describe waves you have observed. Have you ever observed the effects of a wave without being able to see it? Explain. **For more help, refer to the Science Skill Handbook.**

Caption Answer

Figure 7 because they require a medium through which to travel

3 Assess

Reteach

Pair students and give each pair a coiled spring toy. Tie a piece of colored string or yarn around one of the coils. Have students make transverse and then compressional waves in the toy. Ask them to identify what is the same and what is different about the motion of the string with each wave. L1 ELL COOP LEARN IN **Interpersonal**

Challenge

Organize the class into groups of four, and have each group design a product that uses wave motion in some way. Have each group describe its product to the class. Two possible products: Water waves turn a wheel that turns a crank; a spring sets a wheeled toy in motion. L2 ELL COOP LEARN IN **Interpersonal**

Assessment

Process Have students do research on earthquakes. Have them find out how the waves form and why they form in the places they do. Have students make events chains of their findings. Use **Performance Assessment in the Science Classroom,** p. 163. P

Answers to Section Assessment

1. Possible answers include: Water waves are transverse waves. Sound waves are compressional waves.
2. The water is moving up and down, not forward. The boat moves up and down with the wave.
3. Pull the ends of the toy apart and anchor them firmly at both ends. Then, squeeze several coils together at one end and release them.
4. a wave that can travel only through a medium
5. The tide will move unanchored boats.
6. Both waves carry energy. Matter moves up and down in a transverse wave. Matter moves back and forth in a compressional wave.
7. Possible answers: Students in a boat might feel the boat's motion without seeing the waves causing it. You can hear sound waves without seeing them.

SECTION 2

Wave Properties

1 Motivate

Bellringer Transparency

Display the Section Focus Transparency for Section 2. Use the accompanying Transparency Activity Master. L2 ELL

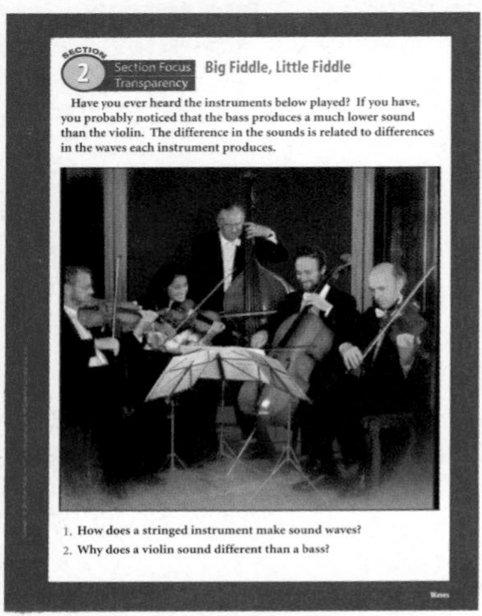
Section 2 Section Focus Transparency — Big Fiddle, Little Fiddle

Have you ever heard the instruments below played? If you have, you probably noticed that the bass produces a much lower sound than the violin. The difference in the sounds is related to differences in the waves each instrument produces.

1. How does a stringed instrument make sound waves?
2. Why does a violin sound different than a bass?

Tie to Prior Knowledge

Have students compare common examples of waves and ask them whether they can identify any similarities among all waves. Tell students that in this section they will learn about the different parts of waves and how these parts determine the amount of energy a wave can carry.

SECTION 

Wave Properties

As You Read

***What* You'll Learn**

- **Compare and contrast** transverse and compressional waves.
- **Describe** the relationship between frequency and wavelength.
- **Explain** how a wave's amplitude is related to the wave's energy.
- **Calculate** wave speed.

Vocabulary

crest	wavelength
trough	frequency
rarefaction	amplitude

***Why* It's Important**

Changing the properties of waves enables them to be used in many ways.

The Parts of a Wave

Besides the fact that sound waves, water waves, and seismic waves travel in different mediums, what makes these waves different from each other? Waves differ in how much energy they carry and in how fast they travel. Waves also have other characteristics that make them different from each other. For example, different waves can look different.

Suppose you shake the end of a rope and make a transverse wave. The transverse wave has alternating high points and low points. **Figure 8A** shows how the highest points of a transverse wave are called the **crests,** and the lowest points are called the **troughs.**

Reading Check *What are the highest and lowest points of a transverse wave?*

On the other hand, a compressional wave has no crests and troughs. When a compressional wave passes through a medium, it creates a region where the medium becomes crowded together and more dense, as in **Figure 8B.** This region is called the compression. When you make compressional waves in a coiled spring, the compression is the region where the coils are close together. **Figure 8B** also shows that the coils in the region next to a compression are spread apart, or less dense. This less-dense region of a compressional wave is called a **rarefaction** (rar uh FAK shun).

Figure 8
Transverse and compressional waves have different characteristics.

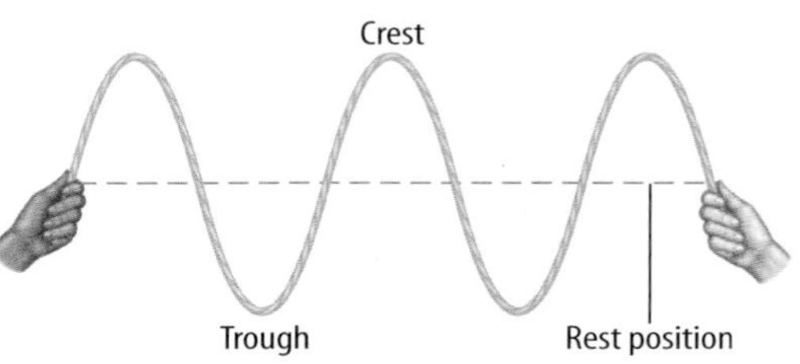

A The highest point of a transverse wave is a crest. The lowest point is a trough.

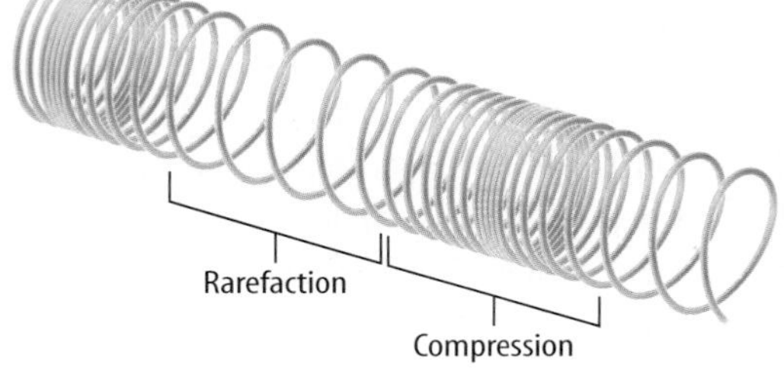

B The densest parts of a compressional wave are compressions. The least dense parts are rarefactions.

Section Assessment Planner

PORTFOLIO
Make a Model, p. 336

PERFORMANCE ASSESSMENT
Try at Home MiniLAB, p. 333
Math Skills Activity, p. 335
Skill Builder Activities, p. 337
See page 354 for more options.

CONTENT ASSESSMENT
Section, p. 337
Challenge, p. 337
Chapter, pp. 354–355

Figure 9
One wavelength starts at any point on a wave and ends at the nearest point just like it.

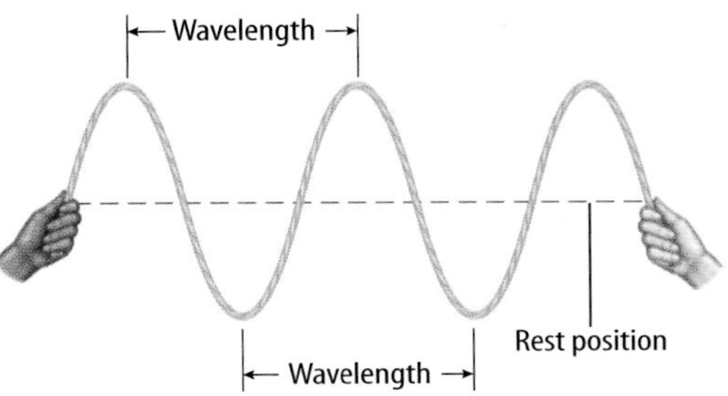

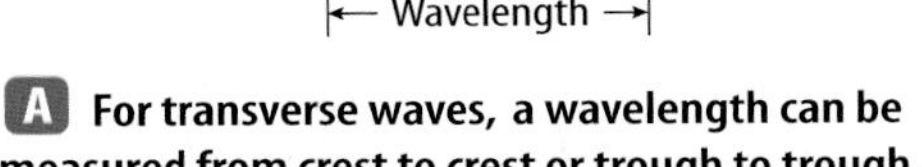

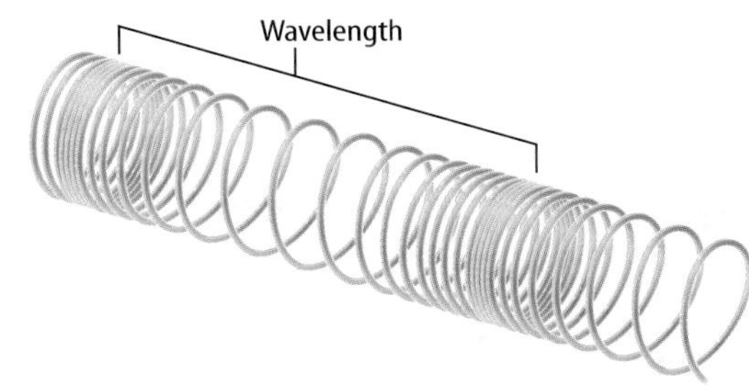

A **For transverse waves, a wavelength can be measured from crest to crest or trough to trough.**

B **The wavelength of a compressional wave can be measured from the start of one compression to the start of the next or the start of one rarefaction to the start of the next.** *How many compressions are in each wavelength?*

Wavelength

Waves also have a property called wavelength. A **wavelength** is the distance between one point on a wave and the nearest point just like it. For example, in transverse waves you can measure wavelength from crest to crest or from trough to trough, as shown in **Figure 9A.**

A wavelength in a compressional wave is the distance between two neighboring compressions or two neighboring rarefactions, as shown in **Figure 9B.** You can measure from the start of one compression to the start of the next compression, or from the start of one rarefaction to the start of the next rarefaction. The wavelengths of sound waves that you can hear range from a few centimeters for the highest-pitched sounds to 20 m to 30 m for the deepest sounds.

Frequency

What is your favorite radio station? When you tune your radio to a station, you are choosing radio waves of a certain frequency. The **frequency** of a wave is how many wavelengths pass a fixed point each second. You can find the frequency of a transverse wave by counting the number of crests or troughs that pass by a point each second. The frequency of a compressional wave is the number of compressions or rarefactions that pass a point every second. Frequency is expressed in hertz (Hz). A frequency of 1 Hz means that one wavelength passes by in 1 s. In SI units, 1 Hz is the same as 1/s.

Reading Check *What does a frequency of 7 Hz mean?*

TRY AT HOME Mini LAB

Observing Wavelength

1. Fill a pie plate or other wide pan with about 2 cm of water.
2. Lightly tap your finger several times per second on the surface of the water and observe the spacing of the water waves.
3. Increase the rate of your tapping, and observe the spacing of the water waves.

Analysis

1. How is the spacing of the water waves related to their wavelength?
2. How do the spacing of the water waves change when the rate of tapping increases?

2 Teach

The Parts of a Wave

Reading Check

Answer highest: crest; lowest; trough

Wavelength

Caption Answer
Figure 9B one

Frequency

Purpose to observe the relationship between the wavelength and frequency of a wave L2 ELL IN Kinesthetic

Materials pie plate, water

Teaching Strategy Suggest students use a watch to measure the rate of tapping.

Analysis

1. The closer the waves, the shorter their wavelength.
2. As the rate of tapping increases, the spacing of the waves decreases.

Assessment

Process Have students draw diagrams of the water waves they formed by tapping at two different rates. Ask students to label the wavelength and their diagrams. Use **PASC,** p. 125.

Teacher FYI

The hertz is named for the German physicist Heinrich Hertz. Hertz showed that radio waves are electromagnetic waves, as is light. He produced and measured electromagnetic waves in his laboratory, and he pioneered broadcasting and receiving radio waves.

Resource Manager 

Chapter Resources Booklet
Transparency Activity, p. 45
Directed Reading for Content Mastery, p. 20
MiniLAB, p. 3

Reading Check

Answer Seven wavelengths pass a fixed point in one second.

Frequency, continued

Quick Demo

Draw transverse waves on the board or on an overhead transparency. Be sure the wavelengths are of equal size. With a meterstick, measure the wavelength of the waves at several heights. Show students that, no matter which two points are chosen to measure wavelength, if the points correspond, the answer is always the same. L2 **LS Visual-Spatial**

Use Science Words

Word Usage Have students use the word *frequency* to refer to something other than waves. Possible answer: He looked at his watch with great frequency, glancing at it three times in one minute. Have students explain how the everyday use of the word frequency relates to its use in describing waves. When something has a greater frequency, it occurs more often within a given time period. When waves have a greater frequency, more of them pass a particular point within a given time period. L2 **LS Linguistic**

Wave Speed

Discussion

Why does sound travel faster in solids than in gases? The particles in solids are close together in a rigid matrix, and they bump into each other more often than do the particles in a gas. **Why does sound travel faster in warm air than it does in cold air?** Gas particles travel faster in warm air than they do in cold air, and they bump into each other more often.

L3 **LS Logical-Mathematical**

Wavelength Is Related to Frequency If you make transverse waves with a rope, you increase the frequency by moving the rope up and down faster. Moving the rope faster also makes the wavelength shorter. This relationship is always true—as frequency increases, wavelength decreases. **Figure 10** compares the wavelengths and frequencies of two different waves.

The frequency of a wave is always equal to the rate of vibration of the source that creates it. If you move the rope up, down, and back up in 1 s, the frequency of the wave you generate is 1 Hz. If you move the rope up, down, and back up five times in 1 s, the resulting wave has a frequency of 5 Hz.

Wave Speed

You're at a large stadium watching a baseball game, but you're high up in the bleachers, far away from the action. The batter swings and you see the ball rising in the air. An instant later you hear the crack of the bat hitting the ball. You see the impact before you hear it because all waves do not travel at the same speed. Light waves travel much faster than sound waves do. Therefore, the light waves reflected from the flying ball reach your eyes before the sound waves created by the crack of the bat reach your ears.

The speed of a wave depends on the properties of the medium it is traveling through. For example, sound waves travel faster in liquids and solids than they do in gases. On the other hand, light waves travel more slowly in liquids and solids than they do in gases or in empty space. Also, sound waves travel faster in a material if the temperature of the material is increased. For example, sound waves travel faster in air at 20°C than in air at 0°C.

Figure 10
The wavelength of a wave decreases as the frequency increases.

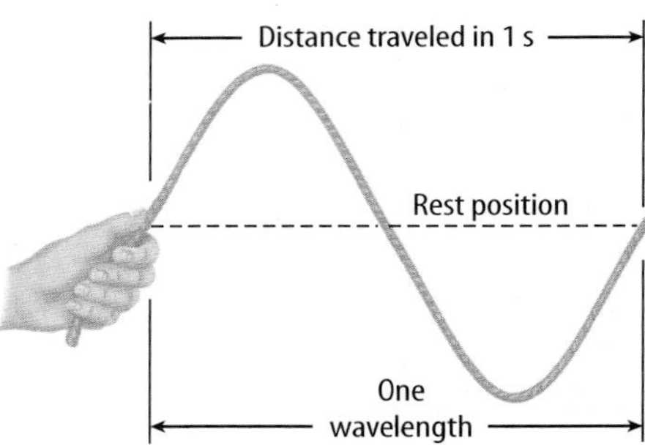

A **The rope is moved up, down, and up again one time in 1 s. One wavelength is created on the rope.**

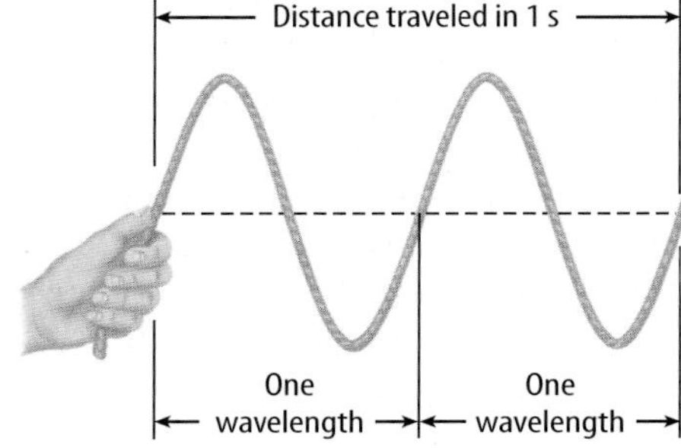

B **The rope is shaken up, down, and up again twice in 1 s. Two wavelengths are created on the rope.**

Visual Learning

Figures 10A and 10B **Why might it be more difficult to measure the exact wavelength of a compressional wave than that of a transverse wave?** It's difficult to determine where compressions begin and where they end. L2 **LS Logical-Mathematical**

Teacher FYI

The first widely accepted value for the speed of light was calculated by Ole Romer in 1676. He realized that the periods of the orbits of Jupiter's moons appeared shorter when Earth approached Jupiter and longer when Earth receded from Jupiter. His value for the speed of light was about three-quarters of the modern value.

Calculating Wave Speed Sometimes people want to know how fast a wave is traveling. For example, earthquakes beneath the ocean floor can produce giant water waves called tidal waves, or tsunamis. Knowing how fast the wave is moving helps determine when the wave will reach land. Wave velocity (v) describes how fast the wave moves forward. You can calculate the velocity of a wave by multiplying its frequency times its wavelength. Wavelength is represented by the Greek letter lambda (λ) and frequency is represented by f.

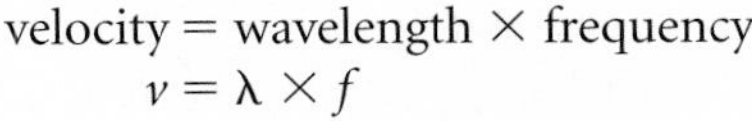

$$\text{velocity} = \text{wavelength} \times \text{frequency}$$
$$v = \lambda \times f$$

For example, what is the speed of a wave with a wavelength of 2 m and a frequency of 3 Hz? Because 3 Hz equals 3 wavelengths/second or 3 × 1/s, the wave's speed is:

$$v = \lambda \times f = 2\text{ m} \times 3\text{ Hz} = 2\text{ m} \times 3/\text{s} = 6\text{ m/s}$$

Earth Science INTEGRATION

Tsunamis can cause serious damage when they hit land. These waves can be up to 30 m tall and can travel more than 700 km/h. Research areas of the world where tsunamis are most likely to occur.

Math Skills Activity

Calculating Wave Speed

Example Problem

A wave is traveling at a velocity of 12 m/s and its wavelength is 3 m. Calculate the wave frequency.

Solution

1. *This is what you know:* velocity (v) = 12 m/s; wavelength (λ) = 3 m
2. *This is what you want to find:* wave frequency (f)
3. *This is the equation you need to use:* $v = \lambda \times f$
4. *Solve for f by substituting the known values in the equation.* $f = v/\lambda$; $f = 12\text{ m/s} / 3\text{ m} = 4 \times 1/\text{s} = 4\text{ Hz}$

Check your answer by substituting the frequency and given wavelength into the original equation. Do you calculate the velocity that was given?

Practice Problem

1. A wave is traveling at a speed of 18 m/s with a frequency of 3 Hz. A second wave is traveling at a speed of 16 m/s with a frequency of 4 Hz. What is the difference between these two wavelengths?

For more help, refer to the Math Skill Handbook.

Earth Science INTEGRATION

Over deep water, tsunami waves have wavelengths of 100 to 200 km, but they rise only half a meter high. They can pass a ship unnoticed. Near shore, however, friction against the increasingly shallow bottom slows down the waves. Frequency is unaffected, so as velocity decreases, so does wavelength. Thus the energy of the wave is concentrated in a smaller volume of water. The height of the wave increases dramatically, creating a towering wall of water. Eighty percent of all tsunamis occur in the Pacific Ocean.

IDENTIFYING Misconceptions

Tsunamis are also called *tidal waves*, which may cause students to think they are related to tides. A tsunami is set off by an underwater geological disturbance; tides are the result of gravitational interactions between Earth, the Moon, and the Sun. Ordinary waves are stirred up by wind. Point out to students that this is a good example of the wide range of disturbances that can transfer energy by waves.

Math Skills Activity

National Math Standards

Correlation to Mathematics Objectives

1,2,9

Answer to Practice Problem

1. $\lambda_1 = 18\text{ m/s} \div 3\text{ Hz} = 6\text{ m}$; $\lambda_2 = 16\text{ m/s} \div 4\text{ Hz} = 4\text{ m}$; $\lambda_1 - \lambda_2 = 6\text{ m} - 4\text{ m} = 2\text{ m}$

Resource Manager

Chapter Resources Booklet

Enrichment, p. 31

Lab Activity, pp. 9–11

Mathematics Skill Activities, p. 9

Curriculum Connection

Math Tell students that as frequency decreases, the wavelength increases if the speed of the wave is constant. Ask students what the relationship between wavelength and frequency is called when the wave speed is constant. They are inversely proportional. L3 LS **Linguistic**

Amplitude and Energy

Visual Learning

Figure 11 Point out to students the areas of compression and rarefaction in each of the waves in **Figure 11. Which wave has denser compressions?** wave A **Which has the less dense rarefactions?** also wave A [L2] LS **Visual-Spatial**

Make a Model

Have students use pennies and 11 x 17 paper to make models of compression waves. Have students divide the paper into twelve equal sections from left to right. Label the sections R (for rarefaction), T (for transition), and C (for compression). The twelve sections in order should be labeled R, T, C, T, R, T, C, T, R, T, C, T. Tell students to fill the areas with pennies to model a compression wave. The areas of compression should have the most pennies and the areas of rarefaction should have the fewest pennies. Ask students how they would need to move the pennies to increase the amplitude of the wave. Move pennies out of the rarefaction section and put them in the compression section. Have students count the pennies in each section and graph the number of pennies on the y-axis against the distance traveled by the wave on the x-axis. [L2] LS **Visual-Spatial** P

Caption Answer

Figure 12 Move the rope only a small distance up and down for lower amplitude, and a larger distance up and down for greater amplitude.

Amplitude and Energy

Why do some earthquakes cause terrible damage, while others are hardly felt? This is because the amount of energy a wave carries can vary. **Amplitude** is a measure of the energy in a wave. The greater the wave's amplitude is, the more energy the wave carries. Amplitude is measured differently for compressional and transverse waves.

Amplitude of Compressional Waves The amplitude of a compressional wave is related to how tightly the medium is pushed together at the compressions. The denser the medium is at the compressions, the larger its amplitude is and the more energy the wave carries. For example, it takes more energy to push the coils in a coiled spring toy tightly together than to barely move them. The closer the coils are in a compression, the farther apart they are in a rarefaction. So the less dense the medium is at the rarefactions, the more energy the wave carries. **Figure 11** shows compressional waves with different amplitudes.

Figure 11
The amplitude of a compressional wave depends on how dense its medium is at each compression. A This coiled spring has the greater amplitude. B This coiled spring has the smaller amplitude.

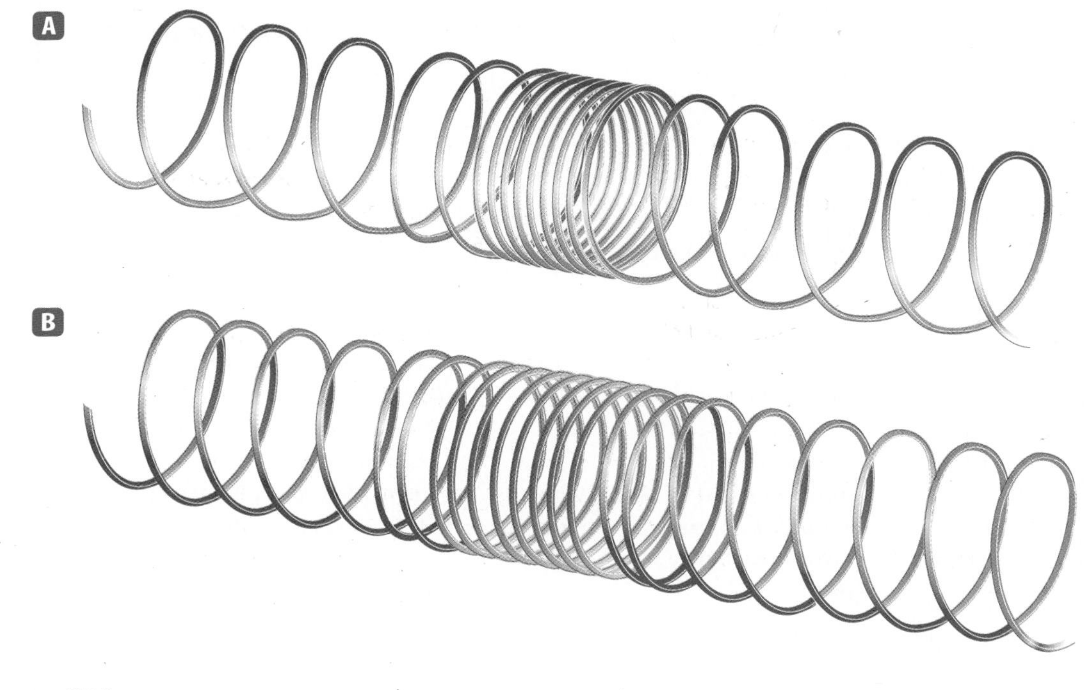

Resource Manager

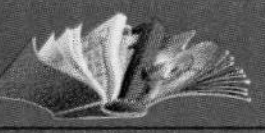

Chapter Resources Booklet

Transparency Activity, pp. 47–48
Reinforcement, p. 28
Activity Worksheet, pp. 5–6

Curriculum Connection

Music Play a recording of a piece of music for students. Make sure the music includes soft sections and loud sections. Ask students to identify the portions of the music in which the sound waves have a large amplitude and those where the sound waves have a lower amplitude. The loud sections have high amplitude waves and the soft sections have low amplitude waves. [L2] LS **Auditory-Musical**

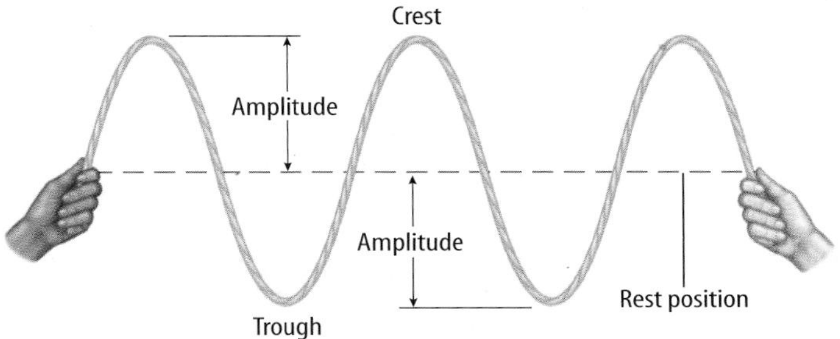

Figure 12
The amplitude of a transverse wave is the distance between a crest or a trough and the position of the medium at rest. *How could you create waves with different amplitudes in a piece of rope?*

Amplitude of Transverse Waves How can you tell the difference between a transverse wave that carries a lot of energy from one that carries little energy? If you've ever been knocked over by an ocean wave, you know that the higher the wave, the more energy it carries. Remember that the amplitude of a wave increases as the energy carried by the wave increases. So a tall ocean wave has a greater amplitude than a short ocean wave does. The amplitude of any transverse wave is the distance from the crest or trough of the wave to the rest position of the medium, as shown in **Figure 12.**

Section  Assessment

1. Sketch a transverse wave and label the crest, trough, wavelength, rest position, and amplitude.
2. How does the wavelength of a wave change when frequency decreases? When frequency increases?
3. How is the density at a compression in a compressional wave like the height of a transverse wave?
4. A wave travels at a speed of 4.0 m/s and has a frequency of 3.5 Hz. What is the wavelength?
5. **Think Critically** Remember that sound waves are compressional waves. Why do you think sound waves travel faster in solids than in gases?

Skill Builder Activities

6. **Concept Mapping** Create a concept map that shows the relationships among the following: *crest, trough, compression, rarefaction, wavelength, wave frequency, amplitude,* and *wave speed.* **For more help, refer to the** Science Skill Handbook.
7. **Drawing Conclusions** The unit *megahertz (MHz)* means "1 million Hertz." Your favorite FM radio station broadcasts at a frequency of 104.1 MHz, or 104.1 million Hz. Your friend prefers a station at 101.9 MHz. If the radio waves from both stations travel at the same speed, which station uses longer wavelengths? Explain. **For more help, refer to the** Science Skill Handbook.

3 Assess

Reteach

Give students a piece of string about 60 cm long. Instruct them to work in pairs to shake the string to form a standing transverse wave. Count the number of waves and measure the average wavelength. Change the wave so it has a greater amplitude, then change it again so it has shorter wavelengths. **What happens to the frequency?** It increases with shorter wavelengths, but it should not change with change in amplitude. L2 ELL COOP LEARN LS **Kinesthetic**

Challenge

Tell students that AM stands for "amplitude modulation" and that FM stands for "frequency modulation." Explain that to modulate means to vary the frequency or amplitude. Ask students what they think is different about how AM and FM radio signals carry information. In AM signals, the amplitude is varied to convey the message; in FM signals, the frequency is varied. L3 LS **Linguistic**

Assessment

Performance Have students shake a coiled spring toy to form a transverse wave, and then determine which variable (amplitude, wavelength, or frequency) cannot be controlled. Wavelength can be controlled only indirectly by changing frequency. Use **PASC,** p. 89.

Answers to Section Assessment

1. Sketches should look like the wave in **Figure 8A.** Students should label clearly the crest, trough, amplitude, rest position, and wavelength.
2. If the speed of the wave remains constant, when frequency decreases, the wavelength increases and when frequency increases the wavelength decreases.
3. Both demonstrate the amplitude of the wave.
4. about 1.1 m
5. Molecules in a solid are closer together and so will bump into each other more frequently.
6. Check student's work.
7. The station at 101.9 MHz uses the longer wavelength. We know that frequency times wavelength = wave speed. Since both waves travel at the same speed, the higher the frequency, the lower the wavelength.

Activity

BENCH TESTED

Purpose Students generate waves in different types of materials and compare and contrast the behavior of these waves. L2 ELL COOP LEARN

LS **Visual-Spatial**

Process Skills observing, comparing and contrasting

Time Required 30 minutes

Alternate Materials Telephone cord can be used to demonstrate the behavior of coiled material.

Teaching Strategies The strips of cloth and string should be about 1 meter long. This will be long enough so that the time for the pulse to move along the strip can be measured. If the strip is too long, the wave energy will die away before the wave reaches the other end.

Troubleshooting If students have difficulty timing the pulses, have them count the wavelengths instead.

Answers to Questions

1. The waves will initially have the same amplitude determined by the movement of the student's hand. The amplitude will decrease in less dense material because of the effects of air or surface friction.
2. The waves travel faster in the less dense material.
3. The speed and amplitude decrease as the waves travel into denser material.
4. From the movement of the student's hand.

Activity

Waves in Different Mediums

Have you ever swum underwater? If so, even with your head underwater, you probably still heard some sounds. Sound waves can travel through more than one medium, including air and water. The noises probably sounded different underwater than they do in air. How do waves change when they pass through different mediums?

What You'll Investigate

How is the speed of a wave affected by the type of material it is traveling through?

Possible Materials

small coiled spring toys (made out of metal and plastic)
rope, both heavy and light
string
long rubber band, such as those used for exercising
strip of heavy cloth, such as a towel
strip of light cloth, such as nylon pantyhose
ribbon
stopwatch

Goals

- **Demonstrate** transverse waves.
- **Compare** the speed of waves traveling through different mediums.

Safety Precautions

Procedure

1. Use pieces of each material that are about the same length. For each material, have a partner hold one end of the material still while you shake the material back and forth between two set points to make a wave.

Identify the points by placing markers or chairs on the floor. Shake each material in the same way.
2. Have someone time how long a pulse takes to reach the opposite end of the material.
3. Tie two different types of rope together or tie a heavy piece of cloth to a lighter piece. **Observe** how the wave changes when it moves from one material to the other.
4. **Observe** compressional waves using coiled spring toys. You can connect two different types of coiled spring toys together to see how a compressional wave changes in different mediums.

Conclude and Apply

1. Did the waves traveling through the different mediums have the same amplitude? Explain why or why not.
2. Did the waves travel at the same speed through the different mediums? **Explain.**
3. **Explain** how the waves changed when they moved from one material to another.
4. Waves carry energy. Where did the waves created in this activity get their energy?

Communicating Your Data

Have students draw diagrams showing the waves they generated in each different material or combination of materials. Each diagram should include the names of the materials used and should have the amplitude, wavelength, and frequency labeled.

Assessment

Process Provide students with a new, different material and ask them to predict the relative amplitude, frequency, and wavelength of the waves they would generate with that material. Give students an opportunity to test their predictions. Use **Performance Assessment in the Science Classroom,** p. 93.

SECTION 3

The Behavior of Waves

Reflection

If you are one of the last people to leave your school building at the end of the day, you'll probably find the hallways quiet and empty. When you close your locker door, the sound echoes down the empty hall. Your footsteps also make a hollow sound. Thinking you're all alone, you may be startled by your own reflection in a classroom window. The echoes and your image looking back at you from the window are caused by wave reflection.

Reflection occurs when a wave strikes an object and bounces off of it. All types of waves—including sound, water, and light waves—can be reflected. How does the reflection of light allow the boy in **Figure 13** to see himself in the mirror? It happens in two steps. First, light strikes his face and bounces off. Then, the light reflected off his face strikes the mirror and is reflected into his eyes.

A similar thing happens to sound waves when your footsteps echo. Sound waves form when your foot hits the floor and the waves travel through the air to both your ears and other objects. Sometimes when the sound waves hit another object, they reflect off it and come back to you. Your ears hear the sound again, a few seconds after you first heard your footstep.

Bats and dolphins use echoes to learn about their surroundings. A dolphin makes a clicking sound and listens to the echoes. These echoes enable the dolphin to locate nearby objects.

As You Read

***What* You'll Learn**

- **Identify** the law of reflection.
- **Recognize** what makes waves bend.
- **Explain** how waves combine.

Vocabulary

refraction
diffraction
interference
standing wave
resonance

***Why* It's Important**

You can check your reflection in a mirror, hear an echo, and see shadows because of how waves behave.

Figure 13
The light that strikes the boy's face is reflected into the mirror. The light then reflects off the mirror into his eyes. *What kinds of waves can be reflected?*

SECTION

The Behavior of Waves

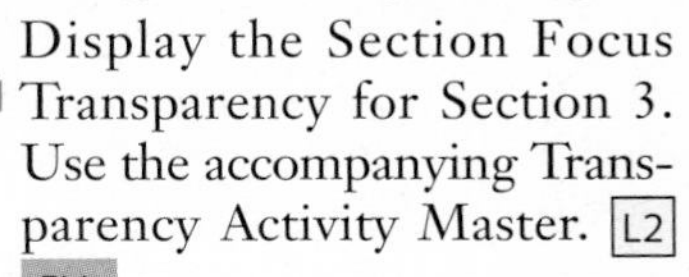

Bellringer Transparency

Display the Section Focus Transparency for Section 3. Use the accompanying Transparency Activity Master. L2 ELL

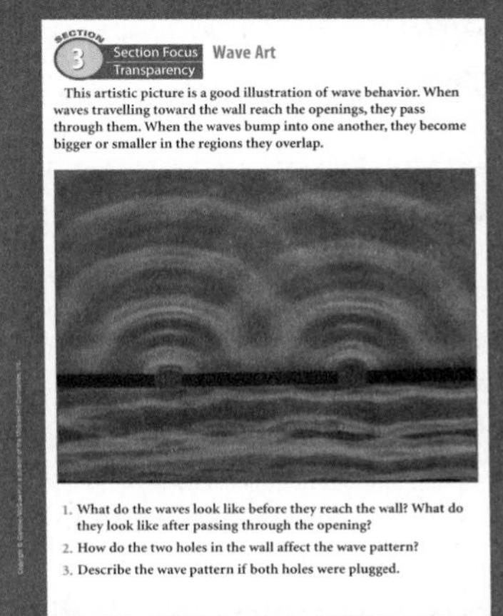

This artistic picture is a good illustration of wave behavior. When waves travelling toward the wall reach the openings, they pass through them. When the waves bump into one another, they become bigger or smaller in the regions they overlap.

1. What do the waves look like before they reach the wall? What do they look like after passing through the opening?
2. How do the two holes in the wall affect the wave pattern?
3. Describe the wave pattern if both holes were plugged.

Tie to Prior Knowledge

Ask students what happens to a ball when it hits a wall. Ask how a ball might travel differently if moving through water. Tell students that in this section they will learn how a wave behaves when it hits something or when it travels through different media.

Section Assessment Planner

Portfolio
Science Journal, p. 340
Curriculum Connection, p. 343

Performance Assessment
MiniLab, p. 347
Skill Builder Activities, p. 347

See page 354 for more options.

Content Assessment
Section, p. 347
Challenge, p. 347
Chapter, pp. 354–355

Resource Manager

Chapter Resources Booklet
Transparency Activity, p. 46
Directed Reading for Content Mastery, pp. 21, 22

2 Teach

Reflection

Activity

Have students sit on the floor and roll a tennis ball against a wall. Have them first roll the ball directly toward the wall and then at increasing angles to the normal. Ask them what they notice about how the ball bounces off the wall as the angle to the normal is increased. The greater the angle between the normal and the ball's path to the wall, the greater the angle to the normal by the ball's path away from the wall. L1 ELL LS **Kinesthetic**

Caption Answer

Figure 13 all kinds

Refraction

Use an Analogy

Ask students whether they've ever ridden on a sled that's moved from snow to ice or mud. If the sled hit the ice or mud at an angle, one of its runners hit the ice or mud before the other. That runner then started moving more quickly or more slowly while the other runner stayed at the original speed, causing the sled to turn. Tell students that this is similar to what happens to a sound, seismic, or light wave when it moves from one medium to another.

Caption Answer

Figure 15 air

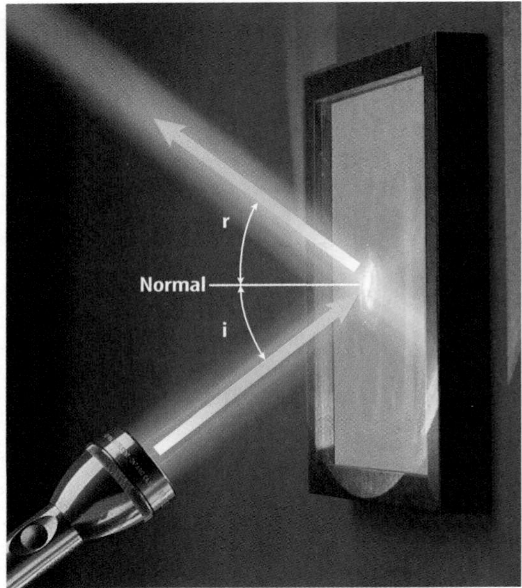

Figure 14
A flashlight beam is made of light waves. When any wave is reflected, the angle of incidence, *i*, equals the angle of reflection, *r*.

The Law of Reflection Look at the two light beams in **Figure 14.** The beam striking the mirror is called the incident beam. The beam that bounces off the mirror is called the reflected beam. The line drawn perpendicular to the surface of the mirror is called the normal. The angle formed by the incident beam and the normal is the angle of incidence, labeled *i*. The angle formed by the reflected beam and the normal is the angle of reflection, labeled *r*. According to the law of reflection, the angle of incidence is equal to the angle of reflection. All reflected waves obey this law. You may have seen objects obey the law of reflection or even used this law without knowing it. For example, suppose you throw a bounce pass while playing basketball. The angle between the ball's direction and the normal to the floor is the same before and after it bounces.

Refraction

Do you notice anything unusual in **Figure 15?** The pencil looks as if it is broken into two pieces. But if you pulled the pencil out of the water, you would see that it is unbroken. This illusion is caused by refraction. How does it work?

Remember that a wave's speed depends on the medium it is moving through. When a wave passes from one medium to another—such as when a light wave passes from air to water—it changes speed. If the wave is traveling at an angle when it passes from one medium to another, it changes direction, or bends, as it changes speed. **Refraction** is the bending of a wave caused by a change in its speed as it moves from one medium to another. The greater the change in speed is, the more the wave bends.

Reading Check *When does refraction occur?*

Figure 16A on the next page shows what happens when a wave passes into a material in which it slows down. The wave is refracted (bent) toward the normal. **Figure 16B** shows what happens when a wave passes into a medium in which it speeds up. Then the wave is refracted away from the normal.

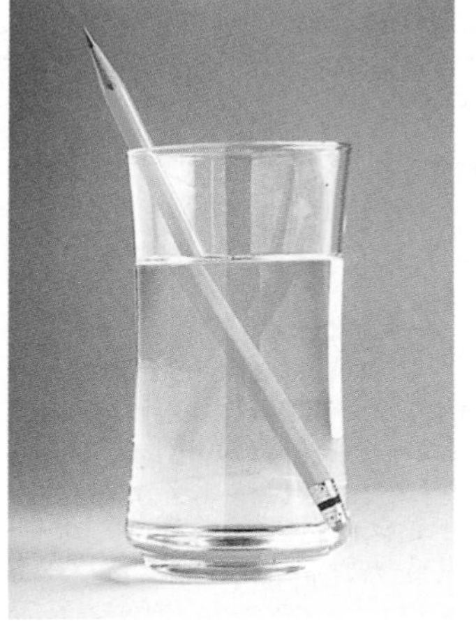

Figure 15
The pencil looks like it is broken at the surface of the water because of refraction. *Does light travel faster in water or air?*

Reading Check

Answer when a wave changes speed as it moves from one medium to another at an angle

Ray Diagrams Have students trace into their Science Journals the two photographs on this page. Then ask them to use the tracings to construct ray diagrams of the reflection and refraction shown in each one. Tell them to be sure to add the line normal to the surface in each diagram and to measure and label the angles. L2 LS **Visual-Spatial** P

Resource Manager

Chapter Resources Booklet
Enrichment, p. 32
Reading and Writing Skill Activities, p. 33

Figure 16
Light travels slower in water than in air.

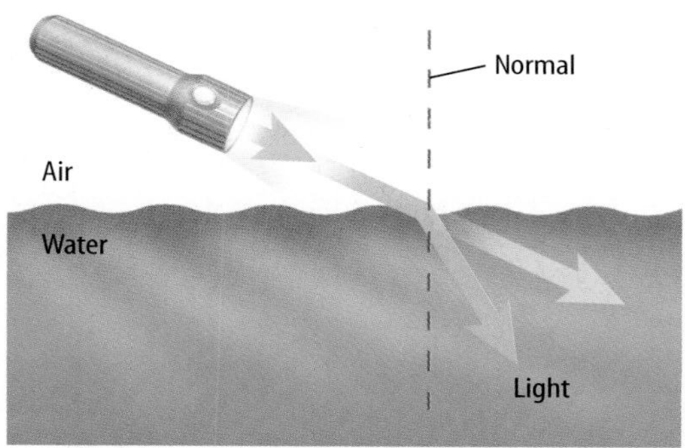

A **When light travels from air to water, it slows down and bends toward the normal.**

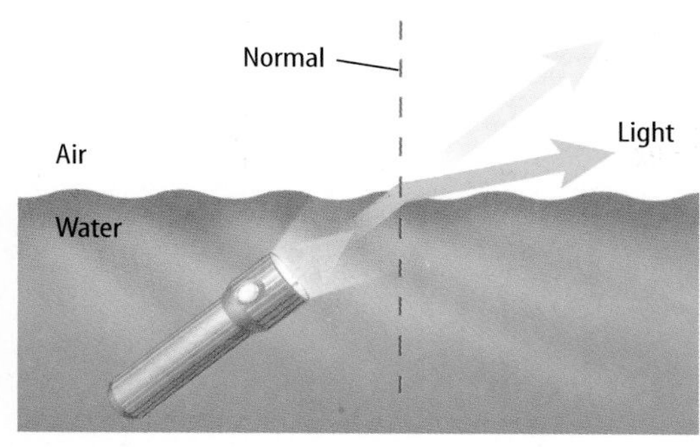

B **When light leaves water and travels to air, it speeds up and bends away from the normal.** *How would the beam bend if the speed were the same in both air and water?*

Refraction of Light in Water You may have noticed that objects that are under water seem closer to the surface than they really are. **Figure 17** shows how refraction causes this illusion. In the figure, the light waves reflected from the swimmer's foot are refracted away from the normal and enter your eyes. However, your brain assumes that all light waves have traveled in a straight line. The light waves that enter your eyes seem to have come from a foot that was higher in the water. This is also why the pencil in **Figure 15** seems broken. The light waves coming from the part of the pencil that is underwater are refracted, but your brain interprets them as if they are not bent. However, the light waves coming from the part of the pencil above the water are not refracted. So, the part of the pencil that is underwater looks as if it has shifted.

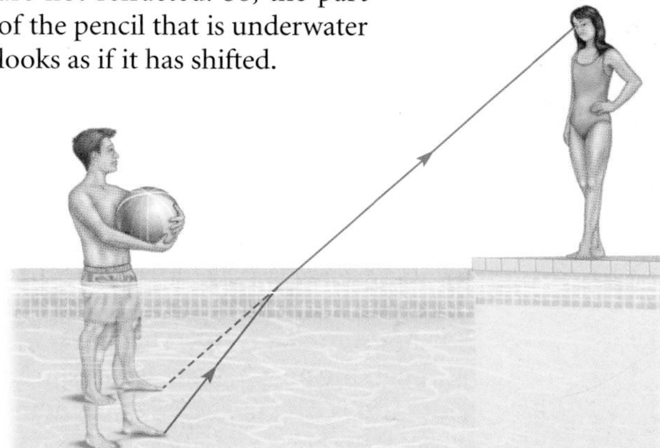

Figure 17
To the observer on the side of the pool, the swimmer's foot looks closer to the surface than it actually is. *When the boy looks down at his feet, will they seem closer to the surface than they really are?*

Caption Answer

Figure 16 The beam wouldn't bend at all. It's the difference in speed that makes the light bend.

Use Science Words

Word Origins Have students look up the word *refraction* or *refract* in a dictionary and find the Latin word from which it is derived and what that word means. **Ask students why this word is appropriate to use to describe refraction.** The word *refract* comes from the Latin word *refringere,* which means "to break up or break open." When you look at the pencil through water, it looks as if it's broken. L2 LS **Linguistic**

Caption Answer

Figure 17 no, because he is looking straight down through the water and not at an angle

Extension

Light travels at a different speed through glass than it does through air. Ask students to find out whether light travels faster or slower in glass than it does in air. slower **Are light waves entering glass refracted toward the normal or away from it?** toward the normal L3 LS **Logical-Mathematical**

Teacher FYI

How much a wave will be refracted when passing from one medium to another depends on the media involved, the angle of the wave, and its frequency. Waves with higher frequencies are refracted more than those with lower frequencies.

Diffraction

Caption Answer

Figure 18 Before they pass the islands, the waves are moving parallel through the water. After they pass the islands, the waves change direction because they are refracted/diffracted, or bent.

Quick Demo

Place a petri dish filled with water on an overhead projector. Using a pencil or pen, make waves in the water. Cut small pieces of cardboard into several different shapes, and place them into the dish, one at a time and in different combinations. Have students observe how each piece or combination of pieces causes a different diffraction pattern. L2 ELL IS **Visual-Spatial**

Answer the bending of waves around an object

Make a Model

Have students use rectangular glass baking dishes and flat pieces of metal or plastic to make a model of the diffraction of water waves through a slit. Have students tape two flat pieces of metal or plastic so they stand vertically across the width of the baking dish. Be sure they leave an open slit between the two pieces. Then have students fill the baking dish with water, use pencils to generate waves, and observe the diffraction. Suggest that students experiment with slit widths until they find the one that diffracts the water waves the most. L2

IS **Kinesthetic**

Figure 18
Ocean waves change direction as they pass a group of islands. *How are the waves different before and after they pass the islands?*

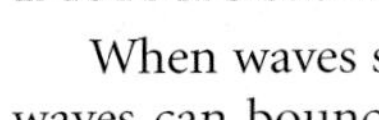

Diffraction

When waves strike an object, several things can happen. The waves can bounce off, or be reflected. If the object is transparent, the waves can be refracted as they pass through it. Sometimes the waves may be both reflected and refracted. If you look into a glass window, sometimes you can see your reflection in the window, as well as objects behind it. Light is passing through the window and is also being reflected at its surface.

Waves also can behave another way when they strike an object. The waves can bend around the object. **Figure 18** shows how ocean waves change direction and bend after they strike an island. **Diffraction** occurs when an object causes a wave to change direction and bend around it. Diffraction and refraction both cause waves to bend. The difference is that refraction occurs when waves pass through an object, while diffraction occurs when waves pass around an object.

Reading Check *What is diffraction?*

Waves also can be diffracted when they pass through a narrow opening, as shown in **Figure 19.** After they pass through the opening, the waves spread out. In this case the waves are bending around the corners of the opening.

Figure 19
When water waves pass through a small opening in a barrier, they diffract and spread out after they pass through the hole.

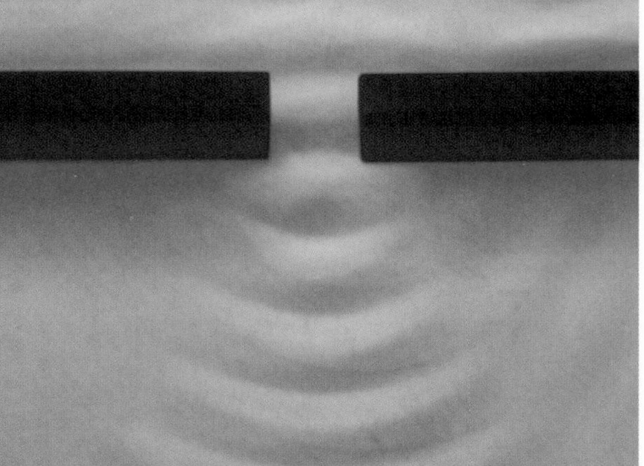

Visual Learning

Figure 19 Why should the hole in the barrier cause a circular wave pattern? The energy the wave sends through the hole is concentrated into one point. It then spreads out evenly in all directions to make the circular pattern. L3 IS **Logical-Mathematical**

Resource Manager

Chapter Resources Booklet
Lab Activity, pp. 13–16

Home and Community Involvement, p. 38

Diffraction and Wavelength How much does a wave bend when it strikes an object or an opening? The amount of diffraction that occurs depends on how big the obstacle or opening is compared to the wavelength. When an obstacle is smaller than the wavelength, it does not cast a shadow because the waves bend around it. But if the obstacle is larger than the wavelength, the waves do not diffract much. In fact, if the obstacle is much larger than the wavelength, almost no diffraction occurs. The obstacle casts a shadow because almost no waves bend around it. The larger the obstacle is compared to the wavelength, the less the waves will diffract, as shown in **Figure 20.**

For example, you're walking down the hallway and you can hear sounds coming from the lunchroom before you reach the open lunchroom door. However, you can't see into the room until you reach the doorway. Why can you hear the sound waves but not see the light waves while you're still in the hallway? The wavelengths of sound waves are similar in size to a door opening. Sound waves diffract around the door and spread out down the hallway. Light waves have a much shorter wavelength. They are hardly diffracted at all by the door. The light waves from the lunchroom bend only slightly around the doorway, and you can't see into the room until you get close to the door.

Radio Waves Diffraction also affects your radio's reception. AM radio waves have longer wavelengths than FM radio waves do. Because of their longer wavelengths, AM radio waves diffract well around obstacles like buildings and mountains. The FM waves with their short wavelengths do not diffract as much. As a result, AM radio reception is often better than FM reception around tall buildings and natural barriers.

SCIENCE Online

Research Visit the Glencoe Science Web site at **science.glencoe.com** for more information about diffraction. Communicate to your class what you learned.

Figure 20
The diffraction of waves around an obstacle depends on the size of the obstacle.

A Less diffraction occurs if the wavelength is smaller than the obstacle.

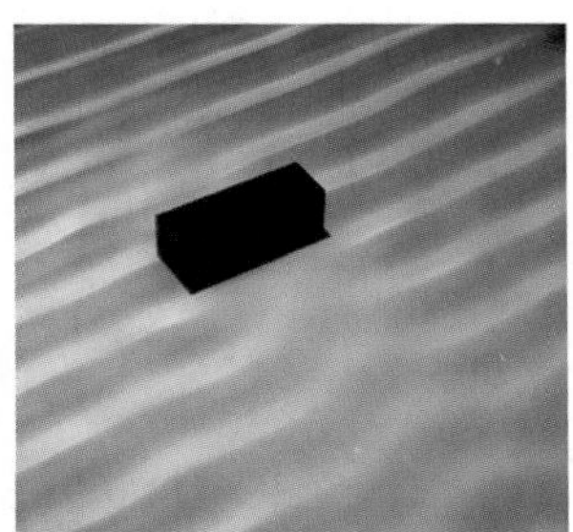

B More diffraction occurs if the wavelength is the same size as the obstacle.

Extension

Light waves also diffract, but the objects that make them diffract are much smaller than those that make sound waves diffract. Have students find out what size objects need to be in order to make light waves diffract. The wavelengths of visible light vary from about $4,300 \times 10^{-10}$ m to about $6,900 \times 10^{-10}$ m. Objects that diffract light must be about the size of these wavelengths. L3 LS **Linguistic**

Teacher FYI

Because the wavelengths of X rays are about the same size as the distances between atoms in crystals, X rays are diffracted by crystals. This phenomenon is exploited in X-ray crystallography, in which crystals are bombarded from different angles by X rays, and the crystal structure is determined by the diffraction of the X rays. This method has been used to determine the structure of thousands of organic, inorganic, organometallic, and biological compounds.

SCIENCE Online

Internet Addresses

Explore the Glencoe Science Web site at **science.glencoe.com** to find out more about topics in this section.

Curriculum Connection

Art Have students use reflection, refraction, and diffraction to create artwork. The art could be as simple as sketching how refraction distorts objects viewed through water or as involved as photographing the diffraction patterns of light waves. Students may wish to research and experiment with how the surface of a CD diffracts light. Have students explain the phenomenon at work in their art. L2 ELL LS **Visual-Spatial** P

Interference

Fun Fact

When we listen to an orchestra, sound waves produced by all the instruments combine and hit our eardrums at the same time. The waves that reach our ears have the amplitude and frequency that result from adding together all of the waves produced by the individual instruments. Our brains and ears, however, are able to separate the wave into its components, and we hear the sounds made by the original instruments. In the same way, our brains interpret the different frequencies of different colors of light waves.

Extension

Radio transmitters use interference to carry information on radio waves. Have students identify and describe the two major ways this is done. The two ways are amplitude modulation (AM) and frequency modulation (FM). To generate an AM signal, a transmitter takes a wave at a given frequency and causes its amplitude to increase or decrease in response to an audio signal. An AM radio receiver then translates these interference patterns to produce the sound you hear. To generate an FM signal, the transmitter causes the frequency of the carrier wave to vary. L3

LS **Logical-Mathematical**

Caption Answer

Figure 21B the sum of the amplitudes of the original waves

Interference

Suppose two waves are traveling toward each other on a long rope as in **Figure 21A.** What will happen when the two waves meet? If you did this experiment, you would find that the two waves pass right through each other, and each one continues to travel in its original direction, as shown in **Figure 21B** and **Figure 21C.** If you look closely at the waves when they meet each other in **Figure 21B,** you see a wave that looks different than either of the two original waves. When the two waves arrive at the same place at the same time, they combine to form a new wave. When two or more waves overlap and combine to form a new wave, the process is called **interference.** This new wave exists only while the two original waves continue to overlap. The two ways that the waves can combine are called constructive interference and destructive interference.

Figure 21
At the ocean, when one wave retreats from shore, it can meet a new wave coming in. The two waves combine to form a new wave. The same thing happens with the waves on this rope.

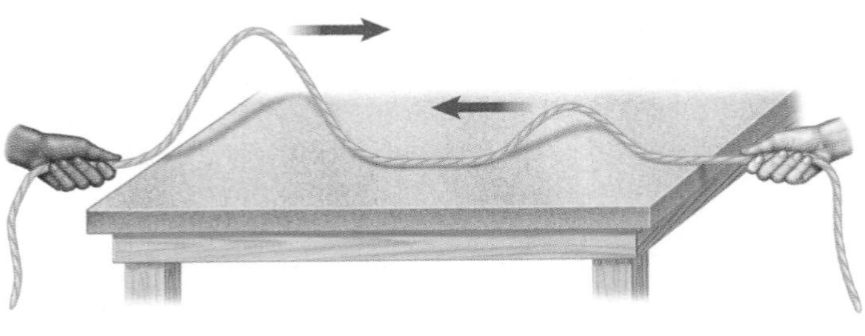

A Two waves move toward each other on a rope.

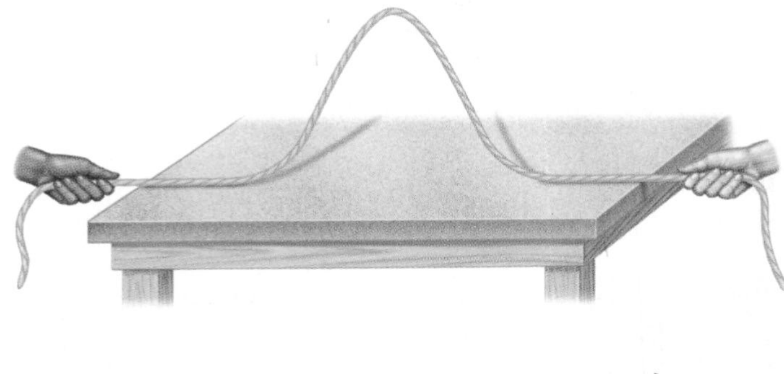

B As the waves overlap, they interfere to form a new wave. *What is the amplitude of the new wave?*

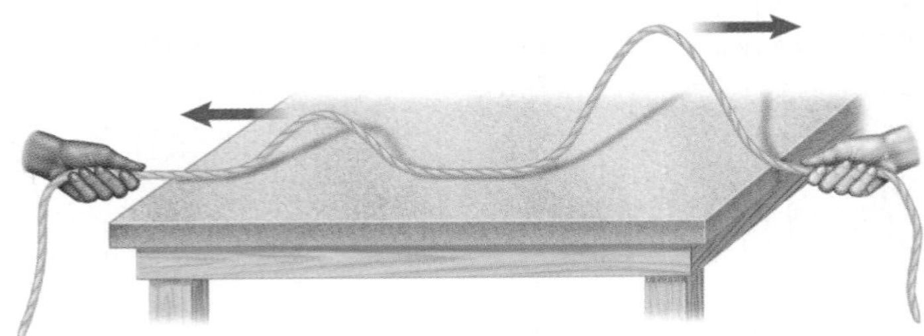

C When the two waves overlap, they move right through each other. Afterward, they continue moving unchanged, as if they had never met.

Cultural Diversity

Mayan Echoes If you clap your hands in the Mayan temple of Kukulkan at Chichen Itza in Central Mexico, you're greeted with a piercing echo. Many believe this echo sounds like the call of a quetzal bird. The bird is native to the region and prized for its bright colors and long tail. Archaeologists are studying the architecture of the temple to determine whether the Maya built it with this effect in mind. The shrieking, birdlike echo is produced by sound waves being diffracted by the gaps in the steps of one of the large staircases. The sound's amplification comes from waves interfering at just the right places.

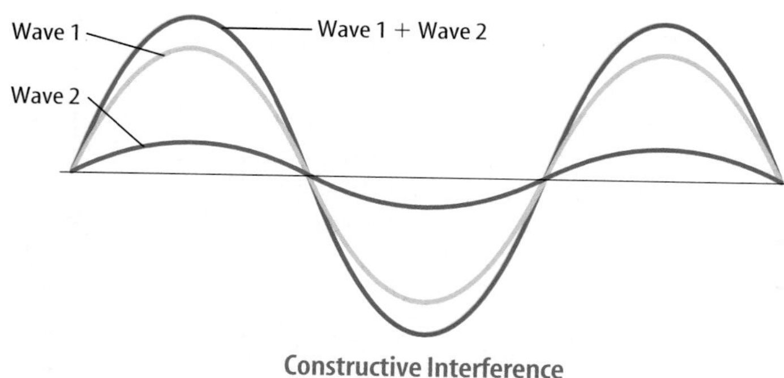

Wave 1
Wave 1 + Wave 2
Wave 2
Destructive Interference

Figure 22
Two types of interference are possible.

A **If Wave 1 and Wave 2 were moving toward each other on a rope, they would constructively interfere and form the green wave. Wave 1 and Wave 2 are in phase.**

B **If Wave 1 and Wave 2 were traveling toward each other on a rope, they would destructively interfere and form the green wave. Wave 1 and Wave 2 are out of phase.**

Constructive Interference In constructive interference, shown in **Figure 22A,** the waves add together. This happens when the crests of two or more transverse waves arrive at the same place at the same time and overlap. The amplitude of the new wave that forms is equal to the sum of the amplitudes of the original waves. Constructive interference also occurs when the compressions of different compressional waves overlap. If the waves are sound waves, for example, constructive interference produces a louder sound. Waves undergoing constructive interference are said to be in phase.

Destructive Interference In destructive interference, the waves subtract from each other as they overlap. This happens when the crests of one transverse wave meet the troughs of another transverse wave, as shown in **Figure 22B.** The amplitude of the new wave is the difference between the amplitudes of the waves that overlapped. With compressional waves, destructive interference occurs when the compression of one wave overlaps with the rarefaction of another wave. The compressions and rarefactions combine and form a wave with reduced amplitude. When destructive interference happens with sound waves, it causes a decrease in loudness. Waves undergoing destructive interference are said to be out of phase.

Health INTEGRATION

People who are exposed to constant loud noises, such as those made by airplane engines, can suffer hearing damage. Scientists are developing ways to reduce loud noises by using destructive interference. Special ear protectors also use destructive interference to cancel damaging noise. With a classmate, list all the jobs you can think of that require ear protectors.

Activity

Position a student at each end of a jump rope, and have them make different interference patterns in the rope. Challenge the students to create both constructive and destructive interference. L2 ELL COOP LEARN
IS **Kinesthetic**

Quick Demo

Ask students who play instruments to bring them in and demonstrate what happens when two notes that have almost the same pitch are played at the same time. Students should be able to hear the beats produced by the interference between the two notes. These pulses of sound disappear when the pitches become equal, so they are used by musicians as they tune their instruments. L2
IS **Auditory-Musical**

Health INTEGRATION

The use of destructive interference to cancel out noise is called active noise control. In active noise control, sounds are generated that exactly cancel out the unwanted sounds. Jobs requiring ear protection include rock concert sound mixer, airport runway worker, and factory worker.

Resource Manager

Performance Assessment in the Science Classroom, p. 52

Cultural Diversity, p. 61

Curriculum Connection

History Scientists first knew that light had wave properties when it could be shown that it produced interference patterns when passed through a slit. Have students find out whose experiments first showed this, and when. Thomas Young in 1801 L3 IS **Linguistic**

Standing Waves

Caption Answer

Figure 23 A point on the waves of a standing wave always cancel each other out.

Resonance

Purpose Students observe resonance and the conditions under which it can occur. L2 ELL LS **Auditory-Musical**

Materials three tuning forks, two of which are at the same frequency, mallet

Teaching Strategy Demonstrate for students the best way to set a tuning fork vibrating. You don't have to hit it hard, but you do have to hit it sharply.

Analysis

The second tuning fork started vibrating, but the third one did not. The natural frequency of the second tuning fork is the same as the frequency of the waves that were hitting it from the first tuning fork, so it resonated. The natural frequency of the third tuning fork is different, so it did not resonate.

Assessment

Process Have students take the tuning forks to different areas of the classroom and see if they can find anything else that resonates with them. Use **Performance Assessment in the Science Classroom**, p. 97.

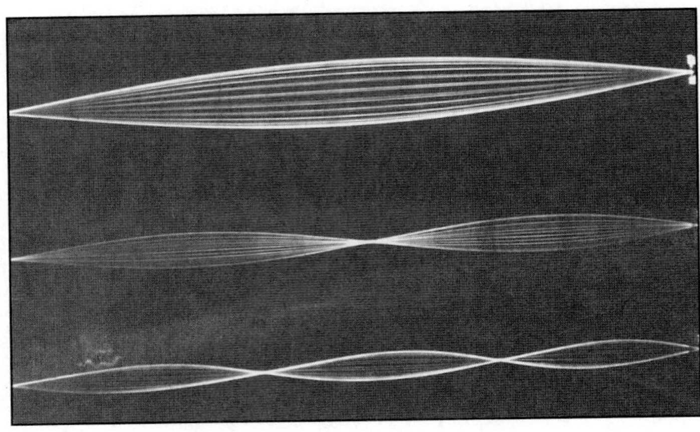

Figure 23
Standing waves seem to stay in the same place. *How do nodes form?*

Standing Waves

When you make transverse waves with a rope, you might shake one end while your friend holds the other end still. What would happen if you both shook the rope continuously to create identical waves moving toward each other? Perhaps you have shaken a jump rope like this so two people could jump at the same time. Interference takes place as the waves from each end overlap along the rope. At any point where a crest meets a crest, a new wave with a larger amplitude forms. But at points where crests meet troughs, the waves cancel each other and no motion occurs.

The interference of the two identical waves makes the rope vibrate in a special way, as shown in **Figure 23.** The waves create a pattern of crests and troughs that do not seem to be moving. Because the wave pattern stays in one place, it is called a standing wave. A **standing wave** is a special type of wave pattern that forms when waves equal in wavelength and amplitude, but traveling in opposite directions, continuously interfere with each other. The places where the two waves always cancel are called nodes. The nodes always stay in the same place on the rope. Meanwhile, the wave vibrates between the nodes.

Standing Waves in Music When the string of a violin is played with a bow, it vibrates and creates standing waves. The standing waves in the string help produce a rich, musical tone. Other instruments also rely on standing waves to produce music. Some instruments, like flutes, create standing waves in a column of air. In other instruments, like drums, a tightly stretched piece of material vibrates in a special way to create standing waves. As the material in a drum vibrates, nodes are created on the surface of the drum.

Visual Learning

Figure 23 Provide pairs of students with jump ropes, and ask them to create standing waves similar to those shown in **Figure 23.** L2 LS **Kinesthetic**

Resource Manager

Chapter Resources Booklet
Reinforcement, p. 29
Activity Worksheet, pp. 7–8
MiniLAB, p. 4

Resonance

You may have noticed that bells of different sizes and shapes create different notes. When you strike a bell, you cause it to vibrate to produce sound. The bell vibrates at a certain frequency called the natural frequency. The note you hear depends on the bell's natural frequency. The natural frequency of vibration depends on the bell's size, shape, and the material it is made from. Other objects, including windows, bridges, and columns of air, also vibrate at their own natural frequencies.

There is another way to make something vibrate at its natural frequency. Suppose you have a tuning fork that has a natural frequency of 440 Hz. Imagine that a sound wave of the same frequency strikes the tuning fork. Because the sound wave has the same frequency as the natural frequency of the tuning fork, the tuning fork will vibrate. The ability of an object to vibrate by absorbing energy at its natural frequency is called **resonance** (RE zun unts).

Sometimes resonance can cause an object to absorb a large amount of energy. What happens to the tuning fork if it continues to absorb energy from the sound wave? Remember that the amplitude of a wave increases as the energy it carries increases. In the same way, an object vibrates more strongly as it continues to absorb energy at its natural frequency. If enough energy is absorbed, the object can vibrate so strongly that it breaks apart.

Experimenting with Resonance

Procedure

1. Strike a **tuning fork** with a **mallet.**
2. Hold the vibrating tuning fork near a **second tuning fork** that has the same frequency.
3. Strike the tuning fork again. Hold it near a **third tuning fork** that has a different frequency.

Analysis

What happened when you held the vibrating tuning fork near each of the other two? Explain.

Section  Assessment

1. Describe how the law of reflection allows you to see your image in a mirror.
2. Sketch a diagram showing what happens when a wave enters a medium and slows down. Also sketch a wave speeding up as it enters a new medium. In each diagram, label the normal, the angle of incidence, and the angle of refraction.
3. What happens when waves overlap?
4. What is resonance?
5. **Think Critically** Aluminum foil is shiny like a mirror, yet you can't see your reflection in a piece of crumpled aluminum foil. Explain.

Skill Builder Activities

6. **Recognizing Cause and Effect** Imagine you are on the shore of a large lake and see waves moving toward you from the center of the lake. However, before reaching shore, the waves pass by a boat dock. The waves then move toward you at a slightly different angle. What would you infer is happening? **For more help, refer to the** Science Skill Handbook.
7. **Using a Word Processor** Use a word processor to make an outline showing important points about constructive interference and destructive interference. **For more help, refer to the** Technology Skill Handbook.

3 Assess

Reteach

Give pairs of students pieces of rope. Ask them to set up standing waves and identify for you the amplitude, wavelength, and frequency of the waves and to point out any nodes. L2 COOP LEARN IS **Kinesthetic**

Challenge

Have students research a musical instrument, such as a guitar, violin, or trumpet, and explain how its shape and features contribute to the sounds it produces. In their reports, students should include the effects of vibrations, resonance, and interference. L2 IS **Linguistic**

Assessment

Performance Have students make up songs describing the reflection, refraction, diffraction, and interference of waves. Use **Performance Assessment in the Science Classroom,** p. 151.

Answers to Section Assessment

1. When you look straight at the mirror, the incident beam and the reflected beam are both normal to the mirror, so your reflection bounces right back to your eyes.
2. Drawings should be similar to **Figure 16.**
3. They combine to form a new wave.
4. the ability of an object to vibrate by absorbing energy at its natural frequency
5. The crumpled foil acts like many tiny mirrors facing different directions, and therefore reflecting light in different directions.
6. The dock has diffracted the waves.
7. The outline should mention that constructive and destructive interference depend upon the point at which the crest of one wave meets the trough of another.

Activity

BENCH TESTED

What You'll Investigate

Purpose

Students will generate transverse waves with a long spring and measure the speed and frequency of the waves.

Process Skills

observing, measuring, recognizing cause and effect, making and using tables, interpreting data

Time Required

45 minutes

Materials

long spring, rope, or hose, meterstick, stopwatch

Safety Precautions

Caution students to keep a firm hold on the spring so it doesn't fly off and hit someone.

Procedure

Teaching Strategy

Suggest to students that they practice the procedures for making and counting waves described in steps 2, 3, and 6 several times before they make their measurements.

Troubleshooting Make sure the spring has no kinks or rough spots places in it, as this will make it difficult for students to produce consistent waves.

Expected Outcome

Wave times measured in steps 2, 3, and 4 should be similar.

Activity

Measuring Wave Properties

Some waves travel through space; others pass through a medium such as air, water, or earth. Each wave has a wavelength, speed, frequency, and amplitude. In this activity you will make waves in the classroom, and observe, measure, and change some of the properties of these waves.

What You'll Investigate

How can the speed of a wave be measured?
How can the wavelength be determined from the frequency?

Materials

long spring, rope, or hose
meterstick
stopwatch

Goals

- **Measure** the speed of a transverse wave.
- **Create** waves with different amplitudes.
- **Measure** the wavelength of a transverse wave.

Safety Precautions

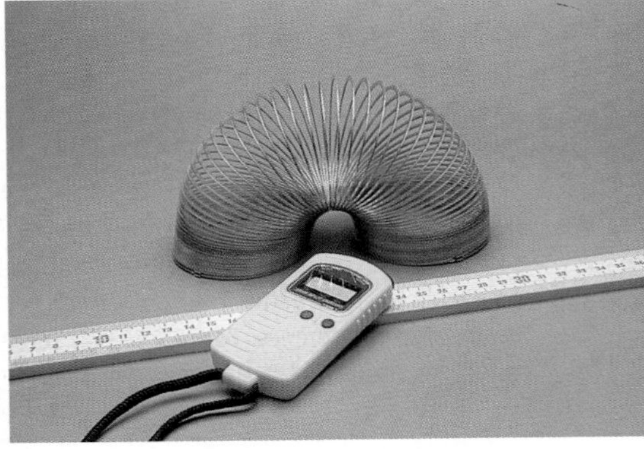

Procedure

1. With a partner, stretch your spring across an open floor and measure the length of the spring. Record this measurement in the data table. Make sure the spring is stretched to the same length for each step.
2. Have your partner hold one end of the spring. Create a single wave pulse by shaking the other end of the spring back and forth.
3. Have a third person use a stopwatch to measure the time needed for the pulse to travel the length of the spring. Record this measurement in the "Wave Time" column of your data table.
4. Repeat steps 2 and 3 two more times.
5. **Calculate** the speed of waves 1, 2, and 3 in your data table by using the formula:

   speed = distance / time

   Average the speeds of waves 1, 2, and 3 to find the speed of waves on your spring.

Inclusion Strategies

Learning Disabled Have these students work in groups with students proficient in the lab. As students do the activity, have them take turns illustrating for each other the wavelength, frequency, and amplitude of waves they generate. Ask them to also create some compressional waves, and compare and contrast them with transverse waves. L1 LS **Linguistic**

348 CHAPTER 11 Waves

6. **Create** a wave with several wavelengths. Have one person stand at the center of the spring. Count the number of wavelengths that pass this student in 10 s. Record this measurement for wave 4 in the Wavelength Count column in your data table.
7. Repeat step 7 two more times. Each time create a wave with a different wavelength by shaking the spring faster or slower.
8. **Calculate** the frequency of waves 4, 5, and 6 by dividing the number of wavelengths by 10 s.

9. Calculate the wavelength of waves 4, 5, and 6 using the formula

wavelength = wave speed / frequency

Use the average speed calculated in step 5 for the wave speed.

Wave Property Measurements

	Spring Length	Wave Time	Wave Speed
Wave 1	5 m	2.33 s	2.15 m/s
Wave 2	5 m	2.25 s	2.22 m/s
Wave 3	5 m	2.61 s	1.92 m/s
	Wavelength Count	**Frequency**	**Wavelength**
Wave 4	4	0.4 Hz	5.24 m
Wave 5	7	0.7 Hz	3.00 m
Wave 6	5	0.5 Hz	4.19 m

Conclude and Apply

1. Was the wave speed different for the three different pulses you created? Why or why not?
2. Why would you average the speeds of the three different pulses to calculate the speed of waves on your spring?
3. How did the wavelength of the waves you created depend on the frequency of the waves?

Communicating Your Data

Ask your teacher to set up a contest between the groups in your class. Have each group compete to determine who can create waves with the longest wavelength, the highest frequency, and the largest wave speed. Record the measurements of each group's efforts on the board. **For more help, refer to the Science Skill Handbook.**

Conclude and Apply

1. Accept all reasonable responses. Wave speed probably varies because it would be difficult to shake the spring exactly the same way each time.
2. to compensate for errors in measurement
3. Wavelength decreased as frequency increased. wavelength = wave speed ÷ frequency

Error Analysis

Have groups compare their data with other students and discuss possible reasons for errors. As they compare their data, make sure students understand that wave times and wave speeds will be different for different springs.

Performance Ask students to repeat the activity, but this time to generate compressional waves. Use **Performance Assessment in the Science Classroom,** p. 97.

Active Reading

Reflective Journal In this strategy, students identify activities and what they learned and record responses to the activities. Have students divide pieces of paper into several columns. Have them record their thoughts under headings such as "What I did," What I learned," "Questions I have," and "Surprises I experienced." Have students write a Reflective Journal entry for this activity.

Communicating Your Data

Help students analyze the data on the board to determine whether there was any relationship between the amplitude, frequency, wavelength, and wave speed of the winning waves.

Content Background

The speed of sound in water was first calculated in 1822. Sound travels much better underwater than light or radio waves. Sailors have long known of whales' songs, which are now known to be as a highly sophisticated communication system.

Piezoelectric crystals discovered in the late 1800s made modern sonar feasible. The crystals are basically the same as those in common sparking devices used to light charcoal grills. If they are compressed, they produce an electrical charge. This enabled the development of transducers that could change the mechanical energy of sound waves into electrical signals.

The first sonar device, called a hydrophone, was used to help calculate the time difference between the sounds of a foghorn and an underwater gong sounded simultaneously by a lightship. The difference in the arrival time of the sounds allowed the distance to the lightship to be determined with greater accuracy.

Active sonar enabled the detection of silent objects by hitting them with a sound and listening for the echo. Increases in power and refinement of frequency generation have led to more sensitive equipment able to produce more detailed images. Sonar is now used to inspect metals for flaws, monitor oceanic temperatures, and determine the gender of unborn babies.

TIME SCIENCE AND HISTORY

SCIENCE CAN CHANGE THE COURSE OF HISTORY!

Making Waves

Sonar Helps Create Deep-Sea Pictures and Save Lives

What is sonar?

Sonar is a device that uses sound waves to find the location and distance of underwater objects. Its name is a shortened version of SOund NAvigation and Ranging.

Sonar was used to find enemy subs during World War II.

How does sonar work?

There are two kinds of sonar—active and passive. Active sonar sends out a ping sound that is reflected back when it hits an underwater object. Since sound travels through water at a constant rate (1,500 m/s), scientists use the time the sound takes to return to calculate the distance. Passive sonar only listens for sounds given off by underwater objects, such as the noise made by a submarine's engines or by torpedoes.

Why was it invented?

Sonar was first developed by scientists in the early twentieth century as a way to detect icebergs and prevent boating disasters. Its technical advancement was hurried by the Allies' need to detect German submarines in World War I. Before 1916, anti-submarine sonar was passive—a series of microphones towed underwater. By 1918, the United States and Britain had developed an active sonar system placed in submarines sent to attack other subs.

The range of early sonar was only 1.6 km. (Today it is more than 16 km.) Even so, in World War II, sonar allowed ships to defend themselves effectively from enemy subs.

350

Resources for Teachers and Students

American Underwater Search & Survey, Ltd., Box 768, Cataumet, MA 02534

Center for Bioacoustics, Texas A&M University-Corpus Christi, Natural Resources Center 3404, 6300 Ocean Drive, Corpus Christi, Texas 78412

National Sonar Association, 40414 Yardley Court, Temecula, CA 92591

Their strategy was to use sonar to find subs and then fire rocket-fueled depth charges from a safe distance. After the war, more silent nuclear submarines were developed. Sonar-absorbing hulls and quiet engines and machinery insured that the subs could partly shield themselves from sonar.

Since the war, sonar has been used to help scientists find schools of fish. It also has been used by oceanographers to map ocean and lake floors. Most dramatically, sonar has been vital in the discovery of submerged wrecks, such as downed airplanes and ships, including the *Titanic*—the passenger liner that sank in 1912.

In 1985, a French and American team used a new type of sonar device called the side-scan sonar to locate the *Titanic.* This kind of sonar projects a tight beam of sound that can create accurate images of the sea bed. Members of the expedition towed this sonar device about 170 m above the sea bed across a section of the Atlantic Ocean where the *Titanic* went down. Although the expedition's ship passed above the *Titanic* early on, the sonar readings were misinterpreted. Weeks later, video cameras finally spotted the wreck. In 1996, a French expedition to the *Titanic* used a special sonar device that produced 3D images of the wreck site. This sonar was also powerful enough to penetrate the 15 m of mud that covered the bow of the ship. It enabled researchers to see how the hull had been damaged when the ship had collided with an iceberg.

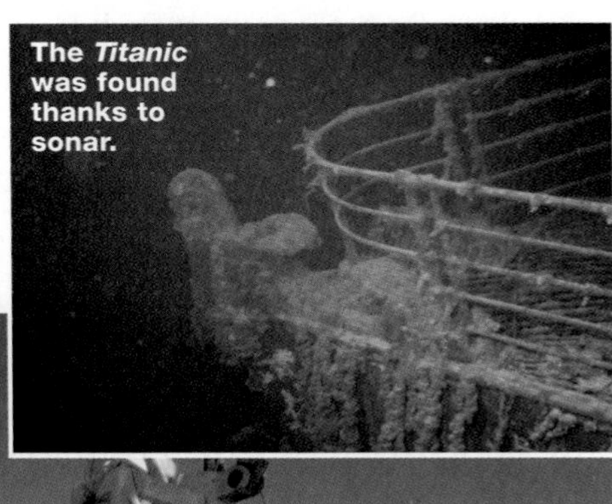

The *Titanic* was found thanks to sonar.

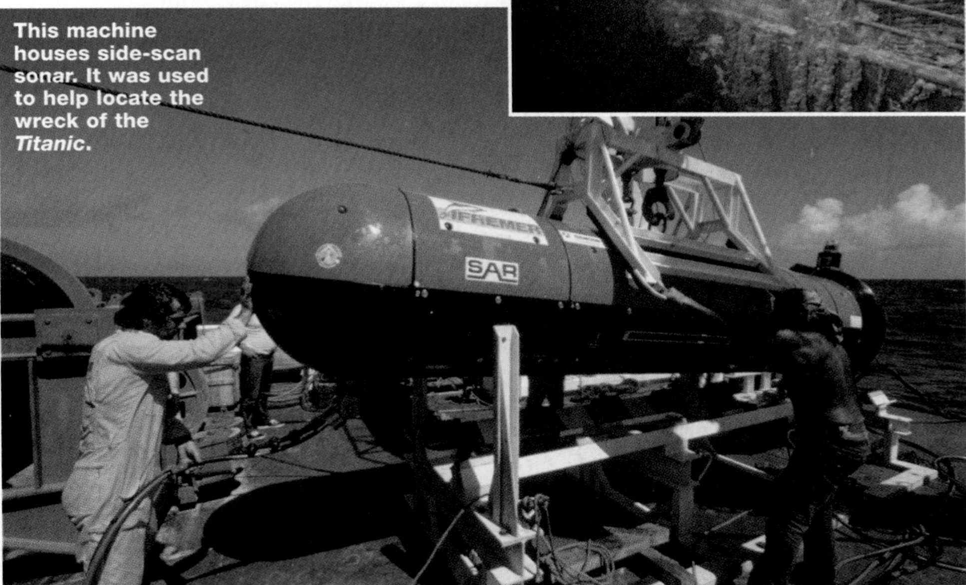

This machine houses side-scan sonar. It was used to help locate the wreck of the *Titanic*.

CONNECTIONS Report **Research how sonar was used by navies in World War I and World War II. Did sonar affect each war's outcome? How did it save lives? What uses can you think of for sonar if it could be used in everyday life?**

SCIENCE *Online*

For more information, visit science.glencoe.com

Discussion

Early anti-submarine sonar consisted of passive hydrophones towed through water. **Would this method be more or less effective than active sonar? Why?** Possible answer: It would be less effective. The submarine could essentially hide by not producing any noise from machinery or propellers, which would give the passive sonar nothing to detect. L2

LS **Logical-Mathematical**

Historical Significance

The development of sonar tremendously increased the safety of shipping. Sonic fathometers enabled the detection of shoal waters allowing deep draft vessels to safely navigate previously hazardous channels. The ability to detect icebergs helped make crossings in the high latitudes safe, lengthening the shipping season. In wartime sonar was a key element in the protection of commercial convoys.

Sonar and related technologies have improved the search for oil, making it possible to look miles below the surface of the ocean and into the seabed. Sonar imaging equipment also makes it possible to locate sunken objects, not only from the recent past but long buried wrecks and structures from antiquity. In addition, ultrasound has improved the quality of medical diagnostics and helped improve the integrity of the structural materials we depend on.

CONNECTIONS

Have students research the modern uses of acoustic technology and make a "Family Tree" chart of all the products and equipment they can discover that perform their primary function through the use or detection of sounds, both audible and inaudible. Through class discussion determine which are directly related to sonar and it basic principles.

SCIENCE *Online*

Internet Addresses

Explore the Glencoe Science Web site at **science.glencoe.com** to find out more about topics in this feature.

Chapter 11 Study Guide

Reviewing Main Ideas

Preview

Students can answer the questions in their Science Journals. Discuss the answers as you go through the chapter. LS **Linguistic**

Review

Students can write their answers, then compare them with those of other students. LS **Interpersonal**

Reteach

Students can look at the illustrations and describe details that support the main ideas of the chapter. LS **Visual-Spatial**

Answers to Chapter Review

Section 1

2. the energy and enthusiasm of the crowd

Section 2

3. by measuring the distance from the crest or trough to the rest position of the medium

Section 3

2. Because of refraction, the fish appears to be closer than it is.

Chapter 11 Study Guide

Reviewing Main Ideas

Section 1 The Nature of Waves

1. Waves are rhythmic disturbances that transfer energy through matter or space.
2. Waves transfer only energy, not matter. *What does a human "wave" in a stadium transfer?*

3. Mechanical waves need matter to travel through. Mechanical waves can be compressional or transverse.
4. When a transverse wave passes through a medium, matter in the medium moves at right angles to the direction the wave travels. For a compressional wave, matter moves back and forth in the same direction as the wave travels. Matters returns to its original position after wave passes.

Section 2 Wave Properties

1. Transverse waves have high points (crests) and low points (troughs). Compressional waves have more dense areas (compressions) and less dense areas (rarefactions).
2. Transverse and compressional waves can be described by their wavelengths, frequencies, and amplitudes. As frequency increases, wavelength always decreases.
3. The greater a wave's amplitude is, the more energy it carries. *How would you measure the amplitude of these ocean waves?*

4. A wave's velocity can be calculated by multiplying its frequency times its wavelength.

Section 3 The Behavior of Waves

1. For all waves, the angle of incidence equals the angle of reflection.
2. A wave is bent, or refracted, when it changes speed as it enters a new medium. *How does refraction affect how this fisher aims with his spear?*

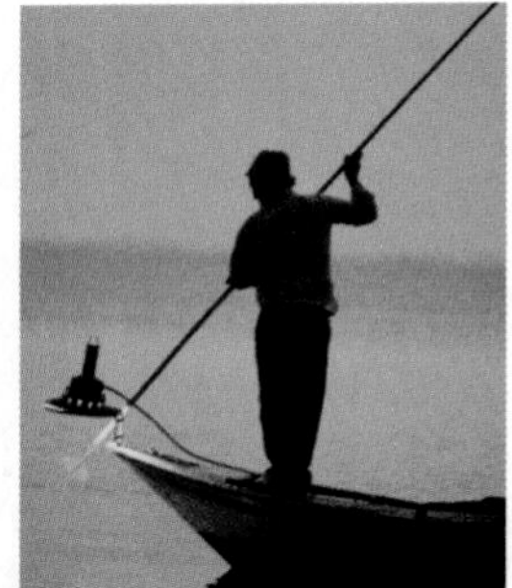

3. When two or more waves overlap, they combine to form a new wave. This process is called interference.

FOLDABLES Reading & Study Skills — After You Read

Use your Foldable to help you review characteristics of light and sound waves.

FOLDABLES Reading & Study Skills — After You Read

After students have read the chapter and completed the Foldable described in Before You Read, have them do the activity on the student page.

Dinah Zike

Visualizing Main Ideas

Complete the following concept map on waves.

Waves
can be: Transverse
matter moves: Back and forth at right angles to direction wave travels
wavelength is measured: From crest to crest or trough to trough
an example is: A wave on a rope

can be: Compressional
matter moves: Back and forth in same direction wave travels
wavelength is measured: From compression to compression or rarefaction to rarefaction
an example is: Coiled spring

Vocabulary Review

Vocabulary Words

a. amplitude
b. compressional wave
c. crest
d. diffraction
e. frequency
f. interference
g. medium
h. rarefaction
i. refraction
j. resonance
k. standing wave
l. transverse wave
m. trough
n. wave
o. wavelength

Study Tip

Use word webs. Write down the main idea of the chapter on a piece of paper and circle it. Connect other related facts to it with lines and arrows.

Using Vocabulary

Answer the following questions using complete sentences.

1. Compare and contrast reflection and refraction.
2. Which type of wave has points called nodes that do not move?
3. Which part of a compressional wave has the lowest density?
4. Find two words in the vocabulary list that describe the bending of a wave.
5. Describe what happens when waves overlap.
6. What is the relationship between amplitude, crest, and trough?
7. What does frequency measure?
8. What does a mechanical wave always travel through?

Chapter 11 Study Guide

Visualizing Main Ideas

See student page.

Vocabulary Review

Using Vocabulary

1. Reflection and refraction both involve waves contacting a surface and changing direction. In reflection, waves bounce off a surface, whereas refraction occurs when waves enter a new medium at an angle, change speed, and are bent.
2. Standing waves have nodes that do not move.
3. The rarefied section of a compressional wave has the lowest density.
4. Refraction and diffraction describe the bending of a wave.
5. When waves overlap, they interfere and form a new wave.
6. The amplitude of any transverse wave is the distance from the crest or trough to the rest position of the medium.
7. Frequency measures how many wavelengths pass a fixed point each second.
8. A mechanical wave always travels through a medium.

IDENTIFYING Misconceptions

Assess

After students have done the activity on page 324F and completed the chapter, have them perform this activity.

Materials corks, pan of water, cup, eyedropper

Procedure Have students work in groups and use the materials provided to design an experiment to see how water waves move corks. Suggest students drop water from the dropper to create the waves.

Expected Outcome Students will realize that the corks are not displaced by the waves. Students should realize that waves travel through a medium without the particles in the medium traveling with the waves.

Chapter 11 Assessment

Checking Concepts

1. B
2. D
3. A
4. A
5. B
6. A
7. C
8. D
9. D
10. D

Thinking Critically

11. No; the water that hits the island is water that already was near the island. Through the wave, it has received energy from the earthquake miles away.
12. No; frequency is independent of amplitude.
13. In a mirror, you can see only objects located at an angle such that their reflected beam bounces toward your eyes.
14. Sound waves have a larger wavelength than light waves. They can diffract around the street corner, but light waves cannot.
15. Possible answers: vocal cords, bell, car engine

Chapter 11 Assessment

Checking Concepts

Choose the word or phrase that best answers the question.

1. Which of the following do waves carry?
   A) matter **C)** matter and energy
   B) energy **D)** the medium
2. When a compressional wave travels through a medium, which way does matter in the medium move?
   A) backward
   B) all directions
   C) at right angles to the direction the wave travels
   D) in the same direction the wave travels
3. What is the formula for calculating wave speed?
   A) $v = \lambda \times f$ **C)** $v = \lambda / f$
   B) $v = f$ **D)** $v = \lambda + f$
4. What is the highest point of a transverse wave called?
   A) crest **C)** wavelength
   B) compression **D)** trough
5. As the frequency of a wave increases, what happens to the wavelength?
   A) It moves forward. **C)** It vibrates.
   B) It decreases. **D)** It increases.
6. What is the amplitude of a wave related to?
   A) the wave's energy **C)** wave speed
   B) frequency **D)** refraction
7. Which term describes the bending of a wave around a barrier?
   A) resonance **C)** diffraction
   B) interference **D)** reflection
8. What types of waves have nodes?
   A) seismic waves **C)** tidal waves
   B) radio waves **D)** standing waves
9. What is equal to the angle of reflection?
   A) refraction angle **C)** bouncing angle
   B) normal angle **D)** angle of incidence
10. When two or more waves arrive at the same place at the same time, what do they do?
    A) turn around
    B) bend toward the normal
    C) stop
    D) combine

Thinking Critically

11. An earthquake on the ocean floor produces a tidal wave that hits a remote island. Is the water that hits the island the same water that was above the earthquake? Explain.
12. When a wave's amplitude increases, does its frequency change? Explain.
13. Use the law of reflection to explain why you see only a portion of the area behind you when you look in a mirror.
14. Explain why you can hear a fire engine coming around a street corner before you can see it.
15. Describe what vibrated to produce three of the sounds you've heard today.

Developing Skills

16. **Forming Hypotheses** In 1981, swaying dancers in the balconies of a Kansas City, Missouri, hotel caused the balconies to collapse. Use what have you learned about wave behavior to form a hypothesis that explains why this happened.
17. **Comparing and Contrasting** Compare and contrast diffraction and refraction.

Chapter Assessment Planner

Portfolio Encourage students to place in their portfolios one or two items of what they consider to be their best work. Examples include:

- Assessment, p. 331
- Make a Model, p. 336
- Science Journal, p. 340
- Curriculum Connection, p. 343

Performance Additional performance assessments, Performance Task Assessment Lists, and rubrics for evaluating these activities can be found in Glencoe's **Performance Assessment in the Science Classroom.**

18. Interpreting Data According to the data in the table below, approximately how many times faster does sound travel in steel than in air?

Sound Transmission	
Substance	**Speed of Sound at 25°C (m/s)**
Air	347
Brick	3,650
Cork	500
Water	1,498
Steel	5,200

19. Making and Using Tables Find newspaper articles describing five recent earthquakes. Construct a table that shows for each earthquake the date, location, magnitude, and whether the damage caused by each earthquake was light, moderate, or heavy.

20. Concept Mapping Design a concept map that shows the characteristics of transverse waves. Include the terms *crest, trough, medium, wavelength, frequency,* and *amplitude.*

Performance Assessment

21. Oral Presentation A seismograph is an instrument that measures the magnitude of earthquakes. Research seismographs, and make an oral presentation explaining how they work.

Technology

Go to the Glencoe Science Web site at **science.glencoe.com** or use the **Glencoe Science CD-ROM** for additional chapter assessment.

The Princeton Review Test Practice

A scientist is studying the formation of ocean waves during windy storms. Her observations are listed in the table below.

Ocean Wave Observations			
Wind Conditions	**Wind Speed (km/hr)**	**Ocean Wave Height (m)**	**Description of Ocean Waves**
Calm	1-5	0.05	Like a Small Lake
Light Breeze	6-11	0.10	Small Wavelets
Gentle Breeze	?	0.25	Small Waves
Mod. Breeze	20-28	0.50	Large Wavelets
Fresh Breeze	29-38	0.75	Mod. Waves
Strong Breeze	39-49	1.00	Large Waves
Gale	62-75	1.50	Breaking Waves

Study the chart and answer the following questions.

1. What wind speeds are considered a "gentle breeze?"
A) 9–17 (km/hr)
B) 10–18 (km/hr)
C) 12–19 (km/hr)
D) 12–20 (km/hr)

2. According to the table, a 33 km/hr wind produced ______.
F) large wavelets
G) moderate waves
H) large waves
J) breaking waves

3. What is the height of a large wave?
A) 1.50
B) 0.25
C) 1.00
D) 0.10

Assessment Resources

Reproducible Masters

Chapter Resources Booklet
Chapter Review, pp. 37–38
Chapter Tests, pp. 39–42
Assessment Transparency Activity, p. 49

Glencoe Science Web site
Interactive Tutor
Chapter Quizzess

Glencoe Technology
Assessment Transparency
Interactive CD-ROM Chapter Quizzes
ExamView Pro Test Bank
Vocabulary PuzzleMaker Software
MindJogger Videoquiz DVD/VHS

Chapter 11 Assessment

The Princeton Review Test Practice

The Test-Taking Tip was written by The Princeton Review, the nation's leader in test preparation.

1. C
2. G
3. C

Developing Skills

16. Vibrations from the dancers created constructive interference, raising the amplitude of the wave and thus increasing the energy pounding on the balconies. The balconies broke just as the crust of the earth can break in an earthquake.

17. Diffraction and refraction both describe changes in a wave upon encountering an object. A diffracted wave changes direction to bend around the object, whereas a refracted wave bends due to a change in wave speed as the wave moves from one medium to another.

18. Sound travels through steel almost 15 times faster than it does through air.

19. Make sure magnitude is given in the same scale for all earthquakes.

20. Check students' work.

Performance Assessment

21. Check students' work. Use **PASC**, p. 143.

Section/Objectives	Standards		Activities/Features
	National	State/Local	
Chapter Opener	See p. 37T for a Key to Standards.		**Explore Activity:** Create music with a ruler, p. 357 **Before You Read,** p. 357
Section 1 **The Nature of Sound** 2 session .5 block 1. **Explain** how sound travels through different mediums. 2. **Identify** what influences the speed of sound. 3. **Describe** how the ear enables you to hear.	National Content Standards: UCP2, A2, B3 (5–8), B6 (9–12), F1 (5–8), F1, (9–12)		**MiniLAB:** Observing Sound in Different Materials, p. 359 **Life Science Integration,** p. 361
Section 2 **Properties of Sound** 1 session 1 block 1. **Recognize** how amplitude, intensity, and loudness are related. 2. **Describe** how sound intensity is measured and what levels can damage hearing. 3. **Explain** the relationship between frequency and pitch. 4. **Discuss** the Doppler effect.	National Content Standards: UCP3, A2, B3 (5–8), B6 (9–12), F1 (5–8), F1, F5(9–12)		**Science Online,** p. 365 **MiniLAB:** Making a Model for Hearing Loss, p. 366 **Astronomy Integration:** p. 367
Section 3 **Music** 2 session 1 block 1. **Distinguish** between noise and music. 2. **Describe** why different instruments have different sound qualities. 3. **Explain** how string, wind, and percussion instruments produce music. 4. **Describe** the formation of beats.	National Content Standards: UCP2, A2, B3 (5–8), B6 (9–12), F1 (5–8), F1 (9–12), G1		**Science Online,** p. 370 **Activity:** Making Music, p. 374
Section 4 **Using Sound** 1 session .5 block 1. **Recognize** some of the factors that determine how a concert hall or theater is designed. 2. **Describe** how some animals use sound waves to hunt and navigate. 3. **Discuss** the uses of sonar. 4. **Explain** how ultrasound is useful in medicine.	National Content Standards: UCP5, A2, B3 (5–8), B6 (9–12), F1, F5 (5–8), F1, F6 (9–12), G1		**Visualizing Bat Echoloation** p.376 **Math Skills Activity:** Calculating with Sonar, p. 378 **Health Integration:** p. 379 **Activity:** Blocking Noise Pollution, p. 380 **Science and Society:** Turning Up the Volume, p. 382

Activity Materials	Reproducible Resources	Section Assessment	Technology
Explore Activity: ruler	**Chapter Resources Booklet** Foldables Worksheet, p. 15 Note-taking Worksheets, pp. 33–35	GLENCOE'S ASSESSMENT ADVANTAGE	
MiniLAB: string, metal object	**Chapter Resources Booklet** Transparency Activity, p. 44 MiniLAB, p. 3 Enrichment, p. 29 Reinforcement, p. 25 Directed Reading, p. 18 Transparency Activity, pp. 49–50	**Portfolio** Extension, p. 360 **Performance** MiniLAB, p. 359 Skill Builder Activities, p. 362 **Content** Section Assessment, p. 362	Section Focus Transparency Teaching Transparency Interactive CD-ROM/DVD Guided Reading Audio Program
MiniLAB: radio, cloth (optional)	**Chapter Resources Booklet** Transparency Activity, p. 45 MiniLAB, p. 4 Enrichment, p. 30 Reinforcement, p. 26 Directed Reading, p. 18 Lab Activity, pp. 9–10	**Portfolio** Assessment, p. 368 **Performance** MiniLAB, p. 366 Skill Building Activities, p. 368 **Content** Section Assessment, p. 368	Section Focus Transparency Interactive CD-ROM/DVD Guided Reading Audio Program
Activity: test tubes, test-tube rack	**Chapter Resources Booklet** Transparency Activity, p. 46 Enrichment, p. 31 Reinforcement, p. 27 Directed Reading, p. 19 Activity Worksheet, pp. 5–6 Lab Activity, pp. 11–14	**Portfolio** Assessment, p. 373 **Performance** Skill Builder Activities, p. 373 **Content** Section Assessment, p. 373	Section Focus Transparency Interactive CD-ROM/DVD Guided Reading Audio Program
Activity: radio, CD player, horn, drum, or other loud noise source; shrubs, trees, concrete walls, brick walls, stone walls, wooden fences, parked cars, or hanging laundry; sound meter; meterstick or metric tape measure	**Chapter Resources Booklet** Transparency Activity, p. 47 Enrichment, p. 32 Reinforcement, p. 28 Directed Reading, pp. 19, 20 Activity Worksheet, pp. 7–8	**Portfolio** Challenge, p. 379 **Performance** Math Skills Activity, p. 378 Skill Builder Activities, p. 379 **Content** Section Assessment, p. 379	Section Focus Transparency Interactive CD-ROM/DVD Guided Reading Audio Program

End of Chapter Assessment

GLENCOE'S ASSESSMENT ADVANTAGE

Blackline Masters	Technology	Professional Series
Chapter Resources Booklet Chapter Review, pp. 37–38 Chapter Tests, pp. 39–42 **Standardized Test Practice by The Princeton Review,** pp. 52–55	MindJogger Videoquiz CD-ROM Explorations and Quizzes Vocabulary Puzzle Makers ExamView Pro Test Bank Interactive Lesson Planner Interactive Teacher's Edition	Performance Assessment in the Science Classroom (PASC)

Transparencies

Section Focus

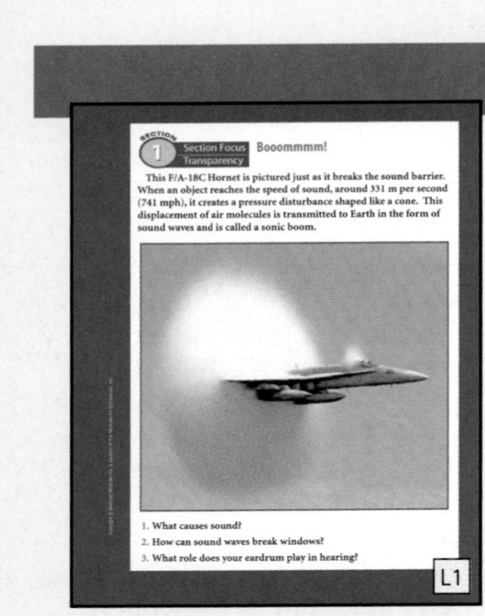
Section 1 Section Focus Transparency — Booommmm!

This F/A-18C Hornet is pictured just as it breaks the sound barrier. When an object reaches the speed of sound, around 331 m per second (741 mph), it creates a pressure disturbance shaped like a cone. This displacement of air molecules is transmitted to Earth in the form of sound waves and is called a sonic boom.

1. What causes sound?
2. How can sound waves break windows?
3. What role does your eardrum play in hearing?

L1

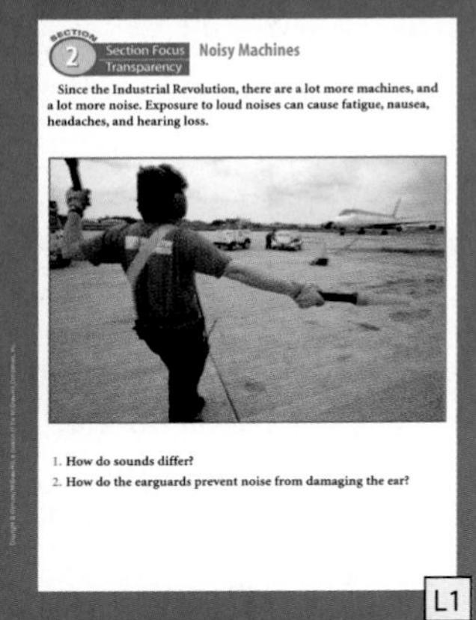
Section 2 Section Focus Transparency — Noisy Machines

Since the Industrial Revolution, there are a lot more machines, and a lot more noise. Exposure to loud noises can cause fatigue, nausea, headaches, and hearing loss.

1. How do sounds differ?
2. How do the earguards prevent noise from damaging the ear?

L1

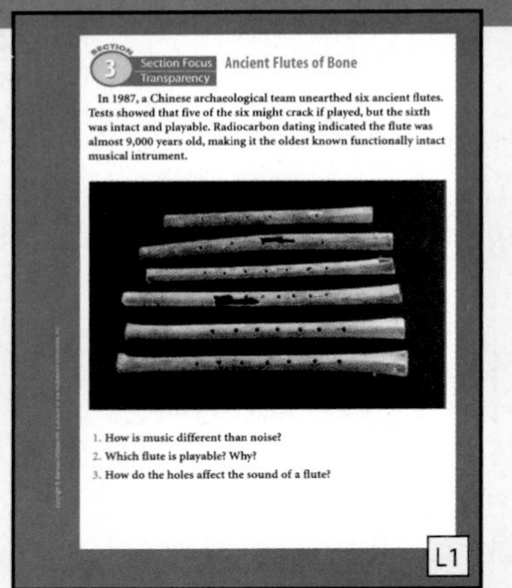
Section 3 Section Focus Transparency — Ancient Flutes of Bone

In 1987, a Chinese archaeological team unearthed six ancient flutes. Tests showed that five of the six might crack if played, but the sixth was intact and playable. Radiocarbon dating indicated the flute was almost 9,000 years old, making it the oldest known functionally intact musical intrument.

1. How is music different than noise?
2. Which flute is playable? Why?
3. How do the holes affect the sound of a flute?

L1

This is a representation of key blackline masters available in the Teacher Classroom Resources. See Resource Manager boxes within the chapter for additional information.

Assessment

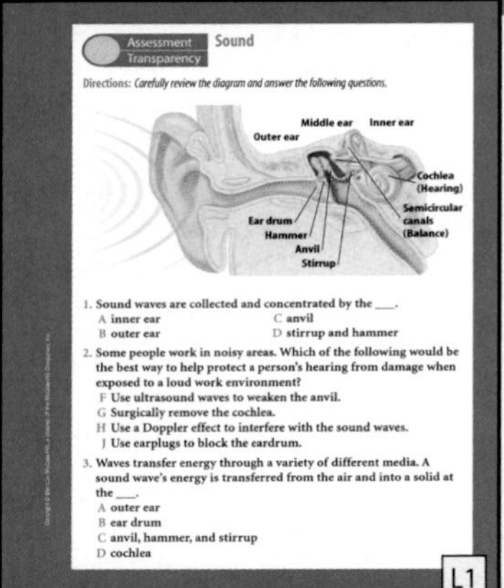
Assessment Transparency — Sound

Directions: *Carefully review the diagram and answer the following questions.*

1. Sound waves are collected and concentrated by the ___.
   A inner ear
   B outer ear
   C anvil
   D stirrup and hammer
2. Some people work in noisy areas. Which of the following would be the best way to help protect a person's hearing from damage when exposed to a loud work environment?
   F Use ultrasound waves to weaken the anvil.
   G Surgically remove the cochlea.
   H Use a Doppler effect to interfere with the sound waves.
   J Use earplugs to block the eardrum.
3. Waves transfer energy through a variety of different media. A sound wave's energy is transferred from the air and into a solid at the ___.
   A outer ear
   B ear drum
   C anvil, hammer, and stirrup
   D cochlea

L1

Teaching

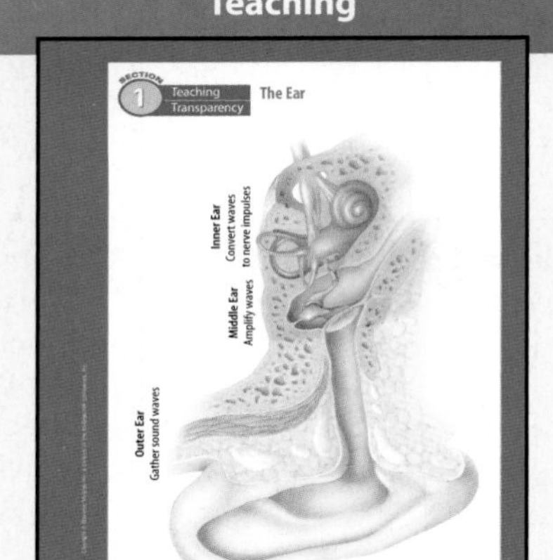
Section 1 Teaching Transparency — The Ear

L1

Key to Teaching Strategies

The following designations will help you decide which activities are appropriate for your students.

- L1 Level 1 activities should be appropriate for students with learning difficulties.
- L2 Level 2 activities should be within the ability range of all students.
- L3 Level 3 activities are designed for above-average students.
- ELL ELL activities should be within the ability range of English Language Learners.
- COOP LEARN Cooperative Learning activities are designed for small group work.
- LS Multiple Learning Styles logos are used throughout to indicate strategies that address different learning styles.
- P These strategies represent student products that can be placed into a best-work portfolio.

Hands-on Activities

Activity Worksheets

Name ___ Date ___ Class ___

Activity — Making Music

Lab Preview

Directions: *Answer these questions before you begin the Activity.*

1. Why do you need to wear an apron or other clothing protection?
2. Do you put the same amount of water in each of the test tubes?

There are many different types of musical instruments. You can also make music using everyday objects that are not formal instruments, such as pots and pot lids, garbage can covers, or boxes of matches. How can you create a musical instrument that requires air to be blown across it in order to make sound?

What You'll Investigate
How can you make different tones using only test tubes and water?

Materials
test tubes
test-tube rack

Goals
- **Demonstrate** how to make music using water and test tubes.
- **Predict** how the tones will change when there is more or less water in the test tubes.

Safety Precautions

Procedure
1. Put different amounts of water into each of the test tubes.
2. **Predict** any differences you expect in how the tones from the different test tubes will sound.
3. Blow across the top of each test tube.
4. In the Data and Observations section, **record** any differences that you noticed in the tones that you heard from each test tube.

Data and Observations
Differences in Tone:

L1

Laboratory Activities

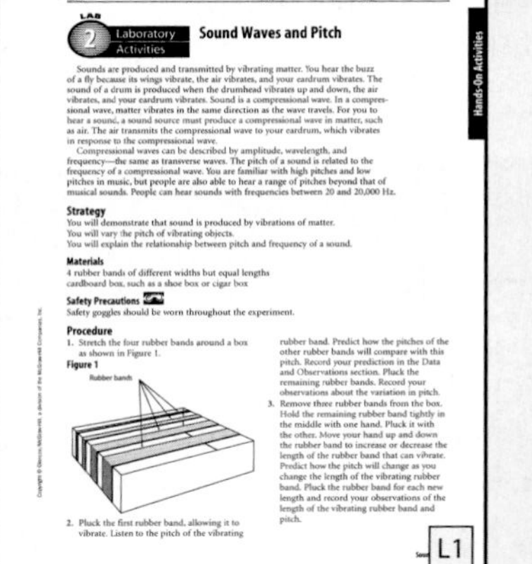
Name ___ Date ___ Class ___

Lab 2 Laboratory Activities — Sound Waves and Pitch

Sounds are produced and transmitted by vibrating matter. You hear the buzz of a fly because its wings vibrate, the air vibrates, and your eardrum vibrates. The sound of a drum is produced when the drumhead vibrates up and down, the air vibrates, and your eardrum vibrates. Sound is a compressional wave. In a compressional wave, matter vibrates in the same direction as the wave travels. For you to hear a sound, a sound source must produce a compressional wave in matter, such as air. The air transmits the compressional wave to your eardrum, which vibrates in response to the compressional wave.

Compressional waves can be described by amplitude, wavelength, and frequency—the same as transverse waves. The pitch of a sound is related to the frequency of a compressional wave. You are familiar with high pitches and low pitches in music, but people are also able to hear a range of pitches beyond that of musical sounds. People can hear sounds with frequencies between 20 and 20,000 Hz.

Strategy
You will demonstrate that sound is produced by vibrations of matter.
You will vary the pitch of vibrating objects.
You will explain the relationship between pitch and frequency of a sound.

Materials
4 rubber bands of different widths but equal lengths
cardboard box, such as a shoe box or cigar box

Safety Precautions
Safety goggles should be worn throughout the experiment.

Procedure
1. Stretch the four rubber bands around a box as shown in Figure 1.

Figure 1

2. Pluck the first rubber band, allowing it to vibrate. Listen to the pitch of the vibrating rubber band. Predict how the pitches of the other rubber bands will compare with this pitch. Record your prediction in the Data and Observations section. Pluck the remaining rubber bands. Record your observations about the variation in pitch.
3. Remove three rubber bands from the box. Hold the remaining rubber band tightly in the middle with one hand. Pluck it with the other. Move your hand up and down the rubber band to increase or decrease the length of the rubber band that can vibrate. Predict how the pitch will change as you change the length of the vibrating rubber band. Pluck the rubber band for each new length and record your observations of the length of the vibrating rubber band and pitch.

L1

Meeting Different Ability Levels

Content Outline

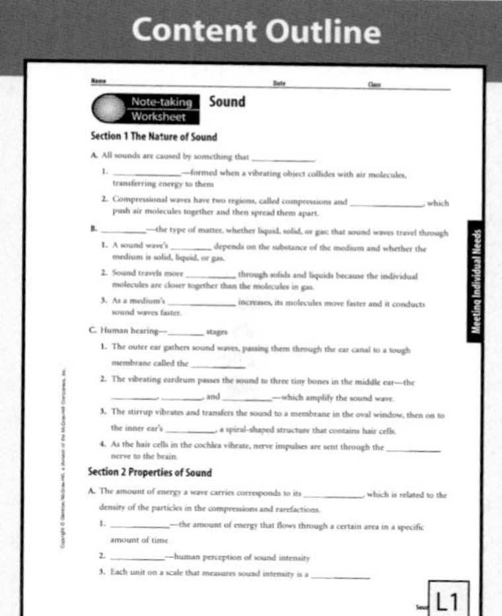

Reinforcement

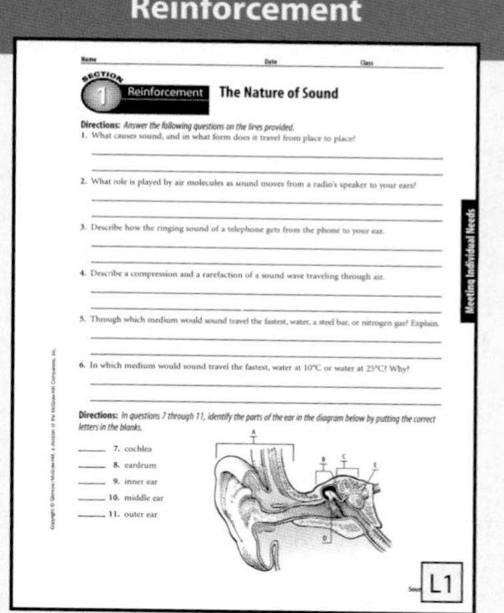

Directed Reading

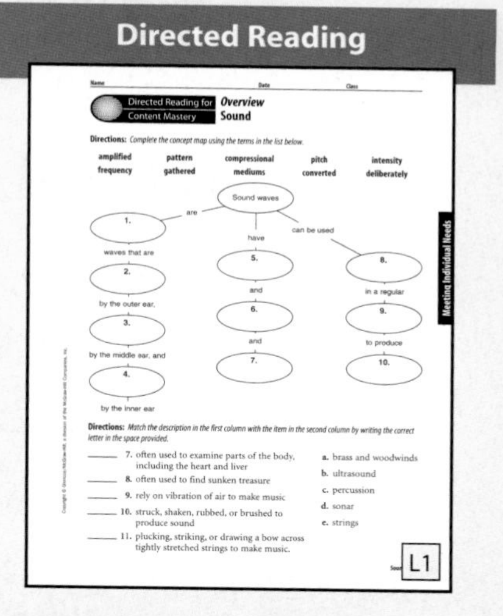

Enrichment

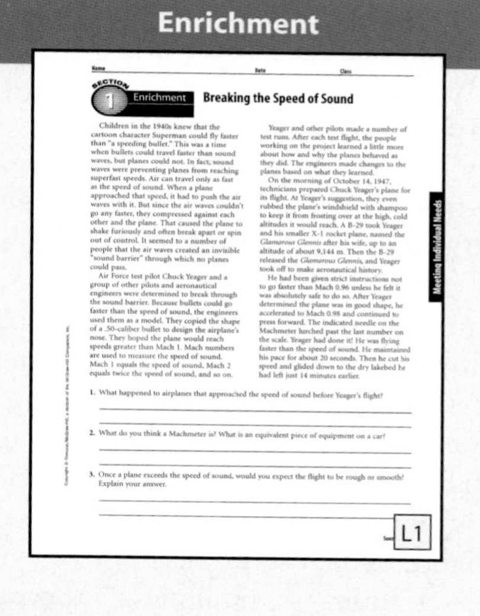

Spanish Directed Reading

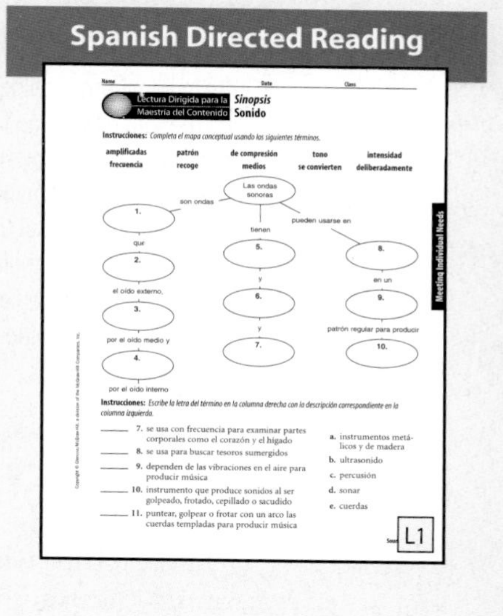

Assessment

Chapter Tests

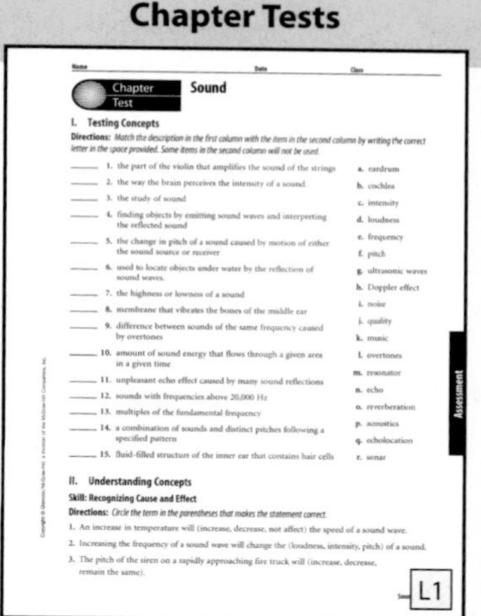

Test Practice Workbook

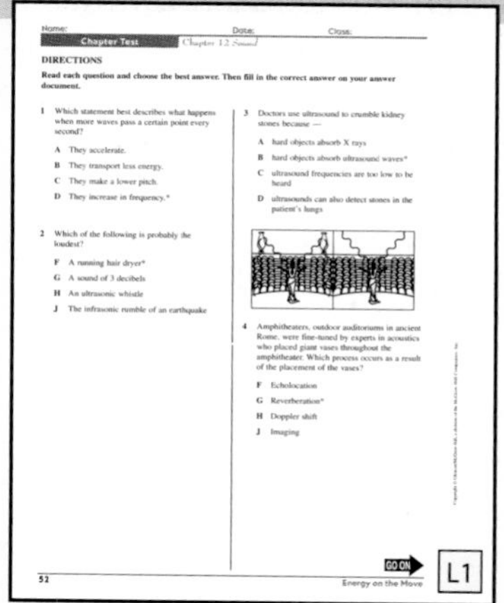

Chapter Review

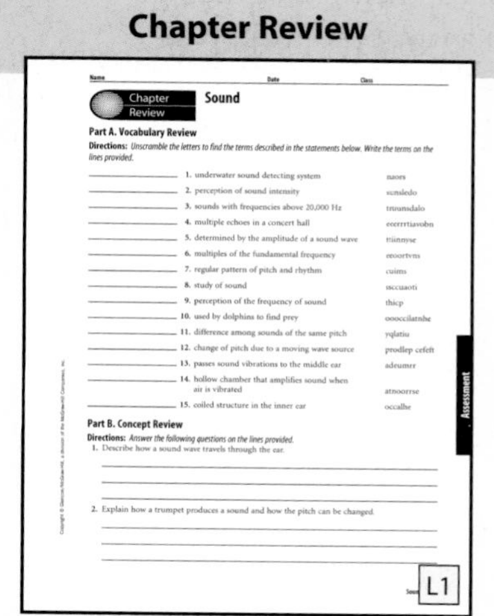

Science Content Background

SECTION 1

The Nature of Sound

Sound Waves

Sound is caused by a type of mechanical waves called compressional or longitudinal waves. The compressions and rarefractions produced cause temporary changes in the pressure of the medium the waves travel through. Our ears respond to this changing pressure and interpret it as sound.

Fun Fact

The "squeaky" voice produced when talking with helium from a balloon results from the sound traveling faster from the speaker's vocal chords than it would in normal air. The pitch made by the vocal cords is not lowered but the different resonance produced results in a different timbre to the voice. Caution: Warn students that breathing helium can be dangerous and is not recommended.

Moving Through Mediums

The speed of sound is how fast sound waves travel through particles. This is quite different from the frequency of a sound wave, which is how often the particles of the medium vibrate back and forth. The approximate speed of sound through air at room temperature is 347 m/s, or 750 miles/hour. Although this is fast, light travels about 900,000 times faster. This explains why we see lightning before we hear it. To calculate how far away lightning is, multiply the speed of sound by the number of seconds between seeing the lightning and hearing the thunder. If this time is three seconds, then the lightning is $3 \text{ s} \times 347 \text{ m/s} = 1{,}041 \text{ m}$ away. For an approximate distance in miles, divide the time by five.

Sound travels about three times faster in helium than it does in air. The more dense the gas, the slower sound travels. This is because dense gases have particles with more mass that resist moving. The speed of sound in air at particular temperatures can be calculated using the equation $v = 331 \text{ m/s} + (0.6 \text{ m/s/°C}) \times t$. So for air at 10°C, sound would pass through at a speed of $331 \text{ m/s} + (0.6 \text{ m/s/°C}) \times 10\text{°C}$ or 337 m/s.

SECTION 2

Properties of Sound

Intensity and Loudness

Sound intensity can be thought of as how much energy passes through a given area in a given amount of time. Because sound waves spread out as they travel, the intensity of a sound decreases as it travels and is proportional to the inverse square of the distance from the source. This means that for every doubling of distance from the source, the intensity of sound is reduced by three-quarters. Humans can detect very low levels of sound. This threshold is defined as 0 dB. A sound of 0 dB will move our eardrums as little as one-billionth of a centimeter, but we can still hear it.

The Doppler Effect

When an airplane going faster than the speed of sound passes over us, it produces a very loud noise called a sonic boom. As in the Doppler effect, the waves, in this case sound waves, are pushed close together. The plane, however, is going so fast that it causes the wavelengths to pile up on each other, producing constructive interference. When these waves reach us, they impart a loud noise.

SECTION 3

Music

What is music?

The sounds produced by different frequencies are referred to as pitch. People with well-trained ears can detect frequency differences of as little as 3 Hz. Constructive and destructive interference make some frequencies sound better together than others do. For example, sounds that are separated by a frequency ratio of 2 to 1 are pleasing. In music these frequencies are said to be separated by an octave.

Sound Quality

Timbre is the musical term to describe sounds with the same frequencies that are perceived differently by our ears.

SECTION 4

Using Sound

Acoustics

A large number of echoes make for a very noisy room. Theaters, music halls, and even restaurants are designed to absorb sound energy rather than reflect it.

Another important task of good acoustics is to make sure that the arrangement of the sound system in a room does not cause destructive interference. Speakers have to be placed in the appropriate positions so that this does not occur.

Fun Fact

Special headphones now exist that produce silence by producing sound. Speakers pick up sound from outside and produce a wave that is a half-cycle out of phase. Thus the produced crests align with the troughs of the outside noise, which results in destructive interference and significant noise reduction.

Echolocation

We can use echolocation to estimate the distance to large objects such as a building. Give a yell and time how long it takes to hear the echo. Because this time represents a round trip journey for the sound waves, you must divide the time by two, and then multiply this number by the speed of sound. For example, if it takes 3 seconds to hear the echo bounce off a building, the distance to the building is 1.5 s ×347 m/s = 520 m.

For additional content background on this topic, go to the Glencoe Science Web site at science.glencoe.com.

Crandall/The Image Works

Sound

Chapter Vocabulary

eardrum
cochlea
intensity
loudness
decibel
pitch
ultrasonic
Doppler effect
music
quality
overtone
resonator
acoustics
echolocation
sonar

What do you think?

Science Journal The photograph shows a person's fingers plucking the strings of a stringed instrument such as a guitar.

CHAPTER 12

Sound

Almost everyone has tried the following experiment. With a friend, you go below the water surface in a swimming pool and scream a message. After you come up for air, you try to guess what was said. Although you heard noises, the sound did not travel effectively. These scuba divers use hand signals to communicate underwater. In this chapter, learn how sound travels and how noise differs from music. Also, learn how musical instruments produce sound, and how sound is used in medicine.

What do you think?

Science Journal Look at the picture below with a classmate. Discuss what this might be or what is happening. Here's a hint: *It's music to your ears.* Write your answer or best guess in your Science Journal.

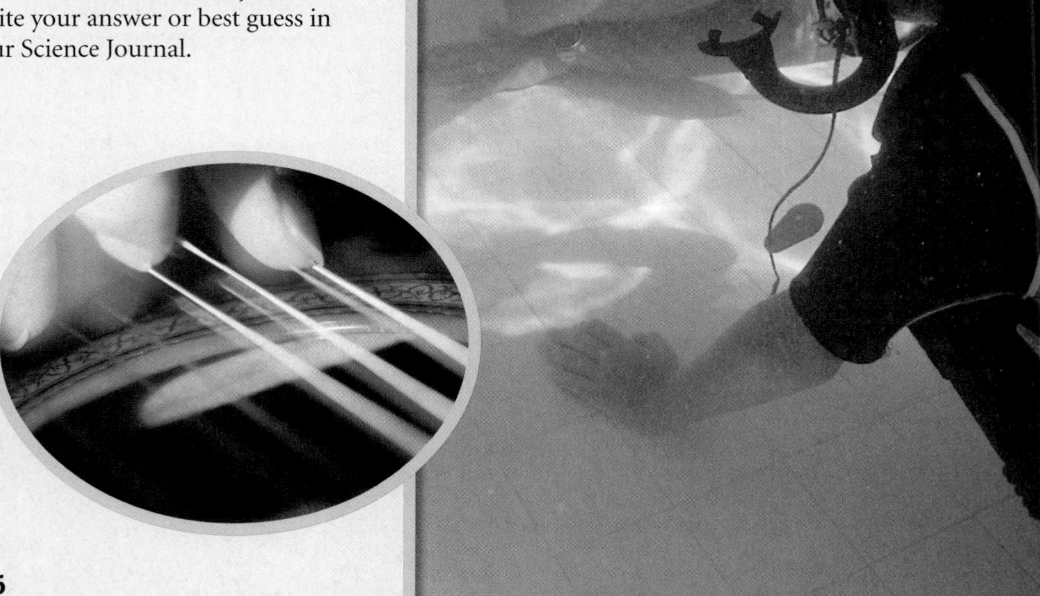

356

Theme Connection

Energy Sound is energy transferred by the collision of molecules in compressional waves. The amount of energy that a wave carries determines the intensity of sound.

Think of all the different kinds of musical instruments you've seen and heard. Some have strings, some have hollow tubes, and others have keys or pedals. Musical instruments come in many shapes and sizes and are played with various techniques. The differences between the instruments give each one a unique sound. What would an instrument made out of a ruler sound like?

Create music with a ruler 

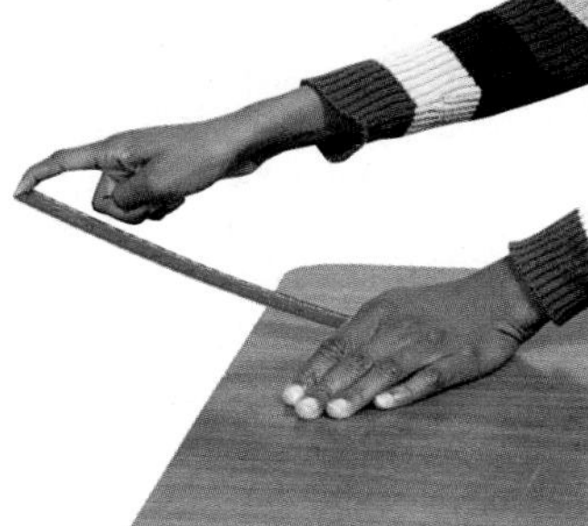

1. Hold one end of a thin ruler firmly down on a desk, allowing the free end to extend beyond the edge of the desk.
2. Gently pull up on and release the end of the ruler. What do you see and hear?
3. Vary the length of the overhanging portion and repeat the experiment several times.

Observe

How does the length of the overhanging part of the ruler affect the sound you hear? In your Science Journal, write a paragraph about how you could write instructions for playing a song with the ruler.

Before You Read

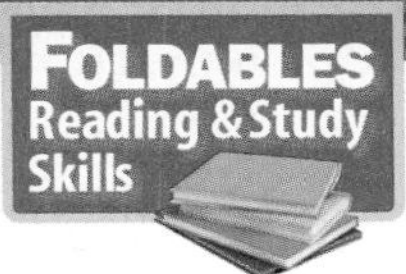

Making a Question Study Fold **Asking yourself questions helps you stay focused and better understand sound when you are reading the chapter.**

1. Place a sheet of paper in front of you so the short side is at the top. Fold the paper in half from the left side to the right side.
2. Fold in the top and the bottom. Unfold the paper so three equal sections show.
3. Through the top thickness of paper, cut along each of the fold lines to the left fold, forming three tabs.
4. Before you read the chapter, write these questions on the tabs: Can sound travel through solids? Can sound travel through liquids? Can sound travel through gases? Now answer each question on the front of the tab.
5. As you read the chapter, write what you learn about how sound travels under the tabs.

Can sound travel through solids?
Can sound travel through liquids?
Can sound travel through gases?

357

Explore Activity

Purpose Use the Explore Activity to introduce students to musical pitches. Explain that as they read the chapter, they will be learning what sound is and what makes sounds different. L1 ELL LS **Auditory-Musical**

Materials thin ruler

Teaching Strategy Suggest that students work in pairs. Have one student describe and record the sounds heard while the other student adjusts and plays the ruler.

Observe

The longer the extending segment of the ruler, the deeper the pitch. There is also a length at which no sound is heard.

Assessment

Content Have students record the tones that occur at different lengths and then try to play a simple song. Use **Performance Assessment in the Science Classroom,** p. 97.

Before You Read

FOLDABLES Reading & Study Skills

Dinah Zike Study Fold

Purpose Students make and use a Foldable to record pre-reading questions and predictions regarding the movement of sound through three differen mediums—solids, liquids, and gases. During reading, students answer the questions and check their predictions.

For additional help, see Foldables Worksheet, p. 15 in **Chapter Resources Booklet,** or go to the Glencoe Science Web site at **science.glencoe.com.** See After You Read in the Study Guide at the end of this chapter.

SECTION 1

The Nature of Sound

1 Motivate

Bellringer Transparency

Display the Section Focus Transparency for Section 1. Use the accompanying Transparency Activity Master. L2 ELL

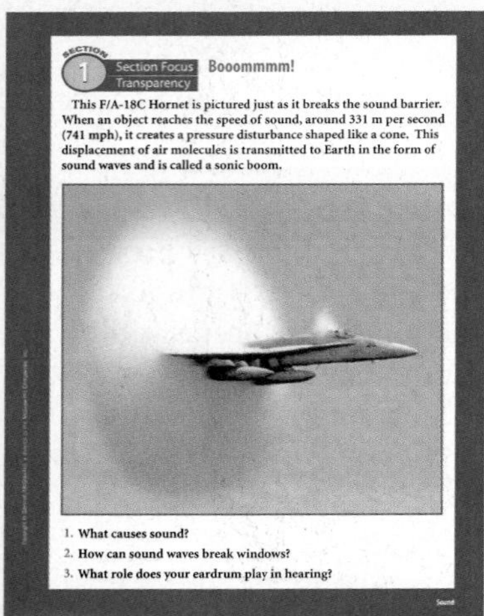
Section 1 Section Focus Transparency Booommmm!

This F/A-18C Hornet is pictured just as it breaks the sound barrier. When an object reaches the speed of sound, around 331 m per second (741 mph), it creates a pressure disturbance shaped like a cone. This displacement of air molecules is transmitted to Earth in the form of sound waves and is called a sonic boom.

1. What causes sound?
2. How can sound waves break windows?
3. What role does your eardrum play in hearing?

Sound

Tie to Prior Knowledge

Ask students to name sounds they have heard today. Can they identify what made each sound? Tell them that all sounds are made by vibrating objects. Human speech is caused by the vibration of vocal cords in the larynx.

SECTION 1

The Nature of Sound

As You Read

***What* You'll Learn**

- **Explain** how sound travels through different mediums.
- **Identify** what influences the speed of sound.
- **Describe** how the ear enables you to hear.

Vocabulary

eardrum
cochlea

***Why* It's Important**

The nature of sound affects how you hear and interpret sounds.

What causes sound?

An amusement park can be a noisy place. With all the racket of carousel music and booming loudspeakers, it can be hard to hear what your friends say. These sounds are all different, but they do have something in common—each sound is produced by an object that vibrates. For example, your friends' voices are produced by the vibrations of their vocal cords, and music from a carousel and voices from a loudspeaker are produced by vibrating speakers. All sounds are created by something that vibrates.

Sound Waves

How does the sound made by a vibrating speaker get to your ears? When an object like a radio speaker vibrates, it collides with nearby molecules in the air, transferring some of its energy to them. These molecules then collide with other molecules in the air and pass the energy on to them. The energy of the vibrating object continues to pass from one molecule to another. This process of collisions and energy transfer forms a sound wave. Eventually, the wave reaches the molecules in the air near your ears and you hear a sound.

Sound Is a Compressional Wave Sound waves are compressional waves. Remember that a compressional wave is made up of two types of regions called compressions and rarefactions. If you look at **Figure 1A,** you'll see that when a radio speaker vibrates outward, the nearby molecules in the air are pushed together to form compressions. As **Figure 1B** shows, when the speaker moves inward, the nearby molecules in the air have room to spread out, and a rarefaction forms. As long as the speaker continues to vibrate back and forth, compressions and rarefactions are formed.

Figure 1
A When the speaker vibrates outward, molecules in the air next to it are pushed together to form a compression. B When the speaker vibrates inward, the molecules spread apart to form a rarefaction.

Section Assessment Planner

Portfolio
Extention, p. 360

Performance Assessment
MiniLab, p. 359
Skill Building Activities, p. 362
See page 386 for more options.

Content Assessment
Section, p. 362
Challenge, p. 362
Chapter, pp. 386–387

Traveling as a Wave Compressions and rarefactions move away from the speaker as molecules in the air collide with their neighbors. As the speaker continues to vibrate, more molecules in the air are alternately pushed together and spread apart. A series of compressions and rarefactions forms that travels from the speaker to your ear. This sound wave is what you hear.

Moving Through Mediums

Most sounds you hear travel through air to reach your ears. However, if you've ever been swimming underwater and heard garbled voices, you know that sound also travels through water. In fact, sound waves can travel through any type of matter—solid, liquid, or gas. The matter that a wave travels through is called a medium. Sound waves create compressions and rarefactions in any medium they travel through.

What would happen if no matter existed to form a medium? Could sound be transmitted without particles of matter to compress, expand, and collide? On the Moon, which has no atmosphere, the energy in sound waves cannot be transmitted from particle to particle because no particles exist. Sound waves cannot travel through empty space. Astronauts must talk to each other using electronic communication equipment.

The Speed of Sound Through Different Mediums

The speed of a sound wave through a medium depends on the substance the medium is made of, and whether it is a solid, liquid, or gas. For example, **Table 1** shows that at room temperature, sound travels at 347 m/s through air, at 1,498 m/s through water, and at 5,200 m/s through steel. In general, sound travels the slowest through gases, faster through liquids, and even faster through solids.

Reading Check *What are two things that affect the speed of sound?*

Liquids and solids conduct sound better than gases do because the individual molecules in a liquid or solid are closer together than the molecules in a gas. When molecules are close together, they can transmit energy from one to another more rapidly. However, the speed of sound doesn't depend on the loudness of the sound. Loud sounds travel through a medium at the same speed as soft sounds.

Table 1 Speed of Sound in Different Mediums

Medium	Speed of Sound (in m/s)
Air	347
Cork	500
Water	1,498
Brick	3,650
Steel	5,200

Mini LAB

Observing Sound in Different Materials

Procedure

1. Tie a piece of **string** on a **metal object,** such as a wire hanger or a spoon, so that you have two long ends of the string.
2. Wrap each string around a finger on each hand.
3. Gently placing the fingers in your ears, let the object swing until it bumps against the edge of a **chair** or **table.** Listen to the sound.
4. Take your fingers out of your ears and listen to the sound made by the collisions.

Analysis

1. Compare and contrast the sounds you hear when your fingers are and are not in your ears.
2. Do sounds travel better through air or the string?

2 Teach

What causes sound?

Activity

Have students place their hands on their throats while talking to feel the vibrations caused by their vocal cords. L2 ELL IS **Kinesthetic**

Moving Through Mediums

Purpose Students listen to sound through different mediums. L1 ELL IS **Auditory-Musical**

Materials metal object such as a spoon, 1.5 m of string

Teaching Strategy Suggest students try a variety of metal objects to obtain different sounds.

Analysis

1. Possible answer: Objects sound deeper and more muffled when your fingers are over your ears.
2. Through the string

Assessment

Content Why does sound travel better through string than air? The molecules are closer to one another. Use **PASC,** p 89.

Reading Check

Answer the substance the medium is made of, and the state of the medium

Inclusion Strategies

Hearing Impaired For many of the activities in this chapter, these students can learn about the sound produced by feeling the vibrations. When they do the MiniLAB, have students feel the vibrations transmitted through the string to their fingers. Using different types of string and metal objects, they can feel how the vibrations differ for various materials. IS **Kinesthetic**

Resource Manager 

Chapter Resources Booklet
- MiniLAB, p. 3
- Transparency Activity, p. 44
- Note-taking Worksheets, pp. 33–35

Moving Through Mediums, continued

Extension

Have students determine the ratio of the speed of light to the speed of sound in air at normal temperature and pressure. The speed of light is 300,000,000 m/s, and the speed of sound is 347 m/s. Therefore, light travels about 865,000 times faster than does sound. L3

LS Logical-Mathematical P

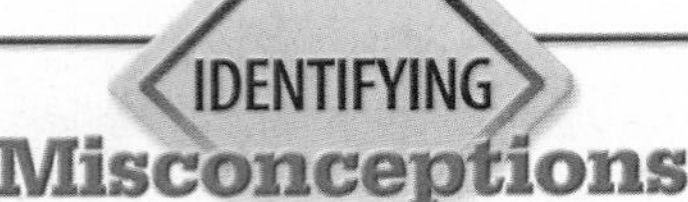

When looking at the pictures of compressions and rarefactions of sound waves, students may think that the molecules travel away from the sound source. Explain that the molecules push on their neighbors and then return to their original position. Only the energy is transported.

Caption Answer

Figure 2B Cork is less rigid than steel. Also, cork is filled with air holes, and sound waves travel more slowly through air. LS **Logical-Mathematical**

Fun Fact

The speed of sound in air is called Mach 1. An object at Mach 2 is traveling at twice the speed of sound. The exact value of the Mach number depends on the speed of sound in a particular medium.

Figure 2
A line of people passing a bucket is like molecules transferring the energy of a sound wave.

A When the people are far away from each other, like the molecules in a gas, it takes a long time to transfer the bucket of water from person to person.

B The bucket travels quickly down the line when the people stand close together. *Why would sound travel more slowly in cork than in steel?*

A Model for Transmitting Sound You can understand why solids and liquids transmit sound well by picturing a large group of people standing in a line. Imagine that they are passing a bucket of water from person to person. If everyone stands far apart, each person has to walk a long distance to transfer the bucket, as in **Figure 2A.** However, if everyone stands close together, as in **Figure 2B,** the bucket quickly moves down the line.

The people standing close to each other are like particles in solids and liquids. Those standing far apart are like gas particles. The closer the particles, the faster they can transfer energy from particle to particle.

Temperature and the Speed of Sound The speed of sound waves also depends on the temperature of a medium. As the temperature of a substance increases, its molecules move faster. This makes them more likely to collide with each other. Remember that sound waves depend on the collisions of particles to transfer energy through a medium. If the particles in a medium are colliding with each other more often, more energy can be transferred in a shorter amount of time. Then sound waves move faster. For example, when the temperature is 0°C, sound travels through the air at only 332 m/s, but at a temperature of 20°C it speeds up to 344 m/s.

Human Hearing

Think of the last conversation you had. Vocal cords and mouths move in many different ways to produce various kinds of compressional waves, but you were somehow able to make sense of these different sound waves. Your ears and brain work together to turn the compressional waves caused by speech, music, and other sources into something that has meaning. Making sense of these waves involves four stages. First, the ear gathers the compressional waves. Next, the ear amplifies the waves. In the ear, the amplified waves are converted to nerve impulses that travel to the brain. Finally, the brain decodes and interprets the nerve impulses.

Teacher FYI

The speed with which sound travels through a material depends on the elasticity of the material as well as on the material's density. Elasticity is the ability of the material to resume its previous shape after being acted on by a force. For example, steel is dense and has high elasticity, so sound travels quickly through steel.

Active Reading

Bubble Map Using a bubble map helps students start ideas flowing about a given topic. Words are clustered to describe a topic or idea that is studied. Students can use a bubble map for a prewriting, to generate ideas before writing in their Journals, or to review for a test. Have students design a bubble map for the concepts about sound discussed in this section.

Gathering Sound Waves—The Outer Ear When you think of your ear, you probably picture just the fleshy, visible, outer part. But, as shown in **Figure 3,** the human ear has three sections called the outer ear, the middle ear, and the inner ear.

The visible part of your ear, the ear canal, and the eardrum make up the outer ear. The outer ear is where sound waves are gathered. The gathering process starts with the outer part of your ear, which is shaped to help capture and direct sound waves into the ear canal. The ear canal is a passageway that is 2-cm to 3-cm long and is a little narrower than your index finger. The sound waves travel along this passageway, which leads to the eardrum. The **eardrum** is a tough membrane about 0.1 mm thick. When incoming sound waves reach the eardrum, they transfer their energy to it and it vibrates.

Reading Check *What makes the eardrum vibrate?*

Amplifying Sound Waves—The Middle Ear When the eardrum vibrates, it passes the sound vibrations into the middle ear, where three tiny bones start to vibrate. These bones are called the hammer, the anvil, and the stirrup. They make a lever system that multiplies the force and pressure exerted by the sound wave. The bones amplify the sound wave. The stirrup is connected to a membrane on a structure called the oval window, which vibrates as the stirrup vibrates.

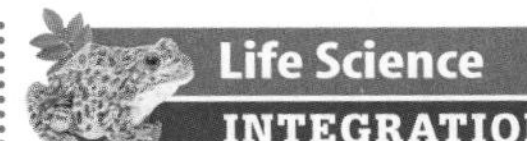

Some types of hearing loss involve damage to the inner ear. The use of a hearing aid often can improve hearing. Research different advertisements for hearing aids. How would you evaluate different companies' claims that they are the best?

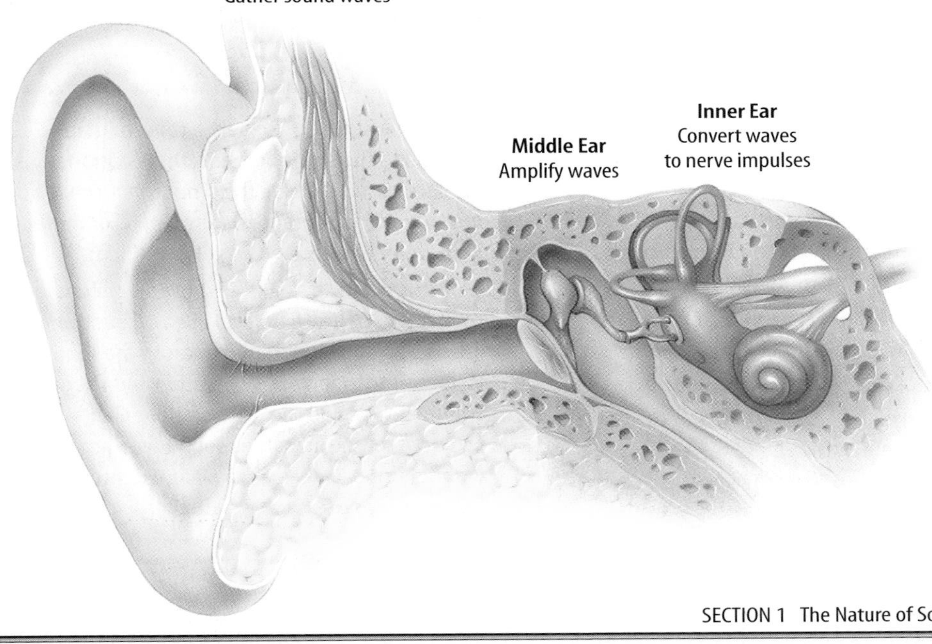

Figure 3
The ear has three regions and each performs specific functions in hearing.

Human Hearing

Accept all reasonable answers.

Fun Fact

The eardrum is also known as the tympanic membrane, from the Latin word tympanum, meaning "drum."

Activity

Have students cup their hands around the backs of their ears to see how they can catch more sound waves. L2 **Kinesthetic**

Reading Check

Answer energy from sound waves

Use an Analogy

The hair cells in the cochlea are like the strings of a piano. Like the thicker, looser low strings on a piano, cells in the wide, flexible part of the cochlea respond more to low-frequency sounds. Like the thinner, stiffer, shorter strings on a piano, the cells in the thin, stiffer part of the cochlea respond more to high-frequency sounds.

Visual Learning

Figure 3 The cochlea is divided down the middle into side-by-side canals. The membrane between these canals contains hair cells. Vibrations in the fluid travel in opposite directions in these canals. The shape of the cochlea determines how hair cells are displaced, enabling you to discern different frequencies. **What happens if the vibration is too strong?** Hair cells can be damaged. L2 **Visual-Spatial**

Resource Manager

Chapter Resources Booklet
- Reinforcement, p. 25
- Enrichment, p. 29
- Directed Reading for Content Mastery, p. 18
- Transparency Activity, pp. 49–50

Human Hearing, continued

Use Science Words

Word Meaning Have students find out why the spiral-shaped structure in the inner ear is called the cochlea. The word *cochlea* comes from the Greek word *kochlias,* meaning "snail shell." L2

LS Linguistic

3 Assess

Reteach

Model an alarm clock ringing on the moon. Place a ringing alarm clock under a bell jar on the pad of a vacuum pump. **What happens as you begin to pump the air out of the jar?** The ringing gets quieter. **What happens as you slowly let air back into the jar?** The ringing returns to normal loudness. L1 ELL

LS Auditory-Musical

Challenge

How do you think you are able to detect the direction from which a sound originates? There are slight differences in the intensity and timing of the signals that reach each of your ears. L3

LS Logical-Mathematical

Assessment

Process Strike a tuning fork and place its handle against various surfaces, such as a wooden desk, a book, a metal surface, and a wall. For each surface, have students explain why the amplified sound is loud or soft. Sounds will be louder for larger, denser, and stiffer surfaces. Use **Performance Assessment in the Science Classroom,** p. 89.

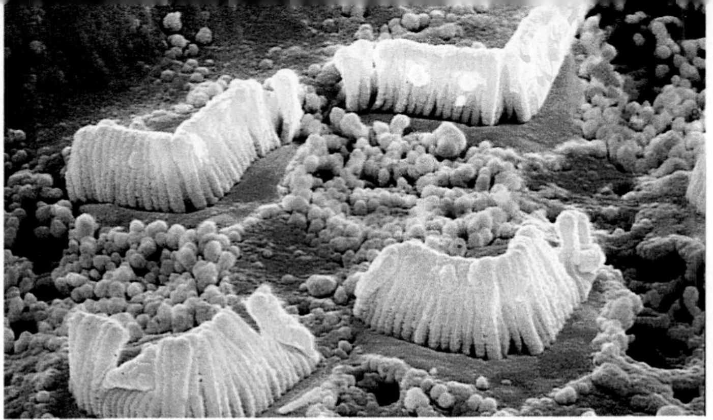

Figure 4
These hair cells in the human ear send nerve impulses to the brain when sound waves cause them to vibrate. In this photo the hair cells are magnified 3,900 times.

Converting Sound Waves—The Inner Ear When the membrane in the oval window vibrates, the sound vibrations are transmitted into the inner ear. The inner ear contains the **cochlea** (KOH klee uh), which is a spiral-shaped structure that is filled with liquid and contains tiny hair cells that are shown in **Figure 4.** When these tiny hair cells in the cochlea begin to vibrate, nerve impulses are sent through the auditory nerve to the brain. It is the cochlea that converts sound waves to nerve impulses.

When someone's hearing is damaged, it's usually because the tiny hair cells in the cochlea are damaged or destroyed, often by a loud sounds. New research suggests that these hair cells may be able to repair themselves.

Section  1 Assessment

1. Explain how sound travels from your vocal cords to your friend's ears when you talk.
2. Compare the speed of sound waves through liquids and air.
3. Explain how the temperature and density of a medium affect the speed of sound waves traveling through it.
4. Describe each section of the human ear and its role in hearing.
5. **Think Critically** Some people hear ringing in their ears, called tinnitus, even when there are no sound waves vibrating their eardrums. Form a hypothesis to explain how this might occur.

Skill Builder Activities

6. **Concept Mapping** Prepare a concept map that shows the series of events that occur to produce sound. Include the terms *rarefaction, medium, vibration,* and *compression.* **For more help, refer to the** Science Skill Handbook.
7. **Communicating** Make a list of 10 different sounds you've heard today. For each sound, identify what was vibrating to cause the sound. Write a description of the vibration and tell whether you could see the vibration. Could you have sensed any of the sounds you heard without using your ears? Explain. **For more help, refer to the** Science Skill Handbook.

Answers to Section Assessment

1. Your vocal cords push on nearby air molecules, causing compressions and rarefactions that travel out in all directions. Some of these waves reach your friend's ear.
2. Sound travels faster in liquids than in air because the molecules in a liquid are closer to one another than are the molecules in air.
3. Sound travels faster through dense materials and through warm materials.
4. The outer ear collects sound waves. Bones in the middle ear amplify sound waves and vibrate the oval window. This causes hairs in the cochlea of the middle ear to vibrate. The cochlea sends information about the vibrations as nerve impulses to the brain.
5. Possible answers: damage to nerves, damage to hair cells in the cochlea
6. Check students' work.
7. Possible answers: You can see guitar strings vibrate to make sounds. You can hear chalk against a board, but you can't see the vibrations.

SECTION

Properties of Sound

Intensity and Loudness

If the phone rings while you're listening to the radio, you might have to turn the radio down to be able to hear the person on the phone. What happens to the sound waves from your radio when you adjust the volume? The notes sound the same as when the volume was higher, but something about the sound changes. The difference is that quieter sound waves do not carry as much energy as louder sound waves do.

Recall that the amount of energy a wave carries corresponds to its amplitude. For a compressional wave, amplitude is related to the density of the particles in the compressions and rarefactions. Look at **Figure 5.** When an object vibrates strongly with a lot of energy, it makes sound waves with tight, dense compressions. When an object vibrates with low energy, it makes sound waves with loose, less dense compressions. The density of particles in the rarefactions behaves in the opposite way. In a loud sound wave, with lots of energy, the particles in its rarefactions are far apart. In quiet sound waves, with low energy, particles in the rarefactions are close together.

As You Read

***What* You'll Learn**

- **Recognize** how amplitude, intensity, and loudness are related.
- **Describe** how sound intensity is measured and what levels can damage hearing.
- **Explain** the relationship between frequency and pitch.
- **Discuss** the Doppler effect.

Vocabulary

intensity
loudness
decibel
pitch
ultrasonic
Doppler effect

***Why* It's Important**

The properties of sound waves determine how things sound to you—from a blaring CD player to someone's whisper.

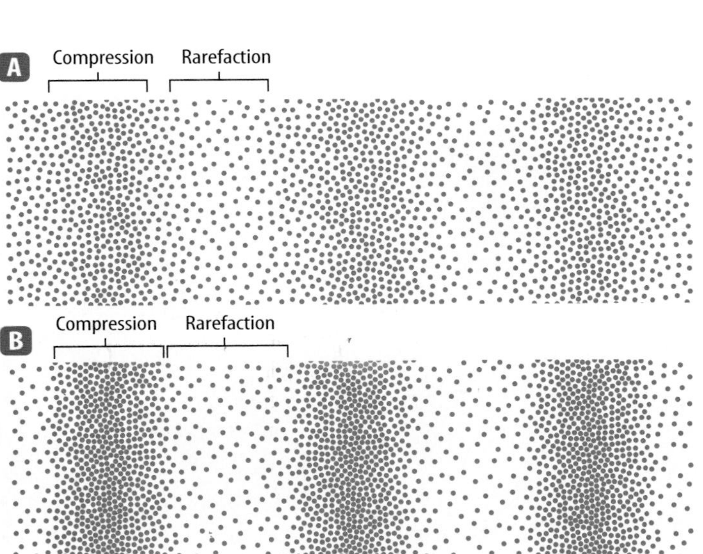

Figure 5
The amplitude of a sound wave depends on how tightly packed molecules are in the compressions and rarefactions. A This sound wave has low amplitude. B This sound wave has a greater amplitude. Molecules are more tightly packed together in compressions, and are farther apart in rarefactions.

Section Assessment Planner

PORTFOLIO
Assessment, p. 368

PERFORMANCE ASSESSMENT
Try at Home MiniLAB, p. 366
Skill Builder Activities, p. 368
See page 386 for more options.

CONTENT ASSESSMENT
Section, p. 368
Challenge, p. 368
Chapter, pp. 386–387

SECTION

Properties of Sound

1 Motivate

Bellringer Transparency

Display the Section Focus Transparency for Section 2. Use the accompanying Transparency Activity Master. L2 ELL

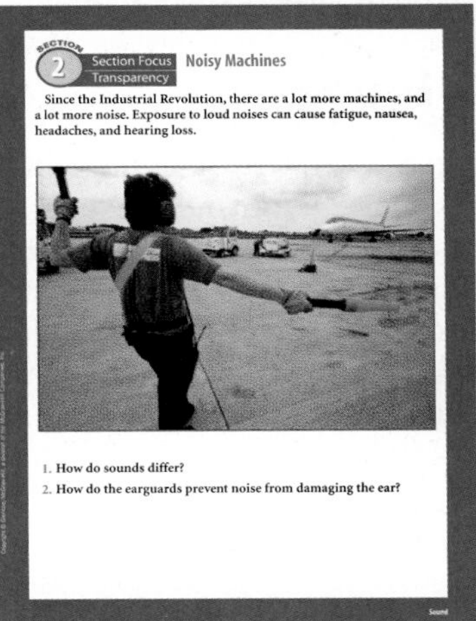
Section Focus Transparency — Noisy Machines

Since the Industrial Revolution, there are a lot more machines, and a lot more noise. Exposure to loud noises can cause fatigue, nausea, headaches, and hearing loss.

1. How do sounds differ?
2. How do the earguards prevent noise from damaging the ear?

Tie to Prior Knowledge

Ask volunteers to make a soft sound, then a loud sound. Can they make a high-pitched sound? How about a low-pitched sound? Tell students that in this section they will learn what causes these differences in sounds.

Resource Manager

Chapter Resources Booklet
Transparency Activity, p. 45
Enrichment, p. 30

2 Teach

Intensity and Loudness

Use an Analogy

The intensity of sound can be visualized by imagining a duck flapping its wings on the surface of a pond. If the duck flaps its wings strongly, large waves will be produced. If it flaps its wings with less intensity, small waves will be produced. The intensity of the flapping is independent of how fast the duck flaps, just as the intensity of sound waves is independent of the frequency of the waves.

Visual Learning

Figure 6 Have students analyze the photograph and the diagram in this figure while you read aloud the description from the text at the top of the page. Then ask a volunteer to explain the concept the figure is illustrating. Intensity of sound decreases as distance from the sound source increases. L2

LS **Auditory-Musical**

Caption Answer

Figure 6 It would be less.

Extension

Play a radio in the classroom at a comfortable volume. Have students place different objects in front of the radio to decrease the intensity of the sound. Objects they could try include a balloon, a pillow, a book, and some paper. Ask students to rank the items they tested in order of how well they decreased the intensity of the sound. Discuss the types of materials that could be used to soundproof buildings. L3 ELL

LS **Auditory-Musical**

Intensity Imagine sound waves moving through the air from your radio to your ear. If you held a square loop between you and the radio, as in **Figure 6,** and could measure how much energy passed through the loop in 1 s, you would measure intensity. **Intensity** is the amount of energy that flows through a certain area in a specific amount of time. When you turn down the volume of your radio, you reduce the energy carried by the sound waves, so you also reduce their intensity.

Intensity influences how far away a sound can be heard. If you and a friend whisper a conversation, the sound waves you create have low intensity and do not travel far. You have to sit close together to hear each other. However, when you shout to each other, you can be much farther apart. The sound waves made by your shouts have high intensity and can travel far.

Intensity influences how far a wave will travel because some of a wave's energy is converted to other forms of energy when it is passed from particle to particle. Think about what happens when you drop a basketball. The ball has potential energy as you hold it above the ground. This potential energy is converted into energy of motion as the ball falls. When the ball hits the ground and bounces up, a small amount of that energy has been transferred to the ground. The ball no longer has enough energy to bounce back to the original level. The ball transfers a small amount of energy with each bounce, until finally the ball has no more energy. If you held the ball higher above the ground, it would have more energy and would bounce for a longer time before it came to a stop. In a similar way, a sound wave of low intensity loses its energy more quickly, and travels a shorter distance than a sound wave of higher intensity.

Figure 6
The intensity of the sound waves from the CD player is related to the amount of energy that passes through the loop in a certain amount of time. *How would the intensity change if the loop were 10 m away from the radio?*

Teacher FYI

The intensity of sound decreases as it travels away from a source not only because the waves lose energy to matter, but also because they radiate out from the source. Sound intensity decreases as $1/r^2$, where r is the distance from the source. For example, the intensity of a sound 100 m from its source is about one-fourth the intensity of the same sound 50 m from its source.

Loudness When you hear different sounds, you do not need special equipment to know which sounds have greater intensity. Your ears and brain can tell the difference. **Loudness** is the human perception of sound intensity. Sound waves with high intensity cause air particles to vibrate strongly. When sound waves of high intensity reach your ear, the vigorously vibrating molecules in the air strike your eardrum with greater force and you hear a loud sound. When waves of lesser intensity reach your eardrum, the molecules in air hit it with less force and you detect a softer sound. As the intensity of a sound wave increases, the loudness of the sound you hear increases.

Reading Check *How are intensity and loudness related?*

A Scale for Loudness It's hard to say how loud too loud is. Two people are unlikely to agree on what is too loud, because people vary in their perception of loudness. A sound that seems fine to you may seem earsplitting to your teacher. Even so, the intensity of sound can be described using a measurement scale. Each unit on the scale for sound intensity is called a **decibel** (DES uh bel), abbreviated dB. On this scale, the faintest sound that most people can hear is 0 dB. Sounds with intensity levels above 120 dB may cause pain and permanent hearing loss. During some rock concerts, sounds reach this damaging intensity level. Wearing ear protection, such as earplugs, around loud sounds can help protect against hearing loss. **Figure 7** shows some sounds and their intensity levels in decibels.

SCIENCE Online

Research Visit the Glencoe Science Web site at **science.glencoe.com** to find a longer list of sounds and their intensities in decibels. Make a table that lists sounds you heard today, from loudest to quietest. In another column, write the intensity level of each sound.

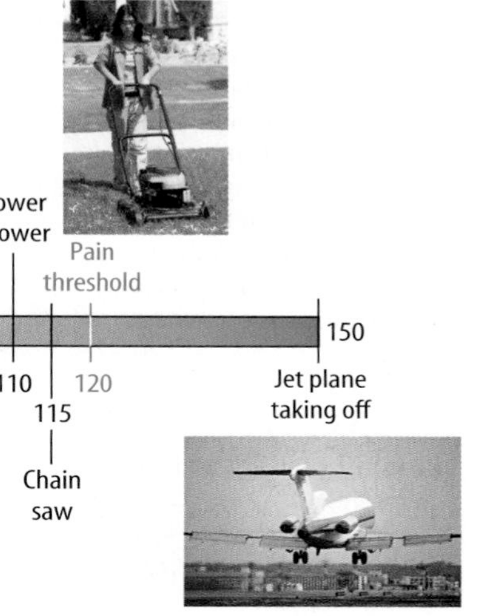

Figure 7
The decibel scale measures the intensity of sound. ***Where would a normal speaking voice fall on the scale?***

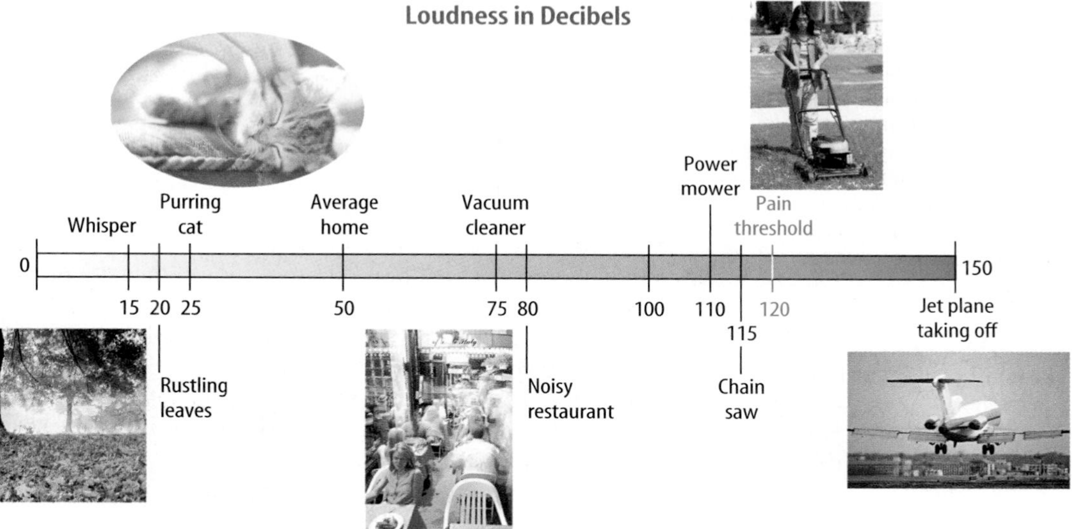

Activity

Have students bring in various whistles. Have them blow the whistles and rank them from loudest to softest. Afterwards, have students examine the whistles to find out what produced the vibration and what feature caused one whistle to be louder than another. L2 ELL
LS **Auditory-Musical**

Reading Check

Answer Intensity is the amount of energy in sound waves that flows through a certain area in a specific amount of time. Loudness is the human perception of this intensity.

Discussion

Why do you think scientists make a distinction between intensity and loudness? Intensity can be measured and agreed upon by everyone. Loudness is experienced differently by different people. A sound that is too loud for one person may be fine for another person. L2
LS **Logical-Mathematical**

Caption Answer

Figure 7 People normally speak at about 60 dB.

Fun Fact

A decibel is one-tenth of a bel, named in honor of Alexander Graham Bell.

SCIENCE Online
Internet Addresses

Explore the Glencoe Science Web site at **science.glencoe.com** to find out more about topics in this section.

Resource Manager

Chapter Resources Booklet
Directed Reading for Content Mastery, p. 18

Physical Science Critical Thinking/Problem Solving, p. 4

Pitch

Quick Demo

Demonstrate the relationships between frequency and pitch by using a microphone attached to an oscilloscope. Have a student volunteer play various pitches on an instrument. Observe the corresponding waveforms on the oscilloscope. L2

LS **Visual-Spatial**

Caption Answer

Figure 8 As frequency increases, pitch becomes higher.

Purpose Students will observe and interpret how hearing loss changees the sounds we hear. L1 ELL COOP LEARN

LS **Auditory-Musical**

Materials radio, thick cloth

Teaching Strategy If students use cloth to muffle their hearing, suggest that they gradually increase the volume of the radio until it is clear, and then take the cloth away from their ears and hear how loud the sound is.

Analysis

1. High pitches are harder to hear. Consonant sounds are harder to hear than vowel sounds.
2. People with hearing losses should be spoken to face-to-face, at a steady, unrushed pace with a slight emphasis on consonant sounds.

Assessment

Performance Have students hypothesize how these results would be affected if the bass were minimized and the treble maximized. Have them test their hypotheses. Sound would be clearer. Use **PASC,** p. 93.

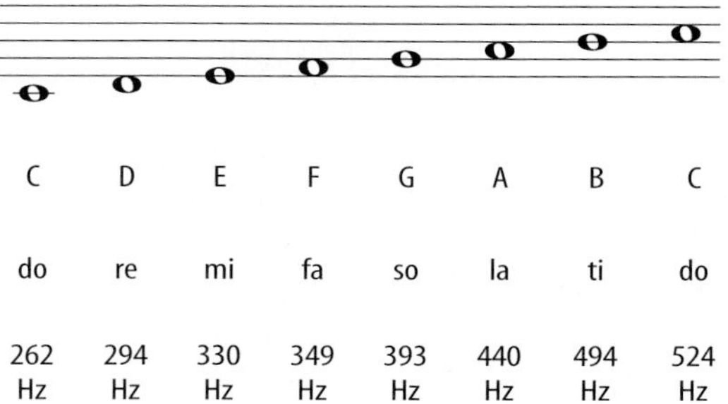

Figure 8
Every note has a different frequency, which gives it a distinct pitch. *How does pitch change when frequency increases?*

Pitch

If you have ever taken a music class, you are probably familiar with the musical scale do, re, mi, fa, so, la, ti, do. If you were to sing this scale, your voice would start low and become higher with each note. You would hear a change in **pitch,** which is how high or low a sound seems to be. The pitch of a sound is related to the frequency of the sound waves.

Frequency and Pitch Frequency is a measure of how many wavelengths pass a particular point each second. For a compressional wave, such as sound, the frequency is the number of compressions or the number of rarefactions that pass by each second. Frequency is measured in hertz (Hz)—1 Hz means that one wavelength passes by in 1 s.

When a sound wave with high frequency hits your ear, many compressions hit your eardrum each second. The wave causes your eardrum and all the other parts of your ear to vibrate more quickly than if a sound wave with a low frequency hit your ear. Your brain interprets these fast vibrations caused by high-frequency waves as a sound with a high pitch. As the frequency of a sound wave decreases, the pitch becomes lower. **Figure 8** shows different notes and their frequencies. For example, a whistle with a frequency of 1,000 Hz has a high pitch, but low-pitched thunder has a frequency of less than 50 Hz.

A healthy human ear can hear sound waves with frequencies from about 20 Hz to 20,000 Hz. The human ear is most sensitive to sounds in the range of 440 Hz to about 7,000 Hz. In this range, most people can hear much fainter sounds than at higher or lower frequencies.

Making a Model for Hearing Loss

Procedure

1. To simulate a hearing loss, tune a **radio** to a news station. Turn the volume down to the lowest level you can hear and understand.
2. Turn the bass to maximum and the treble to minimum. If the radio does not have these controls, hold thick wads of **cloth** over your ears.
3. Observe which sounds are hardest and easiest to hear.

Analysis

1. Are high or low pitches harder to hear? Are vowel or consonant sounds harder to hear?
2. How could you help a person with hearing loss understand what you say?

Ultrasonic and Infrasonic Waves Most people can't hear sound frequencies above 20,000 Hz, which are called **ultrasonic** waves. Dogs can hear sounds with frequencies up to about 25,000 Hz, and bats can detect frequencies as high as 100,000 Hz. Even though humans can't hear ultrasonic waves, they use them for many things. Ultrasonic waves are used in medical diagnosis and treatment. They also are used to estimate the size, shape, and depth of underwater objects.

Infrasonic, or subsonic, waves have frequencies below 20 Hz—too low for most people to hear. These waves are produced by sources that vibrate slowly, such as wind, heavy machinery, and earthquakes. Although you can't hear infrasonic waves, you may feel them as a rumble inside your body.

Science Journal

Feeling Pitch Have students place their hands gently over their necks and sing the musical scale, "do re mi fa sol la ti do." Have them write their observations in their Science Journals. They should be able to tell that their vocal cords vibrate differently as they go up the scale. L2 LS **Kinesthetic**

The Doppler Effect

Imagine that you are standing at the side of a racetrack with race cars zooming past. As they move toward you, the different pitches of their engines becomes higher. As they move away from you, the pitches become lower. The change in pitch or wave frequency due to a moving wave source is called the **Doppler effect. Figure 9** shows how the Doppler effect occurs.

 **Reading Check** *What is the Doppler effect?*

Moving Sound As a race car moves, it sends out sound waves in the form of compressions and rarefactions. In **Figure 9A,** the race car creates a compression, labeled A. Compression A moves through the air toward the flagger standing at the finish line. By the time compression B leaves the race car in **Figure 9B,** the car has moved forward. Because the car has moved since the time it created compression A, compressions A and B are closer together than they would be if the car had stayed still. Because the compressions are closer together, more compressions pass by the flagger each second than if the car were at rest. As a result, the flagger hears a higher pitch. You also can see from **Figure 9B** that the compressions behind the moving car are farther apart, resulting in a lower frequency and a lower pitch after the car passes and moves away from the flagger.

Astronomy INTEGRATION

The Doppler effect can also be observed in light waves emanating from moving sources—although the sources must be moving at tremendous speeds. Astronomers have learned that the universe is expanding by observing the Doppler effect in light waves. Research the phenomenon known as red shift and explain in you Science Journal how it relates to the Doppler effect.

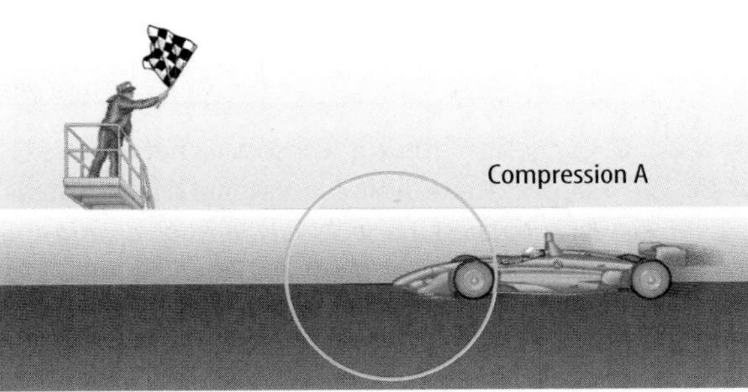

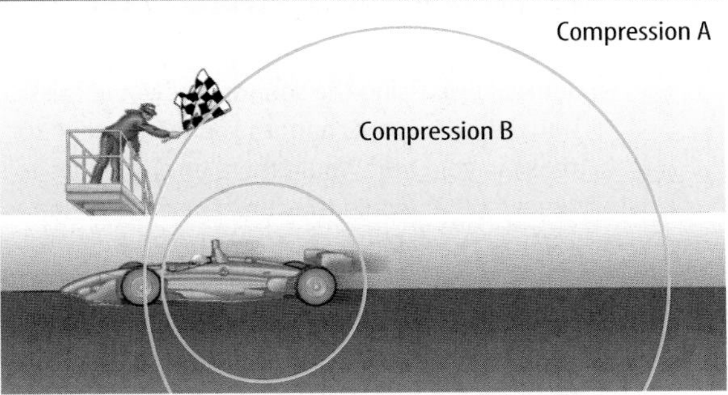

Figure 9
The Doppler effect occurs when the source of a sound wave is moving relative to a listener.

A The race car creates compression A.

B The car is closer to the flagger when it creates compression B. Compressions A and B are closer together in front of the car, so the flagger hears a higher-pitched sound.

The Doppler Effect

Astronomy INTEGRATION

The light from most galaxies is shifted toward the red end of the spectrum because, as these galaxies are moving away from Earth, their light waves become "stretched out." This is known as red shift. The stretching of the light waves is caused by the Doppler effect.

Reading Check

Answer the change in pitch or wave frequency due to a moving wave source

Quick Demo

Cut a small opening in the side of a sponge ball. Place a small electric buzzer connected to a battery inside the opening and tape the opening shut. Throw the ball from the front to the back of the room. The increased and decreased pitches caused by the Doppler effect should be audible. L2
LS **Auditory-Musical**

Visual Learning

Figure 9 Remind students that the sound waves emitted by the car in the figure don't change. It is only the frequency at which they reach the flagger that changes. The car's driver hears no change in pitch at all. Have students draw circles representing sound waves to show how the Doppler effect increases if the speed of the sound source increases. L2 LS **Visual-Spatial**

Curriculum Connection

History When a jet travels faster than the speed of sound, the sound waves it produces trail behind as a cone of pressure disturbances in the air. This Mach cone might be heard as a loud sonic boom as the jet passes by. Have students research the first human-made sonic boom. Chuck Yeager was the first person to break the sound barrier and cause a sonic boom. He did this on October 14, 1947.

Resource Manager

Chapter Resources Booklet
- MiniLAB, p. 4
- Reinforcement, p. 26
- Lab Activity, pp. 9–10

The Doppler Effect, continued

3 Assess

Reteach

Place a clear, shallow container of water on top of an overhead projector to demonstrate various properties of waves. For example, touch the water with a vibrating tuning fork to show low and high intensity. Move the vibrating tuning fork along the surface to show the Doppler effect. L2

LS **Visual-Spatial**

Challenge

Suppose that a car races toward you emitting a sound with a frequency of exactly 440 Hz. Describe what happens to the frequency of the sound you hear if the car slows down and stops just as it approaches you. The frequency you hear will remain above 440 Hz, decreasing to exactly 440 Hz when the car stops. L3

LS **Logical-Mathematical**

Assessment

Portfolio Have students make posters showing pictures of things that produce sound at different frequencies. The pictures should include ultrasonic, infrasonic, and audible frequencies. Use **Performance Assessment in the Science Classroom**, p. 145. P

Figure 10
Doppler radar can show the movement of winds in storms, and, in some cases, can detect the wind rotation that leads to the formation of tornadoes, like the one shown here. This can help provide early warning and reduce the injuries and loss of life caused by tornadoes.

A Moving Observer You also can observe the Doppler effect when you are moving past a sound source that is standing still. Suppose you were riding in a school bus and passed a building with a ringing bell, as in **Figure 10.** The pitch would sound higher as you approached the building and lower as you rode away from it. The Doppler effect happens any time the source of a sound is changing position compared with the observer. It occurs no matter whether it is the sound source or the observer that is moving. The faster the change in position, the greater the change in frequency and pitch.

Using the Doppler Effect The Doppler effect also occurs for other waves besides sound waves. For example, the frequency of electromagnetic waves, such as radar waves, changes if an observer and wave source are moving relative to each other. Radar guns use the Doppler effect to measure the speed of cars. The radar gun sends radar waves toward a moving car. The waves are reflected from the car, and their frequency is shifted, depending on the speed and direction of the car. From the Doppler shift of the reflected waves, the radar gun determines the car's speed. Weather radar also uses the Doppler shift to show the movement of winds in storms, such as the tornado in **Figure 10.**

Section  Assessment

1. When you turn up the volume on a radio, which of the following change: velocity of sound, intensity, pitch, amplitude, frequency, wavelength, or loudness?
2. What does the decibel scale measure? What decibel levels can damage hearing?
3. Compare frequency and pitch.
4. Sketch a diagram that shows why the pitch of an ambulance siren seems to change as the ambulance passes you.
5. **Think Critically** Why is the Doppler effect more dramatic when a race car speeds past you than it is when a police car siren passes you on the street?

Skill Builder Activities

6. **Concept Mapping** Construct a network tree showing how these concepts are related: *intensity, loudness, decibel scale, ultrasonic, infrasonic, pitch,* and *frequency.* **For more help, refer to the Science Skill Handbook.**
7. **Communicating** Imagine how your life would be different if you could not hear sounds at high frequencies. Write a paragraph in your Science Journal discussing the sounds you would miss and describing the changes you would need to make in your life. Would there be any advantages? What would they be? **For more help, refer to the Science Skill Handbook.**

Answers to Section Assessment

1. intensity, amplitude, loudness
2. sound intensity; above 120 dB
3. Frequency is a measure of how many wavelengths pass a point each second. Pitch is how high or low a sound seems to be. As frequency increases, pitch gets higher.
4. Sketches should show that the frequency of compressions increases as the ambulance comes near and decreases as the ambulance goes away.
5. The changes occur faster.
6. Check students' work.
7. Possible answers: Sounds would be muffled and consonant sounds would be hard to distinguish. You would have to listen closely and have people face you when you have conversations. Advantages include the fact that you wouldn't hear annoying high-pitched sounds such as drills.

SECTION 3

Music

What is music?

To someone else, your favorite music might sound like a jumble of noise. Music and noise are caused by vibrations—with some important differences, as shown in **Figure 11.** You can easily make noise—just tap a pencil on a desk. Noise has random patterns and pitches. **Music** is made of sounds that are deliberately used in a regular pattern.

Natural Frequencies Every material has a particular frequency at which it will vibrate, called its natural frequency. No matter how you pluck a guitar string, you hear the same pitch, because the string always vibrates at its natural frequency. The guitar string's natural frequency depends on the string's thickness and length and how tightly it is stretched across the guitar. Each string is tuned to a different natural frequency, which lets you play different notes and make music. Musical instruments contain strings, membranes or columns of air—something that vibrates at its natural frequency to create a pitch.

Resonance In wind instruments, the column of air inside vibrates. The air vibrates because of resonance—the ability of a medium to vibrate by absorbing energy at its own natural frequency. When air is blown into the instrument, reeds or the shape of the mouthpiece create vibrations. The air column absorbs some of this energy and also starts to vibrate. The resonance of the air column amplifies the sound of the instrument. Resonance helps amplify the sound created in many musical instruments.

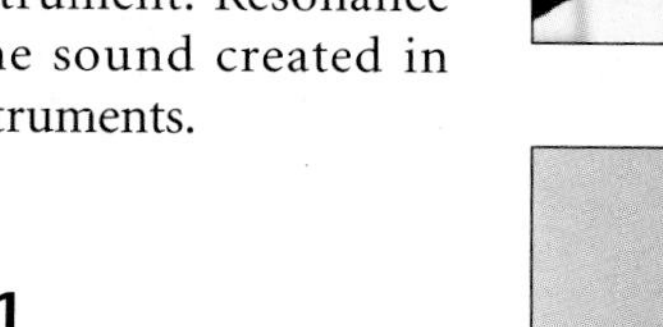

As You Read

***What* You'll Learn**

- **Distinguish** between noise and music.
- **Describe** why different instruments have different sound qualities.
- **Explain** how string, wind, and percussion instruments produce music.
- **Describe** the formation of beats.

Vocabulary

music, quality, overtone, resonator

***Why* It's Important**

Music enhances your enjoyment of life, but noise pollution can interfere with it.

Piano

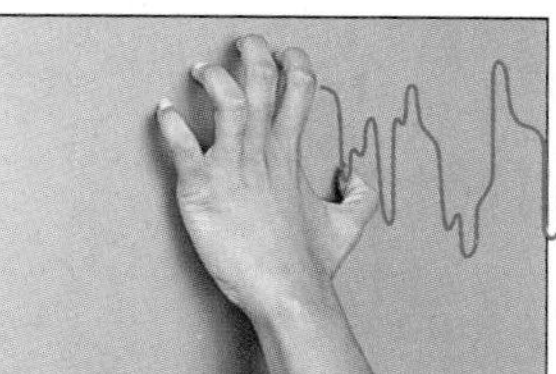

Scraping fingernails

Figure 11
These wave patterns indicate the pitches created by the piano and the scraping fingernails. *Which of these has a regularly repeating pattern?*

SECTION 3

Music

1 Motivate

Bellringer Transparency

Display the Section Focus Transparency for Section 3. Use the accompanying Transparency Activity Master. L2 ELL

SECTION 3 Section Focus Transparency **Ancient Flutes of Bone**

In 1987, a Chinese archaeological team unearthed six ancient flutes. Tests showed that five of the six might crack if played, but the sixth was intact and playable. Radiocarbon dating indicated the flute was almost 9,000 years old, making it the oldest known functionally intact musical intrument.

1. How is music different than noise?
2. Which flute is playable? Why?
3. How do the holes affect the sound of a flute?

Sound

Tie to Prior Knowledge

Ask students to name a musical instrument they play. Tell them that this section explains the science of music.

Caption Answer

Figure 11 the pitches produced by the piano

Section Assessment Planner

PORTFOLIO
Assessment, p. 373

PERFORMANCE ASSESSMENT
Skill Builder Activities, p. 373
See page 386 for more options.

CONTENT ASSESSMENT
Section, p. 373
Challenge, p. 373
Chapter, pp. 386–387

Resource Manager

Chapter Resources Booklet
Transparency Activity, p. 46
Cultural Diversity, p. 61

2 Teach

Sound Quality

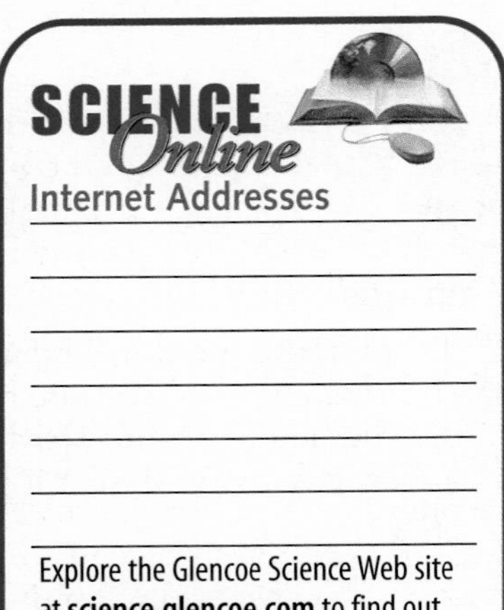

Explore the Glencoe Science Web site at **science.glencoe.com** to find out more about topics in this section.

Reading Check

Answer Differences among sounds of the same pitch and loudness; these are caused by different combinations of frequencies produced by the sources of the sounds.

Visual Learning

Figure 12 A guitar string only vibrates at its fundamental frequency and at integral multiples of that frequency. Have students use lengths of string to show that other frequencies in the string would simply die away L3 LS **Kinesthetic**

Caption Answer

Figure 12 at four times the fundamental frequency

SCIENCE Online

Research Visit the Glencoe Science Web site at **science.glencoe.com** for information about noise pollution. Identify sources of noise pollution that you can help eliminate.

Sound Quality

Suppose your classmate played a note on a flute and then a note of the same pitch and loudness on a piano. Even if you closed your eyes, you could tell the difference between the two instruments. Their sounds wouldn't be the same. Each of these instruments has a unique sound quality. **Quality** of sound describes the differences among sounds of the same pitch and loudness. Objects can be made to vibrate at other frequencies besides their natural frequency. This produces sound waves with more than one frequency. The specific combination of frequencies produced by a musical instrument is what gives it a distinctive quality of sound.

Reading Check *What does sound quality describe and how it is created?*

Overtones Even though an instrument vibrates at many different frequencies at once, you still hear just one note. All of the frequencies are not at the same intensity. The main tone that is played and heard is called the fundamental frequency. On a guitar, for example, the fundamental frequency is produced by the entire string vibrating back and forth, as in **Figure 12A.** In addition to vibrating at the fundamental frequency, the string also vibrates to produce overtones. An **overtone** is a vibration whose frequency is a multiple of the fundamental frequency. The first two of guitar string overtones are shown in **Figure 12B.** These overtones create the rich sounds of a guitar. The number and intensity of overtones vary with each instrument. These overtones produce an instrument's distinct sound quality.

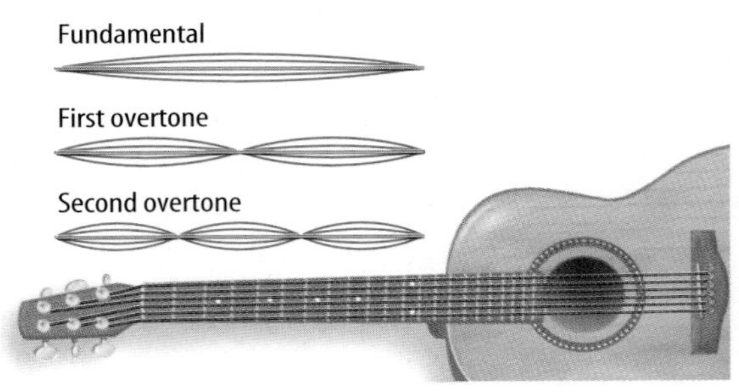

Figure 12
A guitar string can vibrate at more than one frequency at the same time. Here the guitar string vibrations produce the fundamental frequency, and first and second overtones are shown.
How would the string vibrate to produce the third overtone?

Musical Instruments

A musical instrument is any device used to produce a musical sound. Violins, cello, oboes, bassoons, horns, and kettledrums are musical instruments that you might have seen and heard in your school orchestra. These familiar examples are just a small sample of the diverse assortment of instruments people play throughout the world. For example, Australian Aborigines accompany their songs with a woodwind instrument called the didgeridoo (DIH juh ree dew). Caribbean musicians use rubber-tipped mallets to play steel drums, and a flutelike instrument called the nay is played throughout the Arab world.

LAB DEMONSTRATION

Purpose to observe the relationship between resonant wavelength and cavity size

Materials water, 100-mL graduated cylinder, rubber hammer, 440-Hz tuning fork

Procedure Place 20 mL of water in the cylinder. Tap the fork with a rubber hammer and place it horizontally above the cylinder so students can hear the resonant sound produced. Repeat with 40, 60, 80, and 100 mL of water.

Expected Outcome Resonance can't occur if a cavity is less than $\frac{1}{4}$ wavelength long. The wavelength at 440 Hz is about 79 cm, so resonance doesn't occur if the length of the column of air is less than about 20 cm.

Assessment

What was the minimum height of the column of air for which resonance occurred? about 20 cm **Why weren't you able to hear resonance if the column of air was shorter than this?** The cavity wasn't at least $\frac{1}{4}$ wavelength long.

Strings Soft violins, screaming electric guitars, and elegant harps are types of string instruments. In string instruments, sound is produced by plucking, striking, or drawing a bow across tightly stretched strings. Because the sound of a vibrating string is soft, string instruments usually have a resonator, like the violin in **Figure 13.** A **resonator** (RE zen ay tur) is a hollow chamber filled with air that amplifies sound when its air vibrates. For example, if you pluck a guitar string that is stretched tightly between two nails on a board, the sound is much quieter than if the string were on a guitar. When the string is attached to a guitar, the guitar frame and the air inside the instrument begin to vibrate as they absorb energy from the vibrating string. The vibration of the guitar body and the air inside the resonator makes the sound of the string louder and also affects the quality of the sound.

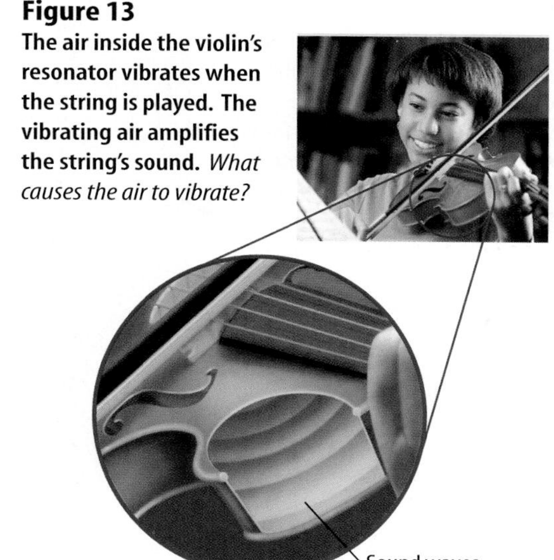

Figure 13
The air inside the violin's resonator vibrates when the string is played. The vibrating air amplifies the string's sound. *What causes the air to vibrate?*

Brass and Woodwinds Brass and woodwind instruments rely on the vibration of air to make music. The many different brass and wind instruments—such as horns, oboes, and flutes—use various methods to make air vibrate inside the instrument. For example, brass instruments have cone-shaped mouthpieces like the one in **Figure 14.** This mouthpiece is inserted into metal tubing, which is the resonator in a brass instrument. As the player blows into the instrument, his or her lips vibrate against the mouthpiece. The air in the resonator also starts to vibrate, producing a pitch. On the other hand, to play a flute, a musician blows a stream of air against the edge of the flute's mouth hole. This causes the air inside the flute to vibrate.

In brass and wind instruments, the length of the vibrating tube of air determines the pitch of the sound produced. For example, in flutes and trumpets, the musician changes the length of the resonator by opening and closing finger holes or valves. In a trombone, however, the tubing slides in and out to become shorter or longer.

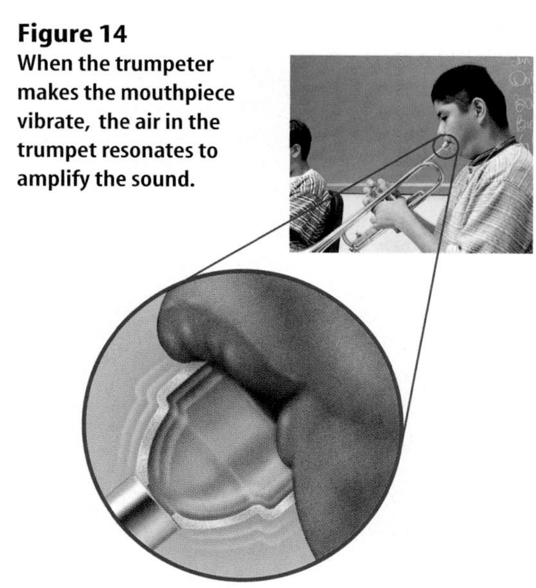

Figure 14
When the trumpeter makes the mouthpiece vibrate, the air in the trumpet resonates to amplify the sound.

Musical Instruments

Caption Answer

Figure 13 It absorbs energy from the vibrating string.

Make a Model

Students can learn more about the importance of resonators by creating a model. Have them cut a circle about 5 cm wide out of the top of a small box. First, they should pluck a stretched rubber band to hear the sound it makes. Next, they should put the rubber band around the box so that it crosses the hole. The rubber band will make a much louder sound when plucked over the hole. L2
ELL LS **Auditory-Musical**

Activity

Have students work in small groups to examine how instruments produce sound. Each group should choose one instrument and examine what vibrates and how it produces a change in pitch. Have groups share their findings with the class. L1
LS **Visual-Spatial**

Teacher FYI

Vibrations in many string instruments, such as the violin (a bowed instrument), are altered by pressing on part of the string. This effectively shortens the length of the vibrating string, so the pitch is higher. Other instruments have fixed string lengths that correspond to different pitches. Examples of this are the harp (a plucked instrument) and the piano (a hammered instrument).

Cultural Diversity

Slack-key Guitar Musicians in Hawaii have a unique way of using a guitar to reflect the spirit and beauty of the island. The *ki ho´ alu*, or slack-key guitar music, is named for the way the strings are loosened and tuned to various pitches. Play recorded slack-key guitar music and have students describe how the sound quality differs from that of other guitar music they have heard. L2 LS **Auditory-Musical**

Resource Manager

Chapter Resources Booklet

Directed Reading for Content Mastery, p. 19
Enrichment, p. 31

Musical Instruments, continued

Caption Answer

Figure 15 The vibrating drum membrane causes the air inside the resonator to vibrate at the same frequency, thereby amplifying the sound.

Activity

Obtain some percussion instruments. If possible, include a snare drum, a kettledrum, and a bass drum, as well as a tambourine and cymbals. Scatter some dry rice on a snare drum's membrane and hit the drum with a drumstick so students can see the vibration. If a kettledrum is available, show students that by pressing on the pedal you can tighten or loosen the membrane and alter the drum's pitch. For each of the different types of drums, have students explore the pitch produced and the way sound is amplified. L2 LS **Auditory-Musical**

Reading Check

Answer to send signals, accompany rituals, and entertain

Caption Answer

Figure 16 Each size resonates at a different frequency.

Beats

Fun Fact

Our ears are capable of hearing beats only if the difference in the frequency of the two notes played is less than 7 Hz.

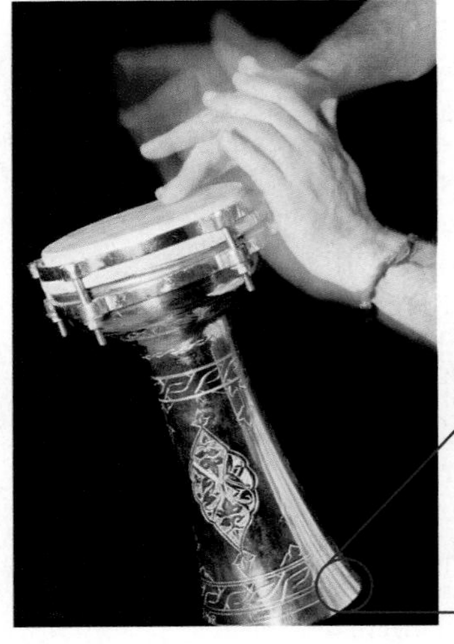

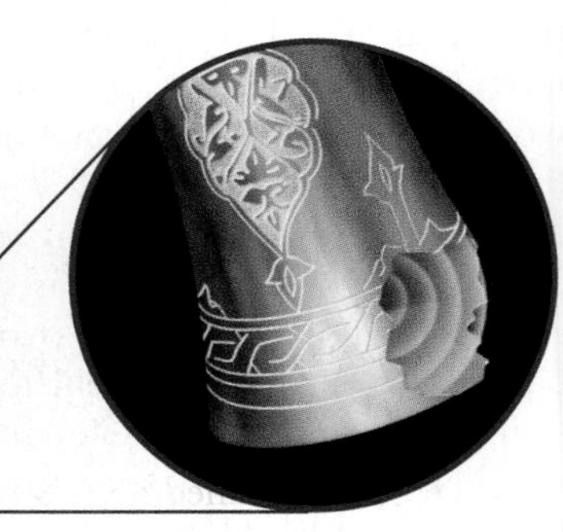

Figure 15
The air inside the resonator of the drum amplifies the sound created when the musician strikes the membrane's surface. *How does the natural frequency of the air in the drum affect the sound it creates?*

Percussion Does the sound of a bass drum make your heart start to pound? Since ancient times, people have used drums and other percussion instruments to send signals, accompany important rituals, and entertain one another. Percussion instruments are struck, shaken, rubbed, or brushed to produce sound. Some, such as kettledrums or the drum shown in **Figure 15,** have a membrane stretched over a resonator. When the drummer strikes the membrane with sticks or hands, the membrane vibrates, and causes the air inside the resonator to vibrate. The resonator amplifies the sound made when the membrane is struck. Some drums have a fixed pitch, but others have a pitch that can be changed by tightening or loosening the membrane.

Caribbean steel drums were developed in the 1940s in Trinidad. As many as 32 different striking surfaces hammered from the ends of 55-gallon oil barrels create clear notes. The side of a drum acts as the resonator.

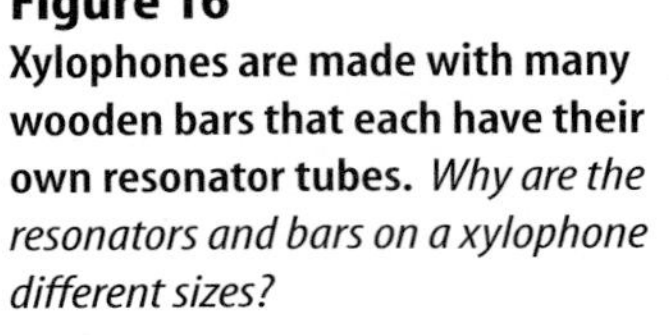

Figure 16
Xylophones are made with many wooden bars that each have their own resonator tubes. *Why are the resonators and bars on a xylophone different sizes?*

Reading Check *How have people used drums?*

The xylophone shown in **Figure 16** is another type of percussion instrument. It has a series of wooden bars, each with its own tube-shaped resonator. The musician strikes the bars with mallets, and the type of mallet affects the sound quality. Hard mallets make crisp sounds, while softer rubber mallets make duller sounds. Other types of percussion instruments include cymbals, rattles, and even old-fashioned washboards.

Science Journal

Sound Effects Several singers, such as Ella Fitzgerald and Enrico Caruso, have reportedly broken crystal glasses by loudly singing a note at a specific frequency. Have students write their speculations about how this happens. The frequency of the singer's voice matches the natural frequency of the glass, causing it to resonate. If the glass vibrates intensely, it will shatter. L2 LS **Logical-Mathematical**

Resource Manager

Chapter Resources Booklet
- Activity Worksheet, pp. 5–6
- Lab Activity, pp. 11–14
- Reinforcement, p. 27

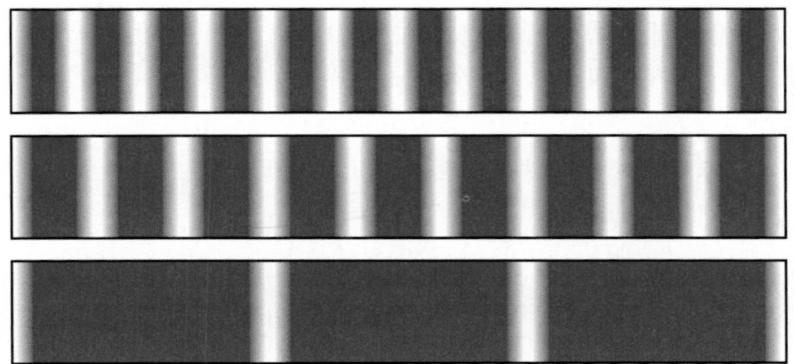

Figure 17
Beats can occur when sound waves of different frequencies, shown in the top two panels, combine. These sound waves interfere with each other, forming a wave with a lower frequency, shown in the bottom panel. This wave causes a listener to hear beats.

Beats

Have you ever heard two flutes play the same note when they weren't properly tuned? The sounds they produce have slightly different frequencies. You may have heard a pulsing variation in loudness called beats.

When two instruments play at the same time, the sound waves produced by each instrument interfere. The amplitudes of the waves add together where compressions overlap and rarefactions overlap, causing an increase in loudness. Where compressions and rarefactions overlap each other, the loudness decreases. Look at **Figure 17.** If two waves of different frequencies interfere, a new wave is produced that has a different frequency. The frequency of this wave is actually the difference in the frequencies of the two waves. The frequency of the beats that you hear decreases as the two waves become closer in frequency. If two flutes that are in tune play the same note, no beats are heard.

Section 3 Assessment

1. Compare and contrast music and noise.
2. Explain how an instrument's overtones contribute to its sound quality.
3. Describe how a flute produces sound.
4. What happens when two instruments that are out of pitch play the same note?
5. **Think Critically** The bull roarer is a blade-shaped, wooden musical instrument. When it is whirled around on a string, it produces a rumbling sound. Explain how this sound might be produced.

Skill Builder Activities

6. **Recognizing Cause and Effect** What causes constructive interference? What is the effect when sound waves constructively interfere? Describe the cause-and-effect sequence for destructive interference. **For more help, refer to the** Science Skill Handbook.
7. **Communicating** In your Science Journal, write a poem about music. Use the terms *resonance, overtone, quality,* and *beat*. **For more help, refer to the** Science Skill Handbook.

Quick Demo

Wrap a rubber band around the tines of a tuning fork to alter its pitch slightly. Hit it and an identical unwrapped fork with a rubber hammer and touch the handles to a desk to amplify the sound. Because the frequencies interfere, students will hear beats.

3 Assess

Reteach

Have students bring in musical instruments and show how they are played, how pitch can be changed, and how they amplify sound. L2

LS **Visual-Spatial**

Challenge

Have students find out the relationship between the difference in frequency and the number of beats produced. The number of beats per second equals the difference in the frequencies of the two waves. **If two flutes play at the same time, one at 440 Hz, and the other at 435 Hz, how often will you hear a beat?** You will hear 5 beats per second. L3

LS **Logical-Mathematical**

Process Show students pictures of various musical instruments. Have them classify each one as a string, brass, woodwind, or percussion instrument. Use **PASC** p. 89.

Answers to Section Assessment

1. Music has definite pitches and sound qualities used in a set pattern; noise has irregular patterns and random pitches.
2. An instrument vibrates at its fundamental frequency and at frequencies that are multiples of this fundamental frequency. The combination of these gives each instrument a distinct sound quality.
3. The musician blows air against the flute's mouth hole causing air to swirl inside the flute. The flute acts as a resonator to amplify the sound.
4. Compressions and rarefactions of the sound waves produced by the instruments interfere destructively. The rise and fall in intensity is called a beat.
5. Air hits against the bull roarer, producing sound waves. Its speed determines pitch.
6. Constructive interference occurs when two instruments play the same note, causing increased amplitude, intensity, and loudness of the sound. Destructive interference happens when compressions from one sound wave overlap the rarefactions of another, so sound intensity and loudness decrease.
7. Check students' poems.

Activity BENCH TESTED

Purpose Students analyze resonance in air columns. L2

LS **Auditory-Musical**

Process Skills observing, inferring, comparing and contrasting, recognizing cause and effect, predicting, communicating

Time Required 30 minutes

Alternate Materials Soda bottles can be used instead of test tubes.

Teaching Strategies Be sure students understand to blow across the top of the tubes instead of directly into them.

Answers to Questions

1. The tone, or quality of sound, is better for test tubes having a larger column of air.
2. A higher column of water produces higher pitch.
3. Only low-frequency sound has room to vibrate in test tubes having long columns of air.
4. Because only frequencies having a node at the bottom of the air column and an antinode at the top will emerge from the tube, the sound is maximized.
5. Shorter air columns have higher frequencies than longer air columns.
6. Both produce sound when air is blown across an opening. The flute is an open-ended resonator. Its air column can be increased or decreased by opening or closing finger holes.

Activity

Making Music

There are many different types of musical instruments. You can also make music using every day objects that are not formal instruments, such as pots and pot lids, garbage can covers or boxes of matches. How can you create a musical instrument that requires air to be blown across it in order to make sound?

What You'll Investigate

How can you make different tones using only test tubes and water?

Materials

test tubes
test-tube rack

Goals

- **Demonstrate** how to make music using water and test tubes.
- **Predict** how the tones will change when there is more or less water in the test tube.

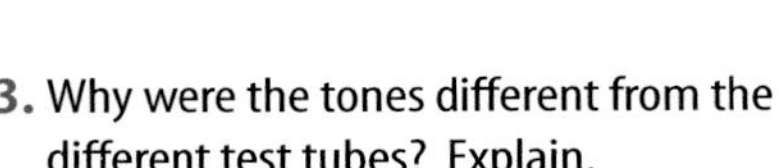

Procedure

1. Put different amounts of water into each of the test tubes.
2. **Predict** any differences you expect in how the tones from the different test tubes will sound.
3. Blow across the top of each test tube.
4. **Record** any differences that you noticed in the tones that you heard from each test tube .

Conclude and Apply

1. **Describe** how the tones changed depending on the amount of water in the test tube.
2. How did the pitch depend on the height of the water?
3. Why were the tones different from the different test tubes? Explain.
4. **Explain** how resonance amplifies the sound from a test tube.
5. **Explain** how the natural frequencies of the columns of air in each of the tubes differ.
6. **Compare and contrast** the way the test tubes make music with the way a flute makes music.

Communicating Your Data

When you are listening to music with family or friends, describe to them what you have learned about how musical instruments produce sound.

Communicating Your Data

Have students draw sketches to show why the sound emerging from the test tubes will have wavelengths that are multiples of $\frac{1}{4}$ the length of the air column.

Assessment

Oral Ask students how the wavelength of a resonator differs if both ends of the cavity, rather than one as in the test tubes, is opened. If the cavity has only one open end, the sound will have wavelengths in multiples of $\frac{1}{4}$ the length of the tube. If both ends are open, the wavelengths will be multiples of $\frac{1}{2}$ the length of the tube. Use **Performance Assessment in the Science Classroom,** p. 89.

SECTION 4

Using Sound

The Uses of Sound

You already know that sound, in the form of music, can provide entertainment. Sounds such as sirens and fire alarms can be warning signals. The bell on a microwave timer tells you when your food is ready. People and animals use sound in a number of important ways.

Acoustics

Think of the last time you heard someone talk into a microphone. Did you hear echoes? When an orchestra is done playing, does it seem as if the sound of its music lingers for a couple of seconds? The sound waves produced by a speaker or an orchestra reflect off the walls and objects around you. The sounds and their reflections reach your ears at different times, so you hear echoes. This echoing effect produced by many reflections of sound is called reverberation (rih vur buh RAY shun).

If you're in the audience at an orchestra performance, reverberation can ruin the sound of the music. To prevent this problem, scientists and engineers who design concert halls must understand how the size, shape, and furnishings of the room affect the reflection of sound waves. These scientists and engineers specialize in **acoustics** (uh KEW stihks), which is the study of sound. They know, for example, that soft, porous materials can reduce excess reverberation, so they may recommend that the walls of concert halls be lined with carpets and draperies. **Figure 18** shows a unique material that can be used to create a good listening environment.

As You Read

What You'll Learn

- **Recognize** some of the factors that determine how a concert hall or theater is designed.
- **Describe** how some animals use sound waves to hunt and navigate.
- **Discuss** the uses of sonar.
- **Explain** how ultrasound is useful in medicine.

Vocabulary
acoustics
sonar
echolocation

Why It's Important

Sound waves have many uses, from discovering sunken treasures to diagnosing and treating diseases.

Figure 18
This concert hall uses cloth drapes to help reduce reverberations. *Do you think the drapes absorb or reflect sound waves?*

Echolocation

At night, bats swoop around in darkness without bumping into anything. They even manage to hunt insects and other prey in the dark. Their senses of sight and smell help them navigate, but many species of bats also depend on echolocation. **Echolocation** is the process of locating objects by emitting sounds and interpreting the sound waves that are reflected back. Look at **Figure 19** to learn how echolocation works.

375

Section Assessment Planner

PORTFOLIO
Challenge, p. 379

PERFORMANCE ASSESSMENT
Math Skills Activity, p. 378
Skill Builder Activities, p. 379
See page 386 for more options.

CONTENT ASSESSMENT
Section, p. 379
Challenge, p. 379
Chapter, pp. 386–387

SECTION 4

Using Sound

1 Motivate

Bellringer Transparency

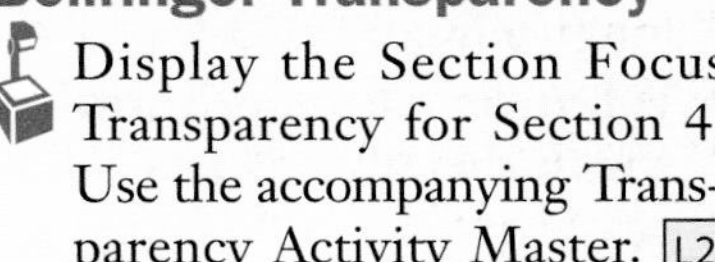

Display the Section Focus Transparency for Section 4. Use the accompanying Transparency Activity Master. L2 ELL

Section Focus Transparency 4 A Late Night Snack

Oilbirds are the world's only nocturnal, fruit-eating birds. Living in South American caves, oilbirds emit high-speed clicks and use the echoes to navigate and feed.

1. How do oilbirds use sound to their advantage?
2. What other creatures use echolocation?
3. What are some technical uses of sound?

Tie to Prior Knowledge

Ask students if they have ever used sounds to figure out where they were. Tell them that in this lesson they will learn how animals use sound to determine location.

Caption Answer

Figure 18 absorb

Resource Manager

Chapter Resources Booklet
Transparency Activity, p. 47
Directed Reading for Content Mastery, pp. 19, 20
Cultural Diversity, p. 51

NATIONAL GEOGRAPHIC

Visualizing Bat Echolocation

Have students examine the pictures and read the captions. Then ask the following questions.

- **What type of wave is the bat emitting transverse or longitudinal?** longitudinal waves
- **What is the medium in which this wave is traveling?** air

  How do bats locate their prey? by sensing the wave that is reflected off of the prey
- **Explain why this moth would be an easy prey to locate.** This moth has a large surface area that will reflect the ultrasonic waves.

Activity

Have pairs of students simulate the compression wave of the bat using a spring toy. Have the students watch for the reflected wave. L2 LS **Kinesthetic**

Extension

Echolocation is very similar to sonar and radar. Have students research these methods that are used by humans to locate objects Students should prepare posters outlining how these methods work and present their posters to their class. L3 LS **Visual-Spatial**

Figure 19

Many bats emit ultrasonic—very high-frequency—sounds. The sound waves bounce off objects, and bats locate prey by using the returning echoes. Known as echolocation, this technique is also used by dolphins, which produce clicking sounds as they hunt. The diagrams below show how a bat uses echolocation to capture a flying insect.

A Sound waves of a bat's ultrasonic cries spread out in front of it.

B Some of the waves strike a moth and bounce back to the bat.

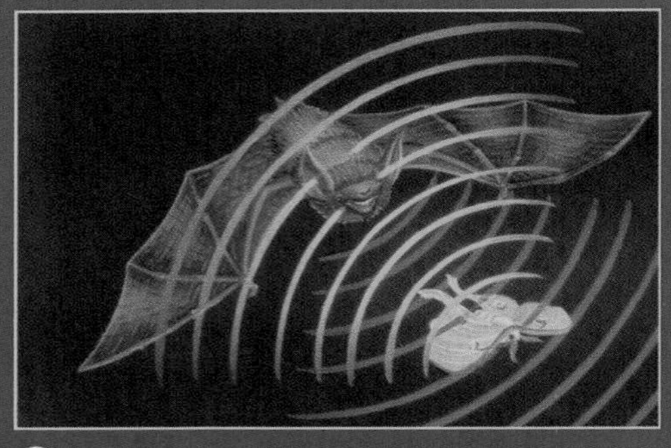

C The bat determines the moth's location by continuing to emit cries, then changes its course to catch the moth.

D By emitting a continuous stream of ultrasonic cries, the bat homes in on the moth and captures its prey.

Resource Manager

Chapter Resources Booklet
Enrichment, p. 32

Mathematics Skill Activities, p. 9

Reading and Writing Skill Activities, p. 7

Sonar

More than 140 years ago, a ship named the *Central America* disappeared in a hurricane off the coast of South Carolina. In its hold lay 21 tons of newly minted gold coins and bars that would be worth $1 billion or more in today's market. When the shipwreck occurred, there was no way to search for the ship in the deep water where it sank. The *Central America* and its treasures lay at the bottom of the ocean until 1988, when crews used sonar to locate the wreck under 2,800 m of water. **Sonar** is a system that uses the reflection of underwater sound waves to detect objects. First, a sound pulse is emitted toward the bottom of the ocean. The sound travels through the water and is reflected when it hits something solid, as shown in **Figure 20.** A sensitive underwater microphone called a hydrophone picks up the reflected signal. Because the speed of sound in water is known, the distance to the object can be calculated by measuring how much time passes between the emitting sound pulse and receiving the reflected signal.

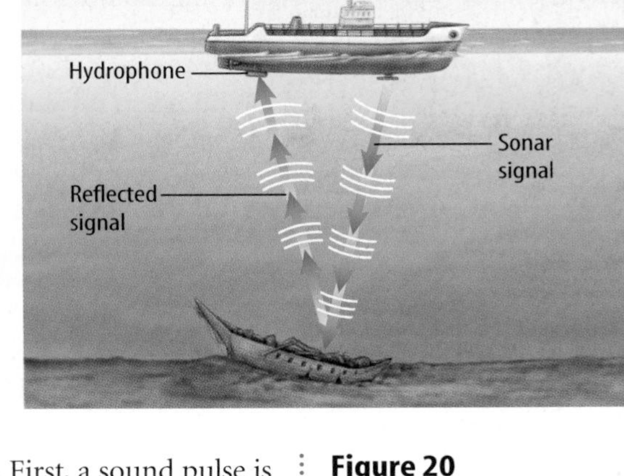

Figure 20
Sonar uses sound waves to find objects that are underwater.
How is sonar like echolocation?

Reading Check *How does sonar detect underwater objects?*

The idea of using sonar to detect underwater objects was first suggested as a way of avoiding icebergs, but many other uses have been developed for it. Navy ships use sonar for detecting, identifying, and locating submarines. Fishing crews also use sonar to find schools of fish, and scientists use it to map the ocean floor. Sonar typically uses ultrasonic frequencies because they are better at revealing small details. This technique can find an object as small as a book at a depth of 7,000 m.

Ultrasound in Medicine

High-frequency sound waves are used in more than just echolocation and sonar. Ultrasonic waves also are used to break up and remove dirt or buildup from jewelry. Chemists sometimes use ultrasonic waves to clean glassware. One of the main uses of ultrasonic waves, though, is in medicine. Using special instruments, medical professionals can send ultrasonic waves into a specific part of a patient's body. Ultrasonic waves are used to diagnose, monitor, and treat conditions such as pregnancy, heart disease, and cancer.

2 Teach

Sonar

Use Science Words

Word Origin Have students find what the letters of the word *sonar* stand for and explain why this is an accurate description. Sonar stands for sound navigation and ranging. This is accurate because sonar directs sound toward a target.

Caption Answer

Figure 20 Both use reflection of sound waves to detect objects.

Teacher FYI

There are three types of sonar systems. An active sonar system sends sound waves toward a target and analyzes the reflected waves. A passive sonar system doesn't emit sound waves; it simply listens for and analyzes sounds made by a target. Sonar systems can also be used for communication by emitting sound waves that are analyzed by a target.

Reading Check

Answer by emitting a sound pulse and measuring the time for the pulse to travel to the object and reflect back

Ultrasound in Medicine

Fun Fact

Ultrasounds are produced by using an electrical signal to induce vibration in a piezoelectric crystal.

Visual Learning

Figure 20 Remind students that the sound waves produced by the sonar signal and the reflected signal spread out in all directions.
L2 LS **Visual-Spatial**

Ultrasound in Medicine, continued

Reading Check

Answer Reflected waves produce electrical signals that are converted by a computer into video images.

Caption Answer

Figure 21 Possible answer: affirming the health of the fetus without the dangers of X rays

Teacher FYI

An ultrasound technician directs the sound waves with a hand-held transducer. The transducer emits an array of ultrasound pulses that vary with time. The density of the target determines the intensity of the pulse that is reflected back to the transducer.

Math Skills Activity

National Math Standards

Correlation to Mathematics Objectives

1, 2, 8, 9

Answer to Practice Problem

1. 719.5 m

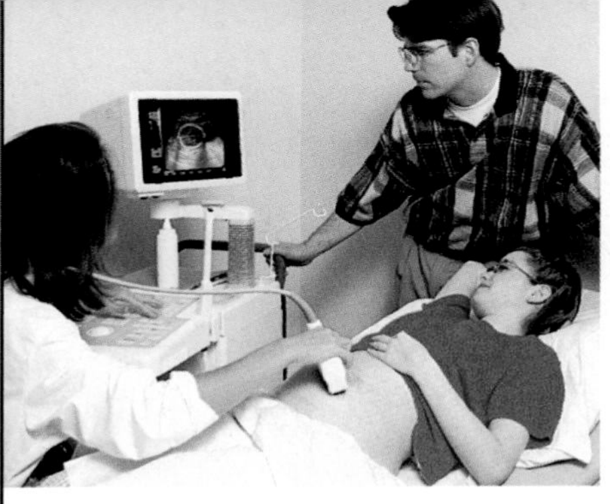

Figure 21
Ultrasonic waves are directed into a pregnant woman's uterus to form images of her fetus.
What benefits can fetal sonograms offer expectant parents?

Ultrasound Imaging Like X rays, ultrasound can be used to produce images of internal structures. A medical ultrasound technician directs the ultrasound waves toward a target area of a patient's body. The sound waves reflect off the targeted organs or tissues, and the reflected waves are used to produce electrical signals. A computer program converts these electrical signals into video images, called sonograms. Physicians trained to interpret sonograms can use them to detect a variety of medical problems.

Reading Check *How does ultrasound imaging use reflected waves?*

Medical professionals use ultrasound to examine many parts of the body, including the heart, liver, gallbladder, pancreas, spleen, kidneys, breast, and eye. Probably the best-known use of ultrasound in medicine is to monitor the development of a fetus in a pregnant woman's uterus, as shown in **Figure 21.** Ultrasound is better than X rays for producing images of soft tissue structures inside the body. However, it is not as good for examining bones and lungs, because hard tissues and air absorb the ultrasonic waves instead of reflecting them.

Math Skills Activity

Calculating Distance with Sonar

Example Problem

You send out a sonar pulse that is returned from a sunken pirate ship in 3 s. How far away is the ship? Hint: *the sonar pulse travels twice the distance from your ship to the sunken ship.*

1. *This is what you know:* speed of sound in water: $v = 1{,}439$ m/s; time: $t = 3$ s
2. *This is what you need to know:* distance: d
3. *This is the equation you need to use:* $d = vt/2$
4. *Substitute the known values:* $d = (1{,}439 \text{ m/s})\ (3 \text{ s}) / 2 = 2{,}158.5$ m

Check your answer by dividing the time and multipling by 2. Do you calculate the same speed of sound that was given?

Practice Problem

When the sonar pulse you emitted returns in 1 s when you are directly over the sunken treasure you were hoping to find. How far away is it?

For more help, refer to the Math Skill Handbook.

Science Journal

Ultrasound Ask students to write in their Science Journals the answer to the following question: **If ultrasound can be used to break up kidney stones, why won't it harm a developing fetus?** The intensity of the sound waves is much higher when ultrasound is used to break up kidney stones. L2 LS **Logical-Mathematical**

Resource Manager

Chapter Resources Booklet
Reinforcement, p. 28

378 CHAPTER 12 Sound

Figure 22
Ultrasonic waves can be used to break apart kidney stones.
What are the benefits of ultrasound therapy for kidney stones?

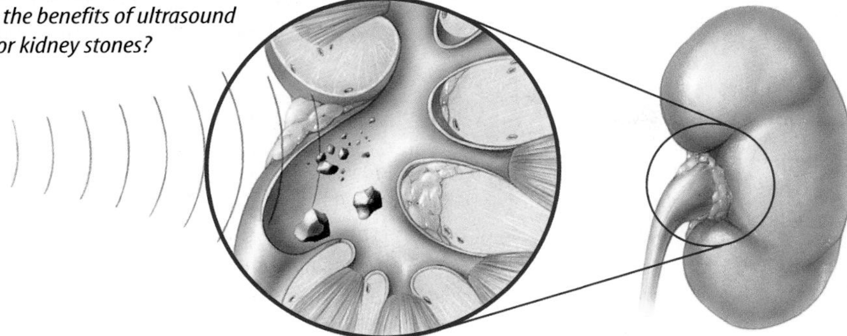

Treating with Ultrasound High-frequency sound waves can be used to treat certain medical problems. For example, sometimes small, hard deposits of calcium compounds or other minerals form in the kidneys, making kidney stones. In the past, physicians had to perform surgery to remove kidney stones. But now ultrasonic treatments are commonly used to break them up instead. Bursts of ultrasound create vibrations that cause the stones to break into small pieces, as shown in **Figure 22.** These fragments then pass out of the body with the urine. A similar treatment is available for gallstones. Patients who are treated successfully with ultrasound recover more quickly than those who have surgery.

Health INTEGRATION

Physicians can measure blood flow by studying the Doppler effect in ultrasonic waves. Brainstorm how the Doppler-shifted waves could help doctors diagnose diseases of the arteries and monitor their healing.

Section 4 Assessment

1. What are some differences between a gym and a concert hall that affect the amount of reverberation you hear in each place?
2. Explain how echolocation helps bats find food and avoid obstacles in the dark.
3. How can sound waves be used to find objects that are underwater?
4. Describe at least three uses of ultrasonic technology in medicine.
5. **Think Critically** How is sonar technology useful in locating deposits of oil and mineral resources?

Skill Builder Activities

6. **Drawing Conclusions** Imagine you are a physician looking at an ultrasound image and an X ray of the same area of a patient's body. A structure that you see on the X ray doesn't appear on the ultrasound image. What can you conclude about the structure? **For more help, refer to the** Science Skill Handbook.
7. **Solving One-Step Equations** Sound travels at about 1,500 m/s in water. How far will a sonar pulse travel in 45 s? **For more help, refer to the** Math Skill Handbook.

Caption Answer

Figure 22 avoiding surgery, faster recovery

Health INTEGRATION

Doctors measure the Doppler effect on ultrasonic waves directed toward the arteries and calculate the rate of blood flow. If blood flow slows down somewhere, there may be problems with the arteries at that point.

3 Assess

Reteach

Illustrate the effect of sound waves on solids by using an ultrasonic cleaner on various substances (jewelry, loosely cemented rocks, dirty or clogged glassware). L2
LS **Visual-Spatial**

Challenge

Have students prepare reports about how concert halls or the music rooms in the school are designed or furnished to provide good acoustics. L2 **LS** **Linguistic**

✔Assessment

Process Have students examine X rays and ultrasound photos of the same body parts and then compare and contrast the films by listing what they can see and identify. Ultrasounds show soft tissue structures better; X rays show bones better. Use **Performance Assessment in the Science Classroom,** p. 97.

Answers to Section Assessment

1. Possible answer: The shape of a concert hall might be designed to reduce reverberation, and it might have carpet and draperies to improve acoustics.
2. Bats emit sound pulses that bounce off prey or obstacles and return to the bat. From the echoes, the bat can determine information about the target, such as its size and velocity.
3. With sonar, a sound pulse is emitted toward the bottom of the ocean. The sound reflects off solid objects, and the reflected signal is detected by an underwater microphone. Using the speed of sound in water, information about the object can be determined.
4. Possible answers: producing sonograms of a developing fetus, breaking up kidney stones, breaking up gallstones
5. Possible answer: The speed of reflection differs depending upon the medium encountered. Knowing the speed for reflected oil or other features would allow explorers to locate them.
6. Possible answer: It might be hard tissue, such as bone, or lungs, because hard tissues and air absorb ultrasonic waves but appear on X rays.
7. 67,500 m

Activity

BENCH TESTED

Recognize the Problem

Purpose

Students will test various sound barriers for effectiveness. L2

LS **Auditory-Musical**

Process Skills

forming a hypothesis, predicting, testing a hypothesis, identifying and manipulating variables, collecting data, interpreting data

Time Required

2 weeks outside of class time

Materials

Many of these barriers are not normally located around a school. Students may need to be provided with a sound meter and a meterstick or metric tape to perform this lab outside of class.

Safety Precautions

Students should have some adult supervision when collecting their data.

Form a Hypothesis

Possible Hypothesis

Most students' hypotheses with reflect that thick concrete walls or thick stone walls are the best sound barriers and hanging laundry is the least effective.

Test Your Hypothesis

Possible Procedures

Students should identify sound barriers in their area. Students should choose a sound that will remain constant for each sound barrier tested such as a radio or CD player at a constant volume. At the location of the sound barrier, students should record the level of the sound using the sound meter at the same distance from the source to the meter both behind the sound barrier and bypassing the sound barrier. These conditions will provide a test with only one variable.

Activity — Design Your Own Experiment

Blocking Noise Pollution

What loud noises do you enjoy, and which ones do you find annoying? Most people enjoy a music concert performed by their favorite artist, booming displays of fireworks on the Fourth of July, and the roar of a crowd when their team scores a goal or touchdown. Although these are loud noises, people enjoy them for short periods of time. Most people find certain loud noises, such as traffic, sirens, and loud talking, annoying. Constant, annoying noises are called noise pollution. What can be done to reduce noise pollution? What types of barriers best block out loud noises?

Recognize the Problem

What types of barriers will best block out noise pollution?

Form a Hypothesis

Based on your experiences with loud noises, form a hypothesis about how effectively different types of barriers block out noise pollution.

Goals

- **Design** an experiment that tests the effectiveness of various types of barriers and materials for blocking out noise pollution.
- **Test** different types of materials and barriers to determine the best noise blockers.

Possible Materials

radio, CD player, horn, drum, or other loud noise source
shrubs, trees, concrete walls, brick walls, stone walls, wooden fences, parked cars, or hanging laundry
sound meter
meterstick or metric tape measure

380

Resource Manager 

Chapter Resources Booklet
Activity Worksheet, pp. 7–8

Test Hypothesis

Plan

1. **Decide** what type of barriers or materials you will test.
2. Describe exactly how you will use these materials.
3. **Identify** the controls and variables you will use in our experiment.
4. **List** the steps you will use and describe each step precisely.
5. **Prepare** a data table in your Science Journal to record your measurements.
6. **Organize** the steps of your experiment in logical order.

Do

1. Ask your teacher to examine your plan and data table before you start.
2. **Conduct** your experiment as planned.
3. **Test** each barrier two or three times.
4. **Record** your test results in your data table in your Science Journal.

Analyze Your Data

1. **Identify** the barriers that most effectively reduced noise pollution.
2. **Identify** the barriers that least effectively reduced noise pollution.
3. **Compare** the effective barriers and identify common characteristics that might explain why they reduced noise pollution.
4. **Compare** the natural barriers you tested with the artificial barriers. Which type of barrier best reduced noise pollution?
5. **Compare** the different types of materials the barriers were made of. Which type of material best reduced noise pollution?

Draw Conclusions

1. Did your results support your hypothesis?
2. **Predict** your results if you had used a louder source of noise such as a siren.
3. Use your results to infer how people living near a busy street could reduce noise pollution.
4. **Identify** major sources of noise pollution in or near your home. How could this be reduced?
5. **Research** how noise pollution can be unhealthy.

Communicating Your Data

Draw a poster illustrating how builders and landscapers could use certain materials to better insulate a home or office from excess noise pollution.

Teaching Strategy

Remind students that it is important for the sound barriers to be tested using the same distance from the sound source to the sound meter in each test.

Expected Outcome

Most results will show that thick concrete walls or thick stone walls are the best sound barriers.

Analyze Your Data

1. Answers may vary but may include concrete and stone walls
2. Answers will vary but may be similar to hanging laundry
3. The effective barriers are thick and dense structures.
4. Answers will vary
5. Answers will vary

Error Analysis

Have students compare their results and their hypotheses and explain why differences occurred.

Draw Conclusions

1. Answers will vary
2. The ranking of sound barriers will be the same.
3. People could build some type of sound barrier between the house and the street.
4. Answers will vary
5. Answers should include eardrum damage.

Assessment

Process Have students write up their procedures and their results for this activity in lab reports. Suggest they include diagrams or photographs of their set ups. Use **Performance Assessment in the Science Classroom,** p. 119.

Communicating Your Data

A gardening book from your local library will be helpful in choosing plants to use in the landscape design.

TIME SCIENCE AND Society

Content Background

Studies suggest that unwanted noise not only can contribute to hearing loss, but also can have other adverse affects on health. Unwanted sounds, even when they are not too loud can be a cause of stress, which can lead to digestive disorders, hypertension, abnormal sleep patterns, and a weakened immune system.

Children are at high risk for health problems due to noise pollution, particularly relating their ability to learn. Reports indicate that school performance is affected when children are exposed to high noise levels. The World Health Organization advises that in order to hear and be heard in a classroom, background noise levels should not exceed 35 dB and playground noise from the environment around the playground should not exceed 55 dB.

Studies also indicate that the intensity, frequency and duration of noise have an affect on the performance of children and adults in tasks at school and in the workplace. Noises that are unpredictable and random tend to distract people more than continuous noise. High frequency or high-pitched noises have similar affects on concentration. Poor performances on reading tests and aural problem solving have been linked to excess noise in the classroom.

It is believed that noise competes with other input channels of information.

TIME SCIENCE AND Society

SCIENCE ISSUES THAT AFFECT YOU!

TURNING UP THE VOLUME

NOISE POLLUTION AND HEARING LOSS

382

Resources for Teachers and Students

National Association of Noise Control Officials
53 Cubberly Rd.
Trenton, NJ 08690

Noise Control Association
104 Cresta Verde Dr.
Rolling Hills Est., CA 90274

Citizens Against Airport Pollution
P. O. Box 26142
San Jose, CA 95159
Contact: Lenora Porcella
Phone: 408-297-9753

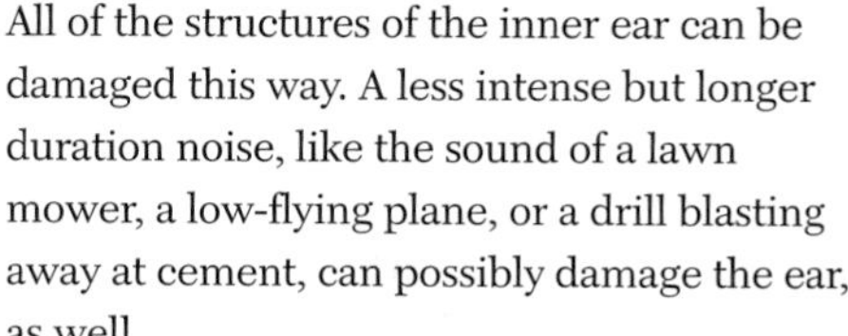

Now hear this: More than 28 million Americans have hearing loss. Six million more people have a condition called tinnitus (TIN uh tus), or ringing in the ears. In at least 10 million of the 28 million cases mentioned above, hearing loss could have been prevented, because it was caused by noise pollution.

People take their music very seriously in the United States. And a lot of people like it loud. So loud, in fact, that it can damage their hearing. The medical term is *auditory overstimulation.* You may have experienced a high-pitched ringing in your ears for days after standing too close to a loudspeaker at a concert. That's how hearing loss starts.

Music isn't the only cause of hearing loss caused by noise pollution. Other kinds of environmental noise can be strong enough to damage the ears, too. Intense, short-duration noise, like the sound of a gunshot or even a thunderclap, can cause some hearing loss. All of the structures of the inner ear can be damaged this way. A less intense but longer duration noise, like the sound of a lawn mower, a low-flying plane, or a drill blasting away at cement, can possibly damage the ear, as well.

All the Better to Hear You

There are 20,000 to 30,000 sensory receptors, or hair cells, located in the inner ear, or the cochlea. When vibrations reach these hair cells, electrical impulses are triggered.

The impulses send messages to the auditory center of the brain. But the human ear was not made to withstand all the very loud sounds of the modern world. Once hair cells are damaged, they don't grow back.

What can you do to avoid hearing damage? Well, the first thing is to turn the volume down on the stereo and TV. And keep the volume low when you've got your earphones on, no matter how tempting it is to blast it. Also, if you go to a rock concert, you can wear earplugs to muffle the sound. You'll still hear everything, but you won't damage your ears. And earplugs are now small enough that they're pretty much undetectable. So enjoy all that music and the street sounds of urban life, but mind your ears.

Did You Know?

Sounds may be measured in terms of their strength (amplitude) or bandwidth (frequency expressed in cycles per second or Hertz). The most often used measure of amplitude is the decibel, dB for short. Conversational speech is between 65 dB and 70 dB. A rock concert can measure up to 140 dB, which is considered beyond the threshold of pain for the ear.

CONNECTIONS Test Put on a blindfold and have a friend test your hearing. Have your friend choose several noise-making objects. (Not so loud, please, and make sure you have your teacher's permission.) Guess what object is making each sound.

SCIENCE *Online*
For more information, visit science.glencoe.com

Discussion

Ask students to sit as quietly as possible and listen to all the noises they hear. After several moments, ask students to name the noises they heard. Possible answer: other students moving, noises in the hall, the heating or electrical systems, traffic or other students outside. L1 LS **Auditory-Musical**

Activity

Tell students to formulate and write a noise pollution ordinance for the classroom or school. The ordinances should include acceptable decibel levels in the classroom and/or other areas of the school, such as the playground, gym, cafeteria and hallways. The ordinances should also propose ways that noise can be reduced in these areas and kept at prescribed levels. L3 LS **Logical-Mathematical**

Investigate the Issue

Tell students that sounds can be classified according to various features, such as pitch, loudness, and duration. Knowing these characteristics enables people to identify harmful noises. Tell students that pitch has to do with bass and treble sounds, loudness involves volume or intensity, and duration relates to length of time.

CONNECTIONS Debate Tell students to think about the three sound characteristics while they are blindfolded. Is the sound high-pitched or low pitched? Loud or soft? Long or short? Ask them whether the size of the object used to make the sound has an affect on its volume or intensity.

SCIENCE *Online*

Internet Addresses

____

____

____

Explore the Glencoe Science Web site at **science.glencoe.com** to find out more about topics in this section.

Chapter 12 Study Guide

Reviewing Main Ideas

Preview

Students can answer the questions in their Science Journals. Discuss the answers as you go through the chapter. LS **Linguistic**

Review

Students can write their answers, then compare them with those of other students. LS **Interpersonal**

Reteach

Students can look at the illustrations and describe details that support the main ideas of the chapter. LS **Visual-Spatial**

Answers to Chapter Review

Section 1

2. summer storm

Section 3

3. by the body of the cello, which acts as a resonator

Section 4

1. too much reverberation

Chapter 12 Study Guide

Reviewing Main Ideas

Section 1 The Nature of Sound

1. Sound is a compressional wave created by something that is vibrating.
2. Sound travels fastest through solids and slowest through gases. The speed of a sound wave also increases as the temperature of the medium increases. *Would the sound of thunder travel faster in a winter or summer storm?*

3. The human ear can be divided into three sections—the outer ear, the middle ear, and the inner ear. Each section plays a specific role in hearing.
4. Hearing involves four stages: gathering sound waves, amplifying them, converting them to nerve impulses, and interpreting the signals in the brain.

Section 2 Properties of Sound

1. Intensity is a measure of how much energy a wave carries. Humans interpret the intensity of sound waves as loudness.
2. The pitch of a sound becomes higher as the frequency increases.
3. The Doppler effect is a change in frequency that occurs when a source of sound is moving relative to a listener.

Section 3 Music

1. Music is made of sounds used deliberately in a regular pattern.
2. Instruments use a variety of methods to produce and amplify sound waves. *How is the sound produced by vibrating strings amplified by this cello?*

3. When sound waves overlap, they can increase or decrease in intensity or form beats.

Section 4 Using Sound

1. Acoustics is the study of sound. *Why would a gym be a poor place for a symphony concert?*

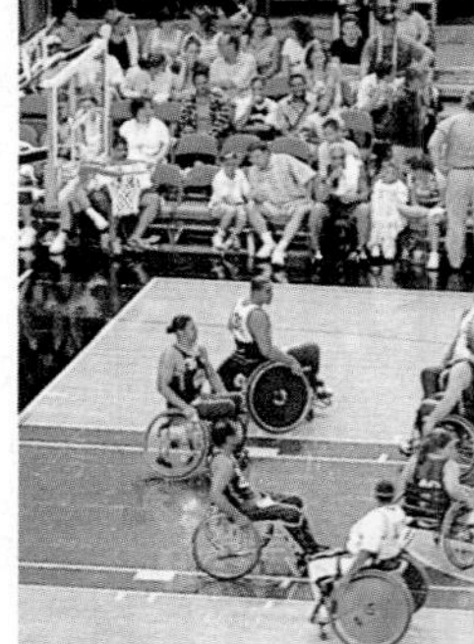

2. Some animals emit sounds and interpret the echoes to navigate and catch prey.
3. Sonar uses reflected sound waves to detect objects.
4. Ultrasound waves can be used for imaging body tissues or treating medical conditions.

FOLDABLES Reading & Study Skills — **After You Read**

Use the information on your Question Study Fold to help explain how the temperature of a solid, liquid, or gas affects how sound moves.

FOLDABLES Reading & Study Skills — **After You Read**

After students have read the chapter and completed the Foldable described in Before You Read, have them do the activity on the student page.

Dinah Zike

384 CHAPTER STUDY GUIDE

Chapter 12 Study Guide

Visualizing Main Ideas

Complete the following table on musical instruments.

Characteristics of Musical Instruments			
	Guitar	Flute	Bongo Drum
How Played	plucked	blown into	struck
Role of Resonator	amplifies sound	amplifies sound	amplifies sound
Type of Instrument	string	wind	percussion

Vocabulary Review

Vocabulary Words

a. acoustics
b. cochlea
c. decibel
d. Doppler effect
e. eardrum
f. echolocation
g. intensity
h. loudness
i. music
j. overtone
k. pitch
l. quality
m. resonator
n. sonar
o. ultrasonic

Study Tip

Take good notes, even during lab. Lab experiments reinforce key concepts, and looking back on these notes can help you better understand what happened and why.

Using Vocabulary

Each of the following sentences is false. Make the sentence true by replacing the underlined word with the correct vocabulary word.

1. The <u>eardrum</u> is filled with fluid and contains tiny hair cells that vibrate.
2. <u>Echolocation</u> is the study of sound.
3. A change in pitch or wave frequency due to a moving wave source is called <u>ultrasonic</u>.
4. <u>Overtone</u> is a combination of sounds and pitches that follows a specified pattern.
5. Differences among sounds of the same pitch and loudness are described as the <u>intensity</u> of sound.
6. <u>Decibel</u> is how humans perceive the intensity of sound.

Chapter 12 Study Guide

Visualizing Main Ideas

See student page.

Vocabulary Review

Using Vocabulary

1. cochlea
2. Acoustics
3. Doppler effect
4. Music
5. quality
6. Loudness

Chapter 12 Assessment

Checking Concepts

1. B
2. D
3. B
4. D
5. A
6. C
7. C
8. C
9. A
10. C

Thinking Critically

11. The train is moving away.
12. The whistle's frequency is outside the range of human hearing but inside the range of the dog's hearing. This means it's between 20,000 and 25,000 Hz.
13. Possible answer: The room would eliminate any sound reflections except those coming directly from the bat's food.
14. The windows resonate with the low-frequency sound waves from the jet engine.
15. The extra strings will resonate and add to the sound of the main strings.

Chapter 12 Assessment

Checking Concepts

Choose the word or phrase that best answers the question.

1. For a sound with a low pitch, what else is always low?
A) amplitude **C)** wavelength
B) frequency **D)** wave velocity

2. Sound intensity decreases when which of the following decreases?
A) wave velocity **C)** quality
B) wavelength **D)** amplitude

3. When specific pitches and sounds are put together in a pattern, what are they called?
A) overtones **C)** white noise
B) music **D)** resonance

4. Sound can travel through all but which of the following?
A) solids **C)** gases
B) liquids **D)** empty space

5. What is the term for variations in the loudness of sound caused by wave interference?
A) beats **C)** pitch
B) standing waves **D)** forced vibrations

6. What does the outer ear do to sound waves?
A) scatter them **C)** gather them
B) amplify them **D)** convert them

7. Which of the following occurs when a sound source moves away from you?
A) The sound's velocity decreases.
B) The sound's loudness increases.
C) The sound's pitch decreases.
D) The sound's frequency increases.

8. Sounds with the same pitch and loudness traveling in the same medium may differ in which of these properties?
A) frequency **C)** quality
B) amplitude **D)** wavelength

9. What part of a musical instrument amplifies sound waves?
A) resonator **C)** mallet
B) string **D)** finger hole

10. What is the name of the method used to find objects that are underwater?
A) sonogram **C)** sonar
B) ultrasonic bath **D)** percussion

Thinking Critically

11. A car comes to a railroad crossing. The driver hears a train's whistle and then hears the whistle's pitch become lower. What can be assumed about how the train is moving?

12. A whistle is blown and a dog responds, even though the person can't hear the whistle. Explain.

13. Acoustic scientists sometimes do research in rooms that absorb all sound waves. How could such a room be used to study how bats find their food?

14. Explain why windows might begin to rattle when an airplane flies overhead.

15. The Indian sitar has extra strings that are tuned to certain pitches but are never played by the musician. Explain why these strings might be present.

Developing Skills

16. Forming Hypotheses Sound travels slower in air at high altitudes than at low altitudes. State a hypothesis to explain this.

17. Identifying a Question Some people say that an ultrasound can harm a fetus. Write a list of questions to ask a doctor about the safety of ultrasound imaging.

Chapter Assessment Planner

Portfolio Encourage students to place in their portfolios one or two items of what they consider to be their best work. Examples include:
- Extension, p. 360
- Assessment, p. 368
- Assessment, p. 373

Performance Additional performance assessments, Performance Task Assessment Lists, and rubrics for evaluating these activities can be found in Glencoe's **Performance Assessment in the Science Classroom.**

18. **Making and Using Tables** You use a lawn mower with a sound level of 100 dB for your lawn-mowing business. Using the table below, determine how many hours a day you can safely work mowing lawns.

Federally Recommended Noise Exposure Limits

Sound Level (dB)	Time Permitted (hours per day)
90	8
95	4
100	2
105	1
110	0.5

19. **Communicating** Some people enjoy using snowmobiles. Others object to the noise that they make. Write a proposal for a policy that seems fair to both groups for the use of snowmobiles in a state park.

20. **Concept Mapping** Design a concept map that shows how the characteristics of sound waves are related. Include these terms: *pitch, compression, medium, speed, loudness, frequency,* and *intensity.*

Performance Assessment

21. **Project** Using materials you have at home, make a musical instrument. Give a demonstration to your class. Explain how you change the pitch of your instrument.

TECHNOLOGY

Go to the Glencoe Science Web site at **science.glencoe.com** or use the **Glencoe Science CD-ROM** for additional chapter assessment.

Test Practice

Lightning and thunder are always associated with each other, but they are very different things. You see lightning, but you hear thunder. Lightning is a large discharge of static electricity. The electrical energy in a lightning bolt ionizes atoms in the atmosphere and produces great amounts of heat. The heat causes air in the bolt's path to expand rapidly producing compressional waves you hear as thunder.

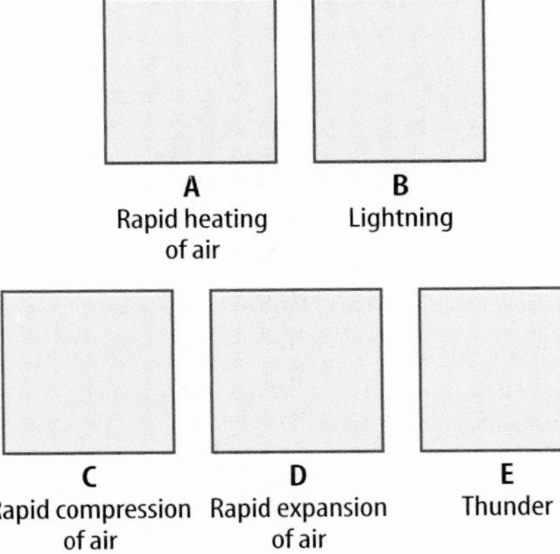

Study the picture and answer the following questions.

1. The different events lead to the creation of thunder. Which of the following shows the correct order of events?
   A) D, A, C, B, E
   B) B, A, D, C, E
   C) A, D, B, C, E
   D) C, A, D, B, E

2. Which of the events above is most closely accompanied by the creation of rarefactions?
   F) B
   G) A
   H) C
   J) E

Chapter 12 Assessment

Test Practice

The Test-Taking Tip was written by The Princeton Review, the nation's leader in test preparation.

1. B
2. H

Developing Skills

16. Air temperature is lower and air is less dense at high altitudes, so the particles do not transfer sound as quickly.
17. Possible questions: Will the fetus feel pain? How long will the fetus be exposed to the sound waves? Have any long-term studies been done on the effects of ultrasound on fetuses? What have they found?
18. 2 hours
19. Proposals might suggest limiting the use of snowmobiles to certain times of the day or to certain areas that are more isolated.
20. Check students' work.

Performance Assessment

21. Possible instruments include a narrow-mouthed bottle with varying amount of water, rubber bands on a box, or metal pans of different sizes. Use **Performance Assessment in the Science Classroom,** p. 117.

Assessment Resources

Reproducible Masters

Chapter Resources Booklet
Chapter Review, pp. 37–38
Chapter Tests, pp. 39–42
Assessment Transparency Activity, p. 51

Glencoe Science Web site
Interactive Tutor
Chapter Quizzess

Glencoe Technology
Assessment Transparency
Interactive CD-ROM Chapter Quizzes
ExamView Pro Test Bank
Vocabulary PuzzleMaker Software
MindJogger Videoquiz DVD/VHS

Section/Objectives	Standards		Activities/Features
	National	State/Local	
Chapter Opener	See p. 37T for a Key to Standards.		**Explore Activity:** Observe damage by ultraviolet waves, p. 389 **Before You Read,** p. 389
Section 1 What are electromagnetic waves? 1 session .5 block 1. **Explain** how vibrating changes produce electromagnetic waves. 2. **Describe** properties of electromagnetic waves	National Content Standards: UCP3, A2, B3 (5–8), B6 (9–12), E2, F5 (5–8), F6 (9–12)		**MiniLAB:** Investigating Electromagnetic Waves, p. 392 **Problem Solving Activity:** What is scientific notation?, p. 393
Section 2 The Electromagnetic Spectrum 2 session 1 block 1. **Compare** the various types of electromagnetic waves 2. **Identify** some useful and some harmful properties of electromagnetic waves	National Content Standards: UCP3, A2, B3 (5–8), B6 (9–12), E2, F1, F3, F5 (5–8), F6 (9–12)		**MiniLAB:** Heating Food with Microwaves, p. 397 **Health Integration,** p. 399 **Activity:** The Shape of Satellite Dishes, p. 402
Section 3 Radio Communication 3 session 1.5 blocks 1. **Explain** how modulating carrier waves makes radio transmissions. 2. **Distinguish** between AM and FM radio. 3. **Identify** various ways of communicating using radio waves.	National Content Standards: UCP3, A2, B3 (5–8), B6 (9–12), E2, F3, F5 (5–8), F5, F6 (9–12)		**Visualizing Radio Broadcasts,** p. 405 **Astronomy Integration,** p. 406 **Science Online,** p. 407 **Science Online,** p. 408 **Activity:** Radio Frequencies, pp. 410–411 **Science and Society:** Cell Phones, p. 412–413

Activity Materials	Reproducible Resources	Section Assessment	Technology
Explore Activity: red construction paper	**Chapter Resources Booklet** Foldables Worksheet, p. 17 Note-taking Worksheets, pp. 33–35	GLENCOE'S ASSESSMENT ADVANTAGE	
MiniLAB: television remote control, a glass, a book, paper, a metal pan	**Chapter Resources Booklet** Transparency Activity, p. 44 MiniLAB, p. 3 Enrichment, p. 30 Reinforcement, p. 27 Directed Reading, p. 20 **Performance Assessment in the Science Classroom,** p. 35 **Science Inquiry Labs,** p. 31	**Portfolio** Assessment, p. 395 **Performance** MiniLAB, p. 392 Problem-Solving Activity, p. 393 Skill Builder Activities, p. 395 **Content** Section Assessment, p. 395	Section Focus Transparency Interactive CD-ROM/DVD Guided Reading Audio Program
MiniLAB: 2 small beakers or baby food jars, 50 mL of dry sand, 20 mL of room-temperature water **Activity:** flashlight, several books, aluminum foil, small, parabolically shaped bowl	**Chapter Resources Booklet** Transparency Activity, p. 45 MiniLAB, p. 4 Enrichment, p. 31 Reinforcement, p. 28 Directed Reading, p. 21 Activity Worksheet, pp. 5–6 Lab Activity, pp. 9–12 Transparency Activity, pp. 47–48 **Reading and Writing Skill Acitivities,** p. 33	**Portfolio** Curriculum Connection, p. 400 Reteach, p. 401 **Performance** MiniLAB, p. 397 Skill Builder Activities, p. 401 **Content** Section Assessment, p. 401	Section Focus Transparency Teaching Transparency Interactive CD-ROM/DVD Guided Reading Audio Program
Need materials? Contact Science Kit at 1-800-828-7777 or www.sciencekit.com on the Internet.	**Chapter Resources Booklet** Transparency Activity, p. 46 Enrichment, p. 32 Reinforcement, p. 29 Directed Reading, pp. 21, 22 Activity Worksheet, pp. 7–8 Lab Activity, pp. 13–16 **Lab Management and Safety,** p. 37 **Earth Science Critical Thinking/Problem Solving,** p. 5	**Portfolio** Science Journal, p. 407 **Performance** Skill Builder Activities, p. 409 **Content** Section Assessment, p. 409	Section Focus Transparency Interactive CD-ROM/DVD Guided Reading Audio Program

End of Chapter Assessment

GLENCOE'S ASSESSMENT ADVANTAGE

Blackline Masters	Technology	Professional Series
Chapter Resources Booklet Chapter Review, pp. 37–38 Chapter Tests, pp. 39–42 **Standardized Test Practice by The Princeton Review,** pp. 56–59	MindJogger Videoquiz CD-ROM Explorations and Quizzes Vocabulary Puzzle Makers ExamView Pro Test Bank Interactive Lesson Planner Interactive Teacher's Edition	Performance Assessment in the Science Classroom (PASC)

Transparencies

Section Focus

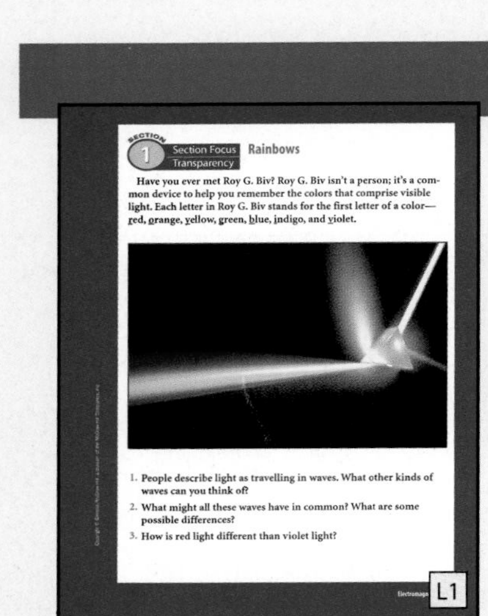
SECTION 1 Section Focus Transparency **Rainbows**

Have you ever met Roy G. Biv? Roy G. Biv isn't a person; it's a common device to help you remember the colors that comprise visible light. Each letter in Roy G. Biv stands for the first letter of a color—red, orange, yellow, green, blue, indigo, and violet.

1. People describe light as travelling in waves. What other kinds of waves can you think of?
2. What might all these waves have in common? What are some possible differences?
3. How is red light different than violet light?

L1

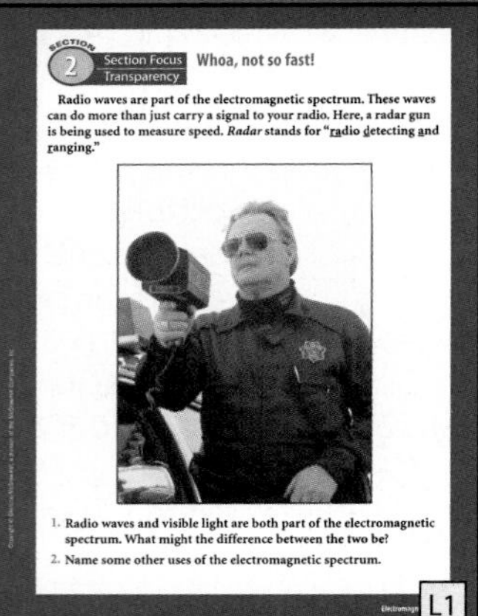
SECTION 2 Section Focus Transparency **Whoa, not so fast!**

Radio waves are part of the electromagnetic spectrum. These waves can do more than just carry a signal to your radio. Here, a radar gun is being used to measure speed. *Radar* stands for "radio detecting and ranging."

1. Radio waves and visible light are both part of the electromagnetic spectrum. What might the difference between the two be?
2. Name some other uses of the electromagnetic spectrum.

L1

SECTION 3 Section Focus Transparency **Could it be a growth spurt?**

A Global Positioning System (GPS) uses electromagnetic waves and satellites to determine locations and measurements on Earth. For example, one group of scientists found that Mount Everest is actually 8,850 m (29,035 feet) tall, 2.1 m higher than the figure accepted since 1954. This man is demonstrating another use of GPS. By connecting it to a computer, he is able to map his location.

1. Name some ways people might use GPSs.
2. How do people use satellites to communicate?
3. Could GPSs function with sound waves? Explain.

L1

This is a representation of key blackline masters available in the Teacher Classroom Resources. See Resource Manager boxes within the chapter for additional information.

Assessment

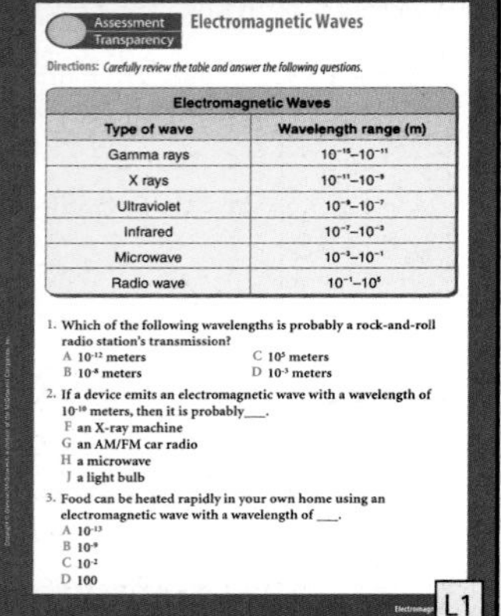
Assessment Transparency **Electromagnetic Waves**

Directions: *Carefully review the table and answer the following questions.*

Electromagnetic Waves	
Type of wave	Wavelength range (m)
Gamma rays	10^{-15}–10^{-11}
X rays	10^{-11}–10^{-8}
Ultraviolet	10^{-8}–10^{-7}
Infrared	10^{-7}–10^{-3}
Microwave	10^{-3}–10^{-1}
Radio wave	10^{-1}–10^{5}

1. Which of the following wavelengths is probably a rock-and-roll radio station's transmission?
   A 10^{-12} meters
   B 10^{-8} meters
   C 10^{5} meters
   D 10^{-3} meters
2. If a device emits an electromagnetic wave with a wavelength of 10^{-10} meters, then it is probably____.
   F an X-ray machine
   G an AM/FM car radio
   H a microwave
   J a light bulb
3. Food can be heated rapidly in your own home using an electromagnetic wave with a wavelength of ____.
   A 10^{-13}
   B 10^{-9}
   C 10^{-2}
   D 100

L1

Teaching

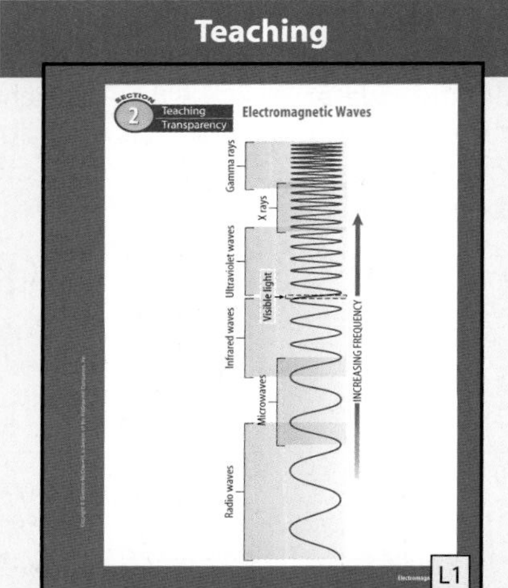
SECTION 2 Teaching Transparency **Electromagnetic Waves**

L1

Key to Teaching Strategies

The following designations will help you decide which activities are appropriate for your students.

- **L1** Level 1 activities should be appropriate for students with learning difficulties.
- **L2** Level 2 activities should be within the ability range of all students.
- **L3** Level 3 activities are designed for above-average students.
- **ELL** ELL activities should be within the ability range of English Language Learners.
- **COOP LEARN** Cooperative Learning activities are designed for small group work.
- **LS** Multiple Learning Styles logos are used throughout to indicate strategies that address different learning styles.
- **P** These strategies represent student products that can be placed into a best-work portfolio.

Hands-on Activities

Activity Worksheets

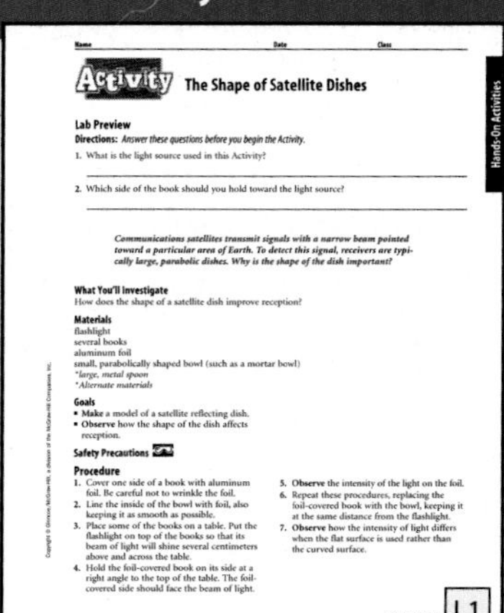
Name Date Class

Activity **The Shape of Satellite Dishes**

Hands-On Activities

Lab Preview

Directions: *Answer these questions before you begin the Activity.*

1. What is the light source used in this Activity?
2. Which side of the book should you hold toward the light source?

Communications satellites transmit signals with a narrow beam pointed toward a particular area of Earth. To detect this signal, receivers are typically large, parabolic dishes. Why is the shape of the dish important?

What You'll Investigate

How does the shape of a satellite dish improve reception?

Materials

flashlight
several books
aluminum foil
small, parabolically shaped bowl (such as a mortar bowl)
**large, metal spoon*
**Alternate materials*

Goals

- **Make** a model of a satellite reflecting dish.
- **Observe** how the shape of the dish affects reception.

Safety Precautions

Procedure

1. Cover one side of a book with aluminum foil. Be careful not to wrinkle the foil.
2. Line the inside of the bowl with foil, also keeping it as smooth as possible.
3. Place some of the books on a table. Put the flashlight on top of the books so that its beam of light will shine several centimeters above and across the table.
4. Hold the foil-covered book on its side at a right angle to the top of the table. The foil-covered side should face the beam of light.
5. **Observe** the intensity of the light on the foil.
6. Repeat these procedures, replacing the foil-covered book with the bowl, keeping it at the same distance from the flashlight.
7. **Observe** how the intensity of light differs when the flat surface is used rather than the curved surface.

L1

Laboratory Activities

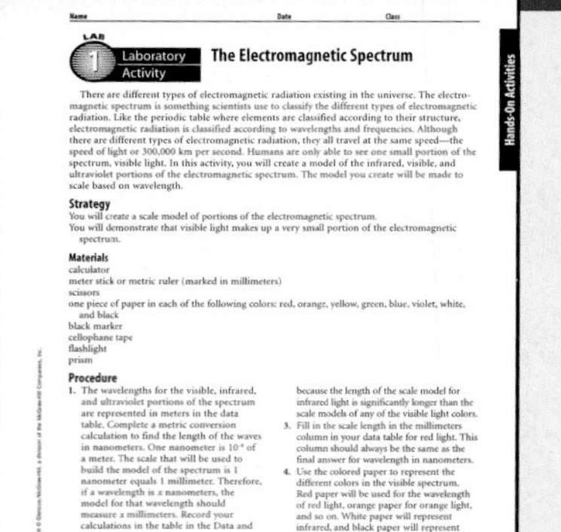
Name Date Class

LAB 1 Laboratory Activity **The Electromagnetic Spectrum**

Hands-On Activities

There are different types of electromagnetic radiation existing in the universe. The electromagnetic spectrum is something scientists use to classify the different types of electromagnetic radiation. Like the periodic table where elements are classified according to their structure, electromagnetic radiation is classified according to wavelengths and frequencies. Although there are different types of electromagnetic radiation, they all travel at the same speed—the speed of light or 300,000 km per second. Humans are only able to see one small portion of the spectrum, visible light. In this activity, you will create a model of the infrared, visible, and ultraviolet portions of the electromagnetic spectrum. The model you create will be made to scale based on wavelength.

Strategy

You will create a scale model of portions of the electromagnetic spectrum.
You will demonstrate that visible light makes up a very small portion of the electromagnetic spectrum.

Materials

calculator
meter stick or metric ruler (marked in millimeters)
scissors
one piece of paper in each of the following colors: red, orange, yellow, green, blue, violet, white, and black
black marker
cellophane tape
flashlight
prism

Procedure

1. The wavelengths for the visible, infrared, and ultraviolet portions of the spectrum are represented in meters in the data table. Complete a metric conversion calculation to find the length of the waves in nanometers. One nanometer is 10^{-9} of a meter. The scale that will be used to build the model of the spectrum is 1 nanometer equals 1 millimeter. Therefore, if a wavelength is x nanometers, the model for that wavelength should measure x millimeters. Record your calculations in the table in the Data and Observations section.
2. Work together as a class on the metric conversion calculation for red light. It is good to begin with red light rather than infrared, which is listed first in the data table, because the length of the scale model for infrared light is significantly longer than the scale models of any of the visible light colors.
3. Fill in the scale length in the millimeters column in your data table for red light. This column should always be the same as the final answer for wavelength in nanometers.
4. Use the colored paper to represent the different colors in the visible spectrum. Red paper will be used for the wavelength of red light, orange paper for orange light, and so on. White paper will represent infrared, and black paper will represent ultraviolet.
5. Cut a strip of red paper that is 2.5 cm wide and the same length as the number you have written in your column for scale length in millimeters.

L1

Meeting Different Ability Levels

Content Outline

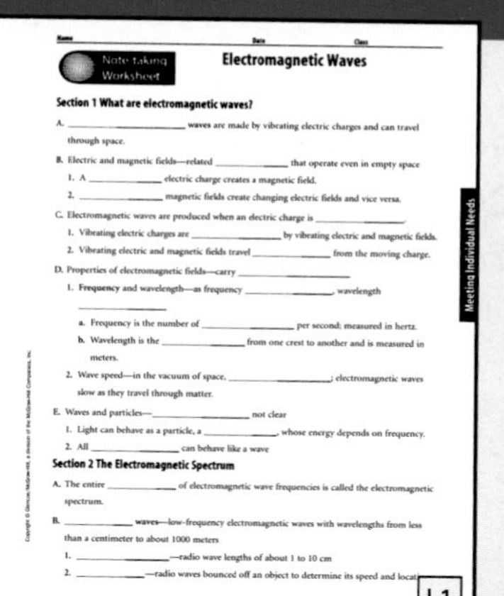

Note-taking Worksheet — Electromagnetic Waves

Section 1 What are electromagnetic waves?

Section 2 The Electromagnetic Spectrum

L1

Reinforcement

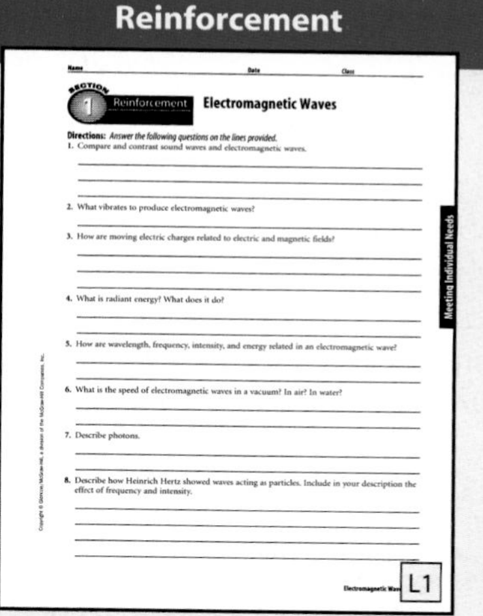

Section 1 Reinforcement — Electromagnetic Waves

Directions: Answer the following questions on the lines provided.

1. Compare and contrast sound waves and electromagnetic waves.
2. What vibrates to produce electromagnetic waves?
3. How are moving electric charges related to electric and magnetic fields?
4. What is radiant energy? What does it do?
5. How are wavelength, frequency, intensity, and energy related in an electromagnetic wave?
6. What is the speed of electromagnetic waves in a vacuum? In air? In water?
7. Describe photons.
8. Describe how Heinrich Hertz showed waves acting as particles. Include in your description the effect of frequency and intensity.

L1

Directed Reading

Content Mastery — Overview — Electromagnetic Waves

Directions: Complete the concept map using the terms in the list below.

radiant, matter, AM, FM, ultraviolet waves, X rays, cordless, cellular, radio waves

Directions: Answer the following questions on the lines provided.

10. Why are sound waves not electromagnetic waves?
11. What are two uses for electromagnetic waves?

L1

Assessment

Chapter Tests

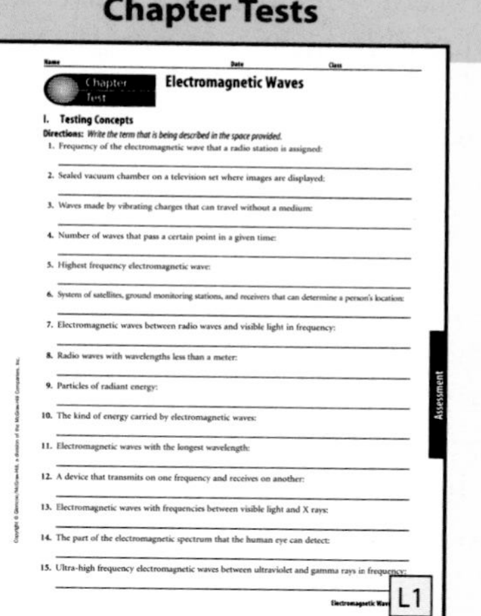

Chapter Test — Electromagnetic Waves

I. Testing Concepts

L1

Enrichment

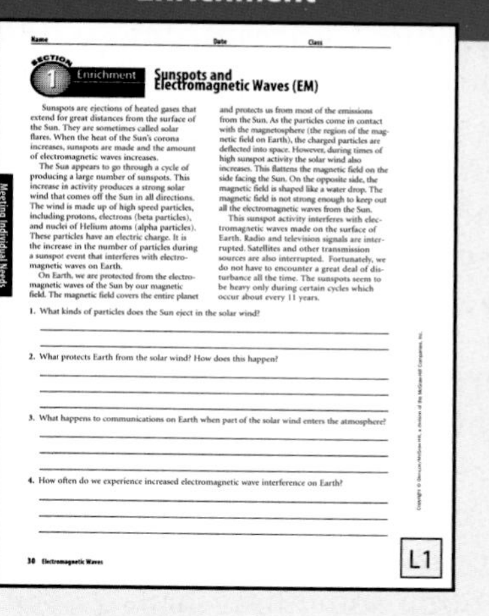

Section 1 Enrichment — Sunspots and Electromagnetic Waves (EM)

L1

Spanish Directed Reading

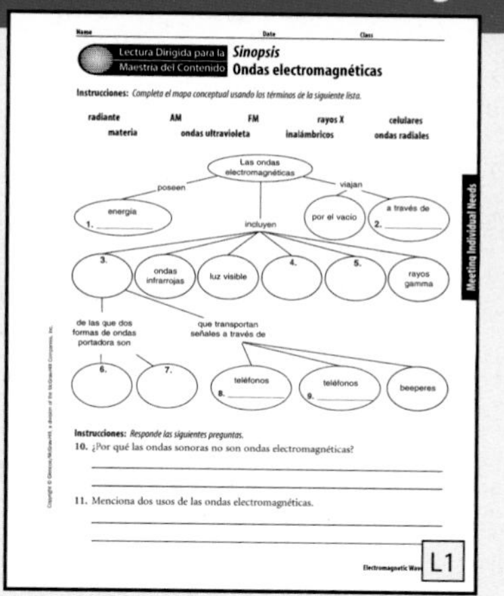

Lectura Dirigida para la Maestría del Contenido — Sinopsis — Ondas electromagnéticas

L1

Test Practice Workbook

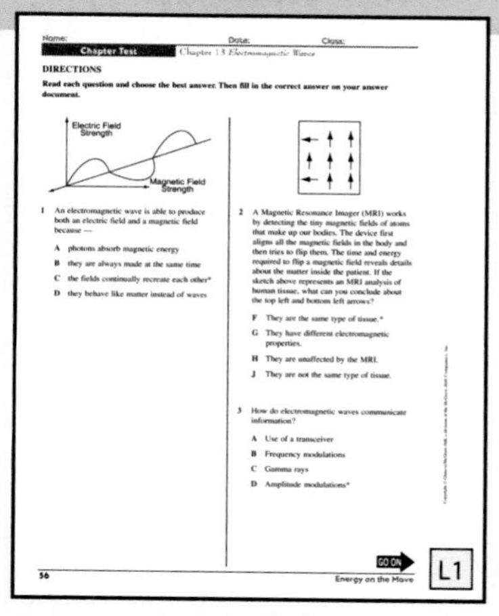

Chapter Test — Chapter 13 Electromagnetic Waves

L1

Chapter Review

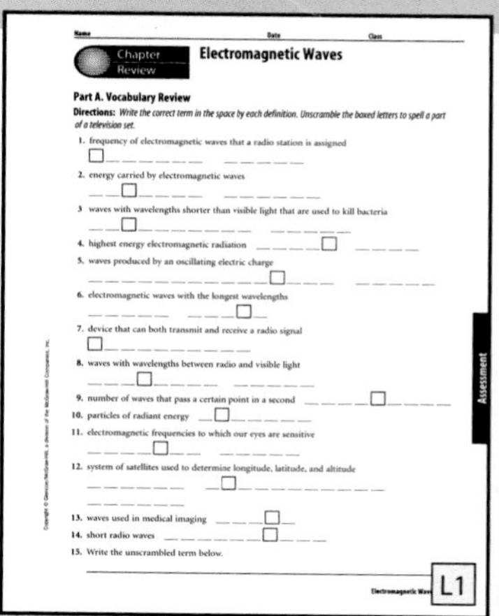

Chapter Review — Electromagnetic Waves

Part A. Vocabulary Review

L1

Science Content Background

SECTION 1

What are electromagnetic waves?

Waves in Space

Throughout history, people have learned about the universe from the visible light that we observe with our eyes. For the past 100 years, people have been able to detect other types of electromagnetic radiation as well. Technologies such as radio telescopes and ultraviolet detectors have made this possible. Some of these instruments, such as NASA's Extreme Ultraviolet Explorer, have been put into space as satellites so Earth's atmosphere does not absorb the radiation before the instrument can analyze it.

Fun Fact

While working with radar in the 1940s, Percy Spencer discovered that the candy in his pockets had melted. He also discovered that directing the radar toward popcorn caused the kernels to pop. From these observations, Spencer went on to develop the microwave oven.

Properties of Electromagnetic Waves

Period and frequency are different but related. The term period always refers to time; in this case, it is the time for one wave to pass a given point. Frequency is how often something happens in a given time. Thus for a wave, frequency is equal to the reciprocal of the period.

SECTION 2

The Electromagnetic Spectrum

Radio Waves

Why is there a metal grid in front of the microwave door? Microwaves can pass through glass but not through metal. The metal grid holes in the grid allow light waves to pass through, but not microwaves.

Infrared Waves

All warm objects emit infrared waves. The warmer an object, the more radiation it emits. Infrared waves are used in heat lamps at fast-food restaurants to keep food warm. The infrared rays used in remote controls are also called "near infrared," because they are near the wavelength of visible light.

Snakes in the pit viper family, which includes rattlesnakes, have "pits" in their heads that allow them to detect infrared radiation. They use this ability when hunting small, warm-blooded mammals in dark tunnels.

Ultraviolet Waves

Skin cells contain melanocytes, which form melanin when exposed to UV rays. Melanin causes people to have a tan, and it blocks some UV radiation. Some insects, such as bees, can see UV radiation.

X Rays and Gamma Rays

Radiation detectors use the tendency of X rays and gamma rays to ionize atoms as a means for detection. Workers who may be exposed to these types of radiation often wear radiation badges. After a few months the badgesm are developed to determine the total amount of radiation the worker has been exposed to.

SECTION 3

Radio Communication

Radio Transmission

Although Guglielmo Marconi was given credit for inventing radio, much of the credit should be given to Nikola Tesla. Tesla invented the means to turn electrical energy into radio waves.

Antennas are made of materials that are good conductors of electricity, so they allow easy movement of electrons. Electrons accelerating up and down a vertical antenna produce radio waves. If an antenna is aligned vertically, incoming radio waves cause the electrons to accelerate up and down the antenna. For a 1.5 million Hz AM radio wave, the electrons move up and down 1.5 million times per second.

AM radio has a relatively small frequency range of 3.2 Mhz, while FM has a range of 20 MHz. The AM band is quite fine for voices, but the FM band is better for listening to music because it produces a much richer sound.

On some nights you can pick up AM stations several hundred miles from where they are broadcast. This is because AM radio waves reflect off the ionosphere. FM radio waves need to travel in a straight line to reach a receiver. This limits their range.

Fun Fact

Although about 1,500 people died on board the ill-fated passenger ship *Titanic,* many think the loss of life would have been even greater if not for Marconi's wireless invention. Indeed, many of the 705 survivors of *Titanic* credited Marconi's invention with saving their lives. Marconi's wireless enabled operators on board the sinking ship to radio other ships for help.

For additional content background on this topic, go to the Glencoe Science Web site at science.glencoe.com.

David Parker/Photo Researchers, Inc.

Electromagnetic Waves

Chapter Vocabulary
electromagnetic waves
radiant energy
frequency
photon
radio wave
microwave
infrared wave
visible light
ultraviolet wave
X ray
gamma ray
carrier wave
cathode-ray tube
transceiver

What do you think?
Science Journal The person in this picture is an engineer climbing inside a microwave tower. Microwaves are a type of electromagnetic wave often used for communication.

CHAPTER 13

Electromagnetic Waves

What do cordless phones and microwave ovens have in common with the stars? Each emits electromagnetic waves. These waves also help your computer read a CD-ROM and they enable quick communication across the globe. The data and information explosion is made possible by manipulating electromagnetic waves. In this chapter, you will learn about the usefulness of the entire spectrum of electromagnetic waves.

What do you think?
Science Journal Look at the picture below with a classmate. Discuss what you think this is. Here's a hint: *Cell phones would be useless without them.* Write your answer or best guess in your Science Journal.

388

Theme Connection
Energy Electromagnetic waves carry energy. The electromagnetic spectrum ranges from low-energy radio waves to high-energy gamma rays. We often use low-energy radio waves for communication.

You often hear about the danger of too much exposure to the Sun's ultraviolet rays, which can damage the cells of your skin. When the exposure isn't too great, your cells can repair themselves, but too much exposure at one time can cause a painful sunburn. Repeated overexposure to the Sun over many years can damage cells and cause skin cancer. In the activity below, observe how energy carried by ultraviolet waves can cause changes in other materials.

Observe damage by ultraviolet waves

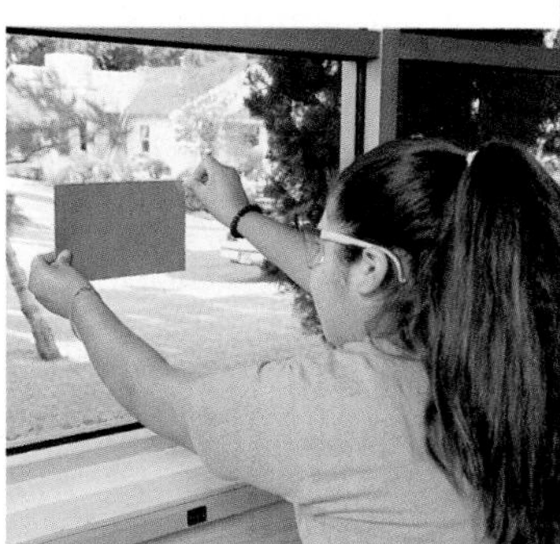

1. Cut a sheet of red construction paper in half.
2. Place one piece in direct sunlight. Place the other in a shaded location.
3. Keep the construction paper in full sunlight for at least 45 min. If possible, allow it to stay there for 3 h or more before taking it down.

Observe

In your Science Journal, describe any differences you notice in the two pieces of construction paper. Comment on your results.

Before You Read

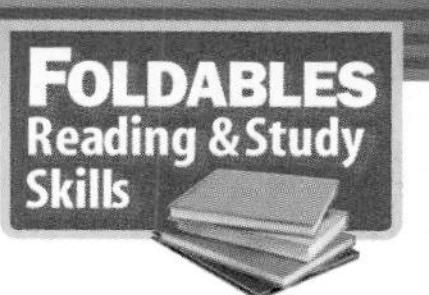

Making a Question Study Fold **Asking yourself questions helps you stay focused and better understand electromagnetic waves when you are reading the chapter.**

1. Place a sheet of paper in front of you so the long side is at the top. Fold the paper in half from the left side to the right side. Fold top to bottom and crease. Then unfold.
2. Through the top thickness of paper, cut along the middle fold line to form two tabs, as shown.
3. Write these questions on the tabs: *How do electromagnetic waves transfer energy with matter? How do electromagnetic waves transfer energy without matter?*
4. As you read the chapter, write answers to the questions under the tabs.

How do electromagnetic waves transfer energy with matter? | How do electromagnetic waves transfer energy without matter?

389

EXPLORE ACTIVITY

Purpose Use the Explore Activity to show students that electromagnetic waves from the Sun can affect things on Earth. L1 ELL IN **Visual-Spatial**

Materials Although any color of construction paper will work for this activity, red will show the most dramatic results. Be sure to use construction paper that has not previously been exposed to sunlight.

Teaching Strategy The construction paper should be exposed to sunlight for as long as possible. If time permits, allow students to observe the effects after different time intervals.

Observe

The color of the construction paper exposed to the Sun is faded compared to that of the paper left in the shade. Ultraviolet waves from the Sun have broken down some of the dye molecules.

✓Assessment

Process Ask students to compare how the ultraviolet waves affected the construction paper with what happens to their skin when they stay out too long in the Sun. Use **Performance Assessment in the Science Classroom,** p. 89.

Before You Read

FOLDABLES Reading & Study Skills

Dinah Zike Study Fold

Purpose Students make and use a Foldable to review what they know about the three most common states of matter before they read the chapter and to list examples and collect information as they read.

For additional help, see Foldables Worksheet, p. 17 in **Chapter Resources Booklet,** or go to the Glencoe Science Web site at **science.glencoe.com.** See After You Read in the Study Guide at the end of this chapter.

SECTION

What are electromagnetic waves?

1 Motivate

Bellringer Transparency

Display the Section Focus Transparency for Section 1. Use the accompanying Transparency Activity Master. L2 ELL

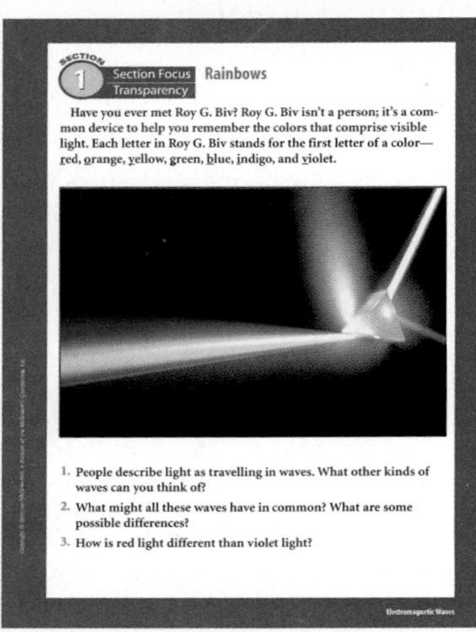

SECTION 1 Section Focus Transparency **Rainbows**

Have you ever met Roy G. Biv? Roy G. Biv isn't a person; it's a common device to help you remember the colors that comprise visible light. Each letter in Roy G. Biv stands for the first letter of a color—red, orange, yellow, green, blue, indigo, and violet.

1. People describe light as travelling in waves. What other kinds of waves can you think of?
2. What might all these waves have in common? What are some possible differences?
3. How is red light different than violet light?

Electromagnetic Waves

Tie to Prior Knowledge

Show students how a magnet pulls on a nearby paper clip, even if they are not touching. Remind students that this is because a magnetic field surrounds the magnet. Tell students that in this section they will learn about magnetic fields and electric fields, and how vibrating electric and magnetic fields create electromagnetic waves.

SECTION 1

What are electromagnetic waves?

As You Read

***What* You'll Learn**

- **Explain** how vibrating charges produce electromagnetic waves.
- **Describe** properties of elecromagnetic waves.

Vocabulary

electromagnetic wave
radiant energy
frequency
photon

***Why* It's Important**

Knowledge of electromagnetic waves helps you understand much of the technology around you.

Waves in Space

Stay calm. Do not panic. As you are reading this sentence, no matter where you are, you are surrounded by electromagnetic waves. Even though you can't feel them, some of these waves are traveling right through your body. They enable you to see. They make your skin feel warm. You use electromagnetic waves when you watch television, talk on a cordless phone, or prepare popcorn in a microwave oven.

Sound and Water Waves Waves are produced by something that vibrates, and they carry energy from one place to another. Look at the sound wave and the water wave in **Figure 1.** Both waves are moving through matter. The sound wave is moving through air and the water wave through water. These waves travel because energy is transferred from particle to particle. Without matter to transfer the energy, they cannot move.

Electromagnetic Waves However, electromagnetic waves do not require matter to transfer energy. **Electromagnetic waves** are made by vibrating electric charges and can travel through space where matter is not present. Instead of transferring energy from particle to particle, electromagnetic waves travel by transferring energy between vibrating electric and magnetic fields.

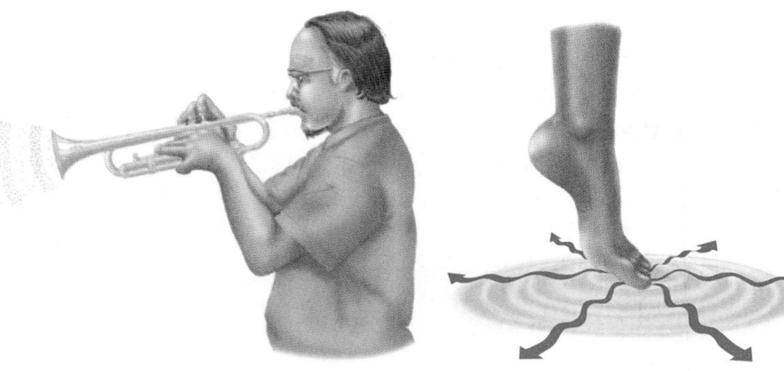

Figure 1
Water waves and sound waves require matter to move through. Energy is transferred from one particle to the next as the wave travels through the matter.

Section Assessment Planner

PORTFOLIO
Assessment, p. 395

PERFORMANCE ASSESSMENT
Try at Home MiniLAB, p. 392
Skill Builder Activities, p. 395
See page 416 for more options.

CONTENT ASSESSMENT
Section, p. 395
Challenge, p. 395
Chapter, pp. 416–417

390 CHAPTER 13 Electromagnetic Waves

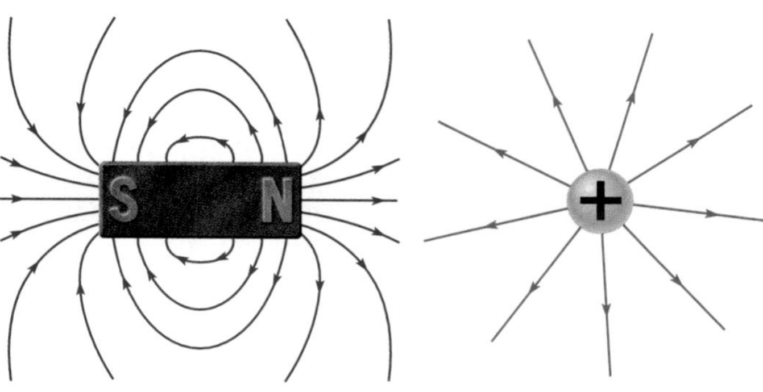

A A magnetic field surrounds all magnets.

B An electric field surrounds all charges.

Figure 2
Fields enable magnets and charges to exert forces at a distance. These fields extend throughout space. *How can you detect a magnetic field?*

Electric and Magnetic Fields

When you bring a magnet near a metal paper clip, the paper clip moves toward the magnet and sticks to it. The paper clip moved because the magnet exerted a force on it. The magnet exerted this force without having to touch the paper clip. The magnet exerts a force without touching the paper clip because all magnets are surrounded by a magnetic field, as shown in **Figure 2A.** Magnetic fields exist around magnets even if the space around the magnet contains no matter.

Just as magnets are surrounded by magnetic fields, electric charges are surrounded by electric fields, as shown in **Figure 2B.** An electric field enables charges to exert forces on each other even when they are far apart. Just as a magnetic field around a magnet can exist in empty space, an electric field exists around an electric charge even if the space around it contains no matter.

Magnetic Fields and Moving Charges In some ways, electricity and magnetism are related. An electric current flowing through a wire is surrounded by a magnetic field, as shown in **Figure 3.** An electric current is created by the movement of electrons in a wire. It is the motion of these electrons that creates the magnetic field around the wire. In fact, any moving electric charge is surrounded by a magnetic field, as well as an electric field.

Figure 3
Electrons moving in a wire are surrounded by a magnetic field. *How would you confirm that a magnetic field exists around a current-carrying wire?*

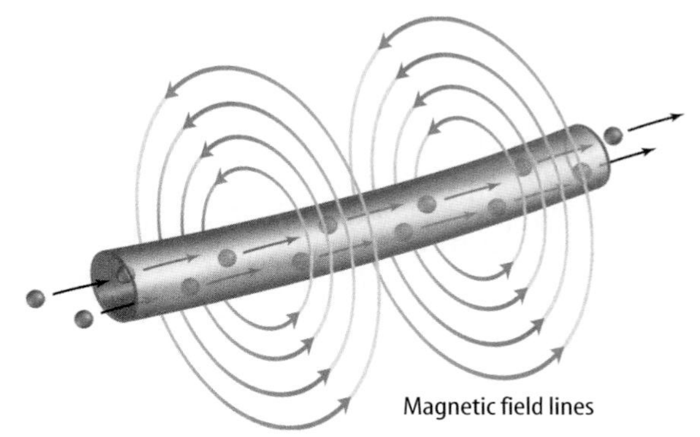

2 Teach

Waves in Space

Discussion

Ask students how they might prove that electromagnetic waves are all around them. Possible answer: Turn on a radio. L3
LS **Logical-Mathematical**

Electric and Magnetic Fields

Caption Answers

Figure 2 with iron-containing metal objects

Figure 3 with a compass

Quick Demo

Use iron filings and a bar magnet to remind students of how a magnetic field surrounds a magnet. Point out that the field drops off rapidly as the distance from the magnet increases. L2 LS **Visual-Spatial**

IDENTIFYING Misconceptions

Students know that an accelerating magnet can induce an electric current. Therefore, they may be confused by the statement that all electromagnetic waves are made by vibrating electric charges. However, magnetism is itself caused by moving charges. In magnetic materials, the electrons move in a way that induces a small magnetic field. These small fields combine to form the macroscopic field. Therefore, the electromagnetic fields caused by vibrating magnets are, in the end, caused by vibrating electric charges.

Resource Manager

Chapter Resources Booklet

Transparency Activity, p. 44
Directed Reading for Content Mastery, p. 20
Note-taking Worksheet, pp. 33–35

Teacher FYI

The fields of an electromagnetic wave are not equal. The electric field is much stronger than the magnetic field, so the electric field has a greater effect on matter.

Making Electromagnetic Waves

Purpose Students investigate the behavior of electromagnetic waves. L2 ELL
LS **Kinesthetic**

Materials television with remote control, glass, book, paper, metal pan

Teaching Strategy Suggest that students hold the objects both very close to the receiver and farther away from it. This will enable them to observe how the beam spreads out and can travel around objects.

Analysis

1. No, because the infrared beam spreads out as it leaves its source.
2. The signal only travels through transparent materials such as glass. However, if the materials are placed away from the receiver, the beam can sometimes travel around and still hit the receiver.

Assessment

Process Ask students to suggest a way they might be able to control the television without pointing the remote directly toward the receiver. Place a mirror so that the electromagnetic waves are reflected back toward the receiver. Use **Performance Assessment in the Science Classroom,** p. 93.

Investigating Electromagnetic Waves

Procedure

1. Point your **television remote control** in different directions and observe whether it will still control the **television.**
2. Place various materials in front of the infrared receiver on the television and observe whether the remote still will control the television. Some materials you might try are **glass, a book, your hand, paper,** and **a metal pan.**

Analysis

1. Was it necessary for the remote to be pointing exactly toward the receiver to control the television? Explain.
2. Did the remote continue to work when the various materials were placed between it and the receiver? Explain why or why not.

Changing Electric and Magnetic Fields The relationship between electricity and magnetism can explain the behavior of electric motors, generators, and transformers. This behavior is the result of the relationship between changing electric and magnetic fields. A changing magnetic field creates a changing electric field. The reverse is also true—a changing electric field creates a changing magnetic field.

Making Electromagnetic Waves

Waves such as sound waves are produced when something vibrates. Electromagnetic waves also are produced when something vibrates—an electric charge that moves back and forth.

Reading Check *What produces an electromagnetic wave?*

Vibrating Fields When an electric charge vibrates, the electric field around it vibrates. Because the electric charge is in motion, it also has a magnetic field around it. This magnetic field is changing as the charge moves back and forth. As a result, the vibrating electric charge is surrounded by vibrating electric and magnetic fields.

How do the vibrating electric and magnetic fields around the charge become a wave that travels through space? The changing electric field around the charge creates a changing magnetic field. This changing magnetic field then creates a changing electric field. This process continues, with the magnetic and electric fields continually creating each other. These vibrating electric and magnetic fields are perpendicular to each other and travel outward from the moving charge, as shown in **Figure 4.**

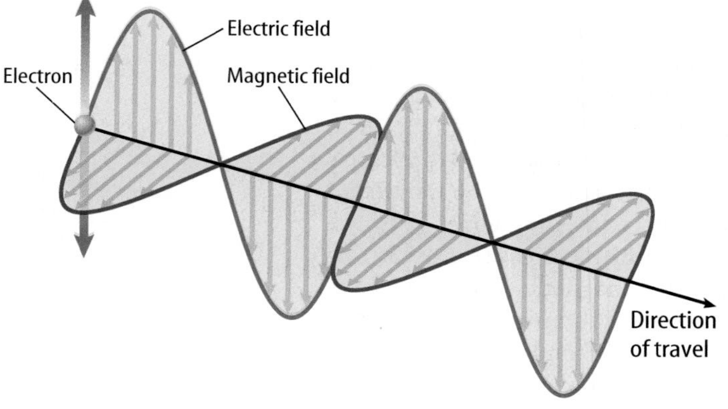

Figure 4
A vibrating electric charge creates an electromagnetic wave that travels outward in all directions from the charge. Only one direction is shown here.

Reading Check

Answer an electric charge moving back and forth

Visual Learning

Figure 4 The electromagnetic wave is shown in one direction to make it easier to visualize. In reality, a vibrating charge causes electromagnetic waves in all directions. An electromagnetic wave is aligned by the vibration of the charge that creates it. The wave shown here is vertically polarized: the electric field oscillates up and down and the magnetic field oscillates right and left. In a horizontal wave, the electric field oscillates right and left and the magnetic field oscillates up and down. Ask students to describe how the amplitude, frequency, and wavelength of the electric and magnetic fields are related. When the amplitude of the electric field is maximum, the amplitude of the magnetic field is minimum, and vice versa. The frequencies and wavelengths of the fields are the same.

Properties of Electromagnetic Waves

Electromagnetic waves travel outward from a vibrating charge in all directions. Recall that a wave transfers energy without transporting matter. How does an electromagnetic wave transfer energy? As an electromagnetic wave moves, its electric and magnetic fields encounter objects. These vibrating fields can exert forces on charged particles and magnetic materials, causing them to move. For example, electromagnetic waves from the Sun cause the charged particles in your skin to vibrate, which you feel as thermal energy, as shown in **Figure 5.** The energy carried by an electromagnetic wave is called **radiant energy.** Radiant energy makes a fire feel warm, and enables you to see.

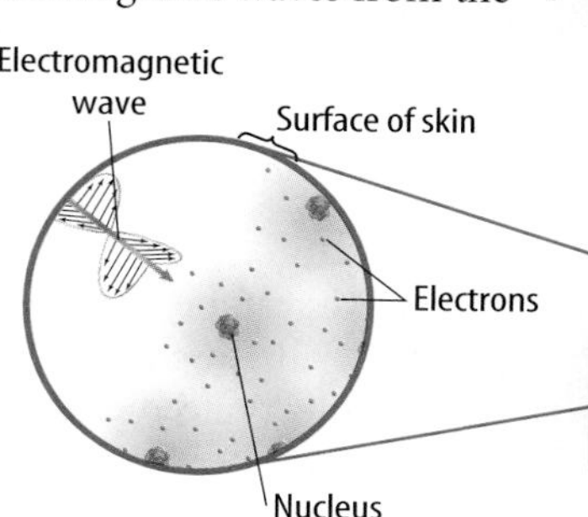

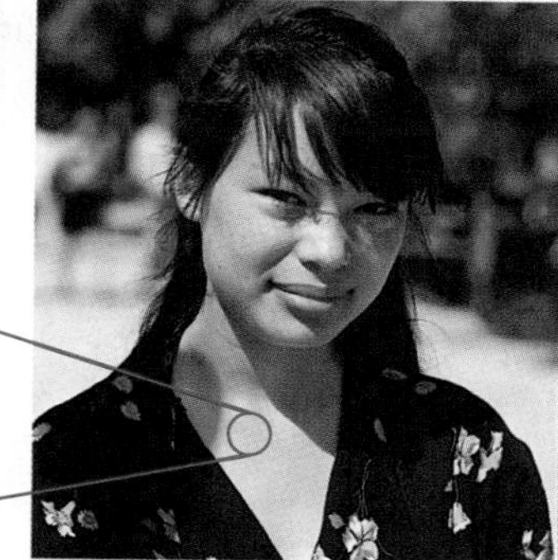

Figure 5
As an electromagnetic wave strikes your skin, electric charges in your skin gain energy from the vibrating electric and magnetic fields.

Problem-Solving Activity

What is scientific notation?

In science, numbers such as the speed of light (300,000,000 m/s) and the size of a gold atoms (0.000,000,000,144 m) are either too large or too small to use easily. By using scientific notation, numbers that are very large or very small can be written in a more compact way. For example, in scientific notation the speed of light is 3.00×10^8 m/s and the size of a gold atom is 1.44×10^{-10} m. Scientific notations follows the form $M \times 10^n$. M is a number with only one number to the left of the decimal point. The number of places the decimal point was moved is represented by n. If the original number is greater than 1, n is positive. If the original number is less than 1, n is negative.

Example Problem

Put the numbers 2,000 and 0.003 into scientific notation.

Solution

1. *For the number 2000, move the decimal point 3 places to the left.*
2. *Because you moved the decimal point 3 places and the number is greater than 1, n equals 3. In scientific notation the number is* 2×10^3.
3. *For the number 0.003, move the decimal point 3 places to the right.*
4. *Because you moved the decimal point 3 places and the number is less than 1, n equals −3. In scientific notation the number is* 3×10^{-3}

Practice Problems

1. Put the following numbers into scientific notation:
   40; 7,000; 100,000.
2. Put the following numbers into scientific notation:
   0.09; 0.000,6; 0.000,005.

Properties of Electromagnetic Waves

Quick Demo

Draw a transverse wave and a longitudinal wave on the board. Tell students that transverse waves oscillate in a direction perpendicular to the direction in which the wave propagates. Longitudinal waves oscillate in the same direction as that in which the wave propagates. Ask students whether electromagnetic waves are transverse waves or longitudinal waves. transverse waves L3 LS **Visual-Spatial**

Problem-Solving Activity

Answers

1. $40 = 4.0 \times 10^1$; $7{,}000 = 7.0 \times 10^3$; $100{,}000 = 1.0 \times 10^5$
2. $0.09 = 9 \times 10^{-2}$; $0.000{,}6 = 6 \times 10^{-4}$; $0.000{,}005 = 5 \times 10^{-6}$

Science Journal

Radiant Energy Warm objects emit more radiant energy than cool objects do. Have students investigate this topic and each write a paragraph summarizing what he/she learns. As an object's temperature increases, the kinetic energy of its atoms increases. The vibrating electrons produce electromagnetic waves. Increasing temperature produces more electromagnetic waves, and these waves have more energy and shorter wavelengths. L3 LS **Logical-Mathematical**

Resource Manager

Chapter Resources Booklet
Enrichment, p. 30
MiniLAB, p. 3
Mathematics Skill Activities, p. 1

Properites of Electromagnetic Waves, continued

Activity

To help students understand how frequency and wavelength are related, have one student draw a series of waves across the board, end to end, each having a similar wavelength. Have another student draw a series of waves with a much longer wavelength below the first set. The drawings should demonstrate that over the same distance, there are more waves with shorter wavelengths and fewer waves with longer wavelengths. L2 LS **Visual-Spatial**

Teacher FYI

There is a rich scientific history leading to the idea that light has both particle and wave nature. In the fifth century B.C., Socrates and Plato thought streams of light were emitted by the eye. Newton formed a particle theory of light in the early eighteenth century, around the same time Huygens concluded that light was a wave. In 1905, Einstein proposed that electromagnetic waves can also behave as particles.

Reading Check

Answer travel through matter or empty space; vary in frequency, wavelength, and speed

Caption Answer

Figure 6 Yes, by varying the number of waves in a given distance

Table 1 Speed of Visible Light

Material	Speed (km/s)
Vacuum	300,000
Air	slightly less than 300,000
Water	226,000
Glass	200,000
Diamond	124,000

Wave Speed Electromagnetic waves travel through space, which is empty, as well as through various materials—and they travel fast. In the time it takes you to blink your eyes, an electromagnetic wave can travel around the entire Earth. All electromagnetic waves travel at 300,000 km/s in the vacuum of space. Because light is an electromagnetic wave, the speed of electromagnetic waves in space is usually called the "speed of light." However, when electromagnetic waves travel through matter, they slow down. The speed of the wave depends upon the material they travel through. Electromagnetic waves usually travel the slowest in solids and the fastest in gases. **Table 1** lists the speed of visible light in various materials.

Frequency and Wavelength Like all waves, electromagnetic waves can be described by their frequency and their wavelength. A vibrating charge produces an electromagnetic wave. A charge can vibrate at different speeds, or frequencies. **Frequency** is the number of vibrations that occur in 1 s. Frequency is measured in hertz. One Hz is one vibration each second. For example, if you clap your hands four times each second, then you are clapping at a frequency of 4 Hz.

The wavelength of an electromagnetic wave, is the distance from one crest to another, as shown in **Figure 6.** Wavelength is measured in meters. The frequency and wavelength of electromagnetic waves are related. As the frequency of the wave increases, the wavelength becomes smaller.

Reading Check *Name some properties of electromagnetic waves.*

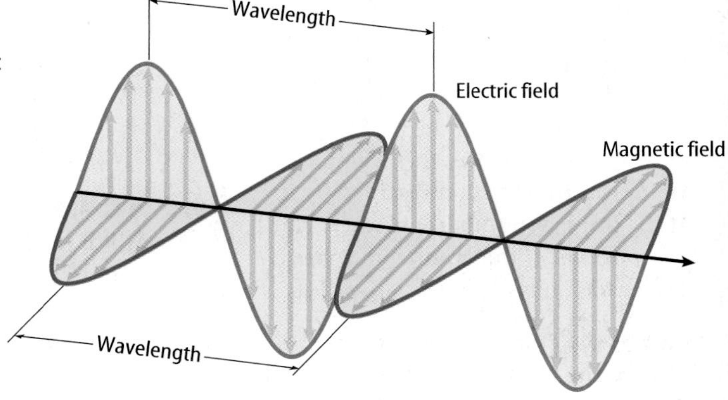

Figure 6
The wavelength of an electromagnetic wave is the distance from one crest to the next one. *Can frequency be represented on this diagram?*

394 CHAPTER 13 Electromagnetic Waves

Active Reading

Metacognition Journal In this strategy, each student analyzes his or her own thought processes. Have students divide the paper in half. On the left, have them record what they have learned about a topic. On the right, have them record the reason they learned it. Have students write a Metacognition Journal about electromagnetic waves.

Resource Manager 

Chapter Resources Booklet
Reinforcement, p. 27
Science Inquiry Labs, p. 31

Performance Assessment in the Science Classroom, p. 35

Waves and Particles

The difference between a wave and a particle might seem obvious—a wave is a disturbance that carries energy, and a particle is a piece of matter that carries energy. However, in reality the difference is not so clear.

Waves as Particles In 1887, Heinrich Hertz found that by shining light on a metal, electrons were ejected from the metal. Hertz found that whether or not electrons were ejected depended on the frequency of the light and not the amplitude. Because the energy carried by a wave depends on its amplitude and not its frequency, this result was mysterious. Years later, Albert Einstein provided an explanation—light can behave as a particle, called a **photon,** whose energy depends on the frequency.

Particles as Waves Because light could behave as a particle, others wondered whether matter could behave as a wave. If a beam of electrons were sprayed at two tiny slits, you might expect that the electrons would strike only the area behind the slits, like the spray paint in **Figure 7A.** Instead, it was found that the electrons formed an interference pattern, as shown in **Figure 7B.** This type of pattern is produced by waves when they pass through two slits and interfere with each other, as the water waves do in **Figure 7C.** This experiment showed that electrons can behave like waves. It is now known that all particles, not only electrons, can behave as a wave.

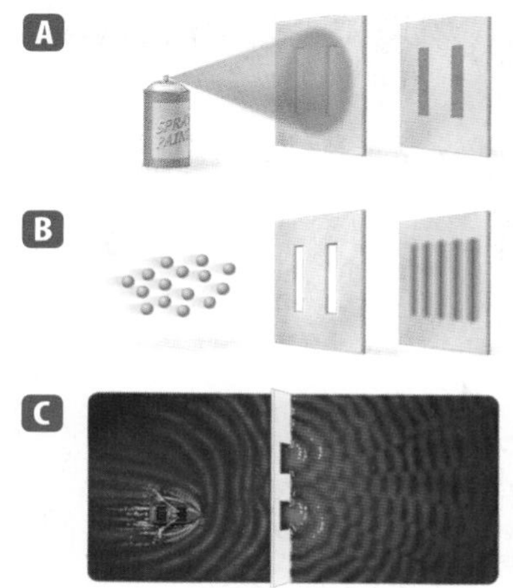

Figure 7
When electrons are sent through two narrow slits, they behave as a wave. A Particles of paint sprayed through two slits coat only the area behind the slits. B Electrons fired at two closely-spaced openings don't strike only the area behind the slits. Instead they form wave-like interference pattern. C Water waves produce interference pattern after passing through two openings.

Section 1 Assessment

1. What produces electromagnetic waves?
2. How is an electromagnetic wave similar to the wave created when a pebble is dropped into a pond?
3. What is the relationship between the frequency and wavelength of electromagnetic waves?
4. **Think Critically** Is it possible to have just an electric-field wave or just a magnetic-field wave? Explain.

Skill Builder Activities

5. **Testing a Hypothesis** Hypothesize that light behaves like water waves. Design an experiment to test your hypothesis. **For more help, refer to the Science Skill Handbook.**
6. **Solving One-Step Equations** When light travels in ethyl alcohol, its speed is about three-fourths its speed in air. What is the speed of light in ethyl alcohol in km/s? **For more help, refer to the Math Skill Handbook.**

Answers to Section Assessment

1. vibrating electric charges
2. Both travel away from the source and are constantly and repeatedly changing from high to low.
3. As the frequency of an electromagnetic wave increases, its wavelength decreases.
4. No; the vibrating electric field will always create a magnetic field, and the vibrating magnetic field will always create an electric field.
5. Possible answer: Design an apparatus to test interference between light waves.
6. $300{,}000 \text{ km/s} \times 0.75 = 225{,}000 \text{ km/s}$

3 Assess

Reteach

Radio waves are long-wavelength, low-frequency electromagnetic waves, and gamma rays are short-wavelength, high-frequency waves. Have students model the relationship between wavelength and frequency of waves by vertically shaking a rope attached to a door handle. First, they can shake it with low frequency to see long wavelengths, then with higher frequency to see shorter wavelengths. L2 ELL LS **Kinesthetic**

Challenge

The idea that electromagnetic waves sometimes behave as waves and sometimes as particles is often confusing to students. Have them form small groups to discuss this concept and then describe it in their own words. L2 LS **Linguistic**

Assessment

Portfolio Have students write several paragraphs that describe how electric and magnetic fields together form electromagnetic waves, and how these waves vary in frequency, wavelength, and speed. Use **Performance Assessment in the Science Classroom,** p. 159. P

SECTION

The Electromagnetic Spectrum

1 Motivate

Bellringer Transparency

Display the Section Focus Transparency for Section 2. Use the accompanying Transparency Activity Master. L2 ELL

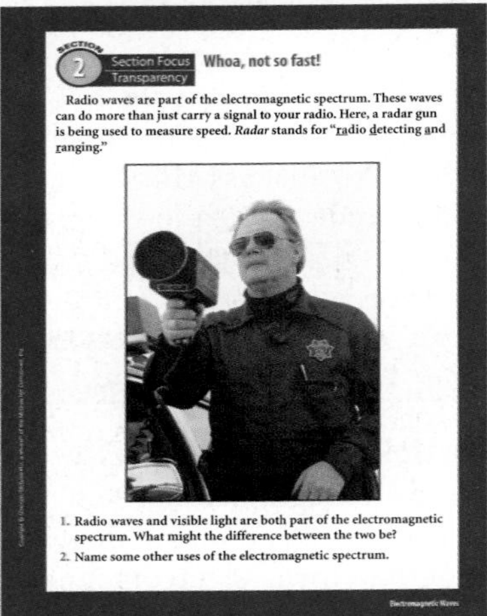

SECTION 2 Section Focus Transparency **Whoa, not so fast!**

Radio waves are part of the electromagnetic spectrum. These waves can do more than just carry a signal to your radio. Here, a radar gun is being used to measure speed. *Radar* stands for "radio detecting and ranging."

1. Radio waves and visible light are both part of the electromagnetic spectrum. What might the difference between the two be?
2. Name some other uses of the electromagnetic spectrum.

Electromagnetic Waves

Tie to Prior Knowledge

Ask students if they have ever had an X-ray image taken by an X-ray technician. X rays are one form of electromagnetic waves that they will be studying in this section.

SECTION

The Electromagnetic Spectrum

As You Read

***What* You'll Learn**

- **Compare** the various types of electromagnetic waves.
- **Identify** some useful and some harmful properties of electromagnetic waves.

Vocabulary

radio wave
microwave
infrared wave
visible light
ultraviolet wave
X ray
gamma ray

***Why* It's Important**

Different types of electromagnetic waves can be usesd in different ways.

A Range of Frequencies

Electromagnetic waves can have a wide variety of frequencies. They might vibrate once each second or have trillions of vibrations each second. The entire range of electromagnetic wave frequencies is known as the electromagnetic spectrum (SPEK trum), shown in **Figure 8.** Various portions of the electromagnetic spectrum interact with matter differently. As a result, they are given different names. The electromagnetic waves that humans can detect with their eyes, called visible light, is a small portion of the entire electromagnetic spectrum. However, devices have been built to detect the other frequencies. For example, the antenna of your radio detects radio waves.

Radio Waves

Stop reading for a moment and look around you. Everywhere you look, **radio waves** are flowing. You can't see or hear them, but they are there. Radio waves carry the signal from a radio station to your radio. It might seem that radio waves should be the same as sound waves. However, sound waves are compressions and expansions of groups of molecules, while radio waves shake electrons, not molecules of air. Therefore, you can't hear radio waves. You can hear sound waves because molecules bump against your eardrums.

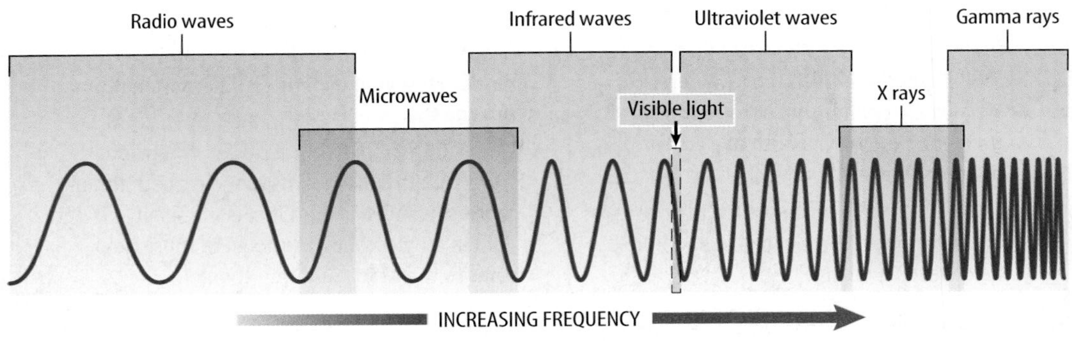

Figure 8
Electromagnetic waves are described by different names depending on their frequency and wavelength.

Section Assessment Planner

Portfolio
Curriculum Connection, p. 400
Reteach, p. 401

Performance Assessment
MiniLAB, p. 397
Skill Building Activities, p. 401
See page 416 for more options.

Content Assessment
Section, p. 401
Challenge, p. 401
Chapter, pp. 416–417

396 CHAPTER 13 Electromagnetic Waves

Figure 9
Microwave ovens use electromagnetic waves to heat food.

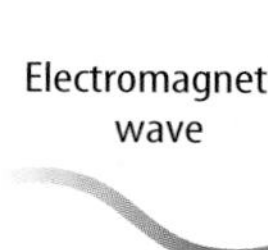

A Normally water molecules are randomly arranged.

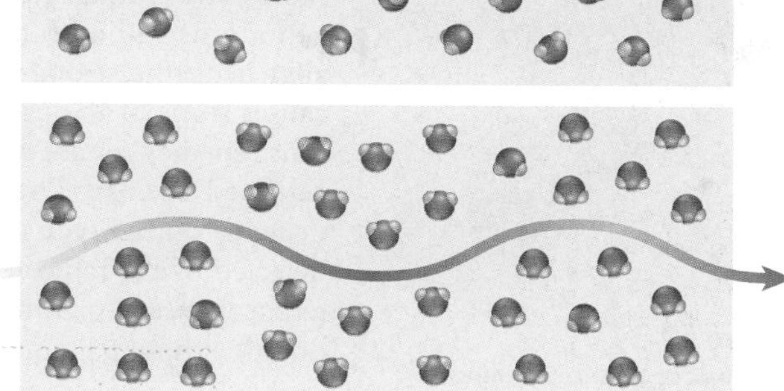

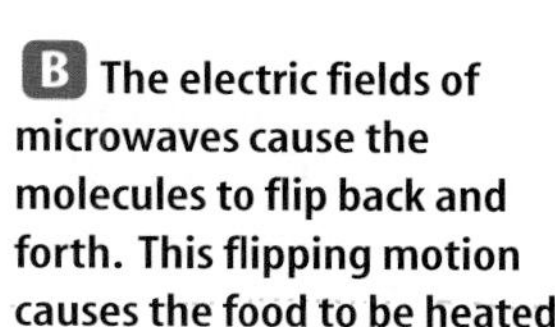

B The electric fields of microwaves cause the molecules to flip back and forth. This flipping motion causes the food to be heated.

Microwaves Radio waves are low-frequency electromagnetic waves with wavelengths from less than 1 cm to about 1,000 m. Radio waves with wavelengths of less than 1 m are called **microwaves**. Microwaves with wavelengths of about 1 cm to 10 cm are widely used for communication, such as for cellular telephones and satellite signals. You are probably most familiar with microwaves because of their use in microwave ovens.

Reading Check *What is the difference between a microwave and a radio wave?*

Microwave ovens heat food when microwaves interact with water molecules in food, as shown in **Figure 9.** Each water molecule is positively charged on one side and negatively charged on the other side. The vibrating electric field in microwaves causes water molecules in food to flip direction billions of times each second. This motion causes the molecules to bump one another. Bumping causes friction between the molecules, changing the microwave's radiant energy into thermal energy. It is the thermal energy that cooks your food.

Radar Another use for radio waves is to find the position and movement of objects by a method called radar. Radar stands for **RA**dio **D**etecting **A**nd **R**anging. With radar, radio waves are transmitted toward an object. By measuring the time required for the waves to bounce off the object and return to a receiving antenna, the speed and location of the object can be found. Law enforcement officers use radar to measure how fast a vehicle is moving. Radar also is used for tracking the movement of aircraft, watercraft, and spacecraft.

Mini LAB

Heating Food with Microwaves

Procedure

1. Obtain two small **beakers or baby food jars.** Place 50 mL of **dry sand** into each. In one of the jars, add 20 mL of **room-temperature water** and stir well.
2. Record the temperature of the sand in each jar.
3. One at a time, **microwave** the jars of sand for 10 s and immediately record the temperature again.

Analysis

1. Compare the initial and final temperatures of the wet and dry sand.
2. Infer why there was a difference.

2 Teach

A Range of Frequencies

Make a Model

Have students use a pan of water to model how altering the frequency of a vibrating object in the water creates waves with different frequencies. L1 ELL LS **Kinesthetic**

Radio Waves

Mini LAB

Purpose students observe how microwave ovens heat food L2 ELL LS **Kinesthetic**

Materials microwave oven, two small beakers or baby food jars, dry sand, water, thermometer

Safety Precautions Be sure students do not overheat the sand.

Analysis

1. Wet sand becomes much hotter than dry sand.
2. The microwaves interact with the water molecules in the wet sand, increasing their kinetic energy. The water molecules transfer some of this energy to the surrounding sand.

Assessment

Process Ask students to infer why the inside of a microwave oven doesn't get hot. It is made of materials that don't interact with microwaves. Use **PASC,** p. 89.

Reading Check

Answer Microwaves are radio waves with wavelengths of less than a meter.

Resource Manager

Chapter Resources Booklet

Transparency Activity, p. 45
Directed Reading for Content Mastery, p. 21
MiniLAB, p. 4

Visual Learning

Figure 9 Point out to students that water molecules are polar. The side with the hydrogen atoms has a slightly positive charge and the side with the oxygen atoms has a slightly negative charge. Because of this polarity, the molecules tend to align themselves with an electric field. The changing electric field in microwaves causes the water molecules to rotate. L2 LS **Visual-Spatial**

Infrared Waves

Teacher FYI

Various celestial objects, including planets, stars, nebulae, and galaxies, give off infrared radiation. The Infrared Astronomical Satellite (IRAS), equipped with an infrared telescope sensitive to wavelengths of 8 to 100 micrometers, was launched in January 1983 to study space objects. IRAS discovered clouds of solid debris around Vega, Fomalhaut, and several other stars. Scientists hypothesize these clouds may indicate the formation of planetary systems around these stars.

Science Words

Word Meanings Ask students to find the meaning of the prefix *infra-* and explain why it is appropriate for describing infrared waves. *Infra-* means "below." It is appropriate because infrared waves have frequencies just below that of red light. [L2] IS **Linguistic**

Extension

Have students find out about other uses of infrared radiation. Possible answers: Organic chemists use infrared spectroscopy to identify molecules; people can see in the dark and in fog using the Forward-Looking Infrared system. [L3] IS **Linguistic**

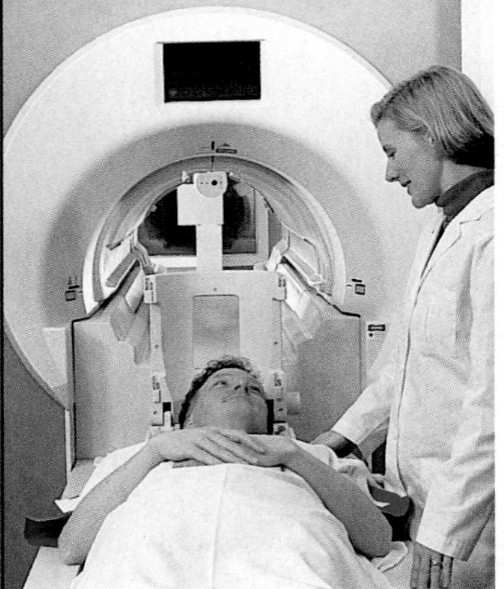

Figure 10
Magnetic resonance imaging technology provides a safe alternative to potentially harmful X-ray imaging.

Magnetic Resonance Imaging (MRI) In the late 1980s, medical researchers developed a technique called Magnetic Resonance Imaging, which uses radio waves to help diagnose illness. The patient lies inside a large cylinder, like the one shown in **Figure 10.** Housed in the cylinder is a powerful magnet, a radio wave emitter, and a radio wave detector. Protons in hydrogen atoms in bones and soft tissue behave like magnets and align with the strong magnetic field. Energy from radio waves causes some of the protons to flip their alignment. As the protons flip, they release radiant energy. A radio receiver detects this released energy. The amount of energy a proton releases depends on the type of tissue it is part of. The released energy detected by the radio receiver is used to create a map of the different tissues. A picture of the inside of the patient's body is produced without pain or risk.

Infrared Waves

Most of the warm air in a fireplace moves up the chimney, yet when you stand in front of a fireplace, you feel the warmth of the blazing fire. Why are you able to feel the heat? The warmth you feel is thermal energy transmitted to you by **infrared waves,** a type of electromagnetic wave with a frequency slightly higher than radio waves.

You use infrared waves every day. A remote control emits infrared waves to communicate with your television. A computer uses infrared waves to read CD-ROMs. In fact, every object emits infrared waves. Hotter objects emit more than cooler objects do. Your world would look strange if you could see infrared waves. It is possible to take photographs called thermograms with a special film that is sensitive to infrared waves. These photographs show cool and warm areas in different colors. Infrared photography is used in many ways. **Figure 11** shows how cities appear different from surrounding vegetation in infrared imagery.

Figure 11
A This visible-light image of the region around San Francisco Bay in California was taken from an aircraft at an altitude of 20,000 m. B This infrared image of the same area was taken from a satellite. In this image, vegetation is red and buildings are gray.

A

B

398

Resource Manager

Chapter Resources Booklet
Enrichment, p. 31
Lab Activity, pp. 9–12
Reading and Writing Skill Activities, p. 33

Imaging Safety Have students write short paragraphs in their Science Journals explaining why Magnetic Resonance Imaging is safer than X rays. The radio waves used for Magnetic Resonance Imaging have much lower energy than X rays, and they do not harm the body. [L2] IS **Linguistic**

Visible Light

Visible light is the range of electromagnetic waves that you can detect with your eyes. Light differs from radio waves and infrared waves only by its frequency and wavelength. Visible light has wavelengths around 390 billionths to 770 billionths of a meter. Your eyes react differently to various wavelengths of visible light, so you see different colors. These colors range from short-wavelength blue to long-wavelength red. If all the colors are present, you see the light as white.

Ultraviolet Waves

Ultraviolet waves are a range of electromagnetic waves with frequencies slightly higher than that of visible light. Ultraviolet waves carry enough energy to enable them to enter skin cells. Overexposure to ultraviolet waves can cause sunburn or even cell damage leading to cancer. People often refer to long-wavelength ultraviolet (UVA) and short-wavelength ultraviolet (UVB) rays. UVB rays are most likely to cause sunburn. UVA rays can cause skin to wrinkle and sag. Too much exposure to the Sun's ultraviolet waves is damaging. Some exposure, however, is necessary because ultraviolet light striking the skin allows your body to make vitamin D. Vitamin D is needed for the development of healthy bones and teeth.

Health INTEGRATION

In certain situations, doctors will perform a CT scan on a patient instead of a traditional X ray. Research to find out more about CT scans. Compare and contrast the CT scan to X rays. What are the advantages and disadvantages of a CT scan? Write a paragraph about your findings in your Science Journal.

Useful UVs A useful property of ultraviolet waves is their ability to kill bacteria on objects such as food or medical supplies. When ultraviolet light enters a cell, it damages protein and DNA molecules. For a single-celled organism like bacteria, damage can mean death, which can be a benefit to health. Ultraviolet waves are also useful because they make some materials fluoresce (floor ES). Fluorescent materials absorb ultraviolet waves and reemit the energy as visible light. As shown in **Figure 12,** police detectives sometimes use fluorescent powder to show fingerprints when solving crimes.

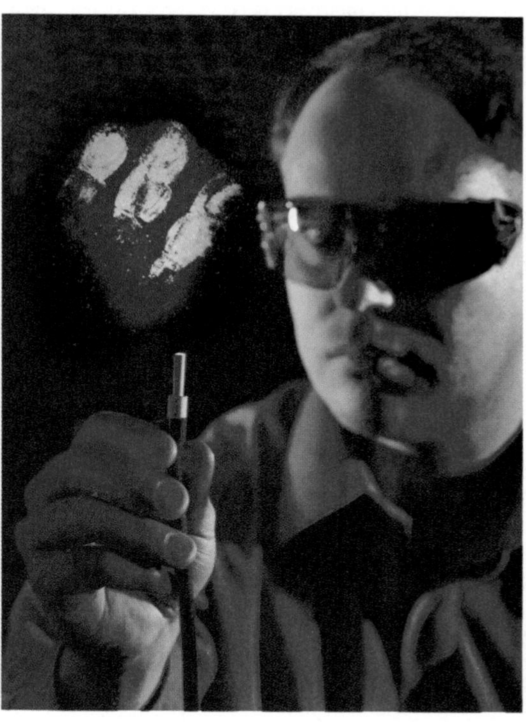

Figure 12
The police detective in this picture is shining ultraviolet light on a fingerprint dusted with fluorescent powder.

Visible Light

Fun Fact

Humans are able to see certain wavelengths of electromagnetic waves because cells called cones and rods in the retina of the human eye absorb those particular wavelengths.

Ultraviolet Waves

Health INTEGRATION

In both traditional X-ray imaging and CT (computerized tomography, also known as CAT, computerized axial tomography) scanning, X-rays are passed through the body to provide an inside view. Traditional X-ray images are not appropriate for some purposes because they show only dense body parts. CT scans provide much clearer cross-sectional images made by rotating an X ray beam around the patient. CT scans are more expensive.

Discussion

Emphasize that electromagnetic waves carry energy, and this energy can be used to do work. Ask students to identify the evidence that electromagnetic waves carry energy if you move a solar-powered calculator away from light. It loses power and stops working. L2

LS **Logical-Mathematical**

LAB DEMONSTRATION

Purpose to demonstrate fluorescence L2
ELL LS **Kinesthetic**

Materials black light bulb, samples of calcite, fluorite, or opal; dry laundry detergent containing whiteners

Procedure In a darkened room, shine the black light on each of the rocks and the laundry detergent. Turn the black light off and on several times. Shine the light on clothing to see if it contains fluorescent whiteners.

CAUTION: *Be careful not to shine ultraviolet light in anyone's eyes.*

Expected Outcome Students will observe the materials fluoresce.

Assessment

Why do the materials fluoresce? When ultraviolet light strikes the materials, the electrons briefly absorb the energy, then reemit it as light at a slightly lower frequency (visible light).

Ultraviolet Waves, continued

Use Science Words

Word Origins Have students find out where the word *ozone* comes from. The word *ozone* comes from the Greek word *ozein* meaning "to smell." Point out that ozone can be formed when electricity or ultraviolet rays pass through oxygen. Its sharp smell can often be detected near electrical machinery or during a thunderstorm. L2 LS **Linguistic**

Environmental Science INTEGRATION

In air conditioners and refrigerators, CFCs are being replaced with HFCs (hydrofluorocarbons), which do not damage the ozone layer, and HCFCs (hydrochlorofluorocarbons), which do less damage than CFCs. Unfortunately, these new compounds are poorer refrigerants than CFCs.

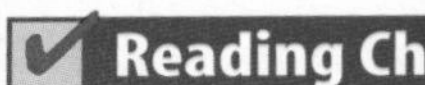

Answer nitric oxides and CFCs

X Rays and Gamma Rays

Discussion

Ask students whether or not they believe there is an upper limit to the energy of electromagnetic waves. Theoretically, there is no upper limit. Gamma rays with energies of billions of electron volts (frequencies of billions of billions of billions of hertz) have been measured. Higher-energy waves are probably absorbed before detectors can measure them. L3 LS **Logical-Mathematical**

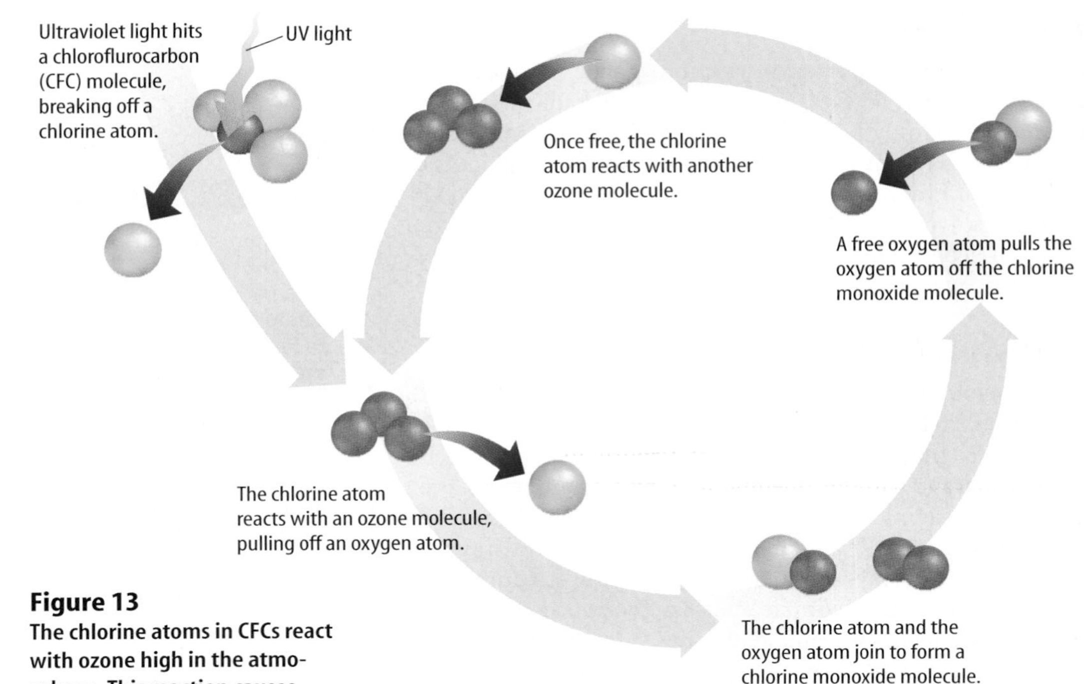

Ultraviolet light hits a chloroflurocarbon (CFC) molecule, breaking off a chlorine atom.
UV light
Once free, the chlorine atom reacts with another ozone molecule.
A free oxygen atom pulls the oxygen atom off the chlorine monoxide molecule.
The chlorine atom reacts with an ozone molecule, pulling off an oxygen atom.
The chlorine atom and the oxygen atom join to form a chlorine monoxide molecule.

Figure 13
The chlorine atoms in CFCs react with ozone high in the atmosphere. This reaction causes ozone molecules to break apart.

The Ozone Layer Far above the surface of Earth is a layer of gas called the ozone layer. Ozone is a molecule composed of three oxygen atoms. It is continually being formed and destroyed high in the atmosphere. The ozone layer is vital to life on Earth because it absorbs most of the Sun's harmful ultraviolet waves. You might have heard of an ozone hole that forms over Antarctica. In fact, thinning of the ozone layer has occurred all over Earth, but is greatest over Antarctica.

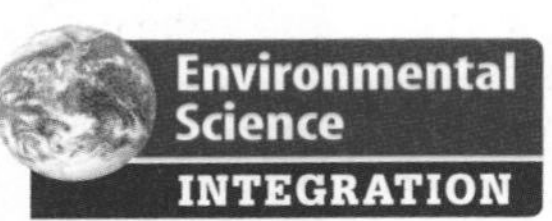

The greatest threat to the ozone layer is from ozone-depleting chemicals, such as nitric oxides and CFCs. CFCs, which stands for chlorofluorocarbons, are used in air conditioners, refrigerators, and as cleaning fluids. When these substances reach the ozone layer, they react chemically with ozone, breaking the ozone molecule apart, as shown in **Figure 13.** One chlorine atom of a CFC molecule will break apart many ozone molecules. To reduce the damage to the ozone layer, many countries in the world are reducing their use of ozone-depleting chemicals.

Reading Check *What chemicals can reduce the amount of ozone in the ozone layer?*

Curriculum Connection

Health Ozone in the stratosphere is necessary to protect life on Earth, but ozone near the ground is harmful. Ozone is a major component in smog produced by chemical pollutants from factories. Ozone also contributes to the greenhouse effect by trapping heat. Have students prepare posters showing useful and harmful effects of ozone. L3 LS **Visual-Spatial** P

Resource Manager

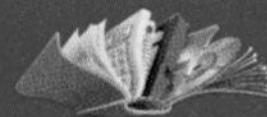

Chapter Resources Booklet
Reinforcement, p. 28
Cultural Diversity, p. 51

X Rays and Gamma Rays

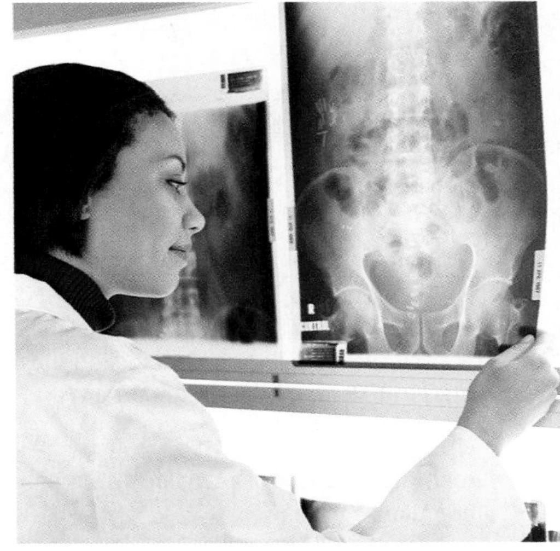

At the far end of the electromagnetic spectrum are **X rays** and **gamma rays.** These ultra-high-frequency electromagnetic waves are so energetic that they can travel through matter, breaking molecular bonds as they go. Doctors and dentists often send low doses of X rays through a patient's body onto photographic film. Dense parts of the body such as bones or teeth absorb more X rays than soft parts do. **Figure 14** shows the shadow image of bones produced by X rays. New techniques are being developed to use gamma rays for more precise medical imaging. X rays are used at airports to inspect luggage without opening it. X rays and gamma rays are used at low doses in industry to check metal objects for cracks and defects.

Radiation therapy is a technique used in medicine for exposing part of a patient's body to X rays or gamma rays to kill diseased cells. X rays and gamma rays have short wavelengths and are highly energetic. When X rays or gamma rays pass through matter, part of the energy damages molecules. This eventually kills cells. However, nearby healthy cells also are damaged by the radiation. By carefully controlling the amount of radiation, the damage to healthy cells is small.

Figure 14
Bones are more dense than surrounding tissues and absorb more X rays. The image of a bone on an X ray is the shadow cast by the bone as X rays pass through the soft tissue.

Section  Assessment

1. Explain how a microwave oven heats food. Draw a diagram to help your explanation.
2. Describe how light you see with your eyes differs from other forms of electromagnetic waves, such as X rays and radio waves.
3. Name some ways that ultraviolet waves are useful and some ways in which they are dangerous.
4. Describe the ozone layer and why damage to the ozone layer could be harmful.
5. **Think Critically** Why are ultraviolet waves, X rays, and gamma rays far more dangerous to humans than other forms of electromagnetic waves?

Skill Builder Activities

6. **Researching Information** Many scientists around the world are studying ozone depletion and how we can solve the problem. Learn about one of these scientists and write a paragraph about the work he or she is doing. **For more help, refer to the** **Science Skill Handbook.**
7. **Using Graphics Software** Use graphics software to create your own version of the electromagnetic spectrum. Be sure to include all of the forms of electromagnetic waves mentioned in this section. Use clip art to represent how each part of the spectrum is used. **For more help, refer to the** **Technology Skill Handbook.**

3 Assess

Reteach

Divide the class into six groups. Ask each group to discuss and make a poster showing various properties and uses of one type of electromagnetic waves. Posters can be displayed in the classroom for reference. L2 COOP LEARN
LS **Visual-Spatial** P

Challenge

Ask students to explain why someone listening on the radio to a live concert many miles away can hear the music slightly sooner than a person sitting at the back of the concert auditorium. To get to the radio, the sound is converted into signals that travel by electromagnetic waves at the speed of light. This is much faster than the speed at which the sound waves travel across the auditorium. L3
LS **Logical-Mathematical**

✔Assessment

Process Ask students to write paragraphs comparing and contrasting MRI and X-ray imaging. Both provide an inside view of a patient. MRI uses radio waves and is safer but more expensive. X-ray imaging uses potentially harmful X rays, but is less expensive. MRI provides clearer images. Use **Performance Assessment in the Science Classroom,** p. 157.

Answers to Section Assessment

1. Microwaves cause water molecules to flip back and forth, which increases their thermal energy and heats the food.
2. Visible light has different frequencies and wavelengths.
3. They can kill bacteria and enable skin cells to make vitamin D. Overexposure can harm plants and animals.
4. It is a layer of O_3 molecules above Earth's surface. Some chemicals used by people thin the ozone layer, so more ultraviolet radiation reaches Earth.
5. They have high energy, so they can enter the body and interact with atomic particles to damage cells.
6. Check students' work.
7. Pictures should include the names of all forms of radiation mentioned in this section, listed in order of wavelength.

Activity

BENCH TESTED

Purpose Students learn how the shape of a satellite dish affects reception. L2 ELL LS **Kinesthetic**

Process Skills observing and inferring, communicating, comparing and contrasting, recognizing cause and effect, making models

Time Required 30 minutes

Alternate Materials Any small parabolic object can be used.

Teaching Strategies For accurate comparison, be sure students have the flashlight at the same distance from the receptor for all measurements.

Answers to Questions

1. The light on the flat surface is spread out, but the light on the curved surface is mostly an intense spot in the middle.
2. The light from the flashlight spreads out as it leaves the flashlight. When it hits a flat surface, this light remains spread out. When it hits a curved surface, the light is focused back to the center, forming the intense spot.
3. This activity uses visible light as a model for the microwaves used in satellite communication, but the general idea is the same. A curved satellite dish focuses the signal so that reception is much better.

Activity

The Shape of Satellite Dishes

Communications satellites transmit signals with a narrow beam pointed toward a particular area of Earth. To detect this signal, receivers are typically large, parabolic dishes. Why is the shape of the dish important?

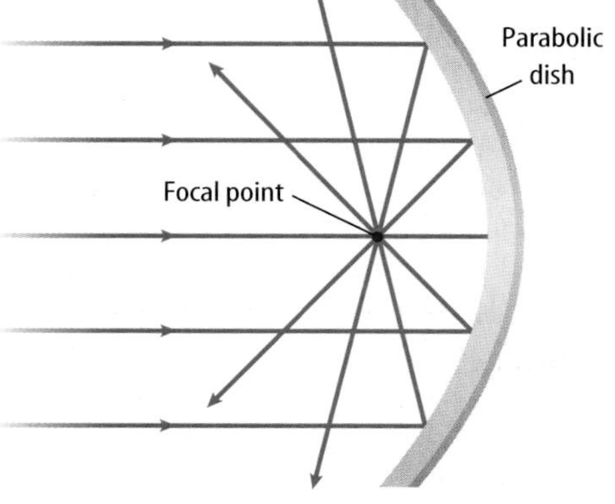

What You'll Investigate

How does the shape of a satellite dish improve reception?

Materials

flashlight
several books
aluminum foil
small, parabolically shaped bowl (such as a mortar bowl)
large, metal spoon
** Alternate materials*

Goals

- **Make** a model of a satellite reflecting dish.
- **Observe** how the shape of the dish affects reception.

Safety Precautions

Procedure

1. Cover one side of a book with aluminum foil. Be careful not to wrinkle the foil.
2. Line the inside of the bowl with foil, also keeping it as smooth as possible.
3. Place some of the books on a table. Put the flashlight on top of the books so that its beam of light will shine several centimeters above and across the table.
4. Hold the foil-covered book on its side at a right angle to the top of the table. The foil-covered side should face the beam of light.
5. **Observe** the intensity of the light on the foil.
6. Repeat these procedures, replacing the foil-covered book with the bowl, keeping it at the same distance from the flashlight.
7. **Observe** how the intensity of light differs when the flat surface is used rather than the curved surface.

Conclude and Apply

1. **Compare** the difference in intensity of light when the two surfaces were used.
2. **Infer** what caused this difference.
3. **Explain** how these results relate to why parabolic dishes are used for satellite signal receivers.

Compare your conclusions with those observed by other students in your class. **For more help, refer to the Science Skill Handbook.**

Resource Manager

Chapter Resources Booklet
Transparency Activity, p. 46
Directed Reading for Content Mastery, pp. 21, 22
Activity Worksheets, pp. 5–6

Earth Science Critical Thinking/Problem Solving, p. 13

Communicating Your Data

Have students use a computer graphics program to prepare sketches of the models they created in this activity. The sketches should show how the light is reflected back from a flat surface, but is reflected toward the center of a curved surface. Have students compare their sketches.

Oral After students have completed the activity, ask them to explain why focusing a satellite signal is important. Focusing increases the intensity of the satellite signal. Use **Performance Assessment in the Science Classroom,** p. 89.

Radio Communication

Radio Transmission

When you listen to the radio, you hear music and words that are produced at a distant location. The music and words are sent to your radio by radio waves. You can't actually hear the radio waves, because they are electromagnetic waves. Ears only detect sound waves. It is the metal antenna of your radio that detects radio waves. As the electromagnetic waves pass by your radio's antenna, the electrons in the metal vibrate, as shown in **Figure 15.** These vibrating electrons produce an electric signal that contains the information about the music and words. An amplifier boosts the signal and sends it to speakers, causing them to vibrate. The speakers vibrate the air and create sound waves that travel to your ears.

Dividing the Radio Spectrum Many radio stations broadcast programs for you to listen to. What is it that allows you to listen to only one station at a time? Each station is assigned to broadcast at one particular radio frequency. Turning the tuning knob on your radio allows you to select a particular frequency to listen to. The specific frequency of the electromagnetic wave that a radio station is assigned is called the **carrier wave.**

The radio station must do more than simply transmit a carrier wave. The station has to send information about the sounds that you are to receive. This information is sent by modifying the carrier wave. The carrier wave is modified to carry information in one of two ways, as shown in **Figure 16.** One way is to vary the amplitude of the carrier wave. This method is called amplitude modulation, or AM. The other way is to vary the frequency of the carrier wave. This method is called frequency modulation, or FM.

As You Read

What **You'll Learn**

- **Explain** how modulating carrier waves makes radio transmissions.
- **Distinguish** between AM and FM radio.
- **Identify** various ways of communicating using radio waves.

Vocabulary

carrier wave
cathode-ray tube
transceiver

Why **It's Important**

Every day you use radio waves to communicate.

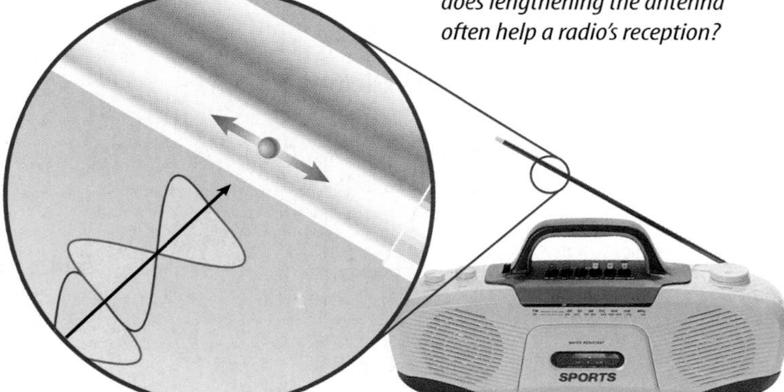

Figure 15
Radio waves exert a force on the electrons in an antenna, causing the electrons to vibrate. *Why does lengthening the antenna often help a radio's reception?*

SECTION 3

Radio Communication

1 Motivate

Bellringer Transparency

Display the Section Focus Transparency for Section 3. Use the accompanying Transparency Activity Master. L2 ELL

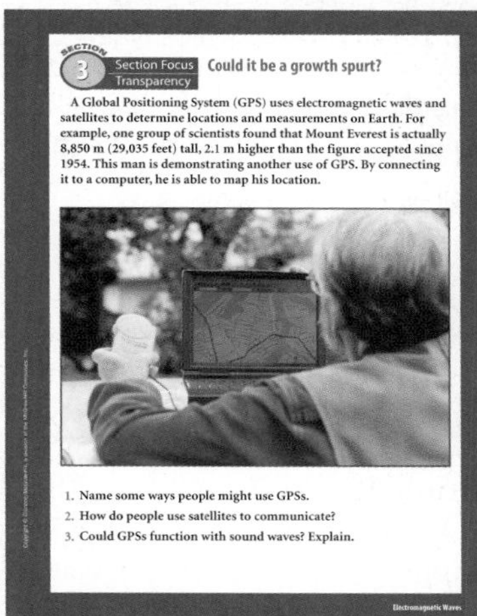
Section Focus Transparency

Could it be a growth spurt?

A Global Positioning System (GPS) uses electromagnetic waves and satellites to determine locations and measurements on Earth. For example, one group of scientists found that Mount Everest is actually 8,850 m (29,035 feet) tall, 2.1 m higher than the figure accepted since 1954. This man is demonstrating another use of GPS. By connecting it to a computer, he is able to map his location.

1. Name some ways people might use GPSs.
2. How do people use satellites to communicate?
3. Could GPSs function with sound waves? Explain.

Tie to Prior Knowledge

Ask students to name different forms of electronic communication. They might mention radio, television, telephone, or the Internet. Tell them much communication relies on the use of radio waves.

Section Assessment Planner

PORTFOLIO
Science Journal, p. 407

PERFORMANCE ASSESSMENT
Skill Builder Activities, p. 409
See page 416 for more options.

CONTENT ASSESSMENT
Section, p. 409
Challenge, p. 409
Chapter, pp. 416–417

2 Teach

Radio Transmission

Use an Analogy

Having a larger sail on a boat increases the amount of wind you catch, so the boat moves faster. Similarly, lengthening a radio's antenna frequently improves reception because more electrons are affected by the incoming radio waves.

Quick Demo

Bring a radio to class and have students tune it to AM and FM stations. Stress that radios are tuned in by the frequency of the carrier wave. List students' favorite radio stations on the board in order of increasing frequency. L2 **Auditory-Musical**

IDENTIFYING Misconceptions

Students might assume that AM stations broadcast with higher-frequency carrier waves than FM stations. For example, a station at 620 AM might seem to have a higher frequency than a station at 98 FM because 620 is greater than 98. Explain that the AM frequencies are in thousands of vibrations per second, while the FM frequencies are in millions of vibrations per second.

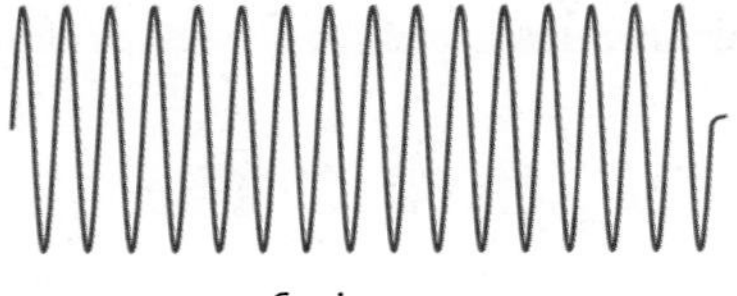

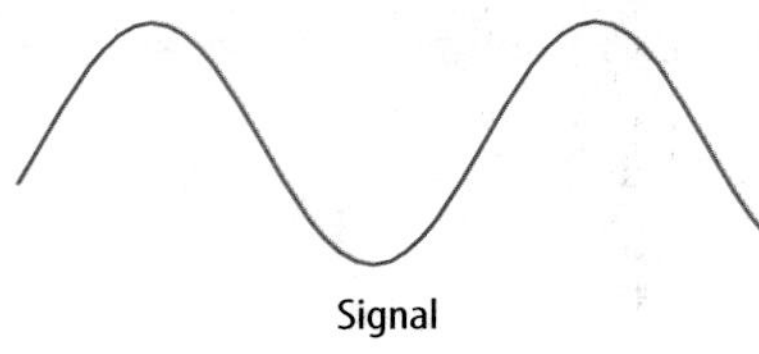

Frequency modulation

Figure 16
A carrier wave broadcast by a radio station can be altered in one of two ways to transmit information, amplitude modulation (AM), or frequency modulation (FM).

AM Radio An AM radio station broadcasts information by varying the amplitude of the carrier wave, as shown in **Figure 16.** Your radio detects the slight variations in amplitude of the carrier wave and makes an electronic signal from these slight variations. The electronic signal is then used to make the speaker vibrate. AM carrier wave frequencies range from 540 to 1,600 thousand vibrations each second.

FM Radio Electronic signals are transmitted by FM radio stations by varying the frequency of the carrier wave, as in **Figure 16.** Your radio detects the slight changes in frequency of the carrier wave. Because the strength of the FM waves is kept fixed, FM signals tend to be more clear than AM signals. FM carrier frequencies range from 88 million to 108 million vibrations each second. This is much higher than AM frequencies, as shown in **Figure 17. Figure 18** shows how radio signals are broadcast.

Figure 17
Radio waves have frequencies that range from 100,000 Hz to more than 1 billion Hz.

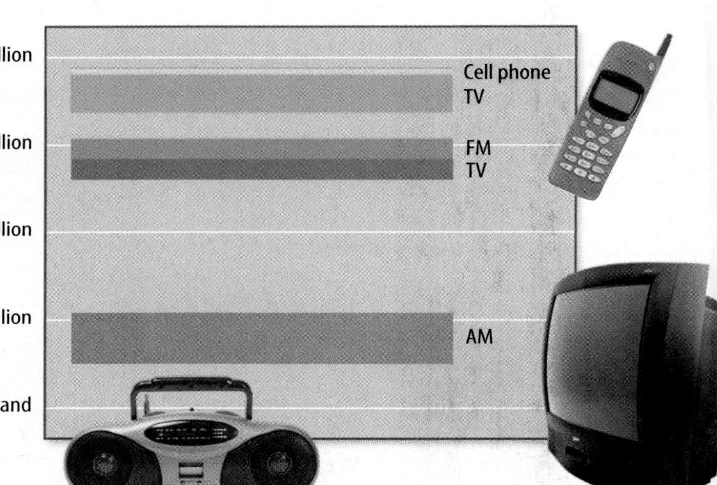

Caption Answer

Figure 15 More electrons are affected by the radio waves, yielding increased current and a stronger signal.

Inclusion Strategies

Learning Disabled To help students understand the meaning of *frequency* and *hertz*, have a student draw high-frequency waves on one end of the board and low-frequency waves on the other. When you list radio stations, write each radio station near the appropriate picture. Point to the pictures often as you use the terms *frequency, vibrations per second,* and *hertz.* L1 ELL

Curriculum Connection

Math The frequencies of AM radio stations are in kilohertz and those of FM stations are in megahertz. Have students use the equation wavelength = c/f to determine the wavelengths of the signals transmitted by local radio stations. (c = 300,000,000 m/s) Possible answer: For 98.6 FM, the wavelength is f = 300,000,000 m/s / 98,600,000 hz = 3.04 m L3 **Logical-Mathematical**

NATIONAL GEOGRAPHIC **VISUALIZING RADIO BROADCASTS**

Figure 18

You flick a switch, turn the dial, and music from your favorite radio station fills the room. Although it seems like magic, sounds are transmitted over great distances by converting sound waves to electromagnetic waves and back again, as shown here.

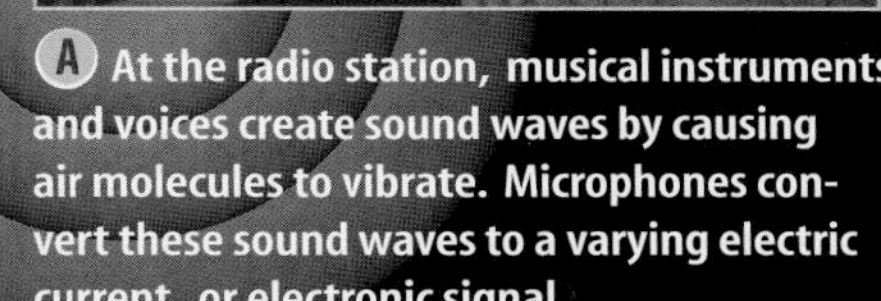

Ⓐ At the radio station, musical instruments and voices create sound waves by causing air molecules to vibrate. Microphones convert these sound waves to a varying electric current, or electronic signal.

Ⓑ This signal then is added to the station's carrier wave. If the station is an AM station, the electronic signal modifies the amplitude of the carrier wave. If the station is a FM station, the electronic signal modifies the frequency of the carrier wave.

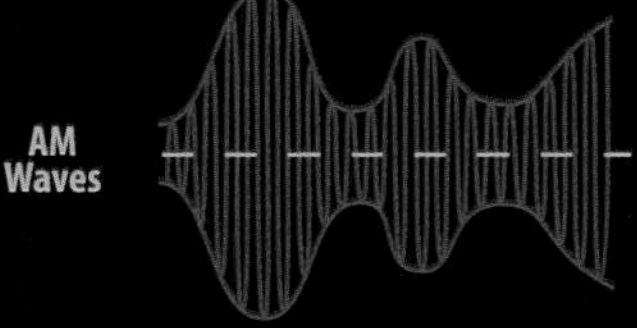

Ⓒ The modified carrier wave is used to vibrate electrons in the station's antenna. These vibrating electrons create a radio wave that travels out in all directions at the speed of light.

Ⓓ The radio wave from the station makes electrons in your radio's antenna vibrate. This creates an electric current. If your radio is tuned to the station's frequency, the carrier wave is removed from the original electronic signal. This signal then makes the radio's speaker vibrate, creating sound waves that you hear as music.

Figure 18

Have students examine the pictures and read the captions. Then ask the following questions.

- **Compare and contrast how electromagnetic waves are modified to create AM and FM radio signals.** Both signals are made by modifying electromagnetic waves and adding them to a carrier wave. The amplitude of the AM carrier wave is modified. The frequency of the FM carrier wave is modified.
- **Explain the roles of antennas in radio transmission and reception.** In transmission, electrons in an antenna are caused to vibrate, sending the electromagnetic wave out in all directions at the speed of light. In reception, the electromagnetic wave makes electrons in an antenna vibrate. The antenna then sends the signal cause by these electrons to a receiver.

Activity

Have students write and perform a skit about the life of a radio wave from birth (original sound wave) to death (final conversion back to a sound wave and then dampened). L2 LS **Kinesthetic**

Extension

Challenge students to find out how radio frequencies are assigned and who regulates and monitors the industry. Have students report the information that they find to their class. FCC L3 LS **Linguistic**

Resource Manager

Chapter Resources Booklet

Enrichment, p. 32

Transparency Activity, p. 46

Directed Reading for Content Mastery, pp. 21, 22

Television

Use an Analogy

Tell students that the tiny rectangles or lines on a television or computer screen form a complete image the same way pieces of a jigsaw puzzle do. Individually the pieces seem meaningless, but when put together they form a picture.

Astronomy INTEGRATION

Learning about objects in distant space requires observing the universe with the entire range of electromagnetic waves. The Compton Gamma Ray Observatory, for example, used gamma rays to look for pulsars at the centers of galaxies. The Chandra X-ray Observatory uses X rays to search for binary stars and black holes. The *Hubble Space Telescope* uses electromagnetic waves from deep ultraviolet to near infrared to look at stars and galaxies.

Teacher FYI

To avoid large cathode-ray tubes, flat-screen televisions and the displays on laptop computers use liquid crystal displays or gas-plasma displays.

Reading Check

Answer a sealed vacuum tube in which one or more beams of electrons are produced

Astronomy INTEGRATION

Do you ever look up at the stars at night and wonder how they were formed? With so many stars and so many galaxies, life might be possible on other planets. Research ways that astronomers use electromagnetic waves to investigate the universe. Choose one project astronomers currently are working on, and write about it in your Science Journal.

Television

What would people hundreds of years ago have thought if they had seen a television? It might seem like magic, but it's not if you know how they work. Television and radio transmissions are similar. At the television station, sound and images are changed into electronic signals. These signals are broadcast by carrier waves. The audio part of television is sent by FM radio waves. Information about the color and brightness is sent at the same time by AM signals.

Cathode-Ray Tubes In many television sets, images are displayed on a cathode-ray tube (CRT), as shown in **Figure 19.** A **cathode-ray tube** is a sealed vacuum tube in which one or more beams of electrons are produced. The CRT in a color TV produces three electron beams that are focused by a magnetic field and strike a coated screen. The screen is speckled with more than 100,000 rectangular spots that are of three types. One type glows red, another glows green, and the third type glows blue when electrons strike it. The spots are grouped together with a red, green, and blue spot in each group.

An image is created when the three electron beams of the CRT sweep back and forth across the screen. Each electron beam controls the brightness of each type of spot, according to the information in the video signal from the TV station. By varying the brightness of each spot in a group, the three spots together can form any color so that you see a full-color image.

Reading Check *What is a cathode-ray tube?*

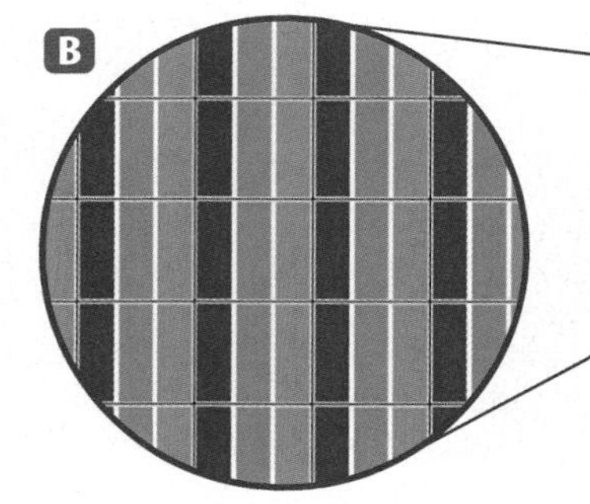

Figure 19
A **Cathode-ray tubes produce the images you see on television.**
B **If you look closely at a television screen, you can see tiny colored rectangles.**

Cultural Diversity

Television As a young boy, Kenjito Takayanagi was a slow learner in school, but hard work enabled him to overcome his difficulties. In 1926, he transmitted the first television signal in Japan. Today he is honored as the founder of Japanese television. Have students make a class time line showing this and other contributions to the invention of television.

Visual Learning

Figure 19 The tiny rectangular spots on a television screen are colored red, green, and blue because these are the primary colors of light. Our eyes combine these into different colors, depending on the intensity of each rectangle. To demonstrate this idea, allow students to experiment with additive color filters or paddles. L2 **LS Visual-Spatial**

Telephones

About 100 years ago, human operators were needed to connect calls between people. Just 20 years ago you never would have seen someone walking down the street talking on a telephone. Today, cell phones are seen everywhere. When you speak into a telephone, a microphone converts sound waves into an electrical signal. In cell phones, this current is used to create radio waves that are transmitted to and from a microwave tower, as shown in **Figure 20.** A cell phone uses one radio signal for sending information to a tower at a base station. It uses another signal for receiving information from the base station. The base stations are several kilometers apart. The area each one covers is called a cell. If you move from one cell to another while using a cell phone, an automated control station transfers your signal to the new cell.

Figure 20
The antenna at the top of a microwave tower receives signals from nearby cell phones. *Are any microwave towers located near your school or home? Where?*

Cordless Telephones Like a cellular telephone, a cordless telephone is a transceiver. A **transceiver** transmits one radio signal and receives another radio signal from a base unit. Having two signals at different frequencies allows you to talk and listen at the same time. Cordless telephones work much like cell phones. With a cordless telephone, however, you must be close to the base unit. Another drawback is that when someone nearby is using a cordless telephone, you could hear that conversation on your phone if the frequencies match. For this reason, many cordless phones have a channel button. This allows you to switch your call to another frequency.

Pagers Another method of transmitting signals is a pager, which allows messages to be sent to a small radio receiver. A caller leaves a message at a central terminal by entering a callback number through a telephone keypad or by entering a text message from a computer. At the terminal, the message is changed into an electronic signal and transmitted by radio waves. Each pager is given a unique number for identification. This identification number is sent along with the message. Your pager receives all messages that are transmitted in the area at its assigned frequency. However, your pager responds only to messages with its particular identification number. Newer pagers can send data as well as receive them.

Research Visit the Glencoe Science Web site at **science.glencoe.com** for recent news or magazine articles about advances in radio wave technology. Communicate to your class what you learn.

Reading Check *How does a pager know when to beep you?*

Telephones

Discussion

Why is there a limit to the number of people who can talk on cell phones in a particular cell at the same time? Each phone uses a different frequency of electromagnetic waves. If all of the assigned frequencies are being used, no other phones can be used at that time. L2 LS **Logical-Mathematical**

Caption Answer

Figure 20 Students should be encouraged to look for microwave towers on both freestanding towers and on other tall objects, such as buildings or water towers.

Discussion

Why is it difficult to talk on a cell phone if you are inside a metal building? The metal blocks the incoming and outgoing microwaves. L2 LS **Logical-Mathematical**

SCIENCE Online

Internet Addresses

Explore the Glencoe Science Web site at **science.glencoe.com** to find out more about topics in this section.

Reading Check

Answer the message has your identification number

Resource Manager

Earth Science Critical Thinking/Problem Solving, p. 5

Science Journal

Telephones of the Future Technology associated with telephones is changing rapidly, and the difference between computers and telecommunication devices is becoming less distinct. Have students write in their Science Journals descriptions of what they think telephones will be like in ten years. L2 LS **Linguistic** P

Communications Satellites

Caption Answer

- **Figure 21** Possible answers: monitor weather conditions, take photographs for military purposes

Use Science Words

Word Meaning The word *satellite* has many meanings. Ask students to look up the origin of the word *satellite* and list various types of satellites. For each one, they should describe why the word satellite is an appropriate term. *Satellite* comes from the Latin word *satelles* meaning "attendant." Possible types: moons, satellite countries.

The Global Positioning System

Activity

Most communication satellites follow a geostationary equatorial orbit (GEO), also called a geosynchronous orbit. This is not the case with satellites for the Global Positioning System (GPS). Have students research the difference between a GEO and a GPS orbit. In a GEO, the satellite orbits Earth directly above the equator once every 24 hours, so that it is always above the same point on the equator. It maintains an altitude of about 35,800 km. In contrast, each of the 24 GPS satellites follows a different, circular orbit that crosses the equator at a 55° angle, circling Earth every 12 hours at an altitude of about 17,500 km. L2

LS **Linguistic**

Figure 21
Currently, more than 2,000 satellites orbit Earth. *Other than communications, what might the satellites be used for?*

Communications Satellites

Since satellites were first developed, thousands have been launched into Earth's orbit. Many of these are used for communication, as shown in **Figure 21.** A station broadcasts a high-frequency microwave signal to the satellite. The satellite receives the signal, amplifies it, and transmits it to a particular region on Earth. To avoid interference, the frequency broadcast by the satellite is different than the frequency broadcast from Earth.

Satellite Telephone Systems If you have a mobile telephone, you can make a phone call when sailing across the ocean. To call on a mobile telephone, the telephone transmits radio waves directly to a satellite. The satellite relays the signal to a ground station, the call is passed on to the telephone network. Satellite links work well for one-way transmissions, but two-way communications can have an annoying delay caused by the large distance the signals travel to and from the satellite.

Television Satellites The satellite-reception dishes that you sometimes see in yards or attached to houses are receivers for television satellite signals. Satellite television is used as an alternative to ground-based transmission. Communications satellites use microwaves rather than the longer-wavelength radio waves used for normal television broadcasts. Short-wavelength microwaves travel more easily through the atmosphere. The waves travel in narrow beams, so the ground receiver dishes are rounded to help focus the beam onto an antenna.

SCIENCE Online

Research Visit the Glencoe Science Web site at **science.glencoe.com** for more information about ways satellites are used for communication. Report to your class what you learn.

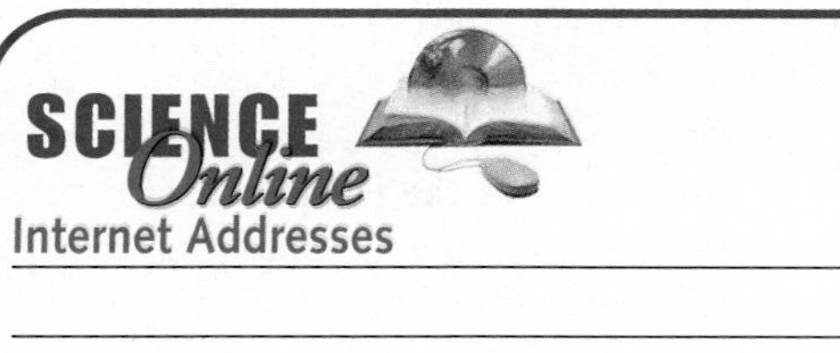

Explore the Glencoe Science Web site at **science.glencoe.com** to find out more about topics in this section.

Resource Manager

Chapter Resources Booklet
Reinforcement, p. 29

408 CHAPTER 13 Electromagnetic Waves

The Global Positioning System

Getting lost while hiking is not uncommon, but if you are carrying a **Global Positioning System** (GPS) receiver, it is much less likely to happen. The GPS is a system of satellites, ground monitoring stations, and receivers that provide details about your exact location at or above Earth's surface. The 24 satellites necessary for 24-hour, around-the-world coverage have been in the sky since the late 1980s. GPS satellites are owned and operated by the United States Department of Defense, but the microwave signals they send out can be used by anyone. As shown in **Figure 22,** signals from the satellites allow a GPS receiver to determine its latitude, longitude, and altitude.

GPS receivers are used in airplanes, ships, cars, and even by hikers. Many police cars, fire trucks, and ambulances have GPS receivers. This allows the closest help to be sent in an emergency. Many automobile GPS receivers come with a high-resolution, color display screen that can show you a map of the area, display mileage to various locations, and provide information on the services provided at the next interstate exit. Can you think of other uses for the Global Positioning System?

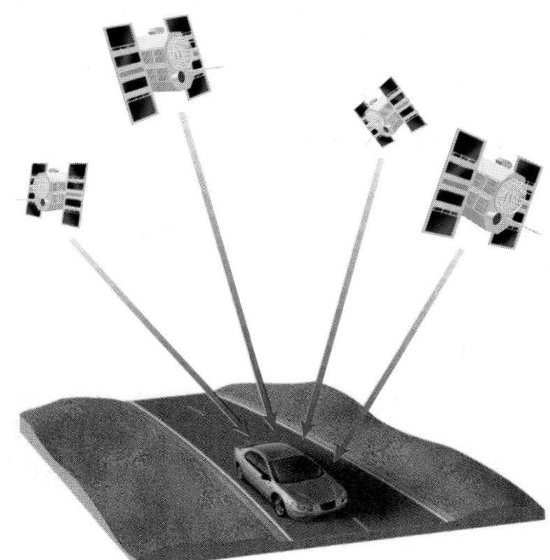

Figure 22
A GPS receiver uses signals from orbiting satellites to determine the user's location. *How would having a GPS receiver in an automobile be useful*

Section  Assessment

1. Explain the difference between AM and FM radio. Make a sketch of how a carrier wave is modulated in AM and FM radio.
2. What is a cathode-ray tube and how is it used in a television?
3. What happens if you are talking on a cell phone while riding in a car and you travel from one cell to another cell?
4. Explain some of the uses of a Global Positioning System. Why might emergency vehicles all be equipped with GPS receivers?
5. **Think Critically** Why do cordless telephones stop working if you move too far from the base unit?

Skill Builder Activities

6. **Researching Information** For a cellular phone system to work, microwave antennas must be spaced every few kilometers throughout the area. Look around your community to see where microwave antennas are located. Draw a map of the area and note where they are. **For more help, refer to the** Science Skill Handbook.
7. **Communicating** Technology using radio waves for communication is changing rapidly. In your Science Journal, write some ways that communication with radio waves might be different in the future. **For more help, refer to the** Science Skill Handbook.

Text Question Answer

Sample answers: hunting, truck driving, military uses, surveying

Caption Answer

- **Figure 22** to determine position

3 Assess

Reteach

Bring a radio or television into your classroom. Have students demonstrate the use of each device with proper physics explanations. They should include explanations about how the radio waves are picked up and what happens when you change the channel. L2 LS **Kinesthetic**

Challenge

The signal detected by a television is a radio wave. How is this changed by the television into sound waves we can hear? The television speakers vibrate in response to changes in the detected radio waves. The speaker movements cause air molecules to vibrate, and the sound waves travel through the air to our ears. L3 LS **Logical-Mathematical**

Assessment

Performance Have students work in pairs to make posters that show how one form of radio communication described in this section works. Posters can be displayed in the classroom to help students remember what they have studied. Use **PASC,** p. 145. L2 COOP LEARN LS **Visual-Spatial**

Answers to Section Assessment

1. For AM, amplitude is modulated. For FM, frequency is modulated. Check students' sketches.
2. A sealed vacuum tube in which beams of electrons are produced; the electron beams hit dots on a coated screen, causing them to glow.
3. A central controller transfers your signal to the base station in the new cell.
4. GPS is used by hikers, airplanes, ships, cars, and others to identify their location on Earth. Emergency vehicles have GPS receivers to help them find places quickly.
5. The handset has trouble detecting the signal.
6. Maps should include antennas on freestanding towers, water towers, etc.
7. Possible answers: Future communication might include handheld video phones, fully interactive television.

Activity

BENCH TESTED

Recognize the Problem

Internet Students will use Internet sites that can be accessed through the Glencoe Science Web site at **science.glencoe.com**. They will investigate AM and FM radio station transmission frequencies and ranges.

Non-Internet Sources Contact the Federal Communications Commission (FCC) for information about station transmission frequencies and ranges.

Time Required

two days

Preparation

Internet Access the Glencoe Science Web site at **science.glencoe.com** to run throught the steps that the students will follow.

Non-Internet Sources Organize FCC information about local radio stations by frequency and range.

Form a Hypothesis

Possible Hypotheses

Students may hypothesize that their favorite AM radio station has a greater broadcast range than their favorite FM radio station.

Test Your Hypothesis

Teaching Strategies

Remind students that AM stations broadcast at a lower frequency than FM stations, which means that AM range is greater than FM range.

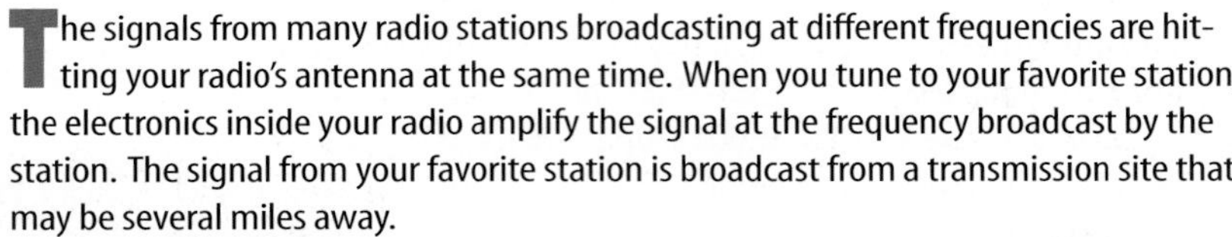

Activity Use the Internet

Radio Frequencies

The signals from many radio stations broadcasting at different frequencies are hitting your radio's antenna at the same time. When you tune to your favorite station, the electronics inside your radio amplify the signal at the frequency broadcast by the station. The signal from your favorite station is broadcast from a transmission site that may be several miles away.

You may have noticed that if you're listening to a radio station while driving in a car, sometimes the station gets fuzzy and you'll hear another station at the same time. Sometimes you lose the station completely. How far can you drive before that happens? Does the distance vary depending on the station you listen to?

Recognize the Problem

What are the ranges of radio stations?

Form a Hypothesis

How far can a radio station transmit? Which type of signal, AM or FM, has a greater range? Form a hypothesis about the range of your favorite radio station.

Goals

- **Research** which frequencies are used by different radio stations.
- **Observe** the reception of your favorite radio station.
- **Make** a chart of your findings and communicate them to other students.

Data Source

SCIENCE *Online* Go to the Glencoe Science Web site at **science.glencoe.com** for more information on radio frequencies, different frequencies of radio stations around the country, and the ranges of AM and FM broadcasts.

SCIENCE *Online*

Internet Addresses

Explore the Glencoe Science Web site at **science.glencoe.com** to find out more about topics in this activity.

Resource Manager

Chapter Resources Booklet

Activity Worksheet, pp. 7–8

Test Your Hypothesis

Plan

1. **Research** what frequencies are used by AM and FM radio stations in your areas and other areas around the country.
2. **Determine** these stations' broadcast locations.
3. **Determine** the broadcast range of radio stations in your area.
4. **Observe** how much the frequencies differ. What is the maximum frequency differences for FM stations in your area? AM stations?

Do

1. Make sure your teacher approves your plan before you start.
2. Visit the Glencoe Science Web site for links to different radio stations.
3. **Compare** the different frequencies of the stations and the locations of the broadcasts.
4. **Determine** the range of radio stations in your area and the power of their broadcast signal in watts.
5. **Record** your data in your Science Journal.

Analyze Your Data

1. **Make** a map of the radio stations in your area. Do the ranges of AM stations differ from FM stations?
2. **Make** a map of different radio stations around the country. Do you see any patterns in the frequencies for stations that are located near each other?
3. **Write** a description that compares how close the frequencies of AM stations are and how close the frequencies of FM stations are. Also compare the power of their broadcast signals and their ranges.
4. **Share** your data by posting it on the Glencoe Science Web site.

Draw Conclusions

1. Compare your findings to those of your classmates and other data that was posted on the Glencoe Science Web site. Do all AM stations and FM stations have different ranges?
2. Look at your map of the country. How close can stations with similar frequencies be? Do AM and FM stations appear to be different in this respect?
3. The power of the broadcast signal also determines its range. How does the power (wattage) of the signals affect your analysis of your data?

Communicating Your Data

Find this *Use the Internet* activity on the Glencoe Science Web site at **science.glencoe.com**. Post your data in the table provided. Compare your data to that of other students. Then combine your data with theirs and make a map for your class that shows all of the data.

Analyze Your Data

1. AM station ranges are different from FM station ranges because AM stations transmit at lower frequencies. Lower frequencies travel farther.
2. If two stations' transmitters are close to each other, their stations' frequencies will not be the same.
3. AM stations have frequencies farther apart than FM stations. FM stations have less interference than AM stations.
4. Students can compare radio stations' ranges and frequencies in different locations around the country.

Draw Conculsions

1. AM stations and FM stations have different ranges. Broadcast range depends on a station's transmitter power.
2. Station transmitters with similar frequencies cannot be very close together because their signals would interfere with one another. AM stations differ from FM stations in how close their transmitters can be, because AM stations have a greater broadcast range than FM stations.
3. Students should use information about signal power and frequency to determine the ranges of radio stations.

Assessment

Performance Show radio stqation transmitter locations on a map of your area. Have students draw each station's range on the map to understand how reception and interference can affect the ability to receive a station's signal. Use **Performance Assessment in the Science Classroom,** p. 127.

Use a spreadsheet program to collect information about radio stations. Include the station's call letters, locations of transmitters, frequency, and power.

Content Background

Apart from the safety issues of driving while talking on cell phones, there has been recent concern that the electromagnetic radiation emitted by handheld cell phones might be linked to the occurrence of certain brain cancers.

The radiation produced by mobile phones is in the form of non-ionizing radiofrequency (RF) energy. This RF energy is different from that of a medical X-ray, which can present a health risk at certain doses.

RF energy, however, also can be dangerous at high levels as it can heat and cook things, including human tissue. Microwaves use RF energy to heat food.

RF energy in a mobile phone emanates from its antennae. The level of radiation and the six-tenths of a watt of power emitted should have virtually no affect on a person, according to currently available data.

To date, studies are inconclusive regarding whether or not increased exposure to these low levels of RF energy leads to increased incidences of brain tumors. However, scientists do believe that more definite answers about the biological effects of cell phone radiation are needed.

TIME SCIENCE AND Society

SCIENCE ISSUES THAT AFFECT YOU!

Can phoning and driving go together safely?

Cell Phones

If you use a cell phone, you're not alone. More than 92 million Americans have them, and 30,000 more new cell phone users sign up each day. Although it seems that you can't eat in a restaurant or ride a train without hearing someone else's cell phone conversation, one of the most popular places for cell phone use is the car. And many people think that's a problem.

412

Resources for Teachers and Students

Cell Phones: Invisible Hazards in the Wireless Age: An Insider's Alarming Discoveries About Cancer and Genetic Damage by George Louis Carlo, Martin Schram, Carroll & Graf (January 5, 2001)

The Cell Phone Handbook : Everything You Wanted to Know About Wireless Telephony (But Didn't Know Who or What to Ask) by Penelope Stetz, Aegis Pub Group (June 1999)

Danger, Danger

According to the National Highway Transportation Safety Board, driver inattention is a factor in half of all accidents. Many people believe that cell phone use distracts drivers, causing accidents. Drivers can get so excited or involved in a phone conversation that they forget they are behind the wheel. Drivers who hold phones (rather than use speaker phones) don't have complete control of the car. Dialing a phone number can make drivers take their eyes off the road.

One study found that people who talk on cell phones while driving are four times more likely to get into a car accident than people who do not. In Oklahoma, accident reports suggest that drivers with cell phones are more likely to speed and swerve between lanes. They are also involved in more fatal accidents. Because of findings such as these, many people think laws should restrict cell phone use by drivers. This is already the case in countries such as Brazil, Sweden, and Australia. Several communities in the United States have restricted cell phone use as well. In Suffolk County, New York, for example, lawmakers have passed a bill making it illegal to use a hand-held cellular phone while driving.

Cellulars Aren't All Bad

Regardless of this evidence, some people feel that singling out cell phones as the cause of accidents is unfair. They say that drivers are inattentive for many reasons. Changing CDs, eating, or looking at maps while driving, can take attention from the road. A driver looking at a digital map display takes his or her eyes off the road about 20 times in a short period, according to one study. This can spell danger in a car speeding down the road at 100 km/h. Yet there are no laws against looking at maps while driving.

Supporters of cell phone use in cars also point out that cellular phones are useful during emergencies. Many drivers have used these phones to report accidents or roadside injuries. These reports have helped people in trouble and have saved lives.

The best course may be to just learn to use car phones more carefully. For example, drivers should pull off the road to make calls. Drivers shouldn't use a hand-held cell phone but should use a speaker phone in order to keep both hands on the steering wheel. But even if people followed those two suggestions, the debate won't end. As cars become more loaded with gadgets that enable drivers to send faxes or even microwave snacks on the road, the question of whether drivers should do anything in the car other than drive will become more important.

CONNECTIONS Survey **With a partner, write a questionnaire on car cell phone use for classmates to answer. Include questions on what they think of cell phone use by drivers, and whether adults in their families use a cell phone while driving. Tabulate the results and post them.**

SCIENCE Online
For more information, visit science.glencoe.com

Discussion

Why have the numbers of cell phone users who drive increased? Possible answers: Because of digital technology, the concept of the office is almost obsolete. More and more people are using their cars, homes and other places as places of business. L2 **LS Logical-Mathematical**

Activity

Explain to students that there are concerns regarding the use of hand-held mobile phones in addition to car safety. One concern is that there may be a link between cell phone use and brain tumors. Tell students that they will be conducting research in groups to find out more information about this. Have each group do research at the school library or on the Internet. Tell them to look at all the evidence they can find and use charts, graphs and signs to present their findings to the rest of the class. L2 COOP LEARN **LS Linguistic**

Investigate the Issue

Ask students whether or not they believe cell phone use in cars should be banned or restricted, and if cell phone use should be restricted, what kinds of restrictions they would place on the use of cell phones in cars and why.

CONNECTIONS Debate Help students write questions for their surveys. Make sure they include questions about passengers' reactions to cell phone use. Students could ask, for example, whether the responsee has ever felt unsafe because of a driver with a cell phone.

SCIENCE Online

Internet Addresses

Explore the Glencoe Science Web site at **science.glencoe.com** to find out more about topics in this feature.

Chapter 13 Study Guide

Reviewing Main Ideas

Preview

Students can answer the questions in their Science Journals. Discuss the answers as you go through the chapter. **L Linguistic**

Review

Students can write their answers, then compare them with those of other students. **L Interpersonal**

Reteach

Students can look at the illustrations and describe details that support the main ideas of the chapter. **L Visual-Spatial**

Answers to Chapter Review

SECTION 1

1. Both are transverse waves. Electromagnetic waves don't require the presence of matter for propagation; water waves do. Electromagnetic waves radiate in three dimensions; water waves radiate in two dimensions.

SECTION 2

1. infrared waves

SECTION 3

1. The carrier wave itself contains no information. The carrier wave has to be modulated to include the information that it is transmitting.

Chapter 13 Study Guide

Reviewing Main Ideas

Section 1 What are electromagnetic waves?

1. A vibrating charge creates electromagnetic waves. *In what ways are electromagnetic waves similar to and different from the waves in this picture?*

2. Electromagnetic waves have radiant energy and travel through a vacuum or through matter.
3. Electromagnetic waves sometimes can behave like particles. The particles are called photons.

Section 2 The Electromagnetic Spectrum

1. Electromagnetic waves with the lowest frequency are called radio waves. Infrared waves have frequencies slightly lower than visible light. *Which type of electromagnetic wave does this viper detect through pits located between its eyes and nostrils?*

2. Human eyes can see electromagnetic waves that span a wavelength range of 390 billionths to 770 billionths of a meter.
3. Ultraviolet waves have frequencies slightly higher than visible light. They have many useful and harmful properties.
4. X rays and gamma rays are two types of ultrahigh-frequency electromagnetic waves that are energetic enough to travel through many materials and destroy living cells.

Section 3 Radio Communication

1. Modulated radio waves are used often for communication. AM and FM are two forms of carrier wave modulation. *Why does a carrier wave have to be modulated before transmission of data?*

2. Television signals are transmitted as a combination of AM and FM waves.
3. Cellular telephones, cordless telephones, and pagers all rely on a type of radio waves for signal transmission. Communications satellites can be used for telephone and television transmissions.
4. The Global Positioning System uses satellites to help people determine their exact locations.

FOLDABLES Reading & Study Skills — After You Read

Make a list of electromagnetic waves that transfer energy with and without matter on the back of the tabs of your Foldable.

FOLDABLES Reading & Study Skills — After You Read

After students have read the chapter and completed the Foldable described in Before You Read, have them do the activity on the student page.

Dinah Zike

Visualizing Main Ideas

Complete the following table about the electromagnetic spectrum.

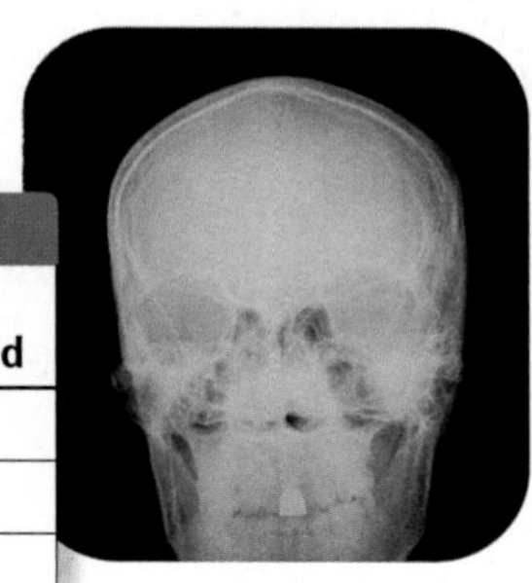

Uses of Electromagnetic Waves

Type of Electromagnetic Waves	Examples of How Electromagnetic Waves Are Used
radio waves	radio, TV transmission
infrared waves	remote control transmitters
visible light	vision
ultraviolet light	fluorescent materials
X rays	medical imaging
gamma rays	destroying harmful cells

Vocabulary Review

Vocabulary Words

a. carrier wave
b. cathode-ray tube
c. electromagnetic wave
d. frequency
e. gamma ray
f. infrared wave
g. microwave
h. photon
i. radiant energy
j. radio wave
k. transceiver
l. ultraviolet wave
m. visible light
n. X ray

THE PRINCETON REVIEW Study Tip

Keep all your homework assignments and reread them from time to time. Make sure you understand any problems you answered incorrectly.

Using Vocabulary

Replace the underlined words with the correct vocabulary word.

1. Gamma rays are a type of electromagnetic wave often used for communication.
2. Visible light and radio waves are used often for medical imaging.
3. A remote control is able to communicate with a television by sending X rays.
4. Electromagnetic waves are composed of massless particles called carrier waves.
5. If you stay outdoors too long, your skin might be burned by exposure to radio waves from the Sun.
6. Microwaves are waves of unique frequencies used by radio stations to broadcast information.

Chapter 13 Study Guide

Visualizing Main Ideas

See student page.

Vocabulary Review

Using Vocabulary

1. radio waves
2. gamma rays and X rays
3. infrared waves
4. photons
5. ultraviolet waves
6. carrier waves

Chapter 13 Assessment

Checking Concepts

1. A
2. C
3. B
4. A
5. C
6. C
7. B
8. D
9. A
10. C

Thinking Critically

11. The molecules of which they are made do not respond to the radiation like the water molecules in food do.
12. They have just the right level of energy to pass through the body's soft tissue and be blocked by hard tissue. This gives good images of the hard tissue on photographic film.
13. The shorter wavelength and higher energy of UVB waves enable them to more easily penetrate and damage skin cells.
14. The wavelengths of visible light range from about 390 to 770 nanometers. These are easily short enough to travel through the holes in the metal door. The wavelength of radiation emitted in microwave ovens is about 5 cm, much too long to escape through the small holes in the metal.
15. The frequency with which the light vibrates is far too fast to visibly affect the compass needle.

Chapter 13 Assessment

Checking Concepts

Choose the word or phrase that best answers the question.

1. Which type of electromagnetic wave is most dangerous to people?
   A) gamma rays **C)** infrared waves
   B) ultraviolet waves **D)** microwaves
2. Electromagnetic waves can behave like what type of particle?
   A) electrons **C)** photons
   B) molecules **D)** atoms
3. Which type of electromagnetic wave enables skin cells to produce vitamin D?
   A) visible light **C)** infrared waves
   B) ultraviolet waves **D)** X rays
4. Which of the following describes X rays?
   A) short wavelength, high frequency
   B) short wavelength, low frequency
   C) long wavelength, high frequency
   D) long wavelength, low frequency
5. Which of the following is changing in an AM radio wave?
   A) speed **C)** amplitude
   B) frequency **D)** wavelength
6. Which type of electromagnetic wave is used to produce a thermogram?
   A) X rays **C)** infrared waves
   B) ultraviolet waves **D)** gamma rays
7. Which type of electromagnetic wave spans wavelengths from less than 1 cm to about 1,000 m?
   A) X rays **C)** gamma rays
   B) radio waves **D)** ultraviolet waves
8. What is the name of the ability of some materials to absorb ultraviolet light and re-emit it as visible light?
   A) modulation **C)** transmission
   B) handoff **D)** fluorescence
9. Which of these colors of visible light has the shortest wavelength?
   A) blue **C)** red
   B) green **D)** white
10. Which type of electromagnetic wave has wavelengths slightly longer than humans can see?
    A) X rays **C)** infrared waves
    B) ultraviolet waves **D)** gamma rays

Thinking Critically

11. When you heat food in a microwave oven, the ceramic, glass, or plastic containers usually remain cool, even though the food can become hot. Why is this?
12. Doctors and dentists often use X rays for medical imaging. Why are X rays useful for this purpose?
13. Why are UVB rays more harmful to people than UVA rays are?
14. The doors of microwave ovens are made of glass covering a metal sheet with many small holes in it. When the microwave oven is in use, a light inside allows you to see the food being heated. What prevents the microwaves from passing through the door just as the light does?

15. Electromagnetic waves consist of vibrating magnetic fields. Why don't you see a compass vibrate when light strikes it?

Developing Skills

16. **Developing Multimedia Presentations** Create a multi-media presentation on how radio waves are used for communication.

Chapter Assessment Planner

Portfolio Encourage students to place in their portfolios one or two items of what they consider to be their best work. Examples include:

- Assessment, p. 395
- Curriculum Connection, p. 400
- Reteach, p. 401
- Science Journal, p. 407

Performance Additional performance assessments, Performance Task Assessment Lists, and rubrics for evaluating these activities can be found in Glencoe's **Performance Assessment in the Science Classroom.**

17. Classifying Look around your home, school, and community. Make a list of the many types of technology that use electromagnetic wave. Beside each item, write the type of electromagnetic wave it uses.

18. Writing a Paper Some people warn that microwaves from cell phones can be harmful. Research this problem and write a paper describing your opinion.

19. Concept Mapping Copy the diagram and fill in the missing events about ozone destruction.

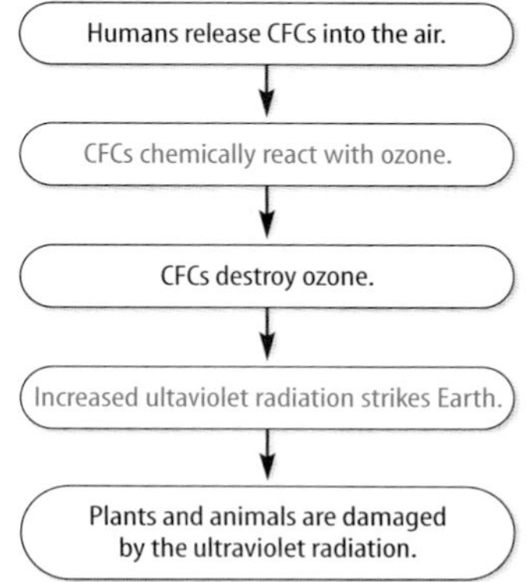
Humans release CFCs into the air.
CFCs chemically react with ozone.
CFCs destroy ozone.
Increased ultaviolet radiation strikes Earth.
Plants and animals are damaged by the ultraviolet radiation.

Performance Assessment

20. Observe and Infer Tune a radio to various AM and FM frequencies. Notice how strong or weak the signals are at various times of the day and night. Record your observations in your Science Journal.

Technology

Go to the Glencoe Science Web site at **science.glencoe.com** or use the **Glencoe Science CD-ROM** for additional chapter assessment.

THE PRINCETON REVIEW Test Practice

Because radio waves can reflect off objects, they are used to detect an object's location. The two rescue ships below are using radio waves to search for a life raft.

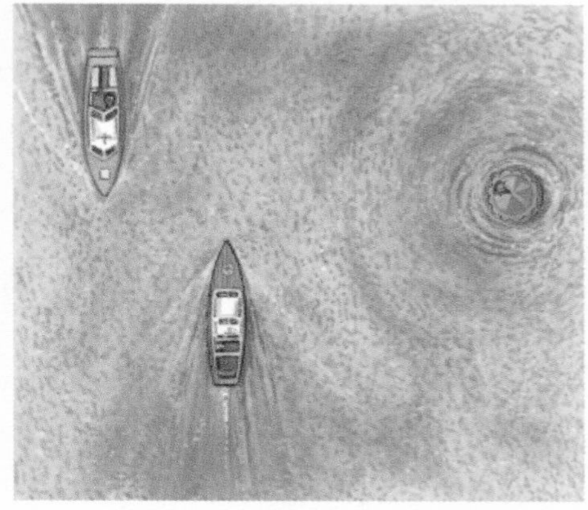
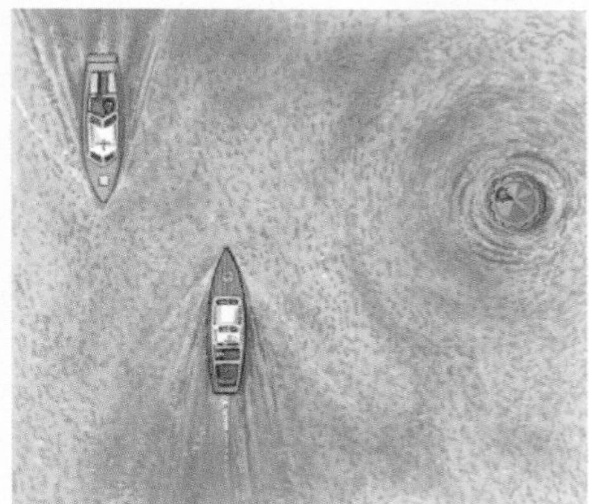

Study the picture and answer the following questions.

1. What do the rescuers know to help them aim toward the life boat?
   A) the strength of the carrier wave
   B) the amplitude and frequency of the radio waves that were sent out
   C) the frequency of the reflected radio waves.
   D) the direction from which the reflected radio waves came.

2. Why will the rescuers detect the reflected radio waves at different times?
   F) The speed of the radio waves leaving each ship is different.
   G) The life boat is a different distance from each ship.
   H) Only one ship is sending radio waves.
   J) the life boat is avoiding detection.

Chapter 13 Assessment

THE PRINCETON REVIEW Test Practice

The Test-Taking Tip was written by The Princeton Review, the nation's leader in test preparation.

1. D
2. G

Developing Skills

16. Presentations should show various forms of communication and the type of electromagnetic waves used with each. Examples are cell phones, satellite communication, and communication with spacecraft.
17. Possible answers: television (radio waves), microwave oven (microwaves), television remote control (infrared waves), cell phone (microwaves)
18. Some people believe that there is no evidence that the low-frequency, non-ionizing radiation used by cell phones causes any adverse health effects if exposure is limited. Others believe that there is sufficient evidence to suggest that cell phone use causes DNA damage and initiates brain tumor growth.
19. See student page.

Performance Assessment

20. Students might notice that FM signals are clearer, but AM signals have greater range, especially at night. Use **PASC,** p. 97.

Assessment Resources

Reproducible Masters

Chapter Resources Booklet
Chapter Review, pp. 37–38
Chapter Tests, pp. 39–42
Assessment Transparency Activity, p. 49

Glencoe Science Web Site
Interactive Tutor
Chapter Quizzes

Glencoe Technology
Assessment Transparency
Interactive CD-ROM Chapter Quizzes
ExamView Pro Test Bank
Vocabulary PuzzleMaker Software
MindJogger Videoquiz DVD/VHS

Section/Objectives	Standards		Activities/Features
	National	State/Local	
Chapter Opener	See p. 37T for a Key to Standards		**Explore Activity:** Make your own rainbow, p. 419 **Before You Read,** p. 419
Section 1 The Behavior of Light 2 sessions 1 block 1. **Describe** the differences among opaque, transparent, and translucent materials. 2. **Explain** how light is reflected. 3. **Discuss** how refraction separates white light.	National Content Standards: UCP5, A1, B1 (5–8), B2, B6		**MiniLAB:** Observing Refraction in Water, p. 423
Section 2 Light and Color 1 session .5 block 1. **Explain** how you see color. 2. **Describe** the difference between light color and pigment color. 3. **Predict** what happens when different colors are mixed.	National Content Standards: UCP5, B6, E2		**Life Science Integration,** p. 428
Section 3 Producing Light 1 session .5 block 1. **Explain** how incandescent and fluorescent lightbulbs work. 2. **Analyze** the advantages and disadvantages of different lighting devices. 3. **Explain** how a laser produces coherent light. 4. **Describe** various uses of lasers	National Content Standards: UCP5, B6, E2, F5 (5–8), F6 (9–12)		**MiniLAB:** Discovering Energy Waste in Lightbulbs, p. 431 **Science Online,** p. 432 **Visualizing Lasers,** p. 433 **Chemistry Integration,** p. 434
Section 4 Using Light 2 sessions 1 block 1. Describe polarized light and the uses of polarizing filters. 2. Apply the concept of total internal reflection to the uses of optical fibers.	National Content Standards: UCP5, B6, E2, F5 (5–8), F6 (9–12)		**Science Online,** p. 437 **Activity:** Make a Light Bender, p. 441 **Activity:** Polarizing Filters, p. 442 **Science and Language Arts:** A Haiku Garden, p. 444

Activity Materials	Reproducible Resources	Section Assessment	Technology
Explore Activity: flashlight, glass prism, pan of water, dishwashing liquid, compact disc	**Chapter Resources Booklet** Foldables Worksheet, p. 17 Note-taking Worksheets, pp. 35–37	GLENCOE'S ASSESSMENT ADVANTAGE	
MiniLAB: penny, short opaque cup, water	**Chapter Resources Booklet** Transparency Activity, p. 46 MiniLAB, p. 3 Enrichment, p. 31 Reinforcement, p. 27 Transparency Activity, pp. 51–52 Directed Reading for Content Mastery, pp. 19–20 **Lab Activity,** pp. 9–12	**Portfolio** Curriculum Connection, p. 421 **Performance** MiniLAB, p. 423 Skill Builder Activities, p. 424 **Content** Section Assessment, p. 424	Section Focus Transparency Teaching Transparency Interactive CD-ROM/DVD Guided Reading Audio Program
	Chapter Resources Booklet Transparency Activity, p. 47 Enrichment, p. 32 Reinforcement, p. 28 Directed Reading for Content Mastery, p. 20 **Physical Science Critical Thinking/Problem Solving,** p. 4	**Portfolio** Activity, p. 428 **Performance** Skill Building Activity, p. 429 **Content** Section Assessment, p. 429	Section Focus Transparency Interactive CD-ROM/DVD Guided Reading Audio Program
MiniLAB: 1 incandescent bulb and 1 fluorescent bulb of identical wattage, power source for bulbs, foam cup, plastic food wrap, thermometetr	**Chapter Resources Booklet** Transparency Activity, p. 48 MiniLAB, p. 4 Enrichment, p. 33 Reinforcement, p. 29 Directed Reading for Content Mastery, p. 21 **Cultural Diversity,** p. 57 **Mathematics Skill Activities,** p. 47	**Portfolio** Assessment, p. 435 **Performance** MiniLAB, p. 431 Skill Builder Activities, p. 435 **Content** Section Assessment, p. 435	Section Focus Transparency Interactive CD-ROM/DVD Guided Reading Audio Program
Activity: light source, pencil, clear rectangular container, water, clay **Activity:** 3 polarizing filters, lamp or flashlight	**Chapter Resources Booklet** Transparency Activity, p. 49 Enrichment, p. 34 Reinforcement, p. 30 Directed Reading for Content Mastery, pp. 21, 22 Lab Activity, pp. 13–16 Activity Worksheet, pp. 5–6, 7–8	**Portfolio** Reteach, p. 440 **Performance** Skill Builder Activities, p. 440 **Content** Section Assessment, p. 440	Section Focus Transparency Interactive CD-ROM/DVD Guided Reading Audio Program

Need materials? Contact Science Kit at 1-800-828-7777 or www.sciencekit.com on the Internet.

End of Chapter Assessment

GLENCOE'S ASSESSMENT ADVANTAGE

Blackline Masters	Technology	Professional Series
Chapter Resources Booklet Chapter Review, pp. 39–40 Chapter Tests, pp. 41–44 **Standardized Test Practice by The Princeton Review,** pp. 60–63	MindJogger Videoquiz CD-ROM Explorations and Quizzes Vocabulary Puzzle Makers ExamView Pro Test Bank Interactive Lesson Planner Interactive Teacher's Edition	Performance Assessment in the Science Classroom (PASC)

Transparencies

Section Focus

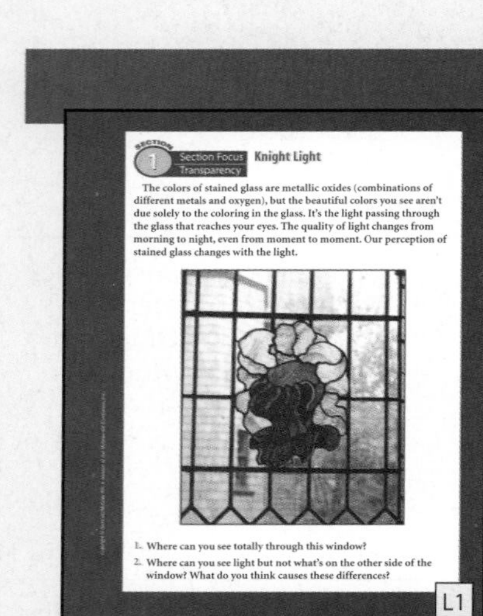
Section 1 Section Focus Transparency **Knight Light**

The colors of stained glass are metallic oxides (combinations of different metals and oxygen), but the beautiful colors you see aren't due solely to the coloring in the glass. It's the light passing through the glass that reaches your eyes. The quality of light changes from morning to night, even from moment to moment. Our perception of stained glass changes with the light.

1. Where can you see totally through this window?
2. Where can you see light but not what's on the other side of the window? What do you think causes these differences?

L1

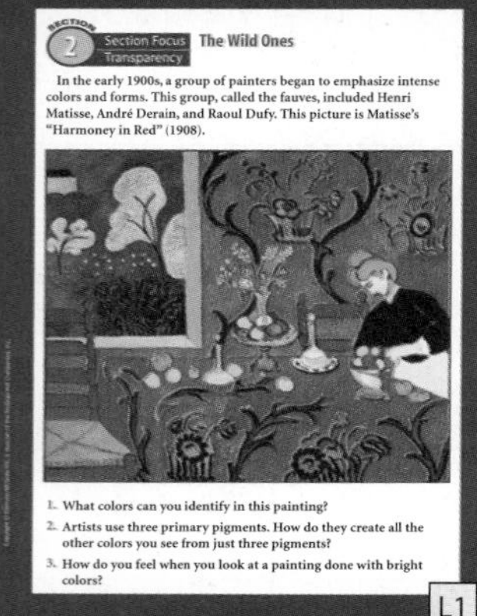
Section 2 Section Focus Transparency **The Wild Ones**

In the early 1900s, a group of painters began to emphasize intense colors and forms. This group, called the fauves, included Henri Matisse, André Derain, and Raoul Dufy. This picture is Matisse's "Harmoney in Red" (1908).

1. What colors can you identify in this painting?
2. Artists use three primary pigments. How do they create all the other colors you see from just three pigments?
3. How do you feel when you look at a painting done with bright colors?

L1

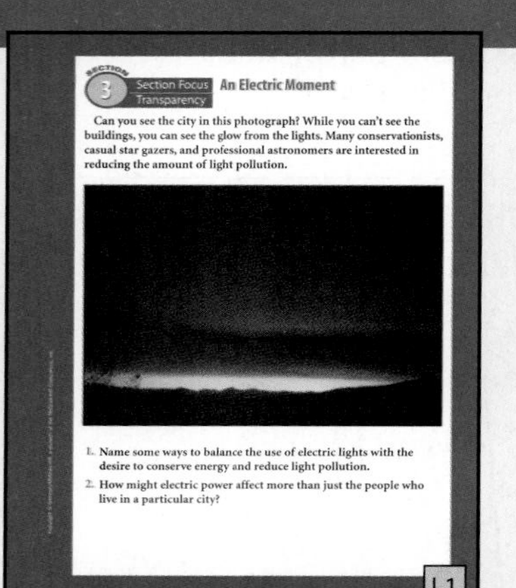
Section 3 Section Focus Transparency **An Electric Moment**

Can you see the city in this photograph? While you can't see the buildings, you can see the glow from the lights. Many conservationists, casual star gazers, and professional astronomers are interested in reducing the amount of light pollution.

1. Name some ways to balance the use of electric lights with the desire to conserve energy and reduce light pollution.
2. How might electric power affect more than just the people who live in a particular city?

L1

This is a representation of key blackline masters available in the Teacher Classroom Resources. See Resource Manager boxes within the chapter for additional information.

Assessment

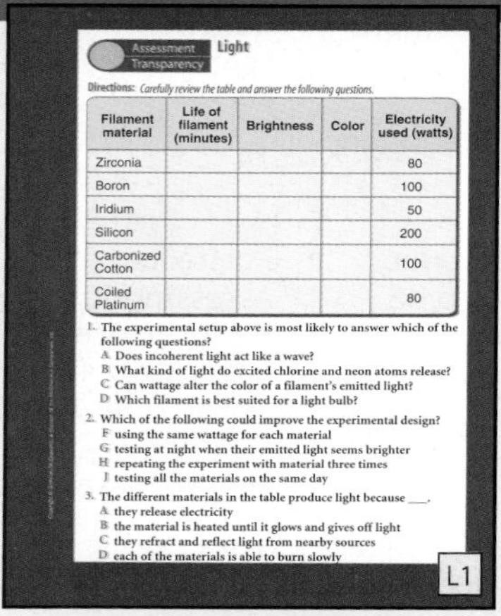

Assessment Transparency **Light**

Directions: Carefully review the table and answer the following questions.

Filament material	Life of filament (minutes)	Brightness	Color	Electricity used (watts)
Zirconia				80
Boron				100
Iridium				50
Silicon				200
Carbonized Cotton				100
Coiled Platinum				80

1. The experimental setup above is most likely to answer which of the following questions?
   A Does incoherent light act like a wave?
   B What kind of light do excited chlorine and neon atoms release?
   C Can wattage alter the color of a filament's emitted light?
   D Which filament is best suited for a light bulb?
2. Which of the following could improve the experimental design?
   F using the same wattage for each material
   G testing at night when their emitted light seems brighter
   H repeating the experiment with material three times
   J testing all the materials on the same day
3. The different materials in the table produce light because ___.
   A they release electricity
   B the material is heated until it glows and gives off light
   C they refract and reflect light from nearby sources
   D each of the materials is able to burn slowly

L1

Teaching

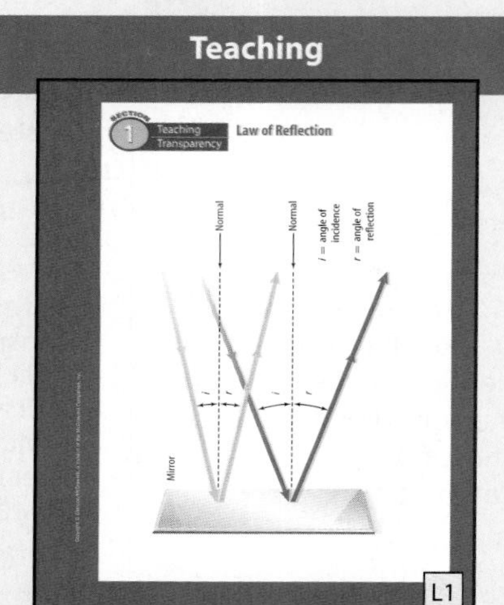
Section 1 Teaching Transparency **Law of Reflection**

L1

Key to Teaching Strategies

The following designations will help you decide which activities are appropriate for your students.

- L1 Level 1 activities should be appropriate for students with learning difficulties.
- L2 Level 2 activities should be within the ability range of all students.
- L3 Level 3 activities are designed for above-average students.
- ELL ELL activities should be within the ability range of English Language Learners.
- COOP LEARN Cooperative Learning activities are designed for small group work.
- LS Multiple Learning Styles logos are used throughout to indicate strategies that address different learning styles.
- P These strategies represent student products that can be placed into a best-work portfolio.

Hands-on Activities

Activity Worksheets

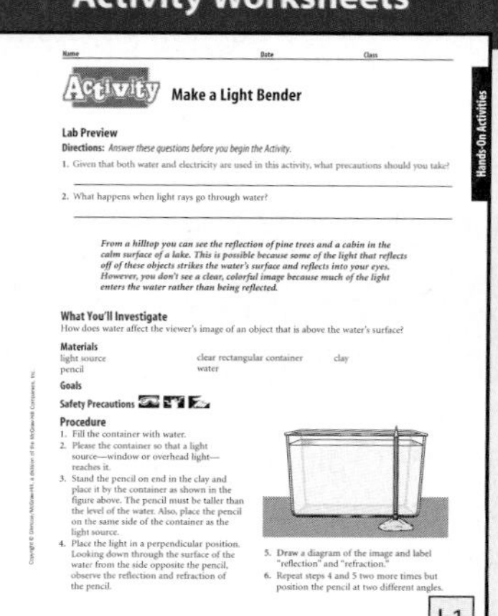
Activity **Make a Light Bender**

Lab Preview

Directions: Answer these questions before you begin the Activity.

1. Given that both water and electricity are used in this activity, what precautions should you take?
2. What happens when light rays go through water?

From a hilltop you can see the reflection of pine trees and a cabin in the calm surface of a lake. This is possible because some of the light that reflects off of these objects strikes the water's surface and reflects into your eyes. However, you don't see a clear, colorful image because much of the light enters the water rather than being reflected.

What You'll Investigate

How does water affect the viewer's image of an object that is above the water's surface?

Materials: light source, pencil, clear rectangular container, water, clay

Goals

Safety Precautions

Procedure

1. Fill the container with water.
2. Place the container so that a light source—window or overhead light—reaches it.
3. Stand the pencil on end in the clay and place it by the container as shown in the figure above. The pencil must be taller than the level of the water. Also, place the pencil on the same side of the container as the light source.
4. Place the light in a perpendicular position. Looking down through the surface of the water from the side opposite the pencil, observe the reflection and refraction of the pencil.
5. Draw a diagram of the image and label "reflection" and "refraction."
6. Repeat steps 4 and 5 two more times but position the pencil at two different angles.

L1

Laboratory Activities

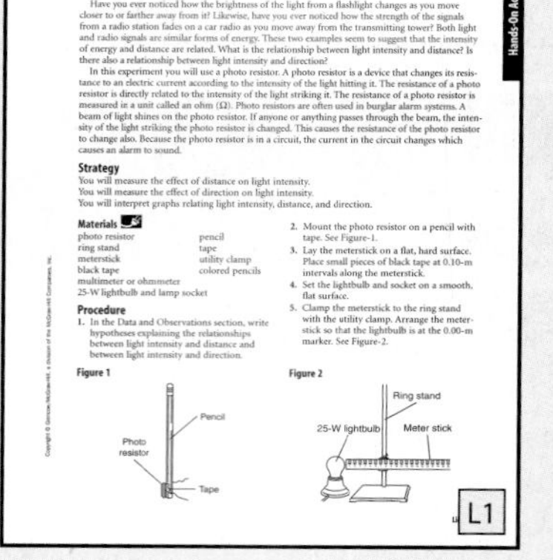
Lab 1 Laboratory Activity **Light Intensity**

Have you ever noticed how the brightness of the light from a flashlight changes as you move closer to or farther away from it? Likewise, have you ever noticed how the strength of the signals from a radio station fades on a car radio as you move away from the transmitting tower? Both light and radio signals are similar forms of energy. These two examples seem to suggest that the intensity of energy and distance are related. What is the relationship between light intensity and distance? Is there also a relationship between light intensity and direction?

Strategy

You will measure the effect of distance on light intensity.
You will measure the effect of direction on light intensity.
You will interpret graphs relating light intensity, distance, and direction.

Materials: photo resistor, ring stand, meterstick, black tape, multimeter or ohmmeter, 25-W lightbulb and lamp socket, pencil, tape, utility clamp, colored pencils

L1

Meeting Different Ability Levels

Content Outline

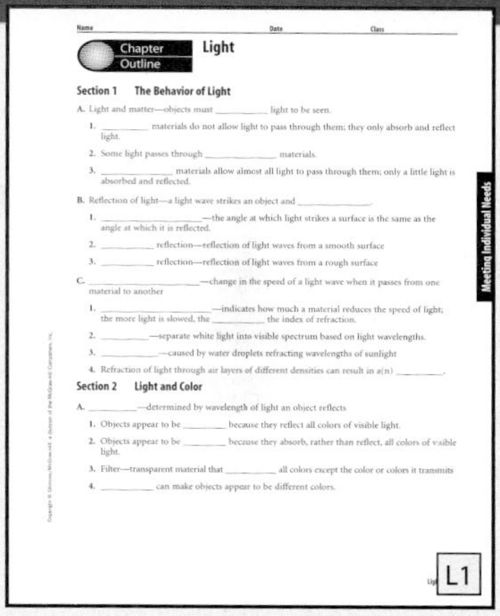
Chapter Outline — Light
Section 1 The Behavior of Light
Section 2 Light and Color
L1

Reinforcement

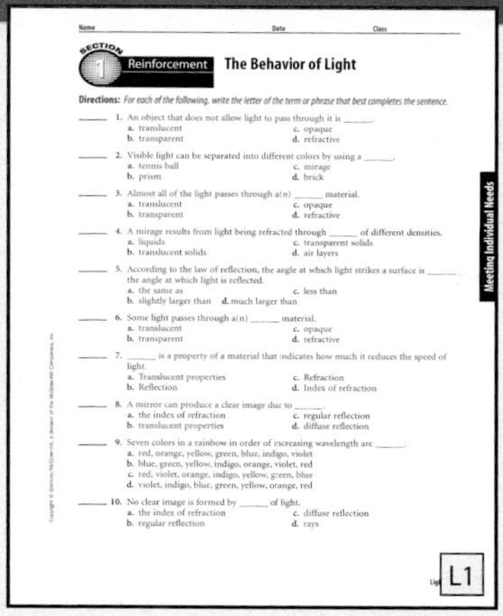
Section 1 Reinforcement — The Behavior of Light
L1

Directed Reading

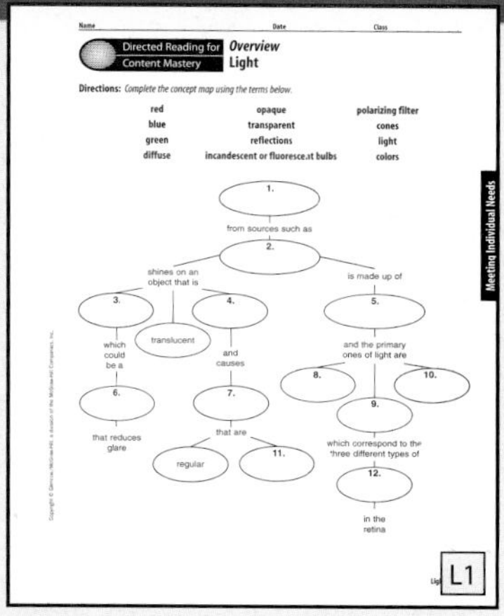
Directed Reading for Content Mastery — Overview — Light
L1

Enrichment

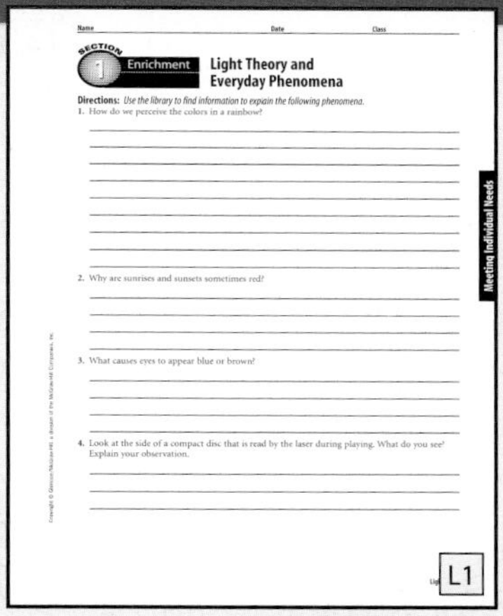
Section 1 Enrichment — Light Theory and Everyday Phenomena
L1

Spanish Directed Reading

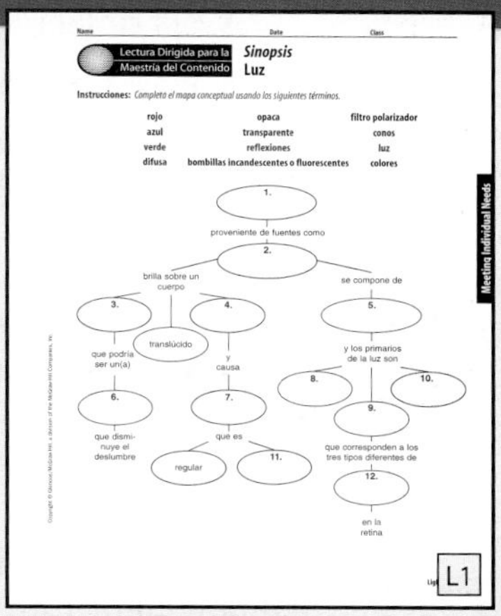
Lectura Dirigida para la Maestría del Contenido — Sinopsis — Luz
L1

Assessment

Chapter Tests

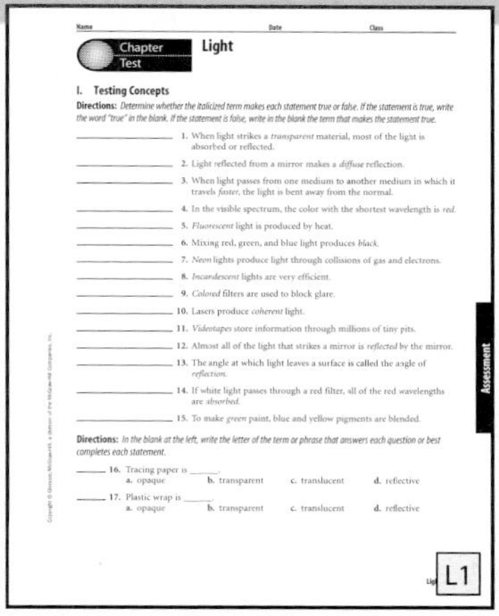
Chapter Test — Light
I. Testing Concepts
L1

Test Practice Workbook

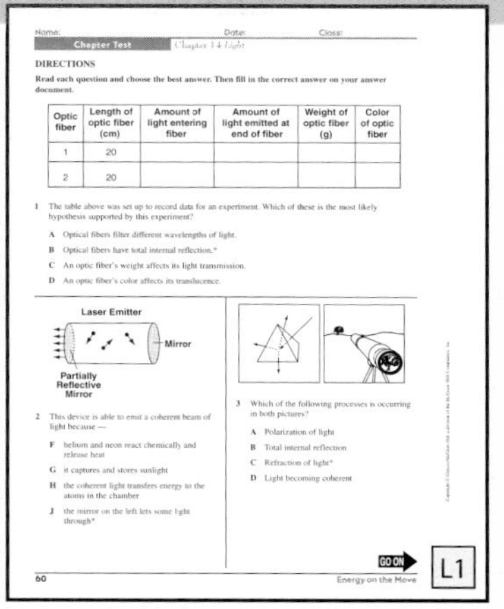
Chapter Test — Chapter 14 Light
L1

Chapter Review

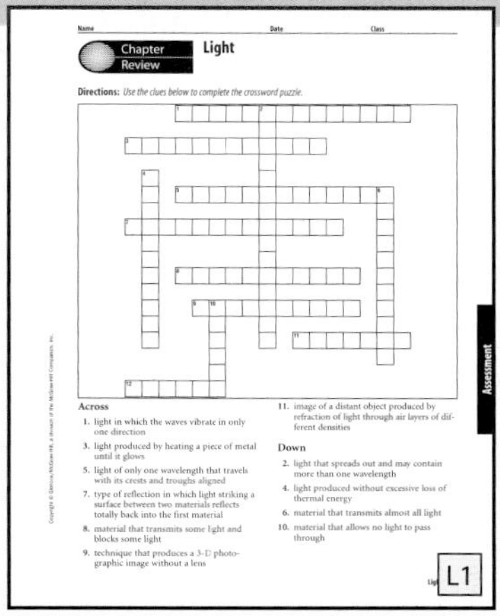
Chapter Review — Light
L1

Science Content Background

SECTION 1

The Behavior of Light

Reflection of Light

The reason we can see objects is that they either emit or reflect light. Most materials don't produce thier own light, so almost everything we see is reflecting light. The reflected light travels to the retina of our eyes where an image is received and sent to the brain.

> **Student Misconception**
>
> Students may think that only special materials reflect light.
>
> **Refer to the facing page for teaching strategies to address this misconception. Refer to pages 421, 425, 426 for content related to this topic.**

Retroflectors, such as those used on bicycle reflectors, reflect light of all angles back to its source. An example of a retroflector is three mirrors arranged at right angles to form a corner. Light strikes one mirror and bounces around and it returns in the direction of the incident rays. A bike's reflector is composed of many of these little "corners." Apollo 11 astronauts set up retroflectors so laser beams would bounce back to their senders.

Refraction of Light

For refraction to occur light must pass at an angle other than 90° into another material with a different optical density. When light moves into a more optically dense material it is refracted towards the normal, when entering a less optically dense material it is refracted away from the normal.

When most people swim underwater without goggles, their vision is not as good. Normally light is refracted when it goes from air into the eye and this is necessary for good vision. Since water has a higher index of refraction than air, light is not refracted enough. Wearing goggles puts air in front of the eye and restores normal vision.

SECTION 2

Light and Color

Mixing Colors

Three types of color dots—red, blue, and green—are repeated throughout the screen of a color TV set. By varying the expression of each, all the colors are achieved.

SECTION 3

Producing Light

Fluorescent Lights

Molecules in black light posters absorb ultraviolet radiation and then emit light in the visible spectrum. In a similar way, chemicals added to some laundry detergents contain molecules that absorb ultraviolet light and emit blue light. This blue makes whites look even whiter.

SECTION 4

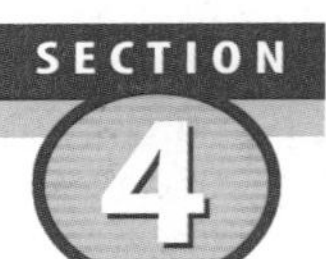

Using Light

Polarized Light

Three-dimensional movies are created by having two cameras record a scene and then two projectors play the recordings back. Through the use of special Polaroid or color lenses, one eye sees the movie from one camera and the other eye sees the movie from the other camera. This creates a very real 3-d effect.

> **SCIENCE Online**
>
> **For additional content background on this topic, go to the Glencoe Science Web site at science.glencoe.com.**

IDENTIFYING Misconceptions

Find Out What Students Think

Students may think that . . .

- **Only special materials reflect light.**

Students are aware that mirrors and shiny metals reflect light. It is not as obvious that other materials also reflect light. Students may not be aware that we can see objects such as trees, rocks, walls, people, moons, and planets because they reflect light. This may seem obvious to most adults, but if a student is not aware of this, it will hinder learning other concepts about light.

Discussion

Write the following question on the board. **Which of the following materials ordinarily reflect light?**

(a) mirror **(b) blue poster paper**
(c) aluminum foil **(d) white cotton sheet**

Ask students to answer the question individually, then have students discuss the question among themselves and attempt to agree upon the answer.

Promote Understanding

Activity

Tell students that they will now have the opportunity to test the materials listed in the question above to see for themselves which ones do or do not reflect light.

Organize the class into groups. Give each group the following:

- a flashlight
- a sheet of white paper
- a mirror
- a sheet of light blue paper
- a piece of aluminum foil
- a section of a white cotton sheet

- Tell students that you will darken the room for the investigations, but that first they must determine how they will conduct their investigations and write down their procedures.
- Procedures will vary but probably most students will shine the flashlight at the material and look for the reflection of light. The white paper can be used to detect the reflected light, especially from the white sheet and the blue paper.
- After students have finished their investigations, have one student from each group write the group's results on the board. Then discuss the results as a class. Make sure students realize that all of the materials tested reflect light.

Assess

After completing the chapter, see *Identifying Misconceptions* in the Study Guide.

CHAPTER 

Light

Chapter Vocabulary

opaque
translucent
transparent
index of refraction
mirage
pigment
incandescent light
fluorescent light
coherent light
incoherent light
polarized light
holography
total internal reflection

What do you think?

Science Journal The photograph shows the pattern produced by light interference on a soap bubble.

CHAPTER 14

Light

A sunrise over the ocean is a spectacle of light and color. As the sun tops the horizon, sea and sky explode into an array of reds, pinks, and oranges. Why does the sky appear red? How are its colors reflected in the water? In this chapter, you will learn about light—how it travels, bends, reflects, and enables you to see different colors. You will also learn how different kinds of bulbs produce light and how light is used by lasers, optical scanners, and optical fibers.

What do you think?

Science Journal Look at the picture below with a classmate. Discuss what this might be or what is happening. Here's a hint: *It's full of air and doesn't last long.* Write your answer or best guess in your Science Journal.

418

Theme Connection

Energy Light is a form of energy that enables us to see the world around us. Energy can change forms. In incandescent lights, fluorescent lights, neon lights, and lasers we produce light from electrical energy and chemical energy.

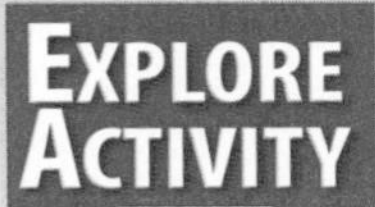

Light passing through a prism can produce exciting patterns of color. Imagine what your surroundings would look like now if humans could see only shades of gray instead of distinct colors. The ability to see color depends on the cells in your eyes that are sensitive to different wavelengths of light. What color is the light produced by a flashlight or the sun?

Make your own rainbow

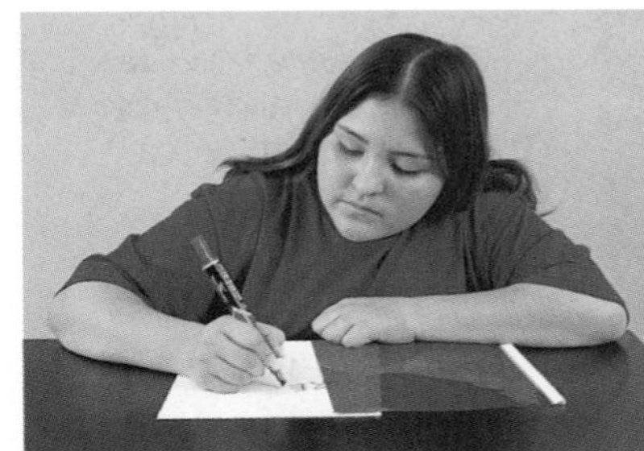

1. In a darkened room, shine a flashlight through a glass prism. Project the resulting colors onto a white wall or ceiling.
2. In a darkened room, shine a flashlight over the surface of some water with dishwashing liquid bubbles in it. What do you see?
3. Aim a flashlight at the surface of a compact disc.

Observe

How did your observations in each case differ? In your Science Journal, explain where you think the colors came from.

Before You Read

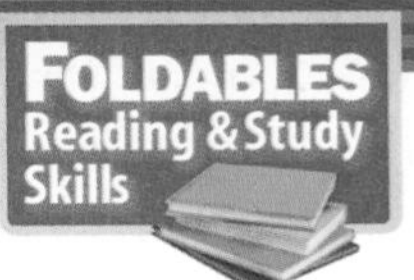

Making a Compare and Contrast Study Fold Make the following Foldable to compare and contrast the characteristics of opaque, translucent, and transparent.

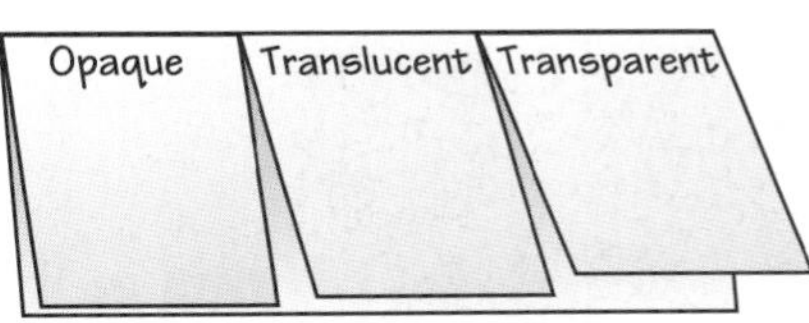

1. Place a sheet of paper in front of you so the short side is at the top. Fold the paper in half from top to bottom.
2. Fold both sides in to divide the paper into equal thirds. Unfold the paper so three sections show.
3. Through one thickness of paper, cut along each of the fold lines to the topfold, forming three tabs. Label each tab *Opaque, Translucent,* and *Transparent* as shown.
4. As you read the chapter, write characteristics of these materials under the tabs, using the words absorb, reflect, and transmit.

Explore Activity

Purpose The Explore Activity introduces students to the reflection and refraction of light. L1 ELL LS **Visual-Spatial**

Preparation Agitate the water and dishwashing liquid to form bubbles.

Materials prism, flashlight, bowl or pan, water, dishwashing liquid, compact disc

Teaching Strategy Darkening the room will make it easier for students to see the colors from the prism, dishwashing liquid, and compact disc.

Observe

In all three observations the student will see colors. The prism refracts the light, which separates it into colors that can be seen on the white wall or ceiling. The thin film on the soap bubbles and the closely spaced grooves on the compact disc cause interference between light waves, causing the colors students observe on their surfaces.

Portfolio Have students prepare a poster that accurately illustrates the light source, how light reached their eye, and color observations in each of the three steps of the Explore Activity. Use **PASC,** p. 145.

Before You Read

FOLDABLES Reading & Study Skills

Dinah Zike Study Fold

Purpose Use this activity and the resulting Foldable to determine what students know about light as they define key terms and find similarities and differences in how materials absorb, reflect, and transmit light.

For additional help, see Foldables Worksheet, p. 17 in **Chapter Resources Booklet,** or go to the Glencoe Science Web site at **science.glencoe.com.** See After You Read in the Study Guide at the end of this chapter.

SECTION

The Behavior of Light

1 Motivate

Bellringer Transparency

Display the Section Focus Transparency for Section 1. Use the accompanying Transparency Activity Master. L2 ELL

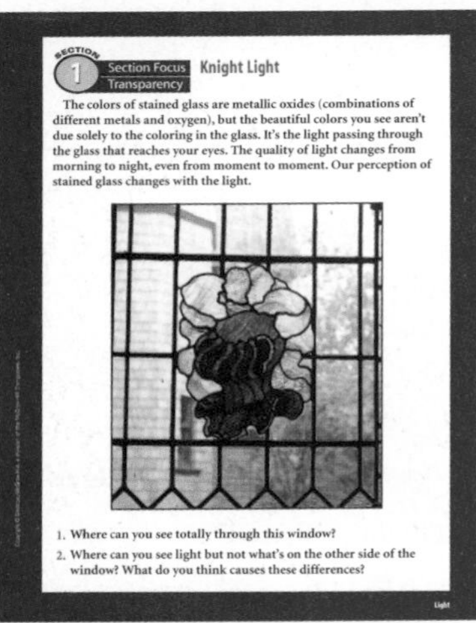

SECTION 1 Section Focus Transparency **Knight Light**

The colors of stained glass are metallic oxides (combinations of different metals and oxygen), but the beautiful colors you see aren't due solely to the coloring in the glass. It's the light passing through the glass that reaches your eyes. The quality of light changes from morning to night, even from moment to moment. Our perception of stained glass changes with the light.

1. Where can you see totally through this window?
2. Where can you see light but not what's on the other side of the window? What do you think causes these differences?

Light

Tie to Prior Knowledge

Ask students how their feet appear if they look at them while their heads are out of the water when they are standing in a swimming pool. They probably will say that they look distorted. This is because the speed of light in water is different from the speed of light in air, causing light to refract, which distorts the image.

SECTION 1

The Behavior of Light

As You Read

***What* You'll Learn**

- **Describe** the differences among opaque, transparent, and translucent materials.
- **Explain** how light is reflected.
- **Discuss** how refraction separates white light.

Vocabulary

opaque, translucent, transparent, index of refraction, mirage

***Why* It's Important**

Knowing how light behaves will help you understand various sights, such as reflections in a store window, rainbows, and mirages.

Light and Matter

Look around your room after turning off the lights at night. At first you can't see anything, but as your eyes adjust to the darkness, you begin to recognize some familiar objects. You know that some of the objects are brightly colored, but they look gray or black in the dim light. Turn on the light, and you clearly can see all the objects in the room, including their colors. What you see depends on the amount of light in the room and the color of the objects. To see an object, it must reflect some light back to your eyes.

Opaque, Transparent, and Translucent Some objects absorb light and others allow light to pass through them. The type of matter in an object determines the amount of light it absorbs, reflects, and transmits. For example, the **opaque** (oh PAYK) material in the candleholder in **Figure 1A,** only absorbs and reflects light—no light passes through it. As a result, you cannot see the candle inside.

Other materials allow some light to pass through, but you cannot see clearly through them. These are **translucent** (trans LEW sunt) materials, like the candleholder in **Figure 1B.**

Transparent materials like the candleholder in **Figure 1C** transmit almost all of the light that strikes them, so you can see objects clearly through them. Only a small amount of light is absorbed and reflected.

Figure 1
These candleholders have different light-transmitting properties.

A Opaque

B Translucent

C Transparent

420 CHAPTER 14 Light

Section Assessment Planner

PORTFOLIO
Curriculum Connection, p. 421

PERFORMANCE ASSESSMENT
Try at Home MiniLAB, p. 423
Skill Builder Activities, p. 424
See page 448 for more options.

CONTENT ASSESSMENT
Section, p. 424
Challenge, p. 424
Chapter, pp. 448–449

Reflection of Light

Just before you left for school this morning, did you take one last glance in a mirror to check your appearance? To see your reflection in the mirror, light had to reflect off you, hit the mirror, and reflect off the mirror into your eye. Reflection occurs when a light wave strikes an object and bounces off.

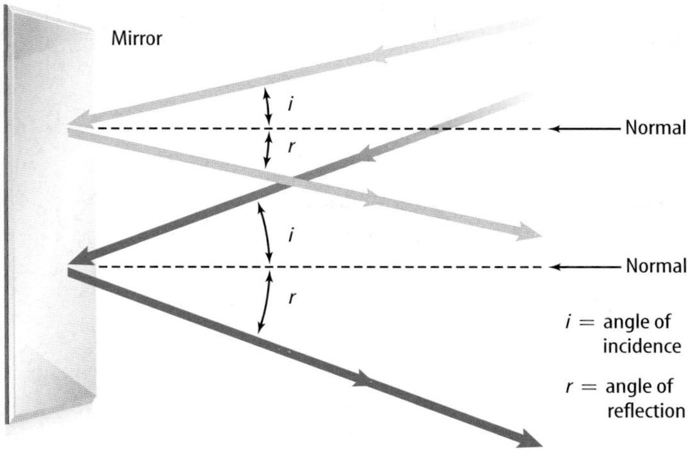

The Law of Reflection

Because light behaves as a wave, it obeys the law of reflection, as shown in **Figure 2.** According to the law of reflection, the angle at which a light wave strikes a surface is the same as the angle at which it is reflected. Light reflected from any surface—a mirror or a sheet of paper—follows this law.

Mirror
Normal
Normal
i
r
i = angle of incidence
r = angle of reflection

Figure 2
Light is reflected according to the law of reflection so that the angle of incidence always equals the angle of reflection.

Regular and Diffuse Reflection Why can you see your reflection in a store window but not in a brick wall? The answer has to do with the smoothness of the surfaces. A smooth, even surface like that of a pane of glass produces a sharp image by reflecting parallel light waves in only one direction. Reflection of light waves from a smooth surface is regular reflection. A brick wall has an uneven surface that causes parallel light waves to be reflected in many directions, as shown in **Figure 3.** Reflection of light from a rough surface is diffuse reflection.

Reading Check *What is diffuse reflection?*

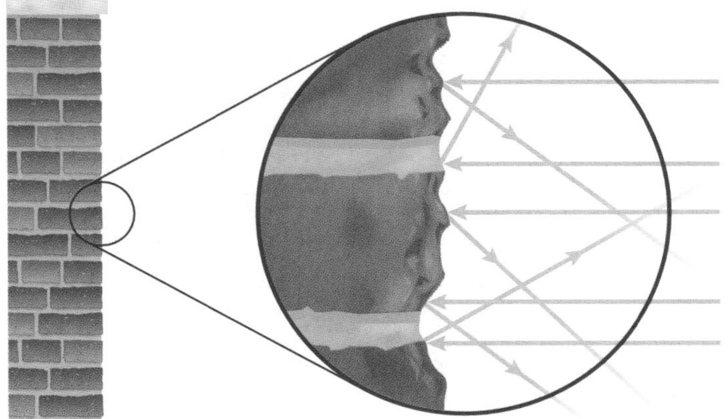

Figure 3
This brick wall has an uneven surface, so it produces a diffuse reflection.

Curriculum Connection

Language Arts Have students write fictitious short stories about why the sky is blue. Then have them research and write the true reason. The short-wavelength violet and blue portions of sunlight interact with air molecules and are scattered. Long-wavelength red light passes straight through to Earth. We see the blue light rather than the violet because our eyes are more sensitive to blue. L3 LS **Linguistic** P

Resource Manager

Chapter Resources Booklet

Note-taking Worksheets, pp. 35–37
Transparency Activity, pp. 51–52
Enrichment, p. 31

2 Teach

Light and Matter

Use Science Words

Word Usage The words *opaque*, *transparent*, and *translucent* describe how well light passes through a material. Have students use these words in sentences that reflect their meanings. Possible answer: I can see through a transparent window, but I can't see through an opaque wall. I can see light but not images through waxed paper, which is translucent. L2 ELL LS **Linguistic**

Reflection of Light

IDENTIFYING Misconceptions

Some students may think that only special materials reflect light. See page 418F for teaching strategies that address this misconception.

Teacher FYI

Materials that are transparent to light are not necessarily transparent to other types of radiation. For example, clear glass transmits long-wavelength ultraviolet rays but blocks most short-wavelength ultraviolet rays. This explains why you are not likely to get a sunburn from light through a window.

Reading Check

Answer reflection of light from a rough surface

Reflection of Light, continued

Use an Analogy

Tell students that reflecting light is similar to a ball bouncing off a wall. If you roll the ball directly toward the wall, it will bounce straight back toward you. If you roll it at an angle, it will bounce so that the angle between the incoming ball and the wall equals the angle between the outgoing ball and the wall. Allow students to roll a ball at a wall from different angles. L2 ELL LS **Kinesthetic**

Refraction of Light

Answer Refraction occurs as a light wave changes speed as it passes from one material to another.

Extension

The index of refraction of a material is the ratio of the speed of light in a vacuum to the speed of light in the material. The higher the index of refraction, the more slowly light travels through the material. Given that the speed of light in a vacuum (c_v) is 300,000 km/s, the following indices of refraction (n), and $v = c_v/n$, have students determine the speed of light through these materials: water, n = 1.33; glass, n = 1.52; diamond, n = 2.42. Approximate values are: water, c_m = 225,000 km/s; glass, c_m = 197,000 km/s; diamond, c_m = 124,000 km/s. **Through which of these materials does light travel the slowest?** diamond L3
LS **Logical-Mathematical**

Figure 4
Although the surface of this pot may seem smooth, it produces a diffuse reflection. At high magnification, the surface is seen to be rough.

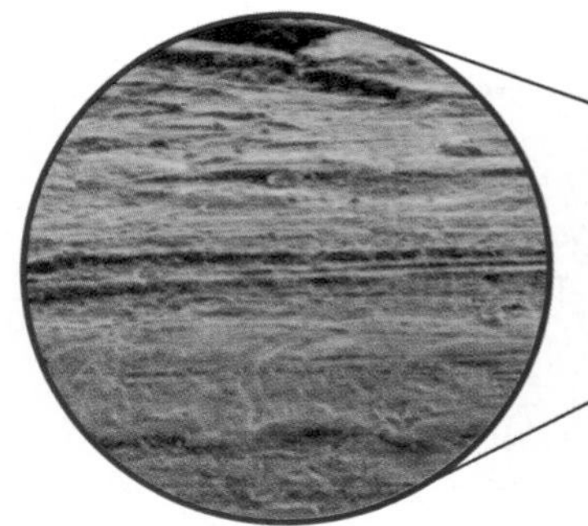

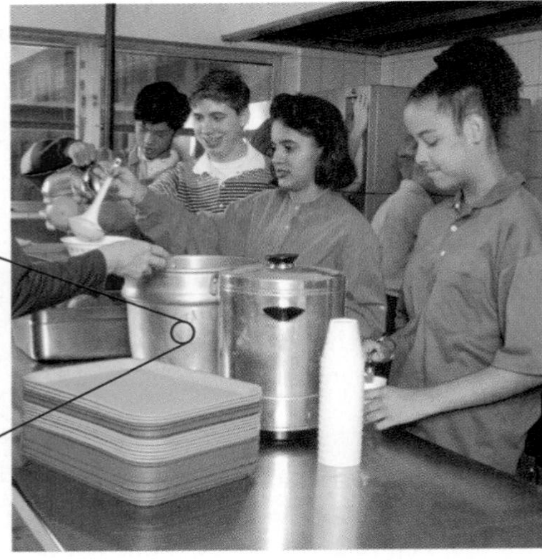

Roughness of Surfaces Even a surface that appears to be smooth can be rough enough to cause diffuse reflection. For example, a metal pot might seem smooth, but at high magnification, the surface shows rough spots, as shown **Figure 4.** To cause a regular reflection, the roughness of the surface must be less than the wavelengths it reflects.

Refraction of Light

What occurs when a light wave passes from one material to another—from air to water, for example? Refraction is caused by a change in the speed of a wave when it passes from one material to another. If the light wave is traveling at an angle and the speed that light travels is different in the two materials, the wave will be bent, or refracted.

Reading Check *How does refraction occur?*

The Index of Refraction The amount of bending that takes place depends on the speed of light in both materials. The greater the difference is, the more the light will be bent as it passes at an angle from one material to the other. **Figure 5** shows an example of refraction. Every material has an **index of refraction**—a property of the material that indicates how much it reduces the speed of light.

The larger the index of refraction, the more light is slowed down in the material. For example, because glass has a larger index of refraction than air, light moves more slowly in glass than air. Many useful devices like eyeglasses, binoculars, cameras, and microscopes form images using refraction.

Figure 5
The spoon looks bent in the water because the light waves are refracted as they change speed when they pass from the water to the air.

Visual Learning

Figure 5 Emphasize that the spoon appears to be broken because of the different paths the light takes as it comes toward your eyes. Light from the spoon in water is bent more than light from the spoon in air, so the light that goes through the water to reach your eyes comes from a different place than it appears. Have students sketch the paths light takes in this picture. L2 ELL LS **Visual-Spatial**

Science Journal

Flattened Sun At the end of a warm, humid day, just as the Sun approaches the horizon, it appears to have a flattened bottom. Have students apply what they have learned about refraction of light to write a paragraph in their Science Journals explaining this phenomenon. Light waves from the bottom part of the Sun are refracted by moisture in the air. L3 LS **Logical-Mathematical**

Prisms A sparkling glass prism hangs in a sunny window, refracting the sunlight and projecting a colorful pattern onto the walls of the room. How does the bending of light create these colors? It occurs because the amount of bending also depends on the wavelength of the light. Wavelengths of visible light range from the longer red waves to the shorter violet waves. White light, such as sunlight, is made up of this whole range of wavelengths.

Figure 6
Refraction causes a prism to separate a beam of white light into different colors.

Figure 6 shows what occurs when white light passes through a prism. The triangular prism refracts the light twice—once when it enters the prism and again when it leaves the prism and reenters the air. Because the longer wavelengths of light are refracted less than the shorter wavelengths are, red light is bent the least. As a result of these different amounts of bending, the different colors are separated when they emerge from the prism. Which color of light would you expect to bend the most?

Rainbows Does the light leaving the prism in **Figure 6** remind you of a rainbow? Like prisms, rain droplets also refract light. The refraction of the different wavelengths can cause white light from the Sun to separate into the individual colors of visible light, as shown in **Figure 7.** A rainbow contains many colors, but typically the human eye can distinguish only about seven colors clearly. In order of decreasing wavelength, these colors are red, orange, yellow, green, blue, indigo, and violet.

Figure 7
As white light passes through the water droplet, the light is refracted into the colors of the visible spectrum.

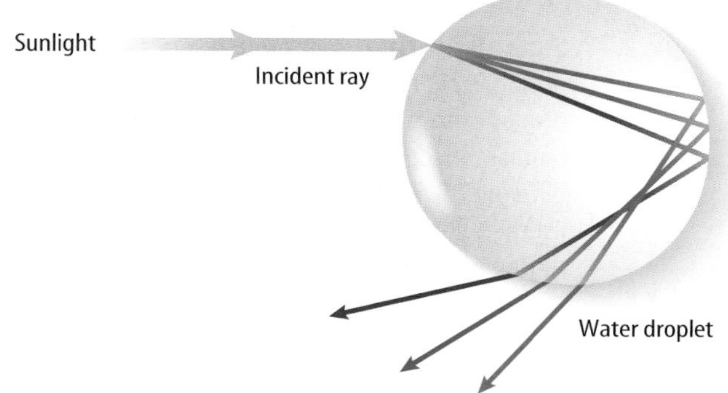

Observing Refraction in Water

Procedure

1. Place a **penny** at the bottom of a **short, opaque cup.** Set it on a **table** in front of you.
2. Have a partner slowly slide the cup away from you until you can't see the penny.
3. Without disturbing the penny or the cup and without moving your position, have your partner slowly pour **water** into the cup until you can see the penny.
4. Reverse roles and repeat the experiment.

Analysis

1. What did you observe? Explain how this is possible.
2. In your **Science Journal,** sketch the light path from the penny to your eye after the water was added.

Text Question Answer

violet

Purpose Students investigate how water bends light. L1 ELL IS **Visual-Spatial**

Materials penny, table, opaque cup, glass of water

Teaching Strategy Have students make a prediction about what may happen as the cup is filled with water.

Analysis

1. The penny became visible as water was added because the light from the penny was bent at the surface of the water.
2. Viewed from the side of the cup, a light ray travels diagonally upward from the penny to the surface of the water. At the surface, the ray is refracted more toward the horizontal.

Assessment

Oral Have students use the results of this MiniLAB to describe what a person sees when underwater in a swimming pool, wearing a mask and looking upward. objects are shifted above their true location Use **PASC,** p. 89.

Inclusion Strategies

Visually Impaired Suggest that visually impaired students work with sighted partners for the MiniLAB. The sighted student should clearly describe what can be seen at each step as the visually impaired student slides the cup away and feels the level of water in the cup. L2 ELL IS **Visual-Spatial**

Resource Manager

Chapter Resources Booklet
MiniLAB, p. 3
Directed Reading for Content Mastery, pp. 19–20
Reinforcement, p. 27
Lab Activity, pp. 9–12

Discussion

Why are mirages likely to appear in the desert? In a desert you can see a long distance over the surface and the air at ground level is much hotter than the air above it.

3 Assess

Reteach

Ask students to draw ray diagrams showing light coming from a flashlight, being refracted as it moves from air to water, being refracted off an object in the water, and being refracted as it moves from the water to air, and then hitting an observer's eye. L2

LS **Visual-Spatial**

Challenge

If you stand in a lighted room at night and look out a window, you can easily see your reflection. If you look out the window during the day, you see through the window instead of seeing your reflection. **Why do you easily see your reflection only at night?** During the day, the reflected light can't be easily seen because of all the light that is transmitted through the window from the outside. L3

LS **Logical-Mathematical**

Assessment

Process Show the class various materials and have students classify them as opaque, transparent, or translucent. Use **PASC,** p. 89.

Figure 8
Mirages result when air near the ground is much warmer or cooler than the air above. This causes some lightwaves reflected from the object to refract, creating one or more additional images.

Mirages When you're riding in a car on a hot day, you might see something that looks like a shimmering pool of water on the road ahead. As you get closer, the water seems to disappear. What you saw was a mirage. A **mirage** is an image of a distant object produced by the refraction of light through air layers of different densities. The density of air increases as the air gets cooler. The greater the difference in densities is, the more the light is refracted. Mirages result when the air at ground level is much warmer or much cooler than the layers of air above it, as **Figure 8** shows. The image you see is always some distance away from the actual object. For example, the water you think you see on a hot road surface is an image of the sky.

Section 1 Assessment

1. Contrast opaque, transparent, and translucent materials. Give at least one example of each.
2. Explain why you can see your reflection in a smooth piece of aluminum foil but not in a crumpled ball of foil.
3. Why are you more likely to see a mirage on a hot day than on a mild day?
4. What happens to white light when it passes through a prism?
5. **Think Critically** Consider the following parts of your body: the lens of your eye, a fingernail, your skin, and a tooth. Decide whether each of these is opaque, transparent, or translucent. Explain.

Skill Builder Activities

6. **Making and Using Tables** Construct a table that shows the light-reflecting or light-absorbing properties of different materials. Use the words *opaque, transparent,* and *translucent.* **For more help, refer to the Science Skill Handbook.**
7. **Communicating** Walk around your classroom noting five reflecting objects. Which objects display diffuse reflection and which display regular reflection? How does the surface differ on each? For each object you note, list the colors the object is absorbing. **For more help, refer to the Science Skill Handbook.**

Answers to Section Assessment

1. Transparent materials (clear glass) transmit all light, opaque materials (a wall) transmit no light, and translucent materials (waxed paper) transmit some light.
2. Smooth surfaces reflect light in one direction; rough surfaces reflect light in many directions.
3. Mirages are caused by refraction of light through air layers of different densities. On a hot day, air near the ground is warmer and less dense than air above it.
4. The different wavelengths of light in it are bent different amounts, causing a rainbow effect.
5. The lens is transparent, the fingernail and skin are translucent, the tooth is opaque.
6. Tables might include plastic wrap (transparent), a table (opaque), or wax paper (translucent).
7. Answers will vary. Students should indicate that most smooth, even surfaces exhibit regular reflection and that most irregular surfaces exhibit diffuse reflection.

SECTION 2

Light and Color

Colors

Why do some apples appear red, while others look green or yellow? An object's color depends on the wavelength of light it reflects. You know that white light is a blend of all colors of visible light. When a red apple is struck by white light, it reflects red light back to your eyes and absorbs all of the other colors. **Figure 9** shows white light striking a green leaf. Only the green light is reflected to your eyes.

Although some objects appear to be black, black isn't a color that is present in visible light. Objects that appear black absorb all colors of light and reflect little or no light back to your eye. White objects appear to be white because they reflect all colors of visible light.

Reading Check *Why does a white object appear white?*

Colored Filters Wearing tinted glasses changes the color of almost everything you look at. If the lenses are yellow, the world takes on a golden glow. If they are rose colored, everything looks rosy. Something similar would occur if you placed a colored, clear plastic sheet over this white page. The paper would appear to be the same color as the plastic. The plastic sheet and the tinted lenses are filters. A filter is a transparent material that transmits one or more colors of light but absorbs all others. The color of a filter is the color of the light that it transmits.

As You Read

***What* You'll Learn**

- **Explain** how you see color.
- **Describe** the difference between light color and pigment color.
- **Predict** what happens when different colors are mixed.

Vocabulary
pigment

***Why* It's Important**

From traffic lights to great works of art, color plays an important role in your world.

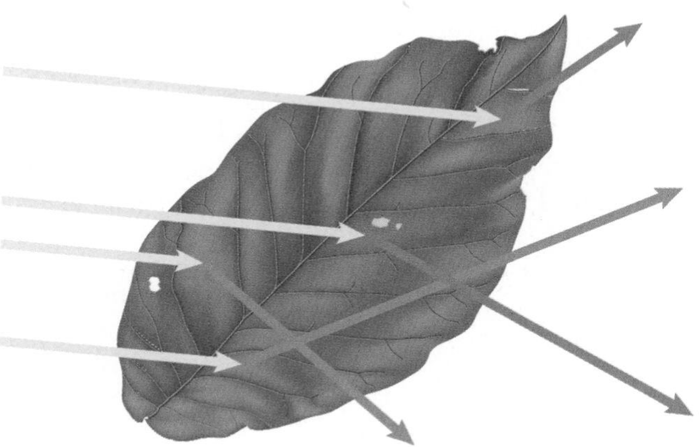

Figure 9
This green leaf absorbs all wavelengths of visible light except green.

Section Assessment Planner

Portfolio
Activity, p. 428

Performance Assessment
Skill Builder Activities, p. 429
See page 448 for more options.

Content Assessment
Section, p. 429
Challenge, p. 429
Chapter, pp. 448–449

SECTION

Light and Color

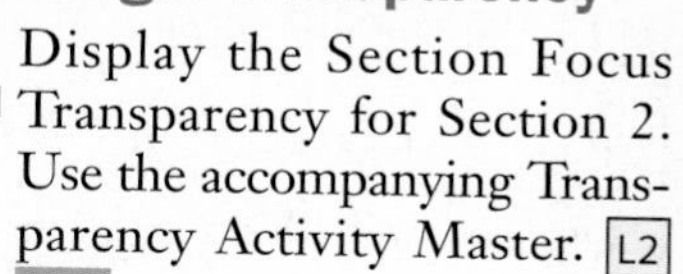

Bellringer Transparency

Display the Section Focus Transparency for Section 2. Use the accompanying Transparency Activity Master. L2 ELL

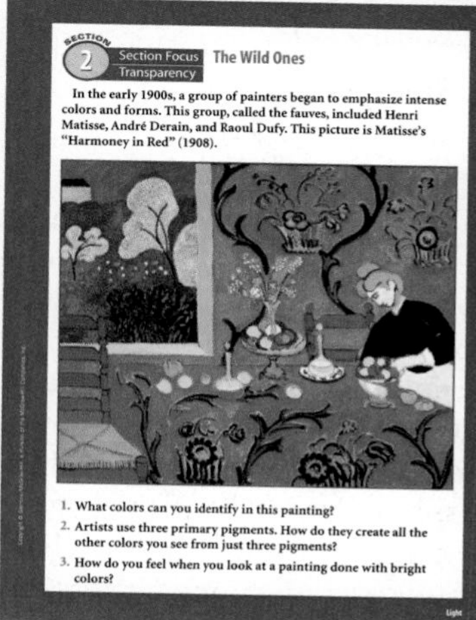

SECTION 2 Section Focus Transparency **The Wild Ones**

In the early 1900s, a group of painters began to emphasize intense colors and forms. This group, called the fauves, included Henri Matisse, André Derain, and Raoul Dufy. This picture is Matisse's "Harmoney in Red" (1908).

1. What colors can you identify in this painting?
2. Artists use three primary pigments. How do they create all the other colors you see from just three pigments?
3. How do you feel when you look at a painting done with bright colors?

Light

Tie to Prior Knowledge

Ask students to find something in the classroom that is red. Do this for orange, yellow, green, blue, and violet also. Tell students that in this section they will learn that the color of an object depends on how it absorbs or reflects light.

Reading Check

Answer It reflects all colors of visible light.

Resource Manager

Chapter Resources Booklet
Transparency Activity, p. 47
Enrichment, p. 32

2 Teach

Colors

Discussion

How is a colored light bulb a filter? The color of the glass on the outside of the bulb determines which color of light is transmitted. The colored glass absorbs the other colors from the white light given off by the filament. L2 IS **Logical-Mathematical**

Quick Demo

Use colored filters to demonstrate the effects shown in **Figure 10** with a colorful object in the classroom. L2 IS **Visual-Spatial**

IDENTIFYING Misconceptions

Students might assume that red, green, and blue are individual wavelengths of light. Explain that each of these is a range of wavelengths that has strongest reflection at a certain wavelength.

Text Question Answer

The cooler absorbs the red light so no color is reflected back to your eyes.

Seeing Color

Discussion

Why do the pupils of our eyes appear black? All light that enters our eyes through the pupils is absorbed by the retina. L3 IS **Logical-Mathematical**

Figure 10
The color of this cooler seems to change under different lighting conditions.

A The blue cooler is shown in white light.

B The cooler appears blue when viewed through a blue filter.

C The cooler appears black through an red filter.

Looking Through Colored Filters **Figure 10** shows what happens when you look at a colored object through various colored filters. In the white light in **Figure 10A,** a blue cooler looks blue because it reflects only the blue light in the white light striking it. It absorbs the light of all other colors. If you look at the cooler through a blue filter as in **Figure 10B,** the cooler still looks blue because the filter transmits the reflected blue light. **Figure 10C** shows how the cooler looks when you examine it through an red filter. Why does it appear to be black?

Seeing Color

As you approach a busy intersection, the color of the traffic light changes from green to yellow to red. On the cross street, the color changes from red to green. At a busy intersection, traffic safety depends on your ability to detect immediate color changes. How do you see colors?

Light and the Eye In a healthy eye, light enters and is focused on the retina, an area on the inside of your eyeball, as shown in **Figure 11A.** The retina is made up of two types of cells that absorb light, as shown in **Figure 11B.** When these cells absorb light energy, chemical reactions convert light energy into nerve impulses that are transmitted to the brain. One type of cell in the retina, called a cone, allows you to distinguish colors and detailed shapes of objects. Cones are most effective in daytime vision. Why?

Curriculum Connection

Theater Arts Plan a trip to your school auditorium or to a theater. Show students what kind of colored lighting is used to illuminate the stage. Investigate the special effects that can be created with lighting. L1 ELL IS **Visual-Spatial**

Cultural Diversity

Names of Colors It may seem obvious to say that the sky is blue and grass is green, but the Mayan people of Mexico have no words that clearly define the two colors. Many other cultures distinguish between colors differently, also. Even in English differences in colors are often difficult to define. Have students bring samples of such colors to class.

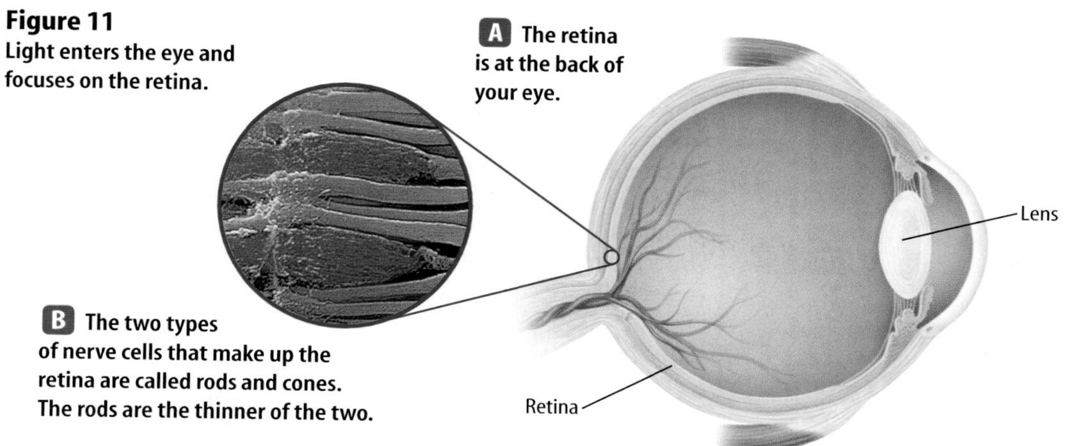

A The retina is at the back of your eye.
Lens
B The two types of nerve cells that make up the retina are called rods and cones. The rods are the thinner of the two.
Retina

Figure 11
Light enters the eye and focuses on the retina.

Cones and Rods Your eyes have three types of cones, each of which absorbs a different range of wavelengths. Red cones absorb mostly red and yellow, green cones absorb mostly yellow and green, and blue cones absorb mostly blue and violet. The second type of cell, called a rod, is more sensitive to dim light and is useful for night vision.

Interpreting Color Why does a banana look yellow? The light reflected by the banana causes the cone cells that are sensitive to both red and green light to send signals to your brain. Your brain would get the same signal if a mixture of red light and green light reached your eye. Again, your red and green cones would respond, and you would see yellow light because your brain can't perceive the difference between incoming yellow light and yellow light produced by combining red and green light. The next time you are at a play or a concert, look at the lighting above the stage. Watch how the colored lights combine to produce effects onstage.

Color Blindness If one or more of your sets of cones did not function properly, you would not be able to distinguish between certain colors. About eight percent of men and one-half percent of women have a form of color blindness. Most people who are said to be color blind are not truly blind to color, but they have difficulty distinguishing between a few colors, most commonly red and green. **Figure 12** shows a plate of a color blindness test. Because these two colors are used in traffic signals, drivers and pedestrians must be able to identify them.

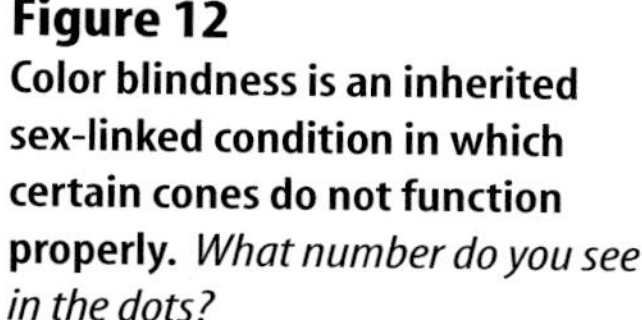

Figure 12
Color blindness is an inherited sex-linked condition in which certain cones do not function properly. *What number do you see in the dots?*

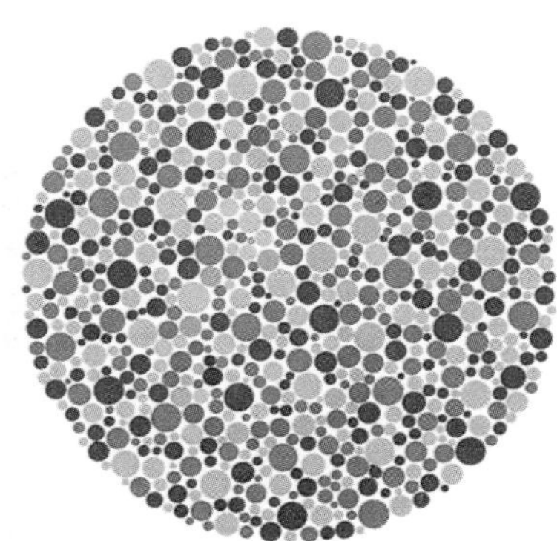

Life Science INTEGRATION

Cones and rods are located near the back of the retina. Cones are located near the center, and rods are located in the peripheral areas. The point at which the optic nerve is connected to the retina has no cones or rods. Your eye is not sensitive to light that falls on this spot.

Extension

Contact lenses that enable a person who is color-blind to distinguish certain colors better are now available. Have students investigate these lenses to find out how they work and their limitations. The lenses are coated with color filters that increase the brightness or darkness of certain colors. This enables the person to distinguish colors better. L3 **LS Linguistic**

Caption Answer

Figure 12 Answers will vary depending on whether the cones of the eye are functioning properly.

Discussion

Are objects still colored in a dark room? Some students may say no because color results from light reflection. Others may say yes, because the property that makes the object reflect light of a certain color is still present, so when the lights are on again, the object will be the same color. L2 **LS Logical-Mathematical**

Visual Learning

Figure 11 Point out the position of the retina. Behind the retina is the optic nerve, which takes information from the rods and cones and sends it to the brain. Humans have many more rod cells than cone cells. Ask students to infer the number of rods in the eyes of nocturnal animals. They have far more rod cells than humans so they can see well at night.

Resource Manager 

Chapter Resources Booklet
Directed Reading for Content Mastery, p. 20
Physical Science Critical Thinking/Problem Solving, p. 4

Mixing Colors

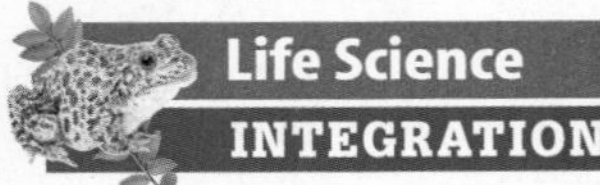

Life Science INTEGRATION

Carotenoids, yellow and orange pigments that include xanthophyll, are always present in green plants. These pigments absorb light in the blue and green wavelengths, which aids plants, especially those growing in low-light conditions, to absorb enough light to make food.

Reading Check

Answer red, green, and blue

Activity

Provide groups of students with red, green, and blue color filters (or colored transparency film) and an overhead projector. Have them use different combinations of filters to produce the colors yellow, magenta, and cyan. Ask them to write down the combination of filters they used to produce each color. Red and green produce yellow. Red and blue produce magenta. Green and blue produce cyan. L2 ELL LS **Visual-Spatial** P

Life Science INTEGRATION

Plant pigments allow plants to select the wavelengths of light they use for photosynthesis. Leaves usually look green due to the pigment chlorophyll. Chlorophyll absorbs most wavelengths of visible light except green, which it reflects. But not all plants are green. Research different plant pigments to find how they allow plant species to survive in diverse habitats.

Mixing Colors

Paint stores display samples of almost every imaginable shade of every color. These choices result from mixtures of pigments. A **pigment** is a colored material that absorbs some colors and reflects others. What would happen if you mixed yellow and blue pigments? Yellow and blue lights? In both instances you would see green, but while mixing lights changes your brain's interpretation of color, mixing pigments actually changes the reflected wavelengths.

Mixing Colored Lights From the glowing orange of a sunset to the deep blue of a mountain lake, all the colors you see can be made by mixing of three colors of light. These three colors—red, green, and blue—are the primary colors of light. They correspond to the three different types of cones in the retina of your eye. When mixed together in equal amounts, they produce white light, as **Figure 13** shows. Mixing the primary colors in different proportions can produce the colors you see.

Reading Check *What are primary colors?*

Paint Pigments If you were to mix equal amounts of red, green, and blue paint, would you get white paint? If mixing colors of paint were like mixing colors of light, you would, but mixing paint is different. Paints are made with pigments. Paint pigments usually are made of chemical compounds such as titanium oxide, a bright white pigment, and lead chromate, which is used for painting yellow lines on highways.

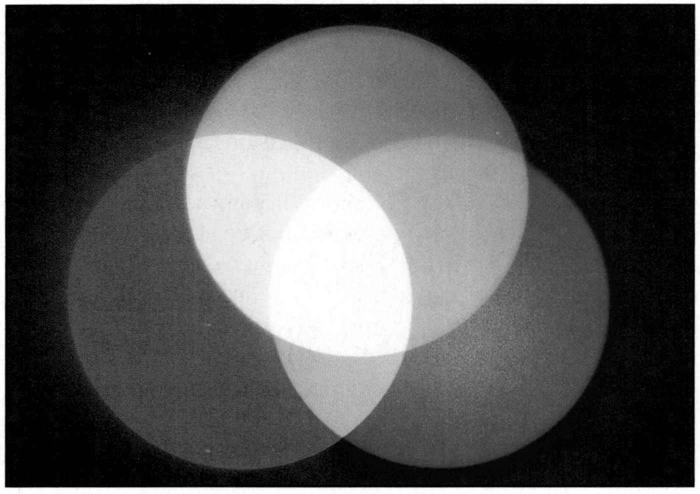

Figure 13
White light is produced when the three primary colors of light are mixed.

Active Reading

Cause and Effect Chart This strategy is used to focus on cause-effect relationships. In the center of a sheet of paper, have students write "Mixing Colors." On the left of the paper, instruct them to write different several combinations of the primary colors of light, followed by combinations of the primary pigments. On the right side, have students record the color that will result from each combination.

Resource Manager

Chapter Resources Booklet
Reinforcement, p. 28

Mixing Pigments You can make any pigment color by mixing different amounts of the three primary pigments—magenta (bluish red), cyan (greenish blue), and yellow. In fact, color printers use those pigments to make full-color prints like the pages in this book. However, color printers also use black ink to produce a true black color. A primary pigment's color depends on the color of light it reflects. Actually, pigments both absorb and reflect a range of colors in sending a single color message to your eye. For example, in white light, the yellow pigment appears yellow because it reflects yellow, red, orange, and green light but absorbs blue and violet light. The color of a mixture of two primary pigments is determined by the primary colors of light that both pigments reflect.

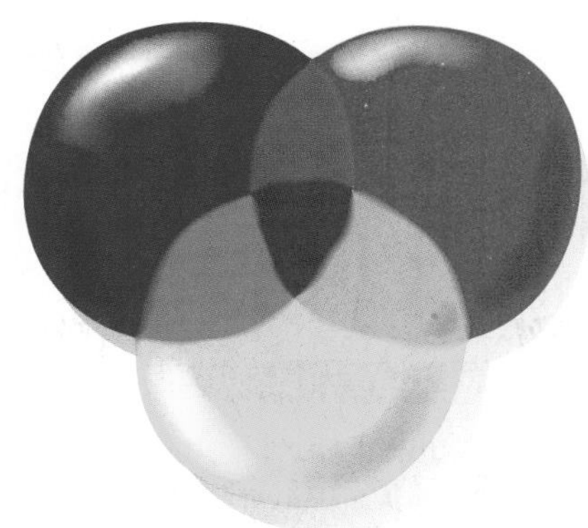

Figure 14
The three primary colors of pigment appear to be black when they are mixed.

Reading Check *What colors are the three primary pigments?*

Look at **Figure 14.** The area in the center where the colors all overlap appears to be black because the three blended primary pigments absorb all the primary colors of light. Recall that the primary colors of light combine to produce white light. They are called additive colors. However, the primary pigment colors combine to produce black. Because black results from the absence of reflected light, the primary pigments are called subtractive colors.

Section 2 Assessment

1. If a white light shines on a red shirt, what colors are reflected and what colors are absorbed?
2. How do the primary colors of light differ from the primary pigment colors?
3. Explain why a person with color blindness can distinguish among some colors but not others.
4. If all colors are present in white light, why does a white fence appear to be white instead of multicolored?
5. **Think Critically** If you had only magenta, cyan, and yellow paints, could you paint a picture of a zebra? Explain why this would or would not be possible.

Skill Builder Activities

6. **Concept Mapping** Design a concept map to show the chain of events that must happen for you to see a blue object. Work with a partner. **For more help, refer to the Science Skill Handbook.**
7. **Researching Information** Research the electromagnetic spectrum to find the wavelength and frequency range of visible light. Make a poster showing the wavelengths for the seven main colors in the visible light spectrum. Explain the units used, and the relationship between wavelength and wave frequency. **For more help, refer to the Science Skill Handbook.**

Reading Check

Answer magenta, cyan, and yellow

3 Assess

Reteach

Have students work in groups to combine small amounts of various primary pigment paints to make other colors. For each color, have them describe which colors are reflected and which are absorbed. Be sure they mix all three primary pigments to produce black. Point out that black pigment absorbs all light and reflects none. L2 ELL COOP LEARN IN **Kinesthetic**

Challenge

Have students stare at a red object for 20 seconds and then look at a white wall. They should see a faint blue/green after image of the object on the wall. Ask them to explain why they think this happens based on how our eyes see color. Their red cones lose sensitivity. When they look at the white wall, the part of their retinas that stared at the red object have only blue and green cones that are sensitive. L3 IN **Logical-Mathematical**

Assessment

Oral Assess students' understanding of colors by asking them to explain why black and white are not true colors. Black is a lack of color that occurs when all light is absorbed. White occurs when all colors are reflected. Use **PASC,** p. 89.

Answers to Section Assessment

1. Red is reflected and all others are absorbed.
2. Primary colors of light are red, green, and blue. Primary colors of pigment are magenta, cyan, and yellow. Primary colors of light transmit the color you see, while primary colors of pigment reflect the color you see.
3. Not all of their cone cells function properly.
4. The fence reflects all colors of visible light. Since all the cones in your eyes are stimulated, you see white.
5. Yes; when you mix them, yellow absorbs blue, cyan absorbs red, and magenta absorbs green. With all color absorbed, you see black. If using white paper, a person could paint a picture of a zebra.
6. The events on the map might be: light shines on an object, the object reflects blue and absorbs other colors, blue cones in your eye absorb the light and convert the light energy into nerve impulses, these impulses are transmitted to the brain.
7. Wavelengths of light are measured in nanometers; one billion nanometers = 1 meter. The wavelengths of visible light increase from about 400 nm (blue) to 700 nm(red). As wavelength increases, frequency decreases.

Producing Light

1 Motivate

Bellringer Transparency

Display the Section Focus Transparency for Section 3. Use the accompanying Transparency Activity Master. L2 ELL

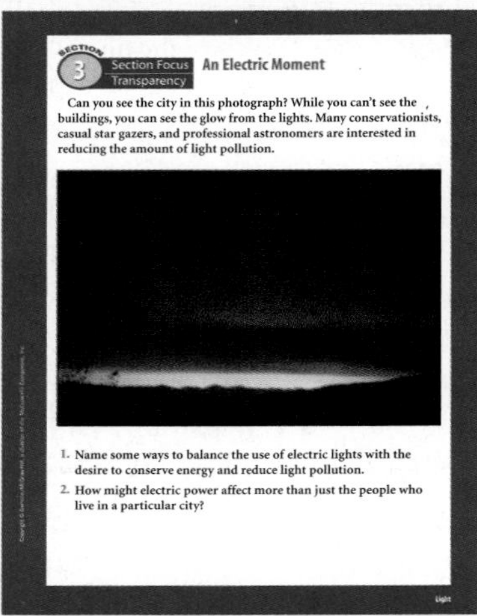
Section 3 Section Focus Transparency **An Electric Moment**

Can you see the city in this photograph? While you can't see the buildings, you can see the glow from the lights. Many conservationists, casual star gazers, and professional astronomers are interested in reducing the amount of light pollution.

1. Name some ways to balance the use of electric lights with the desire to conserve energy and reduce light pollution.
2. How might electric power affect more than just the people who live in a particular city?

Light

Tie to Prior Knowledge

Ask students if they have ever seen a laser light show. Explain that lasers have a very intense, narrow beam of light because of the way the light is produced. In this section students will learn how lasers and other light sources produce light.

Reading Check

Answer More than 80% of the energy it gives off is heat.

Caption Answer

Figure 15 They absorb ultraviolet light and re-emit it as visible light.

Producing Light

As You Read

What **You'll Learn**

- **Explain** how incandescent and fluorescent lightbulbs work.
- **Analyze** the advantages and disadvantages of different lighting devices.
- **Explain** how a laser produces coherent light.
- **Describe** various uses of lasers.

Vocabulary
incandescent light
fluorescent light
coherent light
incoherent light

Why **It's Important**

Knowing how different lighting devices work will help you choose the right one for your needs.

Incandescent Lights

It's only been 100 years or so since lightbulbs became common in households. Their shapes, sizes, and varieties today are a far cry from a single lightbulb swinging from an electric cord over a table. Most of the lightbulbs in your house produce incandescent light. Heating a piece of metal until it glows produces **incandescent light.** If you look into an unlit incandescent lightbulb, you will see a thin wire called the filament. It usually is made of the element tungsten. Turn on the light and electricity flows through the filament and causes it to heat up. When the tungsten filament gets hot, it gives off light. However, if you've ever accidentally touched a lit light bulb, you know that it also produces a great deal of heat. More than 80 percent of the energy given off by incandescent bulbs is in the form of heat.

Reading Check *Why does an incandescent lightbulb get hot?*

Fluorescent Lights

Your house also may have fluorescent (floo RE sunt) lights. A fluorescent bulb, like the one shown in **Figure 15,** is filled with a gas at low pressure. The inside of the bulb is coated with phosphors that emit visible light when they absorb ultraviolet radiation. The tube also contains electrodes at each end. Electrons are given off when the electrodes are connected in a circuit. When these electrons collide with the gas atoms, ultraviolet radiation is emitted. The phosphors on the inside of the bulb absorb this radiation and give off visible light.

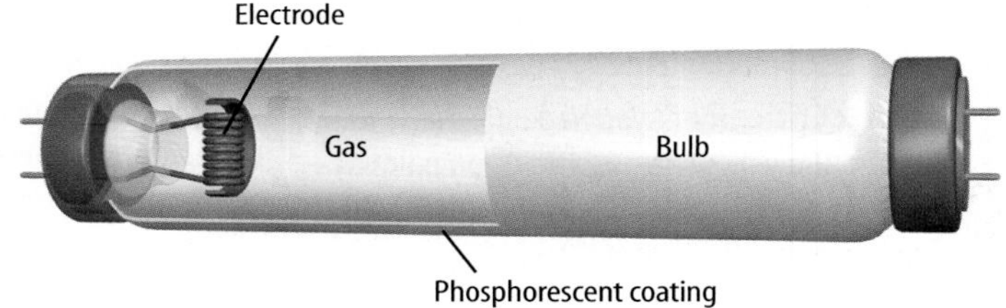

Figure 15
Fluorescent lightbulbs do not use filaments. *What property of phosphors makes them useful in fluorescent bulbs?*

Section Assessment Planner

PORTFOLIO
Assessment, p. 435

PERFORMANCE ASSESSMENT
MiniLAB, p. 431
Skill Builder Activities, p.435
See page 448 for more options.

CONTENT ASSESSMENT
Section, p. 435
Challenge, p. 435
Chapter, pp. 448–449

Efficient Lighting A **fluorescent light** uses phosphors to convert ultraviolet radiation to visible light. Fluorescent lights use as little as one fifth the electrical energy to produce the same amount of light as incandescent bulbs. Fluorescent bulbs also last much longer than incandescent bulbs. This higher efficiency can mean lower energy costs over the life of the bulb. Reduced energy usage could reduce the amount of fossil fuels burned to generate electricity, which also decreases the amount of carbon dioxide and pollutants released into Earth's atmosphere.

Fluorescent bulbs are used widely in hospitals, office buildings, schools, and factories. Compact fluorescent bulbs, which can be screwed into traditional lightbulb sockets, have been developed that are more practical for use in homes.

Neon Lights

The vivid, glowing colors of neon lights, such as those shown in **Figure 16,** make them a popular choice for signs and eye-catching decorations on buildings. These lighting devices are glass tubes filled with gas, typically neon, and work similarly to fluorescent lights. When an electric current flows through the tube, electrons collide with the gas molecules. In this case, however, the collisions produce visible light. If the tube contains only neon, the light is bright red. Different colors can be produced by adding other gases to the tube.

Reading Check *What causes the color in a neon light?*

Mini LAB

Discovering Energy Waste in Lightbulbs

Procedure

1. Obtain an **incandescent bulb** and a **fluorescent bulb** of identical wattage.
2. Make a heat collector by covering the top of a **foam cup** with a piece of **plastic food wrap** to make a window. Carefully make a small hole (diameter less than the thermometer's) in the side of the cup. Push a **thermometer** through the hole.
3. Measure the temperature of the air inside the cup. Then, hold the window of the tester 1 cm from one of the lights for 2 minutes and measure the temperature.
4. Cool the heat collector and thermometer. Repeat step 3 using the second bulb.

Analysis

1. What was the temperature for each bulb?
2. Which bulb appears to give off more heat? Explain why this occurs.

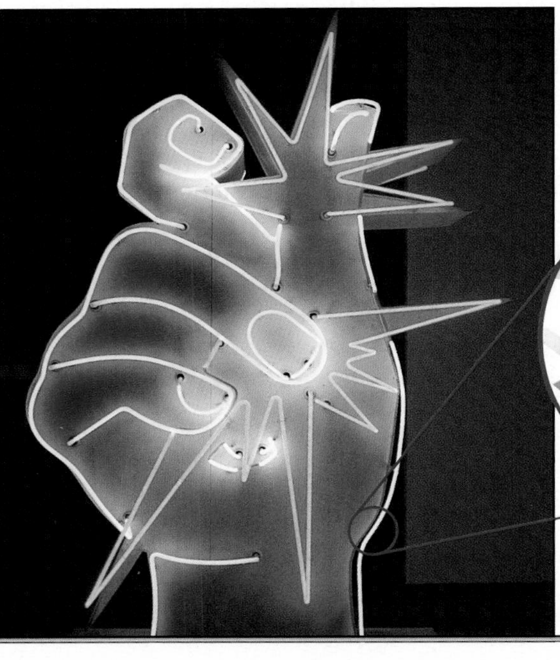

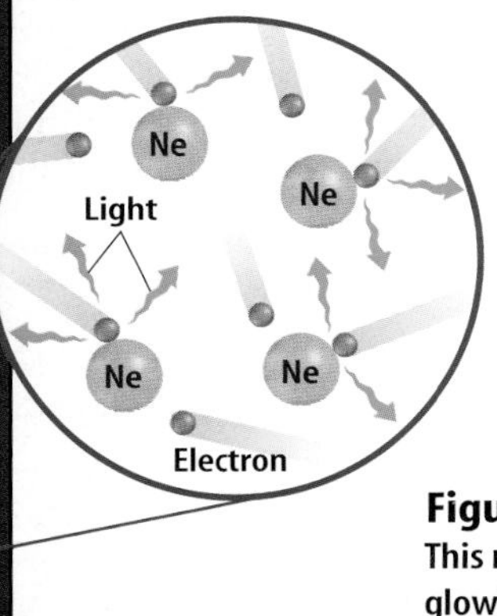

Figure 16
This neon light has vivid, glowing colors.

2 Teach

Flourescent Lights

Purpose Students observe energy wasted by bulbs. L1 COOP LEARN IN **Kinesthetic**

Materials flourescent and incandescent bulbs of same wattage, thermometer, polystyrene foam cup, stopwatch, plastic food wrap

Safety Precautions Caution students not to touch or to allow their heat collectors to touch hot bulbs.

Analysis

1. The temperature should be higher for the incandescent bulb.
2. Incandescent bulb; it produces light by heating a tungsten filament.

Assessment

Oral Ask students which bulb emits high levels of infrared radiation. the incandescent bulb Use **PASC,** p. 89.

Neon Lights

Answer electrons colliding with gas molecules

Teacher FYI

Standard 60- to 75-watt incandescent bulbs can be replaced by 18-watt compact fluorescent bulbs. These bulbs use about 75 percent less electricity to produce the same amount of light.

Resource Manager

Chapter Resources Booklet
Transparency Activity, p. 48
MiniLAB, p. 4

Sodium-Vapor Lights

Activity

Ask students to look around the community at night to find examples of various light sources. Explain that sodium-vapor lights are considered by many to be a good option for decreasing city light pollution. L2 ELL LS **Visual-Spatial**

Lasers

Use Science Words

Word Meaning Laser stands for *L*ight *A*mplification by *S*timulated *E*mission of *R*adiation. Have students explain why this is an appropriate name. A laser amplifies, or magnifies, light by stimulating, or exciting, atoms. This results in the emission of radiation from the atoms as they re-excite. L2 LS **Linguistic**

Reading Check

Answer The partially reflective mirrors reflect most of the light. As the light waves travel back and forth, they stimulate other atoms to emit identical light waves, which produces a beam of laser light.

Figure 17
Sodium-vapor lights emit mostly yellow light. Half of this photo was taken under sunlight and half was taken under sodium-vapor lighting.

Sodium-Vapor Lights

Sodium-vapor lights often are used for streetlights and other outdoor lighting. Like neon lights and fluorescent lights, sodium-vapor lights have a glass shell filled with gas. Most of the gas is neon, but some sodium also is present. When the light is turned on, the neon heats up and glows. The heat from the neon then causes the sodium to turn into vapor, creating a yellow-orange glow, as shown in **Figure 17.**

Tungsten-Halogen Lights

Tungsten-halogen lights sometimes are used to create intensely bright light. Like ordinary incandescent lightbulbs, these lighting devices have a tungsten filament inside a glass bulb or tube. The major difference is that these bulbs are filled with a gas that makes the filaments last longer. The gas contains one of the halogen elements such as fluorine or chlorine. In addition to being used in homes, offices, and public buildings, tungsten-halogen lights are used on movie sets and in underwater photography.

Lasers

From laser surgery to a laser light show, lasers have become a large part of the world you live in. A laser's light begins when a number of light waves are emitted at the same time. To achieve this, a number of identical atoms each must be given the same amount of energy. When they release their energy, each atom sends off an identical light wave. This light wave is reflected between two facing mirrors at opposite ends of the laser. One of the mirrors is coated only partially with reflective material, so it reflects most light but allows some to get through. Some emitted light waves travel back and forth between the mirrors many times, stimulating other atoms to emit identical light waves also. This continual process produces a beam of laser light.

Reading Check *How do mirrors help in creating lasers?*

Lasers can be made with many different materials, including gases, liquids, and solids. One of the most common is the helium-neon laser, which produces a beam of red light. A mixture of helium and neon gases sealed in a tube with mirrors at both ends is excited by a flashtube, as shown in **Figure 18.** The excited atoms then lose their excess energy by emitting coherent light waves.

Research Visit the Glencoe Science Web site at **science.glencoe.com** for more information about sodium vapor lights and light pollution.

Internet Addresses

Explore the Glencoe Science Web site at **science.glencoe.com** to find out more about topics in this section.

Visual Learning

Figure 17 Point out that the sodium-vapor lighting shown on the right allows us to see more detail than the white light in the photo at the left. The yellow-orange light is in the range of wavelengths that our eyes see best. The photo on the right is also clearer because the sodium-vapor lighting produces less glare. L2 ELL LS **Visual-Spatial**

NATIONAL GEOGRAPHIC **VISUALIZING LASERS**

Figure 18

Lasers produce light waves that have the same wavelength. Almost all of these waves travel in the same direction and are in phase, that is, their crests overlap. As a result, beams of laser light transfer more energy than ordinary light. In modern eye surgery, right, lasers have largely replaced the traditional scalpel.

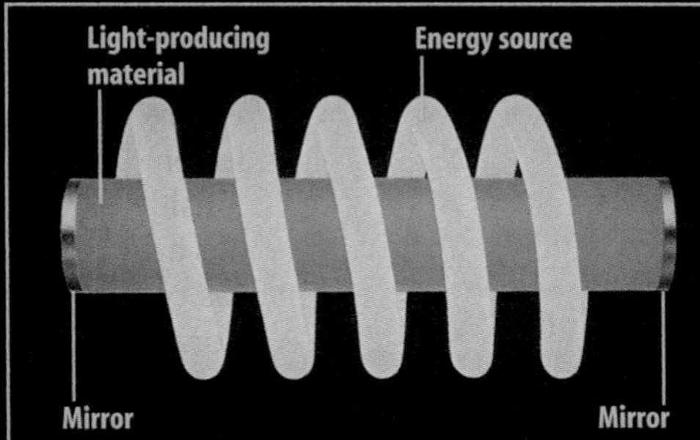

A The key parts of a laser include a material that can be stimulated to produce light, such as a ruby rod, and an energy source. In this example, the energy source is a lamp that spirals around the ruby rod and emits an intense light.

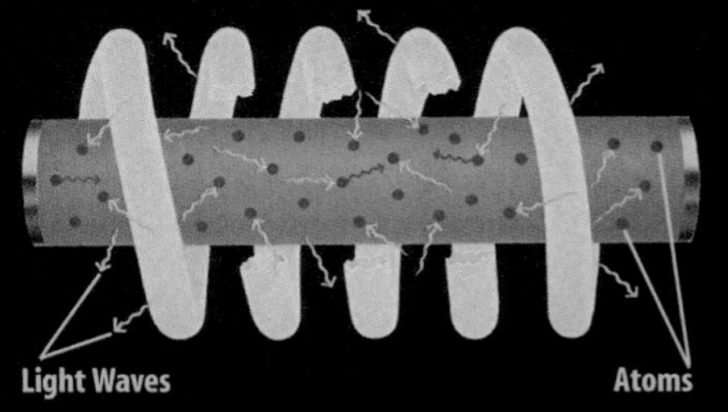

B When the lamp flashes, energy is absorbed by the atoms in the rod. These atoms then re-emit that energy as light waves that are in phase and have the same wavelength.

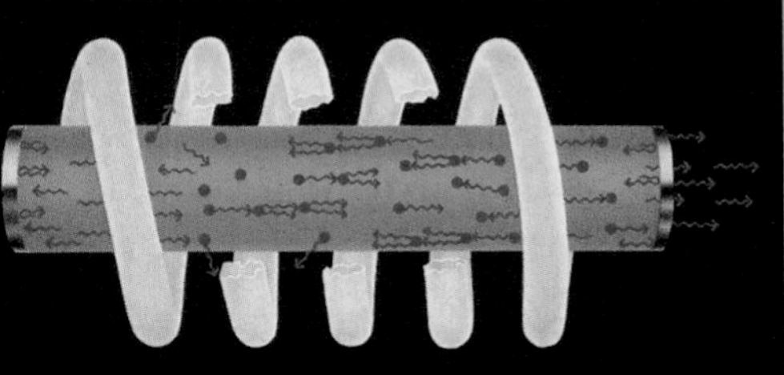

C Most of these waves are reflected between the mirrors located at each end of the laser. One of the mirrors, however, is only partially reflective, allowing one percent of the light waves to pass through it and form a beam.

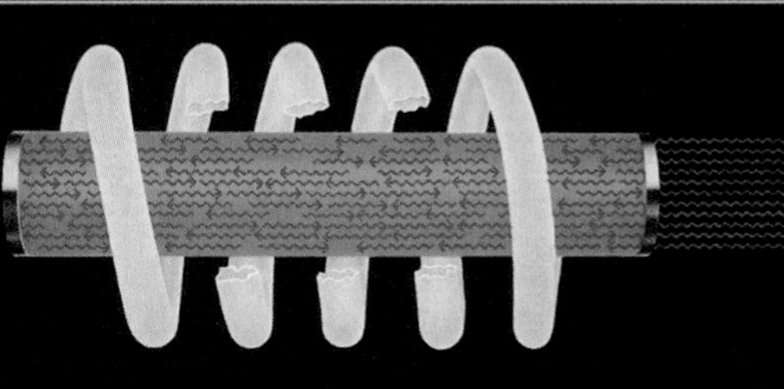

D As the waves travel back and forth between the mirrors, they stimulate other atoms in the ruby rod to emit light waves. In a fraction of a second, billions of identical waves are bouncing between the mirrors. The waves are emitted from the partially reflective mirror in a stream of laser light.

Visualizing Lasers

Have students examine the pictures and read the captions. Then ask the following questions.

- **In a laser, what is the purpose of the energy source?** It provides the energy to stimulate the ruby rod to emit light waves that are of the same wavelength and in phase.
- **What is the effect of allowing only 1% of the light waves through the partially reflective mirror?** The light waves remaining inside the ruby rod stimulate other atoms in the ruby rod to emit light waves, so the energy of the light increases.
- **Why does a laser beam transfer more energy than ordinary light?** The light waves all have the same wavelength and are parallel and in phase.

Quick Demo

Use a laser pointer to show a beam of laser light. Remind students that because the beam is coherent, it spreads out very little and produces an intense spot of light on a faraway wall. You can't see the light until it strikes the wall. The beam is so narrow that it is unlikely to reflect off tiny particles in the air and strike your eyes. If you scatter fine powder, such as chalk dust, in the air, you can see the beam.

L2 ELL IN **Visual-Spatial**

Resource Manager

Chapter Resources Booklet

Enrichment, p. 33

Directed Reading for Content Mastery, p. 21

Lasers, continued

IDENTIFYING Misconceptions

The laser is often thought of as a very powerful and efficient energy source. The typical classroom laser will not burn a hole through your skin, as some students may think, but it should never be directed toward anyone's eyes. Classroom lasers are a very inefficient light source; they are often less than 1% efficient.

Use Science Words

Word Origin The word *coherent* has the prefix *co-*, meaning "together," and the Latin word *haerere*, meaning "to stick." Have each student write a sentence that explains how this definition applies to coherent light. Possible answer: Waves of coherent light have the same wavelength, and they travel together with crests and troughs aligned. L2 LS **Linguistic**

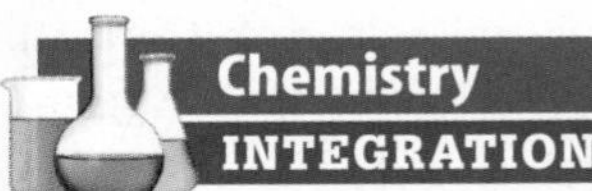

Chemistry INTEGRATION

Helium and neon are located in the far right column of the periodic table. They are noble, or inert, gases. Their valence, or outer, electron orbitals are filled, so these elements are chemically very unreactive. They do not react chemically in lasers.

Figure 19
Light waves can be either coherent or incoherent.

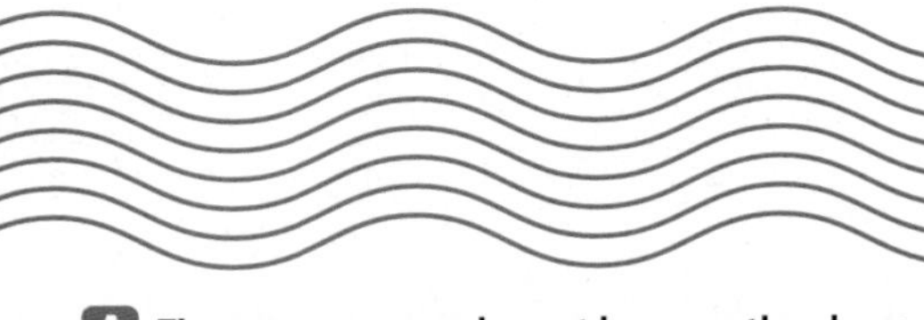

A These waves are coherent because they have the same wavelength and travel with their crests and troughs aligned.

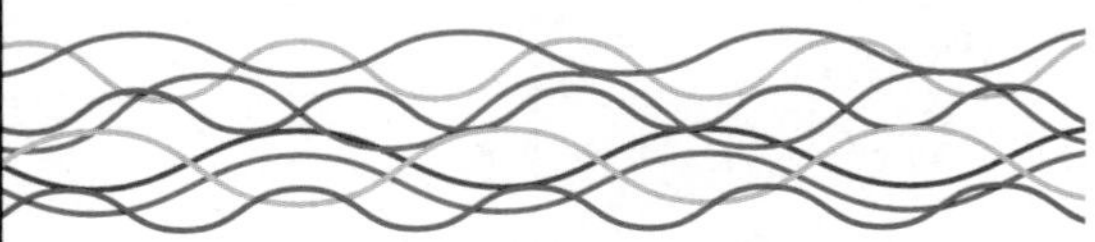

B Incoherent waves such as these can contain more than one wavelength, and do not travel with their crests and troughs aligned.

Coherent Light Lasers produce the narrow beams of light that zip across the stage and through the auditorium during some rock concerts. Beams of laser light do not spread out because laser light is coherent. **Coherent light** is light of only one wavelength that travels with its crests and troughs aligned. The beam does not spread out because all the waves travel in the same direction, as shown in **Figure 19A.** As a result, the energy carried by the beam remains concentrated over a small area.

Incoherent Light Light from an ordinary lightbulb is incoherent. **Incoherent light** can contain more than one wavelength, and its electromagnetic waves are not aligned, as in **Figure 19B.** The waves don't travel in the same direction, so the beam spreads out. The energy carried by the light waves is spread over a large area, so the intensity of the light is much less than that of the laser beam.

Chemistry INTEGRATION

A particular helium-neon laser contains a mixture of 15 percent He and 85 percent Ne. Where are these gases located on the periodic table? Analyze their chemical characteristics. Would you be concerned that a chemical reaction might occur in the laser? Explain.

Using Lasers

Compact disc players, surgical tools, and many other useful devices take advantage of the unique properties of lasers. A laser beam is narrow and does not spread out as it travels over long distances. So lasers can apply large amounts of energy to small areas. In industry, powerful lasers are used for cutting and welding materials. Surveyors and builders use lasers for measuring and leveling. To measure the moon's orbit with great accuracy, scientists use laser light reflected from instruments on the Moon's surface. Information also can be coded in pulses of light from lasers. This makes them useful for communications. In telephone systems, pulses of laser light transmit conversations through long glass fibers called optical fibers.

Lasers in Medicine Lasers are routinely used to remove cataracts, reshape the cornea, and repair the retina. In the eye and other parts of the body, surgeons use lasers in place of scalpels to cut cleanly through body tissues. The energy from the laser seals off blood vessels in the incision and reduces bleeding. Because most lasers do not penetrate deeply through the skin, they can be used to remove small tumors or birthmarks on the surface without damaging deeper tissues. By sending laser light into the body through an optical fiber, physicians can also treat conditions such as ulcers and blocked arteries.

Science Journal

New Uses for Lasers Have each student write a paragraph describing several situations in which lasers are used. Ask them to include new uses that might be found for lasers in the future. Answers might include surgery, surveying, welding, weapons, and so on. L2 LS **Linguistic**

Resource Manager

Chapter Resources Booklet
Reinforcement, p. 29
Mathematics Skill Activities, p. 47

434 CHAPTER 14 Light

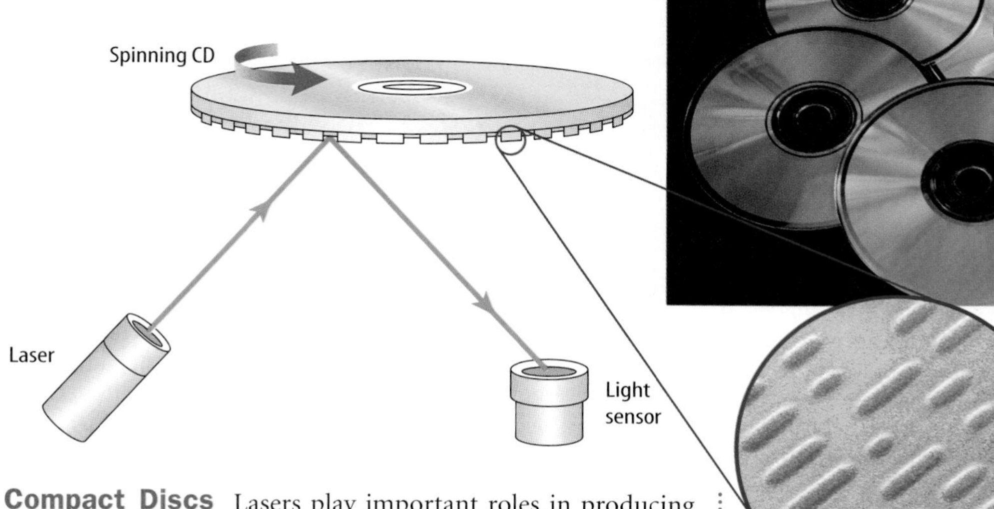

Compact Discs Lasers play important roles in producing and using compact discs, which are aluminum-coated, plastic discs used to store sound, images, and text in digital form. When a CD is produced, the information is burned into the surface of the disc with a laser. The laser creates millions of tiny pits in a spiral pattern that starts at the center of the disc and moves out to the edge. A CD player, shown in **Figure 20,** also uses a laser to read the disc. The laser's beam is aimed at the surface of the disc. As the laser points at a pit or flat spot, different amounts of light reflect back. The reflected light is converted by a processor to an electric signal used by the speakers to create sound.

Figure 20
The blowup shows the pits (blue) on the bottom surface of a CD. A CD player uses a laser to convert the information on the CD to an electric signal.

Section 3 Assessment

1. Explain how light is produced in an ordinary incandescent bulb.
2. What are the advantages and disadvantages of using a fluorescent bulb instead of an incandescent bulb?
3. Describe the difference between coherent and incoherent light.
4. **Think Critically** Which type of lighting device would you use for each of the following needs: an economical light source in a manufacturing plant, an eye-catching sign that will be visible at night, and a baseball stadium? Explain.

Skill Builder Activities

5. **Concept Mapping** Make a concept map showing the sequence of events that occur in a laser to produce coherent light. Begin with the emission of lightwaves from atoms. **For more help, refer to the Science Skill Handbook.**
6. **Using an Electronic Spreadsheet** Create a spreadsheet listing the types of lighting devices described in this chapter. Compare and contrast their features in separate columns. Include a column for how each is used. **For more help, refer to the Technology Skill Handbook.**

3 Assess

Reteach

To reinforce the idea of coherent light, first have students all clap their hands in their own individual rhythms. The sound is scattered and jumbled. Now have everyone clap on the number as you count "one and two and three and . . ." The sound is coherent, or together and more intense. L1 ELL LS **Auditory-Musical**

Challenge

Have students use colored pencils to draw three sketches of light waves. The first sketch should show incoherent light waves (different wavelengths with crests and troughs not aligned). The second should show light of one wavelength with crests and troughs not aligned. The third should show coherent light (one wavelength with crests and troughs aligned). L2 ELL LS **Visual-Spatial**

Assessment

Portfolio Have each student write a letter to the editor explaining why people should or should not switch to using fluorescent rather than incandescent light bulbs in their homes. Students should support their opinions with facts. Use **Performance Assessment in the Science Classroom,** p. 139. P

Answers to Section Assessment

1. Electricity flows through the filament, causing it to heat up and give off light.
2. The fluorescent bulb costs more, but it lasts longer and uses less energy for the same light as an incandescent bulb.
3. Coherent light has only one wavelength and travels with its crests and troughs aligned; incoherent light can contain more than one wavelength, and the waves are not aligned.
4. Manufacturing plant—fluorescent lights; sign at night—neon; baseball stadium—tungsten halogen
5. Energy source emits light that is absorbed by atoms in the laser, which then re-emit the energy as coherent light waves. The light waves bounce between mirrors on either end of the laser, stimulating more atoms to emit coherent light. One of the mirrors allows about one percent of the light to pass through.
6. Spreadsheets might mention gases used, absorption or emission of ultraviolet radiation, and phosphorescence.

SECTION

Using Light

1 Motivate

Bellringer Transparency

Display the Section Focus Transparency for Section 4. Use the accompanying Transparency Activity Master. L2 ELL

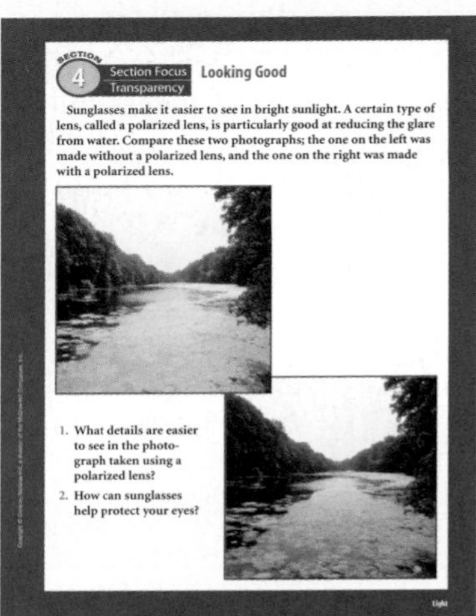

Section 4 Section Focus Transparency — Looking Good

Sunglasses make it easier to see in bright sunlight. A certain type of lens, called a polarized lens, is particularly good at reducing the glare from water. Compare these two photographs; the one on the left was made without a polarized lens, and the one on the right was made with a polarized lens.

1. What details are easier to see in the photograph taken using a polarized lens?
2. How can sunglasses help protect your eyes?

Tie to Prior Knowledge

Ask students if they have ever worn polarized sunglasses. Ask students who have to describe the difference between what they see through regular sunglasses and what they see through polarized sunglasses. Explain that in this section they will learn what polarized light is and how it can be used.

SECTION

Using Light

As You Read

What You'll Learn

- **Describe** polarized light and the uses of polarizing filters.
- **Apply** the concept of total internal reflection to the uses of optical fibers.

Vocabulary

polarized light
holography
total internal reflection

Why It's Important

Light is used in entertainment, medicine, manufacturing, scientific research, communications, and just about every other facet of life.

Polarized Light

You may have a pair of sunglasses with a sticker on them that says polarized. Do you know what makes them different from other sunglasses? The difference has to do with the vibration of light waves. You can make transverse waves in a rope vibrate in any direction—horizontal, vertical, or anywhere in between. Light also is a transverse wave and can vibrate in any direction. In **polarized light,** however, the waves vibrate in only one direction.

Polarizing Filters If the light passes through a special polarizing filter, the light becomes polarized. A polarizing filter acts like a group of parallel slits. Only light waves vibrating in the same direction as the slits can pass through. If a second polarizing filter is lined up with its slits at right angles to those of the first filter, no light can pass through, as **Figure 21** shows.

Polarized lenses are useful for at reducing glare without interfering with your ability to see clearly. When light is reflected from a horizontal surface, such as a lake or a shiny car hood, it becomes partially horizontally polarized. The lenses of polarizing sunglasses have vertically polarizing filters that block out the reflected light that has been polarized horizontally, while allowing vertically polarized light through.

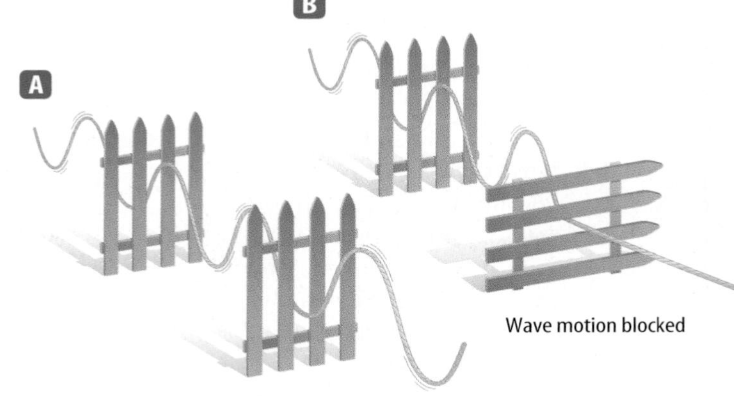

Figure 21
Slats in a fence behave like a polarizing filter for a transverse wave on a rope. A If the slats in the fence are in the same direction, the wave passes through. B If the slats are aligned at right angles to each other, the wave can't pass through.

Section Assessment Planner

PORTFOLIO
Reteach, p. 440

PERFORMANCE ASSESSMENT
Skill Builder Activities, p. 440
See page 448 for more options.

CONTENT ASSESSMENT
Section, p. 440
Challenge, p. 440
Chapter, pp. 448–449

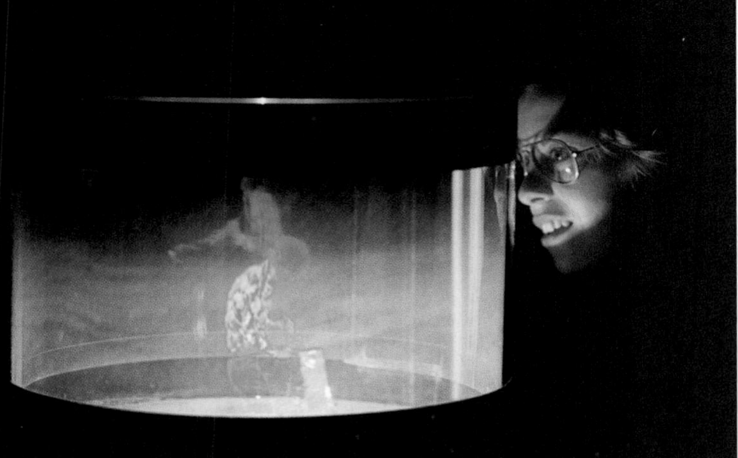

Figure 22
Lasers can be used to make holograms like this one.

Holography

Science museums often have exhibits where a three-dimensional image seems to float in space, like the one shown in **Figure 22.** You can see the image from different angles, just as you would if you passed the real object. Three-dimensional images on credit cards are produced by holography. **Holography** (hoh LAH gruh fee) is a technique that produces a hologram—a complete photographic image of a three-dimensional object.

Making Holograms Illuminating objects with laser light produces holograms. Laser light reflects from the object onto photographic film. At the same time, a second beam split from the laser also is directed at the film. The light from the two beams creates an interference pattern on the film. The pattern looks nothing like the original object, but when laser light shines on the pattern on the film, a holographic image is produced.

Information in Light An ordinary photographic image captures only the brightness or intensity of light reflected from an object's surface, but a hologram records the intensity as well as the direction. As a result, it conveys more information to your eye than a conventional two-dimensional photograph does, but it also is more difficult to copy. Holographic images are used on credit cards, identification cards, and on the labels of some clothing and other products to help prevent counterfeiting. Using X-ray lasers, scientists can produce holographic images of microscopic objects. It may be possible to create three-dimensional views of biological cells.

Reading Check *How are holographic images produced?*

SCIENCE Online

Research Visit the Glencoe Science Web site at **science.glencoe.com** for more information about holograms. Communicate to your class what you learned.

2 Teach

Polarized Light

Make a Model

Have students work in pairs to make model polarizing filters. Using the illustrations below as a guide, have students make two squares of craft sticks, and then glue several sticks in rows inside the square with small spaces between them. Have them use these squares to demonstrate polarized light by attaching a string to a door, running the string through the filters, and moving the string up and down to produce waves. If both filters are aligned vertically, the vibrating string models polarization. If the filters are at right angles, as shown below, the wave motion of the string is stopped, modeling the cancellation of light waves. L2

LS **Kinesthetic**

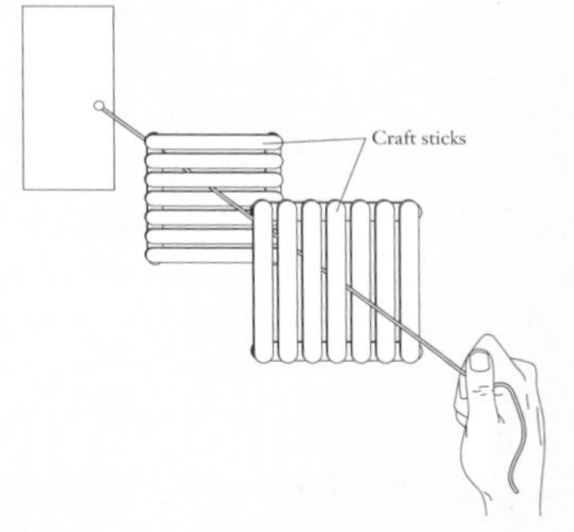

Reading Check

Answer A laser light is reflected from an object onto photographic film. At the same time, a second beam split from the laser is directed at the film. This creates an interference pattern on the film, which produces the holographic image when laser light shines on it.

SCIENCE Online
Internet Addresses

Explore the Glencoe Science Web site at **science.glencoe.com** to find out more about topics in this section.

Resource Manager 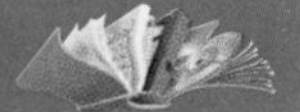

Chapter Resources Booklet
Transparency Activity, p. 49
Enrichment, p. 34

Optical Fibers

Teacher FYI

Since diamonds have a very high index of refraction and many facets, internal reflection allows light to exit only at certain points. As a result, we say that diamonds sparkle.

Activity

Have a physician visit your class to discuss the uses of optical fibers in medical procedures. After the presentation, have students write paragraphs describing one of the procedures. L3 LS **Auditory-Musical**

IDENTIFYING Misconceptions

Students might imagine that the lasers used to transmit telephone or television signals through optical fibers are large. In fact, semiconductor diode lasers smaller than a speck of dust are used.

Reading Check

Answer It occurs when light traveling from one medium to another is completely reflected at the boundary between the two materials.

Optical Fibers

When laser light must travel long distances or be sent into hard-to-reach places, optical fibers often are used. These transparent glass fibers can transmit light from one place to another. A process called total internal reflection makes this possible.

Total Internal Reflection Remember what happens when light speeds up as it travels from one medium to another. For example, when light travels from water to air the direction of the light ray is bent away from the normal, as shown in **Figure 23.** If the underwater light ray makes a larger angle with the normal, the light ray in the air bends closer the surface of the water. At a certain angle, called the critical angle, the refracted ray has been bent so that it is traveling along the surface of the water, as shown in **Figure 23.** For a light ray traveling from water into air, the critical angle is about 48°.

Figure 23 show what happens if the underwater light ray strikes the boundary between the air and water at an angle larger than the critical angle. There is no longer any refraction, and the light ray does not travel in the air. Instead, the light ray is reflected at the boundary, just as if a mirror were there. This behavior of light is called total internal reflection. **Total internal reflection** occurs when light traveling from one medium to another is completely reflected at the boundary between the two materials. Then the light ray obeys the law of reflection. For total internal reflection to occur, light must travel slower in the first medium, and must strike the boundary at an angle greater than the critical angle.

Reading Check *How does total internal reflection occur?*

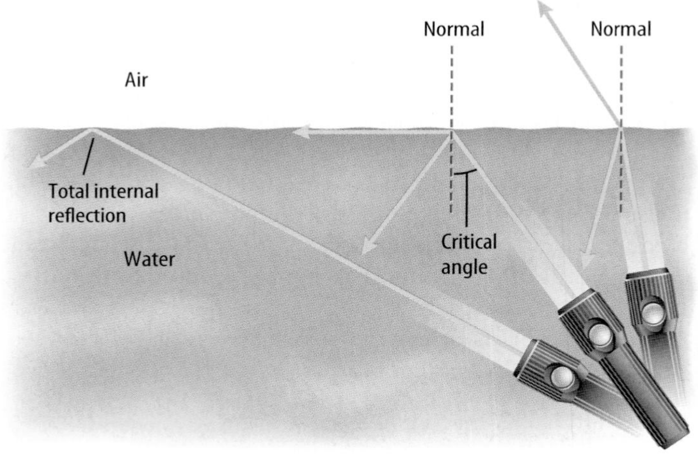

Figure 23
A light wave is bent away from the normal as it passes from water to air. At the critical angle, the refracted wave is traveling along the water surface. At angles greater than the critical angle, total internal reflection occurs.

LAB DEMONSTRATION

Purpose to show how total internal reflection can occur in an optical fiber

Materials laser pointer, 6 plane mirrors with stands (or clay to anchor mirrors), paper

Preparation Make two rows of side-by side mirrors. The lines should be about 2" apart. The mirrors should be facing each other. Tape the paper at the end of the row.

Procedure Darken the room. Shine the laser at an angle on the first mirror so that a series of reflections sends the beam from mirror to mirror through the "fiber" and allows the spot of light to be focused onto the paper at the end of the row.

Expected Outcome Light is reflected and shines on the paper.

Assessment

What happens if light striking the inner surface of the fiber is not totally reflected? The light loses intensity.

Figure 24
Optical fibers make use of total internal reflection.

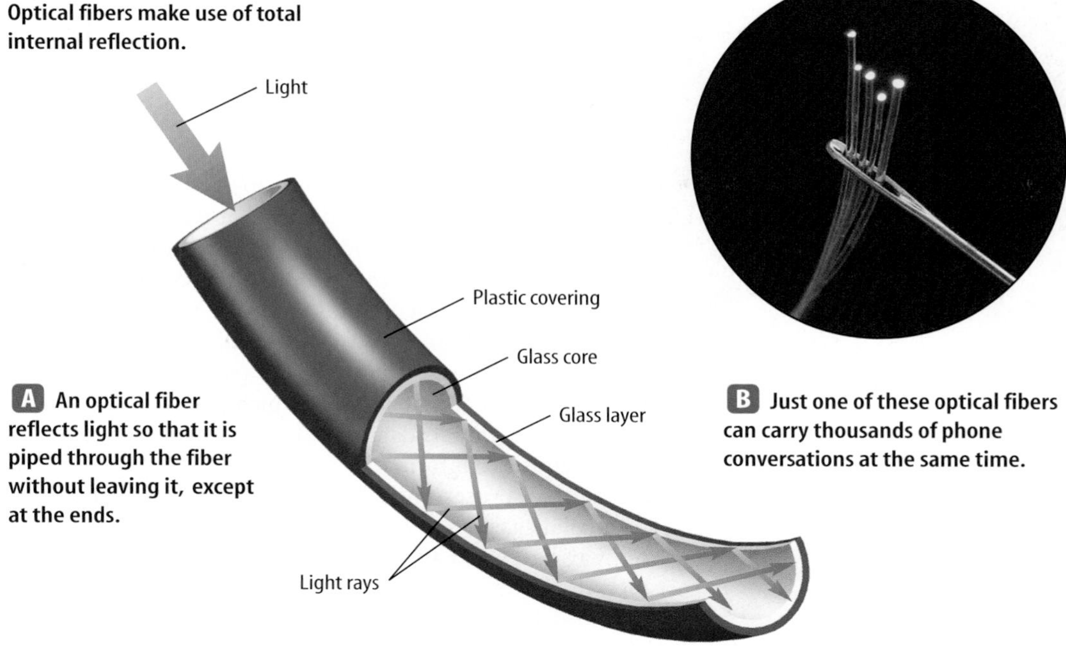

A **An optical fiber reflects light so that it is piped through the fiber without leaving it, except at the ends.**

B **Just one of these optical fibers can carry thousands of phone conversations at the same time.**

Light Pipes Total internal reflection makes light transmission in optical fibers possible. As shown in **Figure 24A,** light entering one end of the fiber is reflected continuously from the sides of the fiber until it emerges from the other end. Like water moves through a pipe, almost no light is lost or absorbed in optical fibers.

Using Optical Fibers Optical fibers are most often used in communications. Telephone conversations, television programs, and computer data can be coded in light beams. Signals can't leak from one fiber to another and interfere with other messages, so the signal is transmitted clearly. To send telephone conversations through an optical fiber, voice signals are converted into digital signals. A laser at one end of the pipe switches on and off several billion times per second. Some systems use multiple lasers, each with its own color to fit multiple signals into the same fiber. You could send a million copies of the play Romeo and Juliet in one second on a single fiber. **Figure 24B** shows the size of typical optical fibers.

Optical fibers also are used to explore the inside of the human body. One bundle of fibers transmits light, while the other carries the reflected light back to the doctor.

Fun Fact

The glass layer surrounding the core of an optical fiber is known as the cladding. The plastic covering is known as the jacket.

IDENTIFYING Misconceptions

Students might assume that because optical fibers are made of glass they are very fragile. Explain that because the fibers are so slender and because the glass core is so pure, optical fibers are instead very flexible. The plastic covering also protects the fibers from damage by preventing them from being bent too sharply.

Activity

Inexpensive optical fibers are available from many scientific supply companies. If possible, bring in fibers for students to see. Have students feel how thin and durable the fibers are. Shine a flashlight near the end of a fiber. Notice how the light doesn't exit through the sides of the fiber. Instead, you see a bright spot of light at the other end of the fiber. L2 ELL LS **Kinesthetic**

Resource Manager

Chapter Resources Booklet

- Directed Reading for Content Mastery, pp. 21, 22
- Lab Activity, pp. 13–16
- Activity Worksheet, pp. 5–6

Visual Learning

Figure 24 To achieve total internal reflection as shown by the arrows, the core of the optical fibers must have a higher index of refraction than the coating. The fiber core must be extremely pure, and the interface between the core and the glass layer must be smooth. **What happens if there is a bubble of air in the core?** The light is scattered. L3 LS **Visual-Spatial**

Optical Scanners

Discussion

Why do you think bar codes are typically black and white? This provides maximum contrast between dark and light areas so the sequence can be read reliably. L2 LS **Logical-Mathematical**

3 Assess

Reteach

Have each student make a concept map for how an optical scanner reads a bar code. The scanner reflects light off the bar code and detects its pattern. The pattern is translated into a digital signal that is compared with a computer database, providing information about the item. L2 LS **Logical-Mathematical P**

Challenge

Have each student use a prism (preferably right-angle) and a laser pointer to demonstrate the concept of total internal reflection. Students should be able to explain how the light behaves as it goes through different sides of the prism depending on the angle of the incident light. Caution students never to look directly into the laser light or point it toward anyone else. L2 LS **Visual-Spatial**

Process Have students work in small groups to hypothesize ways holograms might be used in the future. Use **Performance Assessment in the Science Classroom,** p. 93.

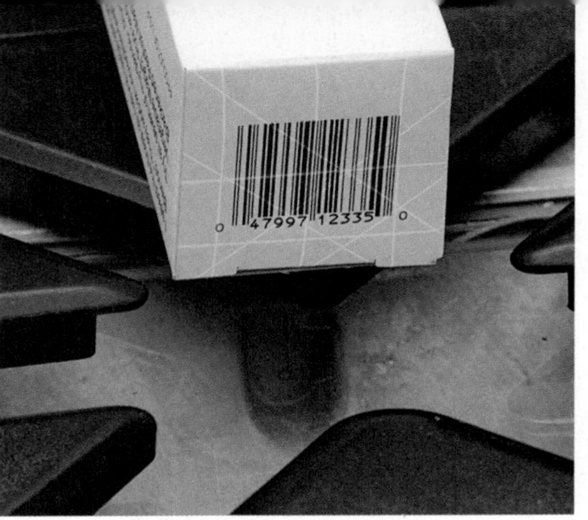

Figure 25
Optical scanners like this one use lasers to find the price of various products.

Optical Scanners

In supermarkets and many other kinds of stores, a cashier passes your purchases over a glass window in the checkout counter or holds a handheld device up to each item, like the one in **Figure 25.** In an instant, the optical scanner beeps and the price of the item appears on a screen. An optical scanner is a device that reads intensities of reflected light and converts the information to digital signals. You may have noticed that somewhere on each item the cashier scans is a pattern of thick and thin stripes called a bar code. An optical scanner detects the pattern and translates it into a digital signal, which goes to a computer. The computer searches its database for a matching item, finds its price, and sends the information to the cash register. The U.S. Postal Service also uses optical scanners to sort mail and keep track of mail delivery.

You may have used another type of optical scanner to convert pictures or text into forms you can use in computer programs. With a flatbed scanner, for example, you lay a document or picture facedown on a sheet of glass and close the cover. An optical scanner passes underneath the glass and reads the pattern of light and dark areas (or colors, if you are scanning a color picture). Some scanners are used with software that can read text on a page and convert the scanned information into a text file that you can work on. Photocopy machines and facsimile (fax) machines also use optical scanners.

Section 4 Assessment

1. What is polarized light?
2. Why is a holographic image three-dimensional?
3. What conditions are necessary for total internal reflection to occur?
4. Explain how an optical fiber is able to transmit light.
5. **Think Critically** Geologists and surveyors often use lasers for aligning equipment, measuring, and mapping. Explain why.

Skill Builder Activities

6. **Comparing and Contrasting** Make a table that compares and contrasts incoherent, coherent, and polarized light. **For more help, refer to the** Science Skill Handbook.
7. **Communicating** Many people wear polarized sunglasses while they are working. Write a list of jobs or occupations in which wearing polarized sunglasses is helpful. Explain why. **For more help, refer to the** Science Skill Handbook.

Answers to Section Assessment

1. light waves vibrating in only one direction
2. A holographic image transmits information about intensity, brightness, and direction of light, not just brightness.
3. Light must travel slower in the first medium, and must strike the boundary at an angle greater than the critical angle.
4. The light moves through the tube by total internal reflection.
5. Coherent light travels in straight paths and doesn't spread out; it can be used to find the direct path and distance between two points.
6. Check students' work.
7. Possible jobs include piloting airplanes and working as forest rangers. People working these jobs expose their eyes to bright sunlight. Polarized sunglasses reduce glare and reflections.

Activity

Make a Light Bender

From a hilltop you can see the reflection of pine trees and a cabin in the calm surface of a lake. This is possible because some of the light that reflects off these objects strikes the water's surface and reflects into your eyes. However, you don't see a clear, colorful image because much of the light enters the water rather than being reflected.

What You'll Investigate
How does water affect the viewer's image of an object that is above the water's surface?

Materials
light source
pencil
clear rectangular container
water
clay

Goals
- Identify reflection of an image in water.
- Identify refraction of an image in water.

Safety Precautions

Procedure
1. Fill the container with water.
2. Place the container so that a light source—window or overhead light—reaches it.
3. Stand the pencil on end in the clay and place it by the container as shown in the figure above. The pencil must be taller than the level of the water. Also, place the pencil on the same side of the container as the light source.

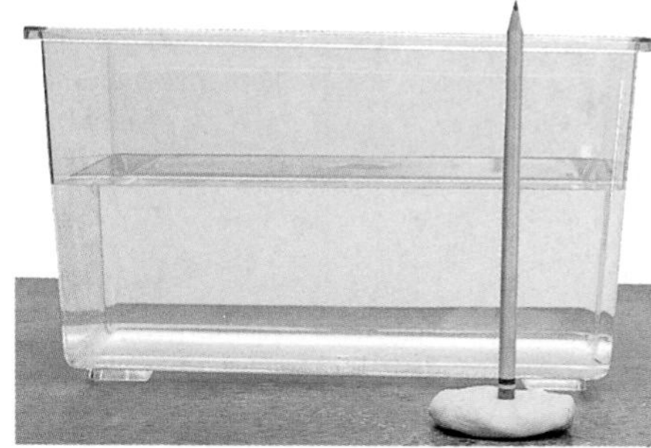

4. Place the light in a perpendicular position. Looking down through the surface of the water from the side opposite the pencil, observe the reflection and refraction of the pencil.
5. **Draw** a diagram of the image and label "reflection" and "refraction."
6. Repeat steps 4 and 5 two more times but position the pencil at two different angles.

Conclude and Apply
1. How would the image you see change or be different if the surface of the water were a mirror?
2. **Predict** how the angles of reflection or refraction would change if the surface of the container were curved. Explain.

Communicating Your Data
Make a poster of your diagrams and use it to explain reflection and refraction of light waves to your class. **For more help, refer to your Science Skill Handbook.**

Resource Manager

Chapter Resources Booklet
Reinforcement, p. 30
Activity Worksheet, pp. 6–7

Communicating Your Data
Have students use computer graphics software to demonstrate this activity, especially noting the angles of reflection and refraction of the light waves.

Activity

BENCH TESTED

Purpose Students observe how light will reflect and refract. L1 ELL COOP LEARN

LS **Interpersonal**

Process experimenting, predicting

Time Required 40 minutes

Alternate Materials A clear baking dish can replace the rectangular container.

Safety Precautions If a standard 120-V AC wall light source is used, caution students about dangerous voltages and shock hazard. Light bulbs can become hot.

Teaching Strategy The light source should be taped so it can't move. The pencil must stand straight up.

Answers to Questions
1. Only the top of the pencil would be visible, as the mirror would block light rays from entering the water, and would reflect them at the same angle as they hit the mirror.
2. For an individual light ray, the angles would not change. For groups of rays, images would be distorted.

Assessment

Oral Ask students to use data they gathered in this experiment to predict and then test to see if they would get the same results if a different clear liquid, such as alcohol or mineral oil, were in the box. The angles of reflected light would change. Use **PASC,** p. 105.

Activity

BENCH TESTED

Recognize the Problem

Purpose

Students will observe the effects of polarizing filters on the passage of light for two then three filters. L2 LS **Visual-Spatial**

Process Skills

forming a hypothesis, predicting, recognize cause and effect, drawing conclusions

Time Required

40 minutes

Materials

polarizing light filters (3), lamp or flashlight

Form a Hypothesis

Possible Hypothesis

For light to pass through the two polarizing filters, the polarizing axes of the filters must be parallel. For no light to pass through, the two polarizing axes must be perpendicular. If the polarizing axes of three filters are parallel, light will pass through. If any two of the axes of the three filters are perpendicular, then no light will pass through.

Activity **Design Your Own Experiment**

Polarizing Filters

Polarizing filters cause light waves to vibrate only in one direction. Wearing polarized sunglasses can help reduce glare while allowing you to see clearly. If you have two polarizing filters on top of one another, when will light shine through and when will it not? What might happen if you added a third filter in between the first two?

Recognize the Problem

How can you demonstrate the effects of polarizing filters?

Form a Hypothesis

Form a hypothesis about how two polarizing filters that are placed on top of one another must be oriented for light to shine through and for no light to shine through.

Goals

- **Demonstrate** when light does and does not shine through a pair of polarizing filters.
- **Predict** what will happen when you add a third polarizing filter.

Possible Materials

polarizing filters (3)
lamp or flashlight

Safety Precautions

Never look directly at the sun, even with a polarizing filter.

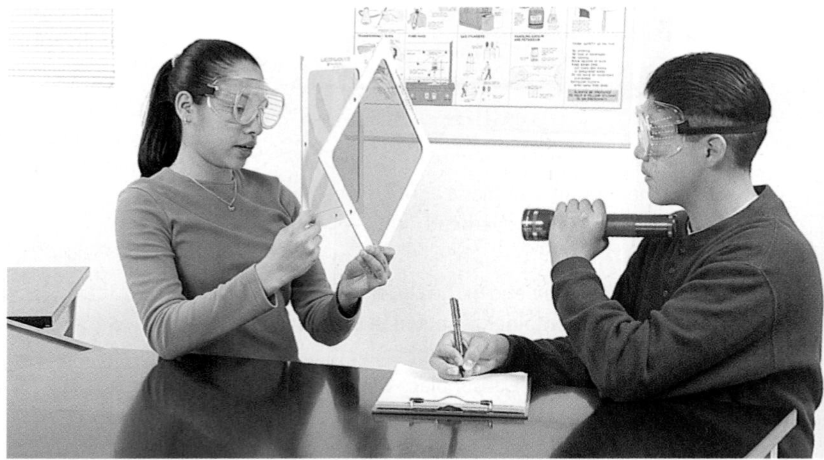

Test Your Hypothesis

Possible Procedures

Align two polarizing filters various ways and record observations. Add a third polarizing filter and again record observations.

Tie to Prior Knowledge

Remind students that light is transmitted by transverse waves. Transverse waves of light that are parallel to the polarizing axis of the filter can pass through. If the axes of two filters are perpendicular, no waves can pass through. If the filters are in any other orientation, the amount of light that passes through will vary.

Test your Hypothesis

Do

1. Using a pair of polarizing filters, choose at least three orientations of the filters to test your hypothesis.
2. When the two filters are oriented to allow the maximum amount of light to shine through, predict how a third filter placed between the two must be oriented for the same results.
3. Repeat step 2 but allow no light to shine through.
4. Make sure that your teacher approves your plan before you start.
5. Using an appropriate light source, test when light does and does not shine through a pair of polarizing filters. Test each of the orientations you planned in step 1. Record the results.
6. Test three orientations of the third filter for allowing the maximum amount of light to pass through. Record the results.
7. Repeat step 6 but allow no light to shine through. Record the results.

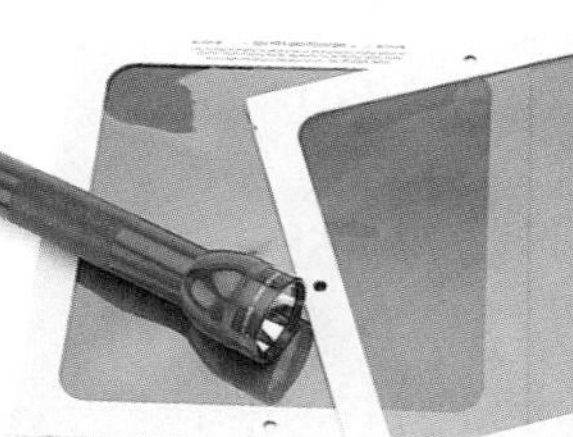

Analyze Your Data

1. **Describe** how the pair of polarizing filters were oriented when light did and did not shine through. In cases where light did shine through, was it always the same amount of light? Or did the amount of light change in different orientations?
2. In each case, describe what happened when you added a third filter between the two. How did the three orientations of the third filter change the amount of light that passed through? Explain.

Draw Conclusions

1. **Explain** why light did or did not shine through two polarizing filters in the various orientations.
2. Was your hypothesis correct? Why or why not?
3. **Explain** why light did or did not shine through various orientations of three polarizing filters.
4. Were your predictions correct? Why or why not?
5. If a polarizing filter reduces the brightness of light reflected from the surface of a lake, what can you conclude about the polarization of reflected light?

Communicating Your Data

The next time you see a family member or friend wearing sunglasses, **explain** to them how polarizing lenses can reduce problems of glare.

Expected Outcome

Students are expected to discover the orientation that the polarizing filters must be in to allow light through and to block it.

Analyze Your Data

1. Parallel: light passes through; perpendicular: light is blocked; the light intensity gradually decreases as the filter is rotated.
2. If the polarizing axes of all three filters are parallel, light will pass through. If any two of the axes of the three filters are perpendicular, then no light will pass through.

Error Analysis

Have students compare their results and their hypotheses and explain why differences occurred.

Draw Conclusions

1. If the polarizing axis of the filter is parallel to the transverse wave, the light can pass through. If the axes of two filters are perpendicular, the waves parallel to the first filter will not pass through the second filter. They cannot pass through the second filter, because they are perpendicular to the polarizing axis. If the filters are in any other orientation, the amount of light that passes through will vary.
2. Answers will vary
3. If the polarizing axes of all three filters are parallel, light will pass through. If any two of the axes of the three filters are perpendicular, then no light will pass through.
4. Answers will vary
5. That part of the reflected light had the same axis as the polarizing filter.

Assessment

Content Have students make posters explaining how polarizing filters work. Students should present their posters to their class. Use **Performance Assessment in the Science Classroom,** p. 145.

Communicating Your Data

Suggest students use their poster to help explain to family members how polarizing filters work.

Science and Language Arts

Pre-Reading Activity

Lead a class discussion about favorite colors. Make a chart on the board with warm colors on one side and cool colors on the other side. Ask students what comes into their minds when they think of certain colors. Ask students to think about what each color represents to them.

Respond to the Reading

Active Reading Strategies

Visualize The simplicity of a haiku allows the reader to use his or her imagination to complete the poet's picture. Students should try to visualize images of the seasons suggested by the haiku as they read. Ask students if a particular color comes to mind when they read each haiku.

Answers to Questions

1. Possible answer: winter is a one-color world because of snow or because so much plant life becomes dormant or dies away.
2. Possible answer: it helps the reader picture the season.
3. Possible answer: lingering indicates that the sun remains longer in the sky each day during spring.

Science and Language Arts

A Haiku Garden:
The Four Seasons in Poems and Prints
by Stephen Addiss with Fumiko and Akira Yamamoto

Respond to the Reading

1. What do the words *one-color world* mean?
2. How do the illustrations help the reader better understand the poems?
3. What do you think is meant by the word *lingering* in the Haiku about spring sunlight?

Withered by winter
the sound of the wind—
one-color world
Basho

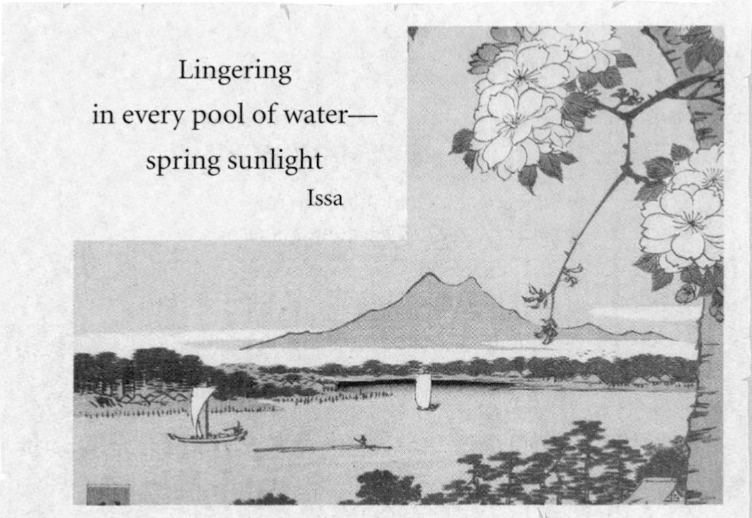

Lingering
in every pool of water—
spring sunlight
Issa

Reading Further

Other sources on this topic include:

The Essential Haiku, ed. and trans. Robert Hass. The Ecco Press. (1994).

The Power of Color, Dr. Morton Walker. Avery Publishing Group. (1991).

Japanese Haiku

Understanding Literature

Japanese Haiku You have just read English translations of two poems from a book that combines Japanese haiku and art. A haiku is a verse that consists of three lines and 17 syllables in the Japanese language. The first and third lines have five syllables each, and the middle line has seven syllables. Using few words, a haiku allows the reader's imagination to complete the picture. For instance, the *sound of the wind* might make you think of the sound of winter wind whipping around the house while you sit snuggly inside.

Science Connection Research has determined that there is a connection between color and mood. For example, the color of a room can affect a person's feelings and behavior. Warm colors have longer wavelengths, and are more stimulating. Cool colors, which have shorter wavelengths, tend to have a calming or soothing effect on people. Light and color have long been used as literary symbols. When the haiku is combined with Japanese prints, do you read it differently? Does the use of color change what you imagine when you read the haiku?

Linking Science and Writing

Writing and Illustrating Haiku Write two haiku poems—one about summer and one about fall. In one poem, use color to help you describe the season. In the other, use light or some property of light to help describe the season. When you have finished, exchange poems with one of your classmates. Read your classmate's haiku and create illustrations to accompany them.

Career Connection

Metamorphosis: III, 1998. Maria Martinez-Cañas. Gelatin silver print, 14 x 11 in.

Photographer

Maria Martinez-Canas uses light in an inventive and exciting way. Martinez-Canas was born in Havana, Cuba and grew up in Puerto Rico. She went to art school in the United States, earning a master of fine arts degree from the School of Art Institute in Chicago. Her innovative technique involves using a type of photographic material that blocks light. She cuts the material into artistic shapes, then prints these shapes on white paper in a manner similar to using stencils. Martinez-Canas lives in Miami and her photography can be seen in art exhibits all over the world.

SCIENCE *Online* To learn more about careers in photography, visit the Glencoe Science Web site at **science.glencoe.com.**

Understanding Literature

Science Connection

The perception of color can have physiological effects on the human body. Not only does the color red convey a mood of excitement, it also causes physiologic changes in the body.

Studies show that upon seeing red, a person's blood pressure increases, breathing becomes more rapid, taste buds become more sensitive and the sense of smell is heightened. Seeing the color blue, on the other hand, slows down the pulse, lowers the body temperature, and reduces the appetite.

Yellow is the first color a person distinguishes when he or she sees something. Studies show that yellow prepares a person for flight or fight, that children are more apt to cry in a yellow room, and allergies flare up more frequently in yellow surroundings. Green, on the other hand, has been shown to help decrease allergic reactions.

Linking Science and Writing

Writing Strategies

Remind students of the number of syllables in each line of a haiku. Suggest students pay attention to the mood they want to convey with their poems, and use color and properties of light appropriately.

Career Connection

There are a variety of career options using photography. Some photographers are artists, and some specialize in taking photographs for advertisements or for newspaper and magazine articles. There are several education options for those choosing photography as a career. An artist might pursue a fine arts degree. Others might pursue programs in commercial photography and in photojournalism.

Internet Addresses

Explore the Glencoe Science Web site at **science.glencoe.com** to find out more about topics in this feature.

Chapter 14 Study Guide

Reviewing Main Ideas

Preview

Students can answer the questions in their Science Journals. Discuss the answers as you go through the chapter. **LS Linguistic**

Review

Students can write their answers, then compare them with those of other students. **LS Interpersonal**

Reteach

Students can look at the illustrations and describe details that support the main ideas of the chapter. **LS Visual-Spatial**

Answers to Chapter Review

Section 1

2. regular

Section 4

1. Use a polarizing filter.

Chapter 14 Study Guide

Reviewing Main Ideas

Section 1 The Behavior of Light

1. You can't see through opaque materials. You can see hazily through translucent materials and clearly through transparent materials.
2. Light behaves as a wave, so it can be reflected. *Is this reflection from the lake regular or diffuse?*

3. Light waves can be refracted, or bent, when a wave changes speed as it travels from one material to another.

Section 2 Light and Color

1. You see color when light is reflected off objects and into your eyes.
2. Specialized cells in your eyes called cones allow you to distinguish colors and shapes of objects. Other cells, called rods, allow you to see in dim light.
3. The three primary colors of light can be mixed to form all other colors.
4. The colors of pigments are determined by the colors they reflect.

Section 3 Producing Light

1. Incandescent bulbs produce light by heating a tungsten filament until it glows brightly.
2. Fluorescent bulbs give off light when ultraviolet radiation produced inside the bulb causes the phosphor coating inside the bulb to glow.
3. Neon lights contain a gas that glows when electricity passes through it.
4. A laser produces coherent light by emitting a beam of light waves that have only one wavelength, with their crests and troughs aligned, and moving in a single direction.

Section 4 Using Light

1. Polarized light consists of transverse waves that vibrate along only one plane. *What could be done to reduce the glare in this photo?*

2. Total internal reflection occurs when a light wave strikes the boundary between two materials at an angle greater than the critical angle.
3. Optical scanners sense reflected light and convert the information to digital signals.

FOLDABLES Reading & Study Skills — After You Read

List examples of common materials that are opaque, transparent, and translucent on the front of your Foldable.

FOLDABLES Reading & Study Skills — After You Read

After students have read the chapter and completed the Foldable described in Before You Read, have them do the activity on the student page.

Dinah Zike

Chapter 14 Study Guide

Visualizing Main Ideas

Complete the following concept map about light.

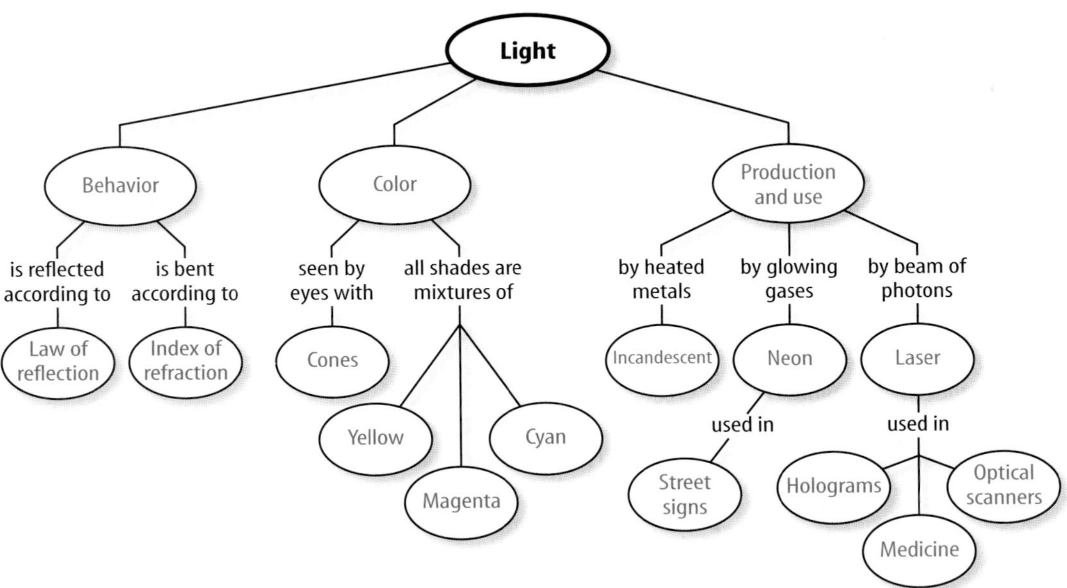

Vocabulary Review

Vocabulary Words

a. coherent light
b. fluorescent light
c. holography
d. incandescent light
e. incoherent light
f. index of refraction
g. mirage
h. opaque
i. pigment
j. polarized light
k. total internal reflection
l. translucent
m. transparent

THE PRINCETON REVIEW Study Tip

Get together with a friend. Quiz each other from textbook and class material.

Using Vocabulary

Answer the following questions using complete sentences.

1. What type of light does heating a filament until it glows produce?
2. What process would you use to produce a complete three-dimensional image of an object?
3. How would you describe an object that you can see through?
4. What process makes it possible for optical fibers to transmit telephone conversations over long distances?
5. What is a false image of a distant object?

IDENTIFYING Misconceptions

Assess

After students have done the activity on page 418F and completed the chapter, have them perform this activity.

Procedure Draw a lit candle, without the light rays, on the board. Explain that the candle is the only light in a room. Have students draw the complete path of a ray of light that allows the person to see the mug.

Expected Outcome We can see materials that don't emit light because they reflect light from other sources.

Visualizing Main Ideas

See student page.

Vocabulary Review

Using Vocabulary

1. Heating a filament until it glows produces incandescent light.
2. You can use holography to produce a complete 3-D image of an object.
3. An object that you can see through is transparent.
4. Total internal reflection makes it possible for optical fibers to transmit telephone conversations over long distances.
5. A false image of a distant object is a mirage.

Chapter 14 Assessment

Checking Concepts

1. B
2. C
3. D
4. A
5. B
6. A
7. D
8. C
9. C
10. B

Thinking Critically

11. The mirror reflects more light. Both reflect all colors of light, but the white shirt is not completely opaque, and allows some light to pass through.
12. Both reflect all the colors of light that hit them. Reflection from a white wall is diffuse while reflection from a mirror is regular.
13. With a blue filter, the shirt would appear blue. With a red or green filter, the shirt would appear black.
14. Violet, because it is bent the most by a prism; the greater the difference in the speed of light in two different media, the more it is refracted.
15. Possible answer: A cat's eye does not have the cone nerve cells that a human's eye does.

Chapter 14 Assessment

Checking Concepts

Choose the word or phrase that best answers the question.

1. Which word describes materials that absorb or reflect all light?
   A) translucent **C)** ultraviolet
   B) opaque **D)** diffuse
2. What is the term for the property of a material that indicates how much light slows down when traveling in the material?
   A) pigment **C)** index of refraction
   B) filter **D)** mirage
3. Which of the following explains why a prism separates white light into the colors of the rainbow?
   A) interference **C)** diffraction
   B) fluorescence **D)** refraction
4. What do you see when noting the color of an object?
   A) the light it reflects
   B) the light it absorbs
   C) polarization
   D) diffuse reflection
5. What do the phosphors inside fluorescent bulbs absorb to create a glow?
   A) incandescent light
   B) ultraviolet radiation
   C) halogens
   D) argon
6. What term describes objects that allow some light, but not a clear image to pass through?
   A) translucent **C)** transparent
   B) reflective **D)** opaque
7. Which light waves are bent most when passing through a prism?
   A) red waves **C)** blue waves
   B) yellow waves **D)** violet waves
8. Which type of cells in your eyes allows you to see the color violet?
   A) red cones **C)** blue cones
   B) green cones **D)** rods
9. What color of light is produced when the three primary colors of light are combined in equal amounts?
   A) black **C)** white
   B) yellow **D)** cyan
10. Which term describes laser light?
    A) incoherent **C)** incandescent
    B) coherent **D)** fluorescent

Thinking Critically

11. Which reflects more, a mirror or a white shirt? Explain the difference.
12. How is the reflection of light from a white wall similar to the reflection of light from a mirror? How is it different?
13. What color would a blue shirt appear to be if a blue filter were placed in front of it? A red filter? A green filter?
14. Which color of light changes speed the most when it passes through a prism? Explain.

Developing Skills

15. **Drawing Conclusions** Most mammals, such as dogs and cats, can't see colors. Infer how a cat's eye might be different from your eye.

Chapter Assessment Planner

Portfolio Encourage students to place in their portfolios one or two items of what they consider to be their best work. Examples include:
- Curriculum Connection, p. 421
- Activity, p. 428
- Assessment, p. 435
- Reteach, p. 440

Performance Additional performance assessments, Performance Task Assessment Lists, and rubrics for evaluating these activities can be found in Glencoe's **Performance Assessment in the Science Classroom.**

16. Concept Mapping Use this blank concept map to show the steps in the production of fluorescent light.

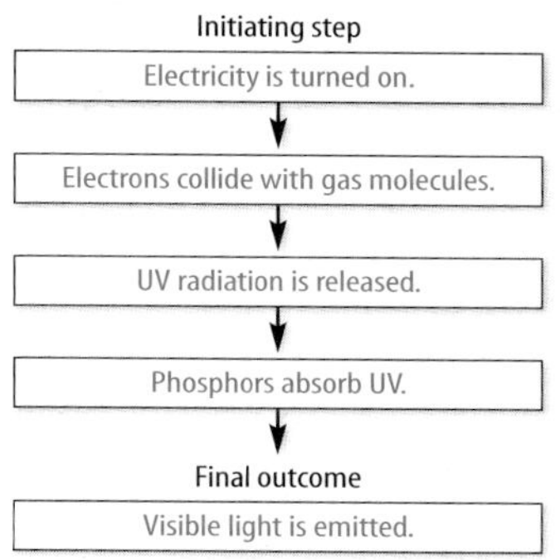
Initiating step
Electricity is turned on.
Electrons collide with gas molecules.
UV radiation is released.
Phosphors absorb UV.
Final outcome
Visible light is emitted.

17. Interpreting Scientific Illustrations Make a drawing that shows how a fluorescent bulb produces light.

18. Drawing Conclusions Why is the inside of a camera painted black?

19. Making and Using Tables Construct a table to show the properties and applications of incandescent, fluorescent, neon, sodium-vapor, and tungsten-halogen lighting devices. For each type of device, include information on how light is produced, typical uses, and its advantages or disadvantages.

Performance Assessment

20. Poster Make a poster to show how the three primary pigments are combined to produce common colors such as blue, red, yellow, green, purple, brown, and black.

Technology

Go to the Glencoe Science Web site at **science.glencoe.com** or use the **Glencoe Science CD-ROM** for additional chapter assessment.

THE PRINCETON REVIEW Test Practice

Judy and Markus are studying light. They have just read about an experiment that shows how light has certain properties and follows certain rules.

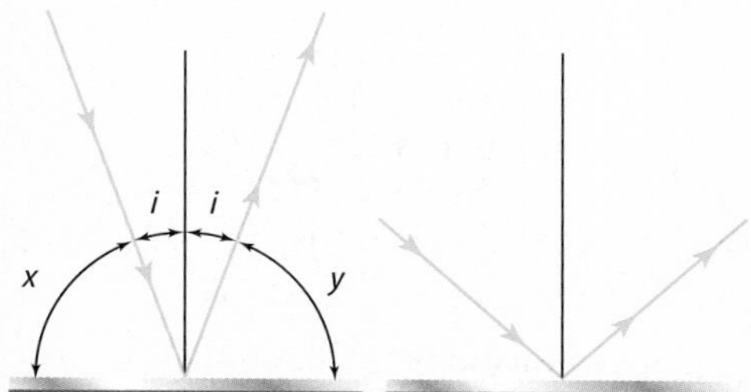
i
i
x
y

Study the pictures above and answer the following questions.

1. Angle *i* measures 20°. Using this information, what is angle *x*?
- **A)** 50°
- **B)** 60°
- **C)** 70°
- **D)** 80°

2. Which of the following is taking place in both of the experiments above?
- **F)** refraction
- **G)** reflection
- **H)** diffusion
- **J)** fluorescence

3. Which of the following statements is true about reflection?
- **A)** $\angle i + \angle x = 100°$
- **B)** $\angle i + \angle x = 60°$
- **C)** $\angle i + \angle x = 80°$
- **D)** $\angle i + \angle x = 90°$

Assessment Resources

Reproducible Masters

Chapter Resources Booklet
- Chapter Review, pp. 39–40
- Chapter Tests, pp. 41–44
- Assessment Transparency Activity, p. 53

Glencoe Science Web site
- Interactive Tutor
- Chapter Quizzess

Glencoe Technology
- Assessment Transparency
- Interactive CD-ROM Chapter Quizzes
- ExamView Pro Test Bank
- Vocabulary PuzzleMaker Software
- MindJogger Videoquiz DVD/VHS

Chapter 14 Assessment

THE PRINCETON REVIEW Test Practice

The Test-Taking Tip was written by The Princeton Review, the nation's leader in test preparation.
1. C
2. G
3. D

Developing Skills

16. See student page.
17. Drawings should show the various parts of a fluorescent bulb, including the gas and the phosphor coating inside the bulb. Details on the drawing should show the steps listed on the concept map of question number 17.
18. The black surface does not reflect any colors, so the camera won't reflect stray light onto the film.
19. Check students' work.

Performance Assessment

20. Posters should show the proper combinations of yellow, magenta, and cyan. Use Performance Assessment in the Science Classroom, p. 145

Section/Objectives	Standards		Activities/Features
	National	State/Local	
Chapter Opener	See p. 37T for a Key to Standards.		**Explore Activity:** Observe objects through a drop of water, p. 451 **Before You Read,** p. 451
Section 1 Mirrors 2 sessions 1 block 1. **Describe** how an image is formed in three types of mirrors. 2. **Explain** the differences between real and virtual images. 3. **Identify** examples and uses of plane, concave, and convex mirrors.	National Content Standards: UCP2, A1, B1 (5–8), B2 (9–12), E1, E2, F5 (6–8)		**Life Science Integration,** p. 453 **MiniLAB:** Observing Images, p. 455 **Activity:** Reflections of Reflections, p. 459
Section 2 Lenses 1 session 5 block 1. **Describe** the shapes of convex and concave lenses. 2. **Explain** how convex and concave lenses refract light to form images. 3. **Explain** how lenses are used to correct vision.	National Content Standards: UCP2, A1, B1 (5–8), B2 (9–12), E1, E2, F5 (6–8), F1 (9–12)		**Problem-Solving Activity:** Comparing Object and Image Distances, p. 462 **Science Online,** p. 464 **Health Integration,** p. 465 **Visualizing the Silicon Retina,** p. 466
Section 3 Title 3 sessions 1.5 blocks 1. **Compare** refracting and reflecting telescopes. 2. **Explain** why a telescope in space would be useful. 3. **Describe** how a microscope uses lenses to magnify small objects. 4. **Explain** how a camera creates an image.	National Content Standards: UCP2, A1, B1 (5–8), B2 (9–12), E1, E2, F5 (6–8)		**Science Online,** p. 470 **MiniLAB:** Experimenting with Focal Lengths, p. 471 **Activity:** Up Close and Personal, p. 474 **Science and Society:** Sight Lines, p. 476

Activity Materials	Reproducible Resources	Section Assessment	Technology
Explore Activity: plastic wrap, newspaper or magazine, water, dropper	**Chapter Resources Booklet** Foldables Worksheet, p. 17 Note-taking Worksheets, pp. 33–35	Glencoe's Assessment Advantage	
MiniLAB: shiny spoon, bright light, poster board **Activity:** 2 plane mirrors, masking tape, protractor, paper clip	**Chapter Resources Booklet** Transparency Activity, p. 44 MiniLAB, p. 3 Enrichment, p. 30 Reinforcement, p. 27 Directed Reading, p. 20 Activity Worksheet, pp. 5–6 **Performance Assessment in the Science Classroom,** p. 52 Lab Activity, pp. 9–12	**Portfolio** Science Journal, p. 456 **Performance** MiniLAB, p. 455 Skill Builder Activities, p. 458 **Content** Section Assessment, p. 458	Section Focus Transparency Interactive CD-ROM/DVD Guided Reading Audio Program
Need materials? Contact Science Kit at 1-800-828-7777 or www.sciencekit.com on the Internet.	**Chapter Resources Booklet** Transparency Activity, p. 45 Enrichment, p. 31 Reinforcement, p. 28 Directed Reading, p. 20 Lab Activity, pp. 13–16 Transparency Activity, pp. 47–48 **Mathematics Skill Activities,** p. 29 **Science Inquiry Labs,** p. 59	**Portfolio** Curriculum Connection, p. 465 **Performance** Problem-Solving Activity, p. 462 Skill Builder Activities, p. 467 **Content** Section Assessment, p. 467	Section Focus Transparency Teaching Transparency Interactive CD-ROM/DVD Guided Reading Audio Program
MiniLAB: test tube, water, test-tube stopper, sheet of paper or note card **Activity:** convex lens with 25–30 cm focal length, convex lens with 2–3 cm focal length, concave lens with 2–3 cm focal length, 2 cardboard tubes that fit snugly one inside the other, clay, scissors	**Chapter Resources Booklet** Transparency Activity, p. 46 MiniLAB, p. 4 Enrichment, p. 32 Reinforcement, p. 29 Activity Worksheet, pp. 7–8 **Cultural Diversity,** p. 51 Directed Reading, pp. 21, 22 **Home and Community Involvement,** p. 39 **Physical Science Critical Thinking/Problem Solving,** p. 4	**Portfolio** Science Journal, p. 470 **Performance** MiniLAB, p. 471 Skill Builder Activities, p. 473 **Content** Section Assessment, p. 473	Section Focus Transparency Interactive CD-ROM/DVD Guided Reading Audio Program

End of Chapter Assessment

Glencoe's Assessment Advantage

Blackline Masters	Technology	Professional Series
Chapter Resources Booklet Chapter Review, pp. 37–38 Chapter Tests, pp. 39–42 **Standardized Test Practice by The Princeton Review,** pp. 64–67	MindJogger Videoquiz CD-ROM Explorations and Quizzes Vocabulary Puzzle Makers ExamView Pro Test Bank Interactive Lesson Planner Interactive Teacher's Edition	Performance Assessment in the Science Classroom (PASC)

Transparencies

Section Focus

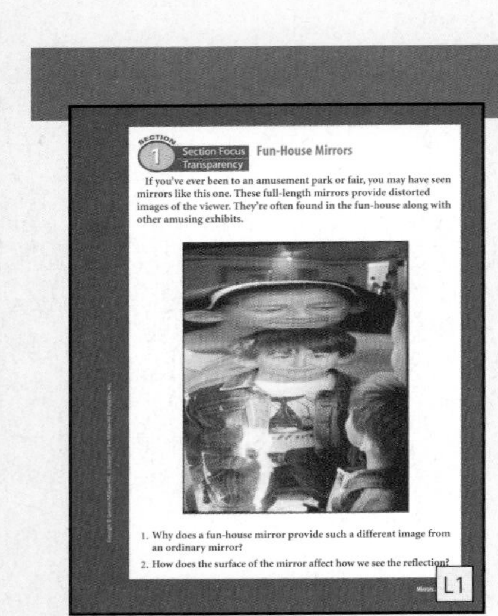
Section 1 Section Focus Transparency **Fun-House Mirrors**

If you've ever been to an amusement park or fair, you may have seen mirrors like this one. These full-length mirrors provide distorted images of the viewer. They're often found in the fun-house along with other amusing exhibits.

1. Why does a fun-house mirror provide such a different image from an ordinary mirror?
2. How does the surface of the mirror affect how we see the reflection?

L1

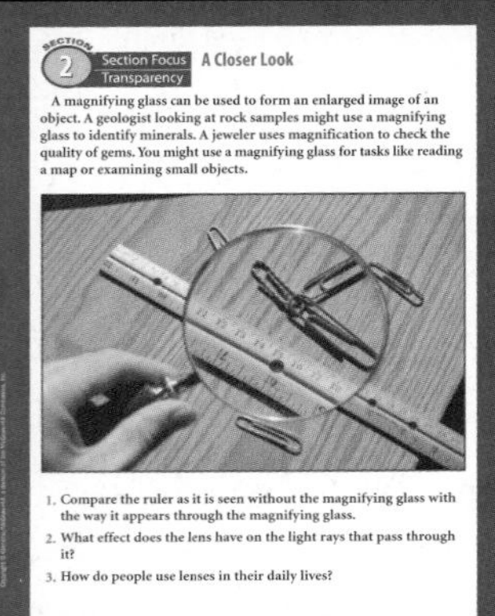
Section 2 Section Focus Transparency **A Closer Look**

A magnifying glass can be used to form an enlarged image of an object. A geologist looking at rock samples might use a magnifying glass to identify minerals. A jeweler uses magnification to check the quality of gems. You might use a magnifying glass for tasks like reading a map or examining small objects.

1. Compare the ruler as it is seen without the magnifying glass with the way it appears through the magnifying glass.
2. What effect does the lens have on the light rays that pass through it?
3. How do people use lenses in their daily lives?

L1

Section 3 Section Focus Transparency **I Spy**

Originally created in 1608 by a Dutch optician named Hans Lippershey, the telescope was put to use by Galileo to observe the Moon and planets. It was soon put to other uses, hence it became known as a "spyglass."

1. Suggest some practical uses to which the instrument was first applied. Why did it earn the name "spyglass"?
2. What modern equivalent of the spyglass can be used at sporting events? How is it an improvement?

L1

This is a representation of key blackline masters available in the Teacher Classroom Resources. See Resource Manager boxes within the chapter for additional information.

Assessment

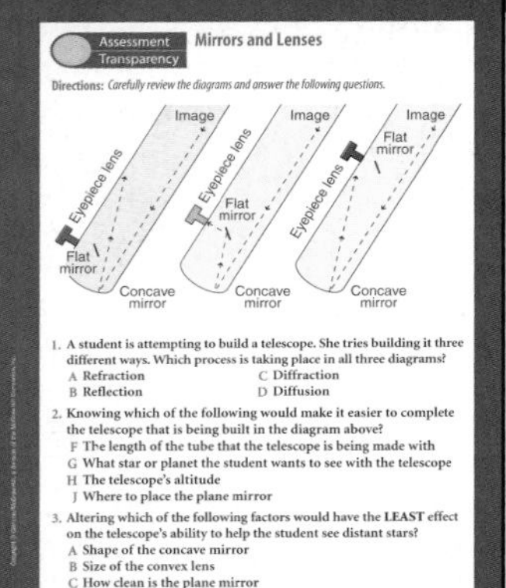
Assessment Transparency **Mirrors and Lenses**

Directions: Carefully review the diagrams and answer the following questions.

1. A student is attempting to build a telescope. She tries building it three different ways. Which process is taking place in all three diagrams?
   A Refraction C Diffraction
   B Reflection D Diffusion
2. Knowing which of the following would make it easier to complete the telescope that is being built in the diagram above?
   F The length of the tube that the telescope is being made with
   G What star or planet the student wants to see with the telescope
   H The telescope's altitude
   J Where to place the plane mirror
3. Altering which of the following factors would have the LEAST effect on the telescope's ability to help the student see distant stars?
   A Shape of the concave mirror
   B Size of the convex lens
   C How clean is the plane mirror
   D Total weight of the tube

L1

Teaching

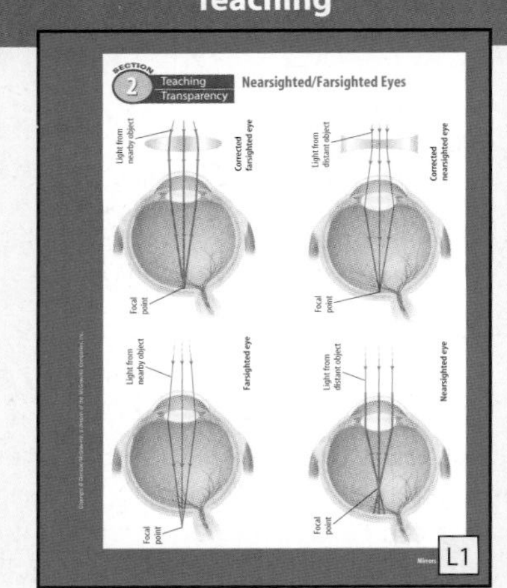
Section 2 Teaching Transparency **Nearsighted/Farsighted Eyes**

L1

Key to Teaching Strategies

The following designations will help you decide which activities are appropriate for your students.

- L1 Level 1 activities should be appropriate for students with learning difficulties.
- L2 Level 2 activities should be within the ability range of all students.
- L3 Level 3 activities are designed for above-average students.
- ELL ELL activities should be within the ability range of English Language Learners.
- COOP LEARN Cooperative Learning activities are designed for small group work.
- LS Multiple Learning Styles logos are used throughout to indicate strategies that address different learning styles.
- P These strategies represent student products that can be placed into a best-work portfolio.

Hands-on Activities

Activity Worksheets

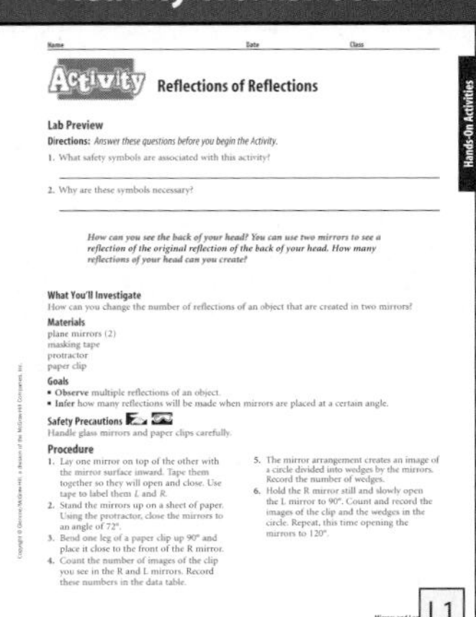
Activity **Reflections of Reflections**

Lab Preview

Directions: Answer these questions before you begin the Activity.

1. What safety symbols are associated with this activity?
2. Why are these symbols necessary?

How can you see the back of your head? You can use two mirrors to see a reflection of the original reflection of the back of your head. How many reflections of your head can you create?

What You'll Investigate

How can you change the number of reflections of an object that are created in two mirrors?

Materials

plane mirrors (2)
masking tape
protractor
paper clip

Goals

- Observe multiple reflections of an object.
- Infer how many reflections will be made when mirrors are placed at a certain angle.

Safety Precautions

Handle glass mirrors and paper clips carefully.

Procedure

1. Lay one mirror on top of the other with the mirror surface inward. Tape them together so they will open and close. Use tape to label them L and R.
2. Stand the mirrors up on a sheet of paper. Using the protractor, close the mirrors to an angle of 72°.
3. Bend one leg of a paper clip up 90° and place it close to the front of the R mirror.
4. Count the number of images of the clip you see in the R and L mirrors. Record these numbers in the data table.
5. The mirror arrangement creates an image of a circle divided into wedges by the mirrors. Record the number of wedges.
6. Hold the R mirror still and slowly open the L mirror to 90°. Count and record the images of the clip and the wedges in the circle. Repeat, this time opening the mirrors to 120°.

L1

Laboratory Activities

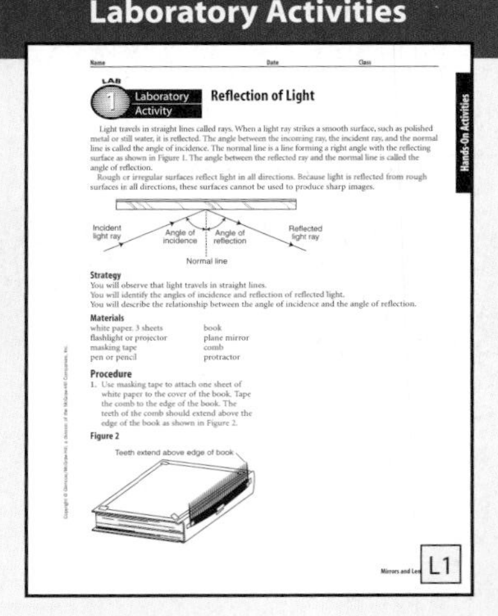
Lab 1 Laboratory Activity **Reflection of Light**

Light travels in straight lines called rays. When a light ray strikes a smooth surface, such as polished metal or still water, it is reflected. The angle between the incoming ray, the incident ray, and the normal line is called the angle of incidence. The normal line is a line forming a right angle with the reflecting surface as shown in Figure 1. The angle between the reflected ray and the normal line is called the angle of reflection.

Rough or irregular surfaces reflect light in all directions. Because light is reflected from rough surfaces in all directions, these surfaces cannot be used to produce sharp images.

Strategy

You will observe that light travels in straight lines.
You will identify the angles of incidence and reflection of reflected light.
You will describe the relationship between the angle of incidence and the angle of reflection.

Materials

white paper, 3 sheets
flashlight or projector
masking tape
pen or pencil
book
plane mirror
comb
protractor

Procedure

1. Use masking tape to attach one sheet of white paper to the cover of the book. Tape the comb to the edge of the book. The teeth of the comb should extend above the edge of the book as shown in Figure 2.

Figure 2

L1

Meeting Different Ability Levels

Content Outline

Note-taking Worksheet — Mirrors and Lenses

L1

Reinforcement

Section 1 Reinforcement — Mirrors

L1

Directed Reading

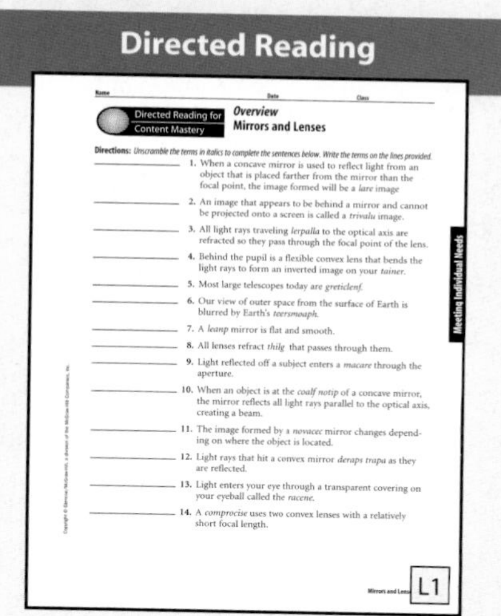

Directed Reading for Content Mastery — Overview: Mirrors and Lenses

L1

Enrichment

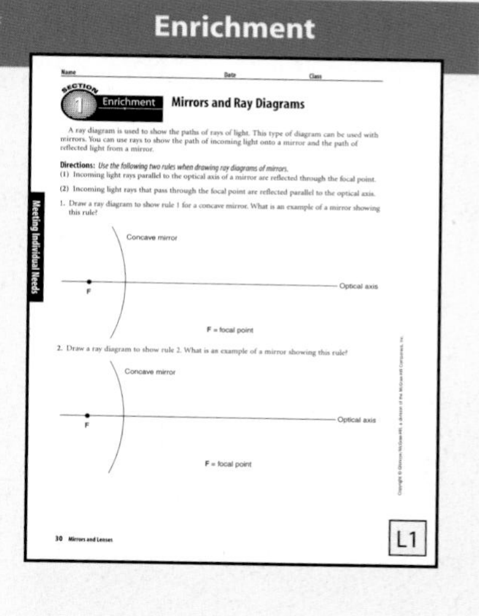

Section 1 Enrichment — Mirrors and Ray Diagrams

L1

Spanish Directed Reading

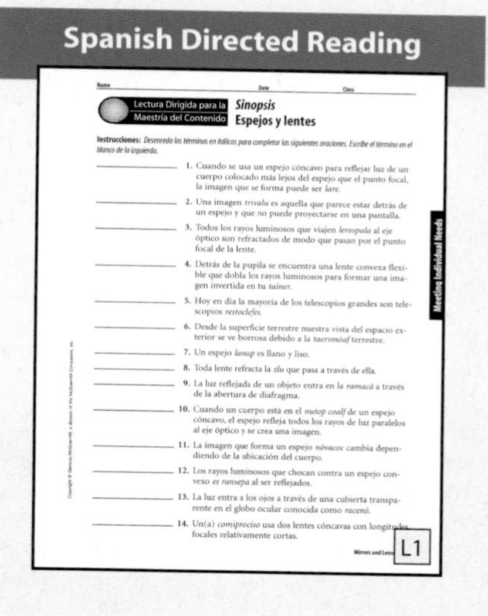

Lectura Dirigida para la Maestría del Contenido — Sinopsis: Espejos y lentes

L1

Assessment

Chapter Tests

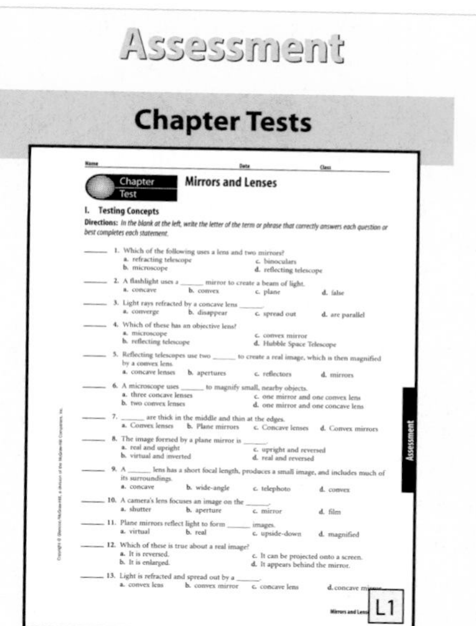

Chapter Test — Mirrors and Lenses

L1

Test Practice Workbook

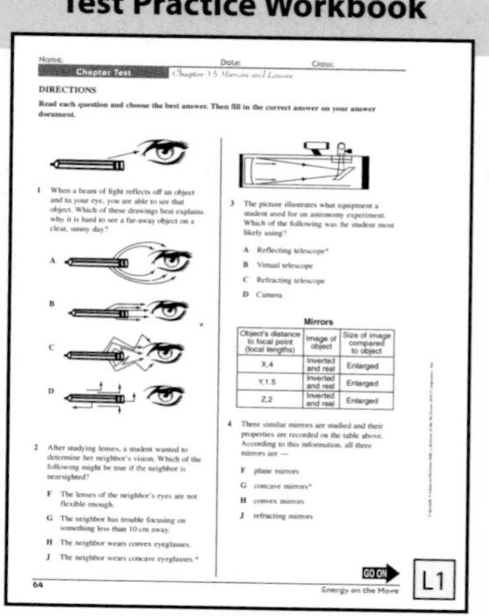

L1

Chapter Review

Chapter Review — Mirrors and Lenses

L1

Science Content Background

SECTION 1

Mirrors

How do you use light to see?

You see objects that reflect light. Mirrors produce orderly reflections; opaque objects such as books produce disordered reflections because they scatter light in many directions.

Seeing with Plane Mirrors

The law of reflection applies whenever light is reflected. The angle of incidence is equal to the angle of reflection. To determine these angles, an imaginary reference line is drawn perpendicular to the reflecting surface. The angle between the incident ray and the reference line is the angle of incidence. The angle between the reflected ray and the reference line is the angle of reflection. The virtual image formed by a plane mirror is upright, but backward. The image appears to be the same distance behind the mirror as the object is in front of the mirror.

The multiple images in a kaleidoscope are produced by three plane mirrors positioned to form a triangle. Through the center of the triangle one can see the reflection of the moving pieces of colored plastic or glass forming the geometric images.

Fun Fact

Familiarity brings contentment. When we frequently view a face, we tend to like it more. When people were shown photographs of a familiar person and the mirror image of that person, they preferred the photograph. But when the person pictured viewed the photographs, he or she tended to prefer the mirror image. Some have hypothesized that this is because people see themselves primarily as a mirror image.

Concave Mirrors

The law of reflection also applies to curved mirrors. Concave mirrors are converging mirrors. The shape of these mirrors causes light rays parallel to the optical axis to be reflected through the focal point. In this manner concave mirrors are more similar to convex lenses than to concave lenses.

Runk/Schoenberger/Grant Heilman Photography, Inc.

SECTION 2 Lenses

What is a lens?

A lens is a curved, transparent device that bends light that passes through the lens. The bending, or refraction, of light requires two conditions: (a) Light must pass from one material through another that has a different optical density, and (b) the light must enter the lens at an angle other than perpendicular.

Convex Lenses

When light hits a convex lens, it bends toward the fatter part of the lens. For a magnifying glass to work, the object being magnified must be closer to the lens than the focal point of the lens.

Lenses and Eyesight

Eyes focus in a process called accommodation. In this process, muscles attached to the eye lens make the lens thinner or thicker to attain sharp focus. Most people with glasses or contact lenses wear concave lenses for myopia, or nearsightedness. This condition has various causes. For instance, a person may genetically have an eyeball that is too long, causing rays of light to be focused in front of, instead of on, the retina.

Optic technology has a long history. Ancient Egyptians and Romans used bowls filled with water to help them read. In the thirteenth century, magnifying glasses were used. Lenses for myopia were developed in the sixteenth century. In the late 1700s, Benjamin Franklin developed bifocal lenses. The first glass contact lenses were developed in the late 1800s by Adolph E. Fick.

SECTION 3 Optical Instruments

Telescopes

Optical telescopes are popular for viewing the night sky. In order to get the best view of the Moon's craters and other features, look near the terminator. The terminator is the line the separates the lighted and dark portions of the Moon.

Cameras

In some cameras, a person moves the lens closer or further away from an object to focus the image. Disposable and other inexpensive cameras are often fixed-focus cameras—the lens does not move. It is set so that most images will be pretty well in focus. Automatic focusing cameras send out an infrared beam that is reflected from the subject. The camera then moves the lens to produce the optimal focus.

For additional content background on this topic, go to the Glencoe Science Web site at science.glencoe.com.

Barry L. Runk/Grant Heilman Photography, Inc.

Mirrors and Lenses

Chapter Vocabulary

plane mirror
virtual image
concave mirror
optical axis
focal point
focal length
real image
convex mirror
convex lens
concave lens
cornea
retina
refracting telescope
reflecting telescope
microscope

What do you think?

Science Journal This photo shows a view of the Lincoln Memorial as seen through a fish eye lens.

Mirrors and Lenses

The dark-tinted glass panes of this office building act as mirrors, reflecting an image of the Iowa State Capitol Building. Why is the image distorted? Depending on whether it is flat or curved, a mirror reflects an object's true size and shape, magnifies the image, or reduces the image. In this chapter, you'll learn about mirrors and lenses and how they are used in cameras, telescopes, microscopes, and your own eyes. You also will learn how the shape of a lens determines the image you see.

What do you think?

Science Journal Look at the picture below with a classmate. Discuss what this might be or what is happening. Here's a hint: *If you could see like this, you would have eyes in the back of your head.* Write your answer or best guess in your Science Journal.

450

Theme Connection

Systems and Interactions Light interacts with mirrors and lenses to produce images. Systems of mirrors and lenses enable us to view distant stars and planets and to magnify tiny objects.

Have you ever used a magnifying glass, a camera, a microscope, or a telescope? If so, you were using a lens to create an image. A lens is a transparent material that bends rays of light. In this activity, you will use water to create a lens.

Observe objects through a drop of water

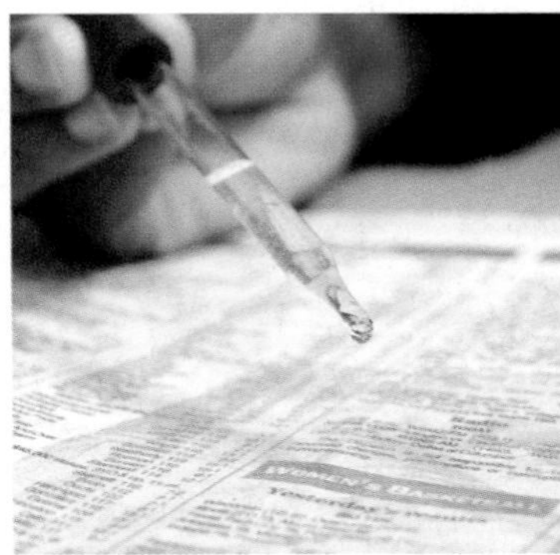

1. Cut a 10-cm × 10-cm piece of plastic wrap. Set it on a page of printed text.
2. Place a small water drop on the plastic. Look at the text through the drop. What do you observe?
3. Make your water drop larger and observe the text through it again.
4. Carefully lift the piece of plastic wrap a few centimeters above the text and look at the text through the water drop again.

Observe

In your Science Journal, describe how the text looked in steps 2, 3, and 4. Why do you think water affects the way the text looks? What other materials might you use to magnify the text?

Before You Read

FOLDABLES Reading & Study Skills

Making a Cause and Effect Study Fold **Make the following Foldable to help you understand the cause and effect relationship of reflections.**

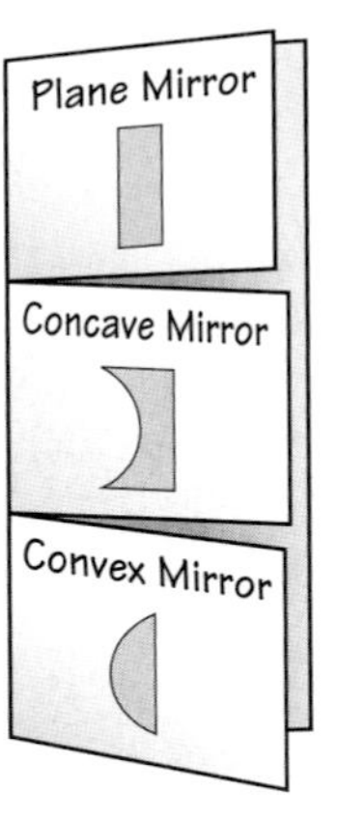

1. Place a sheet of paper in front of you so the short side is at the top. Fold the paper in half from the left side to the right side.
2. Fold in the top and the bottom. Unfold the paper so three sections show.
3. Through the top thickness of paper, cut along each of the fold lines to the left fold, forming three tabs.
4. Label the tabs *Plane Mirror*, *Concave Mirror*, and *Convex Mirror*. Draw examples of the three types of mirrors.
5. As you read the chapter, write under the tabs how each mirror works and how each reflects light differently.

451

EXPLORE ACTIVITY

Purpose Students observe the effects of the refraction of light through a drop of water, which acts as a convex lens. L2 ELL

LS **Visual-Spatial**

Preparation Bring to class samples of printed texts using different type sizes, including some that is very small, for students to observe.

Materials plastic wrap, printed text, water

Teaching Strategies Use an eyedropper to dispense drops of water.

Observe

In step 2 the text looked enlarged and upright. In step 3 it looked larger and still upright. In step 4 the text flipped and looked upside down. As the light reflected from the text moves from the water to the air it is refracted. Other possible materials include plastic, glass, and other transparent liquids and solids.

Assessment

Oral Ask students to make an events chain to describe the path of a light ray from the time it leaves a light source to the time it enters their eyes after passing through the drop of water. The ray moves straight through the air, hits the curved surface of the water and is refracted toward the normal, hits the printed page and is absorbed by the black print and reflected by the white page. The reflected light moves back through the water, and is refracted again as it moves through the curved surface of the water drop, then moves straight to the student's eye. Use **PASC,** p. 163.

Before You Read

FOLDABLES Reading & Study Skills

Dinah Zike Study Fold

Purpose Students will make and use a Foldable to diagram and collect information on three types of mirrors, and explain the cause and effect relationship between each mirror's shape and its reflection.

For additional help, see Foldables Worksheet, p. 17 in **Chapter Resources Booklet,** or go to the Glencoe Science Web site at **science.glencoe.com.** See After You Read in the Study Guide at the end of this chapter.

SECTION 1

Mirrors

1 Motivate

Bellringer Transparency

Display the Section Focus Transparency for Section 1. Use the accompanying Transparency Activity Master. L2 ELL

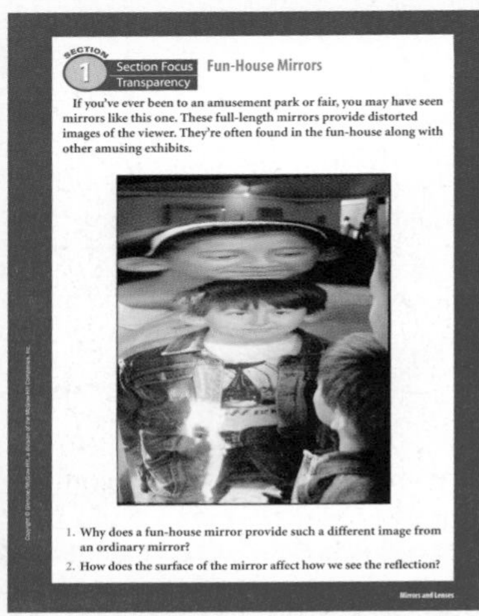

SECTION 1 Section Focus Transparency **Fun-House Mirrors**

If you've ever been to an amusement park or fair, you may have seen mirrors like this one. These full-length mirrors provide distorted images of the viewer. They're often found in the fun-house along with other amusing exhibits.

1. **Why does a fun-house mirror provide such a different image from an ordinary mirror?**
2. **How does the surface of the mirror affect how we see the reflection?**

Mirrors and Lenses

Tie to Prior Knowledge

Ask students whether they have ever looked at a rounded, shiny surface such as a doorknob and noticed that their reflection is distorted. In this section, students will learn how the shape of a mirror determines the type of reflection they see.

SECTION 1

Mirrors

As You Read

***What* You'll Learn**

- **Describe** how an image is formed in three types of mirrors.
- **Explain** the difference between real and virtual images.
- **Identify** examples and uses of plane, concave, and convex mirrors.

Vocabulary

plane mirror, virtual image, concave mirror, optical axis, focal point, focal length, real image, convex mirror

***Why* It's Important**

Mirrors allow you to check your appearance, use flashlights, and see your surroundings.

How do you use light to see?

Have you tried to read a book under the covers with only a small flashlight? Or have you ever tried to find an address number on a house or an apartment at night on a poorly lit street? It's harder to do those activities in the dark than it is when there is plenty of light. Your eyes see by detecting light, so anytime you see something, it is because light has come from that object to your eyes. Light can start from a light source, such as the Sun or a lightbulb, or it can reflect off of an object, such as the page of a book or someone's face. Either way, when light travels from an object to your eye, you see the object. Light can reflect more than once. For example, light can reflect off of an object into a mirror and then reflect into your eyes. When no light is available to reflect off of objects and into your eye, your eyes cannot see anything. This is why it is hard to read a book or see an address in the dark.

Light Rays Light sources send out light waves that travel in all directions. These waves spread out from the light source just as ripples on the surface of water spread out from the point of impact of a pebble.

You also could think of the light coming from the source as being many narrow beams of light. Each narrow beam of light travels in a straight line and is called a light ray. **Figure 1** shows how a light source, such as a candle, gives off light rays that travel away from the source in all directions. Your brain always interprets light rays as if they traveled in a straight line. Because of this, you can use mirrors to see reflections.

Figure 1
A light source, like a candle, sends out light rays in all directions.

Section Assessment Planner

PORTFOLIO
Science Journal, p. 456

PERFORMANCE ASSESSMENT
Try at Home MiniLAB, p. 455
Skill Builder Activities, p. 458
See page 480 for more options.

CONTENT ASSESSMENT
Section, p. 458
Challenge, p. 458
Chapter, pp. 480–481

Some of the light rays then travel toward the mirror and reflect back toward your eyes.
First, when light hits you, it reflects off of each point on your body in many different directions.

Figure 2
Seeing an image of yourself in a mirror involves two sets of reflections.

Seeing with Plane Mirrors

Greek mythology tells the story of a handsome young man named Narcissus who noticed his image in a pond and fell in love with himself. Like pools of water, mirrors are smooth surfaces that reflect light to form images. Just as Narcissus did, you can see yourself as you glance into a quiet pool of water or walk past a shop window. Most of the time, however, you probably look for your image in a flat, smooth mirror called a **plane mirror**.

Reading Check *What is a plane mirror?*

Reflection from Plane Mirrors What do you see when you stand in front of a plane mirror and look straight into it? Your reflection appears to be the same size as you are and is upright. In fact, your reflection is what another person would see if he or she stood where the mirror is and looked at you. **Figure 2** shows how your image is formed by a plane mirror. First, light rays from a light source strike you. Every point that is struck by the light rays reflects these rays so they travel outward in all directions. If your friend were looking at you, these reflected light rays coming from you would enter her eyes so she could see you. However, if a mirror is placed in front of you instead, the light rays are reflected back to your eyes so you can see yourself.

Life Science INTEGRATION

Your left hand and right hand are mirror images of each other. Some of the molecules in your body exist in two forms that are mirror images. However, the chemical reactions that occur in your body use only left-handed mirror-image structures. Using different color gumdrops and toothpicks, make a model of a molecule that has a mirror image.

2 Teach

How do you use light to see?

Quick Demo

To remind students of the basic properties of light, use a laser pointer to reflect light from one mirror to another mirror. Explain that when light reflects off mirrors, the incoming angle equals the outgoing angle. L2 ELL LS **Visual-Spatial**

Seeing with Plane Mirrors

Life Science INTEGRATION

Show students pictures of the L and D isomers of ibuprofen and ask students how they relate to each other. They look like mirror images of each other. Tell students that the L-isomer relieves pain and the D-isomer does not.

Visual Learning

Figure 2 Have students trace the path of light in the picture as you read each caption aloud. Ask students why light rays reflect off your body in many different directions. The surface of the body is rough. As rays of light hit the rough surface, they bounce off in different directions. L1 ELL LS **Visual-Spatial**

Reading Check

Answer a flat, smooth mirror

Use Science Words

Word Meaning Have students explain why a flat mirror is called a *plane* mirror. In mathematics, the word *plane* refers to a flat surface that extends infinitely in all directions, so the word *plane* is frequently used as a synonym for *flat*.

Resource Manager

Chapter Resources Booklet
- Transparency Activity, p. 44
- Directed Reading for Content Mastery, p. 20
- Note-taking Worksheets, pp. 33–35

Curriculum Connection

Social Studies Psychologists sometimes secretly observe animals or people using a two-way mirror, a coated window that only partially transmits light. If one side is in a lighted room, and the other is in a darkened room, the window acts as a mirror on the lighted side and a window on the darkened side. Have students debate whether use of this technology is an invasion of privacy. L3 LS **Linguistic**

Seeing with Plane Mirrors continued

Caption Answer

Figure 3 because that is where the light rays would converge if they actually went behind the mirror

Use Science Words

Word Usage The word *virtual* means having the effect of something without being the thing. Ask students to use this definition to explain the term *virtual image.* When you look in a plane mirror, you see the image of an object, but the rays of light don't actually come together to form an image. The image is virtual, meaning it has the effect of an image, even though the image isn't really there. L2 IS **Linguistic**

Concave Mirrors

Extension

Huge concave mirrors are used as radio telescopes to explore the universe. Have students investigate a radio telescope and prepare posters showing how it works and the types of astronomical objects scientists observe with it. The surface of the mirror focuses radio waves from space onto an antenna at the mirror's focal point. Radio telescopes are used to study quasars, pulsars, supernovas, and interstellar matter, among other things. L3 IS **Linguistic**

Activity

Allow students to experiment with concave mirrors to observe how focusing the image depends on the object's distance from the mirror. Have them observe how the image varies as they move the mirror from side to side. L2 ELL IS **Visual-Spatial**

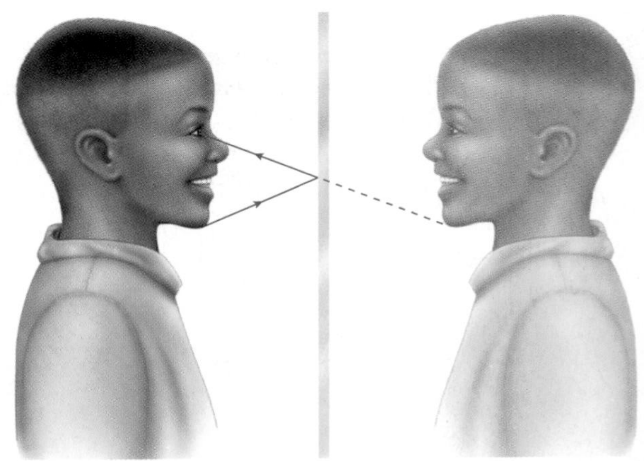

Figure 3
Your brain thinks that the light rays that reflect off of the mirror come from a point behind the mirror. *Why does your reflection seem to be as far behind the mirror as you are in front of it?*

Virtual Images You can understand how your brain interprets your reflection in a mirror by looking at **Figure 3.** The light waves that are reflected off of you travel in all directions. Light rays reflected from your chin strike the mirror at different places. Then, they reflect off of the mirror in different directions. Recall that your brain always interprets light rays as if they have traveled in a straight line. It doesn't realize that the light rays have been reflected and bent. If the reflected light rays were extended back behind the mirror, they would meet at a single point. Your brain thinks that the rays that enter your eye are coming from this point behind the mirror. You seem to see the reflected image of your chin at this point. An image like this, which your brain perceives even though no light rays actually pass through it, is called a **virtual image.** The virtual image formed by a plane mirror is always upright and appears to be as far behind the mirror as the object is in front of it.

Concave Mirrors

Not all mirrors are flat like plane mirrors are. If the surface of a mirror is curved inward, it is called a **concave mirror.** Concave mirrors, like plane mirrors, reflect light waves to form images. The difference is that the curved surface of a concave mirror reflects light in a unique way.

Features of Concave Mirrors A concave mirror has an optical axis. The **optical axis** is an imaginary straight line drawn perpendicular to the surface of the mirror at its center. There is a point on this optical axis that every light ray parallel to the optical axis is reflected through called the **focal point.** Using the focal point and the optical axis, you can diagram how some of the light rays that travel to a concave mirror are reflected, as shown in **Figure 4.** On the other hand, if a light ray passes through the focal point before it hits the mirror, it is reflected parallel to the optical axis. The distance from the center of the mirror to the focal point is called the **focal length.**

Figure 4
A concave mirror has an optical axis, a focal point, and a focal length. When light rays travel toward the mirror parallel to the optical axis, they reflect through the focal point.

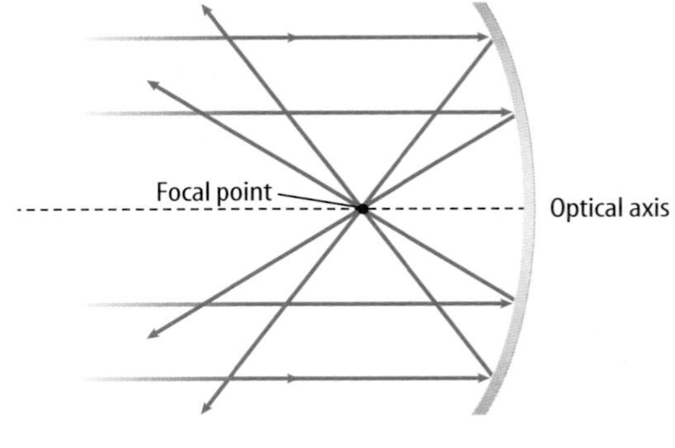

Science Journal

Convergence In biology, convergence is the tendency of different organisms to have some common characteristics when living in the same conditions. Concave mirrors converge light. Ask students to use this information to deduce a definition of *converge* and write it in their Science Journals. A definition from these contexts would be "to come together." L3 IS **Linguistic**

Visual Learning

Figure 4 Have students look at the diagram in **Figure 4.** Explain that one type of concave mirror is called a spherical mirror. In a spherical mirror, if the curve of the mirror extended around it would form a sphere. The center of this imaginary sphere is called the center of curvature. Is the mirror in this diagram a spherical mirror? yes L3 IS **Visual-Spatial**

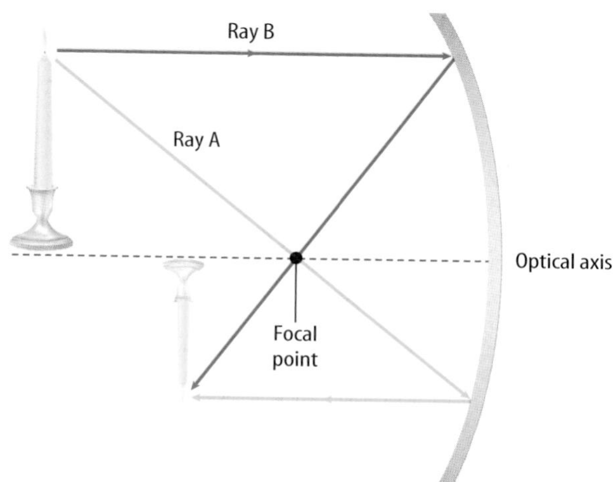

Figure 5
Rays A and B start from the same place on the candle, travel in different directions, and meet again on the reflected image. *How are the other points on the image of the candle formed?*

How a Concave Mirror Works The image that is formed by a concave mirror changes depending on where the object is located realtive to the focal point of the mirror. You can diagram how an image is formed. For example, suppose that the distance between the object, such as the candle in **Figure 5,** and the mirror is a little greater than the focal length. Light rays bounce off of each point on the candle in all directions. One light ray, labeled Ray A, starts from a point on the flame of the candle and passes through the focal point on its way to the mirror. Ray A is then reflected so it travels parallel to the optical axis. Another ray, Ray B, starts from the same point on the candle's flame but travels parallel to the optical axis as it moves toward the mirror. When Ray B is reflected by the mirror, it passes through the focal point. The place where Ray A and Ray B meet after they are reflected forms a point on the flame of the reflected image.

More points on the reflected image can be located in this way. From each point on the pencil, one ray can be drawn that passes through the focal point and is reflected parallel to the optical axis. Another ray can be drawn that travels parallel to the optical axis and passes through the focal point after it is reflected. The point where the two rays meet is on the reflected image.

Real Images Notice that the image that is formed is not virtual. Rays of light pass through the location of the image. A **real image** is formed when light rays converge to form the image. You could hold a sheet of paper at the location of the real image and see the image on the paper. When an object is farther from a concave mirror than the focal point is, the image that is formed is real, enlarged, and upside down, or inverted.

TRY AT HOME Mini LAB

Observing Images

Procedure

1. Look at the inside of a shiny **spoon.** Move it close to your face and then far away. The place where your image changes is the focal point.
2. Hold the inside of the spoon facing a bright **light,** a little farther away than the focal length of the spoon.
3. Place a piece of **poster board** between the light and the spoon without blocking all of the light.
4. Move the poster board between the spoon and the light until you see the reflected light on it.

Analysis
Which of the images you observed were real and which were virtual?

Caption Answer
Figure 5 The rays from the candle that run parallel to the optical axis and those that run through the focal point are reflected by the mirror and meet.

Teacher FYI
Spherical concave mirrors are unable to produce perfectly focused images because rays from the outer edges of the mirror focus slightly closer to the mirror than rays from the middle. This effect, known as spherical aberration, is especially troublesome for large mirrors. To avoid this, large mirrors typically have a parabolic shape, which allows all of the rays to converge at the same point.

TRY AT HOME Mini LAB

Purpose to observe real and virtual images in a spoon L2 ELL IN **Visual-Spatial**

Materials shiny spoon, bright light source, 4" × 4" square of white poster board

Teaching Strategy Folded index cards may be used instead of posterboard.

Troubleshooting Only shiny spoons produce clear images.

Analysis
The up-close images were virtual. The faraway images were real.

Assessment

Oral Ask students why their images changed from upright to inverted. Up close, the student's distance from the mirror was less than the distance from the focal point to the mirror, so they saw a virtual, upright image. Past the focal point, they saw a real, inverted image. Use **PASC,** p. 89.

Resource Manager 

Chapter Resources Booklet
MiniLAB, p. 3

Performance Assessment in the Science Classroom, p. 52

Visual Learning

Figure 5 Have students work in pairs and take turns explaining to each other how rays from all parts of the candle are reflected off the concave mirror to form an image. L1 ELL IN **Visual-Spatial**

Concave Mirrors, continued

Caption Answer

Figure 6 The light source is located at the focal point.

Discussion

How would the reflection of light from a concave mirror be different if the surface of the mirror were rough rather than smooth? At each individual point, the light rays would be reflected so that the angle of incidence equaled the angle of reflection. If the surface were rough, these angles would change from point to point, and the rays would be scattered. You would not see a clear image. L2 LS **Logical-Mathematical**

Activity

Have students open the top of a flashlight to see the shape of the reflector. Explain that if the flashlight had a spherical mirror, the light rays coming out from it wouldn't be parallel. A parabolic reflector has a definite focal point for all rays, so it produces a straighter beam of light. L2 LS **Kinesthetic**

Caption Answer

Figure 7 No light rays pass through the image.

Quick Demo

Obtain a flashlight that has a rotating head that allows you to adjust the divergence of the beam of light. In a darkened room, show students that as you rotate the head, the beam spreads out. Explain that rotating the head moves the light bulb back and forth about the focal point of the reflecting mirror, varying the divergence of the beam. L3 LS **Visual-Spatial**

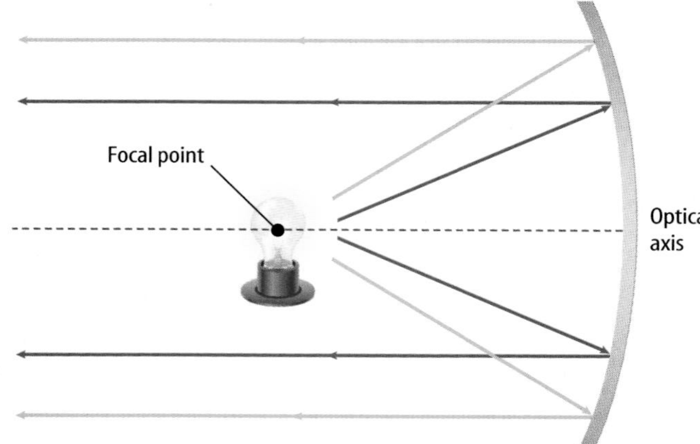

Figure 6
A flashlight uses a concave mirror to create a beam of light. *Why are all of the reflected rays of light in the diagram parallel to each other?*

Creating Light Beams What happens if you place an object exactly at the focal point of the concave mirror? **Figure 6** shows that if the object is at the focal point, the mirror reflects all light rays parallel to the optical axis. No image forms because the rays never meet—not even if the rays are extended back behind the mirror. Therefore, a light placed at the focal point is reflected in a beam. Car headlights, flashlights, lighthouses, spotlights, and other devices use concave mirrors in this way to create concentrated light beams of nearly parallel rays.

Mirrors That Magnify The image formed by a concave mirror changes again when you place an object between it and its focal point. The location of the reflected image again can be found by drawing two rays from each point. **Figure 7** shows that in this case, these rays never meet after they reflect from the mirror. Instead, the reflected light rays spread apart, or diverge. Just as it does with a plane mirror, your brain interprets the light rays as if they met at one point behind the mirror. Because no light rays are behind the mirror where the image seems to be, the image formed is virtual. The image also is upright and enlarged.

Shaving mirrors and makeup mirrors are concave mirrors. They form an enlarged, upright image of a person's face so it's easier to see small details. The bowl of a shiny spoon also forms an enlarged, upright image of your face when it is placed close to your face.

Figure 7
If the pencil is between the mirror and its focal point, the reflected image is enlarged and virtual. *Why couldn't this image be projected on a screen?*

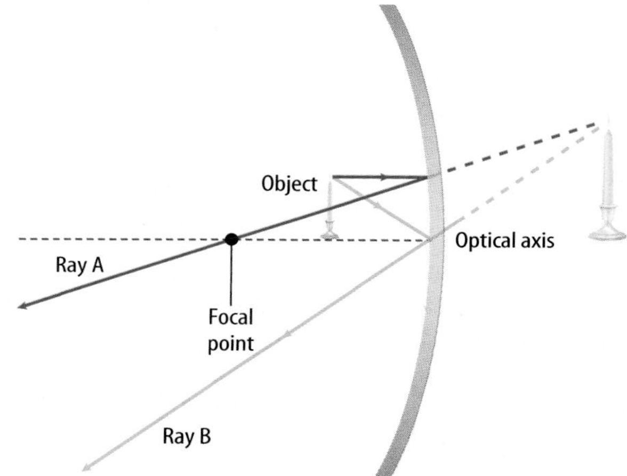

456 CHAPTER 15 Mirrors and Lenses

Science Journal

Solar Furnace Concave mirrors are used in solar furnaces, in which sunlight heats objects. Have students describe in their Science Journals how they think a solar furnace works, and where the object to be heated must be located. At the focal point; the rays that strike the mirror are essentially parallel. By the law of reflection, the rays reflect to the focal point, which becomes intensely hot. L3 LS **Logical-Mathematical** P

Convex Mirrors

Why do you think the security mirrors in banks and stores are shaped the way they are? The next time you are in a store, look up to one of the back corners or at the end of an aisle to see if a large, rounded mirror is mounted there. You can see a large area of the store in the mirror. A mirror that curves outward like the back of a spoon is called a **convex mirror.** Light rays that hit a convex mirror diverge, or spread apart, as they are reflected. Look at **Figure 8** to see how the rays from an object are reflected to form an image. The reflected rays diverge and never meet, the image formed by a convex mirror is a virtual image. The image also is always upright and smaller than the actual object is.

Reading Check *What is a convex mirror, and what happens to light rays that hit it?*

Uses of Convex Mirrors Because convex mirrors spread out the reflected light, they allow large areas to be viewed. In addition to increasing the field of view in places like grocery stores and factories, convex mirrors can widen the view of traffic that can be seen in rearview or side-view mirrors of automobiles. However, because the image created by a convex mirror is smaller than the actual object, your perception of distance can be distorted. Objects look farther away than they truly are in a convex mirror. Distances and sizes seen in a convex mirror are not realistic, so most convex side mirrors carry a printed warning that says "Objects in mirror are closer than they appear."

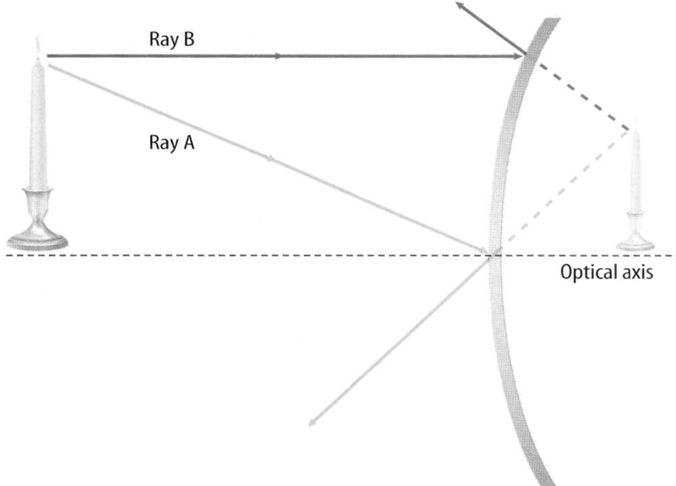

Figure 8
A convex mirror forms a reduced, upright, virtual image. *Why are convex mirrors useful?*

Convex Mirrors

Reading Check

Answer A mirror that curves outward; rays diverge as they are reflected.

Caption Answer

Figure 8 They provide wide-angle views.

Activity

Have students use the information in **Table 1** to make flashcards. Then have them work in pairs and, using their flashcards, quiz one another about the images formed by different types of mirrors. L2 IS **Interpersonal**

Resource Manager

Chapter Resources Booklet
Enrichment, p. 30
Lab Activity, pp. 9–12

Inclusion Strategies

Visually Impaired For all of the activities in this section, have visually impaired students work with sighted students. Make sure the visually impaired students have the opportunity to handle mirrors so they can identify their shapes. Have the sighted students describe in detail everything they do and see as they perform the activities.

3 Assess

Reteach

Have a collection of plane, concave, and convex mirrors for students to experiment with. Ask them to predict for each one whether they will see upright, inverted, enlarged, or diminished images. Then have them look in the mirrors to find out whether they are correct. They should also tell whether the images they see are real or virtual. L2 LS **Visual-Spatial**

Challenge

Tell students that reflecting telescopes use mirrors. Ask students to identify whether the mirror is concave or convex and whether the image is real or virtual, larger or smaller than the object, and right side up or inverted. Concave mirrors are used. The images are real, smaller than the object, and inverted.
L3 LS **Logical-Mathematical**

Assessment

Process Ask each student to draw a ray diagram that represents a person looking into a concave makeup or shaving mirror. Have them include the image seen by the person looking into the mirror. The person's face should be between the mirror and the focal point. The image should be enlarged, upright, and virtual (behind the mirror). They should use rays from the top and bottom of the face. Use **PASC,** p. 127.

Table 1 Images Formed by Mirrors

Mirror Shape		Virtual/ Real	Image Created Upright /Upside Down	Size
Plane		virtual	upright	same as object
Concave	Object beyond focal length	real	upside down	smaller than object
	Object at focal point	none	none	none
	Object within focal length	virtual	upright	larger than object
Convex		virtual	upright	smaller than object

Mirror Images The different shapes of plane, concave, and convex mirrors cause them to reflect light in distinct ways. Each type of mirror has different uses. **Table 1** summarizes the images formed by plane, concave, and convex mirrors.

Section 1 Assessment

1. Contrast the differences between the surfaces of the following types of mirrors: plane, concave, and convex.
2. Diagram how light rays are reflected to form an image in a convex mirror.
3. What is the difference between a real and a virtual image?
4. How are concave mirrors used? Explain.
5. **Think Critically** What kind of mirror would you use to focus light entering a telescope? Explain.

Skill Builder Activities

6. **Recognizing Cause and Effect** You drop a flashlight that has a concave mirror in it. The light is then less intense than it was before you dropped the flashlight. Explain. **For more help, refer to the Science Skill Handbook.**
7. **Communicating** In your Science Journal, list all the mirrors you see during an average day. Describe how each is used, and identify each one as plane, concave, or convex. **For more help, refer to the Science Skill Handbook.**

Answers to Section Assessment

1. plane, flat; concave, curved inward; convex, curved outward
2. Sketches should show the formation of a virtual image behind the mirror.
3. When a real image is formed, reflected light rays converge and actually pass through the image. When a virtual image is formed, reflected light rays diverge and do not actually pass through the image.
4. They are used to produce enlarged images, as in shaving and makeup mirrors.
5. concave; to form real images of far-away objects
6. You might have bent or moved the mirror, so the light is not focused well.
7. Possible answers: plane mirror in washroom; convex mirror for store surveillance; concave flashlight reflector

Activity

Reflections of Reflections

How can you see the back of your head? You can use two mirrors to see a reflection of the original reflection of the back of your head. How many reflections of your head can you create?

What You'll Investigate

How can you change the number of reflections of an object that is created in two mirrors?

Materials

plane mirrors (2)	protractor
masking tape	paper clip

Goals

- **Observe** multiple reflections of an object.
- **Infer** how many reflections will be made when mirrors are placed at a certain angle.

Safety Precautions 

Handle glass mirrors and paper clips carefully.

Procedure

1. Lay one mirror on top of the other with the mirror surface inward. Tape them together so they will open and close. Use tape to label them *L* and *R*.
2. Stand the mirrors up on a sheet of paper. Using the protractor, close the mirrors to an angle of 72°.

Images and Wedges Seen in the Mirrors			
Angle of Mirrors	Number of Paper Clip Images		Number of Wedges
	R	L	
72°	2	2	5
90°	2	1	4
120°	1	1	3

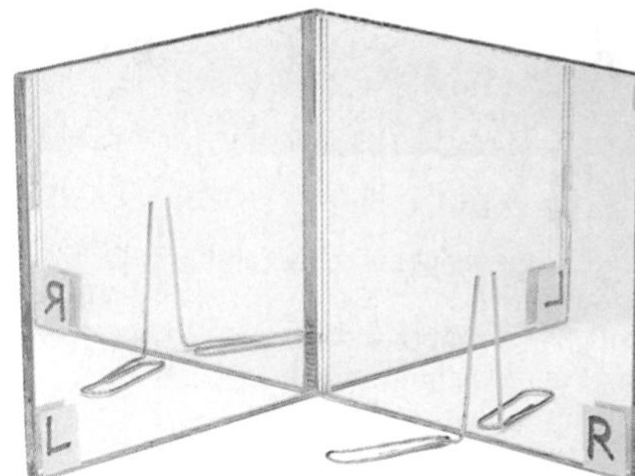

3. Bend one leg of a paper clip up 90° and place it close to the front of the R mirror.
4. **Count** the number of images of the clip you see in the R and L mirrors. Record these numbers in the data table.
5. The mirror arrangement creates an image of a circle divided into wedges by the mirrors. Record the number of wedges.
6. Hold the R mirror still and slowly open the L mirror to 90°. Count and record the images of the clip and the wedges in the circle. Repeat, this time opening the mirrors to 120°.

Conclude and Apply

1. What is the relationship between the number of wedges and paper clip images you can see?
2. What angle would divide a circle into six wedges? Hypothesize how many images would be produced.

Communicating Your Data

Demonstrate for younger students the relationship between the angle of the mirrors and the number of reflections. **For more help, refer to the Science Skill Handbook.**

Resource Manager 

Chapter Resources Booklet
Activity Worksheet, pp. 5–6
Reinforcement, p. 27

Communicating Your Data

Have students draw circles divided into thirds (120°), quarters (90°), fifths (72°), and sixths (60°) and use the circles in their demonstrations to position the mirrors. Then they can use the circles to show younger students how the number of wedges seen relates to the angle between the mirrors.

Activity

Purpose Students will observe image formation by plane mirrors. L1 COOP LEARN

LS **Visual-Spatial**

Process Skills measuring, inferring, recognizing cause and effect, comparing and contrasting, forming operational definitions

Time Required 45 minutes

Teaching Strategies

- Use rectangular mirrors at least 5 cm across. Thin glass is better. Mirror tiles (hardware store) can be cut to size, but sharp edges must be ground or taped.
- Place a protractor on a copy machine and make lab worksheets upon which students can measure the appropriate angles.

Answers to Questions

1. The number of paper clip images is one less than the number of wedges.
2. The angle producing six wedges is $\frac{360}{6} = 60°$. Five images will be produced.

Assessment

Performance Ask students to open the mirrors to an angle of 45° to each other. **How many images of your face do you see?** eight **What about smaller angles?** more images **Larger angles?** fewer images **Explain.** The number of reflections is determined by the angle. This number is 360 divided by the angle. Use **Performance Assessment in the Science Classroom,** p. 89.

SECTION 2

Lenses

1 Motivate

Bellringer Transparency

Display the Section Focus Transparency for Section 2. Use the accompanying Transparency Activity Master. L2 ELL

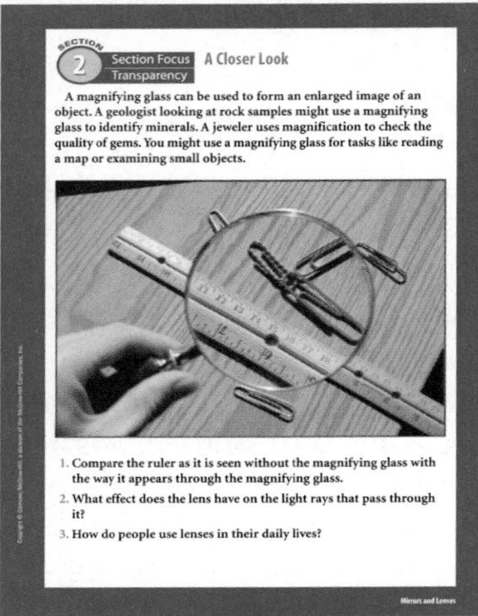
SECTION 2 Section Focus Transparency A Closer Look

A magnifying glass can be used to form an enlarged image of an object. A geologist looking at rock samples might use a magnifying glass to identify minerals. A jeweler uses magnification to check the quality of gems. You might use a magnifying glass for tasks like reading a map or examining small objects.

1. Compare the ruler as it is seen without the magnifying glass with the way it appears through the magnifying glass.
2. What effect does the lens have on the light rays that pass through it?
3. How do people use lenses in their daily lives?

Mirrors and Lenses

Tie to Prior Knowledge

Many students wear corrective lenses, either as eyeglasses or contact lenses. Ask students what the eyeglasses do. They change the light path from the object to your eyes by refracting the light before it enters your eye.

Caption Answer

Figure 9 Glass has a higher index of refraction than air. When light hits glass at an angle, it is refracted toward the optical axis. The lens is curved, so light rays from objects directly in front of it hit the lens at an angle and are refracted.

SECTION 2

Lenses

As You Read

***What* You'll Learn**

- **Describe** the shapes of convex and concave lenses.
- **Explain** how convex and concave lenses refract light to form images.
- **Explain** how lenses are used to correct vision.

Vocabulary

convex lens
concave lens
cornea
retina

***Why* It's Important**

Even if you don't wear glasses or contacts, you rely on lenses to see.

What is a lens?

What do your eyes have in common with cameras, eyeglasses, and microscopes? Each of these things contains at least one lens. A lens is a transparent material with at least one curved surface that causes light rays to bend, or refract, as they pass through. The image that a lens forms depends on the shape of the lens. Like curved mirrors, a lens can be convex or concave.

Convex Lenses

A **convex lens** is thicker in the middle than at the edges. Its optical axis is an imaginary straight line that is perpendicular to the surface of the lens at its thickest point. When light rays approach a convex lens traveling parallel to its optical axis, the rays are refracted toward the center of the lens, as in **Figure 9A.** All light rays traveling parallel to the optical axis are refracted so they pass through a single point, which is the focal point of the lens. The distance from the focal point to the lens, or the focal length of the lens, As the sides of a convex lens become less curved, light rays are bent less. As a result, lenses with flatter sides have longer focal lengths. Light rays that pass through the center of the lens are not bent at all, as shown in **Figure 9B.**

Figure 9
Convex lenses are thicker in the middle than at the edges.

A **A convex lens focuses light rays at a focal point.** *Why does the light bend as it goes through the lens?*

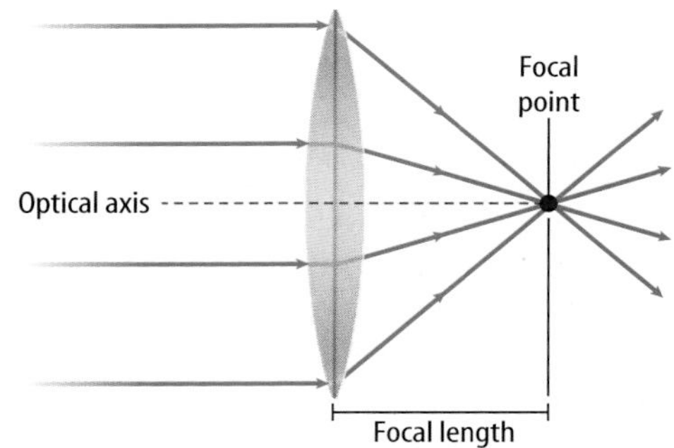

B **The green beam of light is not refracted at all as it passes through the cener of the lens.**

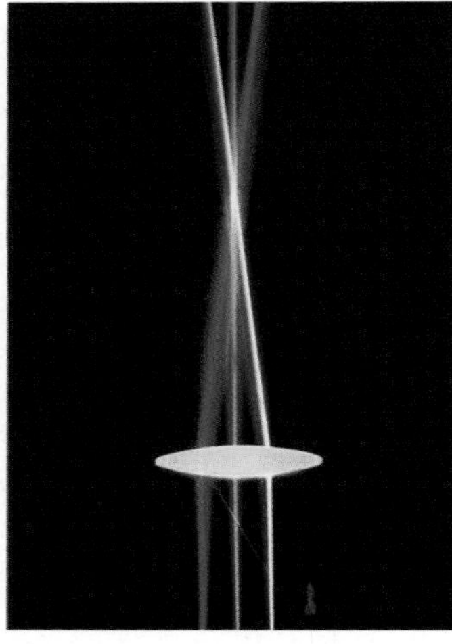

Section Assessment Planner

Portfolio
Curriculum Connection, p. 465

Performance Assessment
Problem-Solving Activity, p. 462
Skill Building Activities, p. 467
See page 480 for more options.

Content Assessment
Section, p. 467
Challenge, p. 467
Chapter, pp. 480–481

Figure 10
The image formed by a convex lens changes depending on where the lens is compared to the object.

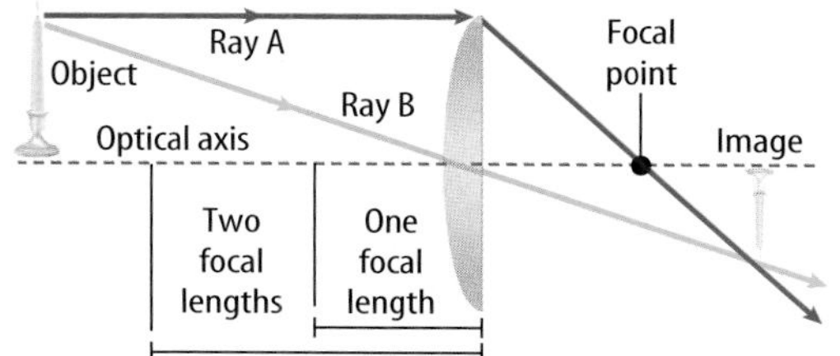

A When the candle is more than two focal lengths away from the lens, its image is real, reduced, and upside down.

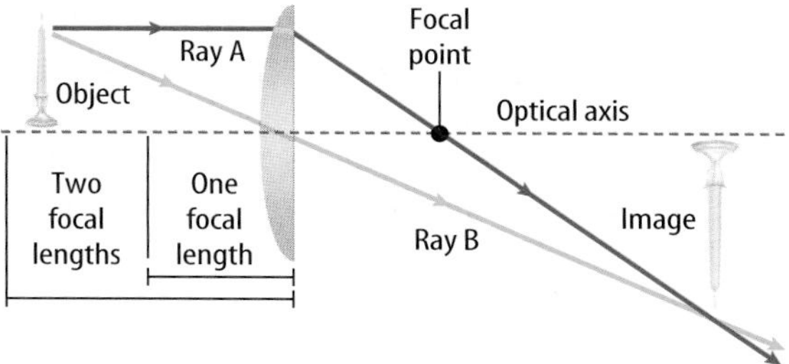

B When the candle is between one and two focal lengths from the lens, its image is real, enlarged, and upside down.

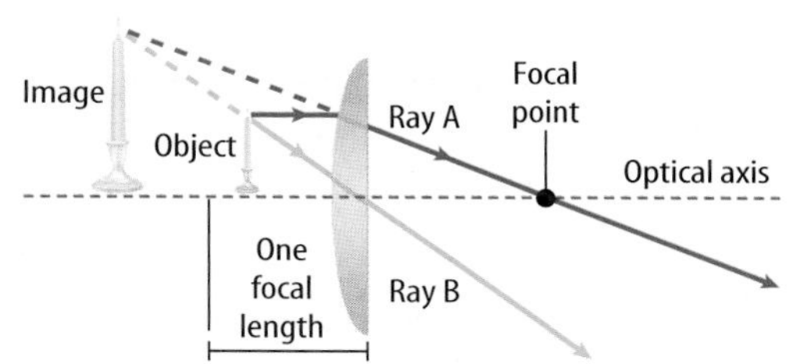

C When the candle is less than one focal length from the lens, its image is virtual, enlarged, and upright.

Forming Images with a Convex Lens The type of image a convex lens forms depends on where the object is relative to the focal point of the lens. If an object is more than two focal lengths from the lens, as in **Figure 10A,** the image is real, reduced, and inverted, and on the opposite side of the lens from the object. As the object moves closer to the lens, the image gets larger. **Figure 10B** shows how the image forms when the object is between one and two focal lengths from the lens. When the object is less than one focal length away from the lens, as in **Figure 10C,** the image seems to be on the same side of the lens as the object. When you use a magnifying glass, you place a convex lens less than one focal length away from an object. The image you see is upright and magnified and appears to be on the same side of the lens as the object you are inspecting.

2 Teach

What is a lens?

Discussion

What is the primary difference between lenses and mirrors? Mirrors reflect light and lenses transmit light.

Use Science Words

Word Origin Lenses were named because of the resemblance of an eye's lens to a small legume called a lentil. The Latin word for lentil is *lenticula*. Bring lentils to class so students can see the resemblance in shape. L2 LS **Visual-Spatial**

Convex Lenses

Activity

Distribute to your class some convex lenses of varying focal lengths. Show students how to find the focal length of a lens by focusing the clearest possible image of an overhead light on a white piece of paper (held by a partner) and measuring the distance from the paper to the lens. L2 LS **Visual-Spatial**

Visual Learning

Figure 10 To help students understand **Figures 10A, 10B,** and **10C,** have them imagine the candle in **Figure 10A** is moving toward the lens. As it does, the image gets larger. When it is at exactly 2 *f*, the image is the same size as the candle. If the candle continues to move, the image becomes larger than the candle. To see this, trace a copy of **Figure 10A** with the candle at 2 *f*. Sketch rays to show how the image forms. L2 LS **Visual-Spatial**

Resource Manager

Chapter Resources Booklet
- Transparency Activity, p. 45
- Directed Reading for Content Mastery, p. 20

Active Reading

Write-Draw-Discuss This strategy encourages students to actively participate in reading and lectures, assimilating content creatively. Have students write about an idea, clarify it, then make an illustration or drawing. Ask students to share responses with the class and display several examples. Have students Write-Draw-Discuss about convex and concave lenses.

Concave Lenses

Caption Answer

Figure 11 A convex mirror; both cause light to diverge and produce virtual images.

Use an Analogy

Convex and concave lenses refract light much like two right-angle prisms joined together. When the prisms are joined at the base so that they are thick at the middle, a beam of light will be refracted downward by the upper prism and upward by the lower prism. This produces the effect of a converging convex lens. When they are joined at the apex, a beam of light will be refracted upward by the upper prism and downward by the lower prism, producing the effect of a diverging concave lens. L2 LS **Visual-Spatial**

Reading Check

Answer thinner in the middle than at the edges

Problem-Solving Activity

Answers

1. Given the same focal length, as the object distance increases, the image distance decreases.
2. $\frac{1}{\text{image distance}} = \frac{1}{15.0} - \frac{1}{60.0} =$

   $0.067 - 0.017 = 0.50$

   $\text{image distance} = \frac{1}{0.50} = 20 \text{ cm}$

Figure 11
A concave lens refracts light rays so they spread out. *Is a concave lens most like a concave mirror or a convex mirror?*

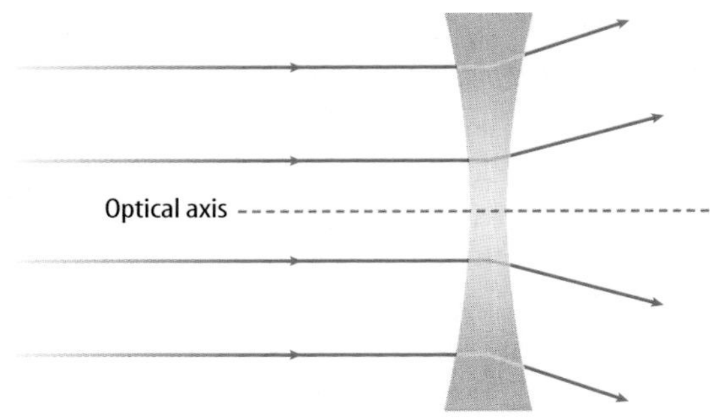

Concave Lenses

A **concave lens** is thinner in the middle and thicker at the edges. As shown in **Figure 11,** light that passes through a concave lens bends outward toward the lens's edges. The rays spread out and never meet at a focal point, so they never form a real image. The image is always virtual, upright, and smaller than the actual object is. Concave lenses are used in some types of eyeglasses and some telescopes. Concave lenses usually are used in combination with other lenses.

Reading Check *What shape is a concave lens?*

Problem-Solving Activity

Comparing Object and Image Distances

The size and orientation of an image formed by a convex lenses depends on the location of the object. What happens to the location of the image formed by a convex lens as the object moves closer to the lens or farther from the lens? The distance from the lens to the object is the object distance, and the distance from the lens to the image is the image distance. How are the focal length, object distance, and image distance related to each other?

Identifying the Problem

A 5-cm-tall object is placed at different lengths from a double convex lens with a focal length of 15 cm. The table below lists the different object and image distances. How are these two measurements related?

Object and Image Distances

Focal Length	Object Distance	Image Distance
15.0 cm	45.0 cm	22.5 cm
15.0 cm	30.0 cm	30.0 cm
15.0 cm	20.0 cm	60.0 cm

Solving the Problem

1. What is the relationship between the object distance and the image distance?
2. The lens equation relates the focal length and the image and object distances: *1/focal length = 1/object distance + 1/image distance.* Using this equation, calculate the image distance of an object placed at a distance of 60.0 cm.

LAB DEMONSTRATION

Purpose to observe images with convex and concave lenses

Materials concave and convex lenses, optical bench with lens holders, tape, pencil

Preparation Place a convex lens in a holder on the bench. Using tape, mark one and two focal lengths.

Procedure Hold a pencil more than two focal lengths from the lens, between one and two focal lengths from the lens, and less than one focal length from the lens. At each position, have students look through the lens. Repeat using a concave lens.

Expected Outcome Students should see real or virtual images through the lens, as shown in **Figures 10** and **11.**

Assessment

When the convex lens is used, why does the image flip as the pencil is moved closer to the lens? The light rays can no longer converge.

Table 2 Images Formed by Lenses				
Lens Shape	**Location of Object**	**Type of Image**		
		Virtual/ Real	**Upright/ Inverted**	**Size**
Convex	**Object beyond 2 focal lengths**	real	inverted	smaller than object
	Object between 1 and 2 focal lengths	real	inverted	larger than object
	Object within 1 focal length	virtual	upright	larger than object
Concave	**Object at any position**	virtual	upright	smaller than object

Lenses and Eyesight

What determines how well you can see the words on this page? Perhaps you wear eyeglasses with lenses like those summarized in **Table 2.** If you don't need eyeglasses, the structure of your eye gives you the ability to focus on these words and other objects around you. Look at **Figure 12.** Light enters your eye through a transparent covering on your eyeball called the **cornea** (KOR nee uh). The light then passes through an opening called the pupil. Behind the pupil is a flexible convex lens. When light rays pass through it, they bend and form an inverted image on your retina. The **retina** (RET nuh) is the inner lining of your eye. It has cells that convert the light image into electrical signals, which are then carried along the optic nerve to your brain to be interpreted.

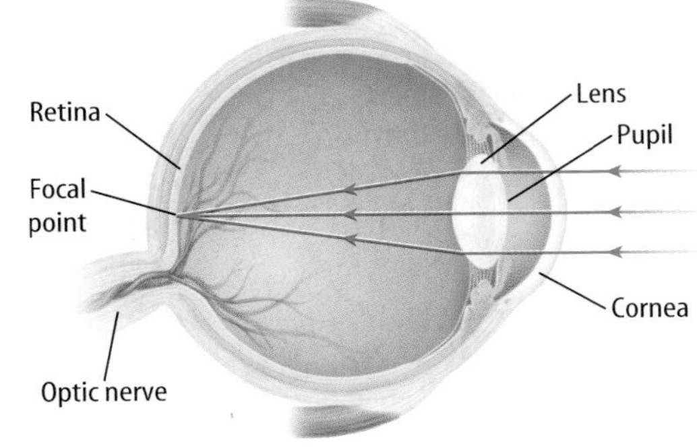

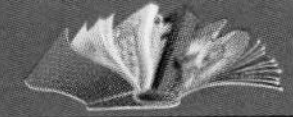

Figure 12
Light bends as it passes through the lens in your eye.
What would happen if the lens were a concave lens?

Fun Fact

The lenses described in this section and summarized in **Table 2,** are thin lenses. One side is curved and one side is flat, so the lenses are called plano-convex and plano-concave. If the opposite sides were also curved, they would be double convex and double concave. Thin lenses can be treated as if they had only one surface—the curved surface facing the object. With thick lenses, the effects of the two surfaces cannot be ignored.

Lenses and Eyesight

IDENTIFYING Misconceptions

Students might assume that rays of light pass through the cornea unaffected. In fact, the cornea does about two-thirds of the focusing and is responsible for most human vision problems. The flexible lens then conducts the fine focusing.

Caption Answer

Figure 12 Light rays would diverge and not focus on the retina.

Resource Manager

Chapter Resources Booklet
Lab Activity, pp. 13–16
Mathematics Skill Activities, p. 29

Teacher FYI

Vertebrates, cephalopods, and some spiders have camera-like eyes with variable focusing. Worms, mollusks, and some crustaceans and insects have simple eyes that can distinguish light and dark. Most arthropods have compound eyes, with many separate lenses, each of which forms its own image.

Lenses and Eyesight, continued

Quick Demo

Bring in a model of the human eye so students can observe the cornea, lens, and retina. Have students explain how light enters through the cornea and is refracted onto the retina. Point out the muscles that adjust the size of the lens, and note the optic nerve, which carries information about images to the brain. L2 LS **Visual-Spatial**

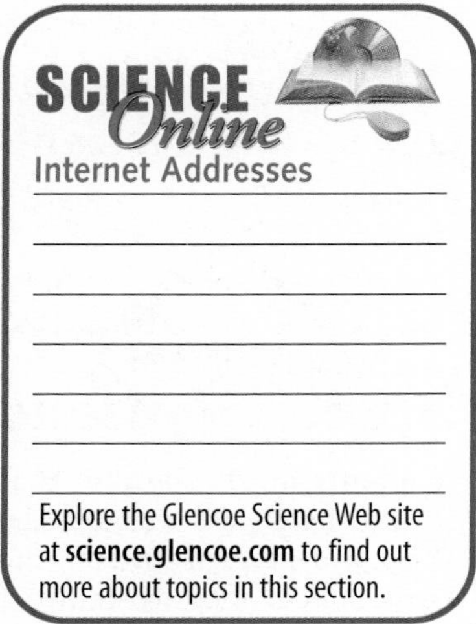

Activity

Normally your eyes change from focusing on nearby objects to focusing on faraway objects without your ever realizing it. It is possible, however, to feel the change. Have students hold a pencil about 10 cm directly in front of their eyes. Tell them to focus on the pencil for a few seconds and then, without moving the pencil, to look beyond it to a distant object. If they do this quickly several times, they will feel a slight strain as their eyes adjust focus.

Answer It changes the focal length.

Research Visit the Glencoe Science Web site at **science.glencoe.com** for information about diseases that affect the retina. Make a poster that shows what you learn.

Focusing on Near and Far How can your eyes focus on close objects, like the watch on your wrist, and distant objects, like a clock across the room? For you to see an object clearly, its image must be focused exactly on your retina. However, the retina is always a fixed distance from the lens. Remember that the location of an image formed by a convex lens depends on the focal length of the lens and the location of the object. For example, look back at **Figure 10.** As an object moves farther from a convex lens, the position of the image moves closer to the lens.

For an image to always be formed on the retina, the focal length of the lens needs to be able to change as the distance of the object changes. The lens in your eye is soft and flexible, and muscles attached to it change its shape and its focal length. This is why you can see objects that are near and far away.

Look at **Figure 13.** As an object gets farther from your eye, the focal length of the lens has to increase. The muscles around the lens stretch it so it has a less convex shape. But when you focus on a nearby object, these muscles make the lens more curved, causing the focal length to decrease.

Reading Check *Why does changing the shape of the lens affect where the image is formed in your eye?*

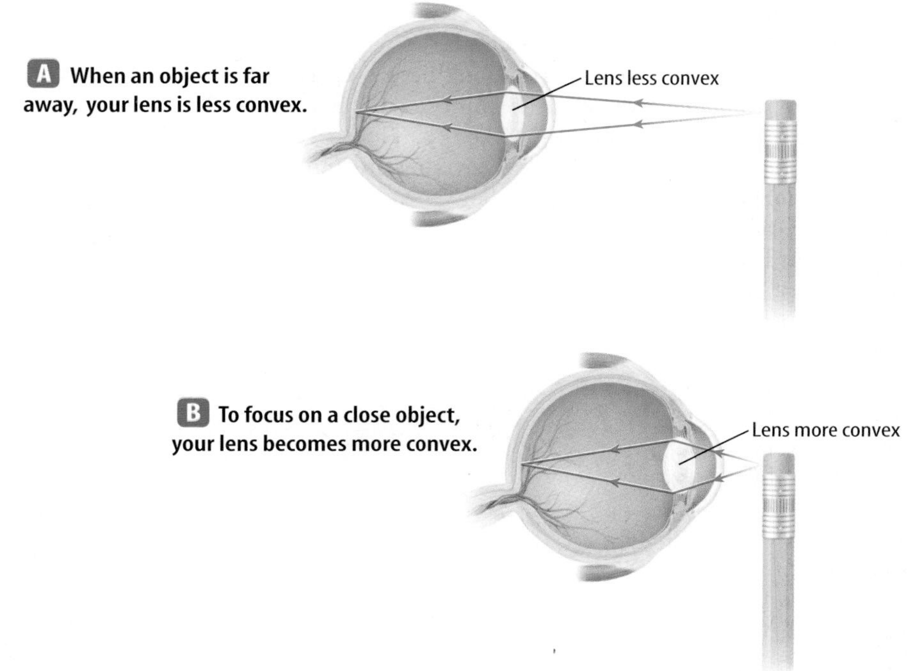

A When an object is far away, your lens is less convex.
Lens less convex
B To focus on a close object, your lens becomes more convex.
Lens more convex

Figure 13
The lens in your eye changes shape so you can focus on objects at different distances.

Cultural Diversity

Arabian Lights One of the greatest early physicists was an Arabian scientist named Abu Ali al-Hasan ibn al-Haytham, better known in the west as Alhazen. His book, *The Optical Thesaurus*, written around 1,000 A.D. was unsurpassed until the appearance of Johannes Kepler's work 600 years later. Among Alhazen's contributions was the theory that vision is based on light coming from a source and being reflected from an object.

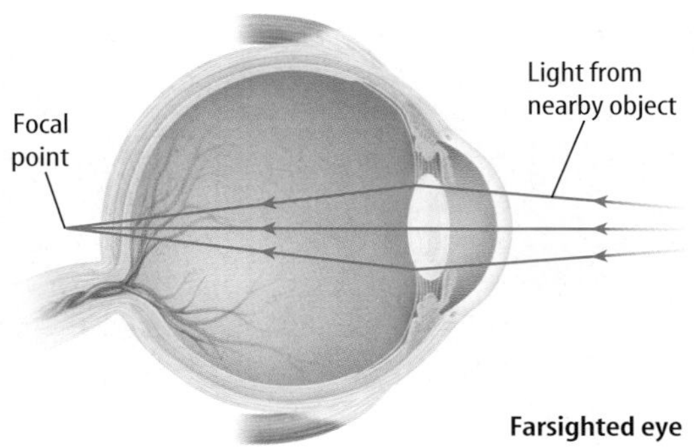

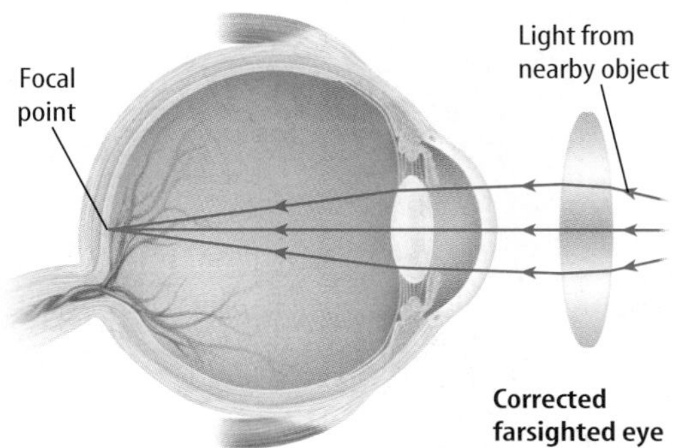

A The lenses in farsighted people's eyes focus the image of a close object behind the retina.

B A convex lens in front of a farsighted eye will help converge the light rays on the retina.

Figure 14
Farsightedness can be corrected by convex lenses.

Vision Problems

If you have healthy vision, you should be able to see objects clearly when they are 25 cm or farther away from your eyes. The image of an object should be formed exactly on your retina. However, for many people, the image is blurry or formed in the wrong place, causing vision problems.

Farsightedness If you can see distant objects clearly, but can't bring nearby objects into focus, then you are farsighted. In farsighted people, the lens doesn't curve enough to form an image of close objects on the retina. The image of a close object would be focused behind the retina, as shown in **Figure 14A.** To correct the problem, convex lenses, as in **Figure 14B,** converge incoming light rays before they enter the eye.

As many people age, their eyes develop a condition that makes them unable to focus on close objects. The lenses in their eyes become less flexible. The muscles around the lenses still contract if they try to focus on a close object. Due to aging, the lenses have become more rigid, and cannot be made curved enough to form an image on the retina. People who are 40 years old might not be able to focus on objects that are closer than 2 m from the eyes. Some vision problems are caused by diseases of the retina. **Figure 15** shows how using new technology allows people with diseased retinas to recover some vision.

Astigmatism Another vision problem, called astigmatism (uh STIHG muh tih zum) occurs when the surface of the cornea is curved unevenly. When people have astigmatism, their corneas are more oval than round in shape. Astigmatism causes blurry vision at all distances. Corrective lenses also have an uneven curvature, canceling out the effect of an uneven cornea.

Health INTEGRATION

If you need eyeglasses, what do the letters and numbers on your eyeglass prescription mean? O.D. specifies right eye, and O.S. specifies left eye. The sphere number tells how nearsighted or farsighted you are. The cylinder and axis numbers are a measure of astigmatism. These numbers allow eyeglasses to be made specifically for your vision problems.

Vision Problems

Fun Fact

Eyeglasses were used as early as the thirteenth century, and gems were used even earlier as natural magnifying glasses by the Greeks and Arabs.

Discussion

Why is it easier to see clear images in good lighting? The pupils of your eyes are smaller, so focusing on objects is easier.

Health INTEGRATION

The abbreviation *O.D.* stands for *oculus dextrus*, which is Latin for "right eye." The abbreviation *O.S.* stands for *oculus sinister*, which is Latin for "left eye." Sometimes the abbreviations *RE* and *LE* are used instead.

Using Science Words

Word Meaning Have students break the word *astigmatism* into its parts and find out what each part means, and what it contributes to the meaning of the whole word. *A-*, in such a state or condition; *stigma-*, scar; *-ism*, state, condition; Astigmatism is in the state or condition of having a scar, the scar being the irregular shape of the lens. L3 **LS Linguistic**

Resource Manager

Chapter Resources Booklet
Enrichment, p. 31
Science Inquiry Labs, p. 59

Curriculum Connection

Language Arts The manufacture of convex and concave lenses for eyeglasses and optical instruments requires high-precision measurements and the use of high-quality glass. Have students write a paper about this process. Students might mention cutting the glass, shaping the convex or concave surface, polishing, and grinding edges so the physical and optical centers match. L2 **LS Linguistic** P

NATIONAL GEOGRAPHIC

Visualizing the Silicon Retina

Have students examine the pictures and read the captions. Then ask the following questions.

- **How do retinitis pigmentosa and macular degeration affect vision differently?** Retinitis pigmentosa causes a lack of peripheral vision, while macular degeration initially affects central vision.
- **How might an artificial retina change a person's life?** Possible answer: A person with improved vision could be more independent, could drive, and could work at jobs and enjoy hobbies and entertainment that rely on vision, such as reading, watching movies, or sewing.

Activity

Have small groups of students research other vision problems that can be helped by implants or other technologies. Have each group prepare a poster illustrating how the technology works. L2 LS **Visual-Spatial**

Extension

Have students research how the silicon retina described in this feature differs from similar devices being developed in Germany and by Harvard Medical School and MIT. Ask students to present brief oral reports on what they learn. L3 LS **Linguistic**

NATIONAL GEOGRAPHIC **VISUALIZING THE SILICON RETINA**

Figure 15

Millions of people worldwide suffer from vision problems associated with diseases of the retina. Until recently, such people had little hope of improving their eyesight. Now, however, scientists are developing specialized silicon chips that convert light into electrical pulses, mimicking the function of the retina. When implanted in the eye, these artificial silicon retinas may restore sight.

Viewed with normal vision

Viewed with retinitis pigmentosa

Viewed with macular degeneration

▲ These three photos show how normal vision can deteriorate as a result of diseases that attack the retina. Retinitis pigmentosa (ret uh NYE tis pig men TOE suh) causes a lack of peripheral vision. Macular degeneration can lead to total blindness.

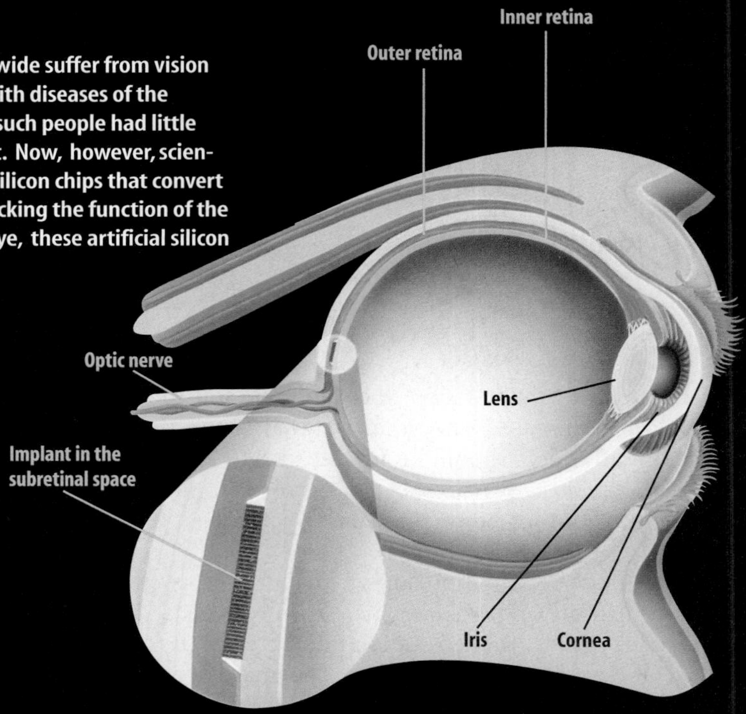

Inner retina
Outer retina
Optic nerve
Lens
Implant in the subretinal space
Iris
Cornea

▲ After making a number of incisions, surgeons implant the artificial silicon retina between the outer and inner retinal layers. Then they reseal the retina over the silicon chip.

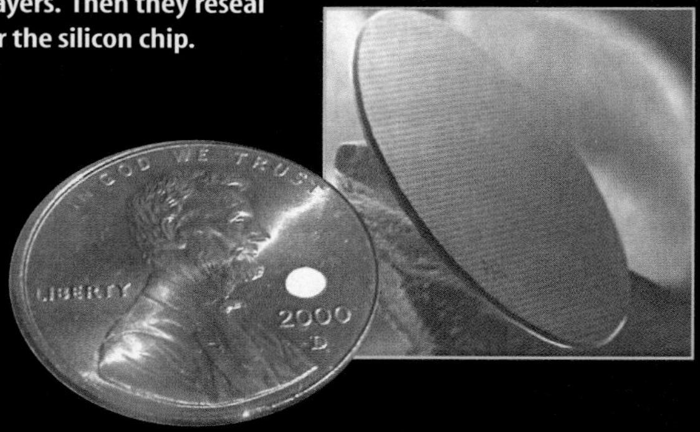

▲ The artificial silicon retina, above right, is thinner than a human hair and only 2 mm in diameter—the same diameter as the white dot on this penny.

466 CHAPTER 15 Mirrors and Lenses

Resource Manager

Chapter Resources Booklet

Transparency Activity, pp. 47–48

Reinforcement, p. 28

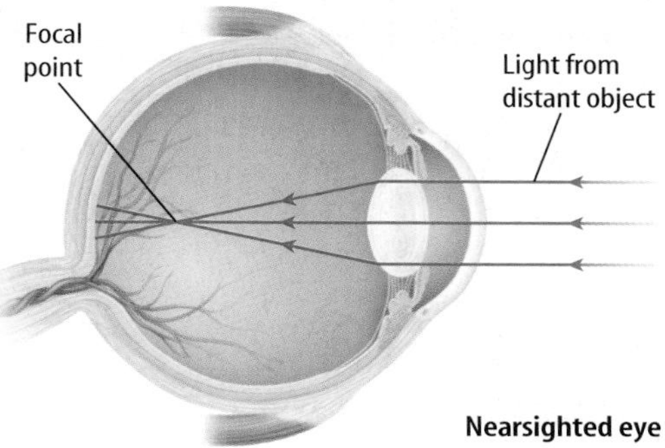

A When a nearsighted person looks at distant objects, the light from the objects is refracted to a focal point that is in front of the retina.

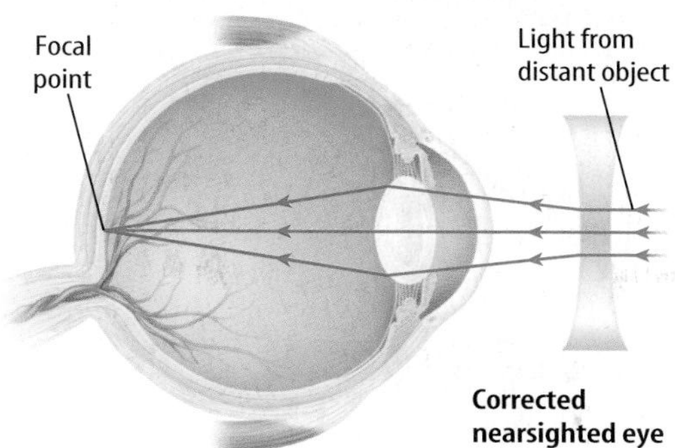

B If the light passes through a concave lens on the way to the nearsighted eye, it will spread apart. It then will be refracted the right amount by the eye's lens so it is focused on the retina.

Nearsightedness If you have nearsighted friends, you know that they can see clearly only when objects are nearby. A nearsighted person's lens cannot be made flat enough to form an image on the retina of an object that is far away. Instead, the image is formed in front of the retina, as in **Figure 16A.** To correct this problem, a nearsighted person can wear concave lenses. **Figure 16B** illustrates how the concave lenses will spread out incoming light rays before they reach the eye. Then when the spread-apart light rays reach the lens, they are refracted the right amount to focus on the retina.

Figure 16
Nearsightedness can be corrected with concave lenses.

Section  Assessment

1. How can you tell the difference between a convex lens and a concave lens?
2. How is light refracted when it passes through a concave lens?
3. What type of lens would you use to examine a tiny spider on your desk?
4. If you have difficulty reading the chalkboard from the back row, what is most likely your vision problem? How can it be corrected?
5. **Think Critically** When using a slide projector, why do you insert the slides in the projector upside down?

Skill Builder Activities

6. **Concept Mapping** Mirrors and lenses are the simplest optical devices. Design a network tree concept map to show some uses for each shape of mirror and lens. **For more help, refer to the Science Skill Handbook.**
7. **Using an Electronic Spreadsheet** Prepare a spreadsheet that organizes the information you have acquired about vision problems. For nearsightedness, astigmatism, and farsightedness, display the following: *the symptom*, *the cause*, and *the method of correction*. **For more help, refer to the Technology Skill Handbook.**

3 Assess

Reteach

Compare eyeglasses that correct nearsightedness and farsightedness. Have students examine near and far objects through each type of lens and explain how each lens corrects vision problems. The convex lens corrects farsightedness and the concave lens corrects nearsightedness. L2 ELL
LS **Visual-Spatial**

Challenge

Challenge students to go back and look over their observations from the Explore Activity. Have each student draw a ray diagram showing what the drop of water does to the light from the text. The virtual image of the text is enlarged and upright because the water acts as a convex lens. L3 LS **Visual-Spatial**

Assessment

Process Ask students to explain why the image you see with a magnifying glass is blurry if you hold the glass too far from the object. The virtual image formed becomes too large to be focused properly with the lens. Use **Performance Assessment in the Science Classroom,** p. 89.

Answers to Section Assessment

1. A convex lens is thicker in the middle, while a concave lens is thicker on the edges.
2. It is bent away from the optical axis.
3. convex
4. nearsightedness; with a concave lens
5. The slides are between one and two focal lengths from a convex lens.
6. Check students' work.
7. Nearsightedness—symptom: can't see faraway objects; cause: lens of the eye can't be made flat enough so image focuses in front of the retina; correction: concave lens. Farsightedness—symptom: can't see close objects; cause: lens of the eye can't be made curved enough so image forms behind the retina; correction: convex lens. Astigmatism—symptom: blurry vision at all distances; cause: irregularly shaped lens; correction: lens with uneven curvature.

SECTION

Optical Instruments

1 Motivate

Bellringer Transparency

Display the Section Focus Transparency for Section 3. Use the accompanying Transparency Activity Master. L2 ELL

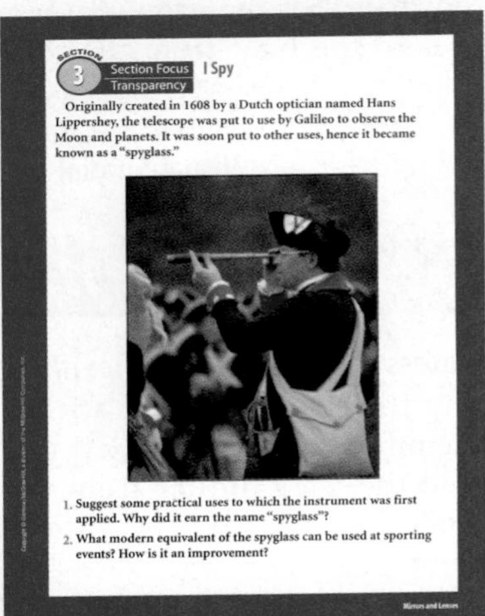

3 Section Focus Transparency | I Spy

Originally created in 1608 by a Dutch optician named Hans Lippershey, the telescope was put to use by Galileo to observe the Moon and planets. It was soon put to other uses, hence it became known as a "spyglass."

1. Suggest some practical uses to which the instrument was first applied. Why did it earn the name "spyglass"?
2. What modern equivalent of the spyglass can be used at sporting events? How is it an improvement?

Tie to Prior Knowledge

Ask students whether they have ever taken a blurry picture with a camera. Have them suggest why this might have happened. The camera or object might have moved, or the lens might not have been focused on the film.

SECTION 3

Optical Instruments

As You Read

***What* You'll Learn**

- **Compare** refracting and reflecting telescopes.
- **Explain** why a telescope in space would be useful.
- **Describe** how a microscope uses lenses to magnify small objects.
- **Explain** how a camera creates an image.

Vocabulary
refracting telescope
reflecting telescope
microscope

***Why* It's Important**

Optical instruments help the human eye see distant and small objects.

Telescopes

Imagine a clear evening when a full moon is just starting to rise. Even though the Moon might seem large and close, it is still too far away for you to see the details on its surface. You know from your own experience that it's hard to see faraway objects clearly. When you look at an object, only some of the light reflected from its surface enters your eye. Much of the light is reflected in other directions. As the object moves farther away, the amount of light entering your eye decreases, as shown in **Figure 17.** As a result, the object appears dimmer and less detailed.

One way to be able to see the Moon's surface clearly would be to go to the Moon and study it up close. Or, if you look at the Moon through a good telescope, you can see the craters and other features on the Moon's surface clearly. A telescope has a system of mirrors and lenses that gather much more light from a faraway object than your eye does. The precise combinations of the lenses and mirrors allow you to see distant objects. Using telescopes, many people have been able to study and gather information about the Moon, the planets, Earth's galaxy, and other galaxies.

Figure 17
The amount of light that reaches the eye decreases as the distance between the eye and the object increases.

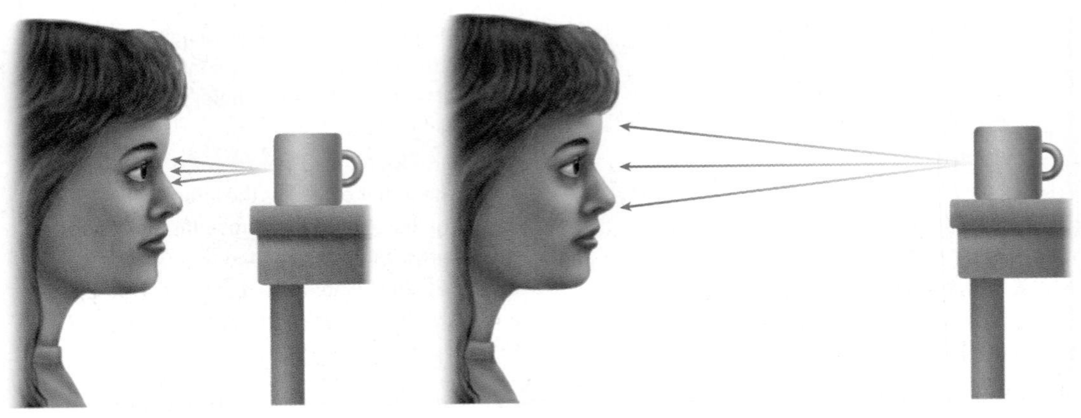

Section Assessment Planner

Portfolio
Science Journal, p. 470

Performance Assessment
MiniLAB, p. 471
Skill Building Activities, p. 473
See page 480 for more options.

Content Assessment
Section, p. 473
Challenge, p. 473
Chapter, pp. 480–481

Refracting Telescopes One common telescope is the refracting telescope. A simple **refracting telescope,** shown in **Figure 18,** uses two convex lenses to gather and focus light from distant objects. Incoming light from distant objects passes through the first lens, called the objective lens. Because the objects are so far away, light rays from these objects are nearly parallel to the optical axis of the lens. As a result, the rays form a real image at the focal point of the lens, within the body of the telescope. The second convex lens, called the eyepiece lens, acts like a magnifying glass and magnifies this real image. When you look through the eyepiece lens, you see an enlarged, inverted, virtual image of the real image formed by the objective lens.

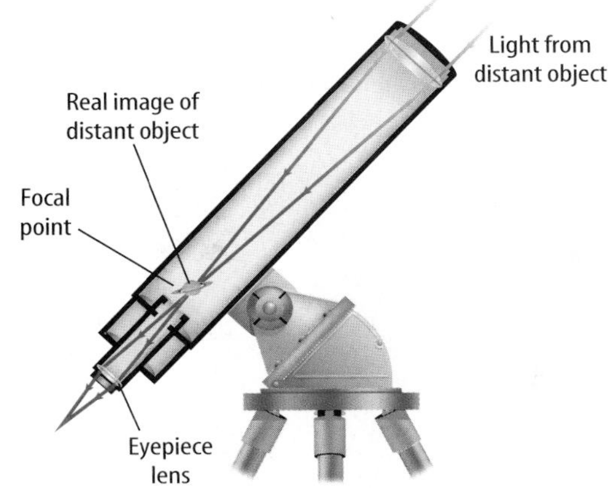

Figure 18
Light from a distant object refracts twice in a refracting telescope to create a large virtual image. *How do you think a refracting telescope could be focused?*

Reading Check *How do the two lenses in a refracting telescope work together?*

Several problems are associated with refracting telescopes. In order to form a detailed image of distant objects, such as planets and galaxies, the objective lens must be as large as possible. A large lens is heavy and can be supported in the telescope tube only around its edge. The lens can sag or flex due to its own weight, distorting the image it forms. Also, these heavy glass lenses are costly and difficult to make.

Reflecting Telescopes Due to the problems with refracting telescopes, most large telescopes today are reflecting telescopes. A **reflecting telescope** uses a concave mirror, a plane mirror, and a convex lens to collect and focus light from distant objects. **Figure 19** shows a reflecting telescope. Light from a distant object enters one end of the telescope and strikes a concave mirror at the opposite end. The light reflects off of this mirror and converges. Before it converges at a focal point, the light hits a plane mirror that is placed at an angle within the telescope tube. The light is reflected from the plane mirror toward the telescope's eyepiece. The light rays converge at the focal point, creating a real image of the distant object. Just as in a refracting telescope, a convex lens in the eyepiece then magnifies this image.

Figure 19
Reflecting telescopes use two mirrors to create a real image, which then is magnified by a convex lens. *Is the final image you see real or virtual?*

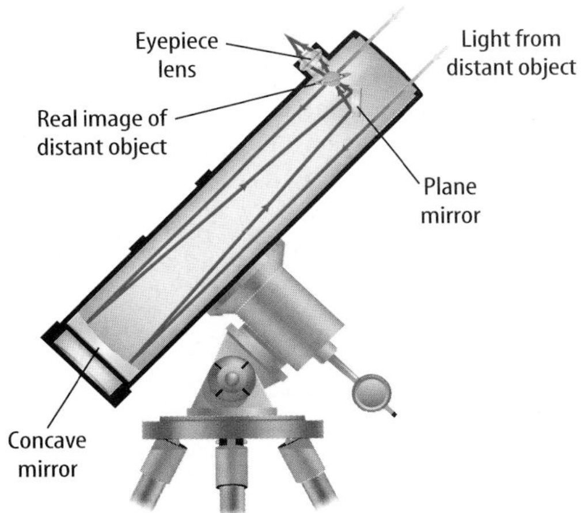

2 Teach

Telescopes

Teacher FYI

The identity of the inventor of the first true telescope is uncertain, but credit is often given to Hans Lippershey of Holland. Galileo heard of Lippershey's "looker" and made an improved version that he used to observe the heavens. Among Galileo's discoveries were sunspots, some moons of Jupiter, and the phases of Venus.

Reading Check

Answer The first forms the real image within the telescope body, and the second magnifies the real image. They work together to produce an enlarged, inverted virtual image of the real image formed by the objective lens.

Caption Answers

Figure 18 by adjusting the distance between the objective and the eyepiece

Figure 19 virtual

Quick Demo

Bring a refracting telescope and a reflecting telescope to class. Allow students to look through both of them at a faraway object. L2 ELL IS **Visual-Spatial**

Fun Fact

A reflecting telescope is often called a Newtonian telescope after its inventor, Isaac Newton.

Resource Manager 

Chapter Resources Booklet
- Directed Reading for Content Mastery, pp. 21, 22
- Transparency Activity, p. 46

Physical Science Critical Thinking/Problem Solving, p. 4

Science Journal

Mystery Element The reflective coating on many mirrors used in telescopes is made of a valuable metallic element. This same element is found in the light-sensitive compounds used in photographic film. Have students write the name of the element, its chemical symbol, and its atomic number in their Science Journals. silver, Ag, atomic number 47 L3 IS **Logical-Mathematical**

Telescopes, continued

Discussion

What are some environmental factors that need to be considered when deciding where to build a new Earth-based telescope? Possible answers: weather, climate, atmospheric pollution, proximity to city lights, ground vibrations, geologic stability
L3 LS **Logical-Mathematical**

Make a Model

Draw a line 2.4 m long to show the diameter of Hubble's primary mirror. The large size allows the telescope to capture much light so that faint, distant stars can be observed. These stars cannot be seen from Earth.
L1 ELL LS **Visual-Spatial**

Quick Demo

Reinforce the idea that the Hubble Space Telescope needs to be above Earth's atmosphere by drawing on the board a circle to represent Earth and a shaded circle around it to represent the atmosphere. L2 ELL
LS **Visual-Spatial**

Fun Fact

The Hubble Space Telescope is 600 km above Earth and orbits it every 95 minutes.

Discussion

What kinds of knowledge might scientists gain from the Hubble Space Telescope? how the universe began and how old it is; how stars form; the dynamics of pulsars, quasars, and black holes; information about planets outside our solar system
L2 LS **Logical-Mathematical**

Reading Check

Answer It is above Earth's atmosphere.

Figure 20
The view from telescopes on Earth is different from the view from telescopes in space.

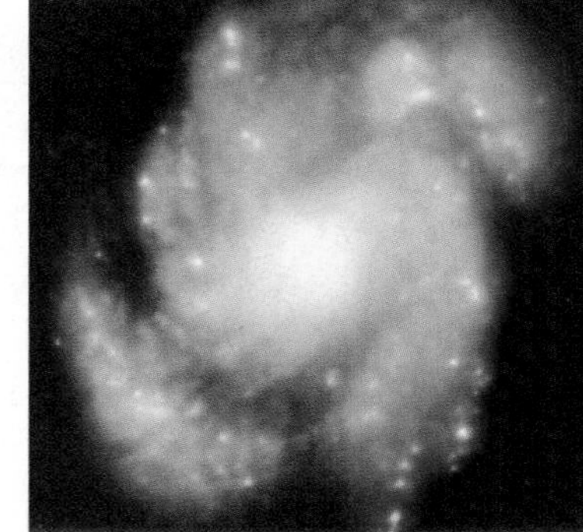

A Telescopes on Earth form blurry images of objects in space due to Earth's atmosphere.

B The *Hubble Space Telescope* is above Earth's atmosphere and forms clearer images of objects in space.

Telescopes from Space Imagine being at the bottom of a swimming pool and trying to read a sign by the pool's edge. The water in the pool would distort your view of any object beyond the water's surface. In a similar way, Earth's atmosphere blurs your view of objects in outer space. To overcome the blurriness of humans' view into space, the National Aeronautics and Space Administration (NASA) built a telescope called the *Hubble Space Telescope* to be placed into space high above Earth's atmosphere. On April 20, 1990, NASA used the space shuttle Discovery to launch this telescope into an orbit about 600 km above Earth. The *Hubble Space Telescope* has produced images much sharper and more detailed than the largest telescopes on Earth can. **Figure 20** shows the difference in the images produced by telescopes on Earth and the *Hubble* telescope. With the *Hubble Space Telescope,* scientists can detect visible light—as well as other types of radiation—from the planets, stars, and distant galaxies that usually is blocked by Earth's atmosphere.

Reading Check *Why is the* **Hubble Space Telescope** *able to produce clearer images than telescopes on Earth?*

The *Hubble* telescope is a type of reflecting telescope that uses two mirrors to collect and focus light to form an image. The primary mirror in the telescope is 2.4 m across. When the *Hubble* was first launched, a defect in this primary mirror caused the telescope to create blurry images. The telescope was repaired by astronauts in December 1993.

SCIENCE Online

Research Visit the Glencoe Science Web site at **science.glencoe.com** for data about the *Hubble Space Telescope.* Do you think the *Hubble Space Telescope* is worthwhile? Prepare a persuasive speech to defend your opinion on whether or not the *Hubble Space Telescope* is useful and important.

SCIENCE Online

Internet Addresses

Explore the Glencoe Science Web site at **science.glencoe.com** to find out more about topics in this section.

Science Journal

Binoculars Most binoculars are like two side-by-side refracting telescopes except that each side also contains two prisms. Have students find out what the prisms do, and in their Science Journals draw diagrams of the light path in binoculars. The prisms reflect the light, allowing the two objective lenses to be farther apart. This gives the viewer more depth perception. L3 LS **Linguistic.** P

Microscopes

A telescope would be useless if you were trying to study the cells in a butterfly wing, a sample of pond scum, or the differences between a human hair and a horse hair. You would need a microscope to look at such small objects. A **microscope** uses two convex lenses with relatively short focal lengths to magnify small, close objects. A microscope, like a telescope, has an objective lens and an eyepiece lens. However, it is designed differently because the objects viewed are not far away.

Figure 21 shows a simple microscope. The object to be viewed is placed on a transparent slide and illuminated from below. The light passes by or through the object on the slide and then travels through the objective lens. The objective lens is a convex lens. It forms a real, enlarged image of the object, because the distance from the object to the lens is between one and two focal lengths. The real image is then magnified again by the eyepiece lens (another convex lens) to create a virtual, enlarged image. This final image can be up to several hundred times larger than the actual object, depending on the magnification powers of the two lenses.

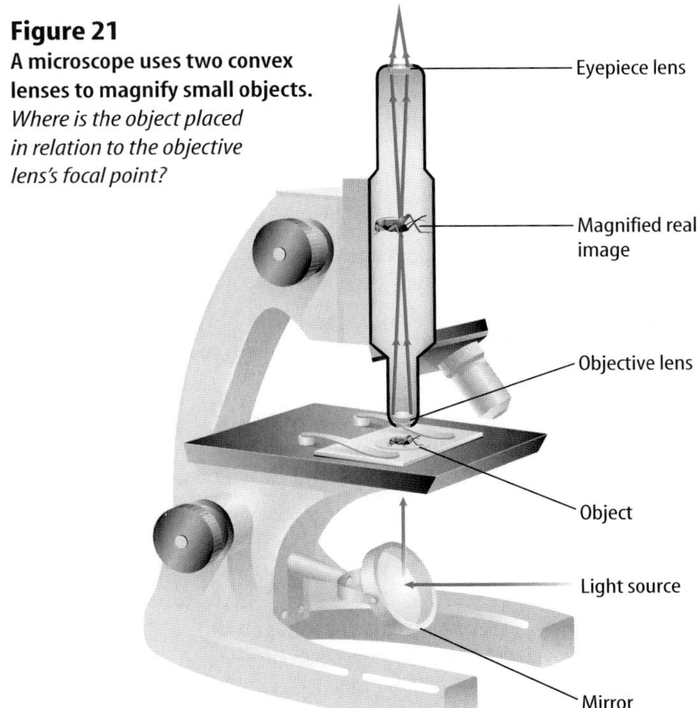

Figure 21
A microscope uses two convex lenses to magnify small objects.
Where is the object placed in relation to the objective lens's focal point?

Mini LAB

Experimenting with Focal Lengths

Procedure

1. Fill a glass **test tube** with **water** and seal it with a **lid or stopper.**
2. Type or print the compound name SULFUR DIOXIDE in capital letters on a piece of **paper or a note card.**
3. Set the test tube horizontally over the words and observe them. What do you notice?
4. Hold the tube 1 cm over the words and observe them again. Record your observations. Repeat, holding the tube at several other heights above the words.

Analysis

1. What were your observations of the words at the different distances? How do you explain your observations?
2. Is the image you see at each height real or virtual?

Microscopes

Purpose Students observe what happens when the distance from a lens to an object is changed.

L1 ELL LS **Visual-Spatial**

Materials glass test tube with lid or stopper, water, paper

Teaching Strategy The words should be printed or typed in capital letters smaller than the test tubes. They can also be in two different colors.

Analysis

1. When the tube is on the paper, the words are slightly magnified. When the tube is about 1 cm above the words, SULFUR is upside down but DIOXIDE unchanged because the letters are symmetrical. The whole image is inverted because the object is beyond the focal length of the lens.
2. The upright, magnified image is virtual. The inverted images are real.

Assessment

Content Ask students to explain whether a magnifying glass (a convex lens) could produce inverted images of the words. yes, if the glass were far enough from the words Use **Performance Assessment in the Science Classroom,** p. 89.

Caption Answer

Figure 21 between one and two focal lengths away

Resource Manager

Chapter Resources Booklet
MiniLAB, p. 4
Enrichment, p. 32
Home and Community Involvement, p. 39

Visual Learning

Figure 21 Point out that although the eyepiece performs as a single convex lens, it is typically a system of multiple lenses. Similarly, the objective is actually a combination of lenses that performs as a single convex lens. Although a single lens for each is possible, the combination of lenses provides clearer images.

Cameras

Activity

Have students find a book on photography and identify the variables in a camera that can be controlled to gain the desired effects in a photograph. Variables include aperture, shutter speed, lenses, film speed, and flashes.
L3 LS **Linguistic**

Extension

A disposable camera provides clear photographs even though the camera can't be focused. Ask students to investigate how this is possible. Have them prepare a presentation showing how disposable cameras work and describing some of their advantages and disadvantages. A disposable camera has a fixed distance between the lens and the film, and the lens is small. When a lens is small, the light rays entering the camera are almost parallel, so the image doesn't require careful focusing. However, the disposable camera collects less light than a conventional camera, so its images are not as precise. L3 LS **Logical-Mathematical**

Caption Answer

Figure 23 Possible answer: when you want to take pictures of a very wide or tall object, such as a skyscraper.

Activity

A camera is easier to focus if it has a small aperture. To demonstrate this, have each student use a pencil to punch a small hole in an index card and look through the hole at a distant object. You can see better through a small opening, especially if you are nearsighted. L2 LS **Visual-Spatial**

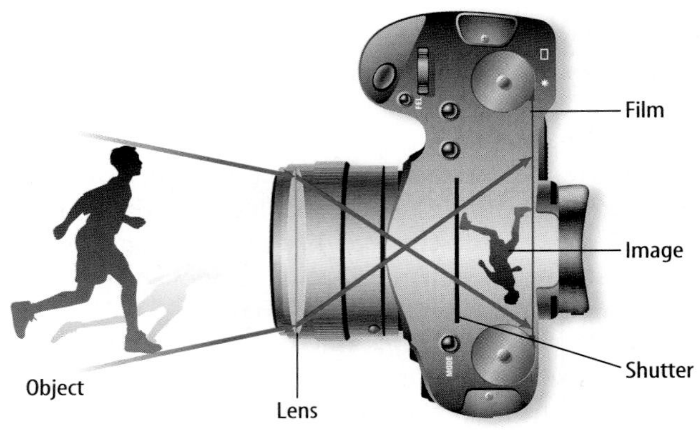

Figure 22
A camera's lens focuses an image on photographic film.

Cameras

Imagine swirls of lavender, gold, and magenta clouds sweeping across the sky at sunset. With the click of a button, you can capture the beautiful scene in a photo. How does a camera make a reduced image of a life-sized scene on film? A camera works by gathering and bending light with a lens. This lens then projects an image onto light-sensitive film to record a scene.

When you take a picture with a camera, a shutter opens to allow light to enter the camera for a specific length of time. The light reflected off your subject enters the camera through an opening called the aperture (AP uh choor). It passes through the camera lens, which focuses the image on the film, as in **Figure 22.** The image is real, inverted, and smaller than the actual object. The size of the image depends upon the focal length of the lens and how close the lens is to the film.

Figure 23
A Each object in the image produced by a wide-angle lens is small. B This allows more of the surroundings to be seen. *What situations would be good for using a wide-angle lens?*

A

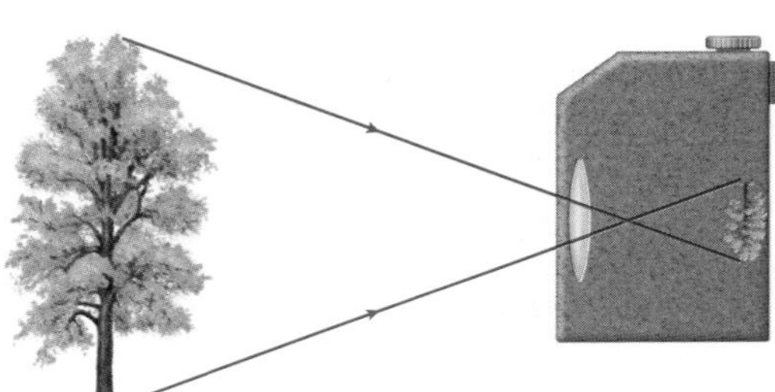

B

Wide-Angle Lenses Suppose you and a friend use two different cameras to photograph the same object at the same distance. If the cameras have different lenses, your pictures will look different. For example, some lenses have short focal lengths that produce a relatively small image of the object but include much of its surroundings. These lenses are called wide-angle lenses, and they must be placed close to the film to focus the image with their short focal length. **Figure 23A** shows how a wide-angle lens works. The photo in **Figure 23B** was taken with a wide-angle lens.

472

Curriculum Connection

Art Photographers have long used photography to produce art. Have students find out about early art photographers, their cameras, and some of the techniques they used to produce their photographs. Have them give multimedia presentations of their findings. Photographers include Edward Weston and Ansel Adams, who used large-format view cameras to produce black and white photographs. L3 LS **Linguistic**

Resource Manager

Chapter Resources Booklet
Reinforcement, p. 29
Activity Worksheet, pp. 7–8
Cultural Diversity, p. 51

Figure 24
A telephoto lens creates a larger image of an object than a wide-angle lens does.

A **The telephoto lens has a long focal length.**

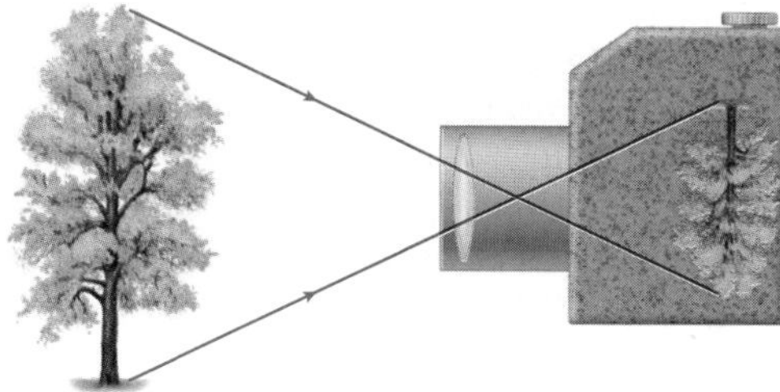

B **Less of the surroundings can be seen, though a close-up of one of the objects can be photographed.** *When would you want to use a telephoto lens?*

Telephoto Lenses Telephoto lenses have longer focal lengths and are located farther from the film than wide-angle lenses are. **Figure 24A** shows how a telephoto lens forms an image. The image you see through a telephoto lens seems enlarged and the object seems closer than it actually is, as shown in **Figure 24B.** Telephoto lenses are easy to recognize because they are usually long. They protrude from the camera to increase the distance between the lens and the film.

Section 3 Assessment

1. Compare and contrast the components of reflecting and refracting telescopes and the images they form.
2. What advantages or disadvantages does the *Hubble Space Telescope* have compared to telescopes on Earth?
3. What does each lens in a microscope do?
4. If you wanted to photograph a single rose on a rosebush, what kind of lens would you use? Explain.
5. **Think Critically** Which optical instrument—a telescope, a microscope, or a camera—forms images in a way most like your eye? Explain.

Skill Builder Activities

6. **Forming Hypotheses** You notice that all the objects in a photograph you've taken are blurry. Use your knowledge of lenses and focal lengths to form a hypothesis that could explain why the photo was blurred and how to correct it. **For more help, refer to the** Science Skill Handbook.
7. **Solving One-Step Equations** Suppose the objective lens in a microscope forms an image that is 100 times the size of an object. The eyepiece lens magnifies this image ten times. What is the total magnification power of the microscope? **For more help, refer to the** Math Skill Handbook.

Answers to Section Assessment

1. Reflecting telescopes form images with a concave mirror, a plane mirror, and a convex lens. Refracting telescopes use two convex lenses. Both form virtual, inverted images.
2. It experiences no distortion caused by Earth's atmosphere.
3. The objective lens forms a real enlarged image and the eyepiece forms a virtual enlarged image.
4. A telephoto lens; it has a longer focal length and allows one object to be enlarged while omitting most surroundings.
5. A camera; both adjust to focus on near and far objects, control the amount of light that enters, form real inverted images, and focus on a light-sensitive surface.
6. Possible answers: lens too close to or too far away from the film; camera not held still while taking the picture, lens dirty or distorted
7. 1000x

Caption Answer

Figure 24B Possible answer: to photograph faraway objects, such as a bird in a tree

3 Assess

Reteach

Point to a distant object that can be seen apart from its surroundings. Ask students to imagine taking two photos of the object, one with a wide-angle lens and one with a telephoto lens. Have them sketch what they might see with each lens. **Which lens has a longer focal length?** telephoto L2 LS **Visual-Spatial**

Challenge

Ask students to describe what you would have to do to change a microscope into a refracting telescope. You would have to make the objective lens bigger so it could gather more light. Having done that, you would have to lengthen the distance between the objective and the eyepiece to accommodate the longer focal distance of the larger objective lens. L2 LS **Logical-Mathematical**

Process Show students sketches of the light paths of some optical instruments mentioned in this section. Have them identify the sketch as a refracting telescope, a reflecting telescope, or a microscope. For each, the student should describe the types of images formed. Use **Performance Assessment in the Science Classroom,** p. 89.

Activity

BENCH TESTED

Recognize the Problem

Purpose

Students build a model of a telescope, estimate the telescope's power, and compare the images formed with different types of lenses. L3 ELL LS **Kinesthetic**

Process Skills

observing, using numbers, measuring, comparing and contrasting, recognizing cause and effect, formulating models

Time Required

45 minutes

Thinking Critically

Discussion

The objective lens is convex and forms a real image of a distant object. The eyepiece then magnifies this image.

The power of the telescope is equal to the ratio of the focal lengths of the lenses.

Possible Materials

A tube from gift wrapping paper will slide smoothly inside the tube from a roll of paper towels.

Duct tape is flexible, but may be hard for students to handle, but small pieces could be cut. Cellophane tape is easier to handle, but may be harder to use to hold the lenses.

Safety Precautions

Remind students not to look directly at the sun with any telescope.

Activity Model and Invent

Up Close and Personal

Galileo used the telescope to enhance his eyesight. It enabled him to see planets and stars beyond the range of his eyes alone. Today more powerful instruments, such as the *Hubble Space Telescope*, are used to learn more about our universe.

Recognize the Problem

How do the lenses in a simple telescope form an image?

Thinking Critically

Galileo found that by combining two lenses, he could magnify distant objects. His telescope used a small convex eyepiece lens and a larger convex objective lens at the other end. How do the lenses in a telescope change the light rays reflected from a distant object to make it appear closer? How do the focal lengths of the eyepiece and objective lenses determine the power of the telescope?

Goals

- **Build** a simple telescope.
- **Estimate** the power of the telescope.
- **Compare** convex and concave eyepieces.

Safety Precautions

WARNING: *Do not look directly at the Sun through a telescope. Permanent eye damage can result.*

Possible Materials

objective lens—convex, 25 cm to 30 cm focal length, about 4 cm diameter

eyepiece lenses—one each convex and concave, 2 cm to 3 cm focal length, about 2.5 cm to 3 cm diameter

cardboard tubes—one with inside diameter of about 4 cm; one with inside diameter of about 3 cm. (The smaller tube should slide inside the larger one with a snug fit.)

clay

**cellophane tape or duct tape* to hold the lenses in place

scissors

**Alternate materials*

Data Source

SCIENCE*Online* Go to the Glencoe Science Web site at **science.glencoe.com** for more information about telescopes.

Inclusion Strategies

Visually Impaired Use one set of tubes and lenses to make a hands-on, cross-sectional display of a telescope for visually impaired students. Cut the tubes in half along their length, fasten the lenses in place, and mount a piece of string from the outer edge of each lens to its focal point. Give visually impaired students the opportunity to handle the telescope to feel the sizes, shapes, and focal lengths of the lenses.

Planning the Model

1. Hold the small, concave eyepiece lens near your eye. Hold the objective lens in front of it and move it away until a distant object appears focused. Note the approximate distance between the two lenses at this point. Subtract half the length of the larger-diameter cardboard tube from this measurement to get the length needed for the smaller tube.
2. **Decide** how you will attach each lens to the tube. You can hold it in place with clay or tape.

Check the Model

1. The lenses must be perpendicular to your line of sight to get the best results. How can you make sure the lenses are in the right position?
2. The smaller-diameter tube must have some room to slide in and out of the larger tube to focus properly on distant objects. Will your calculated length for the shorter tube allow this?
3. Make sure your teacher approves your plan before you start.

Making the Model

1. Cut the smaller-diameter cardboard tube to the calculated length. Make two pieces this size.
2. Attach the objective lens to the end of the larger tube.
3. Attach the convex eyepiece lens to one of the smaller tubes.
4. Slide the smaller tube into the larger one and look through the eyepiece.
5. Move the smaller tube in and out until a distant object is focused clearly.
6. **Estimate** how much larger the image seen through the eyepiece is than the image you see with your unaided eye. Note the appearance of the object.
7. Attach the concave eyepiece to the second smaller tube that you cut.
8. Repeat the observations using the concave eyepiece. Again, note the appearance of the object.

Analyzing and Applying Results

1. How did the image appear when using the convex and concave eyepieces? What happens when you turn the telescope around and look through the objective lens?
2. What was the estimated power of your telescope? How could you change its power?

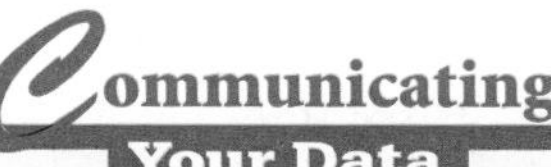

Compare your telescope and its operation with those of other members of your class. Try reading numbers or letters on a distant sign. Which telescope helps you see more detail?

Planning the Model

Teaching Strategies

Have extra quantities of the smaller tube on hand for students who miscut their tubes.

Troubleshooting

Success depends on getting the objective and eyepiece lenses aligned properly. This may be easier if the lenses are slightly larger than the tubes, so they can be taped in place from the outside.

Students should try to keep their fingerprints off the lenses as much as possible to get the sharpest image.

Making the Model

Expected Outcome

The power of the telescope may be estimated by looking at an object alternately with the scope and with the unaided eye, and estimating the change in size of the object. The power can be accurately determined from the ratio of the focal lengths of the lenses.

Analyzing and Applying Results

1. The convex lens gives an inverted image and the concave lens gives an upright image. When you look through the objective lens the image is enlarged and inverted if the distance between the objective lens and the image formed by the eyepiece is between 1 and 2 focal lengths of the objective apart, and enlarged and upright if the distance between the objective lens and the image formed by the eyepiece is less than the focal length of the objective lens.
2. The telescope should magnify the object about 10 *x*. This could be changed by changing the ratio of the focal lengths of the eyepiece and objective lenses.

Assessment

Performance Have students draw two ray diagrams of their telescopes—one with a convex eyepiece and one with a concave eyepiece. Use **Performance Assessment in the Science Classroom,** p. 127.

Have students use a spreadsheet program to put observations from class members' telescopes into a table.

Content Background

Surgery for cataracts was performed in India in 750 B.C. The next real advance in eye surgery was in 1906 when a German surgeon successfully transplanted a human cornea. This enabled the treatment of corneal scarring, but was a last resort procedure. Lasers developed in the 1960s and 70s enabled the removal of tumors and repair of torn retinas, but cornea surgery was not possible with the early lasers. The available laser light colors passed through the transparent cornea and worked by burning, which leaves scars. Radial keratotomy, a surgical procedure to change the shape of the cornea to improve eyesight, was developed at about the same time, but had limited applications. The ultraviolet "excimer laser" was developed in 1977 to cut transparent material. In 1981 it was found that the excimer leaves no scars in tissue and it was developed as a surgical tool. The first excimer technique, called PRK (photo refractive keratectomy), reshaped the cornea by removing corneal tissue, allowing a wider range of defects to be corrected. The draw back was a long recovery time. The procedure described in the article is called LASIK (laser in-situ keratomileusis) which reshapes the cornea in much the same way, but allows the epithelium to be replaced reducing discomfort and shortening recovery time.

TIME SCIENCE AND Society — SCIENCE ISSUES THAT AFFECT YOU!

Sight Lines

Lasers make it possible to throw away eyeglasses

Imagine seeing the world through the eyes of a hawk. With your crystal-clear vision, you could spot a ripple in the grass from hundreds of meters away. This kind of super-hero vision may be possible in the not-so-distant future. Already, scientists have developed ways to improve human eyesight beyond "perfect" 20/20 vision. With this technology, most of the 160 million Americans who wear eyeglasses or contact lenses can kiss them goodbye forever. Poor vision can be changed, permanently.

Laser Eye Surgery

Back in the 1970s, scientists developed a special kind of laser to make microscopic notches in computer chips. The laser is also perfect for eye surgery. It does not generate a lot of heat, so it doesn't damage the delicate tissues of the eye. Plus, the laser is very precise. Eye surgeons like this. They know that one tiny slip-up can cause a lifetime of vision problems.

In a Blink of an Eye . . .

Laser eye surgery only takes about 15 min. The patient is awake the entire time, staring at a red light to keep his or her eyes from moving while the doctor slices through his or her corneas.

Although some people experience complications, such as hazy vision, most couldn't be happier with the results. Soon after the surgery, one patient declared, "When I looked up at the sky I could see the stars clearly—just like that! It's a completely new life for me."

How It Works

A The eye is measured to determine the vision problem. These measurements are fed into the computer that controls the laser.

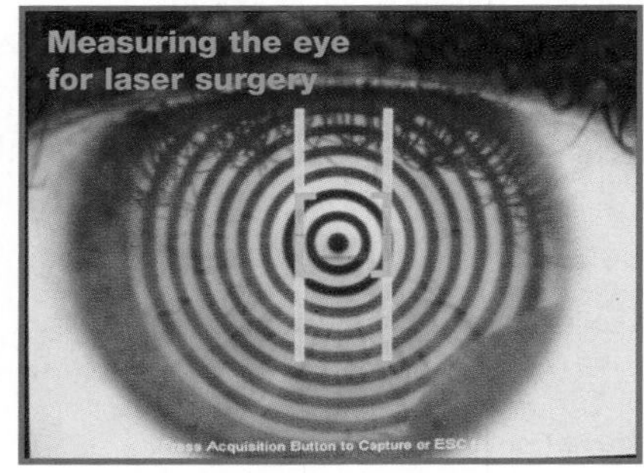

B The doctor numbs the eye with liquid drops, then props the eyelids open. The cornea, the transparent cover in front of the eye, is marked with a special ink before any cutting begins. These marks help the doctor put everything back in the right place.

476

Resources for Teachers and Students

"A Poke in the Eye." by Ann Marsh. *Forbes Magazine*. October 18, 1999

"The excimer laser is no turkey—it gave us scarless eye surgery" *Technology Review* November/December 2000

The Cornea and Laser Eye Institute
Glenpointe Centre East
300 Frank W. Burr Blvd
Teaneck, NJ 07666
201-883-0505

The Cornea and Vision

The cornea is where light begins its journey into the eye. The transparent cornea is a lens that helps focus light that enters the eye. Most of the bending of these light rays occurs when they pass from air into the cornea. They then are bent more by the lens of the eye, which adjusts its shape to focus the light on the retina. Unlike the lens though, the eye doesn't adjust the shape of the cornea.

When someone is nearsighted, light rays are brought to a focus in front of the retina. To focus an image on the retina, the light rays must be bent less. This is usually done by placing a concave lens in front of the eye. However, another way would be to make the shape of the cornea flatter. Then light rays are bent less when they enter the eye.

If someone is farsighted, light rays aren't bent enough to form a focused image on the retina. A convex lens placed in front of the eye causes light rays to be bent before they enter the eye. Light rays also would be bent more if the shape of the cornea were thicker in the center, so it was less flat.

C A suction ring is attached to the eye to hold it steady during surgery.

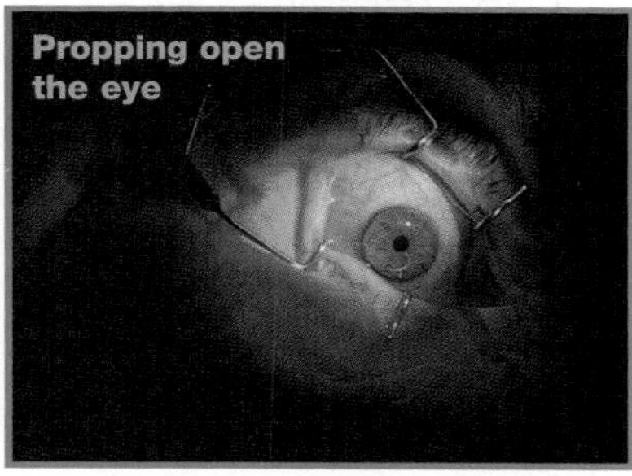

Propping open the eye

D The cutting instrument slices across a guided path through the outer layers of the eye. The blade leaves an uncut section that's lifted until the surgery is completed. Because the eye has been numbed, this procedure is not painful.

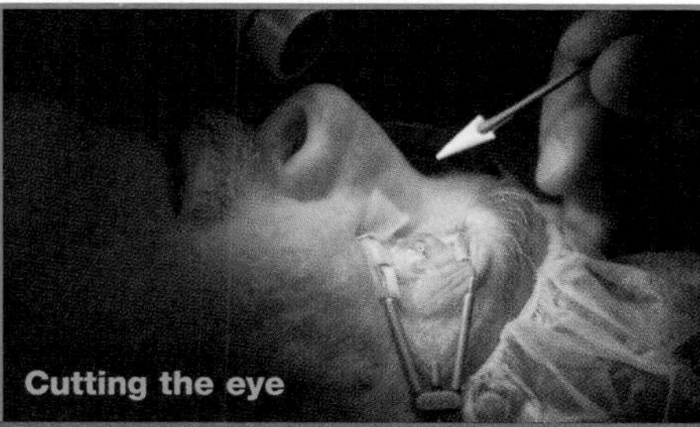

Cutting the eye

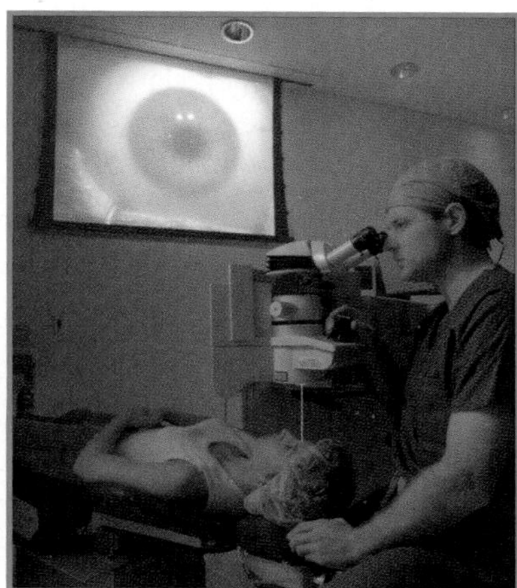

A screen helps this doctor keep tabs on his laser work.

E The blade is taken away and the laser goes to work. For people who are nearsighted—they see near objects clearly—the laser vaporizes the inner cornea, making it flatter. For people who are farsighted—they see far objects clearly—the laser removes a ring of tissue to make the cornea steeper.

CONNECTIONS Interview Opthamalogists are medical doctors who specialize in healing eyes. Optometrists make glasses and check vision. Interview an optometrist or opthamologist to find out how he or she detects eye problems, and how these problems can be corrected.

SCIENCE Online For more information, visit science.glencoe.com

CONNECTIONS Debate It may not be feasible for each student to interview an optometrist or ophthalmologist individually. If possible, arrange to have an ophthalmologist address the class after students have done research and can ask informed questions. Another option might be to compile questions from the class and submit them to an eye doctor who has agreed to correspond with the class.

SCIENCE Online

Internet Addresses

____

____

____

Explore the Glencoe Science Web site at **science.glencoe.com** to find out more about topics in this section.

Discussion

How does removing tissue from the cornea reduce or eliminate the need for glasses? Possible answer: Reshaping the cornea in the proper way has the same light-bending effect as an artificial lens placed in front of the eye.

Activity

Obtain a number of straight-sided clear glass jars of different diameters. Try to make the variation in diameter as great as possible. Fill them with water and place them on a table in a line parallel to the edge about 6 inches apart. Place objects having similar size, shape and color on the opposite side of the table in line with each jar. Have students look at the objects through the jars moving them until they come into focus. For each object they should record the distance from the jar to the object when the object is in focus. For consistent observation they should use the table edge near the jars as a viewing distance. Discuss the results in terms of focal distance and the curvature of the jars. L2

LS **Visual-Spatial**

Investigate the Issue

There are still some concerns about the reliability of PRK and LASIK procedures. Students should research the statistics on these procedures to find the percentage of operations that are a complete success and the percentage of operations in which the patient is left worse than before. L2 LS **Linguistic**

Chapter 15 Study Guide

Reviewing Main Ideas

Preview

Students can answer the questions in their Science Journals. Discuss the answers as you go through the chapter. **LS Linguistic**

Review

Students can write their answers then compare them with those of other students. **LS Interpersonal**

Reteach

Students can look at the illustrations and describe details that support the main ideas of the chapter. **LS Visual-Spatial**

Answers to Chapter Review

Section 1

1. Light rays don't pass through the image.

Section 2

3. to change the focal length so that the light converges on the retina

Section 3

3. virtual

Chapter 15 Study Guide

Reviewing Main Ideas

Section 1 Mirrors

1. Plane mirrors reflect light to form upright, life-sized, virtual images. *Why is the image you see in a plane mirror a virtual image?*

2. Concave mirrors can form various types of images, depending on where an object is relative to the focal point of the mirror. Concave mirrors can be used to magnify objects or create beams of light.
3. Convex mirrors spread out reflected light to form a reduced image. Convex mirrors allow you to see large areas.

Section 2 Lenses

1. Convex lenses converge light rays. Convex lenses can form real or virtual images, depending on the distance from the object to the lens.
2. Concave lenses diverge light rays to form virtual images. They often are used in combination with other lenses.
3. The human eye has a flexible lens that focuses an image on the retina. *Why does the lens in your eye need to change shape when you look at objects at different distances?*

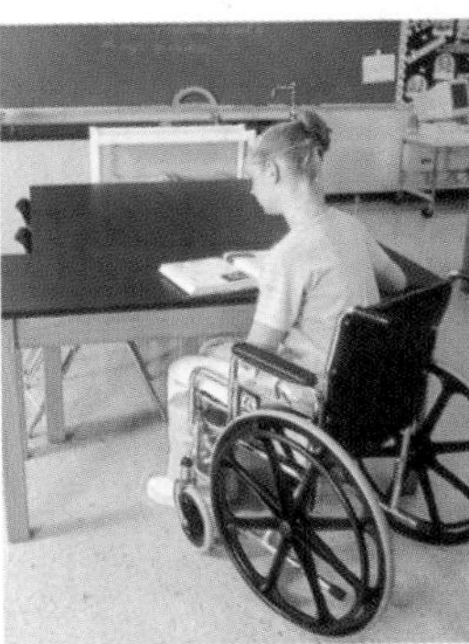

4. People with imperfect vision can use corrective lenses to improve their vision. Farsighted people wear convex lenses, and nearsighted people wear concave lenses.

Section 3 Optical Instruments

1. A refracting telescope uses convex lenses to magnify distant objects. A reflecting telescope uses concave and plane mirrors and a convex lens to magnify distant objects.
2. By avoiding atmospheric distortion, the *Hubble Space Telescope* produces sharper images than telescopes on Earth can.
3. Microscopes use two convex lenses to magnify small objects. *Is the image you see in a microscope real or virtual?*

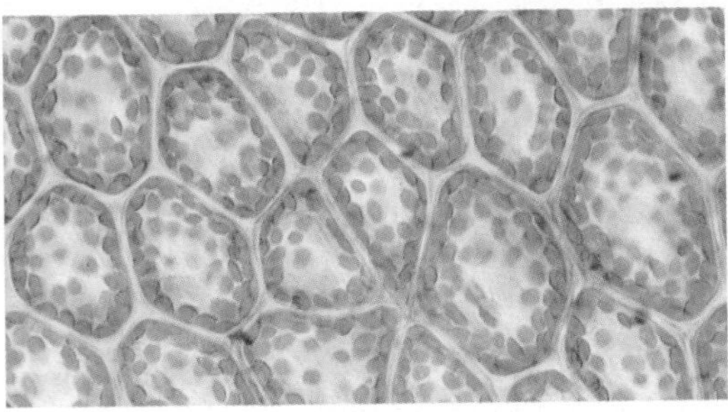

4. Light passing through the lens of a camera is focused on light-sensitive film inside the camera. The image on the film is real, inverted, and reduced.

After You Read

FOLDABLES Reading & Study Skills

On the back of the tabs of your Foldable explain the cause and effect of the reflections of the three types of mirrors.

After You Read

FOLDABLES Reading & Study Skills

After students have read the chapter and completed the Foldable described in Before You Read, have them do the activity on the student page.

Dinah Zike

Chapter 15 Study Guide

Visualizing Main Ideas

Complete the following table about optical instruments.

Types of Optical Instruments		
Optical Instrument	**What is it?**	**How does it work?**
Convex Lens	transparent material that is thicker in the middle than at the edges	causes light rays to converge
Concave Lens	transparent material that is thicker at the edges than in the middle	causes light rays to diverge
Refracting Telescope	tube containing two convex lenses	light gathered by first lens forms an image that is magnified by second lens
Reflecting Telescope	tube containing concave mirror, plane mirror, and convex lens	light gathered by concave mirror is reflected by plane mirror to convex lens
Microscope	tube containing two convex lenses	real image formed by first lens is magnified by second lens

Vocabulary Review

Vocabulary Words

a. concave lens
b. concave mirror
c. convex lens
d. convex mirror
e. cornea
f. focal length
g. focal point
h. microscope
i. optical axis
j. plane mirror
k. real image
l. reflecting telescope
m. refracting telescope
n. retina
o. virtual image

THE PRINCETON REVIEW Study Tip

Write out the full questions and answers to end-of-chapter quizzes, not just the answers. This will help you form complete responses to important questions.

Using Vocabulary

Each of the following sentences is false. Make the sentence true by replacing the underlined word with the correct vocabulary word.

1. A flat, smooth surface that reflects light and forms an image is a convex mirror.
2. A reflecting telescope uses two convex lenses to magnify small, close objects.
3. Every light ray that travels parallel to the optical axis before hitting a concave mirror is reflected to pass through the retina.
4. A concave lens is thicker in the middle than at the edges.
5. The inner lining of the eye that converts light images into electrical signals is called the cornea.

Chapter 15 Study Guide

Visualizing Main Ideas

See student page.

Vocabulary Review

Using Vocabulary

1. plane mirror
2. microscope
3. focal point
4. convex lens
5. retina

Chapter 15 Assessment

Checking Concepts

1. C
2. B
3. C
4. C
5. B
6. C
7. B
8. D
9. B
10. B

Thinking Critically

11. If the object the audience was looking at were really an image in a concave mirror, the magician could make this image disappear by moving the object to the focal point of the mirror, where no image is formed.
12. No; a single concave lens forms an image smaller than the object and the only enlarged upright image formed by a single convex lens is virtual and can't be projected.
13. eyepiece lens; to magnify the image
14. No; the convex mirror would produce a virtual image that could not be magnified by the eyepiece.
15. 1m = 100 cm; magnification = 100 cm / 1 cm = 1

Chapter 15 Assessment

Checking Concepts

Choose the word or phrase that best answers the question.

1. Which of the following types of images is not formed by plane mirrors?
   - **A)** upright
   - **B)** life-sized
   - **C)** enlarged
   - **D)** virtual
2. What object reflects light and curves inward?
   - **A)** plane mirror
   - **B)** concave mirror
   - **C)** convex mirror
   - **D)** concave lens
3. What type of mirror can be used to form a magnified image?
   - **A)** convex
   - **B)** plane
   - **C)** concave
   - **D)** transparent
4. What object is used in a headlight, flashlight, or spotlight to create a beam of light?
   - **A)** concave lens
   - **B)** convex lens
   - **C)** concave mirror
   - **D)** convex mirror
5. What do lenses do?
   - **A)** reflect light
   - **B)** refract light
   - **C)** diffract light
   - **D)** interfere with light
6. Which way does a concave lens bend light?
   - **A)** toward its optical axis
   - **B)** toward its center
   - **C)** toward its edges
   - **D)** toward its focal point
7. What kinds of lenses are most helpful for farsighted people?
   - **A)** flat lenses
   - **B)** convex lenses
   - **C)** concave lenses
   - **D)** plane lenses
8. Which object is not in a reflecting telescope?
   - **A)** plane mirror
   - **B)** concave mirror
   - **C)** convex lens
   - **D)** concave lens
9. Which of the following images do light rays never pass through?
   - **A)** real
   - **B)** virtual
   - **C)** enlarged
   - **D)** reduced
10. Which lens would you use to take a close-up photograph?
    - **A)** lens with a short focal length
    - **B)** lens with a long focal length
    - **C)** a small lens
    - **D)** wide-angle lens

Thinking Critically

11. Magicians often make objects disappear by using trick mirrors. How might a magician seem to make an object disappear by using a concave mirror?
12. A movie or a slide projector projects an image that is magnified and upright. Could such an image be formed by a single lens? Explain why or why not.
13. Which lens in a refracting telescope has a shorter focal length? Why?
14. Would a reflecting telescope work properly if a convex mirror replaced its concave mirror? Explain.
15. The magnification of a refracting telescope can be calculated by dividing the focal length of the objective lens by the focal length of the eyepiece lens. If an objective lens has a focal length of 1 m and the eyepiece has a focal length of 1 cm, what is the magnification of the telescope?

Developing Skills

16. **Classifying** Classify the different types of images formed by plane, concave, and convex mirrors.
17. **Recognizing Cause and Effect** Infer the effects of a hard, rigid eye lens on human vision. Would this make the eye more or less like a simple camera?

Chapter Assessment Planner

Portfolio Encourage students to place in their portfolios one or two items of what they consider to be their best work. Examples include:

- Science Journal, p. 456
- Curriculum Connection, p. 465
- Science Journal, p. 470

Performance Additional performance assessments, Performance Task Assessment Lists, and rubrics for evaluating these activities can be found in Glencoe's **Performance Assessment in the Science Classroom.**

18. Comparing and Contrasting Compare and contrast a microscope and a refracting telescope.

19. Forming Hypotheses Suppose you use a magnifying glass underwater. Propose a hypothesis to explain how the magnification of images would be affected under water.

20. Interpreting Scientific Illustrations Describe the image of the candle seen through the lens.

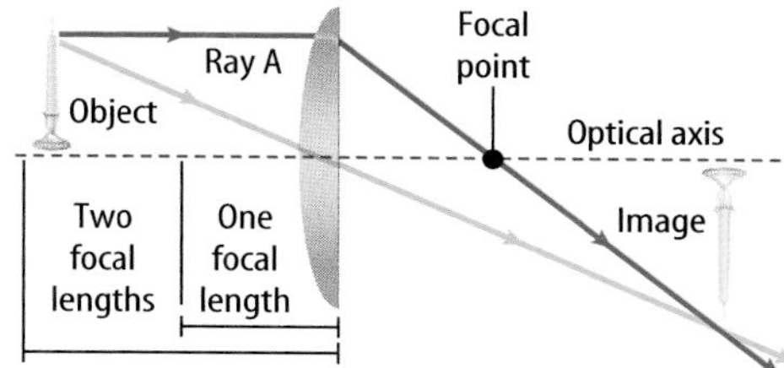

Performance Assessment

21. Writing in Science Write a report tracing the development of the telescope from the time of Galileo to the *Hubble Space Telescope.* Include illustrations with your report.

22. Oral Presentation Investigate the types of mirrors used in fun houses. Explain how these mirrors are formed and why they give distorted images. Demonstrate your findings to the class.

Technology

Go to the Glencoe Science Web site at **science.glencoe.com** or use the **Glencoe Science CD-ROM** for additional chapter assessment.

Test Practice

A student explored the properties of several converging lenses and created the table below.

Exploring Convex Lenses

Lens	Pencil's Distance to Lens	What Image Appears as
1		
2		
3		

Study the table and answer the following questions.

1. The data table could be improved by also recording the _____.
   A) pencil length
   B) lens height
   C) focal length of the lenses
   D) lens temperature

2. Each of the lenses above is able to make the image of the pencil larger. This occurs because _____.
   F) they bend light as light passes through them
   G) light bounces off their surfaces
   H) they create pencils somewhere else nearby
   J) they produce light and send it off in beams to form images

Assessment Resources

Reproducible Masters

Chapter Resources Booklet
Chapter Review, pp. 37–38
Chapter Tests, pp. 39–42
Assessment Transparency Activity, p. 49

Glencoe Science Web site
Interactive Tutor
Chapter Quizzess

Glencoe Technology
Assessment Transparency
Interactive CD-ROM Chapter Quizzes
ExamView Pro Test Bank
Vocabulary PuzzleMaker Software
MindJogger Videoquiz DVD/VHS

Chapter 15 Assessment

Test Practice

The Test-Taking Tip was written by the Princeton Review, the nation's leader in test preparation.

1. C
2. F

Developing Skills

16. Possible answer: Upright images are produced by plane and convex mirrors, and by concave mirrors if the object is within the focal length. Upside-down images are produced by concave mirrors if the object is beyond the focal length. No image is produced if the object is at the focal point of a concave mirror.
17. It would have a fixed focal length and be unable to focus on objects at different distances. It would be more like a simple camera.
18. Both use two convex lenses to create an inverted, virtual image. The object is far from a refracting telescope, so the first lens creates a reduced-sized image. With a microscope, the object is between one and two focal lengths from the lens, so the image is magnified.
19. Possible hypothesis: The difference between the speed of light in water and the speed of light in glass is less than the difference between the speed of light in air and the speed of light in glass, so a magnifying glass used underwater will refract the light less and thus magnify less than if it were used in air
20. The image is real, inverted, and larger than the object.

Performance Assessment

21. Reports might include contributions by Kepler, Newton, and Herschel. Use **PASC**, p. 157.
22. Presentations should show that funhouse mirrors use both concave and convex mirrors to produce distorted images. Use **PASC**, p. 143.

Standardized Test Practice

Reading Comprehension

QUESTION 1: C

Students must recall the explanation provided in the text. Using clues such as how the telescope's first use was to see *distant ships and enemy armies*, students should identify choice C, *could be used to watch other people*.

QUESTION 2: F

Students must use the information in the passage in order to identify a supported conclusion.

QUESTION 3: C

Students must draw a conclusion from the passage.

- Choice A: No; the first refracting telescope was by Lippershey, a Dutchman.
- Choice B: No; Roger Bacon was an English scientist.
- Choice C: Yes; Hooker was an American and the Hooker telescope was his contribution.
- Choice D: No; this is an observation made by Galileo, an Italian scientist.

Teaching Tip

Encourage students to underline the parts of the passage that support their answer choices.

All questions written and validated by The Princeton Review

Standardized Test Practice

Reading Comprehension

Read the passage. Then read each question that follows the passage. Decide which is the best answer to each question.

The History of the Telescope: An International Story

Roger Bacon, an English scientist, first wrote about the basic ideas behind the operation of a telescope in the 1200s. It was not until the early 1600s, however that Han Lippershey, a Dutchman who made spectacles for people with poor vision, made the first telescope. Lippershey noticed that objects appeared closer if he viewed them through a combination of a concave and a convex lens. He placed the lenses in a tube to hold them more easily. This was the world's first refracting telescope.

A few years later, an Italian scientist, Galileo, was the first to point a telescope toward the stars. Galileo first learned of the Dutch invention in 1609. At the time, it was mainly used to see objects on Earth, such as distant ships and enemy armies. This is why the telescope was first called a "spyglass." Galileo made his own telescope and began using it to view the sky. Before this, Galileo had not been particularly interested in astronomy. That quickly changed as he recorded observations of the Moon's surface, spots on the Sun, and four moons circling Jupiter.

Another advance in telescope technology occurred in 1663 when James Gregory, a Scottish scientist, designed the first reflecting telescope. Unfortunately, it would take twenty-five years until Isaac Newton would build the first reflecting telescope. The earliest, most valuable contribution to astronomy made by an American was the construction of the Hooker telescope, a reflecting telescope on Mount Wilson. Completed in 1917, its 100-inch reflecting concave mirror allowed astronomers to see other galaxies clearly for the first time.

Since then, scientists have continued to design and build larger and larger telescopes. The development of the modern telescope is the result of many years of work by many scientists across the world.

Test-Taking Tip As you read the passage, make a timeline of the history of the telescope.

1. The telescope was first called a "spyglass" because it _____.

A) was helpful in observing the Moon and stars
B) was designed by Roger Bacon
C) could be used to watch other people
D) was first made by a Dutchman

2. According to the passage, scientists often _____.

F) use each other's work
G) are slow workers
H) aren't interested in many things
J) never read the work of other scientists

3. The earliest, most valuable contribution to astronomy made by an American was _____.

A) the first refracting telescope built in the 1600s
B) Roger Bacon's basic ideas about the operation of a telescope in the 1200s
C) the construction of the Hooker telescope on Mount Wilson which allowed astronomers to see other galaxies clearly for the first time
D) Using a telescope to view the Moon's surface, spots on the Sun, and four moons circling Jupiter

Reasoning and Skills

Power of a Lens

Lens	Diopter	Focal length (m)
1	1/4	4
2	1/5	5
3	1/6	6
4	1/7	7
5	1/9	?

1. Diopters are one way to measure the strength of a lens. What is the focal length of lens 5?

A) 5
B) 8
C) 9
D) 10

Test-Taking Tip Study the values for the first three lenses and consider how the diopter value is related to the focal length.

Famous Telescopes

Observatory	Mirror's Diameter(m)	Location	Altitude(m)
Roque de los Muchachos	4.2	Spain	2,400
Mauna Kea	10	U.S.(HI)	4,200
Russian Academy	6	Russia	2,070
Cerro Tololo	4	Chile	2,200

2. Reflecting telescopes use large mirrors to view distant objects. To reduce the amount of atmosphere that interferes with observing the stars, they are built atop of mountains. According to the table above, which of these telescopes is at the lowest altitude?

F) Roque de los Muchachos
G) Mauna Kea
H) Russian Academy
J) Cerro Tololo

Test-Taking Tip Read the table's column headings carefully and then reread the question.

CORNEA
RETINA
EYE

3. Which of these belongs with the group above?

A) concave lens
B) convex lens
C) plane mirror
D) convex mirror

Test-Taking Tip In your mind, review the differences between lens and mirrors and between concave and convex.

4. In the last 15 years, the National Aeronautics and Space Administration (NASA) has launched several telescopes into orbit around Earth. From space, these telescopes transmit electronic signals with the images of distant stars, planets and other galaxies. What are the advantages of using a telescope in space?

Test-Taking Tip Think about what has to happen for the light from a distant star to reach a telescope on Earth. Compare that to what has happen to that same light for it to reach a telescope in space.

Standardized Test Practice

Reasoning and Skills

Question 1: C

Students must study the chart and predict that the value of the focal length is the reciprocal of the diopter value.

Question 2: H

Students must study the table to find the data of interest. The *Russian Academy* is the observatory at the *lowest altitude.*

Question 3: A

Students must use their understanding of lenses and mirrors in order to identify that the words in the box are concerned with the human eye, which has a concave lens.

Question 4: Answers will vary.

Students should write a thorough response based on information from this unit.

UNIT 4

Unit Contents

Chapter 16
Solids, Liquids, and Gases
1 Kinetic Theory
2 Properties of Fluids
3 Behavior of Gases

Chapter 17
Classification of Matter
1 Composition of Matter
2 Properties of Matter

Chapter 18
Properties of Atoms and the Periodic Table
1 Structure of the Atom
2 Masses of Atoms
3 The Periodic Table

Chapter 19
Chemical Bonds
1 Stability in Bonding
2 Types of Bonds
3 Writing Formulas and Naming Compounds

Pre-Reading Activity

Have students find and identify any symbols and names of elements in the text.

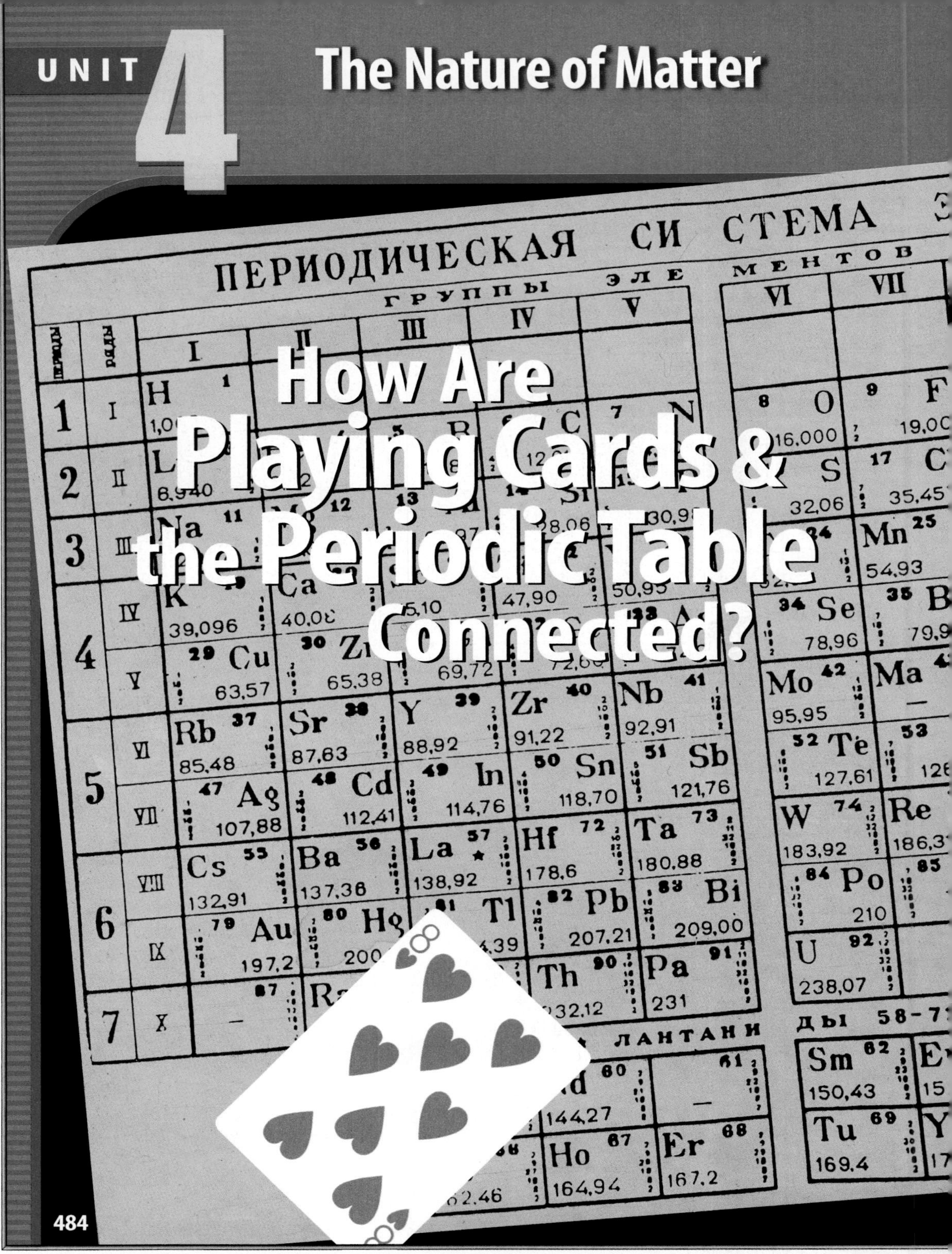

UNIT 4
The Nature of Matter
How Are Playing Cards & the Periodic Table Connected?
484

Teacher to Teacher

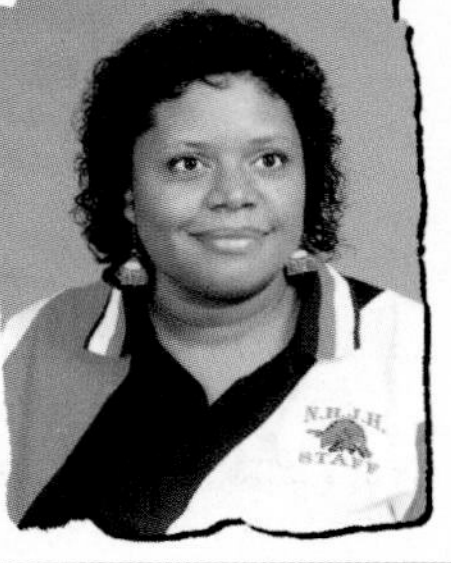

"Multicolored modeling clay is an inexpensive and reusable material for middle school students to use to visualize science concepts. Students use their creativity to make 'atoms' that have touchable protons, neutrons, and electrons."

Petrolia Moss, Teacher
North Heights Junior High
Texarkana, AR

By 1860, scientists knew of about 60 elements. However, they had yet to clearly organize their knowledge. A Russian scientist named Dmitri Mendeleev changed that. Mendeleev loved to play solitaire, a type of card game in which playing cards are arranged into patterns according to their properties. One day, Mendeleev decided to make a set of cards on which he wrote the names and properties of the known elements. Then he began to arrange the cards into rows. The result was a table in which certain chemical properties could be seen to occur periodically—that is, to occur in a repeating pattern. In 1869, Mendeleev published his "periodic table" (seen here in a more advanced version). He left blank spaces in the table where the pattern seemed to call for elements that were not yet known. Over the next several decades, other scientists refined the table, and new elements were added. Modern periodic tables—like the one probably hanging in your classroom—still follow the basic pattern laid out by Mendeleev.

SCIENCE CONNECTION

ELEMENTS Working as a class, investigate all the elements that make up the modern periodic table. Divide up the task so that every student researches 3 to 5 different elements. On index cards, record the name, symbol, and atomic number of each element, as well as whether it is a metal, nonmetal, or metalloid. Also include at least two physical and two chemical properties of each element. Assemble the cards on a bulletin board to create an "enhanced" periodic table.

SCIENCE Online
Internet Addresses

Explore the Glencoe Science Web site at **science.glencoe.com** to find out more about topics in this unit.

NATIONAL GEOGRAPHIC

Introducing the Unit

How Are Playing Cards & the Periodic Table Connected?

- Before class, tape cards from a deck of cards on poster board so that repeating patterns in the cards can be seen. Place all of one suit across a row, from an ace to a king. Ask students how all the cards in a row (period) are alike, and how all the cards in a column (family or group) are alike. They are all of one suit; the same card value is shown.
- Remind students that Mendeleev left blank spaces in his periodic table where elements seemed to be missing. Remove several cards at random from the poster board and ask students what cards belong in the empty spaces. Have them justify their answers and relate them to the empty spaces on Mendeleev's periodic table.

SCIENCE CONNECTION

Activity

Be sure that students receive a variety of elements to investigate. For example, a student might receive an alkali metal, a transition element, a noble gas, and an actinide. Advise them that they should be able to easily find all the required information for most elements, but the properties of some elements might be more difficult to research.

Section/Objectives	Standards		Activities/Features
	National	State/Local	
Chapter Opener	See p. 37T for a Key to Standards		**Explore Activity:** Observe the expansion and contraction of air, p. 487 **Before You Read,** p. 487
Section 1 Kinetic Theory 2 sessions 1 block 1. **Explain** the kinetic theory of matter. 2. **Describe** the particle movement in the four states of matter. 3. **Explain** particle behavior at the melting and boiling points.	National Content Standards: UCP3, UCP4, A2, B1, B3 (5–8), B2, B5, B6 (9–12), D1		**Health Integration,** p. 494 **Activity:** How Thermal Energy Affects Matter, p. 496
Section 2 Properties of Fluids 3 sessions 1.5 blocks 1. **Explain** Archimedes' principle. 2. **Explain** Pascal's principle. 3. **Explain** Bernoulli's principle and explain how we use it.	National Content Standards: UCP3, UCP4, A2, B1, (5–8), B2, B4 (9–12), D1, E1, E2		**MiniLAB:** Observing Density and Buoyancy of Substances, p. 498 **Math Skills Activity:** Calculating Forces Using Pascal's Principle, p. 499 **Science Online,** p. 500 **Earth Science Integration,** p. 501
Section 3 Behavior of Gases 5 sessions 2.5 blocks 1. **Explain** how a gas exerts pressure on its container. 2. **Explain** how a gas is affected when pressure, temperature, or volume is changed.	National Content Standards: UCP3, UCP4, A2, B1, (5–8), B2, B4, B6 (9–12), D1 (5–8), D1 (9–12)		**Visualizing Atmospheric Layers,** p. 503 **Science Online,** p. 505 **Math Skills Activity:** Using Boyle's Law, p. 505 **MiniLAB:** Observing Pressure, p. 506 **Activity:** Testing the Viscosity of Common Liquids, pp. 508–509 **Science Stats:** Hot and Cold, p. 510

Activity Materials	Reproducible Resources	Section Assessment	Technology
Explore Activity: balloon, tape measure, water, large beaker, hot plate	**Chapter Resources Booklet** Foldables Worksheet, p. 19 Note-taking Worksheets, pp. 35–37	GLENCOE'S ASSESSMENT ADVANTAGE	
Activity: 2 beakers, ring clamp, ring stand, wire mesh, Bunsen burner or hot plate, ice, thermometer	**Chapter Resources Booklet** Transparency Activity, p. 46 Enrichment, p. 32 Reinforcement, p. 29 Directed Reading, p. 22 Activity Worksheet, pp. 5–6 Transparency Activity, pp. 49–50	**Portfolio** Curriculum Connection, p. 491 Reteach, p. 495 **Performance** Skill Builder Activities, p. 495 **Content** Section Assessment, p. 495	Section Focus Transparency Teaching Transparency Interactive CD-ROM/DVD Guided Reading Audio Program
MiniLAB: 100-mL beakers (2), corn syrup, vegetable oil, food coloring, stirring straw, 0.5-cm square piece of aluminum foil, steel nut, whole pepper corn	**Chapter Resources Booklet** Transparency Activity, p. 47 MiniLAB, p. 3 Enrichment, p. 33 Reinforcement, p. 30 Directed Reading, p. 22 Lab Activities, pp. 9–11	**Portfolio** Active Reading, p. 498 **Performance** MiniLAB, p. 498 Skill Builder Activities, p. 501 **Content** Section Assessment, p. 501	Section Focus Transparency Interactive CD-ROM/DVD Guided Reading Audio Program
MiniLAB: balloon, beaker filled with ice water **Activity:** room-temperature household liquids such as dish detergent, motor oil, corn syrup, pancake syrup, shampoo, vegetable oil, vinegar, molasses, and water; spheres of known density, such as glass marbles or steel balls; graduated cylinders; ruler; stopwatch	**Chapter Resources Booklet** Transparency Activity, p. 48 MiniLAB, p. 4 Enrichment, p. 34 Reinforcement, p. 31 Directed Reading, pp. 23, 24 Activity Worksheet, pp. 7–8 Lab Activity, pp. 13–18	**Portfolio** Extension, p. 504 **Performance** MiniLAB, p. 506 Skill Builder Activities, p. 507 **Content** Section Assessment, p. 507	Section Focus Transparency Interactive CD-ROM/DVD Guided Reading Audio Program *Need materials?* Contact Science Kit at 1-800-828-7777 or www.sciencekit.com on the Internet.

End of Chapter Assessment

GLENCOE'S ASSESSMENT ADVANTAGE

Blackline Masters	Technology	Professional Series
Chapter Resources Booklet Chapter Review, pp. 39–40 Chapter Tests, pp. 41–44 **Standardized Test Practice by The Princeton Review,** pp. 68–71	MindJogger Videoquiz CD-ROM Explorations and Quizzes Vocabulary Puzzle Makers ExamView Pro Test Bank Interactive Lesson Planner Interactive Teacher's Edition	Performance Assessment in the Science Classroom (PASC)

Transparencies

Section Focus

SECTION 1 Section Focus Transparency **Water Works**

Sculptors use different materials to make works of art. Sculptors who use marble or wood expect their work to last for many years. Sculptors who carve ice know that their art will be short lived.

1. With regard to motion, what happens to molecules of water as ice melts?
2. What happens when water boils? Can water molecules go from the liquid phase to the gaseous phase at temperatures lower than the boiling point? Explain.
3. Does ice float or sink in water? What does that tell you about ice?

Solids, Liquids, L1

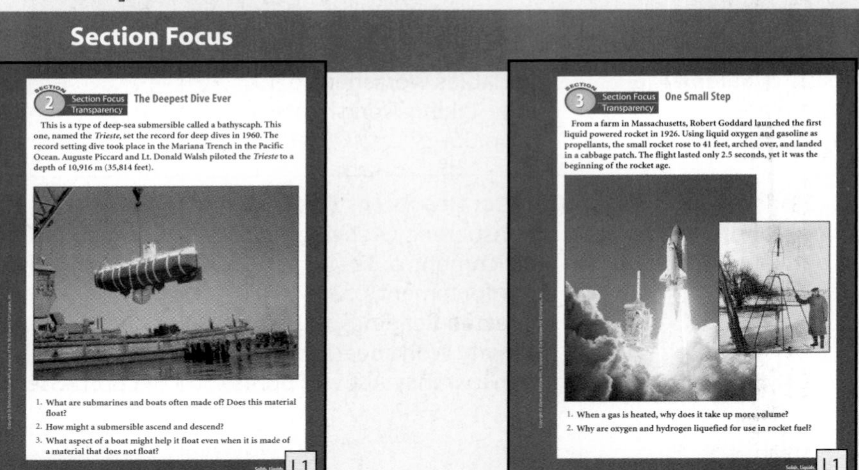

SECTION 2 Section Focus Transparency **The Deepest Dive Ever**

This is a type of deep-sea submersible called a bathyscaph. This one, named the *Trieste*, set the record for deep dives in 1960. The record setting dive took place in the Mariana Trench in the Pacific Ocean. Auguste Piccard and Lt. Donald Walsh piloted the *Trieste* to a depth of 10,916 m (35,814 feet).

1. What are submarines and boats often made of? Does this material float?
2. How might a submersible ascend and descend?
3. What aspect of a boat might help it float even when it is made of a material that does not float?

Solids, Liquids, L1

SECTION 3 Section Focus Transparency **One Small Step**

From a farm in Massachusetts, Robert Goddard launched the first liquid powered rocket in 1926. Using liquid oxygen and gasoline as propellants, the small rocket rose to 41 feet, arched over, and landed in a cabbage patch. The flight lasted only 2.5 seconds, yet it was the beginning of the rocket age.

1. When a gas is heated, why does it take up more volume?
2. Why are oxygen and hydrogen liquefied for use in rocket fuel?

Solids, Liquids, L1

This is a representation of key blackline masters available in the Teacher Classroom Resources. See Resource Manager boxes within the chapter for additional information.

Assessment

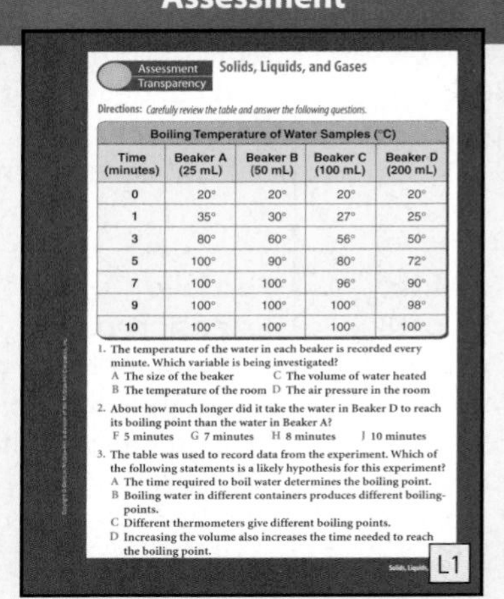

Assessment Transparency **Solids, Liquids, and Gases**

Directions: *Carefully review the table and answer the following questions.*

Boiling Temperature of Water Samples (°C)				
Time (minutes)	Beaker A (25 mL)	Beaker B (50 mL)	Beaker C (100 mL)	Beaker D (200 mL)
0	20°	20°	20°	20°
1	35°	30°	27°	25°
3	80°	60°	56°	50°
5	100°	90°	80°	72°
7	100°	100°	96°	90°
9	100°	100°	100°	98°
10	100°	100°	100°	100°

1. The temperature of the water in each beaker is recorded every minute. Which variable is being investigated?
   A The size of the beaker
   B The temperature of the room
   C The volume of water heated
   D The air pressure in the room
2. About how much longer did it take the water in Beaker D to reach its boiling point than the water in Beaker A?
   F 5 minutes G 7 minutes H 8 minutes J 10 minutes
3. The table was used to record data from the experiment. Which of the following statements is a likely hypothesis for this experiment?
   A The time required to boil water determines the boiling point.
   B Boiling water in different containers produces different boiling-points.
   C Different thermometers give different boiling points.
   D Increasing the volume also increases the time needed to reach the boiling point.

Solids, Liquids, L1

Teaching

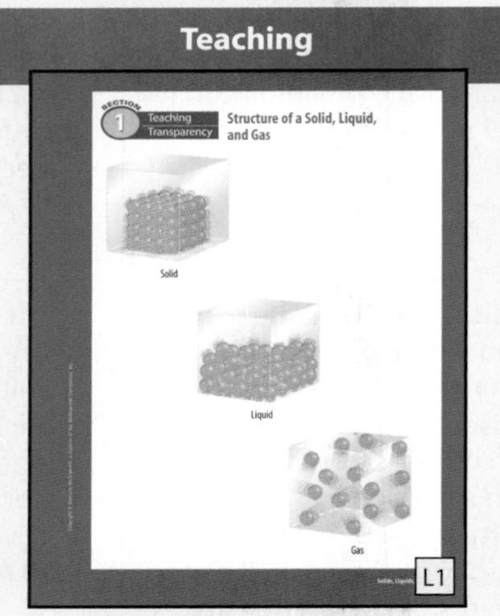

SECTION 1 Teaching Transparency **Structure of a Solid, Liquid, and Gas**

Solids, Liquids, L1

Key to Teaching Strategies

The following designations will help you decide which activities are appropriate for your students.

- L1 Level 1 activities should be appropriate for students with learning difficulties.
- L2 Level 2 activities should be within the ability range of all students.
- L3 Level 3 activities are designed for above-average students.
- ELL ELL activities should be within the ability range of English Language Learners.
- COOP LEARN Cooperative Learning activities are designed for small group work.
- LS Multiple Learning Styles logos are used throughout to indicate strategies that address different learning styles.
- P These strategies represent student products that can be placed into a best-work portfolio.

Hands-on Activities

Activity Worksheets

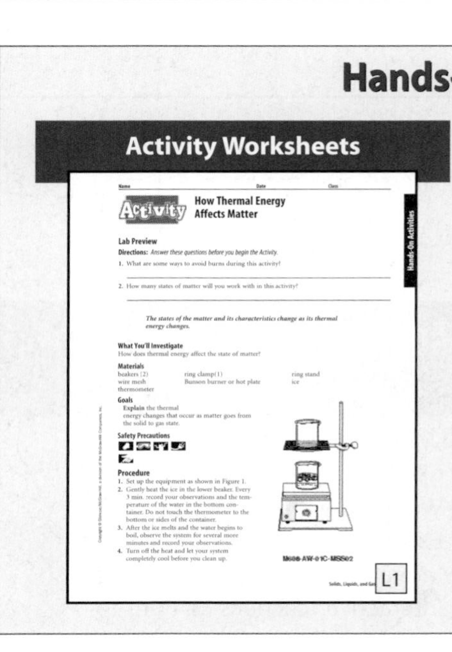

Name Date Class

Activity **How Thermal Energy Affects Matter**

Hands-On Activities

Lab Preview

Directions: *Answer these questions before you begin the Activity.*

1. What are some ways to avoid burns during this activity?
2. How many states of matter will you work with in this activity?

The states of the matter and its characteristics change as its thermal energy changes.

What You'll Investigate

How does thermal energy affect the state of matter?

Materials

beakers (2), wire mesh, thermometer, ring clamp(1), Bunson burner or hot plate, ring stand, ice

Goals

Explain the thermal energy changes that occur as matter goes from the solid to gas state.

Safety Precautions

Procedure

1. Set up the equipment as shown in Figure 1.
2. Gently heat the ice in the lower beaker. Every 3 min. record your observations and the temperature of the water in the bottom container. Do not touch the thermometer to the bottom or sides of the container.
3. After the ice melts and the water begins to boil, observe the system for several more minutes and record your observations.
4. Turn off the heat and let your system completely cool before you clean up.

Solids, Liquids, and Gases L1

Laboratory Activities

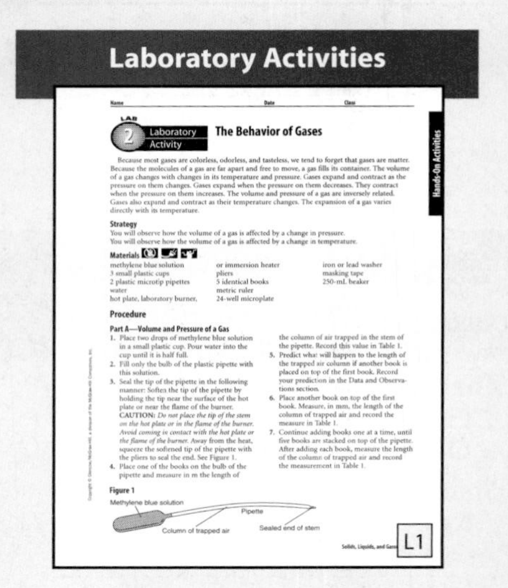

Name Date Class

LAB 2 Laboratory Activity **The Behavior of Gases**

Hands-On Activities

Because most gases are colorless, odorless, and tasteless, we tend to forget that gases are matter. Because the molecules of a gas are far apart and free to move, a gas fills its container. The volume of a gas changes with changes in its temperature and pressure. Gases expand and contract as the pressure on them changes. Gases expand when the pressure on them decreases. They contract when the pressure on them increases. The volume and pressure of a gas are inversely related. Gases also expand and contract as their temperature changes. The expansion of a gas varies directly with its temperature.

Strategy

You will observe how the volume of a gas is affected by a change in pressure.
You will observe how the volume of a gas is affected by a change in temperature.

Materials

methylene blue solution, 3 small plastic cups, 2 plastic microtip pipettes, water, hot plate, laboratory burner, or immersion heater, pliers, 5 identical books, metric ruler, 24-well microplate, iron or lead washer, masking tape, 250-mL beaker

Procedure

Part A—Volume and Pressure of a Gas

1. Place two drops of methylene blue solution in a small plastic cup. Pour water into the cup until it is half full.
2. Fill only the bulb of the plastic pipette with this solution.
3. Seal the tip of the pipette in the following manner: Soften the tip of the pipette by holding the tip near the surface of the hot plate or near the flame of the burner. CAUTION: *Do not place the tip of the stem on the hot plate or in the flame of the burner. Avoid coming in contact with the hot plate or the flame of the burner.* Away from the heat, squeeze the softened tip of the pipette with the pliers to seal the end. See Figure 1.
4. Place one of the books on the bulb of the pipette and measure in m the length of the column of air trapped in the stem of the pipette. Record this value in Table 1.
5. Predict what will happen to the length of the trapped air column if another book is placed on top of the first book. Record your prediction in the Data and Observations section.
6. Place another book on top of the first book. Measure, in mm, the length of the column of trapped air and record the measure in Table 1.
7. Continue adding books one at a time, until five books are stacked on top of the pipette. After adding each book, measure the length of the column of trapped air and record the measurement in Table 1.

Figure 1

Solids, Liquids, and Gases L1

Meeting Different Ability Levels

Content Outline

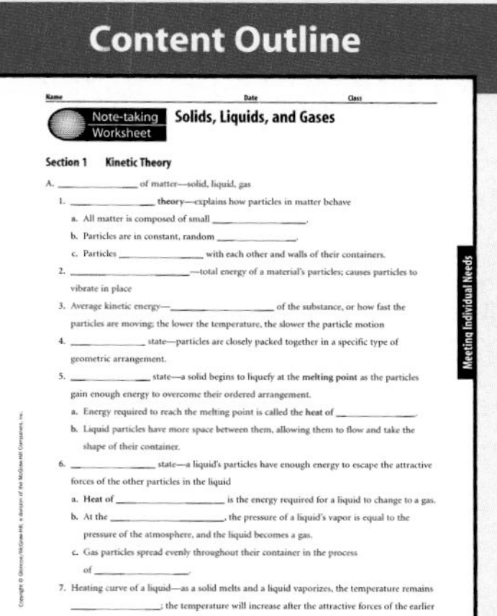
Note-taking Worksheet — Solids, Liquids, and Gases

Section 1 Kinetic Theory

L1

Reinforcement

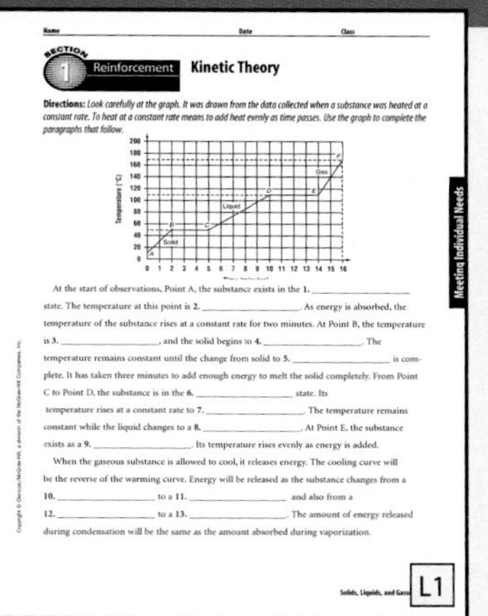
Section 1 Reinforcement — Kinetic Theory

L1

Directed Reading

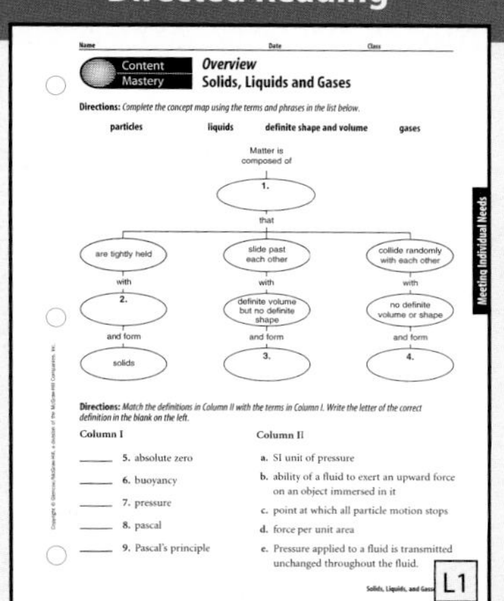
Content Mastery — Overview: Solids, Liquids and Gases

L1

Enrichment

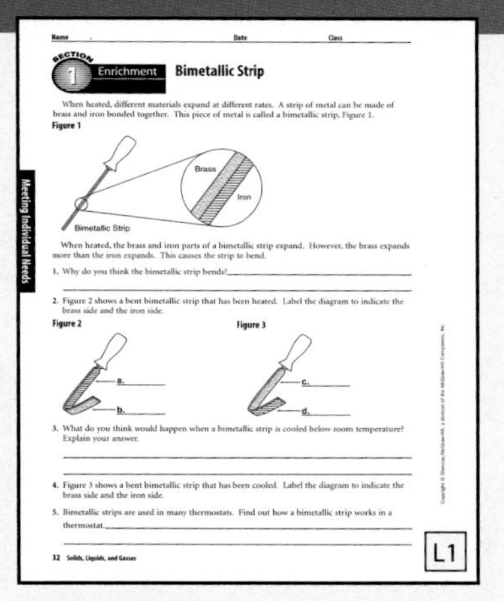
Section 1 Enrichment — Bimetallic Strip

L1

Spanish Directed Reading

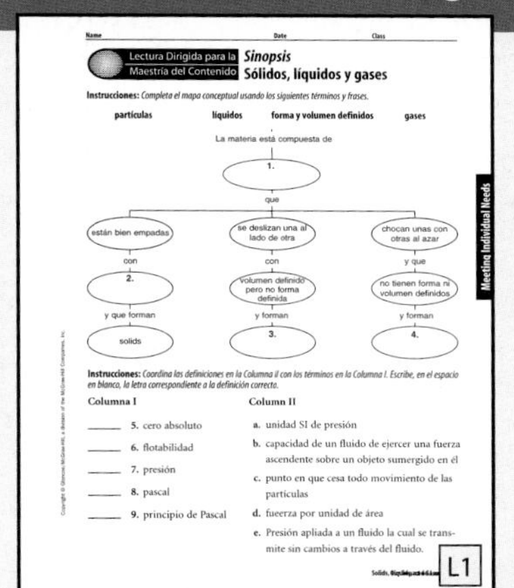
Lectura Dirigida para la Maestría del Contenido — Sinopsis: Sólidos, líquidos y gases

L1

Assessment

Chapter Tests

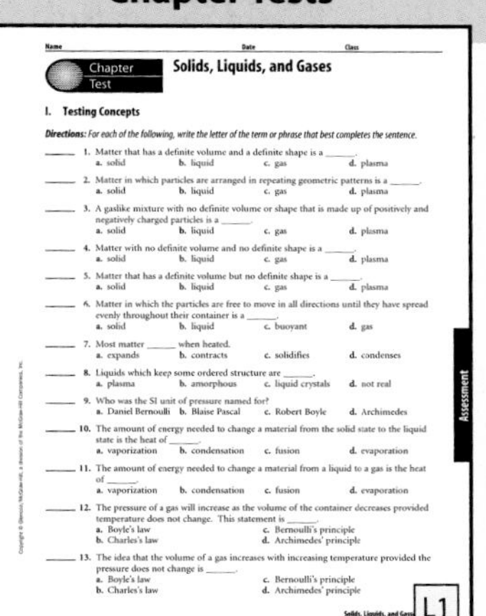
Chapter Test — Solids, Liquids, and Gases

I. Testing Concepts

L1

Test Practice Workbook

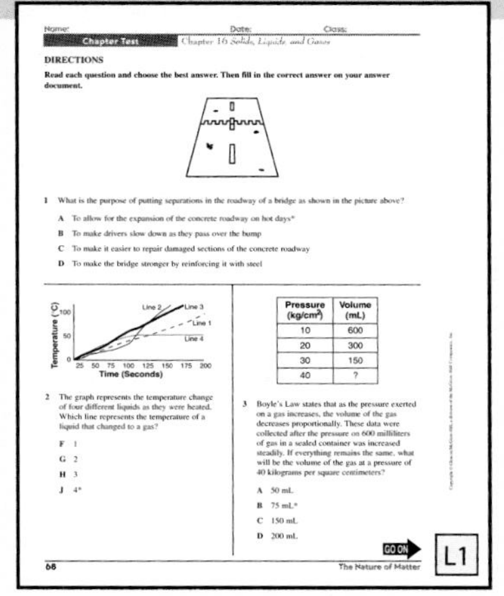
Chapter Test — Chapter 16 Solids, Liquids, and Gases

L1

Chapter Review

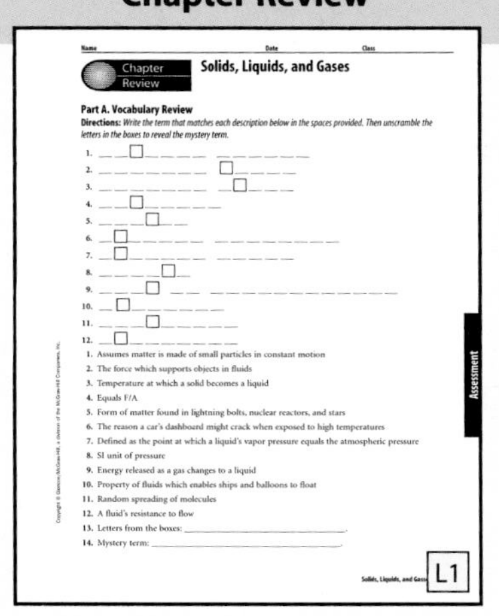
Chapter Review — Solids, Liquids, and Gases

Part A. Vocabulary Review

L1

Science Content Background

SECTION 1 Kinetic Theory

States of Matter

The Kelvin temperature scale begins at absolute zero, or 0 K. Scientists believe that at 0 K matter has no thermal energy. Each degree on the Kelvin scale is the same magnitude as a degree on the Celsius scale. The freezing point of water on the Celsius scale is 0 degrees; the freezing point of water on the Kelvin scale is 273 K. The average kinetic energy of the particles that make up a substance is directly proportional to the Kelvin temperature.

Matter is made of tiny particles separated by distances with nothing between the particles. The particles are in motion. In gases, the separation of the particles is the greatest because these particles are moving the fastest. The amount of space between the particles varies with temperature, volume, and pressure.

Student Misconception

Gases are made of special substances that are not composed of particles like other matter.

Refer to the facing page for teaching strategies to address this misconception. Refer to Section 1 for content related to this topic.

Bonnie Kamin/PhotoEdit

SECTION 2 Properties of Fluids

Bernoulli's Principle

Daniel Bernoulli was born to a family of renowned Swiss mathematicians. Over the course of his career, he worked not only in mathematics but in a number of other disciplines, such as medicine, biology, physiology, mechanics, physics, astronomy, and oceanography. It was for his work in mathematics, however, that Bernoulli was best known. In 1738 he discovered that the pressure in a fluid decreases as the velocity of the fluid increases. That work, called Bernoulli's Principle, remains the basis today for many engineering applications, such as aircraft-wing design. Between 1725 and 1749, Bernoulli won 10 prizes from the Paris Academy of Sciences for his work in astronomy, gravity, tides, magnetism, ocean currents, and the behavior of ships at sea.

SECTION 3 Behavior of Gases

Pressure

The work of Boyle, Charles, and others led to the formulation of a general theory to explain the behavior and properties of gases. This theory is called the kinetic-molecular theory. It ranks with the atomic theory as one of the greatest generalizations of modern science.

The kinetic-molecular theory is based on the motion of gas molecules. A gas that behaves exactly as outlined by the theory is known as an ideal gas. No ideal gases exist, but under certain conditions of temperature and pressure, real gases approach ideal behavior, or at least show only small deviations from it.

SCIENCE Online

For additional content background on this topic, go to the Glencoe Science Web site at science.glencoe.com.

Misconceptions

Find Out What Students Think

Students may think that . . .

- **Gases are made of special substances that are not composed of particles like other matter.**

Since students cannot see gases, they sometimes find it difficult to understand that gas particles exist, and that they are the same kinds of particles that make up solids and liquids.

Discussion

Draw Figure 1 on an overhead. Explain that the box is filled with a gas and that the pump removes some of the gas. Have students choose from Figure 2 the diagram that best represents what the setup looks like before and after the gas is removed. Have students discuss their ideas in small groups.

Figure 1.

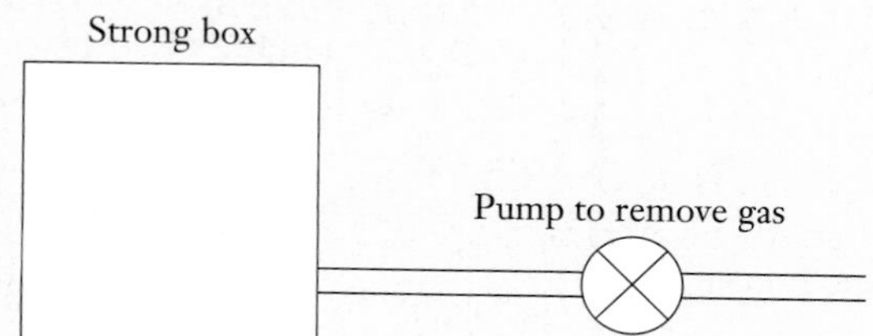

Figure 2.

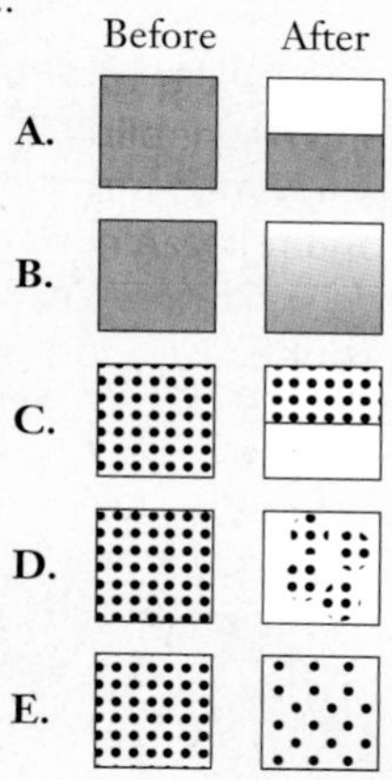

Before After

A.

B.

C.

D.

E.

Promote Understanding

Demonstration

Show students a bottle of vanilla. Open the bottle, and place it on a desk in the front of the room. Have students raise their hands when they can smell the vanilla. When most students can smell the vanilla, ask the following questions: **What did you smell? Did you smell a liquid or a gas? How did the vanilla extract go from being a liquid to being a gas?** Explain that the particles of vanilla that were in the liquid are the same particles that are now in the gas. Ask students to draw liquid vanilla in the bottle as particles, represented by dots. The dots in the bottle should be very close. Then have them draw vanilla as a gas. The dots should be far apart.

Follow up by having students draw the activity and its results as a cartoon strip. Suggest that the first frame show the bottle when it was first opened, the second frame show the scene when the first row of students started to smell the vanilla, and the third frame show the scene when the whole class smelled the vanilla.

Assess

After completing the chapter, see *Identifying Misconceptions* in the Study Guide.

CHAPTER 16

Solids, Liquids, and Gases

Chapter Vocabulary

kinetic theory
melting point
heat of fusion
heat of vaporization
boiling point
diffusion
plasma
thermal expansion
buoyancy
pressure
viscosity
pascal

What do you think?

Science Journal This photograph shows crystals of frost, which is a form of frozen water.

CHAPTER 16

Solids, Liquids, and Gases

If you were traveling on this scenic highway, you couldn't help but notice the lake beside the road and the beautiful snow-capped mountain in the distance. You might even notice the low-lying clouds nestled in the mountain range. This scene provides one of nature's rare opportunities to view water in all of its three states—solid, liquid, and gas.

What do you think?

Science Journal Look at the picture below with a classmate. Discuss what you think this might be. Here's a hint: *It may be on your windows on a cold winter day.* Write your answer or best guess in your Science Journal.

486

Theme Connection

Energy The kinetic energy of the particles in a substance plays a major role in determining whether the substance is in the solid, liquid, or gas state. The kinetic energy of the particles of fluids also helps determine the viscosity and pressure exerted by the fluids.

Why does the mercury in a thermometer rise? Why do sidewalks have cracks? The answer to these questions is heat. Most substances expand when heated and contract when cooled as you will see during this activity.

Saftey Precautions Use caution when handling hot items.

Observe the expansion and contraction of air

1. Blow up a balloon until it is half filled. Use a tape measure to measure the circumference of the balloon.
2. Pour water into a large beaker until it is half full. Place the beaker on a hotplate and wait for the water to boil.
3. Set the balloon on the mouth of beaker and observe for five minutes. Be careful not to allow the balloon to touch the hotplate. Measure the circumference of the balloon.

Observe

Write a paragraph in your Science Journal comparing the changing size of the balloon's diameter. Infer why the balloon's diameter changed.

Before You Read

FOLDABLES Reading & Study Skills

Making a Concept Map Study Fold Make the following Foldable to help you organize information and by diagramming ideas about solids, liquids, and gases.

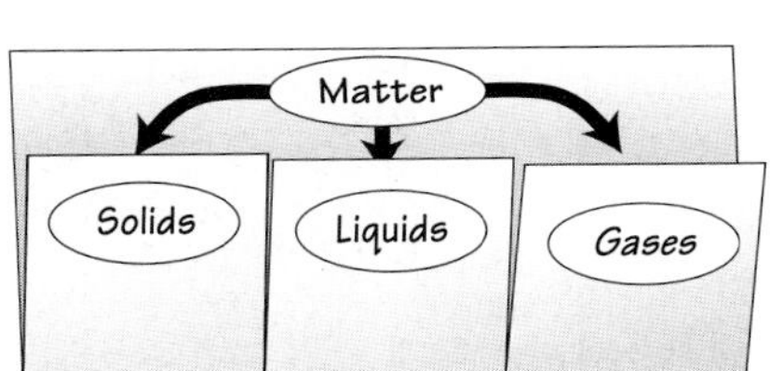

1. Place a sheet of paper in front of you so the long side is at the top. Fold the bottom of the paper to the top, stopping about 4 cm from the top.
2. Draw an oval above the fold. Write *Matter* inside the oval.
3. Fold both sides in and then unfold. Through the top thickness of the paper, cut along each of the fold lines to form three tabs.
4. Label the tabs *Solids, Liquids,* and *Gases* and draw an oval around each word. Draw arrows from the large oval to the smaller ovals.
5. Before you read, list examples of each you already know on the front of the tabs. As you read the chapter, add to your lists.

487

EXPLORE ACTIVITY

Purpose Use the Explore activity to introduce students to the fact that matter changes as temperature changes.

Preparation Before students do this activity, obtain metric tape measures and locate a convenient refrigerator where students can put their balloons.

Materials balloon, tape measure, large beaker, hot plate, water

Teaching Strategy Help students set up data tables in which to record their measurements.

Observe

The balloon expanded when placed over the boiling water. The heat of the steam increased the energy of the air molecules in the balloon, causing them to move faster and make the balloon expand.

Assessment

Process Ask students how the results of this activity would have been different if they had put water in the balloon instead of air. The balloon would not have expanded much when it was heated. Use **Performance Assessment in the Science Classroom,** p. 89.

Before You Read

FOLDABLES Reading & Study Skills

Dinah Zike Study Fold

Purpose Students make and use a Foldable to review what they know about the three most common states of matter before they read the chapter and to list examples and collect information as they read.

For additional help, see Foldables Worksheet, p. 19 in **Chapter Resources Booklet,** or go to the Glencoe Science Web site at **science.glencoe.com.** See After You Read in the Study Guide at the end of this chapter.

SECTION

Kinetic Theory

1 Motivate

Bellringer Transparency

Display the Section Focus Transparency for Section 1. Use the accompanying Transparency Activity Master. L2 ELL

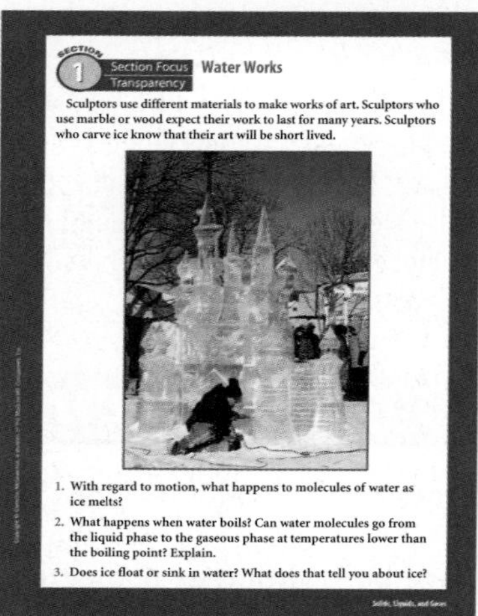

Section 1 Section Focus Transparency Water Works

Sculptors use different materials to make works of art. Sculptors who use marble or wood expect their work to last for many years. Sculptors who carve ice know that their art will be short lived.

1. With regard to motion, what happens to molecules of water as ice melts?
2. What happens when water boils? Can water molecules go from the liquid phase to the gaseous phase at temperatures lower than the boiling point? Explain.
3. Does ice float or sink in water? What does that tell you about ice?

Tie to Prior Knowledge

Ask students if they have ever heard of fuel line freeze-up or vapor lock. With vapor lock, which usually happens in the summer, fuel vaporizes at a hot spot, causing a fuel line to partially fill with vapor. This causes problems for a car's fuel pump, which is designed to pump a liquid, not a vapor. In winter, water from condensation in the gasoline tank can freeze and block the fuel line. Discuss with students how temperature affects the state of matter of the fuel.

SECTION 1

Kinetic Theory

As You Read

What You'll Learn

- **Explain** the kinetic theory of matter.
- **Describe** particle movement in the four states of matter.
- **Explain** particle behavior at the melting and boiling points.

Vocabulary

kinetic theory, melting point, heat of fusion, heat of vaporization, boiling point, diffusion, plasma, thermal expansion

Why It's Important

You can use energy that is lost or gained when a substance changes from one state to another.

States of Matter

If you don't finish lunch quickly, you'll be late for practice. The soup is boiling on the stove. You hastily pour the soup into the bowl, but now it's too hot to eat. You add an ice cube and stir. The soup's temperature drops—now you can eat it without burning your tongue. Does this sound familiar? If you look closely at the situation, as shown in **Figure 1,** you can identify three states or phases of matter—solid, liquid, and gas. The boiling soup on the stove is in the liquid state. The water vapor directly above the boiling soup is the gaseous state. The ice cube you dropped into your soup is in the solid state. Do these states have anything in common? How do they differ? Take a closer look at what is going on at the particle level in the three states of matter.

Kinetic Theory The **kinetic theory** is an explanation of how particles in matter behave. To explain the behavior of particles, it is necessary to make some basic assumptions. The three assumptions of the kinetic theory are as follows:

1. All matter is composed of small particles.
2. These particles are in constant, random motion.
3. These particles are colliding with each other and the walls of their container.

In reality, molecules do lose some energy during collisions with other molecules. But the amount of energy lost is very small and can be neglected in most cases.

To visualize the kinetic theory, think of each particle as a tiny table tennis ball in constant motion. These balls are bouncing and colliding with each other. Mentally visualizing matter in this way can help you understand the movement of particles in matter.

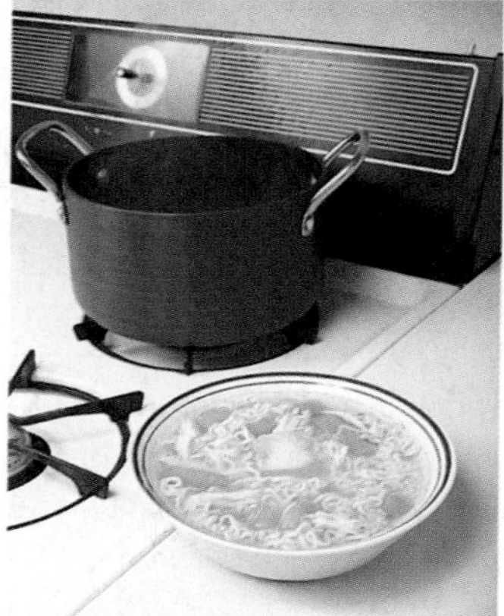

Figure 1
The states of water are present in this photograph.
Can you find the solid, liquid, and gaseous states?

Section Assessment Planner

PORTFOLIO
Curriculum Connection, p. 491
Reteach, p. 495

PERFORMANCE ASSESSMENT
Skill Builder Activities, p. 495
See page 514 for more options.

CONTENT ASSESSMENT
Section, p. 495
Challenge, p. 495
Chapter, pp. 514–515

Thermal Energy Think about the ice cube in the soup. Does the ice cube appear to be moving? How can a frozen, solid ice cube have motion? Remember to focus on the particles. Atoms in solids are held tightly in place by the attraction between the particles. This attraction between the particles gives solids a definite shape and volume. However, the thermal energy in the particles causes them to vibrate in place. Thermal energy is the total energy of a material's particles, including kinetic—vibrations and movement within and between the particles—and potential—resulting from forces that act within or between particles. When the temperature of the substance is lowered, the particles will have less thermal energy and will vibrate more slowly.

Reading Check *What is thermal energy?*

Solid

Figure 2
The particles in a solid are packed together tightly and are constantly vibrating in place.

Average Kinetic Energy Temperature is the term used to explain how hot or cold an object is. In science, temperature means the average kinetic energy in the substance, or how fast the particles are moving. Molecules of frozen water at 0°C will move much slower than molecules of water at 100°C. Therefore, water molecules at 0°C have lower average kinetic energy than the molecules at 100°C. Molecules will have some movement and energy at all temperatures, except at absolute zero. Scientists theorize that absolute zero, or –273.15°C, particle motion is so slow that thermal energy is not present.

Reading Check *How are kinetic energy and temperature related?*

Solid State An ice cube is an example of a solid. The particles of a solid are closely packed together, as shown in **Figure 2.** Most solid materials have a specific type of geometric arrangement in which they form when cooled. The type of geometric arrangement formed by a solid is important. Chemical and physical properties of solids often can be attributed to the type of geometric arrangement that the solid forms. **Figure 3** shows the geometric arrangement of water. Notice that the hydrogen and oxygen atoms are alternately spaced in the arrangement.

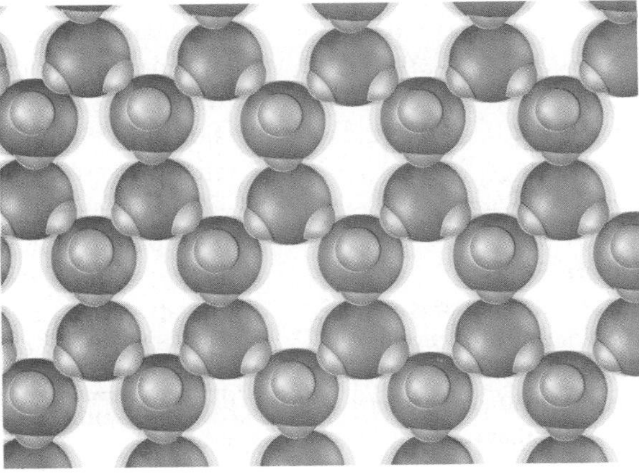

Figure 3
The particles in water align themselves in an ordered geometric pattern. Even though a solid ice cube doesn't look like it is moving, its molecules are vibrating in place.

2 Teach

States of Matter

Caption Answer

Figure 1 All of the hard objects in the photo are solids, including the pot, the bowl, and the stove. Liquids are the water in the pot and the milk in the bowl. Gases are any steam that is pouring off the hot cereal or out of the pot.

Reading Check

Answer the total energy of a material's particles, including both kinetic and potential energy

Quick Demo

Have students observe the regular, cubic shape of salt crystals under a microscope or with a hand lens. L1 ELL
Visual-Spatial

Extension

Cryogenics is the study of matter at low temperatures. Ask interested students to research how the properties of a solid change near absolute zero. Near absolute zero, matter acquires superfluidity, superconductivity, and superdiamagnetism. L3 **Linguistic**

Reading Check

Answer Temperature is the average kinetic energy of the molecules of a substance.

Resource Manager 

Chapter Resources Booklet

- Transparency Activity, p. 46
- Directed Reading for Content Mastery, p. 22
- Note-taking Worksheets, pp. 35–37

Inclusion Strategies

Gifted Have teams of students prepare written statements explaining how oil companies deal with the problems of fuel line freeze-up and vapor lock. Refineries make different gasoline blends for different seasons and different geographical locations. L3
COOP LEARN **Logical-Mathematical**

States of Matter, continued

Reading Check

Answer the amount of energy required to change a substance from the solid state to the liquid state

Use an Analogy

States of matter are like the crowd at a sporting event. When seated, people are like particles in a solid. They can move in place but don't go anywhere. The people in the aisles are like particles in a liquid. They move past each other but aren't free to move far apart. Upon reaching the parking lot, the people are free to move randomly, as are particles in a gas.

Reading Check

Answer 1. The particles in a liquid are far enough apart to allow the particles to flow past each other. 2. The particles have gained enough kinetic energy to escape the attractive forces in the liquid.

Activity

Have a student place five drops of vanilla flavoring into a balloon, blow up the balloon, tie it closed, then smell near the surface of the balloon. Ask students to explain their observations using the kinetic theory. Students will detect the aroma of vanilla as it evaporates inside the balloon. The moving molecules of vanilla passed between the molecules of the stretched balloon. L1 ELL IN **Kinesthetic**

Figure 4
The particles in a liquid are farther apart and moving more freely than the particles in a solid. The extra space between the particles allows liquids to flow.

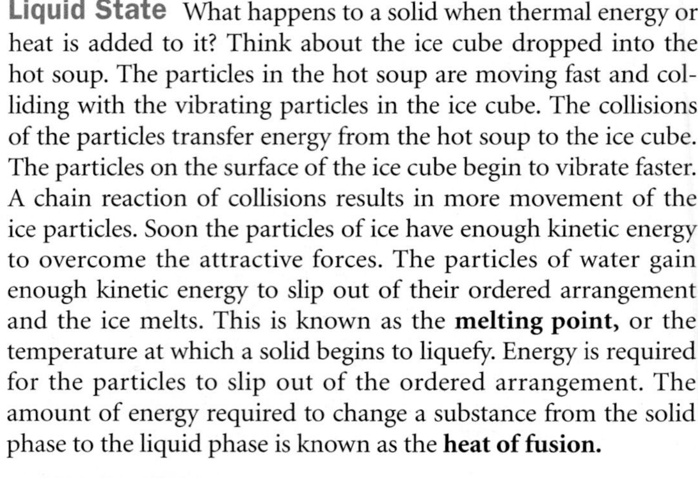

Liquid State What happens to a solid when thermal energy or heat is added to it? Think about the ice cube dropped into the hot soup. The particles in the hot soup are moving fast and colliding with the vibrating particles in the ice cube. The collisions of the particles transfer energy from the hot soup to the ice cube. The particles on the surface of the ice cube begin to vibrate faster. A chain reaction of collisions results in more movement of the ice particles. Soon the particles of ice have enough kinetic energy to overcome the attractive forces. The particles of water gain enough kinetic energy to slip out of their ordered arrangement and the ice melts. This is known as the **melting point,** or the temperature at which a solid begins to liquefy. Energy is required for the particles to slip out of the ordered arrangement. The amount of energy required to change a substance from the solid phase to the liquid phase is known as the **heat of fusion.**

Reading Check *What is heat of fusion?*

Liquids Flow Particles in a liquid, shown in **Figure 4,** are not tightly held in a rigid shape. More space exists between the particles of most liquids than existed between the same particles in solid form. This extra space allows particles to slide past each other allowing liquids to flow and take the shape of their container. The particles in a liquid have some remaining attractive force for each other. This causes the particles to cling together, giving liquids a definite volume.

Reading Check *Why do liquids flow?*

Gaseous State How does a liquid become a gas? According to the kinetic theory, the particles in a gas are in constant motion. If you look at steam rising above a pan on the stove, this movement is not difficult to visualize. The tiny particles of gas are moving quickly and randomly. The particles of a gas are moving faster now than they were in the liquid, and more collisions are taking place. The vapor molecules built up enough energy to escape the attractive forces of the other particles in the liquid, as shown in **Figure 5,** and have escaped into the room. This point is known as the boiling point. **Heat of vaporization** is the amount of energy required for the particles to overcome the attractive forces within the liquid or the energy required to change from a liquid to a gas.

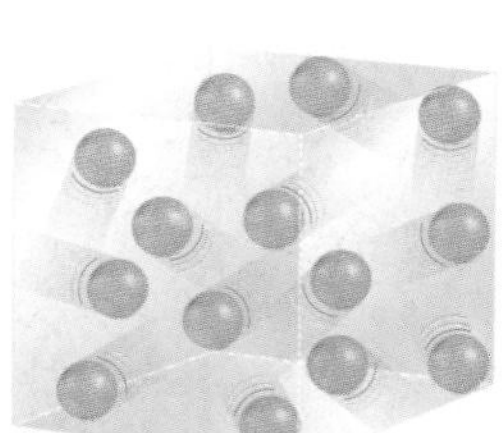

Figure 5
In gases, the particles are far apart and no attractive forces exist between the particles. Gases do not have a definite volume or shape.

Reading Check *What occurs on a molecular level when a liquid begins to boil?*

LAB DEMONSTRATION

Purpose to compare a substance in its solid, liquid, and gas states

Materials moth crystals (naphthalene), test tube, stopper, hot plate, 400-mL beaker, test-tube holder

Safety Precautions Do not allow students to inhale vapors.

Procedure Have students observe moth crystals in a stoppered test tube. Place the unstoppered test tube in boiling water until the crystals melt. Have students observe the liquid. By this time, the distinctive odor of naphthalene vapors will be present.

Expected Outcome Students should observe differences between the states of matter.

Relate the role of energy to melting and vaporization. Adding energy increases the kinetic energy of the particles. If enough energy is added, a solid will melt and a liquid will vaporize.

Boiling Point The **boiling point** of a liquid is the temperature at which the pressure of its vapor is equal to the pressure of the atmosphere. At the boiling point, the gas particles are able to escape the attractive force in the liquid. Atmospheric pressure is a force pushing down upon a liquid, keeping the particles from escaping. The particles require more kinetic energy to overcome this force. The temperature of the liquid must be raised to supply the extra kinetic energy required to overcome the force of the atmosphere. Above sea level, water boils at a lower temperature, due to the decreased atmospheric pressure.

Reading Check *How does atmospheric pressure affect the boiling point of a liquid?*

Gases Fill Their Container What happens to the attractive forces between the particles in a gas? The gas particles are moving so quickly and are so far apart that they have lost the attractive force between them. **Figure 6** shows how the particles of a gas might appear. Because no attractive forces exist between them, gases do not have a definite shape or a definite volume. The rapid movement and lack of attraction between the particles give gases a property known as diffusion. **Diffusion** is the spreading of particles throughout a given volume until they are uniformly distributed. For example, if you spray air freshener in one corner of a room, it's not long before you smell the scent all over the room. The particles of gas have moved, collided, and "filled" their container—the room. The particles have diffused. Gases will fill the container that they are in even if the container is a room. The particles continue to move and collide in a random motion within their container.

Figure 6
As the molecules gain more thermal energy from the heat source, they start moving faster. Soon molecules will have enough energy to escape the attractive forces of the liquid.

Activity

Have students examine the labels of foods such as cake mixes. On Earth, air pressure decreases as altitude increases. Have students determine the effect of altitude on cooking time and temperature for these items. L2 LS **Linguistic**

Reading Check

Answer The higher the atmospheric pressure, the higher the boiling point.

IDENTIFYING Misconceptions

Students may think that gases are made of special substances that are not composed of particles like other matter. See page 486F for teaching strategies that address this misconception.

Fun Fact

At room temperature, oxygen gas molecules have an average speed of 1,700 km/h.

Resource Manager

Chapter Resources Booklet
Enrichment, p. 32
Reading and Writing Skill Activities, p.33

Curriculum Connection

Art Have students visit shopping malls and observe how matter in different states is used to decorate the mall and make shopping more pleasant. Have them write about what they see. Items seen may include fountains (liquid), helium-filled balloons (gas), marble floors (solid), and fluorescent and neon lighting (gases). L2 LS **Visual-Spatial** P

States of Matter, continued

Remind students that even though gases fill the volume of their container, almost all of a gas is empty space. The volume of a container of gas is much greater than the total volume of the gas particles.

Reading Check

Answer The particles are gaining energy and are in the process of changing state.

Use Science Words

Word Meaning Have students find the meaning of the word *plasma* as it is used by biologists and compare that to the meaning as used by physicists. To a biologist, plasma is the colorless fluid part of blood, i.e., blood stripped of red blood cells. To a physicist, plasma is matter in which electrons have been stripped away from the protons and neutrons. L2 ELL LS **Linguistic**

Fun Fact

Unlike most gases, plasmas conduct electricity well and are affected by magnetic fields. Also, while the particles that make up gases move randomly, sometimes the electrons and ions that make up plasmas move together in a wavelike motion.

Reading Check

Answer a gas consisting of positively and negatively charged particles

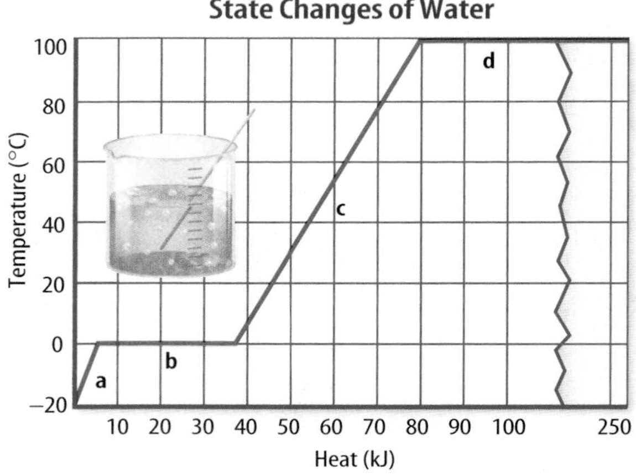

Figure 7
This graph shows the heating curve of water. At A and C the water is increasing in kinetic energy. At B and D the added energy is used to overcome the bonds between the particles.

Heating Curve of a Liquid A graph of water being heated from –20°C to 100°C is shown in **Figure 7.** This type of graph is called a heating curve because it shows the temperature change of water as thermal energy or heat is added. Notice the two areas on the graph where the temperature does not change. At 0°C, ice is melting. All of the energy put into the ice at this temperature is used to overcome the attractive forces between the particles in the solid. The temperature remains constant during melting. After the attractive forces are overcome, particles move more freely and their kinetic energy or temperature increases. At 100°C, water is boiling or vaporizing and the temperature remains constant again. All of the energy that is put into the water goes to overcoming the remaining attractive forces between the water particles. When all of the attractive forces in the water are broken, the energy goes to increasing the kinetic energy or temperature of the particles.

Reading Check ***What is occurring at the two temperatures on the heat curve where the graph is a flat line?***

Plasma State So far, you've learned about the three familiar states of matter—solids, liquids, and gases. But none of these is the most common state of matter in the universe. Scientists estimate that 99 percent of the matter in the universe is plasma. **Plasma** is gas consisting of positively and negatively charge particles. Although this high-temperature gas contains positive and negative particles, the overall charge of the gas is neutral because equal numbers of both charges are present. Recall that particles of matter move faster as the matter is heated to higher temperatures. The faster the particles move the greater the force is with which they collide. The forces produced from high-energy collisions are so great that electrons from the atom are stripped off. This state of matter is called plasma. All of the observed stars including the Sun, shown in **Figure 8,** consist of plasma. Plasma also is found in lightning bolts, neon and fluorescent tubes, and auroras.

Figure 8
Stars including the Sun contain matter that is in the plasma phase. Plasma exists where the temperature is extremely high.

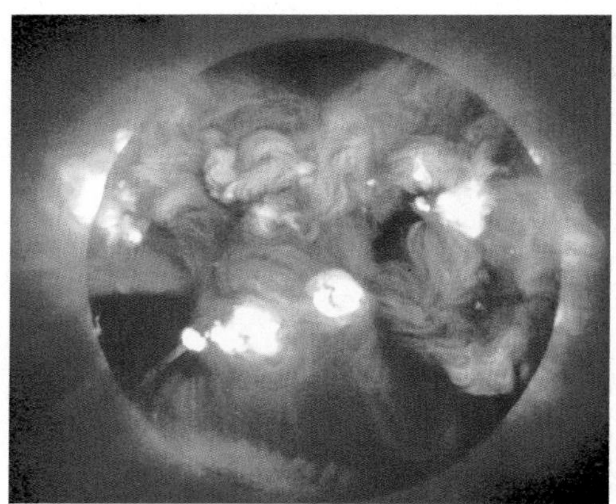

Reading Check ***What is plasma?***

Teacher FYI

At 1 atm, water freezes at 0°C and boils at 100°C. At different pressures, water goes through these changes at different temperatures. In fact, when the pressure is 0.61 kPA and the temperature is 0.01°C, water can exist as a solid, a liquid, and a gas. This point is called the triple point of water.

Visual Learning

Figure 7 Ask a volunteer to read aloud the section of the SE text that describes the graph while the rest of the students follow the graph with their fingers. Discuss with students the effect of adding heat to water at different temperatures. L1 ELL LS **Auditory-Musical**

Thermal Expansion

You have learned how the kinetic theory is used to explain the behavior of molecules in different states of matter. The kinetic theory also explains other characteristics of matter in the world around you. Have you noticed the seams in a concrete driveway or sidewalk? Contractors often will leave a gap between the sections to clearly separate them. These separation lines are called expansion joints. When concrete absorbs heat, it expands. Then when it cools, it contracts. If expansion joints are not used, the concrete will crack when the temperature changes.

Expansion of Matter The kinetic theory can be used to explain this behavior in concrete. Recall that molecules move faster and separate as the temperature rises. This separation of molecules results in an expansion of the entire object known as thermal expansion. **Thermal expansion** is an increase in the size of a substance when the temperature is increased. The kinetic theory can be used to explain the contraction in objects, too. When the temperature of an object is lowered, molecules slow down. The attraction between the molecules increases and the molecules move closer together. The movements of the molecules closer together results in an overall shrinking of the object known as contraction.

Figure 9
As the thermometer is heated, the column of liquid in the thermometer expands. As the temperature cools, the liquid in the thermometer contracts.

Expansion in Liquids Expansion and contraction occurs in most solids, liquids, and gases. A common example of expansion in liquids occurs in thermometers, as shown in **Figure 9.** The addition of energy causes the molecules in the liquid in the thermometer to move faster. The molecules in the liquid in the narrow thermometer tube start to move farther apart as their motion increases. The molecules have to expand only slightly to show a large change on the temperature scale.

Expansion in Gases **Figure 10** is an example of thermal expansion in gases. Hot-air balloons are able to rise due to thermal expansion of air. The air in the balloon is heated, causing the distance between the molecules in the air to expand. As the air in the hot-air balloon expands, the number of molecules per cubic centimeter decreases. This expansion results in a decreased density of the hot air. Because the density of the air in the hot-air balloon is lower than the cool air outside, the balloon will rise.

Figure 10
Heating the air in this hot-air balloon causes the gas molecules in the air to separate creating a lower density inside the balloon.

Thermal Expansion

Quick Demo

Bring to class two identical jars with lids that are sealed and difficult to remove. Have a student attempt to open one of the jars. Place the other lid in hot water for a few minutes. Have the same student attempt to open that jar. Warming the jar lid causes thermal expansion, making the jar easier to open.
L2 ELL LS **Kinesthetic**

Discussion

Sealing food containers is important to preserve freshness and prevent spoilage. Discuss with students two reasons a lid put on a food container when it is warm might become tight as the food cools. Inside the container, warm gases gradually cool, causing the pressure inside the container to drop. Then the pressure outside the container is greater than the pressure inside the container, and the lid has a tighter seal. Also, when the lid placed on the warm container begins to cool, it contracts slightly, causing it to fit more tightly on the container. L3
LS **Logical-Mathematical**

Visual Learning

Figure 9 Most thermometers contain either alcohol or mercury. Ask students how the design of a thermometer depends on the liquid used in it. The size of the bulb and tube are determined by the rate of expansion of the liquid used in the particular thermometer. L2 LS **Logical-Mathematical**

Resource Manager

Science Inquiry Labs, p. 43

Science Journal

Weathering Soils form from the breaking down of rocks. Have students find out and write in their Science Journals the role played by thermal expansion in the weathering of rocks. Rocks are often broken down, or weathered, when water enters cracks in the rocks and then freezes. The expansion of the water as it freezes breaks up the rock. L2
LS **Linguistic**

Thermal Expansion, continued

Visual Learning

Figure 11 Explain to students that the charged parts of the water molecules do not have as much charge as an electron or proton. To show a partial charge, the lowercase Greek letter delta (δ) is used with a sign to show positive (δ^+) or negative (δ^-) charge. Have students draw a picture of a water molecule with partial charges shown. Drawings should show two hydrogen atoms connected to one oxygen atom with a (δ^-) by the oxygen atom, and a (δ^+) by each of the hydrogen atoms. L2

LS Visual-Spatial

Solid or a Liquid?

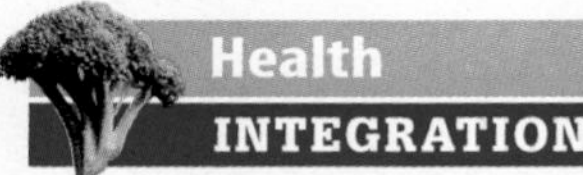

Health INTEGRATION

Answers will vary. Accept all reasonable responses. Bring to class several liquid crystal thermometers. Allow students to place them against their skin to see how the color of the liquid changes as the temperature changes. Ask what advantage liquid crystal thermometers have over mercury thermometers. They eliminate the danger of mercury, which is poisonous.

Reading Check

Answer glass and plastics

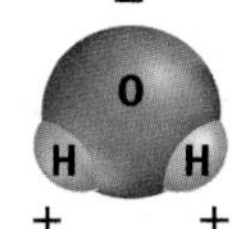

Figure 11
The positively and negatively charged regions on a water molecule interact to create empty spaces in the crystal lattice. These interactions cause water to expand when it is in the solid phase.

The Strange Behavior of Water Normally, substances expand as the temperature rises, because the molecules move farther apart. An exception to this rule, however, is water. Water molecules are unusual in that they have highly positive and highly negative areas. **Figure 11** is a diagram of the water molecule showing these charged regions. These charged regions affect the behavior of water. As the temperature of water drops, the particles move closer together. The unlike charges will be attracted to each other and line up so that only positive and negative zones are near each other. Because the water molecules orient themselves according to charge, empty spaces occur in the structure. These empty spaces are larger in solids than in liquids, so water expands when going from a liquid to a solid state. That is why ice floats on the top of lakes in the winter.

Solid or a Liquid?

There are other substances that have unusual behavior when changing states. Amorphous solids and liquid crystals are two classes of materials that do not react as you would expect when they are changing states. How do these two groups of materials behave?

Amorphous Solids Ice melts at 0°C, gold melts at 1,064°C and lead melts at 327°C. But not all solids have a definite temperature at which they change from solid to liquid. Some solids merely soften and gradually turn into a liquid over a temperature range. There is not an exact temperature like a boiling point where the phase change occurs. These solids lack the highly ordered structure found in crystals. They are known as amorphous solids from the Greek word for "without form."

You are familiar with two amorphous solids—glass and plastics. The particles that make up amorphous solids are typically long, chainlike structures that can get jumbled and twisted instead of being neatly stacked into geometric arrangements. Interactions between the particles occur along the chain, which gives amorphous solids some properties that are very different from crystalline solids.

For example, glass appears to be a solid, but glass windows actually change over time. In old houses if you measure the thickness of the top and bottom windowpane, you will find that the top is thinner than the bottom. Because of the gravitational pull and the lack of crystalline structure, the glass in the windowpane will flow to the bottom over time.

Health INTEGRATION

Some liquid crystals can form thin layers that are one molecule thick. These liquid crystals react to tiny temperature changes by changing color making them useful in determining temperature changes over the surface of the skin such as in a thermometer. In your Science Journal, identify other possible uses for this type of liquid crystal.

Reading Check *What are two examples of amorphous solids?*

Resource Manager

Chapter Resources Booklet
Transparency Activity, pp. 49–50
Cultural Diversity, p. 55

Teacher FYI

Japanese beetles appear to be different colors in different lights because their wings contain liquid crystals.

Liquid Crystals Liquid crystals are another group of materials that do not change states in the usual manner. Normally, the ordered geometric arrangement of the solid is lost when the substance goes from the solid state to the liquid state. Liquid crystals start to flow during the melting phase similar to a liquid, but they do not lose their ordered arrangement completely, as most substances do. Liquid crystals will retain their geometric order in specific directions.

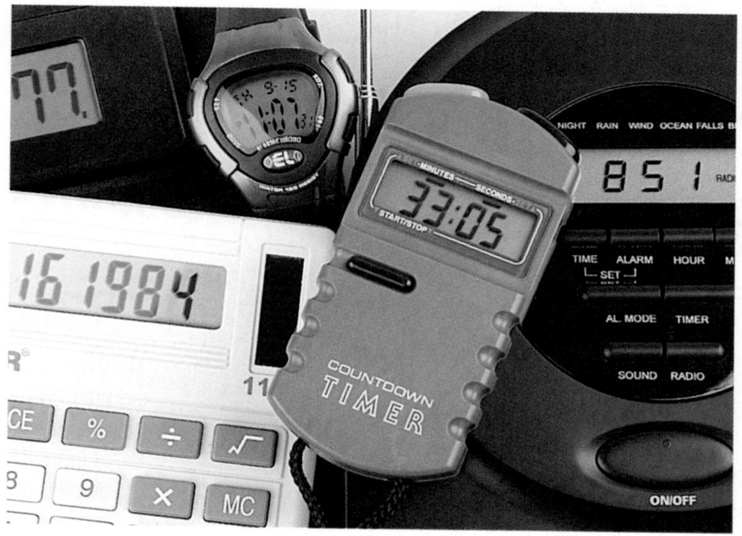

Liquid crystals are placed in classes depending upon the type of order they maintain when they liquefy. They are highly responsive to temperature changes and electric fields. Scientists use these unique properties of liquid crystals to make liquid crystal displays (LCD) in the displays of watches, clocks, calculators, and some notebook computers, as shown in **Figure 12.**

Figure 12
Liquid crystals are used in the displays of watches, clocks, calculators, and some notebook computers because they respond to electric fields.

Reading Check *What unusual property do liquid crystals have when they melt?*

Section 1 Assessment

1. What are the three basic assumptions of the kinetic theory?
2. Describe the movement of the molecules in solids, liquids, and gases.
3. Describe the movement of the molecules at the melting point of a substance.
4. Describe the movement of the molecules at the boiling point of a substance.
5. **Think Critically** Would the boiling point of water be higher or lower on the top of a mountain peak? How would the boiling point be affected in a pressurized boiler system? Explain.

Skill Builder Activities

6. **Interpreting Data** Using the graph in **Figure 7,** describe the energy changes that are occurring when water goes from −15°C to 100°C. **For more help, refer to the** Science Skill Handbook.
7. **Making and Using Graphs** The melting point of acetic acid is 16.6°C and the boiling point is 117.9°C. Draw a graph showing the phase changes for acetic acid similar to the graph in **Figure 7.** Clearly mark the three phases, the boiling point, and the melting point on the graph. **For more help, refer to the** Science Skill Handbook.

Reading Check

Answer The liquid does not lose its ordered arrangement.

3 Assess

Reteach

Have students use pictures from magazines or newspapers to create a collage or bulletin board that illustrates solids, liquids, and gases. L2
LS **Visual-Spatial** P

Challenge

At atmospheric pressure, a few materials, such as iodine and carbon dioxide, change directly from solid to gas without going through a liquid state. Use the kinetic theory to explain what happens when heat is added to solid carbon dioxide (dry ice). The particles increase in energy enough to go from vibrating in place to escaping from the surface of the dry ice. L2
LS **Logical-Mathematical**

Assessment

Process Ask students to draw diagrams illustrating what determines the boiling point of a liquid. At the boiling point, the pressure from molecules leaving the liquid to become gas is equal to the atmospheric pressure above them. Use **Performance Assessment in the Science Classroom,** p. 127.

Answers to Section Assessment

1. All matter is composed of small particles; the particles are in constant motion; these particles collide with each other and with the walls of their container.
2. solid: vibrate in place; liquid: slide past each other; gas: move freely and randomly and collide with one another
3. Molecules slip out of the ordered arrangement they had in the solid.
4. Molecules acquire enough energy to escape the attractions within the liquid.
5. At a mountain top, boiling point would be lower because atmospheric pressure is lower; in a pressurized boiler, boiling point would be higher because the appliance causes the vapor over the liquid to build up more pressure.
6. From −15°C to 0°C, solid water absorbs energy, increasing both the kinetic energy of the particles and the temperature. At 0°C, additional energy breaks attractions in the solid, but the temperature does not rise. After the solid melts, the temperature rises until it reaches 100°C. The temperature does not rise again until all the liquid has become gas.
7. Graphs should show the temperature rising until it reaches 16.6°C, where it plateaus. Then it rises to 117.9°C, where it again plateaus. Finally, it rises once more.

Activity

BENCH TESTED

Purpose Students will heat ice and graph the temperature changes over time. L2
LS **Kinesthetic**

Process collecting data, making and using tables, recording observations, making and using graphs

Time 40 minutes

Safety Precautions Caution students not to use the thermometers as stirring rods and not to allow the thermometers to rest on the bottom of the beaker.

Teaching Strategy Remind students that temperature is defined as the average kinetic energy of a substance.

Answers to Questions

1. Check students' drawings. Encourage them to make the drawings as complete as possible.
2. The gaseous state on the drawing has the greatest amount of thermal energy and the solid state has the least amount.
3. Check students' graphs

Assessment

Process Have students write summaries of their graphs. Make sure they include descriptions of any areas where the temperature did not change quickly or did not change at all. Use **Performance Assessment in the Science Classroom,** p. 113.

Activity

How Thermal Energy Affects Matter

The states of matter and its characteristics change as its thermal energy changes.

What You'll Investigate

How does thermal energy affect the state of matter?

Materials

beakers (2)
ring clamp (1)
ring stand
wire mesh
Bunsen burner or hot plate
ice
thermometer

Goals

- **Explain** the thermal energy changes that occur as matter goes from the solid to gas state.

Safety Precautions

Procedure

1. Set up the equipment as pictured. Prepare a data table in your Science Journal.
2. Gently heat the ice in the lower beaker. Every 3 min record your observations and the temperature of the water in the bottom container. Do not touch the thermometer to the bottom or sides of the container.
3. After the ice in the beaker melts and the water begins to boil, observe the system for several more minutes and record your observations.
4. Turn off the heat and let your system completely cool before you clean up.

Conclude and Apply

1. **Draw** a picture of the system used in this lab in your Science Journal. Label the state the water started at in the lower beaker, the state it changed into in the lower beaker, the state above the lower beaker, and the state on the outside of the upper beaker.
2. Which location on the diagram has the greatest thermal energy and which has the least amount of thermal energy?
3. Make a time-temperature graph using your data for your Science Journal.

Communicating Your Data

Compare your results with other groups in the lab. **For more help, refer to the** Science Skill Handbook.

Communicating Your Data

Students should discuss why their conclusions did or did not agree.

Resource Manager 

Chapter Resources Booklet
Activity Worksheet, pp. 5–6
Reinforcement, p. 29

SECTION 2

Properties of Fluids

How do ships float?

Some ships are so huge that they are like floating cities. For example, aircraft carriers are large enough to allow airplanes to take off and land on their decks. Despite their weight, these ships are able to float. This is because a greater force pushing up on the ship opposes the weight—or force—of the ship pushing down. What is this force? This supporting force is called the buoyant force. **Buoyancy** is the ability of a fluid—a liquid or a gas—to exert an upward force on an object immersed in it. If the buoyant force is greater than the object's weight, the object will float. If the buoyant force is less than the object's weight, the object will sink.

Archimedes' Principle In the third century B.C., a Greek mathematician named Archimedes made a discovery about buoyancy. Archimedes found that the buoyant force on an object is equal to the weight of the fluid displaced by the object. For example, if you place a block of wood in water, it will push water out of the way as it begins to sink—but only until the weight of the water displaced equals or exceeds the block's weight. When the weight of water displaced—the buoyant force—becomes greater than the weight of the block, it floats. If the weight of the water displaced is less than the weight of the block, the object sinks. **Figure 13** shows the forces that affect an object in a fluid.

As You Read

***What* You'll Learn**

- **Explain** Archimedes' principle.
- **Explain** Pascal's principle.
- **Explain** Bernoulli's principle and explain how we use it.

Vocabulary

buoyancy
pressure
viscosity

***Why* It's Important**

Properties of fluids determine the design of ships, airplanes, and hydraulic machines.

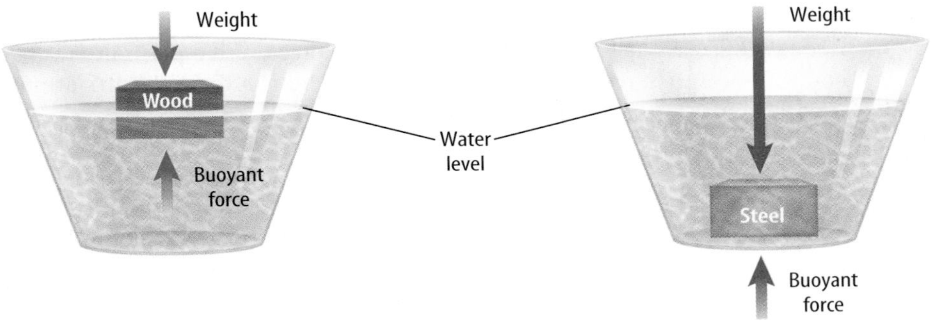

Figure 13
If the buoyant force of the fluid is equal to or greater than the weight of the object, the object floats. If the buoyant force of the fluid is less than the weight of the object, the object sinks.

SECTION 2

Properties of Fluids

1 Motivate

Bellringer Transparency

Display the Section Focus Transparency for Section 2. Use the accompanying Transparency Activity Master. L2 ELL

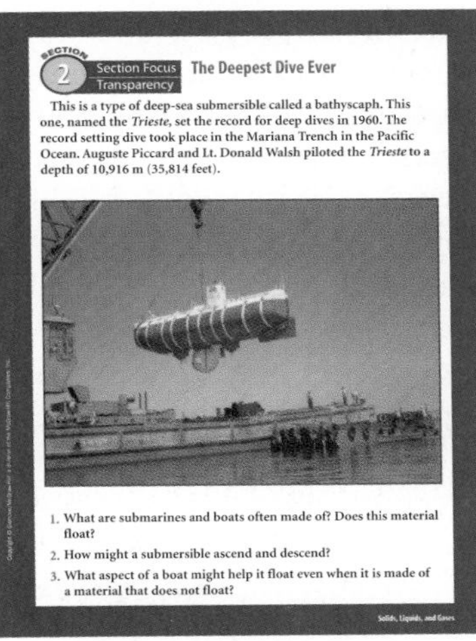

Section 2 Section Focus Transparency — The Deepest Dive Ever

This is a type of deep-sea submersible called a bathyscaph. This one, named the *Trieste*, set the record for deep dives in 1960. The record setting dive took place in the Mariana Trench in the Pacific Ocean. Auguste Piccard and Lt. Donald Walsh piloted the *Trieste* to a depth of 10,916 m (35,814 feet).

1. What are submarines and boats often made of? Does this material float?
2. How might a submersible ascend and descend?
3. What aspect of a boat might help it float even when it is made of a material that does not float?

Solids, Liquids, and Gases

Tie to Prior Knowledge

Ask students to name objects they know that sink or float in water. Have students form a hypothesis about why something as heavy as a boat will float.

Section Assessment Planner

PORTFOLIO
Active Reading, p. 498

PERFORMANCE ASSESSMENT
MiniLAB, p. 498
Skill Builder Activities, p. 501
See page 514 for more options.

CONTENT ASSESSMENT
Section, p. 501
Challenge, p. 501
Chapter, pp. 514–515

2 Teach

How do ships float?

Purpose Students investigate the properties of density and buoyancy. L2 LS **Kinesthetic**

Materials 2 beakers, (100-mL); graduated cylinder; stirring rod; 10 mL each corn syrup, water, and vegetable oil; food coloring; aluminum foil 0.5 cm × 0.5 cm; steel nut; peppercorn

Teaching Strategy Make sure students dispose of steel nuts, aluminum foil, and peppercorns in a trash can, not in the sink.

Safety Precautions Students should wear goggles and a lab apron for this activity.

Analysis

1. The corn syrup (highest density) went to the bottom, the water (medium density) was in the middle, and the oil (lowest density) was on top.
2. The weight of the foil was less than the buoyant force of the oil, so it floated on top of the oil. The weight of the peppercorn was less than the buoyant force of the water and more than the buoyant force of the oil. The weight of the steel nut was more than the buoyant force of any of the liquids, so it sank to the bottom.

Assessment

Process Have students make drawings showing the layers in their beaker. Clearly label each section and item in the drawing. Use **Performance Assessment in the Science Classroom,** p. 127.

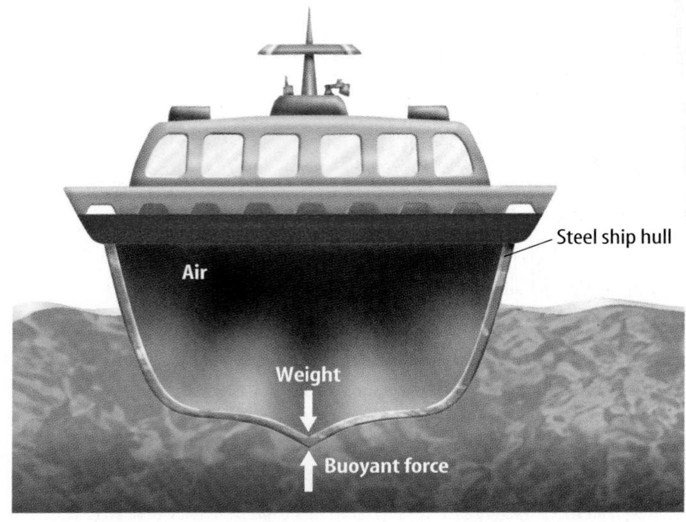

Figure 14
An empty hull of a ship contains mostly air. Its density is much lower than the density of a solid-steel hull. The lower density of the steel and air combination is what allows the ship to float in water.

Observing Density and Buoyancy of Substances

Procedure

1. Pour 10 mL of **corn syrup** into a 100-mL beaker. Add 10 mL of **vegetable oil** to the beaker. In another **beaker,** add 3 to 4 drops of **food coloring** to 10 mL of **water.** Pour the dyed water into the 100-mL beaker containing corn syrup and oil. Gently stir the contents of the beaker.
2. Drop a 0.5 cm square piece of **aluminum foil, a steel nut,** and a **whole pepper corn** into the 100-mL beaker.

Analysis

1. Using the concept of density, explain why the contents of the beaker separated into layers.
2. Using the concept of buoyancy, explain why the foil, steel nut, and pepper corn settled in their places.

Density Would a steel block the same size as a wood block float in water? They both displace the same volume and weight of water when submerged. Therefore, the buoyant force on the blocks is equal. Yet the steel block sinks and the wood block floats. What is different? The volume of the blocks and the volume of the water displaced each have different masses. If the three equal volumes have different masses, they must have different densities. Remember that density is mass per unit volume. The density of the steel block is greater than the density of water. The density of the wood block is less than the density of water. An object will float if its density is less than the density of the fluid it is placed in.

Suppose you formed the steel block into the shape of a hull filled with air as in **Figure 14.** Now the same mass takes up a larger volume. The overall density of the steel boat and air is less than the density of water. The boat will now float.

Pascal's Principle

If you are underwater, you can feel the pressure of the water all around you. **Pressure** is force exerted per unit area. Do you realize that Earth's atmosphere is a fluid? Earth's atmosphere exerts pressure all around you.

Blaise Pascal (1623–1662), a French scientist, discovered a useful property of fluids. According to Pascal's principle, pressure applied to a fluid is transmitted throughout the fluid. For example, when you squeeze one end of a balloon, the balloon expands out on the other end. When you squeeze one end of a toothpaste tube, toothpaste emerges from the other end. The pressure has been transmitted through the fluid toothpaste.

Active Reading

Bubble Map Using a bubble map helps students start ideas flowing about a given topic. Words are clustered to describe a topic or idea that is studied. Students can use a bubble map for a prewriting, to generate ideas before writing in their Journals, or to review for a test. Have students design a bubble map for the properties of fluids discussed in this section. P

498 **CHAPTER 16** Solids, Liquids, and Gases

Applying the Principle Hydraulic machines are machines that move heavy loads in accordance with Pascal's principle. Maybe you've seen a car raised using a hydraulic lift in an auto repair shop. A pipe that is filled with fluid connects small and large cylinders as shown in **Figure 15.** Pressure applied to the small cylinder is transferred through the fluid to the large cylinder. Because pressure remains constant throughout the fluid, according to Pascal's principle, more force is available to lift a heavy load by increasing the surface area. With a hydraulic machine, you could use your weight to lift something much heavier than you are. Do the Math Skills Activity to see how force, pressure, and area are related.

Figure 15
The pressure remains the same throughout the fluid in a hydraulic lift.

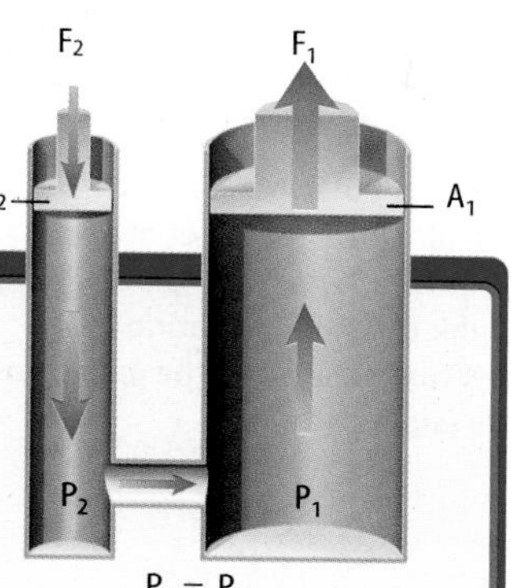

Math Skills Activity

Calculating Forces Using Pascal's Principle

Example Problem

A hydraulic lift is used to lift a heavy machine that is pushing down on a 2.8 m² piston (A_1) with a force (F_1) of 3,700 N. What force (F_2) needs to be exerted on a 0.07 m² piston (A_2) to lift the machine?

Solution

1 *This is what you know:*

$$\text{pressure} = \frac{\text{Force}}{\text{Area}} = \frac{F}{A}$$

$F_1 = 3{,}700$ N

$A_1 = 2.8\ \text{m}^2$

$A_2 = 0.072\ \text{m}^2$

2 *This is what you need to find:* Force needed: F_2

3 *This is the equation that you need to use:* $\frac{F_1}{A_1} = \frac{F_2}{A_2}$

4 *Solve the equation for F_2 and then substitute the known values:*

$$F_2 = \frac{F_1 A_2}{A_1} = \frac{3{,}700\ \text{N} \times 0.072\ m^2}{2.8\ m^2} = 95\ N$$

Check your answer by substituting it and the known values back into the original equation.

Practice Problem

A heavy crate applied a force of 1,500 N on a 25-m² piston. What force needs to be exerted on the 0.8-m² piston to lift the crate?

For more help, refer to the Math Skill Handbook.

Pascal's Principle

Visual Learning

Figure 15 Remind students that pressure is force per unit area. Review with them the pressure and area of each side of the hydraulic machine in this figure and the forces exerted on each side. L2 LS **Visual-Spatial**

Discussion

If the piston on the left in Figure 15 moves down 10 cm, will the piston on the right move up 10 cm, less than 10 cm, or more than 10 cm? less than 10 cm L3
LS **Logical-Mathematical**

Use an Analogy

A hydraulic lift is analogous to a first-class lever in which the fulcrum is closer to the load than it is to the effort force. In both, a relatively small force is moved a long distance to move a heavy load a short distance.

Math Skills Activity

National Math Standards

Correlation to Mathematics Objectives

1, 2, 4, 6, 9

Answer to Practice Problem

$F_2 = \frac{F_1 A_2}{A_1} = 1{,}500\ \text{N}(0.8\ \text{m}^2)/25\ \text{m}^2$

$= 48$ N

Resource Manager

Chapter Resources Booklet

Transparency Activity, p. 47
Directed Reading for Content Mastery, p. 22
MiniLAB, p. 3

Inclusion Strategies

Learning Disabled Review the arithmetic in the Math Skills Activity with these students slowly and carefully. Allow students to use calculators to work through the example problem. Check each number they enter into the calculator to make sure it is correct.

Bernoulli's Principle

Teacher FYI

Fluids flow faster when forced to flow through narrow spaces. The resultant reduction in pressure in these spaces is a special case of Bernoulli's principle. When wind blows between rows of skyscrapers, the reduced air pressure outside of buildings can cause windows to pop out.

Reading Check

Answer The air pressure of the faster-moving air above the wing is less than that of the slower-moving air below the wing. This causes the wing to move up.

Fluid Flow

Earth Science INTEGRATION

A shield volcano is associated with lava that has low viscosity. Lava with higher viscosity produces cones with steeper slopes. Use a runny brand of ketchup and a brand that is more resistant to flow to demonstrate differences in viscosity.

SCIENCE Online

Internet Addresses

Explore the Glencoe Science Web site at science.glencoe.com to find out more about topics in this section.

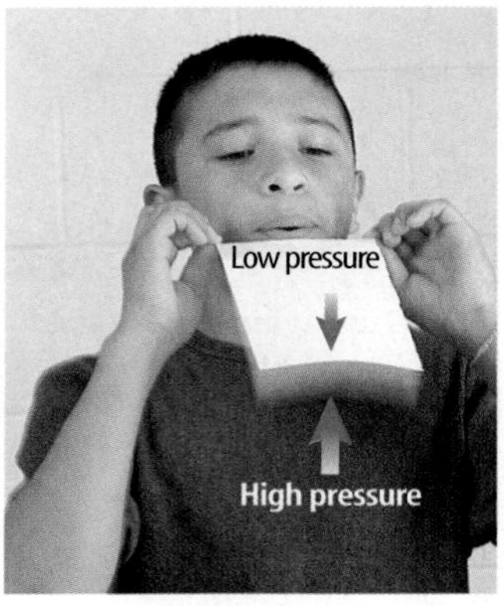

Figure 16
The air above the sheet of paper is moving faster than the air under the paper, creating a low-pressure area above the paper, so the paper rises.

Bernoulli's Principle

It took humans thousands of years to learn to do what birds do instinctively—fly, glide, and soar. It wasn't easy to build a machine that could lift itself off the ground and fly with people aboard. This ability is a property of fluids stated in Bernoulli's principle. Daniel Bernoulli (1700–1782) was a Swiss scientist who studied the properties of moving fluids such as water and air. He published his discovery in 1738. According to Bernoulli's principle, as the velocity of a fluid increases, the pressure exerted by the fluid decreases. One way to demonstrate Bernoulli's principle is to blow across the top surface of a sheet of paper, as in **Figure 16.** The paper will rise. The velocity of the air you blew over the top surface of the paper is greater than that of the quiet air below it. As a result, the air pressure pushing down on the top of the paper is lower than the air pressure pushing up on the paper. The net force below the paper pushes the paper upward.

Now, look at the curvature of the airplane wing in **Figure 17.** As the plane moves forward, the air passing over the wing must travel farther than air passing below it. To take the same time to get to the rear of the wing, air must travel faster over the top of the wing than below it. Thus, the pressure above the wing is less than the pressure below it. The result is a net upward force on the wing, lifting the airplane in flight.

Reading Check *Using Bernoulli's principle, explain how an airplane flies.*

Notice that the airflow over the wing is a smooth path. If the wing encounters air that is rotating, the airplane might not have lift and the plane could crash. It is important for the pilot to be aware of any turbulent airflow, especially when an airplane is landing where there is little room for error.

SCIENCE Online

Research Visit the Glencoe Science Web site at **science.glencoe.com** for information about flying machines. Communicate to your class what you learn.

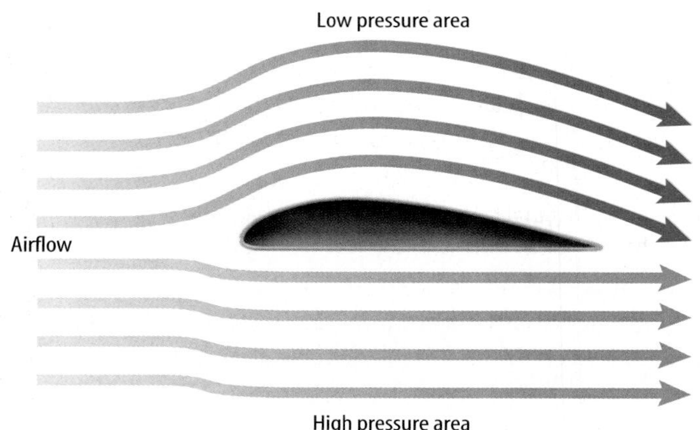

Figure 17
This is a side view of an airplane wing. The air above the wing must travel faster over the wing than under it. This creates a low-pressure area above the wing and the airplane rises.

Cultural Diversity

Boomerangs Several cultures, including some Native Americans, used nonreturning boomerangs to hunt birds and small animals. The most famous boomerangs are those developed by societies in Australia. Have students find out how boomerangs use Bernoulli's principle. A boomerang is like a curved wing. Differences in thickness allow it to fly. L3 LS **Linguistic**

Resource Manager

Chapter Resources Booklet

Enrichment, p. 33
Reinforcement, p. 30
Lab Activity, pp. 9–11

Fluid Flow

Another property exhibited by fluid is its tendency to flow. A resistance to flow by a fluid is called **viscosity.** Fluids vary in their tendency to flow. For example, when you take syrup out of the refrigerator and pour it, the flow of syrup is slow. But if this syrup were heated, it would flow much faster. Water has a low viscosity because it flows easily. Cold syrup has a high viscosity because it flows slowly.

Fluids vary in their tendency to flow because of their molecular structures. When a container of liquid is tilted to allow flow to begin, the falling molecules will transfer energy to the molecules that are stationary. In effect, the flowing molecules are pulling the other molecules causing them to flow, too. If the flowing molecules do not effectively pull the stationary molecules into motion, then the liquid has a high viscosity, or a high resistance to flow. If the molecules pull the stationary molecules in motion easily, then the liquid has low viscosity, or a low resistance to flow.

A rise in temperature increases the movement of molecules in any substance. In substances that are heated, such as the syrup above, the molecules move much faster. If the molecules are moving faster, then energy transfer occurs much faster. Heating the syrup caused the molecules to interact more, resulting in a faster energy transfer and a lower viscosity or a lower resistance to flow.

Reading Check *How does temperature affect viscosity?*

Earth Science INTEGRATION

Magma, or liquefied rock from a volcano, is an example of a liquid with varying viscosity. The viscosity of magma depends upon its composition. The viscosity of the magma flow determines the shape of the volcanic cone. In your Science Journal, infer the type of volcano cone that is created with high- and low-viscosity lava flows.

Section  Assessment

1. Explain what two opposing forces are acting on an object floating in water.
2. What is Archimedes' principle and explain how it enables heavy ships to float?
3. What is Pascal's principle? Explain how it works in a mustard bottle.
4. Using Bernoulli's principle, explain how a helicopter rises.
5. **Think Critically** If you fill a balloon with air, tie it off, and release it, it will fall to the floor. Why does it fall instead of float? What if the balloon contained helium?

Skill Builder Activities

6. **Measuring in SI** The density of water is $1.0\ g/cm^3$. How many kilograms of water does a submerged $120\text{-}cm^3$ block displace? One kilogram weighs 9.8 N. What is the buoyant force on the block? **For more help, refer to the Science Skills Handbook.**
7. **Solving One-Step Equations** If you wanted to lift an object weighing 20,000 N, how much force would you need to exert on the small piston in **Figure 15? For more help, refer to the Math Skills handbook.**

Reading Check

Answer Viscosity decreases as temperature increases.

3 Assess

Reteach

Have students test several objects that sink or float in water. Have students use density, volume, and weight to explain why each object sinks or floats. L2 ELL IS **Logical-Mathematical**

Challenge

Tell students that the Venturi effect is a specific example of the Bernoulli principle. Ask them to find out what the Venturi effect is and build a model to demonstrate it. According to the Venturi effect, a fluid will speed up as it moves through a narrow passageway. Models could include a sand streambed with a narrow section. L3 IS **Kinesthetic**

Assessment

Process Have each student form a hypothesis about what will happen if they blow air between two empty soft drink cans that are placed on their sides 2 cm apart. Have them test their hypotheses. The cans will move closer together. Use **PASC,** p. 93.

Answers to Section Assessment

1. Weight is pushing down and buoyant force is pushing up.
2. Archimedes' principle says that the buoyant force on an object in a fluid is equal to the weight of the fluid displaced by the object. The overall density of an air-filled ship is less than that of water.
3. Pascal's principle states that pressure applied to a fluid is transmitted throughout the fluid. When you squeeze one end of a mustard container, the mustard comes out the other end.
4. The curved, rotating blades of a helicopter create a low pressure area above the helicopter. The higher pressure below the helicopter pushes it up.
5. The air in the balloon is compressed. Thus, its weight exceeds the buoyant force of the surrounding air. Helium is less dense than air, and the balloon would float.
6. The mass of water displaced is $120\ cm^3 \times 1.0\ g/cm^3$, or 120 g, which is 0.12 kg. The buoyant force is $0.12\ kg \times 9.8\ N/kg$, or 1.2 N.
7. $F_2 = \frac{F_1 A_2}{A_1} = \frac{(20{,}000\ N)(0.072\ m^2)}{2.8\ m^2}$
   $= 514\ N$

SECTION

Behavior of Gases

1 Motivate

Bellringer Transparency

Display the Section Focus Transparency for Section 3. Use the accompanying Transparency Activity Master. L2 ELL

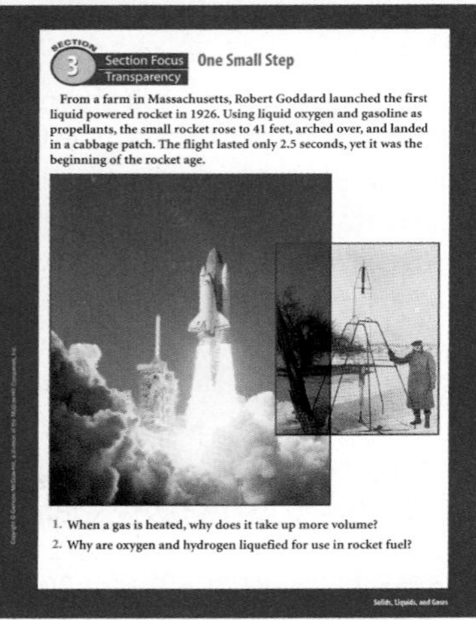

Section Focus Transparency **One Small Step**

From a farm in Massachusetts, Robert Goddard launched the first liquid powered rocket in 1926. Using liquid oxygen and gasoline as propellants, the small rocket rose to 41 feet, arched over, and landed in a cabbage patch. The flight lasted only 2.5 seconds, yet it was the beginning of the rocket age.

1. When a gas is heated, why does it take up more volume?
2. Why are oxygen and hydrogen liquefied for use in rocket fuel?

Solids, Liquids, and Gases

Tie to Prior Knowledge

Ask students if they have ever felt their ears pop as their altitude increased. Discuss the changes in pressure that cause this.

Reading Check

Answer Pressure is the amount of force exerted per unit of area.

SECTION

Behavior of Gases

As You Read

***What* You'll Learn**

- **Explain** how a gas exerts pressure on its container.
- **Explain** how a gas is affected when pressure, temperature, or volume is changed.

Vocabulary
pascal

***Why* It's Important**

Being able to explain and to predict the behavior of gases is useful because you live in a sea of air.

Pressure

Relax and take a deep breath. If the air is clean and fresh, it is primarily a mixture of nitrogen, oxygen, argon, and carbon dioxide. Small amounts of hydrogen, water vapor, and a few other elements are present also. The atmosphere is held in place by the gravitational force on these tiny gas molecules. Without the force of gravity acting on these molecules, it would escape into space. More information about the atmosphere is on the next page in **Figure 18.**

Particle Collisions You learned from kinetic theory that gas molecules are constantly moving and colliding with anything in their path. The collisions of these particles in the air result in atmospheric pressure. Pressure is the amount of force exerted per unit of area, or $P = F/A$. It is measured in units called **pascal** (Pa), the SI unit of pressure. Because pressure is the amount of force divided by area, one pascal of pressure is one Newton per square meter or 1 N/m^2. This is a small pressure unit, so most pressures are given in kilopascals (kPa) or 1,000 pascals. At sea level, atmospheric pressure is 101.3 kPa. This means that at Earth's surface, the atmosphere exerts a force of about 101,300 N on every square meter—about the weight of a large truck.

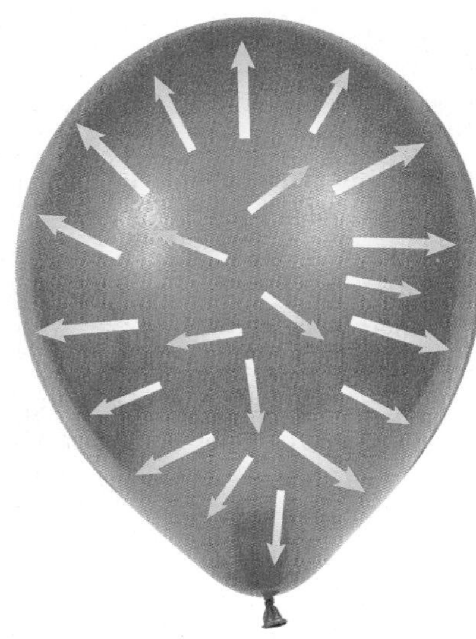

Figure 19
The force created by the many air molecules striking the balloon's walls forces them outward, keeping the balloon inflated.

Often, gases are confined within containers. A balloon and a bicycle tire are considered to be containers. They remain inflated because of collisions the air particles have with the walls of their container, as shown in **Figure 19.** This collection of forces, caused by the collisions of the molecules, pushes the walls of the container outward. If more air is pumped into the balloon, the number of air molecules is increased. This causes more collisions with the walls of the container, which causes it to expand. Since the bicycle tire can't expand, its pressure increases.

Reading Check *How are force, area, and pressure related?*

Section Assessment Planner

Portfolio
Extension, p. 504

Performance Assessment
Try at Home MiniLAB, p. 506
Skill Builder Activities, p. 507
See page 514 for more options.

Content Assessment
Section, p. 507
Challenge, p. 507
Chapter, pp. 514–515

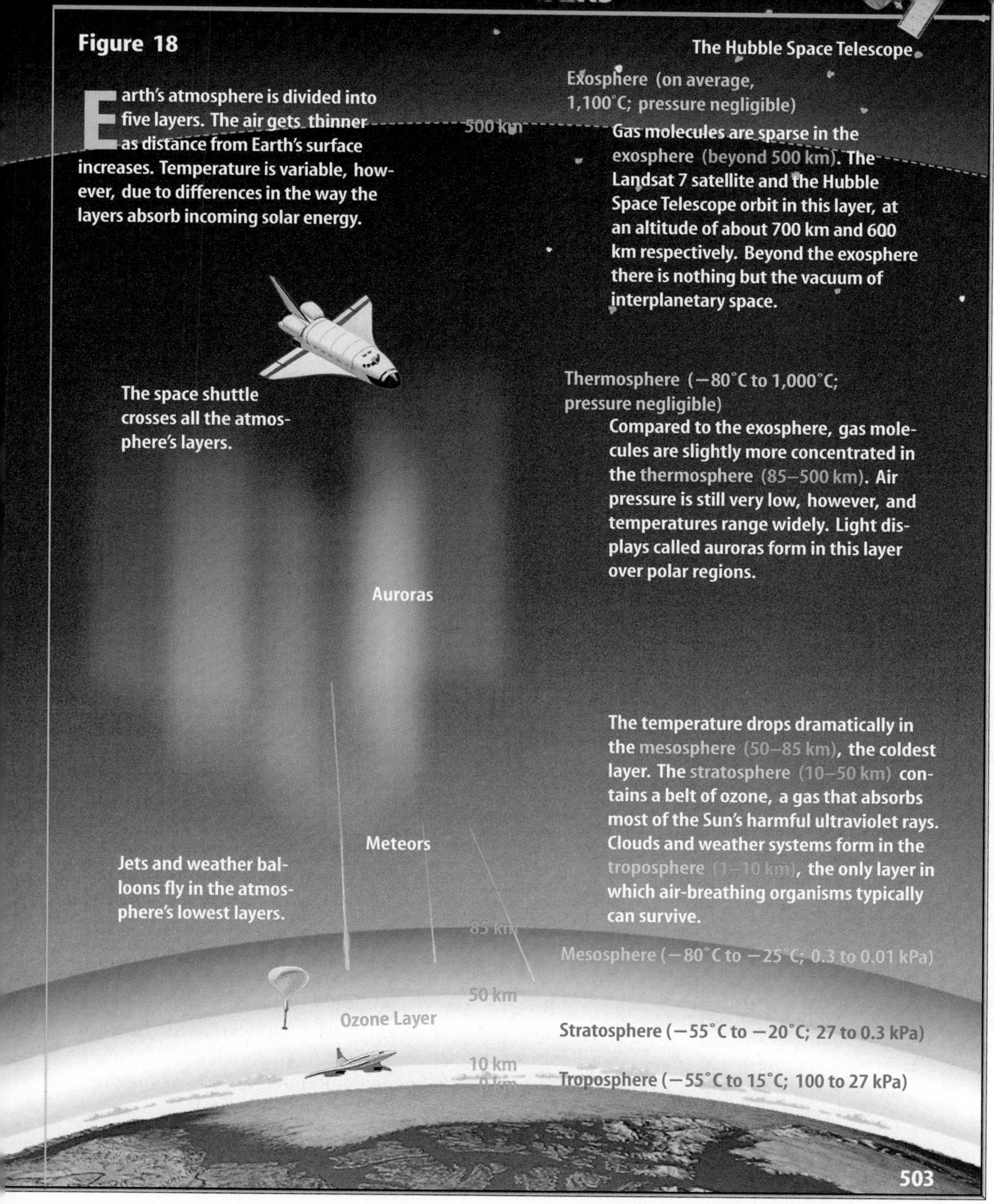

Figure 18

Earth's atmosphere is divided into five layers. The air gets thinner as distance from Earth's surface increases. Temperature is variable, however, due to differences in the way the layers absorb incoming solar energy.

The Hubble Space Telescope

Exosphere (on average, 1,100°C; pressure negligible)

500 km

Gas molecules are sparse in the exosphere (beyond 500 km). The Landsat 7 satellite and the Hubble Space Telescope orbit in this layer, at an altitude of about 700 km and 600 km respectively. Beyond the exosphere there is nothing but the vacuum of interplanetary space.

The space shuttle crosses all the atmosphere's layers.

Thermosphere (−80°C to 1,000°C; pressure negligible)

Compared to the exosphere, gas molecules are slightly more concentrated in the thermosphere (85–500 km). Air pressure is still very low, however, and temperatures range widely. Light displays called auroras form in this layer over polar regions.

Auroras

The temperature drops dramatically in the mesosphere (50–85 km), the coldest layer. The stratosphere (10–50 km) contains a belt of ozone, a gas that absorbs most of the Sun's harmful ultraviolet rays. Clouds and weather systems form in the troposphere (1–10 km), the only layer in which air-breathing organisms typically can survive.

Meteors

Jets and weather balloons fly in the atmosphere's lowest layers.

85 km

Mesosphere (−80°C to −25°C; 0.3 to 0.01 kPa)

50 km

Ozone Layer

Stratosphere (−55°C to −20°C; 27 to 0.3 kPa)

10 km

0 km

Troposphere (−55°C to 15°C; 100 to 27 kPa)

503

Visualizing Atmospheric Layers

Have students examine the pictures and read the captions. Then ask the following questions.

- **Why does the atmosphere get thinner as the distance from the Earth increases?** because the gravitational pull on the molecules in the atmosphere is less
- **Why is the belt of ozone in the stratosphere important to organisms that live on Earth?** the belt of ozone screens out harmful radiation from the Sun
- **Why does the Hubble Space Telescope orbit in the exosphere instead of closer to Earth?** The exosphere has fewer molecules of gas and particles of dust that can limit the visibility of the telescope.

Activity

Have students design a game that involves answering questions about the layers of the atmosphere. L2

LS **Logical-Mathematical**

Extension

Challenge students to make line graphs of the temperature and pressure gradients within each atmospheric level. Color-coding the graphs will make the graphs easier to read and understand. L3 LS **Visual-Spatial**

Resource Manager

Chapter Resources Booklet

Transparency Activity, p. 48

Directed Reading for Content Mastery, pp. 23, 24

Lab Activity, pp. 13–18

2 Teach

Pressure

Activity

Bring a barometer to class. Have students measure and record the pressure and keep a log of weather conditions each day for several days. Ask them to search the data for correlations. They may observe that days of low pressure, tend to be cloudy with precipitation, while days of high pressure are more likely to be clear. L3 ELL
LS Visual-Spat al

Extension

Remind studer hat 1 pascal is 1 N of force e ted over an area of 1 m^2. As em to convert this to find how much force is exerted pascal on 1 cm^2. Th n ask o use their results to calcu e amount of force exerted mospheric pressure on 1 c 1 m^2 = 10,000 cm^2. Therefore, 1 pascal = 1N/10,000 cm^2 = 0.0001 N/cm^2. 1 kPa = 0.1 N/cm^2; therefore, 101.3 kPa exerts a force of 10.13 N/cm^2.
L3 LS L gical-Mat matical P

Boyle's Law

Caption Answer

Figure 21 500 L

Discussion

Why do you think gases used in industry are kept in pressurized containers? to reduce the volume they occupy, which makes them easier to store and transport
L2 LS Logical-Mathematical

Figure 20
Balloons are used to measure the weather conditions at high altitu es. These ballo ns expand as they ise due to decreased pressure.

Boyle's Law

You now know how gas creates pressure in a container. What happens to the gas pressure if you decrease the size of the container? You know that the pressure of a gas depends on how often its particles strike the walls of the container. If you squeeze gas into a smaller space, its particles will strike the walls more often—giving an increased pressure. The opposite is true, too. If you give the gas particles more space, they will hit the walls less often—gas pressure will be reduced. Robert Boyle (1627–1691), a British scientist, described this property of gases. According to Boyle's law, if you decrease the volume of a container of gas and hold the temperature constant, the pressure of the gas will increase. An increase in the volume of the container causes the pressure to drop, if the temperature remains constant.

The behavior of weather balloons, as shown in **Figure 20,** can be explained using Boyle's law. Rubber or neoprene weather balloons are used to carry sensing instruments to high altitudes to detect weather information. The balloons are inflated near Earth's surface with a low-density gas. As the balloon rises, the atmospheric pressure decreases. The balloon gradually expands to a volume of 30 to 200 times its original size. At some point the expanding balloon ruptures. Boyle's law states that as pressure is decreased the volume increases, as demonstrated by the weather balloon. The opposite also is true, as shown by the graph in **Figure 21.** As the pressure is increased, the volume will decrease.

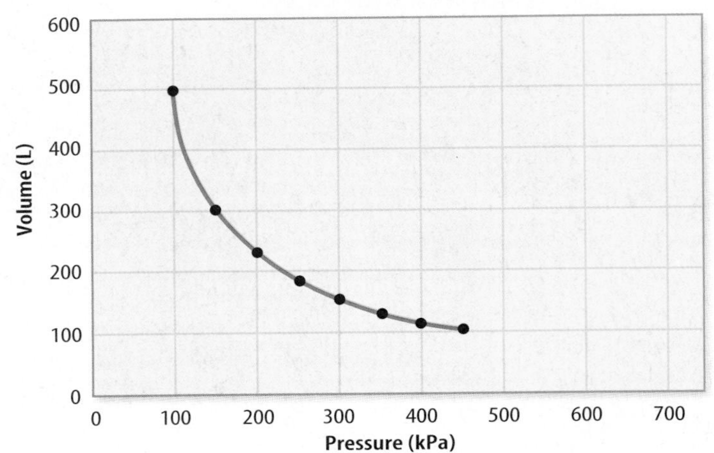

Figure 21
As you can see from the graph, as pressure increases, volume decreases; as pressure decreases, volume increases. *What is the volume of the gas at 100 kPa?*

Visual Learning

Figure 21 Choose several volumes from the graph and have students determine the corresponding pressures. Emphasize that the same volume-pressure relationships hold true no matter what units are used for volume and pressure. L2 ELL LS **Visual-Spatial**

Science Journal

Gases Have students discuss how gases are used in their daily lives. Answers might include breathing, making baked goods rise, filling tires, or determining the weather. L2 LS **Naturalist**

Boyle's Law in Action When Boyle's law is applied to a real life situation, we find that the pressure multiplied by the volume is always equal to a constant if the temperature is constant. As the pressure and volume change indirectly, the constant will remain the same. You can use the equations P_1V_1 = constant = P_2V_2 to express this mathematically. This shows us that the product of the initial pressure and volume—designated with the subscript 1—is equal to the product of the final pressure and volume—designated with the subscript 2. Using this equation, you can find one unknown value, as shown in the example problem below.

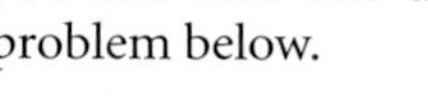

What is $P_1V_1 = P_2V_2$ known as?

SCIENCE Online

Research Visit the Glencoe Science Web site at **science.glencoe.com** for various industrial uses for compressed gases. Communicate to your class what you learn.

Math Skills Activity

Using Boyle's Law

Example Problem

A balloon has a volume of 10.0 L at a pressure of 101 kPa. What will be the new volume when the pressure drops to 43 kPa?

Solution:

1. *This is what you know:* initial pressure: P_1 = 101 kPa; initial volume: V_1 = 10.0 L; final pressure: P_2 = 43 kPa
2. *This is what you need to find:* final volume: V_2
3. *This is the equation you need to use:* $P_1V_1 = P_2V_2$
4. *Solve the equation for V_2:* $V_2 = \frac{P_1V_1}{P_2}$

Substitute the known values: $V_2 = \frac{(101 \text{ kPa})(10.0 \text{ L})}{43 \text{ kPa}} = 23 \text{ L}$

Check your answer by substituting 23 L back into the original equation and solving for P_1. Does the result reflect the theory of Boyle's law—volume increased as the pressure decreased?

Practice Problem

A volume of helium occupies 11 L at 98.0 kPa. What is the new volume if the pressure drops to 86.24 kPa?

For more help, refer to the Math Skill Handbook.

SCIENCE Online

Internet Addresses

Explore the Glencoe Science Web site at **science.glencoe.com** to find out more about topics in this section.

Reading Check

Answer Boyle's law

Use Science Words

Word Origin The word *gas* comes from the Latin word *chaos.* Have students look up *chaos* in the dictionary and explain why it is an appropriate term to explain gases. Chaos is a situation of disorder. Gas particles are in disorder. L2

LS **Linguistic**

Teacher FYI

When the gases in tennis balls are at a high pressure, the balls bounce higher. Tennis balls come in pressurized cans so that the gases contained in the balls do not escape. Once out of the can, the balls will lose gas pressure over time.

Math Skills Activity

National Math Standards

Correlation to Mathematics Objectives

1, 2, 4, 6, 9

Answer to Practice Problem

$V_2 = \frac{P_1V_1}{P_2}$ = 11 L(98.0 kPa) ÷ 86.24 kPa = 12.5 L

Resource Manager

Chapter Resources Booklet

Reinforcement, p. 31

Enrichment, p. 34

Science Inquiry Lab, p. 25

Inclusion Strategies

Learning Disabled Before they solve a gas law problem, have students make a prediction about the answer. After they solve the problem, have them compare their predictions with their answers. For example, when solving a Boyle's law problem in which pressure increases, students should predict that volume decreases. L1

LS **Logical-Mathematical**

Charles's Law

Purpose to demonstrate Charles's law L2 LS **Kinesthetic**

Materials balloon, beaker, ice water

Teaching Strategy Students will need to leave balloons on the beakers for several minutes.

Troubleshooting The balloon will contract faster if it is in contact with the cold water.

Analysis

1. The molecules in the gas slowed down, putting less pressure on the balloon, so it contracted.
2. $V_2 = \frac{(0.5\ L)(358\ K)}{(298\ K)} = 0.6\ L$

Process Have students allow the balloons to return to room temperature and record their observations. Use **PASC,** p. 97.

Students may not understand the relative sizes of temperature units. They may think that 1° K = 1° C = 1° F. While the size of one kelvin unit of temperature does equal the size of one degree Celsius, the size of one degree Fahrenheit is much smaller.

Reading Check

Answer They both explain the behavior of a gas as temperature changes.

Observing Pressure

Safety Precautions

Procedure

1. Blow up a **balloon** to about half its maximum size.
2. Place the balloon on a **beaker** filled with **ice water.**

Analysis

1. Explain what happened to the balloon when you placed it on the beaker.
2. If the volume of the half-filled balloon was 0.5 L at a temperature of 298 K, what would the volume of the balloon be if the temperature increased to 358 K?

Charles's Law

If you've watched a hot air balloon being inflated, you know that gases expand when they are heated. This gas expansion allows the hot air balloon to rise. Jacques Charles (1743–1823) was a French scientist who studied gases. According to Charles's law, the volume of a gas increases with increasing temperature, as long as pressure does not change. As with Boyle's law, the reverse is true, also. The volume of a gas shrinks with decreasing temperature, as shown in **Figure 22.**

Charles's law can be explained using the kinetic theory of matter. As a gas is heated, its particles move faster and faster and its temperature increases. Because the gas particles move faster, they begin to strike the walls of their container more often and with more force. In the hot air balloon, the walls have room to expand so instead of increased pressure, the volume increases. But what happens when the walls of the container cannot expand?

Gay-Lussac's Law Have you ever read the words "keep away from heat" on a pressurized spray canister? What happens if you heat an enclosed gas? The particles of gas will strike the walls of the canister more often. When this happens, pressure increases. If the pressure becomes greater than the canister can hold, it will explode. After the container explodes, the pressure is released and the gas expands.

Joseph Gay-Lussac (1778–1850) was a French scientist that studied gases. His law states that at a constant volume, as temperature is increased, pressure is increased.

Reading Check *What do Charles's law and Gay-Lussac's law have in common?*

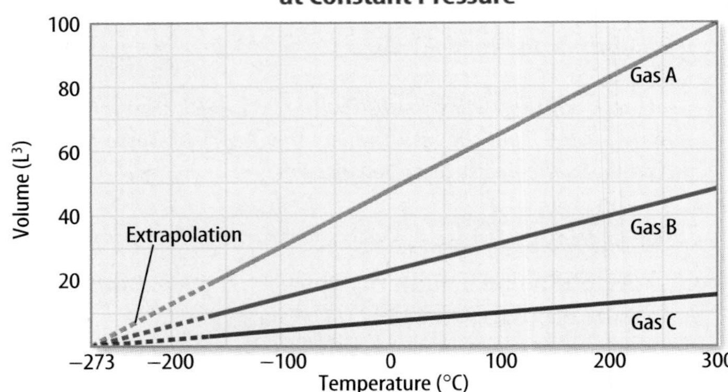

Figure 22
The volume of a gas increases when the temperature increases at constant pressure. Notice that when the graphs are extended to absolute zero, the volume is theoretically zero.

Visual Learning

Figure 22 Give students several different temperatures from the graph and have them read back to you the volume associated with each. L2 ELL LS **Visual-Spatial**

Resource Manager

Chapter Resources Booklet
- Activity Worksheet, pp. 7–8
- MiniLAB, p. 4

Lab Management and Safety, p. 44

Using Charles's Law The formula that relates the variables of temperature to volume shows a direct relationship, $V_1/T_1 = V_2/T_2$, when temperature is given in Kelvin. When using Charles's law, the pressure must be kept constant. What would be the resulting volume of a 2.0-L balloon at 25.0°C that was placed in a container of ice water at 3.0°C, as shown in **Figure 23?**

$V_1 = 2.0\text{ L} \qquad T_1 = 25.0°\text{C} + 273 = 298\text{ K}$

$V_2 = ? \qquad T_2 = 3.0°\text{C} + 273 = 276\text{ K}$

$$\frac{V_1}{T_1} = \frac{V_2}{T_2}$$

$$\frac{2.0\text{ L}}{298\text{ K}} = \frac{V_2}{276\text{ K}}$$

$$V_2 = \frac{(2.0\text{ L})(276\text{ K})}{298\text{ K}}$$

$$V_2 = 1.9\text{ L}$$

As Charles's law predicts, the volume decreased as the temperature of the trapped gas decreased. This assumed no changes in pressure.

Figure 23
Charles's law states that as the temperature is lowered, the volume decreases. *If the balloon in the text was placed in a freezer at 5°C, what would be the new volume?*

Reading Check *According to Charles's law, what happens to the volume of a gas if the temperature increases?*

Section 3 Assessment

1. Why does a gas have pressure?
2. What is the pressure of Earth's atmosphere at sea level?
3. Explain Boyle's law. Give an example of Boyle's law at work.
4. Explain Charles's law. Give an example of Charles's law at work.
5. **Think Critically** Labels on cylinders of compressed gases state the highest temperature to which the cylinder may be exposed. Give a reason for this warning.

Skill Builder Activities

6. **Forming Hypotheses** A bottle of ammonia begins to leak. An hour later, you can smell ammonia almost everywhere, especially near the bottle. State a hypothesis to explain your observations. **For more help, refer to the** Science Skill Handbook.
7. **Solving One-Step Equations** If a 5-L balloon at 25°C was gently heated to 30°C, what new volume would the balloon have? **For more help, refer to the** Math Skill Handbook.

Caption Answer

Figure 23 1.8 L

Reading Check

Answer It increases if pressure stays the same.

3 Assess

Reteach

Have students seal an air sample in a plastic bag and place it in the freezer. Tell them to remove the bag the next day and, with the bag sealed, warm it with a hair dryer or warm water. Ask students to explain their observations. The volume of the air decreased in the freezer and increased as the temperature increased. L2 ELL LS **Visual-Spatial**

Challenge

Put 20 mL of water into an empty aluminum soft-drink can, and place it on a hot plate to boil. After the can has filled with steam, grasp it with tongs or a hot pad and plunge the can inverted into ice water so that it contracts inward. From the results, have students infer the relationship among volume, temperature, and pressure. As temperature decreases, pressure and volume decrease. L2 LS **Visual-Spatial**

Assessment

Content Have students write questions about the behavior of gases. Have other students answer them. Check answers for accuracy. Use **Performance Assessment in the Science Classroom,** p. 91.

Answers to Section Assessment

1. Gas particles move and collide with the sides of their container.
2. 101.3 kPa
3. Assuming the amount and temperature of a gas are constant, when pressure or volume increases, the other quantity decreases. If the volume of a balloon decreases, the pressure of the gas inside it increases.
4. Assuming the amount and pressure of a gas are constant, as temperature or volume increases the other quantity also increases. If the temperature of the gas inside a balloon increases, its volume increases.
5. As temperature increases, pressure increases. The cylinder might explode.
6. The particles of ammonia gas are in constant motion and spread throughout the room.
7. 5 L(303 K/298 K) = 5.1 L

Activity

BENCH TESTED

What You'll Investigate

Purpose

Students observe and measure the movement of a solid through liquids of different viscosities L2 ELL LS **Kinesthetic**

Process Skills

observing, measuring, using numbers, making and using tables, making and using graphs, recognizing cause and effect, controlling variables, interpreting data

Time Required

45 minutes

Materials

Make sure you include materials with a variety of viscosities. Water, alcohol, and corn oil have relatively low viscosities while motor oil and molasses have relatively high viscosities.

Procedure

Teaching Strategies

- This activity will be easier for students to do if they work in pairs.
- Some of these liquids will likely be spilled during the course of the activity. Make sure students clean up their work areas and wash their hands after doing this activity.

Tie to Prior Knowledge

Review with students how the behavior of the particles in matter changes with temperature. As temperature increases, particles move faster.

Activity

Testing the Viscosity of Common Liquids

The resistance to flow of a liquid is called viscosity, and it can be measured and compared. One example of the importance of a liquid's viscosity is motor oil in car engines. The viscosity of motor oil in your family car is very important because it keeps the engine lubricated. It must cling to the moving parts and not run off leaving the parts dry and unlubricated. If the engine is not properly lubricated, it will be damaged eventually. The motor oil must maintain its viscosity in all types of weather from extreme heat in the summer to freezing cold in the winter.

What You'll Investigate

How can you compare the resistance of flow, or viscosity, of common household liquids?

Materials

room temperature household liquids such as:
- dish detergent
- motor oil
- corn syrup
- pancake syrup
- shampoo
- vegetable oil
- vinegar
- molasses
- water

spheres of known density such as glass marbles or steel balls
graduated cylinders
ruler
stopwatch

Goals

- Observe and compare the viscosity of common liquids.

Safety Precautions

Do not pour motor oil into the sink. Dispose of wastes as directed by your teacher.

Active Reading

Reflective Journal In this strategy, students identify activities and what they learned and record responses to the activities. Have students divide pieces of paper into several columns. Have them record their thoughts under headings such as "What I learned," "Questions I have," and "Surprises I experienced." Have each student write a Reflective Journal entry for this activity.

Procedure

1. Measure equal amounts of the liquids to be tested into the graduated cylinders.
2. Measure the depth of the liquid.
3. Copy the data chart into your Science Journal.
4. Place the sphere on the surface of the liquid. Using a stopwatch, measure and record how long it takes for it to travel to the bottom of the liquid.
5. Remove the sphere and repeat step 4 two more times for the same liquid.
6. Rinse and dry the sphere.
7. Repeat steps 4, 5, and 6 for two more liquids.

Sample Data

Viscosity of Common Liquids			
Substance	**Depth of Liquid (cm)**	**Time (s)**	**Velocity (cm/s)**
honey	6.0	9.65	0.62
conditioning shampoo	6.0	6.19	0.97
mint shampoo	6.0	4.01	1.50
hand soap	6.0	4.15	1.45
syrup	6.0	2.44	2.46
corn oil	6.0	0.21	28.13

Conclude and Apply

1. **Graph** the average speed of the sphere for each liquid on a bar graph.
2. Which liquid made the sphere move the fastest? Would that liquid have a high or low viscosity? Explain.
3. Would it matter if you dropped or threw the sphere into the liquid instead of placing it there? Explain your answer.
4. What effect does temperature play in the viscosity of a liquid? What would happen to the viscosity of your fastest liquid if you made it colder? Explain.

Communicating Your Data

Compare your results with other groups and discuss differences noted. Why might these differences have occurred? **For more help, refer to the** **Science Skill Handbook.**

Troubleshooting

- Students may need to use hot water and soap to clean the sphere between liquids.
- Motor oil can be disposed of at a local garage or recycling center.

Conclude and Apply

1. Check students' work. Make sure they have graphed speed and not time.
2. Answers will vary depending on liquids used. The liquid in which the sphere moved fastest has a low viscosity.
3. If you threw the sphere into the liquid it would move faster because the force of your throw gave it an initial velocity.
4. If you cooled the fastest liquid, its viscosity would increase because the particles in it would slow down.

Error Analysis

Problems might occur if students drop or throw the sphere into the liquids or are not careful about observing and timing the sphere's movement.

Assessment

Process Have students hypothesize how their results would have been different if they had used paper clips instead of spheres in the activity. Then have them test their hypotheses using one of the liquids. Use **Performance Assessment in the Science Classroom,** p. 93.

Communicating Your Data

Have students use a computer spread sheet program to compile data from all students in the class and use it to produce class-average bar graphs for the liquids used.

Science Stats

Content Background

Chemical reactions, such as the burning of fuels, either release or absorb energy. The amount of energy released by a chemical reaction is small compared to the energy released during a nuclear reaction, such as those that occur during a supernova. A nuclear reaction involves the conversion of a small amount of mass into a tremendous amount of energy.

Discussion

Oxygen and other gases are removed from liquid air by warming the liquid air until each component reaches its boiling point. At that point, the liquid becomes a gas and can be seaparated from the mixture. The boiling points for several components of air are: oxygen, −183° C; argon, −186° C; nitgrogen, −196° C, and carbon dioxide, −78° C. **In what order will these gases be removed from liquid air?** nitrogen, argon, oxygen, carbon dioxide L2

LS **Logical-Mathematical**

Activity

Have students show that hot and cold are relative terms. Provide students with three bowls of water, one containing very warm water, one containing cold water, and one containing room-temperature water. Have each student place one hand in the warm water and one hand in the cold water for two minutes. Then have them place both hands in the room-temperature water and write a paragraph describing what they felt. L1

LS **Linguistic**

Science Stats

Hot and Cold

Did you know...

. . . The world's coldest substance, liquid helium, is about −269°C. It's used in cryogenics research, which is the study of extremely low temperatures. Cryogenics has enabled physicians to freeze and preserve body parts, such as corneas from human eyes. The freezing keeps cells alive until they are needed.

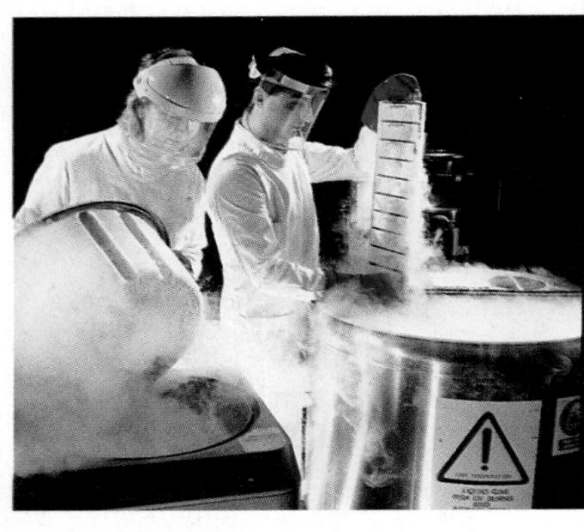

Cryogenics Laboratory

Hot Springs National Park, Arkansas

. . . Hot springs—also called thermal springs—are a popular tourist attraction. Thousands of people visit Hot Springs National Park in Arkansas each year. The average water temperature of the hot springs at the park is about 62°C.

Oxyacetylene Torch

. . . The hottest known flame is made by burning a mixture of oxygen and acetylene. The flame of an oxyacetylene torch can become as hot as 3,300°C. That's more than two times hotter than the melting point of steel.

. . . The hottest temperature in the universe occurs during a supernova—the explosion of a giant star. Temperatures can reach 3,500,000,000 Kelvin. The temperature of the surface of the Sun, by comparison, is about 5,600 K and the temperature of molten lava is 2,000 K.

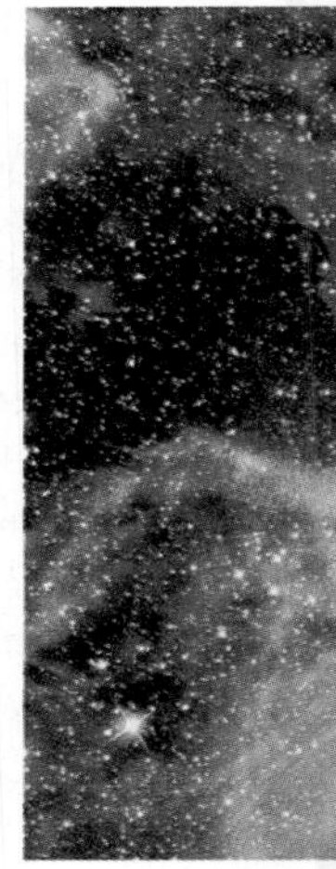

Supernova

Internet Addresses

Explore the Glencoe Science Web site at **science.glencoe.com** to find out more about topics in this feature.

Connecting To Math

. . . Air becomes a liquid at −195°C. Scientists use liquid air to extract liquid oxygen, which is used in high-energy fuels for rocket engines.

. . . The ideal serving temperature of ice cream is between −14°C and −12°C. In this temperature range, the ice cream is firm enough to hold its shape and deliver flavor.

Elements with the Highest Melting Points

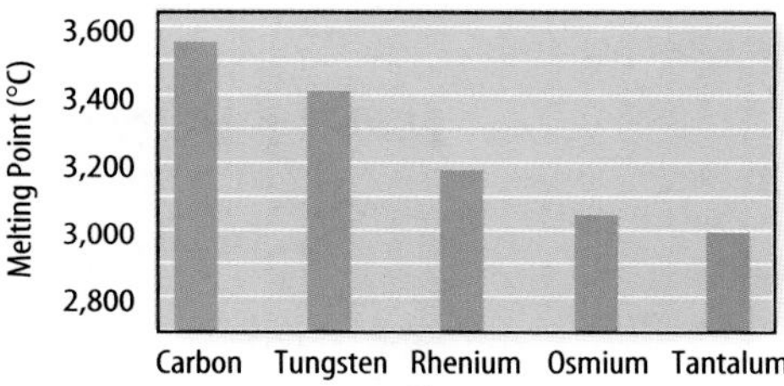

Elements

Do the Math

1. In 1983, the temperature dropped to −89°C in Vostok, Antarctica. How many more degrees Celsius would the temperature need to drop for the air to become a liquid?
2. Make a bar graph that compares the temperature of liquid helium, liquid air, and ice cream at serving temperature.
3. Look at the graph above. List the elements that could be melted by an oxyacetylene torch.

Go Further

Go to **science.glencoe.com** to research the melting points of six metals. Make a bar graph showing the data you find.

Connecting To Math

Do the Math

Teaching Strategies

- Use a number line to help students visually compare temperatures. On the chalkboard, draw a number line that represents Celsius temperatures.
- Have students locate the temperatures mentioned on pages 510–511. Have them first convert any temperatures in Kelvin to Celsius by subtracting 273 from the Kelvin temperature.
- Use the number line to emphasize to students that a negative temperature such as −245° C is colder than a temperature such as −32° C.

Answers

1. 106° C
2. Check students' graphs.
3. rhenium, osmium, and tantalum

Go Further

Remind students that metals are found on the left side of the periodic table. Encourage students to choose metals that noticeably vary in melting point.

Visual Learning

Have students use the graph to answer the following questions. **What is the difference between the melting points of tungsten and tantalum?** approximately 400° C **Carbon and tungsten are elements added to iron to make certain types of steel. How would adding one of these elements to iron affect its melting point?** It would raise it. **Why is tantalum used to make parts for nuclear reactors and missiles?** Both nuclear reactors and missiles can reach extreme temperatures. Tantalum will not melt at these temperatures. **Rhenium is used in aircraft in areas that might reach extremely hot temperatures. Where do you think these areas might be?** Rhenium is used in jet engines.

Chapter 16 Study Guide

Reviewing Main Ideas

Preview

Students can answer the questions in their Science Journals. Discuss the answers as you go through the chapter. LS **Linguistic**

Review

Students can write their answers, then compare them with those of other students. LS **Interpersonal**

Reteach

Students can look at the illustrations and describe details that support the main ideas of the chapter. LS **Visual-Spatial**

Answers to Chapter Review

Section 1

3. It keeps the concrete from cracking when it expands in hot weather and contracts in cold weather.

Section 2

1. Its weight is greater than the buoyant force acting on it.

Section 3

4. The pressure increases.

Chapter 16 Study Guide

Reviewing Main Ideas

Section 1 Kinetic Theory

1. Four states of matter exist: solid, liquid, gas, and plasma.
2. According to the kinetic theory, all matter is made of constantly moving particles that collide without losing energy.
3. Most matter expands when heated and contracts when cooled. *Why is the expansion joint needed in this concrete bridge shown below?*

4. Changes of state can be interpreted in terms of the kinetic theory of matter.

Section 2 Properties of Fluids

1. Archimedes' principle states that the buoyant force of an object in a fluid is equal to the weight of the fluid displaced. *In the photograph on the right, explain why the penny sank in the beaker of water.*

2. Pascal's principle states that pressure applied to a fluid is transmitted unchanged throughout the fluid.
3. Bernoulli's principle states that the pressure exerted by a fluid decreases as its velocity increases.

Section 3 Behavior of Gases

1. Gas pressure results from moving particles colliding with the inside walls of the container.
2. Boyle's law states that the volume of a gas decreases when the pressure increases, at constant temperature.
3. Charles's law states that the volume of a gas increases when the temperature increases, at constant pressure.
4. Gay-Lussac's law states that at constant volume, as the temperature increases, so does the gas pressure. *What happens to the pressure in this cylinder, as the temperature outdoors rises?*

FOLDABLES Reading & Study Skills — After You Read

Under the tabs of your Foldable, write and explain the characteristics of solids, liquids, and gases.

FOLDABLES Reading & Study Skills — After You Read

After students have read the chapter and completed the Foldable described in Before You Read, have them do the activity on the student page.

Dinah Zike

Chapter 16 Study Guide

Visualizing Main Ideas

Complete the following concept map on states of matter.

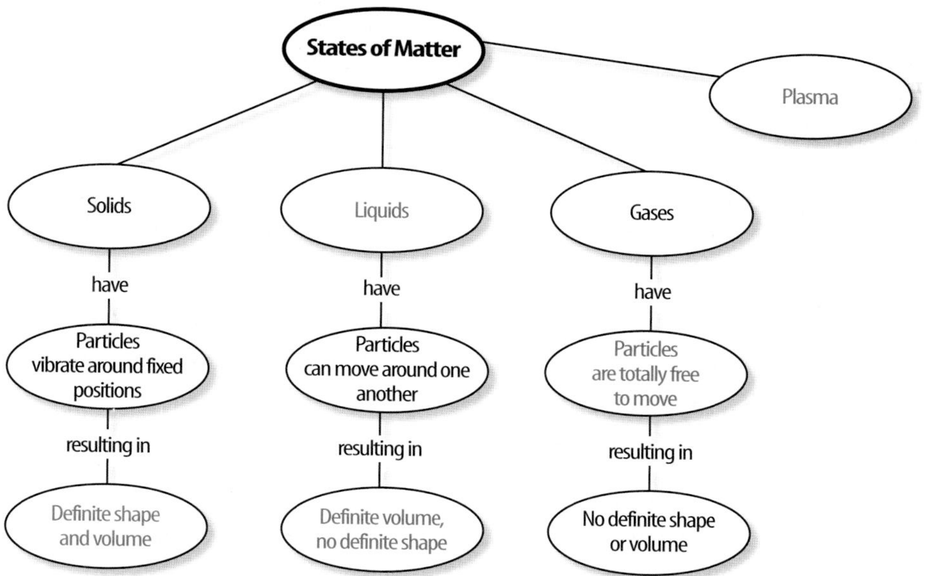

Vocabulary Review

Vocabulary Words

a. boiling point
b. buoyancy
c. diffusion
d. heat of fusion
e. heat of vaporization
f. kinetic theory
g. melting point
h. pascal
i. plasma
j. pressure
k. thermal expansion
l. viscosity

Study Tip

Make flashcards for new vocabulary words. Put the word on one side and the definition on the other. Use them to quiz yourself.

Using Vocabulary

Answer the following questions using complete sentences.

1. What is the property of a fluid that represents its resistance to flow?
2. What is the SI unit of pressure?
3. What term is used to describe the amount of force exerted per unit of area?
4. What is the temperature when a solid begins to liquefy?
5. What is used to explain the behavior of molecules in matter?
6. What is the ability of a fluid to exert an upward force on an object?

IDENTIFYING Misconceptions

Assessment

After doing the activity on page 486F and completing the chapter, have students perform this activity.

Materials rubbing alcohol, cotton wool, well ventilated room

Procedure Using the cotton, dab the backs of students' hands with rubbing alcohol. Ask students to write and explain their observations, including why they could see the rubbing alcohol when it was on their hands but not after it evaporated.

Expected Outcome In the liquid, the particles were close together so students could see the alcohol. When it evaporated the particles became far apart, so students could no longer see it, but the particles were still alcohol particles.

Visualizing Main Ideas

See student page.

Vocabulary Review

Using Vocabulary

1. Viscosity is the resistance of a fluid to flow.
2. The SI unit of pressure is the pascal.
3. Pressure is the amount of force exerted per unit of area.
4. A solid begins to liquefy at its melting point.
5. The kinetic theory is used to explain the behavior of molecules in matter.
6. Buoyancy is the ability of a fluid to exert an upward force on a body immersed in it.

Chapter 16 Assessment

Checking Concepts

1. A
2. A
3. D
4. C
5. B
6. A
7. A
8. D
9. C
10. A

Thinking Critically

11. Gay-Lussac's law states that if the volume of a gas sample remains constant, as the temperature increases, so does the pressure. When the temperature drops, so does the tire pressure. When the temperature rises, so does the tire pressure.
12. The pressure decreases outside of the balloon as the balloon rises, and the helium molecules force the walls of the balloon outward. At some point, the maximum pressure that the walls of the balloon can stand is reached and the balloon ruptures.
13. When temperature increases, pressure increases if volume stays the same. If pressure increases enough, the can might explode.
14. The density of the water is greater than normal because of minerals dissolved in the water. Due to its increased density, the water is able to exert a greater buoyant force on the floating body.

Chapter 16 Assessment

Checking Concepts

Choose the word or phrase that best answers the question.

1. What is the temperature at which all particle motion of matter ceases?
   A) absolute zero **C)** boiling point
   B) melting point **D)** heat of fusion

2. What is the state of matter that has a definite volume and a definite shape?
   A) solid **C)** gas
   B) liquid **D)** plasma

3. What is the most common state of matter in the universe?
   A) solid **C)** gas
   B) liquid **D)** plasma

4. Which of the following would be used to measure pressure?
   A) gram **C)** kilopascals
   B) newtons **D)** kilograms

5. Which of the following uses Pascal's principle?
   A) aerodynamics **C)** buoyancy
   B) hydraulics **D)** changes of state

6. Which of the following uses Bernoulli's principle?
   A) airplanes **C)** boats
   B) pistons **D)** snowboards

7. The particles in which of the following have no attraction for each other?
   A) gas **C)** liquid
   B) solid **D)** plasma

8. Which of the following has the property of diffusion?
   A) solid **C)** plasma
   B) liquid **D)** gas

9. What is the upward force in a liquid?
   A) pressure **C)** buoyancy
   B) kinetic theory **D)** diffusion

10. What is the amount of energy needed to change a solid to a liquid called?
    A) heat of fusion
    B) heat of vaporization
    C) temperature
    D) absolute zero

Thinking Critically

11. Use Gay-Lussac's law to explain why you should check your tire pressure when the temperature changes.
12. Describe the changes that occur inside a helium balloon as it rises from sea level.
13. Why do aerosol cans have a "do not incinerate" warning?
14. In the Dead Sea, the water is so dense that you float on it easily. Explain why you are able to float easily, using the terms *density* and *buoyant force.*

Developing Skills

15. **Making and Using Graphs** A group of students heated ice until it turned to steam. They measured the temperature each minute and graphed the results. Their graph is provided below. Explain what is happening at each letter (a, b, c, d) in the graph.

Temperature v. Time for Heating Water

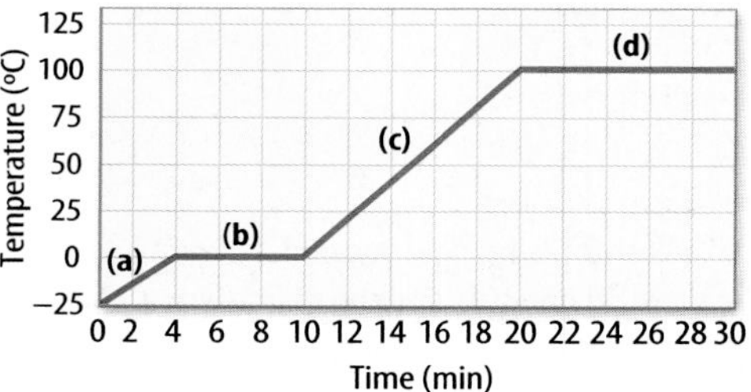

514 CHAPTER ASSESSMENT

Chapter Assessment Planner

Portfolio Encourage students to place in their portfolios one or two items of what they consider to be their best work. Examples include:
- Curriculum Connection, p. 491
- Reteach, p. 495
- Active Reading, p. 498
- Extension, p. 504

Performance Additional performance assessments, Performance Task Assessment Lists, and rubrics for evaluating these activities can be found in Glencoe's **Performance Assessment in the Science Classroom.**

16. Concept Mapping Use a cycle map to show the changes in particles as cool water boils, changes to steam, and then changes back to cool water.

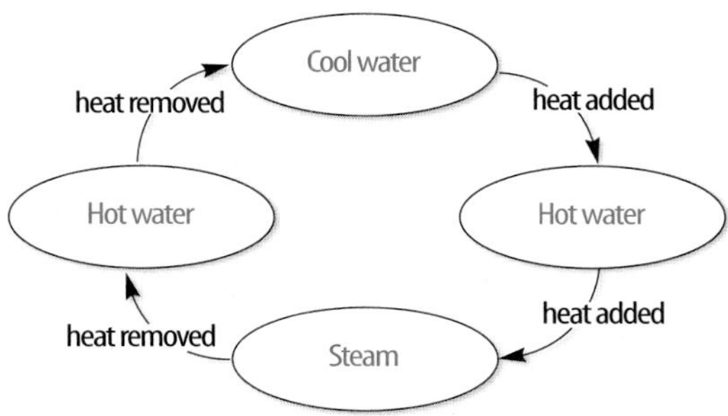

17. Interpreting Data As elevation increases, boiling point decreases. List each of the following locations as *at sea level, above sea level,* or *below sea level.* (Boiling point of water is given in parenthesis.)

Death Valley (100.3°C), Denver (94°C), Madison (99°C), Mt. Everest (76.5°C), Mt. McKinley (79°C), New York City (100°C), Salt Lake City (95.6°C)

Performance Assessment

18. Researching Research the effects of pressure changes on the human body and write a report. Include in your report any precautions that must be taken in dealing with pressure changes in space and when deep-sea diving.

Technology

Go to the Glencoe Science Web site at **science.glencoe.com** or use the **Glencoe Science CD-ROM** for additional chapter assessment.

THE PRINCETON REVIEW Test Practice

A geologist was investigating the effects of the change in seasons on rock formations. One of his observations is shown in the diagram below.

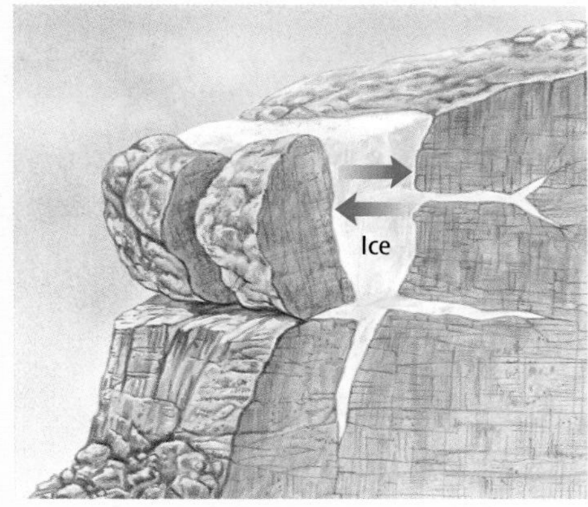

Study the picture and answer the following questions.

1. Which of these is the most likely cause of the rocks being wedged apart?
A) Water contains dissolved chemicals that eat away at rocks.
B) Cold water is more acidic than warm water.
C) Ice is more dense than water.
D) Water expands when it freezes.

2. The ice pushes outward in this manner in response to ______.
F) atmospheric pressure
G) temperature changes
H) glacial movement
J) gravity

Assessment Resources

 **Reproducible Masters**

Chapter Resources Booklet
Chapter Review, pp. 39–40
Chapter Tests, pp. 41–44
Assessment Transparency Activity, p. 51

Glencoe Science Web site
Interactive Tutor
Chapter Quizzess

Glencoe Technology
Assessment Transparency
Interactive CD-ROM Chapter Quizzes
ExamView Pro Test Bank
Vocabulary PuzzleMaker Software
MindJogger Videoquiz DVD/VHS

Chapter 16 Assessment

THE PRINCETON REVIEW Test Practice

The Test-Taking Tip was written by The Princeton Review, the nation's leader in test preparation.

1. D
2. G

Developing Skills

15. **a.** Ice is warming to its melting point. **b.** Ice is absorbing energy and melting. **c.** Liquid water is warming. **d.** Liquid is absorbing energy and boiling.
16. See student page.
17. above sea level: Denver, Madison, Mount Everest, Mount McKinley, Salt Lake City; at sea level: New York City; below sea level: Death Valley

Performance Assessment

18. Look for references to Boyle's and Charles's laws. Use **Performance Assessment in the Science Classroom,** p. 157.

CHAPTER 17 CLASSIFICATION OF MATTER

Section/Objectives	Standards		Activities/Features
	National	State/Local	
Chapter Opener	See p. 37T for a Key to Standards.		**Explore Activity:** Demonstrating the Distillation of Water, p. 517 **Before You Read,** p. 517
Section 1 Composition of Matter 3 sessions 1.5 blocks 1. **Define** substances and mixtures. 2. **Identify** elements and compounds. 3. **Compare and contrast** solutions, colloids, and suspensions.	National Content Standards: UCP2, A1, B1 (5–8), B2, B3, (9–12)		**Visualizing Elements,** p. 519 **MiniLAB:** Separating Mixtures, p. 521 **Activity:** Elements, Compounds, and Mixtures, p. 525
Section 2 Properties of Matter 4 sessions 2 blocks 1. **Identify** substances using physical properties. 2. **Compare and contrast** physical and chemical changes. 3. **Compare and contrast** chemical and physical properties. 4. **Determine** how the law of conservation of mass applies to chemical changes.	National Content Standards: UCP4, A1, B1 (5–8), B2, B3, B5, B6, (9–12)		**Environmental Science Integration,** p. 527 **MiniLAB:** Identifying Changes, p. 528 **Earth Science Integration,** p. 530 **Math Skills Activity:** Calculations with the Law of Conservation of Mass, p. 531 **Science Online,** p. 532 **Activity:** Checking Out Chemical Changes, p. 534 **Science Stats:** Intriguing Elements, p. 536

Activity Materials	Reproducible Resources	Section Assessment	Technology
Explore Activity: 2 beakers, water, red food coloring, hotplate, 15-cm x 15-cm sheet of aluminum foil	**Chapter Resources Booklet** Foldables Worksheet, p. 17 Note-taking Worksheets, pp. 31-32	GLENCOE'S ASSESSMENT ADVANTAGE	
MiniLAB: soil, clay, sand, gravel, pebbles, clear-plastic container, water **Activity:** plastic freezer bag to contain these labeled items: copper wire, small package of salt, pencil, aluminum foil, chalk (calcium carbonate), piece of granite, vial of sugar water	**Chapter Resources Booklet** Transparency Activity, p. 42 MiniLAB, p. 3 Enrichment, p. 29 Reinforcement, p. 27 Activity Worksheet, pp. 5–6 Transparency Activity, p. 45–46 Directed Reading, p. 20 Lab Activity, pp. 9-12 **Cultural Diversity,** p. 67 **Science Inquiry Labs,** p. 43 **Physical Science Critical Thinking/Problem Solving,** p. 9	**Portfolio** Science Journal, p. 520 **Performance** MiniLAB, p. 521 Skill Builder Activities, p. 524 **Content** Section Assessment, p. 524	Section Focus Transparency Teaching Transparency Interactive CD-ROM/DVD Guided Reading Audio Program
MiniLAB: 250-mL beaker, water, 1 crystal of potassium permanganate, 1 g sodium hydrogen sulfite, stirrer **Activity:** baking soda, small evaporating dish, hand lens, 1 *M* HCL, 10-mL graduated cylinder, electric hot plate	**Chapter Resources Booklet** Transparency Activity, p. 43 MiniLAB, p. 4 Enrichment, p. 30 Reinforcement, p. 28 Activity Worksheet, pp. 7–8 Directed Reading, pp. 21, 22 Lab Activity, pp. 13–16 **Science Inquiry Labs,** p. 21 **Home and Community Involvement,** p. 43 **Mathematics Skill Activities,** p. 9	**Portfolio** Science Journal, p. 530 Communicating Your Data, p. 535 **Performance** MiniLAB, p. 528 Math Skills Activity, p. 531 Skill Builder Activities, p. 533 **Content** Section Assessment, p. 533	Section Focus Transparency Interactive CD-ROM/DVD Guided Reading Audio Program

Need materials? Contact Science Kit at 1-800-828-7777 or www.sciencekit.com on the Internet.

End of Chapter Assessment

GLENCOE'S ASSESSMENT ADVANTAGE

Blackline Masters	Technology	Professional Series
Chapter Resources Booklet Chapter Review, pp. 35–36 Chapter Tests, pp. 37–40 **Standardized Test Practice by The Princeton Review,** pp.72–75	MindJogger Videoquiz CD-ROM Explorations and Quizzes Vocabulary Puzzle Makers ExamView Pro Test Bank Interactive Lesson Planner Interactive Teacher's Edition	Performance Assessment in the Science Classroom (PASC)

Transparencies

Section Focus

Section 1 Section Focus Transparency — Brilliant Sunset

What makes some sunsets have such rich, vibrant colors? The color of the sunset depends on the way in which light waves are scattered. Particles in the air scatter light. If the air is relatively free of particles, then the sunset will tend to look yellow. If there are a lot of particles in the air, however, the result is a sunset with fiery reds and oranges.

1. What are some components of air?
2. Why is air called a mixture?
3. How are compounds different than mixtures?

L1

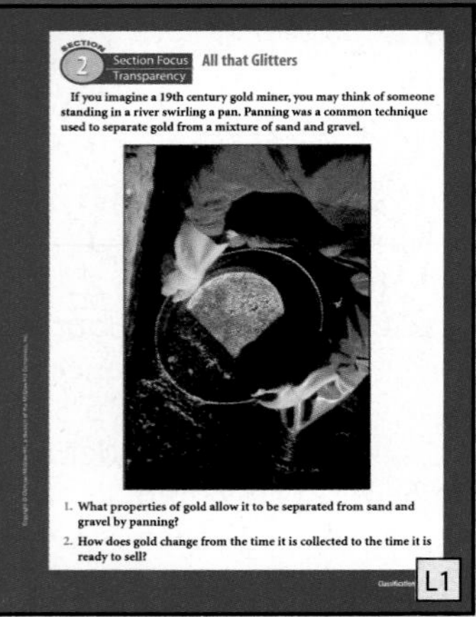
Section 2 Section Focus Transparency — All that Glitters

If you imagine a 19th century gold miner, you may think of someone standing in a river swirling a pan. Panning was a common technique used to separate gold from a mixture of sand and gravel.

1. What properties of gold allow it to be separated from sand and gravel by panning?
2. How does gold change from the time it is collected to the time it is ready to sell?

L1

This is a representation of key blackline masters available in the Teacher Classroom Resources. See Resource Manager boxes within the chapter for additional information.

Assessment

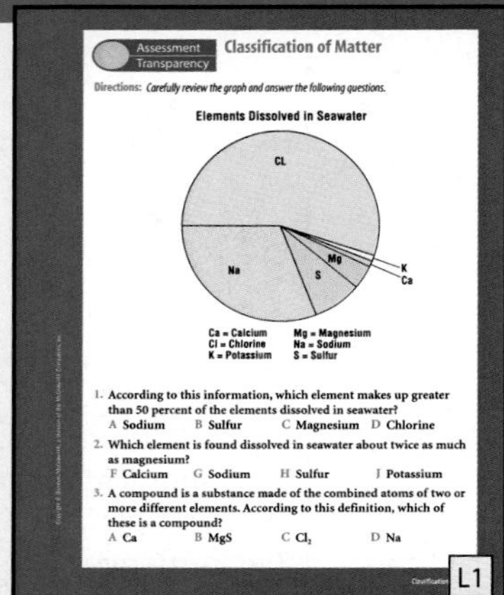
Assessment Transparency — Classification of Matter

Directions: *Carefully review the graph and answer the following questions.*

1. According to this information, which element makes up greater than 50 percent of the elements dissolved in seawater?
A Sodium B Sulfur C Magnesium D Chlorine
2. Which element is found dissolved in seawater about twice as much as magnesium?
F Calcium G Sodium H Sulfur J Potassium
3. A compound is a substance made of the combined atoms of two or more different elements. According to this definition, which of these is a compound?
A Ca B MgS C Cl_2 D Na

L1

Teaching

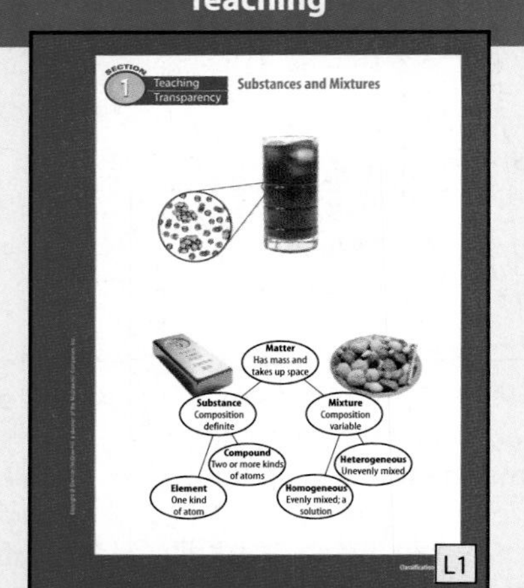
Section 1 Teaching Transparency — Substances and Mixtures

L1

Key to Teaching Strategies

The following designations will help you decide which activities are appropriate for your students.

- L1 Level 1 activities should be appropriate for students with learning difficulties.
- L2 Level 2 activities should be within the ability range of all students.
- L3 Level 3 activities are designed for above-average students.
- ELL ELL activities should be within the ability range of English Language Learners.
- COOP LEARN Cooperative Learning activities are designed for small group work.
- LS Multiple Learning Styles logos are used throughout to indicate strategies that address different learning styles.
- P These strategies represent student products that can be placed into a best-work portfolio.

Hands-on Activities

Activity Worksheets

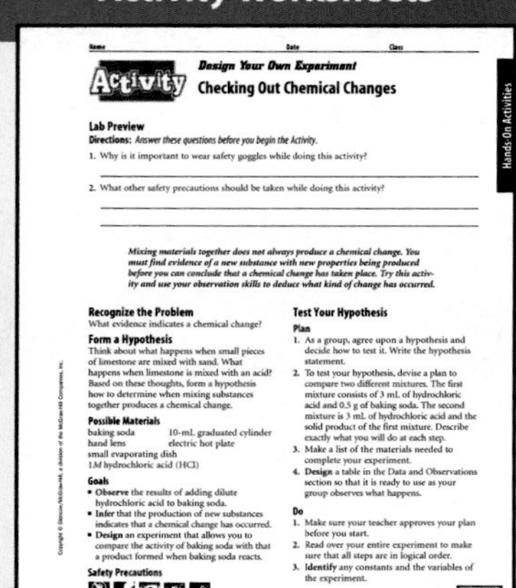
Activity — *Design Your Own Experiment* — Checking Out Chemical Changes

Lab Preview

Directions: *Answer these questions before you begin the Activity.*

1. Why is it important to wear safety goggles while doing this activity?
2. What other safety precautions should be taken while doing this activity?

L1

Laboratory Activities

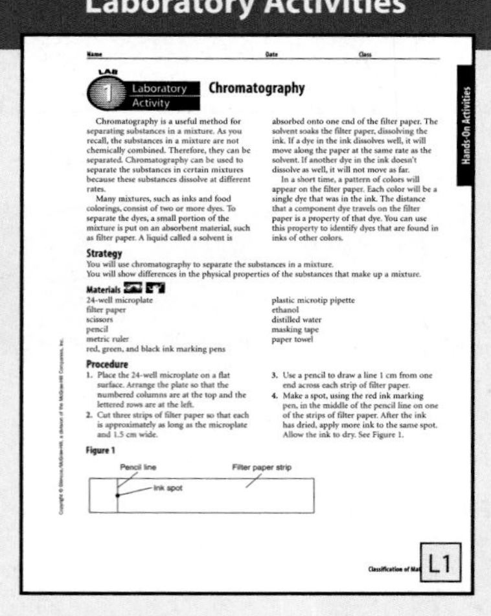
Lab 1 Laboratory Activity — Chromatography

L1

Meeting Different Ability Levels

Content Outline

Name Date Class

Note-taking Worksheet **Classification of Matter**

Section 1 Composition of Matter

A. ______________—either an element or a compound

1. When all the atoms in a substance are alike, the substance is an ______________.
2. A ______________ is a substance with two or more elements combined in a fixed proportion.

B. Two or more substances that can be easily separated by physical means form a ______________.

1. ______________ **mixture**—mixture of different and easily distinguishable materials
2. ______________ **mixture**—contains two or more gaseous, liquid, or solid substances blended evenly; also called a **solution**
3. ______________—heterogeneous mixture with larger particles that never settle; colloids scatter light in the **Tyndall effect**
4. A heterogeneous mixture containing a liquid in which visible particles settle is called a ______________.

Section 2 Properties of Matter

A. ______________—characteristics of a material which can be observed without changing the identity of the substances in the material; examples include color, shape, size, melting point, and boiling point

1. ______________—physical description of a substance
2. ______________—how a substance acts; for example, magnetism, viscosity, ductility
3. Physical properties such as size and magnetism can be used to ______________ mixtures.

B. ______________—change in a substance's size, shape, or state of matter

1. Substance does not change ______________ when it undergoes a physical change
2. ______________ is a process for separating a mixture by evaporating a liquid and condensing its vapor.

C. ______________ **property**—characteristics of a substance indicating that it can change chemically; for example, flammability or light sensitivity of a substance

Meeting Individual Needs

Classification of Matter L1

Reinforcement

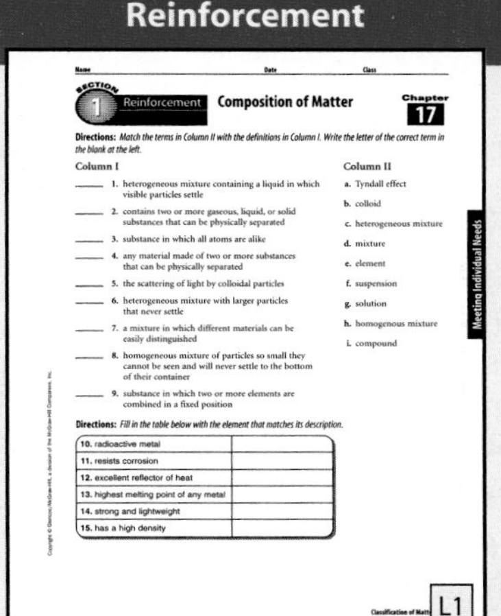
Name Date Class

Section 1 Reinforcement **Composition of Matter** Chapter 17

Directions: *Match the terms in Column II with the definitions in Column I. Write the letter of the correct term in the blank at the left.*

Column I

_____ 1. heterogeneous mixture containing a liquid in which visible particles settle
_____ 2. contains two or more gaseous, liquid, or solid substances that can be physically separated
_____ 3. substance in which all atoms are alike
_____ 4. any material made of two or more substances that can be physically separated
_____ 5. the scattering of light by colloidal particles
_____ 6. heterogeneous mixture with larger particles that never settle
_____ 7. a mixture in which different materials can be easily distinguished
_____ 8. homogeneous mixture of particles so small they cannot be seen and will never settle to the bottom of their container
_____ 9. substance in which two or more elements are combined in a fixed position

Column II

a. Tyndall effect
b. colloid
c. heterogeneous mixture
d. mixture
e. element
f. suspension
g. solution
h. homogeneous mixture
i. compound

Directions: *Fill in the table below with the element that matches its description.*

10. radioactive metal	
11. resists corrosion	
12. excellent reflector of heat	
13. highest melting point of any metal	
14. strong and lightweight	
15. has a high density	

Meeting Individual Needs

Classification of Matter L1

Directed Reading

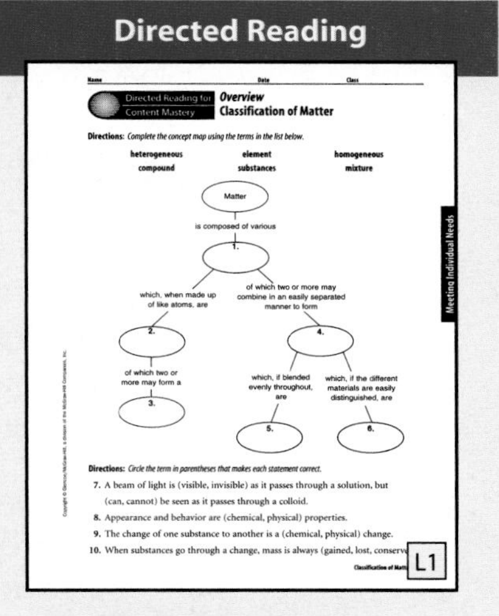
Name Date Class

Directed Reading for Content Mastery *Overview* **Classification of Matter**

Directions: *Complete the concept map using the terms in the list below.*

heterogeneous compound | element substances | homogeneous mixture

Directions: *Circle the term in parentheses that makes each statement correct.*

7. A beam of light is (visible, invisible) as it passes through a solution, but (can, cannot) be seen as it passes through a colloid.
8. Appearance and behavior are (chemical, physical) properties.
9. The change of one substance to another is a (chemical, physical) change.
10. When substances go through a change, mass is always (gained, lost, conserved).

Meeting Individual Needs

Classification of Matter L1

Enrichment

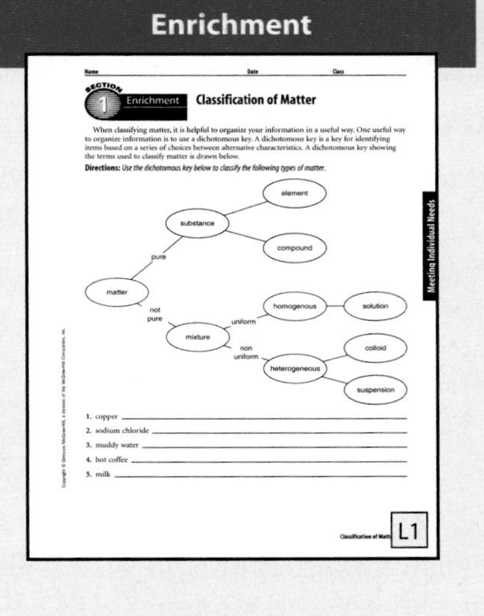
Name Date Class

Section 1 Enrichment **Classification of Matter**

When classifying matter, it is helpful to organize your information in a useful way. One useful way to organize information is to use a dichotomous key. A dichotomous key is a key for identifying items based on a series of choices between alternative characteristics. A dichotomous key showing the terms used to classify matter is drawn below.

Directions: *Use the dichotomous key below to classify the following types of matter.*

1. copper ______________
2. sodium chloride ______________
3. muddy water ______________
4. hot coffee ______________
5. milk ______________

Meeting Individual Needs

Classification of Matter L1

Spanish Directed Reading

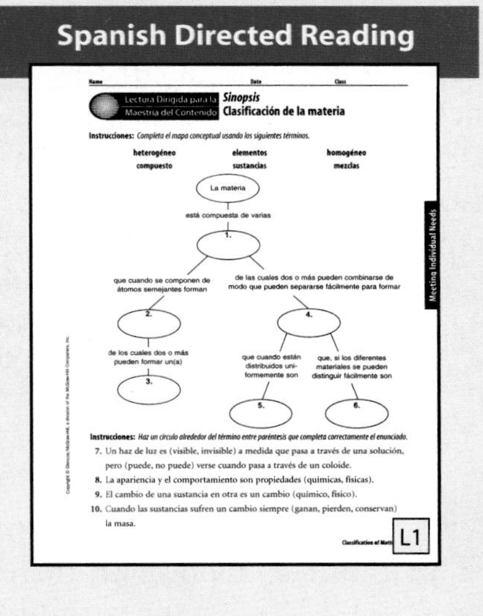
Name Date Class

Lectura Dirigida para la Maestría del Contenido *Sinopsis* **Clasificación de la materia**

Instrucciones: *Completa el mapa conceptual usando los siguientes términos.*

heterogéneo compuesto | elementos sustancias | homogéneo mezclas

Instrucciones: *Haz un círculo alrededor del término entre paréntesis que completa correctamente el enunciado.*

7. Un haz de luz es (visible, invisible) a medida que pasa a través de una solución, pero (puede, no puede) verse cuando pasa a través de un coloide.
8. La apariencia y el comportamiento son propiedades (químicas, físicas).
9. El cambio de una sustancia en otra es un cambio (químico, físico).
10. Cuando las sustancias sufren un cambio siempre (ganan, pierden, conservan) la masa.

Meeting Individual Needs

Classification of Matter L1

Assessment

Chapter Tests

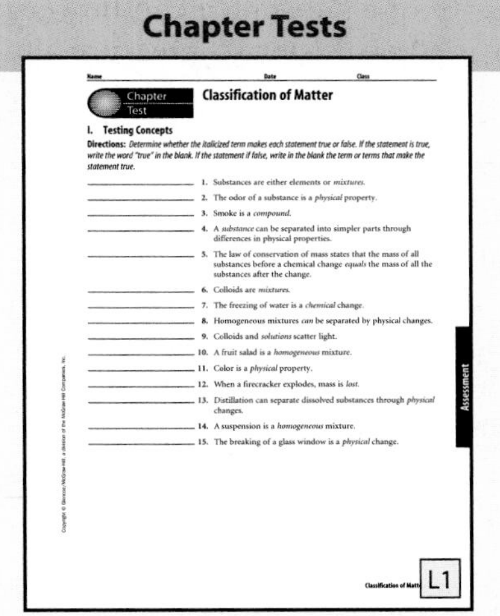
Name Date Class

Chapter Test **Classification of Matter**

I. Testing Concepts

Directions: *Determine whether the italicized term makes each statement true or false. If the statement is true, write the word "true" in the blank. If the statement if false, write in the blank the term or terms that make the statement true.*

______ 1. Substances are either elements or *mixtures*.
______ 2. The odor of a substance is a *physical* property.
______ 3. Smoke is a *compound*.
______ 4. A substance can be separated into simpler parts through differences in physical properties.
______ 5. The law of conservation of mass states that the mass of all substances before a chemical change *equals* the mass of all the substances after the change.
______ 6. Colloids are *mixtures*.
______ 7. The freezing of water is a *chemical* change.
______ 8. Homogeneous mixtures *can* be separated by physical changes.
______ 9. Colloids and *solutions* scatter light.
______ 10. A fruit salad is a *homogeneous* mixture.
______ 11. Color is a physical property.
______ 12. When a firecracker explodes, mass is *lost*.
______ 13. Distillation can separate dissolved substances through *physical* changes.
______ 14. A suspension is a *homogeneous* mixture.
______ 15. The breaking of a glass window is a *physical* change.

Assessment

Classification of Matter L1

Test Practice Workbook

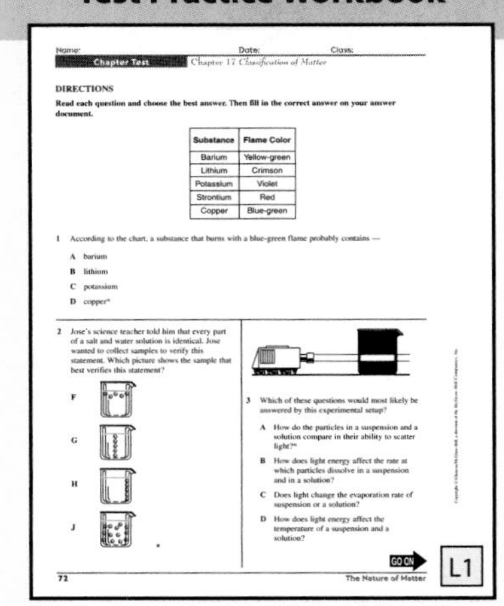
Name: Date: Class:

Chapter Test Chapter 17 Classification of Matter

DIRECTIONS

Read each question and choose the best answer. Then fill in the correct answer on your answer document.

Substance	Flame Color
Barium	Yellow-green
Lithium	Crimson
Potassium	Violet
Strontium	Red
Copper	Blue-green

1 According to the chart, a substance that burns with a blue-green flame probably contains —

A barium
B lithium
C potassium
D copper*

2 Jose's science teacher told him that every part of a salt and water solution is identical. Jose wanted to collect samples to verify this statement. Which picture shows the sample that best verifies this statement?

F
G
H
J

3 Which of these questions would most likely be answered by this experimental setup?

A How do the particles in a suspension and a solution compare in their ability to scatter light?*
B How does light energy affect the rate at which particles dissolve in a suspension and in a solution?
C Does light change the evaporation rate of suspension or a solution?
D How does light energy affect the temperature of a suspension and a solution?

GO ON

72 The Nature of Matter L1

Chapter Review

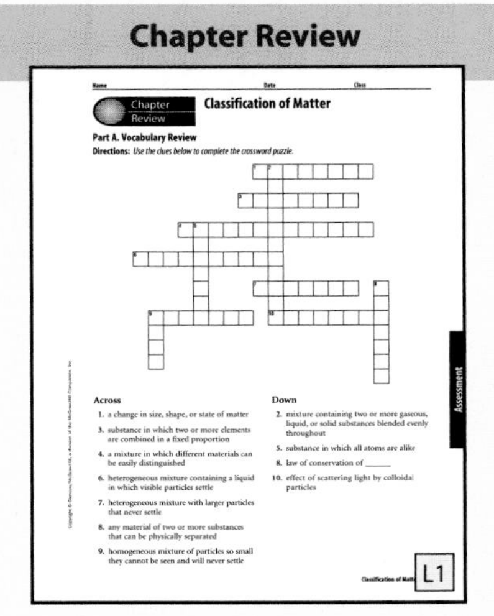
Name Date Class

Chapter Review **Classification of Matter**

Part A. Vocabulary Review

Directions: *Use the clues below to complete the crossword puzzle.*

Across

1. a change in size, shape, or state of matter
3. substance in which two or more elements are combined in a fixed proportion
4. a mixture in which different materials can be easily distinguished
6. heterogeneous mixture containing a liquid in which visible particles settle
7. heterogeneous mixture with larger particles that never settle
8. any material of two or more substances that can be physically separated
9. homogeneous mixture of particles so small they cannot be seen and will never settle

Down

2. mixture containing two or more gaseous, liquid, or solid substances blended evenly throughout
5. substance in which all atoms are alike
8. law of conservation of ______
10. effect of scattering light by colloidal particles

Assessment

Classification of Matter L1

Science Content Background

SECTION 1

Composition of Matter

Pure Substances

All matter can be divided into mixtures and pure substances. Pure substances can be described as either elements or chemical compounds. Mixtures can be either heterogeneous or homogeneous. Homogeneous mixtures are usually called solutions and have a constant composition. Heterogeneous mixtures have regions with visibly different compositions. Homogeneous mixtures tend to be transparent, whereas heterogeneous mixtures are often cloudy and separate on standing.

Student Misconception

Matter is not conserved in physical or chemical changes

Refer to the facing page for teaching strategies to address this misconception. Refer to page 532 for content related to this topic.

Elements

There are 90 naturally occurring elements; however, there are more than 90 different substances found on Earth. All the substances found on the earth are formed when atoms of two or more different elements combine, creating new materials with new properties.

SECTION 2

Properties of Matter

Physical Properties

The characteristics, or properties, that are used to describe matter can be classified in several ways. Physical properties are those that can be determined without changing the chemical composition of the sample, whereas chemical properties are those that do involve a chemical change in the sample. Intensive properties are those that have values that do not depend on the size of the sample. Extensive properties do depend on the size of the sample. Density, the intensive property that relates mass to volume, is one of the most important and useful physical properties. Knowing the density of a substance can be very useful, because it is often easier to measure the volume of a liquid than its mass.

Conservation of Mass

The law of conservation of matter states that matter is not created or destroyed but only converted from one form into another. Thus in a chemical reaction, the amount of matter before the reaction is the same as after the reaction. This is equally true for phase changes. Although a material may turn from a solid to a liquid to a gas, the amount of matter is conserved.

For additional content background on this topic, go to the Glencoe Science Web site at science.glencoe.com.

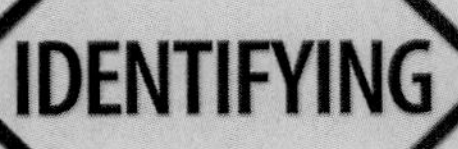

IDENTIFYING Misconceptions

Find Out What Students Think

Students may think that . . .

- **Matter is not conserved in physical or chemical changes.**

Perceptions are often more dominant than logic, and for students it may look as though matter simply vanishes when it turns into an invisible gas. When wood burns in a fire, it is obvious that only ashes remain, but it is not obvious what has happened to the bulk of the wood. For these reasons, students may not recognize the conservation of matter in physical or chemical changes.

Demonstration

Present Figure 1 to students. Tell them that the mass of the jar with everything in it is 500 g. Suppose the magnifying glass is used to light the candle, which then burns in the oxygen-enriched air for about one minute before going out. Ask students to describe any changes that have occurred in the jar. Is the mass of the jar and everything in it now less than, the same as, or greater than 500 g? The mass is still 500 g.

Promote Understanding

Activity

Prior to class fill small plastic soda bottles two-thirds full of water, cap the bottles, and freeze.

On the day of the activity, provide each group of students with one frozen bottle and a paper towel. Then ask students in each group to

- dry the outside of the bottle and find its mass.
- predict what the mass of the bottle will be when the water melts.
- leave the bottles overnight so that the water inside them melts.

On the next day, have students dry the outside of the bottles and find their masses.

Make a table on the board with columns labeled "Mass of Bottle with Frozen Water" And "Mass of Bottle with Liquid Water" and a row for each group. Ask a member of each group to fill in the data for that group. With the class, analyze the data in the table. Discuss why the masses stayed the same. Help students realize that the bottles were closed so no mass was added to or subtracted from them.

Assess

After completing the chapter, see *Identifying Misconceptions* in the Study Guide.

Classification of Matter

Chapter Vocabulary

substance
element
compound
heterogeneous mixture
homogeneous mixture
solution
colloid
Tyndall effect
suspension
physical property
physical change
distillation
chemical property
chemical change
law of conservation of mass

What do you think?

Science Journal This is a close-up view of paints on an artist's palette. Blending makes a heterogeneous mixture. Continued blending will make a homogeneous mixture.

CHAPTER 17

Classification of Matter

Paintings like this one are mixtures that combine many different chemical pigments. They can be mixed skillfully to achieve a well blended color or the artist can intentionally show the individual pigments within one brush stroke. All the materials in a painting can undergo physical and chemical changes with time. In this chapter, you will learn about mixtures and how to separate them. You also will learn about the physical and chemical properties of matter and you'll learn to distinguish between physical and chemical change.

What do you think?

Science Journal Look at the picture below with a classmate. Discuss what you think this might be or what is happening. Here's a hint: *Let the layers settle it.* Write your answer or your best guess in your Science Journal.

516

Theme Connection

Stability and Change Matter can undergo physical and chemical changes. The stability of a substance affects how and when it will change.

Imagine yourself marooned on an island without fresh water. What could you do to get clean drinking water? Could you purify seawater? One way you could do this is distillation. Discover how to purify water in this activity.

Demonstrating the Distillation of Water 

1. Place 200 mL of water in a large beaker and add 20 drops of red food coloring.
2. Place the beaker on a hotplate.
3. Fold a 15 cm × 15 cm sheet of aluminum foil in half to make a tent. Then fold each half diagonally upward to make wings as shown in the photo. The tent should be about 6 cm high at one end and 2 cm at the other.
4. Place the foil tent over the beaker with the low end hanging over the edge.
5. Place a second beaker under the foil overhang.
6. Turn on the hotplate and observe what happens when the water boils.

Observe

Write a paragraph in your Science Journal describing what happens. Comment on how distillation purifies water.

Before You Read

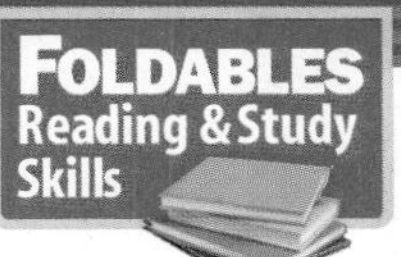

Making a Vocabulary Study Fold **Make the following Foldable to ensure you have understood the content by defining the vocabulary terms from this chapter.**

1. Place a sheet of paper in front of you so the long side is at the top. Fold the paper in half from the left side to the right side.
2. Fold the top and bottom in. Unfold the paper so three sections show.
3. Through the top thickness of the pater, cut along each of the fold lines to fold on the left, forming three tabs. Label *Elements, Compounds,* and *Mixtures* across the front of the tabs as shown.
4. As you read the chapter, define each term and list examples of each under the tabs.

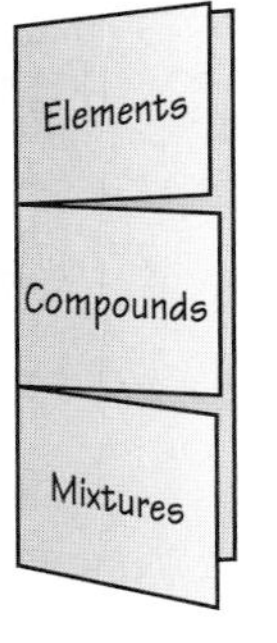

517

Explore Activity

Purpose Use this Explore Activity to demonstrate for students how water can be distilled and purified.

Preparation First try this activity yourself so that you can advise groups on how the aluminum foil should be folded and positioned on the beaker. Set up a hotplate for each group.

Materials two large beakers, water, food dye, sheet of aluminum foil, scissors, and a hotplate for each group

Teaching Strategies To extend this activity, give every student a sheet of aluminum foil and stage a contest to determine who can create a foil design that produces the maximum distillation rate.

Observe

Water droplets from the steam rising from the boiling water will condense on the foil and drip into the second beaker. The water in the second beaker will be clear. The distillation process will separate the water from the food dye.

Assessment

Content Have each group imagine they are marooned on a tropical island without supplies. Ask them what island materials or materials they are wearing could they use to construct an apparatus for distilling water. The lens of a pair of glasses could magnify sunlight on dried grass to produce a fire. Empty coconut shells could replace beakers and large tropical leaves could replace aluminum foil. Use **Performance Assessment in the Science Classroom,** p. 91.

Before You Read

FOLDABLES Reading & Study Skills

Dinah Zike Study Fold

Purpose Make and use a Foldable to determine what students know about elements, compounds, and mixtures before reading the chapter. The Foldable will provide a place for students to define terms and record data while reading.

For additional help, see Foldables Worksheet, p. 17 in **Chapter Resources Booklet,** or go to the Glencoe Science Web site at **science.glencoe.com.** See After You Read in the Study Guide at the end of this chapter.

SECTION

Composition of Matter

1 Motivate

Bellringer Transparency

Display the Section Focus Transparency for Section 1. Use the accompanying Transparency Activity Master. L2 ELL

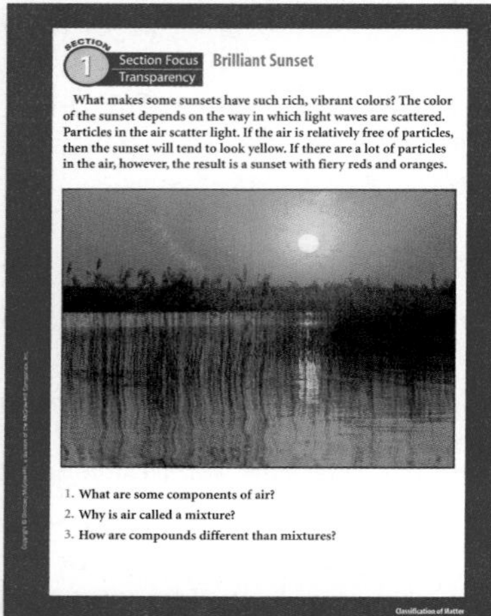
Section Focus Transparency — Brilliant Sunset

What makes some sunsets have such rich, vibrant colors? The color of the sunset depends on the way in which light waves are scattered. Particles in the air scatter light. If the air is relatively free of particles, then the sunset will tend to look yellow. If there are a lot of particles in the air, however, the result is a sunset with fiery reds and oranges.

1. What are some components of air?
2. Why is air called a mixture?
3. How are compounds different than mixtures?

Tie to Prior Knowledge

Ask students to describe the types of substances present in an ice cream soda. Possible answer: liquid and solid ice cream, liquid flavored syrup, liquid soda water, gas carbon dioxide, whipped cream, solid cherry Tell students that the whipped cream is a colloid—a heterogeneous mixture in which the particles are very small.

SECTION

Composition of Matter

As You Read

What You'll Learn

- **Define** substances and mixtures.
- **Identify** elements and compounds
- **Compare and contrast** solutions, colloids, and suspensions.

Vocabulary

substance
element
compound
heterogeneous mixture
homogeneous mixture
solution
colloid
Tyndall effect
suspension

Why It's Important

You can form a better picture of your world when you understand the concepts of elements and compounds.

Pure Substances

Have you ever seen a picture hanging on a wall that looked just like a real painting? Did you have to touch it to find out? If so, the rough or smooth surface told you which it was. Each material has its own properties. The properties of materials can be used to classify them into general categories.

Materials are made of a pure substance or a mixture of substances. A pure **substance,** or merely a substance, is either an element or a compound. Substances cannot be broken down into simpler components and still maintain the properties of the original substance. Some substances you might recognize are helium, aluminum, water, and salt.

Elements All substances are built from atoms. If all the atoms in a substance are alike, that substance is an **element.** The graphite in your pencil point and copper coating of most pennies are examples of elements. In graphite all the atoms are carbon atoms, and in a pure copper sample, all the atoms are copper atoms. The metal substance beneath the copper in the penny is another element—zinc. There are 90 elements found in nature. More than 20 others have been made in laboratories, but most are unstable and exist only for short periods of time. Some elements you might recognize are shown in **Figure 1.** Some less common elements and their properties are shown in **Figure 2.**

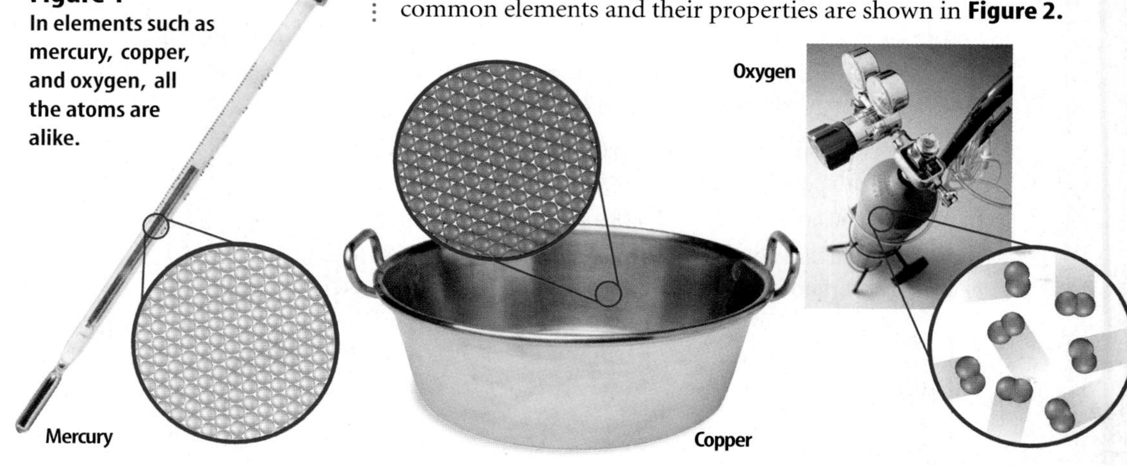

Figure 1
In elements such as mercury, copper, and oxygen, all the atoms are alike.

Section Assessment Planner

PORTFOLIO
Science Journal, p. 520

PERFORMANCE ASSESSMENT
Try at Home MiniLAB, p. 521
Skill Builder Activities, p. 524
See page 540 for more options.

CONTENT ASSESSMENT
Section, p. 524
Challenge, p. 524
Chapter, pp. 540–541

NATIONAL GEOGRAPHIC **VISUALIZING ELEMENTS**

Figure 2

Most of us think of gold as a shiny yellow metal used to make jewelry. However, it is an element that is also used in more unexpected ways, such as in spacecraft parts. On the other hand, some less common elements, such as americium (am-uh-REE-see-um), are used in everyday objects. Some elements and their uses are shown here.

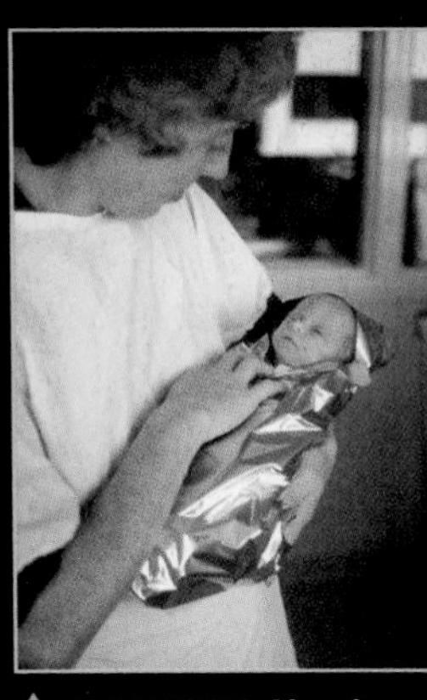

▲ ALUMINUM Aluminum is an excellent reflector of heat. Here, an aluminum plastic laminate is used to retain the body heat of a newborn baby.

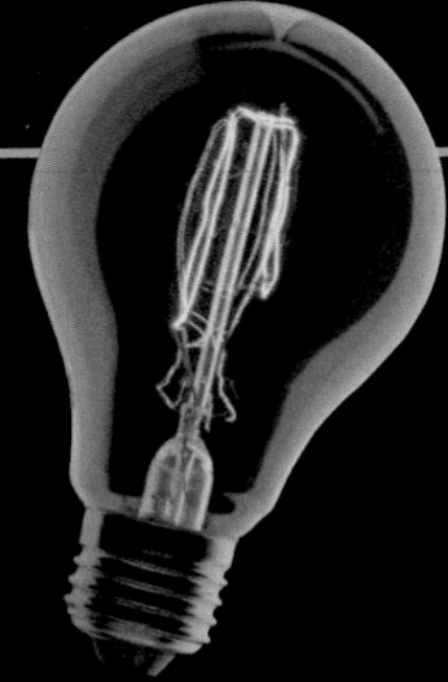

▲ TUNGSTEN Although tungsten can be combined with steel to form a very durable metal, in its pure form it is soft enough to be stretched to form the filament of a lightbulb. Tungsten has the highest melting point of any metal.

▲ TITANIUM (Tie-TAY-nee-um) Parts of the exterior of the Guggenheim Museum in Bilbao, Spain, are made of titanium panels. Strong and lightweight, titanium is also used for body implants.

▲ GOLD Gold's resistance to corrosion and its ability to reflect infrared radiation make it an excellent coating for space vehicles. The electronic box on the six-wheel Sojourner Rover, above, part of NASA's Pathfinder 1997 mission to Mars, is coated with gold.

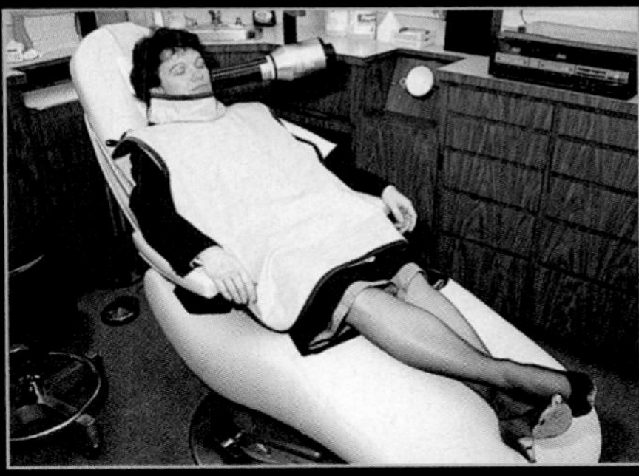

▲ LEAD Because lead has a high density, it is a good barrier to radiation. Dentists drape lead aprons on patients before taking x-rays of the patient's teeth to reduce radiation exposure.

◀ AMERICIUM Named after America, where it was first produced, americium is a component of this smoke detector. It is a radioactive metal that must be handled with care to avoid contact.

SECTION 1 Composition of Matter 519

Figure 2 Visualizing Elements

Have students examine the pictures and read the captions. Then ask the following questions. **Why is pure tungsten used for the filaments of light bulbs?** Because pure tungsten is resistant to electron flow, which is why it glows—gives off light—when current passes through it. **Why is it important to drape the trunk of your body during X rays?** To avoid unnecessary radiation exposure to your vital organs. **Can you think other ways that the reflective properties of aluminum are used?** Answers will vary but may include some of the following: cooking, emergency blankets, and signaling mirrors. **Why would the Sojourner Rover need to reflect infrared radiation?** To protect the equipment inside the box from excessive infrared radiation.

Activity

Have students research and find out why americium is used in smoke detectors. Have the students report their findings to the class.

Extension

Challenge students to find out why titanium is used for body implants and why it is used in aircraft landing gear. The students should report their findings to their class.

Resource Manager 

Chapter Resources Booklet

Note-taking Worksheets, pp. 31–32
Transparency Activity, p. 42
Directed Reading for Content Mastery, p. 20

2 Teach

Pure Substances

Discussion

Describe for students two liquids. Tell them that both liquids contain only hydrogen and oxygen, and both liquids are transparent and colorless. **How can the two liquids have different identities?** They have different combinations of atoms. One liquid is water, H_2O; the other is hydrogen peroxide, H_2O_2. L2 IN **Logical-Mathematical**

Misconceptions

Students may think that any bonding of atoms forms a compound. However, chlorine gas is the diatomic molecule Cl_2. This combination of chlorine atoms is always the same, but this substance is not a compound. Compounds must be made from combinations of different elements.

Use an Analogy

In pedal-powered vehicles, the ratio of one frame to one wheel makes a unicycle. One frame to two wheels forms a bicycle. One frame to three wheels produces a tricycle. Similarly, one carbon to one atom of oxygen makes carbon monoxide. One carbon to two oxygen atoms is carbon dioxide. These compounds do not have the same properties.

Reading Check

Answer Compounds contain two or more elements.

Compounds Two or more elements can combine to form substances called compounds. A **compound** is a substance in which two or more elements are combined in a fixed proportion. For example, water is a compound in which the elements hydrogen and oxygen are combined in the ratio of two hydrogen atoms to one oxygen atom. Chalk contains calcium, carbon and oxygen in the proportion of one atom of calcium and carbon to three of oxygen.

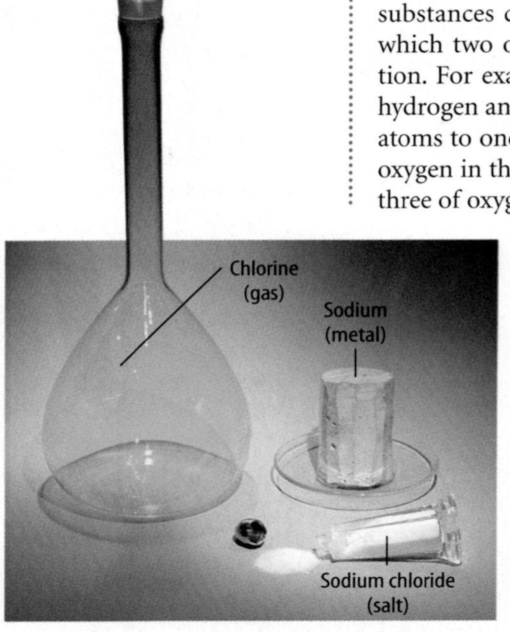

Figure 3
Chlorine gas and sodium metal combine dramatically in the ratio of one to one to form sodium chloride.

Reading Check *How are elements and compounds related?*

Can you imagine yourself putting something made from a silvery metal and a greenish-yellow, poisonous gas on your food? You might have shaken some on your food today—table salt is a chemical compound that fits this description. Even though it looks like white crystals and adds flavor to food, its components—sodium and chlorine—are neither white nor salty, as shown in **Figure 3.** Like salt, compounds usually look different from the elements in them.

Mixtures

Are pizza and a soft drink one of your favorite lunches? If so, you enjoy two foods that are classified as mixtures—but two different kinds of mixtures. A mixture, such as the pizza or soft drink shown in **Figure 4,** is a material made up of two or more substances that can be easily separated by physical means.

Figure 4
Pizza and soft drinks, like most foods, are mixtures.

Science Journal

Elements and Compounds Ask students to list in their Science Journals all the elements and chemical compounds they can think of without looking them up. Have them look up the chemical symbols for the elements and the chemical formulas for the compounds. Have them write the formulas next to the names of the substances. L2 ELL IN **Linguistic** P

Heterogeneous Mixtures Unlike compounds, mixtures do not always contain the same proportions of the substances that make them up—the pizza chef doesn't measure precisely how much of each topping is sprinkled on. You easily can see all the toppings on a pizza. A mixture in which different materials can be distinguished easily is called a **heterogeneous** (het uh ruh JEE nee us) **mixture.** Granite, concrete, and dry soup mixes are other heterogeneous mixtures you can recognize.

You might be wearing another heterogeneous mixture—clothing made of permanent-press fabric like that seen in **Figure 5A.** Such fabric contains fibers of two materials—polyester and cotton. The amounts of polyester and cotton can vary from one article of clothing to another, as shown by the label. Though you might not be able to distinguish the two fibers just by looking at them with your naked eye, you probably could tell using a microscope, as shown in **Figure 5B.** Therefore, a permanent-press fabric is also a heterogeneous mixture.

Most of the substances you come in contact with every day are heterogeneous mixtures. Some components are easy to see, like the ingredients in pizza, but others are not. In fact, the component you see can be a mixture itself. For example, the cheese in pizza is also a mixture, but you cannot see the individual components. Cheese contains many compounds, such as milk proteins, butterfat, colorings, and other food additives.

Separating Mixtures

Procedure

1. Put equal amounts of **soil, clay, sand, gravel,** and **pebbles** in a **clear-plastic container.** Add **water** until the container is almost full. Wash your hands well after handling the materials.
2. Stir or shake the mixture thoroughly. Predict the order in which the materials will settle.
3. Observe what happens and compare your observations to your predictions.

Analysis

1. In what order did the materials settle?
2. Explain why the materials settled in the order they did.

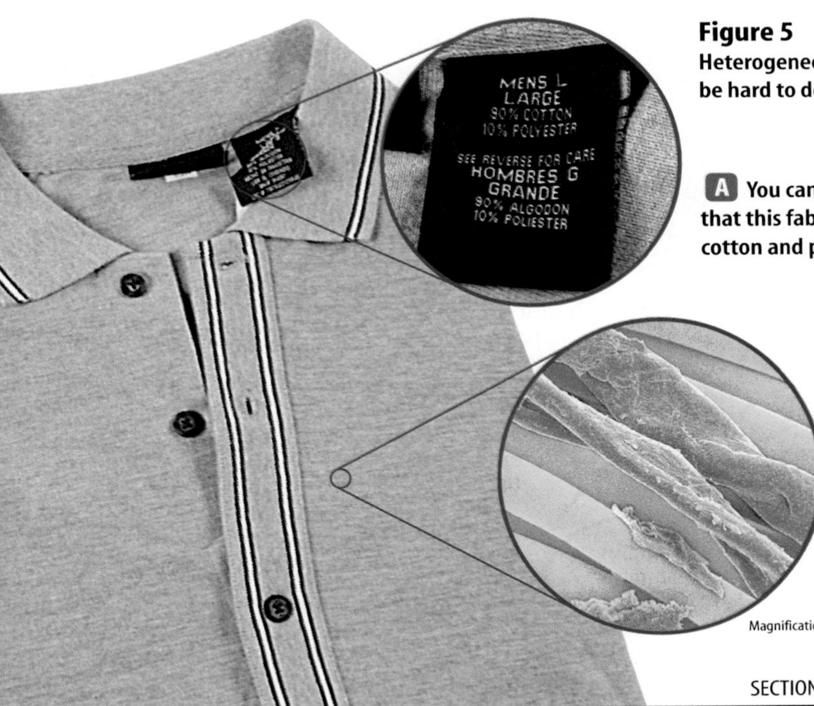

Figure 5
Heterogeneous mixtures can be hard to detect.

A You can't tell at a glance that this fabric is a mixture of cotton and polyester.

B With a microscope however, the difference between the two fibers is clear—the polyester fiber is perfectly smooth and the cotton is rough.

Magnification: 600×

Mixtures

Purpose Students observe that heterogeneous mixtures have identifiable components that do not lose their identities while in the mixture. LS **Kinesthetic**

Materials transparent plastic gallon jar, soil, clay, sand, gravel, small pebbles, water

Teaching Strategy Have students write down their predictions of the order of settling before they make the mixture.

Analysis

1. gravel, pebbles, sand, soil, clay
2. The materials settled out by particle size.

Assessment

Performance Have students use their answers to Question 3 to physically separate the components in the mixture. Use **Performance Assessment in the Science Classroom,** p. 121.

Resource Manager 

Chapter Resources Booklet
Enrichment, p. 29
MiniLAB, p. 3

Physical Science Critical Thinking/ Problem Solving, p. 9

Teacher FYI

Heterogeneous mixtures contain more than one phase. A phase is a region with uniform properties that has a boundary between itself and other areas of uniform properties. For example, the structure, heat capacity, and density of floating ice vary from the liquid water in which it is floating.

Mixtures, continued

Discussion

Remind students that the components of a homogeneous mixture are blended evenly throughout the mixture. Tell students that an alloy can be a solid homogeneous mixture of metals. **How can two solid metals mix homogeneously?** The metals are melted, mixed as liquids, and then allowed to become solid again. L2 IS **Logical-Mathematical**

Activity

Bring four bags to class. Using large lettering, label the bags Element, Compound, Homogeneous, and Heterogeneous. Have students bring objects from home and place each one in the proper bag. After a week, empty the bags and discuss their contents and their classifications with the class. L2 ELL IS **Kinesthetic**

Visual Learning

Figure 7 Bring to class some aluminum foil, cereal with raisins, and liquid made from powdered, flavored drink mix dissolved in water. Have students classify these materials using the chart shown in **Figure 7.** Aluminum foil is an element; raisin cereal is a heterogeneous mixture; powdered, flavored drink mix dissolved in water is a homogeneous mixture. L2 IS **Visual-Spatial**

Answer a homogeneous mixture

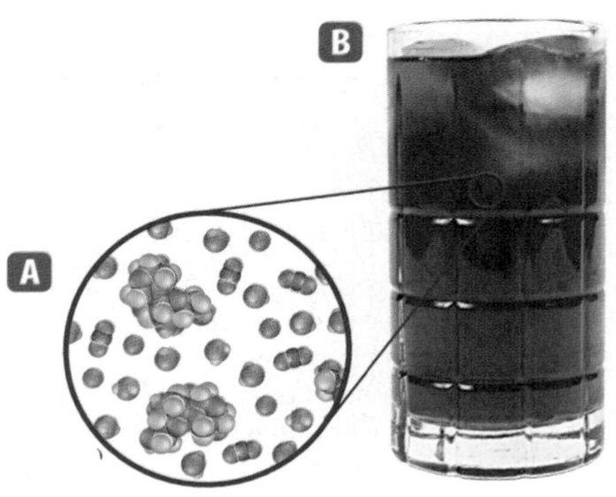

Figure 6
A soft drink can be either heterogeneous or homogeneous.
A As carbon dioxide fizzes out it is a heterogeneous mixture.
B The resulting flat soft drink is a homogeneous mixture of water, sugar, flavor, color and some remaining carbon dioxide.

Homogeneous Mixtures Remember that soft drink you had with your pizza? Regular and diet soft drinks look alike but taste different and contain different amounts of calories.

Cold soft drinks in sealed bottles are examples of homogeneous mixtures. A **homogeneous** (hoh muh JEE nee us) **mixture** contains two or more gaseous, liquid, or solid substances blended evenly throughout. Soft drinks contain water, sugar, flavoring, coloring, and carbon dioxide gas. **Figure 6** will help you to visualize these particles in a liquid soft drink.

Vinegar is another homogeneous mixture. It appears clear even though it is made up of particles of acetic acid mixed with water. Another name for homogeneous mixtures like vinegar and a cold soft drink is solution. A **solution** is a homogeneous mixture of particles so small that they cannot be seen with a microscope and will never settle to the bottom of their container. Solutions remain constantly and uniformly mixed. The differences between substances and mixtures are summarized in **Figure 7.**

Reading Check *What kind of mixture is a solution?*

Colloids Milk is an example of a specific kind of mixture called a colloid. Like a heterogeneous mixture, it contains water, fats, and proteins in varying proportions. Like a solution, its components won't settle if left standing. A **colloid** (KAH loyd) is a heterogeneous mixture that never settles. Its particles are larger than those in solutions but not heavy enough to settle. The word *colloid* comes from a Greek word for glue. The first colloids studied were in gelatin, a source of some types of glue.

Paint is an example of a liquid with suspended colloid particles. Gases and solids can contain colloidal particles, too. For example, fog consists of particles of liquid water suspended in air, and smoke contains solids suspended in air.

Figure 7
All matter can be divided into substances and mixtures.

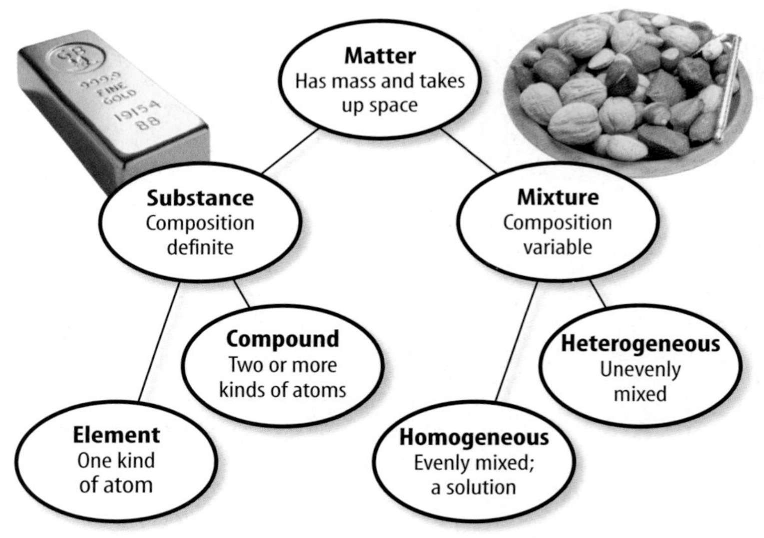

Curriculum Connection

Math Have students express the particle diameter given for solutions (0.000,000,001 m) in exponential notation. 1×10^{-9} m Then, ask them to convert the number to inches and to calculate how many particles it would take to go across one inch. 1×10^{-9} m $\times$ (39.37 inches/1 m) $= 4 \times 10^{-8}$ inches/particle; then, 1 inch/(4×10^{-8} inches/particle) $= 2.5 \times 10^{7}$ particles. L3 IS **Logical-Mathematical**

Resource Manager

Chapter Resources Booklet
Lab Activity, pp. 9–12
Transparency Activity, pp. 45–46

Science Inquiry Labs, p. 43

Figure 8
Fog is a colloid composed of water droplets suspended in air.

A The light from the headlights is scattered by fog.

B The same colloid allows you to see the sunlight as it streams through the trees.

Detecting Colloids One way to distinguish a colloid from a solution is by its appearance. Fog appears white because its particles are large enough to scatter light as shown in **Figure 8.** Sometimes it is not so obvious that a liquid is a colloid. For example, some shampoos and gelatins are colloids called gels that appear almost clear. You can tell for certain if a liquid is a colloid by passing a beam of light through it, as shown in **Figure 9.** A light beam is invisible as it passes through a solution, but can be seen readily as it passes through a colloid. This occurs because the particles in the colloid are large enough to scatter light, but those in the solution are not. This scattering of light by colloidal particles is called the **Tyndall effect.**

Reading Check *How can you distinguish a colloid from a solution?*

Figure 9
Because of the Tyndall effect, a light beam is scattered by the colloid suspension on the right, but passes invisibly through the solution on the left.

Use Science Words

Word Meaning Have students find out the names of colloids in which liquids contain liquids, liquids contain solids, and gases contain liquids or solids. Colloids of liquids in liquids are emulsions, colloids of solids in liquids are gels, colloids of liquids or solids in gases are called aerosols. L3 LS **Linguistic**

Fun Fact

The Tyndall effect is named after Irish scientist John Tyndall, who first described the effect in the mid-1800s.

Quick Demo

Bring a small bright flashlight close to a clear glass containing water. Have students observe the light on the wall as it passes through the water. Then add a couple of drops of milk to the water and shine the light again. Ask students to name the light-scattering effect that they see. the Tyndall effect

Reading Check

Answer Pass a beam of light through it and check for the Tyndall effect.

Active Reading

Learning Journal This strategy encourages student to interact with the reading, allowing personal responses. The left column entries can be research notes, lectures notes, or vocabulary terms. The right column entries are the student's response to, interpretation of, questions about, or analysis of the left column entries. Have students write a Learning Journal related to the composition of matter.

Earth Science INTEGRATION

Another type suspension is found in the meltwater of glaciers. This water has an opaque appearance caused by suspended soil and rock particles that eventually settle out. Ask students what size the particles in meltwater must be. greater than 100 nm

3 Assess

Reteach

Place some NaCl and sand in a clear container and stir them together. Next, place some NaCl and water in a clear beaker and stir them together. Ask the class whether a new compound was formed in either process. no L2 LS **Visual-Spatial**

Challenge

Ask students to determine the connection between beautiful red sunsets and suspensions. The atmosphere around Earth has many suspended particles that scatter light. The more of these particles the light passes through, the redder the light appears. During a sunset, the sun is low in the sky, so we see its light through a large number of scattering particles. Sunsets are particularly beautiful in years in which volcanic eruptions take place. L3 LS **Logical Mathematical**

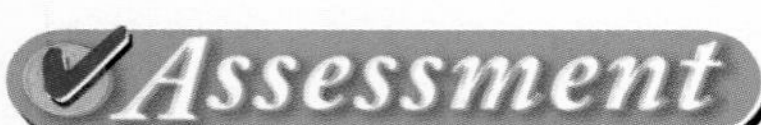

Assessment

Oral Burn a small sample of paper, and ask students to identify any elements, compounds, or mixtures. element: oxygen; compounds: carbon dioxide, the cellulose in the paper; mixtures: air, smoke particles in the air Use **PASC,** p. 89.

Figure 10
Layers of mud build up until they can be thousands of feet thick. The mud deposited by the Mississippi River is said to be more than 10,000 m thick.

Table 1 Comparing Solutions, Colloids, and Suspensions

Description	Solutions	Colloids	Suspensions
Settle upon standing?	no	no	yes
Separate using filter paper?	no	no	yes
Particle Size	0.1–1 nm	1–100 nm	> 100 nm
Scatter Light	no	yes	yes

Suspensions Some mixtures are neither solutions nor colloids. One example is muddy pond water. If pond water stands long enough, some mud particles will fall to the bottom, and the water clears. Pond water is a **suspension,** which is a heterogeneous mixture containing a liquid in which visible particles settle. **Table 1** summarizes the properties of different types of mixtures.

Earth Science INTEGRATION

River deltas are a large scale example of how a suspension settles. Rivers flow swiftly through narrow channels, picking up soil and debris along the way. As the river widens, it flows more slowly. Suspended particles settle forming deltas at the mouth, as shown in **Figure 10.**

Section 1 Assessment

1. How is a compound similar to a homogeneous mixture? How is it different?
2. Distinguish between a substance and a mixture. Give examples.
3. Describe the differences between colloids and suspensions.
4. Why is vinegar considered a solution?
5. **Think Critically** Why do the words "Shake well before using" on a bottle of fruit juice indicate that the fruit juice is a suspension?

Skill Builder Activities

6. **Comparing and Contrasting** In terms of suspensions and colloids, compare and contrast a glass of milk and a glass of fresh-squeezed orange juice. **For more help, refer to the** Science Skill Handbook.
7. **Communicating** In your Science Journal, make a list of the liquid products you find in your home. Classify each as a solution, a colloid, or a suspension. **For more help, refer to the** Science Skill Handbook.

Answers to Section Assessment

1. Both compounds and homogeneous mixtures are made of more than one ingredient and are homogeneous. However, compounds must be made from ingredients in an exact ratio and involve chemical bonds between the substances in them.
2. A substance must be either an element or a compound. Mixtures can be made from combinations of compounds or elements.
3. Colloids do not settle out; suspensions eventually do settle out. Particles in colloids are smaller than particles in suspensions.
4. Vinegar does not settle out into its components. Vinegar does not support the Tyndall effect; it is homogeneous.
5. Because materials in suspensions settle out.
6. Milk is a colloid. Fat globules are small enough to keep from settling out. Orange juice is a suspension.
7. Answers will vary but could include tap water (solution), milk (colloid), and salad dressing (suspension).

Activity

Elements, Compounds, and Mixtures

Elements, compounds, and mixtures all contain atoms. In elements, the atoms all have the same identity. In compounds, two or more elements have been combined in a fixed ratio. In a mixture, the ratio of substances can vary.

What You'll Investigate

What are some differences among elements, compounds, and mixtures?

Materials

plastic freezer bag containing the following labeled items:

copper wire
small package of salt
pencil
aluminum foil
chalk (calcium carbonate)
piece of granite
sugar water in a vial

Goals

- **Determine** whether several materials are elements, compounds, or mixtures.

Safety Precautions

Procedure

1. Copy the data table into your Science Journal and use it to record your observations.
2. Obtain a bag of labeled objects. Identify each object and classify it as an element, compound, heterogeneous mixture, or homogeneous mixture. The elements appear in the periodic table. Compounds are named as examples in Section 1.

Conclude and Apply

1. If you know the name of a substance, how can you find out whether or not it is an element?

Classification of Objects

Object	Identity	Classification
1	copper wire	element
2	salt	compound
3	graphite	element or mixture
4	aluminum foil	element
5	chalk	compound
6	granite	mixture
7	sugar water	mixture

2. **Examine** the contents of your refrigerator at home. Classify what you find as elements, compounds, or mixtures.
3. Then, identify whether the mixtures are homogeneous or heterogeneous, and whether they are colloids or suspensions.

Communicating Your Data

Enter your data in the data table and compare your findings with those of your classmates. **For more help, refer to the Science Skill Handbook.**

Activity

BENCH TESTED

Purpose Students classify materials based on their appearance and chemical makeup. L2 ELL **LS Logical-Mathematical**

Process Skills observing, classifying

Time Required 25 minutes

Teaching Strategy Introduce formulas for the compounds or have students look them up.

Answers to Questions

1. Check the periodic table.
2. Answers could include milk (mixture), water (compound), and soft drinks (mixture). Students will find few, if any, elements.
3. Milk is a heterogeneous mixture that is a colloid; soft drinks are homogeneous mixtures.

Process Have students make homogeneous and heterogeneous mixtures and describe the mixtures and their components. Use **PASC,** p. 89.

Resource Manager

Chapter Resources Booklet
Activity Worksheet, pp. 5–6
Reinforcement, p. 27

Cultural Diversity, p. 67

Communicating Your Data

As a class, discuss reasons for any differences in students' results.

SECTION 2

Properties of Matter

1 Motivate

Bellringer Transparency

Display the Section Focus Transparency for Section 2. Use the accompanying Transparency Activity Master. L2 ELL

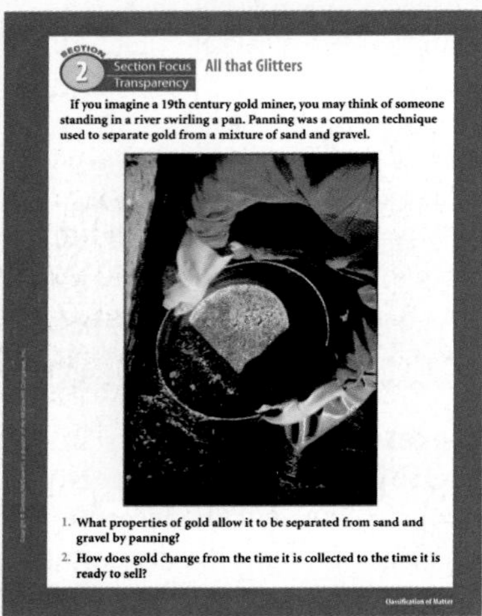
Section Focus Transparency 2 — All that Glitters

If you imagine a 19th century gold miner, you may think of someone standing in a river swirling a pan. Panning was a common technique used to separate gold from a mixture of sand and gravel.

1. What properties of gold allow it to be separated from sand and gravel by panning?
2. How does gold change from the time it is collected to the time it is ready to sell?

Tie to Prior Knowledge

Ask students to describe, without naming it, a place that they have visited. As others try to determine the site, remind students that any description, whether of matter or of a place, requires careful attention to important properties.

Text Question Answer size, shape, color, surface, density, mass

Text Question Answer Mass could be measured with a balance.

SECTION

Properties of Matter

As You Read

***What* You'll Learn**

- **Identify** substances using physical properties.
- **Compare and contrast** physical and chemical changes.
- **Compare and contrast** chemical and physical properties.
- **Determine** how the law of conservation of mass applies to chemical changes.

Vocabulary

physical property
physical change
distillation
chemical property
chemical change
law of conservation of mass

***Why* It's Important**

Understanding chemical and physical properties can help you use materials properly.

Physical Properties

You can stretch a rubber band, but you can't stretch a piece of string very much, if at all. You can bend a piece of wire easily, but you can't bend a matchstick. In each case, the materials change shape, but the identity of the substances—rubber, string, wire, wood—does not change. The abilities to stretch and bend are physical properties. Any characteristic of a material that you can observe or attempt to observe without changing the identity of the substances that make up the material is a **physical property.** Examples of other physical properties are color, shape, size, melting point, and boiling point. What physical properties can you use to describe the items in **Figure 11?**

Appearances How would you describe a tennis ball? You could begin by describing its shape, color, and state of matter. For example, you might describe the tennis ball as a spherical, brightly colored solid. You can measure some physical properties, too. For instance, you could measure the diameter of the ball. What physical property of the ball is measured with a balance?

To describe a soft drink in a cup, you could start by calling it a liquid with a brown color and sweet taste. You could measure its volume and temperature. Each of these characteristics is a physical property of that soft drink.

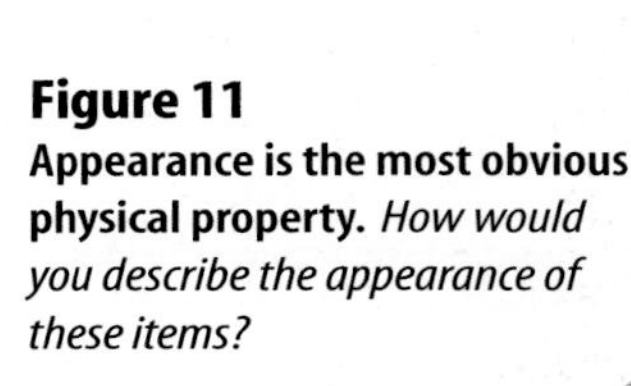

Figure 11
Appearance is the most obvious physical property. *How would you describe the appearance of these items?*

Section Assessment Planner

PORTFOLIO
Science Journal, p. 530
Communicating Your Data, p. 535

PERFORMANCE ASSESSMENT
MiniLAB, p. 528
Math Skills Activity, p. 531
Skill Builder Activities, p. 533
See page 540 for more options.

CONTENT ASSESSMENT
Section, p. 533
Challenge, p. 533
Chapter, pp. 540–541

Figure 12
The best way to separate substances depends on their physical properties.

A Size is the property that helps separate poppy seeds from sunflower seeds.

B Magnetism readily separates iron from sand.

Behavior Some physical properties describe the behavior of a material or a substance. As you might know, objects that contain iron, such as a safety pin, are attracted by a magnet. Attraction to a magnet is a property of the substance iron. Every substance has a specific combination of physical properties that make it useful to certain tasks. Some metals, such as copper, can be drawn out into wires. Others, such as gold, can be pounded into sheets as thin as 0.1 micrometers (μm), about 4 millionths of an inch. This property of gold makes it useful for decorating picture frames and other objects. Gold that has been beaten or flattened in this way is called gold leaf.

Think again about your soft drink. If you knock over the cup, the drink will spread out over the table or floor. If you knock over a jar of molasses however, it does not flow as easily. The ability to flow is a physical property of liquids.

Using Physical Properties to Separate Do you lick the icing from the middle of a sandwich cookie before eating the cookie? If you do, you are using physical properties to identify the icing and separate it from the rest of the cookie. **Figure 12A** shows a mixture of poppy seeds and sunflower seeds. You can identify the two kinds of seeds by differences in color, shape, and size. By sifting the mixture, you can separate the poppy seeds from the sunflower seeds quickly because their sizes differ.

Now look at the mixture of iron filings and sand shown in **Figure 12B.** You probably won't be able to sift out the iron filings because they are similar in size to the sand particles. What you can do is pass a magnet through the mixture. The magnet attracts only the iron filings and pulls them from the sand. This is an example of how a physical property, such as magnetic attraction, can be used to separate substances in a mixture. Something like this is done to separate iron for recycling.

Environmental Science INTEGRATION

Recycling conserves natural resources. In some large recycling projects, it is difficult to separate aluminum metal from scrap iron. What physical properties of the two metals would help separate them?

2 Teach

Physical Properties

Caption Answer

Figure 11 The ball is spherical, fuzzy, all one color, and has a curved line on it. The rock is rough, has many colors, has several dark straight lines, and has an irregular shape.

Discussion

If molasses is cold, it flows more slowly. **Why does the ability of a fluid to flow change with temperature?** At higher temperatures, the particles of the substance have more kinetic energy and are moving faster. L3
IS Logical-Mathematical

Extension

Tell students that viscosity is a measure of a fluid's resistance to flow. Have students contact a service station or an auto parts store and ask about viscosity ratings of motor oils. Higher viscosity oils have more resistance to flow and are used in warm weather, while lower viscosity motor oils flow more easily and are used in cold temperatures. L3
IS Logical-Mathematical

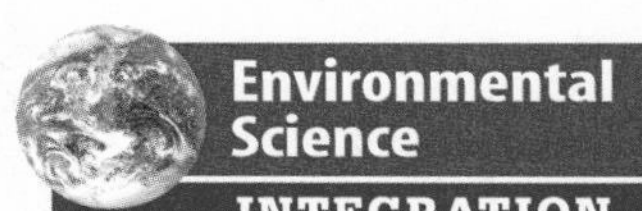

Environmental Science INTEGRATION

Since metallic iron is magnetic and metallic aluminum is not, strong magnets could attract iron from a mixture of iron and aluminum.

Resource Manager

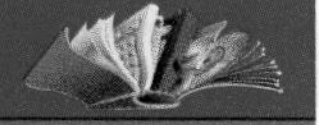

Chapter Resources Booklet

Transparency Activity, p. 43
Directed Reading for Content Mastery, pp. 21, 22
Lab Activity, pp. 13–16

Inclusion Strategies

Learning Disabled Bring a magnet and some iron filings to class. Prepare a mixture of the iron filings and sugar. Ask students how they know the mixture is not the result of a chemical change, and how the mixture can be separated. The mixture looks like the components from which it was made; add water to dissolve the sugar but not the iron, or use a magnet to separate the iron from the sugar particles.

Physical Change

Purpose Students determine whether an observed change is chemical or physical. L2

Kinesthetic

Materials water, potassium permanganate, sodium hydrogen sulfite, 250-mL beaker, stirring rod

Teaching Strategy Have students wear safety goggles and use spatulas to manipulate chemicals.

Analysis

1. physical change
2. The change in color from purple to colorless indicated that new substances were being formed.

Assessment

Oral Ask students what other evidence of a chemical change they might look for. Answers may vary but could include the presence of a gas, the presence of a precipitate, or a change in odor. Use **Performance Assessment in the Science Classroom**, p. 91.

Reading Check

Answer No, the identity of the element or compound remains the same.

Mini LAB

Identifying Changes

Procedure

WARNING: *Clean up any spills promptly. Potassium permanganate can stain clothing.*

1. Add **water** to a **250-mL beaker** until it is half-full.
2. Add a crystal of **potassium permanganate** to the water and observe what happens.
3. Add 1 g of **sodium hydrogen sulfite** to the solution and stir it until the solution becomes colorless.

Analysis

1. Is dissolving a chemical or a physical change?
2. What evidence of a chemical change did you see?

Physical Change

If you break a piece of chewing gum, you change some of its physical properties—its size and shape. However, you have not changed the identity of the materials that make up the gum. Each piece still tastes and chews the same.

The Identity Remains the Same The changes in state that you have studied are all examples of physical changes. When a substance freezes, boils, evaporates, or condenses, it undergoes physical changes. A change in size, shape, or state of matter is called a **physical change.** These changes might involve energy changes, but the kind of substance—the identity of the element or compound—does not change.

Reading Check ***Does a change in state mean that a new substance has formed? Explain.***

Iron is a substance that can change states if it absorbs or releases enough energy—at high temperatures, it melts. However, in both the solid and liquid state, iron has physical properties that identify it as iron. Color changes can accompany a physical change, too. For example, when iron is heated it first glows red. Then, if it is heated to a higher temperature, it turns white, as shown in **Figure 13.**

Using Physical Change to Separate A cool drink of water is something most people take for granted, but in some parts of the world, drinkable water is scarce. Not enough drinkable water can be obtained from wells. Many such areas that lie close to the sea obtain drinking water by using physical properties of water to separate it from the salt. One of these methods, which uses the property of boiling point, is a type of distillation.

Figure 13
Heating iron raises its energy level and it changes color. These energy changes are physical changes because it is still iron.

LAB DEMONSTRATION

Purpose to separate a mixture by a physical property

Materials test tube, water, water-soluble black overhead marker, coffee filter, scissors

Preparation Place a small amount of water in a test tube. Cut a strip of coffee filter that just fits into the tube. Use a marker to draw a line near the bottom of the strip.

Procedure Place the filter paper strip inside the tube. Make sure the ink line is slightly above the water level.

Expected Outcome The water will move up the paper and carry the ink from the line with it. As this happens, the dyes in the black ink will separate and other colors will become visible.

Assessment

What physical property of the dyes causes them to separate? solubility **Are the dyes that move farther more or less soluble in water than the dyes that don't move as far?** more soluble

Distillation **Distillation** is a process for separating substances in a mixture by evaporating a liquid and recondensing its vapor. It usually is done in the laboratory using an apparatus similar to that shown in **Figure 14.** As you can see, the liquid vaporizes and condenses, leaving the solid material behind.

Two liquids having different boiling points can be separated in a similar way. The mixture is heated slowly until it begins to boil. Vapors of the liquid with the lowest boiling point form first and are condensed and collected. Then, the temperature is increased until the second liquid boils, condenses and is collected. Distillation is used often in industry. For instance, natural oils such as mint are distilled.

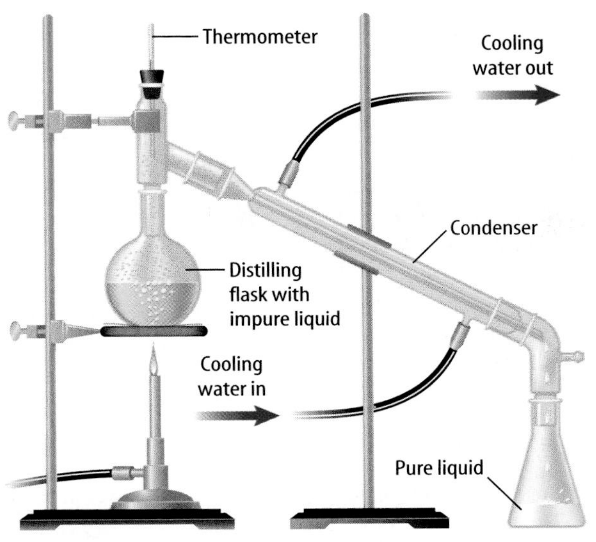

Figure 14
Distillation can easily separate liquids from solids dissolved in them. The liquid is heated until it vaporizes and moves up the column. Then, as it touches the water-cooled surface of the condenser, it becomes liquid again.

Chemical Properties and Changes

You probably have seen warnings on cans of paint thinners and lighter fluids for charcoal grills that say these liquids are flammable (FLA muh buhl). The tendency of a substance to burn or its flammability is an example of a chemical property because burning produces new substances during a chemical change. A **chemical property** is a characteristic of a substance that indicates whether it can undergo a certain chemical change. Many substances used around the home, such as lighter fluids, are flammable. Knowing which ones are flammable helps you to use them safely.

A less dramatic chemical change can affect some medicines. Look at **Figure 15.** You probably have seen bottles like this in a pharmacy. Many medicines are stored in dark bottles because they contain compounds that share chemical properties; that is, they can change chemically if they are exposed to light.

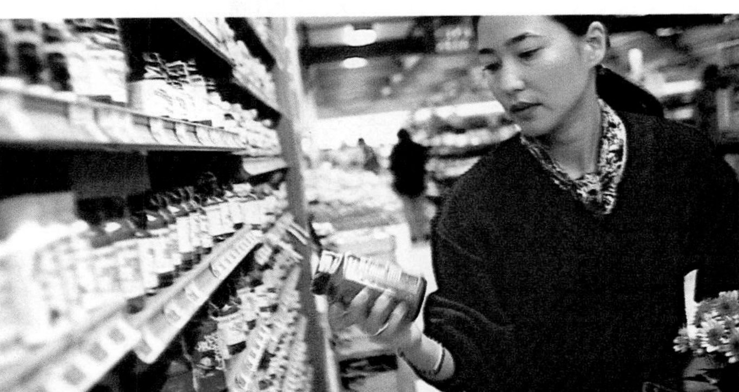

Figure 15
The brown color of these bottles tells you that these vitamins may react to light. Reaction to light is a chemical property.

Visual Learning

Figure 14 Review with students the distillation process, and ask a volunteer to trace the path of water through the apparatus shown in the figure. Explain that the distillate moves through the inner portion of the condenser, while cold water, which helps cool the distillate, runs through the outer portion. L2 LS **Visual-Spatial**

Chemical Properties and Changes

Activity

Ask students to pick a chemical element and use an encyclopedia or Internet source to make a list of its properties. Have them then divide the list into chemical and physical properties. L2 ELL LS **Linguistic**

Resource Manager 

Chapter Resources Booklet
MiniLAB, p. 4
Enrichment, p. 30

Home and Community Involvement, p. 43

Curriculum Connection

History Compounds called nitrates played a major role in the history of Chile. Have students find out what chemical property makes nitrates important and what role they played in Chile. Nitrates can be used to make explosives. Nitrates were Chile's largest export in the late 1800s, giving the country money for economic development. The nitrate market collapsed during World War I, when chemists discovered a way to synthesize nitrates. L3 LS **Linguistic**

Detecting Chemical Change

Ask students why the sound of thunder indicates a physical change rather than a chemical change. To produce thunder, air molecules are driven closer together, then spread apart, setting up a sound wave. The air molecules are not chemically changed in this process.

Reading Check

Answer a change of one substance to another

Quick Demo

Hold the bottom of a glass beaker directly over a burning candle for a few minutes. What clues indicate that a chemical change has taken place? Carbon deposits begin to form on the outside of the beaker caused by the breakdown of the hydrocarbon candle wax. Carbon is released from its bonds with other carbon and hydrogen atoms. L2 LS **Visual-Spatial**

Earth Science INTEGRATION

In a thunderstorm, light and sound tell you that changes have taken place. The pungent smell of ozone indicates that a chemical reaction also took place. Lightning converts oxygen gas, O_2, into ozone, O_3. Ozone is unstable and soon breaks up forming oxygen again.

Detecting Chemical Change

If you leave a pan of chili cooking unattended on the stove for too long, your nose soon tells you that something is wrong. Instead of a spicy aroma, you detect an unpleasant smell that alerts you that something is burning. This burnt odor is a clue telling you that a new substance has formed.

The Identity Changes The smell of rotten eggs and the formation of rust on bikes or car fenders, are signs that a chemical change has taken place. A change of one substance to another is a **chemical change.** The foaming of an antacid tablet in a glass of water and the smell in the air after a thunderstorm are other signs of new substances being produced. In some chemical changes, a rapid release of energy—detected as heat, light, and sound—is a clue that changes are occuring.

Reading Check *What is a chemical change?*

Clues, such as heat, cooling, or the formation of bubbles or solids in a liquid, are helpful indicators that a reaction is taking place. However, the only sure proof is that a new substance is produced. Consider the following example. The heat, light, and sound produced when hydrogen gas combines with oxygen in a rocket engine are clear evidence that a chemical reaction has taken place. But no clues announce the reaction that takes place when iron combines with oxygen to form rust because the reaction takes place so slowly. The only clue that iron has changed into a new substance is the presence of rust. Burning and rusting are chemical changes because new substances form. You sometimes can follow the progress of a chemical reaction visually. For example, you can see silver tarnish being removed in **Figure 16.**

Figure 16
Some reactions are visible only after they take place.

A **Tarnish mars the surface of this silver pitcher.**

B **You can remove the tarnish using another chemical reaction with aluminum foil and baking soda.**

C **The tarnish is gone and no silver is lost.**

Science Journal

Have students keep a log of chemical changes they encounter in a 24-hour period. The logs should describe each change and list clues that helped students conclude that the change was chemical. Answers could include: respiration—oxygen used, carbon dioxide released; combusting gasoline—carbon dioxide produced, heat released; cooking—an egg becomes white and solid. L2 P

Using Chemical Change to Separate One case where you might separate substances using a chemical change is in cleaning tarnished silver. Tarnish is silver sulfide formed from sulfur compounds in the air. It can be changed back into silver using a chemical reaction. To do this you place the tarnished item in a pot of water containing baking soda and some crumpled aluminium foil. Then you heat the pot. The procedure and its results are shown in **Figure 16.**

You don't usually separate substances using chemical changes in the home. In industry and chemical laboratories, however, this kind of separation is common. For example, many metals are separated from their ores and then purified using chemical changes.

Math Skills Activity

Calculations with the Law of Conservation of Mass

When a chemical reaction takes place, the total mass of the reactants equals the total mass of the products. The total number of atoms of reactants also equals the total number of atoms of products.

Example Problem

In the following reaction, 18 g of hydrogen reacts with 639 g of chlorine. How many grams of HCl are formed? $H_2 + Cl_2 \rightarrow 2HCl$

Solution

1. *This is what you know.* — mass H_2 = 18 g; mass Cl_2 = 639 g
2. *This is what you need to find:* — mass of HCl
3. *This is the equation you need to use:* — mass reactants = mass products
4. *Solve for the mass of HCl:* — $(g\ H_2 + g\ Cl_2) = (g\ HCl)$

   Substitute the known values: — $(18\ g + 639\ g) = 657\ g\ HCl$

   Check your answer by subtracting the mass of H_2 from the mass of HCl. Do you obtain the mass of the Cl_2?

Practice Problems

1. In the following reaction, 24 g of CH_4 reacts with 96 g of O_2 to form 66 g of CO_2. How many grams of H_2O are formed? $CH_4 + 2O_2 \rightarrow CO_2 + 2H_2O$
2. In the following equation, 54.0 g of Al reacts with 409.2 g of $ZnCl_2$ to form 196.2 g of Zn metal. How many grams of $AlCl_3$ are formed? $2Al + 3ZnCl_2 \rightarrow 3Zn + 2AlCl_3$

For more help, refer to the Math Skill Handbook.

Quick Demo

Obtain two relatively new pennies. Carefully file away the copper covering from the edge of one. Place both pennies in separate small beakers. Pour about 50 mL of 1 *M* hydrochloric acid over both pennies. Point out the filed edge exposing the zinc metal that makes up the inside of a penny. Ask the class to report their observations of any interaction between the pennies and the acid. The exposed zinc reacts with the acid to form a gas, hydrogen. The other penny has only copper exposed to the acid and shows no reaction. Point out that this difference in chemical properties could be used to separate copper from zinc. L2 LS **Visual-Spatial**

Extension

The extraction of pure metals is a tremendously important process for modern society. Ask students to select a metal and research how it is obtained, any chemical processes used in refining the metal, and how the metal is used. L3 LS **Linguistic**

Math Skills Activity

National Math Standards

Correlation to Mathematics Objectives

1, 2, 9

Teaching Strategies Have students count the atoms of each type of element. The number is the same on both sides of the equation. The total number of atoms of reactants will equal the total number of atoms of products. In the example, there are total of four atoms: two hydrogens on each side.

Answers to questions

1. $(24\ g\ CH_4 + 96\ g\ O_2) = (66\ g\ CO_2 + x\ g\ H_2O)$

   $120\ g = 66\ g + x\ g\ H_2O$

   $120\ g - 66\ g = 54\ g\ H_2O$
2. $(54\ g\ Al + 409.2\ g\ ZnCl_2) = (196.2\ g\ Zn + x\ g\ AlCl_3)$

   $463.2\ g = 196.2\ g + x\ g\ AlCl_3$

   $463.2\ g - 196.2\ g = 267\ g\ AlCl_3$

Resource Manager

Mathematics Skill Activities, p. 9

Physical Science Critical Thinking/Problem Solving, p. 10

Science Inquiry Labs, p. 21

Cultural Diversity

Chinese Chemistry As early as the third century B.C., the Chinese used chemical reactions to separate silver from lead and other impurities. In a process known as cupellation, they used high temperatures and blasts of air to oxidize the lead and other impurities, leaving pure silver behind.

Weathering—Chemical or Physical Change?

Quick Demo

A piece of chalk can be used to show the physical and chemical changes discussed in the text. Have students observe the chalk and note its size, appearance, and color. Next, file the chalk to show bits of it breaking away and reducing its size and form. This illustrates physical changes such as those produced by wind, geological movements, or cracking. Now take the same chalk, and place it in dilute hydrochloric acid. **Caution:** *Avoid direct contact with the acid.* A noticeable gas-producing reaction ensues. This is a chemical change that produces new products, including carbon dioxide gas. L2 ELL

LS **Visual-Spatial**

Students may think that matter is not conserved in physical or chemical changes. Refer to page 516F for teaching strategies that address this misconception.

Reading Check

Answer The mass of all substances present before a chemical change equals the mass of all the substances remaining after the change.

A Flowing water shaped and smoothed these rocks in a physical process.

B Both chemical and physical changes shaped the famous White Cliffs of Dover lining the English Channel.

Figure 17
Weathering can involve physical or chemical change.

SCIENCE Online

Research Visit the Glencoe Science Web site at **science.glencoe.com** to find out more about cave formations. Communicate to your class what you learn.

Weathering—Chemical or Physical Change?

The forces of nature continuously shape Earth's surface. Rocks split, deep canyons are carved out, sand dunes shift, and curious limestone formations decorate caves. Do you think these changes, often referred to as weathering, are physical or chemical? The answer is both. Geologists, who use the same criteria that you have learned in this chapter, say that some weathering changes are physical and some are chemical.

Physical Large rocks can split when water seeps into small cracks, freezes, and expands. However, the smaller pieces of newly exposed rock still have the same properties as the original sample. This is a physical change. Streams can cut through softer rock forming canyons and can smooth and sculpt harder rock, as shown in **Figure 17A.** In each case, the stream carries rock particles far downstream before depositing them. Because the particles are unchanged, the change is a physical one.

Chemical In other cases, the change is chemical. For example, solid calcium carbonate, a compound found in limestone, does not dissolve easily in water. However, when the water is even slightly acidic, as it is when it contains some dissolved carbon dioxide, calcium carbonate reacts. It changes into a new substance, calcium hydrogen carbonate, which does dissolve in water. This change in limestone is a chemical change because the identity of the calcium carbonate changes. The White Cliffs of Dover, shown in **Figure 17B,** are made of limestone and undergo such chemical changes, as well as physical changes. A similar chemical change produces caves and the icicle-shaped rock formations that often are found in them.

Teacher FYI

The weathering of Dover's white cliffs involves the breakdown of limestone into soluble compounds. The formation of stalactites in caves involves the precipitation of limestone from water solutions. Thus, the formation of stalactites is the reverse of the weathering of the cliffs of Dover.

Internet Addresses

Explore the Glencoe Science Web site at **science.glencoe.com** to find out more about topics in this section.

The Conservation of Mass

Figure 18
This reaction appears to be destroying these logs. When it is over, only ashes will remain. Yet you know that nothing is destroyed in a chemical reaction. *How can you explain this?*

Wood is combustible, or burnable. As you just learned this is a chemical property. Suppose you burn a large log in the fireplace, as shown in **Figure 18,** until nothing is left but a small pile of ashes. Smoke, heat, and light are given off and the changes in the appearance of the log confirm that a chemical change took place. At first, you might think that matter was lost during this change because the pile of ashes looks much smaller than the log did. In fact, the mass of the ashes is less than that of the log. However, suppose that you could collect all the oxygen in the air that was combined with the log during the burning and all the smoke and gases that escaped from the burning log and measure their masses, too. Then you would find that no mass was lost after all.

Not only is no mass lost during burning, mass is not gained or lost during any chemical change. In other words, matter is neither created nor destroyed during a chemical change. According to the **law of conservation of mass,** the mass of all substances that are present before a chemical change equals the mass of all the substances that remain after the change.

Reading Check *Explain what is meant by the law of conservation of mass.*

Section 2 Assessment

1. In terms of substances, explain why evaporation of water is a physical change and not a chemical change.
2. Name four physical properties you could use to describe a liquid.
3. Why is flammability a chemical property rather than a physical property?
4. How does the law of conservation of mass apply to chemical changes?
5. **Think Critically** The law of conservation of mass applies to physical changes as well as to chemical changes. How might you demonstrate this law for melting ice and distillation of water?

Skill Builder Activities

6. **Drawing Conclusions** What evidence tells you that chemical and physical changes take place in a candle as it burns? **For more help, refer to the** Science Skill Handbook.
7. **Solving One-Step Equations** Two chemicals with a combined mass of 25.48 g react in a flask that has a mass of 142.05 g. A gas is produced that totally escapes into a flask that has an empty mass of 141.65 g. After the reaction, the first flask and its contents have a mass of 167.16 g. Calculate the total mass of the second flask and gas. **For more help, refer to the** Math Skill Handbook.

Answers to Section Assessment

1. The makeup of the water units is unchanged.
2. color, odor, volume, temperature
3. Burning is a chemical process.
4. The mass of all substances present before a chemical change equals the mass of all the substances remaining after the change.
5. Let the ice melt on a balance, and show that the balance doesn't move.
6. Physical: the candle is getting smaller and some of the solid candle is melting. Chemical: heat, light, and smoke are produced during burning. These indicate that new substances are being formed.
7. $(142.05 + 25.48 = 167.53)$ initially. Later the mass $= 167.16$, so the new gas must have a mass of 0.37 g. The second flask had an initial mass of 141.65. Its final mass will be $141.65 + .37 = 142.02$ g.

Caption Answer

Figure 18 Some of the log's components combine with oxygen to form gases.

3 Assess

Reteach

Place a small open vial of dilute silver nitrate solution carefully inside a large flask containing a dilute solution of sodium chloride. Determine the mass of the entire assembly. Then tip the flask to intentionally spill the contents of the small vial. A white precipitate will quickly form. Re-mass the assembly. Ask students what law is demonstrated when the two masses are in agreement. law of conservation of mass L2 ELL LS **Visual-Spatial**

Challenge

Ask students to find out why the law of conservation of mass is now often known as the law of conservation of mass–energy. Einstein's famous equation, $E = mc^2$, indicates that mass can be changed into energy and vice versa. This occurs in nuclear reactions. Therefore, it is more accurate to acknowledge that mass–energy cannot be created or destroyed. L3 LS **Logical-Mathematical**

Oral Display several similar but slightly different candles. Have a student describe each candle using a minimum number of physical properties. Other students must identify the candle from its physical properties. Use **PASC,** p. 89.

Resource Manager

Chapter Resources Booklet
Reinforcement, p. 28

Activity

BENCH TESTED

Recognize the Problem

Purpose

Students design and carry out an experiment that shows evidence of a chemical change.

Process Skills

observing and inferring, hypothesizing, recognizing cause and effect, interpreting data, and making and using tables

Time Required

45 minutes

Materials

Prepare dilute HCl (4M) by carefully adding 330 mL of stock concentrated HCl (12 M) to 670 mL of distilled water in a well-ventilated area.

Safety Precautions

CAUTION: *Students should avoid any direct contact with HCl, immediately flushing any contacted area with water. They should also avoid inhaling HCl fumes. Use heat-resistant containers for the evaporating dishes.*

Form a Hypothesis

Possible Hypothesis

Mixing baking soda and HCl solution will cause a chemical change, and a new substance will be detected.

Activity Design Your Own Experiment

Checking Out Chemical Changes

Mixing materials together does not always produce a chemical change. You must find evidence of a new substance with new properties being produced before you can conclude that a chemical change has taken place. Try this activity and use your observation skills to deduce what kind of change has occurred.

Recognize the Problem

What evidence indicates a chemical change?

Form a Hypothesis

Think about what happens when small pieces of limestone are mixed with sand. What happens when limestone is mixed with an acid? Based on these thoughts, form a hypothesis about how to determine when mixing substances together produces a chemical change.

Goals

- **Observe** the results of adding dilute hydrochloric acid to baking soda.
- **Infer** that the production of new substances indicates that a chemical change has occurred.
- **Design** an experiment that allows you to compare the activity of baking soda with that of a product formed when baking soda reacts.

Possible Materials

baking soda
small evaporating dish
hand lens
1*M* hydrochloric acid (HCl)
10-mL graduated cylinder
electric hot plate

Safety Precautions

Limestone

Sand

Test Your Hypothesis

Possible Procedures

Place a small amount of baking soda in an evaporating dish. Add 2 mL of dilute hydrochloric acid. Observe. Allow the residue to dry. Add an additional 1 mL of the acid to the residue to see whether the material will react, and compare the response to that of the original baking soda.

Resource Manager

Chapter Resources Booklet

Activity Worksheet, pp. 7–8

Using Scientific Methods

Test Your Hypothesis

Plan

1. As a group, agree upon a hypothesis and decide how to test it. Write the hypothesis statement.
2. To test your hypothesis, devise a plan to compare two different mixtures. The first mixture consists of 3 mL of hydrochloric acid and 0.5 g of baking soda. The second mixture is 3 mL of hydrochloric acid and the solid product of the first mixture. Describe exactly what you will do at each step.
3. Make a list of the materials needed to complete your experiment.
4. **Design** a table for data and observations in your Science Journal so that it is ready to use as your group observes what happens.

Do

1. Make sure your teacher approves your plan before you start.
2. Read over your entire experiment to make sure that all steps are in logical order.
3. **Identify** any constants and the variables of the experiment.
4. Should you run any test more than once? How will observations be summarized?
5. Assemble your materials and carry out the experiment according to your plan. Be sure to record your results as you work.

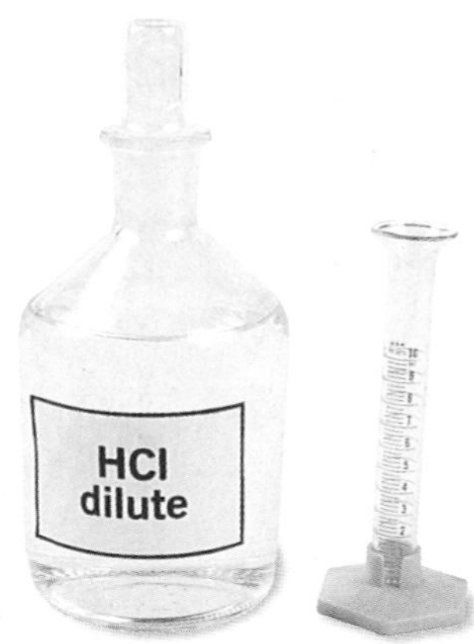

Analyze Your Data

1. What happened to the baking soda? Did anything happen to the product formed from the first mixture? Explain why this occurred.
2. What different properties of any new substances did you observe after adding hydrochloric acid to the baking soda?

Draw Conclusions

1. Did the results support your hypothesis? Explain.
2. If you had used vinegar, which contains acetic acid as the acid, do you think your results would have been different? In what way?

Write a description of your observations in your Science Journal. **Compare** your results with those of other groups. **Discuss** your conclusions.

Teaching Strategies

- The solution should be dried at a low enough temperature to avoid spattering.
- Tell students that baking soda is sodium hydrogen carbonate, $NaHCO_3$.

Expected Outcome

Baking soda will react to produce carbon dioxide gas and, after drying, a white residue will be found. The chemical reaction is $NaHCO_3 + HCl \rightarrow H_2O + CO_2 + NaCl$. The NaCl will not react further with HCl.

Analyze Your Data

1. The baking soda reacted with the HCl solution to form bubbles of carbon dioxide. The product from the first mixture didn't change.
2. The white residue had a different physical appearance, and the new white residue did not react with HCl.

Error Analysis

If too much heat is applied quickly, the acid may not completely react with the baking soda and the residue may contain some NaCl and some unreacted $NaHCO_3$.

Draw Conclusions

1. If the hypothesis was that the HCl and $NaHCO_3$ would react to form new substances, then, the hypothesis is supported.
2. Vinegar contains an acid, so it will react with baking soda to form carbon dioxide. However, the other product of the reaction will be different.

✓Assessment

Performance Have students draw a carbon atom surrounded by three oxygen atoms, with a hydrogen atom near one of the oxygen atoms, and a sodium atom near another oxygen atom. Then, have them draw a hydrogen atom next to a chlorine atom and use scissors to cut apart the molecules and reassemble the atoms as the products of the chemical change. Use **PASC,** p. 127.

Have students write down their observations about chemical changes in their Science Journals. Ask them to include descriptions of clues that led them to believe they witnessed a chemical change. Students can then compare their written notes with those of other students. P

Science Stats

Content Background

Scientists constantly attempt to create or discover new elements. Recently discovered elements do not exist in nature but have been synthesized by bombarding existing elements with high-speed particles. For example, the element seaborgium was synthesized by bombarding the element californium by highly accelerated oxygen nuclei. Most of these synthetic elements are unstable and exist for only a short time.

Discussion

The element oxygen makes up 46 percent of Earth's crust, yet it makes up only 21 percent of Earth's atmosphere. Where is the oxygen that is present in Earth's crust but is not in the atmosphere? Most other oxygen is contained in compounds. For example, sand is silicon dioxide, SiO_2, and water is H_2O.

Activity

Unless an element is radioactive and its nucleus changes, each atom remains the same element. However, elements change form and location. Provide students with the following statements. Have them draw an illustration that uses arrows and the statements to show how the element nitrogen is cycled on Earth. Statements:

- Plants obtain nitrogen from the soil.
- Bacteria on certain plants change atmospheric nitrogen to a useful form.
- Animals eat plants.
- Animals and plants die and decompose.

Science Stats

Intriguing Elements

Did you know...

...Silver-white cobalt, which usually is combined with other elements in nature, is used to create rich paint pigments. It can be used to form powerful magnets, treat cancer patients, build jet engines, and prevent disease in sheep.

Few scientists have seen the rare and elusive element astatine. Earth's supply is lean—probably only about 28 g of astatine total. Chemically, it's similar to iodine.

...You have something in common with diamonds—carbon. Diamonds form from carbon under extremely high pressures and temperatures deep inside Earth. Carbon is an essential element in living organisms, making up about 18 percent of the human body.

Connecting To Math

...Gold is the most ductile (stretchable) of all the elements. Just 29 g of gold—about ten wedding bands—can be pulled into a wire 100 km long. That's long enough to stretch from Toledo, Ohio, to Detroit, Michigan, and beyond.

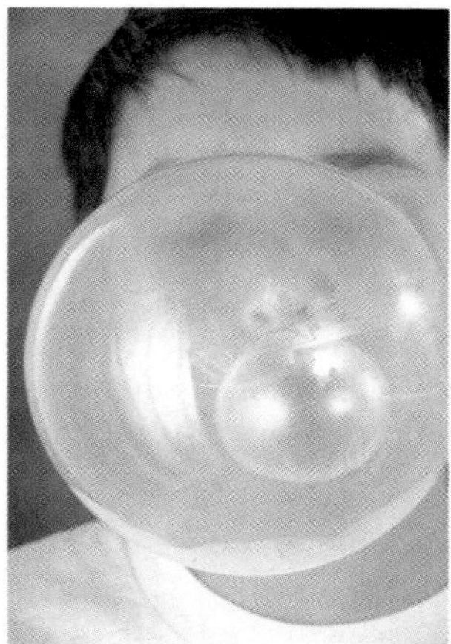

...Zinc makes chewing gum taste better. Up to 0.3 mg of zinc acetate can be added per 1,000 mg of chewing gum to provide a tart, zingy flavor.

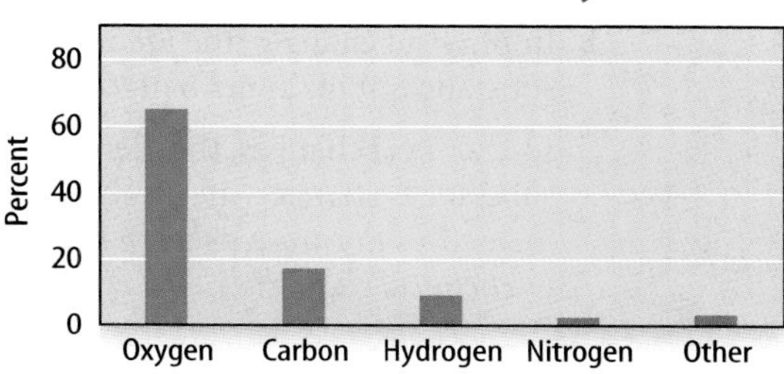

Do the Math

1. For kids, the recommended daily allowance (RDA) of zinc is 10 mg. If chewing gum were your only source of zinc, how many milligrams of gum with the maximum amount of zinc would you have to chew to get your RDA of zinc?
2. If you made the thinnest possible gold wire with 100 g of gold, how long would your wire be?
3. If you had 50 atoms of hydrogen, how many atoms each of oxygen, carbon, and nitrogen would you need to have the elements in the same proportion as they are in your body?

Go Further

What is the element most recently discovered by scientists? Go to the Glencoe Science Web site at **science.glencoe.com** to find out.

Connecting To Math

Do the Math

Teaching Strategies

Show students pictures or examples of aluminum oxide, rubies, and sapphires. Tell them that the only difference in the three materials is trace amounts of compounds of certain elements. If the aluminum oxide contains trace amounts of the compounds FeO and TiO_2, a blue sapphire is formed. Rubies are formed when trace amounts of Cr_2O_3 are present.

Show students examples of wire made from different elements, such as aluminum or copper. Tell them that the ductility of gold is a property shared by most metals.

Answers

1. approximately 33,000 mg
2. 345 km
3. approximately 342 atoms of oxygen, 97 atoms of carbon, and 17 atoms of nitrogen

Go Further

Point out to students that each newly discovered element is given a temporary name based on its atomic number. When an international group of scientists can agree on a name for it, it is assigned a permanent name.

Visual Learning

Have students use the bar graph to create a circle graph that depicts the composition of the human body. Have them multiply the percentages shown on the bar graph by 360° the number of degrees in a circle. The resulting products will provide the number of degrees of the circle represented by each element. Students can use a protractor to divide the circle into the correct number of degrees for each element. Student results should closely agree with the following figures: oxygen, 234°; carbon, 67°; hydrogen, 34°; nitrogen, 12°; and other, 13°. As a check for accuracy, have students be sure their percentages total 100% and their calculated degrees total 360°.

Chapter 17 Study Guide

Reviewing Main Ideas

Preview

Students can answer the questions in their Science Journals. Discuss the answers as you go through the chapter. LS **Linguistic**

Review

Students can write their answers, then compare them with those of other students. LS **Interpersonal**

Reteach

Students can look at the illustrations and describe details that support the main ideas of the chapter. LS **Visual-Spatial**

Answers to Chapter Review

Section 1

3. The white color (or cloudiness) of the liquid indicates that it is a colloid.
5. No; it needs to be shaken to remix the particles.

Section 2

2. The compounds inside the bottle might chemically change if exposed to light.
4. chemical

Chapter 17 Study Guide

Reviewing Main Ideas

Section 1 Composition of Matter

1. Elements and compounds are substances. A mixture is composed of two or more substances.
2. You can distinguish the different materials in a heterogeneous mixture either using your naked eye or using a microscope.
3. Colloids and suspensions are two types of heterogeneous mixtures. The particles in a suspension will settle eventually. Particles of a colloid will not. *What simple observation tells you that the substance shown here is a colloid?*

4. In a homogeneous mixture, the particles are distributed evenly and are not visible, even when using a microscope. Homogeneous mixtures can be composed of solids, liquids, or gases.
5. A solution is another name for a homogeneous mixture that remains constantly and uniformly mixed. *Is this substance a solution? How do you know?*

Section 2 Properties of Matter

1. Physical properties are characteristics of materials that you can observe without changing the identity of the substance.
2. Chemical properties indicate what chemical changes substances can undergo. *What type of chemical change might these bottles prevent?*

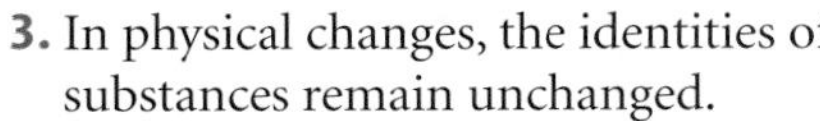

3. In physical changes, the identities of substances remain unchanged.
4. In chemical changes, the identities of substances change—new substances are formed. *Is the process shown here a physical or chemical change?*

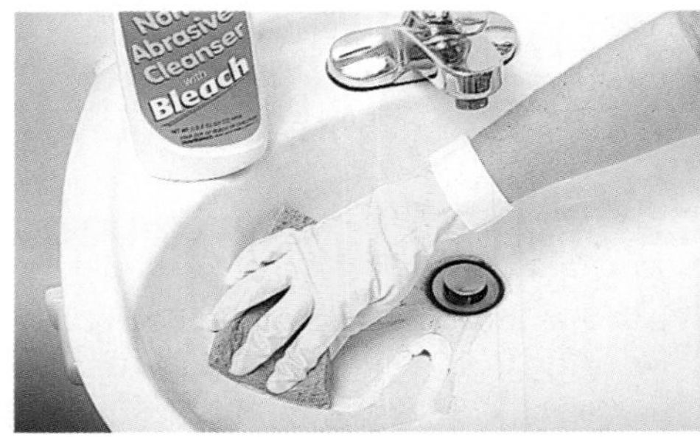

5. The law of conservation of mass states that during any chemical change, matter is neither created nor destroyed.

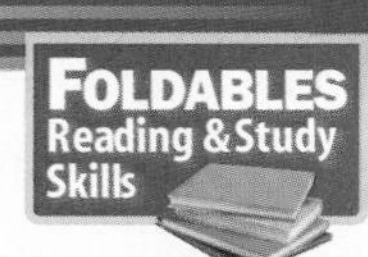

After You Read

To help you review the classifications of matter, use the Vocabulary Study Fold you made at the beginning of the chapter.

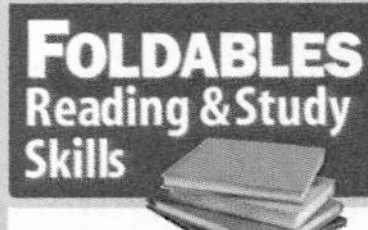

After You Read

After students have read the chapter and completed the Foldable described in Before You Read, have them do the activity on the student page.

Chapter 17 Study Guide

Visualizing Main Ideas

Use the following terms to complete the concept map below:
colloid, mixture, solution, element, heterogeneous

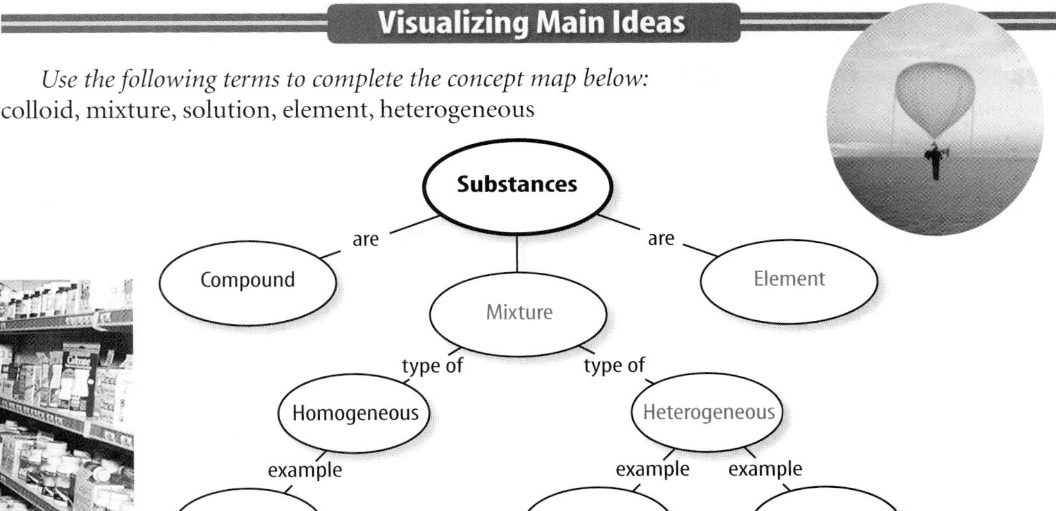

Vocabulary Review

Vocabulary Words

a. chemical change
b. chemical property
c. colloid
d. compound
e. distillation
f. element
g. heterogeneous mixture
h. homogeneous mixture
i. law of conservation of mass
j. physical change
k. physical property
l. solution
m. substance
n. suspension
o. Tyndall effect

Study Tip

Make sure to read over your class notes after each lesson. Reading them will help you better understand what you've learned, as well as prepare you for the next day's lesson.

Using Vocabulary

Replace the underlined words with the correct vocabulary words.

1. Substances formed from atoms of two or more elements are called <u>mixtures</u>.
2. A <u>colloid</u> is a heterogeneous mixture in which visible particles settle.
3. Freezing, boiling, and evaporation are all examples of <u>chemical change</u>.
4. According to the <u>Tyndall effect</u>, matter is neither created nor destroyed during a chemical change.
5. A mixture in which different materials are easily identified is a <u>homogeneous mixture</u>.
6. Compounds are made from the atoms of two or more <u>colloids</u>.
7. Distillation is a process that can separate two liquids using <u>chemical change</u>.

Chapter 17 Study Guide

Visualizing Main Ideas

See student page.

Vocabulary Review

Using Vocabulary

1. compounds
2. suspension
3. physical change
4. law of conservation of mass
5. heterogeneous mixture
6. elements
7. physical change

IDENTIFYING Misconceptions

Assess

After students have done the activity on page 516F and completed the chapter, have them perform this activity.

Materials photograph of a sealed terrarium that contains a plant, an animal, and food for the animal

Procedure Show students the photograph. Explain that the terrarium is completely sealed and nothing gets in or out. Suppose we measure the mass of this terrarium today, leave it for three months in a place where the plant gets enough light, and then measure the mass again. Would the terrarium's mass be greater than, less than, or the same as its original mass?

Expected Outcome Students should realize that the mass of the terrarium would stay the same because it is a closed system.

Chapter 17 Assessment

Checking Concepts

1. B
2. A
3. B
4. A
5. C
6. B
7. D
8. C
9. B
10. B

Thinking Critically

11. Possible description: The carton is made from a wax-coated paper product. It is about 10 cm tall, with a square base of 5 × 5 cm. It is red in color.
12. It can't be separated by physical means; it looks different from the elements that make it up.
13. Some of the first colloids studied were in gelatin, which is a source of glue.
14. The combined mass of the oxygen and the iron before the reaction is equal to the mass of the rust after the reaction.
15. Since ocean water contains dissolved salts it is a saltwater solution. Some ocean water also contains loose sand and other materials in suspension.

Chapter 17 Assessment

Checking Concepts

Choose the word or phrase that best answers the question.

1. Bending a copper wire is an example of what type of property?
   A) chemical **C)** conservation
   B) physical **D)** element
2. Which of the following is NOT an element?
   A) water **C)** oxygen
   B) carbon **D)** hydrogen
3. Which of the following is an example of a chemical change?
   A) boiling **C)** evaporation
   B) burning **D)** melting
4. What type of substance is gelatin?
   A) colloid **C)** substance
   B) solution **D)** suspension
5. A visible sunbeam is an example of which of the following?
   A) an element **C)** a suspension
   B) a solution **D)** the Tyndall effect
6. You start to eat some potato chips from an open bag you found in your locker and notice that they taste unpleasant. What do you think might cause this unpleasant taste?
   A) combustion **C)** physical change
   B) chemical change **D)** melting
7. How would you classify the color of a rose?
   A) chemical change **C)** physical change
   B) chemical property **D)** physical property
8. How would you describe the process of evaporating water from seawater?
   A) chemical change **C)** physical change
   B) chemical property **D)** physical property
9. Which of these warnings refers to a chemical property of the material?
   A) Fragile **C)** Handle with Care
   B) Flammable **D)** Shake Well
10. Which of the following is a substance?
    A) colloid **C)** mixture
    B) element **D)** solution

Thinking Critically

11. Describe a carton of milk using at least four physical properties.
12. Black carbon and the colorless gases hydrogen and oxygen combine to form sugar. How do you know sugar is a compound?
13. The word *colloid* means "gluelike." Why was this term chosen to name certain mixtures?
14. Use a nail rusting in air to explain the law of conservation of mass.
15. Mai says that ocean water is a solution. Tom says that it's a suspension. Can they both be correct? Explain.

Developing Skills

16. **Making and Using Tables** Different colloids can involve different states. For example, gelatin is formed from solid particles in a liquid. Complete this table using these colloids: *smoke, marshmallow, fog,* and *paint.*

Common Colloids

Colloid	Example
Solid in a liquid	Gelatin
Solid in a gas	Smoke
Gas in a solid	Marshmallow
Solid in a liquid	Paint
Liquid in a gas	Fog

17. **Comparing and Contrasting** Give examples of solutions, suspensions, and colloids from your daily life and compare and contrast their properties.

Chapter Assessment Planner

Portfolio Encourage students to place in their portfolios one or two items of what they consider to be their best work. Examples include:

- Science Journal, p. 520
- Science Journal, p. 530
- Communicating Your Data, p. 535

Performance Additional performance assessments, Performance Task Assessment Lists, and rubrics for evaluating these activities can be found in Glencoe's **Performance Assessment in the Science Classroom.**

18. Using Variables, Constants, and Controls Marcos took a 100-cm^3 sample of a suspension, shook it well, and poured equal amounts into four different test tubes. He placed one test tube in a rack, one in hot water, one in warm water, and the fourth in ice water. He then observed the time it took for each suspension to settle. What was the variable in the experiment? What was one constant?

19. Interpreting Data Hannah started with a 25-mL sample of pond water. Without shaking the sample, she poured 5 mL through a piece of filter paper. She repeated this with four more pieces of filter paper. She dried each piece of filter paper and measured the mass of the sediment. Why did the last sample have a higher mass than did the first sample?

20. Concept Mapping Make a network tree to show types of liquid mixtures. Include these terms: *homogeneous mixtures, heterogeneous mixtures, solutions, colloids,* and *suspensions.*

Performance Assessment

21. Design an Experiment Assume that some sugar was put into some rice by mistake. Design an experiment to separate the mixture. In your Science Journal, list your hypothesis and your experimental steps. Then carry out the experiment, and report the results.

Technology

Go to the Glencoe Science Web site at **science.glencoe.com** or use the **Glencoe Science CD-ROM** for additional chapter assessment.

Test Practice

A student did some research about which elements are found in the human body. The information is shown below.

Elements in the Human Body

Element	Percent
Oxygen	65%
Calcium	2.0%
Carbon	18.0%
Hydrogen	10.0%
Phosphorus	1.0%
Other elements	4.0%

Study the table and answer the following questions.

1. Which element makes up 1.0 percent of the human body?
   A) calcium **C)** phosphorus
   B) hydrogen **D)** carbon

2. About how much greater is the percentage of carbon in the human body than hydrogen?
   F) 3 percent **H)** 10 percent
   G) 8 percent **J)** 15 percent

3. Which element together with phosphorous makes up 3 percent of the human body?
   A) hydrogen **C)** calcium
   B) oxygen **D)** nitrogen

4. Which two elements make up three fourths of the human body?
   F) carbon and calcium
   G) oxygen and hydrogen
   H) oxygen and nitrogen
   J) phosphorus and carbon

Assessment Resources

Reproducible Masters

Chapter Resources Booklet
Chapter Review, pp. 35–36
Chapter Tests, pp. 37–40
Assessment Transparency Activity, p. 47

Glencoe Science Web site
Interactive Tutor
Chapter Quizzess

Glencoe Technology

Assessment Transparency
Interactive CD-ROM Chapter Quizzes
ExamView Pro Test Bank
Vocabulary PuzzleMaker Software
MindJogger Videoquiz DVD/VHS

Chapter 17 Assessment

Test Practice

The Test-Taking Tip was written by The Princeton Review, the nation's leader in test preparation.

1. C
2. G
3. C
4. G

Developing Skills

16. See student page.
17. Examples will vary. Solutions are homogeneous. Colloids have large suspended particles that do not settle out. Suspensions have larger suspended particles that can settle out.
18. The variable was temperature. One constant was the amount of suspension put into each tube.
19. The pond water was a suspension in which material had begun to settle out. The first 5 mL came from the top of the water sample, from which much of the suspension had settled out. The last 5 mL came from the bottom and contained settled material.
20. Mixtures include homogeneous mixtures, which are solutions, and heterogeneous mixtures, which include colloids or suspensions.

Performance Assessment

21. Accept all practical responses. Two possible ways of separating rice use particle size and solubility. Use **PASC,** p. 95.

PROPERTIES OF ATOMS AND THE PERIODIC TABLE

Section/Objectives	Standards		Activities/Features
	National	State/Local	
Chapter Opener	See p. 37T for a Key to Standards.		**Explore Activity:** Inferring what you can't observe, p. 543 **Before You Read,** p. 543
Section 1 Structure of the Atom 2 sessions 1 block 1. **Identify** the names and symbols of common elements. 2. **Identify** quarks as subatomic particles of matter. 3. **Describe** the electron cloud model of the atom. 4. **Explain** Explain how electrons are arranged in an atom.	National Content Standards: UCP2, A2, B1 (5–8), B1, B2 (9–12), G2		**Science Online,** p. 545 **MiniLAB:** Modeling an Aluminum Atom, p. 547 **Vizualizing the Atomic Model,** p. 548
Section 2 Masses of Atoms 3 sessions 1.5 blocks 1. **Compute** the atomic mass and mass number of an atom. 2. **Identify** isotopes of common elements. 3. **Interpret** the average atomic mass of an element.	National Content Standards: UCP3, A2, B1 (5–8), B1, B2 (9–12)		**Life Science Integration,** p. 552 **Problem-Solving Activity,** p. 552
Section 3 The Periodic Table 4 sessions 2 blocks 1. **Explain** the composition of the periodic table. 2. **Use** the periodic table to obtain information. 3. **Explain** what the terms *metal, nonmetal,* and *metalloid* mean.	National Content Standards: UCP1, A2, B1 (5–8), B1, B2 (9–12), G3		**MiniLAB:** A Personal Periodic Table, p. 555 **Physics Integration,** p. 558 **Science Online,** p. 559 **Activity:** A Periodic Table of Foods, p. 563 **Activity:** What's in a Name?, pp. 564–565 **Science and History:** A Chilling Story, pp. 566–567

Activity Materials	Reproducible Resources	Section Assessment	Technology
Explore Activity: envelope, dried beans	**Chapter Resources Booklet** Foldables Worksheet, p. 17 Note-taking Worksheets, pp. 33–35	GLENCOE'S ASSESSMENT ADVANTAGE	
MiniLAB: 13 3-cm circles cut from orange paper, 14 3-cm circles cut from blue paper, red paper, hole punch	**Chapter Resources Booklet** Transparency Activity, p. 44 MiniLAB, p. 3 Enrichment, p. 30 Reinforcement, p. 27 Directed Reading, p. 20 Transparency Activity, pp. 47–48 **Reading and Writing Skill Activities,** p. 43	**Portfolio** Challenge, p. 549 **Performance** MiniLAB, p. 547 Skill Builder Activities, p. 549 **Content** Section Assessment, p. 549	Section Focus Transparency Teaching Transparency Interactive CD-ROM/DVD Guided Reading Audio Program
Need materials? Contact Science Kit at 1-800-828-7777 or www.sciencekit.com on the Internet.	**Chapter Resources Booklet** Transparency Activity, p. 45 Enrichment, p. 31 Reinforcement, p. 28 Directed Reading, p. 20 Lab Activity, pp. 9–12 **Mathematics Skill Activities,** p. 7	**Portfolio** Reteach, p. 553 **Performance** Skill Builder Activities, p. 553 **Content** Section Assessment, p. 553	Section Focus Transparency Interactive CD-ROM/DVD Guided Reading Audio Program
MiniLAB: feather, penny, container of water, pencil, dime, strand of hair, container of milk, container of orange juice, container of soda, square of cotton cloth, nickel, crayon, quarter, golf ball, sheet of paper, baseball, marble, leaf, and paper clip **Activity:** 11 x 17 paper, 12- or 18-inch ruler, colored pencils or markers **Activity:** no materials needed	**Chapter Resources Booklet** Transparency Activity, p. 46 MiniLAB, p. 4 Enrichment, p. 32 Reinforcement, p. 29 Directed Reading, pp. 21, 22 Activity Worksheet, pp. 5–6, 7–8 Lab Activity, pp. 13–15 **Reading and Writing Skill Activities,** p. 47 **Home and Community Involvement,** p. 25	**Portfolio** Assessment, p. 555 Science Journal, p. 561 **Performance** MiniLAB, p. 555 Skill Builder Activities, p. 562 **Content** Section Assessment, p. 562	Section Focus Transparency Interactive CD-ROM/DVD Guided Reading Audio Program

End of Chapter Assessment

GLENCOE'S ASSESSMENT ADVANTAGE

Blackline Masters	Technology	Professional Series
Chapter Resources Booklet Chapter Review, pp. 37–38 Chapter Tests, pp. 39–42 **Standardized Test Practice by The Princeton Review,** pp. 76–79	MindJogger Videoquiz CD-ROM Explorations and Quizzes Vocabulary Puzzle Makers ExamView Pro Test Bank Interactive Lesson Planner Interactive Teacher's Edition	Performance Assessment in the Science Classroom (PASC)

Transparencies

Section Focus

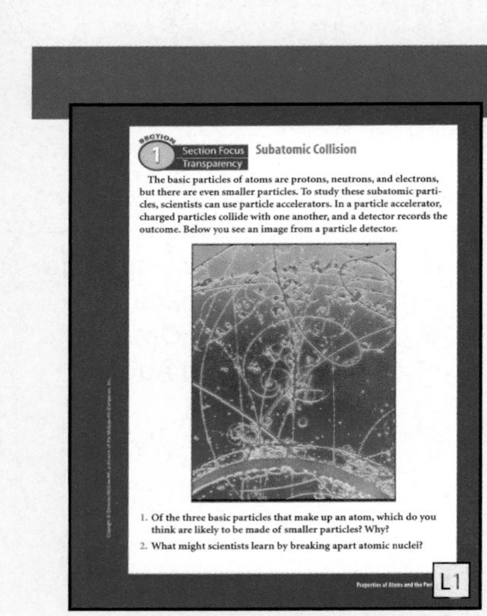

Section Focus Transparency 1 — Subatomic Collision

The basic particles of atoms are protons, neutrons, and electrons, but there are even smaller particles. To study these subatomic particles, scientists can use particle accelerators. In a particle accelerator, charged particles collide with one another, and a detector records the outcome. Below you see an image from a particle detector.

1. Of the three basic particles that make up an atom, which do you think are likely to be made of smaller particles? Why?
2. What might scientists learn by breaking apart atomic nuclei?

L1

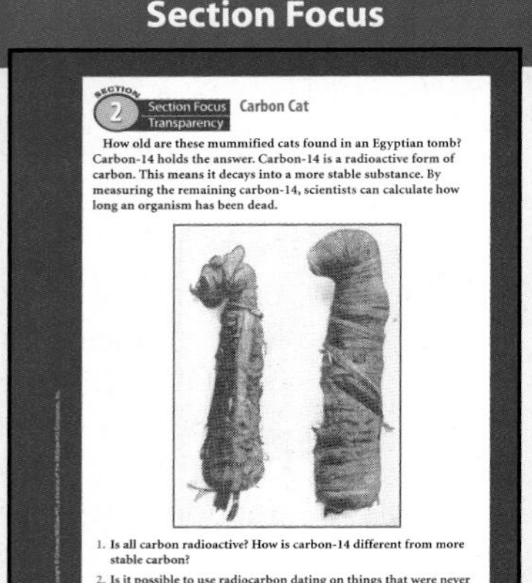

Section Focus Transparency 2 — Carbon Cat

How old are these mummified cats found in an Egyptian tomb? Carbon-14 holds the answer. Carbon-14 is a radioactive form of carbon. This means it decays into a more stable substance. By measuring the remaining carbon-14, scientists can calculate how long an organism has been dead.

1. Is all carbon radioactive? How is carbon-14 different from more stable carbon?
2. Is it possible to use radiocarbon dating on things that were never alive? Why or why not?
3. Why must scientists be careful with the sample they are testing?

L1

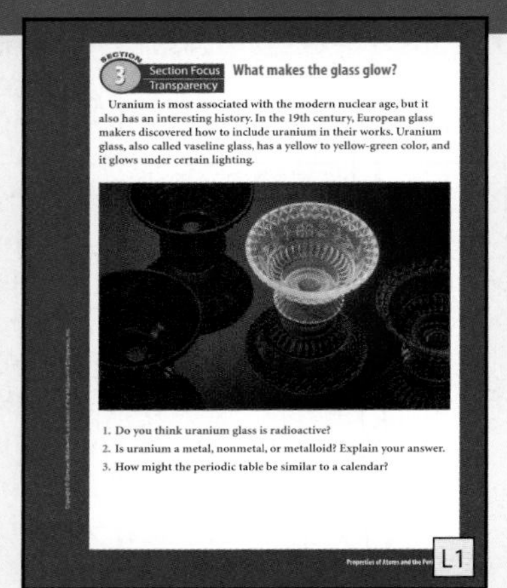

Section Focus Transparency 3 — What makes the glass glow?

Uranium is most associated with the modern nuclear age, but it also has an interesting history. In the 19th century, European glass makers discovered how to include uranium in their works. Uranium glass, also called vaseline glass, has a yellow to yellow-green color, and it glows under certain lighting.

1. Do you think uranium glass is radioactive?
2. Is uranium a metal, nonmetal, or metalloid? Explain your answer.
3. How might the periodic table be similar to a calendar?

L1

This is a representation of key blackline masters available in the Teacher Classroom Resources. See Resource Manager boxes within the chapter for additional information.

Assessment

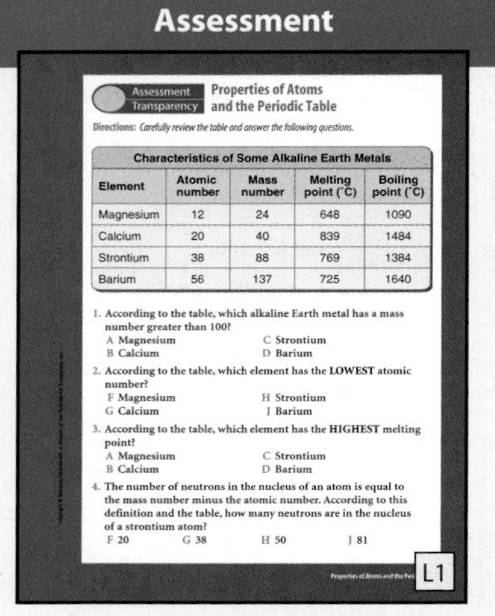

Assessment Transparency — Properties of Atoms and the Periodic Table

Directions: Carefully review the table and answer the following questions.

Characteristics of Some Alkaline Earth Metals

Element	Atomic number	Mass number	Melting point (°C)	Boiling point (°C)
Magnesium	12	24	648	1090
Calcium	20	40	839	1484
Strontium	38	88	769	1384
Barium	56	137	725	1640

1. According to the table, which alkaline Earth metal has a mass number greater than 100?
   A Magnesium C Strontium
   B Calcium D Barium
2. According to the table, which element has the LOWEST atomic number?
   F Magnesium H Strontium
   G Calcium J Barium
3. According to the table, which element has the HIGHEST melting point?
   A Magnesium C Strontium
   B Calcium D Barium
4. The number of neutrons in the nucleus of an atom is equal to the mass number minus the atomic number. According to this definition and the table, how many neutrons are in the nucleus of a strontium atom?
   F 20 G 38 H 50 J 81

L1

Teaching

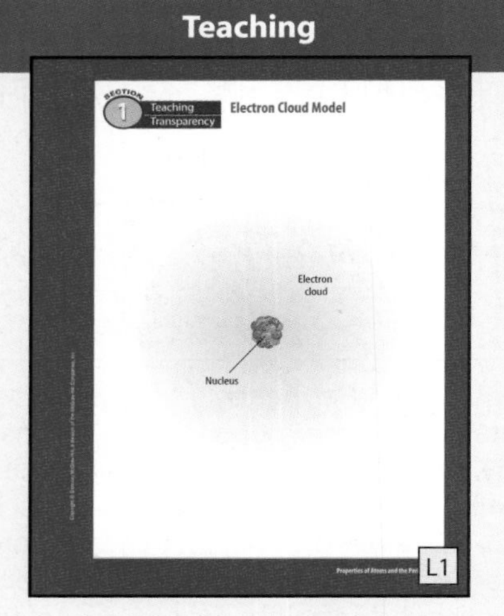

Teaching Transparency 1 — Electron Cloud Model

L1

Key to Teaching Strategies

The following designations will help you decide which activities are appropriate for your students.

- L1 Level 1 activities should be appropriate for students with learning difficulties.
- L2 Level 2 activities should be within the ability range of all students.
- L3 Level 3 activities are designed for above-average students.
- ELL ELL activities should be within the ability range of English Language Learners.
- COOP LEARN Cooperative Learning activities are designed for small group work.
- LS Multiple Learning Styles logos are used throughout to indicate strategies that address different learning styles.
- P These strategies represent student products that can be placed into a best-work portfolio.

Hands-on Activities

Activity Worksheets

Laboratory Activities

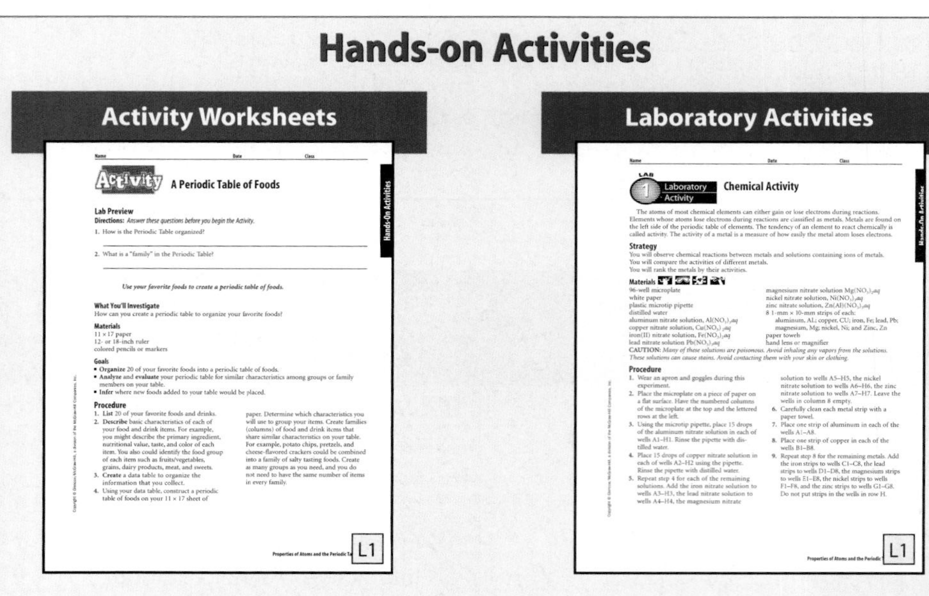

Activity — A Periodic Table of Foods

Lab Preview

Directions: Answer these questions before you begin the Activity.

1. How is the Periodic Table organized?
2. What is a "family" in the Periodic Table?

Use your favorite foods to create a periodic table of foods.

L1

Laboratory Activity 1 — Chemical Activity

L1

Meeting Different Ability Levels

Content Outline

Name Date Class

Note-taking Worksheet

Properties of Atoms and the Periodic Table

Section 1 Structure of the Atom

A. __________ are abbreviated in scientific shorthand—first letter or two of element's name

B. __________—smallest piece of matter that still has the properties of the element

1. __________ have electrical charge of 1+.
2. __________ do not have an electrical charge.
3. __________ have electrical charge of 1-.
4. Protons and neutrons are in the __________ of an atom; electrons surround the nucleus.

C. Protons and neutrons are made up of smaller particles called __________.

1. Quarks are studied by colliding accelerated charged particles with protons, which leave tracks in a __________.
2. Six quarks are known to exist; the sixth is called the ______ quark.

D. Scientists use scaled-up __________ to represent atoms.

1. Early models of atoms used a solid __________.
2. Current __________ model shows electrons traveling in specific energy levels around a nucleus of protons and neutrons.

Meeting Individual Needs

Properties of Atoms and the Periodic Table L1

Reinforcement

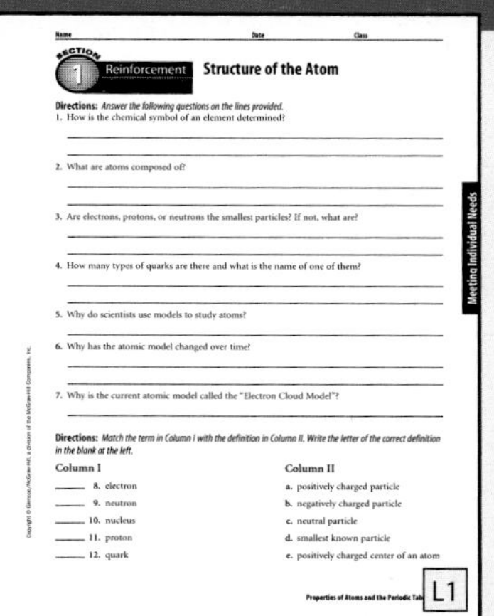

Name Date Class

Section 1 Reinforcement

Structure of the Atom

Directions: Answer the following questions on the lines provided.

1. How is the chemical symbol of an element determined?
2. What are atoms composed of?
3. Are electrons, protons, or neutrons the smallest particles? If not, what are?
4. How many types of quarks are there and what is the name of one of them?
5. Why do scientists use models to study atoms?
6. Why has the atomic model changed over time?
7. Why is the current atomic model called the "Electron Cloud Model"?

Directions: Match the term in Column I with the definition in Column II. Write the letter of the correct definition in the blank at the left.

Column I	Column II
____ 8. electron	a. positively charged particle
____ 9. neutron	b. negatively charged particle
____ 10. nucleus	c. neutral particle
____ 11. proton	d. smallest known particle
____ 12. quark	e. positively charged center of an atom

Meeting Individual Needs

Properties of Atoms and the Periodic Table L1

Directed Reading

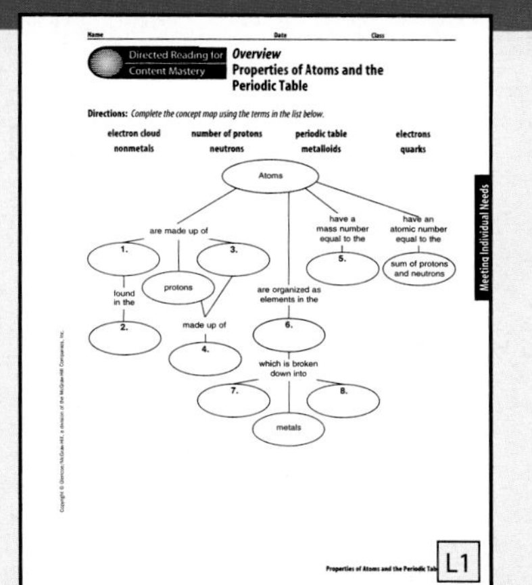

Name Date Class

Directed Reading for Content Mastery

Overview

Properties of Atoms and the Periodic Table

Directions: Complete the concept map using the terms in the list below.

electron cloud, number of protons, periodic table, electrons, nonmetals, neutrons, metalloids, quarks

Meeting Individual Needs

Properties of Atoms and the Periodic Table L1

Enrichment

Name Date Class

Section 1 Enrichment

The Building Blocks of Matter

From experiments involving the high-speed collision of particles, scientists have determined that heavy nuclear particles, such as protons and neutrons, are composed of quarks. The name "quark" was taken from a novel. Quarks are classified into six flavors—up, down, strange, charm, bottom, and top. The flavors are not related to any physical characteristics of the quarks themselves, but are used as classifications. Unlike protons and electrons, which carry whole charges of +1 or −1, quarks carry fractional charges. The following table lists some information about quarks.

Name	Symbol	Charge	Mass	Name	Symbol	Charge
up	u	+2/3	↑	down	d	−1/3
strange	s	−1/3		charm	c	+2/3
bottom	b	−1/3		top	t	+2/3

1. Use the library to find the name of the author and novel from which the word "quark" was taken.
2. Use the library to draw a time line showing the history of quarks.
3. Protons and neutrons are composed of triplets of *up* and *down* quarks. Use the information in the table to determine which of the following quark triplets represents a proton and which represents a neutron.
udd __________ *uud* __________
4. A heavier nuclear particle is composed of a triplet of strange quarks. What is the charge of this particle?

Meeting Individual Needs

30 Properties of Atoms and the Periodic Table L1

Spanish Directed Reading

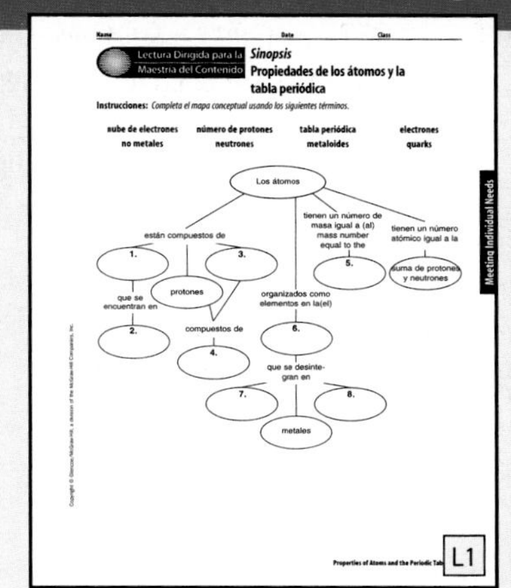

Name Date Class

Lectura Dirigida para la Maestría del Contenido

Sinopsis

Propiedades de los átomos y la tabla periódica

Instrucciones: Completa el mapa conceptual usando los siguientes términos.

nube de electrones, número de protones, tabla periódica, electrones, no metales, neutrones, metaloides, quarks

Meeting Individual Needs

Properties of Atoms and the Periodic Table L1

Assessment

Chapter Tests

Name Date Class

Chapter Test

Atomic Structure and the Periodic Table

I. Testing Concepts

Directions: Determine whether the italicized term makes each statement true or false. If the statement is true, write the word true *in the blank at the left. If the statement is false, write in the blank the term that makes the statement true.*

1. The central core of an atom is called the *hub*.
2. The chart showing the classifications of elements according to their properties and increasing atomic numbers is called the *periodic table*.
3. The mass of an *electron* is about equal to the mass of a proton.
4. Elements arranged in vertical columns in the periodic table are called *periods*.
5. The region around the nucleus occupied by the electrons is called the *negative zone*.
6. The symbol for chlorine is C.
7. The maximum number of electrons in the second energy level of an atom is 4.
8. Two isotopes of carbon are carbon-12 and carbon-14. These isotopes differ from one another by two *electrons*.
9. *Nonmetals* are poor conductors of heat and electricity.
10. Seven electrons in the outermost energy level is characteristic of a *metal*.
11. Quarks can be produced by bombarding *protons* with protons.
12. The number of protons in an atom is called the *atomic mass*.
13. The sum of the number of protons and the number of neutrons in an atom is the *mass number*.
14. The weighted average of the mass numbers of all the isotopes that occur in nature for a particular element is the average *atomic number*.
15. A very stable electron arrangement in the outer energy level is characteristic of *noble gases*.
16. Elements having three or fewer electrons in the outer energy level are classified as *nonmetals*.
17. The atomic masses of the elements are not whole value numbers because of the existence of quarks.
18. The identity of an element is determined by the number of pro...

Assessment

Properties of Atoms and the Periodic Table L1

Test Practice Workbook

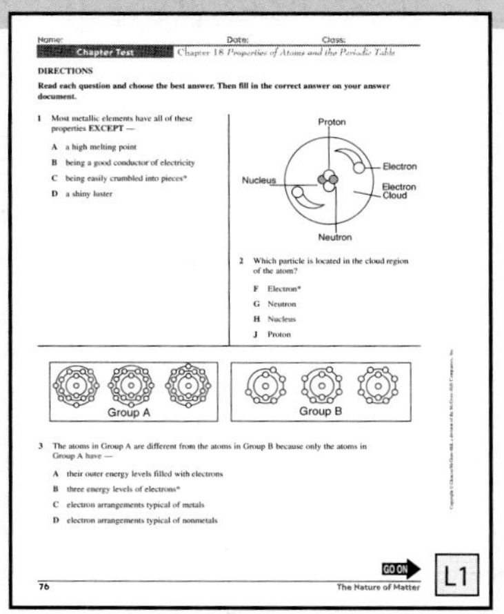

Name: Date: Class:

Chapter Test — Chapter 18 Properties of Atoms and the Periodic Table

DIRECTIONS

Read each question and choose the best answer. Then fill in the correct answer on your answer document.

1 Most metallic elements have all of these properties EXCEPT —
A a high melting point
B being a good conductor of electricity
C being easily crumbled into pieces*
D a shiny luster

2 Which particle is located in the cloud region of the atom?
F Electron*
G Neutron
H Nucleus
J Proton

3 The atoms in Group A are different from the atoms in Group B because only the atoms in Group A have —
A their outer energy levels filled with electrons
B three energy levels of electrons*
C electron arrangements typical of metals
D electron arrangements typical of nonmetals

GO ON

76 The Nature of Matter L1

Chapter Review

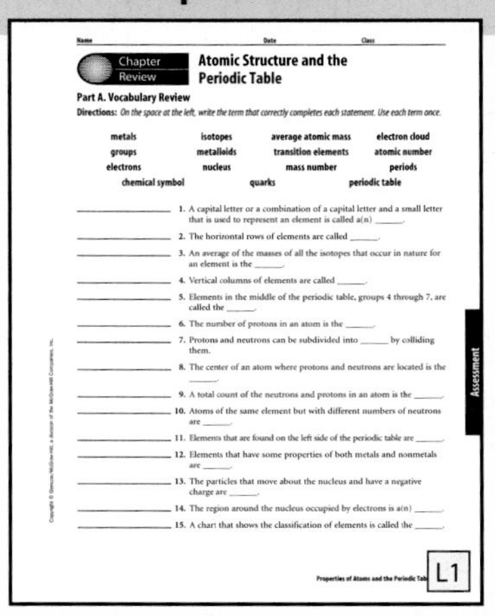

Name Date Class

Chapter Review

Atomic Structure and the Periodic Table

Part A. Vocabulary Review

Directions: On the space at the left, write the term that correctly completes each statement. Use each term once.

metals, isotopes, average atomic mass, electron cloud, groups, metalloids, transition elements, atomic number, electrons, nucleus, mass number, periods, chemical symbol, quarks, periodic table

1. A capital letter or a combination of a capital letter and a small letter that is used to represent an element is called a(n) ______.
2. The horizontal rows of elements are called ______.
3. An average of the masses of all the isotopes that occur in nature for an element is the ______.
4. Vertical columns of elements are called ______.
5. Elements in the middle of the periodic table, groups 4 through 7, are called the ______.
6. The number of protons in an atom is the ______.
7. Protons and neutrons can be subdivided into ______ by colliding them.
8. The center of an atom where protons and neutrons are located is the ______.
9. A total count of the neutrons and protons in an atom is the ______.
10. Atoms of the same element but with different numbers of neutrons are ______.
11. Elements that are found on the left side of the periodic table are ______.
12. Elements that have some properties of both metals and nonmetals are ______.
13. The particles that move about the nucleus and have a negative charge are ______.
14. The region around the nucleus occupied by electrons is a(n) ______.
15. A chart that shows the classification of elements is called the ______.

Assessment

Properties of Atoms and the Periodic Table L1

Science Content Background

SECTION 1 Structure of the Atom

Models—Tools for Scientists

In 1926, Austrian physicist Erwin Schrodinger (1887-1961) proposed the quantum mechanical model of the atom. The model was based on the wavelike properties of the electron. Electrons were no longer seen as small particles moving around the nucleus in a defined path. In fact, it was shown in 1927 by Werner Heisenberg (1901-1976), described in the Heisenberg Uncertainty Principle, that it is impossible to know precisely both an electron's position and path at a given time. Since that time, the behavior of electrons in an atom have been described mathematically by wave functions, or orbitals. Each orbital has a specific energy associated with it and contains information about an electron's position in a specific volume of space.

Fun Fact

Scientists can now "see" individual atoms with a device called a scanning funneling microscope, or STM. This microscope, invented in 1981 by a research team at IBM, has achieved magnifications of up to 10 million X, allowing chemists to look at atoms directly for the first time.

SECTION 2 Masses of Atoms

Isotopes

Isotopes that are radioactive are called radioisotopes. Many radioisotopes, such as carbon-14, occur naturally, and scientists have succeeded in producing many artificial isotopes. In fact, scientists have produced artificial isotopes for all of the elements. Among other applications, radioisotopes are used as tracers in medicine, geology, amd biology research and are used to measure the thickness of materials in industry.

1 H 1.01																	2 He 4.00
3 Li 6.94	4 Be 9.01											5 B 10.8	6 C 12.0	7 N 14.0	8 O 16.0	9 F 19.0	10 Ne 20.2
11 Na 23.0	12 Mg 24.3											13 Al 27.0	14 Si 28.1	15 P 31.0	16 S 32.1	17 Cl 35.5	18 Ar 40.0
19 K 39.1	20 Ca 40.1	21 Sc 45.0	22 Ti 47.9	23 V 50.9	24 Cr 52.0	25 Mn 54.9	26 Fe 55.8	27 Co 58.9	28 Ni 58.7	29 Cu 63.5	30 Zn 65.4	31 Ga 69.7	32 Ge 72.6	33 As 74.9	34 Se 79.0	35 Br 79.9	36 Kr 83.8
37 Rb 85.5	38 Sr 87.6	39 Y 88.9	40 Zr 91.2	41 Nb 92.9	42 Mo 95.9	43 Tc 98	44 Ru 101	45 Rh 103	46 Pd 106	47 Ag 108	48 Cd 112	49 In 115	50 Sn 119	51 Sb 122	52 Te 128	53 I 127	54 Xe 131
55 Cs 133	56 Ba 137	57 La 139	72 Hf 178	73 Ta 181	74 W 184	75 Re 186	76 Os 190	77 Ir 192	78 Pt 195	79 Au 197	80 Hg 201	81 Tl 204	82 Pb 207	83 Bi 209	84 Po 210	85 At 210	86 Rn 222
87 Fr 223	88 Ra 226	89 Ac 227	104 Rf 227	105 Db 262	106 Sg 263	107 Bh 264	108 Hs 265	109 Mt 268	110 Uun 269	111 Uuu 269	112 Uub 277	113	114 Uuq 289	115	116 Uun 289	117	118 Uuo 293
		58 Ce 140	59 Pr 141	60 Nd 144	61 Pm 147	62 Sm 150	63 Eu 152	64 Gd 157	65 Tb 159	66 Dy 163	67 Ho 165	68 Er 167	69 Tm 169	70 Yb 173	71 Lu 175		
		90 Th 232	91 Pa 231	92 U 238	93 Np 237	94 Pu 244	95 Am 243	96 Cm 247	97 Bk 247	98 Cf 251	99 Es 254	100 Fm 257	101 Md 258	102 No 255	103 Lr 256		

color code = light metals -brittle metals -ductile metals -low melting metals -non-metals -noble gases -lanthanides -actinides

SECTION 3

The Periodic Table

Organizing the Elements

In 1817, the German chemist Johann Dobereiner found that he could arrange many elements into groups that he called triads. He noticed for example that lithium, sodium, and potassium react vigorously with water. Similar regularities were uncovered for calcium, strontium, and barium, and for fluorine, chlorine, and bromine.

Dobereiner's early work laid the groundwork for other chemists as they searched for an organizing principle by which to classify elements. In 1864, English chemist John Newlands proposed that when the known elements were arranged according to atomic mass, similarities in chemical properties occurred with every eighth element. He called this regularity the law of octaves.

The modern periodic table didn't come into being until a Dutch physicist, Anton van den Brock, proposed that the elements should be arranged according to nuclear charge rather than atomic mass. Henry Mosely confirmed this hypothesis through studies of the X-ray spectra of a series of elements that had consecutive positions of the table. The change to ordering by atomic number resulted in the reversal of the positions of a few elements.

The Atom and the Periodic Table

The period in which an element appears in the periodic table indicates how many main electron energy levels that are in that atom. For example, oxygen is in the second period, so the oxygen atom has two main energy levels. The group number (for main group elements) indicates how many electrons are in the outermost energy level. Oxygen has six outer or valence electrons, so oxygen is in Group 6A. It is these outermost electrons that determine how an atom reacts.

For every principle quantum number (period or horizontal row), there are sublevels designated by letters, such as *s*, *p*, *d*, and *f*. In the sublevels, electrons pairs are found in orbitals. For each sublevel, there is one *s* orbital, three *p* orbitals, five *d* orbitals, and seven *f* orbitals. As you move across any period of the table, Groups 1 and 2 are filling *s* orbitals with two electrons. Groups 13–18 are filling *p* orbitals with six electrons. In periods 4 through 7, the transition elements, Groups 2–12, are filling five *d* orbitals with ten electrons. The inner transition elements, located below the periodic table, are filling the 4*f* and 5*f* orbitals with 14 electrons.

Fun Fact

Electron dot diagrams are often called Lewis symbols, after American chemist G.N. Lewis (1875–1946), who invented this symbolism.

For additional content background on this topic, go to the Glencoe Science Web site at science.glencoe.com.

Properties of Atoms and the Periodic Table

Chapter Vocabulary

atom
nucleus
electron
proton
neutron
quark
electron cloud
atomic number
mass number
isotope
average atomic mass
periodic table
group
electron dot diagram
period

What do you think?

Science Journal The photograph shows a polarized light micrograph of sulfur crystals.

CHAPTER 18

Properties of Atoms and the Periodic Table

It might surprise you to know that these clouds of Jupiter, your pencil or pen, and you have something in common. Everything in the universe is made up of particles so small they can not even be seen, called atoms. But there are particles even smaller than atoms. What are these tiny pieces of the universe? In this chapter you will learn about atoms and their components—protons, neutrons, and electrons.

What do you think?

Science Journal Look at the picture below with a classmate. Discuss what you think this might be. Here's a hint: *It's a winning combination you couldn't live without.* Write your answer or your best guess in your Science Journal.

542

Theme Connection

Scale and Structure The underlying small-scale structure of atoms determines the properties of elements and their positions on the periodic table of elements.

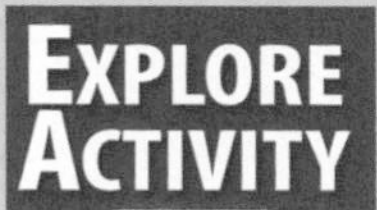

How do detectives solve a crime when no witnesses saw it happen? How do scientists study atoms when they cannot see them? In situations such as these, techniques must be developed to find clues to answer the question. Do the activity below to see how clues might be gathered.

Inferring what you can't observe

1. Take an envelope from your teacher.
2. Place an assortment of dried beans in the envelope and seal it. **WARNING:** *Do not eat any lab materials.*
3. Trade envelopes with another group.
4. Without opening the envelope, try to figure out the types and number of beans that are in the envelope. Record a hypothesis about the contents of the envelope in your Science Journal.
5. After you record your hypothesis, open the envelope and see what is inside.

Observe

How many of each kind of bean did you find? Was your hypothesis correct?

Before You Read

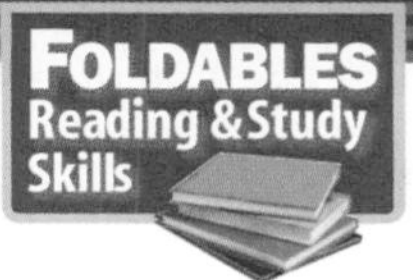

Making a Know-Want-Learn Study Fold Make the following Foldable to help you identify what you already know and what you want to know about properties of atoms.

1. Stack two sheets of paper in front of you so the short side of both sheets is at the top.
2. Slide the top sheet up so that about 4 cm of the bottom sheet shows.
3. Fold both sheets top to bottom to form four tabs and staple along the topfold, as shown.
4. Label the top flap *Atoms.* Then label the other flaps *Know, Want,* and *Learned* as shown. Before you read the chapter, write what you know about atoms on the *Know* tab and what you want to know on the *Want* tab.
5. As you read the chapter, list the things you learn about atoms on the *Learned* tab.

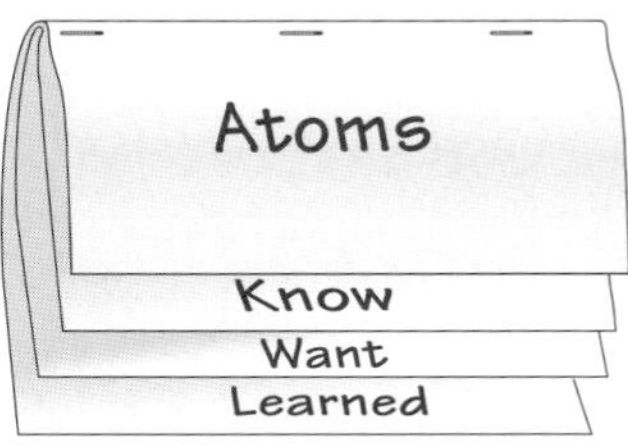

Explore Activity

Purpose Use the Explore Activity to show students how to use inference to describe something they cannot see. L2

LS **Kinesthetic**

Preparation Obtain several varieties of dried beans with different sizes and shapes.

Materials various dried beans, envelopes

Teaching Strategy Suggest that students

- lay a piece of thin paper over the sealed envelope and rub the side of a pencil over the beans.
- hold the envelope up to a bright light to see an outline of the beans.
- shake the envelope from side to side to see whether the beans are flat or round.

Observe

Answers will vary depending on the assortment of beans. The clues students find should be used in their conclusions. For example, aroma could help them identify coffee beans.

✔Assessment

Oral Ask students whether they have ever attempted to guess the contents of a wrapped gift. Have them explain how they used inference to get clues. Finally, ask them to explain how their gift-guessing might be similar to the reasoning used by atomic scientists to determine atomic structure. Use **PASC,** p. 89.

Before You Read

FOLDABLES Reading & Study Skills

Dinah Zike Study Fold

Purpose In this activity, students make a Foldable for recording what they know what they would like to know about atoms before reading the chapter. They again use the Foldable to determine what they have learned about atoms after reading.

For additional help, see Foldables Worksheet, p. 17 in **Chapter Resources Booklet,** or go to the Glencoe Science Web site at **science.glencoe.com.** See After You Read in the Study Guide at the end of this chapter.

SECTION

Structure of the Atom

1 Motivate

Bellringer Transparency

Display the Section Focus Transparency for Section 1. Use the accompanying Transparency Activity Master. L2 ELL

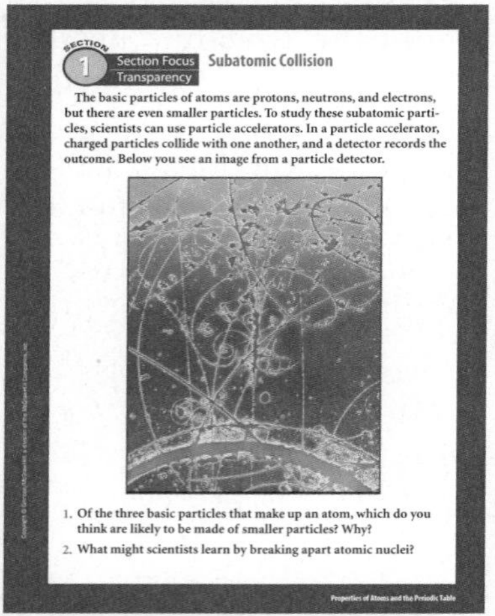

SECTION 1 Section Focus Transparency **Subatomic Collision**

The basic particles of atoms are protons, neutrons, and electrons, but there are even smaller particles. To study these subatomic particles, scientists can use particle accelerators. In a particle accelerator, charged particles collide with one another, and a detector records the outcome. Below you see an image from a particle detector.

1. Of the three basic particles that make up an atom, which do you think are likely to be made of smaller particles? Why?
2. What might scientists learn by breaking apart atomic nuclei?

Properties of Atoms and the Periodic Table

Tie to Prior Knowledge

Have students brainstorm a list of the names of elements that they know without referring to a periodic table. Record the list on the board or on chart paper. Make sure that things like brass or steel, which are mixtures of elements, are not accepted.

SECTION 1

Structure of the Atom

As You Read

What You'll Learn

- **Identify** the names and symbols of common elements.
- **Identify** quarks as subatomic particles of matter.
- **Describe** the electron cloud model of the atom.
- **Explain** how electrons are arranged in an atom.

Vocabulary

atom
nucleus
electron
proton
neutron
quark
electron cloud

Why It's Important

Everything you see, touch, and breathe is composed of tiny atoms.

Scientific Shorthand

Do you have a nickname? Do you use abbreviations for long words or the names of states? Scientists also do this. In fact, scientists have developed their own shorthand for dealing with long, complicated names.

Do the letters C, Al, Ne, and Ag mean anything to you? Each letter or pair of letters is a chemical symbol, which is a short or abbreviated way to write the name of an element. Chemical symbols, such as those in **Table 1,** consist of one capital letter or a capital letter plus one or two small letters. For some elements, the symbol is the first letter of the element's name. For other elements, the symbol is the first letter of the name plus another letter from its name. Some symbols are derived from Latin. For instance, *Argentum* is Latin for "silver." Elements have been named in a variety of ways. Some elements are named to honor scientists, for places, or for their properties. Other elements are named using rules established by an international committee. Regardless of the origin of the name, scientists derived this international system for convenience. It is much easier to write H for hydrogen, O for oxygen, and H_2O for hydrogen oxide (water). Because scientists worldwide use this system, everyone understands what the symbols mean.

Table 1 Symbols of Some Elements

Element	Symbol	Element	Symbol	Element	Symbol
Aluminum	Al	Gold	Au	Mercury	Hg
Calcium	Ca	Helium	He	Nitrogen	N
Carbon	C	Hydrogen	H	Oxygen	O
Chlorine	Cl	Iodine	I	Potassium	K
Copper	Cu	Iron	Fe	Silver	Ag
Fluorine	F	Magnesium	Mg	Sodium	Na

Section Assessment Planner

PORTFOLIO
Challenge, p. 549

PERFORMANCE ASSESSMENT
MiniLAB, p. 547
Skill Builder Activities, p. 549
See page 570 for more options.

CONTENT ASSESSMENT
Section, p. 549
Challenge, p. 549
Chapter, pp. 570–571

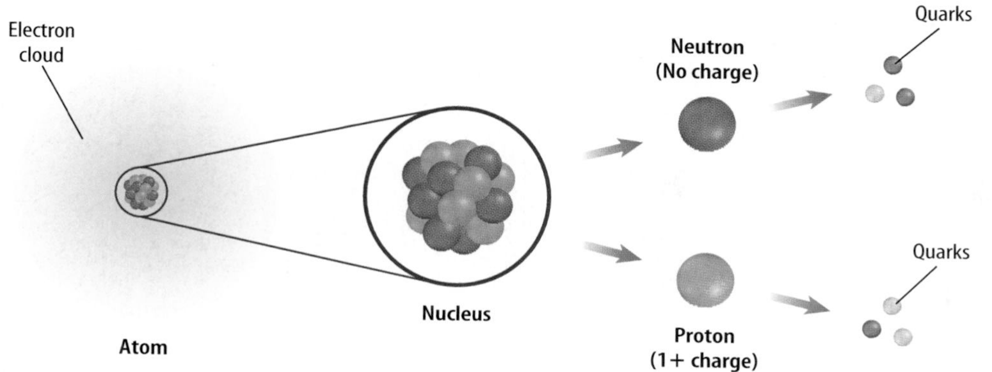

Atomic Components

An element is matter that is composed of one type of **atom,** which is the smallest piece of matter that still retains the property of the element. For example, the element silver is composed of only silver atoms and the element hydrogen is composed of only hydrogen atoms. All atoms are composed of particles called protons, neutrons, and electrons, as shown in **Figure 1.** Protons and neutrons are found in a small, positively-charged center of the atom called the nucleus that is surrounded by a cloud containing electrons. Protons are particles with an electrical charge of 1+. Neutrons are neutral particles that do not have an electrical charge. Electrons are particles with an electrical charge of 1−. Atoms of different elements differ in the number of protons they contain.

Reading Check *What are the particles that make up the atom and where are they located?*

Figure 1
The nucleus of the atom contains protons and neutrons that are composed of quarks. The proton has a positive charge and the neutron has no charge. A cloud of negatively charged electrons surrounds the nucleus of the atom.

Quarks—Even Smaller Particles

Are the protons, electrons, and neutrons that make up atoms the smallest particles that exist? Scientists hypothesize that electrons are not composed of smaller particles and are one of the most basic types of particles. Protons and neutrons, however, are made up of smaller particles called **quarks.** So far, scientists have confirmed the existence of six uniquely different quarks. Scientists theorize that an arrangement of three quarks held together with the strong nuclear force produces a proton. Another arrangement of three quarks produces a neutron. The search for the composition of protons and neutrons is an ongoing effort.

Research Visit the Glencoe Science Web site at **science.glencoe.com** for more information about ongoing research at the Fermi National Accelerator Laboratory. Communicate to your class what you learn.

2 Teach

Atomic Components

Use Science Words

Word Usage Have students compare and contrast the use of the word *nucleus* in biology and in physical science. In biology, *nucleus* refers to the cellular organelle where control of cell functions originates. It is in the interior of the cell, but not necessarily at the center. In physical science the nucleus is also a sort of control area because the number of protons found in the nucleus determines the identity of the atom. The nucleus of an atom, however, is located at the center of the atom. L2 LS **Linguistic**

Reading Check

Answer Particles that make up atoms include protons and neutrons, which are located in the nucleus, and electrons, which are located in a cloud surrounding the nucleus.

Quarks—Even Smaller Particles

Make a Model

Obtain a set of matroshka dolls from an import or department store and place them in front of the room. Ask students what they think is inside. After they respond, open the largest figure and reveal the smaller one. Continue this until you reach the last doll. **How are the dolls similar to the search for smaller nuclear particles?** Scientists thought several times that they had found the smallest particles, but each time they found even smaller particles. Now scientists would say that the last doll is like a quark. L2 LS **Visual-Spatial**

Resource Manager 

Chapter Resources Booklet
- Transparency Activity, p. 44
- Directed Reading for Content Mastery, p. 20
- Note-taking Worksheets, pp. 33–35

SCIENCE Online
Internet Addresses

Explore the Glencoe Science Web site at **science.glencoe.com** to find out more about topics in this section.

Quarks—Even Smaller Particles, continued

Use an Analogy

People walking in snow or skiing down a mountain leave their tracks behind. If there were no snow, tracks of activity would be much more difficult to see. When detecting quarks or other atomic particles, scientists create an environment that helps them see the tracks the moving particles leave behind. In a cloud chamber, a dense cloud condenses to an even denser track when a particle passes through. Just as skiers leave a different track than do snowboarders, an electron moving through the dense cloud leaves a different track than does a proton.

Caption Answer

Figure 2 to accelerate the particles so they will have enough energy to break each other apart when they collide

Quick Demo

Display a large poster in front of the class on which you have made several curved lines using different markers and pens. Tape the markers and pens to the poster board and provide a magnifying lens. Ask students to match the pen with the appropriate line by examining the pen tips with the lens. Next, ask what other method they could use to identify the lines. Make comparison marks with each pen or marker. Tell students that nuclear scientists use both predictions and matching techniques. L2

LS **Visual-Spatial**

Figure 2
The Tevatron is a huge machine. A This aerial photograph of Fermi National Accelerator Laboratory shows the circular outline of the Tevatron particle accelerator. B This close-up photograph of the Tevatron gives you a better view of the tunnel. *Why is such a long tunnel needed?*

A

B

Finding Quarks To study quarks, scientists accelerate charged particles to tremendous speeds and then force them to collide with—or smash into—protons. This collision causes the proton to break apart. The Fermi National Accelerator Laboratory, a research laboratory in Batavia, Illinois, houses a machine that can generate the forces that are required to collide protons. This machine, the Tevatron, shown in **Figure 2,** is approximately 6.4 km in circumference. Electric and magnetic fields are used to accelerate, focus and collide the fast-moving particles.

The particles that result from the collision are detected in a device called a bubble chamber in which the particles leave tracks. Just as police investigators can reconstruct traffic accidents from tire marks and other clues at the scene, scientists are able to examine and gather information from the tracks left after proton collisions, as shown in **Figure 3.** Studying the tracks reveals information about the inner structure of the atom. Scientists then use inference to identify the subatomic particles.

Figure 3
Bubble chambers are used by scientists to study the tracks left by subatomic particles.

The Sixth Quark Finding evidence for the existence of the quarks was not an easy task. Scientists found five quarks and hypothesized that a sixth quark existed. However, it took a team of nearly 450 scientists from around the world several years to find the sixth quark. The tracks of the sixth quark were hard to detect because only about one billionth of a percent of the proton collisions performed showed the presence of a sixth quark—typically referred to as the *top* quark.

Teacher FYI

The first cloud chambers were developed near the beginning of the 1900s by C.T.R. Wilson, a Scottish physicist. He was trying to reproduce weather conditions in a closed chamber. Supersaturated vapor formed in the chamber and formed visible vapor trails when X rays passed through. This led to more sophisticated bubble chambers for detailed study of the vapor trails formed as beta and alpha particles passed through the supersaturated vapor.

Models—Tools for Scientists

Scientists and engineers use models to represent things that are difficult to visualize—or picture in your mind. You might have seen models of buildings, the solar system, or airplanes. These are scaled-down models. Scaled-down models allow you to see either something too large to see all at once, or something that has not been built yet. Scaled-up models are often used to visualize things that are too small to see. Atoms are very small. To give you an idea of how small the atom is, it would take about 62,200 atoms stacked one on top of the other to equal the thickness of a sheet of aluminum foil. To study the atom, scientists have developed scaled-up models that they can use to visualize how the atom is constructed. For the model to be useful, it must support all of the information that is known about matter and the behavior of atoms. As more information about the atom is collected, scientists change their models to include the new information.

Reading Check *Why do scientists use models?*

The Changing Atomic Model You know now that all matter is composed of atoms, but this was not always known. Around 400 B.C., Democritus proposed the idea that atoms make up all substances. However, a famous Greek philosopher, Aristotle, disputed Democritus's theory and proposed that matter was uniform throughout and was not composed of smaller particles. Aristotle's incorrect theory was accepted for 2,100 years—until the seventeenth century. In the 1800s, John Dalton, an English scientist, was able to offer proof that atoms exist.

Dalton's model of the atom, a solid sphere shown in **Figure 4,** was an early model of the atom. As you can see in **Figure 5,** the model has changed somewhat over time. As each scientist performed experiments, and learned a little bit more about the structure of the atom, the model was modified. The model in use today is the accumulated knowledge of almost two hundred years.

Modeling an Aluminum Atom

Procedure

1. Arrange 13 3-cm circles cut from **orange paper** and 14 3-cm circles cut from **blue paper** on a **flat surface** to represent the nucleus of an atom. Each orange circle represents one proton, and each blue circle represents one neutron.
2. Position 2 holes punched from **red paper** about 20 cm from your nucleus.
3. Position 8 punched holes about 40 cm from your nucleus.
4. Position 3 punched holes about 60 cm from your nucleus.

Analysis

1. How many protons, neutrons, and electrons does an aluminum atom have?
2. Explain how your circles model an aluminum atom.
3. Explain why your model does not accurately represent the true size and distances in an aluminum atom.

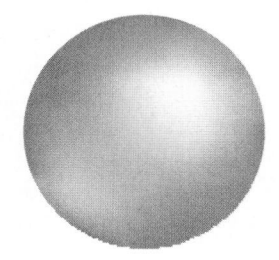

Figure 4
John Dalton's atomic model was a simple sphere.

Models—Tools for Scientists

Mini LAB

Purpose to make a model showing the particles in an atom

Materials blue, orange, and red paper, metric ruler, hole punch

Teaching Strategy To save time, prepare the circles and the punched holes ahead of time.

Analysis

1. 13 protons, 14 neutrons, and 13 electrons.
2. Like an aluminum atom, the model has 13 protons and 14 neutrons. It also has three energy levels with 2 electrons in the first level, 8 in the second, and 3 in the third.
3. In reality, protons and neutrons are more than 1,800 times larger than electrons. This activity does not attempt to model subatomic particle radii nor their exact locations in the cloud. It is merely modeling the grouping that occurs within the cloud.

Assessment

Process Have students use their materials to make models of atoms of as many different elements as they can. Ask them to make lists of the atoms they made, and draw a quick sketch of each one. Use **PASC,** p. 97.

Resource Manager

Chapter Resources Booklet
Enrichment, p. 30
MiniLAB, p. 3
Reading and Writing Skill Activities, p. 43

Visual Learning

Figure 4 Tell students that the wooden sphere atom models that Dalton constructed are on display in the Science Museum in London. Many of his contemporaries ridiculed his idea of atoms simply on the basis that atoms could not be seen and, therefore, did not exist. **What are some other things that exist but can't be seen?** Possible answers: electromagnetic waves, air L2

LS **Visual-Spatial**

Reading Check

Answer Models are less expensive to build than the actual item and they allow the study of things that are difficult to visualize or duplicate.

NATIONAL GEOGRAPHIC

Visualizing The Atomic Model

Have students examine the pictures and read the captions. Then ask the following questions.

- **What significant changes occurred in the atomic model between Figure 5A and Figure 5B?** Scientists found that the atom was not "uncuttable" but was composed of positive and negative particles.
- **What significant changes occurred in the atomic model between Figure 5B and Figure 5C?** Scientists found that the mass of the atom was concentrated in the center instead of throughout the atom and that electrons orbit the nucleus.
- **What significant changes occurred in the atomic model between Figure 5C and Figure 5D?** Scientists found that the orbits of the electrons are not random but are at fixed distances from the nucleus.

Activity

Have students research and find out how Rutherford discovered that the mass of the atom is concentrated primarily in the center of the atom. Ask students to write brief reports in their Science Journals describing Rutherford's experiment. L2 LS **Linguistic**

NATIONAL GEOGRAPHIC **VISUALIZING THE ATOMIC MODEL**

Figure 5

The ancient Greek philosopher Democritus proposed that elements consisted of tiny, solid particles that could not be subdivided (A). He called these particles *atomos,* meaning "uncuttable." This concept of the atom's structure remained largely unchallenged until the 1700s, when researchers began to discover through experiments that atoms were composed of still smaller particles. In the early 1900s, a number of models for atomic structure were proposed (B-D). The currently accepted model (E) evolved from these ideas and the work of many other scientists.

A DEMOCRITUS'S UNCUTTABLE ATOM

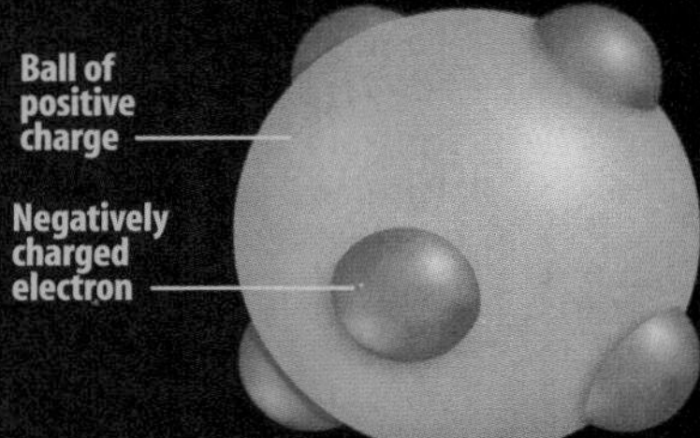

B THOMSON MODEL, 1904 English physicist Joseph John Thomson inferred from his experiments that atoms contained small, negatively charged particles. He thought these "electrons" (in red) were evenly embedded throughout a positively charged sphere, much like chocolate chips in a ball of cookie dough.

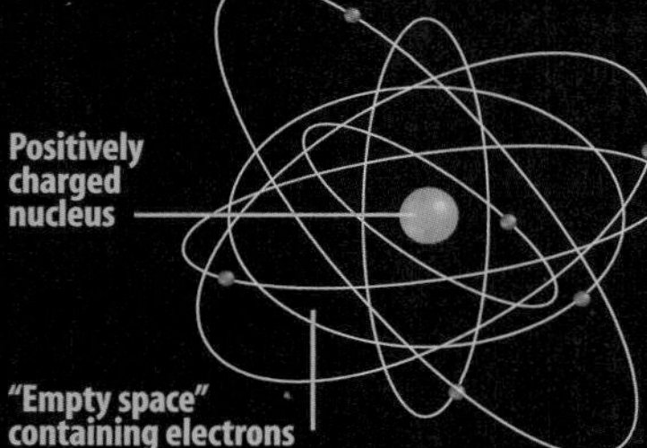

C RUTHERFORD MODEL, 1911 Another British physicist, Ernest Rutherford, proposed that almost all the mass of an atom—and all its positive charges—were concentrated in a central atomic nucleus surrounded by electrons.

D BOHR MODEL, 1913 Danish physicist Niels Bohr hypothesized that electrons traveled in fixed orbits around the atom's nucleus. James Chadwick, a student of Rutherford, concluded that the nucleus contained positive protons and neutral neutrons.

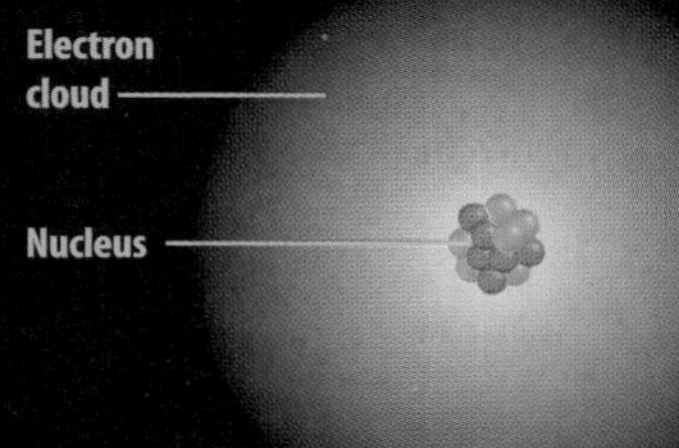

E ELECTRON CLOUD MODEL, CURRENT According to the currently accepted model of atomic structure, electrons do not follow fixed orbits but tend to occur more frequently in certain areas around the nucleus at any given time.

548

Resource Manager

Chapter Resources Booklet
Transparency Activity, pp. 47–48
Reinforcement, p. 27

Physical Science Critical Thinking/ Problem Solving, p. 13

The Electron Cloud Model In 1926, scientists developed the electron cloud model of the atom that is in use today. An **electron cloud** is the area around the nucleus of an atom where its electrons are most likely found. The electron cloud is 100,000 times larger than the diameter of the nucleus. In contrast, each electron in the cloud is much smaller than a single proton.

Because an electron's mass is small and the electron is moving so quickly around the nucleus, it is impossible to describe its exact location in an atom. Picture the spokes on a moving bicycle wheel. They are moving so quickly that you can't pinpoint any single spoke. All you see is a blur that contains all of the spokes somewhere within it. In the same way, an electron cloud is a blur containing all of the electrons of the atom somewhere within it. **Figure 6** illustrates what the electron cloud might look like.

Scientists have determined that the electron cloud is more than just a blur. Each electron travels at an average distance from the nucleus, depending on its energy. These average distances are referred to as energy levels. Energy levels are areas of the cloud where the electrons are more likely to be found.

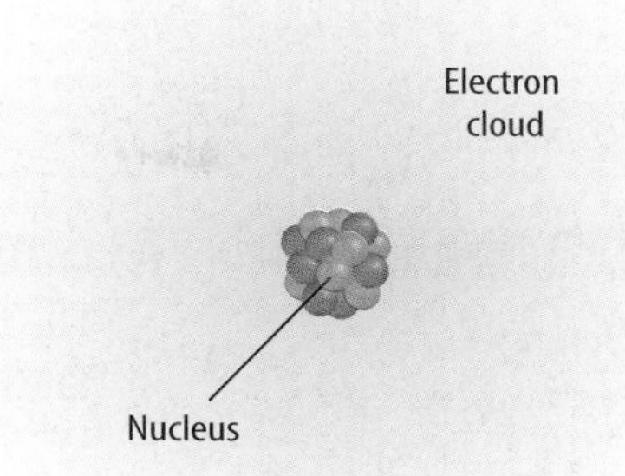

Figure 6
The electrons are located in an electron cloud surrounding the nucleus of the atom.

Section 1 Assessment

1. Write the chemical symbols for the elements carbon, aluminum, hydrogen, oxygen, and sodium.
2. What are the names, charges, and locations of three kinds of particles that make up an atom?
3. What is the smallest particle of matter? How were they discovered?
4. Describe the electron cloud model of the atom.
5. **Think Critically** Explain how a rotating electric fan might be used to model the atom. Explain how the rotating fan is unlike an atom.

Skill Builder Activities

6. **Concept Mapping** Make a concept map for the parts of an atom. Include the following terms: *electron cloud, nucleus, electrons, protons, quarks,* and *neutrons.* Provide the location of each particle in the atom. **For more help, refer to the Science Skill Handbook.**
7. **Calculating Ratios** In the electron cloud model, a maximum of two electrons can be located in the first energy level and eight electrons can be in the second. Using the periodic table, determine the ratio of electrons in the first level to the electrons in the second. **For more help, refer to the Math Skill Handbook.**

3 Assess

Reteach

Place some sesame seeds inside a balloon and carefully (do not breathe in any seeds) inflate and tie off the balloon. As you shake the balloon, ask students how this model could represent electrons in an atom. The seeds are small compared to the balloon, they are constantly moving, their locations are difficult to predict. Ask students how this model does not parallel the electrons in an atom. The balloon has a specific boundary beyond which the seeds cannot move. Electrons can move away from atoms. L2  **Visual-Spatial**

Challenge

Figure 6 shows the sublevels in which electrons may be found in energy levels 1 and 2. These are called the s and p orbitals. Higher energy levels also contain d and f orbitals Have students look up the shapes of the d and f orbitals and make drawings showing each one and how they fit together. L3
LS **Visual-Spatial**

Oral Tell students that a fundamental particle is one that cannot be divided into other particles. Ask whether protons, neutrons, or electrons are fundamental particles. Electrons are fundamental particles. Protons and neutrons are not. Use **Performance Assessment in the Science Classroom,** p. 89.

Answers to Section Assessment

1. C; Al; H; O; Na
2. proton, +1, in the nucleus; neutron, 0, in the nucleus; electron, −1, outside the nucleus
3. quark; by accelerating protons and making them collide with so much force that they broke apart
4. This model says electrons are most likely to be found in a cloud surrounding the nucleus; it is 100,000 times larger than the diameter of the nucleus.
5. The blades on a rotating fan appear as a smooth metal surface around the center hub. The probability area for electrons in an atom also presents a solid appearance. The fan blades are different from electrons because they are much larger and, when the fan stops, can easily be seen.
6. Check students' work.
7. 2 : 8 = 1 : 4

SECTION 2

Masses of Atoms

1 Motivate

Bellringer Transparency

Display the Section Focus Transparency for Section 2. Use the accompanying Transparency Activity Master. L2 ELL

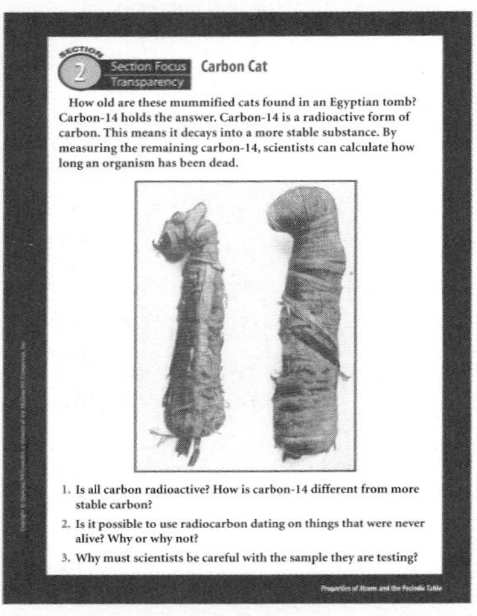
SECTION 2 Section Focus Transparency **Carbon Cat**

How old are these mummified cats found in an Egyptian tomb? Carbon-14 holds the answer. Carbon-14 is a radioactive form of carbon. This means it decays into a more stable substance. By measuring the remaining carbon-14, scientists can calculate how long an organism has been dead.

1. **Is all carbon radioactive? How is carbon-14 different from more stable carbon?**
2. **Is it possible to use radiocarbon dating on things that were never alive? Why or why not?**
3. **Why must scientists be careful with the sample they are testing?**

Properties of Atoms and the Periodic Table

Tie to Prior Knowledge

Ask students to explain the differences between mass, weight, and volume. Mass is the amount of matter in an object, weight is a measure of the force of gravity on an object, and volume is the amount of space the object occupies.

Reading Check

Answer in the nucleus

SECTION 

Masses of Atoms

As You Read

What **You'll Learn**

- **Compute** the atomic mass and mass number of an atom.
- **Identify** isotopes of common elements.
- **Interpret** the average atomic mass of an element.

Vocabulary

atomic number
mass number
isotope
average atomic mass

Why **It's Important**

Most elements exist in more than one form. Some are radioactive, and others are not.

Atomic Mass

The nucleus contains most of the mass of the atom, as shown in **Figure 7,** because protons and neutrons are far more massive than electrons. The mass of a proton is about the same as that of a neutron—approximately 1.67×10^{-24} g, as shown in **Table 2.** The mass of each is approximately 1,836 times greater than the mass of the electron. The electron's mass is so small that it is considered negligible when finding the mass of an atom.

If you were asked to estimate the height of your school building, you probably wouldn't give an answer in kilometers. The number would be too cumbersome to use. Considering the scale of the building, you would more likely give the height in a smaller unit, meters. When thinking about the small masses of atoms, scientists found that even grams were not small enough to use for measurement. Scientists need a unit that results in more manageable numbers. The unit of measurement used for atomic particles is the atomic mass unit (amu). The mass of a proton or a neutron is almost equal to 1 amu. This is not coincidence—the unit was defined that way. The atomic mass unit is defined as one-twelfth the mass of a carbon atom containing six protons and six neutrons. Remember that the mass of the carbon atom is contained almost entirely in the mass of the protons and neutrons that are located in the nucleus. Therefore, each of the 12 particles in the nucleus must have a mass nearly equal to one.

Reading Check ***Where is the majority of the mass of an atom located?***

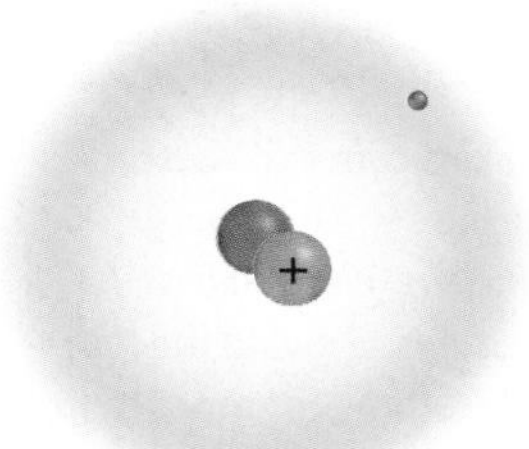

Figure 7
The protons and neutrons in the nucleus of the hydrogen atom are approximately 99.95 percent of the mass of the atom. The mass of the electron is relatively insignificant.

Table 2 Comparison of Particles in an Atom

Particle	Mass (g)	Charge	Location in Atom
Proton	1.67×10^{-24}	+1	Nucleus
Neutron	1.67×10^{-24}	0	Nucleus
Electron	9.11×10^{-28}	−1	Cloud surrounding nucleus

Section Assessment Planner

PORTFOLIO
Reteach, p. 553

PERFORMANCE ASSESSMENT
Skill Builder Activities, p. 553
See page 570 for more options.

CONTENT ASSESSMENT
Section, p. 553
Challenge, p. 553
Chapter, pp. 570–571

550 CHAPTER 18 Properties of Atoms and the Periodic Table

Table 3 Mass Numbers of Some Atoms

Element	Symbol	Atomic Number	Protons	Neutrons	Mass Number	Average Atomic Mass*
Boron	B	5	5	6	11	10.81
Carbon	C	6	6	6	12	12.01
Oxygen	O	8	8	8	16	16.00
Sodium	Na	11	11	12	23	22.99
Copper	Cu	29	29	34	63	63.55

* The atomic mass units are rounded to two decimal places.

Protons Identify the Element You learned earlier that atoms of different elements are different because they have different numbers of protons. In fact, the number of protons tells you what type of atom you have and vice versa. For example, every carbon atom has six protons. Also, all atoms with six protons are carbon atoms. Atoms with eight protons are oxygen atoms. The number of protons in an atom is equal to a number called the **atomic number.** The atomic number of carbon is six. Therefore, if you are given any one of the following—the name of the element, the number of protons in the element, or the atomic number of the element, you can determine the other two.

Reading Check *Which element is an atom with six protons in the nucleus?*

Mass Number The **mass number** of an atom is the sum of the number of protons and the number of neutrons in the nucleus of an atom. Look at **Table 3** and see if this is true.

If you know the mass number and the atomic number of an atom, you can calculate the number of neutrons. The number of neutrons is equal to the atomic number subtracted from the mass number.

number of neutrons = mass number − atomic number

Atoms with different numbers of neutrons can have different properties. For example, carbon with a mass number equal to 12 or carbon-12 is the most common form of carbon. Carbon-14 is present on Earth in much smaller quantities. Carbon-14 is radioactive and carbon-12 is not.

Reading Check *How is the mass number calculated?*

2 Teach

Atomic Mass

Reading Check

Answer carbon

Discussion

How many electrons are found in a neutral atom of carbon? six **What would the charge be on the carbon atom if it lost four electrons? Explain** +4; The atom now has 4 more protons than electrons. **How does neutron count affect atomic charge?** It has no effect.

Teacher FYI

Nearly all elements have isotopes, some of which are radioactive. The mass of an element listed on the periodic table is the weighted average of the masses of the isotopes of that element.

Discussion

Have students determine the number of neutrons, protons, and electrons in neon, potassium, and gold. Ne: 10 protons, 10 neutrons, 10 electrons; K: 19 protons, 20 neutrons, 19 electrons; Au: 79 protons, 118 neutrons, 79 electrons L2

LS **Logical-Mathematical**

Reading Check

Answer mass number = number of protons + number of neutrons

Resource Manager

Chapter Resources Booklet

Transparency Activity, p. 45

Directed Reading for Content Mastery, p. 20

Lab Activity, pp. 9–12

Inclusion Strategies

Visually Impaired If **Table 3** is difficult for some to read, use one type of object, such as small corks, to represent protons and another type, such as rubber stoppers, to represent neutrons. Have students assemble the right numbers of protons and neutrons for the atoms listed in **Table 3.**

Isotopes

Students may think that since many of the lighter elements have the same number of protons as neutrons, all elements have this property. Remind them that this is not true. Large atoms have more neutrons than protons because neutrons play a role in stabilizing the repulsive forces between the protons in the nucleus.

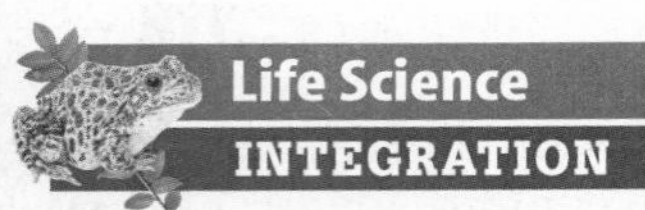

Archaeologists are most interested in carbon-13 and carbon-14 because these isotopes are radioactive. The longer a once-living organism has been dead, the less radioactive it will be per gram of carbon. This gives archaeologists a way to determine the approximate age of once-living organisms.

Reading Check

Answer 146 neutrons

Problem-Solving Activity

National Math Standards

Correlation to Mathematics Objectives
1, 5, 6, 8, 9, 10

Answers

1. 50,000 years; 100,000 years
2. 9,020 million years; lead-209

Life Science INTEGRATION

Living organisms on Earth contain carbon. Carbon-12 makes up 99 percent of this carbon. Carbon-13 and carbon-14 make up the other one percent. Which isotopes are archaeologists most interested in when they determine the age of carbon-containing remains? Explain your answer in your Science Journal.

Isotopes

Not all the atoms of an element have the same number of neutrons. Atoms of the same element that have different numbers of neutrons are called **isotopes.** Suppose you have a sample of the element boron. Naturally occurring atoms of boron have mass numbers of 10 or 11. How many neutrons are in a boron atom? It depends upon the isotope of boron to which you are referring. Obtain the number of protons in boron from the periodic table. Then use the formula on the previous page to calculate the number of neutrons in each boron isotope. You can determine that boron can have five or six neutrons.

Reading Check *Uranium-238 can be found naturally in uranium ore, how many neutrons does it have?*

Problem-Solving Activity

Radioactive Isotopes Help Tell Time

Atoms can be used to measure bones or rock formations that are millions of years old. The time it takes for half of the radioactive atoms in a piece of rock or bone to change into another element is called its half-life. Scientists use the half-lives of radioactive isotopes to measure geologic time.

Half-lives of Radioactive Isotopes

Radioactive Element	Changes to this Radioactive Element	Half-Life
uranium-238	lead-206	4,510 million years
potassium-40	argon-40, calcium-40	1,350 million years
rubidium-87	strontium-87	50,000 years
carbon-14	nitrogen-14	5,730 years

Identifying the Problem

The table above lists the half-lives of a sample of radioactive isotopes and into which elements they change. For example, it would take 5,730 years for half of the carbon-14 atoms in a rock to change into atoms of nitrogen-14. After another 5,730 years, half of the remaining carbon-14 atoms will change, and so on. You can use these radioactive clocks to measure different periods of time.

Solving the Problem

1. How many years would it take half of the rubidium-87 atoms in a piece of rock to change into strontium-87? How many years would it take for 75% of the atoms to change?
2. After a long period, only 25% of the atoms in a rock remained uranium-238. How many years old would you predict the rock to be? The other 75% of the atoms are now which radioactive element?

Visual Learning

Figure 8 Have students draw diagrams in their Science Journals of the nuclei of carbon-12, carbon-13, and carbon-14. Carbon-12 has 6 protons and 6 neutrons, carbon-13 has 6 protons and 7 neutrons, and carbon-14 has 6 protons and 8 neutrons. L2

LS **Visual-Spatial**

Resource Manager 

Chapter Resources Booklet
Reinforcement, p. 28
Enrichment, p. 31

Mathematics Skill Activities, p. 7

552 CHAPTER 18 Properties of Atoms and the Periodic Table

Identifying Isotopes Models of the two isotopes of boron are shown in **Figure 8.** Because the numbers of neutrons in the isotopes are different, the mass numbers are also different. You use the name of the element followed by the mass number of the isotope to identify each isotope: boron-10 and boron-11. Because most elements have more than one isotope, each element is given an average atomic mass. The **average atomic mass** of an element is the weighted-average mass of the mixture of its isotopes. For example, four out of five atoms of boron are boron-11, and one out of five is boron-10. To find the weighted-average or the average atomic mass of boron, you would solve the following equation:

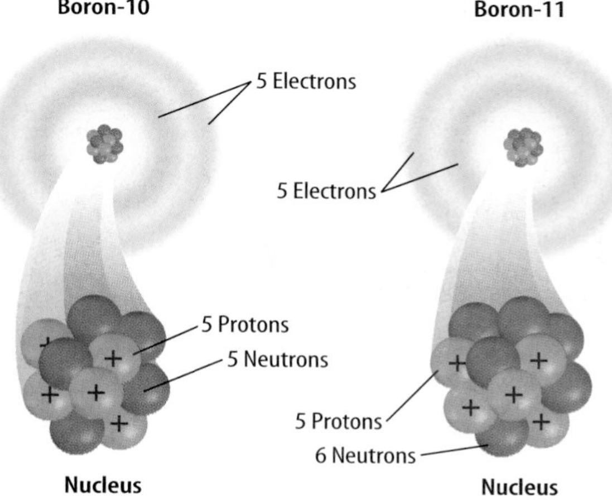

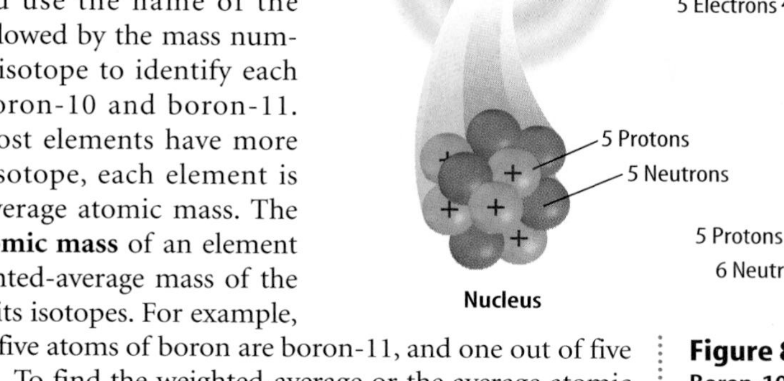

Figure 8
Boron-10 and boron-11 are two isotopes of the boron atom. These two isotopes differ by one neutron.

$$\frac{4}{5}(11 \text{ amu}) + \frac{1}{5}(10 \text{ amu}) = 10.8 \text{ amu}$$

The average atomic mass of the element boron is 10.8 amu. Note that the average atomic mass of boron is close to the mass of its most abundant isotope, boron-11.

Section 2 Assessment

1. A chlorine atom has 17 protons and 18 neutrons. What is its mass number? What is its atomic number?
2. How are the isotopes of an element alike and how are they different?
3. Why is the atomic mass of an element an average mass?
4. How would you calculate the number of neutrons in potassium-40?
5. **Think Critically** Chlorine has an average atomic mass of 35.45 amu. The two naturally occurring isotopes of chlorine are chlorine-35 and chlorine-37. Why does this indicate that most chlorine atoms contain 18 neutrons?

Skill Builder Activities

6. **Comparing and Contrasting** How does the average atomic mass relate to the mass number of an atom? Use an element as an example in your explanation. **For more help, refer to the** Science Skill Handbook.
7. **Using an Electronic Spreadsheet** Use a spreadsheet to construct a table organizing information about the atomic numbers; atomic mass numbers; and the number of protons, neutrons, and electrons in atoms of oxygen-16, oxygen-17, carbon-12, carbon-14, chlorine-35, and chlorine-36. Record your calculations in your Science Journal. **For more help, refer to the** Technology Skill Handbook.

3 Assess

Reteach

Have students calculate the weighted average of student quiz scores if the following results were obtained: 5 students scored 80%; 19 students scored 90%. $(\frac{5}{24} \times 80) + (\frac{19}{24} \times 90) = 88$
L2 LS **Logical-Mathematical**

Challenge

Have students find the names and masses of the three isotopes of hydrogen. **How many neutrons does each one have?** hydrogen, mass = 1, 0 neutrons; deuterium, mass = 2, 1 neutron; tritium, mass = 3, 2 neutrons L3
LS **Linguistic**

Assessment

Oral Place a small plastic container on a table. Have students count as you place colored marbles, representing protons, into the bowl. When you stop, ask them to identify the element. Then ask them to predict the number of neutrons needed for that element, and add the correct number of a different color of marbles. Ask how many small cotton balls, representing electrons, you must lay around the outside of the container to make a neutral atom. Use **Performance Assessment in the Science Classroom,** p. 89.

Answers to Section Assessment

1. Mass number = 35; atomic number = 17
2. Isotopes have the same number of protons but different numbers of neutrons.
3. Elements have several isotopes with different numbers of neutrons, and thus different masses. The average atomic mass is the weighted average of the masses of the element's isotopes.
4. Mass number − atomic number = number of neutrons = 40 − 19 = 21
5. The average of 35.45 lies closer to the 35 mass number than to the 37 mass number.
6. Both the average atomic mass and the mass number are determined by the total number of protons and neutrons in an atom. However the mass number gives this information usually for a specific isotope and the average atomic mass is an average of all of the isotopes.
7. Check students' work.

SECTION 3

The Periodic Table

1 Motivate

Bellringer Transparency

Display the Section Focus Transparency for Section 3. Use the accompanying Transparency Activity Master. L2 ELL

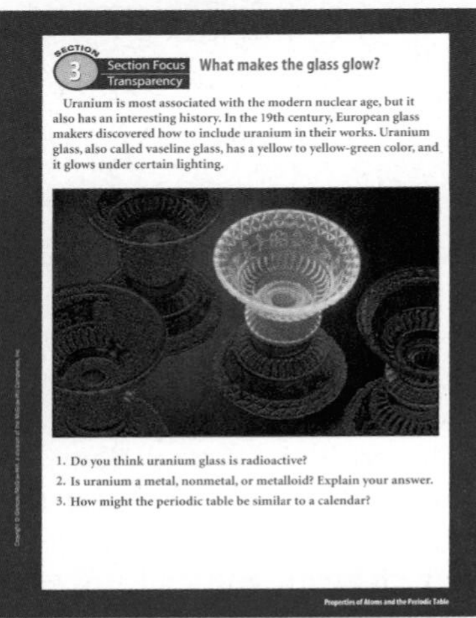
Section 3 Section Focus Transparency — What makes the glass glow?

Uranium is most associated with the modern nuclear age, but it also has an interesting history. In the 19th century, European glass makers discovered how to include uranium in their works. Uranium glass, also called vaseline glass, has a yellow to yellow-green color, and it glows under certain lighting.

1. Do you think uranium glass is radioactive?
2. Is uranium a metal, nonmetal, or metalloid? Explain your answer.
3. How might the periodic table be similar to a calendar?

Tie to Prior Knowledge

Students are already familiar with the repeating pattern of the days of the week. Point out that just as a calendar illustrates the periodic pattern of the days of the week, the periodic table illustrates the periodic patterns of the chemical properties of chemical elements.

SECTION 

The Periodic Table

As You Read

***What* You'll Learn**

- **Explain** the composition of the periodic table.
- **Use** the periodic table to obtain information.
- **Explain** what the terms *metal, nonmetal,* and *metalloid* mean.

Vocabulary

periodic table
group
electron dot diagram
period

***Why* It's Important**

The periodic table is an organized list of the elements that compose all living and nonliving things that are known to exist in the universe.

Organizing the Elements

On a clear evening, you can see one of the various phases of the Moon. Each month, the Moon seems to grow larger, then smaller, in a repeating pattern. This type of change is periodic. *Periodic* means "repeated in a pattern." Look at a calendar. The days of the week are periodic because they repeat themselves every seven days. Months repeat every 12 months. The calendar is a periodic table of days and months. They are used to organize your schedule into a convenient format.

In the late 1800s, Dmitri Mendeleev, a Russian chemist, searched for a way to organize the elements. When he arranged all the elements known at that time in order of increasing atomic masses, he discovered a pattern. **Figure 9** shows Mendeleev's early periodic chart. Chemical properties found in lighter elements could be shown to repeat in heavier elements. Because the pattern repeated, it was considered to be periodic. Today, this arrangement is called a periodic table of elements. In the **periodic table,** the elements are arranged by increasing atomic number resulting in periodic changes in properties.

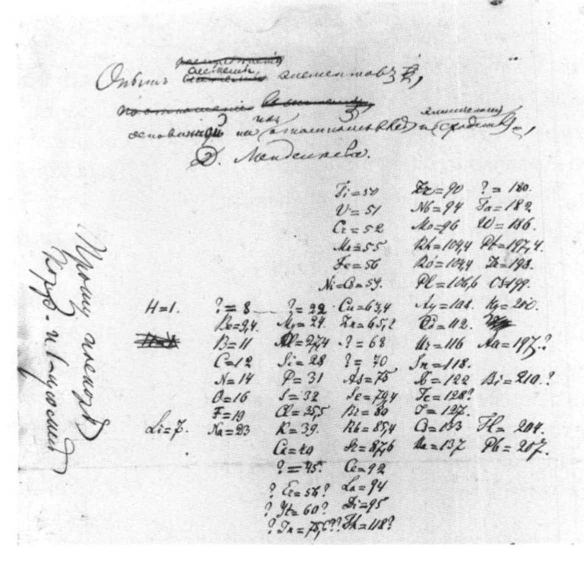

Figure 9
Mendeleev discovered that the elements had a periodic pattern in their chemical properties. Notice the question marks in his chart. These were elements that had not been discovered at that time.

Section Assessment Planner

Portfolio
Assessment, p. 555
Science Journal, p. 561

Performance Assessment
Try at Home MiniLAB p. 555
Skill Builder Activites, p. 562
See page 570 for more options.

Content Assessment
Section, p. 562
Challenge, p. 562
Chapter, pp. 570–571

Table 4 Mendeleev's Predictions

Predicted Properties of Ekasilicon (Es)	Actual Properties of Germanium (Ge)
Predicted Properties	*Actual Properties*
Atomic mass = 72	Atomic mass = 72.61
High melting point	Melting point = 945°C
Density = 5.5 g/cm^3	Density = 5.323 g/cm^3
Dark gray metal	Gray metal
Density of EsO_2 = 4.7 g/cm^3	Density of GeO_2 = 4.7 g/cm^3

Mendeleev's Predictions Mendeleev had to leave blank spaces in his periodic table to keep the elements properly lined up according to their chemical properties. He looked at the properties and atomic masses of the elements surrounding these blank spaces. From this information, he was able to predict the properties and the mass numbers of new elements that had not yet been discovered. **Table 4** shows Mendeleev's predicted properties for germanium, which he called ekasilicon. His predictions proved to be accurate. Scientists later discovered these missing elements and found that their properties were extremely close to what Mendeleev had predicted.

Reading Check *How did Mendeleev organize his periodic chart?*

Improving the Periodic Table Although Mendeleev's arrangement of elements was successful, it did need some changes. On Mendeleev's table, the atomic mass gradually increased from left to right. If you look at the modern periodic table, shown in **Table 5,** you will see several examples, such as cobalt and nickel, where the mass decreases from left to right. You also might notice that the atomic number always increases from left to right. In 1913, the work of Henry G.J. Moseley, a young English scientist, led to the arrangement of elements based on their increasing atomic numbers instead of an arrangement based on atomic masses. This new arrangement seemed to correct the problems that had occurred in the old table. The current periodic table uses Moseley's arrangement of the elements.

Reading Check *How is the modern periodic table arranged?*

A Personal Periodic Table

Procedure

1. Collect as many of the following items as you can find: **feather, penny, container of water, pencil, dime, strand of hair, container of milk, container of orange juice, square of cotton cloth, nickel, crayon, quarter, container of soda, golf ball, sheet of paper, baseball, marble, leaf,** and **paper clip.**
2. Organize these items into several columns based on their similarities to create your own periodic table.

Analysis

1. Explain the system you used to group your items.
2. Were there any items on the list that did not fit into any of your columns?
3. Infer how your activity modeled Mendeleev's work in developing the Periodic Table of the Elements.

2 Teach

Organizing the Elements

Purpose Students classify objects that are very different. L2 LS **Logical-Mathematical**

Materials a variety of objects that can be sorted into several categories

Teaching Strategy A wide variety of objects will force the students to work harder to find common traits.

Analysis

1. Answers will vary but possible groups include metal objects, coins, organic items, spheres, liquids, and writing implements.
2. Answers will vary.
3. Just as Mendeleev searched for similarities and repeating patterns among the elements, students searched for commonalities among the objects to place them in groups.

Assessment

Performance Provide students with an assortment of bolts, screws, and nails. Have them build another periodic table using these items. Use **PASC,** p. 121. P

Resource Manager

Chapter Resources Booklet
Transparency Activity, p. 46
MiniLAB, p. 4

Home and Community Involvement, p. 25

Teacher FYI

Mendeleev predicted several elements in addition to ekasilicon. These included successful predictions of eka-aluminum and eka-boron, which were later found to be gallium and scandium, and unsuccessful predictions of eka-niobium and eka-caesium, which do not exist. The prefix *eka-* is Sanskrit for the numeral one.

Reading Check

- **Answer** He arranged the elements by increasing atomic mass and aligned them in columns based on chemical and physical properties.
- **Answer** by atomic number

Organizing the Elements, continued

Teacher FYI

The elements have an increasing nonmetallic characteristic as you read from left to right across the table. Along the stair-step line are metalloids, which have properties of both metals and nonmetals.

Use an Analogy

Remind students that orderly classification allows them to enter a music store and quickly find a desired selection without examining every CD in the store. The periodic table gives chemists the same advantage when they are looking for elements with particular properties.

Fun Fact

Hydrogen, by its electron arrangement, is part of **Group 1.** However, because it has only one electron energy level that can hold only two electrons, it has its own unique set of properties.

Activity

Have students list the elements in the first six periods that would be out of sequence if the chart were arranged by atomic mass. Ar and K, Co and Ni, Te and I L2 LS **Logical-Mathematical**

PERIODIC TABLE OF THE ELEMENTS

Key: Element — Hydrogen; Atomic number — 1; Symbol — H; Atomic mass — 1.008; State of matter

Period	1A 1	2A 2	3B 3	4B 4	5B 5	6B 6	7B 7	8B 8	9
1	Hydrogen 1 H 1.008								
2	Lithium 3 Li 6.941	Beryllium 4 Be 9.012							
3	Sodium 11 Na 22.990	Magnesium 12 Mg 24.305							
4	Potassium 19 K 39.098	Calcium 20 Ca 40.078	Scandium 21 Sc 44.956	Titanium 22 Ti 47.88	Vanadium 23 V 50.942	Chromium 24 Cr 51.996	Manganese 25 Mn 54.938	Iron 26 Fe 55.847	Cobalt 27 Co 58.933
5	Rubidium 37 Rb 85.468	Strontium 38 Sr 87.62	Yttrium 39 Y 88.906	Zirconium 40 Zr 91.224	Niobium 41 Nb 92.906	Molybdenum 42 Mo 95.94	Technetium 43 Tc 97.907	Ruthenium 44 Ru 101.07	Rhodium 45 Rh 102.906
6	Cesium 55 Cs 132.905	Barium 56 Ba 137.327	Lanthanum 57 La 138.906	Hafnium 72 Hf 178.49	Tantalum 73 Ta 180.948	Tungsten 74 W 183.84	Rhenium 75 Re 186.207	Osmium 76 Os 190.2	Iridium 77 Ir 192.22
7	Francium 87 Fr 223.020	Radium 88 Ra 226.025	Actinium 89 Ac 227.028	Rutherfordium 104 Rf (261)	Dubnium 105 Db (262)	Seaborgium 106 Sg (263)	Bohrium 107 Bh (262)	Hassium 108 Hs (265)	Meitnerium 109 Mt (266)

Series						
Lanthanide series	Cerium 58 Ce 140.115	Praseodymium 59 Pr 140.908	Neodymium 60 Nd 144.24	Promethium 61 Pm 144.913	Samarium 62 Sm 150.36	Europium 63 Eu 151.965
Actinide series	Thorium 90 Th 232.038	Protactinium 91 Pa 231.036	Uranium 92 U 238.029	Neptunium 93 Np 237.048	Plutonium 94 Pu 244.064	Americium 95 Am 243.061

Visual Learning

Table 5 Which element has an average mass greater than 75 but less than 79? selenium **Is it possible to have more than one element that could fit that restriction?** No; based on average masses, there are no missing atomic numbers from 33 to 34 to 35.

Curriculum Connection

Music In music, the syllables do, *re*, *mi*, *fa*, *sol*, *la*, *ti*, *do* give the pitches of the diatonic scale. Have students find out how this scale is similar to the periodic table. The scale do, *re, mi, fa, sol, la, ti, do* can be related to Li, Be, B, C, N, O, F, and Na in the periodic table. Na repeats the properties of Li just as the second *do* is one octave higher than the first *do.* L2 LS **Auditory-Musical**

Resource Manager

Chapter Resources Booklet

Lab Activity, pp. 13–15

Reading and Writing Skill Activities, p. 47

556 CHAPTER 18 Properties of Atoms and the Periodic Table

Metal

Metalloid

Nonmetal

Recently discovered

Gas

Liquid

Solid

Synthetic elements

10	1B 11	2B 12	3A 13	4A 14	5A 15	6A 16	7A 17	8A 18
								Helium 2 He 4.003
			Boron 5 B 10.811	Carbon 6 C 12.011	Nitrogen 7 N 14.007	Oxygen 8 O 15.999	Fluorine 9 F 18.998	Neon 10 Ne 20.180
			Aluminum 13 Al 26.982	Silicon 14 Si 28.086	Phosphorus 15 P 30.974	Sulfur 16 S 32.066	Chlorine 17 Cl 35.453	Argon 18 Ar 39.948
Nickel 28 Ni 58.693	Copper 29 Cu 63.546	Zinc 30 Zn 65.39	Gallium 31 Ga 69.723	Germanium 32 Ge 72.61	Arsenic 33 As 74.922	Selenium 34 Se 78.96	Bromine 35 Br 79.904	Krypton 36 Kr 83.80
Palladium 46 Pd 106.42	Silver 47 Ag 107.868	Cadmium 48 Cd 112.411	Indium 49 In 114.82	Tin 50 Sn 118.710	Antimony 51 Sb 121.757	Tellurium 52 Te 127.60	Iodine 53 I 126.904	Xenon 54 Xe 131.290
Platinum 78 Pt 195.08	Gold 79 Au 196.967	Mercury 80 Hg 200.59	Thallium 81 Tl 204.383	Lead 82 Pb 207.2	Bismuth 83 Bi 208.980	Polonium 84 Po 208.982	Astatine 85 At 209.987	Radon 86 Rn 222.018
Ununnilium * 110 Uun 269	Unununium * 111 Uuu 272	Unumbium * 112 Uub 277		Ununquadium * 114 Uuq 285		Ununhexium * 116 Uuh 289		Ununodium * 118 Uuo 293

* Names not officially assigned. Discovery of elements 114, 116, and 118 recently reported. Further information not yet available.

Gadolinium 64 Gd 157.25	Terbium 65 Tb 158.925	Dysprosium 66 Dy 162.50	Holmium 67 Ho 164.930	Erbium 68 Er 167.26	Thulium 69 Tm 168.934	Ytterbium 70 Yb 173.04	Lutetium 71 Lu 174.967
Curium 96 Cm 247.070	Berkelium 97 Bk 247.070	Californium 98 Cf 251.080	Einsteinium 99 Es 252.083	Fermium 100 Fm 257.095	Mendelevium 101 Md 258.099	Nobelium 102 No 259.101	Lawrencium 103 Lr 260.105

IDENTIFYING Misconceptions

Mendeleev did not have the advantage of knowing atomic structure when he made his periodic chart. Electrons were not discovered until the late 1890s. His chart was based on mass and properties of the elements.

Extension

The chemical symbols for the following elements are not abbreviations of their English names. Have students use reference books to determine the symbols for the following elements and the names upon which the symbols are based: copper (Cu, cuprum); gold (Au, aurum); iron (Fe, ferrum); lead (Pb, plumbum); tin (Sn, stannum); mercury (Hg, hydroargyrum); silver (Ag, argentum) sodium (Na, natrium); potassium (K, kalium); antimony (Sb, stibnum); tungsten (W, wolfram).

L3 IN **Linguistic**

LAB DEMONSTRATION

Purpose to choose a criterion for arranging items

Materials 5 clear plastic cups, water, blue food coloring

Preparation Add an equal amount of water to each cup. Add 1 drop of food coloring to cup 1, 2 drops to cup 2, and so on. Make one with $3\frac{1}{2}$ drops and put it aside.

Procedure Mix the order of the cups and display them. Have students place the cups in a sequence. Display the solution made with $3\frac{1}{2}$ drops of food coloring and ask them to place it in its proper location.

Expected Outcome The sequence may be from dilute to concentrated or the opposite.

How does this activity demonstrate the thinking Mendeleev used for his chart? He made a sequence of chemical elements based on their properties and could tell where new discoveries fit in.

The Atom and the Periodic Table

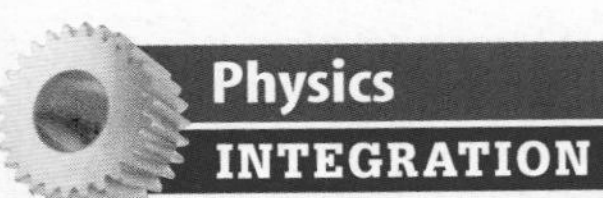

Physics INTEGRATION

Electrons have been removed by the silk as it was rubbed against the rod.

Visual Learning

Figure 10 Point out to students that this diagram is not intended to represent relative sizes of the electrons, atom, or nucleus. Therefore, it does not show that the energy levels get closer together the farther they are from the nucleus.

Extension

Each energy level contains sublevels, which in turn contain atomic orbitals. Have students find out more about the distribution of electrons in sublevels and atomic orbitals. The first energy level has only one sublevel, while the second level has two sublevels, and the third has three. The first sublevel in any level contains one s orbital, which can contain up to two electrons. The second sublevel in any level contains three p orbitals. Each p orbital can contain up to two electrons, so this sublevel can contain a maximum of six electrons. The third sublevel contains five d orbitals, each of which can contain up to two electrons, so this sublevel can contain up to ten electrons. The fourth sublevel contains seven f orbitals, each of which can contain up to two electrons, so this sublevel can contain up to fourteen electrons. L3 LS **Linguistic**

Physics INTEGRATION

When a glass rod is rubbed with silk, the rod becomes positively charged. Infer what type of particle in the atoms in the rod has been removed. Explain your answer in your Science Journal.

The Atom and the Periodic Table

Objects often are sorted or grouped according to the properties they have in common. This also is done in the periodic table. The vertical columns in the periodic table are called **groups,** or families, and are numbered 1 through 18. Elements in each group have similar properties. For example, in Group 11, copper, silver, and gold have similar properties. Each is a shiny metal and a good conductor of electricity and heat. What is responsible for the similar properties? To answer this question, look at the structure of the atom.

Electron Cloud Structure You have learned about the number and location of protons and neutrons in an atom. But where are the electrons located? How many are there? In a neutral atom, the number of electrons is equal to the number of protons. Therefore, a carbon atom, with an atomic number of six, has six protons and six electrons. These electrons are located in the electron cloud surrounding the nucleus.

Scientists have found that electrons within the electron cloud have different amounts of energy. Scientists model the energy differences of the electrons by placing the electrons in energy levels, as in **Figure 10.** Energy levels nearer the nucleus have lower energy than those levels that are farther away. These energy levels fill with electrons from inner levels—closer to the nucleus to outer levels—further from the nucleus.

Elements that are in the same group have the same number of electrons in their outer energy level. It is the number of electrons in the outer energy level that determines the chemical properties of the element. It is important to understand the link between the location on the periodic table, chemical properties, and the structure of the atom.

Figure 10
Energy levels in atoms can be represented by a flight of stairs. Each stair step away from the nucleus represents an increase in the amount of energy within the electrons. The higher energy levels contain more electrons.

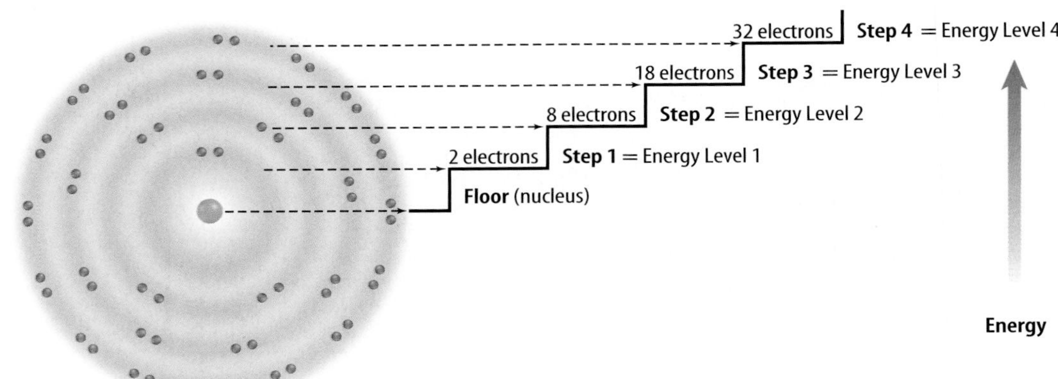

Resource Manager

Chapter Resources Booklet
Enrichment, p. 32
Cultural Diversity, p. 59

Cultural Diversity

Culturally Diverse Elements Have students make a list of elements that are named after countries or cities. magnesium—Magnesia; scandium—Scandinavia; germanium—Germany; yttrium, ytterbium, terbium—town of Ytterby in Sweden; halfnium—Copenhagen; holmium—Stockholm; ruthenium—Russia; polonium—Poland; strontium—Strontian (Scotland); lutetium—Paris

Energy Levels These energy levels are named using numbers one to seven. The maximum number of electrons that can be contained in each of the first four levels is shown in **Figure 10.** For example, energy level one can contain a maximum of two electrons. Energy level two can contain a maximum of eight electrons. Beryllium has four electrons. Two of these electrons are in energy level one, and the remaining two electrons are in energy level two. Therefore, beryllium has two outer electrons.

Reading Check *How many outer electrons does hydrogen have?*

Rows on the Table Remember that the atomic number found on the periodic table is equal to the number of electrons in an atom. Look at **Figure 11.** The first row has hydrogen with one electron and helium with two electrons both in energy level one. Because energy level one is the outermost level containing an electron, hydrogen has one outer electron. Helium has two outer electrons. Recall from **Figure 10** that energy level one can hold only two electrons. Therefore, helium has a full or complete outer energy level. The second row begins with lithium, which has three electrons—two in energy level one and one in energy level two. Lithium has one outer electron. Lithium is followed by beryllium with two outer electrons, boron with three, and so on until you reach neon with eight outer electrons. Again, looking at **Figure 10,** energy level two can only hold eight electrons. Therefore, neon has a complete outer energy level. Do you notice how the row in the periodic table ends when an outer energy level is filled? In the third row of elements, the electrons begin filling energy level three. The row ends with argon, which has a full outer energy level of eight electrons.

SCIENCE Online

Research Visit the Glencoe Science Web site at **science.glencoe.com** for more information about the structure of atomic energy levels. Communicate to your class what you learned.

Figure 11
One proton and one electron are added to each element as you go across the periodic table.

Hydrogen 1 **H**							Helium 2 **He**
Lithium 3 **Li**	Beryllium 4 **Be**	Boron 5 **B**	Carbon 6 **C**	Nitrogen 7 **N**	Oxygen 8 **O**	Fluorine 9 **F**	Neon 10 **Ne**
Sodium 11 **Na**	Magnesium 12 **Mg**	Aluminum 13 **Al**	Silicon 14 **Si**	Phosphorus 15 **P**	Sulfur 16 **S**	Chlorine 17 **Cl**	Argon 18 **Ar**

Fun Fact

The maximum number of electrons in a level is $2n^2$, where n is the level number. For example, when $n = 3$ there can be a maximum of $2(3^2) = 18$ electrons.

Reading Check

Answer one

Discussion

In which row do you find the important metalloid germanium? fourth row **Which row contains the fewest elements?** first row **Which row probably contains the largest atoms on the periodic table?** seventh row
L2 LS **Visual-Spatial**

IDENTIFYING Misconceptions

Students may be confused by the depiction of the last two rows of the periodic table below the rest of the table. These two rows, called the lanthanides and actinides, respectively, are shown below to allow the table to be displayed in a manner that is easy to read.

SCIENCE Online
Internet Addresses

Explore the Glencoe Science Web site at **science.glencoe.com** to find out more about topics in this section.

Inclusion Strategies

Learning Disabled Obtain samples of several elements, such as tin, copper, sulfur, silver, and aluminum. Have students examine and record the characteristics of each element. They should look for such properties as color, hardness, texture, and brittleness. They can play a game in which one student lists the characteristics and another identifies the element.

The Atom and the Periodic Table, continued

Activity

With a periodic table prominently displayed, or while students look at the one in the text, select various elements by name and atomic number. Have students determine the correct number of outer level electrons and write the dot diagram on the board. Do not use the elements from Groups 3–12 for this activity. These groups, called the transition elements, have their new electrons added to a lower energy level. L2

LS **Visual-Spatial**

Use an Analogy

Remind students that when atoms exchange electrons, they become charged, negatively if they gain electrons and positively if they lose electrons, but the atoms retain their identity because the number of protons in the nucleus remains the same. This is analogous to the way a person can wear a hat and easily exchange it with another person's hat without losing his or her identity.

Fun Fact

The elements in **Group 18,** known as the noble gases, had no recognized compounds until 1961 when xenon and fluorine were combined. Since then, other noble gas compounds have been formed. As recently as 2000, argon was found to combine. These are rare cases. In nature, noble gases are found uncombined.

Reading Check

Answer All members of a Group have the same number of electrons in their outer shell.

Figure 12
The elements in Group 1 have one electron in their outer shell. This electron dot diagram represents that one electron.

H•

Li•

Na•

K•

Rb•

Cs•

Fr•

Electron Dot Diagrams Did you notice that hydrogen, lithium, and sodium have one electron in their outer energy level? Elements that are in the same group have the same number of electrons in their outer energy level. These outer electrons are so important in determining the chemical properties of an element that a special way to represent them has been developed. An **electron dot diagram** uses the symbol of the element and dots to represent the electrons in the outer energy level. **Figure 12** shows the electron dot diagram for Group One. Electron dot diagrams are used also to show how the electrons in the outer energy level are bonded when elements combine to form compounds.

Same Group—Similar Properties The elements in Group 17, the halogens, have electron dot diagrams similar to chlorine, shown in **Figure 13.** All halogens have seven electrons in their outer energy levels. Since all of the members of a group on the periodic table have the same number of electrons in their outer shell, group members will undergo chemical reactions in similar ways.

A common property of the halogens is the ability to form compounds readily with elements in Group one. Group one elements have only one electron in their outer energy level. **Figure 13** shows an example of a compound formed by one such reaction. The Group one element, sodium, reacts easily with the Group 17 element, chlorine. The result is the compound sodium chloride, or NaCl—ordinary table salt.

Not all elements will combine readily with other elements. The elements in Group 18 have complete outer energy levels. This special configuration makes Group 18 elements relatively unreactive. You will learn more about why and how bonds form between elements in the later chapters.

Reading Check *Why do elements in a Group undergo similar chemical reactions?*

Figure 13
Electron dot diagrams show the electrons in an element's outer energy level.

A **The electron dot diagram for Group 17 consists of three sets of paired dots and one single dot.**

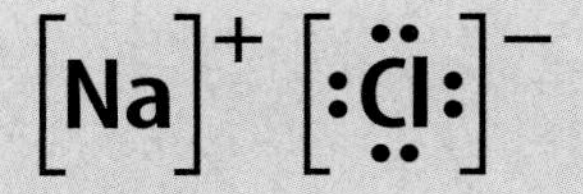

B **Sodium combines with chlorine to give each element a complete outer energy level in the resulting compound.**

C **Neon, a member of Group 18, has a full shell. Neon has eight electrons in its outer energy level making it unreactive.**

Active Reading

Jigsaw In this collaborative learning technique, individuals become experts on a portion of a text and share their expertise with a small group, called their home group. Everyone shares responsibility for learning the assigned reading. Assign each person in each home group an expert number. Have students gather into the expert groups that correspond to the numbers they were assigned. Have them read, discuss, and master chapter concepts and determine how best to teach them to their home groups. Have students return to their home groups and share the content they learned in their expert groups. Have students use the Jigsaw strategy to help them learn about the characteristics of elements and how they are grouped on the periodic table.

560 CHAPTER 18 Properties of Atoms and the Periodic Table

Regions on the Periodic Table

The periodic table has several regions with specific names. The horizontal rows of elements on the periodic table are called **periods.** The elements increase by one proton and one electron as you go from left to right in a period.

All of the elements in the blue squares in **Figure 14** are metals. Iron, zinc, and copper are examples of metals. Most metals exist as solids at room temperature. They are shiny, can be drawn into wires, can be pounded into sheets, and are good conductors of heat and electricity.

Those elements on the right side of the periodic table, in yellow, are classified as nonmetals. Oxygen, bromine, and carbon are examples of nonmetals. Most nonmetals are gases, are brittle, and are poor conductors of heat and electricity at room temperature. The elements in green are metalloids or semimetals. They have some properties of both metals and nonmetals. Boron and silicon are examples of metalloids.

Reading Check *What are the properties of the elements located on the left side of the periodic table?*

A Growing Family Scientists around the world are continuing their research into the synthesis of elements. In 1994, scientists at the Heavy-Ion Research Laboratory in Darmstadt, Germany, discovered element 111. As of 1998, only one isotope of element 111 has been found. This isotope had a life span of 0.003 s. In 1996, element 112 was discovered at the same laboratory. As of 1998, only one isotope of element 112 has been found. The life span of this isotope was 0.00048 s. Both of these elements are produced in the laboratory by joining smaller atoms into a single atom. The search for elements with higher atomic numbers continues. Scientists have hypothesized about the properties of elements beyond 112. However, the actual discovery of many of these elements has not yet occurred.

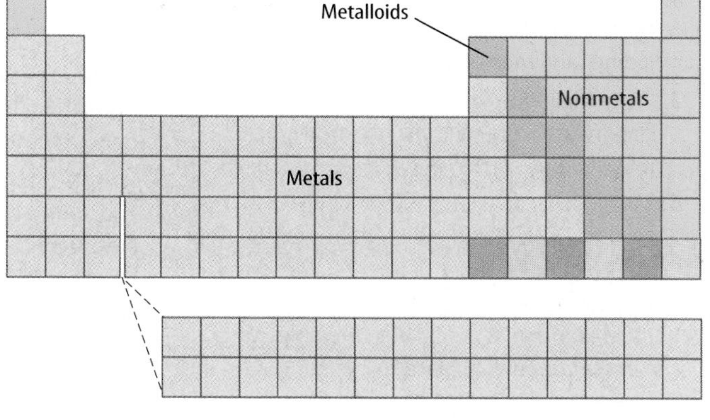

Figure 14
Metalloids are located along the green stair-step line. Metals are located to the left of the metalloids. Nonmetals are located to the right of the metalloids.

SCIENCE Online

Research Visit the Glencoe Science Web site at **science.glencoe.com** for more information about newly discovered elements. Communicate to your class what you learn.

Regions on the Periodic Table

SCIENCE Online

Internet Addresses

Explore the Glencoe Science Web site at **science.glencoe.com** to find out more about topics in this section.

Fun Fact

As a general rule, elements with three or fewer electrons in the outer energy level are considered to be metals, and elements with five or more electrons in the outer energy level are considered to be nonmetals.

Reading Check

Answer The elements on the left side of the table are metals, which are solids at room temperature, shiny, and good conductors of heat and electricity.

Resource Manager

Chapter Resources Booklet

Directed Reading for Content Mastery, pp. 21, 22

Science Journal

New Elements Have students use Internet sources to identify the newest synthesized element. Have them write in their Science Journals the element's name, atomic number, isotope, half-life, and where the element was discovered. L2 LS **Linguistic** P

3 Assess

Reteach

Using a poster-sized periodic table, point to various elements and ask students to identify the group number and period number of each element and classify it as a metal, nonmetal, or metalloid. L2 IS **Visual-Spatial**

Challenge

Ask students to use a reference to assign krypton's 36 electrons to their levels, sublevels, and orbitals. $1s^2, 2s^2, 2p^6, 3s^2, 3p^6, 3d^{10}, 4s^2, 4p^6$. L3 IS **Logical-Mathematical**

Performance Gather pens and pencils from the class and have students suggest ways to group them that place similar ones together. Then have students arrange the pens and pencils by approximate mass in a pencil periodic table. Give students a new pen or pencil and ask them to decide where to place it in the table. **How is this similar to Mendeleev's activities?** He arranged chemical elements by mass and by properties and could predict and classify new elements. Use **PASC,** p. 121.

Resource Manager

Chapter Resources Booklet
Reinforcement, p. 29
Activity Worksheet, pp. 5–6, 7–8

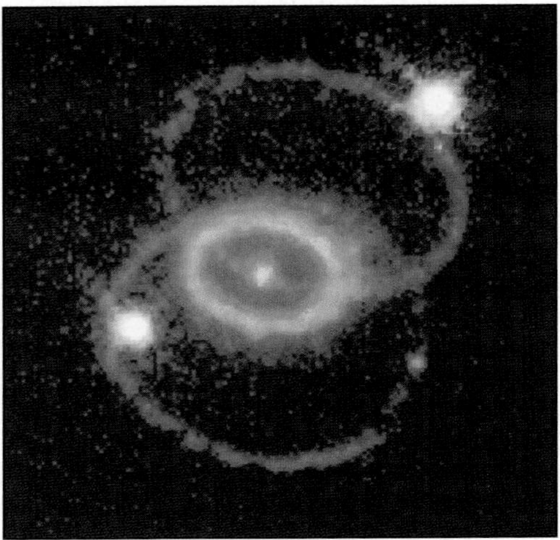

Figure 15
Scientists believe that naturally occurring elements are manufactured within stars.

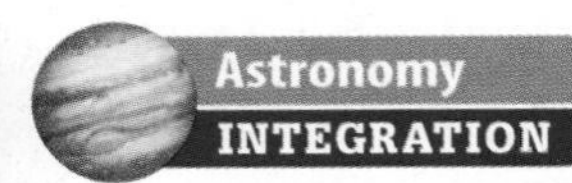

Astronomy INTEGRATION

Elements in the Universe

Are all of the elements throughout the universe the same? Scientists have made giant strides in answering this question. Using the technology that is available today, scientists are finding the same elements throughout the universe. They have been able to study only a small portion of the universe, though, because it is so vast. Many scientists believe that hydrogen and helium are the building blocks of the other naturally occurring elements. Atoms join together within stars to produce elements with atomic numbers greater than 1 or 2—the atomic numbers of hydrogen and helium. Exploding stars, or supernovas, shown in **Figure 15,** give scientists evidence to support this theory. When stars go supernova a mixture of elements, including the heavy elements such as iron, are flung into the galaxy. Many scientists believe that supernovas have spread naturally occurring elements that are found throughout the universe. It is important to note that all of the superheavy elements—those with an atomic number above 92—are human-made and found only in laboratories. Technetium and promethium also do not occur naturally.

Section  Assessment

1. Use the periodic table to find the name, atomic number, and average atomic mass of the following elements: N, Ca, Kr, and W.
2. Give the period and group in which each of these elements is found: nitrogen, sodium, iodine, and mercury.
3. Write the names of these elements and classify each as a metal, a nonmetal, or a metalloid: K, Si, Ba, and S.
4. **Think Critically** The Mendeleev and Moseley periodic charts have gaps for the as-then-undiscovered elements. Why do you think the chart used by Moseley was more accurate at predicting where new elements would be placed?

Skill Builder Activities

5. **Making and Using Graphs** Construct a circle graph showing the percentage of elements classified as metals, metalloids, and nonmetals. Use markers or colored pencils to distinguish clearly between each section on the graph. Record your calculations in your Science Journal. **For more help, refer to the Science Skill Handbook.**
6. **Communicating** Choose a synthetic element and write a brief paragraph about it in your Science Journal. Include information about the element's name, location of the synthesis research, and the people responsible for its discovery. **For more help, refer to the Science Skill Handbook.**

Answers to Section Assessment

1. N, nitrogen, 7, 14.007; Ca, calcium; 20, 40.078; Kr, krypton, 36, 83.80; W, tungsten, 74, 183.85
2. nitrogen, period 2, Group 15; sodium, period 3, Group 1; iodine, period 5, Group 17; mercury, period 6, Group 12
3. K, potassium, metal; Si, silicon, metalloid; Ba, barium, metal; S, sulfur, nonmetal
4. One could not be certain that the gaps in Mendeleev's chart would be filled by only one element. However, Moseley's chart was arranged by number of protons. Therefore, if the gap were between two elements differing by two protons, only one element could fit.
5. The graph should indicate that about 79% of the elements are metals; about 7% are metalloids, and about 14% are nonmetals.
6. Answers will vary.

Activity

A Periodic Table of Foods

Use your favorite foods to create a periodic table of foods.

What You'll Investigate

How can you create a periodic table to organize your favorite foods?

Materials

11 × 17 paper
12- or 18-inch ruler
colored pencils or markers

Goals

- **Organize** 20 of your favorite foods into a periodic table of foods.
- **Analyze** and **evaluate** your periodic table for similar characteristics among groups or family members on your table.
- **Infer** where new foods added to your table would be placed.

Procedure

1. **List** 20 of your favorite foods and drinks.
2. **Describe** basic characteristics of each of your food and drink items. For example, you might describe the primary ingredient, nutritional value, taste, and color of each item. You also could identify the food group of each item such as fruits/vegetables, grains, dairy products, meat, and sweets.
3. **Create** a data table to organize the information that you collect.
4. Using your data table, construct a periodic table of foods on your 11 × 17 sheet of paper. Determine which characteristics you will use to group your items. Create families (columns) of food and drink items that share similar characteristics on your table.

For example, potato chips, pretzels, and cheese-flavored crackers could be combined into a family of salty tasting foods. Create as many groups as you need, and you do not need to have the same number of items in every family.

Conclude and Apply

1. **Evaluate** the characteristics you used to make the groups on your periodic table. Do the characteristics of each group adequately describe all the family members? Do the characteristics of each group distinguish its family members from the family members of the other groups?
2. Analyze the reasons why some items did not fit easily into a group.
3. Infer why chemists have not created a periodic table of compounds.

Communicating Your Data

Construct a bulletin board of the periodic table of foods created by the class. **For more information, refer to the Science Skill Handbook.**

Activity

BENCH TESTED

Purpose Students create a periodic table to organize foods. L2 LS **Logical-Mathematical**

Process Skills classifying, comparing and contrasting, sequencing, making and using tables

Time Required 30 minutes

Teaching Strategies Have references available from which students can find the nutritional content of foods, such as fruits, that have no labels.

Answers to Questions

1. Answers will vary, but food items containing several major ingredients such as pizza or ice cream cones often present classification problems.
2. Individual foods such as mangos or tuna are easily grouped into the major food groups, but when food ingredients are combined into items such as cakes or soups, classification becomes difficult.
3. There are about 115 elements, many with common characteristics. There are millions of compounds, however, which makes a table of compounds impractical to construct and apply.

Assessment

Process Have students repeat the activity using only unprocessed foods. Does this make it easier or more difficult to divide foods into families? Use **Performance Assessment in the Science Classroom,** p. 121.

Communicating Your Data

Students may want to use a spreadsheet program to determine the layout of the class periodic table of foods for the bulletin board.

Activity

BENCH TESTED

Recognize the Problem

Internet Students will gather data from the Internet sites that can be accessed through the Glencoe Science Web site at **science.glencoe.com.** Students can post their findings on the site and get information from other schools around the country.

Non-Internet Sources In its entry for an element, an encyclopedia often will give the history of the discovery and naming of that element. Find books about the history of science, including biographies of famous scientists and descriptions of important discoveries and inventions.

Time Required

about two days

Preparation

Internet Access the Glencoe Science Web site at **science.glencoe.com** to run through the steps that the students will follow.

Non-Internet Sources Bring to class books on the history of chemistry and the history of science that describe how elements were discovered and named.

Form a Hypothesis

Possible Hypothesis

Newly discovered elements are given Latin names, just as they were hundreds of years ago.

Activity Use the Internet

What's in a Name?

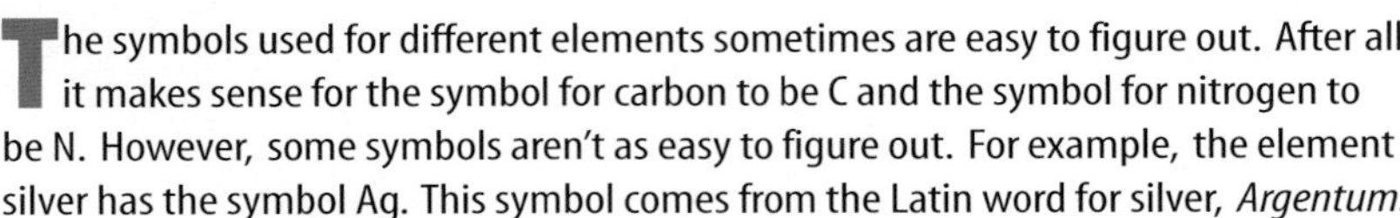

The symbols used for different elements sometimes are easy to figure out. After all, it makes sense for the symbol for carbon to be C and the symbol for nitrogen to be N. However, some symbols aren't as easy to figure out. For example, the element silver has the symbol Ag. This symbol comes from the Latin word for silver, *Argentum*.

Recognize the Problem

How are symbols and names chosen for elements?

Form a Hypothesis

How are elements named? Are newly discovered elements named the same way they were hundreds of years ago? How are the symbols for these elements determined? Form a hypothesis about why certain elements have their names and symbols.

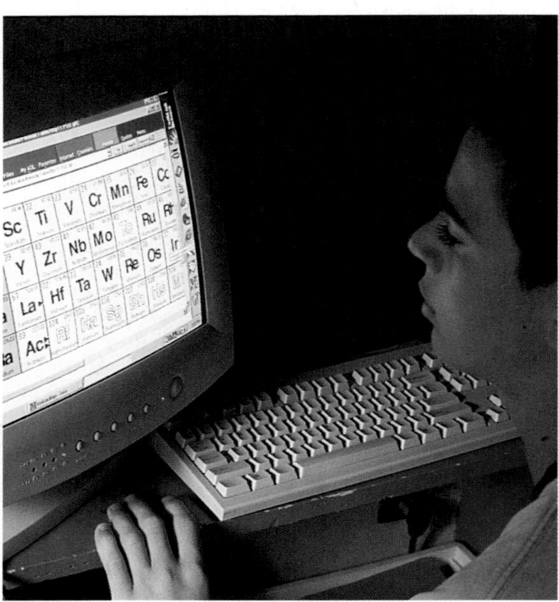

Goals

- **Research** the names and symbols of various elements.
- **Study** the methods that are used to name elements and how they have changed through time.
- **Organize** your data by making your own periodic table.
- **Study** the history of certain elements and their discoveries.
- **Create** a table of your findings and communicate them to other students.

Data Source

SCIENCE *Online* Go to the Glencoe Science Web site at **science.glencoe.com** for more information on naming elements, elements' symbols, and the discovery of new elements, and for data from other students.

SCIENCE Online

Internet Addresses

Explore the Glencoe Science Web site at **science.glencoe.com** to find out more about topics in this activity.

564 CHAPTER 18 Properties of Atoms and the Periodic Table

Test Your Hypothesis

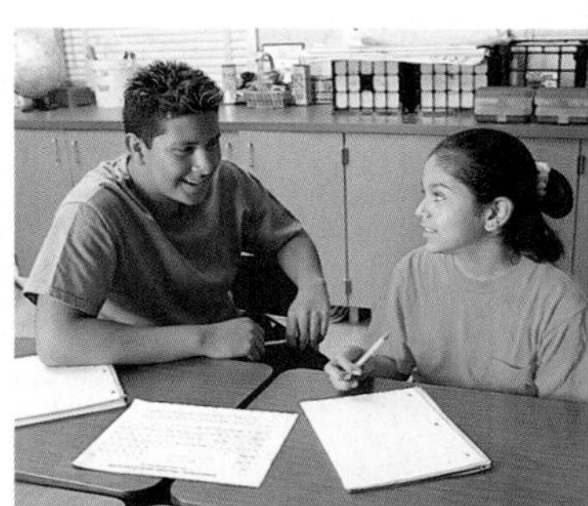

Plan

1. Make a list of particular elements you wish to study.
2. **Compare and contrast** these elements' names to their symbols.
3. **Research** the discovery of these elements. Do their names match their symbols? Were they named after a property of the element, a person, their place of discovery, or a system of nomenclature? What was that system?

Do

1. Make sure your teacher approves your plan before you start.
2. Visit the Glencoe Science Web site for links to different sites about elements, their history, and how they were named.
3. **Research** these elements.
4. Carefully record your data in your Science Journal.

Analyze Your Data

1. **Record** in your Science Journal how the symbols for your elements were chosen. What were your elements named after?
2. Make a periodic table that includes the research information on your elements that you found.
3. Make a chart of your class's findings. Sort the chart by year of discovery for each element.
4. How are the names and symbols for newly discovered elements chosen? Make a chart that shows how the newly discovered elements will be named.

Draw Conclusions

1. **Compare** your findings to those of your classmates. Did anyone's data differ for the same element? Were all the elements in the periodic table covered?
2. What system is used to name the newly discovered elements today?
3. Some elements were assigned symbols based on their name in another language. Do these examples occur for elements discovered today or long ago?

Communicating Your Data

SCIENCE Online Find this *Use the Internet* activity on the Glencoe Science Web site at **science.glencoe.com** and post your data in the table provided. **Compare** your data to those of other students. Combine your data with those of other students to complete your periodic table with all of the elements.

Test Your Hypothesis

Teaching Strategies

- Suggest that students include in their lists of elements to study some elements discovered long ago and some elements discovered more recently.
- Suggest that each student study at least ten elements.
- Have books on Greek and Roman mythology available so students can learn more about the characters from these myths for whom some of the elements are named.

Analyze Your Data

1. Students should report how the names and symbols of the elements were determined.
2. The student's periodic table should resemble the periodic table of the elements.
3. Answers will vary.
4. Different scientific organizations have created naming recommendations for newly discovered elements.

Draw Conclusions

1. Have students write their names next to the elements they researched to see if all the elements were investigated.
2. The International Union of Pure and Applied Chemistry has specific recommendations for giving names and symbols to newly-discovered elements.
3. elements discovered long ago

Communicating Your Data

Students can build an interactive periodic table of the elements. Have them use the computer and an authoring program to display the periodic table. Suggest they design the table so that when an element is clicked, the computer will display information about the origin of the name and symbol for that element.

Assessment

Portfolio Ask students to prepare written reports of their findings about the way elements were named hundreds of years ago and the way they are named today. Have them include in their reports their original hypotheses and discussions of how the information they found proved or disproved their hypotheses. Use **PASC**, p. 157. P

Content Background

Air trapped in ice cores contains traces of whatever the lower atmosphere contained at the time the ice formed. Large increases in the concentration of sulfates indicate volcanic activity. Changes in types of pollen provide clues to general trends in temperature.

Scientists also study tree rings and deep ocean cores to find clues about climate change. Tree rings provide information about localized changes in temperature, rainfall, and soil nutrients. Deep ocean cores give clues about changes in the volume of ice on land, as well as the changes in nutrient content, salinity and directions of ocean currents, which are related to surface temperatures and polar ice cover. When these findings are combined with other data, a picture of changes in the atmosphere over time can be constructed.

These results show that the amount of carbon dioxide in the atmosphere is higher during the warm periods between ice ages. This could support the theory that fossil fuel CO_2 is responsible for the recently observed warming trend in Earth's climate. Some scientists, however, maintain that human activity is only one factor in a natural cycle of warming and cooling.

TIME SCIENCE AND HISTORY

SCIENCE CAN CHANGE THE COURSE OF HISTORY!

A group of people vanish without a trace. Scientists turn to ice for the answer

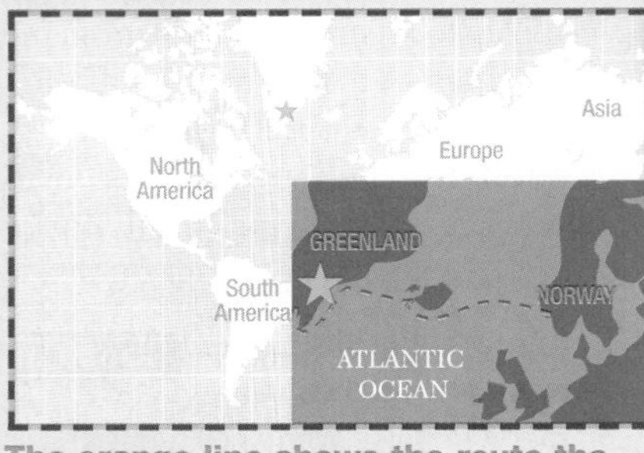

The orange line shows the route the Norse sailed from Norway to Greenland.

A Chilling

A scientist inspects an ice core sample from the Greenland Ice Sheet. The samples are stored in a freezer at −36°C.

566

Resources for Teachers and Students

U.S. National Ice Core Laboratory
United States Geological Survey
MS-975, Box 25046, DFC
Denver, CO 80225

"Science at Sea", *Scientific American*, July 31, 1997

"Global warming: It's happening." *Natural Science* December 4, 1997

Drilling to the bottom of the Greenland Ice Sheet takes place in a deep trench dug in the snow surface, and uses a sophisticated, electronically-controlled drill.

By drilling deep into this ice, scientists can recover an ice core. The core is made up of ice formed from snowfalls going way, way back in time.

By measuring the ratio of oxygen isotopes in the ice core, scientists can estimate Greenland's past air temperatures. The cores provide a detailed climate history going back over 80,000 years. Individual ice layers can be dated much like tree rings to determine their age, and the air bubbles trapped within each layer are used to learn about climate variations. Dust and pollen trapped in the ice also yield clues to ancient climates.

Story

Air bubbles and dirt trapped in ice provide clues to Earth's past climate.

Picture this: It's 1361. A ship from Norway arrives at a Norwegian settlement in Greenland. The ship's crew hopes to trade its cargo with the people living there. The crew gets off the ship. They look around. The settlement is deserted. Some 5,000 people had vanished!

New evidence has shed some light on the mysterious disappearance of the Norse settlers. The evidence came from a place on the Greenland Ice Sheet over 600 km away from the settlement. This part of Greenland is so cold that snow never melts. As new snow falls, the existing snow is buried and turns to ice.

A Little Ice Age

Based on their analysis, scientists think the Norse moved to Greenland during an unusually warm period. Then in the 1300s, the climate started to cool and a period known as the Little Ice Age began. The ways the Norse hunted and farmed were inadequate for survival in this long chill. Since they couldn't adapt to their colder surroundings, the settlers died out.

Examining ice cores fascinates scientists. It gives them an idea of what Earth's climate was like long ago. The ice cores also may help scientists better understand why global temperatures have been rising since the end of the Little Ice Age.

Though life in Greenland ended in a chilling way for the Norse, that hasn't been the story for other people living there. The native Inuit have flourished by finding ways to adapt their lifestyles to their environment—no matter what the weather!

CONNECTIONS Research Report Evidence seems to show that Earth is warming. Rising temperatures could affect our lives. Research global warming to find out how Earth may change. Report to the class.

SCIENCE Online
For more information, visit science.glencoe.com

Discussion

Why do we know more about what caused the Greenland colony to vanish than the people who discovered it was missing? Possible answer: The scientific knowledge and technology to extract and analyze ice cores did not exist until very recently.

Historical Significance

Climate change is not a relic of the past, but a continuing cyclical process. Obtain for the class a cross sectional slab of tree trunk or a large photo of one, approximately three feet in diameter. Make sure you know where the tree grew and when. Have students determine how long the tree lived by counting the rings and then determine where and when it lived. With this knowledge, students can research local temperatures over the lifespan of the tree and plot them using small flags on pins placed at the appropriate rings. Discuss with students the relation between ring size and temperature. Discuss any anomalous variations in ring size and other possible environmental conditions that may have been responsible for them.

CONNECTIONS Global Warming The current warming trend has caused concern regarding its effect on human life and agriculture. Research periods of glaciation over the history of the Earth and discuss the cyles in light of present climate conditions. You might want to construct a timeline for students showing Earth's average temperatures at different points in time and the percentage of Earth's surface covered with ice at those times.

SCIENCE Online

Internet Addresses

Explore the Glencoe Science Web site at **science.glencoe.com** to find out more about topics in this feature.

Chapter 18 Study Guide

Reviewing Main Ideas

Preview

Students can answer the questions in their Science Journals. Discuss the answers as you go through the chapter. **LS Linguistic**

Review

Students can write their answers, then compare them with those of other students. **LS Interpersonal**

Reteach

Students can look at the illustrations and describe details that support the main ideas of the chapter. **LS Visual-Spatial**

Answers to Chapter Review

Section 1

2. 7 protons; 7 neutrons

Section 2

2. 1, 2, and 3

Section 3

3. nonmetals

Chapter 18 Study Guide

Reviewing Main Ideas

Section 1 Structure of the Atom

1. A chemical symbol is a shorthand way of writing the name of an element.

2. An atom consists of a nucleus made of protons and neutrons surrounded by an electron cloud. *In the figure to the right, how many protons and neutrons are in the nucleus?*

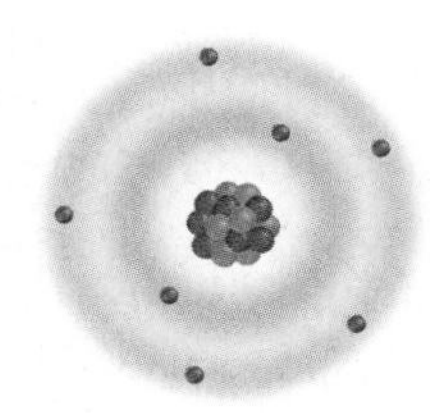

3. Quarks are particles of matter that make up protons and neutrons.

4. The model of the atom changes over time. As new information is discovered, scientists incorporate it into the model.

Section 2 Masses of Atoms

1. The number of neutrons in an atom can be computed by subtracting the atomic number from the mass number.

2. The isotopes of an element are atoms of that same element that have different numbers of neutrons. *What is the mass number of the isotopes below?*

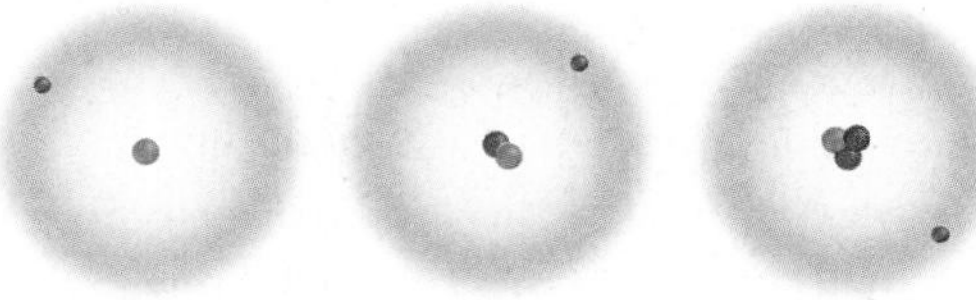

3. The average atomic mass of an element is the weighted-average mass of the mixture of its isotopes. Isotopes are named by using the element name, followed by a dash, and its mass number.

Section 3 The Periodic Table

1. In the periodic table, the elements are arranged by increasing atomic number resulting in periodic changes in properties. Knowing the number of protons, electrons, and atomic number are equal gives you partial composition of the atom.

2. In the periodic table, the elements are arranged in 18 vertical columns, or groups, and seven horizontal rows, or periods.

3. Metals are found at the left of the periodic table, nonmetals at the right, and metalloids along the line that separates the metals from the nonmetals. *In the diagram below, what is the name of the group of elements that is highlighted in blue?*

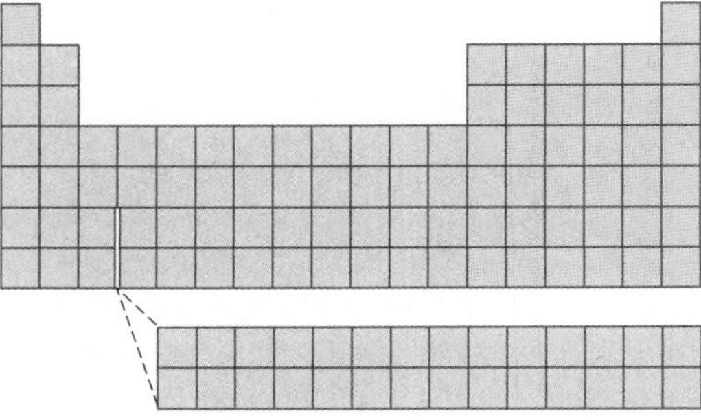

4. Elements are placed on the periodic table in order of increasing atomic number. A new row on the periodic table begins when the outer energy level of the element is filled.

FOLDABLES Reading & Study Skills — **After You Read**

Without looking at the chapter or at your Foldable, write what you learned about atoms on the *Learned* fold of your Foldable.

FOLDABLES Reading & Study Skills — **After You Read**

After students have read the chapter and completed the Foldable described in Before You Read, have them do the activity on the student page.

Dinah Zike

568 CHAPTER STUDY GUIDE

Visualizing Main Ideas

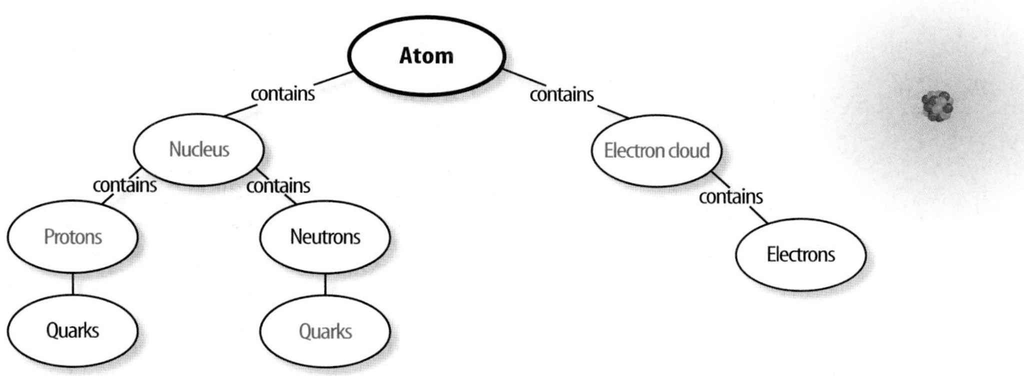

Vocabulary Review

Vocabulary Words

a. atom
b. atomic number
c. average atomic mass
d. electron
e. electron cloud
f. electron dot diagram
g. group
h. isotope
i. mass number
j. neutron
k. nucleus
l. period
m. periodic table
n. proton
o. quark

Study Tip

Don't memorize definitions. Write complete sentences using new vocabulary words to be certain you understand what they mean.

Using Vocabulary

Answer the following questions using complete sentences.

1. What is the name of the organized table of elements that was designed by Mendeleev?

2. What are two elements with the name number of protons but a different number of neutrons called?

3. What is the weighted-average mass of all the known isotopes for an element called?

4. What is the name of the positively charged center of an atom?

5. What are the particles that make up protons and neutrons?

6. What is the name of a horizontal row in the periodic table called?

7. What is the sum of the number of protons and neutrons called?

8. In the current model of the atom, where are the electrons located?

Chapter 18 Study Guide

Visualizing Main Ideas

See student page.

Vocabulary Review

Using Vocabulary

1. The organized table of elements designed by Mendeleev is called the periodic table.
2. Two elements with the same number of protons but different numbers of neutrons are called isotopes.
3. The weighted-average mass of all the known isotopes of an element is called the element's average atomic mass.
4. The positively charged center of an atom is its nucleus.
5. Protons and neutrons are made up of quarks.
6. A horizontal row in the periodic table is called a period.
7. The sum of the number of protons and neutrons in an atom is that atom's mass number.
8. They are located in an electron cloud that surrounds the nucleus.

Chapter 18 Assessment

Checking Concepts

1. D
2. C
3. B
4. B
5. A
6. C
7. D
8. A
9. D
10. B

Thinking Critically

11. Compared to many metals, both lead and mercury have large average atomic masses.
12. Same group
13. 114 will have 4 outer electrons; 116 will have 6, and 118 will have 8. These elements belong to groups that have these numbers of outer electrons.
14. The radioactive nature of Sr can damage human cells. Since Sr is similar to Ca, it could end up in human bones and do damage to cells growing there.

Chapter 18 Assessment

Checking Concepts

Choose the word or phrase that best answers the question.

1. In which state of matter are most of the elements to the left of the stair-step line in the periodic table?
A) gas **C)** plasma
B) liquid **D)** solid

2. Which is a term for a pattern that repeats?
A) isotopic **C)** periodic
B) metallic **D)** transition

3. Which of the following is an element that would have similar properties to those of neon?
A) aluminum **C)** arsenic
B) argon **D)** silver

4. Which of the following terms describes boron?
A) metal **C)** noble gas
B) metalloid **D)** nonmetal

5. How many outer level electrons does lithium and potassium have?
A) 1 **C)** 3
B) 2 **D)** 4

6. Which of the following is NOT found in the nucleus of an atom?
A) proton **C)** electron
B) neutron **D)** quark

7. The halogens are located in which group?
A) 1 **C)** 15
B) 11 **D)** 17

8. In which of the following states is nitrogen found at room temperature?
A) gas **C)** metal
B) metalloid **D)** liquid

9. Which of the elements below is a shiny element that conducts electricity and heat?
A) chlorine **C)** hydrogen
B) sulfur **D)** magnesium

10. The atomic number of Re is 75. The atomic mass of one of its isotopes is 186. How many neutrons are in an atom of this isotope?
A) 75 **C)** 186
B) 111 **D)** 261

Thinking Critically

11. Lead and mercury are two pollutants in the environment. From information about them in the periodic table, determine why they are called heavy metals.

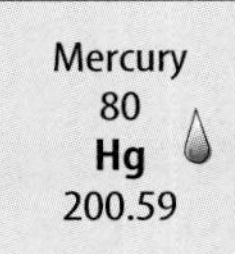

12. Ge and Si are used in making semiconductors. Are these two elements in the same group or the same period?

13. Using the periodic table, predict how many outer level electrons will be in elements 114, 116, and 118. Explain your answer.

14. Ca is used by the body to make bones and teeth. Radioactive Sr is in nuclear waste. Yet one is safe for people and the other is hazardous. Why is Sr hazardous to people?

Developing Skills

15. Making and Using Tables Use the periodic table to list a metal, a metalloid, and a nonmetal each with five outer-level electrons.

16. Comparing and Contrasting From the information found in the periodic table and reference books, compare and contrast the properties of chlorine and bromine.

Chapter Assessment Planner

Portfolio Encourage students to place in their portfolios one or two items of what they consider to be their best work. Examples include:
- Challenge, p. 549
- Reteach, p. 553
- Assessment, p. 555
- Science Journal, p. 561

Performance Additional performance assessments, Performance Task Assessment Lists, and rubrics for evaluating these activities can be found in Glencoe's **Performance Assessment in the Science Classroom.**

18. **Interpreting Data** If scientists have determined that a neutral atom of rubidium has an atomic number of 37 and a mass number of 85, how many protons, neutrons, and electrons does the atom have?

19. **Concept Mapping** As a star dies, it becomes more dense. Its temperature rises to a point where He nuclei are combined with other nuclei. When this happens, the atomic numbers of the other nuclei are increased by 2 because each gains the two protons contained in the He nucleus. For example, Cr fused with He becomes Fe. Complete the concept map showing the first four steps in He fusion.

He → (+He) Be → (+He) C → (+He) O → (+He) Ne

Performance Assessment

20. **Interview** Research the attempts made by Johann Döbereiner and John Newlands to classify the elements. Research the work of these scientists and write your findings in the form of an interview.

21. **Display** Make a display of pictures demonstrating the uses of several elements. List the name, symbol, atomic number, average atomic mass, and several other uses for each element used.

TECHNOLOGY

Go to the Glencoe Science Web site at **science.glencoe.com** or use the **Glencoe Science CD-ROM** for additional chapter assessment.

THE PRINCETON REVIEW Test Practice

Larry researched elements that are nutrients in food. He found that all packaged foods have nutritional labels on them. This makes it very easy to determine the nutritional value of the foods you eat. As he was eating breakfast, he noticed the label on his cereal that is shown below.

Sweet Wheat Cereal Nutrition Facts

Serving Size	About 24 biscuits (59g/2.1 oz.)	
Servings per Container	About 12	
Amount Per Serving	**Cereal**	**Cereal with 1/2 cup fat free milk**
Calories	200	240
Calories from Fat	10	10
	% Daily Value	
Total Fat 1 g	2%	2%
Saturated Fat 0 g	0%	0%
Monounsaturated Fat 0 g		
Polyunsaturated Fat 0.5 g		
Cholesterol 0 mg	0%	0%
Sodium 5 mg	0%	3%
Potassium 200 mg	6%	12%
Total Carbohydrate 48 g	16%	18%
Dietary Fiber 6 g	24%	24%
Sugars 12 g		
Other Carbohydrate 30 g		
Protein 6 g		

Study the chart and answer the following questions.

1. According to the chart, which nutrient is provided only when the cereal is eaten with 1/2 cup of milk?
   A) saturated Fat **C)** potassium
   B) sodium **D)** dietary Fiber

2. If Larry were to eat two servings of this cereal each with 1/2 cup of milk, about how many grams of dietary fiber would he eat?
   F) 48 g **H)** 12 g
   G) 24 g **J)** 6 g

Assessment Resources

Reproducible Masters

Chapter Resources Booklet
Chapter Review, pp. 37–38
Chapter Tests, pp. 39–42
Assessment Transparency Activity, p. 49

Glencoe Science Web site
Interactive Tutor
Chapter Quizzess

Glencoe Technology
Assessment Transparency
Interactive CD-ROM Chapter Quizzes
ExamView Pro Test Bank
Vocabulary PuzzleMaker Software
MindJogger Videoquiz DVD/VHS

Chapter 18 Assessment

Test Practice

The Test-Taking Tip was written by The Princeton Review, the nation's leader in test preparation.

1. B
2. H

Developing Skills

15. metal, Bi; metalloid, As (or Sb); nonmetal, N (or P)
16. The properties of Cl and Br are similar because they are in the same group. At room temperature Br is a liquid, while Cl is a gas. Br atoms have a greater mass than Cl atoms. Br atoms are larger than Cl atoms. Cl is more likely to gain new electrons than Br.
18. 37 protons, 48 neutrons; 37 electrons
19. He→Be→C→O→Ne

Performance Assessment

20. The interview should refer to Dobereiner's triad arrangement of elements and his futile attempt to place all elements in triads. Newland related the musical octave to a Law of Octaves for repeating properties of elements. Use **PASC**, p. 157.
21. Suggest that students make their displays on a bulletin board and present their information to the class. Use **PASC**, p. 135.

Section/Objectives	Standards: National	Standards: State/Local	Activities/Features
Chapter Opener	See p. 37T for a Key to Standards.		**Explore Activity:** Separating liquids, p. 573 **Before You Read,** p. 573
Section 1 Stability in Bonding 2 sessions 1 block 1. **Describe** how a compound differs from its component elements. 2. **Explain** what a chemical formula represents. 3. **State** a reason why chemical bonding occurs.	National Content Standards: UCP2, A2, B1 (5–8), B2, B3 (9–12)		**Science Online,** p. 577 **Activity:** Atomic Trading Cards, p. 579
Section 2 Types of Bonds 3 session 1.5 blocks 1. **Describe** ionic bonds and covalent bonds. 2. **Identify** the particles produced by ionic bonding and by covalent bonding. 3. **Distinguish** between a nonpolar covalent bond and a polar covalent bond.	National Content Standards: UCP3, A1, B1 (5–8), B2, B3 (9–12)		**Life Science Integration,** p. 581 **Science Online,** p. 582 **MiniLAB:** Identifying Bonding Type, p. 584 **Visualizing Polar Molecules,** p. 585
Section 3 Writing Formulas and Naming Compounds 4 sessions 2 blocks 1. **Explain** how to determine oxidation numbers. 2. **Write** formulas and names for ionic compounds. 3. **Describe** hydrates and write their formulas. 4. **Describe** hydrates and write their formulas.	National Content Standards: UCP3, A1, B1 (5–8), B2, B3 (9–12), G1, G2		**Earth Science Integration,** p. 589 **Problem-Solving Activity:** Can you name ionic compounds, p. 590 **MiniLAB:** Making a Hydrate, p. 592 **Activity:** Become a Bond Breaker, pp. 594–595 **Oops! Accidents in Science:** A Sticky Subject, pp. 596–597

Activity Materials	Reproducible Resources	Section Assessment	Technology
Explore Activity: water, vegetable oil, food dye, 100-mL graduated cylinder	**Chapter Resources Booklet** Foldables Worksheet, p. 17 Note-taking Worksheets, pp. 33–35	GLENCOE'S ASSESSMENT ADVANTAGE	
Activity: 4x6-inch cards, periodic table	**Chapter Resources Booklet** Transparency Activity, p. 44 Enrichment, p. 30 Reinforcement, p. 27 Directed Reading, p. 20 Activity Worksheet, pp. 5–6 Lab Activity, pp. 9–12 **Cultural Diversity,** p. 69	**Portfolio** Assessment, p. 578 **Performance** Skill Builder Activities, p. 578 **Content** Section Assessment, p. 578	Section Focus Transparency Interactive CD-ROM/DVD Guided Reading Audio Program
MiniLAB: inflated balloon, wool or fur, running water *Need materials?* Contact Science Kit at 1-800-828-7777 or www.sciencekit.com on the Internet.	**Chapter Resources Booklet** Transparency Activity, p. 45 MiniLAB, p. 3 Enrichment, p. 31 Reinforcement, p. 28 Directed Reading, p. 20 Lab Activity, pp. 13–16 **Science Inquiry Labs,** p. 47	**Portfolio** Science Journal, p. 583 Challenge, p. 586 **Performance** MiniLAB, p. 584 Skill Builder Activities, p. 586 **Content** Section Assessment, p. 586	Section Focus Transparency Interactive CD-ROM/DVD Guided Reading Audio Program
MiniLAB: plaster of paris, water, small bowl, rubber hammer, hair dryer **Activity:** small samples of crushed ice, table salt, and sugar, wire test-tube holder, test tubes, laboratory burner, stopwatch	**Chapter Resources Booklet** Transparency Activity, p. 46 MiniLAB, p. 4 Enrichment, p. 32 Reinforcement, p. 29 Directed Reading, pp. 21, 22 Transparency Activity, pp. 47–48 Activity Worksheet, pp. 7–8 **Mathematics Skill Activities,** p. 29 **Reading and Writing Skill Activities,** p. 41	**Portfolio** Cultural Diversity, p. 592 **Performance** MiniLAB, p. 592 Skill Builder Activities, p. 593 **Content** Section Assessment, p. 593	Section Focus Transparency Teaching Transparency Interactive CD-ROM/DVD Guided Reading Audio Program

End of Chapter Assessment

GLENCOE'S ASSESSMENT ADVANTAGE

Blackline Masters	Technology	Professional Series
Chapter Resources Booklet Chapter Review, pp. 37–38 Chapter Tests, pp. 39–42 **Standardized Test Practice by The Princeton Review,** pp. 80–83	MindJogger Videoquiz CD-ROM Explorations and Quizzes Vocabulary Puzzle Makers ExamView Pro Test Bank Interactive Lesson Planner Interactive Teacher's Edition	Performance Assessment in the Science Classroom (PASC)

Transparencies

Section Focus

Section 1 Section Focus Transparency — Picking Up the Pieces

Jigsaw puzzles can have hundreds of pieces. To complete the puzzle, you need to infer how each piece fits together. Size, shape, and markings all give clues as to how the pieces should be placed.

1. Where do the remaining pieces belong? How do you know?
2. How might a compound and its individual elements compare to a puzzle and its pieces?

L1

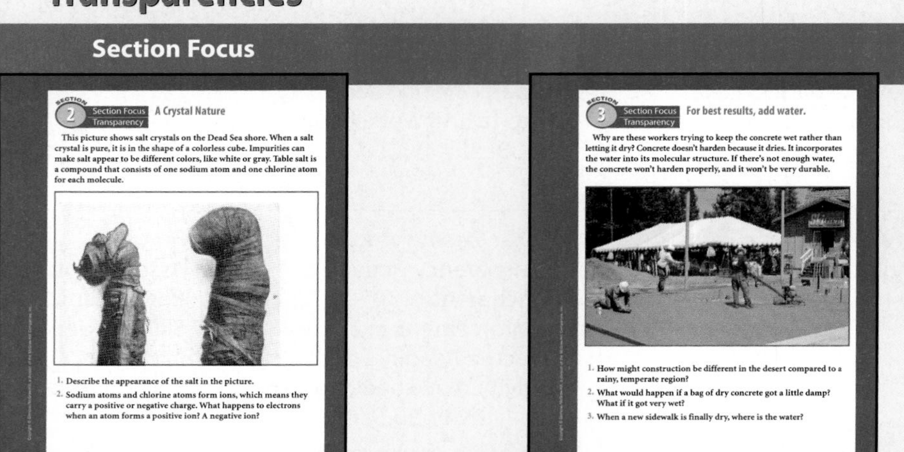

Section 2 Section Focus Transparency — A Crystal Nature

This picture shows salt crystals on the Dead Sea shore. When a salt crystal is pure, it is in the shape of a colorless cube. Impurities can make salt appear to be different colors, like white or gray. Table salt is a compound that consists of one sodium atom and one chlorine atom for each molecule.

1. Describe the appearance of the salt in the picture.
2. Sodium atoms and chlorine atoms form ions, which means they carry a positive or negative charge. What happens to electrons when an atom forms a positive ion? A negative ion?

L1

Section 3 Section Focus Transparency — For best results, add water.

Why are these workers trying to keep the concrete wet rather than letting it dry? Concrete doesn't harden because it dries. It incorporates the water into its molecular structure. If there's not enough water, the concrete won't harden properly, and it won't be very durable.

1. How might construction be different in the desert compared to a rainy, temperate region?
2. What would happen if a bag of dry concrete got a little damp? What if it got very wet?
3. When a new sidewalk is finally dry, where is the water?

L1

This is a representation of key blackline masters available in the Teacher Classroom Resources. See Resource Manager boxes within the chapter for additional information.

Assessment

Assessment Transparency — Chemical Bonds

Directions: Carefully review the tables and answer the following questions.

Group A	
Water	H_2O
Carbon dioxide	CO_2
Ammonia	NH_3
Salt	NaCl
Methane	CH_4

Group B	
Epsom salts	$Mg(OH)_2$
Sugar	$C_{12}H_{22}O_{11}$
Lye	NaOH
Baking soda	$NaHCO_3$
Vinegar	$C_2H_4O_2$

1. The compounds in Group A are different from the compounds in Group B because only the compounds in Group A ____.
   A are gases at room temperature
   B are used in preparing food
   C contain a metal and a nonmetal
   D contain only two different elements
2. According to the chemical formula for lye, all of the following elements are found in a lye molecule **EXCEPT** ____.
   F hydrogen
   G nitrogen
   H oxygen
   J sodium
3. According to the information contained in the both tables, which compound has a total number of atoms greater than 10?
   A Baking soda
   B Methane
   C Sugar
   D Vinegar
4. According to the tables, which compound has the **LEAST** number of total atoms?
   F Ammonia
   G Carbon dioxide
   H Salt
   J Water

L1

Teaching

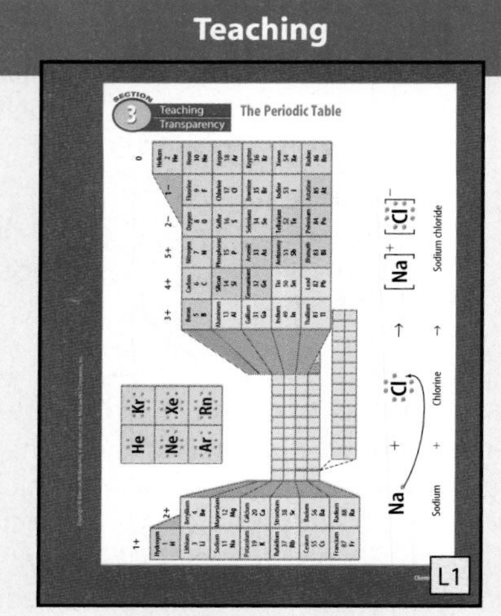

Section 3 Teaching Transparency — The Periodic Table

Key to Teaching Strategies

The following designations will help you decide which activities are appropriate for your students.

- **L1** Level 1 activities should be appropriate for students with learning difficulties.
- **L2** Level 2 activities should be within the ability range of all students.
- **L3** Level 3 activities are designed for above-average students.
- **ELL** ELL activities should be within the ability range of English Language Learners.
- **COOP LEARN** Cooperative Learning activities are designed for small group work.
- **LS** Multiple Learning Styles logos are used throughout to indicate strategies that address different learning styles.
- **P** These strategies represent student products that can be placed into a best-work portfolio.

Hands-on Activities

Activity Worksheets

Laboratory Activities

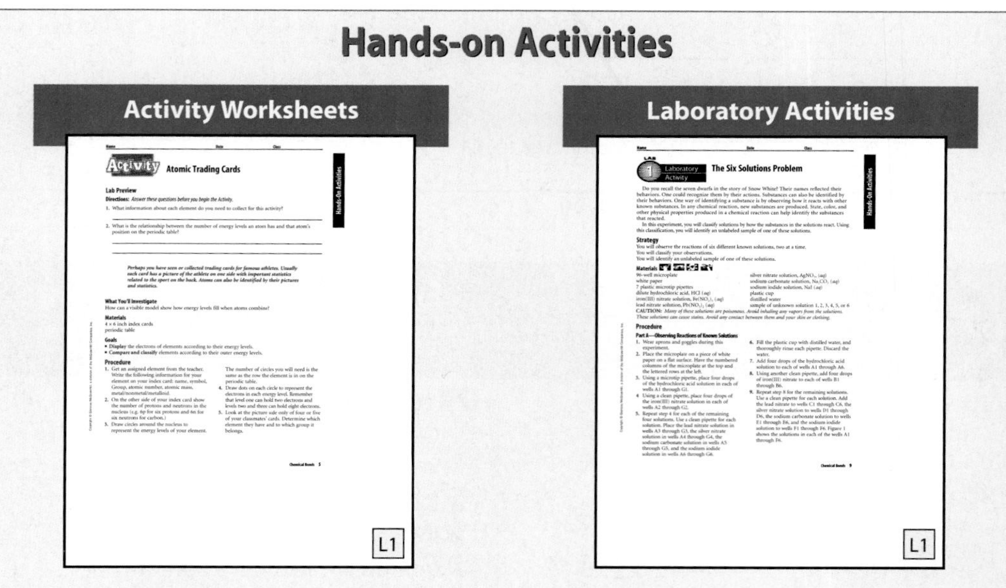

Activity — Atomic Trading Cards

L1

Laboratory Activity 1 — The Six Solutions Problem

L1

Meeting Different Ability Levels

Content Outline

Note-taking Worksheet — Chemical Bonds

L1

Reinforcement

Section 1 Reinforcement — Stability in Bonding

L1

Directed Reading

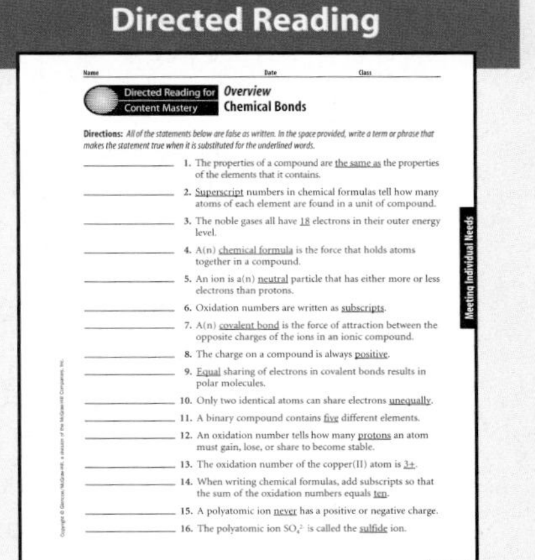

Directed Reading for Content Mastery — Overview: Chemical Bonds

L1

Enrichment

Section 1 Enrichment — Electron Dot Diagrams

L1

Spanish Directed Reading

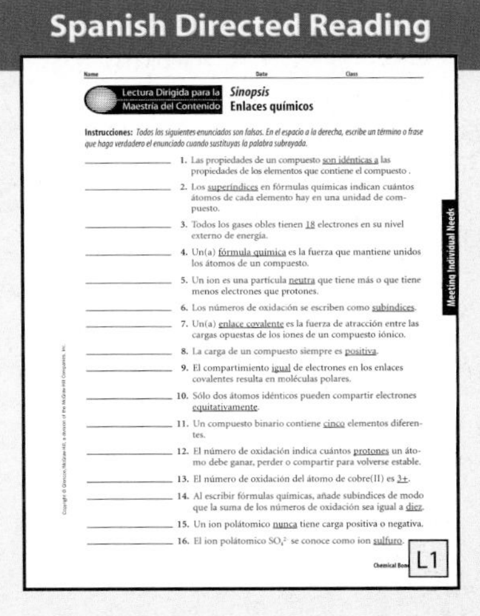

Lectura Dirigida para la Maestría del Contenido — Sinopsis: Enlaces químicos

L1

Assessment

Chapter Tests

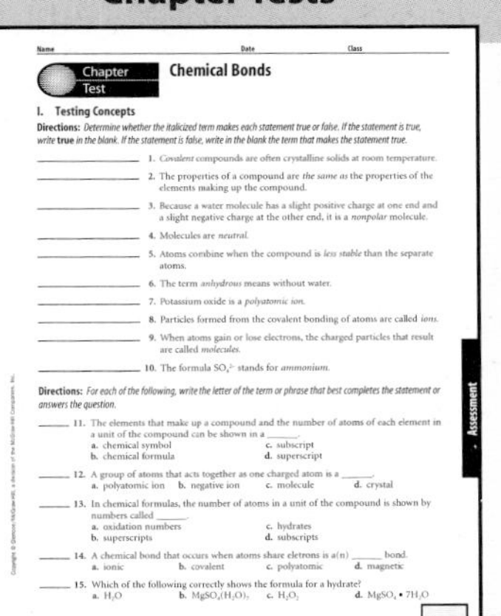

Chapter Test — Chemical Bonds

L1

Test Practice Workbook

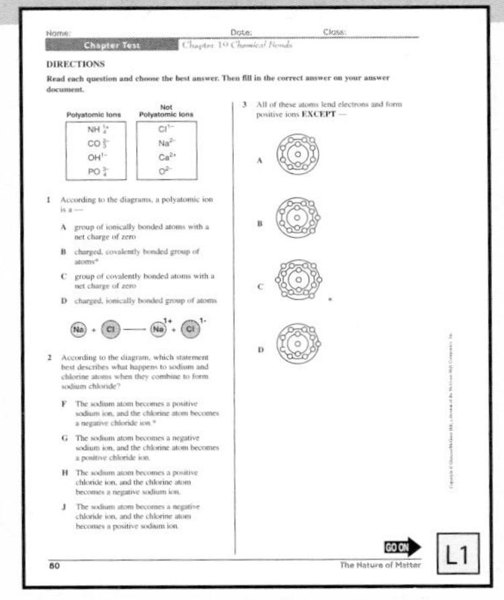

L1

Chapter Review

Chapter Review — Chemical Bonds

L1

Science Content Background

SECTION 1

Stability in Bonding

Atomic Stability

Atoms undergo rearrangements of electrons to become more stable. This concept forms the basis for understanding chemical bonding. The most stable configuration of electrons is found in the noble gases. Atoms gain, lose, or share electrons, some more easily than others, so that they have the same electron configurations as the noble gases. For example, a chlorine atom gains an electron and attains an electron structure like the chemically stable noble gas argon (Cl^-). Sodium loses one of its 11 electrons to attain an electron structure like neon (Na^+). In general, metals tend to form positively charged ions (lose electrons) and nonmetals form negatively charged ions (gain electrons).

Fun Fact

Lithium oxide (Li_2O) is used aboard the space shuttle to remove water from the air.

Barry L. Runk/Grant Heilman Photography, Inc.

SECTION 2

Types of Bonds

Electron Dot Structures

One of the most convenient ways to picture the sharing of electrons between atoms in covalent or polar covalent bonds is to use electron dot structures. Electron dot structures are often called Lewis structures, after American chemist G. N. Lewis (1875-1946), who invented this symbolism. Electron dot structures represent an atom's outer, or valence, electrons by dots. Atoms form covalent bonds by sharing electron pairs, with the resulting molecules drawn by assigning the correct number of valence electrons to each atom. Group 13 atoms have three valence electrons, Group 14 atoms have four valence electrons, and so on across the periodic table.

Group 18 elements, such as neon and argon, rarely form covalent bonds because they have the required eight electrons in their outer energy levels. This is called the octet rule—main group elements tend to undergo reactions that leave them with eight outer-level electrons. In other words, main group elements react so that they attain a noble gas electron configuration in their outer energy level. As a general rule, an atom shares as many of its outer electrons as possible, either until it has no more to share or until it reaches an octet configuration. There are many exceptions to this rule but it useful as a guiding principle.

In molecules such as O_2 and N_2, the atoms share more than one pair of electrons, leading to the formation of multiple covalent bonds. For example, the only way that both oxygen atoms in the O_2 molecule can follow the octet rule is for them to share four electrons or two pairs of electrons, thus producing a double bond. Similarly, the nitrogen atoms in N_2 share six electrons producing a triple bond. Multiple bonds are shorter and stronger than single bonds because there are more electrons holding the nuclei together.

Electronegativity

When two different kinds of atoms share a pair of electrons, a bond forms in which electrons are shared unequally. The attractive force that an atom of an element has for shared electrons in a molecule is known as its electronegativity. Nobel laureate Linus Pauling (1901–1994) developed a scale of relative electronegativities, in which the most electronegative element, fluorine, is assigned a value of 4.0. The higher the electronegativity, the stronger an atom attracts electrons. Electronegativity generally increases from left to right across a period and decreases down a group for typical elements.

Polar or Nonpolar?

A general knowledge of electronegativities can be used to make predictions about bond polarity. A general guideline is that bonds between atoms with the same or similar values are nonpolar covalent, bonds between atoms whose values differ by more than two are substantially ionic, and bonds between atoms whose values differ by less that two are polar covalent. At the extreme, one or more electrons are actually transferred and an ionic bond results. It is important to realize that bonding is a continuum—the difference between ionic and covalent is a gradual change.

SECTION 3 Writing Formulas and Naming Compounds

Hydrates

The best-known hydrates are crystalline solids that lose their structure upon removal of their bound water. Although the number of molecules of water in a given hydrate is fixed, some substances can form several different hydrates. For example, there are four different hydrates of iron (II) sulfate, each with separate and unique physical properties.

Fun Fact

The colorless liquid dimethylhydrazine ($C_2H_8N_2$) is used as a liquid rocket fuel.

For additional content background on this topic, go to the Glencoe Science Web site at science.glencoe.com.

CHAPTER 19

Chemical Bonds

Chapter Vocabulary

chemical formula
chemically stable
chemical bond
ion
ionic bond
molecule
polar molecule
nonpolar molecule
covalent bond
binary compound
oxidation number
polyatomic ion
hydrate

What do you think?

Science Journal This is a photo of iron filings removed with a magnet from dry breakfast cereal. The iron in your body is the same iron you'd find in a nail. In an iron nail, iron has a +3 oxidation number, but in your body, its oxidation number frequently is +2, which gives it very different properties.

CHAPTER 19

Chemical Bonds

Together, holding hands, these sky divers are a stable group instead of separately falling objects. A chemical bond between elements is similar. Atoms combine when the compound formed is more stable than the separate atoms. Like the circle of sky divers, the compounds formed have properties unlike those found in the separate elements. In this chapter, you will read about how chemical bonds form and learn how to write chemical formulas and equations.

What do you think?

Science Journal Look at the picture below with a classmate. Discuss what you think this might be or what is happening. Here's a hint: *Bonds are forming to make something that you can sprinkle on popcorn.* Write your answer or best guess in your Science Journal.

572

Theme Connection

Stability and Change The relationship between an atom's electronic structure and its stability is described in this chapter. Chemical bonding enables compounds to become stable. Chemical changes take place when existing bonds are broken and new bonds form.

You have probably noticed how the liquids in oil and vinegar salad dressings will not stay mixed after the bottle is shaken. Why do some liquids such as water and rubbing alcohol mix together, but others like oil and water do not? The compounds that make up the liquids are different. Some, like water and rubbing alcohol, can attract each other. Others, like water and oil, do not. In this chapter, these different types of compounds will be discussed further.

Separating liquids 

1. Pour 20 mL of water into a 100 mL graduated cylinder.
2. Pour 20 mL of vegetable oil into the same cylinder. Vigorously swirl the two liquids together, and observe for several minutes.
3. Add two drops of food dye and observe.
4. After several minutes, slowly pour 30 mL of rubbing alcohol into the cylinder.
5. Add two more drops of food dye and observe.

Observe

In your Science Journal, write a paragraph describing how the different liquids reacted to each other.

Before You Read

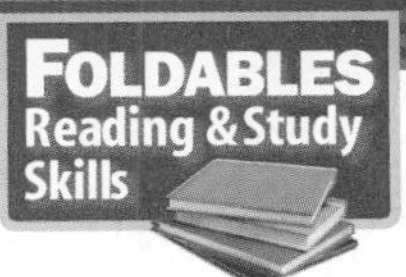

Making a Chemical Formula Study Fold

Make the following Foldable to help you identify chemical formulas from this chapter.

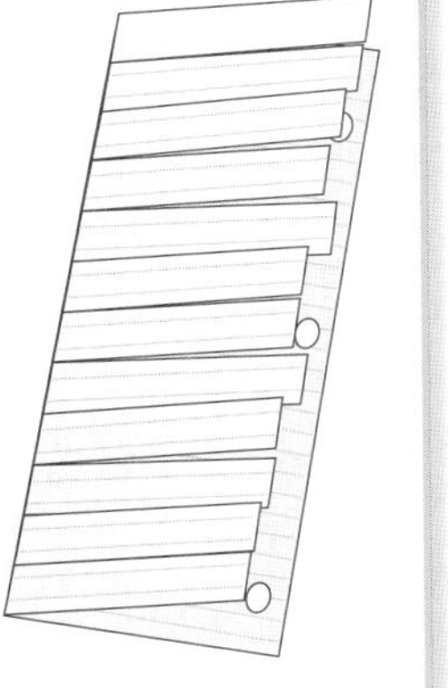

1. Place a sheet of notebook paper in front of you so the short side is at the top and the holes are on the right side. Fold the paper in half from the left side to the right side.
2. Through the top thickness of paper, cut along every third line from the outside edge to the centerfold, forming tabs as shown.
3. Before you read the chapter, collect ten chemical formulas and write them on the front of the tabs. As you read the chapter, write what compound the formula represents under the tabs.

573

EXPLORE ACTIVITY

Purpose Use the Explore Activity to introduce students to the interaction between liquids with polar bonds and liquids with nonpolar bonds. L2

LS **Visual-Spatial**

Preparation Prepare small beakers of each liquid for each group.

Materials two graduated cylinders, water, vegetable oil, rubbing alcohol, food dye, eyedropper

Teaching Strategy Explain that the molecules in water, food dye, and rubbing alcohol have polar chemical bonds, but the molecules in vegetable oil have nonpolar chemical bonds.

Observe

When the oil was added to the water and the cylinder was shaken, the oil formed bubbles that quickly separated from the water when the cylinder was allowed to sit. The oil then sat on top of the water. The drops of food dye moved through the nonpolar oil as droplets. Once the drops of food dye passed through the oil/water boundary, they mixed with the water molecules, exploding with color. The alcohol, which is polar, sat on top of the oil, and the food dye dissolved in it immediately.

✓Assessment

Portfolio Ask students to draw a labeled diagram of their graduated cylinder filled with liquids. Use **Performance Assessment in the Science Classroom,** p. 127.

Before You Read

FOLDABLES Reading & Study Skills

Dinah Zike Study Fold

Purpose Use this activity to expose students before they read, to the "vocabulary" of formulas formed by chemical bonds and to provide a Foldable to collect formulas they discover during reading. The resulting Foldable can be used as an assessment tool and study guide before, during and after reading.

For additional help, see Foldables Worksheet, p. 17 in **Chapter Resources Booklet,** or go to the Glencoe Science Web site at **science.glencoe.com.** See After You Read in the Study Guide at the end of this chapter.

SECTION

Stability in Bonding

1 Motivate

Bellringer Transparency

Display the Section Focus Transparency for Section 1. Use the accompanying Transparency Activity Master. L2 ELL

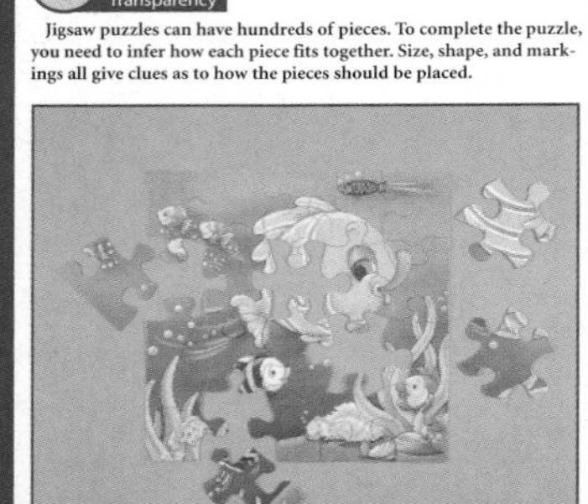

1 Section Focus Transparency — Picking Up the Pieces

Jigsaw puzzles can have hundreds of pieces. To complete the puzzle, you need to infer how each piece fits together. Size, shape, and markings all give clues as to how the pieces should be placed.

1. Where do the remaining pieces belong? How do you know?
2. How might a compound and its individual elements compare to a puzzle and its pieces?

Tie to Prior Knowledge

Have students consider how pieces of a jigsaw puzzle fit together in an orderly, exact way. Explain that it is possible to predict how atoms of different elements fit together in an exact way. As an example, discuss how water forms when two parts hydrogen combine with one part oxygen. The "parts" in this case are atoms that form chemical bonds with one another.

SECTION

Stability in Bonding

As You Read

***What* You'll Learn**

- **Describe** how a compound differs from its component elements.
- **Explain** what a chemical formula represents.
- **State** a reason why chemical bonding occurs.

Vocabulary

chemical formula
chemically stable
chemical bond

***Why* It's Important**

Understanding why atoms form compounds depends on knowing how an atom can become stable.

Combined Elements

Have you ever noticed the color of the Statue of Liberty? Why is it green? Did the sculptor purposely choose green? Why wasn't white, or tan, or even some other color like purple chosen? Was it painted that way? No, the Statue of Liberty was not painted. The Statue of Liberty is made of the metal copper, which is an element. Pennies, too, are made of copper. Wait a minute, you say. Copper isn't green—it's … well, copper colored.

You are right. Uncombined, elemental copper is a bright, shiny copper color. So again the question arises: Why is the Statue of Liberty green?

Some of the matter around you is in the form of uncombined elements such as copper, sulfur, and oxygen. But, like many other sets of elements, these three elements unite chemically to form a compound when the conditions are right. The green coating on the Statue of Liberty and some old pennies is a result of this chemical change. This coating, seen in contrast with elemental copper in **Figure 1,** is a new compound called copper sulfate. Copper sulfate isn't shiny and copper colored like elemental copper. Nor is it a pale-yellow solid like sulfur or a colorless, odorless gas like oxygen. It has its own unique properties.

Figure 1
The difference between the copper metal and the copper sulfate that is formed on the Statue of Liberty is striking. A new compound has formed.

Section Assessment Planner

Portfolio
Assessment, p. 578

Performance Assessment
Skill Builder Activities, p. 578
See page 600 for more options.

Content Assessment
Section, p. 578
Challenge, p. 578
Chapter, pp. 600–601

New Properties One interesting observation you will make is that the compound formed when elements combine often has properties that aren't anything like those of the individual elements. Sodium chloride, for example, shown in **Figure 2,** is a compound made from the elements sodium and chlorine. Sodium is a shiny, soft, silvery metal that reacts violently with water. Chlorine is a poisonous greenish-yellow gas. Would you have guessed that these elements combine to make ordinary table salt?

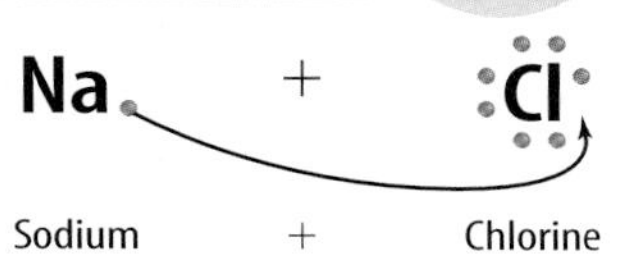

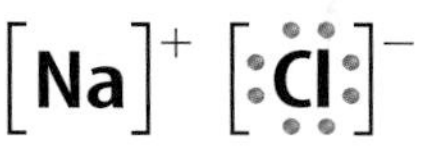

Figure 2
Sodium is a soft, silvery metal that combines with chlorine, a greenish-yellow gas, to form sodium chloride, which is a white crystalline solid. *How are the properties of table salt different from those of sodium and chlorine?*

Formulas

The chemical symbols Na and Cl represent the elements sodium and chlorine. When written as NaCl, the symbols make up a formula, or chemical shorthand, for the compound sodium chloride. A **chemical formula** tells what elements a compound contains and the exact number of the atoms of each element in a unit of that compound. The compound that you are probably most familiar with is H_2O, more commonly known as water. This formula contains the symbols H for the element hydrogen and O for the element oxygen. Notice the subscript number 2 written after the H for hydrogen. *Subscript* means "written below." A subscript written after a symbol tells how many atoms of that element are in a unit of the compound. If a symbol has no subscript, the unit contains only one atom of that element. A unit of H_2O contains two hydrogen atoms and one oxygen atom.

Look at the formulas for each compound listed in **Table 1.** What elements combine to form each compound? How many atoms of each element are required to form each of the compounds?

Table 1 Some Familiar Compounds

Familiar Name	Chemical Name	Formula
Sand	Silicon dioxide	SiO_2
Milk of magnesia	Magnesium hydroxide	$Mg(OH)_2$
Cane sugar	Sucrose	$C_{12}H_{22}O_{11}$
Lime	Calcium oxide	CaO
Vinegar	Acetic acid	$HC_2H_3O_2$
Laughing gas	Dinitrogen oxide	N_2O
Grain alcohol	Ethanol	C_2H_5OH
Battery acid	Sulfuric acid	H_2SO_4
Stomach acid	Hydrochloric acid	HCl

2 Teach

Combined Elements

Caption Answer

Figure 2 Table salt is a stable, white solid. Sodium is very reactive with water, silver in color, soft, and a metal. Chlorine is a poisonous, greenish-yellow gas.

Discussion

Point out that H_2O and H_2O_2 have similar chemical formulas. **Does this mean they are similar compounds? Explain.** They are not similar compounds. The addition of one oxygen atom changes H_2O (water), a substance that is critical for life, into H_2O_2 (hydrogen peroxide), a substance that is used as a disinfectant and quickly reacts with many other compounds. L1

LS **Logical-Mathematical**

Formulas

Text Question Answer

Sand: 1 atom of silicon (Si), 2 of oxygen (O); milk of magnesia: 1 atom of magnesium (Mg), 2 of oxygen (O), 2 of hydrogen (H); cane sugar: 12 atoms of carbon (C), 22 of hydrogen (H), 11 of oxygen (O); lime: 1 atom (ion) of calcium (Ca), 1 of oxygen (O); vinegar: 2 atoms of carbon (C), 2 of oxygen (O), and 4 of hydrogen (H); laughing gas: 2 atoms of nitrogen (N), 1 of oxygen (O); grain alcohol: 2 atoms of carbon (C), 6 of hydrogen (H), 1 of oxygen (O); battery acid: 2 atoms of hydrogen (H), 1 of sulfur (S), 4 of oxygen (O); stomach acid: 1 atom of hydrogen (H), 1 of chlorine (Cl). L2

LS **Logical-Mathematical**

Resource Manager

Chapter Resources Booklet

Transparency Activity, p. 44
Note-taking Worksheets, pp. 33–35
Directed Reading for Content Mastery, p. 20

Teacher FYI

NaCl is an ionic compound. This means that NaCl is not considered to be a molecule. Salt exists as an array of positive sodium ions attracted to negative chloride ions in a crystal lattice. The lattice has an equal number of sodium ions and chloride ions, so the formula for salt is given as NaCl.

Atomic Stability

Visual Learning

Figure 3 Have students predict whether each atom shown would more likely gain or lose electrons to form an octet. An atom with fewer than four electrons in the outer energy level tends to give up electrons, while those with more than four tend to gain electrons to form an octet. L1 **Visual-Spatial**

Use an Analogy

In a cold climate, each person would seek to have two gloves to keep his or her hands warm. Someone with fewer than two would try to get warm by gaining a glove or two. A person with more than two gloves might give up those not needed for warmth. Individuals with exactly two gloves would not be involved in any rearrangements. Similarly, some atoms give up electrons to have eight in their outer energy levels, while others must obtain electrons to have eight. An atom with exactly eight electrons in its outer level does not need to gain or lose electrons, so it does not participate in rearrangements of electrons between atoms. The atoms of all the nonreactive noble gases except helium have eight electrons in their outer energy levels. Helium's outer level is complete with two electrons.

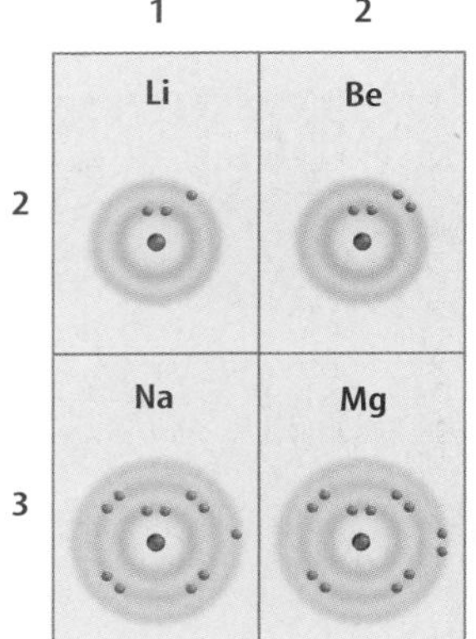

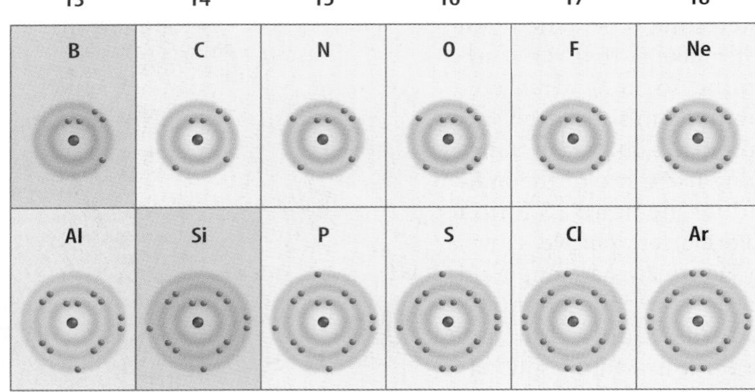

Figure 3
The number of electrons in each group's outer level increases across the table until the noble gases in Group 18 have a complete outer energy level.

Atomic Stability

Why do atoms form compounds? Atoms combine when the compound formed is more stable than the separate atoms. The periodic table on the inside back cover of your book lists 115 elements, most of which can combine with other elements. However, the six noble gases in Group 18 seldom form compounds. Why is this so? Atoms of noble gases are unusually stable. Compounds of these atoms rarely form because they are almost always less stable than the original atoms.

The Unique Noble Gases To understand the stability of the noble gases, you must look at electron dot diagrams. Electron dot diagrams show only the electrons in the outer energy level of an atom. They contain the chemical symbol for the element surrounded by dots representing its outer electrons. How do you know how many dots to make? For Groups 1 and 2 and 13 through 18, you can use a periodic table or the portion of it shown in **Figure 3.** Look at the outer ring of each of the elements. Group 1 has one outer electron. Group 2 has two. Group 13 has three, Group 14, four, and so on to Group 18, the noble gases, which have eight.

What makes the noble gases more stable than other elements? An atom is **chemically stable** when its outer energy level is complete. Recall that the outer energy levels of helium and hydrogen are stable with two electrons. The outer energy levels of all the other elements are stable when they contain eight electrons. The noble gases are stable because they each have a complete outer energy level. **Figure 4** shows electron dot diagrams of some of the noble gases. Notice that eight dots surround Kr, Ne, Xe, Ar, and Rn, and two dots surround He.

Figure 4
Dot diagrams of noble gases show that they all have a stable, filled outer level.

He	Kr
Ne	Xe
Ar	Rn

Teacher FYI

The number of known elements may change during your use of this text. Research teams in Dubna, Russia; Darmstadt, Germany; and Berkeley, California are working to synthesize new elements.

Inclusion Strategies

Gifted Some students will wonder why the text skips elements in Group 3 to Group 12 when talking about outer level electrons. Encourage these students to research and write brief reports about why these transition metals are skipped. The outer energy levels of these elements are similar to those of elements in Groups 1 or 2. As electrons are added, they fill in incomplete lower electron energy levels. L3 LS **Linguistic**

576 CHAPTER 19 Chemical Bonds

Energy Levels and Other Elements How do the dot diagrams represent other elements, and how does that relate to their ability to make compounds? Hydrogen and helium, the elements in row one of the periodic table, can hold a maximum of two electrons in their outer energy levels. Hydrogen contains one electron in its lone energy level. A dot diagram for hydrogen has a single dot next to its symbol. This means that hydrogen's outer energy level is not full. Therefore, it is more stable when it is part of a compound. This is why so many hydrogen-containing compounds, including water, exist on Earth.

In contrast, helium's outer energy level contains two electrons. Its dot diagram has two dots—a pair of electrons—next to its symbol. Helium already has a full outer energy level by itself and is chemically stable. Helium rarely forms compounds but, by itself, the element is a commonly used gas.

When you look at the elements in Groups 13 through 17, you see that each of them falls short of having a stable energy level. Each group contains too many or too few for a stable level of eight electrons. The elements are not stable because of it and commonly form compounds.

Outer Levels—Getting Their Fill As you just learned, hydrogen is an element that does not have a full level. How does hydrogen, or any other element find or get rid of extra electrons? Atoms with partially stable outer energy levels can lose, gain, or share electrons to obtain a stable outer energy level. They do this by combining with other atoms that also have partially complete outer energy levels. As a result, each achieves stability. **Figure 5** shows electron dot diagrams for sodium and chlorine. When they combine, sodium loses one electron and chlorine gains one electron. You can see from the electron dot diagram that chlorine now has a stable outer energy level similar to a noble gas. But what about sodium?

SCIENCE Online

Research Visit the Glencoe Science Web site at **science.glencoe.com** for more information about using dot diagrams to represent outer energy level electrons. Communicate to your class what you learn.

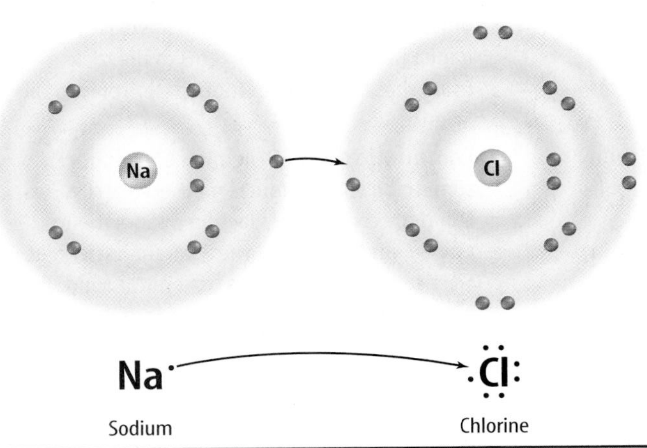

Figure 5
Each of these atoms has the potential of having a stable outer energy level by just adding or taking away one electron.

Quick Demo

Place a pea-sized piece of calcium metal in a small amount of 1 M HCl. Have students note the production of bubbles as H_2 is given off. Carefully evaporate the liquid, leaving $CaCl_2$. On the board, write the dot diagram for the ions contained in this ionic compound. Both Ca^{2+} and Cl^- contain eight outer electrons. (If zinc metal is used instead of Ca, $ZnCl_2$ will form.) L2

LS ELL **Visual-Spatial**

Make a Model

Have students use various colors of modeling clay to make spheres that represent metals and nonmetals. Tell them to use smaller spheres of a specific color to show electrons. Attach the correct number of electrons to each model sphere to represent the outer energy level of the selected atoms. Challenge students to use a periodic table to identify possible elements that each model represents. Then have them explain how the element in each model can obtain eight outer electrons through various combinations with other elements. L2 ELL LS **Kinesthetic**

Text Question Answer

Its outer level is filled, too.

Resource Manager

Chapter Resources Booklet
Lab Activity, pp. 9–12

Cultural Diversity, p. 69

Physical Science Critical Thinking/ Problem Solving, p. 1

SCIENCE Online

Internet Addresses

Explore the Glencoe Science Web site at **science.glencoe.com** to find out more about topics in this section.

Atomic Stability, continued

Reading Check

Answer the force that holds atoms together in a compound

3 Assess

Reteach

Remind students that giving up electrons can sometimes provide a new outer level of eight electrons. Make a poster with sodium's electron distribution written out—two in the first level, eight in the second. Loosely tape a page with the single electron in the third energy level written on it over the poster. Demonstrate that when the outer page is removed (losing the electron), the new outer level is shown to contain eight electrons. Point out that this can occur for several other metals as well. L1 ELL

LS **Visual-Spatial**

Challenge

Ask students to use dot diagrams for one carbon atom and two oxygen atoms and make an arrangement that gives the carbon and both oxygen atoms an octet. Place carbon in the center and make double bonds between the carbon and oxygen atoms. In this arrangement, the carbon atom shares two electrons with one oxygen atom and two with the other. Each oxygen atom shares two electrons with the carbon atom. L3

LS **Visual-Spatial**

Assessment

Performance Have students write out the dot diagrams for two atoms of aluminum and for three atoms of oxygen. Then have them show how this combination gives all atoms eight outer, shared electrons. Use **Performance Assessment in the Science Classroom,** p. 127. P

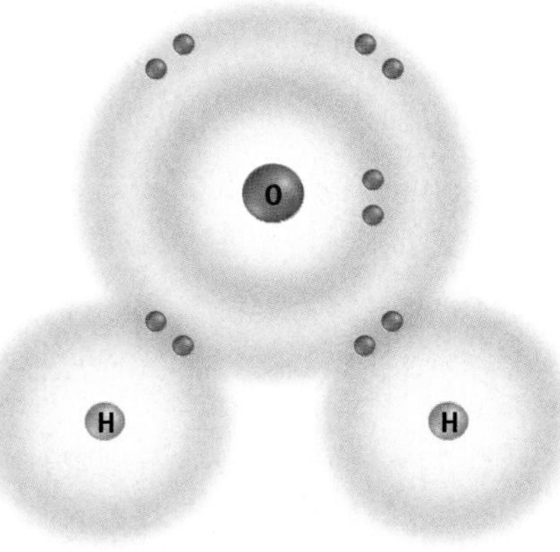

Figure 6
In water, hydrogen contributes one electron and oxygen contributes the other to each hydrogen-oxygen bond. The atoms share those electrons instead of giving them up.

Stability Is Reached Sodium had only one electron in its outer energy level, which it lost to combine with chlorine in sodium chloride. However, look back to the next to the outermost energy level of sodium. This is now the new outer energy level, and it is stable with eight electrons. When the outer electron of sodium is removed, a complete inner energy level is revealed and now becomes the new outer energy level. Sodium and chlorine are stable now because of the exchange of an electron.

In the compound water, each hydrogen atom needs one electron to fill its outer energy level. The oxygen atom needs two electrons for its outer level to be stable with eight electrons. Hydrogen and oxygen become stable and form bonds in a different way than sodium and chlorine. Instead of gaining or losing electrons, they share them. **Figure 6** shows how hydrogen and oxygen share electrons to achieve a more stable arrangement of electrons.

When atoms gain, lose, or share electrons, an attraction forms between the atoms, pulling them together to form a compound. This attraction is called a chemical bond. A **chemical bond** is the force that holds atoms together in a compound. In Section 2 you will learn how these chemical bonds are formed.

Reading Check *What is a chemical bond?*

Section 1 Assessment

1. Describe what happens to the properties of elements when atoms form compounds.
2. What does the formula BaF_2 tell you about this compound?
3. Why are some elements stable on their own while others are more stable in compounds?
4. In what ways can a chemical bond form?
5. **Think Critically** The label on a box of cleanser states that it contains $HC_2H_3O_2$. What elements are in this compound? How many atoms of each element can be found in a unit of $HC_2H_3O_2$?

Skill Builder Activities

6. **Making and Using Tables** The compounds in **Table 1** that contain carbon are classified as organic, and the others are classified as inorganic. Reorganize the contents of the table using these groups. **For more help, refer to the Science Skill Handbook.**
7. **Communicating** A chemical bond is not something you can touch or observe easily. Using the concepts of electron arrangements, energy, and stability, write a paragraph in your Science Journal describing a chemical bond. **For more help, refer to the Science Skill Handbook.**

Answers to Section Assessment

1. They change.
2. The compound is made up of a ratio of one barium atom to two fluorine atoms. Also, since the compound is made up of a metal and a nonmetal, it is likely ionic.
3. If an element has eight electrons in its outer electron energy level, it has a tendency not to react.
4. Atoms can gain or lose electrons or share them.
5. Hydrogen, carbon, and oxygen are in the compound. Each unit contains four hydrogen, two carbon, and two oxygen atoms.
6. Vinegar, grain alcohol, and cane sugar are organic. The other compounds are inorganic.
7. Chemical bonds may form between atoms when the atoms share, gain, or lose outer electrons to become more stable. Stability is reached when the atom's outer energy level is complete.

Activity

Atomic Trading Cards

Perhaps you have seen or collected trading cards for famous athletes. Usually each card has a picture of the athlete on one side with important statistics related to the sport on the back. Atoms can also be identified by their pictures and statistics.

What You'll Investigate

How can a visible model show how energy levels fill when atoms combine?

Materials

4 × 6 inch index cards
periodic table

Goals

- **Display** the electrons of elements according to their energy levels.
- **Compare and classify** elements according to their outer energy levels.

Procedure

1. Get an assigned element from the teacher. Write the following information for your element on your index card: name, symbol, Group, atomic number, atomic mass, metal/nonmetal/metalloid.
2. On the other side of your index card show the number of protons and neutrons in the nucleus (e.g. 6p for six protons and 6n for six neutrons for carbon.)
3. Draw circles around the nucleus to represent the energy levels of your element. The number of circles you will need is the same as the row the element is in on the periodic table.
4. Draw dots on each circle to represent the electrons in each energy level. Remember that level one can hold two electrons and levels two and three can hold eight electrons.
5. Look at the picture side only of four or five of your classmates' cards. Determine which element they have and to which group it belongs.

Conclude and Apply

1. As you classify the elements according to their Group number, what pattern do you see in the number of electrons in the outer energy level?
2. Atoms that give up electrons combine with atoms that gain electrons in order to form compounds. In your Science Journal, predict some pairs of elements that would combine in this way.

Communicating Your Data

Make a graph that relates the groups to the number of electrons in their outer energy level. **For more help, refer to the** **Science Skill Handbook.**

Activity

BENCH TESTED

Purpose Students make models showing the number of electrons in the outer energy levels of atoms of various elements and compare and classify those elements. L2 IN **Visual-Spatial**

Process Skills formulating models, classifying, using numbers, comparing and contrasting, making and using graphs

Time Required 40 minutes

Teaching Strategy To avoid confusion, assign elements from Groups 1, 2, and 13–18 only.

Troubleshooting Emphasize to students that the circles around the nucleus are only representations of the energy levels of electrons. Electrons do not actually move in circles.

Answers to Questions

1. They are the same in each group.
2. Sodium and potassium give up the only electron in their respective outer energy levels to chlorine and iodine, forming the chemically stable compounds sodium chloride and potassium iodide.

Assessment

Oral Ask students to which group carbon and silicon belong and whether these two elements are more likely to gain electrons, lose electrons, or share electrons when they form compounds. Group 14; because they have four electrons in their outer energy levels they most likely share electrons. Use **PASC**, p. 89.

Resource Manager

Chapter Resources Booklet

Enrichment, p. 30
Reinforcement, p. 27
Activity Worksheet, pp. 5–6

Communicating Your Data

Have students enter the number of electrons in the outer energy levels of atoms and the numbers of the groups to which the atoms belong in a computer spreadsheet. Then have them use the spread sheet's graphing function to make the graph.

SECTION

Types of Bonds

1 Motivate

Bellringer Transparency

Display the Section Focus Transparency for Section 2. Use the accompanying Transparency Activity Master. L2 ELL

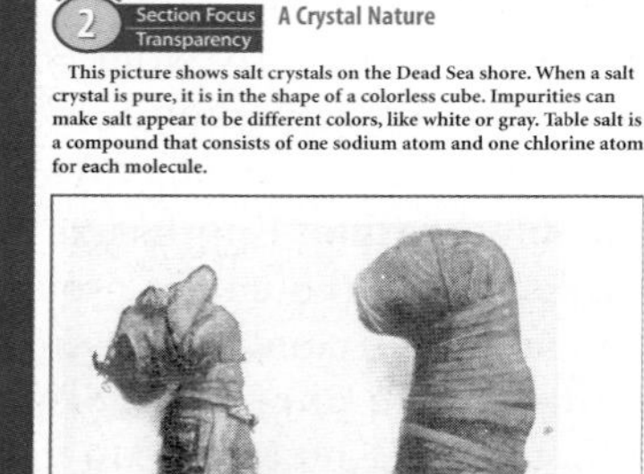

2 Section Focus Transparency **A Crystal Nature**

This picture shows salt crystals on the Dead Sea shore. When a salt crystal is pure, it is in the shape of a colorless cube. Impurities can make salt appear to be different colors, like white or gray. Table salt is a compound that consists of one sodium atom and one chlorine atom for each molecule.

1. **Describe the appearance of the salt in the picture.**
2. **Sodium atoms and chlorine atoms form ions, which means they carry a positive or negative charge. What happens to electrons when an atom forms a positive ion? A negative ion?**

Tie to Prior Knowledge

Ask students if they have ever consumed sports drinks. Explain that the electrolytes that are advertised to be in sports drinks are ions that are found naturally in human blood.

SECTION

Types of Bonds

As You Read

What You'll Learn

- **Describe** ionic bonds and covalent bonds.
- **Identify** the particles produced by ionic bonding and by covalent bonding.
- **Distinguish** between a nonpolar covalent bond and a polar covalent bond.

Vocabulary

ion	polar molecule
ionic bond	nonpolar molecule
molecule	covalent bond

Why It's Important

Bond type determines other properties of the compound.

Gain or Loss of Electrons

When you participate in a sport you might talk about gaining or losing an advantage. To gain an advantage, you want to have a better time than your opponent. It is important that you keep practicing because you don't want to lose that advantage. Gaining or losing an advantage happens as you try to meet a standard for your sport.

Atoms, too, lose or gain to meet a standard—a stable energy level. They do not lose or gain an advantage. Instead, they lose or gain electrons. An atom that has lost or gained electrons is called an ion. An **ion** is a charged particle because it now has either more or fewer electrons than protons. The positive and negative charges are not balanced.

Some of the most common compounds are made by the loss and gain of just one electron. They include an element from Group 1 on the periodic table and an element from Group 17. Some examples are sodium chloride, commonly known as table salt; sodium fluoride, an anticavity ingredient in some toothpastes; and potassium iodide, an ingredient in iodized salt.

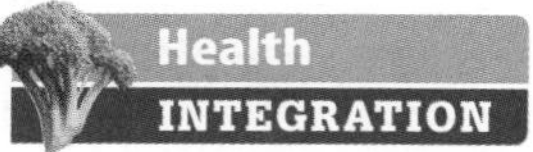

Health INTEGRATION Why do people need iodine? A lack of iodine causes a wide range of problems in the human body. The most obvious is an enlarged thyroid gland shown in **Figure 7,** but the problems can include mental retardation, neurological disorders, and physical problems. In infants the problems can be irreversible and can cause death.

Adding iodide to salt is as easy as spraying it with potassium iodide. However, even though the solution is relatively simple, more countries have iodine deficiency problems than do not. Much progress has been made in the movement to solve this problem, and the work continues.

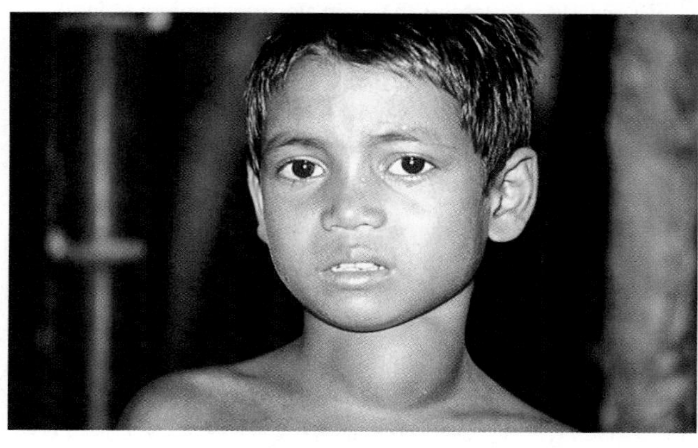

Figure 7
Goiter, a condition that causes an enlargement of the throid gland in the neck, is caused by iodine deficiency.

Section Assessment Planner

PORTFOLIO
Science Journal, p. 583
Challenge, p. 586

PERFORMANCE ASSESSMENT
Try at Home MiniLAB, p. 584
Skill Builder Activities, p. 586
See page 600 for more options.

CONTENT ASSESSMENT
Section, p. 586
Challenge, p. 586
Chapter, pp. 600–601

580 CHAPTER 19 Chemical Bonds

A Bond Forms What happens when potassium and iodine atoms come together? A neutral atom of potassium has one electron in its outer level. This is not a stable outer energy level. When potassium forms a compound with iodine, potassium loses one electron from its fourth level, and the third level becomes a complete outer level. However, the atom is no longer neutral. The potassium atom has become an ion. When a potassium atom loses an electron, the atom becomes positively charged because there is one electron less in the atom than there are protons in the nucleus. The 1+ charge is shown as a superscript written after the element's symbol, K^+, to indicate its charge. *Superscript* means "written above."

The iodine atom in this reaction undergoes change, as well. An iodine atom has seven electrons in its outer energy level. Recall that a stable outer energy level contains eight electrons. During the reaction with potassium, the iodine atom gains an electron, leaving its outer energy level with eight electrons. This atom is no longer neutral because it gained an extra negative particle. It now has a charge of 1– and is called an iodine ion, written as I^-. The compound formed between potassium and iodine is called potassium iodide. The dot diagrams for the process are shown in **Figure 8.**

Reading Check ***What part of an ion's symbol indicates its charge?***

Another way to look at the electron in the outer shell of a potassium atom is as an advertisement to other atoms saying, "Available: One electron to lend." The iodine atom would have the message, "Wanted: One electron to borrow." When the two atoms get together, each becomes a stable ion. Notice that the resulting compound has a neutral charge because the positive and negative charges of the ions cancel each other.

Life Science INTEGRATION

Ions are important in many processes in your body. The movement of muscles is just one of these processes. Muscle movement would be impossible without the movement of ions in and out of nerve cells.

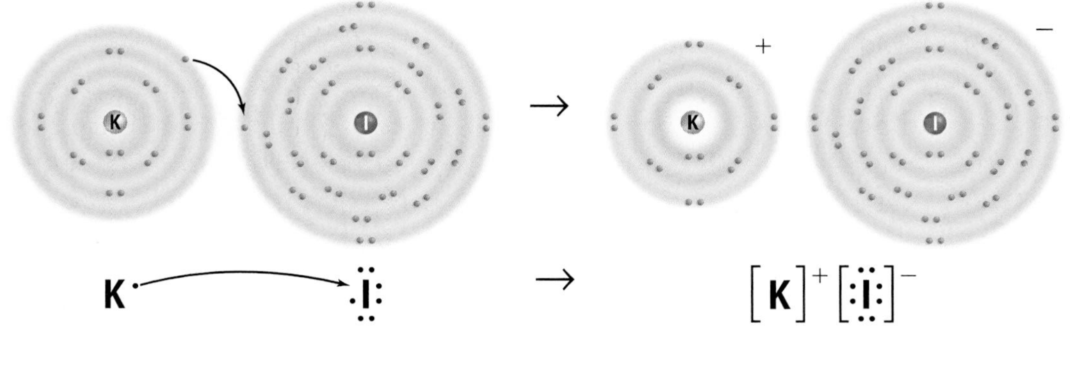

Figure 8
Potassium and iodine must perform a transfer of one electron. Potassium and iodine end up with stable outer energy levels.

2 Teach

Gain or Loss of Electrons

Life Science INTEGRATION

The primary ions needed for nerve impulses are Na^+ and K^+. Remind students that the properties of an ion of an element are different from those of the neutral atom. For example, both sodium and potassium metals react violently with water, while their ions do not.

Discussion

How many protons and electrons are in an atom of chlorine? 17 protons and 17 electrons **How many protons and electrons are in a common ion of Cl?** 17 protons and 18 electrons Remind students that while atoms gain or lose electrons fairly easily, changing the number of protons changes the identity of the atom. L2

LS **Logical-Mathematical**

Reading Check

Answer the superscript written after the element's symbol

Visual Learning

Figure 8 Have students find potassium and iodine on the periodic table. **How many electrons does potassium have?** 19 **How many does iodine have?** 53 Have students count the electrons in each atom and ion in **Figure 8.** Explain that the first energy level in any atom can contain up to 2 electrons, the second level can contain up to 8 electrons, the third level can contain up to 18 electrons, and the fourth level can contain up to 32 electrons. L3 LS **Visual-Spatial**

Resource Manager

Chapter Resources Booklet
- Transparency Activity, p. 45
- Directed Reading for Content Mastery, p. 20

Science Inquiry Labs, p. 47

Inclusion Strategies

Learning Disabled Provide students with two bar magnets. Have them use the magnets to determine that opposite ends (charges) of the magnets attract and like ends (charges) repel. Relate this concept to the attractions that bring opposite ions together. L1 LS **Kinesthetic**

The Ionic Bond

SCIENCE Online

Internet Addresses

Explore the Glencoe Science Web site at science.glencoe.com to find out more about topics in this section.

Discussion

Explain to students that a metal may give up an electron when forming an ionic bond. **What type of charge does the metal have after it loses an electron?** positive L1

LS **Logical-Mathematical**

Activity

Using a classroom periodic table, or the one in the textbook, point out potassium (K) on the left of the table. Ask a volunteer to name a nonmetal that would likely form an ionic bond with that element. Possible answers: O or F (K_2O; KF) Repeat with barium (Ba). Possible answers: Cl or S ($BaCl_2$; BaS) Use this exercise to point out that the metals and nonmetals that form ionic bonds often are located far apart on the periodic table. L2

LS **Logical-Mathematical**

SCIENCE Online

Research Visit the Glencoe Science Web site at **science.glencoe.com** for more information about ionic bonding. Communicate to your class what you learn.

The Ionic Bond

When ions cooperate in this way, a bond is formed. An **ionic bond** is the force of attraction between the opposite charges of the ions in an ionic compound. In an ionic bond, a transfer of electrons takes place. If an element loses electrons, one or more elements must gain an equal number of electrons to maintain the neutral charge of the compound.

Now that you have seen how an ionic bond forms when one electron is involved, see how it works when more than one is involved. The formation of magnesium chloride, $MgCl_2$, is another example of ionic bonding. When magnesium reacts with chlorine, a magnesium atom loses two electrons and becomes a positively charged ion, Mg^{2+}. At the same time, two chlorine atoms gain one electron each and become negatively charged chloride ions, Cl^-. In this case, a magnesium atom has two electrons to lend, but a single chlorine atom needs to borrow only one electron. Therefore, it takes two chlorine atoms, as shown in **Figure 9,** to take the two electrons from the magnesium ion.

Zero Net Charge The result of this bond is a neutral compound. The compound as a whole is neutral because the sum of the charges on the ions is zero. The positive charge of the magnesium ion is exactly equal to the negative charge of the two chloride ions. In other words, when atoms form an ionic compound, their electrons are shifted to other atoms, but the overall number of protons and electrons of the combined atoms remains equal and unchanged. Therefore, the compound is neutral.

Ionic bonds usually are formed by bonding between metals and nonmetals. Looking at the periodic table, you will see that the elements that bond ionically are often across the table from each other. Ionic compounds are often crystalline solids with high melting points.

Figure 9
A magnesium atom gives an electron to each of two chlorine atoms to form $MgCl_2$.

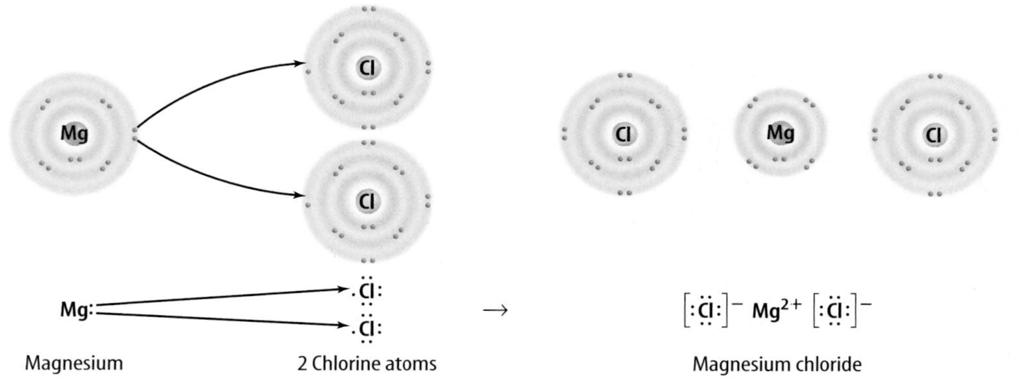

Teacher FYI

A positive ion is always smaller than its original neutral atom, and a negative ion is always larger than its original neutral atom. The charge on an ion acts as though it were located exactly in the center of the ion. Therefore, large ions have less attraction toward other ions; their charge feels farther away. The more highly charged an ion is, the stronger the force around it. The strongest attractions take place between small, highly charged ions such as Al^{3+} and highly negative ions such as O^{2-}. Large, singly charged ions such as K^+ and I^- have less attractive force between them.

Sharing Electrons

Some atoms of nonmetals are unlikely to lose or gain electrons. For example, the elements in Group 4 of the periodic table have four electrons in their outer level. They would have to either gain or lose four electrons in order to have a stable outer level. The loss of this many electrons takes a great deal of energy. Each time an electron is removed, the nucleus holds the remaining electrons even more tightly. Therefore, these atoms become more chemically stable by sharing electrons, rather than by losing or gaining electrons.

In **Figure 6,** you saw how two hydrogen atoms and one oxygen atom share electrons in the compound water. The electrons are attracted to the nuclei of more than one atom at a time. Notice that the electron dot structure, shown in **Figure 10,** shows the compound without charges. This is because the hydrogen and oxygen are not present as ions, but rather as a neutral molecule of water. Neutral particles formed as a result of electron sharing are called **molecules.**

Figure 10
Each of the pairs of electrons between the two hydrogens and the oxygen is shared as each atom contributes one electron to the pair to make the bond.

The Covalent Bond The attraction that forms between atoms when they share electrons is known as a **covalent bond.** Most of the time the atoms in a covalent bond share only one pair of electrons. However, sometimes an atom shares more than one pair of electrons with another atom. Oxygen and nitrogen share more than one pair of electrons, as shown in **Figure 11**. In the case of oxygen, two pairs of electrons are shared by the two oxygen atoms. This is called a double bond. Covalent bonds also form between atoms of nitrogen, the gas that makes up most of air. Two atoms in a molecule of nitrogen share three pairs of electrons, forming three covalent bonds between the atoms. When three pairs of electrons are shared by two atoms, it is called a triple bond.

Covalent bonds form between nonmetallic elements. These elements are close together in the upper right-hand corner of the periodic table. Many covalent compounds are liquids or gases at room temperature.

Reading Check ***What kind of elements form covalent bonds?***

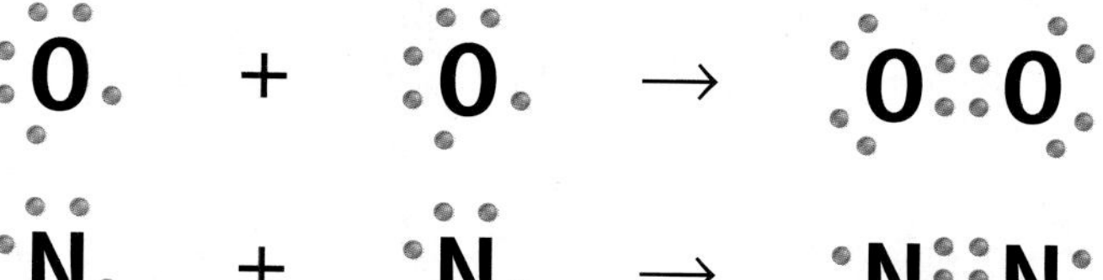

Figure 11
The dot diagram for the formation of oxygen gas, O_2, shows that oxygen atoms share four electrons. The two nitrogen atoms in nitrogen gas share six electrons.

Sharing Electrons

Use an Analogy

The term *cocaptain* is often used to describe the leaders of such things as basketball teams and debate teams. This term implies cooperation and a sharing of responsibilities. This is similar to the situation that occurs to electrons during covalent bonding. When a covalent bond forms, the valence electrons are shared between the atoms in the molecule.

Activity

Point out that in general the closer together reacting elements are on the periodic table, the more likely it is that they will share electrons with one another rather than form ionic bonds. Have students use this information to predict the type of bond that will form between carbon and oxygen. covalent Have them predict the type of bond formed between each of the following: sodium and oxygen, ionic; phosphorus and oxygen, covalent; magnesium and oxygen, ionic; aluminum and oxygen, ionic; chlorine and oxygen, covalent; sulfur and oxygen, covalent. L2
LS **Logical-Mathematical**

Reading Check

Answer nonmetals

Resource Manager

Chapter Resources Booklet
Enrichment, p. 31

Physical Science Critical Thinking/ Problem Solving, p. 13

Science Journal

Dot Diagrams Have students research the work of American chemist Gilbert N. Lewis and write short paragraphs in their Science Journals about his contribution to dot diagrams. The diagrams are called Lewis diagrams because he developed the idea as a way of explaining attractions besides ionic bonding between atoms. The dots allowed him to better explain bonding to his students. L2 LS **Linguistic** P

Sharing Electrons, continued

Purpose Students observe that water molecules are polar. L2

LS **Kinesthetic**

Materials water faucet, balloon, wool

Teaching Strategy Practice to determine the amount of static charge that can be built up on the balloon. High humidity reduces the buildup, causing a smaller deflection of the water stream.

Analysis

1. The balloon acquires a charge when rubbed against the wool. When brought near a thin stream of water, the charge attracts water, causing the stream to bend.
2. The water molecules must also carry some charge. The bond is not ionic, so it must be a polar covalent bond.

Assessment

Oral Explain to students that pentane (C_5H_{12}) is a nonpolar molecule. Ask students to predict whether a stream of pentane would bend if they used the same procedure followed in the MiniLAB. No; pentane is nonpolar and therefore will not be attracted to the static charge on the balloon. Use **Performance Assessment in the Science Classroom**, p. 89. L2

LS **Logical-Mathematical**

Identifing Bonding Type

Procedure

1. Turn on the faucet to produce a thin **stream of water**.
2. Rub an inflated **balloon** with **wool or fur.**
3. Bring the balloon near the stream of water, and describe what you see.

Analysis

1. Explain your observations.
2. Based on your observations, explain what type of bonding is in a water molecule.

Unequal Sharing Electrons are not always shared equally between atoms in a covalent bond. The strength of the attraction of each atom to its electrons is related to the size of the atom, the charge of the nucleus, and the total number of electrons the atom contains. Part of the strength of attraction has to do with how far away from the nucleus the electron being shared is. For example, a magnet has a stronger pull when it is right next to a piece of metal rather than several centimeters away. The other part of the strength of attraction has to do with the size of the positive charge in the nucleus. Using a magnet as an example again, a strong magnet will hold the metal more firmly than a weak magnet.

One example of this unequal sharing is found in a molecule of hydrogen chloride, HCl. In water, HCl is hydrochloric acid, which is used in laboratories, in industry to clean metal, and is found in your stomach where it digests food. Chlorine atoms have a stronger attraction for electrons than hydrogen atoms do. As a result, the electrons shared in hydrogen chloride will spend more time near the chlorine atom than near the hydrogen atom, as shown in **Figure 12.** The chlorine atom has a partial negative charge represented by a lower case Greek symbol delta followed by a negative superscript, δ^-. The hydrogen atom has a partial positive charge represented by a δ^+.

Tug-of-War You might think of the bond as the rope in a tug-of-war, and the shared electrons as the knot in the center of the rope. **Figure 13** illustrates this concept. Each atom in the molecule attracts the electrons that they share. However, sometimes the atoms aren't the same size. The same thing happens in tug-of-war. Sometimes one team is larger or has stronger participants than the other.

When this is true, the knot in the middle of the rope ends up closer to the stronger team. Similarly, the electrons being shared in a molecule are held more closely to the atoms with the stronger pull or larger nucleus.

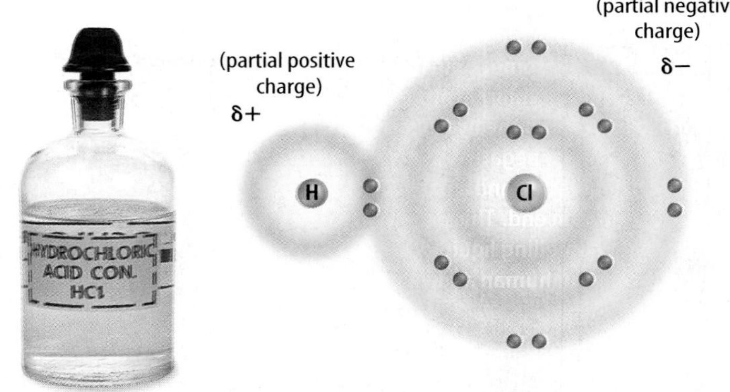

Figure 12
The chlorine atom exerts the greater pull on the electron in hydrogen chloride which forms hydrochloric acid in water.

Inclusion Strategies

Gifted Have students research the electronegativity scale developed by Linus Pauling and relate the information they find to the formation of covalent, polar covalent, and ionic bonds. Pauling's electronegativity scale is a way of ranking the ability of an atom to attract electrons within a bond. Two atoms that have a small or no electronegativity difference form a covalent bond. Those with a great electronegativity difference form an ionic bond. If the difference is moderate, a polar covalent bond forms. Each element is given a numerical ranking, so simple subtraction gives the electronegativity difference. L3 LS **Linguistic**

Figure 13

When playing tug-of-war, if there are more—or stronger—team members on one end of the rope than the other, there is an unequal balance of power. The stronger team can pull harder on the rope and has the advantage. A similar situation exists in polar molecules, in which electrons are attracted more strongly by one type of atom in the molecule than another. Because of this unequal sharing of electrons, polar molecules have a slightly negative end and a slightly positive end, as shown below.

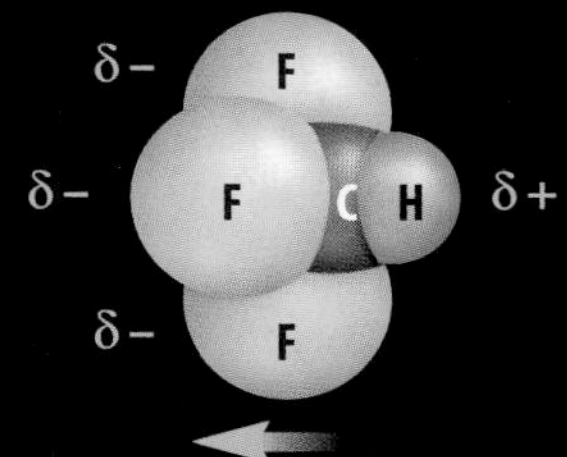

CHLOROFORM In a molecule of chloroform ($CHCl_3$), or trichloromethane (tri klor oh ME thayn), the three chlorine atoms attract electrons more strongly than the hydrogen atom does, creating a partial negative charge on the chlorine end of the molecule and a partial positive charge on the hydrogen end. This polar molecule is a clear, sweet-smelling liquid once widely used as an anesthetic in human and veterinary surgery.

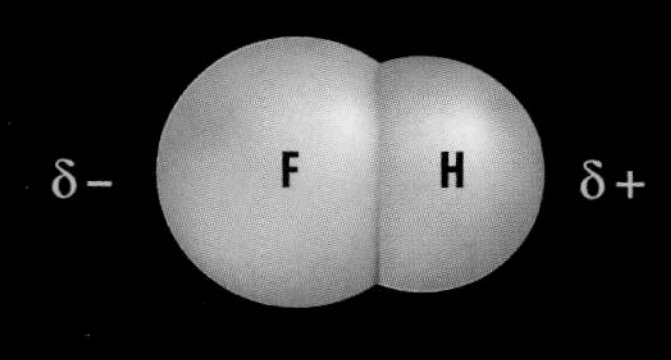

HYDROGEN FLUORIDE Hydrogen and fluorine react to form hydrogen fluoride (HF). In an HF molecule, the two atoms are bound together by a pair of electrons, one contributed by each atom. But the electrons are not shared equally because the fluorine atom attracts them more strongly than the hydrogen atom does. The result is a polar molecule with a slightly positive charge near the hydrogen end and a slightly negative charge near the fluorine end.

SECTION 2 Types of Bonds 585

Visualizing Polar Molecules

Have students examine the pictures and read the captions. Then ask the following questions.

- **In your own words, describe why charge is distributed unevenly in chloroform molecules.** Possible answer: The chlorine molecules have a stronger attraction for electrons than the hydrogen molecule.
- **Why are the hydrogen sides of both chloroform molecules and hydrogen fluoride molecules partially positive?** The electrons have been pulled away, leaving an exposed proton in each hydrogen nucleus.

Activity

Work together as a class to draw on the board the electron dot diagrams for both molecules. Students should easily see that the electrons are concentrated on one side of each molecule, which leads to a partial negative charge on that side. Have students draw these diagrams in their Science Journals. LS **Visual-Spatial**

Extension

Challenge students to find out what an induced dipole is. Direct students to make posters showing examples of induced dipoles and explain their posters to the class. L3 LS **Visual-Spatial**

Resource Manager 

Chapter Resources Booklet
MiniLAB, p. 3
Lab Activity, pp. 13–16
Reinforcement, p. 28

Sharing Electrons, continued

Reading Check

Answer a molecule that has a slightly negative end and a slightly positive end

3 Assess

Reteach

List the formulas for HCl, H_2O, NaCl, and $MgCl_2$ on the board. Have students identify each compound as ionic or covalent. HCl, covalent; H_2O, covalent; NaCl, ionic; $MgCl_2$, ionic. L2 LS **Logical-Mathematical**

Challenge

Ask each student to prepare a chart with two columns labeled *Ionic Compounds* and *Covalent Compounds*. Have students list appropriate properties in each column. **Is an ionic or a covalent compound more likely to conduct electricity?** ionic L3 LS **Logical-Mathematical** P

Assessment

Performance Have each student write the symbol of one of the first 30 elements on a sheet of paper. Now have the student use the periodic table to try to find an element that would form a covalent bond with the first element. Have students repeat the exercise for an ionic compound and explain their choices. Emphasize that both electron configuration and attraction for electrons determine whether two atoms will bond with each other. Use **PASC,** p. 93.

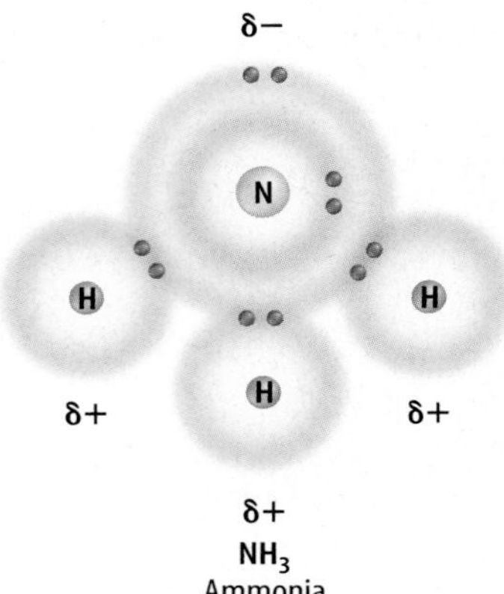

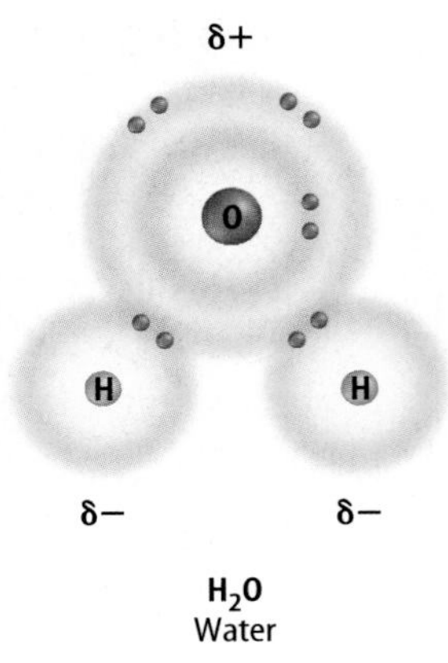

Figure 14
A model of the ammonia molecule illustrates the charge difference as the nitrogen holds the electron more closely. The polarity of water is responsible for many of its unique properties.

Polar or Nonpolar? For the molecule involved in this electron tug-of-war, there is another consequence. Again, look at the molecule of hydrogen chloride. This unequal sharing of electrons gives each chlorine atom a slight negative charge and each hydrogen atom a slight positive charge. The atom holding the electron more closely always will have a slightly negative charge. The charge is balanced but not equally distributed. This type of molecule is called polar. The term *polar* means "having opposite ends." A **polar molecule** is one that has a slightly positive end and a slightly negative end although the overall molecule is neutral. Ammonia and water are examples of a polar molecule, as shown in **Figure 14.**

Reading Check *What is a polar molecule?*

Two atoms that are exactly alike can share their electrons equally, forming a nonpolar molecule. A **nonpolar molecule** is one in which electrons are shared equally in bonds. Such a molecule does not have oppositely charged ends. This is true of molecules made from two identical atoms or molecules that are symmetric, such as CH_4.

Section 2 Assessment

1. Why does an atom make an ionic bond only with certain other atoms?
2. Compare the possession of electrons in ionic and covalent bonds.
3. What types of particles are formed by ionic and covalent bonds?
4. What is the difference between polar and nonpolar molecules?
5. **Think Critically** From the following list of symbols, choose two elements that are likely to form an ionic bond: O, Ne, S, Ca, K. Next, select two elements that would likely form a covalent bond. Explain.

Skill Builder Activities

6. **Concept Mapping** Using the following terms, make a network tree concept map of chemical bonding: *ionic, covalent, ions, positive ions, negative ions, molecules, polar,* and *nonpolar.* **For more help, refer to the** Science Skill Handbook.
7. **Solving One-Step Equations** Aluminum oxide, Al_2O_3, can be produced during space shuttle launches. Show that the sum of the positive and negative charges in a unit of Al_2O_3 equals zero. **For more help, refer to the** Math Skill Handbook.

Answers to Section Assessment

1. In ionic bonds, one atom accepts electrons from another. This happens only among elements having large differences in their attractions for electrons.
2. In ionic bonds one atom accepts an electron from another atom. In covalent bonding electrons are shared, sometimes unequally.
3. Ionic bonds form arrays of evenly spaced, oppositely charged ions. Covalent bonding produces molecules.
4. Polar molecules have one slightly negative end and one slightly positive end because electrons are held more tightly by some atoms. Nonpolar molecules do not have oppositely charged ends.
5. Ionic: Ca–O and K–O, because K and Ca are metals far from O on the periodic table; covalent: S–O because S and O are nonmetals close to each other on the periodic table
6. Check students' work.
7. The charge on Al is +3 and the charge on O is −2. $2(+3) + 3(-2) = 0$

SECTION 3

Writing Formulas and Naming Compounds

Symbols and Shorthand

Does the table in **Figure 15** look like it has anything to do with chemistry? It is an early table of the elements made by alchemists—scientists who tried to make gold from other elements. The alchemist used symbols from a table to write the formulas of substances like silver tarnish. The modern chemist uses symbols from the modern periodic table and writes the formula Ag_2S. When you get to the end of this section, you, too, will name compounds and write their formulas.

As You Read

***What* You'll Learn**

- **Explain** how to determine oxidation numbers.
- **Write** formulas and names for ionic compounds.
- **Describe** hydrates and write their formulas.
- **Write** formulas and names for covalent compounds.

Vocabulary

binary compound
oxidation number
polyatomic ion
hydrate

***Why* It's Important**

The name and formula of a compound convey information about the compound.

Binary Ionic Compounds

The first formulas of compounds you will write are for binary ionic compounds. A **binary compound** is one that is composed of two elements. Potassium iodide, the salt additive discussed in Section 2, is a binary ionic compound. However, before you can write a formula, you must have all the needed information at your fingertips. What all will you need to know?

Are electrons gained or lost? You need to know which elements are involved and what number of electrons they lose, gain, or share in order to become stable. How can you determine this? Section 1 discussed the relationship between an element's position on the periodic table and the number of electrons it gains or loses. This is called the **oxidation number** of an element. An oxidation number tells you how many electrons an atom has gained, lost, or shared to become stable.

For ionic compounds the oxidation number is the same as the charge on the ion. For example, a sodium ion has a charge of 1+ and an oxidation number of 1+. A chlorine ion has a charge of 1− and an oxidation number of 1−.

Figure 15
This old chart of the elements used pictorial symbols to represent elements.

Section Assessment Planner

PORTFOLIO
Cultural Diversity, p. 592

PERFORMANCE ASSESSMENT
MiniLab, p. 592
Skill Builder Activities, p. 593
See page 600 for more options.

CONTENT ASSESSMENT
Section, p. 593
Challenge, p. 593
Chapter, pp. 600–601

SECTION

Writing Formulas and Naming Compounds

1 Motivate

Bellringer Transparency

Display the Section Focus Transparency for Section 3. Use the accompanying Transparency Activity Master. L2 ELL

Section 3 Section Focus Transparency **For best results, add water.**

Why are these workers trying to keep the concrete wet rather than letting it dry? Concrete doesn't harden because it dries. It incorporates the water into its molecular structure. If there's not enough water, the concrete won't harden properly, and it won't be very durable.

1. How might construction be different in the desert compared to a rainy, temperate region?
2. What would happen if a bag of dry concrete got a little damp? What if it got very wet?
3. When a new sidewalk is finally dry, where is the water?

Tie to Prior Knowledge

Bring labels from common substances such as antacids that contain chemical formulas. Identify the substances shown by each formula. Then explain to students that in this section they will discover how to read and interpret such formulas and how to name the compounds they represent.

Resource Manager

Chapter Resources Booklet
Transparency Activity, p. 46
Directed Reading for Content Mastery, pp. 21, 22

2 Teach

Binary Ionic Compounds

Quick Demo

Binary ionic compounds form when oppositely charged ions attract each other. Demonstrate the basic forces involved by placing two 25-cm pieces of cellophane tape side by side on a plastic surface. Pull both up at the same time. As they are brought close together they will repel. Explain that this happens because both pieces of tape have acquired the same charge. Place one piece of tape on the surface and a second piece directly on top of the first. Pull them off the table and separate them. They now attract each other. Why? They have acquired opposite charges, which causes them to attract each other.
L1 **Visual-Spatial**

IDENTIFYING Misconceptions

The use of Roman numerals can be confusing. Copper(II) oxide is CuO, with one copper atom for each oxygen atom. The compound copper(I) oxide is written as Cu_2O, with two copper atoms for each oxygen atom. Remind students that the Roman numeral represents the charge on an atom, while Arabic subscript numbers, such as 2 and 3, show the number of atoms of each element.

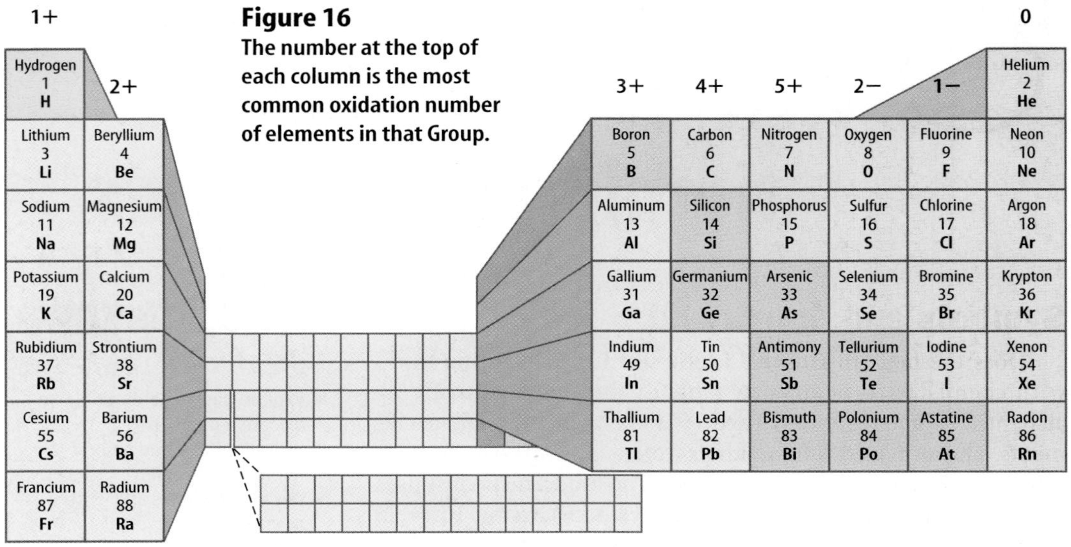

Figure 16
The number at the top of each column is the most common oxidation number of elements in that Group.

1+	2+	3+	4+	5+	2−	1−	0
Hydrogen 1 H							Helium 2 He
Lithium 3 Li	Beryllium 4 Be	Boron 5 B	Carbon 6 C	Nitrogen 7 N	Oxygen 8 O	Fluorine 9 F	Neon 10 Ne
Sodium 11 Na	Magnesium 12 Mg	Aluminum 13 Al	Silicon 14 Si	Phosphorus 15 P	Sulfur 16 S	Chlorine 17 Cl	Argon 18 Ar
Potassium 19 K	Calcium 20 Ca	Gallium 31 Ga	Germanium 32 Ge	Arsenic 33 As	Selenium 34 Se	Bromine 35 Br	Krypton 36 Kr
Rubidium 37 Rb	Strontium 38 Sr	Indium 49 In	Tin 50 Sn	Antimony 51 Sb	Tellurium 52 Te	Iodine 53 I	Xenon 54 Xe
Cesium 55 Cs	Barium 56 Ba	Thallium 81 Tl	Lead 82 Pb	Bismuth 83 Bi	Polonium 84 Po	Astatine 85 At	Radon 86 Rn
Francium 87 Fr	Radium 88 Ra						

Oxidation Numbers The numbers with positive or negative signs in **Figure 16** are the oxidation numbers for these elements. Notice how they fit with the periodic table groupings.

The elements in **Table 2** can have more than one oxidation number. When naming these compounds, the oxidation number is expressed in the name with a roman numeral. For example, the oxidation number of iron in iron(III) oxide is 3+.

Table 2 Special Ions

Name	Oxidation Number
Copper (I)	1+
Copper (II)	2+
Iron (II)	2+
Iron (III)	3+
Chromium (II)	2+
Chromium (III)	3+
Lead (II)	2+
Lead (IV)	4+

Compounds are Neutral When writing formulas it is important to remember that although the individual ions in a compound carry charges, the compound itself is neutral. A formula must have the right number of positive ions and the right number of negative ions so the charges balance. For example, sodium chloride is made up of a sodium ion with a 1+ charge and a chlorine ion with a 1− charge. One of each ion put together makes a neutral compound with the formula NaCl.

However, what if you have a compound like calcium fluoride? A calcium ion has a charge of 2+ and a fluoride ion has a charge of 1−. In this case you need to have two fluoride ions for every calcium ion in order for the charges to cancel and the compound to be neutral with the formula CaF_2.

Some compounds require more figuring. Aluminum oxide contains an ion with a 3+ charge and an ion with a 2− charge. You must find the least common multiple of 3 and 2 in order to determine how many of each ion you need. You need two aluminum ions and three oxygen ions in order to have a 6+ charge and a 6− charge and therefore, the neutral compound Al_2O_3.

Science Journal

Have students use a periodic table to identify the oxidation numbers of the elements in Groups 1, 2, and 13–18. Ask students to make tables containing this information in their Science Journals. L1 LS **Visual-Spatial**

Active Reading

Reflective Journal In this strategy, students identify what they learned from activities. Have students divide sheets of paper into several columns and record their thoughts under headings such as "What I did," "What I learned," "Questions I have," "Surprises I experienced," and "Overall response." Have students write a Reflective Journal for writing formulas.

Writing Formulas After you've learned how to find the oxidation numbers and their least common multiple, you can write formulas for ionic compounds by using the following rules in this order.

1. Write the symbol of the element or polyatomic ion (ions containing more than one atom) that has the positive oxidation number or charge. Hydrogen, the ammonium ion (NH_4^+) and all metals have positive oxidation numbers.
2. Write the symbol of the element or polyatomic ion with the negative oxidation number. Nonmetals other than hydrogen and polyatomic ions other than NH_4^+ have negative oxidation numbers.
3. Use subscripts next to each ion so that the sum of the charges of all the ions in the formula is zero.

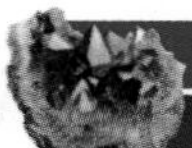

Earth Science INTEGRATION

Farmers must sometimes add lime, which is calcium oxide, to soil in their fields. What is the formula of calcium oxide?

Math Skills Activity

Writing Formulas

Example Problem

What is the formula for lithium nitride?

Solution

1 *This is what you know:*

Write the symbol and oxidation number of the positive element:
Lithium (Li) = 1+
Write the symbol and oxidation number of the negative element:
Nitrogen (N) = 3−
Least common multiple = 3

2 *This is what you need to do:*

Add subscripts so that the sum of the oxidation numbers is zero
3 Li = (3) (1+) = 3+
1 N = 3−
Complete the formula: Li_3N

Check your answer by multiplying each subscript by the oxidation number and compare.

Li_3 gives (3) (1+) = 3+.
N gives (1) (3−) = 3−. (3+) + (3−) = 0.

Practice Problem

What is the formula for lead(IV) phosphide?

For more help, refer to the Math Skill Handbook.

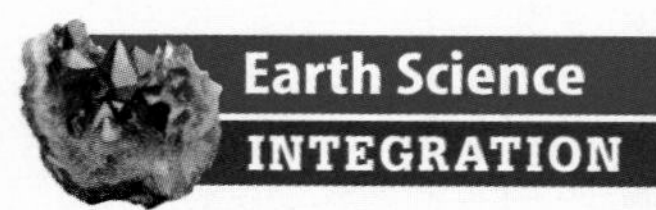

Earth Science INTEGRATION

CaO

Math Skills Activity

National Math Standards

Correlation to Mathematics Objectives

1, 6–10

This is what you know: Write the symbol and oxidation number of the positive element: Lead (Pb) = 4+

Write the symbol and oxidation number of the negative element:

Phosphorus (P) = 3−

Least common multiple = 12

This is what you need to do:

Add subscripts so that the sum of the oxidation numbers is zero.

3Pb = (3) (4+) = 12+;

4P = (4) (3−) = 12−

Complete the formula.

Answer to Practice Problem

Pb_3P_4

Resource Manager

Mathematics Skill Activities, p. 29

Reading and Writing Skill Activities, p. 41

Curriculum Connection

Language Arts The binary ionic compound Fe_3O_4 is the naturally magnetic mineral magnetite. Magnetite was used in the ancient world as a compass; it was called a *lodestone*. Ask students to find out where the name magnetite comes from. Magnetite was named by the ancient Greeks after the place it was originally found, Magnesia in what is now Turkey. L2 LS **Linguistic**

Binary Ionic Compounds, continued

Activity

Organize the class into two teams. Have team one make a list of the names of compounds and write the names on the board. Team two must then write the correct formula next to each compound. Award one point for each correct answer. Then have team two make a list of compound formulas and write them on the board for team one to name. Alternate between the teams until one reaches a score of 10. L2 ELL COOP LEARN LS **Intrapersonal**

Visual Learning

Table 3 **In a binary compound involving oxygen, what name is given to the second part of the compound?** oxide L1
LS **Visual-Spatial**

Problem-Solving Activity

Answers

1. copper (II) oxide
2. aluminum chloride

Writing Names You can name a binary ionic compound from its formula by using these rules.

1. Write the name of the positive ion.
2. Using **Table 2,** check to see if the positive ion is capable of forming more than one oxidation number. If it is, determine the oxidation number of the ion from the formula of the compound. To do this, keep in mind that the overall charge of the compound is zero and the negative ion has only one possible charge. Write charge of the positive ion using roman numerals in parentheses after the ion's name. If the ion has only one possible oxidation number, proceed to step 3.
3. Write the root name of the negative ion. The root is the first part of the element's name. For chlorine the root is *chlor-*. For oxygen it is *ox-*.
4. Add the ending *-ide* to the root. **Table 3** lists several elements and their *-ide* counterparts. For example, BaF_2 is named barium fluoride.

Notice that the subscripts of the positive and negative ion are not part of the name of the compound except when the positive ion has more than one possible charge.

Table 3 Elements in Binary Compounds

Element	-ide Name
Oxygen	oxide
Phosphorus	phosphide
Nitrogen	nitride
Sulfur	sulfide

Problem-Solving Activity

Can you name binary ionic compounds?

What would a chemist name the compound CuCl?

Identifying the problem

There are four simple steps in naming binary ionic compounds.

1. Write the name of the positive ion in the compound. In CuCl, the name of the positive ion is copper.
2. Check **Table 2** to determine if copper is one of the elements that can have more than one oxidation number. Looking at **Table 2,** you can see that copper can have a 1 + or a 2 + oxidation number. You need to determine which to use. Looking at the compound, you see that there is one copper atom and one chlorine atom. You know that the overall charge of the compound is zero and that chlorine only forms a 1− ion. For the charge of the compound to be zero, the charge of the copper ion must be 1+. Write this charge using roman numerals in parentheses after the element's name, copper (I).
3. Write the root name of the negative ion. The negative ion is chlorine and its root is *chlor-*.
4. Add the ending *-ide* to the root, chloride.
5. The full name of the compound CuCl is copper (I) chloride.

Solving the Problem

1. What is the name of CuO?
2. What is the name of $AlCl_3$?

Teacher FYI

Hydrogen is nearly always found with a +1 charge. However, when hydrogen combines with active metals such as those found in Groups 1 and 2, it is assigned a −1 charge. This assignment is made because of the ease with which those metals lose electrons to become +1 ions. Examples include NaH and MgH_2. These compounds are called sodium hydride and magnesium hydride.

Resource Manager

Chapter Resources Booklet
Transparency Activity, pp. 47–48
Home and Community Involvement, p. 46

Compounds with Complex Ions

Not all compounds are binary. Baking soda—used in cooking, as a medicine, and for brushing your teeth—has the formula $NaHCO_3$. This is an example of an ionic compound that is not binary. Which four elements does it contain? Some compounds, including baking soda, are composed of more than two elements. They contain polyatomic ions. The prefix *poly-* means "many," so the term *polyatomic* means "having many atoms." A **polyatomic ion** is a positively or negatively charged, covalently bonded group of atoms. So the compound as a whole contains three or more elements. The polyatomic ion in baking soda is the bicarbonate or hydrogen carbonate ion, HCO_3^-.

Table 4 Polyatomic Ions

Charge	Name	Formula
1+	ammonium	NH_4^+
1–	acetate	$C_2H_3O_2^-$
	chlorate	ClO_3^-
	hydroxide	OH^-
	nitrate	NO_3^-
2–	carbonate	CO_3^{2-}
	sulfate	SO_4^{2-}
3–	phosphate	PO_4^{3-}

Writing Names **Table 4** lists several polyatomic ions. To name a compound that contains one of these ions, first write the name of the positive ion. Use **Table 4** to find the name of a polyatomic ion. Then write the name of the negative ion. For example, K_2SO_4 is potassium sulfate. What is the name of $Sr(OH)_2$? Begin by writing the name of the positive ion, strontium. Then find the name of the polyatomic ion, OH^-. Table 4 lists it as hydroxide. Thus the name is strontium hydroxide.

Writing Formulas To write formulas for these compounds, follow the rules for binary compounds, with one addition. When more than one polyatomic ion is needed, write parentheses around the polyatomic ion before adding the subscript. How would you write the formula of barium chlorate?

First, identify the symbol of the positive ion. Barium has a symbol of Ba and forms a 2+ ion, Ba^{2+}. Next, identify the negative chlorate ion. **Table 4** shows that it is ClO_3^-. Finally, you need to balance the charges of the ions to make the compound neutral. It will take two chlorate ions with a 1– charge to balance the 2+ charge of the barium ion. Since the chlorate ion is polyatomic, you use parentheses before adding the subscript. Therefore, the formula is $Ba(ClO_3)_2$.

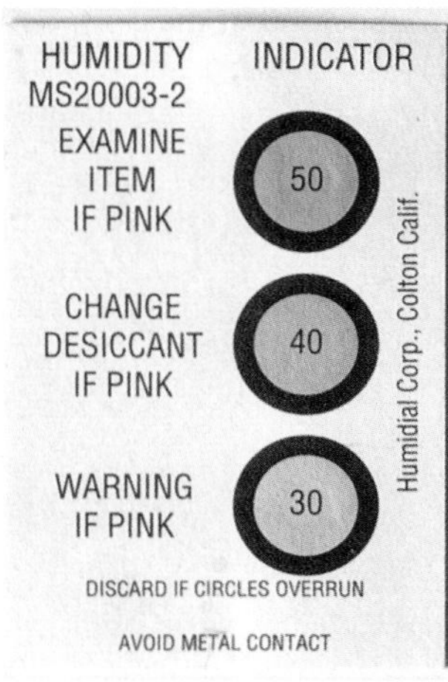

Figure 17
This humidity predictor uses cobalt chloride.

Compounds with Complex Ions

Discussion

Provide practice using polyatomic ions by having students name each of the following compounds and determine the number of atoms of the underlined element in each: $Na_3P\underline{O}_4$, 4 oxygen atoms, sodium phosphate; $Al_2(\underline{C}O_3)_3$, 3 carbon atoms, aluminum carbonate; $Ca(C_2\underline{H}_3O_2)_2$, 6 atoms of hydrogen, calcium acetate L2

LS **Logical-Mathematical**

Extension

Have students find the formulas, names, or charges of the following polyatomic ions: nitrite, NO_2^-; sulfite, SO_3^{2-}; MnO_4^-, permanganate; ClO_2^-, chlorite. L2

LS **Logical-Mathematical**

Fun Fact

Anhydrous compounds such as $CaCl_2$ are sometimes sold as products to reduce humidity. Anhydrous calcium chloride absorbs moisture to become $CaCl_2{\cdot}2H_2O$ hydrate in a moist basement.

LAB DEMONSTRATION

Purpose to observe the difference between a hydrated and a dehydrated compound

Materials copper(II) sulfate pentahydrate, Pyrex test tube, Bunsen burner, water, dropper

Procedure Place a small amount of copper(II) sulfate pentahydrate in the tube and heat it in a strong flame. Have students observe the change. Let the tube cool, then add a few drops of water.

Expected Outcome When heated, the deep blue copper(II) sulfate pentahydrate gradually changes into the white powder of the anhydrous compound. When water is added, the blue hydrate is restored.

Assessment

Write the formula for copper(II) sulfate pentahydrate. $CuSO_4{\cdot}5H_2O$ **What happened when it was heated?** It lost the water of hydration. **Was this a chemical change or a physical change?** A chemical change; it changed the identity of the material.

Compounds with Added Water

Use Science Words

Word Usage Have students use the word *hydrate* in a sentence in a way that describes its meaning. Possible answer: A hydrate forms when water molecules become attached to the ions of a compound. L1 LS **Linguistic**

Purpose Students will create their own hydrates.

Materials plaster of paris, water, small bowl, rubber hammer, hair dryer for each student

Teaching Strategy Ask students to show their final products to the class.

Analysis

1. The plaster should not crack when tapped before it is heated, but it becomes brittle and cracks easily after being heated.
2. Steam will rise from the plaster, and it will easily crumble and become powder. The heat removes water molecules from the hydrated gypsum causing the plaster to lose its strength.

Assessment

Performance Ask students to experiment with different proportions of water and plaster of paris to create hydrates with different heat and stress resistant properties. Use **Performance Assessment in the Science Classroom,** p. 89.

Making a Hydrate

Procedure

1. Mix 150 mL of **plaster of paris** with 75 mL of water in a small **bowl.**
2. Let the plaster dry overnight and take the hardened plaster out of the bowl.
3. Lightly tap the plaster with a **rubber hammer.**
4. Heat the plaster with a **hair dryer** on the hottest setting and observe.
5. Lightly tap the plaster with the hammer after heating it.

Analysis

1. What happened to the plaster when you tapped it before and after heating it?
2. What did you observe happening to the plaster as you heated it? Explain.

Compounds with Added Water

Have you seen weather predictors made from blue paper that turns pink in humid air? **Figure 17** shows some examples of these humidity detectors. What properties allow this change? Some ionic compounds have water molecules as part of their structure. These compounds are called hydrates. A **hydrate** is a compound that has water chemically attached to its ions.

Common Hydrates The term *hydrate* comes from a word that means "water." When a solution of cobalt chloride evaporates, pink crystals that contain six water molecules for each unit of cobalt chloride are formed. The formula for this compound is $CoCl_2 \cdot 6H_2O$ and is called cobalt chloride hexahydrate.

You can remove water from these crystals by heating them. The resulting blue compound is called anhydrous, which means "without water." If you apply this anhydrous compound to paper, the paper will gain water molecules easily. How will this blue paper react to the presence of water vapor?

The plaster of paris shown in **Figure 18** also forms a hydrate when water is added. It becomes calcium sulfate dihydrate, which is also known as gypsum. The water that was added to the powder became a part of the compound.

Naming Binary Covalent Compounds

Covalent compounds are those formed between elements that are nonmetals. Some pairs of nonmetals can form more than one compound with each other. For example, nitrogen and oxygen can form N_2O, NO, NO_2, and N_2O_5. In the system you have learned so far, each of these compounds would be called nitrogen oxide. You would not know from that name what the composition of the compound is.

Figure 18
The presence of water changes this powder into a medium that can be used to create art.

Cultural Diversity

Silicon Dioxide The binary covalent compound silicon dioxide, SiO_2, also known as quartz or rock crystal, has been revered in many cultures since ancient times. Have students report on some of the legends associated with SiO_2. Japanese, ancient Greek, Cherokee Indian, Burmese, Irish, and Scottish are some of the cultures that have legends surrounding SiO_2. P

Text Question Answers

It will turn pink as the hydrate forms.

Resource Manager

Chapter Resources Booklet

Reinforcement, p. 29
Enrichment, p. 32
MiniLAB, p. 4

Using Prefixes Scientists use the Greek prefixes in **Table 5** to indicate how many atoms of each element are in a binary covalent compound. The nitrogen and oxygen compounds N_2O, NO, NO_2, and N_2O_5 would be named dinitrogen oxide, nitrogen oxide, nitrogen dioxide, and dinitrogen pentoxide. Notice that the last vowel of the prefix is dropped when the second element begins with a vowel as in pentoxide. Often the prefix *mono-* is omitted, although it is used for emphasis in some cases. Carbon monoxide is one example.

Reading Check *What prefix would be used for seven atoms of one element in a covalent compound?*

These same prefixes are used when naming the hydrates previously discussed. The main ionic compound is named the regular way, but the number of water molecules in the hydrate is indicated by the Greek prefix.

You have learned how to write formulas of binary ionic compounds and of compounds containing polyatomic ions. Using oxidation numbers to write formulas, you can predict the ratio in which atoms of elements might combine to form compounds. You also have seen how hydrates have water molecules as part of their structures and formulas. Finally, you saw how to use prefixes in naming binary covalent compounds. As you continue to study, you will see many uses of formulas.

Table 5 Prefixes for Covalent Compounds

Number of Atoms	Prefix
1	*mono-*
2	*di-*
3	*tri-*
4	*tetra-*
5	*penta-*
6	*hexa-*
7	*hepta-*
8	*octa-*

Section  Assessment

1. What compounds can be formed from element *X*, with oxidation numbers 3+ and 5+, and element *Z*, with oxidation numbers 2− and 3−? Write their formulas.
2. Write formulas for the following compounds: *potassium iodide, magnesium hydroxide, aluminum sulfate,* and *chlorine heptoxide.*
3. Write the names of these compounds: *KCl, CrO_3, $Ba(ClO_3)_2$, NH_4Cl,* and *PCl_3.*
4. Name $Mg_3(PO_4)_2 \cdot 4H_2O$, and write the formula for calcium nitrate trihydrate.
5. **Think Critically** Explain why sodium and potassium will or will not form a bond.

Skill Builder Activities

6. **Testing a Hypothesis** Design an experiment to distinguish between crystals that are hydrates and those that are not. Include crystals of iron(II) chloride, crystals of copper(II) nitrate, and crystals of sucrose. **For more help, refer to the** Science Skill Handbook.
7. **Solving One-Step Equations** The overall charge on the polyatomic sulfate ion, found in some acids, is 2−. Its formula is SO_4^{2-}. If the oxygen ion has a 2− oxidation number, determine the oxidation number of sulfur in this polyatomic ion. **For more help, refer to the** Math Skill Handbook.

Naming Binary Covalent Compounds

Reading Check

Answer hepta-

3 Assess

Reteach

Ask students why calcium chloride ($CaCl_2$) is named without using the prefix system shown in **Table 5,** while carbon tetrachloride (CCl_4) does use a prefix to designate the number of chlorine atoms. The prefix system is used for covalent compounds between nonmetals. $CaCl_2$ is ionic. L2

LS **Logical-Mathematical**

Challenge

Ask students to determine the type of bonding found in K_2CO_3. The compound has both ionic and covalent bonding. The bond between the K^+ ion and the CO_3^{2-} ion is ionic, and the bonds between carbon and oxygen in the polyatomic ion are covalent. L3

LS **Logical-Mathematical**

Assessment

Performance The common name for $Na_2B_4O_5(OH)_4 \cdot 8H_2O$ is borax. It is used as an important source of boron and can also be used as a washing powder. Ask students to determine the number of oxygen atoms in the molecule. 17 Use **PASC,** p.89

Answers to Section Assessment

1. X_2Z_3; XZ; X_2Z_5; X_3Z_5
2. KI; $Mg(OH)_2$; $Al_2(SO_4)_3$; ClO_7
3. potassium chloride; chromium(VI) oxide; barium chlorate; ammonium chloride; phosphorus trichloride
4. magnesium phosphate tetrahydrate; $Ca(NO_3)_2 \cdot 3H_2O$
5. Sodium and potassium will bond with atoms that are able to easily accept electrons. They would have a difficult time bonding with each other because both tend to lose electrons.
6. Determine the mass of the crystal, and then place it in a dry environment so that any condensation or water adhering to the outside of the crystal dries. Next, heat the dried compound, let it cool, and determine the mass of the cooled compound. If the material has a sharp change in mass, it may be a hydrate, as the drop in mass may indicate a change in the crystal structure, which released the water of hydration. A student also could add water to the heated residues to see whether they reform the original compounds. This would indicate that the original was a hydrate.
7. Oxygen contributes $4 \times -2 = -8$. The total charge is −2, so sulfur must contribute +6.

Activity BENCH TESTED

Recognize the Problem

Purpose

Students design and carry out an experiment to show how the melting properties of a substance relate to the type of bonding found in the substance.
L3 LS **Kinesthetic**

Process Skills

observing, inferring, comparing, making and using tables, forming a hypothesis, designing an experiment, interpreting data, measuring

Time Required

approximately 45 minutes

Safety Precautions

Students should be careful around the hot burner and the heated materials.

Form a Hypothesis

Possible Hypothesis

Students may hypothesize that the more easily a substance melts, the less attraction the particles in the substance have for each other.

Test Your Hypothesis

Possible Procedures

Heat the same amount of each substance. One lab partner can watch for the first sign of melting while the other times the experiment. Students might also note the length of time between the first observable melting and total melting.

Activity Design Your Own Experiment

Become a Bond Breaker

The basic structural units of ionic compounds are ions. For covalent substances, molecules make up the basic units. By using controlled heat to melt substances, you can test various compounds to rate the attractive forces between their basic units. Would a substance that is difficult to melt have strong forces or weak forces holding its basic units together?

Recognize the Problem

How do the attractive forces between ions compare to the attractive forces between molecules?

Form a Hypothesis

Based on what you know about ions and molecules, state a hypothesis about which generally would have stronger attractions between their structural units.

Goals

- **Observe** the effect of heat on melting points of selected substances.
- **Design** an experiment that allows you to make some inferences that relate ease of melting and forces of attraction between particles of a substance.

Possible Materials

small samples of crushed ice, table salt, and sugar
wire test-tube holder
test tubes
laboratory burner
stopwatch

Safety Precautions

Keep a safe distance from the open flame of the lab burner. Wear proper eye protection. Do not continue heating beyond 5 min.

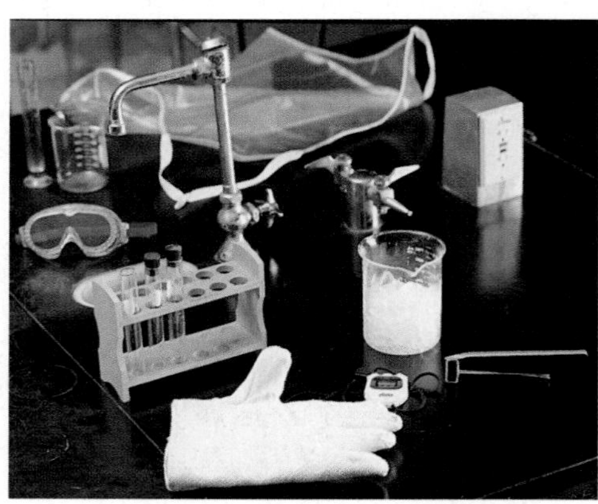

Teaching Strategies

- To avoid melting substances with low melting points too quickly, test tubes should be clean, dry, and at room temperature before starting the experiment.
- Review the chemical formulas of the substances being tested: sugar is $C_{12}H_{22}O_{11}$, water is H_2O, and salt is NaCl.

Data Table

Substance	Ionic or Covalent	Time to Melt
Ice	Covalent	Melts 1st
Salt	Ionic	Doesn't Melt
Sugar	Covalent	Melts 2nd

Test Your Hypothesis

Plan

1. As a group, agree upon and write a hypothesis statement.
2. As a group, write a detailed list of steps that are needed to test your hypothesis. Determine what your control will be.
3. As you heat materials in a test tube, what variables are held constant?
4. How will you time the heating of the individual substances?
5. Will you run any tests more than one time?
6. Make a list of materials that you will need to complete your experiment.
7. **Design** a data table in your Science Journal to record your observations.
8. Make sure your teacher approves your plan before you start.

Do

1. Carry out the experiment exactly as planned.
2. While you are observing the heating of each substance, think about the movement of the particles. Which particles are held together by ionic bonds? Which are made up of covalent molecules? How does that affect their movement?
3. Be sure to write down exactly how long it takes to melt each tested substances.

Analyze Your Data

1. **Compare** your results with those of other groups in the class.
2. **Classify** your tested substances as more likely ionic or covalent.
3. Which substances are generally more difficult to melt?
4. Did you have a control in this experiment? Variables?

Draw Conclusions

1. How did the results of your experiment support or disprove your hypothesis?
2. Sugar is known as a polar covalent compound. Knowing this, infer from your results how polarity affects melting point.

Communicating Your Data

Make a chart showing your results and pointing out ways to distinguish between the different kinds of bonds.

Resource Manager

Chapter Resources Booklet
Activity Worksheet, pp. 7–8

Communicating Your Data

Suggest that students use a computer spreadsheet program for making their charts.

Expected Outcome

The ice will melt first, followed by sugar. NaCl will not melt at temperatures reached by a typical burner.

Analyze Your Data

1. Results should be similar.
2. Ice, covalent; sugar, covalent; salt, ionic
3. Ionic substances are usually more difficult to melt because the network of attractions in an ionic crystal is difficult to break.
4. No, there was no control sample in this experiment. The controlled variables were the amount of the tested substances and constant position of the test tubes in the burner flame. The variable was the bonding of the substances being tested.

Error Analysis

Sources of possible error include using different amounts of each substance and heating the substances differently.

Draw Conclusions

1. Answers will vary depending on student hypotheses.
2. Both sugar and water are polar covalent compounds. Salt is ionic. From the melting of water, sugar, and salt, the student can reach no conclusions about the effect of polarity on melting point.

Assessment

Oral Have students display their data tables and compare the results. Then have them decide where the compound KI would likely fit and what type of bonding it would have. KI is ionic, but has slightly lower melting point than NaCl. Use **Performance Assessment in the Science Classroom**, p. 99.

Content Background

Glue has been around for a long time. Egyptian carvings dating back 3,300 years show figures gluing thin pieces of veneer to sycamore planks. Throughout history, most glues came from a variety of natural sources, including beeswax, flour paste, egg whites, cheese, and extracts from animal horns and fish. Only in the recent century did synthetic glues become more prominent. In addition to cyanoacrylate glues, the common household glues in use today include epoxies and aliphatics (common school glue). Glues work because they are able to seep into the crevices of a surface and form chemical welds to the molecules on that surface. Strong polymer chains give glues their strength and flexibility.

Discussion

Why would you have to be very careful if you used an instant glue to repair a broken object at home? Possible answers: If you spilled any, it could stick other things together, including your fingers. **What would be the advantages of using an instant glue rather than stitches for a cut?** Possible answers: It wouldn't hurt as much; you wouldn't have to have a shot to numb the area like you do before you get stitches.

Oops! Accidents in SCIENCE

SOMETIMES GREAT DISCOVERIES HAPPEN BY ACCIDENT!

A strong adhesive glue was a lucky accident

A Sticky Subject

596

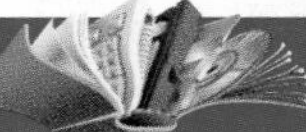

Resources for Teachers and Students

"Adhesion," Encyclopedia Brittanica.

The Encyclopedia of Modelmaking Techniques, by Christopher Payne and P. Quatro, 1996.

The Crafter's Guide to Glues, by Tammy Young, Chilton Book Company Co., 1995.

Sticky, Rigby Interactive Library, 1996.

In 1942, a research team was working on creating a new kind of glass. The group was working with some cyanoacrylate monomers (si uh noh A kruh layt • MAH nuh muhrz) which showed promise, but there was a problem that kept coming up. Everything the monomers touched stuck to everything else!

Cyanoacrylate is the chemical name for instant, super-type glues. The researcher was so focused on finding a different type of glass that at the time nobody recognized an important new adhesive. Not until a few years later.

Super-type glues make it possible to perfectly repair broken objects.

In 1952, a member of the research team, working on new materials for jet plane canopies, made a similar complaint. The ethyl cyanoacrylate they were working with again made everything stick together. This time, the insight stuck to the scientists like, well, like GLUE! "I began gluing everything I could lay my hands on—glass plates, rubber stoppers, metal spatulas, wood, paper, plastic. Everything stuck to everything, almost instantly, and with bonds I could not break apart," recalls the head of the research group.

Stick to It

Most adhesives, commonly called glues, are long chains of bonded molecules called polymers. Cyanoacrylate, however, exists as monomers—single molecules with double bonds. And it stays that way until it hits anything with moisture in it—like air. Yes, even the small amount of moisture in air and on the surfaces of most materials is enough to dissolve the double bonds in the monomers of cyanoacrylate, making them join together in long chains. The chains bond to surfaces as they polymerize.

The discovery of cyanoacrylates had an immediate impact on the automobile and airplane industries. And it soon "held" a spot in almost every household toolbox. Since the 1990s, however, cyanoacrylate glues are also finding a place in the doctor's office. A doctor can apply a thin layer of instant glue instead of putting stitches in a cut. This specially made medical glue was approved by the U.S. Food and Drug Administration in 1998. Cyanoacrylates are also used in dental and eye surgery and to stop bleeding in internal organs.

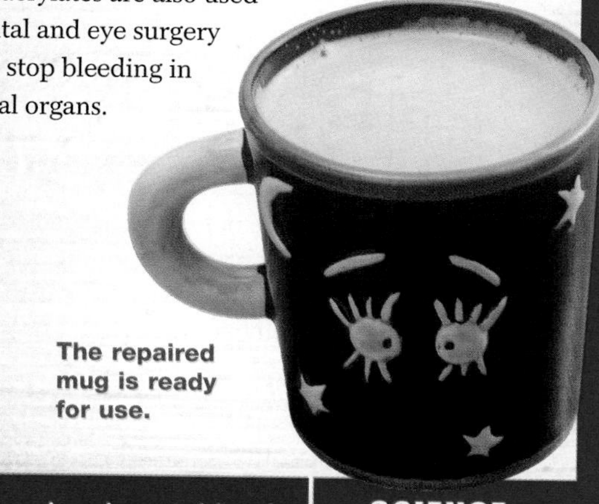

The repaired mug is ready for use.

CONNECTIONS **Take Note** **Visit a store and make a table of different kinds of glues. List their common names, their chemical names, what they are made of, how long it takes them to set, and the types of surfaces for which they are recommended. Note any safety precautions.**

SCIENCE Online
For more information, visit science.glencoe.com

Activity

Let small groups of students experiment with their own glue. Give each group 15 mL of unflavored gelatin in a small beaker. Pour 25 mL of boiling water into the gelatin. CAUTION: Be careful with the hot water. Have students stir the mixture until the gelatin dissolves. Let them use paintbrushes to apply the glue to various types of materials such as paper, wood, and plastic to see which kinds of materials the glue will bond together.

Analyze the Event

Explain to students that Louis Pasteur was a French scientist who discovered, among other things, the rabies vaccine and the pasteurization process for milk. Write the following quote of Pasteur's on the board: "In the field of observation, chance favors only the prepared mind." Ask students to brainstorm what they think the quote means and how it applies to this feature. Possible answers: The first goup of researchers didn't realize the possibilities of the discovery, but the later group did, so the later group had "prepared minds."

CONNECTIONS **Take Note** Tell students to pay careful attention to the recommended uses for each type of glue. Ask students why one glue cannot meet all people's needs. Possible answers: Some glues can be toxic and so wouldn't be useful for gluing drinking cups, as shown in the feature. Some glues might react chemically with paper or wood. Some glues aren't waterproof.

Resource Manager 

Lab Management and Safety, p. 49

Chapter 19 Study Guide

Reviewing Main Ideas

Preview

Students can answer the questions in their Science Journals. Discuss the answers as you go through the chapter. **LS Linguistic**

Review

Students can write their answers, then compare them with those of other students. **LS Interpersonal**

Reteach

Students can look at the illustrations and describe details that support the main ideas of the chapter. **LS Visual-Spatial**

Answers to Chapter Review

Section 1

2. It contains one large oxygen atom bonded to two smaller hydrogen atoms.

Section 2

1. ionic

Section 3

3. calcium carbonate

Chapter 19 Study Guide

Reviewing Main Ideas

Section 1 Stability in Bonding

1. The properties of compounds are generally different from the properties of the elements they contain.
2. A chemical formula for a compound indicates the composition of a unit of the compound. *What can you infer about the composition of water from the model pictured?*

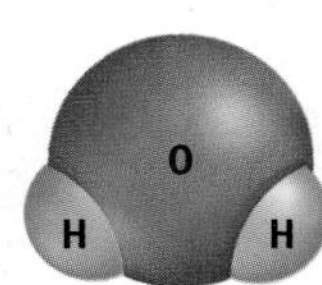

3. Chemical bonding occurs because atoms of most elements become more stable by gaining, losing, or sharing electrons in order to obtain a stable outer energy level.

Section 2 Types of Bonds

1. Ionic bonds between atoms are formed by the attraction between ions. Covalent bonds are formed by the sharing of electrons. *Which kind of bond is shown in the dot diagram?*

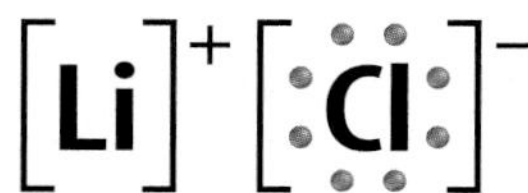

2. Ionic bonding occurs between charged particles called ions and produces ionic compounds. Covalent bonding produces units called molecules and occurs between nonmetallic elements.
3. The unequal sharing of electrons produces compounds that contain polar bonds, and the equal sharing of electrons produces nonpolar compounds.

Section 3 Writing Formulas and Naming Compounds

1. An oxidation number indicates how many electrons an atom has gained, lost, or shared when bonding with other atoms.
2. In the formula of an ionic compound, the element or ion with the positive oxidation number is written first, followed by the one with the negative oxidation number.
3. The name of a binary compound is derived from the names of the two elements that compose the compound. *What is the name of chalk, shown below? It contains the CO_3^- ion and the Ca^{2+} ion.*

4. A hydrate is a compound that has water chemically attached to its ions and written into its formula.
5. Greek prefixes are used in the names of covalent compounds. These indicate the number of each atom present.

FOLDABLES Reading & Study Skills — After You Read

Use the chemical formulas on your Foldable to test your knowledge. See how many you can name and identify as common objects.

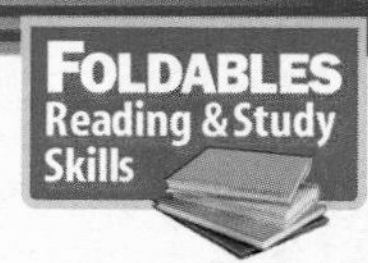

FOLDABLES Reading & Study Skills — After You Read

After students have read the chapter and completed the Foldable described in Before You Read, have them do the activity on the student page.

Dinah Zike

Visualizing Main Ideas

Complete the following concept map.

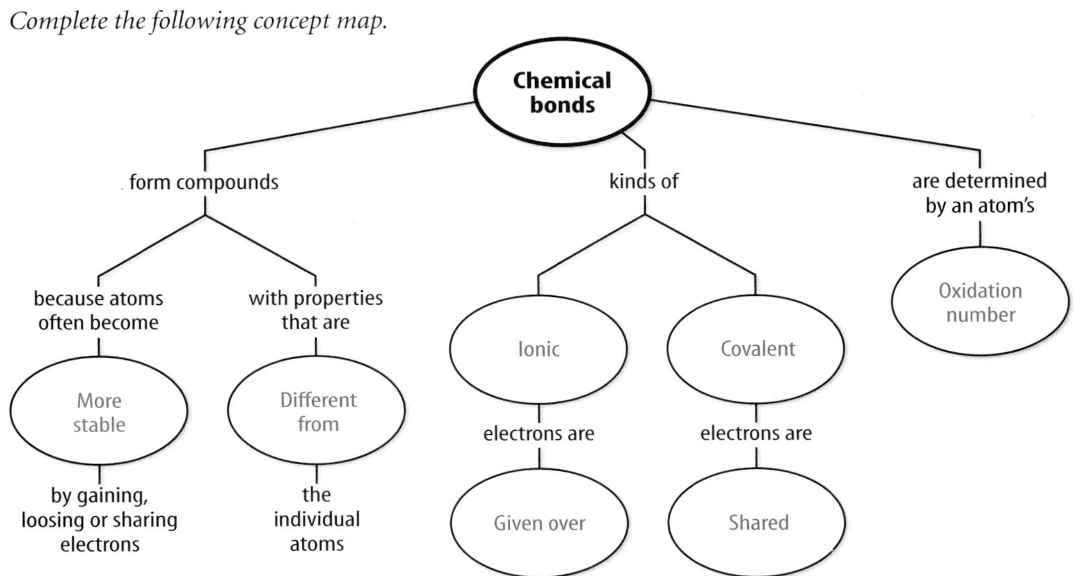

Vocabulary Review

Vocabulary Words

a. binary compound
b. chemical bond
c. chemical formula
d. chemically stable
e. covalent bond
f. hydrate
g. ion
h. ionic bond
i. molecule
j. nonpolar molecule
k. oxidation number
l. polar molecule
m. polyatomic ion

Study Tip

Read the chapters before you go over them in class. Being familiar with the material before your teacher explains it gives you a better understanding and provides you with a good opportunity to ask questions.

Using Vocabulary

Match each phrase with a vocabulary word.

1. a charged group of atoms
2. a compound composed of two elements
3. a molecule with partially charged ends
4. a positively or negatively charged atom
5. a chemical bond between oppositely charged ions
6. a bond formed from shared electrons
7. crystalline substance that contains water
8. outer energy level is filled with electrons
9. shows an element's combining ability
10. tells which elements are in a compound and their ratios

Chapter 19 Study Guide

Visualizing Main Ideas

See student page.

Vocabulary Review

Using Vocabulary

1. polyatomic ion
2. binary compound
3. polar molecule
4. ion
5. ionic bond
6. covalent bond
7. hydrate
8. chemically stable
9. oxidation number
10. chemical formula

Checking Concepts

1. B
2. C
3. C
4. C
5. A
6. D
7. B
8. B
9. A
10. D

Thinking Critically

11. $[:Cl:]^{-}Mg^{2+}[:Cl:]^{-}$
12. $NaHCO_3$; $HC_2H_3O_2$
13. Tl_2CO_3
14. calcium phosphate
15. $(NH_4)_2SO_4$

Chapter 19 Assessment

Checking Concepts

Choose the word or phrase that best answers the question.

1. Which elements are least likely to react with other elements?
   A) metals
   B) noble gases
   C) nonmetals
   D) transition elements
2. What is the oxidation number of Fe in the compound Fe_2S_3?
   A) 1^+
   B) 2^+
   C) 3^+
   D) 4^+
3. What is the name of CuO?
   A) copper oxide
   B) copper(I) oxide
   C) copper(II) oxide
   D) copper(III) oxide
4. What is the formula for copper(II) chlorate?
   A) $CuClO_3$
   B) CuCl
   C) $Cu(ClO_3)_2$
   D) $CuCl_2$
5. Which of the following formulas represents a nonpolar molecule?
   A) N_2
   B) H_2O
   C) NaCl
   D) HCl
6. How many electrons are in the outer energy level of Group 17 elements?
   A) 1
   B) 2
   C) 17
   D) 7
7. Which is a binary ionic compound?
   A) O_2
   B) NaF
   C) H_2SO_4
   D) $Cu(NO_3)_2$
8. Which of these is an example of an anhydrous compound?
   A) H_2O
   B) $CaSO_4$
   C) $CuSO_4 \cdot 5H_2O$
   D) $CaSO_4 \cdot 2H_2O$
9. Which of the following is an atom that has gained an electron?
   A) negative ion
   B) positive ion
   C) polar molecule
   D) nonpolar molecule
10. Which of these is an example of a covalent compound?
    A) sodium chloride
    B) calcium fluoride
    C) calcium chloride
    D) sulfur dioxide

Thinking Critically

11. Anhydrous magnesium chloride is used to make wood fireproof. Draw a dot diagram of magnesium chloride.
12. Baking soda, which is sodium hydrogen carbonate, and vinegar, which contains hydrogen acetate, can be used as household cleaners. Write the chemical formulas for these two compounds.
13. Artificial diamonds are made using thallium carbonate. If thallium has an oxidation number of 1+, what is the formula for the compound?
14. The formula for a compound that composes kidney stones is $Ca_3(PO_4)_2$. What is the chemical name of this compound?
15. Ammonium sulfate is used as a fertilizer. What is its chemical formula?

Developing Skills

16. **Comparing and Contrasting** Compare and contrast polar and nonpolar molecules.
17. **Interpreting Scientific Illustrations** Write the name and formula for the compound illustrated to the right.

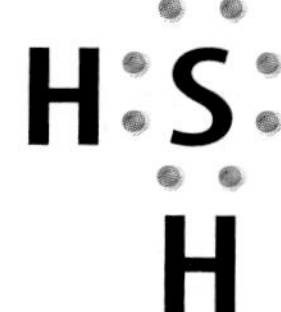

18. **Drawing Conclusions** Ammonia gas and water react to form household ammonia, which contains NH_4^+ and OH^- ions. If the formula for water is H_2O, what is the formula for ammonia gas?

Chapter Assessment Planner

Portfolio Encourage students to place in their portfolios one or two items of what they consider to be their best work. Examples include:

- Assessment, p. 578
- Science Journal, p. 583
- Challenge, p. 586
- Cultural Diversity, p. 592

Performance Additional performance assessments, Performance Task Assessment Lists, and rubrics for evaluating these activities can be found in Glencoe's **Performance Assessment in the Science Classroom.**

Performance Assessment

20. Predicting Elements from one family (vertical row) of the periodic table generally combine with elements from another family and polyatomic ions in the same ratio. For example, one calcium atom combines with two chlorine atoms to give $CaCl_2$ (calcium chloride) as it does with two fluorine atoms to give CaF_2 (calcium fluoride). Using a periodic table as a guide, predict which of the two compounds at the right is more likely to exist, based upon the given formula.

Which compounds exist?

Formula	Possible Compounds
SF_6	AlF_6 or TeF_6
K_2SO_4	Na_2SO_4 or Ba_2SO_4
CO_2	CCl_2 or CS_2
$CaCO_3$	OCO_3 or $BaCO_3$

21. Model One common form of phosphorus, white phosphorus, has the formula P_4 and is formed by four covalently bonded phosphorus atoms. Make a model of this molecule, showing that all four atoms are now chemically stable.

22. Drawing Conclusions You see the name of a compound called copper (II) sulfate written on a bottle. What is the charge of the copper ion? What is charge of the sulfate ion?

TECHNOLOGY

Go to the Glencoe Science Web site at **science.glencoe.com** or use the **Glencoe Science CD-ROM** for additional chapter assessment.

Test Practice

Cindy constructed a graph of ionization energy, which is the energy required to remove one electron and also the number of outer electrons an atom has in relation to its atomic number. Her finished graphs are shown in the diagram below.

Electron Removal Energy v. Atomic Number

Study the diagram and answer the following questions.

1. A reasonable hypothesis based on these data is that as the number of outer electrons increases, the _____.

A) energy required to remove one electron decreases.
B) energy required to remove one electron increases.
C) atomic number decreases.
D) potential to form ions increases.

2. The noble gases have full outer energy levels. Which atomic numbers on the graph represent noble gases?

F) 3 and 11
G) 7 and 15
H) 9 and 17
J) 10 and 18

Chapter 19 Assessment

Test Practice

The Test-Taking Tip was written by The Princeton Review, the nation's leader in test preparation.

1. B
2. J

Developing Skills

16. A polar molecule has opposite charges (positive and negative) on each end because of an unequal sharing of electrons. A nonpolar molecule does not have oppositely charged ends because the electrons involved are shared equally.
17. hydrogen sulfide; H_2S
18. NH_3

Performance Assessment

20. TeF6, Na2SO4, CS2, BaCO3 Use **PASC,** p. 93.
21. :P::P:
:P::P: Use **PASC,** p. 123.
22. copper: 2+; sulfate: 2− Use **PASC,** p. 89.

Assessment Resources

Reproducible Masters

Chapter Resources Booklet
Chapter Review, pp. 37–38
Chapter Tests, pp. 39–42
Assessment Transparency Activity, p. 49

Glencoe Science Web site
Interactive Tutor
Chapter Quizzes

Glencoe Technology
Assessment Transparency
Interactive CD-ROM Chapter Quizzes
ExamView Pro Test Bank
Vocabulary PuzzleMaker Software
MindJogger Videoquiz DVD/VHS

Reading Comprehension

QUESTION 1: C

Students must recall the chronology of events in the passage to identify which answer choice occurred first.

- Choice A: No; this event occurred after Mendeleev made his predictions.
- Choice B: No; this happened much later in the passage.
- Choice C: Yes; this event occurred first in the passage.
- Choice D: No; this happened much later in the passage. **Objective 2**

QUESTION 2: F

Students must use clues from the passage, such as *made . . . in the laboratory*, to identify that the best meaning of the word *artificially* is choice F. **Objective 1**

Teaching Tip

Students should use key words in the questions to locate important information in the passages.

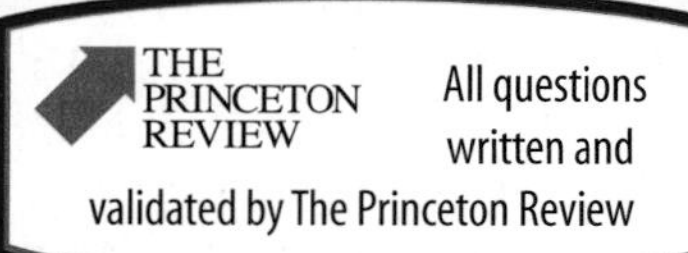

All questions written and validated by The Princeton Review

Standardized Test Practice

Reading Comprehension

Read the passage. Then read each question that follows the passage. Decide which is the best answer to each question.

Mendeleev and the Periodic Table

By 1860, scientists had discovered a total of 63 chemical elements. Dmitri Mendeleev, a Russian chemist, thought that there had to be some order among the elements.

He made a card for each element. On the card, he listed the physical and chemical properties of the element, such as atomic mass, density, color, and melting point. He also wrote each element's combining power, or its ability to form compounds with other elements.

When he arranged the cards in order of increasing atomic mass, Mendeleev noticed that the elements followed a periodic, or repeating, pattern. Every seven cards, the properties repeated. He placed each group of seven cards in rows, one under another so that the elements in a column, or group, had similar chemical and physical properties.

In a few places, Mendeleev had to move his cards one space to the left or right to follow the pattern. This left a few empty spaces. He predicted that these spaces would be filled with elements that were unknown. He even predicted the properties of the unknown elements. Fifteen years later, three new elements were discovered and placed in the empty spaces of the Periodic Table. Their physical and chemical properties agreed with Mendeleev's predictions.

Today there are more than 100 known elements. An extra column has been added for the noble gases, a group of elements not known to exist in Mendeleev's time. Members of this group almost never combine with other elements. As new elements are discovered or are made <u>artificially</u>, scientists can place them in their proper place on the Periodic Table thanks to Mendeleev.

Test-Taking Tip To answer questions about sequence of events, make a timeline of what happened in each paragraph of the passage.

All elements can be organized according to their physical and chemical properties.

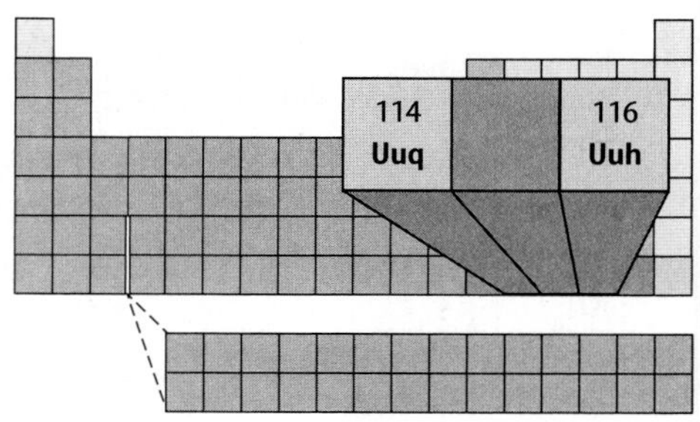

1. Which of the following occurred FIRST in the passage?

A) Three new elements were discovered fifteen years after Mendeleev developed the Periodic Table.
B) The noble gases were discovered and placed in the Periodic Table.
C) Mendeleev predicted properties of the unknown elements.
D) New elements were made in the laboratory and then placed in the Periodic Table.

2. The word <u>artificially</u> in this passage means _____.

F) unnaturally
G) artistically
H) atomically
J) radioactively

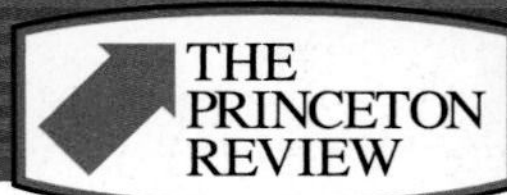

Reasoning and Skills

Read each question and choose the best answer.

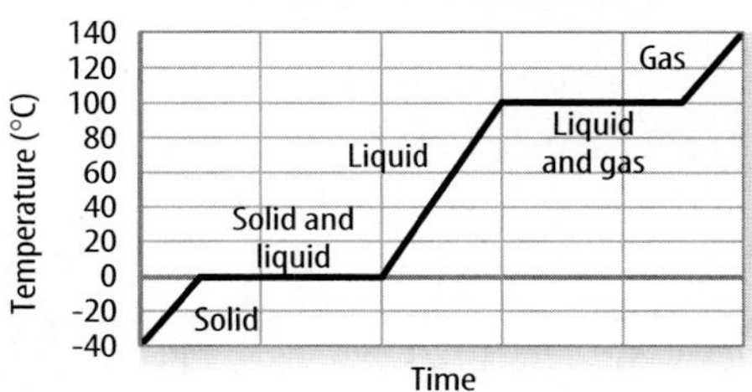

1. The graph shows the change in temperature as ice is heated until it changes completely to gas. How much higher than the starting temperature is the boiling point?

A) 40°C
B) 100°C
C) 140°C
D) 180°C

Test-Taking Tip Boiling point is the flat section of the graph where liquid changes to gas.

2. What is being measured in the illustration?

F) boiling point
G) melting point
H) density
J) flammability

Test-Taking Tip Think about what you might be measuring when you use a thermometer in a liquid that you are heating.

Selected Properties of Selected Pure Substances

Substance	Melting Point (°C)	Boiling Point (°C)	Color
Aluminum	660.4	2467	silver metallic
Argon	-189.2	-185.7	colorless
Mercury	-38.8	356.6	silver metallic
Water	0	100	colorless

3. Room temperature is about 20°C. In the table, which substance is a solid at room temperature?

A) aluminum
B) argon
C) mercury
D) water

Test-Taking Tip Remember that negative temperatures are below zero.

Read this question carefully before writing your answer on a separate sheet of paper.

4. The density of pure water is 1.00 g/cm^3. Since ice floats on water, we know that the density of ice is *less* than that of water. Design an experiment to determine the density of an ice cube. List all the necessary steps.
(Volume = Length × Width × Height;
Density = Mass / Volume.)

Test-Taking Tip Make sure to consider all the information provided in the question.

Standardized Test Practice

Reasoning and Skills

Question 1: C

Students need to retrieve information from the graph in order to identify the correct answer. Since the starting temperature was −40°C and the boiling point is 100°C, the correct answer is choice C.

Question 2: F

Students must look carefully at the diagram. Because the substance in the beaker is already a liquid and appears to be boiling, the correct answer is choice F.

Question 3: A

Students must retrieve information from the table in order to identify the correct answer. Because there is only one substance with a melting point greater than 20°C, the correct answer is choice A.

Question 4: Answers will vary.

Answers should include measuring the length, width, and height of the ice cube with a metric ruler in order to find volume. In addition, the mass of the ice cube should be determined using a triple-beam balance. After these measurements have been determined, students should describe how to calculate volume and density.

UNIT 5

Unit Contents

Pre-Reading Activity

Have students identify things they know to be made of organic compounds.

UNIT 5 Diversity of Matter

How Are Billiards & Bottles Connected?

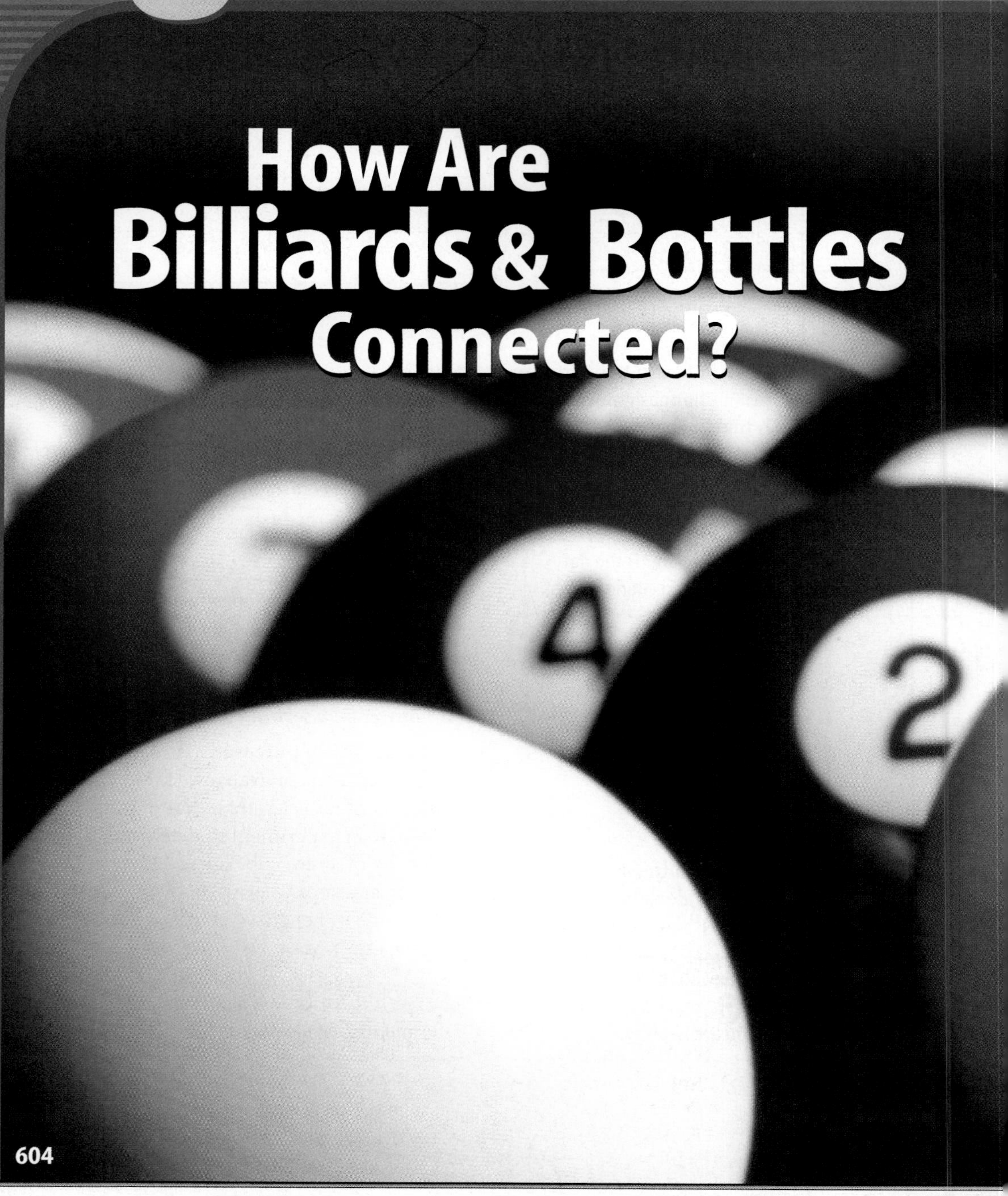

604

Teacher to Teacher

"After introducing the nomenclature for organic compounds, I have students work in pairs to build models of a number of progressively difficult compounds using a kit. You can also use small, different-colored marshmallows and toothpicks."

Tom McCarthy, Ph.D., Teacher
Saint Edward's School
Vero Beach, FL

NATIONAL GEOGRAPHIC

Billiards, a popular table game of the 1800s, used balls carved from ivory. In the 1860s, an ivory shortage prompted one billiard-ball manufacturer to offer a reward of $10,000 to anyone who could come up with a suitable substitute. In an attempt to win the prize, an inventor combined certain organic compounds, put them into a mold, and subjected them to heat and pressure. The result was a hard, shiny lump that sparked a major new industry—the plastics industry. By the mid-1900s, chemists had invented many different kinds of moldable plastic. Today, plastic is made into countless products—everything from car parts to soda bottles.

SCIENCE CONNECTION

POLYMERS Plastics are polymers—long molecules made up of smaller units called monomers. By using different monomers, it's possible to create plastics with different characteristics. Explore your home or school and make a list of plastic items. How do the physical characteristics of different plastics—hardness, flexibility, and so forth—relate to their function? Using your list as a reference, write a description of one part of your day, identifying all the plastics you use.

SCIENCE Online

Internet Addresses

Explore the Glencoe Science Web site at **science.glencoe.com** to find out more about topics in this unit.

Introducing the Unit

How Are Billiards & Bottles Connected?

- Ask students how they can identify plastics. Have them write down their thoughts and revise them as they study more about different types of materials.
- Ask students to define the term *diverse*. Emphasize to students that matter is diverse, and different types of matter can be classified into even more diverse categories.
- Ask students how the plastic in a billiard ball differs from that in a bottle. Point out that the term *plastic* refers to a type of material, not a specific one.

SCIENCE CONNECTION

Activity

Tell students to include on their lists items that contain plastic parts but might not be entirely plastic. Encourage students to use the recycling codes on certain plastics to help classify them. The codes consist of a number contained in a triangle made from three arrows. Not all plastic items are recyclable and contain a code, but many do.

Section/Objectives	Standards		Activities/Features
	National	State/Local	
Chapter Opener	See p. 37T for a Key to Standards.		**Explore Activity:** Observe colorful clues, p. 607 **Before You Read,** p. 607
Section 1 Metals 2 sessions 1 block 1. **Describe** the properties of a typical metal. 2. **Identify** the alkali metals and alkaline earth metals. 3. **Differentiate** among three groups of transition elements.	National Content Standards: UCP5, A1, B1 (5–8), B2 (9–12)		**MiniLAB:** Discovering What's in Cereal, p. 612 **Earth Science Integration,** p. 614
Section 2 Nonmetals 3 sessions 1.5 blocks 1. **Recognize** hydrogen as a nonmetal. 2. **Compare and contrast** properties of the halogens. 3. **Describe** properties and uses of the noble gases.	National Content Standards: UCP5, A1, B1 (5–8), B2, B3, (9–12)		**MiniLAB:** Identifying Chloride in Your Water, p. 618 **Environmental Science Integration,** p. 619 **Activity:** What type is it?, p. 621
Section 3 Mixed Groups 3 sessions 1.5 blocks 1. **Distinguish** among metals, nenmetals, and metalloids. 2. **Describe** the nature of allotropes. 3. **Recognize** the significance of differences in crystal structure in carbon. 4. **Understand** the importance of synthetic elements.	National Content Standards: UCP5, A1, B1 (5–8), B2, B3, (9–12), E2, F5 (5–8), F6 (9–12), G3		**Science Online,** p. 624 **Math Skills Activity:** Using Circle Graphs to Illustrate Data, p. 625 **Visualizing the Discovery of Elements,** p. 628 **Science Online,** p. 629 **Activity:** Slippery Carbon, p. 630 **Science and History:** The Gas that Glows, p. 632

Activity Materials	Reproducible Resources	Section Assessment	Technology
Explore Activity: tongs; paper clip; lab burner; copper (II) sulfate, strontium chloride, and sodium chloride solution	**Chapter Resource Booklet** Foldables Worksheet, p. 17 Note-taking Worksheets, pp. 33–36	GLENCOE'S ASSESSMENT ADVANTAGE	
MiniLAB: tape; magnet; pencil; dry, fortified cold cereal; plastic bag; deep wbowl, water	**Chapter Resource Booklet** Transparency Activity, p. 46 MiniLAB, p. 3 Enrichment, p. 30 Reinforcement, p. 27 Directed Reading, p. 20 **Cultural Diversity,** p. 35 **Science Inquiry Labs,** p. 47	**Portfolio** Assessment, p. 615 **Performance** MiniLAB, p. 612 Skill Builder Activities, p. 615 **Content** Section Assessment, p. 615	Section Focus Transparency Interactive CD-ROM/DVD Guided Reading Audio Program
MiniLAB: 3 test tubes, chloride standard solution, distilled water, drinking water, silver nitrate solution **Activity:** samples of C, Mg, Al, S, and Sn; dish for each sample, conductivity tester, spatula, hammer	**Chapter Resource Booklet** Transparency Activity, p. 47 MiniLAB, p. 4 Enrichment, p. 31 Reinforcement, p. 28 Directed Reading, p. 20 Lab Activity, pp. 9–12 Activity Worksheet, pp. 5–6 **Science Inquiry Labs,** p. 47	**Portfolio** Environmental Science Integration, p. 619 **Performance** MiniLAB, p. 618 Skill Builder Activities, p. 620 **Content** Section Assessment, p. 620	Section Focus Transparency Interactive CD-ROM/DVD Guided Reading Audio Program
Activity: thin spaghetti, small gumdrops, thin polystyrene sheets, flat cardboard, scissors *Need materials?* Contact Science Kit at 1-800-828-7777 or www.sciencekit.com on the Internet.	**Chapter Resource Booklet** Transparency Activity, p. 48 Enrichment, p. 32 Reinforcement, p. 29 Directed Reading, pp. 21, 22 Transparency Activity, pp. 49–51 Lab Activity, pp. 13–16 Activity Worksheet, pp. 7–8 **Mathematics Skill Activities,** p. 5	**Portfolio** Extension, p. 625 **Performance** Math Skills Activity, p. 625 Skill Builder Activities, p. 629 **Content** Section Assessment, p. 629	Section Focus Transparency Teaching Transparency Interactive CD-ROM/DVD Guided Reading Audio Program

End of Chapter Assessment

GLENCOE'S ASSESSMENT ADVANTAGE

Blackline Masters	Technology	Professional Series
Chapter Resources Booklet Chapter Review, pp. 39–40 Chapter Tests, pp. 41–44 **Standardized Test Practice by The Princeton Review,** pp. 84–87	MindJogger Videoquiz CD-ROM Explorations and Quizzes Vocabulary Puzzle Makers ExamView Pro Test Bank Interactive Lesson Planner Interactive Teacher's Edition	Performance Assessment in the Science Classroom (PASC)

Transparencies

Section Focus

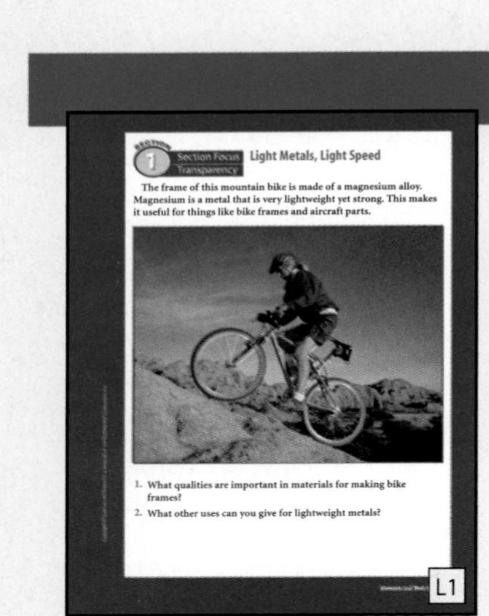
Section Focus Transparency 1 — Light Metals, Light Speed

The frame of this mountain bike is made of a magnesium alloy. Magnesium is a metal that is very lightweight yet strong. This makes it useful for things like bike frames and aircraft parts.

1. What qualities are important in materials for making bike frames?
2. What other uses can you give for lightweight metals?

L1

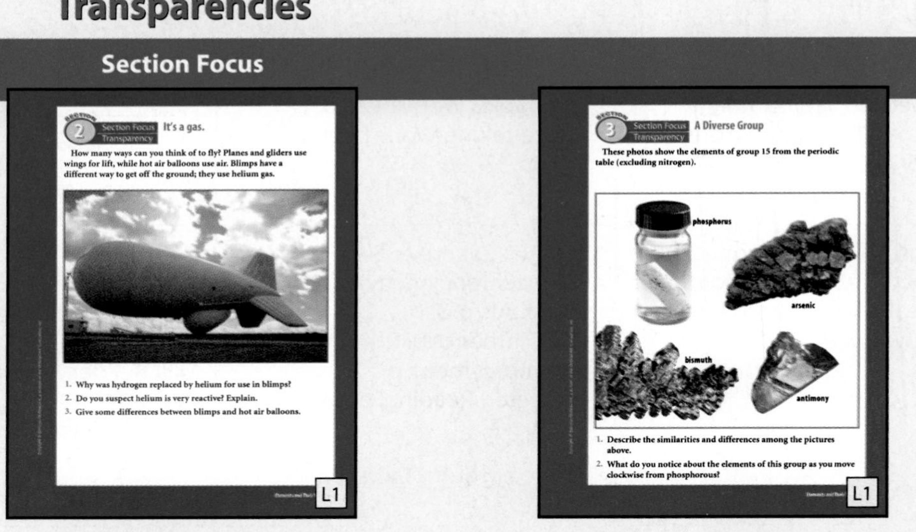
Section Focus Transparency 2 — It's a gas.

How many ways can you think of to fly? Planes and gliders use wings for lift, while hot air balloons use air. Blimps have a different way to get off the ground; they use helium gas.

1. Why was hydrogen replaced by helium for use in blimps?
2. Do you suspect helium is very reactive? Explain.
3. Give some differences between blimps and hot air balloons.

L1

Section Focus Transparency 3 — A Diverse Group

These photos show the elements of group 15 from the periodic table (excluding nitrogen).

1. Describe the similarities and differences among the pictures above.
2. What do you notice about the elements of this group as you move clockwise from phosphorous?

L1

This is a representation of key blackline masters available in the Teacher Classroom Resources. See Resource Manager boxes within the chapter for additional information.

Assessment

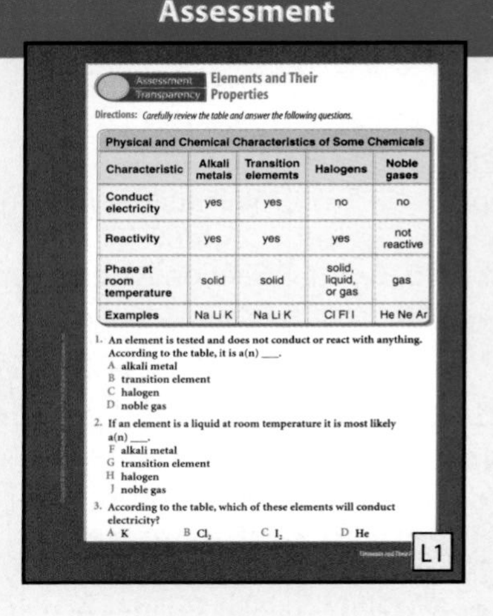
Assessment Transparency — Elements and Their Properties

Directions: *Carefully review the table and answer the following questions.*

Physical and Chemical Characteristics of Some Chemicals				
Characteristic	Alkali metals	Transition elements	Halogens	Noble gases
Conduct electricity	yes	yes	no	no
Reactivity	yes	yes	yes	not reactive
Phase at room temperature	solid	solid	solid, liquid, or gas	gas
Examples	Na Li K	Na Li K	Cl Fl I	He Ne Ar

1. An element is tested and does not conduct or react with anything. According to the table, it is a(n) ___.
   A alkali metal
   B transition element
   C halogen
   D noble gas
2. If an element is a liquid at room temperature it is most likely a(n) ___.
   F alkali metal
   G transition element
   H halogen
   J noble gas
3. According to the table, which of these elements will conduct electricity?
   A K B Cl_2 C I_2 D He

L1

Teaching

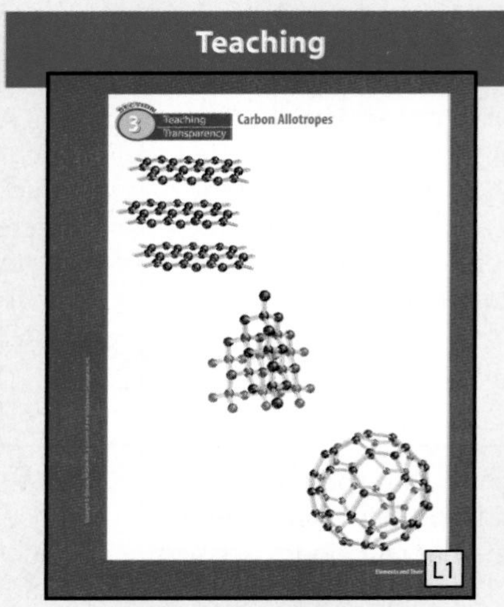
Teaching Transparency 3 — Carbon Allotropes

L1

Key to Teaching Strategies

The following designations will help you decide which activities are appropriate for your students.

- L1 Level 1 activities should be appropriate for students with learning difficulties.
- L2 Level 2 activities should be within the ability range of all students.
- L3 Level 3 activities are designed for above-average students.
- ELL ELL activities should be within the ability range of English Language Learners.
- COOP LEARN Cooperative Learning activities are designed for small group work.
- LS Multiple Learning Styles logos are used throughout to indicate strategies that address different learning styles.
- P These strategies represent student products that can be placed into a best-work portfolio.

Hands-on Activities

Activity Worksheets

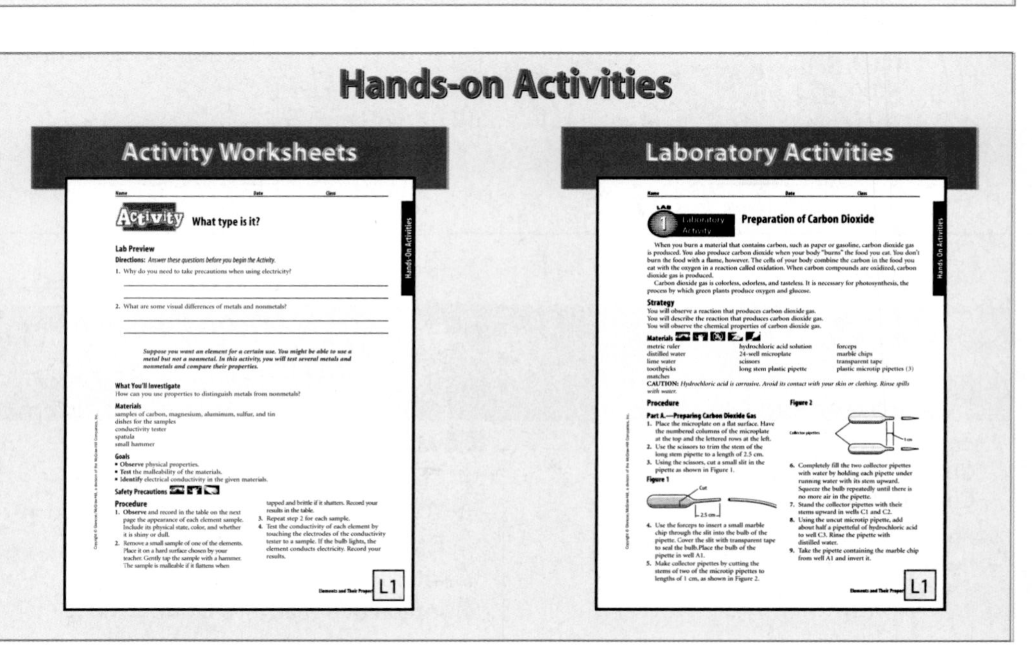
Activity — What type is it?

Lab Preview

Directions: *Answer these questions before you begin the Activity.*

1. Why do you need to take precautions when using electricity?
2. What are some visual differences of metals and nonmetals?

L1

Laboratory Activities

Laboratory Activity 1 — Preparation of Carbon Dioxide

L1

Meeting Different Ability Levels

Content Outline

Note-taking Worksheet — Elements and Their Properties

Section 1 Metals

L1

Reinforcement

Section 1 Reinforcement — Metals

L1

Directed Reading

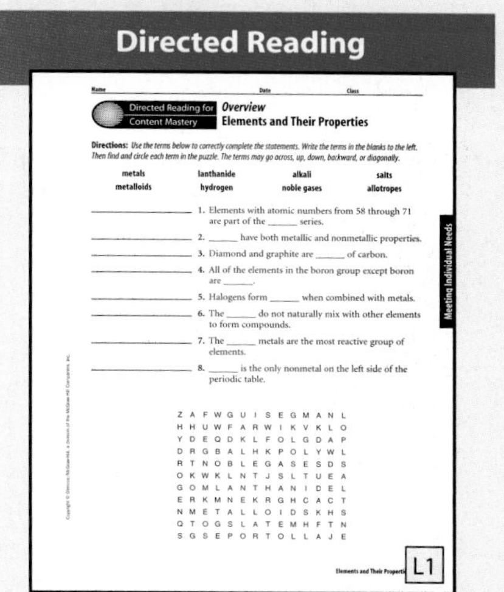

Directed Reading for Content Mastery — Overview — Elements and Their Properties

L1

Enrichment

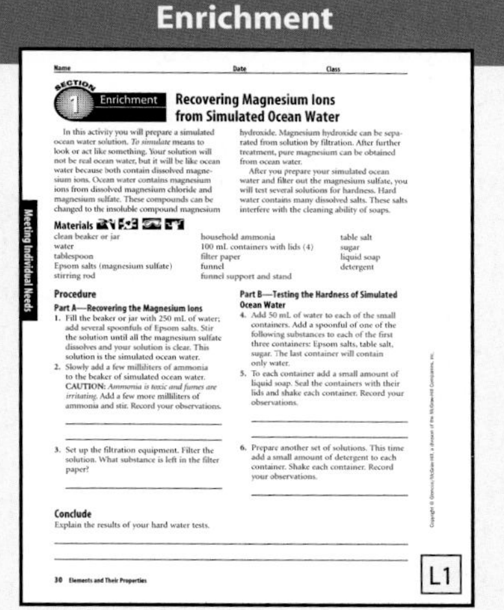

Section 1 Enrichment — Recovering Magnesium Ions from Simulated Ocean Water

L1

Spanish Directed Reading

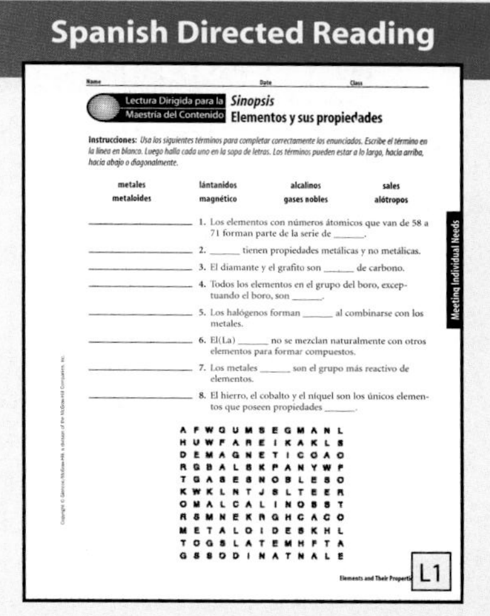

Lectura Dirigida para la Maestría del Contenido — Sinopsis — Elementos y sus propiedades

L1

Assessment

Chapter Tests

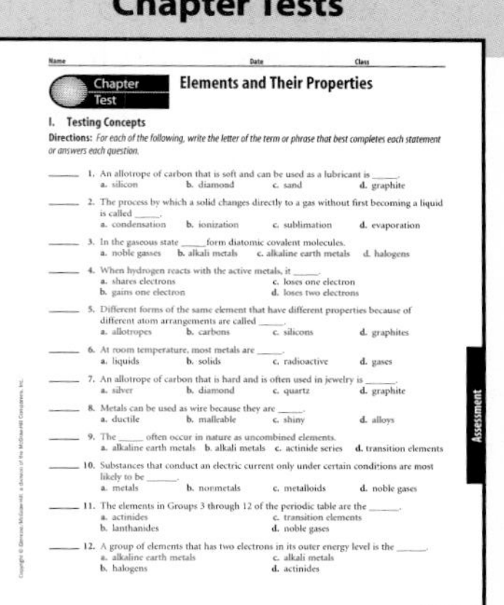

Chapter Test — Elements and Their Properties

I. Testing Concepts

L1

Test Practice Workbook

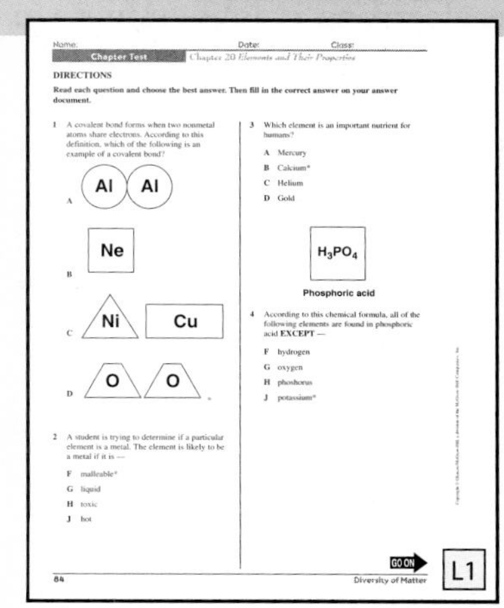

Chapter Test — Chapter 20 Elements and Their Properties

L1

Chapter Review

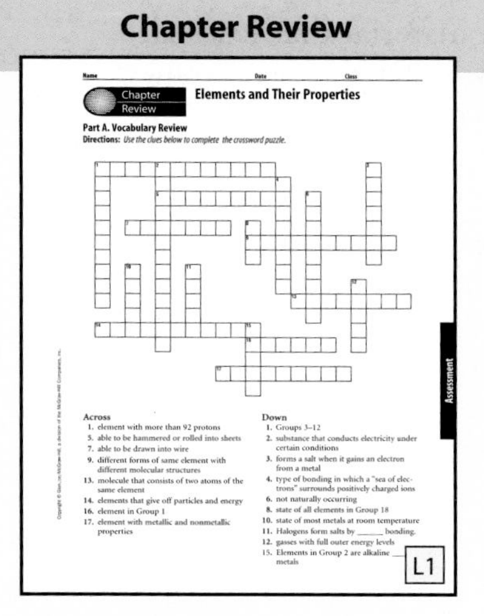

Chapter Review — Elements and Their Properties

Part A. Vocabulary Review

L1

Science Content Background

SECTION 1

Metals

Properties of Metals

The families of elements found on the left side of the periodic table are the metals. Elements whose atoms have identical arrangements of electrons in their highest energy levels have similar properties and make up a family of elements in the periodic table (vertical columns). On Earth, over 90 elements occur naturally. However, the number of known elements, 118 at this time, changes each time scientists create a new one using powerful accelerators.

Fun Fact

Of the 90 or so naturally occurring elements, only four are liquid near room temperature: mercury, gallium, bromine, and cesium.

The sections of the periodic table reflect the electron configurations of the elements and the sublevels occupied by the electrons. It is the electron configuration of the atom that determines its chemical reactivity. For every principle quantum number (period, or horizontal row), there are sublevels designated by letters, such as s, p, d, and f.

Metallic Bonding

Metallic bonding is partly responsible for a metal's ability to conduct electricity. In recent years, much research has been done with superconductivity.

A superconductor is a material that loses all electrical resistance below a characteristic temperature call the superconducting transition temperature. This phenomenon was discovered in 1911 by the Dutch physicist Heike Kamerlingh Onnes, who found that mercury abruptly loses its electrical resistance when it is cooled with liquid helium to 4.2K (−229 degrees Celsius). Below its superconducting transition temperature, a superconductor becomes a perfect conductor, and an electric current, once started, flows indefinitely without loss of energy.

Since 1911, scientists have been searching for materials that superconduct at higher temperatures, and more than 6000 superconductors are now known.

One of the most amazing properties of a superconductor is its ability to levitate a magnet. When a magnet is lowered toward it, the superconductor and magnet repel each other, and the magnet hovers above the superconductor as though suspended in midair. Superconducting magnets are used in magnetic resonance imaging (MRI) instruments, widely used in medical diagnosis.

The Alkali Metals

The alkali metals have one electron in an outer s orbital. This single electron is in a higher energy level than any inner level of electrons, and the inner electrons shield it from the full attractive force of the nucleus. As a result, relatively little energy is needed to remove the electron, and thus ionize the atom to a 1+ state. As you move down the alkali metal group, the outermost s electron is farther and farther from the nucleus and ionization becomes successively easier. As a result, the reactivity of the alkali metals increases down the family.

Alkaline Earth Metals

The alkaline earth metals have two electrons in an outer s orbital. The energy needed to remove both these electrons is low enough to make this group of elements almost as active as the alkali metals. Their chemistry is the chemistry of the 2^+ ion. The trend in reactivity for the oxygen group and the halogens is opposite that of Groups 1 and 2. Fluorine is the most active of the halogens, and activity decreases down the group.

SECTION 2

Nonmetals

Properties of Nonmetals

An elements's position in the periodic table is directly related to the size of the element's atoms. The size of the atoms increases as you go down each column and decreases as you go from left to right. Since the nonmetals are on the right side of the periodic table, it follows that atoms of nonmetals are generally smaller than atoms of metals.

Only seventeen of the known elements are classified as nonmetals. Of those seventeen elements, six belong to the family of noble gases and are considered inert, or nonreactive. As a result, discussions of the chemistry of the nonmetals usually focuses on hydrogen, carbon, nitrogen, oxygen, fluorine, phosphorus, sulfur, chlorine, selenium, bromine, and iodine.

SECTION 3

Mixed Groups

Properties of Metalloids

Metalloids are elements that are neither true metals nor true nonmetals. They have some properties of each group. Metalloids are the elements that touch the line separating the metals from the nonmetals. Aluminum, a metal, is the only exception.

There are eight elements in this group: boron, silicon, germanium, arsenic, antimony, tellurium, polonium, and astatine. These elements often look like metals, but they tend to be brittle, and they are more likely to be semiconductors than conductors of electricity.

One obvious use for elements in this group is for use as semiconductors. However, there are other application in the field of composites and ceremics.

Known since ancient times, ceramics are inorganic, nonmetallic, non-molecular solids. The first ceramics were pottery and porcelain. Modern ceramics materials have high-tech engineering, electronic, and biomedical applications. In many respects, the properties of ceramics are superior to those of metals. Ceramics have higher melting points, and they are stiffer, harder, and more resistant to wear and corrosion. Because ceramics are less dense than steel, they are attractive lightweight, high-temperature materials for replacing metal components in aircraft, space vehicles, and automotive engines. Unfortunately, ceramics are brittle.

Ceramics can be strengthened and toughened by mixing the ceramic with fibers of a second ceramic material, such as carbon, boron, or silicon carbide. The resulting hybrid material, called a ceramic composite, combines the advantageous properties of both components.

Fun Fact

The average adult requires 10 to 18 mg of the element iron every day. If less is taken, the person suffers from anemia; however, and overdose can cause vomiting, diarrhea, shock, coma, and even death. It is thought that heavy metal poisoning is caused by metals inactivating enzymes in the body.

For additional content background on this topic, go to the Glencoe Science Web site at science.glencoe.com.

Elements and Their Properties

Chapter Vocabulary

metals
malleable
ductile
metallic bonding
radioactive element
transition element
nonmetal
diatomic molecule
metalloids
allotrope
semiconductor
transuranium element

What do you think?

Science Journal This photograph shows Krypton lasers being produced. Krypton gas normally glows greenish-blue when excited by an electric current but also has a strong emission line at 647 nm. This is in the red region of the electromagnetic spectrum.

CHAPTER 20

Elements and Their Properties

It takes many different elements to build an airplane like this one. Some of those elements are metals, some are nonmetals, and some are metalloids. Each element has distinct properties. Knowing the properties of elements allows you to use them in a variety of practical ways—from treating diseases to building an airplane. This chapter will describe groups of elements and help you learn how they are related.

What do you think?

Science Journal Look at the picture below with a classmate. Discuss what you think this might be. Here's a hint: *The gas in the tubes stands apart from the crowd.* Write your best guess in your Science Journal.

Theme Connection

Scale and Structure The macroscopic behavior of a substance can be explained by the microscopic structure of its atoms. This is illustrated by the arrangement of elements in the periodic table.

It may be surprising to you that every known physical object is made from one or more of 115 known elements. When they are not attached to atoms of other elements, the atoms of an element have specific, identifiable properties. In this activity, you'll observe how heated atoms of elements gain energy and then in a short time release the absorbed energy, which you see as colored light.

Observe colorful clues

1. Using tongs, carefully hold a clean paper clip in the hottest part of a lab burner flame for 45 seconds.
2. Dip the hot paper clip into a solution of copper(II) sulfate.
3. Using the tongs with the same paper clip, repeat step 1, observing any color change.
4. Repeat all three steps using solutions of strontium chloride and sodium chloride with clean tongs.

Observe

1. Which element—chlorine or strontium—was responsible for the color observed in step 4?
2. In your Science Journal devise a plan to determine whether copper or sulfate was responsible for the color in step 2.

Before You Read

FOLDABLES Reading & Study Skills

Making a Classify Study Fold **Make the following Foldable to help you classify and organize objects into groups based on their common features.**

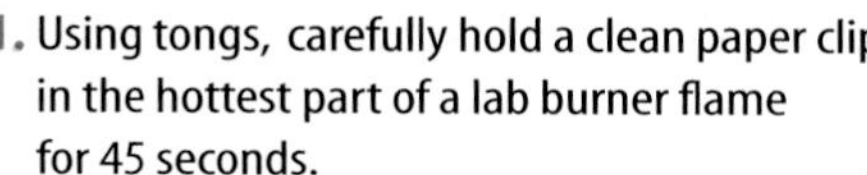

1. Place a sheet of paper in front of you so the long side is at the top. Fold the paper in half from the left side to the right side. Fold top to bottom and crease. Then unfold.
2. Through the top thickness of paper, cut along the middle fold line to form two tabs as shown.
3. Label the tabs *Metals,* and *Nonmetals* as shown.
4. Before you read the chapter, list all the metal and nonmetal elements you know on the front of the tabs. As you read the chapter, check your list and make changes as needed.

607

Before You Read

FOLDABLES Reading & Study Skills

Dinah Zike Study Fold

Purpose Students make and use a Foldable on which to collect information and list examples of metals and nonmetals. They then use what they have learned to compare and contrast the elements listed.

For additional help, see Foldables Worksheet, p. 17 in **Chapter Resources Booklet,** or go to the Glencoe Science Web site at **science.glencoe.com.** See After You Read in the Study Guide at the end of this chapter.

EXPLORE ACTIVITY

Purpose Students will observe that atoms of certain heated elements emit unique colors that can be used to identify the elements. L2 ELL COOP LEARN

Logical-Mathematical

Preparation Before class, make the three concentrated salt solutions. Be sure to use distilled water.

Materials paper clips, tongs, sodium chloride, strontium chloride, copper(II) sulfate, gas burner, distilled water, small beakers

Teaching Strategy It is important that the burner flame be adjusted to the palest blue color. Sodium compounds give a large yellow flame, strontium compounds give a red flame, and copper compounds give a green flame.

Safety Precautions Have students wear goggles and aprons and be cautious when working with open flames. The paper clip will become very hot.

Observe

1. strontium
2. Test a copper compound without sulfate and a sulfate compound without copper.

Assessment

Performance Repeat the procedure with a calcium chloride solution. A red-orange color (similar to the strontium color) will appear. Ask students to explain why flame tests may sometimes be unreliable. Use **PASC,** p. 89.

SECTION

Metals

1 Motivate

Bellringer Transparency

Display the Section Focus Transparency for Section 1. Use the accompanying Transparency Activity Master. L2 ELL

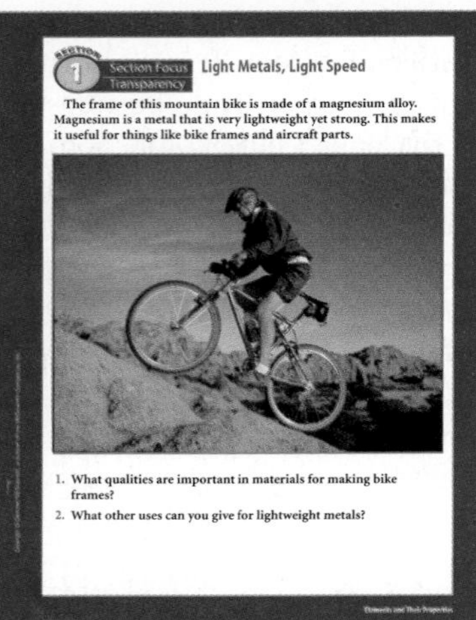

Section Focus Transparency

Light Metals, Light Speed

The frame of this mountain bike is made of a magnesium alloy. Magnesium is a metal that is very lightweight yet strong. This makes it useful for things like bike frames and aircraft parts.

1. What qualities are important in materials for making bike frames?
2. What other uses can you give for lightweight metals?

Tie to Prior Knowledge

Ask students to identify metals they come into contact with on a daily basis. aluminum foil, copper wire, titanium metal in bicycles, and iron in magnets

Caption Answers

- **Figure 1A** Possible answers: shielding (lead), plating (gold), house siding (aluminum)
- **Figure 1B** ductility

SECTION

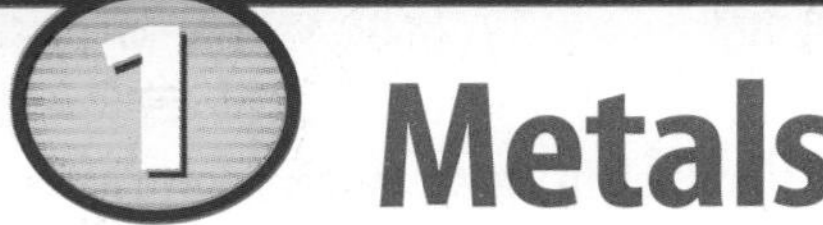

Metals

As You Read

***What* You'll Learn**

- **Describe** the properties of a typical metal.
- **Identify** the alkali metals and alkaline earth metals.
- **Differentiate** among three groups of transition elements.

Vocabulary

metal, malleable, ductile, metallic bonding, radioactive element, transition element

***Why* It's Important**

Metals are a part of your everyday life—from electric cords to the cars you ride in.

Properties of Metals

The first metal used about 8,000 years ago was gold. The use of copper and silver followed a few thousand years later. Then came tin and iron. Aluminum wasn't refined until only about 200 years ago because it must go through a much more complicated refining process that earlier civilizations had not yet developed.

In the periodic table, metals are elements found to the left of the stair-step line. In the table on the inside back cover of your book, the metal element blocks are colored blue. **Metals** usually have common properties—they are good conductors of heat and electricity, and all but one are solid at room temperature. Mercury is the only metal that is not a solid at room temperature. Metals also reflect light. This is a property called luster. Metals are **malleable** (MAH lee uh bul), which means they can be hammered or rolled into sheets, as shown in **Figure 1A.** Metals are also **ductile,** which means they can be drawn into wires like the ones shown in **Figure 1B.** These properties make metals suitable for use in objects ranging from eyeglass frames to computers to building structures.

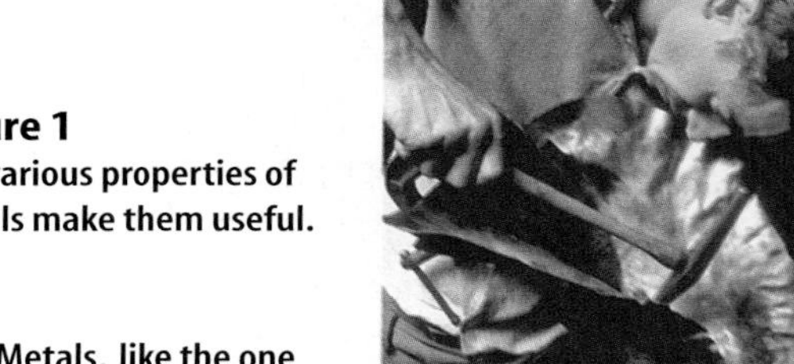

Figure 1
The various properties of metals make them useful.

A Metals, like the one shown, can be hammered into thin sheets. *What is one use for a sheet of metal?*

B Metals can be drawn into wires, like the wire that is being used here. *What is this property of metals called?*

Section Assessment Planner

Portfolio
Assessment, p. 615

Performance Assessment
Try At Home MiniLAB, p. 612
Skill Builder Activities, p. 615
See page 636 for more options.

Content Assessment
Section, p. 615
Challenge, p. 615
Chapter, pp. 636–637

Ionic Bonding in Metals The atoms of metals generally have one to three electrons in their outer energy levels. In chemical reactions, metals tend to give up electrons easily because they are close to having an empty outer energy level. When metals combine with nonmetals, the atoms of the metals tend to lose electrons to the atoms of nonmetals, forming ionic bonds, as shown in **Figure 2.** Both metals and nonmetals become more chemically stable when they form ions. They take on the electron structure of the nearest noble gas.

Metal
Nonmetal
Ag^+
I^-

Figure 2
Metals can form ionic bonds with nonmetals.

Metallic Bonding Another type of bonding, neither ionic nor covalent, occurs among the atoms in a metal. In **metallic bonding,** positively charged metallic ions are surrounded by a cloud of electrons. Outer-level electrons are not held tightly to the nucleus of an atom. Rather, the electrons move freely among many positively charged ions. As shown in **Figure 3,** the electrons form a cloud around the ions of the metal.

The idea of metallic bonding explains many of the properties of metals. For example, when a metal is hammered into a sheet or drawn into a wire, it does not break because the ions are in layers that slide past one another without losing their attraction to the electron-cloud. Metals are also good conductors of electricity because the outer-level electrons are weakly held.

Reading Check *Why do metals conduct electricity?*

Look at the periodic table inside the back cover of your book. How many of the elements in the table are classified as metals? All of the blue-shaded boxes represent metals. Except for hydrogen, all the elements in Groups 1 through 12 are metals, as well as the elements under the stair-step line in Groups 13 through 15. You will learn more about metals in some of these groups throughout this chapter.

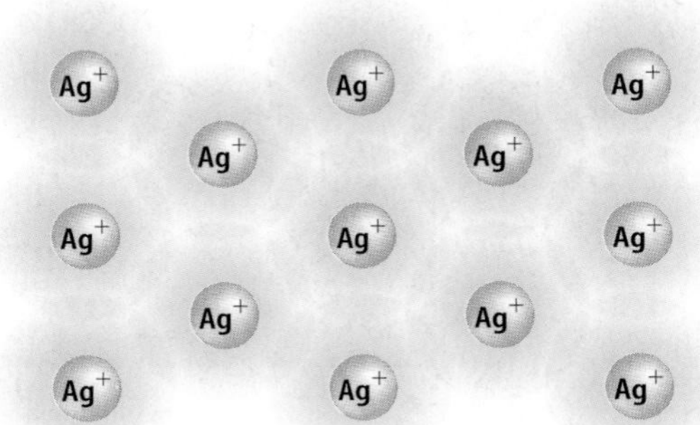

Figure 3
In metallic bonding, the electrons represented by the cloud are not attached to any one silver ion. This allows them to move and conduct electricity.

2 Teach

Properties of Metals

Use an Analogy

The interactions between metal ions and electrons in metallic bonding are analogous to food at a potluck supper. You arrive with your food, as a metal atom arrives with its own electrons. Once people join for dinner, however, the food is shared by all, regardless of who brought which dish. In the same way, the outer electrons of metals are shared, and it matters little with which atom an electron arrived.

IDENTIFYING Misconceptions

Students may think that electrical conductivity is independent of temperature or that it increases as temperature increases. Explain that in metals, conductivity generally increases as temperature decreases.

Reading Check

Answer because their outer-level electrons are weakly held

Visual Learning

Figure 3 Ask students how the metallic bonding shown in this figure is different from covalent bonding. In covalent bonding, electrons are shared between specific atoms, placing the atoms at defined angles, and uniting them into molecules containing a precise number of each atom. In metallic bonding, the atoms share all the valence electrons present, and the electrons are not restricted to specific atoms. This means that no specific molecules form. L3 LS **Visual-Spatial**

Resource Manager

Chapter Resources Booklet
- Transparency Activity, p. 46
- Note-taking Worksheets, pp. 33–36
- Directed Reading for Content Mastery, p. 20

Curriculum Connection

History Have students find out which were the first metals to be used by humans, when they were first used, and how. Copper and bronze, an alloy of copper and tin, were the first metals used by humans. They were used in weapons and tools. The Bronze Age began in the Middle East by about 3500 B.C. L2 LS **Linguistic**

The Alkali Metals

Quick Demo

To show how metal atoms slide over each other to produce the property of malleability, place a clear plastic lid from a container on the overhead projector. Next, layer in metal shot (BBs) to form a layer of rows. Now, show how the rows can be moved from side to side with the movement of a ruler on one side of a layer. L2

LS **Visual-Spatial**

Teacher FYI

Some of the largest atoms on the periodic table are found in the alkali group because of their relatively weak attraction for their outer level electrons. Each atom has only one outer electron, which is held weakly because of repulsion by the underlying level of electrons. Therefore, these metals have relatively low melting points and a soft texture. Cesium melts at a temperature lower than that of the human body. Although it must be done with extreme caution, the metal can be sliced with a knife.

Discussion

Francium occurs in nature in uranium ore. Its most stable isotope, francium-223, has a half-life of about 22 minutes, and is formed from the radioactive decay of actinium-227. **How do scientists know how much francium is in Earth's crust at one time?** They know how much uranium ore is in Earth's crust, and they can calculate the percentage that is francium. L3

LS **Logical-Mathematical**

The Alkali Metals

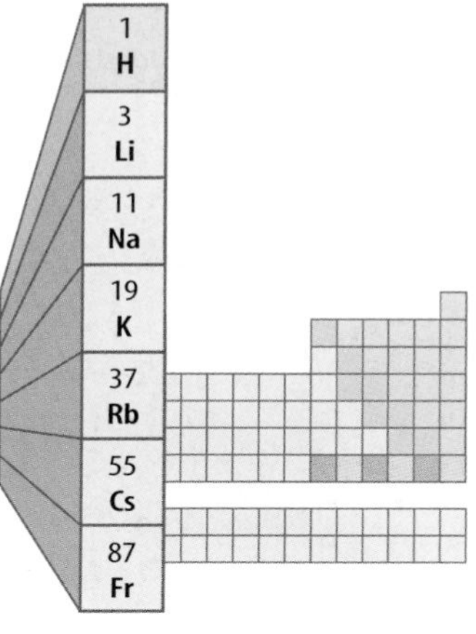

The Alkali Metals

The elements in Group 1 of the periodic table are the alkali (AL kuh li) metals. Like other metals, Group 1 metals are shiny, malleable, and ductile. They are also good conductors of heat and electricity. However, they are softer than most other metals. The alkali metals are the most reactive of all the metals. They react rapidly—sometimes violently—with oxygen and water, as shown in **Figure 4.** Because they combine so readily with other elements, alkali metals don't occur in nature in their elemental form and are stored in substances that are unreactive, such as an oil.

Each atom of an alkali metal has one electron in its outer energy level. This electron is given up when an alkali metal combines with another atom. As a result, the alkali metal becomes a positively charged ion in a compound such as sodium chloride, NaCl, or potassium bromide, KBr.

Alkali metals and their compounds have many uses. You and other living things need potassium and sodium compounds to stay healthy. Doctors use lithium compounds to treat bipolar depression. The lithium keeps chemical levels that are important to mental health within a narrow range. The operation of some photocells depends upon rubidium or cesium compounds. Francium, the last element in Group 1, is extremely rare and radioactive. A **radioactive element** is one in which the nucleus breaks down and gives off particles and energy. Francium can be found in uranium minerals, but only 20 g to 30 g of francium are in all of Earth's crust at one time.

Figure 4
Alkali metals are very reactive.

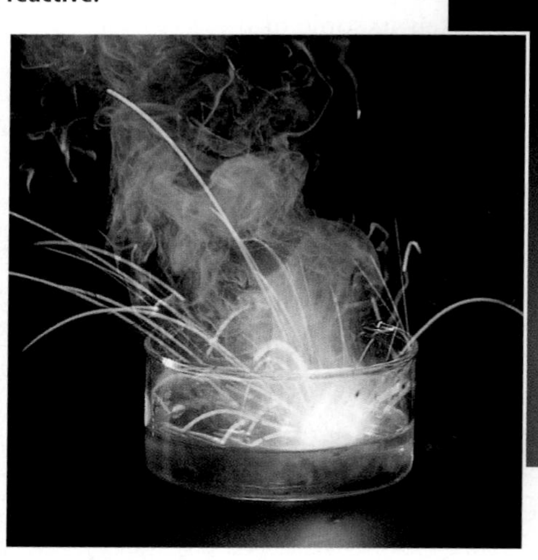

A Potassium reacts strongly in water.

B Sodium will burn in air if it is heated.

Curriculum Connection

Health When doctors prescribe a low-sodium diet, they typically recommend reducing the consumption of salt (NaCl). While some sodium is critical to good health, too much can cause problems. Have students find out why sodium is important to our diets. Na^+ helps conduct nerve impulses. Ask students to bring in labels from foods and drinks to compare sodium content. L2 LS **Linguistic**

Active Reading

Quickwrites This strategy, sometimes called freewrites, lets students use spontaneous writing to discover what they already know. Have students write a list of ideas about a topic, then share these ideas with the class. Next, have students write their ideas freely in a paragraph without worrying about punctuation, spelling, and grammar. Have students use a Quickwrite to share ideas about a group of elements.

The Alkaline Earth Metals

The alkaline earth metals make up Group 2 of the periodic table. Like most metals, these metals are shiny, malleable, and ductile. They are also similar to alkali metals in that they combine so readily with other elements that they are not found as free elements in nature. Each atom of an alkaline earth metal has two electrons in its outer energy level. These electrons are given up when an alkaline earth metal combines with a nonmetal. As a result, the alkaline earth metal becomes a positively charged ion in a compound such as calcium fluoride, CaF_2.

Fireworks and Other Uses Magnesium metal is used to produce the brilliant white color in fireworks like the ones in **Figure 5.** Compounds of strontium produce the bright red flashes. Magnesium's lightness and strength account for its use in cars, planes, and spacecraft. Magnesium also is used in compounds to make such things as household ladders and baseball and softball bats. Most life on Earth depends upon chlorophyll, a magnesium compound that enables plants to make food. Marble statues and some countertops are made of the calcium compound calcium carbonate.

The Alkaline Earth Metals and Your Body Calcium is seldom used as a free metal, but its compounds are needed for life. You may take a vitamin with calcium. Calcium phosphate in your bones helps make them strong.

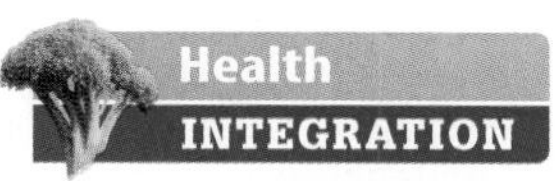

The barium compound $BaSO_4$ is used to diagnose some digestive disorders because it absorbs X-ray radiation well. First, the patient swallows a barium compound. Next, an X ray is taken while the barium compound is going through the digestive tract. A doctor can then see where the barium is in the body. In this way, doctors can diagnose internal abnormalities in the body.

Radium, the last element in Group 2, is radioactive and is found associated with uranium. It was once used to treat cancers. Today, other radioactive elements that are more readily available are replacing radium in cancer therapy.

The Alkaline Earth Metals

4 Be
12 Mg
20 Ca
38 Sr
56 Ba
88 Ra

Figure 5
Alkaline earth metals make spectacular fireworks.

The Alkaline Earth Metals

Extension

Ask students to find the characteristic colors of flames for some alkali and alkaline earth elements not used in the MiniLAB. Possible answers include K, lilac; Ca, red-orange; Ba, yellow-green L3 LS **Linguistic**

Quick Demo

Magnesium burns with an intensely bright white flame. To demonstrate this safely, hold a small strip of magnesium ribbon with tongs in a flame. **CAUTION:** *Be sure to wear gloves.* When the Mg begins to burn, quickly plunge it into a large metallic can. The reflected glare will show students why magnesium has practical use in flares. Adding water to the white, powdery residue of magnesium oxide (MgO) produces a solution with alkaline properties (turns red litmus blue).

Extension

Successful farming depends on the ability of soil to provide crops with the nutrients they need. Have students find out how calcium helps this process. Farmers put CaO, called lime, in the soil. CaO reacts with water to form $Ca(OH)_2$, which neutralizes soil that is too acidic. Maintaining the proper acid level is critical to dissolving soil minerals needed for plant growth. L2 LS **Linguistic**

Use Science Words

Word Usage Elements that are radioactive often decay into other elements. Radium is radioactive. Have students find out what happens to radium during the decay process. Radium releases an alpha particle (helium nucleus) and changes into radon.

Resource Manager

Chapter Resources Booklet
Enrichment, p. 30

Physical Science Critical Thinking/ Problem Solving, p. 19

Earth Science Critical Thinking Problem/ Solving, p. 2

Teacher FYI

Like those in Group 1, the Group 2 metals in water produce hydroxide ions. The reaction (where M represents an alkaline earth metal) is $M + 2H_2O \rightarrow M(OH)_2 + H_2$. The Group 2 metals need two hydroxide ions. The Group 2 metals generally have a 2+ charge in compounds.

Transition Elements

Purpose Students collect iron from breakfast cereal. L1 ELL
LS **Kinesthetic**

Materials plastic bag, high-iron-content cereal, water, pencil, tape, small strong magnet, bowl

Teaching Strategy Provide research materials for students to answer the second question.

Analysis

1. iron
2. Iron is part of hemoglobin and is needed for producing blood.

Oral Ask students why the metal collected is probably iron and not some other transition element. Most metals are not magnetic, and iron is. Use **Performance Assessment in the Science Classroom,** p. 91.

Extension

Other metals are often alloyed with steel to produce metals with particular properties. Have students identify some of these steel alloys and what they are used for. Aluminum added to steel makes it smooth and strong. Chromium steel has hardness, strength, and elasticity that make it useful for automobile and airplane parts. The most widely used alloy of steel is nickel steel, which is extremely strong. Nickel-chromium steel is shock resistant and is used for armor plate. L3 LS **Linguistic**

TRY AT HOME Mini LAB

Discovering What's in Cereal

Procedure

1. **Tape** a small, strong **magnet** to a **pencil** at the eraser end.
2. Place some **dry, fortified, cold cereal** in a **plastic bag.**
3. Thoroughly crush the cereal.
4. Pour the crushed cereal into a **deep bowl** and cover it with **water.**
5. Stir the mixture for about 10 min with your pencil/magnet. Stir slowly for the last minute.
6. Remove the magnet and examine it carefully. Record your observations.

Analysis

1. What common element is attracted to your magnet?
2. Why is this element added to the cereal?

Transition Elements

A titanium bike frame and a glowing tungsten lightbulb filament are examples of objects made from transition elements. **Transition elements** are those elements in Groups 3 through 12 in the periodic table. They are called transition elements because they are considered to be elements in transition between Groups 1 and 2 and Groups 13 through 18. Look at the periodic table inside the back cover of your book. Which elements do you think of as being typical metals? Transition elements are the most familiar because they often occur in nature as uncombined elements, unlike Group 1 and Group 2 metals which are less stable.

Transition elements typically form colored compounds. The gems in **Figure 6** show brightly colored compounds containing chromium. Cadmium yellow and cobalt blue paints are made from compounds of transition elements. However, cadmium and cobalt paints are so toxic that their use is limited.

Iron, Cobalt, and Nickel The first elements in Groups 8, 9, and 10—iron, cobalt, and nickel—form a unique cluster of transition elements. These three are known as the iron triad. All three elements are used in the process to create steel and other metals.

Iron—the main component of steel—is the most widely used of all metals. It is the second most abundant metallic element in Earth's crust after aluminum. Other metals are added to steel to give it various characteristics. Some steels contain cobalt or nickel. Nickel is added to some metals to give them strength. Also, nickel is used to give a shiny, protective coating to other metals.

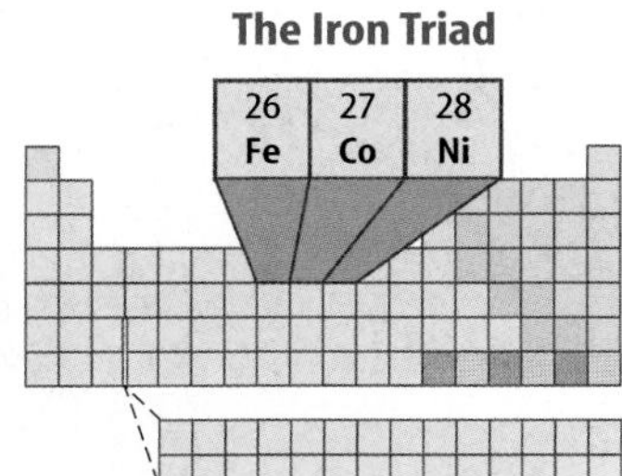

Figure 6
The colors of the ruby and emerald are due to the transition element chromium. The same element causes different colors because rubies and emeralds have different crystal structures.

Science Journal

Transition Metals Ask students to list in their Science Journals metal objects they come in contact with in their daily lives, note the metals from which the objects are made, and put an asterisk beside each that contains transition metals. Possibilities include aluminum cans, iron in steel in an automobile, copper and zinc in brass ornaments, tin in cans, gold and silver in jewelry. L2 LS **Naturalist**

612 CHAPTER 20 Elements and Their Properties

Figure 7
The coinage metals have many uses.

A Because gold and silver are so expensive, copper is more common in coins.

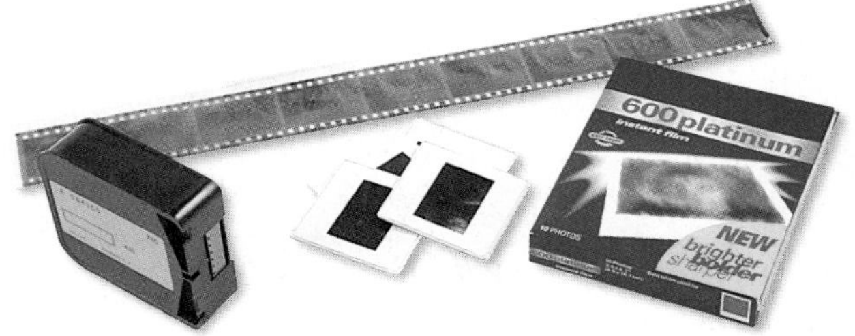

B Silver is used in compounds to make photographic materials.

C Gold frequently is used in jewelry.

Copper, Silver, and Gold The main metals in the objects in **Figure 7** are copper, silver, and gold—the three elements in Group 11. Because they are so stable and malleable and can be found as free elements in nature, these metals were once used widely to make coins. For this reason, they are known as the coinage metals. However, because they are so expensive, silver and gold rarely are used in coins anymore. The United States stopped using gold in the production of its coins in 1934 and silver in 1972. Most coins now are made of nickel and copper.

Copper often is used in electrical wiring because of its superior ability to conduct electricity and its relatively low cost. Can you imagine a world without photographs and movies? Silver iodide and silver bromide break down when exposed to light, producing an image on paper. Consequently, these compounds are used to make photographic film and paper. Silver and gold are used in jewelry because of their attractive color, relative softness, resistance to corrosion, and rarity.

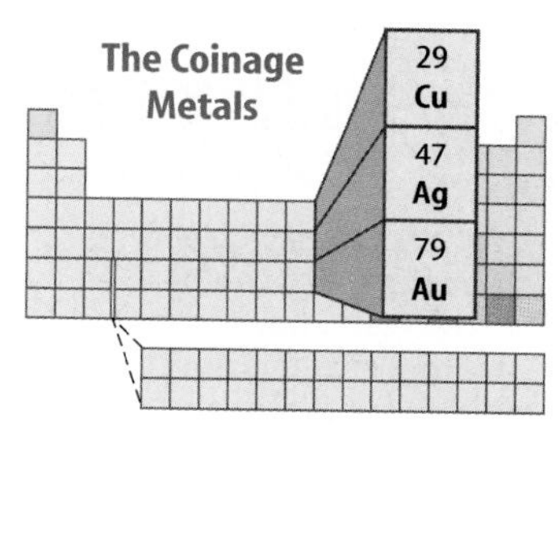

Reading Check *Why does gold's relative softness make it a good choice for jewelry?*

Zinc, Cadmium, and Mercury Zinc, cadmium, and mercury are found in Group 12 of the periodic table. Zinc combines with oxygen in the air to form a thin, protective coating of zinc oxide on its surface. Zinc and cadmium often are used to coat, or plate, other metals such as iron because of this protective quality. Cadmium is used also in rechargeable batteries.

Mercury is a silvery, liquid metal—the only metal that is a liquid at room temperature. For this reason, it is used in thermometers, thermostats, switches, and batteries. Mercury is poisonous and can accumulate in the body. People have died of mercury poisoning after eating fish that lived in mercury-contaminated water.

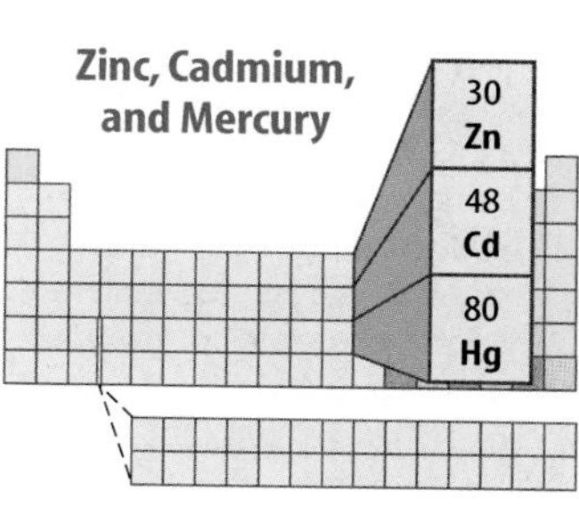

Extension

Have students find out which metal is used in the galvanizing process. zinc **What is the main use of galvanizing?** Zinc, when plated over iron containers, slows down the rusting process, because it oxidizes before the iron does and forms a protective coating. L2 IS **Linguistic**

Reading Check

Answer Gold is soft enough to be delicately shaped.

Activity

Place a large sheet of butcher paper at the front of the room. On it, list the transition elements. Have students add to the list any uses of the elements, or examples of the elements, they encounter during the week. At the end of the week, decide why some elements appear on the sheet more often than others. Possible answers: rarity of the element, cost of manufacture, need for materials that match properties of the element L2 IS **Interpersonal**

Resource Manager

Chapter Resources Booklet
MiniLAB, p. 3

Science Inquiry Labs, p. 47

Cultural Diversity, p. 35

Cultural Diversity

Forms of Money The use of metals for money began in approximately 7000 B.C. In the Middle East, bronze probably was used first, with gold and silver also exchanged. There is evidence that standard weight and value coins were developed in the area of modern Turkey around 640 B.C. Have students discuss characteristics that make a material useful as money. value, portability, rarity, availability, sturdiness L2

IS **Logical-Mathematical**

The Inner Transition Metals

Caption Answer

Figure 8 between Groups 3 and 4 in periods 6 and 7

Earth Science INTEGRATION

Aluminum is extracted from its ore by electrical means. Emphasize to students that the cost of extracting a material affects the price for the material as well as the material's availability. Aluminum, for example, was at one time more valuable than gold because extracting pure aluminum was very expensive.

Discussion

Why are the elements beyond uranium radioactive? As the number of protons increases, so does the repulsive force within the nucleus; this can cause several types of nuclear rearrangements. L2

LS **Logical-Mathematical**

Extension

The identity of an element is based on the number of protons in each of its atoms. When the number of protons changes, the identity of the element changes. Many of the actinides are formed by changing the number of protons in atoms of other elements. Have each student choose one of the actinides and find out how it is formed. Possible answer: When uranium-238 is bombarded with a neutron, it becomes U-239, then decomposes to neptunium-239 and an electron, or beta particle. L2 LS **Linguistic**

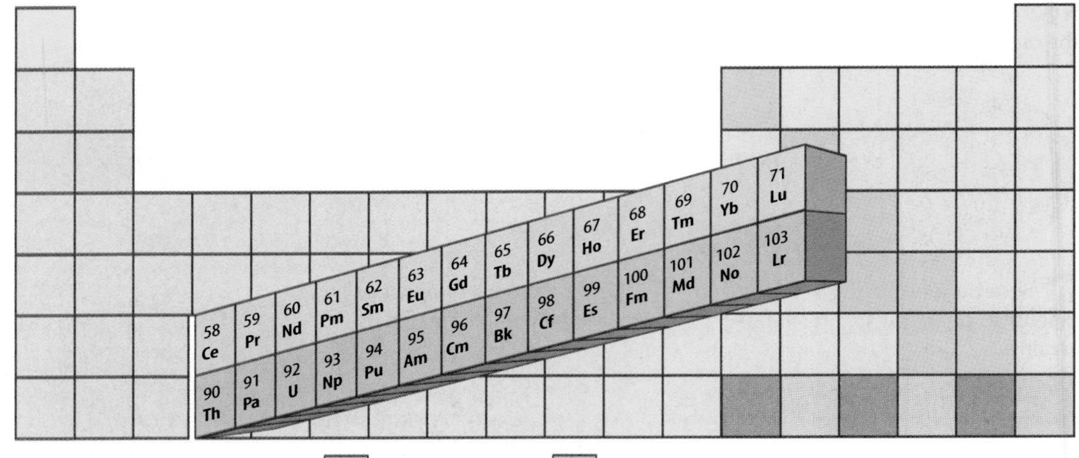

Figure 8
To save space, the periodic table usually isn't shown with the inner transition elements positioned where they should be.
Where are the lanthanide and actinide groups?

The Inner Transition Metals

The two rows of elements that seem to be disconnected from the rest on the periodic table are called the inner transition elements. They are called this because like the transition elements, they fit in the periodic table between Groups 3 and 4 in periods 6 and 7, as shown in **Figure 8.** To save room, they are listed below the table.

The Lanthanides The first row includes a series of elements with atomic numbers of 58 to 71. These elements are called the lanthanide series because they follow the element lanthanum.

Lanthanum, cerium, praseodymium, and samarium are used with carbon to make a compound that is used extensively by the motion picture industry. Europium, gadolinium, and terbium are used to produce the colors you see on your TV screen.

The Actinides The second row of inner transition metals includes elements with atomic numbers ranging from 90 to 103. These elements are called the actinide series because they follow the element actinium. All of the actinides are radioactive and unstable. Their unstable nature makes researching them difficult. Thorium and uranium are the actinides found in the Earth's crust in usable quantities. Thorium is used in making the glass for high-quality camera lenses because it bends light without much distortion. Uranium is best known for its use in nuclear reactors and in weapons applications, but one of its compounds has been used as photographic toner, as well. More will be said about these elements at the end of Section 3.

Earth Science INTEGRATION

Not all materials mined from the Earth can be used in the state they come in. Iron, for example, must be refined from iron ore in large blast furnaces. In these furnaces, charcoal is burned to create carbon monoxide gas that combines with the oxygen in the iron ore and carries it away. Other ways to extract materials from their ores include mixing them in solutions and using electricity. Find examples of metals that are purified from their ores by these two methods.

Curriculum Connection

History Changing one element into another is called transmutation. Transmutation was one of the major goals of alchemists. Ask students to find out what alchemists hoped to transmute. They wanted to change base metals into gold. L3

LS **Linguistic**

Resource Manager

Chapter Resources Booklet
Reinforcement, p. 27

Mathematics Skill Activities, p. 1

Metals in the Crust

Earth's hardened outer layer, called the crust, contains many compounds and a few uncombined metals such as gold and copper. Metals must be mined and separated from their ores, as shown in **Figure 9.**

Some metals are more abundant in one place than in another. Most of the world's platinum is found in South Africa. Chromium is important to the United States because it is used to harden steel, to manufacture stainless steel, and to form other alloys, but the United States imports most of it from South Africa, the Philippines, and Turkey.

Ores: Minerals and Mixtures Metals in Earth's crust that combined with other elements are found as ores. Most ores consist of a metal compound, or mineral, within a mixture of clay or rock. After an ore is mined from Earth's crust, the rock is separated from the mineral. Then the mineral often is converted to another physical form. This step usually involves heat and is called roasting. Finally, the metal is refined into a pure form. Later it can be alloyed with other metals.

Removing the waste rock can be expensive. If the cost of removing the waste rock becomes greater than the value of the desired material, the mineral no longer is classified as an ore.

Figure 9
Copper is mined in the United States at the Bingham Canyon Copper Mine in Utah.

Section  Assessment

1. How would you test a piece of palladium to see whether it is a metal?
2. How does the arrangement of the iron triad differ from the arrangements of coinage metals? Of the zinc group?
3. What characteristics are shared by alkali metals and alkaline earth metals?
4. How do metallic bonds differ from ionic and covalent bonds?
5. **Think Critically** If X stands for a metal, how can you tell from the following formulas—XCl and XCl_2—which compound contains an alkali metal and which contains an alkaline earth metal?

Skill Builder Activities

6. **Interpreting Scientific Illustrations** Draw dot diagrams to show the similarity among the chlorides of three alkali metals: *lithium chloride, sodium chloride,* and *potassium chloride.* **For more help, refer to the Science Skill Handbook.**
7. **Using Percentages** Pennies used to be made of 95 percent copper and 5 percent zinc, and they each weighed 3.11 g. Today, pennies are made of copper-plated zinc, and each weighs 2.5 g. A new penny weighs what percent of an old penny? **For more help, refer to the Math Skill Handbook.**

3 Assess

Reteach

Have students make flash cards with the symbol of a metallic element on one side of each card and the name of the element and whether it is an alkali metal, alkaline earth metal, transition element, or rare earth metal on the other. Have students form small groups and take turns using their cards to quiz the other students in the group. L2

COOP LEARN IS **Interpersonal**

Challenge

Ask students why metallic atoms generally obtain positive charges when combining with nonmetallic elements. Atoms of metals generally have one to three electrons in the outer energy levels, which they give up when they react with nonmetals. This gives them a positive charge. L2 IS **Logical-Mathematical**

✔Assessment

Portfolio Ask each student to draw a diagram that shows how the atoms in a metal are bonded to each other. Diagrams should show a cloud of valence electrons with various nuclei in the cloud. Use **Performance Assessment in the Science Classroom,** p. 127. P

Answers to Section Assessment

1. see if it conducts heat and electricity, reflects light, and is malleable and ductile
2. The iron triad is a horizontal arrangement while the others are vertical.
3. Both groups of metals typically form positive ions. Both give up electrons relatively easily, making them chemically active.
4. Unlike covalent bonds, metallic bonds are nondirectional. Unlike ionic bonds, metallic bonds do not produce inflexible structures. Metallic bonds enable electrical conductivity in the solid state, unlike covalent or ionic bonds.
5. Cl carries a −1 charge when bonded to metals, so the metal in XCl must have a +1 charge to balance it. This means the metal must be from Group 1. To balance the Cl_2 in XCl_2, the X must have a +2 charge, which means it must be from Group 2.
6. Li :C̈l: , Na :C̈l: , K :C̈l: .
7. The weight of a penny is 80% of the weight of an old penny.

Nonmetals

1 Motivate

Bellringer Transparency

Display the Section Focus Transparency for Section 2. Use the accompanying Transparency Activity Master. L2 ELL

Tie to Prior Knowledge

Ask students to name the most abundant elements found in the air they are breathing. nitrogen and oxygen **What are the two most plentiful elements in the universe?** hydrogen and helium Tell students that all of these gases are nonmetals, about which they will learn more in this section.

Nonmetals

As You Read

***What* You'll Learn**

- **Recognize** hydrogen as a nonmetal.
- **Compare and contrast** properties of the halogens.
- **Describe** properties and uses of the noble gases.

Vocabulary

nonmetal
diatomic molecule

***Why* It's Important**

Nonmetals are not only all around you, they are an essential part of your body.

Properties of Nonmetals

Most of your body's mass is made of oxygen, carbon, hydrogen, and nitrogen, as shown in **Figure 10.** Calcium, a metal, and other elements make up the remaining four percent of your body's mass. Phosphorus, sulfur, and chlorine are among these other elements found in your body. These elements are classified as nonmetals. **Nonmetals** are elements that usually are gases or brittle solids at room temperature. Because solid nonmetals are brittle or powdery, they are not malleable or ductile. Most nonmetals do not conduct heat or electricity well, and generally they are not shiny.

In the periodic table, all nonmetals except hydrogen are found at the right of the stair-step line. On the table in the inside back cover of your book, the nonmetal element blocks are colored yellow. The noble gases, Group 18, make up the only group of elements that are all nonmetals. Group 17 elements, except for astatine, are also nonmetals. Other nonmetals, found in Groups 13 through 16, will be discussed later.

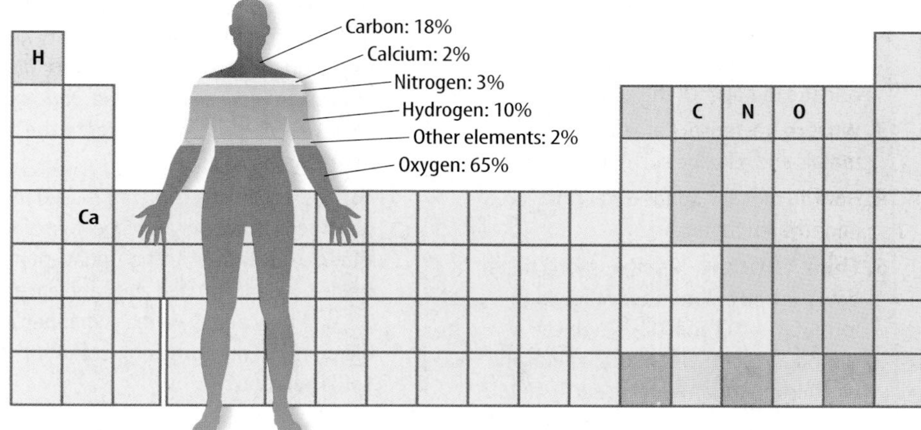

Figure 10
As a percentage of mass, humans are made up of mostly nonmetals.

Resource Manager

Chapter Resources Booklet

Transparency Activity, p. 47
Directed Reading for Content Mastery, p. 20

Section Assessment Planner

PORTFOLIO

Environmental Science Integration, p. 619

PERFORMANCE ASSESSMENT

MiniLab, p. 618
Skill Builder Activities, p. 620
See page 636 for more options.

CONTENT ASSESSMENT

Section, p. 620
Challenge, p. 620
Chapter, pp. 636–637

A Lead and sulfur bond ionically to form lead sulfide, PbS, also known as galena.

B Carbon and oxygen can bond covalently to form carbon dioxide, CO_2.

Figure 11
Nonmetals form ionic bonds with metals and covalent bonds with other nonmetals.

Bonding in Nonmetals The electrons in most nonmetals are strongly attracted to the nucleus of the atom. So, as a group, nonmetals are poor conductors of heat and electricity.

Most nonmetals can form ionic and covalent compounds. Examples of these two kinds of compounds are shown in **Figure 11.**

When nonmetals gain electrons from metals, the nonmetals become negative ions in ionic compounds. An example of such an ionic compound is potassium iodide, KI, which often is added to table salt. KI is formed from the nonmetal iodine and the metal potassium. On the other hand, when bonded with other nonmetals, atoms of nonmetals usually share electrons to form covalent compounds. An example is ammonia, NH_3, the strong, unpleasant-smelling compound you notice when you open a bottle of some household cleaners.

Hydrogen

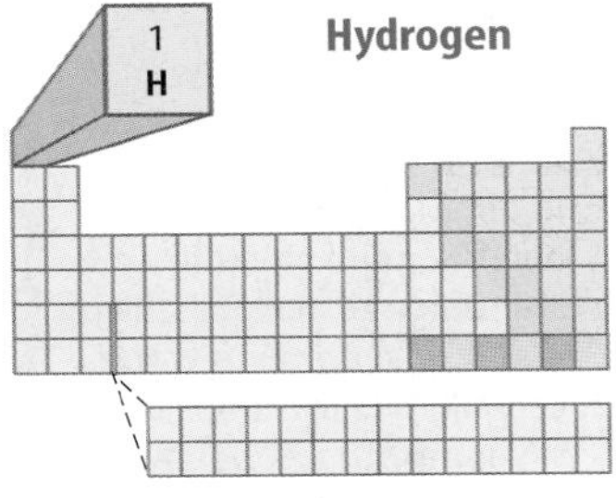

If you could count all the atoms in the universe, you would find that about 90 percent of them are hydrogen. Most hydrogen on Earth is found in the compound water. The word *hydrogen* is derived from the Greek for "water forming". When water is broken down into its elements, hydrogen becomes a gas made up of diatomic molecules. A **diatomic molecule** consists of two atoms of the same element in a covalent bond.

Hydrogen is highly reactive. A hydrogen atom has a single electron, which the atom shares when it combines with other nonmetals. For example, hydrogen burns in oxygen to form water, H_2O, in which hydrogen shares electrons with oxygen.

Hydrogen can gain an electron when it combines with alkali and alkaline earth metals. The compounds formed are hydrides, such as sodium hydride, NaH.

Reading Check *What is a diatomic molecule?*

2 Teach

Properties of Nonmetals

Visual Learning

Figure 11 Point out to students the diagrams showing ionic bonding and covalent bonding. Ask a volunteer to describe the similarities and differences between the two. In ionic bonding, electrons move from one atom to another. In covalent bonding, electrons are shared between atoms. In both types of bonding, the outer electron energy levels are filled. L2 LS **Visual-Spatial**

Teacher FYI

Under normal pressures, nitrogen and oxygen do not become liquids until they reach the very cold temperatures of −196°C and −183°C, respectively.

Hydrogen

Reading Check

Answer A diatomic molecule consists of two atoms of the same element joined by a covalent bond.

LAB DEMONSTRATION

Purpose to prepare a sample of hydrogen and examine its properties

Materials pea-sized sample of zinc metal; two large test tubes; one-holed rubber stopper fitted with 90° bent glass tubing; 6M sulfuric acid

Procedure Place about 4 mL of the acid in one tube. Add the zinc to the acid, and stopper the tube. Collect the H_2 gas by inverting the second tube over the upraised 90° glass bend. Carefully bring the inverted tube containing H_2 near a burning wood splint so that the H_2 ignites. **CAUTION:** *Use an explosion shield and goggles. Never prepare more than this small amount.*

Expected Outcome The reaction is $Zn + H_2SO_4 \rightarrow ZnSO_4 + H_2$. The H_2 then combines with O_2 to form water.

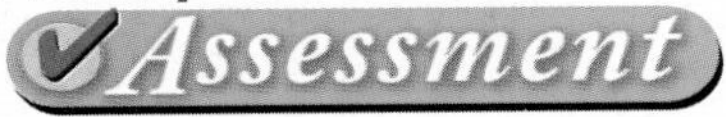

What type of bond do the hydrogen and oxygen make when they combine to form water? covalent

The Halogens

Purpose Students determine the presence of chloride in drinking water. L2

LS **Kinesthetic**

Materials medicine dropper; graduated cylinder; standard chloride comparison compound (0.10 g NaCl in 1 L of distilled water); silver nitrate testing solution (1.7 g $AgNO_3$ in 100 mL of distilled water)

Teaching Strategy

Safety Precaution Remind students to avoid contact with the silver nitrate testing solution.

Analysis

1. Standard chloride will show a white precipitate from the formation of AgCl. Distilled water showed no white precipitate.
2. If the drinking water contains chloride, it will show a white cloudiness similar to that of the standard but not as dense.

Assessment

Performance Have students test a sample of bottled water and determine whether it contains chloride. Read the label to verify results. Use **PASC**, p. 97.

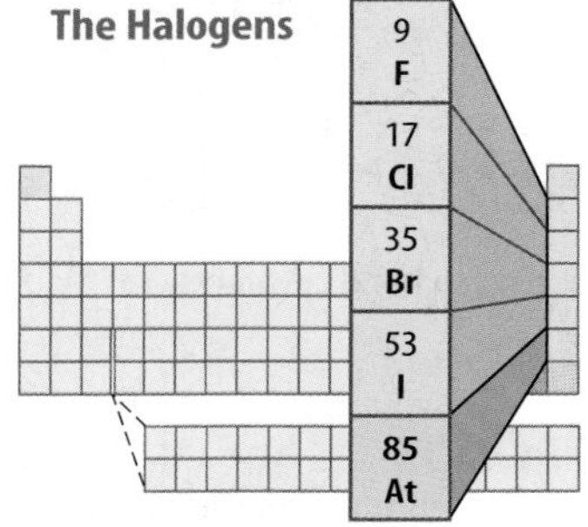

The Halogens

Halogen lights contain small amounts of bromine or iodine. These elements, as well as fluorine, chlorine, and astatine, are called halogens and are in Group 17. They are very reactive in their elemental form, and their compounds have many uses. As shown in **Figure 12,** fluorides are added to toothpastes and to city water systems to prevent tooth decay, chlorine is added to water to disinfect it.

Because an atom of a halogen has seven electrons in its outer energy level, only one electron is needed to complete this energy level. If a halogen gains an electron from a metal, an ionic compound, called a salt, is formed. In the gaseous state, the halogens form reactive diatomic covalent molecules and can be identified by their distinctive colors. Chlorine is greenish yellow, bromine is reddish orange, and iodine is violet.

Fluorine is the most chemically active of all elements. Hydrofluoric acid, a mixture of hydrogen fluoride and water, is used to etch glass and to frost the inner surfaces of lightbulbs.

Mini LAB

Identifying Chloride in Your Water

Procedure

1. In three labeled **test tubes,** obtain 2 mL of **chloride standard solution, distilled water,** and **drinking water.**
2. Carefully add five drops of **silver nitrate solution** to each and stir. **WARNING:** *Avoid contact with the silver nitrate solution.*

Analysis

1. Which solution will definitely show a presence of chloride? How did this result compare to the result with distilled water?
2. Which result most resembled your drinking water?

Figure 12
The halogens have many uses.

A **Chlorine is used in pools to disinfect the water.**

B **Fluoride compounds are used in toothpaste to prevent tooth decay.**

Teacher FYI

The term *halogen* means "salt former." When the atoms of halogens bond to each other, their electrons are shared to form diatomic molecules, such as Cl_2 and Br_2. When bonded to metals, however, they attract electrons so strongly that they form large negative ions.

Inclusion Strategies

Visually Impaired Provide these students with hand lenses to help them see the precipitate in the MiniLAB.

Figure 13
This ocean-salt recovery site uses evaporation to separate the halogen compounds from the water so the salts can be refined further.

Uses of Halogens The odor you sometimes smell near a swimming pool is chlorine. Chlorine compounds are used to disinfect water. Chlorine, the most abundant halogen, is obtained from seawater at ocean-salt recovery sites like the one in **Figure 13.** Household and industrial bleaches used to whiten flour, clothing, and paper also contain chlorine compounds.

Bromine, the only nonmetal that is a liquid at room temperature, also is extracted from compounds in seawater. Other bromine compounds are used as dyes in cosmetics.

Iodine, a shiny purple-gray solid at room temperature, is another halogen obtained from seawater. When heated, iodine changes directly to a purple vapor. The process of a solid changing directly to a vapor without forming a liquid is called sublimation, as shown in **Figure 14.** Iodine is essential in your diet for the production of the hormone thyroxin and to prevent goiter, an enlarging of the thyroid gland in the neck.

Reading Check *What is sublimation?*

Astatine is the last member of Group 17. It is radioactive and rare, but has many properties similar to those of the other halogens. There are no known uses due to its rarity.

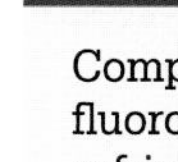

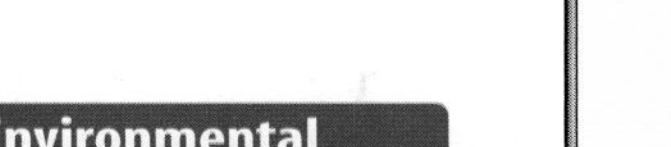

Environmental Science INTEGRATION

Compounds called chlorofluorocarbons are used in refrigeration systems. If released, these compounds destroy ozone in the atmosphere. The ozone protects you from some of the harmful rays from the Sun. Find the advantages and disadvantages of these compounds. Write your answer in your Science Journal.

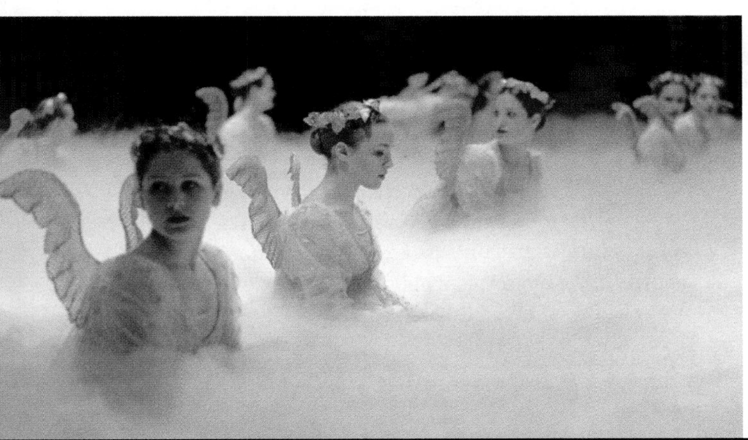

Figure 14
Frozen carbon dioxide, or dry ice, is used to make inexpensive, visible gas for theatrical productions. The carbon dioxide is brought out as a solid, then it sublimes as shown here.

Environmental Science INTEGRATION

Advantages: nontoxic, nonflammable, easily converted from liquid to gas and back, well-suited for many applications; disadvantages: can cause ozone depletion. Have students find the formula of freon and write the electron dot diagram for the molecule. CCl_2F_2 L2 IS **Logical-Mathematical** P

Quick Demo

The process of sublimation can be demonstrated with dry ice. Carefully place a few small pieces of dry ice in a sealed plastic food bag. **CAUTION:** *Wear gloves.* The phase change from solid to gas is observable as the CO_2 gas inflates the bag. Explain to students that solid iodine would do the same if gently heated. However, unlike CO_2 gas, iodine vapor is purple and is potentially harmful. L2 IS **Visual-Spatial**

Reading Check

Answer the process by which a solid changes directly to a gas without forming a liquid

Resource Manager

Chapter Resources Booklet
MiniLAB, p. 4
Enrichment, p. 31
Science Inquiry Labs, p. 45

Cultural Diversity

Seaweed in China As early as the first century B.C., the Chinese recognized that seaweed, which is high in iodine, could be used to treat goiter, a disease of the thyroid. The information was not brought to Europe until the 1100s. Have students find the recommended daily allowance for iodine. The RDA for iodine is 150 mcg. L1 IS **Linguistic**

The Noble Gases

Quick Demo

Bring a pencil-sized laser to class, and demonstrate its use. Have students locate on the periodic table the nonmetal noble gases helium and neon, which are typically used in these lasers. **CAUTION:** *Do not point the laser beam directly into anyone's eyes.* L2 IS **Visual-Spatial**

3 Assess

Reteach

Bring to class magazine, newspaper, and Internet photos of nonmetals in use. Ask students to name each nonmetal and locate it on the periodic table. Examples: lipstick (iodine), bleach (chlorine and oxygen), neon lights (neon). L2 IS **Visual-Spatial**

Challenge

Ask students to use references to find the formulas of these common acids: hydrochloric HCl, nitric HNO_3, sulfuric H_2SO_4, hydrofluoric HF, and carbonic H_2CO_3. Then ask them to determine if the acids are typically formed with atoms of metals or nonmetals. nonmetals L3

IS **Logical-Mathematical**

Assessment

Performance Show students an outline of the periodic table. Point to two elements and ask students to predict the bond type that would form between them. If it is an ionic bond, ask them to predict which element is likely to form a negative ion and which is likely to form a positive ion. If the bond is covalent, ask them to predict the formula. For example, point to Na and F—ionic, Na is positive, F is negative. Point to sulfur and oxygen. The bond is covalent, and the formula is SO_2 or SO_3. Use **PASC**, p. 89. L2 IS **Logical-Mathematical**

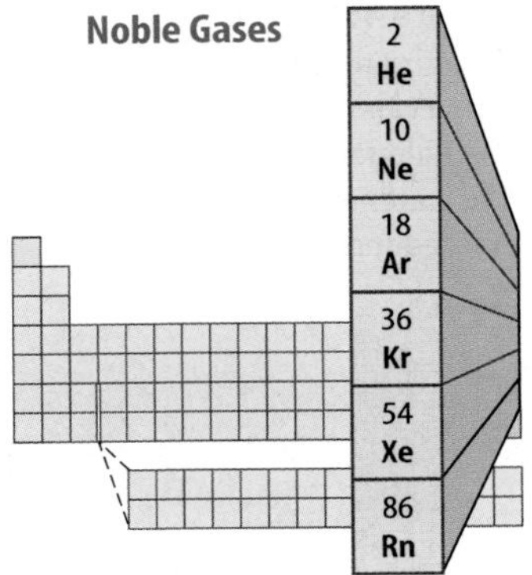

The Noble Gases

The noble gases exist as isolated atoms. They are stable because their outermost energy levels are full. No naturally occurring noble gas compounds are known, but several compounds of xenon and krypton with fluorine have been created in a laboratory.

The stability of noble gases is what makes them useful. In addition, the light weight of helium makes it useful in lighter-than-air blimps and balloons. Neon and argon are used in "neon lights" for advertising. Argon and krypton are used in electric light bulbs to produce light in lasers, as seen in **Figure 15.**

Figure 15
Noble gases are used to produce spectacular laser light shows.

Section 2 Assessment

1. What are two ways in which hydrogen combines with other elements?
2. Rank the following nonmetals from lowest number of electrons in the outer level to highest: Cl^-, H^+, He, and H. What property of noble gases makes them useful?
3. How are solid nonmetals different from solid metals?
4. How can you tell that a gas is a halogen?
5. **Think Critically** What is the process of a solid changing directly into a vapor? Which element observes this process?

Skill Builder Activities

6. **Interpreting Data** Within the following compounds, identify the nonmetal and list its oxidation number: *MgO, NaH,* $AlBr_3$, and *FeS*. **For more help, refer to the** Science Skill Handbook.
7. **Communicating** In your Science Journal, write a paragraph explaining why nonmetals form ionic and covalent compounds, but not metallic bonds. Give some examples of ionic and covalent bonds. **For more help, refer to the** Science Skill Handbook.

Answers to Section Assessment

1. covalently with most nonmetals and ionically with active metals
2. H^+ (zero); H (one); He (two) Cl^- (eight); noble gases don't form compounds naturally, so they are stable.
3. Unlike metals, solid nonmetals typically are not ductile or malleable and do not conduct electricity.
4. By their colors: Cl_2 is greenish-yellow, Br_2 is reddish-orange, and I_2 is violet.
5. sublimation; iodine
6. MgO: oxygen is −2; NaH: H is −1; $AlBr_3$: Br is −1; FeS: S is −2.
7. The atoms of nonmetals are typically small and hold on to their electrons tightly. Also, their outer energy levels contain four or more electrons. These two features combine to make it difficult for electrons in a nonmetal to roam freely, as is necessary in metallic bonds.

620 CHAPTER 20 Elements and Their Properties

Activity

What type is it?

Suppose you want an element for a certain use. You might be able to use a metal but not a nonmetal. In this activity, you will test several metals and nonmetals and compare their properties.

Observing Properties

Element	Appearance	Malleable or Brittle	Electrical Conductivity	Shiny or Dull
Carbon	black solid	B	N	D
Magnesium	silver metal	M	Y	S
Aluminum	silver metal	M	Y	S
Sulfur	yellow solid	B	N	D
Tin	silver metal	M	Y	S

What You'll Investigate

How can you use properties to distinguish metals from nonmetals?

Materials

samples of C, Mg, Al, S, and Sn
dishes for the samples
conductivity tester
spatula
small hammer

Goals

- **Observe** physical properties.
- **Test** the malleability of the materials.
- **Identify** electrical conductivity in the given materials.

Safety Precautions 

Procedure

1. **Prepare** a table in your Science Journal like the one shown.
2. **Observe** and record the appearance of each element sample. Include its physical state, color, and whether it is shiny or dull.
3. Remove a small sample of one of the elements. Place it on a hard surface chosen by your teacher. Gently tap the sample with a hammer. The sample is malleable if it flattens when tapped and brittle if it shatters. Record your results.
4. Repeat step 3 for each sample.
5. Test the conductivity of each element by touching the electrodes of the conductivity tester to a sample, as shown in the photo. If the bulb lights, the element conducts electricity. Record your results.

Conclude and Apply

1. Locate each element you used on the periodic table. Compare your results with what you would expect from an element in that location.
2. Locate palladium, Pd, on the periodic table. Use the results you obtained during the activity to predict some of the properties of palladium.
3. **Infer** why some elements might show properties of metals as well as properties of nonmetals.

Communicating Your Data

Compare your results with those of other students. **For more help, refer to the** Science Skill Handbook.

Resource Manager 

Chapter Resources Booklet
Reinforcement, p. 28
Activity Worksheet, pp. 5–6
Lab Activity, pp. 9–12

Communicating Your Data

Have students display their data tables and share their results with the rest of the class

Activity

BENCH TESTED

Purpose Students will observe properties of metals and nonmetals and use their observations to classify the substances. L2 COOP LEARN IN **Kinesthetic**

Process Skills observing, interpreting data, comparing and contrasting, classifying

Time Required 30 minutes

Safety Precautions Have students wear goggles and use caution when hammering.

Teaching Strategies

Troubleshooting Test the conductivity tester before class. Use amorphous carbon such as charcoal, but not graphite, which is shiny and will conduct a current.

Answers to Questions

1. Elements on the left side of the periodic table should show metallic properties, while those on the right should illustrate nonmetallic properties.
2. Predictions may include that it is shiny, malleable, and a conductor.
3. They are in the area of transition from metallic to nonmetallic elements.

Assessment

Performance Provide a periodic table, and ask students to draw an arrow to indicate the direction of increasing metallic properties. The arrow should move from top to bottom and from right to left. Use **Performance Assessment in the Science Classroom,** p. 89.

Mixed Groups

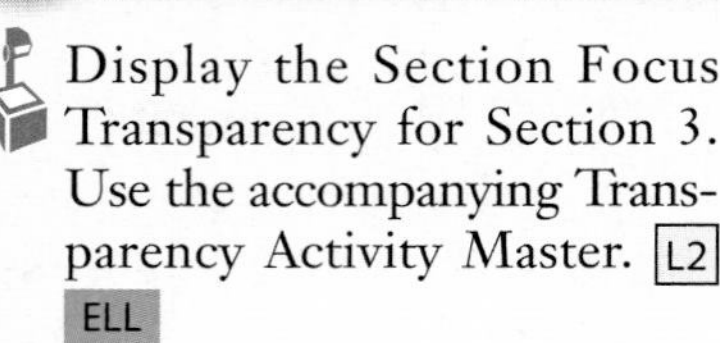

Display the Section Focus Transparency for Section 3. Use the accompanying Transparency Activity Master. L2 ELL

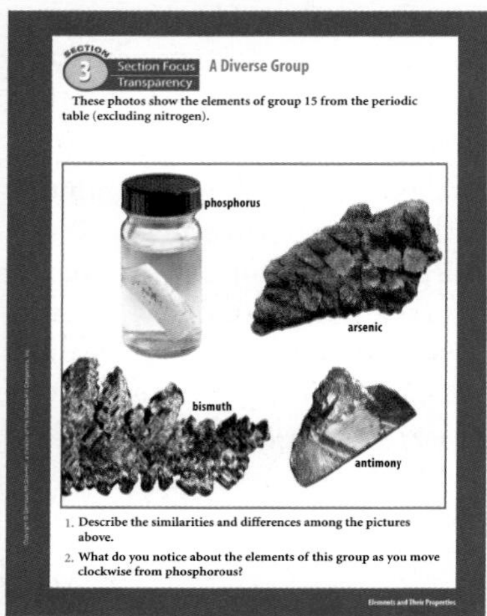

Tie to Prior Knowledge

Ask students what element they typically associate with computers. silicon **Where is this element located on the periodic table?** between metals and nonmetals **What type of properties would you expect silicon to have?** Properties between those of metals and nonmetals; for example, while metals are conductors and nonmetals are nonconductors, silicon is a semiconductor.

Mixed Groups

As You Read

What You'll Learn

- **Distinguish** among metals, nonmetals, and metalloids.
- **Describe** the nature of allotropes.
- **Recognize** the significance of differences in crystal structure in carbon.
- **Understand** the importance of synthetic elements

Vocabulary
metalloid
allotrope
semiconductor
transuranium element

Why It's Important
The elements in mixed groups affect your life every day, because they are in everything from the computer you use to the air you breathe.

Properties of Metalloids

Can an element be a metal and a nonmetal? In a sense, some elements called metalloids are. **Metalloids** share unusual characteristics. Metalloids can form ionic and covalent bonds with other elements. Some metalloids have metallic and nonmetallic properties. They can conduct electricity better than most nonmetals, but not as well as some metals, giving them the name semiconductor. With the exception of aluminum, the metalloids are the elements in the periodic table that are located along the stair-step line. The mixed groups—13, 14, 15, 16, and 17—contain metals, nonmetals, and metalloids. Group 17, the halogens, were discussed in Section two.

The Boron Group

Boron, a metalloid, is the first element in Group 13. Look around your home, you might find two compounds of boron. One of these is borax, which is used in some laundry products to soften water. The other is boric acid, a mild antiseptic. Boron also is used as a grinding material and as boranes, which are compounds used for jet and rocket fuel.

Aluminum, a metal in Group 13, is the most abundant metal in Earth's crust. It is used in soft-drink cans, foil wrap, cooking pans, and as siding. Aluminum is strong and light, and is used in the construction of airplanes such as the one in **Figure 16.**

The Boron Group

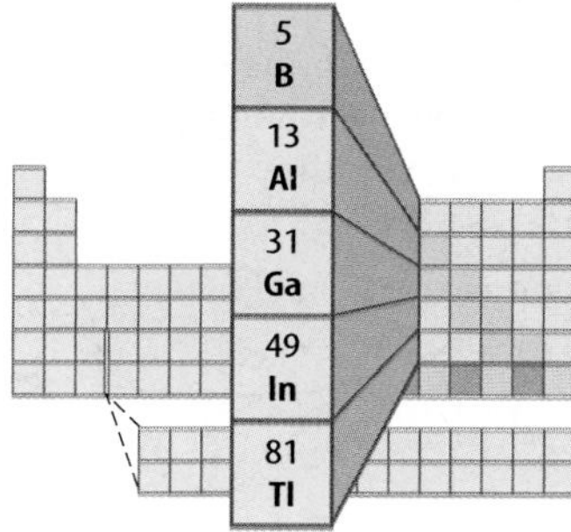

Figure 16
Aluminum is used frequently in the construction of airplanes because it is light and strong.

622 **CHAPTER 20** Elements and Their Properties

Section Assessment Planner

Portfolio
Extension, p. 625

Performance Assessment
Skill Builder Activities, p. 629
See page 636 for more options.

Content Assessment
Section, p. 629
Challenge, p. 629
Chapter, pp. 636–637

Figure 17
Elements in Group 14 have many uses.

A Silicon is used to make the chips that allow this computer to run.

B These tin cans are made of steel with a tin coating.

The Carbon Group

Each element in Group 14, the carbon family, has four electrons in its outer energy level, but this is where much of the similarity ends. Carbon is a nonmetal, silicon and germanium are metalloids, and tin and lead are metals. Carbon occurs as an element in coal and as a compound in oil, natural gas, and foods. Carbon in these materials can combine with oxygen to produce carbon dioxide, CO_2. In the presence of sunlight, plants utilize CO_2 to make food. Carbon compounds, many of which are essential to life, can be found in you and all around you. All organic compounds contain carbon, but not all carbon compounds are organic.

Silicon is second only to oxygen in abundance in Earth's crust. Most silicon is found in sand, SiO_2, and almost all rocks and soil. The crystal structure of silicon dioxide is similar to the structure of diamond. Silicon occurs as two allotropes. **Allotropes,** which are different forms of the same element, have different molecular structures. One allotrope of silicon is a hard, gray substance, and the other is a brown powder.

Reading Check *What are allotropes?*

Silicon is the main component in **semiconductors**—elements that conduct an electric current under certain conditions. Many of the electronics that you use everyday, like the computer in **Figure 17A,** need semiconductors to run. Germanium, the other metalloid in the carbon group, is used along with silicon in making semiconductors. Tin is used to coat other metals to prevent corrosion, like the tin cans in **Figure 17B.** Tin also is combined with other metals to produce bronze and pewter. Lead was used widely in paint at one time, but because it is toxic, lead no longer is used.

The Carbon Group

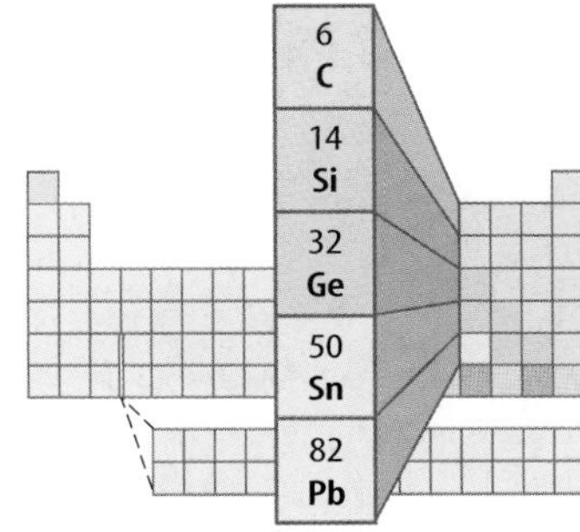

2 Teach

The Carbon Group

Teacher FYI

When solids conduct, valence electrons move from their normal positions to a slightly higher energy level called a conducting band. In metals, the energy gap between the nonconducting band and the conducting band is slight, so metals conduct easily. In metalloids such as Si, the gap between the two states is also small but is larger than in metals. Hence, metalloids do not conduct as well as most metals.

Use Science Words

Word Origin Have students look up the roots of the word *allotrope* and explain how they combine to apply to elements. *Allotrope* comes from the Greek allo-, "other," and *tropos,* "turning or direction." Each allotrope of an element has an other, or different, molecule. L2
LS **Linguistic**

Discussion

Typically, nonmetals gain electrons and a negative charge when reacting while metals lose electrons to obtain positive charges as they react. Ask students to identify the charges atoms in the carbon group have when they react. Those at the top are more likely to become negative. Those near the bottom become positive.

Reading Check

Answer Allotropes are different forms of the same element.

Teacher FYI

Another important property of carbon is its ability to connect with itself to form long chains. This is called catenation, and it enables carbon to make proteins and other large molecules. No other element comes close to carbon in this ability.

Resource Manager

Chapter Resources Booklet

Transparency Activity, p. 48
Directed Reading for Content Mastery, pp. 21, 22
Lab Activity, pp. 13–16

The Carbon Group, continued

Make a Model

Draw an equilateral triangle 5 cm on a side. Make copies, and give each student four. Have each student cut out the triangles, leaving small tabs on each side, and tape the triangles together to form a tetrahedron. Ask students to stack several tetrahedrons to show how tetrahedrons support one another. This interlocking network represents the structure that carbon forms in diamonds. L1 ELL LS **Kinesthetic**

Fun Fact

Soft lead metal was once used for writing black marks on paper. Graphite mixed with clay is less toxic and has replaced lead in pencils for writing. The term *graphite* comes from the Greek word *graphein*, which means "to write."

Research Visit the Glencoe Science Web site at **science.glencoe.com** for more information about buckminsterfullerene. Communicate to your class what you learn.

Allotropes of Carbon What do the diamond in a diamond ring and the graphite in your pencil have in common? They are both carbon. Diamond, graphite, and buckminsterfullerene, shown in **Figure 18,** are allotropes of an element.

A diamond is clear and extremely hard. In a diamond, each carbon atom is bonded to four other carbon atoms at the vertices, or corner points, of a tetrahedron. In turn, many tetrahedrons join together to form a giant molecule in which the atoms are held tightly in a strong crystalline structure. This structure accounts for the hardness of diamond.

Graphite is a black powder that consists of hexagonal layers of carbon atoms. In the hexagons, each carbon atom is bonded to three other carbon atoms. The fourth electron of each atom is bonded weakly to the layer next to it. This structure allows the layers to slide easily past one another, making graphite an excellent lubricant. In the mid 1980s, a new allotrope of carbon called buckminsterfullerene was discovered. This soccer-ball-shaped molecule, informally called a buckyball, was named after the architect-engineer R. Buckminster Fuller, who designed structures with similar shapes.

In 1991, scientists were able to use the buckyballs to synthesize extremely thin, graphitelike tubes. These tubes, called nanotubes, are about 1 billionth of a meter in diameter. That means you could stack tens of thousands of nanotubes just to get the thickness of one piece of paper. Nanotubes might be used someday to make computers that are smaller and faster and to make strong building materials.

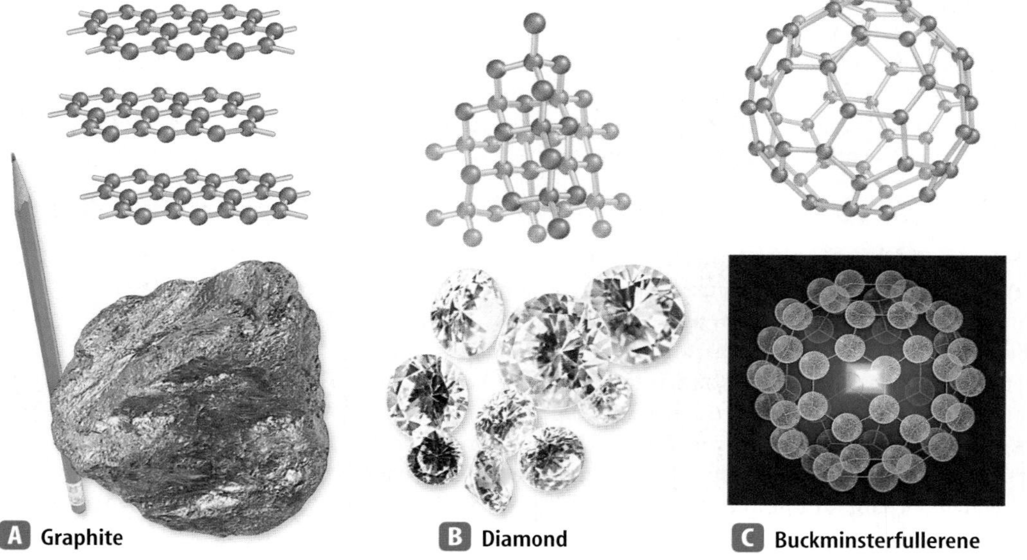

Figure 18
Three allotropes of carbon are depicted here. *What geometric shapes make up each allotrope?*

Caption Answer

Figure 18 graphite, hexagons; diamond, tetrahedrons; buckminsterfullerene, soccer-ball-shaped, made from hexagons and pentagons

Visual Learning

Figure 18 Ask students to examine the structure of buckminsterfullerene and explain why some chemists call it a cage molecule. This molecule is hollow inside, like a cage. **How could the molecule be used as a delivery system?** A substance could be inserted into the cage, the cage could be put in the desired location and then opened, and the contents could be released. L2 LS **Visual-Spatial**

Teacher FYI

Diamonds are crystallized under tremendous heat and pressure, probably in regions of molten rock deep within Earth. Diamonds conduct heat well but are not good conductors of electricity. They are resistant to bases and acids, and burn at about 800°C to form carbon dioxide.

The Nitrogen Group

The nitrogen family makes up Group 15. Each element has five electrons in its outer energy level. These elements tend to share electrons and to form covalent compounds with other elements. Nitrogen often is used to make nitrates and ammonia, NH_3, both of which are used in fertilizers. Nitrogen is the fourth most abundant element in your body. Each breath you take is about 80 percent gaseous nitrogen in the form of diatomic molecules, N_2. Yet you and other animals and plants can't use nitrogen in its diatomic form. The nitrogen must be combined into compounds, such as nitrates—compounds that contain the nitrate ion, NO_3.

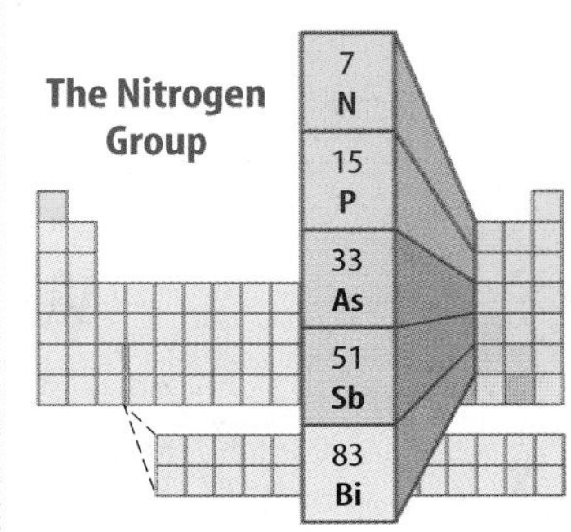

Math Skills Activity

Using Circle Graphs to Illustrate Data

Example Problem

Oxygen, the predominant element in Earth's crust, makes up approximately 46.6 percent of the crust. If you were to show this information on a circle graph, how many degrees would be used to represent oxygen?

Solution

1. *This is what you know:* oxygen = 46.6%; circle contains 360°
2. *This is what you want to find:* the part of 46.6 to 360°
3. *This is the equation you need to use:* $\frac{46.6}{100} = \frac{x}{360°}$
4. *Solve the equation for x:* $x = \frac{46.6 \times 360°}{100} = 167.76°$ or $168°$

Check your answer by dividing your answer by 360, then multiplying by 100.

Practice Problems

1. The percentages of remaining elements in Earth's crust are: silicon, 27.7; aluminum, 8.1; iron, 5.0; calcium, 3.6; sodium, 2.8; potassium, 2.6; magnesium, 2.1; and other elements, 1.5. Illustrate in a circle graph.
2. The approximate percentages of the elements in the body are: oxygen, 65; carbon, 18.5; hydrogen, 9.5; nitrogen, 3.3; calcium, 1.5; phosphorus, 1.0; and other elements which account for 1.2. Illustrate in a circle graph.

For more help, refer to the Math Skill Handbook.

The Nitrogen Group

Make a Model

The general composition of air can be modeled using balloons of two different colors. Have 80% of them one color to represent N_2 and 20% the other color to represent O_2. Bring the inflated and tied balloons to class, and position them in a corner of the room for students to observe. Explain that the balloons show the approximate ratio of nitrogen molecules to oxygen molecules in air. L2 LS **Visual-Spatial**

Extension

In living organisms, phosphorus plays several important roles, one of which is phosphorylation. Have students make posters illustrating the process of phosphorylation in photosynthesis and in respiration. In both photosynthetic phosphorylation and respirational phosphorylation, a phosphate group is added to adenosine diphosphate (ADP) to form adenosine triphosphate (ATP). ATP is used by cells as a source of energy to power cell processes such as the synthesis of proteins. L3 LS **Logical-Mathematical** P

Math Skills Activity

National Math Standards

Correlation to Mathematics Objectives

1, 2, 5, 6, 9, 10

Answers to Practice Problems

1. degrees of the circle needed for each element: O, 167.76; Si, 99.72; Al, 29.16; Fe, 18.00; Ca, 12.96; Na, 10.08; K, 9.36; Mg, 7.56; other, 5.4.
2. degrees of the circle needed for each element: O, 234.00; C, 66.60; H, 34.20; N, 11.88; Ca, 5.40; P, 3.60; other, 4.32.

Inclusion Strategies

Learning Disabled To help students with the math in the Math Skills Activity, draw a circle on the board and divide it into fourths. Ask students how many degrees are in each of the angles between the divisions of the circle. 90° **What percent of the area of the circle is in each division?** 25% Once they see this relationship, work through the math with them: $\frac{25}{100} = \frac{x}{360}$; $x = (25 \times 360) \div 100 = 90$

Resource Manager

Chapter Resources Booklet
Enrichment, p. 32

Life Science Critical Thinking/Problem Solving, p. 22

Mathematics Skill Activities, p. 5

The Nitrogen Group, continued

Reading Check

Answer to lower the melting point of the plug that holds the water in, so heat from a fire will quickly activate the sprinkler

The Oxygen Group

Use an Analogy

A futon is a piece of furniture that can be used as a sofa or laid flat to be used as a bed. These various forms of the same piece of furniture are like the allotropes, or other forms, of the same element.

Fun Fact

Sulfur is one of the oldest known elements. Originally called *brimstone,* meaning "burning stone," it was used by ancient Greeks as a house fumigant. By itself it is odorless, but rotten eggs, skunks, and onions all owe their characteristic odors to compounds of sulfur. Sulfur's main use is in the manufacture of sulfuric acid, which is widely used in making fertilizers.

Extension

Polonium is in the area of the periodic table that might make it seem a metalloid, yet it is typically classed as a metal. Have students find out why. Like metals, polonium conducts electricity better when it is cooled. Metalloids conduct electricity better when they are heated. L3 LS **Logical-Mathematical**

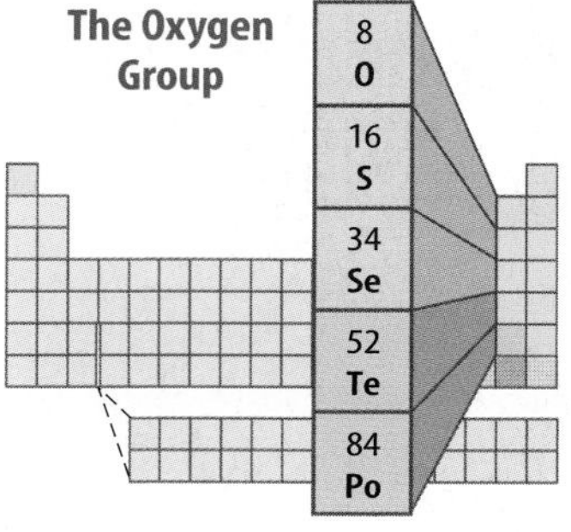

Uses of the Nitrogen Group Phosphorus is a nonmetal that has three allotropes. Phosphorous compounds can be used for many things from water softeners to fertilizers, match heads, and even in fine china. Antimony is a metalloid, and bismuth is a metal. Both elements are used with other metals to lower their melting points. It is because of this property that the metal in automatic fire-sprinkler heads contain bismuth.

Reading Check *Why is bismuth used in fire-sprinkler heads?*

The Oxygen Group

Group 16 on the periodic table is the oxygen group. You can live for only a short time without oxygen, which makes up about 20 percent of air. Oxygen, a nonmetal, exists in the air as diatomic molecules, O_2. During electrical storms, some oxygen molecules, O_2, change into ozone molecules, O_3. Oxygen also has several uses in compound form, including the one shown in **Figure 19A.**

Nearly all living things on Earth need O_2 for respiration. Living things also depend on a layer of O_3 around Earth for protection from some of the Sun's radiation.

The second element in the oxygen group is sulfur. Sulfur is a nonmetal that exists in two allotropic forms as different-shaped crystals and as a noncrystalline solid. Sulfur combines with metals to form sulfides of such distinctive colors that they are used as pigments in paints.

The nonmetal selenium and two metalloids—tellurium and polonium—are the other Group 16 elements. Selenium is the most common of these three. This element is one of several that you need in trace amounts in your diet. Many multivitamins contain this nonmetal as an ingredient. But selenium is toxic if too much of it gets into your system. Selenium also is used in photocopiers like the one in **Figure 19B.**

Figure 19
Group 16 compounds have a variety of uses.

A **Solutions of hydrogen peroxide, H_2O_2, are used to clean minor wounds.**

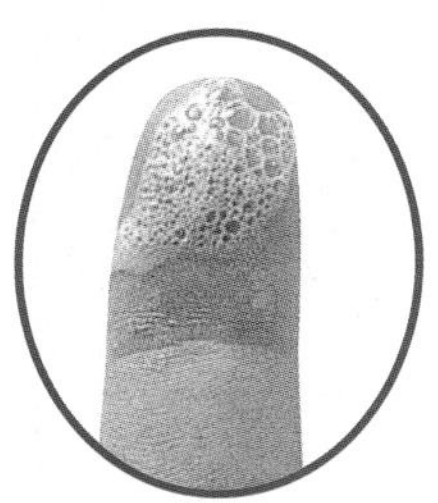

B **Selenium is used in xerography to make photocopies.**

Science Journal

Mystery Element Have students review the work done by Marie and Pierre Curie to discover polonium and write a summary in their Science Journals. Marie Curie noticed that samples of a uranium ore called pitchblende were more radioactive than could be accounted for by their uranium content. She theorized that another element, even more radioactive than uranium, was present in the ore. After reducing and purifying tons of the ore, the Curies succeeded in 1898 in isolating, for the first time ever, the element that is now called polonium after Marie Curie's native country, Poland. L3 LS **Linguistic**

Figure 20
The americium used in smoke detectors is a synthetic element that has saved lives.

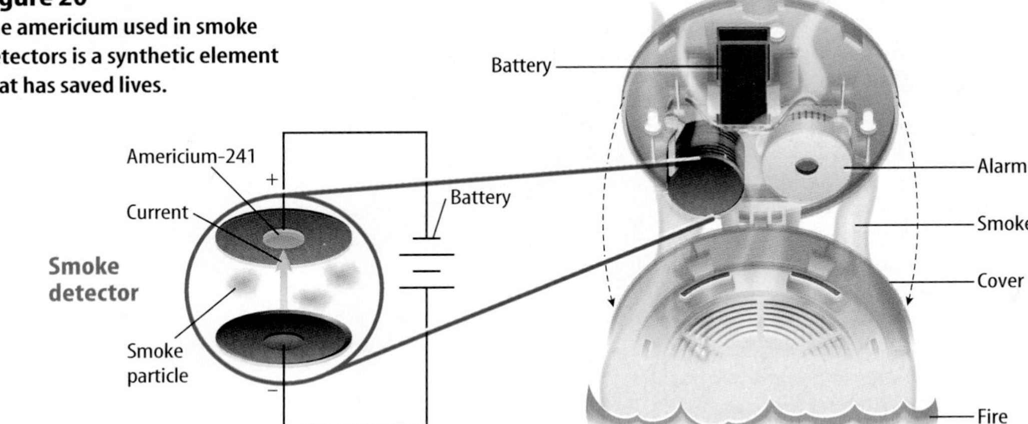

Synthetic Elements

If you made something that always fell apart, you might think you were not successful. However, nuclear scientists are learning to do just that. By smashing existing elements with particles accelerated in a heavy ion accelerator, they have been successful in creating elements not typically found on Earth. Except for technetium 43 and promethium 61, each synthetic element has more than 92 protons.

Bombarding uranium with protons can make neptunium, element 93. Half of the synthesized atoms of neptunium disintegrate in about two days. This may not sound useful, but when neptunium atoms disintegrate, they form plutonium. This highly toxic element has been used in control rods of nuclear reactors and in bombs. Plutonium also can be changed to americium, element 95. This element is used in home smoke detectors such as the one in **Figure 20.** In smoke detectors, a small amount of americium emits harmless, charged particles. An electric plate in the smoke detector attracts some of these charged particles. When a lot of smoke is in the air, it interferes with the electric current, which immediately sets off the alarm in the smoke detector.

Transuranium Elements Elements having more than 92 protons, the atomic number of uranium, are called **transuranium elements.** These elements do not belong exclusively to the metal, nonmetal, or metalloid group. These are the elements toward the bottom of the periodic table. Some are in the actinide series, and some are on the bottom row of the main periodic table. All of the transuranium elements are synthetic and unstable, and many of them disintegrate quickly.

The Transuranium Elements

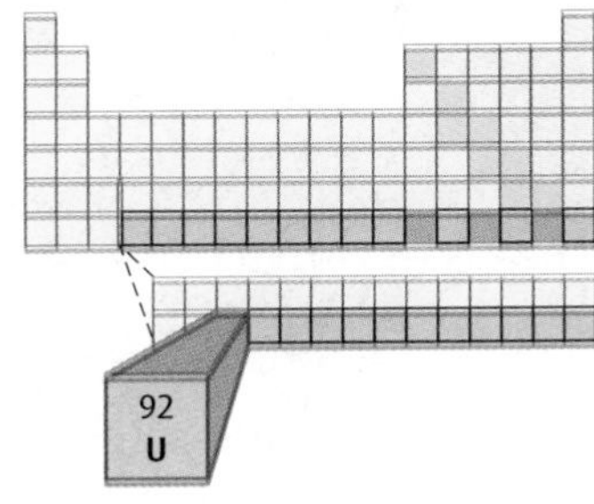

Synthetic Elements

Activity

Assign each student one of the synthetic elements. Ask students to identify the isotopes of their assigned elements and the half-lives of the isotopes. Have students compile the information into a class table. L2
LS **Visual-Spatial**

Extension

Technetium was the first element to be synthesized. The existence of technetium was predicted by the periodic table, but no technetium has been found occurring naturally on Earth. Have students find out how and where technetium was first synthesized and the atomic number and half-life of its most stable isotope. Technetium was first found in 1937 by C. Perrier and E. G. Segré in Italy in a sample of molybdenum that had been bombarded with deuterons at the University of California at Berkeley. Technetium-97 is the most stable isotope. It has a half-life of 2.6 million years. L3
LS **Linguistic**

Use Science Words

Word Origins Ask students to find the origins of the word *radioactive* and determine how the words *radio* and *radioactive* are related. The prefix *radi-* means "radiant energy or radiation," and comes from the Latin word *radius,* meaning "ray." A radio is a device that transmits or receives signals by means of electromagnetic radiation. When used this way, radio is short for radiotelegraphy. L3 LS **Linguistic**

Resource Manager

Chapter Resources Booklet
Transparency Activity, pp. 49–51

Earth Science Critical Thinking/Problem Solving, p. 3

Physical Science Critical Thinking/Problem Solving, p. 13

Science Journal

The Newest Elements What is the newest element? Ask students to use internet sources to determine the current number of known chemical elements and to write their findings in their Science Journals. This could change at any time, as scientists worldwide continue attempting to synthesize new elements. L2 LS **Linguistic**

Section 3 Mixed Groups 627

Visualizing the Discovery of Elements

Have students examine the pictures and read the captions. Then ask the following questions.

Why would gold be a useful material for people to use as early as the Stone Age? Answers will vary, but may be similar to the following response. Gold is soft and easy to process using primitive tools. It also has other desirable properties (namely luster) and is available in limited quantities—giving it monetary value.

Why were so few of the naturally occurring elements still undiscovered as late as 1776? Laboratory methods were still primitive and the technology was not yet available to separate and identify many of the individual elements.

Activity

Have the students write a song about elements and their uses. Have them perform their song for the class.

Extension

Challenge students to research the life and work of Marie and Pierre Curie and their contributions to chemistry. Have them prepare a poster illustrating the important milestones in their careers. Students can share the information that they learn and their poster with the class.

Figure 21

Some elements, such as gold, silver, tin, carbon, copper, and lead, have been known and used for thousands of years. Most others were discovered much more recently. Even at the time of the American Revolution in 1776, only 24 elements were known. The timeline below shows the dates of discovery of selected elements, ancient and modern.

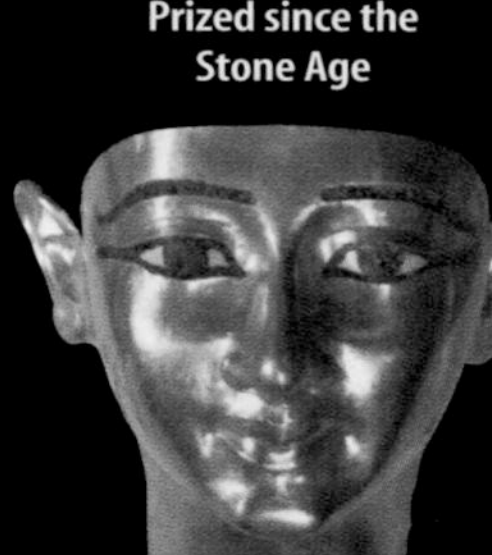

Au - GOLD
Prized since the Stone Age

Ag - SILVER
Found in tombs dating to 4000 B.C.

A.D. 1774
Cl - CHLORINE
Pale green, toxic gas

10,000 B.C. — 1700 A.D.

1817
Cd - CADMIUM
Used to color yellow and red paint

1825
Al - ALUMINUM
Most abundant element in Earth's crust

1868
He - HELIUM
Lighter-than-air gas used to fill balloons

1898
Ne - NEON
Glows when electricity flows through it

1898
Po - POLONIUM and Ra - RADIUM
Radioactive elements discovered by Marie and Pierre Curie

1800 A.D.

1900
Rn - RADON
Radioactive gas that may cause cancer

1952
Es - EINSTEINIUM
Radioactive gas named after Albert Einstein

1981-1996
Ns - NIELSBOHRIUM, Uun - UNUNNILIUM,
Elements isolated by a heavy ion accelerator such as the UNILAC, below

1900 A.D. — 2000 A.D.

Resource Manager

Chapter Resources Booklet
- Reinforcement, p. 29
- Activity Worksheet, pp. 7–8

628 CHAPTER 20 Elements and Their Properties

Why make elements? **Figure 21** shows when some of the elements were discovered throughout history. The processes used to discover these elements have varied widely. The most recently discovered elements are synthetic. By studying how the synthesized elements form and disintegrate, you can gain an understanding of the forces holding the nucleus together. When these atoms disintegrate, they are said to be radioactive.

Radioactive elements can be useful. For example, technetium's radioactivity makes it ideal for many medical applications. At this time, many of the synthetic elements last only small fractions of seconds after they are constructed and can be made only in small amounts. However, the value of applications that might be discovered easily could offset their costs.

Seeking Stability Element 114, discovered in 1999, appears to be much more stable than most synthetic elements of its size. It lasted for 30 s before it broke apart. This may not seem like long, but it lasts 100,000 times longer than an atom of element 112. Perhaps this special combination of 114 protons and 175 neutrons allows the nucleus to hold together despite the enormous repulsion between the protons.

In the 1960s, scientists theorized that stable synthetic elements exist. Finding one might help scientists understand how the forces inside the atom work. Perhaps someday you'll read about some of the everyday uses this discovery has brought.

SCIENCE Online

Data Update For an online update about synthetic elements, visit the Glencoe Science Web site at **science.glencoe.com** and select the appropriate chapter.

Section 3 Assessment

1. Why are Groups 14 and 15 better representatives of mixed groups than Groups 13 and Group 16?
2. Describe how the allotropes of silicon differ in appearance.
3. How is an element classified as a transuranium element?
4. What type of structure does a diamond have? Describe how you would build a model of this.
5. **Think Critically** Graphite and a diamond are both made of the element carbon. Why is graphite a lubricant and diamond the hardest gem known?

Skill Builder Activities

6. **Concept Mapping** Make a concept map for allotropes of carbon using the terms *graphite, diamond, buckminsterfullerene, sphere, hexagon,* and *tetrahedron.* **For more help, refer to the** Science Skill Handbook.
7. **Using a Computerized Card Catalog** Some people are concerned about the use of radioactive elements, such as americium, in smoke detectors and other products. Research smoke detectors and radioactive elements using a computerized card catalog. Summarize what you learn in a table. **For more help, refer to the** Technology Skill Handbook.

SCIENCE Online

Internet Addresses

Explore the Glencoe Science Web site at **science.glencoe.com** to find out more about topics in this section.

3 Assess

Reteach

Display a periodic table on the wall or by using an overhead projector. Point out an element near the bottom of Group 4, 5, or 6. Ask students if the element would more likely have a negative or positive charge in compounds. positive L2 **Visual-Spatial**

Challenge

Ask students to find out why scientists add small amounts of germanium and arsenic to silicon to make different types of computer chips. Arsenic has one more valence electron than silicon, and germanium has one less valence electron than silicon. When silicon is doped with small amounts of these elements, its ability to conduct electricity increases. Chips containing different combinations of these elements can control the current in a circuit. L3 **Logical-Mathematical**

Assessment

Performance Give students blank outlines of the periodic table and have them label as many rows and columns as they can. Then ask them to fill in as many elements as they can. Ask them to include the lines separating the metals, nonmetals, and metalloids. Use **Performance Assessment in the Science Classroom,** p. 109.

Answers to Section Assessment

1. Groups 14 and 15 each contain metals, metalloids, and nonmetals while Group 13 contains metals and a metalloid, and Group 16 contains metalloids and nonmetals.
2. One is a hard gray substance, and the other is a brown powder.
3. The element has an atomic number higher than that of uranium.
4. Tetrahedrons joined in a crystal; answers will vary.
5. Diamond consists of interlocking tetrahedrons that provide support in all directions. Graphite has strong bonds in one direction and weak bonds between flat layers. The layers slide over each other as the weak bonds are easily broken under stress.
6. Make sure students' concept maps link hexagon with graphite, tetrahedron with diamond, and sphere with buckminsterfullerene.
7. Check student tables.

Activity BENCH TESTED

Recognize the Problem

Purpose

Students will make a working model of the layered graphite structure and use the model to determine the cause-and-effect relationship of the bonding between carbon atoms in graphite and graphite's physical properties.

L2 COOP LEARN LS **Kinesthetic**

Process Skills

making and using models, communicating, classifying, recognizing cause and effect, forming a hypothesis, designing an experiment

Time Required

35 minutes

Materials

The polystyrene sheets can be cut from plastic report cover sheets.

Safety Precautions

Advise students to use care when working with scissors, especially when making holes in any of the materials.

Form a Hypothesis

Possible Hypothesis

The weak bonds between layers of graphite allow the layers to slide easily over each other, while the strong bonds within the layers keep the layers intact.

Activity Design Your Own Experiment

Slippery Carbon

Often, a lubricant is needed when two metals touch each other. For example, a sticky lock sometimes works better with the addition of a small amount of graphite. What gives this allotrope of carbon the slippery property of a lubricant?

Recognize the Problem

Why do certain arrangements of atoms in a material cause the material to feel slippery?

Form a Hypothesis

Based on your understanding of how carbon atoms bond, form a hypothesis about the relationship of graphite's molecular structure to its physical properties.

Possible Materials

thin spaghetti
small gumdrops
thin polystyrene sheets
flat cardboard
scissors

Goals

- **Make a model** that will demonstrate the molecular structure of graphite.
- **Compare and contrast** the strength of the different bonds in graphite.
- **Infer** the relationship between bonding and physical properties.

Safety Precautions

Use care when working with scissors and uncooked spaghetti.

630

Test Your Hypothesis

Possible Procedures

1. Use scissors to cut hexagon shapes out of the thin polystyrene or cardboard sheets.
2. Carefully punch small holes near each corner of the hexagons. Insert gum drops in the small holes.
3. Draw lines between the gumdrops on the hexagon to represent bonds between hydrogen atoms.
4. Use the thin spaghetti to connect hexagons to each other by inserting both ends of the spaghetti through gumdrops on different hexagons.
5. Gently push on the connected hexagons to see what happens to the structure.

Test Your Hypothesis

Plan

1. As a group, agree upon a logical hypothesis statement.
2. As a group, sequence and list the steps you need to take to test your hypothesis. Be specific, describing exactly what you will do at each step to make a model of the types of bonding present in graphite.
3. Remember from **Figure 19** that graphite consists of rings of six carbons bonded in a flat hexagon. These rings are bonded to each other. In addition, the flat rings in one layer are weakly attached to other flat layers.
4. List possible materials you plan to use.
5. Read over the experiment to make sure that all steps are in logical order.
6. Will your model be constructed with materials that show weak and strong attractions?

Do

1. Make sure your teacher approves your plan before you start.
2. Have you selected materials to use in your model that demonstrate weak and strong attractions? Carry out the experiment as planned.
3. Once your model has been constructed, list any observations that you make and include a sketch in your Science Journal.

Analyze Your Data

1. **Compare** your model with designs and results of other groups.
2. How does your model illustrate two types of attractions found in the graphite structure?
3. How does the bonding of graphite that you explored in the lab explain graphite's lubricating properties? Write your answer in your Science Journal.

Draw Conclusions

1. Did the results you obtained from your experiment support your hypothesis? Explain.
2. **Describe** why graphite makes a good lubricant.
3. What kinds of bonds do you think a diamond has?

Communicating Your Data

Explain to a friend why graphite makes a good lubricant and how the two types of bonds make a difference. **For more help, refer to the** Science Skill Handbook.

Teaching Strategies

Have students compare lines made by pencils of various ratings (e.g. #2, #2.5). Writing with a pencil illustrates how graphite slides and is sloughed off under applied pressure.

Expected Outcome

- Models should represent six carbon atoms bonded together in a flat, six-sided structure that does not break under pressure. Two flat layers of these structures should be connected by easily broken objects such as thin spaghetti, representing the easily broken bonds between graphite layers.
- When pressure is applied to graphite, the weak bonds between layers break. This change causes the layers to slide over each other while the hexagons remain intact.

Analyze Your Data

1. All should show two different strength bonds between carbon atoms.
2. Attractions within the flat layers are strong and resist change, while the attractions between layers are weak and break easily.
3. The layers of graphite slide easily over each other, so when graphite is placed between two surfaces, it slides between them.

Draw Conclusions

1. Answers will vary. The results should confirm a hypothesis that the weak bonds between layers of graphite molecules allow layers to slide easily over each other, while strong bonds keep the layers intact.
2. Good lubricants need to be fairly unreactive and be able to reduce friction between surfaces. Graphite has both properties.
3. covalent

Assessment

Oral Have students loosen and tighten a nut and bolt with and without graphite. Ask them to explain why the addition of graphite makes this mechanical movement easier. Use **Performance Assessment in the Science Classroom,** p. 89.

Communicating Your Data

If feasible, have students take digital photos of their models before, during, and after the application of stress to their hexagonal structures. These photos can then be posted on the web, or printed out in a time-lapse presentation.

Content Background

Neon was discovered in 1898 by William Ramsay and Morris Travers. Earlier Ramsay had helped isolate argon and predicted the existence of neon. Travers and Ramsay were looking for the missing element. They were testing the products of air liquefaction by bombarding them with electrons in a low-pressure, sealed tube. At some point, one of the elements glowed with an intense red light that had not been seen before. Ramsay named the element neon after the Greek word for new.

Mixing argon and mercury with the neon gas produced color variations. The first neon sign was displayed in Paris in 1910 by Georges Claude, a chemist who soon became a businessman. In 1923 Claude installed the first neon sign in the United States at a Packard dealership in Los Angeles. By 1930 almost every business in America had a neon sign and tube bending was a vibrant trade.

The latter half of the twentieth century saw a decline in the use of neon, which was replaced by plastic signs lit with fluorescent tubes. Neon was put to use in industry and medicine as the primary gas in television tubes, aircraft runway lights and a variety of gas lasers. Neon as decorative lighting was rediscovered by the art community in the 1970s. New fluorescent tube coatings and gas mixtures expanded the color range beyond that available to the old sign makers.

TIME SCIENCE AND HISTORY

SCIENCE CAN CHANGE THE COURSE OF HISTORY!

The GAS that glows

Neon has made the world a more colorful place

"Nothing in the world gave a glow such as we had seen." With these words, two British chemists recorded their discovery of neon in 1898. Neon is a noble gas that emits a spectacular red-orange glow when an electric current is passed through it. It also makes up a tiny portion of the air we breathe.

But neon's presence remained undetected until a technology called spectroscopy allowed the chemists to view that "blaze of crimson light" in their lab—a light that soon lit up the world in fantastical ways.

A neon coffee cup lights up the Seattle night.

A neon sign in the making. Workers carefully twist the light tubes into different shapes.

632

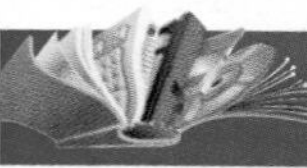

Resources for Teachers and Students

NEON TECHNIQUES: The 4th Edition of the Handbook of Neon Sign and Cold-Cathode Lighting, edited by Wayne Strattman, Cincinnati, Ohio: ST Publications, 1998.

Signs of Change

Pink flamingos, cowboys on bucking broncos, deep-sea fish afloat in the air—neon signs make any building or billboard come alive in a kaleidoscope of colors. Barely a decade after neon was discovered, a chemist developed the first neon sign. The chemist took the air out of a glass tube and replaced it with neon gas. When the gas was jolted with electricity, it glowed like a fiery sunset. The chemist sold the light to a barber, who hung it over his storefront. By the 1920s, neon lights were used to advertise everything from cars to diners.

When a touch of mercury is added to neon, it glows a tropical blue. The other colors seen in "neon lights" actually come from other noble gases. Krypton, for instance, glows yellow. Xenon shines like a bluish-white star.

Elemental Snobs

The noble gases include neon, helium, argon, krypton, xenon, and radon. Scientists called these gases "noble" because that word sometimes implies a snobbish attitude—the perfect description for gases that rarely react with other elements. Like the other noble gases, neon is stable.

For an element to be chemically stable, it needs eight electrons in its outer energy level. Neon has eight electrons in its outer shell—so it doesn't react with other elements because it already has a complete outer energy level. Although scientists have discovered that some noble gases do interact with other elements, thus far, neon remains aloof.

Other Uses for Neon

The vivid light emitted by neon can penetrate the densest fog, making it a natural choice for airplane beacons. Neon also is used to manufacture lasers and television tubes. Neon definitely helps light up our lives!

Neon lights up a Hong Kong, China night.

CONNECTIONS Design a Sign **As a group, brainstorm a new product or business, then design a neon sign to advertise your idea. See if other groups can correctly guess what your sign represents.**

SCIENCE Online
For more information, visit science.glencoe.com

Discussion

Have the students research the noble gases. Why do they emit light when stimulated by electricity? Possible answer: The stable gas molecules form ions when they acquire extra electrons. The ions decay almost immediately and give off light when they return to a stable state.

Historical Significance

Explain that, although neon is the best known of the noble gases, argon, helium, krypton, xenon, and radon are all important in modern tube technology. Neon and argon are the most widely used because they are easier to isolate than the others. Separately and in combination they are used extensively in lighting applications.

Argon is very stable and is used in light bulbs to extend the life of tungsten filaments and to prevent the oxidation of metals during welding. Krypton and xenon are used extensively in gas lasers. Their uses range from delicate eye surgery to cutting the hardest synthetic materials. The discovery of these gases and their use in electrical tubes of all sorts resulted in the rapid development of modern lighting and communication.

CONNECTIONS Based on their research, have students compile a list of devices that use noble gases in some form or another. Make the list as extensive as possible. Discuss ways in which modern life would be different without the listed items. An example might be the airline industry where the uses run from marking runways to the radar screens used by air traffic controllers. The use of lasers in industry and medicine may also be fertile ground for discussion.

SCIENCE Online

Internet Addresses

Explore the Glencoe Science Web site at **science.glencoe.com** to find out more about topics in this feature.

Chapter 20 Study Guide

Reviewing Main Ideas

Preview

Students can answer the questions in their Science Journals. Discuss the answers as you go through the chapter. LS **Linguistic**

Review

Students can write their answers, then compare them with those of other students. LS **Interpersonal**

Reteach

Students can look at the illustrations and describe details that support the main ideas of the chapter. LS **Visual-Spatial**

Answers to Chapter Review

Section 1

2. They are very chemically active and in nature easily combine with other elements.

Section 3

1. The bottom three appear to be metals, while the top three appear to be nonmetals.

Chapter 20 Study Guide

Reviewing Main Ideas

Section 1 Metals

1. A typical metal is a hard, shiny solid that, due to metallic bonding, is malleable, ductile, and a good conductor.
2. Groups 1 and 2 are the alkali and alkaline earth metals, which have some similar and some contrasting properties. *Why aren't Group 1 elements typically found in their elemental form?*

3. The iron triad, the coinage metals, and the elements in Group 12 are examples of transition elements.
4. The lanthanides and actinides have atomic numbers 58 through 71 and 90 through 103, respectively.

Section 2 Nonmetals

1. Nonmetals are typically brittle and dull. They are also poor conductors of electricity.
2. As a typical nonmetal, hydrogen is a gas that forms compounds by sharing electrons with other nonmetals and by forming ionic bonds with metals.
3. All the halogens, Group 17, have seven outer electrons and form covalent and ionic compounds, but each halogen has some properties that are unlike each of the others in the group.
4. The noble gases, Group 18, are elements whose properties and uses are related to their chemical stability.

Section 3 Mixed Groups

1. Groups 13 through 16 include metals, nonmetals, and metalloids. *Which objects below appear to be metallic and which appear to be nonmetallic?*

2. Allotropes are forms of the same element having different molecular structures.
3. The properties of three forms of carbon—graphite, diamond, and buckminsterfullerene—depend upon the differences in their crystal structures.
4. All synthetic elements are short-lived. With two exceptions, they have atomic numbers greater than 92 and are referred to as transuranium elements.

FOLDABLES Reading & Study Skills — After You Read

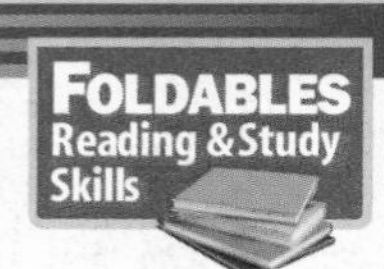

Under the tabs of the Foldable you created, write the common characteristics of metal elements and of nonmetal elements.

FOLDABLES Reading & Study Skills — After You Read

After students have read the chapter and completed the Foldable described in Before You Read, have them do the activity on the student page.

Dinah Zike

Visualizing Main Ideas

Complete the concept map using the following: Transition elements, hydrogen, Metals, Gas or brittle solid at room temperature, Inner transition metals, Metalloids, Noble gases.

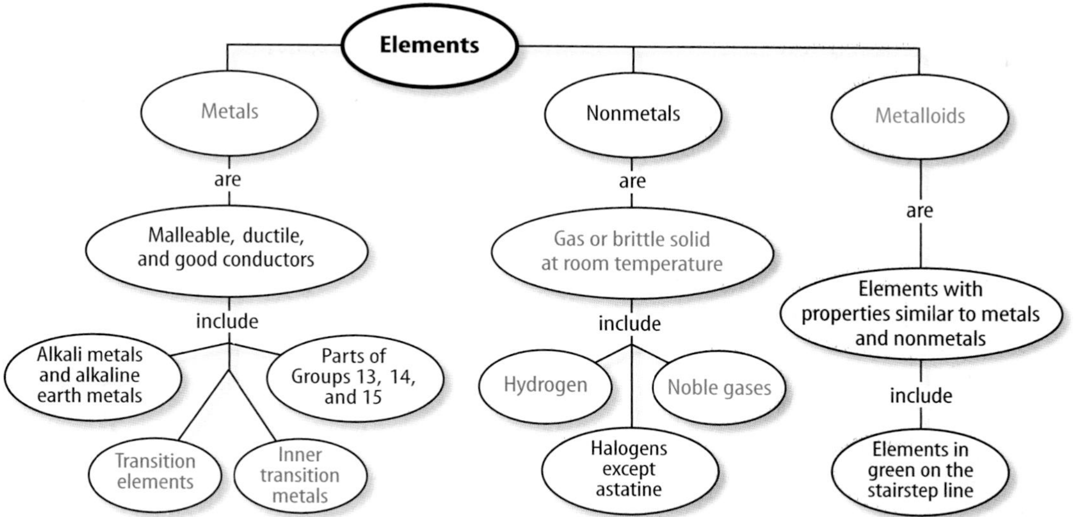

Vocabulary Review

Vocabulary Words

a. allotrope
b. diatomic molecule
c. ductile
d. malleable
e. metal
f. metallic bonding
g. metalloid
h. nonmetal
i. radioactive element
j. semiconductor
k. transition element
l. transuranium element

Study Tip

Outline the chapter to make sure that you're understanding the key ideas. Writing down the main points of the chapter will help you to remember the important details and understand the larger themes.

Using Vocabulary

Each of the following sentences is false. Make the sentence true by replacing the underlined word with a word from the list.

1. The radioactive elements are located to the left of the stair-step line on the periodic table.
2. Different structural forms of the same element are called diatomic molecules.
3. Positively charged ions are surrounded by freely moving electrons in a nonmetal element.
4. An allotrope is a molecule comprised of two atoms.
5. The nonmetals are in Groups 3 through 12 on the periodic table.

Chapter 20 Study Guide

Visualizing Main Ideas

See student page.

Vocabulary Review

Using Vocabulary

1. metals
2. allotropes
3. metallic bonding
4. diatomic molecule
5. transition elements

CHAPTER STUDY GUIDE 635

Chapter 20 Assessment

Checking Concepts

1. B
2. A
3. D
4. C
5. A
6. C
7. C
8. D
9. A
10. D

Thinking Critically

11. Mercury is a liquid at normal temperatures and expands as temperature rises. Mercury is poisonous.
12. Hydrogen is flammable whereas helium is inert.
13. Aluminum, when properly alloyed, has high strength and low density, so the aluminum will weigh less than a comparable amount of steel.
14. Some silver compounds change chemically when exposed to light.
15. Do not exceed recommended doses.

Chapter 20 Assessment

Checking Concepts

Choose the word or phrase that best answers the question.

1. When magnesium and fluorine react, what type of bond is formed?
   A) metallic **C)** covalent
   B) ionic **D)** diatomic
2. What type of bond is found in a piece of pure gold?
   A) metallic **C)** covalent
   B) ionic **D)** diatomic
3. Because electrons move freely in metals, which property describes metals?
   A) brittle **C)** dull
   B) hard **D)** conductors
4. Which set of elements makes up the most reactive group of all metals?
   A) iron triad **C)** alkali metals
   B) coinage metals **D)** alkaline earth metals
5. Which element is the most reactive of all nonmetals?
   A) fluorine **C)** hydrogen
   B) uranium **D)** oxygen
6. Which element is always found in nature combined with other elements?
   A) copper **C)** magnesium
   B) gold **D)** silver
7. Which elements are least reactive?
   A) metals **C)** noble gases
   B) halogens **D)** actinides
8. What element is formed when neptunium atoms fall apart?
   A) ytterbium **C)** americium
   B) promethium **D)** plutonium
9. Which element is an example of a radioactive element?
   A) astatine **C)** chlorine
   B) bromine **D)** fluorine
10. Which is the only group that is completely nonmetallic?
    A) 1 **C)** 17
    B) 2 **D)** 18

Thinking Critically

11. Why was mercury used in clinical thermometers, and why is it no longer used for that purpose?
12. The density of hydrogen is lower than air and can be used to fill balloons. Why is helium used instead of hydrogen?
13. Why is aluminum used instead of steel in building airplanes?
14. Why are various silver compounds used in photography?
15. Like selenium, chromium is poisonous but is needed in trace amounts in your diet. Describe how you would apply this information in order to use vitamin and mineral pills safely.

Developing Skills

16. **Making and Using Tables** Use the periodic table to classify each of the following as a lanthanide or actinide: californium, europium, cerium, nobelium, terbium, and uranium.
17. **Comparing and Contrasting** Aluminum is close to carbon on the periodic table. Explain why aluminum is a metal and carbon is not.
18. **Drawing Conclusions** You are shown two samples of phosphorus. One is white and burns if exposed to air. The other is red and burns if lit. Infer why the properties of two samples of the same element differ.

Chapter Assessment Planner

Portfolio Encourage students to place in their portfolios one or two items of what they consider to be their best work. Examples include:

- Assessment, p. 615
- Environmental Science Integration, p. 619
- Extension, p. 625

Performance Additional performance assessments, Performance Task Assessment Lists, and rubrics for evaluating these activities can be found in Glencoe's **Performance Assessment in the Science Classroom.**

19. Recognizing Cause and Effect Plants need nitrogen compounds. Nitrogen fixing changes free nitrogen into nitrates. Lightning and legumes are possible examples of nitrogen fixing. What are the cause and effect of nitrogen fixing in this example?

20. Concept Mapping Complete the concept map using the following: *Na, Fe, Actinides, Hg, Ba, Alkali,* and *Inner transition.*

Metals
- Alkali
  - K
  - Na
  - Ba
- Inner transition
  - Actinides
  - Lanthanides
- Transition
  - Fe
  - Hg
  - Ag

Performance Assessment

21. Analyze the Data The model made in the two-page activity of this chapter helps explain the lubricating ability of graphite. Use that same model to explain how the graphite in a pencil is able to leave a mark on a piece of paper.

22. Investigate a Controversial Issue Research the pros and cons of using nuclear energy to produce electricity. Prepare a report that includes data as well as your informed opinion on the subject.

Technology

Go to the Glencoe Science Web site at **science.glencoe.com** or use the **Glencoe Science CD-ROM** for additional chapter assessment.

THE PRINCETON REVIEW Test Practice

All of the elements that make up matter can be divided into groups by looking at their different characteristics. Examples of two such groups of elements are listed in Tables A and B below.

Table A
Iron
Silver
Copper

Table B
Helium
Carbon
Sulfur

Study the tables and answer the following questions.

1. The elements in Table A are different from the elements in Table B because only the elements in Table A.
   A) are shiny and malleable
   B) are gases
   C) dissolve instantly in water
   D) are yellow
2. Which of these belongs with Table A?
   F) nitrogen gas
   G) chlorine gas
   H) aluminum foil
   J) water
3. The title of Table A is likely to be _____.
   A) metals
   B) nonmetals
   C) metalloids
   D) elements
4. Which of the following elements does not belong in Table B?
   F) oxygen
   G) helium
   H) sodium
   J) bromine

Chapter 20 Assessment

Test Practice

The Test-Taking Tip was written by The Princeton Review, the nation's leader in test preparation.

1. A
2. H
3. A
4. H

Developing Skills

16. lanthanides: europium, cerium; terbium; actinides: californium, nobelium; uranium
17. Carbon has four electrons in its outer energy level while aluminum has three. Aluminum holds on to its electrons less tightly than carbon, so it can form metallic bonds.
18. They are allotropes.
19. cause: lightning and legumes; effect: changing free nitrogen into nitrates
20. See student page.

Performance Assessment

21. Pressure on the pencil causes the bonds between hexagonal layers to break. This allows the layers to slide past one another so graphite gets pushed onto the paper. Use PASC, p. 99.
22. Pros should include a lack of air pollution and less dependence on other countries for energy sources. Cons should include radioactive waste disposal problems and potential for radiation leakage. Use PASC, p. 137.

Assessment Resources

Reproducible Masters

Chapter Resources Booklet
Chapter Review, pp. 39–40
Chapter Tests, pp. 41–44
Assessment Transparency Activity, p. 51

Glencoe Science Web site
Interactive Tutor
Chapter Quizzess

Glencoe Technology
Assessment Transparency
Interactive CD-ROM Chapter Quizzes
ExamView Pro Test Bank
Vocabulary PuzzleMaker Software
MindJogger Videoquiz DVD/VHS

Section/Objectives	Standards		Activities/Features
	National	State/Local	
Chapter Opener	See p. 37T for a Key to Standards.		**Explore Activity:** Indentify a common element, p. 639 **Before You Read,** p. 639
Section 1 Simple Organic Compounds 2 sessions 1 block 1. **Identify** the difference between organic and inorganic carbon compounds. 2. **Examine** the structures of some organic compounds. 3. **Differentiate** between saturated and unsaturated hydrocarbons. 4. **Identify** isomers of organic compounds.	National Content Standards: UCP5, A1, B1 (5–8), B2 (9–12)		**MiniLAB:** Modeling Structures, p. 643
Section 2 Other Organic Compounds 2 sessions 1 block 1. **Define** atomic compounds. 2. **Identify** the nature of alcohols and acids. 3. **Identify** organic compounds you use in daily life.	National Content Standards: UCP5, A1, B1 (5–8), B2 (9–12), E2, F5 (5–8), F6 (9–12)		**Astronomy Integration,** p. 647 **Activity:** Alcohols and Organic Acids, p. 649
Section 3 Petroleum—A Source of Carbon Compounds 2 sessions 1 block 1. **Explain** how carbon compounds are obtained from petroleum. 2. **Compare and contrast** differences among the various petroleum-based fuels. 3. **Determine** how carbon compounds can form long chains. 4. **Identify** some of the ways petroleum enriches your world.	National Content Standards: UCP2, A1, B1 (5–8), B2, E2, F1, F2, F5 (5–8), F2, F3, F4 (9–12)		**Visualizing Petroleum Products,** p. 652 **MiniLAB:** Visualizing Polymers, p. 653 **Science Online,** p. 654
Section 4 Biological Compounds 2 sessions 1 block 1. **Compare and contrast** proteins, nucleic acids, carbohydrates, and lipids. 2. **Identify** the structure of polymers found in basic food groups. 3. **Identify** the structure of large biological polymers.	National Content Standards: UCP1, A1, B1 (5–8), B2, B6, C5, F1 (5–8), F1, F5, F6 (9–12), G2		**Science Online,** p. 658 **Health Integration,** p. 661 **Activity:** Preparing an Ester, pp. 662–663 **Oops!** Accidents in Science: A Spill for a Spill, pp. 664–665

Activity Materials	Reproducible Resources	Section Assessment	Technology
Explore Activity: no materials needed	**Chapter Resources Booklet** Foldables Worksheet, p. 17 Note-taking Worksheets, pp. 35–38	GLENCOE'S ASSESSMENT ADVANTAGE	
MiniLAB: soft gumdrops, raisins, toothpicks	**Chapter Resources Booklet** Transparency Activity, p. 48 MiniLAB, p. 3 Enrichment, p. 31 Reinforcement, p. 27 Directed Reading, p. 20 Transparency Activity, pp. 53–54	**Portfolio** Science Journal, p. 643 **Performance** MiniLAB, p. 643 Skill Builder Activities, p. 644 **Content** Section Assessment, p. 644	Section Focus Transparency Teaching Transparency Interactive CD-ROM/DVD Guided Reading Audio Program
Activity: large test tube and stopper, 1 mL 0.01 M potassium permanganate solution, 1 mL 6M sodium hydroxide solution, 3 drops ethanol, 10-mL graduated cylinder	**Chapter Resources Booklet** Transparency Activity, p. 49 Enrichment, p. 32 Reinforcement, p. 28 Directed Reading, p. 20 Activity Worksheet, pp. 5–6	**Portfolio** Visual Learning, p. 647 **Performance** Skill Builder Activities, p. 648 **Content** Section Assessment, p. 648	Section Focus Transparency Interactive CD-ROM/DVD Guided Reading Audio Program
MiniLAB: paper clips, 20 strips colored paper *Need materials?* Contact Science Kit at 1-800-828-7777 or www.sciencekit.com on the Internet.	**Chapter Resources Booklet** Transparency Activity, p. 50 MiniLAB, p. 4 Enrichment, p. 33 Reinforcement, p. 29 Directed Reading, p. 21 **Physical Science Critical Thinking/Problem Solving,** p. 14 **Cultural Diversity,** pp. 45, 49	**Portfolio** Science Journal, p. 654 **Performance** MiniLAB, p. 653 Skill Builder Activities, p. 655 **Content** Section Assessment, p. 655	Section Focus Transparency Interactive CD-ROM/DVD Guided Reading Audio Program
Activity: medium-size test tube, test-tube holder, 250-mL beaker, 10-mL graduated cylinder, water, hot plate, ring stand, thermometer, 0.2 g salicylic acid, 2 mL methyl alcohol, 2-3 drops of concentrated sulfuric acid	**Chapter Resources Booklet** Transparency Activity, p. 51 Enrichment, p. 34 Reinforcement, p. 30 Directed Reading, pp. 21, 22 Activity Worksheet, pp. 7–8 Lab Activity, pp. 9–11, 13–15	**Portfolio** Curriculum Connection, p. 660 **Performance** Skill Builder Activities, p. 661 **Content** Section Assessment, p. 661	Section Focus Transparency Interactive CD-ROM/DVD Guided Reading Audio Program

End of Chapter Assessment

GLENCOE'S ASSESSMENT ADVANTAGE

Blackline Masters	Technology	Professional Series
Chapter Resources Booklet Chapter Review, pp. 41–42 Chapter Tests, pp. 43–46 **Standardized Test Practice by The Princeton Review,** pp. 88–91	MindJogger Videoquiz CD-ROM Explorations and Quizzes Vocabulary Puzzle Makers ExamView Pro Test Bank Interactive Lesson Planner Interactive Teacher's Edition	Performance Assessment in the Science Classroom (PASC)

Transparencies

Section Focus

Section 1 Section Focus Transparency **How did I get stuck in this mess?**

Can you imagine what would happen if a sticky mix of oil and tar lurked underneath a little water? You might guess that animals that came to drink the water could get stuck in the tar. At the La Brea tar pits, that's exactly what happened.

1. How are plants and animals involved in the creation of oil?
2. Why do you think carbon chemistry is called organic chemistry, or the chemistry of life?

L1

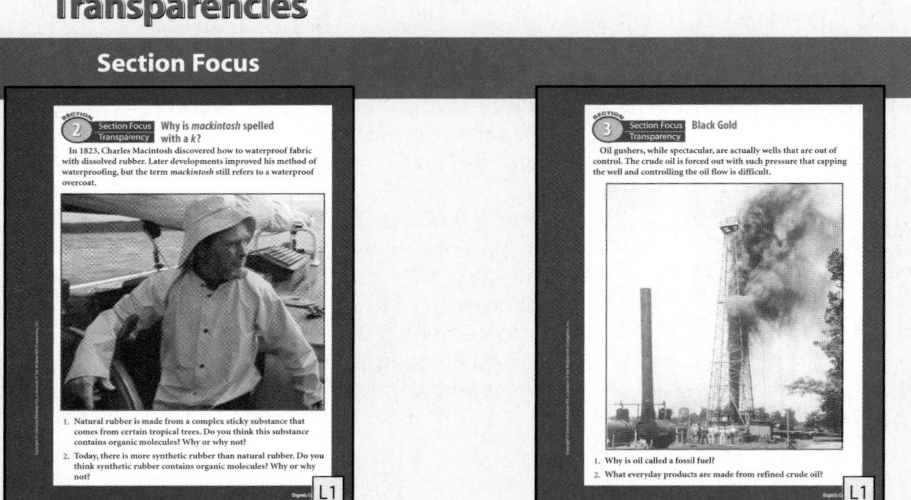
Section 2 Section Focus Transparency **Why is *mackintosh* spelled with a *k*?**

In 1823, Charles Macintosh discovered how to waterproof fabric with dissolved rubber. Later developments improved his method of waterproofing, but the term *mackintosh* still refers to a waterproof overcoat.

1. Natural rubber is made from a complex sticky substance that comes from certain tropical trees. Do you think this substance contains organic molecules? Why or why not?
2. Today, there is more synthetic rubber than natural rubber. Do you think synthetic rubber contains organic molecules? Why or why not?

L1

Section 3 Section Focus Transparency **Black Gold**

Oil gushers, while spectacular, are actually wells that are out of control. The crude oil is forced out with such pressure that capping the well and controlling the oil flow is difficult.

1. Why is oil called a fossil fuel?
2. What everyday products are made from refined crude oil?

L1

This is a representation of key blackline masters available in the Teacher Classroom Resources. See Resource Manager boxes within the chapter for additional information.

Assessment

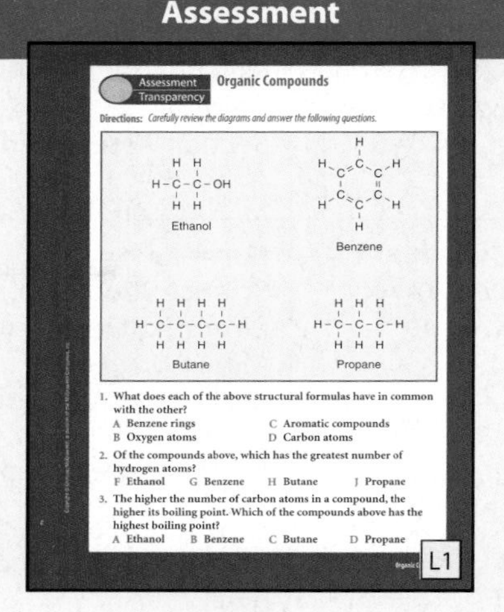
Assessment Transparency **Organic Compounds**

Directions: *Carefully review the diagrams and answer the following questions.*

1. What does each of the above structural formulas have in common with the other?
   A Benzene rings
   B Oxygen atoms
   C Aromatic compounds
   D Carbon atoms
2. Of the compounds above, which has the greatest number of hydrogen atoms?
   F Ethanol G Benzene H Butane J Propane
3. The higher the number of carbon atoms in a compound, the higher its boiling point. Which of the compounds above has the highest boiling point?
   A Ethanol B Benzene C Butane D Propane

L1

Teaching

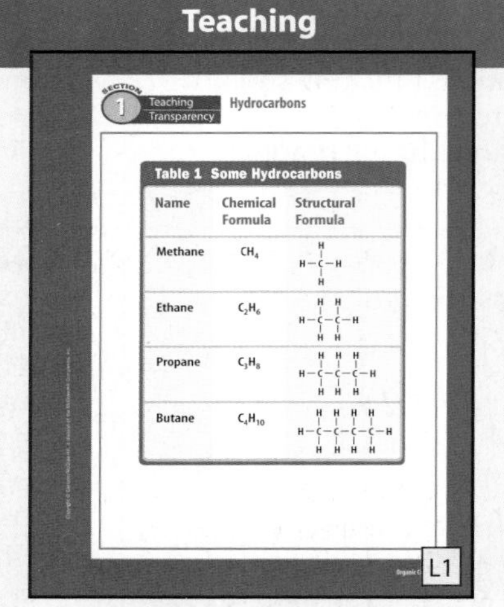
Section 1 Teaching Transparency **Hydrocarbons**

Table 1 Some Hydrocarbons

Name	Chemical Formula	Structural Formula
Methane	CH_4	
Ethane	C_2H_6	
Propane	C_3H_8	
Butane	C_4H_{10}	

L1

Key to Teaching Strategies

The following designations will help you decide which activities are appropriate for your students.

- L1 Level 1 activities should be appropriate for students with learning difficulties.
- L2 Level 2 activities should be within the ability range of all students.
- L3 Level 3 activities are designed for above-average students.
- ELL ELL activities should be within the ability range of English Language Learners.
- COOP LEARN Cooperative Learning activities are designed for small group work.
- LS Multiple Learning Styles logos are used throughout to indicate strategies that address different learning styles.
- P These strategies represent student products that can be placed into a best-work portfolio.

Hands-on Activities

Activity Worksheets

Laboratory Activities

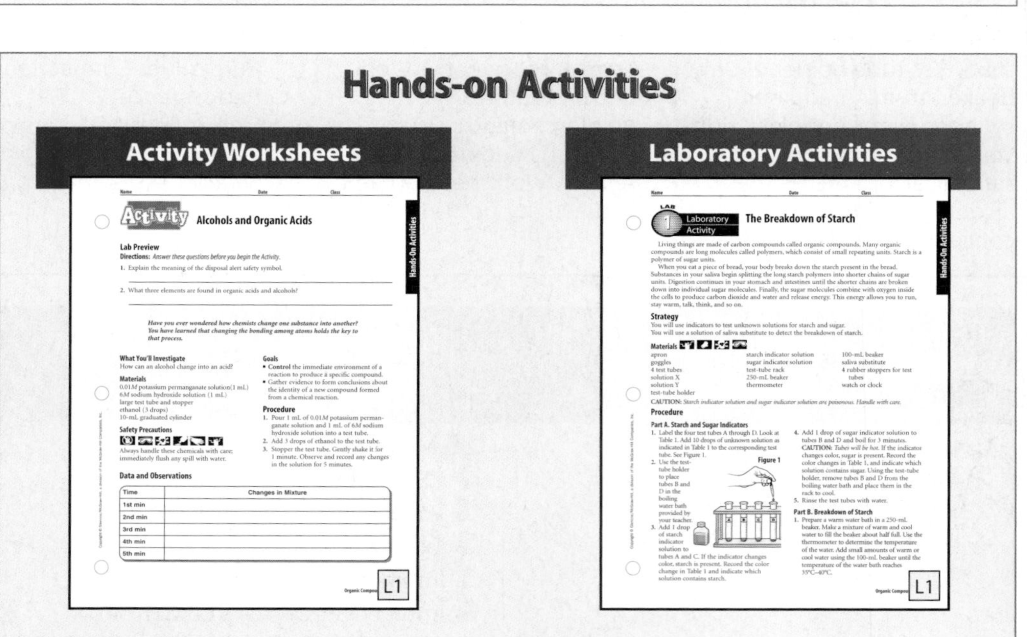
Activity **Alcohols and Organic Acids**

Lab Preview

Directions: *Answer these questions before you begin the Activity.*

1. Explain the meaning of the disposal alert safety symbol.
2. What three elements are found in organic acids and alcohols?

Have you ever wondered how chemists change one substance into another? You have learned that changing the bonding among atoms holds the key to that process.

Data and Observations

Time	Changes in Mixture
1st min	
2nd min	
3rd min	
4th min	
5th min	

L1

Laboratory Activity 1 **The Breakdown of Starch**

L1

Meeting Different Ability Levels

Content Outline

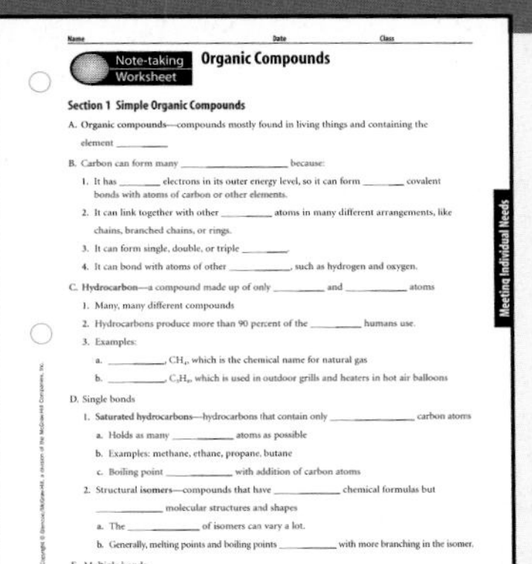

Note-taking Worksheet — Organic Compounds

Section 1 Simple Organic Compounds

L1

Reinforcement

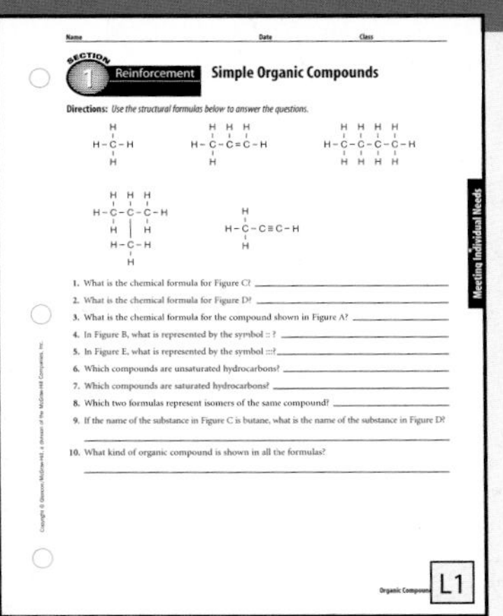

Section 1 Reinforcement — Simple Organic Compounds

Directions: Use the structural formulas below to answer the questions.

L1

Directed Reading

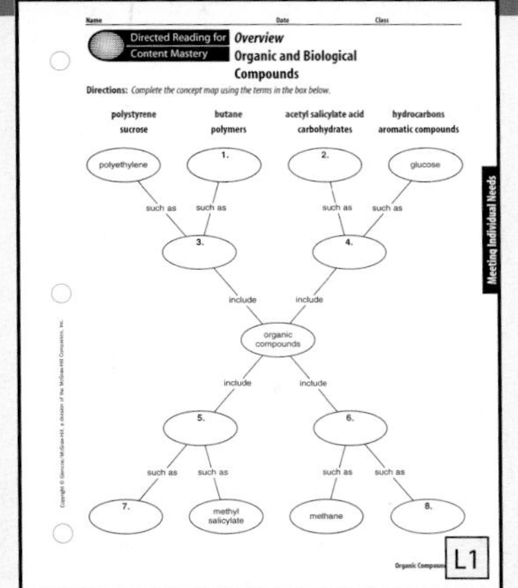

Directed Reading for Content Mastery — Overview: Organic and Biological Compounds

Directions: Complete the concept map using the terms in the box below.

L1

Enrichment

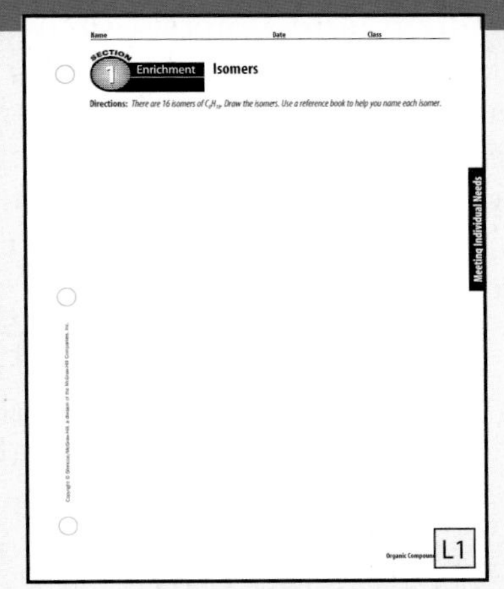

Section 1 Enrichment — Isomers

L1

Spanish Directed Reading

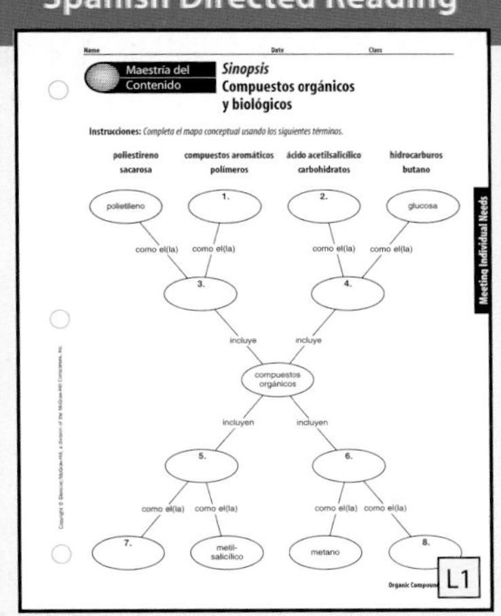

Maestría del Contenido — Sinopsis: Compuestos orgánicos y biológicos

Instrucciones: Completa el mapa conceptual usando los siguientes términos.

L1

Assessment

Chapter Tests

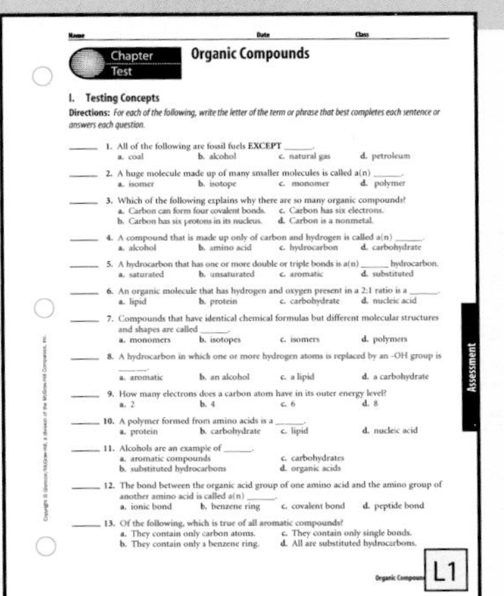

Chapter Test — Organic Compounds

I. Testing Concepts

L1

Test Practice Workbook

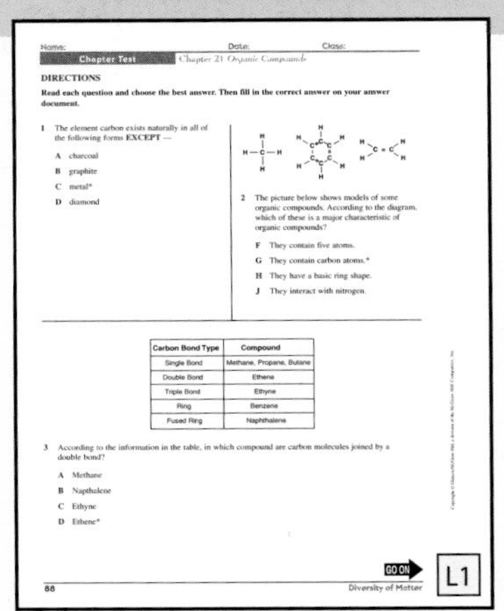

Chapter Test — Chapter 21 Organic Compounds

L1

Chapter Review

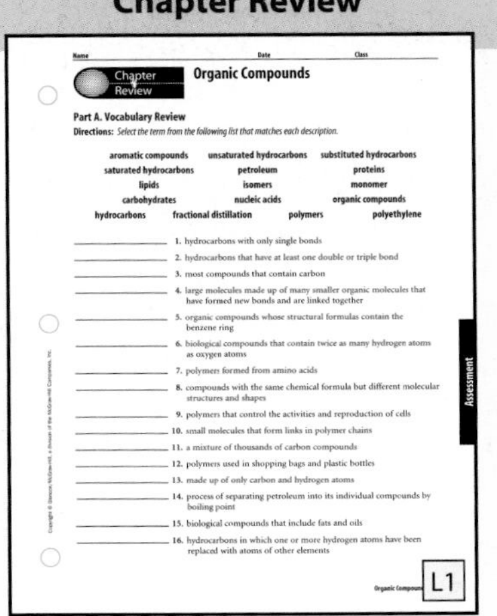

Chapter Review — Organic Compounds

Part A. Vocabulary Review

L1

Science Content Background

SECTION 1 Simple Organic Compounds

Single Bonds

Alkanes, hydrocarbons that contain all single bonds are generally very unreactive. However, they will react with oxygen under certain conditions. The chemical reaction of alkanes with oxygen occurs during combustion in an engine or a furnace when the alkane is burned as a fuel. Carbon dioxide and water are formed as products, and a large amount of heat is released. At room temperature, alkanes with one to four carbons per molecule are gases (methane, propane), five to about sixteen carbons are liquid (gasoline, kerosene), and those with more than sixteen carbons per molecule are solids (wax, petroleum jelly).

Fun Fact

Benzene is a clear liquid that boils at 80.1°C (176.2°F) and solidifies at 5.5°C (41.9°F). Because it is only slightly soluble in water, it makes an excellent solvent for rubber, gums, fats, and a number of resins.

Multiple Bonds

Ethylene, the simplest of the alkenes, is an important commercial organic chemical. Annual United States production of ethylene is more than 20 billion kg. More than half of this amount goes into the manufacture of the plastic, polyethylene. Another 15 percent is converted to ethylene glycol, the major component of antifreeze.

Hans Pfletschinger/Peter Arnold, Inc.

SECTION 2 Other Organic Compounds

Aromatic Hydrocarbons

In the early days of organic chemistry, the word *aromatic* was used to describe certain fragrant substances from natural sources such as fruits and trees. Chemists soon realized, however, that these substances behaved differently from most other organic compounds. Benzene is the simplest aromatic compound, but other compounds such as aspirin, hydrocortisone, and Valium also contain aromatic rings.

Substituted Hydrocarbons

Organic compounds can undergo substitution reactions in which some or all of the hydrogen atoms are replaced with other atoms or group of atoms. For example, when benzene reacts with nitric acid in the presence of sulfuric acid as a catalyst, trinitrotoluene (TNT) is produced. Nitration of aromatic rings is a key step in the synthesis of many important pharmaceutical agents and of many brightly colored dyes used in clothing.

Methanol, the simplest alcohol with one carbon, is also known as wood alcohol because it was once produced by heating wood in the absence of air. Today, almost 1.7 billion gallons of methanol are manufactured each year. Toxic to humans, methanol will cause blindness when ingested in low doses and death when taken in larger amounts. Ethanol, one of the oldest known organic compounds, is an alcohol with two carbons. Sometimes called grain alcohol, ethanol is present in all wines, beers, and distilled liquors.

SECTION 3 Petroleum—A Source of Carbon Compounds

Uses for Petroleum

The gasoline that is distilled directly from petroleum is a poor fuel because it causes engines to "knock." The knock comes from uncontrolled combustion in the engine and can waste fuel and damage the engine. The octane number of gasoline indicates how good or bad the gasoline is as a fuel. Heptane, a straight-chain hydrocarbon and a very bad fuel, is assigned a value of 0. A branched-chain hydrocarbon commonly known as isooctane has a rating of 100. To obtain gasoline, the kerosene fraction which contains hydrocarbons ranging in the number of 12 to 14 carbons, is "cracked" into smaller molecules. The major gasoline products of cracking are branched-chain molecules containing from 7 to 10 carbons. These have high octane ratings. Tetraethlyllead was used for many years to boost a gasoline's octane rating, but now compounds such as ethanol are used.

SECTION 4 Biological Compounds

Proteins

Enzymes are large proteins that act as catalysts for biological reactions. Enzymes are made to catalyze only very specific reactions. The enzyme amylase found in human digestive systems, for example, is able to catalyze the breakdown of starch to yield glucose but has no effect on cellulose, even though the two compounds are similar. This is why humans can digest potatoes but not grass.

Lipids

Steroids are lipids that are made up of tetracyclic (four-ring) hydrocarbons. Three of the rings have six carbons and one has five carbons. Steroids have many diverse roles in both plants and animals. Cholesterol and a variety of hormones have this structure.

Fun Fact

Steroids have long been used for medicinal purposes. The first therapeutic use of steroids dates to the eighteenth century, when foxglove extracts were found to be beneficial for some people with heart conditions. The active ingredient in these preparations, digitalis, is still used today.

For additional content background on this topic, go to the Glencoe Science Web site at science.glencoe.com.

CHAPTER 

Organic Compounds

Chapter Vocabulary

organic compound
hydrocarbon
saturated hydrocarbon
isomer
unsaturated hydrocarbon
aromatic compound
substituted hydrocarbon
alcohol
polymer
monomer
polyethylene
protein
nucleic acid
deoxyribonucleic acid (DNA)
carbohydrate
lipid

What do you think?

Science Journal This is a representation of a DNA double helix looking down on the vertical axis. DNA occurs in an infinite variety of forms.

CHAPTER 21

Organic Compounds

You may not see it, but carbon is everywhere. It is in your clothes, your backpack, your books, and your food. It is even in you. Carbon is an amazing element. In this chapter, you will learn how carbon can form more than a million known compounds. Also, you will see how black, gooey petroleum is transformed into useful substances. You will be introduced to some carbon compounds essential to life itself—among them proteins and DNA.

What do you think?

Science Journal Look at the picture below with a classmate. Discuss what this might be. Here's a hint: *This pattern offers an infinite variety of forms.* Write your answer or best guess in your Science Journal.

Theme Connection

Systems and Interactions This chapter analyzes the structure and interactions of carbon atoms. It discusses how the ability of carbon atoms to interact among themselves in a variety of ways produces the many compounds and polymers that make up the system of organic chemistry.

The element carbon exists in three very different forms. It exists as dull, black charcoal; slippery, gray graphite; and bright, sparkling diamond. However, this is nothing compared with the millions of different compounds that carbon can form. In this activity, you will seek out the carbon hidden in two common substances.

WARNING: *Always use extreme caution around an open flame. Point test tubes away from yourself and others.*

Identify a common element

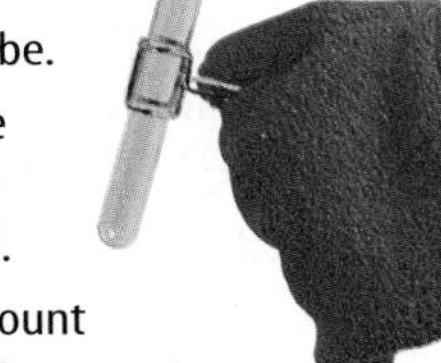

1. Place a small piece of bread in a test tube.
2. Using a test-tube holder, hold the tube over the flame of a laboratory burner until you observe changes in the bread.
3. Using a clean test tube and a small amount of paper instead of bread, repeat step 2.

Observe

1. What happened when you heated the tubes? Did you see anything leave the two samples?
2. What remained in each of the test tubes? Describe it in your Science Journal. What do you think it is?

Before You Read

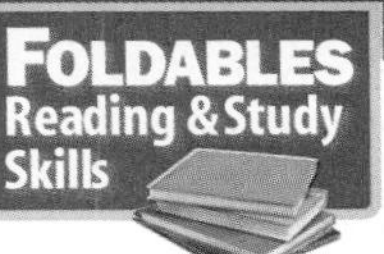

Making a Vocabulary Study Fold **Make the following vocabulary Foldable to ensure you have understood the content by defining the vocabulary terms from this chapter.**

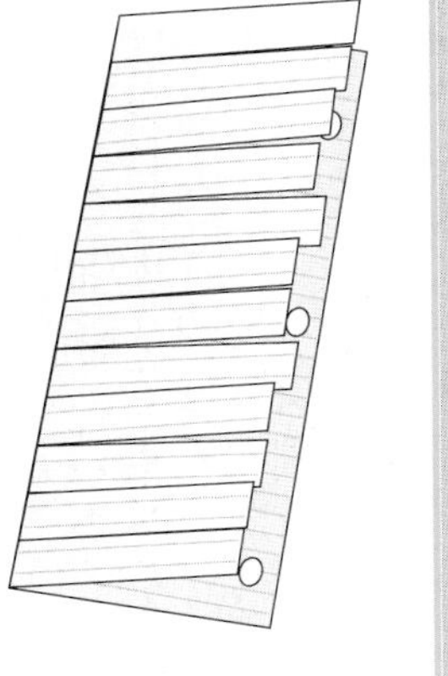

1. Place a sheet of notebook paper in front of you so the short side is at the top. Fold the paper in half from the left side to the right side.
2. Through the top thickness of paper, cut along every third line from the outside edge to the centerfold, forming ten tabs, as shown.
3. On the front of each tab, write a vocabulary word listed on the first page of each section in this chapter. On the back of each tab, define the word.

Explore Activity

Purpose Use the Explore Activity to introduce students to some of the common materials around them that contain carbon. This activity also points out that although two substances can appear very different, their basic makeup may be very similar. L1 ELL LS **Visual-Spatial**

Preparation Cut fresh bread into thin strips, 2 cm long, that will fit into a test tube.

Materials white bread, white paper, laboratory burner, test tubes

Teaching Strategy Bring some carbon ground from charcoal to class and have students examine it before they do this activity.

Observe

1. The bread and paper were reduced to a black ash. Water vapor left the samples.
2. Black ash was left in the test tubes. It is carbon.

Oral After students have done the activity, hold up a burnt piece of bread and ask them if they can identify whether it is bread or paper. Use **Performance Assessment in the Science Classroom,** p. 89

Before You Read

FOLDABLES Reading & Study Skills

Dinah Zike Study Fold

Purpose Expose students to the chapter's content and vocabulary before they read, and encourage them to search for terms and definitions as they read. Have students record answers to their questions in a Foldable, which becomes a study guide after reading.

For additional help, see Foldables Worksheet, p. 17 in **Chapter Resources Booklet,** or go to the Glencoe Science Web site at **science.glencoe.com.** See After You Read in the Study Guide at the end of this chapter.

SECTION 1

Simple Organic Compounds

1 Motivate

Bellringer Transparency

Display the Section Focus Transparency for Section 1. Use the accompanying Transparency Activity Master. L2 ELL

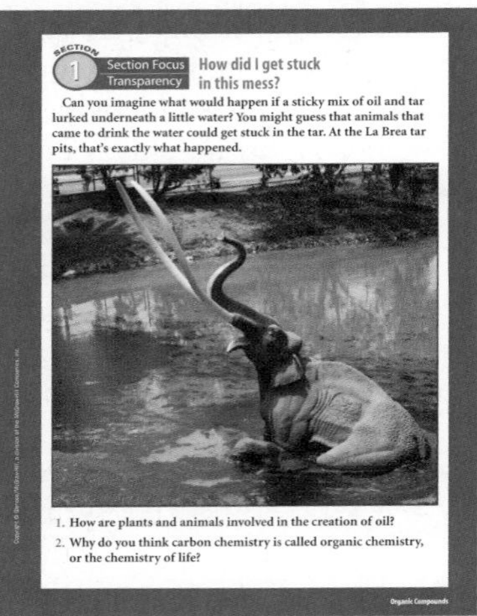

Section Focus Transparency 1

How did I get stuck in this mess?

Can you imagine what would happen if a sticky mix of oil and tar lurked underneath a little water? You might guess that animals that came to drink the water could get stuck in the tar. At the La Brea tar pits, that's exactly what happened.

1. How are plants and animals involved in the creation of oil?
2. Why do you think carbon chemistry is called organic chemistry, or the chemistry of life?

Tie to Prior Knowledge

Ask students to identify forms of carbon that they know. Remind them that diamonds and the graphite in pencils are both forms of carbon. Explain that the element carbon is able to bond with itself and other elements in many different ways.

SECTION 1

Simple Organic Compounds

As You Read

What **You'll Learn**

- **Identify** the difference between organic and inorganic carbon compounds.
- **Examine** the structures of some organic compounds.
- **Differentiate** between saturated and unsaturated hydrocarbons.
- **Identify** isomers of organic compounds.

Vocabulary

organic compound
hydrocarbon
saturated hydrocarbon
isomer
unsaturated hydrocarbon

Why **It's Important**

Carbon compounds surround you—they're in your food, your body, and most materials you use every day.

Organic Compounds

What do you have in common with your athletic shoes, sunglasses, and backpack? All the items shown in **Figure 1** contain compounds of the element carbon—and so do you. Most compounds containing the element carbon are **organic compounds.**

At one time, scientists thought that only living organisms could make organic compounds, which is how they got their name. Did you notice the similarity between the terms *organic* and *organism?* By 1830, scientists could make organic compounds in laboratories, but they continued to call them organic.

Of the millions of carbon compounds known today, more than 90 percent of them are considered organic. The other ten percent, including carbon dioxide and the carbonates, are considered inorganic compounds because they are found in nonliving things, such as air, rocks, and minerals.

Bonding You may wonder why carbon can form so many organic compounds. The main reason is that a carbon atom has four electrons in its outer energy level. This means that each carbon atom can form four covalent bonds with atoms of carbon or with other elements. As you have learned, a covalent bond is formed when two atoms share a pair of electrons. Four is a large number of bonds compared to the number of bonds that atoms of other elements can form. This allows carbon to form many types of compounds ranging from small compounds used as fuel, to complex compounds found in medicines and dyes, and the polymers used in plastics and textile fibers.

Figure 1
Most items used every day contain carbon.

Section Assessment Planner

Portfolio	Content Assessment
Science Journal, p. 643	Section, p. 644
Performance Assessment	Challenge, p. 644
Try at Home MiniLAB, p. 643	Chapter, pp. 668–669
Skill Builder Activities, p. 644	
See p. 668 for more options.	

Arrangement Another reason carbon can form so many compounds is that carbon can link together with other carbon atoms in many different arrangements—chains, branched chains, and even rings. It also can form double and triple bonds as well as single bonds. In addition, carbon can bond with atoms of many other elements, such as hydrogen and oxygen. **Figure 2** shows some possible arrangements for carbon compounds.

Hydrocarbons

Carbon forms an enormous number of compounds with hydrogen alone. A compound made up of only carbon and hydrogen atoms is called a **hydrocarbon.** Does the furnace, stove, or water heater in your home burn natural gas? Almost all the natural gas used for these purposes is the hydrocarbon methane. The chemical formula of methane is CH_4.

Methane can be represented in two other ways, as shown in **Figure 3A.** The structural formula shows that four hydrogen atoms are bonded to one carbon atom in a methane molecule. Each line between atoms represents a single covalent bond. The space-filling model in **Figure 3A** shows a more realistic picture of the size and arrangement of the atoms in the molecule. Chemists might refer to space saving models occasionally, but use chemical and structural formulas to write about reactions.

Another hydrocarbon used as fuel is propane. Some stoves, most outdoor grills, and the heaters in hot-air balloons burn this hydrocarbon, which is found in bottled gas. Propane's structural formula and space-filling model are shown in **Figure 3B.**

Methane and other hydrocarbons produce more than 90 percent of the energy humans use. More importantly, carbon compounds are found in medicines, foods, and clothing. To understand how carbon can play so many roles, you must understand how it forms bonds.

Figure 2
A Carbon atoms bond to form chains, as in heptane found in gasoline. **B** The chains can be branched, as in isoprene, found in natural rubber. **C** The chains also can be rings, as in vanillin, found in vanilla flavor.

A

B

C

Figure 3
A Natural gas is mostly methane, CH_4. **B** Bottled gas is mostly propane, C_3H_8.

A

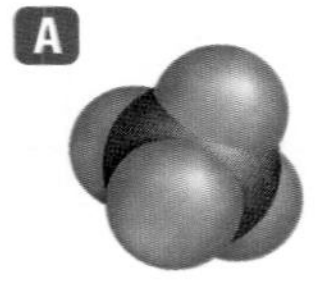

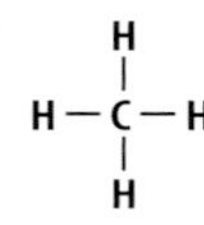

Methane
CH_4

B

Propane
C_3H_8

2 Teach

Organic Compounds

Extension

It was once believed that organic compounds were found only in living systems. The work of Friedrich Wöhler helped change this. Ask students to research Wöhler's work and report on it to the class. In 1828 Wöhler synthesized urea, an organic compound, from inorganic materials. L3 LS **Linguistic**

Hydrocarbons

Teacher FYI

Alkanes are extremely unreactive compounds. Their most notable reaction is combustion, in which the products are CO_2 and H_2O. The amount of heat released by burning is also known as the heat of combustion. The heats of combustion for some short-chain alkanes are: methane: 890.8 kJ/mol; ethane, 1560.7 kJ/mol; propane: 2,219.2 kJ/mol; butane: 2,877.6 kJ/mol; pentane: 3,509.0 kJ/mol; hexane: 4,163.2 kJ/mol; and heptane: 4,817.0 kJ/mol.

Resource Manager

Chapter Resources Booklet

Transparency Activity, p. 48
Note-taking Worksheets, pp. 35–38
Directed Reading for Content Mastery, p. 20

Visual Learning

Figure 2 Point out to students that in this figure, each line between atoms represents a single bond and each double line represents a double bond. Ask students to count the number of double bonds in heptane 0, isoprene 2, and vanillin 4. Point out that in vanillin, carbon is attached to oxygen atoms as well as to hydrogen atoms. L1 ELL LS **Visual-Spatial**

Single Bonds

✔ Reading Check

Answer hydrocarbons in which all of the bonds are single covalent bonds

Use Science Words

Word Origin Explain to students that in the word *isomer* the prefix *iso-* means "equal." Ask students what is equal about different isomers. their chemical formulas Have students name other words they know that have the prefix *iso-*, and tell what the words mean. Possible answers: *isobar*—line of equal pressure; *isotherm*—line of equal temperature; *isotope*—atoms with the same atomic number but different numbers of neutrons. L2 LS **Linguistic**

Visual Learning

Figure 4 Have students look at the graph and determine the boiling point of propane. ~-40° C Ask them to use the data in the graph to estimate the boiling point of octane. Accept 100 to 125° C. L2 ELL LS **Visual-Spatial**

Table 1 Some Hydrocarbons

<table>
<tr><th>Name</th><th>Chemical Formula</th><th>Structural Formula</th></tr>
<tr><td>Methane</td><td>CH_4</td><td><pre>
   H
   |
H—C—H
   |
   H
</pre></td></tr>
<tr><td>Ethane</td><td>C_2H_6</td><td><pre>
   H H
   | |
H—C—C—H
   | |
   H H
</pre></td></tr>
<tr><td>Propane</td><td>C_3H_8</td><td><pre>
   H H H
   | | |
H—C—C—C—H
   | | |
   H H H
</pre></td></tr>
<tr><td>Butane</td><td>C_4H_{10}</td><td><pre>
   H H H H
   | | | |
H—C—C—C—C—H
   | | | |
   H H H H
</pre></td></tr>
</table>

Single Bonds

In some hydrocarbons, the carbon atoms are joined by single covalent bonds. Hydrocarbons containing only single-bonded carbon atoms are called **saturated hydrocarbons.** Saturated means that a compound holds as many hydrogen atoms as possible—it is saturated with hydrogen atoms.

✔ Reading Check *What are saturated hydrocarbons?*

Table 1 lists four saturated hydrocarbons. Notice how each carbon atom appears to be a link in a chain connected by single covalent bonds. **Figure 4** shows a graph of the boiling points of some hydrocarbons. Notice the relationship between boiling points and the addition of carbon atoms.

Structural Isomers Perhaps you have seen or know about butane, which is a gas that sometimes is burned in camping stoves and lighters. The chemical formula of butane is C_4H_{10}. Another hydrocarbon called isobutane has exactly the same chemical formula. How can this be? The answer lies in the arrangement of the four carbon atoms. Look at **Figure 5.** In a molecule of butane, the carbon atoms form a straight chain. The carbon chain of isobutane is branched. The arrangement of carbon atoms in each compound changes the shape of the molecule. Isobutane and butane are isomers.

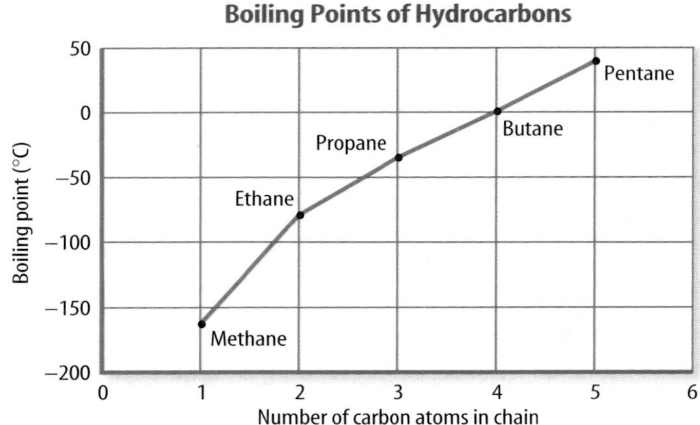

Figure 4
Boiling points of hydrocarbons increase as the number of carbon atoms in the chain increases.

Inclusion Strategies

Learning Disabled Ask students to make models of organic compounds. Have them paint polystyrene foam balls different colors to represent specific elements (carbon–black, hydrogen–yellow, etc.). Have them combine the atoms to form models of some of the compounds shown in this chapter. L1 ELL LS **Kinesthetic**

Resource Manager

Chapter Resources Booklet
- MiniLAB, p. 3
- Transparency Activity, p. 53–54
- Reinforcement, p. 27
- Enrichment, p. 31

A

B

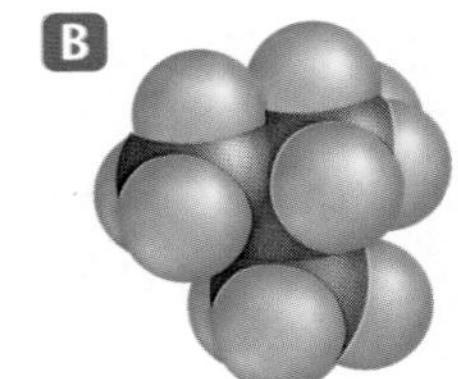

Figure 5
Butane has two isomers. **A** One isomer has a straight chain. **B** The other isomer has a branched chain.

```
    H   H   H   H
    |   |   |   |
H — C — C — C — C — H
    |   |   |   |
    H   H   H   H
```

Butane
C_4H_{10}

```
    H   H   H
    |   |   |
H — C — C — C — H
    |   |   |
    H   |   H
        |
    H — C — H
        |
        H
```

Isobutane
C_4H_{10}

Isomers are compounds that have identical chemical formulas but different molecular structures and shapes. Thousands of isomers exist among the hydrocarbons. Generally, melting points and boiling points decrease as the amount of branching in an isomer increases. You can see this pattern in **Table 2,** which lists properties of butane and isobutane.

Sometimes properties of isomers can vary amazingly. For example, the isomer of octane having all eight carbons in a straight chain melts at −56.8°C, but the most branched octane melts at 100.7°C. In this case, the high melting point results from the symmetry of the molecule and its globular shape. Look for this isomer when you do the Try at Home MiniLAB.

Other Isomers There are many other kinds of isomers in organic and inorganic chemistry. Some isomers differ only slightly in how their atoms are arranged in space. Such isomers form what is often called right- and left-handed molecules, like mirror images. Two such isomers may have identical physical and chemical properties.

Table 2 Properties of Butane Isomers

Property	Butane	Isobutane
Description	Colorless gas	Colorless gas
Density	0.60 kg/L	0.62 kg/L
Melting Point	−138°C	−160°C
Boiling Point	−0.5°C	−12°C

Modeling Structures of Octane

Procedure

1. To model octane, C_8H_{18}, a hydrocarbon found in gasoline, use soft **gumdrops** to represent carbon atoms.
2. Use **raisins** to represent hydrogen atoms.
3. Use **toothpicks** for chemical bonds.

Analysis

1. How do you distinguish one structure from another?
2. What was the total number of different molecules found in your class?

Single Bonds, continued

Purpose Students use models to determine the structures of isomers of octane. L2 ELL
LS **Kinesthetic**

Materials gumdrops of one color, raisins, toothpicks

Teaching Strategies Start by having each student build the straight-chain isomer of octane. This ensures that everyone will have all carbons and hydrogens in correct relative positions.

Safety Precaution Remind students that toothpicks are sharp and to use care when piercing gumdrops.

Troubleshooting Monitor the structure comparisons so students do not consider identical structures to be different because they are oriented differently.

Analysis

1. by the positions and arrangements of the carbon atoms
2. There can be a maximum of 18 different structures.

Oral Have students explain why different structures have different properties. Some shapes form stronger intermolecular bonds than others. Use **PASC,** p. 89.

Science Journal

Isomers Have students draw and label in their Science Journals all the isomers of the short-chain hydrocarbons methane, ethane, propane, butane, pentane, hexane, and heptane. After students have drawn the isomers, have them check carefully and cross out any isomers that are equivalent to ones they have already drawn. Ask students to record the number of different isomers possible for each compound. methane: 1; ethane: 1; propane: 1; butane: 2; pentane: 3; hexane: 5; heptane: 9 L3 ELL
LS **Logical-Mathematical** P

Multiple Bonds

Reading Check

Answer ethylene

3 Assess

Reteach

Use a propane torch and a small butane lighter to carefully demonstrate that these two hydrocarbons are good fuels. Write the formulas of the compounds on the board. propane: C_3H_8; butane: C_4H_{10} Use this as a starting point for discussing the structure, naming, and bonding of hydrocarbons. L1 ELL
LS **Visual-Spatial**

Challenge

Ask students to predict whether changing a single bond in an alkane molecule to a double bond increases or decreases the amount of heat released when the substance burns. After they have made their predictions, have them do research to find the answer. Changing a single bond to a double bond decreases the amount of heat released during combustion.
L3 LS **Logical-Mathematical**

Performance Provide the boiling points and structural formulas of the three isomers of pentane, n-pentane: 36.0°C; isopentane: 27.8°C, and neopentane: 9.4°C. Have students graph the boiling points and use the graph to infer a relationship between branching and boiling points. The greater the branching, the lower the boiling point. Use **Performance Assessment in the Science Classroom,** p. 111.

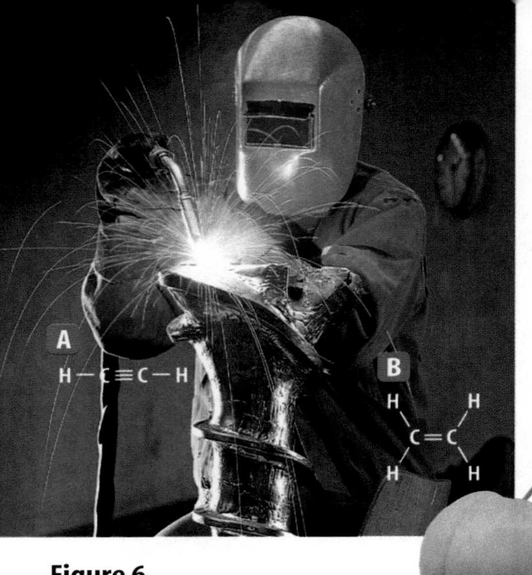

Figure 6
Hydrocarbons can contain double or triple bonds between carbon atoms. A Ethyne, also called acetylene, is used in torches for welding. B Ethene or ethylene gas ripens fruit.

Multiple Bonds

Peaches are among the many fruits that can form small quantities of ethylene gas, which aids in ripening. Ethylene is another name for the hydrocarbon ethene, C_2H_4. This contains one double bond in which two carbon atoms share two pairs of electrons. The hydrocarbon ethyne contains a triple bond in which three pairs of electrons are shared. Hydrocarbons, such as ethene and ethyne, that contain at least one double or triple bond are called **unsaturated hydrocarbons.** They are shown in **Figure 6.**

Reading Check ***What is another name for ethene?***

Remember that saturated hydrocarbons contain only single bonds and have as many hydrogen atoms as possible. Hydrocarbons having more than one double or triple bond are called polyunsaturated, because the prefix *poly* means many.

Section 1 Assessment

1. Explain why carbon can form so many organic compounds?
2. Compare and contrast *ethane*, *ethene*, and *ethyne*.
3. How is an unsaturated hydrocarbon different from a saturated hydrocarbon?
4. How did organic compounds get this name?
5. **Think Critically** Cyclopropane is a saturated hydrocarbon containing three carbon atoms. In this compound, each carbon atom is bonded to two other carbon atoms. Draw its structural formula. Are cyclopropane and propane isomers? Explain. Carbon can form single, double, and triple bonds easily. How many electrons are shared between two carbon atoms joined in a triple bond?

Skill Builder Activities

6. **Making and Using Graphs** Make a graph of **Table 1.** For each compound, plot the number of carbon atoms on one axis and the number of hydrogen atoms on the other axis. Use the graph to predict the formula of hexane, which has six carbon atoms. **For more help, refer to the Science Skill Handbook.**
7. **Solving One-Step Equations** Compare the formulas of three saturated hydrocarbons: C_2H_6, C_3H_8, and C_4H_{10}. What mathematical relationship do you see between the number of carbon atoms and the number of hydrogen atoms in each? Compare the number of carbon and the number of hydrogen atoms in the unsaturated hydrocarbons C_2H_4, C_3H_6, and C_4H_8. **For more help, refer to the Math Skill Handbook.**

Answers to Section Assessment

1. Each atom of carbon can form four covalent bonds with other atoms. This enables them to form long, branched chains. The bonds can be single, double, or triple.
2. They are hydrocarbons with two carbon atoms each. Ethane has a single bond between the two carbon atoms, ethene has a double bond, and ethyne has a triple bond.
3. A saturated hydrocarbon has only single bonds between carbon atoms. An unsaturated hydrocarbon has one or more double or triple bonds between carbon atoms.
4. Organic refers to living. Originally it was thought that these carbon-based compounds came only from living organisms.
5. No; cyclopropane, C_3H_6, is not an isomer of propane, C_3H_8, because it has a different chemical formula. Six electrons are shared by two carbons joined by a triple bond.
6. Check student work
7. saturated: C_xH_{2x+2}; unsaturated: C_xH_{2x}

Other Organic Compounds

Aromatic Compounds

Chewing flavored gum or dissolving a candy mint in your mouth releases pleasant flavors and aromas. Many chemical compounds produce pleasant odors but others have less pleasant flavors and smells. For example, aspirin, which has an unpleasant, sour taste, is shown in **Figure 7A.** The compound that produces the fresh fragrance of wintergreen is shown in **Figure 7B.** Both of these compounds are considered aromatic compounds. In addition to the fragrances mentioned here, aromatic compounds contribute to the smell of cloves, cinnamon, anise, and vanilla.

You might assume that aromatic compounds are so named because they are smelly—and most of them are. However, smell is not what makes a compound aromatic in the chemical sense. To a chemist, an **aromatic compound** is one that contains a benzene structure having a ring with six carbons.

Reading Check *What structure is found in all aromatic compounds?*

As You Read

What You'll Learn

- **Define** aromatic compounds.
- **Identify** the nature of alcohols and acids.
- **Identify** organic compounds you use in daily life.

Vocabulary

aromatic compound
substituted hydrocarbon
alcohol

Why It's Important

Aromatic compounds are building blocks of thousands of useful compounds, such as flavorings and medicines.

Figure 7
You can see the six-carbon benzene ring in these aromatic compounds. **A** Aspirin is acetyl salicylic acid. **B** Wintergreen is methyl salicylate.

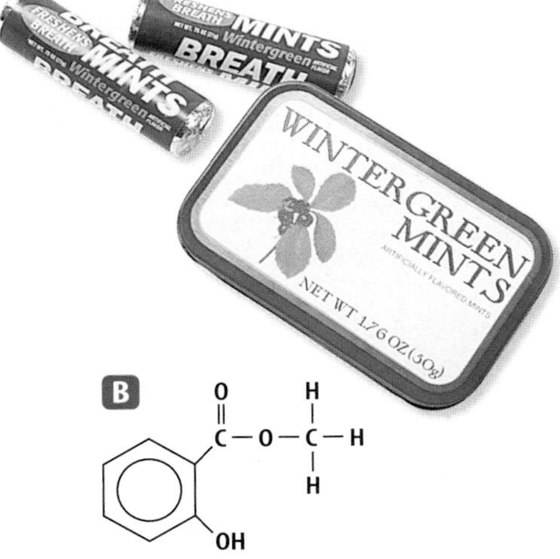

A
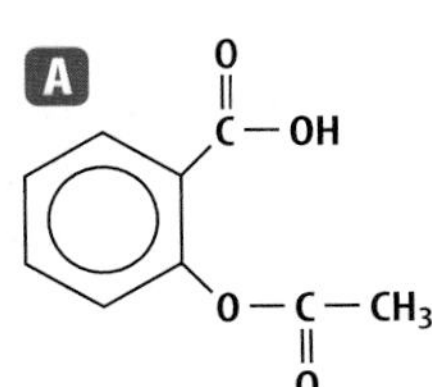

B

Section Assessment Planner

PORTFOLIO
Visual Learning, p. 647

PERFORMANCE ASSESSMENT
Skill Builder Activities, p. 648
See p. 668 for more options.

CONTENT ASSESSMENT
Section, p. 648
Challenge, p. 648
Chapter, pp. 668–669

SECTION 2

Other Organic Compounds

1 Motivate

Bellringer Transparency

Display the Section Focus Transparency for Section 2. Use the accompanying Transparency Activity Master. L2 ELL

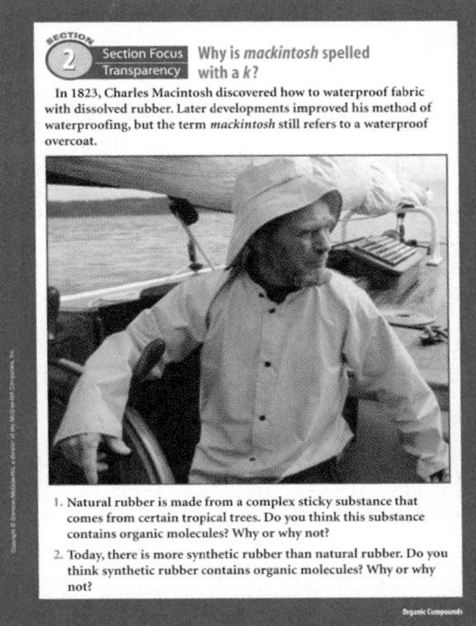

Section Focus Transparency 2 — Why is *mackintosh* spelled with a *k*?

In 1823, Charles Macintosh discovered how to waterproof fabric with dissolved rubber. Later developments improved his method of waterproofing, but the term *mackintosh* still refers to a waterproof overcoat.

1. Natural rubber is made from a complex sticky substance that comes from certain tropical trees. Do you think this substance contains organic molecules? Why or why not?
2. Today, there is more synthetic rubber than natural rubber. Do you think synthetic rubber contains organic molecules? Why or why not?

Tie to Prior Knowledge

Remind students that organic compounds contain carbon. Review principles of bonding with students before beginning this section.

Reading Check

Answer benzene ring structure

Resource Manager

Chapter Resources Booklet
Transparency Activity, p. 49
Enrichment, p. 32
Directed Reading for Content Mastery, p. 20

2 Teach

Aromatic Compounds

Reading Check

Answer the equal sharing of electrons by the 6 carbon atoms of the benzene ring

Substituted Hydrocarbons

Fun Fact

Substituted hydrocarbons are generally more reactive than unsubstituted hydrocarbons.

Quick Demo

Use a model or drawing of a benzene ring. Remove, or erase one H and replace it with an –OH group. This forms the disinfectant phenol. Explain to students that chemists with proper training cause this substitution on billions of molecules during synthesis reactions.

L1 ELL IS **Visual-Spatial**

Figure 8
Benzene, C_6H_6, can be represented by a A space-filling model, B a structural formula, or C the benzene symbol.

A
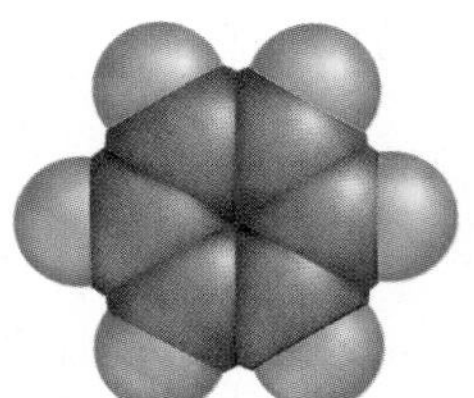
Benzene C_6H_6

B
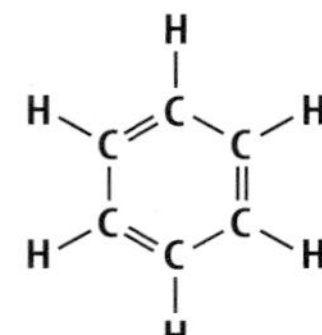

C
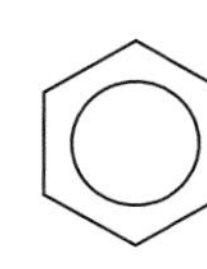

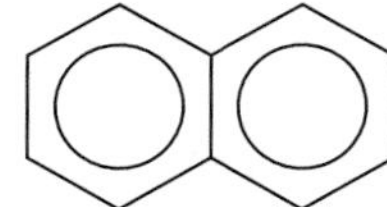
Naphthalene
$C_{10}H_8$

Figure 9
Naphthalene used in moth crystals is an example of a fused-ring system.

Benzene Look at a model of benzene, C_6H_6, and its structural formula in **Figure 8.** As you can see, the benzene molecule has six carbon atoms bonded into a ring. The electrons shown as alternating double and single bonds that form the ring are shared by all six carbon atoms in the ring. This equal sharing of electrons is represented by the special symbol shown in **Figure 8C.** The sharing of these electrons causes the benzene molecule to be very stable because all six carbon atoms are bound in a rigid, flat structure. Many compounds contain this stable ring structure. The stable ring acts as a framework upon which new molecules can be built.

Reading Check *What is responsible for the stability of the benzene ring?*

Fused Rings Moth crystals have a distinct odor. One type of moth crystal is made of naphthalene (NAF thuh leen). This is a different type of aromatic compound that is made up of two ring structures fused together, as shown in **Figure 9.** Many known compounds contain three or more rings fused together. Tetracycline (te truh SI kleen) antibiotics are based on a fused ring system containing four fused rings.

Substituted Hydrocarbons

Usually a cheeseburger is a hamburger covered with melted American cheese and served on a bun. However, you can make a cheeseburger with Swiss cheese and serve it on toast. Such substitutions would affect the taste of this cheeseburger.

In a similar way chemists change hydrocarbons into other compounds having different physical and chemical properties. They may include a double or triple bond or add different atoms or groups of atoms to compounds. These changed compounds are called substituted hydrocarbons.

LAB DEMONSTRATION

Purpose to show the odorous compounds that result when an organic acid reacts with an organic alcohol

Materials concentrated sulfuric acid, acetic acid, ethanol, isopentanol, 1-octanol, test tubes, warm water bath

Safety Acid is corrosive; alcohols are flammable. Check aromas by using a wafting motion to direct fumes toward your nose.

Procedure Put 6 mL each of the acid and alcohol combinations listed below in a test tube. Add 5 drops of sulfuric acid, mix, and heat in a warm water bath.

Expected Outcome acetic acid + ethanol = apple; acetic acid + isopentanol = banana; acetic acid + 1-octanol = orange

How do you know chemical changes took place in these reactions? New substances with new characteristics were formed.

A **substituted hydrocarbon** has one or more of its hydrogen atoms replaced by atoms or groups of other elements. Depending on what properties are needed, chemists decide what to add. Examples of substituted hydrocarbons are shown in **Figure 10.**

Alcohols and Acids Rubbing alcohol gets its name from the fact that it was used for rubbing on aching muscles. Rubbing alcohol is a substituted hydrocarbon. Alcohols are an important group of organic compounds. They serve often as solvents and disinfectants, and more importantly can be used as pieces to assemble larger molecules. An **alcohol** is formed when –OH groups replace one or more hydrogen atoms in a hydrocarbon. **Figure 10A** shows ethanol, an alcohol produced by the fermentation of sugar in grains and fruit.

Reading Check *Why are alcohols considered substituted hydrocarbons?*

Organic acids form when a carboxyl group, –COOH, is substituted for one of the hydrogen atoms attached to a carbon atom. Look at **Figure 10.** The structures of ethane, ethanol, and acetic acid are similar. Do you see that acetic acid, found in vinegar, is a substituted hydrocarbon? You know some other organic acids, too—citric acid found in citrus fruits, such as oranges and lemons, and lactic acid found in sour milk.

Astronomy INTEGRATION

Carbon compounds also are found in space. About five percent of meteorites contain water and carbon compounds. Carbon compounds, such as formic acid and a form of acetylene, have been detected in outer space using radio telescopes. The areas where they are found are thought to be regions of space where new stars are forming.

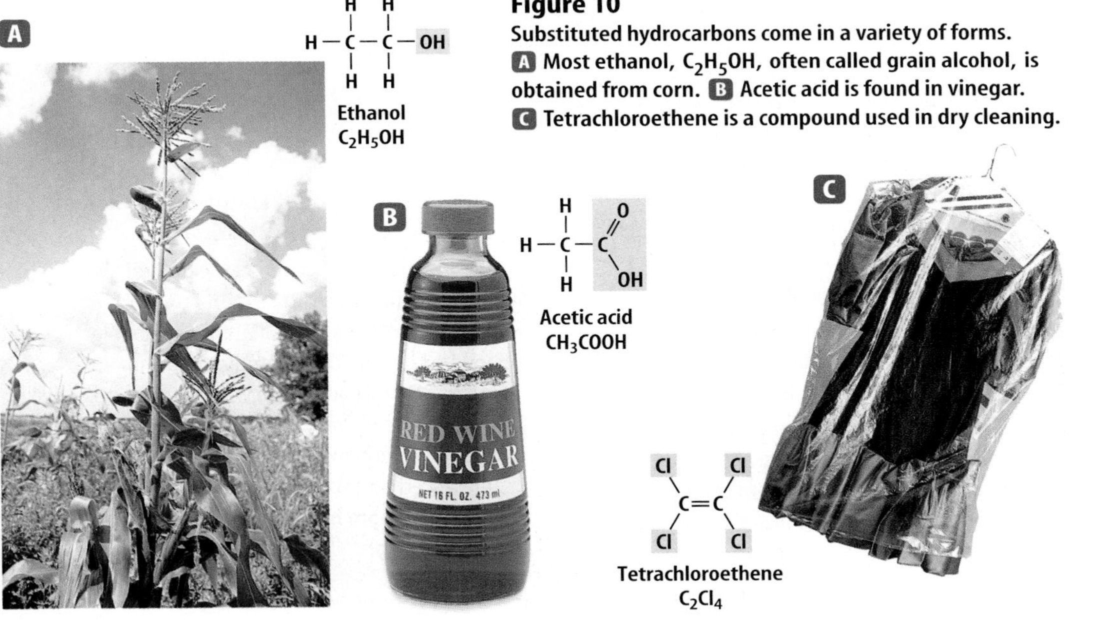

Figure 10
Substituted hydrocarbons come in a variety of forms.
A **Most ethanol, C_2H_5OH, often called grain alcohol, is obtained from corn.** **B** **Acetic acid is found in vinegar.** **C** **Tetrachloroethene is a compound used in dry cleaning.**

Astronomy INTEGRATION

Carbonaceous chondrites are stony meteorites that contain material associated with life, such as amino acids and hydrocarbons. They are similar in texture to volcanic tuffs, a type of terrestrial rock. This indicates that they have been fragmented and re-cemented.

Reading Check

Answer They are formed when hydrogen atoms are replaced by atoms or groups of atoms of other elements.

Visual Learning

Figure 10 Have students copy the formulas from the examples on this page, then have them circle the basic hydrocarbon chain in each formula. This will help students identify the parts that have been substituted onto the chain. L1 ELL IN **Visual-Spatial** P

Discussion

In the process of fermentation, one glucose molecule, $C_6H_{12}O_6$, is broken down into two molecules of ethanol, C_2H_5OH. **What else is produced?** two molecules of CO_2

Teacher FYI

Lactic Acid Students may have heard of lactic acid $C_3H_6O_3$. This organic acid builds up in muscle tissue during exercise. Also, as milk spoils, the lactose it contains is converted to lactic acid. Lactic acid has three carbon atoms. The middle carbon has an –OH group attached, and one end carbon has a double bonded oxygen and an –OH group.

Active Reading

Write-Draw-Discuss This strategy encourages students to actively participate in reading and lectures, assimilating content creatively. Have students write about an idea, clarify it, then make an illustration or drawing. Ask students to share responses with the class and display several examples. Have students Write-Draw-Discuss as they read about aromatic compounds and substituted hydrocarbons.

Resource Manager

Chapter Resources Booklet
Reinforcement, p. 28
Home and Community Involvement, p. 42

3 Assess

Reteach

Have students reuse the gumdrop models to form other substituted hydrocarbons. For example, formic acid, HCOOH, the compound that provides the sting in some insect stings, could be assembled along with others pictured in the text. L1

ELL LS **Kinesthetic**

Challenge

Isopropyl alcohol (rubbing alcohol) is an example of an isomer of a substituted hydrocarbon. Challenge students to show two ways that a three-carbon chain can have an –OH group attached. 2-propanol and n-propanol **How many isomers of butanol are there?** two L2

LS **Logical-Mathematical**

Oral Ask students to report the number of bonds made to each carbon atom in every structure they have studied in this section. 4 **Use Performance Assessment in the Science Classroom,** p. 89

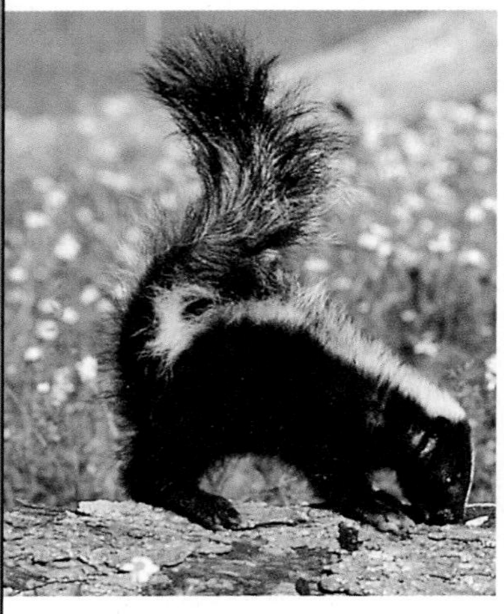

Figure 11
Strangely, small concentrations of foul-smelling compounds are often found in pleasant-smelling substances. For example, the mercaptan in skunk spray is among the 834 components of coffee aroma.

Substituting Other Elements Other atoms besides hydrogen and oxygen can be added to hydrocarbons. One is chlorine. When four chlorine atoms replace four hydrogen atoms in ethylene, the result is tetrachloroethene (teh truh klor uh eth EEN), a solvent used in dry cleaning. It is shown in **Figure 10C.** Adding four fluorine atoms to ethylene makes a compound that can be transformed into the black, shiny material called Teflon, used for nonstick surfaces in cookware. Among other possible substituted hydrocarbons are molecules containing nitrogen, bromine, and sulfur.

When sulfur replaces oxygen in the –OH group of an alcohol, the resulting compound is called a thiol, or more commonly a mercaptan. Most mercaptans have unpleasant odors. This can be useful to animals like the skunk shown in **Figure 11.**

Mercaptan odors are not only unpleasant, they are also powerful. You can smell skunk spray even in concentrations as low as 0.5 parts per million. Though you might not think so, such a powerful stink can be an asset, and not just for skunks. In fact, smelly mercaptans can save lives. As you know natural gas has no odor of its own so it is impossible to smell a gas leak. For this reason, gas companies add small amounts of a bad-smelling mercaptan to the gas to make people aware of any leaks before gas can accumulate to dangerous levels.

Section  Assessment

1. What do the structures of all aromatic compounds have in common?
2. How is each of the following a substituted hydrocarbon: *tetrachloroethene, ethanol,* and *acetic acid?*
3. What elements other than oxygen could be added to a hydrocarbon to produce a substituted hydrocarbon?
4. Explain why chemists might want to prepare substituted hydrocarbons. Give two examples of possible substitutions.
5. **Think Critically** Chloroethane, C_2H_5Cl, can be used as a spray-on anesthetic for localized injuries. How does chloroethane fit the definition of a substituted hydro-carbon? Diagram its structure.

Skill Builder Activities

6. **Interpreting Scientific Illustrations** Formic acid, HCOOH, is the simplest organic acid. Draw its structural formula by referring to the structure of acetic acid in **Figure 10B.** **For more help, refer to the** Science Skill Handbook.
7. **Communicating** Examine the different ways a benzene molecule can be represented, as shown in **Figure 8**. Do you think the double bonds in the structural formula shown in **Figure 8B** must always be written in the positions shown? In your Science Journal, explain your answer and discuss why benzene can be represented by a six-sided figure containing a circle. **For more help, refer to the** Science Skill Handbook.

Answers to Section Assessment

1. a benzene structure having a ring with six carbons
2. tetrachloroethene: chlorine atoms have replaced four hydrogen atoms; ethanol:–OH group has replaced a hydrogen atom; acetic acid:–COOH group has replaced a hydrogen atom
3. chlorine, fluorine, bromine, nitrogen, and sulfur
4. To make compounds with properties they want; substituted compounds carbon tetrachloride, CCl_4, and phenol, C_6H_5OH.
5. Ethane is C_2H_6. In chloroethane a hydrogen atom has been replaced with a chlorine atom.
6. Check students' work.
7. No; they could be put in the places that now have single bonds and the single bonds could be moved to the places that now have double bonds. Benzene has six carbon atoms, which all share the double-bonded electrons.

Resource Manager

Chapter Resources Booklet
Activity Worksheet, pp. 5–6
Reinforcement, p. 28

Activity

Alcohols and Organic Acids

Have you ever wondered how chemists change one substance into another? You have learned that changing the bonding among atoms holds the key to that process.

What You'll Investigate

How can an alcohol change into an acid?

Materials

large test tube and stopper
0.01*M* potassium permanganate solution (1 mL)
6*M* sodium hydroxide solution (1 mL)
ethanol (3 drops)
10-mL graduated cylinder

Safety Precautions

Always handle these chemicals with care; immediately flush any spill with water.

Goals

- **Control** the immediate environment of a reaction to produce a specific compound.
- Gather evidence to form conclusions about the identity of a new compound formed from a chemical reaction.

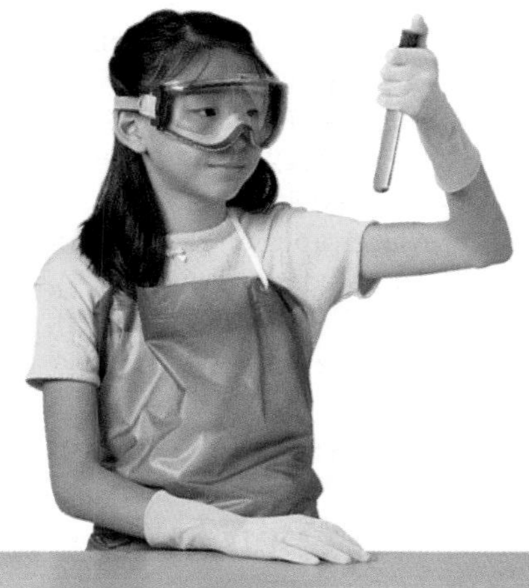

Procedure

1. Pour 1 mL of 0.01*M* potassium permanganate solution and 1 mL of 6*M* sodium hydroxide solution into a test tube.
2. Add 3 drops of ethanol to the test tube.
3. Stopper the test tube. Gently shake it for 1 minute. Observe and record any changes in the solution for 5 minutes.

Conclude and Apply

1. What is the structural formula for ethanol?
2. What part of a molecule identifies a compound as an alcohol?
3. What part of a molecule identifies a compound as an organic acid?
4. **Explain** how you know that a chemical change took place in the test tube.
5. In the presence of potassium permanganate, an alcohol may undergo a chemical change into an acid. If ethanol is used, predict the formula of the acid produced.
6. The acid from ethanol is found in a common household product—vinegar. What is the acid's chemical name?

Communicating Your Data

Design a table and record what changes take place in the color of the solution. Compare your observations with those of other students in your class. **For more help, refer to the** Science Skill Handbook.

Activity

BENCH TESTED

Purpose Students recognize the evidence of the chemical reaction of an organic compound. L2 **LS Visual-Spatial**

Process Skills observing, predicting, classifying, recognizing cause and effect, interpreting data

Time Required 25 minutes

Safety Precautions Caution students against spilling, skin contact with, or inhaling fumes of any chemicals used. If a spill does occur, immediately rinse the area with water.

Teaching Strategies

- Show students how to shake a tube by holding it at the lip with the fingers of one hand while swinging it gently against the palm of the other hand.
- Prepare 6.0 M NaOH by dissolving 24 grams of solid NaOH in 100 mL distilled water. **CAUTION:** Sodium hydroxide is caustic, and the solution will become hot. Prepare only in a heat-resistant glass container.
- Prepare 0.01 M $KMnO_4$ by dissolving 0.16 g $KMnO_4$ in 100 mL distilled water.

Answers to Questions

1.
```
     H   H
     |   |
 H — C — C — OH
     |   |
     H   H
```
2. the –OH group attached to a carbon not attached to any other O
3. the carboxyl group, –COOH
4. The color of the solution changed from purple to green to brown.
5. CH_3COOH
6. acetic acid

Assessment

Process Write the formulas C_3H_8O and $C_3H_6O_2$ on the board and ask students to explain how to determine which formula is for an acid and which is for an alcohol. Organic acids must have at least two oxygen atoms per molecule. Use **Performance Assessment in the Science Classroom,** p. 89.

Communicating Your Data

Students may want to use an electronic spreadsheet to generate the Data Table.

SECTION 3

Petroleum—A Source of Carbon Compounds

1 Motivate

Bellringer Transparency

Display the Section Focus Transparency for Section 3. Use the accompanying Transparency Activity Master. L2 ELL

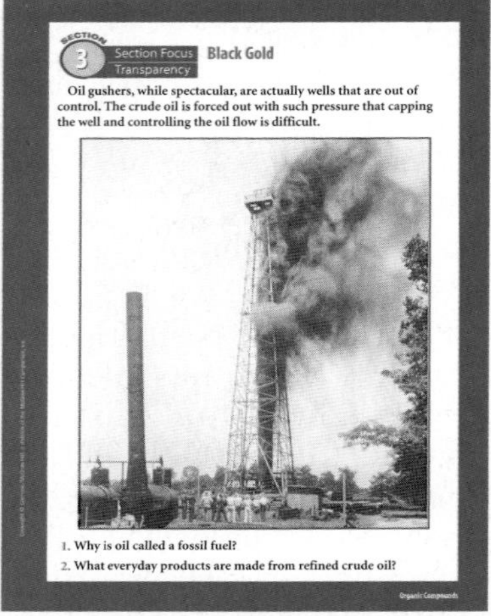

Tie to Prior Knowledge

Ask students if they have ever seen string confetti. Get a can and spray a string from the can. Tell students that the string is made of a polymer—many molecules attached together to form a long string.

SECTION

Petroleum—A Source of Carbon Compounds

As You Read

What You'll Learn

- **Explain** how carbon compounds are obtained from petroleum.
- **Compare and contrast** differences among the various petroleum-based fuels.
- **Determine** how carbon compounds can form long chains.
- **Identify** some of the ways petroleum enriches your world.

Vocabulary

polymer
monomer
polyethylene

Why It's Important

Petroleum gives us fuels, plastics, clothing, and many other products.

What is petroleum?

Do you carry a comb in your pocket or purse? What is it made from? If you answer plastic, you are probably right, but do you know where that plastic came from? Chances are it came from petroleum—a dark, flammable liquid, often called crude oil, that is found deep within Earth. Like coal and natural gas, this dark, foul-smelling substance is formed from the remains of fossilized material. For this reason these substances often are called fossil fuels.

How can a thick, dark liquid like petroleum be transformed into a hard, brightly colored, useful object like a comb? The answer lies in the nature of petroleum. Petroleum is a mixture of thousands of carbon compounds. To make items such as combs, the first step is to extract the crude oil from its underground source, as shown in **Figure 12.** Then, chemists and engineers separate it into its individual compounds using a physical property that you have learned about. This property is the boiling point. Even though petroleum contains a large number of compounds, each compound has its own boiling point.

Figure 12
Drilling for petroleum beneath the ocean floor requires huge platforms.

Separating Petroleum Compounds The separation process is known as fractional distillation. It takes place in petroleum refineries. If you have ever driven past a refinery, you may have seen these big, metal towers called fractionating towers. They often rise as high as 35 m and can be 18 m wide and have pipes and metal scaffolding attached to the outside.

Section Assessment Planner

PORTFOLIO
Science Journal, p. 654

PERFORMANCE ASSESSMENT
MiniLAB, p. 653
Skill-Builder Activities, p. 655
See p. 668 for more options.

CONTENT ASSESSMENT
Section, p. 655
Challenge, p. 655
Chapter, pp. 668–669

The Tower Inside the tower is a series of metal plates arranged like the floors of a building. These plates have small holes so that vapors can pass through. On the outside you can see a maze of pipes at various levels. The tower separates crude oil into fractions containing compounds having a range of boiling points. Within a fraction, boiling points may range more than 100°C.

How It Happens The crude petroleum at the base of the tower is heated to more than 350°C. At this temperature most hydrocarbons in the mixture become vapor and start to rise. The higher boiling fractions reach only the lower plates before they condense, forming shallow pools that drain off through pipes on the sides of the tower and are collected.

Fractions with lower boiling points may climb higher to the middle plates before condensing. Finally, those with the lowest boiling points condense on the topmost plates or never condense at all and are collected as gases at the top of the tower. **Figure 13** shows some typical fractions and how they are used.

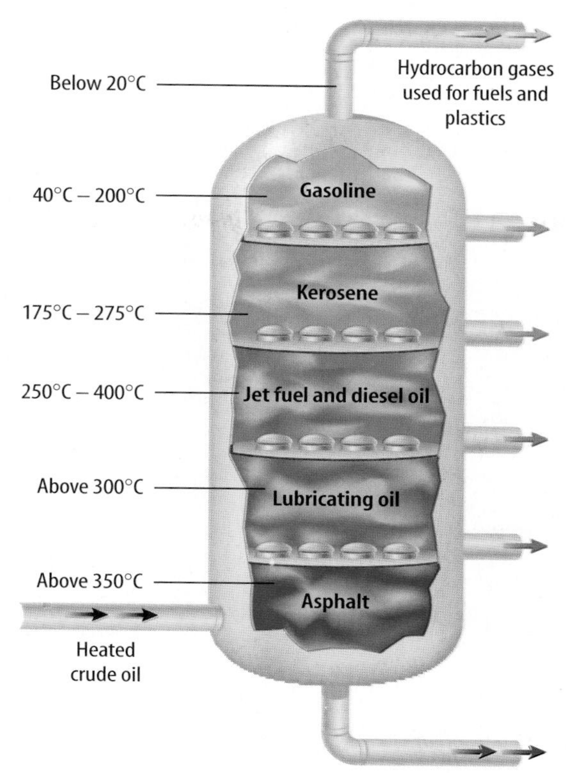

Figure 13
Typical fractions separated by a fractionating tower and their boiling points and uses.

Why don't the condensed liquids fall back through the holes? The reason is that pressure from the rising vapors prevents this. In fact, the separation of the fractions is improved by the interaction of rising vapors with condensed liquid. The processes involved vary. For example, some towers add steam at the bottom to aid vaporization. The design and process used depend on the type of crude oil and on the fractions desired.

Uses for Petroleum Compounds

Some fractions are used directly for fuel—the lightest fractions from the top of the tower include butane and propane. The fractions that condense on the upper plates and contain from five to ten carbons are used for gasoline and solvents. Below these are fractions with 12 to 18 carbons that are used for kerosene and jet fuel. The bottom fractions go into lubricating oil, and the residue is used for paving asphalt. **Figure 14** shows the variety of useful products that can be obtained from petroleum, in addition to its use as a fuel.

2 Teach

What is petroleum?

Quick Demo

Mix three colors of food coloring liquid together before class. In front of the class, put a rectangular piece of filter paper into a beaker filled with the food coloring liquid to a depth of 1 cm. As the liquids rise up the filter paper, the food coloring will separate into its three components. This illustrates how components can be separated from a mixture. L2 ELL

LS **Visual-Spatial**

Discussion

Bring in a label from a bottle of distilled water. Ask students to describe the distillation of water and compare it to the distillation of petroleum. Distilled water has been separated by distillation from any materials dissolved in it. The water was boiled off and collected, separating it from the non-boiling or higher-boiling materials. The distillation of petroleum also separates components in the crude oil mixture through the differences in boiling points. L2

LS **Logical-Mathematical**

Uses for Petroleum Compounds

Teacher FYI

Another process used in petroleum refining is to break the larger hydrocarbon molecules into smaller ones that can be used in gasoline. This process is called cracking. In this way the gasoline yield from a petroleum sample can be increased.

Resource Manager

Chapter Resources Booklet
Transparency Activity, p. 50
Directed Reading for Content Mastery, p. 21
Physical Science Critical Thinking/ Problem Solving, p. 14

Visual Learning

Figure 13 Ask students to explain which hydrocarbons would be found and removed from the top of a fractionating tower. butane, propane, and ethylene, which have the lowest boiling points

Visualizing Petroleum Products

Have students examine the pictures and read the captions. Then ask the following questions.

- **All of the products in the figures are made from petroleum, so which elements would you expect them to include?** carbon and hydrogen
- **Look at all of the products around you that are made from petroleum. Why is it important for us to have a reliable supply of crude oil?** Without crude oil, we would not have any of these things.

Activity

Have students research how crude oil is refined and what items are manufactured from some of the refined components. L2 LS **Linguistic**

Extension

Challenge students to find out the process by which crude oil is refined. Ask them to make posters explaining the process and share their posters with the class. L2 LS **Visual-Spatial**

NATIONAL GEOGRAPHIC **VISUALIZING PETROLEUM PRODUCTS**

Figure 14

Petroleum, or crude oil, provides the raw material for a huge number of products that have become essential to modern life. After it has been refined, petroleum can be used to make various types of fuel, plastics, and synthetic fibers, as well as paint, dyes, and medicines.

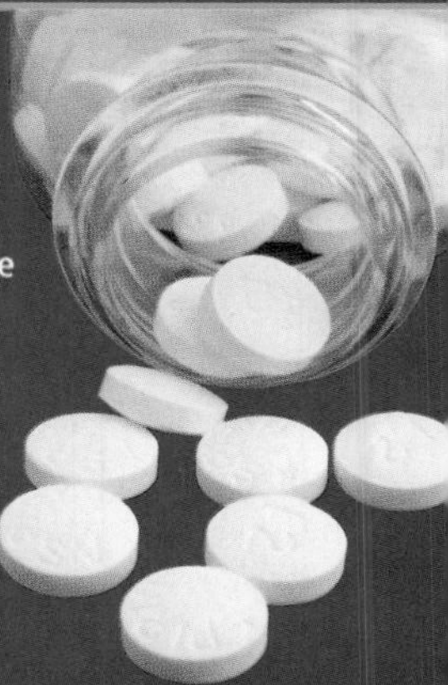

MEDICINES The active ingredient in aspirin used to be extracted from the bark of willow trees. Today it is manufactured from petroleum.

FABRICS Like the fleece used to make these gloves, many modern fabrics are made from synthetic, rather than natural, fibers. Some of the most popular synthetic fibers—polyester, nylon, and rayon—are petroleum-based.

PRINTING INK The ink used in newspapers is made from carbon black, another product from petroleum.

FUELS This commuter jet is being refueled at an airport. Most of the world's petroleum is still used in the form of fuel.

PLASTICS The durability of hard plastic makes it the ideal material for a cell phone keypad.

652

Resource Manager 

Chapter Resources Booklet
MiniLAB, p. 4
Enrichment, p. 33
Cultural Diversity, p. 45

Polymers

Did you ever loop together strips of paper to make paper chains for decorations, or have you ever strung paper clips together? A paper chain can represent the structure of a polymer as shown in **Figure 15.** Some of the smaller molecules from petroleum can act like links in a chain. When these links are hooked together, they make new, extremely large molecules known as **polymers.** The small molecule, which forms a link in the polymer chain, is called a **monomer.** *Mono* means one.

Reading Check *How are polymers similar to paper chains or linked paper clips?*

Common Polymers One common polymer or plastic is made from the monomer ethene or ethylene. Under standard room-temperature conditions, this small hydrocarbon is a gas. However, when ethylene combines with itself repeatedly, it forms a polymer called **polyethylene.** Polyethylene (pah lee EH thuh leen) is used widely in shopping bags and plastic bottles. Another common polymer is polypropylene (pah lee PRO puh leen) used to make glues and carpets. Often two or more different monomers, known as copolymers, combine to make one polymer molecule.

Polymers can be made light and flexible or so strong that they can be used to make plastic pipes, boats, and even some auto bodies. In many cases, they have replaced natural building materials, such as wood and metal. Because so many things used today are made of synthetic polymers, some people call this "The Age of Plastics."

Mini LAB

Visualizing Polymers

Procedure

1. Use **paper clips** to represent monomers in a synthetic polymer. Hook about 20 together to make a chain.
2. Cut 20 **strips of colored paper** and mark each with a different letter of the alphabet from A to T.
3. Assemble these strips in random order to make a paper chain.

Analysis

1. Imagine both chains extended to contain 10,000 or more units. Compare them in terms of ease of construction and degree of complexity.
2. Compare the paper chains made by your class. How many different combinations of letters are there?

Figure 15
Imagine this paper chain extended by 10,000 units. Then imagine each link as a monomer. Now you have an idea of what a typical polymer used to make plastic looks like.

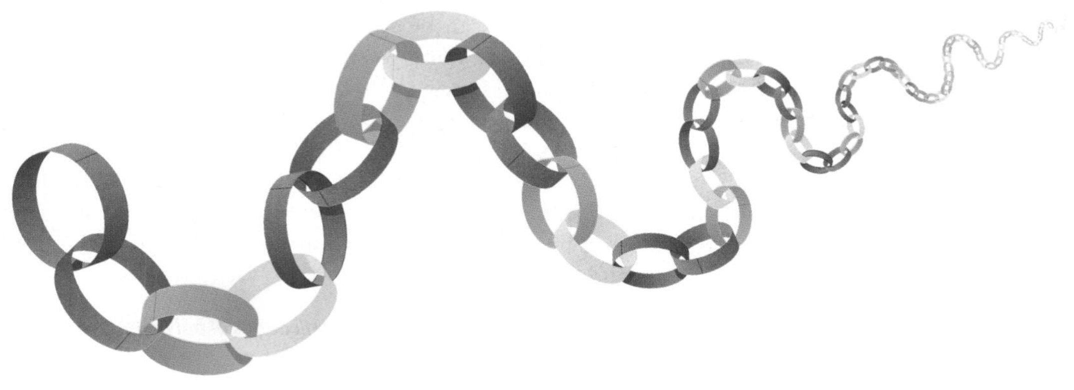

Polymers

Reading Check

Answer They are made of many identical small parts linked together.

Purpose Students model the bonding between monomers found in synthetic and natural polymers. L1 ELL
LS **Kinesthetic**

Materials markers, scissors, tape or stapler, colored paper, paper clips

Teaching Strategy Explain that the pieces of colored paper could represent amino acids in a protein.

Analysis

1. They would both be easy to construct, but the paper chain would be more complex.
2. There are probably as many arrangements as there are class members. There are 20! (20 factorial) possibilities.

Assessment

Process Give students pieces of construction paper of four different colors. Ask students to link the pieces of paper in different orders to make as many different 4-link paper chains as they can, using each color only once in each chain. Ask them how many different chains they can make. 4! or 24 Use **PASC**, p. 97.

Curriculum Connection

Geography Have students locate on a world map areas that have high concentrations of crude oil. Countries having high concentrations of crude oil include Saudi Arabia, the United States (Alaska), Russia, Iraq, Iran, Venezuela, Kuwait, United Arab Emirates, Egypt, Mexico, China, Canada, and Libya. High concentrations are also claimed by England and Norway in the North Sea.

Inclusion Strategies

Visually Impaired For the MiniLAB, pair visually impaired students with students who see well. Make sure the visually impaired students have the opportunity to run the paper clip polymer and the paper chain polymer through their hands. Have the sighted student name the colors of the paper chain in order.

Polymers, continued

Use An Analogy

Have each student assume the role of a monomer. Have students loop their arms together to form polymers. Have several 5- or 6-member polymer chains in the room. Have students move around to show how monomers can twist and turn and one chain can get intertwined with another chain. Now place one student between two chains and have the student hold on to one chain with one hand and on to the other chain with the other hand. This mimics cross-linking in polymers. This limits the flexibility of both chains, much the same way cross-linking limits the flexibility of chains in true polymers. L1 ELL IS **Kinesthetic**

Extension

Tell students that there are two basic types of polymers, addition polymers and condensation polymers. Have students research these designations and name some polymers of each type. In addition polymers such as polyethylene, the monomer is identical with the repeating unit of the polymer. In condensation polymers, such as polyesters, the monomer has lost atoms to form the polymer. L3 IS **Intrapersonal**

Reading Check

Answer suitcases, back packs, bullet-proof vests, spandex exercise garments

Figure 16
Processing can modify a polymer's properties. A Polystyrene used in CD cases is clear, hard, and brittle. B Polystyrene used in cups is opaque, light-weight, and foamy.

A

B

Designing Polymers The properties of polymers depend mostly on which monomers are used to make them. Also, like hydrocarbons, polymers can have branches in their chains. The amount of branching and the shape of the polymer greatly affect its properties.

Polymer materials can be shaped in many ways. Some are molded to make containers or other rigid materials. Sometimes the same polymer can take two completely different forms. For example, polystyrene (pah lee STI reen) that is made from styrene, shown in **Figure 16,** forms brittle, transparent cases for CDs but also lightweight, opaque plastic foam cups and packing materials. To make this transformation, a gas such as carbon dioxide is blown into melted polystyrene as it is molded. Bubbles remain within the polymer when it cools, making polystyrene foam an efficient insulator.

Other polymers can be spun into threads, which are used to make clothing or items such as suitcases and backpacks. Fibers can be made strong and durable for products that receive wear and tear. Others can resist strong impacts. For example, bullet-proof vests are made of a tightly woven, synthetic polymer. Polymer fibers also can be made stretchy and resilient for products like spandex exercise garments. Some polymers remain rigid when heated, but others become soft and pliable when heated and harden again when cooled.

SCIENCE Online
Research Visit the Glencoe Science Web site at **science.glencoe.com** to learn more about polymers. Communicate to your class what you learn.

Reading Check ***Name some applications of polymer fibers.***

Science Journal

Fullerene Buckminsterfullerene is a form of carbon first discovered in the late 1900s. Have students find out what it is and who Buckminster Fuller was, and write their findings in their Science Journals. The molecule contains 60 carbon atoms arranged in the shape of a ball, not unlike a soccer ball or a geodesic dome, which is a structure Buckminster Fuller developed. L3 IS **Linguistic** P

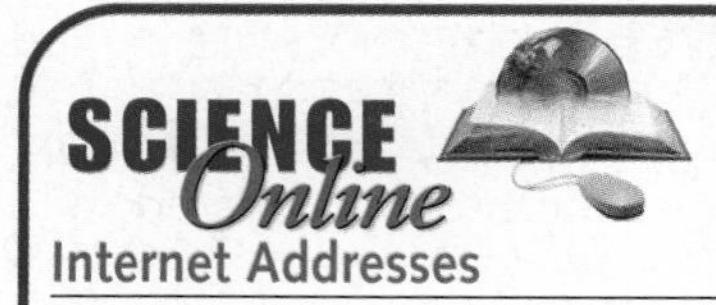

SCIENCE Online
Internet Addresses

Explore the Glencoe Science Web site at **science.glencoe.com** to find out more about topics in this section.

Other Petroleum Products

Other fractions obtained from fractional distillation of petroleum may be purified further by different techniques to isolate individual compounds. After these are separated, they can be converted into substituted hydrocarbons, as you learned in the last section. Chemists use these to make products ranging from medicines such as aspirin to dyes, insecticides, printers' ink, and flavorings.

Many of the products that come from petroleum are aromatic compounds. For example, the sweetener saccharin is related to toluene, a substituted benzene molecule. It has from 200 to 700 times the sweetening power of sugar, but no calories. In fact, it passes unchanged through the digestive tract. Although other sweeteners are available today, saccharin still is used widely in many diet foods and to sweeten mouthwash, as shown in **Figure 17.**

Also, aromatic dyes have replaced natural dyes, such as indigo and alizarin, almost completely. The first synthetic dye was a bright purple called mauve that was discovered accidentally in coal tar compounds. Today, most dyes come from petroleum.

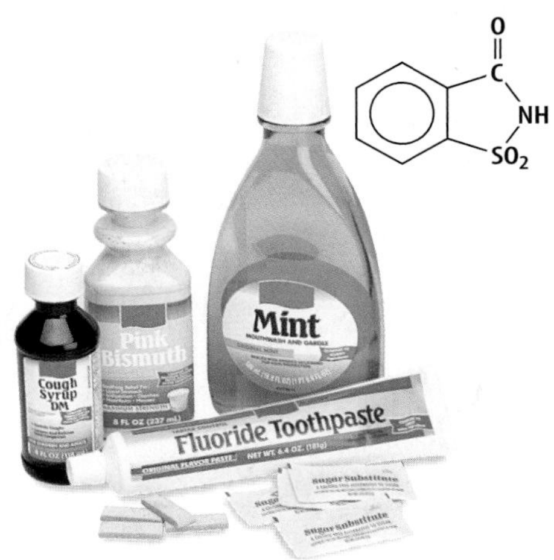

Figure 17
Saccharin is used as a sweetener because it doesn't damage teeth like sugar can.

Section 3 Assessment

1. What is petroleum and where does it come from?
2. Why are some fuels referred to as fossil fuels?
3. Which fractions of petroleum are used directly for fuel? How are they obtained from petroleum?
4. What is the name for substances made from thousands of small molecules that are linked together? What are the small molecules called?
5. **Think Critically** Petroleum fractions obtained by fractional distillation contain many individual compounds. How might these mixtures be separated further? What physical property could be used?

Skill Builder Activities

6. **Predicting** Based on the names of the polymers and monomers in this section, what do you think polymers made from the monomers terpene and urethane would be called? **For more help, refer to the** Science Skill Handbook.
7. **Communicating** Research at least two synthetic polymers other than those mentioned in this section. Write in your Science Journal *which monomers they include, the approximate length of their chains, and how they are used.* Describe their properties and, if possible, how they are related to polymer structure. Report your findings to your class. **For more help, refer to the** Science Skill Handbook.

3 Assess

Reteach

Use the recycling of plastics to start a review of polymers. 1 PETE is polyethyl terephtalate, 2 HDPE is high-density polyethylene, 3 V is polyvinyl chloride, 4 LDPE is low-density polyethylene, and 5 PP is polypropylene. Pass samples around and ask students to notice the properties of the polymers. L1 ELL **Kinesthetic**

Challenge

One of the most famous early synthetic polymers was nylon, which was synthesized by Dr. Wallace Carothers of the DuPont Corporation. Ask student to find the structures of the two different monomers used and to explain how the monomers are joined. This example is found in most high school chemistry textbooks as a classic example of polymer synthesis. The two monomers are adipoyl chloride and hexamethylenediamine. L3 LS **Logical-Mathematical**

Assessment

Oral Ask students to name materials or fibers that contain *poly-* as a prefix. Possibilities include polyvinyl chloride (PVC), polypropylene, polyester, polystyrene, polyvinyl alcohol (used to absorb water in some disposable diapers), polyethylene terephthalate (PETE) soft drink bottles, and polybutadiene used in automobile tires. Use **PASC,** p. 89.

Answers to Section Assessment

1. Petroleum is a dark, smelly substance often called crude oil formed from fossilized material
2. They are formed from fossilized remains.
3. The lightest fractions with up to ten carbon atoms per molecule; they are obtained from the condensed vapors of petroleum mixtures separated by fractional distillation in fractionating towers.
4. polymers; monomers
5. Each fraction could be redistilled separately; boiling point.
6. polyterpene, polyurethane
7. Possible synthetic polymers to investigate include Teflon, Acrilan, Dunel, Mylar, nylon and rayon.

Resource Manager

Chapter Resources Booklet
Reinforcement, p. 29
Cultural Diversity, p. 49

SECTION

Biological Compounds

1 Motivate

Bellringer Transparency

Display the Section Focus Transparency for Section 4. Use the accompanying Transparency Activity Master. L2 ELL

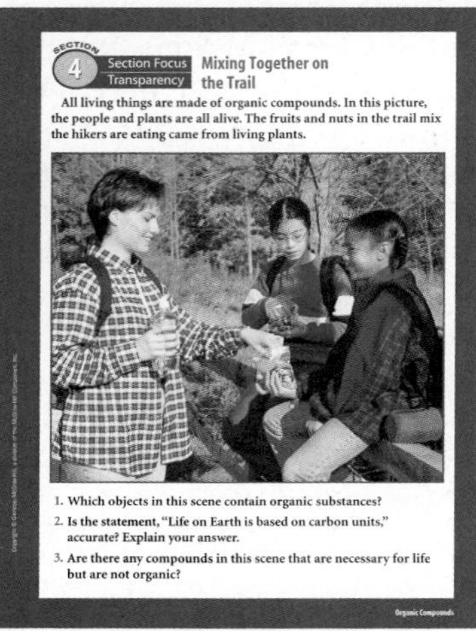

Tie to Prior Knowledge

Discuss with students what they already know about proteins and how they are used by the body. Remind them that proteins form cartilage, muscle, tendons and hair. Explain that proteins are polymers made up of hundreds of amino acids strung together.

SECTION

Biological Compounds

As You Read

What You'll Learn

- **Compare and contrast** proteins, nucleic acids, carbohydrates, and lipids.
- **Identify** the structure of polymers found in basic food groups.
- **Identify** the structure of large biological polymers.

Vocabulary

protein
nucleic acid
deoxyribonucleic acid (DNA)
carbohydrate
lipid

Why It's Important

All life processes depend on large biological compounds.

Biological Polymers

Like the polymers that are used to make the plastics and fibers, biological polymers are huge molecules. Also, they are made of many smaller monomers that are linked together. The monomers of biological polymers are usually larger and more complex in structure. Still, you can picture a biological monomer as one link in a very long chain.

Many of the important biological compounds in your body are polymers. Among them are the proteins, which often contain hundreds of units.

Proteins

Proteins are large organic polymers formed from organic monomers called amino acids. Even though only 20 amino acids are commonly found in nature, they can be arranged in so many ways that millions of different proteins exist. Proteins come in numerous forms and make up many of the tissues in your body, such as muscles and tendons, as well as your hair and fingernails. In fact, proteins account for 15 percent of your total body weight.

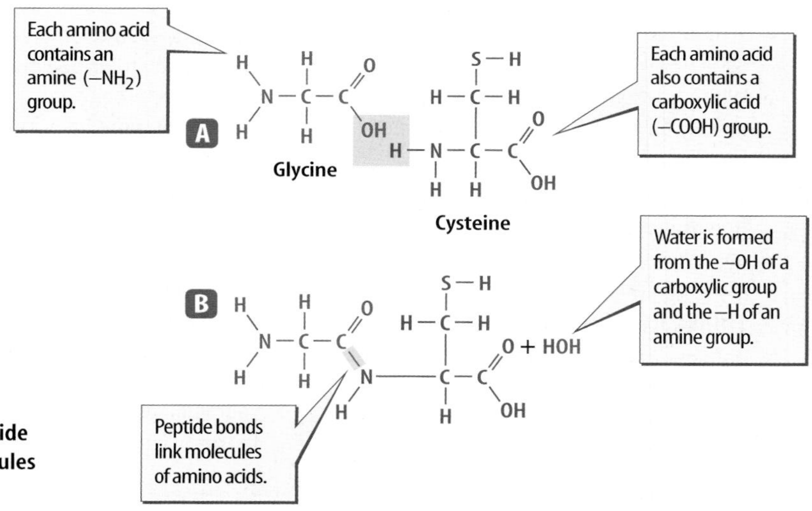

Figure 18
In a protein polymer, peptide bonds link together molecules of amino acids.

Section Assessment Planner

PORTFOLIO
Curriculum Connection, p. 660

PERFORMANCE ASSESSMENT
Problem-Solving Activity, p. 658
Skill-Builder Activities, p. 661
See p. 668 for other options.

CONTENT ASSESSMENT
Section, p. 661
Challenge, p. 661
Chapter, pp. 668–669

Figure 19
Four peptide chains coil around each other in the protein polymer hemoglobin. Each chain has an atom of iron, which carries oxygen.

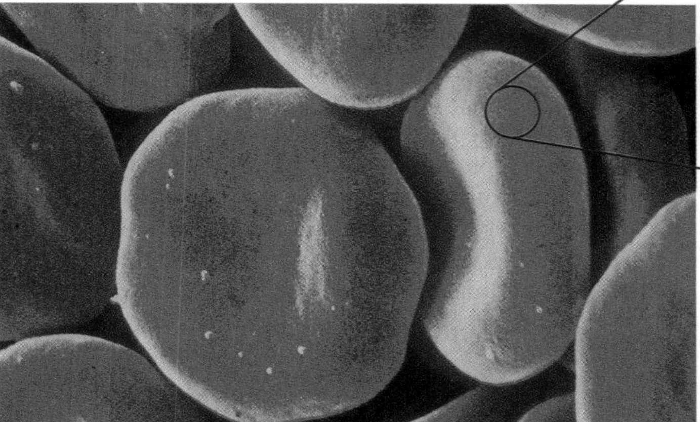

Protein Monomers Amino acids are the monomers that combine to form proteins. Two amino acids are shown in **Figure 18A.** The $-NH_2$ group is the amine group and the –COOH group is the carboxylic acid group. Both groups appear in every amino acid.

Amine groups of one amino acid can combine with the carboxylic acid group of another amino acid, linking them together to form a compound called a peptide as shown in **Figure 18B.** The bond joining them is known as a peptide bond. When a peptide contains a large number of amino acids—about 100 or more—the molecule is called a protein.

Reading Check *Approximately how many amino acid units does a protein contain?*

Protein Structure Long protein molecules tend to twist and coil in a manner unique to each protein. For example, hemoglobin, which carries oxygen in your blood, has four chains that coil around each other as shown in **Figure 19.** Each chain contains an iron atom that carries the oxygen. If you look closely, you can see all four iron atoms in hemoglobin.

When you eat foods that contain proteins, such as meat, dairy products, and some vegetables, your body breaks down the proteins into their amino acid monomers. Then your body uses these amino acids to make new proteins that form muscles, blood, and other body tissues.

2 Teach

Proteins

Extension

Amino acids are found in plants and animals. Our bodies can synthesize some amino acids but not others. The ones that we cannot make are called essential amino acids. Have students research to find the names and food sources of the essential amino acids. Have them display their findings in class. L3
LS **Linguistic**

Teacher FYI

About one-half of the body's proteins are used as catalysts for biochemical processes. These proteins are called enzymes.

IDENTIFYING Misconceptions

The artificial sweetener marketed as Nutrasweet is not made from any kind of sugar. It is made from two amino acids, aspartic acid and phenylalanine. They are combined by a peptide bond.

Reading Check

Answer more than 100

Resource Manager

Chapter Resources Booklet
Transparency Activity, p. 51
Directed Reading for Content Mastery, pp. 21, 22
Mathematics Skill Activities, p. 23

Inclusion Strategies

Gifted Have students report how results on the mapping of human chromosomes have enabled the detection and possible treatment of some diseases. L3 LS **Linguistic**

Nucleic Acids

SCIENCE Online

Internet Addresses

Explore the Glencoe Science Web site at science.glencoe.com to find out more about topics in this section.

Fun Fact

The two organic bases cytosine, C, and guanine, G, attract each other when they are aligned on opposite strands of a DNA molecule. Thymine, T, and adenine, A, do the same. The attractive forces between these base pairs hold the two strands of DNA together.

Problem-Solving Activity

National Math Standards

Correlation to Mathematics Objectives

1, 5, 6, 8, 9, 10

Answers

1. Protein: cheddar cheese, hamburger, soybeans, wheat; carbohydrates: wheat, potato chips; they would give you too much fat.
2. Possible answers: soybeans are rich in protein, soybean products are low in fat; people with lactose intolerance may eat them for protein.

SCIENCE Online

Data Update Visit the Glencoe Science Web site at **science.glencoe.com** for recent news of magazine articles about DNA fingerprinting. Communicate to your class what you learn.

Nucleic Acids

The **nucleic acids** are another important group of organic polymers that are essential for life. They control the activities and reproduction of cells. One kind of nucleic acid, called **deoxyribonucleic** (dee AHK sih ri boh noo klay ihk) **acid** or DNA, is found in the nuclei of cells where it codes and stores genetic information. This is known as the genetic code.

Nucleic Acid Monomers The monomers that make up DNA are called nucleotides. Nucleotides are complex molecules containing an organic base, a sugar, and a phosphoric acid unit. In DNA two nucleotide chains twist around each other forming what resembles a twisted ladder or what is called the double helix. Human DNA contains only four different organic bases, but they can form millions of combinations. The bases on one side of the ladder pair with bases on the other side, as shown in **Figure 20.** The genetic code gives instructions for making other nucleotides and proteins needed by your body.

Problem-Solving Activity

Selecting a Balanced Diet

What do you like to eat? You probably choose your foods by how good they taste. A better way might be to look at their nutritional value. Your body needs nutrients like proteins, carbohydrates, and fats to give it energy and help it build cells. Almost every food has some of these nutrients in it. The trick is to pick your foods so you don't get too much of one thing and not enough of another.

Identifying the Problem

The table on the right lists some basic nutrients for a variety of foods. The amount of the protein, carbohydrate, and fat is recorded as the number of grams in 100 g of the food. By examining these data, can you select the foods that best provide each nutrient?

Solving the Problem

1. Using the table, list the foods that supply the most protein and carbohydrates. What might be the problem with eating too many potato chips?
2. In countries where meat and dairy products are hard to get, people eat a lot of food made from soybeans. Can you think of reasons why people might wish to substitute meat and dairy products with soybean based products?

Nutritional Values for Some Common Foods

Food (100 g)	Protein (g)	Carbohydrate (g)	Fat (g)
Cheddar cheese	25	1	33
Hamburger	17	23	17
Soybeans	13	11	7
Wheat	15	68	2
Potato chips	7	53	35

Cultural Diversity

Hold the Cheese! Lactase is an enzyme that allows us to break down lactose, the sugar in milk. Normally, infants produce lactase, but lactase production stops in humans as we age. This causes a condition know as lactose intolerance. If a person lacks lactase, digesting milk products is difficult. Only about 18% of adult Americans of northern European ancestry are lactose intolerant, but about 80% of African American adults and 60% of Mexican-American adults do not produce lactase. In some Asian populations, such as Thai, as many as 98% do not produce lactase. Scientists suggest that populations that have used dairy farming as in important food resource for thousands of years have adapted by retaining the ability to produce lactase into adulthood.

DNA Fingerprinting Human DNA contains more than 5 billion base pairs. The DNA of each person differs in some way from that of everyone else, except for identical twins, who would share the same DNA. The unique nature of DNA offers crime investigators a way to identify criminals from hair or fluids left at a crime scene. DNA from bloodstains or cells in saliva found on a cigarette can be extracted in the laboratory. Then, chemists can break up the DNA into its nucleotide components and use radioactive and X-ray methods to obtain a picture of the nucleotide pattern. Comparing this pattern to one made from the DNA of a suspect can link that suspect to the crime scene.

Carbohydrates

If you hear the word *carbohydrate,* you may think of bread, cookies, or pasta. Have you heard of carbohydrate loading by athletes? Runners, for example, often prepare for a long-distance race by eating, or loading up on, carbohydrates in foods such as vegetables and pasta. **Carbohydrates** are compounds containing carbon, hydrogen, and oxygen, that have twice as many hydrogen atoms as oxygen atoms. Carbohydrates include the sugars and starches.

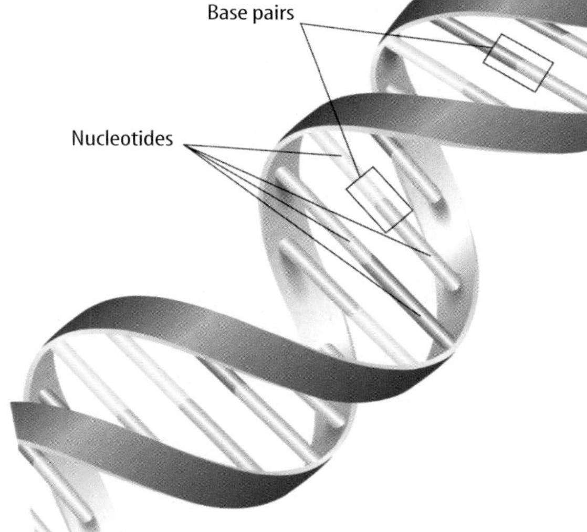

Figure 20
DNA models show how nucleotides are arranged in DNA. Each nucleotide looks like half of a ladder rung with an attached side piece. As you can see, each pair of nucleotides forms a rung on the ladder, while the side pieces give the ladder a little twist that gave it the name double helix.

Make a Model

Have students make 3-D models of the DNA twisted helix. Detail could vary, but could include the phosphate and sugar groups that make up the structure along with the four bases of guanine, cytosine, thymine and adenine. L2
LS **Visual-Spatial**

Activity

Nucleic acids are polymer chains that are cross-linked. You can demonstrate cross-linking by having students place 10 mL of white school glue in a small disposable cup. Then add about 1 to 2 mL of a saturated solution of borax (made by dissolving 4 g of sodium borate in 96 mL of water). As students stir and squeeze the substances together, the borax cross-links the polymer chains of the glue into a more connected rubberlike polymer. After the excess borax is washed away, the glue polymer will bounce. L2 ELL
LS **Kinesthetic**

Carbohydrates

Teacher FYI

The process of breaking down carbohydrates into CO_2 and H_2O provides most of the energy used by living things. Most plants store the carbohydrates they need in the form of starch. Starch contains more than ten thousand glucose monomers. Animals store carbohydrates in the form of glycogen. Glycogen contains fewer glucose units than starch and has more branches, which allows them to be broken faster to release the energy animals need to move.

Resource Manager

Chapter Resources Booklet
Enrichment, p. 34
Lab Activity, pp. 9–11
Science Inquiry Labs, p. 17

Science Journal

Sickle-Cell Anemia Have students research the genetic disease sickle cell anemia and write a report in their Science Journals on their findings. The genetic basis for the disease is in a change in only two of the more than 500 amino acids in hemoglobin. If both parents carry the gene for this disease, it is likely to be passed on to children. L2 LS **Linguistic**

Carbohydrates
continued

Caption Answer

Figure 21 because they are organic compounds with twice as many hydrogen atoms as oxygen atoms

Visual Learning

Figure 21 Point out the structure of glucose. Explain to students that fructose also has the formula $C_6H_{12}O_6$, but differs in the position of the oxygen atom in the ring.

Activity

Safety Precaution Before doing this activity, check to see if any students have dietary restrictions.

During digestion, enzymes break down starch into monomers of glucose, a simple sugar. Give each student a small piece of cracker. Have students chew the cracker many times without swallowing until they notice a taste change. The taste change shows that the enzyme ptyalin in the mouth's saliva is beginning the process of breaking the starch polymer into monomers of glucose. L1 ELL IS **Kinesthetic**

Lipids

Extension

Have students compare labels on various margarine and butter products. Have them report the percent of unsaturated and saturated fats in each one. Then have them research why saturated fats have been associated with circulation problems. L2 IS **Linguistic**

Reading Check

Answer They contain the same elements as carbohydrates but in different proportions.

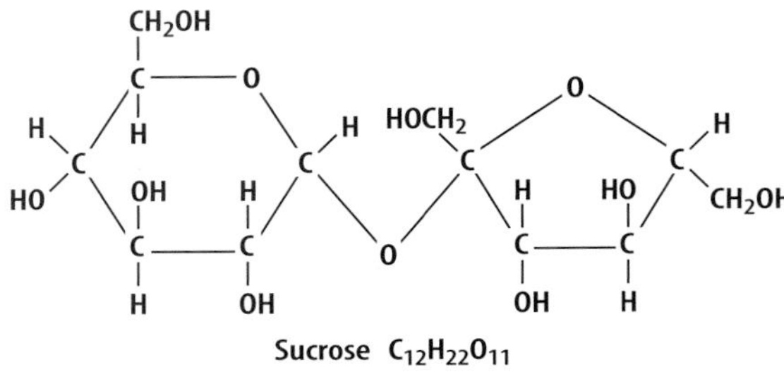

Sucrose $C_{12}H_{22}O_{11}$

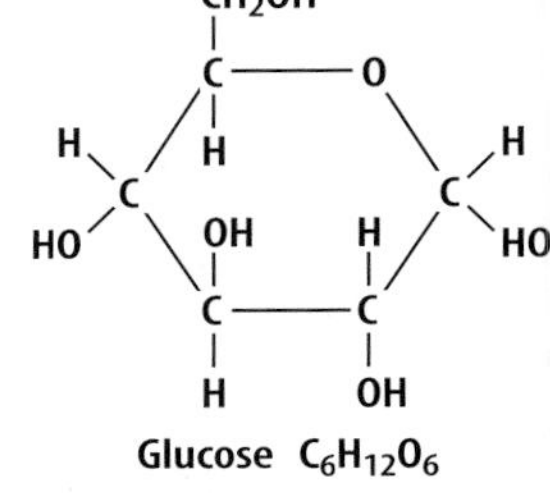

Glucose $C_6H_{12}O_6$

Figure 21
Sucrose and glucose are sugars found in foods. Fruits contain glucose and another simple sugar called fructose. *Why are sugars carbohydrates?*

Sugars Sugars are a major group of carbohydrates, as shown in **Figure 21.** The sugar glucose is found in your blood and also in many sweet foods such as grapes and honey. Common table sugar, known as sucrose, is broken down by digestion into two simpler sugars—fructose, often called fruit sugar, and glucose. Unlike starches, sugars provide quick energy soon after eating.

Starches Starch, shown in **Figure 22,** is a carbohydrate that is also a polymer. It is made of units or monomers of the sugar glucose. During digestion, the starch is broken down into smaller molecules of glucose and other similar sugars, which release energy in your body cells.

Athletes, especially long distance runners, use starches to provide high-energy, long-lasting fuel for the body. The energy from starches can be stored in liver and muscle cells in the form of a compound called glycogen. During a long race, this stored energy is released giving the athlete a fresh burst of power.

Figure 22
Starch is the major component of pasta.

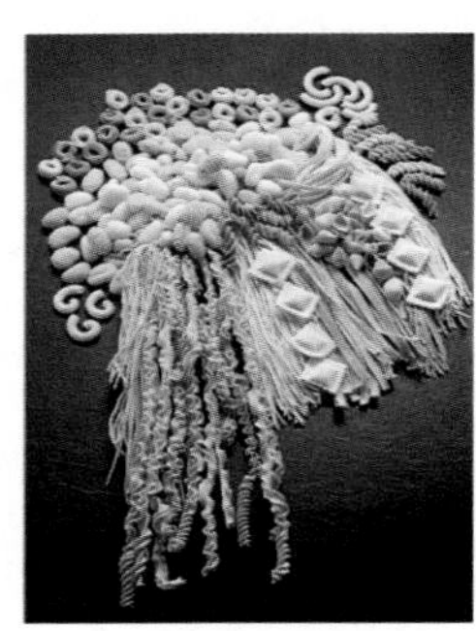

Lipids

Fats, oils, and related compounds make up a group of organic compounds known as **lipids.** Lipids include animal fats such as butter and vegetable oils, such as corn oil. Lipids contain the same elements as carbohydrates but in different proportions. For example, lipids have fewer oxygen atoms and contain carboxylic acid groups.

Reading Check *How are lipids like carbohydrates? How are they different?*

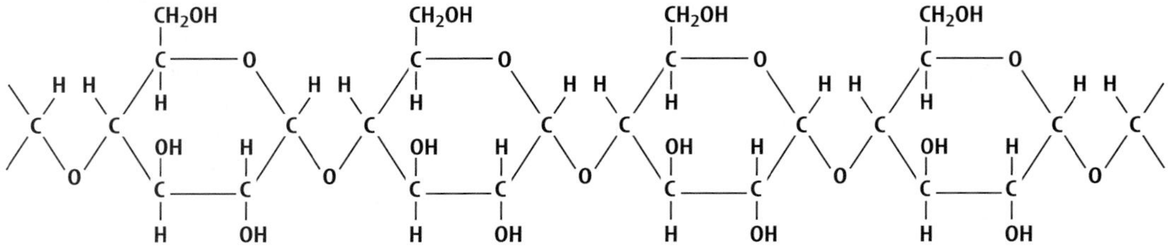

Curriculum Connection

Language Arts Steroids are one type of lipid. Percy Lavon Julian (1899–1975) synthesized the steroids progesterone, testosterone, and cortisone. Have students research the medical uses of steroids and the effects of using steroids in sports and body-building. Students should write reports documenting their findings. Steroids are used to treat inflammation and for estrogen replacement therapy during menopause. P

Resource Manager

Chapter Resources Booklet
Reinforcement, p. 30
Lab Activity, pp. 13–15

Fats and Oils These substances are similar in structure to hydrocarbons. They can be classified as saturated or unsaturated, according to the types of bonds in their carbon chains. Saturated fats contain only single bonds between carbon atoms. Unsaturated fats having one double bond are called monounsaturated, and those having two or more double bonds are called polyunsaturated. Animal lipids or fats tend to be saturated and are solids at room temperature. Plant lipids called oils are unsaturated and are usually liquids, as shown in **Figure 23.** Sometimes hydrogen is added to vegetable oils to form more saturated solid compounds known as hydrogenated vegetable shortenings.

Have you heard that eating too much fat can be unhealthy? Evidence shows that too much saturated fat and cholesterol in the diet may contribute to some heart disease and that unsaturated fats may help to prevent heart disease. It appears that saturated fats are more likely to be converted to substances that can block the arteries leading to the heart. A balanced diet includes some fats, just as it includes proteins and carbohydrates.

Cholesterol Another lipid that is often in the news is cholesterol, which is found in meats, eggs, butter, cheese, and fish. Even if you never eat foods containing cholesterol, your body makes its own. Some cholesterol is needed by the body to build cell membranes. It is also found in bile, a digestive fluid. Too much cholesterol, may cause serious damage to heart and blood vessels, similar to the damage caused by saturated fats.

Figure 23
At room temperature, fats are normally solids, and oils are usually liquids.

Health INTEGRATION

Check the label on any available container of milk. What percentage of fat is in the milk? Infer any advantages of drinking low-fat milk.

Section 4 Assessment

1. What is a polymer? Why are polymers important organic compounds? Give some specific examples.
2. Compare and contrast proteins and nucleic acids in terms of their structures and their functions in your body.
3. Where does your body get the amino acids it needs to build proteins?
4. Explain the difference between saturated and unsaturated fats and oils. Which type is considered healthier in foods?
5. **Think Critically** Is ethanol a carbohydrate? Explain.

Skill Builder Activities

6. **Comparing and Contrasting** In terms of DNA fingerprinting, compare and contrast identical twins and two people who are not identical twins. **For more help, refer to the Science Skill Handbook.**
7. **Solving One-Step Equations** Changing just one amino acid in a chain changes the function of the entire protein. If the letters G, L, C, and I represent four amino acids, how many different peptides containing four amino acids can be made? **For more help, refer to the Math Skill Handbook.**

Health INTEGRATION

Consuming too much saturated fat can lead to heart disease.

3 Assess

Reteach

To show where carbohydrates got their name, write the formula for glucose as $C_6H_{12}O_6$ and as $C_6(H_2O)_6$. The second way emphasizes the carbon, and shows that the hydrogen to oxygen ratio is the same as that in water (hydra). Explain that, contrary to their name, carbohydrates are not actually hydrates of carbon. L1 ELL LS **Linguistic**

Challenge

Have students research the pros and cons of DNA testing and screening of humans for health concerns. Possible answers: DNA screening may help assess possible risks of certain diseases. This could help people seek earlier treatment. DNA testing could be used by employers to keep some people from being hired if the employer thinks it is too risky. L3 LS **Linguistic**

Assessment

Content Have each student make a small poster identifying the monomers in each of the biologically important polymers described in this section. The poster should include the structures of the monomers and examples of the polymers that show how the monomers connect. Use **PASC,** p. 145.

Answers to Section Assessment

1. Polymers are large molecules made up of smaller units called monomers. Polymers have many useful properties. Plastics and synthetic fibers are polymers.
2. Proteins are formed when amino acids form polymers; they are used to make body tissues and enzymes. Nucleic acids are polymers of nucleotides that contain a code that controls cell activities.
3. Some amino acids can be synthesized in our bodies, but others must come from our diet of plants or animals that contain needed amino acids.
4. Saturated fats have only single bonds between carbon atoms. Unsaturated fats have one or more double or triple bonds between carbon atoms. Unsaturated fats are healthier.
5. Ethanol is not a carbohydrate. Its hydrogen to oxygen ratio is too high.
6. Identical twins have the same DNA; other people have DNA that is unique to them alone.
7. $4! = 4 \times 3 \times 2 \times 1 = 24$

Activity

BENCH TESTED

What You'll Investigate

Purpose

Students investigate the reaction between an acid and an alcohol to produce an ester. They will determine the presence of the ester by detecting its aroma. L2

COOP LEARN LS **Kinesthetic**

Process Skills

observing, experimenting

Time Required

25 minutes

Safety Precautions

CAUTION: Sulfuric acid is caustic. Avoid all skin contact. Detect aromas carefully. Gently waft a current of air from the tube toward the direction of your nose.

Procedure

Teaching Strategies

Have students work in pairs. Have one student in the pair get the acid, while the other obtains the alcohol.

Tie to Prior Knowledge

Before the experiment, tell students that the aroma of this ester is one that they have detected before. During the experiment ask them to report where they have smelled this aroma before.

Troubleshooting

Demonstrate the correct wafting technique for detecting aromas.

Activity

Preparing an Ester

Are esters aromatic compounds? Organic compounds known as acids and alcohols react to form another type of organic compound called an ester. Esters frequently produce a recognizable and often pleasant fragrance, even though they are not aromatic in the chemical sense—they might not contain a benzene ring. Esters are responsible for many fruit flavors, such as apple, pineapple, pear, and banana.

What You'll Investigate

How do an acid and an alcohol combine to produce a compound with different characteristics? Can the presence of the new compound formed be detected by its odor?

Goals

- Prepare an ester from an alcohol and an acid.
- Detect the results of the reaction by the odor of the product.

Materials

medium-size test tube
test-tube holder
250-mL beaker
10-mL graduated cylinder
water
hot plate
ring stand
thermometer
salicylic acid (0.2 g)
methyl alcohol (2 mL)
concentrated sulfuric acid (2 or 3 drops to be added by teacher)

Safety Precautions

WARNING: *Sulfuric acid is caustic. Avoid all contact. Mix all the contents together using a glass stirring rod.*

Inclusion Strategies

Behaviorally Disordered Tell these students several days in advance that they will be doing this activity. Give them copies of the procedure so they can get accustomed to what they will be expected to do. Tell them to read through the procedure and ask any questions they have about what they will be doing. When they do the activity, pair them with students who work well in the lab.

Resource Manager

Chapter Resources Booklet
Activity Worksheet, pp. 7–8

Procedure

WARNING: *Any compound you can smell has entered your body, and unknown compounds can be toxic or caustic. To detect an aroma safely, hold the container about 10 cm in front of your face and wave your hand over the opening to direct air currents to your nose.* See the illustration below for the proper way to detect odors in the laboratory.

1. Add about 150 mL of water to the beaker and heat it on the hot plate to 70°C.
2. Place approximately 0.2 g of salicylic acid in a test tube. Does this solution have an odor?
3. Add 2 mL of methyl alcohol to the test tube. Before adding it, check to see if this compound has an odor. If so, try to remember what it smells like.
4. Ask your teacher to add carefully three to five drops of concentrated sulfuric acid.
5. Place the test tube in the hot water and leave it untouched for about 12 to 15 minutes.
6. Remove the tube from the hot water using a test-tube holder and allow it to cool. Check to see if you can detect a new aroma.

Conclude and Apply

1. What did you smell in step 6?
2. Look closely at the surface of the liquid in the test tube. Do you see any small droplets of an oily substance? What do you think it is?
3. Look at the equation for the reaction below. One product is given. What do you think is the second product formed in this reaction?

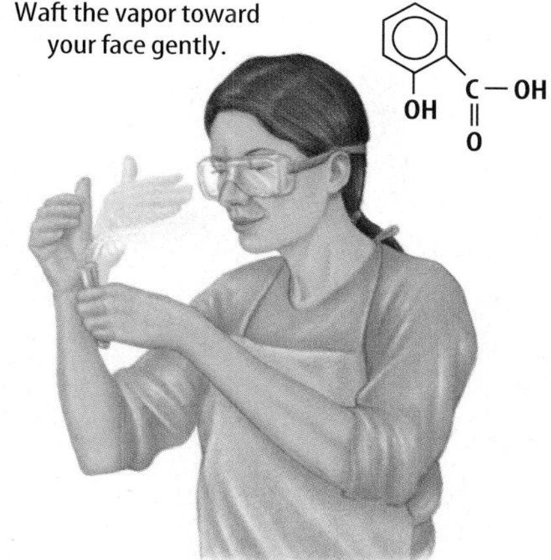
Waft the vapor toward your face gently.

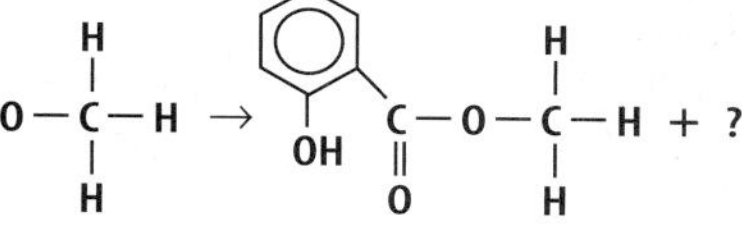

Communicating Your Data

Write a description of your experiment in your Science Journal. Suggest how you might modify the experiment to produce a different ester. **For more help, refer to the Science Skill Handbook.**

Expected Outcome

The aroma of wintergreen should appear soon after the mixture is heated.

Conclude and Apply

1. wintergreen (methyl salicylate)
2. Yes; it is the ester; the ester is not very polar, so it does not dissolve in the polar water solvent.
3. water

Error Analysis

If the wintergreen aroma is not detected, too much heating may have decomposed the ester or driven it out of the tube.

Content Have students examine the structures of both reactants, and predict the formulas of the products. Use **Performance Assessment in the Science Classroom,** p. 93.

Communicating Your Data

Have selected students share their ideas for modifying the experiment with the class. L1 **IN Interpersonal**

Oops!

Oops! Accidents in SCIENCE

SOMETIMES GREAT DISCOVERIES HAPPEN BY ACCIDENT!

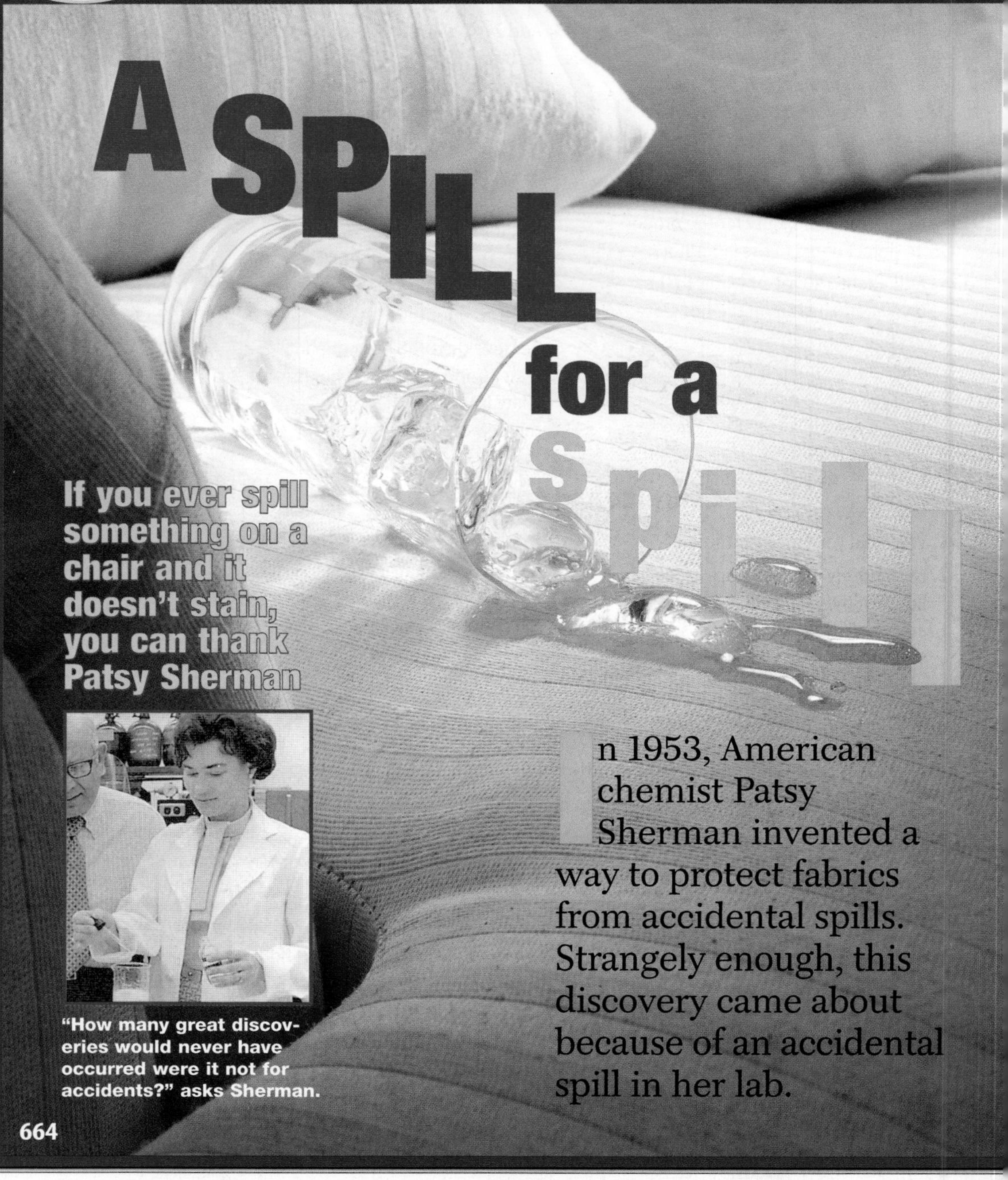

Content Background

Today, Patsy Sherman's fabric-protecting chemical comes in many forms, each engineered for a particular type of surface. It is composed of rubbery molecules containing hydrogen, carbon, oxygen, chlorine, and fluorine. What is really special about these molecules, however, is that they are sticky on one side and slippery on the other. This allows one side to stick to the surface of a fabric while the other side repels molecules that potentially might stain the fabric. But, if carpets and clothing are to remain stain repellant in the future, some chemist will have to come up with a new chemical soon. Due to perceived environmental hazards, Sherman's chemical will be taken off the market. Experts predict it may take as many as seven years for scientists to come up with a suitable alternative.

Discussion

What kinds of items would you want to be coated with a fabric protector that repelled water and stains? Possible answers: Tents to make them waterproof for camping; raingear; baby bibs; dog beds.

What kinds of items would you not want to be coated with water and stain repellent? Why not? Possible answers: Towels, wash cloths, and sponges because they would not absorb water.

A SPILL for a Spill

If you ever spill something on a chair and it doesn't stain, you can thank Patsy Sherman

"How many great discoveries would never have occurred were it not for accidents?" asks Sherman.

In 1953, American chemist Patsy Sherman invented a way to protect fabrics from accidental spills. Strangely enough, this discovery came about because of an accidental spill in her lab.

664

Resources for Teachers and Students

Serendipity Accidental Discoveries in Science, by Royston M. Roberts, John Wiley & Sons, Inc., 1989.

"We were trying to develop a new kind of rubber for jet aircraft fuel lines," Sherman once explained, "when one of the lab assistants accidentally dropped a glass bottle that contained a batch of synthetic latex I had made. Some of the latex mixture splashed on the assistant's canvas tennis shoe and the result was remarkable."

The latex mixture didn't stain the shoe or change it in any way. But it simply would not come off.

Neither soap nor alcohol nor any other cleaning material could remove the stubborn mixture from the shoe. In fact, the mixture actually made water bead and run off the shoe in much the same way that water runs off a duck's back.

Perfecting the Product

Although the lab assistant was frustrated by the mixture's staying power, Sherman was inspired. She realized that it could be used to protect fabrics from oil, water, and dirt. She spent three years working with another chemist to perfect the product, which came on the market in 1956. The substituted hydrocarbon compound that Sherman developed makes fabrics more durable as well as stain resistant. It bonds to the fibers in the fabric and protects them like an invisible shield. Today, the carpet in your home, the fabric that covers the couch in your living room, and some of the clothes that you wear are likely treated with the fabric protector invented by Sherman. Her product is especially useful on uniforms for people who spend a lot of time outdoors in difficult, dirty, or messy situations, such as firefighters, police officers, and military personnel.

Encouraging Young Inventors

Sherman had a successful career as a chemist and inventor before she retired in 1992. She often speaks to students about the life of an inventor and encourages them to pursue their dreams. Sherman stresses that a creative mind is a scientist's best tool. "Anyone can become an inventor," she insists, "as long as they keep an open and inquiring mind and never overlook the possible significance of an accident or apparent failure."

Patsy Sherman and her team have made mud on the rug easier to deal with.

CONNECTIONS **Experiment** Pour a small amount of water on a piece of cloth that has been treated with fabric protector. Do the same to a piece of untreated cloth. What happened to the water in both cases? What happened to the pieces of cloth?

SCIENCE Online For more information, visit science.glencoe.com

Activity

Have students put drops of tap water and water that has food coloring added to it on small pieces of construction paper and waxed paper. Allow the water to sit for one minute, then have students blot it up with a paper towel. **Which paper was protected against wetness and staining?** the waxed paper Explain to students that some companies manufacture coats and hats that have wax applied to their outer surfaces. **How does applying wax to act as a fabric protector?** It keeps water from soaking into the fabric.

Analyze the Event

There is some irony in Sherman's discovery, since she never went on to find the new rubber for jet airplane fuel lines she had originally been searching for. **What characteristics do you think Patsy Sherman or any scientist must have to take advantage of an accidental discovery?** Possible answers: a good imagination, the ability to recognize a potential opportunity for a discovery, even though it is not related to what the scientist is investigating.

CONNECTIONS **How People Responded** Students should see the water on the treated cloth bead up and not soak into the cloth. The water should soak into the untreated cloth.

SCIENCE Online

Internet Addresses

Explore the Glencoe Science Web site at **science.glencoe.com** to find out more about topics in this feature.

Chapter 21 Study Guide

Reviewing Main Ideas

Preview

Students can answer the questions in their Science Journals. Discuss the answers as you go through the chapter. LS **Linguistic**

Review

Students can write their answers, then compare them with those of other students. LS **Interpersonal**

Reteach

Students can look at the illustrations and describe details that support the main ideas of the chapter. LS **Visual-Spatial**

Answers to Chapter Review

Section 1

3. 4

Section 2

2. substituted hydrocarbons

Section 3

4. elasticity

Section 4

3. amino acids

Chapter 21 Study Guide

Reviewing Main Ideas

Section 1 Simple Organic Compounds

1. Carbon is an element with a structure that enables it to form a large number of compounds, known as organic compounds.
2. Saturated hydrocarbons contain only single bonds between carbon atoms. Unsaturated hydrocarbons contain double or triple bonds.
3. Many camp stoves burn butane. *How many carbon atoms are in a butane molecule?*

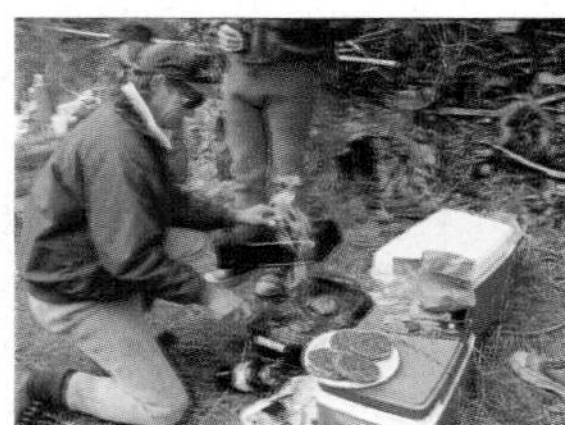

4. Isomers of organic compounds have identical formulas but different molecular shapes.

Section 2 Other Organic Compounds

1. Aromatic compounds, many of which have odors, contain the benzene ring structure.
2. Cookware often has a nonstick coating. This coating is a hydrocarbon polymer in which fluorine replaces some hydrogen atoms. *What are such hydrocarbons called?*

3. Benzene rings are stable because all six carbon atoms are bound tightly on one plane.
4. Aromatic compounds include those having two or more rings fused together.

Section 3 Petroleum—A Source of Carbon Compounds

1. Petroleum is a mixture of thousands of carbon compounds.
2. A fractionating tower separates petroleum into groups of compounds or fractions based on their boiling points.
3. Small hydrocarbons obtained from petroleum can be combined to make long chains called polymers, which are used for plastics.
4. Polymers can be spun into fibers designed to have specific properties. *What property is important in spandex fibers?*

Section 4 Biological Compounds

1. Proteins, nucleic acids, carbohydrates, and lipids are major groups of biological organic compounds.
2. Many important biological compounds are polymers, huge organic molecules made of smaller units, or monomers.
3. The pain-producing components of wasp venom are peptides. *What are the monomers of peptides?*

FOLDABLES Reading & Study Skills — After You Read

Use each of the vocabulary words on your Foldable in a complete sentence that explains something about the organic compounds discussed in this chapter.

FOLDABLES Reading & Study Skills — After You Read

After students have read the chapter and completed the Foldable described in Before You Read, have them do the activity on the student page.

Dinah Zike

Chapter 21 Study Guide

Visualizing Main Ideas

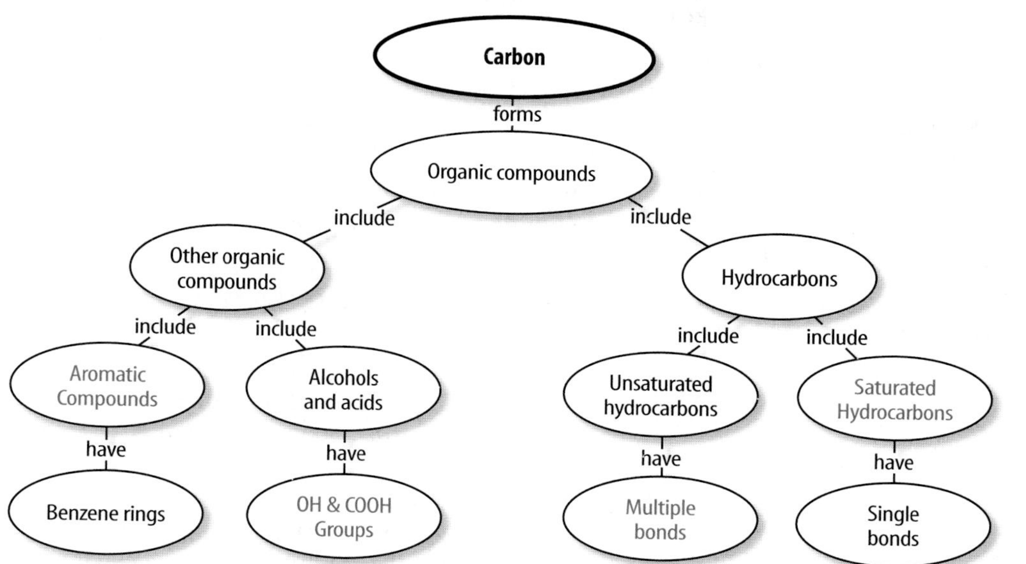

Vocabulary Review

Vocabulary Words

a. alcohol
b. aromatic compound
c. carbohydrate
d. deoxyribonucleic acid (DNA)
e. hydrocarbon
f. isomer
g. lipid
h. monomer
i. nucleic acid
j. organic compound
k. polyethylene
l. polymer
m. protein
n. saturated hydrocarbon
o. substituted hydrocarbon
p. unsaturated hydrocarbon

Study Tip

Think of other ways that you might design an experiment to prove scientific principles. Consider controls and variables.

Using Vocabulary

Replace the underlined words with the correct vocabulary words.

1. Isomers are compounds that contain the element carbon.
2. A peptide forms a link in a polymer chain.
3. Protein is the nucleic acid that contains your genetic information.
4. An unsaturated hydrocarbon contains the benzene ring-structure.
5. Organic compounds such as sugars and starches are called proteins.
6. Organic compounds such as fats and oils are called isomers.
7. Polyethylene is the process of separating petroleum compounds.

Chapter 21 Study Guide

Visualizing Main Ideas

See student page.

Vocabulary Review

Using Vocabulary

1. organic compound
2. monomer
3. deoxyribonucleic acid (DNA)
4. aromatic compound
5. carbohydrates
6. lipids
7. protein

CHAPTER STUDY GUIDE 667

Checking Concepts

1. B
2. C
3. A
4. D
5. D
6. B
7. C
8. D
9. D
10. C

Thinking Critically

11. Saturated fats contain only single bonds between carbon atoms. Unsaturated fats have one or more double or triple bonds between carbon atoms.
12. In isopropyl alcohol the –OH is on the middle carbon atom. In propyl alcohol the –OH is on one of the end carbon atoms.
13. Single bond—two atoms share a pair of electrons; double bond—atoms share two electron pairs; triple bond—three electron pairs are shared. Student diagrams should show four bonds for each carbon atom.

H H H H
H–C–C–C=C–C–C≡C–H
H H H H

Single bond Double bond Triple bond

14. A fraction is a portion of crude oil separated by fractional distillation from petroleum. In fractional distillation, petroleum is heated and the portions with different boiling points that separate out are collected in a fractionating tower.

Chapter 21 Assessment

Checking Concepts

Choose the word or phrase that best answers the question.

1. How would you describe a benzene ring?
   A) rare **B)** stable **C)** unstable **D)** saturated
2. How would you classify hydrocarbons, such as alcohols and organic acids?
   A) aromatic **B)** saturated **C)** substituted **D)** unsaturated
3. What are the small units that make up polymers called?
   A) monomers **B)** isomers **C)** plastics **D)** carbohydrates
4. What type of compound is hemoglobin found in red blood cells?
   A) carbohydrate **B)** lipid **C)** nucleic acid **D)** protein
5. RNA tells your body how to make proteins. What does DNA code and store?
   A) lipids **B)** nucleic acids **C)** protein **D)** genetic information
6. What type of compounds form the DNA molecule?
   A) amino acids **B)** nucleotides **C)** polymers **D)** carbohydrates
7. Glucose and fructose both have the formula $C_6H_{12}O_6$. What are such compounds called?
   A) amino acids **B)** alcohols **C)** isomers **D)** polymers
8. If a carbohydrate has 16 oxygen atoms, how many hydrogen atoms does it have?
   A) 4 **B)** 8 **C)** 16 **D)** 32
9. What type of compound is cholesterol?
   A) sugar **B)** starch **C)** protein **D)** lipid
10. Which petroleum fractions are collected at the top of a fractionating tower?
    A) highest boiling **B)** liquid **C)** lowest boiling **D)** polymer

Thinking Critically

11. Too much saturated or unsaturated fat in your diet is unhealthful. How do they differ in composition?
12. Propyl alcohol and isopropyl alcohol have the formula C_3H_80. How might their structures differ?
13. Draw a diagram to explain single, double, and triple bonds in hydrocarbons. Draw a chain of carbon atoms that shows each type of bond.
14. Explain the term *fraction* when used to describe the products produced during petroleum refining. Describe the process by which these products are obtained.

Developing Skills

15. **Making and Using Graphs** Using the following table, plot the number of carbon atoms on one axis and the boiling point on the other axis on a graph. Use the graph to predict the boiling points of butane, octane, and dodecane ($C_{12}H_{26}$).

Hydrocarbons

Name	Formula	Boiling Point (°C)
Methane	CH_4	–162
Ethane	C_2H_6	–89
Propane	C_3H_8	–42

16. **Recognizing Cause and Effect** Anthracene is a compound containing three fused rings similar to the benzene ring. How would you explain the stability of this compound?

Chapter Assessment Planner

Portfolio Encourage students to place in their portfolios one or two items that they consider to be their best work. Examples include:

- Science Journal, p. 643
- Visual Learning, p. 647
- Science Journal, p. 654
- Curriculum Connection, p. 660

Performance Additional performance assessments, Performance Task Assessment Lists, and rubrics for evaluating these activities can be found in Glencoe's **Performance Assessment in the Science Classroom.**

668 CHAPTER ASSESSMENT

17. Interpreting Scientific Illustrations Which of the following terms apply to the illustration below: *alcohol, aromatic, carbohydrate, hydrocarbon, lipid, organic compound, polymer, saturated,* and *substituted hydrocarbon.*

```
H       H   H
 \      |   |
  C  =  C - C - H
 /          |
H           H
```

18. Concept Mapping Make a network tree to describe types of fats. Include the terms *saturated fats, unsaturated fats, single bonds,* and *double bonds.*

19. Hypothesizing A weight-reduction diet allows no food other than lettuce and fresh fruit for three days a week. What is the problem with such a diet?

Performance Assessment

20. Scientific Drawing Research three hydrocarbons containing five carbon atoms. Draw diagrams of their structures, name them, and tell their uses.

21. Surveying and Graphing Record the fiber content of your clothing, noting whether it is synthetic or natural. Make a circle graph comparing the percentage of natural and synthetic fibers.

TECHNOLOGY

Go to the Glencoe Science Web site at **science.glencoe.com** or use the **Glencoe Science CD-ROM** for additional chapter assessment.

Test Practice

The common alcohol methanol is represented by the following chemical symbol:

CH_3OH

Methanol

Study the chemical formula above and answer the following questions.

1. According to this chemical formula, all of the following elements are found in methanol EXCEPT ________.
   A) carbon
   B) nitrogen
   C) hydrogen
   D) oxygen

2. How many carbon atoms are there in the compound methanol?
   F) one
   G) two
   H) three
   J) four

3. How many electrons are shared in each of the bonds linking the carbon atom in methanol to the three hydrogen atoms?
   A) one
   B) two
   C) three
   D) four

Assessment Resources

Reproducible Masters

Chapter Resources Booklet
Chapter Review, pp. 41–42
Chapter Tests, pp. 43–46
Assessment Transparency Activity, p. 55

Glencoe Science Web site
Interactive Tutor
Chapter Quizzes

Glencoe Technology
Assessment Transparency
Interactive CD-ROM Chapter Quizzes
ExamView Pro Test Bank
Vocabulary PuzzleMaker Software
MindJogger Videoquiz DVD/VHS

Chapter 21 Assessment

THE PRINCETON REVIEW Test Practice

The Test-Taking Tip was written by The Princeton Review, the nation's leader in test preparation.

1. B
2. F
3. B

Developing Skills

15. Answers should be close to −1°C, 126°C, and 216°C, respectively.
16. It should be very stable.
17. organic compound, unsaturated, hydrocarbon
18. Concept maps should show that fats consist of saturated fats, which contain only single bonds, and unsaturated fats, which contain double as well as single bonds.
19. Possible answer: dieters will not get all the nutrients they need.

Performance Assessment

20. The compounds will be various isomers of pentane, pentene, and pentyne. The pentanes are used for fuel. The pentenes and pentynes are used for synthesizing various other organic chemicals. Answers may also include cyclopentane. Use **PASC,** p. 127.
21. Answers will vary considerably. Have each student put his or her data in a table. Make sure the circle graphs accurately represent the data in the tables. Use **PASC,** p. 111.

Section/Objectives	Standards		Activities/Features
	National	State/Local	
Chapter Opener	See p. 37T for a Key to Standards.		**Explore Activity:** Compare Properties, p. 671 **Before You Read,** p. 671
Section 1 Materials with a Past 1 session .5 block 1. **Identify** how different alloys are used. 2. **Explain** how the properties of alloys determine their use.	National Content Standards: UCP5, A2, B1 (58), B2 (9–12), E2, F5 (58), F6 (9–12)		**MiniLAB:** Observing Properties of Alloys, p. 673 **Earth Science Integration,** p. 674 **Science Online,** p. 676
Section 2 Versatile Materials 1 session .5 block 1. **Examine** the versatile properties of ceramics. 2. **Identify** how ceramic materials are used. 3. **Explain** what a semiconductor is.	National Content Standards: UCP5, A2, B1 (58), B2 (9–12), E2, F5 (58), F6 (9–12)		**MiniLAB:** Modeling a Composite Material, p. 679 **Problem-Solving Activity:** Can you choose the right material? p. 680 **Visualizing the History of Computers,** p. 683 **Science Online,** p. 684
Section 3 Polymers and Composites 2 sessions 1 block 1. **Identify** what a polymer is and the variety of polymers around us. 2. **Explain** what a composite material is and why composites are used.	National Content Standards: UCP5, A2, B1 (58), B2 (9–12), E2, F5 (58), F6 (9–12), G3		**Environmental Science Integration,** p. 686 **Science Online,** p. 687 **Science Online,** p. 689 **Activity:** What can you do with this stuff? p. 691 **Activity:** Can polymer composites be stronger than steel? p. 692 **Science and Society:** Wonder Fiber, p. 694

Activity Materials	Reproducible Resources	Section Assessment	Technology
Explore Activity: tongs, 2 pieces of 5-cm steel wire, lab burner, beaker of cold water, heat-proof surface	**Chapter Resources Booklet** Foldables Worksheet, p. 17 Note-taking Worksheets, pp. 33–35	GLENCOE'S ASSESSMENT ADVANTAGE	
MiniLAB: aluminum foil, conductivity tester, paper, pencil, ink pen, paper clip	**Chapter Resources Booklet** Transparency Activity, p. 44 Enrichment, p. 30 Reinforcement, p. 27 Directed Reading, p. 20 MiniLAB, p. 3 Transparency Activity, pp. 47–48 Lab Activity, pp. 9–11	**Portfolio** Curriculum Connection, p. 673 **Performance** MiniLAB, p. 673 Skill Builder Activities, p. 677 **Content** Section Assessment, p. 677	Section Focus Transparency Teaching Transparency 1 Interactive CD-ROM/DVD Guided Reading Audio Program
MiniLAB: goggles, apron, sand, aquarium gravel or small pebbles, white glue, water *Need materials?* Contact Science Kit at 1-800-828-7777 or www.sciencekit.com on the Internet.	**Chapter Resources Booklet** Transparency Activity, p. 45 MiniLAB, p. 4 Enrichment, p. 31 Reinforcement, p. 28 Directed Reading, p. 21 **Cultural Diversity,** p. 49 **Science Inquiry Labs,** pp. 45, 49	**Portfolio** Science Journal, p. 682 **Performance** MiniLAB, p. 679 Problem-Solving Activity, p. 680 Skill Builder Activities, p. 684 **Content** Section Assessment, p. 684	Section Focus Transparency 2 Interactive CD-ROM/DVD Guided Reading Audio Program
Activity: white glue, borax laundry soap, warm water, 250-mL beaker or cup, 100-mL beaker or cup, graduated cylinder, popsicle or craft stick for mixing **Activity:** meterstick, spring scale, 0–12 kg range and 0–2 kg range wood, steel, fiberglass composite rods, 6.35 mm in diameter by 50 cm long supports, graph paper	**Chapter Resources Booklet** Transparency Activity, p. 46 Enrichment, p. 32 Reinforcement, p. 29 Directed Reading, pp. 21, 22 Activity Worksheet, pp. 5–6, 7–8 Lab Activity, pp. 13–16 Transparency Activity, pp. 47–48	**Portfolio** Activity, p. 687 **Performance** Skill Builder Activities, p. 690 **Content** Section Assessment, p. 690	Section Focus Transparency 3 Teaching Transparency Interactive CD-ROM/DVD Guided Reading Audio Program

End of Chapter Assessment

GLENCOE'S ASSESSMENT ADVANTAGE

Blackline Masters	Technology	Professional Series
Chapter Resources Booklet Chapter Review, pp. 37–38 Chapter Tests, pp. 39–42 **Standardized Test Practice by The Princeton Review,** pp. 92–95	MindJogger Videoquiz CD-ROM Explorations and Quizzes Vocabulary Puzzle Makers ExamView Pro Test Bank Interactive Lesson Planner Interactive Teacher's Edition	Performance Assessment in the Science Classroom (PASC)

Transparencies

Section Focus

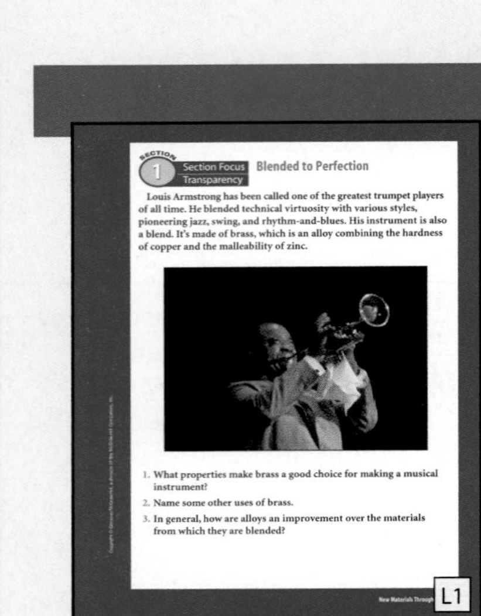
Section 1 Section Focus Transparency — Blended to Perfection

Louis Armstrong has been called one of the greatest trumpet players of all time. He blended technical virtuosity with various styles, pioneering jazz, swing, and rhythm-and-blues. His instrument is also a blend. It's made of brass, which is an alloy combining the hardness of copper and the malleability of zinc.

1. What properties make brass a good choice for making a musical instrument?
2. Name some other uses of brass.
3. In general, how are alloys an improvement over the materials from which they are blended?

L1

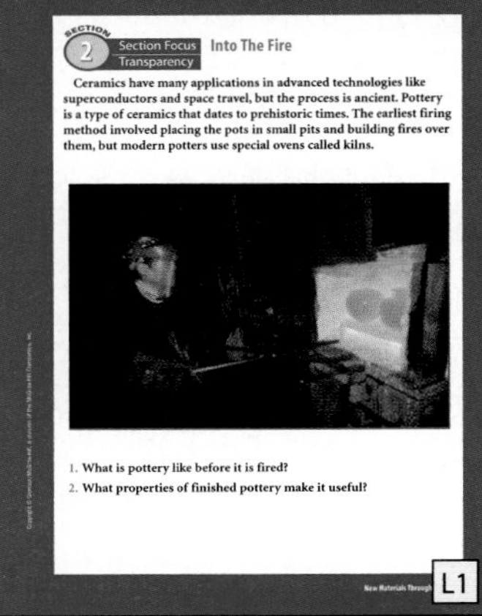
Section 2 Section Focus Transparency — Into The Fire

Ceramics have many applications in advanced technologies like superconductors and space travel, but the process is ancient. Pottery is a type of ceramics that dates to prehistoric times. The earliest firing method involved placing the pots in small pits and building fires over them, but modern potters use special ovens called kilns.

1. What is pottery like before it is fired?
2. What properties of finished pottery make it useful?

L1

Section 3 Section Focus Transparency — Get a Grip

Mountain climbers face many hazards, including extreme temperatures and massive crevasses. During the twentieth century, the development of modern synthetic materials drastically changed a climber's ability to cope with these dangers.

1. Describe the equipment this climber is using. Where did the material to make this gear come from?
2. Why is nylon rope an improvement over rope made of hemp?
3. If you were designing a tent, what characteristics would you look for in a fabric?

L1

This is a representation of key blackline masters available in the Teacher Classroom Resources. See Resource Manager boxes within the chapter for additional information.

Assessment

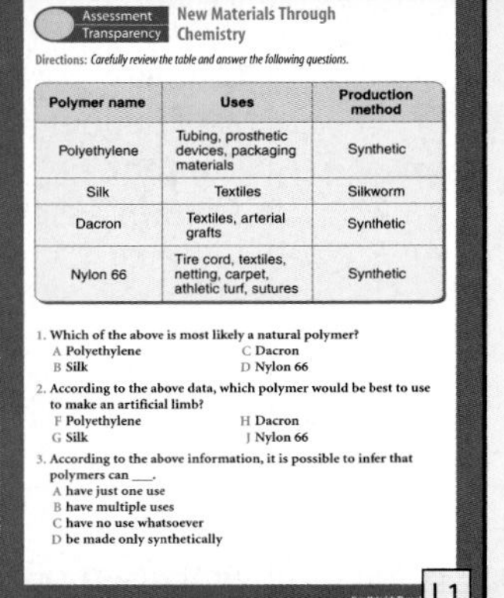
Assessment Transparency — New Materials Through Chemistry

Directions: Carefully review the table and answer the following questions.

Polymer name	Uses	Production method
Polyethylene	Tubing, prosthetic devices, packaging materials	Synthetic
Silk	Textiles	Silkworm
Dacron	Textiles, arterial grafts	Synthetic
Nylon 66	Tire cord, textiles, netting, carpet, athletic turf, sutures	Synthetic

1. Which of the above is most likely a natural polymer?
   A Polyethylene C Dacron
   B Silk D Nylon 66
2. According to the above data, which polymer would be best to use to make an artificial limb?
   F Polyethylene H Dacron
   G Silk J Nylon 66
3. According to the above information, it is possible to infer that polymers can ___.
   A have just one use
   B have multiple uses
   C have no use whatsoever
   D be made only synthetically

L1

Teaching

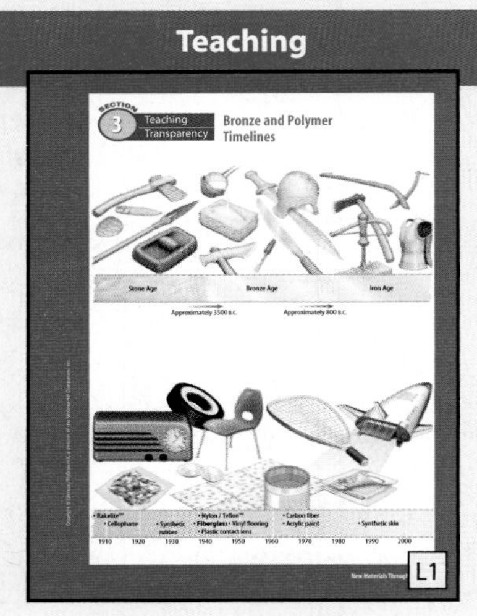
Section 3 Teaching Transparency — Bronze and Polymer Timelines

L1

Key to Teaching Strategies

The following designations will help you decide which activities are appropriate for your students.

L1 Level 1 activities should be appropriate for students with learning difficulties.

L2 Level 2 activities should be within the ability range of all students.

L3 Level 3 activities are designed for above-average students.

ELL ELL activities should be within the ability range of English Language Learners.

COOP LEARN Cooperative Learning activities are designed for small group work.

LS Multiple Learning Styles logos are used throughout to indicate strategies that address different learning styles.

P These strategies represent student products that can be placed into a best-work portfolio.

Hands-on Activities

Activity Worksheets

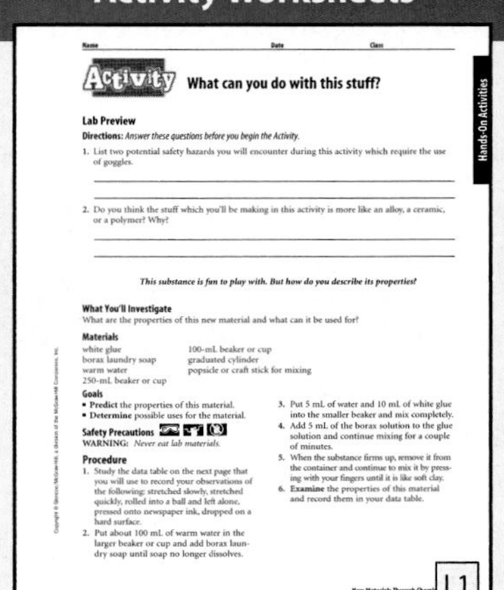
Activity — What can you do with this stuff?

L1

Laboratory Activities

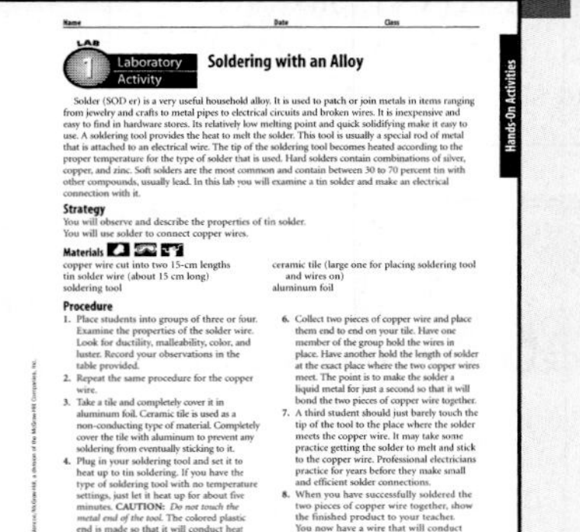
Laboratory Activity 1 — Soldering with an Alloy

L1

Meeting Different Ability Levels

Content Outline

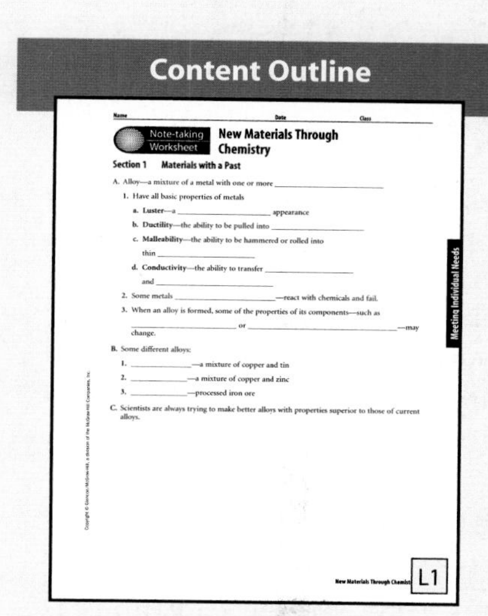
Note-taking Worksheet — New Materials Through Chemistry

Section 1 Materials with a Past

A. Alloy—a mixture of a metal with one or more ______
1. Have all basic properties of metals
   a. Luster—a ______ appearance
   b. Ductility—the ability to be pulled into ______
   c. Malleability—the ability to be hammered or rolled into thin ______
   d. Conductivity—the ability to transfer ______ and ______
2. Some metals ______—react with chemicals and fail.
3. When an alloy is formed, some of the properties of its components—such as ______ or ______—may change.

B. Some different alloys:
1. ______—a mixture of copper and tin
2. ______—a mixture of copper and zinc
3. ______—processed iron ore

C. Scientists are always trying to make better alloys with properties superior to those of current alloys.

L1

Reinforcement

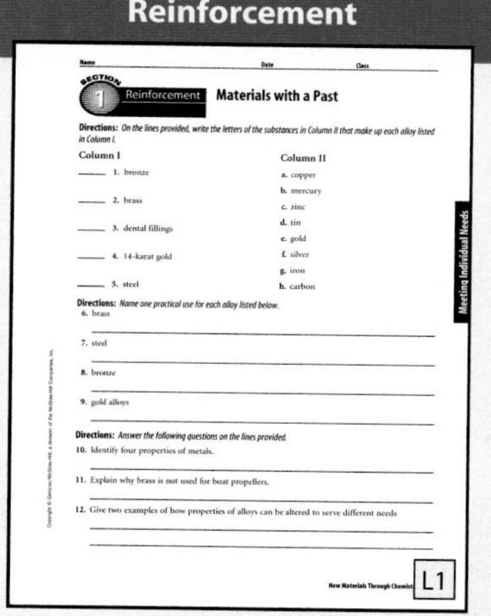
Section 1 Reinforcement — Materials with a Past

Directions: On the lines provided, write the letters of the substances in Column II that make up each alloy listed in Column I.

Column I	Column II
____ 1. bronze	a. copper
____ 2. brass	b. mercury
	c. zinc
____ 3. dental fillings	d. tin
	e. gold
____ 4. 14-karat gold	f. silver
	g. iron
____ 5. steel	h. carbon

Directions: Name one practical use for each alloy listed below.
6. brass
7. steel
8. bronze
9. gold alloys

Directions: Answer the following questions on the lines provided.
10. Identify four properties of metals.
11. Explain why brass is not used for boat propellers.
12. Give two examples of how properties of alloys can be altered to serve different needs.

L1

Directed Reading

Directed Reading for Content Mastery — Overview — New Materials Through Chemistry

Directions: Complete the graphic organizer below by listing the composition, properties, examples, and uses of alloys, polymers, and ceramics.

Properties of Material	Alloys	Polymers	Ceramics
Composition	1.	4.	clay, sand, feldspar, compounds of other elements
Properties	luster, ductility, malleability, conductivity	5.	7.
Examples	2.	plastic, PVC, acrylic, nylon, adhesives	8.
Uses	3.	6.	computers, toys, medical, glass, pottery, dental, construction

Directions: Answer the following questions on the lines provided.
4. Name at least four industries or activities that are benefitting from new materials technology.
5. Select one of your responses and explain how it has been changed by technology.

L1

Assessment

Chapter Tests

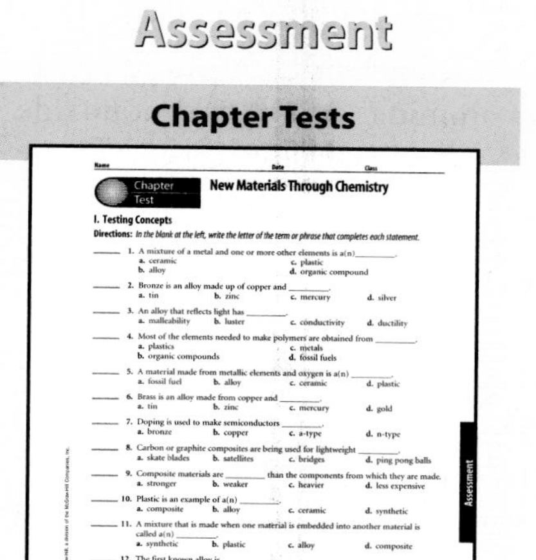
Chapter Test — New Materials Through Chemistry

I. Testing Concepts

Directions: In the blank at the left, write the letter of the term or phrase that completes each statement.

1. A mixture of a metal and one or more other elements is a(n) ______. a. ceramic b. alloy c. plastic d. organic compound
2. Bronze is an alloy made up of copper and ______. a. tin b. zinc c. mercury d. silver
3. An alloy that reflects light has ______. a. malleability b. luster c. conductivity d. ductility
4. Most of the elements needed to make polymers are obtained from ______. a. plastics b. organic compounds c. metals d. fossil fuels
5. A material made from metallic elements and oxygen is a(n) ______. a. fossil fuel b. alloy c. ceramic d. plastic
6. Brass is an alloy made from copper and ______. a. tin b. zinc c. mercury d. gold
7. Doping is used to make semiconductors ______. a. bronze b. copper c. a-type d. n-type
8. Carbon or graphite composites are being used for lightweight ______. a. skate blades b. satellites c. bridges d. ping pong balls
9. Composite materials are ______ than the components from which they are made. a. stronger b. weaker c. heavier d. less expensive
10. Plastic is an example of a(n) ______. a. composite b. alloy c. ceramic d. synthetic
11. A mixture that is made when one material is embedded into another material is called a(n) ______. a. synthetic b. plastic c. alloy d. composite
12. The first known alloy is ______. a. bronze b. brass c. fossil fuels d. iron
13. Office buildings, bridges, and over passes are built using ______. a. plastic b. iron c. steel d. bronze
14. The gold alloy that is often used to make jewelry is made up of gold and ______. a. silver b. steel c. copper d. aluminum
15. Fiberglass is an example of a(n) ______. a. alloy b. composite c. cermet d. plastic

L1

Enrichment

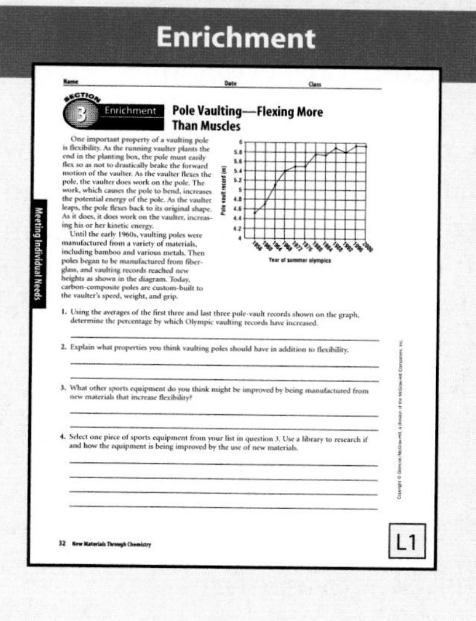
Section 3 Enrichment — Pole Vaulting—Flexing More Than Muscles

One important property of a vaulting pole is flexibility. As the running vaulter plants the end in the planting box, the pole must easily flex so as not to drastically brake the forward motion of the vaulter. As the vaulter flexes the pole, the vaulter does work on the pole. The work, which causes the pole to bend, increases the potential energy of the pole. As the vaulter leaps, the pole flexes back to its original shape. As it does, it does work on the vaulter, increasing his or her kinetic energy.

Until the early 1960s, vaulting poles were manufactured from a variety of materials, including bamboo and various metals. Then poles began to be manufactured from fiberglass, and vaulting records reached new heights as shown in the diagram. Today, carbon-composite poles are custom-built to the vaulter's speed, weight, and grip.

1. Using the averages of the first three and last three pole-vault records shown on the graph, determine the percentage by which Olympic vaulting records have increased.
2. Explain what properties you think vaulting poles should have in addition to flexibility.
3. What other sports equipment do you think might be improved by being manufactured from new materials that increase flexibility?
4. Select one piece of sports equipment from your list in question 3. Use a library to research if and how the equipment is being improved by the use of new materials.

L1

Spanish Directed Reading

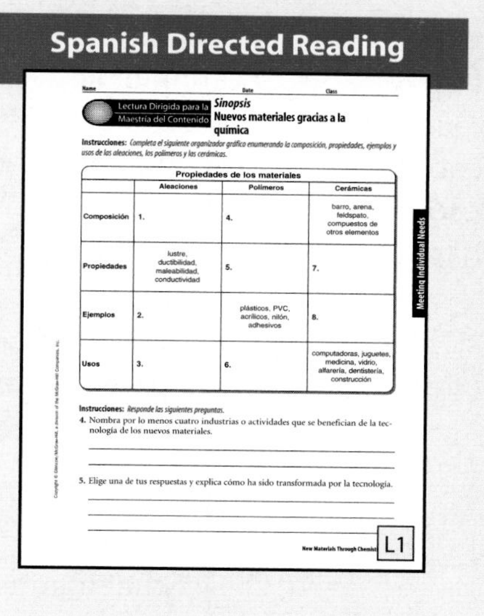
Lectura Dirigida para la Maestría del Contenido — Sinopsis — Nuevos materiales gracias a la química

Instrucciones: Completa el siguiente organizador gráfico enumerando la composición, propiedades, ejemplos y usos de las aleaciones, los polímeros y las cerámicas.

Propiedades de los materiales	Aleaciones	Polímeros	Cerámicas
Composición	1.	4.	barro, arena, feldespato, compuestos de otros elementos
Propiedades	lustre, ductibilidad, maleabilidad, conductividad	5.	7.
Ejemplos	2.	plásticos, PVC, acrílicos, nilón, adhesivos	8.
Usos	3.	6.	computadoras, juguetes, medicina, vidrio, alfarería, dentistería, construcción

Instrucciones: Responde las siguientes preguntas.
4. Nombra por lo menos cuatro industrias o actividades que se benefician de la tecnología de los nuevos materiales.
5. Elige una de tus respuestas y explica cómo ha sido transformada por la tecnología.

L1

Test Practice Workbook

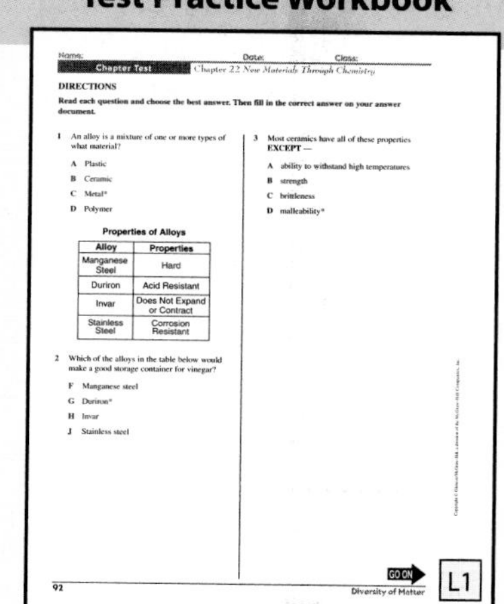
Chapter Test — Chapter 22 New Materials Through Chemistry

DIRECTIONS

Read each question and choose the best answer. Then fill in the correct answer on your answer document.

1 An alloy is a mixture of one or more types of what material?
A Plastic
B Ceramic
C Metal*
D Polymer

Properties of Alloys

Alloy	Properties
Manganese Steel	Hard
Duriron	Acid Resistant
Invar	Does Not Expand or Contract
Stainless Steel	Corrosion Resistant

2 Which of the alloys in the table below would make a good storage container for vinegar?
F Manganese steel
G Duriron*
H Invar
J Stainless steel

3 Most ceramics have all of these properties EXCEPT—
A ability to withstand high temperatures
B strength
C brittleness
D malleability*

GO ON

L1

Chapter Review

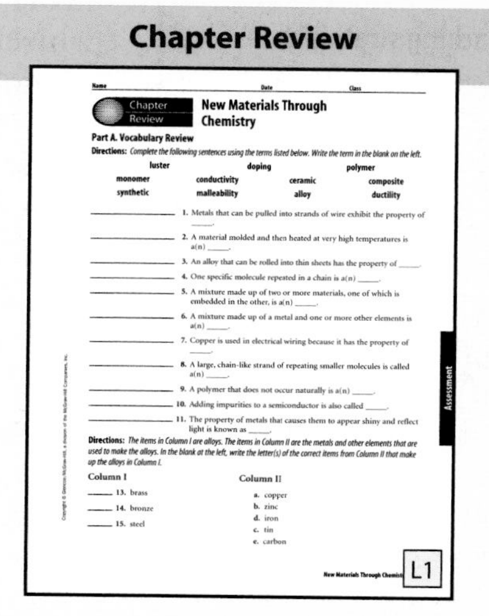
Chapter Review — New Materials Through Chemistry

Part A. Vocabulary Review

Directions: Complete the following sentences using the terms listed below. Write the term in the blank on the left.

luster, doping, polymer, monomer, conductivity, ceramic, composite, synthetic, malleability, alloy, ductility

1. Metals that can be pulled into strands of wire exhibit the property of ______.
2. A material molded and then heated at very high temperatures is a(n) ______.
3. An alloy that can be rolled into thin sheets has the property of ______.
4. One specific molecule repeated in a chain is a(n) ______.
5. A mixture made up of two or more materials, one of which is embedded in the other, is a(n) ______.
6. A mixture made up of a metal and one or more other elements is a(n) ______.
7. Copper is used in electrical wiring because it has the property of ______.
8. A large, chain-like strand of repeating smaller molecules is called a(n) ______.
9. A polymer that does not occur naturally is a(n) ______.
10. Adding impurities to a semiconductor is also called ______.
11. The property of metals that causes them to appear shiny and reflect light is known as ______.

Directions: The items in Column I are alloys. The items in Column II are the metals and other elements that are used to make the alloys. In the blank at the left, write the letter(s) of the correct items from Column II that make up the alloys in Column I.

Column I	Column II
____ 13. brass	a. copper
____ 14. bronze	b. zinc
____ 15. steel	d. iron
	c. tin
	e. carbon

L1

Science Content Background

SECTION 1 Materials with a Past

Alloys

Iron is separated from iron ore in a huge chimney-like oven called a blast furnace. The raw materials that go into the furnace are iron ore (iron oxide), carbon, and limestone (calcium carbonate). The iron from the blast furnace, called pig iron, has a fairly low melting point, so it is easily cast into molds - hence the name cast iron. Cast iron is brittle, and still has many impurities, so most cast iron is converted to steel. In another furnace, pressurized oxygen reacts with impurities still left in the iron. Properties of steel can be made to vary over a wide range by adjusting the amount of carbon in it. Low carbon steel is ductile and malleable, whereas high carbon steel is hard and strong.

Steel is commonly alloyed with other metals to give it special properties. For example, tungsten imparts high temperature strength, manganese imparts hardness, and additions of chromium and nickel produce stainless steel.

> **Student Misconception**
>
> Students may think that the goals of the engineering model of experimentation are the same as the goals of the scientific model of experimentation.
>
> **Refer to the facing page for teaching strategies to address this misconception.**

Pure science is often contrasted with applied science. Pure science seeks to extend what is known, regardless of whether it will produce something beneficial. Applied science seeks to create things to benefit people. The boundary between pure and applied sciences is very blurry. Some scientists do pure science, others do applied science, and some do both. Engineering, like medicine and computer science, is a field that investigates how to apply science. It focuses on developing, applying, or adapting a technology for a particular outcome. Therefore, the engineering model of investigation usually focuses on producing a specific outcome, and the scientific model frequently focuses on understanding cause and effect relationships.

SECTION 2 Versatile Materials

Ceramics

One type of new ceramics is called advanced ceramics. Advanced ceramics are ceramics that have high-tech engineering, electronic, and biomedical applications. These ceramics include oxide ceramics such as alumina (Al_2O_3) and nonoxide ceramics such as silicon carbide (SiC). These ceramics have melting points 500 to 1500 °C higher than steel, are almost twice as hard, and much less elastic.

SECTION 3 Polymers and Composites

Composites

Composites are hybrid materials that have been strengthened and toughened by mixing ceramic powder with fibers of a second ceramic material, such as carbon, boron, or silicon carbide. An example is the composite consisting of fine grains of alumina reinforced with single crystals, or whiskers, of silicon carbide. Silicon carbide-reinforced alumina possesses high strength and high shock resistance, even at high temperatures, and is used to make high-speed cutting tools for machining very hard steel.

For additional content background on this topic, go to the Glencoe Science Web site at science.glencoe.com.

Misconceptions

Find Out What Students Think

Students may think that . . .

- **The goals of the engineering model of experimentation are the same as the goals of the scientific model of experimentation.**

Technology pervades our lives. For some people the pursuit of science is justified solely by its delivery of technology, and thus the words science and technology are often used interchangeably. This may obscure the distinction between the goals of engineering and the goals of science.

Demonstration

Have students do a Two-Minute Essay. Give each students a sheet of paper and ask them to describe the differences between a pure scientist and an engineer.

Promote Understanding

Activity

Prior to class:

- Explore the Web site of your nearest research university, and find descriptions of the research being done by the science faculty and the engineering faculty. For example, if you live near Texas A&M University, you can go to the Chemistry Department's Internet link.
- Print the descriptions of three faculty engaged in pure science research and three engaged in applied science research.

In class:

- Describe to students the differences between the goals and methods of pure science and those of applied science.
- Distribute the descriptions you printed from the Internet.
- Ask students to classify the work of each faculty member as either pure or applied research.
- Discuss students' classifications and any reasons for different opinions.

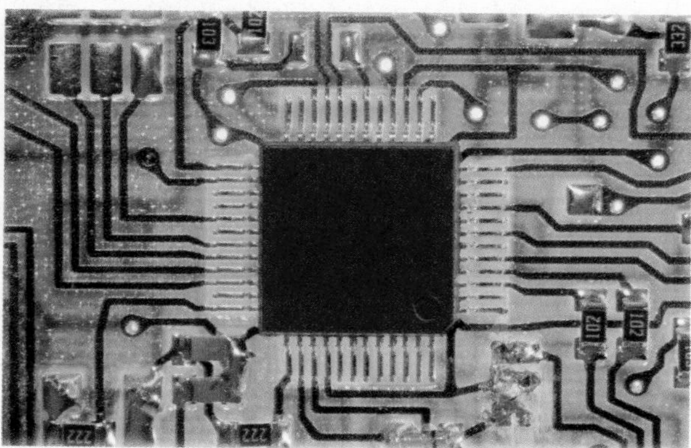

Jeffrey Sylvester/FPG International

Assess

After completing the chapter, see *Identifying Misconceptions* in the Study Guide.

CHAPTER 

New Materials Through Chemistry

Chapter Vocabulary

alloy
luster
ductility
malleability
conductivity
ceramics
semiconductors
integrated circuit
polymer
monomer
synthetic
composite

What do you think?

Science Journal This is a microscopic view of nylon fibers. Nylon is used often to make durable lightweight clothing.

CHAPTER 

New Materials Through Chemistry

This *X-33* test aircraft is testing a new heat protection system made from nickel and hydrogen holding tanks made from a carbon reinforced plasticlike material. If the tests are successful, a future aircraft will carry payloads to the *International Space Station.* In this chapter, you will learn about various types of materials—old, new, and improved.

What do you think?

Science Journal Look at the picture below with a classmate. Discuss what this might be. Here's a hint: *It is a strong and lightweight material.* Write your answer or best guess in your Science Journal.

Theme Connection

Stability and Change The arrangement of the basic particles in the alloys, ceramics, and polymer structures described in this chapter makes these materials stable. However, when the basic particles are altered or substituted, the properties of the materials can change.

When an engineer designs a vehicle, bridge, or building, the materials used for construction must be selected. Can the manufacturing process affect a material's performance?

Safety Precautions:

WARNING: *Use proper protection when handling hot objects or near an open flame. Tie back hair; roll up sleeves.*

Compare Properties

1. Using tongs, hold a 5-cm piece of steel wire in a lab burner flame until the wire glows red-hot for 30 seconds.
2. Quickly drop the hot wire into a beaker of cold water.
3. Repeat step 1 with another 5-cm piece of steel wire, but place this hot wire on a heat-proof surface to cool instead of in water.
4. After both pieces of wire are cool, compare the flexibility of each wire.

Observe

In your Science Journal, write what you observe about the flexibility of the two wires. Suggest reasons.

Before You Read

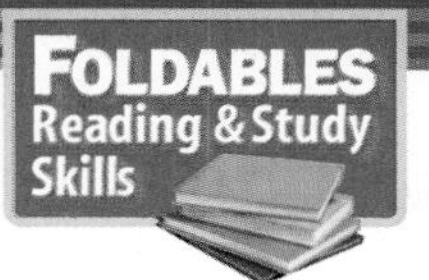

Making a Classify Study Fold **Make the following Foldable to help you organize objects into groups based on their common features.**

1. Place a sheet of paper in front of you so the long side is at the top. Fold the paper in half from the left side to the right side and then unfold.
2. Fold each side in to the centerfold line to divide the paper into fourths. Fold the paper in half from top to bottom and unfold.
3. Through the top thickness of paper, cut along both of the middle fold lines to form four tabs as shown. Label the tabs *Alloys*, *Ceramics*, *Polymers*, and *Composites*.
4. As you read the chapter, list three or more examples of common materials around you under the tab for each group.

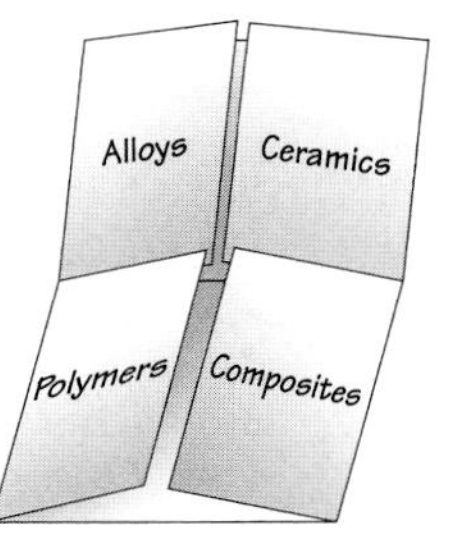

671

Explore Activity

Purpose To investigate how metals may respond to fast and slow temperature changes L2 ELL LS **Kinesthetic**

Preparation Prepare several beakers of ice water.

Materials lab burner, tongs, pieces of thin steel wire, ice water

Teaching Strategies

- Point out that both wire pieces are heated to the same temperature, so the only variable is the rate at which they cool.
- Remind students that heating metals to high temperature and then allowing them to cool occurs in engines and heating elements.

Observe

Before heating, both wires were somewhat flexible. After being heated to red-hot, then cooled, the wire that cooled slowly was still somewhat flexible. However, the wire that was cooled quickly became brittle and snapped easily when bent.

Assessment

Oral What happened to the atoms in the metal as it was heated? The atoms began to move faster and their relationship to each other changed and weakened. **Why might cooling quickly not restore the flexibility to the metal wire?** The heated atoms were not given time to return to their original stable positions. Use **PASC,** p. 89.

Before You Read

FOLDABLES Reading & Study Skills

Dinah Zike Study Fold

Purpose Before reading the chapter, ask students what they know about new materials made through chemistry. Then, during reading, have students provide a Foldable for recording and organizing notes on alloys, ceramics, polymers, and composites.

For additional help, see Foldables Worksheet, p. 17 in **Chapter Resources Booklet,** or go to the Glencoe Science Web site at **science.glencoe.com.** See After You Read in the Study Guide at the end of this chapter.

SECTION

Materials with a Past

1 Motivate

Bellringer Transparency

Display the Section Focus Transparency for Section 1. Use the accompanying Transparency Activity Master. L1 ELL

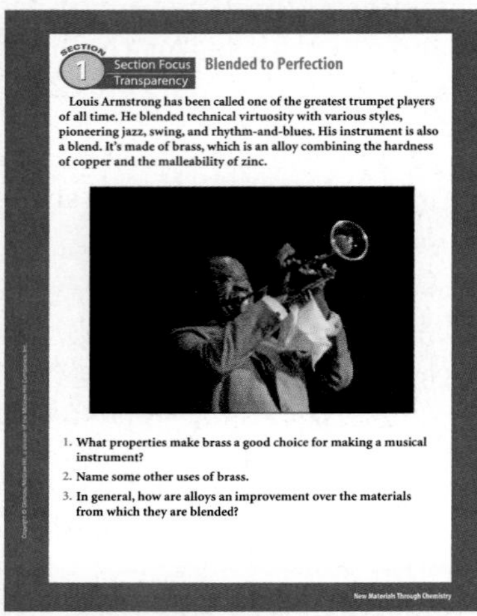

SECTION 1 Section Focus Transparency **Blended to Perfection**

Louis Armstrong has been called one of the greatest trumpet players of all time. He blended technical virtuosity with various styles, pioneering jazz, swing, and rhythm-and-blues. His instrument is also a blend. It's made of brass, which is an alloy combining the hardness of copper and the malleability of zinc.

1. What properties make brass a good choice for making a musical instrument?
2. Name some other uses of brass.
3. In general, how are alloys an improvement over the materials from which they are blended?

New Materials Through Chemistry

Tie to Prior Knowledge

Ask students to name things that are made of metal and the elements that make up these metals. Possible answers: steel supports in buildings and bridges (mostly iron), wire (copper, among others), pots, pans, and bicycle frames (aluminum, among others) Explain that brass and bronze are metal alloys—metal solutions whose properties depend on the ratio of the elements each contains.

SECTION

Materials with a Past

As You Read

What You'll Learn

- **Identify** how different alloys are used.
- **Explain** how the properties of alloys determine their use.

Vocabulary

alloy, luster, ductility, malleability, conductivity

Why It's Important

Alloys make modern cities, space travel, and many other things possible.

Alloys

For ages, people have searched for better materials to use to make their lives more comfortable and their tasks easier. Ancient cultures used stone tools until methods for processing metals became known. Today, advances in metal processing are still occurring as scientists continue to improve the art of blending metals, or making alloys, to make better metal products. An **alloy** is a mixture of a metal with one or more other elements where the mixture retains the properties of the metal. Alloys are produced to obtain a material with improved properties such as greater hardness, strength, lightness, or durability. This idea of creating better materials to make better tools is not new, as you will soon learn.

Alloys Through Time In about 3500 B.C., historians believe that ancient Sumerians in the Tigris-Euphrates Valley (now Iraq) accidentally discovered bronze. They believe that Sumerians used rocks rich in copper and tin ore to make fire rings to keep their campfires from spreading. The hot campfire melted the copper and tin ores within the rocks, creating bronze. This first known mixture of metals became so popular and widely used that a 2,000-year span of history is known as the Bronze Age.

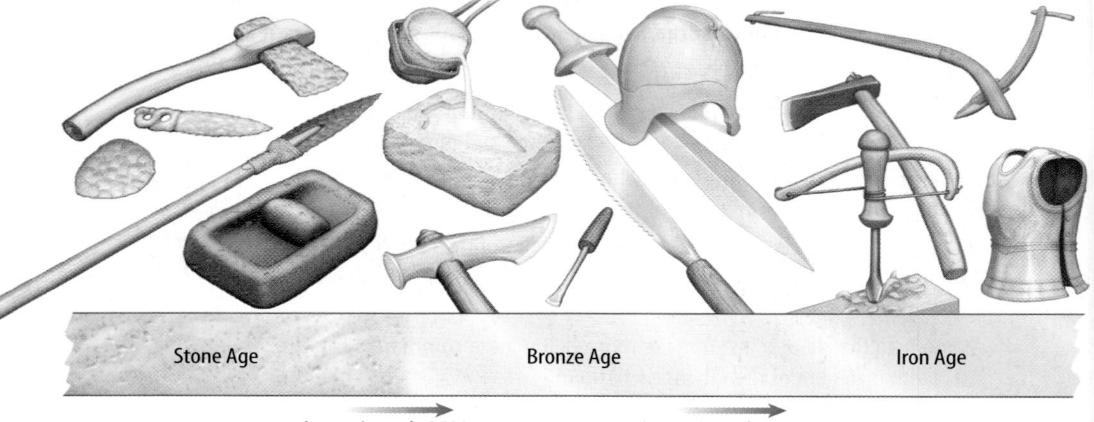

Figure 1
This historic time line shows the Stone Age, Bronze Age, and Iron Age. Some artifacts common from those times are shown above the time line.

Section Assessment Planner

PORTFOLIO
Curriculum Connection, p. 673

PERFORMANCE ASSESSMENT
MiniLAB, p. 673
Assessment, p. 677
See page 698 for more options.

CONTENT ASSESSMENT
Section, p. 677
Challenge, p. 677
Chapter, pp. 698–699

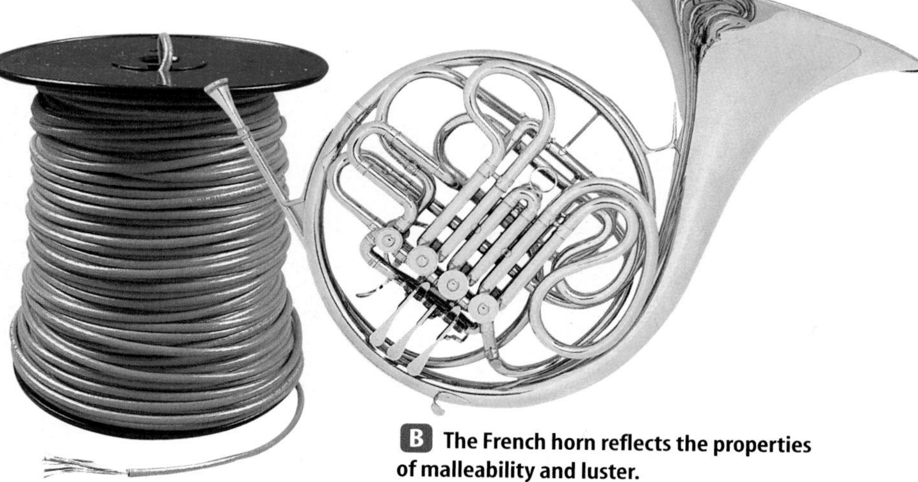

Figure 2

A This roll of copper wire reflects the metallic properties of luster, ductility, and conductivity.

B The French horn reflects the properties of malleability and luster.

Materials Change Typical objects from the Bronze Age and the following Iron Age are shown in **Figure 1.** Bronze and iron are still used today, but it is doubtful that these ancient people would recognize them. The methods of processing these alloys have undergone many changes. Other alloys also have been developed through the ages giving people a large selection of materials to choose from today.

Properties of Metals and Alloys Alloys retain the properties of metals, as shown in **Figure 2,** but what are the properties of metals? Metals have **luster,** which means they reflect light or have a shiny appearance. The shiny appearance of aluminum foil and copper wire demonstrates the property of luster. **Ductility** (duk TIH luh tee) means the metal can be pulled into wires. The copper electrical wire in your home demonstrates the ductility of metals and alloys. **Malleability** (ma lee uh BIH luh tee) is the property that allows metals and alloys to be hammered or rolled into thin sheets. Aluminum foil that is used in food preparation and food storage demonstrates the malleability of aluminum. The French horn above demonstrates the luster and malleability of brass. **Conductivity** (kahn duk TIH vuh tee) means that heat or electrical charges can move easily through the material. Metals and alloys have high conductivity because some of their electrons are not tightly held by their atoms. Metals and alloys usually are good conductors of heat and electricity because of these loosely bound electrons. Copper is used to carry electricity because it is conductive and ductile.

Reading Check *What are five other examples of items that you know of that have metallic properties?*

Mini LAB

Observing Properties of Alloys

Safety Precautions:

Procedure
1. Observe a small sheet of **aluminum foil.**
2. Using a **conductivity tester,** test the following items for their ability to conduct electric current: aluminum foil, **paper, pencil, ink pen,** and **paper clip.**

Analysis
1. What metallic properties of the foil do you observe?
2. Explain why each item was or was not able to conduct electric current.

2 Teach

Alloys

Mini LAB

Purpose Students observe properties of aluminum and compare the conductivity of several common materials. L2 LS **Kinesthetic**

Materials conductivity tester, paper, pencil, ink pen, and paper clip, aluminum foil

Teaching Strategy Inexpensive, continuity testers that are available in hardware stores can be substituted for the conductivity tester.

Safety Precautions Some conductivity testers have sharp points.

Analysis
1. ductility, malleability, and conductivity
2. conductors: aluminum foil and paper clip; nonconductors: paper, pencil; nonconductors are made from nonmetals. The ink pen may conduct current if it is constructed of a metallic material.

Assessment

Process Have students make a list of ten items in their homes—five conductors and five nonconductors. Ask them to hypothesize the materials used to make each item. Use **PASC,** p. 93.

Curriculum Connection

Language Arts Have students write science fiction stories involving a new alloy with unusual properties. Have students tell how the alloy is made and what its properties are. An example is the legend surrounding frontiersman Jim Bowie's knife. It was said to be made from the metal of a meteorite he found. The blade was said to be indestructible and never to need sharpening. L2 LS **Linguistic** P

Resource Manager

Chapter Resources Booklet
Transparency Activity, p. 44
MiniLAB, p. 3
Directed Reading for Content Mastery, p. 20

Reading Check

Answer Possible answers include coins, silver or gold jewelry, toasters, keys, and paper clips.

Earth Science INTEGRATION

Gold is not soluble in water and is very dense (19.3 g/cm^3), so it sinks in water. Prospectors panned for gold by scooping up dirt and soil samples thought to contain gold and washing water over them. Less dense materials floated away, leaving the bright yellow and very dense particles of gold in the bottom of the pan.

Activity

Have students locate copper, zinc, and tin on the periodic table and find the melting point of each. Cu 1,085°C, Zn 420°C, Sn 232°C L2 LS **Linguistic**

Visual Learning

Figure 3 Explain to students that one karat is one-twenty-fourth part of pure gold. Therefore pure gold is 24-karat. Have students express the amount of gold in each ring in twenty-fourths. 22 karat ring is $\frac{22}{24} = \frac{11}{12}$; 14 karat ring is $\frac{14}{24} = \frac{7}{12}$; 12 karat ring is $\frac{12}{24} = \frac{1}{2}$ L2 LS **Logical-Mathematical**

Make a Model

Have students bring to class plastic molds for making ice cubes. Then, have them mix water with a colored solution, such as fruit juice, and pour it into the molds. Next freeze the molds and later remove the solid material to display. Tell students that mixing the liquids represents the mixing of copper and zinc to make brass. Pouring the solution into molds represents the process by which various doorknobs, plumbing fixtures, bronze jewelry, and wrought iron fences are made. L2 ELL LS **Kinesthetic**

Figure 3
These gold rings appear to look alike, but they vary in the amount of copper that has been added to the gold. The composition of the alloy that was used to make the ring will determine its properties.

Earth Science INTEGRATION

During the California gold rush, prospectors obtained gold by panning. Panning is a process in which dirt and gravel are washed away with water, leaving gold in the bottom of the pan. In your Science Journal describe the properties of gold that were important in making this technique useful.

Choosing an Alloy What properties of an alloy are most important? The answer depends upon how the alloy will be used and which characteristics are the most desirable. Look at the characteristics of familiar objects made from alloys such as the gold jewelry shown in **Figure 3.** The rings appear to be made of pure gold, but they are made from alloys.

Gold is a bright, expensive metal that is soft and bends easily. Copper, on the other hand, is an inexpensive metal that is harder than gold. When gold and copper are melted, mixed, and allowed to cool, an alloy forms. The properties will vary depending upon the amount of each metal that is added. A ring made with a higher percentage of gold will bend easily due to gold's softness. This ring will be more valuable because it contains a higher percentage of gold. A ring with a higher percentage of copper will not bend as easily because copper is harder than gold. This ring will be less valuable because it contains more copper, a less-expensive metal.

Which properties are needed? Choosing the alloy to make a piece of jewelry and deciding which alloy to use to manufacture a drill bit do not appear to have much in common. However, the characteristics of the final product must be considered in both situations before the product is constructed.

How hard does the alloy have to be to prevent the object from breaking when it is used? Will the object be exposed to chemicals that will react with the alloy and cause the alloy to fail? These questions relate to the properties of the alloy and its intended use. This represents only two of the many possible questions that must be answered while a product is being designed.

Cultural Diversity

K. Aslihan Yener was born in Turkey. She became interested in archeology and applied chemical technology to archeology in the "analysis of lead isotopes found in the mines and metals located throughout the Near East." Yener knew that the ratio of lead isotopes to other metals in Bronze Age objects would be like fingerprints. This insight enabled Yener to match the objects to the mine from which the metal originated. By doing this, Yener not only found large industrial parks in the Taurus Mountains of Turkey; but she also located a subterranean city built into the mountainside. Have students explain how determining which mine a metal came from enabled Yener to find those Bronze Age industrial parks.

674 CHAPTER 22 New Materials Through Chemistry

Uses of Alloys Alloys are used in a variety of products, as shown in **Table 1.** If you see an object that looks metallic, it is most likely an alloy. Alloys that are exceptionally strong are used to manufacture industrial machinery, construction beams, and railroad cars and rails. Automobile and aircraft bodies that require strong materials are constructed of alloys that are corrosion resistant and lightweight but able to carry heavy loads. Other types of alloys are used in products such as food cans, carving knives, and roller skates. **Figure 4** shows some additional examples of alloys.

Table 1 Common Alloys

Name	Composition	Use
Bronze	copper, tin	jewelry, marine hardware
Brass	copper, zinc	hardware, musical instruments
Sterling Silver	silver, copper	tableware
Pewter	tin, copper, antimony	tableware
Solder	lead, tin	plumbing
Wrought Iron	iron, lead, copper, magnesium	porch railings, fences

If you have a tooth filling, your dentist might have used a silver and mercury alloy to fill it, preventing further tooth decay. Other alloys that are resistant to tissue rejection can be used inside the human body. Special pins and screws made from alloys are used by surgeons to connect broken bones, as shown in **Figure 5.** Alloys also are used as metal plates to repair damage to the skull. These plates protect the brain from injury, and are safe to use inside the body.

Reading Check *What are several uses for alloys?*

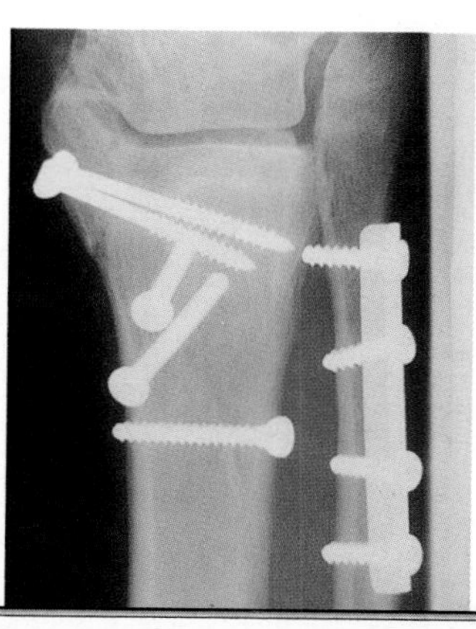

Figure 5
Surgical steel can be used to join bones. *What properties of this type of steel are most important?*

Figure 4
The fork and saw blade are both steel alloys, but they vary in chemical composition.

IDENTIFYING Misconceptions

Not every alloy is made to produce a stronger substance. An alloy called Wood's metal is actually a soft metal that melts around 70°C. It is made from bismuth, lead, tin, and cadmium. Its low melting point makes Wood's metal a good material to use in overhead sprinkler systems. A fire would heat the metal alloy to its melting point, when it would no longer hold back the water in a sprinkler system.

Quick Demo

Obtain small samples of copper, zinc, and brass. Place the samples in individual large test tubes that contain 0.5 M hydrochloric acid. Zinc will quickly react in the acid forming hydrogen gas, but copper will not. **CAUTION:** Exercise care with the acid, using only small amounts well below the top of the tube. Use pea-sized pieces of the metals and do not pressurize the hydrogen gas.

Reading Check

Answer Possible answers include bronze jewelry, brass door handles, sterling silver spoons, wrought iron fences, and steel automobile bodies.

Caption Answer

Figure 5 resistance to tissue rejection, strength, and the ability to resist corrosion

Inclusion Strategies

Learning Disabled Give students a photocopy of The Periodic Table. Use vertical, horizontal, and diagonal hash marks of different colors to shade in elements used to make alloys. For example, the metals used to make bronze could be colored in with vertical red lines. Point out how some elements are used over and over.
L1 LS **Visual-Spatial**

Resource Manager 

Chapter Resources Booklet
Note-taking Worksheets, pp. 33–35
Enrichment, p. 30
Transparency Activity, pp. 47–48

Alloys, continued

Teacher FYI

Steel is recycled easily. The magnetic properties of iron in steel products make it easy to separate from other wastes. Steel also can withstand the high temperatures used to clean old steel objects. Approximately 65 percent of steel made annually is made from recycled steel.

Use an Analogy

Remind students that steel is mostly iron, but with the addition of even small amounts of other elements the properties of the resulting alloy can be changed. This situation also occurs in flavoring soft drinks. A soft drink is mostly carbonated water. However, the flavor can be greatly changed by the addition of small amounts of other compounds.

Reading Check

Answer It is strong.

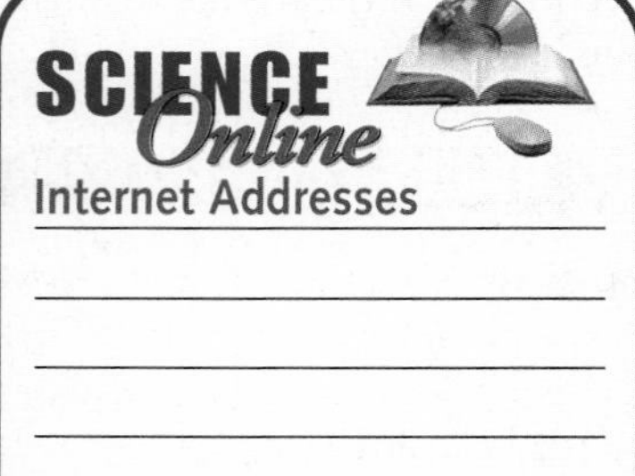

SCIENCE Online

Internet Addresses

Explore the Glencoe Science Web site at science.glencoe.com to find out more about topics in this section.

Steel—An Important Alloy There are various classes of steel. They are classified by the amount of carbon and other elements present, as well as by the manufacturing process that is used to refine the iron ore. The classes of steel have different properties and therefore different uses. Steel is a strong alloy and is used often if a great deal of strength is required. Office buildings have steel beams to support the weight of the structure. Bridges, overpasses, and streets also are reinforced with steel. Ship hulls, bedsprings, and automobile gears and axles are made from steel. Another class of steel, called stainless steel, is used in surgical instruments, cooking utensils, and large vessels where food products are prepared.

SCIENCE Online

Research Visit the Glencoe Science Web site at **science.glencoe.com** for recent news on research for new materials that can be used for space travel. Communicate what you learn to your class.

Reading Check *Why is steel an important alloy?*

New Aluminum Alloys Steel is not the only common type of alloy. Aluminum is familiar because it is used to make soda cans and cooking foil. Did you know that engineers also are using new aluminum and titanium alloys to build large commercial aircraft? The aircraft shown in **Figure 6** shows how extensively alloys are used in new aircraft construction. The new alloys are strong, lightweight and last longer than alloys used in the past. Also, a lighter plane is less expensive to fly.

Space Age Alloys Titanium alloy panels, developed for the space shuttle heat shield, will be used also on future reusable launch vehicles that are designed to carry payloads to the *International Space Station.* The *X-33* experimental aircraft, shown at the beginning of the chapter, is the test vehicle for this technology.

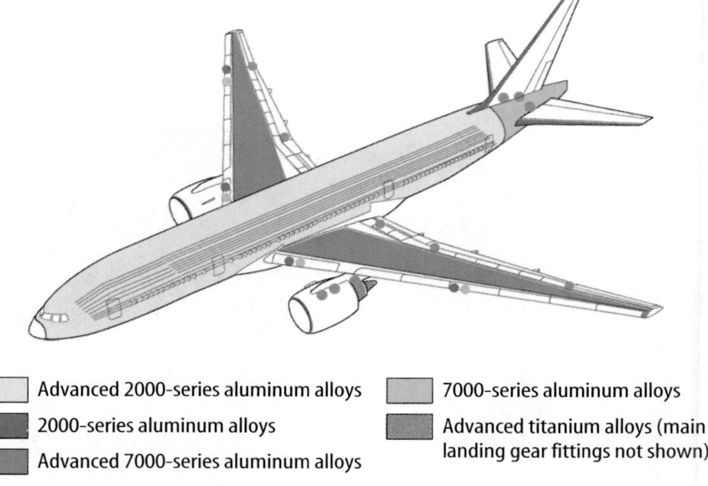

Figure 6
This commercial aircraft uses new alloys in its construction. Notice that the aircraft skin is mostly alloy construction.

Curriculum Connection

Math Students can calculate the small amount of carbon used in a sample of steel. High-carbon steel, used to make tools and springs, may contain only 0.7 percent carbon. Calculate the grams of carbon needed to make 1.0 kg of high-carbon steel. 0.007 × 1,000 grams = 7 grams

L2 LS **Logical-Mathematical**

Resource Manager

Chapter Resources Booklet

Reinforcement, p. 27

Lab Activity, pp. 9–11

Physical Science Critical Thinking/Problem Solving, p. 23

New Titanium Alloy Heat Shield The original heat shield on the space shuttle, shown in **Figure 7A,** uses ceramic tiles that are prone to cracking as a result of the high temperature and stress they experience during reentry into Earth's atmosphere. Each broken ceramic tile must be removed carefully and a new one glued into place.

The new titanium alloy panels, **7B,** are much larger and easier to attach to the heat shield than the ceramic tiles are. A lower maintenance cost for the heat shield is expected by using the new alloy. Scientists and engineers also predict that the new alloy will protect the space shuttle as well as the old ceramic tiles did.

Figure 7
New alloys are being tested for use on the space shuttle.
A The ceramic heat shield is constructed of small tiles, which are glued in place. They are more difficult to replace if damage occurs. B The shell of this test aircraft is made up of almost entirely of titanium alloy panels.

Reading Check *Why is the new heat shield desirable?*

Section 1 Assessment

1. Give two medical uses of alloys.
2. What are the properties of metals and alloys?
3. How are steels classified?
4. Why must the property of a material be considered before it is used to make a product?
5. **Think Critically** If you were designing a skyscraper in an earthquake zone, what properties would the structural materials need?

Skill Builder Activities

6. **Comparing and Contrasting** Compare and contrast ceramic tiles and titanium alloys used on the space shuttle heat shield. **For more help, refer to the** Science Skill Handbook.
7. **Solving One-Step Equations** Use the information from **Figure 3** to calculate the actual amount of gold in a 65-g, 14-karat gold necklace. How many grams of copper are in the necklace? **For more help, refer to the** Math Skill Handbook.

Answers to Section Assessment

1. Possible answers include tooth fillings and protective metal plates in the skull.
2. They are malleable and ductile and conduct electricity and heat. They also have luster.
3. by the amount of carbon and other elements present
4. to make sure the product will be able to do what it is needed to do
5. strength to support the weight of the structure and the flexibility to withstand the forces generated by seismic shaking
6. Ceramic tiles resist heat as do the newer titanium alloys. However, ceramic tiles tend to crack more easily. Titanium panels are easier to attach than the smaller ceramic tiles.
7. $65\ g \times 0.58 = 38\ g$ of gold
   $65\ g \times 0.42 = 27\ g$ of copper

Reading Check

Answer It is easier to attach and costs less to maintain.

3 Assess

Reteach

Bring a pewter object to class. Explain to students that pewter is an alloy. Ask whether that means pewter is a type of solution. yes Ask students to locate the positions of tin, antimony, and copper on the periodic table. These are the ingredients in pewter. L2 IS **Visual-Spatial**

Challenge

The properties of many types of brass depend on the ratio of copper to zinc and the presence of other metals. Have students identify some of the most common brasses, the metals they contain, and what they are used for. Common brasses include cartridge brass (70 percent copper, 30 percent zinc), used for plumbing fixtures, naval brass (contains less than 2 percent tin), used in naval construction, and Dutch metal (80–85 percent copper, 15–20 percent zinc), used as a substitute for gold leaf. L3 IS **Linguistic**

Assessment

Oral The strongest known permanent magnet is an alloy. Ask students what they know about the magnet when they know it is an alloy. It is made from more than one type of metallic element. The alloy metals are neodymium, iron, and boron. Have students locate the metals on the periodic table by their atomic numbers. Nd is 60; Fe is 26, B is 5. Use **PASC,** p. 121.

SECTION

Versatile Materials

1 Motivate

Bellringer Transparency

Display the Section Focus Transparency for Section 2. Use the accompanying Transparency Activity Master. L2 ELL

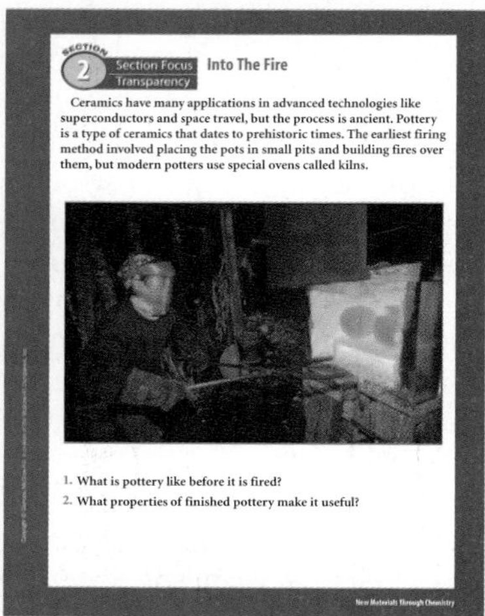

Section 2 Section Focus Transparency **Into The Fire**

Ceramics have many applications in advanced technologies like superconductors and space travel, but the process is ancient. Pottery is a type of ceramics that dates to prehistoric times. The earliest firing method involved placing the pots in small pits and building fires over them, but modern potters use special ovens called kilns.

1. What is pottery like before it is fired?
2. What properties of finished pottery make it useful?

New Materials Through Chemistry

Tie to Prior Knowledge

Most students have seen painted ceramic figurines. Bring some examples to class. Students are also familiar with glass. Explain that glass is a type of ceramic that doesn't have a consistent crystal structure.

SECTION

Versatile Materials

As You Read

***What* You'll Learn**

- **Examine** the versatile properties of ceramics.
- **Identify** how ceramic materials are used.
- **Explain** what a semiconductor is.

Vocabulary

ceramics
doping
integrated circuit
semiconductor

***Why* It's Important**

Ceramics and semiconductors are classes of materials with versatile properties that are used in many modern devices.

Ceramics

Do you think of floor tiles or pottery when you see the word *ceramic?* **Ceramics** are materials made from dried clay or clay-like mixtures. Ceramics have been around for centuries—in fact, pieces of clay pottery from 10,000 B.C. have been found. The first walled town, Jericho, was built about 8,000 B.C. The wall surrounding Jericho, as well as the homes inside the walls were constructed of bricks made from mud and straw that were baked in the Sun. Around 1,500 B.C., the first glass vessels were made and kilns were used to fire and glaze pottery. By 50 B.C. the Romans developed concrete and used it as a building material. Some of the structures built by the Romans still stand today. About the same time that Romans were developing concrete, the Syrians were developing glass-blowing techniques to make glass vessels. Pottery, bricks, glass, and concrete are examples of ceramics.

How are ceramics made? Traditional ceramics are made from easily obtainable raw materials—clay, silica (sand), and feldspar (crystalline rocks). These raw materials were used by ancient civilizations to make ceramic materials and still are used today. However, some of the more recent ceramics are made from compounds of metallic elements and carbon, nitrogen, or sulfur.

Reading Check *What raw materials are used to make traditional ceramic objects?*

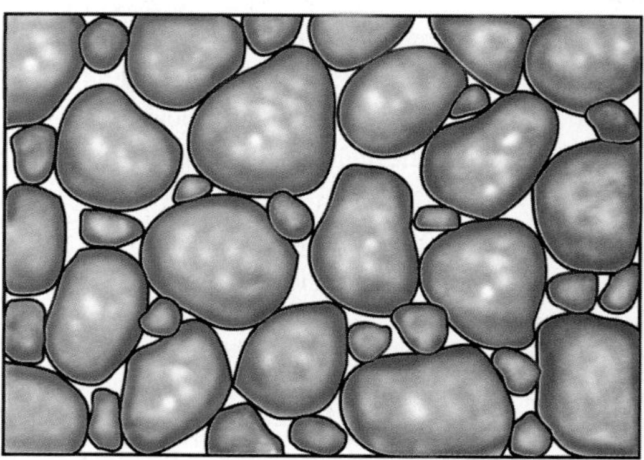

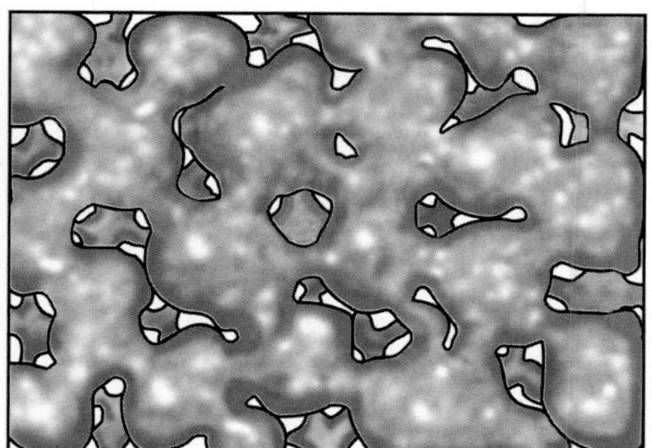

Figure 8
Ceramics are molded and then heated to high temperatures to force the particles to merge. The object shrinks and the structure becomes more dense.

Section Assessment Planner

Portfolio
Science Journal, p. 682

Performance Assessment
Try At Home MiniLAB, p. 679
Problem-Solving Activity, p. 680
Assessment, p. 678
See page 698 for more options.

Content Assessment
Section, p. 684
Challenge, p. 684
Chapter, pp. 698–699

Resource Manager

Chapter Resources Booklet
Transparency Activity, p. 45
Directed Reading for Content Mastery, p. 21
MiniLAB, p. 4

678 CHAPTER 22 New Materials Through Chemistry

Figure 9
Ceramic materials are used for a wide range of products. Glass, pottery, bricks, and tile are all made from ceramics.

Firing Ceramics After the raw materials are processed, ceramics are usually made by molding the ceramic into the desired shape, then heating it to temperatures between 1,000°C and 1,700°C. The heating process, called firing, causes the spaces between the particles to shrink, as shown in **Figure 8.** The entire object shrinks as the spaces become smaller. This extremely dense internal structure gives ceramics their strength. This is demonstrated by the use of ceramics on the space shuttle heat shield. They are able to withstand the high temperatures and stress of reentry into Earth's atmosphere. However, these same ceramics also are fragile and will break if they are dropped or if the temperature changes too quickly.

Traditional Ceramics Ceramics are known also for their chemical resistance to oxygen, water, acids, bases, salts, and strong solvents. These qualities make ceramics useful for applications where they may encounter these substances. For instance, ceramics are used for tableware because your foods contain acids, water, and salts. Ceramic tableware is not damaged by contact with foods containing these substances.

Traditional ceramics are used also as insulators because they do not conduct heat or electricity. You may have seen electric wires attached to poles or posts with ceramic insulators. These insulators keep the current flowing through the wire instead of into the ground.

The properties of ceramics can be customized which makes them useful for a wide variety of applications as shown in **Figure 9.** Changing the composition of the raw materials or the manufacturing process changes the properties of the ceramic. Manufacturing ceramics is similar to manufacturing alloys because scientists which properties are required and then attempt to create a ceramic material with the desired properties.

TRY AT HOME Mini LAB

Modeling a Composite Material

Safety Precautions

WARNING: *Wear goggles and an apron while doing lab. Wash your hands before leaving the lab.*

Procedure

1. Mix four tablespoons of **sand,** four tablespoons of **aquarium gravel or small pebbles,** and six tablespoons of **white glue** in a paper cup.
2. Add enough water to thoroughly mix the ingredients.
3. Stir the mixture until it is smooth.
4. Allow the mixture to sit for several days and observe.
5. Dispose of the cup as instructed by your teacher.

Analysis

1. Describe what happened to your mixture after several days? Is it a ceramic?
2. How is your mixture similar to concrete?
3. What are some of the properties of your product?

2 Teach

Ceramics

Reading Check

clay, silica, and feldspar

Purpose Students make concrete. L2 LS **Kinesthetic**

Materials sand, aquarium gravel, white glue, water, paper cup, and large spoon

Analysis

1. The mixture hardened into a stone-like material and is a ceramic.
2. Both mix sand, gravel, and a sticking agent with water to form a rock-hard material.
3. Answers will vary, but should describe the appearance and apparent strength of the material.

Assessment

Oral Ask students how life might be different had concrete and other stone building materials never been developed. Answers will vary but could include that stone building materials were necessry to construct the large, permanent cities where culture developed. Use **PASC,** p. 89.

Curriculum Connection

Art If possible, invite the school art teacher to demonstrate for the class the properties of clay before and after kiln firing to show how the clay becomes brittle. L1 LS **Visual-Spatial**

Fun Fact

The color of an unglazed ceramic is very likely to be white or brown if it was made from the pure clay called kaolinite, $Al_2Si_2O_5(OH)_4$. Red brick ceramic gets its color from additional iron oxide present in the clay.

Ceramics, continued

Teacher FYI

Firing ceramics must be done very carefully. The rate of heating and of cooling can influence the small structural relationships among the fine particles. Microwave heating can be better controlled than flame heating and is used for making some specialty ceramics. If ceramics are not heated gradually, the sudden application of heat causes the internal water to vaporize with enough pressure to shatter the ceramic object.

Problem-Solving Activity

Answers

1. Ceramic A; it does not wear out easily, and would not likely react with fuel chemicals. In addition, it could withstand the high temperatures often found in engines. The overall mass of the engine needs to be kept low, so the density of the ceramic could be a factor.
2. Ignoring cost, ceramic D or C would possibly provide the qualities of electrical conductivity needed in some computer parts. Neither appears to have corrosion problems.
3. cost and availability of the materials and how well the material could withstand impacts that occur in collisions

Figure 10
This ceramic hip socket is used to replace damaged ones in the human body.

Modern Ceramics Ceramics can be customized to have nontraditional properties, too. For instance, ceramics traditionally are used as insulators, but there are exceptions. For instance, chromium dioxide conducts electricity as well as most metals and some copper-based ceramics have superconductive properties. One application of nontraditional ceramics uses a transparent, electrically conductive ceramic in aircraft windshields to keep them free of ice and snow.

Ceramics have medical uses too. **Figure 10** shows a ceramic replacement hip socket for use in the human body. Ceramics can be used in the body because they are strong and resistant to body fluids, which can damage other materials. In the medical field, surgeons use ceramics for the repair and replacement of joints such as hips, knees, shoulders, elbows, fingers, and wrists. Dentists use ceramics for tooth replacements, repair, and braces.

Problem-Solving Activity

Can you choose the right material?

Scientists are learning about atoms and how they bond at a rapid pace. With this new knowledge, technology also is advancing quickly. Chemists today are able to create substances with a wide range of properties. This is especially evident in the production of specialized ceramics.

Ceramic Properties

Material	Wear Resistant	Conducts Electricity	Reacts with Chemicals	Melting Point
ceramic A	highly resistant	no	no	3,000°C
ceramic B	wears easily	no	yes	100°C
ceramic C	moderately resistant	yes	no	1,500°C
ceramic D	resistant	yes	no	500°C

Identifying the Problem

As an engineer working on the design of a new car, you need to select the right ceramic materials to build parts of the car's engine and its onboard computer. The table above shows the materials you have to choose from. Using the properties given in the table, decide which materials should be used for the engine parts and the onboard computer. Be prepared to explain your answer.

Solving the Problem

1. Which of the above materials would you use when you build the engine? Explain the factors that you considered to make your decision.
2. Which of the above materials would you select when building the onboard computer? Explain your selection.
3. If you had to choose a material for building the car's bumper, what factors would you consider? Do you think that a ceramic material would be the best choice? Explain your answer.

LAB DEMONSTRATION

Purpose To show that ceramics are strong and brittle

Materials small ceramic tiles (from a home improvement store), hammer, heavy cloth, container for the wrapped tile

Preparation Obtain tile that can demonstrate breakage without undue force from the hammer.

Procedure Demonstrate strength: stand on a tile. Demonstrate brittleness: wrap a tile in heavy cloth, place it in a container, and strike the wrapped tile with a hammer. Unwrap the tile and observe.

Expected Outcome The tile can support heavy objects without cracking, but the blow shatters the tile.

Assessment

If ceramics are so brittle why are they used in some places instead of metal? Ceramics can withstand extremely high temperatures at which most metals would melt. Also, they may be cheaper or less massive than metal.

Semiconductors

Another class of versatile materials is semiconductors. **Semiconductors** are the materials that make computers and other electronic devices possible.

The Periodic Table What are semiconductors? To answer this question, think about the periodic table. The elements on the left side and in the center of the table are metals. Metals are good conductors of electricity. Nonmetals, on the right side of the table, are poor conductors of electricity and are electrical insulators. The small number of elements found along the staircase-shaped border shown in **Figure 11** between the metals and nonmetals are metalloids. Some metalloids, such as silicon and germanium, are semiconductors. Semiconductors are poorer conductors of electricity than metals but better conductors than nonmetals, and their electrical conductivity can be controlled. It is this property that makes semiconductor devices useful and versatile.

Controlling Conductivity Adding impurities to some metalloids will alter their conductive properties. For example, silicon is used to make semiconductor devices. Its electrical conductivity can be increased by introducing impurities, such as atoms of arsenic or gallium, into its crystal structure, as shown in **Figure 12.** Adding even a single atom of one of these elements to a million silicon atoms significantly changes the conductivity. By controlling the type and amount of elements that are added, the conductivity of silicon can be made to vary over a wide range.

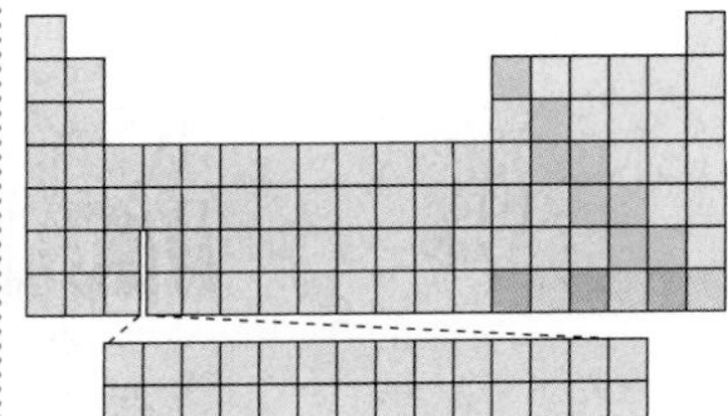

Figure 11
This outline of the periodic table clearly shows the metalloids, which appear in green.

Figure 12
Pure silicon is a poor conductor of electricity. Adding an impurity to the crystal changes the conductivity.

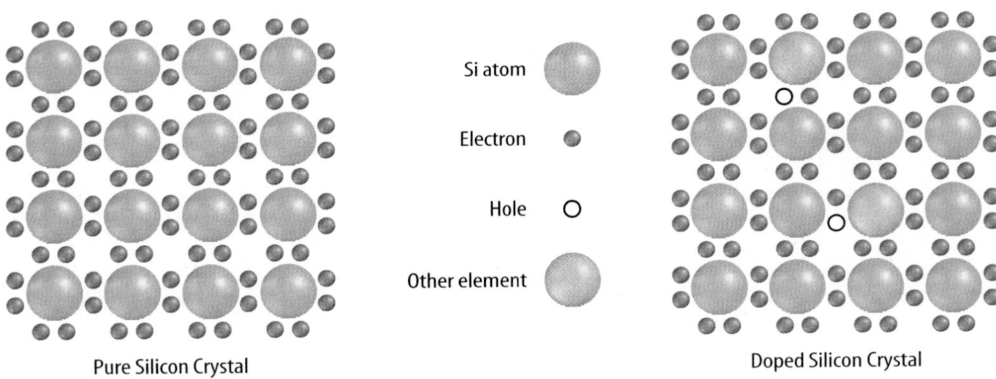

Semiconductors

Visual Learning

Figure 12 Ask a volunteer to point out the holes in the doped semiconductor, and to describe the movement of electrons and holes in it. L2 LS **Visual-Spatial**

Extension

The first semiconductor materials used were the elements germanium, silicon, and a form of tin known as gray tin. Now some compounds are also used as semiconductors. Have students find out what some of these compounds are. Gallium arsenide, indium antimonide, and aluminum phosphide are three compounds used as semiconductors. L3 LS **Linguistic**

Discussion

Why would silicon be a popular and inexpensive material for making semiconductors? It is found in most rocks and is one of the most plentiful elements on Earth. In addition, its conductive properties can be changed by adding impurities to the crystalline structure. L2 LS **Logical-Mathematical**

Resource Manager

Reading and Writing Skill Activities, p. 9

Cultural Diversity, p. 49

Inclusion Strategies

Visually Impaired As they examine computer chips, ask sighted students to describe to visually impaired students what is on the chips and how small they are. Suggest that they describe size by using analogies to items whose size can be determined by touch.

Semiconductors, continued

Use Science Words

Word Meaning Tell students that the word *integrate* means "to blend into a functioning or unified whole." Ask students to explain how this applies to integrated circuits. In an integrated circuit, all the components are blended into a functioning whole on a single chip of semiconductor material. L2 LS **Linguistic**

Activity

Have some microchips with integrated circuits on them available for students to observe and examine through a microscope. They should realize how tiny the components can be and still be effective. L2 LS **Visual-Spatial**

Extension

Transistors form the backbone of the logic circuits used in computers. Have students find out about logic circuits and how they work. Logic circuits process binary information, such as electric signals that can be in one of two states, either on or off. Logic circuits include AND gates, OR gates, and NOT gates. L3 LS **Logical-Mathematical**

Fun Fact

A transistor is a semiconductor that amplifies or strenghtens an electric signal or acts as a tiny electric on-off switch. Transistors, which have been used in electronic circuits as amplifiers, rectifiers, detectors, or switches, paved the way for the development of the integrated circuit used in today's myriad of electronic devices.

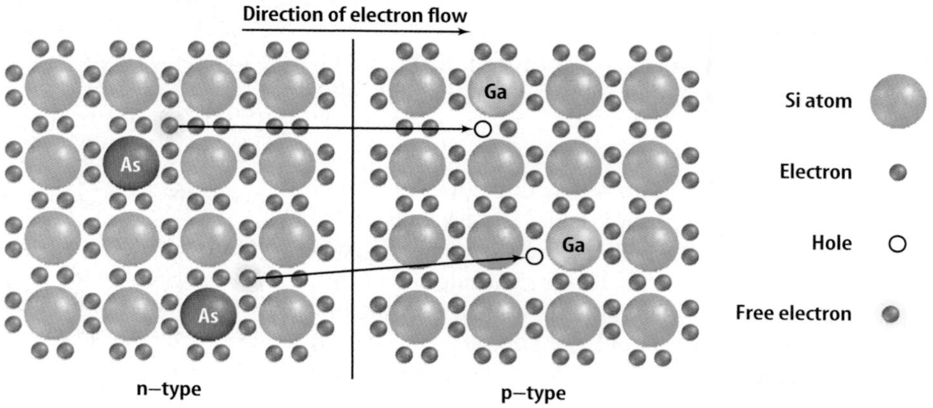

Direction of electron flow

As, As, Ga, Ga

n–type, p–type

Si atom, Electron, Hole, Free electron

Figure 13
The electrons flow from the arsenic doped silicon to the germanium doped silicon, filling the available holes. The electron flow is controlled by the sequence of n-type or p-type semiconductors.

Doping The process of adding impurities or other elements to a semiconductor to increase the conductivity is called **doping.** Depending on the element added, the overall number of electrons in the semiconductor is increased or decreased. If the impurity causes the overall number of electrons to increase, the semiconductor is called an *n-type* semiconductor. If doping reduces the overall number of electrons, the semiconductor is called a *p-type* semiconductor.

Integrated Circuits By placing n-type and p-type semiconductors together, semiconductor devices such as transistors and diodes can be made. These devices are used to control the flow of electrons in electrical circuits, as shown in **Figure 13.** During the 1960s, methods were developed for making these components extremely small. At the same time the integrated circuit was developed.

An **integrated circuit** contains many semiconducting devices. Integrated circuits as small as 1 cm on a side can contain millions of semiconducting devices. Because of their small size, integrated circuits are sometimes called microchips. **Figure 14** shows how small an integrated chip can be.

Being able to pack so many circuit components onto a tiny integrated circuit was a technological breakthrough. This makes it possible for today's televisions, radios, calculators, and other devices to be smaller in size, cheaper to manufacture and capable of more advanced functions than older ones. Also because the circuit components are so close together, it takes less time for electric current to travel through the circuit. This enables electronic signals to be processed more rapidly by computers, cell phones, and other electronic appliances. **Figure 15** demonstrates how integrated circuits have given us faster, smaller, and more capable computers since the 1940s.

Figure 14
A single integrated circuit is tiny. This allows computers and other electronic devices to be compact.

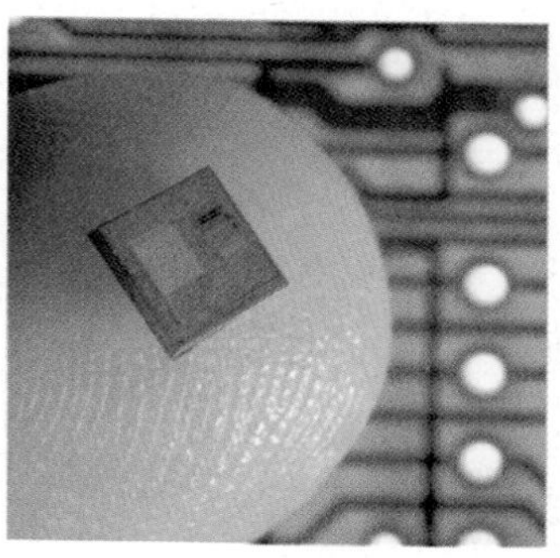

Science Journal

Integrated Circuits Have students make note of all the devices they use in a week that contain integrated circuits. Ask students to write their lists in their Science Journals. Devices include computers, printers, televisions, calculators, VCRs, automobiles, digital watches, radios, CD players, microwave ovens, and cellular phones. L2 LS **Visual-Spatial** P

Resource Manager

Chapter Resources Booklet
Reinforcement, p. 28
Enrichment, p. 31
Science Inquiry Labs, p. 45

682 CHAPTER 22 New Materials Through Chemistry

NATIONAL GEOGRAPHIC **VISUALIZING THE HISTORY OF COMPUTERS**

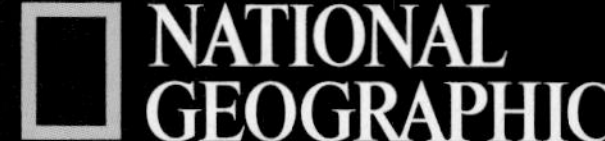

Figure 15

The earliest, room-size computers relied on vacuum tubes to store data. Today's computers use microchips, tiny flakes of silicon engraved with millions of circuit components. A selection of computers is shown here, beginning with the Electronic Numerical Integrator and Computer (ENIAC), developed by the Army in 1946.

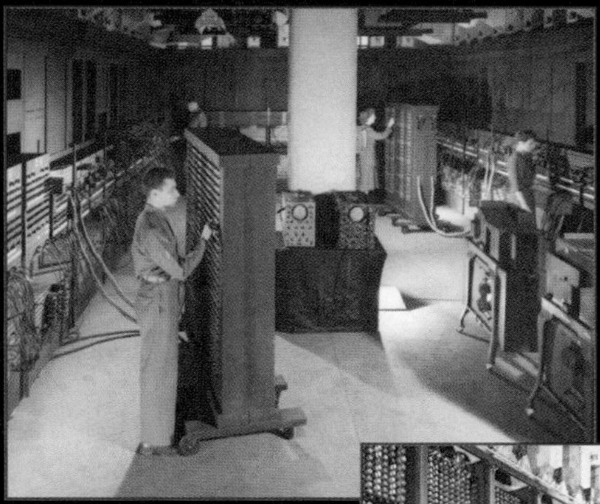

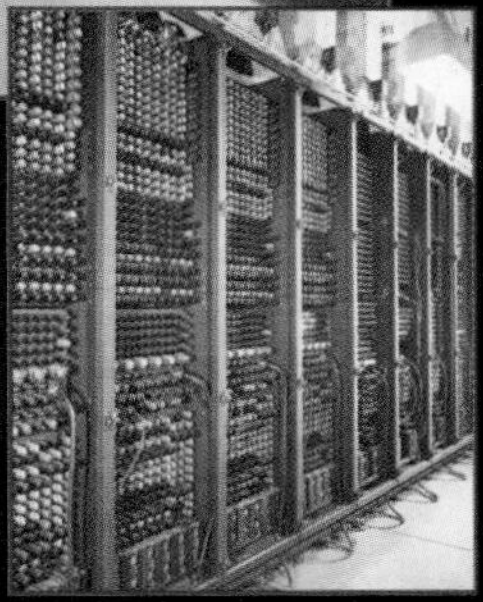

Ⓐ A technician programs the ENIAC, the first electronic computer. Some of the 19,000 vacuum tubes that ran the ENIAC are shown at right.

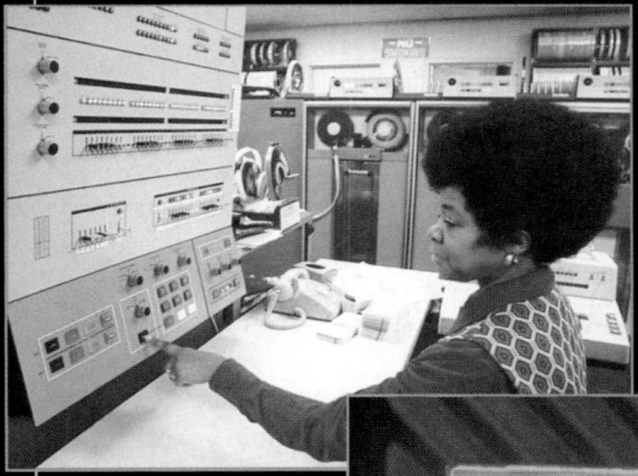

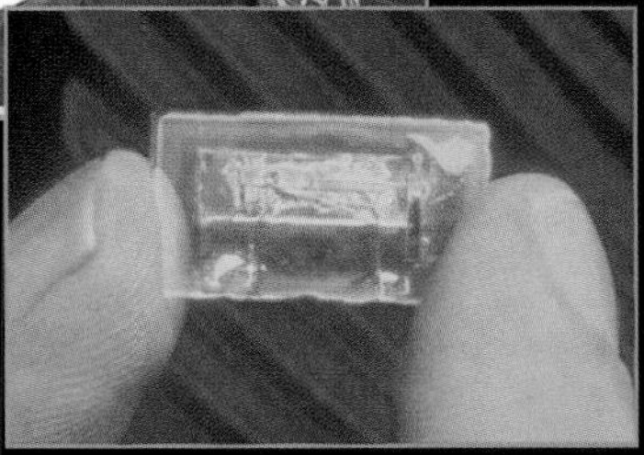

Ⓑ A young woman operates a 1960s-era computer. The inset photo shows an integrated circuit from such a computer.

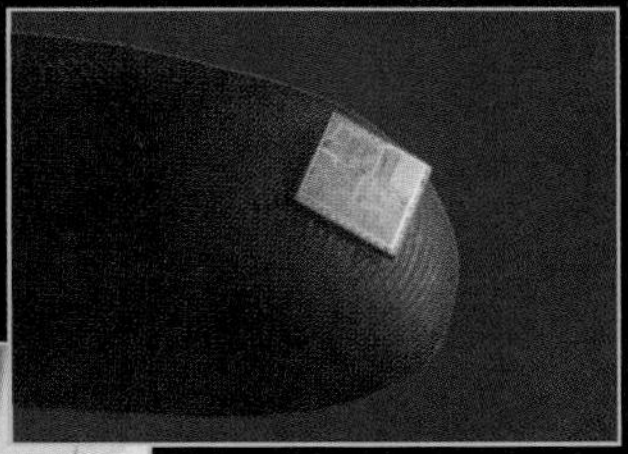

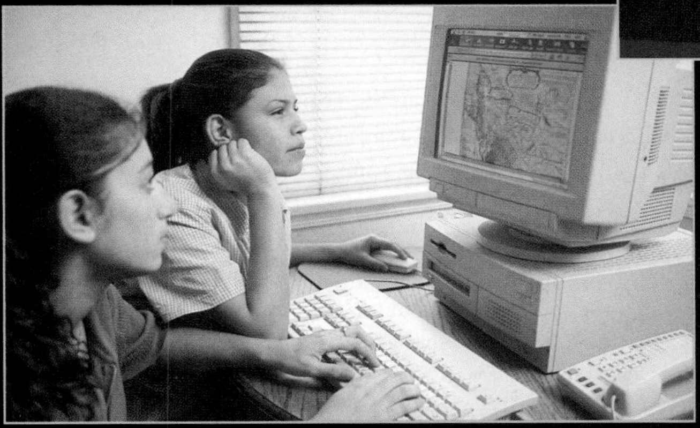

Ⓒ Teenagers surf the Internet on a modern personal computer. The microchips that store computer programs are now smaller than a fingernail.

683

NATIONAL GEOGRAPHIC

Visualizing the History of Computers

Have students examine the pictures and read the captions. Then ask the following questions.

- **How have the changes in the size of computers affected their use?** Possible answer: Old computers were too large to be used in schools, homes, and many offices.
- **How might your lives be different if personal computers had not been developed?** Possible answer: You wouldn't be able to do research on the Internet; e-mail friends and family; do homework on the computer; play computer games.

Activity

Divide the class into four groups. Assign each group one of the following topics: business and industry; government and law enforcement; engineering and science; medicine and health. Have students in each group research how computers are being used in the area they were assigned. Each group should present an oral report to the class. L2 COOP LEARN **Linguistic**

Extension

Have students research the manufacturing of microchips. Ask students to make posters that show how microchips are made and explain the processes involved. L3 **Visual-Spatial**

Active Reading

Learning Journal The Learning Journal encourages students to interact with the reading, allowing personal responses. Students should draw a vertical line down each page of their Learning Journal. The left column entries can be research notes, lecture notes, or vocabulary terms. The right column entries can be the student's response to, interpretation of, question about, or analysis of the left column entries. Have students write a Learning Journal related to the Versatile Materials described in this section.

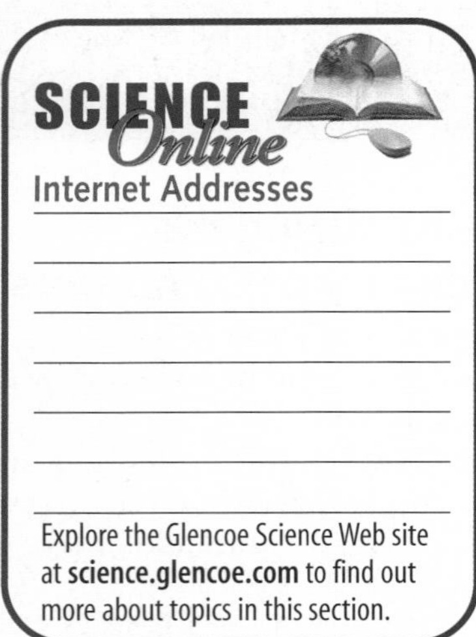

3 Assess

Reteach

Bring a spark plug from a car engine to class. Ask students to identify the metal component of the plug. The tip is metallic. Show them the white ceramic part and ask students for its properties. nonconductor, withstands high heat surrounding the plug L2 ELL

LS **Visual-Spatial**

Challenge

Have students find out about ceramics that are being studied for their superconductivity properties. The ceramics contain ytterium, barium, copper, mercury, and oxygen. Their electrical resistance is extremely low, so little heat is lost during conduction. L3 LS **Linguistic**

Oral Describe how semiconductors control the flow of electrons in integrated circuits. Electrons only flow from n-type to p-type semiconductors. Use **PASC,** p. 89.

Figure 16
Desktop computers use semiconductors to perform their tasks.

SCIENCE Online

Research Visit the Glencoe Science Web site at **science.glencoe.com** to learn more about semiconductors and computers. Communicate what you learn to your class.

Semiconductors and Computers Semiconductors make our computers possible. A desktop computer is an example of a device that uses semiconductors. A computer has three main jobs. First, it must be able to receive and store the information that is needed to solve a problem. Next, it must be able to follow instructions to perform tasks in a logical way. Finally, a computer must communicate information to the outside world. All three jobs can be done with a combination of hardware and software components.

Computer hardware refers to the major permanent components of a computer, such as the keyboard, monitor, and central processing unit, CPU. These components are shown in **Figure 16.** Software refers to the instructions that tell the computer what to do. When a computer system is functioning properly, the hardware and software work together to perform tasks.

Section 2 Assessment

1. Describe how ceramic materials are made.
2. List five uses of ceramic materials.
3. Describe electrical conductivity of ceramics.
4. Explain what semiconductors are and where they are used.
5. **Think Critically** Computers and software have changed the way in which businesses operate. If you operated a distribution center for a manufacturer, how would you use computers to assist you?

Skill Builder Activities

6. **Drawing Conclusions** What properties of ceramics are useful in coffee mugs? **For more help, refer to the** Science Skill Handbook.
7. **Communicating** In your Science Journal, explain how computers aid scientists and engineers in their profession. Include information about problem solving and communicating in your explanation. **For more help, refer to the Science Skill Handbook.**

Answers to Section Assessment

1. They are molded into form and heated to force the particles to merge.
2. Answers may include engine parts, insulators, floor tile, containers, and replacement joints and teeth.
3. Some ceramics do not conduct, those that contain chromium dioxide conduct well, and those containing copper are superconductors.
4. metalloids such as silicon and germanium that are poorer conductors of electricity than metals but better conductors than nonmetals; they are used in computer chips, integrated circuits, and computers.
5. to track inventories, check customer credit, transfer funds electronically.
6. They don't conduct heat well; they are strong and dense and hold liquids without leaking; they are resistant to the chemical action of strong coffee.
7. Accept all reasonable answers.

684 CHAPTER 22 New Materials Through Chemistry

SECTION 3

Polymers and Composites

Polymers

Polymers are similar to alloys and ceramics because they represent another class of materials. **Polymers** are a class of natural or manufactured substances that are composed of molecules arranged in large chains with small, simple, repeating units called monomers. Each link in the chain is a monomer. A **monomer** is one specific molecule that is repeated in the polymer chain. Polypropylene, for example, might have 50,000 to 200,000 monomers in its chain. Several examples of manufactured polymers are shown in **Table 2.** Not all polymers are manufactured. Some polymers occur naturally. Proteins, cellulose, and nucleic acids are polymers found in living things. In this section, the focus will be on manufactured polymers or synthetic polymers. **Synthetic** means that the polymer does not occur naturally, but it was manufactured in a laboratory or chemical plant.

✔ Reading Check *What are some similarities and differences between monomers and polymers?*

As You Read

What You'll Learn

- **Identify** what a polymer is and the variety of polymers around us.
- **Explain** what a composite material is and why composites are used.

Vocabulary

polymer, synthetic, monomer, composite

Why It's Important

Polymers and composite materials can replace natural materials such as metal, wood, and paper.

Table 2 Common Polymers

Polymer	Monomer	Uses
Polyethylene	$-[CH_2-CH_2]-$	bottles, garment bags
Polyvinyl Chloride (PVC)	$-[CH_2-CHCl]-$	pipe, bottles, compact discs, computer housing
Polypropylene	$-[CH_2-CH(CH_3)]-$	rope, luggage, carpet, film
Polystyrene	$-[CH-CH_2]-$ with benzene ring on CH	toys, packaging, egg cartons, flotation devices
Polytetrafluoroethylene	$-[CF_2-CF_2]-$	nonstick cookware, gaskets, bearings

Section ✔Assessment Planner

PORTFOLIO
Activity, p. 687

PERFORMANCE ASSESSMENT
Assessment, p. 690
See page 698 for more options.

CONTENT ASSESSMENT
Section, p. 690
Challenge, p. 690
Chapter, pp. 698–699

SECTION 3

New Materials

1 Motivate

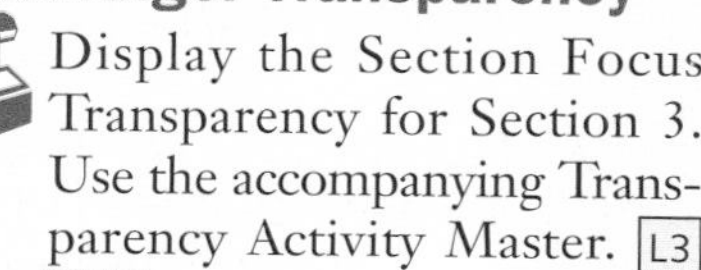

Bellringer Transparency

Display the Section Focus Transparency for Section 3. Use the accompanying Transparency Activity Master. L3 ELL

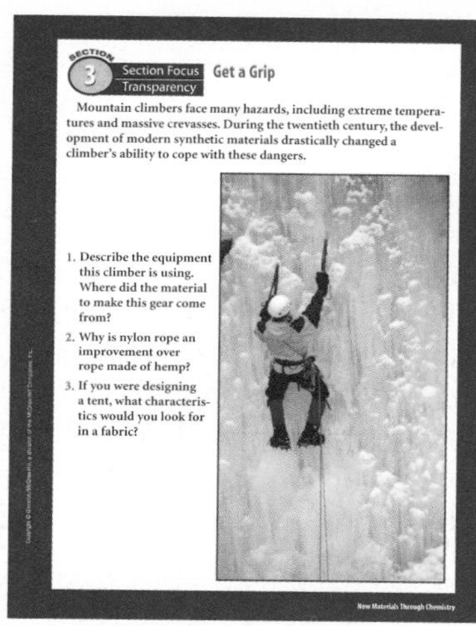

SECTION 3 Section Focus Transparency **Get a Grip**

Mountain climbers face many hazards, including extreme temperatures and massive crevasses. During the twentieth century, the development of modern synthetic materials drastically changed a climber's ability to cope with these dangers.

1. Describe the equipment this climber is using. Where did the material to make this gear come from?
2. Why is nylon rope an improvement over rope made of hemp?
3. If you were designing a tent, what characteristics would you look for in a fabric?

New Materials Through Chemistry

Tie to Prior Knowledge

Bring labels from clothing and other items made of materials whose names start with *poly-* (for example, polyester and polypropylene). Explain to students that the materials used to make these items are polymers. In this section they will learn more about what polymers are and how they are used.

Resource Manager

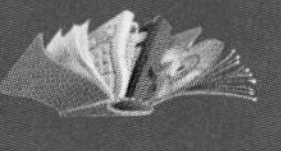

Chapter Resources Booklet
Transparency Activity, p. 46
Directed Reading for Content Mastery, pp. 21, 22

Reading and Writing Skill Activities, p. 17

2 Teach

Polymers

Reading Check

Answer Polymers are large chains of small, repeating molecules; monomers are molecules repeated in the polymer chain.

Activity

Have students bring in plastic products. Arrange them from soft to rigid as a display representing the various properties of polymers. Have students identify the names of the polymers and their monomers. Possible polymers include those listed in **Table 2**. L2 LS **Visual-Spatial**

Make a Model

Using a molecular modeling kit or colored gumdrops and chenille sticks, make a class model of polyethylene. Have each student make a polyethylene monomer, then join the monomers together to make a polyethylene chain. Discuss with students the formation of polymers and show how the chain could have many twists and turns. L2 ELL LS **Kinesthetic**

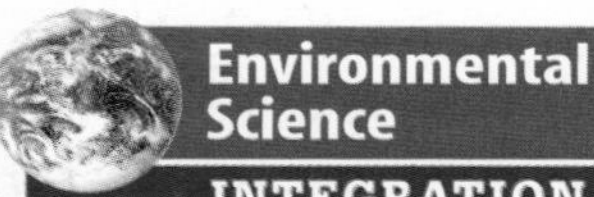

Environmental Science INTEGRATION

Students may want to contact a local landfill agency and obtain comments about the synthetic polymers being placed there. **Why are the polymers so stable?** When they polymerize, the monomers form new bonds that are very stable.

Environmental Science INTEGRATION

Synthetic polymers are used to make many of our disposable items such as plates, diapers, trash bags, and utensils. These items are used once then thrown away. Most synthetic polymers do not decompose in our landfills. In your Science Journal, infer the problems that this might cause and suggest solutions to these problems.

History of Synthetic Polymers Humankind has used natural polymers for centuries. The ancient Egyptians soaked their burial wrappings in natural resins to help preserve their dead. Animal horns and turtle shells, which contain natural resins, were used to make combs and buttons for many years. In the 1800s, scientists began developing processes to improve natural polymers and to create new ones in the laboratory.

In 1839, Charles Goodyear, an American inventor, found that heating sulfur and natural rubber together improved the qualities of natural rubber. By treating the rubber with sulfur, the natural rubber was no longer brittle when it became cold or soft when it became hot. In 1862, John Hyatt, a British inventor, developed celluloid as a replacement for ivory in billiard balls. Celluloid was used in other products such as umbrella handles and toys. These early polymers had many drawbacks, but they were the beginning of the development of a huge class of materials now referred to as polymers. Today, so many types of synthetic polymers exist that they tend to be divided into groups such as plastics, synthetic fibers, adhesives, surface coatings, and natural and synthetic rubbers. **Figure 17** shows a time line of when some of these materials were created.

Hydrocarbons Today, synthetic polymers usually are made from fossil fuels such as oil, coal, or natural gas. Fossil fuels are composed primarily of carbon and hydrogen and are referred to as hydrocarbons. Because synthetic polymers are made from hydrocarbons, carbon and hydrogen are the primary components of most synthetic polymers.

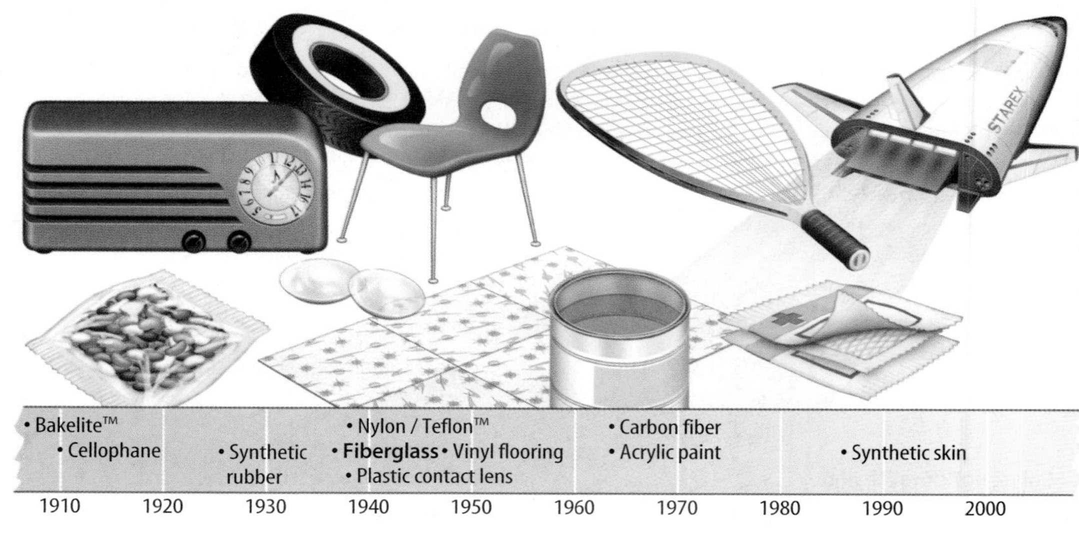

Figure 17
Polymers were developed in the late 1800s, but they did not become widely used until after World War II in 1945.

Cultural Diversity

South American Rubber Rubber was first used by Native Americans in Central and South America. They harvested rubber from local trees and used it for balls, containers, and shoes and for waterproofing fabrics. Later, rubber was harvested from pará rubber trees found in Brazil's Amazon basin. Have students find out about the history of rubber in Brazil. In the late nineteenth century, the need for electrical insulation and the invention of pneumatic tires dramatically increased the world's demand for rubber. Most of the world's rubber came from Brazil's Amazon basin, which went through a rubber boom from 1880–1910. After 1910, competition from Asian rubber decreased the importance of Brazil's rubber, and the development of relatively inexpensive synthetic rubber during World War II made natural rubber unnecessary. L3

Changing Properties Polymers are a class of materials with a wide range of uses. The reason that polymers can be used for so many applications is directly related to the ease in which their properties can be modified. Polymers are long chains of monomers. If the composition or arrangement of monomers is changed, then the properties of the material will change.

Figure 18 shows how the monomer ethylene can be modified to produce a polymer with different properties and uses. Ethylene has only two carbon atoms and six bonding sites. The number of carbon atoms in the polymer can be high, and each bonding site represents a possibility of a change in properties. Polyethylene can be high density or low density depending upon how the molecules are attached to the monomer. One of the substances on the monomer can be replaced by another substance or a group of substances and the properties will change, too. The possibilities for creating new materials are almost limitless.

Science Online

Research Visit the Glencoe Science Web site at **science.glencoe.com** to learn more about how changing the monomer changes the properties of the polymer. Communicate what you learn to your class.

The Plastics Group Plastics are widely used for many products because they have desirable properties. Plastics are usually lightweight, strong, impact resistant, waterproof, moldable, chemical resistant, and inexpensive. Examples of plastics are easy to find. They are used to make toys, computer housing, telephones, containers, plates, and so on. The properties of plastics vary widely within this group. Some plastics are clear, some melt at high temperature, and some are flexible. Transparency, melting temperature, and flexibility are properties of plastics that relate to the composition of the polymer.

Figure 18
The arrangement of the branches along the chain can affect the properties of the polymer.

A Low-Density Polyethylene, LDPE, is flexible, tough, and chemical resistant. The chain has a great deal of side-branching, which causes low density.

B High-Density Polyethylene, HDPE, is firmer, stronger, and less translucent than LDPE. This chain has little side-branching, which allows the chain to pack closer together, thus giving it a higher density and different properties.

C Polyvinyl chloride (PVC) is used in building materials. The substitution of chlorine for a hydrogen in the polyethylene chain makes the polymer harder and more heat resistant.

Science Online

Internet Addresses

Explore the Glencoe Science Web site at **science.glencoe.com** to find out more about topics in this section.

Resource Manager

Chapter Resources Booklet
Enrichment, p. 32
Lab Activity, pp. 13–16
Transparency Activity, pp. 47–48

Activity

Have students find out how polypropylene forms and make posters with drawings and explanations to display their findings. Polypropylene is made from propene, a three-carbon monomer with one double bond. To start the polymer chain, one propene molecule joins another at the double bond, reducing the bond to a single bond. Each succeeding propene monomer adds to the chain at the double bond, which changes to a single bond. L3 LS **Visual-Spatial** P

Teacher FYI

Plastics that soften when heated are called thermo-plastics. Examples are PVC, styrene and Lucite. Thermosetting plastics contain cross-links between polymer chains and become rigid when heated as more cross-links form. As these plastics cool, they harden.

Visual Learning

Figure 18 Draw on the board a polyethylene chain with many side branches to illustrate low-density polyethylene. Draw three polyethylene chains with few side branches and show how these chains can pack together to form high-density polyethylene. L2 ELL LS **Visual-Spatial**

Quick Demo

Place some fingernail polish remover in a small dish. Keep it away from flames. Set a Styrofoam cup in the fingernail polish remover. The acetone in the fingernail polish remover breaks down some of the Styrofoam, which reforms into a small puddle. Tell students that Styrofoam is polystyrene that has been puffed into a lightweight form. The Styrofoam cup contains very little polystyrene. L2 ELL LS **Visual-Spatial**

Polymers, continued

Quick Demo

To make nylon, pour about 5 ml of hexanedioxyl dichloride into a small beaker. Carefully pour about 2 ml of diaminohexane on top, making sure that the two solutions do not mix. The reaction occurs where the two liquids meet. You should be able to see a new layer being formed. Take a pair of forceps and pull out a thread from this layer. Wind the thread around a glass rod. By turning the rod gently you should be able to get a long thread of nylon. You can continue until the two reactants are used up. L2 LS **Visual-Spatial**

Discussion

How can synthetic fibers provide greater versatility in clothing? Synthetic fibers can be developed to meet specific needs, such as warmth, weight, and durability. In addition, they can be combined with natural fibers. L1
LS **Logical-Mathematical**

Reading Check

Answer Adhesives are used in the manufacture of automobile parts, home building, window and door sealant, braces, pressure-sensitive tape.

Resource Manager

Chapter Resources Booklet
Reinforcement, p. 29

Physical Science Critical Thinking/Problem Solving, p. 5

Mathematics Skill Activities, p. 19

Figure 19
Some synthetic polymers are used in hazardous conditions.
A This aramid is a fiber that is fire proof. Clothing made from this fabric is used by firefighters and flight crews. B Survival cells are manufactured from another aramid for use in Indy race cars. C A survival cell in an Indy car provides protection for the driver during a crash.

A

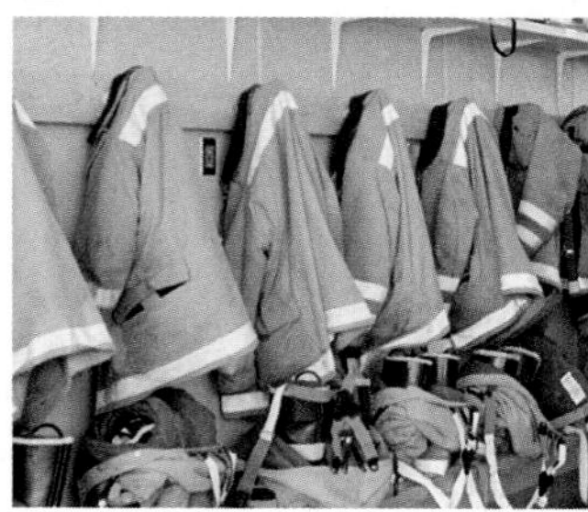

B

C

Synthetic Fibers Nylon, polyester, acrylic, and polypropylene are examples of polymers that can be manufactured as fibers. Most synthetic fibers are composed of carbon chains because they are produced from petroleum or natural gas. Synthetic fibers can be mass-produced to almost any set of desired properties. Nylon is often used in wind and water-resistant clothing such as lightweight jackets. Polyester and polyester blended with natural fibers such as cotton often are used in clothing. Polyester fiber also is used to fill pillows and quilts. Polyurethane is the foam used in mattresses and pillows.

Special fibers called aramids are a family of nylons with special properties. **Figure 19** shows some uses for these fabrics. Aramids are used to make fireproof clothing. Firefighters, military pilots, and race car drivers are examples of professionals that make use of this special fabric. Another aramid is used to make bulletproof vests, Indy race car survival cells, puncture-resistant gloves, and motorcycle clothing. Although they are light, these aramids are five times stronger than steel.

Adhesives Synthetic polymers are used to make adhesives that can be modified to provide the best properties for a particular application. Contact cements are used in the manufacture of automobile parts, furniture, leather goods, and decorative laminates. They bond instantly with the bond getting stronger after it dries. Structural adhesives are used in construction projects. One structural adhesive, silicone, is used to seal windows and doors to prevent heat loss in homes and other buildings. Ultraviolet-cured adhesives are used by orthodontists to adhere brace brackets to teeth. These adhesives bond after exposure to ultraviolet light. Other types of adhesives are hot-melt and transparent, pressure-sensitive tape.

Reading Check ***What are five uses of adhesives?***

Teacher FYI

For an adhesive to stick to an object, the surface of the adhesive must contact the surface of the object. The surfaces bond to each other by mechanical adhesion or by chemical reaction. During bonding, the adhesive must change from a liquid to a tough, nonflowing solid. The exact nature of these bonds is a matter of continuing scientific research. There are two main types of adhesives, thermoplastic and thermosetting. Thermoplastic adhesives set on cooling or evaporation of a solvent, whereas thermosetting adhesives set on heating or when mixed with a catalyst.

Figure 20
Composite materials are used to make some cars and boats. A The glass fiber embedded in the plastic reinforces the plastic structure. B This composite material is strong, lightweight, and corrosion resistant.

Surface Coatings and Elastic Polymers Many surface coatings use synthetic polymers. Polyurethane is a popular polymer that is used to protect and enhance wood surfaces. Many paints use synthetic polymers in their composition, too.

Synthetic rubber is a synthetic elastic polymer. It is used to manufacture tires, gaskets, belts, and hoses. The soles of some shoes also are made from this rubber.

Taking a Cue from Nature Spinning long fibers into threads and fabrics is not an original idea. Spiders spun fibers for their webs long before humans copied the idea and began spinning fibers themselves. Nylon fiber is another idea borrowed from nature. The silkworm produces a highly desirable fiber that is woven into fabric for items such as blouses and stockings. Can you imagine how long it would take a silkworm to produce enough silk for one blouse? Nylon was produced in the laboratory as a possible substitute for silk. Why do you think natural silk fabric is more expensive than nylon fabric?

Composites

The properties of a synthetic polymer can be altered by using more than one material. A **composite** is a mixture of two or more materials—one embedded or layered in the other. Composite materials of plastic are used to construct boat and car bodies, as shown in **Figure 20.** These bodies are made of a glass-fiber composite that is a mixture of small threads or fibers of glass embedded in a plastic. The structure of the fiberglass reinforces the plastic, making a strong, lightweight composite. If a substance is light but brittle, such as some plastics, embedding flexible fibers into it can alter the brittleness property. After the substance has the flexible fibers embedded, the product is less brittle and can withstand greater forces before it breaks. Glass fibers are used often to reinforce plastics because glass is inexpensive, but other materials can be used, as well.

Research Visit the Glencoe Science Web site at **science.glencoe.com** for recent news on newly created polymers and new uses for older ones. Write a short passage in your Science Journal about the information that you find.

Inclusion Strategies

Gifted Have students research and write reports on the material used to replace natural ivory in piano keys. Reports should include why the ivory needed to be replaced and what problems had to be overcome. The material is a polymer composite made of polyester mixed with polyethylene glycol. It was developed when it became illegal to use elephant ivory. Creating something with the feel and texture of ivory was difficult.

Text Question Answer

Its supply is limited.

SCIENCE *Online*

Internet Addresses

Explore the Glencoe Science Web site at **science.glencoe.com** to find out more about topics in this section.

Use Science Words

Word Origins The word *composite* can be broken down into the parts *com-* and *-posit.* Have students find the origins and meanings of these word parts. *Com-* comes from Latin and means "with." *-Posit* comes from the Latin word *ponere,* meaning "to put or place." Thus the word *composite* means to put or place together. L3 LS **Linguistic**

Composites

Quick Demo

Make two batches of transparent gelatin dessert. Follow the printed directions for making the dessert for the first batch. Before the gel sets in the second batch, add short pieces of uncooked spaghetti. Bring the gelatin to class and have students compare the rigidity and density of both products. Discuss how embedding one material in another results in a change in the properties. L2 ELL LS **Visual-Spatial**

Reading Check

Answer Composite materials are strong and lightweight. Reduced weight reduces the amount of fuel required. Composites provide corrosion resistance and are simple to repair.

3 Assess

Reteach

Bring to class an article of sports equipment that is manufactured from a known composite (graphite tennis racquet, fishing rod, golf club, etc.). Tell students the object is a composite and demonstrate one of its properties (flexibility, strength, corrosion resistance, etc.). Ask students what they can determine about the object knowing it is a composite. The material it is made of is a combination of different materials. L2 LS **Visual-Spatial**

Challenge

Cross-linking changes the properties of polymers. Have students define cross-linking and name some cross-linked polymers. Cross-linking is the formation of bridges between chains of polymers. Vulcanization cross-links rubber by forming sulfur bridges between the chains. L3 ELL LS **Linguistic**

Assessment

Oral Ask students to give examples and explain the benefits of composites. They combine the qualities, such as flexibility and strength, of the different materials used to make them. Use **PASC**, p. 89

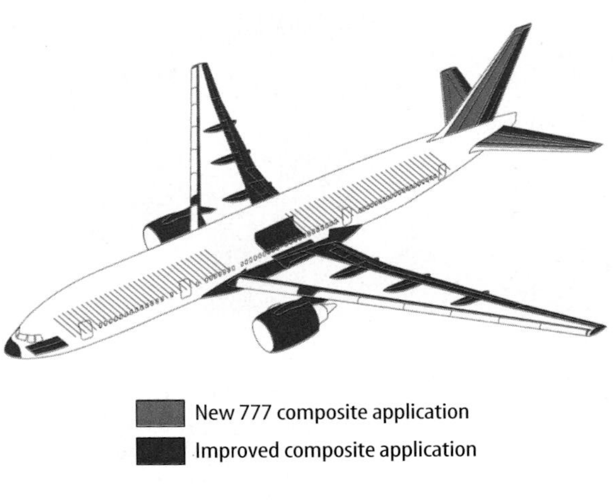

Figure 21
Commercial aircraft use composite materials in some locations. Composites provide corrosion resistance and are simple to repair.

Composites in Flight Composite materials are used in the construction of satellites. Lighter-weight satellites are less expensive to launch into orbit, yet the structure is able to withstand the stress of the launch. Carbon fibers are used to strengthen the plastic body, creating a material that is four times more firm and 40 percent stronger than aluminum. Satellites made of graphite composites are about 13 percent lighter than satellites made of aluminum. The composite material is stronger and lighter in weight than aluminum, therefore, it is less expensive to launch and can endure the stress of the launch better.

Commercial aircraft use composite materials in their construction, as shown in **Figure 21.** Aircraft made of composites also benefit from the strong yet lightweight properties of composite materials. The weight of this aircraft was reduced by more than 2,600 kg by using advanced alloys and composite materials. The lower weight results in cost savings by reducing the amount of fuel required to operate the aircraft.

Reading Check *Why are composites used in aircraft?*

Section 3 Assessment

1. Explain what a polymer is and give three examples of items that are made from polymers.
2. What are the raw materials that are used to make most synthetic polymers?
3. Explain what a composite material is and give three examples of items that are made from composites.
4. Synthetic polymers can be separated into groups based upon their uses, what are some of these groups?
5. **Thinking Critically** How are synthetic polymers creating waste-disposal problems? Discuss possible solutions to this problem.

Skill Builder Activities

6. **Classifying** Make a list of 20 items in your home that are made of polymers. Group the items based on the following properties: elastic, heat resistant, and shatterproof. Did any of your items have all three properties? Why or why not? **For more help, refer to the** Science Skill Handbook.
7. **Communicating** You've created a new synthetic polymer. In your Science Journal, describe the properties of your polymer and suggest uses for it. **For more help, refer to the** Science Skill Handbook.

Answers to Section Assessment

1. a large molecule made from joining smaller molecules, monomers, into chains; packaging, carpet, toys
2. fossil fuels, such as oil, coal, natural gas
3. a material made from two or more materials that have been mixed so that one material is embedded in the other; boat and car bodies, parts for commercial aircraft
4. Synthetic polymer groups include plastics, synthetic fibers, adhesives, surface coatings, and synthetic rubbers.
5. Some synthetic materials resist the breakdown action of bacteria in land fills. This can cause the volume of the landfill waste to increase rapidly. One possible solution is to recycle plastic materials.
6. Lists may include sports equipment (heat resistant, elastic), insulators (heat resistant), and plastic table tops (heat resistant, shatterproof). Some plastics fit several categories.
7. Possible answer: a polymer that is flexible and durable, but when lightly sprayed with an initiating chemical becomes susceptible to bacterial breakdown in a landfill

Activity

What can you do with this stuff?

This substance is fun to play with. But how do you describe its properties?

What You'll Investigate

What are the properties of this new material and what can it be used for?

Materials

white glue
borax laundry soap
warm water
250-mL beaker or cup
100-mL beaker or cup
graduated cylinder
popsicle or craft stick for mixing

Goals

- **Predict** the properties of this material.
- **Determine** possible uses for the material.

Safety Precautions

WARNING: *Never eat lab materials.*

Procedure

1. Prepare a data table to record your observations of the following: stretched slowly, stretched quickly, rolled into a ball and left alone, pressed onto newspaper ink, dropped on a hard surface.
2. Put about 100 mL of warm water in the larger beaker and add Borax laundry soap until soap no longer dissolves.
3. Put 5 mL of water and 10 mL of white glue into the smaller beaker and mix completely.
4. Add 5 mL of the borax solution to the glue solution and continue mixing for a couple of minutes.

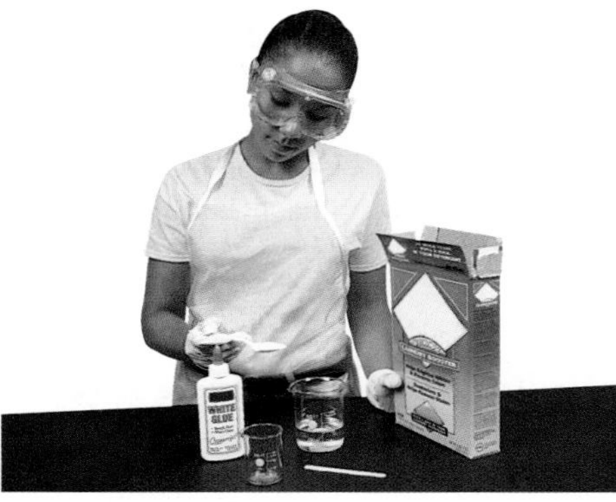

5. When the substance firms up, remove it from the container and continue to mix it by pressing with your fingers until it is like soft clay.
6. **Examine** the properties of this material and record them in your data table.

Conclude and Apply

1. What were the properties of this material?
2. Get together with other students and brainstorm. What could this material be used for, and which of its properties would make it useful for that purpose?
3. You're in charge of marketing this product. Prepare an advertisement with text and graphics on a sheet of notebook paper. Which magazine would you place this ad in and why?

Communicating Your Data

Compare your conclusions with other students in your class. **For more help, refer to the Science Skill Handbook.**

Activity

BENCH TESTED

Purpose To produce a new material and learn to investigate its properties

Process Skills observing, predicting, classifying, recognizing cause and effect, interpreting data

Time Required 35 minutes

Alternative Materials Try various brands of white glue to see which one works best.

Safety Precautions The materials should never be tasted.

Teaching Strategies

- Color the material made by adding food coloring to the glue mixture.
- The new material will mold within a few minutes.
- The new material can leave water spots on wooden surfaces.

Troubleshooting Make sure students squeeze any pockets of solution from the polymer. The liquid pockets interfere with the final product.

Conclude and Apply

1. The material was a puttylike substance. It had form but could be easily molded. It bounced like a ball.
2. The product could be a new toy, or it could be an insulator that would harden after being poured like a liquid into small cracks.
3. Possible answer: Solquid! Is it a liquid or a solid or a new phase of matter? Advertise it in magazines that appeal to young people.

Communicating Your Data

Put a large version of the student data table on the board. Have students put their observations on the large summary board.

Assessment

Process Have students vary the ratio of glue to borax solution. **What properties appear when there is too much glue for the borax?** The material is more liquid-like. Use **Performance Assessment in the Science Classroom,** p. 97.

Activity

BENCH TESTED

Recognize the Problem

Purpose Students will measure the flexibility of various rods. L2

 **Kinesthetic**

Process Skills collecting data, measuring, making and using tables, recording data, interpreting data

Time Required 80 minutes

Thinking Critically

The properties of a material are very important to consider when deciding which material to use for a particular application. Strength and flexibility are two factors that are very important. For instance, fiberglass would not be a good choice for bridge construction; steel would be a better choice. This lab will provide students with an opportunity to test materials and decide which material would be best for a particular application.

Materials

Wood and steel rods are available as 1/4" × 36" rods from a hardware store. Fiberglass rods that are used as supports for driveway reflectors also are available in hardware stores.

Safety Precautions

It is extremely important that during this lab everyone in the classroom be wearing safety goggles. It is possible that rods will break and fly across the room.

Activity

Can polymer composites be stronger than steel?

Why are composite materials used instead of wood or metal in high performance applications? Scientists and engineers test many materials before selecting the best one for a specific use. Composites are used in aircraft parts, sports equipment, and space vehicles because of their strength and low weight. What other factors might be important? How do you measure performance?

Recognize the Problem

How can you compare the performance of a composite with other materials?

Thinking Critically

How do you choose the best material for an application?

Goals

- **Model** appropriate equipment to test wood, steel, and fiberglass composite rods.
- **Measure** the force required to flex the test rods.
- **Calculate** the relative flexibility of each rod.
- **Estimate** the performance of each material.

Possible Materials

meterstick
spring scale, 0–12-kg range and 0–2-kg range
wood, steel, and fiberglass composite rods, 6.35 mm in diameter by 50 cm long
supports to hold the test rods
graph paper

Safety Precautions

WARNING: *Wear safety goggles at all times during this lab.*

Material	Distance Flexed (cm)	Force Required (kg)
composite	1	1.0
composite	2	2.0
composite	3	3.5
steel	1	4.5
steel	2	9.0
steel	3	12.0
wood	1	0.34
wood	2	0.80
wood	3	1.0

Inclusion Strategies

Learning Disabled These students can work with other students to make the calculations and generate the graphs. All students should construct graphs and make the calculations.

692 CHAPTER 22 New Materials Through Chemistry

Planning the Model

1. To test the model, hook the spring scale to the center of the fiberglass rod. Have a team member pull down on the spring scale until the top of the test rod moves down 1 cm from the zero point. Record the scale reading on the data table. Pull down on the spring scale until the rod flexes 2 cm, then 3 cm. Record both of the spring scale readings on the data chart.
2. Repeat the tests on the steel and wood rods. Record the data in your table.

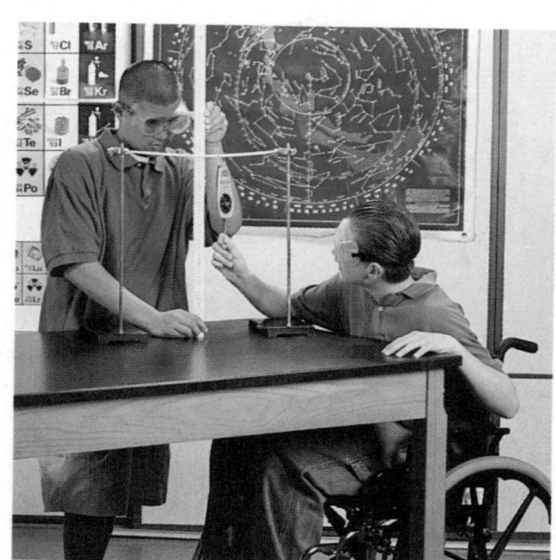

Analyzing and Applying Results

1. For each of the rods, graph the force measured on the *y*-axis and the distances on the *x*-axis. Calculate the slope of each line in kilograms per centimeter. The slope is a relative measure of the flexibility of the samples.
2. Divide the slope of each line by the density of the corresponding material to get a specific performance number, which may be used to compare different materials. Use the following values for the densities: composite = 1.2, steel = 7.9, and wood = 0.5 g/cm^3.
3. **Determine** which rod had the highest specific performance number. What is meant by the statement that a polymer composite is twice as strong as steel?
4. **Analyze** which variables could affect the flexibility measurement.

Making the Model

1. Using the data that you have gathered, create a model exhibit showing possible construction uses for each of these materials.
2. Indicate the reason the specific material was chosen.

Communicating Your Data

Give an oral presentation on choosing the best material for a specific application to another class of students using your model.

BENCH TESTED

Planning the Model

Teaching Strategy

Have students work in pairs to collect data. One student should hold the meterstick in place while the other student flexes the rod and reads the spring scale.

Analyzing and Applying Results

1. Check students' graphs
2. The slopes of the lines will be approximately: steel: 4 kg/cm; fiberglass: 1.1 kg/cm; and wood: 0.3 kg/cm.
3. The specific performance numbers are fiberglass: 916; wood: 600; and steel: 506. Polymer composites are about twice as strong as steel on a per mass basis.
4. Possible answers: The type of material tested. The diameter of the material tested.

Making the Model

Expected Outcome

Most results will show that steel has the least flex and fiberglass has the most. The applications that the students choose should take this into consideration.

Assessment

Oral What advantages would fiberglass have over steel in some applications? Possible answers: Flexibility is an advantage in some applications. Fiberglass does not rust. It is inexpensive to produce. It can be molded into the desired shape. Use **PASC,** p. 89.

Resource Manager

Chapter Resources Booklet
Activity Worksheet, pp. 5–6, 7–8

Physical Science Critical Thinking/Problem Solving, p. 15

Communicating Your Data

Students may want to make posters as visual aids for their presentations.

Content Background

Stephanie Kwolek's discovery of aramid polymers in 1964 had an impact far beyond the original purpose of the investigation. DuPont was searching for a product to replace steel in belted automobile tires. The research lab was working with a number of polymer compounds and attempting to create others.

Most plastics are polymers or polymer-based. Polymers are carbon-based substances formed by molecules that bond together end to end in long chains. The longer the chain gets before the molecule turns back on itself, the stronger the material. The immense strength of the aramid polymers derives from exceptional molecular length plus a unique characteristic. When aramid molecules bend they form a crystalline structure making them very hard.

The features that make Kevlar® strong also make it difficult to produce and form into useful shapes. Impervious to solvents, it is difficult to dissolve and, with a melting point of 500°C, molding it with heat is not practical. As a result it took almost ten years for the first Kevlar® products to reach the public. Since then its uses and those of its descendants seem to have no end. Kevlar® is now used in applications as diverse as space exploration, automobile brakes, bridge suspension cables and, as was originally intended, belting for tires.

TIME SCIENCE AND Society

SCIENCE ISSUES THAT AFFECT YOU!

Wonder Fiber

In 1964, Stephanie Kwolek was a chemist working at a research laboratory. Her assignment? Create a new type of tough, lightweight fiber. Kwolek's routine at the lab was about the same each day. She combined different substances in test tubes. She stirred them. She heated them. Then she would have any new substance spun into fibers. The idea was to get a fiber that was both strong and lightweight. But coming up with a new superfiber was difficult.

This police dog can thank Stephanie Kwolek for its bulletproof vest!

A close-up view of fiber-optic cables wrapped in Kwolek's discovery.

694

Resources for Teachers and Students

Mothers of Invention; From the Bra to the Bomb: Forgotten Women and Their Unforgettable Ideas. By Ethlie Ann Vare and Greg Ptacek. NY,NY: Morrow (1988)

From Indian Corn to Outer Space: Women Invent in America. by Ellen H. Showell and Fred M. B. Amram Peterborough, NH: Cobblestone Publishing, Inc (1995)

College of Science and Technology The School of Polymers and High Performance Materials University of Southern Mississippi Box 5165 Hattiesburg, MS 39406-5165

Stephanie Kwolek

A Shocking Discovery

At one point, Kwolek was working with two polymers. She wanted to use heat to combine them, but they would not melt. So she decided to use a solvent to dissolve them. But when she poured the solvent onto one of the polymers, she got something unlike anything she had ever seen. Not only did it look different, it behaved differently when she stirred it. It separated into two distinct layers.

Kwolek thought this strange liquid might be something special. She asked one of her coworkers to spin it into fibers using a machine called a spinneret. The other chemist refused at first, saying the liquid wouldn't form fibers. And besides, it would probably gum up the equipment. But Kwolek had a hunch about this liquid. So she persisted. Finally, after several days, the other chemist agreed to try to spin the liquid into fibers.

A New Type of Fiber

What they found shocked Kwolek and everyone else in the lab. The fibers that formed in the spinneret were very lightweight but also extremely stiff and strong. Kwolek had accidentally discovered a new type of synthetic fiber—a fiber made from a new substance called a liquid-crystal solution.

This new fiber was five times stronger than steel, and over the decades since its discovery, it has been put to many uses. It is found in a number of products where a material that is light but very strong is needed. These products include bulletproof vests, boat hulls, fiber-optic cables, cut-resistant gloves, airplane parts, skis, tennis rackets, and parts of spacecraft.

The discovery was a huge accomplishment for Kwolek, but an even more important one for the world. The fiber she discovered 40 years ago has benefited many people and saved many lives, from the creation of bulletproof vests used by police officers to the tough clothing used by firefighters.

CONNECTIONS Research Use resources in your school's media center or the Glencoe Science Web site to find out more about the superfiber Kwolek discovered. List as many of the possible uses as you can. Compare what you uncover with what others in the class find.

SCIENCE Online
For more information, visit science.glencoe.com

Discussion

Are there any examples of naturally occurring polymers? Possible Answer: Yes. Many polymers occur naturally. Tree sap, honey, and the slime that help snails glide are examples. Modern polymer chemistry began in 1839 when Charles Goodyear developed vulcanization, a way to harden natural rubber in molded shapes without losing its flexibility

Activity

Form students into parallel, single file lines of five to eight students each. Placing their right hand on the shoulder of the person in front of them they should try walking around the classroom. Re-form them in the starting position, but add the additional link of placing their left hand on the right shoulder of the person next to them. Have them try moving in this formation. The first exercise is similar to single polymer chains, the second to cross-linked polymers. Lessened mobility equates to higher material strength.

Investigate the Issue

Have the teams from the exercise above find examples of simple polymers and cross-linked polymers. Provide an appropriate reward for the team with the longest list. Allow the teams to challenge each other's lists before determining a winner.

CONNECTION While researching Kevlar® students will come across information about other polymers and their development. Some were discovered accidentally, while searching for synthetic replacements for natural substances with quite different uses. Two of these were Bakelite and Teflon. Have students discuss the similarities and differences between these materials and compare the uses of each.

SCIENCE Online

Internet Addresses

Explore the Glencoe Science Web site at **science.glencoe.com** to find out more about topics in this feature.

Chapter 22 Study Guide

Reviewing Main Ideas

Preview

Students can answer the questions in their Science Journals. Discuss the answers as you go through the chapter. LS **Linguistic**

Review

Students can write their answers, then compare them with those of other students. LS **Interpersonal**

Reteach

Students can look at the illustrations and describe details that support the main ideas of the chapter. LS **Visual-Spatial**

Answers to Chapter Review

Section 1

2. malleability

Section 2

1. transparency and electrical conductivity

Section 3

3. wear resistance, resistance to warping under different weather conditions, and likely is probably lighter than a wooden skateboard

Chapter 22 Study Guide

Reviewing Main Ideas

Section 1 Materials with a Past

1. People have been making and using alloys for thousands of years. Some common alloys include bronze, brass, and various alloys of iron.

2. An alloy is a mixture of a metal with one or more other elements. Metals and alloys have the properties of luster, ductility, malleability, and conductivity. *Which property or properties does the figure above demonstrate?*

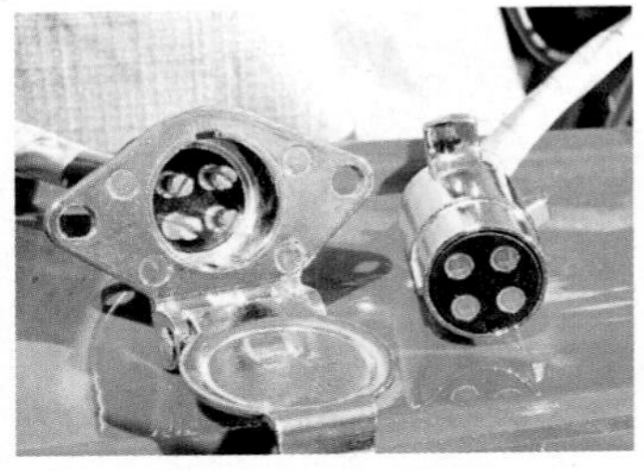

Section 2 Versatile Materials

1. Ceramics are used in a wide range of products. This is due to the ability of scientists to customize the properties of ceramics. *What properties does this ceramic material in the windshield have?*

2. Semiconductors are made from silicon doped with other elements.

3. Ceramic materials are made by molding the object, and then heating the object to high temperatures. This process increases the density of the material.

4. Integrated circuits contain n-type and p-type semiconducting devices.

Section 3 Polymers and Composites

1. Polymers are a class of natural or human-made substances that are composed of molecules that are in large chains with simple repeating units called monomers.

2. Synthetic polymers can be produced in many forms, ranging from thin films to thick slabs or blocks. Synthetic fibers are produced in thin strands that can be woven into fabrics.

3. A composite is a mixture of two materials, one embedded in the other. Reinforced concrete and fiberglass are examples of composites. The skateboard in the figure to the right is constructed of a fiberglass composite. *What advantages would composite construction have over wood construction?*

FOLDABLES Reading & Study Skills

After You Read

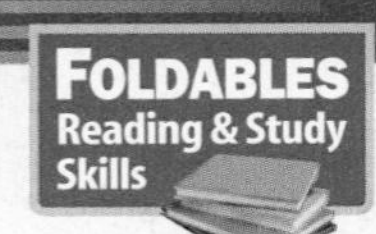

Number the tabs on your Foldable in the order the materials were discovered. Predict new materials of the future.

FOLDABLES Reading & Study Skills

After You Read

After students have read the chapter and completed the Foldable described in Before You Read, have them do the activity on the student page.

Dinah Zike

Visualizing Main Ideas

Complete the following concept map on materials.

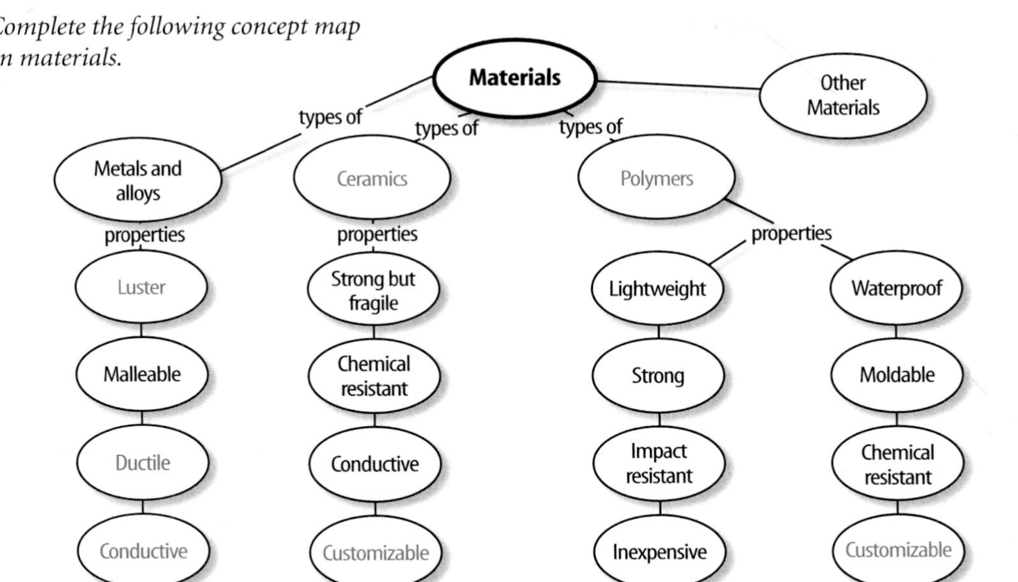

Vocabulary Review

Vocabulary Words

a. alloy
b. ceramics
c. composite
d. conductivity
e. doping
f. ductility
g. integrated circuit
h. luster
i. malleability
j. monomer
k. polymer
l. semiconductor
m. synthetic

Using Vocabulary

Replace the underlined words with the correct vocabulary word(s).

1. The ability to be hammered or rolled into thin sheets is a property of metals and alloys.
2. Compounds made from clay, silica, and feldspar are used on the space shuttle heat shield and are being replaced by an alloy.
3. Fiberglass is a humanmade material that is used to make boats and skateboards.
4. Fiberglass is a mixture of two materials.
5. A chrome bumper has a reflective surface.
6. A molecule that is formed by a long chain of repeating units is used to make food storage containers.

Study Tip

After each day's lesson, make a practice quiz for yourself. Later, when you're studying for the test, take the practice quizzes that you created.

IDENTIFYING Misconceptions

Assess

After students have done the activity on page 670F and completed the chapter, have them perform this activity.

Materials paper and pencil

Procedure Have each student divide a sheet of paper into two columns, one labeled Pure Science and the other labeled Applied Science, and place the following in the appropriate columns: (a) finding the best electrical material to use in a computer, (b) researching the causes of cancer, (c) finding how chimpanzees communicate, (d) finding a non-flammable alternative to hydrogen for balloon travel, (e) isolating new forms of carbon.

Expected Outcome Examples (a) and (d) are applied science while (b), (c), and (e) are pure science.

Chapter 22 Study Guide

Visualizing Main Ideas

See student page.

Vocabulary Review

Using Vocabulary

1. malleability
2. ceramics
3. synthetic
4. composite
5. luster
6. polymer

Chapter 22 Assessment

Checking Concepts

1. D
2. A
3. D
4. A
5. D
6. B
7. C
8. D
9. D
10. D

Thinking Critically

11. Gold that is 10-karat would be less likely to bend out of shape.
12. Answers will vary. One example could be that composite tennis racquets allow players to stroke the ball faster due to the lighter mass of the newer racquets. This gives an advantage to a strong server. Lighter racquets may add so much serve power that other aspects of the game are overshadowed. This may require rule changes such as a higher net that would de-emphasize the importance of a powerful serve.
13. The synthetic material may not decompose, thus adding more volume to overcrowded landfills.

Chapter 22 Assessment

Checking Concepts

Choose the word or phrase that best answers the question.

1. Which metal replaces bronze as a widely used metal?
   A) copper **C)** zinc
   B) tin **D)** iron
2. Why are metals and alloys good conductors of heat and electricity?
   A) They have loosely bound electrons within the atom.
   B) They have luster and malleability.
   C) They are composed of mixtures.
   D) They have a shiny appearance.
3. An alloy of steel will contain iron and what element?
   A) mercury **C)** zinc
   B) tin **D)** carbon
4. What raw materials are many synthetic polymers made from?
   A) hydrocarbons **C)** fiberglass
   B) iron ore **D)** ceramics
5. What type of fibers are used to reinforce polymers in some automobile bodies?
   A) ceramic **C)** hydrocarbon
   B) metal alloy **D)** glass
6. Which element below is found in both brass and bronze?
   A) mercury **C)** tin
   B) copper **D)** zinc
7. Which of the following is a natural fiber?
   A) nylon **C)** silk
   B) polyester **D)** acrylic
8. Which group of materials below is not classified as synthetic?
   A) ceramics **C)** composites
   B) alloys **D)** metal ores
9. Customizing properties is NOT likely in which of the following?
   A) alloys
   B) synthetic polymers
   C) ceramics
   D) pure metals
10. Which of the following elements is used to dope silicon crystals?
    A) carbon **C)** copper
    B) zinc **D)** gallium

Thinking Critically

11. A lower karat gold has less gold in it than a higher karat gold. Why might you prefer a ring that is 10-karat gold over a ring that is 20-karat gold?

12. Explain the advantages and disadvantages of using composites in the world of sports.
13. A synthetic fiber might be preferred over a natural fiber for use outdoors because it will not rot. Explain how this could negatively affect the environment.

Developing Skills

14. **Interpreting Scientific Illustrations** Look at the polymer below. Draw the monomer upon which the polymer is based.

```
[ H   H   H   H   H   H  ]
[ |   |   |   |   |   |  ]
[ C — C — C — C — C — C  ]
[ |   |   |   |   |   |  ]
[ H   CN  H   CN  H   CN ]
```

15. **Measuring in SI** A bronze trophy has a mass of 952 g. If the bronze is 85 percent copper, how many grams of tin are contained in the trophy?

Chapter Assessment Planner

Portfolio Encourage students to place in their portfolios one or two items of what they consider to be their best work. Examples include:

- Curriculum Connection, p. 673
- Science Journal, p. 682
- Activity, p. 687

Performance Additional performance assessments, Performance Task Assessment Lists, and rubrics for evaluating these activities can be found in Glencoe's **Performance Assessment in the Science Classroom.**

16. Comparing and Contrasting Compare and contrast alloys and ceramics.

17. Recognizing Cause and Effect A student performing the two-page lab did not see any difference in the flexing of the rods. What are some possible causes of this result?

18. Concept Mapping Draw a network tree about polymers, moving from the most general term to the most specific. Use the terms *composites, hydrocarbons, product groups, polymers, adhesives, plastics, synthetic fibers,* and *surface coatings and elastic polymers.*

Polymers
usually made of
Hydrocarbons
Product groups
Surface coatings & elastic polymers
Plastics
Composites
Synthetic fibers
Adhesives

Performance Assessment

21. Project Research the production of silk fabric and compare it with production of synthetic fabrics such as nylon. Display samples of each.

TECHNOLOGY

Go to the Glencoe Science Web site at **science.glencoe.com** or use the **Glencoe Science CD-ROM** for additional chapter assessment.

THE PRINCETON REVIEW Test Practice

An engineer studied various composite materials and created the table below.

Thermal Properties of Composite Ceramics

Material	Melting Temperature (°C)	Thermal Conductivity (W/m•K)
Alumina	2,050	30.00
Fused Silica	1,650	2.00
Soda-lime Glass	700	1.70
Polyethylene	120	0.38

Use this table and answer the following questions.

1. According to the table, what is the thermal conductivity of Fused Silica?
A) 30 W/m•K
B) 2.0 W/m•K
C) 1.7 W/m•K
D) 0.38 W/m•K

2. According to this table, which composite ceramic will melt first if heated?
F) Alumina
G) Fused Silica
H) Soda-Lime Glass
J) Polyethylene

Chapter 22 Assessment

THE PRINCETON REVIEW Test Practice

The Test-Taking Tip was written by The Princeton Review, the nation's leader in test preparation.

1. B
2. J

Developing Skills

14. Check students' work.
15. 952 g × (1 − 0.85) = 142.8 g, or approximately 143 g
16. Alloys and ceramics are made from more than one substance in varying ratios. Alloys are made from a metal and one or more other elements. Ceramics are made from metallic elements and oxygen, nitrogen, and sulfur. Alloys are typically less brittle than ceramics.
17. The rods were cooled at the same rate.
18. Student concept maps should show materials broken down into substances and mixtures; under substances should be elements and compounds. Under mixtures should be solutions. Solutions should be check-marked, and mixtures underlined.

Performance Assessment

21. Students' research should reflect the role of the silkworm in silk production compared to the industrialized production of synthetic materials. Students could compare the cost, available starting materials, and associated environmental impact. Use **PASC,** p. 135.

Assessment Resources

Reproducible Masters

Chapter Resources Booklet
Chapter Review, pp. 37–38
Chapter Tests, pp. 39–42
Assessment Transparency Activity, p. 49

Glencoe Science Web site
Interactive Tutor
Chapter Quizzes

Glencoe Technology
Assessment Transparency
Interactive CD-ROM Chapter Quizzes
ExamView Pro Test Bank
Vocabulary PuzzleMaker Software
MindJogger Videoquiz DVD/VHS

Standardized Test Practice

Reading Comprehension

QUESTION 1: D

Students must use context clues in the passage to identify the correct answer choice. They should reread the sentences surrounding the underlined word in order to locate these clues. Using context clues, students should be able to identify choice D as the correct choice.

QUESTION 2: H

Students must use information in the passage to identify which answer choice is the best supported conclusion.

- Choice F: No; this is not supported by the passage.
- Choice G: No; this is not supported by the passage.
- Choice H: Yes; this is supported by the passage.
- Choice J: No; this is not supported by the passage.

QUESTION 3: C

Students must use clues in the passage, such as *because it is so rare, medications would need to be made from synthesized Germanium*, in order to identify the correct answer choice.

Teaching Tip

Students should always choose the answer that is best supported by information in the passage.

Standardized Test Practice

Reading Comprehension

Read the passage. Then read each question that follows the passage. Decide which is the best answer to each question.

Medicine and Synthetic Compounds

In the constant battle to develop new treatments for fatal illnesses such as cancer and AIDS, scientists have studied the possibilities provided by synthetic compounds.

Synthetic compounds are man-made, and as a result, can be adapted to suit multiple needs and purposes. For example, a doctor discovered that a rare metalloid, Germanium, improves patients' stamina and endurance. This could increase the quality of life for both cancer and AIDS patients. But because it is so rare, medications would need to be made from synthesized Germanium.

Other research has shown that medicine containing synthetic opiates might be able to limit the growth of the HIV virus as well as limit the development of secondary infections.

Having learned about the effectiveness of synthetic polyanionic compounds in treating cancer and developing antibiotics, a research team is now working to use synthetic polyanionic compounds to treat AIDS.

In addition to these cases, many other studies are being conducted to learn about the medicinal benefits of synthetics. From plastics in computers to non-stick surfaces on our pots and pans, synthetic compounds are assisting our quality of life.

Test-Taking Tip Consider how the title of the passage relates to the main idea of the passage.

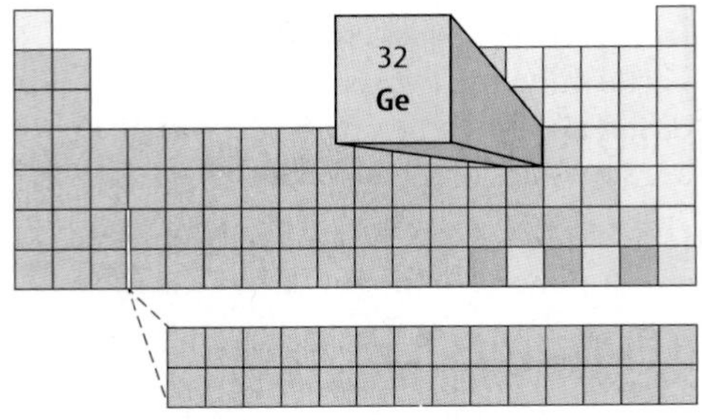

Scientists are studying the medicinal benefits of synthetic Germanium.

1. You can tell from the passage that synthetic means _____.
- **A)** natural
- **B)** rare
- **C)** helpful
- **D)** man-made

2. Based on the information in the passage, the reader can conclude that _____.
- **F)** synthetics are only being studied for their possible medicinal purposes
- **G)** medicines made out of plastic could help cancer and AIDS patients
- **H)** synthetic medicines could improve the quality of life for patients
- **J)** Germanium is a common element found in Earth's crust

3. According to the passage, why would medications need to be made from synthesized Germanium?
- **A)** because natural Germanium is very dangerous
- **B)** because natural Germanium is not as effective as synthesized Germanium
- **C)** because natural Germanium is rare
- **D)** because synthesized Germanium is very hard to produce

Standardized Test Practice

Reasoning and Skills

Read each question and choose the best answer.

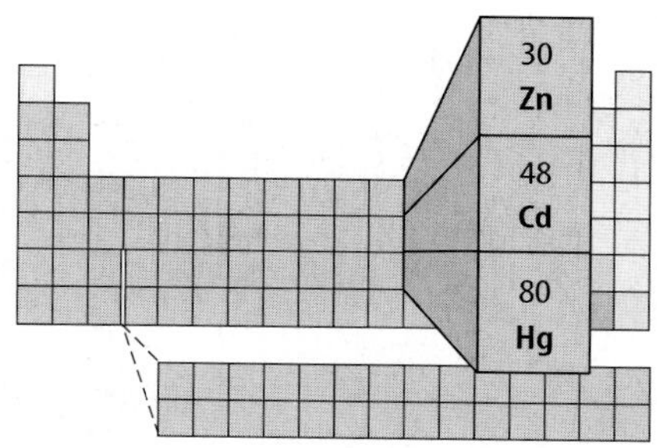

1. Zinc, Cadmium & Mercury are examples of _____.
A) synthetic elements
B) metals
C) nonmetals
D) metalloids

Test-Taking Tip Review the information about groups in the periodic table.

Nutrients Found in Certain Foods	
Food	**Nutrient**
Fruits	Sugars
Pasta, Bread Cookies	Starches
Vegetables	Vitamins & Minerals
Meat & Fish	Cholesterol

2. According to the chart, spaghetti would be a good source of _____.
F) sugars
G) starches
H) vitamins and minerals
J) cholesterol

Test-Taking Tip Review carbohydrates and lipids.

3. Ceramics are made from clay, sand, and/or crystalline rocks. According to this information, which of the following is a ceramic?

A) 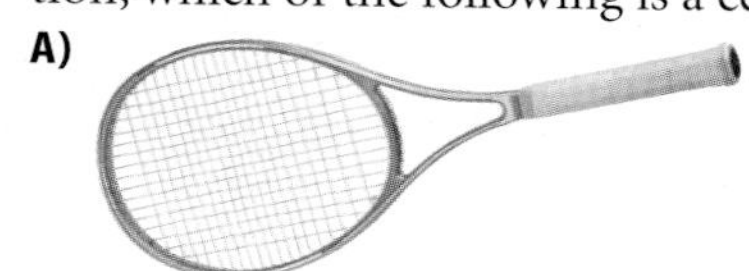

B) 

C)  **D)** 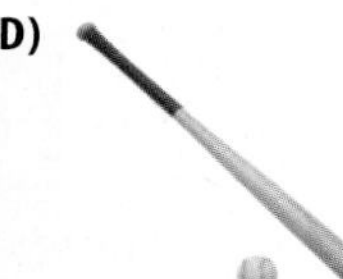

Test-Taking Tip Carefully consider the information in both the graphic and the question before answering the question.

Consider this question carefully before writing your answer on a separate sheet of paper.

4. Spandex, plastic, and Kevlar are all examples of synthetic polymers. Discuss the benefits of developing synthetic polymers.

Test-Taking Tip Review the history and specialized uses of synthetic polymers.

Standardized Test Practice

Reasoning and Skills

Question 1: C

Students must use their understandings of the elements in Group 12 of the periodic table to identify the correct answer choice. Choices A, B, and D do not belong to Group 12. Only choice C belongs to Group 12.

Question 2: G

Student must carefully consider the information in the table in order to identify the correct answer choice.

- Choice F: No; fruits are a source of sugars.
- Choice G: Yes; spaghetti is a source of starches.
- Choice H: No; vegetables are a source of vitamins and minerals.
- Choice J : No; meat and fish are a source of cholesterol.

Question 3: D

Students must carefully read the question to identify which choice is an exception. Choices A, B, and C are all mixtures of two materials and, therefore, are all composites. Only choice D is not a composite.

Question 4: Answers will vary.

Students need to use their understanding of the history and specialized uses of synthetic polymers in order to write a thorough response.

Teaching Tip

Students should review their answers to these practice science questions in preparation for the test.

UNIT 6

Unit Contents

Pre-Reading Activity

Have students recall the difference between physical and chemical changes.

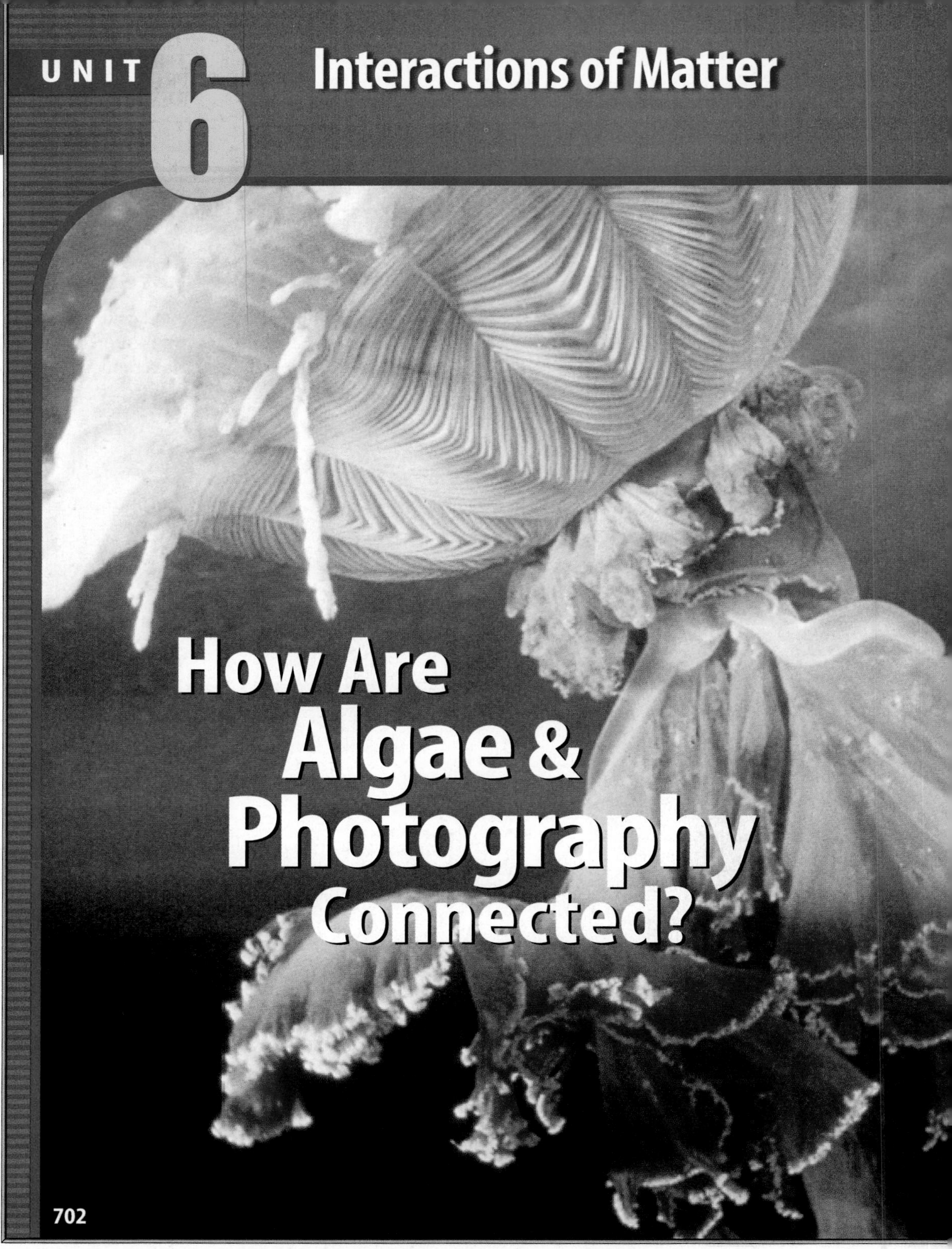

UNIT 6 Interactions of Matter

How Are Algae & Photography Connected?

702

Teacher to Teacher

"Students need to talk while working together during labs, but the noise level can get loud. I solve this problem by playing music during the lab activity. If the students cannot hear the music, they know they are too loud. Believe it or not, this works!"

Catherine C. Walker, Teacher
Martin Middle School
Raleigh, NC

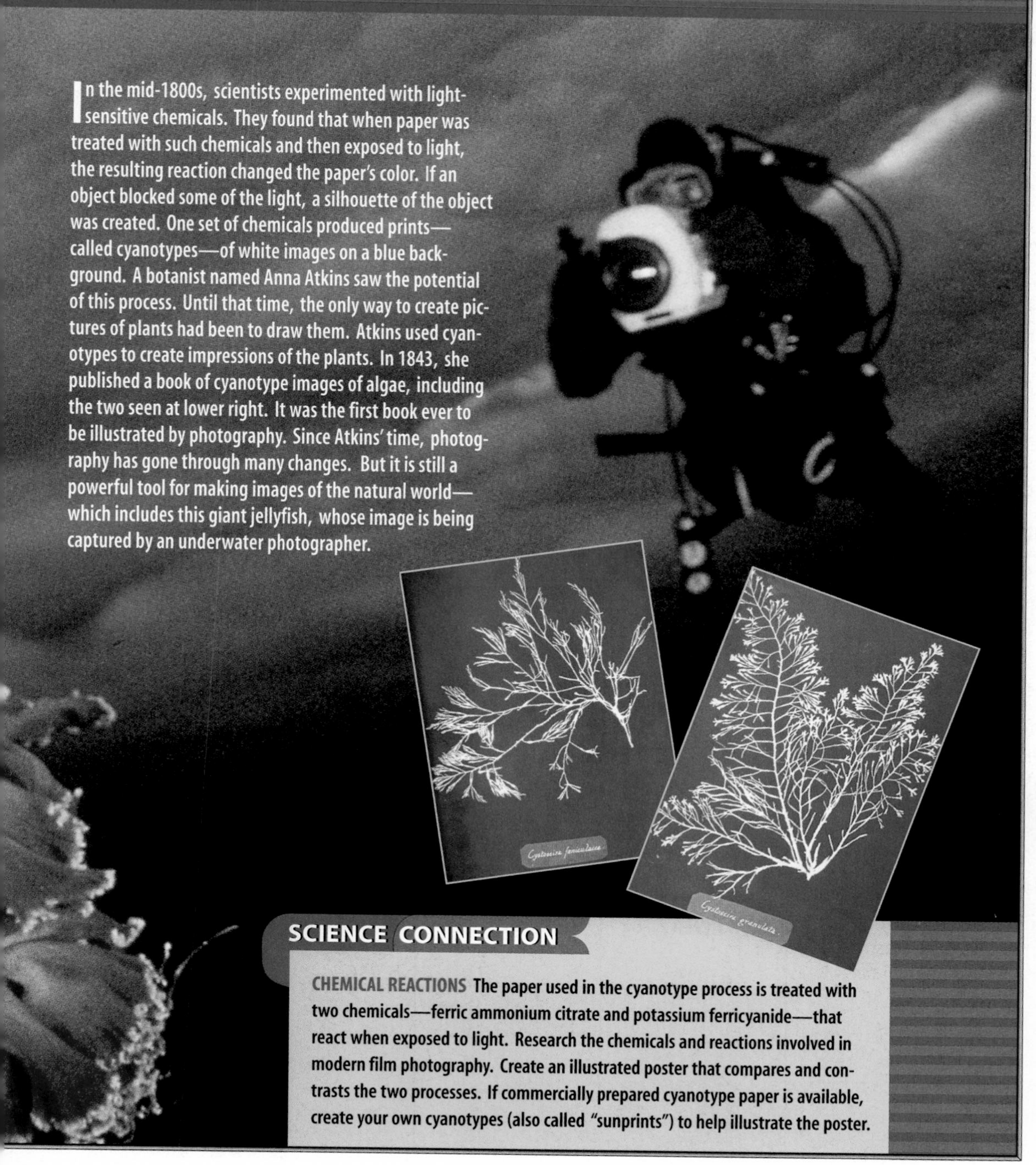

NATIONAL GEOGRAPHIC

In the mid-1800s, scientists experimented with light-sensitive chemicals. They found that when paper was treated with such chemicals and then exposed to light, the resulting reaction changed the paper's color. If an object blocked some of the light, a silhouette of the object was created. One set of chemicals produced prints—called cyanotypes—of white images on a blue background. A botanist named Anna Atkins saw the potential of this process. Until that time, the only way to create pictures of plants had been to draw them. Atkins used cyanotypes to create impressions of the plants. In 1843, she published a book of cyanotype images of algae, including the two seen at lower right. It was the first book ever to be illustrated by photography. Since Atkins' time, photography has gone through many changes. But it is still a powerful tool for making images of the natural world—which includes this giant jellyfish, whose image is being captured by an underwater photographer.

SCIENCE CONNECTION

CHEMICAL REACTIONS The paper used in the cyanotype process is treated with two chemicals—ferric ammonium citrate and potassium ferricyanide—that react when exposed to light. Research the chemicals and reactions involved in modern film photography. Create an illustrated poster that compares and contrasts the two processes. If commercially prepared cyanotype paper is available, create your own cyanotypes (also called "sunprints") to help illustrate the poster.

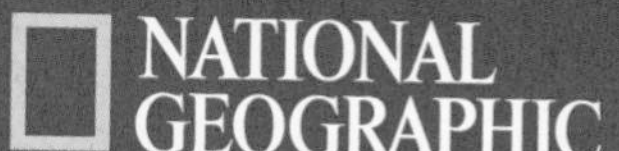

Introducing the Unit

How Are Algae & Photography Connected?

- Students are probably familiar with a specific application of the cyanotype process—blueprints. If any of their families have blueprints of their homes, have students share them with the class.
- Ask students to hypothesize how cyanotypes can be used to photocopy something. The item to be photocopied can be placed over treated paper, then exposed to light. Tell students that this type of copying was first done in the mid-1800s.
- Tell students that they will study many such interactions of matter and energy. All chemical reactions involve energy transfer.

SCIENCE CONNECTION

Activity

Students should determine that both early and modern photographic methods involve exposing photosensitive materials to light. Current photosensitive materials include silver compounds, including silver bromide. Exposure to light reduces the silver ions present to metallic silver.

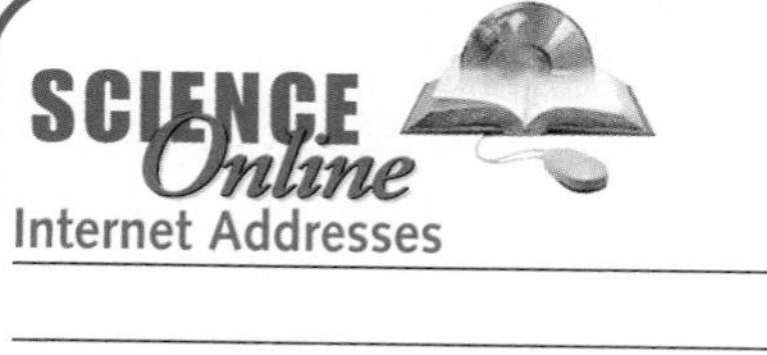

Internet Addresses

Explore the Glencoe Science Web site at **science.glencoe.com** to find out more about topics in this unit.

Section/Objectives	Standards		Activities/Features
	National	State/Local	
Chapter Opener	See p. 37T for a Key to Standards.		**Explore Activity:** Identify the solution by solvent subtraction, p. 705 **Before You Read,** p. 705
Section 1 How Solutions Form 2 sessions 1 block 1. **Identify** three types of solutions. 2. **Determine** how things dissolve. 3. **Examine** the factors that affect the rates at which solids and gases dissolve.	National Content Standards: UCP2, A1, B1 (5–8), B2, B3, B5 (9–12)		**Visualizing Metal Alloys,** p. 708 **MiniLAB:** Observing the Effect of Surface Area, p. 710 **Math Skills Activity:** Calculating Surface Area, p. 711
Section 2 Dissolving Without Water 2 sessions 1 block 1. **Identify** the kinds of solutes that do not dissolve well in water. 2. **Explain** how solvents work. 3. **Determine** how to choose the right solvent for the job.	National Content Standards: UCP2, A1, B1 (5–8), B2, B3, B5 (9–12)		**MiniLAB:** Clinging Molecules, p. 715 **Science Online,** p. 716 **Health Integration,** p. 717
Section 3 Solubility and Concentration 1 session .5 block 1. **Determine** how temperature affects solubility. 2. **Identify** how to express the concentration of solutions. 3. **Compare and contrast** saturated, unsaturated, and supersaturated solutions.	National Content Standards: UCP2, B1 (5–8), B2, B3, B5 (9–12)		
Section 4 Particles in Solution 3 sessions 1.5 blocks 1. **Examine** how solutes break apart in water solutions to form positively and negatively charged particles. 2. **Determine** how some solutions conduct electricity. 3. **Describe** how antifreeze works.	National Content Standards: UCP2, A1, B1 (5–8), B2, B3, B5 (9–12), E2		**Life Science Integration,** p. 725 **Activity:** Boiling Points of Solutions, p. 727 **Activity:** Saturated Solutions, p. 728 **Science Stats:** Weird Solutions, p. 730

Activity Materials	Reproducible Resources	Section Assessment	Technology
Explore Activity: bottled water, 2 different brands of sports drinks, 100-mL beakers (3), hot plate, thermal mitt	**Chapter Resources Booklet** Foldables Worksheet, p. 17 Note-taking Worksheets, pp. 35–37	Glencoe's Assessment Advantage	
MiniLAB: 2 ground sugar cubes, 2 whole sugar cubes, 2 medium-sized glasses, distilled water	**Chapter Resources Booklet** Transparency Activity, p. 46 MiniLAB, p. 3 Enrichment, p. 31 Reinforcement, p. 27 Directed Reading, p. 20 Lab Activity, pp. 9–12	**Portfolio** Science Journal, p. 707 **Performance** MiniLAB, p. 710 Math Skills Activity, p. 711 Skill Builder Activities, p. 712 **Content** Section Assessment, p. 712	Section Focus Transparency Interactive CD-ROM/DVD Guided Reading Audio Program
MiniLAB: 2 clean pennies, paper towel, water, dropper, rubbing alcohol	**Chapter Resources Booklet** Transparency Activity, p. 47 MiniLAB, p. 4 Enrichment, p. 32 Reinforcement, p. 28 Directed Reading, p. 21	**Portfolio** Health Integration, p. 716 **Performance** MiniLAB, p. 715 Skill Builder Activities, p. 717 **Content** Section Assessment, p. 717	Section Focus Transparency Interactive CD-ROM/DVD Guided Reading Audio Program
Need materials? Contact Science Kit at 1-800-828-7777 or www.sciencekit.com on the Internet.	**Chapter Resources Booklet** Transparency Activity, p. 48 Transparency Activity, pp. 51–52 Enrichment, p. 33 Reinforcement, p. 29 Directed Reading, p. 20 Lab Activity, pp. 13–16	**Portfolio** Science Journal, p.719 **Performance** Skill Builder Activities, p. 722 **Content** Section Assessment, p. 722	Section Focus Transparency Teaching Transparency Interactive CD-ROM/DVD Guided Reading Audio Program
Activity: distilled water, thermometer, 72 g salt, ring stand, hot plate, 250-mL beaker **Activity:** distilled water, large test tubes, thermometer, table sugar, copper wire stirrer (bent into a spiral), test-tube holder, 10-mL graduated cylinder, 250-mL beaker, 150 mL water, hot plate, test-tube rack, ring stand	**Chapter Resources Booklet** Transparency Activity, p. 49 Enrichment, p. 34 Reinforcement, p. 30 Directed Reading, pp. 20, 22 Activity Worksheet, pp. 5–6, 7–8	**Portfolio** Science Journal, p. 725 **Performance** Skill Builder Activities, p. 726 **Content** Section Assessment, p. 726	Section Focus Transparency Interactive CD-ROM/DVD Guided Reading Audio Program

End of Chapter Assessment

Glencoe's Assessment Advantage

Blackline Masters	Technology	Professional Series
Chapter Resources Booklet Chapter Review, pp. 39–40 Chapter Tests, pp. 41–44 **Standardized Test Practice by The Princeton Review,** pp. 96–99	MindJogger Videoquiz CD-ROM Explorations and Quizzes Vocabulary Puzzle Makers ExamView Pro Test Bank Interactive Lesson Planner Interactive Teacher's Edition	Performance Assessment in the Science Classroom (PASC)

Transparencies

Section Focus

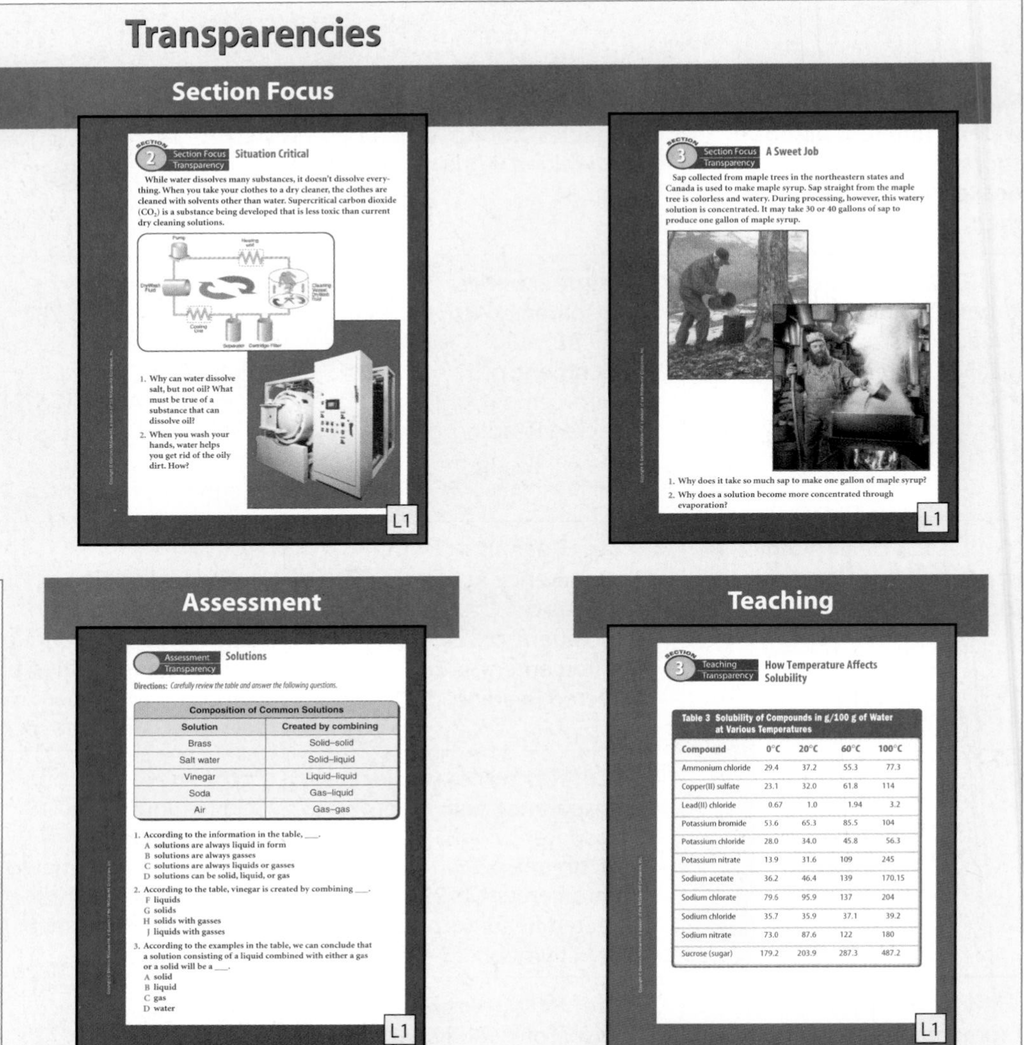

Assessment

Teaching

This is a representation of key blackline masters available in the Teacher Classroom Resources. See Resource Manager boxes within the chapter for additional information.

Key to Teaching Strategies

The following designations will help you decide which activities are appropriate for your students.

L1 Level 1 activities should be appropriate for students with learning difficulties.

L2 Level 2 activities should be within the ability range of all students.

L3 Level 3 activities are designed for above-average students.

ELL ELL activities should be within the ability range of English Language Learners.

COOP LEARN Cooperative Learning activities are designed for small group work.

LS Multiple Learning Styles logos are used throughout to indicate strategies that address different learning styles.

P These strategies represent student products that can be placed into a best-work portfolio.

Hands-on Activities

Activity Worksheets

Laboratory Activities

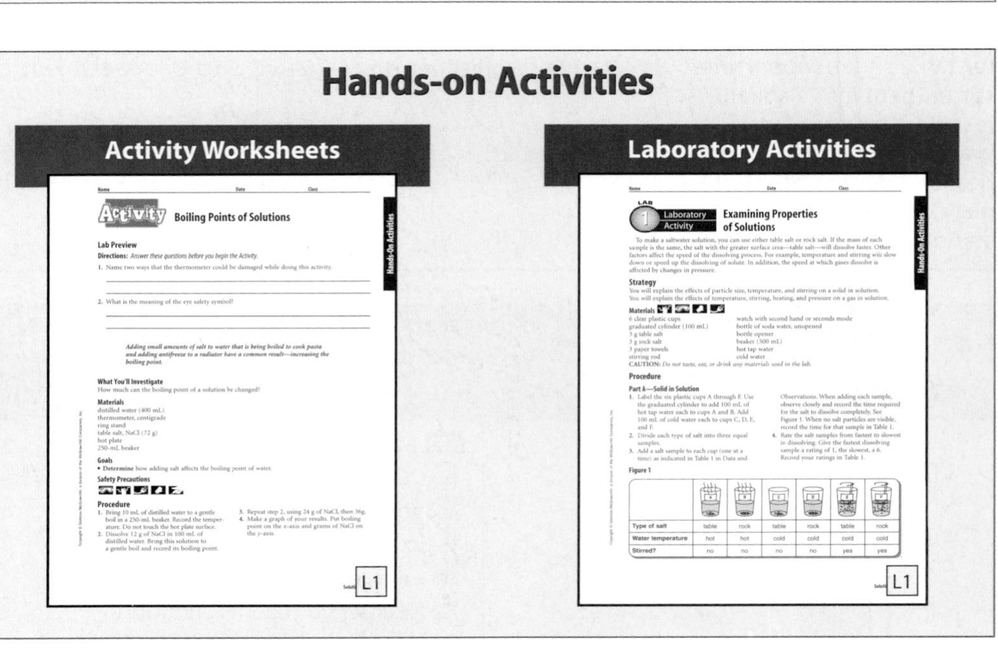

Meeting Different Ability Levels

Content Outline

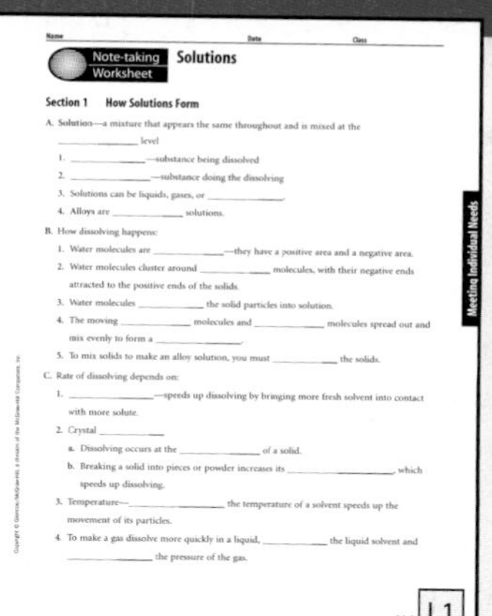

Reinforcement

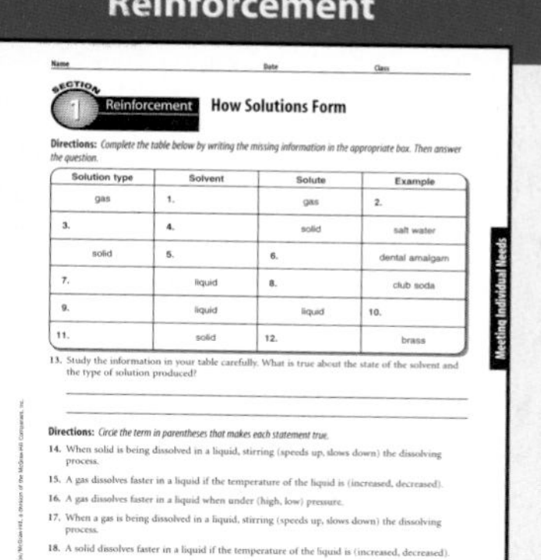

Directed Reading

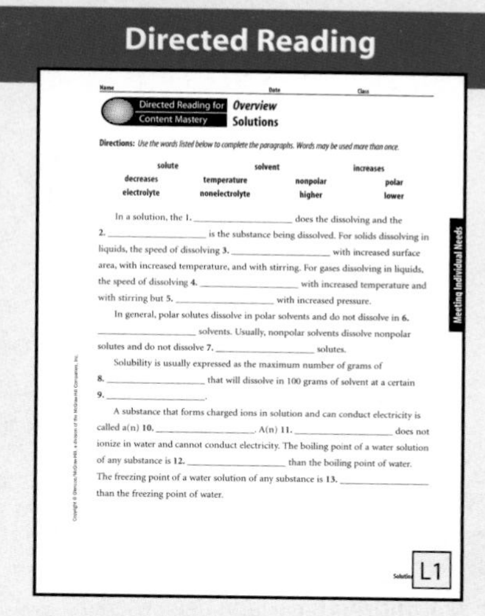

Enrichment

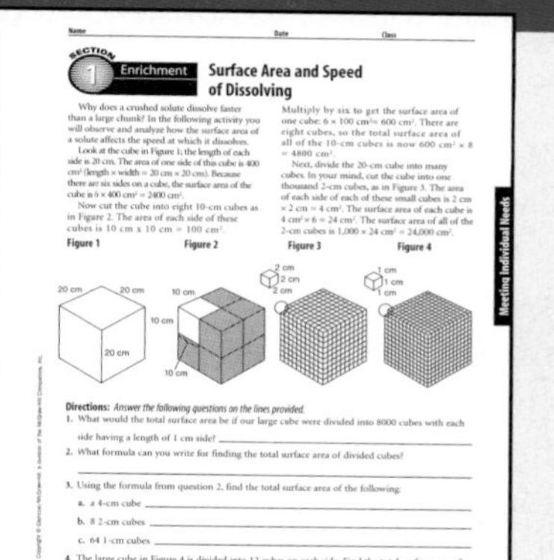

Spanish Directed Reading

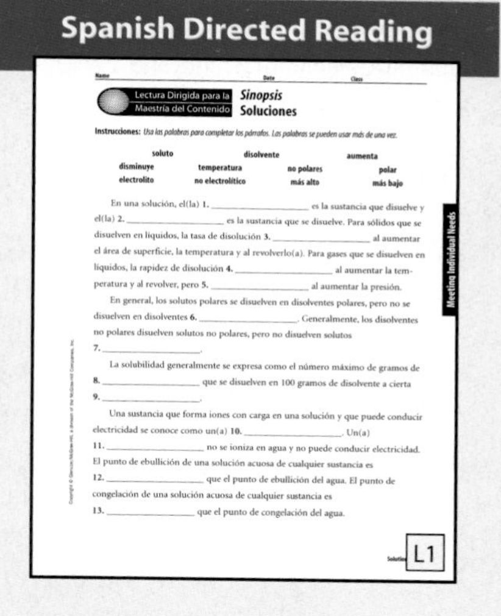

Assessment

Chapter Tests

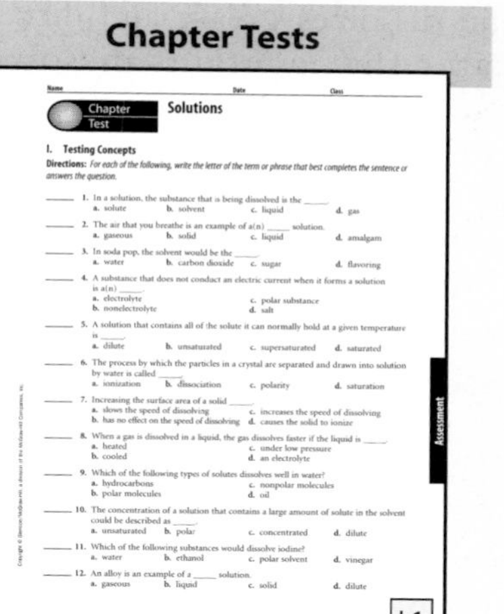

Test Practice Workbook

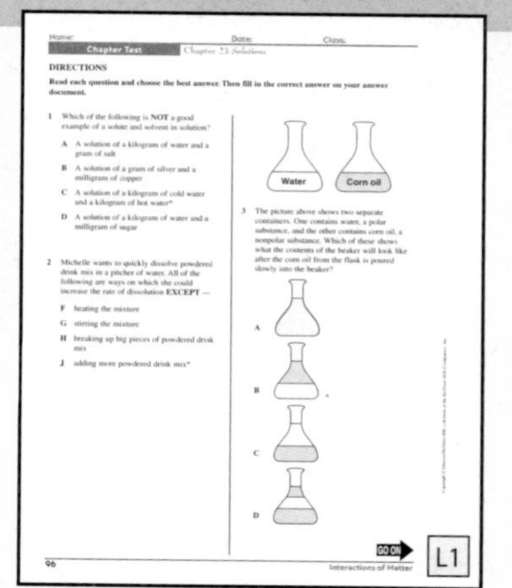

Chapter Review

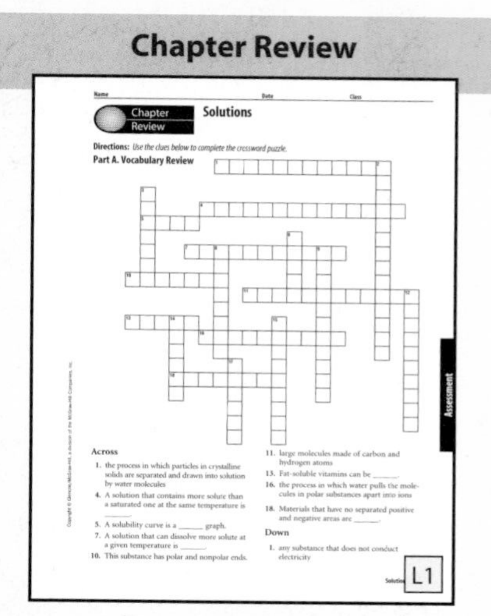

Science Content Background

SECTION 1 How Solutions Form

What is a solution?

Attractive forces between the atoms, ions, or molecules of a substance hold liquid and solid substances together. When a substance is surrounded by a solvent, particles of the substance may be attracted to the solvent molecules by various forces. If the attractive forces of the solvent molecules are strong enough to overcome the internal attractive forces of the solute, the substance will be soluble to some extent. A substance with an extremely low solubility is usually said to be insoluble.

Fun Fact

Moisturizers have long been used to protect and rehydrate the skin. These products contain compounds called humectants and emollients that increase the water content of the skin in different ways. Humectants add water to the skin by attracting water vapor from the air. Emollients cover the skin with a layer of material that is immiscible with water. This prevents water from within the skin from evaporating.

Dissolving

The process of dissolving, called dissolution, involves energy. Energy is absorbed when the structure of a molecular solid or liquid is broken down or the ions of an ionic crystal are separated. Energy is released when the particles of solute form new bonds with the solvent. In the cold packs used by athletic trainers, more energy is absorbed in the first part of the dissolution process than released in the second. For that reason, the overall process is endothermic, and the liquid becomes colder.

SECTION 2 Dissolving Without Water

Useful Nonpolar Molecules

One nonpolar solvent with which many people are familiar is turpentine, which is used to dissolve oil-based paint. Turpentine is made up of a mixture of cyclic monoterpene hydrocarbons with the molecular formula C10H16. About 85 percent of the turpentine made in the United States is sulfate turpentine, produced in the process that converts wood from longleaf and slash pines into pulp.

The molecules contained in soap and detergent have both a polar and a nonpolar end. The polar end makes them soluble in water while the nonpolar end dissolves grease and dirt. In hard water, water that contains dissolved calcium and magnesium salts, ordinary soap reacts with the calcium and magnesium ions to form an insoluble greasy scum. Detergents, however, do not form precipitates with hard water and have excellent cleaning ability. Hard water is also undesirable because it causes "scale" to form on the walls of water heaters, teakettles, coffee pots, and irons, which greatly reduces their efficiency. Hard water can be "softened" by distillation, precipitating the calcium and magnesium, ion exchange, and demineralization.

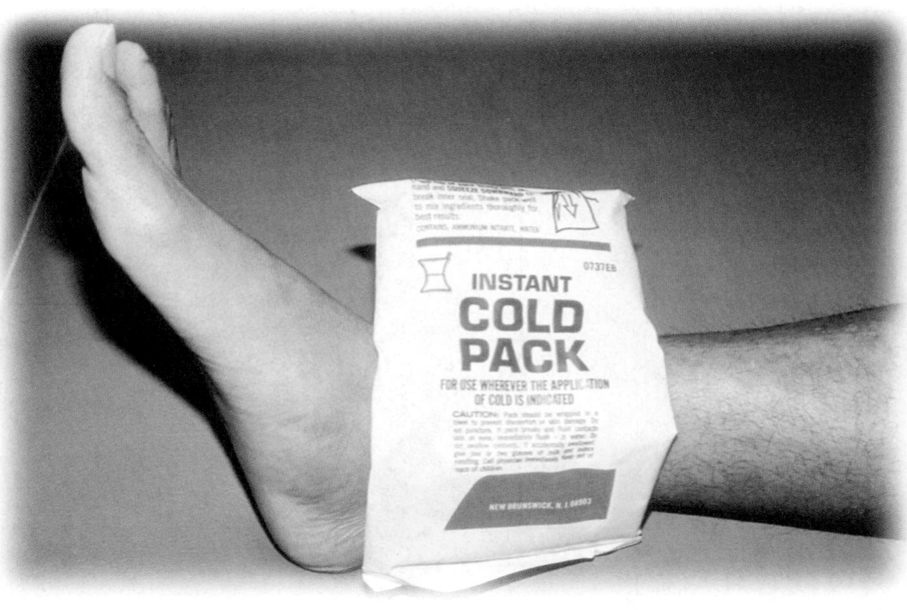

David R. Frazier/Photo Researchers, Inc.

SECTION 3

Solubility and Concentration

Types of Solutions

A solution is saturated when equilibrium between the undissolved solute and dissolved solute is established at a particular temperature. It is important to state the temperature of a saturated solution. This is because a solution that is saturated at one temperature may not be saturated at another temperature. In the state known as solution equilibrium, the solute is dissolving into the solution and coming our of solution at exactly the same rate.

If a solution contains more dissolved solute than it usually can hold at a given temperature, the solution is supersaturated. Supersaturated solutions are unstable and disturbances such as jarring, stirring, scratching the walls of the container, or dropping in a "seed" crystal cause the solution to return to the saturated state.

Particles in Solution

Particles With a Charge

It was the British scientists William Nicholson and Anthony Carlisle who in 1800 first used electricity to decompose aqueous solutions of common salts, thus producing electrolytes. It was Michael Faraday (1791–1867) who first used the term *electrolyte*, as well as the terms *ion*, *cation*, *anion*, *cathode*, *anode*, and *electrode*. In 1884, Svante Arrhenius (1859–1927) introduced the idea that salt ions dissociate as soon as they are dissolved in water, without the aid of electrical current.

Fun Fact

Compounds that absorb water are useful as drying agents and are called desiccants. Bags of drying agents are often enclosed in packages containing iron or steel parts to absorb moisture and prevent rusting. Magnesium sulfate, sodium sulfate, calcium sulfate, and silica gel are some of the compounds commonly used for drying liquids and gases that contain small amounts of moisture.

For additional content background on this topic, go to the Glencoe Science Web site at science.glencoe.com.

CHAPTER 23

Solutions

Chapter Vocabulary

solution
solute
solvent
alloy
polar
nonpolar
solubility
saturated solution
unsaturated solution
supersaturated solution
ion
electrolyte
ionization
nonelectrolyte
dissociation

What do you think?

Science Journal This photograph shows a precipitate of sodium acetate coming out of a supersaturated solution. This phenomenon is explained in the caption for **Figure 15.**

CHAPTER 23

Solutions

What do lemonade, seawater, and suntan lotion have in common? Not only are they all liquids, they are all solutions. In this chapter, you will learn about solutions—how they form and why some form faster than others. You'll learn why something like lemon juice forms a solution with water while something like suntan lotion does not. In addition, you'll learn about the properties of some solutions and how you apply them to your everyday life.

What do you think?

Science Journal Look at the picture below with a classmate. Discuss what you think this might be or what is happening. Here's a hint: *It's not snow, but it's closer to snow than you realize.* Write your best guess in your Science Journal.

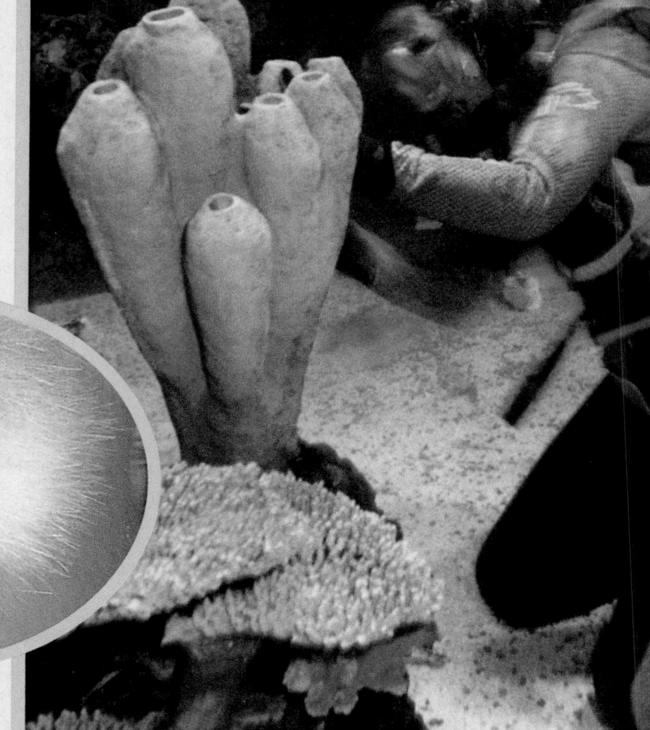

704

Theme Connection

Systems and Interactions Solutions are systems whose properties are determined by the interactions between the molecules or ions of the solute and the molecules or ions of the solvent.

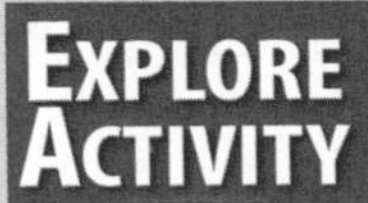

What do you like to drink when you're thirsty? Do you prefer water from the faucet, bottled water, or a sports drink that contains substances added to replace those lost during sweating? What do these thirst quenchers contain? Try the following activity to find out.

Identify the solution by solvent subtraction

1. Obtain three solution samples from your teacher and place equal amounts of all three in separate, marked 100-mL beakers.
2. Carefully, boil each solution on a hot plate. As soon as the liquid is gone, remove each beaker to a heat-proof surface using a thermal mitt. Let cool.
3. Examine the inside of your cooled beakers. What do you see? Try to guess the identity of the three solutions.

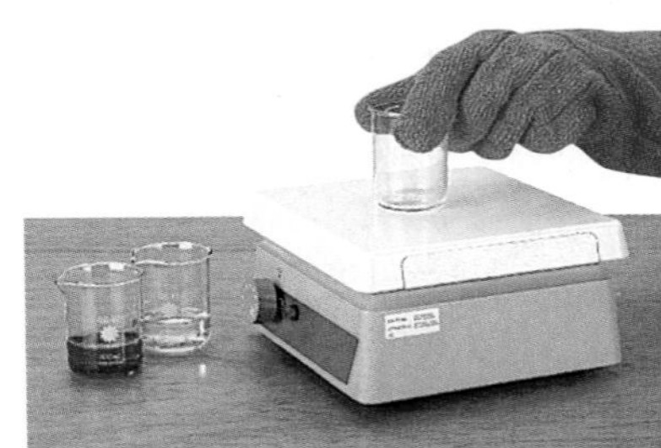

Observe

Describe in your Science Journal what remained in each of the three containers and explain how solutions may look alike but contain different substances.

Before You Read

FOLDABLES Reading & Study Skills

Making a Venn Diagram Study Fold Make the following Foldable to compare and contrast the characteristics of solvents and solutes.

Solvents | Both | Solutes

1. Place a sheet of paper in front of you so the short side is at the top. Fold the paper in half from top to bottom.
2. Fold both sides in to divide the paper into thirds. Unfold the paper so three sections show.
3. Through the top thickness of paper, cut along each of the fold lines to the topfold, forming three tabs. Label each tab *Solvents, Both,* and *Solutes* as shown.
4. Draw circles across the front of the paper as shown. Before you read the chapter, define the terms and list characteristics of each under their tabs.

Explore Activity

Purpose Students will investigate the solid solute content of liquid samples. L2 ELL

LS **Visual-Spatial**

Preparation Purchase samples of bottled water and common sports drinks.

Materials three small beakers per group, hot plate, oven mitt

Teaching Strategy Display the labels of the bottled water and sports drink. Ask students to note the amounts of dissolved solutes.

Observe

Results will vary depending on the minerals dissolved in local tap water and the bottled water and sports drinks used. The sports drink will likely produce the most precipitate, which will have a dark color. Because solutes are dissolved, it is impossible to tell by looking at a solution how much solute is present.

Assessment

Process Show two types of sweetened drinks. Ask students how they might decide which had the most dissolved solute without heating the samples. Determine the density of both. The one with more dissolved solute is denser. Use **Performance Assessment in the Science Classroom,** p. 95.

Before You Read

FOLDABLES Reading & Study Skills

Dinah Zike Study Fold

Purpose Have students define terms and list what they already know about solutions and how they are formed. Students use their Venn diagram Foldable to collect information and examples as they read the chapter.

For additional help, see Foldables Worksheet, p. 17 in **Chapter Resources Booklet,** or go to the Glencoe Science Web site at **science.glencoe.com.** See After You Read in the Study Guide at the end of this chapter.

SECTION

How Solutions Form

1 Motivate

Bellringer Transparency

Display the Section Focus Transparency for Section 1. Use the accompanying Transparency Activity Master. L2 ELL

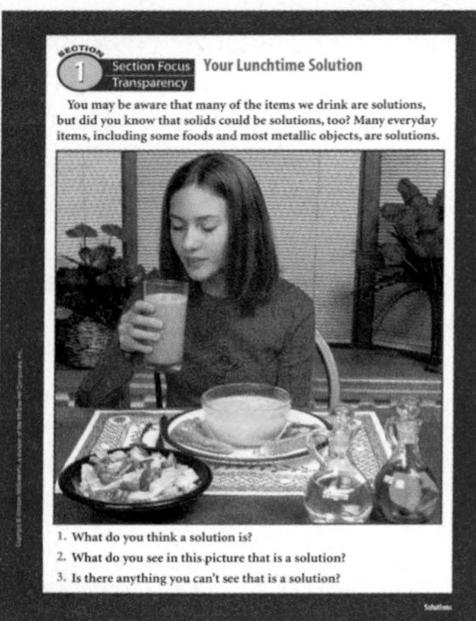

Section Focus Transparency 1
Your Lunchtime Solution
You may be aware that many of the items we drink are solutions, but did you know that solids could be solutions, too? Many everyday items, including some foods and most metallic objects, are solutions.
1. What do you think a solution is?
2. What do you see in this picture that is a solution?
3. Is there anything you can't see that is a solution?

Tie to Prior Knowledge

Have students recall what they know about heterogeneous and homogeneous mixtures. In a homogeneous mixture, the particles are distributed evenly throughout. In a heterogeneous mixture, the mixed materials are not distributed evenly. A solution is a homogeneous mixture in which the particles are distributed evenly at the molecular or ionic level.

SECTION

How Solutions Form

As You Read

***What* You'll Learn**

- **Identify** three types of solutions.
- **Determine** how things dissolve.
- **Examine** the factors that affect the rates at which solids and gases dissolve in liquids.

Vocabulary

solution
solute
solvent
alloy
polar

***Why* It's Important**

Many chemical reactions take place in solution—the food you eat is digested, or chemically changed, in the solution that is in your stomach.

What is a solution?

Hummingbirds are fascinating creatures. They can hover for long periods while they sip nectar from flowers through their long beaks. To attract hummingbirds, many people use feeder bottles containing a red liquid. The liquid is a solution of sugar and red food coloring in water.

Suppose you are making some hummingbird food. When you add sugar to water and stir, the sugar crystals disappear. When you add a few drops of red food coloring and stir, the color spreads evenly throughout the sugar water. Why does this happen?

Hummingbird food is one of many solutions. A **solution** is a mixture that has the same composition, color, density, and even taste throughout. The reason you no longer see the sugar crystals and the reason the red dye spreads out evenly is that they have formed a completely homogeneous mixture. The sugar crystals broke up into sugar molecules, the red dye into its molecules, and both mixed evenly among the water molecules.

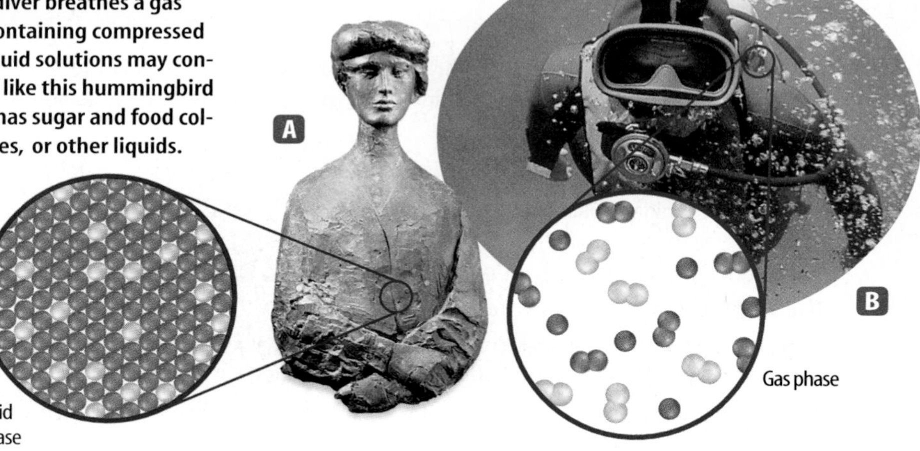

A
B
Solid phase
Gas phase

Figure 1
Three phases of solutions exist—solid, gas, and liquid. A Bronze is a solid solution of copper and tin. B A diver breathes a gas solution containing compressed air. C Liquid solutions may contain solids like this hummingbird food that has sugar and food coloring, gases, or other liquids.

Section Assessment Planner

PORTFOLIO
Science Journal, p. 707

PERFORMANCE ASSESSMENT
MiniLAB, p. 710
Math Skills Activity, p. 711
Skill Builder Activities, p. 712
See page 734 for more options.

CONTENT ASSESSMENT
Section, p. 712
Challenge, p. 712
Chapter, pp. 734–735

Solutes and Solvents

To describe a solution, you may say that one substance is dissolved in another. The substance being dissolved is the **solute,** and the substance doing the dissolving is the **solvent.** When a solid dissolves in a liquid, the solid is the solute and the liquid is the solvent. Thus, in salt water, salt is the solute and water is the solvent. In carbonated soft drinks, carbon dioxide gas is one of the solutes and water is the solvent. When a liquid dissolves in another liquid, the substance present in the larger amount is usually called the solvent.

Reading Check *How do you know which substance is the solute in a solution?*

Solutions can also be gaseous or even solid. Examples of all three solution phases are shown in **Figure 1.** Did you know that the air you breathe is a solution? In fact, all mixtures of gases are solutions. Air is a solution of 78 percent nitrogen, 20 percent oxygen, and small amounts of other gases such as argon, carbon dioxide and hydrogen. The sterling silver and brass used in musical instruments is an example of a solid solution. The sterling silver contains 92.5 percent silver and 7.5 percent copper. The brass is a solution of copper and zinc metals. Solid solutions are known as **alloys.** They are made by melting the metal solute and solvent together. Most coins, as shown in **Figure 2,** are alloys.

C

2 Teach

What is a solution?

Quick Demo

Partially fill a petri dish with water and place it on the overhead projector. Place a crystal of potassium permanganate in the water. The purple color will stream out from the crystal as it dissolves. L1 ELL
LS **Visual-Spatial**

Activity

Have students stir table salt into 50 mL of water until no more salt dissolves. Then have them add 5 mL of powdered chalk and stir again. Have them pour the liquid through filter paper. They should observe the chalk on the filter paper. Have them evaporate the filtered liquid and observe the residue remaining (salt). Explain that if filter paper can separate a substance out of a liquid, the substance was not dissolved. The chalk did not dissolve; the salt did. L2 ELL LS **Visual-Spatial**

Solutes and Solvents

Teacher FYI

Steel is an alloy of mostly iron with various other metals and semimetals added. Chromium, carbon, and nickel are solutes added to molten iron, which is cooled to make an alloy.

Resource Manager

Chapter Resources Booklet

Transparency Activity, p. 46
Note-taking Worksheets, pp. 35–37
Directed Reading for Content Mastery, p. 20

Science Journal

Everyday Solvents and Solutes Have students recall that solvents and solutes are all around them. Ask them to list in their Science Journals solvents and solutes they encounter in their daily lives. Their bodies contain solutes dissolved in water. Paint thinner, alcohol, spot removers, and nail polish remover are all solvents that do not contain water. L2
LS **Linguistic** P

Reading Check

Answer It is the substance being dissolved and is usually the substance that is present in the lesser amount.

NATIONAL GEOGRAPHIC

Visualizing Metal Alloys

Have students examine the pictures and read the captions. Then ask the following questions.

- **Why is it necessary for vending machines to be able to recognize a coin by its size, weight, and electrical conductivity?** All three properties are difficult to duplicate in counterfeit coins or slugs.
- **Look at the photograph of the two types of dollars. Do they appear to be made from the same alloy?** No, the Susan B. Anthony dollar appears to be made of a material such as nickel or silver that is silver in color. The Sacagawea dollar is copper in color similar to the element copper.

Activity

Have students find the composition of the Susan B. Anthony dollar and construct circle graphs for the Susan B. Anthony dollar similar to the one shown in the text for the Sacagawea dollar. L2

LS **Logical-Mathematical**

Extension

Challenge students to find out how vending machines check the size, weight, and electrical conductivity of coins. Have students report their findings to their class. L3 LS **Linguistic**

Figure 2

Have you ever accidentally put a non-United States coin into a vending machine? Of course, the vending machine didn't accept it. If a vending machine is that selective, how can it be fooled by two coins that look and feel very different? This is exactly the case with the silver Susan B. Anthony dollar and the new golden Sacagawea dollar. Vending machines can't tell them apart.

Vending machines recognize coins by size, weight, and electrical conductivity. The size and weight of the Susan B. Anthony coin were easy to copy. Copying the coin's electrical conductivity was more difficult.

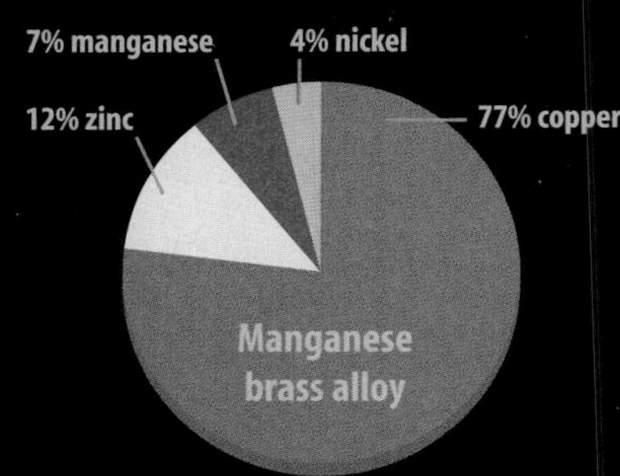

The dollar's copper core is half the coin's thickness. It is sandwiched between two layers of manganese brass alloy.

Over 30,000 samples of coin coatings were tested to find an alloy and thickness that would copy the conductivity of the Susan B. Anthony dollar. The final composition of the alloy is shown in the graph above. The key ingredient? Manganese.

708 CHAPTER 23

Resource Manager

Chapter Resources Booklet
Enrichment, p. 31
Lab Activity, pp. 9–12

Reading and Writing Skill Activities, p. 17

Dissolving

Fruit drinks and sports drinks are examples of solutions made by dissolving solids in liquids. Like hummingbird food, both contain sugar as well as other substances that add color and flavor. How do solids such as sugar dissolve in water?

The dissolving of a solid in a liquid occurs at the surface of the solid. To understand how water solutions form, keep in mind two things you have learned about water. Like the particles of any substance, water molecules are constantly moving. Also, water molecules are **polar,** which means they have a positive area and a negative area. Molecules of sugar are also polar.

How It Happens **Figure 3** shows molecules of sugar dissolving in water. First, in **Figure 3A,** water molecules cluster around sugar molecules with their negative ends attracted to the positive ends of the sugar. Then, in **Figure 3B,** the water molecules pull the sugar molecules into solution. Finally, in **Figure 3C,** the water molecules and the sugar molecules mix evenly, forming a solution.

Reading Check *How do water molecules help sugar molecules dissolve?*

The process described in **Figure 3** repeats as layer after layer of sugar molecules moves away from the crystal, until all the molecules are evenly spread out. The same three steps occur for any solid solute dissolving in a liquid solvent.

Dissolving Liquids and Gases A similar but more complex process takes place when a gas dissolves in a liquid. Particles of liquids and gases move much more freely than do particles of solids. When gases dissolve in gases or when liquids dissolve in liquids, this movement spreads solutes evenly throughout the solvent.

Dissolving Solids in Solids How can you mix solids to make alloys? Although solid particles do move a little, this movement is not enough to spread them evenly throughout the mixture. The solid metals are first melted and then mixed together. In this liquid state, the metal atoms can spread out evenly and will remain mixed when cooled.

Figure 3
The dissolving of sugar in water can be thought of as a three-step process.

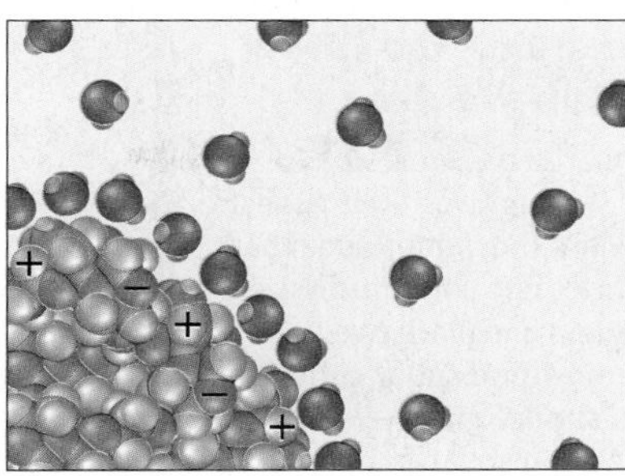

A **The moving water molecules cluster around the sugar molecules as their negative ends are attracted to the positive ends of the sugar molecules.**

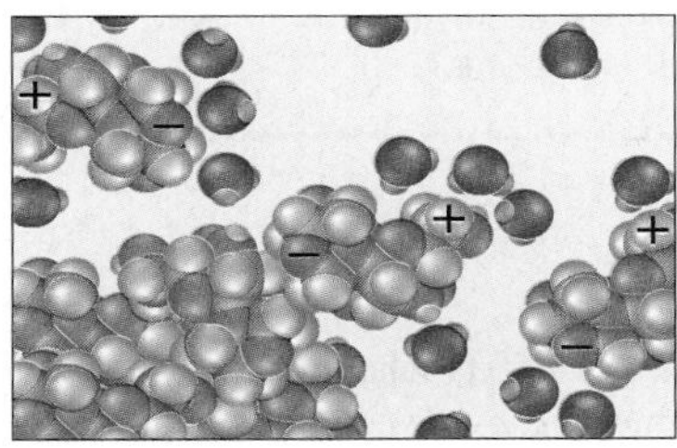

B **The water molecules pull the sugar molecules into solution.**

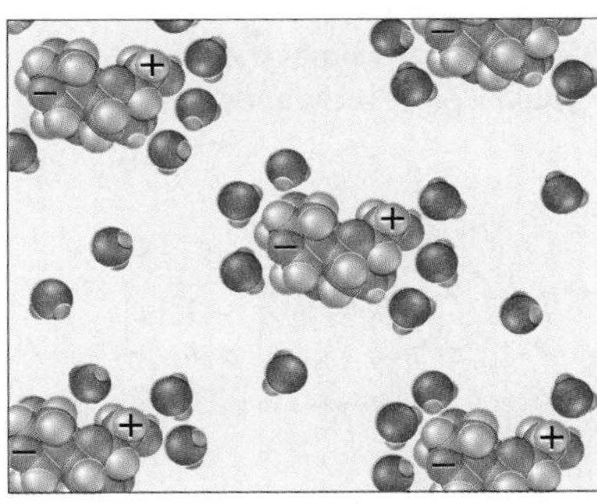

C **The water molecules and sugar molecules spread out to form a homogeneous mixture.**

Dissolving

Visual Learning

Figure 3 Place a box of styrofoam spheres in the center of a group of students who have linked arms. Tell students that they are solvent particles and the spheres are solute particles. In order for a sphere to dissove, it must be held by a student. Discuss the three dissolving steps presented on the page. Then have students act out the steps with the spheres as you call out Step 1, Step 2, and Step 3. The activity can also be used to discuss the advantage of making the solute more available by stirring it among the solvent particles. L2 ELL
LS **Kinesthetic**

Reading Check

Answer The negative ends of the water molecules pull on the positive ends of sugar molecules.

Quick Demo

To show the polarity of water, blow up a balloon and rub its surface with a wool cloth or piece of fur. Turn on the water faucet so it delivers a thin steady stream. Bring the statically charged balloon near the stream, but do not touch the balloon to it. Have students observe that the stream bends dramatically. L2 ELL
LS **Visual-Spatial**

Cultural Diversity

Sandbox Trees The sap from the tall sandbox trees, found in the jungles of Central and South America, is acidic. Fishermen throw this sap into lakes and streams, which have been dammed, to stun the fish so they can gather them for food. Then, they remove the dams. The sap becomes sufficiently dilute, and the fish recover completely.

Inclusion Strategies

Learning Disabled As you do the various demonstrations, help students follow what you are doing by moving slowly and deliberately through each step and explaining what you are doing as you do it. Make sure all students can see what you do and can see the results. Make sure you describe the results to the class. L1 ELL **Auditory-Musical**

Rate of Dissolving

Purpose Students observe differences in the rates of dissolution of crushed and uncrushed sugar cubes. L2

ELL LS **Visual-Spatial**

Materials four sugar cubes, distilled water, two glasses, two stirring rods per group

Teaching Strategy Have students do the activity twice, once stirring the sugar and once not stirring. Stirring increases rate of dissolving.

Analysis

1. The granules dissolved faster than the cubes when they were treated identically.
2. The greater the surface area of the solute, the faster it dissolves.

Oral Have students use their MiniLAB results and Figure 4 to explain how the surface area of the two cubes increases when they are ground. Use **PASC,** p. 89.

Discussion

Discuss with students how rapidly surface area increases as an object is divided into smaller pieces. Have students calculate the surface area of a 2-cm cube. $6 \times 4\text{ cm}^2 = 24\text{ cm}^2$ Ask students to predict how much larger the surface area would be if the cube were divided into 1-cm cubes. **How many 1-cm cubes would there be?** 8 **What is their surface area?** $8 \times 6 \times 1\text{ cm}^2 = 48\text{ cm}^2$

Mini LAB

Observing the Effect of Surface Area

Procedure

1. Grind up two **sugar cubes.**
2. Place the ground sugar particles into a **medium-sized glass** and place two **unground sugar cubes** into a **similar glass.**
3. Add an equal amount of **distilled water** at room temperature to each glass.

Analysis

1. Compare the times required to dissolve each.
2. What do you conclude about the dissolving rate and surface area?

Rate of Dissolving

How can you speed up the dissolving process? Think about how you make a drink from a powdered mix. After you add the mix to water, you stir it. Stirring a solution speeds up dissolving because it brings more fresh solvent into contact with more solute. The fresh solvent attracts the particles of solute, causing the solid solute to dissolve faster.

Crystal Size A second way to speed the dissolving of a solid in a liquid is to grind large crystals into smaller ones. Suppose you have to use a 5-g crystal of rock candy to sweeten your lemonade. If you put the whole crystal into a glass of lemonade, it might take several minutes to dissolve, even with stirring. However, if you first grind the crystal of rock candy into a powder, it will dissolve in the same amount of lemonade in a few seconds.

Why does breaking up a solid cause it to dissolve faster? Breaking the solid into smaller pieces greatly increases its surface area, as you can see in **Figure 4.** Because dissolving takes place at the surface of the solid, increasing the surface area allows more solvent to come into contact with more solid solute. Therefore, the speed of the dissolving process increases.

Temperature A third way to increase the rate at which most solids dissolve is to increase the temperature of the solvent. Think about making hot chocolate from a mix. You can make the sugar in the chocolate mix dissolve faster by putting it in hot water instead of cold water. Increasing the temperature of a solvent speeds up the movement of its particles. This increase causes more solvent particles to bump into the solute. As a result, solute particles break loose and dissolve faster.

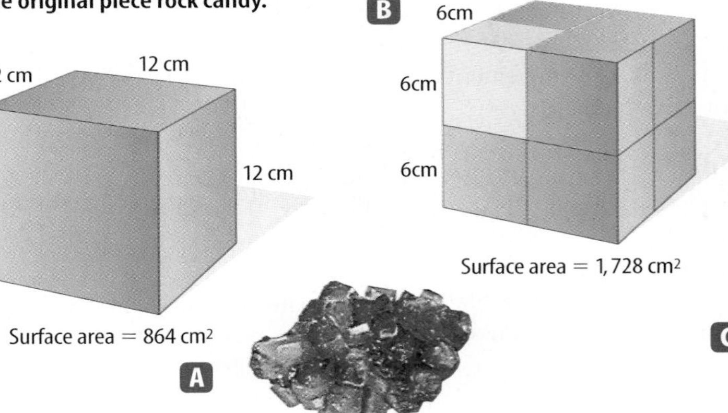

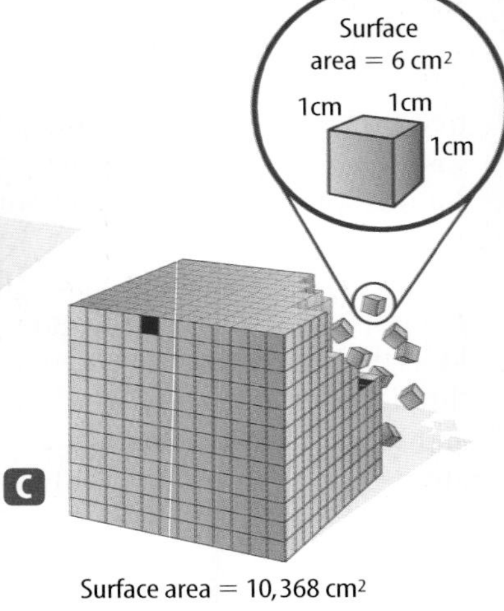

Figure 4
Crystal size affects solubility.
A **Large crystals of sugar called rock candy dissolve in water slowly because the surface area is limited.** **B** **Crushing the crystal increases its surface area.**
C **Further crushing produces a surface area many times that of the original piece rock candy.**

Active Reading

Quickwrites Let students spontaneously discover what they already know about solutions, solvents, and solutes. Have students list their ideas and thoughts about these topics freely in a paragraph. Then, during or after a learning experience, share those ideas and thoughts with the class.

Math Skills Activity

Calculating Surface Area

Example Problem

The length, height, and width of a cube are each 1 cm. If the cube is cut in half to form two rectangular solids, what is the total surface area of the new pieces?

Solution

1. *This is what you know:*
   The cube has dimensions of $l = h = w = 1$ cm.
   The rectangular solid has a width $w = 0.5$ cm.
   The rectangular solid has length and height $l = h = 1$ cm each.
2. *This is what you want to find:* The total surface area of the two rectangular solids
3. *Here is how you get the equation you need:* The cube and the rectangular solid have six faces.

   Front and back = $(h \times w)$
   Left and right = $(h \times l)$
   Top and bottom = $(w \times l)$
   The total surface area of the cube or the rectangular solid is the sum of these areas, or
   $2(h \times w) + 2(h \times l) + 2(w \times l)$ = total surface area.

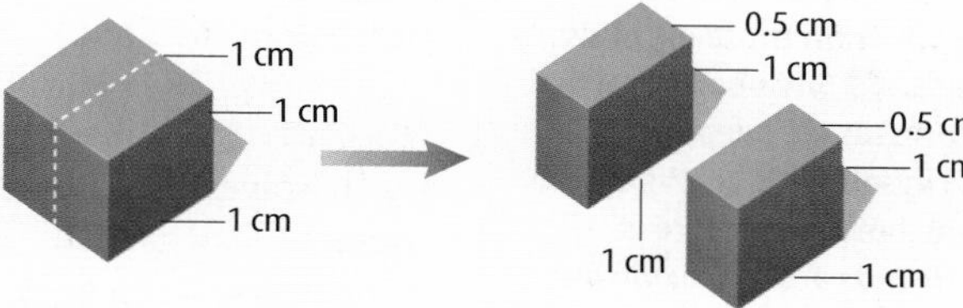

4. *Solve the equation by substituting the appropriate numbers.*

   Total surface area of the cube is:
   $2(1\text{ cm} \times 1\text{ cm}) + 2(1\text{ cm} \times 1\text{ cm}) + 2(1\text{ cm} \times 1\text{ cm}) = 6\text{ cm}^2$

   Total surface area of the rectangular solid is:
   $2(1\text{ cm} \times 0.5\text{ cm}) + 2(1\text{ cm} \times 1\text{ cm}) + 2(0.5\text{ cm} \times 1\text{ cm}) = 4\text{ cm}^2$

   Because there are two rectangular solids, their combined surface area is:
   $4\text{ cm}^2 + 4\text{ cm}^2 = 8\text{ cm}^2$

   To find out how much new surface area has been created, compare the two results:
   $8\text{ cm}^2 - 6\text{ cm}^2 = 2\text{ cm}^2$

   Check your answer by considering what you've done by splitting the cube in two. You have created two new faces, each with a surface area of 1 cm². Can you think of a way to simplify the equation for the total surface area of the cube?

Practice Problem

A cube of salt with a length, height, and width of 5 cm is attached along a face to another cube of salt with the same dimensions. What is the combined surface area of the new rectangular solid? How much surface area has been lost?

Extension

In most cases, dissolving a solid solute in a liquid solvent requires energy. This energy comes from the thermal energy of the solution. In these cases, the temperature of the liquid decreases as the solute dissolves in it. However, when solid $CaCl_2$ dissolves in water, the temperature of the liquid increases. **What does this mean?** Dissolving $CaCl_2$ in water gives off energy. The bonds formed between the dissolved particles are stronger than the bonds between atoms in the original $CaCl_2$. L3

LS **Analytical-Mathematical**

Math Skills Activity

National Math Standards

Correlation to Mathematics Objectives

1, 2, 3, 4, 6, 8, 9

Answers to Practice Problems

1. Solve the equations

- For the attached cubes: h = 5 cm, l = 5 cm, w = 10 cm
  $2(5\text{ cm} \times 10\text{ cm}) + 2(5\text{ cm} \times 5\text{ cm}) + 2(10\text{ cm} \times 5\text{ cm}) = 250\text{ cm}^2$
- For the original cubes: h = l = w = 5 cm
  $2(5\text{ cm} \times 5\text{ cm}) + 2(5\text{ cm} \times 5\text{ cm}) + 2(5\text{ cm} \times 5\text{ cm}) = 150\text{ cm}^2$
- Because there were two cubes, $150\text{ cm}^2 + 150\text{ cm}^2 = 300\text{ cm}^2$, so 50 cm^2 of surface area was lost.

Resource Manager

Chapter Resources Booklet
MiniLAB, p. 3
Reinforcement, p. 27

Mathematics Skill Activities, p. 13

3 Assess

Reteach

Bring in hot and cold packs used in sports medicine. Demonstrate that by breaking an inner seal, the solute comes in contact with the solvent and either produces heat or absorbs heat. Alternatively, you could add solid ammonium nitrate to 100 mL of water in one beaker, and add solid calcium chloride to 100 mL of water in another beaker. Record the water temperatures of both before and after the solutes have dissolved. The temperature of the ammonium chloride solution will decrease and the temperature of the calcium chloride solution will increase. L2 LS **Visual-Spatial**

Challenge

Air is a solution of gases. **After oxygen and nitrogen, what are the most abundant gases in air?** Argon is next, then carbon dioxide. Nitrogen and oxygen account for 99.03% of air, argon accounts for 0.934%, and carbon dioxide accounts for approximately 0.033%. L2

LS **Analytical-Mathematical**

Content Have students work in groups of two or three to write a story or a poem about what happens to one NaCl crystal as it is put into water and dissolves. Use **Performance Assessment in the Science Classroom,** p. 151.

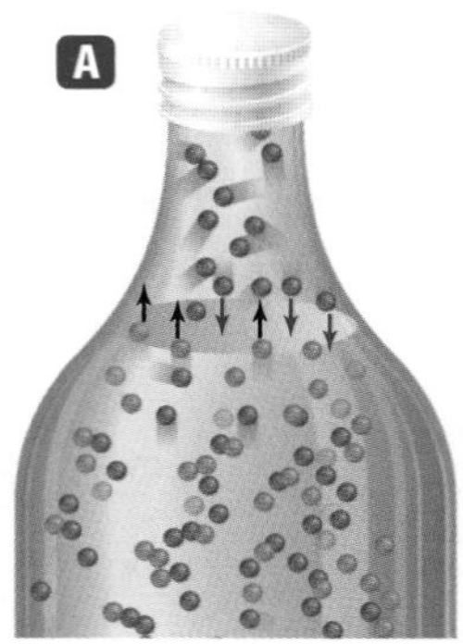

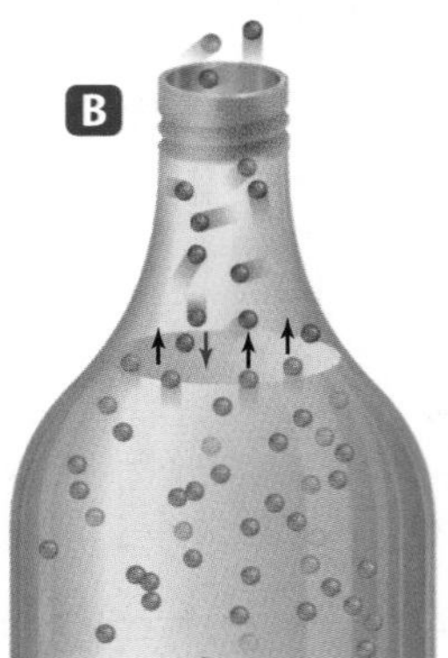

Figure 5
Solutions of gases behave differently from those of solids or liquids. A Soda pop is bottled under pressure to keep carbon dioxide in solution. B When you open the bottle, pressure is released and carbon dioxide bubbles out of solution.

Gases in Solution

When you shake an opened bottle of soda, it bubbles up and may squirt out. Shaking or pouring a solution of a gas in a liquid causes gas to come out of solution. Agitating the solution exposes more gas molecules to the surface, where they escape from the liquid.

Pressure What might you do if you want a gas to dissolve faster in a liquid? One thing you can do is increase the pressure of that gas over the liquid. Soft drinks are bottled under increased pressure. This also increases the amount of carbon dioxide that dissolves in the liquid.

Temperature Another way to increase the rate at which a gas dissolves in a liquid to is cool the liquid. This is just the opposite of what you do to increase the speed at which most solids dissolve in a liquid. In **Figure 5,** you can see what happens to the carbon dioxide when a bottle of soft drink is opened. Even more carbon dioxide will bubble out of a soft drink as it gets warmer.

Section 1 Assessment

1. Name three phases of solutions. Give an example of each type.
2. What three methods can increase the rate of dissolving a solid in a liquid?
3. How can you keep a bottle of soda from going "flat"?
4. How are the metals in an alloy mixed so that they are evenly distributed?
5. **Think Critically** Amalgams, which are sometimes used in tooth fillings, are alloys of mercury with other metals. Is an amalgam a solution? Explain.

Skill Builder Activities

6. **Comparing and Contrasting** Compare and contrast the effects on the rate of dissolving (1) a solid in a liquid and (2) a gas in a liquid, when the solution (a) is cooled, (b) is stirred, and (c) the pressure on it is lowered. **For more help, refer to the Science Skill Handbook.**
7. **Communicating** Write a paragraph in your Science Journal explaining why many fish aquariums have a device that bubbles air into the water. **For more help, refer to the Science Skill Handbook.**

Answers to Section Assessment

1. Possible answer: liquid/liquid, solid/liquid, gas/liquid, gas/gas, solid/solid; examples will vary.
2. increase temperature, stir or shake solution, break solute into small particles
3. Keep the container tightly sealed. Once it is opened, keep the temperature low.
4. Metals are melted, mixed evenly, then cooled to a solid.
5. Yes, alloys are solutions.
6. (a) When a solid in a liquid is cooled, usually less solid dissolves. When a gas in a liquid is cooled, more solute dissolves. (b) When a solid in a liquid is stirred, the rate of dissolving increases. When a gas in a liquid is stirred, the gas dissolves less. (c) Lowering the pressure on a solid in a liquid typically has no measurable effect. Lowering the pressure on gas in a liquid causes less gas to dissolve
7. Air leaves the surface easily, so to keep enough air in the water for the fish, new air must be bubbled into the tank.

Dissolving Without Water

When Water Won't Work

Water often is referred to as the universal solvent because it can dissolve so many things. However, there are some things it can't do. For example, it can't dissolve a lipstick stain on a linen napkin or clean an oil-soaked seabird. To explain why water can't dissolve some materials, you must know what these materials are and how they differ from water.

The reason water can't dissolve some things is its polarity. As you learned in the first section, water has positive and negative areas that allow it to attract polar solutes. However, **nonpolar** materials have no separated positive and negative areas. Because of this, they do not attract polar molecules, which means they do not attract water molecules. Nonpolar molecules do not dissolve in water except to a small extent, if at all.

Nonpolar Solutes An example of a nonpolar substance that does not dissolve in water can be seen on many dinner tables. The vinegar-and-oil salad dressing shown in **Figure 6** has two distinct layers—the bottom layer is vinegar, which is a solution of acetic acid in water, and the top layer is salad oil.

Most salad oils contain large molecules made of carbon and hydrogen atoms, which are called hydrocarbons. In hydrocarbons, carbon and hydrogen atoms share electrons in a nearly equal manner.

This equal distribution of electrons means that the molecule has no positive and negative charge separation. Because it has no charge separation, the nonpolar oil molecule is not attracted to the polar water molecules in the vinegar solution. That's why you must shake this kind of dressing to mix it just before you pour it on your salad.

Figure 6
Oil and vinegar do not form a solution, so you must shake this salad dressing before using it.

As You Read

***What* You'll Learn**

- **Identify** the kinds of solutes that do not dissolve well in water.
- **Explain** how solvents work.
- **Determine** how to choose the right solvent for the job.

Vocabulary
nonpolar

***Why* It's Important**
Many solutes do not dissolve in water.

Section Assessment Planner

Portfolio
Health Integration, p. 716

Performance Assessment
Try at Home MiniLAB, p. 715
Skill Builder Activities, p. 717
See page 734 for more options.

Content Assessment
Section, p. 717
Challenge, p. 717
Chapter, pp. 734–735

SECTION 2

Dissolving Without Water

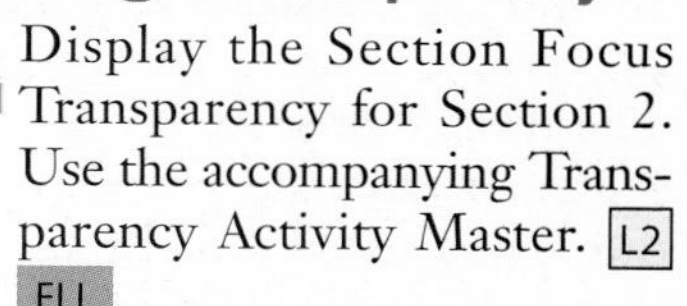

1 Motivate

Bellringer Transparency

Display the Section Focus Transparency for Section 2. Use the accompanying Transparency Activity Master. L2 ELL

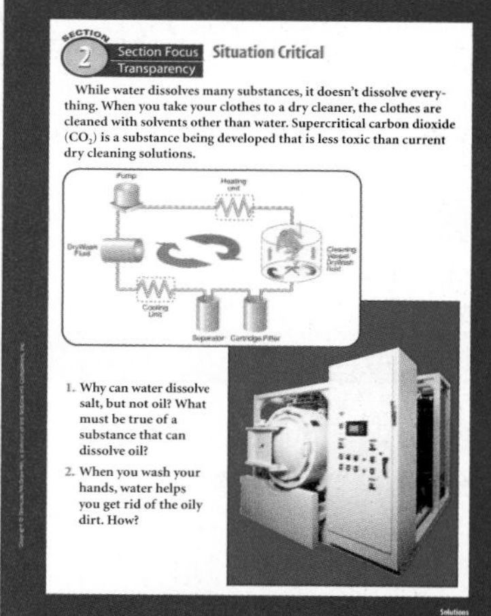

Section 2 Section Focus Transparency
Situation Critical
While water dissolves many substances, it doesn't dissolve everything. When you take your clothes to a dry cleaner, the clothes are cleaned with solvents other than water. Supercritical carbon dioxide (CO_2) is a substance being developed that is less toxic than current dry cleaning solutions.
Pump
Heating unit
Cooling Unit
Separator
Cartridge Filter
1. Why can water dissolve salt, but not oil? What must be true of a substance that can dissolve oil?
2. When you wash your hands, water helps you get rid of the oily dirt. How?
Solutions

Tie to Prior Knowledge

Ask students if they have ever had to clean paint brushes with a solvent other than water. Explain that some paints are not water soluble.

Resource Manager

Chapter Resources Booklet
Transparency Activity, p. 47
Directed Reading for Content Mastery, p. 21

2 Teach

When Water Won't Work

Activity

Tell students how to make a "pet" drop. Obtain a small vial with a very tight-sealing screw cap. Pour water tinted with food coloring into the vial until it is half full. Add rubbing alcohol until the vial is nearly full. Then add a large drop of cooking oil. The drop should float near the center of the vial. As you move the vial, the oil will float and change locations. (Do not shake the mixture.) The density of the water-alcohol solution allows the oil to hover near the center of the solution. The nonpolar oil will not dissolve in the polar water-alcohol solution. L2

ELL **Kinesthetic**

Reading Check

Answer The molecule has both a polar end and a nonpolar end.

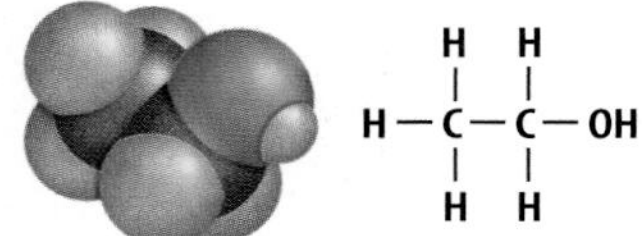

Figure 7
Ethanol, C_2H_5OH, has a polar $-OH$ group at one end but the $-C_2H_5$ section is nonpolar.

Versatile Alcohol Some substances form solutions with polar as well as nonpolar solutes because their molecules have a polar and a nonpolar end. Ethanol, shown in **Figure 7,** is such a molecule. The polar end dissolves polar substances, and the nonpolar end dissolves nonpolar substances. For example, ethanol dissolves iodine, which is nonpolar, as well as water, which is polar.

Reading Check *How can alcohol dissolve both polar and nonpolar substances?*

Useful Nonpolar Molecules

Some materials around your house may be useful as nonpolar solvents. For example, mineral oil may be used as a solvent to remove candle wax from glass or metal candleholders. Both the mineral oil and the candle wax are nonpolar materials. Mineral oil can also aid in removing bubble gum from some surfaces for the same reason. Oil-based paints contain pigments that are dissolved in oils. In order to thin or remove such paints, a nonpolar solvent must be used. The gasoline you use in your car and lawnmower is a solution of hydrocarbons, which are nonpolar substances.

Dry cleaners use nonpolar solvents when removing oily stains. The word *dry* refers to the fact that no water is used in the process. Molecules of a nonpolar solute can slip easily among molecules of a nonpolar solvent. That is why dry cleaning can remove stains of grease and oil that you cannot clean easily yourself. A general statement that describes which substance dissolves which is the phrase "like dissolves like."

Many nonpolar solvents are connected with specific jobs. People who paint pictures using oil-based paints probably used the solvent turpentine. It comes from the sap of a pine tree. **Figure 8** shows how well turpentine dissolves nonpolar paint.

Figure 8
With no polarity to interfere, paint molecules slide smoothly among molecules of turpentine.

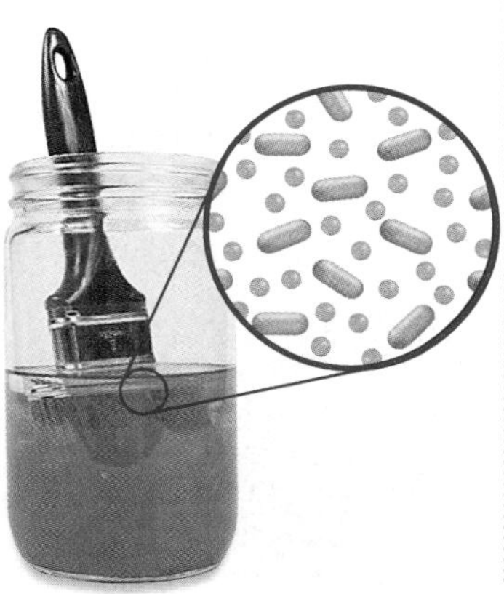

Toxicity Although nonpolar solvents have many uses, they have some drawbacks, too. First, many nonpolar solvents are flammable. Also, some are toxic, which means that contact with the skin or inhaling vapors of many solvents can be dangerous. For these reasons, you must always be careful when handling these materials and never use them in a closed area. Good ventilation is critical, because nonpolar solvents tend to evaporate more readily than water, and even small amounts of a nonpolar liquid can produce high concentrations of harmful vapor in the air.

Teacher FYI

The solvent acetone has three carbons joined in a chain. The middle carbon is double-bonded to an oxygen atom. Both end carbons have three hydrogen atoms attached. These bonds have very little polarity. These small nonpolar molecules do not cling to each other, so they evaporate easily.

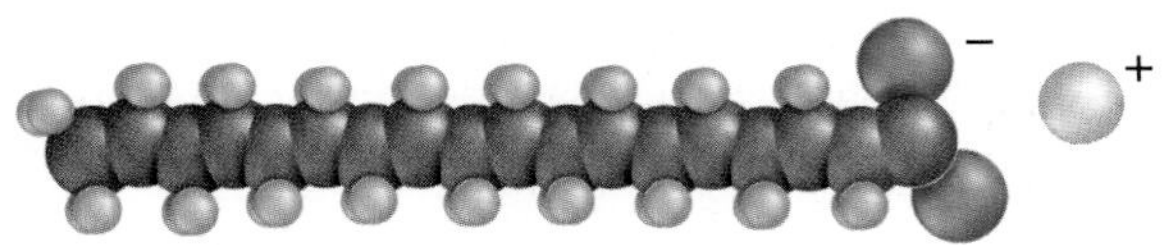

Figure 9
The long hydrocarbon tail of sodium stearate is nonpolar. The head is ionic.

How Soap Works The oils on human skin and hair keep them from drying out, but the oils can also attract and hold dirt. The oily dirt is a nonpolar mixture, so washing with water alone won't clean away the dirt. This is where soap comes in. Soaps, you might say, have a split personality. They are substances that have polar and nonpolar properties. Soaps are salts of fatty acids, which are long hydrocarbon molecules with a carboxylic acid group –COOH at one end. When a soap is made, the hydrogen atom of the acid group is removed, leaving a negative charge behind, and a positive ion of sodium or potassium is attached. This is shown in **Figure 9.**

Reading Check *Why doesn't water alone clean oily dirt?*

Thus, soap has an ionic end that will dissolve in water and a long hydrocarbon portion that will dissolve in oily dirt. In this way, the dirt is removed from your skin, hair, or a fabric, suspended in the wash water and washed away, as shown in **Figure 10.**

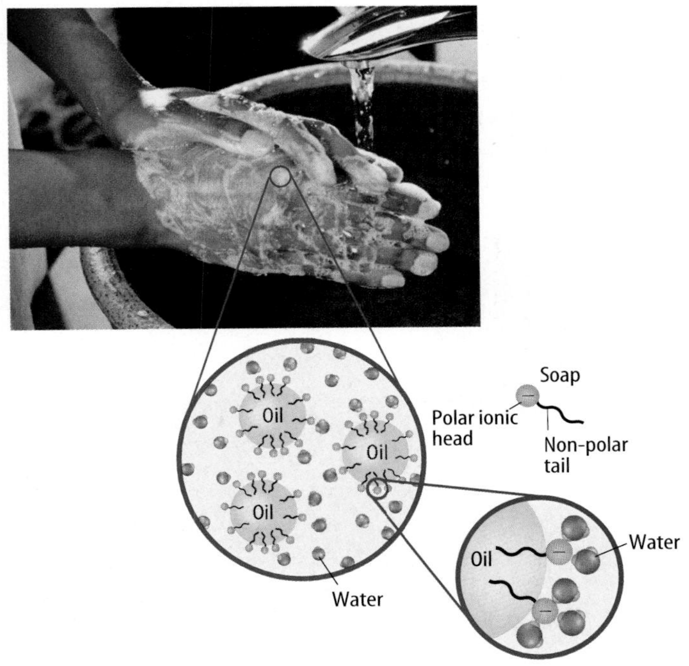

Figure 10
Soap cleans because its nonpolar hydrocarbon part dissolves in oily dirt and its ionic part interacts srongly with water. The oil and water mix and the dirt is washed away.

Clinging Molecules

Procedure

1. Lay **two clean pennies** side by side and heads up on a **paper towel.**
2. Slowly place drops of **water** from a **dropper** onto the head of one penny. Count each drop and continue until the accumulated water spills off the edge of the penny.
3. With adult supervision, repeat step 2 using **rubbing alcohol,** which is approximately 30 percent isopropyl, and the other penny.

Analysis

1. Which penny held the most drops before liquid spilled over the edge of the penny?
2. Isopropyl alcohol has the formula C_3H_7OH. How polar do you think it is?
3. How do the results of the experiment support the concept of polarity and molecules sticking to each other?

Useful Nonpolar Molecules

Reading Check

Answer Oily dirt won't dissolve in water because it is nonpolar.

Purpose Students compare the clinging ability of polar molecules with that of nonpolar molecules. L2 ELL

LS **Kinesthetic**

Materials two clean pennies, paper towel, two droppers, water, rubbing alcohol

Teaching Strategy Tell students to hold the dropper close to but not touching the penny or liquid surface. Remind them that the distance used with water should be the same as that used with the alcohol.

Analysis

1. the penny containing water drops
2. slightly polar, but not as polar as water
3. The polar water molecules stick to each other better than the less polar alcohol molecules.

Assessment

Process Have students describe the variables that may cause different students to have different answers. Possible answers: size of opening in droppers, distance between dropper and surface, cleanliness of the pennies Use **Performance Assessment in the Science Classroom,** p. 89.

Inclusion Strategies

Physically Disabled Suggest that any student who cannot manipulate the dropper work with a partner who can.

Resource Manager 

Chapter Resources Booklet
MiniLAB, p. 4

Science Inquiry Labs, p. 51

Polarity and Vitamins

Extension

Have students find the solubilities in water of alcohols with different hydrocarbon chains. Ask them to use the information to infer the relationship between the length of the carbon chain and solubility.

- Methanol, CH_3OH: soluble
- Ethanol, CH_3CH_2OH: soluble
- Propanol, $CH_3CH_2CH_2OH$: soluble
- Butanol, $CH_3(CH_2)_2CH_2OH$: 8 g/100 g water
- Pentanol, $CH_3(CH_2)_3CH_2OH$: 2.6 g/100 g water
- Hexanol, $CH_3(CH_2)_4CH_2OH$: 0.6 g/100 g water

The greater the number of carbons in the chain, the lower the ability of the alcohol to dissolve in polar water. L3

LS **Logical-Mathematical**

science.glencoe.com

Access this Web site for activities and the **Content Mastery** booklet to reinforce chapter content and vocabulary.

vitamin B-6: nerve damage causing changes in touch sensation; vitamin D: nausea, vomiting, headache, dizziness; niacin: headache, nausea, flushing, rashes, tingling, liver damage, glucose intolerance, cramping, eye damage, heart injury L2

LS **Linguistic** P

SCIENCE Online

Research Visit the Glencoe Science Web site at **science.glencoe.com** for more information about vitamins. Prepare a report on your research.

Polarity and Vitamins

Having the right kinds and amounts of vitamins is important for your health. The B vitamins and vitamin C are polar compounds. They dissolve readily in the water present in cells throughout your body. Because water is passing constantly through your system, these dissolved vitamins can be flushed out before they are used. For this reason, you must replace these vitamins by eating enough of the foods that contain them or by taking vitamin supplements. Look at **Table 1** for some good sources of vitamin C.

When you look at the structure of vitamin C, shown in **Figure 11,** you will see that it has several carbon-to-carbon bonds. This might make you think that it is nonpolar. But, if you look again, you will see that it also has several oxygen-to-hydrogen bonds that resemble those found in water. This makes it polar. That is why water dissolves vitamin C.

Fat is stored in various specialized cells of your body. Fat molecules consist of long chains of carbon atoms bonded to each other by nonpolar bonds. This makes them nonpolar. Therefore, fat molecules do not dissolve in the water around them.

Table 1 Sources of Vitamin C

Food	Amount	mg
Orange juice, fresh	1 cup	124
Green peppers, raw	1/2 cup	96
Broccoli, raw	1/2 cup	70
Cantaloupe	1/4 melon	70
Strawberries	1/2 cup	42

Figure 11
Vitamin C helps heal wounds and helps the body absorb iron.
A Although it has carbon-to-carbon bonds, it also has polar groups and is water soluble. B These foods are good sources of vitamin C as you can see in Table 1.

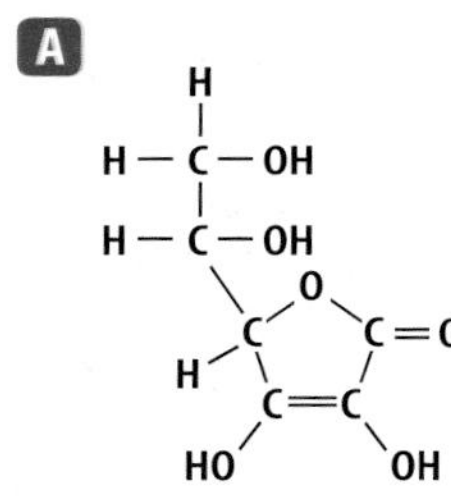

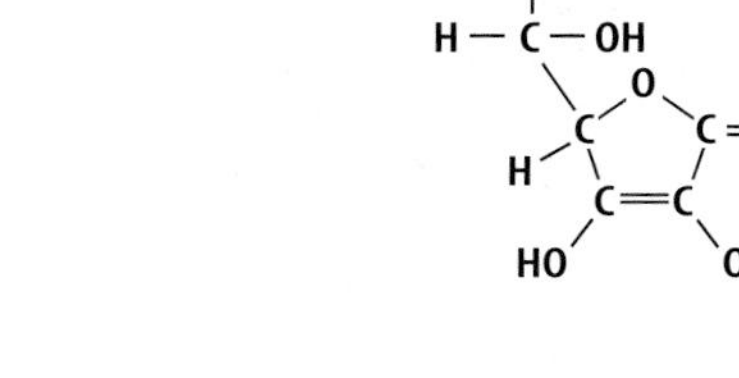

Resource Manager

Chapter Resources Booklet
Enrichment, p. 32
Reinforcement, p. 28

Visual Learning

Figure 11 How does cooking in water affect foods that contain vitamin C? Vitamin C is water soluble, so cooking in water removes some of the vitamin from the food. Explain that vitamin C deficiency (scurvy) was the first deficiency disease identified in humans. In 1753, Scottish naval surgeon James Lind showed that scurvy could be cured and prevented by eating citrus fruits.

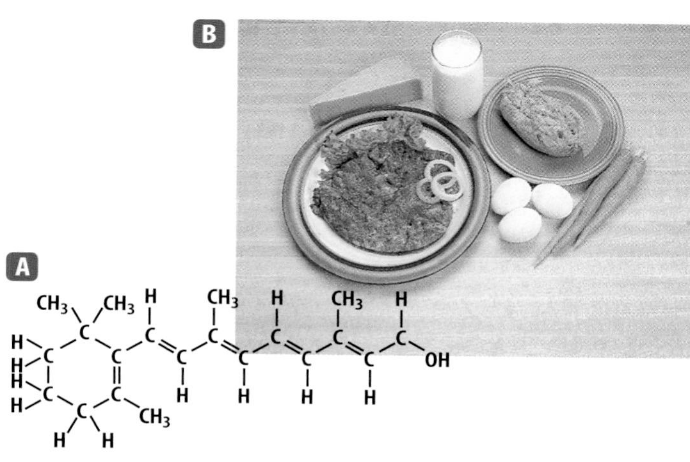

Figure 12
Vitamin A is a nonpolar, fat-soluble vitamin. A You can see the long hydrocarbon chain that makes it nonpolar in this structural formula. B These foods are good sources of vitamin A.

Vitamin Dosage Some of the vitamins you need, such as vitamin A shown in **Figure 12,** are also nonpolar and can dissolve in fat. Because they do not wash away with water, fat-soluble vitamins are not easily eliminated and they can accumulate in our tissues. Some of these vitamins are toxic in high concentrations, so taking large doses can be dangerous. In general, the best way to stay healthy is to eat a variety of healthy foods. Such a diet will supply all the vitamins you need with no risk of overdoses. Vitamins D, E, and K are also fat-soluble.

Reading Check ***Why do you need to replace some of the vitamins used in your body?***

Health INTEGRATION

Gulping too much carrot juice, which is rich in beta carotene, a substance related to vitamin A, can cause the palms of your hands and soles of your feet to turn orange. Though this condition is not serious and the color fades in time, taking too much of several vitamins can be dangerous. *Research what might result from taking too much of vitamin B-6, vitamin D, and niacin.*

Section  Assessment

1. What general statement describes which solutes will dissolve in which solvents?
2. Explain the phrase "like dissolves like" and give an example of two "like" substances.
3. Explain how soap cleans grease from hands.
4. Some small engines require a mixture of oil and gasoline. Gasoline evaporates easily. What conclusion can be drawn about the polarity of the engine oil?
5. **Think Critically** What might happen to your skin if you washed with soap too often?

Skill Builder Activities

6. **Drawing Conclusions** Some people believe in taking large doses of vitamin C to prevent colds. How does the polarity of vitamin C aid in preventing accumulation of this vitamin? Explain your reasoning. **For more help, refer to the** Science Skill Handbook.
7. **Communicating** Make a survey of your home and list in your Science Journal the nonpolar solvents you find. Read the labels. What precautions should be observed while using them? **For more help, refer to the** Science Skill Handbook.

Fun Fact

All of the B vitamins are water soluble, as is vitamin C. Vitamins E, D, and A are fat soluble.

Reading Check

Answer Vitamins that are water soluble are eliminated with body wastes and therefore need to be constantly replaced.

3 Assess

Reteach

Ask students to explain how nonpolar solvents dissolve nonpolar solutes. The nonpolar molecules have no attraction for one another, so the nonpolar solute can slip easily among the molecules of a nonpolar solvent. L1 LS **Linguistic**

Challenge

Micelles are the structures in soap that enable soap to dissolve both polar and nonpolar substances. Have students find out about the structures of micelles. A micelle is made up of a group of 50 to 100 molecules, each of which has a polar head and a nonpolar part. L3 LS **Logical-Mathematical**

Assessment

Performance Have students examine the molecular structure of antifreeze (ethylene glycol) and write newspaper articles describing why it dissolves so well in water. It has two –OH groups, one on each of the two carbon atoms. These make it very polar. Use **PASC,** p. 141.

Answers to Section Assessment

1. Like dissolves like.
2. Polar substances dissolve in polar solvents and nonpolar substances dissolve in nonpolar solvents. Water and alcohol are two like substances because they are polar.
3. Soap has one polar end and one nonpolar end. Grease dissolves in the nonpolar end and is carried away because the polar end of the soap is dissolved in water.
4. Since gasoline easily evaporates, it is probably nonpolar. Engine oil dissolves in gasoline, so engine oil must also be nonpolar.
5. You would lose natural oils.
6. Vitamin C is water soluble, so it leaves the body easily.
7. Answers will vary. Paint thinners and fingernail polish remover are typical examples. Care should be used because nonpolar solvents can easily evaporate, producing potentially high levels of vapor. They are also often highly flammable.

SECTION 3

Solubility and Concentration

1 Motivate

Bellringer Transparency

Display the Section Focus Transparency for Section 3. Use the accompanying Transparency Activity Master. L2 ELL

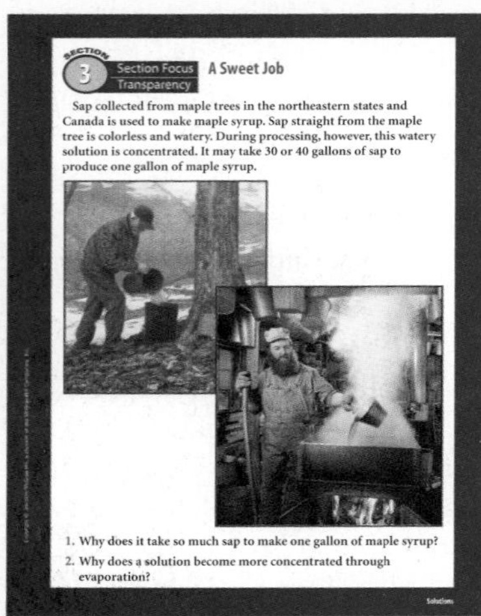

SECTION 3 Section Focus Transparency **A Sweet Job**

Sap collected from maple trees in the northeastern states and Canada is used to make maple syrup. Sap straight from the maple tree is colorless and watery. During processing, however, this watery solution is concentrated. It may take 30 or 40 gallons of sap to produce one gallon of maple syrup.

1. Why does it take so much sap to make one gallon of maple syrup?
2. Why does a solution become more concentrated through evaporation?

Solutions

Tie to Prior Knowledge

Students are familiar with milk as a nutritious food. Bring in a milk carton and go over the percent concentrations of various nutrients dissolved in the milk. Point out that solute percentages can provide important information.

SECTION 3

Solubility and Concentration

As You Read

What **You'll Learn**

- **Determine** how temperature affects solubility.
- **Identify** how to express the concentration of solutions.
- **Compare and contrast** saturated, unsaturated, and supersaturated solutions.

Vocabulary

solubility
saturated solution
unsaturated solution
supersaturated solution

Why **It's Important**

Many products that we use and foods that we eat are in the form of solutions.

How much can dissolve?

Sugar, as you know, dissolves easily in water. To make extra sweet lemonade, you stir two, three, four, or more teaspoons of sugar into a glass of lemon and water. It all dissolves. You try adding more sugar, but eventually, no more sugar dissolves, and the excess granules sink to the bottom of the glass. You now see how soluble sugar is in water. **Solubility** (sol yuh BIHL ih tee) is the maximum amount of a solute that can be dissolved in a given amount of solvent at a given temperature.

Reading Check *What is solubility?*

Comparing Solubilities The amount of a substance that can dissolve in a solvent depends on the nature of these substances. To determine the solubility of two substances, A and B, you stir 1 g of substance A into a beaker containing 100 mL of water. All of substance A dissolves. But, when you try to add more of substance A to that beaker, it doesn't dissolve. Then you stir 1 g of substance B into another beaker containing 100 mL of water. Substance B dissolves completely. You add more of substance B, and find that you can add two more grams before no more will dissolve. If the temperature of the water is the same in both beakers, you can conclude that substance B is more soluble than substance A as shown in **Figure 13.** Another way to state this is that substance B has a higher solubility in water than substance A does.

Table 2 shows how the solubility of several substances varies at 20°C. For solutes that are gases, the pressure also must be given.

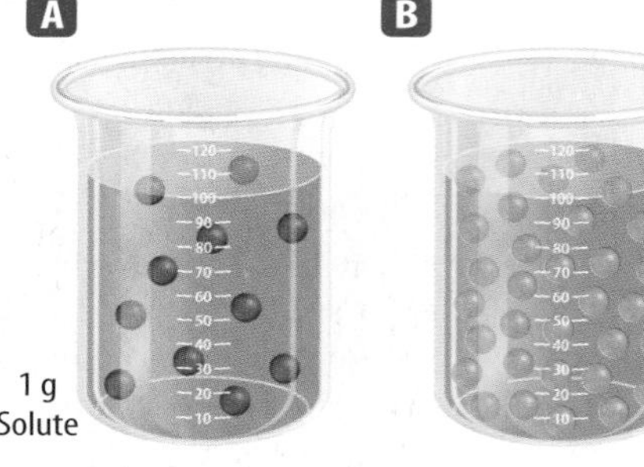

Figure 13
Only 1 g of A dissolves in 100 mL of water, but more than 3 g of B dissolves in the same amount of water at the same temperature. Substance B is more soluble in water than substance A.

Section Assessment Planner

PORTFOLIO
Science Journal, p. 719

PERFORMANCE ASSESSMENT
Skill Builder Activities, p. 722
See page 734 for more options.

CONTENT ASSESSMENT
Section, p. 722
Challenge, p. 722
Chapter, pp. 734–735

Concentration

Suppose you add one teaspoon of lemon juice to a glass of water to make lemonade. Your friend adds four teaspoons of lemon juice to another glass of water the same size. You could say that your glass of lemonade is dilute and your friend's lemonade is concentrated, because your friend's drink now has more lemon flavor than yours. A concentrated solution is one in which a large amount of solute is dissolved in the solvent. A dilute solution is one that has a small amount of solute in the solvent.

Precise Concentrations How much real fruit juice is there in one of those boxed fruit drinks? You can read the label to find out. *Concentrated* and *dilute* are not precise terms. However, concentrations of solutions can be described precisely. One way is to state the percentage by volume of the solute. The percentage by volume of the juice in the drink shown in **Figure 14** is ten percent. Adding 10 mL of juice to 90 mL of water makes 100 mL of this drink. Commonly, fruit-flavored drinks can contain from ten percent to 100 percent fruit juice. Generally, if two or more liquids are being mixed, the concentration is given in percentage by volume, stated in number of milliliters of solute plus enough solvent to make 100 mL of solution.

Table 2 Solubility of Substances in Water at 20°C

Substance	Solubility in g/100 g of Water
Solid Substances	
Salt (sodium chloride)	35.9
Baking soda (sodium bicarbonate)	9.6
Washing soda (sodium carbonate)	21.4
Lye (sodium hydroxide)	109.0
Sugar (sucrose)	203.9
Gaseous Substances*	
Hydrogen	0.00017
Oxygen	0.005
Carbon dioxide	0.16

*at normal atmospheric pressure

Figure 14
The concentrations of fruit juices often are given in percent by volume like these. Concentrations can range from ten percent to 100 percent juice.

2 Teach

How much can dissolve?

Reading Check

Answer the maximum amount of solute that can be dissolved in a given amount of solvent at a given temperature

Concentration

Some people think that all concentrated acids are 100% acid. Bring sealed, labeled bottles of concentrated acids and display the labels. Point out that concentrated hydrochloric acid is 37% HCl, concentrated nitric acid is 70% HNO_3, and sulfuric acid is 96% H_2SO_4.

Activity

Bring a colored drink to class and dilute it into several glasses of equal volume but different concentration. Have students place the solutions in sequence from low to high concentration. (The basis for the sequencing is the intensity of the color.) Once the students are satisfied with the sequence, tell them the concentrations of the solutions in %v/v. L1 ELL IN **Visual-Spatial**

Resource Manager

Chapter Resources Booklet
- Transparency Activity, p. 48
- Directed Reading for Content Mastery, p. 20

Physical Science Critical Thinking/Problem Solving, p. 1

Science Journal

General and Precise Terms In general terms, solutions can be described as *concentrated* or *dilute*. Precise concentrations are expressed in other terms. Have students record in their Science Journals some other examples in which general and precise terms can be used. A baseball player may be described as a "good hitter" or by batting average, "a 320 hitter." L2  **Linguistic** P

Types of Solutions

Make a Model

On the chalkboard draw three identical oversized beakers. Draw the same number of small circles in each beaker. These represent particles of a solvent. Ask students to copy your drawings and add, using a different color of pen or pencil, circles in the beakers to represent unsaturated, saturated, and supersaturated solutions. The unsaturated example should have the fewest solute circles, all dissolved; the saturated example should have more solute than the first, perhaps even one or two on the bottom; the supersaturated example should have a larger number of solute particles dissolved than the saturated example has. L1 LS **Analytical-Mathematical**

Visual Learning

Table 3 Prepare 50 mL of a saturated solution of any substance from **Table 3** except lead (II) chloride and barium hydroxide. Place a small amount of this solution in a petri dish. Place a small amount of the same solution in a second petri dish and add water to make it unsaturated. Place both petri dishes on the overhead projector. Have a student drop a crystal of the salt into each dish and slowly stir both solutions. The crystal will dissolve in the unsaturated solution, but it will remain visible in the saturated solution. L2 ELL LS **Visual-Spatial**

Types of Solutions

How much solute can dissolve in a given amount of solvent? That depends on a number of factors, including the solubility of the solute. Here you will examine the types of solutions based on the amount of a solute dissolved.

Saturated Solutions If you add 35 g of copper(II) sulfate, $CuSO_4$, to 100 g of water at 20°C, only 32 g will dissolve. You have a saturated solution because no more copper(II) sulfate can dissolve. A **saturated solution** is a solution that contains all the solute it can hold at a given temperature. However, if you heat the mixture to a higher temperature, more copper(II) sulfate can dissolve. As a rule, as the temperature of a liquid solvent increases, the amount of solid solute that can dissolve in it also increases. **Table 3** shows the amounts of a few solutes that can dissolve in 100 g of water at different temperatures, forming saturated solutions. Some of these data also are shown on the accompanying graph.

Table 3 Solubility of Compounds in g/100 g of Water at Various Temperatures

Compound	0°C	20°C	60°C	100°C
Ammonium chloride	29.4	37.2	55.3	77.3
Copper(II) sulfate	23.1	32.0	61.8	114
Lead(II) chloride	0.67	1.0	1.94	3.2
Potassium bromide	53.6	65.3	85.5	104
Potassium chloride	28.0	34.0	45.8	56.3
Potassium nitrate	13.9	31.6	109	245
Sodium acetate	36.2	46.4	139	170.15
Sodium chlorate	79.6	95.9	137	204
Sodium chloride	35.7	35.9	37.1	39.2
Sodium nitrate	73.0	87.6	122	180
Sucrose (sugar)	179.2	203.9	287.3	487.2

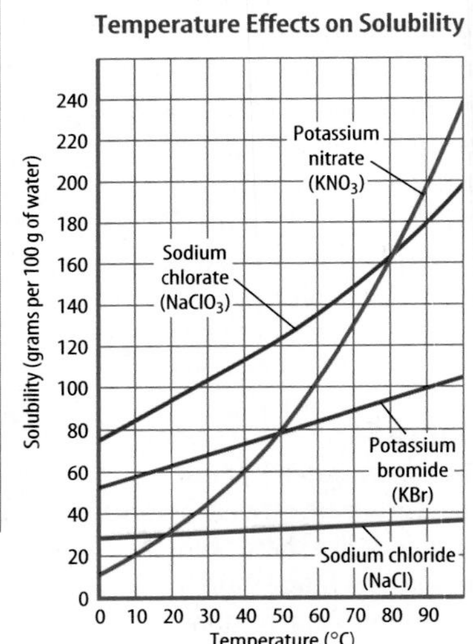

Curriculum Connection

Math Ask students to refer to **Table 3** and answer the following question. **If you were to graph the solubility of a solute on the *y* axis and the temperature of the solution on the *x* axis, which solute would have the line with the steepest slope, ammonium chloride, potassium chloride, or sodium chloride?** ammonium chloride

Solubility Curves Each line on the graph is called a solubility curve for a particular substance. You can use a curve to figure out how much solute will dissolve at any temperature given on the graph. For example, about 78 g of KBr (potassium bromide) will form a saturated solution in 100 g of water at 47°C. How much NaCl will form a saturated solution with 100 g of water at the same temperature?

Unsaturated Solutions An **unsaturated solution** is any solution that can dissolve more solute at a given temperature. Each time a saturated solution is heated to a higher temperature, it becomes unsaturated. The term *unsaturated* isn't precise. If you look at **Table 3,** you'll see that at 20°C, 37.2 g of NH_4Cl (ammonium chloride) forms a saturated solution in 100 g of water. However, an unsaturated solution of NH_4Cl could be any amount less than 37.2 g in 100 g of water at 20°C.

Reading Check *What happens to a saturated solution if it is heated?*

Supersaturated Solutions If you make a saturated solution of potassium nitrate at 100°C and then let it cool to 20°C, part of the solute comes out of solution. This is because, at the lower temperature, the solvent cannot hold as much solute. Most other saturated solutions behave in a similar way when cooled. However, if you cool a saturated solution of sodium acetate from 100°C to 20°C without disturbing it, no solute comes out. At this point, the solution is supersaturated. A **supersaturated solution** is one that contains more solute than a saturated one at the same temperature. If a seed crystal of sodium acetate is dropped into the supersaturated solution, excess sodium acetate crystallizes out, as in **Figure 15.**

Figure 15
A supersaturated solution is unstable. (A) When a seed crystal of sodium acetate is added to a supersaturated solution of sodium acetate, (B) (C) excess solute immediately crystallizes from solution.

Text Question Answer

approximately 37 g of NaCl

Teacher FYI

Most solid solutes dissolve better as the solution is warmed. However, the solubility of some solids decreases as temperature increases. Calcium acetate, $Ca(C_2H_3O_2)_2$, has a solubility of 37.4 g/100 mL of water at 0° C, but at 100° C, only 29.7 g dissolve per 100 mL of water.

Reading Check

Answer It may become unsaturated.

Quick Demo

Open a small bottle of ammonia in the back of the room without telling students. Ask if anyone can detect any type of chemical aroma. As the ammonia fumes mix in the air, point out to students that the air is diluting the ammonia. Insects detect molecules dissolved in the air, sometimes in very dilute solutions. Some insects can detect sex pheromones at only a few molecules per milliliter, which is 1 part per billion parts of air! L1 ELL IN **Kinesthetic**

Resource Manager

Chapter Resources Booklet
Transparency Activity, pp. 51–52
Lab Activity, pp. 13–16
Cultural Diversity, p. 37

Science Journal

The Solution Is in the Solution Have students imagine they have a crystal and a solution of zinc chloride. Have them explain how to use the crystal to tell whether the solution is unsaturated, saturated, or supersaturated. Drop the crystal into the solution. If it dissolves, the solution is unsaturated; if not, the solution is saturated; if the solution crystallizes, it is supersaturated. L2 IN **Linguistic**

3 Assess

Reteach

Describe, or bring to class if available, an old jar of honey. Ask students to describe why there are crystals of sugar forming in the previously smooth solution. As the water evaporates from the solution, the dissolved sugar becomes more concentrated. As the concentration exceeds the saturation limit, sugar will begin to precipitate, crystallizing out of the solution. L2 LS **Linguistic**

Challenge

Ask students to calculate the grams of potassium nitrate, KNO_3, needed to make 50 mL of water into a solution that is 50% KNO_3 by weight. 50g. **If the temperature of the solution was 25° C would the solution be unsaturated, saturated, or supersaturated?** 100 g/100 g H_2O would be super saturated at 25° C.

L3 LS **Analytical-Mathematical**

Assessment

Performance Have students use the data in **Table 3** to plot solubility versus temperature for sucrose. Have them use a different color and sketch a line on the same graph that they think would show qualitatively how the solubility of oxygen gas in water changes with temperature. The first line slopes up, and the second line slopes down. Use **Performance Assessment in the Science Classroom,** p. 111.

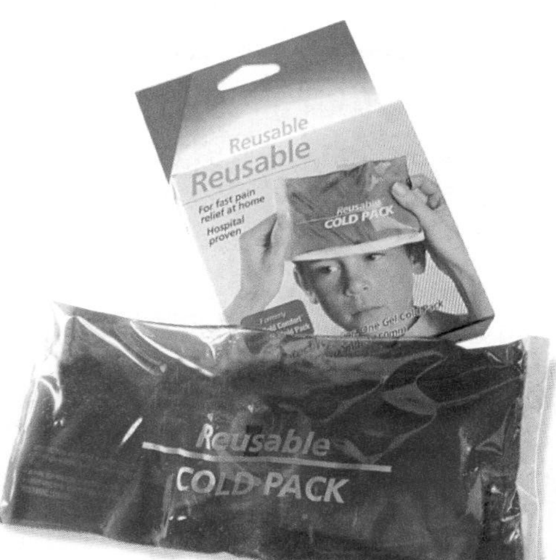

Figure 16
In this cold pack there are sealed bags of water and ammonium nitrate. When the pack is squeezed, the inner bags break and the water and ammonium nitrate mix. As the ammonium nitrate dissolves, the pack cools.

Solution Energy As the supersaturated solution of sodium acetate crystallizes, the solution becomes hot. Energy is given off as new bonds form between the ions and the water molecules. Some portable heat packs use crystallization from supersaturated solutions to produce heat. After crystallization, the heat pack can be reused by heating it to again dissolve all the solute.

You may have seen a "cold pack," like the one shown in **Figure 16,** applied to a sport's injury to reduce swelling. Some substances, such as ammonium nitrate, *need* energy to dissolve. The energy needed is taken from the surroundings, so the temperature of the water will drop several degrees.

Section 3 Assessment

1. Do all solutes dissolve to the same extent in the same solvent? How do you know?
2. Using **Table 3** state the following: the mass of $NaNO_3$ (sodium nitrate) that would have to be dissolved in 100 g of water to form a saturated, an unsaturated, and a supersaturated solution of $NaNO_3$ at 20°C.
3. Suppose you add a solute crystal to a solution of the solute. After the solution is stirred, the crystal is on the bottom of the container. What do you know about the solution?
4. **Think Critically** By volume, orange drink is ten percent each of orange juice and corn syrup. A 1.5-L can of the drink costs $0.95. A 1.5-L can of orange juice is $1.49, and 1.5 L of corn syrup is $1.69. Does it cost less to make your own orange drink or buy it ?

Skill Builder Activities

5. **Making and Using Graphs** Using **Table 3,** make a graph of solubility versus temperature for $CuSO_4$ (copper(II) sulfate) and $NaNO_3$ (sodium nitrate). How would you make a saturated solution of each substance at 80°C? **For more help, refer to the** **Math Skill Handbook.**
6. **Using an Electronic Spreadsheet** Use **Table 3** to prepare a spreadsheet showing the number of grams of solute needed to make 10 mL, 50 mL, 100 mL, 500 mL, and 1,000 mL of a saturated solution at 20°C of the following compounds: *ammonium chloride, lead(II) chloride, sodium chlorate,* and *sucrose.* **For more help, refer to the** **Technology Skill Handbook.**

Resource Manager

Chapter Resources Booklet
Enrichment, p. 33
Reinforcement, p. 29

Answers to Section Assessment

1. No; you can determine this experimentally.
2. Unsaturated: mass less than 87.6 g; saturated: 87.6 g; supersaturated: mass greater than 87.6 g
3. The solution is saturated.
4. Making it is cheaper. If you were making 1,500 mL of orange drink you would need 150 mL of orange juice @ $1.49/1,500 mL = 14.9 cents per 150 mL; 150 mL of syrup @ $1.69/1,500 mL = 16.9 cents per 150 mL; so, to make 1,500 mL of drink you need only 14.9 + 16.9 cents = 31.8 cents of ingredients per 1,500 mL of drink
5. $CuSO_4$: use approximately 87g per 100 g of water. $NaNO_3$; use approximately 150 g of solute per 100 g of water.
6. Use the following algorithm: mL asked × (grams for saturated/100 g water at 20° C) = grams needed to dissolve for saturated solution at 20° C.

SECTION

Particles in Solution

Particles With a Charge

Did you know that there are charged particles in your body that conduct electricity? In fact, you could not live without them. Some help nerve cells transmit messages. Each time you blink your eyes or wave your hand nerves control how muscles will respond. These charged particles, called **ions,** are in the fluids that are in and around all the cells in your body. The compounds that produce solutions of ions that conduct electricity in water are known as **electrolytes.** Some substances, like sodium chloride, are strong electrolytes and produce a strong current. Strong electrolytes exist completely in the form of ions in solution. Other substances, like the acetic acid in vinegar, remain mainly in the form of molecules when they dissolve in water. They produce few ions and conduct current only weakly. They are called weak electrolytes. Substances that form no ions in water and cannot conduct electricity are called **nonelectrolytes.** Among these are organic molecules like ethyl alcohol and sucrose.

Reading Check *What is a nonelectrolyte?*

How Ions Form

Electrolytes form ions in two different ways. Electrolytes, such as hydrogen chloride, are molecules made up of neutral atoms. To form ions, the molecules must be broken apart in such a way that the atoms take on a charge. This process of forming ions is called **ionization.** The process is shown in **Figure 17,** using hydrogen chloride as a model. Both hydrogen chloride and water are polar molecules. Water surrounds the hydrogen chloride molecules and pulls them apart, forming positive hydrogen ions and negative chloride ions. The hydrogen chloride is a strong electrolyte because it exists completely as ions in water.

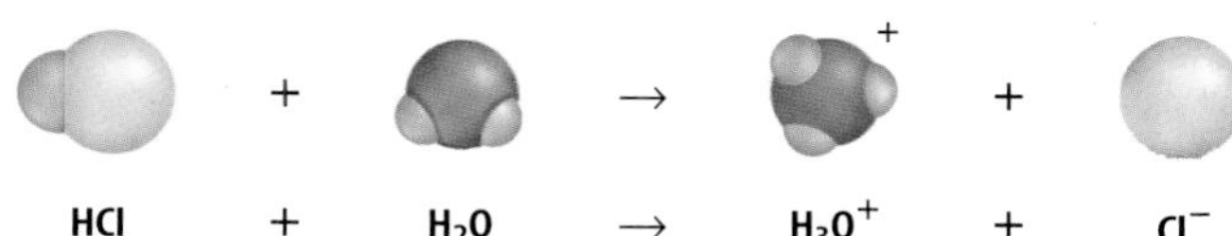

As You Read

What **You'll Learn**

- **Examine** how some solutes break apart in water solutions to form positively and negatively charged particles.
- **Determine** how some solutions conduct electricity.
- **Describe** how antifreeze works.

Vocabulary

ion
electrolyte
ionization
nonelectrolyte
dissociation

Why **It's Important**

We use the properties of solutes every day.

Figure 17
When hydrogen chloride dissolves in water, H_2O molecules surround and pull apart the HCl molecules, forming chloride and hydrogen ions, which are often shown as H_3O^+ to emphasize the role water plays in ionization.

Section Assessment Planner

Portfolio
Science Journal, p. 725

Performance Assessment
Skill Builder Activities, p. 726
See page 734 for more options.

Content Assessment
Section, p. 726
Challenge, p. 726
Chapter, pp. 734–735

SECTION

Particles in Solution

1 Motivate

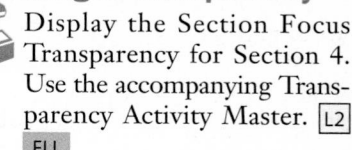

Bellringer Transparency

Display the Section Focus Transparency for Section 4. Use the accompanying Transparency Activity Master. L2 ELL

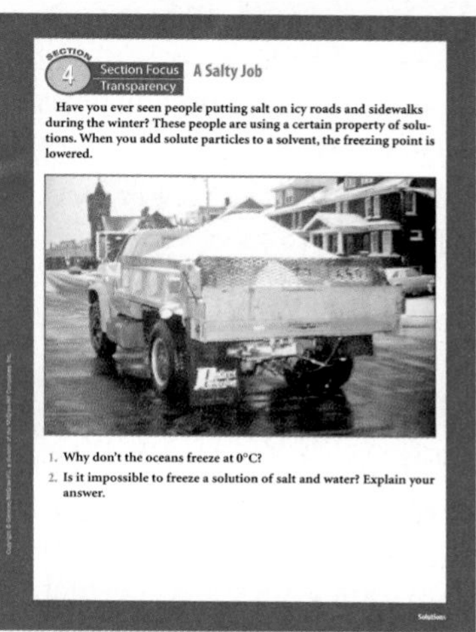

Tie to Prior Knowledge

Ask students to describe situations in which the boiling point or the freezing point of a material was changed. If they have trouble, explain that adding antifreeze to automobile radiators raises the boiling point. Explain that they will learn how this process works.

2 Teach

Particles With a Charge

Reading Check

Answer a substances that doesn't ionize in water and can't conduct electricity

How Ions Form

Visual Learning

Figure 19 Have students follow the dissolution process as you read the caption aloud. Emphasize that ionization is a process in which particles obtain a charge, while dissociation is a process in which already charged particles are separated from one another.

Teacher FYI

The osmosis of solutions is directly affected by the amount of dissolved solute in a solution. That is, dissolved solute particles on one side of a membrane slow down the rate at which a solvent can pass through a membrane. This fact is important in plant and animal cells.

Reading Check

Answer dissociation: particles are separated from other particles; ionization: process that forms ions

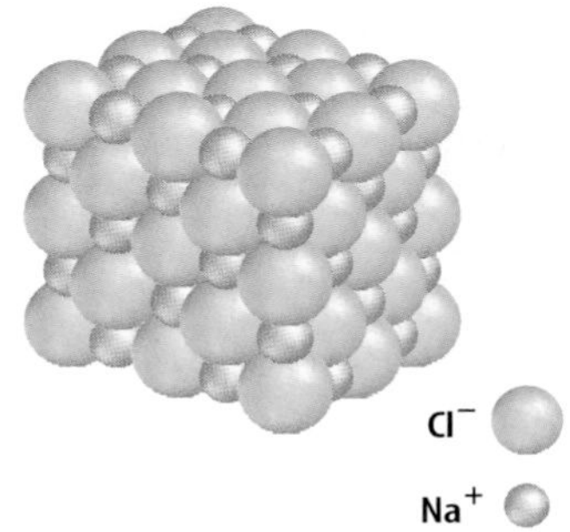

Figure 18
This is a model of a sodium chloride crystal. Each chloride atom is surrounded by six sodium atoms and vice versa.

Dissociation The second way that electrolytes form ions is by dissociation. The ions already exist in the ionic compound and are attracted into the solution by the surrounding polar water molecules. **Dissociation** is the process in which an ionic solid, such as sodium chloride, separates into its positive and negative ions. A model of a sodium chloride crystal is shown in **Figure 18.** In the crystal, each positive sodium ion is attracted to six negative chloride ions. Each of the negative chloride ions is attracted to six sodium ions, a pattern that exists throughout the crystal.

When placed in water, the crystal begins to break apart under the influence of water molecules. Remember that water is polar, which means that the positive areas of the water molecules are attracted to the negative chloride ions. Likewise the negative oxygen part of the water molecules is attracted to the sodium ions.

In **Figure 19,** water molecules are approaching the sodium and chloride ions in the crystal. The water molecules surround the sodium and chloride ions, having pulled them away from the crystal and into solution. The sodium and chloride ions have dissociated from one another. The solution now consists of sodium and chloride ions mixed with water. The ions move freely through the solution and are capable of conducting an electric current.

Reading Check *What are the differences and similarities between dissociation and ionization?*

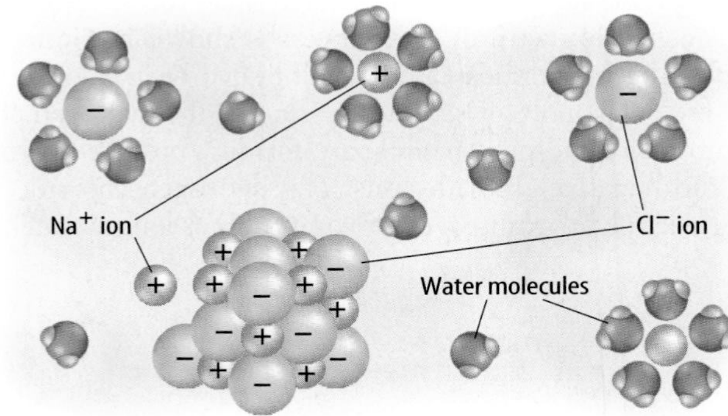

Figure 19
Sodium chloride dissociates as water molecules attract and pull the sodium and chloride ions from the crystal. Water molecules then surround and separate the Na^+ and Cl^- ions.

LAB DEMONSTRATION

Purpose to show that dissolved ionic compounds conduct an electrical current

Materials conductivity tester, distilled water, NaCl, Epsom salt, rubbing alcohol, sugar

Preparation List the solutes on the chalkboard. Dissolve each in distilled water.

Procedure Test the conductivity of each solution. Make sure students can see the results of each test.

Expected Outcome NaCl and Epsom salt solutions will conduct electricity; alcohol and sugar solutions will not.

Assessment

What occurs in the conducting solutions? Ions are moving out of crystals and into water where they can move in the solution and conduct electricity. **Why don't the other solutions conduct electricity?** The solutes in the other solutions don't form ions.

Effects of Solute Particles

All solute particles—polar and nonpolar, electrolyte and nonelectrolyte—affect the physical properties of the solvent, such as its freezing point and its boiling point. These effects can be useful. For example, antifreeze that you may add to water in a car radiator keeps the radiator fluid from freezing. Sugar and salt would do the same thing, but they are not used for obvious reasons. The effect that a solute has on the freezing point or boiling point of a solvent depends on the *number* of solute particles in solution, not on the chemical nature of the particles.

Lowering Freezing Point Adding a solute such as antifreeze to a solvent lowers the freezing point of the solvent. How much the freezing point goes down depends upon how many solute particles you add. How does this work?

As a substance freezes, its particles arrange themselves in an orderly pattern. The added solute particles interfere with the formation of this pattern, making it harder for the solvent to freeze as shown in **Figure 20.** To overcome this interference, a lower temperature is needed to freeze the solvent.

Raising Boiling Point Surprisingly, antifreeze also raises the boiling point of the water. How can it do this? The amount the boiling point is raised depends upon the number of solute molecules present. Solute particles interfere with the evaporation of solvent particles. Thus, more energy is needed for the solvent particles to escape from the liquid surface, and so the boiling point of the solution will be higher than the boiling point of solvent alone.

Life Science INTEGRATION

Certain animals that live in extremely cold climates have their own kind of antifreeze. Caribou, for example, contain substances in the lower section of their legs that prevent freezing in subzero temperatures. The caribou can stand for long periods of time in snow and ice with no harm to their legs.

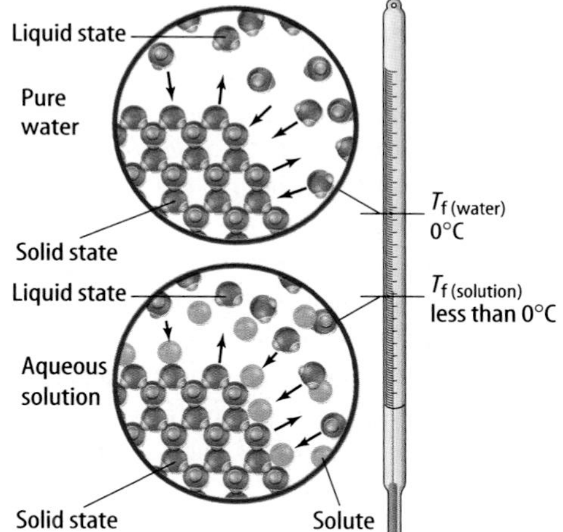

Figure 20
Solute molecules interfere with the freezing process by blocking molecules of solvent as they try to join the growing crystal lattice. For example, antifreeze molecules added to water block the formation of ice crystals.

Resource Manager

Chapter Resources Booklet
- Transparency Activity, p. 49
- Directed Reading for Content Mastery, pp. 20, 22
- Enrichment, p. 34

Science Journal

Have students write a paragraph describing why adding salt or other deicing agents to icy sidewalks on cold days helps keep the sidewalks clear of ice. At first the salt dissolves a bit in the small amount of water present, then the solution that forms has a lower freezing point than the original water on the sidewalk. P

Effects of Solute Particles

Life Science INTEGRATION

Many insects also have a type of antifreeze in their fluids. This allows them to survive extreme winter conditions without freezing.

IDENTIFYING Misconceptions

The antifreeze used in automobiles is ethylene glycol, which has a freezing point of about −13° C. Some people think the antifreeze lowers the freezing point in the car's cooling system because it has a lower freezing point than water. Actually, the ethylene glycol molecules interfere with the crystallization process of water, making it more difficult for water to solidify. A 50% solution with water has a freezing point of −37°C.

Use Science Words

Word Usage Have students find out why the word *electrolyte* is used when discussing sports drinks and the contents of batteries. Sports drinks contain electrolytes (sodium and potassium ions) that transport signals in the body. Batteries contain electrolytes (ammonium ions, sulfate ions, hydrogen ions) that conduct electricity in the battery. They all conduct electricity, but they contain different elements. L2 ELL

LS **Linguistic**

Reteach

To emphasize that the number of solute particles is the major factor in changing freezing and boiling points, have students predict the number of solute particles expected per starting particle of:

- $NaCl \rightarrow Na^{+} + Cl^{-}$ two
- $CaCl_2 \rightarrow Ca^{2+} + 2Cl^{-}$ three
- $Mg(OH)_2 \rightarrow Mg^{2+} + 2\ OH^{-}$ three
- $C_6H_{12}O_6 \rightarrow C_6H_{12}O_6$ one, nonelectrolyte

L1 LS **Analytical-Mathematical**

Challenge

Ask students to research and find out what happens to electrolytes when their concentration in a solution is very high. As polar water molecules surround each ion, the ions are held apart from each other. However, when many ions are present, there are fewer water molecules available per ion to keep the ions apart. The ions could draw back together, reducing the percent of ionization. L3 LS **Analytical-Mathematical**

Content Have students draw and label diagrams showing the process of dissociation of an ionic salt. Use **Performance Assessment in the Science Classroom,** p. 127.

Figure 21
Solute molecules raise the boiling point of a solution. A Solvent molecules vaporize freely from the surface. B Solute molecules block part of the surface, making it more difficult for solvent to vaporize.

Car Radiators The beaker in **Figure 21** represents a car radiator when it contains water molecules only—no antifreeze. Some of those molecules on the surface will vaporize, and the number of molecules that do vaporize depends upon the temperature of the solvent. As temperature increases, solvent molecules move faster, and more molecules vaporize. Finally, when the pressure of the solvent vapor equals atmospheric pressure, the solvent boils. Have you ever seen a vehicle at the side of the road with vapors rising from the radiator?

The result of adding antifreeze is shown in **Figure 21.** Molecules of solute are distributed evenly throughout the solution, including the surface area. Now fewer solvent molecules can reach the surface and evaporate, making the vapor pressure of the solution lower than that of the solvent. This means that it will take a higher temperature to make the car's radiator boil over.

Section  Assessment

1. Explain (a) how ionization is different from dissociation and (b) how the two processes are similar.
2. What kinds of solute particles are present in water solutions of electrolytes and nonelectrolytes?
3. Describe how an ionic substance dissociates in water.
4. How does the concentration of a solution influence its boiling point?
5. **Think Critically** In cold weather, people often put salt on ice that forms on sidewalks and driveways. The salt helps melt the ice, forming a saltwater solution. Explain why this solution may not refreeze.

Skill Builder Activities

6. **Concept Mapping** Draw a concept map to show the relationship among the following terms: *electrolytes, nonelectrolytes, dissociation, ionization, ionic compounds, certain polar compounds,* and *other polar compounds.* **For more help, refer to the Science Skill Handbook.**
7. **Communicating** Many insect eggs can survive extremely cold temperatures. What can you conclude about the fluids in these eggs? Research chicken eggs. What temperatures can they withstand? Summarize your conclusions in your Science Journal. **For more help, refer to the Science Skill Handbook.**

Resource Manager

Chapter Resources Booklet
Reinforcement, p. 30
Activity Worksheet, pp. 5–6
Science Inquiry Labs, p. 21

Answers to Section Assessment

1. (a) Ionization: the process of forming ions; dissociation: the process of separating ions (b) Both processes can yield electrolytic solutions.
2. electrolytes: ions; nonelectrolytes: molecules
3. The particles in the crystal are separated and drawn into solution by water molecules.
4. As the concentration rises, the boiling point increases until saturation is reached.
5. The ions from the salt have disrupted the crystal lattice formed by water when it freezes. The temperature will have to be lower for the molecules of water to freeze.
6. Check students' work.
7. The fluids in the eggs contain a solute that lowers the freezing point enough to keep the eggs from freezing in cold temperatures. Chicken eggs are usually stored at about 45°F, but can be frozen out of the shell at –9°F.

Activity

Boiling Points of Solutions

Adding small amounts of salt to water that is being boiled to cook pasta and adding antifreeze to a radiator have a common result—increasing the boiling point.

What You'll Investigate

How much can the boiling point of a solution be changed?

Materials

distilled water (400 mL)
Celsius thermometer,
table salt, NaCl (72 g)
ring stand
hot plate
250-mL beaker

Safety Precautions

Goals

- **Determine** how adding salt affects the boiling point of water.

Procedure

1. Bring 10 mL of distilled water to a gentle boil in a 250-mL beaker. Record the temperature. Do not touch the hot plate surface.
2. Dissolve 12 g of NaCl in 100 mL of distilled water. Bring this solution to a gentle boil and record its boiling point.
3. Repeat step 2, using 24 g of NaCl, then 36 g.
4. Make a graph of your results. Put boiling point on the *x*-axis and grams of NaCl on the *y*-axis.

The Effects of Solute on Boiling Point

Grams of NaCl Solute	Boiling Point (°C)
0	~100°C
12	~102°C
24	~104°C
36	~106°C

Conclude and Apply

1. **Explain** the difference between the boiling points of pure water and a water solution.
2. Instead of doubling the amount of NaCl in step 3, what would have been the effect of doubling the amount of water?
3. **Predict** what would happen if you continued to add more salt. Would your graph continue in the same pattern or eventually level off? Explain your prediction.

Communicating Your Data

Compare your results with those of other groups and discuss any differences in the results obtained. **For more help, refer to the** Science Skill Handbook.

Activity

BENCH TESTED

Purpose Students will determine the effect of added solute on the boiling point of a solution. L3 ELL **Analytical-Mathematical**

Process Skills observing, predicting, classifying, recognizing cause and effect, interpreting data

Time Required 35 minutes

Safety Precautions Students should not let the thermometer touch the sides or bottom of the beaker. Have them use care around boiling solutions.

Teaching Strategies

- Have one student measure out the next amount of solute while the other heats the solution.
- Start the graph at 90°C.

Troubleshooting Make sure the thermometer bulb is submerged during temperature readings.

Answers to Questions

1. The boiling points of solutions are higher.
2. The boiling point would still have been higher than that of pure water, but not as high as before.
3. The boiling point would continue to rise until the solution was saturated, then the boiling point would level off.

Assessment

Process Have students use their graphs to predict the boiling point of a solution that contains 18 g NaCl. about 103° C Use **Performance Assessment in the Science Classroom,** p. 101.

Communicating Your Data

Some differences arise because lab grade thermometers may vary and measurements of water and salt may vary. Also, as solutions boil, they become more concentrated, so variations in the length of time they boil can cause differences.

Activity

BENCH TESTED

What You'll Investigate

Purpose

Students compare the solubility of a solute at various temperatures. L2 ELL

LS **Logical-Mathematical**

Process Skills

measuring, using numbers, communicating, making and using graphs, making and using tables, inferring

Time Required

40 minutes

Alternate Materials

In addition to sugar, other solutes such as $CuSO_4$ (**CAUTION:** toxic) or KBr could be used.

Safety Precautions

CAUTION: Students should use test tube holders when handling hot test tubes. They should not stir solutions with a thermometer.

Activity

Saturated Solutions

Two major factors to consider when you are dissolving a solute in water are temperature and the ratio of solute to solvent. What happens to a solution as the temperature changes? To be able to draw conclusions about the effect of temperature, you must keep other variables constant. For example, you must be sure to stir each solution in a similar manner.

What You'll Investigate

How does solubility change as temperature is increased?

Materials

distilled water at room temperature
large test tubes
Celsius thermometer
table sugar
copper wire stirrer, bent into a spiral as shown
test-tube holder
graduated cylinder (10 mL)
beaker (250 mL) with 150 mL of water
electric hot plate
test-tube rack
ring stand

Goals

- **Observe** the effects of temperature on the amount of solute that dissolves.

Safety Precautions

WARNING: *Do NOT touch the test tubes or hot plate surface when hot plate is turned on or cooling down. When heating a solution in a test tube, keep it pointed away from yourself and others. Do NOT remove goggles until clean up including washing hands is completed.*

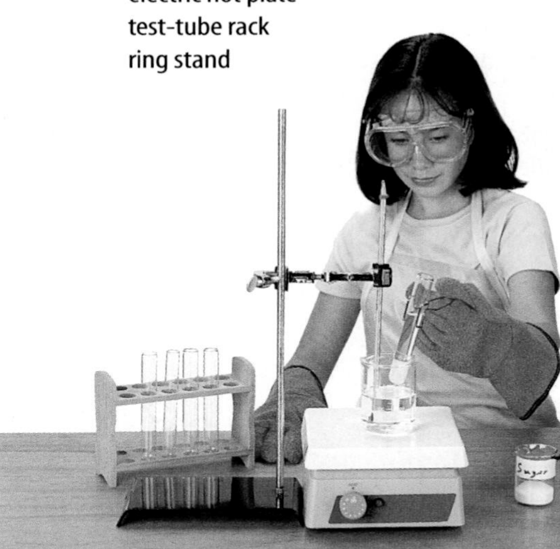

Resource Manager

Chapter Resources Booklet
Activity Worksheet, pp. 7–8

Performance Assessment in the Science Classroom, p. 41

Inclusion Strategies

Visually Impaired Pair students who have difficulty reading temperatures, measuring mass, and recording results with a partner who can describe the steps and results as the activity is carried out.

Procedure

1. Place 20 mL of distilled water in a test tube.
2. Add 30 g of sugar.
3. Stir. Does this dissolve?
4. If it dissolves completely, add another 5 g of sugar to the test tube. Does it dissolve?
5. Continue adding 5-g amounts of sugar until no more sugar dissolves.
6. Now place the beaker of water on the hot plate and hang the thermometer from the ring stand so that the bulb is immersed about halfway into the beaker, making sure it does not touch the sides or bottom. Record the starting temperature.
7. Using a test-tube holder, place the test tube into the water.
8. Gradually increase the temperature of the hot plate, while stirring the solution in the tube, until all the sugar dissolves.
9. Note the temperature at which this happens.
10. Add another 5 g of sugar and continue. Note the temperature at which this additional sugar dissolves.
11. Continue in this manner until you have at least four data points. Note the total amount of sugar that has dissolved. Record your data on the data table.

Dissolving Sugar in Water

Temperature	Total Grams of Sugar Dissolved
20°C–25°C	about 40 g
30°C–35°C	about 45 g
50°C	about 50 g
55°C–60°C	about 55 g

Conclude and Apply

1. How did the saturation change as the temperature was increased?
2. **Graph** your results using a line graph. Place grams of solute per 100 g of water (multiply the number of grams by five because you used only 20 mL of water) on the *y*-axis and place temperature on the *x*-axis.
3. Using your graph, estimate the solubility of sugar at 100°C and at 0°C, the boiling and freezing point of water, respectively.
4. **Compare** your results with those given in **Table 3.**

Compare your results with those of other groups and discuss any differences noted. Why might these differences have occurred? **For more help, refer to the** Science Skill Handbook.

Procedure

Teaching Strategy

Keep the hot plate setting low so the temperature changes will be slow.

Tie to Prior Knowledge

Remind students about dissolving sugar in hot tea versus cold tea.

Troubleshooting

Experiment with making the copper stirrers before the lab. Coil the copper wire around a pencil and check to be sure the coil fits into the test tubes being used.

Expected Outcome

At higher temperatures, more sugar will dissolve.

Draw Conclusions

1. The amount of solute needed to cause saturation was higher at each higher temperature.
2. Check student graphs against their results for accuracy.
3. approximately 490 g per 100mL at 100° C and 179 g per 100 mL at 0° C
4. Answers will vary.

Error Analysis

It may be difficult to tell whether the solute is dissolved when the solution is near saturation. Be sure students pause at each temperature long enough to give the solute time to dissolve. Otherwise, the amount of solute may be less than expected for saturation.

Assessment

Oral Have students explain how the relationship between saturation and temperature shown in this activity can be used in making candy. Large amounts of sugar may be dissolved at a very high temperature, then cooled quickly to form sugar crystals used in candy making. Students should also observe how stirring influences crystal size. Use **Performance Assessment in the Science Classroom,** p. 93.

Keeping the temperature constant while observing possible saturation is difficult. It is easy to go beyond the saturation level without knowing it. If the temperature increases at different rates, results will be different.

Science Stats

Content Background

The stomach is also protected from stomach acid by a mucous layer that coats the stomach walls. Ulcers can result if this layer does not completely cover the stomach lining.

Many mixtures are heterogeneous but contain solutions. For example, blood is heterogeneous because it contains blood cells that are not dissolved in it. However, the dissolved solids and gases in blood plasma form a solution. Seawater is another example. If all material suspended in seawater is allowed to settle, seawater is a solution. However, most samples of seawater contain particles of sea organisms or sediments that keep it from being a true solution.

Discussion

Water is the solvent in many glues, such as the washable school glue used by younger students. **When would you need to use glue that contains a solvent that is not water?** When items that are being glued will be exposed to moisture, water should not be the solvent.

Activity

For each of the solutions listed except that in the light stick, have students name the solute and the solvent. With the exception of steel, water is the solvent; iron is the solvent in steel. Solutes listed for steel are carbon, chromium, and nickel; for stomach acid, hydrochloric acid; for salt water, salt; and for natural glues, animal proteins and plant carbohydrates.

Science Stats

Weird Solutions

Did you know...

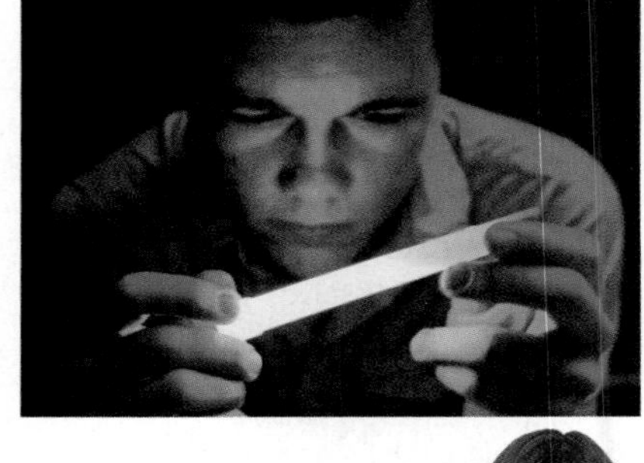

. . . The "brightest" solutions can glow like a streetlight. Glowing rods called light sticks are an example. Each rod contains two liquids that are kept apart using glass or plastic containers. When you flex the rod, the containers break, and the solutions mix and react to produce luminescence, or glowing light. A similar process called bioluminescence allows some living organisms, like fireflies and squid, to glow.

. . . One of the hardest solutions is steel, a solid solution of iron, carbon, and other elements. When you add some chromium and nickel to the mix, you get stainless steel, which is a tough, rust-resistant solution. In 1998, the United States produced nearly 100 million metric tons of raw steel—enough to make more than 18,000 Empire State Buildings.

. . . One of the strongest acids around is the solution found in your stomach. Stomach acid contains hydrochloric acid and is about 10 times stronger than vinegar. Vinegar is 10 times more acidic than fresh tomatoes. Fortunately, chemical buffers in the stomach neutralize the hydrochloric acid when it touches the stomach walls.

SCIENCE Online

Internet Addresses

Explore the Glencoe Science Web site at **science.glencoe.com** to find out more about topics in this feature.

Connecting To Math

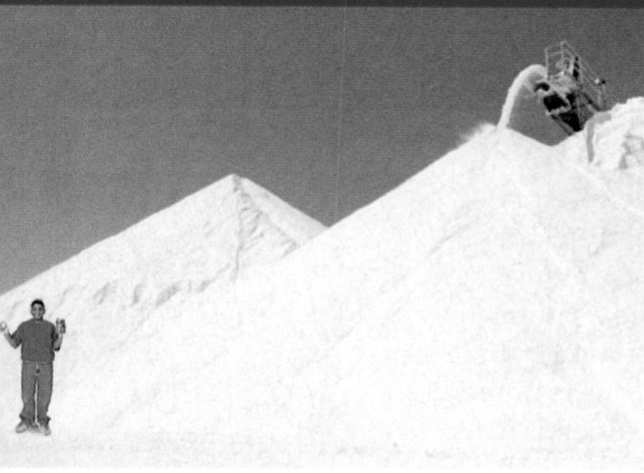

. . . The saltiest and largest body of solution in the western hemisphere is the Great Salt Lake in Utah. If all the salt in the lake dried out and hardened, the result would be a rock with a mass of about $4\frac{1}{2}$ trillion kg—as heavy as 300,000 large trucks.

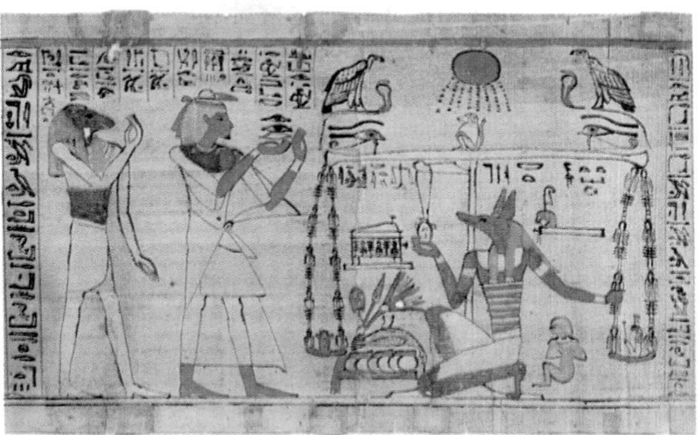

. . . Some of the stickiest solutions are glues. Gluing is nothing new. Papyrus—ancient Egyptian paper—was held together with glues. Natural adhesives come from animal proteins and plant carbohydrates. During the twentieth century, chemists developed many synthetic adhesives.

Do the Math

1. Great Salt Lake's salinity is 5 percent when the water is highest and 30 percent when the water is lowest. What is the lake's salinity when the water level is halfway between its highest and lowest levels?
2. Glow sticks shine for about 10 h. If you kept a glow stick glowing continuously in your window for seven days, how many sticks would you need?
3. One formula for making stainless steel is 1 percent carbon, 54 percent iron, and twice as much chromium as nickel. Calculate the percentage of chromium used.

Go Further

The human body contains many solutions. On **science.glencoe.com,** find out how many liters of solutions are in an average adult body.

Connecting To Math

Do the Math

Teaching Strategies

For question 1, review with students how to interpolate values between two known values.

For question 3, suggest students first set up an equation that relates the amount of chromium to the amount of nickel in stainless steel, then incorporate that in an equation that includes the total percentage of material needed to complete the stainless steel.

Answers

1. $30\% - 5\% = 25\%; \frac{1}{2} \times 25\% = 12.5\%; 5\% + 12.5\% = 17.5\%$
2. $\frac{(7 \times 24)}{10} = 16.8 = 17$ glow sticks
3. 1% carbon $+ 54\%$ iron $= 55\%$, leaving 45% nickel and chromium; if the amount of nickel $= x$, and the amount of chromium $= y$; $x + y = 45\%; 2x = y; 2x + x = 45\%; 3x = 45\%; x = 15\% =$ amount of nickel; amount of chromium $= 2x = 30\%$

Go Further

Before finding the volume of the solutions in the human body, have students brainstorm the types of solutions present. Such solutions include blood plasma, lymph, saliva, urine, and stomach acid.

Visual Learning

The acidity of a solution is measured by what is called pH. The pH scale ranges from 0 to 14, and the lower the pH, the more acidic the solution. Each unit on the pH scale indicates that a solution is 10 times more acidic than the next higher number. For example, if a solution has a pH of 4, it is 10 times more acidic than a solution that has a pH of 5. Have students read about the solution that is present in the stomach. Ask them to determine the pH of vinegar and the pH of tomatoes if the pH of stomach acid is 2. The pH of vinegar is 3; the pH of tomatoes is 4.

Chapter 23 Study Guide

Reviewing Main Ideas

Preview

Students can answer the questions in their Science Journals. Discuss the answers as you go through the chapter. **LS Linguistic**

Review

Students can write their answers, then compare them with those of other students. **LS Interpersonal**

Reteach

Students can look at the illustrations and describe details that support the main ideas of the chapter. **LS Visual-Spatial**

Answers to Chapter Review

SECTION 2

4. Never use them in an enclosed area.

SECTION 3

4. an unsaturated solution

Chapter 23 Study Guide

Reviewing Main Ideas

Section 1 How Solutions Form

1. A solution is a mixture that has the same composition, color, density, and taste throughout.
2. The substance being dissolved is called a solute, and the substance that does the dissolving is called a solvent.
3. The rate of dissolving can be increased by stirring or increasing temperature.
4. Under similar conditions, small particles of solute dissolve faster than large particles.

Section 2 Dissolving Without Water

1. Water cannot dissolve all solutes.
2. Nonpolar solvents are needed to dissolve nonpolar solutes.
3. Some vitamins are nonpolar and dissolve in the fat contained in some body cells.
4. Nonpolar solvents can be dangerous as well as helpful. *What precautions are needed when using substances like these?*

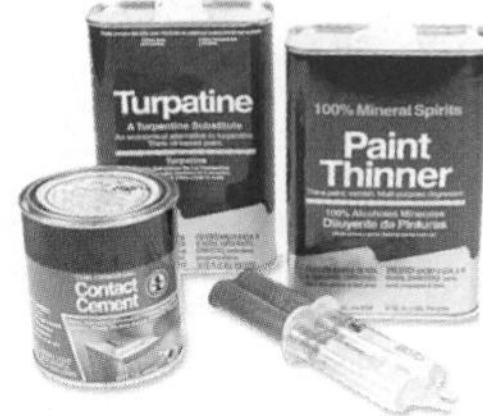

Section 3 Solubility and Concentration

1. Some compounds are more soluble than others, and this can be measured.
2. *Concentrated* and *dilute* are not precise terms used to describe concentration of solutions.
3. Concentrations can be expressed as percent by volume.
4. An unsaturated solution can dissolve more solute, and a saturated solution cannot. A supersaturated solution is made by raising the temperature of a saturated solution and adding more solute. If it is cooled carefully, the supersaturated solution will retain the dissolved solute. *Is this tea unsaturated, saturated, or supersaturated with sugar? Explain.*

Section 4 Particles in Solution

1. Substances that dissolve in water to produce solutions that conduct electricity are called electrolytes.
2. When water pulls apart the molecules of a polar substance, forming ions, the process is called ionization.
3. When ionic solids dissolve in water, the process is called dissociation, because the ions are already present in the solid.

FOLDABLES Reading & Study Skills — After You Read

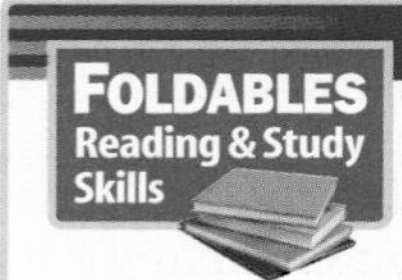

Use your Foldable to determine what characteristics solvents and solutes have in common.

FOLDABLES Reading & Study Skills — After You Read

After students have read the chapter and completed the Foldable described in Before You Read, have them do the activity on the student page.

Dinah Zike

Visualizing Main Ideas

Complete the following concept map on solutions.

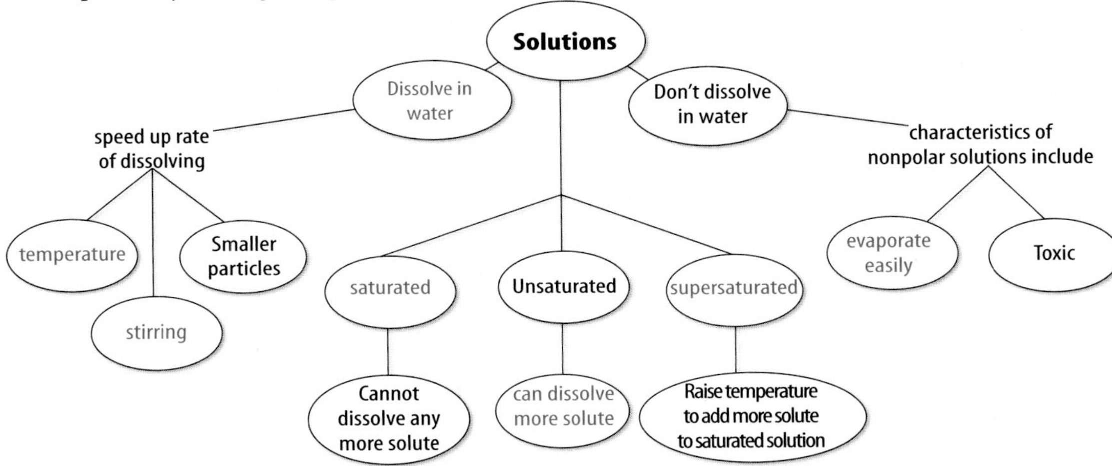

Vocabulary Review

Vocabulary words

a. alloy
b. dissociation
c. electrolyte
d. ion
e. ionization
f. nonelectrolyte
g. nonpolar
h. polar
i. saturated solution
j. solubility
k. solution
l. solute
m. solvent
n. supersaturated solution
o. unsaturated solution

Using Vocabulary

The sentences below include terms that are used incorrectly. Change the incorrect terms so that the sentence reads correctly. Underline your change.

1. In lemonade, sugar is the solvent and water is the solution.
2. During ionization, particles in an ionic solid are separated and drawn into solution.
3. If more of substance B dissolves in water than substance A, then substance B has a higher dissociation than substance A.
4. Adding a seed crystal may cause solute to crystallize from an unsaturated solution.
5. More solute can be added to a saturated solution.
6. A substance that does not form ions in water is a solute.

THE PRINCETON REVIEW Study Tip

Pay attention to the chapter's illustrations. Try to figure out exactly what point the picture is trying to stress.

Chapter 23 Study Guide

Visualizing Main Ideas

See student page.

Vocabulary Review

Using Vocabulary

1. solute and solvent
2. dissociation
3. solubility
4. supersaturated solution
5. unsaturated solution
6. nonelectrolyte

Chapter 23 Assessment

Checking Concepts

1. D
2. A
3. B
4. A
5. B
6. B
7. B
8. A
9. B
10. C

Thinking Critically

11. The salted water boils at a slightly higher temperature than unsalted water because of the presence of dissolved ions. At the higher temperature, the potatoes cook more quickly.
12. It dissociates into Cu^{2+} and SO_4^{2-} ions that are attracted to the polar water molecules.
13. Concentrated merely indicates a large amount of solute; dilute indicates not much solute.
14. Place 25 mL of concentrated apple juice in 75 mL of water.
15. Water can be the solute in a solution.

Chapter 23 Assessment

Checking Concepts

Choose the word or phrase that best answers the question.

1. Which of the following is NOT a solution?
   A) glass of soda **C)** bronze alloy
   B) air in a SCUBA tank **D)** mud in water
2. What term is NOT appropriate to use when describing solutions?
   A) heterogeneous **C)** liquid
   B) gaseous **D)** solid
3. When iodine is dissolved in alcohol, what term is used to describe the alcohol?
   A) alloy **C)** solution
   B) solvent **D)** solute
4. What word is used to describe a mixture that is 85 percent copper and 15 percent tin?
   A) alloy **C)** saturated
   B) solvent **D)** solute
5. Solvents, such as paint thinner and gasoline evaporate more readily than water because they are what type of compounds?
   A) ionic **C)** dilute
   B) nonpolar **D)** polar
6. What can a polar solvent dissolve?
   A) any solute **C)** a nonpolar solute
   B) a polar solute **D)** no solute
7. If a water solution conducts electricity, what must the solute be?
   A) gas **C)** liquid
   B) electrolyte **D)** nonelectrolyte
8. In forming a water solution, what process does an ionic compound undergo?
   A) dissociation **C)** ionization
   B) electrolysis **D)** no change
9. What can you increase to make a gas more soluble in a liquid?
   A) particle size **C)** stirring
   B) pressure **D)** temperature
10. If a solute comes out of a solution, what kind of solution might it be?
   A) unsaturated **C)** supersaturated
   B) saturated **D)** dilute

Thinking Critically

11. Why might potatoes cook more quickly in salted water than in unsalted water?
12. Explain what happens when an ionic compound such as copper(II) sulfate, $CuSO_4$, dissolves in water.
13. Why are *concentrated* and *dilute* not precise?
14. Explain how you would make a 25 percent solution by volume of apple juice.
15. Why is the statement, "Water is the solvent in a solution," not always true?

Developing Skills

16. **Making and Using Tables** Using the data in **Table 3,** fill in the following table. Use the terms *saturated, unsaturated,* and *supersaturated* to describe the type of solution.

Limits of Solubility

Compound	Type of Solution	Solubility in 100 g Water at 20°C
$CuSO_4$	saturated	32.0 g
KCl	supersaturated	45.8 g
KNO_3	saturated	31.6 g
$NaClO_3$	unsaturated	79.6 g

Chapter Assessment Planner

Portfolio Encourage students to place in their portfolios one or two items of what they consider to be their best work. Examples include:

- Science Journal, p. 707
- Health Integration, p. 716
- Science Journal, p. 719
- Science Journal, p. 725

Performance Additional performance assessments, Performance Task Assessment Lists, and rubrics for evaluating these activities can be found in Glencoe's **Performance Assessment in the Science Classroom.**

Formation of electrolytes
- from → ionic componds → is called → dissociation
- from → molecular compounds → is called → ionization

17. Concept Mapping Compare and contrast the processes of ionization and dissociation in the concept map above.

18. Measuring in SI 153 g of potassium nitrate have been dissolved in enough water to make 1 L of this solution. You use a graduated cylinder to measure 80 mL of solution. What mass of potassium nitrate is in the 80-mL sample?

Performance Assessment

19. Wise consumer Visit a grocery store and identify 20 examples of solutions. Classify them according to the type of solution—gas, liquid, or solid. Present your results to your class.

Technology

Go to the Glencoe Science Web site at **science.glencoe.com** or use the **Glencoe Science CD-ROM** for additional chapter assessment.

Test Practice

Pictured below are a scoop of cherry drink mix, a glass of water, and a glass of cherry drink made by adding the mix to the water.

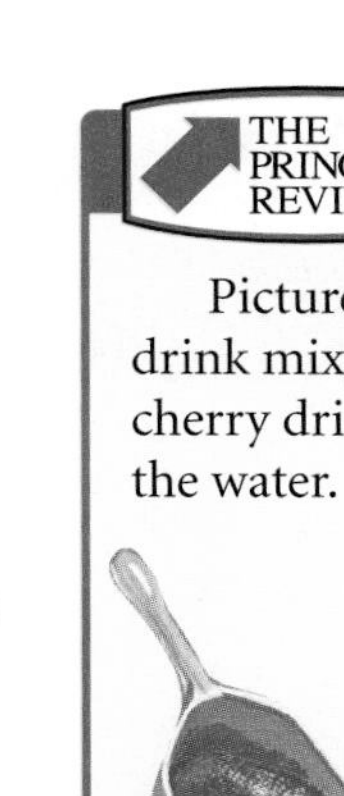
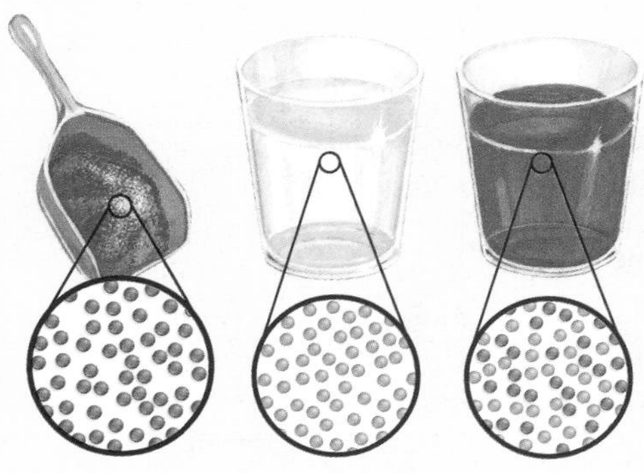

1. Which of the following best describes what happens when the cherry drink mix is added to the water?

A) The size and number of cherry drink mix particles increases.
B) The particles reject the cherry drink mix particles.
C) The cherry drink mix particles become evenly mixed with the water particles.
D) Each cherry drink particle enters a water particle.

2. Which of the following best represents a solution that contains a high level of cherry drink mix?

F) 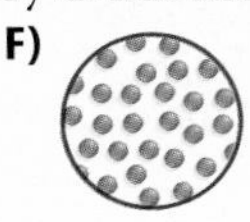
H) 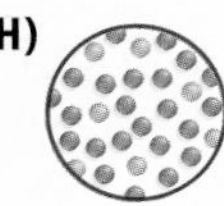
G) 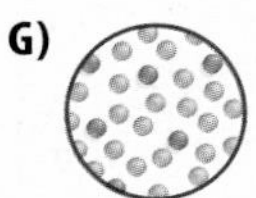
J) 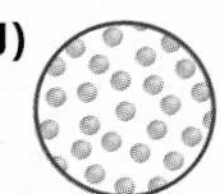

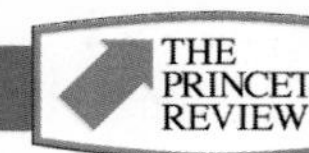

Test Practice

The Test-Taking Tip was written by The Princeton Review, the nation's leader in test preparation.

1. C
2. H

Developing Skills

16. See student page.

17. Ionization refers to the formation of ions. Dissociation refers to the process of separating ions in an ionic solid through interaction with water.

18. 153 g/1000 mL $\times$ 80.0 mL $= 12.2$ g KNO_3

Performance Assessment

19. Answers will vary. Use **PASC**, pp. 97 and 99.

Assessment Resources

Reproducible Masters

Chapter Review, pp. 39–40
Chapter Tests, pp. 41–44
Assessment Transparency Activity, p. 53

Glencoe Science Web site
Interactive Tutor
Chapter Quizzes

Glencoe Technology
- Assessment Transparency
- Interactive CD-ROM Chapter Quizzes
- ExamView Pro Test Bank
- Vocabulary PuzzleMaker Software
- MindJogger Videoquiz DVD/VHS

<table>
<tr><th>Section/Objectives</th><th colspan="2">Standards</th><th>Activities/Features</th></tr>
<tr><td rowspan="2">Chapter Opener</td><td>National</td><td>State/Local</td><td rowspan="2">Explore Activity: Observe which metals reacts, p. 737
Before You Read, p. 737</td></tr>
<tr><td>See p. 26T for a Key to Standards.</td><td></td></tr>
<tr><td>Section 1 Chemical Changes
1 session 1 block
1. Identify the reactants and products in a chemical reaction.
2. Determine how a chemical reaction satisfies the law of conservation of mass.
3. Determine how chemists express chemical changes using equations.</td><td>National Content Standards: UCP3, A1, B1 (5–7), B3, B5 (9–12)</td><td></td><td>Science Online, p. 739
MiniLAB: Designing a Team Equation, p. 741</td></tr>
<tr><td>Section 2 Chemical Equations
2 sessions 1 block
1. Identify what is meant by a balanced chemical equation.
2. Determine how to write balanced chemical equations.</td><td>National Content Standards: UCP3, B1 (5–7), B3, B5 (9–12)</td><td></td><td>Science Online, p. 744</td></tr>
<tr><td>Section 3 Classifying Chemical Reactions
2 sessions 1 block
1. Identify the four general types of chemical reactions.
2. Predict which metals will replace other metals in compounds.</td><td>National Content Standards: UCP3, B1 (5–7), B3, B5 (9–12)</td><td></td><td>Math Skills Activity, p. 748</td></tr>
<tr><td>Section 4 Chemical Reactions and Energy
3 sessions 1.5 blocks
1. Identify the source of energy changes in chemical reactions.
2. Compare and contrast exergonic and endergonic reactions.
3. Examine the effects of catalysts on the speed of chemical reactions.</td><td>National Content Standards: UCP3, A1, B1 (5–7), B3, B5 (9–12), E2, F4, F5 (5–8), F3, F4, F5, F6 (9–12), G1, G3</td><td></td><td>Visualizing Chemical Energy, p. 751
MiniLAB, p. 752
Environmental Science Integration, p. 754
Activity: Catalyzed Reaction, p. 755
Activity: Fossil Fuels and Greenhouse Gases, pp. 756–757
Oops! Accidents in Science: A Clumsy Move Pays Off, pp. 758–759</td></tr>
</table>

Activity Materials	Reproducible Resources	Section Assessment	Technology
Explore Activity: clean iron nail, piece of aluminum metal, petri dishes containing agar gel and small amounts of two indicators	**Chapter Resources Booklet** Foldables Worksheet, p. 17 Note-taking Worksheets, pp. 35–37	GLENCOE'S ASSESSMENT ADVANTAGE	
MiniLAB: 15 index cards	**Chapter Resources Booklet** Transparency Activity, p. 46 MiniLAB, p. 3 Enrichment, p. 31 Reinforcement, p. 27 Directed Reading, p. 20 Transparency Activities, pp. 51–52 Lab Activity, pp. 9–11	**Portfolio** Curriculum Connection, p. 739 **Performance** MiniLAB, p. 741 Skill Builder Activities, p. 742 **Content** Section Assessment, p. 742	Section Focus Transparency Teaching Transparency Interactive CD-ROM/DVD Guided Reading Audio Program
	Chapter Resources Booklet Transparency Activity, p. 47 Enrichment, p. 32 Reinforcement, p. 28 Directed Reading, p. 20 Lab Activity, pp. 13–16	**Portfolio** Assessment, p. 745 **Performance** Skill Builder Activities, p. 745 **Content** Section Assessment, p. 745	Section Focus Transparency Interactive CD-ROM/DVD Guided Reading Audio Program
	Chapter Resources Booklet Transparency Activity, p. 48 Enrichment, p. 33 Reinforcement, p. 29 Directed Reading, p. 21 **Science Inquiry Labs,** p. 15	**Portfolio** Challenge, p. 749 **Performance** Skill Builder Activities, p. 749 **Content** Section Assessment, p. 749	Section Focus Transparency Interactive CD-ROM/DVD Guided Reading Audio Program
MiniLAB: 5 mL water, test tube, copper(II) bromide **Activity:** 3 test tubes, test-tube stand, 3% hydrogen peroxide, H_2O_2 (15 mL), 10-mL graduated cylinder, small plastic teaspoon, 1/4-teaspoon sand, hot plate, wooden splint, beaker of hot water, 1/4 teaspoon manganese dioxide MnO_2 **Activity:** Internet and other resource on fossil fuels and greenhouse gases	**Chapter Resources Booklet** Transparency Activity, p. 49 MiniLAB, p. 4 Enrichment, p. 34 Reinforcement, p. 30 Directed Reading, pp. 21, 22 Activity Worksheet, pp. 5–6, 7–8 **Cultural Diversity,** p. 63 **Physical Science Critical Thinking/Problem Solving,** p. 14	**Portfolio** Active Reading, p. 753 **Performance** MiniLAB, p. 752 Skill Builder Activities, p. 754 **Content** Section Assessment, p. 754	Section Focus Transparency Interactive CD-ROM/DVD Guided Reading Audio Program

Need materials? Contact Science Kit at 1-800-828-7777 or www.sciencekit.com on the Internet.

End of Chapter Assessment

GLENCOE'S ASSESSMENT ADVANTAGE

Blackline Masters	Technology	Professional Series
Chapter Resources Booklet Chapter Review, pp. 39–40 Chapter Tests, pp. 41–44 **Standardized Test Practice by The Princeton Review,** pp. 100–103	MindJogger Videoquiz CD-ROM Explorations and Quizzes Vocabulary Puzzle Makers ExamView Pro Test Bank Interactive Lesson Planner Interactive Teacher's Edition	Performance Assessment in the Science Classroom (PASC)

Transparencies

Section Focus

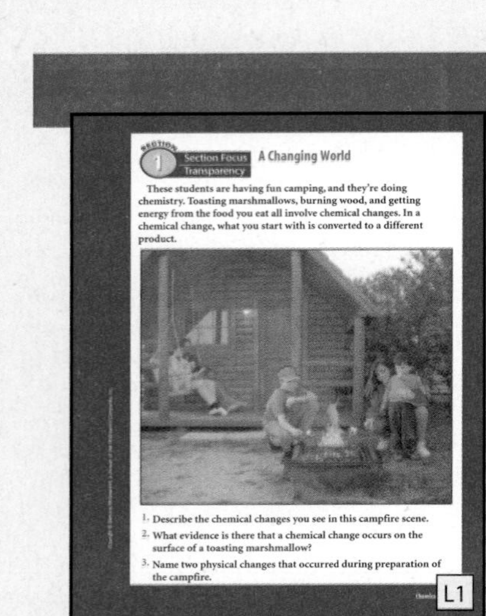

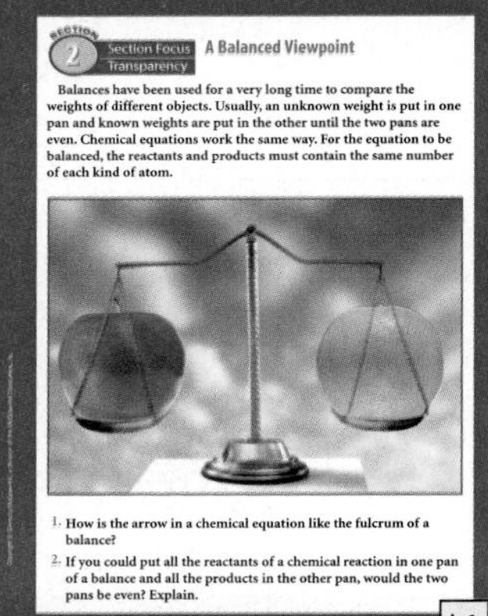

Assessment

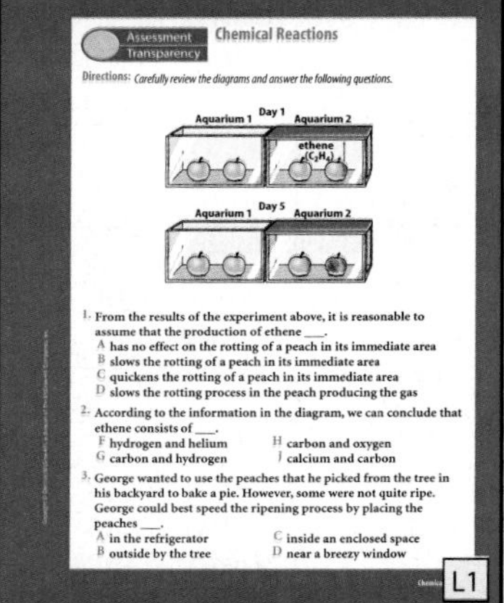

Teaching

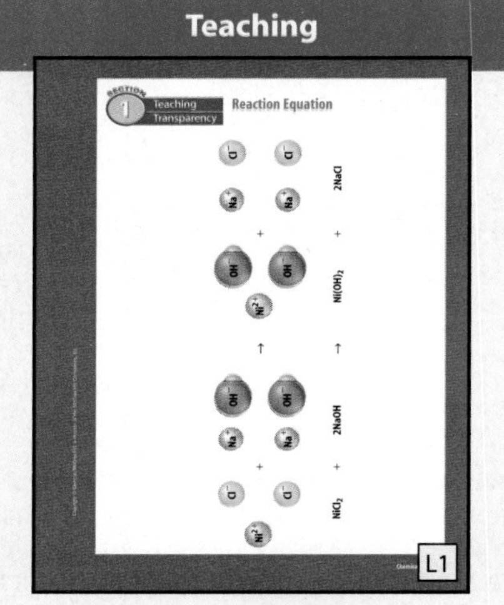

This is a representation of key blackline masters available in the Teacher Classroom Resources. See Resource Manager boxes within the chapter for additional information.

Key to Teaching Strategies

The following designations will help you decide which activities are appropriate for your students.

L1 Level 1 activities should be appropriate for students with learning difficulties.

L2 Level 2 activities should be within the ability range of all students.

L3 Level 3 activities are designed for above-average students.

ELL ELL activities should be within the ability range of English Language Learners.

COOP LEARN Cooperative Learning activities are designed for small group work.

LS Multiple Learning Styles logos are used throughout to indicate strategies that address different learning styles.

P These strategies represent student products that can be placed into a best-work portfolio.

Hands-on Activities

Activity Worksheets

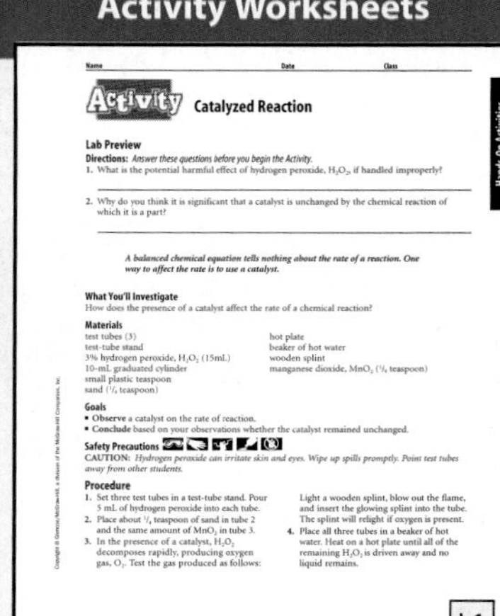

Laboratory Activities

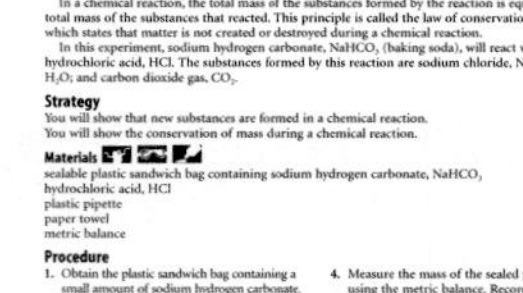

Meeting Different Ability Levels

Content Outline

Note-taking Worksheet — Chemical Reactions

Section 1 Chemical Changes in Matter

L1

Reinforcement

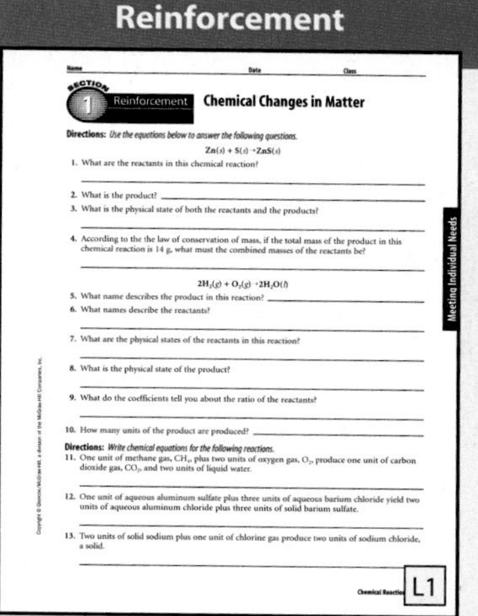

Section 1 Reinforcement — Chemical Changes in Matter

L1

Directed Reading

Directed Reading for Content Mastery — Overview: Chemical Reactions

L1

Enrichment

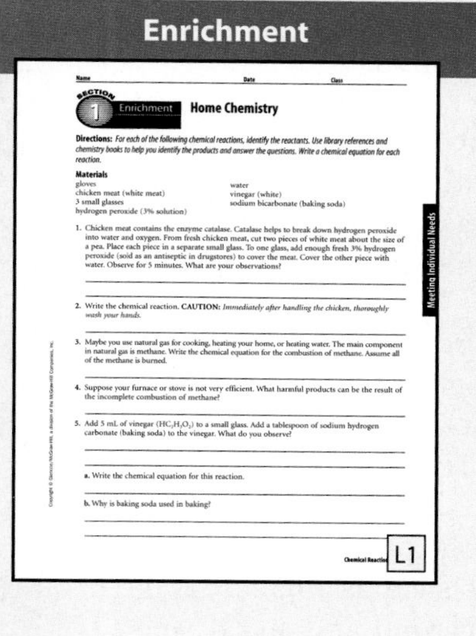

Section 1 Enrichment — Home Chemistry

L1

Spanish Directed Reading

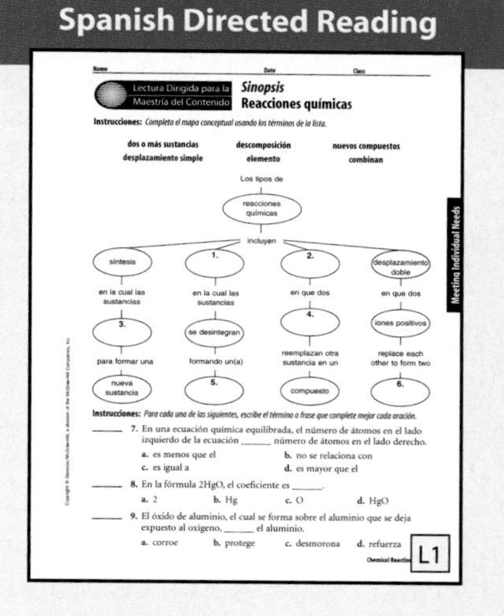

Lectura Dirigida para la Maestría del Contenido — Sinopsis: Reacciones químicas

L1

Assessment

Chapter Tests

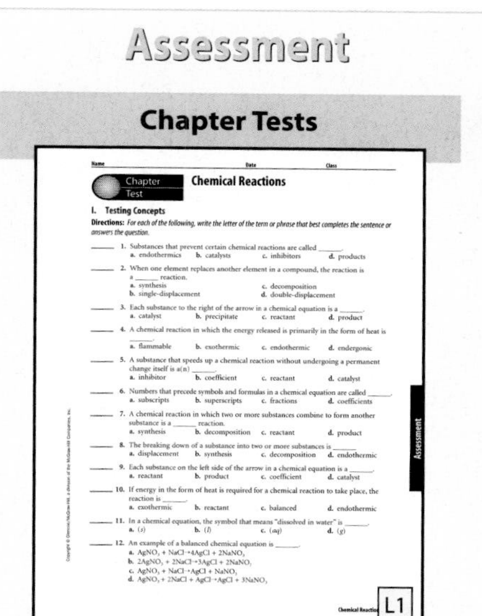

Chapter Test — Chemical Reactions

I. Testing Concepts

L1

Test Practice Workbook

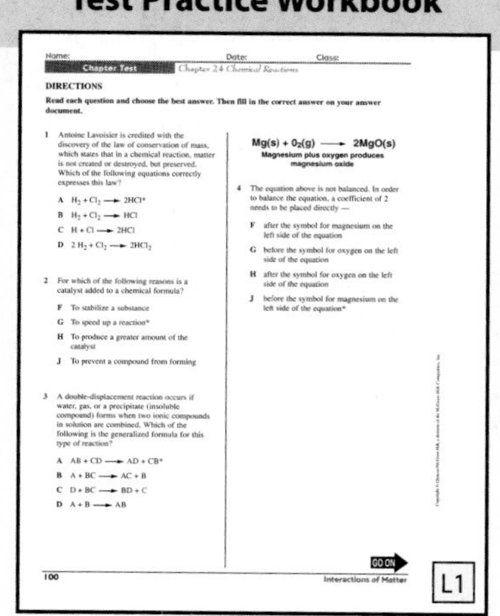

Chapter Test — Chapter 24 Chemical Reactions

L1

Chapter Review

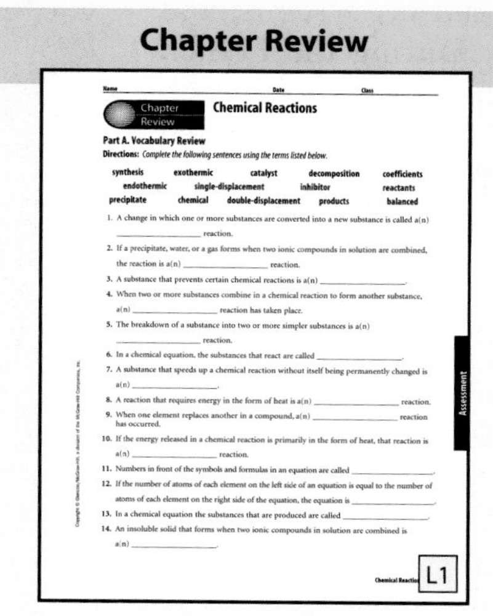

Chapter Review — Chemical Reactions

Part A. Vocabulary Review

L1

Science Content Background

SECTION 1

Chemical Changes

Conservation of Mass

For his work on conservation of mass, many consider eighteenth century French scientist Antoine-Laurent Lavoisier to be the founder of modern chemistry. Lavoisier's work, done during the late 1700s, included some of the first quantitative chemical experiments ever performed. He showed that the quantity of matter is the same at the end of a chemical reaction as it is at the beginning of the reaction.

Fun Fact

Antoine-Laurent Lavoisier was secretary and treasurer of a commission appointed in 1790 to secure the uniformity of weights and measures throughout France. That work led to the establishment of the metric system.

While most of Lavoisier's experiments centered on combustion, he also investigated the composition of water. In fact, he named the two components of water, hydrogen and oxygen. With the help of other scientists, he devised a chemical naming system that served as the basis of the modern system.

Lavoisier held many public offices in France, working in areas such as finance, economics, agriculture, education, and social welfare. In these capacities, he attempted to introduce various reforms, among them changes in the French monetary and tax systems, and also in farming methods. During the French Revolution, he and other influential French leaders fell out of favor. Lavoisier was arrested in 1793. On May 8, 1794, after a trial that lasted less than a day, Lavoisier and 27 others were beheaded.

SECTION 2

Chemical Equations

Balanced Equations

A chemical equation must show the identities and relative amounts of the reactants and products. However, it can also indicate the physical states of the reactants and products, whether energy is released or absorbed, and whether a catalyst is used. A chemical equation is not accurate unless the formulas are correct and the equation is balanced.

Charles D. Winters/Photo Researchers

SECTION 3

Classifying Chemical Reactions

Types of Reactions

Most chemical reactions can be classified as one of five types of reactions: synthesis, decomposition, single-displacement, double-displacement, and combustion. In a double-displacement reaction, two elements replace one another in two different compounds. Double-displacement reactions occur only in solution and only if a precipitate or water is formed.

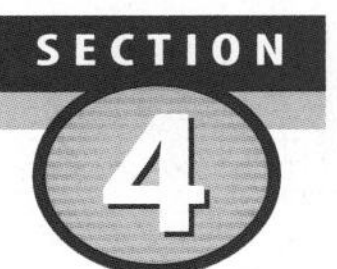

Chemical Reactions and Energy

Chemical Reaction—Energy Exchanges

Every reaction has a rate, or speed at which it proceeds. The study of reaction rates and reaction mechanisms is known as chemical kinetics. Temperature, concentration, particle size, catalysts, and the nature of the reactants determine the reaction rate. The rate of a reaction is not constant throughout the course of the reaction because the rate is proportional to reactant concentration. The concentration of reactants decreases as reactants are converted to products. In other words, as the reactants are used up to form products, the reactants cannot find one another as often as they could in the beginning of the reaction. In turn this decreases the rate of reaction. To counteract this slow down, an excess of one reactant is often used to keep the reaction from becoming impractically slow.

For additional content background on this topic, go to the Glencoe Science Web site at science.glencoe.com.

In 1888, the French chemist Henri Le Chatelier (1850–1936) set forth a simple important generalization on the behavior of equilibrium systems. This generalization, known as Le Chatelier's principle, states that "if a stress is applied to a system of equilibrium, the system will respond in such a way as to relieve that stress and restore equilibrium under a new set of conditions." The application of Le Chatelier's principle helps in predicting the effect of concentration, temperature, and volume on the rate of chemical reactions.

More Energy In

Catalysts are extremely important to industrial chemistry. Most industrial processes use catalysts to lower reaction temperatures, thus reducing energy costs.Once suitable catalysts are found, chemical reactions that are otherwise too slow to be of practical value become cost-effective.

Enzymes are large proteins that act as catalysts for biological reactions. The enzyme amylase found in human digestive systems is able to catalyze the breakdown of starch to yield glucose but has no effect on cellulose, even though the two compounds are similar. This is why humans can digest a hamburger bun, but not the grass that fed the cow.

John Paul Endress/The Stock Market

Chemical Reactions

Chapter Vocabulary

chemical reaction
reactant
product
chemical equation
coefficient
balanced chemical equation
synthesis reaction
decomposition reaction
single-displacement reaction
double-displacement reaction
precipitate
exergonic reaction
exothermic reaction
endergonic reaction
endothermic reaction
catalyst
inhibitor

What do you think?

Science Journal This photograph shows a chemical reaction that forms a gas.

Chemical Reactions

Ohhhh! Ahhhh! The crowd gasps as fireworks explode overhead into patterns of brightly colored sparks. Deafening booms split the air and children squeal with delight. All these effects are produced by chemical reactions with oxygen. The colors come from small amounts of metal ions—blue from copper, red from lithium, gold from sodium, and green from barium. In this chapter, you will learn about chemical reactions—what they are, how to describe them, and how they release or absorb energy.

What do you think?

Science Journal Look at the picture below with a classmate. Discuss what you think this might be or what is happening. Here's a hint: *These bubbles are lighter than air.* Write down your best guess in your Science Journal.

736

Theme Connection

Systems and Interactions Chemical reactions depend on interactions among chemical compounds. A chemical reaction can be considered to be a system into and out of which energy flows.

Like exploding fireworks, rusting is a chemical reaction in which iron metal combines with oxygen. Other metals combine with oxygen, too—some more readily than others. In this activity, you will compare how iron and aluminum react with oxygen.

Safety Precautions 

Observe which metal reacts

1. Place a clean, iron nail in one of the dishes that your teacher has prepared. These dishes contain agar gel and small amounts of two indicators.
2. One indicator turns pink when aluminum is changed by oxygen. The other turns blue when iron is changed.
3. Place a piece of aluminum metal in the second dish.
4. Carefully examine both of the nails the next day. Where are the pink areas around the nails? Where are the blue areas?

Observe

How readily does aluminum react with oxygen? Describe in your Science Journal how this compares with how iron reacts with oxygen.

Before You Read

FOLDABLES Reading & Study Skills

Making a Cause and Effect Study Fold **Make the following Foldable to help you understand the cause and effect relationship of chemical reactions.**

1. Place a sheet of paper in front of you so the short side is at the top. Fold the paper in half from the left side to the right side.
2. Now fold the paper in half from top to bottom. Then fold it in half again top to bottom. Unfold the last two folds you did.
3. Through one thickness of paper, cut along each of the fold lines to form four tabs as shown.
4. Label the four sections "R" for reactants, "⟶" for produce, and "P" for products as shown. As you read the chapter, record examples of chemical reactions under the tabs.

737

EXPLORE ACTIVITY

Purpose Use this activity to introduce students to chemical reactions and to the evidence that a chemical change has occurred. L2 ELL LS **Visual-Spatial**

Preparation Bring 1 L of water to a gentle boil, add 10 g of powdered agar mix, and stir until the mix is dissolved. While the mixture is warm, add 1 g of phenolphthalein powder or 25 drops of a 0.1% phenolphthalein solution. Next, add 3 mL of iron oxidation indicator (3 g of potassium ferricyanide in 100 mL of water).

Materials agar mixture, petri dishes, aluminum metal, iron nails

Teaching Strategy Ask students how we know when a chemical change has taken place. evidence such as color changes

Observe

The blue color in the agar indicates that iron was oxidized. The lack of color surrounding the nail in the other dish indicates that aluminum reacted with oxygen.

Process Have students diagram the two petri dishes, using colored markers to indicate the two different chemical reactions that took place. Use **PASC,** p. 127.

Before You Read

Dinah Zike Study Fold

Purpose Students make and use a Foldable to determine what they know about chemical reactions. They then list on the Foldable examples of chemical reactions, and describe them using descriptive sentences and chemical equations.

For additional help, see Foldables Worksheet, p. 17 in **Chapter Resources Booklet,** or go to the Glencoe Science Web site at **science.glencoe.com.** See After You Read in the Study Guide at the end of this chapter.

SECTION

Chemical Changes

1 Motivate

Bellringer Transparency

Display the Section Focus Transparency for Section 1. Use the accompanying Transparency Activity Master. L2 ELL

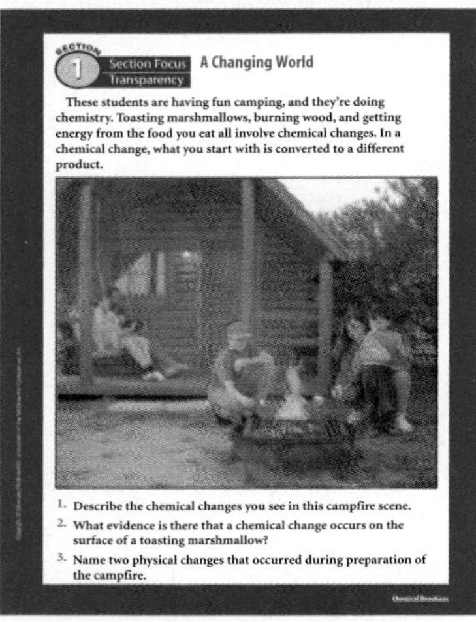

Section 1 Section Focus Transparency **A Changing World**

These students are having fun camping, and they're doing chemistry. Toasting marshmallows, burning wood, and getting energy from the food you eat all involve chemical changes. In a chemical change, what you start with is converted to a different product.

1. Describe the chemical changes you see in this campfire scene.
2. What evidence is there that a chemical change occurs on the surface of a toasting marshmallow?
3. Name two physical changes that occurred during preparation of the campfire.

Chemical Reactions

Tie to Prior Knowledge

Ask students to describe evidence they have observed of chemical reactions. Examples will vary but could include evolution of a gas—baking soda and vinegar; production of heat and light—burning a fuel; color change—cooking a hot dog over a fire; formation of a precipitate—spoiling of milk.

SECTION 1

Chemical Changes

As You Read

***What* You'll Learn**

- **Identify** the reactants and products in a chemical reaction.
- **Determine** how a chemical reaction satisfies the law of conservation of mass.
- **Determine** how chemists express chemical changes using equations.

Vocabulary

chemical reaction, chemical equation, coefficient, reactant, product

***Why* It's Important**

Chemical reactions cook our food, warm our homes, and provide energy to our bodies.

Describing Chemical Reactions

Dark mysterious mixtures react, gas bubbles up and expands, and powerful aromas waft through the air. Where are you? Are you in a chemical laboratory carrying out a crucial experiment? No. You are in the kitchen baking a chocolate cake. Nowhere in the house do so many chemical reactions take place as in the kitchen.

Actually, chemical reactions are taking place all around you and even within you. A **chemical reaction** is a change in which one or more substances are converted into new substances. The substances that react are called **reactants.** The new substances produced are called **products.** This relationship can be written as follows:

$$\text{reactants} \xrightarrow{\text{produce}} \text{products}$$

Conservation of Mass

By the 1770s, chemistry was changing from the art of alchemy to a true science. Chemical reactions were studied carefully. Through such study, the French chemist Antoine Lavoisier established that the mass of the products always equals the mass of the reactants. This principle is demonstrated in **Figure 1.**

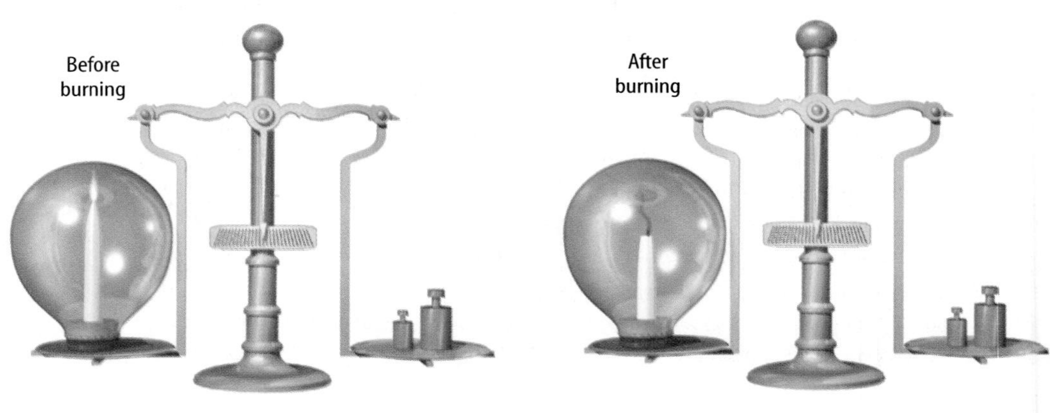

Figure 1
The mass of the candles and oxygen before burning is exactly equal to the mass of the remaining candle and gaseous products.

Section Assessment Planner

PORTFOLIO

Curriculum Connection, p. 739

PERFORMANCE ASSESSMENT

Try at Home MiniLAB, p. 741

Skill Builder Activities, p. 742

See page 762 for more options.

CONTENT ASSESSMENT

Section, p. 742

Challenge, p. 742

Chapter, pp. 762–763

738 CHAPTER 24 Chemical Reactions

Figure 2 Antoine Lavoisier's wife, Marie-Anne, drew this view of Lavoisier in his laboratory performing studies on oxygen. She depicted herself at the right taking notes.

Describing Chemical Reactions

In one experiment, Lavoisier placed a carefully measured mass of solid mercury(II) oxide, which he knew as mercury calyx, into a sealed container. When he heated this container, he noted a dramatic change. The red powder had been transformed into a silvery liquid that he recognized as mercury metal, and a gas was produced. When he determined the mass of the liquid mercury and gas, their combined masses were exactly the same as the mass of the red powder he had started with.

mercury(II) oxide	produces	oxygen	plus	mercury
10.0 g	=	0.7 g	+	9.3 g

Lavoisier also established that the gas produced by heating mercury oxide, which we call oxygen, was a component of air. He did this by heating mercury metal with air and saw that a portion of the air combined to give red mercury oxide. He studied the effect of this gas on living animals, including himself. Hundreds of experiments carried out in his laboratory, shown in **Figure 2,** confirmed that in a chemical reaction, matter is not created or destroyed, but is conserved. This principle became known as the law of conservation of mass. This means that the starting mass of the reactants equals the final mass of the products.

Reading Check *What does the law of conservation of mass state?*

This principle is the basis for modern chemistry. It made it possible for chemists to see clearly what happens in chemical reactions. More importantly, the concept of balance between reactants and products led to a valuable tool of chemistry—chemical equations.

SCIENCE Online

Research Visit the Glencoe Science Web site at **science.glencoe.com** for more information about Antoine Lavoisier and his contributions to chemistry. Communicate to your class what you learn.

2 Teach

Describing Chemical Reactions

Use an Analogy

Lavoisier's background included tax collecting and auditing. Balancing a ledger is somewhat like balancing a chemical equation. One must carefully consider what goes in and what come out without losing anything.

SCIENCE Online

Internet Addresses

Explore the Glencoe Science Web site at **science.glencoe.com** to find out more about topics in this section.

Quick Demo

Obtain a camera with removable flashcubes. In class, determine the mass of a flashcube before and after it has been used. Explain that the flash and the appearance of whitish powder show that a chemical change has occurred. The fact that the mass of the flashcube remains constant indicates that mass is conserved. L2 ELL LS **Visual-Spatial**

Reading Check

Answer In a chemical reaction matter is not created or destroyed.

Resource Manager

Chapter Resources Booklet

Transparency Activity, p. 46

Directed Reading for Content Mastery, p. 20

Enrichment, p. 31

Curriculum Connection

History Have students research and write a short report about the time period in which Laviosier lived (mid- to late-eighteenth century). L2

 **Linguistic** P

Writing Equations

Use an Analogy

Have a baseball coach or interested student bring in a scorer's record book from a baseball game. The records are kept for each inning with accepted symbols for events such as strikeout (K), home run (HR), infield out made by throw from third to first base (3-5), etc. The symbols in baseball allow a great deal of information to be recorded accurately in a small space. Chemical equations do this as well. L2

LS **Logical-Mathematical**

Discussion

Burning a piece of copper in a flame will produce a product that has a greater mass than the original copper. **Why doesn't this violate the conservation of mass?** The mass of oxygen participating in the burning process must be included as part of the mass of the reactants. L2 LS **Logical-Mathematical**

Fun Fact

Lavoisier was an early advocate of the use of chemical equations. He used symbols to show both the identity and quantity of materials in reactions and thought that algebra was the best language for expressing scientific information. He wrote, "In order to show at a glance the results of what happens . . . I have constituted formulae of a kind that could at first be taken for algebraic formulae . . ."

Table 1 Symbols Used in Chemical Equations

Symbol	Meaning
$\rightarrow$	produces or forms
+	plus
(*s*)	solid
(*l*)	liquid
(*g*)	gas
(*aq*)	aqueous, a substance is dissolved in water
heat $\rightarrow$	the reactants are heated
light $\rightarrow$	the reactants are exposed to light
elec. $\rightarrow$	an electric current is applied to the reactants

Writing Equations

If you wanted to describe the chemical reaction shown in **Figure 3,** you might write something like this:

nickel(II) chloride, dissolved in water, plus sodium hydroxide, dissolved in water, produces solid nickel(II) hydroxide plus sodium chloride, dissolved in water

This series of words is rather cumbersome, but all of the information is important. The same is true of descriptions of most chemical reactions. Many words are needed to state all the important information. As a result, scientists have developed a shorthand method to describe chemical reactions. A **chemical equation** is a way to describe a chemical reaction using chemical formulas and other symbols. Some of the symbols used in chemical equations are listed in **Table 1.**

The chemical equation for the reaction described above in words and shown in **Figure 3** looks like this:

$$NiCl_2(aq) + 2NaOH(aq) \rightarrow Ni(OH)_2(s) + 2NaCl(aq)$$

It is much easier to tell what is happening by writing the information in this form. Later, you will learn how chemical equations make it easier to calculate the quantities of reactants that are needed and the quantities of products that are formed.

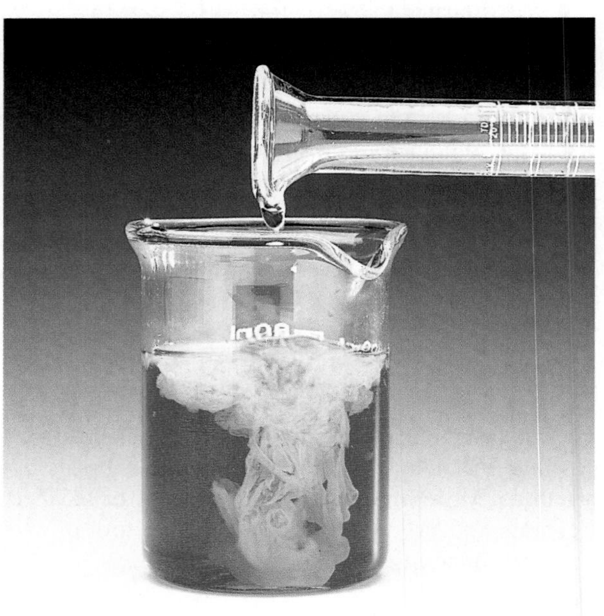

Figure 3
A white precipitate of nickel(II) hydroxide forms when sodium hydroxide is added to a green solution of nickel(II) chloride. Sodium chloride, the other product formed, is in the solution.

Teacher FYI

Some chemists use the symbol (cr) to represent solids that are crystals and (amor) to represent solids that have no definite structure.

Resource Manager

Chapter Resources Booklet
MiniLAB, p. 3
Reinforcement, p. 27
Transparency Activities, pp. 51–52

Unit Managers

What do the numbers to the left of the formulas for reactants and products mean? Remember that according to the law of conservation of mass, matter is neither made nor lost during chemical reactions. Atoms are rearranged but never lost or destroyed. These numbers, called **coefficients,** represent the number of units of each substance taking part in a reaction. Coefficients can be thought of as unit managers.

Reading Check ***What is the function of coefficients in a chemical equation?***

Imagine that you are responsible for making sandwiches for a picnic. You have been told to make a certain number of three kinds of sandwiches, and that no substitutions can be made. You would have to figure out exactly how much food to buy so that you had enough. You might need two loaves of bread, four packages of turkey, four packages of cheese, two heads of lettuce, and ten tomatoes. With these supplies you could make exactly the right number of turkey, cheese, lettuce, and tomato sandwiches.

In a way, your sandwich-making effort is like a chemical reaction. The reactants are your bread, turkey, cheese, lettuce, and tomatoes. The number of units of each ingredient are like the coefficients of the reactants in an equation. The sandwiches are like the products, and the numbers of each kind of sandwich are like coefficients, also.

Knowing the number of units of reactants enables chemists to add the correct amounts of reactants to a reaction. Also, these units, or coefficients, tell them exactly how much product will form. An example of this is the reaction of one unit of $NiCl_2$ with two units of NaOH to produce one unit of $Ni(OH)_2$ and two units of NaCl. You can see these units in **Figure 4.**

Designing a Team Equation

Procedure

1. Obtain **15 index cards** and mark each as follows: five with *guard*, five with *forward*, and five with *center*.
2. Group them to form as many complete basketball teams as possible. Each team needs two guards, two forwards, and one center.

Analysis

1. Write the formula for a team. Write the formation of a team as an equation. Use coefficients in front of each type of player needed for a team.
2. How is this equation like a chemical equation? Why can't you use the remaining cards?

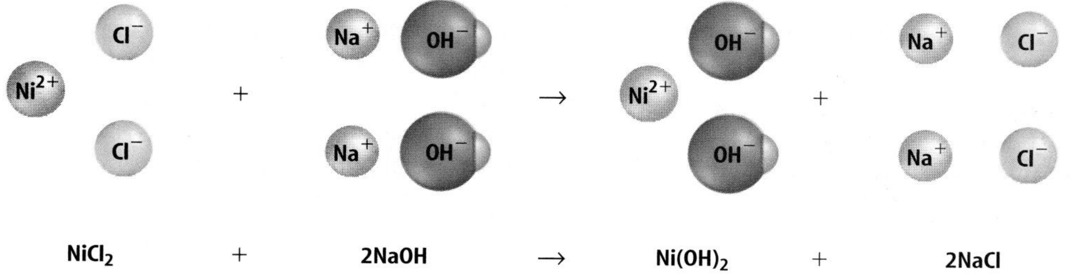

$NiCl_2 + 2NaOH \rightarrow Ni(OH)_2 + 2NaCl$

Figure 4
Each coefficient in the equation represents the number of units of each type in this reaction.

Unit Managers

Purpose Students see that coefficients are not conserved in a chemical equation but that mass is. L2

Logical-Mathematical

Materials 15 index cards per student, markers

Teaching Strategy Suggest students redo the activity, varying the composition of a team.

Analysis

1. 2 guards + 2 forwards + 1 center → 1 team
2. The equation uses coefficients like a chemical equation, and it shows conservation of mass. Only a specific number of each type of player can be used per team. Those left over sit on the bench (cannot be used).

Assessment

Oral Ask students how many guards would be needed to make four teams. $4 \times 2 = 8$ **How many complete teams could be made around 5 centers?** $5 \times 1 = 5$ teams **How many players would be left over when the following players assembled to make teams: 10 guards, 9 forwards, and 5 centers?** $\frac{9}{2} = 4$ teams with 1 extra forward 1 extra center, 2 extra guards Use **PASC,** p. 101.

Visual Learning

Figure 4 Have students count the atoms in the illustration and match them with the formulas in the equation. Point out which atoms combine to form each product. L2 **Visual-Spatial**

Soda Coefficients Have students calculate the total amount of soft drink in two 2-L bottles, three six-packs of 355-mL cans, and one case of 355-mL cans. Total = 4,000 + 6,390 + 8,520 = 18,910 mL. The coefficients in *2 bottles, 3 six-packs,* and *1 case* indicate the number of packaged units. Coefficients in a chemical equation indicate the number of units of atoms.

Reading Check

Answer They act as unit managers, representing the number of units of each substance taking part in a reaction.

3 Assess

Reteach

Show that the balanced equation for the decomposition of water is $2H_2O \rightarrow 2H_2 + O_2$. Ask students to use the coefficients to determine the number of hydrogen and oxygen atoms on each side of the equation. 4 hydrogens and 2 oxygens on the left side and 4 hydrogens and 2 oxygens on the right side L1

LS **Logical-Mathematical**

Challenge

Photographs are made using a chemical reaction driven by exposure to light. Ask students to find out what metal is typically involved in the process. Silver ions in silver bromide (AgBr) can be changed to silver metal when exposed to light. L3 LS **Linguistic**

Assessment

Performance Have students examine the unbalanced equation for the rusting of iron ($Fe + O_2 + H_2O \rightarrow Fe_2O_3{\cdot}3H_2O$) to determine the products and reactants and use coefficients to balance the equation. The dot between Fe_2O_3 and $3H_2O$ shows that three water molecules are contained in the product. $4Fe + 3O_2 + 6H_2O \rightarrow 2Fe_2O_3{\cdot}3H_2O$ Use **PASC,** p. 101.

Metals and the Atmosphere

When iron is exposed to air and moisture, it corrodes or rusts, forming hydrated iron(III) oxide. Rust can seriously damage iron structures because it crumbles and exposes more iron to the air. This leads to more oxidation and eventually can destroy the structure. However, not all reactions of metals with the atmosphere are damaging like rust. Some are helpful.

Aluminum also reacts with oxygen in the air to form aluminum oxide. Unlike rust, aluminum oxide adheres to the aluminum surface, forming an extremely thin layer that protects the aluminum from further attack. You can see this thin layer of aluminum oxide on aluminum outdoor furniture. It makes the once shiny aluminum look dull.

Copper is another metal that corrodes when it is exposed to air forming a blue-green coating called a patina. You can see this type of corrosion on many public monuments and also on the Statue of Liberty, shown in **Figure 5.**

Figure 5
The blue-green patina that coats the Statue of Liberty contains copper(II) sulfate among other copper corrosion products.

Section 1 Assessment

1. Identify the reactants and the products in the following chemical equation.
   $Cd(NO_3)_2(aq) + H_2S(g) \rightarrow CdS(s) + 2HNO_3(aq)$
2. What is the name and state of matter of each substance in the following reaction?
   $Zn(s) + 2HCl(aq) \rightarrow H_2(g) + ZnCl_2(aq)$
3. Why is the reaction of oxygen with iron a problem, but the reaction of oxygen with aluminum is not?
4. What is the importance of the law of conservation of mass?
5. **Think Critically** Why do you think the copper patina was kept when the Statue of Liberty was restored?

Skill Builder Activities

6. **Recognizing Cause and Effect** Lavoisier heated mercury(II) oxide in a sealed flask. Explain the effect on Lavoisier's conclusions about the law of conservation of mass if he had used an open container. **For more help, refer to the** Science Skill Handbook.
7. **Solving One-Step Equations** When making soap, if 890 g of a specific fat react completely with 120 g of sodium hydroxide, the products formed are soap and 92 g of glycerin. Calculate the mass of soap formed to satisfy the law of conservation of mass. **For more help, refer to the** Math Skill Handbook.

Answers to Section Assessment

1. reactants: $Cd(NO_3)_2$ and H_2S; products: CdS and HNO_3
2. Zn is a solid, HCl is dissolved in water, H_2 is a gas, and ZnCl is dissolved in water.
3. Iron and oxygen form a compound that flakes off and eventually destroys the iron structure. The aluminum-oxygen compound is resistant to further reaction and adheres to the original aluminum, forming a protective coat.
4. What appears to be the creation of new matter is actually the rearrangement of existing particles. It allows scientists to study reactions.
5. It protects the statue.
6. With an open container, the released oxygen would have escaped, and Lavoisier likely would have thought that the products of the reaction had less mass than the reactants.
7. $890 + 120 = 1{,}010$ g of reactant, which must equal 1,010 g of product; $1{,}010 - 92 = 918$ g of soap.

SECTION

2 Chemical Equations

Balanced Equations

Lavoisier heated mercury(II) oxide—HgO—and obtained mercury and oxygen. When written as a chemical equation, it is:

$$HgO(s) \xrightarrow{\text{heat}} Hg(l) + O_2\,(g)$$

Notice that the number of mercury atoms is the same on both sides of the equation but that the number of oxygen atoms is not the same. One oxygen atom appears on the reactant side of the equation and two appear on the product side

Atoms	HgO	→	Hg	+	O_2
Hg	1		1		
O	1				2

Now wait a minute, you say. The law of conservation of mass states that atoms are neither created nor destroyed in a chemical reaction. One oxygen atom can't just become two. Are the formulas wrong? Can you fix this problem simply by adding the subscript 2 and writing HgO_2 instead of HgO?

Think for a moment about water, H_2O, and hydrogen peroxide, H_2O_2. Although their formulas are similar, they are very different compounds. Similarly, the formulas HgO_2 and HgO do not represent the same compound. In fact, HgO_2 does not exist. In Lavoisier's experiment, he heated HgO, not HgO_2. The formulas in a chemical equation must accurately represent the compounds that react. They can't be changed to something different.

Reading Check *Why can't you change the subscripts in a chemical equation?*

If you can't change the subscripts in an equation, how can you fix Lavoisier's equation so that the number of oxygen atoms is the same on both sides? Fixing this equation requires a process called balancing. Balancing an equation doesn't change what happens in a reaction—it simply changes the way the reaction is represented. The balancing process involves changing coefficients in a reaction to achieve the same number of atoms of each element on both sides of the equation. A **balanced chemical equation** has the same number of atoms of each element on both sides of the equation.

As You Read

***What* You'll Learn**

- **Identify** what is meant by a balanced chemical equation.
- **Determine** how to write balanced chemical equations.

Vocabulary

balanced chemical equation

***Why* It's Important**

Chemical equations are the language used to describe chemical change.

Figure 6
Mercury metal forms when mercury oxide is heated.

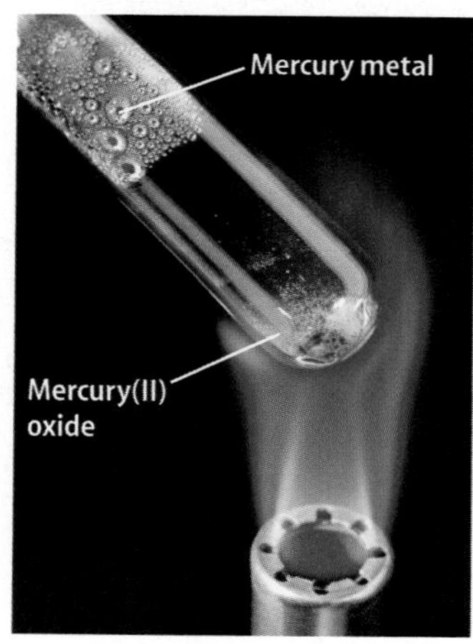

Section Assessment Planner

PORTFOLIO
Assessment, p. 745

PERFORMANCE ASSESSMENT
Skill Builder Activities, p. 745
See page 762 for more options.

CONTENT ASSESSMENT
Section, p. 745
Challenge, p. 745
Chapter, pp. 762–763

SECTION

Chemical Equations

1 Motivate

Bellringer Transparency

Display the Section Focus Transparency for Section 2. Use the accompanying Transparency Activity Master. L2 ELL

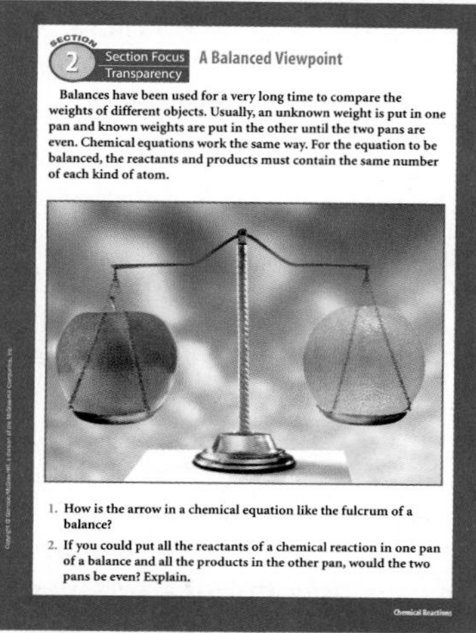

Section 2 Section Focus Transparency **A Balanced Viewpoint**

Balances have been used for a very long time to compare the weights of different objects. Usually, an unknown weight is put in one pan and known weights are put in the other until the two pans are even. Chemical equations work the same way. For the equation to be balanced, the reactants and products must contain the same number of each kind of atom.

1. **How is the arrow in a chemical equation like the fulcrum of a balance?**
2. **If you could put all the reactants of a chemical reaction in one pan of a balance and all the products in the other pan, would the two pans be even? Explain.**

Chemical Reactions

Tie to Prior Knowledge

Ask students if they remember attachable plastic building blocks. Remind students that the structures could be disassembled to make different objects from the same blocks. In a similar way, a balanced chemical equation represents the rearrangement of a set of atoms into new compounds.

Resource Manager

Chapter Resources Booklet
Transparency Activity, p. 47
Lab Activity, pp. 13–16

Balanced Equations

Reading Check

Answer because that would change the compounds involved in the reaction

Extension

Safety air bags in automobiles depend on a chemical reaction to inflate. Have students supply the coefficients needed to balance the equation: $NaN_3(s) \rightarrow Na(g) + N_2(g)$

$2NaN_3(s) \rightarrow 2Na(g) + 3N_2(g)$

Air bags should really be called nitrogen bags. They are not filled with air, but with nitrogen.

L3 LS **Logical-Mathematical**

Teacher FYI

Fractions can be used to balance chemical equations. $Na + Cl_2 \rightarrow NaCl$ can be balanced as $2Na + Cl_2 \rightarrow 2NaCl$ or as $Na + \frac{1}{2}Cl_2 \rightarrow NaCl$. Fractions are used mainly when the calculations involve the formation of only one unit of a product.

Research Visit the Glencoe Science Web site at **science.glencoe.com** for more information on balancing chemical equations. Communicate to your class what you learned.

Choosing Coefficients Finding out which coefficients to use to balance an equation is often a trial-and-error process, but with practice the process becomes easier. In the equation for Lavoisier's experiment, the number of mercury atoms is balanced, but one oxygen atom is on the left and two are on the right. Therefore, this equation isn't balanced. If you put a coefficient of 2 before the mercury(II) oxide on the left, the oxygen atoms will be balanced. However, you have two mercury atoms on the left and only one on the right. To correct this, put a 2 in front of mercury on the right. The equation is now balanced.

Atoms	$2HgO$	$\rightarrow$	$2Hg$	+	O_2
Hg	2		2		
O	2				2

Try Your Balancing Act Magnesium burns with such a brilliant, white light that it is often used in emergency flares as shown in **Figure 7.** Burning leaves a white powder called magnesium oxide. To write a balanced chemical equation for this and most other reactions, follow these four steps.

Step 1 Write a chemical equation for the reaction using formulas and symbols. Review how to write formulas for compounds. Recall that oxygen gas is a diatomic molecule.

$$Mg(s) + O_2(g) \rightarrow MgO(s)$$

Step 2 Check the equation for atom balance.

Atoms	Mg	+	O_2	$\rightarrow$	MgO
Mg	1				1
O			2		1

The magnesium atoms are balanced, but the oxygen atoms are not. Therefore, this equation isn't balanced.

Step 3 Choose coefficients that balance the equation. Remember, never change subscripts of a correct formula to balance an equation. Try putting a coefficient of 2 before MgO.

$$Mg(s) + O_2(g) \rightarrow 2MgO(s)$$

Step 4 Recheck the numbers of each atom on each side of the equation and adjust coefficients again if necessary.

Now two Mg atoms are on the right side and only one is on the left side. So a coefficient of 2 is needed for Mg also.

$$2Mg(s) + O_2(g) \rightarrow 2MgO(s)$$

The equation is now balanced.

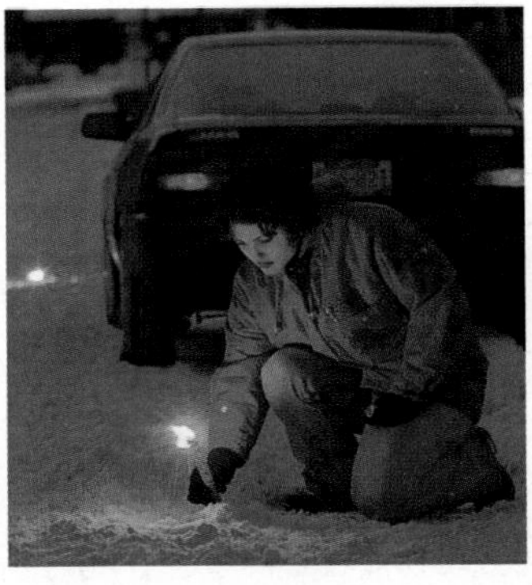

Figure 7
Magnesium combines with oxygen giving an intense white light.

Internet Addresses

Explore the Glencoe Science Web site at **science.glencoe.com** to find out more about topics in this section.

Resource Manager

Chapter Resources Booklet
- Reinforcement, p. 28
- Enrichment, p. 32
- Directed Reading for Content Mastery, p. 20

Home and Community Involvement, p. 46

Polish Your Skill When lithium metal is treated with water, hydrogen gas and lithium hydroxide are produced, as shown in **Figure 8.**

Step 1 Write the chemical equation.

$$Li(s) + H_2O \rightarrow H_2(g) + LiOH(aq)$$

Step 2 Check for balance by counting the atoms.

Atoms	Li	+	H_2O	→	LiOH	+	H_2
Li	1				1		
H			2		1		2
O			1		1		

This equation is not balanced. There are three hydrogen atoms on the right and only two on the left. Complete steps 3 and 4 to balance the equation. After each step, count the atoms of each element. When equal numbers of atoms of each element are on both sides, the equation is balanced.

Just as in the first example, this balancing does not change the reaction that took place between lithium and water. It just states what happened more accurately. This accurate statement tells chemists how much lithium metal to use to produce a certain amount of hydrogen gas.

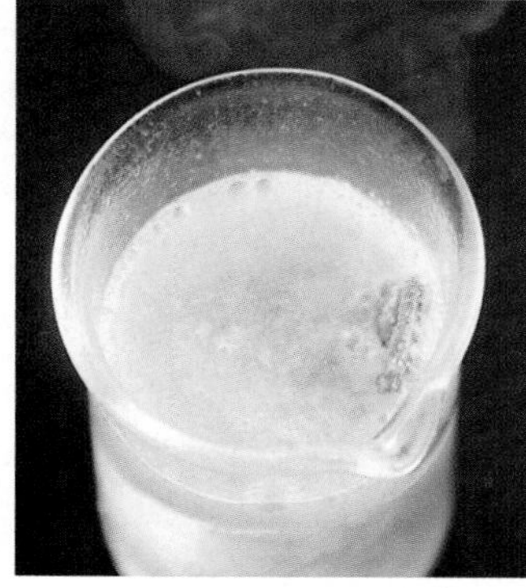

Figure 8
When lithium metal is added to water, it reacts, producing a solution of lithium hydroxide and bubbles of hydrogen gas.

Section  Assessment

1. Give two reasons for balancing equations for chemical reactions.
2. Write a balanced chemical equation for each of the following reactions.
   - **a.** Iron metal plus oxygen produces iron(II) oxide.
   - **b.** Sodium metal plus water produces sodium hydroxide plus hydrogen gas.
3. Explain why oxygen gas must always be written as O_2 in a chemical equation.
4. What is understood if no coefficient is written before a formula in a chemical equation?
5. **Think Critically** Explain why the sum of the coefficients on the reactant side of a balanced equation does not have to equal the sum of the coefficients on the product side of the equation.

Skill Builder Activities

6. **Predicting** Silver tarnish, Ag_2S, forms from sulfur compounds in the air and in some foods, such as eggs. Polishing removes this tarnish. Why might people not wish to polish their silverware very frequently? How might they prevent tarnish from forming and thereby reduce how often they need to polish? **For more help, refer to the Science Skill Handbook.**
7. **Using an Electronic Spreadsheet** Use a spreadsheet and design a table for the reaction of $CaCO_3$ with HCl to form CO_2, $CaCl_2$, and water. Remember that equal numbers of each element must be on both sides of a balanced equation. **For more help, refer to the Technology Skill Handbook.**

Answers to Section Assessment

1. Conservation of mass requires that the number of atoms of an element on the left side equals the number of atoms on the right side. Balanced equations accurately depict chemical changes.
2. a) $2Fe(s) + O_2(g) \rightarrow 2FeO(s)$; b) $2Na(s) + 2H_2O \rightarrow 2NaOH(s) + H_2(g)$
3. Oxygen gas exists as a diatomic molecule.
4. The coefficient is understood to be 1.
5. The coefficients represent the number of units of a compound, not the number of atoms.
6. Each time they polish, they lose silver. To prevent tarnish from forming, they could wrap silver so it doesn't come in contact with air.
7. The balanced equation is $CaCO_3(s) + 2HCl(aq) \rightarrow CO_2(g) + CaCl_2(aq) + H_2O(l)$

Extension

Have students do research to find out when the symbols we use for elements in chemical equations were first introduced and by whom. Have them write their findings in their Science Journals They were introduced in 1813 by the Swedish chemist Jöns Jakob Berzelius. L3 IS **Linguistic**

3 Assess

Reteach

Using the style of **Figure 4,** draw on the chalkboard the molecules $Ca(OH)_2$, H_3PO_4, $Ca_3(PO_4)_2$, and H_2O. Tell students that calcium hydroxide reacts with hydrogen phosphate to produce calcium phosphate and water. Ask students to write the balanced chemical equation for this reaction. $3Ca(OH)_2 + 2H_3PO_4 \rightarrow Ca_3(PO_4)_2 + 6H_2O$ L2

IS **Visual-Spatial**

Challenge

Bring a disposable butane lighter to class. Write the formula for butane, C_4H_{10}, on the chalkboard, and as you light the lighter, ask students to identify the chemical reaction taking place. Oxygen is combining with the carbon and hydrogen to produce water and carbon dioxide. Have them write and balance the equation for the reaction. $2C_4H_{10} + 13O_2 \rightarrow 8CO_2 + 10\,H_2O$ L3

IS **Logical-Mathematical**

Assessment

Performance Have students draw Venn diagrams to contrast the changes in chemical reactions with those in nuclear reactions. In a chemical change, the atoms do not change their basic identity. In nuclear changes, the identity of an atom is often changed. Use **PASC,** p. 167. P

SECTION 3

Classifying Chemical Reactions

1 Motivate

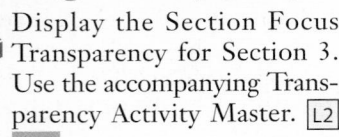

Bellringer Transparency

Display the Section Focus Transparency for Section 3. Use the accompanying Transparency Activity Master. L2 ELL

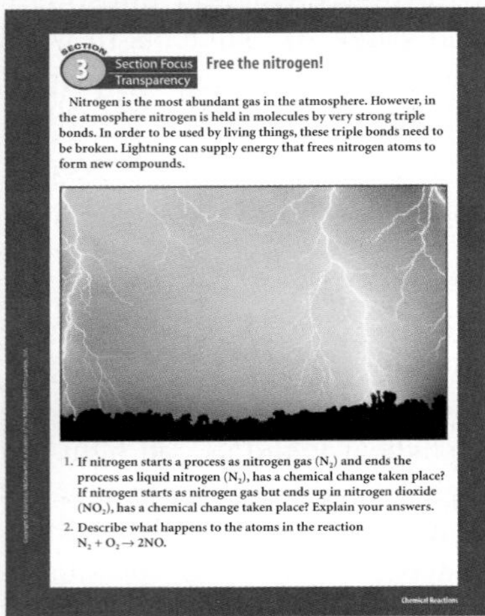

SECTION 3 Section Focus Transparency **Free the nitrogen!**

Nitrogen is the most abundant gas in the atmosphere. However, in the atmosphere nitrogen is held in molecules by very strong triple bonds. In order to be used by living things, these triple bonds need to be broken. Lightning can supply energy that frees nitrogen atoms to form new compounds.

1. If nitrogen starts a process as nitrogen gas (N_2) and ends the process as liquid nitrogen (N_2), has a chemical change taken place? If nitrogen starts as nitrogen gas but ends up in nitrogen dioxide (NO_2), has a chemical change taken place? Explain your answers.
2. Describe what happens to the atoms in the reaction $N_2 + O_2 \rightarrow 2NO$.

Chemical Reactions

Tie to Prior Knowledge

The four general types of chemical reactions are synthesis, decomposition, single displacement and double displacement. Ask students to think of situations they know in which these terms are used. Synthesis—bringing together carbon dioxide and water; decomposition—one substance converting to others as it falls apart, such as grass or leaves decomposing; single and double displacement—similar to substituting one food item for another or substituting two food items for two others on a restaurant menu

SECTION 3

Classifying Chemical Reactions

As You Read

What **You'll Learn**

- **Identify** the four general types of chemical reactions.
- **Predict** which metals will replace other metals in compounds.

Vocabulary

synthesis reaction
decomposition reaction
single-displacement reaction
double-displacement reaction
precipitate

Why **It's Important**

Classifying reactions helps you understand what is happening and predict the outcome of reactions.

Types of Reactions

You might have begun to notice that there are all sorts of chemical reactions. You could just memorize them, but that would be difficult. Fortunately there is a better way.

Imagine if the public library shelved its books without any order. Every time you wanted a particular book you would have to search through all the books or remember where you had seen it last. Fortunately libraries classify books into groups, such as biography, history, and fiction. This way you know exactly where to look.

You can do the same thing with chemical reactions. Also, once a chemical reaction is placed into a certain type, you can learn a great deal by comparing it to others of that type. One system is based upon the way the compounds interact. Most reactions can be divided into four main types—synthesis, decomposition, single displacement, and double displacement.

Synthesis Reactions One of the easiest reaction types to recognize is a synthesis reaction. In a **synthesis reaction,** two or more substances combine to form another substance. The generalized formula for this reaction type is as follows.

$$A + B \rightarrow AB$$

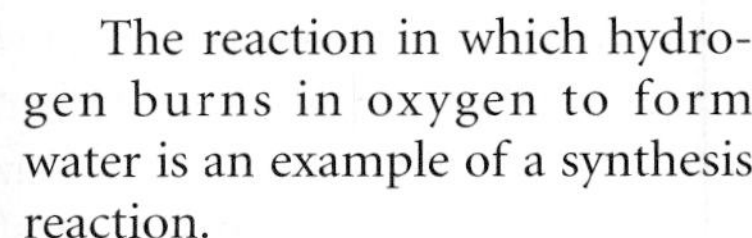

The reaction in which hydrogen burns in oxygen to form water is an example of a synthesis reaction.

$$2H_2(g) + O_2(g) \rightarrow 2H_2O(g)$$

This reaction is used to power some types of rockets. Another synthesis reaction is the combination of oxygen with iron to form hydrated iron(II) oxide or rust. This reaction, shown in **Figure 9,** is a much slower process.

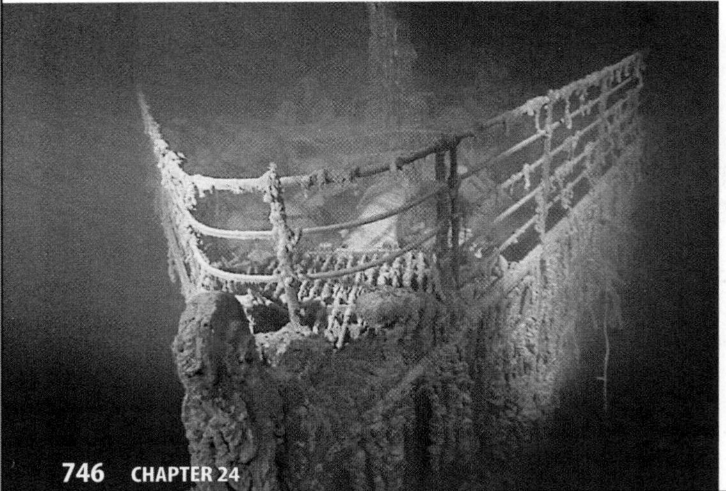

Figure 9
Rust has accumulated on the *Titanic* since it sank in 1912.

746 CHAPTER 24

Section Assessment Planner

PORTFOLIO
Challenge, p. 749

PERFORMANCE ASSESSMENT
Math Skills Activity, p. 748
Skill Builder Activities, p. 749
See page 762 for more options.

CONTENT ASSESSMENT
Section, p. 749
Challenge, p. 749
Chapter, pp. 762–763

Decomposition Reactions A decomposition reaction is just the opposite of a synthesis. Instead of two substances coming together to form a third, a **decomposition reaction** occurs when one substance breaks down, or decomposes, into two or more substances. The general formula for this type of reaction can be expressed as follows:

$$AB \rightarrow A + B$$

Most decomposition reactions require the use of heat, light, or electricity. For example, an electric current passed through water produces hydrogen and oxygen as shown in **Figure 10.**

$$2H_2O(l) \xrightarrow{\text{elec.}} 2H_2(g) + O_2(g)$$

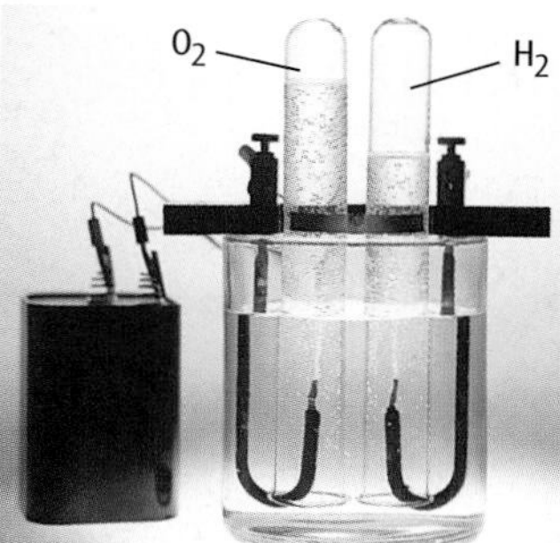

Figure 10
Water decomposes into hydrogen and oxygen when an electric current is passed through it. A small amount of sulfuric acid is added to increase conductivity. Notice the proportions of the gases collected. ***How is this related to the coefficients of the products in the equation?***

Single Displacement When one element replaces another element in a compound, it is called a **single-displacement reaction.** There are two generalized types of this reaction.

In the first case, A replaces B as follows:

$$A + BC \rightarrow AC + B$$

In the second case, D replaces C:

$$D + BC \rightarrow BD + C$$

The first case is illustrated in **Figure 11,** where a copper wire is put into a solution of silver nitrate. Because copper is a more active metal than silver, it replaces the silver, forming a blue copper(II) nitrate solution. The silver, which is not soluble, forms on the wire.

$$Cu(s) + 2AgNO_3(aq) \rightarrow Cu(NO_3)_2\,(aq) + 2Ag(s)$$

Reading Check ***Describe a single-displacement reaction.***

Sometimes single displacement reactions can cause problems. For example, if iron-containing vegetables such as spinach are cooked in aluminum pans, aluminum can displace iron from the vegetable. This causes a black deposit of iron to form on the sides of the pan. For this reason it is better to use stainless steel or enamel cookware when cooking spinach.

Figure 11
Copper in a wire replaces silver in silver nitrate, forming a blue solution of copper(II) nitrate.

2 Teach

Types of Reactions

Teacher FYI

Scientists are researching the possibility of using the synthesis of water to power automobiles. The reaction is considered a clean reaction because the product is water instead of greenhouse gases or petroleum products.

Caption Question Answer

Figure 10 It is the same.

Reading Check

Answer One element replaces another in a compound.

Resource Manager

Chapter Resources Booklet

Transparency Activity, p. 48

Directed Reading for Content Mastery, p. 21

Home and Community Involvement, p. 33

Visual Learning

Figure 11 Ask students if the copper replacement of silver could have any practical use. It is a good way to retrieve silver for recycling. L2

LS **Logical-Mathematical**

Types of Reactions, continued

Use an Analogy

Before a basketball game, the coach assembles the players and selects five to form the starting team. **Which one of the four reactions does this resemble?** synthesis One of the starting players on the basketball team fouls out of the game. The coach then substitutes a player from the bench into the game. **Which one of the four reaction types does this resemble?** single displacement L2

LS **Logical-Mathematical**

Math Skills Activity

National Math Standards

Correlation to Mathematics Objectives

1, 2, 6, 9, 10

Answer to Practice Problem

1. $2HCl + Na_2CO_3 \rightarrow 2NaCl + H_2O + CO_2$

Make a Model

A quick model for a double-displacement reaction can be prepared with two large, different colored, capped marking pens. Hold the two pens up for the class to see, then remove the caps and place them on the opposite pens. L2 ELL LS **Visual-Spatial**

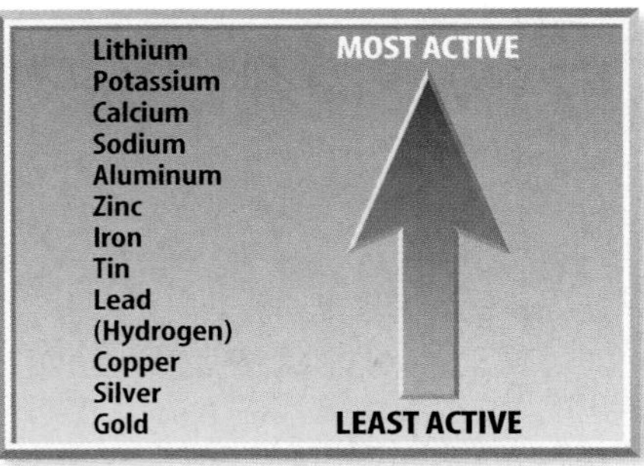

Figure 12
This figure shows the Activity Series of Metals. A metal will replace any other metal that is less active.

The Activity Series We can predict which metal will replace another using the diagram shown in **Figure 12,** which lists metals according to how active they are. A metal will replace any less active metal. Notice that copper, silver, and gold are the least active metals on the list. That is why these elements often occur as deposits of the relatively pure element. For example, gold is sometimes found as veins in quartz rock, and copper is found in pure lumps known as native copper. Other metals occur as compounds.

Math Skills Activity

Using Coefficients to Balance Chemical Equations

Example Problem

A sample of barium sulfate is placed on a piece of paper, which is then ignited. Barium sulfate reacts with the carbon from the burned paper producing barium sulfide and carbon monoxide. Write a balanced chemical equation for this reaction.

Solution

1. *Write a chemical equation using formulas and symbols:*

$BaSO_4(s) + C(s) \rightarrow BaS(s) + CO(g)$

2. *Check the equation for atom balance by setting up a table:*

Kind of Atom	Number of Atoms Before Reaction	Number of Atoms After Reaction
Ba	1	1
S	1	1
O	4	1
C	1	1

The oxygen atoms are not equal—this equation is not balanced.

3. *Choose coefficients that balance the equation. Try putting a 4 in front of CO. Now you have 4 oxygens, but 4 carbons also, so add another 4 in front of the C in the reactants to balance the remaining elements.*

$BaSO_4(s) + 4C(s) \rightarrow BaS(s) + 4CO(g)$

Practice Problem

1. HCl is slowly added to aqueous $NaCO_3$ forming NaCl, H_2O, and CO_2. Follow the steps above to write a balanced equation for this reaction.

For more help with solving equations, refer to the Math Skill Handbook.

748 CHAPTER 24 Chemical Reactions

Cultural Diversity

Japanese Chemistry In 1908, the Japanese chemist Ikeda Kikunae (1864–1936) used chemical reactions to make monosodium glutamate from hydrolyzed kelp protein. This synthesis became the foundation of Japan's first major chemical industry.

Resource Manager

Chapter Resources Booklet
Enrichment, p. 33
Reinforcement, p. 29
Science Inquiry Labs, p. 15

Double Displacement A **double-displacement reaction** takes place if a precipitate, water, or a gas forms when two ionic compounds in solution are combined. A **precipitate** is an insoluble compound that comes out of solution during this type of reaction. In a double-displacement reaction, the positive ion of one compound replaces the positive ion of the other to form two new compounds. The generalized formula for this type of reaction is as follows.

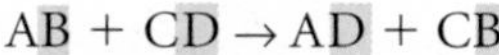

$$AB + CD \rightarrow AD + CB$$

The reaction of barium with potassium sulfate is an example of this type of reaction. A precipitate—barium sulfate—forms, as shown in **Figure 13.** The chemical equation is as follows:

$$Ba(NO_3)_2(aq) + K_2SO_4(aq) \rightarrow BaSO_4(s) + 2KNO_3(aq)$$

These are a few examples of chemical reactions classified into types. Many more reactions of each type occur around you.

Reading Check *What type of reaction produces a precipitate?*

Figure 13
A precipitate of barium sulfate settles to the bottom of a test tube containing potassium nitrate. Because it is opaque to X rays, barium sulfate is used to take X-ray photographs of the intestinal tract.

Section  3 Assessment

1. Classify each of the following reactions:
   a. $CaO(s) + H_2O \rightarrow Ca(OH)_2\ (aq)$
   b. $Fe(s) + CuSO_4(aq) \rightarrow FeSO_4(aq) + Cu(s)$
   c. $NH_4NO_3(s) \rightarrow N_2O(g) + 2H_2O(g)$
2. Sulfur trioxide, (SO_3), a pollutant released by coal-burning plants, can react with water in the atmosphere to produce sulfuric acid, H_2SO_4. Write a balanced equation for this reaction.
3. Explain the difference between synthesis and decomposition reactions.
4. Why can't you change the subscripts of reactants and products when balancing a chemical equation?
5. **Think Critically** Balance the following equation and identify the reaction type.
   $Au(CN)_2^-\ (aq) + Zn(s) \rightarrow Au(s) + Zn(CN)_4^{2-}(aq)$

Skill Builder Activities

6. **Forming Hypotheses** Group 1 metals replace hydrogen in water in reactions that are often violent. This sample equation shows what happens when potassium reacts with water.
   $2K(s) + 2HOH(l) \rightarrow 2KOH(aq) + H_2(g)$
   Use **Figure 12** to help you hypothesize why these metals are often stored in kerosene. **For more help, refer to the** Science Skill Handbook.
7. **Using Proportions** The following equation, showing the formation of iron oxide, is balanced, but the coefficients used are larger than necessary. Rewrite this equation using the smallest coefficients that give a balanced equation. **For more help, refer to the** Math Skill Handbook.
   $9Fe(s) + 12H_2O(g) \rightarrow 3Fe_3O_4(s) + 12H_2(g)$

Reading Check

Answer Double-displacement reactions frequently produce a precipitate.

3 Assess

Reteach

Ask students to review the four kinds of chemical reactions by using colored note cards. Synthesis: Tape two different colored cards together. Decomposition: Two cards that are taped could be pulled apart. Single-displacement: Two different cards are taped together and a third colored card replaces one of them. Double-displacement: Two cards, from each of two sets of two different colored, taped cards are traded. L2 ELL LS **Kinesthetic**

Challenge

Many single-displacement reactions involve oxidation and reduction. Challenge students to determine the importance of the two terms in determining the activity of a metal. Oxidation refers to losing electrons; reduction refers to gaining electrons. Chemical activity for metals usually involves the exchange of electrons. Active metals give up their electrons, or oxidize, easily. L3 LS **Linguistic** P

Assessment

Performance Have students complete and balance the following single-displacement reaction:

$K + AlCl_3 \rightarrow$ _____ + _____
$3K + AlCl_3 \rightarrow 3KCl + Al$

Use **PASC,** p. 101.

Answers to Section Assessment

1. (a) synthesis (b) single displacement (c) decomposition
2. $SO_3 + H_2O \rightarrow H_2SO_4$
3. Synthesis involves bringing elements or compounds together. Decomposition involves breaking compounds down.
4. The subscripts identify the combination of atoms that form a specific compound. Different subscripts indicate different compounds.
5. $2Au(CN)_2^-(aq) + Zn(s) \rightarrow 2Au(s) + Zn(CN)_4^{2-}(aq)$; single displacement
6. Kerosene is a nonpolar solvent (polar water is typically not present) that prevents the metal from being exposed to water in the air.
7. $3Fe(s) + 4H_2O(l) \rightarrow Fe_3O_4(s) + 4H_2(g)$.

Chemical Reactions and Energy

1 Motivate

Bellringer Transparency

Display the Section Focus Transparency for Section 4. Use the accompanying Transparency Activity Master. L2 ELL

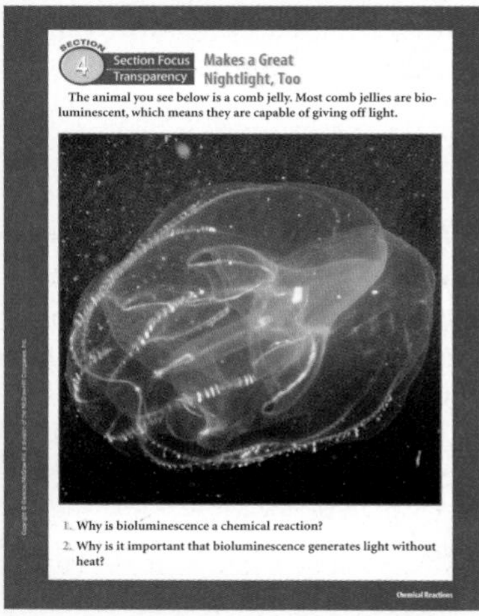

Tie to Prior Knowledge

Students realize that they obtain energy from eating food. Ask them how the energy is obtained from food. Chemical bonds in proteins, carbohydrates, and fats store energy. During digestion, those bonds are broken and new ones form. The energy required to break bonds is less than the energy released when new bonds form, so the net result is the release of energy.

Chemical Reactions and Energy

As You Read

What **You'll Learn**

- **Identify** the source of energy changes in chemical reactions.
- **Compare and contrast** exergonic and endergonic reactions.
- **Examine** the effects of catalysts and inhibitors on the speed of chemical reactions.

Vocabulary

exergonic reaction
exothermic reaction
endergonic reaction
endothermic reaction
catalyst
inhibitor

Why **It's Important**

Chemical reactions provide energy to cook your food, keep you warm, and transform the food you eat into substances you need to live and grow.

Chemical Reactions—Energy Exchanges

Often a crowd gathers to watch a building being demolished using dynamite. In a few breathtaking seconds, tremendous structures of steel and cement that took a year or more to build are reduced to rubble and a large cloud of dust. A dynamite explosion, as shown in **Figure 14,** is an example of a rapid chemical reaction.

Most chemical reactions proceed more slowly, but all chemical reactions release or absorb energy. This energy can take many forms, such as heat, light, sound and electricity. The heat produced by a wood fire and the light emitted by a candle are two examples of reactions that release energy.

Chemical bonds are the source of this energy. When most chemical reactions take place, some chemical bonds in the reactants must be broken, and breaking these bonds takes energy. In order for products to be produced, new bonds must form. Bond formation releases energy. Reactions such as dynamite combustion require much less energy to break chemical bonds than the energy released when new bonds are formed. The result is a release of energy and sometimes a loud explosion. Another release of energy is used to power rockets, as shown in **Figure 15.**

Figure 14
When its usefulness is over, a building is sometimes demolished using dynamite. Dynamite charges must be placed carefully so that the building collapses inward, where it cannot harm people or property.

Section Assessment Planner

PORTFOLIO
Active Reading, p. 753

PERFORMANCE ASSESSMENT
MiniLAB, p. 752
Skill Builder Activities, p. 754
See page 762 for more options.

CONTENT ASSESSMENT
Section, p. 754
Challenge, p. 754
Chapter, pp. 762–763

NATIONAL GEOGRAPHIC VISUALIZING CHEMICAL ENERGY

Figure 15

Rockets burn fuel to provide the thrust necessary to propel them upward. In 1926, engineer Robert Goddard used gasoline and liquid oxygen to propel the first ever liquid-fueled rocket. Although many people at the time ridiculed Goddard's space travel theories, his rockets eventually served as models for those that have gone to the Moon and beyond. A selection of rockets—including Goddard's—is shown here. The number below each craft indicates the amount of thrust—expressed in newtons (N)—produced during launch.

◀ SPACE SHUTTLE The main engines produce enormous amounts of energy by combining liquid hydrogen and oxygen. Coupled with solid rocket boosters, they produce over 32.5 million newtons (N) of thrust to lift the system's 2 million kg off the ground.

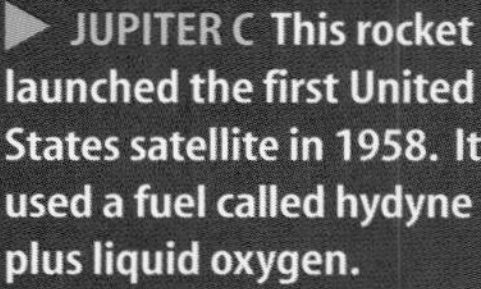

▶ JUPITER C This rocket launched the first United States satellite in 1958. It used a fuel called hydyne plus liquid oxygen.

▼ GODDARD'S MODEL ROCKET Although his first rocket rose only 12.6 m, Goddard successfully launched 35 rockets in his lifetime. The highest reached an altitude of 2.7 km.

▼ LUNAR MODULE Smaller rocket engines, like those used by the Lunar Module to leave the Moon, use hydrazine-peroxide fuels. The number shown below indicates the fixed thrust from one of the module's two engines; the other engine's thrust was adjustable.

400 N | 369,350 N | 32,500,000 N | 15,920 N

751

NATIONAL GEOGRAPHIC

Visualizing Chemical Energy

Have students examine the pictures and read the captions. Then ask the following questions.

- **How much more thrust did the Jupiter C rocket produce than Goddard's rocket?** 369,500 N/400 N = 923.75 times more thrust
- **Why does the Space Shuttle require so much thrust to launch it into orbit?** because it has so much mass
- **Why do you think it was desirable to have adjustable thrust on the Lunar Module?** so the astronauts could have more control over the Lunar Module's flight

Activity

Have students research the development of rocket technology throughout history and prepare timeline posters showing the major milestones in this technology. L2 **Visual-Spatial**

Extension

Challenge students to research new developments in rocket technology and the projected dates that the new technology will be used. Ask students to give short oral reports to the class describing what they learn.

Resource Manager

Chapter Resources Booklet

Transparency Activity, p. 49

Directed Reading for Content Mastery, pp. 21, 22

Enrichment, p. 34

More Energy Out

Purpose to observe evidence of a chemical reaction L2

LS ELL **Visual Spatial**

Materials water, test tube, copper(II) bromide

Teaching Strategies The chemical reaction that occurs is

1. $CuBr_2 + 4H_2O \rightarrow Cu(H_2O)_4^{+2}$ $2 + 2Br^-$
2. $Cu(H_2O)_4^{+2} + H_2O \rightarrow Cu(H_2O)_3OH^{+1} + H_3O^+$

Analysis

1. brown
2. blue
3. A chemical reaction occurred.

Performance Have students repeat the activity and look for signs of energy absorbed or released by the reaction. Use **PASC,** p. 97.

Reading Check

Answer The energy given off by the reaction is primarily in the form of heat.

Mini LAB

Colorful Chemical Reaction

Procedure

1. Pour 5 mL of **water** into a **test tube.**
2. Sprinkle a few crystals of **copper(II) bromide** into the test tube and observe the color change of the crystals.
3. Slowly add more water and observe what happens.

Analysis

1. What color were the copper(II) bromide crystals after you added them to the test tube of water?
2. What color were they when you added more water?
3. What caused this color change?

More Energy Out

You have probably seen many reactions that release energy. Chemical reactions that release energy are called **exergonic** (ek sur GAH nihk) **reactions.** In these reactions less energy is required to break the original bonds than is released when new bonds form. As a result, some form of energy, such as light or heat, is given off by the reaction. The familiar glow from the reaction inside a glow stick, shown in **Figure 16,** is an example of an exergonic reaction, which produces visible light. In other reactions however, the energy given off can produce heat. This is the case with heat packs that are used to treat muscle aches and other problems that require heat.

When the energy given off in a reaction is primarily in the form of heat, the reaction is called an **exothermic reaction.** The burning of wood and the explosion of dynamite are exothermic reactions. Iron rusting is also exothermic, but the reaction proceeds so slowly that it's difficult to detect any temperature change.

Reading Check *Why is a log fire considered to be an exothermic reaction?*

Exothermic reactions provide most of the power used in homes and industries. Fossil fuels that contain carbon, such as coal, petroleum, and natural gas, combine with oxygen to yield carbon dioxide gas and energy. Unfortunately impurities in these fuels, such as sulfur, burn as well, producing pollutants such as sulfur dioxide. Producing too much carbon dioxide can be a problem also, and has been blamed for global warming.

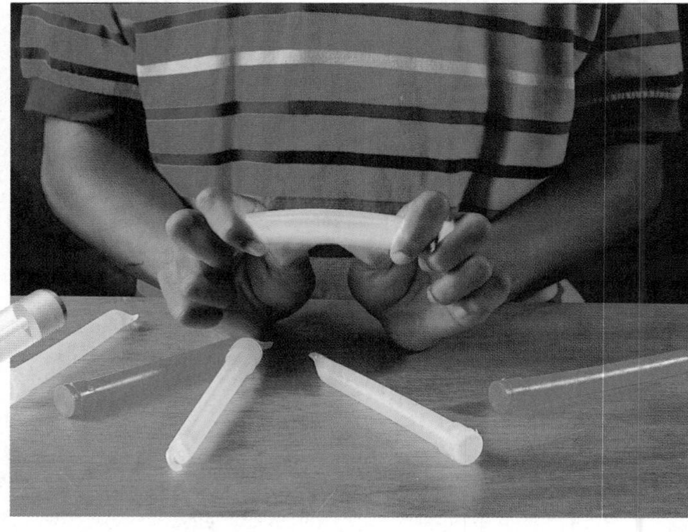

Figure 16
Light sticks contain three different chemicals—an ester and a dye in the outer section and hydrogen peroxide in a center glass tube. Bending the stick breaks the tube and mixes the three components.

LAB DEMONSTRATION

Purpose to demonstrate an exothermic process

Materials supersaturated solution of sodium acetate, sodium acetate crystal

Preparation Make a saturated solution of sodium acetate. Leave excess crystals in the bottom of the flask. Heat and stir until the crystals dissolve. Cool undisturbed to room temperature.

Procedure Drop an additional crystal of sodium acetate into the solution. Have students watch the solution and carefully feel the outside of the flask.

Expected Outcome The solution will crystallize, and the flask will become hot.

Why did the solution heat up? The amount of energy required to break the bonds in the solution is less than the energy needed to form crystals. The excess energy is released as heat.

752 CHAPTER 24 Chemical Reactions

More Energy In

Sometimes a chemical reaction requires more energy to break bonds than is released when new ones are formed. These reactions are called **endergonic reactions.** The energy provided may be in the form of light, heat, or electricity.

Electricity is often used to supply energy to endergonic reactions. For example, electroplating deposits a coating of metal on a surface, as shown in **Figure 17.** Also, aluminum metal is obtained from its ore using the following endergonic reaction.

$$2Al_2O_3(l) \xrightarrow{\text{elec.}} 4Al(l) + 3O_2(g)$$

In this case, electrical energy provides the energy needed to keep the reaction going.

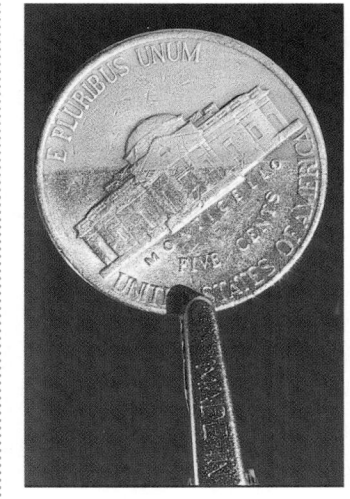

Figure 17 Electroplating of a metal is an endergonic reaction that requires electricity. A coating of copper is being plated onto this coin.

Heat Absorption When the energy needed is in the form of heat, the reaction is called an **endothermic reaction.** Some endothermic reactions absorb so little heat that you would need a sensitive thermometer to detect it. Other endothermic reactions absorb so much heat that the cooling is readily noticeable. If you ever had to soak a swollen ankle in an Epsom salt solution, you probably noticed that when you mixed the solution, it became cold. The dissolving of Epsom salt absorbs heat and thus is an endothermic process.

Cold packs also use endothermic processes, as shown in **Figure 18.** They contain ammonium nitrate crystals and a water container. When the water container is ruptured, water mixes with the ammonium nitrate. Almost immediately the pack cools dramatically.

B

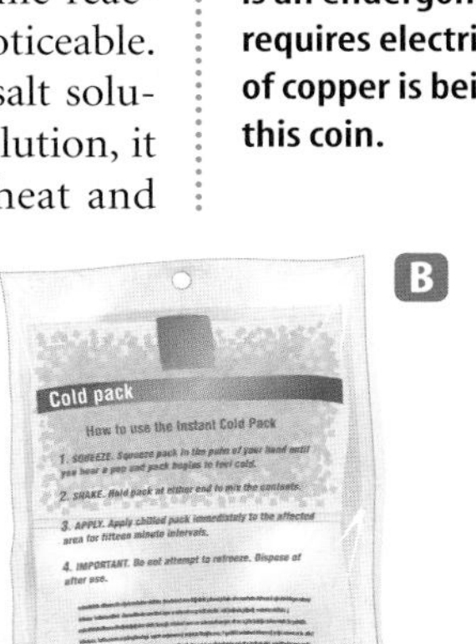

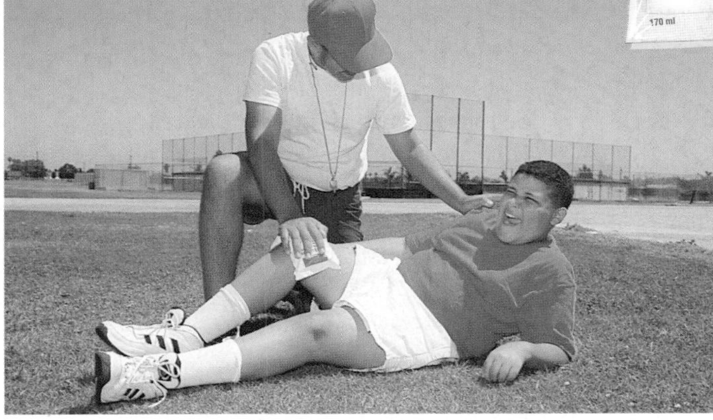

Figure 18 Cold packs are often used in sports. A Because they cool so quickly, it's like carrying an instant bag of ice. They are handy for treating athletic injuries on the field. B They start to work only when you press the pack breaking a container of water that mixes with ammonium nitrate crystals in a process that absorbs heat.

Activity

Obtain several packaged hand warmers used for outdoor activities from a sports supply store. Have students carefully follow the directions and observe the results. Place the hand warmers around a small beaker of water and measure the temperature change in the water. **What causes heat to be released ?** Many such packaged devices have a sealed sample of iron that slowly combines with oxygen (rusts) after the seal is broken and releases more heat than is required to get the reaction started. L2

ELL **Kinesthetic**

More Energy In

Use Science Words

Word Meanings Ask students to break the words *endergonic* and *exergonic* down into parts, and find out what each part means. Have them then explain why the words are appropriate for describing chemical processes that release or require energy. Ex-ergon-ic: ex- out of , ergo- work, -ic - having the character of: End-ergon-ic: end - into, ergo- work, -ic - having the character of. An exergonic reaction produces energy that can do work. An endergonic reaction requires energy, or work, in order to occur. L2

Linguistic

Teacher FYI

A cold pack absorbs heat as ammonium nitrate dissolves. The dissolving process is usually considered a physical change, not a chemical reaction. In most changes, the energy can be tracked as it moves from the system to the surroundings and vice versa. In the cold pack, the system is the chemical dissolving in water. The surroundings are the plastic bag, the air, any injured body area, etc.

Resource Manager

Chapter Resources Booklet
MiniLAB, p. 4
Earth Science Critical Thinking/Problem Solving, p. 17
Cultural Diversity, p. 63

Active Reading

Bubble Map Using a bubble map helps students start ideas flowing about a given topic. Words are clustered to describe a topic or idea that is studied. Students can use a bubble map for a prewriting, to generate ideas before writing in their Journals, or to review for a test. Have students design a bubble map for energy exchanges in chemical reactions. P

More Energy In,

continued

Environmental Science
INTEGRATION

The metals in exhaust catalysis help break down the unused hydrocarbon fuel molecules into less harmful compounds.

Reading Check

Answer to speed up the reaction

3 Assess

Reteach

Write the following two equations on the board:

$A + B \rightarrow C + \text{energy}$

$X + Y + \text{energy} \rightarrow Z$

Which equation depicts an endothermic reaction? second one **Which depicts an exothermic reaction?** first one L2 **LS Logical-Mathematical**

Challenge

One familiar unit of energy is the calorie. Ask students to find the definition of the calorie. heat needed to raise 1 g H_2O 1°C Have them compare a food Calorie to a chemical calorie. 1 food Calorie = 1000 cal (c) Ask them to find another label for energy used in chemistry. the joule: 4.184 J = 1 cal L3 **LS Linguistic**

Assessment

Oral Ask students to suppose that they are each holding a test tube that has a chemical change taking place inside. The tube is beginning to feel colder. **Is the process in the tube endothermic or exothermic?** Endothermic; the system is gaining energy from the surroundings—your hand. Use **PASC,** p. 89.

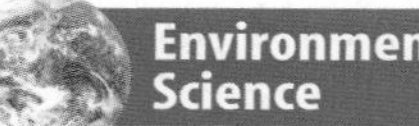

Environmental Science
INTEGRATION

Metals, such as platinum and palladium, are used as catalysts in the exhaust systems of automobiles. What reactions do you think they catalyze?

Catalysts and Inhibitors Some reactions proceed too slowly to be useful. To speed them up, a catalyst can be added. A **catalyst** is a substance that speeds up a chemical reaction without being permanently changed itself. When you add a catalyst to a reaction, the mass of the product that is formed remains the same, but it will form more rapidly. The catalyst remains unchanged and often is recovered and reused. Catalysts are used to speed many reactions in industry, such as polymerization to make plastics and fibers.

Reading Check *Why would a catalyst be needed for a chemical reaction?*

At times, it is worthwhile to prevent certain reactions from occurring. Substances called **inhibitors** are used to combine with one of the reactants. This ties up the reactant and prevents it from undergoing the original reaction. The food preservatives BHT and BHA are inhibitors that prevent spoilage of certain foods, such as cereals and crackers.

Sometimes you might want to inhibit a catalyst. For example, the cut surfaces of fruits darken rapidly due to an enzyme-catalyzed reaction with air. Brushing or spraying the surfaces with lemon juice prevents the catalyst from acting.

One thing to remember when thinking about catalysts and inhibitors is that they do not change the amount of product produced. They only change the rate of production. Catalysts increase the rate and inhibitors decrease the rate. Therefore, foods containing preservatives will spoil eventually, but preservatives are inhibitors that often add months or even years to the shelf time.

Section 4 Assessment

1. Discuss the difference between exergonic and endergonic reactions.
2. What happens to a catalyst in a reaction?
3. Crackers containing BHT stay fresh longer than those without it. Explain why.
4. Classify the reaction that makes a firefly glow in terms of energy input or output.
5. **Think Critically** To develop a product that warms people's hands, would you choose an exothermic or endothermic reaction to use? Why?

Skill Builder Activities

6. **Concept Mapping** Construct a concept map to show the relationship between energy and bond formation and bond breakage. **For more help, refer to the** Science Skill Handbook.
7. **Communicating** In your Science Journal, compare the profit or loss in an investment or a business deal with the gain or loss of energy in a chemical reaction. **For more help, refer to the** Science Skill Handbook.

Answers to Section Assessment

1. Exergonic reactions give off more energy than they take in. Endergonic reactions take in more energy than they give off.
2. A catalyst does not become permanently changed.
3. BHT is an inhibitor that slows spoilage of the cracker.
4. exergonic
5. Exothermic; it would release energy to warm people's hands.
6. Check students' work.
7. In a business deal, a profit occurs when more money comes in than goes out. This is like a gain of energy in a chemical reaction. Both the business and the chemical reaction have the resources to continue. After a loss of money, a business doesn't have as many resources to stay in business, just as after losing energy, chemicals have to take resources from their surroundings to continue reacting.

Activity

Catalyzed Reaction

A balanced chemical equation tells nothing about the rate of a reaction. One way to affect the rate is to use a catalyst.

What You'll Investigate

How does the presence of a catalyst affect the rate of a chemical reaction?

Materials

test tubes (3)
test-tube stand
3% hydrogen peroxide, H_2O_2 (15 mL)
10-mL graduated cylinder
small plastic teaspoon
sand (¼ teaspoon)
hot plate
wooden splint
beaker of hot water
manganese dioxide, MnO_2 (¼ teaspoon)

Goals

- **Observe** a catalyst on the rate of reaction.
- **Conclude** based on your observations whether the catalyst remained unchanged.

Safety Precautions

WARNING: *Hydrogen peroxide can irritate skin and eyes. Wipe up spills promptly. Point test tubes away from other students.*

Procedure

1. Set three test tubes in a test-tube stand. Pour 5 mL of hydrogen peroxide into each tube.
2. Place about ¼ teaspoon of sand in tube 2 and the same amount of MnO_2 in tube 3.
3. In the presence of a catalyst, H_2O_2 decomposes rapidly producing oxygen gas, O_2. Test the gas produced as follows: Light a wooden splint, blow out the flame, and insert the glowing splint into the tube. The splint will relight if oxygen is present.

4. Place all three tubes in a beaker of hot water. Heat on a hot plate until all of the remaining H_2O_2 is driven away and no liquid remains.

Conclude and Apply

1. What changes did you observe when the solids were added to the tubes?
2. In which tube was oxygen produced rapidly, and how do you know?
3. Which substance, sand or MnO_2, caused the rapid production of gas from the H_2O_2?
4. What remained in each tube after the H_2O_2 was driven away?

Communicating Your Data

Compare your results with those of your classmates and discuss any differences observed. **For more help refer to the** Science Skill Handbook.

Activity

BENCH TESTED

Purpose Students operationally define a catalyst and observe its action. L2 LS **Kinesthetic**

Process Skills observing, inferring, forming operational definitions, classifying, recognizing cause and effect

Time Required 30 minutes

Teaching Strategy Demonstrate the glowing splint test for students.

Answers to Questions

1. There was no observable change from the addition of sand, but the MnO_2 increased the rate of oxygen production.
2. The tube containing MnO_2; it produced oxygen bubbles fastest.
3. manganese dioxide
4. the sand in one tube, the MnO_2 in the other tube

Resource Manager

Chapter Resources Booklet
Activity Worksheet, pp. 5–6
Physical Science Critical Thinking/Problem Solving, p. 14
Science Inquiry Labs, p. 39

Assessment

Performance Have students repeat the test with a small piece of liver instead of MnO_2. Ask what was in the liver to cause increased O_2 production. an enzyme Use **Performance Assessment in the Science Classroom,** p. 97.

Communicating Your Data

Have students draw illustrations showing each test tube at each step of the procedure.

Activity

BENCH TESTED

Recognize the Problem

Internet Students will use Internet sites that can be accessed through the Glencoe Science Web site at **science. glencoe. com.** They will investigate activities in their daily lives that contribute to the production of greenhouse gases.

Non-Internet Sources Contact the Environmental Protection Agency (EPA) and other environmental groups for information about the production of greenhouse gases.

Time Required

about two days

Preparation

Internet Access the Glencoe Science Web site at **science. glencoe.com** to run through the steps that the students will follow.

Non-Internet Sources Collect information about the greenhouse gases and how the burning of fossil fuels produces them.

Form a Hypothesis

Possible Hypothesis

Students should think about everyday activities that burn fossil fuels and result in the production of greenhouse gases. For example, using a gasoline-powered lawn mower burns a fossil fuel, producing greenhouse gases.

Activity Use the Internet

Fossil Fuels and Greenhouse Gases

You've probably heard a lot about global warming and the greenhouse effect. According to one theory, certain gases in the atmosphere might be causing Earth's average global temperature to rise. The gases carbon dioxide, nitrous oxide, and methane, known as greenhouse gases, result from chemical reactions with oxygen when fossil fuels, such as coal, oil, and gas, are burned. What are some everyday activities that you do that might produce greenhouse gases?

Recognize the Problem

What do you do to produce greenhouse gases?

Form a Hypothesis

Think of the different ways you use fossil fuels every day. Why are fossil fuels important? Form a hypothesis about how certain activities add greenhouse gases to our atmosphere.

Goals

- **Observe** how you use fossil fuels in your daily life.
- **Gather data** on the process of burning fossil fuels and how greenhouse gases are released.
- **Research** the chemical reactions that produce greenhouse gases.
- **Identify** the importance of fossil fuels and their effect on the environment.
- **Communicate** your findings to other students.

Data Source

SCIENCE *Online* Go to the Glencoe Science Web site at **science.glencoe. com** for more information about fossil fuels, the chemical reactions that produce greenhouse gases, uses of fossil fuels, their effects on the environment, and data from other students.

756 CHAPTER 24 Chemical Reactions

Test Your Hypothesis

Teaching Strategies

Have students work in small groups ot brainstorm different activities that burn fossil fuels. Ask them to make a list of fossil fuels, which should include coal and oil.

SCIENCE Online

Internet Addresses

Explore the Glencoe Science Web site at **science.glencoe.com** to find out more about topics in this activity.

Test Your Hypothesis

Plan

1. **Observe** your activities in your daily life. How do you use energy from fossil fuels each day?
2. **Develop** a way to categorize the different chemical reactions and the greenhouse gases they produce.
3. **Search** reference sources to learn what chemical reactions produce greenhouse gases.
4. What are some of the most common uses of fossil fuels? Is it possible to never use fossil fuels?

Do

1. Make sure your teacher approves your plan before you start.

2. **Research** the different greenhouse gases and the chemical reactions that produce them.
3. **Compare** the different reactions and their products.
4. **Record** your data in your Science Journal.

Analyze Your Data

1. **Record** in your Science Journal what activities contribute to the greatest amount of greenhouse gases in our atmosphere.
2. **Analyze** the types of chemical reactions that produce greenhouse gases. What type of reactions are they?
3. **Compare** your results with other students. What greenhouse gas is most often released?
4. Make a table of your data.

Draw Conclusions

1. How do you think your data would be affected if you had performed this experiment 100 years ago?
2. What processes in nature might also contribute to the release of greenhouse gases? Compare their impact to that made by fossil fuels.

Communicating Your Data

SCIENCE Online Find this *Use the Internet* activity on the Glencoe Web site at **science.glencoe.com.** Post your data in the table provided. Compare your data to that of other students. Combine your data with that of other students and write an entry in your Science Journal that explains how the production of greenhouse gases could be reduced.

Analyze Your Data

1. Answers may vary. Activities that result in the production of greenhouse gases include the burning of fossil fuels, deforestation, and volcanic activity. Methane, which is also a greenhouse gas, is produced in the intestines of animals such as cows and termites.
2. Combustion reactions produce the largest amount of greenhouse gases in the atmosphere.
3. Carbon dioxide is most often released as a greenhouse gas. Methane and water vapor are also commonly-released greenhouse gases.
4. Student's tables should include information on the type of greenhouse gas, the chemical reaction that produces it, and activity that involves the chemical reaction.

Draw Conclusions

1. Accept all reasonable answers.
2. Respiration of plants and animals releases both carbon dioxide and water vapor into the air, but in smaller quantities than are released by the combustion of fossil fuels.

Performance Have students write reports describing how the activity they investigated produces greenhouse gases. Make sure they include descriptions of the activity, the fossil fuel it burns, the chemical reaction that happens, and the gases that are produced. Use **Performance Assessment in the Science Classroom,** p. 157.

Resource Manager 

Chapter Resources Booklet
Activity Worksheet, pp. 7–8
Reinforcement, p. 30

Communicating Your Data

Have students make flowcharts showing how their everyday activities produce greenhouse gases. Flowcharts should include descriptions of the process and illustrations to show how the activities lead to greenhouse gas production.

Oops! Accidents in SCIENCE

SOMETIMES GREAT DISCOVERIES HAPPEN BY ACCIDENT!

A Clumsy Move Pays Off

Hillaire de Chardonnet

Clumsy (KLUM zee)—lacking physical coordination

Procrastinate (proh KRAS tuh nayt)—to put off doing something until later

Most people might not think that a person who had the two qualities described above would make a great scientific discovery. But they never met a chemist named Hillaire de Chardonnet (hee LAYR • duh • shar doh NAY). In 1878, Chardonnet accidentally knocked over some nitrate chemicals. He put off cleaning up the mess—and ended up inventing artificial silk.

Silk is produced naturally by silkworms. In the mid-1800s, though, silkworms were dying from disease and the silk industry was suffering. Businesses were going under and people were put out of work. Many scientists were working to develop a solution to this problem.

Silkworms at work—spinning their cocoons

758

Content Background

Chardonnet made his discovery in 1878. At the time, the great French scientist Louis Pasteur was actively trying to save the French silk industry by looking into what was causing the silkworms to die off. Chardonnet was taking a different route by trying to develop a replacement for silk. He derived the solution from which he finally produced his artificial silk from the pulp of mulberry leaves, the natural food of silkworms. When he displayed the product at the Paris Exposition in 1891, he got backing for it immediately. It wasn't called rayon until about 1924.

Discussion

Students can discuss the following questions as a class or in small groups. **Why do you think it was obvious to Chardonnet that his accident could lead to an artificial silk?** because he had been searching for an artificial silk all along **How might this give you a new perspective on making mistakes?** It tells that, even if you make a mistake, you should look at what has happened and try to learn from it. The mistake could give a whole new outlook on a problem.

Resources for Teachers and Students

"*Chardonnet*" in Random House Dictionary of Scientists, Random House, 1997.

To help prevent counterfeiting, dollars are printed on paper which contains red and blue rayon fibers. If you can scratch off the red or blue, that means it's ink—and your bill is counterfeit. If you can pick out the red or blue fiber with a needle, it's a real bill.

Chardonnet had been searching for a silk substitute for years—he just didn't plan to find it by knocking it over!

A Messy Discovery

Chardonnet was in his darkroom developing photographs when the accidental spill took place. He decided to clean up the spill later—and finish what he was working on. By the time he returned to wipe up the spill, the chemical solution had turned into a thick, gooey mess. When he pulled the cleaning cloth away, the goop formed long, thin strands of fiber that stuck to the cloth. The chemicals had reacted with the cellulose in the wooden table and liquefied it. The strands of fiber looked just like the raw silk made by silkworms.

Within six years, Chardonnet had developed a way to make the fibers into an artificial silk. Other scientists extended his work, developing a fiber called rayon—"ray" for its shiny appearance, and "on" to remind people of the word "cotton." The rayon we wear on our backs today, called viscose rayon, is made with sodium hydroxide. The sodium hydroxide is mixed with wood fibers. The wood turns into a liquid that can be squeezed through tiny holes to make strands or fibers. The fibers are then woven together to make cloth.

Polymers

Rayon is a polymer. A polymer is a big molecule made up of smaller molecules that are linked together to form a straight chain, a twisting ladder, or a branching tree, depending on how the smaller molecules link together. The cellulose in plant cells is a natural polymer, as is the DNA in your body. To make artificial polymers, such as rubber or plastics, scientists studied natural polymers and then tried to mimic their structure in the lab.

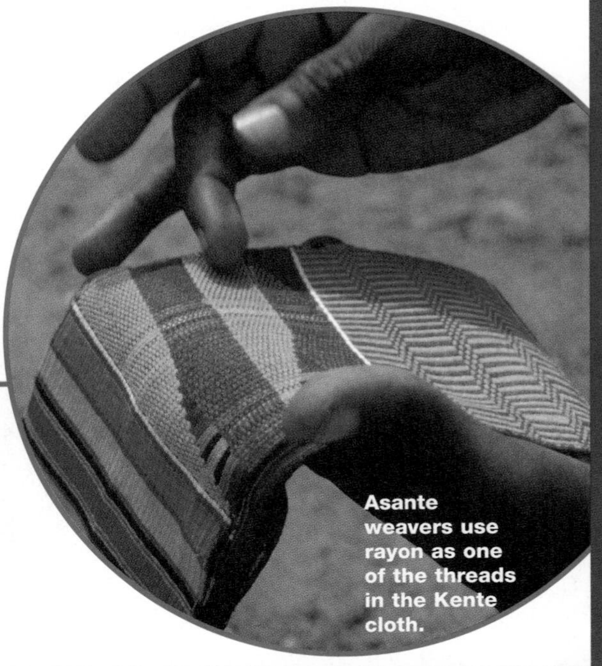

Asante weavers use rayon as one of the threads in the Kente cloth.

CONNECTIONS Create Make a data table. Work with a partner to examine the labels on the inside collars of your clothes. These labels list the different materials found in the clothes. Research the materials, then make a data table that identifies their characteristics.

SCIENCE Online For more information, visit science.glencoe.com

Activity

To help students understand polymers better, do the following activity. Pour acetone into a large beaker until it is about half full. Have a student throw packing peanuts into the beaker and try to fill it up. The peanuts will almost instantly disintegrate. Using a glass stirring rod, draw out the long, thin polymer strands that have formed. Explain that to make the packing peanuts, the molecules making up the long, thin strands cluster around themselves, like a piece of string being crumpled into a ball. Have students draw pictures showing how polymers can be used to make fabrics and things like packing peanuts. L2
LS **Visual-Spatial**

Analyze the Event

Eventually, the diseases striking silkworms were identified and controlled. **Why do you think Chardonnet's artificial silk remained so popular?** Possible answers: because now the amount of silk produced could be easily controlled. As much or as little fabric could be made as was necessary to meet demand. No longer did people have to worry about silkworms getting sick. **Can you think of any other natural products that have synthetic counterparts?** Possible answers include rubber, oils, glues, and some foods.

CONNECTIONS What's the Weather? Suggest students include in their tables information on the weather conditions for which each piece of clothing is used. Ask students to examine the textures and elasticity of the clothing and hypothesize how the polymers must be arranged.

SCIENCE Online

Internet Addresses

Explore the Glencoe Science Web site at **science.glencoe.com** to find out more about topics in this feature.

Chapter 24 Study Guide

Reviewing Main Ideas

Preview

Students can answer the questions in their Science Journals. Discuss the answers as you go through the chapter. LS **Linguistic**

Review

Students can write their answers, then compare them with those of other students. LS **Interpersonal**

Reteach

Students can look at the illustrations and describe details that support the main ideas of the chapter. LS **Visual-Spatial**

Answers to Chapter Review

SECTION 1

2. carbon dioxide

SECTION 3

2. NaCl

SECTION 4

1. heat and light

Chapter 24 Study Guide

Reviewing Main Ideas

Section 1 Chemical Changes in Matter

1. In a chemical reaction, one or more substances are changed to new substances.
2. The substances that react are called reactants, and new substances formed are called products. Charcoal, the reactant shown below, is almost pure carbon. *What is the major product formed?*

3. The law of conservation of mass states that in chemical reactions, matter is neither created nor destroyed, just rearranged.
4. Chemical equations efficiently describe what happens in chemical reactions.

Section 2 Chemical Equations

1. A balanced chemical equation has the same number of atoms of each element on both sides of the equation.
2. A balanced equation tells the ratio of products and reactants.
3. When balancing equations, change only the coefficients of the formulas, never the subscripts.

Section 3 Classifying Chemical Reactions

1. In synthesis reactions, two or more substances combine to form another substance.
2. When laundry bleach—sodium hypochlorite (NaClO)—decomposes, it forms oxygen and another product. *What common household substance is the other product?*

3. In single displacement reactions one element replaces another in a compound.
4. In double displacement reactions, ions in two compounds switch places, often forming a gas or insoluble compound.

Section 4 Chemical Reactions and Energy

1. Energy in the form of light, heat, sound or electricity is released from some chemical reactions known as exergonic reactions. *What types of energy are produced in the reaction shown here?*

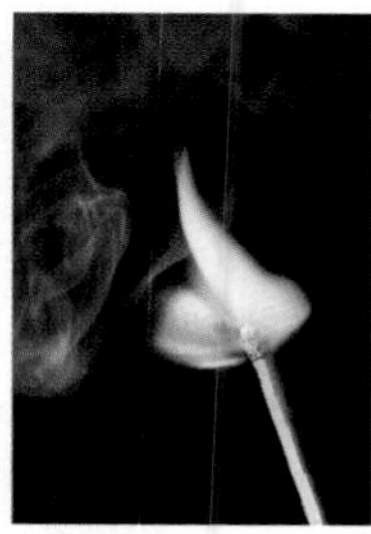

2. Reactions that need energy to proceed are called endergonic reactions.
3. Reactions may be sped up by adding catalysts and slowed down by adding inhibitors.
4. When energy released in the form of heat, the reaction is exothermic.

FOLDABLES Reading & Study Skills

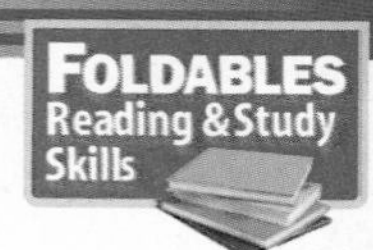

After You Read

Under the tabs of your Foldable write the chemical reactions you recorded using a sentence or chemical equation.

FOLDABLES Reading & Study Skills

After You Read

After students have read the chapter and completed the Foldable described in Before You Read, have them do the activity on the student page.

Dinah Zike

Chapter 24 Study Guide

Visualizing Main Ideas

Complete the spider map about chemical reactions.

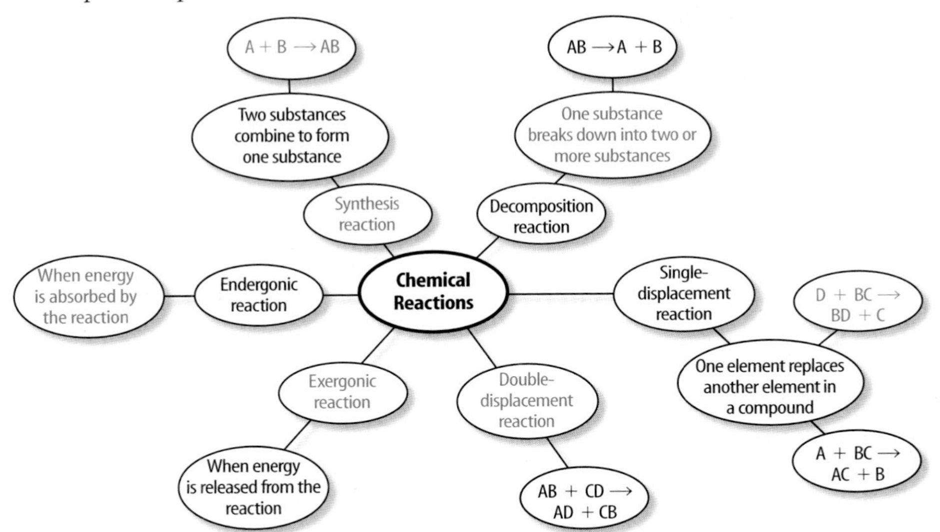

Vocabulary Review

Vocabulary Words

a. balanced chemical equation
b. chemical equation
c. catalyst
d. chemical reaction
e. coefficient
f. decomposition reaction
g. double-displacement reaction
h. endergonic reaction
i. endothermic reaction
j. exergonic reaction
k. exothermic reaction
l. inhibitor
m. precipitate
n. product
o. reactant
p. single-displacement reaction
q. synthesis reaction

Using Vocabulary

For each set of vocabulary words below, explain the relationship that exists.

1. coefficient, balanced chemical equation
2. synthesis reaction, decomposition reaction
3. reactant, product
4. catalyst, inhibitor
5. exothermic reaction, endothermic reaction
6. chemical reaction, product
7. endergonic reaction, exergonic reaction
8. single-displacement reaction, double-displacement reaction
9. chemical reaction, synthesis reaction

THE PRINCETON REVIEW — Study Tip

Use acronyms to help you remember important facts. For example, the acronym SDSD will help you remember the types of chemical reactions—Synthesis, Decomposition, Single Displacement, and Double Displacement.

Chapter 24 Study Guide

Visualizing Main Ideas

See student page.

Vocabulary Review

Using Vocabulary

1. Coefficients are whole numbers used in front of chemical units in a balanced chemical equation.
2. In a synthesis reaction substances are put together; in a decomposition reaction they are taken apart.
3. In a chemical change, reactants change into products.
4. Catalysts speed up chemical reactions, while inhibitors slow them down.
5. Exothermic reactions release heat to the surroundings, while endothermic reactions absorb heat from the surroundings.
6. Chemical reactions are processes in which new substances, called products, are formed.
7. Endergonic reactions absorb more energy than they give off to their surroundings. Exergonic reactions give off more energy to their surroundings than they take in.
8. In single-displacement reactions, only one element of one compound is replaced by another element. In double-displacement reactions, two elements in two compounds change places.
9. A chemical reaction that involves bringing two or more elements or compounds together to form a new product is called a synthesis reaction.

Chapter 24 Assessment

Checking Concepts

1. D
2. B
3. A
4. C
5. A
6. C
7. A
8. D
9. D
10. D

Thinking Critically

11. 52 grams
12. $C_3H_8(g) + 5O_2(g) \rightarrow 3CO_2(g) + 4H_2O(g)$
13. Using the example above, the reactant side mass = 204; the product side mass = 204 (adding the masses of all atoms on each side).
14. Zinc reacts in the solution of copper nitrate and displaces copper to form $Zn(NO_3)_2$. In the second solution, no reaction is observed.
15. exothermic

Developing Skills

16. Fructose and glucose; the acid is a catalyst.
17. Chemical Reactions
    I. Synthesis Reaction
    a. Two or more elements or compounds combine.
    b. Example: $2H_2 + O_2 \rightarrow 2H_2O$
    II. Decomposition
    a. A compound is broken down into its elements or other compounds.
    b. Example: $2H_2O \rightarrow 2H_2 + O_2$
    III. Single displacement
    a. An element in one compound is replaced by another element .
    b. Example: $Cu + 2AgNO_3 \rightarrow Cu(NO_3)_2 + 2Ag$
    IV. Double displacement
    a. Two elements from two different compounds replace each other.
    b. Example: $Ba(NO_3)_2 + K_2SO_4 \rightarrow BaSO_4 + 2KNO_3$
    Accept all reasonable examples.

Chapter 24 Assessment

Checking Concepts

Choose the word or phrase that best answers the question.

1. Oxygen gas is always written as O_2 in chemical equations because it exists in what form?
   A) product **C)** catalyst
   B) atomic molecule **D)** diatomic molecule
2. What law is based on the experiments of Lavoisier?
   A) chemical reaction **C)** coefficients
   B) conservation of mass **D)** gravity
3. What must an element be in order to replace another element in a compound?
   A) more active **C)** more inhibiting
   B) a catalyst **D)** more soluble
4. How do you indicate that a substance in an equation is a solid?
   A) *(l)* **C)** *(s)*
   B) *(g)* **D)** *(aq)*
5. What term is used to describe the 4 in the expression 4 $Ca(NO_3)_2$?
   A) coefficient **C)** subscript
   B) formula **D)** symbol
6. What type of compound is the food additive BHA?
   A) catalyst **C)** inhibitor
   B) formula **D)** CFC
7. How do you show that a substance is dissolved in water when writing an equation?
   A) *(aq)* **C)** *(g)*
   B) *(s)* **D)** *(l)*
8. What word would you use to describe HgO in the reaction that Lavoisier used to show conservation of mass?
   A) catalyst **C)** product
   B) inhibitor **D)** reactant
9. When hydrogen burns, what is oxygen's role?
   A) catalyst **C)** product
   B) inhibitor **D)** reactant
10. Give an example of a chemical reaction.
    A) bending **C)** melting
    B) evaporation **D)** photosynthesis

Thinking Critically

11. Chromium is produced by reacting its oxide with aluminum. If 76 g of Cr_2O_3 and 27 g of Al react to form 51 g of Al_2O_3, how many grams of Cr are formed?
12. Propane, $C_3H_8(g)$, burns in oxygen to form carbon dioxide and water vapor. Write a balanced equation for burning propane.
13. Use the balanced chemical equation from question 12 to explain the law of conservation of mass.
14. If Zn is placed in a solution of $Cu(NO_3)_2$, and Cu is placed in a $Zn(NO_3)_2$ solution, what reaction takes place? Explain.
15. If lye, NaOH*(s)*, is put in water, the solution gets hot. What kind of energy process is this?

Developing Skills

16. **Recognizing Cause and Effect** Sucrose, or table sugar, is a disaccharide. This means that sucrose is composed of two simple sugars chemically bonded together. Sucrose can be separated into its components by heating it in an aqueous sulfuric acid solution. Research what products are formed by breaking up sucrose. What role does the acid play?
17. **Classifying** Make an outline with the general heading "Chemical Reactions." Include the four types of reactions, with a description and example of each.

Chapter Assessment Planner

Portfolio Encourage students to place in their portfolios one or two items of what they consider to be their best work. Examples include:

- Curriculum Connection, p. 739
- Assessment, p. 745
- Challenge, p. 749
- Active Reading, p. 753

Performance Additional performance assessments, Performance Task Assessment Lists, and rubrics for evaluating these activities can be found in Glencoe's **Performance Assessment in the Science Classroom.**

Chapter 24 Assessment

18. Concept Mapping The arrow in a chemical equation tells the reaction direction. Some reactions are reversible. Sometimes, the bond formed is weak, and a product breaks apart as it's formed. Double arrows are used in the equation to indicate this reaction. Fill in the concept map, using the words *product(s)* and *reactant(s)*. In the blank in the center, fill in the formulas for the substances appearing in the reversible reaction.

$$H_2(g) + I_2(g) \rightleftarrows 2HI(g)$$

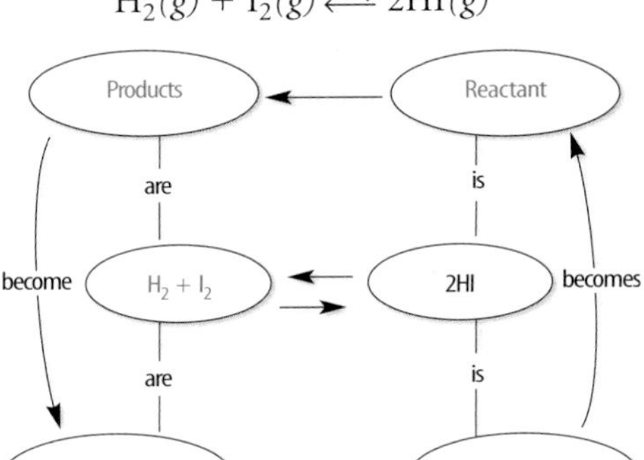

19. Interpreting Data When 46 g of sodium were exposed to dry air, 62 g of sodium oxide formed. How many grams of oxygen from the air were used?

Performance Assessment

20. Portfolio List five chemical reactions you have observed. Illustrate them using diagrams or photos. Include a brief description of the compounds involved.

Technology

Go to the Glencoe Science Web site at **science.glencoe.com** or use the **Glencoe Science CD-ROM** for additional chapter assessment.

THE PRINCETON REVIEW Test Practice

Students were studying how to balance chemical equations. The table below shows some equations they wrote for the reaction of sulfuric acid with potassium hydroxide.

1	$H_2SO_4 + KOH \rightarrow K_2SO_4 + H_2O$
2	$H_2SO_4 + 2KOH \rightarrow K_2SO_4 + H_2O$
3	$H_2SO_4 + 2KOH \rightarrow K_2SO_4 + 2H_2O$
4	$2H_2SO_4 + 4KOH \rightarrow K_2SO_4 + H_2O$

Study the table above and answer the following questions:

1. Which of the equations in the table is correctly balanced?
- **A)** one
- **B)** two
- **C)** three
- **D)** four

2. All of the chemical reactions in the table show ______.
- **F)** reactants combining with products to produce new substances
- **G)** reactants not being changed by the chemical reaction
- **H)** reactants combining to produce new products
- **J)** products combining to produce new reactants

Chapter 24 Assessment

THE PRINCETON REVIEW Test Practice

The Test-Taking Tip was written by The Princeton Review, the nation's leader in test preparation.

1. C
2. H

Developing Skills

18. See student page.
19. $62\text{ g} - 46\text{ g} = 16\text{ g of } O_2$

Performance Assessment

20. Check students' work.
Use **PASC**, p. 135.

Assessment Resources

 **Reproducible Masters**

Chapter Resources Booklet
Chapter Review, pp. 39–40
Chapter Tests, pp. 41–44
Assessment Transparency Activity, p. 53

Glencoe Science Web site
Interactive Tutor
Chapter Quizzes

Glencoe Technology
Assessment Transparency
Interactive CD-ROM Chapter Quizzes
ExamView Pro Test Bank
Vocabulary PuzzleMaker Software
MindJogger Videoquiz DVD/VHS

<table>
<tr><th rowspan="2">Section/Objectives</th><th colspan="2">Standards</th><th rowspan="2">Activities/Features</th></tr>
<tr><th>National</th><th>State/Local</th></tr>
<tr><td>Chapter Opener</td><td>See p. 37T for a Key to Standards.</td><td></td><td>Explore Activity: Determine how acid rain affects limestone and marble, p. 765
Before You Read, p. 765</td></tr>
<tr><td>Section 1 Acids and Bases
3 sessions
1.50 blocks
1. Compare and contrast acids and bases, and identify the characteristics they have.
2. Examine some formulas and uses of acids and bases you encounter every day.
3. Determine how the processes of ionization and dissociation apply to acids and bases.</td><td>National Content Standards: UCP3, A1, B1 (5-8), B2, B3 (9–12), E2, F5 (5–8), F6 (9–12)</td><td></td><td>MiniLAB: Observing Acid Relief, p. 768
Life Science Integration, p. 770
Science Online, p. 771</td></tr>
<tr><td>Section 2 Strength of Acids and Bases
2 sessions
1 block
1. Determine what is responsible for the strength of an acid or a base.
2. Compare and contrast strength and concentration of acids and bases.
3. Determine the meaning of pH.
4. Examine the relationship between pH and acid or base strength.</td><td>National Content Standards: UCP3, A1, B1 (5-8), B2, B3 (9–12), E2, F5 (5–8), F6 (9–12)</td><td></td><td>Activity: Strong and Weak Acids, p. 776
Need materials? Contact Science Kit at 1-800-828-7777 or www.sciencekit.com on the Internet.</td></tr>
<tr><td>Section 3 Salts
4 sessions
2 blocks
1. Identify a neutralization reaction.
2. Determine what a salt is and how salts form.
3. Compare and contrast soaps and detergents.
4. Examine how esters are made and what they are used for.</td><td>National Content Standards: UCP3, A1, B1 (5-8), B2, B3 (9–12), E2, F4, F5 (5–8), F5, F6 (9–12)</td><td></td><td>Visualizing Salt, p. 779
Science Online, p. 780
MiniLAB: Testing a Grape Juice Indicator, p. 781
Problem-Solving Activity: How can you handle an upsetting situation?, p. 781
Environmental Science Integration, p. 783
Activity: Be a Soda Scientist, p. 786
Science and Society: Acid Rain, p. 788</td></tr>
</table>

Activity Materials	Reproducible Resources	Section Assessment	Technology
Explore Activity: 5 g of classroom chalk; 100-mL beaker; 50 mL plain, bottled carbonated water; paper filter; glass funnel	**Chapter Resource Booklet** Foldables Worksheet, p. 17 Note-taking Worksheets, pp. 33–35	GLENCOE'S ASSESSMENT ADVANTAGE	
MiniLAB: 150 mL water, 250–mL beaker, 1 M Hcl, 12 drops of universal indicator, antacid tablet	**Chapter Resource Booklet** Transparency Activity, p. 44 MiniLAB, p. 3 Enrichment, p. 30 Reinforcement, p. 27 Directed Reading, p. 20 Transparency Activity, pp. 47–48 **Science Inquiry Labs,** p. 7	**Portfolio** Curriculum Connection, p. 767 Assessment, p. 768 **Performance** MiniLAB, p. 768 Skill Builder Activities, p. 771 **Content** Section Assessment, p. 771	Section Focus Transparency Teaching Transparency Interactive CD-ROM/DVD Guided Reading Audio Program
Activity: typing paper, thick cardboard, scissors, 2 test tubes, 2 droppers, dilute hydrochloric acid, dilute acetic acid, pH paper, timer with a second hand	**Chapter Resource Booklet** Transparency Activity, p. 45 Enrichment, p. 31 Reinforcement, p. 28 Directed Reading, p. 20 Lab Activity, pp. 9–11 Activity Worksheet, pp. 5–6 **Science Inquiry Labs,** p. 53	**Portfolio** Science Journal, p. 774 **Performance** Skill Builder Activities, p. 775 **Content** Section Assessment, p. 775	Section Focus Transparency Interactive CD-ROM/DVD Guided Reading Audio Program
MiniLAB: water, 2 small glasses, purple grape juice, measuring spoons, baking soda, white vinegar **Activity:** goggles, 2 test tubes, 2 different colorless soft drinks, graduated cylinder, 2 droppers, dilute NaOH solution 1% phenolphthalein indicator solution	**Chapter Resource Booklet** Transparency Activity, p. 46 MiniLAB Worksheet, p. 4 Enrichment, p. 32 Reinforcement, p. 29 Directed Reading, p. 21, 22 Transparency Activity, pp. 47–48 Lab Activity, p. 13–16 Activity Worksheet, pp. 7–8 **Cultural Diversity,** p. 37	**Portfolio** Cultural Diversity, p. 782 **Performance** MiniLAB, p. 781 Problem-Solving Activity, p. 781 Skill Builder Activities, p. 785 **Content** Section Assessment, p. 785	Section Focus Transparency Teaching Transparency Interactive CD-ROM/DVD Guided Reading Audio Program

End of Chapter Assessment

GLENCOE'S ASSESSMENT ADVANTAGE

Blackline Masters	Technology	Professional Series
Chapter Resources Booklet Chapter Review, pp. 37–38 Chapter Tests, pp. 39–42 **Standardized Test Practice by The Princeton Review,** pp. 104–107	MindJogger Videoquiz CD-ROM Explorations and Quizzes Vocabulary Puzzle Makers ExamView Pro Test Bank Interactive Lesson Planner Interactive Teacher's Edition	Performance Assessment in the Science Classroom (PASC)

Transparencies

Section Focus

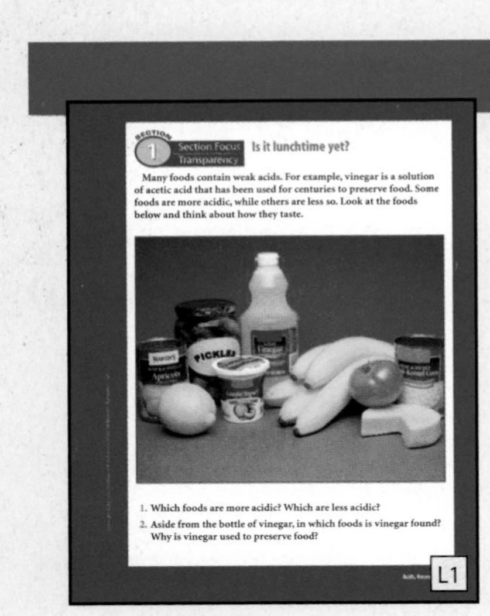
Section 1 Section Focus Transparency **Is it lunchtime yet?**

Many foods contain weak acids. For example, vinegar is a solution of acetic acid that has been used for centuries to preserve food. Some foods are more acidic, while others are less so. Look at the foods below and think about how they taste.

1. Which foods are more acidic? Which are less acidic?
2. Aside from the bottle of vinegar, in which foods is vinegar found? Why is vinegar used to preserve food?

L1

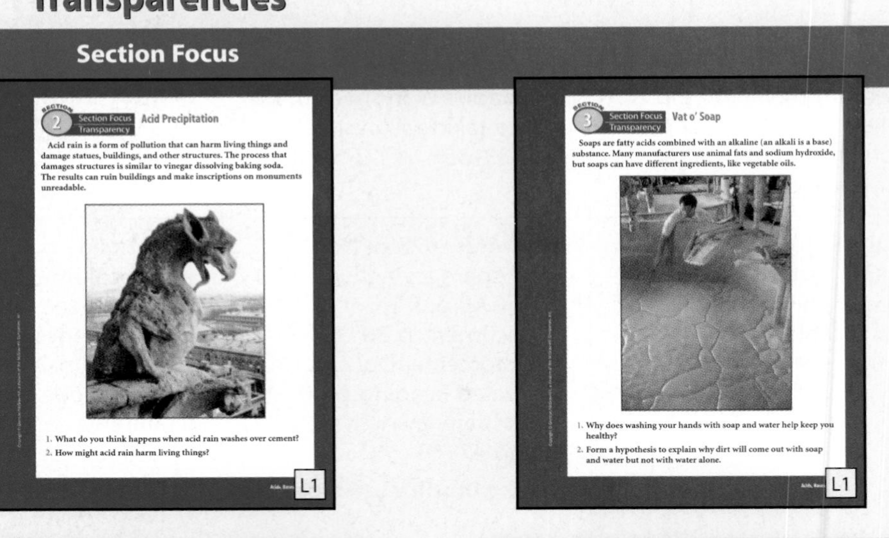
Section 2 Section Focus Transparency **Acid Precipitation**

Acid rain is a form of pollution that can harm living things and damage statues, buildings, and other structures. The process that damages structures is similar to vinegar dissolving baking soda. The results can ruin buildings and make inscriptions on monuments unreadable.

1. What do you think happens when acid rain washes over cement?
2. How might acid rain harm living things?

L1

Section 3 Section Focus Transparency **Vat o' Soap**

Soaps are fatty acids combined with an alkaline (an alkali is a base) substance. Many manufacturers use animal fats and sodium hydroxide, but soaps can have different ingredients, like vegetable oils.

1. Why does washing your hands with soap and water help keep you healthy?
2. Form a hypothesis to explain why dirt will come out with soap and water but not with water alone.

L1

This is a representation of key blackline masters available in the Teacher Classroom Resources. See Resource Manager boxes within the chapter for additional information.

Assessment

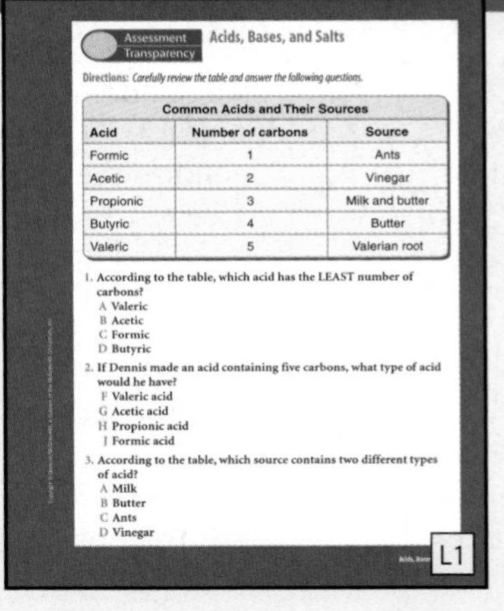
Assessment Transparency **Acids, Bases, and Salts**

Directions: Carefully review the table and answer the following questions.

Common Acids and Their Sources		
Acid	Number of carbons	Source
Formic	1	Ants
Acetic	2	Vinegar
Propionic	3	Milk and butter
Butyric	4	Butter
Valeric	5	Valerian root

1. According to the table, which acid has the LEAST number of carbons?
   A Valeric
   B Acetic
   C Formic
   D Butyric
2. If Dennis made an acid containing five carbons, what type of acid would he have?
   F Valeric acid
   G Acetic acid
   H Propionic acid
   J Formic acid
3. According to the table, which source contains two different types of acid?
   A Milk
   B Butter
   C Ants
   D Vinegar

L1

Teaching

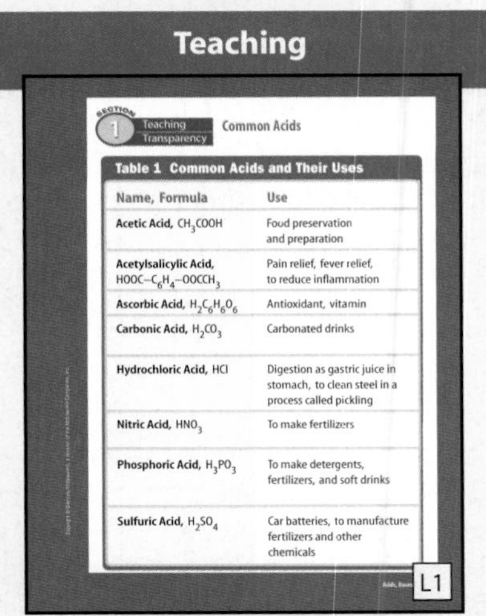
Section 1 Teaching Transparency **Common Acids**

Table 1 Common Acids and Their Uses	
Name, Formula	Use
Acetic Acid, CH_3COOH	Food preservation and preparation
Acetylsalicylic Acid, $HOOC{-}C_6H_4{-}OOCCH_3$	Pain relief, fever relief, to reduce inflammation
Ascorbic Acid, $H_2C_6H_6O_6$	Antioxidant, vitamin
Carbonic Acid, H_2CO_3	Carbonated drinks
Hydrochloric Acid, HCl	Digestion as gastric juice in stomach, to clean steel in a process called pickling
Nitric Acid, HNO_3	To make fertilizers
Phosphoric Acid, H_3PO_4	To make detergents, fertilizers, and soft drinks
Sulfuric Acid, H_2SO_4	Car batteries, to manufacture fertilizers and other chemicals

L1

Key to Teaching Strategies

The following designations will help you decide which activities are appropriate for your students.

L1 Level 1 activities should be appropriate for students with learning difficulties.

L2 Level 2 activities should be within the ability range of all students.

L3 Level 3 activities are designed for above-average students.

ELL ELL activities should be within the ability range of English Language Learners.

COOP LEARN Cooperative Learning activities are designed for small group work.

LS Multiple Learning Styles logos are used throughout to indicate strategies that address different learning styles.

P These strategies represent student products that can be placed into a best-work portfolio.

Hands-on Activities

Activity Worksheets

Laboratory Activities

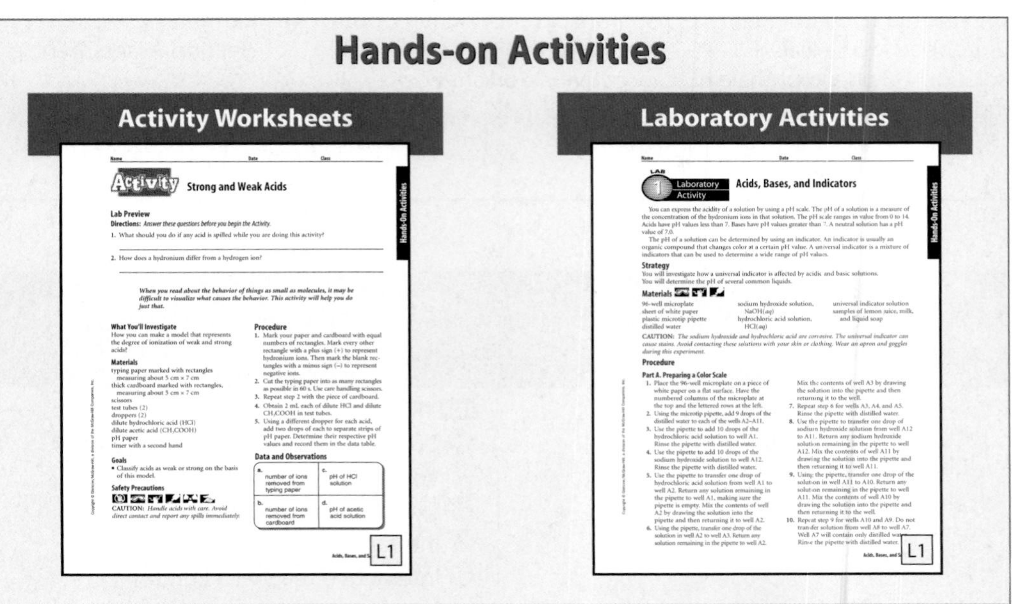
Activity **Strong and Weak Acids**

Lab Preview

Directions: Answer these questions before you begin the Activity.

1. What should you do if any acid is spilled while you are doing this activity?
2. How does a hydronium ion differ from a hydrogen ion?

When you read about the behavior of things as small as molecules, it may be difficult to visualize what causes the behavior. This activity will help you do just that.

What You'll Investigate

Procedure

Data and Observations

L1

Laboratory Activity 1 **Acids, Bases, and Indicators**

Strategy

Materials

Procedure

Part A. Preparing a Color Scale

L1

Meeting Different Ability Levels

Content Outline

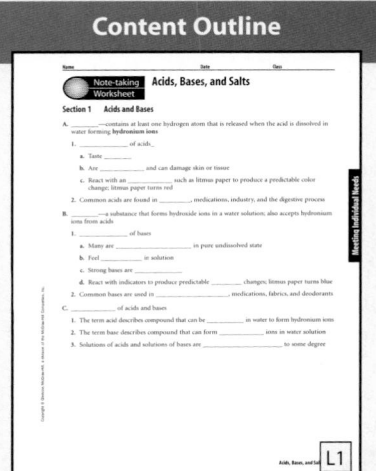

Reinforcement

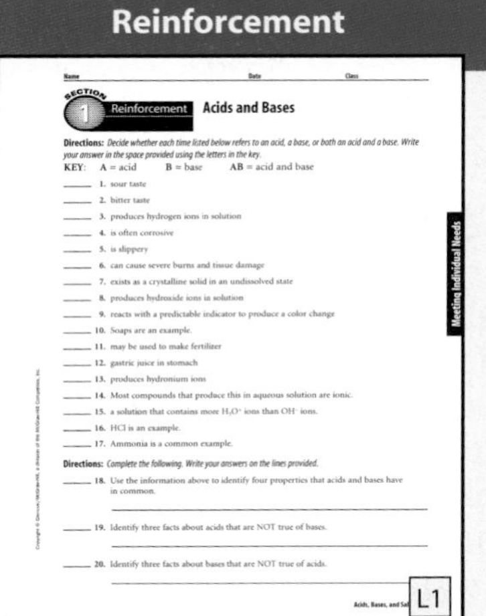

Directed Reading

Chapter Tests

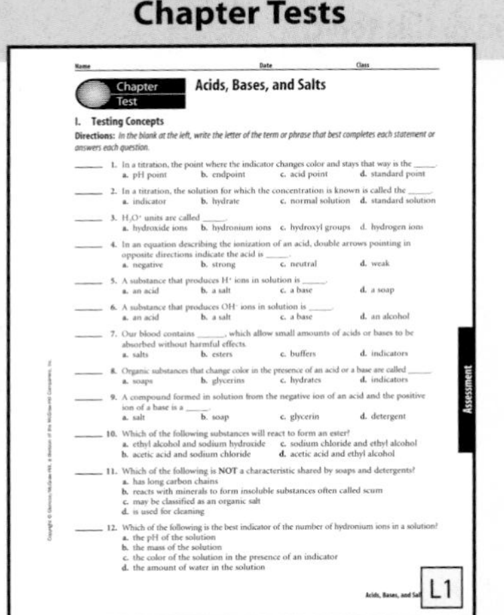

Enrichment

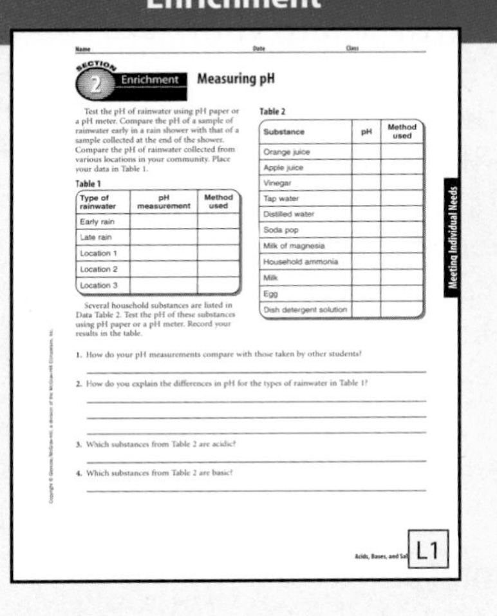

Spanish Directed Reading

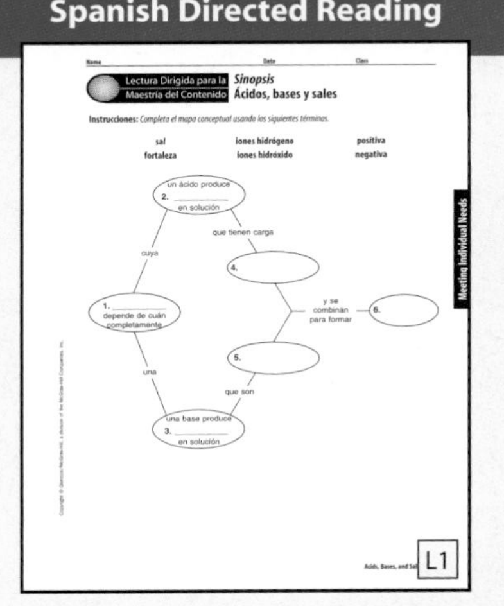

Test Practice Workbook

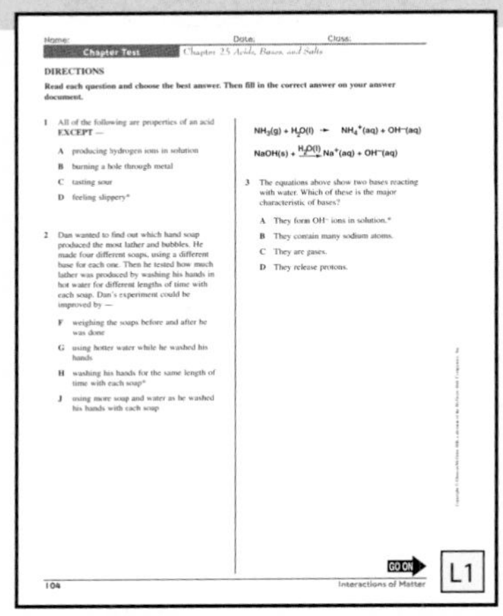

Chapter Review

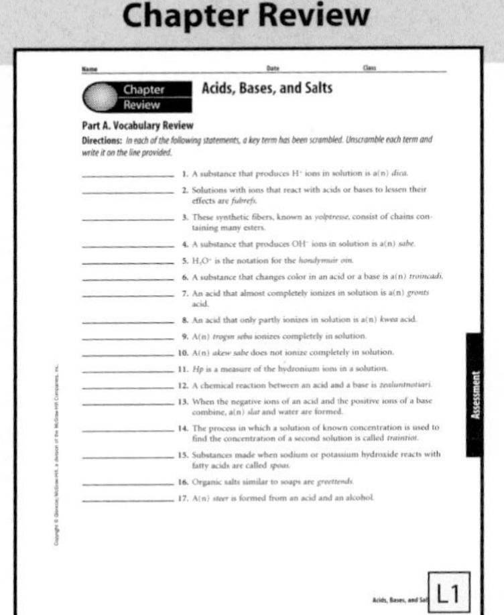

Science Content Background

SECTION 1

Acids and Bases

Solutions of Acids and Bases

A good operational definition of acids and bases is that acids increase the concentration of hydrogen ions when dissolved in water and bases increase the concentration of hydroxide ions when dissolved in water. Other characteristics come from work by Robert Boyle in the 1600s. Acids have a sour taste, are corrosive, turn litmus from red to blue, and lose their acidity when they react with alkaline (basic) materials. Bases feel slippery, change litmus from blue to red, and become less *alkaline* when they react with bases. The word alkaline became synonymous with basic because alkalines are the "basis" for making salts.

Fun Fact

Hydrochloric acid is essential for digestion and is secreted by the lining of the stomach in quantities of 1.2 to 1.5 L per day.

SECTION 2

Strength of Acids and Bases

pH of a Solution

The term pH is derived from the French *puissance d'hydrogène* (power of hydrogen) and refers to the power of 10 used to express the molar H_3O^+ concentration. The approximate pH of a solution can be determined by using an acid-base indicator. Bromothymol blue, for instance, changes color in the pH range 6.0–7.6 from yellow in its acid form to blue in its base form. Phenolphthalein changes in the pH range of 8.2–9.8 from colorless in its acid form to pink in its base form. A mixture of indicators called universal indicator can be used that measures the range of pH from 3–10.

Student Misconception

Students may think that pH is only a measure of the degree of acidity.

Refer to the facing page for teaching strategies to address this misconception. Refer to pages 774–775 for content related to this topic.

Salts

SECTION 3

Salts

A salt is an ionic compound that is formed when an acid neutralizes a base. Salt solutions can be neutral, acidic, or basic, depending on the acid-base properties of the constituents. As a general rule, salts formed by the reaction of a strong acid with a strong base are neutral, salts formed by reaction of a strong acid with a weak base are acidic, and salts formed by the reaction of a weak acid with a strong base are basic.

SCIENCE Online

For additional content background on this topic, go to the Glencoe Science Web site at science.glencoe.com.

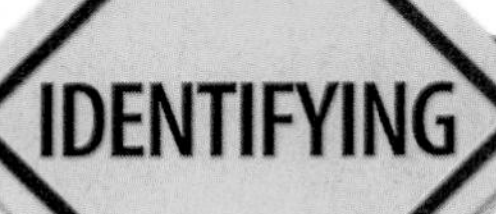

Misconceptions

Find Out What Students Think

Students may think that . . .

- **pH is only a measure of the degree of acidity.**

From lemon juice to vinegar, examples of acids seem common in our lives. Thus it is no wonder that students think of pH in terms of acidity and neglect the basic or alkaline components of pH. Even most adults have an easier time giving the names of acids than bases.

Activity

Ask students to record their responses as you read each statement:

- Explain what is meant by pH.
- List three materials that have a pH between 1 and 6.
- List three materials that have a pH between 8 and 14.

Promote Understanding

Activity

Before class:

- Place small amounts of each of the following materials into beakers: bleach, clear ammonia, milk of magnesia, Pine Sol, baking soda in water, vinegar, lemon juice, and orange juice.
- Create stations with these solutions. Have a glass rod in each beaker and a small plate at each station. Place caution signs at the bleach and ammonia stations.
- Have water available in case chemicals contact the body.

In class:

- Draw a scale from 0 to 14 on the board. Directly over the number 7, write HOH. Explain that a material with a pH of 7 is neutral. Pure water, HOH, is neutral. It is not acidic or basic. It has an equal number of Hs and Ohs.
- Write H+ above the numbers 0–6 and OH- above the numbers 8–14. Explain that solutions with a pH of 0 to 6 have more H+ ions than OH- ions in water. These solutions are acidic.
- Hydrochloric acid is a very acidic material. It has a pH of 1. Write *hydrochloric acid* above 1 on the scale.
- Solutions with a pH of 8 to 14 have more OH^- ions than H^+ ions in water. These solutions are basic. A very basic material is drain cleaner, with a pH of 14. Write *drain cleaner* above 14.
- Some dishwasher detergents have a pH of 13. Write this above the number 13 on the scale.

Tell students they will work in groups to test the pH of materials and find one material for each number of the pH scale. Materials have already been found for the numbers 1, 7, 13, and 14.

- Distribute universal pH strips, and explain how they are used.
- Distribute goggles and aprons to each student.
- Instruct students to put the pH strip on the plate and add one drop of liquid. Have them leave the pH test strips on the plates for you to dispose of later.
- If needed, students can use their textbooks, the library, and the Internet to find remaining materials and their pH values.

Assess

After completing the chapter, see *Identifying Misconceptions* in the Study Guide.

CHAPTER 

Acids, Bases, and Salts

Chapter Vocabulary

acid
hydronium ion
indicator
base
strong acid
weak acid
strong base
weak base
pH
buffer
neutralization
salt
titration
soap

What do you think?

Science Journal The photo shows a close-up view of a salt crystal on a pretzel. Salts are formed in the neutralization reaction that occurs when an acid is mixed with a base.

CHAPTER 

Acids, Bases, and Salts

Salt is essential for most animals including humans. Farmers often provide salt to livestock, and many wild animals get salt from natural salt licks. Butterflies like those shown here suck salt from moist ground—a behavior known as puddling. In this chapter you'll learn about this specific salt—sodium chloride—among other salts and about the acids and bases that react to form them.

What do you think?

Science Journal Look at the picture below with a classmate. Discuss what you think this might be. Here's a hint: *These and many more like them keep the oceans from being big lakes.* Write your answer in your Science Journal.

764

Theme Connection

Systems and Interactions Acids and bases react with each other to produce chemical changes. This interaction is predictable, and one product—a salt— is classified as a separate group of compounds. An acid-base reaction forms a system.

Many limestone caves and rock formations are shaped by water containing carbon dioxide. Higher levels of carbon dioxide in acid rain can damage marble structures. Observe this reaction using soda water to represent acid rain and chalk, which like limestone and marble is calcium carbonate.

Determine how acid rain affects limestone and marble

1. Measure approximately 5 g of classroom chalk.
2. Crush it slightly and place it in a 100-mL beaker.
3. Add 50 mL of plain, bottled carbonated water to the beaker.
4. After several minutes, stir the mixture.
5. When the mixture stops reacting, filter it using a paper filter in a glass funnel.
6. Dry the residue overnight and determine its mass.

Observe

1. How did the mass change?
2. In your Science Journal, write your conclusions about the effect that acid rain can have on marble buildings and monuments.

Before You Read

Making a Venn Diagram Study Fold A Venn Diagram can be used to compare and contrast the characteristics of acids and bases.

1. Place a sheet of paper in front of you so the short side is at the top. Fold the paper in half from top to bottom.
2. Draw and label *Acids, Salts,* and *Bases* across the front of the paper, as shown. Fold both sides in.
3. Unfold the paper so that three columns show.
4. Through the top thickness of paper, cut along each of the fold lines to the topfold, forming three tabs.
5. As you read the chapter, collect information about each and write it under its tab.

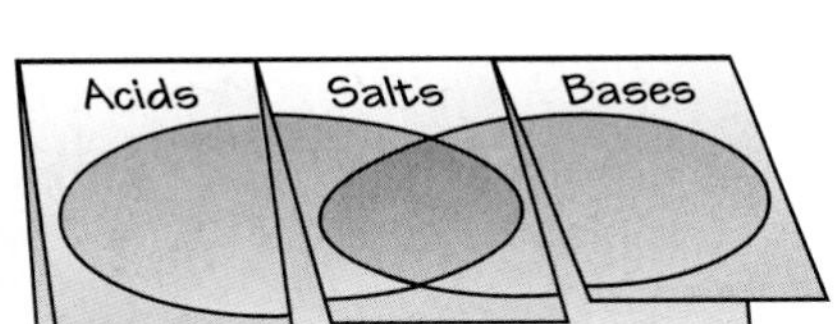

765

Explore Activity

Purpose Use the Explore Activity to shows evidence of a chemical reaction between the carbonic acid in soda and the base calcium carbonate. L2 **Kinesthetic**

Preparation Chalk pieces may be massed ahead of time and placed in beakers, each labeled with the mass of the chalk. Keep soda water sealed until immediately before use.

Materials classroom chalk, mortar and pestle to crush the chalk, several bottles of fresh soda water, 100-mL beakers, 50-mL or 100-mL graduated cylinder, funnels, filter paper

Teaching Strategies

- Provide the filter paper folded into funnels.
- The residue may be dried in the air overnight or with an electric heater.

Observe

1. The mass of the residue is less than the mass of the chalk.
2. Acid rain can dissolve limestone.

Oral Ask students to draw diagrams showing how increasing the level of acidity in rainwater would affect ancient marble sculptures. More acid in rainwater would cause marble sculptures to decompose more quickly. Use **Performance Assessment in the Science Classroom,** p. 127.

Before You Read

FOLDABLES Reading & Study Skills

Dinah Zike Study Fold

Purpose Students each make a Foldable to help them determine what they know about acids, bases, and salts. They then record data on their Foldables as they read and learn more about acids, bases, and salts.

For additional help, see Foldables Worksheet, p. 17 in **Chapter Resources Booklet,** or go to the Glencoe Science Web site at **science.glencoe.com.** See After You Read in the Study Guide at the end of this chapter.

SECTION 1

Acids and Bases

1 Motivate

Bellringer Transparency

Display the Section Focus Transparency for Section 1. Use the accompanying Transparency Activity Master. L2 ELL

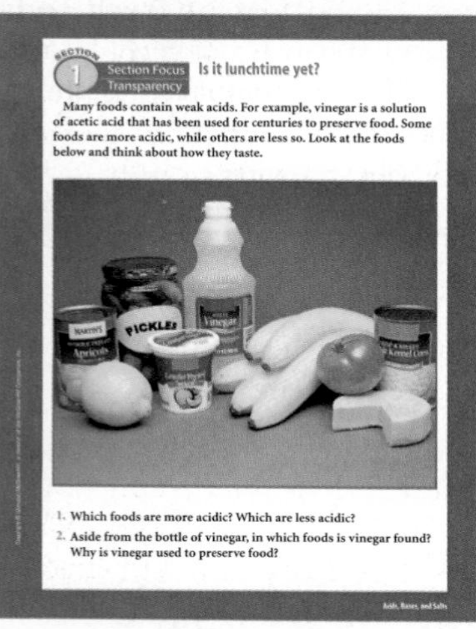
Section Focus Transparency 1 — Is it lunchtime yet?

Many foods contain weak acids. For example, vinegar is a solution of acetic acid that has been used for centuries to preserve food. Some foods are more acidic, while others are less so. Look at the foods below and think about how they taste.

1. Which foods are more acidic? Which are less acidic?
2. Aside from the bottle of vinegar, in which foods is vinegar found? Why is vinegar used to preserve food?

Tie to Prior Knowledge

Ask students whether they have heard of someone using an antacid for an upset stomach. **What does this indicate about the contents of our stomachs?** Our stomachs must contain an acid. Medical antacid preparations typically contain weak bases.

Caption Answer

Figure 1 Yogurt and buttermilk contain lactic acid; lemons contain citric acid.

SECTION 

Acids and Bases

As You Read

What **You'll Learn**

- **Compare** and **contrast** acids and bases and identify the characteristics they have.
- **Examine** some formulas and uses of acids and bases you encounter every day.
- **Determine** how the processes of ionization and dissociation apply to acids and bases.

Vocabulary

acid, indicator, hydronium ion, base

Why **It's Important**

Acids and bases are found almost everywhere—from fruit juice and gastric juice to soaps.

Acids

What comes to mind when you hear the word *acid?* Do you think of a substance that can burn your skin or even burn a hole through a piece of metal? Do you think about sour foods like those shown in **Figure 1?** Does your mouth water when you think about biting into a sour pickle or sinking your teeth into a lemon? Although some acids can burn and are dangerous to handle, the acids in foods are safe to eat. What all acids have in common, however, is that they contain at least one hydrogen atom that can be removed when the acid is dissolved in water.

Properties of Acids

When an acid dissolves in water, some of the hydrogen is released as hydrogen ions, H^+. An **acid** is a substance that produces hydrogen ions in a water solution. It is the ability to produce these ions that gives acids their characteristic properties. When an acid dissolves in water, H^+ ions interact with water molecules to form H_3O^+ ions, which are called **hydronium ions** (hi DROH nee um • I ahnz).

Acids have several common properties. For one thing, all acids taste sour. The familiar sour taste of many foods is due to the presence of acids. However, taste never should be used to test for the presence of acids. Some acids can damage tissue by producing painful burns.

Figure 1
Pickles contain acetic acid.
Can you guess which of these foods contain lactic and citric acids?

Acids are corrosive. Some acids react strongly with certain metals, seeming to eat away the metals as metallic compounds and hydrogen gas form. Acids also react with indicators to produce predictable changes in color. An **indicator** is an organic compound that changes color in acid and base. For example, the indicator litmus paper turns red in acid.

Section Assessment Planner

PORTFOLIO
Curriculum Connection, p. 767
Assessment, p. 768

PERFORMANCE ASSESSMENT
MiniLAB, p. 768
Skill Builder Activities, p. 771
See page 792 for more options.

CONTENT ASSESSMENT
Section, p. 771
Challenge, p. 771
Chapter, pp. 792–793

Common Acids

Many foods contain acids. In addition to citric acid in citrus fruits, lactic acid is found in yogurt and buttermilk, and any pickled food contains vinegar or acetic acid. Your stomach uses hydrochloric acid to help digest your food. Four acids are vital to industry—sulfuric, phosphoric, nitric and hydrochloric.

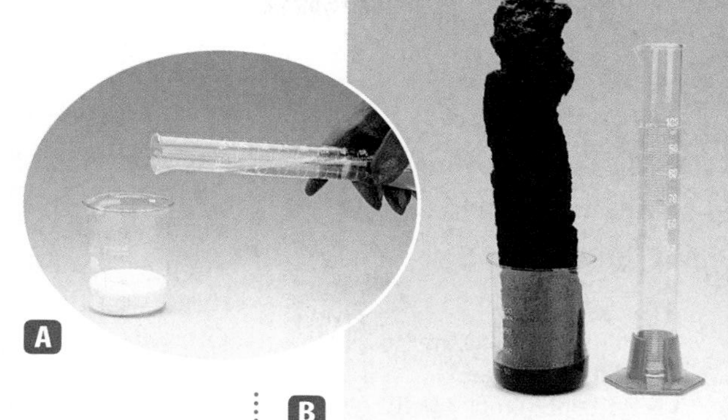

Figure 2
A When sulfuric acid is added to sugar **B** the mixture foams, removing hydrogen and oxygen atoms as water and leaving air-filled carbon.

Reading Check ***Which four acids are important for industry?***

Table 1 lists the names and formulas of a few acids, their uses, and some properties. Three acids are used to make fertilizers—most nitric and sulfuric acid and 80 percent of phosphoric acid are used for this purpose. Many acids can burn, but sulfuric acid can burn by removing water from your skin as easily as it takes water from sugar, as shown in **Figure 2.**

Table 1 Common Acids and Their Uses

Name, Formula	Use	Other Information
Acetic Acid, CH_3COOH	Food preservation and preparation	When in solution with water, it is known as vinegar.
Acetylsalicylic Acid, $HOOC{-}C_6H_4{-}OOCCH_3$	Pain relief, fever relief, to reduce inflammation	Known as aspirin
Ascorbic Acid, $H_2C_6H_6O_6$	Antioxidant, vitamin	Called vitamin C
Carbonic Acid, H_2CO_3	Carbonated drinks	Involved in cave, stalactite, and stalagmite formation and acid rain
Hydrochloric Acid, HCl	Digestion as gastric juice in stomach, to clean steel in a process called pickling	Commonly called muriatic acid
Nitric Acid, HNO_3	To make fertilizers	Colorless, yet yellows when exposed to light
Phosphoric Acid, H_3PO_3	To make detergents, fertilizers, and soft drinks	Slightly sour but pleasant taste, detergents containing phosphates cause water pollution
Sulfuric Acid, H_2SO_4	Car batteries, to manufacture fertilizers and other chemicals	Dehydrating agent, causes burns by removing water from body cells

2 Teach

Properties of Acids

Activity

Have students note the formulas of the inorganic acids listed in **Table 1.** Ask what they observe about the way formulas of these acids are typically written. Chemists commonly indicate that a compound is an acid by writing the formula with "H" as the first element. L2 LS **Logical-mathematical**

Use Science Words

Word Meaning Have students use the word *indicator* in a sentence, and then explain how the meaning of *indicator* in their sentence parallels its meaning in the context of acid and base identification. L2 LS **Linguistic**

Common Acids

Visual Learning

Table 1 If an acid contains a structure that includes COOH, it is an organic acid. Other acids, including H_2CO_3, are inorganic. Have students work in small groups to classify the acids from **Table 1** as organic or inorganic. All are inorganic except acetic acid and acetylsalicylic acid. L2 LS **Linguistic**

Reading Check

Answer sulfuric, phosphoric, nitric, and hydrochloric acids

Resource Manager

Chapter Resources Booklet
- Transparency Activity, p. 44
- Note-taking Worksheets, pp. 33–35
- Directed Reading for Content Mastery, p. 20

Curriculum Connection

Art Etching is using the reaction between an acid and a metal to make a piece of art. Have students find out more about this process and make posters illustrating it. A metal plate, usually copper or zinc, is coated with acid-resistant resin. The artist draws lines through the resin, then puts the plate in an acid bath. The acid reacts with the metal exposed by the drawing and not through the resin. L2 LS **Visual-Spatial** P

Bases

Use an Analogy

In a football game, a quarterback holding the ball cannot complete a pass unless a receiver catches the ball. An H^+ ion from an acid is like the football. The quarterback (the acid) must have a receiver (the base) to receive the football (the H^+ ion) to complete the pass (the reaction between the acid and the base). This could be demonstrated in class with a foam football labeled H^+. L1 ELL

LS **Kinesthetic**

Properties of Bases

Quick Demo

Bring some drain cleaner to class and add a small amount to distilled water. Test the solution with litmus to demonstrate the base properties of the cleaner. **CAUTION:** *Keep the solution out of reach of students. Dispose of it properly.* L2 ELL

LS **Visual-Spatial**

Caption Answer

Figure 3 slipperiness, bitter taste

Purpose to observe how an indicator changes color as a base is neutralized L2 ELL

LS **Kinesthetic**

Materials water, 250-mL beaker, 1 M HCl, universal indicator, antacid tablets, graduated cylinder, dropper

Teaching Strategy A blue or violet color may occur when the HCl is added, depending on the brand of antacid used.

Analysis

1. The color changed from red to orange to yellow to green.
2. The base neutralized the HCl, changing the color of the indicator.

Observing Acid Relief

Procedure

1. Add 150 mL of **water** to a **250-mL beaker.**
2. Add three drops **1 M HCl** and 12 drops of **universal indicator.**
3. Observe the color of the solution.
4. Add an **antacid tablet** and observe for 15 minutes.

Analysis

1. Describe any changes that took place in the solution.
2. Explain why these changes occurred.

Bases

You might not be as familiar with bases as you are with acids. Although you can eat some foods that contain acids, you don't consume many bases. Some foods, such as egg whites, are slightly basic. Other basic materials you might consume are baking powder and weak bases, such as caffeine and amines found in some foods. Medicines, such as milk of magnesia and antacids are basic too. Still, you come in contact with many bases every day. For example, each time you wash your hands using soap, you are using a base. One characteristic of bases is that they feel slippery, like soapy water. Bases are important in many types of cleaning materials, as shown in **Figure 3.** Bases are important in industry, also. For example, sodium hydroxide is used in the paper industry to separate fibers of cellulose from wood pulp. The freed cellulose fibers are made into paper.

Bases can be defined in two ways. Any substance that forms hydroxide ions, OH^-, in a water solution is a **base.** In addition, a base is any substance that accepts H^+ from acids. The definitions are related, because the OH^- ions produced by some bases do accept H^+ ions.

Properties of Bases

One way to think about bases is as the complements or opposites of acids. Although acids and bases share some common features, the bases have their own characteristic properties.

In the pure, undissolved state, many bases are crystalline solids. In solution, bases feel slippery and have a bitter taste. Like strong acids, strong bases are corrosive, and contact with skin can result in severe burns. Therefore, taste and touch never should be used to test for the presence of a base. Finally, like acids, bases react with indicators to produce changes in color. The indicator litmus turns blue in bases.

Figure 3
Bases are commonly found in many cleaning products used around the home.
What property of bases is evident in soaps?

Assessment

Portfolio Have students write complete lab reports of this activity in their Science Journals. Encourage them to include both diagrams and written descriptions. Make sure they include the materials used, the procedure, and all of their observations. Use **Performance Assessment in the Science Classroom,** p. 119. P

Teacher FYI

All bases attract H^+ to a pair of unshared electrons in their structures. OH^- ions have a negative charge, which helps attract positive H^+ ions. Bases containing nitrogen have an unshared pair of electrons around the nitrogen. Typically, nitrogen-containing bases are not as strong as OH^--containing bases.

Figure 4
Two applications of bases are shown here.

A Aluminum hydroxide is a base used in water-treatment plants. Its sticky surface collects impurities, making them easier to filter.

B Some drain cleaners contain NaOH, which dissolves grease, and small pieces of aluminum. The aluminum reacts with NaOH, producing hydrogen and dislodging solids, such as hair.

Common Bases

You probably are familiar with many common bases because they are found in cleaning products used in the home. These and some other bases are shown in **Table 2,** which also includes their uses and some information about them. **Figure 4** shows two uses of bases that you might not be familiar with.

Table 2 Common Bases and Their Uses

Name, Formula	Use	Other Information
Aluminum Hydroxide, $Al(OH)_3$	Deodorant, antacid, water purification as shown in **Figure 4A**	Sticky gel that collects suspended clay and dirt particles on its surface
Calcium Hydroxide, $Ca(OH)_2$	Leather-making, mortar and plaster, lessen acidity of soil	Called caustic lime
Magnesium Hydroxide, $Mg(OH)_2$	Laxative, antacid	Called milk of magnesia
Sodium Hydroxide, NaOH	To make soap, oven cleaner, drain cleaner, textiles, and paper	Called lye and caustic soda; generates heat (exothermic) when combined with water, reacts with metals to form hydrogen
Ammonia, NH_3	Cleaners, fertilizer, to make rayon and nylon	Irritating odor that is damaging to nasal passages and lungs

Common Bases

IDENTIFYING Misconceptions

The bases examined in this section have OH bonded to a metal. Students may have seen the OH symbols connected to other compounds called alcohols. This does not make alcohols fit the definition of a base. The—OH in an alcohol is called a hydroxyl group and is not the same thing as the hydroxide ion, OH^-.

Quick Demo

Bring some milk of magnesia to class to test with litmus. Call students' attention to the list in **Table 2** for the formula of magnesium hydroxide. Remind students that litmus turns blue in the presence of bases, and then test the magnesium hydroxide. Ask why this compound might be found in some antacid preparations. Because it is a base, it would help neutralize stomach acid. L2 ELL

LS **Visual-Spatial**

Fun Fact

The formula for caffeine, the stimulant found in coffee, tea, and many soft drinks, is $C_8H_{10}N_4O_2$. Since caffeine has nitrogen atoms in a position to accept H^+ ions, it fits the definition of a base, although it is a weak one.

Resource Manager

Chapter Resources Booklet
MiniLAB, p. 3
Transparency Activity, pp. 47–48
Home and Community Involvement, p. 36

Solutions of Acids and Bases

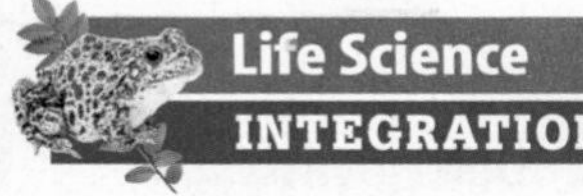

Life Science INTEGRATION

HCOOH, formic acid, has the simplest structure of the organic acids. One of the first preparations of this acid included the crushing and heating of ants and the recovery of the vapor that contained the acid.

Make a Model

To illustrate the ionization that takes place when an acid is dissolved in water, have students hold a capped ink pen in the right hand. On your signal, have them use the left hand to remove the cap and cover it in that hand. In this model, water (the left hand) detaches H^+ (the pen cap) from an acid (the pen) and surrounds and holds it. This same process takes place with billions of acid molecules as they ionize in water. L1 ELL

LS **Kinesthetic**

Visual Learning

Figure 5 With students, review the two parts of the illustration. Draw a diagram on the chalkboard showing how hydrogen chloride gas molecules form hydronium ions in water. Draw a similar diagram for formic acid. L2

LS **Visual-Spatial**

Reading Check

Answer NH_3 removes H^+ from water to leave behind OH^- ions and form NH_4^+.

Life Science INTEGRATION

Some ants add sting to their bite by injecting a solution of formic acid. In fact, formic acid was named for ants, which make up the genus *Formica*. Still ants are considered tasty treats by many animals. For example, one woodpecker called a flicker has saliva that is basic enough to take the sting out of ants.

Solutions of Acids and Bases

You have learned that substances such as HCl, HNO_3, and H_2SO_4 are acids because of their ability to produce H^+ ions. This ionization process is shown in **Figure 5A,** using HCl as an example. When a polar molecule, such as HCl, is dissolved in water, the negatively charged area of nearby water molecules attracts the positively charged area of the polar molecule. The H^+ is removed from the polar molecule, and a hydronium ion (H_3O^+) is formed. Thus, acid describes any compound that can be ionized in water to form hydronium ions. When an organic acid ionizes, the H at the end of the $-COOH$ group separates as H^+ and combines with water to form the hydronium ion as shown in **Figure 5B.**

Bases Compounds that can form hydroxide ions (OH^-) in solution are classified as bases. If you look at **Table 2,** you will find that most of the substances that are listed contain OH in their formulas. Except for ammonia, inorganic compounds that produce bases in aqueous solution are ionic compounds—that is, they already are made up of ions. As the following equation shows, when such a compound dissolves in water, the ions dissociate and exist as individual ions in solution.

$$NaOH(s) \xrightarrow{H_2O} Na^+(aq) + OH^-(aq)$$

These substances release OH^- ions in water. If a solution contains more OH^- ions than H_3O^+ ions, it is referred to as a basic solution.

Figure 5
Both inorganic and organic acids form hydronium ions in water.

A Hydrogen chloride gas dissolves in water and ionizes to produce hydronium ions and chloride ions.

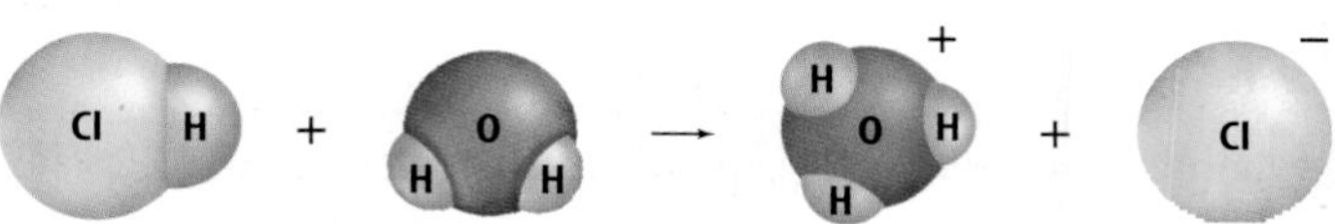

B Organic acids also form hydronium ions when they dissolve in water. Here, formic acid forms hydronium ions and formate ions.

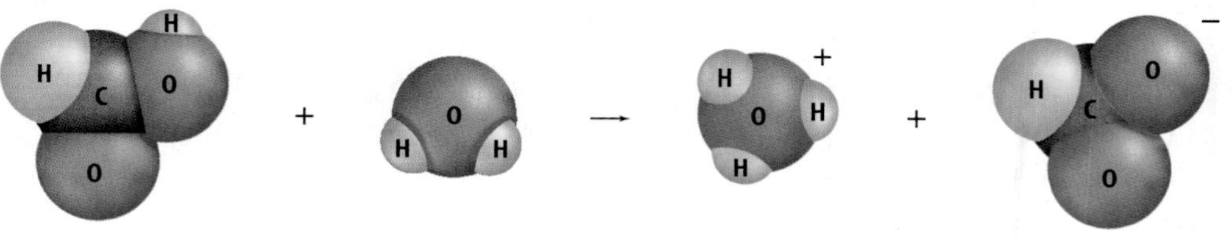

Science Journal

Oil of Vitriol Sulfate compounds used to be called vitriols because the compounds look glassy. The old name for sulfuric acid was *oil of vitriol.* The words *vitriol* and *vitriolic* have taken on broader meanings. Ask students to write the meaning of *vitriol* in their Science Journals and explain how it is connected to sulfuric acid. *Vitriol* means something caustic, or virulence of feeling or speech.

Resource Manager

Chapter Resources Booklet
- Reinforcement, p. 27
- Enrichment, p. 30

Science Inquiry Labs, p. 7

Figure 6
Even though ammonia is not a hydroxide, it reacts with water to produce some hydroxide ions. Therefore, it is a base.

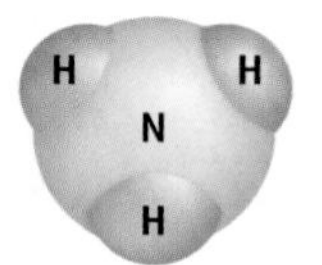

+

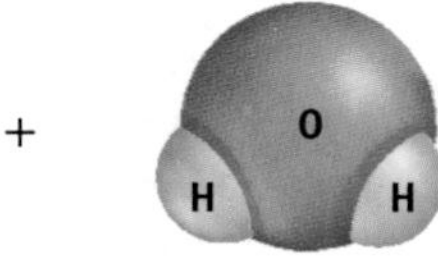

→

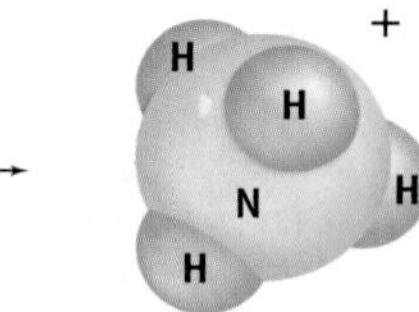

+

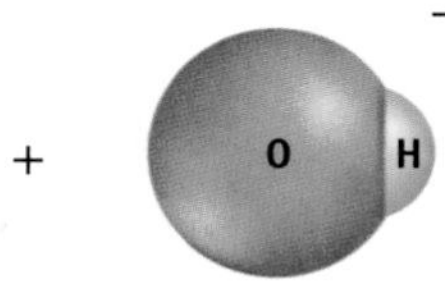

Ammonia Ammonia is a polar compound. In a water solution, ionization takes place when the ammonia molecule attracts a hydrogen ion from a water molecule, forming an ammonium ion. This leaves a hydroxide ion, as shown in **Figure 6.**

Reading Check *How does ammonia react in a water solution?*

Ammonia is a popular household cleaner. However, products containing ammonia never should be used with other cleaners that contain hydrochloric acid or chlorine, such as some bathroom bowl cleaners and bleach. A reaction between vapors of hydrogen chloride and ammonia produces fine particles of the solid compound ammonium chloride suspended in the air. Breathing these particles can severely damage lung tissues.

Solutions of both acids and bases produce some ions that are capable of carrying electric current to some extent. Thus, they are said to be conductors.

Research Visit the Glencoe Science Web site at **science.glencoe.com** for more information about the dangers of mixing ammonia cleaners with chlorine or hydrochloric acid cleaners. Communicate to your class what you learn.

Section 1 Assessment

1. Name three important acids and three important bases and describe their uses.
2. What is an indicator?
3. What metallic compound would you predict forms when sulfuric acid reacts with magnesium metal?
4. If an acid donates H^+ and a base produces OH^-, what compound is likely to be produced when acids react with bases?
5. **Think Critically** Vinegar contains acetic acid, CH_3COOH. Is acetic acid organic or inorganic? How do you know? Write an equation showing how acetic acid ionizes.

Skill Builder Activities

6. **Predicting** Remember that solutions of acids and bases produce ions that can conduct electric current. Name two substances found in your home that could conduct electricity. Explain why. **For more help, refer to the Science Skill Handbook.**
7. **Using a Database** Make a database that compares acids and bases. Include the following: *home and commercial uses, properties, where they are found,* and *what ions they form in solution.* **For more help, refer to the Technology Skill Handbook.**

Answers to Section Assessment

1. Accept all reasonable responses.
2. an organic compound that changes color in acid or base
3. magnesium sulfate
4. HOH, which is water
5. Acetic acid is organic. It has a COOH group. $CH_3COOH \rightarrow CH_3COO^- + H^+$
6. Possible substances: ammonia, water; accept all reasonable answers.
7. Check students' work.

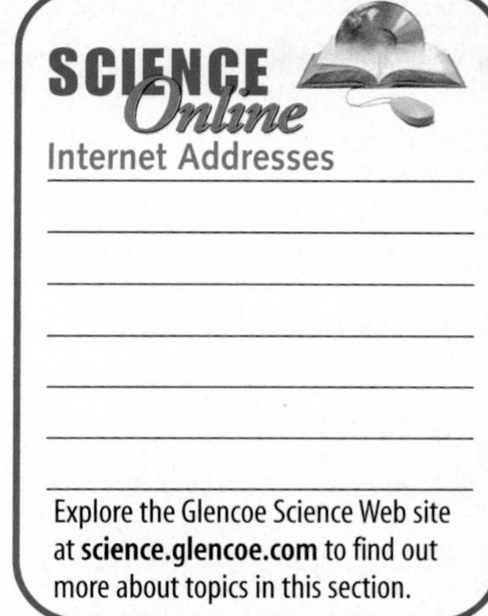

3 Assess

Reteach

Provide several unlabeled dilute solutions of acids and bases. Give students litmus paper to test the solutions to determine which are acids and which are bases. Litmus is red in an acid and blue in a base. L2

LS **Visual-Spatial**

Challenge

Amino acids make up the building blocks of proteins. Write out the structure of the amino acid glycine, $NH_2CH COOH$. Ask students to identify the areas of the molecule that cause it to have acid properties. The H at the end of COOH can be donated to produce H^+ ions. Also ask students to look for another area that allows it to have base properties. The N atom has unshared electrons that can attract and accept H^+ ions, as bases do. L3

LS **Logical-Mathematical**

Performance Ask students to write the balanced chemical equation for the reaction of an aqueous solution of ammonia with vapors of hydrogen chloride. $NH_4OH + HCl \rightarrow NH_4Cl + H_2O$. Use **PASC,** p. 101.

SECTION

Strength of Acids and Bases

1 Motivate

Bellringer Transparency

Display the Section Focus Transparency for Section 2. Use the accompanying Transparency Activity Master. L2 ELL

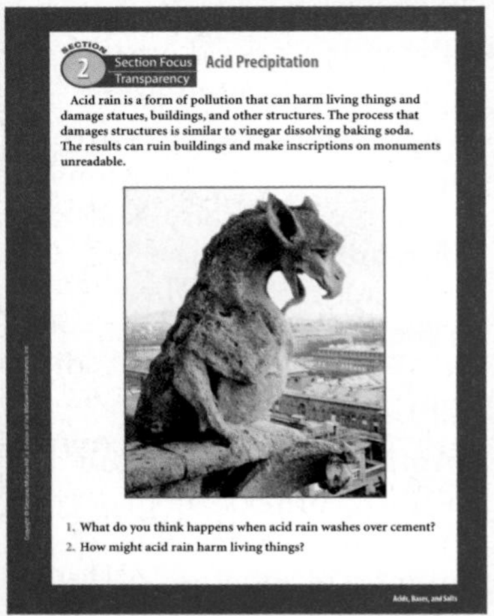

Tie to Prior Knowledge

Ask students to name acids they have encountered that weren't harmful and acids that were. Possible answers: Fruit juices with weak acids are not harmful; battery acid is harmful. Tell students that in this section, they will learn why some acids are stronger than others.

SECTION 2

Strength of Acids and Bases

As You Read

***What* You'll Learn**

- **Determine** what is responsible for the strength of an acid or a base.
- **Compare and contrast** strength and concentration of acids and bases.
- **Determine** the meaning of pH.
- **Examine** the relationship between pH and acid or base strength.

Vocabulary

strong acid, weak acid, strong base, weak base, pH, buffer

***Why* It's Important**

Understanding the strength of acids and bases helps you use them safely.

Strong and Weak Acids and Bases

Some acids must be handled with great care. For example, sulfuric acid found in car batteries can burn your finger, yet you drink acids such as citric acid in orange juice and carbonic acid in soft drinks. Obviously, some acids are stronger than others. One measure of acid strength is the ability to ionize in solution.

The strength of an acid or base depends on how completely a compound separates into ions when dissolved in water. An acid that ionizes almost completely in solution is a **strong acid.** HCl, HNO_3, and H_2SO_4 are strong acids. Conversely, an acid that only partly ionizes in solution is a **weak acid.** Acetic acid and carbonic acid are weak acids.

Ions in solution can carry electric current. **Figure 7** shows how strengths of acids can be compared using conductivity. When more ions are present, more electricity can be conducted.

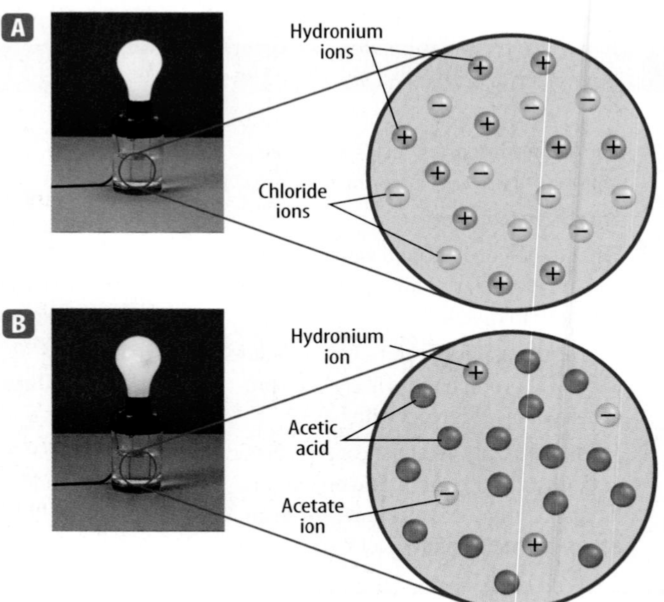

Figure 7
This test compares the conductivity of two acids that are prepared in the same concentration. A HCl, a strong acid, ionizes completely, so the bulb burns brightly. B Acetic acid, a weak acid, produces fewer ions to carry the current so the bulb is dimmer.

Section Assessment Planner

PORTFOLIO
Science Journal, p. 774

PERFORMANCE ASSESSMENT
Skill Builder Activities, p. 775
See page 792 for more options.

CONTENT ASSESSMENT
Section, p. 775
Challenge, p. 775
Chapter, pp. 792–793

Acids Equations describing ionization can be written in two ways. In strong acids, such as HCl, nearly all the acid ionizes. This is shown by writing the equation using a single arrow pointing toward the ions that are formed.

$$HCl(g) + H_2O(l) \longrightarrow H_3O^+(aq) + Cl^-(aq)$$

Almost 100 percent of the particles in solution are H_3O^+ and Cl^- ions, and only a negligible number of HCl molecules are present. Equations describing the ionization of weak acids, such as acetic acid, are written using double arrows pointing in opposite directions. This means that only some of the CH_3COOH ionizes. Thus, the reaction is incomplete.

$$CH_3COOH(l) + H_2O(l) \rightleftarrows H_3O^+(aq) + CH_3COO^-(aq)$$

Double arrows usually indicate that the reaction proceeds in both directions and that the forward reaction does not go to completion. In an acetic acid solution, most of the particles are CH_3COOH molecules, and only a few CH_3COO^- and H^+ ions are in solution.

Bases Remember that many bases are ionic compounds that dissociate to produce ions when they dissolve. A **strong base** dissociates completely in solution. The following equation shows the dissociation of sodium hydroxide, a strong base.

$$NaOH(s) + H_2O \longrightarrow Na^+(aq) + OH^-(aq)$$

The ionization of ammonia, which is a weak base, is shown using double arrows to indicate that not all the ammonia ionizes. A **weak base** is one that does not ionize completely.

$$NH_3(aq) + H_2O(l) \rightleftarrows NH_4^+(aq) + OH^-(aq)$$

Because ammonia produces only a few ions and most of the ammonia remains in the form of NH_3, ammonia is a weak base.

Strength and Concentration Sometimes, when talking about acids and bases, the terms *strength* and *concentration* can be confused. The terms *strong* and *weak* are used to classify acids and bases. The terms refer to the ease with which an acid or base dissociates in solution. *Strong* acids and bases dissociate completely; *weak* acids and bases dissociate only partially. In contrast, the terms *dilute* and *concentrated* are used to indicate the concentration of a solution, which is the amount of acid or base dissolved in the solution. It is possible to have dilute concentrations of strong acids and bases and concentrated solutions of weak acids and bases, as shown in **Figure 8.**

Figure 8
You can have a dilute solution of a strong acid and a concentrated solution of a weak acid.

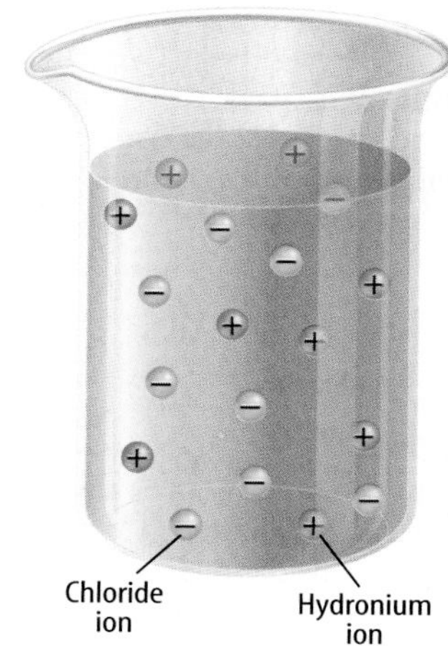

A This is a dilute solution of HCl.

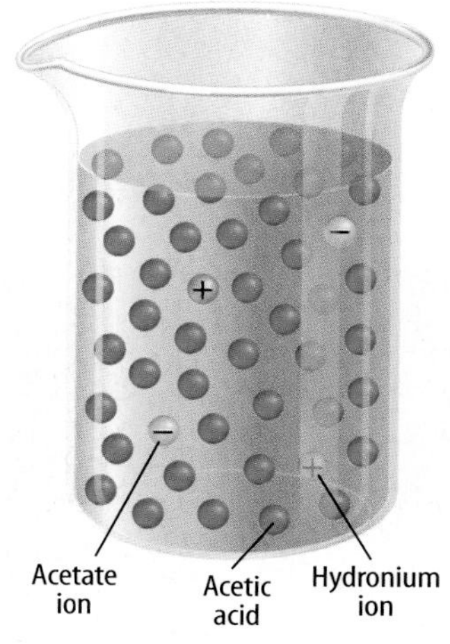

B This is a concentrated solution of acetic acid.

2 Teach

Strong and Weak Acids and Bases

Visual Learning

Figure 7 How could the solutions in Figure 7 be adjusted to cause both lightbulbs to glow with the same intensity? Increase the concentration of the weaker acid or decrease the concentration of the stronger acid. L2
LS **Logical-Mathematical**

IDENTIFYING Misconceptions

In connection with acid, the word *strong* means that the acid forms ions easily. Some students may confuse the concept, thinking it is a contradiction to use the word *strong* with something that comes apart easily.

Use Science Words

Word Usage Have students complete the following sentence: A ____________ will have little ionization because its molecules have a strong hold on their H atoms. weak acid L1 ELL
LS **Linguistic**

Resource Manager

Chapter Resources Booklet

Transparency Activity, p. 45
Directed Reading for Content Mastery, p. 20
Enrichment, p. 31

pH of a Solution

Activity

Provide samples, other than those shown in **Figure 9,** with which students can measure pH using universal pH paper. Examples may include spoiled milk, lemon juice, soap solutions, and dissolved antacids. L2 ELL LS **Visual-Spatial**

Teacher FYI

The value of pH is based on a logarithmic scale. Each unit increment is a tenfold change in hydrogen ion concentration. In other words, if one solution has a pH of 3 and another has a pH of 2, the second one is 10 times more acidic than the first.

Quick Demo

Use litmus paper or universal indicator paper to show that vinegar has an acidic pH value. Then add a small amount of milk of magnesia to the vinegar. Check the pH again to see whether it has changed. Remind students that vinegar produces H^+ ions in solution, so the pH should be low. As the milk of magnesia is added, OH^- is brought into the solution. OH^- ions react with the H^+ ions, so the pH should rise. Continue adding milk of magnesia until this effect is noticed on the pH indicator. If one is available, do this demonstration with a pH meter. L2 ELL LS **Visual-Spatial**

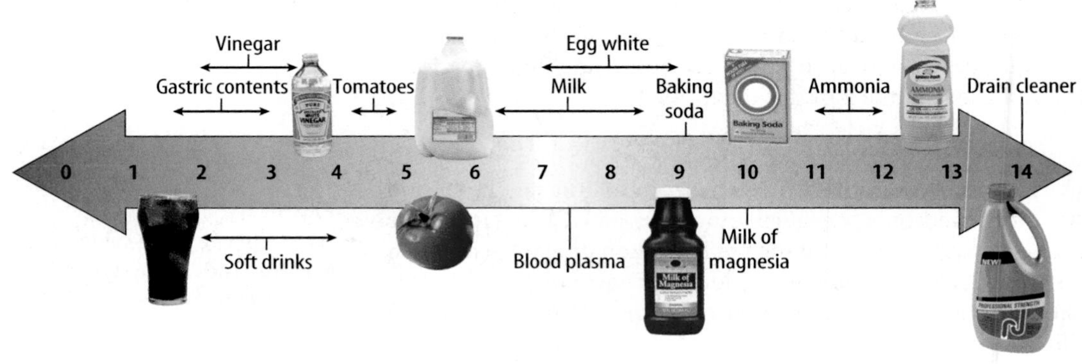

Figure 9
The pH scale helps you classify solutions as acidic or basic.

Figure 10
The pH of a sample can be measured in several ways. A Indicator paper gives an approximate value quickly. B A pH meter is quick and more precise.

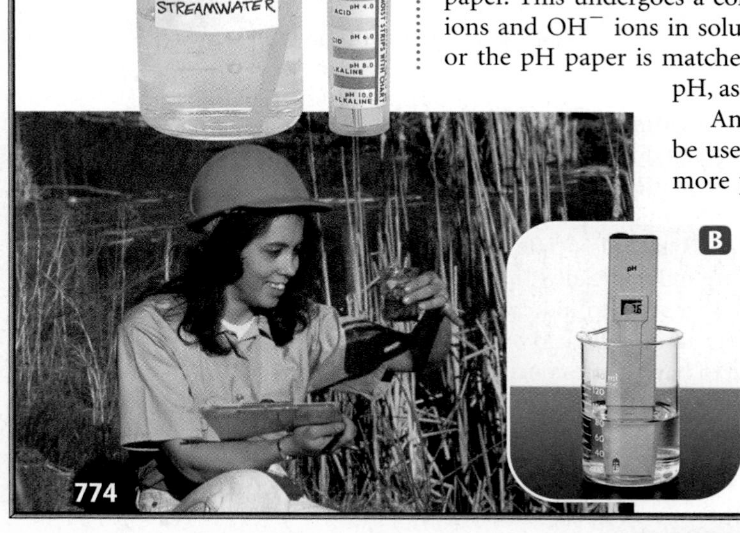

pH of a Solution

If you have a swimming pool or keep tropical fish, you know that the pH of the water must be controlled. Also, many products such as shampoos claim to control pH so it suits your type of hair. The **pH** of a solution is a measure of the concentration of H^+ ions in it. The greater the H^+ concentration is, the lower the pH is and the more acidic the substance is. The pH measures how acidic or basic a substance is. To indicate pH, a scale ranging from 0 to 14 has been devised, as shown in **Figure 9.**

As the scale shows, solutions with a pH lower than 7 are described as acidic, and the lower the value is, the more acidic the solution is. Solutions with a pH greater than 7 are basic, and the higher the pH is, the more basic the solution is. A solution with a pH of exactly 7 indicates that the concentration of H^+ ions and OH^- ions is equal. These solutions are considered neutral. Pure water at 25°C has a pH of 7.

One way to determine pH is by using a universal indicator paper. This undergoes a color change in the presence of H_3O^+ ions and OH^- ions in solution. The final color of the solution or the pH paper is matched with colors in a chart to find the pH, as shown in **Figure 10A.**

An instrument called a pH meter can be used to determine the pH of a solution more precisely. This meter is operated by immersing the electrodes in the solution to be tested and reading the dial. Small, battery-operated pH meters with digital readouts are convenient for use outside the laboratory when testing the pH of soils and streams, as shown in **Figure 10B.**

774

Identifying Misconceptions

Students may think that pH is only a measure of degree of acidity. See page 764F for teaching strategies that address this misconception.

Science Journal

Sour Milk Have students describe the changes in pH that occur in milk as it spoils. They may need to examine the process in a nutrition reference or biology source. Lactose, commonly called milk sugar, is changed through bacterial action into lactic acid. This change lowers the pH of the solution. L2 LS **Logical-Mathematical** P

Resource Manager

Chapter Resources Booklet
Lab Activity, pp. 9–11
Reinforcement, p. 28

Physical Science Critical Thinking/ Problem Solving, p. 16

Blood pH Your blood circulates throughout your body carrying oxygen, removing carbon dioxide, and absorbing nutrients from food that you have eaten. In order to carry out its many functions properly, the pH of blood must remain between 7.0 and 7.8. The main reason for this is that enzymes, the protein molecules that act as catalysts for many reactions in the body, cannot work outside this pH range. Yet you can eat foods that are acidic without changing the pH of your blood. How can this be? The answer is that your blood contains compounds called buffers that enable small amounts of acids or bases to be absorbed without harmful effects.

Buffers are solutions containing ions that react with additional acids or bases to minimize their effects on pH. The buffer ions in blood are bicarbonate ions, HCO_3^-. Because of these buffer systems, adding even a small amount of concentrated acid will not change pH much, as shown in **Figure 11.** Buffers help keep your blood close to a nearly constant pH of 7.4.

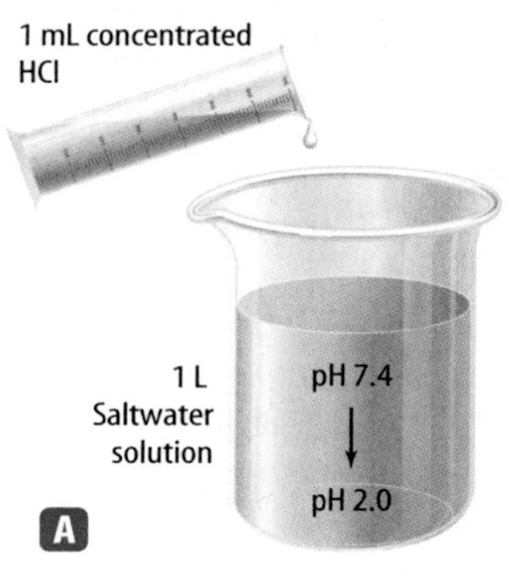

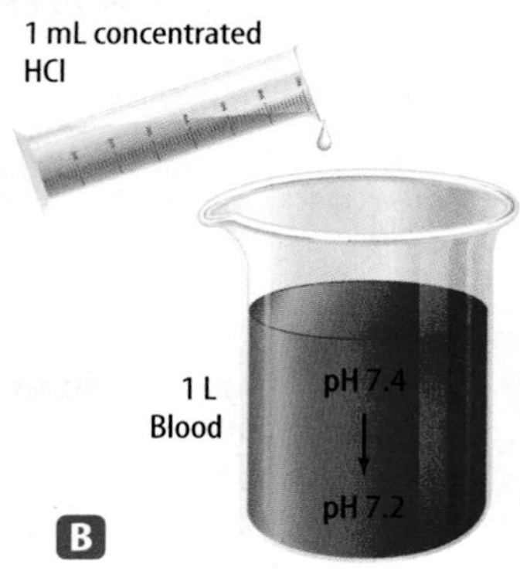

Figure 11
This experiment shows how well blood acts as a buffer. A Adding 1 mL of concentrated HCl to 1 L of salt water changes pH from 7.4 to 2.0. B Adding the same amount of concentrated HCl to 1 L of blood changes the pH from 7.4 to 7.2.

Reading Check *What are buffers and how are they important for health?*

Section  Assessment

1. What determines the strength of an acid? A base?
2. How can you make a dilute solution of a strong acid? Include an example.
3. Explain the meaning of pH.
4. Describe pH values of 9.1, 1.2, and 5.7 as basic, acidic, or very acidic.
5. **Think Critically** The proper pH range for a swimming pool is between 7.2 and 7.8. Most pools use two substances, Na_2CO_3 and HCl, to maintain this range. How would you adjust the pH if you found it was 8.2? What would you do if it was 6.9?

Skill Builder Activities

6. **Concept Mapping** Make a concept map of pH values. Start with three boxes labeled *Acidic, Neutral,* and *Basic* and indicate the pH range of each box. Below each box, give some examples of solutions that belong in each pH range. **For more help, refer to the** Science Skill Handbook.
7. **Communicating** In your Science Journal, explain why a weak acid in solution has a higher pH than a strong acid of the same concentration. Extend your explanation to include strong and weak bases. **For more help, refer to the** Science Skill Handbook.

Answers to Section Assessment

1. The strength of an acid is determined by its ability to produce H^+ ions in solution. The strength of a base is determined by its ability to produce OH^- ions in solution.
2. You can dilute hydrochloric acid, a strong acid, by adding a small amount of acid to a much larger amount of water.
3. pH is a measure of the concentration of H^+ ions.
4. 9.1–basic; 1.2–very acidic; 5.7–acidic
5. pH of 8.2: add HCl; pH of 6.9: add Na_2CO_3
6. Acidic: 0 to 7; Neutral: 7; Basic: 7 to 14; check examples for accuracy.
7. A weak acid produces only a few H^+ ions. A strong acid at the same concentration produces more H^+ ions. Therefore, the pH of the weak acid is higher than that of the strong acid.

Reading Check

Answer Buffers are solutions containing ions that react with acids or bases to minimize their effects. This is important because our blood needs to maintain a pH of about 7.4.

3 Assess

Reteach

Place a small piece of magnesium ribbon in a petri dish and add a few drops of 1 *M* HCl. Note that the reaction produces hydrogen gas. Repeat the activity with another small piece of magnesium metal, but use a few drops of 1*M* acetic acid. Ask which is a strong acid and which is a weak acid. The HCl is a strong acid because it reacts with magnesium to produce more hydrogen than acetic acid does. L2 LS **Visual-Spatial**

Challenge

Have students write chemical equations that show HCO_3^- acting to neutralize the addition of OH^- ions and the addition of H^+ ions. This would show how one of the blood buffers works. $HCO_3^- + OH^- \rightarrow H_2O + CO_3^{2-}$; $HCO_3^- + H^+ \rightarrow H_2CO_3$ L3
LS **Logical-Mathematical**

Assessment

Oral Sometimes soil pH must be changed to encourage plant growth. Ask students whether adding $Ca(OH)_2$, sometimes referred to as slaked lime, would raise or lower the pH of soil. The OH^- ions released by $Ca(OH)_2$ would raise the pH. Use **PASC,** p. 89.

Activity

BENCH TESTED

Purpose Students compare the ease of ionization of weak and strong acids with a model. L2

LS **Kinesthetic**

Process Skills using models, comparing and contrasting, forming operational definitions, interpreting scientific illustrations

Time Required approximately 20 minutes

Safety Precautions Caution students to use scissors with care and to avoid direct contact with the acid solutions.

Teaching Strategies

- To save time, have the rectangles marked on the paper and cardboard before class starts.
- To prepare 0.1 M acetic acid, add 5.9 mL of 17 M glacial acetic acid to 1.0 L of water. **CAUTION:** *Avoid direct contact with the acid.*
- To prepare 0.1 M HCl, add 8.4 mL of 12 M HCl to 1.0 L of water. **CAUTION:** *Avoid direct contact with the acid.*

Answers to Questions

1. typing paper
2. HCl; its pH was lower than that of acetic acid.
3. HCl; it produced more H^+ ions.
4. Typing paper; it let go of its pieces (ions) more easily.

Assessment

Process If an acid were weak, would its negative ions have strong or weak attractions for H^+? The attraction would be strong. The acid does not ionize easily in water because it has a strong attraction for its H^+ ions. Use **Performance Assessment in the Science Classroom,** p. 89.

Activity

Strong and Weak Acids

When you read about the behavior of things as small as molecules, it may be difficult to visualize what causes the behavior. This activity will help you do just that.

What You'll Investigate

How can you make a model that represents the degree of ionization of weak and strong acids?

Materials

typing paper marked with rectangles measuring about 5 cm × 7 cm
thick cardboard marked with rectangles measuring about 5 cm × 7 cm
scissors
test tubes (2)
droppers (2)
dilute hydrochloric acid (HCl)
dilute acetic acid (CH_3COOH)
pH paper
timer with a second hand

Goals

- **Classify** acids as weak or strong on the basis of this model.

Safety Precautions

WARNING: *Handle acids with care. Avoid direct contact and report any spills immediately.*

Procedure

1. Mark your paper and cardboard with equal numbers of rectangles. Mark every other rectangle with a plus sign (+) to represent hydronium ions. Then mark the blank rectangles with a minus sign (−) to represent negative ions.
2. Cut the typing paper into as many rectangles as possible in 60 s. Use care handling scissors.
3. Repeat step 2 with the piece of cardboard.
4. Obtain 2 mL each of dilute HCl and dilute CH_3COOH in test tubes.
5. Using a different dropper for each acid, add two drops of each to separate strips of pH paper. Determine their respective pH values and record them in the data table.

Comparing Cutting Difficulty to Ease of Ionization

Number of Ions Removed		pH of Solution	
from typing paper	8–12	pH of HCl solution	1
from cardboard	4–6	pH of acetic acid solution	2

Conclude and Apply

1. Was the typing paper or the cardboard easier to cut into pieces?
2. Which acid formed ions more easily? How do you know?
3. Which acid is stronger—HCl or CH_3COOH? How do you know?
4. Does the typing paper or the cardboard represent the stronger acid? Explain.

Communicating Your Data

Compare your results with those of other students in your class. **For more help, refer to the Science Skill Handbook.**

776 **CHAPTER 25** Acids, Bases, and Salts

Communicating Your Data

Set up a classroom data table on the chalkboard and have students enter their results. Average the results to find the trend for the whole class.

Resource Manager 

Chapter Resources Booklet
Activity Worksheet, pp. 5–6
Science Inquiry Labs, p. 53

SECTION 3

Salts

Neutralization

Advertisements for antacids describe how effectively these products neutralize excess stomach acid that causes indigestion. What does this mean? Normally, gastric juice in your stomach contains a dilute solution of hydrochloric acid. Too much of the acid can produce discomfort. Antacids contain bases or other compounds containing sodium, potassium, calcium, magnesium, or aluminum, that react with acids and lower acid concentration. **Figure 12** shows what happens when you take an antacid tablet containing sodium bicarbonate—$NaHCO_3$. The equation is:

$$HCl(aq) + NaHCO_3(s) \longrightarrow NaCl(aq) + CO_2(g) + H_2O(l)$$

Too many H^+ ions can cause indigestion. Therefore, the important part of this reaction for a person suffering from indigestion is the cancelling or neutralizing of these ions.

Neutralization is a chemical reaction between an acid and a base that takes place in a water solution. For example, when HCl is neutralized by NaOH, hydronium ions from the acid combine with hydroxide ions from the base to produce neutral water.

$$H_3O^+(aq) + OH^- \longrightarrow 2H_2O(l)$$

Salt Formation The equation above accounts for only half of the ions present in the solution. What happens to the remaining ions? They react to form a salt. A **salt** is a compound formed when the negative ions from an acid combine with the positive ions from a base. In the reaction above the salt formed in water solution is sodium chloride.

$$Na^+(aq) + Cl^- \longrightarrow NaCl(aq)$$

Acid-base reactions in water can be represented by the general equation:

$$\text{acid} + \text{base} \longrightarrow \text{salt} + \text{water}$$

Another neutralization reaction occurs between HCl, an acid and $Ca(OH)_2$, a base.

$$2HCl(aq) + Ca(OH)_2(aq) \longrightarrow CaCl_2(aq) + 2H_2O(l)$$

The products are water and the salt $CaCl_2$.

As You Read

What **You'll Learn**

- **Identify** a neutralization reaction.
- **Determine** what a salt is and how salts form.
- **Compare and contrast** soaps and detergents.
- **Examine** how esters are made and what they are used for.

Vocabulary
neutralization
salt
titration
soap

Why **It's Important**

You need salt to live and soaps and detergents to keep yourself and your clothing clean.

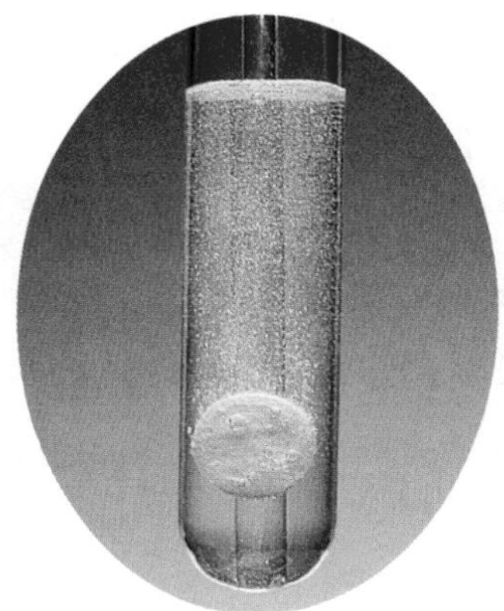

Figure 12
An antacid tablet reacts in your stomach much as it does in this dilute HCl. Usually, people chew antacid tablets before swallowing them. *How would this affect the rate of the reaction?*

Section Assessment Planner

PORTFOLIO
Cultural Diversity, p. 782

PERFORMANCE ASSESSMENT
Try at Home MiniLAB, p. 781
Problem-Solving Activity, p. 781
Skill Builder Activities, p. 785
See page 792 for more options.

CONTENT ASSESSMENT
Section, p. 785
Challenge, p. 785
Chapter, pp. 792–793

SECTION

Salts

1 Motivate

Bellringer Transparency

Display the Section Focus Transparency for Section 3. Use the accompanying Transparency Activity Master. L2 ELL

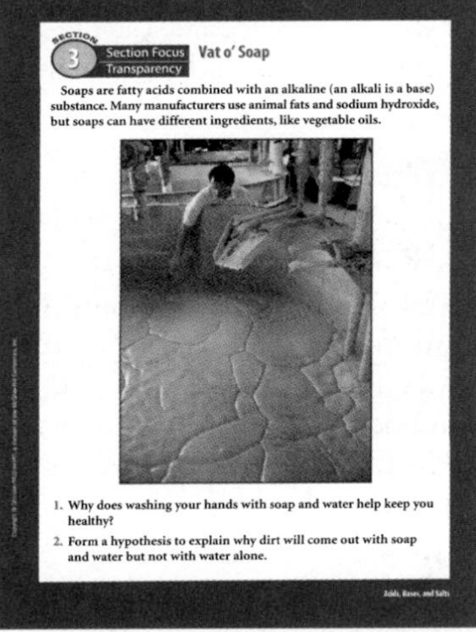

Tie to Prior Knowledge

Bring several antacid medications to class and show students the labels. Ask them which acid is being neutralized when a person uses an antacid. HCl

Caption Answer

Figure 12 It would speed it up by providing more surface area, allowing more of the antacid to come in contact quickly with stomach acid.

2 Teach

Neutralization

Quick Demo

Place a pea-size piece of zinc metal in a medium-sized test tube. Add 1 M HCl to the zinc metal. Using a test-tube holder, invert another test tube over the first to collect the gas (H_2) that is generated. Then bring a lighted splint near the mouth of the second tube. The hydrogen will give a small "bark" as the hydrogen and oxygen react. Ask students to balance the equation and name the salt that is produced. $Zn + 2HCl \rightarrow H_2 + ZnCl_2$; zinc chloride L3

LS **Logical Mathematical**

Salts

Discussion

Ask students to use the information in **Table 3** to predict the acid and base that most likely produced each salt.

$NaCl$: $NaOH$; HCl
$NaHCO_3$: $NaOH$; H_2CO_3
$CaCO_3$: $Ca(OH)_2$; H_2CO_3
KNO_3: KOH; HNO_3
K_2CO_3: KOH; H_2CO_3
Na_3PO_4: $NaOH$; H_3PO_4
NH_4Cl: NH_3; HCl

Figure 13
Like many animals, elephants get salt from natural deposits. Salt helps to maintain body processes.

Salts

Salt is essential for many animals large and small. Some animals find it at natural deposits, as shown in **Figure 13.** Even insects, such as butterflies, need salt and often are found clustered on moist ground as you saw earlier. You need salt too, especially because you lose salt in perspiration. How humans obtain one salt—sodium chloride—is shown in **Figure 14.**

There are many other salts, however, a few of which are shown in **Table 3.** Most salts are composed of a positive metal ion and an ion with a negative charge, such as Cl^- or CO_3^-. Ammonium salts contain the ammonium ion, NH_4^+, rather than a metal.

Salts also form when acids react with metals. These are single-displacement reactions in which a metal displaces hydrogen from the acid. For example, zinc displaces hydrogen from sulfuric acid forming hydrogen gas and zinc sulfate.

$$H_2SO_4(aq) + Zn(s) \longrightarrow ZnSO_4(aq) + H_2(g)$$

Table 3 Some Common Salts and Their Uses

Name, Formula	Common Name	Uses
Sodium Chloride, $NaCl$	Salt	Food preparation, manufacture of chemicals
Sodium Hydrogen Carbonate, $NaHCO_3$	Sodium bicarbonate Baking soda	Food preparation, antacids
Calcium Carbonate, $CaCO_3$	Calcite, chalk	Manufacture of paint and rubber tires
Potassium Nitrate, KNO_3	Saltpeter	Fertilizers
Potassium Carbonate, K_2CO_3	Potash	Manufacture of soap and glass
Sodium Phosphate, Na_3PO_4	TSP	Detergents
Ammonium Chloride, NH_4Cl	Sal ammoniac	Dry-cell batteries

Science Journal

Epsom Salt Another salt students may know is Epsom salt. Have them find out the chemical formula for Epsom salt, what it is used for, and how it was named. Have them record their findings in their Science Journals. Epsom salt is $MgSO_4 \cdot 7H_2O$. It is used for soaking bruises and sprains. It was named after the mineral-rich waters of Epsom, England, which contained magnesium sulfate. L2 LS **Linguistic**

Inclusion Strategies

Learning Disabled React a small amount of dilute HCl with the same amount of dilute NaOH. Gently boil away the liquid. Collect the white residue and show the resulting salt (NaCl) of the neutralization reaction. **CAUTION:** *Do not taste the salt as it may contain impurities.*

LS **Visual-Spatial**

778 CHAPTER 25 Acids, Bases, and Salts

VISUALIZING SALT

Figure 14

The salt you use every day comes from both the land and the sea. Some salt can be mined from the ground in much the same way as coal, or salt can be obtained by the process of evaporation in crystallizing ponds.

▲ MINING SALT Underground salt deposits are found where there was once a sea. Salt mines can be located deep underground or near Earth's surface in salt domes. Salt domes, such as the one above on Avery Island, Louisiana, form when pressure from Earth pushes buried salt deposits close to the surface, where they are easily mined.

◀ EVAPORATION PROCESS Workers fill evaporation ponds, like these near San Francisco Bay, California, with salt water, or brine. They move the brine from pond to pond as it becomes saltier through evaporation. (Red-tinted ponds have a higher salt content.) The saltiest water is then pumped from evaporation ponds into crystallizing ponds, where the remaining water is drained off. In the five years it takes to produce a crop of salt, brine may move through as many as 23 different ponds.

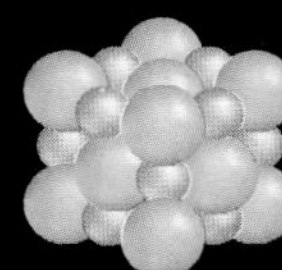

Unit cell of sodium chloride (NaCl)

◀ TABLE SALT Raw sodium chloride is washed in chemicals and water to remove impurities before it appears on your dining-room table as salt. Iodine is added to table salt to ensure against iodine deficiency in the diet.

▼ SALT MOUNDS When the crystallizing ponds are drained, the result is huge piles of salt, like these on the Caribbean island of Bonaire.

NATIONAL GEOGRAPHIC

Visualizing Salt

Have students examine the pictures and read the captions. Then ask the following questions.

- **In which geographic locations would the evaporation process be an obvious choice for obtaining salt?** areas that are located near oceans or other salt water sources
- **What are some of the advantages and disadvantages of each process?** Answers will vary but may include: removing salt from a mine is a much faster process than evaporation. The evaporation process requires a lot of land for evaporation ponds.
- **Would the land near San Francisco Bay that is used for the evaporation process be useful for farming should the salt evaporation process cease?** No, because the concentration of salt in the soil is too high.

Activity

Challenge students to find the areas throughout the world where salt mining occurs. Use a world map and mark these locations. Ask them to find out what these locations have common. L2 LS **Visual-Spatial**

Extension

Challenge students to research how salt was used to pay soldiers in ancient times and report to the class the information they find. L2 LS **Linguistic**

Resource Manager

Chapter Resources Booklet

- Transparency Activity, p. 46
- Directed Reading for Content Mastery, pp. 21, 22
- Transparency Activity, pp. 47–48

Titration

Use an Analogy

Finding the concentration of an acid or base by titration can be compared with balancing a seesaw. If on one end of a seesaw we had an unknown mass, we could carefully add known masses to the other side until the seesaw was balanced. In a titration, one solution has an unknown concentration. We carefully add reacting molecules until they exactly balance the unknown concentration of molecules in the solution. By knowing the amount added, we may calculate the unknown concentration. L2 **Logical-Mathematical**

Caption Answer

Figure 15 Subtract the initial reading on a buret from the final reading. The difference is the volume of solution added.

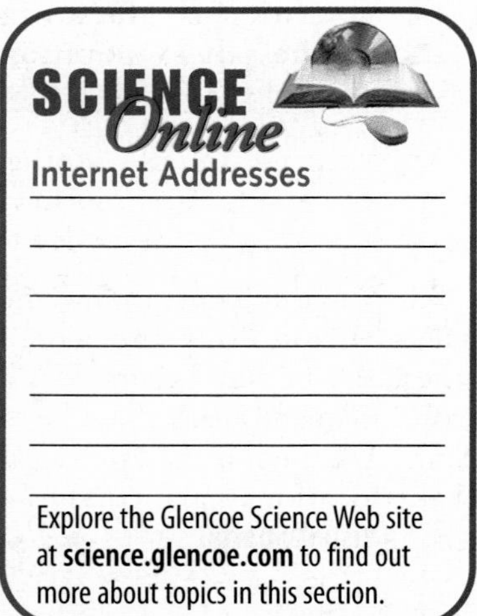

SCIENCE Online

Research Visit the Glencoe Science Web site at **science.glencoe.com** for more information about acids, bases, and indicators. Communicate to your class what you learn.

Titration

Sometimes you need to know the concentration of an acidic or basic solution; for example, to determine the purity of a commercial product. This can be done using a process called **titration** (ti TRAY shun), in which a solution of known concentration is used to determine the concentration of another solution. **Figure 15** shows a titration experiment.

A titration uses a solution of known concentration, called the standard solution. This is added slowly and carefully to a solution of unknown concentration to which an acid/base indicator has been added. If the solution of unknown concentration is a base, a standard acid solution is used. If the unknown is an acid, a standard base solution is used.

The Endpoint Has a Color The titration shown in **Figure 15** shows how you could find the concentration of an acid solution. First, you would add a few drops of an indicator, such as phenolphthalein (fee nul THAY leen), to a carefully measured amount of the solution of unknown concentration. Phenolphthalein is colorless in an acid but turns bright pink in the presence of a base.

Then, you would slowly and carefully add a base solution of known concentration to this acid-and-indicator mixture. Toward the end of the titration you must add base drop by drop until one last drop of the base turns the solution pink and the color persists. The point at which the color persists is known as the end point, the point at which the acid is completely neutralized by the base. When you know what volume of base was used, you use that value and the known concentration of the base to calculate the concentration of the acid solution.

Figure 15
In this titration, a base of known concentration is being added to an acid of unknown concentration. The swirl of pink color shows that the endpoint is near. *How would you calculate the volume of standard solution that you had added?*

Teacher FYI

The most common method for expressing the concentration of solutions in chemistry is molarity (M). Molarity is the ratio between the number of moles of solute dissolved in the solution and the volume of the solution. A mole of any substance is 6.02×10^{23} units, typically molecules. In an acid-base titration, the number of moles of acid required to neutralize the unknown solution is equal to the number of moles of base in the unknown solution. If the volume, in liters, of a solution is multiplied by the molarity, the number of moles can be determined.

Figure 16
Natural indicators include red cabbage, radishes, and roses.

Many natural substances are acid/base indicators. In fact, the indicator litmus comes from a lichen—a combination of a fungus and an algae or a cyanobacterium. Flowers that are indicators include hydrangeas, which produce blue blossoms when the pH of the soil is acidic and pink blossoms when the soil is basic. Strangely, this is just the opposite of litmus.

Other natural indicators possess a range of color. For example, the color of red cabbage varies from deep red at pH 1 to lavender at pH 7 and yellowish green at pH 10. Grape juice is also an indicator, as you can find out by doing the Try at Home Minilab.

TRY AT HOME Mini LAB

Testing a Grape Juice Indicator

Procedure

1. Add one-half cup of **water** to each of **two small glasses.**
2. Add 1 tablespoon of **purple grape juice** to each glass.
3. To one glass, add 1 teaspoon of **baking soda.** Stir.
4. To the other glass add 1 teaspoon of **white vinegar.**
5. Note the color after each addition in steps 2, 3, and 4.

Analysis

1. Did the color change when you added baking soda? Why?
2. Did the color change when you added vinegar? Did your grape juice contain any citric or ascorbic acid? How would this affect your experiment?

Problem-Solving Activity

How can you handle an upsetting situation?

Most of us have, at some time, experienced an upset stomach. Often, the cause is the excess acid within our stomachs. For digestive purposes, our stomachs contain dilute hydrochloric acid with a pH between 1.6 and 3.0. A doctor might recommend an antacid treatment for an upset stomach. What type of compound is "anti acid"?

Identifying the Problem

You have learned that neutralization reactions change acids and bases into salts. Antacids typically contain small amounts of $Ca(OH)_2$, $Al(OH)_3$, or $NaHCO_3$, which are bases. Whereas having an excess of acid lowers the pH of your stomach contents, these compounds raise the pH of your stomach contents. How does this change of pH make you feel better?

Solving the Problem

1. What compounds are produced from a reaction of HCl and $Mg(OH)_2$?
2. Why is it important to have some acid in your stomach?
3. How could you compare how well antacid products neutralize acid? Describe the procedure you would use.

TRY AT HOME Mini LAB

Purpose Students use an acid-base indicator to demonstrate a change in the pH of a solution. L2 IS **Kinesthetic**

Materials 2 water glasses, grape juice, baking soda, white vinegar

Safety Precaution Remind students not to taste chemicals used in the lab.

Analysis

1. Yes; from the original red-purple to a blue tone to a greenish tone. The solution became more basic.
2. The color became reddish. Acids lower the pH, so the addition of a base has less effect on the color because the acid already present neutralizes the added hydrogen carbonate.

Assessment

Performance Provide another unknown solution, and have students use the grape juice to determine whether it is an acid or a base. A soap solution should register as basic. Use **PASC,** p. 97.

Problem-Solving Activity

Answers

1. water and magnesium chloride, $MgCl_2$
2. Acid in your stomach is needed for the digestion of protein.
3. You would need an indicator to change color when the HCl was neutralized. To make the test fair, you would have to have a constant amount of acid and carefully measure the mass of the antacid tablets that were needed to neutralize that amount of acid. Also, you would have to ensure that the time needed for complete neutralization was adequate.

Active Reading

Reflective Journal In this strategy, students record responses to an activity. Have students divide sheets of paper into columns. Have them record their thoughts under headings such as "What I did," "What I learned," "What questions I have," "What surprises I experienced," and "Overall response." Have students write a Reflective Journal entry for the Mini-LAB on this page.

Resource Manager

Chapter Resources Booklet
Enrichment, p. 32
MiniLAB, p. 4

Physical Science Critical Thinking/ Problem Solving, p. 15

Soaps and Detergents

Extension

What causes polarity and nonpolarity in molecules? In some chemical bonds, some of the electrons of the bonded atoms spend more time around one atom than around the other. Because an electron carries a negative charge, the atom where electrons spend more time carries a slight negative charge. The other atom has a slight positive charge. The uneven charge distribution results in a polar bond. When electrons are shared almost equally between bonded atoms, the result is nonpolarity. L3

LS **Logical-Mathematical**

Quick Demo

To show the effect of soap on other nonpolar substances, pour 4% (whole) milk into a petri dish. Place one drop of each of four different food dyes in different areas around the edges of the dish. Next, dip a toothpick into some detergent. Touch the surface of the milk with the toothpick. The detergent changes the attractions between the water molecules and interacts with the nonpolar fat molecules. The resulting motion in the milk can be seen as the food dyes begin to mix. L2 ELL

LS **Visual-Spatial**

Figure 17
Soaps that contain sodium like this one made from stearic acid are solids, those that contain potassium are liquids.

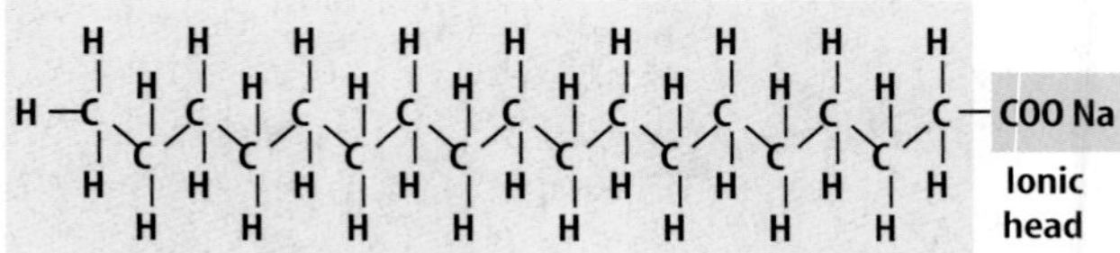

Soaps and Detergents

The next time you are in a supermarket, go to the aisle with soaps and detergents. You'll see all kinds of products—solid soaps, liquid soaps, and detergents for washing clothes and dishes. What are all these products? Do they differ from one another? Yes, they do differ slightly in how they are made and in the ingredients included for color and aroma. Still, all these products are classified into two types—soaps and detergents.

Soaps The reason soaps clean so well is explained by polar and nonpolar molecules. **Soaps** are organic salts. They have a nonpolar organic chain of carbon atoms on one end and either a sodium or potassium salt of a carboxylic acid (kar bahk SIHL ihk), $-COOH$, group at the other end. Look at **Figure 17.** The nonpolar, hydrocarbon end interacts with oils and dirt so that they can be removed readily, and the ionic end, $COONa$ or $COOK$, helps them dissolve in water.

To make an effective soap, the acid must contain ten to 18 carbon atoms. If it contains fewer than ten atoms, it will not be able to mix well with and clean oily dirt. If it has too many carbon atoms, its sodium or potassium salt will not be soluble in water. **Figure 18** shows how soap interacts with dirt particles to clean your hands.

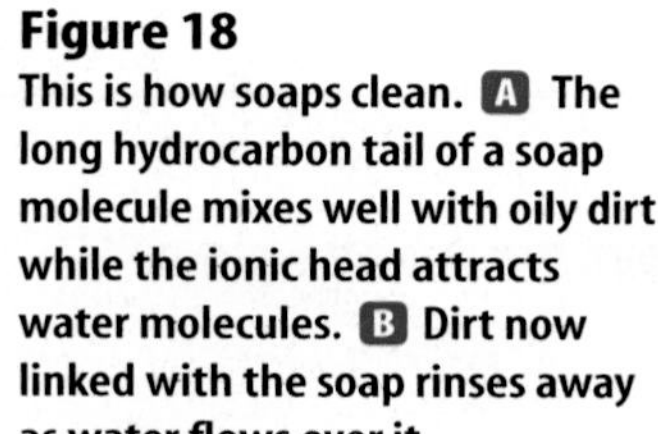

Figure 18
This is how soaps clean. A The long hydrocarbon tail of a soap molecule mixes well with oily dirt while the ionic head attracts water molecules. B Dirt now linked with the soap rinses away as water flows over it.

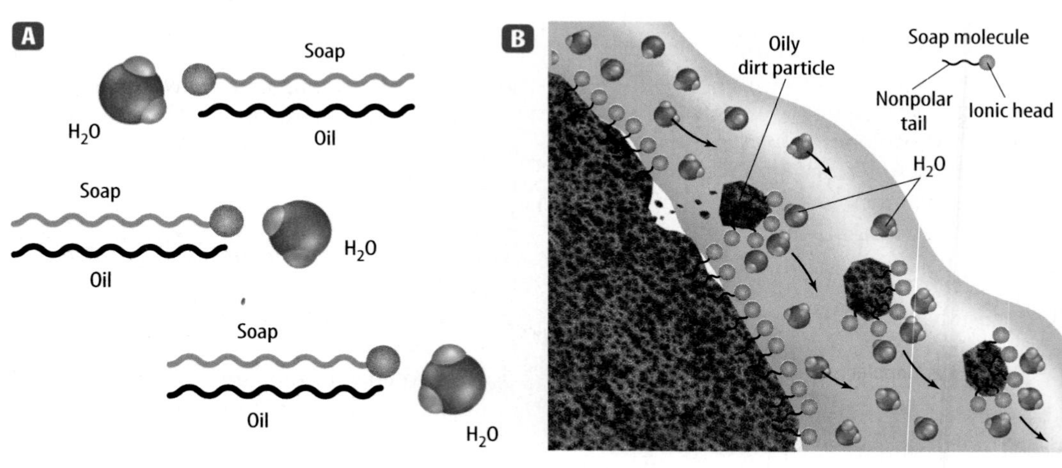

Cultural Diversity

Soap Science African American scientist George Washington Carver made many discoveries in the late 1800s and early 1900s. Have students make miniposters illustrating his contribution to the making of soap. He found a way to extract peanut oil and convert the oil to soap, using lye, $NaOH$. L3 LS **Linguistic** P

Resource Manager

Mathematics Skill Activities, p. 1

Cultural Diversity, p. 37

Performance Assessment in the Science Classroom, p. 40

782 CHAPTER 25 Acids, Bases, and Salts

Commercial Soaps A simple soap like the one shown in **Figure 17** can be made by reacting a long-chain fatty acid with sodium or potassium hydroxide. The fatty acids used to make commercial soaps come from natural sources, such as cottonseed, palm, and coconut oils. One problem with all soaps, however, is that the sodium and potassium ions can be replaced by ions of calcium, magnesium, and iron found in some water known as hard water. When this happens, the salts formed are insoluble. They precipitate out of solution in the form of soap scum. Detergents were developed to avoid this problem.

Reading Check *How are simple soaps made?*

Detergents Like soaps, detergents have long hydrocarbon chains, but instead of a carboxylic acid group (−COOH) at the end, they contain either a sulfonic acid or phosphoric acid group. These acids form more soluble salts with the ions in hard water and thereby lessen the problem of soap scum. They can also be used in cold water. Most detergents contain other substances called builders to further improve cleaning in hard water.

Detergents introduce other problems, however. For example, phosphates act as fertilizers that cause overgrowth of vegetation in streams. For this reason, many states limit the amount of phosphates that can be used in detergents. Also, one form of sulfonic acid detergent causes excessive foaming in water-treatment plants and streams, as shown in **Figure 19B.** These detergents are not degraded or broken down easily by bacteria. They stay in the environment over long periods. Most detergents now in use resemble the one shown in **Figure 19A.**

Figure 19
Some detergents can have adverse effects on the environment.

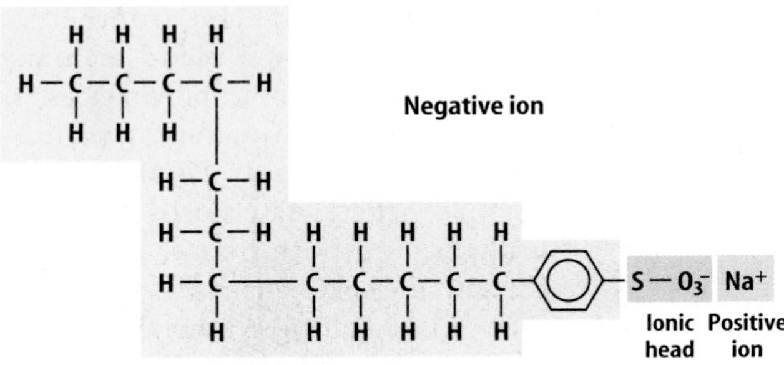

A **Newer, biodegradable detergents like the one shown here do not produce excess foam.**

Environmental Science INTEGRATION

When phosphates are added to detergents and washed into streams, they can act like a strong fertilizer. This can cause algae and water plants to grow uncontrollably. Research to find if this is a problem in your area. Communicate your findings to your class.

B **Foam from nonbiodegradable detergents can build up in waterways.**

Environmental Science INTEGRATION

Some detergents produce large amounts of foam that stay on the surface of wastewater. When the wastewater enters sewage systems, the foam prevents the degradation of organic compounds in the sewage. Research in the 1960s led to changes in detergents so that they are more easily broken down by bacteria.

Reading Check

Answer by reacting long-chain fatty acids with NaOH or KOH

Activity

Have students place 10 mL of hard water and 10 mL of soft water in separate test tubes. Have them add 1 mL of cooking oil to each, add 5 drops of soap to each, then stopper the tubes and shake them vigorously to see which produces more suds. Then have them drain the water and allow the moist tubes to dry. Compare the residues left behind. Soft water produces more suds and leaves less residue. L1 ELL

LS **Kinesthetic**

Visual Learning

Figure 19 A sulfonic acid is an organic compound with an $-SO_3H$ group. Point out the sulfonic acid group in the detergent in this figure.

LAB DEMONSTRATION

Purpose to show the soap-making process

Materials solid vegetable shortening, ethanol, NaOH, NaCl, water, cheescloth

Procedure Place 25 g of solid vegetable shortening, 10 mL of ethanol, and 5 mL of 6 M NaOH in a 250-mL beaker. Heat the mixture on a hot plate and stir for 15 minutes. **CAUTION:** *Ethanol is flammable.* Cool the mixture in an ice water bath. Add 25 mL of water and 25 mL of saturated NaCl solution. Usable soap will begin to appear as curds. Filter the soap through cheesecloth and press it into a dish. Allow the soap to dry for a few days.

Assessment

Which ingredients reacted to form the soap? vegetable shortening and sodium hydroxide

Why were the NaCl and water added? NaCl was added to make the soap precipitate, and water was added to wash out the excess hydroxide.

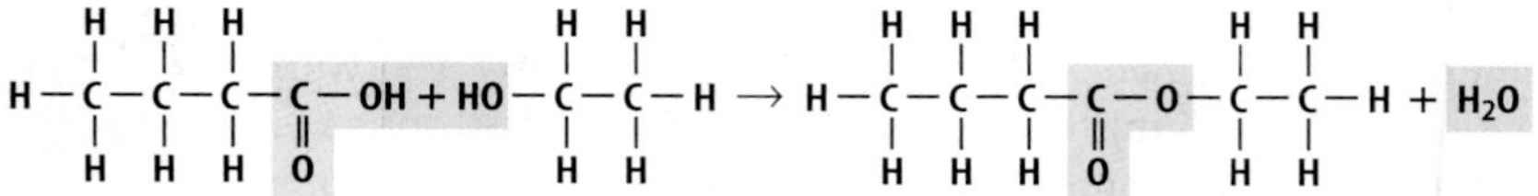

Versatile Esters

Caption Answer

Figure 20 butyl alcohol (C_4H_7OH)

Answer soaps, flavors and perfumes, and fibers

Extension

Aromas are detected when molecules or particles interact with receptors inside our noses. Research has shown that the shape of an aroma molecule plays a major role in its detection. The receptors are often in cavities into which the aroma molecule must fit to cause a sensation. Ask students to compare the shapes of the esters that cause the aroma of bananas and the aroma of wintergreen. The banana aroma is related to 3-methylbutyl acetate, which is a 4-carbon chain. The aroma of wintergreen comes from methyl salicylate, which has a benzene ring. L3 **LS Visual-Spatial**

Discussion

The reverse reaction to the formation of an ester is hydrolysis, which splits the ester into its acid and base components. The compound pentyl butyrate is associated with apricots. Ask students to determine what acid and base would result from the hydrolysis of this ester. The pentyl part comes from pentanol, C_5H_9OH; the acid part comes from butanoic acid, C_3H_7COOH. L2

LS Logical-Mathematical

Butyric acid + Ethyl alcohol → Ethyl butyrate + Water (H_2O)

Figure 20
This structural equation shows the formation of the ester ethyl butyrate, an ester that tastes and smells like pineapple. *Which alcohol would you use to prepare butyl butyrate?*

Versatile Esters

In a way esters can be thought of as the organic counterparts of salts. Like salts esters are made from acids, and water is formed in the reaction used to prepare them. The difference is that salts are made from bases and esters come from alcohols that are not bases but have a hydroxyl group.

Esters have many different applications. Esters of the alcohol glycerine are used commercially to make soaps. Other esters are used widely in flavors and perfumes, and still others can be transformed into fibers to make clothing.

Reading Check *What are three types of products that are made from esters?*

Esters for Flavor Many fruit-flavored soft drinks and desserts taste like the real fruit. If you look at the label though, you might be surprised to find that no fruit was used—only artificial flavor. Most likely this artificial flavor contains some esters.

The reaction to prepare esters involves removing a molecule of water from an acid and an alcohol. Often concentrated sulfuric acid is added to aid this reaction. **Figure 20** shows the reaction of butyric (byew TIHR ihk) acid and ethyl alcohol to produce water and the ester, ethyl butyrate, which is a component in pineapple flavor.

Although natural and artificial flavors often contain a blend of many esters, the odor of some individual esters immediately makes you think of particular fruits, as shown in **Figure 21.** For example, octyl acetate smells much like oranges, and both pentyl and butyl acetates smell like bananas.

Making realistic synthetic flavors is an art, in which chemists vary the composition to achieve the desired taste. Strawberry flavor, for example, may contain several esters.

Figure 21
These esters have strong fruity aromas.

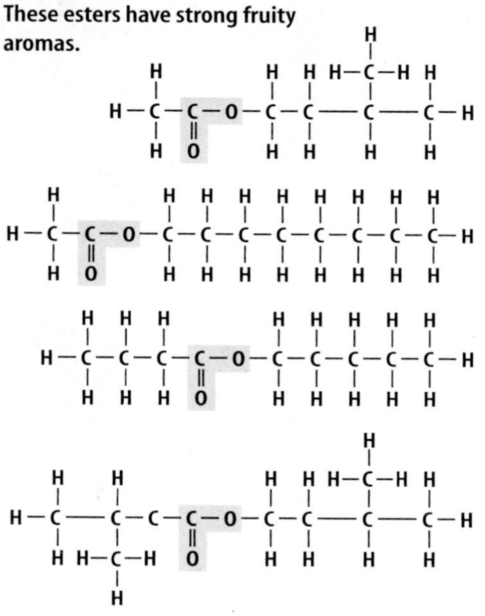

Banana

Orange

Apricot

Apple

Resource Manager

Chapter Resources Booklet
Activity Worksheet, pp. 7–8
Lab Activity, pp. 13–16
Reinforcement, p. 29

Figure 22
Polyesters and nylons are polymers most often used for clothing fibers.

$$HO-\overset{O}{\overset{\|}{C}}-C_6H_4-\overset{O}{\overset{\|}{C}}-OH + HO-CH_2-CH_2-OH \rightarrow \sim\!\left[\overset{O}{\overset{\|}{C}}-C_6H_4-\overset{O}{\overset{\|}{C}}-O-CH_2-CH_2-O\right]\!\sim + 2H_2O$$

Organic acid · Alcohol · Polymer (1 unit) · Water

A **Polyesters contain long, nonpolar chains that tend to repel water.**

Polyesters Synthetic fibers known as polyesters are polymers; that is, they are chains containing many or *poly* esters. They are made from an organic acid that has two $-COOH$ groups and an alcohol that has two $-OH$ groups, as shown in **Figure 22A.** The two compounds form long chains that are closely packed together. This adds strength to the polymer fiber. Many varieties of polyesters are made, depending on what alcohols and acids are used. They can be woven or knitted into fabrics that are durable, colorfast, and do not wrinkle easily. Because of their low moisture content however, they tend to build up a static electric charge that causes them to cling. Polyesters often are combined with natural fibers, as shown in **Figure 22B.**

B **Blends of polyester and cotton fibers make comfortable activewear.**

Section 3 Assessment

1. What is a neutralization reaction? What are the products of such reactions?
2. In a titration experiment, what is the purpose of an indicator?
3. How does the composition of detergents differ from that of soaps?
4. What small molecule is produced in the reaction between an alcohol and an acid to form an ester?
5. **Think Critically** Give the names and formulas of the salts formed in these neutralizations: sulfuric acid and calcium hydroxide, nitric acid and potassium hydroxide, and carbonic acid and aluminum hydroxide.

Skill Builder Activities

6. **Interpreting Data** Three salts—calcium sulfate, sodium chloride, and potassium nitrate—were obtained in reactions of the acid-base pairs shown here. Match each salt with the acid-base pair that produced it. **For more help, refer to the** Science Skill Handbook.

   $HCl + NaOH$; $HNO_3 + KOH$; $H_2SO_4 + Ca(OH)_2$

7. **Calculating Ratios** In the following reaction:

   $2HCl(aq) + Ca(OH)_2(aq) \longrightarrow CaCl_2(aq) + 2H_2O(l)$

   acid reacts with base in what ratio? How many molecules of HCl are needed to produce four molecules of H_2O? **For more help, refer to the** Math Skill Handbook.

3 Assess

Reteach

The formula OH has been seen on three types of compounds. Write the following compounds on the chalkboard, and have students determine which is an acid, which is a base, and which is an alcohol. $Ca(OH)_2$ base; C_2H_5COOH acid; $CH_3CH_2CH_2OH$ alcohol
L2 **Logical-Mathematical**

Challenge

Mylar is a polyester that many students have seen as the material helium-filled balloons are made of. Challenge students to find other uses for mylar and to describe the properties of the polyester that make it useful. Mylar is also used in videotapes. It is nonpolar, which keeps it from reacting with water, and it can be made into a smooth fabric with only tiny pores. L3
LS **Linguistic**

Assessment

Performance Bring several well-known antacid products to class and write components from the labels on the chalkboard. Do the same for some soap and detergent samples. Ask students to identify which compounds most likely are from an antacid, which are from a soap, and which are from a detergent. Use **PASC,** p. 89.

Answers to Section Assessment

1. A reaction between an acid and a base; water and a salt are produced.
2. The indicator changes color when the substance of unknown concentration has completely reacted with the substance of known concentration.
3. They contain a sulfonic acid or phosphoric acid group at the end of their hydrocarbon chains.
4. water
5. **(a)** calcium sulfate, $CaSO_4$ **(b)** potassium nitrate, KNO_3 **(c)** aluminum carbonate, $Al_2(CO_3)_3$
6. calcium sulfate from calcium hydroxide + sulfuric acid; sodium chloride from sodium hydroxide + hydrochloric acid; potassium nitrate from potassium hydroxide + nitric acid
7. One molecule of base reacts with two molecules of acid. Four molecules of HCl produce four molecules of H_2O.

Activity

BENCH TESTED

Recognize the Problem

Purpose

Students will design and carry out an experiment to find the level of acidity in soft drinks. L2

COOP LEARN **Interpersonal**

Process Skills

observing, comparing, measuring, communicating, making and using tables, recognizing cause and effect, forming a hypothesis, designing an experiment, separating and controlling variables, interpreting data, measuring

Time Required

45 minutes

Materials

To prepare a 0.2 *M* NaOH solution, dissolve 8.0 g of NaOH pellets in enough water to make 1.0 L of solution. **CAUTION:** *Sodium hydroxide is highly caustic. Do not touch the pellets or the solution.* Be sure the carbonated beverages are freshly opened so that the escape of CO_2 does not affect the acidity.

Safety Precautions

Students should avoid direct contact with NaOH. Wash any affected area immediately. Make sure students do not drink any of the beverages.

Activity **Design Your Own Experiment**

Be a Soda Scientist

Carbonated soft drinks contain carbonic acid and sometimes phosphoric acid. You have learned that bases can neutralize acids. Using a proper indicator and a base solution, how could you compare the acidity levels in soft drinks?

Recognize the Problem

How can the acidity level of soft drinks be compared effectively?

Form a Hypothesis

Based on observations about acids and bases, develop a hypothesis about how neutralization reactions can be used to rank the acidity of soft drinks.

Possible Materials

different colorless soft drinks (2)
test tubes (2)
25-mL graduated cylinder
droppers (2)
1% phenolphthalein indicator solution
dilute NaOH solution

Goals

- **Observe** evidence of a neutralization reaction using an indicator.
- **Compare** the acidity levels in two different soft drinks.
- **Design** an experiment that uses the independent variable of acid content of soft drinks and the dependent variable of amount of base added to the soft drinks to determine the acidity of the drinks.

Safety Precautions

WARNING: *Sodium hydroxide is caustic. Wear eye protection and avoid any skin contact with the solution. Flush thoroughly under a stream of water if any of the NaOH touches your skin. Keep your hands away from your face.*

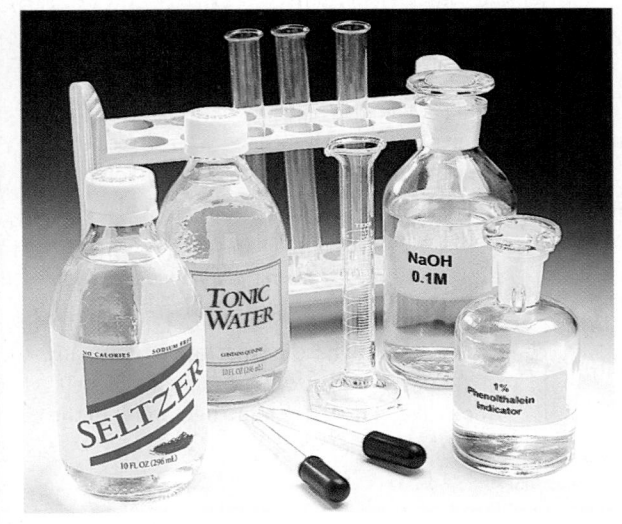

Form a Hypothesis

Possible Hypotheses

- A neutralization reaction can be used as a method of comparing acid levels in solutions.
- The NaOH solution will neutralize the acidity of soft drinks. The number of drops of NaOH solution needed for neutralization is proportional to the acidity level of the soft drinks.

Test Your Hypothesis

Possible Procedures

- Mix the solutions well after each addition of NaOH.
- The pink color can be seen best if the test tubes are held against a piece of white paper.
- For most carbonated beverages, about 15–25 drops of the NaOH solution will neutralize 5 mL.

Test Your Hypothesis

Plan

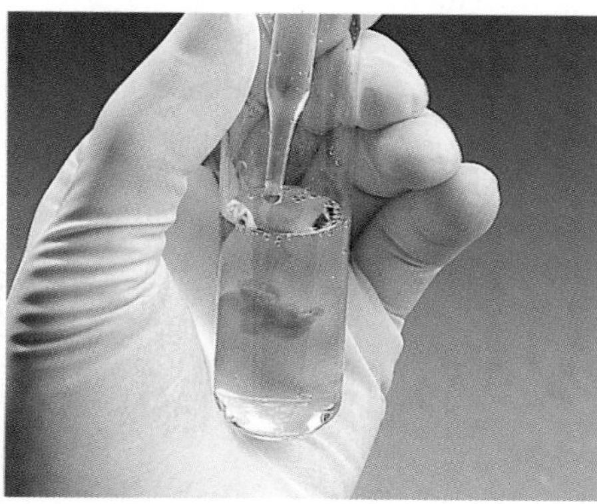

1. As a group, agree upon and write the hypothesis statement.
2. In a logical manner, list the specific steps that you will use to test your hypothesis.
3. **List** all of the materials that you will need to test your hypothesis.
4. **Design** a data table in your Science Journal that will allow you to record the amount of NaOH that was required to neutralize each soda sample.
5. **Decide** the amount of soda to be tested in each trial as a control. Decide also how many times to repeat each trial.
6. **Predict** whether you can test only colorless solutions with this procedure and explain why.

Do

1. Make sure your teacher approves your plan before you start.
2. What color change does the indicator phenolphthalein undergo in a solution that changes from an acidic pH to a basic pH?
3. While doing the experiment, write your observations and complete the data table in your Science Journal.

Analyze Your Data

1. **Classify** the sodas you tested based on their acidities. Rank them in the order of most acidic to least acidic.
2. Can your acidity values be compared with those of other groups if they used different amounts of soda?

Draw Conclusions

1. Did the results support your hypothesis? Explain why or why not.
2. At warmer temperatures less gas dissolves in a liquid. How would this affect the results of an experiment comparing two sodas stored at different temperatures?

Communicating Your Data

Compare your soda rankings with those of other class groups. **Discuss** possible reasons for any differences observed.

Teaching Strategies

Be sure to test the selected beverages ahead of time to ensure that there is a measurable difference in the number of NaOH drops required.

Expected Outcome

The acidity of a carbonated soda is directly related to the number of drops of NaOH solution needed to neutralize the acid. When the NaOH has no more acid to neutralize, the phenolphthalein stays pink.

Analyze Your Data

1. Answers between groups should be similar although not necessarily identical.
2. only if drops used per milliliter of soda are reported

Error Analysis

Different droppers may produce slightly different volumes in the drops, causing slightly different results. The judgment that the acid has been neutralized and that it is time to stop the addition of NaOH may not be consistent from group to group.

Draw Conclusions

1. Answers will vary.
2. Warmer sodas tend to lose CO_2 gas, which lowers the acidity of the soda. Thus, the same soda at a warmer temperature may require fewer drops of NaOH solution for neutralization.

Assessment

Performance Have one student from each group demonstrate the procedure the group used to compare the soft drinks. Use **Performance Assessment in the Science Classroom,** p. 143.

Communicating Your Data

Make a chart on the board showing the results of the different groups. Combine the data to get a class average for each soft drink.

Content Background

Acid rain is caused by water falling through polluted air. A number of factors determine the severity of the effects of acid rain. Among them are the amount and type of chemicals contained in the clouds and the contours and composition of the soil on which it falls. Some scientists evaluate the effect of acid rain by calculating the "critical load" capacity of the soil. This is an estimate of the amount of a particular pollutant a given volume of soil can contain before harmful effects on plants and water quality are observed.

Soils formed over limestone or chalk can tolerate much higher levels of acid than those based on granite or sandstone. The alkalinity of limestone and chalk neutralizes acids before they can have a corrosive effect. Quartzite granite does not react with the acids, leaving them in the soil to be washed into streams and lakes. An additional consequence is the acids' extraction of heavy metals, such as lead, aluminum, cadmium and copper, from the soil that also collect in surface and ground water. Northern and high altitude areas have the added problem of acid snow. Snow melt causes a rapid influx of low pH water into lakes and streams in a very short period of time. This heightens the short-term exposure of new plant growth and young animals. There is some disagreement over the extent of the harm caused by acid rain, but not over the fact that it is harmful.

SCIENCE AND Society

SCIENCE ISSUES THAT AFFECT YOU!

Acid Rain

Protecting Earth from the damaging effects of chemically-loaded precipitation

In a forest in eastern Canada, the trees grow slower than normal. It's the height of summer, but their leaves are brown and spotted. In a nearby lake, dead fish rise to the surface of the water. The trees and the fish are victims of a form of pollution known as acid rain.

788

Resources for Teachers and Students

US EPA
Clean Air Markets Division
1200 Pennsylvania Avenue, NW
Mail Code 6204N
Washington, DC 20460

National Park Service
Air Resources Division
1849 C Street NW
Washington, DC 20240
Phone: (202) 208-6843

U.S. Department of the Interior
U.S. Geological Survey
12201 Sunrise Valley Drive, Reston, VA
2019212201

Acid rain is rain, snow or sleet that is more acidic than unpolluted precipitation. It's caused by the burning of fossil fuels, such as coal, oil, and natural gas. In the United States, most gasoline and electricity come from fossil fuels. People burn fossil fuels each time they drive a car, heat a building, or turn on a light.

Normally, raindrops pick up particles and natural chemicals in the air. When rain falls it mixes with the carbon dioxide in the atmosphere, giving clean rain a slightly acidic pH of 5.6. Then natural chemicals found in the air and soil balance out the acidity, giving most lakes and streams a pH between six and eight. But when pollutants are introduced, this delicate balance is upset. This upset can affect entire ecosystems.

The burning of fossil fuels releases sulfur dioxide and nitrogen oxides into the air. In the clouds these chemicals combine with moisture to form mild solutions of sulfuric acid and nitric acid.

The natural chemicals, or bases, that balance clean rain's acidity are not strong enough to neutralize these solutions. Wind can carry this acidic moisture for hundreds of miles before it falls to Earth as acid rain. That's why even an isolated forest in Canada, lying far from the nearest power plant, can be devastated by acid rain. And that's why acid rain is a worldwide problem.

Eating Away at History

Like all acids, acid rain can corrode, or eat away at, substances. Many historical monuments, such as the Mayan temples in Mexico, and the Parthenon in Greece, have been slowly but steadily damaged by acid rain. The Environmental Protection Agency (EPA) notes that this kind of damage can be fixed, though it costs billions of dollars. But if ancient monuments and buildings, like the Colosseum in Rome, are destroyed, they can never be replaced.

Some Solutions

In some countries, high acid levels in lakes and streams have been lowered by adding lime to the water. Lime, a natural base, balances out the damaging chemicals. In the United States, all new cars must have catalytic converters, which help reduce the amount of exhaust pollution that vehicles give off. Also, coal-burning power plants can use scrubbers that wash sulfur out of the coal during or after burning. This, too, helps reduce air pollution.

Ride a bike! It saves fuel, is non-polluting, and helps preserve the environment.

You also can make a difference. Turning off the lights when you are not using them, means a power plant does not have to produce as much electricity. By car-pooling, using public transportation, and walking, there is less pollution from cars. The results of all these individual actions can make a huge difference in preserving our environment.

CONNECTIONS List Go to a local park or forest. List any effects of acid rain that you see. Make a list of the things you do that use energy or cause pollution. Did you turn lights out? How do you go to school? Think about what your family can do to reduce pollution and save energy. Share your list with a parent.

SCIENCE Online

For more information, visit .science.glencoe.com

Discussion

Discuss the feasibility of the solutions being used to counter the acid rain problem that were proposed in the article. **Which do you think is the least effective in the long run?** Possible Answer: The neutralization of acidic lakes with lime while immediately effective does not address the source of the problem and must be undertaken at regular intervals to maintain water quality. L2 **LS Logical-Mathematical**

Activity

Give each student a clean glass container. Assign a location in the community for each container and label them accordingly. Students should place their containers at the assigned location prior to an expected rainstorm. Collect the rain samples and check each using pH paper. Hang a local map in the classroom and have students mark on it with colored pins the location of their samples and the pH. Suggest they use blue for basic, white for neutral and red for acidic. L2 **LS Kinesthetic**

Investigate the Issue

Research the patterns of acid rain across the country and the presumed sources. Note them on a national map and use it to discuss how the local are is affected. Find out whether you are in an area of acid rainfall, a source area or both.

CONNECTIONS Debate If your local park shows symptoms of acid rain try to determine the source of the acid rain. In many cases the sources of acid rain are also major contributors to the local economy. Find out if the economic activity of your community produces acid rain-causing pollutants and what steps local industries and government have taken to address the problem.

Internet Addresses

Explore the Glencoe Science Web site at **science.glencoe.com** to find out more about topics in this feature.

Chapter 25 Study Guide

Reviewing Main Ideas

Preview

Students can answer the questions in their Science Journals. Discuss the answers as you go through the chapter. LS **Linguistic**

Review

Students can write their answers, then compare them with those of other students. LS **Interpersonal**

Reteach

Students can look at the illustrations and describe details that support the main ideas of the chapter. LS **Visual-Spatial**

Answers to Chapter Review

Section 1

2. lemons, apples

Section 3

3. soap

Chapter 25 Study Guide

Reviewing Main Ideas

Section 1 Acids and Bases

1. An acid is a substance that produces hydrogen ions, H^+, in solution. A base produces hydroxide ions, OH^-, in solution.
2. Properties of acids and bases are due, in part, to the presence of the H^+ and OH^- ions. *Which of the foods shown here are acidic?*

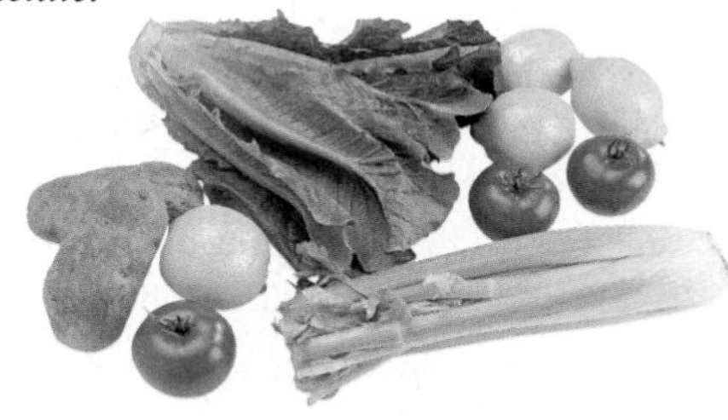

3. Common acids include hydrochloric acid, sulfuric acid, nitric acid, and phosphoric acid. Common bases include sodium hydroxide, calcium hydroxide, and ammonia.
4. Acidic solutions form when certain polar compounds ionize as they dissolve in water. Except for ammonia, basic solutions form when certain ionic compounds dissociate upon dissolving in water.

Section 2 Strength of Acids and Bases

1. The strength of an acid or base is determined by how completely it forms ions when it is in solution.
2. Strength and concentration are not the same thing. Concentration involves the relative amounts of solvent and solute in a solution, whereas strength is related to the extent to which a substance ionizes.
3. pH measures the concentration of hydronium ions in water solution using a scale ranging from 1 to 14.
4. For acidic solutions of equal concentration, the stronger the acid is, the lower its pH is. For basic solutions of equal concentration, the stronger the base is, the higher its pH is.

Section 3 Salts

1. In a neutralization reaction, the H_3O^+ ions from an acid react with the OH^- ions from a base to produce water molecules. The products of a neutralization reaction are a salt and water.
2. Salts form when negative ions from an acid combine with positive ions from a base.
3. Soaps and detergents are organic salts. Unlike soaps, detergents do not react with compounds in hard water to form soap scum. *Which type of product was used to wash materials in this sink?*

4. Esters are organic compounds formed by the reaction of an organic acid and an alcohol.

FOLDABLES Reading & Study Skills — **After You Read**

List examples of acids, bases, and salts on the front of your Venn Diagram study fold. Contrast the properties of acids and bases. Explain how salts are formed from acids and bases.

FOLDABLES Reading & Study Skills — **After You Read**

After students have read the chapter and completed the Foldable described in Before You Read, have them do the activity on the student page.

Dinah Zike

790 CHAPTER STUDY GUIDE

Chapter 25 Study Guide

Visualizing Main Ideas

Complete the concept map using the following: salt, slippery feel, pH less than 7, tastes sour, forms hydroxide ions in solution, water, forms hydrogen ions in solution, pH higher than 7, corrosive, *and* bitter taste.

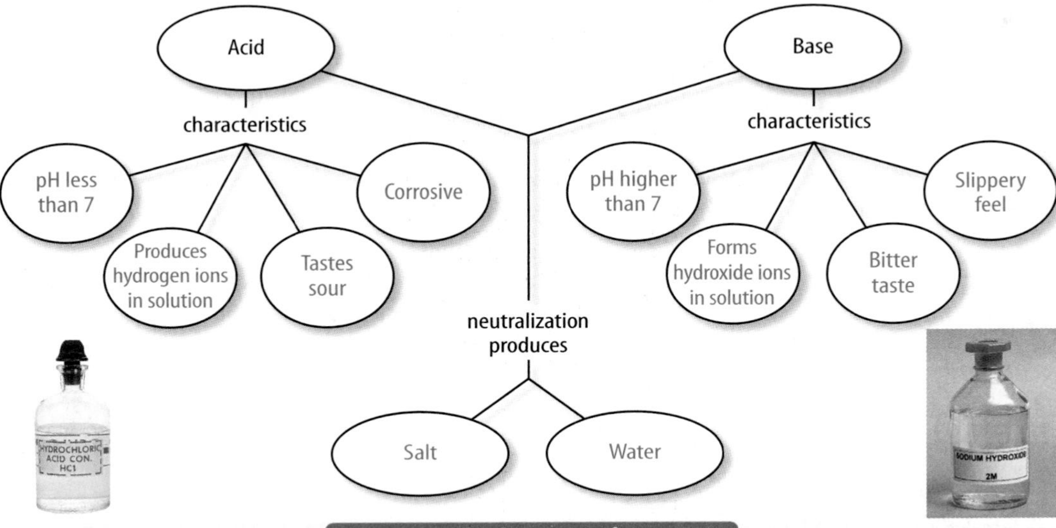

Vocabulary Review

Vocabulary Words

a. acid
b. base
c. buffer
d. hydronium ion
e. indicator
f. neutralization
g. pH
h. salt
i. soap
j. strong acid
k. strong base
l. titration
m. weak acid
n. weak base

THE PRINCETON REVIEW Study Tip

Take good notes, even during lab. Lab experiments reinforce key concepts, and looking back on these notes can help you better understand what happened and why.

Using Vocabulary

Explain the differences between each set of vocabulary words given below. Then explain how the words are related.

1. acid, base
2. acid, salt
3. salt, soap
4. base, soap
5. neutralization, salt
6. strong acid, pH
7. hydronium ion, acid
8. indicator, titration
9. pH, buffer
10. weak base, strong base

IDENTIFYING Misconceptions

Assess

After students have done the activity on page 764F and completed the chapter, have them perform this activity.

Materials paper and pencil

Procedure Have students make cartoon posters of a basketball game between the Acids and the Bases. Each team should have five players, which will be the names of acids or bases. Each player's number will be its pH value.

Expected Outcome Students should realize that the pH scale includes both acids and bases.

Chapter 25 Study Guide

Visualizing Main Ideas

See student page.

Vocabulary Review

Using Vocabulary

1. An acid produces hydrogen ions in solutions. A base forms hydroxide ions in solutions and accepts hydrogen ions from acids.
2. A salt forms when an acid and base combine.
3. Soaps are organic salts.
4. Soaps are organic salts. Salts are formed when an acid and base combine.
5. Neutrilization reactions produce salts.
6. A strong acid has a low pH.
7. When acids dissolve in water, hydronium ions are formed.
8. Titrations and indicators are used to determine the concentration of acid or base solutions.
9. pH is a measure of the concentration of hydronium ions in a solution. A buffer is a solution that contains ions that react with additional acids and bases to minimize their effects.
10. A strong base ionizes completely in solution. A weak base does not.

Checking Concepts

1. A
2. C
3. B
4. D
5. C
6. A
7. C
8. B
9. D
10. C

Thinking Critically

11. Water interacts forming H_3O^+ and Cl^- ions in the ionization process.
12. OH^- is part of an ionic compound that dissociates in water. The OH found in alcohol molecules is covalently bonded to a carbon atom and does not ionize or dissociate in water.
13. Ammonia can accept H^+ ions from water, forming NH_4^+ ions and thus producing OH^- in water. It is a weak base.
14. A concentrated acid has a large amount of acid dissolved in a solution. A strong acid easily donates H^+ ions. A concentrated acid could be a large amount of weak acid in a solution.
15. They soaked the ashes in water, dissolving the OH^-, and then combined them with fatty acids found in animal products to form soap.

Chapter 25 Assessment

Checking Concepts

Choose the word or phrase that best answers the question.

1. What best describes solutions of equal concentrations of HCl and CH_3COOH.
A) do not have the same pH
B) will react the same with metals
C) will make the same salts
D) have the same amount of ionization

2. What is hydrochloric acid also known as?
A) battery acid **C)** stomach acid
B) citric acid **D)** vinegar

3. What is 80 percent of phosphoric acid used to produce?
A) batteries **C)** petroleum products
B) fertilizer **D)** plastics

4. Which of the following is an acid that is vital to industry?
A) acetic **C)** citric
B) lactic **D)** sulfuric

5. Which of the following is another name for sodium hydroxide (NaOH)?
A) ammonia **C)** lye
B) caustic lime **D)** milk of magnesia

6. Carrots have a pH of 5.0, so how would you describe them?
A) acidic **C)** neutral
B) basic **D)** an indicator

7. What is the pH of pure water at 25°C?
A) 0 **C)** 7
B) 5.2 **D)** 14

8. A change of what property permits certain materials to act as indicators?
A) acidity **C)** concentration
B) color **D)** taste

9. What type of substance is KBr?
A) acid **C)** indicator
B) base **D)** salt

10. Which of the following might you use to titrate an oxalic acid solution?
A) HBr **C)** NaOH
B) $Ca(NO_3)_2$ **D)** NH_4Cl

Thinking Critically

11. When hydrogen chloride, HCl, is dissolved in water to form hydrochloric acid, what happens to the HCl?

12. Explain how the hydroxide ion differs from the −OH group in an alcohol.

13. Why is ammonia considered a base, even though it contains no hydroxide ions? Is it a strong or weak base?

14. Explain why a concentrated acid is not necessarily a strong acid.

15. Ashes from a wood fire are basic. Explain how this helped early settlers to make soap.

Developing Skills

16. Comparing and Contrasting How would the pH of a dilute solution of HCl compare with the pH of a concentrated solution of the same acid?

17. Recognizing Cause and Effect Ramon often saw his mother cleaning her teakettle using vinegar. When she added vinegar, bubbles formed. When she finished, all the white deposits inside the kettle were gone. What do you think these white deposits might be? Do you think dish detergent would have worked as well?

18. Interpreting Data A soil test indicates that the pH of the soil in a field is 4.8. To neutralize this soil, would you add a substance that contained H_3PO_4 or a substance that contained $Ca(OH)_2$? Explain.

Chapter Assessment Planner

Portfolio Encourage students to place in their portfolios one or two items of what they consider to be their best work. Examples include:
- Curriculum Connection, p. 767
- Assessment, p. 768
- Science Journal, p. 774
- Cultural Diversity, p. 782

Performance Additional performance assessments, Performance Task Assessment Lists, and rubrics for evaluating these activities can be found in Glencoe's **Performance Assessment in the Science Classroom.**

792 CHAPTER ASSESSMENT

19. Comparing and Contrasting Compare and contrast the reactions that would occur when a marshmallow is burned and when acid in paper causes damage over time.

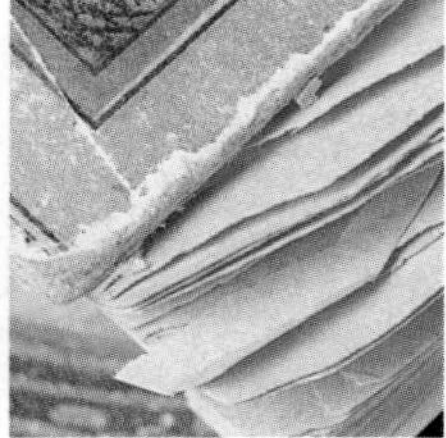

20. Drawing Conclusions You have equal amounts of three colorless liquids: A, B, and C. You add several drops of phenolphthalein to each liquid. A and B remain colorless, but C turns pink. Next, you add some C to A and the pink color disappears. Then, you add the rest of C to B and the mixture remains pink. What can you infer about each of these liquids? Which original liquid probably had a pH of 7?

Performance Assessment

21. Display Make a display and write a report about common household acids and bases, their uses, and cautions to be taken.

22. Lab Report Do research to find out how acids and bases are used in making fertilizer. Name several acids and one base, tell why each is needed, and explain how their proportions can vary.

Technology

Go to the Glencoe Science Web site at **science.glencoe.com** or use the **Glencoe Science CD-ROM** for additional chapter assessment.

THE PRINCETON REVIEW Test Practice

A chemist is measuring the pH levels of several different substances. The table below lists some common substances and their average pH values.

pH Readings

Substance	pH
Battery acid	1.5
Lemon juice	2.5
Apple	3
Milk	6.7
Sea water	8.5
Ammonia	12

Study the table and answer the following questions.

1. The chemist measures a pH of 8.4 for an unknown substance. What is the substance likely to be?

A) Apples **C)** Lemon juice
B) Sea water **D)** Milk

2. According to this information, what is an unknown substance with a pH of 3.1 likely to be?

F) ammonia **H)** an apple
G) lemon juice **J)** battery acid

3. Among the substances listed in the table, which one would be most effective for neutralizing battery acid?

A) seawater **C)** lemon juice
B) ammonia **D)** milk

4. Which of the substances listed in the table has a pH value that is closest to being neutral?

F) apple **H)** milk
G) seawater **J)** ammonia

Assessment Resources

Reproducible Masters

Chapter Resources Booklet
Chapter Review, pp. 37–38
Chapter Tests, pp. 39–42
Assessment Transparency Activity, p. 49

Glencoe Science Web site
Interactive Tutor
Chapter Quizzes

Glencoe Technology
Assessment Transparency
Interactive CD-ROM Chapter Quizzes
ExamView Pro Test Bank
Vocabulary PuzzleMaker Software
MindJogger Videoquiz DVD/VHS

THE PRINCETON REVIEW Test Practice

The Test-Taking Tip was written by The Princeton Review, the nation's leader in test preparation.

1. B
2. H
3. B
4. H

Developing Skills

16. A concentrated solution of HCl has a low pH. A dilute solution has a higher pH that is still below 7.
17. It is likely that the deposits contained carbonate and the gas was carbon dioxide. Detergent would have had little effect on the white deposits.
18. Add $Ca(OH)_2$ because the soil is acidic and $Ca(OH)_2$ is a base.
19. Both reactions break down hydrocarbons. Sulfuric acid removes the hydrogen and oxygen atoms from the paper, leaving behind carbon. Burning combines oxygen with the marshmallow to form CO_2 and H_2O.
20. Liquid A is acidic. Liquid B is likely near neutral. Liquid C is basic. Liquid A contains more acid than a small amount of liquid C can neutralize. Liquid B contains less acid than liquid A and could have a pH near 7.

Performance Assessment

21. Check students' work. Use **PASC,** p. 135
22. The most common acid used to make fertilizer is sulfuric acid. It is used to break up phosphate-containing rock. Ca(H2PO4)2 and NH4H2PO4 are commonly found in fertilizers. Use **PASC,** p. 119

Standardized Test Practice

Reading Comprehension

QUESTION 1: B

Students must use information in the passage to identify the cause in the cause-and-effect relationship.

- Choice A: No; information in the passage indicates that the scientists were familiar with the compounds.
- Choice B: Yes; this is the correct cause.
- Choice C: No; information in the passage suggests that the process was difficult, not simple.
- Choice D: No; this is not the correct cause. **Objective 4**

QUESTION 2: H

Students must use information in the passage to identify the cause in a cause-and-effect relationship. Only choice H is the reason that historians knew that ancient Greeks and Romans used "wet chemistry." **Objective 4**

Teaching Tip

Point out to students that incorrect answer choices can often be eliminated, as can choices A, C, and D for question 1, because these choices contradict information in the passage.

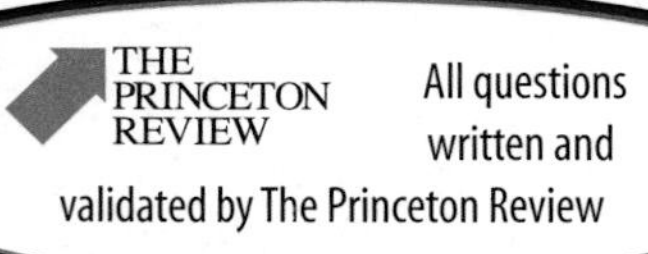

All questions written and validated by The Princeton Review

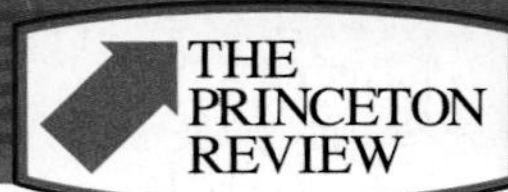

Standardized Test Practice

Reading Comprehension

Read the passage. Then read each question that follows the passage. Decide which is the best answer to each question.

Test-Taking Tip Remember that clues and information can always be found in the passage.

The Eyes Have It

If you've ever seen ancient Egyptian paintings, then you were probably struck by the dramatic appearance of the dark-rimmed eyes of their subjects. Anthropologists know from the records of ancient scribes that the Egyptians achieved this effect in real life by using cosmetics. However, until recently, they were unaware of the sophisticated chemistry that went into the ancient Egyptians' creation of these early cosmetics.

The Louvre Museum in Paris has an extensive collection of ancient Egyptian makeup containers. Amazingly, many of them still retain remnants of their original contents. When the technology to analyze the remains of the Egyptians' creams and powders became available, French scientists went to work. They found that the cosmetics contained several lead-based chemicals. Two of them, lead sulfide (PbS) and lead carbonate ($PbCO_3$), are common in nature. However, two of the others found in the makeup are not. (PbOHCl) and ($Pb_2Cl_2CO_3$) are formed only when lead minerals oxidize in a combination of chlorinated and carbonated water. Scientists believe that the Egyptians created these compounds artificially, using a sophisticated process called "wet chemistry" to synthesize their molecules.

Scientists had already found written records indicating that the ancient Greeks and Romans used wet chemistry. However, the Egyptian discovery pushes the date of the first known use of this technique back to 2000 B.C., more than 1,000 years before the birth of Cleopatra.

This painting reflects regular use of cosmetics by ancient Egyptians.

1. Scientists believe that Egyptians created two of the compounds found in the ancient cosmetics artificially because _____.
   - **A)** scientists had never seen these compounds before
   - **B)** they are not often found in nature
   - **C)** the process used to make them was simple
   - **D)** only artificially created compounds could survive such a long time
2. Historians knew that ancient Greeks and Romans used "wet chemistry" because _____.
   - **F)** they had found samples of cosmetics for testing
   - **G)** they saw evidence of the use of cosmetics in their artwork
   - **H)** surviving text from the period indicates the use of "wet chemisty"
   - **J)** the Greek and Roman civilizations followed the Egyptian model

Standardized Test Practice

Reasoning and Skills

Read each question and choose the best answer.

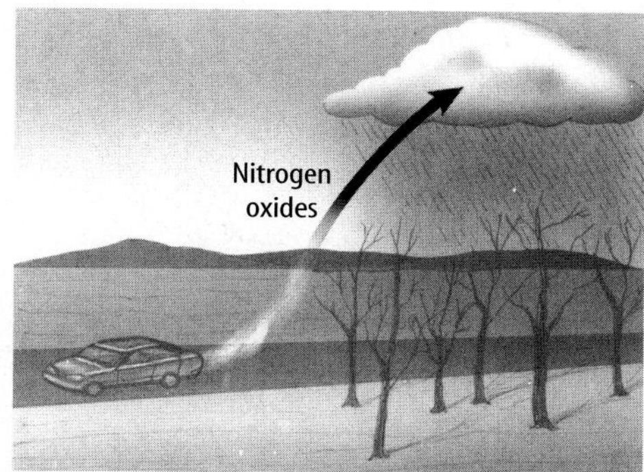

1. This picture indicates that the tree is probably losing its leaves because of _____.
   A) soil erosion
   B) acid rain
   C) nutrient-poor soil
   D) over-watering

Test-Taking Tip The best answer is always supported by any information in a chart or graphic.

2. What is the source of the nitrogen oxides?
   F) the soil
   G) the air
   H) the car exhaust
   J) the cloud

Common Bases and Applications	
Bases	**Product**
Sodium hydroxide	Drain cleaner
Magnesium hydroxide	Laxative
Ammonium hydroxide	Window cleaner
Aluminum hydroxide	Deodorant

3. According to the information on the chart, ammonium hydroxide is used in the manufacturing of _____.
   A) window cleaner
   B) laxative
   C) drain clearer
   D) deodorant

Test-Taking Tip Always consider every answer choice as you work through a question.

4. A balanced chemical equation has the same number of atoms of each element on both sides of the equation. Which of the following is a balanced equation?
   F) $2Al + 3Ag_2S \rightarrow Al_2S_3 + Ag$
   G) $2H_2CO_3 \rightarrow H_2O + CO_2$
   H) $Fe + O_2 \rightarrow Fe_2O_3$
   J) $2Ag + H_2S \rightarrow Ag_2S + H_2$

Test-Taking Tip Double-check that you have identified the correct answer by making sure that the other answer choices are not balanced equations.

Consider this question carefully before writing your answer on a separate sheet of paper.

5. Touch and litmus tests can be used to help determine if a substance is a base. Discuss how each of these tests indicates the presence of a base. Also, discuss the possible benefits or drawbacks of using that type of test.

Test-Taking Tip Consider the different types of experiments that you have done in class or have read about in your textbooks as you answer this question.

Standardized Test Practice

Reasoning and Skills

QUESTION 1: B

This question tests students' abilities to draw a conclusion based on information provided in an illustration.

QUESTION 2: H

Students must use knowledge of pollution in order to answer this question.

QUESTION 3: A

This question tests students' abilities to locate information in a chart. Students should use the key word *Ammonium hydroxide* to identify the correct answer.

QUESTION 4: J

This question requires students to demonstrate a familiarity with balancing chemical equations.

Teaching Tip

Students should use any information that the test provides—graphs, pictures, or charts—to identify the correct answer.

QUESTION 5: Answers will vary.

Students must use knowledge of bases and testing bases to answer this question thoroughly.

Student Resources

CONTENTS

Skill Handbooks 798

Reference Handbook 826

Organizing Information

As you study science, you will make many observations and conduct investigations and experiments. You will also research information that is available from many sources. These activities will involve organizing and recording data. The quality of the data you collect and the way you organize it will determine how well others can understand and use it. In **Figure 1,** the student is obtaining and recording information using a thermometer.

Putting your observations in writing is an important way of communicating to others the information you have found and the results of your investigations and experiments.

Researching Information

Scientists work to build on and add to human knowledge of the world. Before moving in a new direction, it is important to gather the information that already is known about a subject. You will look for such information in various reference sources. Follow these steps to research information on a scientific subject:

Step 1 Determine exactly what you need to know about the subject. For instance, you might want to find out about one of the elements in the periodic table.

Step 2 Make a list of questions, such as: Who discovered the element? When was it discovered? What makes the element useful or interesting?

Step 3 Use multiple sources such as textbooks, encyclopedias, government documents, professional journals, science magazines, and the Internet.

Step 4 List where you found the sources. Make sure the sources you use are reliable and the most current available.

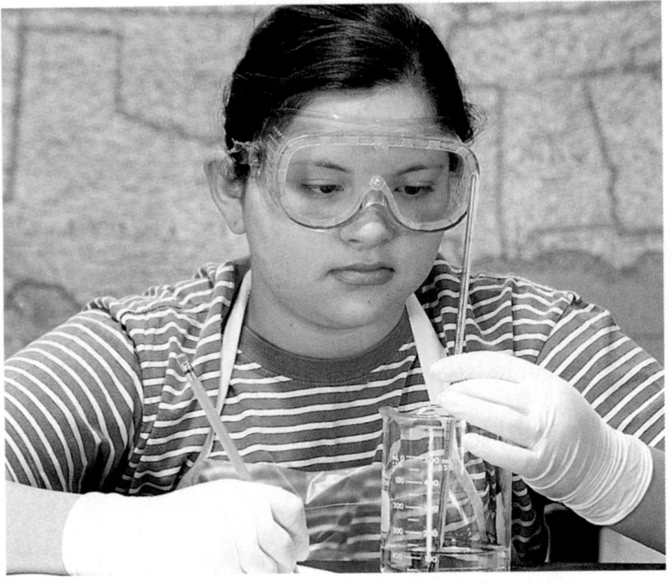

Figure 1
Making an observation is one way to gather information directly.

Evaluating Print and Nonprint Sources

Not all sources of information are reliable. Evaluate the sources you use for information, and use only those you know to be dependable. For example, suppose you want to find ways to make your home more energy efficient. You might find two Web sites on how to save energy in your home. One Web site contains "Energy-Saving Tips" written by a company that sells a new type of weatherproofing material you put around your door frames. The other is a Web page on "Conserving Energy in Your Home" written by the U.S. Department of Energy. You would choose the second Web site as the more reliable source of information.

In science, information can change rapidly. Always consult the most current sources. A 1985 source about saving energy would not reflect the most recent research or findings.

Interpreting Scientific Illustrations

As you research a science topic, you will see drawings, diagrams, and photographs. Illustrations help you understand what you read. Some illustrations are included to help you understand an idea that you can't see easily by yourself. For instance, you can't see the tiny particles in an atom, but you can look at a diagram of an atom as labeled in **Figure 2** that helps you understand something about it. Visualizing a drawing helps many people remember details more easily. Illustrations also provide examples that clarify difficult concepts or give additional information about the topic you are studying.

Most illustrations have a label or caption that identifies the illustration or provides additional information to better explain it. Can you find the caption or labels in **Figure 2?**

Figure 2
This drawing shows an atom of carbon with its six protons, six neutrons, and six electrons.

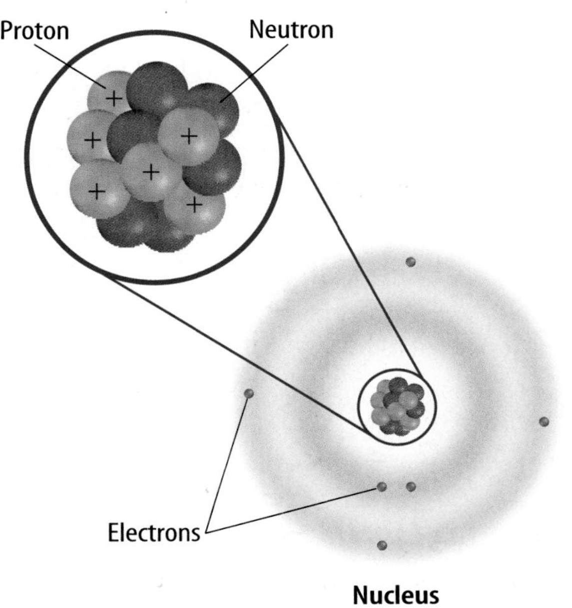

Concept Mapping

If you were taking a car trip, you might take some sort of road map. By using a map, you begin to learn where you are in relation to other places on the map.

A concept map is similar to a road map, but a concept map shows relationships among ideas (or concepts) rather than places. It is a diagram that visually shows how concepts are related. Because a concept map shows relationships among ideas, it can make the meanings of ideas and terms clear and help you understand what you are studying.

Overall, concept maps are useful for breaking large concepts down into smaller parts, making learning easier.

Venn Diagram

Although it is not a concept map, a Venn diagram illustrates how two subjects compare and contrast. In other words, you can see the characteristics that the subjects have in common and those that they do not.

The Venn diagram in **Figure 3** shows the relationship between two different substances made from the element carbon. However, due to the way their atoms are arranged, one substance is the gemstone diamond, and the other is the graphite found in pencils.

Figure 3
A Venn diagram shows how objects or concepts are alike and how they are different.

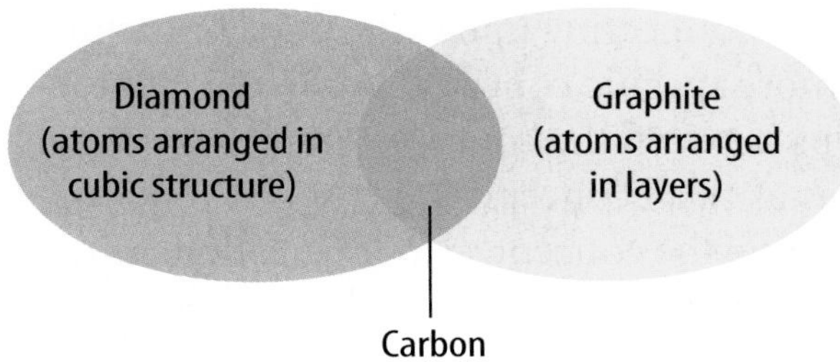

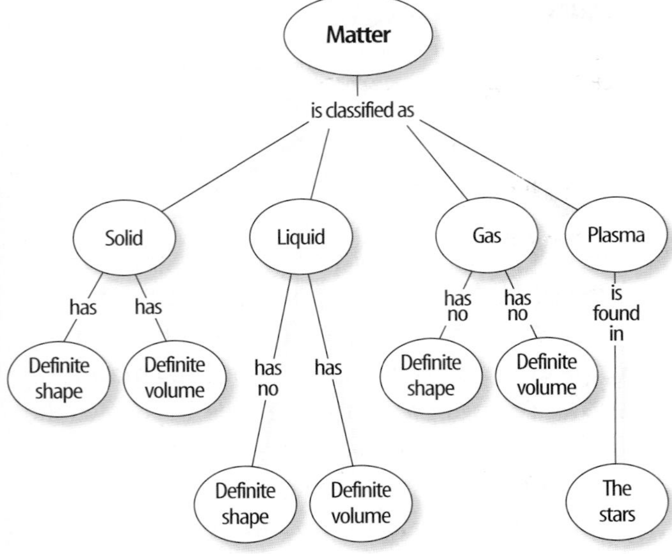

Figure 4
A network tree shows how concepts or objects are related.

Network Tree Look at the concept map in **Figure 4,** that describes the different types of matter. This is called a network tree concept map. Notice how some words are in ovals while others are written across connecting lines. The words inside the ovals are science terms or concepts. The words written on the connecting lines describe the relationships between the concepts.

When constructing a network tree, write the topic on a note card or piece of paper. Write the major concepts related to that topic on separate note cards or pieces of paper. Then arrange them in order from general to specific. Branch the related concepts from the major concept and describe the relationships on the connecting lines. Continue branching to more specific concepts. Write the relationships between the concepts on the connecting lines until all concepts are mapped. Then examine the concept map for relationships that cross branches, and add them to the concept map.

Events Chain An events chain is another type of concept map. It models the order of items or their sequence. In science, an events chain can be used to describe a sequence of events, the steps in a procedure, or the stages of a process.

When making an events chain, first find the one event that starts the chain. This event is called the *initiating event.* Then, find the next event in the chain and continue until you reach an outcome. Suppose you are asked to describe why and how a sound might make an echo. You might draw an events chain such as the one in **Figure 5.** Notice that connecting words are not necessary in an events chain.

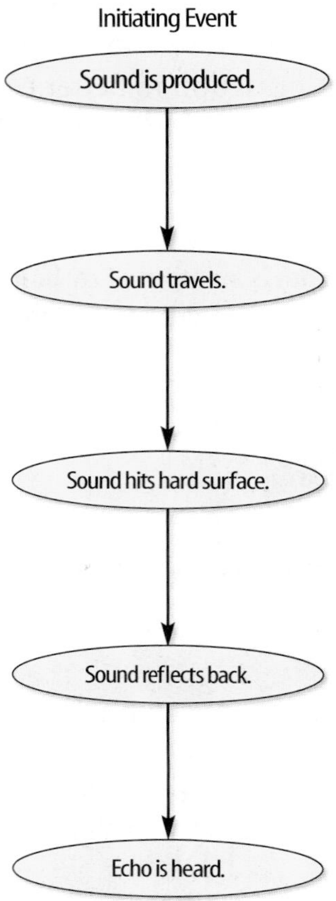

Figure 5
Events chains show the order of steps in a process or event.

Cycle Map A cycle concept map is a specific type of events chain map. In a cycle concept map, the series of events does not produce a final outcome. Instead, the last event in the chain relates back to the beginning event.

You first decide what event will be used as the beginning event. Once that is decided, you list events in order that occur after it. Words are written between events that describe what happens from one event to the next. The last event in a cycle concept map relates back to the beginning event. The number of events in a cycle concept varies, but is usually three or more. Look at the cycle map, as shown in **Figure 6.**

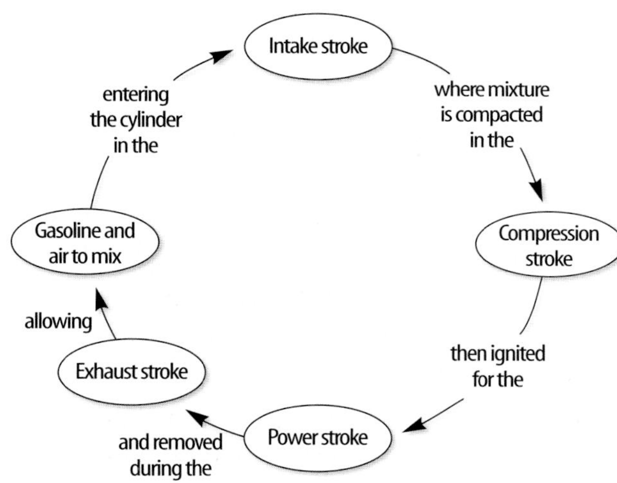

Figure 6
A cycle map shows events that occur in a cycle.

Spider Map A type of concept map that you can use for brainstorming is the spider map. When you have a central idea, you might find you have a jumble of ideas that relate to it but are not necessarily clearly related to each other. The spider map on sound in **Figure 7** shows that if you write these ideas outside the main concept, then you can begin to separate and group unrelated terms so they become more useful.

Figure 7
A spider map allows you to list ideas that relate to a central topic but not necessarily to one another.

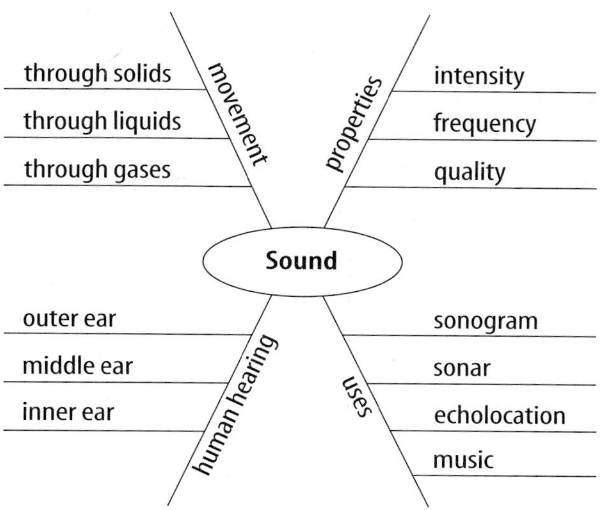

Writing a Paper

You will write papers often when researching science topics or reporting the results of investigations or experiments. Scientists frequently write papers to share their data and conclusions with other scientists and the public. When writing a paper, use these steps.

Step 1 Assemble your data by using graphs, tables, or a concept map. Create an outline.

Step 2 Start with an introduction that contains a clear statement of purpose and what you intend to discuss or prove.

Step 3 Organize the body into paragraphs. Each paragraph should start with a topic sentence, and the remaining sentences in that paragraph should support your point.

Step 4 Position data to help support your points.

Step 5 Summarize the main points and finish with a conclusion statement.

Step 6 Use tables, graphs, charts, and illustrations whenever possible.

Investigating and Experimenting

You might say the work of a scientist is to solve problems. When you decide to find out why your neighbor's hydrangeas produce blue flowers while yours are pink, you are problem solving, too. You might also observe that your neighbor's azaleas are healthier than yours are and decide to see whether differences in the soil explain the differences in these plants.

Scientists use orderly approaches to solve problems. The methods scientists use include identifying a question, making observations, forming a hypothesis, testing a hypothesis, analyzing results, and drawing conclusions.

Scientific investigations involve careful observation under controlled conditions. Such observation of an object or a process can suggest new and interesting questions about it. These questions sometimes lead to the formation of a hypothesis. Scientific investigations are designed to test a hypothesis.

Identifying a Question

The first step in a scientific investigation or experiment is to identify a question to be answered or a problem to be solved. You might be interested in knowing how beams of laser light like the ones in **Figure 8** look the way they do.

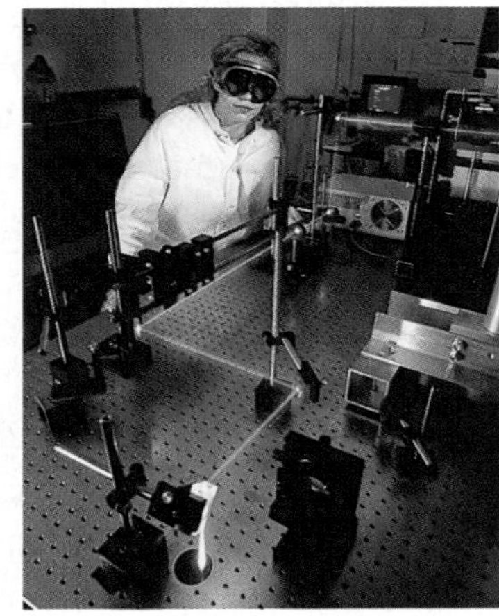

Figure 8
When you see lasers being used for scientific research, you might ask yourself, "Are these lasers different from those that are used for surgery?"

Forming Hypotheses

Hypotheses are based on observations that have been made. A hypothesis is a possible explanation based on previous knowledge and observations.

Perhaps a scientist has observed that certain substances dissolve faster in warm water than in cold. Based on these observations, the scientist can make a statement that he or she can test. The statement is a hypothesis. The hypothesis could be: *A substance dissolves in warm water faster.* A hypothesis has to be something you can test by using an investigation. A testable hypothesis is a valid hypothesis.

Predicting

When you apply a hypothesis, or general explanation, to a specific situation, you predict something about that situation. First, you must identify which hypothesis fits the situation you are considering. People use predictions to make everyday decisions. Based on previous observations and experiences, you might form a prediction that if substances dissolve in warm water faster, then heating the water will shorten mixing time for powdered fruit drinks. Someone could use this prediction to save time in preparing a fruit punch for a party.

Testing a Hypothesis

To test a hypothesis, you need a procedure. A procedure is the plan you follow in your experiment. A procedure tells you what materials to use, as well as how and in what order to use them. When you follow a procedure, data are generated that support or do not support the original hypothesis statement.

For example, premium gasoline costs more than regular gasoline. Does premium gasoline increase the efficiency or fuel mileage of your family car? You decide to test the hypothesis: "If premium gasoline is more efficient, then it should increase the fuel mileage of my family's car." Then you write the procedure shown in **Figure 9** for your experiment and generate the data presented in the table below.

Figure 9
A procedure tells you what to do step by step.

Procedure

1. Use regular gasoline for two weeks.
2. Record the number of kilometers between fill-ups and the amount of gasoline used.
3. Switch to premium gasoline for two weeks.
4. Record the number of kilometers between fill-ups and the amount of gasoline used.

Gasoline Data

Type of Gasoline	Kilometers Traveled	Liters Used	Liters per Kilometer
Regular	762	45.34	0.059
Premium	661	42.30	0.064

These data show that premium gasoline is less efficient than regular gasoline in one particular car. It took more gasoline to travel 1 km (0.064) using premium gasoline than it did to travel 1 km using regular gasoline (0.059). This conclusion does not support the hypothesis.

Are all investigations alike? Keep in mind as you perform investigations in science that a hypothesis can be tested in many ways. Not every investigation makes use of all the ways that are described on these pages, and not all hypotheses are tested by investigations. Scientists encounter many variations in the methods that are used when they perform experiments. The skills in this handbook are here for you to use and practice.

Identifying and Manipulating Variables and Controls

In any experiment, it is important to keep everything the same except for the item you are testing. The one factor you change is called the independent variable. The factor that changes as a result of the independent variable is called the dependent variable. Always make sure you have only one independent variable. If you allow more than one, you will not know what causes the changes you observe in the dependent variable. Many experiments also have controls—individual instances or experimental subjects for which the independent variable is not changed. You can then compare the test results to the control results.

For example, in the fuel-mileage experiment, you made everything the same except the type of gasoline that was used. The driver, the type of automobile, and the type of driving did not change. In this way, you could be sure that any mileage differences were caused by the type of fuel—the independent variable. The amount of fuel per kilometer was the dependent variable.

If you could repeat the experiment using several automobiles of the same type on a standard driving track with the same driver, you could make one automobile a control by using regular gasoline over the four-week period.

Collecting Data

Whether you are carrying out an investigation or a short observational experiment, you will collect data, or information. Scientists collect data accurately as numbers and descriptions and organize it in specific ways.

Observing Scientists observe items and events, then record what they see. When they use only words to describe an observation, it is called qualitative data. For example, a scientist might describe the color, texture, or odor of a substance produced in a chemical reaction. Scientists' observations also can describe how much there is of something. These observations use numbers, as well as words, in the description and are called quantitative data. For example, if a sample of the element gold is described as being "shiny and very dense," the data are clearly qualitative. Quantitative data on this sample of gold might include "a mass of 30 g and a density of 19.3 g/cm^3." Quantitative data often are organized into tables. Then, from information in the table, a graph can be drawn. Graphs can reveal relationships that exist in experimental data.

When you make observations in science, you should examine the entire object or situation first, then look carefully for details. If you're looking at an element sample, for instance, check the general color and pattern of the sample before using a hand lens to examine its surface for any smaller details or characteristics. Remember to record accurately everything you see.

Scientists try to make careful and accurate observations. When possible, they use instruments such as microscopes, metric rulers, graduated cylinders, thermometers, and balances. Measurements provide numerical data that can be repeated and checked.

Sampling When working with large numbers of objects or a large population, scientists usually cannot observe or study every one of them. Instead, they use a sample or a portion of the total number. To *sample* is to take a small, representative portion of the objects or organisms of a population for research. By making careful observations or manipulating variables within a portion of a group, information is discovered and conclusions are drawn that might apply to the whole population.

Estimating Scientific work also involves estimating. To *estimate* is to make a judgment about the amount of something or the number of something without measuring every part of an object or counting every member of a population. Scientists first measure or count the amount or number in a small sample. A geologist, for example, might remove a 10-g sample from a large rock that is rich in copper ore, as in **Figure 10.** Then a chemist would determine the percentage of copper by mass and multiply that percentage by the total mass of the rock to estimate the total mass of copper in that large rock.

Figure 10
Determining the percentage of copper by mass in a piece from a large rock that is rich in copper ore, can help estimate the total mass of copper ore in the large rock.

Measuring in SI

The metric system of measurement was developed in 1795. A modern form of the metric system, called the International System, or SI, was adopted in 1960. SI provides standard measurements that all scientists around the world can understand.

The metric system is convenient because unit sizes vary by multiples of 10. When changing from smaller units to larger units, divide by a multiple of 10. When changing from larger units to smaller, multiply by a multiple of 10. To convert millimeters to centimeters, divide the millimeters by 10. To convert 30 mm to centimeters, divide 30 by 10 (30 mm equal 3 cm).

Prefixes are used to name units. Look at the table below for some common metric prefixes and their meanings. Do you see how the prefix *kilo-* attached to the unit *gram* is *kilogram*, or 1,000 g?

Metric Prefixes

Prefix	Symbol	Meaning	
kilo-	k	1,000	thousand
hecto-	h	100	hundred
deka-	da	10	ten
deci-	d	0.1	tenth
centi-	c	0.01	hundredth
milli-	m	0.001	thousandth

Now look at the metric ruler shown in **Figure 11.** The centimeter lines are the long, numbered lines, and the shorter lines are millimeter lines.

When using a metric ruler, line up the 0-cm mark with the end of the object being measured, and read the number of the unit where the object ends, in this instance it would be 4.5 cm.

Figure 11
This metric ruler has centimeter and millimeter divisions.

Liquid Volume In some science activities, you will measure liquids. The unit that is used to measure liquids is the liter. A liter has the volume of 1,000 cm^3. The prefix *milli-* means "thousandth (0.001)." A milliliter is one thousandth of 1 L, and 1 L has the volume of 1,000 mL. One milliliter of liquid completely fills a cube measuring 1 cm on each side. Therefore, 1 mL equals 1 cm^3.

You will use beakers and graduated cylinders to measure liquid volume. A graduated cylinder, as illustrated in **Figure 12,** is marked from bottom to top in milliliters. This one contains 79 mL of a liquid.

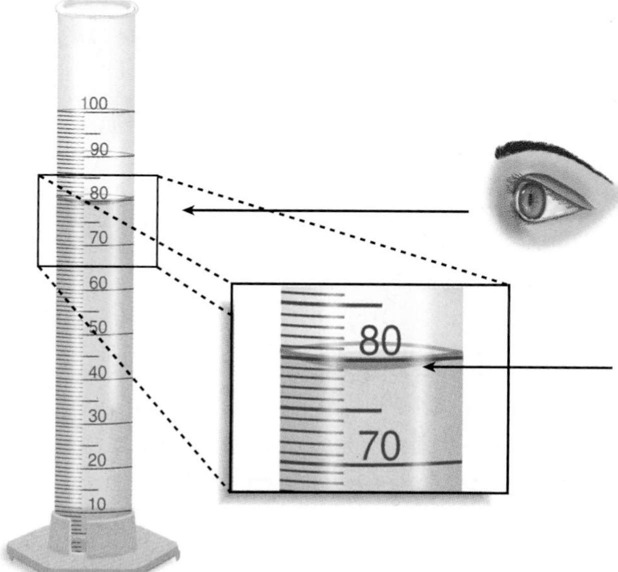

Figure 12
Graduated cylinders measure liquid volume.

Mass Scientists measure mass in grams. You might use a beam balance similar to the one shown in **Figure 13.** The balance has a pan on one side and a set of beams on the other side. Each beam has a rider that slides on the beam.

Before you find the mass of an object, slide all the riders back to the zero point. Check the pointer on the right to make sure it swings an equal distance above and below the zero point. If the swing is unequal, find and turn the adjusting screw until you have an equal swing.

Place an object on the pan. Slide the largest rider along its beam until the pointer drops below zero. Then move it back one notch. Repeat the process on each beam until the pointer swings an equal distance above and below the zero point. Sum the masses on each beam to find the mass of the object. Move all riders back to zero when finished.

Figure 13
A triple beam balance is used to determine the mass of an object.

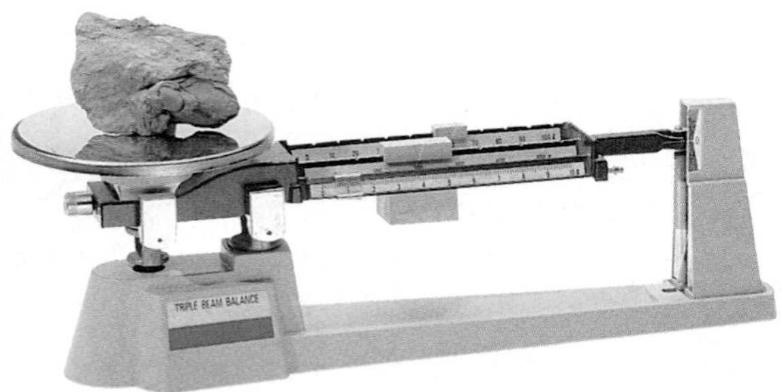

You should never place a hot object on the pan or pour chemicals directly onto the pan. Instead, find the mass of a clean container. Remove the container from the pan, then place the chemicals in the container. Find the mass of the container with the chemicals in it. To find the mass of the chemicals, subtract the mass of the empty container from the mass of the filled container.

Making and Using Tables

Browse through your textbook and you will see tables in the text and in the activities. In a table, data, or information, are arranged so that they are easier to understand. Activity tables help organize the data you collect during an activity so results can be interpreted.

Making Tables To make a table, list the items to be compared in the first column and the characteristics to be compared in the first row. The title should clearly indicate the content of the table, and the column or row heads should tell the reader what information is found in there. The table below lists materials collected for recycling on three weekly pick-up days. The inclusion of kilograms in parentheses also identifies for the reader that the figures are mass units.

Recyclable Materials Collected During Week

Day of Week	Paper (kg)	Aluminum (kg)	Glass (kg)
Monday	5.0	4.0	12.0
Wednesday	4.0	1.0	10.0
Friday	2.5	2.0	10.0

Using Tables How much paper, in kilograms, is being recycled on Wednesday? Locate the column labeled "Paper (kg)" and the row "Wednesday." The information in the box where the column and row intersect is the answer. Did you answer "4.0"? How much aluminum, in kilograms, is being recycled on Friday? If you answered "2.0," you understand how to read the table. How much glass is collected for recycling each week? Locate the column labeled "Glass (kg)" and add the figures for all three rows. If you answered "32.0," then you know how to locate and use the data provided in the table.

Recording Data

To be useful, the data you collect must be recorded carefully. Accuracy is key. A well-thought-out experiment includes a way to record procedures, observations, and results accurately. Data tables are one way to organize and record results. Set up the tables you will need ahead of time so you can record the data right away.

Record information properly and neatly. Never put unidentified data on scraps of paper. Instead, data should be written in a notebook like the one in **Figure 14.** Write in pencil so information isn't lost if your data gets wet. At each point in the experiment, record your data and label it. That way, your information will be accurate and you will not have to determine what the figures mean when you look at your notes later.

Figure 14
Record data neatly and clearly so it is easy to understand.

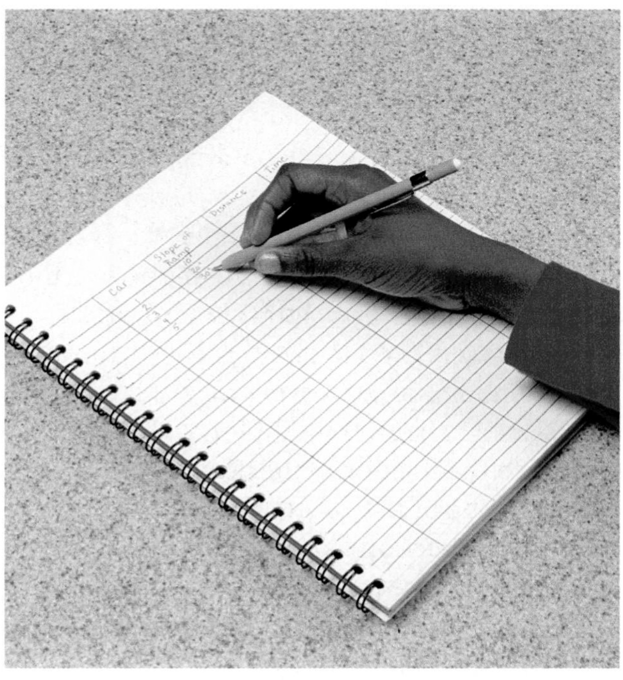

Recording Observations

It is important to record observations accurately and completely. That is why you always should record observations in your notes immediately as you make them. It is easy to miss details or make mistakes when recording results from memory. Do not include your personal thoughts when you record your data. Record only what you observe to eliminate bias. For example, when you record the time required for five students to climb the same set of stairs, you would note which student took the longest time. However, you would not refer to that student's time as "the worst time of all the students in the group."

Making Models

You can organize the observations and other data you collect and record in many ways. Making models is one way to help you better understand the parts of a structure you have been observing or the way a process for which you have been taking various measurements works.

Models often show things that are too large or too small for normal viewing. For example, you normally won't see the inside of an atom. However, you can understand the structure of the atom better by making a three-dimensional model of an atom. The relative sizes, the positions, and the movements of protons, neutrons, and electrons can be explained in words. An atomic model made of a plastic-ball nucleus and pipe-cleaner electron shells can help you visualize how the parts of the atom relate to each other.

Other models can be devised on a computer. Some models, such as those that illustrate the chemical combinations of different elements, are mathematical and are represented by equations.

Skill Handbooks

Making and Using Graphs

After scientists organize data in tables, they might display the data in a graph that shows the relationship of one variable to another. A graph makes interpretation and analysis of data easier. Three types of graphs are the line graph, the bar graph, and the circle graph.

Line Graphs A line graph like in **Figure 15** is used to show the relationship between two variables. The variables being compared go on two axes of the graph. For data from an experiment, the independent variable always goes on the horizontal axis, called the *x*-axis. The dependent variable always goes on the vertical axis, called the *y*-axis. After drawing your axes, label each with a scale. Next, plot the data points.

A data point is the intersection of the recorded value of the dependent variable for each tested value of the independent variable. After all the points are plotted, connect them.

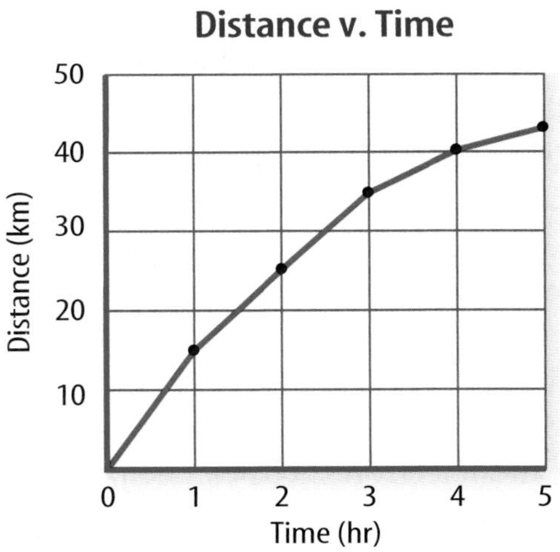

Distance v. Time

Distance (km): 10, 20, 30, 40, 50

Time (hr): 0, 1, 2, 3, 4, 5

Figure 15
This line graph shows the relationship between distance and time during a bicycle ride lasting several hours.

Bar Graphs Bar graphs compare data that do not change continuously. Vertical bars show the relationships among data.

To make a bar graph, set up the *y*-axis as you did for the line graph. Draw vertical bars of equal size from the *x*-axis up to the point on the *y*-axis that represents value of *x*.

Figure 16
The amount of aluminum collected for recycling during one week can be shown as a bar graph or circle graph.

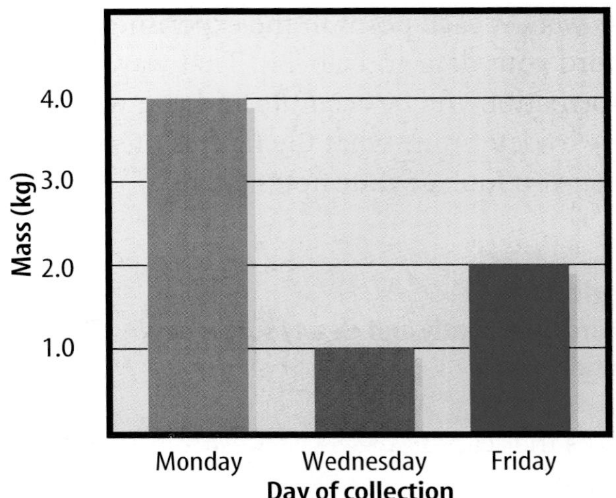

Circle Graphs A circle graph uses a circle divided into sections to display data as parts (fractions or percentages) of a whole. The size of each section corresponds to the fraction or percentage of the data that the section represents. So, the entire circle represents 100 percent, one-half represents 50 percent, one-fifth represents 20 percent, and so on.

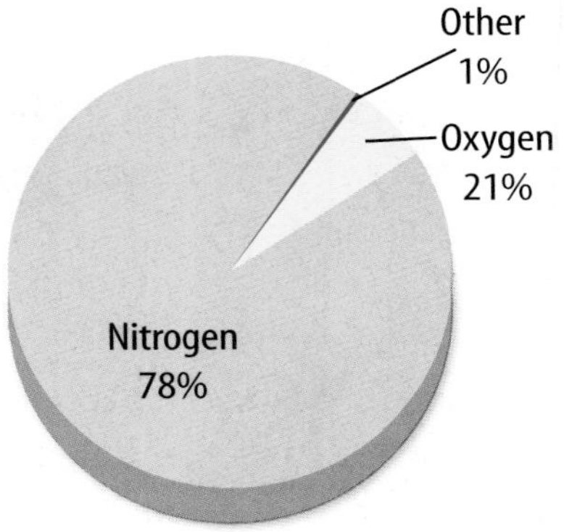

Other 1%
Oxygen 21%
Nitrogen 78%

Analyzing Results

To determine the meaning of your observations and investigation results, you will need to look for patterns in the data. You can organize your information in several of the ways that are discussed in this handbook. Then you must think critically to determine what the data mean. Scientists use several approaches when they analyze the data they have collected and recorded. Each approach is useful for identifying specific patterns in the data.

Forming Operational Definitions

An operational definition defines an object by showing how it functions, works, or behaves. Such definitions are written in terms of how an object works or how it can be used; that is, they describe its job or purpose.

For example, a ruler can be defined as a tool that measures the length of an object (how it can be used). A ruler also can be defined as something that contains a series of marks that can be used as a standard when measuring (how it works).

Classifying

Classifying is the process of sorting objects or events into groups based on common features. When classifying, first observe the objects or events to be classified. Then select one feature that is shared by some members in the group but not by all. Place those members that share that feature into a subgroup. You can classify members into smaller and smaller subgroups based on characteristics.

How might you classify a group of chemicals? You might first classify them by state of matter, putting solids, liquids, and gases into separate groups. Within each group, you could then look for another common feature by which to further classify members of the group, such as color or how reactive they are.

Remember that when you classify, you are grouping objects or events for a purpose. For example, classifying chemicals can be the first step in organizing them for storage. Both at home and at school, poisonous or highly reactive chemicals should all be stored in a safe location where they are not easily accessible to small children or animals. Solids, liquids, and gases each have specific storage requirements that may include waterproof, airtight, or pressurized containers. Are the dangerous chemicals in your home stored in the right place? Keep your purpose in mind as you select the features to form groups and subgroups.

Figure 17
Color is one of many characteristics that are used to classify chemicals.

Comparing and Contrasting

Observations can be analyzed by noting the similarities and differences between two or more objects or events that you observe. When you look at objects or events to see how they are similar, you are comparing them. Contrasting is looking for differences in objects or events. The table below compares and contrasts the characteristics of two elements.

Elemental Characteristics		
Element	Aluminum	Gold
Color	silver	gold
Classification	metal	metal
Density (g/cm^3)	2.7	19.3
Melting Point (°C)	660	1064

Recognizing Cause and Effect

Have you ever heard a loud pop right before the power went out and then suggested that an electric transformer probably blew out? If so, you have observed an effect and inferred a cause. The event is the effect, and the reason for the event is the cause.

When scientists are unsure of the cause of a certain event, they design controlled experiments to determine what caused it.

Interpreting Data

The word *interpret* means "to explain the meaning of something." Look at the problem originally being explored in an experiment and figure out what the data show. Identify the control group and the test group so you can see whether or not changes in the independent variable have had an effect. Look for differences in the dependent variable between the control and test groups.

These differences you observe can be qualitative or quantitative. You would be able to describe a qualitative difference using only words, whereas you would measure a quantitative difference and describe it using numbers. If there are differences, the independent variable that is being tested could have had an effect. If no differences are found between the control and test groups, the variable that is being tested apparently had no effect.

For example, suppose that three beakers each contain 100 mL of water. The beakers are placed on hot plates, and two of the hot plates are turned on, but the third is left off for a period of 5 min. Suppose you are then asked to describe any differences in the water in the three beakers. A qualitative difference might be the appearance of bubbles rising to the top in the water that is being heated but no rising bubbles in the unheated water. A quantitative difference might be a difference in the amount of water that is present in the beakers.

Inferring Scientists often make inferences based on their observations. An inference is an attempt to explain, or interpret, observations or to indicate what caused what you observed. An inference is a type of conclusion.

When making an inference, be certain to use accurate data and accurately described observations. Analyze all of the data that you've collected. Then, based on everything you know, explain or interpret what you've observed.

Drawing Conclusions

When scientists have analyzed the data they collected, they proceed to draw conclusions about what the data mean. These conclusions are sometimes stated using words similar to those found in the hypothesis formed earlier in the process.

Conclusions To analyze your data, you must review all of the observations and measurements that you made and recorded. Recheck all data for accuracy. After your data are rechecked and organized, you are almost ready to draw a conclusion such as "salt water boils at a higher temperature than freshwater."

Before you can draw a conclusion, however, you must determine whether the data allow you to come to a conclusion that supports a hypothesis. Sometimes that will be the case, other times it will not.

If your data do not support a hypothesis, it does not mean that the hypothesis is wrong. It means only that the results of the investigation did not support the hypothesis. Maybe the experiment needs to be redesigned, but very likely, some of the initial observations on which the hypothesis was based were incomplete or biased. Perhaps more observation or research is needed to refine the hypothesis.

Avoiding Bias Sometimes drawing a conclusion involves making judgments. When you make a judgment, you form an opinion about what your data mean. It is important to be honest and to avoid reaching a conclusion if there were no supporting evidence for it or if it were based on a small sample. It also is important not to allow any expectations of results to bias your judgments. If possible, it is a good idea to collect additional data. Scientists do this all the time.

For example, the *Hubble Space Telescope* was sent into space in April, 1990, to provide scientists with clearer views of the universe. The *Hubble* is the size of a school bus and has a 2.4-m-diameter mirror. The *Hubble* helped scientists answer questions about the planet Pluto.

For many years, scientists had only been able to hypothesize about the surface of the planet Pluto. The *Hubble* has now provided pictures of Pluto's surface that show a rough texture with light and dark regions on it. This might be the best information about Pluto scientists will have until they are able to send a space probe to it.

Evaluating Others' Data and Conclusions

Sometimes scientists have to use data that they did not collect themselves, or they have to rely on observations and conclusions drawn by other researchers. In cases such as these, the data must be evaluated carefully.

How were the data obtained? How was the investigation done? Was it carried out properly? Has it been duplicated by other researchers? Were they able to follow the exact procedure? Did they come up with the same results? Look at the conclusion, as well. Would you reach the same conclusion from these results? Only when you have confidence in the data of others can you believe it is true and feel comfortable using it.

Communicating

The communication of ideas is an important part of the work of scientists. A discovery that is not reported will not advance the scientific community's understanding or knowledge. Communication among scientists also is important as a way of improving their investigations.

Scientists communicate in many ways, from writing articles in journals and magazines that explain their investigations and experiments, to announcing important discoveries on television and radio, to sharing ideas with colleagues on the Internet or presenting them as lectures.

Computer Skills

People who study science rely on computers to record and store data and to analyze results from investigations. Whether you work in a laboratory or just need to write a lab report with tables, good computer skills are a necessity.

Using a Word Processor

Suppose your teacher has assigned a written report. After you've completed your research and decided how you want to write the information, you need to put all that information on paper. The easiest way to do this is with a word processing application on a computer.

A computer application that allows you to type your information, change it as many times as you need to, and then print it out so that it looks neat and clean is called a word processing application. You also can use this type of application to create tables and columns, add bullets or cartoon art to your page, include page numbers, and check your spelling.

Helpful Hints

- If you aren't sure how to do something using your word processing program, look in the help menu. You will find a list of topics there to click on for help. After you locate the help topic you need, just follow the step-by-step instructions you see on your screen.
- Just because you've spell checked your report doesn't mean that the spelling is perfect. The spell check feature can't catch misspelled words that look like other words. If you've accidentally typed *cold* instead of *gold*, the spell checker won't know the difference. Always reread your report to make sure you didn't miss any mistakes.

Figure 18
You can use computer programs to make graphs and tables.

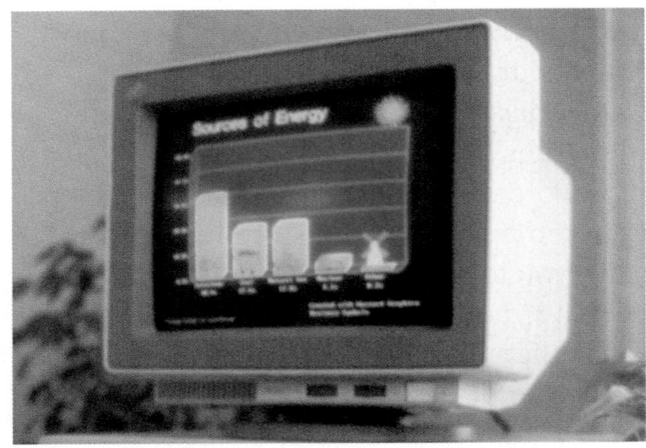

Using a Database

Imagine you're in the middle of a research project, busily gathering facts and information. You soon realize that it's becoming more difficult to organize and keep track of all the information. The tool to use to solve information overload is a database. Just as a file cabinet organizes paper records, a database organizes computer records. However, a database is more powerful than a simple file cabinet because at the click of a mouse, the contents can be reshuffled and reorganized. At computer-quick speeds, databases can sort information by any characteristics and filter data into multiple categories.

Helpful Hints

- Before setting up a database, take some time to learn the features of your database software by practicing with established database software.
- Periodically save your database as you enter data. That way, if something happens such as your computer malfunctions or the power goes off, you won't lose all of your work.

Doing a Database Search

When searching for information in a database, use the following search strategies to get the best results. These are the same search methods used for searching internet databases.

- Place the word *and* between two words in your search if you want the database to look for any entries that have both the words. For example, "gold *and* silver" would give you information that mentions both gold and silver.
- Place the word *or* between two words if you want the database to show entries that have at least one of the words. For example "gold *or* silver" would show you information that mentions either gold or silver.
- Place the word *not* between two words if you want the database to look for entries that have the first word but do not have the second word. For example, "gold *not* jewelry" would show you information that mentions gold but does not mention jewelry.

In summary, databases can be used to store large amounts of information about a particular subject. Databases allow biologists, Earth scientists, and physical scientists to search for information quickly and accurately.

Using an Electronic Spreadsheet

Your science fair experiment has produced lots of numbers. How do you keep track of all the data, and how can you easily work out all the calculations needed? You can use a computer program called a spreadsheet to record data that involve numbers. A spreadsheet is an electronic mathematical worksheet.

Type your data in rows and columns, just as they would look in a data table on a sheet of paper. A spreadsheet uses simple math to do data calculations. For example, you could add, subtract, divide, or multiply any of the values in the spreadsheet by another number. You also could set up a series of math steps you want to apply to the data. If you want to add 12 to all the numbers and then multiply all the numbers by 10, the computer does all the calculations for you in the spreadsheet. Below is an example of a spreadsheet that records test car data.

Helpful Hints

- Before you set up the spreadsheet, identify how you want to organize the data. Include any formulas you will need to use.
- Make sure you have entered the correct data into the correct rows and columns.
- You also can display your results in a graph. Pick the style of graph that best represents the data with which you are working.

Figure 19
A spreadsheet allows you to display large amounts of data and do calculations automatically.

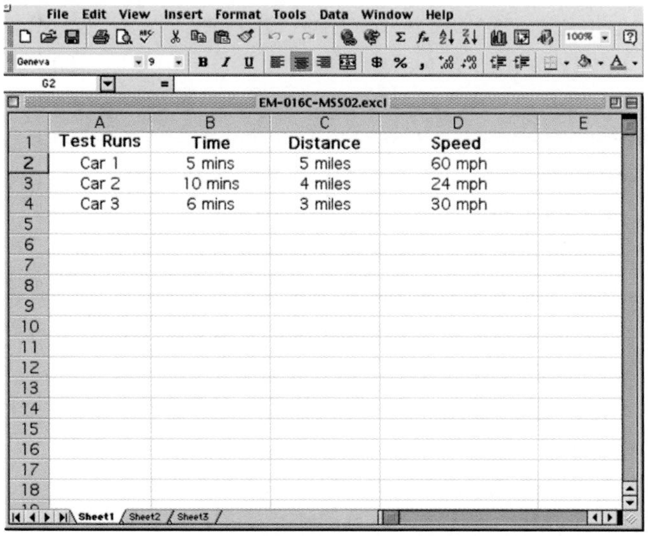

EM-016C-MSS02.excl

	A	B	C	D	E
1	Test Runs	Time	Distance	Speed	
2	Car 1	5 mins	5 miles	60 mph	
3	Car 2	10 mins	4 miles	24 mph	
4	Car 3	6 mins	3 miles	30 mph	

Using a Computerized Card Catalog

When you have a report or paper to research, you probably go to the library. To find the information you need in the library, you might have to use a computerized card catalog. This type of card catalog allows you to search for information by subject, by title, or by author. The computer then will display all the holdings the library has on the subject, title, or author requested.

A library's holdings can include books, magazines, databases, videos, and audio materials. When you have chosen something from this list, the computer will show whether an item is available and where in the library to find it.

Helpful Hints

- Remember that you can use the computer to search by subject, author, or title. If you know a book's author but not the title, you can search for all the books the library has by that author.
- When searching by subject, it's often most helpful to narrow your search by using specific search terms, such as *and, or,* and *not.* If you don't find enough sources this way, you can broaden your search.
- Pay attention to the type of materials found in your search. If you need a book, you can eliminate any videos or other resources that come up in your search.
- Knowing how your library is arranged can save you a lot of time. If you need help, the librarian will show you where certain types of materials are kept and how to find specific holdings.

Using Graphics Software

Are you having trouble finding that exact piece of art you're looking for? Do you have a picture in your mind of what you want but can't seem to find the right graphic to represent your ideas? To solve these problems, you can use graphics software. Graphics software allows you to create and change images and diagrams in almost unlimited ways. Typical uses for graphics software include arranging clip art, changing scanned images, and constructing pictures from scratch. Most graphics software applications work in similar ways. They use the same basic tools and functions. Once you master one graphics application, you can use other graphics applications.

Figure 20
Graphics software can use your data to draw bar graphs.

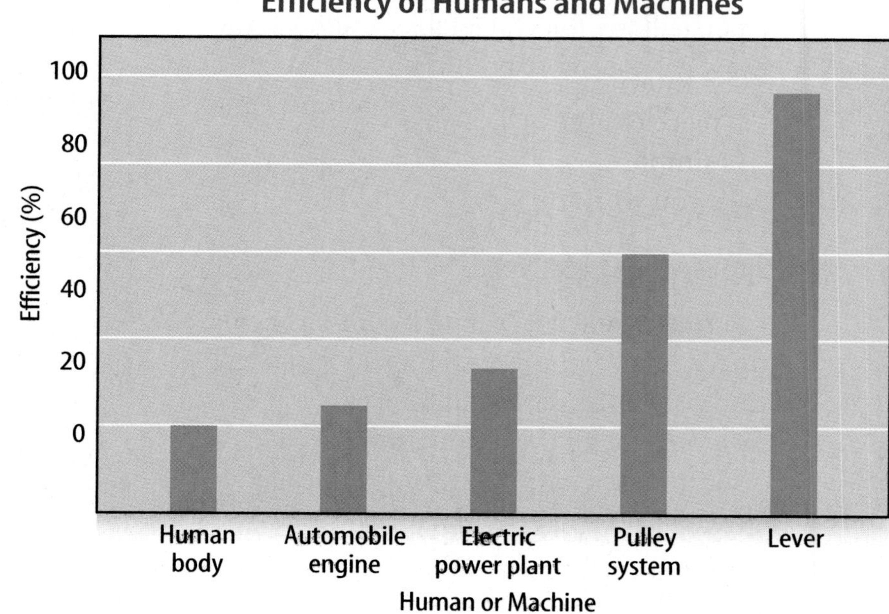

Figure 21
Graphics software can use your data to draw circle graphs.

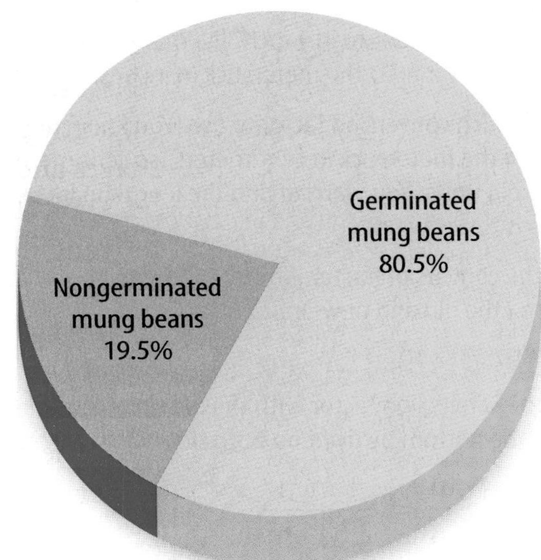

Helpful Hints

- As with any method of drawing, the more you practice using the graphics software, the better your results will be.
- Start by using the software to manipulate existing drawings. Once you master this, making your own illustrations will be easier.
- Clip art is available on CD-ROMs and the Internet. With these resources, finding a piece of clip art to suit your purposes is simple.
- As you work on a drawing, save it often.

Developing Multimedia Presentations

It's your turn—you have to present your science report to the entire class. How do you do it? You can use many different sources of information to get the class excited about your presentation. Posters, videos, photographs, sound, computers, and the Internet can help show your ideas.

First, determine what important points you want to make in your presentation. Then, write an outline of what materials and types of media would best illustrate those points. Maybe you could start with an outline on an overhead projector, then show a video, followed by something from the Internet or a slide show accompanied by music or recorded voices. You might choose to use a presentation builder computer application that can combine all these elements into one presentation. Make sure the presentation is well constructed to make the most impact on the audience.

Figure 22
Multimedia presentations use many types of print and electronic materials.

Helpful Hints

- Carefully consider what media will best communicate the point you are trying to make.
- Make sure you know how to use any equipment you will be using in your presentation.
- Practice the presentation several times.
- If possible, set up all of the equipment ahead of time. Make sure everything is working correctly.

Math Skill Handbook

Use this Math Skill Handbook to help solve problems you are given in this text. You might find it useful to review topics in this Math Skill Handbook first.

Skill Handbooks

Converting Units

In science, quantities such as length, mass, and time sometimes are measured using different units. Suppose you want to know how many miles are in 12.7 km?

Conversion factors are used to change from one unit of measure to another. A conversion factor is a ratio that is equal to one. For example, there are 1,000 mL in 1 L, so 1,000 mL equals 1 L, or:

$$1{,}000 \text{ mL} = 1 \text{ L}$$

If both sides are divided by 1 L, this equation becomes:

$$\frac{1{,}000 \text{ mL}}{1 \text{ L}} = 1$$

The **ratio** on the left side of this equation is equal to one and is a conversion factor. You can make another conversion factor by dividing both sides of the top equation by 1,000 mL:

$$1 = \frac{1 \text{ L}}{1{,}000 \text{ mL}}$$

To **convert units,** you multiply by the appropriate conversion factor. For example, how many milliliters are in 1.255 L? To convert 1.255 L to milliliters, multiply 1.255 L by a conversion factor.

Use the **conversion factor** with new units (mL) in the numerator and the old units (L) in the denominator.

$$1.255 \cancel{\text{L}} \times \frac{1{,}000 \text{ mL}}{1 \cancel{\text{L}}} = 1{,}255 \text{ mL}$$

The unit L divides in this equation, just as if it were a number.

Example 1 There are 2.54 cm in 1 inch. If a meterstick has a length of 100 cm, how long is the meterstick in inches?

Step 1 Decide which conversion factor to use. You know the length of the meterstick in centimeters, so centimeters are the old units. You want to find the length in inches, so inch is the new unit.

Step 2 Form the conversion factor. Start with the relationship between the old and new units.

$$2.54 \text{ cm} = 1 \text{ inch}$$

Step 3 Form the conversion factor with the old unit (centimeter) on the bottom by dividing both sides by 2.54 cm.

$$1 = \frac{2.54 \text{ cm}}{2.54 \text{ cm}} = \frac{1 \text{ inch}}{2.54 \text{ cm}}$$

Step 4 Multiply the old measurement by the conversion factor.

$$100 \cancel{\text{cm}} \times \frac{1 \text{ inch}}{2.54 \cancel{\text{cm}}} = 39.37 \text{ inches}$$

The meter stick is 39.37 inches long.

Example 2 There are 365 days in one year. If a person is 14 years old, what is his or her age in days? (Ignore leap years)

Step 1 Decide which conversion factor to use. You want to convert years to days.

Step 2 Form the conversion factor. Start with the relation between the old and new units.

$$1 \text{ year} = 365 \text{ days}$$

Step 3 Form the conversion factor with the old unit (year) on the bottom by dividing both sides by 1 year.

$$1 = \frac{1 \text{ year}}{1 \text{ year}} = \frac{365 \text{ days}}{1 \text{ year}}$$

Step 4 Multiply the old measurement by the conversion factor:

$$14 \cancel{\text{years}} \times \frac{365 \text{ days}}{1 \cancel{\text{year}}} = 5{,}110 \text{ days}$$

The person's age is 5,110 days.

Practice Problem A book has a mass of 2.31 kg. If there are 1,000 g in 1 kg, what is the mass of the book in grams?

Using Fractions

A **fraction** is a number that compares a part to the whole. For example, in the fraction $\frac{2}{3}$, the 2 represents the part and the 3 represents the whole. In the fraction $\frac{2}{3}$, the top number, 2, is called the numerator. The bottom number, 3, is called the denominator.

Sometimes fractions are not written in their simplest form. To determine a fraction's **simplest form,** you must find the greatest common factor (GCF) of the numerator and denominator. The greatest common factor is the largest common factor of all the factors the two numbers have in common.

For example, because the number 3 divides into 12 and 30 evenly, it is a common factor of 12 and 30. However, because the number 6 is the largest number that evenly divides into 12 and 30, it is the **greatest common factor.**

After you find the greatest common factor, you can write a fraction in its simplest form. Divide both the numerator and the denominator by the greatest common factor. The number that results is the fraction in its **simplest form.**

Example Twelve of the 20 chemicals used in the science lab are in powder form. What fraction of the chemicals used in the lab are in powder form?

Step 1 Write the fraction.

$$\frac{\text{part}}{\text{whole}} = \frac{12}{20}$$

Step 2 To find the GCF of the numerator and denominator, list all of the factors of each number.

Factors of 12: 1, 2, 3, 4, 6, 12 (the numbers that divide evenly into 12)

Factors of 20: 1, 2, 4, 5, 10, 20 (the numbers that divide evenly into 20)

Step 3 List the common factors.

1, 2, 4.

Step 4 Choose the greatest factor in the list of common factors.

The GCF of 12 and 20 is 4.

Step 5 Divide the numerator and denominator by the GCF.

$$\frac{12 \div 4}{20 \div 4} = \frac{3}{5}$$

In the lab, $\frac{3}{5}$ of the chemicals are in powder form.

Practice Problem There are 90 rides at an amusement park. Of those rides, 66 have a height restriction. What fraction of the rides has a height restriction? Write the fraction in simplest form. 11/15

Calculating Ratios

A **ratio** is a comparison of two numbers by division.

Ratios can be written 3 to 5 or 3:5. Ratios also can be written as fractions, such as $\frac{3}{5}$. Ratios, like fractions, can be written in simplest form. Recall that a fraction is in **simplest form** when the greatest common factor (GCF) of the numerator and denominator is 1.

Example A chemical solution contains 40 g of salt and 64 g of baking soda. What is the ratio of salt to baking soda as a fraction in simplest form?

Step 1 Write the ratio as a fraction. $\frac{\text{salt}}{\text{baking soda}} = \frac{40}{64}$

Step 2 Express the fraction in simplest form. The GCF of 40 and 64 is 8.

$$\frac{40}{64} = \frac{40 \div 8}{64 \div 8} = \frac{5}{8}$$

The ratio of salt to baking soda in the solution is $\frac{5}{8}$.

Practice Problem Two metal rods measure 100 cm and 144 cm in length. What is the ratio of their lengths in simplest fraction form? 25/36

Using Decimals

A **decimal** is a fraction with a denominator of 10, 100, 1,000, or another power of 10. For example, 0.854 is the same as the fraction $\frac{854}{1,000}$.

In a decimal, the decimal point separates the ones place and the tenths place. For example, 0.27 means twenty-seven hundredths, or $\frac{27}{100}$, where 27 is the **number of units** out of 100 units. Any fraction can be written as a decimal using division.

Example Write $\frac{5}{8}$ as a decimal.

Step 1 Write a division problem with the numerator, 5, as the dividend and the denominator, 8, as the divisor. Write 5 as 5.000.

Step 2 Solve the problem.

$$\begin{array}{r} 0.625 \\ 8\overline{)5.000} \\ \underline{48} \\ 20 \\ \underline{16} \\ 40 \\ \underline{40} \\ 0 \end{array}$$

Therefore, $\frac{5}{8} = 0.625$.

Practice Problem Write $\frac{19}{25}$ as a decimal. 0.76

Using Percentages

The word *percent* means "out of one hundred." A **percent** is a ratio that compares a number to 100. Suppose you read that 77 percent of Earth's surface is covered by water. That is the same as reading that the fraction of Earth's surface covered by water is $\frac{77}{100}$. To express a fraction as a percent, first find an equivalent decimal for the fraction. Then, multiply the decimal by 100 and add the percent symbol. For example, $\frac{1}{2} = 1 \div 2 = 0.5$. Then $0.5 = 0.50 = 50\%$.

Example Express $\frac{13}{20}$ as a percent.

Step 1 Find the equivalent decimal for the fraction.

$$\begin{array}{r} 0.65 \\ 20\overline{)13.00} \\ \underline{12\,0} \\ 100 \\ \underline{100} \\ 0 \end{array}$$

Step 2 Rewrite the fraction $\frac{13}{20}$ as 0.65.

Step 3 Multiply 0.65 by 100 and add the % sign.

$0.65 \cdot 100 = 65 = 65\%$

So, $\frac{13}{20} = 65\%$.

Practice Problem In one year, 73 of 365 days were rainy in one city. What percent of the days in that city were rainy? 20%

Using Precision and Significant Digits

When you make a **measurement,** the value you record depends on the precision of the measuring instrument. When adding or subtracting numbers with different precision, the answer is rounded to the smallest number of decimal places of any number in the sum or difference. When multiplying or dividing, the answer is rounded to the smallest number of significant figures of any number being multiplied or divided. When counting the number of **significant figures,** all digits are counted except zeros at the end of a number with no decimal such as 2,500, and zeros at the beginning of a decimal such as 0.03020.

Example The lengths 5.28 and 5.2 are measured in meters. Find the sum of these lengths and report the sum using the least precise measurement.

Step 1 Find the sum.

$$\begin{array}{rl} 5.28\text{ m} & \text{2 digits after the decimal} \\ +\ 5.2\ \ \text{m} & \text{1 digit after the decimal} \\ \hline 10.48\text{ m} & \end{array}$$

Step 2 Round to one digit after the decimal because the least number of digits after the decimal of the numbers being added is 1.

The sum is 10.5 m.

Practice Problem Multiply the numbers in the example using the rule for multiplying and dividing. Report the answer with the correct number of significant figures. 27.5 m^2

Skill Handbooks

Solving One-Step Equations

An **equation** is a statement that two things are equal. For example, $A = B$ is an equation that states that A is equal to B.

Sometimes one side of the equation will contain a **variable** whose value is not known. In the equation $3x = 12$, the variable is x.

The equation is solved when the variable is replaced with a value that makes both sides of the equation equal to each other. For example, the solution of the equation $3x = 12$ is $x = 4$. If the x is replaced with 4, then the equation becomes $3 \cdot 4 = 12$, or $12 = 12$.

To solve an equation such as $8x = 40$, divide both sides of the equation by the number that multiplies the variable.

$$8x = 40$$
$$\frac{8x}{8} = \frac{40}{8}$$
$$x = 5$$

You can check your answer by replacing the variable with your solution and seeing if both sides of the equation are the same.

$$8x = 8 \cdot 5 = 40$$

The left and right sides of the equation are the same, so $x = 5$ is the solution.

Sometimes an equation is written in this way: $a = bc$. This also is called a **formula.** The letters can be replaced by numbers, but the numbers must still make both sides of the equation the same.

Example 1 Solve the equation $10x = 35$.

Step 1 Find the solution by dividing each side of the equation by 10.

$$10x = 35 \qquad \frac{10x}{10} = \frac{35}{10} \qquad x = 3.5$$

Step 2 Check the solution.

$$10x = 35 \qquad 10 \times 3.5 = 35 \qquad 35 = 35$$

Both sides of the equation are equal, so $x = 3.5$ is the solution to the equation.

Example 2 In the formula $a = bc$, find the value of c if $a = 20$ and $b = 2$.

Step 1 Rearrange the formula so the unknown value is by itself on one side of the equation by dividing both sides by b.

$$a = bc$$
$$\frac{a}{b} = \frac{bc}{b}$$
$$\frac{a}{b} = c$$

Step 2 Replace the variables a and b with the values that are given.

$$\frac{a}{b} = c$$
$$\frac{20}{2} = c$$
$$10 = c$$

Step 3 Check the solution.

$$a = bc$$
$$20 = 2 \times 10$$
$$20 = 20$$

Both sides of the equation are equal, so $c = 10$ is the solution when $a = 20$ and $b = 2$.

Practice Problem In the formula $h = gd$, find the value of d if $g = 12.3$ and $h = 17.4$. $d = 1.4$

Using Proportions

A **proportion** is an equation that shows that two ratios are equivalent. The ratios $\frac{2}{4}$ and $\frac{5}{10}$ are equivalent, so they can be written as $\frac{2}{4} = \frac{5}{10}$. This equation is an example of a proportion.

When two ratios form a proportion, the **cross products** are equal. To find the cross products in the proportion $\frac{2}{4} = \frac{5}{10}$, multiply the 2 and the 10, and the 4 and the 5. Therefore **$2 \cdot 10 = 4 \cdot 5$, or $20 = 20$.**

Because you know that both proportions are equal, you can use cross products to find a missing term in a proportion. This is known as **solving the proportion.** Solving a proportion is similar to solving an equation.

Example The heights of a tree and a pole are proportional to the lengths of their shadows. The tree casts a shadow of 24 m at the same time that a 6-m pole casts a shadow of 4 m. What is the height of the tree?

Step 1 Write a proportion.

$$\frac{\text{height of tree}}{\text{height of pole}} = \frac{\text{length of tree's shadow}}{\text{length of pole's shadow}}$$

Step 2 Substitute the known values into the proportion. Let *h* represent the unknown value, the height of the tree.

$$\frac{h}{6} = \frac{24}{4}$$

Step 3 Find the cross products.

$$h \cdot 4 = 6 \cdot 24$$

Step 4 Simplify the equation.

$$4h = 144$$

Step 5 Divide each side by 4.

$$\frac{4h}{4} = \frac{144}{4}$$

$$h = 36$$

The height of the tree is 36 m.

Practice Problem The ratios of the weights of two objects on the Moon and on Earth are in proportion. A rock weighing 3 N on the Moon weighs 18 N on Earth. How much would a rock that weighs 5 N on the Moon weigh on Earth?

Using Statistics

Statistics is the branch of mathematics that deals with collecting, analyzing, and presenting data. In statistics, there are three common ways to summarize the data with a single number—the mean, the median, and the mode.

The **mean** of a set of data is the arithmetic average. It is found by adding the numbers in the data set and dividing by the number of items in the set.

The **median** is the middle number in a set of data when the data are arranged in numerical order. If there were an even number of data points, the median would be the mean of the two middle numbers.

The **mode** of a set of data is the number or item that appears most often.

Another number that often is used to describe a set of data is the range. The **range** is the difference between the largest number and the smallest number in a set of data.

A **frequency table** shows how many times each piece of data occurs, usually in a survey. The frequency table below shows the results of a student survey on favorite color.

Color	Tally	Frequency
red	||||	4
blue	卌	5
black	||	2
green	|||	3
purple	卌 ||	7
yellow	卌 |	6

Based on the frequency table data, which color is the favorite?

Example The speeds (in m/s) for a race car during five different time trials are 39, 37, 44, 36, and 44.

To find the mean:

Step 1 Find the sum of the numbers.

$$39 + 37 + 44 + 36 + 44 = 200$$

Step 2 Divide the sum by the number of items, which is 5.

$$200 \div 5 = 40$$

The mean measure is 40 m/s.

To find the median:

Step 1 Arrange the measures from least to greatest.

$$36,\ 37,\ \underline{39},\ 44,\ 44$$

Step 2 Determine the middle measure.

The median measure is 39 m/s.

To find the mode:

Step 1 Group the numbers that are the same together.

$$44, 44, 36, 37, 39$$

Step 2 Determine the number that occurs most in the set.

$$\underline{44, 44}, 36, 37, 39$$

The mode measure is 44 m/s.

To find the range:

Step 1 Arrange the measures from largest to smallest.

$$44, 44, 39, 37, 36$$

Step 2 Determine the largest and smallest measures in the set.

$$\underline{44}, 44, 39, 37, \underline{36}$$

Step 3 Find the difference between the largest and smallest measures.

$$44 - 36 = 8$$

The range is 8 m/s.

Practice Problem Find the mean, median, mode, and range for the data set 8, 4, 12, 8, 11, 14, 16.

mean, 10; median, 11; mode, 8; range, 12

List of Formulas

Chapter 2 Motion

$$\text{Speed (m/s)} = \frac{\text{distance (m)}}{\text{time (s)}}$$

$$s = \frac{d}{t}$$

$$\text{Acceleration (m/s}^2\text{)} = \frac{\text{change in speed (m/s)}}{\text{time(s)}}$$

$$= \frac{\text{final speed} - \text{initial speed}}{\text{time}}$$

$$a = \frac{v_f - v_i}{t}$$

Chapter 3 Forces

$$\text{Acceleration (m/s}^2\text{)} = \frac{\text{net force (N)}}{\text{mass (kg)}}$$

$$a = \frac{f}{m}$$

$$\text{Weight (N)} = \text{mass (kg)} \times \text{acceleration due to gravity (m/s}^2\text{)}$$

$$W = m \times g$$

$$\text{Momentum (kg m/s)} = \text{mass (kg)} \times \text{speed (m/s)}$$

$$p = m \times v$$

Chapter 4 Energy

$$\text{Kinetic energy (J)} = \frac{1}{2}\text{mass (kg)} \times \text{velocity (m/s)} \times \text{velocity (m/s)}$$

$$KE = \frac{1}{2} \times m \times v^2$$

$$\text{Gravitational potential energy (J)} = \text{weight (N)} \times \text{height (m)}$$

$$GPE = W \times h$$

$$\text{Gravitational potential energy (J)} = \text{mass (kg)} \times \text{gravitational acceleration (m/s}^2\text{)} \times \text{height (m)}$$

$$GPE = m \times g \times h$$

Chapter 5 Work and Machines

$$\text{Work (J)} = \text{force (N)} \times \text{distance (m)}$$

$$W = F \times d$$

$$\text{Power (W)} = \frac{\text{work (J)}}{\text{time (s)}}$$

$$P = \frac{W}{t}$$

Mechanical advantage = resistance force (N) / effort force (N)

$$MA = \frac{F_r}{F_e}$$

$$\text{efficiency} = 100\% \times \frac{\text{output work (J)}}{\text{input work (J)}}$$

$$= \frac{W_{out}}{W_{in}} \times 100\%$$

Chapter 6 Thermal Energy

Change in thermal energy (J) =
mass (kg) × change in temperature (K) × specific heat (J/kg · K)

$$Q = m \times (T_{final} - T_{initial}) \times C$$

Chapter 7 Solids, Liquids, and Gases

$$\text{Pressure (N/m}^2) = \frac{\text{Force (N)}}{\text{area (m}^2)}$$

$$P = \frac{F}{A}$$

Chapter 17 Electricity

Voltage (V) = current (A) × resistance (ohms)

$$V = I \times R$$

Electrical power (W) = current (A) × Voltage (V)

$$P = I \times V$$

Electrical energy used (kWh) = electric power(kW) × time (h)

$$E = P \times t$$

Chapter 21 Waves

Wave speed (m/s)= frequency (1/s) × wavelength (m)

$$V = f \times \lambda$$

Practice Problems

Chapter 2

1. It took you 6.5 h to drive 550 km. What was your speed?
2. You are riding in a train that is traveling at a speed of 120 km/h. How long will it take to travel 950 km?
3. A car goes from rest to a speed of 90 km/h in 10 s. What is the car's acceleration in m/s^2?
4. A cart rolling at a speed of 10 m/s comes to a stop in 2 s. What is the cart's acceleration?

Chapter 3

1. A book with a mass of 1 kg is sliding on a table. If the frictional force on the book is 5 N, calculate the book's acceleration. Is it speeding up or slowing down?
2. What is the weight of a person with a mass of 80 kg?
3. A car with a mass of 1,200 kg has a speed of 30 m/s. What is the car's momentum?

Chapter 4

1. A car with a mass of 900 kg is traveling at a speed of 25 m/s. What is the kinetic energy of the car in joules?
2. What is the gravitational potential energy of a diver with a mass of 60 kg who is 10 m above the water?
3. If your weight is 500 N, and you are standing on a floor that is 20 m above the ground, what is your gravitational potential energy?

Chapter 5

1. By applying a force of 50 N, a pulley system can lift a box with a mass of 20 kg. What is the mechanical advantage of the pulley system?
2. A person pushes a box up a ramp that is 3 m long, and 1 m high. If the box has a mass of 20 kg, and the person pushes with a force of 80 N, what is the efficiency of the ramp?
3. A first-class lever has a mechanical advantage of 5. How large would a force need to be to lift a rock with a mass of 100 kg?
4. If a person has a mass of 50 kg, how much power is used to climb a flight of stairs in 5 s if the stairs are 4 m high?

Chapter 6

1. How much heat is needed to raise the temperature of 100 g of water by 50 K, if the specific heat of water is 4,184 J/kg·K?
2. A sample of an unknown metal has a mass of 0.5 kg. Adding 1,985 J of heat to the metal raises its temperature by 10 K. What is the specific heat of the metal?

Chapter 7

1. A skater has a weight of 500 N. The skate blades are in contact with the ice over an area of 0.001 m^2. What is the pressure exerted on the ice by the skater?
2. A piston applies a pressure of 5000 N/m^2. If the piston has a surface area of 0.1 m^2, how much force can the piston apply?

Chapter 17

1. What is the resistance of a lightbulb that draws 0.5 amp of current when plugged into an outlet of voltage 120 V?
2. How much current flows through a 100-W lightbulb that is plugged into a 120-V outlet?
3. 8 amps of current flow through a hair dryer connected to a 120-V outlet. How much electrical power does the hairdryer use?
4. Compare the electrical energy that is used by a 100-W lightbulb that burns for 10 h, and a 1,200-W hair drier that is used for 15 min.

Chapter 21

1. A sound wave has a wavelength of 50 m and a frequency of 22 cycles per second. What is the speed of the sound wave?
2. A tidal wave, or tsunami, travels across the ocean at a speed of 500 km/h. If the distance between wave crests is 200 km, what is the frequency of the waves?

Safety in the Science Classroom

1. Always obtain your teacher's permission to begin an investigation.
2. Study the procedure. If you have questions, ask your teacher. Be sure you understand any safety symbols shown on the page.
3. Use the safety equipment provided for you. Goggles and a safety apron should be worn during most investigations.
4. Always slant test tubes away from yourself and others when heating them or adding substances to them.
5. Never eat or drink in the lab, and never use lab glassware as food or drink containers. Never inhale chemicals. Do not taste any substances or draw any material into a tube with your mouth.
6. Report any spill, accident, or injury, no matter how small, immediately to your teacher, then follow his or her instructions.
7. Know the location and proper use of the fire extinguisher, safety shower, fire blanket, first aid kit, and fire alarm.
8. Keep all materials away from open flames. Tie back long hair and tie down loose clothing.
9. If your clothing should catch fire, smother it with the fire blanket, or get under a safety shower. NEVER RUN.
10. If a fire should occur, turn off the gas then leave the room according to established procedures.

Follow these procedures as you clean up your work area

1. Turn off the water and gas. Disconnect electrical devices.
2. Clean all pieces of equipment and return all materials to their proper places.
3. Dispose of chemicals and other materials as directed by your teacher. Place broken glass and solid substances in the proper containers. Make sure never to discard materials in the sink.
4. Clean your work area. Wash your hands thoroughly after working in the laboratory.

First Aid

Injury	Safe Response ALWAYS NOTIFY YOUR TEACHER IMMEDIATELY
Burns	Apply cold water.
Cuts and Bruises	Stop any bleeding by applying direct pressure. Cover cuts with a clean dressing. Apply ice packs or cold compresses to bruises.
Fainting	Leave the person lying down. Loosen any tight clothing and keep crowds away.
Foreign Matter in Eye	Flush with plenty of water. Use eyewash bottle or fountain.
Poisoning	Note the suspected poisoning agent.
Any Spills on Skin	Flush with large amounts of water or use safety shower.

SI—Metric/English, English/Metric Conversions

	When you want to convert:	To:	Multiply by:
Length	inches	centimeters	2.54
	centimeters	inches	0.39
	yards	meters	0.91
	meters	yards	1.09
	miles	kilometers	1.61
	kilometers	miles	0.62
Mass and Weight*	ounces	grams	28.35
	grams	ounces	0.04
	pounds	kilograms	0.45
	kilograms	pounds	2.2
	tons (short)	tonnes (metric tons)	0.91
	tonnes (metric tons)	tons (short)	1.10
	pounds	newtons	4.45
	newtons	pounds	0.22
Volume	cubic inches	cubic centimeters	16.39
	cubic centimeters	cubic inches	0.06
	liters	quarts	1.06
	quarts	liters	0.95
	gallons	liters	3.78
Area	square inches	square centimeters	6.45
	square centimeters	square inches	0.16
	square yards	square meters	0.83
	square meters	square yards	1.19
	square miles	square kilometers	2.59
	square kilometers	square miles	0.39
	hectares	acres	2.47
	acres	hectares	0.40
Temperature	To convert °Celsius to °Fahrenheit		$°C \times 9/5 + 32$
	To convert °Fahrenheit to °Celsius		$5/9\ (°F - 32)$

*Weight is measured in standard Earth gravity.

PERIODIC TABLE OF THE ELEMENTS

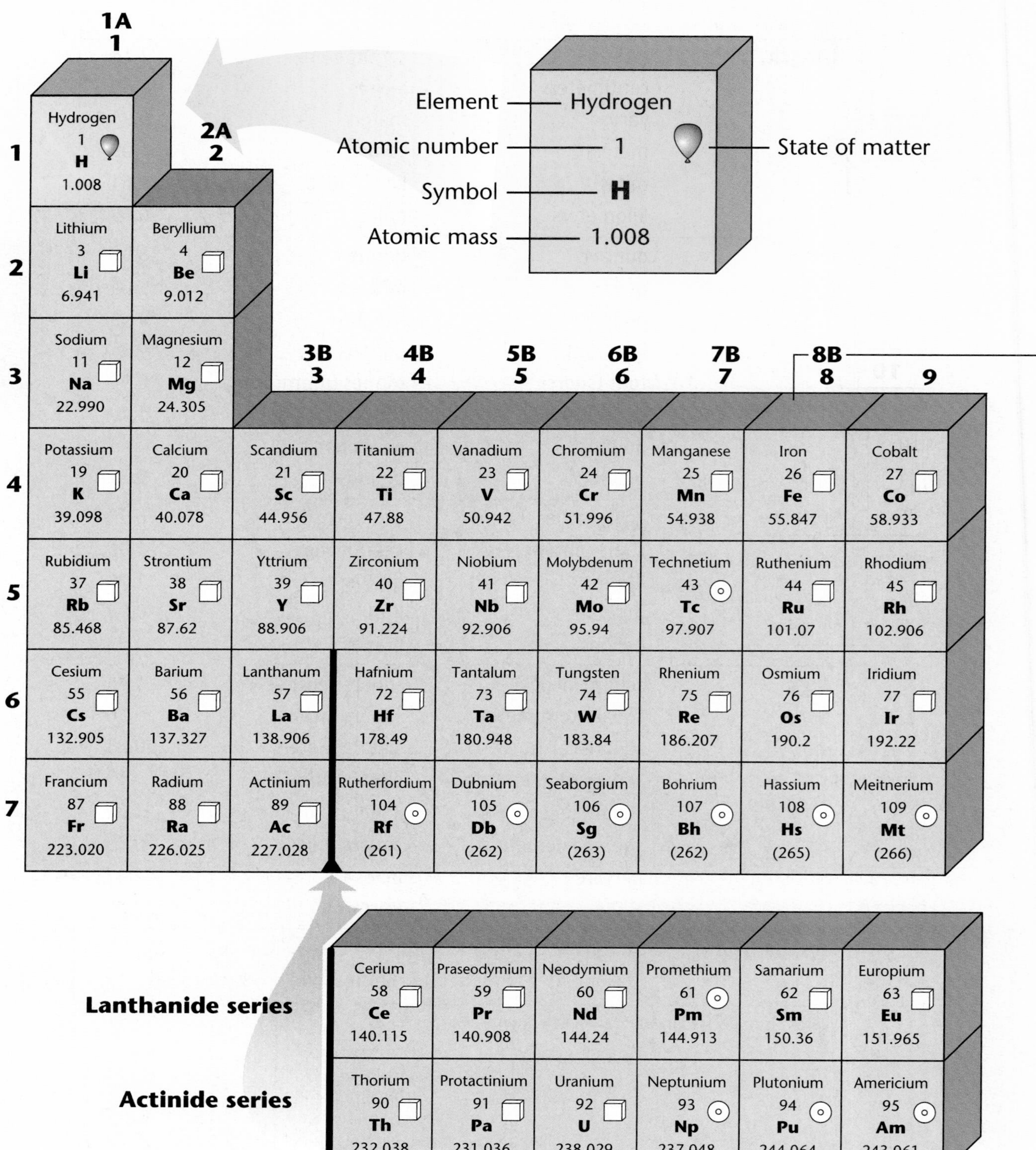

Period	1A 1	2A 2	3B 3	4B 4	5B 5	6B 6	7B 7	8B 8	9
1	Hydrogen 1 **H** 1.008								
2	Lithium 3 **Li** 6.941	Beryllium 4 **Be** 9.012							
3	Sodium 11 **Na** 22.990	Magnesium 12 **Mg** 24.305							
4	Potassium 19 **K** 39.098	Calcium 20 **Ca** 40.078	Scandium 21 **Sc** 44.956	Titanium 22 **Ti** 47.88	Vanadium 23 **V** 50.942	Chromium 24 **Cr** 51.996	Manganese 25 **Mn** 54.938	Iron 26 **Fe** 55.847	Cobalt 27 **Co** 58.933
5	Rubidium 37 **Rb** 85.468	Strontium 38 **Sr** 87.62	Yttrium 39 **Y** 88.906	Zirconium 40 **Zr** 91.224	Niobium 41 **Nb** 92.906	Molybdenum 42 **Mo** 95.94	Technetium 43 **Tc** 97.907	Ruthenium 44 **Ru** 101.07	Rhodium 45 **Rh** 102.906
6	Cesium 55 **Cs** 132.905	Barium 56 **Ba** 137.327	Lanthanum 57 **La** 138.906	Hafnium 72 **Hf** 178.49	Tantalum 73 **Ta** 180.948	Tungsten 74 **W** 183.84	Rhenium 75 **Re** 186.207	Osmium 76 **Os** 190.2	Iridium 77 **Ir** 192.22
7	Francium 87 **Fr** 223.020	Radium 88 **Ra** 226.025	Actinium 89 **Ac** 227.028	Rutherfordium 104 **Rf** (261)	Dubnium 105 **Db** (262)	Seaborgium 106 **Sg** (263)	Bohrium 107 **Bh** (262)	Hassium 108 **Hs** (265)	Meitnerium 109 **Mt** (266)

Series						
Lanthanide series	Cerium 58 **Ce** 140.115	Praseodymium 59 **Pr** 140.908	Neodymium 60 **Nd** 144.24	Promethium 61 **Pm** 144.913	Samarium 62 **Sm** 150.36	Europium 63 **Eu** 151.965
Actinide series	Thorium 90 **Th** 232.038	Protactinium 91 **Pa** 231.036	Uranium 92 **U** 238.029	Neptunium 93 **Np** 237.048	Plutonium 94 **Pu** 244.064	Americium 95 **Am** 243.061

Reference Handbook C

Metal

Metalloid

Nonmetal

Recently discovered

Gas

Liquid

Solid

Synthetic elements

10	1B 11	2B 12	3A 13	4A 14	5A 15	6A 16	7A 17	8A 18
								Helium 2 **He** 4.003
			Boron 5 **B** 10.811	Carbon 6 **C** 12.011	Nitrogen 7 **N** 14.007	Oxygen 8 **O** 15.999	Fluorine 9 **F** 18.998	Neon 10 **Ne** 20.180
			Aluminum 13 **Al** 26.982	Silicon 14 **Si** 28.086	Phosphorus 15 **P** 30.974	Sulfur 16 **S** 32.066	Chlorine 17 **Cl** 35.453	Argon 18 **Ar** 39.948
Nickel 28 **Ni** 58.693	Copper 29 **Cu** 63.546	Zinc 30 **Zn** 65.39	Gallium 31 **Ga** 69.723	Germanium 32 **Ge** 72.61	Arsenic 33 **As** 74.922	Selenium 34 **Se** 78.96	Bromine 35 **Br** 79.904	Krypton 36 **Kr** 83.80
Palladium 46 **Pd** 106.42	Silver 47 **Ag** 107.868	Cadmium 48 **Cd** 112.411	Indium 49 **In** 114.82	Tin 50 **Sn** 118.710	Antimony 51 **Sb** 121.757	Tellurium 52 **Te** 127.60	Iodine 53 **I** 126.904	Xenon 54 **Xe** 131.290
Platinum 78 **Pt** 195.08	Gold 79 **Au** 196.967	Mercury 80 **Hg** 200.59	Thallium 81 **Tl** 204.383	Lead 82 **Pb** 207.2	Bismuth 83 **Bi** 208.980	Polonium 84 **Po** 208.982	Astatine 85 **At** 209.987	Radon 86 **Rn** 222.018
Ununnilium * 110 **Uun** 269	Unununium * 111 **Uuu** 272	Unumbium * 112 **Uub** 277		Ununquadium * 114 **Uuq** 285		Ununhexium * 116 **Uuh** 289		Ununodium * 118 **Uuo** 293

*** Names not officially assigned. Discovery of elements 114, 116, and 118 recently reported. Further information not yet available.**

Gadolinium 64 **Gd** 157.25	Terbium 65 **Tb** 158.925	Dysprosium 66 **Dy** 162.50	Holmium 67 **Ho** 164.930	Erbium 68 **Er** 167.26	Thulium 69 **Tm** 168.934	Ytterbium 70 **Yb** 173.04	Lutetium 71 **Lu** 174.967
Curium 96 **Cm** 247.070	Berkelium 97 **Bk** 247.070	Californium 98 **Cf** 251.080	Einsteinium 99 **Es** 252.083	Fermium 100 **Fm** 257.095	Mendelevium 101 **Md** 258.099	Nobelium 102 **No** 259.101	Lawrencium 103 **Lr** 260.105

English Glossary

This glossary defines each key term that appears in bold type in the text. It also shows the chapter, section, and page number where you can find the word used.

A

acceleration: rate of change of velocity, which occurs if an object speeds up, changes direction, or slows down. (Chap. 2, Sec. 2, p. 47)

acid: any substance that produces hydrogen ions, H+, in a water solution. (Chap. 25, Sec. 1, p. 766)

acoustics (uh KEW stihks): the study of sound. (Chap. 12, Sec. 4, p. 375)

alcohol: compound, such as ethanol, that is formed when −OH groups replace one or more hydrogen atoms in a hydrocarbon. (Chap. 21, Sec. 3, p. 647)

allotropes: different forms of the same element having different molecular structures. (Chap. 20, Sec. 3, p. 623)

alloy: mixture of a metal with one or more elements that retains the original properties of the metal. (Chap. 22, Sec. 1, p. 672; Chap. 23, Sec. 1, p. 707)

alpha particle: particle with a +2 electrical charge and atomic mass of 4 that is made of two protons and two neutrons and is emitted from a decaying atomic nucleus. (Chap. 9, Sec. 2, p. 263)

alternating current (AC): electric current that reverses its direction regularly and is used to run appliances. (Chap. 8, Sec. 3, p. 244)

amplitude: a measure of the energy carried by a wave. (Chap. 11, Sec. 2, p. 336)

aromatic compound: compound that contains the benzene ring structure and can have a pleasant or unpleasant odor and flavor. (Chap. 21, Sec. 2, p. 645)

atom: the smallest piece of matter. (Chap. 18, Sec. 1, p. 545)

atomic number: number of protons in an atom's nucleus. (Chap. 18, Sec. 2, p. 551)

average atomic mass: weighted-average mass of the mixture of an element's isotopes. (Chap. 18, Sec. 2, p. 553)

average speed: total distance that an object travels divided by the total time it takes to travel that distance. (Chap. 2, Sec. 1, p. 41)

B

balanced chemical equation: chemical equation with the same number of atoms of each element on both sides of the equation. (Chap. 24, Sec. 2, p. 743)

balanced forces forces on a body that are equal in size and opposite in direction and do not change the motion of the body. (Chap. 2, Sec. 3, p. 53)

base: any substance that forms hydroxide ions, OH^-, in a water solution. (Chap. 25, Sec. 1, p. 768)

beta particle: electron with an atomic mass of 0 and a –1 electrical charge that is emitted at high speed from a decaying atomic nucleus. (Chap. 9, Sec. 2, p. 265)

bias: occurs when a scientist's expectations change how the results of an experiment are viewed. (Chap. 1, Sec. 1, p. 10)

binary compound: compound that is composed of two elements. (Chap. 19, Sec. 3, p. 587)

biomass: renewable organic matter from plants and animals, such as wood and animal manure, that can be burned to heat water and produce electricity. (Chap. 10, Sec. 3, p. 310)

boiling point: temperature at which the pressure of the atmosphere is equal to the pressure of a liquid's vapor, and gas molecules can escape the attractive force between the molecules. (Chap. 16, Sec. 1, p. 491)

bubble chamber: a type of tool that uses superheated liquid to detect and monitor the paths of nuclear particles. (Chap. 9, Sec. 3, p. 269)

buffer: solution containing ions that react with added acids or bases and minimize their effects on pH. (Chap. 25, Sec. 2, p. 775)

buoyancy: ability of a fluid to exert an upward force on an object immersed in the fluid. (Chap. 16, Sec. 2, p. 497)

C

carbohydrates: group of biological compounds, such as sugars and starches, with twice as many hydrogen atoms as oxygen atoms. (Chap. 21, Sec. 4, p. 659)

carrier wave: specific electromagnetic wave frequency that a radio station is assigned. (Chap. 13, Sec. 3, p. 403)

catalyst: substance that speeds up a chemical reaction without being permanently changed itself. (Chap. 24, Sec. 4, p. 754)

cathode-ray tube: sealed vacuum tube that uses one or more beams of electrons that strike tiny colored rectangles on a screen and produce full-color images on a TV. (Chap. 13, Sec. 3, p. 406)

centripetal acceleration: acceleration of an object toward the center of a curved or circular path. (Chap. 3, Sec. 2, p. 81)

ceramics: versatile materials with customizable properties; produced by a process in which an object is molded and then heated to high temperatures, increasing its density. (Chap. 22, Sec. 2, p. 678)

chain reaction: ongoing series of fission reactions. (Chap. 9, Sec. 4, p. 274)

charging by contact: process of transferring charge between objects by touching or rubbing. (Chap. 7, Sec. 1, p. 197)

charging by induction: process of transferring charge between objects by bringing a charged object near a neutral object. (Chap. 7, Sec. 1, p. 198)

chemical bond: force that holds atoms together in a compound. (Chap. 19, Sec. 1, p. 578)

chemical change: change of one substance into a new substance. (Chap. 17, Sec. 2, p. 530)

chemical equation: shorthand method to describe chemical reactions using chemical formulas and other symbols. (Chap. 24, Sec. 1, p. 740)

chemical formula: chemical shorthand that uses symbols to tell what elements are in a compound and their ratios. (Chap. 19, Sec. 1, p. 575)

chemical potential energy: energy stored in chemical bonds. (Chap. 4, Sec. 1, p. 103)

chemical property: any characteristic of a substance, such as flammability, that indicates whether it can undergo a certain chemical change. (Chap. 17, Sec. 2, p. 529)

chemical reaction: process in which one or more substances are changed into new substances. (Chap. 24, Sec. 1, p. 738)

chemically stable: describes an atom whose outer energy level is completely filled with all the electrons allowed in that level. (Chap. 19, Sec. 1, p. 576)

circuit: closed conducting loop through which an electric current can flow. (Chap. 7, Sec. 2, p. 203)

cloud chamber: a type of tool that uses water or ethanol vapor to detect alpha and beta particle radiation. (Chap. 9, Sec. 3, p. 268)

cochlea (KAHK lee uh): spiral-shaped, fluid-filled structure in the inner ear that converts sounds waves to nerve impulses. (Chap. 12, Sec. 1, p. 362)

coefficient: number in a chemical equation that represents the number of units of each substance taking part in a chemical reaction. (Chap. 24, Sec. 1, p. 741)

coherent light: light of a single wavelength that travels with its crests and troughs aligned in the same direction. (Chap. 14, Sec. 3, p. 434)

colloid (KAHL oyd): heterogeneous mixture whose particles never settle. (Chap. 17, Sec. 1, p. 522)

composite: mixture of two materials, one of which is embedded in the other. (Chap. 22, Sec. 3, p. 689)

compound: substance formed from two or more elements in which the exact combination and proportion of elements is always the same. (Chap. 17, Sec. 1, p. 520)

compound machine: combination of two or more simple machines. (Chap. 5, Sec. 3, p. 146)

compressional wave: a type of wave where the matter in the medium moves back and forth in the same direction that the wave travels; has compressions and rarefactions. (Chap. 11, Sec. 1, p. 328)

concave lens: diverges light rays to form reduced, upright, virtual images; is thinner in the middle and thicker at the edges and is usually used in combination with other lenses. (Chap. 15, Sec. 2, p. 462)

concave mirror: reflects light from a surface that curves inward and can magnify objects or create beams of light. (Chap. 15, Sec. 1, p. 454)

conduction: transfer of energy through matter by colliding particles; takes place because the particles are in constant motion. (Chap. 6, Sec. 2, p. 164)

conductivity (kahn duk TIHV ut ee): property of metals and alloys that allows them to be good conductors of heat and electricity. (Chap. 22, Sec. 1, p. 673)

conductor: material, such as copper wire, through which an excess of electrons can move easily. (Chap. 7, Sec. 1, p. 196)

constant: in an experiment, a variable that does not change when other variables change. (Chap. 1, Sec. 1, p. 9)

control: standard used for comparison of test results in an experiment. (Chap. 1, Sec. 1, p. 9)

convection: transfer of energy by the motion of heated particles in a fluid. (Chap. 6, Sec. 2, p. 165)

convex lens: converges light rays, is thicker in the middle than at the edges, and can form real or virtual images. (Chap. 15, Sec. 2, p. 460)

convex mirror: reflects light from a surface that curves outward and forms a reduced, upright, virtual image. (Chap. 15, Sec. 1, p. 457)

cornea: transparent covering on the eyeball through which light enters. (Chap. 15, Sec. 2, p. 463)

covalent bond: attraction formed between atoms when they share electrons. (Chap. 19, Sec. 2, p. 583)

crest: highest point of a transverse wave. (Chap. 11, Sec. 2, p. 332)

critical mass: amount of fissionable material required so that each fission reaction produces approximately one more fission reaction. (Chap. 9, Sec. 4, p. 274)

D

decibel (DES uh bel): unit on the scale for sound intensity, abbreviated dB. (Chap. 12, Sec. 2, p. 365)

decomposition reaction: chemical reaction in which one substance breaks down into two or more substances. (Chap. 24, Sec. 3, p. 747)

density: mass per unit volume of a material. (Chap. 1, Sec. 2, p. 19)

deoxyribonucleic (dee AHK sih ri boh noo klay ihk) **acid:** a type of essential biological compound that codes and stores genetic information, controls the production of RNA, and is found in the nuclei of cells. (Chap. 21, Sec. 4, p. 658)

dependent variable: factor that changes as the independent variable changes. (Chap. 1, Sec. 3, p. 6)

derived unit: unit, such as cubic meter (m^3), that is obtained by combining different SI units. (Chap. 1, Sec. 2, p. 19)

diatomic molecule: a molecule that consists of two atoms of the same element. (Chap. 20, Sec. 2, p. 617)

diffraction: describes the bending of waves around a barrier; can also occur when waves pass through a narrow opening. (Chap. 11, Sec. 3, p. 342)

diffusion: spreading of particles throughout a given volume until they are uniformly distributed. (Chap. 16, Sec. 1, p. 491)

direct current (DC): electric current that flows through a wire in only one direction. (Chap. 8, Sec. 3, p. 244)

displacement: distance and direction of an object's change in position from the starting point. (Chap. 2, Sec. 1, p. 39)

dissociation: process in which ions are separated from a crystal and drawn into solution. (Chap. 23, Sec. 4, p. 724)

distance: how far an object moves. (Chap. 2, Sec. 1, p. 39)

distillation: process than can separate two substances in a mixture by evaporating a liquid and recondensing its vapor. (Chap. 17, Sec. 2, p. 529)

doping: process of adding impurities to a semiconductor to increase its conductivity. (Chap. 22, Sec. 2, p. 682)

Doppler effect: change in pitch or frequency that occurs when the source of a sound wave is moving relative to an observer. (Chap. 12, Sec. 2, p. 367)

double-displacement reaction: chemical reaction that produces a precipitate, water, or a gas when two ionic compounds in solution are combined. (Chap. 24, Sec. 3, p. 749)

ductile: ability of metals to be drawn into wires. (Chap. 20, Sec. 1, p. 608)

ductility (duk TIHL uh tee): ability of metals or alloys to be pulled into wires. (Chap. 22, Sec. 1, p. 673)

E

eardrum: tough membrane in the outer ear that is about 0.1 mm thick and passes sound vibrations into the middle ear. (Chap. 12, Sec. 1, p. 361)

echolocation: process in which objects are located by emitting sounds and interpreting sound waves that are reflected back. (Chap. 12, Sec. 4, p. 375)

efficiency: measure of how much of the work put into a machine is changed into work done by a machine. (Chap. 5, Sec. 2, p. 136)

effort force: force exerted on a machine that is used to do work. (Chap. 5, Sec. 2, p. 134)

elastic potential energy: energy stored by things that stretch or twist or compress. (Chap. 4, Sec. 1, p. 103)

electric current: flow of electric charge through a wire or any conductor; measured in amperes (A) in a circuit. (Chap. 7, Sec. 2, p. 203)

electric motor: device that converts electrical energy to mechanical energy to do work; basically has a power supply, a permanent magnet, and an electromagnet that can rotate. (Chap. 8, Sec. 2, p. 237)

electrical power: rate at which electrical energy is converted to another form of energy; expressed in watts (W). (Chap. 7, Sec. 3, p. 212)

electrolyte: compound that breaks apart in water, forming charged particles (ions) that can conduct electricity. (Chap. 23, Sec. 4, p. 723)

electromagnet (ih lek troh MAG nut): temporary magnet made by placing an iron core inside a current-carrying coil of wire and whose strength can be increased by adding more turns to the wire loop or by increasing the amount of current passing through the wire. (Chap. 8, Sec. 2, p. 234)

electromagnetic induction (ih lek troh mag NET ihk • ihn DUK shun): process in which electric current is produced by moving a wire loop through a magnetic field or by moving a magnet through a loop of wire. (Chap. 8, Sec. 3, p. 240)

electromagnetic waves: waves created by vibrating electric charges; can travel through a vacuum or through matter and can have a wide variety of frequencies and wavelengths. (Chap. 13, Sec. 1, p. 390)

electron: negatively charged particles surrounding the center of an atom. (Chap. 18, Sec. 1, p. 545)

electron cloud: area around the nucleus of an atom where the atom's electrons are most likely to be found. (Chap. 18, Sec. 1, p. 549)

electron dot diagram: uses the symbol for an element and dots representing the number of electrons in the element's outer energy level. (Chap. 18, Sec. 3, p. 560)

element: substance with atoms that are all alike. (Chap. 17, Sec. 1, p. 518)

endergonic reaction: chemical reaction; requires energy to proceed. (Chap. 24, Sec. 4, p. 753)

endothermic reaction: chemical reaction that requires heat energy to proceed. (Chap. 24, Sec. 4, p. 753)

exergonic reaction: chemical reaction that releases some form of energy, such as light or heat. (Chap. 24, Sec. 4, p. 752)

exothermic reaction: chemical reaction in which energy is primarily given off in the form of heat. (Chap. 24, Sec. 4, p. 752)

experiment: organized procedure for testing a hypothesis that tests the effect of one thing on another under controlled conditions. (Chap. 1, Sec. 1, p. 8)

F

fluorescent light: light that results when ultraviolet radiation produced inside a fluorescent bulb causes the phosphor coating in-side the bulb to glow. (Chap 14, Sec. 3, p. 431)

focal length: distance from the center of a lens or mirror to the focal point. (Chap. 15, Sec. 1, p. 454)

focal point: a single point on the optical axis of a concave mirror or convex lens where light rays pass through. (Chap. 15, Sec. 1, p. 454)

force: push or pull that one body exerts on another. (Chap. 2, Sec. 3, p. 52)

fossil fuels: nonrenewable energy resources, such as oil, natural gas, and coal, that are formed from the decayed remains of ancient plants and animals; can be burned to supply energy and generate electricity. (Chap. 10, Sec. 1, p. 291)

fractional distillation: the separation of compounds in petroleum. (Chap. 10, Sec. 1, p. 293)

frequency: measures how many wavelengths pass a fixed point each second and is expressed in hertz (Hz). (Chap. 11, Sec. 2, p. 333; Chap. 13, Sec. 1, p. 394)

friction: force that opposes motion between two touching surfaces. (Chap. 3, Sec. 1, p. 70)

G

galvanometer (gal vuh NAHM ut ur): instrument that uses an electromagnet to measure electric current. (Chap. 8, Sec. 2, p. 236)

gamma ray: electromagnetic wave with no mass and no charge that travels at the speed of light and is usually emitted with alpha or beta particles. (Chap. 9, Sec. 2, p. 265; Chap. 13, Sec. 2, p. 401)

Geiger counter: device that measures radioactivity by producing an electric current when radiation is present; emits a clicking sound or flashing light. (Chap. 9, Sec. 3, p. 270)

generator: device that converts mechanical energy to electrical energy by rotating a wire coil through the magnetic field of a permanent magnet. (Chap. 8, Sec. 3, p. 240)

geothermal energy: thermal energy contained in hot magma; can be converted by a power plant into electrical energy. (Chap. 10, Sec. 3, p. 309)

Global Positioning System (GPS): uses satellites, ground monitoring systems, and receivers to help people determine their exact location at or above Earth's surface. (Chap. 13, Sec. 3, p. 409)

graph: visual display of information or data that can provide a quick way to communicate a lot of information clearly in a small amount of space. (Chap. 1, Sec. 3, p. 22)

gravitational potential energy: energy stored by things attracted to each other by the force of gravity. (Chap. 4, Sec. 1, p. 104)

group: vertical column in the periodic table. (Chap. 18, Sec. 3, p. 558)

H

half-life: amount of time it takes for half the nuclei in a sample of a radioactive isotope to decay. (Chap. 9, Sec. 2, p. 266)
heat engine: device that converts thermal energy produced by combustion into mechanical energy. (Chap. 6, Sec. 3, p. 176)
heat mover: device, such as a refrigerator, that removes thermal energy from one place and transfers it to another place at a different temperature. (Chap. 6, Sec. 3, p. 177)
heat of fusion: amount of energy required to change a substance from the solid phase to the liquid phase. (Chap. 16, Sec. 1, p. 490)
heat of vaporization: amount of energy required for liquid particles to escape the attractive forces within the liquid or the energy required to change from a liquid to a gas. (Chap. 16, Sec. 1, p. 490)
heat: thermal energy that flows from a warmer material to a cooler material; is measured in joules (J). (Chap. 6, Sec. 1, p. 160)
heterogeneous (het uh ruh JEE nee us) **mixture:** mixture, such as concrete or a dry soup mix, in which different materials are unevenly distributed and are easily identified. (Chap. 17, Sec. 1, p. 521)
holography: technique that produces a complete photographic image of a three-dimensional object. (Chap. 14, Sec. 4, p. 437)
homogeneous (hoh moh JEE nee us) **mixture:** solid, liquid, or gas that contains two or more substances blended evenly throughout. (Chap. 17, Sec. 1, p. 522)
hydrate: compound that has water chemically attached to its ions and written into its chemical formula. (Chap. 19, Sec. 3, p. 591)
hydrocarbon: saturated or unsaturated compound containing only carbon and hydrogen atoms. (Chap. 21, Sec. 1, p. 641)
hydroelectricity: electricity produced from the energy of moving water. (Chap. 10, Sec. 3, p. 307)
hydronium ions (hi DROH nee um • I ahnz): H_3O^+ ions, which form when an acid dissolves in water and H^+ ions interact with water. (Chap. 25, Sec. 1, p. 766)
hypothesis: educated guess using what you know and what you observe. (Chap. 1, Sec. 1, p. 8)

I

incandescent light: light produced by heating a piece of metal, usually tungsten, until it glows. (Chap. 14, Sec. 3, p. 430)
inclined plane: simple machine that consists of a sloping surface, such as a ramp, that reduces the amount of force needed to lift something by increasing the distance over which the force is applied. (Chap. 5, Sec. 3, p. 144)
incoherent light: light that contains more than one wavelength and does not travel with its crests and troughs aligned in the same direction. (Chap. 14, Sec. 3, p. 434)
independent variable: factor that, as it changes, affects the measure of another variable. (Chap. 1, Sec. 3, p. 6)
index of refraction: property of a material indicating how much light slows down when traveling in the material. (Chap. 14, Sec. 1, p. 422)
indicator: organic compound that changes color in acids and bases. (Chap. 25, Sec. 1, p. 766)
inertia (ihn UR shuh)**:** resistance of an object to a change in its motion. (Chap. 2, Sec. 3, p. 54)
infrared wave: electromagnetic wave that has a frequency slightly lower than visible light, transmits thermal energy, and is used in television remote controls and bar code scanners. (Chap. 13, Sec. 2, p. 398)
inhibitor: substance that slows down a chemical reaction or prevents it from occurring by combining with a reactant. (Chap. 24, Sec. 4, p. 754)

instantaneous speed: speed of an object at a given point in time, which is constant for an object moving with constant speed and is different at each point in time for an object that is slowing down or speeding up. (Chap. 2, Sec. 1, p. 41)

insulator: material that doesn't allow electrons to move through it easily. (Chap. 7, Sec. 1, p. 197)

insulators: materials, such as fleece or fiberglass, that do not allow heat to move easily through them. (Chap. 6, Sec. 2, p. 169)

integrated circuit: tiny chip of semiconductor material that can contain millions of transistors, diodes, and other components. (Chap. 22, Sec. 2, p. 682)

intensity: amount of energy a sound wave carries, which can be measured in decibels (dB). (Chap. 12, Sec. 2, p. 364)

interference: occurs when two or more waves overlap and combine to form a new wave; can form a larger wave (constructive interference) or a smaller wave (destructive interference). (Chap. 11, Sec. 3, p. 344)

internal combustion engine: a type of heat engine that burns fuel inside the engine. (Chap. 6, Sec. 3, p. 176)

ion: charged particle that has either more or fewer electrons than protons. (Chap. 19, Sec. 2, p. 580)

ionic bond: attraction formed between oppositely charged ions in an ionic compound. (Chap. 19, Sec. 2, p. 582)

ionization: process in which electrolytes dissolve in water and separate into charged particles. (Chap. 23, Sec. 4, p. 723)

isomers: compounds with identical chemical formulas but different molecular structures and shapes, which can affect physical properties such as melting points. (Chap. 21, Sec. 1, p. 643)

isotopes: atoms of the same element that have different numbers of neutrons. (Chap. 18, Sec. 2, p. 552)

J

joule (JEWL)**:** SI unit of energy. (Chap. 4, Sec. 1, p. 102)

K

kilowatt-hour: unit of electrical energy, which is 1000 W of power used for one hour. (Chap. 7, Sec. 3, p. 215)

kinetic energy: energy in the form of motion; depends on the mass and velocity of the object. (Chap. 4, Sec. 1, p. 102)

kinetic theory: explanation of the behavior of molecules in matter; states that all matter is made of constantly moving particles that collide without losing energy. (Chap. 16, Sec. 1, p. 488)

L

law of conservation of charge: states that charge can be transferred from one object to another but cannot be created or destroyed. (Chap. 7, Sec. 1, p. 195)

law of conservation of energy: states that energy can never be created or destroyed. (Chap. 4, Sec. 2, p. 111)

law of conservation of mass: states that the mass of all substances that are present before a chemical change equals the mass of all the substances that are remaining after the change. (Chap. 17, Sec. 2, p. 533)

law of gravitation: states that any two masses exert an attractive force on each other, the amount of which depends on the mass of the two objects and the distance between them. (Chap. 3, Sec. 2, p. 75)

lever: simple machine made from a bar that is free to pivot about a fixed point. (Chap. 5, Sec. 3, p. 138)

lipids: group of biological compounds that contains the same elements as carbohydrates but in different arrangements and combinations, and includes saturated and unsaturated fats and oils. (Chap. 21, Sec. 4, p. 660)

loudness: describes how humans perceive sound intensity. (Chap. 12, Sec. 2, p. 365)

luster: property of metals and alloys that describes having a shiny appearance or reflecting light. (Chap. 22, Sec. 1, p. 673)

M

machine: device that makes doing work easier by increasing the force applied to an object, by changing the direction of an applied force, or by increasing the distance over which a force can be applied. (Chap. 5, Sec. 2, p. 133)

magnetic domain: group of atoms having aligned magnetic poles. (Chap. 8, Sec. 1, p. 231)

magnetic pole: region where a magnet's magnetic force is strongest; like poles repel and opposite poles attract. (Chap. 8, Sec. 1, p. 227)

magnetism: the properties and interactions of magnets. (Chap. 8, Sec. 1, p. 226)

malleability (mal yuh BIHL yt ee)**:** ability of metals and alloys to be rolled into thin sheets or hammered. (Chap. 22, Sec. 1, p. 673)

malleable (MAH lee uh bul): ability of metals to be hammered or rolled into thin sheets. (Chap. 20, Sec. 1, p. 608)

mass: amount of matter in an object. (Chap. 1, Sec. 2, p. 19)

mass number: sum of the number of protons and neutrons in an atom's nucleus. (Chap. 18, Sec. 2, p. 551)

mechanical advantage (MA): number of times a machine multiplies the effort force applied to it. (Chap. 5, Sec. 2, p. 136)

mechanical energy: sum of potential and kinetic energy in a system. (Chap. 4, Sec. 2, p. 108)

medium: any material—a solid, liquid, gas, or combination of these—that a wave transfers energy through. (Chap. 11, Sec. 1, p. 327)

melting point: temperature at which a solid begins to liquefy. (Chap. 16, Sec. 1, p. 490)

metal: element that typically is a hard, shiny solid, is malleable, and is a good conductor of heat and electricity. (Chap. 20, Sec. 1, p. 608)

metallic bonding: occurs because electrons move freely among a metal's positively charged ions and explains properties such as ductility and the ability to conduct electricity. (Chap. 20, Sec. 1, p. 609)

metalloid: element that shares some properties with metals and some with nonmetals. (Chap. 20, Sec. 3, p. 622)

microscope: uses convex lenses to magnify small, close objects. (Chap. 15, Sec. 3, p. 471)

microwave: radio wave with a wavelength of less than 1 m. (Chap. 13, Sec. 2, p. 397)

mirage: image of a distant object that results when air at ground level is much warmer or cooler than the air layers above it, which makes the image refract and appear at a different location from where it actually is. (Chap. 14, Sec. 1, p. 424)

model: can be used to represent an idea, object, or event that is too big, too small, too complex, or too dangerous to observe or test directly. (Chap. 1, Sec. 1, p. 11)

momentum: property that a moving object has because of its mass and velocity. (Chap. 3, Sec. 3, p. 86)

monomer: small molecule that forms a link in the polymer chain and can be made to combine with itself repeatedly. (Chap. 21, Sec. 3, p. 653; Chap. 22, Sec. 3, p. 685)

music: sound created using specific pitches and sound qualities used in a set pattern. (Chap. 12, Sec. 3, p. 363)

N

net force: sum of the forces that are acting on an object. (Chap. 2, Sec. 3, p. 53)

neutralization: chemical reaction that occurs when the H_3O^+ ions from an acid react with the OH^- ions from a base to produce water molecules. (Chap. 25, Sec. 3, p. 777)

neutron: neutral particle, composed of quarks, inside the nucleus of an atom. (Chap. 18, Sec. 1, p. 545)

Newton's second law of motion: states that a net force acting on an object causes the object to accelerate in the direction of the net force. (Chap. 3, Sec. 1, p. 69)

Newton's third law of motion: describes action-reaction pairs—to every action force there is an equal and opposite reaction force. (Chap. 3, Sec. 3, p. 83)

nonelectrolyte: substance that does not ionize in water and cannot conduct electricity. (Chap. 23, Sec. 4, p. 723)

nonmetal: element that usually is a gas or brittle solid at room temperature, is not malleable or ductile, is a poor conductor of heat and electricity, and typically is not shiny. (Chap. 20, Sec. 2, p. 616)

nonpolar: material that has no separated positive and negative areas, does not attract water molecules, and does not dissolve easily in water. (Chap. 23, Sec. 2, p. 713)

nonpolar molecule: molecule that shares electrons equally and does not have oppositely charged ends. (Chap. 19, Sec. 2, p. 586)

nonrenewable resources: any natural resources, such as all fossil fuels, that cannot be replaced by natural processes as quickly as they are used. (Chap. 10, Sec. 1, p. 297)

nuclear fission: process of splitting a large atomic nucleus into two nuclei with smaller masses. (Chap. 9, Sec. 4, p. 273)

nuclear fusion: process of fusing together two atomic nuclei with low masses to form one nucleus with a larger mass. (Chap. 9, Sec. 4, p. 275)

nuclear reactor: uses energy from a controlled nuclear chain reaction to generate electricity. (Chap. 10, Sec. 2, p. 298)

nuclear waste: any radioactive by-product that results when radioactive materials are used; must be stored safely away from human activity. (Chap. 10, Sec. 2, p. 302)

nucleic acids: essential organic polymers that control the activities and reproduction of cells. (Chap. 21, Sec. 4, p. 658)

nucleotides: complex, organic molecules that make up RNA and DNA; contain an organic base, a phosphoric acid unit, and a sugar. (Chap. 21, Sec. 4, p. 658)

nucleus: positively charged center of an atom that contains protons and neutrons and is surrounded by a cloud of electrons. (Chap. 18, Sec. 1, p. 545)

O

Ohm's law: states that the current in a circuit equals the voltage difference divided by the resistance. (Chap. 7, Sec. 2, p. 207)

opaque (oh PAYK): material that absorbs or reflects all light. (Chap. 14, Sec. 1, p. 420)

optical axis: imaginary straight line on a concave mirror or convex lens that contains the focal point. (Chap. 15, Sec. 1, p. 454)

organic compounds: large number of compounds containing the element carbon. (Chap. 21, Sec. 1, p. 640)

overtone: vibration whose frequency is a multiple of the fundamental frequency, or main tone. (Chap. 12, Sec. 3, p. 364)

oxidation number: positive or negative number that indicates how many electrons an atom has gained, lost, or shared to become stable. (Chap. 19, Sec. 3, p. 587)

P

parallel circuit: circuit in which electric current has more than one path to follow. (Chap. 7, Sec. 3, p. 210)

pascal: SI unit of pressure. (Chap. 16, Sec. 3, p. 502)

period: horizontal row in the periodic table. (Chap. 18, Sec. 3, p. 561)

periodic table: organized list of all known elements that are arranged according to repeated changes in properties. (Chap. 18, Sec. 3, p. 554)

petroleum: crude oil—a highly flammable fossil fuel formed from decayed remains of ancient organisms; contains hydrocarbons and can be refined into fuels and used to make plastics. (Chap. 10, Sec. 1, p. 293)

pH: a measure of the concentration of hydronium ions in a solution using a scale ranging from 0 to 14, with 0 being the most acidic and 14 being the most basic. (Chap. 25, Sec. 2, p. 774)

photon: a type of particle that can describe light. (Chap. 13, Sec. 1, p. 395)

photovoltaic cell: device that converts solar energy into electricity; also called a solar cell. (Chap. 10, Sec. 3, p. 305)

physical change: any change in size, shape, or state of matter in which the identity of the substance remains the same. (Chap. 17, Sec. 2, p. 528)

physical property: any characteristic of a material, such as size or shape, that you can observe or attempt to observe without changing the identity of the material. (Chap. 17, Sec. 2, p. 526)

pigment: colored material that absorbs some colors and reflects others. (Chap. 14, Sec. 2, p. 428)

pitch: how high or low a sound appears to be, which is related to the frequency of the sound waves. (Chap. 12, Sec. 2, p. 366)

plane mirror: flat, smooth mirror that reflects light to form upright, life-sized, virtual images. (Chap. 15, Sec. 1, p. 453)

plasma: high-temperature gas with an overall neutral charge that is the most common state of matter in the universe. (Chap. 16, Sec. 1, p. 492)

polar molecule: molecule with a slightly positive end and a slightly negative end as a result of electrons being shared unequally. (Chap. 19, Sec. 2, p. 586)

polarized light: light in which transverse waves vibrate in only one direction. (Chap. 14, Sec. 4, p. 436)

polyatomic ion: positively or negatively charged, covalently bonded group of atoms. (Chap. 19, Sec. 3, p. 591)

polyethylene: polymer formed from a chain containing many ethylene units; often used in plastic bags and plastic bottles. (Chap. 21, Sec. 3, p. 653)

polymer: new, huge molecule made up of many monomers linked together to form a long chain that can be spun into fibers and used for plastics. (Chap. 21, Sec. 3, p. 653; Chap. 22, Sec. 3, p. 685)

potential energy: stored energy due to position; can be converted to kinetic energy when something acts to release it. (Chap. 4, Sec. 1, p. 103)

power: amount of work done, or the amount of energy transferred, in a certain amount of time; measured in watts (W). (Chap. 5, Sec. 1, p. 129)

precipitate: insoluble compound that comes out of solution during a double-displacement reaction. (Chap. 24, Sec. 3, p. 749)

pressure: amount of force exerted per unit area; SI unit is the pascal (Pa). (Chap. 16, Sec. 3, p. 502)

product: in a chemical reaction, the new substance that is formed. (Chap. 24, Sec. 1, p. 738)

projectile: an object that is thrown or shot through the air. (Chap. 3, Sec. 2, p. 79)

proteins: large, complex, biological polymers formed from amino acids; make up many body tissues such as muscles, tendons, hair, and fingernails. (Chap. 21, Sec. 4, p. 656)

proton: positively charged particle, composed of quarks, inside the nucleus of an atom. (Chap. 18, Sec. 1, p. 545)

pulley: simple machine that consists of a grooved wheel with a rope, chain, or cable that runs along a groove, changes the direction of the effort force, and can be either fixed or movable. (Chap. 5, Sec. 3, p. 141)

Q

quality: describes the differences among sounds having the same pitch and loudness. (Chap. 12, Sec. 3, p. 370)

quarks: particles of matter that make up protons and neutrons. (Chap. 18, Sec. 1, p. 545)

R

radiant energy: energy carried by an electromagnetic wave. (Chap. 13, Sec. 1, p. 393)

radiation: transfer of energy in the form of electromagnetic waves. (Chap. 6, Sec. 2, p. 166)

radiator: device with a large surface area that warms the surrounding air by conduction. (Chap. 6, Sec. 3, p. 173)

radio wave: low-frequency, electromagnetic wave with a wavelength from less than 1 cm to about 1,000 m that can carry the signal from a radio station to a radio. (Chap. 13, Sec. 2, p. 396)

radioactive element: element, such as radium, whose nucleus breaks down and emits particles and energy. (Chap. 20, Sec. 1, p. 610)

radioactivity: process of nuclear decay that takes place when the strong force is not able to hold unstable nuclei together permanently. (Chap. 9, Sec. 1, p. 260)

rarefaction (rar uh FAK shun): the least dense region of a compressional wave. (Chap. 11, Sec. 2, p. 332)

reactant: in a chemical reaction, the substance that reacts. (Chap. 24, Sec. 1, p. 738)

real image: upside-down, optical image formed when light rays pass through an object. (Chap. 15, Sec. 1, p. 455)

reflecting telescope: uses a concave mirror, a plane mirror, and a convex lens to collect and focus light from distant objects. (Chap. 15, Sec. 3, p. 469)

refracting telescope: uses two convex lenses to gather and focus light from distant objects. (Chap. 15, Sec. 3, p. 469)

refraction: bending of a wave as it changes speed, moving from one medium to another. (Chap. 11, Sec. 3, p. 340)

renewable resource: energy source, such as solar energy, that is replaced almost as quickly as it is used. (Chap. 10, Sec. 3, p. 305)

resistance: tendency for a material to oppose electron flow and change electrical energy into thermal energy and light; measured in ohms. (Chap. 7, Sec. 2, p. 205)

resistance force: force applied by a machine to overcome resistance. (Chap. 5, Sec. 2, p. 134)

resonance (RE zun unts)**:** ability of an object to vibrate by absorbing energy at its natural frequency. (Chap. 11, Sec. 3, p. 347)

resonator (RE zen ay tur)**:** hollow, air-filled chamber of a stringed instrument that amplifies sound when its air vibrates. (Chap. 12, Sec. 3, p. 371)

retina: inner lining of the eye that has cells that convert light images into electrical signals. (Chap. 15, Sec. 2, p. 463)

S

salt: compound formed when negative ions from an acid combine with positive ions from a base. (Chap. 25, Sec. 3, p. 777)

saturated hydrocarbon: compound, such as propane or methane, that contains only single bonds between carbon atoms. (Chap. 21, Sec. 1, p. 642)

saturated solution: any solution that contains all the solute it can hold at a given temperature. (Chap. 23, Sec. 3, p. 720)

scientific law: statement about how things work in nature that seems to be true all the time. (Chap. 1, Sec. 1, p. 12)

scientific method: organized set of investigation procedures that can include stating a problem, forming a hypotheses, researching and gathering information, testing a hypothesis, analyzing data, and drawing conclusions. (Chap. 1, Sec. 1, p. 8)

screw: simple machine that consists of an inclined plane wrapped in a spiral around a cylindrical post. (Chap. 5, Sec. 3, p. 145)

semiconductors: elements (silicon and germanium) that will conduct an electric current under certain conditions. (Chap. 20, Sec. 3, p. 623)

series circuit: circuit in which electric current has only one path to follow. (Chap. 7, Sec. 3, p. 209)

SI: International System of Units—the improved, universally accepted version of the metric system that is based on multiples of ten and includes the meter (m), liter (L), and kilogram (kg). (Chap. 1, Sec. 2, p. 15)

simple machine: machine that does work with only one movement; includes the lever, pulley, wheel and axle, inclined plane, screw, and wedge. (Chap. 5, Sec. 3, p. 138)

single-displacement reaction: chemical reaction in which one element replaces another element in a compound. (Chap. 24, Sec. 3, p. 747)

soaps: organic salts with nonpolar, hydrocarbon ends that interact with oils and dirt and polar ends that helps them dissolve in water. (Chap. 25, Sec. 3, p. 782)

solar collector: solar heating system device that absorbs radiant energy from the Sun. (Chap. 6, Sec. 3, p. 175)

solar energy: energy from the Sun that is free, renewable, and can be used to heat homes and buildings. (Chap. 6, Sec. 3, p. 174)

solubility: maximum amount of a solute that can be dissolved in a given amount of solvent at a given temperature. (Chap. 23, Sec. 3, p. 718)

solute: in a solution, the substance being dissolved. (Chap. 23, Sec. 1, p. 707)

solution: mixture that appears to have the same composition, color, density, and taste throughout and is mixed at the atomic or molecular level. (Chap. 17, Sec. 1, p. 522; Chap. 23, Sec. 1, p. 706)

solvent: in a solution, the substance in which the solute is dissolved. (Chap. 23, Sec. 1, p. 707)

sonar: system that uses the reflection of sound waves to find objects that are underwater. (Chap. 12, Sec. 4, p. 377)

specific heat: amount of energy needed to raise the temperature of 1 kg of a material 1 K (Chap. 6, Sec. 1, p. 161)

speed: distance an object travels per unit of time, which can be calculated by $v = d/t$, where v = speed, d = distance, and t equals time. (Chap. 2, Sec. 1, p. 39)

standard: exact, agreed-upon quantity used for comparison. (Chap. 1, Sec. 2, p. 14)

standing wave: a type of wave that forms when waves of equal wavelength and amplitude, but traveling in opposite directions, continuously interfere with each other; has points called nodes that do not move. (Chap. 11, Sec. 3, p. 346)

static electricity: electricity generated when more of one type of charge is on an object. (Chap. 7, Sec. 1, p. 194)

strong acid: any acid that ionizes almost completely in solution. (Chap. 25, Sec. 2, p. 772)

strong base: any base that ionizes completely in solution. (Chap. 25, Sec. 2, p. 773)

strong force: force that acts between protons and neutrons in an atomic nucleus and keeps them together. (Chap. 9, Sec. 1, p. 259)

substance: element or compound that cannot be broken down into simpler components and maintain the properties of the original substance. (Chap. 17, Sec. 1, p. 518)

substituted hydrocarbon: hydrocarbon with one or more of its hydrogen atoms replaced by atoms or groups of other elements. (Chap. 21, Sec. 2, p. 647)

supersaturated solution: any solution that contains more solute than a saturated solution at the same temperature. (Chap. 23, Sec. 3, p. 721)

suspension: heterogeneous mixture containing a liquid in which visible particles settle. (Chap. 17, Sec. 1, p. 524)

synthesis reaction: chemical reaction in which two or more substances combine to form a different substance. (Chap. 24, Sec. 3, p. 746)

synthetic: describes polymers, such as plastics, adhesives, and surface coatings, that are made from hydrocarbons. (Chap. 22, Sec. 3, p. 685)

T

technology: application of science to help people. (Chap. 1, Sec. 1, p. 13)

temperature: a measure of the average kinetic energy of all the particles in an object. (Chap. 6, Sec. 1, p. 159)

theory: explanation of things or events that is based on knowledge gained from many observations and experiments. (Chap. 1, Sec. 1, p. 12)

thermal energy: total energy, including kinetic and potential energy, of the particles that make up a material; is transferred by conduction, convection, and radiation. (Chap. 6, Sec. 1, p. 159)

thermal expansion: increase in the size of a substance that results from the separation of its molecules when the temperature is increased. (Chap. 16, Sec. 1, p. 493)

titration (ti TRAY shun)**:** process in which a solution of known concentration is used to determine the concentration of another solution. (Chap. 25, Sec. 3, p. 780)

total internal reflection: occurs when light strikes a surface between two materials and completely reflects back into the first material. (Chap. 14, Sec. 4, p. 438)

tracer: a radioisotope that is used to find or keep track of molecules in an organism. (Chap. 9, Sec. 4, p. 276)

transceiver: transmits one radio signal and receives another radio signal from a base unit, allowing a cordless phone user to talk and listen at the same time. (Chap. 13, Sec. 3, p. 407)

transformer: device that increases or decreases alternating current generated by a power plant so that it can enter homes safely. (Chap. 8, Sec. 3, p. 244)

transition elements: elements in Groups 3 through 12 of the periodic table, occur in nature as uncombined elements, and include the iron triad and coinage metals. (Chap. 20, Sec. 1, p. 612)

translucent (trans LEWS unt)**:** material that allows some light to pass through but not enough to see objects clearly through it. (Chap. 14, Sec. 1, p. 420)

transmutation: process of changing one element to another through radioactive decay. (Chap. 9, Sec. 2, p. 264)

transparent: material that transmits almost all the light striking it so that objects can be seen clearly through it. (Chap. 14, Sec. 1, p. 420)

transuranium element: elements having more than 92 protons. (Chap. 20, Sec. 3, p. 627)

transverse wave: a type of wave, such as a water wave, where the matter in the medium moves back and forth at right angles to the direction that the wave travels; has crests and troughs. (Chap. 11, Sec. 1, p. 328)

trough: lowest point of a transverse wave. (Chap. 11, Sec. 2, p. 332)

turbine: large wheel that rotates when pushed by steam, wind, or water and that provides mechanical energy to a generator. (Chap. 8, Sec. 3, p. 242)

Tyndall effect: scattering of a light beam as it passes through a colloid. (Chap. 17, Sec. 1, p. 523)

U

ultrasonic: sound waves with frequencies above 20,000 Hz. (Chap. 12, Sec. 2, p. 366)

ultraviolet wave: electromagnetic wave with frequencies slightly higher than visible light that can have useful and harmful effects. (Chap. 13, Sec. 2, p. 399)

unsaturated hydrocarbon: compound, such as ethene or ethyne, that contains at least one double or triple bond between carbon atoms. (Chap. 21, Sec. 1, p. 644)

unsaturated solution: any solution that can dissolve more solute at a given temperature. (Chap. 23, Sec. 3, p. 721)

V

variable: factor that cacn cause a change in the results of an experiment. (Chap. 1, Sec. 1, p. 9)

velocity: describes the speed and direction of a moving object. (Chap. 2, Sec. 1, p. 44)

virtual image: upright, reflected image that is perceived by your brain even though no light rays pass through the image. (Chap. 15, Sec. 1, p. 454)

viscosity: a fluid's resistance to flow. (Chap. 16, Sec. 2, p. 501)

visible light: electromagnetic waves with wavelengths 390 billionths to 770 billionths of a meter that can be seen by human eyes. (Chap. 13, Sec. 2, p. 399)

voltage difference: push that causes electrical charges to flow through a conductor; measured in volts (V). (Chap. 7, Sec. 2, p. 202)

volume: amount of space occupied by an object. (Chap. 1, Sec. 2, p. 18)

W

wave: a rhythmic disturbance that transfers energy through matter or space; exists only as long as it has energy to carry. (Chap. 11, Sec. 1, p. 326)

wavelength: distance between one point on a wave and the nearest point just like it on the following wave; as frequency increases, wavelength always decreases. (Chap. 11, Sec. 2, p. 333)

weak acid: any acid that only partly ionizes in solution. (Chap. 25, Sec. 2, p. 772)

weak base: any base that does not ionize completely in solution. (Chap. 25, Sec. 2, p. 773)

wedge: simple machine that consists of an inclined plane with one or two sloping sides. (Chap. 5, Sec. 3, p. 145)

weight: gravitational force exerted on an object by Earth. (Chap. 3, Sec. 2, p. 77)

wheel and axle: simple machine that consists of two different-sized wheels that rotate together. (Chap. 5, Sec. 3, p. 143)

work: transfer of energy that occurs when a force makes an object move; measured in joules. (Chap. 5, Sec. 1, p. 126)

X

X ray: ultrahigh-frequency, energetic electromagnetic wave that can travel through matter and is often used for medical imaging. (Chap. 13, Sec. 2, p. 401)

Spanish Glossary

Este glossario define cada término clave que aparece en negrillas en el texto. También muestra el capítulo y el número de página en donde se usa dicho término.

A

acceleration / aceleración: tasa de cambio de la velocidad, la cual ocurre si un objeto acelera, cambia de dirección o decelera. (Cap. 2, Sec. 2, pág. 47)

acid / ácido: toda sustancia que produce iones hidrógeno, H+, en una solución acuosa. (Cap. 25, Sec. 1, pág. 766)

acoustics / acústica: estudio del sonido. (Cap. 12, Sec. 4, pág. 375)

alcohol / alcohol: compuesto como el etanol, que se forma cuando los grupos –OH reemplazan uno o más átomos de hidrógeno en un hidrocarburo. (Cap. 21, Sec. 3, pág. 647)

allotropes / formas alotrópicas: formas diferentes del mismo elemento que poseen distintas estructuras moleculares. (Cap. 20, Sec. 3, pág. 623)

alloy / aleación: mezcla de un metal con uno o más elementos, la cual retiene las propiedades originales del metal. (Cap. 22, Sec. 1, pág. 672; Cap. 23, Sec. 1, pág. 707)

alpha particle / partícula alfa: partícula con una carga eléctrica de +2 y una masa atómica de 4 compuesta por dos protones y dos neutrones y que se emite desde un núcleo atómico en desintegración. (Cap. 9, Sec. 2, pág. 263)

alternating current (AC) / corriente alterna (CA): corriente eléctrica que invierte su dirección regularmente y que se usa en el funcionamiento de electrodomésticos. (Cap. 8, Sec. 3, pág. 244)

amplitude / amplitud: medida de la energía que transporta una onda. (Cap. 11, Sec. 2, pág. 336)

aromatic compound / compuesto aromático: compuesto que contiene la estructura de anillo bencénico y que puede tener un olor y sabor agradables o desagradables. (Cap. 21, Sec. 2, pág. 645)

atom / átomo: la parte más pequeña de la materia. (Cap. 18, Sec. 1, pág. 545)

atomic number / número atómico: número de protones en el núcleo de un átomo. (Cap. 18, Sec. 2, pág. 551)

average atomic mass / masa atómica promedio: masa media ponderada de la mezcla de los isótopos de un elemento. (Cap. 18, Sec. 2, pág. 553)

average speed / rapidez promedio: distancia total que viaja un objeto dividida entre el tiempo total que le lleva viajar tal distancia. (Cap. 2, Sec. 1, pág. 41)

B

balanced chemical equation / ecuación química equilibrada: ecuación química que posee el mismo número de átomos de cada elemento en ambos lados de la ecuación. (Cap. 24, Sec. 2, pág. 743)

balanced forces / fuerzas equilibradas: fuerzas sobre un cuerpo que son iguales en tamaño, pero opuestas en dirección y que no alteran el movimiento del cuerpo. (Cap. 2, Sec. 3, pág. 53)

base / base: toda sustancia que forma iones hidróxido, OH^-, en una solución acuosa. (Cap. 25, Sec. 1, pág. (768)

beta particle / partícula beta: electrón con una masa atómica de 0 y una carga eléctrica de –1 que se emite a gran velocidad desde un núcleo atómico en desintegración. (Cap. 9, Sec. 2, pág. 265)

bias / sesgo: se presenta cuando las expectativas de un científico cambian el modo en que se enfocan los resultados de un experimento. (Cap. 1, Sec. 1, pág. 10)

Spanish Glossary

binary compound / compuesto binario: compuesto formado por dos elementos. (Cap. 19, Sec. 3, pág. 587)
biomass / biomasa: materia orgánica renovable proveniente de plantas y animales, como por ejemplo, el abono vegetal y animal, que se puede quemar para calentar agua y producir electricidad. (Cap. 10, Sec. 3, pág. 310)
boiling point / punto de ebullición: temperatura a la cual la presión de la atmósfera es igual a la presión del vapor de un líquido, y las moléculas gaseosas pueden escapar de la fuerza de atracción entre las moléculas. (Cap. 16, Sec. 1, pág. 491)
bubble chamber / cámara de burbujas: tipo de instrumento que utiliza un líquido supercalentado con el fin de detectar y monitorear las trayectorias de partículas nucleares. (Cap. 9, Sec. 3, pág. 269)
buffer / tampón: solución que contiene iones que reaccionan con ácidos o bases que se le añaden y minimiza sus efectos sobre el pH. (Cap. 25, Sec. 2, pág. 775)
buoyancy / flotabilidad: capacidad que tiene un líquido de ejercer una fuerza ascendente sobre un cuerpo inmerso en tal líquido. (Cap. 16, Sec. 2, pág. 497)

C

carbohydrates / carbohidratos: grupo de compuestos biológicos que poseen el doble de átomos de hidrógeno que de oxígeno, por ejemplo, los azúcares y almidones. (Cap. 21, Sec. 4, pág. 659)
carrier wave / onda portadora: frecuencia de onda electromagnética específica que se le asigna a una radioemisora. (Cap. 13, Sec. 3, pág. 403)
catalyst / catalizador: sustancia que acelera una reacción química sin cambiar ella misma permanentemente. (Cap. 24, Sec. 4, pág. 754)
cathode-ray tube / tubo de rayos catódicos: tubo sellado al vacío que utiliza uno o más haces de electrones que dirigen e impactan diminutos rectángulos coloreados sobre una pantalla y producen imágenes a todo color en un televisor. (Cap. 13, Sec. 3, pág. 406)
centripetal acceleration / aceleración centrípeta: aceleración de un cuerpo hacia el centro de una trayectoria curva o circular. (Cap. 3 Sec. 2, pág. 81)
ceramics / cerámica: materiales versátiles cuyas propiedades son adaptables; se producen mediante un proceso en el cual un objeto se moldea y luego se calienta a altas temperaturas, aumentando su densidad. (Cap. 22, Sec. 2, pág. 678)
chain reaction / reacción en cadena: serie progresiva de reacciones de fisión nuclear. (Cap. 9, Sec. 4, pág. 274)
charging by contact / cargar por contacto: proceso de transferir cargas entre objetos al tocarlos o frotarlos. (Cap. 7, Sec. 1, pág. 197)
charging by induction / cargar por inducción: proceso de transferir cargas entre objetos al acercar un objeto con carga a un objeto neutro. (Cap. 7, Sec. 1, pág. 198)
chemical bond / enlace químico: fuerza que mantiene unidos a los átomos de un compuesto. (Cap. 19, Sec. 1, pág. 578)
chemical change / cambio químico: cambio de una sustancia a una nueva sustancia. (Cap. 17, Sec. 2, pág. 530)
chemical equation / ecuación química: método abreviado de describir reacciones químicas usando fórmulas químicas y otros símbolos. (Cap. 24, Sec. 1, pág. 740)
chemical formula / fórmula química: abreviación química que usa símbolos para indicar los elementos presentes en un compuesto y sus razones. (Cap. 19, Sec. 1, pág. 575)
chemical potential energy / energía potencial química: energía almacenada en enlaces químicos. (Cap. 4, Sec. 1, pág. 103)

chemical property / propiedad química: cualquier característica de una sustancia, como la combustibilidad, que indica si puede sufrir cierto cambio químico. (Cap. 17, Sec. 2, pág. 529)

chemical reaction / reacción química: proceso en el cual una o más sustancias se transforman en nuevas sustancias. (Cap. 24, Sec. 1, pág. 738)

chemically stable / químicamente estable: describe un átomo cuyo nivel de energía externo está completamente lleno con todos los electrones que se permiten a ese nivel. (Cap. 19, Sec. 1, pág. 576)

circuit / circuito: bucle conductor cerrado a través del cual puede fluir una corriente eléctrica. (Cap. 7, Sec. 2, pág. 203)

cloud chamber / cámara de niebla: tipo de instrumento que utiliza agua o vapor de etanol con el fin de detectar la radiación de partículas alfa y beta. (Cap. 9, Sec. 3, pág. 268)

cochlea / cóclea: estructura en forma de espiral y llena de líquido ubicada en el oído interno, la cual convierte las ondas sonoras en impulsos nerviosos. (Cap. 12, Sec. 1, pág. 362)

coefficient / coeficiente: número en una ecuación química que representa el número de unidades de cada sustancia que participa en una reacción química. (Cap. 24, Sec. 1, pág. 741)

coherent light / luz coherente: luz de una longitud de onda individual que viaja con sus crestas y senos alineados en la misma dirección. (Cap. 14, Sec. 3, pág. 434)

colloid / coloide: mezcla heterogénea cuyas partículas nunca se asientan. (Cap. 17, Sec. 1, pág. 522)

composite / compuesto: mezcla de dos materiales, uno de los cuales está incrustado en el otro. (Cap. 22, Sec. 3, pág. 689)

compound / compuesto: sustancia que se forma a partir de dos o más elementos, en la cual la combinación y proporción exactas de elementos es siempre la misma. (Cap. 17, Sec. 1, pág. 520)

compound machine / máquina compuesta: combinación de dos o más máquinas simples. (Cap. 5, Sec. 3, pág. 146)

compressional wave / onda de compresión: tipo de onda donde la materia del medio poseen un movimiento de vaivén en la misma dirección en que viaja la onda; tiene compresiones y rarefacciones. (Cap. 11, Sec. 1, pág. 328)

concave lens / lente cóncava: desvía los rayos luminosos para formar imágenes reducidas, verticales y virtuales; es más delgada en el centro y más gruesa en los bordes y, por lo general, se utiliza conjuntamente con otras lentes. (Cap. 15, Sec. 2, pág. 462)

concave mirror / espejo cóncavo: refleja la luz desde una superficie que se curva hacia adentro y puede aumentar objetos o crear haces de luz. (Cap. 15, Sec. 1, pág. 454)

conduction / conducción: transferencia de energía a través de la materia debido a partículas que chocan; se lleva a cabo porque las partículas se encuentran en constante movimiento. (Cap. 6, Sec. 2, pág. 164)

conductivity / conductividad: dícese de la propiedad de los metales y aleaciones que les permite ser buenos conductores de calor y electricidad. (Cap. 22, Sec. 1, pág. 673)

conductor / conductor: material, como el alambre de cobre, a través del cual puede moverse fácilmente un exceso de electrones. (Cap. 7, Sec. 1, pág. 196)

constant / constante: en un experimento, una variable que no cambia cuando cambian otras variables. (Cap. 1, Sec. 1, pág. 9)

control / control: estándar que se usa para efectos de comparar los resultados de las pruebas en un experimento. (Cap. 1, Sec. 1, pág. 9)

convection / convección: transferencia de energía debido al movimiento de partículas calentadas en un líquido. (Cap. 6, Sec. 2, pág. 165)

convex lens / lente convexa: converge rayos luminosos, es más gruesa en el centro que en los bordes y puede formar imágenes reales o virtuales. (Cap. 15, Sec. 2, pág. 460)

convex mirror / espejo convexo: refleja la luz desde una superficie que se curva hacia afuera y forma una imagen reducida, vertical y virtual. (Cap. 15, Sec. 1, pág. 457)

cornea / córnea: cubierta transparente en el globo ocular por la cual entra la luz. (Cap. 15, Sec. 2, pág. 463)

covalent bond / enlace covalente: atracción que se presenta entre los átomos cuando comparten electrones. (Cap. 19, Sec. 2, pág. 583)

crest / cresta: el punto más alto de una onda transversal. (Cap. 11, Sec. 2, pág. 332)

critical mass / masa crítica: cantidad de materia fisible que se requiere para que cada reacción nuclear produzca aproximadamente una reacción nuclear más. (Cap. 9, Sec. 4, pág. 274)

D

decibel / decibel: unidad de la escala de intensidad sonora, abreviada dB. (Cap. 12, Sec. 2, pág. 365)

decomposition reaction / reacción de descomposición: reacción química en la cual una sustancia se descompone en dos o más sustancias. (Cap. 24, Sec. 3, pág. 747)

density / densidad: masa por unidad de volumen de un material. (Cap. 1, Sec. 2, pág. 19)

deoxyribonucleic acid / ácido desoxirribonucleico: tipo de compuesto biológico esencial que codifica y almacena información genética, controla la producción de RNA y se encuentra en el núcleo de las células. (Cap. 21, Sec. 4, pág. 658)

dependent variable / variable dependiente: factor que cambia conforme cambia la variable independiente. (Cap. 1, Sec. 3, pág. 6)

derived unit / unidad derivada: unidad, como el metro cúbico (m^3), que se obtiene combinando diferentes unidades SI. (Cap. 1, Sec. 2, pág. 19)

diatomic molecule / molécula diatómica: molécula formada por dos átomos del mismo elemento. (Cap. 20, Sec. 2, pág. 617)

diffraction / difracción: describe la flexión de las ondas alrededor de un obstáculo; también puede ocurrir cuando las ondas atraviesan una abertura estrecha. (Cap. 11, Sec. 3, pág. 342)

diffusion / difusión: propagación de partículas a través de un volumen dado hasta que su distribución es uniforme. (Cap. 16, Sec. 1, pág. 491)

direct current (DC) / corriente directa (CD): corriente eléctrica que fluye a través de un alambre en una sola dirección. (Cap. 8, Sec. 3, pág. 244)

displacement / desplazamiento: distancia y dirección del cambio de posición de un cuerpo desde el punto de partida. (Cap. 2, Sec. 1, pág. 39)

dissociation / disociación: proceso en el cual se separan los iones de un cristal para llevarlos a una solución. (Cap. 23, Sec. 4, pág. 724)

distance / distancia: el recorrido o trayecto que se mueve un cuerpo. (Cap. 2, Sec. 1, pág. 39)

distillation / destilación: proceso que puede separar dos sustancias en una mezcla al evaporar un líquido y recondensar su vapor. (Cap. 17, Sec. 2, pág. 529)

doping / doping o adulteración: proceso de añadir impurificaciones a un semiconductor para aumentar su conductividad. (Cap. 22, Sec. 2, pág. 682)

Doppler effect / efecto Doppler: cambio de tono o frecuencia que ocurre cuando la fuente de una onda sonora se mueve en relación con el observador. (Cap. 12, Sec. 2, pág. 367)

double-displacement reaction / reacción de desplazamiento doble: reacción química que produce un precipitado, agua o un gas cuando se combinan dos compuestos iónicos en solución. (Cap. 24, Sec. 3, pág. 749)

ductile / dúctil: propiedad de los metales de extenderse en alambres. (Cap. 20, Sec. 1, pág. 608)

ductility / ductilidad: capacidad de los metales o aleaciones de extenderse en alambres. (Cap. 22, Sec. 1, pág. 673)

E

eardrum / tímpano: membrana resistente del oído externo de aproximadamente 0.1 mm de grosor y que transmite las vibraciones sonoras al oído medio. (Cap. 12, Sec. 1, pág. 361)

echolocation / ecolocalización: proceso en el cual se localizan objetos emitiendo sonidos e interpretando las ondas sonoras que regresan y son reflejadas de nuevo. (Cap. 12, Sec. 4, pág. 375)

efficiency / rendimiento: mide la cantidad de trabajo realizado por una máquina, en comparación con el trabajo que se le pone a la máquina. (Cap. 5, Sec. 2, pág. 136)

effort force / fuerza de esfuerzo: fuerza ejercida sobre una máquina que se utiliza para hacer trabajo. (Cap. 5, Sec. 2, pág. 134)

elastic potential energy / energía potencial elástica: energía almacenada por cuerpos que se estiran, torsionan o comprimen. (Cap. 4, Sec. 1, pág. 103)

electric current / corriente eléctrica: flujo de carga eléctrica a través de un alambre o cualquier otro conductor, medido en amperios (A), en un circuito. (Cap. 7, Sec. 2, pág. 203)

electric motor / motor eléctrico: dispositivo que convierte la energía eléctrica en energía mecánica para hacer trabajo; básicamente consta de una fuente de potencia, un imán permanente y un electroimán que puede girar. (Cap. 8, Sec. 2, pág. 237)

electrical power / potencia eléctrica: tasa a la cual la energía eléctrica se convierte en otra forma de energía; se expresa en vatios (W). (Cap. 7, Sec. 3, pág. 212)

electrolyte / electrólito: compuesto que se descompone en el agua formando partículas con carga eléctrica (iones) que pueden conducir electricidad. (Cap. 23, Sec. 4, pág. 723)

electromagnet / electroimán: imán temporal que se fabrica colocando un núcleo de hierro dentro de un rollo de alambre que transporta corriente y cuya fuerza se puede aumentar añadiendo más vueltas de alambre o aumentando la cantidad de corriente que pasa por el alambre. (Cap. 8, Sec. 2, pág. 234)

electromagnetic induction / inducción electromagnética: proceso de producción de corriente eléctrica mediante el movimiento de un bucle de alambre a través de un campo magnético o al mover un imán a través de un bucle de alambre. (Cap. 8, Sec. 3, pág. 240)

electromagnetic waves / ondas electromagnéticas: ondas creadas por la vibración de cargas eléctricas; pueden viajar a través del vacío o de la materia y pueden tener una amplia variedad de frecuencias y longitudes de onda. (Cap. 13, Sec. 1, pág. 390)

electron / electrón: partícula cargada negativamente que rodea el centro de un átomo. (Cap. 18, Sec. 1, pág. 545)

electron cloud / nube electrónica: área

alrededor del núcleo de un átomo donde es más probable que se hallen los electrones del átomo. (Cap. 18, Sec. 1, pág. 549)

electron dot diagram / diagrama de puntos electrónicos: utiliza el símbolo para un elemento y los puntos representan el número de electrones que se hallan en el nivel de energía externo del elemento. (Cap. 18, Sec. 3, pág. 560)

element / elemento: sustancia cuyos átomos son todos semejantes. (Cap. 17, Sec. 1, pág. 518)

endergonic reaction / reacción endergónica: reacción química que requiere energía con el fin de seguir su curso. (Cap. 24, Sec. 4, pág. 753)

endothermic reaction / reacción endotérmica: reacción química que requiere energía térmica con el fin de seguir su curso. (Cap. 24, Sec. 4, pág. 753)

exergonic reaction / reacción exergónica: reacción química que libera algún tipo de energía, como por ejemplo, energía luminosa o energía calórica. (Cap. 24, Sec. 4, pág. 752)

exothermic reaction / reacción exotérmica: reacción química en la cual la energía es emitida primordialmente en forma de calor. (Cap. 24, Sec. 4, pág. 752)

experiment / experimento: procedimiento organizado para probar una hipótesis que prueba el efecto de un fenómeno sobre otro bajo condiciones controladas. (Cap. 1, Sec. 1, pág. 8)

F

fluorescent light / luz fluorescente: luz que resulta cuando la radiación ultravioleta producida dentro de un bombillo fluorescente hace brillar el revestimiento fosforescente dentro del bombillo. (Cap. 14, Sec. 3, pág. 431)

focal length / distancia focal: distancia desde el centro de una lente o espejo hasta el punto focal. (Cap. 15, Sec. 1, pág. 454)

focal point / punto focal: punto individual en el eje óptico de un espejo cóncavo o de una lente convexa por donde pasan los rayos luminosos. (Cap. 15, Sec. 1, pág. 454)

force / fuerza: empuje o halón que un cuerpo ejerce sobre otro. (Cap. 2, Sec. 3, pág. 52)

fossil fuel / combustible fósil: recursos energéticos no renovables, como el petróleo, el gas natural y el carbón, que se forman a partir de los restos descompuestos de plantas y animales antiguos; se pueden quemar para suministrar energía y generar electricidad. (Cap. 10, Sec. 1, pág. 291)

fractional destillation / destilación fraccional: la separación de los compuestos del petróleo. (Cap. 10, Sec. 1, pág. 293)

frequency / frecuencia: mide el número de longitudes de onda que pasan por un punto fijo cada segundo y se expresa en hertz (Hz). (Cap. 11, Sec. 2, pág. 333; Cap. 13, Sec. 1, pág. 394)

friction / fricción: fuerza que resiste el movimiento entre dos superficies en contacto. (Cap. 3 Sec. 1, pág. 70)

G

galvanometer / galvanómetro: instrumento que usa un electroimán para medir la corriente eléctrica. (Cap. 8, Sec. 2, pág. 236)

gamma ray / rayo gamma: onda electromagnética que no posee masa ni carga, la cual puede viajar a la velocidad de la luz y que por lo general es emitida por partículas alfa o beta. (Cap. 9, Sec. 2, pág. 265; Cap. 13, Sec. 2, pág. 401)

Geiger counter / contador Geiger: dispositivo que mide la radiactividad al producir una corriente eléctrica cuando detecta radiación; emite un clic o una luz centelleante. (Cap. 9, Sec. 3, pág. 270)

generator / generador: dispositivo que convierte la energía mecánica en energía eléctrica al rotar un rollo de alambre a través del campo magnético de un imán permanente. (Cap. 8, Sec. 3, pág. 240)

geothermal energy / energía geotérmica: energía térmica presente en el magma caliente; una planta eléctrica puede convertirla en energía eléctrica. (Cap. 10, Sec. 3, pág. 309)

Global Positioning System (GPS) / Sistema global de posicionamiento: utiliza satélites, sistemas de monitoreo desde tierra y receptores para ayudar a la gente a determinar su ubicación o posición exacta ya sea en o encima de la superficie terrestre. (Cap. 13, Sec. 3, pág. 409)

graph / gráfica: exhibición visual de información o de datos que puede ofrecer una manera rápida de comunicar, de manera clara, una gran cantidad de información, en una cantidad pequeña de espacio. (Cap. 1, Sec. 3, pág. 22)

gravitational potential energy / energía potencial gravitatoria: energía almacenada por cuerpos que se atraen entre sí debido a la fuerza de gravedad. (Cap. 4, Sec. 1, pág. 104)

group / grupo: columna vertical en la tabla periódica. (Cap. 18, Sec. 3, pág. 558)

H

half-life / media vida: cantidad de tiempo que tarda en desintegrarse la mitad de los núcleos en una muestra de un isótopo radioactivo. (Cap. 9, Sec. 2, pág. 266)

heat / calor: energía térmica que fluye de un material con mayor temperatura a otro con menor temperatura; se mide en julios (J). (Cap. 6, Sec. 1, pág. 160)

heat engine / motor térmico: dispositivo que convierte, en energía mecánica, la energía térmica producida por combustión. (Cap. 6, Sec. 3, pág. 176)

heat mover / máquina térmica: dispositivo, como el refrigerador, que extrae energía térmica de un lugar y la transfiere a otro a una temperatura diferente. (Cap. 6, Sec. 3, pág. 177)

heat of fusion / calor de fusión: cantidad de energía que se requiere para cambiar una sustancia de la fase sólida a la fase líquida. (Cap. 16, sec. 1, pág. 490)

heat of vaporization / calor de vaporización: cantidad de energía que se requiere para que las partículas de un líquido escapen de las fuerzas de atracción dentro del líquido o la energía que se requiere para cambiar de líquido a gas. (Cap. 16, Sec. 1, pág. 490)

heterogeneous mixture / mezcla heterogénea: mezcla, como el concreto o una mezcla de sopa seca, en la cual diferentes materiales se hallan distribuidos desigualmente y se pueden identificar con facilidad. (Cap. 17, Sec. 1, pág. 521)

holography / holografía: técnica que produce una imagen fotográfica completa de un objeto tridimensional. (Cap. 14, Sec. 4, pág. 437)

homogeneous mixture / mezcla homogénea: sólido, líquido o gas que contiene dos o más sustancias combinadas uniformemente. (Cap. 17, Sec. 1, pág. 522)

hydrate / hidrato: compuesto que contiene agua añadida químicamente a sus iones y que se indica en su fórmula química. (Cap. 19, Sec. 3, pág. 591)

hydrocarbon / hidrocarburo: compuesto saturado o no saturado que contiene sólo átomos de carbono e hidrógeno. (Cap. 21, Sec. 1, pág. 641)

hydroelectricity / hidroelectricidad: electricidad producida por la energía del agua en movimiento. (Cap. 10, Sec. 3, pág. 307)

hydronium ions / iones hidronio: iones H_3O^+, que se forman cuando un ácido se disuelve en agua y los iones H^+ interactúan con el agua. (Cap. 25, Sec. 1, pág. 766)

hypothesis / hipótesis: estimación razonada o bien fundada que usa el conocimiento y la observación. (Cap. 1, Sec. 1, pág. 84)

I

incandescent light/ luz incandescente: luz producida al calentar un trozo de metal, por lo general tungsteno, hasta que brille. (Cap. 14, Sec. 3, pág. 430)

inclined plane / plano inclinado: máquina simple que consta de una superficie inclinada, como una rampa, que reduce la cantidad de fuerza que se necesita para levantar algo al aumentar la distancia sobre la cual se aplica la fuerza. (Cap. 5, Sec. 3, pág. 144)

incoherent light / luz incoherente: luz que contiene más de una longitud de onda y que no viaja con sus crestas y senos alineados en la misma dirección. (Cap. 14, Sec. 3, pág. 434)

independent variable / variable independiente: factor que a medida que cambia, afecta la medida de otra variable. (Cap. 1, Sec. 3, pág. 6)

index of refraction / índice de refracción: propiedad de un material que indica cuánto aminora la velocidad de la luz cuando viaja por el material. (Cap. 14, Sec. 1, pág. 422)

indicator / indicador: compuesto orgánico que cambia de color en ácidos y bases. (Cap. 25, Sec. 1, pág. 766)

inertia / inercia: resistencia de un cuerpo a un cambio en su movimiento. (Cap. 2, Sec. 3, pág. 54)

infrared wave / onda infrarroja: onda electromagnética con una frecuencia ligeramente menor que la frecuencia de la luz visible, transmite energía térmica y se usa en los controles remotos de los televisores y en lectores o escáneres de código de barras. (Cap. 13, Sec. 2, pág. 398)

inhibitor / inhibidor: sustancia que retarda una reacción química o evita que ocurra al combinarse con un reactivo. (Cap. 24, Sec. 4, pág. 754)

instantaneous speed / rapidez instantánea: rapidez de un objeto en un punto dado en el tiempo, la cual es constante para un objeto que se mueve a velocidad constante y diferente en cada punto del tiempo, para un objeto que decelera o acelera. (Cap. 2, Sec. 1, pág. 41)

insulator / aislante: material que no permite que los electrones se muevan fácilmente a través de él. (Cap. 7, Sec. 1, pág. 197)

insulators / aisladores: materiales, como por ejemplo, el vellocino o la fibra de vidrio, que no permiten el movimiento fácil del calor a través de ellos. (Cap. 6, Sec. 2, pág. 169)

integrated circuit / circuito integrado: microplaqueta de material semiconductor que puede contener millones de transistores, diodos y otros componentes. (Cap. 22, Sec. 2, pág. 682)

intensity / intensidad: cantidad de energía que transporta una onda sonora, la cual se puede medir en decibeles (dB). (Cap. 12, Sec. 2, pág. 634)

interference / interferencia: ocurre cuando dos o más ondas se traslapan y se combinan para formar una nueva onda; puede formar una onda más grande (interferencia constructiva) o una onda más pequeña (interferencia destructiva). (Cap. 11, Sec. 3, pág. 344)

internal combustion engine / motor de combustión interna: tipo de motor térmico que quema el combustible dentro del motor. (Cap. 6, Sec. 3, pág. 176)

ion / ion: partícula cargada que posee o más o menos electrones que protones. (Cap. 19, Sec. 2, pág. 580)

ionic bond / enlace iónico: atracción que se presenta entre iones de carga opuesta en un compuesto iónico. (Cap. 19, Sec. 2, pág. 582)

ionization / ionización: proceso en el cual los electrólitos se disuelven en agua y se separan en partículas con carga. (Cap. 23, Sec. 4, pág. 723)

isomers / isómeros: compuestos con fórmulas químicas idénticas, pero diferentes estructuras y formas moleculares, los cuales pueden afectar las propiedades físicas como el punto de fusión. (Cap. 21, Sec. 1, pág. 643)

isotopes / isótopos: átomos de un mismo elemento que poseen diferentes números de neutrones. (Cap. 18, Sec. 2, pág. 552)

J

joule / julio: unidad SI de energía. (Cap. 4, Sec. 1, pág. 102)

K

kilowatt-hour / kilovatio-hora: unidad de energía eléctrica, que corresponde a 1000 vatios de potencia usados durante una hora. (Cap. 7, Sec. 3, pág. 215)

kinetic energy / energía cinética: energía en forma de movimiento; depende de la masa y velocidad del cuerpo. (Cap. 4, Sec. 1, pág. 102)

kinetic theory / teoría cinética: explicación del comportamiento de las moléculas en la materia; establece que toda la materia se compone de partículas en constante movimiento que chocan sin perder energía. (Cap. 16, Sec. 1, pág. 488)

L

law of conservation of charge / ley de conservación de cargas: establece que las cargas se pueden transferir de un objeto a otro, pero que no se puede crear o destruir. (Cap. 7, Sec. 1, pág. 195)

law of conservation of energy / ley de conservación de la energía: establece que la energía no se crea ni se destruye. (Cap. 4, Sec. 2, pág. 111)

law of conservation of mass / ley de conservación de la masa: establece que la masa de todas las sustancias, presente antes de un cambio químico, equivale a la masa de todas las sustancias que quedan después del cambio. (Cap. 17, Sec. 2, pág. 533)

law of gravitation / ley de gravitación: establece que cualquier par de masas ejercen una fuerza de atracción entre sí, la cantidad de la cual depende de la masa de los dos cuerpos y la distancia entre ellos. (Cap. 3 Sec. 2, pág. 75)

lever / palanca: máquina simple hecha de una barra libre para girar sobre un punto fijo. (Cap. 5, Sec. 3, pág. 138)

lipids / lípidos: grupo de compuestos biológicos que contiene los mismos elementos que los carbohidratos, pero en arreglos y combinaciones diferentes; incluye las grasas y los aceites saturados e insaturados. (Cap. 21, Sec. 4, pág. 660)

loudness / volumen: describe cómo los seres humanos perciben la intensidad sonora. (Cap. 12, Sec. 2, pág. 365)

luster / lustre: propiedad de metales y aleaciones que describe su apariencia brillante o la propiedad de reflejar la luz. (Cap. 22, Sec. 1, pág. 673)

M

machine / máquina: dispositivo que facilita el trabajo aumentando la fuerza aplicada a un cuerpo, cambiando la dirección de una fuerza aplicada o aumentando la distancia sobre la cual se puede aplicar una fuerza. (Cap. 5, Sec. 2, pág. 133)

magnetic domain / dominio magnético: grupo de átomos cuyos polos magnéticos están alineados. (Cap. 8, Sec. 1, pág. 231)

magnetic pole / polo magnético: región donde la fuerza magnética de un imán es más fuerte; los polos iguales se repelen y los polos opuestos se atraen. (Cap. 8, Sec. 1, pág. 227)

magnetism / magnetismo: las propiedades e interacciones de los imanes. (Cap. 8, Sec. 1, pág. 226)

malleability / maleabilidad: propiedad de los metales y aleaciones de extenderse en láminas delgadas o de poder martillarse. (Cap. 22, Sec. 1, pág. 673)

malleable / maleable: propiedad de los metales de ser martillados o extenderse en láminas delgadas. (Cap. 20, Sec. 1, pág. 608)

mass / masa: cantidad de materia que posee un cuerpo. (Cap. 1, Sec. 2, pág. 19)

mass number / número de masa: suma del número de protones y neutrones en el núcleo de un átomo. (Cap. 18, Sec. 2, pág. 551)

mechanical advantage (MA) / ventaja mecánica (VM): número de veces que una máquina multiplica la fuerza de esfuerzo que se le aplica. (Cap. 5, Sec. 2, pág. 136)

mechanical energy / energía mecánica: suma de la energía potencial y la cinética de un sistema. (Cap. 4, Sec. 2, pág. 108)

medium / medio: cualquier material, ya sea sólido, líquido, gas o una combinación de estos tres, a través del cual una onda transfiere energía. (Cap. 11, Sec. 1, pág. 327)

melting point / punto de fusión: temperatura a la cual un sólido comienza a volverse líquido. (Cap. 16, Sec. 1, pág. 490)

metal / metal: elemento que típicamente es un sólido duro, brillante y maleable y que es un buen conductor del calor y la electricidad. (Cap. 20, Sec. 1, pág. 608)

metallic bonding / enlace metálico: se presenta debido al movimiento libre de los electrones entre iones de un metal cargados positivamente y explica las propiedades como la ductibilidad y la capacidad de conducir electricidad. (Cap. 20, Sec. 1, pág. 609)

metalloid / metaloide: elemento que comparte algunas propiedades con los metales y algunas con los no metales. (Cap. 20, Sec. 3, pág. 622)

microscope / microscopio: utiliza lentes convexas para aumentar objetos pequeños cercanos. (Cap. 15, Sec. 3, pág. 471)

microwave / microondas: onda radial con una longitud de onda menor que 1 m. (Cap. 13, Sec. 2, pág. 397)

mirage / espejismo: imagen de un objeto lejano que resulta cuando el aire a nivel del suelo es más caliente o más frío que las capas de aire por encima, lo cual hace que la imagen se refracte y aparezca en una ubicación diferente de la cual se encuentra en realidad. (Cap. 14, Sec. 1, pág. 424)

model / modelo: se puede utilizar para representar una idea, un objeto o un evento que es demasiado grande, demasiado pequeño, demasiado complejo o demasiado peligroso para ser observado o probado directamente. (Cap. 1, Sec. 1, pág. 11)

momentum / momento: propiedad que posee un cuerpo en movimiento debido a su masa y velocidad. (Cap. 3 Sec. 3, pág. 86)

monomer / monómero: molécula pequeña que forma un enlace en una cadena polímera y que se puede combinar consigo misma repetidamente. (Cap. 21, Sec. 3, pág. 653; Cap. 22, Sec. 3, pág. 685)

music / música: sonido creado al usar tonos específicos y cualidades sonoras que se utilizan en un patrón fijo. (Cap. 12, Sec. 3, pág. 363)

N

net force / fuerza neta: suma de las fuerzas que actúan sobre un cuerpo. (Cap. 2, Sec. 3, pág. 53)

neutralization / neutralización: reacción

química que ocurre cuando los iones H_3O^+ de un ácido reaccionan con los iones OH^- de una base para producir moléculas de agua. (Cap. 25, Sec. 3, pág. 777)

neutron / neutrón: partícula neutra, compuesta de quarks, en el interior del núcleo de un átomo. (Cap. 18, Sec. 1, pág. 545)

Newton's second law of motion / segunda ley del movimiento de Newton: establece que una fuerza neta que actúa sobre un cuerpo hace que éste acelere en la dirección de la fuerza neta. (Cap. 3 Sec. 1, pág. 69)

Newton's third law of motion / tercera ley del movimiento de Newton: describe pares de acción y reacción: por cada fuerza de acción existe una fuerza de reacción igual y opuesta. (Cap. 3 Sec. 3, pág. 83)

nonelectrolyte / no electrólito: sustancia que no se ioniza en el agua y que no puede conducir electricidad. (Cap. 23, Sec. 4, pág. 723)

nonmetal / no metal: elemento que por lo general es un gas o un sólido frágil a temperatura ambiente, no es maleable o dúctil, es mal conductor de calor y electricidad y típicamente no es brillante. (Cap. 20, Sec. 2, pág. 616)

nonpolar / no polar: material que no posee áreas positivas y negativas separadas, no atrae las moléculas de agua y no se disuelve con facilidad en el agua. (Cap. 23, Sec. 2, pág. 713)

nonpolar molecule / molécula no polar: molécula que comparte electrones equitativamente y que no posee extremos con carga opuesta. (Cap. 19, Sec. 2, pág. 586)

nonrenewable resources / recursos no renovables: todos los recursos naturales, como los combustibles fósiles, que los procesos naturales no pueden reemplazar con la misma rapidez con que se utilizan. (Cap. 10, Sec. 1, pág. 297)

nuclear fission / fisión nuclear: proceso que separa un núcleo atómico grande en dos núcleos de menor masa. (Cap. 9, Sec. 4, pág. 273)

nuclear fusion / fusión nuclear: proceso que une dos núcleos atómicos de menor masa para formar un núcleo con una masa mayor. (Cap. 9, Sec. 4, pág. 275)

nuclear reactor / reactor nuclear: utiliza energía de una reacción nuclear en cadena controlada con el fin de generar electricidad. (Cap. 10, Sec. 2, pág. 298)

nuclear waste / desecho nuclear: todo subproducto radiactivo que resulta cuando se usan materiales radiactivos; se deben almacenar de manera segura lejos de la actividad humana. (Cap. 10, Sec. 2, pág. 302)

nucleic acids / ácidos nucleicos: polímeros orgánicos esenciales que controlan las actividades y reproducción de las células. (Cap. 21, Sec. 4, pág. 658)

nucleotides / nucleótidos: moléculas orgánicas complejas que componen el RNA y el DNA; contienen una base orgánica, una unidad de ácido fosfórico y un azúcar. (Cap. 21, Sec. 4, pág. 658)

nucleus / núcleo: centro de un átomo, cargado positivamente, que contiene protones y neutrones y que se halla rodeado de una nube electrónica. (Cap. 18, Sec. 1, pág. 545)

O

Ohm's law / ley de Ohm: establece que la corriente de un circuito equivale a la diferencia de potencial dividida entre la resistencia. (Cap. 7. Sec. 2, pág. 207)

opaque / opaco: material que absorbe o refleja la luz en su totalidad. (Cap. 14, Sec. 1, pág. 420)

optical axis / eje óptico: recta imaginaria en un espejo cóncavo o una lente convexa que contiene el punto focal. (Cap. 15, Sec. 1, pág. 454)

organic compounds / compuestos orgánicos: extenso número de compuestos que contienen el elemento carbono. (Cap. 21, Sec. 1, pág. 640)

overtone / armónico: vibración cuya frecuencia es un múltiplo de la frecuencia fundamental o tono principal. (Cap. 12, Sec. 3, pág. 364)

oxidation number / número de oxidación: número positivo o negativo que indica la cantidad de electrones que un átomo ha ganado, perdido o compartido para poder estabilizarse. (Cap. 19, Sec. 3, pág. 587)

P

parallel circuit / circuito paralelo: circuito en el cual la corriente eléctrica tiene más de una trayectoria que puede seguir. (Cap. 7, Sec. 3, pág. 210)

pascal / pascal: unidad SI de presión. (Cap. 16, Sec. 3, pág. 502)

period / período: hilera horizontal en la tabla periódica. (Cap. 18, Sec. 3, pág. 561)

periodic table / tabla periódica: lista organizada de todos los elementos conocidos que están ordenados según cambios repetidos de propiedades. (Cap. 18, Sec. 3, pág. 554)

petroleum / petróleo bruto: petróleo crudo, un combustible fósil altamente inflamable que se formó a partir de los restos de organismos antiguos; contiene hidrocarburos, se puede refinar para producir combustibles y se utiliza en la elaboración de plásticos. (Cap. 10, Sec. 1, pág. 293)

pH / pH: medida de la concentración de iones hidronio en una solución que usa una escala que va de 0 a 14, donde 0 denota la mayor acidez y 14 denota la mayor basicidad. (Cap. 25, Sec. 2, pág. 774)

photon / fotón: un tipo de partícula que puede describir la luz. (Cap. 13, Sec. 1, pág. 395)

photovoltaic cell / célula fotovoltaica: dispositivo que convierte la energía solar en electricidad; también recibe el nombre de célula solar. (Cap. 10, Sec. 3, pág. 305)

physical change / cambio físico: todo cambio de tamaño, forma o estado de la materia en el cual no cambia la identidad de la sustancia. (Cap. 17, Sec. 2, pág. 528)

physical property / propiedad física: cualquier característica de un material, como el tamaño o la forma, que se puede observar o intentar observar sin alterar la identidad del material. (Cap. 17, Sec. 2, pág. 526)

pigment / pigmento: material coloreado que absorbe algunos colores y refleja otros. (Cap. 14, Sec. 2, pág. 428)

pitch / tono: agudeza o gravedad de un sonido, el cual se relaciona con la frecuencia de las ondas sonoras. (Cap. 12, Sec. 2, pág. 366)

plane mirror / espejo plano: espejo liso que refleja la luz para formar imágenes verticales, virtuales y de tamaño real. (Cap. 15, Sec. 1, pág. 453)

plasma / plasma: gas de alta temperatura con una carga neutra total que es el estado de materia más común en el universo. (Cap. 16, Sec. 1, pág. 492)

polar molecule / molécula polar: molécula que tiene un extremo ligeramente positivo y un extremo ligeramente negativo, como resultado de compartir electrones desigualmente. (Cap. 19, Sec. 2, pág. 586)

polarized light / luz polarizada: luz en la cual las ondas transversales vibran en una sola dirección. (Cap. 14, Sec. 4, pág. 436)

polyatomic ion / ion poliatómico: grupo de átomos cargados positiva o negativamente y que están enlazados covalentemente. (Cap. 19, Sec. 3, pág. 591)

polyethylene / polietileno: polímero formado a partir de una cadena que contiene muchas unidades de etileno; se usa a menudo en la fabricación de bolsas y botellas plásticas. (Cap. 21, Sec. 3, pág. 653)

polymer / polímero: nueva molécula enorme compuesta de muchos monómeros enlazados entre sí para formar una cadena larga que puede hilarse en fibras y ser usada para los plásticos. (Cap. 21, Sec. 3, pág. 653; Cap. 22, Sec. 3, pág. 685)

potential energy / energía potencial: energía almacenada debido a la posición de los cuerpos; se puede convertir en energía cinética cuando algo actúa para liberarla. (Cap. 4, Sec. 1, pág. 103)

power / potencia: cantidad de trabajo realizado, o la cantidad de energía transferida, en cierta cantidad de tiempo; se mide en vatios (W). (Cap. 5, Sec. 1, pág. 129)

precipitate / precipitado: compuesto insoluble que proviene de una solución durante una reacción de desplazamiento doble. (Cap. 24, Sec. 3, pág. 749)

pressure / presión: cantidad de fuerza ejercida por área unitaria o unidad de superficie; la unidad SI es el pascal (Pa). (Cap. 16, Sec. 3, pág. 502)

product / producto: en una reacción química, la nueva sustancia que se forma. (Cap. 24, Sec. 1, pág. 738)

projectile / proyectil: objeto que se lanza o que se dispara por el aire. (Cap. 3, Sec. 2, pág. 79)

proteins / proteínas: polímeros biológicos complejos y grandes formados a partir de aminoácidos; las proteínas son los constituyentes de muchos tejidos corporales, como los músculos, los tendones, el cabello y las uñas. (Cap. 21, Sec. 4, pág. 656)

proton / protón: partícula cargada positivamente, compuesta de quarks, que se halla en el interior de un átomo. (Cap. 18, Sec. 1, pág. 545)

pulley / polea: máquina simple compuesta de una rueda acanalada con una cuerda, cadena, o cable que corre a lo largo de una ranura; una polea cambia la dirección de la fuerza de esfuerzo y puede ser fija o movible. (Cap. 5, Sec. 3, pág. 141)

Q

quality / calidad: describe las diferencias entre sonidos que poseen el mismo tono y volumen sonoro. (Cap. 12, Sec. 3, pág. 370)

quarks / quarks: partículas de materia que son los constituyentes de los protones y neutrones. (Cap. 18, Sec. 1, pág. 545)

R

radiant energy / energía radiante: energía transmitida por una onda electromagnética. (Cap. 13, Sec. 1, pág. 393)

radiation / radiación: transferencia de energía en forma de ondas electromagnéticas. (Cap. 6, Sec. 2, pág. 166)

radiator / radiador: dispositivo con un área de superficie grande que calienta, por conducción, el aire que lo rodea. (Cap. 6, Sec. 3, pág. 173)

radio wave / onda radial: onda electromagnética de baja frecuencia cuya longitud de onda varía entre menos de 1 cm hasta unos 1,000 m y que puede portar la señal desde una radioemisora a un radiorreceptor. (Cap. 13, Sec. 2, pág. 396)

radioactive element / elemento radiactivo: elemento, como el radio, cuyo núcleo se desintegra y emite partículas y energía. (Cap. 20, Sec. 1, pág. 610)

radioactivity / radiactividad: proceso de desintegración nuclear que ocurre cuando la fuerza fuerte no es capaz de mantener juntos los núcleos inestables de manera permanente. (Cap. 9, Sec. 1, pág. 260)

rarefaction / rarefacción: la región menos densa de una onda de compresión. (Cap. 11, Sec. 2, pág. 332)

reactant / reactante: en una reacción química, la sustancia que reacciona. (Cap. 24, Sec. 1, pág. 738)

real image / imagen real: imagen óptica invertida que se forma cuando los rayos

Spanish Glossary

luminosos atraviesan un cuerpo. (Cap. 15, Sec. 1, pág. 455)

reflecting telescope / telescopio reflector: utiliza un espejo cóncavo, un espejo plano y una lente convexa para recoger y enfocar la luz de cuerpos distantes. (Cap. 15, Sec. 3, pág. 469)

refracting telescope / telescopio refractor: utiliza dos lentes convexas para recoger y enfocar la luz de cuerpos distantes. (Cap. 15, Sec. 3, pág. 469)

refraction / refracción: flexión de una onda a medida que cambia de rapidez, al moverse de un medio a otro. (Cap. 11, Sec. 3, pág. 340)

renewable resource / recurso renovable: fuente energética, como la energía solar, que se recupera o se reproduce casi al mismo ritmo con que se utiliza. (Cap. 10, Sec. 3, pág. 305)

resistance / resistencia: la tendencia de un material a oponerse al flujo de electrones y a transformar la energía eléctrica en energía térmica y luminosa; se mide en ohmios. (Cap. 7, Sec. 2, pág. 205)

resistance force / fuerza de resistencia: fuerza que aplica una máquina para vencer una resistencia. (Cap. 5, Sec. 2, pág. 134)

resonance / resonancia: capacidad que tiene un objeto de vibrar al absorber energía a su frecuencia natural. (Cap. 11, Sec. 3, pág. 347)

resonator / resonador: cámara hueca y llena de aire de un instrumento de cuerda que amplifica el sonido cuando su aire vibra. (Cap. 12, Sec. 3, pág. 371)

retina / retina: revestimiento interno del ojo que tiene células que convierten las imágenes luminosas en señales eléctricas. (Cap. 15, Sec. 2, pág. 463)

S

salt / sal: compuesto que se forma cuando los iones negativos de un ácido se combinan con los iones positivos de una base. (Cap. 25, Sec. 3, pág. 777)

saturated hydrocarbon / hidrocarburo saturado: compuesto que contiene sólo enlaces sencillos entre los átomos de carbono, como el propano o el metano. (Cap. 21, Sec. 1, pág. 642)

saturated solution / solución saturada: solución que contiene todo el soluto que puede sostener a una temperatura dada. (Cap. 23, Sec. 3, pág. 720)

scientific law / ley científica: enunciado sobre cómo funcionan los elementos en la naturaleza, el cual parece ser siempre cierto. (Cap. 1, Sec. 1, pág. 12)

scientific method / método científico: conjunto organizado de procedimientos de investigación que puede incluir la enunciación de un problema, la formulación de una hipótesis, la investigación y la recopilación de información, el someter a prueba una hipótesis, el análisis de datos y el sacar conclusiones. (Cap. 1, Sec. 1, pág. 8)

screw / tornillo: máquina simple que consta de un plano inclinado enrollado en espiral alrededor de un poste cilíndrico. (Cap. 5, Sec. 3, pág. 145)

semiconductors / semiconductores: elementos (silicio y germanio) que pueden conducir una corriente eléctrica bajo ciertas condiciones. (Cap. 20, Sec. 3, pág. 623)

series circuit / circuito en serie: circuito en el cual la corriente eléctrica tiene solamente una trayectoria que puede seguir. (Cap. 7, Sec. 3, pág. 209)

SI International System of Units / SI (Sistema internacional de unidades): la versión mejorada y universalmente aceptada del sistema métrico que se basa en múltiplos de diez e incluye el metro (m), el litro (L) y el kilogramo (kg). (Cap. 1, Sec. 2, pág. 15)

simple machine / máquina simple: máquina que realiza trabajo con un movimiento solamente; incluye la palanca, la polea, la rueda y eje, el plano inclinado, el tornillo y la cuña. (Cap. 5, Sec. 3, pág. 138)

single-displacement reaction / reacción de desplazamiento simple: reacción química en la cual un elemento reemplaza a otro elemento en un compuesto. (Cap. 24, Sec. 3, pág. 747)

soaps / jabones: sales orgánicas con extremos no polares hidrocarburos que interactúan con los aceites y la suciedad y extremos polares que les ayudan a disolverse en el agua. (Cap. 25, Sec. 3, pág. 782)

solar collector / colector solar: dispositivo de sistemas de calefacción solar que absorbe la energía radiante del Sol. (Cap. 6, Sec. 3, pág. 175)

solar energy / energía solar: energía proveniente del Sol que es gratis, renovable y se puede utilizar para calentar hogares y otros inmuebles. (Cap. 6, Sec. 3, pág. 174)

solubility / solubilidad: cantidad máxima de un soluto que se puede disolver en una cantidad dada de disolvente a una temperatura dada. (Cap. 23, Sec. 3, pág. 718)

solute / soluto: en una solución, la sustancia que se disuelve. (Cap. 23, Sec. 1, pág. 707)

solution / solución: mezcla que parece tener la misma composición, color, densidad y sabor y que se mezcla a nivel molecular o atómico. (Cap. 17, Sec. 1, pág. 522; Cap. 23, Sec. 1, pág. 706)

solvent / disolvente: en una solución, la sustancia en la cual se disuelve el soluto. (Cap. 23, Sec. 1, pág. 707)

sonar / sonar: sistema que utiliza el reflejo de las ondas sonoras para hallar objetos debajo del agua. (Cap. 12, Sec. 4, pág. 377)

specific heat / calor específico: cantidad de energía que se necesita para elevar en 1 K la temperatura de 1 kg de material. (Cap. 6, Sec. 1, pág. 161)

speed / rapidez: distancia que viaja un objeto por unidad de tiempo, la cual se puede calcular por $v = d/t$, donde v = rapidez, d = distancia y t es igual a tiempo. (Cap. 2, Sec. 1, pág. 39)

standard / estándar: cantidad exacta que se ha acordado y que se usa para efectos de comparación. (Cap. 1, Sec. 2, pág. 14)

standing wave / onda estacionaria: tipo de onda que se forma cuando las ondas con longitud de onda y amplitud idénticas, pero que viajan en direcciones opuestas, interfieren continuamente entre sí; posee puntos llamados nodos que no se mueven. (Cap. 11, Sec. 3, pág. 346)

static electricity / electricidad estática: electricidad que se genera cuando hay más de un tipo de carga en un objeto. (Cap. 7, Sec. 1, pág. 194)

strong acid / ácido fuerte: todo ácido que se ioniza casi totalmente en una solución. (Cap. 25, Sec. 2, pág. 772)

strong base / base fuerte: toda base que se ioniza totalmente en una solución. (Cap. 25, Sec. 2, pág. 773)

strong force / fuerza fuerte: fuerza que actúa entre protones y neutrones en un núcleo atómico para mantenerlos juntos. (Cap. 9, Sec. 1, pág. 259)

substance / sustancia: elemento o compuesto que no se puede descomponer en componentes más simples y mantener las propiedades de la sustancia original. (Cap. 17, Sec. 1, pág. 518)

substituted hydrocarbon / hidrocarburo de sustitución: hidrocarburo en que uno o más de sus átomos de hidrógeno son reemplazados por átomos o grupos de otros elementos. (Cap. 21, Sec. 2, pág. 647)

supersaturated solution / solución supersaturada: toda solución que contiene más soluto que una solución saturada a igual temperatura. (Cap. 23, Sec. 3, pág. 721)

suspension / suspensión: mezcla heterogénea que contiene un líquido en el cual se asientan partículas visibles. (Cap. 17, Sec. 1, pág. 524)

synthesis reaction / reacción de síntesis: reacción química en la cual dos o más sustancias se combinan para formar una sustancia diferente. (Cap. 24, Sec. 3, pág. 746)

synthetic / sintético: describe a los polímeros, como los plásticos, los adhesivos y los revestimientos de superficies, que están hechos de hidrocarburos. (Cap. 22, Sec. 3, pág. 685)

T

technology / tecnología: aplicación de la ciencia para ayudar a la gente. (Cap. 1, Sec. 1, pág. 13)

temperature / temperatura: medida de la energía cinética promedio de todas las partículas de un cuerpo. (Cap. 6, Sec. 1, pág. 159)

theory / teoría: explicación de fenómenos o eventos que se basa en el conocimiento adquirido a través de la observación y la experimentación. (Cap. 1, Sec. 1, pág. 12)

thermal energy / energía térmica: energía total, que incluye la energía cinética y la energía potencial, de las partículas que forman un material; se transfiere por conducción, convección y radiación. (Cap. 6, Sec. 1, pág. 159)

thermal expansion / expansión térmica: aumento en el tamaño de una sustancia como resultado de la separación de sus moléculas, al aumentar la temperatura. (Cap. 16, Sec. 1, pág. 493)

titration / titulación o análisis volumétrico: proceso en el cual una solución de concentración conocida se usa para determinar la concentración de otra solución. (Cap. 25, Sec. 3, pág. 780)

total internal reflection / reflexión interna total: se produce cuando la luz choca contra una superficie entre dos materiales y se vuelve a reflejar completamente en el primer material. (Cap. 14, Sec. 4, pág. 438)

tracer / indicador radiactivo: radioisótopo que se utiliza para encontrar o rastrear moléculas en un organismo. (Cap. 9, Sec. 4, pág. 276)

transceiver / transceptor: transmite una señal de radio y recibe otra señal de radio desde una unidad base, lo cual le permite al usuario de teléfonos inalámbricos hablar y escuchar al mismo tiempo. (Cap. 13, Sec. 3, pág. 407)

transformer / transformador: dispositivo que aumenta o disminuye la corriente alterna generada por una planta eléctrica, de modo que pueda entrar en las casas sin presentar peligros. (Cap. 8, Sec. 3, pág. 244)

transition elements / elementos de transición: elementos de los Grupos 3 al 12 en la tabla periódica; se presentan en la naturaleza como elementos libres e incluyen la tríada del hierro y los metales de acuñación. (Cap. 20, Sec. 1, pág. 612)

translucent / traslúcido: material a través del cual pasa la luz pero no en suficiente cantidad como para ver cuerpos claramente a través de él. (Cap. 14, Sec. 1, pág. 420)

transmutation / transmutación: proceso que transforma un elemento en otro por medio de la desintegración radiactiva. (Cap. 9, Sec. 2, pág. 264)

transparent / transparente: material que transmite casi toda la luz que choca contra él y a través del cual pueden verse de forma clara los cuerpos. (Cap. 14, Sec. 1, pág. 420)

transuranium element / elemento transuránico: elementos con más de 92 protones. (Cap. 20, Sec. 3, pág. 627)

transverse wave / onda transversal: tipo de onda, como la ola, en que la materia del medio se mueve de un lado a otro formando ángulos rectos a la dirección en que viaja la onda; posee crestas y senos. (Cap. 11, Sec. 1, pág. 328)

trough / seno: el punto más bajo de una onda transversal. (Cap. 11, Sec. 2, pág. 332)

turbine / turbina: rueda grande que gira cuando es empujada por el vapor, por el viento o por el agua y que provee energía mecánica a un generador. (Cap. 8, Sec. 3, pág. 242)

Tyndall effect / efecto de Tyndall: dispersión de un haz luminoso conforme atraviesa un coloide. (Cap. 17, Sec. 1, pág. 523)

U

ultrasonic / ultrasónico: ondas sonoras con frecuencias por encima de 20,000 Hz. (Cap. 12, Sec. 2, pág. 366)

ultraviolet wave / onda ultravioleta: onda electromagnética con frecuencias ligeramente más altas que la luz visible y la cual puede presentar efectos tanto útiles como perjudiciales. (Cap. 13, Sec. 2, pág. 399)

unsaturated hydrocarbon / hidrocarburo insaturado: compuesto, como el eteno o el etino, que contiene por lo menos un enlace doble o triple entre los átomos de carbono. (Cap. 21, Sec. 1, pág. 644)

unsaturated solution / solución no saturada: toda solución que puede disolver más soluto a una temperatura dada. (Cap. 23, Sec. 3, pág. 721)

V

variable / variable: factor que puede causar un cambio en los resultados de un experimento. (Cap. 1, Sec. 1, pág. 9)

velocity / velocidad: describe tanto la rapidez como la dirección de un cuerpo en movimiento. (Cap. 2, Sec. 1, pág. 44)

virtual image / imagen virtual: imagen vertical y reflejada que percibe el encéfalo aunque ningún rayo luminoso atraviese la imagen. (Cap. 15, Sec. 1, pág. 454)

viscosity / viscosidad: resistencia de un líquido a fluir. (Cap. 16, Sec. 2, pág. 501)

visible light / luz visible: ondas electromagnéticas con longitudes de onda de 390 a 770 billonésimas de metro que el ojo humano puede observar. (Cap. 13, Sec. 2, pág. 399)

voltage difference / diferencia de voltaje: empuje que hace que las cargas eléctricas fluyan por un conductor; se mide en voltios (V). (Cap. 7, Sec. 2, pág. 202)

volume / volumen: cantidad de espacio que ocupa un cuerpo. (Cap. 1, Sec. 2, pág. 18)

W

wave / onda: perturbación rítmica que transfiere energía a través de la materia o del espacio; existe solamente mientras posea energía para transportar. (Cap. 11, Sec. 1, pág. 326)

wavelength / longitud de onda: distancia entre un punto en una onda y el punto más cercano semejante en la onda siguiente; a medida que aumenta la frecuencia, la longitud de onda siempre disminuye. (Cap. 11, Sec. 2, pág. 333)

weak acid / ácido débil: todo ácido que sólo se ioniza parcialmente en una solución. (Cap. 25, Sec. 2, pág. 772)

weak base / base débil: toda base que no se ioniza totalmente en una solución. (Cap. 25, Sec. 2, pág. 773)

wedge / cuña: máquina simple que comprende un plano inclinado con uno o dos lados inclinados. (Cap. 5, Sec. 3, pág. 145)

weight / peso: fuerza gravitatoria que la Tierra ejerce sobre un cuerpo. (Cap. 3 Sec. 2, pág. 77)

wheel and axle / rueda y eje: máquina simple que consta de dos ruedas de diferente tamaño que giran juntas. (Cap. 5, Sec. 3, pág. 143)

work / trabajo: transferencia de energía que ocurre cuando una fuerza causa el movimiento de un cuerpo; se mide en julios. (Cap. 5, Sec. 1, pág. 126)

X

X ray / rayos X: onda electromagnética de hiperfrecuencia que puede viajar a través de la materia y que se utiliza a menudo en la formación de imágenes médicas. (Cap. 13, Sec. 2, pág. 401)

Index

The index for *Glencoe Physical Science* will help you locate major topics in the book quickly and easily. Each entry in the index is followed by the number of the pages on which the entry is discussed. A page number given in boldfaced type indicates the page on which that entry is defined. A page number given in italic type indicates a page on which the entry is used in an illustration or photograph. The abbreviation *act.* indicates a page on which the entry is used in an activity.

A

D

E

Index

F

Index

I

J

K

L

M

Index

Index

Index

Index

T

Index

Credits

Art Credits

Glencoe would like to acknowledge the artists and agencies who participated in illustrating this program: Absolute Science Illustration; Andrew Evansen; Argosy; Articulate Graphics; Craig Attebery represented by Frank & Jeff Lavaty; CHK America; Gagliano Graphics; Pedro Julio Gonzalez represented by Melissa Turk & The Artist Network; Robert Hynes represented by Mendola Ltd.; Morgan Cain & Associates; JTH Illustration; Laurie O'Keefe; Matthew Pippin represented by Beranbaum Artist's Representative; Precision Graphics; Publisher's Art; Rolin Graphics, Inc.; Wendy Smith represented by Melissa Turk & The Artist Network; Kevin Torline represented by Berendsen and Associates, Inc.; WILDlife ART; Phil Wilson represented by Cliff Knecht Artist Representative; Zoo Botanica.

Photo Credits

Abbreviation Key: AH=Aaron Haupt; AP=Amanita Pictures; CB=CORBIS; BD=Bob Daemmrich; DM=Doug Martin; FI=First Image; FP=Fundamental Photographs; GB=Geoff Butler; GH=Grant Heilman Photography; IS=Index Stock; KS=KS Studios; LA=Liaison Agency; MM=Matt Meadows; PA=Peter Arnold, Inc.; PD=PhotoDisc; PE=PhotoEdit; PQ=PictureQuest; PR=Photo Researchers; PT=PhotoTake NYC; RM=Richard Megna; SB=Stock Boston; SPL=Science Photo Library; SS=SuperStock; TIB=The Image Bank; TIW=The Image Works; TSA=Tom Stack & Associates; TSM=The Stock Market; VU=Visuals Unlimited.

Cover (l)PD; (r)RM/FP; **x** John S. Shelton; **xiv** Hank Morgan/Science Source/PR; **xvi** MM; **xvii** Dale Sloat/PT/PQ; **xviii** Walter H. Hodge/PA; **xix** MM; **xx** Mark E. Gibson/VU; **xxii** Ray Ellis/PR; **1** Tony Walker/PE; **2-3** John Terence Turner/FPG; **3** (t)Artville, (b)Charles L. Perrin; **4** GH; **4-5** AFP/CB; **5** FI; **6** Shuttle Mission Imagery/LA; **7** Will McIntyre/PR; **9** James L. Amos/CB; **10** David Young-Wolff/PE; **11** (l)Roger Ressmeyer/CB, (r)Douglas Mesney/TSM; **12** J. Marshall/TIW; **13** (t)Jonathan Nourok/PE, (b)Tony Freeman/PE; **14** FI; **15** Courtesy Bureau International Des Poids et Mesures; **16** MM; **17** (t)AP, (bl)Runk/Schoenberger from GH, (br)CB; **20** Stephen R. Wagner; **24** FI; **26** (l)Stock Montage, (r)North Wind Picture Archives; **28** BD; **29** Icon Images; **30** (l)Rosalie Winard, (r)courtesy Temple Grandin; **31** NASA; **32** (l)TSADO/NCDC/NOAA/TSA, (r)David Ball/TSM; **34** Clement Mok/PQ; **35** AP: **36** Alan Towse/Ecoscene/CB; **36-37** Robert Mathena/FP; **37** Frank Lane/Parfitt/Stone; **38** Icon Images; **41** Paul Silverman/FP; **42** A. & J. Verkaik/Skyart/TSM; **43** Terje Rakke/TIB; **44** (t)SS, (b)Robert Homes/CB; **49** (t)RDF/VU, (c)Ron Kimball, (b)RM/FP; **50** (l)The Image Finders, (r)Richard Hutchings; **51** Bill Aaron/PE; **52** Holway & Lobel Globus; **53** BD; **54** Rob Nelson/SB/PQ; **55** (t)Paul Kennedy/LA, (b)Courtesy Insurance Institute for Highway Safety; **56** Donald Johnston/Stone; **57** FI; **58** (t)Rod Joslin, (b)Icon Images; **59** Icon Images; **60** Sylvain Grandadam/Stone; **61** Andreas Fechner; **62** (t)Tony Freeman/PE, (c)Peter Newton/Stone, (b)Tony Freeman/PE; **63** (l)Don C. Nieman, (r)Jim Steinberg/PR; **64** Duomo; **66** NASA; **66-67** Tim Wright/CB; **67** Dominic Oldershaw; **68** David Young-Wolff/PE; **70** (t)Pictor, (c)M.W. Davidson/PR, (b)PD; **71** BD; **72** (t)BD, (b)Peter Fownes/Stock South/PQ; **73** (t)Michael Newman/PE, (b)James Sugar/Black Star/PQ; **74** Keith Kent/PA; **76** CB; **77** Peticolas-Megna/FP; **78** NASA; **80** (tl)KS, (tr)David Young-Wolff/PE, (b)RM/FP; **81** Pictor; **83** Steven Sutton/Duomo; **84** Philip Bailey/TSM; **85** (t)North American Rockwell, (cl)NASA, (cr)Teledyne Ryan Aeronautical, (b)North American Rockwell; **86** StockTrek/CB; **87** (t)Tony Freeman/PE, (bl)Jeff Smith/Fotosmith, (br)RM/FP; **88** AP; 90 MM; **91** John Evans; **92** Bettmann/CB; **92-93** CB; **93** (l)CB, (r)George Hall/CB; **94** (t)Mark Burnett, (c)Robert Brenner/PE, (b)Dominic Oldershaw; **95** (l)Dominic Oldershaw, (r)Gunter Marx/CB; **96** Mary Ann McDonald/CB; **98** Alfred Pasieka/PA; **98-99** SS; **99** GB; **100** (l)Runk/Schoenberger from GH, (c)Michael Newman/PE, (r)Richard Clintsman/Stone; **101** (tl)Tony Walker/PE, (tr)D. Boone/CB, (b)AH; **105** MM; **109** Walter H. Hodge/PA; **110** RFD/VU; **114** Rudi Von Briel; **117** MM; **118** Maurites Escher; **119** (l)Brompton Studios, (r)Hank Morgan/PR; **120** (t)SS, (c)Telegraph Colour Library/FPG, (b)Jana R. Jirak/VU; **122** Courtesy Six Flags Amusement Parks; **124** Tom Pantages; **124-125** Eduardo Di Baia/AP/Wide World Photos; **125** Timothy Fuller; **126 127** Michael Newman/PE; **129** Michelle Bridwell/PE; **131** Jules Frazier/PD; **132** Michael Newman/PE; **133** (t)Mark Burnett, (b)Tony Freeman/PE; **134** Joseph P. Sinnot/FP; **135** RM/FP; **138** Yoav Levy/PT; **139** (tl)Tom Pantages, (tr)Mark Burnett, (b)Tony Freeman/PE; **140** (t)Richard T. Nowitz, (c)David Madison/Stone, (b)John Henley/TSM; **141** A.J. Copley/VU; **143** Mark Burnett; **144** Tom Pantages; **145** (tl tc)file photo, (tr)Mark Burnett, (b)AP; **146** SS; **147** Mark Burnett; **148** Bruno P. Zehnder/PA; **149** Hickson-Bender; **150** Joe Lertola; **151** (t)Sandia National Laboratory, (b)courtesy D. Carr & H. Craighead, Cornell University; **152** (t)Ed Lallo/LA, (bl)file photo, (br)C Squared Studios/PD; **153** (t bl)Siede Preis/PD, (br)Glenn Mitsui/PD; **156** Stone; **156-157** Charles E. Rotkin/CB; **157** Dominic Oldershaw; **160** AH; **165** Peter Ardito/IS; **166** (t)Earth Imaging/Stone, (bl)K&K Arman/Bruce Coleman, Inc./PQ, (br)Charles & Josette Lenars/CB; **168** (l)Doug Cheeseman/PA, (c)Tim Davis/TSM, (r)Ed Reschke/PA; **169** David Madison; **171** Leonard Lee Rue III/Bruce Coleman, Inc./PQ; **173** Steve Callahan/VU; **175** Stu Rosner/SB; **182** (t)NASA, (c)Roy Johnson/TSA, (b)NASA; **182-183** StockTrek/PD; **183** (t)Michael Newman/PE, (b)NASA; **184** (t)Dean Conger/CB, (c)Myrleen Ferguson Cate/PE, (b)MM; **185** Sami Sarkis/PD; **188** Tony Freeman/PE; **190** Digital Stock; **190-191** K. Yamashita/Panoramic Images; **192** Kip Peticolas/FP; **192-193** Richard Pasley/SB/PQ; **193** Michael Newman/PD; **195** GB; **197 198** KS; **199** T. Wiewandt/DRK Photo; **200** Dale Sloat/PT/PQ; **205** Ray Ellis/PR; **206** Thomas Veneklasen; **208 209 210** GB; **212** (l)GB, (r)Tony Freeman/PE; **213** AH; **216** GB; **217** GB; **218** B. Gotfryd/Woodfin Camp & Associates; **219** Courtesy Carnegie Mellon University, School of Computer Science; **220** (t)file photo, (bl)Lester Lefkowitz/TSM, (br)Harold Stucker/Black Star; **224** Yoav Levy/PT; **224-225** Steele Hill/NASA; **225** Thomas Veneklasen; **227 228** RM/FP; **231** (l)Stephen Frisch/SB, (c)Mark Burnett, (r)Stephen Frisch/SB; **232** Mark Burnett; **235** Icon Images; **242** (t)Tom Campbell/FPG, (b)Russell D. Curtis/PR; **243** (l, t to b)Clement Mok/PQ, Tim Ridley/DK Images, Brian Gordon Green, (r, t to b) Joseph Palmieri/Pictor, Robin Adshead/Military Picture Library/CB, Tim Ridley/DK Images; **244** Mark Burnett; **247 248 249** KS; **250** Laurence Dutton/Stone; **251** (l)Brian Blauser/Stock Shop, (r)Mehau Kulyk/PR; **252** (t)Mark Burnett, (c)Jeff Greenberg/PA, (b)Michael Newman/PE; **256** Timothy Fuller; **256-257** NASA/LA; **257** Dominic Oldershaw; **258** (l)FI, (r)David Frazier/TIW; **262** American Institute of Physics; **264** AP; **268** (l)courtesy Supersaturated Environments, (r)SPL/PR; **269** (t)CERN, P. Loiez/SPL/PR, (b)RM/FP; **270** Glen Allison/PD; **271** Hank Morgan/PR; **276** Oliver Meckes/Nicole Ottawa/PR; **277** (t)Davis Meltzer, (b)UCLA School of Medicine; **278** J.L. Carson/Custom Medical Stock Photo; **279** Dominic Oldershaw; **280** (t)Fermilab/VU, (b)MM; **281** MM; **282** Hulton-Getty/LA; **283** (t)Nicholas Veasey/Stone, (b)Rob Maass/Sipa Press; **284** (t)Photri/TSM, (b)Martha Cooper/PA; **285** Richard Green/PR; **286** Oliver Meckes/Nicole Ottawa/PR; **288** Joseph Sohm/ChromoSohm, Inc./CB; **288-289** Andy Sacks/Stone; **289** MM; **290** (l)Jan Halaska/PR, (c)James Sugar/Black Star, (r)Bill Heinsohn/Stone; **292** Robert E. Pratt; **293** AP; **294** (t)Digital Vision/PQ, (b)DM; **298** Robert Essel/TSM; **299** PR; **302** AFP/CB; **303** Tim Wright/CB; **305** AP; **307** S.K. Patrick/TSA; **308** (t)John Elk III/SB, (b)Lester Lefkowitz/TSM; **310** Martin Bond/SPL/PR; **312** Timothy Fuller; **313** Dominic Oldershaw; **314** (l)Sally A. Morgan/Ecoscene/CB, (r)Lester Lefkowitz/TSM; **315** (t)Ahmet Sel/Sipa Press, (b)CB Sygma; **316** (t)AP, (c)Kathy Ferguson/PE, (b)Jose Azel/Aurora/PQ; **317** (l)Paul A. Souders/CB, (r)Mark Newham/Eye Ubiquitous/CB; **318** Lester Lefkowitz/TSM; **320** Robert Holmes/CB; **322** John Eastcott & Yva Momatiuk/Woodfin Camp & Associates; **322-323** Nonstock Inc.; **324** Francois Gohier/PR; **324-325** Will Dickey, Florida Times Union/AP/Wide World; **325** MM; **326** James H. Karales/PA; **328** SS; **330** (t)Galen Rowell, (b)Stephen R. Wagner; **338** DM; **339** Richard Hutchings/PR; **340** (t)RM/FP, (b)SIU/VU; **342** (t)John S. Shelton, (b)RM/FP; **343** RM/FP; **346** Kodansha; **348 349** DM; **350** US Naval Institute; **351** (t)Ralph White/CB, (b)Ralph White/CB; **352** (tl)Stan Osolinski/TSM, (tr)Bruce Heinemann/PD, (b)Kevin Fleming/CB; **356** TSM; **356-357** Jonathan Blair/CB; **357** Mark Burnett; **360** AH; **362** Prof. P.l. Motta/Dept. of Anatomy/University la Sapienza, Rome/SPL/PR; **364** Michael Newman/PE; **365** (tl)Ian O'Leary/Stone, (tr)David Young-Wolff, (bl)Mark A. Schneider/VU, (bc)Rafael Macia/PR, (br)SS; **368** NOAA/OAR/ERL/National Severe Storms Laboratory (NSSL); **369** (t)Jean Miele/TSM, (b)FI; **371** (t)Charles Gupton/Stone, (b)Will Hart/PE; **372** (t)Nick Rowe/PD, (b)Derick A. Thomas, Dat's Jazz/CB; **374** DM; **375** Araldo de Luca/CB; **376** (tl)Gary W. Carter/CB, (tr)Merlin D. Tuttle, (b)Stephen R. Wagner; **378** DM; **380** (t)Hisham F. Ibrahim/PD, (b)John Wang/PD; **381** David Young-Wolff/PE; **382** (t)Zig Leszczynski/Earth Scenes, (cl)Australian Picture Library/CB, (c)PD, (cr)CB, (bl)David Sacks, (br)Ethan Miller/CB; **384** (tl)Planet Earth Pictures/FPG, (tr)CMCD/PD, (b)Robert Brenner/PE; **385** (l)Steve Cole/PD, (c)C Squared Studios/PD, (r)CMCD/PD; **386** KS; **388** Vince Streano/CB; **388-389** VCG/FPG; **389** Spencer Grant/PE;

393 Matt Jacob/TIW; **398** (t)Pete Saloutos/TSM, (bl)NASA/GSFC/JPL, MISR and AirMISR Teams, (br)NASA/GSFC/MITI/ERSDAC/JAROS, and USA/Japan ASTER Science Team; **399** AP/Wide World Photos; **401** Telegraph Colour Library/FPG; **403** StudiOhio; **404** (t bl)FI, (br)PD; **405** (t)Mark Richards/PE/PQ, (c)Stephen Frisch/SB/PQ, (bl)CB, (bc)Dorling Kindersley, (br)Michael Newman/PE/PQ; **406** Nino Mascardi/TIB; **407** Photolink/PD; **408** VCG/FPG; **410** Len Delessio/IS; **411** Jim Wark/IS; **412-413** It Stock International/IS; **414** (tl)Martin Dohrn/SPL/PR, (tr)Mickey Pfleger/Photo 20-20, (b)Joe McDonald/TSA; **415** (t)Susan Leavises/PR, (c)Alain Evrard/LA, (b)Myrleen Ferguson; **416** Shaun Egan/Stone; **418** Mickey Pfleger/Photo 20-20/PQ; **418-419** Richard During/Stone; **419** Dominic Oldershaw; **420** FI; **422** (tl)Bruce Iverson, (tr)Myrleen Cate/IS/PQ, (b)Stephen Frisch/SB/PQ; **423** David Parker/SPL/PR; **424** Charles O'Rear/CB; **426** FI; **427** (t)Ralph C. Eagle, Jr./PR, (b)Diane Hirsch/FP; **428** MM; **431** Ginger Chih/PA; **432** FI; **433** (t)Will & Deni McIntyre/PR, (others)Marvin J. Fryer; **435** (t)Paul Silverman/FP, (b)Andrew Syred/SPL/PR; **437** Larry Mulvehill/PR; **439** Paul Silverman/FP; **440** David Young-Wolff/PE; **441** DM; **442** (t)Timothy Fuller, (b)Dominic Oldershaw; **443** Dominic Oldershaw; **444** (t)Archivo Iconografico, S.A./CB, (b)Ashmolean Museum, Oxford, UK/Bridgeman Art Library, London/NY; **445** Courtesy Maria Martinez-Cañas and Fredric Snitzer Gallery; **446** (l)Dick Poe/VU; (r)Timothy Fuller; **448** AH; **450** Bob Rowan/Progressive Image/CB; **450-451** John Elk III/SB/PQ; **451** Mark Burnett; **452** CB; **453** Jeff Greenberg/VU; **456** George B. Diebold/TSM; **457** Paul A. Souders/CB; **459** MM; **460** David Parker/SPL/PR; **466** (tr)Stephen R. Wagner, (bc br)courtesy Optobionics Corp., (others) National Eye Institute, National Institutes of Health; **470** NASA/Consolidated News Pictures/Archive Photos; **472 473** Breck P. Kent/Earth Scenes; **474** (t)NASA, (b)Dominic Oldershaw; **475** Dominic Oldershaw; **476** Hemsey/LA; **477** (tl)Max Aquilera-Hellweg/Timepix, (tr)AFP/CB, (b)Louis Psihoyos/Matrix; **478** (t)David Young-Wolff/PE, (c)John Durham/SPL/PR, (b)Mark Burnett; **479** (l)DM, (r)Croan Studio; **484-485** (foreground) National Geographic Society, (background)Granger Collection, NY; **486** Alfred Pasieka/PA; **486-487** TSM; **487** MM; **488** Icon Images; **491** DM; **492** JISAS/Lockheed/SPL/PR; **493** (t)CB, (b)Mark E. Gibson/VU; **495** AP; **496** MM; **500** BD; **502** file photo; **504** Mark Burnett/PR; **507** MM; **508** John Evans; **510** (t)Geoff Tomkinson/SPL/PR, (c)BD/SB, (b)Michael Dwyer/SB; **510-511** StockTrek/PD; **511** (l)StockTrek/PD, (r)Jules Frazier/PD; **512** (t)Breck P. Kent/Animals Animals, (c)AH, (b)Icon Images; **516** MM; **516-517** Michael Newman/PE; **517** Mark Burnett; **518** (l)Siede Pries/PD, (c)Ryan McVay/PD, (r)PD; **519** (tl)Yann Arthus-Bertrand/CB, (tc)James L. Amos/CB, (tr)Stockbyte/PQ, (c)CalTech, (bl)Robert Fried/SB/PQ, (br)Dorling Kindersley; **520** (t)RM/FP, (b)Icon Images; **521** (t)Icon Images, (b)Andrew Syred/SPL/PR; **522** (t)Icon Images, (bl)PD, (br)C Squared Studios/PD; **523** (tl)Chuck Keeler, Jr./TSM, (tr)Kaj R. Svensson/SPL/PR, (b)RM/FP; **524** Larry Mayer/LA; **525** Icon Images; **526** MM; **527** (t)AP, (b)DM; **528** RM/FP; **529** Jed & Kaoru Share/Stone; **530** Tim Courlas; **532** (l)M. Romesser, (r)SS; **533** Chris Rogers/TSM;

534 (t)MM, (b)Icon Images; **535** Icon Images; **536** (tl)Dominic Oldershaw, (tr)George Hall/CB, (b)The Denver Post/AP/Wide World Photos; **536-537** (br)Peter Johnson/CB; **537** (l)DM, (r)Frank Siteman/SB/PQ; **538** (tl)Icon Images, (tr)Will Ryan/TSM, (c)Icon Images, (b)Tony Freeman/PE; **539** (l)Mary Kate Denny/PE, (r)Dean Conger/CB; **542** PR; **542-543** CB; **543** Icon Images; **546** (tl)SPL/PR, (tr)Hank Morgan/Science Source/PR, (b)PR; **547** Sheila Terry/SPL/PR; **548** file photo; **554** (l)Bettmann/CB, (r)Science Museum/Science & Society Picture Library; **562** CB; **563** TIB; **564** Tom Pantages; **565** PE; **566** Roger Ressmeyer/CB; **567** (t)John Bolzan, (b)Maria Stenzel/National Geographic Image Collection; **572** Yoav Levy/PT/PQ; **572-573** Aerial Focus/IS; **573** AP; **574** (l)John Evans, (r)CB; **575** (l)Runk/Schoenberger from GH, (c)RM/FP, (r)TIW; **579** FI; **580** John Paul Kay/PA; **584** John Evans; **585** (t)Patricia Lanza, (bl br)file photo; **587** Bettmann/CB; **591** Courtesy Süd-Chemie Performance Packaging; **592** AP; **594** (t)AP, (b)Richard Hutchings; **595** Richard Hutchings; **596 597** Daniel Belknap; **598** AP; **603** Yoav Levy/PT; **604-605** Jon Feingersh/TSM; **605** Dorling Kindersley; **606** Dan McCoy from Rainbow/PQ; **606-607** Georg Gerster/PR; **607** KS; **608** (l)Henry Groskinsky/TimePix, (r)Nubar Alexanian/CB; **610** (l)Stephen Frisch/SB, (r)Jerry Mason/SPL/PR; **611** Firefly Productions/TSM; **612** Mark Burnett/PR; **613** (tl)MM, (tr)Icon Images, (b)Jeff J. Daly/FP; **615** Melvyn P. Lawes/Papilio/CB; **617** (l to r)Russ Lappa/Science Source/PR, Gregory G. Dimijian/PR, Stephen Frisch/SB, Andrew J. Martinez/PR, DM, Charles Gupton/SB; **618** (t)Spencer Grant/PE/PQ, (b)Dick Frank/TSM; **619** (t)Norris Blake/VU, (b)Steven Senne/AP/Wide World; **620** Gene J. Puskar/AP/Wide World Photos; **622** George Hall/CB; **623** (l)Icon Images, (r)Charles D. Winters/PR; **624** (l)AH, (c)Rick Gayle Studio/TSM, (r)Alfred Pasieka/SPL/PR; **626** (l)RMIP/Richard Haynes, (r)PD; **628** (tl)Gianni Dagli Orti/CB, (tc)Jonathan Blair/CB, (tr)Patricia Lanza, (cl)CB, (ccl)Tony Freeman/CB, (c)PD, (ccr)Paul A. Souders/CB, (cr)Bettmann/CB, (bl)Steve Cole/CB, (bc)Artville, (br)Achim Zschau; **630** (t)Charles D. Winters/PR, (b)Richard Hutchings; **631** Richard Hutchings; **632** (t)Ken Reid/FPG, (b)Lynn Johnson/Aurora; **633** Flip Chalfant/TIB; **634** (tl)Charles D. Winters/PR, (tcl)Stephen Frisch/SB, (tcr)Charles E. Zirkle, (tr)DM, (bl)Russ Lappa/Science Source/PR, (br)Karl Hartmann/Sachs/PT; **638** Ken Eward/Science Source/PR; **638-639** KS; **639 640** KS; **642** (tl)courtesy Land's End, Inc., (tr)CB, (c)Bernard Roussel/TIB, (bl)George Hall/Check Six/PQ, (br)PD; **644** (l)Jens Jorgen Jensen/TSM, (r)PD; **645** (l)AH, (r)FI; **646** Ken Frick; **647** (l)AH, (c r)Timothy Fuller; **648** Lynn M. Stone/IS; **649** KS; **654** (l)GB, (r)Charles D. Winters/PR; **655** AP; **657** David M. Phillips/VU; **660** (t)Bob Mullenix, (b)Diana Calder/TSM; **661** Ken Frick; **662** MM; **664 665** Courtesy 3M; **666** (tl)Francis & Donna Caldwell/VU, (tr)Richard Hutchings/PR, (bl)PD, (br)IS; **670** Meckes/Ottawa/PR; **670-671** NASA/LA; **671** MM; **673** (l)Icon Images, (r)IS; **674** Icon Images; **675** (t)Mark Thomas/FoodPix, (bl)SIU/VU, (br)Jonathan Blair/CB; **676** Courtesy Boeing; **677** (l)James L. Amos/PA, (r)NASA; **679** KS; **680** Courtesy Zimmer, Inc.; **682** Michael Philip Manheim/Photo Network/PQ; **683** (t)Bettmann/CB, (cl)L. Mulvehill/PR, (c)courtesy Texas Instruments, (cr)Bettmann/CB, (bl)David Young-Wolff/PE, (br)Charles O'Rear/CB; **684** AP; **687** (l)Leonard Lessin/PA, (c)Myrleen Ferguson/PE, (r)Robert Rathe/SB; **688** (t)Doug Wilson/CB, (bl)courtesy Dallara, (br)Jon Eisberg/FPG; **689** (l)Herb Charles Ohlemeyer/Fran Heyl Associates, (r)Cindy Lewis; **690** Courtesy Boeing; **691** AH; **692** Icon Images; **693** Timothy Fuller; **694** (l)Steve Taylor/Stone, (r)Steve Labadessa/Timepix; **694-695** Bernard Roussel/TIB; **695** Courtesy 3M; **696** (t)Tony Freeman/PE, (bl)Mark Wagner/Stone, (br)Flexdex Skateboards www.flexdex.com. Photo by John Durant Photography; **698** KS; **701** (t)Elaine Shay, (c)Ken Frick, (bl)Phillip A. Harrington/PA, (br)Jules Frazier/PD; **702-703** Norbert Wu; **703** Spencer Collection, NY Public Library, Astor, Lenox & Tilden; **704** RM/FP; **704-705** Michael Pogany/Columbus Zoo; **705** MM; **706** (l)Christie's Images, (r)Flip Schulke/Black Star; **707** Annie Grifiths Belt/CB; **708** (tl)Bettmann/CB, (tr)Brian Gordon Green, (b)Michael Newman/PE/PQ; **710 713 714** Icon Images; **715** Steve Mason/PD; **716 717** KS; **719** Mark Thayer; **721** RM/FP; **722** David Young-Wolff/PE; **727 728 729** MM; **730** (t)Tony Freeman/PE, (bl)AISI/VU, (br)John Evans; **730-731** CB; **731** (t)Standard-Examiner, Kort Duce/AP/Wide World Photos, (b)Alinari/Art Resource, NY; **732** Icon Images; **736** RM/FP; **736-737** Transglobe/IS; **737** MM; **739** Mansell Collection/TimePix; **740** RM/FP; **742** CB; **743** RM/FP; **744** DM/PR; **745** RM/FP; **746** Emory Kristof/National Geographic Image Collection; **747** (t)Charles D. Winters/PR, (b)Stephen Frisch/SB/PQ; **749** RM/FP; **750** Tim Matsui/LA; **751** (t)Roger Ressmeyer/NASA/CB, (c)Bettmann/CB, (bl)Bettmann/CB, (br)NASA/CB; **752** MM; **753** (t)Jeff J. Daly/FP, (b)Spencer Grant/PE; **755** Timothy Fuller; **756** UNEP-Topham/TIW; **757** Michael Newman/PE; **758** (t)Bibliotheque du Museum D'Histoire Naturelle, (b)Paul Chesley/Stone; **759** (t)Brad Maushart/Graphistock, (b)Owen Franken/CB; **760** (t)Icon Images, (c)Charles D. Winters/PR, (b)Joseph P. Sinnot/FP; **764** Michael Dalton/FP; **764-765** Luiz C. Marigo/PA; **765** Bjorn Bolstad/PA; **766** KS; **767** MM; **768** GB; **769** Rick Poley/IS; **772** MM; **774** (vinegar)Elaine Shay, (milk)Brent Turner/BLT Productions, (baking soda)MM, (ammonia) Elaine Shay, (cola, tomato)CB, (milk of magnesia)Icon Images, (drain cleaner)StudiOhio, (c)Mark Burnett/SB/PQ, (bl)Dominic Oldershaw, (br)MM; **777** Charles D. Winters/PR; **778** The Purcell Team/CB; **779** (t)Wolkmar Wentzel, (cl)Kevin Schafer/CB, (cr)CB, (b)Kevin Schafer/CB; **780** RM/FP; **781** (l)MM, (r)AP; **783** Chinch Gryniewicz/Ecoscene/CB; **784** AP; **785** PD; **786** (t)Bill Lyons/LA, (b)RM/FP; **787** RM/FP; **790** (l)KS, (r)MM; **791** (l)John Evans, (r)Martyn F. Chillmaid/SPL/PR; **793** (l)Mike & Carol Werner/SB/PQ, (r)Paul Silverman/FP; **794** Egyptian National Museum, Cairo, Egypt/SS; **796-797** PD; **798** Timothy Fuller; **802** Roger Ball/TSM; **804** (l)GB, (r)Coco McCoy from Rainbow/PQ; **805** Dominic Oldershaw; **806** StudiOhio; **807** FI; **809** MM; **812** Paul Barton/TSM; **815** Davis Barber/PE.

PERIODIC TABLE OF THE ELEMENTS

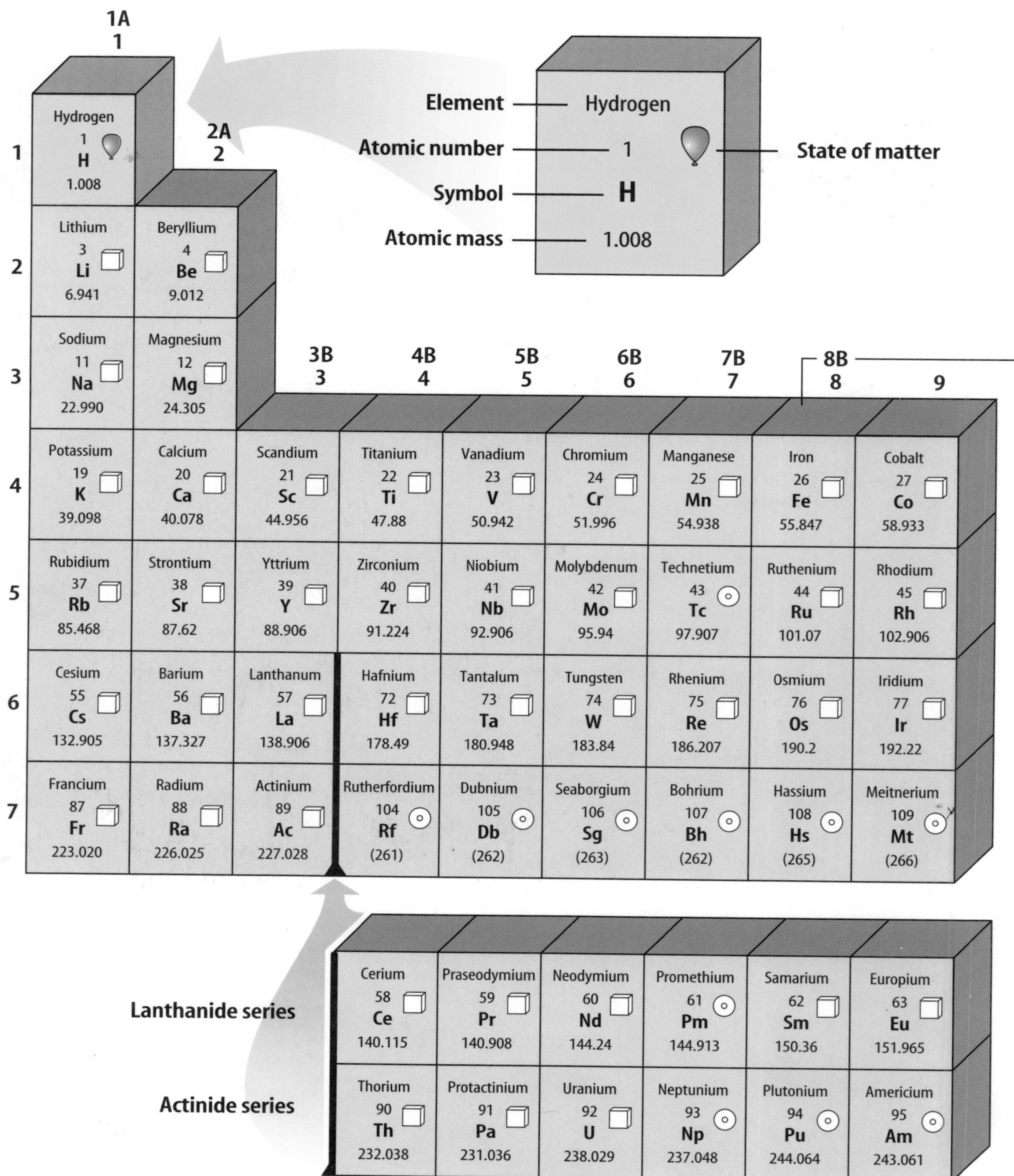

Element
Hydrogen
Atomic number
1
State of matter
Symbol
H
Atomic mass
1.008
1A
1
2A
2
3B
3
4B
4
5B
5
6B
6
7B
7
8B
8
9
1
2
3
4
5
6
7
Hydrogen 1 H 1.008
Lithium 3 Li 6.941
Beryllium 4 Be 9.012
Sodium 11 Na 22.990
Magnesium 12 Mg 24.305
Potassium 19 K 39.098
Calcium 20 Ca 40.078
Scandium 21 Sc 44.956
Titanium 22 Ti 47.88
Vanadium 23 V 50.942
Chromium 24 Cr 51.996
Manganese 25 Mn 54.938
Iron 26 Fe 55.847
Cobalt 27 Co 58.933
Rubidium 37 Rb 85.468
Strontium 38 Sr 87.62
Yttrium 39 Y 88.906
Zirconium 40 Zr 91.224
Niobium 41 Nb 92.906
Molybdenum 42 Mo 95.94
Technetium 43 Tc 97.907
Ruthenium 44 Ru 101.07
Rhodium 45 Rh 102.906
Cesium 55 Cs 132.905
Barium 56 Ba 137.327
Lanthanum 57 La 138.906
Hafnium 72 Hf 178.49
Tantalum 73 Ta 180.948
Tungsten 74 W 183.84
Rhenium 75 Re 186.207
Osmium 76 Os 190.2
Iridium 77 Ir 192.22
Francium 87 Fr 223.020
Radium 88 Ra 226.025
Actinium 89 Ac 227.028
Rutherfordium 104 Rf (261)
Dubnium 105 Db (262)
Seaborgium 106 Sg (263)
Bohrium 107 Bh (262)
Hassium 108 Hs (265)
Meitnerium 109 Mt (266)
Lanthanide series
Actinide series
Cerium 58 Ce 140.115
Praseodymium 59 Pr 140.908
Neodymium 60 Nd 144.24
Promethium 61 Pm 144.913
Samarium 62 Sm 150.36
Europium 63 Eu 151.965
Thorium 90 Th 232.038
Protactinium 91 Pa 231.036
Uranium 92 U 238.029
Neptunium 93 Np 237.048
Plutonium 94 Pu 244.064
Americium 95 Am 243.061